RANDOM HOUSE

WEBSTER'S

COLLEGE

THESAURUS

Original Edition Edited by

JESS STEIN

and

STUART BERG FLEXNER

Revised and Updated by

FRASER SUTHERLAND

RANDOM HOUSE

WEBSTER'S

COLLEGE

THESAURUS

RANDOM HOUSE
New York

This is a completely revised, updated, and retypeset edition of the *Random House Thesaurus*, originally published in 1984.

Based upon the Reader's Digest *Family Word Finder*, Copyright © 1975 The Reader's Digest Association, Inc. Copyright © 1975 The Reader's Digest Association (Canada) Ltd.

Random House Webster's college thesaurus / edited by Jess Stein and
 Stuart Berg Flexner ; revised and updated by Fraser Sutherland.
     p.   cm.
   Rev. ed. of: The Random House thesaurus. College ed. 1984.
   ISBN 0-679-45280-X (hc). -- ISBN 0-679-77375-4 (pb)
   1. English language--Synonyms and antonynms. I. Stein, Jess M.
 II. Flexner, Stuart Berg. III. Sutherland, Fraser. IV. Random
 House (Firm) V. Random House thesaurus.
 PE1591.R314   1996
 423'.1--dc20   96-29480
                                                           CIP

 ISBN   0-679-45280-X hc
           0-679-77375-4 pb

Random House Web address http://www.randomhouse.com/
Typeset and Printed in the United States of America
Revised and Updated Edition
9 8 7 6 5 4 3 2 1

New York   Toronto   London   Sydney   Auckland

TO THE READER

Words, words; they surround us. And we like to think we can surround and manipulate them. But more often than we would wish, we're at a loss for the right word. It's on the tip of our tongue or the back of our mind. Sometimes we don't know what we're thinking until we write it down, and even then we're faced with blanks. Or if we more or less know what we mean and know at least an approximate word, it's not the word we *want*. This is when the *Random House Webster's College Thesaurus* can help, with its succinctly organized list of choices.

If you do know the right word but not the meaning, you can look it up in the *Random House Webster's College Dictionary*. But vital though it is, a dictionary is only half the story. The *Random House Webster's College Thesaurus* supplies the other half. Not only does it give you synonyms, words closely related in meaning, but also antonyms, words opposite in meaning. Just browsing through it brings rewards, extending and enriching your thoughts, adding to your hoard of words.

Although it was not the first one and was far from being the last, the most famous thesaurus was put together by an Englishman, Peter Mark Roget (1779-1869). A physician and scientist, Roget was one of those Victorians who really thought he could know everything. He developed a system of organizing the world of knowledge under headings, subheadings, and lists. Much to his surprise, people looked to his book not to find out how the universe and its contents were organized, but for its system of classifying words—because inside that system were the words they wanted to use. The Roget system has been around for a long time. Indeed, because *Roget's* is not in copyright, you often see it in the titles of thesauruses today. But, impressive though it is, one problem with a Roget-type thesaurus is that it requires you to consult a long and sometimes baffling index, and to play catch-as-catch-can inside the text. It induces severe eye strain trying to solve a crossword puzzle.

The alphabet is more familiar to us, which is why it is the organizing principle for phone books and dictionaries. The *Random House Webster's College Thesaurus* also uses alphabetical order, with all the main entry words in **boldface** type.

Following that word comes a label for the part of speech, including the noun (n.) and verb (v.), the adjective (adj.) and adverb (adv.), and, less commonly, preposition (prep.), conjunction (conj.), and interjection (interj.). When a main entry word has more than one part of speech, each part is listed separately.

Also separated under the main entry word are different clusters of meaning, each group having its own boldfaced number and list of synonyms. Each is introduced with one or more example sentences to shed light on meaning and show you how the word is used in context. The synonyms are arranged so that the most common ones, and the ones closest in meaning to the main entry word, come first. Sometimes semicolons distinguish whole clusters of synonyms so as to separate shades of meaning or levels of use. Lastly comes a list of antonyms: when needed, each list has a number that matches a list of related synonyms.

Few synonyms in English are truly identical in meaning and even apparently exact synonyms may differ in use. Words that come from Latin or French are often more formal than those deriving from Old English. Thus, although *perspire (French)* and *sweat (Old English)* mean the same thing, the former is considered a bit more genteel. Then we have differences among branches of English. *Autumn* and *fall* tend to be, respectively, British English and American. But far more important than these subtleties are all the aspects and refinements of meaning that related words can have, which is why, under **road,** you'll find *boulevard, highway, street,* and *path.* The *Random House Webster's College Thesaurus* further recognizes that sometimes you want not a synonym but a subset—something that is part of a larger unit: *wood* and *coal* are subsets of **fuel.** For these it uses the label *(variously).*

But *(variously)* isn't the only label *Random House* uses to help you to navigate through the maze of usage. Here and there you'll find labels like *(Informal), (Slang),* etc., to keep you from committing a contextual faux pas; *(medical), (nautical),* etc., to show that the word belongs to a specific field of knowledge or endeavor; and *(French), (Latin),* etc., to indicate that, although used in English, the word or phrase is mainly foreign.

Let us put it all together.

> **insane** adj. *1 The psychiatrists declared the killer insane. The letter made her insane with jealousy:* mentally deranged, not sane, not of sound mind, mad, crazed, crazy, lunatic, unsound, demented, maniacal, out of one's mind, bereft of reason, not in touch with reality, mentally disordered, unbalanced; (variously) psychotic, manic, schizophrenic, paranoiac; *Informal* out of one's wits, out of one's head, touched, mad as a hatter, mad as a March hare, stark staring mad, unhinged; *Slang* loco, teched, bats, batty, nuts, bats in the belfry, nutty, nutty as a fruitcake, balmy, loony, off one's rocker, cracked, zany; British daft, around the bend, off one's chump, potty, bonkers; raving, frenzied, wild, berserk. *2 It's insane to fly in this weather:* idiotic, senseless, unreasonable, foolish, dumb, imbecilic, mad, crazy; imprudent, injudicious; absurd, ridiculous, insensate; bizarre, eccentric.
> *Ant.* 1, 2 sane, sensible, judicious, wise, sapient, prudent, sound, reasonable.

To the **antonyms** for *insane* you may wish to add *Random House Webster's College Thesaurus.* It can't think, write, or speak for you. But, with eminent sanity, it can help you do these things a good deal better.

ACKNOWLEDGMENTS

This project has had, over the years, the benefit of many outstanding contributors who have worked with exceptional care and devotion. Eugene F. Shewmaker, Gloria Mihalyi Solomon, Robert L. Hurtgen, Dorothy Gerner Stein, Regina B. Wilson, and Keith Hollaman contributed much to the original project. We would also like to express our appreciation to Eric Stein, Sharon Leong, and Rose M. Price. We have had the advantage of access to much of the material in *The Family Word Finder* published by Reader's Digest, for which we are very grateful. The Random House Reference & Information Publishing staff has been generous with its help and guidance and checked the manuscript for accuracy and ease of use.

abaft *adv. The other vessel was abaft ours:* Nautical aft, astern, behind.

abandon *v.* **1.** *She abandoned her child on the doorstep of the church. Abandon ship!:* desert, forsake, leave, depart from, leave behind, withdraw from, evacuate; give up, quit, relinquish, jilt, run out on, let go, cast aside, turn one's back on, forswear, abdicate, renounce, repudiate. **2.** *The scientist abandoned his research for lack of funds:* discontinue, give up, drop, stop, cease, forgo, waive, discard, junk, wash one's hands of, get rid of, relinquish, forfeit, surrender, scrap. —*n.* **3.** *The Gypsies danced with abandon:* unrestraint, freedom; immoderation, intemperance; recklessness, wantonness, impulsiveness, impetuosity, spontaneity; enthusiasm, gusto, élan, exuberance, spirit, dash, verve, ardor, animation. —**Ant.** 1 claim, take; keep, hold, possess. 2 continue, maintain. 3 restraint, control, caution, prudence; moderation, tameness, deliberation.

abandoned *adj.* **1.** *The abandoned house was finally torn down:* deserted, forsaken, vacant, desolate, unoccupied; discarded, cast aside, cast away, relinquished, rejected, jilted, left behind, marooned, neglected. **2.** *The pleasure-seeker led an abandoned life:* debauched, debased, dissipated, dissolute, licentious, degraded, profligate, reprobate, shameless, immoral, disreputable, sinful, wild, wicked, loose, wanton, unprincipled; impure, unchaste, lewd; irreformable, irreclaimable, incorrigible, unrepentant. —**Ant.** 1 occupied; well-kept, kept, claimed. 2 virtuous, reputable, respectable, upright, high-principled, worthy, elevated, healthy, conscientious; moral, sinless, pure, chaste; reformed, redeemed, penitent, regenerate.

abandonment *n.* **1.** *Abandonment of spouses and children is a grave social problem:* desertion, forsaking, dereliction, jilting. **2.** *Starvation could only mean the city's abandonment:* evacuation, quitting. **3.** *The queen's exile followed abandonment of her throne:* relinquishment, abdication, renunciation. **4.** *The railroad decided on the branch line's abandonment:* discontinuation, dropping.

abase *v.* *The Bible says that the proud man shall be abased:* humble, bring low, cast down; *Informal* put down, badmouth, bring down a peg, cut down to size; humiliate, disgrace, dishonor, defame, discredit, belittle, malign, vilify, denigrate, vitiate; downgrade, degrade, demean, cheapen, devaluate, besmirch, debase; shame, mock, mortify. —**Ant.** elevate, raise, exalt, uplift, lift; dignify, honor, acclaim, praise, laud, extol; promote, upgrade, inflate.

abasement *n.* *The way he begged forgiveness suggested total abasement:* humbling, humiliation, dishonor, downgrading, debasement, demotion, reduction, shame, belittlement.

abashed *adj.* *He was abashed at forgetting his wife's birthday:* embarrassed, ashamed, chagrined, mortified, humiliated, humbled, selfconscious, dismayed, taken aback, bewildered, confused, dumbfounded, nonplussed, disconcerted,

disheartened, daunted, confounded, fazed; shy, bashful, cowed, overawed, subdued, crushed, intimidated. —**Ant.** proud, pleased, elated, exalted, buoyed; confident, poised, heartened, undaunted, emboldened, reassured.

abate *v.* *The wind abated after the storm:* decrease, diminish, reduce, lessen, subside, decline, fade, fade away, recede, dwindle, moderate, mitigate, weaken, wane, ebb, curtail, slack, slacken, go down, lower, fall off, fall away, taper off, lighten, soften, quiet, quell, slow, slow down, slake off, temper, cool, blunt; ease, relieve, alleviate, assuage, pacify, soothe, allay, mollify, palliate, dull; dampen, restrain, restrict. —**Ant.** increase, intensify, magnify, enhance, heighten, aggravate, amplify, grow; multiply, rise, come up, strengthen, sharpen, heat up; quicken, accelerate, hurry, speed, speed up; prolong, extend.

abatement *n.* **1.** *The next budget may give us a tax abatement:* alleviation, mitigation, lessening, letup, diminution, decrease, slackening. **2.** *Thicker walls contribute to noise abatement:* suppression, termination, ending, end, cessation. **3.** *The abatement of flooding resulted from drier weather:* subsidence, decline, sinking, way, ebb, slack, fade-out, fading. —**Ant.** 1 intensification, increase.

abbey *n.* *The monks live in their abbey in the mountains. Westminster Abbey is in London:* monastery, friary, cloister, priory, hermitage, cenoby; convent, nunnery; seminary; church, cathedral, chapel.

abbreviate *v.* *You can abbreviate the word "Mister" as "Mr." As time was short, he abbreviated his visit:* shorten, abridge, curtail, condense, compress, summarize, synopsize, contract, reduce, diminish; cut, cut down, cut short, boil down, trim, clip, truncate. —**Ant.** lengthen, extend, elongate, stretch, stretch out, draw out; expand, enlarge, amplify, increase, inflate, augment, add to, pad out; prolong, protract; write out, write in full.

abbreviation *n.* *"Mr." is the abbreviation of "Mister." The current edition is an abbreviation of an originally longer work:* shortened form, short form, shortening, condensed form, reduced form, compressed form, contracted form, cut-down form; reduction, contraction, diminution, abridgment, condensation, compression, abstraction, digest, synopsis, summary, abstract, brief; lessening, trimming, curtailment, cutting, clipping, pruning. —**Ant.** full form, written-out form; lengthening, extending, extension, elongation, stretching, stretching out, drawing out; expansion, enlargement, amplification, increase, increasing, augmentation, prolongation.

ABC's *n.* **1.** *Children must learn their ABC's:* alphabet, letters of alphabet. **2.** *The manual will give you the ABC's of engine repair:* essentials, rudiments, basics, fundamentals, principles, grammar, elements.

abdicate v. *Edward VIII of England abdicated to marry a commoner. He abdicated his throne:* renounce, resign, vacate the throne; re-linquish, give up, abnegate, abandon, surrender, abjure, quit, forgo, cede, waive, yield. —**Ant.** accede to the throne; claim, possess, usurp, assume, seize; keep.

abdication n. *The abdication of Edward VIII from his throne made headlines everywhere:* renunciation, disclaimer, disavowal, repudiation, resignation, retirement, quittance; abandonment, surrender, cession, waiver. —**Ant.** commitment.

abdomen n. *She tried various exercises to flatten her abdomen:* stomach, visceral cavity, venter, epigastrium; belly, tummy; gut, paunch, breadbasket, bay window, pot, pot belly.

abduct v. *Kidnappers abducted the child:* kidnap, carry off, make off with, run off with, steal, take away, bear off, seize. —**Ant.** return, bring back; free, set free; restore, relinquish, surrender.

abduction n. *Several people witnessed the abduction of the little girl:* kidnapping, capture, ravishment, seizure, rape.

abductor n. *Kidnap victims sometimes make friends with their abductors:* kidnapper, captor, ravisher, seizer, rapist.

aberrant adj. **1.** *The planet's orbit was plainly aberrant:* straying, stray, deviating, deviate, wandering, errant, erring, devious, erratic, rambling, diverging, divergent. **2.** *Aberrant behavior led to his confinement:* abnormal, irregular, unusual, odd, eccentric, peculiar, exceptional, weird, queer, curious, singular, strange; unconforming, nonconforming, anomalous. —**Ant.** 1 direct. 2 normal.

aberration n. **1.** *The flaw in a lens that doesn't focus properly is called spherical aberration. The new rules were confusing and full of aberrations:* irregularity, deviation, exception, departure, abnormality, anomaly, incongruity, divergence, digression, aberrance, aberrancy; wandering, rambling, straying, lapse. **2.** *His only aberration was an occasional lapse of memory:* minor mental disorder, mental lapse, abnormality, curiosity, quirk, peculiarity, idiosyncrasy, eccentricity, unconformity, nonconformity, oddity, singularity, strangeness, distortion, mutation; illusion, delusion, self-deception, hallucination; madness, insanity, lunacy, derangement. —**Ant.** 1, 2 normality, regularity, uniformity, conformity. 2 sanity, soundness of mind.

abet v. *The criminal was aided and abetted by his brother:* encourage, support, endorse, sustain, back, give moral support to, sanction, advocate, promote, advance, uphold, urge, urge on, goad, spur, incite, instigate; lead on, egg on; assist, help, aid, second, join with. —**Ant.** discourage, talk out of, dissuade, expose, denounce; deter, stop, check, hinder, impede, undermine, thwart, obstruct, balk.

abeyance n. *The building project will be held in abeyance until spring:* postponement, suspen-sion, intermission, remission, deferral, adjournment, discontinuance, inaction, dormancy, latency; pause, delay, cessation, quiescence, recess, hiatus, waiting period, in a holding pattern; in cold storage, on ice, on a back burner. —**Ant.** continuance, continuation, continuity, ceaselessness.

abhor v. *Nature abhors a vacuum. She abhors snakes:* detest, hate, loathe, dislike, despise, disdain, scorn, shun, abominate, execrate; feel aversion toward, be revolted by, find repulsive, shudder at, recoil at, shrink from, regard with repugnance, view with horror, eschew, can't stand, can't stomach, be nauseated by. —**Ant.** love, adore, like, delight in, dote on, cherish, relish, treasure, prize, value, enjoy, admire; desire, crave, covet.

abhorrence n. *She looked with abhorrence at bad table manners:* hate, hatred, loathing, execration, odium, abomination, aversion, repugnance, revulsion, disgust, horror, antipathy, detestation, animosity, enmity. —**Ant.** love.

abhorrent adj. **1.** *The brutal attack was abhorrent to everyone:* hateful, loathsome, antipathetic, detestable. **2.** *Torture of prisoners is abhorrent:* horrible, horrifying, shocking, disgusting, revolting, sickening, nauseating, repugnant, repulsive, odious; hateful, detestable, abominable, invidious. —**Ant.** 1 amiable, lovable.

abide v. **1.** *I can't abide loud noise:* bear, stand, tolerate, put up with, endure, last, stomach, brook; suffer, submit to, accept, stand for. **2.** *Abide with me a while longer:* stay, remain, tarry, linger, stop; live, reside, dwell; visit, sojourn, sit; *Slang* stick with, stick around. —**Ant.** 2 go, leave, quit, depart; escape, flee, fly; abandon, shun, avoid; move, migrate, journey.

abiding adj. *Abraham Lincoln had an abiding faith in the Union:* lasting, everlasting, enduring, eternal, unending, continuing, permanent, durable, firm, fast; changeless, unchanging, steadfast, constant, steady, unshakable, wholehearted, unquestioning, immutable, indissoluble. —**Ant.** temporary, passing, momentary, impermanent, ephemeral; weak, shaky, failing; changeable, fickle.

ability n. *A good salesman has the ability to sell anything:* capability, capacity, power, facility, faculty, aptitude, potential, potentiality, proficiency, knack, competence, qualification; skill, talent, knowhow, expertise, adeptness, adroitness, acumen; flair, genius, gift, mind for, bent. —**Ant.** inability, incapacity, incapability, inaptitude, incompetence, maladroitness; weakness, inadequacy, powerlessness, helplessness.

abject adj. **1.** *The old couple lived in abject poverty:* hopeless, inescapable, complete, thorough; wretched, miserable, deplorable, terrible, horrible. **2.** *The soldier deserted like an abject coward:* lacking courage, spiritless, cringing, groveling; contemptible, despicable, vile, base, mean, low, ignoble, sordid. —**Ant.** 1 hopeful; partial; dignified, honorable. 2 courageous, spirited, bold, staunch; manly, domineering, vain, arrogant, haughty, insolent; admirable, respected, esteemed, worthy.

abjectness n. **1.** *The abjectness of the ghetto cried out for drastic measures:* wretchedness, misery, destitution, forlornness, hopelessness. **2.** *The spectacle of the soldier's abjectness only made punishment more severe:* Cringing, groveling, spiritlessness, cowardice, contemptability, despicableness, vileness, baseness, meanness, ignobility.

abjure v. **1.** *Pacifism abjures the use of deadly force:* disclaim, disallow, repudiate, disavow, reject. **2.** *Some of the prisoners abjured their heresies and lived:* renounce, abandon, relinquish, desert, give up, forswear, recant. **—Ant.** maintain, embrace, swear by, uphold.

ablaze adj. **1.** *The house was completely ablaze when the fire trucks arrived:* burning, blazing, on fire, afire, conflagrant, flaming, aflame, in flames; ignited, alight; fiery, glowing. **2.** *The students were ablaze with enthusiasm after the coach's pep talk:* eager, excited, fervent, fervid, zealous, impassioned; feverish, flushed, intoxicated; red-hot, passionate, ardent; turned-on, hopped-up, switched-on.

able adj. **1.** *Our case was handled by two able lawyers:* skillful, proficient, capable, competent, expert, good, talented, highly qualified, accomplished, masterful, effective, efficient, adroit, adept, apt; experienced, practiced, learned. **2.** *The starving man was barely able to walk. We are not able to grant your request:* capable, fit, fitted, competent, having the means; equal to, adequate, qualified. **—Ant.** 1 unskillful, incapable, incompetent, inexpert, inept, inefficient, ineffective, amateurish; mediocre, indifferent, fair. 2 incapable, unfit, incompetent, inadequate, unqualified.

able-bodied adj. *We need four able-bodied men to move the piano:* muscular, brawny, robust, strong, vigorous, well-built, athletic, thewy, beefy, herculean, strapping, rugged, hardy, sturdy, stalwart, hearty, lusty, broad-shouldered. **—Ant.** weak, puny, flabby, feeble, frail, infirm.

ablution n. **1.** *After ablutions in the river, the holy man continued on his way:* ceremonial washing, ritualistic washing; bathing, cleansing, purification. **2.** *He had no time for his morning ablutions:* washing, bathing, cleaning, lavation; wash, bath.

abnegation n. *In a mood of abnegation, he gave up sweets and midnight snacks:* self-denial, sacrifice, renunciation, relinquishment, surrender, resignation, giving up, eschewal, forbearance, forbearing; abstinence, temperance, continence; rejection, refusal. **—Ant.** self-indulgence, indulgence, abandon; intemperance, incontinence; affirmation, concession.

abnormal adj. *That cat has an abnormal fear of birds. An abnormal amount of snow fell in October:* unnatural, atypical, unusual, irregular, aberrant, deviant, anomalous; uncommon, unconventional, exceptional, extraordinary, unexpected, unaccustomed, inordinate; strange, peculiar, rare, queer, odd, freakish, eccentric, bizarre, curious, outlandish, unheard of, gro-

tesque, weird, monstrous, deformed. **—Ant.** normal, natural, typical, usual, ordinary, common; conventional, routine, regular, expected, customary, familiar, unexceptional.

abnormality n. *A clubfoot is an abnormality that can often be corrected by surgery:* deformity, malformation; irregularity, aberration, aberrance, anomaly, deviation, perversion; oddity, curiosity, peculiarity, idiosyncrasy, eccentricity, unconformity.

abode n. *The hermit's abode was a cave:* residence, place of residence, dwelling place, habitat, dwelling, habitation; house, home, living quarters, domicile, lodging, address, *Slang* pad, nest.

abolish v. *Prohibition was abolished in 1933:* eliminate, eradicate, erase, obliterate, extinguish, exterminate, annihilate, extirpate, terminate, end, put an end to, wipe out, stamp out, blot out, do away with, squelch, quash; repeal, revoke, annul, nullify, invalidate, declare null and void, rescind, cancel; abrogate, vitiate, set aside, repudiate. **—Ant.** establish, institute, introduce, create, inaugurate, build, found; support, promote, increase, sustain, continue; revive, reinstate, renew, repair, restore, reintroduce; authorize, legalize, enact.

abolition n. *The senator fought for abolition of the income tax:* elimination, ending, termination, eradication, dissolution, extinction, abolishment, invalidation, vitiation; repeal, annulment, nullification, revocation, cancellation, recantation, retraction, rescinding, repudiation, abrogation. **—Ant.** establishment, institution, introduction, creation, inauguration, founding; authorization, legalization, enactment, passing; promotion; continuation; reinstatement, restoration, reintroduction.

abominable adj. **1.** *Murder is the most abominable crime:* detestable, despicable, contemptible, reprehensible, loathsome, hateful, abhorrent, execrable, disgusting, revolting, repulsive, repugnant, repellent, odious; vile, base, wretched, heinous, ignominious, villainous, infamous, atrocious, horrid, horrible, foul, hellish, damnable, evil, cursed, accursed. **2.** *The weather was abominable:* very unpleasant, disagreeable, miserable, terrible, deplorable, foul, extremely bad, unsuitable, awful, *Informal* lousy. **—Ant.** 1 laudable, praiseworthy, commendable, admirable, respectable, desirable, applaudable; satisfactory, gratifying, charming, enchanting, likable. 2 pleasant, agreeable, enjoyable, pleasing, delightful, good, wonderful, charming, suitable, *Informal* beautiful.

abominate v. *We abominate cruel practical jokes:* abhor, regard with aversion, detest, hate, loathe, execrate, contemn, despise, regard with repugnance, view with horror, shrink from, shudder at, bear malice *or* spleen. **—Ant.** like, love, enjoy.

abomination n. **1.** *The dirty streets of this city are an abomination!:* abhorrence, anathema, evil, obscenity, horror, disgrace, torment, defilement, plague, affliction, annoyance, bugbear, *French* bête noire. **2.** *My feeling of abomination* for concentration camps has never changed: revulsion, loathing, repugnance, disgust, detestation, hate, hatred, abhorrence, antipathy, aversion. —**Ant.** 1 delight, joy, pleasure, treat; benefit, blessing, boon, satisfaction, gratification. 2 love, liking, affection, fondness, relish, regard; admiration, appreciation, respect, approval, esteem.

aboriginal adj. The Indians were the aboriginal people of America: native, indigenous, original, endemic, autochthonous; earliest, first, ancient, primordial, primeval, primitive, primary, prime. —**Ant.** alien, foreign, immigrant, imported, exotic; late, recent, subsequent, successive, modern.

aborigine n. The Australian aborigines still hunt with spears: original inhabitant, primitive inhabitant, indigenous person; native, aboriginal. —**Ant.** alien, foreigner, immigrant; newcomer, late arrival, Johnny-come-lately.

abort v. **1.** Cows with Bang's disease often abort their calves: miscarry, terminate the pregnancy of. **2.** The astronauts aborted the space flight when their oxygen began to run low: terminate, end, halt, stop, call off; fail, fail to develop fully. —**Ant.** 1 give birth, bear, deliver. 2 carry through, see through, conclude, complete, finish; execute, perform, effect, achieve.

abortion n. **1.** Her pregnancy ended in an abortion: miscarriage, termination of pregnancy. **2.** The attempt to redesign the airplane was an abortion: failure, unsuccessful attempt, fruitless attempt, fiasco, disaster; halting, calling off, ending, termination. —**Ant.** 1 childbirth, parturition, giving birth, delivery. 2 success, successful completion, realization, achievement.

abortive adj. **1.** The abortive raid on the port led to many casualties: failing, unsuccessful, miscarrying, immature, premature. **2.** The fetus had only abortive limbs: undeveloped, underdeveloped, rudimentary, primitive. **3.** (medicine) Some crudely abortive methods can lead to infection: abortifacient. **4.** (pathology) Her cold proved to be abortive: short, mild, without symptoms. —**Ant.** 1 consummate.

abound v. Our garden abounds with roses. Tulips abound in Holland: teem, overflow, spill over, be flooded, be filled, have plenty of, luxuriate, be well supplied, be rich in, swarm, run wild, proliferate, superabound; exist in great numbers, be plentiful, flourish, thrive, be numerous; Informal gush. —**Ant.** lack, want, have too few, be deficient in, fall short, be scant; be in short supply.

abounding adj. The abounding crops of the countryside astonished onlookers: plentiful, abundant, bountiful, prolific, teeming, profuse, full, ample, lavish.

about prep. **1.** The debate was about whether to raise taxes: of, concerning, in regard to, respecting, with regard or respect or reference to, relating or relative to; connected with, in connection with, relating or relative to. **2.** It's nice to have a pet about the house: near, around, round, not far from, close to. **3.** That will cost you about three dollars: near, close to, approxi-

mately, almost. **4.** There was a moat about the castle: around, circling, encircling, inclosing, enclosing, surrounding **5.** Do you have any loose change about you?: on one's person, having in one's possession. **6.** I'm about ready to go: on the point of, ready, prepared. **7.** Unable to sleep, he paced about the house: here and there, in, on, hither and yon, to and fro, back and forth, hither and thither. —adv. **8.** She was about exhausted: near, approximately, nearly, almost, well-nigh. **9.** She is somewhere about: nearby, close, not far, around. **10.** We were ringed about by enemies: on every side, in every direction, all around, everywhere, every, all over. **11.** Turn about and you'll see who's following: half round, reversed, backwards, opposite direction. **12.** We shared the task turn and turn about: in succession, alternately, in rotation.

about-face n. The senator did an about-face on his support of tax cuts: reversal, rightabout, turnaround, tergiversation, reverse, turnabout, switch, shift, French volte-face; change of heart, disavowal, recantation, retraction.

above adv. **1.** Window-cleaners were working above our heads: overhead, aloft, on high, atop, on top of. **2.** Costs were above the estimate: higher, beyond, over, superior, surpassing. **3.** The meaning was clearer in the paragraph above: before, prior, earlier, sooner, previous, first. **4.** To some, God reigns above us: in heaven, on high, in excelsis. —prep. **5.** She valued dignity above comfort: over, in a higher than, higher than, superior to. **6.** The cat was above average in weight: more, greater than, more than, exceeding. **7.** She considered herself above mundane concerns: superior to, beyond, surpassing. —adj. **8.** The above clause in the contract is ambiguous: supra, said, written, mentioned previously, foregoing, preceding.

aboveboard adj. All of his criticisms seemed fair and aboveboard: candid, open, honest, truthful, forthright, straightforward, sincere, frank, straight, square-dealing, plain-dealing, straight-shooting, undissembling, on the up and up, square, foursquare; guileless, ingenuous, artless; blunt, direct, plain, unconcealed. —**Ant.** devious, roundabout, evasive, underhand.

abracadabra n. You may have to use some abracadabra to get that lock to work: hocus-pocus, mumbo-jumbo, open sesame; witchcraft, sorcery, voodoo, magic, magic spell, incantation, invocation, spell, charm, exorcism.

abrade v. Constant use had abraded the doorstep: wear off, wear down, scrape off; erode, wear away, rub off.

abrasion n. **1.** The abrasion on his knee soon healed: scraped spot, scrape; scratch, lesion. **2.** Years of abrasion had worn the stones smooth: scraping, grating, rubbing, friction, excoriation, scouring, chafing; erosion, wearing away, wearing down.

abrasive n. **1.** Use sandpaper or some other abrasive to remove the paint: scraping material, grinding material, scouring material; smoothing substance. —*adj.* **2.** *The speaker's abrasive re-marks insulted the audience:* harsh, coarse, annoying, irritating, excoriating; rasping, grating, rough, caustic, sharp, cutting, biting, nasty, hurtful, galling, chafing. —**Ant.** 2 mild, soothing, healing, comforting, gentle, pleasant, agreeable.

abreast *adv., adj. The soldiers marched three abreast:* side by side, in a line across, in rank, aligned, in alignment. —**Ant.** one behind another, one after another, in single file, Indian file.

abridge *v.* **1.** *The book was abridged to a more readable length:* shorten, condense, reduce, compress, digest, abbreviate, cut, cut down, scale down, pare down, trim, telescope, truncate. **2.** *No one can abridge your legal rights:* restrict, limit, curtail, diminish, lessen, reduce, decrease; deprive one of, take away. —**Ant.** 1 expand, enlarge, lengthen, increase, extend, amplify; prolong; augment, add to, supplement. 2 increase, augment, add to.

abridgment *n.* **1.** *Have you seen the new abridgment of Gibbon's Roman history?:* shortened form, condensed form, condensation, abbreviation, digest, truncation. **2.** *The city council voted for an abridgment of the mayor's power:* restriction, limitation, restraint, curtailment, reduction, lessening, decrease, diminishing, diminution. —**Ant.** 1 lengthened version. 2 expansion, enlargement, amplification, increase, augmentation, extension, inflation.

abroad *adv.* **1.** *On our trip abroad we visited relatives in England:* overseas, out of the country. **2.** *It's unsafe to be abroad at night in some parts of New York City:* out of doors, outside, out, out of the house, forth, out in the open air. **3.** *A thousand rumors were abroad:* in circulation, at large, making the rounds, all around, round and about; spread far and wide, rife, astir. —**Ant.** 1 nearby, near home; in one's native land, within the country. 2 indoors, inside, in, in the house, at home, within four walls; *French* chez soi, *German* zuhause.

abrogate *v. Congress must abrogate the new tax law:* abolish, cancel, terminate, put an end to, end, do away with, quash; repeal, revoke, rescind, annul, nullify, void, invalidate, set aside, override, reverse, undo, negate, dissolve, vitiate; retract, countermand, recall withdraw, repudiate, renounce, abjure; *Informal* junk, throw out. —**Ant.** institute, establish, create, found; enact, ratify, fix; confirm, sustain, uphold, support, sanction; continue; revive, renew.

abrogation *n. Tension between the countries led to abrogation of their treaty:* abolition, cancellation, annulment, repeal, disannulment, revocation, rescission, nullification, invalidation. —**Ant.** establishment.

abrupt *adj.* **1.** *The car came to an abrupt stop at the barricade:* sudden, unexpected, unforeseen, unanticipated, impulsive, unlooked for, unannounced; hasty, quick, rapid, swift, instantaneous, precipitate. **2.** *His abrupt reply hurt our feelings:* curt, brusque, blunt, brisk, gruff, short, crisp; discourteous, impolite, uncivil, ungra-

cious, unceremonious, rude, rough. **3.** *The cliff made an abrupt descent to the sea:* steep, sheer, sharp, precipitous. —**Ant.** 1 anticipated, expected, foreseen; gradual, leisurely, unhurried, deliberate, slow, easy. 2 courteous, polite, gracious, thoughtful, civil; gentle, easy. 3 gradual, smooth, easy, slow.

abscond *v. The thief absconded with the jewels:* flee, take flight, fly, vanish, disappear, depart hastily, leave suddenly; take off, make off, steal off, steal away; escape, run away, run off; *Informal* skip; *Slang* split.

absence *n.* **1.** *The teacher noted the student's absence:* not being present, nonattendance, nonpresence, nonappearance, absenteeism; truancy, cut. **2.** *He shows an absence of initiative:* lack, unavailability, nonexistence; scarcity, deficiency, insufficiency, scantiness, want, dearth. —**Ant.** 1 presence, attendance, appearance. 2 existence, supply; abundance, plenty, sufficiency, adequacy, surfeit, plethora.

absent *adj.* **1.** *Why were you absent from class yesterday?:* not present, nonpresent, nonattendant; away, gone, missing, out, truant. **2.** *He gave her an absent look:* inattentive, unthinking, heedless, oblivious, unaware, unconscious, absent-minded, preoccupied, distracted; vacant, blank, faraway, removed, empty, vague, dreamy, musing; *Slang* out of it, tuned out, out to lunch. —*v.* **3.** *Why did you absent yourself from the meeting yesterday?:* cause to be not present, fail to attend, not appear, stay away, keep away, play truant, *Informal* not show up, cut. —**Ant.** 1 present, in attendance, attendant. 2 attentive, thoughtful, meaningful, conscious, aware, alert; *Slang* with it, tuned in. 3 attend, appear at, show up.

absentee *n. There was a sharp rise in the number of absentees during the summer holidays:* truant, deserter, runaway; apostate, renegade, backslider; slacker, shirker, malingerer, quitter.

absenteeism *n. Absenteeism was chronic at the defense plant:* truancy, nonattendance, defection, absence, desertion.

absently *adv. She stared absently into the middle distance:* vacantly, abstractedly, distractedly, inattentively, bemusedly.

absent-minded *adj. He's so absent-minded he's lost three hats:* forgetful, distracted, withdrawn, unheeding, unmindful, preoccupied, absent, faraway, woolgathering, oblivious, engrossed, absorbed, lost in thought, daydreaming, distrait; out of it, not with it. —**Ant.** attentive, alert, heedful, observant; with it, hip.

absolute *adj.* **1.** *The emperor was an absolute monarch:* unrestricted, unrestrained, unlimited, unconditional, unqualified, unbounded; complete, supreme, pure, full, *Informal* out-and-out. **2.** *His story was an absolute lie:* complete, pure, total, definite, thorough, unqualified, unrestricted, unadulterated, unmitigated, utter, sheer, unlimited; perfect, consummate, outright; *Informal* out-and-out, through and through. **3.** *The police have absolute proof of his guilt:* positive, definite, conclusive, sheer, certain, sure, decisive; real, genuine, reliable, unqualified, unmitigated, unquestionable, undeniable, confirmed, infallible, unequivocal. —**Ant.** 1 restricted, restrained, conditional, limited, provisional, qualified; constitutional. 2, 3 qualified, limited, partial, conditional, provisional, questionable, dubious, unconfirmed, equivocal; not complete, incomplete.

absolutely adv. **1.** I am absolutely sure he was the one who held up the bank: entirely, completely, thoroughly, wholly, utterly, definitely, positively; unconditionally, without limitation. **2.** Good nutrition is absolutely essential for your health: positively, certainly, utterly, definitely, decidedly, truly, really, indeed; undoubtedly, unquestionably, unequivocally, indubitably. —**Ant.** 1 somewhat, fairly, reasonably, approximately. 2 probably, conditionally.

absoluteness n. **1.** Only some philosophies pretend to absoluteness: wholeness, perfection, consummateness, totality, purity. **2.** The absoluteness of her conviction persuaded us: certainty, conviction, conclusiveness, infallibility, positiveness, decidedness. **3.** The absoluteness of the chairman's regime allowed no room for critical comment: tyranny, unquestionability, arbitrariness, supremacy, despotism.

absolution n. The pilgrims came to the shrine, seeking absolution for their sins: pardon, amnesty, forgiveness, mercy, deliverance, vindication, quittance, exculpation, exoneration, remission, acquittal, clearance, dispensation, indulgence, liberation, release. —**Ant.** blame, censure, condemnation, conviction, prosecution.

absolutism n. Absolutism was the mark of the last dynasty: totalitarianism, autarchy, autocracy, dictatorship, tyranny.

absolve v. **1.** The priest absolved their sins: pardon, forgive, shrive, declare removed. **2.** The jury absolved him of the crime: acquit, find not guilty, judge innocent; exonerate, vindicate, exculpate, clear. **3.** I was absolved of having to pay my partner's debts: release, free, set free, excuse from, exempt, discharge, loose, deliver. —**Ant.** 1 accuse, blame; condemn. 2 convict, charge, find guilty. 3 obligate, oblige, bind, hold to, be held responsible.

absorb v. **1.** The sponge absorbed all the spilled water: soak up, take up, suck up, swallow up, drink in, sponge up. **2.** Can the students absorb this lesson in an hour?: take in completely, assimilate, incorporate, digest, ingest; Informal drink in, make part of oneself. **3.** I was so absorbed in this book that I didn't hear you: engross, immerse, occupy, preoccupy, consume, engage, enwrap; arrest, rivet, fix, fascinate. —**Ant.** 1 exude, eject, cast off, cast out, disperse, dispel; drip. 2 give out, disperse, impart. 3 unoccupy; distract.

absorbent adj. Blotting paper and terry cloth are extremely absorbent materials: permeable, spongy, penetrable, absorptive, porous, thirsty, pervious, bibulous, osmotic, assimilative. —**Ant.** moistureproof, waterproof, water-repellent, impermeable, watertight, impenetrable.

absorbing adj. Boys find Tom Sawyer an absorbing book: fascinating, interesting, engrossing, captivating, intriguing, engaging; exciting, thrilling.

absorption n. A new pill aided the body's absorption of nutrients: assimilation, incorporation, osmosis, consumption, digestion, imbibing, ingestion, intake, saturation.

abstain v. Vegetarians abstain from eating meat: refrain, desist, forbear, eschew, avoid, forgo, hold back, decline, refuse; deny oneself, resist. —**Ant.** partake of, indulge in, yield to, surrender, give in to; overdo, abandon oneself to, make a slave of oneself to.

abstemious adj. His abstemious habits allowed him few pleasures: abstinent, ascetic, austere, temperate, continent, nonindulgent, teetotal, self-denying, sparing, self-disciplined, abstentious. —**Ant.** self-indulgent, abandoned, undisciplined, uncontrolled, hedonistic, profligate, licentious, unrestrained, immoderate.

abstention n. Vegetarians are known for their abstention from eating meat: abstaining, nonindulgence, refraining, desisting, holding back, forbearance, eschewing, eschewal, avoidance, refusal; nonparticipation, denying oneself, resist-ance. —**Ant.** indulgence, abandon.

abstinence n. I admire Quakers for their abstinence: nonindulgence, self-denial, self-restraint, self-control, discipline, forbearance, abstention; (variously) temperance, sobriety; continence, chastity. —**Ant.** indulgence, self-indulgence, abandon, excess; (variously) intemperance, dissipation; wantonness; gorging, gluttony; greediness, covetousness, graspingness, acquisitiveness.

abstinent adj. The abstinent members swore off every form of stimulant: abstemious, temperate, moderate, self-controlled, self-restraining, self-denying, forbearing, temperate. —**Ant.** self-indulgent.

abstract adj. **1.** Abstract ideas may lead to concrete plans: theoretical, theoretic, conceptual, unapplied, general, generalized, imaginary, visionary, intangible, hypothetical, indefinite, nonspecific, remote, impractical; subtle, profound, abstruse, obscure, esoteric, recondite, arcane, intellectual. —n. **2.** Please write an abstract of this scientific article: summary, synopsis, précis, résumé, brief, recapitulation; digest, extract, condensation, abridgment; outline. —v. **3.** This machine abstracts salt from sea water: extract, remove, withdraw, take out, take; separate, dissociate, isolate. **4.** Please abstract this scientific article: summarize, synopsize; digest, condense, abridge, compress; outline. —**Ant.** 1 concrete, obvious, specific, clear, uncomplicated, material; practical; factual, definite, real, actual. 2 amplification, enlargement, expansion. 3 add, inject; mix, unite, combine.

abstraction n. Even in a crowded room, she showed great powers of abstraction: detachment, pensiveness, preoccupation, remoteness, reflection, pensiveness, aloofness, contemplation, reverie, ruminating.

absurd adj. It's absurd to believe that the earth

is flat. The clown wore an absurd costume: unreasonable, illogical, irrational, preposterous, senseless; ridiculous, foolish, inane, silly, stupid, ludicrous, idiotic, nonsensical, asinine, comical, farcical; funny, laughable; *Informal* crazy, wild; *Slang* screwy, kooky. **—Ant.** reasonable, logical, sensible, rational, sound; smart, intelligent, sagacious, judicious, prudent, wise.

absurdity *n. His story of being kidnapped by little green men was sheer absurdity. The absurdities of the playful little monkeys amused us:* nonsense, unreasonableness, unbelievability, idiocy, inanity, asininity, irrationality, ridiculousness, drivel; falsehood, fallacy, delusion; foolishness, buffoonery, comicalness, silliness. **—Ant.** truth; reasonableness, credibility; wisdom, sagacity.

abtruse *adj. Mathematics can be an abstruse subject:* hard to understand, obscure, incomprehensible, unfathomable, complex, complicated, puzzling, perplexing, arcane, enigmatic; profound, deep, subtle, abstract, remote, esoteric, recondite. **—Ant.** simple, direct, easy, obvious, straightforward, clear, uncomplicated; superficial, light, amusing, entertaining.

abundance *n. There was such an abundance of food that we all overate:* ample amount, great supply, full measure, profusion, sufficiency; excess, more than enough, plenty, surplus, glut, plenitude, repletion, plethora, surfeit, cornucopia, copiousness; heap, flood, bounty, wealth, richness. **—Ant.** scarcity, deficiency, lack, dearth, scantiness, sparseness, paucity.

abundant *adj. There is abundant water despite the dry spell:* ample, sufficient, enough, plenty, more than enough, profuse, copious, prolific, bounteous, bountiful, abounding, lavish, rich, luxuriant, brimming, teeming; rife, replete, galore. **—Ant.** insufficient, scant, sparse, meager, uncommon, scarce, skimpy, sparing.

abuse *v.* **1.** *A good workman doesn't abuse his tools. Stop abusing that dog!:* misuse, use improperly, exploit, take advantage of, ill-use; mistreat, maltreat, ill-treat; harm, hurt, injure, torment, excoriate; impose upon. **2.** *The old shrew abused everyone in a loud voice:* insult, speak ill of, scold, berate, carp at, rail at, revile, vilify, castigate; speak harshly to, reproach, criticize, censure, bawl out, upbraid; belittle, deride, malign, ridicule, slur, denigrate; curse, slander, *Slang* badmouth, denounce, defame, disparage, inveigh against. **—***n.* **3.** *Borrowing money is sometimes an abuse of friendship:* misuse, unfair use, improper use, misapplication, misemployment; exploitation, imposition. **4.** *Child abuse is a punishable offense:* mistreatment, maltreatment, oppression, ill-use, torment, cruelty; injury, harming, beating, assault. **5.** *I'll listen to no more of your abuse!:* insulting language, insults, harsh language, torments; berating, railing, invective, tirade; reproach, criticism, tongue-lashing, censure, scolding, upbraiding, castigation, diatribe, carping; belittling, sneering, disparagement, slander, ridicule, derision, vilification; cursing, defamatory remarks, defamation. **—Ant.** 1 respect, protect, care for.

2 praise, speak well of, compliment, extol, laud, flatter, sweet-talk, acclaim. 5 praise, compliment, acclaim; flattery.

abusive *adj.* **1.** *Please don't use such abusive language:* insulting, harsh, vituperative, mean railing, acrimonious; offensive, obscene, foulmouthed, vile, rude, gross; derogatory, disparaging, defamatory, scurrilous, deprecatory, castigating, critical, censorious, slanderous, reviling, maligning, vilifying, scornful. **2.** *He was arrested for his abusive treatment of the dog:* cruel, improper; harmful, hurtful, injurious. **—Ant.** 1 laudatory, flattering, complimentary, praising, extolling, mild, courteous, respectful, polite. 2 kind; just.

abut *v. There is a fence where the two yards abut:* meet end to end, meet, join, adjoin, touch; border, be contiguous, be adjacent to, be next to.

abysmal *adj. The serfs were maintained in a state of abysmal ignorance:* thorough, endless, unending, complete; bottomless, boundless, incredible, unbelievable, unimaginable, unfathomable, deep, profound, enormous, extreme, vast, stupendous, immense.

abyss *n. One slip on this mountain and you'll fall into the abyss:* bottomless pit, vast chasm, crevasse, fissure, gorge, gully; void, depth, nadir, gulf. **—Ant.** elevation, height; mountain, hill, mount; summit, zenith.

academic *adj.* **1.** *He remembered his academic days fondly:* school, scholastic, educational; collegiate, university. **2.** *A good historian must have an academic mind:* scholarly, studious, learned, educated, erudite; pedantic, bookish. **3.** *One brother went to an academic high school, the other to a trade school:* general, liberal-arts, scholastic, college-preparatory; nontechnical, nonvocational, nonspecialized. **4.** *How to talk to a Martian is rather an academic question:* theoretical, hypothetical, abstract, moot, speculative, conjectural, suppositional, presumptive; not practical, remote, ivory-towered. **—Ant.** 2 nonscholarly, nonstudious, unpedantic; uneducated, unschooled, untaught, unlettered, unlearned. 3 technical, vocational, trade, specialized. 4 practical, realistic, immediate, common-sense; everyday, functional, ordinary, matter-of-course, matter-of-fact.

accede *v.* **1.** *The mayor acceded to the citizens' demands:* consent to, approve, agree to, grant, assent to, accept, concur with; concede, permit, yield to, submit to, defer to, acquiesce, surrender to; subscribe to, abide by, comply with, conform to; admit, acknowledge, endorse. **2.** *When the king dies, the crown prince will accede to the throne:* succeed to, inherit. **—Ant.** 1 reject, refuse, disallow, spurn, decline, veto; oppose, object to, resist, protest, disapprove, demur; shy away from, balk at.

accelerate *v.* **1.** *The car suddenly accelerated:* to go faster, to move faster, speed up, pick up speed, quicken pace. **2.** *Fertilizer will accelerate the growth of these tomato plants:* speed up, hurry, quicken, hasten, rush, step up, augment, spur; expedite, further, promote, advance, precipitate, facilitate, intensify, impel. —**Ant.** 1, 2 slow, slow down, decelerate, brake. 2 delay, retard, slacken, hinder, impede, hamper, obstruct.

acceleration *n. The car had rapid acceleration:* speeding up, stepping up, quickening, hurrying, hastening, dispatch, expedition.

accent *n.* **1.** *The word "woman" has its accent on the first syllable:* stress, emphasis; primary accent, primary stress. **2.** *She speaks with a German accent:* pronunciation, enunciation, articulation, inflection, manner of speaking, twang, drawl; intonation, tone, modulation, tonality. **3.** *The room was all white with a few red accents:* hint, touch, embellishment, detail; ornament, adornment, trimming. —*v* **4.** *Accent the word "woman" on the first syllable:* stress, emphasize, accentuate, punctuate, give prominence to; underline, underscore, feature, spotlight, highlight.

accept *v.* **1.** *She accepted his invitation to dance:* take something offered, receive willingly, receive with favor. **2.** *I accept your apology. The police accepted his story as true:* agree to, consent to, grant as satisfactory, accede to, go along with, assent to, receive with approval, acknowledge; *Slang* swallow, buy, fall for. **3.** *The boy accepted full responsibility for breaking the window:* assume, undertake, bear, acknowledge, admit, avow. —**Ant.** 1, 2 refuse, reject, decline, spurn, turn down, resist. 3 disown, repudiate; deny, disavow, disacknowledge.

acceptable *adj.* **1.** *The lawyers found the contract acceptable:* capable of being accepted, agreeable, proper, suitable, admissible, satisfactory; worthy, good. **2.** *His grades are acceptable, but he's not on the honor roll:* adequate, suitable, passable, tolerable, allowable, fair; barely satisfactory, *Informal* so-so. —**Ant.** 1, 2 unacceptable, unsatisfactory, unsuitable, inadmissible, substandard.

acceptance *n.* **1.** *His acceptance of bribes led to his arrest:* accepting, taking, receiving; receipt, reception. **2.** *The employer gave his acceptance to the worker's suggestions:* approval, consent, agreement, permission, concession, acquiescence; *Informal* O.K., stamp of approval; sanction, endorsement, affirmation. **3.** *It took years for Einstein's theory to gain acceptance:* approval, approbation, belief, recognition, acknowledgment; affirmation, confirmation. —**Ant.** 1, 2 rejection, refusal, repudiation; disapproval. 3 rejection; disavowal.

accepted *adj. Camels are an accepted means of transportation in the desert:* agreed upon, approved, acceptable, confirmed, acknowledged, established; common, normal, usual, conventional, standard, regular, customary, universal, time-honored.

access *n.* **1.** *How could the thief have gained access to the vault? The senator has access to the President:* admittance; entrance, entrée. **2.** *Switzerland has access to the sea via the Rhine River:* a means of reaching, an approach, passage, passageway, gateway, entrance, entry; road, path, way, avenue, course.

accessible *adj.* **1.** *A doctor must have a tele-*phone accessible at all times: available, ready, at hand, on hand, handy, within reach, nearby; obtainable, attainable, reachable, possible. **2.** *The principal was always accessible to the students:* available, approachable, reachable. —**Ant.** 1 unavailable, far-off, unobtainable, impossible, beyond reach; hidden, hidden away, se-creted. 2 unapproachable, unavailable, inaccessible, unreachable, standoffish, forbidding.

accession *n. Her accession to the throne nearly caused a civil war:* assumption, induction, installation, investment, inheritance, inauguration, taking over, arrogation; seizure, usurpation. —**Ant.** abdication, deposition, resignation, renunciation.

accessory *n.* **1.** *The new auditorium was a welcome accessory to the school:* addition, supplement, plus; adjunct, attachment, component, extension, auxiliary. **2.** *This belt makes a beautiful accessory to your dress:* accompaniment, adornment, decoration; complement, accent, detail. **3.** *The getaway driver was convicted as an accessory in the robbery:* accomplice, confederate, partner; associate, cohort, colleague, assistant, contributor, auxiliary.

accident *n.* **1.** *Columbus discovered America by accident:* chance, fluke, happenstance; luck, fate, good fortune, fortuity, serendipity. **2.** *An ambulance rushed to the scene of the accident. He broke his leg in a skiing accident:* collision, crash, wreck, smashup; mishap, misadventure, mischance; bit of bad luck, misfortune. —**Ant.** 1 plan, intention, intent, design, calculation, purpose.

accidental *adj. Our meeting on the street was purely accidental:* unplanned, unintentional, unpremeditated, uncalculated, unwitting, unforeseen; unexpected, unanticipated, fortuitous, serendipitous; chance, haphazard, random, incidental, inadvert. —**Ant.** planned, intentional, intended, premeditated, calculated; foreseen, expected; prepared, designed, projected.

acclaim *v.* **1.** *Critics acclaimed the new play:* praise, loudly approve, applaud, cheer, hail; laud, extol, commend, sing the praises of, exalt, cheer, compliment, eulogize; honor, celebrate, salute. **2.** *The people acclaimed him king:* name by acclamation. —*n.* **3.** *The new opera was greeted with acclaim:* great praise, loud approval, applause, plaudits, kudos, bravos, cheering, ovation, acclamation, endorsement, rejoicing, enthusiasm. —**Ant.** 1 criticize, denounce, condemn, disapprove, *Informal* pan, boo, hiss, heckle, shout down, give the raspberry, give the Bronx cheer; *Slang* razz. 3 criticism, condemnation, disapproval, *Informal* panning, booing, hissing, heckling; *Slang* razzing.

acclaimed *adj. The acclaimed Shakespearean actor triumphed in his first Broadway role:* praised, honored, famed, renowned, celebrated, prominent, world-renowned, world-famous, stellar.

acclamation *n. The queen received an acclamation from the crowd. He was elected president of the union by acclamation:* ovation, burst of applause, cheering, shout of approval, salutation; acclaim, homage, tribute, approbation, plaudits, adulation; cheers, hurrahs, hosannas. —**Ant.** booing, hissing, Bronx cheers; disapproval, denunciation, censure, disapprobation, execration, excoriation.

acclimate v. In a few days you'll be acclimated to the cold weather: get used to, accustom, adapt, adjust, reconcile, habituate, become seasoned to, accommodate, inure.

accolade n. The Nobel prize is the highest accolade a writer can receive: award, honor, tribute, prize, trophy, decoration, citation, testimonial; praise, compliment, commendation, acclaim, recognition, admiration.

accommodate v. **1.** Can you accommodate me with a loan?: do a kindness for, do a favor for; oblige, help, aid, assist; supply, provide, furnish, lend a hand. **2.** This hotel can accommodate 500 guests: have capacity for, furnish room for, house, billet, quarter, shelter, board, bed down; entertain; hold, contain; lodge, put up. **3.** You'll have to accommodate yourself to the situation: adapt, adjust, fit, acclimate, accustom, bring into line; conform, modify, harmonize; reconcile, Informal get used to. —**Ant.** 1 inconvenience, disoblige, trouble.

accommodating adj. The cab driver was very accommodating: obliging, helpful, considerate, kind, hospitable, Informal neighborly; polite, courteous, gracious; conciliatory, yielding. —**Ant.** disobliging, inconsiderate; rude, churlish.

accommodation n. **1.** What kind of accommodations did you have on the ship?: rooms, quarters, lodgings, housing; arrangements. **2.** If labor and management don't reach an accommodation there will be a strike: compromise, settlement, adjustment; agreement, concord, reconciliation.

accompany v. **1.** My daughter accompanied me on the trip. Secret Service agents accompany the President everywhere: go in company with, go along with, attend; conduct; escort, chaperon, convoy, usher, guard, Informal back up, support, attend. **2.** Suffering accompanies war: to occur with, go together with, go hand in hand with, go hand in glove with, be connected with, coexist with, follow. **3.** The pianist accompanied her singing: play accompaniment for, supply music for, provide background or harmony for, back up.

accomplice n. The butler was an accomplice in the robbery: confederate, accessory, partner, collaborator, co-conspirator, partner-in-crime, Informal crony; associate, cohort, colleague, ally, comrade, Informal henchman, sidekick; assistant subordinate, aide, helper, supporter, abettor, Slang stooge; participant.

accomplish v. **1.** Henry Ford accomplished what he set out to do: achieve, succeed at, carry out, do; perform, realize, execute, attain, fulfill; bring about, produce, expedite, Slang knock off. **2.** If you organize your work you'll accomplish more: do, get done, finish, complete, achieve, realize, Slang knock off. —**Ant.** 1 fail, fall

short, miss the mark; give up, forsake. 2 leave undone.

accomplished adj. **1.** Space flight is an accomplished fact: existing, realized, effected, completed, consummated; established, accepted, proven, proved, concluded. **2.** Van Cliburn is an accomplished pianist: expert, able, proficient, capable, fine, skilled, skillful; masterly, practiced, well-trained, finished, experienced, seasoned, eminent, polished, cultivated; talented, gifted, brilliant, adroit, deft, apt, qualified. —**Ant.** 1 nonexistent, unrealized, unestablished, unproven. 2 unskilled, poor, incompetent, incapable, inept, inexpert; inexperienced; unpolished, crude; untalented, amateurish, clumsy.

accomplishment n. **1.** All nations must work for the accomplishment of peace: achievement, realization, execution, attainment, triumph, victory, fulfillment, success, carrying out; culmination, consummation. **2.** Developing the supersonic jet was quite an accomplishment: achievement, feat, tour de force, success, attainment, exploit, triumph, victory; deed, act. **3.** Playing the piano is but one of her accomplishments: achievement, feat, skill; talent, gift, proficiency, capability. —**Ant.** 1 failure. 2 failure, blunder. 3 lack, deficiency, lacuna, incapacity.

accord v. **1.** The views of the President and Vice President accord on the new tax bill: agree, concur; conform, correspond, be in unison, match, comply with, tally, jibe, harmonize; Informal square, be in tune, go along with. **2.** High honors were accorded him when he graduated: grant, present, give, bestow, award, render, tender, bequeath, vouchsafe; concede, allow, cede. —n. **3.** Our views on politics are not in accord: agreement, harmony, accordance, mutual understanding, concurrence, unison, concert, unanimity, uniformity, conformity, consonance; rapport, sympathy. —**Ant.** 1 differ, disagree, conflict, clash, collide, contrast. 2 withhold, deny, refuse, hold back. 3 conflict, discord, disagreement, dissidence, dissension; variance, contention.

accordingly adv. **1.** I'm an adult and I expect to be treated accordingly: in accordance with the fact, correspondingly, suitably, conformably. **2.** This furnace cost a lot of money; accordingly, it should perform perfectly: therefore, thus, so, hence, wherefore, whereupon, consequently, as a result, ergo; in which case, then, whence, thence, in due course. —**Ant.** 1 conversely.

accost v. A beggar accosted me in front of the hotel: hail, call to, speak to suddenly, greet, salute, address; confront, approach, buttonhole, waylay, Informal nab, stop, halt; solicit, make an appeal to, proposition. —**Ant.** evade, avoid, ignore, overlook; slight, shun.

account n. **1.** Give us a full account of your vacation: description, report; story, history, record, chronicle, tale, narrative, narration, commentary; explanation, version, statement, enumeration, recital, Slang megillah. **2.** The student disobeyed the rules and on this account is being *expelled from school:* reason, cause, grounds, basis, sake, consideration, regard, *Informal* score. **3.** *These old letters are of no account:* importance, import, worth, significance, consequence, note; value, use, merit; esteem, honor, repute, distinction, dignity, standing, rank. **4.** *My wife handles our household accounts:* financial record, financial statement, bookkeeping, books, accounting. —*v.* **5.** *He accounts himself lucky to be alive after that accident:* consider, regard, believe, look upon as, view as, think, judge, count, deem, hold, take to be; rate, estimate, calculate, reckon, value, appraise, weigh, gauge. **6.** *Can you account for your strange behavior?:* explain, justify, clarify, illuminate, give a reason for, show cause.

accountable *adj. You will be held accountable if any of the money is missing:* liable, answerable, responsible, obligated, chargeable, to blame, guilty, at fault, culpable, blameworthy. —**Ant.** blameless, exempt, innocent, guiltless, excused, clear.

accountant *n. An accountant helped me fill out my income tax form:* certified public accountant, CPA; bookkeeper, auditor, actuary.

accredit *v.* **1.** *The new ambassador is fully accredited by his government:* furnish with credentials, certify, license, endorse, guarantee, commission, authorize, sanction, officially recognize; empower. **2.** *The invention of the electric light is accredited to Thomas Alva Edison:* attribute, ascribe, assign, credit.

accretion *n. The coral reef was built up by accretions over thousands of years:* increase, addition, supplement, increment, augmentation, rise, accumulation, accrual, growth, extension, expansion, enlargement, amplification. —**Ant.** loss, decrease, diminution, shrinkage, reduction.

accrue *v. Interest on money in a savings account accrues regularly:* accumulate, collect, build up, amass, pile up, add up; grow, increase. —**Ant.** dwindle, decrease, diminish, lessen, wane, dissipate, dribble away.

accumulate *v. Snow accumulated on the ground. He accumulated a fortune buying and selling used cars:* gather, gather together, pile up, heap up, amass, collect, accrue, assemble, aggregate; grow, congregate, cumulate, garner; save up, store up, hoard. —**Ant.** scatter, disperse, distribute; dissipate, waste, get rid of.

accumulation *n.* **1.** *Let's throw out that accumulation of junk in the attic:* collection, assemblage, conglomeration; mass, heap, pile, stack, hoard, stockpile, store; stock, supply, pile-up, aggregation, accrual. **2.** *The accumulation of rare books is his pastime:* collecting, amassing, gathering; acquiring, agglomerating, hoarding. —**Ant.** 2 distribution, dispersing, dispersal, scattering.

accuracy *n. The Internal Revenue Service checks tax returns for accuracy:* accurateness, correctness, freedom from error; exactness, exactitude, precision; truth, truthfulness, verity, fidelity, faithfulness. —**Ant.** error, inaccuracy,

incorrectness, carelessness, slovenliness; lies, lying, fallaciousness.

accurate *adj. The drawing of the house is accurate in every detail. He is an accurate mathematician:* correct, without error, unerring, true, truthful, faithful, perfect, authentic, faultless, exact, right, precise, scrupulous, punctilious, meticulous, careful. —**Ant.** incorrect, wrong, inaccurate, fallacious; inexact, defective, imperfect, faulty; careless, slipshod, slovenly, sloppy.

accusation *n. Your accusation that I lied is untrue. The accusation is grand larceny:* charge, allegation, insinuation, complaint, imputation, incrimination, citation, indictment. —**Ant.** reply, answer, plea; denial, rebuttal; vindication, exoneration.

accuse *v.* **1.** *The prosecutor accused the defendant of murder:* charge, lodge a complaint against, arraign, indict, cite. **2.** *You can't accuse him of laziness:* charge, reproach, take to task, call to account, upbraid; blame. —**Ant.** 1, 2 reply, answer, plea, rebut; deny, defend; acquit, absolve, vindicate, exonerate.

accustomed *adj.* **1.** *Painting barns red is an accustomed practice:* usual, common, normal, regular, general, customary, habitual, established, conventional, set, routine, commonplace, ordinary, familiar, everyday, well-known, prevailing, prevalent, fixed, ingrained; hackneyed, trite, cliché, expected. **2.** *Alaskans are accustomed to cold weather:* used to, acclimated, seasoned, familiarized, acquainted with, inured, in the habit of, given to, habituated, hardened, wonted, prone. —**Ant.** 1 unusual, uncommon, rare, strange, unfamiliar, foreign, exotic; singular, infrequent, occasional; peculiar, abnormal, unconventional, odd, queer, erratic. 2 unused, unaccustomed.

ace *n.* **1.** *He was an ace at any sport he took up:* champion, winner, master, victor, star, headliner, medalist, expert. —*adj.* **2.** *She became an ace driver in the stock-car races:* outstanding, top, top-rated, crack, front-ranking, excellent. —**Ant.** 1 failure, disaster, fiasco, dud, klutz.

acerbic *adj.* **1.** *The wine was much too acerbic:* acidic, astringent, sour, tart, sharp. **2.** *Her acerbic remark killed the conversation:* sarcastic, mordant, sardonic, ironic, wry, satiric, caustic, biting, scathing, sour, vinegary, vinegarish. —**Ant.** 2 sweet, dulcet, generous, upbeat, Pollyannaish, goody-goody.

acerbity *n.* **1.** *The Smiths received the uninvited callers with acerbity:* ill-tempered manner, brusqueness, sarcastic irritability, sarcasm, irascibility, acrimony, pointed rudeness, nastiness, sharpness. **2.** *The acerbity of some wines is such as to make them an acquired taste:* acidity, sourness, tartness, bitterness, astringency, pungency, acridity. —**Ant.** 1 good nature, cordiality, good humor, affability, pleasantness, mellowness, complai-sance. 2 blandness, tastelessness, lifelessness, indifference.

ache *n.* **1.** *A dentist can fix that ache:* pain, throb, twinge, pang, hurt, discomfort, soreness. —*v.* **2.** *The blow made my head ache:* hurt, feel pain, be sore, smart, throb. **3.** *She was aching for her dead husband:* grieve, mourn, lament, suffer, sorrow, agonize, lament. **4.** *The child ached for a bicycle:* desire, want, crave, need, hunger, yearn, hanker, covet, long for.

achieve *v.* **1.** *The Community Chest has achieved its goal of collecting one million dollars:* accomplish, attain, realize, reach, complete, finish, arrive at, fulfill; bring to pass, bring about, carry out, effect, effectuate, succeed in, do, dispatch. **2.** *Can a mere mortal achieve perfect happiness?:* attain, obtain, realize, reach, gain, get, earn, win, acquire, procure. —**Ant.** 1 fail to, fall short of. 2 lose, be deprived of.

achievement *n.* **1.** *Man's first walk on the moon was a stunning technological achievement:* accomplishment, attainment, realization, fulfillment; fear, coup, tour de force, exploit, effort, act, deed. **2.** *Playing the piano is just one of her achievements:* accomplishment, attainment, acquirement; skill, mastery, expertise, command. —**Ant.** 1 failure, defeat, frustration, fiasco.

acid *adj.* **1.** *These lemons are more acid than usual:* sour, tart, astringent, pungent, sharp, biting, harsh, vinegary, vinegarish. **2.** *That movie critic has an acid wit:* acerbic, acrimonious, acidulous, sharp, biting, stinging, cutting, scalding, harsh, scathing, bitter, acrid, caustic, nasty, vitriolic, crabbed; sarcastic, satirical, irascible, ironic. —**Ant.** 1 sweet, succulent; alkaline; pleasant-tasting, mild, gentle, bland. 2 kindly, gentle, sweet, mild, soft; pleasant; friendly, warmhearted, benign, compassionate.

acidulous *adj.* *A drop of vinegar had turned the milk acidulous:* acidic, sour, acerbic, sharp, tart.

acknowledge *v.* **1.** *The losing candidate acknowledged his defeat. We acknowledge that night must follow day:* recognize, accept, admit, own, own up to, confess, allow, grant, concede, accede, concur, yield, assent. **2.** *The chairman acknowledges the delegate from Ohio:* recognize, extend cognizance to, take notice of; call upon, call upon to speak, call upon to vote. **3.** *Did he acknowledge your greeting?:* respond to, reply to, answer; express appreciation for, thank for. —**Ant.** 1 disclaim, repudiate, reject, renounce, contradict; deny, disavow. 2, 3 ignore, disregard, disdain, slight, spurn, reject; deny.

acknowledgment *n.* **1.** *He gave his wife full acknowledgment for her help in starting the business:* recognition, recognizance, credit. **2.** *His acknowledgment that he stole the necklace cleared his sister of blame:* affirmation, admission, confession, concession. **3.** *Accept our grateful acknowledgment with this note:* thanks, gratitude, appreciation; response, answer, reply. —**Ant.** 1, 2 denial, disavowal, disclaimer, demurrer.

acme *n.* *Opening on Broadway was the acme of his theatrical career:* height, peak, pinnacle, zenith, high point, highest point, climax, summit; heyday, flowering; crown, crest, apex, culmination, apogee. —**Ant.** depth, low point, worst point, bottom, nadir, abyss.

acolyte *n.* **1.** *Two acolytes attended the priest*

at Mass: altar boy; novice, ministerial assistant. **2.** *The famous movie director arrived, surrounded by his acolytes:* follower, admirer, adherent, devotee, *Informal* fan, *Slang* groupie; assistant, helper, attendant.

acquaint *v.* **1.** *Have you two just met, or were you acquainted before? Our minister believes in getting acquainted with everybody in town:* introduce, make known socially, meet. **2.** *It takes time to acquaint yourself with a new job. Let me acquaint you with the facts in the matter:* familiarize, apprise, disclose, reveal, advise, tell, inform, notify, enlighten, make aware, divulge to. —**Ant.** 2 hide, conceal, keep secret, keep private; withhold, reserve, retain, hold back.

acquaintance *n.* **1.** *He's not really a friend, just an acquaintance:* person slightly known, distant friend. **2.** *We had a brief acquaintance with her a while back:* friendship, relationship, association, dealings. **3.** *The school's curriculum stresses acquaintance with the sciences:* familiarity, awareness, knowledge, conversance, cognizance. —**Ant.** 1 stranger; good friend, intimate, bosom buddy. 3 unfamiliarity, ignorance.

acquiesce *v.* *I don't like the idea, but I will acquiesce to it:* consent, agree, assent, accede, allow; bow to, yield, submit, capitulate, give in; admit, concede, grant, comply, concur, conform, fall in with; resign oneself, reconcile oneself. —**Ant.** resist, fight, contest, refuse, balk at, veto; protest, object, disagree, dissent, demur.

acquire *v.* *John Paul Getty acquired a fortune in the oil business. She has acquired a working knowledge of French:* get, obtain, attain, gain, secure, procure, capture; achieve, realize; earn, win, pick up; cultivate. —**Ant.** lose, be deprived of; relinquish, give up, forgo.

acquisition *n.* **1.** *This painting is the museum's most recent acquisition:* acquirement, procurement, possession, property, gain, purchase, prize. **2.** *Leonardo devoted his life to the acquisition of knowledge:* attainment, obtainment, achievement, acquirement, procurement, gain.

acquisitive *adj.* *She is an acquisitive person, always wanting things:* covetous, grasping, greedy, avaricious; possessive, materialistic, selfish. —**Ant.** self-denying, abstemious, nonpossessive; altruistic; generous.

acquit *v.* **1.** *The jury acquitted the defendant of all charges:* declare not guilty, declare innocent, clear; exonerate, vindicate, exculpate, absolve, let off, discharge, release, relieve, reprieve, deliver, liberate, pardon, set free; exempt, excuse. **2.** *A gentleman must acquit himself well in any situation:* conduct, behave, comport, act. —**Ant.** 1 charge, indict, blame; convict, declare guilty; condemn, damn, doom.

acrid *adj.* **1.** *The burning rubber gave off acrid smoke:* caustic, harsh, sharp, bitter, burning, stinging, irritating, biting, pungent; smelly, foul-smelling, malodorous. **2.** *A political cartoonist must have an acrid sense of humor:* harsh, sharp, biting, bitter, nasty, acrimonious, vitriolic, acid; sarcastic, ironic, satirical. —**Ant.** 1 sweet, pleasing; fragrant, aromatic. 2 kindly, gentle, sweet, sweet-natured, good-natured; benign, compassionate.

acrimonious *adj. You may not like my decision, but don't be acrimonious about it:* sarcastic, spiteful, rancorous, bitter, peevish, testy, ill-natured, nasty, *Slang* bitchy; venomous, vitriolic, caustic, corrosive, sour, cutting, biting, splenetic, irascible. **—Ant.** forgiving, benign, benignant, pleasant, agreeable, good-humored, kindhearted, civil, polite.

acrimony *n. The election campaign led to bitter acrimony between the candidates:* ill will, hard feelings, rancor, anger, bitterness; animosity, hostility, derision, spitefulness, antagonism, asperity, malignity, spite, scorn, malignancy, spleen, animus. **—Ant.** good will, good feelings, love, liking, friendliness, politeness, civility.

acrobat *n. The acrobat hung from the trapeze by one foot:* aerialist, athlete, balancer, contortionist, dancer, funambulist, gymnast, stunt man *or* woman, tumbler.

across *adj.* **1.** *We walked across the field:* athwart, crosswise, over, transversely, traversing, to the other side of. *—prep.* **2.** *Her house was across from ours:* opposite from, opposite to, facing, in front of.

act *n.* **1.** *He was criticized for one careless act:* deed, action, performance, step, move; feat, exploit, accomplishment, achievement. **2.** *The thief was caught in the act:* action, process of doing. **3.** *This area was declared a National Park by an act of Congress:* official decision, law, edict, decree, enactment, legislation, bill, resolution, statute, mandate, ordinance, measure, order. **4.** *Romeo dies in the last act of* Romeo and Juliet. *His song and dance act was a sensation in vaudeville:* segment of a play, main division of a play; short performance, routine, *Informal* skit, bit, *Slang* gig. **5.** *Her sickness is just an act to get sympathy:* pretense, front, pose, posture, fake, pretension, insincere act, affectation, show, performance, *Informal* put-on, stance. *—v.* **6.** *Act now and save money during our annual sale:* do it, perform, do, function, go about, execute, carry out, operate, move; press on, put forth; commit oneself. **7.** *Act your age! The car acted as if it was about to run out of gas. Mr. Smith will act as chairman of the committee:* behave, conduct oneself, comport oneself; work, operate, function. **8.** *When you see the gift, act surprised:* pretend to be, feign, fake, affect, simulate, counterfeit. **9.** *He has acted the part of Hamlet three times:* perform, play, portray, enact; represent; impersonate. **—Ant.** 1 inactivity, inaction. 6 stay, stop, rest, procrastinate, put off.

acting *adj.* **1.** *Mr. Smith will be acting mayor until new elections are held:* temporary, substitute, surrogate, deputy, provisional, officiating, interim; simulated, ersatz. *—n.* **2.** *Acting can be a difficult profession:* dramatics, thespianism, stage playing; theater, dramaturgy, stagecraft. **—Ant.** 1 permanent; real, true.

action *n.* **1.** *The action of this crank turns the wheel:* power, force, work, effort; effect, influence; movement, motion. **2.** *The fire department was called into action when the alarm sounded:* operation, activity, functioning, performing, performance; process; production. **3.** *The tax increase was an unpopular action:* act, deed, step, move, endeavor, enterprise; exploit, feat, achievement. **4.** *We expect action on our complaint before next Friday:* activity, work, effort, exertion, movement, enterprise; committed attention, achievement, accomplishment, progress, execution. **5.** *The general has seen action in three wars:* combat, battle, fighting, conflict, warfare. **6.** *It was a boring movie with no action:* movement, excitement, adventure. **7.** *My lawyer will take action against you in the courts:* legal proceedings, prosecution, suit, judicial redress. **—Ant.** 2 inaction, inactivity, rest. 4 complacency. 6 dialogue, exposition.

activate *v. These push buttons activate the elevator:* start, turn on, actuate, put into action, set going, stimulate, propel, prompt; drive, impel, motivate, energize; vitalize, mobilize, *Informal* stir. **—Ant.** deactivate, immobilize, paralyze, deaden; stop, turn off, halt, check.

active *adj.* **1.** *No one is more active than a teenager. He is the most active member of the team:* energetic, vigorous, lively, animated, frisky, peppy, spirited, indefatigable; busy, on the go, occupied, engaged, industrious, enterprising, ambitious, go-getting, forceful, assertive, aggressive, zealous. **2.** *Skiing is an active sport:* strenuous, energetic; vigorous; lively, animated. **3.** *Invitations went to all active members of the club. Mount Vesuvius is an active volcano:* functioning, actively operative, working, acting, effectual, productive; in force, at work. **4.** *She may be eighty, but she has an active mind:* alert, quick, vigorous, alive, lively; agile, spry, nimble, sprightly, animated, imaginative; industrious, diligent. **—Ant.** 1–4 inactive. 1 unoccupied; torpid, sluggish, indolent, idle, lazy. 2 sedentary; dull. 3 nonfunctioning, inoperative; dormant. 4 sluggish, slow, dull; unimaginative.

activity *n.* **1.** *The schoolroom was full of bustling activity:* action, movement; enterprise; commotion, hustle, bustle, tumult, agitation, flurry, stir, fuss, hurly-burly; sprightliness, vivacity, liveliness, animation, *Informal* goings on. **2.** *We need a little activity to keep ourselves warm:* exercise, exertion, movement. **3.** *What school activities interest you?:* undertaking, pursuit, enterprise, function, venture, endeavor, project, avocation, occupation, assignment. **—Ant.** 1 inactivity, immobility, torpor, dullness. 2 relaxation, rest, stillness, serenity.

actor *n.* **1.** *A good actor can play any role:* performer, thespian, dramatic artist, trouper, player, *Slang* ham; (*variously*) star, feature actor, supporting actor, character actor, working actor, bit player, walk on; starlet. **2.** *We are all actors in the drama of life:* participant, doer, functionary, perpetrator.

actual *adj.* **1.** *This book is based on an actual case:* real, existing, *Informal* true-to-life, factual, true, genuine, bona fide, authentic, legitimate, confirmed. **2.** *What is the actual location of the* *ship now?:* real, physical, corporeal, existent, existing, concrete, tangible, verifiable, certain, sure; current, present, prevailing. —**Ant.** 1 fictional, fictitious, made-up; hypothetical, theoretical. 2 probable, supposed, projected, conjectured.

actuality *n. In actuality he never liked her at all:* reality, fact, truth, point of fact, plain fact, brutal fact, verity, substance. —**Ant.** pretense, falseness, make-believe, illusion.

actually *adv. The events depicted in the movie did not actually take place:* in fact, really, truly, verily, genuinely, literally, indeed.

actuate *v.* **1.** See ACTIVATE. **2.** *Everything he does is actuated by greed:* motivate, prompt, cause, induce, stimulate, instigate, incite, bring about, move, drive, impel, trigger, arouse, rouse; influence, inspire, excite, stir, animate. —**Ant.** 1 See ACTIVATE. 2 check, curb, restrain, hinder, deter, dampen, damper, inhibit, thwart.

acumen *n. His business acumen will help the company:* keenness, acuteness, smartness, astuteness, shrewdness, cleverness; discernment, intelligence, wisdom, sound judgment; perspicacity, clearheadedness, sagacity, insight, perception, ingenuity. —**Ant.** obtuseness, dullness, ignorance, stupidity, folly, bad judgment.

acute *adj.* **1.** *Angles of less than 90° are called acute angles:* sharply pointed, sharp, peaked, needle-shaped. **2.** *She had an acute headache. He's suffering from acute appendicitis:* severe, intense, fierce, powerful, very great, very bad, critical; excruciating, distressing, piercing, agonizing. **3.** *Einstein was a man of uncommonly acute intelligence:* keen, penetrating, piercing, sharp; discriminating, discerning, perceptive, intuitive, sensitive, clever, ingenious. —**Ant.** 1 obtuse, dull, blunt, blunted. 2 mild, moderate, *Medical* chronic. 3 obtuse, dull, dense, stolid.

adage *n. "Live and let live" is an old adage:* saying, proverb, maxim, axiom, motto, aphorism, epigram; dictum, truism, wise observation, precept, platitude, cliché, *Informal* saw, old saw, quip.

adamant *adj. Her mother is adamant in demanding she be home by eleven:* insistent, unyielding, inflexible, rigid, fixed, set, firm, tough, immovable, uncompromising, unbending, resolute, intransigent, determined, stubborn, *Informal* hard as rock, obdurate, inexorable, *Slang* uptight. —**Ant.** yielding, flexible, lax, undemanding, easy-going, indifferent, *Slang* loose; submissive, capitulating, pliant, compliant, compromising.

adapt *v.* **1.** *The chameleon adapts to its surroundings by changing color:* adjust, conform, accommodate, acclimate, fit, suit, assimilate, acculturate, coordinate, harmonize, reconcile, attune to. **2.** *The play is adapted from a short story:* reshape, shape, fashion, frame, transform, rework, convert, adjust, make suitable, make fit, recompose, remodel, modify, change, alter.

adaptable *adj.* **1.** *An adaptable person is at ease anywhere:* flexible, pliant, compliant, unrigid, open-minded, easygoing; obliging, ac-

commodating, conformable, malleable, tractable, amenable. **2.** *The new auditorium is adaptable for either theatrical or sports events:* usable, serv-iceable, applicable, accommodative; changeable, adjustable, alterable. —**Ant.** 1 inflexible, rigid, fixed, closed-minded, *Slang* uptight. 2 inflexible, nonadjustable, unalterable; unusable, unserviceable.

adaptation *n.* **1.** *The building is undergoing adaptation from garage to living quarters:* alteration, modification, remodeling, conversion, metamorphosis; refitting; adjustment, change, shift. **2.** *The TV series is an adaptation of a novel:* altered version, modification, reworking, revision, reshaping.

add *v.* **1.** *Let's add up the cost of all our purchases:* total, sum up, count up, figure up, compute, calculate, reckon; combine. **2.** *Add one more item to the list. May I add a point or two?:* include, attach, append, affix, join, join on, tack on; offer in addition, supplement, increase by, enlarge by. —**Ant.** 1 subtract, deduct. 2 remove, exclude, eliminate, withdraw; take, take away, reduce.

addendum *n. The report has an addendum clarifying certain points:* added section, supplement, addition, codicil, postscript; appendage, afterthought, attachment.

addict *n.* **1.** *Addicts must be identified and treated at once:* drug addict; *Slang* junkie, user, head, freak, dope fiend. **2.** *She's an opera addict:* devotee, fan, adherent, habitué, acolyte, votary; *Slang* nut, hound, buff. —*v.* **3.** *Don't addict yourself to sweets:* give (oneself) habitually, yield obsessively, surrender, indulge in, submit; *Slang* hook, turn on. —**Ant.** 3 withdraw, break the habit, *Slang* kick the habit; renounce, give up, eschew.

addiction *n. His addiction to drugs nearly ruined his life:* addictedness, obsession, enslavement, fixation, enthrallment, mania, compulsion, craze, fetish, quirk, hangup, preoccupation; alcoholism, dipsomania, barbiturism, cocainism, morphinism.

addition *n.* **1.** *Addition is taught before subtraction:* mathematical summation, totaling, counting up, summing up, summation, reckoning, enumeration. **2.** *The addition of a baby to the household changed our lives. The addition of a porch will increase the value of the house:* adding, including, encompassing, embracing; joining, adjoining, annexing, appending, attaching; extending, increasing. **3.** *The addition in cost over last year's tuition is $200:* increase, increment; extension, enlargement, extra, additive, augmentation, expansion. **4.** *The addition to the town library will double its size:* annex, wing, extension, appendage; adjunct, appurtenance, addendum, added contribution. —**Ant.** 1–3 subtraction. 2 subtracting, removing, removal, detaching, detachment. 3 decrease, reduction, deduction, lessening, diminution.

additional *adj. The charge for the delivery of the furniture is additional:* extra, spare, added, added on, supplementary, appended, over-and-above.

additionally *adv. Additionally, we were tired and fed up:* in addition, again, also, as well, besides, moreover, over, to boot, too, withal, yet, farther, further, beyond.

additive *n. Food coloring was one additive to canned tomatoes:* addition, supplement.

addled *adj. The witness became addled by the cross-examination. My brain may be old, but it's not addled:* confused, mixed-up, muddled, befuddled, nonplused; foolish, silly.

address *n.* **1.** *Please print your name and address:* street number, city, and state; mailing address, postal address, street address, street number; place of residence, dwelling, place of business; location, locality. **2.** *The Presidential address will be broadcast at 8 o'clock:* speech, talk, statement, oration, discourse. *—v.* **3.** *Address this letter to the Attorney General:* write for delivery to, put an address on. **4.** *The general addressed his troops before the battle:* give a formal talk, talk to, speak to, orate, lecture, greet, salute in words; write to.

adept *adj. She's adept at organizational work. He's adept in needlecraft:* skilled, skillful, expert, proficient, accomplished, master, masterful, ingenious, practiced; good, apt, able, adroit, dexterous, gifted. *—Ant.* amateurish, beginning; unskilled, inept, unaccomplished, clumsy, awkward.

adequate *adj. Our hotel room wasn't luxurious, but it was adequate:* suitable, satisfactory, sufficient, equal to need, passable, tolerable, fitting, fit; enough, ample, *Informal* so-so. *—Ant.* inadequate, unsuitable, unsatisfactory, insufficient; imperfect, defective; too little, not enough.

adequately *adv. We were supplied adequately:* sufficiently, suitably, satisfactorily, acceptably, appropriately, decently, fittingly, presentably, tolerably, enough, well enough.

adhere *v.* **1.** *The decal doesn't adhere to the window:* stick, stick fast, hold, cling, cleave; glue, glue on, paste, cement; fix, fasten. **2.** *He adhered to the faith of his fathers:* be faithful, be loyal, be constant, be true, keep, keep to, hold closely, maintain, cling, stick, cleave, stand by, abide by, remain fixed. *—Ant.* 1 come unstuck, come loose, come unglued; detach, unfasten. 2 break with, part from, separate from, leave, be disloyal, be untrue.

adherence *n.* **1.** *Put more glue on the wallpaper to increase its adherence:* adhesion, adhesiveness, stickiness. **2.** *The teacher demanded adherence to the rules:* strict observance, attachment, keeping to, obedience; loyalty, fealty, faithfulness, fidelity, constancy, allegiance, devotion. *—Ant.* 1 looseness; slickness. 2 breaking, disobedience, disloyalty, unfaithfulness, infidelity.

adherent *n.* **1.** *He is a leader with many adherents:* follower, supporter, advocate, disciple, upholder; devotee, partisan, champion, ally, fan; acolyte, pupil. *—adj.* **2.** *Scrape off that adherent substance with a razor blade:* adhesive, sticky, sticking, gummy, viscous, viscid, clinging, adhering, holding fast. *—Ant.* 1 opponent, detractor. 2 slick; watery.

adhesive *adj.* **1.** *Glue and paste are adhesive substances:* adherent, adhering, sticky, sticking, clinging; gummy, mucilaginous; gummed. *—n.* **2.** *You need an adhesive to hold these cutouts in place:* sticky substance, adhering substance, gummy substance; glue, paste, rubber cement, cement, epoxy, solder, mortar, stickum. *—Ant.* 2 solvent.

adieu *n.* **1.** *When we said adieu, I never expected to see her again:* goodby, so long, see you later, take it easy, godspeed, farewell, by-by, *Hawaiian* aloha, *Italian* ciao, *German* Auf Wiedersehen, *Spanish* adios; *French* au revoir, à demain, à bientôt; *Brit.* cheerio, ta-ta, good day, toodle-oo. **2.** *Their adieus were cordial, but I sensed a coolness in their manner:* goodby, leavetaking, farewell, valediction.

ad infinitum *He talks about his new computer ad infinitum:* ceaselessly, continuously, endlessly, unendingly, unceasingly; interminably; infinitely, limitlessly, boundlessly. *—Ant.* occasionally, on occasion, sporadically, now and again, off and on; never, not at all, at no time; seldom, infrequently, rarely.

adjacent *adj. Our farm is adjacent to yours:* next to, beside, right beside, abutting, touching, bordering, tangential, next door to; contiguous with, conterminous, proximate, juxtaposed. *—Ant.* far from, remote from, distant from, separated from.

adjoining *adj. The two sisters had adjoining rooms at the hotel:* joining, joined, touching, connected, interconnected, contiguous, next-door. *—Ant.* separate, detached, individual.

adjourn *v.* **1.** *He adjourned the meeting until tomorrow at 10 A.M.:* recess, suspend, interrupt, discontinue, break off, put off, postpone; close, end, dismiss, dissolve. **2.** *Dinner finished, they adjourned to the living room:* repair, remove, withdraw, move; depart for. *—Ant.* 1 convene, be in session, call to order, open, reopen; assemble, gather, convoke, continue. 2 remain, stay, stay put.

adjournment *n. Both lawyers sought an adjournment:* recess, suspension, break, delay, stay, pause, interruption, deferment, deferral, discontinuation, intermission, postponement, prorogation.

adjudge *v. The justices sought precedents before adjudging the case:* decide, determine, consider, adjudicate, settle, rule, arbitrate, rule on, issue a decree; ordain, decree, pronounce; referee, umpire.

adjudicate *v. She was brought in to adjudicate the dispute:* judge, adjudge, arbitrate, decide, settle, determine, mediate, referee, umpire.

adjunct *n. The Civil War was the first to see railroads used as an adjunct to military operations:* accessory, supplement, complement, auxiliary part, subsidiary, secondary feature; incidental, appurtenance.

adjust *v.* **1.** *It's cold in here; can you adjust the thermostat?:* set, fix, move, regulate, change, order. **2.** *My eyes haven't adjusted to the dark yet:* accustom, acclimate, accommodate, adapt, attune, reconcile, conform; fix, alter, modify, regulate. —**Ant.** 1 leave as is, let remain as is, leave alone.

adjustment *n.* **1.** *These eyeglasses need adjustment:* adjusting, alignment, straightening; fixing, regulation, regulating, modification, alteration; bringing into agreement, justification, reconciliation, rectification; focusing. **2.** *This knob on the TV set is the vertical adjustment:* control, regulator, adjusting device; setting. **3.** *The newlyweds need a period of adjustment:* settling in, settlement, acclimation, adapting, *Informal* getting used to; orientation.

adjutant *n.* *The general chose the major as his adjutant:* assisting staff officer, aide, assistant, right-hand man, right hand, aide-de-camp.

ad-lib *n.* **1.** *The comedian's ad-libs were quoted in the newspaper:* extemporaneous wisecrack, improvisation. —*v.* **2.** *If you forget your speech, just ad-lib:* improvise, extemporize, speak extemporaneously, speak off the cuff, speak impromptu, make up. —**Ant.** 2 follow the script, speak from notes.

administer *v.* **1.** *It takes brains to administer a large corporation:* manage, run, direct, *Informal* boss, administrate, govern, supervise, superintend, preside over, oversee. **2.** *Administer the salve to the sunburned area with a cotton swab:* dispense, apply, give, tender.

administration *n.* **1.** *The administration of justice is difficult:* administering, application, execution, management; dispensation, distribution, tendering. **2.** *An executive should be experienced in administration:* management, executive duty, superintendence, leadership, overseeing; governing, government. **3.** *The teachers are responsible to the dean and the administration:* officers, executives, *Slang* brass; governing body, management, managerial organization, government.

administrative *adj.* *How best to expand the factory is an administrative problem:* executive, managerial, management, supervisory, organizational.

administrator *n.* *Running a small company had made him a competent administrator:* manager, director, superintendent, supervisor, overseer, custodian, authority, controller, executive, leader, organizer.

admirable *adj.* *His honesty is admirable:* worthy of admiration, commendable, praiseworthy, laudable, estimable, venerable. —**Ant.** deplorable, reprehensible, censurable, disappointing; bad, untrustworthy, worthless, faulty.

admiration *n.* *My admiration for his courage knows no bounds:* high regard, high opinion, esteem; veneration, honor, commendation, praise, approval, respect. —**Ant.** low regard, low opinion, disdain.

admire *v.* *I admire your courage. He's so conceited he stops to admire himself in front of every mirror:* view with approval, hold in high regard, hold in esteem, think highly of, respect, esteem, praise, value, prize, take pleasure in. —**Ant.** hold in low regard, hold a low opinion of, view with disapproval, disdain, abhor.

admissible *adj.* *Only a few errors are admissi-* ble. *Hearsay is not admissible evidence in court:* capable of being admitted, permitted, allowed, allowable, permissible, acceptable, legitimate, admittable, tolerated, tolerable, passable. —**Ant.** inadmissible, unacceptable, disallowed, nonpermissible, intolerable.

admission *n.* **1.** *Admission is limited to persons whose names appear on the guest list:* admittance, permission to enter, entry, entrance, entrée, access. **2.** *Admission to the lecture is $3.00:* price of admission, entrance fee; ticket; fee, charge, tariff. **3.** *Your admission of guilt will reduce the court's sentence:* acknowledgment, confession, profession, concession, declaration; assent, affirmation. —**Ant.** 3 denial, disavowal; rejection, negation.

admit *v.* **1.** *Please admit the guests of honor. Only 15 new lawyers were admitted to the bar:* let in, allow to enter, let enter, give access to, grant entrance; appoint, induct, invest; receive, welcome. **2.** *Did the thief admit his guilt?:* acknowledge, confess, concede, profess, declare, *Informal* own up. **3.** *The rules of checkers do not admit touching a piece without moving it:* allow, permit, grant, let. —**Ant.** 1 exclude, keep out, debar; dismiss, reject. 2 deny, disavow, reject, negate. 3 prohibit, forbid, disallow.

admittance *n.* *The applicant gained admittance to head office:* entrance, admission, introduction; access, reception.

admixture *n.* *The face powder is an admixture of nonallergenic ingredients:* blend, amalgam, combination, compound, composite, amalgamation, mixture, intermixture, intermingling, mélange, medley, commingling, commixture; hodgepodge, confusion, conglomeration, jumble, mess, mishmash, potpourri, salmagundi, gallimaufry.

admonish *v.* **1.** *The captain admonished the guards to be on the alert:* warn, caution, put on guard, tip off; advise, counsel, enjoin. **2.** *The preacher admonished his congregation for failure to attend weekly services:* reprove, censure, reprimand, rebuke, reproach, remonstrate, chide, chasten, scold, upbraid, criticize, take to task, call to account, rap on the knuckles. —**Ant.** 2 praise, compliment, commend.

admonition *n.* *The judge gave the careless driver an admonition to watch for one-way streets but did not fine him:* reprimand, mild reproof, scolding, reproach, remonstrance, rebuke, rap on the knuckles; warning, chiding, cautionary reminder, advice. —**Ant.** compliment, commendation, bit of praise, pat on the back.

ado *n.* *There was a lot of ado in preparation for the President's visit:* bustle, commotion, stir, bother, flurry, flutter, pother, fuss, trouble; to-do, turmoil, agitation, tumult, hurlyburly, hubbub, confusion, uproar, furore, racket, fracas. —**Ant.** tranquillity, serenity, calm, calmness, peace, peacefulness.

adolescent *n.* **1.** *Most of today's adolescents will finish high school:* teenager, teen, young teen, young man or woman, minor, youth, schoolboy, schoolgirl, lad, lass, lassie; stripling, fledgling. **—adj. 2.** *The movie's attitude toward life is adolescent:* for a teenager, befitting a teenager, not adult; immature, sophomoric, puerile, pubescent, juvenile; callow, undeveloped; youthful, boyish, girlish; childish, babyish. **—Ant.** 1 adult; child. 2 adult, grownup, mature.

adopt *v.* **1.** *Many childless couples adopt children:* become the legal parent of, take as one's own child. **2.** *We've adopted a motto for our club. The schools must adopt new methods of teaching foreign languages:* formally approve, accept, choose, appropriate, take up, follow, embrace, espouse; utilize, employ, assume, affect, use; acknowledge, conform to. **—Ant.** 1 give up for adoption, place; disinherit. 2 give up, cast aside, cast off; spurn, forswear, repudiate, reject, disclaim; annul, abrogate.

adoption *n. Adoption of his motion came after heated debate:* approval, acceptance, adopting, approbation, appropriation, confirmation, endorsement, espousal, ratification, enactment.

adorable *adj. The little girl was adorable. There is the most adorable dress on sale at the store!:* lovable, delightful, precious, darling, likable, pleasing, divine; appealing, charming, winsome, captivating, engaging, fetching, irresistible. **—Ant.** hateful, unlovable, unlikable, hard to like, despicable; displeasing, unappealing.

adoration *n. The monks devote their lives to the adoration of God:* worship, worshiping, glorification, exaltation, veneration, reverence, adulation, devotion; honor, idolization, magnification. **—Ant.** blasphemy, denunciation, reviling, execration, belittling.

adore *v.* **1.** *He adores his wife and children. I just adore your new hat:* love, hold dear, cherish; *Informal* worship, revere, glorify; fancy, like, prize, dote on; admire. **2.** *O, come let us adore Him:* worship, glorify, exalt, revere, venerate, idolize. **—Ant.** 1 hate, dislike, abhor, loathe, despise. 2 blaspheme, revile, denounce, execrate, belittle.

adorn *v. A simple gold pin adorned her dress:* ornament, decorate, embellish, array, bedeck, bejewel, *Informal* deck out; beautify, set off to advantage, furbish. **—Ant.** strip, bare; simplify.

adornment *n. They said her greatest adornment was her beauty:* ornament, ornamentation, decoration, jewelry, embellishment; finery, attire.

adrift *adj.* **1.** *The boat was adrift on the outgoing tide:* drifting, afloat, unmoored, aweigh, unanchored. **2.** *After college he was adrift for several years:* confused, lost, uncertain, bewildered, unstable, at sea, perplexed, irresolute, unsettled. **—Ant.** 1 moored, fastened, secured, anchored. 2 stable, certain, resolute, sure, confident.

adroit *adj. A sculptor must have adroit hands. Politicians must be adroit speakers:* dexterous, nimble; deft, apt, proficient, skilled, skillful, expert, masterful; clever, artful, facile, cunning, slick. **—Ant.** clumsy, awkward, unhandy.

adulation *n. The official adulation of Stalin in the Soviet Union ended suddenly after his death:* flattery, adoration, fawning, fulsome praise. **—Ant.** condemnation, denunciation, defamation, aspersion, abuse, vituperation, censure, ridicule; hatred, dislike, loathing.

adult *n.* **1.** *Many of the adults had lived in the area since childhood:* grownup, man, woman; father, mother, parent; elder, oldster, senior citizen; grandfather, grandpa, grandmother, grandma, granny. **—adj. 2.** *The clothing comes in adult sizes only:* mature, big, of age, full-grown, grownup, senior; seasoned, experienced, developed. **—Ant.** 1 child, baby, infant, adolescent. 2 immature, raw, green, inexperienced, callow.

adulterate *v. The ancient Greeks often adulterated their wine with water:* contaminate, thin, water, water down; depreciate, *Informal* cut.

adultery *n. In some states adultery is theoretically punishable by a prison sentence:* unfaithfulness, fornication, marital infidelity, illicit intercourse, cuckoldry, carnality, unchastity, promiscuity, extramarital relations, violation of the marriage bed, criminal conversation. **—Ant.** fidelity, faithfulness, steadfastness, constancy.

advance *v.* **1.** *The troops advanced twenty miles. We will advance hard workers to the head of the class:* go forward, come forward, bring forward, send forward, progress, bring up, move up, send up, move onward, press on, propel; put up front, promote. **2.** *The biologist advanced a new theory of life:* proffer, bring forward, offer, bring to notice, bring to attention, lay down, assign. **3.** *The Apollo landings advanced our knowledge of the moon:* bring forward, further, increase, improve, upgrade, promote, add to, multiply, further the growth of, take a step forward. **4.** *My boss advanced me $50 against next week's salary:* pay beforehand, give beforehand; pay on account, pay now. **—n. 5.** *The enemy advance must be stopped!:* forward movement, progress, onward movement. **6.** *Discovering a cure for cancer would be a major medical advance. His advance in the firm led him from stockboy to president:* improvement, advancement, progress, furthering, promotion, step, breakthrough, growth, gain. **7.** *The plumber wanted an advance of $50 before he started work:* prepayment, down payment; binder. **8.** *If you don't stop making advances to all the girls, you'll get your face slapped!:* pass, amorous overture, overture; proposition. **—adj. 9.** *The advance troops have sighted the enemy:* forward, foremost, before all others, in front, up front. **10.** *The advance sale of tickets made the play a success despite the bad reviews:* preliminary, previous, prior, before the fact, *Informal* pre. **—Ant.** 1 retreat, go backward, regress, retrogress, move back, withdraw; demote, degrade. 2 hide, keep secret, withhold, suppress, hold back, keep under wraps; recall. 3 decrease, lessen, diminish, subtract from, set back, retard, weaken. 4 defer payment, withhold payment. 5 retreat, withdrawal, regression, retrogression. 6 worsening, regression, retrogression, setback. 7 deferred payment. 9 rear, hindmost, in back.

advanced *adj. She was very advanced for her*

age: ahead, forward-looking, progressive, leading, higher, imaginative, avant-garde, *Informal* cutting-edge. **—Ant.** backward, behind, retarded, undeveloped.

advancement *n. He eagerly sought advancement in the company:* growth, improvement, progress, betterment, headway, development, gain, promotion, maturation, advance, amelioration, elevation, rise, upgrading. **—Ant.** demotion, retardation.

advantage *n.* **1.** *Being able to speak French is a great advantage on a trip to Europe:* asset, help, benefit, aid, service, profit; blessing, boon, support, comfort, convenience. **2.** *The taller team has an advantage in a basketball game:* edge, upper hand, initial supremacy, *Slang* clout, precedence, dominance; superiority, success. **—Ant.** 1, 2 disadvantage. 1 hindrance, difficulty, drawback, deterrent, disservice, curse; discomfort, inconvenience. 2 handicap, *Slang* short end of the stick.

advantageous *adj.* **1.** *You'll find it advantageous to learn Spanish before visiting South America:* helpful, beneficial, useful, valuable, profitable, of assistance, of service. **2.** *Taking his opponent's queen put the chess player in an advantageous position:* superior, favorable, dominating, auspicious, enviable, fortunate. **—Ant.** 1 unhelpful, useless, detrimental; harmful, injurious. 2 inferior, unfavorable, unfortunate; *Informal* behind the eight ball, up the creek.

advent *n. The advent of the railroad opened up transcontinental travel:* coming, arrival, onset, beginning, occurrence, commencement, start, appearance, bowing in, appearing, opening up. **—Ant.** end, conclusion, finish, demise, expiration.

adventure *n. Have you read about the adventures of Marco Polo?:* enterprise, undertaking, venture, *Poetic* emprise, quest, escapade.

adventurer *n. There's a little bit of the adventurer in every man:* daredevil, dragonslayer, vagabond, romantic, giant-killer, hero, heroine, soldier of fortune, buccaneer, swashbuckler.

adventurous *adj.* **1.** *Her father was an adventurous man, unafraid of risks:* seeking excitement, eager for experience, daring, bold, venturesome, audacious; brave, courageous, valiant, intrepid. **2.** *The trip promised to be long but adventurous:* challenging, risky, hazardous, dangerous, perilous. **—Ant.** 1 unadventurous, cautious, hesitant. 2 dull, boring, routine; completely safe.

adversary *n. UCLA and Stanford are adversaries on the football field:* opponent, rival, competitor, foe, antagonist, enemy. **—Ant.** ally, accomplice, colleague, teammate; friend.

adverse *adj. Adverse winds prevented our plane from arriving on time. Don't be discouraged by adverse criticism:* unfavorable, contrary, opposing, unpropitious, detrimental, negative, difficult; hostile, antagonistic, unfriendly, inimical; pernicious, harmful, injurious. **—Ant.** favorable, helpful, beneficial, supporting, agreeable; auspicious.

adversity *n. She tried to be brave in the face of adversity:* unfavorable circumstances, misfortune, calamity, disaster, ill-fortune, bad luck, catastrophe, hardship, suffering, mishap; affliction, trouble, distress, trial, tribulation, woe. **—Ant.** good fortune, success, blessings.

advertise *v. If you want to sell your product, you must advertise it. Don't advertise your shortcomings:* publicize, call attention to, give public notice of, proclaim, broadcast, vaunt, tout, noise abroad; display, reveal, show. **—Ant.** hide, conceal, keep hidden, keep under cover, keep secret, keep under wraps.

advertisement *n. I saw your advertisement for the used car:* want ad, classified ad, announcement, flier, handbill, poster, placard, public notice, leaflet, circular, broadside, throwaway, commercial, trailer.

advice *n.* **1.** *Get a lawyer's advice on the matter:* recommendation, counsel, suggestion, opinion, view; advisement, guidance. **2.** *Advice from abroad indicates that war is about to begin:* information, intelligence, communication, word, tidings, news, report, notification, message, account.

advisable *adj. It's advisable for all children to have polio shots:* recommendable; prudent, judicious, wise, smart; suitable, seemly, expedient, sound, proper, fitting, fit; *Informal* best, a good bet. **—Ant.** unsuitable, unsound, improper; inexpedient, stupid, silly; unfitting.

advise *v.* **1.** *I advise you to reconsider your decision:* counsel, recommend, recommend to, suggest, suggest to, offer an opinion, offer the opinion that; commend, urge, encourage, enjoin; caution, warn, admonish, exhort. **2.** *We have been advised that the roads are too icy for the trip:* inform, tell, notify, apprise, report, give notice, make known, communicate.

adviser or **advisor** *n.* **1.** *The doctor is chief medical adviser to the health department:* consultant, counselor, idea person, resource person; aide, surrogate, assistant. **2.** *Each student has a faculty adviser to help in planning a career:* counselor, guide, mentor, preceptor, monitor, admonitor, director, coach; instructor, teacher, tutor.

advisory *adj. Several experts were hired in an advisory capacity:* informational, informative, consultatory, consultative, counseling, instructive, guiding; admonitory, cautionary, warning.

advocacy *n. Susan B. Anthony was famed for her advocacy of equal rights for women:* championship, campaigning for, pleading the case of, speaking out for, support, patronage, supporting, backing, espousal, pressing for, advancement, furthering, promotion, propagation; recommendation, endorsement, defense. **—Ant.** opposition; combatting, assault, attacking.

advocate *v.* **1.** *The committee is advocating revision of the draft laws:* recommend, advise, propose, prescribe; champion, urge, promote, campaign for, plead the cause of, argue for, speak out for, stand up for, push for; encourage, endorse, favor, support, back, press for, espouse; advance, further, propagate. **—n. 2.**

The forest ranger is an advocate of environmental protection laws: champion, backer, supporter, proponent, promoter, spokesman for; believer, upholder, apostle, patron; defender, pleader, apologist, propagandist. **3.** *He hired the best advocate he could find to represent him in court:* lawyer, attorney, legal adviser, counsel, counselor, attorney-at-law, barrister, solicitor, *Slang* mouthpiece. —**Ant.** 1 oppose, combat, attack, assail, impugn. 2 opponent, adversary, enemy, antagonist, detractor; attacker, accuser.

aegis *n. The concert was presented under the aegis of the Chamber of Commerce:* sponsorship, auspices, protection, patronage, guard, favor, wing, shelter, backing, support, guardianship, championship, guaranty, surety.

aerial *n.* **1.** *If you had a rooftop aerial, you could get distant stations on your TV set:* antenna. —*adj.* **2.** *Seagulls glided overhead on aerial currents:* air, in the air, from the air, by air, airborne; by aircraft, of aircraft, flying, capable of flight; atmospheric, airy, wind-created. **3.** *These aerial notions of yours are just daydreams:* dreamy, ethereal, ephemeral, airy, lofty, unsubstantial, unreal, fanciful, soaring, visionary, imaginary; elusive, tenuous, impractical. —**Ant.** 2 land, on the ground; by land. 3 down to earth, real, realistic, practical, pragmatic.

aesthete or **esthete** *n. After an afternoon at the National Gallery, the tourists considered themselves aesthetes:* connoisseur, collector, expert, virtuoso.

aesthetic See ESTHETIC.

affable *adj. The elderly woman proved an affable companion:* amiable, genial, congenial, agreeable, friendly, cordial, gracious, sociable, compatible; good-natured, good-humored, pleasant, warm, easygoing, open; courteous, civil, mannerly. —**Ant.** unfriendly, disagreeable, unsociable, unapproachable, inaccessible, distant, haughty, *Informal* standoffish; ill-humored, unpleasant, cold; discourteous, uncivil, ungracious, rude, brusque, curt, surly.

affair *n.* **1.** *What I do in my spare time is my own affair:* personal business, private matter, concern, business; personal problem, interest, pursuit. **2.** *The Department of State handles international affairs. Running a household is a complex affair:* undertaking, activity, matter, business, operation, function, transaction, effort; incident, occurrence, episode, event, happening, proceeding, circumstance, adventure. **3.** *Christmas was a gala affair:* celebration, festivity, party, social gathering, social function, occasion, *Slang* shindig. **4.** *The affair between the two movie stars caused a scandal:* love affair, romance, relationship, liaison, intrigue, amour.

affect[1] *v.* **1.** *The rain will affect our plans for a picnic:* influence, be of importance to, impinge on, act on, produce an effect on, alter, change, modify; concern, relate to, pertain to, interest, regard. **2.** *The speech deeply affected the audience:* have an emotional effect on, move, touch, stir, impress. —**Ant.** 2 leave unmoved, *Informal* leave cold; bore.

affect[2] *v. She's from Chicago, but she affects a British accent:* make a pretense of, feign, fake, put on, pretend to, assume, adopt, imitate, counterfeit, simulate; fancy, show a preference for, tend toward, embrace, be inclined toward. —**Ant.** repudiate, scorn, reject, shed, *Informal* cast aside, cast off.

affectation *n. Her finishing-school accent is just an affectation:* false mannerism, pretense, pretension, sham, façade; airs, false air, insincerity, artificiality, *Slang* put-on. —**Ant.** the genuine article; naturalness, sincerity, genuineness, artlessness, simplicity.

affected[1] *adj.* **1.** *The affected workers said the layoff was unfair:* acted upon, concerned, pertinent, interested; influenced, changed. **2.** *The sad story left him deeply affected:* moved, touched, stirred, impressed; grieved, sorry, sorrowful, troubled, upset, distressed, afflicted. **3.** *The disease left his sense of hearing affected:* upset, harmed, injured, impaired. —**Ant.** 1–3 unaffected. 1 unconcerned, uninter-ested. 2 unmoved, untouched, *Informal* cold. 3 healed, cured; unharmed, uninjured, untouched.

affected[2] *adj. Wealth and fame have made him so affected that I don't like him any more:* pretentious, pompous, conceited, vainglorious, vain; artificial, unnatural, mannered, unreal, not genuine, phony, assumed, contrived, studied. —**Ant.** natural, unpretentious, genuine, real; modest.

affecting *adj. Her affecting performance moved many in the audience to tears:* touching, pathetic, piteous, moving, impressive.

affection *n.* **1.** *He feels great affection for his parents:* emotional attachment, love, fondness, tenderness, warmth; liking, kind disposition, proclivity. **2.** *Chopin died of a consumptive affection:* sickness, illness, disease, ailment, malady, disorder, physical complaint. —**Ant.** 1 hate, loathing, antipathy, enmity; dislike, coldness, coolness. 2 healthiness, well-being, healthfulness, salubriousness.

affectionate *adj. The affectionate child loved to be cuddled. She has an affectionate relationship with her grandparents:* loving, demonstrative; warm, warmhearted, tender, tenderhearted, fond, doting, caring; ardent. —**Ant.** cold, cool, undemonstrative, impassive, stolid; apathetic, callous.

affectless *adj. In showing little remorse, psychopaths are said to be affectless:* unemotional, unfeeling, remote, numb, dead, distant, passionless, dispassionate, detached, disinterested, indifferent, lukewarm, impersonal, cold, cool, cold-blooded, self-absorbed, impassive, untouchable. —**Ant.** interested, involved, passionate, ardent, committed.

affiance *v. The king affianced his daughter to a neighboring prince:* engage to marry, betroth, pledge, solemnly promise.

affidavit *n. She swore an affidavit that she was not responsible:* sworn statement, testimony, affirmation, declaration, oath.

affiliate v. **1.** *Businessmen should affiliate themselves with the local Chamber of Commerce:* associate, connect; join, unite, amalgamate, ally, incorporate, band together, merge; fraternize, consort. —n. **2.** *Our company is an affiliate of a large corporation:* close associate, legally connected associate, colleague; branch, chapter, part, arm, division, subdivision. —**Ant.** l disassociate; leave, quit, resign from.

affiliation n. *The two hospitals have a close affiliation, sometimes sharing equipment:* association, relationship, alliance, connection, union.

affinity n. **1.** *Many classical musicians have an affinity for jazz:* natural liking, partiality, fancy, penchant, liking, fondness; leaning, bent, tendency, proclivity, propensity, inclination; sympathy, rapport. **2.** *There is a close affinity between lemons and limes:* family resemblance, similarity, likeness, parallelism, homology; relation, connection, compatibility. —**Ant.** 1 aversion, repulsion, antipathy, disliking. 2 dissimilarity.

affirm v. **1.** *We affirm these statements to be true:* declare, assert, aver, avow, maintain, proclaim; profess, allege, hold, contend, claim. **2.** *Congress affirmed the treaty the President had made:* confirm, sustain, ratify, validate, endorse, approve, uphold, support, warrant. —**Ant.** 1 deny, refute, repudiate, disavow, renounce. 2 reject, deny, rescind, nullify, veto, disallow, contravene, forswear.

affirmation n. **1.** *The Pledge of Allegiance is a formal affirmation of Americanism:* strong assertion, avowal, declaration. **2.** *The President is awaiting Congressional affirmation of his nominee:* confirmation, ratification, approval, consent, endorsement, certification. —**Ant.** 1 denial, refutation, repudiation, disavowal, renunciation. 2 rejection, nullification, veto.

affirmative adj. **1.** *Please give an affirmative answer if you agree:* yes, assenting, positive, affirmatory; approving, concurring, confirmatory. **2.** *The medical tests are affirmative:* positive, confirming, confirmatory, corroborative, ratifying, affirming, concurring; emphatic, conclusive, categorical. —n. **3.** *Our debating team gave the arguments for the affirmative:* side in favor of a question; positive side, optimistic side. —adv. **4.** *When asked if the water supply seemed adequate, the astronaut replied "Affirmative!":* yes. —**Ant.** 1–4 negative. 1 negating, no. 2 nonconfirming; inconclusive, doubtful. 4 no.

affix v. *Affix the inspection sticker to your windshield:* attach, fasten, fix, add on, tack on, put on; set to, seal, stick, glue, paste, tag. —**Ant.** detach, unfasten, take off; unglue.

afflict v. *Famine and war still afflict mankind:* distress, oppress, torment, plague, beset. —**Ant.** relieve, comfort, console, solace, assuage; bless, delight.

affliction n. *Faith permitted him to endure every affliction:* distress, hardship, trouble, trial, tribulation, torment, oppression, adversity, misfortune, ordeal, calamity, pain, anguish, misery, wretchedness, curse. —**Ant.** relief, comfort, consolation, solace; blessing, joy, delight.

affluent adj. *In a truly affluent society there's* more than enough for all: rich, wealthy, prosperous, well-to-do, moneyed, well-off, *Slang* loaded, well-heeled, well-fixed. —**Ant.** poor, impoverished, impecunious; destitute, indigent.

afford v. **1.** *We can afford the house if we save our pennies:* have the money for, meet the expense of, manage, bear, support. **2.** *A mountain climber can't afford to take chances with inferior equipment:* bear the consequences of, bear, sustain; risk, chance. **3.** *A four-day work week will afford us more leisure time. The terrace affords a fine view:* give, provide, offer, supply, furnish, command, grant, yield, lend, impart.

affray n. *The police broke up an affray in the waterfront bar:* fight, brawl, row, donnybrook, fracas, free-for-all, altercation, row, melee, scuffle, ruction, rumpus, scrap, set-to, battle royal, skirmish, tussle, wrangle, commotion, squabble.

affront v. **1.** *Don't affront the speaker by asking rude questions:* offend, insult, provoke, cause umbrage to. —n. **2.** *His rejection of my plan was a personal affront!:* offense, insult, slur, slight, indignity; rudeness, discourtesy, insolence, impertinence, contemptuousness; outrage, dishonor, disgrace, ignominy, humiliation, *Slang* put-down, mortification; wrong, abuse, injury, ill-treatment. —**Ant.** 1 pamper, flatter, humor, indulge, gratify; honor, please; appease, smooth the feathers of. 2 courtesy, deference, compliment, honor; apology.

afraid adj. **1.** *I'm afraid of lightning:* scared, fearful, frightened, terrified, terror-stricken, alarmed, anxious, anxiety-ridden, apprehensive, timorous, panicky, panic-stricken; fainthearted, cowardly; *Informal* lily-livered, chicken-livered, chickenhearted; *Slang* chicken. **2.** *I'm afraid I can't come to your party:* regretful, sorry, apologetic, unhappy; disappointed. —**Ant.** 1 fearless; bold, audacious, venturesome; indifferent. 2 happy, pleased.

afresh adv. *He tore up the unsatisfactory manuscript and started afresh:* anew, again, over, once more, another time; again and again, over and over.

after prep. **1.** *One after another they came in:* following, behind. —adv. **2.** *They lived happily ever after:* subsequently, afterwards, thereafter, later. —adj. **3.** *We never heard from him in after years:* following, ensuing, later. —**Ant.** 1 before. 3 previously, earlier, sooner.

aftermath n. *The picnic had an unfortunate aftermath--we all had poison ivy the next day:* consequence, outcome, result; sequel, follow-up, upshot, offshoot, byproduct, *Slang* payoff.

afternoon n. *We spent the afternoon at home:* cocktail hour, p.m., post meridian, *Informal* sun down over the yardarm.

afterthought n. *As an afterthought he asked about her health:* reconsideration, review, second thought.

afterward adv. *We enjoyed the tennis match but afterward we were tired:* later, after, subsequently, in a while, a while later, by and by, eventually, following, next, then, ultimately, thereafter.

again adv. They hoped never to do this again: another time, once more, afresh, anew, encore, freshly, newly, over, repeatedly, ditto.

agape adv. **1.** She just stood there with her mouth agape, not knowing what to say: wide open, gaping. **2.** The symphony left the audience agape: wonderstruck, spellbound, dumbstruck, dumbfounded, stupefied, amazed, astonished, awestruck, flabbergasted, agog.

age n. **1.** The child was about three years of age. The age of man is three score and ten: period of existence, duration of life, life span; lifetime, generation. **2.** His face was wrinkled with age. You can't get a driver's license until you're of age: old age, advanced age, seniority; adulthood. **3.** Geologists say this valley was formed by the last ice age. We reach middle age before we know it: era, epoch, period, phase, date; stage of time, stage of life. **4.** It seemed an age before he arrived: a long time, eon, millennium; forever. —v. **5.** Children seem to age before our eyes. The tragedy has aged him: advance in age, grow older, mature, develop; make old. **6.** The cheese was aged for two years before being ready for market: mature, ripen, mellow, season, develop. —**Ant.** 2 youth, childhood, adolescence. 4 short time, instant, second.

aged adj. **1.** The tribe was ruled by an aged and venerable man: old, elderly, of advanced age, advanced in years, ancient. **2.** A pretty little girl, aged 3: of the age of, as old as, having lived for. **3.** Do you have any aged cheddar cheese?: mature, ripe, ripened, mellow. —**Ant.** 1 young, youthful, juvenile. 3 unripe, immature.

agency n. **1.** I got the job through an employment agency: service organization, bureau, department. **2.** The hero was granted a pension through the agency of the king: power, action, activity, operation; intervention, mediation, force, influence, charge, means, instrument, instrumentality.

agenda n. What's on your agenda today?: list of things to be done, schedule, docket, program, timetable; items of business.

agent n. **1.** She's not a good actress, but she gets a lot of parts because she has a good agent: representative; emissary, envoy, deputy, advocate; intermediary, negotiator, go-between. **2.** Gravity is the agent that draws objects to earth: force, power, agency, mover, effective principle; means, instrument, cause, author, vehicle. **3.** General Grant was a leading agent of the South's defeat: doer, perpetrator, performer, practitioner, worker, mover, operator, executor. —**Ant.** 2 counteragent, counteractor, opponent, neutralizer.

agglomerate v. She agglomerated the silk threads into a large ball: gather, assemble, amass, cluster, condense, collect, accumulate, conglomerate, heap together, lump together, pile up, heap up, bunch, clump, gather into a mass; rally, muster, mobilize. —**Ant.** disperse, scatter, unwind.

aggrandize v. His being elected mayor aggrandized his standing in the community: enlarge, increase, amplify, magnify, extend, inflate, blow up, build up, expand, broaden, widen; strengthen, intensify, beef up; stretch, bloat, puff up, distend, dilate. —**Ant.** decrease, diminish, contract, constrict, deflate, collapse, crunch.

aggravate v. **1.** Don't scratch--you'll only aggravate the itch: make worse, worsen, make more severe; intensify, inflame, irritate, exacerbate, increase, heighten. **2.** His bossy attitude aggravates me: irritate, annoy, exasperate, anger, vex, rile, nettle, affront. —**Ant.** 1 improve; soothe, relieve, assuage, alleviate, ease; lessen, mitigate, pacify. 2 please; soothe, calm, placate, ease.

aggravation n. **1.** Nuisance phone calls only added to his aggravation: irritation, exasperation, annoyance, provocation, affliction, bother, difficulty, vexation, worry. **2.** Putting weight on his foot caused more aggravation of the strain: worsening, intensification, exacerbation, exaggeration, heightening, increase, inflammation, magnification. —**Ant.** 2 amelioration.

aggregate n. The final plan was an aggregate of all our ideas: composite, compound, union, combination, gathering, accumulation, collection, amassing, bringing together, summation, mixture, mix, blend, mass, conglomeration, conglomerate.

aggression n. Deer show less aggression than tigers. Sinking our ship was an act of open aggression: hostile behavior, hostility, fighting spirit, active anger, viciousness, pugnacity, belligerence, combativeness; act of war, hostile act, assault, invasion, raid, offense. —**Ant.** peacefulness, friendliness, submissiveness; peace, pacification.

aggressive adj. **1.** Aggressive nations must turn to peace. Dogs can become aggressive if provoked: hostile, belligerent, combative, assailant, pugnacious, vicious, tending to attack, contentious, warring. **2.** An aggressive young man can go far in this firm: self-assertive, forceful, competitive, bold; enterprising, ambitious, energetic, zealous. —**Ant.** 1 peaceful, friendly; submissive. 2 retiring, quiet, shy, bashful, mild; lazy.

aggrieved adj. She couldn't help feeling aggrieved at the slight: sorrowful, saddened, troubled, pained, disturbed; sad, grieving, griefstricken, tearful, mournful; offended, affronted, wronged, hurt, stung, wounded, injured, abused, ill-treated, maltreated, put upon, persecuted, distressed, imposed upon.

aghast adj. **1.** We were completely aghast at his failure: astonished, amazed, stunned, astounded, thunderstruck. **2.** She was aghast at the brutal way prisoners were treated: filled with horror, horrified, terrified, horror-struck, shocked, appalled; fear-struck, frightened. —**Ant.** 1 expectant, expecting, confident; nonplussed. 2 pleased, calmed; indifferent, unmoved, unaffected, unexcited.

agile adj. With an agile leap, the boy escaped his captor. The job requires an agile mind: nimble, spry, supple, limber, lithe, dexterous, athletic, graceful; quick, swift, fleet, clever, alert, keen, active. **—Ant.** clumsy, awkward, heavy, ponderous; slow, sluggish, lethargic, inactive, torpid.

agility n. The gymnast showed great agility: dexterity, suppleness, adroitness, acuteness, alertness, cleverness, quickness.

aging adj. **1.** Good wine requires careful aging: maturing, mellowing. **2.** Her aging parents retired from their jobs: waning, declining, senescent, getting on.

agitate v. **1.** A mixer agitates the cement until it is ready to pour: stir, stir up, shake, shake up, churn, mix; beat, rock, jar. **2.** The fiery speech agitated the crowd: upset, excite, work up, bring to a fever pitch; provoke, goad, disquiet, trouble, disturb, alarm, foment. **—Ant.** 2 calm, calm down, soothe, pacify, quiet, compose, still.

agitation n. **1.** The feverish patient showed much agitation: agitating, shaking, jarring, disturbing. **2.** The period was marked by protests, riots, and other agitation: disturbance, excitement, turmoil, tumult, storm; unrest, disquiet; struggle, conflict; perturbation, flurry, ado, to-do. **3.** After much agitation from the public, the government withdrew its legislation: urging, persistence; debate, discussion, dispute, argument, campaign. **—Ant.** 2 serenity, calm, tranquility.

agitator n. Local agitators were accused of disrupting the meeting: inciter, instigator, fomentor, provoker, troublemaker, provocateur, French agent provocateur, incendiary, rabble-rouser, mischief-maker, inflamer, firebrand, revolutionary.

agnostic n. He calls himself an agnostic, because he's just not interested in religion: nonbeliever, unbeliever; doubter, skeptic, secularist, doubting Thomas, free spirit, freethinker, empiricist; disbeliever, heathen, heretic, infidel, pagan, atheist.

ago adv. It occurred long ago: before, back, back when, gone, since, past.

agog adj. The teenagers were agog at the sight of the movie star: openmouthed, awestruck, enthralled, thrilled, excited, worked up, astir, eagerly expectant. **—Ant.** indifferent, uninterested; bored.

agonize v. The man agonized over the guilt he felt: feel pain, be in agony, suffer, anguish, be tormented, be tortured, be distressed; worry, strain, struggle, labor, wrestle, Slang sweat. **—Ant.** enjoy, exhilarate; relax.

agony n. **1.** This country must not again go through the agony of war: suffering, pain, torment, throes, torture; anguish, distress, misery, affliction, woe; sorrow, anxiety. **2.** She went through agonies finishing her term paper: effort, striving, struggle, strain; trial, tribulation. **—Ant.** 1, 2 pleasure, joy, enjoyment; comfort, ease; relief, consolation.

agrarian adj. North Dakota is primarily an agrarian state: agricultural, farming, crop-raising, agronomical. **—Ant.** manufacturing, industrial.

agree v. **1.** I can't agree to the terms of this contract: assent, consent, accede, go along with; think alike, be of one mind, side with, support, subscribe, come to the same conclusion, admit, grant, concede, accept, allow. **2.** Since the two stories don't agree, someone is lying: concur, accord, coincide, conform, correspond; jibe, match, square, harmonize, chime, tally. **3.** The union and management have agreed on a new contract: settle, come to an understanding, see eye to eye. **—Ant.** 1–3 disagree, differ. 1 dissent, dispute, refute, deny, oppose. 2 contradict.

agreeable adj. **1.** The new neighbor was an agreeable person. I hope you will find your room agreeable: pleasing, pleasant, gratifying, congenial; to one's liking, to one's taste, acceptable, suitable, appropriate, fitting. **2.** Are you agreeable to my plans for a picnic?: in accord, consenting, complying, amenable, going along with; approving, concurring. **—Ant.** 1 disagreeable, unpleasant, displeasing, unlikable, offensive; unacceptable, unsuitable, inappropriate, unfitting. 2 disapproving.

agreement n. **1.** The meeting ended in friendly agreement: mutual understanding, accord; concord, concordance, alliance, harmony, concert, meeting of the minds. **2.** The decorations were in agreement with the holiday season. There is so much agreement between the term papers, that the teacher suspects plagiarism: harmony, in keeping, compliance, conformance, conformity, compatibility, accordance, affinity; similarity, analogy, correspondence. **3.** They made an agreement to rent the house: promise, contract, compact, pact, arrangement, settlement, covenant, Informal deal, bargain. **—Ant.** 1, 2 disagreement, discord. 1 dissension. 2 inconsistency, dissonance, difference, dissimilarity, discrepancy.

agricultural adj. Oats and barley were the main crops in that agricultural area: agrarian, farming, rural, rustic.

agriculture n. Better methods of agriculture are needed to feed the world's population: farming, husbandry, crop-raising, cultivation, tillage, market gardening; agronomy, agronomics, geoponics.

aground adj., adv. The ship was aground in shallow water: stranded, grounded, foundered, stuck, beached, ashore. **—Ant.** afloat.

ahead adv. He took courses as a way to get ahead: forward, in front, advancing, advanced, along, ante, first, fore, foremost, leading, progressing, superior, triumphant. **—Ant.** behind, trailing, last.

aid v. **1.** At Christmas, many organizations aid the poor: help, assist, abet, lend assistance, give a helping hand; support, give support to, sustain, minister to, serve, accommodate; contribute, give alms to. **2.** A good dictionary can aid language learning: foster, further, promote, advance; facilitate, make easy, serve. **—n. 3.** The stranded climbers needed aid to get back down the mountain: help, assistance, helping hand; support. **4.** The United States spent millions in foreign aid after World War II. The family lived on government aid for two years: relief, dole; charity, donation, contribution, assistance; subsidy, allowance. **5.** Usually **aide.** *His political aides worked hard during the election campaign:* assistant, right-hand man, associate, subordinate, adjutant, auxiliary, girl Friday, man Friday; helper, abettor; follower, adherent, retainer; *Religious* acolyte, *Military* aide-de-camp. —**Ant.** 1 hurt, harm, injure; oppose, hinder. 2 hinder, obstruct, block, *Informal* hold up; oppose, discourage, thwart, impede, detract from. 3 hindrance. 5 superior, boss; leader.

aide *n. She worked several years as a teacher's aide:* assistant, aid, helper, supporter, attendant, deputy.

ail *v.* **1.** *What's ailing you today?:* bother, annoy, trouble, distress, worry, upset; be the matter with, afflict, sicken, make ill; pain. **2.** *My grandmother is ailing again:* be sick, be ill, be unwell, be indisposed; fail in health, be infirm; *Slang* be on the sick list. —**Ant.** 1 make happy; comfort, solace, console. 2 be in good health, make well; be strong, thrive, flourish.

ailing *adj. The ailing woman suffered from hypertension and diabetes:* sickly, sick, ill, unwell. —**Ant.** healthy, well.

ailment *n. Back pains and an upset stomach are just two of his ailments:* disorder, complaint, malady, infirmity, discomfort, affliction, disability; illness, sickness, disease, infection; indisposition, weakness. —**Ant.** good health, healthy sign; fitness.

aim *v.* **1.** *Aim the gun at the target:* point, direct, level, slant, beam, train on; take aim, sight, focus. **2.** *We aim to please. He aimed for the presidency:* try, strive, aspire to, work toward, endeavor, seek, attempt, be after; intend, mean, want, wish, desire, essay, have in mind; have in view, have an eye to. —*n.* **3.** *The gunner's aim was on target:* aiming, line of sighting; marksmanship. **4.** *His aim is to retire to Florida:* desire, wish, intention, intent; aspiration, goal, ambition, target, purpose, object; plan, scheme, design.

aimless *adj. The critic characterized the music as "aimless tootling":* directionless, undirected, unorganized, erratic, unsystematic, unguided, rudderless; pointless, purposeless, unfocused; wayward, frivolous, chance, unpredictable, haphazard, accidental, random, indiscriminate, hit-or-miss, inconsistent. —**Ant.** well-organized, purposeful, systematic, methodical, discriminating, consistent.

air *n.* **1.** *Air is composed mainly of oxygen, nitrogen, carbon dioxide, and water vapor:* the air we breathe, *Slang* ozone. **2.** *The glider soared high in the air:* atmosphere, stratosphere, sky. **3.** *Cold air blew in through the open window:* wind, breeze, draft, air current, air flow, blast, puff, zephyr, whiff, waft, breath of air. **4.** *An air of mystery pervaded the abandoned house. She has a certain air of sadness all the time:* atmosphere, aura, mood, spirit, feeling, tone, ambience; quality, manner, style, look, appearance. **5. airs.** *Don't put on airs with me!:* affectations, affectedness, pretensions, pretense, artificial manners; haughtiness, hauteur, arrogance, su-

perciliousness, swank. **6.** *The child sang a delightful air:* tune, ditty, melody, song, strain; ballad, lay, carol. —*v.* **7.** *The blankets were aired on the line:* ventilate, expose to air, aerate. **8.** *The gubernatorial candidates aired their views on television:* voice, express, declare, vent, tell, utter; proclaim, make public, reveal, disclose, divulge, display, exhibit, publicize, expose. —**Ant.** 8 keep silent; suppress, repress, hide, conceal.

aircraft *n. The aircraft stopped to refuel:* airplane, plane.

airplane *n. The airplanes flew overhead in V-formation:* plane, aircraft, heavier-than-air craft, *British* aeroplane; *(variously)* jet, prop-jet, propeller-driven plane; *Slang* bird, crate, flying jenny; *Obsolete* airship.

airport *n. Be at the airport a half hour before the plane leaves:* airfield, landing field, flying field, field; airstrip, landing strip; airdrome, *British* aerodrome; air base, jet base.

airship *n. The airship floated over the trees:* lighter-than-air craft; *(variously)* dirigible, blimp, balloon.

airtight *adj. The experiment required an airtight jar:* closed, impenetrable, impermeable, sealed, shut.

airy *adj.* **1.** *The castle halls were large and airy:* open to the air, well-ventilated, sunny, spacious; windy, breezy, drafty. **2.** *The little goats hopped about in an airy way. The band played an airy tune:* jaunty, sprightly, lively, frolicsome; light-hearted, light, light-of-heart, merry, cheerful, cheery. **3.** *His head was full of airy thoughts:* imaginary, fanciful, dreamy, ethereal, gossamer, unsubstantial, immaterial, unrealistic, illusory, idealized. —**Ant.** 1 airless, stifling; gloomy, dark, dank. 2 ponderous, heavy, sluggish, clumsy, slow; cheerless, doleful. 3 material, substantial, factual, realistic; solid, hard.

aisle *n. The aisle was crammed with people:* passageway, passage; walkway, walk, path, way, corridor, avenue, lane, alley; ambulatory, cloister.

ajar *adv. The door was left ajar:* partly open; open, unclosed, agape, gaping.

akin *adj., adv.* **1.** *Wolves and dogs are closely akin:* related by blood, related, kin, kindred; of the same stock, having a common ancestor, consanguineous; connected, allied, affiliated. **2.** *Her thoughts on the subject are akin to mine:* alike, like, identical, uniform; similar, resembling, parallel, comparable, corresponding, analogous; agreeing, congenial, correlative. —**Ant.** 1, 2 unrelated, unconnected; foreign, alien. 2 unlike, different, divergent, dissimilar, disparate; disagreeing, noncongenial.

alacrity *n.* **1.** *She answered his call for assistance with alacrity:* willingness, enthusiasm, eagerness, fervor, zeal, avidity; alertness, promptness, dispatch, readiness. **2.** *Despite his 80 years, he moved with alacrity:* liveliness, briskness, sprightliness; agility, nimbleness. —**Ant.** 1 unwillingness, indifference, unconcern, apathy, impassiveness, reluctance, disinclination;

languor, lethargy, dullness. 2 slowness, sluggishness.

alarm *n.* **1.** *The building was evacuated at the first alarm:* warning, danger signal, alert. **2.** *An alert guard gave the alarm to the troops:* call to arms, summons to arms, war cry; hue and cry, beat of drum. **3.** *She responded with alarm to the news:* apprehension, trepidation, consternation, agitation, dismay, distress, perturbation, misgiving; fear, fright, affright, panic, terror. —*v.* **4.** *The sight of smoke alarmed them. I am alarmed by your irresponsible attitude:* unnerve, frighten, scare, terrify; panic; dismay, disturb, make uneasy, distress, trouble, make anxious, make nervous, agitate, appall. —**Ant.** 1 all clear. 3 composure, self-possession, equanimity, sangfroid, calmness, coolness, serenity, tranquillity. 4 give courage; calm, assure, relieve, comfort.

album *n.* *They pasted the photos in the album:* scrapbook, book, portfolio; register.

alcohol *n.* *She had not touched alcohol since her accident:* drink, intoxicant, alcoholic beverage, liquor, *Informal* booze, *Slang* firewater.

alcoholic *adj.* **1.** *It is against the law to serve alcoholic beverages to minors:* intoxicating, inebriating, inebriative, spirituous, hard, strong; fermented, distilled; *Slang* with a kick. —*n.* **2.** *He became an alcoholic and lost his job:* drunkard, drunk, dipsomaniac, inebriate; hard drinker, sot, rummy, guzzler, tippler, imbiber, toper; *Slang* lush, souse, barfly, soak, boozer, whiskey head. —**Ant.** 1 nonalcoholic, nonintoxicating, soft. 2 teetotaler, abstainer.

alcoholism *n.* *She can't hold a job because of her alcoholism:* acute alcoholism, chronic alcoholism, dipsomania, pathological drunkenness, alcoholic psychosis, oenomania; delirium tremens, DT's, intemperance, chronic intoxication, chronic drunkenness.

alcove *n.* *The living room had a dining alcove at one end:* recess, niche, nook, bay; cubicle, compartment, corner, opening.

alert *adj.* **1.** *For a two-month-old, the baby was exceptionally alert:* aware, attentive, wide-awake, observant, perceptive, intelligent; active, quick, lively, sprightly, nimble. **2.** *The alert guard foiled the robbery:* watchful, vigilant, diligent, attentive, keen-eyed, wary, on guard, careful, heedful. —*n.* **3.** *The air raid alert sounded at noon:* alarm, siren; warning, signal. —*v.* **4.** *The sign alerted us to the thin ice:* warn, forewarn, make aware of, signal, notify, inform. —**Ant.** 1 unaware, oblivious, half-asleep; slow, listless, sluggish, inactive, lethargic, languid. 2 unwary, off guard, careless, heedless, lackadaisical, unconcerned, dilatory. 3 all clear. 4 lull.

alias *n.* *To avoid reporters, the movie star registered under the alias of Pete Jones:* assumed name, pseudonym, nom de guerre.

alibi *n.* *The defendant had no alibi for the night of the crime:* defense of being elsewhere; excuse, explanation, justification, pretext, *Slang* out.

alien *n.* **1.** *During World War II, all aliens had to register with the government:* resident foreigner,

foreigner, outsider, outlander, stranger; immigrant, newcomer. —*adj.* **2.** *Orange trees are alien to Canada:* foreign, not native, strange; remote, distant, outlandish, exotic. **3.** *Cheating is alien to my nature:* contrary, opposed, contradictory, inconsistent, incompatible, conflicting; unlike, different, dissimilar, unconnected, unrelated, incongruous; separated, estranged. —**Ant.** 1 citizen, natural, subject, countryman; native. 2 native, indigenous. 3 in accordance with, agreeable, compatible, consistent, congenial; like, related, relevant, congruous.

alienate *v.* *His increasing belligerence alienated him from his old friends:* estrange, separate, keep at a distance, come between, divorce, turn away, set against. —**Ant.** make friendly, draw close, unite; reunite, reconcile, turn to.

alienation *n.* *Lack of communication led to their alienation:* estrangement, breach, breaking off, rupture, separation, divorce.

alight *v.* *No one was waiting for her when she alighted from the bus:* come down, get down, dismount, descend, land, touch down, thump down, climb down, get off, disembark, detrain, deplane.

align *v.* **1.** *She neatly aligned the flower pots on the window sill:* arrange in line, line up; straighten, even, even up; make parallel, put in a row. **2.** *He aligned himself with those who voted against the tax bill:* join, ally, side, go along with, cast one's lot with; associate, affiliate.

alike *adj.* **1.** *He and his brother are very much alike:* same, identical, uniform, equal, even, of a piece, akin, one and the same, kindred; parallel, corresponding, equivalent, synonymous, homogeneous, analogous. —*adv.* **2.** *Good teachers treat all their students alike:* equally, in the same way, similarly, identically, evenly, uniformly. —**Ant.** 1 different, unlike, dissimilar, distinct, separate, divergent, diverse. 2 differently, unequally, unevenly, distinctly, separately, disparately, diversely.

alimony *n.* *The court ordered $300 a month in alimony:* maintenance, keep, upkeep, provision, subsistence.

alive *adj.* **1.** *My brother is alive and well in Mexico. Despite the hard winter, the rose bush is still alive:* living, among the living, animate, breathing, subsisting, *Archaic* quick, *Informal* alive and kicking, above ground. **2.** *My grandmother is more alive than a lot of young people:* full of life, vital, lively, active, vivacious, animated, vigorous, energetic, spry; aware, eager, alert, spirited. **3.** *Our plans to remodel the house are still alive:* in existence, extant, in force, operative, in operation; not dead, unextinguished, unquenched; possible, viable. —**Ant.** 1 dead, deceased, expired, defunct, lifeless, departed, no more; inanimate. 2 lifeless, unanimated, dispirited, spiritless, apathetic; inactive, unaware. 3 extinct, inactive, inoperative, inoperable; gone, lost, down the drain.

alkaline *adj.* *Tests showed the soil was alkaline:* antacid, alkali, basic, salty.

all *adj.* **1.** *We drank all the coffee:* the whole of, the total of; the entire contents of, every part of. **2.** *All children must be asleep before Santa Claus comes:* every one of, each of, each and every one of, every single one of; any of, any one of; the whole number of, the total of, the sum of; to a man. **3.** *In all fairness I have to warn you of his plans:* complete, total, full, entire, perfect, utter, utmost, the greatest possible. —*adv.* **4.** *This shirt is all worn out. She's all excited about going to the party:* completely, entirely, totally, utterly, wholly, altogether; very, exceedingly, in the highest degree, fully. —*pron.* **5.** *Is that all you can carry?:* everything, every item; the whole quantity, the greatest number, the whole amount, the greatest amount, the total, the entirety, the utmost possible. **6.** *All of us overate!:* everyone, each, every member. —**Ant.** 1, 2 none of; some. 3 partial. 4 somewhat, partially, a little. 5 nothing, none; some. 6 no one, none; some.

all-around *adj. He's an all-around ballplayer who can play any position:* versatile, many-sided, multifaceted, well-rounded, all-round; adaptable, gifted, flexible, adroit, ambidextrous.

allay *v.* **1.** *His reassuring words allayed my fears:* calm, quiet, put to rest, soothe; subdue, cause to subside, quell, hush, smooth, appease, pacify, mollify. **2.** *This medicine will allay the pain:* relieve, ease, alleviate, lessen, assuage, reduce, diminish, check; lighten, soften, mitigate, mollify; blunt, dull, moderate, slake, slacken, subdue, quiet, quench. —**Ant.** 1 arouse, awake, kindle, stir, stir up, excite, provoke; stimulate, fan. 1, 2 make worse, aggravate, increase, intensify, heighten, enhance, magnify, multiply.

allegation *n. Your allegation that the mayor is corrupt must be proved:* assertion, declaration, claim, avowal, profession, contention, statement; charge, accusation, indictment. —**Ant.** retraction; denial, disavowal, refutation.

allege *v. The newspaper article alleges that the mayor is corrupt:* claim, declare, state, assert, maintain, say, avow, contend, affirm, aver, profess, impute; charge, accuse, impugn. —**Ant.** retract; disclaim, deny, disavow, refute.

alleged *adj. She was extradited for the alleged offence:* supposed, asserted, ostensible, pretended, professed, purported, so-called, stated, declared.

allegiance *n. I'm proud to pledge allegiance to the flag and to my country. My first allegiance is to my family, then to my friends:* loyalty, faithfulness, fidelity, fealty, adherence, constancy; deference, devotion, obedience, homage. —**Ant.** disloyalty, betrayal, treachery, perfidy, deceit, faithlessness; treason, traitorousness, sedition, rebellion; alienation.

allegorical *adj. The figures in the mural were allegorical:* symbolic, symbolizing, emblematic, figurative, illustrative, metaphorical, typifying, representative.

allegory *n. George Orwell's* Animal Farm *is generally interpreted as an allegory about the Russian Revolution:* fable, parable. —**Ant.** true story, history.

alleviate *v. This medication will alleviate the soreness:* relieve, ease, allay, assuage; lessen, reduce, abate, diminish, check, temper, lighten, soften, mitigate, mollify; blunt, dull, moderate, slake, slacken, subdue, quit, quench. —**Ant.** make worse, aggravate, increase, intensify, heighten, enhance, magnify, multiply.

alley *n. There was a boulevard in front of the house and an alley behind it:* narrow back street, byway; passageway, passage, pathway, lane.

alliance *n.* **1.** *England and France formed an alliance against Germany:* agreement, pact, compact, treaty, concordat, entente cordiale. **2.** *The American colonies joined in an alliance against the British:* association, partnership, affiliation, league, company; confederation, confederacy, federation, union, coalition. —**Ant.** 2 separation, secession.

allied *adj.* **1.** *The allied armies of the United States, Canada, Britain, and France invaded Hitler's Europe:* joint, combined, united; associated; federated, affiliated; incorporated, corporate, amalgamated. **2.** *Music and drama are allied arts:* related, kindred, akin, cognate; similar, resembling, alike, like. —**Ant.** 1 unallied, uncombined, disunited; individual. 2 alien, foreign to each other, unrelated; different, dissimilar, unalike, disparate; divergent.

allocate *v. The town allocated funds for the new school:* set aside, designate, earmark, allot, assign, allow, apportion; budget, appropriate. —**Ant.** withhold, hold back, deny, refuse, veto.

allot *v. The factory alloted a parking space to each employee:* assign, allocate, earmark, give out, appoint, consign, grant, allow, dispense; apportion, portion out, distribute, parcel out, dole out, divide up, mete out, provide. —**Ant.** withhold, retain, keep; deny, refuse.

allotment *n. When food is scarce, rationing will assure that each person gets a fair allotment. The company gives me an allotment of $15 a day for traveling expenses:* share, portion, quota, measure, apportionment, allocation, ration, consignment; allowance, appropriation, grant, dispensation.

all-out *adj. With an all-out effort, we can put the fund over the top:* full-out, unstinted, unreserved, full-scale, total, complete, maximum, thoroughgoing, intensive, exhaustive, unqualified, out-and-out, unremitting, unlimited. —**Ant.** half-hearted, indifferent, perfunctory, lukewarm.

allow *v.* **1.** *My salary doesn't allow me to live extravagantly. The teacher allowed us to leave school early:* permit, let, give permission to, give leave to; authorize, concede to, sanction, agree to, approve. **2.** *Allow yourself an hour to get to the airport:* allot, allocate, assign, grant, give, provide. —**Ant.** 1 forbid, refuse, prohibit, disallow, deny.

allowance *n.* **1.** *When I was a boy, my allowance was 50¢ a week. Disabled veterans deserve a government allowance:* allotment, ration, subsidy, stipend, grant, payment, bounty; annuity, income, pension. **2.** *Trade in your old* car and you'll get an allowance on the new one: discount, deduction, reduction, concession, subtraction. **—Ant.** 2 increase, addition.

alloy n. **1.** Brass is an alloy of copper and zinc: fusion, compound, amalgam, mixture, admixture, synthesis, commixture, blend, composite. —v. **2.** Bronze is made by alloying tin with copper: mix, admix, commix, interblend, combine, conglomerate, intermix; impair, adulterate, dilute.

all right adj., adv. **1.** She felt all right in spite of her accident: well, healthy, in good health, hale, hearty; safe, uninjured, unharmed, unimpaired, Informal O.K. **2.** The new cake recipe turned out all right: satisfactorily, acceptably, fair, Informal O.K.; correctly, properly. **3.** All right, I'll do as you wish: yes, very well, Informal O.K.; certainly, absolutely. **—Ant.** 1 bad, poorly, in bad health, incapacitated; injured, harmed. 2 badly, poorly, unsatisfactorily, unacceptably; incorrectly. 3 no, not at all; absolutely not.

allude v. He frequently alluded to his childhood on the farm: mention, refer, speak of, touch upon; hint, suggest, intimate. **—Ant.** keep secret, keep quiet about, be closemouthed about.

allure v. **1.** He was allured by her wealth and sophistication: lure, attract, entice, tempt, lead on, bait, seduce; fascinate, beguile, charm, enchant, intrigue, captivate. —n. **2.** The allure of foreign travel tempted him to join the Navy: attraction, enticement, lure, temptation; fascination, enchantment, charm, glamour, intrigue. **—Ant.** 1 repel, alienate, drive away, deter, damp one's enthusiasm, Slang turn off; bore, be indifferent to.

allusion n. The book on American history makes a brief allusion to the ancient Greek concept of democracy: reference, mention; hint, suggestion.

ally n. **1.** The United States was an ally of Great Britain in two world wars: partner, associate, confederate, affiliate; collaborator, accomplice, accessory; colleague, confrere. —v. **2.** The townspeople allied themselves in the fight for lower taxes: unite, join together, join forces, band together, combine, bind together; affiliate, confederate, league. **—Ant.** 1 enemy, foe, adversary, opponent; rival, competitor, antagonist. 2 go separate ways; separate.

almanac n. She found her horoscope in the almanac: annual, yearbook, calendar, chronicle, journal, record, register, registry.

almighty adj. **1.** Judaism was the first religion to teach the existence of a supreme deity having almighty power: unlimited, absolute, sovereign, supreme, infinite, transcendent, invincible, omnipotent, all-powerful. —n. **2. The Almighty.** See GOD.

almost adv. She almost fell off her horse. It's almost ten miles from here to downtown Cleveland: nearly, very nearly, about, just about, practically, approximately, close to, all but, not quite, not far from, on the verge of, within an inch of, well-nigh. **—Ant.** exactly, definitely; certainly, surely.

alms n. The tourists were besieged by beggars demanding alms: donation, gift, contribution, offering, gratuity, present, handout, baksheesh, pittance; assistance, aid, charity, benefaction, dole, relief, mercy, subsidy, largess, beneficence, tribute.

aloft adv. The glider soared aloft. They held their heads aloft: in the air, above, overhead, in the sky, in the clouds, skyward, heavenward; up, high up, way up, on high; in a higher place. **—Ant.** down, low, low down; lower, below, beneath; earthward.

alone adv., adj. **1.** She's too young to go to the party alone. The house stood alone on the hill: by oneself, without others, unaccompanied, separately, singly, solitarily; single, solitary, isolated; unescorted, unattended, unchaperoned. **2.** It's too big a job for one man to do alone. The President alone has the power to appoint a member of the U.S. cabinet: without help, unaided, unassisted, single-handedly, with one's own two hands; all by oneself, only, on one's own, solely, sole. **3.** Mount Everest stands alone in its magnificence: unique, uniquely, singular, singularly; unsurpassed, unequalled, unrivaled, unmatched, matchless, peerless, without peers, unparalleled, nonpareil, incomparable. **4.** After her husband's death she felt terribly alone: lonely, lonesome, friendless; forsaken, deserted, abandoned, isolated, separated; forlorn, desolate. **—Ant.** 1 accompanied, with others, jointly; escorted, attended, chaperoned. 2 with assistance, assisted, with help, helped, aided; jointly, together, with others. 3 among others, equally, equalled; surpassed, overshadowed.

aloof adj. **1.** Her aloof manner gained her few friends: cool, cold, chilly, detached, indifferent, standoffish, distant, remote, unsociable, reserved, unapproachable, unsympathetic, uninterested, unconcerned, unresponsive, haughty, high-hat, formal. **2.** The royal family usually stands aloof from politics: apart, at a distance, above. **—Ant.** 1 warm, friendly, familiar, open, sociable, gregarious, neighborly; interested, sympathetic, compassionate.

aloud adv. If you want to say it aloud, don't be bashful. The ancients were in the habit of reading aloud even when alone: not in a whisper; in a normal speaking voice, audibly. **—Ant.** whispered, in a whisper; inaudibly, silently.

alphabet n. The invention of the alphabet changed humanity: writing system, ABCs, characters, letters, hieroglyphics, script, signs, symbols.

alpine adj. We went hiking through the alpine country of Switzerland: mountainous, towering, lofty, elevated, aerial, alpen; alpestrine, subalpine; cloud-capped, snow-capped, snow-clad; heaven-touching, sky-kissing, cloud-touching, cloud-piercing.

also adv. A year later her sister was also admitted to the bar: in addition, additionally, including, too, further, besides, moreover, furthermore, ditto, to boot.

alter v. The blonde wig completely altered her appearance: change, transform, make different, amend, revise, remodel, convert; modify, vary, recast. —**Ant.** keep, retain, *Informal* stick to.

alteration *n.* *If we remodel the store we'll have to close for alterations:* change, modification, remodeling; transformation, transmutation, conversion; adjustment. —**Ant.** permanence, changelessness, stability.

altercation *n.* *Their frequent altercations destroyed their friendship:* dispute, argument, controversy, quarrel, spat, row, *Informal* scene, wrangling; discord, falling-out, disagreement; fight, bickering, scrape, fracas, scuffle, affray, rumpus, brawl, melee, *Slang* broil. —**Ant.** agreement, accord, concord, harmony; peace; making-up.

altered *adj.* *Their altered plans signified a reduced budget:* modified, adjusted, changed, converted, redone, refitted, remodelled, renovated, reshaped, revised, doctored.

alter ego *n.* *A close friend is sometimes called one's alter ego:* twin, other self, second self, *doppelgänger*, double, counterpart, other likeness, other image; simulacrum, semblable, duplicate, complement, match.

alternate *v.* **1.** *My sister and I alternate in washing the supper dishes. The desert temperatures alternate from 120° at noon to 40° at night:* take turns, perform by turns, rotate; interchange, intersperse; vary, change, alter. —*adj.* **2.** *Each of the two druggists works on alternate Sundays. The awning had alternate red and white stripes:* every other, every second; alternating, reciprocal, consecutive, successive. **3.** *If the main road is closed, take an alternate route:* another, substitute, second, backup. —*n.* **4.** *He attended the Republican National Convention not as a delegate but as an alternate:* substitute, surrogate, sub, second, standby, backup, understudy, *Informal* stand-in, pinch hitter; deputy, proxy.

alternative *n.* *If he wants to get to Chicago by tonight, he has no alternative but to go by plane:* choice, other choice, option, recourse, way out; selection, substitute.

although *conj.* *Although she was partly deaf, she was a gifted pianist:* though, even though, notwithstanding, even if, albeit.

altitude *n.* *At that altitude most people have trouble breathing:* height, elevation; tallness, loftiness; prominence, eminence, sublimity; apex, zenith, vertex. —**Ant.** depth, pit, abyss.

altogether *adv.* **1.** *The actor gave an altogether magnificent performance:* completely, entirely, utterly; absolutely, totally, wholly, thoroughly, perfectly, fully, out and out; in general, on the whole, quite. **2.** *The bill came to $67 altogether:* in all, as a whole, in toto, in sum total; collectively, all inclusive. **3.** *Altogether, I'm glad we're moving:* all told, all in all, on the whole, in sum, *Informal* when all is said and done. —**Ant.** 1 partially, partly, incompletely. 2 in part; separately, individually. 3 partially, partly; somewhat.

altruism *n.* *A man of great altruism, he spent his life helping the poor:* selflessness, magnanimity, generosity, unselfishness, large-heartedness, beneficence, humanitarianism, philanthropy, benefaction, benevolence, liberality, humanity. —**Ant.** selfishness, misanthropy, self-centeredness, self-servingness.

altruistic *adj.* *Her altruistic deeds helped many people:* unselfish; generous, benevolent, large-hearted; humanitarian, charitable, philanthropic, public-spirited. —**Ant.** selfish, self-seeking, covetous, greedy; egoistic, egocentric, self-centered; malevolent, mean, grudging.

alumnus *v.* *He was an alumnus of the University of Missouri:* male graduate, former student.

always *adv.* **1.** *Work always begins at nine:* every time, on every occasion, without exception; regularly, invariably, consistently. **2.** *Will you love me always?:* forever, forever and ever, for all time, eternally, everlastingly, perpetually, evermore; continually, unceasingly, unremittingly, incessantly. —**Ant.** 1 never; rarely.

amalgam *n.* *Her character is a curious amalgam of charm and aggressiveness:* mixture, blend, fusion, combination, amalgamation, union, merger, compound, admixture, commixture, composite, intermixture, alloy; assemblage, joining, alliance, league; *Slang* combo, mishmash.

amalgamate *v.* *Silver must be amalgamated with a harder material to make durable jewelry. The two shipping companies amalgamated into one:* combine, blend, merge, fuse, mix, commingle; unite, unify, join together, consolidate, coalesce, incorporate, federate, integrate, synthesize. —**Ant.** separate, part, divide, disunite.

amass *v.* *The campers amassed a large pile of branches before starting their fire. He amassed a fortune in the oil business:* accumulate, gather, collect, acquire, assemble, compile, heap up, pile up, round up. —**Ant.** scatter, disperse, distribute, dispense.

amateur *n.* **1.** *Amateurs are not allowed to play in most professional golf tournaments. An amateur shouldn't play poker for high stakes:* nonprofessional, dabbler, hobbyist, dilettante; beginner, novice, neophyte, greenhorn, tyro. —*adj.* **2.** *Acting with an amateur theatrical group can be fun:* nonprofessional; unprofessional, unpolished, inexperienced; unskilled, inexpert. —**Ant.** 1, 2 professional, expert. 2 experienced, practiced, polished, finished; skilled.

amatory *adj.* *His amatory glances made her extremely uncomfortable:* amorous, passionate, ardent, impassioned, romantic, infatuated, doting, loverlike, loving, adoring, languishing, devoted, tender, fond, lovesick, fervent, rapturous, yearning; erotic, libidinal, lascivious, sensual, hot, steamy, sexy, sexual, sexed-up. —**Ant.** hateful, mean, spiteful, vindictive, contemptuous.

amaze *v.* *Her rapid progress in karate amazed the teacher:* surprise, astonish, astound; flabbergast, awe, daze, shock, dumbfound, stupefy, stun, stagger. —**Ant.** expect, anticipate.

amazement *n.* *Imagine my amazement when the 70-year-old man beat me at tennis:* astonishment, surprise, shock, stupefaction; disbelief, incredulity, bewilderment; wonder, awe. —**Ant.**

anticipation, expectation; calmness, composure, indifference.

ambassador n. The President appointed him ambassador to Chad: ambassadress (fem.), diplomat, representative, minister, envoy, agent, deputy, emissary, consul, legate, nuncio, go-between, intermediary, courier, Brit. diplomatist, minister plenipotentiary, consul general, attaché, career diplomat.

ambience n. The food wasn't much, but the restaurant had a nice ambience: atmosphere, environment, surroundings, climate, milieu, setting; character, mood, temper, flavor, spirit, tenor.

ambiguity n. The ambiguities of his statement led us to suspect he might be lying: equivocation, vagueness, abstruseness, uncertainty, doubtfulness, indefiniteness. —**Ant.** clarity, clearness, explicitness, definiteness, certainty.

ambiguous adj. "Indian" is an ambiguous word because it can refer to an American Indian or a native of India: equivocal, vague, unclear, cryptic, enigmatic, puzzling, indefinite, uncertain, doubtful; misleading, having a double meaning. —**Ant.** explicit, definite, specific, direct, conclusive; clear, plain, frank, unmistakable, obvious, simple, lucid; unquestionable, honest.

ambition n. **1.** An executive has to have a lot of ambition to reach the top: drive, zeal, desire, push, striving. **2.** Her ambition is to be a lawyer: aspiration, goal, aim, intent, objective, purpose, plan, design; desire, dream, hope, longing, yearning. —**Ant.** 1 indifference; indolence, sloth.

ambitious adj. **1.** Ambitious students make the best grades: aspiring; zealous, eager, intent, desirous, ardent, avid, determined. **2.** Building your own garage is a rather ambitious undertaking: grandiose, enterprising, industrious, energetic; strenuous, difficult, arduous. —**Ant.** 1 unambitious, unaspiring; apathetic, indolent, slothful, lazy. 2 modest, humble, lowly; easy, simple.

ambivalent adj. I have ambivalent thoughts on where to spend my vacation: contradictory, conflicting, opposing, clashing, warring; confused, undecided, unfocused, mixed, wavering, fluctuating, vacillating, Informal wishy-washy. —**Ant.** definite, positive; unwavering.

amble v. We ambled across the meadow, enjoying the fresh air: stroll, walk leisurely, wander aimlessly, ramble, meander, saunter. —**Ant.** rush, run, race.

ambulatory adj. The doctor says your leg is healing well and you'll be ambulatory in another week: up and about, not confined to bed; walking, moving, mobile, peripatetic. —**Ant.** bedridden; not walking, immobile.

ambush n. **1.** The robbers lay in ambush as the stagecoach approached: concealment, cover, hiding, ambuscade, hiding place, hideaway, blind, stalking-horse. —v. **2.** The soldiers were ordered to ambush the enemy patrol: waylay, surprise, trap, entrap, lay for, attack, assault.

ameliorate v. **1.** The council met to consider ways of ameliorating the foreign situation: im-

prove, better, help, heal, fix up, patch up, correct, rectify; amend, reform, revise, improve upon, make an improvement upon; advance, promote. **2.** Doctors say the patient's condition has ameliorated: improve, get better, grow better, perk up, pick up, progress, come along, mend, show improvement. —**Ant.** 1 ruin, botch, queer, screw up, wreck, destroy. 2 deteriorate, go downhill, decline, weaken, worsen.

amen interj. All Christian and Jewish prayers end with an "Amen!": so be it, it is so, let it be so, so shall it be, would that it were so; truly, verily; Informal hear hear, yes indeed.

amenable adj. The committee is amenable to any suggestions. Are you amenable to having the meeting next Tuesday?: agreeable, willing to agree, willing to listen, responsive, cooperative; favorably disposed, cordial, persuadable, tractable, open, open-minded, acquiescent, willing, obliging, complaisant, sympathetic, yielding, submissive. —**Ant.** closed-minded, obstinate, stubborn, headstrong, truculent, recalcitrant, autocratic, autonomous.

amend v. **1.** The members of the club voted to amend the constitution: change, revise, modify, alter, emend. **2.** I would advise you to amend your manners: improve, better, perfect, develop, polish, enhance; emend, correct, rectify, reform, remedy, mend, fix. —**Ant.** 2 corrupt, spoil, damage, harm, injure, hurt, impair, blemish; vitiate.

amendment n. **1.** The first ten amendments to the U.S. Constitution are called the Bill of Rights: addition, adjunct. **2.** Amendments must be made to the blueprints before the builder will accept them: revision, modification, change, alteration, emendation; improvement, correction, rectification, reform.

amends n. Is there any way I can make amends for ruining your party?: apology, defense, justification, explanation, vindication; redress, restitution, recompense, retribution, compensation, reparation, indemnification, restoration, payment, requital, expiation, Informal peace offering; atonement, acknowledgment, satisfaction.

amenity n. **1.** amenities. Children should be taught the social amenities: good manners, politeness, courtesies, niceties, gallantries, bits of etiquette; refinement, gentility. **2.** The host greeted his guests with amenity: geniality, amiability, affability, agreeableness, pleasantness, graciousness, friendliness, civility; gentleness, mildness. —**Ant.** 1 bad manners, impoliteness, discourtesy, rudeness, boorishness. 2 unpleasantness, surliness, incivility.

amiable adj. Amiable neighbors help make a house a home. He has an amiable personality: friendly, agreeable, amicable, pleasant, congenial, good-natured, kindly, obliging, cordial, sociable, affable; pleasing, attractive, engaging, winning, charming; polite, genial, gracious. —**Ant.** unfriendly, hostile, disagreeable, unpleasant, ill-humored, sullen, surly, sour; displeasing, unattractive, repellent, repugnant, loathsome, offensive.

amicable adj. If wars are to end, nations must

learn amicable means of settling their disputes: friendly, peaceable, agreeable, amiable, amenable, harmonious, cordial, civil, polite, courteous, kind, kindly, kindhearted, benevolent; sociable, neighborly. —**Ant.** unfriendly, hostile, belligerent, antagonistic, contentious, pugnacious, bellicose, quarrelsome; disagreeable, nasty, unsociable, unkind, cold.

amid prep. Amid the flying bricks and bottles, the riot police kept calm: among, amidst, amongst, surrounded by, in the middle of, in the midst of.

amiss adj. **1.** I knew something was amiss from her startled expression: wrong, awry, askew, inappropriate, unsuitable, improper, out of order, Slang off base; faulty, mistaken, incorrect, erroneous; false, fallacious, mixed-up; untoward. —adv. **2.** Did I speak amiss when I mentioned the surprise?: wrongly, wrong, inappropriately, unsuitably, improperly, mistakenly, untowardly, out of order, Informal out of line; incorrectly, erroneously, falsely, faultily, inaccurately, awry, astray. —**Ant.** 1 right, proper, appropriate, suitable, Informal perfect, O.K., in good shape; in order; correct, true. 2 rightly, properly, appropriately, suitably; correctly, truly.

amity n. Canada and the United States have lived side by side in amity for generations: friendship, harmony, good will, understanding, sympathy; cooperation, agreement, accord, concord; cordiality, fellowship, fraternity, brotherhood. —**Ant.** enmity, antagonism, hostility, animosity, conflict, contention, ill will; disagreement, dissension, discord, strife.

amnesty n. The king granted amnesty to the rebels: pardon, reprieve; forgiveness, absolution, reconciliation; immunity.

among prep. Among the trash, we found real gems: amid, amongst, between, in the midst of, surrounded by, between, with.

amorous adj. The young man gave his fiancée an amorous glance: loving, enamored, lovesick; ardent, passionate, impassioned; fond, affectionate, tender, doting. —**Ant.** unloving, indifferent, uncaring, cold, frigid; hateful.

amorphous adj. An amorphous haze hung over the city: shapeless, formless, undefined, undelineated, unshapen; vague, nondescript, indeterminate, characterless, anomalous.

amount n. **1.** What is the amount of my bill?: total, sum, sum total, aggregate; extent, magnitude. **2.** The recipe calls for a small amount of sugar: quantity, measure; volume, bulk, mass.

amour n. He's always bragging about his amours: love affair, affair, romance, intrigue, liaison.

ample adj. **1.** This country has an ample supply of fuel oil if we don't waste any. We have ample time for a leisurely lunch: enough, sufficient, adequate, satisfactory; substantial, capacious, more than enough, plenty, abundant, plentiful, bountiful, profuse, copious, generous, liberal. **2.** A wrestler must have ample muscles: large, big, immense, huge, vast; wide, broad, extensive, expansive, outspread, extended, roomy, spacious, voluminous, commodious. —**Ant.** 1 in-

sufficient, inadequate, unsatisfactory; limited, restricted; scant, scanty, sparse, meager, skimpy, scrimpy; niggardly, stingy. 2 small, little, minute, wee.

amplification n. **1.** The amplification of the project will take more time: enlargement, expansion, increasing, development, extension, aggrandizement; heightening, broadening, widening. **2.** His story needs amplification: elaboration, rounding out, developing, augmentation, added detail, fleshing out. —**Ant.** 1 reduction, decreasing, curtailment, contraction, cutting down, paring down; narrowing. 2 simplification, simplifying; condensing, abridging, cutting, boiling down.

amplify v. **1.** We must amplify our effort by working a lot harder: increase, intensify, strengthen, heighten, raise; expand, broaden, extend, enlarge, widen, lengthen, deepen. **2.** Please amplify your remarks by giving us some examples: elaborate on, illustrate, expatiate on; expand, develop, add to, augment, supplement, fill out, complete. —**Ant.** 1 reduce, decrease, curtail, cut down, pare down. 2 simplify, condense, abbreviate, abridge; summarize, boil down.

amplitude n. **1.** The amplitude of the universe is awesome: magnitude, extent, size; vastness, largeness, bigness; spaciousness, capaciousness; dimension, breadth, width; bulk, volume, mass. **2.** Leonardo da Vinci is remembered for the great amplitude of his creative powers: range, scope, extent, compass, sweep, reach; expanse; completeness, fullness, richness; abundance, profusion, plenitude, copiousness, plethora. —**Ant.** 1 smallness. 2 limitation, narrowness, restriction, circumscription.

amply adv. The troops were amply supplied with provisions: adequately, sufficiently, satisfactorily, thoroughly, completely, fully; more than enough, abundantly, plentifully, profusely, copiously, bountifully, generously, liberally, lavishly, richly, unstintingly. —**Ant.** inadequately, insufficiently; scantily, meagerly, skimpily.

amputate v. The surgeon had to amputate the patient's leg: cut off, sever, dismember, excise, remove; Informal lop off.

amuck adv. The escaped lunatic ran amuck through the hospital, waving a hatchet: amok, wildly, insanely, murderously, uncontrollably, maniacally, in a frenzy, ferociously, frenziedly, berserk; Slang nuts, crackers, bonkers.

amulet n. The witch doctor wore an amulet on a string around his neck: charm, talisman, fetish, lucky piece.

amuse v. We amused ourselves by playing games: entertain, divert, occupy; interest, engross, absorb, beguile; please, gladden, cheer, enliven. —**Ant.** bore; tire, weary; vex, annoy.

amusement n. **1.** Reading is my favorite amusement. There is a time for work and a time for amusement: pastime, diversion, pleasure, distraction; entertainment, recreation, avocation, hobby; fun, play, game, revel. **2.** He smiled with amusement at the child's prank: merriment, pleasure, delight, enjoyment.

—**Ant.** 1 bore, boredom, tedium, monotony, ennui. 2 sadness; displeasure, disgust.

amusing *adj.* **1.** *Charades is an amusing game:* entertaining, diverting, interesting, beguiling, engrossing, absorbing; pleasant, delightful, pleas-urable, pleasing, cheering. **2.** *His jokes were amusing:* funny, comical, humorous, witty, droll, farcical, waggish. —**Ant.** 1 boring, dull, tedious, monotonous. 2 sad, depressing.

analgesic *n.* *The most common analgesic is aspirin:* painkiller, anodyne; (*variously*) anesthetic, narcotic, opiate, drug. —**Ant.** irritant.

analogous *adj.* *The heart is analogous to a pump:* similar, like, comparable, akin, equivalent, parallel, correlative, corresponding. —**Ant.** dissimilar, unlike; different, divergent.

analogy *n.* *The doctor pointed out the analogy between the heart and a pump:* similarity, likeness, resemblance, similitude; comparison, correspondence, parallelism, correlation, equivalence; simile, metaphor. —**Ant.** dissimilarity, difference.

analysis *n.* **1.** *Chemical analysis of water yields hydrogen and oxygen:* separation, breakdown, breakup, reduction, dissection, resolution, partition, dissociation. **2.** *The F.B.I. wants a complete analysis of how the crime was committed:* examination, investigation, inquiry, observation, study, test, search. **3.** *The newscaster's analysis of the election results was interesting:* judgment, evaluation, diagnosis, reasoning, thinking, interpretation, speculation, estimation, assay, appraisal; summary, review, outline, synopsis, abstract, précis, digest, brief. **4.** *The psychiatrist recommended analysis:* psychoanalysis, psychotherapy, therapy. —**Ant.** 1 synthesis, uniting, union, combining, combination.

analyst *n.* **1.** *The neurotic patient was sent to an analyst:* psychoanalyst; *Slang* headshrinker, shrink. **2.** *A football coach has to be a good analyst of his players' abilities:* judge, evaluator, estimator, appraiser; examiner, investigator, observer, tester.

analytic or **analytical** *adj.* *A chess player must have an analytic mind:* logical, rational, systematic, organized, problem-solving; inquiring, studious, searching, testing, diagnostic. —**Ant.** illogical, disorganized, unsystematic, chaotic.

analyze *v.* **1.** *The doctor analyzed the blood sample for anemia:* separate and examine the parts of. **2.** *The mathematician analyzed his figures again:* examine, study, investigate, question, search, assay, appraise; evaluate, diagnose, consider, judge, think through, reason out. —**Ant.** 2 ignore, overlook, pay no heed to, shut one's eyes to; neglect, slight, pass over, brush aside.

anarchist *n.* *Anarchists burned down the palace:* rebel, revolutionary, insurgent, terrorist, mutineer; syndicalist; nihilist. —**Ant.** loyalist, tory, conservative; disciplinarian.

anarchy *n.* **1.** *Any form of government is better than anarchy:* absence of government, disorder, lawlessness, chaos. **2.** *Anarchists dream of an ideal state of anarchy in which people will be* completely free: utopia, the millennium. —**Ant.** 1 order, discipline, authority; government, organization, control; regimentation, subjection.

anathema *n.* **1.** *That traitor's name is anathema in this house!:* abomination, taboo, unmentionable. **2.** *The papal anathema was pronounced chiefly against heretics:* curse, malediction; excommunication, ban, censure, proscription; denunciation, condemnation. —**Ant.** 1 beloved; welcomed. 2 blessing, benediction.

anathematize *v.* *We declare him excommunicated and anathematized and we judge him condemned to eternal fire:* excommunicate, maledict, damn; condemn, accurse, execrate, abominate, hold in abomination.

ancestor *n.* **1.** *His ancestors were pioneers:* forefather, forebear; progenitor, procreator, begetter. **2.** *The icebox is the ancestor of the refrigerator:* forerunner, predecessor, antecedent, precursor, prototype. —**Ant.** 1 descendant, inheritor; progeny, scion, issue, offspring. 2 successor.

ancestry *n.* **1.** *Many Mexicans are of Spanish ancestry:* descent, extraction, derivation; origin, stock, heredity, race. **2.** *My aunt has always made much of her ancestry:* ancestors, lineage, progenitors; family, line, parentage, house; genealogy, pedigree, blood line, family tree. —**Ant.** 1 posterity. 2 descendants, progeny, issue.

anchor *n.* **1.** *Drop the anchor when the boat passes the sandbar: Informal* hook; ground tackle, mooring. **2.** *The Bible is the anchor of our faith:* mainstay, support, bulwark, strong point, basis, foundation; safeguard, security, defense. —*v.* **3.** *They anchored their boat in the outer bay:* secure by anchor, moor; drop anchor, cast anchor, ride at anchor. **4.** *We anchored the hammock to the trees:* secure, fix, affix, fasten. —**Ant.** 3 lift anchor, weigh anchor, break free.

anchorage *n.* *The breakwater provided an anchorage for the sailboats:* harbor, roadstead, port, mooring, harborage, berth, seaport, dock, marina, quay, key, jetty, bund, dockage.

ancient *adj.* **1.** *The pyramids were built in ancient times:* long past, remote, olden, old; early, primeval, primitive, prehistoric; *Historical use* Greco-Roman, classical, prior to A.D. 476. **2.** *Canada's Laurentian Mountains are the most ancient on the continent. He drives an ancient Packard:* old, very old, aged, age-old; antique, timeworn, hoary. **3.** *That the woman's place is only in the home is an ancient idea:* out-of-date, old-fashioned, out-of-fashion, outmoded, antiquated, passé, bygone, *Informal* old hat; obsolete, obsolescent, archaic, fossilized. —**Ant.** 1 recent, late. 2 new, brand new, spanking new, young. 3 modern, fresh, novel, modernistic; current, up-to-date, newfangled, new-fashioned, in vogue, modish, *Slang* with it.

ancillary *adj.* *The main clause of the contract concerns the amount of money to be paid, and all the whens and wherefores are ancillary to it:*

supplementary, auxiliary, accessory, contributory, adjunct; secondary, subordinate, subsidiary, additional; minor, dependent, subservient, inferior. —**Ant.** main, major, primary, prime; independent; counteractive, contrary, at odds with.

anecdote *n. Public speakers often begin their talks with humorous anecdotes:* story, tale, yarn, short narrative, brief account, sketch, reminiscence.

anemic or **anaemic** *adj.* **1.** *He felt weak because he was anemic:* deficient in hemoglobin, thin-blooded. **2.** *That anemic-looking room needs some bright paint:* pale, pallid, wan, dull, colorless, subdued, quiet; weak, feeble, characterless. —**Ant.** 2 bright, colorful, florid, loud, flashy; strong, powerful.

anesthesia or **anaesthesia** *n. His state of anesthesia lasted several hours after the operation:* insensibility to sensations, loss of feeling, insentience, numbness; unconsciousness, stupor.

anesthetic or **anaesthetic** *n. The doctor used a new anesthetic on the patient:* painkiller, analgesic, narcotic, opiate, drug. —**Ant.** stimulant, analeptic.

anew *adv. After the applause the performers began anew. If the experiment doesn't work this time, you'll have to begin your research anew:* again, once more, over again; from scratch, in a new way, afresh, newly. —**Ant.** never again, nevermore.

angel *n.* **1.** *The angel Gabriel is mentioned in the Bible in Daniel 8:16 and Luke 1:26:* messenger of God, heavenly spirit, celestial being; (*variously*) seraph, cherub, throne, domination, virtue, power, principality, archangel. **2.** *I married an angel:* angelic person, *Slang* doll, gem, jewel, treasure, saint. **3.** *He's an angel of the new play on Broadway:* financial backer, patron, benefactor, sponsor, underwriter. —**Ant.** 1 devil.

angelic *adj.* **1.** *The music had an angelic quality:* ethereal, celestial, heavenly, divine, spiritual, saintly, beatific; seraphic, cherubic. **2.** *What an angelic child!:* angellike, good, ideal, pure, innocent; beautiful, lovely, enrapturing, rapturous, entrancing, adorable. —**Ant.** 1, 2 demonic. 1 hellish, netherworld. 2 diabolical, fiendish; ugly, ugly as sin, repulsive.

anger *n.* **1.** *My anger grew as he continued his insults:* rage, outrage, fury, wrath, ire, temper, gall, bile, choler, spleen, pique, dander; indignation, resentment, exasperation, petulance, vexation, irritation, annoyance, displeasure, umbrage, disapprobation; antagonism, animosity, hostility, hatred, enmity, acrimony; ill temper, hot temper. —*v.* **2.** *I did not mean to anger you:* infuriate, enrage, outrage, madden, incense, inflame, pique, rile, gall, nettle, chafe, exacerbate; provoke, exasperate, vex, irritate, rankle, annoy, displease; antagonize, embitter, cause ill feelings; *Informal* make bad blood, ruffle one's feathers, get one's dander up. —**Ant.** 1 love, liking, fondness; good will, peaceful-ness, mildness, amiability; approval, acceptance, condona-

tion; calmness, equanimity; pleasure, gratification; forgiveness. 2 placate, appease, pacify, mollify, propitiate, calm, soothe; please, delight, gladden, gratify, *Informal* tickle.

angle *n.* **1.** *A vertical line will meet a horizontal line at an angle of 90°: Geometry* space between two lines or planes that meet; divergence. **2.** *The road makes a sharp angle just over that hill:* bend, turn, corner, edge, cusp. **3.** *Try to look at the situation from my angle. The view of the valley is beautiful from this angle:* point of view, viewpoint, standpoint, position, side, aspect, slant; outlook, focus, perspective.

angry *adj. Her rudeness makes me angry. She's in an angry mood:* mad, furious, infuriated, enraged, outraged, raging, fuming, boiling, turbulent, incensed, inflamed, irate, indignant, exasperated, resentful, vexed, piqued, riled, nettled, galled, *Slang* burnt up; provoked, irritated, annoyed, displeased, offended, affronted; hostile, hateful, antagonistic, acrimonious, embittered; ill-tempered, petulant, irascible, splenetic, huffy. —**Ant.** loving, fond, friendly; calm, soothing, peaceful, mild, complaisant, agreeable, pleasant, amiable; happy, pleased, pleasing, gratified, gratifying; good-natured, even-tempered; apologetic, forgiving, unresentful, placating.

anguish *n. The mother waited in anguish for news of her missing child:* distress, pain, agony, suffering, torment, despair, misery; anxiety, heartache, grief, woe; remorse, sorrow. —**Ant.** comfort, ease; relief, solace, consolation, alleviation.

angular *adj.* **1.** *The mountain trail is angular and difficult to travel:* sharp-cornered, bent, crooked, jagged. **2.** *The old mountaineer had an angular face:* bony, gaunt, spare, lean, rawboned, scrawny, lanky, lank. —**Ant.** 1 straight; rounded. 2 chubby, fleshy, rotund, plump, stout, portly.

animal *n.* **1.** *Human beings are social animals. Corals are compound animals:* living being, creature, organism, biological system. **2.** *No animals are allowed in the restaurant:* nonhuman; (*variously*) wild animal, beast, farm animal, pet. **3.** *The zoo has collections of animals, birds, and reptiles:* mammal, quadruped. **4.** *Those teenage hoodlums behaved just like animals:* brute, beast.

animate *v.* **1.** *All living forms are animated by a mysterious force sometimes known as the "life force":* make alive, vivify, vitalize, quicken. **2.** *Her gaiety animated the entire group:* make lively, enliven, invigorate, give energy to, add spirit to, energize; excite, fire, fire up, warm. **3.** *She was animated by the best of intentions:* stimulate, arouse, stir, inspire, spur on, move, impel, set on, incite, instigate, activate, actuate; goad, urge, prompt, provoke, work up. —*adj.* **4.** *Do you think animate beings exist on Mars?:* alive, having life; moving. —**Ant.** 1 kill, deaden, make lifeless, devitalize. 2 depress, dishearten, cool, put a damper on, dull; bore. 3 discourage, dampen; deter, restrain, inhibit, curb, check. 4 inanimate, dead, lifeless.

animated *adj. The party was filled with ani-*

mated conversation: lively, spirited, active, vivacious, vigorous, zestful, invigorating, energetic, exciting, elated, vibrant, dynamic, vivid, bright, fervent, ebullient, ardent, zealous, passionate, hot, glowing, buoyant, airy, sprightly, quick, brisk, breezy, blithe, gay, sportive. —**Ant.** dull, deadly, lifeless, boring, monotonous; depressed, dejected; inactive, listless, spiritless, lethargic, torpid, slow, apathetic, passive; dispirited.

animation *n. The children sparkled with animation:* liveliness, life, spirit, high spirit, good spirit, animal spirit, blithe spirit, vivacity, vitality, vital power, zest, vigor, vim, verve, exhilaration, eagerness, enthusiasm, ebullience; excitement, ardor, elation, glow, vibrancy, fire, alertness, brightness, alacrity, sprightliness, buoyancy, briskness, gaiety, good cheer, sportiveness; action, activity. —**Ant.** lifelessness, dullness, spiritlessness; lethargy, apathy, passivity, inertness, stolidity, sluggishness, dejection, depression, low spirits.

animosity *n. The animosity between Alexander Hamilton and Aaron Burr finally resulted in a duel:* ill will, antagonism, bitterness, dislike, unfriendliness, malice, malevolence, malignity, hatred, hate, hostility, enmity, antipathy, anger, strife, resentment, rancor, acrimony. —**Ant.** good will, love, friendship, friendliness, harmony, congeniality, kindness, sympathy.

animus *n. I have no animus toward him; I just don't like being around him:* animosity, hatred, hostility, enmity, ill will, antagonism, dislike, bad blood, antipathy, ill feeling, rancor, venom. —**Ant.** friendliness, harmony, affection, good will, amicability, friendship.

annals *n. We found the information in the 1945 annals of the society. Never in the annals of crime has there been such a daring robbery:* yearly records, chronological records; chronicles, historical rolls, records, registers, archives; history, chronology; minutes.

annex *v.* **1.** *The city annexed the area across the river:* attach, add, incorporate, acquire, appropriate, expropriate, seize, merge, connect, join, subjoin, adjoin, affix, append, tack on, *Informal* grab. —*n.* **2.** *A new annex is being added to the school:* addition, attachment, appendage. —**Ant.** 1 detach, separate, disconnect, remove, disengage. 2 separation, detachment.

annihilate *v. Hitler sought to annihilate resistance movements throughout Europe:* wipe out, exterminate, liquidate, *Slang* waste; demolish, destroy completely, reduce to nothing, lay waste, decimate, obliterate, extinguish, end, abolish, eradicate, erase, extirpate. —**Ant.** let live; build, construct, create, make.

anniversary *n. Helen wants to go to Paris on our anniversary:* commemoration, fete, celebration, holiday, feast day; name day, birthday; centennial *or* centenary, sesquicentennial, bicentennial *or* bicentenary.

annotate *v. The famous classicist Richard Porson annotated the plays of Aeschylus in 1795:* explicate, commentate, elucidate, interpret, expound; construe, explain, comment, remark; gloss, footnote.

annotation *n. The annotations were printed in italics:* note, footnote, gloss, marginalia; remark, comment, observation; commentary, elucidation, interpretation, explication, *explication de texte,* exegesis, *apparatus criticus.* —**Ant.** main text, text.

announce *v.* **1.** *The President announced his cabinet appointments:* publish, promulgate, proclaim, declare; broadcast, advertise, disseminate, give out, sound abroad, trumpet; disclose, divulge, reveal. **2.** *The dark clouds announced the coming of a storm:* herald, harbinger, foretell, presage, augur, betoken, portend, signify, signal. —**Ant.** 1, 2 suppress, secrete, hide, cover up, conceal, bury, withhold, hush, keep back, keep secret, repress; hold back, reserve.

annoy *v. You children must stop annoying me by asking for candy all day long. I'm annoyed every day by the slow bus service in this town:* disturb, bother, pester, badger, harry, harass, nag, heckle, tax, hector, tease; trouble, worry, torment, plague, inconvenience, distract; irritate, provoke, exasperate, vex, gall, irk, ruffle, rile, nettle. —**Ant.** calm, soothe, comfort, relieve, solace, console; please, gratify; appease, mollify.

annul *v. The contract was annulled because it had not been legally signed by both parties:* render null and void, nullify, negate, invalidate, cancel, void; abrogate, revoke, rescind, retract, recall, repeal, reverse; abolish, dissolve, undo. —**Ant.** validate; enact, perform.

annulment *n. The marriage annulment was granted by the judge:* nullification, invalidation, cancellation, voiding; abrogation, revocation, retraction, recall, repeal, reversal; dissolution, undoing, repudiation, abolition. —**Ant.** validation.

anoint *v.* **1.** *She anointed herself with suntan lotion:* put oil on, smear with oily liquid, pour oil on, oil. **2.** *And the men of Judah came, and there they anointed David king:* crown, ordain, consecrate by unction, make holy by anointing, sanctify by anointing.

anomalous *adj.* **1.** *An Eskimo in native dress would cut an anomalous figure in Rio:* odd, strange, peculiar, incongruous, out of keeping, bizarre. **2.** *Cats with six toes are anomalous but not uncommon:* irregular, abnormal, atypical; monstrous. —**Ant.** 1 common, usual, standard, typical, familiar, unexceptional, ordinary, natural, normal, regular, conventional, customary. 2 normal, typical.

anomaly *n. His mature behavior was an anomaly for someone so young:* irregularity, exception to the rule; oddity, rarity; abnormality, deviation, aberration; eccentricity, peculiarity, incongruity. —**Ant.** the norm, the rule, the common thing.

anonymous *adj. They did not know whom to thank for the anonymous gift:* nameless, unnamed, bearing no name, unsigned; unidentified, unacknowledged, of unknown authorship. —**Ant.** named, signed; identified, acknowledged, known.

answer n. **1.** *Please send an answer to my letter soon:* reply, response, acknowledgment, rejoinder. **2.** *How many students had the correct answer?:* solution, explanation, resolution. —v. **3.** *Answer your sister's letter when you have the time. Please answer the doorbell:* reply, respond, acknowledge, react to; write, say, rejoin, retort. **4.** *I answered the problems on the test quickly and got them all right:* give a solution to, solve, resolve. **5.** (usually followed by **for**) *He will answer for his mistakes:* be responsible, be accountable, be liable; pay for, suffer for, make amends for, atone for, expiate. **6.** *His qualifications answer the requirements of the job:* meet, fill, fulfill, serve, suit; be sufficient, be adequate, be enough, pass muster, be satisfactory, do well enough; conform, correspond, be similar, be like, be equivalent, be the counterpart of, be correlated. —**Ant.** 1 question, query, inquiry, interrogation; summoning, summons, call, challenge. 2 problem. 3 question, ask, query, inquire, interrogate; summon, call, challenge. 4 ask. 6 fail; differ.

answerable *adj. All 18-year-olds are answerable for their behavior:* accountable, responsible, liable. —**Ant.** excused, exempt, unaccountable, not responsible.

antagonism n. *The unfairness of the will caused antagonism between the brothers:* hostility, opposition, conflict, friction, clashing, discord, strife; animosity, enmity, antipathy, rivalry, dissension; animus, bitterness, rancor, spite, resentment; hatred, dislike, aversion, detestation. —**Ant.** love, friendship, friendliness, amity, liking; peacefulness, agreement, accord, concord, harmony; sympathy, understanding.

antagonist n. *His antagonist in the debate was smarter than he:* opponent, adversary, rival, competitor, opposer, contestant, disputant; enemy, foe, attacker, assailant. —**Ant.** ally, partner, colleague, teammate; supporter, patron, defender; friend.

antagonize v. *His rude remarks antagonized the guests:* alienate, estrange, repel, offend. —**Ant.** conciliate, placate, pacify, appease, mollify, propitiate.

ante n. *He thinks nothing of a game where $100 is the ante and $500 the limit:* stake, bet, beginning bet, wager, pot.

antecedent *adj.* **1.** *The harpsichord was antecedent to the pianoforte:* precursory, preexistent, anterior, precedent, previous, prior. —n. **2.** *The horse and buggy was the antecedent of the automobile:* precursor, forerunner, predecessor, precedent, ancestor; harbinger, herald, pioneer. **3. antecedents.** *My antecedents were all pioneers:* ancestors, forefathers, forebears, family, predecessors, ancestry; family tree, lin-eage, pedigree, stock, house, extraction, progeniture. —**Ant.** 1 subsequent, following, posterior; later, after. 2 successor, sequel; consequence, result, aftermath, upshot. 3 descendants, progeny, issue, offspring.

antedate v. *The American Revolution antedated the French Revolution by 14 years:* precede, come first, be of older date than, occur earlier than, predate, go before, happen before, anticipate, antecede. —**Ant.** follow, succeed, come after, postdate.

antediluvian *adj. Uncle Jim's antediluvian business methods prevented him from ever making any money:* antiquated, antique, archaic, obsolete.

anterior *adj.* **1.** *Architects often embellish the anterior wall of a building and leave the rear wall blank:* front, in front, forward, placed before. **2.** *The Magna Carta is anterior to the U.S. Constitution by more than 500 years:* previous, precedent, prior, antecedent. —**Ant.** 1 posterior, rear, back. 2 subsequent, posterior.

anthology n. *He bought an anthology of Edgar Allan Poe's stories:* collection, compendium, compilation, choice; treasury, chapbook, garland, florilegium; digest, selections, extracts, miscellanea, scrapbook, commonplace book, miscellany, analects, gleanings, collectanea.

antic n. usually **antics.** *The clown's lively antics made the children laugh:* pranks, tricks, monkeyshines, tomfoolery, clownishness, buffoonery, sport, practical jokes; playful behavior, fanciful acts, shenanigans, ridiculous acts, skylarking, larks, escapades. —**Ant.** seriousness, solemnity, gravity.

anticipate v. *We anticipate a lot of snow this winter:* expect, look for, await; count on, prepare oneself for, look toward; look forward to, long for, pin hope on; foresee, forecast, predict, envision, foretell. —**Ant.** despair of, doubt; dread, fear; remember, recollect.

anticipation n. **1.** *As Christmas drew near, the children were filled with anticipation:* expectation, expectancy, hope. **2.** *The soldier shined his boots in anticipation of the inspection:* expectation, preparation.

anticlimax n. *After the excitement of the campaign, election day was an anticlimax:* letdown, comedown, disappointment, dull ending. —**Ant.** exciting climax, lofty ending.

antidote n. **1.** *Doctors rushed an antidote to the boy who had been bitten by the snake:* antipoison, counterpoison, countervenom, antitoxin, counteragent. **2.** *A hobby is a good antidote for boredom:* remedy, cure, countermeasure, corrective.

antipathy n. *I try to be broadminded but do feel antipathy toward people who are dirty and unkempt:* dislike, aversion, distaste; disgust, repulsion, loathing, repugnance, abhorrence; antagonism, animosity, ill will, enmity, rancor, hostility, unfriendliness. —**Ant.** affinity, fellow feeling, regard, sympathy, attraction, partiality; love, affection, attachment.

antiquated *adj. Grandmother has antiquated ideas about etiquette:* antique, old-fashioned, outmoded, passé, dated, out-of-date, outdated, of the old school; obsolete, archaic, obsolescent. —**Ant.** modern, new, young, current, recent, fresh, novel; up-to-date, new-fashioned, fashionable, newfangled, stylish, modish, smart.

antique *adj.* **1.** *She has a fine collection of antique furniture:* old, antiquated. —n. **2.** *The museum has a display of valuable antiques:* relic, rarity, curio, memorabile, objet d'art, bibelot, trinket. —**Ant.** 1 modern, new, fashionable, recent, current.

antiquity n. **1.** The vase in the museum is valuable because of its great antiquity: ancientness, great age, oldness. **2.** "Classical Antiquity" refers to the period of the ancient Greeks and Romans: ancient times. **3. antiquities.** We went to the British Museum to look at the Elgin Marbles and other antiquities: relics, monuments, artifacts. —**Ant.** 1 modernity, newness. 2 modern times, the present, today.

antiseptic n. **1.** You'd better put an antiseptic on that cut: disinfectant, germicide, germ killer, bactericide, prophylactic. —adj. **2.** The operating room must be antiseptic before the heart transplant begins: sterile, germ-free, aseptic.

antisocial adj. **1.** I don't know whether he's antisocial or just shy: unfriendly, unsociable, retiring; unsocial, asocial, misanthropic. **2.** Someday his antisocial behavior will land him in jail: hostile, menacing, antagonistic, belligerent; alienated, disruptive, rebellious, sociopathic. —**Ant.** 1 gregarious, friendly, sociable, genial, social. 2 cooperative, conformist, well-adjusted, normal.

antithesis n. **1.** Good is the antithesis of bad: direct opposite, reverse, inverse, converse, opposite extreme, contrary, contrast, antipode. **2.** "To be or not to be" is an example of literary antithesis: opposition of one idea against another in the same sentence, stating opposites in one sentence, setting of one clause against another in a sentence.

antonym n. An antonym is a word that is opposite in meaning to another: antithesis, opposite; abbreviation ant.

anxiety n. Our anxiety grew when the mountain climbers hadn't returned by nightfall: uneasiness, unease, worry, apprehension, misgiving, foreboding, distress, concern, tension, anguish, angst, suspense, fretfulness, disquiet, disquietude; dread, fear, alarm; solicitude. —**Ant.** relief; assurance, certainty, confidence; calmness, tranquility, serenity, composure, self-possession, aplomb.

anxious adj. **1.** She was anxious about her friend's illness: uneasy, distressed, apprehensive, tense, Slang uptight, disturbed, worried, troubled, disquieted, concerned, fretful, fraught with anxiety, anguished, fearful, alarmed, overwrought. **2.** The children are anxious to go to the party: eager, impatient, desirous, wanting, itching, yearning, expectant; earnest, intent, keen, ardent, fervent, avid, zealous. —**Ant.** 1 relieved, assured, sure, confident; calm, composed, cool, collected, unruffled, unperturbed, nonchalant. 2 reluctant, averse, hesitant, loath, disinclined, indisposed.

anyhow adv. See ANYWAY.

anyway adv. **1.** The weather was uncertain but we went hiking anyway: anyhow, nevertheless, nonetheless, just the same, regardless. **2.** It's too cool to go swimming anyway: in any case, in any event, at any rate, anyhow. **3.** A well-groomed woman can't fix her hair just anyway: carelessly, haphazardly, indifferently, anyhow,

without concern, sloppily. —**Ant.** 3 with care, carefully, perfectly, neatly.

apace adv. He galloped apace to warn of the enemy's approach: fast, quickly, rapidly, swiftly, hastily, precipitately, speedily, posthaste, Mil. on the double, expeditiously, at top speed, flat-out, lickety-split, double-quick, at a good clip, hell-bent for leather. —**Ant.** slow, slowly, dawdlingly, lackadaisically, listlessly.

apart adv. **1.** The toy fell apart the first time the child played with it: into pieces, into parts, asunder. **2.** The two stores are a block apart. Our birthdays are only a week apart: distant, one from another, afar; separately. **3.** The shy child sat apart from the other children: aside, to one side, by oneself, by itself, alone, aloof; isolated, separate, cut off, divorced. —**Ant.** 1 together. 2 near; together, adjoining. 3 in the midst of, surrounded.

apartment n. **1.** The couple moved into a new three-room apartment: set of rooms, suite, flat, Slang pad. **2.** There are sixteen units in the new apartment on Putnam Avenue: apartment building, multiple-dwelling building.

apathetic adj. Today's students are not apathetic about religion. The castaways lost hope and grew apathetic: indifferent, unconcerned, uninterested, unresponsive, uncommitted, disengaged, impassive, impossible, unmoved; unemotional, emotionless, unfeeling, cold, passionless, phlegmatic, spiritless. —**Ant.** concerned, interested, responsive, committed, active; stirred, aroused, roused, excited; emotional, passionate, zealous, vehement, hot.

apathy n. Public apathy can lead to bad government: indifference, unconcern, lack of interest, inattention, unresponsiveness, passiveness, lethargy, lassitude; lack of feeling, numbness, emotionlessness, coolness, impassibility, impassivity. —**Ant.** concern, interest, attention, responsiveness, action; emotion, feeling, excitement, passion, zeal, vehemence, enthusiasm, fervor.

ape n. **1.** Gorillas are the largest of the apes: tailless monkey, primate, (loosely) monkey. —v. **2.** He apes everything his older brother does: mimic, imitate, copy, echo, parrot, mirror, emulate, follow; mock, parody, caricature, burlesque, travesty.

aperture n. The light came in through an aperture in the roof: opening, hole, orifice, slit, space, interstice, slot; rift, rent, cleft, gap; chink, fissure, breach. —**Ant.** closure.

apex n. The apex of the pyramid looms 80 feet above the desert. Winning the Nobel prize was the apex of William Faulkner's career: summit, highest point, pinnacle, peak, height, tip, zenith, crest, vertex, crown, crowning point, cap; climax, acme, apogee, culmination, consummation. —**Ant.** bottom, base, foot; lowest point, low point, depth, nadir, perigee.

aphorism n. The statement "A man is known by the company he keeps" is an aphorism: maxim, epigram, proverb, adage, axiom, slogan, apothegm, dictum, saying, truism, Slang old saw.

aphrodisiac n. **1.** Doctors say the mind is the

most effective of all aphrodisiacs: love potion, philter, magic potion, cantharis, cantharides. —adj. **2.** All aphrodisiac literature was banned from the dormitory: erotic, sexually stimulating, prurient, sexy, fleshly, carnal, raunchy.

apiece adv. The rings cost thirty dollars apiece. Father gave us two cupcakes apiece: each, individually, severally, respectively. —**Ant.** together, all together, overall, collectively, en masse, as a group.

aplomb n. A good hostess can handle an embarrassing situation with great aplomb: composure, poise, self-composure, self-possession, calmness, coolness, equanimity, levelheadedness, stability, balance, imperturbability; self-assurance, self-confidence, confidence, intrepidity, savoir faire, sang-froid. —**Ant.** awkwardness, confusion; embarrassment.

apocalyptic adj. His apocalyptic views seemed to doom the human race: prophetical, prophetic, oracular, predictive, revelational, revealing, revelatory, far-seeing, prescient, disclosing, eye-opening, prognosticative.

apocryphal adj. Historians consider the story of George Washington's cutting down a cherry tree to be apocryphal: probably untrue, doubtful, questionable, dubious, unauthentic; mythical, fictitious, fabricated, unauthenticated, unverified, unsubstantiated, disputed; unauthorized, unofficial, uncanonical, spurious. —**Ant.** undisputed, unquestionable, without a doubt, authentic, creditable, true, factual; verified, authenticated, substantiated, attested; authorized, approved, official, sanctioned, canonical.

apogee n. Verdi, at 80, was at the apogee of his powers: farthest point, highest point, most distant point; vertex, apex, zenith, meridian, acme; top, crest, pinnacle, summit, peak; climax, culmination. —**Ant.** nadir, bottom, lowest point, weakest point.

apologetic adj. **1.** If you're truly apologetic, why not say you're sorry?: regretful, sorry, contrite, remorseful, self-reproachful, penitent. **2.** Good students don't need to be apologetic about their grades: making excuses, defensive, excusatory, extenuatory, vindicatory, justificatory, exonerative, mitigatory, apologetical. —**Ant.** 2 proud.

apologize v. He apologized for his rude behavior: express regret, make apology, beg pardon, say one is sorry.

apology n. **1.** She made an apology for breaking the glass: expression of regret, saying one is sorry, begging pardon; acknowledgment of error. **2.** The writer's autobiography was really an apology for the way he had lived: explanation, justification, defense, vindication, excuse.

apostate n. Julian "the Apostate" attempted to replace Christianity with worship of the old gods: heretic, dissenter, dissident, traitor, defector, deserter, backslider, renegade, seceder, tergiversator, recanter, turncoat, turnabout, recusant, bolter, nonconformist.

apostle n. **1.** Paul was an apostle of Christ. Dr. Thomas Dooley won fame as an apostle of democracy in Laos: missionary, evangelist, prose-

lytizer, disciple, witness; envoy, emissary, messenger, zealot, preacher. **2.** Thomas Paine was an apostle of free speech: advocate, pioneer, supporter, proponent, exponent, spokesperson, propagator, propagandist, activist, zealot. —**Ant.** opponent, detractor.

apotheosis n. To the public he was the apotheosis of the self-made man: immortalization, deification, exaltation, glorification, magnification, enshrinement, idealization, canonization, elevation, consecration, dignification; quintessence, embodiment, epitome, essence.

appall v. The sinking of the Lusitania by a German U-boat in 1915 appalled all Americans: horrify, dismay, shock, offend, outrage; disgust, sicken, repel, revolt, nauseate; stun, terrify, alarm, unnerve, dishearten, abash, frighten. —**Ant.** please, gladden; attract; reassure, calm, comfort, console.

appalling adj. The plight of the starving natives is appalling: dreadful, horrible, horrifying, horrific, awful, terrible, dire, grim, dismaying, horrid, frightful, fearful, ghastly, shocking, outrageous, intolerable, insufferable, abominable; disgusting, sickening, revolting, nauseating, repulsive, repellent; alarming, disheartening, terrifying, frightening. —**Ant.** pleasing, pleasant; reassuring, comforting.

apparatus n. **1.** This apparatus can purify a thousand gallons of water a minute: equipment, machinery, mechanism, machine, contraption, device, contrivance, appliance, gadget, Informal gismo; tools, implements, instruments, utensils, gear, paraphernalia, outfit, tackle; materials, material. **2.** The apparatus of government must not be choked with red tape: system, organization, setup.

apparel n. The new apparel for this spring features bright plaids. The nun packed all her apparel in one small suitcase: clothing, clothes, garments, dress, attire, Slang duds, threads, togs; vestments, vesture, raiment, robes, habit, garb, costume; equipment, gear, array, trappings, accouterments.

apparent adj. **1.** Her love for the child was apparent. The correct answer is apparent: obvious, evident, manifest, self-evident, plain, open, patent, marked, overt, blatant, conspicuous, clear, clear as day, clear-cut; understandable, unmistakable, unequivocal. **2.** It was an apparent stroke, but the doctors aren't certain yet: probable, seeming, according to appearances, likely, presumable, ostensible. **3.** The boat slowly became apparent through the fog: visible, discernible, perceivable, perceptible, conspicuous, distinct. —**Ant.** 1 unclear, uncertain, doubtful, ambiguous; hidden, covered up, veiled, disguised. 2 improbable, doubtful, unlikely, obscure. 3 invisible, hidden, concealed, indiscernible, imperceptible; dim, fuzzy.

apparition n. **1.** After hearing the ghost stories, the children thought they saw an apparition: ghost, phantom, specter, spirit, phantasm, wraith, shade, revenant, spook; materialization, manifestation, presence. **2.** Snow is quite an ap-

parition in Florida: unusual sight, strange spectacle, phenomenon.

appeal *n.* **1.** *The appeal for funds for the flooded city was highly successful:* plea, request, entreaty, petition, supplication, solicitation, adju-ration, suit, *Informal* S.O.S. **2.** *The kitten's appeal was hard to resist:* attraction, charm, fascination, interest, allure, charisma, *Informal* pull. —*v.* **3.** *The besieged nation appealed to the United Nations for aid:* plead, entreat, implore, call upon, petition, apply, solicit, beseech, invoke, adjure, sue to, beg, supplicate. **4.** *The idea of learning to ski appeals to me:* attract, interest, allure, entice, invite, tempt, fascinate, excite, charm, engage, *Slang* turn one on. —**Ant.** 1 refusal, rejection, repudiation, denial. 2 repulsiveness, alienation. 3 refuse, reject, repudiate, deny, rebuff. 4 repel, repulse, alienate, revolt, disgust, sicken, *Slang* turn one off; bore.

appear *v.* **1.** *Dark clouds appeared on the horizon:* come into view, become visible, show, show up, turn up, crop up, loom up, come to light; materialize, emerge, arise, surface. **2.** *She appears older than she is:* look, seem, strike one as being. **3.** *It appears that supper will be late:* be evident, be apparent, be obvious, be clear, be plain, be manifest, be patent. **4.** *The ad will appear in tomorrow's paper. Roberta Peters has appeared in concert halls all over the world:* be published, come out, be placed before the public; be on the stage, come before the public, perform. —**Ant.** 1 disappear, disappear from sight, vanish. 3 be uncertain, be unclear, be unknown; be doubtful.

appearance *n.* **1.** *The sudden appearance of the bear terrified the hikers. After the cold winter everyone looked forward to the appearance of spring:* appearing, coming into view, showing up, turning up; arrival, coming, advent, emergence, materialization, manifestation. **2.** *A job applicant should try to have a neat appearance:* look, aspect, image. **3.** *He gave the appearance that he was doing well until he flunked:* outward show, pretense, guise, pretext, impression. —**Ant.** 1 disappearance, vanishing; departure, passing.

appease *v.* **1.** *Nothing would appease the crying baby:* calm, make peaceful, pacify, quiet, soothe, solace, mollify, lull, compose, placate. **2.** *That sandwich appeased my appetite:* satisfy, ease, allay, abate, assuage, alleviate, temper, mitigate, relieve; slake, quench, quell, blunt, still, quiet, dull. **3.** *Chamberlain should never have tried to appease Hitler:* conciliate, accommodate, propitiate. —**Ant.** 1–3 aggravate, provoke, inflame, arouse. 1 disturb, upset, bother, annoy, dissatisfy, perturb. 3 anger, enrage, infuriate; antagonize, *Informal* cross.

appeasement *n.* **1.** *Is appeasement of an enemy better than war?:* acceding to demands, conciliation, propitiation, accommodation; submission, giving in. **2.** *All dieters have the problem of appetite appeasement. Music is an appeasement to shattered nerves:* means of quieting, means of calming, pacification, easing; alleviation, allaying, abating, mollification, as-

suagement, assuasion, mitigation, abatement, dulling, blunting, quenching; satisfaction, gratification. —**Ant.** aggravation, provocation, arousal; disturbance, annoyance.

appellation *n.* *Richard I was given the appellation "The Lion-Hearted":* name, title, designation, epithet, cognomen, sobriquet, nom de guerre, *Slang* handle, moniker, tag.

append *v.* *The professor will append a glossary to his new book:* add, affix, attach, join, subjoin, tack on, supplement; suspend, hang on. —**Ant.** remove, omit, leave out; subtract, take away, detach, disconnect, disengage, separate.

appendage *n.* **1.** *The porch wasn't part of the original house but was added later as an appendage:* addition, attachment, adjunct, extension; supplement, auxiliary, accessory. **2.** *The insect had lost one of its appendages and moved awkwardly:* extremity, member, projecting part, offshoot; (variously) branch, limb, arm, leg, feeler, tentacle, tail. —**Ant.** 1 main body. 2 body.

appendix *n.* *The book's appendix included a list of important dates in history:* supplement, codicil, back matter; addendum, addition, postscript. —**Ant.** front matter, introductory material; main body, body of the text.

appertain *v.* *The responsibilities that appertain to parenthood were discussed at the meeting:* belong to, be part of, pertain to, be characteristic of, inhere in; relate to, apply to, concern, be proper to, refer to, touch upon, bear upon. —**Ant.** be unrelated, be irrelevant, have no bearing upon.

appetite *n.* **1.** *The diet pills made him lose his appetite:* hunger, thirst. **2.** *He has an enormous appetite for classical music:* desire, craving, yearning, passion, inclination, penchant, proclivity; relish, zest, gusto, fondness, liking, stomach. —**Ant.** 2 surfeit, fill; distaste, aversion, dislike, detestation, disgust, loathing, revulsion, repugnance, repulsion.

appetizer *n.* *After so many appetizers we passed up the main course:* cocktail; tidbit, savory, dainty, delicacy; *French* apéritif, canapé, bonne bouche, hors d'oeuvre; *Italian* antipasto.

appetizing *adj.* *The smell of the overcooked food was not very appetizing:* mouth-watering, appealing, tempting, inviting, enticing, alluring, tantalizing; attractive; savory, palatable, succulent. —**Ant.** unappetizing; nauseating, sickening, repulsive; unpalatable, unsavory, distasteful.

applaud *v.* **1.** *Please don't applaud until everyone has performed:* clap. **2.** *The mayor applauded the fire fighter's bravery in his speech:* praise, laud, congratulate, commend, compliment; acclaim, hail, extol, sing the praises of, eulogize. —**Ant.** 1 boo, hiss, *Slang* give the raspberry, give the Bronx cheer. 2 criticize, censure; disparage, deride, ridicule, decry, deprecate, belittle.

applause *n.* **1.** *The applause for the pianist was deafening:* clapping, ovation. **2.** *Critics seldom give playwrights the applause they want:* praise, accolades, acclaim, plaudits, compliments, kudos, approval. —**Ant.** 1 booing, hissing, *Infor-*

mal raspberries, Bronx cheers. 2 criticism, condemnation, derision, ridicule.

appliance *n. The kitchen is equipped with modern appliances:* device, apparatus, fixture, machine, mechanism, contraption, contrivance, implement; equipment, gear.

applicable *adj. Yesterday's solutions are not always applicable to today's problems:* relevant, pertinent, adaptable, germane, apt, useful, suitable, fit, befitting, fitting, apropos. —**Ant.** inapplicable, inappropriate, wrong, useless, unsuitable, unfit, irrelevant.

applicant *n. There were three applicants for the job:* candidate, aspirant, hopeful; job seeker, office seeker; petitioner, suppliant, claimant.

application *n.* **1.** *The burn needs an application of ointment three times a day:* spreading on, putting on. **2.** *The liquid application was less effective against sunburn than the cream:* ointment, salve, unguent, lotion, balm, wash, solution, poultice, dressing, emollient. **3.** *The application of French cooking terms to American cooking is open to debate:* relevance, pertinence, germaneness, suitability, appositeness. **4.** *Have you made out your application for a passport?:* request, requisition, form; petition, claim, appeal, suit, entreaty, solicitation. **5.** *His application to his studies was rewarded by an A:* attention, attentiveness, diligence, industry, perseverance, persistence, dedication, commitment, assiduity. —**Ant.** 5 inattention, *Slang* goofing off; laxness, indolence.

apply *v.* **1.** *Apply two coats of varnish to the wood:* put on, lay on, spread on. **2.** *He applied what he had learned in class to the experiment:* use, utilize, employ, exercise, practice, implement, adapt, bring to bear. **3.** *The rules of safe driving apply to everyone:* be applicable, refer, pertain, relate, have bearing upon, be appropriate, fit, suit. **4.** *Job seekers should apply at the personnel office:* make application, request, petition. **5.** *It's difficult to apply oneself to a boring task:* devote, dedicate, direct, address. —**Ant.** 1 remove, take off. 3 be inapplicable, be irrelevant, be inappropriate, be unsuitable.

appoint *v.* **1.** *The President appointed a new cabinet member:* name, designate, assign, deputize, commission, delegate; select, nominate, engage. **2.** *Let's appoint a time for our next meeting:* designate, set, fix, determine, establish, prescribe; decide on, choose, settle, arrange. **3.** *The decorator appointed the new hotel with ultramodern furnishings:* furnish, equip, fit out, provide, supply. —**Ant.** 1 dismiss, discharge, cashier, fire. 2 cancel; change, rearrange. 3 strip, divest, denude, dismantle.

appointment *n.* **1.** *The cabinet appointments will be announced Tuesday:* designation, assignment, placement, commissioning; naming, selection, choosing, nomination. **2.** *The appointment as ambassador will be difficult for one with no experience:* assignment, position, office, situation, post, job, station, spot, place, berth. **3.** *What time is your lunch appointment?:* meeting, engagement, date, rendezvous; meeting time, meeting place. **4. appointments.** *The*

room's appointments were in Early American style: furnishings, furniture; accouterments, outfit, equipment, equipage, gear. —**Ant.** 1 dismissal. 3 accidental meeting; cancellation.

apportion *v. Apportion your income so that 25 percent goes for housing and 10 percent for food:* allocate, allot, distribute proportionally, prorate, portion out, parcel out, measure out, mete out, deal out, dole out, ration; divide, disperse, consign, partition, share. —**Ant.** collect, receive, gather, assemble; keep, retain; give all, dispense all at once.

apposite *adj. His remarks were amusing but not apposite to the topic:* appropriate, suitable, fitting, apropos, applicable, pertinent, apt, relevant, germane, material. —**Ant.** unsuitable, inappropriate, irrelevant, inapt.

appraisal *n.* **1.** *What's your appraisal of the situation?:* evaluation, judgment, estimate, assessment. **2.** *Before granting mortgage money the bank must make an appraisal on the house:* monetary evaluation, estimated value, valuation; assessment.

appraise *v.* **1.** *The house is appraised at $25,000 for tax purposes:* value, estimate to be worth, assay; assess. **2.** *The personnel director personally appraises each job applicant:* evaluate, judge, examine, inspect, review, *Informal* size up, assess.

appreciable *adj. There is an appreciable difference between the two cars:* noticeable, obvious, evident, definite, clear-cut, substantial, significant, pronounced; recognizable, perceptible, perceivable, discernible, detectable, ascertainable. —**Ant.** unnoticeable, imperceptible, immaterial, unsubstantial, indistinguishable, undetectable; minor, small.

appreciate *v.* **1.** *I appreciate all you've done for me:* be grateful for, be thankful for, regard highly, feel indebted; acknowledge. **2.** *Van Gogh's paintings weren't appreciated until after his death. You don't have to be a connoisseur to appreciate good wine:* realize the worth of, estimate justly; value, rate highly, hold in high regard, esteem, prize, cherish, relish, treasure, savor; like, admire, respect. **3.** *Many men don't appreciate how much work it takes to keep house and cook three meals a day:* realize, understand, comprehend, recognize, perceive, sympathize, be conscious of, be aware of, be cognizant of; acknowledge. **4.** *Land will continue to appreciate in the years ahead:* rise in value, inflate, improve, enhance. —**Ant.** 1 be ungrateful. 2 undervalue, underrate, underestimate; belittle, disparage, scorn, disdain, ignore. 3 be unaware, be insensitive to; misunderstand, misjudge, misconceive. 4 depreciate; devaluate, deflate.

appreciation *n.* **1.** *How can we express our appreciation for your help?:* gratitude, gratefulness, thankfulness, thanks, regard. **2.** *An educated person should have an appreciation of good music:* awareness, understanding, comprehension, clear perception, cognizance, recognition of worth; admiration, relish, liking, sympathy. **3.** *The appreciation of real estate* values has been phenomenal: increase in value; growth, rise, elevation, advance. —**Ant.** 1 ingratitude; disregard. 2 ignorance, incomprehension; dislike, antipathy, aversion. 3 depreciation, devaluation; fall, decline, drop.

apprehend v. **1.** The police expect to apprehend the kidnappers before nightfall: arrest, take into custody, take prisoner; catch, seize, capture, Informal nab, bag, Slang collar. **2.** The public doesn't fully apprehend the complexity of space flight: comprehend, understand, perceive, discern, see, grasp; realize, recognize, know, sense. —**Ant.** 1 release, free, let go; discharge; liberate. 2 be unaware of, be unconscious of; misunderstand, misconceive, miss, lose.

apprehension n. **1.** He was filled with apprehension about the future: foreboding, uneasiness, misgiving, dread, dismay, anxiety, alarm, suspicion, mistrust, disquiet, apprehensiveness; worry, concern, distress; presentiment of evil, premonition of trouble. **2.** The apprehension of the murderer was announced by the police chief: arrest, capture, seizure. **3.** Quickness of apprehension is the mark of a good student: comprehension, perception, understanding. —**Ant.** 1 confidence, assurance; tranquillity, trust; unconcern, nonchalance, composure. 2 release, freeing; discharge; liberation. 3 incomprehension, lack of understanding.

apprehensive adj. The prospect of major surgery would make anyone apprehensive: uneasy, filled with misgiving, anxious, disquieted, distressed, alarmed, worried, concerned, fearful, afraid, Informal scared; nervous, jittery; suspicious, distrustful. —**Ant.** confident, assured, calm, at ease, cool, composed, unruffled, nonchalant; unafraid.

apprentice n. My grandfather learned shoemaking as an apprentice to a master craftsman: indentured assistant, learner, student, pupil; beginner, novice, tyro, neophyte. —**Ant.** expert, master, professional, Informal pro.

apprise v. Police should apprise an arrested person of his or her rights to remain silent and to be represented by a lawyer: inform, notify, advise, tell, make acquainted, make aware, make cognizant of, disclose, enlighten. —**Ant.** keep secret, keep quiet about.

approach v. **1.** The car slowed as it approached the corner. Summer is approaching. John is approaching manhood: come, near, come near, draw near, come nearer to, come close, move toward, gain upon. **2.** Few actors approach Laurence Olivier in ability: come close to, approximate; equal, match, compare, be like, resemble. **3.** The superintendent of schools has approached several educators about filling the principal's job: make overtures to, broach a subject to, make advances to, solicit, make a proposal to, sound out. **4.** Approach each new job with enthusiasm: embark on, undertake, set about, enter upon, begin, begin work on, initiate. —n. **5.** The dog's barking announced our approach: drawing near, coming nearer, advance. **6.** The approach to the castle leads

through the woods: access, way; road, avenue, passage, passageway. **7.** His whole approach to the problem is wrong: way of handling, method of attack, attitude; method, procedure, modus operandi, technique, system. —**Ant.** 1 leave, go, draw away; retreat, withdraw, retire, go back. 2 be different, diverge. 3 ignore, overlook, pass over, pass by. 4 leave, finish, end. 5 departure, leaving, withdrawal. 6 exit.

approbation n. The architect received approbation for his new office building design: praise, congratulation, compliment, good word, applause, acclaim; approval, acceptance, support, endorsement, ratification, commendation, laudation, official sanction. —**Ant.** censure, condemnation, criticism; disapproval, dissatisfaction, protest, rejection, veto.

appropriate adj. **1.** A long dress is appropriate for a formal wedding: suitable, proper, well-suited, congruous, fitting, befitting, correct, seemly, apt, apropos, well-chosen; characteristic, belonging, pertinent, relevant, germane, to the purpose, to the point, opportune. —v. **2.** The city will appropriate money for two new schools: allocate, set apart, allot, apportion, assign, earmark. **3.** The county should appropriate land for a new highway: take possession of, take, confiscate, expropriate. —**Ant.** 1 inappropriate, improper, ill-suited, unsuitable, unsuited, unfitting, incongruous, unbefitting, unseemly, incorrect, wrong, inconsonant, incompatible, outré; uncharacteristic, out of place, inopportune, irrelevant. 2 withhold. 3 give, bestow, donate; relinquish, cede, dispose of.

appropriation n. **1.** The mayor approved the appropriation for the new building: allocation, money set aside, apportionment of funds, allotment. **2.** The treasurer was jailed for his appropriation of company funds: taking for one's own use, taking, misappropriation, expropriation, arrogation, confiscation, usurpation. —**Ant.** 1 withholding of funds. 2 return, reimbursement, repayment, paying back, recompense.

approval n. **1.** He studied hard to win his teacher's approval: good opinion, regard, admiration, acceptance, respect, esteem, acclaim, appreciation, approbation, acknowledgment, favor, liking. **2.** In this state, parental approval is necessary before a 17-year-old can obtain a driver's license: permission, consent, endorsement, concurrence, agreement, confirmation, compliance, acquiescence, leave, sanction, countenance, license; authorization, mandate. —**Ant.** 1 disapproval, disfavor, dislike, dissatisfaction, displeasure, censure, criticism, rebuke, reproof, reproach, disparagement. 2 refusal, disapproval, objection; denial, refutation, veto.

approve v. **1.** The family approves of her new fiancé: consider favorably, judge as good, regard as worthy, think highly of, have a good opinion of, be pleased with, receive with favor; esteem, respect, appreciate, praise, like, accept; believe in. **2.** No teacher can approve of cheating on exams: permit, allow, consent to, condone, countenance, assent to, concur in, accede to, advocate, uphold, go along with, subscribe to, defend, second. **3.** *The Senate approved the new housing bill:* confirm, affirm, sustain, uphold, ratify, pass, endorse, sanction, rubber-stamp; permit, allow. **—Ant.** 1 disapprove, dislike; criticize, disparage, condemn. 2 disallow, repudiate, reject, object to, refute. 3 reject, disapprove, veto.

approximate *adj.* **1.** *The approximate time of our arrival will be two o'clock:* rough, very near, estimated, relative; nearly accurate, almost exact, inexact. **—v. 2.** *The color of these curtains approximates that of the rug:* almost match, approach, come close to, border on, verge on, nearly equal; look like, closely resemble. **3.** *The TV repairman approximated the cost at fifty dollars:* estimate, figure roughly; reckon, guess, make a stab at. **—Ant.** 1 exact, precise, correct, accurate; definite, specific. 2 differ completely, be nowhere near.

approximately *adv.* *The time is approximately ten o'clock:* just about, almost, around, more or less, very nearly, close to, not far from, in the vicinity of, in the neighborhood of, circa, generally. **—Ant.** exactly, precisely, on the dot; definitely, specifically.

apropos *adj.* *The speaker's jokes were not apropos for such a solemn occasion:* appropriate, fitting, befitting, suitable, well-suited, opportune, just the thing, congruous, correct, seemly, apt; pertinent, relevant, germane, applicable, related, to the point. **—Ant.** inappropriate, unsuitable, ill-suited, unsuited, inapt, unfitting, unseemly, incorrect, wrong, incongruous, out of place, inopportune, irrelevant, untimely, unrelated.

apt *adj.* **1.** *That dog is apt to bite if he's teased:* likely, liable; inclined, prone, given to, disposed to, predisposed. **2.** *Alert children are usually apt students:* bright, clever, intelligent, gifted. **3.** *The doctor made a few apt remarks about nutrition and health:* appropriate, suitable, well-suited, proper, fitting, befitting, congruous, seemly, apropos; pertinent, relevant, germane, opportune. **—Ant.** 1 unlikely; averse, disinclined. 2 slow to learn, slow, dull. 3 inappropriate, unsuitable, ill-suited, unsuited, improper, unfitting, incongruous, unseemly; irrelevant, inopportune.

aptitude *n.* *She has a natural aptitude for music:* ability, capacity, capability, talent, gift, faculty, genius, knack, flair, facility, proficiency, endowment, quickness, cleverness; inclination, tendency, predisposition, leaning, turn, bent, propensity, penchant, proclivity, proneness, predilection. **—Ant.** inaptitude, ineptitude; aversion, disinclination.

aquatic *adj.* **1.** *Ducks are aquatic creatures:* at home in water, living in or near water, growing in water; marine (*salt water*), oceanic, pelagic (*open sea*), thalassic (*seagoing*), lacustrine (*lake-dwelling*), fluvial, fluviatile (*river and stream*), littoral, neritic (*offshore*), abyssal (*deepest parts of the ocean*). **2.** *Water-skiing is a popular aquatic sport:* occurring on water, carried on in water. **—Ant.** 1 land, terrestrial.

aqueduct *n.* *The Romans built aqueducts to transport water from the mountains:* conduit, channel, artificial waterway, watercourse, duct, race.

aqueous *adj.* *The human eye is filled with aqueous humor:* watery, liquid, moist, waterish, lymphatic, hydrous, damp, serous.

arable *adj.* *The land is too rocky to be arable:* cultivable, farmable, plowable, tillable; productive, fruitful, fertile, fecund. **—Ant.** uncultivable, unfarmable, untillable; unproductive, barren, unfertile.

arbiter *n.* *Emily Post was an arbiter of good manners:* judge, referee, umpire, arbitrator; authority, connoisseur, pundit.

arbitrary *adj.* **1.** *A judge can't make arbitrary decisions--he must follow the rules of law:* subjective, personal, willful, chance, random, summary; capricious, frivolous, whimsical, fanciful, inconsistent. **2.** *Dictators are arbitrary rulers:* absolute, unlimited, unrestrained, peremptory, uncontrolled, imperious, autocratic, despotic. **—Ant.** 1 objective, impersonal. 2 constitutional, lawful.

arbitrate *v.* **1.** *The United Nations will try to arbitrate the international dispute:* decide, settle, mediate, reconcile, bring to terms, sit in judgment; judge, adjudge, adjudicate; umpire, referee. **2.** *The union agreed to arbitrate its differences with the company:* submit to arbitration, allow to be decided by an arbitrator. **—Ant.** negotiate.

arbitrator *n.* *If negotiations are deadlocked, an arbitrator must be called in:* mediator, arbiter, adjudicator, judge; referee, umpire; (*loosely*) negotiator, moderator, intermediary, go-between.

arbor *n.* *We walked through the arbor, tasting the newly ripened grapes:* vine-covered bower, shaded walk, pavilion, grotto, pergola; summerhouse, kiosk, gazebo, belvedere, *Brit.* folly.

arc *n.* *The rainbow formed a beautiful arc in the sky:* curve, arch, semicircle, crescent, halfmoon, bow.

arcade *n.* *The twin towers are connected by an arcade lined with elegant boutiques:* colonnade, archway, cloister, gallery, loggia, *Brit.* piazza, peristyle, covered passageway, vaulted passage; areaway, breezeway, underpass, overpass, skywalk.

arcane *adj.* *Astrology is an arcane subject:* mysterious, enigmatic, esoteric, occult, abstruse, recondite, obscure, hermetic, mystic, mystical. **—Ant.** clear, obvious, evident, understood, known, well-known, open, revealed.

arch[1] *n.* **1.** *The arch of the ceiling spans 50 feet:* curved span, vault, dome. **2.** *Her eyebrows have a naturally high arch:* curvature, curve, arc, bow shape, bend. **—v. 3.** *The trees arched over the garden path:* span, curve, bend. **4.** *The cat arched its back:* curve, bend. **—Ant.** 2 straightness. 4 straighten out, unbend.

arch[2] *adj.* **1.** *The butler was the arch villain of the piece:* chief, primary, principal, main, major. **2.** *She gave him an arch look:* mischievous, sly, wily, roguish, saucy, designing, cunning.

—**Ant.** 1 minor, petty, lesser. 2 frank, open, forthright.

archaic *adj. Hitching posts have been archaic for years:* antiquated, obsolete, obsolescent, gone out of use, out-of-date, old-fashioned, bygone, passé, behind the times; ancient, antique. —**Ant.** modern, current; new, fresh, novel, up-to-date, fashionable, newfangled, modish, *Slang* trendy.

archenemy *n. Sherlock Holmes enjoyed matching wits with his archenemy Moriarty:* foe, adversary, archfoe, nemesis, antagonist, opponent; assailant, combatant, disputant; bugbear, *French* bête noire, scourge. —**Ant.** friend, companion, comrade, champion, defender, ally, supporter, benefactor.

archetype *n. Satan is the archetype of evildoers:* original, prototype, classic, model, exemplar, prime example.

architect *n.* **1.** *Frank Lloyd Wright is my favorite architect:* building designer, master builder. **2.** *Thomas Jefferson was the prime architect of the Constitution of the United States:* engineer, originator, creator, author, designer, planner, draftsman, deviser, contriver, founder, artificer; instigator, prime mover, shaper, innovator.

architecture *n.* **1.** *The study of architecture includes both engineering and aesthetics:* science of building, art of designing buildings; structural design, construction, architectonics. **2.** *I like the wood and glass architecture of our West Coast homes:* design, construction, structuring, style.

archives *n. pl.* **1.** *The Fidelio sketchbook is in the Beethoven archives in Bonn, West Germany:* depository, library, museum. **2.** *The museum's Civil War archives are valuable:* documents, papers, records, annals, chronicles, memorabilia.

arctic *adj.* **1.** *Permafrost occurs only in arctic regions:* north of the Arctic Circle, near the North Pole; polar, far-northern; septentrional, hyperborean. **2.** *Napoleon's army bogged down in the arctic Russian winter:* bitter, icy, frigid, ice-cold, glacial, freezing, frostbound, icebound, frozen, gelid. —*n.* **3. Arctic.** *Admiral Byrd explored the Arctic:* region north of the Arctic Circle, North Pole, north polar region. —**Ant.** 2 torrid, hot, warm, summery. 3 Antarctica, the Antarctic, South Pole.

ardent *adj. Nathan Hale was an ardent patriot. Don Juan was an ardent lover:* impassioned, passionate, zealous, eager, fervent, fervid, fiery, tempestuous, vehement, emotional, enthusiastic, intense, fierce, keen, earnest; lusty, spirited, feverish. —**Ant.** indifferent, half-hearted, nonchalant, dispassionate, unenthusiastic, apathetic, impassive, phlegmatic, detached; unloving, unamorous, cold, cool, frigid.

ardor *n.* **1.** *Van Gogh began each new painting with great ardor:* feeling, passion, fervor, intensity, gusto, zeal, vehemence, fierceness, warmth, excitement, eagerness, enthusiasm, spirit, feverishness, animation, vigor, verve. **2.** *Women spoke of Rudolph Valentino with ardor:* passion, rapture, amorousness, devotion, love, warmth. —**Ant.** 1 indifference, unconcern, dis-

interestedness, apathy, detachment, dispassion, languor, languidness; coldness, coolness, frigidity.

arduous *adj. Crossing the continent in a covered wagon was an arduous undertaking:* difficult, hard, laborious, toilsome, wearisome, exhausting, fatiguing, tiring, burdensome, heavy, tough, troublesome, onerous, trying, full of hardships, formidable, severe, Herculean; vigorous, strenuous, energetic. —**Ant.** light, facile, easy, simple, effortless, smooth.

area *n.* **1.** *The pineapple plantation occupies a large area of the island:* expanse, extent, stretch, portion, zone, space. **2.** *Alligators are found in marshy areas:* region, locality, terrain, territory, *Slang* turf, section, tract, range, district, precinct. **3.** *France has always excelled in the area of the arts:* field, sphere, realm, domain, province, arena, scope.

arena *n.* **1.** *The city built a new sports arena:* coliseum, stadium, amphitheater, bowl, gymnasium, field, hippodrome, circus; ring, stage, platform. **2.** *After World War II Japan entered the arena of international trade:* field, realm, area, province, territory, domain, sphere, scene, theater, stage; battleground, battlefield, sector, lists, playing field, marketplace.

argot *n. Damon Runyon used the argot of pickpockets in some of his stories:* criminal jargon, cant; (*loosely*) lingo, vernacular, idiom, slang, patois.

argue *v.* **1.** *The local merchants argued that a new municipal parking lot was necessary:* reason, contend, maintain, assert, claim, hold, plead, expostulate, remonstrate. **2.** *The children argued about whose turn it was to sit in the front seat:* have an argument, quarrel, dispute, debate, bicker, quibble, wrangle. **3.** *Her flower arrangements argue her artistic tastes:* show, indicate, exhibit, display, manifest, demonstrate, evince; express, imply, denote, point to. —**Ant.** 2 agree, concur. 3 hide, conceal; raise doubt, disprove.

argument *n.* **1.** *Arguments about matters of taste are futile:* quarrel, bickering, squabble, row, clash, altercation, fight, spat, tiff, imbroglio, embroilment; disagreement, dispute, debate, controversy, heated discussion, war of words. **2.** *The city has a powerful argument for turning the land into a park:* reason, line of reasoning, case, line of argument, argumentation. **3.** *It used to be the custom to print the argument of a play before the main text:* outline, abstract, summary, plot, synopsis, story, central idea, contents, gist. —**Ant.** 1 agreement, accord, concord, concurrence, harmony. 2 rebuttal, refutation, retort, rejoinder, response, answer.

argumentative *adj. He's so argumentative it's hard to get him to agree that it's a nice day:* quarrelsome, contentious, belligerent, combative, disputatious, litigious, scrappy; cantankerous, snappish, fractious, querulous, peevish, testy, petulant, contrary. —**Ant.** congenial, amenable, cordial, sympathetic.

aria *n. The aria she sang from "Tosca" was my favorite:* solo, song, tune, melody, air; selection, number, section, excerpt; *Italian* arietta, canzonetta, aria cantabile.

arid *adj.* **1.** *Mormons in Utah made a garden out of an arid waste:* dry, dried-up, waterless, parched, drought-scourged, desertlike; barren. **2.** *Mark Twain's table talk was never arid:* dull, tedious, lifeless, colorless, uninteresting, dreary, vapid, uninspired, unimaginative, jejune, dry as dust; pedantic. **—Ant.** 1 well-watered; lush, verdant. 2 lively, full of life, interesting, exciting, spirited, imaginative, pithy.

arise *v.* **1.** *The President arises at six every morning. I arose from the chair to answer the doorbell:* get out of bed, awake, wake, wake up; get up, rise, stand up. **2.** *A plume of smoke arose from the volcano:* rise, move upward, ascend, go up, mount, climb. **3.** *Resentment can arise between two men who want the same job. Accidents can arise from carelessness:* come into being, occur, spring up, crop up, set in, emanate, ensue; originate, stem from, start, begin, commence, dawn, result, appear, make its appearance, emerge, show itself, come to light. **—Ant.** 1 retire, lie down, go to bed, recline; sit, sit down, kneel. 2 descend, come down, fall. 3 cease, stop, end, die; disappear, go away, fade away, be suppressed, be hidden.

aristocracy *n.* *The highest-ranking members of the Spanish aristocracy are the grandees:* nobility, peerage, patricians; upper class, high society, society, beau monde, elite, *haut monde*, upper crust, gentry. **—Ant.** commons, common people, bourgeoisie, demos, plebs, commoners, populace, masses; lower classes, working class, proletariat, hoi polloi, riffraff, rabble, canaille.

aristocrat *n.* *Jockey Club membership was once limited to aristocrats:* noble, nobleman, noblewoman, lord, peer, grandee; gentleman, gentlewoman, Brahmin, blue blood, silk stocking, patrician. **—Ant.** commoner, bourgeois, plebeian, proletarian, peasant.

aristocratic *adj.* *She comes from an aristocratic family. The senator had an aristocratic bearing:* noble, titled, lordly, royal, regal, courtly, blue-blooded; highborn, wellborn, highbred, of gentle blood, of high rank, patrician, gentlemanly, silk-stocking, upper-class; genteel, refined, dignified. **—Ant.** common; bourgeois, middle-class, lower-class, working-class, plebeian, lowbred; unrefined, crude.

arm *n.* **1.** *Put the bracelet back on your arm. He broke his arm. Most starfish have five arms:* (of humans) upper limb, forearm, upper arm; (of certain animals) anterior limb. **2.** *The English Channel is an arm of the sea:* appendage, offshoot, branch, projection. **3.** *The Secret Service is an arm of the U.S. Treasury Department:* branch, division, department, section, sector, detachment. **4. arms.** *The army can't advance until the new shipment of arms arrives:* firearms, guns, weapons; ordnance, weaponry, armament, matériel. **5.** *The procession was led by a soldier carrying the royal arms:* coat of arms, heraldic emblem, insignia, crest, blazonry. **—v. 6.** *The cowboys armed themselves to fight the*

rustlers. *During World War II the United States armed many of its allies:* take up arms, obtain arms; furnish with weapons, prepare for war. **7.** *He armed himself for the long night's drive by drinking black coffee:* prepare, make ready, prime, forearm; equip, outfit, fortify, strengthen, protect, brace. **—Ant.** 6 disarm.

armada *n.* *The armada was lined up off the coast, ready for battle:* fleet, flotilla, squadron, escadrille, navy.

armament *n.* **1.** *The battleship's armament included cannon, rocket launchers, antiaircraft guns, and six inches of steel plating:* weapons, arms, guns, ordnance, equipment, outfitting, munitions. **2.** *The armament of any of the great powers could destroy civilization:* military might, war-making machine, weaponry.

armistice *n.* *Armistice was declared on November 11, 1918:* suspension of hostilities, cease-fire, truce; peace. **—Ant.** outbreak of war, attack; war, hostilities.

armor *n.* **1.** *Bulletproof cars are sheathed in armor. The priest felt protected by the armor of his faith:* protective covering, protection, shield, bulwark. **2.** *Knights fought in armor:* suit of armor, coat of mail, mail, chain.

armory *n.* *Many old armories are now used to house reserve units:* arsenal, arms depot, ordnance depot.

army *n.* **1.** *The Allied Army invaded Nazi-occupied France on June 6, 1944:* military force, military machine, military; land forces, land force, troops, soldiers, soldiery, fighting men, legions, legion, militia. **2.** *An army of ants swarmed over the sandhill:* host, horde, swarm, pack, multitude, legion, throng, congregation, force, crowd, mob, band, gang, crew, bevy; mass, aggregation. **—Ant.** 1 civilians. 2 small number.

aroma *n.* *The aroma of cooking made me hungry:* good smell, pleasant odor, scent, fragrance, bouquet, redolence, savor. **—Ant.** stench, stink.

aromatic *adj.* *He smokes an aromatic pipe tobacco:* fragrant, sweet-smelling, sweet-scented, scented, perfumed, odoriferous, odorous, redolent; piquant, spicy, pungent. **—Ant.** nonaromatic, unscented; bad-smelling, stinking, malodorous, noisome, rank, putrid, fetid, acrid.

arouse *v.* **1.** *She aroused the children from their nap:* awaken, wake up, waken, rouse, bestir. **2.** *A walk before dinner will arouse your appetite. Don't arouse my anger!:* summon up, call forth, excite, stimulate, provoke, spur, incite, kindle, stir up, foster, foment, move, quicken; pique, sharpen, whet, goad, fan, heat up, warm. **—Ant.** 1 put to sleep, lull. 2 end, kill, still, quench; damp, dampen, dull, calm, quell, quiet, allay, mitigate, assuage, alleviate, relieve, pacify, moderate, placate, mollify.

arraign *v.* **1.** *The district attorney asked that the suspect be arraigned immediately:* indict, charge. **2.** *The medical association met to arraign the doctor for his unethical behavior:* accuse, charge, indict; call to account, take to task, denounce, censure, criticize, find fault with, impute. **—Ant.** 2 withdraw charges, drop charges; exonerate, absolve, excuse, pardon, exculpate, overlook; defend, vindicate; condone, approve, support, praise, acclaim.

arrange v. **1.** *She arranged the flowers beautifully. The books were arranged in alphabetical order:* group, array, set out, range, pose; order, set in order, organize, sort, assort, assign places to, file, classify, marshal, rank, line up, systematize, methodize. **2.** *The travel agent arranged the trip with a stopover in Rome:* plan, schedule, map out, lay out, prepare, devise, contrive, plot, provide, design, fix up; settle, agree to. **3.** *The musician arranged the symphony so it could be performed without violins by a marching band:* orchestrate, score, adapt. **—Ant.** 1 disorganize, disarrange, jumble, disturb, mess up; scatter, disperse.

arrangement n. **1.** *Flower arrangement can be made an art. The arrangement of the files makes it easy to find what one needs:* grouping, arraying, disposal, assortment, distribution, ordering; order, organization, systematization, classification, categorization, methodization. **2.** Often **arrangements.** *The bride's family is responsible for the wedding arrangements. The arrangements for a truce were made at last:* plans, preparations, measures, provisions; settlement, agreement, terms, compact. **3.** *The symphony orchestra played a special arrangement of "Silent Night":* orchestration, score, adaptation. **—Ant.** 1 disorder, disorganization, disarray, topsy-turviness.

arrant adj. *My uncle was an arrant bachelor. The highwayman is an arrant knave:* thorough, thoroughgoing, utter, confirmed, outright, downright, egregious, unmitigated, flagrant, out-and-out, rank, extreme, notorious; undisguised. **—Ant.** partial, sometimes, incomplete, inconsistent, modified.

array n. **1.** *The stores have set out their array of Christmas merchandise:* display, exhibition, arrangement, disposition, marshaling, order, show, parade, pageantry; collection, assortment, supply. **2.** *The women were decked out in their best array for the charity ball:* finery, fine clothes, attire, clothing, apparel, raiment, garments, dress, garb, *Informal* glad rags, Sunday best. **—v. 3.** *Array the paintings so everyone can see them:* arrange, group, order, organize, marshal, align, range, rank; set out, place, display, deploy, pose. **4.** *The child was arrayed in silk and lace for its christening:* clothe, attire, dress, adorn, bedeck, deck, fit out, outfit, robe, wrap. **—Ant.** 1 disarray, hodgepodge, odds and ends. 2 rags. 3 disarrange, mix up, mess up.

arrears n. *He hasn't paid the arrears on his mortgage yet:* overdue debt, unpaid debt, outstanding debt; indebtedness, liability, obligation, debit, balance due. **—Ant.** prepayment, early payment.

arrest v. **1.** *The police arrested the suspect a block away from the scene of the crime:* take into custody, apprehend, catch, seize, capture, take prisoner, collar; detain, hold, secure, *Slang* bust, nab, pinch. **2.** *A speck on the horizon ar-*

rested the navigator's attention: catch, attract; fix, hold, seize, capture, occupy, engage, rivet, absorb, engross. **3.** *The new drug arrested the spread of the disease:* check, block, stay, halt, stop, end, bring to a standstill; delay, slow, retard, inhibit, hold back, restrain, hinder, stall, suppress, interrupt. **—n. 4.** *Fingerprints on the safe led to the robber's arrest:* apprehension, capture, seizure, taking into custody, *Slang* bust, roust. **5.** *The arrest of the floodwaters saved many homes:* stopping, stoppage, halt, blocking, checking, staying; slowing, inhibiting, holding back, retention. **—Ant.** 1 release, free, set free, let go. 2 be ignored, be passed over. 3 encourage, quicken, speed up. 4 releasing, freeing. 5 quickening.

arrival n. **1.** *The President's arrival was greeted with loud cheers:* arriving, coming, advent, appearance, approach, entrance. **2.** *The motel had no rooms for late arrivals:* comer, visitor, visitant, newcomer, entrant. **—Ant.** 1 departure, leaving, going, withdrawal.

arrive v. **1.** *Fire fighters arrived at the house within ten minutes of the alarm. The plane is arriving now:* come, reach, get to, appear, show up, turn up, reach a destination; approach, near, draw near, go toward. **2.** *Good weather has arrived at last:* come, occur, happen, befall, take place, come to pass, appear. **3.** *With the movie's huge success, the leading actor has really arrived:* achieve recognition, succeed, make good, reach the top. **—Ant.** 1, 2 depart, go, go away, leave, withdraw, retire, *Slang* scram, beat it, cut out, make tracks; set out, set forth, be off. 3 fail, fall.

arrogance n. *The arrogance of the aristocracy helped bring on the French Revolution:* overbearing pride, haughtiness, assurance, presumption, pretension, loftiness, imperiousness; vanity, conceit, egoism, bluster, swagger, vainglory, self-importance, braggadocio; insolence, disdain, contempt, scorn, lordliness. **—Ant.** humility, modesty, simplicity, politeness, self-deprecation, self-effacement, diffidence, bashfulness, meekness, shyness.

arrogant adj. *The boss's son was arrogant to all the employees:* overbearing, haughty, presumptuous, pretentious, imperious, overweening, high-and-mighty; vain, conceited, egoistical, vainglorious, self-important, self-assuming, swaggering; insolent, disdainful, contemptuous, scornful, lordly, pompous, supercilious. **—Ant.** unassuming, polite, considerate, modest, diffident, deferential; self-effacing, bashful, meek, shy.

arrogate v. *The President tried to arrogate to himself the powers of Congress:* take over, claim, appropriate, seize, preempt, usurp, commandeer, assume, adopt, help oneself to, make free with. **—Ant.** cede, relinquish, surrender, yield, resign, renounce.

arsenal n. **1.** *The gun collector's home looked like an arsenal. This arsenal produces two tons of gunpowder a day:* armory, arms depot, ordnance depot, military storehouse; ammunition dump, magazine; arms factory, munitions factory. **2.** *The police found an arsenal in the trunk of the robbers' car:* cache of weapons, weapon collection, weapons, military stores.

art *n.* **1.** *Music and ballet are my favorite forms of art:* artistic activity, creative work, artistry. **2.** *The museum has a fine collection of modern art:* works of art, objects of art. **3.** *Caruso's great art is demonstrated in this recording:* artistry, genius, mastery, expertise, skill, facility, virtuosity, dexterity. **4.** *I received my bachelor of arts degree:* liberal arts, humanities. **5.** *She is accomplished in the art of flattery:* craft, technique, methods, principles, strategy; fine points, subtleties, finesse, knack. **—Ant.** 1 science. 2 junk, worthless objects. 3 lack of skill, ineptitude, incompetence, inability.

artful *adj.* **1.** *He used an artful excuse to get out of doing the work:* cunning, crafty, sly, wily, foxy, strategic, diplomatic, politic, scheming, designing, contriving, machinating, maneuvering; deceitful, deceptive, underhand, disingenuous, shifty, tricky. **2.** *William Jennings Bryan was an artful lawyer:* skillful, smart, clever, shrewd, sharp, astute, quick, adroit, deft, resourceful, ingenious, inventive, imaginative, nimble-minded, dexterous, knowing, subtle; able, apt, adept, masterly, proficient, gifted, talented. **—Ant.** 1 artless; simple, natural, candid, open, frank, straightforward, unsophisticated, ingenuous, naïve. 2 dull, clumsy, plodding; ungifted, untalented, unadept, unskilled.

article *n.* **1.** *Today's newspaper has an article about soil conservation:* piece, write-up, story, item, essay, paper, theme, sketch, commentary, review. **2.** *Every article in the store is on sale:* item, thing, piece, object, product, commodity; substance, matter. **3.** *We discussed every article of business on the agenda. The negotiators agreed to all the articles of the settlement:* item, piece, point, count, particular, matter, detail; clause, paragraph, part, division, portion; term, condition, stipulation, proposition, provision, proviso.

articulate *adj.* **1.** *The lecturer stated that the first human language consisted of "articulate cries":* enunciated, intelligible, meaningful, speechlike, expressive. **2.** *Porpoises communicate with one another but are not truly articulate:* capable of speech. **3.** *He's a highly articulate speaker. They engaged in an articulate argument:* eloquent, expressive, fluent, facile; clearly expressed. **—v. 4.** *Please articulate clearly so that everyone can hear you:* enunciate, utter, pronounce, enounce. **5.** *A good debater must articulate his ideas well enough to convince others:* express, convey, state, voice; formulate, organize. **6.** *The hand articulates with the forearm at the wrist:* hinge, connect, join, fit together, hook up. **—Ant.** 1–3 inarticulate. 1 unintelligible, incomprehensible, indistinct. 2 dumb, mute, aphasic. 3 inexpressive, nonfluent. 4 mumble, murmur, swallow words.

articulation *n.* **1.** *Clear articulation was the first thing we worked on in the speech class:* utterance, enunciation, pronunciation; diction, elocu-

tion. **2.** *The knee joint forms a ball-and-socket articulation:* joint, juncture, connection, hinge.

artifice *n.* **1.** *Being able to palm a card is an artifice every magician must know:* trick, device, tactic, stratagem, maneuver, contrivance; subterfuge, ruse, dodge, feint, wile; hoax, blind, trap. **2.** *A master spy must be full of artifice:* cunning, craftiness, guile, slyness, wiliness, artfulness, intrigue, trickery, machination, scheming, foxiness; deceit, deception, duplicity, imposture, falsehood; ingenuity, inventiveness, invention, cleverness. **—Ant.** 2 frankness, candor, openness, artlessness, ingenuousness, sincerity; truthfulness, honesty.

artificial *adj.* **1.** *The new dam will form a large artificial lake behind it. Fill the vase with artificial flowers:* manmade, manufactured, synthetic, nonnatural; imitation, simulated, fake, counterfeit, false, sham, phony, mock, spurious, specious, ersatz. **2.** *The movie star flashed an artificial smile at the crowd:* insincere, feigned, pretended, phony, forced, labored, unnatural, affected, mannered, stilted, factitious, theatrical, stagy. **—Ant.** 1 natural, real, genuine, authentic, bona fide, true, actual. 2 sincere, natural, honest, frank, candid, open; unaffected.

artillery *n.* *General Grant had numerical superiority in troops and artillery:* cannon, big guns, mounted guns, ordnance.

artisan *n.* *The carpenter was a talented artisan:* craftsman, handicraftsman; skilled worker, technician; master, master craftsman.

artist *n.* **1.** *The artist's works were displayed at the museum. Joan Sutherland is an operatic artist:* practitioner of a fine art. **2.** *He's an artist in the kitchen:* master, expert, virtuoso. **—Ant.** 2 amateur, beginner, tyro, novice.

artistic *adj.* **1.** *The museum has high artistic standards:* aesthetic. **2.** *Picasso's artistic ability was apparent in his early youth:* befitting an artist, of an artist, of art, in art. **3.** *The flower arrangement is very artistic:* elegant, exquisite, attractive, handsome, tasteful, aesthetic, stylish, graceful. **—Ant.** 1 inartistic, unaesthetic. 3 tasteless, inelegant, unattractive; unpolished, uncultured, unrefined; unaccomplished, untalented, inexpert.

artistry *n.* *Duke Ellington's artistry will long be admired:* artistic ability, mastery, talent, proficiency, sensibility, taste, touch; accomplishment, virtuosity.

artless *adj.* **1.** *Her love was as artless as a child's:* frank, candid, open, honest, true, guileless, innocent, naïve, simple, humble, straightforward; sincere, unpretentious, trusting, undesigning, open-hearted, ingenuous, unsophisticated, unaffected, unself-conscious. **2.** *Nothing can compare to the artless beauty of a waterfall:* natural, pure, unadorned, plain, simple, primitive, crude. **3.** *The painting was completely artless:* inartistic, lacking art; without artistic talent, untalented. **—Ant.** 1 cunning, crafty, sly, wily, dishonest, deceitful, designing, artful, insincere, pretended, faked, phony, false, counterfeit; sophisticated, affected, self-conscious; suspicious, distrustful. 2 artificial, unnatural, synthetic. 3 artistic, aesthetic.

arty adj. The photography of the film was so arty we couldn't follow the story: precious, highbrow, affected, pretentious, overnice, overrefined, bluestocking, overblown, high-sounding; effeminate, foppish, dainty, dandified, artsy-craftsy.

ascend v. 1. The balloon ascended quickly. The climbers slowly ascended the mountain: rise; climb, mount, scale. 2. Queen Elizabeth II ascended the throne when her father died: succeed to, inherit. —**Ant.** 1 descend; fall.

ascendancy also **ascendance** n. The Labour party is gaining ascendancy in Parliament: power, control, domination, dominance, predominance, superiority, supremacy, preeminence, leadership, mastery, advantage, edge, sway, upper hand, whip hand; command, authority, influence, rule, reign, sovereignty. —**Ant.** inferiority, weakness, subordination, subjection, servility; disadvantage, defeat.

ascension n. There's a balloon ascension every year at the county fair. The climber's ascension of the mountain was difficult: ascent, ascendancy; rising, mounting, climbing, scaling.

ascent n. 1. The steeplejack made a careful ascent up the roof of the building: ascension, climb, climbing, scaling, mounting, rise, rising, upward movement. 2. The road made a sharp ascent to the top of the hill: gradient, upgrade, grade, incline, slope. 3. His ascent from office boy to president of the company took fifteen years: advancement, advance, rise, progress, progression, climb, ascension. —**Ant.** descent. 3 fall, retrogression.

ascertain v. The insurance adjuster had to ascertain the exact value of the missing jewels: find out, establish, verify, determine, certify, learn, discover, detect, unearth, ferret out.

ascetic n. 1. Most of the early saints were extreme ascetics: self-denier, abstainer, self-mortifier; hermit, recluse, solitary, eremite, anchorite, celibate, cenobite; religious, monk, nun, flagellant; yogi, fakir, dervish. —adj. 2. Trappist monks lead an ascetic existence: austere, self-denying, abstemious, strict, stern, Spartan, rigorous, self-mortifying. —**Ant.** 1 hedonist, sensualist, voluptuary, sybarite, bon vivant. 2 self-indulgent, indulgent, pampered, luxurious, comfortable; abandoned, dissolute, voluptuous, sensuous, sensual, sybaritic.

ascribe v. Scholars ascribe the unsigned painting to Rubens. He ascribes his good health to proper diet and exercise: attribute, credit, accredit, charge to, assign, impute, trace to, relate. —**Ant.** discredit, deny, discount; dissociate.

ashamed adj. He was ashamed of his bad manners. Modern women aren't ashamed to wear slacks in public: feeling shame, put to shame, mortified, embarrassed, humiliated, chagrined, discomfited, disconcerted, abashed, distressed, crestfallen, chapfallen, shamefaced; shy, bashful, prudish, squeamish; guilt-stricken, conscience-stricken. —**Ant.** proud, honored;

arrogant, vain; gratified, satisfied, pleased, comforted.

ashen adj. The sick woman had an ashen complexion: wan, pale, pallid, pasty, gray, leaden, blanched, livid, anemic. —**Ant.** bright, vivid, colorful, warm-hued; rosy, red-cheeked, blushing, robust.

ashore adv. All ashore that's going ashore! The wreckage of the boat washed ashore: to shore, onto the shore, on shore, on land, on dry land. —**Ant.** on board, at sea, sailing; to the sea, on the sea, in the sea.

asinine adj. It's asinine to build a house so close to a river that floods every year: stupid, foolish, silly, ridiculous, absurd, senseless, brainless, idiotic, moronic, imbecilic, feeble-minded, witless, half-witted, insane, lame-brained, simpleminded, irrational, muddle-headed, dunderheaded, thickheaded, thick-skulled, thick-witted. —**Ant.** smart, wise, intelligent, clever, sage; sensible, rational, reasonable, sane.

ask v. 1. May we ask where you've been all this time? The driver asked directions from the gas-station attendant: inquire, query, request an answer to; request information about, request information from, question, interrogate, quiz, pump, grill, sound out. 2. Ask the Johnsons to come to dinner tomorrow: invite, request, bid, summon, call, send for. 3. I asked for a bicycle for Christmas. Don't ask for a raise. Ask for help: express a desire for, seek, request, call, apply, petition, solicit, sue, appeal, plead, urge, implore, entreat, beseech, beg, supplicate, press. 4. The antique dealer is asking $25 for that old watch: state as a price, charge, demand, claim; request, desire, seek, expect. —**Ant.** 1 answer, inform, supply information. 2 ignore, pass over; blackball; accept; refuse, decline, reject. 3 grant, give; refuse, reject, deny, spurn. 4 declare not for sale; offer, pay, give, shell out.

askance adv. The shopkeeper looked askance at the crowd of young rowdies who entered his store: skeptically, distrustfully, mistrustfully, suspiciously; disdainfully, disapprovingly. —**Ant.** trustfully, unsuspiciously.

askew adv., adj. His tie was hanging askew: crooked, crookedly, awry, lopsided, aslant, Slang cockeyed. —**Ant.** straight, centered, even, right, true, in line, in a line, aligned, plumb, Informal straight as an arrow.

asleep adj., adv. The little boy was asleep before the bedtime story was finished: sleeping, slumbering; (variously) sound asleep, fast asleep, dead to the world, dozing, napping, taking a siesta. —**Ant.** awake, wide awake; up.

aspect n. 1. The valley took on a mysterious aspect at dusk: look, air, appearance. 2. Consider the financial aspects of owning your own house: feature, point, side, facet, angle, consideration.

asperity n. With some asperity I told him I didn't need his help: crossness, crankiness, acerbity, acrimony, churlishness, crabbedness, irritability, irascibility, sullenness, surliness, bitterness, harshness, tartness, waspiness, testiness, shirtiness, snappishness, captiousness. —**Ant.** affability, cheerfulness, geniality, amiability.

aspersion n. It's not fair to cast aspersions on someone you know nothing about: slur, abuse, smear, slander, deprecation, disparagement, detraction, defamation, reproach, censure, vilification, railing, reviling, calumny, obloquy. —**Ant.** praise, laudatory remark, plaudit, compliment, commendation, Informal pat on the back.

asphyxiate v. Carbon monoxide asphyxiates dozens of people every year: suffocate, smother, stifle, choke, strangulate. —**Ant.** breathe, inhale, take in oxygen.

aspiration n. Simon Bolivar's aspiration was to establish democracy in South America: ambition, object, objective, daydream, end, mark, endeavor, design, purpose, intent, intention, hope, desire, longing, wish, yearning, craving, hankering.

aspire v. As a model, Marilyn Monroe always aspired to an acting career: desire, wish for, hope for, long for, yearn for, crave, covet, hanker after, thirst after, hunger over, pine for, pant after; seek, pursue, aim at.

ass n. **1.** The asses were hitched to the cart: donkey, male jackass; burro. **2.** Don't be an ass and quit your job without having another: jackass, fool, idiot, numskull, dolt, blockhead, bonehead, lamebrain, nitwit, nincompoop, ninny, Slang jerk, half-wit, moron, imbecile, dunce, dunderhead, lunkhead, booby, dum-dum. —**Ant.** 2 sage; brain, genius.

assail v. A mugger assailed him on the dark street: attack, assault; set upon, lunge at, pitch into, fly at, descend upon. —**Ant.** defend, support, champion; retreat, withdraw.

assailant n. The assailant was identified by the man he had beaten: attacker, mugger, assaulter, assailer, molester, aggressor.

assassin n. John Wilkes Booth was Lincoln's assassin: killer, murderer, slayer, executioner, Slang hit man.

assassinate v. President John F. Kennedy was assassinated in Dallas in 1963: kill, murder, slay, exterminate, liquidate, put to death, do to death, Slang bump off, rub out.

assault n. **1.** The Battle of Britain was an air assault that lasted many months. The stickup man was charged with robbery and assault with a deadly weapon: attack, onslaught, assailing, aggression; (variously) raid, strike, foray, charge, sally, lunge, thrust, drive, push, offense, invasion, storming, bombardment, siege. —v. **2.** The king's troops assaulted the castle on all sides: attack, assail, set upon, strike at, fall upon, lunge at, fly at, lash out at, (variously) raid, strike, charge, thrust at, invade, storm, bombard, besiege. —**Ant.** 1 defense, resistance, protection; retreat, withdrawal. 2 defend, protect, resist, withstand; retreat, withdraw.

assay v. **1.** The teacher assayed to explain the hidden meaning of the story: try, attempt, endeavor, undertake, essay. **2.** The ore assayed

75 percent gold. Historians have not yet seriously assayed the space programs of the 1960's: analyze, assess, evaluate, appraise, rate, estimate; test, try, prove.

assemblage n. The zoo has a remarkable assemblage of animals: collection, gathering, assembly, aggregation, aggregate, congregation, amassment, accumulation; bunch, group, body, company, store, stock, throng, conclave, flock, herd, pack, cluster, clump, mass, pile, heap, batch.

assemble v. **1.** The club members assembled in the meeting room: gather, convene, come together, congregate, meet, rally, convoke, flock; call together, summon. **2.** Assemble your papers and put them in this file: gather, collect, accumulate, round up, bring together, group together, amass, muster, marshal, compile, heap up, pile up. **3.** It took two hours to assemble the bicycle: put together, fit together, construct, fabricate; join, connect. —**Ant.** 1 disperse, scatter, go separate ways; disband, adjourn, dismiss. 2 disperse, scatter, distribute, divide, dispense. 3 disassemble, dismantle, take apart, Informal knock down.

assembly n. **1.** The assembly of doctors discussed the latest medical research: assemblage, gathering, company, congregation, convocation, group, body, conclave, crowd, throng, flock, herd, pack, troop; collection, aggregate, aggregation, cluster, mass. **2.** Usually **Assembly.** The State Assembly passed a new highway bill: lower house of a legislature, state house of representatives, chamber of deputies; legislature, congress, council. —**Ant.** 1 dispersion, dismissal, disunion, disruption. 2 upper house, Senate.

assent v. **1.** The majority assented to my views on the matter: agree, concur, accept, subscribe to, fall in with, concede, approve, allow, grant; acquiesce, defer to, consent, comply, yield, accord, permit. —n. **2.** The teacher answered with a brief nod of assent: agreement, concurrence, acceptance, consent, approval, compliance, acquiescence, accord, concession, confirmation, approbation, admission, affirmation, ratification, endorsement, sanction, acknowledgment, recognition, corroboration, verification. —**Ant.** 1 dissent, disagree, differ, disapprove, protest, object, reject, refuse, deny, negate, spurn, disallow. 2 disagreement, dissent, dissension, difference, disapproval, protest, objection; refusal, rejection, unacceptance; denial, negation, disavowal, disallowance, veto.

assert v. The old man asserts that eating garlic prevents rheumatism: maintain, contend, insist, avow, claim, uphold, affirm, swear, declare, state, aver, profess, propound, advocate, argue, advance, put forward, set forth, avouch; stress, accent, emphasize. —**Ant.** deny, disavow, disclaim, refute, negate, repudiate; laugh off, Informal put down; retract, take back.

assertion n. The assertion that gout is caused by eating rich foods has not been proved: claim, contention, declaration, statement, dictum, upholding, maintaining, argument, protestation; avowal, averment, allegation. —**Ant.** denial, disavowal, disclaimer, negation, repudiation; retraction.

assertive *adj. A good army officer must be assertive:* positive, forceful, decisive, strong-willed, confident, self-assured, self-assertive, insistent, emphatic; aggressive, domineering, pushy, outspoken, cocksure. —**Ant.** retiring, reserved, shy, bashful, meek, timid, timorous, submissive; hesitant, uncertain, fearful.

assess *v.* **1.** *The house was assessed at $30,000:* value for taxation, estimate, appraise, value. **2.** *The club assessed each member $100 to rebuild the clubhouse:* levy a charge on, tax. **3.** *The general assessed the situation and called for reinforcements:* judge, evaluate, appraise, look over, consider.

assessment *n.* **1.** *The homeowner protested the high assessment on his house:* value for taxation, rate; appraisal. **2.** *The city levied an assessment on each property owner when it put in the new sewers:* tax, tariff, impost, fine, toll, charge, fee, dues. **3.** *The critic's assessment of the book is that it is beautifully written:* judgment, evaluation, appraisal, estimation.

asset *n.* **1.** *A knowledge of French can be a great asset when traveling in Europe:* benefit, advantage, help, aid, service, boon, plus. **2. assets.** *This bank has assets of more than $1 billion:* financial resources, means, wealth; money and cashable possessions; (*loosely*) cash, property, effects, possessions, belongings, capital, money, reserves. —**Ant.** 1 liability, handicap, disadvantage, disservice, drawback, hindrance. 2 liabilities, debts.

asseverate *v. The witness asseverated that he had never met the defendant:* avow, state, avouch, assert, declare, aver, affirm, declare solemnly, attest, swear, contend, certify. —**Ant.** deny, disavow, repudiate, take back, retract.

assiduous *adj. It takes assiduous work to learn Russian. I admire an assiduous student:* diligent, industrious, hardworking, laborious, unremitting, determined, persistent, persevering, earnest, steadfast, constant, tenacious, dogged, untiring, tireless, unflagging, indefatigable, sedulous. —**Ant.** indolent, lazy, idle; haphazard, casual, cavalier, lax, hit-or-miss, undetermined, inconstant, happy-go-lucky.

assign *v.* **1.** *A locker was assigned to each student:* allot, allocate, consign, set apart, distribute, apportion, mete out; dispense, grant, give. **2.** *The reporter was assigned to cover international news:* designate, name, appoint, commission, delegate, choose; charge, entrust, invest. **3.** *Let's assign a day for the next meeting:* name, fix, set, appoint, specify, designate, stipulate, prescribe, determine. —**Ant.** 2 dismiss, discharge, divest, relieve. 3 keep open, hold in abeyance.

assignation *n. Their assignation had to be kept a secret:* tryst, date, rendezvous, meeting, appointment.

assignment *n.* **1.** *The student's assignment was to write a book report:* homework, lesson, exercise, chore, task, job, duty. **2.** *The ambassador's next assignment will be to India:* post, appointment, designation, commission. **3.** *The foreman is responsible for the assignment of jobs:* distribution, apportionment, parceling out, dealing out, doling out, allotment, allocation.

assimilate *v. What we eat is assimilated into our systems. A good student assimilates knowledge quickly:* absorb, take in, digest, metabolize, incorporate, integrate, imbibe, ingest. —**Ant.** keep out, reject; keep apart, segregate, isolate.

assist *v.* **1.** *The nurse assisted the doctor in the operating room:* help, aid, abet, serve, accommodate, work for, lend a hand, wait on; work with, collaborate, cooperate, support, benefit, sustain, uphold, back up, reinforce. —*n.* **2.** *Give me an assist in lifting this trunk:* helping hand, hand, aid, boost. —**Ant.** 1 hinder, hamper, impede, obstruct; oppose, counteract.

assistance *n.* **1.** *The pilot needed the copilot's assistance in landing the plane:* help, aid, support, helping hand, service; collaboration, cooperation, reinforcement. **2.** *The public's assistance is needed to build the orphanage:* financial support, contribution, charity, alms, relief, subsidy, sustenance, stipend. —**Ant.** 1 hindrance, obstruction; opposition, resistance, counteraction.

assistant *n. The boss's new assistant is a hard worker:* helper, subordinate, aide, second-in-command, subaltern, lieutenant, adjutant, associate, sidekick, auxiliary, apprentice, aid, aider, helping hand; colleague, co-worker, collaborator, partner, accessory, confederate, accomplice, cooperator, ally, supporter.

associate *v.* **1.** *In the children's minds summer is associated with picnics:* identify, relate, link, connect, affiliate, ally, league, couple; pair, bind, tie, yoke, combine, unite, merge, join, correlate. **2.** *They associate with all the right people socially:* fraternize, be friends, consort, mix, mingle, club, run around, pal around, hobnob, hang out, rub elbows. —*n.* **3.** *The doctor's associates agreed that the operation was necessary:* colleague, confrere, collaborator, co-worker, peer, fellow, partner, confederate, ally, intimate, confidant, accomplice, sidekick. **4.** *My associates on the hike included my brother and three neighbors:* comrade, companion, fellow, friend, pal, buddy, chum, mate, crony. —*adj.* **5.** *He became an associate member of the club. They appointed her an associate professor:* subordinate; closely connected, affiliated, related, allied, fellow. —**Ant.** 1 separate, disconnect, dissociate, divorce; distinguish. 2 avoid, ignore; alienate, estrange. 4 stranger. 5 major, main, leading, chief; unaffiliated, unrelated, unallied.

association *n.* **1.** *The local farmers' association markets all our produce:* organization, federation, confederation, confederacy, alliance, league, union, combine, syndicate, coalition, fraternity, society, body, group, club, clique; company, corporation, partnership. **2.** *The salesman's association with the firm lasted 20 years. My association with Tom goes back to our days in high school:* affiliation, connection, alliance, participation, membership, relation, relationship, relations, collaboration; friendship, acquaintance, familiarity, intimacy, friendliness, fraternization, companionship, fellowship, camaraderie. **3.** *In the United States, fireworks have a strong association with the 4th of July, but in China, fireworks are associated with New Year's:* identification, connection, relation, correlation, linkage, bond, tie, affiliation, alliance. **4.** *The football team was a rare association of brains and brawn:* combination, mixture, blend, meld, mingling, union, assemblage, community. —**Ant.** 2 disassociation, dissociation, separation, independence; alienation, estrangement.

assorted *adj. The jar contained assorted hard candies:* mixed, various, varied, diverse, diversified, sundry, miscellaneous, motley, different, heterogeneous. —**Ant.** identical, uniform, like, unvaried, all the same, homogeneous.

assortment *n.* **1.** *Modern drugstores have a wide assortment of merchandise:* variety, mixture, selection, conglomeration, diversity, miscellany, motley, medley, potpourri, hodgepodge, mélange; array, collection, stock, store, quantity. **2.** *The back room of the post office was used for the assortment of mail:* assorting, sorting, grouping, classifying, classification, arrangement, arranging, disposition. —**Ant.** 1 uniformity, sameness, monotony. 2 mixing, heaping together, disarrangement.

assuage *v. Liniment will assuage the pain, but soaking in hot water does the injury more good:* allay, ease, relieve, mitigate; lighten, lessen, soften; mollify, alleviate, soothe, calm, quiet, still, pacify, appease, temper, take the edge off, tone down. —**Ant.** intensify, aggravate, irritate, exacerbate, heighten, sharpen, increase, augment; provoke, excite, arouse, kindle, inflame.

assume *v.* **1.** *I assume I'll see you at the meeting Tuesday. Scientists assume there is no life on Mars:* take for granted, suppose, presume, suspect, believe, think, understand, guess, imagine, gather, fancy; infer, postulate, theorize, deduce, hypothesize, surmise, speculate, conjecture, judge. **2.** *The new buyer assumed the mortgage on the house. The new admiral will assume command of the Pacific fleet:* take on, take up, take over, become responsible for, take care of, shoulder, attend to, accept, enter upon, undertake, set about. **3.** *The Bolsheviks assumed power by means of the October Revolution:* seize, take, appropriate, usurp, arrogate, commandeer, expropriate. —**Ant.** 1 know, prove. 2, 3 relinquish, renounce, abandon, give up, give over, hand over, put aside, divest oneself of, leave.

assumed *adj.* **1.** *The reporter agreed to quote his informant under an assumed name:* pseudonymous, pseudonymic, fictitious, make-believe, made-up, phony, bogus, falsified, fake, false. **2.** *The assumed time of his arrival was 2 P.M.:* supposed, presupposed, presumed. —**Ant.** 1 real, authentic, actual, true, original, natural. 2 stated, known, proved; positive, absolute.

assuming *adj. Her assuming airs annoyed eve-*

ryone she met: presumptuous, forward, brazen, audacious, nervy, bold, cheeky, presuming; overbearing, pushy, self-assertive, haughty, arrogant, insolent. —**Ant.** meek, mild, retiring, reticent, modest, humble, soft-spoken.

assumption *n.* **1.** *They rented the old house on the assumption that the landlord would paint it. A basic assumption of physics is that all celestial objects have gravitational fields:* belief, supposition, presumption, presupposition, premise, theory, hypothesis, postulate, postulation. **2.** *His assumption of his father's debts was admirable. The new governor's assumption of office takes place next Tuesday:* taking on, taking up, becoming responsible for, assuming, shouldering, accepting, acceptance, entering upon, undertaking. **3.** *The general's assumption of power was the start of a dictatorship:* seizure, taking, appropriating, usurpation, arrogation.

assurance *n.* **1.** *The plumber gave us his assurance that he would fix the pipes tomorrow. The customer said he would be back with a check for the car and left $50 assurance:* pledge, promise, word of honor, vow, oath, profession, averment, affirmation; guarantee, warranty, binder. **2.** *Theodore Roosevelt had the natural assurance of a born leader:* self-assurance, assuredness, confidence, self-confidence, self-possession, certitude, certainty, sureness, poise, coolness; boldness, aggressiveness, self-reliance. —**Ant.** 1 lie, fib, falsehood, fiction, tall story, cock-and-bull story, fish story, whopper; doubt, uncertainty, skepticism, suspicion, distrust, dis-belief. 2 shyness, timidity, bashfulness; timor-ousness, self-doubt, uncertainty, hesitancy; nervousness, apprehension.

assure *v.* **1.** *The witness assured the judge that he was telling the truth. The office manager assured the secretary that she would receive a raise:* vow to, promise, pledge to, give one's word to, guarantee. **2.** *If you want to assure that a job gets done right, do it yourself. One more touchdown will assure victory:* make sure, make certain, guarantee, ensure; clinch, secure, confirm. —**Ant.** 1 deny, refute, disavow, disclaim; lie, fib; doubt, express doubt, disbelieve. 2 be uncertain, be unsure, be up in the air; make doubtful.

assured *adj.* **1.** *The old family retainer had an assured position for life. After he won the Academy Award the actor's next movie was an assured success:* guaranteed, certain, sure, secure, dependable, settled, fixed, positive; undoubted, unquestionable, irrefutable, indisputable, indubitable. **2.** *General Patton was an assured man:* self-assured, self-confident, self-possessed, confident, secure, poised. —**Ant.** 1 uncertain, unsure, insecure, unsettled; questionable, doubtful, disputable, dubious. 2 timid, timorous, shy, bashful; self-doubting, uncertain; nervous, apprehensive, fearful.

astern *adv. The tugboat drew astern of the ship:* to the stern, toward the stern, aft, abaft, to the rear, behind. —**Ant.** fore, afore, forward; ahead, before, in front.

astir *adj., adv. The campers were astir at dawn:*

awake, roused, out of bed, up, up and about, afoot, moving about, on the move, in motion, active, bustling about. **—Ant.** asleep, napping, in bed, lying down, reclining; quiet, still.

astonish *v. The magician's next trick will astonish you:* surprise, astound, amaze, overwhelm, take aback; startle, stun, shock, electrify, stupefy, daze, dazzle, stagger, strike dumb, dumfound, flabbergast, make one's eyes pop, take one's breath away; perplex, bewilder, confound, confuse. **—Ant.** come as no surprise, be expected, anticipate, foresee, count upon; bore.

astonishing *adj. The small store had an astonishing selection of watches for sale:* surprising, astounding, amazing, overwhelming, overpowering; startling, breathtaking, staggering, striking, impressive, shocking, electrifying, stupefying, dazzling; perplexing, bewildering, confounding, confusing. **—Ant.** expected, anticipated, foreseen, looked for.

astonishment *n. Imagine the astonishment of prehistoric man when a comet appeared in the sky:* amazement, surprise, shock, wonder, wonderment, awe; bewilderment, perplexity, confusion, stupefaction. **—Ant.** calmness, indifference; boredom.

astound *v. Alexander Graham Bell astounded the world with his invention of the telephone:* astonish, amaze, overwhelm, stun, startle, electrify, shock, stupefy, stagger, dazzle, daze, strike dumb, dumfound, flabbergast, surprise, take back, make one's eyes pop, take one's breath away.

astray *adj., adv. We went astray at the crossroads and were lost. The police were led astray by false clues:* off the right track, off the course, off the mark, amiss, afield, off, into error. **—Ant.** on the right track, on course.

astringent *adj.* **1.** *Use an astringent lotion after shaving to firm up the skin:* tonic, invigorating, bracing, restorative, salutary, salubrious, curative; styptic, contracting. **2.** *His astringent remarks made us reconsider the proposal:* stern, severe, austere; incisive, sharp, penetrating, keen; biting, stabbing, piercing. **—Ant.** 1 bland, mild. 2 noncommittal, unclear, ambiguous, indecisive, pussyfooting.

astute *adj. Sam is an astute judge of character. You'd better hire an astute businessperson:* shrewd, smart, sagacious, clever, keen, keen-minded, sharp, acute, bright, able, intelligent, perceptive, discerning, perspicacious, knowing, penetrating, subtle; cunning, sly, foxy, wily, crafty; adroit, Machiavellian, artful, politic, designing, calculating. **—Ant.** dull, slow, thick, unknowing, unintelligent, stupid, dumb, gullible, naïve.

asunder *adj., adv. The election debate tore the country asunder:* apart, into pieces, to shreds; in pieces, rent, torn apart, broken apart.

asylum *n.* **1.** *It is no longer customary to call a mental hospital an asylum. The abandoned children were put into an asylum:* institution, home; *(variously)* sanitarium, sanatorium, mental hospital, mental institution, state hospital, insane asylum, madhouse, poorhouse, almshouse, el-eemosynary institution, orphanage, children's home. **2.** *The United States granted asylum to the political refugees:* refuge, haven, harbor; shelter, home; place of immunity, retreat, sanctuary, preserve.

atheism *n. The minister was shocked by the youth's atheism:* disbelief, unbelief, godlessness, irreligion, apostasy. **—Ant.** religion, belief.

atheist *n. I believe in God but my brother is an atheist:* disbeliever, unbeliever, nonbeliever, denier of God's existence, godless person, infidel. **—Ant.** believer, religionist, God-fearing person.

athlete *n. American athletes won twenty gold medals in the Olympics:* person active in physical exercise and sports, *Slang* jock, sportsman, game player; contestant, contender, champion.

athletic *adj.* **1.** *Teddy Roosevelt was sickly as a youth but built himself up into an athletic man:* strong, able-bodied, muscular, brawny, powerful, sturdy, strapping, hardy, robust, husky, stalwart, burly; manly, masculine, virile. **2.** *In the old days sailors led athletic lives:* physically active, vigorous, hardy. **—Ant.** 1 frail, weak, puny, fragile, delicate, feeble, run down, out of shape, flabby, sickly. 2 sedentary, inactive.

athletics *n. pl. A well-rounded student should like both intellectual pursuits and athletics:* exercise, exercises, sports, gymnastics, physical training.

athwart *adv., prep. Our defensive position lay athwart the enemy's line of advance:* across, astride; crosswise, crossways, sidewise, sideways, transversely, from side to side of, at a right angle to. **—Ant.** parallel to, to the side of.

atmosphere *n.* **1.** *Man must stop polluting the earth's atmosphere:* gaseous envelope, air. **2.** *We all love the cheerful atmosphere of Christmas:* mood, spirit, feeling, feel, ambience, aura, quality, tone, color; environment, surroundings.

atom *n.* **1.** *The splitting of the atom was a milestone in the history of science:* smallest part of a chemical element; *(loosely)* indivisible particle. **2.** *There was not an atom of evidence to convict him:* particle, scrap, shred, speck, grain, iota, *Informal* smidgen, bit, whit, jot, trace, mite, dot, morsel, crumb, fragment, scintilla, tittle, smithereen, mote. **—Ant.** 1 compound; subatomic particle. 2 mass, load, quantity, heap.

atomic *adj.* **1.** *The university received a grant for atomic research. The new missile delivers a cluster of atomic bombs:* nuclear, fission, fissionable, thermonuclear; uranium, plutonium, hydrogen, cobalt, neutron, superatomic. **2.** *The physicists have designed elaborate machinery to analyze atomic particles:* subatomic, microscopic, microcosmic, infinitesimal, molecular; imperceptible, impalpable, indiscernible, unseeable.

atone *v. The errant father promised to atone for the way he had neglected his children:* repent, do penance for, make amends for, make up for, make expiation, expiate, pay for, compensate, recompense, remunerate, make reparation for, render satisfaction for, redeem, shrive.

atonement *n. The criminal reformed and promised atonement for his acts:* repentance, penance, penitential act, amends, satisfaction, shrift, expiation, redress, reparation, compensation, recompense, redemption.

atrocious *adj.* **1.** *Murder is the most atrocious crime of all:* cruel, brutal, inhuman, heinous, monstrous, horrible, terrible, villainous, outrageous, nefarious, enormous, infamous, grievous, pitiless, merciless, ruthless, flagrant, vile, evil, bad, savage, barbarous, vicious, fiendish, diabolical, hellish, infernal, black, dark. **2.** *It was an atrocious play:* bad, dreadful, execrable, terrible, tasteless, uncouth, vulgar, tawdry, vile, rude, low. **—Ant.** 1 humane, kind, benevolent, generous, merciful, gentle, tender, civilized; virtuous, honorable; admirable, wonderful. 2 good, fine, elegant, tasteful, high-class.

atrocity *n. The mercenaries ravaged the countryside, committing one atrocity after another:* crime against humanity, savage deed, atrocious deed, outrage, horror, villainy, enormity; barbarity, barbarism, brutality, inhumanity, heinousness, savagery. **—Ant.** humaneness, kindness, benevolence, mercifulness, gentleness, tenderness; good deed, kind act.

atrophy *n. Bedridden people should exercise to prevent atrophy of their muscles:* wasting away, withering, degeneration, deterioration, emaciation, shriveling, drying up, decaying, decline; lack of development, lack of use. **—Ant.** growth, development, strengthening; exercise, use.

attach *v.* **1.** *Attach the trailer to the car. Attach a stamp to the envelope and mail it:* fasten to, make fast, join, connect, couple; affix, fix, secure; append, annex. **2.** *The submarine was attached to the Pacific fleet:* assign, allocate, allot, designate, detail, destine, earmark; associate, affiliate, connect. **3.** *The boy was so attached to the new puppy that he refused to leave it:* be fond of, be devoted to, be in love with; feel affection for, be bound by love of, feel regard for. **—Ant.** 1 detach, unattach, unfasten, disconnect, unconnect, remove, release, separate, disengage. 2 withdrawn, recall; disassociate, dissociate, separate, retire.

attaché *n. An attaché from the American Embassy helped me get the visa:* diplomat, consul, envoy, emissary, minister, consul general, ambassador, ambassadress, vice consul, military attaché, *Brit.* diplomatist, Foreign Service officer; aide, assistant, adjutant, subordinate.

attachment *n.* **1.** *The attachment of the new engine to the train took but a few minutes:* attaching, fastening, coupling, connection; affixing, fixing, securing. **2.** *She has a great attachment to her sister:* love, devotion, affection, fondness, tenderness, bond, affinity, predilection; friendship, liking, regard, respect. **3.** *The vacuum cleaner has four different attachments. The attachment to the contract must be signed by two witnesses:* accessory, fixture; supplement, addition, adjunct, appendage, addendum, appendix. **—Ant.** 1 separation, unfastening, detachment, parting. 2 aversion, antipathy, ha-

tred, animosity, enmity, dislike; estrangement, alienation, indifference, coolness.

attack *v.* **1.** *The Japanese attacked Pearl Harbor on December 7, 1941. Good chess players must always attack their opponent's king:* assault, assail, strike, take the offensive, begin hostilities against, set upon, fall upon, bear down upon, descend upon, charge, fly at, lunge at, pitch into. **2.** *The book attacks the Navy for being unprepared for World War II:* censure, denounce, disparage, damn, denigrate, impugn, blame, criticize, fault. **3.** *Attack each new task with enthusiasm:* set about, undertake, go to work on, go at, tackle. **—n. 4.** *The enemy attack came at dawn:* offensive, offense, assault, invasion, onslaught, incursion, aggression, charge, onset. **5.** *The newspaper's attack on the mayor's plans aroused public indignation:* censure, impugnment, denigration, abuse, disparagement, criticism. **6.** *His attack was brought on by overexcitement:* seizure, stroke, fit, spasm, paroxysm, spell. **—Ant.** 1 withdraw, retreat; defend, guard, protect, resist. 2 defend, support, uphold, sustain, vindicate, excuse, whitewash. 4 retreat, withdrawal; defense, resistance. 5 defense, support, vindication, excuse, whitewash.

attain *v. He attained success through hard work:* achieve, gain, procure, win, earn, obtain, secure; accomplish, effect, acquire, reach, realize, reap, bring off. **—Ant.** lose, let go, give up, forfeit; fail at, fall short of.

attainment *n.* **1.** *The attainment of an engineering degree is no easy task:* attaining, obtaining, gaining, getting, winning, earning, securing, acquirement, acquiring, acquisition, procuring, procurement, realization, fulfillment. **2.** *She's a woman of great attainments in several fields:* achievement, accomplishment, success, acquirement; proficiency, competence, mastery, skill, talent.

attempt *v.* **1.** *The expedition will attempt to climb the mountain:* try, strive, endeavor, venture, undertake, seek, essay, aim, work at, make an effort, have a go at, take a whack at, take a crack at, tackle, hazard. **—n. 2.** *Hannibal's attempt to invade Italy by crossing the Alps was successful:* effort, undertaking, try, endeavor, venture, essay, aim. **3.** *An unsuccessful attempt was made on President Truman's life:* assault, attack, onslaught.

attend *v.* **1.** *All students must attend classes the day before Thanksgiving:* be present at, go to, appear at, show up, frequent; visit. **2.** *I'll attend to the work tomorrow. The nurse is attending the patient now:* take care of, tend to, look after, mind, serve, service, be attendant on, minister to, wait upon, care for, provide for. **3.** *Each child must be attended by a parent:* accompany, conduct, escort, convoy, squire, usher, watch over, oversee, superintend, have charge of. **4.** *Her illness was attended by weakness:* accompany, be associated with, be connected with, go hand-in-hand with; follow. **5.** *Attend to my words of warning:* heed, mind, listen to, harken to, give thought to, consider, pay attention to, note, observe, mark, take to heart. **—Ant.** 1

absent oneself from, be absent, play truant, miss, *Informal* cut, skip. **2** ignore, disregard, neglect, slight. **4** disassociate, dissociate, be unrelated to. **5** ignore, disregard, turn a deaf ear to.

attendance *n.* **1.** *Your attendance at the club meeting is necessary:* presence, attending, being there, appearance. **2.** *The teacher took attend-ance. The employee's attendance was so poor he was fired:* record of attendance. **3.** *The attendance at the Super Bowl was more than 90,000:* number present, audience, crowd, assemblage, house, gate. —**Ant. 1** absence, nonattendance.

attendant *n.* **1.** *The queen was always surrounded by her attendants:* servant, underling, menial, lackey, flunky, aid, assistant, helper; companion, escort, chaperon; follower, adherent. —*adj.* **2.** *We always dread winter and its attendant hardships:* accompanying, associated, related; accessory, consequent.

attention *n.* **1.** *Nobody paid any attention to the warning:* heed, regard, note, notice, mind, concern, consideration; observance, alertness, vigilance, wariness. **2.** *A scientist must give full attention to any problem he or she wants to solve:* concentration, diligence, alertness, thought, thoughtfulness, deliberation, contemplation. **3.** *The attention of the host pleased the guests:* courtesy, civility, thoughtfulness, politeness, deference, respect; service, care, homage. **4.** *The young man showered his attentions on his fiancée:* devotion, suit, court, wooing; gallantries, compliments, assiduities. —**Ant. 1–4** inattention, disregard, neglect, negligence, indifference, unconcern. **3** distraction, thoughtlessness, carelessness. **3** thoughtlessness, discourtesy, incivility, rudeness, impoliteness.

attentive *adj.* **1.** *A good speaker deserves an attentive audience:* heedful, mindful, considerate, intent, awake, wide awake, alert, listening, observant. **2.** *She's always an attentive hostess:* thoughtful, considerate, obliging, accommodating, courteous, respectful, deferential, polite; dedicated, devoted, diligent, painstaking, zealous. —**Ant. 1** inattentive, indifferent, unconcerned, heedless, neglectful. **2** thoughtless, inconsiderate, unaccommodating; discourteous, impolite, rude; negligent, remiss, careless.

attenuate *v.* **1.** *The silversmith attenuated the ingot into one long thread:* draw out, make thin, make fine, make slender, spin out. **2.** *Aspirin only attenuated the pain:* weaken, reduce, diminish, lessen, decrease; dilute, water down, adulterate, impair, enervate, enfeeble. —**Ant. 1** broaden, make thick, make coarse, make fat, enlarge, expand. **2** increase, amplify, intensify, augment, strengthen, develop.

attest *v.* *The lawyer attested to the validity of the will. The success of the operation attests the surgeon's skill:* testify, swear to, verify, confirm, corroborate, vouch for, certify, warrant, affirm, assert, evince, assure, declare; prove, demonstrate, exhibit, show, display, support, substantiate, give evidence, bear witness, bear out. —**Ant.** refute, deny, disavow; controvert, contradict, disprove, gainsay, belie, cut the ground from under.

attic *n.* *The Christmas decorations were put in boxes and returned to the attic:* garret, loft, clerestory, cockloft, mansard, *French* grenier, *Spanish* guardilla, *German* Dachboden.

attire *v.* **1.** *The mourners were attired in black:* dress, clothe, garb, robe, gown, deck out, array, bedeck, costume, don, invest, fit out, turn out, rig out. —*n.* **2.** *Her wedding attire was all satin and lace:* dress, garments, apparel, clothing, clothes, costume, outfit, garb, wardrobe, habiliments, raiment, vestments, *Slang* duds, togs; finery, array, glad rags. —**Ant. 1** undress, disrobe, unclothe, strip, bare, denude.

attitude *n.* **1.** *Why do you have such a belligerent attitude?:* disposition, frame of mind, outlook, point of view, perspective, manner, demeanor, air. **2.** *The listeners stood in an attentive attitude:* posture, stance, pose, position.

attorney *n.* *The defendant was represented by his attorney:* lawyer, counsel, counselor, legal adviser, attorney at law, member of the bar, *British* barrister, solicitor, advocate; *Slang* mouthpiece, beak, ambulance chaser.

attract *v.* **1.** *Sugar attracts flies. The zoo attracted many visitors:* draw, lure, allure, entice, invite, beckon, pull; interest, appeal to, fascinate; captivate, charm, enchant, bewitch. **2.** *Try not to attract attention:* draw, induce, provoke, cause, bring about, precipitate, evoke. —**Ant. 1** repel, repulse; disgust, antagonize, affront, offend, outrage.

attraction *n.* *Suspense novels hold a special attraction for me:* appeal, fascination, allure, lure, enticement, inducement, magnetism, charisma, drawing power, pull, temptation, enchantment, captivation, tendency, affinity; charm, glamour, attractiveness. —**Ant.** repulsion, repugnance; aversion, disinclination, indifference, apathy.

attractive *adj.* *The new dress styles are very attractive:* appealing, pleasing, likable, agreeable, pleasant; charming, delightful, enchanting, engaging, charismatic, winning; lovely, beautiful, pretty, handsome, becoming, fetching, fair, sightly, chic, elegant, tasteful; inviting, tempting, enticing, fascinating, alluring, bewitching, captivating, seductive. —**Ant.** unappealing, displeasing, unlikable, unpleasant, unpleasing, offensive, repellent, repugnant, repulsive, revolting, obnoxious, distasteful; ugly, unbecoming, inelegant; uninviting.

attribute *v.* **1.** *The automobile accident was attributed to faulty brakes:* ascribe, credit, assign, allege to belong; charge to, set down to, lay to, account for, impute, trace to, blame on, bring home to, saddle with, lay at the door of; cause by, derive from. —*n.* **2.** *Generosity is but one of her many fine attributes:* characteristic, trait, quality, virtue, aspect, facet, feature, character, property; accomplishment, acquirement, attainment, faculty, ability, distinction, grace, gift, talent, endowment.

attrition *n.* **1.** *Attrition over thousands of years* formed a cave in the rocks: wearing down, wearing away, friction, abrasion, erosion, disintegration, grinding, scraping. **2.** *No one will be fired, but the staff will be reduced by natural attrition:* decrease, reduction, decimation, loss.

attune *v. Astronauts have to attune themselves to weightlessness in space:* adapt, accustom, adjust, acclimate, acclimatize, tailor. **—Ant.** resist, fight against; alienate.

atypical *adj. Seasickness is an atypical ailment among experienced sailors:* unusual, uncommon, untypical, nontypical, anomalous, unrepresentative, out of keeping, unlooked for, contrary, abnormal, unnatural, irregular, uncustomary. **—Ant.** typical, representative; common, familiar, ordinary, usual, customary, in keeping, normal, natural, regular, expected.

auburn *adj.* **1.** *She now has auburn hair:* reddish-brown, golden-brown, tawny, chestnut-colored, nut brown, cinnamon, russet, rust-colored, copper-colored, henna. **—n.** **2.** *She darkened her hair to auburn:* reddish-brown, golden-brown, nut brown, russet, henna.

audacious *adj.* **1.** *Napoleon was an audacious leader:* bold, daring, adventurous, venturesome, enterprising; brave, courageous, fearless, unafraid, valiant, intrepid, dauntless, stouthearted, lionhearted, stalwart, valorous, plucky, *Slang* gutsy. **2.** *We admired the audacious feats of the trapeze artists:* bold, daring, reckless, rash, risky, daredevil, devil-may-care, death-defying, breakneck; heedless, foolhardy, injudicious, imprudent, desperate, hotheaded, self-willed, wild. **3.** *Her audacious behavior shocked us all:* impudent, impertinent, insolent, brazen, fresh, shameless, outrageous, defiant, unabashed, presumptuous, assuming, forward, saucy, cheeky, bossy, pert; disrespectful, rude, discourteous. **—Ant.** 1 unadventurous, unenterprising; cowardly, fainthearted, craven, frightened, timid, pusillanimous, *Slang* yellow, chickenhearted, lily-livered. 2 careful, guarded, discreet; prudent, circumspect, cautious, judicious. 3 tactful, gracious, unassuming, cordial, amiable, ingratiating, deferential, reverential, obsequious, *Informal* kowtowing; polite, courteous, mannerly, well-mannered, gentlemanly, ladylike, refined, polished, formal.

audacity *n.* **1.** *Skydiving takes both audacity and skill:* boldness, daring, nerve, spunk, grit, pluck, mettle, *Slang* guts, backbone; derring-do, venturesomeness; fearlessness, valor, bravery, courage; recklessness, temerity, rashness, foolhardiness. **2.** *She had the audacity to walk out on the sermon:* impudence, impertinence, insolence, brashness, effrontery, brazenness, brass, shamelessness, cheek, gall, *Slang* chutzpah, presumption, forwardness, bumptiousness. **—Ant.** discretion, prudence, caution, wariness, circumspection; cowardice, faintheartedness, timidity, timorousness.

audible *adj. The music was barely audible. He heaved an audible sigh:* loud enough to be heard, heard, perceptible, discernible, clear, distinct. **—Ant.** inaudible, muffled, faint.

audience *n.* **1.** *The audience applauded the* performance: listeners, spectators, onlookers, assembly, congregation, house. **2.** *Shakespeare has always had a large audience:* public, following, readership, market; constituency. **3.** *They requested an audience with the Pope:* interview, personal meeting, hearing, audition, reception; conference, discussion, consultation, talk, parley.

audit *v.* **1.** *Accountants audit the company's books every year:* examine, inspect, check, go over, investigate, scrutinize; verify, balance, review, take stock of. **—n.** **2.** *The stockholder demanded an audit of the firm's accounts:* examination, inspection, investigation, scruti-nizing; verification, review.

audition *n.* **1.** *The actor's audition landed him a role in the new play:* tryout, hearing, test performance. **—v.** **2.** *The opera company is auditioning new singers for the chorus:* try out, give a test performance.

auditor *n.* **1.** *The auditor checked the firm's books:* financial examiner; (*loosely*) accountant, bookkeeper, comptroller. **2.** *I'm not a regular student but just an auditor of the course:* one who listens, listener.

auditorium *n. The graduation exercises took place in the school auditorium:* assembly hall, lecture hall, concert hall, meeting hall, auditory; arena, theater, coliseum.

aught[1] *n. Eight followed by three aughts represents the number 8,000:* zero, naught; a cipher (0); nothing, null, *Slang* goose egg, zip, horse collar; *Tennis* love.

aught[2] *pron. For aught I know, she's gone, and for aught I care, she can stay:* all.

augment *v. The boy augmented his allowance by mowing lawns:* add to, increase, enlarge, expand, extend, raise, boost, swell, inflate, amplify, magnify, intensify, build up, flesh out; heighten, lengthen, widen, deepen. **—Ant.** decrease, reduce, diminish, lessen, lower; curtail, cut back, abridge, shorten, narrow, contract, shrink, moderate, subside.

augur *n.* **1.** *Roman augurs predicted the future by interpreting flights of birds and other natural occurrences:* oracle, prophet, seer; diviner, prognosticator, soothsayer. **—v.** **2.** *Dark clouds augured the coming of the thunderstorm:* prophesy, predict, prognosticate, presage, bode, intimate, be an omen of; be a sign of, signify, portend, forecast, foretell, herald, forewarn, foreshadow, promise.

augury *n.* **1.** *Augury was commonly performed by inspecting the flight of birds or the entrails of sacrificial victims:* prophecy, divination, prognostication, soothsaying, fortunetelling; auspice, sortilege. **2.** *The rainbow was an augury of clear weather:* omen, portent, sign, token, warning, forewarning, indication; herald, forerunner, precursor, promise, harbinger.

august *adj. George Washington is one of the most august figures in American history:* awe-inspiring, monumental, majestic, magnificent, impressive, imposing, sublime, grand, grandiose, noble, dignified, distinguished, eminent, illustrious, stately, solemn, venerable, exalted, estimable, glorious, supreme, superb, lofty, high-ranking, regal. **—Ant.** unawesome, unimpressive, unimposing, uninspiring; mean, common, commonplace, undistinguished, undignified, unstately, ignoble, unmajestic, unexalted; paltry, insignificant; ridiculous, comic.

aura n. *There was an aura of glamour about her:* atmosphere, ambience, mood, feeling, feel, character, quality, suggestion, air, essence, aroma, emanation.

auspice n. **1.** *The break in the clouds was an auspice of better weather to come:* indication, sign, portent, omen, warning, augury, prognostication. **2. auspices.** *The free concerts were offered under the auspices of the opera company:* sponsorship, patronage, support, advocacy, aegis, championship; care, charge, authority, control, countenance, guidance, influence, protection.

auspicious adj. **1.** *The amount of business the new store did on its first day was most auspicious:* being a good omen, encouraging, favorable, promising, propitious, heartening, reassuring, hopeful. **2.** *On this auspicious occasion I would like to toast the bride and groom:* happy, felicitous, benign, good, fortunate, successful, lucky, opportune, timely, red-letter. **—Ant.** inauspicious. 1 ill-omened, ominous, sinister, discouraging, unfavorable, unpromising, unpropitious, disheartening, adverse, unsatisfactory. 2 sad, unhappy, sorrowful, baleful, melancholy, cheerless, joyless, pathetic, dismal; unfortunate, unlucky, black.

austere adj. **1.** *In the old days, schoolmasters were thought of as austere men:* stern, strict, severe, forbidding, ascetic. **2.** *The Puritans led austere lives:* rigorous, rigid, Spartan, ascetic, self-denying, abstemious, strict, simple, spare, stark, strait-laced, chaste. **—Ant.** 1 permissive, lenient, indulgent, easy, flexible, lax; frivolous, gay, cheerful, joyful, merry, lighthearted, jovial, jolly, jaunty, nonchalant, lively, exuberant, vivacious, effervescent, high-spirited, playful, convivial; kindly, kind, sweet, genial. 2 luxurious, lush, comfortable, easy; sophisticated, cosmopolitan; loose, corrupt, dissolute, dissipated, debauched, degenerate, depraved, wanton, abandoned, self-gratifying, free-and-easy, immoral, wicked, evil, sinful, impure, lewd, licentious, lascivious.

austerity n. **1.** *After several years of austerity, goods were once again abundant:* severity, rigor, rigorousness, sternness, strictness, harshness, rigidity, inflexibility, stiffness **2.** *The monks practiced extreme austerity:* asceticism, restraint, reserve, self-denial, self-discipline. **—Ant.** 1 lenience, flexibility.

authentic adj. **1.** *This is an authentic Persian rug:* genuine, real, true, actual, bona fide, legitimate, original. **2.** *This book tells the authentic story of a doctor's life:* true, actual, real; factual, accurate, faithful, veritable, valid; verified, authenticated, attested, accredited, unquestioned, pure, unadulterated; reliable, dependable, trustworthy, authoritative. **—Ant.** 1 imitation, counterfeit, simulated, synthetic, fake, sham, phony, bogus, mock, specious. 2 unreal, false, untrue,

inaccurate, unfaithful; fictitious, pretended, make-believe, hypothetical, supposed, unverified, unreliable, untrustworthy, undependable; deceptive, misleading, fraudulent, corrupt, adulterated.

authenticate v. *The lawyer authenticated the will:* establish as genuine, document, verify, confirm, corroborate, attest, vouch for, avouch, validate, substantiate, certify, guarantee, warrant, endorse. **—Ant.** impugn, gainsay, invalidate, disprove, discredit, negate, contravene; repudiate, deny, refute, reject, spurn.

author n. **1.** *Mark Twain is the author of* Tom Sawyer: writer; (*variously*) novelist, short-story writer, poet, essayist, playwright. **2.** *The secretary of state is one of the authors of present U.S. foreign policy:* creator, originator, maker, prime mover, innovator, initiator, inventor, father, framer; founder, producer, planner, organizer.

authoritarian adj. **1.** *Their country has an authoritarian government:* favoring authority, repressing individual freedom; strict, harsh, severe, unyielding, inflexible, uncompromising, austere, disciplinary, disciplinarian, dogmatic, doctrinaire; dictatorial, tyrannical, fascist; by the rule, by the book. **—**n. **2.** *The drill sergeant was a strict authoritarian:* disciplinarian, rule follower; martinet, autocrat, tyrant, little dictator. **—Ant.** 1 revolutionary, insurgent, mutinous, dissenting, nonconformist; lenient, permissive, flexible. 2 anarchist, rebel, revolutionary, insurgent, mutineer; malcontent, dissenter, nonconformist.

authoritative adj. **1.** *Is this an authoritative order from the general or merely a personal request?:* official, sanctioned, commanding, commanding obedience; administrative, sovereign, ruling. **2.** *He was a small man but there was an authoritative tone in his voice:* showing authority, commanding, imperative, decisive, masterful, imposing, impressive, peremptory; arrogant, lordly, autocratic, dogmatic, dictatorial, tyrannical. **3.** *Read a good, authoritative book on the Civil War:* trustworthy, reliable, dependable, sound, valid, authentic, definitive, factual, scholarly, learned. **—Ant.** 1 unofficial, unsanctioned, unauthorized, without authority; facetious, frivolous. 2 subservient, servile; weak, indecisive, meek, timid, humble, modest. 3 untrustworthy, unreliable, undependable, invalid; deceptive, misleading.

authority n. **1.** *The sheriff's authority ends at the county line. Speak to someone in a position of authority:* command, control, power, sway, force, weight, rule, supremacy, domination, dominion, strength, might, influence, importance, *Slang* clout, respect, prestige, esteem; jurisdiction, administration. **2. authorities.** *You had better notify the authorities that the child is missing:* powers that be, government administration; officialdom, police. **3.** *A leading agricultural authority predicts farm prices will hold firm:* expert, specialist, scholar, mastermind, pundit, connoisseur; accepted source, trustworthy source. **—Ant.** 1 servility, servitude, weakness. 2 follower; public, masses.

authorize v. **1.** *The law authorizes police officers to carry revolvers:* give authority to, empower, permit, allow, commission, license, entitle, invest, charter, enable, give leave. **2.** *The firm's bookkeeper has to authorize all payments:* give authority for, approve, sanction, confirm; certify, accredit, warrant, vouch for. **—Ant.** 1 enjoin, prohibit, forbid, proscribe, preclude, interdict; prevent, disallow.

autocracy n. *Nazi Germany was an autocracy where absolute power was vested in one person, Adolf Hitler:* dictatorship, monocracy, totalitarian regime, autarchy, absolute monarchy; despotism, absolutism, tyrannical rule, tyranny, totalitarianism, czarism, Hitlerism, Stalinism, Bonapartism, Caesarism, kaiserism.

autocrat n. *One of the Czar's titles was "Autocrat of all the Russias." My father was the autocrat in our house:* absolute ruler, ruler, dictator, monarch, overlord; tyrant, despot.

autocratic adj. *The emperor was an autocratic ruler. The warden had an autocratic attitude toward his prisoners:* having absolute power, dictatorial, monarchical, czaristic; tyrannical, tyrannous, despotic, imperious, authoritarian, repressive, oppressive, iron-handed. **—Ant.** limited, constitutional, democratic, egalitarian; lenient, permissive, indulgent, forbearing, tolerant.

autograph n. *She asked the President to put his autograph in her album:* signature, John Hancock, John Henry, X, mark, sign, endorsement, inscription, handwriting, countersignature.

automatic adj. **1.** *Mother bought an automatic dishwasher:* self-operating, self-acting, self-moving, self-propelling, electric, mechanical, push-button, automated. **2.** *Breathing and blinking are automatic reactions:* occurring independently, involuntary, reflex, instinctive, unconscious, spontaneous, natural, nonvolitional, uncontrolled, unwilled, inherent; mechanical, routine, habitual. **—Ant.** 1 manual. 2 voluntary, conscious, intentional, controlled, deliberate.

automation n. *We're living in the age of automation:* automatic machinery, machine-operated machinery, robotism.

automaton n. *Computer-controlled automatons are widely used in industry:* robot, machine, android; puppet, marionette, *Italian* fantoccino; pawn, cat's-paw, tool, stooge, patsy, fall guy.

automobile n. See CAR.

autonomous adj. *The school of adult education was an autonomous extension of the university:* self-governing, self-determined; self-sufficient, self-reliant, independent, sovereign, free. **—Ant.** governed, dependent, subject.

autonomy n. *After World War II, Britain granted many of its colonies autonomy:* self-government, home rule, self-rule, self-determination; independence; sovereignty, freedom, liberation. **—Ant.** foreign rule, dependency; colonial status.

autumn n. *Autumn usually begins on September 21st:* fall, Indian summer, harvest time; autumnal equinox.

auxiliary adj. **1.** *If the main power line fails, the hospital will use its auxiliary generator:* supplementary, ancillary, subordinate, secondary, subsidiary, accessory; reserve, emergency, backup. **—n. 2.** *The helicopters will serve as an auxiliary to the fast reconnaissance planes:* supplement, subsidiary, accessory; partner, companion, accomplice, associate; helper, assistant, giver of aid, helping hand; reserve, backup. **—Ant.** 1 main, chief, primary, first-line. 2 main body, major item; opponent, antagonist, hindrance, drawback.

avail n. **1.** *Efforts to save the sinking ship were of no avail:* use, usefulness, advantage, purpose, service, benefit, success, profit; help, aid. **—v. 2.** *Avail yourself of every opportunity to get a good education. Our efforts to save the burning building availed us little:* use, utilize, profit from, take advantage of; benefit, help, aid, assist, serve, be of use, be of advantage, profit. **—Ant.** 1 detriment, disadvantage, disservice, harm. 2 overlook, neglect, ignore, slight, pass up, spurn; hinder, harm, hurt, be useless.

available adj. *The motel had no available rooms. Is there a doctor available?:* ready for use, ready for service, free, open, obtainable, accessible, at one's disposal, convenient, on hand, in reserve, at hand, handy, at one's elbow, on tap, up for grabs. **—Ant.** unavailable, unobtainable, in use, occupied, spoken for, taken; inconvenient, inaccessible; unusable, unserviceable.

avalanche n. **1.** *The avalanche trapped the climbers:* snowslide; earthslide, rockslide. **2.** *The post office expects an avalanche of mail at Christmas:* overwhelming amount, barrage, bombardment, flood, deluge, inundation, cataclysm, torrent, cascade, blizzard, heap, pile, mass. **—Ant.** 2 paucity, scantiness; dearth, lack, deficiency, insufficiency, shortage, drought, famine.

avant-garde n. *In the 1920's Picasso was still considered a member of the avant-garde:* artistic innovators, advance guard, vanguard, trailblazers, trendsetters, pioneers, tastemakers, leaders, forerunners, originators.

avarice n. *His avarice led him into unethical business deals:* lust for money, greed, greediness, money-grubbing, rapacity, venality, graspingness, covetousness, worship of the golden calf; miserliness, stinginess, parsimony, penury, niggardliness, penny-pinching, close-fistedness. **—Ant.** generosity, benevolence, magnanimity, munificence, charitableness, unselfishness; extravagance, liberality, open-handedness.

avenge v. *The settlers avenged the burning of the fort by destroying an Indian village:* take vengeance for, wreak vengeance, revenge, retaliate, get even for, *Informal* get back at, repay, punish, exact satisfaction for, inflict injury for, injure, exact an eye for an eye. **—Ant.** excuse, forgive, pardon, overlook; accept, be resigned to, tolerate.

avenue n. **1.** *The avenue was lined with modern shops:* boulevard, thoroughfare, broad street; parkway, tree-lined road, esplanade, concourse. **2.** *The only avenue to escape is over that mountain:* way, route, road, course, path, pathway, passage, passageway, direction; opportunity, chance, means, access, approach, gate, gateway, outlet. **—Ant.** l alley, lane.

aver v. *The witness averred that he had seen the suspect at the scene of the crime:* assert, declare, affirm, state, avow, avouch, maintain, swear, insist, emphasize, contend, profess, represent, proclaim, pronounce, protest, asseverate; certify, verify, guarantee. **—Ant.** deny, disavow, disclaim, repudiate; doubt, be uncertain, gainsay.

average n. **1.** *The average of 2, 3, and 7 is 4. He maintained a .283 batting average. She hopes to graduate with a B average:* arithmetical mean, mean amount; (*loosely*) mean, median, ratio, medium, norm, midpoint, par; standing, accomplishment. **2.** *He bowls better than average:* the ordinary, the standard, the typical, the general, the usual, normal, the run of the mill, the rule. *—adj.* **3.** *Including stops for gas and a traffic jam, our average speed was still 40 miles an hour:* mean, par; (*loosely*) medium, median, medial. **4.** *Yesterday was an average working day. He is of average height. It was only an average movie:* typical, ordinary, common, normal, usual, standard, moderate; fair, passable, so-so, tolerable, mediocre, indifferent, not bad, run-of-the-mill, betwixt and between, rank and file. **—Ant.** 1, 3 maximum; minimum. 4 unusual, uncommon, different, special, remarkable, exceptional, extraordinary, extreme, abnormal; memorable, conspicuous, noticeable, prominent; outstanding, superlative, surpassing, excellent, wonderful, terrific, stupendous, tremendous, great, fine, good; awful, bad, dreadful, terrible, horrible, lousy.

averse adj. *I don't approve of whiskey but I'm not averse to a glass of wine now and then:* opposed, loath, disinclined, unwilling, reluctant, indisposed, ill-disposed, unfavorable, recalcitrant, antipathetic, unamenable, inimical. **—Ant.** agreeable, amenable, willing, inclined, disposed, favorable; eager, avid, ardent, desirous, intent, keen.

aversion n. *Cats have an aversion to getting wet:* dislike, unwillingness, reluctance, antipathy, disinclination; distaste, repugnance, prejudice against, opposition; abhorrence, loathing, hatred, disgust, detestation, revulsion, repulsion, animosity, hostility, horror. **—Ant.** willingness, inclination; eagerness, desire, love, liking.

avert v. **1.** *She averted her head so we couldn't see her face:* turn aside, turn away, turn, deflect, shift. **2.** *The quick arrival of fire fighters averted a major forest fire:* prevent, forestall, deter, avoid, preclude, ward off, stave off, keep off, fend off, beat off, keep at bay, nip in the bud, frustrate, sidetrack. **—Ant.** 1 hold steady. 2 allow, permit, let.

aviation n. *The Wright brothers were pioneers in aviation:* flying, flight, aeronautics, aerodynamics.

aviator, Fem. **aviatrix** n. *Eddie Rickenbacker was the most famous American aviator of World War I:* pilot, flyer, airman, *Slang* birdman, bird, fly-boy.

avid adj. **1.** *People who are too avid for success may miss some of the joys of life:* eager, greedy, avaricious, insatiable, hungry, desirous, keen, anxious; grasping, covetous, acquisitive, voracious, rapacious. **2.** *He was an avid football fan:* devoted, enthusiastic, ardent, intense, zealous, rabid, fanatic. **—Ant.** indifferent, apathetic 1 unconcerned, disdainful; indisposed, disinclined, loath. 2 reluctant, recalcitrant, unwilling.

avocation n. *The doctor's avocation was painting:* sideline, secondary occupation; hobby, diversion, pastime, distraction, recreation, entertainment. **—Ant.** vocation, occupation, work, business, *Informal* line.

avoid v. *How did the burglars avoid the guards? Avoid fried foods for a while:* evade, elude, dodge, escape, avert, sidestep, skirt, fight shy of; keep away from, shun, keep clear of, steer clear of, refrain from, eschew, forsake, forbear, boycott. **—Ant.** meet, face, confront, incur, contact; approach, find, seek out, invite, solicit; pursue, embrace.

avoidance n. *Constant avoidance of exercise is unhealthy:* keeping away from, shunning, evasion, eluding, shirking, skirting. **—Ant.** search, invitation, soliciting; pursuit, embrace; meeting, facing, confronting.

avouch v. *The authenticity of the painting was avouched by several experts:* declare, own, affirm, assert, aver, announce, asseverate, swear, certify, confirm; admit, confess, acknowledge. **—Ant.** deny, repudiate, recant, controvert, gainsay, disclaim, disavow.

avow v. *He avowed his love to her:* declare, admit, announce, confess, own, disclose, reveal, proclaim, profess, affirm, acknowledge; assert, state, swear, aver. **—Ant.** disavow, disclaim, deny, repudiate; keep hidden, keep secret.

avowal n. *The criminal's avowal of guilt closed the case:* admission, confession, profession, declaration, proclamation, acknowledgment; affirmation, assertion, statement, protestation, assurance, word, averment. **—Ant.** disavowal, disclaimer, repudiation; hiding, keeping secret.

avowed adj. *George Bernard Shaw was an avowed vegetarian:* self-declared, professed, self-proclaimed, confessed, sworn; acknowledged, declared, admitted. **—Ant.** secret, undisclosed, unrevealed, private, closet, clandestine, surreptitious, furtive.

await v. *The audience eagerly awaited the speaker's arrival. Your Highness, your coach awaits:* wait for, look for, look forward to, anticipate, expect; be in readiness for, be in waiting, attend.

awake v. **1.** *We awake every morning at six. The alarm awoke everyone in the house:* wake, wake up, awaken, raise from sleep. **2.** *The fuel shortage awoke the country to the need for developing alternate sources of energy:* make awake, arouse, incite, inspire, stimulate, spark, excite, provoke, bestir, alert, make aware, make heedful. —*adj.* **3.** *The campers lay awake, listening to the night sounds:* not sleeping, wide-awake, open-eyed. **4.** *A pilot must be awake to changes in the weather:* alert, aware, attentive, watchful, vigilant, heedful, mindful, conscious, wide-awake, alive to. —**Ant.** 1 sleep, go to sleep; doze, nap. 2 put to sleep, make unaware; dull. 3 asleep, sleeping, dozing, napping; dormant, hibernating. 4 unaware, inattentive, unmindful, unconscious.

awaken *v.* **1.** *The parents were awakened by the child's coughing:* wake, wake up, awake, rouse from sleep. **2.** *Seeing the Lincoln Memorial awakened my interest in the Civil War:* arouse, kindle, call forth, make aware, stimulate, stir up, excite; revive, fan, fire, give new life to. —**Ant.** 1 go to sleep, put to sleep. 2 quiet, dampen, dull, subdue, check.

awakening *n.* **1.** *After an early awakening, we had a big breakfast:* awaking, waking, waking up; arising, getting up, rising from sleep. **2.** *If you think this is an easy job, you're in for a rude awakening. The child had a gradual awakening to the joys of music:* arousal, stimulation, stirring, sparking.

award *v.* **1.** *They award a scholarship to the student with the highest grades. The grandparents were awarded custody of the children:* grant, accord, confer on, bestow, give; assign, allot, allow, concede; decree, appoint. —*n.* **2.** *The Academy Awards are given out once a year:* prize, trophy; medal, decoration, laurels, honor, citation, tribute. —**Ant.** 1 withhold; refuse, disallow; deny. 2 booby prize.

aware *adj.* *Everyone should be aware of the dangers of cigarette smoking:* conscious, cognizant, familiar with, acquainted with, informed, apprised, enlightened on, knowledgeable, sensible, sentient, conversant, *au courant,* mindful, awake to, alert to, alive to, *Slang* tuned in to, with it. —**Ant.** unaware, unfamiliar with, unacquainted with, uninformed about, ignorant, unknowledgeable, nonconversant, unmindful, insensible, unconscious, oblivious, unenlightened on.

awareness *n.* *A good senator must have an awareness of what the people back home want:* realization, recognition, cognizance, familiarity, sensibility, understanding, mindfulness, acquaintance, appraisal, alertness, consciousness, perception, acuteness; knowledge, information. —**Ant.** unawareness, unfamiliarity, insensibility, obliviousness, ignorance, unenlightenment.

awe *n.* **1.** *The sight of Notre Dame Cathedral filled the tourists with awe:* wonder, reverence, veneration, solemnity, exaltation, respect, adoration, amazement, astonishment, abashment. **2.** *The approaching tornado struck awe in our hearts:* fright, fear, terror, dread, panic, dismay, alarm, apprehension, consternation, disquietude, perturbation, trepidation, shock, horror, trembling, quaking, quivering. —*v.* **3.** *The natives of New Guinea were awed when they saw*

their first airplane: strike with wonder, amaze, astonish, abash, overawe, cow, intimidate, fill with reverence; frighten, beset by fear, terrify, fill with dread, panic, dismay, alarm, disquiet, perturb, shock. —**Ant.** 1 contempt, scorn, disdain; irreverence, disrespect, insolence, arrogance, superciliousness, levity. 2 scorn, disdain. 3 take in stride.

awesome *adj.* *The eruption of a volcano is an awesome sight:* solemn, inspiring, majestic, magnificent, wondrous, formidable, astonishing, amazing, awe-inspiring, breathtaking, overwhelming, stupefying; fearsome, fearful, frightening, terrifying, dreadful, alarming, disquieting, perturbing, intimidating.

awful *adj.* **1.** *What awful weather! She gave me an awful book. He was guilty of the awful crime of murder:* bad, dreadful, terrible, horrible, horrendous, deplorable, distressing, lousy, unpleasant, disagreeable, displeasing, appalling, frightful, ghastly, fearful, horrifying, hideous, ugly, gruesome, monstrous, shocking, revolting, reprehensible, despicable, contemptible, mean, low, base, heinous; dire, redoubtable, formidable, alarming. **2.** *The astronauts know the awful expanse of the solar system:* awe-inspiring, awesome; wondrous, solemn, majestic, amazing, stupefying; fearsome, terrifying, dreadful, disquieting. —**Ant.** 1 good, fine, O.K., wonderful, terrific, tremendous, pleasant, pleasing; attractive, beautiful, pretty; admirable, likable.

awfully *adv.* *It's awfully cold today:* very, extremely, quite, exceptionally, terribly, horribly, dreadfully, immensely, excessively. —**Ant.** somewhat.

awkward *adj.* **1.** *She was an awkward skier:* clumsy, uncoordinated, without grace, graceless, ungainly; inexpert, unskillful, inept, bungling, blundering, gauche, maladroit. **2.** *The heavy ax was awkward to use:* unwieldy, unhandy, cumbersome, inconvenient, troublesome, difficult, unmanageable. **3.** *The scandal was an awkward situation for the entire family:* embarrassing, unpleasant, trying, difficult, uncomfortable, disconcerting, ticklish, touchy, delicate, troublesome, inconvenient. —**Ant.** 1 graceful, well-coordinated, effortless, dexterous; skillful, adept. 2 handy, convenient. 3 proud; pleasing, pleasant, easy, comfortable.

awry *adj., adv.* **1.** *The picture is hanging awry:* askew, crooked, crookedly, unevenly, uneven, turned to one side, twisted, out of kilter, obliquely. **2.** *The game was supposed to start at two, but something went awry and it didn't start until three:* wrong, amiss, askew, astray. —**Ant.** 1 straight, even, evenly, in line, true; horizontally, vertically. 2 right, perfectly.

axiom *n.* *The statement that all men are created equal is an axiom of democracy:* basic, principle, postulate, assumption, precept, fundamental law. —**Ant.** contradiction, paradox; absurdity.

axiomatic *adj.* *It is axiomatic that absolute power corrupts absolutely:* assumed, accepted, generally understood, demonstrable, apodictic, self-evident, incontestable, indisputable, manifest, unquestioned, given; platitudinous, aphoristic, epigrammatic; banal, cliché. —**Ant.** debatable, questionable, moot, controversial, arguable.

axis *n.* **1.** *The globe spun on its axis:* line around which a rotating body turns, line of rotation, line of symmetry, center line; shaft, spindle, stem; pivot, pivotal point. **2.** *Germany, Italy, and Japan formed an axis against the Allies in World War II:* alliance, coalition, alignment, affiliation, confederation, compact, entente.

aye *n.* *All those in favor, say "Aye." The ayes have it:* yes, yea; affirmative vote. —**Ant.** nay, no; negative vote.

azure *n.* **1.** *Azure goes well with her blond hair:* sky blue, clear blue, cerulean, cobalt, lapis lazuli. —*adj.* **2.** *The ship sailed under azure skies:* clear blue, sky blue, cobalt, cerulean, lapis; cloudless.

B

babble *n.* **1.** *The salesman kept up his babble until we shut the door in his face:* gabble, drivel, twaddle, blabber, blab, gab, jabber, jabbering, prattle, chitchat, chitter-chatter. **2.** *The speaker shouted over the babble of the crowd:* murmur, clamor, hubbub, hum, din. **3.** *We could hear the babble of a brook:* murmur, murmuring, babbling, burble, gurgle. —*v.* **4.** *The baby babbled happily:* gurgle, murmur, gibber, coo. **5.** *Don't babble on the phone all day:* talk, talk incoherently, talk foolishly, prattle, jabber, chatter, chitchat, blabber, blather, blab, gab, gabble, prate, rattle on, run off at the mouth. **6.** *The brook babbled merrily:* murmur, gurgle. —**Ant.** 2 silence, stillness, quietness. 4 articulate, enunciate.

babe *n.* *The mother cuddled the babe in her arms:* baby, infant, child, tot.

babel Sometimes **Babel** *n.* *The convention became a babel of conflicting opinions:* tumult, confusion, turmoil, uproar, pandemonium, bedlam, hullabaloo, clamor, hubbub, din. —**Ant.** stillness, silence, quiet, quietness; calm, tranquillity.

baby *n.* **1.** *The baby slept in its crib:* infant, babe, babe in arms, newborn child, neonate. **2.** *Dr. Anderson is the baby of our bridge club:* youngster; junior member, youngest member, newest member. **3.** *Take your medicine and don't be such a baby about it:* sniveler, crybaby, coward. —*v.* **4.** *Her older sisters always babied her:* pamper, indulge, overindulge, spoil, coddle, mollycoddle, humor. —*adj.* **5.** *The baby bird fell out of the nest. Her garden is full of baby marigolds:* young; small, diminutive, miniature, tiny, little, minute, petite, wee, midget, pygmy, dwarf, dwarfish, bantam, pocket-sized. —**Ant.** 1 adult; elder, oldster, old man, old woman, ancient. 2 oldest, oldster, senior member, oldest member. 3 adult; stoic, good sport. 4 mistreat, abuse. 5 adult, mature; giant, large, great, huge, enormous.

babyish *adj.* *The actress was known for her babyish temper tantrums:* childish, infantile, immature, juvenile, puerile; babylike.

bacchanal *n.* *That New Year's Eve party was a real bacchanal!:* drunken party, spree, orgy, debauch, debauchery, carouse, carousal, revel, wassail, revelry, Saturnalia; festival, carnival, frolic, merrymaking, feast.

bachelor *n.* *Distrusting women, he remained a bachelor all his life:* unmarried man, single man. —**Ant.** husband; bridegroom, groom.

back *n.* **1.** *Lie flat on your back. You were lucky you didn't break your back in the accident:* rear part of the body; backbone, spine, spinal column, dorsum; hindquarters. **2.** *Did you paint the back of the bookcase? Please move to the back of the bus:* rear, rear end, posterior, hind part, tail, far end, afterpart; reverse, reverse side, far side. —*v.* **3.** *Back the car out of the ga-*rage. *The trainer backed away from the enraged tiger:* move backward; move away, retreat, retire, withdraw, pull back, fall back, draw back, back down, back off, turn tail, beat a retreat; reverse, retract, revert, retrogress, recede, ebb; return, rebound, recoil, spring back. **4.** *Which candidate will you back in the election? Can you back your story with facts?:* help, assist, support, aid, abet, sustain, maintain; endorse, sponsor, vouch for, advocate, promote, encourage, sanction, uphold, countenance, second, reinforce, corroborate, substantiate, confirm, bear witness, attest, testify for, validate, certify, affirm, verify, bolster, hold up, take sides with; praise, protect, guard, succor; patronize, finance, subsidize, underwrite, warrant. —*adj.* **5.** *The dog stood up and begged on its back legs. Put this flowerpot on the back porch:* rear, hindmost, hind, hinder, behind, after; posterior, dorsal, caudal, tail, tail end, tergal; furthermost, farthermost. **6.** *Turn off the highway and drive down this back road:* minor, unimportant; secluded, unpopulated, untraveled, undeveloped, rural, countrified, countryside, backwoods, remote, distant. **7.** *The library has 50 years of the newspaper's back issues:* past, previous, former, earlier; out-of-date, obsolete, expired, elapsed, behind, bygone, gone. **8.** *He owed three months' back rent:* overdue, tardy, late, belated, delayed, past, elapsed; in arrears, not paid. —**Ant.** 1 front; face, stomach. 2 front, head, fore. 3 move forward, move ahead, move toward, approach, advance, progress; attack. 4 hinder, oppose, resist, combat, block; repudiate, invalidate, negate, weaken, undermine, subvert, *Slang* knock. 5 front, fore. 6 major, main, important; busy, urban, populated. 7 future, late. 8 advance.

backbiting *adj.* **1.** *The candidate resorted to backbiting attacks on his opponent:* belittling, detracting, deprecating, abusive, maligning, slanderous, libeling, defamatory, calumnious, scandalous, disparaging, censuring, hurtful, injurious, derogating, denigrating, vilifying, malicious, catty, gossipy, scandal-mongering. —*n.* **2.** *Character assassination and backbiting were useful to him in his writing:* reviling, scurrility, vilification, traduction, vituperation, contumely, invective, calumny, calumniation, gossip, slander, defamation, aspersion, malice, maliciousness, traducement, abuse, obloquy, detraction, cattiness, belittling, disparagement, *Slang* bad-mouthing, backstabbing, bitchiness.

backbone *n.* **1.** *Good posture results from holding the backbone straight:* spine, spinal column, vertebrae, vertebral column, back; chine, dorsum. **2.** *Do you have the backbone to overcome hard luck?:* strength of character, character, fortitude, resolve, resoluteness, resolution, strength, mettle, tenacity, spunk, pluck, nerve, firmness, spirit, grit, sand, guts, intrepidity, steadfastness; bravery, courage, dauntlessness, manliness. **3.** *The cotton industry was the backbone of the Southern United States:* mainstay; basis, foundation, strength. —**Ant.** 2 spinelessness; cowardliness, cowardice.

backer *n. To win the election you'll need some powerful political backers. The backers of the play doubled their money:* supporter, champion, advocate, promoter; adherent, ally, follower, well-wisher; sponsor, patron, guarantor, angel, underwriter, investor, financier. **—Ant.** detractor; hinderer, enemy, competitor, adversary, opponent.

backfire *v. Even our most carefully laid plans may backfire:* miscarry, go awry, come to naught, come to nothing, fall through, boomerang, ricochet, backlash, flop, fizzle, crash, lay an egg, bounce back, come to grief, miss, disappoint. **—Ant.** thrive, work out, succeed, come off, make it, *Slang* click.

background *n.* **1.** *The painting showed trees in the foreground and mountains in the background:* distance, rear, landscape, *Theater* mise-en-scène, backdrop, setting, set, flats. **2.** *Lincoln came from an impoverished background. Her background qualifies her for this office:* environment, circumstances, milieu, context; upbringing, rearing, family connections, antecedents, breeding, heritage, life story; training, experience, education, preparation, grounding, past, history, credentials. **—Ant.** 1 foreground; fore, forefront. 2 future.

backing *n.* **1.** *The bill won't pass Congress without the President's backing:* help, support, aid, assistance; endorsement, sanction, sponsorship, patronage, advocacy, championing, encouragement, prompting, aegis, sustenance, succor, cooperation, helping hand. **2.** *The plaster wall has a backing of asbestos:* back, interior, core, inner layer. **—Ant.** 1 discouragement, hindrance, opposition, detraction, resistance; repudiation, subversion, ill will. 2 front, covering, cover, exterior, outer layer.

backlash *v.* **1.** *Her efforts to force culture on the town quickly backlashed:* boomerang, snap back, ricochet, backfire, rebound, bounce back, recoil, kick back, snag, ravel, come to nothing, come to naught, come to grief, miscarry, go away, fall through, fizzle, flop, crash. *—n.* **2.** *The threat of nuclear destruction triggered a backlash among conservatives:* negative reaction, resistance, recalcitrance, recoil, reversion, counteraction, antagonism, animosity, hostility, opposition. **—Ant.** 2 agreement, sympathy, cooperation, support, concurrence.

backlog *n. They held a sale to dispose of their backlog of typewriters:* inventory, supply, reserve, stock, reserve supply, store, backlist, hoard, stockpile, accumulation, amassment, excess, abundance, superabundance, assets, savings, nest egg, reservoir. **—Ant.** shortage, dearth, lack, deficiency, shortfall, scarcity, want.

backside *n. The chief thing I remember about ice skating is my sore backside:* posterior, rump, buttocks, derriere, behind, rear, rear end, sitter; *Slang* setter, settee, tail, duff, fanny, prat, buns, keister; *Vulgar* butt.

back talk *n. When I tell you to do something I don't want to hear any back talk:* sass, lip, negative response, jaw, guff, impudence, sassiness, sauciness, cheek, insolence, pertness, imperti-

nence. **—Ant.** concurrence, agreement, respect, diffidence.

backward also **backwards** *adv.* **1.** *Take two steps backward:* toward the rear, rearward, to the rear, back, in reverse, back away from, in retreat. **2.** *Can you somersault backward? Your shirt's on backward. You did the job backward from the way I wanted:* with the back first, back; (*variously*) upside down, inside out, wrong side out, topsy-turvy, wrong, improperly, disorderly, chaotically, messily. **3.** *Count backward from 10 to 1. You can't turn the clock backward:* in reverse, toward the past, to the past. *—adj.* **4.** *She gave the homestead a sad backward glance:* turned away from the front, turned toward the back, reversed, inverted. **5.** *He's a little backward in his studies:* slow, slow-paced, retarded, behind, undeveloped, remiss, tardy, impeded, sluggish, laggard; slow-witted, dull, dense. **6.** *Why do you act so backward with strangers?:* shy, bashful, timid, withdrawn, reserved, reticent, uncommunicative. **7.** *We watched the backward flow of the tide:* reverse, ebbing, receding, retreating, withdrawing, returning, retrograde, regressive, retrogressive. **—Ant.** 1 forward, frontward. 2 right side up, right side out; properly, correctly. 3 forward. 5 advanced, ahead. 6 forward, bold, brazen, brash, precocious; eager, willing. 7 forward.

backwash *n.* **1.** *The newspaper was caught in an unfavorable backwash from its endorsement of isolationism:* aftermath, wake, consequence, aftereffect, outcome, upshot, result. **2.** *She admitted she came from some little backwash in the Midwest:* hinterland, backwater, boondocks, *Slang* boonies, backcountry, provinces, upcountry, frontier; *Slang* sticks; tank town, burg.

backwater *n. The town was such a backwater, you couldn't buy a book:* back country, hinterland, outback, back woods, bush, sticks, boondocks, boonies, middle of nowhere.

backwoods *n. Lincoln grew up in the backwoods of Indiana and Kentucky:* remote area, unpopulated area, hinterland, country, rural area, wilds; woodland, countryside; *Slang* sticks, boondocks, boonies. **—Ant.** city, metropolis, metropolitan area, urban area, populated area.

bacteria *n. Some bacteria are beneficial, as in cheesemaking:* germ, microbe, microorganism, virus, *Slang* bug; bacillus, pathogen.

bad *adj.* **1.** *She's a very bad singer. Your car won't start if the battery is bad. We expect bad weather. She gets bad grades:* not good, poor, inferior, wretched, awful, terrible, dreadful, below standard, substandard, below par, secondrate, lousy; faulty, defective, imperfect, deficient, lacking, inadequate, valueless, useless, unproductive, unfit, baneful. **2.** *Lying is a bad thing to do:* immoral, unethical, sinful, evil, wicked, naughty, wrong, offensive, corrupt, unprincipled, opprobrious, villainous, false, disreputable, criminal, detestable, deplorable, perfidious, reprehensible, base, mean, vile, nefarious, beastly, rotten. **3.** *You exercised bad judgment. Her bad spelling kept her from becoming a secretary:* erroneous, wrong, incorrect, not correct, imperfect, unsound, fallacious, faulty, questionable; inefficient, ineffective, poor. **4.** *Too much candy is bad for your teeth:* harmful, unhealthy, hurtful, injurious, detrimental, distractive; disadvantageous, troublesome, nonproductive; risky, dangerous, hazardous, menacing. **5.** *We were prepared for bad news. He's in a bad mood:* unpleasant, unwelcome, disagreeable, disappointing, distressed, distressing, discouraged, sorry, discouraging, disturbing, regrettable, troubled, troubling; gloomy, glum, melancholy, joyless, grim, disheartening, unnerving, dreadful, obnoxious; cross, angry, short-tempered, offensive, irascible, irritable, touchy. **6.** *Don't feel bad about breaking the glass. I feel bad about not being able to help you:* sorry, sad, regretful, remorseful, contrite, guilty, conscience-stricken, terrible. **7.** *Bad milk can make you sick:* spoiled, rotten, decayed, foul, decomposed, sour, rancid, turned, rank, putrescent, moldy, mildewed; contaminated, polluted, tainted. **8.** *What's that bad smell?:* disagreeable, unpleasant, sickening, loathsome, odious, nasty, distasteful, foul, disgusting, nauseating, putrid, fetid, unpalatable, bitter, acrid, sour, revolting, repulsive, vile, repugnant, noxious. **9.** *I feel bad enough to go to the hospital:* ill, sick, sickly, unwell, ailing, infirm, indisposed, unhealthy, under the weather. **10.** *He has a bad toothache. They were in a bad accident:* severe, harsh, terrible, serious, grave, disastrous, painful, acute, frightful, dreadful, calamitous, dire, tragic; agonizing, distressing, searing, excruciating, grievous, wretched, miserable. —*n.* **11.** *You must learn to take the bad with the good:* harmful things, sad events, disappointment, misfortune. **12.** *The bad people can be forgiven by God:* evil, wickedness, immorality, sin, offenses, wrongs, villainy, crimes. —**Ant.** 1–9, 11, 12 good. 1 fine, excellent, above average, superior, first-rate. 2 virtuous, moral, ethical, right, righteous, exemplary, highminded. 3 correct, right, perfect, sound, intelligent. 4 beneficial, healthful, salubrious; harmless, safe. 5 pleasant, welcome, heartening, encouraging, promising, hopeful, cheerful, cheering, happy, joyful, joyous, sweet, smiling, good-tempered, sweet-tempered. 7 fresh, sweet, uncontaminated. 8 agreeable, pleasant, fragrant, aromatic, sweet. 9 well, healthy, sound, fit. 10 mild, light, frivolous, trivial, unimportant, minor.

badge *n.* *The police officer wore her badge proudly. The war veteran considers his scar a badge of honor:* emblem, insignia, medallion, ensign, shield, seal, brand, device; symbol, sign, hallmark, mark, earmark, token, stamp.

badger *v.* *You can't badger me into going to the party!:* goad, bully, provoke, bait, pester, nag, harass, hector, harry, hound, persecute, tease, annoy, vex, irritate, nettle, chafe, trouble, torment, plague, coerce, beset.

badly *adv.* **1.** *He did the work very badly. You judged him badly:* poorly, improperly, incorrectly, not well, in an inferior way, wretchedly, shoddily, imperfectly, defectively, deficiently, inadequately, erroneously, wrong, wrongly, fault-ily, unsoundly, unsatisfactorily, incompetently, ineptly, carelessly, sloppily. **2.** *The army behaved badly toward the war prisoners:* immorally, unethically, sinfully, wickedly, wrongly, offensively, corruptly, without principle, villainously, disreputably, criminally, basely, vilely, nefariously. **3.** *The boy wants a new bicycle badly. The tooth hurts badly:* very much, greatly, exceedingly, extremely, desperately; intensely, severely, acutely, sorely, horribly, terribly, dreadfully, frightfully. —**Ant.** 1 well, fine, excellently, superbly; properly, correctly, perfectly, competently, ably, splendidly, satisfactorily; right, rightly. 2 well, morally, ethically, virtuously, righteously.

baffle *v.* **1.** *The thick walls baffled the street noises:* stop, restrain, inhibit, thwart, foil, bar, check; deaden, dull, minimize, reduce. **2.** *The unexpected news baffled us:* confuse, bewilder, perplex, mystify, confound, befuddle, stump, puzzle, muddle, nonplus; daze, astonish, astound, disconcert, dumfound, amaze, surprise. —**Ant.** 1 admit, allow; transmit. 2 clarify to, explain to, elucidate to, clear up for.

bag *n.* **1.** *We brought home three bags of groceries:* sack, paper bag; packet, bundle, pouch, receptacle. **2.** See SUITCASE. **3.** See PURSE. —*v.* **4.** *Since you've lost weight that suit bags on you:* sag, droop, hang loosely; bulge, swell out, protrude. **5.** *The hunters bagged three deer:* kill in hunting, shoot; capture, catch, trap, entrap, snare, ensnare; get, take, collect, obtain, acquire.

baggage *n.* **1.** *Customs officers examined all baggage at the airport:* luggage, suitcases, bags, bundles, packages, traveling bags, valises, grips, trunks. **2.** *The king's army traveled with much baggage:* equipment, movables, gear, paraphernalia, accouterments, trappings, apparatus, impedimenta; belongings, effects.

baggy *adj.* **1.** *Circus clowns always wear baggy pants:* sagging, droopy, loose, loose-fitting, slack, limp; unshapely, unpressed. **2.** *His jowls are baggy with fatigue:* flabby, flaccid, paunchy, bulbous, swollen, bloated, puffed. —**Ant.** 1 tight, tight-fitting, close-fitting; well-cut, shapely; neat, pressed.

bail[1] *n.* **1.** *The accused are being held on $5,000 bail:* bond, surety, guarantee. —*v.* **2.** *The accused's brother bailed him out of jail:* post bond for, post bail for.

bail[2] *v.* *Bail the water out of the boat:* scoop, ladle, lade, dip, spoon.

bailiwick *n.* *The kitchen's my bailiwick so don't try to tell me how to cook:* domain, province, realm, dominion, department, sphere; neighborhood, place, territory, area, beat, arena, *Slang* turf, orbit, compass.

bait *n.* **1.** *Worms are good bait for catfish:* lure. **2.** *The store offered a free gift as bait to get customers:* lure, allure, allurement, inducement, enticement, temptation, attraction, magnet, bribe, come-on. —*v.* **3.** *Bait your hook with a worm:* put bait on. **4.** *He baited his sister unmercifully:* tease, torment, tantalize, antagonize, provoke, annoy, vex, harry, heckle, harass, hound, hector, badger, worry; *Slang* needle, ride.

bake *v. Bake the bread in a hot oven for 40 minutes. I'll have a week to bake in the tropical sun:* cook, roast, oven-bake, toast, sauté, sear, braise, fry, grill, pan-fry, parboil, simmer, stew, boil; swelter, scorch, burn.

balance *n.* **1.** Also **balances.** *Weigh that side of beef on the balance:* scales, scale. **2.** *A counterweight keeps the machine in balance:* equilibrium, stability, equipoise, counterpoise, weight, equality, equalization; symmetry, parity. **3.** *The speech struck a perfect balance between humor and seriousness:* equilibrium, ratio, proportion, harmony; middle ground, mean. **4.** *She's young but she has a great deal of emotional balance:* stability, steadiness, poise, aplomb, composure, *Slang* cool, equanimity, equilibrium, equipoise, self-possession, level-headedness, imperturbability, unflappability, coolness, presence, judgment, judiciousness. **5.** *On balance, his accomplishments outweigh his faults:* comparison, evaluation, consideration, appraisal, estimate, opinion. **6.** *The balance on your account is $5.00. Leave the balance of the work until tomorrow:* amount owed, amount credited, sum minus payment; remainder, rest, leftover, residue, remnant, outstanding portion. —*v.* **7.** *Can you balance on one foot? Balance that big rock with these two small ones:* steady, keep steady, hold equilibrium, stabilize, poise, counterpoise; make level, level off, parallel. **8.** *The good balances the bad:* offset, set off, counterbalance, equate, counteract, neutralize, compensate for. **9.** *We balanced the benefits against the costs of medical insurance:* compare, contrast, juxtapose, evaluate, weigh; consider, estimate, deliberate, reflect, ponder, cogitate, sum up. **10.** *The company balances its accounts every month:* compute, calculate, sum up, total, tally, reckon, tot up, square; pay. —**Ant.** 3 imbalance, disproportion. 4 instability, flightiness, self-doubt, uncertainty, irrationality, incertitude, shakiness. 8 upset, overbalance, outweigh, underbalance.

balanced *adj. The book gives a balanced account of the Carter administration:* fair, equitable, just, impartial, unprejudiced, disinterested. —**Ant.** one-sided, lopsided, prejudiced, biased, slanted, distorted, unfair.

balcony *n.* **1.** *Many of the old New Orleans houses have wrought-iron balconies:* deck, veranda, upstairs porch, portico, loggia, terrace. **2.** *We had cheap seats in the balcony of the theater:* mezzanine, loges, upper circle, boxes; upper floor, foyer.

bald *adj.* **1.** *When he grew bald he bought a toupee:* baldheaded, baldpated, hairless, depilated, smooth, glabrous. **2.** *The mountain is bald above the tree line:* bare, without cover, treeless, denuded, naked, barren. **3.** *That is a bald falsehood!:* open, bare, undisguised, flagrant, blunt, flat, obvious, unadorned, stark, naked, straightforward, plain, simple, unvarnished, unembellished; outright, out-and-out, categorical, unequivocal, unqualified, utter. —**Ant.** 1 hairy, hirsute, coiffed. 2 overgrown, forested. 3

elaborate, complicated, embellished, fancy; hidden, disguised, devious, roundabout, underhanded, surreptitious.

balderdash *n. That story is 10 percent fact and 90 percent balderdash:* nonsense, poppycock, tommyrot, tomfoolery, stuff and nonsense, drivel, trash, rot, claptrap, bunk, buncombe (or bunkum), bosh, twaddle, *Slang* bull, hot air, crock; gibberish, double-talk, obfuscation, flummery. —**Ant.** sense, good sense; truth, fact.

bale *n. The farmers loaded the cotton bales onto the river boat:* bound bundle, bundle, pack, packet, parcel, package, case; load.

baleful *adj. She gave him a baleful stare:* sinister, ominous, threatening; evil, malignant, malign, malevolent, malicious, baneful, venomous, spiteful, dire, furious, cold, cold-hearted, icy; hurtful, deadly, harmful. —**Ant.** kindly, friendly, benevolent, beneficent, benign, salutary, warm; favorable.

balk *v.* **1.** *The burro balked at climbing the path:* shirk, refuse, resist, demur, recoil, draw back, hang back, shrink from, shun, evade, hesitate, eschew. **2.** *The kidnapping attempt was balked by the police:* thwart, stall, forestall, stymie, frustrate, prevent, hinder, defeat, check, baffle, foil, impede, block, obstruct, bar, spike, inhibit, derail. —**Ant.** 1 accept willingly, do eagerly, submit; relent, yield, acquiesce. 2 aid, help, assist, abet; further, promote, advance, support, encourage, expedite, facilitate, smooth; allow, permit.

balky *adj. That mule is too balky to pull a plow:* contrary, stubborn, obstinate, recalcitrant, perverse, ornery; unmanageable, unruly, rebellious, restive, refractory, disobedient, willful, intractable, fractious, wayward, mulish, pigheaded. —**Ant.** obedient, submissive, willing, cooperative, amenable; tame, docile, subdued, tractable.

ball[1] *n.* **1.** *The cat played with the ball of twine:* round mass, sphere, spheroid, pellet, globe, globule, orb. **2.** *Four boys were playing ball in the field:* game of ball, ball game. **3.** *The muskets were loaded with powder and ball:* shot, bullets, projectiles. —**Ant.** 1 cube.

ball[2] *n. The banquet was followed by a ball:* dance, dancing party, cotillion; promenade, prom, soiree, *Slang* hop.

ballad *n.* **1.** *He read the class one of the great Scottish ballads:* narrative poem, narrative verse, rhyming story. **2.** *We sat around the campfire, while a folk singer sang ballads:* folk song, song, lay; ditty, chanty, carol.

ballast *n. The ship carried bags of sand as ballast:* stabilizing material, counterweight, counterpoise, weight, dead weight; makeweight; balance, counterbalance, ballasting, control, equipoise, stabilizer.

balloon *n.* **1.** *The child's balloon floated into the air. The weather balloon carried scientific instruments several miles above the clouds:* air-filled bag, gas-filled bag, inflatable bag. —*v.* **2.** *His coat ballooned in the high wind:* billow, swell out, puff out, fill with air, inflate, fill out, blow up, distend, increase, expand, belly, bloat, enlarge, grow, dilate. **—Ant.** 2 deflate, collapse, shrink, flatten.

ballot *n.* **1.** *Three candidates for mayor are listed on the ballot:* list of candidates to be voted on, ticket, slate. **2.** *He won the nomination on the third ballot:* vote, round of voting, voting, poll, polling.

ballyhoo *n.* **1.** *Weeks of ballyhoo preceded the movie's premiere:* promotion, publicity, advertising, public relations, propaganda, hoopla, buildup, puffery, hullabaloo; *Slang* hype. **—v. 2.** *The ads ballyhooed the movie's virtues:* publicize, promote, advertise, tout, push, trumpet, proclaim, herald; *Slang* puff, hype. **—Ant.** 2 keep secret, hide, obscure.

balm *n.* **1.** *You'd better put some balm on that sunburn:* ointment, salve, unguent, emollient, lotion, cream, balsam. **2.** *The music was balm for his jangled nerves:* solace, comforter, comfort, restorative, curative, anodyne, palliative, narcotic, sedative, tranquilizer. **—Ant.** 1 irritant, abrasive. 2 annoyance, nuisance, vexation, affliction, stimulant.

balmy *adj.* **1.** *By April the weather had turned balmy. The rain brought a balmy breeze:* gentle, mild, soft, fair, clement, bland, temperate, summery, warm, pleasant, refreshing, agreeable; calm, calming, easing, soothing, salubrious. **2.** *A balmy aroma came from the evergreen forest:* fragrant, sweet-smelling, aromatic, perfumed, ambrosial, refreshing, redolent. **3.** *He was balmy to try swimming across the lake at night:* eccentric, weird, odd, *Slang* kooky. **—Ant.** 1 harsh, raw, strong, intense, severe, inclement, rough, discomforting, irksome, vexing, annoying; stormy, unseasonable. 2 stinking, smelly, malodorous, foul, offensive, rank, fetid, putrid, putrescent.

baluster *n.* *The balcony railing is supported by a series of vase-shaped balusters:* post, support, upright, rail, column, pillar, pilaster.

bamboozle *v.* *The con man bamboozled him out of $500:* dupe, deceive, trick, cheat, swindle, victimize, defraud, cozen, gull, rook, gyp; delude, mislead, hoodwink, fool, hoax; lure, beguile, coax, con, *Slang* take.

ban *v.* **1.** *Bicycles are banned from the new superhighway. They threatened to ban the book:* prohibit, bar, exclude, banish, debar, disallow, enjoin, forbid; proscribe, suppress, interdict. **—n. 2.** *The police lifted the ban against parking on this street:* prohibition, forbiddance, barring, proscription, taboo, interdiction, interdict, exclusion, restriction, restraint, censorship, embargo, banishment, stoppage. **—Ant.** 1 allow, permit, let, approve, authorize, O.K., countenance, endorse, sanction. 2 approval, permission, allowance.

banal *adj.* *There were no new ideas in his banal lecture:* stale, trite, unoriginal, hackneyed, ordinary, commonplace, prosaic, pedestrian, unexciting, unimaginative, everyday, stock, humdrum, dull, uninteresting, conventional, stereotyped, insipid, threadbare, shopworn, tired, corny, cliché-ridden, vapid, platitudinous, bromidic, jejune. **—Ant.** original, new, novel,

unique, exciting, fresh, unusual, extraordinary, innovative, distinctive, stimulating, stimulative, gripping, provocative, challenging, imaginative, interesting.

band[1] *n.* **1.** *A band of students brought their grievances before the dean:* group, company, party, body, troop, crowd, caucus, gang, junta, party, pack, bunch, throng, assembly, multitude; confederacy, confederation, association, society, clique, crew, fellowship, league, club, set, circle, brotherhood, sisterhood. **2.** *The band played until midnight:* orchestra, ensemble, group. **—v. 3.** *If we band together we can give our argument strength:* unite, join, consolidate, gather, group. **—Ant.** 3 split up, divide, disperse.

band[2] *n.* *Her hair was held in place by a velvet band. A dark band of clouds was on the horizon:* strip, stripe, streak, ring, fillet, circlet, strap, hoop, binding; ribbon, sash, belt, collar, bandeau, thong, girdle, swath, surcingle, cincture.

bandage *n.* **1.** *Wrap the bandage around your injured arm:* dressing, binding, compress, plaster. **—v. 2.** *Disinfect the wound before you bandage it:* cover with a bandage, dress, bind.

bandanna or **bandana** *n.* *She put a bandanna on her head to keep her hair from blowing:* kerchief, neckerchief, silk square, handkerchief, scarf.

bandit *n.* *The stagecoach was held up by two bandits:* outlaw, robber, desperado, highwayman, badman, thief, brigand, burglar, crook, thug, ladrone; *Obsolete* road agent, blackleg, footpad.

bandy *v.* *We can't take you seriously when you just bandy words:* toss back and forth, trade, swap, exchange, interchange, barter, shuffle, play with, toss about.

bane *n.* **1.** *Dirt and noise from the nearby highway were the bane of her existence:* plague, curse, scourge, torment, nuisance; affliction, blight, burden, woe, canker, poison, ruin, ruination; pain in the neck, thorn in the side, fly in the ointment; disaster, calamity, tragedy, detriment, destroyer, downfall. **2.** *Beware, my lord—there's bane in that cup:* poison, toxin, venom. **—Ant.** 1 blessing, treasure, treat, prize, bright spot, joy, pleasure; comfort, consolation, solace, balm, apple of one's eye. 2 antitoxin.

bang *n.* **1.** *The balloon burst with a bang. He closed the door with a bang:* loud sound, sudden noise, report, boom, pop, clap, burst, slam, crash, explosion. **2.** *The falling branch gave her a terrific bang on the head:* blow, hit, knock, smack, clout, rap, box, wallop, whack, tap, slap, cuff, thwack, thump, lick, buffet, *Slang* sock. **3.** *Slang. We got a bang out of seeing the movie star:* thrill, excitement, pleasure, enjoyment, delight, good time, *Slang* charge, kick. **—v. 4.** *The baby kept banging his spoon on the plate. Don't bang the door!:* strike noisily, beat, close loudly, slam. **—adv. 5.** *The car rolled bang into the telephone pole:* headlong, suddenly, smack, slap, crashingly.

bangle *n.* *I lost one of the bangles on my charm bracelet:* fob, charm, ornament, bauble, trinket, knickknack, gewgaw, fribble, tinsel, gimcrack, bibelot; wristlet, bracelet, chain; costume jewelry, junk jewelry.

banish v. **1.** *The king banished the traitor from the realm:* exile, expel, eject, evict, outlaw, deport, extradite, cast out, turn out, drive out, send away, dismiss, send to Coventry; excommunicate. **2.** *Banish gloom from your thoughts:* ban, shut out, bar, dismiss, put away, exclude; cast out, drive out, eliminate, remove, get rid of, shake off, erase, cast away, send away, drop, dispel, dislodge, discharge, eradicate, evict, oust, discard, eject, reject. —**Ant.** 1, 2 invite, admit, accept, receive, receive with open arms, welcome, entertain; harbor, shelter; foster, nourish, cherish.

bank[1] n. **1.** *A high bank of earth surrounded the fortress:* embankment, mound, heap, pile, mass; ridge, rise, hill, knoll, dune, dike, parapet, barrow, terrace. **2.** *The boaters picnicked on the bank of the river:* shore, side, edge, margin, strand, brink. **3.** *The fishing boats headed for the Grand Banks of Newfoundland:* shoal, reef, shallow, bar, shelf, sandbank, flat. —v. **4.** *The plow banked the snow along the side of the road:* pile up, heap, stack, amass. **5.** *The highway banks sharply on that curve:* have one side higher than the other, slope, slant, tilt, tip. —**Ant.** 1 ditch, trench; valley, dip. 3 deep water, depths. 4, 5 level, plane, smooth out.

bank[2] n. *A bank of spotlights lit up the scene:* row, tier, rank, line, file, string, lineup, series, array, keyboard, succession, train, chain.

bank[3] n. **1.** *The bank cashed his check:* banking house, financial institution; trust company, savings bank, commercial bank; exchequer. **2.** *The hospital maintained its own blood bank:* repository, depository, storehouse; store, stockpile, supply, accumulation, fund, savings, reserve, reservoir. —v. **3.** *I bank at the First National. She banks $10 a week:* transact business with a bank; deposit money in a bank, save, keep.

bankrupt adj. *Severe business losses left the company bankrupt:* ruined, failed, without funds, unable to pay debts, insolvent, broke, wiped out; destitute, indigent, penniless, impoverished, depleted, exhausted, in the red, *Slang* busted. —**Ant.** solvent, sound; prosperous.

bankruptcy n. *Overspending led to bankruptcy:* failure, ruin, insolvency, default.

banner n. **1.** *The king's banner showed his coat of arms. Welcoming banners hung from the balconies:* standard, flag, colors, ensign, pennant, pendant, streamer, burgee. —adj. **2.** *Farmers had a banner year:* outstanding, most successful, notable, leading, record, red-letter; profitable, winning.

banquet n. **1.** *A victory banquet was served in the royal dining room:* feast, repast, dinner, symposium. —v. **2.** *The guests banqueted until midnight:* feast, dine, eat one's fill, revel. —**Ant.** 1 snack, light meal; fasting, starvation; abstinence. 2 fast, starve; abstain.

bantam adj. *The boy is a bantam edition of his father:* miniature, small, tiny, little, diminutive, minute, petite; stunted, dwarf, dwarfed, pocket-size, pocket-sized, runty, wee, weeny, teeny, teeny-weeny; Lilliputian. —**Ant.** large, enlarged, blown-up, overgrown, big, giant, colossal.

banter n. **1.** *We laughed at the banter of the two old friends:* kidding, joking, ribbing, joshing, jesting, teasing, repartee, word play, waggery, raillery, ragging, badinage, chaff, chaffing. —v. **2.** *He stood on the corner, bantering with friends:* kid, josh, rib, taunt, mock, jolly, twit, chaff, dish, ride, needle, tease.

baptism n. **1.** *The baptism of new members of the church will take place tomorrow:* Christian sacrament of initiation; sprinkling, immersion; spiritual rebirth, purification. **2.** *The battle was his baptism as a soldier:* initiation, rite of passage; introduction, beginning. —**Ant.** 2 last act; farewell.

baptize v. **1.** *The minister baptized the baby:* administer the Christian sacrament of baptism to. **2.** *The child was baptized Robert:* christen, name, dub.

bar n. **1.** *The monkey rattled the bars of his cage:* pole, rod, stick, stake, rail, pale, paling, grating, rib; (*variously*) crosspiece, crossbar, lever, crowbar, jimmy, spar, sprit. **2.** *The bar of soap slipped from his grasp:* block, ingot, cake. **3.** *The boat ran aground on the bar:* sandbar, reef, shoal, shallow, spit, bank, shelf, flat. **4.** *We had a sandwich and a beer at a neighborhood bar. He opened a snack bar. Put your glass on the bar:* tavern, saloon, taproom, cocktail lounge, lounge; public house, pub, alehouse; speakeasy; serving counter, long table; canteen, lunchroom, sandwich bar. **5.** *A bar of light fell across the darkened room:* band, strip, stripe, ribbon, streak, stroke, beam, belt, slice, line. **6.** *Nearsightedness is a bar to becoming a pilot:* obstacle, barrier, obstruction, impediment, stumbling block, block, check, curb, barricade, snag, catch, hindrance, constraint, restraint, restriction, injunction, limitation, taboo. **7.** *After finishing law school she was admitted to the bar:* legal profession, legal fraternity, body of lawyers. **8.** *His misbehavior brought him before the bar of public opinion:* court, tribunal, forum; judgment. **9.** *The song is 24 bars long:* measure. —v. **10.** *Bar the barn door so the cows can't get out:* put a bar across, lock, bolt, fasten, secure; block up, close up, barricade. **11.** *He has been barred from practicing medicine:* ban, prohibit, enjoin, stay, stop, restrain, prevent, forbid, obstruct, block, blacklist, blackball, debar, disallow, restrict, limit, exclude, preclude, impede. **12.** *Reporters were barred from the courtroom:* exclude, shut out, lock out; banish, expel, evict, eject, exile, oust, cast out. —**Ant.** 3 deep water, depths. 6 aid, help, advantage, boon, benefit, edge. 10 open, unlock, clear. 11, 12 allow, permit, let, accept; admit, invite, welcome, receive.

barb n. **1.** *The fishhook has a barb at the tip:* spur, backward point, point, spike, prong, tine, snag, bristle, nib, cusp, prickle, barbule, spicule. **2.** *We're tired of your nasty barbs:* disagreeable remark, sarcasm, insult, complaint, criticism, affront, badmouthing, dig, jibe, cut, *Slang* put-down.

barbarian *n.* **1.** *The city barricaded itself against the invading barbarians:* savage, alien, outlander. **2.** *Young barbarians have defaced public buildings:* hoodlum, roughneck, ruffian, rowdy, tough, punk, hood, hooligan, delinquent, vandal, bully, lout. **3.** *Barbarians in the audience jeered the composer's new work:* anti-intellectual, lowbrow, philistine, peasant, vulgarian, illiterate, ignoramus, know-nothing, troglodyte, yahoo, boor. *—adj.* **4.** *The emperor commanded a great wall to be built against barbarian invaders:* savage, alien. **5.** *The artist accused the public of having barbarian tastes:* uncultivated, uncultured, lowbrow, crude, philistine, unsophisticated, provincial, uncouth, boorish. *—Ant.* 1 native, citizen. 3 highbrow, intellectual, connoisseur, sophisticate; *plural* literati, cognoscenti. 5 cultivated, cultured, highbrow, intellectual; refined, literate, humane, liberal.

barbaric *adj.* **1.** *The Huns were notorious for their barbaric cruelty. The tribal dance was a spectacle of barbaric splendor:* barbarian, uncivilized, untamed, barbarous, savage, wild. **2.** *His behavior to the guests was barbaric and embarrassing:* coarse, uncouth, crude, ill-mannered, vulgar, rude, unpolished, uncivilized, boorish. *—Ant.* civilized, cultivated, gentlemanly, gracious, polite.

barbarism *n.* **1.** *The civil war brought one barbarism after another:* savagery, inhumanity, barbarity, atrocity, cruelty. **2.** *There were numerous barbarisms in his writing style:* vulgarism, corruption, impropriety.

barbarity *n.* *The pirates treated their captives with barbarity:* savageness, cruelty, brutality, ruthlessness. *—Ant.* humaneness, gentleness, mildness.

barbarous *adj.* **1.** *It's barbarous to keep a large dog cooped up like that:* cruel, brutal, mean, inhuman, vicious, harsh, barbaric, outrageous. **2.** *The crank letter was written in barbarous English:* coarse, crude, rough, vulgar, crass, impolite. *—Ant.* 1 humane, merciful, compassionate, lenient, humanitarian, benevolent, benign.

barbecue *n.* **1.** *We'll have a barbecue in the backyard:* cookout, party, picnic, weeny roast. **2.** *She put steaks on the barbecue:* grill, charcoal grill, gas grill. *—v.* **3.** *Fish takes little time to barbecue:* grill, broil, sear.

barber *n.* **1.** *My barber recommended a new hair tonic:* haircutter, hairdresser. *—v.* **2.** *You need to barber that beard of yours:* cut, trim, tonsure, shave; dress, arrange, style.

bard *n.* **1.** *The Homeric poems were composed and sung by bards:* poet-singer, epic poet, poet. **2.** *A local bard read his poetry to the audience:* narrative poet, writer, versifier, rhymer, rhymester, poetaster, poetizer; minstrel, troubador.

bare *adj.* **1.** *The engineers worked bare to the waist in the broiling sun:* stripped, naked, nude, undressed, unclothed, unrobed, disrobed, uncovered, unclad, *Slang* in the raw, exposed, peeled. **2.** *Let's hang up some paintings on those bare walls. The cupboard was bare:* empty, without contents, void, vacant, blank; unadorned, unembellished, naked, undecorated, unornamented; austere, stark, plain. **3.** *The carpet was worn bare from years of use:* threadbare, bald, thin, hapless, worn. **4.** *We existed on nothing but the bare necessities:* just sufficient, just enough, scant, mere, marginal, meager, supportable, endurable. **5.** *The detective outlined the bare facts of the case. Let's have the bare truth:* plain, undisguised, stark, bald, simple, fundamental, basic, essential, elementary, unelaborated, straightforward, unadorned, unembellished, unvarnished, uncolored. *—v.* **6.** *Bare your head when the flag is raised:* uncover, undress, strip, unveil, undrape; unsheathe, denude. **7.** *The poet bared his heart to the world:* open, reveal, uncover, show, expose, divest, unmask, offer. *—Ant.* 1 clothed, dressed, clad, covered, attired, robed, appareled. 2 full, overflowing, well-stocked, crammed; adorned, embellished, ornamented, dressed up. 3 thick. 4 abundant, profuse, copious, plentiful, bounteous, ample. 6 cover, clothe, dress, veil, robe. 7 hide, conceal, mask; suppress.

barefaced *adj.* *He persisted in the most barefaced lies about the accident:* brazen, impudent, shameless; transparent, palpable, bald; bold, unabashed, insolent, brash, fresh, cheeky, sassy, forward, flippant, flip, *Slang* snotty. *—Ant.* modest, reticent, shy.

barefoot *adj.* *The sign asks you not to come into the store if you're barefoot:* barefooted, unshod, shoeless, unsandaled, discalced, discalceate.

barely *adv.* *When the rescuers found the castaway he was barely alive. A pound of sugar is barely enough for a week:* almost not, only just, just, scarcely, hardly, no more than, just about, almost, slightly, sparingly, scantly, meagerly, faintly; by the skin of one's teeth. *—Ant.* fully, completely; abundantly, amply, copiously, profusely.

bareness *n.* *Devoid of vegetation, the land spoke only of bareness:* starkness, unadornment, nakedness.

bargain *n.* **1.** *We made a bargain that I would do the work and you would supply the materials:* agreement, compact, pact, promise, pledge, accord, understanding, settlement, arrangement, contract, transaction, covenant, treaty, entente. **2.** *At that low price the house is a bargain:* good deal, good buy; *Slang* steal. *—v.* **3.** *I refuse to bargain over the price:* negotiate, haggle, dicker, barter, higgle, deal. *—Ant.* 2 extravagance, white elephant, swindle.

bark¹ *n.* **1.** *The bark of a dog sounded in the night:* yelp, yip, yap, howl, howling, bay, cry; woof, arf-arf, bow-wow. *—v.* **2.** *The dog barks at strangers:* yelp, yip, yap, howl, bay. **3.** *The captain barked a command at the troops:* shout, bellow, yell, roar, holler, cry out. *—Ant.* 3 whisper, murmur, mutter.

bark² *n.* **1.** *Beavers had stripped away the tree's bark:* covering, husk, sheathing, skin, casing, rind, peel, crust, hide, hull, *Scientific* periderm.

—v. **2.** *He barked his shins on the doorjamb:* scrape, skin, abrade, scale, rub, flay, strip.

baroque *adj. The mansion was built in a baroque style:* extravagant, florid, ornate, flamboyant. —**Ant.** classical, simple.

barracks *n. After sentencing, the soldier was confined to barracks:* garrison, cantonment, army camp, quarters.

barrage *n.* **1.** *The cannons kept up a barrage over the enemy lines:* bombardment, shelling, salvo, volley, cannonade, fusillade, battery, curtain of fire, *Slang* ack-ack. **2.** *The reporters fired a barrage of questions at the mayor:* volley, salvo, fusillade, deluge, torrent, outpouring; blast, burst, stream, shower, spray.

barrel *n.* **1.** *The old store offered barrels full of crackers and pickles. We bought a barrel of apples:* cask, keg, tub, vat, hogshead, butt, drum, tun; *the amount a barrel can hold,* (*in technical use*) 31 gallons of liquid or 105 dry quarts. **2.** *The rifle barrel was hot:* tube, tubular part (as of a gun or a pen).

barren *adj.* **1.** *The farmer was cheated when he bought a barren cow:* infertile, sterile, infecund, (*of cows*) farrow. **2.** *No one could raise crops on this barren land:* infertile, unproductive, unfruitful, depleted, waste, desolate, austere; arid, dry. **3.** *It's a barren topic, not worth discussion:* unproductive, unfruitful, fruitless, unrewarding, ineffectual, useless, futile; uninteresting, dull, prosaic, uninformative, lackluster, uninstructive, uninspiring, stale. —**Ant.** productive, fertile. 1 fecund, prolific. 2 lush, rich, luxuriant. 3 useful, worthwhile, fruitful, profitable, interesting, instructive.

barricade *n.* **1.** *The rebels fired from behind barricades:* barrier, rampart, bulwark, blockade, obstruction, impediment, obstacle, fence. —v. **2.** *The police barricaded the streets:* block, obstruct, protect or shut in with a barrier.

barrier *n.* **1.** *The stallion leaped over the wooden barrier. The castle's defensive barrier was 20 feet deep:* obstruction; (*variously*) obstacle, barricade, blockade, fortification, rampart, fence, wall, hedge; ditch, trench, moat. **2.** *Not knowing a foreign language is a barrier to enjoying travel abroad. The country set up trade barriers against imported goods:* obstacle, obstruction, impediment, hindrance, handicap, bar, difficulty, restriction, limitation, stumbling block, hurdle. —**Ant.** 1 entrance, opening, passage, passageway, way. 2 aid, help, advantage; encouragement, spur.

barter *v. The Indians would barter beaver pelts for weapons:* trade, swap, exchange, interchange.

basal *adj.* **1.** *The animals have been classified by their most basal characteristics:* basic, fundamental, necessary, essential, intrinsic, prerequisite, indispensable, key, cardinal, vital. **2.** *We are developing a series of basal readers for the lower grades:* elementary, primary, lower-level, rudimentary, initial, beginning; easy, simple, simplified. —**Ant.** 1 superfluous, ancillary, supplementary, extra, accessory.

base[1] *n.* **1.** *The lamp stands on a circular base:* support, pedestal, stand, bottom, foundation, underpinning, substructure, ground, groundwork, bed. **2.** *The base of his argument is that our price is too high:* foundation, basis, essence, principle, root, core, backbone, heart, key, rudiment, ground, source. **3.** *The soup has a tomato base:* essential ingredient, principal constituent. **4.** *The weary troops marched back to the base:* camp, station, post, billet, installation, garrison. —v. **5.** *This song is based on an old folk tune:* derive from, model on, found on. **6.** *The company's headquarters is based in Paris. The 3rd Armored Division was based at Fort Knox:* station, garrison, locate, situate, install, billet, ground, establish, place. —**Ant.** 1 top, summit, apex, zenith, peak, pinnacle; superstructure. 2, 3 nonessentials, frills.

base[2] *adj.* **1.** *Zinc and brass are base metals:* inferior, poor quality; alloyed, impure, debased, adulterated, spurious. **2.** *Cheating at cards is a base practice:* mean, vile, low, contemptible, despicable, ignoble, shameful, immoral, bad, scoundrelly, villainous, sinful, wicked, dishonorable, dastardly, scurvy, iniquitous, depraved, degenerate, vulgar, gross, cowardly, corrupt, sordid, craven, foul, faithless, nefarious, infamous, dissolute, debased, degraded, ignominious, unworthy, disgraceful, black-hearted, evil-minded, unprincipled, insidious, detestable, reprehensible, discreditable, disreputable, abject, petty, sneaky, *Slang* dirty, scrubby. —**Ant.** 1 precious, valuable, rare; pure, unadulterated, unalloyed. 2 virtuous, honorable, honest, just, aboveboard, righteous, upright, moral, ethical, lofty, good, admirable, heroic.

baseless *adj. The story is founded on a baseless rumor:* unfounded, groundless, ungrounded, without basis, unsupported, unsubstantiated, uncorroborated, unfactual, unjustified, unjustifiable, unsound. —**Ant.** well-founded, well-grounded, supported, substantiated, corroborated, factual, documented.

bashful *adj. She is too bashful to speak to strangers:* shy, timid, easily embarrassed, demure, retiring, unconfident, timorous, modest, overly modest, diffident, reticent, reserved, shrinking, constrained, uncertain, shamefaced, sheepish, skittish, blushing. —**Ant.** aggressive, brash, bold, brazen, impudent, immodest, forward, shameless, intrepid; conceited, egoistic, egotistic, confident, self-assured, fearless, arrogant.

basic *adj.* **1.** *The basic ingredient of the dish is hamburger:* fundamental, elementary, vital, essential, intrinsic, rudimentary, key, core, base, prime, primary, foundational. —n. **2.** *Reading ability is one of the basics of education:* fundamental, prerequisite, essential, core, rudiment, base, foundation, underpinning, bedrock. —**Ant.** 1 accompanying, supporting, supplementary, complementary, secondary; unimportant, trivial, minor. 2 unessential; frill, frivolity, triviality.

basin *n.* **1.** *She washed her hands in a basin of warm water:* bowl, washbowl, pan, tub, washtub, vat, tureen, washbasin, lavatory, washstand, lavabo, sink, dishpan; finger bowl, porringer; font, stoup. **2.** *Torrential rains caused flooding in the basin:* valley, dale, dell, glen, gulch, gully, ravine, crater, hollow, sinkhole, depression, bowl.

basis *n., pl.* **bases** *Charity toward others is the basis of her philosophy:* base, starting point, underpinning, root, ground, foundation, touchstone, bedrock, cornerstone, fundamental, essential, principle.

bask *v.* **1.** *The skiers basked by the fire:* warm oneself, toast oneself, soak up warmth; sunbathe. **2.** *He basked in his wife's admiration:* revel, wallow, luxuriate, delight, relish, savor.

bastard *n.* **1.** *The king sired three bastards:* illegitimate child, natural child, love child. —*adj.* **2.** *He managed to speak a kind of bastard French:* impure, irregular, imperfect, inferior, spurious.

bastion *n.* **1.** *Foot soldiers stormed the mighty bastion:* fortress, fort, citadel; rampart, breastwork, barbette. **2.** *The university is a bastion of intellectual freedom:* bulwark, stronghold, citadel, tower, pillar.

bat *n.* **1.** *The player swung with his bat but missed the ball:* club, mallet, baton, stick; cane, staff, mace; cudgel, shillelagh, blackjack, truncheon, billy, bludgeon, rod. —*v.* **2.** *We batted the shuttlecock back and forth across the net a few times:* hit, strike, smack, knock, cuff, clobber, wallop, whack, thwack, sock, slug, clip, buffet.

batch *n.* *The first batch of cookies was burnt. The prisoners were led out in batches and shot:* group, bunch, lot, amount, stock, collection, crowd, number, aggregate, quantity.

bath *n.* *Once a week I allow myself the luxury of a long, uninterrupted bath:* cleansing, ablution, shower, showerbath, wash, tub, douche, washing, sponge bath, sauna, Turkish bath, steam bath, sitz bath, hip bath, dip, lavement, irrigation, immersion.

bathe *v.* *We bathed in a cool mountain stream. She bathed the child in a plastic basin:* wash, cleanse, shower, soak, lave, dip, wet, douse, *Slang* douche, sponge, irrigate, *Brit.* tub.

bathos *n.* *The play is full of melodramatic bathos:* sentimentality, sentimentalism, mawkishness, false pathos, maudlinism, soppiness, slush, slushiness, mush, mushiness, corn, schmaltz.

bathroom *n.* *He's in the bathroom, washing his socks. The child wants to use the bathroom:* washroom, men's room, ladies' room, *Brit.* lavatory, *Brit. Slang* loo, water closet, W.C., toilet, commode, facility, powder room, restroom, *Slang* john, *Slang* can, *Baby Talk* biffy, little girls' room, little boys' room, *Navy Slang* head, *Army* latrine.

baton *n.* *The drum majorettes twirled their batons in advance of the marching band:* staff, mace, crook, scepter, crosier, rod, wand; fasces, caduceus; stick, nightstick, cudgel, truncheon, shillelagh, war club, bludgeon, billy, billy club, bat.

battalion *n.* *The battalion retreated under*

heavy fire: contingent, force, horde, host, legion, multitude, mass, throng, unit.

batten *v.* *"Batten down the hatches" is an old nautical term:* secure, fix, fasten, clamp down, nail down.

batter *v.* **1.** *Enemy fire battered the walls of the fort:* beat, buffet, smash against, pound, pummel, smite, lash, *Slang* clobber. **2.** *Police battered down the door to the thieves' hideout:* pound, smash, break, beat, shatter; crush. **3.** *The old hat was battered beyond recognition:* beat up, maul, mangle, knock out of shape.

battery *n.* **1.** *Students were subjected to a battery of tests. The battleship bombarded the enemy's shore battery:* group, pack, set, series, block, band, suite; troop, force, brigade, team, legion, company, army, convoy, spearhead, phalanx, lineup; cannon, cannonry, ordnance, armament; outfit, section, division, squadron, cadre. **2.** *He was arrested on charges of assault and battery:* hitting, wounding, maiming, hurting, thrashing, beating, clubbing, caning, strapping, drubbing, flogging, whipping, cudgeling.

battle *n.* **1.** *The Battle of Waterloo was decisive. The two boxers had a championship battle:* combat, clash, campaign, siege, war, warfare, skirmish, firefight, fight; contest, encounter, affray, fray, conflict, engagement, action; duel, bout. **2.** *Martin Luther King led the battle for equal rights for blacks:* struggle, fight, contest; dispute, controversy, altercation, agitation, debate, confrontation, crusade. —*v.* **3.** *The two armies battled all night. The two boxers battled until the final bell. He battled the decision all the way to the Supreme Court:* war, fight, clash, skirmish, duel, meet, engage; struggle, contend, contest, combat, brawl, tussle, pitch into each other; quarrel, argue, feud, dispute, debate. —**Ant.** 1 armistice, peace, truce; concord, agreement. 2 agreement, accord.

battlefield *n.* *The opposing armies met on the battlefield at dawn:* battleground, theater of war, field of battle, battle line, the front, front line, no man's land, theater of operations, scene of battle, war arena.

bawdy *adj.* *The old drinking song was bawdy but amusing:* earthy, lusty, risqué, ribald, indecent, coarse, gross, licentious, off-color, blue, suggestive, sexual, sexy, indecorous, immodest, improper, indelicate, vulgar, lewd, dirty, raunchy. —**Ant.** decent, modest, delicate, clean.

bawl *v.* **1.** *The babies were bawling in the nursery:* cry, wail, howl, yowl, squall, blubber, weep. **2.** *The captain bawled for the sergeant:* shout, bellow, yell, roar, cry out, howl, call, call out, clamor. —**Ant.** 1 laugh. 2 whisper, murmur, mutter.

bay[1] *n.* *The ship dropped anchor in a quiet bay:* cove, inlet, estuary, strait, narrows, arm of the sea, sound, gulf, bayou, basin, natural harbor; firth, fiord, bight, road, lagoon.

bay[2] *n.* *A small table and chair stood in the dining bay:* alcove, nook, niche, recess, compartment.

bay[3] *n.* **1.** *The fox hunters followed the bay of the hounds:* barking, howling, bellowing, cry, clamor, yelping, yapping, yelling. **2. at bay.** *bear at bay is very dangerous:* cornered, trapped, forced to stand and fight. —*v.* **3.** *The hound bayed mournfully:* howl, bellow, bark, yelp, yap, cry.

bazaar or **bazar** *n.* **1.** *We bought this rug at the bazaar in Marrakesh:* market, marketplace, outdoor market, mart, shopping quarter, trade center, exchange. **2.** *Mother baked this cake for the church bazaar:* charity fair, charity sale; fair, carnival.

be *v.* **1.** *There are five of us in our family:* exist, live, subsist. **2.** *The party will be in a week:* occur, happen, come to pass, take place, befall. **3.** *Will you be at the party after I get there?* Gone with the Wind *will always be my favorite movie:* be present, endure, last, continue, remain, stay, persist.

beach *n.* *The waves receded from the beach:* shore, seashore, strand, coast, littoral, water's edge.

beached *adj.* *After the hurricane almost all the boats were beached:* grounded, marooned, aground, ashore, stranded.

beacon *n.* *The ship's crew watched for the flashing beacon of home port:* light, beam, signal; (*variously*) lighthouse, lighted buoy, landmark, seamark, watchtower, pharos; watch fire, bale- fire.

bead *n.* **1.** *She wore a string of beads around her neck:* small pieces of glass, stones, wood, etc., used for ornament, as on a necklace. **2.** *Beads of sweat covered his brow. Beads of gold dust covered the counter top:* drop, droplet, globule, little ball, blob, pellet, spherule, bubble; speck, particle, dot, pill.

beam *n.* **1.** *The carpenter was raising the roof beam:* (*in technical use*) horizontal support; structural support, prop, girder, rafter, joist, brace, spar, stud, trestle, timber. **2.** *A beam of light penetrated the darkness:* ray, streak, stream, gleam, glimmer, glint, glow, radiation. **3.** *The ship was very broad in the beam:* widest part, width, expanse, breadth. —*v.* **4.** *Television and radio stations beamed the news to the country. A searchlight beamed in the distance:* transmit, emit, radiate, broadcast; gleam, glimmer, glitter, glow, glare, shine. **5.** *Her entire face beamed with happiness:* shine, gleam, glow, radiate.

bear *v.* **1.** *These columns bear the weight of the roof. Our office bears the brunt of the work. He bears responsibility well:* support, sustain, maintain, carry, uphold, shoulder, take on, endure, hold up under, tolerate; underpin, brace, bolster. **2.** *Donkeys bore supplies up the steep mountain trail. Bear this gentleman to his quarters:* transport, carry, tote, convoy, bring, haul, take; accompany, lead, escort, conduct, go with, convey, deliver, transfer. **3.** *She did bear three fine sons:* give birth to, bring into being, bring forth, produce, deliver; reproduce, propagate, germinate, spawn, hatch, whelp, drop. **4.** *Apple trees bear blossoms in early spring:* produce, develop, bring forth, give, yield; engender, create, generate, render. **5.** *Bear these*

thoughts with you as you go out into the world: maintain, carry, keep in mind, hold close, harbor, cherish, take. **6.** *She can't bear the sound of chalk scraping on a blackboard:* tolerate, abide, endure, stand, put up with, stomach, brook, take, undergo, submit to, suffer, brave. **7.** *This information bears strongly on the matter under discussion:* pertain, relate, apply, refer, appertain, concern, be pertinent to, affect, have bearing on, have respect to, touch upon. **8.** *This matter bears investigation:* warrant, invite, admit, be susceptible to, permit, allow, encourage. **9.** *You bear a strong likeness to my sister. The letter bears the salutation "Dear Sir":* exhibit, manifest, display, show, have, carry, contain, possess, be marked with, be equipped with, be furnished with, wear. **10.** *To get this door open you have to bear hard against it:* press, push, bear down, force, drive. **11.** *Bear right at the intersection:* go in the direction of, aim for, turn, tend, bend, curve, diverge, deviate. —**Ant.** 1 rest on; reject, cast off, throw off. 2 put down; leave. 4 shed, drop, loose. 5 put aside, forget; relinquish. 9 hide, conceal. 10 pull.

beard *n.* **1.** *The prospector had a long beard. John sported a two-day growth of beard:* whiskers; bristles, stubble, five-o'clock shadow. —*v.* **2.** *Daniel bearded the lion in its den:* corner, bring to bay, trap, confront, face, defy, brave, dare.

bearded *adj.* *The penny shows Lincoln with a bearded face:* bewhiskered, whiskered, unshaven, hairy, hirsute, shaggy, bushy, bristly. —**Ant.** clean-shaven, smooth-shaven.

bearing *n.* **1.** *The old judge has a regal bearing:* carriage, mien, manner, air, presence; demeanor, behavior, attitude, comportment, deportment, port. **2.** *Your remarks have no bearing on our discussion:* relevance, pertinence, significance, reference, application, applicability, connection, concern, relation, relationship, association; sense, meaning, meaningfulness, import, importance. **3.** *These fruit trees are past bearing:* reproducing, reproduction, giving birth, germination, procreation, propagation, producing, breeding, conception. **4. bearings.** *We lost our bearings in the darkness:* sense of direction, orientation, direction, way, course, position. —**Ant.** 2 irrelevance, insignificance.

beast *n.* **1.** *The lion is the king of beasts:* animal, creature, mammal, quadruped, brute. **2.** *You were a beast to insult her needlessly:* brute, savage, barbarian, ogre, cad, swine, pig, cur, rat. —**Ant.** 1 human being. 2 gentleman, lady; *Informal* angel, sweetheart, gem.

beastly *adj.* *The weather has been beastly. He's a beastly little man:* unpleasant, disgusting, disagreeable, nasty, vile, loathsome, abominable, contemptible; cruel, brutal, monstrous, inhuman, bestial, brutish, savage, barbarous, gross, coarse, degraded, swinish; bad, terrible, awful, dreadful, deplorable, *Slang* lousy. —**Ant.** pleasant, agreeable, appealing, admirable; humane, sweet, sensitive, gentlemanly, ladylike; good, fine, wonderful.

beat *v.* **1.** *Stop beating on the door! Listen to*

him beat that drum: hit, strike, pound, wallop, whack, thwack, knock, smack, punch, slap, smite, clout, flail, bat, tap, rap, bang, hammer. **2.** *They beat him to within an inch of his life:* thrash, pummel, batter, maul, trounce; whip, flog, flail, scourge, switch, strap, club, cane. **3.** *Alexander the Great beat every opponent between Greece and India:* defeat, be victorious over, triumph over, win over, overcome, overpower, vanquish, best; conquer, crush, rout, destroy, repel, repulse, quell, put down, master, subdue, whip, lick, clobber, trounce, drub. **4.** *He beat all competition in the elections:* win out over, excel over, surpass, outdo, prevail over, predominate, eclipse, overcome, shellac, carry all before one. **5.** *Her heart beat madly with fright. The sea gull beat its wings against the air:* pulsate, pulse, throb, pound, palpitate, flutter, quiver, fluctuate, vibrate, quake, shake, twitch, go pit-a-pat; flap, flop. **6.** *Beat the egg whites until they are stiff:* whip; stir vigorously, mix. **—***n.* **7.** *The room resounded with each beat of the gong:* blow, stroke, strike, hit, whack, rap, slap. **8.** *The music had the familiar beat of a waltz:* cadence, time, rhythm, meter, count, pulse, pulsation, stress, accent. **9.** *They felt safer knowing that the police officer was on his beat:* route, rounds, circuit, path, course, way; area, zone, territory, domain, realm. **—Ant.** 1, 2 caress, stroke, pat, pet; soothe, comfort; shield, protect, guard. 3, 4 lose, suffer defeat, go down in defeat, surrender; fall, fail, get the worst of, go under.

beatific *adj. The Madonna's smile was beatific:* blissful, serene, heavenly, divine, sublime, glorious, exalted, transcendental, angelic, saintly; enraptured, rapturous, rapt, ecstatic. **—Ant.** worldly, sophisticated; mundane, common, coarse, crude.

beatitude *n. Prolonged meditation had given him an aura of beatitude:* bliss, felicity, blessedness, saintliness; exaltation, exaltedness, transcendence, transfiguration; rapture, ecstasy, euphoria. **—Ant.** despair, hopelessness, dolor.

beau *n., pl.* **beaux** **1.** *Do you think Helen will marry her new beau?:* boyfriend, sweetheart, young man, steady, fellow, suitor, *Informal* guy, admirer, flame, gentleman caller *or* friend, squire, swain; fiancé, betrothed; love, beloved, lover. **2.** *The young beau flirted with all the ladies:* ladies' man, cavalier, dandy, fop, swell, playboy, gay blade, Romeo, Don Juan, blade; young blood, popinjay, coxcomb; nob, spark, dude, stud, buck, toff.

beautiful *adj.* **1.** *His sister is a beautiful woman. The music is beautiful:* pretty, handsome, good-looking, fine-looking, lovely, gorgeous, attractive, exquisite, ravishing, comely, fair, bonny, seemly, beauteous, radiant, pulchritudinous, resplendent; pleasing, enjoyable, captivating, alluring. **2.** *You did a beautiful job of cleaning up the kitchen:* very good, excellent, first-rate, superb, wonderful, fine, splendid, admirable, great, stupendous, commendable, estimable, worthy. **—Ant.** 1 ugly, unattractive, bad-looking, hideous, grotesque; unpleasant, bad,

awful, disgusting, repulsive, repugnant, revolting. 2 bad, awful, terrible, lousy, second-rate.

beautifully *adv. She swam beautifully:* excellently, pleasingly, splendidly, wonderfully, attractively, elegantly, gracefully.

beautify *v. Planting flowers along the boulevards will help to beautify the town:* enhance, embellish, adorn, ornament, glamorize, improve, grace, dress up, smarten up, do up, *Slang* gussy up. **—Ant.** spoil, mar, disfigure, deface, besmirch.

beauty *n.* **1.** *Paris is a city of great beauty:* loveliness, handsomeness, good looks, pulchritude, attractiveness, splendor, resplendence, magnificence, radiance. **2.** *The actress is one of the great beauties of our time:* beautiful woman, beautiful girl, belle, goddess, Venus; *Slang* knockout, beaut, doll, stunner, eyeful, good-looker, looker. **3.** *One of the beauties of the plan is its simplicity:* advantage, asset, attraction, feature, good thing, excellence, benefit, grace, boon. **—Ant.** 1 ugliness, repulsiveness, unpleasantness. 2 *Slang* witch, bag, dog, pig. 3 disadvantage, detraction, shortcoming, flaw.

because *conj. She can't attend because she has a cold:* as, since, for, inasmuch as, for the reason that, in consequence of.

beckon *v.* **1.** *The leader beckoned the others to follow him:* signal, motion, wave at, wave on, gesture, gesticulate, crook a finger at. **2.** *The romance of the sea beckoned the old sailor:* entice, lure, allure, invite, attract, draw, pull, call, summon, coax. **—Ant.** 2 repel, repulse, *Informal* put off.

becloud *v. Don't try to becloud the basic issues by launching a personal attack on your opponent:* obscure, befog, confuse, obfuscate, hide, confound, muddle, cover up, camouflage, eclipse, screen, overcast, veil, shroud, overshadow.

become *v.* **1.** *My eyes become tired after so much reading:* get, begin to be, grow, turn, come to be, get to be, turn out to be, commence to be, be converted into, be reduced to, settle into. **2.** *Lavender always becomes you. Compassionate behavior becomes a leader:* suit, go with, flatter, complement, agree with, enhance; accord with, harmonize with, be proper to, be consistent with. **—Ant.** 2 clash with, conflict with, disagree with, detract from.

becoming *adj.* **1.** *His behavior was not very becoming for a gentleman:* suitable, appropriate, proper, seemly, fit, fitting, befitting, worthy, meet, congruous, consistent, in keeping. **2.** *Blue is a very becoming color on you:* flattering, enhancing, attractive, pretty, good-looking; apt, harmonious, congenial, compatible. **—Ant.** unbecoming. 1 unsuitable, inappropriate, improper, unseemly, unfit, unfitting, unbefitting, unworthy, incongruous, inconsistent with, out of keeping, indecorous. 2 ugly, unattractive.

bed *n.* **1.** *The bed needs a new mattress. The cowboy made a bed on the ground out of his saddle and blankets:* bedstead, place to sleep, bunk, pallet, berth, cot; *Slang* sack, hay; (*for infants*) cradle, crib. **2.** *Serve the shrimp cocktail*

on a bed of lettuce: base, bottom, floor, foundation. **3.** *There's a bed of anthracite coal in this
mountain:* layer, stratum, band, belt, zone;
seam, deposit, lode. **4.** *Plant a bed of roses by
the garage:* plot, patch, bank.

bedazzle *v.* **1.** *The bright lights bedazzled her:*
daze, confuse, dumfound, bewilder, stupefy,
nonplus, disconcert, befuddle, fluster. **2.** *Her
charm bedazzled him:* dazzle, confound, astound, stagger, flabbergast, overwhelm, overpower, enchant, captivate, sweep one off one's
feet.

bedevil *v.* *Several mischievous youngsters be-
deviled his first day of teaching:* afflict, pester,
annoy, plague, nag, harass, harry, worry, beleaguer, bother, beset, trouble, vex, torment, try,
persecute, hassle.

bedim *v.* *Clouds bedimmed the sky:* darken,
dim, obscure, cloud, becloud. —**Ant.** brighten.

bedlam *n.* *The argument turned the party into a
bedlam:* scene of wild confusion, uproar, pandemonium, chaos, madhouse, tumult, turmoil.

bedraggled *adj.* *The bedraggled children always looked hungry and undernourished:* unkempt, untidy, sloppy, dirty, soiled, messy, disordered, dowdy, tattered, seedy, threadbare,
down-at-the-heels, tacky, *Brit.* tatty, ragtag, out-
at-the-elbows, draggletailed; frumpy, frumpish,
sluttish, slatternly. —**Ant.** neat, dapper, well-
groomed, immaculate.

bedroom *n.* *The house has three bedrooms:*
sleeping room, bedchamber, boudoir.

beehive *n.* **1.** *The bees followed their queen to
the new beehive:* hive, apiary. **2.** *The office is a
beehive of activity:* busy place, powerhouse.

beer *n.* *He ordered a cheese sandwich and a
bottle of beer:* (variously) lager, ale, stout, porter, malt liquor, dark, bitter, light, near beer,
bock beer; *Slang* brew, suds.

befall *v.* *Bad luck may befall at any time:* happen, occur, come to pass, ensue, materialize,
chance, fall, follow, betide.

befitting *adj.* *A formal gown is befitting the diplomatic reception:* suitable, appropriate, fitting,
fit, proper, apt, seemly, right, decent, becoming;
relevant. —**Ant.** unsuitable, inappropriate, unfit, unfitting, unbecoming, improper, unseemly,
wrong; irrelevant, meaningless.

beforehand *adv.* *If you wanted soup for lunch
you should have told me beforehand:* earlier,
sooner, before, before now, ahead of time, in
advance, before the fact, in time. —**Ant.** afterwards, after.

befriend *v.* *Will Rogers befriended every
stranger he met:* make friends with, get acquainted with, associate with, consort with, fraternize with; assist, help, help out, give aid to,
succor, comfort, minister to, protect, defend,
hold out a helping hand to, look after, sympathize with, embrace, welcome, support, sustain,
stick by, stand by, side with, uphold, take under
one's wing. —**Ant.** alienate, estrange.

befuddle *v.* **1.** *The new arrival was befuddled by
the rapid-fire conversation:* confuse, perplex,
bewilder, puzzle, baffle, confound, disorganize,
daze, unsettle, rattle, fluster, muddle, mix up,

knock off balance, disorient. **2.** *The wine had
befuddled him:* addle, stupefy, make groggy, intoxicate, make drunk, make tipsy, inebriate.
—**Ant.** 1 make clear to, illuminate, bring into
focus. 2 sober, clear one's head.

beg *v.* **1.** *During the Depression, many men had
to beg for a living:* seek charity, solicit, panhandle, mooch, *Informal* cadge, sponge, bum, hustle, go from door to door, be on one's uppers.
2. *The accused begged for the court's understanding:* plead, entreat, implore, beseech, supplicate, sue, appeal to, petition, importune,
pray. **3.** *Your reply begs the question:* evade,
avoid, dodge, shirk, shun, escape, avert, eschew, parry, fend off, sidestep, steer clear of,
shy away from. —**Ant.** 1 give, contribute, present, bestow, donate, confer. 2 demand, exact,
insist, grant, give, accord.

beget *v.* **1.** *The old patriarch is said to have be-
gotten more than 200 children in his lifetime:*
father, sire, get, propagate, breed, engender,
procreate, spawn. **2.** *Evil deeds may beget dire
consequences:* bring about, result in, cause, effect, occasion, lead to, produce, give rise to, call
forth, engender, generate. —**Ant.** 2 prevent,
forestall, foil, block, ward off, deter, save.

beggar *n.* **1.** *A street beggar held out his hand,
asking for a coin:* almsman, mendicant, panhandler, tramp; *Slang* sponger, bum, moocher.
2. *The poor beggar looked silly trying to portray
the role of Hamlet:* fellow, chap, guy, *Slang*
devil. —*v.* **3.** *Her hat was so funny it beggars
description:* make inadequate, be beyond, surpass; challenge, baffle. —**Ant.** 1 giver, contributor, bestower, donor, donator, benefactor, philanthropist.

begin *v.* **1.** *Please begin work. School vacation
begins on Monday:* start, commence, initiate,
set out, embark on, take the first step. **2.** *This
has been true since the world began. He began
a new business last year:* come into existence,
bring into existence, be born, start, commence,
initiate, undertake; originate, establish, introduce, found, institute, launch, inaugurate;
emerge, arise, burst forth, break out, crop up,
set in motion. —**Ant.** 1, 2 end, finish, terminate, conclude, complete; stop, cease, quit.

beginner *n.* **1.** *I'm just a beginner in woodworking:* novice, neophyte, student, tyro,
learner, fledgling, tenderfoot, greenhorn, rookie,
freshman, apprentice, *Slang* babe, babe in the
woods. **2.** *Eli Whitney was one of the beginners
of American industry. My grandfather was the
beginner of this business:* founder, father, originator, initiator, creator, starter, inaugurator,
prime mover, author, organizer. —**Ant.** 1 expert, professional, master, authority, virtuoso,
old hand.

beginning *n.* **1.** *Start at the beginning and play
the piece again. This is only the beginning!:*
start, commencement, starting point, onset,
outset, zero hour. **2.** *The beginning of the scandal was a small item in the newspaper:* origin,
source, foundation, fountainhead, wellspring,
spring, springboard; embryo, inauguration,
birth, inception, seed, germ, introduction,

launching, kickoff. —*adj.* **3.** *For a beginning chess player, she plays quite well:* novice, neophyte, student, inexperienced, untried, new, preliminary, embryonic, incipient. —**Ant.** 1, 2 end, ending, conclusion, finish, closing, termination, expiration. 3 experienced, accomplished, finished, skilled, learned, expert, master.

begone *v. Begone with you!:* go away, away, be off, get out, out, depart, leave, *Slang* scram, vamoose, beat it, scat, shoo, get lost. —**Ant.** come here, come.

begrudge *v. Why do you begrudge him his success?:* grudge, resent, hold against; envy, covet, be jealous of. —**Ant.** congratulate, wish well; be happy for.

beguile *v.* **1.** *The boy was beguiled into thinking he could become a famous singer:* delude, lead astray, deceive, dupe, bamboozle, ensnare, lure, trick, cheat, hoodwink, hoax. **2.** *Beguiled by the warm day, the students fell to daydreaming:* lull, distract, enchant, charm, bewitch, captivate, please, cheer; entertain, divert, amuse, occupy. —**Ant.** 1 enlighten, disabuse, make weary, *Informal* wise up. 2 alert, alarm, bring to one's senses, jar.

behave *v.* **1.** *Why can't that child behave?:* conduct oneself properly, comport oneself well, act correctly, control oneself. **2.** *You behave as if you'd been wronged:* act, conduct oneself, comport oneself, deport oneself, acquit oneself. —**Ant.** 1 misbehave.

behavior *n.* **1.** *His behavior under stress is admirable:* conduct, manner, attitude, control, self-control, comportment, deportment, bearing, demeanor. **2.** *The compass is showing strange behavior:* response, reaction, functioning, conduct, operation, action, performance. **3.** *The naturalist studied the behavior of lions in their natural habitat:* acts, deeds, actions, activity, conduct, practice, habits.

behead *v. Henry VIII gave the order to behead Anne Boleyn:* decapitate, send to the ax, bring to the block; guillotine, decollate.

behest *n. At the attorney general's behest I am sending you a transcript of the trial:* order, direction, command, instruction, mandate, dictate, charge, say-so, injunction, bidding; decree, ruling, fiat, edict, ultimatum.

behold *v. The strollers could behold the beautiful sunset. Behold, the new king is crowned!:* look, look at, look upon, observe, note, see, gaze at, stare at, view, discern, survey, regard, watch, examine, inspect, notice, scan, scrutinize, witness, *Slang* get a load of; attend, pay attention, heed, mark, contemplate. —**Ant.** overlook, disregard, ignore, miss.

beholden *adj. Your help has made us beholden to you:* under obligation, obligated, obliged, indebted, in one's debt, bound, liable; answerable, accountable, responsible.

behoove *v. It would behoove you to take better care of your health:* be advantageous, benefit, be advisable, be wise; be fitting, befit, become, suit, be proper, be necessary, be apt, be appropriate.

being *n.* **1.** *A new world came into being:* exist-ence, existing, occurrence, reality, actuality, life, living, subsistence. **2.** *His very being felt the need of love:* nature, soul, spirit, psyche, essence, true being, core, inner person, persona. **3.** *Can there be beings on other planets?:* living creature, creature, human being, human, person, fellow creature, mortal, individual. —**Ant.** 1 nothingness, nonexistence, nullity.

belabor *v. We all see your point; there's no need to belabor it:* hammer away at, dwell on, go on (and on) about, repeat, rehash, reiterate, recapitulate, pound away at; beat a dead horse.

belated *adj. Our good wishes are belated but sincere:* late, tardy, past due, overdue, behind, behind time, slow, delayed, deferred, unpunctual, after the fact, behindhand. —**Ant.** early, ahead of time, beforehand, before the fact.

belch *v.* **1.** *After the feast the king belched hugely:* burp, eruct. **2.** *The volcano belched fire:* emit, discharge, spew, spout, spurt, eject, issue, send forth, gush, roar forth, expel, erupt, disgorge, vomit, vent, cough up. —*n.* **3.** *The gluttonous king gave forth a belch:* burp, eructation. **4.** *A belch of flame came from the rocket's exhaust:* emission, discharge, spurt, spout, gush, ejection, issuing, eruption.

beleaguer *v.* **1.** *Enemy troops beleaguered the city:* besiege, surround, blockade, bombard, assail. **2.** *He beleaguered her with pleas for forgiveness:* harass, badger, pester, bother, annoy, assail, hector, vex, bombard, besiege, plague.

belfry *n. Mischievous boys climbed up to the belfry and rang the bells at midnight:* bell tower, campanile; (*loosely*) steeple, spire, dome.

belie *v.* **1.** *The facts belie your story:* disprove, refute, contradict, controvert, repudiate, show to be false, give the lie to, invalidate, gainsay, negate, betray, deny, defy. **2.** *The author's smile belied his anger with the critic:* misrepresent, falsify; disguise, camouflage, mask, conceal, cloak. —**Ant.** 1 prove, verify, attest to, validate, support, confirm, corroborate. 2 represent, reveal, disclose, indicate.

belief *n.* **1.** *The prevailing belief is that Mars is uninhabited. It is my belief that it's going to rain:* conviction, firm notion, opinion, view, theory, persuasion; conclusion; assumption, supposition, presumption, feeling, expectation, judgment, impression, hypothesis, deduction, inference, guess. **2.** *I have complete belief in my friends:* confidence, trust, faith, assurance, reliance, certitude. **3.** Often **beliefs**. *Could you defend your political beliefs?:* conviction, persuasion, principle, way of thinking; morality, morals, teachings, ethics; faith, creed, dogma, doctrine, tenet, canon, gospel. —**Ant.** 2 distrust, mistrust, doubt. 3 disbelief, unbelief, skepticism; denial, disavowal.

believable *adj. The story is hardly believable:* plausible, credible, convincing, possible, imaginable, acceptable. —**Ant.** unbelievable, incredible, doubtful, dubious, unconvincing, implausible, questionable; unacceptable; fabulous.

believe *v.* **1.** *Don't believe everything you hear. We all believe in good, free education for our children:* trust, put faith in, place confidence in, be certain of, credit, rely on, depend on; presume true, accept as true, hold, be assured by, be convinced by, be persuaded by, judge accurate, count on, be sure of, swear by; swallow, fall for. **2.** *I believe it's going to rain:* presume, think, imagine, guess, surmise, suspect, judge, suppose, assume, consider, speculate, conjecture, presuppose; theorize, hypothesize, deduce, infer; maintain, hold. **—Ant.** 1 doubt, question, distrust, mistrust, discredit, disbelieve. 2 know, know for sure.

believer *n.* *The car's performance made a believer of him:* adherent, follower, devotee, disciple.

belittle *v.* *Don't belittle her piano playing just because you're jealous:* make light of, disparage, deride, scorn, disdain, sneer at, malign, cast aspersions on, deprecate, play down, minimize, mitigate, underrate, undervalue, underestimate, depreciate; *Slang* knock, run down, put down, pooh-pooh. **—Ant.** overpraise, praise, vaunt, glorify, elevate, exalt, play up, magnify; boast about, crow over, make a big fuss over.

bell *n.* *The church bells called the worshipers to prayer. The fire bell woke us in the middle of the night:* tocsin, chime, carillon, gong; peal of bells, peal, ringing, tintinnabulation.

belle *n.* *The movie is about Southern belles and their dashing Confederate beaux. That gown will make you the belle of the ball:* beautiful girl, beautiful woman, beauty; most beautiful woman, most beautiful girl, star, queen; charmer; *Slang* heart-stopper.

bellicose *adj.* See BELLIGERENT.

belligerence also **belligerency** *n.* *The two hostile nations regarded each other with belligerence:* warlike attitude, hostility, aggressiveness, combativeness, pugnacity, antagonism, unfriendliness, animosity. **—Ant.** peacefulness, friendliness.

belligerent *adj.* **1.** *Why do nations maintain belligerent attitudes toward each other?:* warlike, warring, hostile, antagonistic, aggressive, combative, martial, bellicose. **2.** *Why do you have such belligerent feelings toward your neighbors?:* unfriendly, hostile, antagonistic, bellicose, pugnacious, quarrelsome, contentious, irritable, bad-tempered, cantankerous, irascible, inimical, truculent. *—n.* **3.** *Switzerland was not a belligerent in World War II. The larger nation was the belligerent:* warring country, nation at war, combatant, fighter, adversary; aggressor, attacker, antagonist. **—Ant.** 1, 2 peaceful, peaceable. 1 pacific; neutral. 2 friendly, amicable, neighborly. 3 neutral, noncombatant; the attacked, defender.

bellow *v.* **1.** *The bull bellowed with rage. The captain bellowed a command at the troops:* roar; shout, yell, bawl, holler, scream, shriek, whoop. *—n.* **2.** *The wrestler gave a loud bellow and attacked his opponent:* roar, shout, yell, shriek, scream, whoop. **—Ant.** 1, 2 whisper. 1 murmur, mutter.

bellwether *n.* *What we need is a bellwether to take the initiative on this project:* leader, guide, pilot, lead, doyen, pacesetter, standard-bearer; shepherd, conductor, director; precursor, forerunner, guidepost.

belly *n.* **1.** *Eating green apples gave the boy a pain in the belly:* stomach, tummy, abdomen, paunch, vitals, *Slang* gut, guts, midriff, breadbasket. **2.** *He has no belly for adventure:* liking, desire, appetite, stomach, hunger, taste, yen. **3.** *The luggage is in the belly of the plane:* bowels, depths, recesses, interior, insides.

belong *v.* **1.** *These boots belong in the closet. Do these woods belong to the property that's for sale?:* have as a proper place; be part of, attach to, go with; concern, pertain to, be connected with. **2.** *This book belongs to the school:* be the property of, be owned by, be held by. **3.** *We belong to the country club:* be a member of, be included in; be associated with, be allied to.

belongings *n.* *Pack up your belongings and leave!:* possessions, effects, personal property, movables, goods; gear, paraphernalia, accouterments, things, stuff, *Slang* junk.

beloved *adj.* **1.** *It was given me by a beloved friend:* loved, cherished, dear, precious, treasured, adored, darling, endeared; respected, admired, highly valued, esteemed, revered. *—n.* **2.** *He received a long letter from his beloved:* sweetheart, loved one, love, dearest, precious; (variously) steady, lover, boyfriend, beau, girl friend, betrothed, fiancé, fiancée, spouse, husband, wife.

below *prep.* *His marks were below average:* under, lower, subordinate, lesser, inferior, less.

belt *n.* **1.** *This dress comes with a red leather belt:* sash, band, cinch, waistband, cummerbund, girdle. **2.** *A belt of trees encircled the field:* circle, band, strip, stripe, layer. **3.** *The drought damaged crops in the corn belt:* area, district, region, zone, country, land. *—v.* **4.** *The coat is belted at the waist:* encircle by a belt, fasten with a belt, cinch, girdle, encircle.

bemoan *v.* *Stop bemoaning the loss of your job and go look for a new one:* grieve over, weep over, cry over, whine over, lament, bewail, mourn, regret, rue. **—Ant.** laugh at; celebrate, exult.

bemused *adj.* **1.** *He gave the child a bemused look:* preoccupied, absent-minded, engrossed, thoughtful. **2.** *The wine left him somewhat bemused:* confused, muddled, bewildered, fuzzy, dull-witted, stupefied, dazed, stunned. **—Ant.** 1 angry, stern, unsympathetic. 2 clearheaded, perceptive, *Slang* sharp.

bench *n.* **1.** *The old man sat on the park bench and fed the pigeons:* seat, settee, pew, rigid couch, backless couch, backless chair, stool. **2.** *The carpenter's bench was covered with tools:* workbench, worktable, counter, trestle, board, table. **3.** *The accused will be brought before the bench:* court, tribunal, judiciary, seat of justice; judge's chair. **4.** *The championship will be won by the team with the best bench:* substitute players, substitutes, second team, second string. *—v.* **5.** *The first baseman has been benched for the season:* remove from active play, remove from the game, take out, sideline.

benchmark *n.* *After more than 50 years the*

Rosa Ponselle recording still remains the benchmark: standard, yardstick, measure, gauge, criterion, touchstone, model, guide, exemplar, paradigm; reference, norm, principle, prototype, example.

bend *v.* **1.** *Be careful or you'll bend that spoon. The mountain road bends treacherously:* twist, make crooked, become crooked, warp, buckle, contort; curve, arc, loop, turn, wind. **2.** *Bend at the knee when you ski downhill:* flex; crouch, stoop, lean; bow, buckle, genuflect. **3.** *We will not bend to the will of a tyrant. No tyrant can bend us to his will:* bow down, submit, yield, give in, defer, accede, relent, succumb, be subjugated, surrender, capitulate, *Informal* knuckle under; force to submit, cause to yield, cause to give in, cause to defer, cause to relent, force to surrender, force, compel, coerce, control, shape, mold, influence, sway. **4.** *The welder bent to his work with determination:* apply oneself, attend, give oneself to, buckle down, put one's heart into. —*n.* **5.** *Steer around that bend in the river:* curve, turn, crook, arc, hook, twist. —**Ant.** 1, 2 straighten; stiffen.

benediction *n. At the end of the service the bishop gave the benediction:* blessing, prayer, benison, consecration, invocation, closing prayer. —**Ant.** malediction, curse, imprecation; censure.

benefactor *n. The new wing of the hospital is the gift of a generous benefactor:* supporter, patron, donor, sponsor, upholder, backer, helper, friend, angel, fairy godmother; contributor.

beneficial *adj. Exercise is beneficial to good health:* helpful, advantageous, propitious, useful, valuable, contributive, favorable, profitable, productive; healthful, healing, good for. —**Ant.** useless, detrimental, detractive, disadvantageous; unfavorable, harmful, pernicious, unwholesome.

beneficiary *n. Fill in the name of your beneficiary on the insurance policy:* inheritor, legatee, heir, heiress; receiver, recipient, grantee.

benefit *n.* **1.** *Your advice was of great benefit to me. The new factory will be a great benefit to the town:* help, aid, service, use, avail, profit, value, gain, worth, advantage, asset, good, betterment, blessing; behalf, interest. **2.** *The theater benefit collected $100,000:* charity affair, charity performance. —*v.* **3.** *The new hospital will benefit the entire community. I benefited from my father's advice:* help, aid, assist, serve, be useful to, be an advantage to, do good for, advance, better, profit; be helped, be aided, be served, gain, profit from. —**Ant.** 1 damage, harm, injury, impairment, privation; loss, disservice, disadvantage, drawback. 3 harm, injure, hurt, damage, impair, deprive; lose, detract from, be useless to, be bad for, worsen, hold back.

benevolence *n.* **1.** *The playground director smiled with benevolence at the noisy children:* good will, kindliness, kindheartedness, kindness, compassion, benignity. **2.** *The Community Chest depends on the public's benevolence:* generosity, charity, charitableness, humanitari-

anism, bountifulness, liberality. —**Ant.** 1 ill will, unkindness, unkindliness, malevolence, malignity. 2 selfishness, greediness; stinginess, illiberality, niggardliness.

benevolent *adj.* **1.** *The old woman had a benevolent feeling toward all cats. He gave her a benevolent gaze:* kindhearted, warmhearted, kind, compassionate, tender, full of good will, benign, benignant, considerate, humane. **2.** *The church women are forming a Benevolent Society. The club received a benevolent donation:* unselfish, charitable, philanthropic, humanitarian; generous, liberal, considerable, bountiful, bounteous, bighearted. —**Ant.** 1 unkind, cruel, malevolent, malicious, malignant. 2 selfish, greedy; stingy, miserly, niggardly, illiberal.

benighted *adj. Anthropologists discovered a primitive, benighted tribe living in the mountain's caves:* ignorant, backward, unenlightened, untutored, primitive, uncivilized, uncultivated, uncultured, illiterate, unlettered, crude, uneducated, unschooled, uninformed, untaught; know-nothing, empty-headed, dumb, *Slang* unhip. —**Ant.** cultured, educated, schooled, civilized, informed, cultivated.

benign *adj.* **1.** *The benign uncle tended to spoil the boy:* kind, kindly, genial, kindhearted, tender, tender-hearted, soft-hearted, soft, gentle, benevolent, humane; gracious, affable. **2.** *The decrease of the patient's fever was a benign sign:* good, favorable, salutary, auspicious, encouraging, propitious, lucky. **3.** *Los Angeles has a benign climate:* temperate, mild, balmy, pleasant, nice; healthful, harmless, innocuous. —**Ant.** 1 unkind, unkindly, hard-hearted, harsh, stern, malicious, malevolent, hateful, malign, inhumane, ungracious. 2 bad, unfavorable, discouraging, threatening, ominous, unlucky. 3 harsh, severe, extreme, unpleasant.

bent *adj.* **1.** *At 80 my grandfather was wizened and bent. I can't use that bent pin:* angled, twisted, crooked, curved, arched, contorted, stooped, hunched, bowed. —*n.* **2.** *If the boy has a bent for music, give him piano lessons:* leaning, tendency, inclination, propensity, penchant, proclivity, disposition, predisposition; mind, liking, fondness, bias, partiality, attraction, predilection; talent, gift, flair, knack, faculty, facility, ability, aptness, capacity, endowment, aptitude, genius. —**Ant.** 1 unbent, straight, straight as an arrow, rigid, uncurved, unbowed. 2 aversion, disinclination, dislike, antipathy, hate, hatred, abhorrence.

bequeath *v. Most people bequeath their property to their spouses and children:* will, leave, hand down, impart, consign, endow.

bequest *n. Grandfather left a bequest to each of the grandchildren:* legacy, inheritance, endowment, bestowal, settlement.

berate *v. The principal berated the student for his tardiness:* scold, upbraid, reprimand, rebuke, reprove, reproach, criticize, castigate, take to task, rail at, bawl out, chew out, tongue-lash. —**Ant.** praise, compliment, laud, thank, congratulate.

bereave *v. The accident bereaved Jane of her

husband. The refugees arrived bereft of their possessions. The looters behaved as if altogether bereft of their senses: deprive, rob, strip, dispossess, divest.

bereavement n. She wore black after her bereavement: deprivation, affliction, sorrow, loss, tribulation.

bereft adj. The shipwrecked passengers were bereft of food and clothing: bereaved, deprived, lacking, devoid, divested, impoverished, shorn, without, wanting.

berserk adj. The man was berserk, throwing rocks at anyone who came near him: maniacal, frenzied, amok, wild, violent, out of control, frantic, wild-eyed; deranged, insane, demented, crazy; distracted, distraught, desperate. —**Ant.** calm, serene, tranquil, collected, pacific.

berth n. **1.** Have you ever slept in the upper berth of a Pullman car?: bunk, bed, sleeping place. **2.** The ship rested in its berth: dock, pier, slip, quay, anchorage, wharf; haven, resting place. **3.** The saleswoman found a new berth with a shoe company: job, position, situation, place, office, post, spot, niche, appointment, employ, billet.

beseech v. I beseech you to forgive me: beg, plead with, implore, entreat, adjure, supplicate, pray.

beset v. **1.** The Complaints Department was beset by angry customers: attack on all sides, besiege, surround, hem in, assail, set upon; beleaguer, bedevil, plague, pester, badger, harass, hound, annoy, worry, dog. **2.** The crown was beset with rubies, emeralds, and pearls: set, stud, array, deck, embellish, bead; set upon, place upon.

besides adv. **1.** I don't want to go; besides, I don't feel well: moreover, in addition, furthermore, else, otherwise, too, also, yet, further. —prep. **2.** Besides lots of food, we were given plenty to drink: over and above, in addition to, except, other than, save, distinct from.

besiege v. **1.** The troops besieged the fort: lay siege to, surround and attack, beleaguer; assail, assault. **2.** He was besieged with requests for money: beset, plague, pester, badger, harass, hound, bedevil, annoy, dog.

besmirch v. He never forgave the reporter for besmirching his family's name: smear, taint, tarnish, corrupt, stain, sully, soil, defile, blacken; slander, dishonor, disgrace, degrade, discredit, defame, debauch. —**Ant.** respect, honor, do homage to, exalt, praise.

best adj. **1.** This movie was voted the best picture of the year. What's the best medicine for a cold?: most excellent, superior, finest, choice, highest quality, topnotch, unrivaled, unsurpassed, unexcelled, unequaled; most helpful, most desirable. **2.** It rained for the best part of a week: largest, greatest, most. —adv. **3.** Which vacuum cleaner picks up dirt best? Which coat do you like best? Which job pays best?: most excellently, most successfully, beyond all others; in the highest degree; most, most of all, above all others; most profitably, most advantageously, to the greatest advantage. **4.** The com-

pany hired the person best able to do the job: to the highest degree, most fully, most, most of all. —n. **5.** Even the best of us make mistakes. The dog won a prize for being the best of the breed: finest, most excellent, choice, elite, greatest, foremost, pick, cream, top. **6.** Do the best you can: utmost, hardest, all that one can, the most that can be done, highest endeavor. **7.** I'm not at my best unless I've had a good night's sleep: most pleasant, nicest, loveliest, most competent, highest perfection. **8.** Aunt Ellen sent her best to all: best wishes, kindest regards, greetings, compliments. —**Ant.** 1, 3, 6, 7 worst. 2, 4, 6 least. 1 poorest. 3 most poorly.

bestial adj. The prisoners received bestial treatment: brutal, cruel, beastly, ruthless, merciless, barbaric, barbarous, savage, depraved, inhumane. —**Ant.** tender, humane; kind, gentle, merciful.

bestow v. **1.** The country bestowed its highest medal on the war hero: grant, confer, present, give, award, accord, render, impart, mete, dispense, Slang lay on; give away, donate, hand out, consign, turn over to, deliver, settle upon, apportion, deal out. **2.** You should bestow more time to work and less to daydreaming: apply, expend, devote, occupy; use, utilize, employ, spend, consume. —**Ant.** 1 get, receive, acquire, procure, obtain, gain, earn, take, collect. 2 waste, lose, fritter away.

bet v. **1.** Over $1 million were bet on the Kentucky Derby last year: wager, gamble, make a bet, stake, risk, venture, speculate, chance, hazard, plunge. —n. **2.** Put your bet down before the wheel stops spinning: wager, stake, speculation, gamble, ante.

betray v. **1.** Benedict Arnold betrayed his country: be disloyal, be treacherous, be unfaithful, break faith with, sell out, inform against, play false with, double-cross, two-time, play Judas; deceive, trick, dupe; abandon, jilt. **2.** Don't ever betray a confidence. Her eyes betrayed her sadness: violate, let down; reveal, disclose, divulge, expose, uncover, show, tell, tell on, unmask, give away, lay bare, let slip, blurt out, Slang rat on, fink, squeal. —**Ant.** 1 be loyal, be faithful, be true, keep the faith. 2 keep, guard, safeguard; preserve, hide, conceal, cover, mask.

betrayal n. **1.** The Bible tells of the betrayal of Christ by Judas: treachery, treason, sedition, disloyalty, unfaithfulness, falseness, breach of faith, bad faith, perfidy, double-dealing, double-cross, two-timing; deception, chicanery, duplicity, trickery. **2.** Nothing is worse than the betrayal of a confidence: revelation, disclosure, divulgence, telling, giving away, blurting out, violation. —**Ant.** 1 loyalty, faithfulness. 2 keeping, guarding, safeguarding; preserving.

betroth v. She is betrothed to her childhood sweetheart: engage, affiance, promise, pledge, espouse, contract, commit.

betrothal n. A feud between their two families prevented Romeo and Juliet's betrothal: engagement, affiancing, troth, betrothing, espousal.

better adj. **1.** She's a better dancer than I. A down-filled jacket is better than a wool one for really cold weather: superior, finer, more excellent, of higher quality, greater; preferable, more useful, of greater value, more suitable, more desirable, more acceptable. **2.** The better part of the day was spent working: greater, larger, longer, bigger. **3.** The patient is better today: healthier, more healthy, stronger, fitter; improving, improved, mending, progressing, recovering. —adv. **4.** Learn to play the violin a little better before joining the orchestra. You understand the problem better than I do: in a superior way, more completely, more thoroughly. **5.** It takes better than an hour to get to work. The soldiers marched better than twenty miles today: more, greater; longer, farther. —v. **6.** He tried to better himself by going to night school: improve, advance, further, forward, raise, upgrade, uplift, elevate, enhance, enrich, cultivate, refine, promote, increase, heighten, strengthen. **7.** The pole vaulter bettered the world's record by six inches: surpass, exceed, outdo, outstrip, top. —**Ant.** 1, 3, 4 worse, poorer. 1 inferior, lesser. 2 lesser, smaller; shorter. 3 sicker, weaker; failing, sinking. 5 less, under. 6 worsen, lessen, weaken; lower, downgrade, devaluate, depress, impoverish.

betterment n. Science should work for the betterment of humanity: improvement, advancement, amelioration, promotion, enrichment; correction, amendment, revision, regeneration, reform, reconstruction, rectification. —**Ant.** debasement, degeneration, decline, ruination, nemesis, destruction.

between prep. Her apartment was between two larger ones: betwixt, mid, among, amid, amidst, halfway, midway, inserted, surrounded by, enclosed by, separating.

beverage n. We had a choice of hot or cold beverages: drink, libation, liquid, draft, brew, liquor, potation.

bevy n. **1.** The hunters flushed a bevy of quail: flock, flight; group, coterie, covey, (loosely) brood, herd, pack, drove, swarm, clutch, gaggle, school, shoal. **2.** A bevy of beautiful women was in the beauty contest: company, body, crowd, assemblage, gathering, collection, group, coterie, multitude, horde, band, party, host, throng.

bewail v. The boy bewailed the loss of his dog: lament, mourn, grieve over, bemoan, moan over, cry over, weep over; regret, rue, deplore. —**Ant.** rejoice over, laugh over, celebrate, delight in.

beware v. Beware of the dog. Caesar was warned to beware the Ides of March: look out, look out for, watch out for, take warning, guard against, take care, take precautions, be on the alert, be careful, be cautious, be wary, take heed, mind. —**Ant.** ignore, pay no attention to.

bewilder v. The motorist was bewildered by the conflicting road signs: confuse, puzzle, perplex, bemuse, baffle, befuddle, mix up, muddle, addle, disconcert, nonplus, mystify, stupefy, fluster. —**Ant.** enlighten, inform, instruct, edify, educate, straighten out, advise, set straight, awaken.

bewildered adj. The odd question bewildered us: confused, disoriented, perplexed, puzzled, baffled, addled, dumbfounded, muddled, mystified, nonplussed.

bewilderment n. Imagine my bewilderment when the plane landed in the wrong city!: confusion, puzzlement, perplexity, mystification, frustration. —**Ant.** enlightenment, edification.

bewitch v. **1.** Half the village accused Goodwife Osborne of having bewitched the cow: put under a spell, cast a spell on, Informal jinx, spook; bedevil. **2.** Shirley Temple bewitched a generation of moviegoers: charm, enchant, entrance, captivate, fascinate, beguile, delight, enrapture, Slang turn on. —**Ant.** 2 repulse; repel, disgust, displease, Slang turn off.

bewitchment n. Her prowess on the stage was a form of bewitchment: witchery, enchantment, entrancement, possession.

beyond adv. Beyond the village lay the forest: farther, further, past, away from, after, apart from, behind, besides, clear of, more remote, outside, yonder, on the other side, over there, out of range.

bias n. **1.** Some people have a bias against foreigners. The pianist has a bias for Chopin: prejudice, leaning, inclination, bent, predilection, proneness, propensity, proclivity, tendency, feeling; fixed idea, preconceived idea, preconception, narrow view, slant, one-sidedness, unfairness, narrow-mindedness; bigotry, intolerance; partiality. **2.** The dress was cut on the bias: angle, slant, diagonal line. —v. **3.** Don't let his insults bias you against her: prejudice, predispose, sway. —**Ant.** 1 fairness, impartiality, dispassionateness, objectivity; open-mindedness, tolerance.

Bible n. **1.** We studied the Bible in Sunday school: the Holy Scriptures (Hebrew and Christian); the Scriptures, Holy Writ, the Good Book, the Book, Gospel. **2.** bible. To spell well, let a dictionary be your bible: authority, guide; guidebook, reference book, handbook, manual.

bicker v. The children constantly bicker over their toys: squabble, wrangle, quarrel, argue, spat, spar, dispute, haggle, disagree, fight. —**Ant.** agree, concur, accord, be of one mind; assent, consent, concede, acquiesce.

bicycle n. **1.** It's dangerous to ride a bicycle on the highway: bike, two-wheeler, cycle, moped. —v. **2.** In Europe, many workers bicycle to work: bike, cycle, ride.

bid v. **1.** The queen bids all her subjects to pay the tax. I bid you join our party: command, order, direct, require, charge, call upon, enjoin, insist, instruct, demand, ordain; invite, summon, ask, request, call, beckon. **2.** He bade us farewell: tell, say, wish, greet. **3.** The antique dealer bid $200 for the rug. The aircraft company bid for the Air Force contract: offer, proffer, tender, propose; submit an offer. —n. **4.** What was the highest bid for the painting? Every senior will receive a bid to the prom: offer, offering, proposal, bidding; invitation. **5.** McGov-

ern's bid for the presidency failed: try, attempt, effort, endeavor. **—Ant.** 1 forbid, prohibit, disallow, ban, bar.

bidding *n.* **1.** *The dog came at his master's bidding:* command, order, request, behest, demand, direction, charge, injunction, instruction, mandate, dictate; summons, summoning, invitation, bid, call, beck. **2.** *The bidding at the auction reached $500 for one antique chair:* offer, offering, offers, proffering, tendering, proposal.

bide *v.* **1.** *Bide with us awhile:* remain, wait, stay, tarry, linger, abide, dwell. **2.** *Aunt Mary could never bide children:* endure, put up with, suffer, tolerate, stand. **—Ant.** 1 go, depart, leave. 2 resist, rebel against, abominate.

big *adj.* **1.** *Brazil is a big country. Farmers expect a big corn crop this year. Wrestlers have to be big:* large, huge, enormous, vast, immense, gigantic, mammoth, great, colossal, monumental, grandiose; considerable, sizable, substantial, abundant, ample, prodigious; strapping, husky, bulky, hulking, heavy, massive. **2.** *The president has a big decision to make. Clark Gable was a big star in his day:* important, vital, major, consequential, significant, momentous, weighty; prominent, leading, eminent, notable, top, great, chief, main, prime, head, high. **3.** *No one likes his big talk:* pretentious, arrogant, pompous, boastful, conceited, bragging, haughty. **4.** *Your charitable contribution shows that you have a big heart. It takes a big man to admit his mistakes:* generous, magnanimous, benevolent, liberal, gracious, kind; noble, humane, honorable, just, princely, high-minded, chivalrous, heroic, great. **5.** *You're a big boy now:* mature, grown, grown-up, adult. **—Ant.** 1 little, small, diminutive, microscopic, wee, tiny, petite, minute, miniature, bantam, pygmy, dwarf, pocket-sized, teeny, teeny-weeny, itsy-bitsy. 2 unimportant, insignificant, inconsequential, minor; low-ranking, subordinate, unknown. 3 ordinary, commonplace, modest, humble, unassuming, meek, unpretentious, mild, unpresuming, reserved, restrained, diffident. 4 stingy, cheap, petty, dishonorable, unjust, unchivalrous; ignoble, inhumane, unkind, cruel. 5 little, young, immature.

big-hearted *adj.* *The concert season looked hopeless, but a big-hearted donor came to our rescue:* generous, unselfish, liberal, open-handed, free-handed, benevolent, unstinting, magnanimous, charitable, beneficent, open-hearted; bounteous, bountiful, lavish, prodigal, princely, handsome. **—Ant.** miserly, niggardly, stingy, tight-fisted, penny-pinching.

bigot *n.* *Rejecting some of the applicants proved he was a bigot:* racist, prejudiced person, jingoist, segregationist, *Slang* redneck.

bigoted *adj.* *Bigoted people can never bring themselves to admit that the other fellow might be right, too:* prejudiced, intolerant, biased, narrow-minded, closed-minded. **—Ant.** unbigoted, unprejudiced, tolerant, unbiased, broad-minded, open-minded.

bigotry *n.* *At one time or another, every race and religion has been the object of bigotry:* prejudice, intolerance, bias, narrow-mindedness, closed-mindedness; racism, discrimination, unfairness. **—Ant.** tolerance, open-mindedness, broad-mindedness.

big shot *n.* *The board of directors is composed of big shots from the world of business: Slang* wheel, big gun, big deal, wheeler-dealer, bigwig, big cheese, fat cat, VIP, high-muck-a-muck; mogul, nabob, magnate, dignitary, tycoon, somebody, name, personage. **—Ant.** nobody, nothing, cipher, nebbish, underling, minion, follower.

bilge *n.* *His speech was full of the same old bilge about big government gobbling up the little fellow:* nonsense, drivel, rubbish, stuff and nonsense, foolishness, gibberish, jabber; *Slang* bosh, bull, hogwash, twaddle, jabberwocky, balderdash, tosh, hooey, bunk, malarkey, piffle, humbug, baloney, rot, horsefeathers, tripe.

bilious *adj.* **1.** *That hot dog gave me a bilious feeling:* sick, queasy, nauseous, green at the gills, sickly, sickening; greenish, bilelike. **2.** *The boss was in a bilious mood today:* irritable, peevish, ill-tempered, ill-humored, angry, grumpy, nasty, cranky, crabby, cross, grouchy, petulant, testy, touchy, snappish, short-tempered, cantankerous, huffy, out of sorts. **—Ant.** 1 good, fine, healthy; attractive. 2 happy, pleasant, good-tempered, amicable, genial, cordial, gentle, mild, warm; agreeable, sympathetic, compliant, winsome.

bilk *v.* *The lad was bilked out of his inheritance:* swindle, cheat, defraud, victimize, trick, dupe, deceive, bamboozle, hoodwink, fleece, gyp, rook, gull, cozen, *Slang* take, rip off.

bill *n.* **1.** *Did you pay the phone bill?:* statement, invoice, account, chit, charge, charges, fee, reckoning, tally. **2.** *A dollar bill doesn't buy much nowadays:* banknote, treasury note, treasury bill, greenback, silver certificate. **3.** *How many bills are before Congress this session?:* piece of legislation, proposal; measure, act; law, statute, regulation, ordinance, decree. **4.** *On the wall was a sign reading "Post no bills":* poster, placard, advertisement, bulletin; handbill, leaflet, circular, brochure. **5.** *The Palace Theater used to have the best vaudeville bill. The waiter brought us a bill of fare:* program, schedule, list, agenda, card, roster, calendar, catalog, inventory, ticket, register, docket.

billet *n.* **1.** *The town fathers agreed to find billets for the soldiers:* quarters, lodging, lodgment, residence, dwelling, *Slang* digs. **2.** *He found a billet as a typist at the auto factory:* job, post, situation, berth, position, office, place, appointment. **—***v.* **3.** *Headquarters said to billet the soldiers with the townspeople:* lodge, house, quarter, put up, domicile.

billfold *n.* See WALLET.

billow *n.* **1.** *The sailboat was tossed by the billows:* wave, swell, breaker; surge, crest. **2.** *A billow of steam rose from the basement:* wave, cloud, surge. **—***v.* **3.** *The sails billowed in the wind:* swell, puff up, balloon, belly; surge, roll. **—Ant.** 1 trough. 3 deflate, collapse.

bind *v.* **1.** *Bind those boxes together with a*

rope. *Bind the layers of wood together with glue:* fasten, secure, tie, tie up, truss, gird, strap, rope, lash, hitch; join, attach, affix, stick, glue, paste. **2.** *The doctor bound the wound with gauze. The book was bound in red leather:* bandage, swathe; cover, encase, wrap. **3.** *The contract binds the company to pay royalties to the inventor:* obligate, require, necessitate, oblige, compel, coerce, force, prescribe. **4.** *The seamstress bound the hem of the dress with a ruffle:* border, edge, trim, rim, frame, fringe. **5.** *This tight jacket binds under the arms:* confine, encumber, cramp; chafe. **—Ant.** 1 untie, unbind, unfasten, unloose, loosen; free, set free, separate. 2 unbandage; unwrap, uncover. 3 free, release, exempt, absolve.

binding *adj.* **1.** *Management and the union reached a binding agreement:* mandatory, necessary, obligatory, incumbent on, required. **2.** *The binding cables couldn't be released:* restraining, confining, constraining, limiting, tying. **—n. 3.** *The book was given a new binding:* wrapper, adhesive, fastener. **—Ant.** 1 optional, discretionary, unforced. 2 free, noncompulsory.

binge *n. He went on a three-day binge and his friends couldn't locate him: Slang* drunken spree, spree, bender, blast, jag, fling, tear, bust, toot; carousal, orgy, bacchanalia.

birth *n.* **1.** *The child's birth occurred at 2 A.M. The mother had a difficult birth:* being born; childbirth, bearing, delivery, parturition, confinement. **2.** *The impostor claimed to be of royal birth:* descent, ancestry, family, parentage, extraction, lineage, derivation, breeding, genealogy, blood, stock, strain, origin, beginnings, background. **3.** *The birth of jazz took place in New Orleans:* start, beginning, commencement, origin, source, inception, genesis, emergence. **—Ant.** 1 death; miscarriage, abortion. 3 conclusion, finale, end, finish, death.

bisect *v. The new highway bisects the town:* cut in two, cut in half, divide in two, split, split down the middle; intersect, cross.

bit *n.* **1.** *The glass broke into bits:* small piece, piece, fragment, particle, smithereen, chip. **2.** *A bit of carrot fell on the floor:* small amount, trace, scrap, morsel, speck, dab, pinch, whit, iota, mite, smidgen, trifle, crumb, shred, snip, paring, shaving, grain, granule, drop, droplet, sprinkling, dollop. **3.** *Stay a bit longer:* short while, little while, short time, spell, brief period, moment. **—Ant.** 1 whole, entity, aggregation. 2 lot, mass, hunk, block, heap, the lion's share. 3 long time.

bitchy *adj. Maybe it is true, but it was a bitchy thing to say:* spiteful, mean, vicious, malicious, malevolent, nasty, vindictive, cruel, wicked, heartless, hateful, backbiting, *Slang* catty.

bite *v.* **1.** *Be careful, that dog bites! A mosquito just bit me:* seize with the teeth, eat into, nip, gnash, champ, gnaw, nibble; sting, pierce, prick. **2.** *The tires bit into the snow and we were on our way:* take hold, dig, grip. **—n. 3.** *I just want a bite of that pie:* small portion, small piece, mouthful, bit, speck, morsel, taste, scrap, crumb, shred, dab, snip. **4.** *The dog gave the*

mail carrier a nasty bite. He was scratching an insect bite:* tooth wound, nip; sting, prick. **5.** *The cold bite of the wind drove us indoors:* sting, stinging, nip, smart.

biting *adj.* **1.** *The biting cold froze the sailor's hands:* stinging, piercing, sharp, harsh, smarting, nipping, cutting, bitter. **2.** *She loves to make biting remarks:* sarcastic, trenchant, mordant, sharp-tongued, cutting, stinging, piercing; caustic, withering, scathing. **—Ant.** 1 mild. 2 pleasant, gentle, soothing, genial, flattering, complimentary.

bitter *adj.* **1.** *Vinegar has a bitter taste:* sour, acid, acerbic, acrid, tart, sharp, caustic, biting, stinging, harsh, astringent. **2.** *The children shouldn't be outdoors in this bitter cold:* stinging, smarting, piercing, sharp, biting, severe. **3.** *Flunking math was a bitter blow to the boy's pride:* grievous, cruel, harsh, painful, wretched, distressing. **4.** *Being left out of his father's will made him bitter. The brothers had a bitter argument:* resentful, sullen, morose, spiteful, crabbed, sour, rancorous, scornful, mean, angry. **—Ant.** 1 sweet, sugary, saccharine, cloying; bland, mild, insipid, flat, dull. 2 mild, gentle, balmy. 3 happy, joyful, delightful, pleasant, gay; fortunate, lucky. 4 grateful, thankful, appreciative; friendly, amiable, genial, pleasant.

bitterness *n.* **1.** *The bitterness of the wild apples passed belief:* tartness, acidity, brackishness, astringency, brininess. **2.** *Her friend's ingratitude led to bitterness:* painfulness, resentment, anguish, rancor, acrimony, asperity, mordancy, venom, virulence.

bizarre *adj. Children like to wear bizarre costumes at Halloween:* strange, fantastic, weird, queer, freakish, grotesque, outlandish, odd, unusual, *Slang* kooky, kinky. **—Ant.** subdued, ordinary.

blabber *n.* **1.** *It was hard to concentrate with blabber on all sides:* chatter, jabber, prattle, drivel, palaver, babble, gab; *Slang* gabble, twaddle, blather, blah-blah, gobbledegook, mumbo-jumbo, gas, bull. **—v. 2.** *They never get tired of blabbering about their hard life: Slang* gab, prattle, prate, blab, yak, blather, gibber, gabble.

blabbermouth *n. He's such a blabbermouth you daren't tell him anything:* gossip, gossiper, chatterbox, scandalmonger, gossipmonger, rumormonger, tattletale, busybody, talebearer, chatterer, informer, prattler, prater, jabberer, gabber, quidnunc; *Slang* blabber, bigmouth, liverlip.

black *adj.* **1.** *A black cat crossed our path:* coal-black, jet, raven, ebony, sable, inky, swarthy. **2.** *It was a cold, black night:* dark, murky, lightless, stygian, sunless, moonless, unilluminated, unlighted. **3.** *Often* **Black.** *Jackie Robinson was the first black major-league baseball player:* Negro, colored, dark-skinned. **4.** *Cynics have a black outlook on the state of the world:* gloomy, grim, dismal, somber, dim, calamitous. **5.** *The bus driver stopped short and gave the pedestrian a black look:* sullen, hostile, dark, furious, angry, threatening. **6.** *The villain had a black heart:* evil, wicked, bad, nefarious. **—n. 7.** *Black* *is the most somber color:* ebony, jet, raven, sable. **8.** Often **Black.** *Martin Luther King, Jr., was the first American Black to win the Nobel prize:* Negro, Afro-American, black person, colored person, person of color. **—Ant.** 1 white, snowwhite, chalky, whitish. 2 bright, light, sunny, moonlit, illuminated, lighted, well-lighted, lit. 3 white, Caucasian. 4 optimistic, bright, happy, gay. 5 friendly, amiable, amicable, congenial, warm, pleased. 6 good, virtuous, wholesome, righteous, moral, honorable, upright, exemplary, pure. 7 white. 8 white, white person, Caucasian.

blackball *v. He never knew why they blackballed him from the club:* ban, ostracize, banish, outlaw, proscribe, blacklist, boycott, exclude, debar, turn down, reject, vote against; snub, cut, cold-shoulder, send to Coventry. **—Ant.** welcome, invite, entice, ask, entreat, bid.

blacken *v.* **1.** *The commandos blackened their faces with charcoal:* make black, become black; darken, black. **2.** *Don't blacken my name by spreading rumors:* defame, dishonor, defile, disgrace, discredit, denigrate, stigmatize, tarnish, sully, stain, smear, befoul, besmirch, revile, slander, vilify, libel. **—Ant.** 1 lighten, whiten; clear. 2 exalt, honor, credit, uplift, eulogize, praise.

blackguard *n. In the old play, the blackguard was outwitted by the hero:* villain, scoundrel, knave, rogue, rascal, cad, scamp, miscreant, rat, *Slang* louse, bastard, SOB. **—Ant.** hero; gentleman.

blacklist *v. Communists were blacklisted from working in the motion-picture industry:* blackball, bar, debar, shut out, lock out, ban, preclude, exclude, reject, ostracize, shun. **—Ant.** welcome, accept, invite, meet with open arms.

blackmail *n.* **1.** *For not turning the evidence over to the police, she demanded $10,000 blackmail from him:* hush money, extortion, shakedown, payoff, tribute. **—v. 2.** *Threatening a scandal, he blackmailed the firm into paying him for keeping quiet:* extort, shake down, demand a payoff; threaten, force, coerce, *Slang* squeeze.

blade *n.* **1.** *The blade needs sharpening:* cutting edge, cutter; (*variously*) sword, knife, scalpel, razor; skate runner, sled runner. **2.** *The boy chewed on a blade of grass:* leaf, frond, needle, switch.

blah *n.* **1.** *It was the same old blah you've heard a hundred times before:* nonsense, bunkum, humbug, hooey, bosh, blather, eyewash, balderdash, twaddle, gibberish, hot air, guff, claptrap. **—adj. 2.** *Everyone seems to feel blah on Monday morning. The play was terribly earnest but rather blah:* lifeless, listless, nothing; tedious, dull, pedestrian, bland, dreary, characterless, uninteresting, unimaginative, humdrum, monotonous. **—Ant.** 2 vivacious, energetic, alive; trenchant, gripping, dynamic.

blame *v.* **1.** *The police blame the accident on the driver who was attempting to pass. I don't blame you for being angry:* hold responsible, accuse, charge; fault, find fault with, reproach,

reprove, censure, condemn, rebuke, castigate, criticize, disapprove. **—n. 2.** *The accountant accepted the blame for the error. Mother's going to put all the blame on me:* responsibility, accountability, liability, guilt, onus, fault, culpability, burden; accusation, charge, recrimination; reproach, censure, condemnation, reproof, rebuke, criticism, denunciation, castigation, remonstrance. **—Ant.** 1 exonerate, vindicate, absolve, acquit, clear, exculpate; excuse, justify, forgive; praise, laud, acclaim, commend, compliment, approve of. 2 exoneration, vindication, absolution; excuse, alibi; praise, acclaim, commendation, compliment, congratulations, tribute, credit, honor, glory, distinction.

blameless *adj. The grand jury found the building contractor blameless. She's always had a blameless reputation:* not responsible, not at fault, guiltless, not guilty, innocent, unblamable, clear, inculpable; irreproachable, spotless, unspotted, unsullied, untainted, unstained, unblemished, uncorrupted, unimpeachable. **—Ant.** responsible, at fault, guilty, implicated, culpable; sullied, tainted, censurable, reprovable.

blanch *v. Blanch celery by keeping it in a dark place. He blanched with fright:* whiten, turn pale; bleach, fade, lighten. **—Ant.** darken, blacken; brighten, color, stain, dye.

bland *adj.* **1.** *They put him on a bland diet. What a bland movie!:* uninteresting, unexciting, dull, uninspiring, unstimulating, tedious, tiresome, monotonous, humdrum, flat, vapid, prosaic, *Slang* blah, nothing. **2.** *These bland spring days are meant for daydreaming:* mild, balmy, calm, calming, tranquil, quiet, moderate, temperate, unruffled, even, smooth, soothing, benign, peaceful, peaceable, untroubled, nonirritating. **—Ant.** 1 interesting, exciting, electrifying, sensational, thrilling, astonishing, stimulating, inspiring, stirring, rousing, overpowering, moving. 2 turbulent, tempestuous, excited, volatile, explosive; harsh, severe, rough, irritating, annoying.

blandishment Often **blandishments** *n. Even her blandishments couldn't win him over:* flattery, cajolery, coaxing, wheedling, inveiglement, ingratiation, blarney, sweet talk. **—Ant.** intimidation, threats, scolding, insults, bullying, browbeating.

blank *adj.* **1.** *Take a blank sheet of paper and write your name at the top. Never sign a blank check:* not written on, clean, unmarked, unused, not filled out, not filled in; empty, vacant, clear, plain. **2.** *The stranger returned my greeting with a blank look:* vacant, empty, inexpressive, expressionless, unrecognizing, inane, uninterested, thoughtless, dull, vacuous, hollow, void. **3.** *The invalid spent long blank days alone:* empty, idle, meaningless, futile, wasted, unrewarding, useless, worthless, valueless, inconsequential, insignificant, profitless, unprofitable, fruitless, unproductive. **—n. 4.** *Fill in the blanks to complete the word puzzle. My memory is a blank!:* empty space, space, void, gap; emptiness, hollowness, vacuum, vacancy. **—Ant.** 1

marked, filled out, filled in, full, completed. **2** thoughtful, interested, meaningful, expressive, intelligent, alert, sharp. **3** full, filled, busy; rewarding, valuable, worthwhile, useful, meaningful, significant, consequential, profitable, fruitful, productive.

blanket n. **1.** *Put another blanket on the bed:* comforter, coverlet, quilt; throw, Afghan. **2.** *A blanket of snow covered the ground:* covering, cover, coating, coat, mantle, carpet, overlay, film, veneer. —v. **3.** *Confetti blanketed the ballroom floor:* cover, carpet, coat, overlay, cloak.

blare v. *The loudspeaker blared the music over the park. The horns blared:* sound loudly, blast, resound, scream, bellow, roar; trumpet, make a fanfare, peal, honk. —**Ant.** mute, stifle; hum, murmur, whisper.

blarney n. *He was a ladies' man with quite a line of blarney:* flattery, fawning, overpraise, honeyed words, sweet words, line; cajolery, wheedling, inveigling, coaxing, blandishments; fanciful talk, exaggeration, overstatement, hyperbole, stories, fibs, *Slang* hot air, pitch, snow job, *Informal* spiel. —**Ant.** truth, frankness, candidness, guilelessness, directness.

blasé adj. *Don't be so blasé about your good fortune:* bored, unexcited, unenthusiastic, unconcerned, uninterested, indifferent, insouciant, nonchalant, world-weary, spiritless, unmovable, apathetic; jaded, surfeited, gorged, full, glutted, saturated, satisfied. —**Ant.** enthusiastic, excited, interested, concerned, spirited.

blasphemous adj. *"God is dead" is a blasphemous statement:* irreverent, profane, sacrilegious, irreligious, impious, ungodly, godless. —**Ant.** reverent, religious, pious, godly.

blasphemy n. *Taking the name of the Lord in vain is pure blasphemy:* profanity, profanation, irreverence, sacrilege, impiety, impiousness; cursing, swearing. —**Ant.** prayer, praying; veneration, reverence, adoration; blessing, benediction, thanksgiving.

blast n. **1.** *A blast of wind shook the house:* gust, gale, surge, burst, rush, roar. **2.** *The blast of the factory whistle could be heard for miles:* loud noise, blare, scream, roar, bellow, bleat, shriek, toot, honk, peal. **3.** *The blast completely demolished the building:* explosion, detonation, report, burst, boom, discharge, eruption. —v. **4.** *Music blasted from the little radio:* sound loudly, blare, resound, scream, shriek, roar, bellow, honk, peal, toot. **5.** *The construction crew blasted a tunnel through the mountain. Heavy bombers blasted the enemy positions:* explode, dynamite, torpedo, bomb, shell; burst, level, blow up, bore.

blatant adj. **1.** *There's a blatant error in this bill:* obvious, unmistakable, clear, conspicuous, prominent, glaring, overt, flagrant. **2.** *He's so blatant no one wants anything to do with him:* loud, obtrusive, offensive, crude, uncouth, gross, crass, coarse, vulgar, undignified, indelicate, cheap, tawdry, brazen, ill-mannered, unrefined, tasteless, unsubtle, ungenteel, unpolished; noisy, blaring, clamorous, harsh, ear-splitting, deafening, piercing. —**Ant.** incon-

spicuous, subtle. **1** unnoticeable, hidden. **2** unobtrusive, agreeable, acquiescent, refined, genteel, dignified, delicate, well-mannered, tasteful, in good taste, cultured, polished, high- class, *Informal* classy; quiet, subdued, soft.

blaze n. **1.** *The ice skaters huddled around the blaze of the bonfire:* fire, flame, flames, conflagration. **2.** *The blaze of sunlight on the water was breathtaking:* glow, gleam, shimmer, glitter, flash, shine, glare, flare, beam, ray; radiance, brilliance, brightness, effulgence, resplendence. **3.** *The troublemaker stalked out in a blaze of anger:* outburst, burst, blast, flash, rush; eruption, outbreak, torrent, explosion. —v. **4.** *The fire blazed all night:* burn brightly, burn, flame. **5.** *Her eyes blazed with happiness:* glow, gleam, shine, glisten, glitter, shimmer, be resplendent, be bright, be brilliant; flash, beam, glare, flame, flare.

bleach v. *The sun bleached the lifeguard's hair:* whiten, blanch, lighten, fade, make pale, wash out. —**Ant.** blacken, darken; color, stain, dye.

bleak adj. **1.** *Northern Scotland is bleak and damp:* bare, barren, windswept, weather-beaten, desolate. **2.** *The world situation seems bleak. Saturday was a bleak wintry day:* gloomy, dreary, dismal, grim, depressing, cheerless; unpromising, distressing, somber, forbidding. **3.** *A bleak wind blew from the north:* bitter, raw, cold, icy, piercing, biting, nipping, frosty, chill, wintry. —**Ant.** **1** covered with vegetation, wooded, forested; sheltered, protected, warm, cheerful, comfortable. **2** bright, cheerful, cheery, sunny; pleasant, genial; promising, encouraging. **3** mild, balmy, soft, warm, springlike.

blemish n. **1.** *Because of the blemish in the wood, the table was half price. A pimple is a skin blemish:* flaw, imperfection, defect, disfigurement; spot, blotch, blot, mark, stain, taint, *Slang* zit. —v. **2.** *The one loss blemished the team's otherwise perfect record:* flaw, mar, spoil, tarnish, sully, taint, stain, smudge, smirch; spot, mark, blot, blotch, blur, disfigure. —**Ant.** **1** perfection, improvement; decoration, ornament, complement, refinement. **2** perfect, improve, complete, refine, enhance; purify, purge, reclaim, restore, rectify, correct.

blend v. **1.** *Blue and yellow blend to make green:* mix, merge, combine, unite, mingle, intermingle; fuse, compound, melt together, incorporate, coalesce, amalgamate. **2.** *The drapes blend with the rug:* harmonize, go well, complement. —n. **3.** *Mocha icing is a blend of coffee and chocolate:* mixture, mix, combination, merger, mergence, mingling, concoction; compound, amalgam, fusion. —**Ant.** **1** separate, divide. **2** clash. **3** separation, division.

bless v. **1.** *The bishop blessed the new chapel:* make holy, consecrate, sanctify, hallow, dedicate, give benediction; anoint, baptize. **2.** *Fate blessed him with great talent:* favor, oblige, honor, benefit, endow, bestow, ordain, grace, give. **3.** *God bless you:* guard, protect, watch over, support. —**Ant.** **1** curse, anathematize. **2** curse, condemn, disfavor; handicap, harm, injure.

blessed *adj.* **1.** *He prayed to the Blessed Virgin:* revered, holy, hallowed, sacred, sanctified, consecrated, adored, venerated. **2.** *The birth of a baby is truly a blessed event:* joyous, joyful, happy, felicitous, blissful, wonderful. **3.** *Having a healthy body and a sound mind, I consider myself twice-blessed:* fortunate, favored, lucky, endowed, graced. **—Ant.** 1 cursed, accursed, anathematized. 2 unhappy, sad, unfortunate, grievous. 3 condemned, deprived.

blessing *n.* **1.** *The rabbi officiated at the blessing of the new temple. Do you say a blessing before meals?:* consecration, sanctification, dedication, hallowing, invocation, benediction; grace, prayer of thanks, thanksgiving. **2.** *He knew the blessings of a happy childhood:* advantage, benefit, good, good fortune, favor, gift, bounty, gain, profit. **3.** *The engaged couple had the blessing of their families:* approval, consent, concurrence, permission, leave, support, sanction, backing, good wishes, favor, regard. **—Ant.** curse. 1 imprecation, malediction, anathema. 2 deprivation, misfortune, disadvantage, detriment, drawback, harm, injury, damage. 3 disapproval, objection, disapprobation, condemnation, denunciation, censure, reproof; ill will, disfavor.

blight *n.* **1.** *A mysterious blight destroyed the corn crop:* plant disease, pestilence; *(loosely)* dry rot, rot, rust, fungus, mildew, decay. **2.** *Greed is a blight on humanity:* affliction, cancer, curse, plague, scourge, pestilence, canker, contamination, corruption, *Slang* pox. **—v. 3.** *Lack of education blighted his chances of success:* spoil, ruin, wreck, kill, destroy, smash, demolish, blast, crush; wither, shrivel, cripple, thwart, rot, injure, harm, frustrate. **—Ant.** 2 blessing, good, favor, service, boon, bounty. 3 benefit, help, aid, improve, better, advance, further, foster, promote.

blind *adj.* **1.** *Helen Keller was born deaf and blind:* sightless, unable to see, without vision, unseeing. **2.** *The teacher was blind to the fact that some students were cheating. We must not be blind to the suffering of others:* ignorant, unaware, unknowing, unobserving, unobserv-ant, incognizant, uncomprehending, uncon-scious of, unenlightened, unseeing, obtuse; unmindful, unfeeling, dull, insensitive, unper-ceptive or imperceptive, undiscerning, indifferent, neglectful, inattentive, heedless, unconcerned, uninterested, insouciant. **3.** *The argument put him in a blind rage:* uncontrolled, uncontrollable, unthinking, mindless, unreasonable, irrational, senseless, insane. **4.** *A car entered the highway from the blind drive:* hidden, concealed, obscure, unnoticeable, unnoticed. **—n. 5.** *The blinds keep the sun out:* shade, sun shield. **6.** *The duck hunters fired from the blind. The nightclub was just a blind for the gambling casino:* cover, screen, front, subterfuge, disguise, masquerade, camouflage; dodge, ruse, pretext, deception, *Informal* smoke screen. **—Ant.** 1 sighted, seeing. 2 aware, conscious, knowledgeable, observant, cognizant, alive to, awake to; mindful, sensitive, discerning, attentive, heedful,

concerned. 3 controlled, controllable, rational. 4 in plain sight, obvious, noticeable, open.

blindly *adv. She blindly searched among the coats:* indiscriminately, confusedly, aimlessly, at random, heedlessly, instinctively, purposelessly, wildly.

blink *v.* **1.** *He bet me he could hold my gaze without blinking:* wink, nictitate, squint, bat the eyes; waver, vacillate, falter, flinch. **2.** *In the distance an airport beacon blinked:* twinkle, flash, flicker, sparkle, glimmer, shine, shimmer.

bliss *n. Being home again was pure bliss:* happiness, joy, ecstasy, delight, rapture, glee, gladness, luxury, heaven, paradise; exhilaration, exaltation, jubilation. **—Ant.** misery, agony, anguish, torment, distress; sorrow, sadness, grief, unhappiness; dejection, depression, gloom.

blissful *adj. All was blissful on their honeymoon:* happy, felicitous, delightful, rapturous, joyful, ecstatic, euphoric.

blister *n. Not wearing gloves, she developed a blister:* sore, boil, cyst, abscess, canker, pimple, pustule, ulcer.

blithe *adj.* **1.** *The child had a wonderfully blithe personality:* joyous, merry, happy, cheery, cheerful, gay, sunny, radiant, glad, gleeful, jolly, jovial, mirthful; carefree, light-hearted, frolicking, debonair, sprightly, jaunty, lively, ebullient, exaltant, airy, blithesome. **2.** *Don't act with such a blithe disregard of others:* heedless, careless, thoughtless, unmindful, insensitive, unconscious, uncaring, unfeeling, indifferent, unconcerned, blind, casual, inconsiderate. **—Ant.** 1 sad, unhappy, sorrowful, dejected, depressed, gloomy, cheerless, glum, morose, dour, melancholy, heavy-hearted. 2 thoughtful, considerate, concerned, solicitous, obliging, kindhearted.

blizzard *n. The blizzard brought 60-mile-an-hour winds and 2 feet of snow:* snowstorm, tempest, blow, squall, blast, gale, snow blast, snow squall, flurry, snowfall, winter storm.

bloat *v. The cow's stomach was bloated from eating the wet fodder:* distend, swell, puff up, expand, dilate, inflate, blow up, balloon, enlarge. **—Ant.** shrink, contract, shrivel.

bloc *n. The farm bloc greatly influenced the election:* faction, group, wing, body, clique, ring, cabal; alliance, coalition, combination, combine, union.

block *n.* **1.** *The garage was made of concrete blocks:* brick, bar, cube, square. **2.** *The filibuster was a block to passage of the bill:* obstruction, barrier, obstacle, blockade, bar, impediment; hindrance, interference, blockage. **—v. 3.** *Snowdrifts blocked our progress:* obstruct, blockade, bar, choke, stop up, jam; hinder, impede, check, halt, prevent, thwart. **4.** *Hats cleaned and blocked:* shape, form, mold; reshape, re-form. **—Ant.** 3 clear, unblock, unbar, open, free; advance, further, forward, promote, foster, facilitate.

blockade *n. Ships could not get past the blockade to supply their allies:* block, blockage, roadblock, barrier, barricade, impediment, hindrance, obstruction, hurdle, stoppage, bar, restriction, check, *Mil.* checkpoint; dam, fortification, stockade, dike, earthworks, levee, parapet.

blockhead *n. Nobody but a blockhead would invest in that stock:* fool, dunce, nitwit, nincompoop, simpleton, booby, klutz, mushhead, noodlehead, *Ger.* dummkopf, dum-dum, *Yiddish* yutz, featherbrain, dolt, dummy, harebrain, jackass, fathead; imbecile, moron.

blond or **blonde** *adj.* **1.** *He has blond hair and blue eyes:* light-colored, yellowish, yellow, gold, golden, flaxen. **2.** *The Nordic peoples tend to be blond rather than dark:* fair, fair-skinned, light-complexioned, light, pale, fair-haired. —*n.* **3.** *Blond is a fashionable color for furniture:* light tan, yellowish tan, whitish brown. **4.** *Do gentlemen really prefer blondes?:* blond-haired woman; person having fair skin and hair. —**Ant.** brunette, brunet. 1 dark, black. 2 dark, dark-skinned, olive-complexioned.

blood *n.* **1.** *The boxer had blood running down his nose:* life fluid, vital fluid, gore. **2.** *Tolerance of others is the very blood of democracy:* lifeblood, source, vital principle, vital force, vitality. **3.** *He's a terror when his blood is up:* temper, passion, temperament, spirit. **4.** *The king must marry a woman of noble blood:* extraction, lineage, descent, ancestry, heritage, stock, family, family line, birth, consanguinity.

bloodshed *n. War has always been an excuse for unconscionable bloodshed:* carnage, killing, slaying, spilling of blood, slaughter, massacre, pogrom, bloodletting, butchery, manslaughter, murder, mass murder, blood feud, blood bath, gore.

bloodthirsty *adj. The bloodthirsty killer was hunted by police in seven states:* murderous, homicidal, savage, inhuman, brutal, murdering, barbarous, ruthless, bestial, bloody, cutthroat, sanguinary, sanguineous.

bloody *adj.* **1.** *Both boxers were bloody by the end of the round:* bleeding, bloodstained, wounded, ensanguined, gory. **2.** *The bloody reign of the tyrant ended abruptly:* savage, murderous, cruel, bloodthirsty, savage, barbarous, ferocious, fierce, homicidal, murderous, ruthless.

bloom *n.* **1.** *This plant has one white bloom. The dogwood had a heavy bloom this spring:* blossom, flower, bud; flowerage, blossoming, florescence. **2.** *Her face shone with the bloom of youth:* glow, flush, rosiness, radiance, luster, shine, beauty, vigor, zest, strength, prime, heyday; flowering, blossoming, flourishing. —*v.* **3.** *The century plant blooms only once in its lifetime:* flower, blossom, burgeon, sprout, bear fruit, fructify. **4.** *Musical talent usually blooms at an early age:* flourish, thrive, fare well, prosper, succeed, bear fruit, germinate, burgeon; develop, grow, flare. —**Ant.** 2 pallor, grayness, wanness, ashenness; decay, decadence, blight. 3 wither, die; be sterile. 4 wither, fade, fail, wane.

blooper *n. Everyone laughed when the speaker made a blooper:* mistake, error, blunder, lapse, slip, gaffe; *Slang* goof, booboo, fluff, bobble, boner, screwup, botch.

blossom *n.* **1.** *Orange blossoms have a lovely odor:* flower, bloom. —*v.* **2.** *Did the wisteria blossom this year?:* flower, bloom, burgeon. **3.** *Their romance was blossoming:* bloom, grow, develop; flourish, thrive, burgeon, progress. —**Ant.** 2 wither, die, be sterile. 3 wither, fade, fail, diminish.

blot *n.* **1.** *Will that ink blot come out?:* blotch, spot, splotch, smudge, smear, stain, mark, discoloration. **2.** *The one poor grade was a blot on the student's record:* blemish, flaw, blotch, taint, stain, stigma, bad mark, smirch. —*v.* **3.** *The ink blotted on the paper:* smear, smudge, splotch, blotch; spot, stain, besmirch. **4.** *Blot the wet ink with a clean blotter:* soak up, absorb, take up; remove, dry. —**Ant.** 2 credit, distinction, honor, feather in one's cap.

blotch *n. The measles gave him red blotches all over his face:* spot, splotch, mark, blot.

blow *n.* **1.** *The fighter was punch-drunk from too many blows on the head:* hit, knock, punch, smack, whack, clout, thump, sock, wallop, box, jab, bash, crack, bang, belt, cuff. **2.** *The failure of his business was a terrible blow to him:* shock, jolt, upset, disappointment, rebuff, reversal, detriment; tragedy, disaster, calamity, misfortune, catastrophe, affliction. **3.** *The weather forecast says to prepare for a big blow:* gale, squall, tempest, windstorm, storm, wind, gust of wind, blast. —*v.* **4.** *The leaves are blowing away. The wind is blowing:* move by wind; gust, puff. **5.** *Blow on your hands to keep them warm:* exhale, breathe, expel air, puff. **6.** *Little Boy Blue, come blow your horn:* sound, toot, honk, whistle, blast, play. **7.** *The left tire blew. The explosion blew the bridge to smithereens. My curling iron always blows a fuse:* burst, explode, blow out, pop, burn out. —**Ant.** 1 caress, pat. 2 comfort, relief, blessing, consolation; achievement, victory. 3 calm. 4 still. 5 inhale.

blowhard *n. His tales of conquest convinced us he was a blowhard:* braggart, bragger, boaster, blusterer, self-advertiser, self-promoter, blower, vaunter, *Slang* windbag, gasbag. —**Ant.** introvert, milquetoast, *Slang* shrinking violet.

blue *adj.* **1.** *The sky is very blue today:* bluish, azure, cerulean, sky blue, cobalt blue, cobalt, Prussian blue, navy blue, navy, robin's-egg blue, powder blue, sapphire, lapis lazuli, indigo, aqua, aquamarine, ultramarine, turquoise. **2.** *She feels homesick and blue:* depressed, dejected, sad, gloomy, despondent, downcast, low, downhearted, disconsolate, morose, melancholy, doleful, down, down in the dumps, down in the mouth. —**Ant.** 2 elated, exultant, excited, exhilarated, jubilant, happy, overjoyed, joyful, pleased, delighted, blithe, glad, gay, merry, jolly, up, up in the clouds, in high spirits.

blueprint *n. The architect's staff drew up a blueprint for the plant:* draft, design, model, prototype, plan, outline, scheme, schema, diagram, paradigm.

bluff[1] *adj.* **1.** *Teddy Roosevelt had a bluff and hearty nature:* outspoken, plain-spoken, blunt, frank, open, unceremonious, candid, direct, straightforward, forthright, bold, headlong; abrupt, brusque, curt, rough, crusty. —*n.* **2.** *The farm was perched on a bluff high above the river:* promontory, cliff, palisade, headland, bank, ridge, precipice, escarpment, crag, peak. —**Ant.** 1 retiring, reticent, repressed, hesitant, unsure, mealymouthed, shy; indirect, roundabout, deceptive; formal, ceremonious, mannered, tactful.

bluff² *v.* **1.** *The poker player bluffed his opponents into thinking he had a good hand. He's just bluffing about his raise:* deceive, delude, humbug, mislead, fool, bamboozle, dupe, *Slang* fake out; fake, sham, lie, counterfeit, pretend, hoax. —*n.* **2.** *The bully's claim to be a professional boxer was just a bluff to scare you:* pretense, fake, sham, fraud, lie, humbug, deception, subterfuge; idle boast, boast, bragging. **3.** *Her foolish talk of being wealthy shows she's just a big bluff:* bluffer, pretender, fraud, faker; liar, boaster, braggadocio. —**Ant.** 2 truth, fact.

blunder *n.* **1.** *Sending the bill to the wrong customer was a terrible blunder. His remark was a social blunder:* mistake, error, slip; impropriety, indiscretion, gaucherie, gaffe, faux pas; *Slang* boner, goof, booboo. —*v.* **2.** *The clerk blundered when he added up the bill:* make a mistake, be in error, be at fault, slip up, *Slang* goof, make a booboo. **3.** *How did you manage to blunder onto the wrong airplane?:* flounder, bumble, bungle, stumble, stagger. —**Ant.** 1 achievement, success. 2 be correct, be accurate, be exact. 3 go alertly, move purposely.

blunt *adj.* **1.** *It's hard to carve a roast with a blunt knife:* dull, dulled, unsharpened; thick, edgeless, unpointed. **2.** *You can hurt people's feelings by being too blunt:* frank, open, outspoken, candid, straightforward, explicit, to the point; curt, abrupt, brusque, rough, tactless, insensitive. —*v.* **3.** *Lack of sleep blunted his thinking:* dull, numb, benumb, weaken, deaden, make insensitive, stupefy; moderate, mitigate, soften, lighten. —**Ant.** 1 sharp, keen, acute; edged, serrated, pointed. 2 tactful, subtle, diplomatic, politic, sensitive, polite, courteous, polished. 3 sharpen, hone, put an edge on, make keen; stimulate, excite, animate, vitalize.

blur *v.* **1.** *Mist often blurs the landscape:* cloud, becloud, fog, befog, make hazy, dim, bedim, darken, obscure, veil, make indistinct. **2.** *The damp paper caused the ink to blur:* smear, smudge, blotch, spread, run, blot. —*n.* **3.** *The water made a blur on the paper:* smudge, smear, blotch, splotch, blot. **4.** *I was so exhausted the evening was just a blur:* confusion, fog, haze, cloud, obscurity. —**Ant.** 1 clear, brighten, outline, spotlight.

blush *v.* **1.** *She blushes every time a boy talks to her:* flush, redden, turn red, color, grow red. —*n.* **2.** *At the first blush of dawn, the rooster will crow:* reddening, rosy tint, pinkish tinge. —**Ant.** 1 blanch, turn pale, pale, turn ashen.

bluster *v.* **1.** *He blusters so much it's hard to believe him:* boast, swagger, rant, brag, crow, gloat; protest, threaten, storm, bully. —*n.* **2.** *His bragging and bluster made him unpopular:* bluff, swagger, swaggering, bravado, bombast,

boasting, ranting, gloating, crowing, boisterousness, noisy talk, noise. —**Ant.** 1 be retiring, be reticent, be shy. 2 shyness, meekness, mildness, reticence.

board *n.* **1.** *Saw this board in half:* plank, piece of lumber; slat, clapboard, panel, deal, batten. **2.** *How much is room and board?:* meals, daily meals, food. **3.** *The founder of the company is chairman of the board:* board of directors, directors, council, tribunal. —*v.* **4.** *The ranch boards vacationers during the summer:* lodge, house, quarter, put up; billet, bed; feed. **5.** *The passengers boarded the plane at noon:* enter, get on, go onto, embark. —**Ant.** 5 leave, get off or out of, disembark, deplane, detrain.

boast *v.* **1.** *He boasted that he was the best swimmer in school:* brag, crow; vaunt, talk big, blow one's own horn. **2.** *The city boasted two new schools:* be proud of, speak proudly of, show off, exhibit, flaunt; have, contain, possess. —*n.* **3.** *Mother's favorite boast was that no one had more beautiful children:* brag, vaunt. —**Ant.** 1 disclaim, disavow, deprecate, depreciate. 2 be ashamed, cover up. 3 disclaimer, disavowal.

boastful *adj.* *The team's quarterback is extremely boastful. Discount his boastful claim:* conceited, cocky, vainglorious, puffed up, full of swagger, pretentious, pompous, cocksure, bragging, braggadocio; vaunting, crowing, exaggerated, inflated, swollen. —**Ant.** modest, self-disparaging, deprecating, self-belittling.

boat *n.* *The fishing boat left the dock at dawn:* vessel, craft, ship.

bob¹ *v.* *The skiff bobbed in the water. A boxer learns to bob and weave:* move up and down; bounce, hop, leap, jump about, dance; duck, nod.

bob² *v.* *Women began to bob their hair in the 1920's:* crop, shorten, cut, clip, shear, trim; dock.

body *n.* **1.** *When a body meets a body coming through the rye. The house faces a body of water. Stars are heavenly bodies:* person, being, thing, quantity, mass. **2.** *He developed a muscular body. The wings are soldered to the body of the airplane:* physique, figure, build, form, shape; frame, main part, torso, trunk. **3.** *The police took the body to the morgue:* corpse, remains, deceased, cadaver, carcass, *Slang* stiff. **4.** *The body of the populace supported the mayor. A large body of people attended the outdoor concert:* majority, bulk, mass, group, throng, mob, multitude. **5.** *New York State's governing body meets in Albany:* assembly, confederation, federation, congress, council, faction, bloc, coalition, combine, league, society, force, brotherhood. **6.** *Flour will give the gravy more body:* consistency, thickness, stiffness, cohesion. —**Ant.** 2 soul, spirit; mind, intellect, intelligence, psyche; limb, wing, protuberance. 4 minority; handful, scattering, few.

bog *n.* **1.** *Walking is difficult in the bog:* marsh, marshland, swamp, swampland, wetlands, mire, fen, spongy ground, quagmire, morass. —*v.* **2.** *The car was bogged down in the mud:* be stuck, mire, sink, be partially buried, be partially immersed. **—Ant.** 1 dry ground, firm ground.

bogus *adj. The teller was reprimanded for not spotting the bogus check. She wore the bogus diamonds and left the real ones in the vault:* counterfeit, fraudulent, spurious, forged; artificial, synthetic, pseudo, fake, imitation, simulated, fake, phony, dummy, sham, false, feigned, make-believe, pretend, ersatz. **—Ant.** genuine, real, authentic, legitimate, true, bona fide, actual, natural.

Bohemian or **bohemian** *n.* **1.** *Greenwich Village is the home of many artists and bohemians:* nonconformist, hippie, beatnik. **—adj. 2.** *The poet lived a bohemian life in Paris:* nonconformist, unconventional, unorthodox. **—Ant.** 1 conformist, *Slang* square, straight. 2 conventional, conformist, *Slang* square, straight.

boil *v.* **1.** *Boil the water for the tea:* simmer, seethe, brew; parboil, stew. **2.** *The waves boiled around the ship:* bubble, froth, foam, churn, well up, toss, simmer. **3.** *His rudeness made me boil with anger:* rage, rave, storm, seethe, fume, fulminate, rant, burn, sizzle, smolder, foam, quiver, chafe, bristle. **—n. 4.** *The doctor had to lance the boil:* sore, abscess, fester, pustule, carbuncle, furuncle. **—Ant.** 1 freeze; cool, gel. 2 subside, calm. 3 calm, appease, assuage, simmer down.

boiling *adj. He took the boiling kettle off the stove:* steaming, bubbling, simmering, cooking, stewing, percolating.

boisterous *adj. The children became boisterous when their mother left the room:* clamorous, uproarious, noisy, loud; disorderly, wild, rowdy, unruly, obstreperous, out-of-hand, unrestrained. **—Ant.** quiet, silent, still, calm, peaceful, tranquil, serene, sedate; well-behaved, restrained.

bold *adj.* **1.** *Sergeant York was a very bold soldier. The engineer had a bold plan to build a bridge over the English Channel:* brave, courageous, valiant, unafraid, fearless, heroic, valorous, stalwart, dauntless, indomitable, stouthearted, lionhearted, intrepid, unshrinking; daring, audacious, adventuresome, daredevil, imaginative, creative. **2.** *I was offended by his bold remarks:* rude, impudent, fresh, insolent; brazen, impertinent, defiant, cheeky, saucy, brash, forward; fiery, spirited. **3.** *The room was decorated in bold colors:* colorful, loud, eye-catching, hot, vivid, striking, flashy. **—Ant.** 1 cowardly, fainthearted, fearful, shrinking, flinching; *Slang* chicken, chickenhearted, yellow; mundane, ordinary, modest, unimaginative, uncreative or noncreative. 2 meek, timid, timorous, retiring, bashful, shy; courteous, polite, gracious, tactful. 3 pale, dull, soft, colorless, pastel, conservative, cold, cool.

boldness *n.* **1.** *The boldness of the attack surprised the enemy:* bravery, fearlessness, courageousness, audacity. **2.** *Their child's boldness led to his being banished from the table:* impertinence, impudence, gall, insolence, effrontery, insubordination.

bolster *v.* **1.** *More timbers are needed to bolster the roof of the mine:* support, brace, prop up,

hold up, buttress, reinforce, maintain, sustain, shore up, shoulder, cradle. **2.** *More facts are needed to bolster your argument:* support, uphold, sustain, strengthen, reinforce, add to, help, aid, assist. **—n. 3.** *Put the bolster on the couch:* cushion, pillow. **—Ant.** 1 weigh down. 2 diminish, lessen, weaken, tear down.

bolt *n.* **1.** *Is the bolt on the door closed?:* sliding bar, bar, catch, fastener, rod, latch, lock. **2.** *The engine is held in place by two strong bolts:* fastening rod, pin, peg, dowel, rivet. **3.** *The suspect made a bolt for the door:* dash, rush, run, scoot, sprint; spring, jump, leap. **4.** *It took two bolts of cloth to make the draperies:* roll, length. **5.** *A bolt of lightning lit up the sky:* thunderbolt, firebolt, shaft, dart, stroke, flash, brand. **—v. 6.** *Bolt the windows before you leave:* bar, latch, lock, fasten, secure. **7.** *He bolted out of the room in a rage:* dash, rush, run, fly, speed, hasten, hurry, scoot, flee, tear, hurtle, sprint; spring, jump, leap, bound. **8.** *Eat slowly and don't bolt your food:* eat rapidly, gobble, gulp, swallow whole, wolf. **—Ant.** 6 unbolt, unlatch, unbar, unlock, unfasten, open. 7 saunter, stroll, amble, creep, sneak.

bomb *n.* **1.** *The warplane carries 5,000 pounds of bombs:* explosive device, explosive missile, grenade, mine, *Slang* egg. **2.** *(Slang) The play was such a bomb it closed on opening night:* failure, fiasco, flop, dud, *Slang* lemon, bust, washout. **—v. 3.** *The rebels bombed the munitions factory:* set off a bomb in, drop a bomb on, throw a bomb at, bombard. **4.** *(Slang) The movie bombed at the box office:* fail, flop, fizzle, *Slang* wash out.

bombard *v.* **1.** *Planes, ships, and artillery bombarded the enemy port:* rain explosives upon, fire upon, batter, pepper, open fire on, shell, bomb, cannonade, strafe. **2.** *During the storm the phone company was bombarded with reports of downed wires:* barrage, besiege, beset, pepper, assail, assault, attack; harass, pester, hound, worry.

bombastic *adj. No one believed his bombastic claims:* grandiloquent, pompous, windy, padded, inflated, magniloquent, tumid, turgid, verbose, wordy. **—Ant.** temperate, unpretentious, modest, natural, simple, unaffected, deflated, quiet.

bona fide *adj. This is a bona fide $100 bill. He made a bona fide offer and I accepted:* genuine, real, actual, true, authentic, legitimate; honest, sincere, in good faith, honorable, lawful, legal. **—Ant.** counterfeit, fraudulent, spurious, forged; artificial, synthetic, imitation, simulated, fake, phony, sham, bogus, false, feigned, make-believe, pretended.

bonanza *n. His modest investment grew into a bonanza:* windfall, sudden profit, gold mine. **—Ant.** disaster, loss.

bond *n.* **1.** Usually **bonds.** *The captive could not break his bonds:* bindings, fastenings; *(variously)* rope, cord, chains, shackles, manacles, handcuffs, irons, fetters. **2.** *There is a strong bond between the two brothers:* tie, affinity, allegiance, union, connection, knot, link, attachment. **3.** *An honest man's word is his bond:* guarantee, pledge, compact, agreement, obligation, stipulation, promise. **4.** *Stocks and bonds can be good investments:* promissory note, security, certificate; scrip.

bondage *n. Lincoln freed the slaves from bondage:* slavery, servitude, enslavement, vassalage, serfdom, captivity, yoke; bonds, shackles, chains, fetters. **—Ant.** freedom, liberty, emancipation, independence, liberation.

bonhomie *n. The host greeted us with smiles and bonhomie:* good humor, good-humoredness, affability, cordiality, geniality, hospitality, warmth, graciousness, heartiness, neighborliness, friendliness, congeniality, sociability. **—Ant.** unfriendliness, surliness, enmity.

bonus *n. The workers are expecting a large Christmas bonus. If you order three books you will receive a fourth one as a bonus:* gratuity, gift, premium, dividend, honorarium, prize, reward, benefit, bounty. **—Ant.** fine, penalty, withholding.

book *n.* **1.** *The best way to get a child to read is to have many books in the house:* volume, written work, bound work, tome, opus, treatise, publication. **2.** *You should keep an address book. Write in my autograph book:* notebook; album, tablet. *—v.* **3.** *The travel agent booked our vacation cruise. The night club has booked an excellent floor show:* reserve, make reservations, arrange for, engage, procure, schedule, program, slate, line up, bill. **4.** *The police booked him for suspicion of robbery:* register, list, record, enter, put down, write down, mark down, note, insert, post, enroll; file, catalog, index; charge, accuse, indict. **—Ant.** 3 cancel, disengage.

boom[1] *n.* **1.** *The boom of the explosion could be heard for miles:* bang, roar, rumble, blast, thunder. **2.** *After the depression, there was a business boom:* prosperous period, successful period, good times; upsurge, upturn, boost, spurt, thrust, push, expansion, growth, development, increase, gain, improvement, advance. *—v.* **3.** *The drums boomed:* bang, rumble, roar, blast, thunder. **4.** *The frontier town boomed when gold was discovered nearby:* thrive, flourish, prosper, increase, grow, develop, spurt. **—Ant.** 2 depression, recession, bad times, hard times, slump, downturn, decrease, bust, burst. 4 fail, slump.

boom[2] *n. Lower the boom and take in the sail:* horizontal pole, spar; beam, shaft, bar.

boomerang *v. His incautious remarks boomeranged:* rebound, return, bounce back, come back, recoil, rebound, backfire, backlash.

boondocks *n. He finished his novel while teaching at a small school in the boondocks:* backwater, backwoods, hinterland, backcountry, frontier, provinces; *Slang* boonies, bush, outback, veld, sticks, Podunk, squaresville, nowheresville.

boor *n. He's a clumsy boor:* lout, oaf, yokel, churl, bumpkin, clodhopper, guttersnipe, peasant, rube, hick, hayseed, rustic; vulgarian, brute,

philistine. **—Ant.** sophisticate, cosmopolitan; gentleman, gallant, lady.

boorish *adj. She considers the peasants boorish:* crude, rude, coarse, vulgar, unrefined, unpolished, uncouth, gauche, loutish, oafish, rustic, peasantlike. **—Ant.** genteel, polite, polished, cultured, refined, cultivated, gentlemanly, courtly, gallant, lady-like; sophisticated, urbane, cosmopolitan.

boost *v.* **1.** *Boost me up so I can look in the window:* lift, raise, heave, hoist, elevate, push, shove, pitch, give a leg up. **2.** *The new assembly line boosted production by 20 percent:* increase, raise, advance, raise upward, add to, enlarge, expand, advance, develop, improve. **3.** *The Chamber of Commerce boosts local business:* promote, advance, foster, further, forward, support, sustain, nurture; speak well of, propound, praise, extol, acclaim, laud, urge on, root for, put in a good word for, stick up for. *—n.* **4.** *Give me a boost onto the horse:* lift, heave, hoist, raise, shove, push. **5.** *I received a pay boost. Last month saw a boost in sales:* increase, raise, hike, addition, increment; growth, development, enlargement, expansion, advance, improvement, rise, pickup, upsurge, upswing, upturn, upward trend. **6.** *The charity bazaar got a boost in the local newspaper:* favorable mention, good word, good review, free ad, *Informal* plug, promotion, praise, compliment, applause. **—Ant.** 1, 2 lower, let down, push down, drop. 2 decrease, reduce, diminish, lessen, subtract from, deduct, cut, curtail, crop, pare, whittle down, scale down, moderate, ease. 3 hinder, hold back, condemn, criticize, *Informal* knock. 5 decrease, reduction, cutback, curtailment, lessening, decline, fall, falling off, diminution, dwindling, wane, ebb, deterioration. 6 condemnation, criticism, *Informal* knock.

booth *n.* **1.** *She called from a phone booth. Each voter went into a voting booth:* compartment, enclosure, cubbyhole, nook; hutch, coop, pen. **2.** *I won a kewpie doll at the ringtoss booth at the fair:* stall, stand, counter, table; tent.

booty *n. The pirates buried their booty on a desert island:* loot, plunder, spoils, pillage, takings, pickings; prize, gain, winnings, *Slang* boodle. **—Ant.** fine, forfeiture.

border *n.* **1.** *Summer cottages were built all around the border of the lake. The bedspread had a fringed border:* edge, rim, periphery, perimeter, circumference, extremity, verge, margin, brim, brink, curb, hem, skirt, frame, outskirt, fringe, pale, limit. **2.** *Do you need a passport to cross the Mexican border?:* frontier, boundary, line. *—v.* **3.** *California borders the Pacific Ocean:* be next to, adjoin, join, flank, touch, neighbor on, abut, skirt, verge upon. **4.** *The seamstress bordered the dress with flowers:* edge, trim, fringe, befringe, frame, bind, rim, hem, skirt. **—Ant.** 1 interior, inside, middle, center.

borderline *adj. He's not certifiably insane, but he's a borderline case:* marginal, halfway, problematic, open, indefinite, unclear, uncertain, ambivalent, indefinable, obscure, indeterminate, equivocal, inexact, undecided, vague, ambiguous, unsettled. **—Ant.** decisive, unambiguous, clear, precise, positive, definite.

bore¹ v. **1.** *Long stories about "the good old days" bore me:* be tedious to, tire, weary, fatigue, exhaust, tax one's patience, wear out, *Slang* be a drag. —n. **2.** *The guest speaker turned out to be a deadly bore:* dull person, tiresome thing, *Slang* drag, drip, wet blanket. **—Ant.** 1 excite, interest, amuse, stimulate, delight. 2 life of the party, *Slang* ball, gas.

bore² v. **1.** *To reach the iron-ore deposit, engineers had to bore through solid rock:* drill, tunnel, hollow out, gouge out, sink, pierce, burrow, drive. —n. **2.** *In general, rifles have smaller bores than shotguns:* inside diameter, caliber. **—Ant.** 1 fill, plug.

boredom n. *The patient spent long days of boredom in the hospital:* dullness, tedium, ennui, monotony, tediousness, doldrums, weariness. **—Ant.** excitement, interest, stimulation; amusement, entertainment, diversion.

boring adj. *Playing bridge all evening can be boring:* dull, unexciting, uninteresting, tiresome, monotonous, humdrum, repetitious, tedious, wearisome, flat, stale, insipid, tiring. **—Ant.** exciting, interesting, stimulating, exhilarating; amusing, entertaining.

born adj. **1.** *Charles Dickens was born in 1812:* given birth to, brought forth, delivered. **2.** *George Gershwin was a born musician:* natural, innate, intuitive; endowed from birth.

borrow v. **1.** *May I borrow your car?:* use, take on loan, take and return. **2.** *The playwright borrowed the essence of the plot from Shakespeare:* appropriate, take, get, obtain, acquire, copy, use, usurp; filch, pirate, plagiarize, pilfer, steal, commandeer. **—Ant.** lend. 1 return. 2 contribute, give, present.

bosom n. **1.** *She clutched the child to her bosom:* breast, bust, chest. **2.** *Conflicting emotions wrestled in his bosom:* heart, innermost being, inmost nature, soul, spirit, core, breast, center. **3.** *Every young man must leave the bosom of his family to seek his own fortune:* midst, inner circle, heart, center, nucleus, core. —adj. **4.** *They have been bosom buddies for years:* close, intimate, cherished, dear, beloved. **—Ant.** 4 distant, remote.

boss n. **1.** *A good boss tries to keep his workers happy:* employer, supervisor, foreman, manager, superintendent, administrator, executive, chief, leader, head, master, *Slang* kingpin, big cheese. —v. **2.** *Don't try to boss me around!:* order, command, *Informal* push. **—Ant.** 1 employee, worker, man in the ranks, subordinate, underling; follower.

botch v. **1.** *The typist botched the job and had to start over:* spoil, muff, bungle, make a mess of, ruin, do unskillfully, butcher, mar, mismanage; blunder, fail, err, fumble, flub, *Slang* louse up, foul up, goof, blow. —n. **2.** *The new cook made a botch of the dinner:* mess, bungle, blunder, failure, hash, fumble, butchery, flop. **—Ant.** 1 master, perfect, do well at, do skill-

fully, make a success of, triumph at. 2 success, triumph, achievement, *Informal* hit.

bother v. **1.** *My cold still bothers me:* annoy, trouble, distress, inconvenience, dismay, disquiet, worry, disturb, upset, pester, nag, harass, harry, aggravate, fret, vex, irk, try, irritate, tax, strain. **2.** *She didn't even bother to say she was sorry:* trouble, attempt, make an effort. —n. **3.** *Having an extra guest at dinner will be no bother at all. Don't make such a bother over which dress to wear:* inconvenience, problem, trouble, difficulty, hardship, strain, stress, load, tax, onus, encumbrance, nuisance, trial, affliction, *Slang* drag; hindrance, impediment, worry, responsibility, care, aggravation, vexation, irritation, *Informal* headache, pain in the neck; fuss, disturbance, commotion, tumult, stir, ado, flurry, rumpus, racket. **—Ant.** 1 convenience, help, aid, comfort, solace, console, calm, quiet, appease, placate, pacify, mollify. 2 neglect. 3 convenience, help, aid, solution, answer, cinch; pleasure, delight, comfort.

bothersome adj. *Being without a car for the day was bothersome:* troublesome, annoying, inconvenient, aggravating, vexing, taxing, distressing, disturbing, worrisome, disquieting. **—Ant.** convenient, helpful, comforting, consoling; pleasant, delightful, comfortable.

bottle n. *Remember when milk came in bottles instead of cardboard containers?:* glass container, vessel; (*variously*) phial, vial, jar, canteen, carafe, flask, flagon.

bottleneck n. *A bottleneck at the bridge stopped traffic in all directions:* block, barrier, bar, impediment, jam, gridlock, obstacle, obstruction, blockage, clog, congestion, detour, stop, stoppage; *Med.* thrombus, embolus, infarction, embolism; costiveness, constipation.

bottom n. **1.** *Attach the cord to the bottom of the lamp. The mine entrance is at the bottom of the mountain:* base, foot, pedestal, foundation. **2.** *The shoes are in the bottom of the trunk:* lowest part, deepest part. **3.** *Is that chewing gum stuck to the bottom of your shoe?:* underside, underpart, lower side, belly, sole. **4.** *The ship sank to the bottom:* ocean floor, riverbed, depths. **5.** *She spanked the child on its bottom:* rump, backside, buttocks, seat, fundament; *Slang* fanny, can. **6.** *Let's get to the bottom of this mystery:* basis, base, root, heart, core, center, substance, essence, principle; gist, quintessence, foundation, source, origin, beginning, cause, ground, rudiments, mainspring, spring, wellspring. —adj. **7.** *The cat slept on the bottom step of the stairs:* lowest, lower; deepest, deeper. **—Ant.** 1–4, 7 top. 1 crown, peak, summit, height, acme, apex; cover, lid. 4 surface. 7 highest, uppermost, higher, upper.

bough n. *During the storm a bough broke off the tree:* branch, limb.

boulevard n. *The parade route led down the main boulevard of the city:* avenue, wide street, tree-lined street, parkway, concourse. **—Ant.** alley, back street.

bounce v. **1.** *The ball bounced against the wall:* rebound, ricochet, bound, recoil, bob, jounce, bump, thump. —*n.* **2.** *In tennis you must return the ball before the second bounce:* rebound, bound, hop. **3.** *A good night club entertainer has to have a lot of bounce:* vitality, liveliness, pep, animation, vivacity, vigor, verve, energy, life, dynamism, spirit. —**Ant.** 3 staidness, calmness, calm, tranquillity, composure; weariness, tiredness.

bound[1] *adj.* **1.** *Bound newspapers will be collected for the scrap paper drive:* tied, tied up, fastened, secured, tethered, trussed, lashed together; in bonds. **2.** *The author gave his manuscripts and bound books to the local library:* encased, wrapped, covered. **3.** *The roses are bound to die in this frost:* sure, certain, fated, destined, doomed. **4.** *The borrower is bound by contract to pay off the debt in two years:* required, obliged, restrained, confined, limited, liable, beholden, forced; determined, resolved, resolute, committed. —**Ant.** 1 unbound, untied, loose. 3 unsure, uncertain; avoidable, escapable. 4 free, unlimited, unrestrained; irresolute.

bound[2] *n.* **1.** *There are a hunting lodge and an orchard within the bounds of the estate. Her flashy evening gown oversteps the bounds of good taste:* limit, boundary, border, confine, demarcation, line; periphery, extremity, rim, pale. **2.** *Rangers are hunting for the lost hikers somewhere in the vast bounds of Yellowstone Park:* area, territory, region, compass, range, domain, province, district; realm, bailiwick, orb, orbit. —*v.* **3.** *A stone wall bounds the property:* surround, enclose, encircle, circumscribe, border, edge, hedge, fringe; mark, define, limit, confine, demarcate.

bound[3] *v.* **1.** *The dog bounded out of the house:* leap, jump, vault, spring; bounce, bob, prance, dance, gambol, romp, flounce. —*n.* **2.** *In one bound, the boy jumped the fence:* leap, jump, vault, spring; bounce, rebound, flounce, bob. —**Ant.** 1 crawl, creep, amble, hobble, limp.

bound[4] *adj.* *We're Alabama bound:* going to, heading for, destined.

boundary *n.* *The Ohio River forms the boundary between Kentucky and Indiana:* border, dividing line, line, demarcation, frontier, barrier; landmark, rim, edge, margin, pale, periphery, extremity.

bounded *adj.* *Their property was bounded by a fence:* limited, enclosed, circumscribed, compassed, encompassed, encircled, fenced, belted, rimmed, bordered, girdled, hedged, restricted, ringed, surrounded. —**Ant.** unlimited, unbounded.

boundless *adj.* *Teenagers seem to have boundless appetites:* vast, immense; limitless, unlimited, unbounded, endless, inexhaustible, measureless, immeasurable, infinite, incalculable, without end, unending, everlasting, perpetual, unrestricted. —**Ant.** limited, restricted, bounded, circumscribed; small, little.

bounteous *adj.* **1.** *The crops were bounteous this year:* abundant, plentiful, plenteous, bountiful, profuse, copious, ample, prolific, lavish, large, rich, full, teeming, overflowing, abound-ing. **2.** *Many bounteous donors contributed to the charity drive:* generous, bountiful, munificent, unstinting, unsparing, magnanimous, charitable, beneficent, liberal, free, large, philanthropic, benevolent. —**Ant.** 1 sparse, spare, meager, scant, scanty, scrimpy, lean, slender, modest, small, limited, restricted, inadequate. 2 stingy, miserly, niggardly, sparing, stinting, close, penurious, uncharitable, frugal, parsimonious; greedy, covetous, avaricious.

bountiful *adj.* See BOUNTEOUS.

bounty *n.* **1.** *In olden days the poor had to depend on the parish's bounty:* generosity, benevolence, munificence, charitableness, charity, philanthropy, assistance, aid, help, giving, liberality, openhandedness, almsgiving. **2.** *Every soldier was promised ten acres of land as a bounty:* grant, reward, recompense, bonus, tribute, bestowal, benefaction, endowment; gift, present, favor, gratuity, donation, contribution. —**Ant.** 1 stinginess, closeness, niggardliness, miserliness; greed, covetousness, avarice.

bouquet *n.* **1.** *The bride carried a bouquet of white roses:* bunch of flowers, garland, spray, nosegay; boutonniere. **2.** *The wine has a marvelous bouquet:* aroma, scent, odor, fragrance, perfume, essence.

bourgeois *n.* **1.** *The princess was ostracized for marrying a rich bourgeois:* member of the middle class, commoner, burgher, (*disparagingly*) Babbitt. —*adj.* **2.** *The furnishings were in bourgeois taste:* middle-class, conventional, ordinary, unimaginative, *Slang* square.

bout *n.* **1.** *I've never attended a championship bout:* fight, boxing match, match, battle, contest, tourney, conflict, struggle, fray, brush, tilt, skirmish, embroilment, scuffle, clash, encounter, engagement, contention, affair, *Informal* go-round, set-to. **2.** *I just had a bout of the flu:* spell, session, turn, course, interval, period, term, siege, spree, series, cycle.

bow[1] *v.* **1.** *The duke bowed and kissed her hand. Bow your head when the flag passes:* bend, salaam, stoop, genuflect; (*of a female*) curtsy. **2.** *The City Council refused to bow to the wishes of the mayor:* yield, give in, submit, surrender, capitulate, succumb, defer, comply, relent, agree, acquiesce, concede, knuckle under, kowtow. —*n.* **3.** *The conductor made a deep bow to the audience:* bend, salaam, genuflection; (*of a female*) curtsy. —**Ant.** 2 fight, battle, contest, resist, stand fast.

bow[2] *n.* *The captain walked toward the bow of the ship:* forward end, front, prow. —**Ant.** stern.

bowels *n.* **1.** *He ran his sword through the bowels of the villain:* guts, intestines, entrails, innards, stomach, vitals, viscera, vital organs. **2.** *The miners were forced to work in the bowels of the earth:* depths, innermost part, interior, abyss, insides, guts, innards, core, pit, hollow, heart, midst, bosom, womb.

bowl *n.* **1.** *What lovely salad bowls! Would you like another bowl of soup?:* deep dish, vessel, container, receptacle; (*variously*) tureen, porringer, boat; bowlful, dishful, portion, helping. **2.**

Unless there is rain, the entire area will be a dust bowl. The bathroom has no washbowl: basin; hollow, depression, cavity, valley. **3.** *Outdoor concerts are given in the Hollywood Bowl:* stadium, amphitheater, coliseum, arena.

box[1] *n.* **1.** *He bought me a box of candy:* carton, cardboard container, container, receptacle; crate, chest, caddy; coffer. **2.** *We have a box at the opera:* stall, compartment, booth.

box[2] *v.* **1.** *Father used to box our ears when we were bad:* cuff, slap, bat, hit, rap, belt, strike, punch, whack, thwack, buffet. **2.** *The champion was asked to box in an exhibition bout:* fight, spar, exchange blows, engage in fisticuffs. —*n.* **3.** *One more smart-aleck remark and you'll get a box on the ears!:* cuff, slap, whack, thwack, hit, rap; buffet, thumping.

boy *n. We have two boys and a girl:* male child; man child, lad, youth, stripling, youngster.

boycott *n.* **1.** *Housewives organized a meat boycott to protest high prices:* refusal to buy, rejection, spurning, exclusion, ostracism, blacklisting, blackballing. —*v.* **2.** *The townspeople boycotted the overpriced store:* refuse to have dealings with, reject, spurn, ostracize, exclude, blacklist, blackball. —**Ant.** 1 mass patronage, group support, usage, acceptance. 2 patronize, support, welcome, use, accept.

boyfriend *n. In college she had a new boyfriend every few weeks:* beau, fellow, young man, escort, cavalier, date, companion, gentleman caller, swain, admirer, suitor, wooer, steady; lover, beloved, truelove, sweetheart, paramour, inamorato, man, flame, Don Juan, Lothario, old man.

boyhood *n. His boyhood was solitary:* youth, adolescence, childhood, young manhood.

boyish *adj. The actor had boyish good looks. He was punished for a boyish prank:* youthful, boylike, juvenile, innocent, fresh, tender; childish, childlike, immature, puerile; sophomoric, callow, boyey. —**Ant.** manly, rugged; adult, mature, grown-up, experienced, sophisticated, worldly.

brace *n.* **1.** *The table is shaky because the braces are loose:* reinforcement, support, bracket, prop, stanchion, stay, strut, truss, bracer. **2.** *We caught a brace of squab:* pair, couple, duo, twosome. —*v.* **3.** *Brace those sagging shelves with more crosspieces. Brace yourself for some bad news:* reinforce, strengthen, steady, prop, prop up, shore, shore up, bolster, fortify, buttress, support, sustain, hold up, prepare. —**Ant.** 3 weaken, loosen; let fall.

bracelet *n. She's wearing a beautiful charm bracelet:* armlet, bangle.

bracer *n. She needed a bracer to get started in the morning:* reviver, refresher.

bracing *adj. A steam bath followed by a cold shower is very bracing:* invigorating, stimulating, energizing, exhilarating, restorative, refreshing, arousing; strengthening, fortifying, reviving. —**Ant.** soporific, restful, dulling, depressing; weakening, debilitating, enervating.

bracket *n.* **1.** *The shelf was supported by a bracket at each end:* support, brace, stay, strut,

prop, stanchion. **2.** *What tax bracket are you in?:* group, grouping, class, classification, category, range, division, rank, designation, status. —*v.* **3.** *You'd better bracket those shelves with two-by-fours:* support, brace; prop, prop up, shore, shore up, truss. **4.** *All able-bodied men will be bracketed as 1-A in the military draft:* class, classify, group, rank, categorize, designate.

brackish *adj. The water is too brackish to drink:* salty, briny, saline, salt. —**Ant.** fresh, clear, sweet.

brag *v.* **1.** *He constantly brags about how well he plays golf:* boast, extol oneself, vaunt, crow, talk big, puff oneself up, exaggerate, blow one's own horn, pat oneself on the back. —*n.* **2.** *People who are really good bridge players don't have to make brags about it:* boast, boasting, boastfulness, bragging, self-praise, big talk, exaggeration, crowing. —**Ant.** 1 be humble, be self-deprecating, deprecate, depreciate, disclaim, disavow; be ashamed, cover up. 2 humility, humbleness, modesty, self-deprecation, disclaimer, disavowal, self-criticism, shame.

braggart *n. He's so proud of his success that he's become a braggart:* bragger, boaster, big talker, self-trumpeter, *Slang* blowhard. —**Ant.** humble person, self-effacing person, modest person.

braid *v. The mother braided the girl's hair into two pigtails:* plait, weave, intertwine, entwine, twine, interlace, twist, ravel, lace, knit, wreathe.

brains *n. pl. The simple puzzle took little brains to understand:* understanding, intelligence, mind, intellect, sense, reason; capacity. —**Ant.** stupidity.

brainwash *v. The cult brainwashed him into accepting its beliefs:* indoctrinate, condition, instill, catechize.

brake *n.* **1.** *This car has four-wheel brakes. Higher taxes will put a brake on inflation:* stopping device; curb, constraint, restraint, control, rein, check, drag. —*v.* **2.** *Don't brake the car abruptly on an icy road. The increase in the crime rate must be braked:* stop, halt, arrest, stay, check; reduce speed, slow; curb, control. —**Ant.** 1 starter, accelerator, gas pedal; acceleration, stimulus; freedom. 2 start; move, accelerate, speed up, hasten, quicken, expedite.

bramble *n. Brambles tore our pants as we ran through them:* burr, brier, gorse, thorn.

branch *n.* **1.** *There's a robin's nest in the branch of that tree:* limb, bough, spray. **2.** *There's good fishing in the west branch of the river:* leg, prong, channel, tributary, feeder; extension, offshoot, section, part. **3.** *The local branch of the union is very small. Theater is a branch of the arts:* section, part, segment, component, arm, wing, member, extension, division, subdivision, chapter, offshoot; bureau, office, branch office, department, agency. —*v.* **4.** *The highway branches into three local roads up ahead:* divide, diverge, radiate, separate, fork, shoot off, ramify, bifurcate. —**Ant.** 1 trunk. 2 main channel. 4 complex, composite, mass, conglomerate, union, affiliation, alliance; main office, home office.

brand *n.* **1.** *The ranch's brand is an X. The store removed the brands from the dresses so it could sell them at a discount:* branding iron; mark made by branding; label, mark, emblem, stamp, sign, trademark. **2.** *Which brand of peanut butter is cheapest?:* brand name, make, manufacture; type, kind, sort, variety, grade, class, quality. **3.** *After the scandal he carried the brand of an informer wherever he went:* stigma, stain, mark, disgrace, smirch, smear, slur, taint, spot, blot, imputation, blemish. —*v.* **4.** *The cowboys branded a hundred calves in the roundup:* mark with a branding iron, mark, sear, burn in. **5.** *His criminal record branded him for life:* stigmatize, mark, stain, taint, besmirch, spot, blemish, disgrace, discredit. —**Ant. 3** trophy, laurel, honor. **5** bring honor to, commemorate.

brandish *v.* *The cavalry officer brandished his sword and the charge began:* flourish, wave, shake, swing, wield, waggle; flaunt, display, exhibit, show off. —**Ant.** sheathe, put away; put down, lower.

brash *adj.* **1.** *Buying the house without having it appraised was very brash:* rash, reckless, incautious, foolhardy, imprudent, careless; unconsidered, impetuous, madcap, hasty, too quick, precipitous. **2.** *He's such a brash young man:* impudent, impertinent, brazen, forward, rude, cheeky, sassy, *Slang* fresh; bold, heedless, overconfident, know-it-all, *Slang* smart-alecky. —**Ant. 1** cautious, prudent, careful, well-considered, thoughtful, circumspect. **2** respectful, deferential, polite, reserved; hesitant, uncertain, timid, timorous.

brassy *adj.* *The job requires someone who's a bit brassy and doesn't mind dealing with the public:* brazen, bold, impudent, saucy, insolent, sassy, forward, overbold, shameless, barefaced, unblushing, unabashed, brash, outspoken, impertinent, arrogant, cocky. —**Ant.** shy, modest, retiring, reticent, self-effacing.

brat *n.* *That little brat needs spanking:* spoiled child, rude child, hoyden, whelp, chit, rascal, imp. —**Ant.** little angel, little darling.

bravado *n.* *His bravado hides his real fear:* show of courage, swaggering, swagger, braggadocio, bravura, boasting, boastfulness, bragging, big talk, crowing, bombast, cockiness, bluster, puffery, blowing. —**Ant.** nervousness, trembling, quaking; shame.

brave *adj.* **1.** *A brave fire fighter rescued the woman:* courageous, valiant, valorous, heroic, fearless, dauntless, undaunted, stouthearted, lionhearted, intrepid, unafraid, unflinching, unshrinking; plucky, spunky, gritty, game, doughty, stalwart, *Slang* gutsy. —*v.* **2.** *The Coast Guard braved the storm to reach the sinking ship:* dare, confront, challenge, face, defy, outbrazen, breast, stand up to, look in the eye; endure, bear, withstand, tolerate, take, put up with, suffer, sustain, stand, weather, brook, abide, stomach, undergo. —**Ant. 1** cowardly, cringing, frightened, fearful, afraid, craven, fainthearted, *Slang* chicken, chickenhearted, yellow, yellow-

livered; timid, timorous, shrinking. **2** retreat from, back away from, give in to, surrender to, give up in the face of, *Informal* turn tail.

bravery *n.* *The police officers showed great bravery in the face of danger:* courage, valor, heroism, fearlessness, intrepidity, dauntlessness; boldness, daring, pluck, spunk, audacity, spirit, mettle, *Slang* grit. —**Ant.** cowardice, fright, fearfulness, faintheartedness, timidity, *Slang* chickenheartedness, yellowness.

brawl *n.* *Most cowboy movies include a scene with a barroom brawl:* fight, scuffle, fracas, fray, melee, row, ruckus, scrap, broil, clash, set-to, battle, uproar, rumpus, embroilment, altercation, imbroglio; quarrel, squabble, tiff, dispute, wrangle.

brawn *n.* *It takes brawn to be a weight lifter:* brawniness, muscles, muscular development, robustness, huskiness, beefiness, sturdiness, stamina, ruggedness; strength, might, power. —**Ant.** slightness, scrawniness, leanness, thinness, skinniness, slenderness; weakness, feebleness, fragility.

brawny *adj.* *Most wrestlers are very brawny:* muscular, burly, robust, husky, rugged, sturdy, strapping, strong, powerful, mighty. —**Ant.** scrawny, gaunt, slender, slight, skinny, thin, slim, lean, lanky, lank; weak, feeble, fragile, delicate.

brazen *adj.* *How can you believe such a brazen lie?:* brassy, impudent, shameless, bold, bold-faced, barefaced, brash, unabashed, insolent, saucy, forward, immodest, audacious; open, arrogant, cheeky. —**Ant.** reserved, reticent, diffident, respectful, decorous, well-mannered, mannerly, polite; cautious, modest, timid, timorous, shy, bashful; underhand, secret, stealthy, surreptitious.

breach *n.* **1.** *The explosion made a breach in the dam. Armored units poured through the breach in the enemy's lines:* opening, break, hole, rift, gap, gash, rent, crack, split, chink, cleft, crevice, slit, rupture, fissure. **2.** *If the ballplayer isn't paid he'll sue the team for breach of contract. Police arrested the brawlers for committing a breach of the peace:* violation, infringement, infraction, transgression, disobedience, trespass, defiance; nonobservance, noncompliance, disregard, neglect, dereliction, failure. —**Ant. 1** closure; stoppage, blockage. **2** adherence to, observance, compliance with, obedience, fidelity to; attention, heed, regard.

breadth *n.* **1.** *Everyone knows the length of a football field is 100 yards, but few know its breadth is 160 feet:* width, wideness, broadness, latitude. **2.** *Thomas Jefferson, writer, politician, architect, and farmer, had a mind of great breadth. We were stunned by the breadth of the mountain range:* broadness, scope, range, reach, spread, compass, stretch, span, expanse, extent, extensiveness; size, area, dimensions, measure. —**Ant. 1** length, longness, longitude. **2** narrowness, confinement, circumscription, restrictedness, slightness, scantiness.

break *v.* **1.** *If you break that vase you'll have to pay for it. I broke my leg skiing:* shatter, fragment, burst, crack, fracture, rupture, snap, split, chip, splinter, *Slang* bust; smash, crush, pulverize, granulate, powder, disintegrate, demolish. **2.** Often **break off, break away.** *Break off a piece of licorice for me. The mainmast broke away in the storm:* detach, separate, pull off, tear off, wrench away, sever, divide, cleave, sunder, rive, rend, disjoint, disconnect, dismember. **3.** *The TV set is broken again:* be inoperative, work improperly, become useless; ruin, destroy. **4.** Usually **break off.** *The union broke off negotiations and called a strike:* end, stop, cease, halt, suspend, shut down, interrupt, discontinue. **5.** *Who's going to break the bad news to her?:* disclose, reveal, divulge, announce, proclaim, tell, inform, make public, give out. **6.** *When the storm breaks, run for the house. The audience broke into applause:* erupt, burst out, come forth suddenly; happen, occur, appear. **7.** *Mustangs must be broken before they can be ridden. You must break yourself of the cigarette habit:* tame, train, master, discipline, control, subdue, overcome, bend to one's will. **8.** *Paying for the house will just about break me:* bankrupt, ruin, wipe out, cripple financially, strap for funds, impoverish, make insolvent, make impoverished, take all one's money, put on the rocks. **9.** *The net broke the acrobat's fall:* take the force of, soften, diminish, cushion, weaken, lessen, lighten. **10.** *This winter broke the record for snowfall:* surpass, exceed, better, top, outdo, outstrip, overcome, overshadow, beat, cap, excel, go beyond, transcend, eclipse. **11.** *The convict broke out of jail. The fullback broke through the defensive line and scored a touchdown:* escape, get away from, make a getaway, slip away, take to one's heels, fly the coop; flee, run, run away, fly, dash, make a dash, take flight. **12.** *Did you ever break a law? I hate to break my promise:* violate, be guilty of infraction of, infringe on, transgress against, disobey, defy; disregard, ignore, pay no heed to, be derelict in, neglect, shirk, fall back on, renege on. —*n.* **13.** *We heard the break and saw the glass fall out of the window. Water seeped through the break in the basement wall:* shattering, breaking, burst, snap, fracturing, cracking, splitting; breach, opening, rupture, fissure, hole, rent, crack, fracture, gap, gash, rift, tear, split, cleft, division, separation. **14.** *Let's take a short break for lunch:* interruption, interlude, recess, interval, intermission, hiatus, lapse, rest, respite, pause. **15.** *The actress's big break came when she substituted for the ailing star:* stroke of luck, opportunity, chance, fortune, opening. —**Ant.** 1 repair, fix, mend, heal. 2 connect, join, unite, fasten, secure, attach, bind, weld. 3 repair, fix. 4 start, begin, commence, open; continue, preserve, prolong. 5 keep quiet about, conceal, hide, secrete, cover up. 6 end, stop, cease, halt; die down, die away, diminish. 7 submit to, yield to, acquiesce; free. 8 make wealthy, make prosperous, enrich, fill one's pockets, feather one's nest, give one money to burn. 9 increase. 10 fall short of, be under, be lower than. 11 capture, catch. 12 obey, adhere to, comply with;

heed, observe, regard. 13 mending, repair, fixing, healing; closing, stopping, blockage. 14 continuation, resumption.

breakable *adj. Those plates are too breakable for everyday use:* fragile, delicate, brittle, crumbly, frail, flimsy, shaky. —**Ant.** unbreakable, sturdy, strong.

breakdown *n.* **1.** *The train had a breakdown outside of Denver. I hear she had a nervous breakdown:* failure, collapse; disorder, mishap, deterioration, decline, *Slang* crackup. **2.** *Give me a complete breakdown of all the supplies you need:* division, categorization, detailed list, item-by-item count, step-by-step instructions; analysis.

breaker *n. After the storm, big breakers continued all the next day:* wave, comber, surge, whitecap, roller; bore, eagre.

breakthrough *n. Learning how to speak after his stroke was the first breakthrough:* progress, advance, step forward, discovery, invention.

breakup *n. The ship can't get through until the breakup of the ice in the spring. The argument between the friends led to their breakup:* separation, breaking, dispersal, split, splitting, disintegration, crackup.

breast *n.* **1.** *He beat his breast in agony:* chest, bust, bosom. **2.** *The father's breast was full of pride over his son's accomplishments:* heart, innermost self, very marrow, core.

breath *n.* **1.** *It's so cold you can see your breath:* air breathed in and out. **2.** *The patient's breath grew stronger:* breathing, respiration, wind, inhalation, exhalation. **3.** *The puppets were so real they seemed to have the very breath of life:* spirit, vital spirit, vital spark, divine spark, life force, lifeblood, animation, vitalization.

breathe *v.* **1.** *Breathe that clear mountain air!:* draw breath, draw in air, inhale and exhale, respire; gasp, pant, puff, huff. **2.** *Don't breathe a word of this to anyone:* whisper, murmur, impart, utter.

breathtaking *adj. The trapeze artists performed breathtaking feats:* exciting, awesome, amazing, astonishing, startling, surprising.

breech *n.* **1.** *"Breech" is an old-fashioned word for "backside":* buttocks, rump, seat, behind, posterior, fundament; hindquarters, hind part, haunches. **2. breeches.** *Jodhpurs are a type of riding breeches:* knee breeches; (*loosely*) trousers, pants.

breed *v.* **1.** *Mosquitoes breed in stagnant water. Iowa farmers breed the best hogs in the world:* reproduce, propagate, beget, multiply, procreate, produce offspring, bear, spawn, bring forth, give forth; raise, grow, proliferate. **2.** *Familiarity breeds contempt:* foster, nurture, develop, cultivate, promote, mother, father; generate, produce, spawn, give rise to, cause, lead to, occasion, sire. —*n.* **3.** *The collie is a beautiful breed of dog:* species, strain, race, stock, order, family, variety, type, sort, kind. —**Ant.** 2 destroy, extinguish, kill, wipe out, eradicate, erase, demolish, extirpate; stifle, hinder, harm, injure, block, obstruct, stop, stay.

breeding *n.* **1.** *Cattle breeding is a big business. Tsetse-fly breeding is reduced by draining swamps:* raising, producing, production, growing; reproduction, propagation, begetting, multiplying, mating, procreation, generation, germination, bearing, spawning, hatching, bringing forth. **2.** *The value of a race horse depends on its breeding:* lineage, bloodline, line, heredity, ancestry, parentage, extraction, pedigree, family tree, descent, genealogy. **3.** *People of good breeding seldom lose their tempers:* manners, refinement, polish, gentility, background, politeness, courtesy, grace, cultivation; upbringing, training, rearing.

breeze *n.* **1.** *A warm breeze blew from the south:* gentle wind, light wind, current of air, puff of wind, light gust, zephyr, waft. —*v.* **2.** *She breezed out of the room without a backward glance:* move in a carefree manner, sweep, sail, glide, flit, float, coast, waft, pass.

breezy *adj.* **1.** *It's breezy out on deck today:* windy, windswept, gusty, blowy, blustery, squally. **2.** *The speaker's short breezy talk cheered up the audience:* light, carefree, free and easy, casual, blithesome, buoyant, lively, animated, vivacious, gay, cheerful, sunny, merry, jaunty, pert, debonair, fresh, airy, brisk, peppy, spry, frisky, sprightly, spirited, energetic, bouncy, resilient. —**Ant.** 1 calm, still, windless. 2 heavy, careworn, depressed, dull, sad, mournful, morose, lifeless, inanimate, unspirited; serious, pompous, heavy-handed.

brevity *n.* *Brevity is the opposite of prolixity. The brevity of life should make one live each day to the fullest:* briefness, shortness, quickness, conciseness, pithiness, succinctness, terseness; impermanence, transience, ephemerality. —**Ant.** long-windedness, prolixity; lengthiness.

brew *v.* **1.** *Brew the tea a little longer. To make beer, grain, hops, and malt must be brewed:* boil, steep, seethe, cook; ferment, soak. **2.** *The children are brewing a surprise for your birthday. A storm is brewing on the horizon:* concoct, contrive, scheme, plot, devise, plan, think up, arrange, prepare, make, produce, foment, *Informal* cook up; originate, initiate, germinate, hatch, start, begin, form, formulate, gather, ripen. —*n.* **3.** *Milk with honey and an egg yolk is a delicious brew. In English pubs, brew is ordered by the pint or half-pint:* beverage, drink, concoction, mixture; (*variously*) beer, ale, stout, porter, malt liquor. —**Ant.** 1 chill; drain, distill. 2 cancel, disperse, break up, die away.

bribe *n.* **1.** *The inspector was accused of accepting a bribe:* payoff, hush money, illegal gift, graft, inducement, *Slang* payola, grease. —*v.* **2.** *The traffic offender tried to bribe the police officer:* buy off, pay off, suborn, *Informal* grease the palm of, grease the hand of.

bric-a-brac *n.* *Her home is filled with bric-a-brac:* baubles, trinkets, ornaments, bibelots, knickknacks, gimcracks, gewgaws, kickshaws.

bridal *adj.* *Her bridal gown was of pure silk. The bridal party arrived at the church:* bride's; wedding, marriage, matrimonial, nuptial.

bridge *n.* **1.** *The Golden Gate Bridge crosses the strait leading into San Francisco Bay. They built a bridge over the highway:* span, overpass, passageway; viaduct, catwalk. **2.** *We must build a strong bridge of friendship with Europe:* bond, link, tie, band, connection, union, association, alliance, liaison. —*v.* **3.** *A wooden plank bridged the stream. Both parents and teenagers must try to bridge the generation gap between them:* span, cross, cross over, traverse, go over, extend across, reach across; link, connect, bind, band, unify. —**Ant.** 2 separation, division, schism, split, break, disassociation. 3 widen, separate, divide, split, break.

bridle *n.* **1.** *Grab the horse by the bridle:* head harness; (*loosely*) bit and brace, restraint, muzzle, check, curb. —*v.* **2.** *Bridle the horses:* put on the head harness; harness. **3.** *You must learn to bridle your temper:* curb, check, restrain, control, restrict, suppress, repress, constrain, inhibit, hinder, arrest, muzzle, gag; master, manage, harness, direct, rule. **4.** *Anyone would bridle at such insults:* thrust up one's head, rear up, draw up; recoil, draw back, flinch. —**Ant.** 2 unbridle, unharness. 3 express, voice, utter, air, vent, let out, let go, free. 4 cringe, cower, grovel.

brief *adj.* **1.** *There will be a brief stop for lunch:* short, short-lived, momentary, temporary, quick, hasty, swift, fleeting, transient, transitory. **2.** *Each student is to write a brief outline of the book:* short, concise, succinct, terse, pithy, compact, thumbnail; abbreviated, condensed, abridged, compressed, limited, shortened, curtailed, summarized, summary. —*v.* **3.** *The secretary of defense briefed the President on the enemy's strength:* inform, inform quickly, give the high spots, fill in on, give the details of, describe to, advise, instruct, prepare. —*n.* **4.** *The law journal printed the brief of the case:* legal summary; (*loosely*) argument, contention, case, defense; précis, abstract, capsule, abridgment, résumé. —**Ant.** 1, 2 long, lengthy, extended, prolonged, protracted, extended, extensive. 3 keep uninformed, conceal, keep secret, hide, cover up.

brigade *n.* **1.** *A brigade is usually commanded by a brigadier general:* (*technically, two or more*) regiments, battalions, army groups, squadrons; (*loosely*) military unit, unit, legion, contingent, body of troops, detachment. **2.** *The little town has a volunteer fire brigade:* company, corps, unit, force, squad, team, contingent, outfit, crew, group, organization.

brigand *n.* *In the Old West, masked brigands plundered farmhouses and held up stagecoaches:* outlaw, bandit, desperado, ruffian, cutthroat, gunman, hoodlum; marauder, plunderer, looter, vandal, pillager, spoiler, despoiler, pilferer; (*variously*) highwayman, robber, thief, rustler, pirate, buccaneer, privateer, corsair.

bright *adj.* **1.** *The bright lights hurt my eyes. Children love bright colors:* brilliant, blazing, dazzling, shimmering, vivid, intense, shining, glowing, gleaming, beaming, radiant, sparkling, glittering, resplendent; luminous, lustrous, lambent, effulgent; illuminated, light-filled, sunny, warm. **2.** *Only bright students are given scholarships. He came up with a bright idea:* intelligent, smart, brainy, brilliant; wise, profound, sage, sagacious, shrewd, keen, clever, inventive, resourceful, ingenious, perceptive, discerning, alert, wide-awake, clearheaded, aware, quick, quick-witted, sharp, acute, astute; talented, gifted, capable, competent, proficient, masterful, excellent, great, illustrious, grand, magnificent, outstanding, remarkable, splendid. **3.** *The children's bright laughter could be heard throughout the house:* merry, gay, blithe, happy, joyous, joyful, cheerful, glad; jolly, lively, exhilarating, sparkling. **4.** *The young lawyer has a bright future ahead of him:* promising, favorable, auspicious, propitious, hopeful, optimistic, exciting, rosy; successful, prosperous, happy, healthy, sunny, excellent, grand, good. **—Ant.** dull. 1 dim, pale, subdued, dark, drab, gloomy, murky, obscure, dusky, cloudy, misty, cool. 2 dumb, stupid, muddleheaded, slow-witted, witless, brainless, simple-minded, simple, foolish, foolheaded, unwise, rattlebrained, featherbrained, doltish, oafish, dunderheaded, moronic, idiotic, imbecilic, half-witted, asinine, thick, slow, retarded, lethargic, sluggish, ignorant; untalented, ungifted, incapable, incompetent. 3 sad, glum, dreary, joyless, gloomy, forlorn, unhappy, dismal, cheerless, grim, depressed, dejected, doleful, melancholy, downcast, downhearted, heavyhearted. 4 unpromising, inauspicious, hopeless, pessimistic, dim, grim; failing, unsuccessful, unhappy, cloudy, bad, awful, terrible, poor.

brighten *v.* **1.** *Brighten the kitchen by painting it yellow:* make brighter, lighten, enliven, perk up; illuminate, light. **2.** *Your visit brightened my day:* gladden, cheer, make happy, perk up, buoy up, lift, lift up, boost, enliven, animate, stimulate. **—Ant.** 1 darken, dull, blacken. 2 sadden, depress, make downcast.

brilliance also **brilliancy** *n.* **1.** *The diamond glowed with a pure white brilliance:* brightness, radiance, sparkle, glitter, luster, gleam, glow, shine, sheen, shimmer, dazzle, blaze, resplendence, splendor, luminosity, effulgence, intensity, vividness. **2.** *The brilliance of Louis Pasteur led to important advances in medicine and chemistry:* intelligence, smartness, braininess, wisdom, profundity, sagacity, shrewdness, keenness, cleverness, inventiveness, resourcefulness, ingenuity, perception, discernment, alertness, clearheadedness, awareness, quickness, sharpness, acuity; genius, talent, gift, capability, competence, proficiency, masterfulness, excellence, greatness, illustriousness, magnificence, grandeur, distinction. **—Ant.** 1 dullness, dimness, paleness, darkness, drabness, obscurity. 2 stupidity, dumbness, dullness, idiocy, asininity, imbecility, thickness, simple-mindedness, doltishness, oafishness, folly, silliness; inanity, ineptitude, incompetence, mediocrity.

brilliant *adj.* **1.** *The crown was brilliant with jewels:* See BRIGHT, def. **1**. **2.** *Einstein had a brilliant mind. Rachmaninoff was a brilliant pianist:*

See BRIGHT, def. **2.** **—Ant.** See BRIGHT, Antonym list 1 and 2.

brim *n.* **1.** *Fill the cup to the brim:* upper edge, brink, rim, ledge, border, margin, verge; projecting rim, lip. **—v. 2.** *Her eyes brimmed with tears:* fill, fill up, well up, overflow, flood.

brimming *adj. Each cow produced a brimming pail of milk:* brimful, full, level with, loaded, awash.

brine *n. To make dill pickles, soak cucumbers in brine:* salt water, salt solution, saline solution, pickling solution; the sea, sea water. **—Ant.** fresh water, clear water.

bring *v.* **1.** *Bring the dessert to the table:* carry, convey, bear, tote, fetch, deliver, transport, take; accompany. **2.** *April showers bring May flowers. On Tuesday, the district attorney will bring charges:* bring about, cause, induce, effect, institute, begin, start, initiate, usher in, result in; create, engender, generate, originate, produce. **3.** *I just can't bring myself to apologize:* compel, force, make, persuade, convince. **4.** *How much did the house bring on the market?:* sell for; fetch. **—Ant.** 1 take away, send, remove. 2 quash, kill, prevent, suppress, quell, crush, repress, extinguish, put down, squelch, squash, dispel, nullify, abolish, void, revoke.

brink *n. The tree grew on the brink of the cliff. The world is on the brink of war:* edge, margin, rim, brim, verge, border, skirt, shore, bank; threshold, point.

brisk *adj.* **1.** *The hikers kept up a brisk pace:* quick, swift, lively, active, sprightly, spry, energetic, vigorous, snappy, peppy, alert, animated, spirited, vivacious, chipper, breezy, bustling, busy, dynamic. **2.** *It's great to work outdoors during brisk fall days:* bracing, invigorating, refreshing, fresh, stimulating, stirring, rousing, exhilarating, vivifying. **—Ant.** 1 sluggish, torpid, lethargic, lazy, indolent, slothful, inactive, unenergetic, heavy, dull. 2 tiring, exhausting, fatiguing, wearisome; boring, monotonous, dull.

brittle *adj. This chalk is too brittle to write with:* breakable, fragile, frangible, crumbly, friable. **—Ant.** strong, sturdy, supple, elastic, resilient, flexible; unbreakable.

broach *v. He's been dating her for years but has never broached the subject of marriage:* mention, suggest, introduce, bring up, touch on, pose, propose, advance, submit, institute, open up, launch. **—Ant.** repress, suppress, keep hidden, conceal, secrete; close, end.

broad *adj.* **1.** *He was tall and had broad shoulders:* wide; outspread. **2.** *Can you imagine crossing the broad plains of the West in a covered wagon?:* expansive, extensive, extended, spacious, immense, capacious, roomy, rangy, large, ample, sizable, thick. **3.** *A zookeeper has to have a broad knowledge of the animal kingdom:* extensive, comprehensive, sweeping, general, inclusive, far-reaching, encyclopedic, universal, wide, wide-ranging, all-embracing, immense, unlimited; nonspecific, undetailed. **4.** *Give me a broad hint. They robbed the bank in broad daylight:* full, plain, open, clear, obvious. **—Ant.** narrow. 1 long, lengthy. 2, 3 limited, confined, circumscribed, restricted, small, slight, scant. **3** specific, detailed. **4** partial, veiled, obscure, hidden, enigmatical.

broadcast v. **1.** *The World Series is broadcast to Europe, Asia, and South America:* transmit, send out, beam, put on the air, radio, televise, relay, cable; distribute, disseminate. —n. **2.** *The special election broadcast will be on the local station at eight tonight:* program, show; announcement, talk, statement.

broadcasting n. *Broadcasting was regulated by a government act:* transmission, transmitting, telecasting, televising, airing, air time.

broaden v. *The road was broadened into a four-lane highway. The company broadened its line by adding three new items to sell to supermarkets:* widen, spread out, stretch, enlarge, expand, extend, distend, dilate, swell; increase, raise, boost, build up, amplify, augment, supplement, develop, advance, improve, strengthen, reinforce, intensify. —**Ant.** narrow, squeeze, contract, decrease; reduce, simplify, subtract from, diminish.

broad-minded adj. *The new priest is a flexible and broad-minded man:* open-minded, tolerant, catholic, unprejudiced, unbiased, unbigoted, undogmatic, liberal, flexible, unprovincial, charitable, amenable, receptive, magnanimous. —**Ant.** narrow-minded, closed-minded, intolerant, prejudiced, biased, bigoted, inflexible, dogmatic, provincial, uncharitable.

brochure n. *The store sent out an advertising brochure:* pamphlet, leaflet, circular, flier, handbill, throwaway, booklet, folder.

broil v. **1.** *Don't fry the steaks; broil them:* cook by direct heat. **2.** *This sun will broil you:* make very hot, burn, scorch, sear, cook, blister, bake, roast, fry, toast, parch.

broke adj. *The company went broke in 1929:* without funds, bankrupt, penniless, insolvent, wiped out, impoverished, strapped, strapped for funds. —**Ant.** wealthy, rich, prosperous, affluent, solvent.

broken-hearted adj. *She was broken-hearted when she and her boyfriend split up:* heartbroken, melancholy, gloomy, wretched, miserable, sad, woebegone, mournful, forlorn, dejected, depressed, despairing, crushed, long-faced, disconsolate. —**Ant.** cheerful, elated, lighthearted, merry, jolly, carefree.

broker n. *My broker suggested that I buy the stock:* brokerage, agent, intermediary, intermediate, middleman, go-between, mediator.

bronze adj. *The lifeguard's skin was bronze from the sun:* reddish-brown, copper-colored, chestnut, reddish-tan, tan, brownish.

brooch n. *The dress was ornamented with a brooch on the lapel:* pin, clasp.

brood n. **1.** *The hen drove the intruders away from her brood:* hatchlings, chicks, young, offspring, litter, spawn, family, children. —v. **2.** *The hen is brooding her eggs:* sit upon, incubate, hatch, cover. **3.** *Don't brood over lost opportunities:* worry, fret, agonize, mope, sulk, dwell, mull, chew.

brook[1] n. *There are trout in this brook:* stream, streamlet, creek, rivulet, rill, run.

brook[2] v. *I will not brook any more of your insolence!:* take, stand, abide, allow, accept, tolerate, bear, put up with, suffer, endure, stomach. —**Ant.** reject, refuse, dismiss, forbear, forbid, prohibit, disallow, bar, banish, resist, repudiate, rebuff, renounce.

broth n. *Instead of coffee try a cup of beef broth for breakfast:* stock, clear soup, bouillon, consommé.

brothel n. *New Orleans was once notorious for its brothels:* whorehouse, house of prostitution, sporting house, fancy house, bawdy house, house of ill repute, house of ill fame, house, bordello, bordel, bagnio, stew, *Slang* cathouse; *French* maison de passe, maison close.

brother n. **1.** *Jakob and Wilhelm Grimm were the scientist brothers who collected fairy tales:* male sibling, blood brother. **2.** *We are all brothers under the skin. Joe was my fraternity brother. The soldiers were brothers in arms:* fellow member, kinsman, peer; fellowman, fellow citizen, countryman, landsman; comrade, companion; colleague, confrere, associate, partner, *Informal* pal, buddy, chum. **3.** *Trappist brothers take vows of silence:* monk, friar, monastic, cleric. —**Ant.** 1 sister, female sibling. 2 nonmember, foreigner, stranger.

brotherhood n. *Brotherhood was not advanced by rivalry on the golf course:* fraternity, clan, clique, coterie guild, league; friendliness, friendship, fellowship, intimacy, kinship, comradeship, camaraderie.

brotherly adj. *Turning him out into the cold wasn't a brotherly act:* benevolent, generous, kindly, charitable, philanthropic, neighborly, comradely.

brow n. **1.** *The blacksmith wiped the sweat from his brow:* forehead. **2.** *The lighthouse is on the brow of the cliff:* edge, brink, brim, rim, periphery, verge, margin, side, border, boundary.

browbeat v. *The lawyer browbeat the witness into confessing he had seen the crime committed:* bully, intimidate, cow, cower, domineer, tyrannize, abash, henpeck, *Slang* bulldoze; badger, harass, hector; threaten, terrorize, frighten. —**Ant.** coax, persuade, flatter, invite, charm, beguile, seduce.

brown adj. **1.** *Pot roast with brown gravy is delicious:* brownish, brunet, brunette, chocolate, cocoa, coffee, mahogany, walnut, nut brown, drab, khaki, greenish-brown, olive drab, dirt-colored, liver-colored, chestnut, tawny, sorrel, hazel, bay, purplish-brown, puce, umber, reddish-brown, terra-cotta, rust, russet, roan, bronze, yellow-brown, buff, golden-brown, copper, auburn, light brown, dun, sand-colored, cinnamon, toast, ginger, tan, camel, fawn, beige. —v. **2.** *Brown the meat and onions together:* sauté, fry, cook.

brownie n. *The fairy tale featured a brownie:* goblin, fairy, elf, pixie, leprechaun, nix, nixie, sprite, imp.

browse v. **1.** *Two cows were browsing in the field:* graze, pasture, nibble, feed, eat. **2.** *I just* browsed through the paper. We browsed through the bookstore: peruse, look through, look over, glance through, examine cursorily, check over, skim, scan, survey, dip into; wander through.

bruise v. **1.** I was cut and bruised by the fall. Don't bruise the tomatoes: discolor, mark, blacken, mar, blemish; injure, wound, hurt, damage. **2.** The insult bruised her feelings: offend, wound, hurt, injure, abuse. —n. **3.** The blow caused a large bruise on his arm: contusion, black mark, discoloration, mark, blemish; injury, wound.

brunet or **brunette** adj. **1.** She prefers brunet men to blonds: dark-haired, brown-haired; brown-haired and brown-eyed, dark, olive-skinned. —n. **2.** She was a brunette until she dyed her hair red. He is a brunet: a dark-haired woman or girl; a dark-haired man or boy. —**Ant.** blond, blonde. 1 fair, light, light-haired, light-skinned.

brunt n. The Florida Keys bore the brunt of the hurricane: full force, force, impact, thrust, main shock, violence, stress.

brush[1] n. **1.** Paint goes on more slowly with a brush than with a roller: bristled tool; (variously) paintbrush, whisk, whiskbroom, duster, clothes brush, hairbrush, nailbrush, scrub brush, wash brush, toothbrush, shoe brush. **2.** She removed the speck of dust with a brush of her hand: brushing, sweep, whisk, flick, grazing, dusting; touch, stroke. **3.** The arrest for speeding was his first brush with the law: encounter, meeting, confrontation, skirmish, engagement, fracas, scuffle, battle, set-to, run-in. —v. **4.** Brush your teeth three times a day: use a brush on; (variously) wash, clean, cleanse, scrub, dust, groom, paint, polish, shine, varnish. **5.** He brushed the papers aside. The spider web brushed my forehead: sweep, whisk, flick; graze, touch, stroke, caress.

brush[2] n. The rabbit disappeared into the brush: underbrush, brushwood, undergrowth, bush, bushes, shrubbery, shrubs; thicket, bracken, fern, copse, sedge, scrub, forest, woodland, woodlands, bush country.

brush-off n. When I saw him again years later, he gave me the brush-off: rejection, cold shoulder, rebuff, snub, repudiation, disregard, slight, squelch, cut; Slang brush, put-down.

brusque adj. Being busy is no excuse for being brusque: abrupt, curt, short, gruff, bearish, crusty, blunt, bluff, harsh, rough, tart; rude, impolite, ungracious, unceremonious, discourteous, ungentle. —**Ant.** civil, considerate, patient, gentle, courteous, polite, gracious, cordial, genial.

brutal adj. In Peter Pan, Captain Hook is a brutal pirate. Murder is a brutal crime: cruel, vicious, savage, inhuman, barbaric, barbarous, ruthless, hardhearted, heartless, pitiless, merciless, remorseless, unfeeling, bloody, brutish, fierce, demoniacal, bloodthirsty, atrocious, hellish; harsh, crude, coarse. —**Ant.** humane, gentle, sweet, kind, softhearted, merciful, sympathetic, sensitive; noble, civilized, refined.

brutality n. The kidnappers subjected their prisoners to extreme brutality: cruelty, viciousness, savagery, savageness, inhumanity, ruthlessness, barbarity, brutishness, ferocity, harshness. —**Ant.** humaneness, gentleness, kindness, tenderness.

brute n. **1.** Hunger can turn people into brutes: savage, barbarian, cruel person, monster, demon, fiend, devil, swine. **2.** Alexander Pope said that man is "the middle link between angels and brutes": beast, wild animal, animal, dumb creature, beast of the field. —**Ant.** 1 gentleman, angel. 2 angel; human, man.

bubble n. **1.** A bubble of paint ruined the smooth wall. Children love to blow bubbles: air ball, globule, droplet, blister, bleb. **2. bubbles.** foam, froth, fizz, effervescence. —v. **3.** The water began to bubble in the teapot: boil, percolate, seethe; foam, froth, fizz, fizzle, effervesce, sparkle, gurgle, burble. —**Ant.** 3 be flat.

bubbly adj. **1.** The bubbly wine gave us a headache: frothy, foamy, effervescent, sparkling, carbonated. **2.** Her bubbly greeting put us in a good mood: high-spirited, vivacious, animated, lively, bouncy, effusive, energetic, sprightly, effervescent, sparky, perky, pert, peppy, frisky. —**Ant.** 1 flat, colorless.

buccaneer n. Buccaneers attacked Spanish treasure galleons in the Caribbean: pirate, privateer, freebooter, corsair.

bucket n. The water bucket leaks: pail, tub, can, cask, container, pitcher, receptacle, vessel; scoop, scuttle, hod; bucketful, pailful.

buckle n. **1.** The cowboy wore a wide belt with a large silver buckle: clasp, hasp, fastener, catch, clip. —v. **2.** Buckle the strap tighter: clasp, fasten, catch, secure, hook, couple. **3.** The walls of the building buckled during the fire: bend, belly out, bulge, sag, warp, curl, crinkle, wrinkle, contort, distort; collapse, cave in, crumple. —**Ant.** 2 unbuckle, unfasten, unhook, uncouple, release, loosen. 3 straighten.

bud n. **1.** The plant's first buds will open soon: unopened flower; shoot, sprout. —v. **2.** The rosebushes are budding: put forth shoots, sprout, open; begin to grow, begin to bloom, blossom, flower, develop, burgeon.

budding adj. The budding plants promised a good show by midsummer: burgeoning, developing, germinating, blossoming, bursting forth, incipient, embryonic, fledgling, flowering, nascent.

buddy n. He had a beer or two with some of his buddies: friend, pal, Brit. mate, chum, comrade, associate, companion, crony, sidekick, partner, fellow, intimate, colleague, confidant, Spanish amigo, confederate, confrere, brother. —**Ant.** foe, enemy, opponent, rival, adversary.

budge v. **1.** We couldn't budge the heavy rock: stir, move, shift, dislodge, dislocate, push, slide, roll. **2.** Once Dad had made a decision, no one could budge him: move, change, shift, influence, persuade, sway, convince. —**Ant.** 1 stick, remain, stay.

budget n. **1.** The federal budget must be approved by Congress. Our household budget is

$50 a week: financial plan, spending plan, financial statement; allowance, allotment, allocation, `funds, moneys, resources, means, cost. *—v.* **2.** *Smart people budget their income:* allocate, schedule, plan, apportion, portion out, arrange, ration.

buff *n.* **1.** *I bought a jacket made of buff:* leather, buffalo hide. **2.** *The boys went swimming in the buff:* nakedness, bare skin, *Informal* the raw. **3.** *Where's the buff that came with the bottle of shoe polish?:* polisher; swab, dauber. **4.** *(Informal) She is an ardent opera buff:* devotee, admirer, fan, enthusiast, follower, connoisseur, mavin, *Slang* nut, bug, freak. *—adj.* **5.** *The child has buff-colored hair:* yellowish-brown, tan, tawny; straw, sandy, yellowish. *—v.* **6.** *She buffed the wood until it shone:* polish, rub, burnish, smooth.

buffer *n.* *After World War I several small countries were created to serve as buffers between major powers:* shield, cushion, protector, bumper.

buffet *v.* *The boxer buffeted his opponent about the head. The wind buffeted the sails:* hit, strike, beat, box, jab, wallop, cuff, slap, knock, baste, pound, thump, bang, rap, thwack, pummel, thrash; push, bump, shove.

buffoon *n.* *The class buffoon made funny faces while the teacher was lecturing:* clown, jester, joker, prankster, trickster, funnyman, mimic, zany, silly-billy, comedian, comic, merry-andrew, madcap, wag; fool, harlequin, pantaloon, punchinello, Punch, Scaramouch, Pierrot.

bug *n.* **1.** *The campers were plagued by bugs:* insect, *(in technical use)* Hemiptera, Heteroptera. **2.** *A lot of people have the flu bug now:* virus, germ. **3.** *The plan contained too many bugs to be effective:* defect, drawback, flaw, fault, weakness. *—v.* **4.** *Stop bugging me!:* bother, annoy, pester, nag, badger. **5.** *He suspected the phone had been bugged:* wiretap, eavesdrop, listen in.

build *v.* **1.** *The school is building a new gym. This factory builds cars:* construct, erect, make, put up, set up, put together, fabricate, fashion, manufacture, produce, forge. **2.** *My father built this business with years of hard work. You must build up your strength again:* increase, enlarge, greaten, extend, develop, raise, enhance, build up, improve, intensify, multiply, augment, supplement, amplify, strengthen, renew, reinforce, harden, steel, brace; establish, found, originate, launch, institute, begin, start, initiate, inaugurate, set up, open, embark on, undertake. **3.** *The army tries to build men and women:* form, shape, mold, produce, create. *—n.* **4.** *His build is too small for playing football:* physique, form, figure, body, construction, structure, shape. *—Ant.* 1–3 demolish, tear down, dismantle, destroy. 2 decrease, diminish, reduce, lessen, lower, contract, attenuate, curtail, shrink, scale down; weaken, dilute, deplete, decline, impair, sap, undermine, debilitate, cripple, harm, injure; end, stop, terminate, finish, conclude, wind up, close, discontinue, suspend, relinquish.

building *n.* *This building was designed by Frank Lloyd Wright:* structure, edifice, construction.

buildup *n.* *The buildup of arms continued yet fighting did not begin:* accumulation, accretion, growth, increase, stockpile, enlargement, escalation, expansion, gain.

built-in *adj.* *The sporty vehicle even had a built-in picnic basket:* inherent, ingrained, innate, congenital, deep-seated, implicit, inborn, incorporated, integral.

bulb *n.* *One clown squeezed the bulb of a horn:* knob, nub, nodule, protuberance, swelling.

bulge *n.* **1.** *What's that bulge in your pocket?:* lump, bump, protuberance, protrusion, projection, swelling, prominence, curve; sagging, bagginess, excess. *—v.* **2.** *The Christmas stocking bulged with goodies:* swell, swell out, puff out, protrude, distend, project, stand out, stick out, bag, sag. *—Ant.* 1 hollow, cavity, hole, pocket. 2 shrink, cave in, collapse.

bulk *n.* **1.** *The sheer bulk of an elephant is startling:* mass, massiveness, largeness, bigness, amplitude, magnitude, size, volume, weight, dimensions, proportions, extent, quantity, measure, substance, greatness, hugeness, enormity. **2.** *He left the bulk of his estate to his wife:* main part, major part, greater part, principal part, better part, lion's share, body, most, majority, preponderance, plurality. *—Ant.* 2 lesser part, minor part, smaller part.

bulky *adj.* *The package is light but it's too bulky to carry:* cumbersome, unwieldy, clumsy, awkward, unhandy, ungainly, unmanageable, lumpish; large, big, huge, massive, immense, voluminous, enormous, hulking, extensive, capacious, sizable. *—Ant.* handy, manageable, wieldy, small, little, petite, diminutive, slim.

bull *n.* *The elephant herd contained three bulls and seven cows:* male; *(variously)* male bovine, ox, male elephant, male whale, male seal, male elk, male moose.

bulldoze *v.* **1.** *The heavy machinery bulldozed a path through the forest:* drive, thrust, push, force, press, shoulder, bump, jostle, propel, shove; rage, fell, level, flatten. **2.** *He bulldozed the other committee members into agreeing with him:* browbeat, intimidate, cow, *Slang* buffalo, bully, dragoon, hector, coerce, bludgeon, subdue.

bullet *n.* *The bullet lodged in the wall behind us:* slug, shot, ammo, ammunition, ball, cartridge, pellet.

bulletin *n.* *The TV program was interrupted by a news bulletin:* brief announcement, news report, report, dispatch, release, account, communiqué, communication, statement, message, notification, note.

bully *n.* **1.** *The bully terrorized the small boys:* tormentor, intimidator, browbeater, petty tyrant, despot, oppressor, coercer; tough, ruffian. *—v.* **2.** *He loved to bully his younger brother:* intimidate, cow, browbeat, bulldoze, tyrannize, domineer, terrorize, frighten, coerce, harass, annoy, ride over, tread on. *—interj.* **3.** *Bully for our team!:* hurray, hurrah, cheers, good, well done,

Slang swell, right on. —**Ant.** 2 lure, entice, flatter, coax, cajole, urge, persuade.

bulwark *n.* **1.** *A bulwark surrounded the old fort. Aswan Dam stands as a bulwark against flooding of the Nile:* defensive wall, earthwork, embankment, rampart, parapet; barrier, guard. **2.** *The town meeting was the bulwark of New England democracy:* support, mainstay. —**Ant.** 2 weakness, weak link.

bum *n.* **1.** (*Informal*) *The bum begged in the daytime and slept in a doorway at night. A ski bum spends more time skiing than working:* tramp, hobo, derelict, vagrant, vagabond; loafer, idler, drifter. —*v.* **2.** *Buy your own cigarettes instead of bumming them from me!:* beg, borrow, cadge, *Slang* grub, mooch, sponge.

bump *v.* **1.** *The child bumped his head on the table. The two cars bumped together:* hit, strike, knock, slam, bang, smack, whack, crack, thump, rap; collide, crash into, crash, smash into, run into, butt, buffet, clash. **2.** *The old truck bumped along the rocky road:* bounce, jolt, jar, jounce, jostle; shake, rattle. —*n.* **3.** *His amnesia was caused by a bump on the head:* blow, rap, knock, impact, hit, whack, wallop, slam, smack, sock, smash, bang, crack, slap, punch, crash, jolt, collision; *Slang* poke. **4.** *His legs were covered with bumps and bruises. Watch that bump in the road:* lump, swelling, node; hump, knob, protuberance, bulge, excrescence, gnarl, knot, nodule. —**Ant.** 2 roll, glide, sail, flow, slide, slip, glissade, coast.

bumptious *adj.* *He's a bumptious young man who has more than his share of self-confidence:* overbearing, aggressive, pushy, self-assertive, impudent, insolent, cocky, cocksure, overconfident, impertinent, brazen, obtrusive, forward, presumptuous, *Dial.* bodacious; arrogant, haughty, conceited, swaggering, boastful. —**Ant.** shy, retiring, self-effacing, demure, timid, modest, bashful.

bun *n.* **1.** *Cinnamon buns are good for breakfast:* roll, soft roll, sweet roll. **2.** *Aunt Mary always wore her hair in a bun:* coil, knot.

bunch *n.* **1.** *A bunch of grapes makes a pretty centerpiece. Let's throw out that old bunch of newspapers:* cluster, clump; bundle, batch, collection, assortment, accumulation, array, stack, heap, pile, quantity, lot, mass, number, amount; shock, knot. **2.** *A bunch of children surrounded the ice-cream vendor:* group, band, flock, bevy, troop, pack, multitude, crowd, host, company, gang, tribe, team, mob, string, gathering; assembly. —*v.* **3.** *We bunched around the fire for warmth:* huddle, crowd, gather, cluster, group, mass, collect, draw together, congregate, assemble, pack, flock, herd, cram together. —**Ant.** 3 separate, disperse, scatter, leave.

bundle *n.* **1.** *The Christmas shopper was loaded down with bundles. A bundle of books was donated to the library:* package, parcel, packet; bale, sheaf, pack, stack, heap, pile, array, bunch, batch, collection, assortment, accumulation, multitude; mass, group, lot, amount, quantity. —*v.* **2.** *Newspapers were bundled on*

the truck: tie together, wrap, package, bind, truss, bale, stack. —**Ant.** 2 disperse, scatter.

bungle *v.* *The plumber bungled the job and now the pipe leaks. I bungled in thinking $100 would be enough for the vacation:* blunder, botch, miff, mismanage, do badly, spoil, ruin, mar, butcher, mess up, make a mess of, miscalculate, misreckon, misestimate, miscompute, misjudge; *Slang* foul up, louse up, goof, screw up, *Informal* flub. —**Ant.** succeed, accomplish, effect, carry off, carry out, triumph.

bunk[1] *n.* *First-class passengers sleep in staterooms, third-class sleep in bunks:* berth, built-in bed, platform bed, bed, pallet, cot.

bunk[2] *n.* (*Informal*) *His claiming to be a good swimmer is a lot of bunk:* poppycock, baloney, hokum, tommyrot, rot, hogwash, claptrap, humbug, hooey, malarky, spinach, applesauce, hot air, stuff and nonsense, stuff, bull, bunkum, balderdash, blather; nonsense, foolishness, inanity, bombast, ridiculousness.

buoy *n.* **1.** *The Coast Guard replaced the buoy in the channel:* floating marker, bellbuoy, float, beacon, bell. —*v.* **2.** *Flotation collars are used to buoy space capsules that land in the sea:* keep afloat, keep from sinking. **3.** *There's nothing like a good joke to buoy one's spirits:* lift, uplift, raise, boost, elevate, lighten, cheer, cheer up, gladden, brighten. —**Ant.** 2 sink, drown. 3 lower, crush, dash, cast down, depress, deject, deaden, sadden, dull, darken, chill, damp, dampen.

buoyancy also **buoyance** *n.* **1.** *Modern life preservers have a great deal of buoyancy:* floatability, floatiness; lightness, weightlessness. **2.** *The host's buoyancy ensured that the guests had a good time:* good spirits, animation, vivacity, enthusiasm, exhilaration, good humor, cheerfulness, cheeriness, gladness, joyousness, sunniness, brightness, glee, gaiety, lightheartedness, joviality, jollity. —**Ant.** 2 depression, dejection, low spirits, bad humor, cheerlessness, sadness, gloominess, melancholy, tears; dullness, lethargy.

buoyant *adj.* **1.** *Taking a deep breath and holding it can keep a person buoyant in the water:* afloat, floating, floatable; light, weightless. **2.** *Her buoyant personality made many friends for her:* animated, vivacious, enthusiastic, exhilarated, elated, cheerful, happy, glad, joyful, joyous, sunny, bright, gay, light, lighthearted, blithesome, merry, jolly; optimistic, hopeful, carefree, free and easy, breezy, sportive; energetic, peppy, lively, sprightly. —**Ant.** 2 gloomy, glum, dour, sullen, moody, sad, joyless, cheerless, unhappy, tearful, depressed, dejected, morose, doleful, melancholy, despondent; pessimistic, careworn; forlorn, hopeless, despairing; dull, lethargic.

burden *n.* **1.** *A horse can easily carry a burden of several hundred pounds:* load, weight; cargo, freight, pack. **2.** *She bore the burden of raising two children alone:* weight, load, strain, stress, care, responsibility, onus, trouble, anxiety; encumbrance, hardship. —*v.* **3.** *The hiker was burdened with a heavy pack. I don't like being bur-*

dened with someone else's problems: weigh down, load with, load, overload; make responsible for, obligate, saddle with, trouble, encumber, try, tax, vex, press down, afflict, handicap, oppress, hamper, strain, hinder. —**Ant.** 2 freedom, ease. 3 lighten, free, ease.

bureau *n.* **1.** *Put the clean shirts in the top drawer of the bureau:* chest of drawers, dresser, chiffonier, cabinet, commode. **2.** *The Weather Bureau has issued a storm warning:* agency, department, office, division, station, administration, branch, service.

bureaucracy *n. Every year the bureaucracy lost effectiveness:* officials, officialdom, administration, government, public service, civil service, directorate, ministry, management; routine, regulations, *Informal* red tape.

bureaucrat *n. I couldn't get a definite answer out of any of those bureaucrats at City Hall:* civil servant, public servant, functionary, *Russian* apparatchik, officeholder, official, *Slang* penpusher, politician, politico, rubber stamp, mandarin.

burgeon *v. Housing developments are burgeoning on all sides. Spring has begun to burgeon in every valley and glade:* thrive, flourish, expand, enlarge, grow, develop, mushroom, escalate, wax, increase, spring up, shoot up, proliferate, augment, spread; bloom, blossom, flower, blow, effloresce, open, fructify, bear fruit.

burglar *n. The burglar has robbed eight houses in two weeks:* housebreaker, prowler; robber, thief, pilferer, purloiner; second-story man, cracksman, *Slang* yegg.

burglary *n. The burglary took place when no one was home:* breaking and entering, break-in, theft, robbery, housebreaking, burglarizing, stealing, larceny, felony; filching, pilfering, purloining.

burial *n. The burial was held at a nonsectarian cemetery:* inhumation, interment, entombment; funeral, obsequies, rites. —**Ant.** exhumation, disinterment.

burlesque *n. The senior class show contained a burlesque on absent-minded professors:* satire, parody, farce, takeoff, spoof, caricature, mockery, ridicule, travesty; comedy, slapstick comedy, buffoonery. —**Ant.** factual representation, history, portrait; tragedy.

burly *adj. The wrestler was a burly man:* sturdy, strapping, hefty, bulky, brawny, beefy, stocky, thickset, big, large, sizable, strong, ponderous, hulking. —**Ant.** puny, weak, thin, slim, skinny, scrawny, lean, spare, lanky, gaunt, angular, rawboned; small, diminutive.

burn *v.* **1.** *The building burned as crowds watched helplessly. The lights in the kitchen burned all night:* be on fire, blaze, be ablaze, flame, be in flames, smoke, smolder; incandesce, glow, flare, flash, flicker. **2.** *Wet wood won't burn. Rake up the leaves and burn them. The toast burned:* ignite, kindle, fire; set on fire, set fire to, incinerate, consume with flames, reduce to ashes, cremate; char, scorch, sear, scald, singe, blister, oxidize, wither, shrivel, parch. **3.** *This car burns too much gas:* use as

fuel, consume. **4.** *The child burned with fever:* be feverish, be hot, swelter, be flushed. **5.** *The cut burns from the iodine. Holding the rope burned his hands:* pain, hurt, smart, sting, tingle, prickle, prick, bite, nip; chafe, abrade, scrape, skin, blister, irritate, nettle. **6.** *I burn too easily to stay on the beach for long:* sunburn, tan, suntan, brown, bronze. —*n.* **7.** *The fire fighter suffered severe burns. The burn of the antiseptic made him wince. The lariat gave me a rope burn:* (*variously*) first-degree burn, reddening, second-degree burn, blistering, blister, third-degree burn, charring; smart, sting, tingle, pain, prickle, bite; abrasion, chafe, scrape, irritation. **8.** *I smell the burn of rubber:* incineration, burning, fire, flames, smoke, smoldering, kindling. —**Ant.** 1, 2 extinguish, put out, go out, burn out, smother. 4 be cold, shiver, have a chill, chill. 5 tickle, cool, assuage, soothe. 6 whiten, pale, fade.

burning *adj.* **1.** *The burning building gave off an eerie light:* flaming, aflame, afire, blazing, fiery, ignited, kindled, smoldering, smoking, raging, sizzling, glowing, flaring, flickering, flashing. **2.** *She had a burning desire to be an actress:* all-consuming, raging, fervent, fervid, passionate, impassioned, ardent, eager, fanatic, zealous, intense, frantic, frenzied, fiery, red-hot, glowing, boiling, hot, heated, aglow; resolute, compelling, sincere, earnest. **3.** *The hot mustard left a burning sensation on his tongue:* stinging, smarting, piercing, irritating, prickling, tingling; painful, caustic, biting, sharp, astringent, acrid, corroding, pungent. —**Ant.** 2 half-hearted, indifferent, lukewarm, mild, perfunctory, faint, passive, apathetic, lethargic, laconic, phlegmatic, lackadaisical. 3 soothing, cooling, numbing.

burnish *v. The silver bracelet was burnished to a bright finish:* polish, wax, buff, shine, smooth, rub up. —**Ant.** abrade, scratch, mar.

burrow *n.* **1.** *The rabbit's burrow is under the flower bed:* hole, furrow, dugout, den, lair, tunnel, cave, covert. —*v.* **2.** *The steam shovel burrowed into the soft ground:* dig, tunnel, excavate, scoop out, hollow out. —**Ant.** 2 fill in, cover over.

bursar *n. Tuition checks are made out to the college bursar:* treasurer, purser, cashier, cashkeeper, paymaster.

burst *v.* **1.** *The balloon burst. He watched the bombs bursting in air. This dress is so tight the seams are bursting:* break, break open, shatter, fly apart, fragment, disintegrate; explode, blow up, blast, detonate, discharge, pop; rupture, fracture, split, crack, splinter, pull apart, tear apart, separate, detach, divide, sunder, rend, disjoin, disconnect. **2.** *She burst into tears. He burst into the room ranting and raving:* erupt, break, break out, gush forth, spout; rush, run, spring forth, barge, fly, *Slang* bust. —*n.* **3.** *The soldiers heard the burst of guns in the distance:* explosion, detonation, discharge, blast, bang, pop; breaking, shattering, crashing, cracking, splitting. **4.** *With a great burst of speed the airplane took off:* outburst, outpouring, outbreak, eruption, rush, torrent. —**Ant.** 1 put together, hold together, connect, join, unite, fasten, secure, attach. 4 cessation, stopping; slowing down, deceleration.

bury v. **1.** *John F. Kennedy is buried in Arlington Cemetery:* inter, entomb, inhume, lay in the grave, consign to the grave, deposit in the earth. **2.** *The letter was buried under a pile of papers on the desk:* hide, conceal, secrete, cache, cover, cover up, submerge, submerse, immerse, engulf, enclose, encase. —**Ant.** 1 exhume, disinter; resurrect. 2 unearth, uncover, discover, find, bring to light, reveal, expose, show, exhibit, display.

bush n. **1.** *The yard was bordered by neatly trimmed bushes:* plant, shrub, shrubbery, hedge. **2.** *The safari headed off into the bush:* woods, woodlands, veld, barrens, forest, jungle, brush.

bushy adj. *The bushy hedge required pruning:* shaggy, thick, unruly, unkempt, furry, prickly, rough, rumpled, bristly.

busily adv. *They occupied themselves busily in the kitchen:* energetically, industriously, ardently, assiduously, diligently, expeditiously, fervently, indefatigably, strenuously, unremittingly, vigorously, zealously.

business n. **1.** *What business are you in?:* job, profession, vocation, occupation, career, calling, pursuit; work, employment, line, industry, trade, field, activity, specialty, specialization, function, duty, position, place, province, assignment, mission, livelihood, living, means of support, walk of life, bread and butter, *Slang* racket. **2.** *A financier must have a keen understanding of business:* commerce, industry, manufacturing, trade, buying and selling, merchandising; dealing, transaction, negotiation, bargaining, affairs. **3.** *My father owns a small business in St. Louis:* firm, establishment, concern, store, shop, factory, office, enterprise, venture, undertaking; corporation, company, partnership. **4.** *My personal life is none of your business! Let's get down to the business at hand:* concern, affair, problem, question, responsibility; matter, job, task, duty, chore, situation, procedure, case, subject, topic, point. —**Ant.** 1 unemployment, inactivity; avocation, hobby, entertainment, relaxation.

businesslike adj. *Let's conduct this meeting in a businesslike manner:* orderly, organized, systematic, methodical, regular, efficient, practical, professional, correct; serious, careful, thorough, diligent, industrious, sedulous, assiduous, painstaking. —**Ant.** disorderly, disorganized, unorganized, unsystematic, irregular, miscellaneous, catch-as-catch-can, frivolous; inefficient, unprofessional, impractical, careless, sloppy, messy, untidy, slipshod.

bust n. **1.** *The sweater had red sleeves and a blue stripe across the bust:* bosom, breast, chest. **2.** *The sculptor made a bust of Beethoven:* head, sculpture.

bustle v. **1.** *The clerk bustled about trying to wait on three customers at once:* scurry, hurry, rush, hustle, scamper, dash, scramble, tear, fly,

flit, scuttle, flutter, fluster; stir, bestir, be active, press on, make haste, be quick, make the most of one's time, work against time, not let the grass grow under one's feet. —n. **2.** *The bustle of New York City is very confusing:* commotion, flurry, tumult, hustle, stir, agitation, hurly-burly, activity, fuss, hurry, excitement; pother, to-do, ado. —**Ant.** 1 move slowly, crawl, creep, drag one's feet, procrastinate, waste time; loaf, relax, rest. 2 inactivity, quiet, peacefulness, tranquillity.

busy adj. **1.** *The secretary was busy all day typing the reports:* occupied, active, engaged, employed, working, hard at work, laboring, toiling, industrious, slaving, on duty, in harness; engrossed, absorbed, intent. **2.** *This is one of my busy days:* active, strenuous, full, bustling. —v. **3.** *Grandmother busied herself with sewing:* occupy, keep occupied, engage, employ, work at, labor at, be engrossed in, be absorbed in. —**Ant.** 1, 2 idle, inactive, unoccupied, unemployed, at leisure, lackadaisical, off duty. 2 lazy, slothful, sluggish, indolent, relaxed, slack.

busybody n. *That old busybody wants to know everyone's business:* meddler, snoop, pry, Paul Pry; gossip, scandalmonger, telltale, tattletale, blabbermouth, blabber, chatterbox, newsmonger, talebearer.

but conj. **1.** *She was tall but her brother was very short:* however, nevertheless, yet, further, moreover, still. **2.** *Overcome by misery, the dog could do nothing but howl:* excepting, save, except. —prep. **3.** *We had nothing left but a dry biscuit:* excepting, except, save, excluding, disregarding. —adv. **4.** *There is but one excuse for his conduct:* only, just, no more than.

butcher v. **1.** *Roving patrols were accused of butchering many of the villagers:* massacre, murder, kill, assassinate, slaughter, exterminate, liquidate, slay, decimate, purge, annihilate. **2.** *The band proceeded to butcher every selection on the program:* botch, ruin, spoil, mess up, bungle, manhandle, mishandle, fumble, boggle; *Slang* louse up, screw up, goof, muff. —n. **3.** *The inmates knew him as the Butcher of Buchenwald:* killer, murderer, mass-murderer, assassin, slaughterer, liquidator, exterminator, bloodshedder, homicide, hatchet man, hit man, homicidal maniac.

butt[1] n. *Pork butt makes a delicious roast. The rifle barrel is firmly attached to the butt:* end, blunt end, bottom, shank, stub, stump. —**Ant.** front, top.

butt[2] n. *It's no fun to be the butt of a joke:* target, victim, mark, object, laughingstock, dupe, *Slang* goat.

butt[3] v. *The rams butted each other playfully:* (with the head or horns) push, shove, bump, knock, hit, strike, bunt, smack, thump, thwack, rap, ram, buck, thrust, buffet, jostle, jab, slap.

buttocks n. *The pants are too tight across the buttocks:* posterior, rump, seat, rear, rear end, backside, bottom, derrière, *Informal* fanny, keister, *Slang* behind, butt; fundament, nates, hindquarters, haunches.

buttress n. **1.** *The north wall of the cathedral had a beautiful stone buttress:* support, brace, prop, stanchion, abutment, arch, stay, shoulder. —*v.* **2.** *Buttress that fence with some two-by-fours. You'd better buttress your argument with more facts:* prop, prop up, brace, shore, shore up, reinforce, strengthen, bolster, support, boost, steel.

buxom *adj. Some women prefer to be thin rather than buxom:* (of women) plump, robust, well-developed, strapping, chesty, large-breasted, bosomy, voluptuous, *Yiddish* zaftig. —**Ant.** frail, delicate, thin, slender, skinny, lean; pale, wan.

buy *v.* **1.** *Many families buy a new car every two years:* purchase, put money into, pay for, invest in, acquire, procure, obtain, gain, get. **2.** *Honest politicians cannot be bought:* bribe, buy off, corrupt, influence, suborn. —*n.* **3.** *The coat was a good buy at $39:* bargain, worthy purchase. —**Ant.** l sell, vend, retail, auction, hawk; rent, lease.

buzz *n.* **1.** *The audience made such a buzz, I couldn't hear the play. The buzz in the room stopped when he got up and spoke:* murmur, whisper; buzzing, hum, humming sound. —*v.* **2.** *Insects buzzed around the flowers:* hum, drone, whir.

by *adv.* **1.** *The bus drove by them:* near, close, at hand, handy, in reach. —*prep.* **2.** *Their home was by the shopping center:* next to, near, nigh, nearby, close to, beside, along, alongside. **3.** *She arrived by plane:* by means of, on, through, with, via.

bygone *adj. The old man told stories of bygone days:* gone by, past, earlier, previous, former, departed, of yore, olden, ancient. —**Ant.** future, to come, coming, prospective, subsequent, succeeding, later, unborn.

bypass *v. Route 80 bypasses Cleveland to avoid city traffic:* go around, go by, circumvent, detour around, avoid, dodge, avert. —**Ant.** go through, bisect, cross, meet, confront.

bypath *n. We took the bypath through the woods and arrived ahead of the others:* back road, side road, secondary road, lane, trail, dirt road, byway, bypass, footway, footpath, alley, way, track, pathway, garden path, shortcut, walkway, bridle path, towpath, beaten path.

bystander *n. The boy wasn't involved in the fight—he was just an innocent bystander:* onlooker, looker-on, spectator, witness, observer, beholder, viewer, watcher, attender; passerby. —**Ant.** participant, principal.

byword *n. From now on, "Haste makes waste" is going to be my byword:* rule, dictum, principle, precept, law, truth; pet phrase, slogan, motto, saying, maxim, proverb, axiom, adage, watchword, aphorism, apothegm, catchword, shibboleth, saw.

C

cab n. Don't wait for a bus; hail a cab: taxi, taxi-cab, hack.

cabal n. **1.** The government was toppled by a cabal of dissident generals: junta, faction, combination, band, ring, league. **2.** The Russian émigrés were constantly engaged in anti-Soviet cabals: intrigue, conspiracy, plot, design, scheme, plan, machination, connivance.

cabalistic adj. It was an ancient philosophy featuring cabalistic interpretations of the Scriptures: obscure, occult, mysterious, supernatural, abstruse, esoteric, arcane, secret, mystic; impenetrable, unknowable, inscrutable, unfathomable, incomprehensible. **—Ant.** obvious, apparent, unmistakable, self-evident, crystal-clear.

cabaret n. Cabarets are full on New Year's Eve: supper club, nightclub, bistro, café, Informal club.

cabin n. **1.** Abraham Lincoln was born in a cabin. Many fishermen own cabins along the lake: log cabin, hut, shack, shanty, hutch; lodge, cottage, bungalow. **2.** The captain's cabin is near the bridge of the ship: stateroom, quarters, room; compartment. **—Ant.** 1 mansion, palace, castle.

cabinet n. **1.** The secretary of state is an important member of the federal cabinet: council, group of counselors, official advisers, advisory board, ministry. **2.** Put the dishes in the cabinet: cupboard, kitchen cabinet, china closet, china cabinet, breakfront, bureau; case, chest, chest of drawers, file, box, receptacle.

cable n. **1.** The telephone company laid their cables beneath the streets. The tarpaulin was held in place by two cables: bundle of wires, electric wire, wires, wire line, line, wire rope; rope, cord, twisted strand; chain, mooring, hawser; fastening. **2.** Send a cable to our overseas office: cablegram, overseas telegram, wire.

cache n. **1.** The rebels had a cache of firearms in the mountains: store, stockpile, stock, secret repository, hoard, heap. **2.** Pirates buried their gold in a cache near here: hiding place, hideaway, secret place. **—Ant.** 2 display, exhibition, show, array.

cacophonous adj. The cacophonous sounds of the street came through the open window: dissonant, inharmonious, harsh, raucous, discordant, unmusical, unmelodious, strident, screechy, jarring, grating, disharmonious, nonmelodious; out of tune, off-key, off-pitch.

cad n. Only a cad would strike a woman: dishonorable man, bounder, rotter, lout, churl, dastard, Slang cur, louse, heel, rat; villain, scoundrel, rascal, knave, rogue, caitiff. **—Ant.** gentleman, cavalier; hero, champion, worthy, Informal prince.

cadaver n. The cadaver was taken to the morgue: corpse, dead body, body, remains, deceased, Slang stiff.

cadaverous adj. His long illness gave him a cadaverous appearance: corpselike, deathlike, deathly; ghastly, gaunt, pale, ashen, chalky, pallid, bloodless, blanched.

cadence n. The soldiers marched to the cadence of the band: rhythmic pattern, beat, tempo, swing, lilt, throb, pulse, accent, measure, meter, rhythm.

café n. We ate in a little sidewalk café overlooking the Seine: restaurant, bistro, coffeehouse, inn, tavern, bar and grill, cafeteria, luncheonette, automat, diner, chophouse, lunchroom; Slang eatery, hash house, beanery; night club, supper club, discotheque, cabaret, nitery.

cage n. **1.** The lion paced back and forth in his cage: barred enclosure, enclosure, pen, coop. **—v. 2.** In modern zoos animals are not caged but are confined by walls and moats: lock up, shut in, pen, pen in, coop up, encage, impound, imprison; confine, restrict, restrain. **—Ant.** 2 let out, free, liberate.

cagey adj. The cagey deer avoided the hunter's traps: wary, cautious, chary, careful, prudent, alert, watchful, heedful, discreet, leery; wily, cunning, crafty, shifty, sly, foxy, artful, shrewd, sharp, keen. **—Ant.** unwary, careless, heedless, reckless, rash, unthinking, unguarded, trusting, imprudent, indiscreet; dense, dull, slow-witted, stolid.

cajole v. The cat cajoled her into giving it a sardine: wheedle, coax, beguile, entice, inveigle, flatter, soft-soap, sweet-talk, blandish.

cajolery n. The mother used threats and cajolery to get the child to eat his spinach: wheedling, coaxing, inveigling, enticement, beguilement, promises, Informal sweet talk, Slang soft soap; persuasion; flattery, fawning, adulation, blandishment, blarney. **—Ant.** threats, extortion, coercion, force.

cake n. **1.** The birthday cake had chocolate icing: (variously) layer cake, loaf cake, cupcake, gateau; (loosely) pastry, sweet rolls, buns, tortes, éclairs, cookies. **2.** Cakes of ice floated downstream. Buy a cake of soap: block, bar; mass, lump. **—v. 3.** The mud caked on the side of the car: harden, solidify, dry, coagulate, congeal, thicken, crust; mass, compress, consolidate.

calamitous adj. A drought would be calamitous to the region's crops: disastrous, catastrophic, fatal, ruinous, cataclysmic, adverse, destructive, detrimental, harmful, deleterious, pernicious, blighting; tragic, distressful, dreadful, woeful, baleful, unfortunate, unlucky. **—Ant.** beneficial, advantageous, favorable, helpful, valuable, fortunate, good, convenient.

calamity n. The recent flooding in the South was a calamity: disaster, catastrophe, tragedy, cataclysm, adversity, affliction, hardship, misfortune, tribulation, trial, undoing, downfall, reverse, blow, failure, scourge, ruin; mishap, mischance, ill fortune, bad luck, stroke of ill luck; distress, misery, trouble, woe, sea of troubles, ill, ill wind. **—Ant.** benefit, blessing, advantage, help, aid, boon, good fortune, good luck, piece of luck, windfall.

calculate *v.* **1.** *Income tax is calculated on a percentage of net income minus exemptions and deductions:* compute, figure, reckon, determine, ascertain, work out; count, sum up, add up, measure. **2.** *I calculate we'll be in San Diego in six more hours:* judge, estimate, figure, reckon, surmise, predict, conjecture. **3.** *The President's speech was calculated to ease world tensions:* design, intend, plan, devise, project, mean, aim at.

calculating *adj.* *He's a cold, calculating man who will do anything to get to the top:* scheming, designing, plotting, contriving, intriguing, Machiavellian, crafty, manipulative, devious, cunning, wily, tricky, artful; shrewd, foxy, sly. —**Ant.** open, candid, frank, direct, plainspoken, sincere, aboveboard, honest; naïve, artless, guileless, ingenuous, undesigning.

calculation *n.* **1.** *The scientist's calculations proved exactly right:* computation, figuring, reckoning; answer, result. **2.** *By my calculations, Ohio State will win the game by one touchdown:* judgment, estimation, reckoning.

calendar *n.* **1.** *The calendar showed that Christmas fell on a Tuesday:* chart of days, weeks, and months. **2.** *The executive noted the appointment on his calendar:* agenda, day book, diary, schedule, list, register, docket, program, table.

caliber *n.* **1.** *The caliber of a gun determines the weight of its projectile:* bore, inside diameter. **2.** *His character was of the highest caliber:* worth, merit, excellence, quality, ability, competence, capability, capacity, talent, gifts, skill, power, scope; stature, reputation, repute, importance, prominence, prestige, eminence, distinction, estimation, achievement, position, rank, place.

call *v.* **1.** *Did you hear someone call for help? Please stand when the teacher calls your name:* call out, cry out, cry, shout, yell, bellow, scream, roar, clamor, bawl, speak loudly, holler, hail, halloo. **2.** *Call the children in for supper. Call a meeting of the club members:* summon, ask, bid, invite, order, command, demand, require, direct, instruct, charge; call together, convene, assemble, convoke, muster, collect, gather, rally. **3.** *The hospital calls on everyone to support the fund-raising drive:* appeal to, ask, ask for, call upon, entreat, bid, request, petition, invoke, summon, invite, supplicate, pray to. **4.** *Some old friends came to call. Our sales representative will call to pick up the order:* visit, pay a visit, look in on, drop in, stop off, stop by. **5.** *The union called a strike:* proclaim, announce, declare, decree, order, command, convoke. **6.** *Just call me Bob. The publisher decided to call the book* The Golden Flower. *The play was called a masterpiece:* name, dub, christen, title, entitle, term, identify, designate, style, label, tag, characterize, describe as, know as, specify. **7.** *I'll call you long distance tonight:* telephone, phone, contact, *Informal* buzz, *Chiefly British* ring. —*n.* **8.** *Did you hear a call?:* outcry, crying out, cry, shout, yell, scream, bellow, clamor; hail, halloo, *Informal* holler. **9.** *He got a call for jury duty. The President issued a call to arms. The explorer answered the call of the wild:* summons, order, notice, command, demand, direction, instruction, charge; invitation, request, bid, appeal, entreaty, petition, supplication, plea; announcement, proclamation, declaration, decree. **10.** *Let's make a call on the Johnsons. The doctor doesn't make house calls:* visit, stop. **11.** *The secretary took all calls:* telephone call, phone call, telephone message. **12.** *You had no call to do that. There's no call for us to take skis on our vacation this year:* right, need, cause, reason, grounds, claim, occasion, justification, excuse, warrant. —**Ant.** 1 be silent, be still, be quiet; whisper, murmur. 2 excuse, dismiss, release, disperse, scatter. 3 grant, give. 5 call off, cancel, renounce. 8 whisper, murmur. 9 excuse, dismissal, release.

calling *n.* **1.** *We could hear him calling to us from a block away:* calling out, crying out, outcry, crying, shouting, yelling, screaming, bellowing, hailing, hallooing. **2.** *Math is her calling:* main interest, mission, first love, attachment, dedication, devotion, passion, enthusiasm, preferred pursuit, province, forte, specialty, specialization, métier; life's work, career, profession, vocation, occupation, employment, business, job, work, line, field, trade, craft, activity, function, assignment, livelihood, living, means of support, walk of life, bread and butter. —**Ant.** 1 whispering, murmuring. 2 hobby, avocation; bane, nuisance, affliction, scourge, curse, plague, aversion, dislike, anathema, abomination, bane of one's existence, thorn in the flesh.

callous *adj.* **1.** *The farmer's hands were callous from years of toil:* callused, hard, hardened, horny, tough, thick-skinned, pachydermatous. **2.** *Years of pain made her callous to the suffering of others:* unsympathetic, unfeeling, insensitive, uncaring, cold, hard, hardened, inured, hard-hearted, heartless, cruel, apathetic, dispassionate, unresponsive, indifferent. —**Ant.** 1 tender, soft, thin-skinned. 2 compassionate, sympathetic, sensitive, soft, soft-hearted, warmhearted, caring, responsive, gentle.

callow *adj.* *The callow youth didn't know enough to be polite to the old man:* immature, inexperienced, unseasoned, untried, green, raw, unschooled, uninitiated, uninformed, ignorant, shallow, awkward, unsophisticated, naïve, crude, artless; childish, juvenile, infantile, puerile, sophomoric. —**Ant.** mature, grown-up, adult, experienced, tried and true, finished; informed, sophisticated, polished.

calm *adj.* **1.** *The water was so calm it looked like glass:* motionless, smooth, quiet, still, unruffled, undisturbed, placid, mild, balmy, bland, pacific, gentle, tranquil, serene, halcyon. **2.** *The defendant remained calm throughout the trial:* unperturbed, unshaken, unruffled, unexcited, composed, self-possessed, unagitated, collected, cool, cool-headed, impassive, sedate; passionless, imperturbable, untroubled, relaxed, serene, placid, peaceful, tranquil; *Slang* unflappable. —*n.* **3.** *Peace and calm are the only cure for jangled nerves. Her calm in the face of dis-*

aster is amazing: calmness, quiet, quietness, peacefulness, tranquillity, serenity, restfulness, stillness, smoothness; windlessness, stormlessness; composure, self-control, placidity, repose, self-possession, impassivity, imperturbability, coolness, *Slang* cool. —*v.* **4.** *She had to calm herself after all the excitement:* calm down, compose, collect, quiet, pacify, cool off, becalm, *Slang* simmer down. **5.** *This ointment will calm the pain:* allay, assuage, soothe, quell, mollify, mitigate, relieve, alleviate, moderate, subdue, cause to subside, placate, tranquilize, ease, lessen, diminish, reduce. —**Ant.** 1, 2 agitated, disturbed, ruffled, violent, raging, fierce, wild. 1 turbulent, stormy, rough. 2 excited, aroused, hotheaded, heated, passionate; tense, troubled, perturbed, worried, upset, uncollected, discomposed, shaken, jolted, rocked, frantic, frenzied. 3 disturbance, agitation, violence, fierceness, wildness, tempestuousness. 4 excite, agitate, disturb, arouse, work up. 5 irritate, aggravate, intensify, inflame.

calumny *n. The calumnies in his speech were obviously aimed at his opponent:* slander, libel, defamation, backstabbing, vilification, depreciation, backbiting, deprecation, disparagement, derogation, animadversion, revilement, calumniation, malice, innuendo, denigration; slur, smear, insinuation, barb. —**Ant.** praise, acclaim, kudos, encomium, eulogy.

camaraderie *n. She never forgot the easy camaraderie of her college days:* conviviality, good-fellowship, sociability, good will, friendliness, affability, jollity, companionship, clubbiness, congeniality, brotherhood, comradeship, esprit de corps, bonhomie. —**Ant.** hostility, enmity, animosity, rancor, hatred.

camouflage *n.* **1.** *The tanks' camouflage prevented enemy planes from seeing them. His friendliness is just camouflage to get us off our guard:* deceptive markings, deceptive covering, disguise; mask, masquerade, subterfuge, false appearance, blind, front, cover, screen, cloak, concealment. —*v.* **2.** *A chameleon camouflages itself by changing color:* cover with a disguise, disguise, give a false appearance to; mask, screen, cloak, conceal, hide, cover up, veil, shroud. —**Ant.** 2 show, expose, display, exhibit.

camp *n.* **1.** *The hikers set up camp for the night. The army camp wasn't far from town:* encampment, campground, temporary shelter, tents, tent, bivouac, lodging, quarters; army base, barracks. —*v.* **2.** *Our family camped in Yellowstone National Park this summer:* lodge in temporary quarters, encamp, pitch a tent; bivouac; rough it.

campaign *n.* **1.** *The desert campaign was won with tanks and armed vehicles:* military operation, operation, offensive, regional battle, battle series, action. **2.** *The company started a new sales campaign:* drive, effort, push, movement, endeavor, offensive, crusade, action. —*v.* **3.** *The President is campaigning for reelection:* electioneer, solicit votes, compete for office, run,

stump, whistle-stop, beat the drums, stump the countryside.

can *v.* **1.** *I can run a mile. They can erect a fence. We can enter the building whenever we like:* know how to, be able to, have the ability to, have the right to, have the power to, have the means to, have qualifications to. —*n.* **2.** *First, open a can of tuna:* tin, container, canister, receptacle.

canal *n.* **1.** *The Panama Canal connects the Atlantic and Pacific Oceans:* artificial waterway, manmade waterway; channel, conduit, aqueduct; arm of the sea. **2.** *Food is digested in the alimentary canal:* duct, tube, passage, channel.

cancel *v.* **1.** *We canceled our hotel reservations and stayed with friends. The general canceled all military leaves:* call off, set aside, quash, do away with, dispense with, abolish, revoke, recall, call back, rescind, repeal, countermand, retract, recant, blue-pencil, vitiate; annul, nullify, invalidate, abrogate, repudiate, void, declare null and void, delete. **2.** *This show of kindness cancels the cruelty shown yesterday:* offset, make up for, compensate for, counterbalance, balance out, neutralize, erase. —**Ant.** 1, 2 confirm, affirm, reaffirm, ratify; implement, enact, enforce, uphold, sustain, maintain.

cancer *n.* **1.** *Cigarette smoking can cause lung cancer:* malignant growth, malignancy, malignant tumor, carcinoma, sarcoma, neoplasm. **2.** *By the early 1930's, the cancer of Hitlerism was widespread in Germany:* malignancy, plague, sickness, rot, scourge.

candid *adj.* **1.** *To be candid, I don't think you have the talent to be a great violinist:* frank, open, honest, truthful, sincere, genuine, blunt, straightforward, forthright, plain-spoken, outspoken, direct, plain, outright, downright, free, unvarnished, fair, just. **2.** *Candid photographs can be very revealing:* impromptu, spontaneous, unposed, extemporaneous, informal, relaxed, natural. —**Ant.** 1 diplomatic, flattering, fawning, honeyed, subtle, mealy-mouthed, complimentary, kind. 2 formal, posed.

candidacy *n. She announced her candidacy for president:* candidature, running for, standing for.

candidate *n. There are three candidates for the foreman's job. Who will be the Republicans' presidential candidate?:* applicant, nominee, aspirant, eligible, possibility, hopeful, competitor, contender, contestant; office seeker, job seeker.

candle *n. The candles gave a warm glow to the room:* taper; *Archaic and Literary* tallow, light, rush light, wax, dip, bougie, *French* cierge.

candlestick *n. Before the dinner party, the host put fresh candles in the candlesticks:* candleholder, candelabrum, sconce, chandelier, girandole; *Eastern Orthodox Church* dikerion, trikerion; *Judaism* menorah.

candor *n. A good critic must be a man of great candor:* frankness, openness, honesty, truthfulness, sincerity, bluntness, straightforwardness, forthrightness, plainspokenness, directness, artlessness, fairness, justness, impartiality, freedom from prejudice. —**Ant.** diplomacy, flattery, subtlety, evasiveness, deceit, artfulness, dishonesty, insincerity, hypocrisy, unfairness, partiality, bias, prejudice.

candy n. *The children's Christmas stockings were filled with candy:* sugar candy, confection, confectionary, dainty, sweet, sweets, sweetmeat; (*variously*) hard candy, filled candy, chocolate, kiss, bonbon, fudge, cream, jelly, toffee, taffy, caramel, nougat, fondant, comfit, candy bar, lollipop, all-day sucker, candy cane, peanut brittle, brittle, praline, gumdrop, jellybean.

cane n. **1.** *Since he broke his hip, he's had to walk with a cane:* walking stick, stick, staff, rod. —v. **2.** *Schoolmasters used to cane disobedient students:* (with a cane) flog, thrash, beat, whip, flail, trounce, baste, drub, tan, lash, switch; strike, hit, whack, wallop, rap, smite.

canker n. **1.** *The canker caused her lip to swell:* mouth sore; lesion, inflammation, ulcer, sore. **2.** *Organized crime, the speaker said, is a canker in our way of life:* source of corruption, cancer, blight.

canny adj. *The old senator was a canny politician:* artful, skillful; knowing, wise, astute, shrewd, sharp, clever, subtle, convincing, cunning, crafty, foxy, wily, cagey; wary, careful, judicious, sagacious, intelligent, perspicacious, circumspect. —**Ant.** unskilled, inept, dumb, obtuse, blatant; bumbling, fumbling.

canon n. **1.** *The canons of the Roman Catholic Church permit divorce only by dispensation:* doctrine, dogma, decree, edict. **2.** *The canons of good behavior apply to everyone:* rule, principle, precept, code, model, pattern, standard, yardstick, criterion, bench mark, touchstone; regulation; order, ordinance, law, decree, statute.

canonical adj. *Only canonical texts will be used in the course:* accepted, authorized, sanctioned, orthodox, recognized, authoritative, approved, legitimate, authentic, proper, conventional, customary. —**Ant.** freakish, bizarre, outlandish, eccentric.

canonize v. *The saint was canonized in 1637:* sanctify, glorify, beatify, bless, consecrate, dedicate.

canopy n. *A canopy shaded the entrance to the building:* awning, covering, cover, tester, hood.

cant n. **1.** *The thief's claim that he was going to give the money to the poor was just a lot of cant:* hypocrisy, insincerity, humbug, pretentiousness, pretense, sham, sanctimoniousness, lip service. **2.** *Thieves' cant is unintelligible to outsiders:* jargon, lingo, talk, parlance, slang, argot, vernacular.

cantankerous adj. *When the team loses, the coach is in a cantankerous mood:* quarrelsome, argumentative, contentious, contrary, testy, touchy, peevish, fretful, huffy, ill-tempered, ill-natured, ill-humored, disagreeable, grouchy, grumpy, irascible, irritable, cranky, cross, bearish, surly, churlish, snappish, waspish, crabbed, morose, sullen, sulky, short, crusty, mean, choleric, splenetic. —**Ant.** agreeable, good-humored, good-natured, pleasant; amiable, affable, genial, kindly; placid, calm, complaisant,

mellow; merry, gay, happy, jolly, jaunty, breezy, vivacious, cheerful, lighthearted.

canteen n. **1.** *Each Boy Scout took a canteen of water on the hike:* flask, pocket flask, bottle. **2.** *The sergeant bought a razor at the base canteen:* commissary, post exchange, PX, club.

canvas n. **1.** *Gym shoes are made of canvas. The canvas protected the baseball field from the rain:* sailcloth, tent cloth, duck; tarpaulin. **2.** *The artist set his canvas on the easel:* painting, picture (*on canvas*).

canvass v. **1.** *The marketing specialists canvassed the buying habits of the local householders:* survey, analyze, examine, scrutinize, investigate, scan, explore, inquire into, take stock of, give thought to. —n. **2.** *After the canvass of voters, each party was forecasting victory:* poll, investigation, survey, tally, evaluation, analysis, study, enumeration, inquiry, exploration, scrutiny.

canyon n. *A narrow trail led down into the canyon:* gorge, gully, pass, ravine, chasm, gap, col, valley, corridor, gulch, defile, coulee, draw, water gap, wash, crevasse, arroyo, *Arabic* wadi; cut, break, cleft, fissure, divide, crack, opening, notch.

cap n. **1.** *The nurse wore a pleated cap on her head:* brimless hat, visored hat, headdress, headgear. **2.** *Put the cap back on the bottle of soda:* top, lid, cover, seal. —v. **3.** *The Wright brothers capped their first flight with many longer ones:* better, surpass, exceed, outdo, outstrip, top off.

capability n. *Only pilots of the highest capability are chosen to become test pilots. The country has the capability to defeat any aggressor:* ability, competency, competence, attainment, proficiency, facility, faculty, capacity, skill, art, know-how, qualification; power, efficacy, potential, potentiality, talent, gift, flair, knack. —**Ant.** incompetence, ineptitude, inadequacy, inability, inefficiency, impotency, powerlessness.

capable adj. *Napoleon was one of the most capable generals in history:* able, competent, expert, skillful, skilled, masterly, accomplished, gifted, talented, proficient, adept, apt, deft, adroit, effective, efficacious; clever, intelligent, artful, ingenious. —**Ant.** incapable, incompetent, unaccomplished, unqualified, inexpert, unskilled, inept, ineffective, amateurish.

capacious adj. *She seemed to carry all her belongings in that capacious leather handbag:* roomy, spacious, commodious, ample, extensive, expansive, broad, wide, expandable, amplitudinous, voluminous; big, large, vast, mammoth, gigantic, massive, huge, tremendous. —**Ant.** small, confined, narrow, cramped, restricted.

capacity n. **1.** *The hot water tank has a fifty-gallon capacity:* maximum contents, limit, extent, volume, size, amplitude, room, space. **2.** *The United States has the capacity to outproduce all other nations:* ability, power, capability, faculty, facility, strength, might; scope, range. **3.** *Einstein was a man of overwhelming mental capacity:* ability, endowment, talent, gifts, faculty, aptitude, potential; intelligence, intellect, sagacity, brain power, mind; perspicacity, discernment, judgment. **4.** *In his capacity as Commander in Chief, the President is head of the armed forces:* role, function, position. —**Ant.** 2, 3 inability, incapacity.

cape *n.* **1.** *The West Point dress uniform includes a cape:* cloak, mantle, shawl, manta, pelisse, tabard, poncho, serape. **2.** *Steer the boat around the cape and into the harbor:* peninsula, point, promontory, headland, tongue, spit.

caper *v.* **1.** *The fawns capered about in the forest:* prance, gambol, frisk, cavort, romp, frolic; leap, jump, hop, skip, bounce, bound. —*n.* **2.** *The students' latest caper was putting frogs in all the drinking fountains:* lark, escapade, caprice, adventure, spree, fling, frolic; trick, prank, practical joke, antic, stunt, shenanigans, high jinks, carrying on, jape, monkey business.

capital *n.* **1.** *London is the capital of England. Detroit is the capital of the automotive industry:* seat of government; chief city, first city, center, headquarters. **2.** *The child wrote his name in capitals:* capital letter, upper-case letter, large letter, majuscule. **3.** *The corporation had enough capital to build another factory:* investment funds, working capital, income-producing property, resources, available means, money, cash, cash on hand, wealth, riches, financing, principal, working assets, wherewithal. —*adj.* **4.** *It was a capital idea!:* excellent, supreme, great, fine, super, superb, first-rate, first-class, matchless. —**Ant.** 2 small letter, lower-case letter, minuscule. 3 debts, debits, red ink. 4 bad, poor, inferior, awful, lousy, second-rate.

capitalism *n.* *Under capitalism, we can own our own business:* free enterprise, private ownership. —**Ant.** socialism, communism, collectivism.

capitalist *n.* **1.** *Small capitalists own most of America's businesses:* investor, businessperson. **2.** *The Rockefellers and the DuPonts are leading capitalists:* financier, tycoon, plutocrat, mogul. —**Ant.** worker, laborer, proletariat; socialist, communist, collectivist.

capitalize *v.* **1.** *The producers capitalized the new musical production at a million dollars:* bankroll, finance, fund, back, stake, subsidize, support; foot the bill, put up the money. **2.** *She capitalized on the resurgent market to sell her stocks and bonds:* take advantage of, profit by, make capital of, exploit, utilize, cash in on, avail oneself of, trade on, put to advantage, make the most of, turn to account, make a good thing of; make hay while the sun shines, strike while the iron is hot, turn an honest penny.

capitol *n.* *The Capitol is one of the most beautiful structures in Washington:* legislative building; statehouse, government house.

capitulate *v.* *Lee capitulated to Grant at Appomattox Courthouse:* surrender, submit, acknowledge defeat, give up, give in, yield, acquiesce, accede, succumb, lay down one's arms, relent, come to terms, sue for peace, cry quits, hoist the white flag. —**Ant.** defeat, win over, be victorious.

caprice *n.* *Is your decision to become a vegetarian serious or just a caprice?:* whim, fancy, quirk, notion, impulse; eccentricity, idiosyncrasy, oddity, peculiarity, crotchet, erraticism, vagary; lark, escapade, caper, stunt, prank, antic, spree, fling; craze, fad.

capricious *adj.* *The capricious man bought and exchanged three shirts in a week:* changeable, fickle, variable, impulsive, erratic, flighty, skittish, mercurial, fanciful, faddish; indecisive, undecided, irresolute, uncertain, wavering, vacillating, shilly-shallying; irresponsible, inconsistent, unsteady, unstable, fitful, uneven, eccentric, quirky. —**Ant.** consistent, unchangeable, inflexible, unmovable, firm, fixed, unwavering, invariable, unswerving; resolute, determined, steadfast, certain, decided, decisive; serious, responsible, steady, stable, even.

capsize *v.* *The boat capsized when all the cargo shifted to one side:* overturn, turn over, keel over, tip over, flip over, invert, upset, turn turtle. —**Ant.** right, upright.

capsule *adj.* **1.** *We got a capsule summary of the news:* condensed, abridged, shortened, brief —*n.* **2.** *The doctor prescribed one capsule after meals:* pill, cap, pellet, dose, lozenge, tablet.

captain *n.* **1.** *William Bligh was the captain of the* Bounty *when the crew mutinied:* commanding officer, commander, master, skipper, *Slang* old man; pilot. **2.** *Six first lieutenants were promoted to captains:* company commander, commanding officer, commandant, chief officer. **3.** *Robin Hood was the captain of a famous robber band:* leader, headman, chief, chieftain, head, boss. —**Ant.** 1 able seaman, deckhand. 3 follower, member.

caption *n.* *The caption did not match its picture:* heading, head, inscription, legend, subtitle, title.

captious *adj.* *He's a captious critic who makes jokes at the performers' expense:* carping, nitpicking, hypercritical, faultfinding, caviling, picayune, niggling, censorious, querulous, deprecating, picky, cutting, belittling; peevish, testy, snappish, petulant; perverse, contrary, ornery, fractious, mean, cantankerous. —**Ant.** flattering, laudatory, approving, appreciative, fawning.

captivate *v.* *The actor's talent and good looks captivated the audience:* fascinate, charm, enchant, bewitch, dazzle, hypnotize, mesmerize, enthrall, delight, enrapture, transport, carry away, win over, lure, seduce, attract, infatuate, enamor, take the fancy of, turn the head of. —**Ant.** repulse, repel, alienate, turn away, disenchant, antagonize; disgust, nauseate, make sick.

captive *n.* **1.** *Captives were kept in POW camps until the war was over:* prisoner, internee; hostage. —*adj.* **2.** *The captive fliers were released after the war. The captive peoples of Europe formed guerrilla groups to fight the Nazis:* imprisoned, incarcerated, confined, penned, caged, locked up; subjugated, enslaved, oppressed. —**Ant.** 1 captor, guard; free person. 2 free, unconfined, at liberty; freed, liberated, independent, emancipated.

captivity *n. They prayed to be released from captivity:* bondage, servitude, slavery, thralldom, serfdom, subjection; imprisonment, confinement, incarceration, detention. —**Ant.** freedom.

capture *v.* **1.** *The army captured the town. The boys captured a hawk. The police captured the criminal:* seize, take, grasp, grab, procure; take prisoner, take captive, catch, trap, ensnare, snare, bag, snag, lay hold of; arrest, apprehend, take into custody, *Slang* pinch, collar, nab, bust. —*n.* **2.** *The capture of the white whale was Captain Ahab's obsession:* seizure, taking, capturing, taking prisoner, taking captive, catching, trapping, snaring, ensnaring, bagging, collaring, laying hold of; arrest, apprehension. —**Ant.** 1 release, free, let go, liberate. 2 release, freeing, liberation; escape.

car *n.* **1.** *The new car had disc brakes:* automobile, auto, motorcar, motor, machine, vehicle, motor vehicle, *Slang* jalopy, heap, flivver, tin lizzie, wheels, buggy, hot rod. **2.** *The railroad bought 200 new cars:* railway car; *(variously)* coach, carriage, parlor car, sleeping car, Pullman car, sleeper, dining car, diner, baggage car, freight car, boxcar, cattle car, coal car; streetcar, cable car, horsecar.

caravan *n. The caravan of old cars celebrated the town's 100th anniversary:* procession, parade, column, cortege, train, string, file, motorcade, wagon train, company, cavalcade, line, band, queue, convoy, retinue, entourage, troop; coffle, chain gang.

carcass *n.* **1.** *They found the carcass of the poisoned cow lying by the stream:* body, corpse, cadaver. **2.** *The next day we picked at the carcass of the turkey:* framework, skeleton, remains.

card *n.* **1.** *In bridge, each player is dealt thirteen cards:* playing card. **2.** *Amy mailed a card from France:* postcard, *(variously)* picture postcard, greeting card, birthday card, Christmas card, anniversary card, New Year's card, Eastercard, Valentine's Day card, Valentine, get-wellcard. **3.** *The sales representative left his card:* *(variously)* business card, calling card. **4.** *The vaudeville card included a stand-up comedian and two singers:* program, bill, ticket.

cardinal *n.* **1.** *The Pope appointed the archbishop cardinal:* Roman Catholic Church member of the college of cardinals. —*adj.* **2.** *Decorum was the cardinal rule in the office:* first, foremost, basic, prime, primary, fundamental, elementary, chief, main, key, principal, central, leading, most important, paramount, highest, greatest, outstanding, dominant, predominant, preeminent, uppermost, top, head, underlying; vital, necessary, essential, indispen-sable, intrinsic. **3.** *The king wore a cardinal robe trimmed with ermine:* deep red, cherry, blood-red, carmine, wine-colored, claret, scarlet. —**Ant.** 2 second, secondary, subordinate, insignificant, least important, unessential, unnecessary, irrelevant, immaterial, extraneous, dispensable; lowest, smallest.

care *n.* **1.** *Handle these fragile glasses with care. Answer all the questions with care:* carefulness, caution, precaution, circumspection, diligence, attention, attentiveness, heed, watchfulness, vigilance, thought; regard, concern, effort, pains, consideration, discrimination, solicitude, conscientiousness, application, fastidiousness, meticulousness, exactness, scrupulousness. **2.** *He doesn't have a care in the world. The mother's major care was the safety of her children:* concern, worry, responsibility, load, anxiety, strain, stress, pressure; bother, annoyance, nuisance, vexation, tribulation, heartache, distress, trouble, hardship, affliction, sorrow, grief, misery, anguish, sadness, unhappiness. **3.** *The sick man is still under the doctor's care:* ministration, attention, supervision, custody, control, management, charge, keeping, responsibility, protection. —*v.* **4.** *Do you care what happens to the house?:* be concerned, be interested in, be worried, mind, regard, bother about, trouble about. **5.** *The guests didn't care to have coffee after dinner:* want, wish, desire. —**Ant.** 1 carelessness, neglect, negligence, abandon, recklessness, unconcern, disregard, inattention, thoughtlessness, heedlessness, indifference. 2 relaxation; pleasure, delight, happiness. 4 disregard, forget about. 5 dislike, hate, detest, abhor, loathe; reject.

careen *v. The motorbike careened around the corner:* sway, lurch, lean, heel over, swing, roll, rock, wobble, reel, weave, waver.

career *n. Florence Nightingale made nursing her life's career:* profession, vocation, calling, occupation, employment, work, job, business, livelihood, lifework, activity, line, pursuit, walk of life. —**Ant.** hobby, avocation, sideline, diversion, entertainment, relaxation.

carefree *adj. Oh, to be young and carefree again!:* free of care, careless, without worry, without a worry in the world, untroubled, happy-go-lucky, light-hearted, relaxed, easygoing, free-and-easy; in high spirits, joyous, elated, jaunty, optimistic, buoyant, jubilant, breezy; happy, cheerful, sunny, glad, laughing, smiling, radiant, full of life, gleeful, jolly, gay. —**Ant.** careworn, heavy-hearted, worried; unhappy, sad, sorrowful, joyless, cheerless, melancholy, crestfallen, blue, gloomy, dismal, dreary, depressed, dejected, disconsolate, desolate, despondent.

careful *adj.* **1.** *Be careful crossing the street. My mother was careful to show no favoritism:* cautious, watchful, wary, guarded, chary, alert, observant, attentive, on guard, vigilant, diligent, concerned, thoughtful, mindful, regardful, heedful, prudent, painstaking, scrupulous; circumspect, discreet, tactful, judicious, solicitous. **2.** *The teacher has a careful handwriting:* precise, punctilious, exact, fastidious, particular, meticulous, conscientious, fussy, painstaking, fine, nice, scrupulous, accurate, correct. —**Ant.** 1 careless, reckless, rash, abandoned, slack, lax, neglectful, negligent, remiss, heedless, perfunctory, thoughtless, unthinking, inattentive, unconcerned, improvident. 2 careless, sloppy, slipshod, slovenly, slapdash, casual; inexact, imprecise, inaccurate; unrigorous, slack.

caregiver n. *Each caregiver at the nursing home took a course:* protector, safekeeper, guardian, caretaker, attendant, custodian, warden, nurse.

careless adj. **1.** *A careless mistake cost the company millions of dollars. Careless remarks hurt the girl's feelings:* thoughtless, unthinking, heedless, mindless, unmindful, absent-minded, sloppy, slipshod, lax, slack, negligent, rash; inconsiderate. **2.** *The student was careless about his personal appearance:* nonchalant, offhand, indifferent, heedless, thoughtless, unconcerned, devil-may-care, forgetful, negligent, neglectful, lackadaisical, carefree, untroubled, casual, lax, slack, slipshod, slapdash; untidy, slovenly, sloppy, messy, disorderly; inexact, imprecise, incorrect, inaccurate. **3.** See CAREFREE. —**Ant.** 1 careful, cautious, wary, alert, attentive, diligent, watchful, mindful, concerned. 2 careful, fastidious, neat, tidy, meticulous, fussy, painstaking, orderly; scrupulous, correct, precise, exact, accurate.

caress n. **1.** *The grandmother gave each of the children a kiss and a caress:* gentle touch, stroking, pat, petting, fondling; embrace, hug. —v. **2.** *The old man thoughtfully caressed his beard:* stroke, fondle, toy with, pet, pat, touch; embrace, hug, clasp; cuddle. —**Ant.** 1 hit, blow, slap, cuff, box. 2 hit, beat, thrash, slap, cuff, box.

caretaker n. *John was the caretaker of the old mansion:* custodian, keeper, overseer, curator, concierge, steward, warden; superintendent, janitor, porter; watchman, gatekeeper.

careworn adj. *Years of toil had made her shrunken and careworn:* exhausted, weary, drawn, worn, worn-down, strained, haggard, hollow-eyed, ravaged, woebegone.

cargo n. *The cargo was put in the hold of the ship:* freight, shipment, consignment, load, lading, burden; goods, merchandise.

caricature n. **1.** *The comedian's caricature of a fat man running for a bus was very amusing:* lampoon, takeoff, burlesque, parody, satire, travesty, mockery; distortion, absurdity, exaggeration. —v. **2.** *The cartoonist caricatured senators sleeping on the job:* lampoon, burlesque, parody, satirize, mock.

carnage n. *Those who have seen the carnage of war will never forget:* slaughter, butchery, blood bath, great bloodshed, mass killing, massacre.

carnal adj. *A chaste mind has no room for carnal thoughts:* sexual, sensual, erotic, voluptuous, sensuous, prurient, lustful, libidinous, fleshly, unchaste, lewd, lascivious, lecherous, salacious, immoral, sinful, impure, venereal, wanton. —**Ant.** chaste, modest, virginal, pure.

carnival n. **1.** *Two circuses and a carnival came to town each year:* small circus, traveling sideshow. **2.** *The neighborhood held a street carnival:* fair, festival, jamboree, celebration, jubilee, fete, gala; Mardi Gras; holiday.

carnivorous adj. *Lions are carnivorous animals:* meat-eating, flesh-eating, predatory, predaceous. —**Ant.** herbivorous; vegetarian.

carol n. *"Silent Night" is a favorite carol:* Christmas carol, noel; hymn, canticle, paean, song of praise, song of joy. —**Ant.** dirge, lament.

carouse v. *The sailors caroused in the pub:* revel, make merry, *Informal* live it up, make whoopee, *Slang* party; drink, tipple, imbibe, guzzle, quaff, wassail, *Informal* go on a binge.

carp v. *The man carped continually about the hotel's service:* complain, find fault, fault-find, nag, cavil, criticize, disapprove, deride, belittle, knock, condemn, deprecate, disparage, chide, decry, reproach, censure, impugn, pick on, jibe at, pull to pieces. —**Ant.** compliment, praise, applaud, laud, approve.

carpet n. **1.** *Our living room is covered with a wall-to-wall carpet:* rug; matting, mat. **2.** *A carpet of leaves covered the ground:* blanket, layer, covering, sheet.

carriage n. **1.** *The queen rode in an ornate carriage pulled by four white horses:* coach, horse-drawn coach; wagon, buggy, rig; vehicle, conveyance. **2.** *The prima ballerina was a woman of erect and handsome carriage:* bearing, posture, comportment; demeanor, mien, attitude, appearance, air, poise, aspect; presence, manner, behavior, deportment.

carrion n. *Vultures fed on the carrion left from the lions' feast:* remains, bones, corpse, cadaver, dead body, carcass, putrefying flesh, *Slang* crowbait, *Law* corpus delicti; refuse, garbage, offal, waste, wastage, leavings.

carry v. **1.** *The bellhops carried the luggage upstairs:* take, bring, tote, bear, fetch, haul, lug, cart, lift; move, transport, transmit, convey, transfer, conduct, shift, displace, ship, deliver. **2.** *The money will carry me through the week. The walls carry the weight of the roof:* support, sustain, maintain, bear, uphold, hold up, prop, brace, shoulder, lift. **3.** *All the newspapers carried the story:* communicate, transmit, disseminate, publish, run, print, broadcast, release, offer. **4.** *The shop carries only name brands:* supply, stock, keep on hand, display, offer. —**Ant.** 1 throw down, drop, let go. 3 withhold, reject, delete, censor; cover up, keep secret.

cart n. **1.** *The farmer sold fresh corn from his roadside cart:* wagon, truck, tumbrel, dumpcart, curricle, trap; two-wheeler, dogcart, gig, dray, tipcart; go-cart, pushcart, handcart, barrow, wheelbarrow, handbarrow. —v. **2.** *Trucks carted the garbage to the city dump:* transport, haul, lug, tote, carry, truck; *Slang* schlepp; bear, move; take, bring, fetch, convey, transmit, transfer, transplant.

carte blanche n. *The interior decorator was given carte blanche in decorating the house:* a free hand, free reign, full authority, unconditional power, blank check, license, open sanction.

cartel n. *The government accused the cartel of restraining trade:* monopoly, trust, syndicate, consortium, combine, chain, pool, corporation, federation.

carton n. *The books were packed in cartons:* box, cardboard box, container, cardboard container; packing case, case, packing crate, crate.

cartoon *n. The new cartoon had us laughing outright:* caricature, animated cartoon, animation, caricature, comic book, comic strip, sketch, *Informal* funny pictures.

carve *v.* **1.** *The statue was carved from marble. The boys carved their initials in the tree:* sculpture, sculpt, chisel, hew, block out; shape, mold, model, fashion, pattern, form, work, turn; engrave, etch, incise. **2.** *Dad carved the Thanksgiving turkey:* slice, cut up, dissever, saw, hack, slash; cleve, rend, split, divide, quarter, apportion, allot.

Casanova *n. From the time he discovered girls he was known as a Casanova:* ladies' man, Lothario, Don Juan, Romeo, lover boy; admirer, suitor, wooer, lover, swain, gallant, cavalier, beau, paramour; womanizer, lady-killer, philanderer, chaser, wolf, libertine, profligate, roué, lecher, *Slang* lech, bounder, cad, rounder, rip.

cascade *n.* **1.** *The water formed a cascade down the mountain:* waterfall, falls, cataract, Niagara; rapids, chute. —*v.* **2.** *The water cascaded over the cliff:* surge, pour, gush, plunge, rush, fall, tumble. —**Ant.** 2 trickle, dribble, drip, drop, seep.

case[1] *n.* **1.** *In this case, no action is necessary. It was a case of love at first sight:* instance, incidence, incident, occurrence, situation, event, episode, happening, condition, example, illustration, circumstance; matter, business, affair, concern. **2.** *The case was brought before a jury:* lawsuit, suit, litigation, action; dispute, controversy, debate, argument, inquiry, hearing, proceeding; plea, appeal, cause. **3.** *A doctor attended the case:* patient, sick person, invalid, victim, sufferer; disease, injury.

case[2] *n.* **1.** *Put the books in a packing case. The thieves took a jewel case:* box, crate, carton, chest, container, receptacle; tray, cabinet, display case, bin. **2.** *The credit card was protected by a plastic case:* wrapper, cover, covering, sheath, sheathing, jacket, envelope, overlay, housing, protection.

cash *n.* **1.** *The purchases were paid for with cash:* money, currency, legal tender, paper money, bank notes, bills, coins, change; *Slang* bread, dough; coin of the realm, cash on the barrelhead. —*v.* **2.** *The store will cash your check:* turn into money, give cash for, obtain cash for; redeem, exchange, change. —**Ant.** 1 check; charge, chit, promissory note, note, IOU.

cashier *n. Please pay the cashier:* cash keeper; teller, bank teller; bursar, purser, treasurer, banker.

cask *n. The wine was fermented in large casks:* vat, barrel, keg, hogshead, tub, butt, tun, pipe.

casket *n.* **1.** *Six pallbearers carried the casket to the grave:* coffin, sarcophagus, pall. **2.** *Caskets of jewels were found in the pirate's cave:* jewel box, chest, coffer, case.

cast *v.* **1.** *Let him who is without sin cast the first stone:* pitch, toss, fling, hurl, throw, let fly, sling, heave; propel, launch, fire, shoot, discharge, project, catapult. **2.** *The candles cast a warm glow on the table:* shed, spread, diffuse, direct, deposit, scatter, disseminate, disperse, distribute, circulate, broadcast, sow. **3.** *The director cast leading actors in the play:* assign, appoint, pick, choose, give parts to. **4.** *The statue was cast from bronze:* mold, form, shape, model, set, sculpt; mint. —*n.* **5.** *The fisherman caught a trout on the first cast:* pitch, toss, throw; fling, hurl, heave, sling; propulsion, launch, launching. **6.** *The play's cast was given a standing ovation:* performers, actors, company, troupe, players; list of characters, dramatis personae. **7.** *The plaster was poured into a bronze cast:* mold, form, shape, pattern, casting, casing, impression, stamp, set, model. **8.** *Her face has a distinctly Oriental cast:* look, appearance, semblance, mien, set, stamp.

castaway *n. The mission was a haven for the castaways of society:* outcast, pariah, Ishmael, offscouring, unperson, leper, untouchable, nonperson; outlaw, exile, expatriate, renegade, deportee; vagrant, rover, wanderer, vagabond, nomad, hobo, knight-of-the-road, beachcomber, derelict, down-and-outer, stray, waif, foundling, *Slang* bum.

caste *n. Hindu society is based on a system of castes:* hereditary social class, lineage, rank, position, status, condition, station.

castigate *v. The principal castigated the students for their unruly behavior:* chastise, upbraid, rebuke, censure, reprimand, reproach, chasten, reprove, berate, scold, admonish, criticize, chide, call on the carpet, bawl out, chew out, dress down, haul over the coals, take to task; punish, discipline, correct, penalize. —**Ant.** praise, laud, compliment, honor; reward, encourage.

castle *n. The king's castle stood on a hill:* palace, mansion, hall, manor, villa, chateau; fortified residence, stronghold, citadel, fortress, tower, keep.

castrate *v. After weaning, the bull calves were castrated:* emasculate, geld, neuter, alter, change, cut, sterilize, *Informal* fix.

casual *adj.* **1.** *The two old friends had a casual meeting:* chance, unexpected, accidental, fortuitous, serendipitous, unplanned, unarranged, unforeseen, unpremeditated, unintentional, undesigned, unlooked for. **2.** *I have a casual interest in golf:* incidental, informal, haphazard, random, undirected, offhand, vague, so-so, half-hearted, indiscriminate, passing, relaxed, cool, easygoing, lackadaisical, blasé, nonchalant, indifferent. **3.** *The guests wore casual attire:* informal, nondressy, sporty; haphazard, random. —**Ant.** formal. 1 intentional, calculated, planned, fixed, arranged, designed, deliberate, intentional, premeditated, foreseen, expected; studied, considered, well-advised. 2 serious, committed, concerned, specific, direct, systematic, professional; all-consuming, wholehearted, fanatic, passionate, enthusiastic. 3 dressy, ceremonial.

casualty *n. The earthquake caused many casualties:* injured, victim, wounded or dead person; injury, fatality.

casuistry *n. If I can follow his casuistry, our defeat was really a victory:* sophistry, sophism, speciousness, deceptiveness, equivocation, pettifoggery, sophistication, fallacy, Jesuitism; quibbling, nitpicking, hair-splitting, guile, subtlety, deceit.

cat *n.* **1.** *The neighbors have a dog and a cat:* feline, house cat, pussycat, pussy, puss, tabby, tabby cat, mouser; (*young*) kitten, kitty; (*male*) tomcat, tom. **2.** *At the zoo, the bears are next to the cats:* (*loosely*) lions and tigers; (*variously*) lion, tiger, leopard, panther, cougar, lynx, ocelot, wildcat, bobcat.

cataclysm *n.* *The weakened government could not withstand another cataclysm:* catastrophe, calamity, disaster, debacle, upheaval, devastation, blow. **—Ant.** triumph, victory, success; benefit, good fortune, boon.

catalog or **catalogue** *n.* **1.** *The farmer ordered new boots from the store's catalog:* list, listing, inventory, file, record, index, roll, roster, register, directory, syllabus. **—v. 2.** *The librarian catalogs the books alphabetically:* list, inventory, classify, enumerate, tabulate, file, record, post, index, register.

catapult *n.* **1.** *The catapult hurled the missile two hundred yards:* hurling engine, sling, slingshot. **—v. 2.** *The shove catapulted the boy into the room:* hurl, be hurled, hurtle, fling, throw, propel, heave, pitch, cast, toss, shoot.

cataract *n.* **1.** *Only experienced canoers should attempt riding over the cataracts of the Colorado River:* rapids, falls, waterfall, cascade. **2.** *A cataract of rain washed out the road:* deluge, torrent, downpour; flood, inundation.

catastrophe *n.* *The Mississippi flood of 1973 was a major catastrophe:* disaster, calamity, misfortune, mishap, tragedy; affliction, scourge, cataclysm, devastation, havoc, debacle, ravage, blow. **—Ant.** benefit, good fortune, boon.

catcall *n.* *The auditorium was filled with catcalls from the hostile audience:* boo, hiss, hoot, whistle, jeer, gibe, heckling; *Slang* raspberry, Bronx cheer. **—Ant.** applause, cheering; hurrah, huzzah.

catch *v.* **1.** *The children learned to catch lightning bugs and put them in a jar. The police caught the thief:* seize, seize and hold, capture, take captive, take, lay hold of, trap, snare, bag, grab, snag, hook, corner, corral; arrest, apprehend, take into custody, collar, snatch, nab; *Slang* bust. **2.** *The winning runner caught his opponent at the finish line. Leave now if you want to catch the train:* overtake, reach, get to, intercept, make. **3.** *The thief was caught in the act:* discover, detect, come upon, discern, expose, find out, spot, descry; surprise, take off guard, unmask. **4.** *I was caught by his false promises:* deceive, fool, trick, dupe, take in, delude, mislead, betray, play false, hoodwink, bamboozle; lure, trap, ensnare, bait. **5.** *A snowball caught the passerby in the shoulder:* strike, hit, belt, bang, bump, bat, buffet, whack, smack, smite. **6.** *Children catch cold easily:* contract, get, come down with, become infected with, break out with. **7.** *The charming child caught the group's fancy:* captivate, attract, allure, charm, enchant, bewitch, enthrall, transport, carry away; delight, dazzle, enrapture; *Slang*

turn on. **8.** *I caught something of his sadness from the tremor in his voice:* sense, feel, discern, grasp, understand, perceive, recognize, comprehend, fathom. **9.** *This belt buckle doesn't catch:* fasten, hook, latch, clasp, lock. **—n. 10.** *The center fielder made a good catch of a line drive:* catching, seizure, snatch, snap, grab, grasp, snare, capture. **11.** *The fisherman's catch was two trout:* take, haul, bag, capture, seizure, find, pickings, yield, prize, booty. **12.** *The catch on the screen door is loose:* fastening, latch, hook, clasp, hasp, closure, coupling, lock. **13.** *It looks so easy; there must be a catch:* hitch, snag, drawback, stumbling block, disadvantage, trick, hoax, deceit, *Informal* kicker, *Slang* gimmick. **14.** *There was a catch in the speaker's voice when he spoke of the tragedy:* break, crack, rasping. **—Ant.** 1 free, release, loose, let go, give up, liberate; drop, fumble. 2 miss. 3 to be undetected, to be undiscovered. 4 undeceive, untrick, undupe, undelude. 5 miss. 6 avoid, evade; be resistant to. 7 repel, alienate, turn away; *Slang* turn off. 9 unfasten, unhook, unlatch, unlock. 10 drop; fumble. 11 loss, losings. 13 advantage, benefit, boon, reward.

catching *adj.* *Chicken pox is catching. Her laughter was so catching we all joined in:* contagious, communicable, infectious, transmittable. **—Ant.** noncatching, noncontagious, uncommunicable, noninfectious, nontransmittable.

catchword *n.* **1.** *Children know all the catchwords used in television commercials:* slogan, pet phrase, cliché, motto, byword, watchword, password, shibboleth; war cry, battle cry. **2.** *The catchwords at the top of the page make it easier to find entries in a dictionary:* guide word.

categorical *adj.* *The politician made a categorical denial of the charges that he had taken bribes:* absolute, unconditional, unqualified, unequivocal, unmistakable, unreserved, express, flat, sure, certain, emphatic, explicit, pronounced, definite. **—Ant.** conditional, qualified, equivocal, ambiguous, vague, dubious, doubtful, questionable, indefinite, unsure, uncertain, hesitant, enigmatic.

categorize *v.* *They categorized the outburst as outrageous:* class, classify, group, peg, pigeonhole, sort.

category *n.* *The social services department has specialists for each welfare category:* classification, class, grouping, division.

cater *v.* *The doting husband catered to his wife's every wish:* humor, pamper, indulge, pander; satisfy, gratify, please.

caterwaul *v.* *The caterwauling of the cats kept the neighborhood awake all night:* howl, wail, cry, scream, shriek, screech, whine, yelp, squawk, squeal, bawl, clamor, rend the air.

catharsis *n.* *Aristotle said that tragic drama provides catharsis for the audience by arousing people's pity and fear:* purification, cleansing, purging, release, venting.

cathedral *n.* *Bells summoned the faithful to the cathedral:* church, sanctuary, basilica, minster, holy place, temple.

catholic *adj.* **1.** *Catholic. My son attends a Catholic school:* Roman Catholic. **2.** *Pope John XXIII aimed for a truly catholic ecumenical Christianity:* universal, world-wide, all-inclusive, all-embracing. **3.** *Our young people distinguish themselves with more catholic sympathies and tastes than ever before:* broad, comprehensive, universal, liberal. —**Ant.** 1 non-Catholic. 2, 3 sectarian, parochial, provincial, narrow, exclusive, limited.

cattle *n. Cowboys tend herds of beef cattle:* livestock, stock, cows, *Archaic* kine; (*male*) bulls, bullocks, steers, beefs, beeves, oxen; (*female*) cows, milk cows, dairy cattle; (*young*) calves, dogies.

catty *adj.* **1.** *That gossip always has something catty to say about others:* spiteful, malicious, mean, malignant, malevolent. **2.** *The room had a catty smell:* catlike.

caucus *n. The delegates held a caucus to elect a chairman before the convention:* assembly, meeting, conclave, council, conference, parley, *Informal* powwow, session.

causation *n. Causation of the symptoms has not been determined:* origin, genesis, cause, etiology, source, mainspring, root, reason, stimulus, antecedent, determinant, origination, conception, invention, inspiration; author, inventor, originator, generator, creator. —**Ant.** result, aftermath, effect, consequence, outcome, causatum.

cause *v.* **1.** *Icy roads cause many accidents:* bring about, lead to, give rise to, bring to pass, produce, generate, create, effect, make, provoke, incline, precipitate; motivate, incite, stimulate, stir up, impel, inspire. —*n.* **2.** *Differences over money were the cause of the argument:* reason, source, root, prime mover; provocation, inducement, motivation, motive, grounds, incentive, instigation, inspiration, initiation, occasion, stimulus, foundation, origin, mainspring, spring, genesis, etiology. **3.** *Patrick Henry spoke for the cause of liberty:* goal, aspiration, object, purpose, principle, ideal, belief, conviction, tenet, persuasion, side. —**Ant.** 1 prevent, forestall, deter, inhibit, ward off, stop, foil. 2 effect, result, end result, consequence, fruit, outcome, final outgrowth, end.

caustic *adj.* **1.** *Acid is caustic:* burning, corrosive, corroding, erosive; astringent, stinging, biting, gnawing, sharp. **2.** *His caustic remarks hurt our feelings:* sarcastic, biting, stinging, cutting, scathing, sharp, harsh, acrid, acrimonious, tart, bitter. —**Ant.** 1 soothing, healing; bland, mild. 2 flattering, complimentary; sweet, kind, loving, pleasant, pleasing, gentle, gracious, agreeable, mild, bland.

caution *n.* **1.** *Cross the street with caution:* care, carefulness, wariness, alertness, watchfulness, vigilance, prudence, precaution, heed, heedfulness, concern, thought, regard, discretion, restraint, circumspection, deliberation, guardedness, mindfulness. **2.** *The flashing red light served as a caution of trouble ahead:* warning, forewarning, alarm, tip-off, admonition, caveat. —*v.* **3.** *The state trooper cautioned us about the icy roads:* warn, forewarn, alert, put on one's guard, tip off, admonish, exhort, advise; alarm, notify. —**Ant.** 1 carelessness, recklessness, foolhardiness, rashness, heedlessness, imprudence, indiscretion, daring, daredevilry. 2 put off one's guard; dare.

cautious *adj. Be cautious when swimming in deep water:* careful, wary, cagey, alert, watchful, vigilant, attentive, guarded, prudent, circumspect, discreet, judicious. —**Ant.** careless, reckless, rash, foolhardy, heedless, inattentive; daring, impetuous, adventurous, venturous, venturesome.

cavalcade *n. The circus cavalcade marched around the ring before the show:* parade, procession, column, retinue, troop; caravan.

cavalier *n.* **1.** *The Queen's Horse Guard had 20 cavaliers:* cavalryman, mounted soldier, horse soldier, horse trooper, horseman; lancer, dragoon, hussar. **2.** *Beau Brummel was the epitome of a cavalier:* gallant, courtier, courtly man, fine gentleman, beau; dandy, swell, fop; man about town, playboy, gay blade, blade. —*adj.* **3.** *Don Juan was known for his cavalier treatment of women's deeper feelings:* disdainful, uncaring, offhand, thoughtless, cursory, indifferent, easygoing, nonchalant; arrogant, haughty, cocky. —**Ant.** 1 infantryman, foot soldier. 2 bum, tramp. 3 conscientious, considerate, diligent, caring, thoughtful, sincere.

cavalry *n. My father joined the cavalry because he loved horses:* mounted troops, horse soldiers, horse troops, mounted men; lancers, dragoons, hussars. —**Ant.** infantry, foot soldiers.

cave *n. Bears often hibernate in caves:* underground chamber, cavern, grotto; dugout, hollow, den, cavity.

caveat *n. I needed no caveat to know the water should be tested before we drank it:* warning, caution, forewarning, admonition, alarm, tip-off, alert, red light, red flag, aviso, admonishment, word to the wise, flea in the ear, handwriting on the wall, high sign, danger sign, yellow jack.

cavern *n. The Carlsbad Caverns attract many tourists:* large cave, large underground chamber.

cavernous *adj. It was one of those English country houses with cavernous rooms:* vast, huge, yawning, gaping, cavelike, chasmal, spacious, roomy, enormous, immense, tremendous. —**Ant.** small, cramped, crowded, confined, restricted.

cavil *v. My boss cavils at the least detail:* complain, find fault, faultfind, criticize, disparage, deprecate, belittle, discredit, deride, quibble, pick to pieces, *Informal* nitpick. —**Ant.** praise, applaud, compliment, flatter, approve.

cavity *n. There was a large cavity in the ground where the meteor had hit:* crater, concavity, depression, hole, excavation, basin, hollow, pit, sink, dent, pocket, dip, vacuity; tunnel, burrow, bore, orifice, aperture, opening, niche.

cavort *v. The ponies cavorted in the corral:* caper, prance, frisk, frolic, gambol, bound, romp, play.

cay *n. They sailed among the cays:* key, bar, sandbank, sandbar.

cease *v. The general ordered his troops to cease fire. The music ceased:* stop, halt, leave off, desist, quit, conclude, end, bring to an end, finish, terminate, forbear, break off, adjourn, discontinue, suspend, pause, refrain from, abstain from; die away, pass, surcease, abate, come to a standstill. **—Ant.** begin, commence, start, initiate, continue, persist.

ceaseless *adj. We had ceaseless rain during those three days:* endless, uninterrupted, incessant, continuous, unending, unceasing, perpetual, interminable, everlasting, constant, enduring, protracted, never-ending, eternal, permanent, unremitting. **—Ant.** fitful, transitory, intermittent, spasmodic, fleeting.

cede *v. Mexico ceded New Mexico to the United States in 1848:* yield, grant, deliver, deliver up, hand over, surrender, give, tender, relinquish, release, abandon, leave, transfer. **—Ant.** keep, retain, withhold, hold back, maintain.

celebrated *adj. Robert Frost was a celebrated New England poet:* famous, famed, renowned, well-known, prominent, important, distinguished, acclaimed, noted, notable, outstanding, eminent, illustrious, respected, revered, venerable, honored, treasured, prized, lionized. **—Ant.** unknown, little-known, forgotten, undistinguished, unacclaimed, unnotable, insignificant, trivial, paltry; dishonored, degraded, unpopular.

celebration *n. The birthday celebration went on all day:* celebrating, party, festivity, festival, feast, gala, fete, jubilee, carnival, revelry; commemoration, ritual, observance, ceremony, ceremonial, solemnization, hallowing, memorialization, sanctification.

celebrity *n.* **1.** *Diamond Jim Brady was a leading celebrity of his day:* famous person, star, notable, luminary, personality, name; dignitary, personage, person of note; *Slang* big shot, bigwig, wheel. **2.** *Babe Ruth gained celebrity by hitting home runs:* fame, stardom, renown, note, notoriety, notability, distinction, glory, prominence, eminence, popularity, a name for oneself. **—Ant.** 1 unknown, nobody; has-been. 2 obscurity, oblivion.

celerity *n. The order must be carried out with celerity:* haste, swiftness, dispatch, briskness, quickness, speed, speediness, rapidity, expedition, alacrity, legerity, expeditiousness, hurry, hustle, precipitance, fastness, snappiness, lightning speed, fast clip. **—Ant.** slowness, laxness, sluggishness, languidness, torpor.

celestial *adj.* **1.** *As a child, the saint had the celestial beauty of an angel:* heavenly, divine, angelic, seraphic, blissful, hallowed, sublime, beatific, ethereal, elysian, otherworldly, unearthly, empyrean, paradisiacal. **2.** *A celestial map shows the positions of the planets:* astral, astronomical, solar, planetary, stellar; sky. **—Ant.** 1 earthy, earthly, mundane, worldly, mortal; hellish, infernal, satanic. 2 earthly, terrestrial.

celibacy *n. Priests must take vows of celibacy:* chastity, virginity, continence, abstinence; bachelorhood, spinsterhood.

celibate *adj. Unlike priests, preachers need not lead celibate lives:* unmarried, unwed, single, bachelor, spinster; chaste, virginal, continent, abstinent, pure. **—Ant.** married, wed, wedded; unchaste, incontinent, impure; promiscuous, loose, wanton.

cell *n.* **1.** *The cell proved to be malignant:* nucleus, germ, corpuscle, ectoplasm, egg, embryo. **2.** *The hermit retreated to his cell:* chamber, vault, crypt, pen, cage, coop, booth, compartment, cubicle, hold, keep, lockup.

cellar *n. The furnace is down in the cellar. Do you keep a wine cellar? We're building a storm cellar:* basement, downstairs; underground room, subterranean room; cave, den, dugout. **—Ant.** attic, garret; upstairs.

cement *n.* **1.** *The kids wrote their initials in the cement before it dried. Paste the picture in the album with rubber cement:* (*loosely*) concrete, mortar; glue, paste. **—v.** **2.** *Let's cement the parts together:* glue, paste, stick, fix, seal, weld, set; unite, join, bind, fuse, secure.

cemetery *n. We went to the cemetery to visit Grandfather's grave:* graveyard, burial ground, memorial park, churchyard, burying ground, necropolis, catacomb, ossuary, (*of paupers*) potter's field; *Slang* boneyard, Boot Hill.

censor *n.* **1.** *After the local censors finished with the play it was all but unrecognizable:* inspector, custodian of morals, examiner, reviewer, investigator, judge, scrutinizer, guardian of the public morals, expurgator, amender, bowdlerizer. **—v.** **2.** *The dictator censors all news reports leaving the country:* expurgate, blue-pencil, amend, clean up, edit, bowdlerize, blip, purge, excise, black out, suppress.

censorious *adj. The newspaper critics were especially censorious about the play:* disapproving, critical, condemnatory, condemning, chiding, complaining, disparaging, faultfinding, reproaching.

censorship *n. The novelist naturally opposed censorship of his work:* suppression, restriction, control, ban.

censure *n.* **1.** *The sleeping sentry received a strong censure from his commanding officer:* reprimand, reproof, upbraiding, rebuke, reprobation, reproach, admonition, castigation, scolding, chiding, remonstrance, criticism, complaint, condemnation, disapproval, disapprobation, dressing-down, bawling-out, chewing-out, tongue-lashing. **—v.** **2.** *The dean censured the students for breaking curfew:* rebuke, reprimand, admonish, upbraid, reproach, castigate, denounce, condemn, chide, berate, disapprove, criticize, reprove, scold, reprehend; *Slang* bawl out, chew out, take over the coals, rap on the knuckles, pan, rap. **—Ant.** praise. 1 approval, eulogy, commendation, compliment, encouragement. 2 commend, applaud, compliment, eulogize, laud.

center or (*esp. Brit.*) **centre** *n.* **1.** *He hit the center of the target:* middle point, dead center, hub; middle, mid, central part; core, heart, interior, pivot, axis, nucleus. **2.** *Broadway is the theatrical center of the United States:* focal point, focus, main point, main place, hub, heart, crux, essence. —*v.* **3.** *Please center your attention on the front of the room:* concentrate, direct, address, fix, focus, converge, gather. —**Ant.** 1 exterior, outside; perimeter, edge, rim, circumference. 3 diffuse, scatter, disperse.

central *adj.* **1.** *The capital is in the central part of the state:* in the center, middle, middlemost, midmost, interior, inner, inmost. **2.** *The firm's central office is in Toronto. The President is the central figure in the government:* major, main, principal, most important, chief, key, leading, primary, paramount, prime, dominant, predominant, foremost, focal, pivotal, basic, fundamental, essential. —**Ant.** 1 outermost, outside, outer, exterior. 2 minor, subordinate, subsidiary, secondary.

centralize *v.* *For years the performing arts were centralized in New York City:* focus, concentrate, consolidate, coalesce, center, center on, converge, congregate, gather, collect, unify, compact, integrate. —**Ant.** disperse, scatter, dispel, spread, dissipate, disband.

centrifugal *adj.* *The centrifugal force was tremendous:* outward, radiant, radiating, spiral.

ceremonial *adj.* **1.** *The king loved to behave in a very ceremonial manner:* formal, ceremonious, ritualistic. **2.** *Bach wrote the ceremonial music for the Easter service:* used in ceremonies, liturgical. —*n.* **3.** *Mother enjoys the ceremonial of the mass:* ritual, rite, service, ceremony, liturgy, sacrament; formality, celebration, observance. —**Ant.** 1 informal, relaxed, casual, down-to-earth, plain, simple.

ceremonious *adj.* *The host's greetings were too ceremonious to be friendly:* formal, stiff, correct, overly polite, proper, starched, rigid, meticulous, careful, precise, methodical, exact, punctilious, fussy; solemn, dignified, pompous. —**Ant.** unceremonious, informal, relaxed, casual, down-to-earth, plain, simple.

ceremony *n.* **1.** *The inauguration ceremony was brief:* rite, ritual, service, observance, ceremonial, celebration, pageant, function, formalities, commemoration. **2.** *Lack of ceremony caused the conference to break up in chaos:* formality, formal behavior, etiquette, politeness, decorum, protocol, propriety, custom, conventionality; nicety, amenity. —**Ant.** 2 informality.

certain *adj.* **1.** *I'm certain I put the book on the table:* sure, positive, confident, convinced, undoubting, undoubtful, satisfied, secure, assured, cocksure. **2.** *After the Boston Tea Party, war with England seemed certain. That the diamonds are real is certain:* definite, inevitable, positive, inescapable, bound to happen, settled, sure; conclusive, indubitable, unequivocal, unmistakable, unquestionable; unqualified, indisputable, undisputed, undeniable, incontrovertible, incontestable, irrefutable, reliable, absolute, unalterable, unchangeable, unshakable, well-grounded, valid. **3.** *A certain person has been asking questions about you:* specific, particular, individual, special, express. —**Ant.**

1 uncertain, doubtful, dubious, unconvinced. 2 doubtful, unlikely, questionable, unclear, unsure, unsettled, indefinite, inconclusive, undecided, disputable, unreliable, unfounded; equivocal, qualified, fallible.

certainty *n.* **1.** *The forecast of rain was given with such certainty that everyone carried an umbrella:* positiveness, confidence, certitude, assurance, surety, sureness, conclusiveness; conviction, belief, trust, faith, presumption, authoritativeness. **2.** *It is a certainty that the new highway will be built:* fact, reality, actuality, inevitability, inescapability, sure thing, sure bet. —**Ant.** uncertainty. 1 indecision, inconclusiveness, unsureness; skepticism, disbelief, faithlessness, doubt.

certificate *n.* *Do you have a certificate of ownership for this car?:* document, certification, credential, permit, license, deed, affidavit, voucher, authorization, authentication, warranty, testimonial, diploma.

certify *v.* *Two witnesses must certify that this is your legal signature. Ask the bank manager to certify this check:* confirm, corroborate, attest, substantiate, validate, verify, witness, testify to, vouch, swear, guarantee, warrant, endorse, authorize, ratify, underwrite, notarize, second, support, sanction, authenticate, assure, declare, aver, give one's word. —**Ant.** repudiate, disavow, deny, question, disprove.

cessation *n.* *The warring nations agreed to a cessation of hostilities:* stopping, stop, ceasing, halting, halt, desisting, quitting, ending, end, concluding, termination, surcease, leaving off, breaking off; discontinuing, discontinuance, suspension, adjournment, stay, pause, respite, interruption, recess. —**Ant.** starting, start, beginning, commencement, initiation; continuance, continuation, persistence; resumption.

chafe *v.* **1.** *The tight collar chafed his neck:* rub, scratch, scrape, rasp, abrade. **2.** *The bus driver chafed at the slow traffic:* be irritated, be exasperated, be annoyed, rage, rankle, seethe, boil, burn, fume, foam. —**Ant.** 1 soothe, cool, heal, protect. 2 pacify.

chaff *n.* **1.** *Threshers had to separate the wheat from the chaff:* husks, hulls, shells, pods, shucks, remnant, leavings, residue, sweepings; waste, rubbish, refuse, debris, trash, litter, rubble; dross, slag, junk, shoddy. —*v.* **2.** *The other kids liked to chaff him about his big ears:* rib, kid, razz, josh, jolly, twit, rag, ride, bug, ridicule.

chagrin *n.* *The man resigned his job with chagrin, admitting he could not do the work:* shame, humiliation, embarrassment, mortification, distress, dismay. —**Ant.** pride, glory, triumph, exultation.

chain *n.* **1.** *Where can I buy a bicycle chain? Grandfather always wore a watch chain:* linked cable, metal links; fob. **2.** Usually **chains.** *The prisoners were put in chains:* shackles, fetters, bonds, irons; manacles, handcuffs, leg irons. **3.** **chains.** *The Civil War freed the slaves from their chains:* bondage, subjugation, enslavement, slavery, servitude, serfdom, thralldom. **4.** *A bizarre chain of events caused the accident on the*

Orient Express: series, sequence, succession, string, train. —*v.* **5.** *Chain the dog securely to the fence:* shackle, fetter, fasten, tie, tie up, secure, bind, lash, tether, moor; put in irons, manacle. —**Ant.** 5 unchain, unfasten, untie, unshackle, unstrap; free, let go, let loose, liberate.

chair *n.* **1.** *There weren't enough chairs at the table:* perch, seat. **2.** *The chair adjourned the meeting early:* chairman, chairperson, chairwoman, moderator, authority, speaker, director, leader, master, principal.

chairman *n.* *The president of the company will become the next chairman of the board:* presiding officer, head, administrator, executive, director, manager, supervisor, chairwoman, chairlady, chairperson; chair, moderator, master of ceremonies, *Slang* emcee, speaker, leader, toastmaster.

chairperson *n.* *She was elected chairperson of the committee:* chair, chairman, chairwoman.

chairwoman *n.* *For the first time, the conference has a chairwoman:* chair, chairperson.

chalice *n.* *The priest poured wine into the chalice:* goblet, cup, vessel.

challenge *n.* **1.** *He received a challenge to a duel. The champion issued a challenge to all other boxers to fight him:* summons, dare, defiant, bid, hostile invitation, demand. **2.** *Mt. Everest is the supreme challenge to a mountain climber:* test, trial, *Archaic* gage. —*v.* **3.** *The fathers challenged the sons to a race:* dare, summon, bid, invite to compete, defy, fling down the gauntlet. **4.** *I challenge the truth of your story:* question, impute, dispute, take exception to, doubt. **5.** *The new job challenged his skill:* test, try, tax. —**Ant.** 4 accept, believe, agree with; concede, yield, acquiesce.

chamber *n.* **1.** *The lawyers met in the judge's chambers. The senators debated in the chambers of Congress:* room, inner room, office; apartment; hall. **2.** *The king retired to his chamber:* bedroom, boudoir; sitting room, parlor, drawing room, salon. **3.** *The Senate chamber approved the amendment:* legislative body; council, assembly, congress, board, diet, house; court.

champion *n.* **1.** *Joe Louis was the world's heavy-weight boxing champion for many years:* title holder, contest winner; victor, winner, conqueror, vanquisher; master, laureate, paragon. **2.** *Mahatma Gandhi was a champion of peaceful relations among all countries:* upholder, advocate, protagonist, defender, supporter, protector, backer, promoter. —*v.* **3.** *Teddy Roosevelt championed the establishment of national parks:* fight for, battle for, uphold, support, back, defend, stand up for, promote, advocate, aid, abet, speak for, espouse. —**Ant.** 1 loser; contender. 2 opponent, enemy, detractor. 3 oppose, combat; hinder.

chance *n.* **1.** *The two friends met by chance on the street:* accident, happenstance; fortune, luck, destiny, fate, providence. **2.** *There's a chance of rain today:* possibility, likelihood, likeliness, probability. **3.** *Candidates who fail the*

driver's test will have another chance next month: opportunity, try, attempt, occasion, possibility. **4.** *Don't take chances by driving too fast:* risk, danger, hazard; gamble, speculation, jeopardy. —*v.* **5.** *It chanced someone found the lost ring:* happen, occur, come to pass, come about, turn out, fall, befall, fall to one's lot. **6.** *Should we chance making it home before it snows?:* take a chance, risk, hazard, venture, gamble, try, attempt, rely on fortune. —*adj.* **7.** *A chance meeting brought the two old friends together again:* accidental, unintentional, unexpected, unlooked for, unplanned, unforeseen, random, undesigned, unpremeditated, fortuitous, fortunate, lucky. —**Ant.** 1 plan, design, intent, intention, premeditation. 2 unlikelihood, impossibility, improbability, certainty. 4 surety, certainty, sure thing. 7 intentional, planned, premeditated; designed, arranged, expected, foreseen, looked for.

chancy *adj.* *The prospect of your making a profit is chancy at best:* risky, precarious, dubious, doubtful, uncertain, unpredictable, hazardous, problematical, speculative, venturesome, capricious, erratic, whimsical, touchy, unsound, tricky; *Slang* dicey, iffy. —**Ant.** sure, safe, infallible, predictable, certain, unmistakable.

change *v.* **1.** *Rain made us change our plans for the picnic. The caterpillar changed into a butterfly:* alter, modify, make different, shift, vary, recast, restyle, remodel, reorganize, reform, revolutionize; transfer, transmute, mutate, transform, turn, convert, metamorphose. **2.** *You'd better change that shirt for a larger one:* exchange, replace, substitute, swap, trade, switch, shift, interchange, shuffle; remove and replace. —*n.* **3.** *After the warm days, this cold weather is quite a change. The new owner made a lot of changes in the business:* difference, modification, switch, shift, variation, deviation, variety, fluctuation, veering; alteration, conversion, substitution, swapping, reform, reformation, revolution, reorganization, remodeling, restyling; metamorphosis, transformation, transposition, turn about, conversion, transmutation, transfiguration. **4.** *Let's eat out for a change:* novelty, something different, exception, switch; diversion, variety. **5.** *Do you have change for the tip?:* coins, small coins, silver, pocket money, pin money. —**Ant.** 1 hold, keep, bide, stay, remain. 2 keep. 3 uniformity, permanence, immutability, fixedness, constancy, stability, invariability, unchangeableness, monotony. 5 bills, paper money.

changeable *adj.* *Her moods are as changeable as the weather:* variable, varying, erratic, irregular, alternating, deviating, inconstant, fickle, flighty, volatile, fluctuating, mercurial, capricious, fitful, vacillating, unsteady, uncertain, unstable, capricious; mutable, reversible, transformable, modifiable, convertible. —**Ant.** unchangeable, invariable, regular, undeviating, constant, steady, certain, reliable, stable, immutable, irreversible, inconvertible.

channel *n.* **1.** *We sailed across the English Channel:* strait, passage, watercourse, narrows.

2. *Heavy rains wore a channel in the yard:* groove, furrow, trough, gash, cut, gutter. **3.** *It takes a week for a memo to reach the boss by the normal channels:* route, course, avenue of communication. —*v.* **4.** *The requests for transfers are channeled through the personnel office:* route, direct, send, convey, guide, steer, lead.

chant *n.* **1.** *After dinner they entertained us with native chants and dancing:* song, hymn, melody, lied, strain, theme, chanson; psalm, doxology, plainsong, canticle, offertory, Gregorian chant, chorale, Gloria Patri, descant; dirge, threnody, elegy, ode, monody, monophony, homophony. —*v.* **2.** *The monks chanted softly as they filed in for vespers:* sing, croon, intone, vocalize, carol, descant, troll, trill, chorus.

chaos *n.* *Without rules, people would live in a state of chaos:* turmoil, upheaval, confusion, agitation, tumult, uproar, furor, bedlam, pandemonium, turbulence, commotion; disorder, disarray, disorganization, disarrangement, mess, muddle, jumble, discomposure. —**Ant.** order, organization, routine, efficiency; calmness, calm; quiet, composure, peacefulness.

chaotic *adj.* *Looting and rioting made the scene chaotic:* confused, upset, tumultuous, turbulent, disordered, unruly, disorderly, anarchic, scattered, disarrayed, higgledy-piggledy. —**Ant.** organized, orderly.

chaperon or **chaperone** *n.* **1.** *The teenagers needed a chaperon for their house party:* adult overseer, adult attendant; guardian, protector, custodian, attendant, duenna. —*v.* **2.** *A group of parents chaperoned the high-school dance:* oversee, keep an eye on, shepherd; guard, safeguard, watch, accompany, escort.

chaplain *n.* *In the army the company chaplain had arranged an emergency leave for him:* priest, minister, rabbi, padre, father, reverend; *Military Slang* sky pilot, Holy Joe; cleric, churchman, ecclesiastic, curate, abbé, vicar, pastor, rector, parson, preacher.

chapter *n.* **1.** *Read chapters 1 through 5 of the textbook. The Civil War was an important chapter in United States history:* part, section, division, subdivision, portion; episode; clause, period, span, phase, era. **2.** *The fraternity has local chapters all over the country:* branch, affiliate, group, division, subdivision; body, unit.

char *v.* *The sparks from the fireplace charred the carpet:* singe, scorch, sear, burn; incinerate, reduce to charcoal, carbonize.

character *n.* **1.** *Each individual should be judged by his own character:* qualities, traits, attributes, nature, self, being, makeup, individuality, distinctiveness. **2.** *A person who cheats has little character:* honor, integrity, moral strength, morality, honesty, goodness, rectitude, uprightness. **3.** *The police were tracking a suspicious character:* person, individual, specimen, being, personality. **4.** *My old aunt is a priceless character:* odd person, eccentric, original, one-of-a-kind; *Slang* weirdo, oddball. **5.** *Ophelia is the main female character in Shakespeare's Hamlet:* fictional person, person, persona; role, part;

(*plural*) dramatis personae. —**Ant.** 2 dishonor, dishonesty, moral weakness.

characteristic *adj.* **1.** *Windy days are characteristic of March:* typical, representative, indicative, symbolic, emblematic, distinctive, distinguishing. —*n.* **2.** *Tactfulness is one of his nicest characteristics:* attribute, trait, quality, aspect, feature, property, mark, earmark; mannerism, peculiarity, specialty, trademark. —**Ant.** 1 uncharacteristic, unusual, atypical, unrepresentative, rare.

characterization *n.* *The characterization of librarians as old maids is unfair and untrue. The actress's characterization of Juliet was superb:* representing, representation, portrayal, portrait, picturing, depiction; delineation, description.

characterize *v.* *They characterized the gathering as unruly:* describe, portray, delineate, define, designate, differentiate, distinguish, identify, personalize, portray, represent, stamp, typify, mark, brand, dub, tag.

charade *n.* *The ostensibly serious discussion ended up as a charade:* farce, mockery, travesty, make-believe, deception, mimicry, pretense, put-on.

charge *v.* **1.** *The hotel charges thirty dollars a day for this room:* fix as a price, put a value on, ask, demand, require, exact, price; request payment, assess, levy. **2.** *Did the customer pay cash for the shoes or charge them?:* put on one's account, incur a debit, take credit, delay payment; debit. **3.** *The air was charged with electricity:* load, fill, lade, pack, stuff; pile, stack, heap. **4.** *The major charged his soldiers to stand firm:* command, order, direct, instruct, bid, call upon, summon, enjoin. **5.** *The insurance investigator charged the fire to a faulty heater. The suspect was charged with reckless driving:* attribute, ascribe, fix responsibility for, lay the blame for, impute, assign; accuse, incriminate, blame, indict, lodge a complaint against, prefer charges against. **6.** *The cavalry charged the enemy fort:* rush, attack, storm, come at, make a dash at, beset, assail, assault, make an onslaught. —*n.* **7.** *The charge for admission is three dollars:* fee, cost, price, expense, assessment, rate, amount, payment; payment due, toll, duty. **8.** *Teddy Roosevelt led the charge up San Juan Hill:* attack, onslaught, assault, storming, rush, onset, sortie. **9.** *The children are in the charge of a nursemaid:* care, custody, keeping, safekeeping, guardianship, protection; jurisdiction, superintendence, supervision, administration, control, command, management. **10.** *The suspect was booked on a charge of theft:* allegation, accusation, complaint; arraignment, indictment. **11.** *The judge made a brief charge to the jury:* direction, advice, instruction, injunction; order, command, bidding, dictate, enjoining; rule of conduct. —**Ant.** 1 give away, give. 2 pay, pay cash. 3 empty, unload. 5 absolve, exculpate; vindicate, exonerate, pardon, acquit. 6 retreat, withdraw. 8 retreat, withdrawal. 10 absolution, vindication, exoneration; acquittal, pardon.

charisma *n.* *The charisma of Garbo in those*

old movies is irresistible: charm, appeal, magnetism, presence, fascination, glamour, allure, bewitchery, enchantment, witchery, attractiveness, sex appeal.

charismatic *adj. The charismatic speaker attracted big crowds:* alluring, attractive, fascinating, magnetic, captivating, spellbinding, beguiling, glamorous, entrancing, riveting, bewitching.

charitable *adj.* **1.** *The Community Chest asks us to be charitable in our gifts this year. The foundling home is a charitable organization:* generous, giving, bountiful, bounteous, munificent, open-handed; philanthropic, almsgiving, eleemosynary, benevolent. **2.** *A more charitable person would forgive the boy's errors:* forgiving, understanding, sympathetic, sympathizing, kindly, kind, kindhearted, benevolent, warmhearted, gracious, considerate, magnanimous; lenient, liberal, tolerant, indulgent. **—Ant.** 1 uncharitable, stingy, parsimonious, miserly, ungiving, ungenerous. 2 unforgiving, strict, rigid, unkind, malevolent, unsympathetic, hardhearted, cold-hearted, inconsiderate.

charity *n.* **1.** *The orphanage is supported by the charity of the townspeople. The Red Cross is my favorite charity:* philanthropy, contributions, donations, donating, alms, alms-giving, giving, financial help, help, aid, gift, assistance, offering, endowment, benefaction, fundraising, handout; generosity, munificence, openhandedness, bounty, benefaction; charitable institution, fund. **2.** *Faith, hope, and charity can make the world a better place:* good will, love of mankind, altruism, love, humanity, compassion, sympathy, kindness, goodness, benevolence, benignity, tolerance, graciousness. **—Ant.** 1 uncharitableness, stinginess, parsimony. 2 malice, ill will, hate, hatred, selfishness, cruelty, intolerance.

charlatan *n. It's been proved that fortune-tellers are charlatans:* fake, fraud, deceiver, quack, impostor, cheat, swindler, trickster, cozener, confidence artist, mountebank.

charm *n.* **1.** *The host of a TV talk show must have lots of charm. The girl's warm personality is her greatest charm:* power to please, charisma, fascination, enchantment, allure, allurement, attraction, magnetism, lure, draw. **2.** *The fairy godmother's magic charm turned Cinderella's rags into a beautiful gown:* spell, incantation, conjuration; sorcery, magic. **3.** *Some people used to carry a rabbit's foot as a charm:* lucky piece; amulet, talisman; trinket, bauble, ornament. **—v. 4.** *Everyone was charmed by the child's graciousness:* please, give pleasure, delight, gratify, make happy, enrapture, enthrall; fascinate, attract, allure, engage, entrance, enchant, grip, captivate, take, bewitch, *Slang* turn on. **5.** *His daughter charmed him into buying her a car:* lure, seduce, cajole, win over, beguile, bewitch. **6.** *The witch charmed the prince into a frog:* change by magic, work magic on, cast a spell, conjure. **—Ant.** 1 unattractiveness, repulsiveness. 4 repel, alienate, disgust, displease; *Slang* turn off.

charming *adj. She gave us a charming smile.*

Jim has developed a charming personality: attractive, pleasing, charismatic, delightful, agreeable, lovely, graceful, winning, winsome, likable; entrancing, fascinating, captivating, engaging, enthralling, bewitching, enchanting, fetching, enticing, magnetic, irresistible, alluring. **—Ant.** unattractive, unpleasing, unpleasant, unlikable, repulsive, repellent, disgusting.

chart *n.* **1.** *The navigator plotted the ship's course on the chart. The chart showed the decline in the company's sales during the year:* map, navigator's map, mariner's map; diagram, graph, table, tabulation; blueprint, scheme, plan, outline, sketch. **—v. 2.** *The pilot charted the plane's course. The committee charted the annual fund-raising drive:* map, map out, draw up, diagram; plot, draft, plan, delineate, design, outline, sketch, lay out.

charter *n.* **1.** *The organization operates under federal charter:* permit, license, authority, franchise, agreement, contract, compact, covenant, deed, concession, sanction. **—v. 2.** *The state chartered the university fifty years ago:* establish by charter, license, commission, grant, authorize. **3.** *The vacationers chartered a boat to go fishing:* rent, hire, lease, let, engage, commission, employ.

chary *adj. After so much criticism he was chary about endorsing any more worthy causes:* wary, suspicious, leery, cautious, circumspect, careful, prudent, watchful, vigilant, heedful, guarded, alert, *Slang* cagey, distrustful, shy. **—Ant.** reckless, rash, headstrong, daring, heedless, bold.

chase *v.* **1.** *The police officer chased the thief down the street. Hunters chased the deer silently:* pursue, go in pursuit of, go after, run after, try to overtake, try to catch up with; hunt, stalk, trail, track, follow, tail, dog, hound, shadow. **2.** *Mother chased the cat from the bedroom:* drive, put to flight; evict, oust, send away, drive away, rout, shoo, send packing, cast out; scatter, dispel, repulse. **—n. 3.** *Many hunters find the chase more exciting than the kill:* hunt, hunting, quest, pursuit, pursuing, following, stalking, tracking. **—Ant.** 1 let go, let escape, lose, lose track of, escape, flee, elude.

chasm *n. The earthquake left a deep chasm in the earth's surface:* abyss, fissure, rift, split, gorge, ravine, gap, crevasse, divide, gulch, gulf, break, cleft, crack, breach; pit, crater, hold, cavity.

chaste *adj.* **1.** *Boy Scouts are enjoined to remain chaste in mind and body:* virginal, pure, continent. **2.** *The elderly couple were hardworking and chaste:* clean-living, wholesome, decent, virtuous, sinless, clean, righteous, untainted, uncorrupted, unsullied, immaculate. **3.** *The author's chaste style is elegant but boring:* pure, classic, restrained, modest, austere, severe, strict, precise; unadorned, unornamented, unembellished. **—Ant.** 1 unchaste, incontinent, impure, lewd, obscene, wanton, promiscuous, licentious, ribald; married, wed. 2 corrupt, unwholesome, dishonorable, immoral, sinful, immodest; impure, unclean, tainted, sullied, soiled, dirty, blemished, tarnished. 3 ornate, flashy, gaudy, unrestrained, self-indulgent, vulgar.

chasten See CHASTISE.

chastise v. *The teacher chastised the child for arriving late:* punish, discipline, penalize, beat, whip, spank, thrash, flog, strap; reprimand, scold, castigate, upbraid, rebuke, reproach, admonish, chasten, reprove, correct, censure, criticize, chide, call down, berate, scourge, roast, take to task, fulminate against, call on the carpet, give a tongue-lashing to, haul over the coals. —**Ant.** reward, honor, praise, compliment, applaud, commend, congratulate, give kudos to.

chastity n. *Nuns must take vows of chastity:* celibacy, purity, virginity, innocence, continence, abstinence, abstemiousness; singleness, bachelorhood, spinsterhood. —**Ant.** incontinence; promiscuity, lewdness, wantonness, licentiousness; marriage.

chat v. **1.** *Stop and chat a while:* talk, converse, chatter, gab, chitchat, prate, prattle, palaver, chew the rag, chew the fat, *Slang* rap. —n. **2.** *Call me tomorrow and we'll have a chat:* talk, conversation; chitchat, palaver, confabulation, talk session, heart-to-heart talk, *Slang* rap session.

chattel n. *The will says that "all goods and chattels" are left to his brother:* personal possessions, personal effects, belongings, effects, movable property, movables; paraphernalia, gear, things, trappings, accouterments.

chatter v. **1.** *The guests chattered as they waited for dinner:* talk, talk idly, babble, jabber, prattle, prate, gabble, chitchat, palaver, confabulate, gossip, twaddle, blather, chitterchatter, blab, patter, *Slang* gas. **2.** *My teeth are chattering from the cold:* clatter, click, clank. —n. **3.** *The children's constant chatter was irritating:* jabber, gibber, babble, talk, talking, gossip, chitchat, chitterchatter, gabble, palaver, twaddle, blather, blabbing, blabber, patter, idle talk.

chatterbox n. *My seatmate on the plane was a chatterbox from my old hometown:* talker, jabberer, gabber, blatherskite, chatterer, chatterbasket, babbler, prattler; *Slang* windbag, gasbag, blabbermouth, hot-air artist; gossip, talebearer, tattletale, tattler, telltale.

chatty adj. *While Mother was in a chatty mood she told me some interesting stories about her girlhood:* talkative, talky, effusive, voluble, chatting; garrulous, gabby, gushing, gushy, babbling, long-winded, loquacious, prating, jabbering, verbose, windy, gassy; gossipy, blabbering, tongue-wagging, loose-tongued, loose-lipped. —**Ant.** quiet, close-mouthed, secretive, uncommunicative, taciturn.

chauvinism n. *The senator's chauvinism made him intolerant of other countries:* superpatriotism, ethnocentricity, blind patriotism, flag-waving, jingoism, militarism, nationalism.

cheap adj. **1.** *Chicken is not as cheap as it was:* inexpensive, low-priced, economical, reasonable. **2.** *Talk is cheap:* effortless, costless, easy. **3.** *The coat may be expensive but it looks cheap:* shoddy, shabby, inferior, worthless, poor, second-rate, trashy, meager, paltry, gimcrack; flashy, gaudy, in bad taste, tawdry, tacky, common, inelegant. **4.** *Spreading gossip is a cheap thing to do:* contemptible, petty, despicable, sordid, ignoble, wretched, mean, base, *Slang* two-bit; vulgar, immoral, indecent. **5.** *He's too cheap to pick up the check:* tight, stingy, miserly, penurious, tightfisted, close. —**Ant.** 1 expensive, costly, high-priced, high, overpriced. 2 worthwhile, valuable; difficult, troublesome. 3 superior, good, fine, first-rate, worthy; in good taste, tasteful, high-class, classy, elegant, chic, smart. 4 admirable, commendable; moral, decent. 5 generous, charitable, openhanded.

cheapen v. *Inflation cheapened the currency:* devalue, depreciate, abase, corrupt, debase, degrade, demean, denigrate, diminish, discredit, downgrade, lose value, lower, mark down, minimize, reduce.

cheat v. **1.** *Her uncle cheated her out of her inheritance:* swindle, defraud, trick, bilk, gyp, fleece; *Slang* take, rook; deceive, dupe, victimize, betray, delude, hoodwink, bamboozle, humbug, cozen, hoax, gull; *Slang* con. **2.** *Only a cad would cheat at cards:* practice fraud, practice trickery, break the rules, act unfairly. **3.** *You can't cheat fate for long:* escape, thwart, foil, circumvent, outwit, frustrate, baffle, fool, shortchange, mislead, defeat. —n. **4.** *That cheat would defraud his own mother!:* swindler, trickster, con artist, shark, double-crosser, deceiver; fraud, charlatan, mountebank, crook; quack, fake, impostor, chiseler, dodger.

check v. **1.** *Inflation must be checked if the dollar is to have any value. The sandbags will check the floodwaters temporarily:* stop, bring to a standstill, stay, halt, restrain, slow, hold back, curb, limit, brake, inhibit, arrest, constrain, rein in, rein, harness, bridle, stall; impede, obstruct, choke, prevent, suppress, block, muzzle, retard, smother, frustrate, thwart, circumvent, hold, gag. **2.** *Please check the broken light switch. Did you check your purse for the keys?:* inspect, look at, test, examine; search, look into, peruse, explore. **3.** *Check on the problem and report the results at the next meeting:* investigate, study, take stock of, review, probe, inspect, survey, look over, examine, scrutinize, explore. **4.** *His alibi checks with the information we have:* agree, correspond, fit, tally, conform, jibe, mesh, chime, harmonize, be uniform. —n. **5.** *A system of checks and balances keeps the three branches of the U.S. government equal. The anchor served as a check to the boat's forward progress:* restraint, limit, limitation, restriction, control, curb, prevention, prohibition, constraint, hindrance, impediment, barrier, bar, block, obstacle, obstruction, repression, bridle; stop, stoppage, halt, end, stay, cessation. **6.** *The plumber made a careful check of the pipes:* test, inspection, scrutiny, examination, survey, search, perusal, probe, investigation, exploration, study. —**Ant.** 1 begin, initiate, start; accelerate, speed up, spur, let loose, give free rein, unleash, release; foster, encourage, further, urge on; help, abet, aid, support. 2, 3 ignore, overlook, disregard. **4** disagree, contradict, jar. **5** accelerator, spur, encouragement, fostering, furthering, help, aid; start, beginning.

checked adj. A checked tablecloth was brought out: checkered, parquet, plaid, tartan.

checkered adj. **1.** The table had a red and white checkered tablecloth. The fields were checkered with patches of light and shade: checked, parti-colored, variegated, motley, mottled, dappled, piebald, pied. **2.** He had a checkered career of failure and success: varied, uneven, motley, inconstant, irregular, fitful, fluctuating, vacillating, up-and-down, seesaw. —**Ant. 1** solid. **2** consistent, constant, unvarying, unvaried, unvariable, unchanging, steady, stable, even, smooth.

cheek n. **1.** Don't put too much rouge on your cheeks: jowl, side of the face. **2.** I wouldn't have the cheek to go to a party uninvited: impudence, impertinence, nerve, insolence, arrogance, effrontery, audacity, brazenness, brass, boldness, forwardness, brashness, temerity. —**Ant. 2** reserve, reticence, shyness, bashfulness, timidity, timorousness, humility, self-effacement.

cheer n. **1.** The touchdown brought loud cheers from the crowd: approving shout, encouraging cry, acclamation, acclaim, hooray, huzzah, bravo, yell, shriek. **2.** The nurse always had words of cheer for the patients: assurance, reassurance, encouragement, comfort, hopefulness, hope; optimism, buoyancy. **3.** The party sparkled with cheer: gaiety, fun, merriment, animation, joy, joviality, liveliness, revelry, gladness, high spirits, vivacity, buoyance, joyfulness, delight, pleasure, glee, geniality, rejoicing, jubilation, merrymaking, festivity. —v. **4.** The hometown fans cheered the team to victory: root, hail, encourage, hurrah, shout, yell, cry. **5.** A vase of roses cheered the room. The minister's words cheered the family: brighten, enliven, gladden, animate; assure, reassure, encourage, comfort, hearten, warm, inspire, fortify, buoy up, uplift. —**Ant. 1** boo, catcall, hiss, Bronx cheer, raspberry. **2** gloom, discouragement, hopelessness, pessimism. **3** gloom, sadness, despair, depression, despondency. **4** deride, discourage, taunt, ridicule, boo, hiss. **5** darken, sadden; discourage, dispirit, depress, dishearten.

cheerful adj. **1.** It's wonderful to see you so cheerful: cheery, gay, joyful, joyous, light-hearted, happy, glad, gladsome, merry, sunny, high-spirited, in high humor, jovial, buoyant, elated, gleeful, jolly, agreeable, pleasant; breezy, jaunty, blithe, optimistic, airy, lively, sprightly. **2.** Yellow is a cheerful color: bright, lively, cheery, gay, sparkling, sunny. —**Ant. 1** cheerless, glum, gloomy, sullen, dour, morose, dejected, depressed, depressing, downcast, downhearted, melancholy, sad, doleful, despondent, disconsolate, dismal, rueful, unhappy, joyless, miserable; dispiriting, unpleasant; lifeless, dull. **2** cheerless, dull, somber, lifeless, depressing.

cheering adj. Her cheering words aided his re-

covery: encouraging, uplifting, comforting, auspicious, heartening, hopeful, promising, propitious.

cheerless adj. The host's cheerless mood cast a pall on the party. It was a cheerless fall day: gloomy, downcast, dreary, glum, dispirited, despondent, dolorous, forlorn, downhearted, funereal, doleful, spiritless, dejected, joyless, desolate, heavy-hearted, solemn, austere, grim, saturnine, morose, sullen, sad, melancholy, miserable, mournful, lugubrious, woebegone, unhappy, disconsolate, rueful, woeful; bleak, gray, dull, sunless, somber, dismal, uninviting, depressing, comfortless. —**Ant.** cheerful, gay, joyful, light-hearted, happy, merry, jolly, gleeful, elated.

cherish v. **1.** Some people cherish possessions more than friends: love, hold dear, revere, treasure, value, prize, dote on, appreciate, venerate, honor, esteem, idolize, nurse, nourish, nurture, sustain, shelter. **2.** The bride and groom promised to cherish each other through sickness and health: care for, take care of, sustain, succor, nurture. —**Ant. 1** hate, dislike, scorn, despise, disdain. **2** desert, forsake, abandon, renounce, neglect, ignore.

chest n. **1.** Across his chest was a string of medals: breast, bosom, torso, upper trunk, thorax. **2.** You will find the blankets at the bottom of the chest: cabinet, bureau, coffer, bin, box, commode, strongbox, trunk.

chew v. Chew your food slowly: masticate; champ, gnaw, crunch, munch, nibble, grind, crush; ruminate.

chic adj. The movie star wore a very chic dress: fashionable, stylish, smart, elegant; modish, voguish, natty, Informal swank, swanky, Slang classy, ritzy, snazzy. —**Ant.** unfashionable, unstylish, passé; dowdy, inelegant, shabby, shoddy.

chicanery n. There was some chicanery with our reservations, and we complained to the travel agent: deception, trickery, fraud, deceit, cozenage, gulling, guile, hocus-pocus, double-dealing, duplicity, duping, subterfuge, hoodwinking, pettifoggery, humbuggery; knavery, roguery, rascality, villainy.

chichi adj. **1.** Their chichi house was fitted with every bit of bric-a-brac that money could buy: showy, ostentatious, flashy, frilly, gimcrack, splashy, flamboyant, garish, vulgar; pompous, pretentious, grandiose, affected. **2.** It was a bit of chichi acting that one critic called an ego trip: precious, fussy, arty, arty-tarty, artsy-craftsy, finicky, overnice, nasty-nice, overrefined; prissy, sissyish. —**Ant. 1** plain, simple, uncomplicated, natural, unaffected.

chide v. Mother chided me for being late: admonish, reprimand, scold, chasten, rebuke, reproach, reprove, upbraid, berate, take to task; find fault, criticize, censure, denounce. —**Ant.** praise, commend, laud, extol, applaud, compliment.

chief n. **1.** The chief of the Italian delegation addressed the U.N.: head, leader, director, chairman; boss, overseer, administrator, superintendent, supervisor; commander, captain; ring-leader, master; ruler, chieftain, monarch, overlord, lord, sovereign, potentate. —*adj.* **2.** *His patient's well-being was the doctor's chief concern:* major, main, prime, primary, first, number-one, foremost, cardinal, highest-ranking, greatest, dominant, predominant, paramount, uppermost, prevailing, highest, supreme, principal, preponderant, key, leading, outstanding; governing, ruling, crowning. —**Ant.** 1 subordinate, underling, follower, hanger-on; subject. 2 minor, least, last, subordinate, secondary, subsidiary.

chiefly *adv. Shakespeare thought of himself chiefly as a poet but is admired above all as a playwright:* primarily, principally, mainly, in the main, first, mostly, most of all, predominantly, particularly, above all, expressly, especially. —**Ant.** least, last, least of all, in a small way.

child *n. The child is only six years old. The average family has two children:* youth, youngster, juvenile, kid, boy, lad, girl, lass, *Informal* tad; baby, infant, tot, little one, tyke, toddler, moppet; son, daughter, offspring. —**Ant.** adult, grownup, man, woman; parent.

childbirth *n. Many obstetricians encourage some form of natural childbirth:* childbearing, giving birth, delivery, parturition; confinement.

childhood *n. A happy childhood helps give children security:* youth, boyhood, girlhood; nursery days, school days, adolescence. —**Ant.** adulthood, maturity.

childish *adj. Her behavior is extremely childish:* immature, childlike, infantile, puerile, juvenile, callow, adolescent, babyish; silly, foolish, naïve, simple, asinine. —**Ant.** mature, grown-up, adult, sophisticated; manly, manful, womanly, womanlike.

childlike *adj. Her childlike behavior was endearing:* artless, naive, guileless, ingenuous, trusting, childish, credulous, innocent, unaffected.

children *n. Their children included two boys and three girls:* offspring, descendants, progeny, line, issue.

chill *n.* **1.** *There's a chill in the air this morning:* chilliness, coolness, iciness, frostiness, frigidity; crispness, sharpness, nip, bite, rawness. **2.** *He caught a chill from being out in the rain:* cold; fever. —*adj.* **3.** Also **chilly.** *A chill wind blew from the North:* chilling, cold, wintry, arctic, icy, frigid, frosty, penetrating, cool; brisk, biting, bitter, raw, keen, shivery, crisp, sharp, cutting, nippy. **4.** *We received a chill greeting from our opponents:* icy, frigid, cold, aloof, hostile, unfriendly, stony, callous, indifferent, uncaring, unresponsive, stiff, unfeeling, passionless, forbidding, harsh. —**Ant.** 1 warmth, warmness. 3 warm, warming, hot, tropical, balmy, mild. 4 warm, friendly, cordial, congenial, emotional.

chime *n.* **1.** *Our church's chimes are more than 200 years old:* set of bells, carillon. **2.** *I love to listen to the chime of the bells:* peal, pealing, ring, ringing, toll, tollings, sound, knell, tinkling, jingle, ding-dong, gong, tintinnabulation. —*v.* **3.** *The bells chimed as the bride and groom left*

the church: peal, ring, sound, toll, knell, tintinnabulate, jingle, tinkle.

chimera *n. His greatest consolation was the chimera that one day he would write a novel:* delusion, illusion, dream, fantasy, fancy, idle whim, pipe dream, bubble, daydream, self-deception, self-deceit, figment of one's imagination, mirage, hallucination, castle in the air, castle in Spain, fool's paradise, will-o'-the-wisp.

china *n. Set the table with the good china:* dishes, cups and saucers, plates, tableware, chinaware; pottery, crockery, earthenware, stoneware, porcelain, ceramic ware.

chink[1] *n. The rain came in through a chink in the roof:* crack, slit, rift, rent, crevice, cleft, fault, breach, fissure, cut, split, gap, gash, cut, break; hole, opening, aperture.

chink[2] *v. The coins chinked in my pocket:* clink, jingle, jangle, clank, tinkle, ring, rattle.

chintzy *adj.* **1.** *The furniture was chintzy, but the rent was cheap:* shabby, sleazy, tacky, *Slang* schlocky, dowdy, *Brit.* tatty, frowzy, frumpy. **2.** *She's never chintzy when she spends money on herself:* stingy, cheap, tight, miserly, close, grudging, niggardly, closefisted, stinting, parsimonious, penny-pinching, penurious. —**Ant.** 1 stylish, elegant, chic, classy, ritzy, fashionable.

chip *n.* **1.** *Gather some wood chips for the fire. Buy a package of potato chips:* small piece, fragment, scrap, sliver, chunk, shaving, splinter, shred, slice, paring, cutting; flake, crumb, morsel, bit, wafer. **2.** *This glass has a chip:* nick, gash. —*v.* **3.** *I chipped the dish when I dropped it:* nick, gash, split, splinter. **4.** *The sculptor chipped away at the block of marble:* hew, chop, cut, whittle, hack, chisel.

chipper *adj. After being ill so long, he's looking chipper again:* lively, animated, spirited, alive, sprightly, cheerful, jaunty, peppy, pert, spry, carefree, high-spirited, energetic, light-hearted, gay, easygoing, frisky, vivacious. —**Ant.** downhearted, sad, morose; sluggish, lethargic.

chirp *v.* **1.** *Listen to the birds chirping:* chirrup, tweet, twitter, sing, chitter, cheep, peep. —*n.* **2.** *The chirps of the crickets keep us awake:* chirrup, tweet, twitter, chitter, cheep, peeping, cheeping, chirr.

chivalrous *adj. Chivalrous men treat women with great respect:* gallant, courtly; polite, mannerly. —**Ant.** ungallant, loutish, boorish, discourteous, rude, unmannerly, disloyal, untrustworthy, inconstant, dishonorable; cruel.

chivalry *n. His considerate treatment of his fiancée shows that chivalry isn't dead:* knighthood; gallantry, courtliness, politeness, courtesy. —**Ant.** loutishness, boorishness, rudeness, impoliteness, unmannerliness, discourtesy, disloyalty, inconstancy; cruelty, inhumanity.

choice *n.* **1.** *The worker left the job of his own choice. The child had no choice but to go to bed:* choosing, decision, deciding, discretion, opting, determination; alternative, option, voice, vote, say. **2.** *My choice for dessert is ice cream:* selection, preference, pick, appointment. **3.** *The store has a poor choice of dresses:* selection, variety, pick, stock, supply, store, collection, assemblage, assortment, array, display. —*adj.* **4.** *The market only carries choice fruits and vegetables:* select, well-chosen, superior, first-rate, first-class, A-one, best, better, prime, prize, preferred, preferable, exclusive, special, excellent, fine; exceptional, superlative, elite, top drawer, tip-top, extraordinary, consummate. —**Ant.** 1 coercion, force; command, order. 4 poor, inferior, worse, second-rate, second-class, mediocre, fair, average, common, ordinary, indifferent.

choke *v.* **1.** *The Boston Strangler choked his victims. The rescuers were choking from the heavy smoke:* strangle, garrote, throttle; smother, asphyxiate, suffocate, gag, stifle. **2.** *Ice choked the river:* stop up, clog, obstruct, constrict, blockade, block, congest, plug, plug up, dam, dam up, stuff; impede, retard, hold back, arrest, check, hinder, constrain, restrain, hamper, inhibit, bridle, suppress, repress. —**Ant.** 2 clear, unclog, unstop, unblock, unplug; spur, speed, accelerate, aid, help, encourage.

choleric *adj.* *She grew more choleric with the years until she was impossible to please:* cranky, dyspeptic, cantankerous, testy, *Brit.* shirty, snappish, peevish, irate, mad, angry, irascible, wrathful, indignant, hot-tempered, ill-tempered, touchy, quick-tempered, short-tempered, thin-skinned, infuriated, short-fused, sour-tempered, furious, vexed, waspish, enraged. —**Ant.** placid, cool, tranquil, easygoing, nonchalant, serene.

choose *v.* **1.** *What dress did the girl choose?:* select, pick out, pick, take, decide on, settle on, fix upon, single out, opt for, call out, extract; make up one's mind, resolve, espouse, embrace, adopt. **2.** *President Lyndon Johnson chose not to run for a second full term:* decide, determine, resolve, prefer, commit oneself, opt, elect, intend, see fit, desire, wish, be inclined, like. —**Ant.** 1 reject, eschew, refuse, decline, spurn, repudiate, cast away, cast out, leave, throw aside, disclaim, dismiss; forgo, forbear.

choosy *adj.* *Dieters must be very choosy about the food they eat:* fussy, finicky, particular, fastidious, picky, discriminating, selective.

chop *v.* **1.** *George Washington chopped down the cherry tree. Chop some wood for the fire:* cut, fell; sunder, hew, hack, split, cleave, slash, gash, lop, crop. **2.** *Chop the carrots for the stew:* cut up, dice, mince, chip, cube; pulverize, fragment. —*n.* **3.** *The lumberjack gave the tree one last chop and it fell:* stroke, whack, blow, hit, cut, hack, swipe. **4.** *Pork chops and greens are a great combination:* cutlet, rib slice, slice, cut, *French* côtelette.

choppy *adj.* *They paddled through choppy water:* rough, inclement, tempestuous, violent, windswept, squally, broken, wild. —**Ant.** calm, smooth, windless.

chore *n.* **1.** *Children should help with the household chores:* household task, domestic work, farm task, small job, task, job, duty, responsibility, work, assignment, stint, errand. **2.** *Filling out complicated tax forms is a real chore:* unpleasant task, difficult job, strain, burden, tedious job, exacting task.

chortle *v.* **1.** *Father used to chortle over the funny papers every Sunday:* chuckle, snort merrily, laugh. —*n.* **2.** *The child gave a merry chortle:* chuckle, merry snort, laugh, gleeful whoop.

chorus *n.* **1.** *Sing the last chorus again:* refrain, antiphony, response. **2.** *The chorus sang Christmas carols:* choir, singing group, glee club, choral society, vocal ensemble; line of dancers; group of speakers. **3.** *The union members shouted their assent in chorus:* concert, unison, unity, one voice; accord, concord, concordance, consensus, unanimity.

chosen *adj.* *The chosen soldiers took an officers' course:* select, selected, elite, elected, picked, named, preferred, favored.

christen *v.* *The baby was christened in St. Patrick's Cathedral:* baptize, sprinkle, dip, immerse; name, designate, dub, dedicate, launch.

chronic *adj.* *She's developed a chronic cough. He's become a chronic complainer:* habitual, longstanding, continual, continuous, constant, persistent, persisting, enduring, lasting, abiding, confirmed, inveterate, perennial, ingrained, deep-seated, deep-rooted; recurring, recurrent, periodic, intermittent. —**Ant.** temporary, infrequent, once-in-a-lifetime, fleeting.

chronicle *n.* **1.** *The Anglo-Saxon Chronicle is one of the earliest written records of England:* record, history, chronology, journal, diary, account, log, annals, archives; narrative, story, epic, saga. —*v.* **2.** *The historian chronicled the main events of the decade:* record, set down, list, docket, log, note, post, enter; recount, relate, report, narrate.

chronological *adj.* *Put the biographies in chronological sequence by the subject's date of birth:* consecutive, successive, ordered, progressive, serial, dated, time-ordered, sequent, succeeding, sequential, chronometric, chronoscopic, chronographic.

chubby *adj.* *He's gotten quite chubby since he learned how to cook:* pudgy, stocky, podgy, plump, thickset, stout, portly, paunchy, tubby, fat, corpulent, flabby, overweight, fleshy, rotund, heavyset, buxom; *Slang* zaftig, roly-poly. —**Ant.** lean, skinny, gaunt, bony, thin, emaciated, underweight.

chuck *v.* **1.** *He chucked the child under the chin:* poke lovingly, pat, tap, pet, tickle. **2.** *Chuck the suitcase onto the back seat:* toss, fling, sling, cast, throw, heave, pitch.

chuckle *v., n.* *A cartoon should make us at least chuckle. The so-called comedy offered only the occasional chuckle:* laugh, giggle, titter, snicker. —**Ant.** cry, sob.

chum *n.* *Bobby and I were childhood chums:* friend, close friend, pal, buddy, bosom buddy, companion, comrade, cohort, intimate, confidant, crony, *Slang* sidekick; playmate, playfellow. —**Ant.** stranger, casual acquaintance; enemy, antagonist.

chummy *adj.* *The two girls seemed very chummy:* friendly, close, intimate, familiar, congenial, affectionate, devoted; *Slang* palsy, palsy-walsy, buddy-buddy. **—Ant.** estranged, alienated, unfriendly, antagonistic, distant, aloof, cool.

chunk n. Chunks of ice were floating in the cold water: lump, hunk, piece, mass, batch, clod, block, square, wad, gob, nugget.

chunky adj. "Chunky" is a more polite way of describing someone who's short and fat: stocky, thickset, beefy, pudgy, stubby, squat, chubby, dumpy, thick-bodied, heavyset, stodgy, portly, squabby. **—Ant.** slim, slender, gangling, scrawny, lithe, lanky.

church n. **1.** St. Peter's in Rome is the largest church in the Christian world: house of worship, house of God, Lord's house, tabernacle, chapel, temple; cathedral, basilica, mosque, synagogue. **2.** Did you attend church last Sunday?: religious service; service, divine worship, devotions. **3.** I belong to the Episcopal Church: religion, denomination, faith, affiliation, persuasion, belief, sect, cult.

churlish adj. Many people tend to be churlish before they've had breakfast: surly, grouchy, sullen, crabbed, bearish, brusque, crusty, quarrelsome, ill-tempered, irascible, petulant, testy, irritable, rancorous, bilious, choleric, splenetic, captious, waspish, sour, tart; uncivil, ill-mannered, unmannerly, rude, boorish, impolite, insulting, discourteous; ill-bred, crude, uncouth, dastardly, obnoxious, contemptible, arrogant, impudent, insolent. **—Ant.** pleasant, agreeable, amiable, easygoing, sweet, kind, good-humored, even-tempered; civil, polite, courteous, gallant, mannerly; well-bred, noble, admirable, cultivated, gentlemanly, humble.

churn v. Butter is made by churning cream. The sea was churning furiously: beat, whisk, whip, shake, shake up, stir up, agitate, vibrate; toss, heave, swirl, roll, roil, foam, rage, convulse, disturb, pulsate, palpitate.

chute n. The grain came tumbling down the chute: incline, ramp, funnel, slide, slope, sluice, channel, course, runway, trough.

chutzpah n. To ask such a price for shoddy goods takes chutzpah: audacity, brashness, boldness, temerity, effrontery, presumption, presumptuousness, brazenness, impudence, nerve, cheek, gall. **—Ant.** timidity, modesty, self-effacement.

cinder n. A cinder blew into my eye. The chimney sweep cleaned the cinders from the chimney: ember, ash; piece of burned coal or wood or iron slag; (also in plural) embers, ashes, clinkers, scoria, slag, dross.

cinema n. Mary Pickford was one of the first stars of the cinema: motion pictures, moving pictures, movies, films, flicks.

cinematography n. The film won her awards for cinematography: camera work, footage, motion-picture photography.

cipher n. **1.** One followed by two ciphers is 100: zero, naught, aught; nothing, nil; Slang goose egg, zip. **2.** He was determined not to remain a cipher all his life: nobody, nonentity, nullity, nothing, naught, obscurity. **3.** The spy's report was written in cipher: code, secret writing; cryptogram, cryptograph; anagram, acrostic. **—Ant.** 1 infinity, something. 2 somebody, something, notable, personage, star.

circa prep. The saint died circa 1150: about, around, approximately, near, roughly.

circle n. **1.** The children gathered around in a circle. There's a circle of haze around the moon tonight: ring, circuit; halo, corona, orb, hoop, belt, girdle, cordon, circlet, ringlet, girt, girth. **2.** He is not in my circle of friends. Sports are not within my circle of interests: group, set, coterie, clique, society, cabal, knot, crowd, company; sphere, orbit, field, realm, compass, circuit, bounds, region, domain, range, reach, arena, theater, sweep, swing, province, dominion, territory, bailiwick. **3.** He farmed throughout the circle of the seasons: cycle, round, revolution, turn, swing, circuit, course, sequence, progression. **—v. 4.** The fence circles the yard: encircle, surround, ring, ring around, border, enclose, hedge in, hem in, border, circuit, belt, gird, girdle, wind about, loop, bound, envelop, encompass, circumscribe. **5.** Our plane circled the airport for an hour before landing. The children circled around and around: revolve around, curve around, move around, circumnavigate, circumrotate; revolve, pivot, reel, curve, curl, turn. **—Ant.** 1 square.

circuit n. **1.** The circuit of the earth around the sun takes about a year: circling, orbiting, revolving; revolution, course, pivoting. **2.** It rained within a fifty mile circuit of the center of the storm: circumference, perimeter, sphere, compass, area, distance around; border, bounds, limit, confine, extremity, edge, margin, frontier. **3.** The mail carrier walks the same circuit everyday: beat, route, round, course, run, territory, tour, lap; journey, jaunt, excursion, trek, walk.

circuitous adj. We took a circuitous path. I couldn't follow his circuitous reasoning: circular, winding, roundabout, circumlocutory, indirect, devious, meandering, rambling; tortuous, twisting, turning, serpentine, labyrinthine. **—Ant.** direct, straight, undeviating, as the crow flies.

circular adj. **1.** The kitchen has a circular table. A circular drive leads to the house: round, rounded, ring-shaped, curved, winding, circuitous. **2.** The circular motion of the merry-go-round made the girl dizzy: turning, rotary, revolving, spinning, twirling, winding, pivoting, spiraling, coiling, curling, swiveling, gyrating; rolling, rocking. **—n. 3.** The store printed a circular advertising the sale: handbill, bill, flier, leaflet, throwaway, advertisement, bulletin, notice, announcement. **—Ant.** 1 square, rectangular, straight. 2 linear.

circulate v. **1.** Blood circulates in the veins and arteries. Waiters serving champagne circulated among the guests: flow, circle, move around, pass through, course, radiate; go around, make the rounds, move about; travel, journey, get abroad, go forth, visit around. **2.** Pictures of the criminals were circulated to police around the country: distribute, disperse, disseminate, pass around, issue, put forward, put about, give out;

make public, spread, scatter, strew, publicize, announce, broadcast, make known, publish. **—Ant.** l stop, stagnate. 2 keep, hold back; keep secret, hide, conceal, suppress.

circulation n. **1.** *The 17th-century English physician William Harvey discovered the circulation of the blood:* flow, flowing, circling, rotation, motion. **2.** *The half eagle, or five-dollar gold piece, is no longer in circulation. The local newspaper has a circulation of 10,000 copies a day:* distribution, dissemination, dispersion, diffusion, radiation, propagation, transmission, promulgation. **—Ant.** l stagnation.

circumference n. *The circumference of a circle is equal to pi times the diameter. We sailed around the entire circumference of the island:* distance around, periphery, perimeter, circuit; boundary, bounds, extremity, border, edge, margin, rim, girdle, girth, outline, compass, limits, fringe. **—Ant.** center, interior.

circumlocution n. *The speaker's point could have been made with less circumlocution:* roundaboutness, roundabout expression, wordiness, meandering, verbiage, garrulity, verbosity, discursiveness, long-windedness, rambling, digression. **—Ant.** directness, conciseness, terseness, succinctness, brevity, briefness.

circumscribe v. **1.** *On this map, major cities are circumscribed in red:* circle, encircle, outline, delineate, define; surround, enclose, encompass. **2.** *His illness circumscribed his activities:* limit, proscribe, restrict, restrain, confine, constrain, impede, hem in, check, curb, bridle, corset, fix. **—Ant.** 2 expand, extend, enlarge, open, throw open, unfetter.

circumspect adj. *Be circumspect in making important decisions:* careful, cautious, guarded, vigilant, alert, wide-awake; watchful, discreet, deliberate, wary, thoughtful, judicious, prudent, sagacious, sage, discriminating, contemplative, discerning, particular, perspicacious. **—Ant.** rash, reckless, foolhardy, heedless, careless; audacious, adventurous, venturous, daring, venturesome, bold.

circumstance n. **1.** *Bad weather is a circumstance we cannot control:* fact, factor, occurrence, happenstance, event, incident, happening, phenomenon, condition, state of affairs, vicissitude, detail, particular, item, thing, point, element, matter. **2.** *The king's coronation was an occasion for much pomp and circumstance:* ceremony, pageantry, ritual, formality; splendor, resplendence, magnificence, brilliance.

circumstantial adj. **1.** *She seems to have been convicted on circumstantial evidence:* presumed, inferred, inferential, conjectural, evidential, implied, deduced, hearsay; incidental, provisional, secondary; nonessential, extraneous. **2.** *He gave a circumstantial account of the accident that was harrowing:* detailed, precise, accurate, explicit, exhaustive, full, complete, unabridged, thorough, blow-by-blow, particular, minute. **—Ant.** 2 short, abridged; cursory, superficial; terse, pithy.

circumvent v. *The pilot circumvented the storm by flying farther south. The swindler tried*

to circumvent the law: circle, circumnavigate, go around, bypass, skirt; escape, avoid, elude, evade, keep away from, shun, miss, dodge, thwart, outwit, frustrate. **—Ant.** face, confront, meet, meet head on, go through; follow, conform to.

circus n. *Clowns and acrobats vied for attention at the circus:* fair, spectacle, big top.

citadel n. *Soldiers took up defensive positions behind the walls of the citadel:* fortress, fort, stronghold, bastion, fortification, rampart.

citation n. **1.** *The* Oxford English Dictionary *contains citations of the written language to illustrate how words have been used:* quotation, quote, excerpt, passage, extract, cite; illustration, example, instance. **2.** *The soldier won two citations for bravery:* commendation, official praise; medal, award, honor, kudos.

cite v. **1.** *The lawyer cited a previous case to support her argument:* allude to, refer to, specify, quote, mention, note, bring forward, indicate, give as example, advance, present, exemplify, document, enumerate. **2.** *The corporal was cited for bravery in battle:* commend, praise, honor, mention, name. **—Ant.** l ignore, disregard; conceal, keep secret. 2 condemn, rebuke, chastise, chasten, criticize; dishonor.

citizen n. *Only citizens of the United States may vote in the election. The citizens of Paris live in a beautiful city:* national, subject; inhabitant, resident, denizen, native. **—Ant.** alien, foreigner; nonresident, visitor, transient, tourist, out-of-towner.

city n. **1.** *The city is an exciting place to live:* town, big town, metropolitan area, megalopolis, metropolis; incorporated town, municipality, township, *Slang* burg. **2.** *The entire city turned out for the celebration:* population of a city, townspeople, inhabitants, residents, denizens.

civic adj. **1.** *Voting is your civic duty:* citizen's, public. **2.** *Keeping your lawn clean should be part of civic pride:* communal, community, local, public.

civil adj. **1.** *Martin Luther King devoted his life to civil rights:* citizen, citizen's, individual. **2.** *The governors met to discuss civil problems:* community, communal, state, city, municipal, civic, public. **3.** *Public education is under civil rather than religious control:* communal, secular, lay, civic, public; nonmilitary. **4.** *It was all I could do to be civil to the rude man:* polite, courteous, well-mannered, mannerly, respectful, gentlemanly; affable, gracious, cordial, neighborly, amiable, obliging, conciliatory, genial, decorous, civilized. **—Ant.** l state. 3 religious; military. 4 uncivil, impolite, rude, discourteous, ill-mannered, unmannerly; uncordial, ungracious.

civilian n. *What does it feel like to be a civilian after 20 years in the army?:* private citizen, non-military person, nonuniformed person; lay person. **—Ant.** soldier, member of the military; uniformed fire fighter, uniformed police officer.

civility n. *Even though angry, he treated us with civility:* politeness, courtesy, courteousness, good manners, manners, respect, respectfulness, tact; graciousness, agreeableness, affability, amiability, cordiality, good temper, pleasantness. **—Ant.** impoliteness, discourtesy, discourteousness, bad manners, disrespect; unfriendliness, hostility, unpleasantness, disagreeableness, ungraciousness.

civilization *n.* **1.** *The missionary returned to civilization after two years in the jungle:* civilized life or society. **2.** *Ancient Greek civilization was one of the highest humanity has achieved:* culture, cultivation, enlightenment, refinement, sophistication, worldliness. **—Ant.** 1, 2 ignorance; barbarism, barbarity, barbarousness, savagery.

civilize *v.* *The missionaries hoped to civilize the natives:* refine, culture, educate, teach, train, instruct, inform, enlighten, cultivate, humanize, edify, polish, acculturate, elevate, develop, sophisticate.

clad *adj.* *The beggar was clad in rags:* clothed, dressed, attired, outfitted, garbed, arrayed. **—Ant.** undressed, unclothed, naked.

claim *v.* **1.** *She claimed the ring was stolen, not lost:* assert, profess, declare, maintain, proclaim, avow, allege, affirm, charge. **2.** *Has anyone claimed the gloves you found?:* lay claim to, seek as due, demand, exact, command, insist on; call for, collect, pick up, ask, request, take. *—n.* **3.** *The jury believed the defendant's claim of innocence:* assertion, avowal, affirmation, declaration, profession, protestation, postulation, statement, proclamation, plea, allegation. **4.** *The doctor's work makes too many claims on her time. His claim to the property was declared valid:* demand, call, requirement, exaction, request; right, title, ownership, access, pretension. **—Ant.** 1 disavow, deny. 2 disclaim, renounce, disown, reject, repudiate, refuse, relinquish, forgo, abnegate, abjure, waive, cede. 3 disclaimer, disavowal, denial, repudiation.

clairvoyant *adj.* *She said she was clairvoyant and offered to help find the kidnapped boy:* telepathic, psychic, extrasensory, prescient, precognitive, prophetic, divining, oracular, telekinetic, psychokinetic, psychometric, foreknowing, second-sighted.

clammy *adj.* *She has a chill and her hands are clammy:* cold and damp, damp, sticky, slimy, pasty; wet, sweaty, perspiring. **—Ant.** dry, cool.

clamor *n.* **1.** *The clamor of the traffic gave me a headache:* noise, uproar, din, blast, hubbub, brouhaha, hullabaloo, jangle, racket, clangor, tumult, rumpus, commotion, chaos, bedlam, shouting. **2.** *A clamor of protest went up from the crowd:* cry, outcry, hue and cry, shout, call, bellow, yell, howl, wild chorus, storm, thunder. *—v.* **3.** *The audience clamored for the show to begin:* shout, cry out, cry, call out, call, bellow, howl, yell, vociferate, bluster, make a racket. **—Ant.** 1–3 whisper, murmur. 1 silence, quiet.

clamp *n.* **1.** *Hold the parts together with a clamp until the glue hardens:* clip, clasp, grip, vise, fastener, brace, bracket. *—v.* **2.** *Clamp the two-by-fours together securely. He clamped his jaws in anger:* clinch, clench, clip, clasp, fasten, secure.

clan *n.* **1.** *What clan do your Scottish ancestors belong to?:* tribal family, family group, house, dynasty; line, lineage, lineal group, strain, stock, pedigree, breed. **2.** *The same clan of actors always spend their vacation at this resort:* circle, group, gang, party, alliance, ring, knot, crowd, company; society, brotherhood, cabal, guild, fraternity, league, affiliation, association.

clandestine *adj.* *The spy had a clandestine meeting to receive confidential information:* secret, undercover, hidden, covert, cloaked, secretive, masked, underground, veiled, concealed; private, confidential, secluded, undisclosed, unrevealed; stealthy, sneaking, surreptitious, furtive, underhand, underhanded. **—Ant.** open, out in the open, public, aboveboard, disclosed, revealed, unconcealed; straightforward, forthright, frank, candid.

clang *v.* **1.** *The bells clanged:* ring loudly, resound, peal, bong, gong, chime, toll, knell, jangle. *—n.* **2.** *The clang of pots and pans woke us:* clash, clashing, din, clangor, clank; ringing, resounding, peal, tolling, knell, bong, gong, jangle, chime.

clank *n.* **1.** *The woman heard the pots and pans clanking in the kitchen:* rattle, clang, clash, clashing, clink, clangor, chink, jangle. *—v.* **2.** *The snow chains clanked every time the car moved:* rattle, clang, clink, chink, jangle, clash, clatter.

clannish *adj.* *The older families in town are very clannish and have little to do with newcomers:* cliquish, exclusive, snobbish, unreceptive, cold, aloof, distant, unfriendly; sectarian, narrow, restricted, provincial, parochial, insular. **—Ant.** open, friendly, hospitable, receptive, warm.

clap *v.* **1.** *The audience stood and clapped at the end of the performance:* applaud. **2.** *The victorious players clapped each other on the back:* slap, smack, rap, strike, whack, thump, swat, hit, smite, thwack; bump, buffet, bang, crack, clatter. **3.** *A detective clapped the handcuffs on the suspect. He clapped the door shut:* set suddenly, cast, thrust, slam, hurl, rush, propel, pitch, fling, force, dash, toss, push, shove, drive, plunge. *—n.* **4.** *I received a sudden clap on the shoulder:* slap, slam, rap, bat, tap, smack, swat, hit, whack, strike, cuff, thump, crack, wallop, thwack. **5.** *The clap of thunder woke everyone:* peal, burst, roar, crack, bang, clack, clatter, slam, explosion. **—Ant.** 1 boo, hiss, give a Bronx cheer, give the raspberry.

claptrap *n.* *It was an old-fashioned melodrama, full of bombast and claptrap:* pretentiousness, humbug, sham, fustian, tomfoolery, staginess, tinsel, gaudiness, quackery, affectation, tawdriness, hokum, nonsense, blarney, twaddle; *Slang* bull, baloney, flapdoodle, bosh, tripe, bilge.

clarification *n.* *The press release required clarification:* illumination, elucidation, simplification, explanation, exposition, unravelling. **—Ant.** obfuscation.

clarify *v.* **1.** *How do you clarify syrup?:* clear, purify, refine, purge. **2.** *His explanation clarified the mystery:* explain, clear up, make clear, resolve, solve, disentangle, illuminate, elucidate, explicate, lay open, make plain, make understandable, bring to light, shed light on. **—Ant.** 1 cloud, muddy. 2 obscure, confuse, mix up, entangle, cloud, muddle.

clarion adj. The clarion call of a bugle rent the air: clear, shrill, high-pitched, ringing, sharp, acute, piercing, blaring; resonant, sonorous; distinct, stirring, compelling, commanding, imperative. **—Ant.** dull, muted, muffled, soft; low.

clarity n. **1.** The news commentator analyzed the situation with clarity: clearness, lucidity, intelligibility, comprehensibility, plainness, simplicity, directness; precision, exactness, explicitness. **2.** The clarity of the spring water was amazing: clearness, transparency, purity, translucence, lucidity; brightness, brilliance, glassiness, luminosity, radiance, effulgence. **—Ant.** 1 obscurity, confusion; imprecision, complexity. 2 cloudiness, muddiness, murkiness; dullness, opaqueness.

clash v. **1.** The garbage cans clashed as the men unloaded them: crash, clang, clank, bang, rattle, clatter, crash. **2.** The two armies clashed on the plains below the city: battle, fight, contest, contend, combat, grapple, skirmish, tussle, cross swords, exchange blows. **3.** The two lawyers clashed in court: argue, dispute, quarrel, wrangle, squabble, boil, altercate, tiff, feud, lock horns. **—**n. **4.** The clash of swords signaled the start of the battle: crash, crashing, clang, clank, rattle, clatter, clangor, jangle. **5.** The clash between the armies occurred at dawn: battle, fight, combat, conflict, contest, fray, skirmish, encounter, struggle; fracas, set-to. **6.** The clash of opinions caused tension in the room: conflict, disagreement, difference, opposition, discord, dissidence, disharmony, jarring, friction, antagonism. **—Ant.** 2 make peace. 3 agree, concur; make up. 5 peace, truce. 6 concord, accord, harmony, agreement.

clasp n. **1.** The bracelet has a gold clasp: fastening, fastener, catch, latch, grip, hook, coupler, hasp, link, clinch, bolt, clamp, buckle, lock, snap. **2.** He held her in a tight clasp: hold, grip, embrace, hug, grasp, clutch, squeeze. **—**v. **3.** Clasp the necklace with the safety catch: latch, catch, hook, clamp, lock, hasp, buckle, clinch, link, couple, secure, fasten, clip, snap. **4.** The child clasped the doll tightly: hold, grip, grasp, hug, embrace, clutch, grapple, press, squeeze. **—Ant.** 3 unclasp, unfasten, open, unlock, unlatch, unhook, unbuckle, uncouple, unsnap. 4 let go, drop; release, give up.

class n. **1.** Pine trees belong to the evergreen class: classification, category, group, type, kind, sort, order, variety, division, genre, breed, pedigree, species, genus. **2.** The senior class graduates in June: set of pupils, graduating group, grade, form, group, section. **3.** Professor Johnson takes the nine o'clock history class: course, session, section; lesson. **4.** She was born into the middle class. Royalty comprise the ruling class: social stratum, social rank, station, status, position, caste, condition, sphere, state; circle, clique, set, group. **—**v. **5.** Jackson Pollack is

classed as an abstract expressionist: classify, group, categorize, designate, departmentalize, type, rank, codify, rate, brand, label, pigeonhole; catalog, arrange, index, order; grade, size, number.

classic adj. Also **classical 1.** Carl Sandburg wrote a classic biography of Lincoln. Sneezing and a sore throat are classic symptoms of a cold: definitive, authoritative, absolute, accepted, traditional, model, archetypal, prototypal, exemplary; excellent, outstanding, distinguished, distinguishing, first-class, first-rate, consummate, masterly, ageless, heroic, enduring, epic. **2.** Latin is a classical language. Caesar was a hero of classical antiquity: ancient Greek or Roman; Greco-Roman. **—**n. **3.** Dickens's A Tale of Two Cities is a literary classic: masterpiece, standard work; prototype, archetype, model, first-class example, paragon. **—Ant.** 1 bad, poor, inferior, awful, terrible, lousy, second-rate; unrepresentative, atypical. 2 modern. 3 piece of junk, trash.

classification n. **1.** The classification of books in the library follows the Dewey Decimal System: grouping, categorization, categorizing, classing, arrangement, arranging, gradation, organization, organizing, ordering, codification, labeling, systematization, taxonomy, assortment, disposition. **2.** Aspirin belongs to the classification of nonprescription drugs: group, grouping, class, category, division, section, designation, order, rank, series, family, species, genus, kind, sort, type.

classify v. Eggs are classified according to size: organize, class, grade, type, rank, rate, distinguish, categorize, group, assort, range, arrange, pigeonhole, segregate; label, catalog, index, brand, list, codify, tag, ticket; size, number, order.

classy adj. It was a classy affair, with waiters serving champagne to all the guests: smart, elegant, fashionable, high-class, aristocratic, stylish, modish, chic, opulent, genteel, refined, ultrasmart; Slang posh, swell, ritzy, swank, tony, nifty, spiffy, dressy, swanky, Brit. nobby. **—Ant.** shabby, wretched, miserable, tacky, Slang unclassy.

clatter v. **1.** The shutters clattered in the wind: clash, clack, rattle, bang, clump, crash, clang, clank, clink, jangle. **—**n. **2.** The shop was filled with the clatter of machinery: clattering, clack, clank, rattling, racket, jangle, crashing, clamor, chatter.

clause n. **1.** In general, a grammatical clause contains a subject and a predicate: simple sentence or part of a sentence. **2.** The third clause of the contract specifies when payments are due: provision, proviso, stipulation, specification, term, condition, article, covenant, proposition.

claw n. **1.** The cat tore the chair with its claws: talon, animal nail. **2.** The animal's claw was caught in the trap. The boy was gnawing on a lobster claw: paw, foot; clawed hand, pincer. **—**v. **3.** He clawed at the door trying to open it:

tear, maul, lacerate, slash, scratch, scrape; clutch, seize, grip.

clean *adj.* **1.** *Put on a clean shirt. I like a clean room:* unsoiled, spotless, immaculate, sanitary, unblemished, unstained, unspotted; cleaned, cleansed, washed, scrubbed, bathed, scoured, laundered, fresh; neat, tidy, orderly. **2.** *The cabinetmaker did a clean job:* perfect, flawless, faultless, neat, fine, trim, well-made. **3.** *In the country we breathed clean air:* unpolluted, pure, clear, uncontaminated, unadulterated, untainted, uninfected, undefiled. **4.** *He leads a clean life:* wholesome, honorable, upright, virtuous, moral, decent, decorous, innocent, healthy, chaste, unsoiled, exemplary, untainted, stainless, unsullied, unblemished, unspotted. —*v.* **5.** *The curtains cleaned beautifully. Clean your room before going to school:* cleanse, wash, scour, scrub, launder, bathe, shampoo; sweep, vacuum, mop, dust; tidy, tidy up, order, neaten. —**Ant.** 1 dirty, filthy, soiled, stained, spotted; unwashed, unbathed; messy, untidy, disorderly. 2 flawed, imperfect, faulty, crude, ragged, awkward, sloppy, messy. 3 contaminated, polluted, impure, infected, tainted. 4 unwholesome, dishonorable, indecorous, immoral, indecent, stained, unhealthy, tainted, sullied, blemished; evil, wicked, depraved. 5 soil, dirty, stain; mess up, disorder.

clean-cut *adj.* **1.** *His clean-cut looks helped make him a movie star:* sharp, definite, chiselled, clear, etched, well-defined. **2.** *Her new boyfriend is soft-spoken, polite, and clean-cut:* neat, wholesome, sound.

cleanse *v.* **1.** *Cleanse your face thoroughly before going to bed:* clean, wash, bathe, launder, scrub, scour, shampoo. **2.** *The minister's soothing words cleansed my heart of guilt:* rid, free, expunge, expurgate, clear, flush, sweep out, erase, absolve; release, unburden, deliver. —**Ant.** 1 soil, dirty, befoul, stain. 2 burden, weigh down, charge, fill, load.

cleanser *n.* *The cleanser failed to remove the stain:* detergent, antiseptic, disinfectant, purifier, scourer, soap, abrasive.

clear *adj.* **1.** *The day dawned with a clear sky. The water in the bay was clear as glass:* unclouded, cloudless, unobscured, fair, halcyon, serene, sunny; bright, brilliant, radiant, gleaming, dazzling, luminous, shining light, glistening, glowing, sparkling; lucid, transparent, translucent, crystalline, pellucid; gauzy, diaphanous. **2.** *The singing was loud and clear:* distinct, audible, intelligible, distinguishable, plain, recognizable, articulate. **3.** *His meaning was as clear as the nose on your face:* plain, obvious, unmistakable, evident, self-evident, manifest, comprehensible, clear-cut, undisguised, unambiguous, straightforward, explicit, inescapable, apparent, unhidden, unconcealed, positive, certain, definite, unequivocal, unqualified, undeniable, pronounced, patent, express. **4.** *This problem requires clear thinking:* unconfused, unmuddled, unencumbered, alert, keen, wide-awake, sharp, discerning. **5.** *The path was clear:* open, free, unobstructed, unimpeded, unblocked. —*adv.* **6.**

The message came over the wireless loud and clear: clearly, distinctly, plainly, audibly, articulately. **7.** *The jogger ran clear to the end of the island:* entirely, wholly, completely, all the way. —*v.* **8.** *The skies finally cleared:* become unclouded, brighten, lighten; become fair. **9.** *The snowplows cleared the streets. Machines have cleared the way for progress:* unblock, unstop, empty, rid, clean, open; remove, free, remove obstacles from. **10.** *The small plane cleared the trees easily:* pass over, fly over; vault over, leap over, skip over, hop over, bound over, *Informal* make. **11.** *A surprise witness cleared him of the crime:* vindicate, exculpate, exonerate, free, absolve, acquit. —**Ant.** 1 cloudy, clouded, obscured; hazy, stormy, murky, muddy, un-clear, opaque. 2 inaudible, unclear, indistinguishable, indistinct, unrecognizable, unarticulate. 3 unclear, ambiguous, uncertain, hidden. 4 confused, muddled. 5 obstructed, blocked, barricaded, clogged, closed. 6 unclearly, indistinctly, inarticulately. 8 cloud, darken. 9 obstruct, block, clog, close. 11 convict; accuse, blame.

clear-cut *adj.* *He gave us a clear-cut explanation of the causes leading to the Reformation:* exact, precise, distinct, manifest, definite, well-defined, explicit, lucid, plain, express, detailed, unambiguous, crystal-clear, unequivocal, understandable, unmistakable, unconfused. —**Ant.** hazy, vague, muddled, indefinite, ambiguous, unclear, confused.

clearheaded *adj.* *If you're not clearheaded on this job, your life could be in danger:* awake, alert, clear-sighted, clear-witted, sensible, realistic, astute, perspicacious, practical, discerning, rational; *Slang* on the ball, on the stick, on one's toes. —**Ant.** unrealistic, foolish, irrational, impractical, *Slang* dopey.

clearing *n.* *In the clearing stood two deer:* clearance, glade, opening, open space, dell.

clearly *adv.* *The country is clearly in the midst of a drought:* undoubtedly, beyond doubt, beyond question, unquestionably, decidedly, palpably, undeniably, certainly, plainly, evidently, unmistakably, assuredly, recognizably, patently, distinctly, noticeably, unequivocally, indubitably, perceptibly, surely, obviously, manifestly, observably, markedly.

cleavage *n.* *Opposing views led to a cleavage in the party:* split, break, chasm, cleft, division, fracture, gap, rift, schism.

cleave[1] *v.* *His wet shirt cleaved to his back. Honest people always cleave to their principles:* cling, stick, hold, hold fast, adhere, fuse, be joined, unite; be faithful, be constant, be true, stand by, abide by, uphold. —**Ant.** separate, come loose, slip off; let go, release, free; forsake, abandon, relinquish.

cleave[2] *v.* **1.** *With one blow of his ax, the forester cleaved the tree stump down the center. The ice breaker cleaved a passage through the frozen river:* split, divide, bisect, halve, rend, slit, slice, part, crack, rive; cut, slash, chop, hack, hew, lay open, open, plow, furrow, tear. **2.** *The butcher cleaved the bones from the side of beef:* sever, cut off, disjoin, sunder, detach, separate, chop off, disengage, dismember, break off. —**Ant.** 1, 2 unite, join. 2 attach, affix.

cleft n. **1.** The mountain climbers found shelter in a cleft in the ice: split, crack, crevice, crevasse, rift, fissure, rent, cranny, opening, aperture, break, breach, divide, gap, cleavage, division, separation, notch, indentation, slit, furrow, trough, trench. —adj. **2.** Swine have cleft feet. The boys built a tree house on a cleft branch of the tree: divided, cloven, bisected, split, slotted, notched; forked, branched.

clemency n. **1.** The defendant was grateful for the judge's clemency: mercy, mercifulness, charity, forbearance, forgivingness, magnanimity, tolerance, sympathy, compassion, humanity, benevolence, kindness, indulgence, leniency. **2.** Southern California is known for the clemency of its weather: mildness, moderation, softness, pleasantness, temperance. —**Ant.** 1 sternness, strictness; cruelty, mercilessness, hardheartedness. 2 harshness, severity.

clement adj. The weather report forecast clement weather: fair, fine, balmy, clear, mild, warm, temperate.

clench v. **1.** The boy clenched his fists in anger: close tightly, set, set firmly, tighten, stiffen, tense, strain tight. **2.** The patient clenched the arms of the dentist's chair: grasp firmly, clinch, clasp, clutch, fasten on, grip, hold fast. —**Ant.** 1 unclench, loose, loosen, relax. 2 unclench, unclasp, release, let go.

clergy n. Many members of the clergy went to Rome for the ecumenical council: ministry, priesthood, pastorate, rabbinate, the cloth, the pulpit, the church, the first estate; clergymen, preachers, churchmen, ministers, pastors, prelates, clerics, clericals, priests, rabbis.

clergyman n. Only a clergyman can help you with your religious problems: member of the clergy, minister, priest, reverend, rabbi, father; preacher, pastor, chaplain, parson, cleric, prelate, man of the cloth, churchman; Slang padre, sky pilot. —**Ant.** lay person.

clerical adj. **1.** The new employee must be good at filing and other clerical work: of clerks, of general office work, clerkly, office; (variously) bookkeeping, accounting, record-keeping, filing, typing. **2.** The priest donned his clerical robes: ecclesiastical, churchly, cleric, pastoral, ministerial, priestly, rabbinical. —**Ant.** 2 lay, secular.

clerk n. **1.** The new clerk is an excellent typist: clerical worker, office worker; (variously) file clerk, bookkeeper, typist. **2.** The store needs more clerks to wait on customers: salesclerk, salesperson, salesman, saleswoman.

clever adj. **1.** A clever student should have no trouble with math: smart, bright, intelligent, sharp, keen, astute, quick, quick-witted, able, adroit. **2.** He has a clever plan. We laughed at her clever remark: inventive, ingenious, imaginative, creative, original, deft, adroit, artful, crafty, shrewd, resourceful, expert; cute, humorous, witty, keen, acute, sharp, smart. —**Ant.** 1 dull, stupid, witless, dim-witted, dense, obtuse, inept, incompetent, slow-witted, unaccomplished. 2 clumsy, awkward, maladroit, Slang

klutzy; unimaginative, uninventive, unresourceful, boring, tedious, dull.

cleverly adv. The escape was cleverly executed: ingeniously, inventively, imaginatively, creatively, craftily, artfully, adroitly, sharply, expertly, deftly, intelligently, smartly; wittily, humorously. —**Ant.** unimaginatively, inexpertly, stupidly, clumsily, awkwardly.

cleverness n. Cleverness is not enough; one must work hard: intelligence, skill, smartness, adroitness, astuteness, brains, brightness, dexterity, ingenuity, wit, resourcefulness, sharpness, shrewdness.

cliché n. "Her lips are as red as roses" is a cliché: hackneyed expression, saw, old saw, old story, stereotype, banality, platitude, trite phrase, bromide.

click n. **1.** I heard the click of a key in the door: sharp sound, clack, clink, snap. —v. **2.** The lock clicked shut. The dancer clicked her castanets: clack, clink, clap, crack, crackle, snap, tap, rattle.

client n. The lawyer believed in his client's innocence. The fur shop has many wealthy clients: person represented, advisee; patron, customer, buyer, purchaser, shopper.

clientele n. The clientele were dissatisfied with shoddy service: customers, market, patrons, public, audience.

cliff n. The castle was perched on the top of a cliff: bluff, palisade, precipice, promontory; ledge, crag, tor.

climactic adj. It proved to be the climactic victory of Word War II: decisive, crucial, critical, central, main, supreme, paramount, peak.

climate n. **1.** The Virgin Islands have a mild climate. Retirees often move to a warm climate: usual weather, weather pattern, weather; weather region, weather zone. **2.** After the revolution, the climate of the country remained tense: general feeling, mood, atmosphere, disposition, condition, pulse, frame of mind, attitude, spirit, tone, character, temper, quality, air, ambience.

climax n. **1.** Seeing the Vatican was the climax of our trip: highest point, high point, culmination, supreme moment, crowning point, best part, height, acme, summit, peak, pinnacle, apex, crown. **2.** The climax of the play came in the last act: turning point, decisive point, critical point, crisis, moment of revelation, denouement, point of highest development. —**Ant.** 1 nadir, bottom. 2 anticlimax.

climb v. **1.** The cat climbed the tree. The plane climbed to 40,000 feet: ascend, mount, clamber up, scramble up, scale, rise hand over hand; rise, go up, come up. —n. **2.** The climb to the mountain top took ten hours: ascent, climbing. —**Ant.** 1 descend, go down, come down, climb down. 2 descent.

clinch v. **1.** A fourth-quarter touchdown clinched the game. The executive clinched the deal with a handshake: make sure of winning, win, ensure victory; make sure of obtaining, obtain, make sure, assure, settle, cinch, secure, decide; close, conclude, establish, fix, bind, verify, confirm, cap, crown, complete, culminate, wind up, finish off. **2.** *Clinch the boards together:* nail, screw, clamp, bolt, couple, fasten, make fast. **3.** *The boxer clinched his opponent:* clasp, clutch, grab hold of, grasp, grip, grapple, hold firmly, seize and hold.

cling *v. Wet clothes cling to the body. The shy child clung to his mother. Always cling to your beliefs:* stick, hold, hold fast, adhere, cleave, fuse; stay close; grasp, grip, hang on to, hold on to, clasp, hug, clutch, grab hold of; be faithful, be constant, be true, stand by, maintain. **—Ant.** separate, come loose, slip off; let go, release, free; forsake, abandon, relinquish, give up.

clinic *n. The public health clinic is giving free x-rays this week:* medical center, outpatients' ward, polyclinic; infirmary.

clink *n.* **1.** *The keys clinked in his pocket:* jangle, clank, jingle, tinkle, ring sharply; click, clack; rattle. **—n.** **2.** *The diners toasted with a clink of glasses:* tinkle, ting, jingle, jangle, sharp ring, clank, click, clack.

clip[1] *v.* **1.** *The gardener clipped the shrubbery:* cut off, cut short, cut out, shorten, trim, crop, bob, snip, shear. **—n.** **2.** *The veterinarian gave the dog a close clip:* clipping, trim, crop, cropping, cut, bob, shearing, cutting, snipping, paring.

clip[2] *v.* **1.** *Please clip these cards together:* clamp, staple, fasten, couple, attach, fix, secure, clinch. **—n.** **2.** *My hair clip came unfastened:* fastener, hook, grip, clasp, buckle, clinch. **—Ant.** 1 unclip, unstaple, unfasten, uncouple, separate.

clique *n. The summer visitors have their own clique and seldom mingle with townspeople:* group, coterie, circle, set, faction, clan, crowd, gang.

cloak *n.* **1.** *The queen wore an ermine cloak:* cape, mantle, robe, tunic, burnoose, pelisse. **2.** *The invaders attacked under a cloak of fog. The negotiations were conducted under a cloak of secrecy:* cover, screen, curtain, shield, concealment, camouflage, mantle, veil, curtain. **—v.** **3.** *The magician was cloaked in black silk:* robe, shroud, wrap. **4.** *The soldiers cloaked their fear with joking and bravado:* hide, mask, screen, veil, conceal, secrete, disguise, camouflage. **—Ant.** 4 reveal, show, display, expose, bare, uncover.

clobber *v. The champion clobbered the challenger in the second round:* thrash, wallop, whip, batter, beat up, hit, punch, strike, whack, lick, clout, trim, smash, beat the tar out of; *Slang* belt, slug, sock, shellac, smear, lambaste.

clock *n. The clock on the mantle showed the right time:* timepiece, watch, horologe, chronometer.

clockwork *n. All the tasks were performed like clockwork:* precision, accuracy, consistency, perfect timing.

clod *n.* **1.** *Some clods of dirt stuck to the uprooted plants:* lump, clump, chunk, wad, hunk, glob. **2.** *That clod wouldn't know a gentleman if he saw one:* boor, yokel, rube, bumpkin, lout;

dolt, oaf, dope, blockhead, clown, dunce, moron, imbecile, ignoramus, numskull, simpleton, *Informal* dummy, fathead. **—Ant.** 2 sophisticate, gentleman; genius, savant.

clodhopper *n. You may think he's just a clodhopper, but he's very shrewd:* hick, yokel, provincial, rube, rustic, bumpkin, plowboy, oaf, clod, lout, booby, hayseed, lubber, lummox, clown, galoot, lunkhead, slob, clodpole, hillbilly, redneck.

clog *v.* **1.** *Leaves and twigs clogged the gutter:* stop up, stop, block, obstruct, choke, congest, close, dam up. **—n.** **2.** *There's a clog somewhere in the drainpipe:* stoppage, obstruction, block, blockage; obstacle, impediment, barrier, restraint, check. **—Ant.** 1 unclog, unblock, clear, free, open.

cloister *n.* **1.** *My cousin spent his life in prayer and study in a cloister:* monastery, abbey, friary; *(female)* convent, nunnery. **2.** *The arches in the cloister date back to the 12th century:* colonnade, gallery, arcade, portico, stoa, ambulatory, walkway, courtyard, promenade. **—v.** **3.** *The two aging sisters had cloistered themselves from the world many years ago:* confine, sequester, shut away, shut up, seclude, closet, embower, coop up, immure, wall up, hole up, conceal.

cloistered *adj. The child led a cloistered life, seeing only her guardian and tutor:* secluded, sheltered, insulated, isolated, withdrawn, dissociated, aloof, recluse, sequestered, closeted, confined, immured, solitary, alone, separate, apart, detached; hidden, concealed, secreted. **—Ant.** public, social, gregarious.

close *v.* **1.** *Close the door tightly. The handyman closed the hole in the wall with plaster. The stableboy closed the horse in the stall:* shut, secure; close up, stop up, stop, fill up, fill, fill in, stuff, clog, clog up, plug, plug up, shut off, blockade, block, obstruct, seal off; shut in, shut up, confine, pen in, enclose, pen, coop up. **2.** *The soldiers closed ranks. The surgeon closed the two edges of the incision with surgical thread:* join, link, connect, couple, unite, fuse, bring together. **3.** *The pianist closed the concert with a Gershwin medley. Schools closed for the Christmas holiday:* end, finish, conclude, terminate, stop, halt, cease, bring to an end, wind up; adjourn, recess, suspend, discontinue, dismiss, leave off, break off, shut down. **—adj.** **4.** *The house is close to the park. The migration of the ducks southward showed that winter was close:* near, nearby, next to, neighboring, approximate, hard by; imminent, at hand, impending, forthcoming, nigh. **5.** *Keep a close grip on your purse. Keep a close watch on the children:* tight, firm, secure, fast, fixed, solid; alert, intense, intent, watchful, careful, attentive, vigilant, keen, sharp, thorough. **6.** *Living in such close quarters makes privacy difficult. The fabric was of a close weave:* congested, crowded, teeming, swarming, populous; tight, cramped, confined, narrow, restricted, compact, compressed, pinched, stuffed, squeezed, jammed; dense, solid, impenetrable, impermeable. **7.**

The air in this room is very close: stuffy, suffocating, stagnant, unventilated; muggy, humid, stifling, sweltering, uncomfortable, hot, warm. **8.** *The two brothers are very close:* attached, friendly, intimate, familiar, loving, warm, devoted; inseparable, allied, *Informal* thick as thieves, *Slang* tight. **9.** *The color is close to what I want, but the style is wrong. It was a close race:* near, similar, akin, almost like, almost alike, much the same as, resembling, approaching; nearly even, nearly equal, well-matched, nip-and-tuck. **10.** *He's as close with his money as Scrooge:* stingy, miserly, tight, tight-fisted, close-fisted, penurious, parsimonious, niggardly, stinting, scrimping, penny-pinching, ungenerous, grudging. **11.** *A straight razor gives a close shave:* near to the skin, smooth, trim, neat, short. —*n.* **12.** *The crowd began to leave before the close of the game:* end, finish, conclusion, termination, windup, completion; closing, ending, finale. —*adv.* **13.** *Come close so I can see you:* near, nearby, in proximity. —**Ant.** 1–3, 5, 6, 10 open. 1 unstop, unplug, unclog; free, release, let out. 2 widen, spread, expand; separate, part, divide, disunite. 3 begin, start, commence, inaugurate, initiate. 4 far, far off, distant, a long way off. 5 loose, weak, relaxed; careless, inattentive. 6 spacious, roomy, uncrowded, uncongested, vacant, empty; open wide, spread out, unrestricted, unconfined; loose, porous, lacy. 7 fresh, refreshing; cool, airy. 8 unfriendly, estranged, alienated, distant, detached, aloof, cold, cool, indifferent, hateful. 9 far, dissimilar; unequal, uneven, unmatched. 10 extravagant, generous, open-handed, free, liberal, unstinting, magnanimous, charitable, bountiful, lavish. 12 beginning, start, commencement, opening, initiation, inauguration, inception. 13 far, far away.

closed *adj.* **1.** *The closed park was off-limits to us:* shut, shut down, fastened, locked, not open, sealed. **2.** *The country club was a closed world:* exclusive, restricted, self-contained, self-sufficient, self-sustaining. **3.** *The police declared the case closed:* settled, concluded, terminated, decided, ended, finished, over, resolved.

close-fisted *adj. Old Scrooge was the most close-fisted of people:* stingy, miserly, tight, niggardly, parsimonious, penurious, penny-pinching, mingy, close-handed, tight-fisted, ungenerous, grudging, mean. —**Ant.** generous, open-handed, prodigal, profligate, lavish.

closely *adv. Listen closely to the instructions:* carefully, diligently, attentively, heedfully, alertly, intently, sharply, keenly, watchfully, vigilantly; intensely, vigorously. —**Ant.** carelessly, inattentively.

close-mouthed *adj. He's close-mouthed about his personal affairs, but that's not such a bad trait:* tight-lipped, uncommunicative, diffident, cool, reticent, retiring, reserved, taciturn, secretive, terse, shy, distant, bashful, withdrawn. —**Ant.** open, frank, candid, forthright, talkative, outgoing.

closet *n. Her closet was crammed with shoes:* wardrobe, cabinet, repository, storage, locker, depository, armoire, cupboard.

closure *n.* **1.** *A small closure protected the contents of the container:* plug, stopper, cork, bung; cover, lid; faucet, tap, spigot. **2.** *The closure of the bronze doors meant the bank was shut for the day:* shutting, sealing, securing, bringing together, locking, barring, bolting, stoppering. **3.** *The chairman announced the closure of debate on the proposal:* termination, conclusion, ending, cessation, stop, closing, finish, cloture, discontinuance, stoppage, discontinuation. —**Ant.** 3 commencement, beginning, opening, start, onset, kickoff.

clot *n.* **1.** *The medication dissolved the blood clot:* embolism, occlusion, coagulation, gob, mass, lump, thrombus. —*v.* **2.** *In hemophilia the blood doesn't clot properly:* coagulate, congeal, thicken, solidify.

cloth *n. Two yards of cloth will be enough for the dress:* fabric, dry goods, piece goods, yard goods, goods, material, textile.

clothe *v.* **1.** *After showering, I clothed myself for the party. The charity feeds and clothes the needy:* dress, attire, robe, garb, array, drape, accouter, cloak, don; deck, deck out, bedeck, outfit, bedizen, rig out, costume. **2.** *A dense fog clothed the road:* cover, envelop, wrap, enwrap, sheathe, shroud, encase, case, swaddle, cloak, coat, screen, cloud, veil. —**Ant.** 1 undress, disrobe, strip, unclothe; divest, dismantle. 2 uncover, lay bare, denude, expose, exhibit.

clothes *n. pl. The fashion designer made all his own clothes:* clothing, wearing apparel, apparel, garments, wardrobe, wear, attire, habiliments, dress, raiment, garb, costume, ensemble, finery, regalia, *Slang* duds, togs, rags.

clothing *n.* See CLOTHES.

cloud *v.* **1.** *The sunny sky suddenly clouded. Fog clouded the road ahead:* grow cloudy, overcast, darken, dim; overshadow, shadow, shade, eclipse; obscure, blur, shroud, cover, veil, cloak, screen, conceal, hide, curtain. **2.** *A foolish misunderstanding clouded his good name:* place under suspicion, call to question, cast doubt on, discredit, tarnish, sully. **3.** *Personal involvement clouded her sense of fair play:* impair, distort, upset, mar, disturb; confuse, muddle, muddy, blind, make vague. —**Ant.** 1 clear, uncloud; uncover, unveil, show, reveal, uncloak. 2 recommend, honor, confirm, second; clear, exonerate. 3 clear, clarify, purify; restore, cure.

cloudy *adj.* **1.** *Cloudy skies drove the bathers off the beach:* clouded, overclouded, overcast, dark, gray, leaden, dreary, gloomy, hazy, murky, sunless. **2.** *The reason for her anger is rather cloudy:* unclear, vague, confused, confusing, nebulous, hazy, indefinite, undefined, mysterious, obscure, veiled. —**Ant.** 1 uncloudy, clear, bright, fair, sunny, sunfilled. 2 clear, transparent, plain, obvious, straightforward, distinct, definite, well-defined.

clown *n.* **1.** *Emmett Kelly was the most famous circus clown of his time. The boy plays the clown to get attention:* buffoon, jester, harlequin, comic, comedian, comedienne, fool, mime, zany, funny person, joker, madcap; merry-andrew; wit, wag, card, humorist. —*v.* **2.** *Don't clown around anymore—it's time to get down to business:* joke, jest, cut up, kid around, fool around.

cloy *v. Our tolerance for whimsy soon became cloyed by her cuteness:* glut, satiate, surfeit, sate, pall, saturate, overdo; weary, bore, tire, benumb, tire, exhaust; nauseate, choke, gag.

club *n.* **1.** *The police officer walked down the street swinging his club:* truncheon, bludgeon, stick, bat, billyclub, billy, shillelagh, cudgel. **2.** *The bridge club meets every Wednesday:* group, society, league, association, affiliation, union, alliance, guild; fraternity, sorority, brotherhood, sisterhood, lodge. **3.** *Dances were held at the club twice a year:* clubhouse; country club. —*v.* **4.** *The farmer clubbed the snake with a stick:* beat, strike, hit, pommel, pummel, slug, bat, batter, bash, buffet, cudgel, bludgeon, flail, flog, lay on.

clue *n. The pirates left no clues as to where the treasure was hidden:* sign, hint, trace, cue, indication, evidence, mark, key, scent, glimmer, inkling; guide, indicator, pointer; intimation, inference, suggestion, insinuation.

clump *n.* **1.** *Clumps of daisies grew wild in the field:* cluster, group, mass, batch, shock, bunch, assemblage, collection, aggregate; thicket, grove, copse. **2.** *The plow kicked up clumps of soil:* lump, mass; bump, knot, knob, bulb. **3.** *The book fell from the table with a clump:* thump, thud, clunk, clomp, plunk, bump. —*v.* **4.** *The skiers clumped into the lodge in their heavy boots:* tramp, stomp, stamp, plunk, clunk; plod, lumber.

clumsy *adj.* **1.** *The clumsy waiter spilled the soup:* blundering, bungling, maladroit, careless, butterfingered, heavy-handed, unhandy, like a bull in a china shop, inept, graceless, ungraceful, awkward, gawky, *Slang* klutzy. **2.** *The toy windmill was a clumsy package to carry. The carpenter did a clumsy piece of work repairing the banister:* unhandy, cumbersome, bulky, unwieldy, unmanageable, ungainly; awkward, crude, rough, unskilled, inept, ill-contrived, makeshift, careless. —**Ant.** 1 dexterous, deft, handy, adroit, careful; graceful, smooth. 2 handy; professional, expert, skillful.

cluster *n.* **1.** *Clusters of four-leaf clovers grew in the yard. People were standing in a cluster at the bus stop:* clump, bunch, sheaf, batch, shock, mass; group, crowd, block, knot, band, collection, assemblage, throng, aggregate, congregation, company, swarm, herd, pack, bevy, accumulation, agglomeration, conglomeration. —*v.* **2.** *The Boy Scouts clustered around the bonfire for warmth:* gather, group, crowd, bunch, collect, congregate, assemble, throng, swarm, muster, flock, herd, converge; mass, amass, heap, pile, accumulate, aggregate. —**Ant.** 2 disperse, scatter, fan out.

clutch *v.* **1.** *The little girl clutched her doll tightly:* grasp, clasp, hold, grip, clench, hug, embrace, squeeze, hang on to, cling to. —*n.* **2.** *The man held the money in a tight clutch:* grasp, hold, grip, clasp, hug, embrace. —**Ant.** 1 let go, let loose, loose, free.

clutter *v.* **1.** *The child cluttered his room with toys and pictures:* strew, scatter, litter, fill, pile, heap. —*n.* **2.** *A clutter of dirty dishes filled the sink. The clutter in this room is disgraceful:* pile, heap, mess, litter, hodgepodge, jumble, tangle, disorder, disarray, confusion, chaos. —**Ant.** 1 straighten, straighten up, tidy, arrange, order, organize, clean. 2 neatness, tidiness, order, orderliness, organization.

coach *n.* **1.** *Cinderella rode to the ball in a coach pulled by white horses:* carriage, four-wheeler, four-in-hand; stagecoach, stage. **2.** *The train was made up of an engine and four coaches. The bus company is putting new coaches on all its routes:* railroad passenger car; motor coach, bus, omnibus; automobile, sedan, limousine. **3.** *Did you take a Pullman or a coach?:* second class, inexpensive accommodation, economy class. **4.** *A football team needs a good coach. The professor agreed to be the boy's math coach:* trainer, athletic director; tutor, private teacher, preceptor, mentor. —*v.* **5.** *I coach a Little League baseball team during the spring:* train, instruct, tutor, teach, drill; advise, guide, direct. —**Ant.** 3 first class; Pullman, sleeping car. 4 player; student. 5 learn.

coagulate *v. Certain drugs cause blood to coagulate:* clot, congeal; solidify, set, gel, jell, jellify, harden, curdle; thicken. —**Ant.** liquefy, melt, dissolve, soften.

coalesce *v. The flour and milk coalesced into a pasty batter. The Liberal and Democratic parties coalesced to back one candidate:* unite, unify, combine, integrate, fuse, meld, form, join, amalgamate, agglutinate, mix, blend; join forces, band together, come together, cohere, form an alliance, ally, consolidate, become one, merge. —**Ant.** separate, divide, disunite, part; split, disintegrate, dissolve.

coalition *n. The United Fund is a coalition of several charities:* union, alliance, partnership, league, affiliation, federation, association, confederacy, combination, syndicate, society; fusion, consolidation, conglomeration, amalgamation, agglomeration.

coarse *adj.* **1.** *The recipe calls for coarse salt. Father has a heavy, coarse beard:* coarse-grained, unrefined; rough, rough-textured, harsh, scratchy, prickly, nubbly, shaggy, bristly, bristling, *Slang* sandpaper. **2.** *He was a coarse, loud-mouthed man:* crude, crass, unrefined, lacking taste, rough, unpolished; ungentlemanly, unladylike, ill-bred, uncouth, boorish, loutish, inelegant, common, brutish, rude, impolite, ill-mannered; vulgar, indelicate, indecent, improper, indecorous, offensive, gross, foul-mouthed, obscene, dirty, lewd, licentious, lascivious, ribald; sordid, odious, repulsive, revolting, scurrilous, vile, disgusting. —**Ant.** 1 fine-grained, fine, refined, smooth, soft, silky, satiny. 2 refined, gentlemanly, ladylike, genteel, well-bred, cultivated, cultured, civilized, polished, elegant; polite, well-mannered, mannerly; decent, delicate, proper, decorous, inoffensive, clean; pleasant, pleasing, appetizing.

coarseness *n. Coarseness marked the comedian's spiel:* vulgarity, bawdiness, crudity, indelicacy, rawness, rudeness, earthiness, ribaldry.

coast *n.* **1.** *Fishing boats were anchored all along the coast:* seacoast, shore, littoral, strand, shoreline, seashore, seaside; seaboard. *—v.* **2.** *The glider coasted down onto the landing strip. The sled coasted down the slope:* glide, glissade, float, drift, waft, sweep, skim; slide, slip. *—Ant.* 1 interior, midlands, hinterland.

coat *n.* **1.** *It's very cold, so wear a heavy coat:* topcoat, overcoat, wrap; raincoat, slicker, mackinaw, mackintosh; jacket, sports coat, blazer. **2.** *The horse's coat was kept shiny by brushing:* hair, fur, hide, pelt. **3.** *Two coats of paint were needed to cover the old color:* coating, covering; layer, overlay. *—v.* **4.** *Coat the table top with a thin layer of varnish. The furniture was coated with dust:* cover, spread, overlay, smear; envelop, encase, encrust; (*variously*) paint, enamel, lacquer, glaze, whitewash, plaster, laminate. *—Ant.* 4 remove, uncover, clear; clean, wash, dust, scrape, dissolve.

coating *n. The walk was covered with a thin coating of snow:* coat, covering, layer, overlay, film, sheet, veneer, skin, envelope.

coax *v. John coaxed his father to let him use the family car:* wheedle, cajole; inveigle, talk into; *Informal* soft-soap, butter up, sweet-talk. *—Ant.* intimidate, cow, threaten, menace, pressure, bully, bulldoze, browbeat; coerce, force, compel.

cobbler *n.* **1.** *The cobbler repaired the shoes:* shoemaker, shoe repairer, bootmaker. **2.** *Dessert was a delicious peach cobbler:* deep-dish fruit pie, pie.

cock *n.* **1.** *The cock crowed in the barnyard:* cockerel, chanticleer, rooster; male bird. **2.** *Turn the cock to increase the flow of oil:* valve, faucet, handle, knob. *—v.* **3.** *The soldiers cocked their rifles:* draw back the hammer, raise the hammer of. **4.** *The puppy cocked its ear at the sound of footsteps:* turn to one side, raise, tip, stand up, perk up; set erect, bristle up. *—Ant.* 1 hen; chick. 3 uncock.

cockeyed *adj.* **1.** *He had dressed hastily and his hat was cockeyed:* awry, aslant, askew, off-center, crooked, twisted, asymmetrical, tilted, lopsided, sideways, unbalanced, irregular, *Slang* out of whack. **2.** *Having a different bicycle for every day of the week is just another of his cockeyed ideas:* ridiculous, absurd, foolish, inane, preposterous, senseless, nonsensical; mad, insane, crazy; *Slang* nutty, goofy, cockamamie, wild, weird. *—Ant.* 1 straight, symmetrical, centered, even. 2 plausible, sensible, reasonable, commendable.

cocksure *adj. He was so cocksure, he could never admit he'd been mistaken:* cocky, overconfident, conceited, arrogant, brash, vain, smug, bumptious, overbearing, swaggering, pert, swell-headed, self-assured; assertive, aggressive, audacious; *Slang* pushy, cheeky,

snooty. *—Ant.* humble, shy, self-effacing, deferential, timid.

cocktail *n. The cocktail was too strong for us:* mixed drink, highball, long drink, punch.

cocoon *v. Luxury and privacy cocooned the pair:* insulate, cushion, swathe, pad, protect, swaddle, encase, envelop.

coddle *v.* **1.** *His parents coddled him because he was an only child:* pamper, spoil, indulge, baby, mollycoddle, humor, dote on. **2.** *The mother coddled the baby in her arms:* fondle, cuddle, caress, pet, pat. *—Ant.* 1 neglect, ignore, deny.

code *n.* **1.** *The spy sent his message in code:* secret writing, secret language, cipher; cryptogram, cryptograph. **2.** *The club's code of dress requires men to wear ties at dinner:* laws, rules, regulations, guidelines, standards, principles, proprieties, precepts; statute, ordinance.

codicil *n. A codicil was attached to the will:* added clause, addendum, rider; postscript, subscript; addition, supplement, extension, appendix.

codify *v. We used the computer to codify the data according to place and time of occurrence:* classify, catalog, categorize, systematize, order, arrange, organize, tabulate, index, methodize, coordinate, group, regularize, grade, rank, rate.

coerce *v. Prisoners of war were coerced into writing letters praising their captors:* force, pressure, compel, constrain, drive, oblige, make, intimidate, cow, dragoon, bully, browbeat, bulldoze, threaten, strong-arm. *—Ant.* free, allow, permit; coax, cajole, flatter.

coercion *n. The boy attended school only under coercion:* force, pressure, compulsion, intimidation, constraint, threats, duress, bullying, browbeating. *—Ant.* by choice, by one's own free will, volition, desire, by preference, self-motivation.

coexistence *n. Some countries prospered under peaceful coexistence:* simultaneousness, concurrence, conjunction; accord, harmony, order.

coffer *n.* **1.** *A coffer of gold coins was found in the pirate's cave:* repository, depository, chest, treasure chest, box, strongbox, case. **2.** **coffers.** *The nation's coffers are empty:* treasury, money supply, vaults, safes, cash boxes.

coffin *n. The coffin was transported to the cemetery in a hearse:* casket, pall, box, catafalque, sarcophagus.

cogency *n. We were impressed by the cogency of her remarks:* force, soundness, persuasiveness, potency, strength, power, point, bearing, pertinence, relevance, validity.

cogent *adj. He gave us several cogent reasons why the plan would inevitably fail:* compelling, valid, persuasive, forceful, powerful, potent, trenchant, convincing, well-founded, incontrovertible, sound, meritorious, weighty, effective, undeniable, well-grounded. *—Ant.* unconvincing, unsound, dubious, implausible, improbable.

cogitate *v. The professor cogitated in front of the fire for hours. I need a few days to cogitate* *the problem:* think, ponder, contemplate, deliberate, ruminate, meditate, reflect; think about, think over, reflect upon, deliberate on, mull over, consider thoroughly, study, concentrate upon, weigh.

cogitation *n. Further cogitation led to making a decision:* deliberation, thought, consideration, contemplation, meditation, reflection, rumination.

cognate *adj.* **1.** *We were cognate on our mothers' sides. French and Italian are cognate languages:* related, akin, kindred, relative, consanguine, familial, affiliate. **2.** *Jogging and bicycling are cognate forms of exercise:* similar, like, alike, parallel, close. —*n.* **3.** Kaiser *and* Czar *are German and Russian cognates of the Latin* Caesar: word that is related to another word or words by derivation, borrowing, or descent. —**Ant.** 1, 2 unrelated. 2 unlike, unalike, dissimilar, different, opposite, contrary, contradicting, conflicting; unallied, unassociated, unaffiliated, diverse.

cognition *n. Psychologists seek to understand the process of cognition:* understanding, reasoning, recognition, cognizance, comprehension, discernment, insight, intelligence, knowledge, mind, observation, perception, regard.

cognizance *n.* **1.** *Most tourists take little cognizance of European flowers:* notice, note, heed, attention, recognition, cognition, awareness; regard, observation, scrutiny. **2.** *Cognizance of all available facts was necessary to solve the mystery:* knowledge, awareness, cognition, familiarity; apprehension, comprehension, grasp, perception, understanding; sensibility, consciousness. —**Ant.** 1 inattention, disregard, nonobservance, neglect, oversight. 2 ignorance, unfamiliarity, unawareness, incomprehension; insensibility, unconsciousness.

cognizant *adj. Is the prisoner cognizant of her rights?:* aware, informed, knowledgeable, knowing, familiar, acquainted, conversant, no stranger to, understanding, enlightened, versed in, instructed, posted, mindful, conscious. —**Ant.** unaware, uninformed, ignorant, unfamiliar, unknowledgeable, unknowing, unacquainted, unenlightened, unapprised, oblivious, unconscious, insensible.

cohabit *v. They cohabited for three years before marriage:* live together, room together, share an address, *Slang* shack up.

cohere *v.* **1.** *The powdery snow wouldn't cohere into snowballs:* stick together, hold together, unite, join, fuse, cling, bind, cement, glue, stick, hold, combine, coalesce, consolidate; set, solidify, congeal, coagulate. **2.** *The witnesses' accounts didn't cohere:* agree, coincide, correspond, match, fit, tally, synchronize, harmonize, conform, concur, be consistent, jibe, square, dovetail; be related, be connected. —**Ant.** 1 separate, fall apart, come apart, unstick, detach, disjoin; scatter, disperse. 2 disagree, differ, diverge, be inconsistent, be at odds, be unlike; be disconnected, be unrelated.

coherence *n. Though we disagreed with her conclusion, we admired the coherence of her argument:* consistency, cohesion, congruity, conformity, rationality, clarity, organization, logic, accordance; unity, harmony, concord, consonance. —**Ant.** confusion, chaos, incoherence, muddle, inconsistency.

coherent *adj. A good reporter can write a coherent account of confusing events:* logical, meaningful, intelligible, articulate, rational, clear, lucid, connected, comprehensible, understandable; organized, orderly, systematic; consistent, cohesive, harmonious, corresponding, congruous, in agreement, in keeping. —**Ant.** disjointed, disconnected, rambling, inconsistent, incongruous; irrational, illogical, meaningless, confusing, chaotic, vague, hazy, unintelligible, incomprehensible.

cohesive *adj. Tar is a cohesive substance:* coherent, cohering, viscous, sticky, sticking, agglutinative; inseparable, connected, consolidated, solid, cemented, indivisible, set.

cohort *n. He and his cohorts play bridge every Friday night:* companion, friend, comrade, fellow, chum, pal, buddy, crony, associate; accomplice, follower, myrmidon.

coiffure *n. The hairdresser created a dramatic new coiffure for her:* hairdo, haircut, hairstyle, *Slang* coif; wave, permanent wave, cold wave, home permanent, *Brit. Slang* perm, blowcut, shag, bob, comb-out, beehive, pompadour, upsweep, bun, pageboy, *Slang* Afro, cornrows; flattop, G.I. trim, ducktail, D.A.

coil *v.* **1.** *Vines coiled around the oak tree:* wind, spiral, loop, twist, twine; entwine, circle, encircle, curl, writhe. —*n.* **2.** *The sailor tripped over a coil of rope:* loop, spiral, ring, circle, curl, roll, braid.

coin *n.* **1.** *The silver dollar has become a rare coin in our day. The bank teller counted out five dollars in coin:* metal piece of money, piece; change, silver. —*v.* **2.** *These pennies were coined at the mint in Denver:* mint, strike. **3.** *Who coined the phrase "Life is not a bowl of cherries"?:* create, make up, conceive, originate, fabricate, invent, devise, concoct, think up, dream up, hatch.

coincide *v.* **1.** *The two paths coincide a few yards above the beach. My birthday coincides with my wedding anniversary:* meet, come together, converge, synchronize, cross; be concurrent, occur simultaneously. **2.** *Does the witness's story coincide with that of the defendant?:* agree, concur, accord, harmonize, correspond, match, tally, fit, conform, jibe, square, dovetail. —**Ant.** 1 diverge, separate, divide, part, split. 2 disagree, differ, contradict, counter, be unlike, be at odds, be inconsistent.

coincidence *n.* **1.** *Running into Mother at the store was pure coincidence:* chance, accident, luck, fate, happenstance. **2.** *The coincidence of smoking and cancer suggests that the disease may be caused by the habit:* simultaneous occurrence, concurrence, synchronism. —**Ant.** 1 design, plan, premeditation, purpose.

coincidental *adj.* **1.** *These meetings happen too often to be coincidental:* accidental, unplanned, chance, happenstance. **2.** *The drop in the* *stock market was coincidental with the bad news from abroad:* simultaneous, synchronous, synchronal, contiguous, concomitant.

cold *adj.* **1.** *Would you like a glass of cold milk? The coffee is cold:* cool, cooled, chilled, chilly, icy, ice-cold, gelid, frosty, frosted, frigid; unheated, unwarmed. **2.** *The rain brought a cold wind. Last week we had some cold weather:* wintry, freezing, chilling, chilly, chill, cool, icy, ice-cold, frigid, glacial, arctic, polar, brisk, crisp, snappy, nippy, nipping, bitter, sharp, harsh, severe, cutting, biting, penetrating, piercing, stinging, marrow-chilling, bone-chilling, teeth-chattering. **3.** *You must be cold without a coat:* chilled, chilly, cool, ice-cold, chilled to the bone, chilled to the marrow, freezing, frozen, frozen stiff, numbed. **4.** *Her brother was a cold person. His wife gave us a cold reception:* unemotional, passionless, frigid, unresponsive, unfeeling, undemonstrative, unmoved, unimpressionable, impervious, passive, impassive, unexcitable, stiff, unstirred; apathetic, antipathetic; unsympathetic, unconcerned, uninterested, indifferent, phlegmatic, uncaring, unloving; unfriendly, reserved, detached, distant, remote, aloof, haughty, supercilious, disdainful, reticent, uncommunicative, inaccessible, un-approachable, forbidding, steely, stony, heart-less, cold-hearted, cold-blooded, cruel, hard, hardened, inured, harsh, callous. **5.** *The news item was cold by morning. The scent of the fox was cold:* old, stale, flat, uninteresting; faint, faded, dead. **6.** *(Informal) The fighter was knocked cold:* unconscious, insensible, insensate. —*n.* **7.** *Some people feel the cold more than others:* coldness, coolness, chill. —**Ant.** 1–5 hot, warm. 1 red-hot, steaming; heated, warmed. 2 sweltering, scorching, warming, balmy, mild, summery, sunny. 3 sweltering, roasting, perspiring, sweating. 4 emotional, passionate, ardent, fervent, responsive, demonstrative, alive, vital, animated, excitable, spirited, gay; sympathetic, compassionate, concerned, caring, interested; loving, friendly, open, unreserved, warm-hearted. 5 new, fresh; sharp, strong. 6 conscious; semiconscious. 7 heat, warmth.

cold-blooded *adj.* **1.** *Few people could have made the difficult decision in such a cold-blooded way:* cold, unfeeling, unemotional, heartless, cold-hearted, hard-hearted, passionless, unimpassioned, unsympathetic, implacable, unfriendly, reserved, formal, stiff, unresponsive, insensitive; unconcerned, uninterested, detached, disinterested, indifferent, uncaring, unmoved, unimpressible, unimpressionable, impervious, passive, impassive, unexcitable, unstirred; contemptuous, disdainful; calculating, deliberate; steely, flinty, stony, hard, cruel, callous, hardened, inured, harsh. **2.** *The cold-blooded murder shocked the town:* brutal, inhuman, inhumane, bloodthirsty, savage, barba-rous, fiendish, ruthless, merciless, unmerciful, unpitying, pitiless, diabolical, demonic, satanic, evil, villainous. —**Ant.** 1 warm, feeling, emotional, heartfelt, kindhearted, soft-hearted, passionate, excitable, impassioned, sympathetic, compas-

sionate, friendly, open, responsive, sensitive, concerned, interested, involved, caring, loving, kind, gentle, humane. 2 humane, civilized, merciful, benevolent, charitable.

coliseum *n.* *A new sports coliseum was built for the football team:* stadium, arena, amphitheater, bowl; hippodrome, theater, circus; exhibition hall.

collaborate *v.* **1.** *Rodgers and Hammerstein collaborated on many Broadway musicals:* work together, work side by side, team up, join forces, create together, cooperate, unite. **2.** *Few townspeople collaborated with the occupying army:* cooperate, collude, join, assist.

collaborator *n.* **1.** *Gilbert and Sullivan were collaborators on* The Mikado: associate, colleague, confederate, co-worker, teammate, co-partner, ally. **2.** *Following the liberation of Paris, many collaborators were executed:* collaborationist, puppet, quisling, traitor.

collapse *v.* **1.** *The earthquake caused many buildings to collapse:* cave in, fall, buckle, fall to pieces, give way, break apart, disintegrate, crumple. **2.** *The negotiations collapsed when no agreement could be reached:* break down, disintegrate, fail, fall through, come to nothing, be in vain, flounder, run aground, *Slang* flop, fizzle, fold. **3.** *The fire fighter collapsed from smoke inhalation. We collapsed with laughter:* fall prostrate, become unconscious, swoon, *Slang* keel over; take sick, be stricken, become ill, suffer a breakdown; fall helpless, give way, break up. —*n.* **4.** *The collapse of the old bridge forced the ferry back into operation. The collapse of the government left the country in chaos:* fall, falling apart, disintegration, downfall, breakdown, failure, cave-in, buckling, giving way. **5.** *The actress's collapse was brought on by overwork:* breakdown, sudden illness, crack-up, seizure, attack; fall, faint, swoon; coma. —**Ant.** 1 stand. 2 succeed, triumph, flourish. 3 stand up; get well, recover. 5 good health.

collate *v.* *The separate pages had to be collated:* arrange, sort, assemble, gather, group, match, order, relate, compare, compose.

collateral *n.* **1.** *The house served as collateral for the loan:* security, pledge, warranty, warrant, guarantee, insurance, bond, surety, endorsement. —*adj.* **2.** *The information was collateral to the main issue but still important. The student needs collateral tutoring in math:* secondary, subordinate, incidental; auxiliary, supplementary, ancillary, accessory, additional, extra, supporting, supportive, contributory, parallel. —**Ant.** 2 superior, overshadowing; primary, essential, fundamental, basic, chief, key.

colleague *n.* *The judge was highly respected by his colleagues:* confrere, associate, fellow; partner, co-partner, co-worker, fellow worker, confederate, teammate, collaborator, mate. —**Ant.** rival, competitor, opponent, adversary, antagonist.

collect *v.* **1.** *A crowd collected to watch the fight:* gather, assemble, congregate, flock together, cluster around, herd together, rally, meet, come together, get together, draw together, convene, bring together. **2.** *Dust collects on the furniture overnight:* accumulate, concentrate, amass, pile up, heap up, aggregate, compile. **3.** *The Fresh Air Fund collected $10,000 in town this year:* raise, obtain, receive, solicit, amass, get, scrape up, scrape together, muster, assemble. **4.** *The sanitation men collect the garbage every Wednesday:* pick up, call for, gather up. **5.** *Give the speaker a few minutes to collect herself and then begin the program:* compose, calm, control, get hold of, get together, pull together, summon; prepare, muster, rally, marshal. **—Ant.** 1–4 disperse, scatter. 3, 4 distribute, disperse.

collected *adj. The witness was remarkably collected under the cross-examination:* self-controlled, self-assured, self-possessed, composed, confident, poised, calm, cool, cool-headed, restrained, level-headed, steady, even-tempered; quiet, serene, tranquil, peaceful, placid, unruffled, unperturbed, undisturbed, unemotional, unflappable. **—Ant.** nervous, perturbed, disturbed, ruffled, unsteady, shaky, troubled, distressed; unpoised, uncontrolled, excitable, irritable, emotional.

collection *n.* **1.** *A strange collection of people attended the party. A collection of old books filled the attic:* group, gathering, assembly, assemblage, aggregation, crowd, bunch, pack, body, throng, mob, drove, swarm, hoard, flock, bevy; accumulation, assortment, array, jumble, clutter, miscellany, hodgepodge, variety, heap, pile, cluster, clump, mass. **2.** *As a child I had a stamp collection. She has written a collection of short stories:* assemblage, aggregation, compilation, treasury, store, anthology, corpus. **3.** *The church collection was taken before the last hymn:* collecting, gathering, amassing, accumulating, muster, receiving, soliciting; gift, offertory, oblation.

collective *adj. If the team makes a strong collective effort, we'll win the game:* unified, united, joint, combined, cooperative, mutual, common, integrated; collected, gathered, aggregate, cumulative, accumulated, composite. **—Ant.** individual, separate, divided, uncombined, uncooperative, fragmented, piecemeal.

college *n. She went to college direct from high school:* university, seminary, academy, institute, lyceum.

collide *v.* **1.** *The cars collided at the intersection:* run into one another, crash, hit, smash, meet, meet head on, crack up; strike against, hurtle against, beat against, knock into, bump into. **2.** *The brothers' political views usually collide:* disagree, conflict, clash, diverge. **—Ant.** 1 miss; avoid, evade. 2 agree, coincide, accord, harmonize, mesh, jibe, fit, square.

collision *n.* **1.** *There was a three-car collision on the highway. The collision could be heard for blocks:* crash, smash-up, accident; impact, smash, clash, bump, striking together. **2.** *The collision of the opposing armies ravaged the countryside:* conflict, clash of arms, battle, combat, fight, encounter, engagement, skirmish, struggle.

colloquial *adj. The politician's colloquial language endeared him to small-town voters:* folksy, homespun, homey, chatty, ordinary, vernacular, idiomatic, common, everyday, workaday, plain, informal, casual, unsophisticated, conversational, familiar. **—Ant.** formal; sophisticated, literary, cultured, refined.

colloquy *n. A colloquy was arranged between the two ambassadors:* talk, conversation, dialogue, conference, seminar, discussion, parley, chat, discourse, commerce, council, caucus, converse, congress, intercourse, palaver, confabulation, communion, *Slang* rap session, interchange.

collusion *n. The diplomat was arrested for acting in collusion with the enemy:* secret agreement, conspiracy, collaboration, intrigue, guilty association, connivance, complicity; treason; fraud.

colonial *adj. France's colonial empire peaked in the nineteenth century:* colonized, territorial, transplanted; provincial, unsettled, uncivilized, unsophisticated, pioneer.

colonization *n. Exploration led directly to colonization:* settlement, settling, peopling, populating, expansion, founding, opening up.

colony *n.* **1.** *New York was originally a Dutch colony:* settlement, province, territory, dependency, dominion, protectorate, possession, mandate, satellite state. **2.** *A colony of gulls and terns inhabits the island:* community, group, body, set, band, swarm, flock.

color *n.* **1.** *Children love bright colors. Many artists mix their own colors:* coloring, coloration, tint, hue, shade, tone, tinge, cast; pigment, pigmentation, paint, dye, dyestuff. **2.** *A few weeks in the country brought back her healthy color:* natural complexion, skin hue; bloom, rosiness, glow, blush, redness, flush. **3.** *It wasn't the words so much as the color of his criticism that hurt her:* tone, feeling, spirit, mood, aspect, intent, intention, force, stress, effect, implication, insinuation, intimation, connotation, import, significance, sense, meaning, drift. *—v.* **4.** *Let's color the walls green and the ceiling white:* paint, stain, dye, tint, pigment, tinge, crayon, chalk, wash. **5.** *A judge can't let personal feelings color his decisions:* prejudice, influence, affect, bias, distort, slant, warp, twist, pervert, taint. **6.** *Her face colored when she was embarrassed:* redden, blush, flame, burn, flush, glow, go crimson, become florid; change color. **—Ant.** 2 paleness, pallor, wanness, sallowness, whiteness. 3 denotation. 6 blanch, go white.

colorful *adj.* **1.** *Colorful wallpaper would brighten up the room:* brightly colored, bright, brilliant, vibrant, full-toned, gay, florid, loud, showy; multicolored, many-colored, particolored, variegated. **2.** *He wrote of the colorful characters he met on his trip:* picturesque, interesting; unusual, distinctive, unique; graphic, vivid, vivacious, animated, spirited, vigorous, zestful, dynamic, forceful, compelling. **—Ant.** 1 dull, drab, dingy, dreary, monotonous, dark, gray, faded, washed out, pale. 2 dull, uninteresting, colorless, unexciting, lifeless, flat, boring.

colorless adj. **1.** *Continuous washings gave the shirt a colorless appearance:* without color, undyed, natural, neutral; white, whitened, grayed, pale, bleached, faded, washed out, dull, drab, dingy, dreary. **2.** *Her colorless skin could use a bit of rouge:* pale, pallid, ashen, ashy, wan, blanched, white, sallow, pasty, anemic, bloodless, sickly, cadaverous, ghastly, ghostly. **3.** *Her boyfriend has a colorless personality:* dull, unexciting, uninteresting, lifeless, monotonous, boring, dreary, drab, lackluster, flat, unanimated, spiritless, uninspired, ordinary, commonplace, prosaic, neutral, vapid, insipid, pale, anemic, bloodless. **—Ant.** 1 bright, brilliant, lustrous, colorful. 2 ruddy, glowing, healthy, robust. 3 colorful, bright, exciting, interesting, lively, full of life, animated, spirited, vigorous, dynamic, forceful, compelling, strong; unusual, unique, distinctive.

colossal adj. *Samson was feared for his colossal strength. I just made a colossal blunder:* extremely large, huge, vast, immense, massive, enormous, gigantic, giant, titanic, mammoth, great, grand, mighty, extreme, exceeding, excessive, extravagant, tremendous, spectacular, prodigious, inordinate, incredible, overwhelming, imposing, awe-inspiring, monumental. **—Ant.** small, little, tiny, minute, diminutive, miniature; slight, weak, feeble; ordinary, common, average, so-so.

column n. **1.** *The dome was supported by white marble columns:* pillar, support, upright, post, shaft, pilaster, pylon. **2.** *The accounting ledger had many columns for entries:* vertical row, vertical list; row, line. **3.** *A column of soldiers marched down the road:* row, line, queue, file, string; procession, formation, parade, caravan, cavalcade, train, phalanx.

comatose adj. **1.** *The doctor said the patient was comatose all week:* unconscious, insensible, cataleptic, catatonic; stuporous, drugged, narcotized. **2.** *The stock market has been comatose all winter:* sluggish, leaden, dull, lifeless, torpid, languid, lethargic, listless, phlegmatic, spiritless, inactive, inert; apathetic, unconcerned, passive, indifferent, unresponsive; lazy, indolent, slothful, idle, lax. **—Ant.** 2 brisk, energetic, active, lively, industrious.

comb n. **1.** *Bring me the comb and brush:* hair comb, toilet comb, dressing comb, fine-tooth comb; card, currycomb. **2.** *The rooster had a red comb:* cockscomb, topknot, head tuft; tuft, plume, panache. **—v. 3.** *The mother combed the child's hair:* dress, groom, untangle; style, arrange; curry, card. **4.** *Police combed the house for clues:* search, hunt over, seek through, look through, rummage through, scour, ransack, cast about, explore.

combat n. **1.** *The enemy battleship was sunk in combat:* military action, action, fighting, battle, engagement, clash, skirmish. **2.** *Republicans and Democrats are engaged in a combat over the new housing bill:* conflict, battle, clash, struggle, fight, fighting, encounter, confrontation, contest, contention. **—v. 3.** *The nation will combat all invaders. The Salk vaccine did much*

to combat polio: fight, battle, do battle with, war against, wage war, go to war, make warfare, attack, contest, march against, grapple with, come to blows, struggle; resist, oppose, work against, contest against, make a stand against. **—Ant.** 1 peacetime, peace; armistice, truce; surrender, capitulation. 2 agreement, accord, concord, compliance, concurrence, acquiescence. 3 make peace, declare a truce; surrender, capitulate, give up; support, uphold, accept, comply, assent, concur, acquiesce, welcome.

combatant n. *How many combatants were killed during D-Day?:* fighting man, soldier, serviceman, man-at-arms, warrior, fighter. **—Ant.** noncombatant, nonfighting man; civilian.

combative adj. *The combative dog put his rivals to flight:* belligerent, militant, bellicose, contentious, truculent, scrappy, antagonistic, aggressive, hawkish, ornery, quarrelsome, warlike.

combination n. **1.** *The actress had the right combination of looks and talent to become a star. The combination of yellow and blue forms green:* combining, mixture, mix, mixing, blend, blending, pooling, union, joining, composition, compound, composite, synthesis, amalgamation, amalgam, alloy, fusion; medley, variety, assortment. **2.** *The combination of the 50 states forms the United States:* union, federation, confederation, confederacy, merger, alliance, association, coalition, league, joining, combining, coalescing. **—Ant.** 1, 2 division, separation; dissolution, dissolving.

combine v. *Combine catsup and horseradish to make the shrimp sauce. The two boys combined their resources to buy a bicycle:* unite, unify, join, bring together, put together, merge, consolidate, couple, pool, lump together, league; mix, blend, mingle, commingle, compound, amalgamate, incorporate, fuse, synthesize. **—Ant.** separate, divide, part, sever, sunder, detach; dissolve, dissociate, disunite.

combustible adj. *Gasoline is highly combustible:* flammable, inflammable, incendiary, conflagrative, burnable, combustive, ignitable.

combustion n. *The spontaneous combustion of the oil-soaked rags caused the barn to catch fire:* burning, ignition, kindling, incineration, conflagration, flaming, firing.

come v. **1.** *Come here!:* move toward, go toward, approach, draw near, advance; present oneself. **2.** *What time are the guests coming?:* arrive, reach a destination; appear, show up, turn up, drop in. **3.** *Father's birthday comes on September 6. Spring is coming:* take place, fall, occur, happen, come about, come to pass, rise, arise, emerge, appear, materialize, arrive, spring forth, rear its head; advance, approach, be imminent, impend, loom, be in the wind, be on the horizon, bear down upon. **4.** *The belt came unbuckled. Dreams can come true:* become; be, grow to be. **5.** *John Kennedy came from Boston. This radio comes from Japan:* be a resident, be a native; issue, spring, arise, descend, follow; bud, germinate; be a product of, originate in, emanate. **6.** *The curtains come just* *to the window sill:* reach, extend, go, stretch, range, spread. **7.** *The blouse comes in all colors:* be made, be produced, be available, be offered. —**Ant.** 1–3 go, go away, depart, leave, withdraw, retreat.

comeback *n.* **1.** *He was unable to make a comeback after that insult:* riposte, retort, rejoinder, repartee, reply, response, retaliation. **2.** *After retirement, the boxer decided on a comeback:* rally, revival, rebound, recovery, resurgence, return.

comedian *n.* *The star of the show was a very funny comedian:* comic, (*fem.*) comedienne, joker, jokester, humorist, wag; clown, funny person, jester, buffoon, fool, madcap, zany, prankster, cutup, practical joker; comic actor.

comedown *n.* *Digging ditches after being an executive was quite a comedown:* reversal, reverse, disappointment, defeat, downfall, failure, blow, collapse, comeuppance, crash, letdown, setback, humiliation.

comedy *n.* **1.** *Shakespeare wrote comedies, histories, and tragedies:* play with a happy ending, farce, satire, light entertainment; travesty, burlesque. **2.** *The seriousness of the situation left no room for comedy:* joking, jesting, humor, wit, drollery, banter, pleasantry, raillery; fun, silliness, pranks, foolery, tomfoolery, fooling around, cutting up, buffoonery, horseplay. —**Ant.** 1 tragedy, tragic drama, high drama, serious play, melodrama; opera. 2 seriousness, solemnity, sobriety; tears, sadness, melancholy.

comely *adj.* **1.** *The prince fell in love with a comely young maiden:* pretty, fair, sightly, well-favored, attractive, bonny, winsome, fetching, pleasing, engaging, winning; wholesome, blooming. **2.** *The girl's comely behavior was a delight to her parents:* seemly, becoming, suitable, tasteful, proper, decorous, nice, correct, fitting; appealing, pleasing, pleasant, agreeable, engaging, winning, charming; natural, simple, unaffected. —**Ant.** 1 ugly, homely, plain, unsightly, unlovely, unattractive, ill-favored, repulsive, disagreeable; jaded, faded. 2 unseemly, unbecoming, unsuitable, tasteless, distasteful, tactless, indecorous, inappropriate, unfitting, improper, scandalous; disagreeable, unappealing, unpleasant, repellent, repulsive; unnatural, affected, pretentious.

come-on *n.* *The ad was just a come-on to get customers into the store:* lure, enticement, inveiglement, temptation, attraction, magnet, allurement, seducement, seduction, bewitchery, bait, decoy, snare, trap, hook.

comfort *v.* **1.** *The mother comforted the crying child:* console, solace, soothe, quiet, calm, compose, ease, reassure, lighten one's burden, quiet one's fears; cheer, cheer up, hearten, encourage, bolster up, bolster one's spirits. —*n.* **2.** *After the disaster, he found comfort in his old friends:* solace, succor, reassurance, consolation, serenity, composure, peace, calm, cheering up, encouragement, help, relief. **3.** *The child is a great comfort to his grandparents:* consolation, solace, satisfaction, pleasure, source of serenity, source of encouragement,

comforter. **4.** *The hotel provides all the comforts of home:* creature comforts, ease, satisfaction, pleasure, gratification, well-being, contentment, warmth, coziness, snugness, relaxation, freedom from distress; luxury, opulence. —**Ant.** 1–4 discomfort, distress, torment, bother, burden, trouble. 1 aggravate, annoy, irk, rile, ruffle, stir up, excite; sadden, depress, dishearten, discourage. 2–4 aggravation, irritation, annoyance, sadness, discouragement, dissatisfaction, displeasure. 3 bane. 4 poverty, hardship, inconvenience.

comfortable *adj.* **1.** *Air conditioning makes for a comfortable house:* providing comfort, giving ease; pleasurable, pleasant, congenial, agreeable, gratifying; suitable, satisfactory, adequate. **2.** *Make yourself comfortable. Shy people don't feel comfortable with strangers:* at ease, easy, at home, relaxed, contented, cozy, serene, untroubled, undisturbed; free from distress. —**Ant.** uncomfortable. 1 unsatisfactory, unsuitable, displeasing, unpleasaat, disagreeable, uncongenial. 2 uneasy, nervous, tense, fretful, worried, troubled, disturbed, distressed, miserable, wretched, discontented.

comforting *adj.* *The comforting hot milk and honey soothed our aches:* consoling, solacing, soothing, succoring, abating, alleviating, assuaging, cheering, encouraging, mitigating, reassuring, relieving, sustaining, warming. —**Ant.** upsetting, alarming, disturbing, perplexing, worrying.

comic also **comical** *adj.* *It was such a comic state of affairs we had to laugh:* funny, humorous, laughable, amusing, ridiculous, ludicrous, silly, farcical, absurd, nonsensical, mirthful, merry, risible, whimsical, jocose, jocular, jovial, nimble-witted, droll, witty, rich, facetious. —**Ant.** tragic; serious, grave, solemn, sober; pathetic, touching, poignant, melancholy; sad, depressing, doleful, dolorous.

coming *n.* **1.** *The dark clouds foretold the coming of rain:* arrival, arriving, approach, approaching, imminence, nearing, proximity; appearance, advent, occurrence, emergence, materializing. —*adj.* **2.** *The new hospital will be built in the coming year:* next, forthcoming, subsequent, arriving, advancing, approaching; future, imminent, impending, to come, prospective, on the way, in view, on the horizon, in the wind. —**Ant.** 1 departure, withdrawal, disappearance. 2 departing; past, previous, prior.

command *v.* **1.** *The king commanded the guards to raise the drawbridge:* order, direct, bid, charge, require, adjure, call upon, instruct, decree; call for, summon, ordain, enjoin. **2.** *General Patton commanded the 7th Army in World War II:* direct, lead, head, have authority over, have charge of, be master of, rule, boss, govern; guide, conduct, manage, supervise, superintend, administer. **3.** *Toscanini commanded the admiration of music lovers all over the world:* call forth, elicit, receive, get, deserve, compel, draw, extract, evoke, induce, prompt, provoke, inspire, motivate, kindle, incite. —*n.* **4.** *Who issued the command to fire?:* order, commandment, fiat, direction, directive, ordinance, injunction, demand, charge, ultimatum, summons, behest, bid, call, instruction, edict, decree. **5.** *The dictator assumed command of the country:* control, domination, rule, grip, grasp, hold, power, authority; direction, charge, conduct, governing, leadership, management, administration, supervision. **6.** *The teacher had a good command of French:* mastery, comprehension, understanding, grasp, knowledge, familiarity. **—Ant.** 1 plead, beg, supplicate; obey. 2 follow. 3 repel; deter, discourage.

commandeer *v. The police officers commandeered a taxi to chase the robbers:* appropriate, expropriate, seize, take, usurp, shanghai.

commander *n. General Eisenhower was commander of the Allied forces during World War II:* commanding officer, commander-in-chief; chief, leader, head; ruler, director, conductor, manager, boss. **—Ant.** subordinate, follower; inferior.

commanding *adj.* **1.** *The speaker's commanding manner quieted the crowd:* authoritative, imposing, forceful, compelling, powerful, strong, dynamic, gripping, arresting; impressive, important, striking; distinguished, stately, grand, lofty. **2.** *The soldier reported directly to his commanding officer:* in command, directing, controlling, leading, governing; chief, head, ruling, ranking, senior. **3.** *The penthouse offered a commanding view of the city:* dominating, towering, imposing, prominent, significant, overshadowing. **—Ant.** 1 shrinking, retiring, timid, shy, modest, weak; unimposing, unimpressive. 2 subordinate, subservient, junior.

commandingly *adv. She spoke commandingly in class:* by order, by command, imperatively.

commemorate *v.* **1.** *The monument commemorates local war heroes:* memorialize, honor, pay homage to, pay tribute to, acclaim, hallow. **2.** *The bicentennial will commemorate the town's first 200 years:* celebrate, observe, salute, hail, mark, acknowledge, show respect for, glorify, extol, solemnize, revere, venerate. **—Ant.** 1, 2 dishonor, shame, degrade. 2 overlook, ignore, pass over, forget.

commemoration *n. The fallen hero received a full commemoration:* memorial, memorial service, remembrance, celebration, observance, tribute.

commemorative *adj. A commemorative coin was struck in her honor:* celebratory, commemoratory, in honor, in memory, in remembrance.

commence *v. The dancing will commence right after dinner:* begin, start, get started, get going; inaugurate, initiate, originate. **—Ant.** end, conclude, finish, stop, halt, terminate.

commencement *n.* **1.** *The commencement of World War II for the United States was December 7, 1941:* beginning, start, initiation, inauguration, outset, dawn, morning; onset, inception, genesis, birth, origination; first step. **2.** *The dean gave a short speech at commencement:* graduation, graduation day, graduation ceremonies, commencement exercises. **—Ant.** 1 end, ending, close, conclusion, finish.

commend *v.* **1.** *The student's teachers commended her to her prospective employers. The critics commended the director's new movie:* recommend, endorse, put in a good word for, support, back, stand by; speak highly of, laud, praise, extol, approve, acclaim, *Informal* O.K. **2.** *The old man commended his business responsibilities to his grandson:* entrust, give over, hand over, leave in the hands of, give, commit, consign, confer, convey, pass over, relegate, delegate, transfer. **—Ant.** 1 denounce, renounce, condemn, blackball; criticize, censure, deride, attack. 2 withhold, keep; withdraw.

commendable *adj. Perseverance is a commendable trait:* to be commended, worthy, praiseworthy, admirable, laudable, meritorious, honorable, creditable, notable, exemplary, deserving, estimable. **—Ant.** unworthy, dishonorable, discreditable, disreputable, undeserving.

commendation *n. For the superb dinner the chef received commendations. Bravery in battle earned him a commendation:* recommendation, praise, approval, approbation, applause; medal. **—Ant.** censure, blame.

commensurate also **commensurable** *adj. Her salary is commensurate with her ability and experience:* in accord, consistent, in agreement, suitable, fitting, appropriate, compatible, corresponding, proportionate, comparable, on a proper scale, relative, equal, equivalent, even, balanced, meet, parallel, relative, square. **—Ant.** inconsistent, unsuitable, inappropriate, unfitting, incompatible, disproportionate, dissimilar, incomparable, unequal, discordant.

comment *n.* **1.** *The teacher wrote his comments in the margin of the composition:* commentary, criticism, remark, explanation, observation, reflection, elucidation, clarification, explication, exemplification; note, annotation. **2.** *The councilor's proposal drew angry comments from the crowd:* remark, statement, commentary, observation, reflection; word, utterance, expression, assertion. **—v. 3.** *Would the mayor care to comment on why she voted against the new housing project?:* explain, clarify, elucidate, expound, expand on, shed light, touch upon; discuss, talk about, remark, make a statement.

commentary *n.* **1.** *Students were asked to write a commentary on one of Shakespeare's plays:* series of comments, explanatory essay, critique, explanation, explication, exposition, interpretation, review, criticism; treatise, dissertation, scholium. **2.** See COMMENT (senses **1, 2**).

commentator *n. The TV sports commentator said our team won fairly:* newscaster, news analyst, columnist, critic, reviewer; reporter, explainer, interpreter, speaker, writer; panelist.

commerce *n. Overseas commerce increased 20 percent in the last quarter:* business, trade, traffic, trading, buying and selling, exchange, barter, mercantilism; industry.

commercial *adj.* **1.** *He wanted to make his living in the arts rather than in the commercial world. Christmas has become too commercial:* business, trade, mercantile, buying-and-selling, sales, profit-making. **—n. 2.** *The TV show was* interrupted by too many commercials: advertisement, ad, Informal sales pitch. —**Ant.** 1 artistic, professional; nonprofit-making, charitable, philanthropic, eleemosynary.

commingle v. The perfumes of various flowers were commingled in the air of the garden: intermingle, interjoin, intermix, amalgamate, blend, combine, compound, integrate, mingle, join, merge, unite.

commiserate v. Friends commiserated with the bereaved family: feel for, express sorrow, sympathize with, show pity, have compassion for, express fellow feeling, grieve with, lament with, send one's condolences, share one's sorrow.

commission n. **1.** He was indicted for the commission of a felony: committing, committal, carrying out, act, acting out, performing, performance, doing, perpetration, transacting, exercise, conduct. **2.** The ambassador was given the commission to negotiate the treaty: authority, authorization, power, capacity, mandate, charge, duty, task, appointment, mission, assignment, office, function, role, deputation, warrant, license, proxy, commitment, entrusting, trust. **3.** ROTC graduates are granted lieutenant's commissions in the Army: officer's rank, rank, position, appointment, office; appointment papers, document, certificate, written orders. **4.** All tenant complaints should be sent to the Housing Commission: commissioners, board, agency, council, committee; delegation, representatives, deputation. **5.** The insurance agent earned a commission on every policy she sold: percentage, cut, portion, piece, fee; allotment, allowance, dividend, stipend; Slang rake-off, piece of the action. —v. **6.** An architect was commissioned to design the new building: authorize, empower, appoint, assign, name, delegate, charge, bid, order, direct, give the go-ahead, engage, employ, hire, contract, charter. **7.** Annapolis graduates are commissioned as naval officers: grant officer's rank, appoint; give a document, certify. —**Ant.** 1 noncommission, omission, noncommittal, nonperformance. 5 salary, straight salary. 6 release, fire, let go.

commit v. **1.** He was accused of committing robbery: perform, carry out, do, act, enact, transact, practice, perpetrate, execute, effect, pursue, participate in; Slang pull, pull off. **2.** The company committed its profits to building new factories. The court committed the man to an insane asylum: consign, put in the custody of, give over, put in the hands of, deliver, entrust, transfer, place, put, assign, deposit; confine, intern, institutionalize. **3.** The government committed itself to spending $10 million on new roads: obligate, bind, make liable, engage, decide, determine, resolve. —**Ant.** 1 omit. 2 withhold, hold back, take from; receive, accept; release, free. 3 disavow, disregard; waver, vacillate, shilly-shally.

commitment n. **1.** The factory requested a larger commitment of coal for its needs. The prisoner's period of commitment to the penitentiary lasted five years: consignment, assignment, delivery, dispatching, transfer, giving over; con-

finement, internment, institutionalizing, imprisonment, detention, incarceration, restraint. **2.** Citizens have a commitment to defend their country. By signing the lease you made a commitment to pay $300 a month rent: obligation, liability, responsibility; bond, guarantee, warranty, pledge, assurance, vow, word, promise; resolution, decision, determination, stand. —**Ant.** 1 withholding; release, freeing, liberation. 2 negation, disavowal, reneging; indecisiveness, wavering, vacillation, shilly-shallying.

committee n. A committee of three ran the company: panel, jury, board, commission, council, advisory group, cabinet.

commodious adj. Is the house commodious enough for a large family?: roomy, spacious, capacious, large, ample, unconfining, uncramped. —**Ant.** cramped, confining, small, narrow.

commodity n. **1.** Wheat is a valuable commodity: article of trade, article of commerce, merchandise, product, ware, goods, stock, staple. **2.** A good reputation is a valuable commodity: asset, possession, property, chattel, belonging, holding, convenience, advantage. —**Ant.** 2 liability, handicap, disadvantage, hindrance, burden.

common adj. **1.** We must all work for the common good. That the couple argue a lot is common knowledge: public, general, joint, shared, collective, communal; widespread, universal. **2.** Automobile accidents are far too common. "Haste makes waste" is a common saying: commonplace, ordinary, frequent, often met with, routine, regular; customary, conventional, standard, settled, established, familiar, everyday, well-known, widely known, popular, traditional, oft-repeated, pervasive; stock, garden-variety, household, homespun, prosaic, threadbare, moth-eaten, old-hat, worn-out, worn thin; infor-mal, colloquial. **3.** He wasn't a hero but just a common man: ordinary, plain, simple, average, normal, middling; Slang workaday, garden-variety, dime-a-dozen; undistinguished, obscure, unknown, nameless, unnoticed, inglorious, ignoble, unexalted, middle-class, plebeian, bourgeois; without rank, unimportant, insignificant, lowly, low, minor, lesser, subordinate, mediocre. **4.** His common manners repulsed her: coarse, crude, crass, uncouth, insensitive, callous, brutal, boorish, loutish, brash, brazen, shameless, shameful, unblushing, disagreeable, unrefined, uncultured, unpolished, tasteless, gross, base, mean, cheap, tawdry, bad, deficient; rude, impolite, ill-mannered, ill-bred, low-bred, ignoble; vulgar, despicable, obnoxious, offensive, contemptible, vile, disgraceful, low-minded, lewd, smutty, obscene, ribald. —**Ant.** 1 private, personal, individual, separate, secret. 2 uncommon, unusual, rare, infrequent, strange, unique, odd, abnormal, exceptional, unfamiliar, extraordinary, unpopular, unorthodox, unconventional, unheard of, scarce, unknown, little-known; formal, sophisticated; literary. 3 superior, outstanding, exceptional, extraordinary, important; distinguished, famous, renowned, noble, ranking, noteworthy, glorious, exalted. **4** polished, refined, cultured, gentle, delicate, sensitive, gentlemanly, ladylike, gallant, noble; polite, well-mannered, well-bred, becoming, pleasing, modest, unassuming.

commonly *adv. Barbara was commonly known as Babs:* usually, ordinarily, generally, normally, customarily, of course, regularly, routinely, traditionally, conventionally, habitually, frequently, often, most often, repeatedly, in most instances, by and large, in general, as a rule, for the most part, generally speaking, as a matter of course, by force of habit, popularly, widely; familiarly, informally. **—Ant.** rarely, seldom, infrequently, scarcely; privately, secretly; formally, politely.

commonplace *adj.* **1.** *Horses and buggies were commonplace sights in 1900:* common, ordinary, usual, routine, everyday, familiar, regular, standard, traditional, customary, general, widespread. **2.** *The movie's commonplace plot bored the audience:* common, dull, banal, run-of-the-mill, pedestrian, humdrum, uninteresting, unimaginative, unoriginal, trite, hackneyed, stereotyped, stale, old, old-hat, oft-repeated, worn-out, worn thin, threadbare, moth-eaten. **—n. 3.** *"East, West, home's best" is a well-known commonplace:* hackneyed expression, banality, platitude, cliché, adage, bromide, received idea, truism. **—Ant.** 1, 2 uncommon, unusual, unfamiliar, rare, strange, unique, odd, extraordinary, exceptional, infrequent. 2 exciting, interesting, imaginative; original, new, distinguished.

common sense *n. Though he wasn't schooled, his common sense guided him through life:* native reason, good sense, good judgment, natural sagacity, basic intelligence, mother wit, *Slang* horse sense.

common-sense lso **commonsensical** *adj. She proposed a common-sense solution:* practical, commonsensical, sensible, realistic, judicious, down-to-earth, levelheaded. **—Ant.** impractical, foolish, unwise.

commotion *n. What's all the commotion about?:* hullabaloo, fuss, bustle, stir, ado, to-do; excitement, tumult, furor, uproar, turmoil, disturbance, agitation, perturbation, fussing and fuming, racket, clatter, *Informal* ruckus. **—Ant.** peace, tranquillity, calm, calmness, serenity; quiet, quietness.

communal *adj. The park was communal property:* community, common, collective, mutual, joint, shared, public. **—Ant.** private, personal, individual.

commune *v. It was said that St. Francis was able to commune with the birds:* communicate, talk, converse, confer, discourse, parley, chat, visit, chatter, palaver, confabulate, prattle, babble; *Slang* rap, chin, yak, gossip, gab, schmooze, chew the fat, chew the rag, shoot the breeze, powwow.

communicable *adj. Measles is a communicable disease:* contagious, catching, infectious, transmittable, transmissible, transferable. **—Ant.** uncontagious.

communicate *v.* **1.** *The radio stations communicated the storm warnings to the islanders:* make known, inform of, announce, apprise of, tell, notify, advise, pass on, convey, disclose, divulge, reveal, relate, bring word, proclaim, broadcast, publish, publicize; state, declare, say, mention; show, exhibit, signify. **2.** *Schoolchildren often communicate colds to each other:* give, transmit, impart, pass on; convey. **3.** *The two friends hadn't communicated with each other for years:* exchange information, express feelings; converse, speak together, talk, correspond, write. **—Ant.** 1 keep secret, hush up, suppress, repress, withhold, hold back, cover up.

communication *n.* **1.** *There can be no mutual understanding without communication between people:* exchanging information, expressing feelings; rapport, liaison; conversation, speaking, correspondence, writing. **2.** *The latest communication from the ship indicates the danger has passed:* notices, report, message, news, information; intelligence, communiqué, liaison; (*variously*) bulletin, directive, statement, declaration, proclamation; correspondence, letter, missive, missal, dispatch, document, note; telephone call, telegram, wire, cablegram, cable, radio message, broadcast.

communicative *adj. If he were more communicative we would know his true feelings. This letter is not very communicative:* talkative, freespoken, unreserved, loquacious, voluble, chatty, outgoing, sociable, friendly, open, candid, frank, forthright; informative, expressive, revelatory, revealing. **—Ant.** uncommunicative, untalkative, quiet, reserved, introverted, unsociable, secretive, guarded; uninformative.

communion *n.* **1.** Often **Communion.** *The family took Communion at midday Mass:* Holy Communion, the Eucharist. **2.** *The old couple had a perfect communion of thoughts:* sharing, harmony, concord, accord, agreement, affinity, sympathy. **3.** *The woodsman spent the day in communion with nature:* spiritual concentration, contemplation, rapport, communication. **—Ant.** 2 alienation, disunion, division, separation; disharmony, discord, disagreement.

communiqué *n. The latest communiqué from our ambassador says that negotiations are continuing:* bulletin, dispatch, message, communication, announcement, missive, notice, statement, notification, letter, epistle, memorandum, note, report, aviso, flash; cable, telegram, wire.

Communism *adj. Under Communism, all banks were nationalized:* Bolshevism, dictatorship of the proletariat, Marxism, state socialism.

community *n.* **1.** *This is a good community in which to bring up children:* neighborhood, district, locale, area, vicinity, quarter, residential suburb, environs; environment, surroundings. **2.** *The entire community is behind the charity drive. The scholarly community welcomed the new library:* group, social group, interest group; populace, population, citizenry, public, people, folk, society. **3.** *Archeologists and anthropologists share somewhat the same community of interest:* area, sphere, field, range, realm, scope, province, arena, commonwealth; sameness, similarity, likeness, affinity, agreement.

—**Ant.** 3 difference, dissimilarity, disparity, disagreement, conflict.

commute v. *The governor commuted the convict's sentence to life imprisonment. Medieval alchemists tried to commute base metals into gold:* change, reverse, exchange, substitute, adjust, alter, replace, switch, supersede; alleviate, soften, mitigate, diminish; transmute, transform, transpose, redeem, convert, metamorphose, transfigure, transmogrify.

compact[1] *adj.* **1.** *The primitive hut was made of compact mud and branches:* compressed, pressed, tightly packed, dense, concentrated, clustered, crammed, stuffed. **2.** *The apartment has a compact but well-equipped kitchen:* small, little, snug, close, tidy. —*v.* **3.** *Try to compact the sand into the mold:* pack closely, compress, press, pack, stuff, cram, squeeze. —**Ant.** 1 loosely packed, loose, spread-out, dispersed, scattered, sprawling. 2 spacious, rambling, roomy, large, big, huge. 3 disperse, loosen; separate.

compact[2] *n. The two nations made a compact to preserve the peace:* agreement, pact, treaty, covenant, contract, concordat, bond; understanding, arrangement, alliance, bargain, deal.

companion *n.* **1.** *Bad companions can lead a youth astray:* associate, friend, comrade, crony, chum, pal, buddy, mate. **2.** *The doctor recommended hiring a companion for the elderly woman:* attendant, helper, assistant, escort. —**Ant.** 1 stranger; enemy, foe.

companionable *adj. The newcomers were most companionable:* sociable, friendly, affable, amicable, convivial, cordial, genial, good-natured, gregarious, neighborly.

companionate *adj. In her later years she looked forward to a companionate marriage:* harmonious, suitable, providing companionship, compatible, consonant, concordant, accordant; nonsexual, platonic, passionless, non-physical, unfleshly, spiritual; companionable, friendly, easygoing, amicable, cordial, agreeable, warm, affectionate, genial, warm-hearted. —**Ant.** antagonistic, discordant, inharmonious, clashing, conflicting, incompatible.

companionship *n. The lonely man longed for companionship:* friendship, friendly relations, close acquaintance, fellowship, comradeship, camaraderie, sociability, familiarity; friends, companions, company, associates, comrades, chums, pals, buddies. —**Ant.** isolation, solitude, loneliness, aloneness.

company *n.* **1.** *Company is coming for dinner:* guest, guests, visitor, visitors, callers. **2.** *I enjoy her company. Dad didn't want any company around when he was working:* presence, companionship, friendship, fellowship, comradeship, camaraderie, society, sociability; people, friends, comrades, companions. **3.** *There are advantages in working for a large company:* business concern, concern, firm, business corporation, syndicate, conglomerate, establishment; *Slang* outfit. **4.** *A large company of men gathered around the courthouse:* assembly, assemblage, congregation, gathering, group, band, mob,

multitude, throng, bunch, party, gang. —**Ant.** 1 host, hostess. 2 isolation, solitude, loneliness, aloneness.

comparable *adj. Being granted a yearly bonus can be considered comparable to getting a raise in pay. This dinner is comparable to the best French cooking:* similar, like, equal, equivalent, as good as, on a par with, akin to, roughly the same as, analogous, tantamount, commensurable, commensurate; parallel, approximate, approaching, close, a match for, in a class with, up to. —**Ant.** incomparable, different, unlike, dissimilar, incommensurable, incommensurate, unequal.

comparative *adj. I'm a comparative newcomer:* relative, by comparison; near, approximate.

compare *v.* **1.** *Compare food costs today with those of a year ago:* note the similarities of, note the differences of, contrast, balance against. **2.** *Many people compared Marilyn Monroe to Jean Harlow:* liken, equate, describe as similar, draw a parallel between, correlate, relate, identify with. **3.** *This canned soup can't compare to homemade:* be comparable, match, equal, compete with, approach, be as good as, bear comparison, hold a candle to, vie with, come near to, be in a class with, be on a par with, be up to. —**Ant.** 3 bear no comparison, be unlike, be dissimilar, be incomparable, be unequal.

comparison *n.* **1.** *The traveler made a comparison between the Alps and the Rocky Mountains:* comparative estimate, selective judgment, notation of similarities and differences, contrast. **2.** *There was no comparison between the two voices:* similarity, comparability, likeness, resemblance, equality, analogy, relation, correlation, parallel, kinship, connection. —**Ant.** 2 difference, dissimilarity, inequality, discrepancy.

compartment *n. On the dashboard is a compartment for gloves, maps, and other small objects:* cubicle, niche, alcove, hole, nook, pigeonhole, cubbyhole, cell, pew, section, booth, box, crib, crypt, stall, vault; berth, room, cabin, closet, anteroom, chamber, antechamber, roomette, bunker, hold, brig.

compassion *n. The nurse had great compassion for her patients:* sympathy, empathy, commiseration, feeling, fellow feeling, pity, tenderness, tender-heartedness, heart, humanity. —**Ant.** apathy, unconcern, indifference, detachment, disdain; cold-heartedness, hardheartedness.

compassionate *adj. The compassionate judge gave the young offender a light sentence:* sympathetic, pitying, humane, merciful, kindhearted, kind, benevolent, tender-hearted, charitable. —**Ant.** uncompassionate, inhumane, unfeeling, unsympathetic, unpitying, pitiless.

compatibility *n. The couple attributed their happy marriage to complete compatibility:* affinity, harmony, rapport, agreement, accord, unanimity, like-mindedness, congeniality, concord. —**Ant.** incompatibility, disharmony, disagreement, disaccord, discord.

compatible *adj. The two sisters couldn't live to-*

gether because they weren't compatible. Giggling is not compatible with a serious discussion: in harmony, like-minded, congenial, mutually sympathetic; fitting, fit, suitable, in accord, in keeping, seemly, apt, appropriate. —**Ant.** incompatible, unharmonious, uncongenial; contradictory, unfitting, unsuitable, out of keeping, unseemly, inapt, inappropriate, inconsistent, counter.

compel v. Bad health compelled him to resign from his job: force, drive, require, necessitate, oblige, make, give no choice but. —**Ant.** stop, deter, thwart, hinder, prevent.

compendium n. It was fascinating to browse through the compendium of quotations: digest, abridgment, condensation, abstract, brief, epitome, overview, précis, summary.

compensate v. **1.** The firm compensated the injured worker for the time lost: recompense, reimburse, make restitution, pay back, repay, make up, cover, redress, redeem, make compensation, indemnify; pay, remunerate. **2.** The marvelous acting compensated for the play's weak script: make up, offset, balance, counterbalance, make amends, square. —**Ant.** 2 emphasize, exaggerate, worsen, add insult to injury.

compensation n. **1.** The injured man was granted $10,000 in compensation: recompense, reimbursement, restitution, repayment, redress, indemnity; benefits, settlement, satisfaction, consideration. **2.** The job is hard but the compensation is good: pay, payment, salary, wages, fee, remuneration, income, earnings; reward, profit, gratuity, return, gain. —**Ant.** 1, 2 loss, expenditure, time and trouble.

compete v. Professional football teams compete for the best college players: contend, contest, vie, match strength, match wits, oppose, be rivals; fight, combat, battle, lock horns, strive against. —**Ant.** surrender, give up, yield.

competence n. The young surgeon showed exceptional competence: ability, ableness, capability, competency, proficiency, skill, expertness, mastery, expertise, know-how; Slang the goods, what it takes. —**Ant.** incompetence, inability, incapacity, inadequacy.

competent adj. Be sure to get a competent electrician for the job: skilled, skillful, expert, proficient, efficient; qualified, fit, trained, practiced, experienced, versed, dependable, responsible, trustworthy. —**Ant.** incompetent, incapable, unskilled, unskillful, inexpert; unqualified, unfit, inexperienced, inadequate, undependable, irresponsible, untrustworthy.

competition n. **1.** Competition between business firms keeps prices down: competing, rivalry, contention, opposition, struggle, conflict. **2.** Who will be the team's competition in next week's game?: opposition, rival, opponent, contender. **3.** The figure-skating competition was judged by an international panel: contest, event, match, tournament, tourney. —**Ant.** 1 cooperation, collaboration, concert, joint effort, teamwork. 2 partner, helper, aider, abettor.

competitive adj. The city asked for competitive

bids on the housing project. An athlete must have a competitive spirit: competing, opposing, contending; fighting, combative, striving, aggressive. —**Ant.** cooperative, mutual, joint; noncombative, unaggressive.

competitor n. The firm's largest competitor is going out of business. The heavyweight champion is fighting an unknown competitor: rival, opposition, opponent, adversary, contestant, contender, fighter. —**Ant.** ally, partner, collaborator.

compilation n. **1.** The compilation of data for the report took six months: compiling, collecting, gathering, accumulating, collating, mustering, marshaling, garnering, assembling, aggregating, drawing together. **2.** The newspaper published a compilation of local recipes: assemblage, group, collection, aggregation, body; assortment, compendium, accumulation. —**Ant.** 1 distribution, dispersal, scattering, disbanding, dispelling, dissipation.

compile v. Doctors compiled thousands of case histories to prove the relationship between smoking and cancer: collect, accumulate, assemble, amass, collate, heap up, gather, muster, marshal, bring together, draw together, garner. —**Ant.** distribute, disperse, scatter.

complacent adj. Ever since he got a raise he's been too complacent to work hard: self-secure, content, contented, self-satisfied, smug; untroubled, unbothered, at ease. —**Ant.** unsatisfied, insecure, discontent, discontented, troubled, uneasy, soul-searching, self-questioning.

complain v. The tenants complained that there was not enough hot water: state a grievance, express dissatisfaction, find fault, criticize, carp, cavil, nag, whine, pick; Informal beef, gripe, kick, grouse, grouch, grumble, Slang bellyache, squawk. —**Ant.** compliment, praise, laud, commend; approve, appreciate.

complaint n. **1.** The store has a special department to handle customer complaints: grievance, dissatisfaction, criticism, faultfinding, protest, objection, tirade; Informal beef, gripe, kick, squawk. **2.** Arthritis is a common complaint among the elderly: disorder, malady, infirmity, debility, ailment, impairment, sickness, illness. —**Ant.** 1 compliment, praise, commendation; approval, appreciation. 2 remedy, salve, balm, ointment.

complaisant adj. The host's complaisant manner made everyone feel welcome: obliging, solicitous, pleasing, agreeable, compliant, cordial, congenial, affable, warm, gracious, friendly, pleasant, amiable, good-natured, good-humored, easygoing. —**Ant.** unobliging, contrary, unsolicitous, uncooperative, indifferent; disagreeable, unpleasant, cold, unfriendly, ungracious.

complement n. **1.** Travel can be an excellent complement to one's education: completion, consummation, rounding-out; supplement, companion, counterpart, balance, parallel. **2.** The farm was sold along with its complement of livestock: full amount, full number, total, ensemble, aggregate; completion, whole, entirety;

required number, necessary amount. —*v.* **3.** *A flaming dessert complemented the dinner:* make complete, round out, perfect, crown, cap, consummate; match, serve as a companion, supplement.

complementary *adj. The period costume calls for a complementary hair style:* integral, corresponding, correspondent, interrelated, compatible, companion, matched, correlative. **—Ant.** uncomplementary, incompatible, incongruous, inconsistent; different, diverse; contradictory.

complete *adj.* **1.** *The library has a complete set of Robert Louis Stevenson's books:* entire, whole, full, plenary, unabridged, unbroken, intact, undivided. **2.** *Our triumph was complete:* thorough, absolute, total, utter, conclusive, perfect, consummated, fully realized, accomplished, achieved, performed, executed, carried out, settled. —*v.* **3.** *The workers haven't completed the house yet:* make complete, make whole; finish, end, conclude, terminate, make an end of, accomplish, achieve, perform, execute, carry out, fulfill, discharge, settle, consummate; *Informal* polish off, wrap up. **4.** *A good brandy completes a fine meal:* complement, round out, perfect, crown, cap. **—Ant.** 1, 2 incomplete, partial. 2 inconclusive, imperfect, deficient, spoiled, marred, blemished, tainted, unfinished, unsettled, unachieved, unaccomplished, undone. 3 start, begin, commence, initiate; undo. 4 spoil, ruin, mar, taint.

completely *adv. She trusted him completely:* entirely, totally, wholly, absolutely, all, altogether, comprehensively, thoroughly, fully, in all, in entirety, in toto, utterly, without exception, without omission, without reservation, perfectly.

completion *n.* **1.** *The completion of the new road is scheduled for June:* completing, finishing; concluding, ending, closing, terminating, windup. **2.** *The teacher retired at the completion of the school year:* conclusion, end, close, termination, finish, expiration, windup; fulfillment, consummation. **—Ant.** 1 beginning, starting, initiating, commencing. 2 start, beginning, commencement, initiation.

complex *adj.* **1.** *The new mayor must deal with many complex problems:* complicated, intricate, involved, difficult, perplexing, bewildering, puzzling, enigmatic; composite, compound, manifold, multiple, multifarious, variegated, mixed, tangled, knotty, labyrinthian, labyrinthine. —*n.* **2.** *We live in a large apartment complex. President Eisenhower warned against the military-industrial complex:* system, network, aggregate, conglomerate, maze. **3.** *Don't let him give you an inferiority complex:* subconscious idea, fixed idea, psychological feeling; obsession, preoccupation. **—Ant.** 1 simple, uncomplicated, easy, uninvolved, clear, obvious, unconfused.

complexion *n.* **1.** *Blondes often have fair complexions:* skin coloring, coloring, pigmentation, coloration, color, hue, tone; skin texture. **2.** *Knowing that one of the witnesses lied puts a different complexion on the case:* appearance, impression, aspect, look, outlook, guise, slant, image, countenance, character.

complexity *n. The complexity of the problem has occupied the country's top minds:* complication, intricacy, elaboration, involution, crabbedness, involvement; perplexity, bafflement, entanglement, inextricability, puzzle; obscurity, incomprehensibility, unintelligibility. **—Ant.** simplicity, clearness, clarity, obviousness, unmistakability.

compliance *n. Compliance with the traffic laws is necessary for safe driving. Yes-men are known for their compliance:* conformity, conforming, obedience, yielding, giving in, submission, deference; assent, acquiescence, complaisance, pliancy, nonresistance, passivity, docility, meekness. **—Ant.** noncompliance, nonconformity, disobedience, resistance, rebelliousness, assertiveness, individuality, stubbornness; obstinacy.

complicate *v. Don't complicate the problem by raising new issues:* make complex, make intricate, make difficult, involve, confound, confuse, muddle, entangle, knot, snarl, ravel, tangle. **—Ant.** uncomplicate, simplify, clarify, unsnarl, untangle, disentangle, unknot, clear up.

complicated *adj. It was the most complicated crossword puzzle she'd ever seen:* complex, Byzantine, difficult, hard, circuitous, convoluted, elaborate, entangled, intricate, involved, labyrinthine. **—Ant.** clear, uncomplicated, easy, simple, uncomplicated, uninvolved.

complication *n. Bad flying conditions were an unexpected complication:* problem, difficulty, aggravation, disadvantage, handicap, drawback, hitch, snag, obstacle, obstruction, stumbling block, hindrance, impediment, quandary, dilemma, predicament, perplexity. **—Ant.** answer, solution; boon, bonus, help, aid, asset, advantage, benefit, boost.

complicity *n. The jury had to decide on the extent of her complicity in the crime:* connivance, conspiracy, collusion, intrigue, confederacy, scheming, finagling, contrivance, plotting, schemery, abetment; entanglement, involvement, implication.

compliment *n.* **1.** *The hostess received glowing compliments on the dinner:* expression of praise, approving remark, commendation, praise, kudos, laudation, adulation, flattery, acclamation, tribute, honor, homage, congratulation. **2.** **compliments.** *Please give my compliments to your parents:* regards, respects, good wishes, best wishes, best, greetings, felicitations, salutations; congratulations, praise, homage; salute, toast. —*v.* **3.** *The mayor complimented the city on the good voting turnout:* pay a compliment to, praise, pay tribute to, laud, applaud, salute, toast, commend; speak highly of, sing the praises of, extol, exalt. **—Ant.** 1 insult, denunciation, condemnation, criticism, deprecation, disparagement, reproach, complaint; *Informal* beef, gripe, kick, squawk. 3 insult, criticize, denounce, decry, disparage, condemn, censure, reprehend, reproach.

complimentary *adj.* **1.** *The reviews were full of complimentary remarks on the actress's performance:* commendatory, praising, praiseful, admiring, laudatory, plauditory, extolling, panegyric; appreciative, congratulatory, flattering, adulatory. **2.** *Each player was given four complimentary tickets to the game:* free, gratis, gratuitous, without charge. —**Ant.** 1 uncomplimentary, disparaging, abusive, insulting, critical, disapproving, unflattering.

comply *v. Visitors to the factory must comply with the rules:* conform, accede, adhere, abide by, follow, obey, mind, observe, fulfill, meet, satisfy, be faithful to; surrender, submit, yield, give in, defer, consent, acquiesce, bow, bend. —**Ant.** disobey, break, reject, repudiate, spurn, disregard, ignore; resist, fight, oppose.

component *adj.* **1.** *Iron and carbon are two component elements of steel:* constituent, ingredient, modular, member, composing, material, fundamental, elementary, intrinsic, essential, elemental. —*n.* **2.** *A component had to be replaced in the stereo system:* part, component part, constituent, module, member, element, ingredient, segment, piece, item; detail, particular. —**Ant.** 1, 2 whole, complex, compound.

comport *v. The prisoner of war comported himself with dignity:* conduct, carry, deport, bear; behave, acquit.

compose *v.* **1.** *The poet composed a new sonnet:* create, make, conceive, form, formulate, frame, shape, fashion, devise, write. **2.** *England, Scotland, and Wales compose the island of Great Britain:* be part of, be a portion of, make up, form, comprise, constitute, belong to. **3.** *Compose yourself before answering that nasty letter:* calm, settle, collect, pull oneself together, get hold of oneself, quiet, relax, lull, soothe, pacify, placate, quell, modulate, smooth down one's feathers. —**Ant.** 1 destroy, demolish, obliterate, tear up. 2 contain, include, embrace, enfold, encompass, comprise, embody. 3 excite, upset, agitate, rouse, stir up, antagonize, inflame, become nervous, fly off the handle, lose one's cool.

composed *adj. The captain remained composed throughout the raging storm:* calm, serene, at ease, placid, peaceful, tranquil, sedate, quiet, quiescent, cool, cool-headed, collected, poised, controlled, steady, level-headed, even-tempered, unflappable, imperturbable, unperturbed, unagitated, undisturbed, unexcited, unruffled, untroubled, unemotional, restrained, dispassionate, undemonstrative. —**Ant.** hotheaded, unpoised, uncontrolled, perturbed, agitated, disturbed, anxious, upset, *Slang* uptight; distraught, nervous, uneasy, ruffled, excited, stirred up, steamed up, inflamed.

composer *n. Brahms was her favorite composer:* orchestrator, arranger, scorer.

composite *adj. The artist made a composite drawing of the two faces:* combined, compound, compounded, blended, mosaic. —**Ant.** uncombined, single, uncompounded, unmixed, unblended.

composition *n.* **1.** *The orchestra played a modern composition:* work, opus, piece, creation; concoction, production, product, exercise, essay, etude. **2.** *The composition of the report*

took two months: composing, forming, formulation, creating, creation, making, framing, shaping, fashioning, preparation, devising, compilation, organizing, organization. **3.** *The composition of the painting is very graceful. The composition of brass includes copper and zinc:* structure, design, configuration, arrangement, form, organization, framework, layout; make-up, constitution, combination.

compost *n. All the kitchen scraps went into the compost bin:* mulch, humus, manure, admixture.

composure *n. The speaker retained her composure throughout the heckling:* poise, aplomb, calm, calmness, serenity, ease, cool, coolness, cool-headedness, sang-froid, control, self-control, self-possession, self-restraint, even-temperedness, self-assurance, equanimity, levelheadedness, patience, dignity, unexcitability, imperturbability, unflappability. —**Ant.** discomposure, nervousness, uneasiness, disquiet, impatience, excitability, agitation, hotheadedness, perturbation, unrestraint, instability.

compound *adj.* **1.** *Bronze is a compound metal made of copper and tin:* combined, complex, complicated, composite, conglomerate, mixed, blended. —*n.* **2.** *Water is a compound of hydrogen and oxygen:* combination, composition, composite, blend, mixture, union, fusion, amalgam, alloy, conglomeration. —*v.* **3.** *The chemist compounded several elements to form the antidote:* put together; combine, blend, mix, mingle, unite, fuse, alloy, incorporate, formulate, prepare, devise, make, concoct, fabricate, synthesize. **4.** *The speeder compounded his mistake by arguing with the police officer:* add to, augment, increase, heighten, enlarge, magnify, amplify, reinforce, boost. —**Ant.** 1 single, simple, pure, unmixed, unblended, uncompounded. 2 element. 3 separate, part, divide, disunite, divorce, split; isolate, segregate, sift. 4 lessen, decrease, ameliorate, palliate, mitigate, modify, minimize, moderate.

comprehend *v. The child couldn't comprehend the advanced textbook:* understand, grasp, fathom, make out, perceive, conceive, penetrate, absorb, assimilate, digest, appreciate; *Informal* savvy, get, catch, *Slang* dig. —**Ant.** misunderstand, mistake, misapprehend, misinterpret, misconceive, miss the point of.

comprehension *n. The teacher had no comprehension of the boy's problems at home:* understanding, conception, grasp, perception, insight, apprehension, realization, awareness, consciousness, appreciation, acquaintance. —**Ant.** misunderstanding, misconception, incomprehension, misapprehension, unawareness.

comprehensive *adj. The book is a comprehensive study of the 1930's:* all-inclusive, all-embracing, overall, extensive, expansive, broad, sweeping, widespread, universal, general; exhaustive, complete, thorough, full, copious, compendious. —**Ant.** limited, restricted, narrow, specialized, specific; exclusive, incomplete.

compress *v. Compress this clay into a small*

ball. Can you compress your speech into five minutes?: press, squeeze, compact, cram, pack; condense, reduce, shrink, shorten, curtail, abbreviate, abridge. **—Ant.** stretch, spread, expand, enlarge, increase, lengthen.

comprise v. **1.** *Our country is comprised of 50 states. A full deck comprises 52 cards:* include, contain, be composed of, consist of, be made of. **2.** *Some 20,000 readers comprised the English upper-class reading public in Jane Austen's day:* constitute, make up, form, compose.

compromise n. **1.** *A compromise was finally reached after days of arbitration:* mutual concession, accommodation, agreement, settlement, conciliation, adjustment, arrangement, rapprochement; balance, happy medium; truce, compact. **—v. 2.** *Let's compromise and each pay half the damages:* make mutual concessions, adjust differences, come to an understanding, strike a bargain, come to terms, make a deal, settle, agree, meet halfway; *Slang* split the difference. **3.** *The malicious rumors compromised his good reputation:* endanger, jeopardize, imperil, risk; discredit, prejudice, undercut, make suspect, make vulnerable, implicate, embarrass. **—Ant.** 1 difference, dispute, disagreement, contention, controversy, quarrel, strife. 2 differ, disagree, dispute, contest, argue, quarrel. 3 enhance, support, boost; establish, assure, save.

compulsion n. *The suspect said he signed the confession under compulsion. It took a lot of compulsion to get Dad to wear a tuxedo:* coercion, duress, force, pressure, domineering; obligation, necessity, requirement, demand; strong inducement, urging. **—Ant.** choice, free will, option.

compulsive adj. **1.** *The pregnant woman had a compulsive craving for pickles. An organization has been formed to help compulsive gamblers:* unable to resist, uncontrollable, obsessive, fanatic, compelled, compelling, driving, driven, addicted, habitual; *Slang* hooked. **2.** See COMPULSORY. **—Ant.** 1 noncompulsive, resistible, controllable, uncompelling; weak, wishy-washy.

compulsory adj. *The nation has compulsory education for everyone between the ages of six and sixteen:* mandatory, obligatory, required, imperative, requisite, demanded, prescriptive, binding, unavoidable; enforced, compulsive, coercive, forcible. **—Ant.** voluntary, optional, discretionary, nonobligatory, nonrequired, nonrequisite, unimperative, unnecessary, nonbinding.

compunction n. *The student seemed to have no compunctions about cheating:* pang of conscience, qualm, demur, misgiving, regret, anxiety, shame, concern, contrition, unease, remorse, distress of mind, scruple. **—Ant.** pride, self-respect, righteousness; shamelessness.

computation n. *Estimating costs required much computation:* computing, calculation, counting, estimation, figuring.

compute v. *Ask the waiter to compute the bill. Can you compute the distance of the moon from the earth?:* add, add up, total, sum up, count up, tally; calculate, determine mathemati-

cally, reckon, ascertain, figure out, work out. **—Ant.** guess, suppose, conjecture, surmise, estimate, approximate, make a stab at.

comrade n. *The boys have been comrades since kindergarten days:* companion, boon companion, friend, crony, confrere, intimate, pal, chum, buddy, bosom buddy, confidant; colleague, fellow member, associate, helpmate, co-worker, ally, partner, confederate, collaborator. **—Ant.** stranger; enemy, foe, antagonist.

con n. **1.** *The shell game was his favorite con:* cheat, swindle, fraud, dupe, graft, bluff, deception. **—v. 2.** *She was conned out of her inheritance:* cheat, deceive, defraud, swindle, fool, dupe, bamboozle, bilk, cheat, hoax, hoodwink, rook, trick.

concatenation n. *Due to a concatenation of events, the friends found themselves on the same train:* joining, connection, union, junction, conjunction, link, hookup, coupling, linking, bracketing, confluence, reunion, intercommunication, interconnection, interlinking, interassociation.

concave adj. *His concave cheeks emphasized his thinness:* curving inward, sunken, hollow, depressed, indented. **—Ant.** convex, protuberant, rounded.

conceal v. *The robber concealed the weapon under his coat. You can't conceal the truth forever:* hide, cover, cover up, keep out of sight, secrete, keep secret, disguise, mask, shield, screen, cloak, camouflage, obscure. **—Ant.** reveal, disclose, divulge, expose, exhibit, display, show, lay bare, uncover, unmask, uncloak, unveil, flash.

concealed adj. *The concealed object was at last uncovered:* camouflaged, buried, cached, covered up, covert, guarded, hidden, incognito, masked, obscured, secreted, shrouded, ulterior, under wraps, unseen, veiled, screened.

concealment n. **1.** *Concealment of evidence is against the law:* concealing, hiding, covering, covering up, secreting, secretion, masking, screening. **2.** *The boy remained in concealment until the bully went away:* hiding, hiding place, hideaway, hideout, under cover, cover, secret place. **—Ant.** 1 disclosure, developing, revealing, revelation, exposure, exhibition, displaying, display, showing, show, uncovering.

concede v. **1.** *I concede that your request is reasonable:* grant, agree, acknowledge, be persuaded, vouchsafe, acquiesce, accept, recognize, own, allow, confess, admit. **2.** *After his queen was captured, the chess player conceded the game to his opponent:* surrender, give up, yield, abandon, relinquish, resign, cede, hand over, deliver, tender. **—Ant.** 1 deny, refute, reject, repudiate, disclaim, disavow, dissent, contest, protest, contradict, controvert, debate, dispute, argue. 2 make a stand, fight to the last man; win, defeat, beat.

conceit n. *Her conceit about her good looks is unbearable:* vanity, pride, vainglory, egotism, self-love, self-esteem, self-importance, *Slang* ego trip; bragging, boastfulness. **—Ant.** humility, modesty; self-deprecation.

conceited *adj. The conceited actor thinks he's better than John Barrymore:* vain, overproud, arrogant, egotistical, self-important, swell-headed, vainglorious, puffed up, *Informal* stuck-up; boasting, bragging, bombastic, strutting, smug. **—Ant.** humble, modest, unassuming, unaffected; self-effacing.

conceivable *adj. There is no conceivable way to raise a thousand dollars:* imaginable, thinkable, possible, perceivable, knowable, believable, credible, supposable. **—Ant.** inconceivable, unthinkable, unimaginable, unbelievable, incredible.

conceive *v.* **1.** *The Chamber of Commerce conceived a plan to encourage business:* think up, produce, form, create, hatch, contrive, frame, concoct, invent, dream up; initiate, originate, start. **2.** *Most Americans couldn't conceive of living without a telephone:* imagine, envision, envisage, understand, comprehend; think of, consider.

concentrate *v.* **1.** *The enemy concentrated its attack on the right flank. Please concentrate on the lesson:* focus, center, converge, bring to bear, direct toward, close in, hem in; give full attention to, pay attention to, fasten on, pay heed, consider closely, attend to, be engrossed in, put one's mind to. **2.** *Many retirement villages are concentrated on Florida's west coast:* mass, amass, congregate, converge, accumulate, assemble, gather, cluster, bunch, heap up. **3.** *Concentrate the broth by boiling it:* reduce, condense, thicken. **—Ant.** 1 spread out, deploy, dissipate; let one's mind wander, pay no attention. 2 scatter, spread, spread out, disperse, diffuse. 3 dilute, water down, thin.

concentrated *adj. Her recipe called for concentrated orange juice:* reduced, boiled down, condensed, potent, rich, strong, thickened, unadulterated, undiluted, telescoped.

concentration *n.* **1.** *Chess requires great concentration:* concentrating, close attention, fixed regard, mental application, deep thought, intentness, absorption, engrossment, diligence. **2.** *There's a concentration of colleges in the Boston area:* mass, cluster, assemblage, collection, accumulation, aggregation, gathering; centralization, convergence, consolidation, focus; boiling down, reduction, thickening. **—Ant.** 1 inattention, inattentiveness, disregard, distraction, absent-mindedness. 2 scattering, spreading out, dispersion, diffusion, divergence; dilution, thinning.

concept *n. The astronomer presented a new concept of the beginning of the universe:* idea, thought, conception, theory, hypothesis, postulate, notion, surmise, supposition, impression, image, view; opinion, belief, conviction.

conception *n.* **1.** *The conception of the plan occurred at a meeting of scientists:* conceiving, envisioning, imagining, forming, formation, formulation, concocting, devising, creating, originating; inception, genesis, birth, invention, initiation, start, beginning, hatching, launching. **2.** *The architect's conception of the building was a glass skyscraper. Have you any conception of how I feel?:* idea, image, picture, concept; perception, understanding, apprehension, notion, inkling. **3.** *Conception occurred in Europe but the baby was born in America:* becoming pregnant, getting with child, fertilization, inception of pregnancy. **—Ant.** 1 completion, finish, ending, termination; outcome, result, issue.

concern *v.* **1.** *Good government concerns every citizen:* affect, touch, bear upon, involve, be relevant to, relate to, pertain to, appertain to, apply to, interest, occupy, be one's business. **2.** *The boy's poor health concerned his parents:* worry, trouble, disturb, make anxious, distress, disconcert. **—n.** **3.** *Earning a living was her first concern:* consideration, business, interest, matter, affair, involvement, thing of moment; job, duty, chore, charge, mission. **4.** *The teacher began to feel concern about the child's frequent absences. He showed concern for the feelings of others:* worry, anxiety, apprehension, trouble, care, distress, disturbance; thoughtfulness, regard, solicitude, consideration, heed, attention. **5.** *The two banking concerns merged:* firm, establishment, company, corporation, business, enterprise, undertaking; store, house. **—Ant.** 1 be irrelevant to, be unrelated to, disinterest. 4 unconcern, indifference, disregard, inattention, heedlessness, carelessness.

concerned *adj.* **1.** *Good citizens must be concerned in civic affairs:* involved, committed, engaged, participating, active; caring, interested, solicitous, attentive. **2.** *The sailor was concerned about the approaching storm:* worried, anxious, uneasy, disturbed, troubled, distressed, upset. **—Ant.** 1 unconcerned, indifferent, aloof, detached, uninterested; neglectful, remiss. 2 undisturbed, untroubled, carefree, without a care.

concert *n. Working in concert, the scientists completed the experiment and announced their discovery:* unity, harmony, collaboration, accord, union, concord, agreement, teamwork, cooperation, association, complicity, unanimity, accordance, congruity, correspondence. **—Ant.** opposition, discord, disruption, disunity.

concerted *adj. The team made a concerted effort to win the game:* united, joint, cooperative, by assent; planned, predetermined, prearranged, premeditated, agreed upon. **—Ant.** disunited, separate, individual, uncooperative; unplanned, unpremeditated, uncontrived.

concession *n.* **1.** *The lawyer's concession on that point will help your case:* admission, acknowledgment, assent, acquiescence. **2.** *The union made concessions at the bargaining table:* compromise, adjustment, modification; yielding, giving in, indulgence. **3.** *Joe's Diner received the hot-dog concession at the ball park:* franchise, lease, privilege. **—Ant.** 1 denial, disavowal, dissent.

conciliate *v. I would like to conciliate the warring parties:* appease, placate, win over, soothe, propitiate; reconcile, pacify. **—Ant.** alienate, antagonize.

conciliatory *adj. One conciliatory remark would make them friends again:* peacemaking, reconciling, friendly, reassuring, placatory, pacifying, mollifying, accommodative, appeasing. —**Ant.** antagonistic, hostile, unfriendly, unforgiving.

concise adj. Write a concise summary of the book: terse, to the point, succinct, pithy, condensed, compact, brief, short, abbreviated. —**Ant.** rambling, discursive, wordy, verbose.

conciseness n. Her short stories were marked by extreme conciseness: brevity, laconicism, summary, terseness, pithiness. —**Ant.** wordiness, length, verbosity, turgidity, prolixity.

conclave n. The committee members held a conclave before the public meeting: private meeting, secret council, private gathering; meeting, convocation, assembly, council, conference, session, convention, parley, Informal powwow.

conclude v. **1.** The pianist concluded the recital with a Chopin étude: close, draw to a close, finish, end, complete; discontinue, stop, terminate, halt, break off, ring down the curtain on. **2.** The peace negotiations were successfully concluded: settle, decide, resolve, arrange; effect, accomplish, bring to pass, carry out. **3.** After waiting an hour they concluded that she wasn't coming: decide, determine, judge; deduce, reason, surmise, infer, gather. —**Ant.** 1 begin, commence, start, initiate, inaugurate, open; prolong, protract, extend.

conclusion n. **1.** The lovers are united at the conclusion of the play: end, finish, close, completion, windup, termination, finale, final part, denouement, resolution. **2.** The company announced the conclusion of a new union contract: arrangement, settlement, resolution, agreement, working out, completion. **3.** The astronomer's conclusion was that the moon was never part of the earth. One conclusion of the meeting was that the club must raise its dues: finding, determination, decision, judgment, summation, deduction, inference, presumption; result, outcome, resolution, upshot. —**Ant.** 1 beginning, commencement, start, initiation, inauguration, opening.

conclusive adj. Fingerprints on the gun were conclusive evidence that the suspect was guilty: decisive, determining, compelling, convincing, definite, absolute, clinching, certain, categorical; undeniable, irrefutable, incontrovertible, unquestionable, incontestable, inescapable, unanswerable, unimpeachable; clear, demonstrable, manifest, obvious, patent, palpable. —**Ant.** inconclusive, indecisive, unconvincing, indefinite, uncertain; deniable, refutable, doubtful, dubious, questionable, disputable, contestable, impeachable; vague, obscured, confused.

concoct v. The cook concocted a delicious stew. He'll concoct some excuse to keep from cutting the grass: cook up, mix, brew, compound, formulate; make up, think up, create, invent, fabricate, frame, devise, contrive, hatch.

concoction n. The dessert was a concoction of bananas, custard, and bread crumbs. The story was a fantastic concoction of lies: mixture, brew, conglomeration, potpourri, blend, medley, compound, jumble, creation, invention, fabrication, contrivance.

concomitant adj. His wit was a concomitant reason for his success: attendant, accompanying, contributing, additional, related, connected, corollary, secondary, accessory, complementary, supplemental. —**Ant.** unattendant, noncontributory, unconnected.

concord n. Canada and the United States have lived in concord for many years: peace, harmony, agreement, cooperation, mutual understanding, goodwill, cordial relations, accord; amity, friendship, amicability. —**Ant.** discord, conflict, strife, disagreement, dissension, contention; animosity, ill will.

concourse n. Hours before the Pope appeared, there was a tremendous concourse of people into the square: flocking together, confluence, meeting, association, junction, conglomeration, flowing together, concursion, linkage, joining, assembling, congregation, convergence, focalization, conflux, aggregation, concentration, amassment. —**Ant.** separation, dispersal, spreading, division, disjunction, fragmentation.

concrete n. **1.** The walk was paved with concrete: fused stones, alloyed rocks, (loosely) cement; (technical use) mixture of cement, sand, and water. —adj. **2.** The lawyer had concrete evidence of her client's innocence. The remark was a concrete example of his rudeness: real, material, tangible, solid, factual, substantial; definite, specific, precise, explicit, distinct, express, particular. —**Ant.** 2 theoretical, abstract, immaterial, intangible, insubstantial; vague, indefinite, inexplicit, nonspecified.

concupiscence n. We were shocked by the concupiscence of many of his poems: sexual desire, lechery, lustfulness, lust, randiness, lasciviousness, lewdness, libertinism, lecherousness, libidinousness, wantonness, prurience, lubricity, satyrism; Slang horniness, goatishness, hot pants, itch; passion, desire, craving, longing, appetite.

concur v. My political views concur with his. The two accounts concur in all major points: agree, be in accord, correspond, coincide, conform, be uniform, tally, square, match, go hand in hand, go along with, hold with. —**Ant.** disagree, differ, diverge, be at odds.

concurrence also **concurrency** n. **1.** When the two parties reach concurrence, they will sign a contract: agreement, accord, concord, harmony, unanimity, mutual consent, consensus, meeting of the minds; cooperation, collaboration, working together. **2.** The concurrence of the two events made for a fun-filled day: simultaneous occurrence, happening at the same time, coincidence, correspondence, conformity, conjuncture, coexistence, synchronism. —**Ant.** 1 disagreement, discord, difference, divergence, disharmony.

concurrent adj. **1.** Our views of popular music are concurrent: agreeing, in agreement, in accordance, of the same mind, at one, harmonious; commensurate, consonant, correspondent, aligned; allied, congenial, sympathetic, compatible; matching, congruous, coincident. **2.** *New Year's Day and the Rose Bowl game are concurrent. The concurrent political rallies caused a traffic jam:* occurring at the same time, coinciding, simultaneous, synchronous, coexisting; contemporary, contemporaneous. **—Ant.** 1 in disagreement, different, unsympathetic, incompatible.

condemn *v.* **1.** *In 1915 women were condemned for wearing short skirts:* censure, disapprove, criticize, decry, denounce, reprehend, rebuke. **2.** *The thief was condemned to a year of hard labor. The refugee was condemned to a life of wandering:* sentence, doom, damn, proscribe. **—Ant.** 1 praise, compliment, commend, applaud, acclaim, laud, extol, condone, approve. 2 free, liberate.

condemnation *n.* **1.** *Cheating deserves our harshest condemnation:* censure, disapproval, criticism, reprehension, reproach, reproof, rebuke, denunciation, disapprobation. **2.** *The jury's condemnation was a shock to the suspect:* pronouncement of guilt, conviction, judgment; punishment, sentence. **—Ant.** 1 praise, compliment, commendation, approval, acclaim, lauding, extolling. 2 acquittal, exoneration, exculpation, vindication.

condensation *n.* *The magazine published a condensation of the new novel:* abridgment, condensed version, digest, shortened form, reduction.

condense *v.* **1.** *Moisture in the atmosphere condensed into dew during the night:* liquefy, precipitate. **2.** *The editors condensed the manuscript to half its original length:* abridge, digest, shorten, abbreviate, reduce, cut, trim, pare down, boil down, blue-pencil. **3.** *Condense the mixture by boiling off some of the liquid:* thicken, concentrate, reduce, boil down; compress, compact, consolidate, contract. **—Ant.** 1 evaporate, vaporize. 2 expand, lengthen, enlarge, increase, round out, piece out, beef up. 3 dilute, water down; amplify.

condescend *v.* **1.** *The director condescended to take advice from the stagehand:* humble oneself, lower oneself, deign, stoop, submit, descend, *Informal* unbend, come down a peg, come down off one's high horse. **2.** *Don't condescend to me!:* patronize, talk down to, look down on, disdain, *Informal* get on one's high horse with. **—Ant.** 1 scorn, spurn, disdain. 2 accept, treat as an equal, respect.

condescending *adj. I dislike his condescending manner toward his employees:* patronizing, superior, disdainful, overbearing, *Informal* highhat.

condescension *n.* **1.** *I admire the king's condescension toward his subjects:* assumption of equality, self-effacement, humbleness, humility, modesty, self-abasement, graciousness, deference. **2.** *The duke's condescension infuriates me:* haughtiness, loftiness, disdain, hauteur, patronizing attitude; *Informal* high-and-mighty attitude, airs. **—Ant.** 1 arrogance, haughtiness, superiority, pride.

condign *adj. Under the circumstances, impris-*

onment seemed like condign punishment: fitting, appropriate, suitable, fair, just, right, merited, earned, due, proper, warranted, deserved, worthy, meet. **—Ant.** unjust, unwarranted, unmerited, inappropriate.

condition *n.* **1.** *The business is in good financial condition:* state, situation, circumstances, state of affairs, shape, standing, position, status. **2.** *The doctor says your condition is better. She has a heart condition:* state of health, state, physical fitness, shape, fettle; ailment, malfunction, malady, complaint, problem. **3.** *What are the conditions of the contract? We agreed to rent the house on condition that the roof be repaired:* term, provision, proviso, stipulation, demand, arrangement, agreement; prerequisite, requisite, contingency; qualification, restriction, limitation, reservation. **—v. 4.** *Jogging conditioned her for skiing:* prepare, ready, train, equip, fit, put in shape, tone up, accustom, adapt, make used to. **—Ant.** 4 disqualify, incapacitate; unaccustom.

conditional *adj. The warring nations agreed to a conditional truce:* provisional, tentative, with reservations, qualified, limited, restricted, contingent, stipulative, dependent. **—Ant.** unconditional, absolute, unlimited, unrestricted, categorical.

condolence *n.* *The widow received many letters of condolence:* sympathy, commiseration, solace, comfort, compassion, consolation, pity. **—Ant.** congratulation, felicitation.

condone *v. Parents must not condone their children's bad behavior:* overlook, let pass, ignore, disregard, put up with, wink at; forgive, excuse, pardon, justify, absolve, forget. **—Ant.** condemn, denounce, censure, disapprove; punish, castigate.

conducive *adj. Exercise is conducive to good health:* contributive, contributory, favorable, instrumental, calculated to produce, helpful in bringing about, helpful, expeditious, promotive, beneficial; salutary. **—Ant.** harmful, hurtful, deleterious, damaging.

conduct *n.* **1.** *The student's conduct in class was disruptive:* behavior, comportment, deportment, ways, manner, action, deeds. **2.** *His conduct of the business was very successful:* management, administration, direction, guidance, supervision, leadership, control, government, generalship. **—v. 3.** *The mayor conducted the visitors through town. He should learn how to conduct a meeting:* guide, lead, escort, usher, convey, convoy, pilot, steer, marshal, attend, accompany; preside over, chair. **4.** *The children conducted themselves well at the party:* behave, comport, act, carry, bear. **5.** *The oldest son conducts the family's business affairs:* manage, administer, direct, guide, regulate, rule, control, govern, superintend, supervise; perform, transact, carry on, carry out, discharge, dispatch, execute, operate, enact, look after. **—Ant.** 3 follow, trail.

conduit *n.* *The water flows through this underground conduit:* main, pipe, duct, tube, canal, channel, passage; (variously) watercourse, flume, aqueduct, sewer, gutter, trough, drain.

confederacy n. **1.** The Spanish seaports formed a confederacy against pirates: alliance, league, coalition, association, federation, confederation, union, combine, fusion; guild, society, band, bloc, syndicate. **2. the Confederacy.** General Lee commanded the forces of the Confederacy: the Confederate States of America, the C.S.A., the Southern Confederacy, the Southern states, the South, the secessionist states.

confederate n. Tom Sawyer was Huck's confederate in various pranks: ally, colleague, partner, associate, collaborator, accomplice, co-worker, fellow-conspirator, cohort, accessory, helper, abettor, cooperator, comrade, companion, right hand, helping hand. —**Ant.** opponent, rival, enemy, foe.

confederation n. The United Nations is a confederation of many countries: league, association, alliance, coalition, federation, confederacy, union, combine, fusion; society, band, guild, syndicate.

confer v. **1.** Diplomas were conferred on members of the graduating class: present to, bestow upon, award, accord, give. **2.** The two lawyers conferred on the best way to handle the case: consult, discuss, hold a conference, deliberate together, parley, talk together, converse, compare notes, palaver. —**Ant.** 1 withdraw, take away; withhold, deny.

conference n. The teacher had a conference with each student during the term. The annual conference of lawyers will be held in Chicago this year: discussion, talk, consultation, deliberation, parley; meeting, convention, symposium, seminar, conclave, council.

confess v. The murderer confessed his crime to the police. He confessed his love to the girl: admit, acknowledge, reveal, disclose, divulge, make known, bring to light, expose, lay bare, declare, avow, blurt out, make a clean breast of, unbosom one's self, own up; Slang come clean, sing. —**Ant.** disavow, repudiate, disown; deny, hide, conceal, cover; remain silent, keep mum, button one's lips.

confession n. **1.** The thief's confession of guilt closed the case: admission, acknowledgment, revelation, disclosure, divulgence, declaration, avowal. **2.** He made his confession at St. Patrick's: priestly confession, confessional, acknowledgment of one's sins, Archaic shrift. —**Ant.** 1 denial, disavowal, refutation, concealment, hiding.

confidant or (fem.) **confidante** n. She is my closest confidante: intimate, friend, trusty companion, crony, bosom buddy.

confide v. Did she confide her plans to you?: tell secretly, tell privately, reveal, disclose, make known, impart, divulge, let know, let in on; confess, lay bare, unbosom oneself. —**Ant.** keep one's own counsel, keep secret, remain silent, keep mum, button one's lips; deny, repudiate.

confidence n. **1.** The bank manager has complete confidence in the tellers: trust, faith, conviction, belief, reliance, credence. **2.** He would

be a good pianist if he had more confidence: self-confidence, self-assurance, faith in oneself, certainty, certitude; self-reliance, courage, intrepidity, mettle, spirit, nerve, boldness, daring, audacity; Informal spunk, pluck, grit, Slang guts. **3.** The old friends exchanged confidences: secret, intimacy, private matter, confidential matter, inside information. —**Ant.** 1 distrust, mistrust, doubt, misgiving, apprehension, disbelief. 2 self-doubt, uncertainty, timidity, bashfulness, shyness.

confident adj. **1.** The team is confident that it will win the game: convinced, certain, sure, positive, secure, assured, optimistic, expectant. **2.** A champion bridge player must be very confident: self-confident, self-assured, cocksure, sure of oneself, self-reliant, intrepid, dauntless, daring, bold, cocky. —**Ant.** 1 unconfident, uncertain, unsure, distrustful, dubious, doubtful, apprehensive, fearful, pessimistic. 2 self-doubting, unsure of oneself, insecure, hesitant, nervous, jittery.

confidential adj. Please lock up these confidential reports: secret, private, not to be disclosed, privy, undisclosed, off-the-record, top-secret, classified, Informal hush-hush. —**Ant.** public, open; published, publicized.

confidentially adv. She told me the news confidentially: in strict confidence, in secret, secretly, privately, behind closed doors, between ourselves, sub rosa, just between you and me. —**Ant.** openly, publicly.

confine v. **1.** Please confine your remarks to the topic under discussion: limit, restrict, restrain, keep, regulate, govern. **2.** The dog was confined in a fenced enclosure. The prisoner was confined in a windowless room: keep in, shut in, shut up, coop up, hold, fence in, cage, pen, tie, bind; imprison, jail, incarcerate, hold in custody, lock up, impound, sequester. —**Ant.** 1 extend, expand, amplify. 2 release, free, liberate, loose, let out.

confined adj. The confined prisoners squabbled over minor things: bound, circumscribed, bottled up, compassed, encompassed, enclosed, cramped, grounded, imprisoned, incarcerated, indisposed, locked up, restrained, restricted, sealed up, shut in, immured, Informal cooped up.

confinement n. **1.** Expectant mothers used to spend a long time in confinement: lying in, accouchement, childbirth, parturition. **2.** His doctor recommended confinement to a bland diet: restriction, limitation, restraint, circumscription. **3.** The unruly prisoner was put in solitary confinement: detention, constraint, custody, shutting in, cooping up, imprisonment, incarceration. —**Ant.** 2, 3 release, freeing, liberation.

confines n. pl. The lost colt must be somewhere within the confines of this ranch: limits, border, bounds, boundaries, precinct, edge, margins, circumference.

confirm v. **1.** The witnesses' testimony confirmed the suspect's story: corroborate, bear out, uphold, sustain, verify, validate, substantiate, authenticate, establish, prove, clinch. **2.** The hotel confirmed our reservations by tele-

gram: acknowledge, agree to, approve, accept; make firm, make certain, make binding; validate, authorize, certify, ratify. **—Ant.** 1 contradict, refute, repudiate, deny, disavow, disprove, impugn, contravene, controvert. 2 cancel, reject, refuse; annul, abrogate, repeal.

confirmation *n.* **1.** *The newspaper received confirmation of the story:* substantiation, verification, corroboration, affirmation, authentication, validation, proof. **2.** *The executive committee's choice of location requires confirmation by a majority of club members:* acceptance, approval, endorsement, ratification, sanction; assent, agreement. **—Ant.** 1 denial, repudiation, refutation, contradiction, disavowal, recantation. 2 rejection, refusal, disapproval, cancellation, annulment.

confirmed *adj.* **1.** *Confirmed reports from the front tell of a great victory:* corroborated, substantiated, authenticated, verified, proven true, validated, established. **2.** *My brother is a confirmed bachelor:* established, inveterate, ingrained, chronic, set, fixed, dyed-in-the-wool, deep-seated, deep-rooted, hardened. **—Ant.** 1 unconfirmed, unsubstantiated, unverified, unproven; contradicted, refuted, repudiated, denied. 2 temporary, sometimes, occasional, on-and-off, now-and-then.

confiscate *v. The customs officer confiscated the smuggled goods:* seize, commandeer, appropriate, possess, preempt, take, take over, impound, sequester, expropriate. **—Ant.** release, return, restore.

conflagration *n. The conflagration destroyed several blocks in the downtown section:* fire, blaze, wildfire, inferno, firestorm, holocaust, bonfire, wall of fire, sheet of flame, sea of flames, raging fire, brush fire, forest fire.

conflict *v.* **1.** *Our political views conflict:* disagree, oppose, be contrary, clash, collide, be inharmonious, be contradictory. *—n.* **2.** *Nations must not settle their differences by armed conflict:* fight, combat, battle, struggle, clash, warfare, hostility, encounter, confrontation, action, skirmish, engagement, fray, scuffle, melee, set-to, fracas, tussle. **3.** *The conflict between the brothers' political views caused a row:* disagreement, difference, discord, division, variance, dissent, dissension; antagonism, friction, strife. **—Ant.** 1 agree, harmonize, coincide, reconcile. 2 peace; truce, treaty. 3 agreement, harmony, accord, concord.

conflicting *adj. She found they had conflicting opinions:* opposite, contradictory, contrary, converse, hostile, antagonistic, antipodal, antithetical, clashing, counter, discordant, discrepant, dissonant, incompatible, irreconcilable, inconsistent, opposed, paradoxical, polar, vacillating, wavering, ambivalent, unresolved, equivocal, unresolved. **—Ant.** harmonious, agreeing, compatible, congruous.

confluence *n. St. Louis is located at the confluence of the Mississippi and Missouri rivers:* conflux, convergence, coming together, junction, concourse, union, meeting, linkage, gathering, juncture, flowing together, joining, concursion, assembling, concentration, association.

conform *v.* **1.** *All students must conform to the rules:* follow, comply with, obey, submit to, be guided by, adhere to, acquiesce in, fall in with, act in agreement with. **2.** *The seamstress made the dress conform to the pattern. He conformed the plans to the new specifications:* correspond to, agree with, tally with, square with, fit, jibe with; reconcile, adjust, adapt. **—Ant.** 1 disobey, oppose, diverge, differ. 2 differ, be dissimilar.

conformation *n. The horse had the conformation of a thoroughbred:* form, shape, formation, configuration, build, figure, structure, framework, arrangement, anatomy.

conformity *n. Everyone must live in conformity with his own beliefs. There is too much conformity in the design of these houses:* agreement, harmony, accord, compliance, observance, acquiescence, assent, obedience, submission; uniformity, conventionality, resemblance, likeness, correspondence, similarity. **—Ant.** disagreement, disharmony, discord, disobedience, opposition, rebellion; difference, dissimilitude, divergence.

confound *v. The patient's unusual symptoms confounded the doctor:* perplex, confuse, baffle, bewilder, puzzle, mystify, mix up, disconcert, unsettle, nonplus, rattle, fluster, throw off the scent; amaze, astound, astonish, surprise, startle, dumfound, flabbergast, strike with wonder. **—Ant.** enlighten, explain, solve, clear up, clarify.

confront *v. We must confront the future with optimism. The boy confronted his accuser and denied the charges:* face, face up to, meet, encounter, cope with; withstand, challenge, dare, brave, defy. **—Ant.** avoid, evade, flee, turn tail; surrender to, yield to.

confrontation *n. A confrontation with government forces led to the destruction of the rebel army:* showdown, opposition, encounter, eyeball-to-eyeball encounter, contest, face-to-face meeting, face-off, conflict, battle, run-in, set-to, skirmish, clash, engagement.

confuse *v.* **1.** *The road signs confused the driver:* perplex, bewilder, baffle, puzzle, stump, mystify, fluster, rattle, muddle, addle, befuddle, mix up, confound, disconcert, unsettle, nonplus, discompose. **2.** *You confused me with my twin brother. This new clue confuses the case against him:* mix up, mistake; confound, make perplexing, make baffling, make unclear, muddle, befog, throw into disorder. **—Ant.** 1 enlighten. 2 differentiate, untangle; explain, solve, clarify, clear up.

confusion *n.* **1.** *Imagine our confusion when we found the party was the following week:* bewilderment, stupefaction, bafflement, perplexity, puzzlement, mystification; disconcertment, discomposure, abashment. **2.** *The room was in a state of confusion. The painting was a confusion of colors:* chaos, disorder, disarrangement, disarray, disorganization, untidiness, shambles, upheaval, mess; muddle, clutter, jumble, hodgepodge, snarl, tangle; riot, tumult, madhouse, turmoil, pandemonium, hullabaloo, hubbub, commotion, ferment, disturbance, bedlam, uproar. **—Ant.** 1 enlightenment, explanation, solution, clarification; composure, calm. 2 organization, order, orderliness, arrangement, tidiness, neatness.

confute v. In her next article she confuted his argument: invalidate, nullify, negate, disprove, confound, controvert, overthrow, overturn, prove false, prove wrong, rebut, refute, set aside, vanquish, subvert, impugn. **—Ant.** confirm, prove.

congeal v. The gelatin will congeal quickly in the refrigerator: harden, set, stiffen, solidify, thicken, curdle, clot, coagulate, jell, gelatinize; freeze. **—Ant.** dissolve, soften, melt, thaw.

congenial adj. **1.** The two friends had congenial tastes: similar, compatible, kindred, harmonious, well-suited, consistent, like, agreeing, related, sympathetic, corresponding. **2.** The girl has a warm, congenial disposition: agreeable, pleasing, pleasant, amenable, gracious, affable, genial, cordial, companionable, social, sociable, convivial. **—Ant.** 1 dissimilar, different, incompatible, opposite, unrelated, unlike. 2 disagreeable, displeasing, unpleasant, ungracious.

congenital adj. Left-handedness is a congenital trait: innate, inherent, inborn, inbred, intrinsic, hereditary, inherited, ingrained; natural, native. **—Ant.** acquired, extrinsic, assumed, learned.

congested adj. The roads are becoming more and more congested: crowded, overcrowded, filled, packed, jammed, gorged, saturated. **—Ant.** uncongested, empty, uncrowded, free.

congestion n. The congestion at the beach on weekends is unbelievable: crowding, overcrowding, jam, mass, mob, pile-up, obstruction, bottleneck, snarl. **—Ant.** uncrowding, emptiness, desertedness.

conglomeration n. The stew was a conglomeration of fish, potatoes, and leftover vegetables: mixture, collection, assortment, combination, aggregate, aggregation, potpourri, medley, agglomeration; jumble, hodgepodge, mishmash.

congratulate v. I congratulate you on your 20th anniversary: give one's best wishes, wish one joy, salute, felicitate, hail, compliment, rejoice with, wish many happy returns of the day. **—Ant.** rebuke, reprove, censure, condemn, criticize, reprehend.

congratulations n. pl. Let's telegraph our congratulations to the new parents: best wishes, good wishes, greetings, well-wishing, salute, felicitations, blessings, many happy returns of the day. **—Ant.** rebuke, reproof, censure, condemnation, criticism, reprehension.

congregate v. A crowd congregated around the soapbox orator: assemble, gather, collect, cluster, come together, crowd together, mass, amass, throng, flock, swarm. **—Ant.** disperse, scatter, separate, part.

congregation n. **1.** The guru spoke before a large congregation: audience, assembly, gathering, crowd, group, throng, multitude, horde, flock. **2.** The congregation welcomed its new minister: church membership, religious assembly, parishioners, parish, brethren, laity.

congress n. **1.** A congress of heart specialists is meeting in Chicago: conference, convention, assembly, council, gathering, caucus, discussion group; delegates, representatives. **2.** usually **Congress.** The United States Congress handles over 200 bills a session: legislature, legislative body, national council, federal council; (variously) parliament, chamber of deputies, diet.

congruent adj. He learned about congruent angles in geometry: harmonious, consonant, similar, corresponding, coinciding, compatible, concurring, conforming, consistent.

conical adj. The hilltop was conical: tapered, tapering, funnel-shaped, coned, cylindrical, pointed.

conjectural adj. His reconstruction of the ancient city was, he admitted, entirely conjectural: theoretical, speculative, hypothetical, surmised, putative, suppositional, abstract, doubtful, supposed, inferential, reputed, supposititious. **—Ant.** factual, certain, actual, evidential, literal, proven.

conjecture n. **1.** Do you know for sure or is it only conjecture?: guesswork, supposition, inference, deduction, surmise, guess, view, judgment, speculation, suspicion, opinion, notion, idea, theory, hypothesis, assumption, augury, Informal shot in the dark, Slang guesstimate. **—v. 2.** The old man conjectured that it would be an unusually cold winter: guess, suppose, think, calculate, reckon, surmise, theorize, imagine, infer, forecast, speculate, hypothesize, presume, presuppose, judge, fancy. **—Ant.** 1 fact, surety, certainty. 2 know.

conjoin v. The separate departments eventually conjoined: associate, unite, join, combine, connect. **—Ant.** disjoin, dissociate.

conjugal adj. There is a vast difference between infatuation and conjugal love: marital, wedded, married, matrimonial, nuptial, connubial, spousal. **—Ant.** single, unmarried, unwedded.

conjunction n. The conjunction of heavy rains and high winds caused flooding: combination, union, joining, meeting, association, concurrence, coincidence.

conjure v. Witches are supposed to be able to conjure the Devil: call forth, call upon, make appear, summon, raise, command, invoke; call away, make disappear, allay; practice sorcery, bewitch, charm, enchant, cast a spell.

connect v. **1.** Please connect the two wires: join, attach, unite, fasten together; couple, tie, hinge, combine, merge. **2.** A good student must connect what she reads with what she sees around her: associate, relate, compare, correlate, combine. **—Ant.** 1 disconnect, detach, unfasten, disjoin, sunder, separate, divide, part. 2 dissociate, separate.

connected adj. The connected rooms shared a hallway: joined, linked, affiliated, associated, banded together, bracketed, coupled, pertinent, related, undivided, allied, akin.

connection n. **1.** The connection between the throttle and the carburetor is broken: coupling, coupler, fastening, link, bond, linkage, connector, attachment, nexus, tie, junction. **2.** *There is no connection between the two incidents:* relation, relationship, interrelation, association, correlation, affinity, attachment, alliance. **3.** *They have the same last name but are not connections of ours. He's just a business connection:* relative, relation, family, kin, kinfolk, kinsfolk, kinsman, kith and kin, flesh and blood; friend, associate, acquaintance, contact. —**Ant.** 1 disconnection, detachment. 2 detachment, dissociation. 3 stranger.

connive *v.* *The two gangs connived in the smuggling of goods:* conspire, plan, plot, cooperate secretly, participate surreptitiously, collude, be a party to, be accessory to, be in collusion with, lend oneself to, aid, abet; allow, shut one's eyes to, wink at. —**Ant.** have no part, be innocent of, deter, resist; censure, deplore, condemn, expose.

connoisseur *n.* *The old gentleman was a connoisseur of fine wines:* expert, judge, authority, mavin, person of good taste, cognoscente; epicure, gourmet.

connotation *n.* *The word "winter" has the connotation of ice skating and skiing. His speech wasn't openly contemptuous, but its connotations were insulting:* suggested meaning, suggestion, implication, undertone, insinuation, import, significance, coloring, intimation, spirit, drift, evocation. —**Ant.** denotation, basic meaning, literal meaning.

connote *v.* *To her the word "home" always connoted warmth, gaiety, and contentment:* imply, suggest, hint at, intimate, insinuate, bring to mind.

connubial *adj.* *The couple celebrated their tenth anniversary of connubial bliss:* conjugal, wedded, married, marital, matrimonial, nuptial. —**Ant.** single, unmarried, unwedded.

conquer *v.* **1.** *The Allies conquered Germany in World War II:* defeat, vanquish, win over, overcome, overpower, triumph over, prevail over, beat, whip, thrash, drub, trim, rout, lick, best, floor, subdue, subjugate, humble; occupy, possess, rule. **2.** *You must conquer your fear of heights:* overcome, surmount, master, rise above, prevail over, get the better of, get the upper hand of, quell. —**Ant.** 1 be defeated, be beaten, lose, surrender, capitulate, give up, bow to. 2 give in, yield to, surrender to.

conqueror *n.* *The conqueror marched into the defeated country:* victor, vanquisher, conquistador, subjugator, subduer, winner; champion. —**Ant.** conquered, conquest, defeated, vanquished, subjugated, loser.

conquest *n.* **1.** *Faith will help in your conquest of fear:* conquering, defeat, vanquishment, mastery, overcoming, victory, triumph, winning, ascendancy, subjugation, domination, upper hand, sway, whip hand. **2.** *In World War II much of China was Japan's conquest. Her beauty won her many conquests:* captured territory, captive, acquisition; adherent, follower, fan, lover, adorer. —**Ant.** 1 failure, surrender, submission, loss.

consanguinity *n.* *The consanguinity of the cousins was obvious:* blood relationship, brotherhood, connection, affiliation, affinity, family, family tie, filiation, kin, kinship, lineage, shared race.

conscience *n.* *George Washington's conscience would not let him lie:* moral sense, sense of right and wrong, ethical feelings, scruples, principles.

conscientious *adj.* *A conscientious worker arrives on time and leaves no mess behind:* conscionable, high-principled, dutiful, upright, scrupulous, responsible, honest, ethical, trustworthy; painstaking, careful, exact, particular, meticulous, fastidious. —**Ant.** unconscientious, unprincipled, unscrupulous, unreliable, untrustworthy; careless, neglectful, remiss, negligent, heedless, thoughtless, slack, lax, feckless, irresponsible.

conscious *adj.* **1.** *Is the patient conscious yet?:* able to feel and think, sentient, sensible, having awareness. **2.** *Were you conscious of his hostility?:* aware, cognizant, discerning, knowledgeable, perceiving, noticing, observing, apperceptive, awake to, alert to, alive to, in the know. **3.** *His rudeness was conscious, not accidental:* deliberate, calculated, studied, premeditated. —**Ant.** 1–3 unconscious. 2 unaware, ignorant, insensible, oblivious.

consciousness *n.* **1.** *The accident victim never lost consciousness:* awareness, sensibility, mental activity. **2.** *That people on the other side of the world are starving never entered his consciousness:* awareness, cognizance, perception, mind, thoughts, senses, feelings, discernment. —**Ant.** 1 unconsciousness; unawareness, insensibility.

conscript *v.* **1.** *The armed forces did not conscript farmers until the war was nearly over:* draft, induct, call up, impress, select, conscribe, mobilize, recruit, enlist, register, muster, enroll, levy, *Navy* shanghai; hire, engage, take on, employ. —*n.* **2.** *All conscripts were ordered to report to the town square:* draftee, inductee, rookie, recruit, selectee, enlistee; private, buck private, P.F.C., boot, seaman.

consecrate *v.* *The shrine was consecrated by the Church:* declare sacred, make sacred, sanctify, hallow, bless, glorify, immortalize. —**Ant.** desecrate, profane, defile.

consecutive *adj.* *The streets of New York City are numbered in consecutive order:* successive, following one another, progressive, sequential, serial, continuous, uninterrupted, unbroken, in turn. —**Ant.** nonconsecutive, random, haphazard, hit-or-miss, disordered.

consensus *n.* *The consensus of the voters was to defeat the referendum. A large group will seldom have a consensus of opinion:* general agreement, majority opinion, general opinion; common consent, unanimity, concord, accord, concurrence. —**Ant.** minority opinion; disagreement, discord, difference.

consent *v.* **1.** *The firm will consent to your taking a leave of absence:* agree, concur, assent, approve, accept, accede, acquiesce, concede;

yield, submit, fall in with, permit, allow, sanction, confirm, ratify, endorse. **—n. 2.** *The President appoints cabinet members with the Senate's advice and consent:* agreement, concurrence, assent, approval, acceptance, willingness, permission, sanction, confirmation, ratification, endorsement, accord, concord, acquiescence. **—Ant.** 1 dissent, refuse, disallow, decline, resist, balk, demur, disagree, disapprove. 2 refusal, unacceptance, unwillingness, disapproval, dissent, disagreement, discount.

consequence *n.* **1.** *As a consequence of his laziness, he was fired:* result, outcome, development, upshot, outgrowth, issue, aftermath, end, sequel, fruit. **2.** *An event of great consequence took place in 1914:* importance, import, significance, note, moment, magnitude, distinction, prominence, notability, seriousness, gravity, influence, avail, worth, value, account, usefulness. **—Ant.** 1 prelude, source, root, cause, determinant, reason. 2 insignificance, unimportance, paltriness, triviality.

conservation *n.* *The world will run out of oil unless it practices conservation:* preservation, husbandry, care, careful use, safekeeping, protection, maintenance, upkeep. **—Ant.** waste, destruction, decay, loss, neglect.

conservative *adj.* **1.** *Lord Tweedsmuir reflected the conservative views of his day. The professor is a radical in politics but a conservative dresser:* nonliberal, unprogressive, traditional, right-wing, reactionary, unchanging; old-line, cautious, orthodox, undaring, quiet, *Slang* square. **—n. 2.** *The conservatives voted against building the new road:* opponent of change, champion of the status quo, middle-of-the-roader, moderate, right-winger, reactionary, *Slang* square. **—Ant.** 1 radical, liberal, progressive, revolutionary; innovative, avant-garde, imaginative, speculative, faddish. 2 radical, innovator, changer, progressive.

conservatory *n.* **1.** *Orchids grow all year in the conservatory:* greenhouse, hothouse, nursery, glasshouse; arboretum. **2.** *The pianist is a graduate of the local conservatory:* music school, music academy, conservatoire.

conserve *v.* *The public must conserve electricity to prevent brownouts:* preserve, save, use less, use sparingly, husband, not waste, cut back; maintain, care for, safeguard, guard. **—Ant.** waste, squander.

consider *v.* **1.** *Consider the consequences before deciding:* think about, reflect on, envision, contemplate, regard, weigh, appraise, gauge, examine, review, mull over, ponder, turn over in one's mind, study, cogitate on, deliberate on, bear in mind, be aware of, note, pay heed; respect, honor, make allowances for. **2.** *The critics considered the play excellent:* regard, hold to be, judge, deem, think, believe, hold, opine. **—Ant.** 1 ignore, neglect, overlook, disregard.

considerable *adj.* *Graduating summa cum laude is a considerable achievement:* sizable, substantial, large, great, goodly, tidy, of some size, ample, not small, a good deal of; of some importance, significant, notable, noticeable, es-

timable, noteworthy, remarkable, impressive. **—Ant.** insubstantial, meager, small, insignificant; ordinary, average, unimportant, workaday, unremarkable, inestimable.

considerably *adv.* *Losing 30 pounds changed his appearance considerably:* substantially, significantly, noticeably, notably, sizably, largely, greatly, amply, abundantly, estimably, remarkably. **—Ant.** minimally, unnoticeably, insignificantly, little.

considerate *adj.* *It was very considerate of you to send me a get-well card:* thoughtful, kind, kindly, solicitous, attentive, concerned, obliging, mindful. **—Ant.** inconsiderate, thoughtless, unfeeling, oblivious, heedless, selfish.

consideration *n.* **1.** *Please give this suggestion serious consideration:* thought, regard, attention, concern, heed, notice, deliberation, contemplation, meditation, cogitation, reflection, judgment, advisement, study, review, examination. **2.** *Consideration of others is the basis of good manners:* thoughtfulness, regard, considerateness, respect, solicitude, tact, honor, kindliness. **3.** *Cost is a major consideration in buying a new car:* factor, point, concern, interest; inducement, motive, reason, cause, ground. **—Ant.** 1 disregard, inattention. 2 thoughtlessness, heedlessness, selfishness.

considered *adj.* *In her considered opinion he was an idiot:* thoughtful, thought-out, thought-about, contemplated, weighed, deliberate, intentional, premeditated, studied, weighed, examined.

consign *v.* *The father consigned his property to his eldest son:* hand over, transfer, deliver, entrust, commit, deposit with, convey, remit, remand, assign, relegate, delegate, commend to. **—Ant.** receive; keep, retain, withhold.

consignment *n.* **1.** *The consignment of the property to the new owners will take place tomorrow:* transfer, delivery, committing, depositing, assignment, handing over, consigning, entrusting, relegation, delegation, committing. **2.** *The consignment of merchandise arrived on time:* shipment, goods shipped, goods for sale, goods sent on approval. **—Ant.** 1 reception, receiving; keeping, retention.

consist *v.* **1.** *This fudge consists largely of chocolate and sugar:* to be composed of, be made up of, contain, include. **2.** *Happiness consists in appreciating what you have:* lie, to be found in, reside.

consistency also **consistence** *n.* **1.** *This sauce has a thin consistency:* texture, viscosity, density, thickness, firmness, stiffness, compactness; body, composition, construction, structure, makeup. **2.** *A good ball player must prove consistency throughout the season:* constant performance, undeviating behavior, steady effort, uniform standards, persistence; steadfastness, faithfulness. **3.** *There is no consistency in the furniture styles in this room:* harmony, congruity, unity, uniformity, conformity, agreement, accordance, coherence, correspondence, connection, compatibility. **—Ant.** 2 inconsistency, erratic behavior, volatility. 3 inconsistency, disharmony, incongruity, disagreement, discordance, incompatibility.

consistent *adj.* **1.** *A golf champion must be a consistent winner:* constant, steady, regular, persistent, unchanging, undeviating, conforming to type. **2.** *Choose furniture that's consistent with the modern style of the house:* harmonious, consonant, in agreement, agreeing, of a piece, unified, compatible, congenial, meet, correspondent, congruous, suitable. **—Ant.** 1 inconsistent, irregular, erratic, nonuniform, changing, deviating. 2 inconsistent, in disagreement, incompatible, noncongenial, incongruous, discordant, contradictory, contrary, unsuitable.

consolation *n.* *Words are little consolation when tragedy strikes:* solace, comfort, relief, succor, assuagement, help, alleviation, soothing, easement, support, encouragement, cheer; condolence, sympathy. **—Ant.** depression, discomfort, discouragement.

console *v.* *The mother consoled the boy, then bandaged his scuffed knee:* soothe, comfort, calm, succor, cheer, ease, support, sustain; condole with, commiserate with, lament with, express sorrow, express sympathy for, sympathize. **—Ant.** distress, trouble, discompose, upset, annoy, disturb, perturb, agitate, aggravate, grieve, sadden, hurt, wound, disquiet.

consolidate *v.* **1.** *The two railroads were consolidated into one line:* combine, unify, centralize, incorporate, unite, merge, bring together, band together, join, fuse, amalgamate, coalesce, league, integrate, federate, compress, condense, concentrate. **2.** *The team's victory consolidated its chance for the championship:* strengthen, fortify, solidify, make solid, make sure, make firm. **—Ant.** 1 separate, divide, part, sever, sunder; dissolve. 2 weaken, make uncertain, leave up in the air.

consonance *n.* *We studied the organism to determine the consonance of its various parts:* harmony, agreement, accord, accordance, correspondence, compatibility, consistency, coherence, concord, concordance, congruity, congruence, consonancy, unison, conformity, unanimity, like-mindedness, homogeneity, oneness. **—Ant.** conflict, disagreement, dissonance, disparity, inconsistency, discrepancy, discord.

consonant *n.* **1.** *If it's a, e, i, o, or u it's not a consonant:* sonorant, fricative, stop, plosive, continuant. **—adj. 2.** *Your view is consonant with my understanding of the situation:* in agreement, concordant, consistent, harmonious, compatible, congruous, conformant, suitable. **—Ant.** 1 vowel 2 discordant, inconsistent.

consort *n.* **1.** *Prince Albert was the consort of England's Queen Victoria:* spouse, mate, husband, wife, *Informal* other half; partner, companion, associate, *Slang* sidekick. **—v. 2.** *The police suspect him because he consorts with known criminals:* keep company, accompany, pal around, go around, fraternize, mingle, mix, pair off, club, hang out, rub elbows. **—Ant.** 2 dissociate, separate, part, estrange.

conspicuous *adj.* **1.** *That red hat makes you conspicuous. The Borgia family were conspicuous violators of the laws of God and men:* standing out, easily seen, easily noticed, highly visible, obvious, striking; plain, clear, evident, manifest, patent, distinct, glaring, prominent, arresting, flagrant. **2.** *The first moon landing was a conspicuous achievement:* outstanding, striking, notorious, remarkable, notable, illustrious, distinguished, glorious, memorable, celebrated, prominent, eminent, renowned, famous, well-known, splendid, brilliant, great. **—Ant.** 1 inconspicuous, unnoticeable, concealed, hidden, unseen, invisible, imperceptible, unapparent, indiscernible. 2 inconspicuous, undistinguished, trifling, unmemorable, common, ordinary, modest, humble; mediocre, average, commonplace.

conspiracy *n.* *Those who planned the rebellion were indicted for conspiracy against the king:* criminal plan, treasonous plan, secret plan, plot, intrigue, collusion, connivance, machination; sedition, treason, treachery.

conspirator *n.* *Those who signed the Declaration of Independence were considered conspirators against the British crown:* plotter, schemer, conniver, traitor, subversive, intriguer.

conspire *v.* **1.** *John Brown and his associates were tried for conspiring to overthrow the slave states:* scheme, intrigue, collude, connive, machinate, plot treason. **2.** *Bad weather and car trouble conspired to ruin our vacation:* contribute jointly, combine, unite, cooperate, concur, work together.

constancy *n.* *The teacher's constancy in the face of obstacles was remarkable:* determination, fidelity, firmness, fortitude, resolution, inflexibility, decision, tenacity, steadfastness, faithfulness, fealty, devotion, loyalty; regularity, stability, immutability, uniformity, permanence, sameness, consistency. **—Ant.** randomness, faithlessness, irregularity, instability.

constant *adj.* **1.** *Keep the chemicals at a constant temperature of 40 degrees:* fixed, uniform, steady, regular, even, unchanging, invariable, unalterable, unvaried, undeviating, permanent, stable, immutable, unswerving, unfailing. **2.** *Her constant nagging drives me crazy:* incessant, unceasing, ceaseless, unrelenting, continual, endless, never-ending, everlasting, eternal, interminable, perpetual, persistent, unbroken, uninterrupted, sustained. **3.** *The seeing-eye dog was the blind man's constant companion:* loyal, devoted, faithful, true, tried-and-true, trustworthy, trusty, steadfast, staunch, dependable, diligent, resolute, abiding, unflagging, unwavering, enduring, stalwart. **—Ant.** 1 variable, fluctuating, changing, changeable, erratic, irregular, uneven, unfixed, deviating, alterable, unstable. 2 occasional, intermittent, irregular, spasmodic, sporadic, fitful, random, unsustained. 3 inconstant, disloyal, unfaithful, faithless, false, perfidious; untrustworthy, undependable, irresolute, wavering, flagging, fickle.

constellation *n.* *The Big Dipper is the easiest constellation to locate. The gallery opening attracted the usual constellation of celebrities:* configuration, pattern, assemblage, cluster, group, gathering, collection; galaxy, nebula, spi-ral, spiral nebula, island universe; company, group, circle, rally, host, throng.

consternation n. To their complete consterna-tion the swimmers saw a shark approaching: paralyzing fear, panic, shock, terror, horror, fright, alarm; dismay, apprehension, trepidation. —**Ant.** composure, calmness, equanimity, aplomb, self-possession, sang-froid, presence of mind; fearlessness, boldness.

constituency n. There were three main ethnic groups in his constituency: voters, voting public, body politic, public, district, electorate, electors, people, precinct, province, voters.

constituent adj. **1.** The constituent elements were all in place: component, constituting, ele-mental, fundamental, integral. **2.** The constitu-ent assembly elected a leader: electing, elec-toral, voting. —n. **3.** One constituent was egg-white: part, portion, component, factor, ingredient, element, unit. **4.** voter, elector.

constitute v. **1.** Meat, milk, vegetables, fruit, and starches constitute a balanced diet: form, compose, make up, make, produce, compound. **2.** A committee was constituted to investigate rising prices: establish, create, set up, institute, found; appoint, delegate, commission, author-ize, empower, name, invest.

constitution n. **1.** The fabric's open-weave con-stitution makes it unsuitable for drapes: compo-sition, make-up, construction, structure, config-uration, figuration, formation, texture. **2.** The old man still has a strong constitution: physical condition, physique, figure, health, strength, mettle, stamina, vitality. **3.** The legislators voted to amend the Constitution: governing charter, charter, fundamental principles, basic laws.

constitutional adj. **1.** His limp is constitutional, not the result of an accident: organic, physical, internal, congenital, natural, inborn, inherent, intrinsic. **2.** Freedom of speech is a Constitu-tional guarantee: of the Constitution, chartered, basic, fundamental, vested. —n. **3.** My father takes a daily constitutional: walk, stroll, ramble, turn. —**Ant.** 1 inorganic, nonphysical, external, fortuitous; foreign, alien, extraneous, extrinsic, acquired, environmental, accidental. 2 unconsti-tutional, unlawful, illegal.

constrain v. **1.** His conscience constrained him to apologize: force, compel, coerce, oblige, urge, drive, necessitate, strong-arm, enforce, pressure, Slang put the screws on. **2.** She con-strained her impulse to tell him her secret: re-strain, curb, fight down, suppress, repress, check, quash, put down, squelch, crush, sub-due. —**Ant.** 1 beg, implore, ask, request, plead. 2 free, loose, unleash, release, let go, lib-erate.

constraint n. **1.** The manufacturer was forced to return the money under constraint of law: force, obligation, coercion, pressure, compul-sion, necessity, duress, enforcement. **2.** He stopped shouting and began to speak with con-straint: restraint, reserve, suppressed feelings, inhibition, diffidence. —**Ant.** 1 free will; desire,

wish. 2 naturalness, openness, frankness, bold-ness.

constrict v. Doesn't that tight bracelet constrict your arm?: squeeze, cramp, pinch, strangle, strangulate, choke, bind; contract, compress, shrink. —**Ant.** free, release, loosen, unbind, untie; distend, swell.

constriction n. Constriction in the patient's chest made breathing difficult: tightness, com-pression, contraction, narrowing, stricture, con-straint; squeezing, cramping, choking, pinching, binding, shrinking, strangling. —**Ant.** loosen-ing, freeing, releasing, unbending; expansion, widening, dilation, distension, swelling.

construct v. To construct a building. To con-struct a plan: build, erect, make, fabricate, set up; create, formulate, form, frame, design, de-vise, fashion, shape, organize, arrange. —**Ant.** demolish, destroy, raze, tear down, take apart.

construction n. **1.** The construction of the bridge took two years: constructing, building, putting together, erecting, rearing, raising, fabri-cation, fashioning, creation, production, manu-facture. **2.** The construction will be used to store farm equipment: building, structure, edi-fice. **3.** The construction of the new school is simple and modern: style, form, configuration, build, conformation, composition, format, make. **4.** The witness's construction of the crime is very confusing: rendition, version, ex-planation, interpretation, explication, elucida-tion, reading. —**Ant.** 1 demolition, razing, de-struction, tearing down.

constructive adj. The painter gave the art stu-dents constructive criticism of their work: help-ful, productive, practical, handy, useful, benefi-cial, advantageous, valuable. —**Ant.** de-structive, unhelpful, useless.

construe v. Do you construe that remark as fa-vorable or critical?: interpret, understand, com-prehend, take, read, decipher, translate, make out, figure out; explain, elucidate.

consul n. The French consul in Toronto will stamp your visa: diplomatic agent, representa-tive, foreign officer, minister, envoy, emissary.

consult v. **1.** Did anyone consult the boss about this job?: refer to, inquire of, ask advice of, seek counsel from, seek the opinion of; take into ac-count, consider, regard, have an eye to. **2.** The two lawyers consulted on the case: confer, ex-change views, deliberate together, talk over, dis-cuss together, parley, compare notes. —**Ant.** 1 ignore, disregard, bypass.

consultation n. The doctor is in consultation with a patient: meeting, conference, council, de-liberation, hearing, discussion, palaver, inter-view.

consume v. **1.** The small car consumed very lit-tle gas: use up, expend, spend, deplete, ex-haust, drain; waste, squander, dissipate, fritter away. **2.** The children consumed all the hot dogs and hamburgers: eat, devour, eat up, swallow up, gulp, guzzle, drink up. **3.** The entire building was consumed by fire: destroy, lay waste, ravage, devastate, demolish, annihilate. **4.** He was consumed with envy: absorb, engross, eat up, devour. **—Ant.** I conserve, preserve, save; provide, supply.

consumer n. **1.** *Consumers want better, safer products:* user, customer, buyer, purchaser, patron, client. **2.** *Worry is a great consumer of energy:* user, spender, drain; waster, dissipater, squanderer. **—Ant.** 1 manufacturer, maker, seller. 2 saver, preserver, conserver; supplier, provider.

consummate v. **1.** *It took weeks of bargaining to consummate the deal:* complete, perfect, fulfill, execute, accomplish, achieve, realize, effect, finish, bring about, carry out, perform, do. **—adj. 2.** *After years of study and practice he is a consummate pianist:* finished, complete, accomplished, faultless, perfect; thorough, absolute, utter, unquestioned, unconditional, undisputed, supreme, unmitigated, sheer, total, through-and-through, 100 percent. **—Ant.** 1 begin, start, initiate, conceive, inaugurate. 2 unfinished, incomplete, imperfect, deficient; crude, rough, raw; partial, conditional.

consummation n. *At the consummation of the negotiations the premier signed the treaty:* achievement, realization, fulfillment, attainment, execution, accomplishment; completion, finish, conclusion, close, culmination, end. **—Ant.** beginning, inception, start, initiation; failure, breakdown.

consumption n. **1.** *Increased consumption of paper is depleting our forests:* use, using up, consuming, utilization; expenditure, depletion, exhaustion, exploitation. **2.** *In the 19th century consumption was a frightening disease:* tuberculosis, TB. **—Ant.** 1 conservation, preservation, saving.

contact n. **1.** *The car turned over when the rear wheels lost contact with the road:* touch, connection; meeting, touching, junction, union, adjacency, abutment. **2.** *The pilot lost contact with the control tower:* communication, connection, association. **—v. 3.** *When these two wires contact, the machine starts:* touch, meet, connect, join. **4.** *I finally contacted him by phone:* communicate with, reach, get in touch with, get hold of.

contagion n. *The contagion spread through several districts:* pestilence, contamination, plague, illness, infection, virus, bane.

contagious adj. *Chicken pox is a contagious disease:* catching, infectious, communicable, transmittable, spreading, spreadable. **—Ant.** noncontagious, noncatching, noninfectious.

contain v. **1.** *The suitcase contained nothing but dirty clothes. The story contained some humorous passages:* hold, include, enclose; accommodate, incorporate, embody, embrace, involve. **2.** *Try to contain your anger:* control, hold back, hold in, suppress, repress, restrain, inhibit, keep within bounds, curb, check, keep back, *Slang* keep the lid on. **—Ant.** 2 express, vent, release, let out.

container n. *Is that container large enough to hold all the books?:* receptacle, holder; (*variously*) vessel, carton, box, bag, can, bucket, pail, bottle, jar, vat, barrel.

contaminate v. *The oil spill contaminated the river:* taint, pollute, dirty, soil, infect, foul, befoul, make impure, spoil, blight, poison, corrupt, defile, adulterate, debase, besmirch. **—Ant.** purify, clean, cleanse, purge.

contamination n. *The contamination of the water made it unfit to drink:* polluting, dirtying, soiling, fouling, poisoning, defilement, spoiling, adulteration; impurity, pollution, dirtiness, foulness, uncleanness, filth, putridity. **—Ant.** purity, cleanness.

contemplate v. **1.** *The Roman augurs contemplated the stars for signs of things to come:* regard, survey, examine, inspect, scan, note, look at fixedly, view attentively, stare at, gaze at, observe. **2.** *Contemplate the problem before making a final decision:* ponder, mull over, reflect upon, think about, consider fully, deliberate on, cogitate on, weigh, meditate on, speculate about, muse about, ruminate. **3.** *The travel agent contemplates trouble in obtaining hotel reservations. Our neighbor contemplates moving to Chicago:* expect, anticipate, envision, imagine, project; plan, intend, look forward to, think of, aspire to, have in view. **—Ant.** 1 disregard, overlook, ignore.

contemplation n. **1.** *The tourists' contemplation of the Alps was obstructed by fog:* viewing, observation, inspection, examination, seeing, survey, scanning, looking, gazing. **2.** *The governor reached his decision after a great deal of contemplation:* thought, thinking, reflection, cogitation, pondering, meditation, study, deliberation, consideration, musing, rumination, reverie.

contemplative adj. *De Gaulle personified the "man of action," so we were surprised by the contemplative tone of his writings:* thoughtful, reflective, meditative, musing, ruminating, cogitative, pensive, speculative, introspective, studious, engrossed, lost in thought. **—Ant.** active, practical, pragmatic; thoughtless, impetuous, impulsive.

contemporary adj. **1.** *Do you prefer contemporary furniture?:* modern, up-to-date, up-to-the-minute, current, present-day, recent, late, new, newfangled, brand-new, ultra-modern, advanced, *Slang* with-it. **2.** *Hitler was contemporary with Mussolini:* of the same time, coexistent, concurrent, contemporaneous, coincident, simultaneous. **—Ant.** 1 antique, old-fashioned, old, early, out-of-date, archaic, obsolete.

contempt n. *Traitors have always been treated with contempt:* scorn, disdain, derision, ridicule, shame, humiliation, disgrace, dishonor, ignominy; disrepute, disfavor, disregard, disgust, distaste, repugnance, revulsion, aversion, detestation, loathing, hatred, hate, abhorrence, antipathy. **—Ant.** honor, respect, esteem, admiration, regard; liking, love.

contemptible adj. *Spreading ugly gossip is contemptible:* mean, vile, low, base, shameful, ignominious, miserable, wretched, unworthy, abject, cheap, shabby, paltry; disgusting, repugnant, revolting, despicable, detestable. **—Ant.** honorable, respectful, admirable, laudable, praiseworthy, worthy; pleasant, attractive, appealing.

contemptuous *adj. Snobs are usually contemptuous of people they feel to be beneath them:* scornful, disrespectful, insolent, disdainful, arrogant, snobbish, condescending, haughty, lordly, pompous, supercilious, derisive. —**Ant.** humble, awestruck; respectful, deferential, civil, obliging, gracious, amicable, admiring.

contend *v.* **1.** *It is hard to contend with poverty. Three students contended for the prize:* fight, struggle, strive, contest, combat, battle, war, wrestle, grapple, tussle, jostle, spar, clash, skirmish; compete, vie, be a rival. **2.** *The suspect contended that the witness was lying:* assert, declare, avow, aver, claim, insist, hold, maintain, put forward, allege, propound; argue, quarrel, debate, dispute. —**Ant.** 1 concede, yield, surrender, give up. 2 deny, disavow, refute.

content¹ *n.* **1.** (*Often plural*) *Empty out the contents of your purse. The content of this can is seven ounces of tuna fish:* thing contained, insides, load; capacity, volume, area, size. **2.** *The content of his argument was weak:* substance, essence, heart, core, thoughts, ideas, matter, meaning, gist, thesis, text.

content² *adj.* **1.** *Many people are content with a routine life:* satisfied, contented, gratified, wanting no more, pleased, happy, comfortable, complacent; untroubled, unconcerned, unmoved, at ease, serene, at rest. —*v.* **2.** *The cozy fire and good company contented him:* satisfy, suffice, comfort, gratify, please, make easy, cheer, set at ease, appease. —*n.* **3.** *The children ate to their heart's content:* satisfaction, contentment, gratification, comfort, peace of mind, peace, serenity, pleasure, happiness. —**Ant.** 1–3 discontent. 1 dissatisfied, unsatisfied, unhappy, displeased, uncomfortable; troubled, concerned, worried, restless. 2 dissatisfy, displease, provoke, pique, upset, annoy. 3 dissatisfaction, discomfort, unhappiness, displeasure.

contented *adj. Are you contented with things as they are?:* satisfied, content, gratified, pleased, happy; comfortable, at ease, serene, at peace. —**Ant.** discontented, discontent, dissatisfied, displeased, uncomfortable, uneasy, worried, troubled, concerned, annoyed, piqued.

contention *n.* **1.** *Border raiding led to even more contention:* struggle, strife, conflict, combat, altercation, feud, wrangle, rivalry, contest; argument, debate, dispute, disagreement, controversy, dispute, dissension, falling out, opposition, discord. **2.** *It was his contention that she was lazy:* allegation, charge, assertion, claim, position, point. —**Ant.** 1 peace; accord, agreement.

contentment *n. The baby finished his milk with a smile of contentment:* satisfaction, content, contentedness, gratification, happiness, pleasure, peace, ease, serenity, comfort. —**Ant.** discontent, dissatisfaction, unhappiness, displeasure, discomfort.

contest *n.* **1.** *It was a bitter contest of wills. She will enter the beauty contest:* conflict, struggle, fight, battle, combat, war, encounter, bout, engagement, dispute; competition, match, tournament, tourney, rivalry, game. —*v.* **2.** *The soldiers contested the valley to the end:* fight for, battle for, combat for, struggle for, compete for, contend for, vie for. **3.** *The referee's decision was contested by the loser:* dispute, call in question, argue against, challenge, debate, oppose, controvert, object to. —**Ant.** 1 agreement, accord, peace. 2 relinquish, surrender, yield, give up. 3 accept, agree to, approve, support, maintain.

contestant *n. There were seven contestants in the race:* candidate, competitor, contender, contester, challenger, adversary, antagonist, aspirant, entrant, participant, player.

context *n. The election can be understood only in the context of the country's history:* framework, setting, frame of reference, ambience, situation, environment, surroundings, circumstances, background, connection, relationship, conditions, precincts, milieu, climate, atmosphere, meaning.

contiguous *adj. Their farms were contiguous, and the families were great friends:* adjoining, bordering, abutting, adjacent, next-door, neighboring, tangent, touching, conterminous; nearby, close, close-by, handy. —**Ant.** remote, distant, far-off, faraway.

continence *n. The minister advised continence:* self-restraint, forbearance, abstinence, moderation; (*variously*) purity, chastity, sobriety, temperance. —**Ant.** incontinence, abandon, self-indulgence, excess; licentiousness, wantonness, drunkenness.

contingency *n. We must be prepared for any contingency:* emergency, unforeseen event, likelihood, possibility, accident; extremity, urgency, predicament.

contingent *adj. Whether the picnic is held or not is contingent on the weather:* dependent, subject to, controlled by, conditioned. —**Ant.** independent, uncontrolled, unrelated.

continual *adj.* **1.** *Traffic passed in a long, continual flow:* ceaseless, unceasing, continuous, constant, incessant, unremitting, perpetual, perennial, never-ending, unending, endless, interminable, everlasting, eternal, unbroken, uninterrupted. **2.** *She was tired by the continual trips to the grocery, school, and office:* frequent, habitual, constant, recurring, persistent, oft-repeated. —**Ant.** 1 ceasing, terminable, broken, fitful, spasmodic, intermittent, irregular. 2 infrequent, rare, occasional, sporadic, spasmodic, exceptional.

continuance *n. Investors hope for a continuance of prosperity:* continuation, continuing, persistence, perseverance, lasting, permanence, stay, extension, protraction, prolongation. —**Ant.** end, cessation, stopping, termination.

continuation *n. This new stretch of road is just a continuation of the old highway:* addition, continuance, continuing, extension, prolongation, protraction, sequence, sequel, supplement. —**Ant.** end, cessation, termination.

continue *v.* **1.** *The rain continued all day. After the detour, the road continues all the way to*

Boston: keep on, keep up, go on, proceed, persist, persevere, last, endure, extend, carry on, drag on; resume. **2.** *Mr. Keppel will continue as principal of the school:* remain, stay, stay on, keep on, carry on, abide. **—Ant.** 1 discontinue, stop, cease, desist, quit, pause, stay. 2 leave, resign, retire, quit, step down.

continuity *n. When the typist got sick, another typist was employed to keep up the continuity of the work:* flow, progression, succession, continuation, continuance, continuum, chain.

continuous *adj.* **1.** *A continuous line of cars stretched as far as the eye could see:* unbroken, successive, progressive, consecutive; linked, connected. **2.** *This continuous hot weather is oppressive:* unremitting, constant, uninterrupted, unceasing, incessant, interminable, continual, continuing, lasting, ceaseless, steady, endless, perpetual, everlasting, eternal, persistent, persevering, enduring, extensive, protracted, prolonged. **—Ant.** 1 intermittent, broken, disconnected. 2 passing, spasmodic, sporadic, occasional; inconstant, interrupted, ending, ceasing.

contort *v. His face contorted with rage:* twist, bend, distort, deform, warp, be misshapen. **—Ant.** straighten, unbend.

contour *n. The chair follows the contour of the body:* outline, profile, shape, form, silhouette, figure, lines, physiognomy.

contraband *n. Customs agents checked the ship for contraband:* prohibited articles, illegal imports, illegal exports, smuggled goods, unlicensed goods, unlawful trafficking, bootlegging, black-marketeering.

contract *n.* **1.** *The lawyer drew up a binding contract:* written agreement, legal document, compact, pact, treaty, covenant, arrangement. *—v.* **2.** *When you bend your elbow, the muscles of the arm contract:* draw together, become smaller, compress, tighten, constrict; shorten, narrow, shrink, dwindle, condense, reduce. **3.** *He contracted huge debts by rash spending:* acquire, incur, get, take, develop, assume, absorb, enter into, engender. **4.** *The firm contracted to deliver the merchandise in six months:* sign an agreement, agree, pledge, promise, make a bargain, undertake, negotiate, come to terms. **—Ant.** 2 expand, stretch, distend, enlarge, dilate, swell, lengthen, widen, grow, increase. 3 avoid, evade, elude, escape, shun, eschew; avert, ward off. 4 disagree, refuse.

contraction *n. Cold weather causes a contraction of two inches in the bridge:* drawing in, constriction, compression, tightening, shrinkage, shriveling, decrease, reduction, lessening, shortening, narrowing, condensation, abbreviation. **—Ant.** expansion, extension, increase, stretching, swelling, enlargement, lengthening, widening, broadening.

contradict *v. The witness contradicted the defendant's testimony:* refute, deny, confute, controvert, impugn, oppose, counter, dispute, be contrary to, disagree with, gainsay, rebut; disprove, belie. **—Ant.** corroborate, confirm, verify, substantiate, authenticate, agree with, affirm, sustain, support, endorse.

contradiction *n. One story is a direct contradiction of the other. The chairman wouldn't listen to any contradiction of his opinions:* refutation, denial, confutation, disagreement, rebuttal, counter, negation. **—Ant.** corroboration, confirmation, verification, substantiation, affirmation, support, endorsement; agreement, accord.

contradictory *adj. The two experts had contradictory views on the matter:* conflicting, opposing, dissenting, contrary, disagreeing, countervailing, antithetical, discrepant, irreconcilable, refutatory, inconsistent. **—Ant.** similar, like, parallel, agreeing.

contrary *adj.* **1.** *Lying is contrary to my beliefs. The boy was swimming in a direction contrary to the current:* opposed, opposite, contradictory, counter, at variance, at cross purposes, conflicting, incompatible, antithetical, inimical, converse, discordant, disparate. **2.** *Don't be so contrary!:* disagreeing, contradictory, unaccommodating, stubborn, obstinate, intractable, refractory, balky, recalcitrant, willful, headstrong, froward, wayward; hostile, antagonistic. **3.** *Oranges won't grow in a contrary climate:* unfavorable, adverse, disagreeable, unpropitious, untoward, inauspicious, unsuitable, unfitting. **—Ant.** 1 consistent, parallel, accordant. 2 complaisant, compliant, obliging, accommodating, acquiescent, tractable, agreeing, unassuming, submissive; good-natured, agreeable, pleasant, peaceful. 3 favorable, propitious, auspicious, suitable, fitting.

contrast *v.* **1.** *Contrast Keats's poetry with Dylan Thomas's. This cold weather contrasts with last week's heat:* differentiate, set in opposition; differ, diverge, deviate, depart, disagree with. *—n.* **2.** *In contrast to our old house, the new one is a mansion! There's a remarkable contrast between England and Scotland:* comparing differences, comparison, differentiation; difference, dissimilarity, unlikeness, variance, disparity, divergence, distinction. **—Ant.** 1 liken, compare, resemble, parallel. 2 similarity, likeness, comparison, parallelism, sameness, similitude, agreement.

contravene *v.* **1.** *He didn't realize he had contravened one of the tribe's most stringent laws:* infringe on, violate, transgress, trespass against, act against, breach, disobey, overreach, overstep, infract, offend, encroach upon. **2.** *We felt that one of the proposals had to be contravened:* oppose, deny, contradict, gainsay, fight, combat, repudiate, spurn, reject, abjure, exclude, resist, disclaim, disown; nullify, abrogate, annul. **—Ant.** 1 observe, respect, comply with, adhere to. 2 endorse, support, go along with, agree with, second.

contribute *v.* **1.** *Every household contributed to the Community Chest:* give, donate, bestow, grant, confer, hand out, present, endow. **2.** *Air pollution contributes to respiratory diseases:* advance, influence, lead to, help bring about, forward, be conducive to, have a hand in, bear a part. **—Ant.** 1 take, receive; withhold, deny. 2 curb, check, slow, impede, detract.

contribution n. Each five-dollar contribution will buy the orphans milk for a week: donation, gift, bestowal, endowment, grant, benefaction, dispensation, subsidy, offering; charity, alms.

contrite adj. His contrite manner made us forgive him: conscience-stricken, sorrowful, regretful, repentant, rueful, penitent, remorseful, apologetic, chastened, humbled. **—Ant.** proud, pleased, uncontrite, unrepentant, unapologetic.

contrition n. Did Judas feel contrition for his betrayal of Christ?: self-reproach, regret, remorse, qualms of conscience, compunction; repentance, penitence, penance, atonement.

contrivance n. **1.** This contrivance peels and cores apples: device, contraption, gadget, instrument, apparatus, implement, tool, machine, mechanism, invention; Slang gizmo, doodad, thingamajig. **2.** The boy tried every contrivance to get the puppy to follow him home: plan, trick, stratagem, plot, artifice, intrigue, measure, design, machination.

contrive v. **1.** She contrived a bookcase out of bricks and boards: devise, create, concoct, improvise, invent, design. **2.** The youths contrived to stow away on the ship: scheme, plot, plan, devise a plan; maneuver, manage, effect by stratagem.

control v. **1.** The pilot controls the plane from the cockpit. The treasurer controls the expenditure of funds: command, govern, rule, master, regulate, manipulate, manage, have charge of, superintend, supervise, steer; dominate, reign over. **2.** Control your temper: restrain, restrict, repress, subdue, contain, curb, master, bridle. **—n. 3.** The small island was under the control of Great Britain. The driver lost control of the car: command, management, mastery, regulation, direction, sway, rule, dominion, domination, jurisdiction, authority, supervision, charge. **4.** Aspirin serves as an effective control for most headaches: curb, restraint, suppressant, brake. **—Ant.** 2 free, release, let loose, give vent.

controversial adj. James Joyce's Ulysses was a controversial book. Abortion is a highly controversial matter: widely discussed, causing debate; polemical, debatable, disputable, arguable, open to discussion, questionable, at issue. **—Ant.** noncontroversial, undebatable, indisputable, incontrovertible, unquestionable, proven, sure, certain.

controversy n. There was a huge controversy over the plans for the new school: debate, discussion, dispute, contention, argument, quarrel, wrangle, squabble, altercation; disagreement, dissension. **—Ant.** agreement, unanimity, accord.

controvert v. He was able to controvert the argument point by point: deny, disprove, contradict, oppose, refute, dispute, rebut, confute, confound, contravene, gainsay, disaffirm; challenge, question, protest. **—Ant.** corroborate, prove, affirm, demonstrate, uphold, verify.

contumacious adj. She was too contumacious ever to take anyone's advice: contrary, perverse, rebellious, froward, factious, disobedient, mutinous, seditious, refractory, fractious, unruly, disrespectful, ungovernable, unmanageable, insolent, insubordinate, intractable, headstrong. **—Ant.** compliant, acquiescent, obedient, submissive, amenable, tractable, docile.

contumely n. Hamlet found it difficult to bear "the proud man's contumely": abuse, contempt, rudeness, insolence, scorn, disdain, brusqueness, obloquy, reproach, opprobrium, invective, vituperation, scurrility, billingsgate; arrogance, pomposity, overbearingness, haughtiness. **—Ant.** civility, politeness, regard, respect, consideration, esteem.

contusion n. The accident wasn't serious; we only suffered a few contusions: bruise, discoloration, black-and-blue mark; abrasion, injury, hurt, sore, black eye; Slang mouse, shiner.

conundrum n. No one in the room could find the answer to the conundrum: puzzle, riddle, enigma, mystery, poser, puzzler, paradox, arcanum, brain-teaser, stumper, stopper, Chinese puzzle, rebus, problem.

convalescence n. Fresh air and sunshine helped the patient's convalescence: recovery, recuperation, restoration, return to health, Archaic recruit.

convene v. The club convenes every month. The chairman convened the committee to put the issue to a vote: gather, come together, assemble, hold a session, bring together, summon, call together, convoke, muster, collect, round up. **—Ant.** adjourn, disperse, dissolve, dismiss, disband.

convenience n. **1.** The campers missed the convenience of a refrigerator: usefulness, utility, service, benefit; handiness, accessibility, availability. **2.** The new house has every modern convenience: comfort, accommodation, facility; appliance, work saver. **3.** Shopping bags are provided for the customers' convenience: accommodation, use, ease, enjoyment, pleasure, satisfaction. **4.** Please call at your earliest convenience: opportunity, chance, convenient time, suitable time. **—Ant.** 1 inconvenience, nuisance, uselessness, hardship. 2 nuisance. 3 inconvenience, dissatisfaction, discomfort, annoyance.

convenient adj. **1.** The height of this lamp isn't convenient for reading: suitable, suited, useful, helpful, adapted, easy to use, handy, serviceable, advantageous, beneficial. **2.** The parking lot is convenient to the office: easily accessible, nearby, at hand. **—Ant.** 1 inconvenient, unsuitable, awkward, unwieldy, useless, unhandy. 2 inconvenient, inaccessible, distant.

convent n. The religious girl wanted to join a convent: society of nuns, nunnery, cloister.

convention n. **1.** The Republican presidential candidate will be chosen at the national convention: assembly, conference, congress, convocation, conclave, caucus, meeting, gathering. **2.** Youth often questions the conventions of society: custom, social rule, standard, code, precept, practice, propriety, protocol, formality.

conventional adj. White is the conventional

color of a wedding gown: traditional, customary, accepted, proper, orthodox; normal, standard, regular, common, routine, usual. —**Ant.** unconventional, unorthodox, extraordinary, uncommon, abnormal.

converge *v. The Mississippi and Missouri rivers converge at St. Louis. A lens converges light rays:* come together, meet, approach; focus, concentrate, bring together. —**Ant.** diverge, separate, part, scatter, disperse.

conversant *adj. We need someone who's at least conversant with storage systems:* familiar, acquainted, knowledgeable of, well-informed, up on, proficient, tutored, erudite, skilled, practiced, privy to, on good terms with; *French* au fait, au courant. —**Ant.** ignorant, unversed, unfamiliar, uninformed.

conversation *n. We had a long telephone conversation:* talk, discourse, dialogue, chat, chit-chat, tête-à-tête, palaver, confabulation; *Slang* gabfest, rap, bull session.

converse[1] *v. We conversed for hours on the phone:* talk, speak together, engage in conversation, chat, chitchat, confabulate, palaver; *Slang* gab, chin, jaw, chew the rag, chew the fat, shoot the breeze, rap.

converse[2] *n. His political views are the converse of mine:* opposite, reverse, contrary, antithesis. —**Ant.** identical, same.

conversion *n.* **1.** *The conversion of a caterpillar into a butterfly is miraculous:* change, transformation, modification, transfiguration, metamorphosis, transmutation. **2.** *Saint Patrick is traditionally regarded as responsible for Ireland's conversion to Christianity:* change, change of religion, changeover, change of heart, change in beliefs.

convert *v.* **1.** *The plant converts crude oil into gasoline:* change, transform, modify, turn. **2.** *He converted to Judaism. The explanation converted him to our point of view:* change one's religion, change one's belief; cause a change of opinion, proselytize. —*n.* **3.** *He is a convert to Buddhism:* converted person; proselyte, neophyte, novice.

convex *adj. The outside of an eyeglass lens is convex:* curved outward, rounded, protuberant, bulging. —**Ant.** concave, sunken, hollowed out.

convey *v.* **1.** *The pipeline conveys natural gas to the Midwest:* carry, transport, bear, conduct, bring, move, transmit. **2.** *Please convey my best wishes to your parents:* communicate, make known, impart, transmit, dispatch, relate, give, tell, disclose, reveal, divulge, confide to. **3.** *The old man conveyed the family farm to his son:* transfer, deliver over, cede, deed, consign, grant; will, bequeath, leave. —**Ant.** 2 conceal, hide, receive, listen. 3 retain, keep, hold on to, cling to.

conveyance *n.* **1.** *The trucking firm handles the conveyance of lumber to building sites:* conveying, transport, transportation, carrying, transfer, carriage, movement, transmission. **2.** *What kind of conveyance does the dairy use to deliver the milk?:* transportation, vehicle; (*variously*)

bus, car, truck, rig, carriage, van, wagon, cart, buggy.

convict *v.* **1.** *He was convicted of manslaughter:* declare guilty, prove guilty, find guilty; condemn, doom. —*n.* **2.** *The convicts complained bitterly about prison conditions:* prisoner, felon; *Slang* jailbird, yardbird, con. —**Ant.** 1 acquit, find innocent.

conviction *n.* **1.** *His political convictions are very radical:* belief, view, viewpoint, opinion, judgment, principle, tenet, faith, persuasion, position, creed, doctrine, dogma. **2.** *The audience was swayed by the speaker's conviction:* certainty, certitude, assurance, firm persuasion, steadfastness, intensity, ardor, earnestness, fervor, fever, zeal. —**Ant.** 2 doubt, uncertainty, misgiving, hesitation.

convince *v. The politician's speech convinced the voters he was the person for the job:* persuade, prevail upon, sway, win over, bring around, influence, assure, satisfy.

convincing *adj. They thought that she presented a convincing argument:* conclusive, persuasive, credible, authentic, believable, credible, plausible, likely, satisfying, trustworthy, trusty, valid, powerful, solid, telling. —**Ant.** dubious, far-fetched, implausible, inconclusive, incredible, unlikely.

convivial *adj. It's fun to take a tour with convivial people:* sociable, friendly, companionable, genial, affable, agreeable, fun-loving, merry, jovial, gregarious, festive. —**Ant.** unsociable, unfriendly, reserved, reticent, serious, sober, grave, sedate, solemn.

convocation *n. A convocation of experts was called to debate the issue:* convention, congress, conference, caucus, council, conclave, assembly, gathering, ingathering, meeting, roundup, roster, muster. —**Ant.** adjournment, dismissal, disbanding.

convolution *n. The children were fascinated by the convolutions of the snake:* coiling, coil, twisting, twist, winding, undulation, contortion; sinuosity, sinuousness, tortuousness; maze, labyrinth. —**Ant.** uncoiling, unwinding.

convoy *v.* **1.** *A Coast Guard cutter convoyed the ship into the port:* escort, conduct, usher, accompany, go along with. —*n.* **2.** *Seven destroyers formed the troop ship's convoy:* escort, protection, safeguard, armed guard; (*variously*) column, fleet, formation.

convulsion *n.* **1.** *The patient had an epileptic convulsion:* spasm, fit, contortion, seizure, paroxysm. **2.** *The audience broke into convulsions of laughter:* outburst, fit, spasm; commotion, disturbance, tumult, agitation.

cool *adj.* **1.** *Today was a cool day for July:* slightly cold, somewhat cold, chill, chilly, not warm. **2.** *The announcer had a cool, unruffled manner:* calm, unexcited, composed, unflappable, imperturbable, self-possessed, collected, deliberate, cool-headed, undisturbed, untroubled, unemotional, dispassionate, impassive, serene. **3.** *He seemed so cool I feared I had offended him:* unfriendly, uncordial, unsociable, distant, reserved, aloof, standoffish, offish, unresponsive, indifferent, nonchalant, cold, icy, frosty. —*v.* **4.** *Cool the soup before freezing it:* make cool, become cool, chill, lose heat. —**Ant.** 1 warm, *Informal* warmish. 2 excited, frenzied, frantic, wild, delirious, impassioned, high-strung, nervous, tense, wrought-up, over-wrought, hysterical, agitated, perturbed, disturbed, troubled, upset. 3 friendly, cordial, warm, responsive. 4 warm, heat.

cooperate *v. Please cooperate with us in evacuating the island quickly:* work together, participate, collaborate, unite, act jointly, join, join forces, take part, share in, pitch in, work side by side, go along, bear part in, stand shoulder to shoulder, join hands, pull together. —**Ant.** oppose, fight, conflict, rival; counteract, negate, neutralize, nullify.

cooperation *n. With the cooperation of all the employees the work was done on time:* cooperating, working together, participation, collaboration, joint action, teamwork, give and take, pulling together; concurrence, agreement, accordance, concert, détente. —**Ant.** opposition, hindrance, conflicting, rivalry, dissension, infighting; disagreement, discord.

cooperative *adj. The cooperative children helped with the dishes:* helpful, supportive, assisting, pitching in, reciprocal, coordinated, collaborative, collective, collegial, combining, common, concerted, concurring, harmonious, in league, interdependent, joint, shared, symbiotic, synergetic, united, accommodating.

coordinate *v.* **1.** *Try to coordinate the work so that the plasterers are finished before the painters arrive:* organize, order, arrange, systematize, correlate, relate, match, mesh, harmonize. —*adj.* **2.** *The army, navy, and air force are coordinate branches of the armed services:* equal, coequal, parallel, equally important, correlative. —**Ant.** 1 disorganize, muddle. 2 unequal, disparate.

cope *v. An executive has to cope with many business problems every day:* contend, spar, wrestle, face, strive, struggle, tussle, hold one's own; manage, hurdle.

copious *adj. The secretary took copious notes on everything that was said at the meeting:* profuse, plentiful, abundant, bountiful, extensive, full, ample, liberal, generous, lavish, plenteous. —**Ant.** skimpy, sparse, meager, scanty, scant, spare.

copiousness *n. After such copiousness, we were unaccustomed to going without:* plenty, plentifulness, abundance, affluence, bountifulness, bounty, cornucopia, lavishness, luxuriance.

copulate *v. The cats copulated in the back yard:* mate, have sex, breed, fornicate, conjugate, couple, have relations, make love, sleep together.

copy *n.* **1.** *The copy of the painting is very close to the original:* reproduction, facsimile, likeness, duplicate, carbon copy, replica, clone, representation; imitation, counterfeit, forgery, fake, sham. **2.** *The reporter's copy was due at four:* text, story, written material, reportage, manu-

script. —*v.* **3.** *Please copy this letter in triplicate:* make a copy of, reproduce, duplicate, clone; photostat, Xerox. **4.** *Don't copy everything your older brother does!:* emulate, follow, imitate, mimic, ape, parody, mirror, repeat. —**Ant.** 1 original, archetype, prototype, model, pattern. 3 originate, create.

coquette *n. Be careful that little coquette doesn't steal your boyfriend:* flirt, vamp, heartbreaker, *Slang* tease.

cord *n. Wrap the cord tightly around the box:* twine, thin rope, braid, heavy string.

cordial *adj. The hostess gave each guest a cordial greeting:* friendly, gracious, genial, amiable, affable, warm, affectionate, sincere, heartfelt, wholehearted, hearty, good-natured. —**Ant.** unfriendly, ungracious, cool, cold, frigid, indifferent, distant, detached, reserved, aloof, formal, ceremonious.

cordiality *n. She greeted her guests with the utmost cordiality:* friendliness, warmth, affability, amiability, geniality, agreeableness, heartiness, amicability, graciousness, earnestness, sincerity, goodwill, affection. —**Ant.** coldness, insincerity, disagreeableness, ill will.

core *n.* **1.** *Cut out the core of the apple:* kernel, center, central part, innermost part, nucleus. **2.** *Let's get to the core of the matter:* essence, essential part, gist, heart, center, pith, substance, sum and substance, crux, nub, meat; *Slang* guts, brass tacks, nitty-gritty.

corner 1. *If he corners you, he'll tell you all his problems:* trap, grab, seize, back into a corner; *Slang* nail, pigeonhole, collar, nab. —*n.* **2.** *He put plants in all four corners of the room:* angle, bend, nook. **3.** *He got himself into a corner with so many debts:* predicament, dilemma, plight, impasse, awkward position, dead end, blind alley; *Slang* fix, jam, pickle, spot, hole, scrape.

corny *adj. He thinks it's corny to have the guests play Chinese checkers:* hackneyed, trite, commonplace, banal, stale, insipid, stereotyped, platitudinous, ordinary, square, old-fashioned, bromidic, unsophisticated, inane, fatuous, *Slang* hokey. —**Ant.** original, fresh, unhackneyed, sophisticated, unique.

coronet *n. The duke wore his coronet and ceremonial robes:* small crown, diadem; chaplet, tiara, circlet.

corporal *adj. I don't believe in corporal punishment, but I'd love to give that boy a spanking:* bodily, physical, *Archaic* corporeal.

corporation *n. The corporation has branch offices in several cities:* incorporated group, corporate body, association, legal entity; (*loosely*) company, holding company, association, syndicate, combine, conglomeration.

corporeal *adj. Spiritualists believe that an aura surrounds our corporeal being:* physical, bodily; mortal, worldly, nonspiritual, material, perceptible. —**Ant.** spiritual, heavenly, ethereal, religious; intellectual, mental.

corps *n.* **1.** *His father served in the signal corps during the First World War:* military branch; organized body of troops, combat unit, squad, outfit. **2.** *A corps of doctors arrived to inoculate* *the recruits:* team, crew, force, troop, party, band.

corpse *n. The coroner was called to examine the corpse:* dead body, body, cadaver, remains; *Slang* stiff.

corpulent *adj. Overeating had made him corpulent:* fat, obese, overweight, rotund, fleshy, portly, stout, plump, well-padded, chubby, pudgy, roly-poly, chunky; well-fed, hefty; dumpy, lumpish. —**Ant.** emaciated, thin, slender, slim, lean, gaunt, skinny, scrawny; rawboned, lanky.

corpus *n. The corpus of his work was not large:* collection, compilation, core, body, oeuvre, whole, aggregation.

correct *v.* **1.** *Please correct any misspellings in this letter. Wearing glasses should correct your vision:* make right, remove the errors of, amend, rectify, repair, remedy, improve; alter, change, adjust, modify; regulate, fix; rework, revamp, revise. **2.** *His father corrected him when he misbehaved:* chasten, reprimand, admonish, berate, scold, rebuke, censure, reprove, lecture, chide, dress down, take to task, haul over the coals, read the riot act to; punish, castigate, discipline, chastise. —*adj.* **3.** *Each correct answer was worth ten points on the exam:* free from error, accurate, right, faultless, flawless, perfect; exact, precise, true, factual, unerring. **4.** *Correct behavior should be taught in the home:* proper, fitting, fit, appropriate, suitable, seemly, becoming; conventional, acceptable. —**Ant.** 1 spoil, mar, ruin, damage, harm, hurt, injure, impair. 2 excuse, condone, praise, compliment, laud. 3 incorrect, wrong, inaccurate, false, untrue. 4 improper, inappropriate, unfitting, unsuitable, unseemly, unbecoming, unconventional.

correction *n.* **1.** *Make any final corrections before handing in your examination papers. The navigator made a correction to bring the ship back on course:* rectification, improvement, emendation; alteration, change, revision, modification, adjustment. **2.** *The juvenile offenders were sent to a school of correction:* discipline, punishment, reformation, chastisement, castigation.

corrective *adj. The upsurge in crime calls for strong corrective measures. A hearing aid is a corrective device:* counter, counteractive, counterbalancing; reformatory, rectifying; improving, ameliorative, therapeutic, remedial, compensatory; restorative, palliative.

correctly *adv. It often takes time to do something correctly:* properly, rightly, fitly, fittingly, accurately, befittingly, decently, decorously, justly, nicely, well.

correctness *n.* **1.** *They questioned the correctness of his findings:* accuracy, exactitude, truth. **2.** *She was a model of correctness:* properness, propriety, seemliness, civility, decency, decorousness, decorum, fitness, good breeding, orderliness, order.

correlate *v. The attorney tried to correlate the testimony of the two witnesses:* relate, show relationship between, bring together, compare, connect, correspond, parallel. —**Ant.** disconnect, contradict, oppose.

correlation *n. They found little correlation between the two events:* reciprocity, relationship, interrelationship, match, parallel, correspondence, equivalence, interconnection, interdependence.

correspond *v.* **1.** *The two sisters correspond every week:* exchange letters, write letters, communicate, keep in touch, drop a line to. **2.** *The news report doesn't correspond with the facts. His sporty clothes don't correspond with his shy behavior:* agree, conform, concur, coincide, accord, parallel, harmonize, equate, match, fit, suit, tally, dovetail, jibe, square; be similar, be like, be equivalent, be complementary. —**Ant.** 2 differ, disagree, belie, diverge.

correspondence *n.* **1.** *Our correspondence is limited to a few friendly letters. The latest correspondence from the front tells of a great victory:* mail, letters, missives, epistles; dispatches, bulletins, communiqués. **2.** *There is no correspondence between the two stories:* similarity, resemblance, relation, analogy, association.

corresponding *adj. A corresponding act occurred later:* correspondent, correlative, akin, alike, comparable, equivalent, like, matching, parallel, reciprocal, similar, analogous.

corridor *n. Each office opens onto the corridor:* hallway, hall, passageway; passage, aisle; approach, way, road, artery.

corroborate *v. Recent experiments seem to corroborate Einstein's theory:* prove, verify, confirm, uphold, support, sustain, substantiate, affirm, validate, bear out, vindicate, authenticate, certify, endorse, back, back up. —**Ant.** disprove, contradict, refute, nullify, negate, invalidate.

corrode *v. Battery acid had corroded the inside of the flashlight:* eat away, wear away, erode, disintegrate; rust, oxidize.

corrosive *adj. The spilled acid had a corrosive effect:* corroding, eroding, erosive, oxidizing, caustic, biting, cutting.

corrugated *adj. The box is made of corrugated cardboard:* bent into folds, ridged, furrowed, crenelated, puckered, pleated, fluted, grooved, creased, wrinkled, crinkled.

corrupt *adj.* **1.** *Corrupt politicians must be thrown out of office:* dishonest, dishonorable, crooked, shady, unscrupulous, fraudulent, unethical, unprincipled. **2.** *Corrupt friends led him astray:* wicked, immoral, depraved, debased, iniquitous, base, mean, low, sinful, evil. —*v.* **3.** *Criminal parents could corrupt any child:* make immoral, deprave, debase, subvert, lead astray, debauch; contaminate, poison; pervert, seduce. —**Ant.** 1 honest, honorable, upright, ethical, principled, scrupulous, righteous, moral; *Slang* straight. 2 virtuous, moral, ethical, righteous, noble, high-minded. 3 reform, uplift.

corruption *n.* **1.** *Our police department seems free of corruption:* dishonest practices, dishonesty, graft, bribery, fraud, malfeasance, shady dealings. **2.** *The Bible warns against sin and corruption:* wickedness, depravity, evil ways, immorality, iniquity, sinfulness, debauchery, perversion, turpitude, vice, wrongdoing, degeneracy, decadence, looseness. **—Ant.** 1 honesty, righteousness, scrupulousness, trustworthiness, integrity. 2 goodness, good, righteousness, morality, nobility, purity.

corsair *n. Setting sail from Algiers, the ship was set upon by a band of corsairs:* pirate, privateer, buccaneer, sea rover, sea robber, picaroon, freebooter, marauder, plunderer, sea dog, sea wolf, viking, sea looter; Long John Silver, Blackbeard, Captain Kidd.

corset *n. She needs a corset to control her ample figure:* girdle, foundation garment, corselet, laces.

cortege *n. The mourners headed a cortege that stretched for more than a mile:* funeral procession, train, entourage, escort, retinue, company, attendants, staff, suite, column, string, caravan, line, motorcade, parade, cavalcade, following.

cosmetic *n.* **1.** *The actor applied cosmetics before going on stage:* makeup, greasepaint, cover-up, paint, rouge, foundation, pancake; *Informal* war paint. *—adj.* **2.** *She got the full cosmetic treatment at the beauty salon:* beautifying, decorative, enhancing, improving, corrective. **3.** *Mildew on the wallboard showed the renovation was merely cosmetic:* superficial, surface, shallow, cursory, passing, skin-deep.

cosmic *adj.* **1.** *Our science library has a history of cosmic theory since Galileo. Without math and physics, cosmic space and time can't be understood:* of the universe, (*especially*) extraterrestrial, of outer space, interplanetary, interstellar. **2.** *This is a matter of cosmic importance:* vast, immense, enormous, widespread, colossal, stupendous, grandiose; infinite, universal. **—Ant.** 2 minor, small, minute, infinitesimal, microscopic, minuscule.

cosmopolitan *adj.* **1.** *San Francisco is a very cosmopolitan city:* sophisticated, broad-minded, worldly, worldly-wise, urbane, international, not provincial. *—n.* **2.** *A true cosmopolitan is as much at home in Tokyo as in London:* man of the world, sophisticate, cosmopolite, citizen of the world, world traveler, globe trotter. **—Ant.** 1 provincial, insular, parochial, narrow-minded, bigoted, hidebound, rigid, isolated; rustic, countrified. 2 provincial, rustic, boor.

cosmos *n. There may be other intelligent life elsewhere in the cosmos:* universe, interstellar system, macrocosm, earth and the heavens, the whole wide world; heavenly bodies, starry host, vault of heaven, stars.

cost *n.* **1.** *What's the cost of a European vacation?:* price, charge, amount, outlay, expense, expenditure, market price, bill, tab, toll, fee; worth, value, face value, valuation. **2.** *The soldiers captured the hill at great cost:* loss, sacrifice; expense, price, penalty; pain, distress, suffering, hurt, harm, injury, damage. *—v.* **3.** *This mink coat costs $3,000:* sell for, be priced at, go for, fetch, bring in, take, amount to, come to, *Informal* run, set back. **4.** *That mistake will certainly cost you!:* harm, injure, hurt, damage, burden, weigh down; cause suffering to, cause to lose, make sacrifice.

costly *adj.* **1.** *The house is too costly for us to buy:* expensive, high-priced, extravagant, dear, precious, stiff, steep, exorbitant. **2.** *The general's decision to invade was a costly mistake:* causing much loss, disastrous, catastrophic; harmful, damaging, deleterious. **—Ant.** 1 cheap, inexpensive; reasonable, fair.

costume *n. The peasants danced in their native costumes:* national dress, indigenous garb, historical dress; outfit, attire, dress, garb, raiment, apparel, garments, clothing, clothes; uniform, livery.

coterie *n. The literary coterie lunches at the hotel every Thursday:* set, clique, faction, camp, circle, crowd, group, band, clan, crew, club, gang.

cottage *n. The old wood-carver lived in a cottage on the side of the hill:* simple house, rustic house, cot, bungalow; lodge, chalet; hut, shack. **—Ant.** palace, castle, château, mansion, manor house, town house.

couch *n.* **1.** *Sit beside me on the couch:* sofa, divan, davenport, settee; (*variously*) lounge, chesterfield, love seat, daybed. *—v.* **2.** *He couched his demands in careful, polite language:* express, voice, word, utter, put, state, set forth, phrase, frame; draw up, draft.

cough *n.* **1.** *With her cold came a nasty cough:* bark, hack, whoop *—v.* **2.** *He coughed to restore silence:* bark, hack, hawk, hem.

council *n.* **1.** *A council of leading educators is meeting in Memphis:* convention, conference, congress, conclave, assembly, convocation, colloquy, synod; gathering, congregation. **2.** *The city council met to discuss the new proposal:* legislative body, assembly, governing body, representatives; cabinet, privy council, chamber, ministry, board, panel, committee.

counsel *n.* **1.** *Seek an architect's counsel before building the house:* advice, opinion, guidance, recommendation, suggestion; consultation, advisement. **2.** *On advice of counsel they settled out of court:* lawyer, legal adviser, counselor, counselor-at-law, attorney; *British* barrister, solicitor. *—v.* **3.** *The teacher counseled the boy to study harder:* advise, recommend, suggest, advocate, prompt, urge, charge, call for, instruct; warn, admonish, caution.

counselor or **counsellor** *n.* **1.** *Each student has a counselor to guide in the choice of classes. The queen met with her counselor:* adviser, instructor, tutor, mentor; cabinet member, minister. **2.** *The counselor for the defense asked that the case be dismissed:* legal adviser, lawyer, attorney, counsel, counselor-at-law, advocate; *British* barrister, solicitor.

count *v.* **1.** *Count from one to ten:* add one by one, number, enumerate, numerate, tick off; add up, total. **2.** *Six people are on the trip if you count the children. The old friend was counted as a member of the family:* include, take into account, consider; regard, look on, ascribe, attribute, impute. **3.** *Count yourself lucky to have escaped serious injury:* consider, regard, deem, hold, look upon, rate, reckon, estimate, judge. **4.** *Every penny counts:* matter, be worthwhile, tell, be effective, carry weight, be important, enter into consideration, add to the number. **5.** *According to my count there are 27 people present:* total, tally, calculation, enumeration, computation, reckoning, numbering, numeration. **—Ant.** 2 exclude, except, leave out, ignore.

countenance *n.* **1.** *He may have aged since I last saw him, but I'd recognize his countenance anywhere:* expression, look, mien, appearance, air, aspect, presence, visage, traits; profile, silhouette, face, features, contours, build, physiognomy. **2.** *The mayor will give his countenance to the new tax proposal:* approval, sanction, approbation, moral support, advocacy, auspices, encouragement, championship; assistance, help, aid, promotion. **—v. 3.** *The navy will countenance longer shore leave for all personnel:* permit, approve, sanction, endorse, condone; advocate, support, promote, further, advance, uphold, forward, favor, champion, back, work for. **—Ant.** 2 disapproval, discouragement, disapprobation, disfavor, opposition. 3 prohibit, disapprove, oppose, condemn; discourage, hinder, thwart, frustrate, block.

counter[1] *n.* **1.** *Take your groceries to the checkout counter. Watches are at the jewelry counter. Let's eat at a lunch counter:* table, stand, display case; bar, fountain, soda fountain, buffet. **2.** *In Monopoly each player receives $200 when his counter passes "Go":* playing piece, piece, disk, man.

counter[2] *adv., adj.* **1.** *The election results are running counter to all predictions:* contrary, contrary to, contra, contradictory, in the opposite way, at variance, in defiance of, opposite, opposed, against, conflicting, in conflict. **—v. 2.** *After being hit by a left, the boxer countered with a left of his own:* retaliate, strike back, fight back, hit back, get even, pay back; oppose, offset, reverse, resist, defy. **—Ant.** 1 in agreement, similar to, parallel to, in unison with, as planned, as expected, accordant with, coincident with, consonant with. 2 accept, take; yield, give in, give up, surrender.

counteract *v.* *This medicine should counteract the fever:* act against, nullify, negate, neutralize, undo, offset, counterbalance, contravene; fight, oppose, check, thwart, frustrate, hinder, restrain, repress, curb, resist; alleviate, assuage; clash with, conflict with, counterattack; overpower, overcome, defeat, annihilate. **—Ant.** aid, assist, abet, reinforce, support, help, cooperate with, promote, advance, forward, further, encourage.

counterbalance *v.* *In general the virtues of the book counterbalanced its shortcomings:* offset, compensate for, atone for, make up for, correct, amend, rectify, check, balance, equalize, neutralize, recompense, make good, make compensation, counteract, counterweigh, countervail, counterpoise, outweigh, outbalance, set off, redeem.

counterfeit *adj.* **1.** *The counterfeit money fooled many bank tellers:* forged, fake, phony, not genuine, bogus, sham, fraudulent, imitation,

simulated, artificial, ersatz, spurious, feigned, make-believe. **—n. 2.** *The painting is not really a Rembrandt but a counterfeit:* forgery, fake, phony, fraud, sham, imitation, facsimile, substitute, copy. **—Ant.** 1 genuine, authentic, real, the real McCoy, good, original.

countermand *v.* *The second order the soldiers received seemed to countermand the first:* revoke, rescind, cancel, abrogate, overrule, call back, abolish, recall, withdraw, retract, annul, void, quash, nullify, disestablish, repeal, disenact, do away with, write off, declare null and void, reverse, set aside, render null and void. **—Ant.** endorse, support, reinforce, second, reiterate.

counterpart *n.* *Canada's Prime Minister is the counterpart of the U.S. President. The two cars are exact counterparts in make, model, and color:* equal, one comparable to another, correspondent, correlative, parallel; match, twin, double, fellow, duplicate, copy, mate, the spitting image, doppelgänger. **—Ant.** antithesis, opposite, contradiction, contrast.

countless *adj.* *There are countless stars in the sky:* innumerable, numberless, infinite, endless, myriad, multitudinous, unlimited, limitless, untold, immeasurable, measureless, unnumbered, incalculable. **—Ant.** finite, limited, enumerable.

country *n.* **1.** *The plane flew over mountainous country:* terrain, land, area, region, district, territory; countryside, landscape, scenery. **2.** *Over 130 countries are members of the United Nations:* nation, state, kingdom, commonwealth, realm. **3.** *The country will elect a new president this year:* nation, population, populace, inhabitants, citizens, people, natives, public, community, countrymen. **4.** *His father's country was Czechoslovakia:* native country, native land, mother country, homeland, fatherland, native soil; nationality. **5.** *City people often dream of buying a house in the country:* rural areas, countryside, hinterlands, farming area, wide open spaces; *Slang* sticks, boondocks, backwoods, boonies. **—adj. 6.** *She was born in a little country town out West:* rural, farming, farm, provincial, rustic, back-country; unsophisticated, simple. **—Ant.** 5 city, town, urban area, metropolis. 6 urban, cosmopolitan, city, urbane, sophisticated, citified.

countryman *n.* **1.** *"Friends, Romans, countrymen, lend me your ears":* compatriot, fellow citizen, fellow countryman, landsman. **2.** *The city slicker tried to outwit the innocent countryman:* rustic, farmer, peasant, provincial; *Slang* yokel, hick, hayseed, country bumpkin, rube, clodhopper. **—Ant.** 1 alien, foreigner, stranger. 2 city dweller, townsman, urbanite, metropolitan, cosmopolitan, city slicker.

countryside *n.* *They looked for a picnic spot in the countryside:* country, rural district, farm country, farmland, grassland, grazing country, meadows, pastures, the country, woodland, woods, fields, agricultural region, arable land.

county *n.* *They could only find a liquor store in the next county:* shire, canton, constituency.

coup de grâce *After the firing squad finished, an officer administered the coup de grace with a pistol:* deathblow, finishing stroke, mercy stroke, decisive blow.

coup d'état *Army leaders ousted the president in the latest coup d'état:* overthrow, rebellion, revolution, palace revolution; subversion, uprising, mutiny.

couple *n.* **1.** *Arrange the chairs in couples:* pair, two of a kind, combination of two, doublet. **2.** *Mr. and Mrs. Cutler are a nice-looking couple:* twosome, pair, duo; man and wife, husband and wife, married pair, engaged pair, dating pair, man and woman. —*v.* **3.** *The caboose is coupled to the last freight car:* connect, join, link, fasten, hitch, tie, bind, yoke. —**Ant.** 3 detach, separate, disconnect, part, unfasten, unhitch, untie.

coupon *n.* *The store offered a gift coupon with every purchase:* certificate, slip, chit, token, voucher.

courage *n.* *He received many medals for his courage in battle:* bravery, valor, fearlessness, dauntlessness, stout-heartedness, intrepidity, daring, boldness, nerve, derring-do, fortitude; *Slang* guts, pluck, spunk, mettle, grit, sand. —**Ant.** cowardice, faintheartedness, pusillanimousness, timidity; terror, fear, dread.

courageous *adj.* *Jumping into the icy water to save the child was certainly a courageous act:* brave, valiant, bold, fearless, dauntless, stronghearted, intrepid, unafraid, chivalrous, manly, dashing, valorous, doughty, dogged, gallant, resolute, indomitable, stalwart, bold-spirited, heroic. —**Ant.** cowardly, fainthearted, craven, timid, fearful, apprehensive.

courier *n.* *The courier picked up the dispatch in New York and delivered it in London the next day:* messenger, emissary, runner, dispatch bearer, go-between, dispatch rider, postrider, pony-expressman; herald, Mercury, herald angel, harbinger, Gabriel; envoy, legate, internuncio; postman, letter carrier, mailman, mail carrier.

course *n.* **1.** *The ship was 200 miles off course:* route, direction, path, channel, passage, road, track, way; orbit, trajectory. **2.** *In the course of the discussion many views were heard:* progression, development, sequence, onward movement, unfolding, flow, march. **3.** *Your best course would be to accept his offer:* procedure, action, conduct, method, mode, policy, behavior. **4.** *The college offers courses in science and in the humanities:* classes, lessons, lectures; course of study, curriculum, study program, subject. **5.** *The country club has a golf course. The race was run on the turf course:* circuit, circle, round, run; racecourse, track. —*v.* **6.** *The trout stream courses over the rocks:* run, flow, race, pour, surge, gush, stream.

court *n.* **1.** *Some of Shakespeare's plays were performed before the court of Queen Elizabeth I:* royal household, staff, entourage, retinue, train, advisers, council, following, cortege, attendants. **2.** *The king held court every day:* audience, hearing, assembly, session, meeting. **3.** *Hampton Court was the country home of England's Henry VIII:* royal residence, palace, castle, château, hall, manor. **4.** *The apartment house is built around a court:* courtyard, yard, enclosed area, atrium, plaza, quadrangle, quad. **5.** *The knight paid court to his fair lady:* courtship, homage, respects, courtesies, address, solicitations, flattering attention; suit, wooing. **6.** *The young lawyer made her first appearance before the court:* court of law, court of justice, bench, bar, judicial tribunal. —*v.* **7.** *Some companies court only wealthy clients:* curry favor with, fawn upon, pander to, flatter, blandish; woo, pay suit to, pay one's addresses to; pursue, run after. **8.** *Don't court disaster by driving too fast:* invite, attract, induce, provoke, seek. —**Ant.** 7 avoid, shun, ignore, refuse, repudiate, reject, turn down, turn away.

courteous *adj.* *They wrote us a courteous thank-you note. Bill is always a courteous youth:* polite, well-mannered, mannerly, well-behaved, refined, well-bred, civil, respectful, tactful, diplomatic, kind, gracious, considerate; soft-spoken, mild. —**Ant.** discourteous, impolite, rude, uncivil, curt, ill-mannered, unmannerly, insolent, disrespectful, unkind, ungracious.

courtesy *n.* **1.** *Friend or foe, king or fool, treat everyone with courtesy:* politeness, courteousness, good manners, manners, good behavior, civility, respect, deference, kindly consideration, graciousness, gentility, gentle breeding, cultivation, refinement, courtliness, gallantry. **2.** *Each woman shopper was given a rose, by courtesy of the management:* courteous act, favor, considerate gesture, kindness, consideration, indulgence; regards, respects. —**Ant.** 1, 2 discourtesy. 1 impoliteness, discourteousness, bad manners, unmannerliness, rudeness, incivility, disrespect, insolence; churlishness, boorishness.

courtly *adj.* *The old man was esteemed for his courtly manners:* refined, genteel, polished, elegant, decorous, civilized, gallant, chivalrous, suave, debonair, dignified, stately; aristocratic, blue-blooded, highbred, silk-stockinged; polite, courteous, mannerly, gentlemanly, ladylike. —**Ant.** unrefined, inelegant, ungentlemanly, unladylike, undignified, unpolished, impolite; coarse, vulgar, base, low, boorish, loutish, plebeian; ill-mannered, discourteous, rude, uncivil.

courtship *n.* *They were married after a courtship of nine years:* wooing, courting, suit, engagement period, keeping company.

cove *n.* *The boat was anchored in the cove:* bay, inlet, lagoon, estuary.

covenant *n.* *The Old Testament tells of the covenant the Jews made with God:* solemn agreement, pledge, vow, promise, oath, bond; pact, treaty, contract, bargain.

cover *v.* **1.** *Grandmother always covered the table with a lace cloth:* put on, put over, lay on, overlay, blanket, clothe, sheathe, shroud, envelop, wrap, enwrap. **2.** *The tent covered the campers from the rain:* protect, shield, guard, shelter, defend. **3.** *She covered her face with her hands:* hide, conceal, obscure, secrete; cloak, veil, hood, screen; mask, disguise, camouflage. **4.** *The history book covers the years of Eisenhower's presidency. The reporter covered the convention for the local newspaper:* deal with, include, involve, contain; embrace, encompass, embody, comprise, take in, comprehend; report, tell of, describe, chronicle, write up. **5.** *We covered three states in two days:* travel through, pass over, pass through, traverse, cross. —*n.* **6.** *The jewel box had a carved wooden cover. Don't judge a book by its cover:* lid, top, cap, covering; wrapper, case, encasement, envelope, jacket, sheath, binding. **7.** *Do you want another cover on the bed?:* blanket, comforter, quilt, coverlet, eiderdown. **8.** *When the rain started, we took cover under a large tree:* shelter, protection, shield, guard, defense; asylum, refuge, sanctuary, concealment, hiding place. —**Ant.** 1 uncover, remove, take off; unclothe, unwrap, expose. 2 expose. 3 uncover, reveal, exhibit, show, unmask, expose. 4 exclude, omit, leave out. 6 base, bottom, stand. 8 exposure.

coverage *n.* **1.** *This insurance policy provides coverage for all types of accidents:* protection, indemnity; payment, reimbursement. **2.** *The newscaster received an award for her coverage of the election:* reporting, description, analysis; publishing, broadcasting.

covering *n.* **1.** *The lampshade was wrapped in a cellophane covering:* cover, wrapper, wrapping, casing, envelope, sheath. —*adj.* **2.** *Send a covering letter with your résumé:* descriptive, explanatory, introductory.

covert *adj.* *The FBI had a covert meeting with the kidnappers to arrange for release of the captive:* secret, clandestine, hidden, concealed, sub rosa, surreptitious, unknown, veiled, disguised. —**Ant.** overt, known, open, public; candid, frank, plain, clear, evident, obvious.

covertly *adv.* *The negative campaign was waged covertly:* furtively, by stealth, clandestinely, secretly, slyly, stealthily, surreptitiously, undercover, underhandedly.

covet *v.* *The assistant coveted the boss's job:* desire, desire greedily, crave, lust after, yearn for, want, long for, aspire to, have an eye on, fancy, hanker after. —**Ant.** reject, forswear, decline, refuse, renounce, relinquish.

covetous *adj.* *Poverty made him covetous of others' wealth:* craving, desirous, lustful, yearning; greedy, avaricious, rapacious, grasping, mercenary, selfish; envious, jealous. —**Ant.** self-denying, self-abnegating, forswearing, renouncing, abjuring; liberal, generous, bountiful, unselfish.

cow *v.* *The smaller boys were cowed by the class bully:* intimidate, frighten, threaten, make cringe, terrorize, terrify, scare, browbeat, bully, bulldoze; dishearten, dismay, abash, discourage, deter. —**Ant.** calm, soothe, quiet, encourage, support, embolden.

coward *n.* *Only a coward would run from danger:* uncourageous person, dastard, sissy, cad, caitiff, craven, poltroon; *Slang* chicken, yellowbelly; milksop, mollycoddle, Milquetoast.

—**Ant.** brave person, hero, champion, daredevil.

cowardice *n.* *Running away was his first act of cowardice:* fearfulness, poltroonery, dastardliness, timidity. —**Ant.** boldness, bravery, temerity.

cowardly *adj.* *Sending anonymous letters is a cowardly act:* uncourageous, fainthearted, timorous, timid, dastardly, craven, pusillanimous; showing the white feather; *Slang* chickenhearted, yellow, yellow-bellied, lily-livered, gutless; frightened, afraid, fearful, apprehensive, anxious, nervous, shaky, tremulous. —**Ant.** brave, courageous, valiant, valorous, dauntless, stout-hearted, lionhearted, plucky, spunky; bold, daring, audacious, intrepid, doughty.

cowboy *n.* *Following the roundup, the cowboys branded all the newborn calves:* cowpoke, broncobuster, cowpuncher, cowhand, buckaroo, roughrider, cattle-herder, drover, cowherd; *Spanish* gaucho, vaquero; *Brit.* cowman; *Fem.* cowgirl.

cower *v.* *The serfs cowered before the lord of the manor:* crouch in fear, cringe, draw back, shrink, recoil, flinch, quail, tremble; grovel, crawl, truckle, bootlick, toady. —**Ant.** swagger, strut, stand tall; intimidate, bully, terrorize, cow, browbeat.

coxcomb *n.* *A fancy vest was one sign of the London coxcomb:* dandy, fop, dude, exquisite, beau, popinjay, jackanapes.

coy *adj.* *He always gets coy when asked to recite:* shy, modest, bashful, sheepish, shrinking, timid, diffident, timorous, skittish; overmodest, prudish, blushing, demure; pretending to be shy, coquettish, kittenish. —**Ant.** brash, brazen, bold, forward, impudent, impertinent, flippant, flip, pert, saucy, immodest.

cozy *adj.* *We spent a cozy evening chatting by the fire:* snug, snugly warm, comfortable, comfy, relaxing, easy, restful, snug as a bug in a rug; homelike, homey, *Spanish* simpático, *German* gemütlich.

crack *v.* **1.** *The whip cracked as the wagon master started the horses:* sound sharply, snap, pop, crackle, clap, thunder; strike sharply. **2.** *The plate cracked when I dropped it:* split, fracture, cleave, chip, splinter, break partially. **3.** *Anyone can crack under pressure:* break, break down, give way, lose control, become irrational, go to pieces. —*n.* **4.** *There was a crack of rifle fire in the distance:* sharp sound, report, burst, snap, pop, clap, crackle. **5.** *The earthquake caused huge cracks in the earth:* split, fissure, rift, rent, cleft, slit, gash, crevice, rupture. **6.** *Don't make any cracks about her funny-looking hat:* wisecrack, joke, quip, gag, jest, jab, gibe, funny remark, teasing remark, witticism; insult, critical remark, smart-alecky remark, taunt.

crackpot *n.* **1.** *All public figures have to deal with the crackpots who accost them:* eccentric, fool, crackbrain, maniac, lunatic, madman, crank, character; *Slang* nut, screwball, kook, weirdo, freak, dingbat, loony, wacko, oddball. —*adj.* **2.** *He's full of crackpot ideas on how to live to be 300 years old:* insane, crackbrained, foolish, odd, eccentric, impractical; *Slang* weirdo, wacko, kooky, nutty, balmy, kinky, freaky. **—Ant.** 2 rational, sensible, sane, sound, clear-headed.

crackup *n.* **1.** *The crackup on the thruway stopped traffic for more than an hour:* collision, smashup, pileup, smash, wreck, accident; disaster, calamity, catastrophe, debacle, mishap. **2.** *The soldier suffered a crackup after being under fire for a week:* nervous breakdown, nervous collapse, prostration, battle fatigue, exhaustion, combat fatigue, *Archaic* shellshock.

cradle *n.* **1.** *The child slept soundly in her cradle:* bed on rockers, baby's bed; (*loosely*) crib, bassinet. **2.** *Ancient Athens was the cradle of democracy:* beginning place, birthplace, nursery, source, origin, fountain, fountainhead, font, wellspring, spring. *—v.* **3.** *The nurse cradled the infant in her arms:* rock, cuddle, snuggle, enfold, hug, clasp tenderly.

craft *n.* **1.** *Making stained-glass windows requires great craft:* skill, ability, adeptness, deftness, fineness, proficiency, adroitness, knack, competency, expertise, expertness, know-how, technique, mastery. **2.** *Weaving was the town's chief craft:* trade, business, occupation, vocation, employment; industry, commerce, pursuit, calling; handicraft, art. **3.** *Magicians use craft to hoodwink an audience:* craftiness, cunning, artifice, artfulness, ruse, wile, trickery, chicanery; deception, guile, duplicity, deceit, perfidy; intrigue, sharp practice. **4.** *The small craft skimmed over the water:* ship, boat, vessel; aircraft, airplane, plane. **—Ant.** 1 inaptitude, unskillfulness, maladroitness, inaptness, ineptitude, ineptness, inability, incompetency, clumsiness. 2 manual labor; intellectual pursuit. 3 openness, candor, frankness, straightforwardness, sincerity, ingenuousness.

craftsman *n.* *Attention to detail showed that he was a craftsman:* artisan, artificer, craftsperson, craftswoman, handicraftsman, workman.

crafty *adj.* *The crafty business partner wound up with all the money:* cunning, shrewd, sharp, wily, foxy, tricky, sly, guileful, artful, shifty, underhand, devious, deceptive, deceitful, perfidious, unethical, dishonest; intriguing, scheming, designing, calculating, plotting; astute, canny, suspicious. **—Ant.** honest, open, candid, frank, aboveboard, ethical; naive, innocent, simple, ingenuous.

craggy *adj.* *We spent many pleasant summers along the craggy coast of Maine:* rocky, stony, cragged, rugged, rough, rockbound, bouldery, scraggy, jagged, ragged, snaggy, rock-ribbed; steep, precipitous, sheer, abrupt. **—Ant.** smooth, even, regular, level, straight, flat.

cram *v.* **1.** *He couldn't cram any more into the bulging suitcase:* jam, pack, stuff, fill, fill to overflowing, crowd, overcrowd, congest; force, press, compress, squeeze, ram. **2.** *(Informal) The student had to cram for her history test:* study hastily, study hard, grind. **—Ant.** 1 empty, deplete, drain, exhaust, clear.

cramp *n.* **1.** *She got a cramp in her leg while swimming:* muscular contraction, spasm, seizure, stitch, crick, charley horse; sharp pain, pang. *—v.* **2.** *A lack of education cramped his chances of getting a good job:* hamper, hold back, restrict, limit, check, prevent, hinder, thwart, restrain, frustrate, handicap, obstruct, block, stymie. **—Ant.** 2 help, aid, advance, forward, expand, increase; free, release, loose.

cramped *adj.* *She decided to give up the cramped apartment:* overcrowded, crowded, congested, awkward, circumscribed, close, closed in, confined, hemmed in, incommodious, packed, squeezed, tight. **—Ant.** uncrowded, roomy, spacious, capacious, open.

cranky *adj.* *My husband is always cranky in the morning until he's had his coffee:* grouchy, cross, bearish, crabby, crotchety, ill-tempered, ill-humored, out of sorts, irascible, captious, splenetic, cantankerous, peevish, waspish, testy, touchy, petulant. **—Ant.** good-natured, good-humored, even-tempered, cheerful, gay, happy, amiable, agreeable, complaisant; placid, calm, serene.

cranny *n.* *We searched every cranny of the cave:* niche, breach, chink, cleft, crack, crevice, fissure, gap, hole, interstice, nook.

crash *v.* **1.** *The flowerpot crashed to the sidewalk:* fall heavily, dash, strike noisily, smash, shatter, clatter; topple, hurtle, tumble, plunge. **2.** *The two cars crashed at the intersection:* collide, strike together, dash together, hit together, smash, bump, bang. **3.** *Five boys tried to crash her birthday party:* enter without invitation, come uninvited to, enter without a ticket, slip in, sneak in, invade, intrude. *—n.* **4.** *We could hear the crash of pots and pans in the kitchen:* clatter, bang, din, racket, clangor, crack, boom; noisy breaking, shattering, smashing; noisy striking, hitting, bumping; heavy falling, toppling, tumbling. **5.** *Several persons were injured in the car crash:* collision, smashup, crackup, accident, wreck, pileup. **6.** *The stock market crash of 1929 ruined many people:* financial collapse, financial disaster, failure, bankruptcy, ruin; (*loosely*) depression, recession, slump, decline, setback. **—Ant.** 4 silence; murmur, whisper. 6 prosperity, upsurge, flourishing, success.

crass *adj.* *His crass manners made others dislike him:* coarse, crude, vulgar, gross, unrefined, unpolished, inelegant; uncaring, insensitive, boorish, oafish, unsympathetic, unfeeling, hardhearted, cruel. **—Ant.** refined, polished, elegant; deferential, obliging, sympathetic, kind, warmhearted, soft-hearted.

crave *v.* *Since going on the diet, she craves sweets:* pine for, sigh for, wish for, hope for, desire, want, long for, yearn for, hunger for, thirst for, hanker after, have a fancy for, have a yen for, lust after, covet; require, need. **—Ant.** reject, spurn, repudiate, renounce, scorn, refuse, decline; detest, abominate, loathe, hate, despise, abhor.

craven *adj.* *Refusing to stand and fight was a craven thing to do:* cowardly, dastardly, pusillanimous; timid, timorous, fearful, frightened, scared; *Slang* yellow, lily-livered, chickenhearted; mean-spirited, base, low, lowdown.

—Ant. brave, courageous, heroic, fearless, valorous, valiant, dauntless; bold, daring, audacious.

craving *n. I have a great craving for a hamburger:* yearning, longing, urge, yen, hankering, appetite, desire, hunger, itch, lust, thirst.

crawl *v.* **1.** *The caterpillar crawled across the rock:* move by dragging the body, creep, slither, squirm, wiggle, wriggle, writhe, worm; move on hands and knees, go on all fours. **2.** *The holiday traffic crawled along the highway:* go at a snail's pace, inch, drag, worm, poke, mosey. **—Ant.** 1 walk; run. 2 race, rush, dash, dart, spurt, hurry, hasten, tear, fly, go like sixty, go lickety-split, go like the wind.

craze *v.* **1.** *The shipwrecked men were crazed with thirst:* drive mad, make crazy, make insane, drive wild, make berserk, derange, dement, unhinge, cause to run amuck. *—n.* **2.** *Hula hoops were a craze some years ago:* fad, rage, furor, polular whim, mania, passion, infatuation. **—Ant.** 1 calm, soothe, ease.

crazy *adj.* **1.** *Not all the crazy people are in asylums:* insane, mad, demented, deranged, maniacal, daft, berserk, unbalanced, unhinged; *Slang* cracked, touched, nuts, nutty, out of one's head, mad as a hatter, mad as a March hare. **2.** *She always wears a crazy hat:* bizarre, weird, odd, unusual, peculiar, strange, uncommon, silly, absurd, outrageous, laughable; *Slang* far-out. **3.** *You children are crazy to get married so young:* foolish, imprudent, unwise, foolhardy; senseless, stupid, silly, ridiculous, idiotic, absurd. **4.** *All the girls are crazy about the good-looking football hero:* mad, smitten with, taken with, fanatical, wild, keen, rabid, avid, zealous, frantic, hysterical, excited; very fond, infatuated, passionate, enthusiastic, gaga, *Slang* nuts. **—Ant.** 1 sane, mentally sound, rational, reasonable, sensible, well-balanced. 2 sensible, practical; acceptable, conservative, common, average, usual, run-of-the-mill. 3 smart, wise, prudent, sensible. 4 unenthusiastic, uncaring, unexcited, cool, indifferent.

creak *v. The rusty hinges creaked when the gate opened:* rasp, squeak, screech, screak, grate, grind, scrape.

cream *n.* **1.** *The cream will soften your skin:* ointment, salve, unguent, lotion, cosmetic, emulsion, paste. **2.** *The cream of the paintings went to the highest bidder:* best, finest, pick, elite, choice, favorite, flower, top.

creamy *adj. The creamy milk made excellent eggnog:* rich, smooth, velvety, buttery, milky, oily.

crease *n.* **1.** *Iron the creases out of this blouse:* fold, wrinkle, ridge, crinkle, rumple, pucker, corrugation, furrow. *—v.* **2.** *Years of worry had creased his brow:* wrinkle, pucker, crinkle, ruffle, rumple, crimple, corrugate, furrow; fold, pleat, crimp. **—Ant.** 2 smooth, flatten, straighten out.

create *v.* **1.** *The chemist worked for years to create a waterproof glue:* originate, invent, develop, devise, formulate, make, concoct, contrive, fashion, fabricate, design, form, mold, erect, construct, conceive, bring into being, give birth to; cause, bring to pass. **2.** *The government has created a new agency for agriculture:* found, establish, set up, institute, form, organize, appoint. **—Ant.** 1 destroy, demolish, annihilate. 2 close, shut down.

creation *n.* **1.** *The whale is the largest mammal in creation:* the world, the universe, nature; all things, all living things. **2.** *The creation of new playgrounds will benefit the local children:* creating, making, institution, origination, development, devising, establishment, founding, production, bringing into existence, formation; building, construction, fabrication, fashioning, erection. **3.** *The designer's latest creation is a backless evening dress:* original work, imaginative work, invention, conception, brainchild, concoction, production, handiwork. **—Ant.** 2 destruction, demolition, annihilation.

creative *adj. James Joyce was one of Ireland's most creative writers:* original, imaginative, ingenious, inventive, resourceful, fanciful.

creator *n.* **1.** *Thomas Jefferson was one of the creators of the U.S. Constitution:* originator, author, framer, designer, producer, architect, maker, initiator, inventor, founder, father, generator, begetter. **2. the Creator.** See GOD.

creature *n. All creatures great and small inhabit the earth:* living being, living thing, earthling; animal, lower animal, beast, critter, dumb animal; (*variously*) quadruped, vertebrate, invertebrate, mammal, bird, fish, reptile, insect; human being, human, mortal, man, person, individual.

credence *n. Try not to lend credence to rumors of war:* belief, confidence, trust, reliance, credibility, creditability, faith, trustworthiness, credit; reliability, dependableness, acceptableness; certainty, certitude. **—Ant.** doubt, mistrust, disbelief, skepticism, distrust, incredulity.

credentials *n. The new ambassador will present his credentials to the foreign minister this morning. A scholar's publications are the best credentials:* (*diplomatic*) letter of credence; (*general*) written proof of status or qualifications, certificate, diploma, reference, letter of recommendation, testimonial, authorization, voucher, permit, license.

credibility *n. When he lied about something so important, he lost all credibility:* believability, plausibility, trustworthiness, validity, likelihood, probability, reliability, validity, soundness, tenability. **—Ant.** implausibility.

credible *adj. Is the witness's story credible?:* believable, plausible, reasonable, likely, possible, probable, tenable; conceivable, thinkable, imaginable; reliable, trustworthy, dependable. **—Ant.** incredible, unbelievable, implausible, unreasonable, unlikely, improbable, inconceivable; unreliable, untrustworthy, dubious, doubtful, questionable, unthinkable.

credit *n.* **1.** *The photographer was given credit in the program:* recognition, acknowledgment; honor, high regard, esteem, glory, acclaim, commendation. **2.** *We bought the sofa on credit:* the installment plan, charge account, time. **3.** *You have a credit of $10 toward your next purchase:* allowance, prepayment. *—v.* **4.** *Edison is credited with the invention of the phonograph:* attribute, ascribe, assign, acknowledge, recognize; honor, acclaim. **5.** *How could you credit such a wild story?:* believe, trust, have faith in, put confidence in, rely on, accept; *Informal* swallow, fall for, buy. **—Ant.** 1 disgrace, shame, censure, ignominy. 2 cash, cash on the barrelhead. 3 debit, charge. 5 doubt, disbelieve, distrust, question.

creditable *adj. The coach did a creditable job in bringing the team to the championship:* admirable, commendable, praiseworthy, meritorious, laudable; reputable, estimable, respectable, worthy. **—Ant.** blamable, censurable, discreditable; disreputable, dishonorable.

credo *n. His credo is "Work hard and save every penny":* creed, set of beliefs, set of principles, doctrine, tenet, code, rule, maxim, motto, philosophy.

credulous *adj. Anne is so credulous she'll believe anything you tell her:* ready to believe, easily convinced, gullible, trusting, believing; naive, unsophisticated, too trustful, overtrustful, unsuspecting, unsuspicious, unquestioning. **—Ant.** incredulous, unbelieving; suspicious, suspecting, wary, cynical.

creed *n. The minister explained the church's creed to the visitors:* religious belief, belief, profession of faith, doctrine, dogma, set of principles, set of beliefs, credo, group of tenets, canons, gospel.

creek *n. The children love to wade in the creek:* stream, brook, small river, rivulet, rill, freshet, branch, run, spring, millstream.

creep *v.* **1.** *The snake crept along the garden wall:* crawl, slither, writhe, worm, wriggle, squirm. **2.** *The hunter crept up as close to the deer as possible:* advance secretly, walk stealthily, come unnoticed, sneak, steal. **3.** *The old car crept down the road:* move slowly, inch, crawl, dawdle, poke along, go at a snail's pace. **—Ant.** 1 run. 2 blunder, bluster, trample. 3 race, rush, fly, tear, hasten, hurry, sprint, dart, dash, go like sixty, go lickety-split, go like the wind.

creepy *adj. Remembering the creepy movie kept him awake:* disturbing, eerie, scary, ghoulish, threatening, disturbing, frightening, gruesome, macabre, ominous, sinister, weird, *Informal* hair-raising, skin-crawling.

cremate *v. His remains were cremated the day after his death:* reduce to ashes, burn, incinerate; char, sear, burn to a cinder, scorch, consume by fire, conflagrate, roast; set fire to, ignite, set on fire, enkindle, fire, kindle.

crescent *adj.* **1.** *The crescent rolls were delicious:* bowed, bow-shaped, concave, convex, curved, semicircular. *—n.* **2.** *At that juncture the river became a crescent:* bow, bend, curve, arc, arch, semicircle.

crest *n.* **1.** *The bird has a crest of white feathers:* tuft, topknot, comb, plume, crown. **2.** *The lookout tower is on the crest of the hill:* top, summit, pinnacle, highest point, peak, tip, apex,

height. **3.** *They proudly displayed their family crest above the mantel:* emblem, coat of arms, arms, armorial bearings, escutcheon. **—Ant.** 2 bottom, base.

crestfallen *adj. The team was crestfallen after losing the game:* downhearted, downcast, dejected, depressed, disappointed; discouraged, disheartened, dispirited, low-spirited, despondent, woebegone. **—Ant.** elated, exuberant, happy, joyful, up in the clouds, on cloud nine, in seventh heaven; encouraged, heartened, uplifted.

crevice *n. A huge crevice split the iceberg almost in two:* fissure, crack, cleft, split, fracture, rift, breach, rent, slit; chasm, crevasse.

crew *n.* **1.** *The wrecking crew began to demolish the building:* work gang, squad, corps, force, team, company, party. **2.** *The ship's crew mutinied:* work force, company of sailors, company, complement, hands, sailors, mariners, seafarers, seamen; air crew, plane crew. **3.** *The rebels were a motley crew:* band, body, pack, group, mob, throng, troop, horde; assemblage, multitude, mass, herd. **—Ant.** 2 officers.

crick *n. She winced from the crick in her neck:* cramp, ache, twinge, kink, pain, spasm, stitch, wrench, *Informal* charley horse.

crime *n.* **1.** *He was convicted of the crime of embezzling:* unlawful act, violation of the law, lawbreaking, foul play, offense; *(variously)* capital crime, tort, felony, misdemeanor, malfeasance. **2.** *It's a crime to waste so much food:* wrong, wrongdoing, misdeed, blameworthy action, misconduct; senseless act, wasteful act, outrage, villainy, abomination; sin, transgression, iniquity. **—Ant.** 1 lawful act; retribution, pardon. 2 good deed, right, virtue, virtuous act; benefit, boon.

criminal *adj.* **1.** *Robbery is a criminal act:* illegal, unlawful, lawbreaking, lawless, indictable, felonious, illicit, crooked, guilty, culpable, delinquent. **2.** *It's criminal to let such a fine garden go to ruin:* wrong, blameworthy; senseless, wasteful; disgraceful, outrageous, villainous, abominable. *—n.* **3.** *The criminal was sent to prison for ten years:* guilty person, person convicted of a crime; culprit, lawbreaker, outlaw, felon; *Informal* hood, crook; wrongdoer, transgressor, malefactor, offender. **—Ant.** 1 lawful, legal, licit; honest, law-abiding; innocent. 2 right, just, commendable, admirable, meritorious, honorable, praiseworthy. 3 innocent person.

crimp *v. The skirt was crimped at the hem:* crease, wrinkle, ruck, scrunch, wave, coil, curl, crinkle, fold, pleat.

cringe *v. The child cringed every time the father raised his voice:* cower, flinch, shrink, quail, blench, recoil, dodge, duck; grovel, be servile, toady, truckle. **—Ant.** strut, swagger.

crinkly *adj. We made some party decorations with the crinkly paper:* wrinkly, wrinkled, crimped, crimpy, crimpled, crimply, puckered, puckery, cockled, rumpled, shriveled; twisted, kinky, ruffled; curly, wavy; frizzy, frizzled. **—Ant.** smooth, straight, flat, even, unwrinkled.

cripple *n.* **1.** *Before the Salk vaccine, infantile paralysis made cripples of many people:* lame person, the disabled, the handicapped, the impaired; *Slang* gimp. —*v.* **2.** *The accident crippled her permanently:* make lame, disable, incapacitate; impair, damage, harm, maim. **3.** *The snowstorm crippled rail transportation:* impair, disable, incapacitate, render impotent, paralyze, debilitate, hamstring, inactivate; stop, halt, bring to a standstill. —**Ant.** 3 help, aid, assist, ease, facilitate.

crippled *adj. Suffering several direct hits, the crippled plane went down:* incapacitated, disabled, handicapped, impaired, lame, paralyzed.

crisis *n. Negotiations between the two countries are approaching a crisis:* turning point, climax; emergency, critical stage.

crisp *adj.* **1.** *These potato chips are not very crisp:* crispy, brittle, snappy, crunchy. **2.** *It was a delightful evening of crisp conversation:* brisk, sharp, pointed, snappy, incisive, candid, terse; vivacious, energetic, lively, sparkling, witty. **3.** *Yesterday was a crisp fall day:* brisk, pleasantly cool, chilly, nippy, bracing, refreshing, fresh, invigorating. —**Ant.** 1 limp, soft, wilted. 2 dull, slow, cautious, insipid. 3 warm, balmy.

criterion *n. What is the major criterion for judging a symphony?:* standard, measure, gauge, yardstick, guidepost, rule, principle, law, norm; model, precedent, example, touchstone.

critic *n.* **1.** *I like painting, but I'm no critic of modern art:* judge, connoisseur, expert, authority, mavin, cognoscente, virtuoso; evaluator, analyst, arbiter; professional reviewer, commentator. **2.** *The senator called a press conference to answer his critics:* detractor, antagonist, attacker, faultfinder, censor, criticizer; carper, scold, backbiter, reviler, vilifier; *Informal* knocker, rapper.

critical *adj.* **1.** *Don't be so critical of everyone else:* censorious, faultfinding, disparaging, derogatory, picky, fussy, nagging, caviling, carping, nitpicking, disapproving, finicky, hairsplitting. **2.** *It takes years to develop one's critical abilities:* judging, discriminating, analytical, diagnostic; perspicacious, judicious. **3.** *This is a critical time in the nation's history:* decisive, crucial, grave, serious, sensitive, urgent, momentous, pressing, vital; dangerous, perilous, precarious, hazardous, harrowing, risky, *Slang* hairy. —**Ant.** 1–3 uncritical. 1 complimentary, approving, laudatory; inexact, haphazard, permissive. 2 undiscriminating, unanalytical, shallow. 3 secure, settled, calm, tranquil; safe.

criticism *n.* **1.** *The height of the public sculpture aroused much criticism:* censure, faultfinding, stricture, animadversion, reflection. **2.** *She claimed that current Dickens criticism was not scholarly:* review, critique, comment.

criticize *v. She's always criticizing her husband for being sloppy:* find fault with, disapprove of, disparage, cast aspersions on, reprove, reproach, denounce, censure; nag at, fuss, carp, cavil, pick, nitpick. —**Ant.** compliment, praise, commend, laud, extol, applaud.

critique *n. The students were required to write*

a critique of a Hemingway novel: critical essay, criticism, critical commentary, critical examination, analysis; review.

croak *v. The raven croaked briefly, then flew off:* squawk, caw, gasp, grunt, wheeze.

crony *n. Frank and his cronies get together for poker every Thursday night:* friend, companion, pal, chum, associate, acquaintance, *Brit.* mate, comrade, buddy, sidekick, bosom buddy; shipmate, bunkmate, *Slang* bunkie; ally, cohort, confederate, accomplice, collaborator, *Law* accessory, coconspirator.

crook *n.* **1.** *The cottage is just past the crook in the road:* bend, curve, turn, twist, angle, curvature; hook, arc, bow. **2.** *Only a crook would charge for work and not do it:* cheat, dishonest person, knave, criminal, robber, thief, bandit, swindler, embezzler; outlaw, thug, burglar, robber.

crooked *adj.* **1.** *Please straighten that crooked picture. The old mill is on a crooked road:* askew, awry, not straight; curved, twisted, twisting, winding, meandering, tortuous, sinuous, serpentine, zigzag, spiral; bent, bowed, hooked; distorted, deformed, warped, out of shape. **2.** *The mayor was suspected of crooked dealings:* dishonest, corrupt, unscrupulous, dishonorable, criminal, unlawful; deceptive, fraudulent, unethical, underhanded, deceitful, perfidious, nefarious; sneaky, shifty, shady, wily, crafty. —**Ant.** 1 straight, straight as an arrow; flat. 2 honest, legal, lawful, ethical, scrupulous, honorable, fair, aboveboard, upright.

crop *n.* **1.** *This year's corn crop will set a new record:* harvest, yield, production, growth, gleaning, gathering, reaping. —*v.* **2.** *His hair was cropped when he entered the army:* cut short, clip, shear, trim, lop, snip, cut, bob, prune.

cross *n.* **1.** *The church has a cross on top of its steeple:* crux, rood, crucifix. **2.** *Her illness is a cross she will have to bear:* burden, misfortune; affliction, distress, suffering, ordeal, adversity, difficulty, trial, tribulation, trouble. **3.** *The mule is a cross between a female horse and a male donkey:* crossbreed, hybrid, half-breed; blend, combination, amalgam. —*v.* **4.** *Cross the eggs off the grocery list:* delete, erase, strike out, cancel, cross out, obliterate. **5.** *We crossed the river in a rowboat:* go across, traverse, cut across, go over, pass over, travel over, ford, travel through; intersect, meet, crisscross. **6.** *They tried to cross a beagle with a Saint Bernard:* crossbreed, interbreed, mix, intermix; hybridize, cross-pollinate, cross-fertilize. —*adj.* **7.** *The roof is supported by cross timbers:* intersecting, lying crosswise; athwart, transverse, oblique. **8.** *Why is Mother so cross today?:* angry, mad, ill-tempered, annoyed, in a bad mood, cranky, petulant, surly, disagreeable, ill-humored, grouchy, peevish, touchy, snappish, shirty, churlish, gruff, out of sorts, irritable, waspish, irascible, testy, choleric, cantankerous, crotchety, captious, splenetic; contrary, querulous, intractable. —**Ant.** 2 relief, respite; boon, benefit. 3 thoroughbred. 4 write down, add, include. **8** good-humored, good-natured, good-tempered; agreeable, amenable, sweet.

crossing *n. There was a guard at the crossing:* crossroad, crosswalk, crossway, intersection, junction, portage, underpass, overpass, bridge.

crosswise *adj. To make a paper plane, first fold the sheet crosswise:* crossways, diagonally, across, aslant, athwart, crisscross, sideways, transversely.

crotchet *n. It was his crotchet to begin a meal with dessert:* quirk, eccentricity, idiosyncrasy, whim, peculiarity, quiddity, vagary, caprice, whimsy, oddity, irregularity, bent; characteristic, mannerism, trait, habit, foible, *Slang* hang-up.

crotchety *adj. Grandfather has grown crotchety with age:* cranky, contrary, fussy, grouchy; eccentric, odd, peculiar, erratic.

crouch *v. The hunters crouched in the reeds, waiting for the geese to fly over:* bend, stoop, squat, scrunch down, hunker down, hunch over, *Slang* scrooch down; cower, cringe, shrink, recoil, duck.

crow *v.* **1.** *The rooster crows at daybreak:* utter the cry of a rooster, cackle, cock-a-doodle-doo. **2.** *I wish he would stop crowing about his new promotion:* gloat, boast, brag, strut, swagger, vaunt; *Slang* blow; exult, rejoice, jubilate, triumph, trumpet.

crowd *n.* **1.** *Shop early and avoid the crowd:* throng, multitude, horde, mob, swarm, crush, herd, flock, host, legion; gathering, assemblage, congregation. **2.** *She's started to go around with a rather fast crowd:* set, circle, circle of friends, clique, claque, group, gang, coterie. —*v.* **3.** *We crowded around the platform to hear the speaker:* congregate, flock, swarm, gather, assemble; cluster, mass, herd, throng, huddle, concentrate. **4.** *The eager spectators crowded into the stadium:* shove, push, press, cram, jam, squeeze, swarm, surge, elbow in. —**Ant.** 3 disperse, scatter; draw back, draw away, retreat.

crowded *adj. Times Square is always crowded on New Year's Eve:* crammed, jammed, jam-packed, packed, full, filled, mobbed, congested, teeming, swarming, thronged, overflowing. —**Ant.** empty; half-full.

crown *n.* **1.** *The queen wore a crown encrusted with diamonds:* coronet, tiara, diadem, circlet. **2.** *The winning athlete was given a crown of laurel leaves:* wreath, garland, circlet, chaplet. **3.** *The ambassador is a representative of the British Crown:* royalty, sovereignty, monarchy, royal dominion. **4.** *The crown of the hat is covered with lace:* highest part, top, summit, pinnacle, peak, crest, apex, zenith, acme. **5.** *Jack fell down and broke his crown:* top of the head, pate, head; *Slang* noodle, noggin. —*v.* **6.** *British kings are crowned in Westminster Abbey:* invest with a crown, give royal power to, put a crown upon. **7.** *Winning an Academy Award crowned the actor's career:* top, top off, bring to the highest point, climax, complete, cap, fulfill, perfect, round out, reach a peak. —**Ant.** 4 bottom, base, foot. 6 dethrone, depose.

crowning *adj. Her throwing a drink in his face was the crowning touch:* ultimate, climactic,

consummate, culminating, paramount, supreme, final.

crucial *adj. Father made all the crucial decisions in our family:* decisive, critical, determining, significant, momentous, weighty, important, essential, pressing, knotty, urgent; grave, serious.

crucify *v. If the media heard about his affair, they would crucify him:* torment, torture, execute, kill, martyr, persecute, rack.

crude *adj.* **1.** *The crude sugar was shipped to the refinery:* raw, unrefined, unprocessed, unprepared; coarse. **2.** *The client was shown the crude sketches of the architect's plans:* uncompleted, incomplete, unfinished, rough, undeveloped, sketchy, imperfect. **3.** *I've never appreciated his crude sense of humor:* vulgar, obscene, unrefined, coarse, tasteless, crass, gross, uncouth, unpolished. —**Ant.** 1 refined, processed, prepared; fine, fine-grained. 2 final, finished, completed. 3 refined, polished, tasteful, subtle.

cruel *adj. Attila the Hun was a cruel tyrant:* inhuman, inhumane, sadistic, brutal, vicious, savage, merciless, unmerciful; heartless, pitiless, uncompassionate, unfeeling, hardhearted, ruthless, remorseless, cold-blooded. —**Ant.** humane, benevolent, merciful, compassionate, kind, warmhearted, sympathetic, tender, gentle, mild.

cruelty *n. She could not stand cruelty to animals:* harshness, brutality, ruthlessness, barbarity, inhumanity, atrocity. —**Ant.** kindness, benevolence.

cruise *v. We cruised from Piraeus to Istanbul via the Dardanelles:* sail, navigate, float, glide, coast, drift, stream, sweep, skim, scud, travel the bounding main, sail the seas, go by ship, seafare, ply the seas, go down to the sea in ships, sail the ocean blue, voyage.

crumb *n. Slicing the bread left crumbs all over the table:* scrap, shred, bit, morsel, sliver, minute portion, particle, fragment, speck, grain.

crumble *v.* **1.** *Crumble graham crackers to make the piecrust:* break into crumbs, fragment, splinter; crush, grind, pulverize, powder, grate. **2.** *After years of neglect the house began to crumble:* decay, disintegrate, fall apart, break up, waste away, wear away, decompose, go to wrack and ruin.

crumbly *adj. The peanut butter cookies were crumbly:* powdery, breakable, brittle, deteriorated, disintegrated, fragile, frail, friable.

crumple *v.* **1.** *The new synthetic fabrics won't crumple when folded:* wrinkle, rumple, crease, crinkle, crush; pucker, corrugate, crimple. **2.** *The staircase crumpled under his weight:* collapse, give way, cave in, fall, fall to pieces, break up.

crunch *v. The squirrels crunched on the nuts:* chew noisily, chomp, gnaw, gnash, grind, munch; chew, masticate.

crusade *n.* **1.** *often* **Crusade.** *The First Crusade departed for the Holy Land in 1096:* military expedition against non-Christians. **2.** *The city is launching a crusade to clean up the slums:* reform movement, idealistic campaign, movement, drive; rally, mass meeting.

crush v. **1.** *To make wine, you first crush the grapes:* mash, squash, squeeze, press, compress; crumble, crumple, pulverize, break, shatter, granulate. **2.** *The hero crushed the heroine in his arms:* hug tightly, hold closely, embrace, enfold, squeeze, press. **3.** *The army quickly crushed the uprising:* subdue, suppress, quash, smash, squash, squelch, put down, quell; overcome, overpower, overwhelm; quench, extinguish.

crusty adj. *Our crusty old neighbor complains every time the dog barks:* peevish, gruff, shirty, testy, waspish, brusque, sullen, surly, short-tempered, ill-tempered, ill-natured, curt, abrupt, blunt, short, snappish, cranky, splenetic, choleric, irascible, crabby, snippy, snippety. **—Ant.** agreeable, sweet-tempered, good-natured, placid, patient, understanding.

crux n. *The crux of the matter is that he's going to resign:* main point, decisive point, essence, essential, basis, heart, core, nub, gist, central issue; *Slang* brass tacks, nitty-gritty.

cry v. **1.** *Many mourners were crying at the funeral:* weep, shed tears, sob, bawl, blubber, snivel, boohoo; keen, mourn, lament, whimper, moan, wail, howl, groan. **2.** *He cried a warning just as the boat struck the rocks:* cry out, call, call out, shout, yell, scream, roar, bellow, shriek, howl, screech, exclaim, utter; whoop, cheer; hurrah, huzzah. **3.** *The prisoner cried for mercy:* beg, plead, implore, importune; appeal, sue, petition. **4.** *The hawker cried his wares throughout the town:* proclaim, make public, call out, blare, trumpet, hawk, blazon; advertise, promulgate. **—n. 5.** *He gave a cry of alarm:* call, shout, yell, scream, yelp, screech, roar, bellow, shriek, howl, exclamation; outcry, camor, whoop, cheer; hurrah, huzzah. **6.** *Hear our cry, O Lord!:* plea, entreaty, appeal, supplication, petition, prayer; request, solicitation, adjuration. **—Ant.** 1 laugh, snicker, giggle. 2, 5 whisper, murmur, mutter.

crying adj. **1.** *The crying baby kept his mother awake:* weeping, wailing, whimpering. **2.** *Some say that it's a crying shame more people don't vote:* flagrant, notorious, demanding, urgent, important, great, enormous. **—Ant.** 1 laughing. 2 nugatory, trifling.

crypt n. *The bishop was buried in a crypt beneath the altar:* underground chamber, vault, tomb, sepulcher, mausoleum, catacomb.

cryptic adj. *The old fortune-teller kept muttering cryptic warnings:* puzzling, perplexing, enigmatical, mysterious, obscure; ambiguous, vague; secret, hidden, mystical, strange, dark, cabalistic, arcane, occult, esoteric.

crystalline adj. *The stream was crystalline:* pellucid, transparent, clear, crystal clear, lucid, luminous.

cuddle v. **1.** *The little girl cuddled the rabbit:* hug tenderly, embrace, hold warmly, snuggle, nuzzle, cling to, clasp; caress, fondle, pet. **2.** *The children cuddled up in the warm bed:* snuggle, nestle, huddle, lie snug, draw close, curl up.

cuddly adj. *She took the cuddly teddy bear to bed with her:* snuggly, huggable, embraceable, lovable, cozy.

cudgel n. *The old peddler always carried a cudgel for protection:* club, bludgeon, shillelagh, truncheon, staff, stick, billy club, blackjack, quarterstaff, baton.

cue n. *Her wink was my cue to suggest we leave the party:* actor's signal; signal, sign, hint, clue, key, intimation, insinuation, suggestion, tip, inkling.

cull v. **1.** *The gallery owners culled enough of her paintings to make an interesting exhibition:* choose, select, pick out, gather, garner, collect, single out, take, extract, winnow, sift, glean, sort out, separate, divide, set apart, segregate. **—n. 2.** *Put the good berries in this bowl, the culls in that one:* scrap, reject, discard, castoff, scouring, leaving, second; jetsam, junk, trash, dross, waste.

culminate v. **1.** *A giant fireworks display culminated the Fourth of July festivities:* top, top off, climax, cap, crown, complete, consummate, provide the high point of. **2.** *Their disagreement culminated in a fight:* conclude, end, end up, result, wind up, terminate, finish.

culmination n. *Her victory was the culmination of much hard work:* finish, end, climax, apex, apogee, completion, conclusion, consummation, zenith, finale, height, peak, pinnacle, summit, top.

culpable adj. *The insurance company is trying to find out which driver is culpable:* guilty, at fault, liable, blameworthy, blamable, censurable, to blame. **—Ant.** innocent, blameless.

culprit n. *Police apprehended the culprit two blocks from the scene of the crime:* guilty party, offender; lawbreaker, criminal, felon; malefactor, miscreant, evildoer, sinner, transgressor, wrongdoer.

cult n. **1.** *The evangelist broke with his church and formed his own cult:* religious rites, religious observances; sect, religious group, faction. **2.** *The youth cult places emphasis on good intentions rather than on hard work:* devotion, admiration; devotees, admirers, zealots, followers, disciples.

cultivate v. **1.** *They moved to the country to cultivate the soil:* till, farm, raise crops from, garden; plow, hoe, spade, dig, weed; sow, plant, grow. **2.** *She cultivated her mind by reading many books:* develop, improve, enrich, enhance, elevate, advance. **3.** *Get out more and cultivate new friends:* acquire, develop, seek, court; ingratiate oneself with, run after. **—Ant.** 1 be fallow. 2 impoverish, bankrupt.

cultivation n. **1.** *Most of the land is devoted to cultivation:* agriculture, farming, agronomy, husbandry, gardening; tilling, planting, sowing. **2.** *They are people of great wealth and cultivation:* culture, refinement, polish, elevation, gentility, manners, grace, good breeding, good taste.

culture n. **1.** *A child should be exposed to culture at an early age:* art, music, and literature; the arts; good taste, enrichment, enlightenment, learning, accomplishments, erudition, knowledge. **2.** *Ancient Egypt had an advanced culture:* civilization, state of refinement, level of progress.

cultured *adj.* **1.** *One doesn't have to be cultured to enjoy good music:* well-educated, artistically knowledgeable, learned, well-read, erudite, enlightened. **2.** *She learned her cultured manners in a European finishing school:* cultivated, sophisticated, refined, polished, accomplished, genteel, elegant, well-bred. —**Ant.** 1 uncultured, uncultivated, unenlightened, uneducated. 2 uncultivated, unrefined, unpolished, inelegant, coarse, crass, low-bred, common, vulgar.

culvert *n.* *The heavy rain had flooded the culvert:* ditch, drain, gutter, conduit, canal, channel.

cumbersome *adj.* *The packages are too cumbersome to carry:* unwieldy, clumsy, cumbrous, unmanageable, awkward, ungainly, bulky, hefty; ponderous. —**Ant.** compact, manageable, wieldy.

cumulative *adj.* *Obesity is the cumulative result of years of overeating:* accumulative, collective, aggregate, conglomerate, amassed, additive, heaped up, *Informal* piled up.

cunning *n.* **1.** *The prime minister retained power by great cunning:* craftiness, slyness, shrewdness, guile, artifice, wiliness, foxiness, artfulness; deviousness, duplicity, deception, deceit, trickery, chicanery. **2.** *The inlaid desk had been made with great cunning:* cleverness, art, craft, skill, dexterity, adroitness, deftness, finesse, subtlety; ability, aptitude, expertness, knack, talent, genius. —*adj.* **3.** *By a cunning trick he became the queen's confidant:* shrewd, crafty, sly, artful, canny, ingenious, guileful, wily, foxy, Machiavellian, deceptive, deceitful, devious, shifty, underhand, tricky. —**Ant.** 1 sincerity, candor, ingenuousness. 2 clumsiness. 3 ingenuous, artless.

cupboard *n.* *There's another box of salt in the cupboard:* kitchen cabinet, cabinet, closet; buffet, sideboard, china closet, storeroom; bureau, chiffonier, armoire, clothespress.

cupidity *n.* *Nothing excited his cupidity so much as being in the company of rich people:* greed, avarice, covetousness, graspingness, avidity, acquisitiveness, concupiscence, greediness, rapacity, insatiability, selfishness, rapaciousness, avariciousness.

cur *n.* **1.** *You'd better put a muzzle on that cur before he bites someone:* mean dog, unfriendly dog; mongrel, mutt, varmint. **2.** *Only a cur would treat a woman like that!:* blackguard, scoundrel, villain, varlet, rascal, cad, rogue, wretch.

curable *adj.* *The disease was curable:* improvable, mendable, correctable, fixable, restorable.

curative *adj.* *She spent a curative week at the spa:* curing, medicinal, healing, restorative, healthful, alleviative, beneficial, helpful, invigorating, remedying, salutary, therapeutic, tonic, remedial, corrective, rejuvenating.

curb *n.* **1.** *Park your car parallel to the curb:* edge of a sidewalk, curbstone; edge, rim, border, ledge, brink. **2.** *The nation must put a curb on its spending to balance the economy:* restraint, restriction, control, check, bridle, harness, halter, rein, hindrance, limitation, retardation. —*v.* **3.** *Try to curb your wild enthusiasm:* restrain, restrict, check, control, bridle, harness; repress, suppress, inhibit, limit, moderate, retard, slow down, slow up, hold back; slacken, decelerate.

curdle *v.* *After about a week the cream will begin to curdle:* clabber, clot, curd, thicken, coagulate, solidify, congeal; turn, go off, ferment, sour, spoil, go bad; putrefy, putresce, rot, decay, deteriorate.

cure *v.* **1.** *Moving to Arizona cured her of asthma:* restore to health, make well, heal, eradicate sickness from, rid of an illness. **2.** *The hams were cured over a hickory fire:* preserve, smoke, dry, salt. —*n.* **3.** *Scientists are working on a cure for the common cold:* remedy, corrective, curative treatment, means of healing, antidote.

cure-all *n.* *He claimed that the medicine was a cure-all for every known disease:* universal remedy, sovereign remedy, cure, relief, nostrum, elixir, panacea.

curiosity *n.* **1.** *She's full of curiosity about our new house:* inquisitiveness, interest, questioning; prying; *Slang* nosiness. **2.** *This red and yellow striped seashell is quite a curiosity:* rare object, rarity, curio, novelty; phenomenon, marvel, wonder, sight, oddity, freak. —**Ant.** 1 indifference, apathy, disregard.

curious *adj.* **1.** *Humans are naturally curious about the universe:* inquisitive, interested in, eager to learn, anxious to know, inquiring, questioning, searching; nosy, snooping, prying. **2.** *She has a curious way of talking:* unusual, odd, peculiar, bizarre, strange, queer, weird, *Informal* funny; novel, quaint, singular, uncommon, unique, rare. —**Ant.** 1 incurious, uninterested, unconcerned, indifferent, apathetic. 2 customary, commonplace, common, usual, familiar, average, everyday.

curl *v.* **1.** *Her mother curled her hair:* form into ringlets, coil, wave; twist, frizz, frizzle, crimp. **2.** *Smoke curled from the chimney:* coil, curve, swirl, wind, twist, twirl, spiral. —*n.* **3.** *The little boy had blond curls:* ringlet, coil of hair, lock. **4.** *Curls of wood lay on the workshop floor:* coil, spiral, twist, curlicue, wave, corkscrew, scallop.

curly *adj.* *She combed her curly brown hair:* curled, curling, kinky, coiled, corkscrew, crimped, crimpy, crinkling, crinkly, frizzed, frizzy, looped, looping, spiralled, waved, wavy, coiled, wound.

curmudgeon *n.* *The old curmudgeon never smiled at anyone:* grouch, grumbler, crank, gruff person, irritable person, irascible person; *Slang* grump, crab, sourball.

currency *n.* **1.** *The pound sterling is the currency of Great Britain:* medium of exchange, legal tender, money; cash, bills, coin, coinage, bank notes, paper money, ready money. **2.** *That style enjoyed great currency in the 1920's:* popularity, vogue, acceptance, prevalence, predominance, universality.

current *adj.* **1.** *Current fashions are more casual than those of the 1950's:* present, present-day, up-to-date, contemporary, modern, existing; popular, prevailing, prevalent, in vogue, in style; *Slang* now, with-it. —*n.* **2.** *The glider soared upward on a current of air:* flow, stream, tide; draft, flux. **3.** *There was a current of unrest among the students:* undercurrent, tendency, inclination, drift, trend, *German* zeitgeist; feeling, mood, spirit, atmosphere. —**Ant.** 1 past, out-of-date; old-fashioned, out-of-style, outmoded, obsolete, passé, archaic.

curse *n.* **1.** *The witch put a curse on the princess:* evil spell, evil eye; *Slang* whammy; damnation, execration, malediction, denunciation, anathema, imprecation. **2.** *His curse made her blush:* swearing, oath; expletive, profanity, blasphemy, obscenity, *Informal* cuss. **3.** *Housework was the curse of her life:* burden, ordeal, affliction, misfortune, trouble, trial, tribulation, bane, annoyance, torment, vexation, plague, scourge, cross, crown of thorns. —*v.* **4.** *When angry, he cursed everyone in sight:* swear at, swear, utter a profanity, utter a blasphemy, utter an obscenity, *Informal* cuss; damn, blast, denounce, condemn, execrate; invoke evil on, anathematize. **5.** *The family has been cursed with poor health:* afflict, trouble, burden, torment, vex, plague, scourge. —**Ant.** 1, 2 blessing, benediction. 3 joy, boon, benefit; relief, respite. 4 compliment, praise, laud, extol; bless. 5 benefit, relieve, help, aid.

cursed *adj.* **1.** *The cursed fig tree withered:* damned, accursed, banned, blighted. **2.** *I've got this cursed cold again:* execrable, damnable, hateful, abominable, nasty. —**Ant.** 1 blessed.

cursory *adj.* *He gave the report a cursory glance and tossed it aside:* quick, hasty, hurried, swift, brief, passing, perfunctory, random, haphazard, casual, offhand, superficial, desultory, careless, inattentive. —**Ant.** slow, careful, painstaking, meticulous, scrupulous, searching, profound, elaborate, minute.

curt *adj.* *I was surprised at his curt reply:* abrupt, blunt, bluff, brusque, short, terse, summary, peremptory; petulant, snappy, gruff, crusty, rude. —**Ant.** warm, friendly, courteous, polite.

curtail *v.* *The trip was curtailed because of bad weather:* cut short, cut, shorten, pare down, clip, trim; reduce, decrease, diminish, abridge, abbreviate, condense, contract. —**Ant.** lengthen, extend, prolong, elongate, protract, expand.

curtain *n.* **1.** *She drew the curtain aside to let the sun stream in:* drape, drapery, hanging, portiere, valance, blind, shade, shutter, shutters. **2.** *Under a curtain of darkness, the thieves approached the house:* cover, concealment. —**Ant.** 1 window.

curvaceous *adj.* *A curvaceous actress was chosen for the role in the movie:* shapely, curvy, rounded, voluptuous.

curvature *n.* *The lens had an extreme curvature:* curve, arc, arch, bend, bow, flexure.

curve *n.* **1.** *This road is full of sharp curves:* bend, turn, crook, arc, arch, bow, curvature, loop. —*v.* **2.** *The ball curved to the right:* turn, bend, hook, curl, wind, arch, twist, swerve, coil, spiral.

curved *adj.* *The curved line was a hallmark of his drawing style:* rounded, round, curvilinear, curvaceous, arced, arched, bent, circular, elliptical, humped, looped, loopy, serpentine, sinuous, snaky, sweeping, swirly, twisted, wreathed, bowed.

cushion *n.* **1.** *The children sat on cushions on the floor:* pillow, pad, bolster, mat. —*v.* **2.** *The catcher's chest protector cushions the blow:* soften, suppress, damp, dampen, stifle; muffle, quiet, deaden.

custodian *n.* **1.** *The museum's custodian locked the doors promptly at five:* caretaker, janitor, superintendent, attendant, concierge, watchman. **2.** *Who is the child's custodian?:* guardian, keeper, warden; chaperon, duenna.

custody *n.* **1.** *The mother was given custody of the children:* guardianship, charge, care, trusteeship, safekeeping, protection, watch; preservation, conservation. **2.** *The police have taken the suspect into custody:* detention, confinement; possession.

custom *n.* **1.** *It is the custom for gentlemen to remove their hats in elevators:* habitual practice, convention, usage, fashion, mode, form, habit. **2. customs** *We had to pay customs on the camera equipment we bought abroad:* duty, import tax, tariff, levy, excise; toll, assessment; national customs department, customhouse. —**Ant.** 1 rarity, phenomenon, curiosity.

customary *adj.* *He arrived with his customary promptness:* usual, habitual, normal, regular, routine, wonted, typical, accustomed, conventional, traditional, general, common, ordinary, everyday. —**Ant.** unusual, uncommon, rare, exceptional; occasional, infrequent, irregular, sporadic.

customer *n.* *The store has more customers than it can take care of:* patron, shopper, buyer, purchaser; client, habitué.

cut *v.* **1.** *He cut his chin while shaving. Cut the cake:* lacerate, incise, pierce, gash, slash, hack, nick, lance, slit; slice, carve, saw, chop, dice, cube, mince; divide, section, split, dissect; sever, sunder, rive. **2.** *It's time to cut the lawn again:* trim, clip, shear; mow, prune, pare, crop, snip, shave. **3.** *Cut the report to four pages:* condense, abridge, contract, abbreviate, pare down, reduce, diminish, curtail, decrease; leave out, delete. **4.** *We spoke to her, but she cut us:* snub, ignore, refuse to recognize, refuse to greet, turn one's back on, give one the cold shoulder. **5.** *The road cuts through the forest:* cross, intersect, bisect, divide, go through, go across, move, change direction. —*n.* **6.** *Put a bandage on that cut. The bulldozer made a cut for the railroad tracks:* incision, wound, gash, nick; slit, rent, opening; hollow, furrow, indentation, trench, excavation, channel, passage, course. **7.** *This is a good lean cut of beef. The actor's agent gets a 10 percent cut:* piece, portion, share, slice, section, segment, part. **8.** *Some auto makers have announced a price cut:* reduction, decrease, abatement, decline, fall, diminution, contraction, shortening, shrinkage, curtailment, lessening. —**Ant.** 3 expand, enlarge, increase, lengthen. 4 welcome, greet. 8 increase, rise, surge; expansion, enlargement.

cute *adj. The baby wore a cute dress:* pretty, dainty, adorable, darling, sweet, precious, beautiful, handsome, attractive, lovable.

cutlery *n. They bought a set of cutlery:* flatware, silverware.

cutting *adj.* **1.** *That north wind is cutting:* piercing, sharp, harsh, stinging, nipping, biting, penetrating, smarting; cold, raw, bitter. **2.** *He replied with a cutting remark:* harsh, sharp, caustic, stringent, stinging, scathing, searing, biting, bitter, sarcastic, disparaging, acrimonious, acerbic, derisive. —**Ant.** 1 balmy, soothing, pleasant. 2 gratifying, flattering; soothing, consoling, kind, mild.

cycle *n. We studied the cycle of events leading to Hitler's downfall:* series, connected group, progression, sequence, succession, run.

cynic *n. A cynic attributes selfish motives to all acts:* skeptic, scoffer, misanthrope, faultfinder, misogynist; pessimist. —**Ant.** humanitarian; optimist.

cynical *adj. With that cynical outlook, he doesn't trust anyone:* misanthropic, misogynic, skeptical, sneering, sardonic, scornful, scoffing, derisive, sarcastic. —**Ant.** philanthropic, humanitarian; hopeful, optimistic; credulous, ingenuous.

cyst *n. They removed a cyst from his eye:* sac, sore, blister, growth, wen.

czar or **tsar** *n. The czar of Russia was overthrown in 1917:* emperor, ruler, potentate, overlord; (*loosely*) monarch, sovereign, caesar, king; despot, tyrant, dictator.

D

dab *v.* **1.** *She dabbed some cold cream on her face:* pat, tap, apply gently. —*n.* **2.** *Put a dab of butter on your toast:* pat, bit, small quantity, smidgen, soupçon; small lump, little chunk. **3.** *She applied her makeup with quick dabs:* pat, stroke, tap, light slap.

dabble *v.* **1.** *The child dabbled in her bath. We dabbled our feet in the brook:* splash, slosh, spatter, sprinkle; play in water; dip in and out of water. **2.** *He dabbles in politics:* putter, do something superficially, work on something casually, fiddle, flirt with, toy with, *Informal* fool around.

dabbler *adj.* *A dabbler in many fields, he was unable to settle on a steady occupation:* nonprofessional, amateur, dilettante, putterer, trifler, dallier. —**Ant.** professional, expert, adept.

daft *adj.* *The daft stunt driver roared off the cliff:* silly, daffy, foolish, absurd, asinine, crazy, demented, deranged, idiotic, lunatic, mad, ridiculous, stupid, witless, unbalanced, *Informal* nuts, bonkers.

daily *adj.* *He does daily exercises to help control his weight:* on each day, day in day out, day by day, from day to day, of each and every day, every weekday; diurnal, everyday, quotidian, circadian, per diem.

dainty *adj.* **1.** *The tiny statue has dainty hands:* delicate, fine, refined, lovely, pretty, beautiful, exquisite; attractive, pleasing, elegant. **2.** *Old people are often dainty eaters:* fussy, choosy, fastidious, particular. **3.** *Dainty pastries were served with tea:* delicious, choice, tasty, savory. —**Ant.** 1 gross, coarse, vulgar. 2 easily satisfied. 3 bad tasting.

dally *v.* **1.** *Come straight home from school and don't dally:* dawdle, dillydally, trifle, loiter, waste time, fritter away time. **2.** *In the novel, the prince dallied with the servant girl:* flirt, toy, play, trifle, fool around. —**Ant.** 1 hurry, hasten, speed.

dam[1] *n.* **1.** *The beavers built a dam across the stream:* barrier, wall, obstruction, hindrance. —*v.* **2.** *A wall of sandbags was thrown up to dam the floodwaters:* block, bar, stop, barricade, hinder, obstruct, impede, inhibit, check, stanch, hold back, confine, stop up, clog, hold in, bridle, restrain, repress, block up, blockade, stuff up, plug, congest, plug up, stopper. —**Ant.** free, loose, release, unleash, let go, let out.

dam[2] *n.* *The word* cow *is used to indicate the dam of some animals, such as elephants or moose:* female parent of an animal. —**Ant.** sire.

damage *n.* **1.** *The flood caused great damage to the town:* injury, harm, hurt, impairment, destruction, despoliation, loss. **2.** *The court ordered the defendant to pay $1,000 in damages for the accident:* cost, compensation for a loss. —*v.* **3.** *The fire damaged our house:* injure, hurt, harm, mar, impair, ravage. —**Ant.** 1 improvement, betterment; reparation. 3 improve, repair, mend, better.

damaged *adj.* *The truck was damaged beyond repair:* impaired, marred, injured, hurt, beat-up, bent, blemished, broken, busted, cooked, flawed, fouled up, not working, run down, spoiled.

damaging *adj.* *Damaging testimony came on the second day:* harmful, hurtful, injurious, detrimental, prejudicial. —**Ant.** favorable, advantageous, valuable.

damn *v.* **1.** *The reviewer damned the new novel:* condemn, blast, criticize, censure, disparage, denounce, bring condemnation on, inveigh against, rail at. **2.** *Should all sinners be damned?:* doom, condemn, sentence to hell. —**Ant.** 1 commend, praise, laud, applaud, speak well of, declare successful. 2 redeem, bless.

damnable *adj.* *The invaders performed one damnable deed after another:* wicked, sinful, despicable, hateful, cursed, accursed, wicked, abhorrent, abominable, detestable, execrable, hateful, offensive, odious. —**Ant.** exemplary, worthy, admirable, commendable.

damned *adj.* **1.** *No matter what she did, she was damned:* cursed, accursed, infamous, damnable, despicable, detestable, execrable, hateful, damnable, revolting, unhappy, unwelcome, doomed. **2.** *I've got the damned flu:* bad, undesirable, regrettable, *Informal* lousy.

damp *adj.* **1.** *My clothes are damp from the rain:* moist, wet, wettish, soggy, clammy, sodden, soaked, sopping, dripping. **2.** *It was a cold, damp day:* humid, muggy, dank, wet, rainy, drizzly, foggy, misty, dewy. —*n.* **3.** *The damp is bad for my rheumatism:* moisture, humidity, mist; clamminess, mugginess, dankness. **4.** *The sad story put a damp on our happy feelings:* curb, check, discouragement, restraint. —*v.* **5.** *His loss didn't damp his zest for living:* check, curb, restrain, hinder, hamper, inhibit; spoil, dash, discourage, depress; reduce, diminish, dull, deaden. —**Ant.** 1, 2 dry. 1 watertight. 2 arid, without rain. 3 dryness, aridity, aridness.

dampen *v.* **1.** *She dampened a sponge and cleaned the counter:* moisten, wet, wet down; make damp. **2.** See DAMP, sense **5**.

damsel *n.* *The novel tells about a man who enjoys rescuing damsels in distress:* young lady, girl, lass, maiden.

dance *v.* **1.** *The couple danced a polka:* move the feet and body to music, perform. **2.** *We danced with glee at the good news:* leap, skip, jump, cavort, bounce, prance, frolic, gambol. —*n.* **3.** *Do you know any new dances?:* rhythmical steps or motions, usually to music; a specific set of steps or motions (fox-trot, Charleston, jitterbug, lindy, cakewalk, twist, polka, etc.); choreography. **4.** *Do you know Beethoven's German Dances?:* dance music, music to dance to. **5.** *He studied dance:* the art of dancing. **6.** *They're having a dance Saturday night at the club:* ball, party; prom, hop.

dandified *adj.* *A cravat and imported hat made*

for a dandified appearance: foppish, dandyish, ultrasmart, fashionable, ultrafashionable, dapper, dressy, natty, spruce, chic, chichi, showy, flamboyant, peacockish, affected, preening. —**Ant.** plain, dowdy, frumpy.

dandy *n.* **1.** *Beau Brummel was a famous English dandy:* fop, clotheshorse, beau, coxcomb, fashion plate, man of fashion; dude, peacock; sharp dresser. **2.** *My new car is a dandy:* beauty, beaut; fine thing, something first-rate. —*adj.* **3.** *She thinks giving a party is a dandy idea:* fine, great, excellent, superb; swell, terrific, super; first-rate, very good. —**Ant.** 1 slob, sloppy person. 3 bad, terrible, awful.

danger *n.* *A firefighter's life is full of danger:* peril, risk, hazard, threat, menace, jeopardy, endangerment; exposure to injury, state of being exposed to harm. —**Ant.** security, safety, immunity, exemption; safeguarding, safeguard, protection.

dangerous *adj.* *It's dangerous to skate on thin ice:* risky, perilous, hazardous, chancy, unsafe, precarious, treacherous, menacing, threatening; apt to harm, full of risk, *Slang* hairy. —**Ant.** safe, steady, secure; shielded.

dangerously *adv.* *They decided to live dangerously and take up hang-gliding:* hazardously, perilously, carelessly, precariously, recklessly, riskily.

dangle *v.* *An elegant silk handkerchief dangled from his breast pocket:* hang, suspend, depend, swing, oscillate, sway, hang down, drag, droop, sag, draggle, trail, hang over, hang out.

dank *adj.* *The bear entered the dark, dank cave:* damp, moist, wet; humid, muggy, clammy, sticky, soggy, sodden; chilly, cold.

dapper *adj.* *The tailored jacket made him look particularly dapper today:* smart, neat, trim, spruce, modish, stylish, sporty, jaunty, natty, well-groomed, *Slang* spiffy.

dappled *adj.* *The children rode on a dappled mare:* spotted, mottled, flecked, variegated.

dare *v.* **1.** *She dared to walk the tightrope without a net:* venture, have the courage or nerve. **2.** *I dare you to jump across the brook:* challenge, defy. —*n.* **3.** *On a dare I jumped off the high diving board:* challenge, bet; provocation; taunt.

daredevil *n.* **1.** *The daredevil drove his motorcycle across the high wire:* stuntman, stuntwoman, desperado, adventurer. —*adj.* **2.** *Niagara Falls has often invited daredevil stunts:* rash, adventurous, risk-taking, reckless, heedless, foolhardy, wild, devil-may-care, venturesome, nervy.

daring *n.* **1.** *Amelia Earhart's daring made her a famous pilot:* boldness, courage, bravery; audaciousness, audacity, adventurousness. —*adj.* **2.** *The soldier was decorated for daring acts behind enemy lines:* bold, gallant, valiant, courageous, brave, adventurous, venturesome, dauntless, undaunted, intrepid; plucky, game; audacious. —**Ant.** 1 cowardice, timidity, timorousness. 2 cowardly, uncourageous.

dark *adj.* **1.** *The streets were dark during the blackout:* black, obscure, opaque, dim, dusky,

shadowy, shady; overcast, murky, inky, dingy; sunless; without light. **2.** *She had beautiful big dark eyes:* deeply colored, not light, not pale. **3.** *The war was a dark period for us:* gloomy, dismal, bleak, dreary, joyless, sorrowful, somber; disheartening, discouraging, hopeless. **4.** *The witch in the story practiced the dark arts of sorcery:* evil, wicked, sinister. **5.** *His dark expression showed his mood:* angry, sullen, somber, gloomy, frowning; forbidding, ominous, bleak, sinister, threatening. **6.** *There seemed to be some dark meaning in his remark:* hidden, concealed, secret; obscure, dim, deep. —*n.* **7.** *It was hard to find a seat in the dark of the theater:* darkness; absence of light, partial absence of light. **8.** *The children got home before dark:* nightfall, night, nighttime; evening, twilight, eventide. —**Ant.** 1–3, 5, 7, 8 light. 1–3, 5 bright. 1 luminous, lit, illumined, illuminated; dazzling, radiant. 2 pale, fair, white. 3 happy, joyful, hopeful. 5 happy, joyful, cheerful. 6 open, known; clear, lucid, plain, transparent; comprehensible. 7 lightness, brightness. 8 dawn, morning, daytime, daybreak, afternoon.

darken *v.* **1.** *We closed the curtains and darkened the room:* dim, blacken, obscure, make dark, make darker, make dim, exclude light from. **2.** *She used a tint to darken her hair:* color, dye, tint; make less pale or fair; color deeper, shade a deeper hue. **3.** *The argument darkened her mood:* cloud, dispirit, sadden; make despondent, make gloomy, fill with gloom, cast a pall over. —**Ant.** 1, 2, 3 lighten, brighten. 3 make happy.

darkness *n.* **1.** *Darkness comes early in winter:* nighttime, night, dark; evening, twilight, dusk, nightfall, eventide. **2.** *The interior of the cave was in complete darkness:* dark, blackness, dimness, shade.

darling *n.* **1.** *Darling, we'll be married in June!:* beloved, dear, dearest, sweetheart, love. —*adj.* **2.** *My darling wife and I are going to Europe:* beloved, dear, dearest; precious, loved, lovable, adored, cherished; sweet, charming, enchanting, lovely. **3.** *I bought a darling hat:* cute, attractive; charming, enchanting, captivating; adorable.

dart *n.* **1.** *We each threw two darts at the target:* missile, spear, javelin, projectile; small arrow. **2.** *With a dart, she escaped from the room:* dash, rush, sprint, run; spurt, leap, jump, bound, fling; sudden movement. —*v.* **3.** *The bird darted from branch to branch:* dash, rush, bolt, tear, run, race, sprint; hurry, hasten; spring, leap, jump, bound; flit; fly quickly, move quickly.

dash *v.* **1.** *She dashed the plate against the door in anger:* hurl, throw, fling, thrust, slam, smash, shatter, crash, splinter. **2.** *Upon hearing the scream, he dashed out of the room and up the stairs:* dart, bolt, zip, tear, race, rush, run, bound, speed, hurry, hasten. **3.** *Don't dash the paint on the wall like that:* splash, splatter, spatter. **4.** *The rain dashed our plans for hiking:* ruin, spoil; thwart, frustrate, foil; discourage, disappoint, throw a damper on, dampen. —*n.* **5.** *He made a dash for the train just as it began to* leave the station: dart, bolt, race, rush, run, sprint. **6.** *The contestants lined up for the 100-yard dash:* sprint, short race; trial of speed. **7.** *A dash of vinegar might help the salad:* pinch, bit, a drop, touch, small addition, slight amount, soupçon. **8.** *She conducted the orchestra with a great deal of fire and dash:* verve, vigor, spirit, flair, panache, zeal, exuberance, animation, élan, vivacity, energy, *Slang* pizazz, oomph.

dashing *adj.* *He always played dashing buccaneer types in the movies:* impetuous, daring, audacious, bold, swashbuckling, gallant, spirited; brave, courageous, fearless, plucky, unafraid.

dastardly *adj.* *A hit-and-run driver has got to be a dastardly person:* cowardly, mean, sneaky, base, vile, despicable, atrocious, shameful, low. —**Ant.** gallant, valiant, valorous, brave, courageous.

data *n. pl.* *The data on the company's progress was incomplete:* information, facts, figures; documents, evidence, dossier, *Slang* info, dope.

date *n.* **1.** *The date of the attack on Pearl Harbor was December 7, 1941:* particular point or period of time, day, month, or year. **2.** *The date of the Renaissance is sometimes considered to be from the 14th to the 17th centuries:* period, age, era, stage, epoch, historical period. **3.** *Didn't we have a date for lunch today?:* appointment, engagement, rendezvous, agreement to meet. **4.** *Who's your date for the dance?:* escort, companion, partner. —*v.* **5.** *The cathedral of Notre Dame dates from the 12th century:* originate, to exist from, bear a date. **6.** *Please date all your business letters. This statue has been dated as 5th century B.C.:* put a date on, affix a date to, mark with a date, ascertain the date of, fix the time of. **7.** *He's been dating Thelma for two years:* escort, court, go out on dates with, take out, keep company with.

dated *adj.* **1.** *Clothing styles become dated very quickly:* old-fashioned, unfashionable, out-of-date, outmoded, passé, antiquated, obsolete, *Slang* old hat. **2.** *We bought a dated engraving by Rembrandt:* showing a date, having a date.

daub *v.* **1.** *First daub the surface with plaster, then paint:* coat, cover, smear, paint. **2.** *The walls were daubed with finger marks:* smear, smudge, spot, soil, dirty, stain, smirch. —*n.* **3.** *The child's clothes were covered with daubs of mud:* blot, blotch, spot, splotch, stain.

daunt *v.* *Crossing the country in wagons did not daunt the early pioneers:* intimidate, dismay, faze, discourage, dishearten, deject, depress, dash, unnerve, subdue, browbeat, cow, abash, menace, threaten; frighten, scare, alarm, affright. —**Ant.** embolden, encourage, cheer, animate, enliven.

dauntless *adj.* *The dauntless troops charged the enemy stronghold:* fearless, unafraid, bold, courageous, brave, valiant, valorous, heroic, gallant, daring, resolute, stouthearted, undaunted, *Slang* gutsy. —**Ant.** cowardly, fearful, afraid, apprehensive, fainthearted, irresolute.

dawdle *v.* *If you dawdle on the way home, you won't have time for your schoolwork:* dally, dilly-dally, idle, loiter, loaf, delay; procrastinate; putter around, loll around, fool around; kill time, waste time, fritter away time. —**Ant.** hurry, hasten, speed.

dawn *n.* **1.** *Did you hear the cock crow at dawn?:* daybreak, sunrise, sunup, daylight, dawning. **2.** *The book is about the dawn of civilization:* beginning, commencement, birth, rise, inception, origin, advent, start, emergence, unfolding; first appearance; early development. —*v.* **3.** *Day will dawn at 5:03 A.M. tomorrow:* begin to grow light in the morning. **4.** *A new age for humankind is dawning:* begin, appear, rise, commence; develop, unfold, emerge. **5.** *It dawned on me that I'd left the oven on:* occur, strike, come to one's mind, begin to see or understand, begin to make an impression.

day *n.* **1.** *She never goes out during the day:* time between sunrise and sunset, from dawn to dusk; period of 12 daylight hours; period of 24 hours. **2.** *What day is her birthday?:* date; particular day. **3.** *The day of the horse and buggy is long past:* heyday, period, time, epoch, age; period of ascendancy. **4.** *Do you still work an 8-hour day?:* workday, period of activity. **5.** *Mexico is three days from here by bus:* day's journey, distance that can be traveled in a day. —**Ant.** 1 night, nighttime.

daybreak *n.* *He was up at daybreak:* dawn, break of day; sunrise, sunup.

daydream *v.* **1.** *She daydreamed about a carefree vacation:* muse, imagine, fantasize, fancy; wool-gather, dream. —*n.* **2.** *His daydream is to retire to a tropical island:* fantasy, dream, reverie, pipe dream, castle in the air.

daylight *n.* **1.** *Wear these dark glasses in the daylight:* sunlight, sunshine; light of day. **2.** *A farmer must finish the chores during daylight:* daytime, day; the period between sunrise and sunset, the period between dawn and dusk, the daylight hours, the period of 12 daylight hours. **3.** *In winter he feeds the livestock before daylight:* dawn, daybreak, crack of dawn, sunrise, sunup, morning; beginning of day. **4.** *Certain facts in the case have not been brought into the daylight:* public attention, full view; openness.

daze *v.* **1.** *The blow dazed me, but I wasn't hurt:* stun, shock, stupefy; stagger, confuse, bewilder, disorient, discombobulate; numb, benumb. **2.** *The natural beauty of the Grand Canyon dazed all of us:* amaze, astound, astonish, surprise, dazzle, startle, stun, flabbergast, *Slang* blow one's mind; excite, electrify. —*n.* **3.** *After the accident, she walked around in a daze:* stupor, muddle, shock, bewilderment; astonishment, surprise.

dazzle *v.* **1.** *The bright array of candles dazzled the crowd:* daze, blind, confuse, blur; blind temporarily, as with strong light; dim the vision. **2.** *The glamorous movie star dazzled us:* awe, overawe, overwhelm, overpower; excite, electrify; impress greatly.

dead *adj.* **1.** *The doctor pronounced him dead on arrival at the hospital:* deceased, expired, perished, lifeless; no longer living, having no life. **2.** *Scientists believe that Mercury is a dead* *planet:* lifeless, inorganic, inanimate; incapable of life; devoid of life, having no life. **3.** *A language that is no longer spoken is called a dead language:* defunct; extinct; obsolete; no longer in use. **4.** *The battery was dead and the car wouldn't start:* inoperative, inactive; not working, not responsive; out of operation. **5.** *That color looks dead next to your skin. This town is dead after 10 P.M.:* dull, lackluster, unexciting, vapid, flat, insipid. **6.** *The arrow hit at dead center:* exact, unerring, precise. **7.** *The company's lack of profits is the result of too much dead capital:* unproductive, ineffectual, unused, useless; unemployed, unprofitable, stagnant. **8.** *There was a dead silence after the announcement:* total, complete, utter, absolute, thorough, entire. **9.** *After a day of shopping, I'm usually dead:* exhausted, tired, spent; worn-out, *Slang* beat. —*n.* **10.** *The furnace broke down in the dead of winter:* midst, depth, middle; period of greatest darkness, cold, quiet, or gloom. **11. the dead.** *We must pray for the dead:* dead people; those who have died. —*adv.* **12.** *The deer stopped dead in her tracks:* abruptly, suddenly. **13.** *I am dead certain that I saw him:* absolutely; completely, entirely, utterly. —**Ant.** 1 alive, living, live, animate; breathing. 2 living, animate. 3 existing, living, in use. 4 working, responsive, operative, operating, active, in motion; alive. 5 lively, vivacious, exciting. 6 inaccurate, inexact. 7 productive, effective, useful. 8 partial, incomplete. 9 active, energetic.

deaden *v. Two of these pills will deaden the ache. A new muffler will deaden the noise your car's exhaust makes:* blunt, dull, diminish, subdue, moderate, mitigate; abate, lessen, weaken; soothe, assuage, alleviate; numb, drug, anesthetize, dope; muffle, smother, mute.

deadlock *n. The negotiations reached a deadlock after two hours:* standstill; standoff, impasse, stalemate.

deadly *adj.* **1.** *Cancer is often a deadly disease:* fatal, lethal, mortal, death-dealing, deathly; malignant; destructive, baneful. **2.** *He has become my deadly enemy:* dangerous enough to kill, destroy, or harm; relentless, unrelenting, implacable. **3.** *Her deadly appearance was due to long illness:* deathlike, cadaverous, ghostly, ashen, pallid, wan. **4.** *A deadly silence filled the auditorium:* excessive, extreme, inordinate; very great; undue. **5.** *The lecture is deadly—let's leave:* boring, dull, tedious, wearisome, tiresome; terrible, awful, dreadful. —*adv.* **6.** *It was a deadly boring play:* completely, entirely, fully, thoroughly, totally; terribly, awfully, horribly. —**Ant.** 1 vital, wholesome, life-giving, benign, harmless. 2 relenting, appeasable, conciliatory, placable. 3 healthy, glowing. 5 exciting.

deal *v.* **1.** *Next time the problem comes up, I'll deal with it:* treat, handle, oversee; attend to, see to, take care of, cope with, dispose of. **2.** *His book dealt with the life of George Washington:* concern, consider; have to do with, be occupied with. **3.** *It is important to know how to deal effectively with one's co-workers:* act, behave. **4.** *This gallery deals in 19th-century paint-*

ings: trade, market, buy and sell; do business. **5.** *The challenger dealt the champion a swift blow:* give, deliver, administer. **6.** *The person on the left deals the cards now:* distribute, dispense, apportion, give out, mete out, parcel out, dole out. —*n.* **7.** *The deal rotates clockwise. I lost on that last deal:* distribution, apportionment, round, hand, single game. **8.** *The terms are agreeable—it's a deal:* bargain, agreement, arrangement. —**Ant.** 1 ignore, overlook, disregard; neglect, leave undone. 6 receive, gather, collect, take back.

dealer *n. We found the right dealer downtown:* merchant, merchandiser, vendor, marketer, trader, tradesman, businessman, retailer, trafficker.

dealing *n.* **1.** Usually **dealings.** *We have dealings with their firm from time to time:* relations, transactions, traffic, trade; business. **2.** *She has a reputation for honest dealing:* treatment, practice; method or manner of conduct.

dear *adj.* **1.** *She's very dear to us. Letters often begin "Dear Sir or Madam":* precious, beloved, loved, cherished, much loved, fondly regarded, favorite; esteemed, respected, highly regarded (used in a salutation: "Dear Dr. Jones"). **2.** *Diamonds are very dear:* expensive, costly, high-priced; at a premium. —*n.* **3.** *You're a dear to look after the children for me:* darling, sweetheart, love, angel, good person, kind person, generous person. —**Ant.** 1 hated, abhorred, disliked. 2 inexpensive, cheap, low-priced; common; worthless.

dearly *adv.* **1.** *He dearly loved his wife:* fondly, affectionately, devotedly, lovingly, tenderly. **2.** *She dearly paid for her adventure:* very, greatly, extremely.

dearth *n. There is a dearth of skilled workers in this area:* scarcity, lack, shortage, paucity; deficiency; insufficient supply. —**Ant.** abundance, superabundance, plethora, plenty; adequate supply.

death *n.* **1.** *He mourned the death of his best friend:* dying, demise, passing, departure, decease, expiration; loss of life. **2. Death.** *Death is often pictured as a skeleton carrying a scythe:* grim reaper, angel of death. —**Ant.** 1 life; birth, beginning, rise, growth.

deathbed *n. She made a new will on her deathbed:* last breath, death struggle, death rattle, death groan, death throes, deathwatch, dying breath, last rites, final extremity, last agony.

deathless *adj. Only the body dies—the soul is deathless:* immortal, eternal, perpetual, everlasting, not subject to death. —**Ant.** mortal; perishable; transitory; passing.

deathly *adj.* **1.** *The deathly aura of the old house frightened us:* deathlike, resembling death. **2.** *I have a deathly fear of snakes:* extreme, terrible, intense, overwhelming. —*adv.* **3.** *The man is deathly ill:* extremely, very. —**Ant.** 1 lifelike, lively.

debacle *n. The teams were so mismatched that the game turned into a debacle:* disaster, catastrophe, devastation, ruination, collapse, overthrow, rout, vanquishment, cataclysm, havoc, ruin, downfall, bankruptcy, dissolution, disintegration, wreck, breakdown. —**Ant.** success, victory, conquest, achievement, triumph.

debar v. **1.** *She was debarred from the premises:* exclude, shut out, blackball. **2.** *Besides facing a heavy fine, the lawyer was debarred from practising his profession:* prevent, prohibit, hinder, interdict, outlaw. —**Ant.** 1 include, welcome 2 encourage, support.

debase v. *Inflation has debased the country's currency. Don't debase yourself by accepting a bribe:* lower, degrade, defile, disgrace, dishonor; befoul, desecrate, corrupt, deteriorate; adulterate; impair the worth of, reduce the quality of. —**Ant.** enhance, elevate, uplift, improve, heighten.

debatable adj. *It's debatable whether I will go to Europe this summer:* questionable, doubtful, dubious, undecided, uncertain, unsure; problem-atical, arguable, disputable; *Informal* iffy. —**Ant.** certain, sure, settled, decided, beyond question.

debate n. **1.** *The two college teams will have a debate on Saturday:* argument, discussion, dispute; formal discussion of opposing points of view. **2.** *After much debate, I refused their offer:* deliberation, consideration, reflection, meditation, cogitation. —v. **3.** *The senate debated whether the new highway should be built or not:* argue, dispute, discuss, *Slang* hash over. **4.** *I debated whether to accept the job:* deliberate, consider, reflect, ponder, think about, meditate upon, cogitate.

debauch v. *He debauched every woman he could find:* seduce, ravish, deprave, violate, abuse, corrupt, debase, defile, lead astray.

debauched adj. *He retained some youthful good looks, rather like a debauched choirboy:* depraved, corrupted, debased, perverted, licentious, lascivious, lewd, libidinous, lecherous, wanton, vitiated, led astray, dissipated, dissolute, immoral, profligate, degraded. —**Ant.** pure, moral, good, saintly, virtuous, high-minded.

debauchery n. *The carnival nights were full of rioting and debauchery:* excess, intemperance, immoderation, self-indulgence, dissipation.

debilitate v. *She was debilitated by a bad cold:* weaken, devitalize, enervate; make feeble, deprive of strength, wear out. —**Ant.** strengthen, invigorate, energize, vitalize; rejuvenate, renew, restore.

debility n. *A bout with the flu left her with a feeling of debility for weeks:* weakness, infirmity, feebleness, asthenia, frailty, invalidism, prostration, decrepitude, sickliness, senility; lassitude, exhaustion, fatigue, enervation. —**Ant.** vigor, stamina, robustness, vitality, energy.

debonair adj. **1.** *The debonair gentleman always had a smile for everyone:* charming, urbane, gracious, suave; refined, elegant, well-bred, sophisticated, genteel. **2.** *We recognized him by his debonair walk:* carefree, lighthearted, jaunty, dapper, buoyant, sprightly, free and

easy. —**Ant.** 1 awkward, rude, gauche, uncivil. 2 serious, gloomy.

debris n. *The explosion reduced the building to debris in seconds:* rubble, trash, junk, rubbish, scrap, detritus, clutter, wreckage, litter, ruins, waste, dregs, garbage, dross, fragments, shards; *Slang* dreck, crap.

debt n. *I'll pay off all my debts with this check:* liability, obligation, debit, bill, arrears, deferred payment; that which is owed.

debunk v. *The newspaper debunked the youth cult as the tool of a foreign government:* expose, uncover, bare, uncloak, deflate, show up, strip, unmask, disparage, demystify, demythologize; ridicule, satirize, burlesque, lampoon; *Slang* send up, take off.

debut or **début** n. **1.** *The young actress made her debut in the new comedy:* first public appearance. **2.** *She made her debut at the annual ball:* coming out, presentation, formal introduction into society.

decadence n. *A long period of decadence preceded the fall of the Roman Empire:* decline, deterioration, decay, corruption, immorality, degeneration, degeneracy, debasement.

decadent adj. *The country eliminated its powerful, rich, and decadent aristocracy:* corrupt, immoral, decaying, degenerate, debased, depraved, debauched, perverse, perverted, dissolute.

decamp v. **1.** *The army decamped during the night:* depart from camp, break camp; move off, march off. **2.** *The treasurer decamped with part of the company's payroll:* depart suddenly, leave quickly or secretly, make off quickly, run away, sneak off, take off.

decay v. **1.** *The tree began to decay as soon as it was cut down:* rot, decompose, disintegrate, spoil, putrefy; corrode. —n. **2.** *The decay of the meat could have been prevented by proper refrigeration:* decomposition, rot, rotting, putrefaction; spoiling. —**Ant.** 1 flourish, flower, expand, grow, increase.

decayed adj. *Left out, the vegetables quickly decayed:* rotted, rotten, decomposed, gangrenous, putrid, rank, spoiled, corroded.

deceased adj. See DEAD.

deceit n. *There is too much deceit practiced against consumers:* deception, cheating, fraud, fraudulence, dishonesty, deceitfulness; double-dealing, duplicity, trickiness trickery, underhandedness; misrepresentation. —**Ant.** honesty, frankness, sincerity, openness, candor, forthrightness; truthfulness; fair dealing.

deceitful adj. *Her saying one thing and doing the opposite shows she's deceitful:* untrustworthy, insincere, hypocritical; underhanded, false, dishonest, deceptive, treacherous; sneaky, duplicitous, double-dealing; tricky, cunning, crafty.

deceive v. *He deceived me by pretending to be a famous movie star:* mislead, delude, trick, fool, cheat; swindle, defraud, *Slang* con, put on. —**Ant.** enlighten; guide; tell the truth to, be true to, be honest to.

decency n. *Please have the decency to apolo-*

gize: propriety, decorum; respectability, modesty, appropriateness; quality of being decent. —**Ant.** indecency.

decent *adj.* **1.** *I'm not sure the movie is decent enough for the children:* proper, suitable, fitting, appropriate; seemly, correct. **2.** *He is rather fat, but he has a decent face:* fair; fairly attractive. **3.** *The workers went on strike for decent working conditions:* adequate, satisfactory, acceptable; passable, fair; ample, sufficient, reasonably satisfying. **4.** *He was decent enough to say thank you:* courteous, accommodating, obliging, gracious, nice. —**Ant.** 1 improper, unsuitable, inappropriate, unseemly, incorrect, unbecoming; immodest, indecent, obscene, lewd. 3 inadequate, unsatisfactory, unfair, intolerable. 4 awkward, gauche, inept, maladroit, clumsy, crude; discourteous.

deception *n.* **1.** *There was deception in the salesperson's claims:* deceit, deceitfulness, deceptiveness, fraud, fraudulence; trickery, trickiness; duplicity, insincerity, double-dealing; treachery; cunning. **2.** *The magician's disappearing act was done by deception:* trick, artifice, illusion. —**Ant.** 1 candor, honesty, sincerity, truthfulness.

deceptive *adj.* *The magazine won't accept any deceptive ads:* misleading, dishonest, deceitful, fraudulent, *Informal* phony. —**Ant.** truthful, honest, trustworthy.

decide *v.* **1.** *I have decided to learn shorthand. We've decided to buy the house in the country:* determine, resolve, settle; choose, elect, select; make up one's mind. **2.** *The court decided against the defendant:* settle, decree, rule; judge; come to a decision; make a decision. —**Ant.** 1 vacillate, waver, hesitate, falter, fluctuate.

decided *adj.* **1.** *It was a decided win for our team:* clear-cut, certain, unquestionable, unmistakable, definite, indisputable; beyond all question. **2.** *She coped with the problems in a decided manner:* determined, decisive, definite, unhesitating, unwavering, resolute, deliberate, emphatic, assertive, firm, strong-willed. —**Ant.** 1 dubious, doubtful, questionable, ambiguous. 2 undetermined, indecisive, hesitating, wavering, irresolute, weak, weak-willed.

deciding *adj.* *The deciding factor was its low cost:* crucial, significant, chief, conclusive, critical, decisive, determining, important, necessary, prime, principal, influential.

decipher *v.* *Deciphering the enemy's messages hastened the war's end. It's always a problem deciphering her handwriting:* decode, decrypt, cryptanalyze, translate, construe, explain, render, interpret, deduce, puzzle out, figure out, unravel, untangle, solve, make out, *Slang* dope out.

decision *n.* **1.** *After much debate, I came to a decision to accept the job:* conclusion, judgment, verdict; resolution; determination; result arrived at after consideration. **2.** *The court's decision will be made known tomorrow:* verdict, finding, outcome, decree; pronouncement by a court. **3.** *The job demands a man of*

decision: determination, decisiveness, decidedness, resolution, resoluteness, resolve, purpose, purposefulness. —**Ant.** 3 indecision, uncertainty, vacillation, vagueness.

decisive *adj.* **1.** *The last battle made the victory decisive:* conclusive, undeniable, indisputable, final, convincing, definitive. **2.** *A decisive person is needed to deal with this situation:* resolute, determined, decided, positive, definite, absolute; firm. —**Ant.** 1 inconclusive, disputable, dubious, moot. 2 indecisive, irresolute, wavering, fluctuating; hesitant, reluctant.

deck *v.* *The women decked themselves in the finest silks and furs:* decorate, adorn, dress, clothe, garb, apparel, accouter, outfit, array, bedeck, ornament, trim, embellish, festoon, garnish, furbish, beautify, enrich, bedizen, deck out, prank, spruce up, gussy up, doll up, tog out. —**Ant.** strip, divest, denude, uncover, expose, lay bare.

declaim *v.* **1.** *Mark Antony declaimed over the body of Caesar:* orate, recite, utter aloud in rhetorical manner, make a formal speech, sermonize, pontificate. **2.** *The senator declaimed against higher taxes:* rail, inveigh.

declaration *n.* **1.** *His signed declaration presented the facts as he knew them:* statement, affirmation; attestation, testimony, deposition; avowal, acknowledgment, assertion. **2.** *We read the declaration posted on the bulletin board:* announcement, proclamation; notification, notice, publication, document. —**Ant.** 1 denial; disavowal, retraction.

declare *v.* **1.** *The governor declared a state of emergency:* proclaim, pronounce, announce. **2.** *Their appearance at the meeting declared their willingness to compromise:* affirm; reveal, show, express, give evidence of. —**Ant.** 1 suppress, withhold. 2 hide, conceal.

decline *v.* **1.** *I declined to go along with such a wild scheme:* refuse, reject, eschew, spurn; fail to accept, turn down, balk at. **2.** *The road declines sharply at this point:* slope downward, incline downward, slope down. **3.** *Her health has been declining these past months. The dollar declined on the open market. His popularity declined after the 1950's and he retired:* weaken, fail, flag, sink, deteriorate, worsen; ebb, wane, diminish, dwindle, decrease, lessen. —*n.* **4.** *The path follows a sharp decline to the lake:* downgrade, declivity, drop; downward incline, downward slope. **5.** *We are studying the decline of ancient Rome:* downfall, deterioration, decay. **6.** *Our business has gone into a decline this year:* slump, downswing, downfall, downward tendency. **7.** *With his life in decline, he waited for death:* last part, period close to the end. —**Ant.** 1 accept, consent. 2 rise. 3 improve, increase, strengthen. 5, 6 rise, advancement, improvement. 7 first part.

decompose *v.* **1.** *The dead tree decomposed and had to be uprooted:* rot, decay, putrefy, spoil; disintegrate; go to pieces. **2.** *Salt decomposes into sodium and chlorine:* separate; break up, disintegrate, break down.

decomposition *n.* *The hot weather aided the*

decomposition: putrefaction, rot, corruption, decay, disintegration, dissolution, breakdown.

decontaminate *v. The laboratory was sprayed with chemicals to decontaminate it:* purify, sterilize, disinfect. **—Ant.** contaminate, infect.

decor or **décor** *n. The decor in the room was French Provincial:* decoration, ornamentation; style of decorating.

decorate *v.* **1.** *We decorated the house for the holidays:* ornament, adorn, beautify, bedeck, deck, array, trim, garnish, embellish, festoon. **2.** *The soldier was decorated for bravery:* honor; award a decoration to, confer distinction upon.

decoration *n.* **1.** *He specializes in the decoration of private estates:* adornment, ornamentation, beautification, embellishment. **2.** *The decorations for the party were bright and cheery:* ornament, ornamentation, trimming, trim, embellishment, adornment, garnish. **3.** *The admiral's uniform was covered with decorations:* medal, award, emblem, ribbon, badge.

decorative *adj. The architect added some decorative elements:* ornate, embellished, florid, gilt, ornamental.

decorous *adj. The inauguration is an occasion calling for decorous behavior:* proper, correct, suitable, dignified, becoming, seemly, fit, appropriate; decent, polite, mannerly, respectful. **—Ant.** improper, unfit, unbecoming, unsuitable, undignified.

decorum *n. Jennifer always acts with decorum:* propriety, politeness; tact, gentility, respectability, dignity, taste; good form. **—Ant.** impropriety, inappropriate behavior, bad manners.

decoy *n.* **1.** *The hunters used wooden ducks as decoys to attract the flock. The Trojan Horse was a decoy:* enticement, bait, lure, snare, inducement; smoke screen, *Slang* plant, come-on; deceptive stratagem. *—v.* **2.** *He used a whistle to decoy the birds within range:* bait, entice, lure, snare, allure; attract by some deceptive device.

decrease *v.* **1.** *Water consumption decreased during the summer:* diminish, lessen, reduce, dwindle, drop, subside, de-escalate; slacken, ease, abate, taper, decline. *—n.* **2.** *A big decrease in sales caused the store to close:* reduction, lessening, loss, decline, abatement, diminution, dwindling, cutback, de-escalation; falloff. **—Ant.** 1 increase, augment, enlarge, extend, lengthen, expand. 2 growth, extension, expansion, swelling.

decree *n.* **1.** *The king issued a decree that all prisoners would be granted amnesty:* order, command, proclamation, dictum, statute, law, edict, ruling, mandate. *—v.* **2.** *The king decreed an amnesty:* order, authorize, command, proclaim.

decrepit *adj. This decrepit building shows many years of negligence:* broken-down, dilapidated, battered, rickety.

decry *v. The king decried the lack of support he received from the people:* criticize, denounce, rail against, condemn; disparage, deprecate, censure. **—Ant.** extol, acclaim, laud, commend, praise.

dedicate *v.* **1.** *She dedicated herself to conserving our natural resources:* devote, commit, pledge; give completely. **2.** *The school dedicated the new building on Sunday:* launch, present; devote to a special use. **3.** *She dedicated the novel to her husband:* inscribe, address.

dedicated *adj. The dedicated nurse worked overtime:* committed, single-minded, whole-hearted, devoted, enthusiastic, loyal, sworn. **—Ant.** unconcerned, indifferent, uncaring.

dedication *n.* **1.** *The archbishop attended the dedication of the new church:* ceremony or act of dedicating for a specific use. **2.** *His dedication to teaching gained the respect of his peers:* devotion, devotedness, commitment. **3.** *The book's dedication reads "To Mother":* prefatory inscription or address.

deduce *v. From her conversation, I deduced that she had a large family:* conclude, reason, gather, infer, comprehend, understand.

deducible *adj. From what happened, the result was deducible:* consequent, following, provable, inferable, inferential, derivable, deductive, reasoned, traceable, understandable.

deduct *v. They deducted the cost of the broken window from his allowance:* subtract, remove, take, withdraw; decrease by, take from. **—Ant.** add, enlarge, amplify; add to.

deduction *n.* **1.** *It was the inspector's deduction that the crime was an inside job:* conclusion, inference, assumption, presumption, judgment, supposition, interpretation, analysis, calculation; understanding, comprehension, reflection, guess, speculation, consideration. **2.** *The store allows a deduction of 10 percent for cash payment:* reduction, discount, markdown, rebate, concession, abatement, rollback, allowance, exemption, subtraction, credit. **—Ant.** 2 increase, addition, increment, raise, appreciation.

deed *n.* **1.** *He is remembered for his many good deeds:* act, action, feat, achievement, accomplishment; effort. **2.** *Do you have the deed to the house?:* legal document showing ownership of property.

deem *v. I deem it advisable to buy property now:* think, believe, judge, regard, consider, hold, view.

deep *adj.* **1.** *Don't go into deep water unless you can swim. They drilled a deep hole in the earth's crust:* of great depth, far below the surface, extending far downward. **2.** *A deep closet can hold two rods. She went deep into the woods:* far in or back, extending inward from front to back. **3.** *Rip Van Winkle was in a deep sleep for many years:* intense, profound, extreme. **4.** *The child sat there deep in thought:* absorbed, involved, immersed, engrossed; lost. **5.** *He's certainly a deep thinker:* intelligent, astute, sagacious, discerning, wise, learned; profound, philosophical. **6.** *The matching skirt is in deep blue:* dark, strong, intense; rich, vivid. **7.** *Don't you love his deep, rich voice?:* resonant, sonorous; low in pitch, not high, not sharp. *—n.* **8.** *The ill-fated* Titanic *rests in the deep:* ocean, sea. **9.** *They were lost in the deep of the forest:* midst; inmost part, part of greatest intensity.

—adv. 10. *They dug deep for the treasure:* deeply; far down. **11.** *The rescuers worked deep into the night:* far, late. **—Ant.** 1, 2 shallow. 3 light. 4 uninvolved. 5 superficial; slow. 6 light, pale, faded; dull. 7 high, sharp; light. 9 shallowest part.

deepen *v.* **1.** *They deepened the trench:* dig, dig out, dredge, excavate, extend, hollow, scoop out. **2.** *Re-reading the book deepened our awareness:* intensify, extend, aggravate, develop, enhance, expand, grow, heighten, increase, magnify, reinforce, strengthen.

deeply *adv.* **1.** *How deeply did the submarine dive?:* deep; far below the surface, far down. **2.** *I was deeply moved by her testimony:* greatly, profoundly, intensely; passionately; acutely; completely, thoroughly, entirely. **3.** *Who can gaze deeply into the future?:* far on in time or place. **4.** *He spoke deeply in a masculine voice:* resonantly, sonorously; with a deep tone, at a low pitch. **5.** *The fabric is deeply tinted in red:* vividly, intensely, richly. **6.** *I'm amazed to learn he's deeply in debt:* seriously, gravely; over one's head. **—Ant.** 1 shallowly. 2 hardly, very little. 4 with a high tone, at a high pitch. 5 lightly, dully. 6 not seriously.

deface *v.* *He defaced the book by writing on it:* mar, damage, disfigure, impair; spoil, injure, bruise, mark, scar. **—Ant.** beautify; improve the looks of.

de facto 1. *Though the king had absolute authority, the noblemen ruled their own lands de facto:* actually, really; in fact. **2.** *Elections meant nothing--he was the de facto head of state:* actual, real, in existence.

defamation *n.* *He sued the newspaper for defamation of his character:* slander, libel, disparagement, calumny, vilification.

defamatory *adj.* *I won't stand for any more of his defamatory remarks:* libelous, slanderous, disparaging, derogatory, calumnious, vilifying.

defame *v.* *We expect politicians to defame each other in an election year:* slander, libel, malign, disparage, discredit, denigrate, degrade, derogate, vilify, calumniate; speak ill of, attack the good reputation of. **—Ant.** praise, laud, applaud, extol.

default *n.* **1.** *If the team doesn't show up, they will lose by default:* failure to appear or act. **2.** *His car was repossessed because of default of the monthly installment:* nonpayment; failure to pay.

defeat *v.* **1.** *A British fleet defeated the French at Trafalgar:* overcome, conquer, overthrow, rout, vanquish, overpower, overwhelm, quell, crush, trounce, *Slang* shellac, cream; gain a victory over an opponent, prevail over. **2.** *This kind of problem always defeats me:* confound, baffle, thwart, foil, frustrate; elude, get the better of. **—n. 3.** *The new housing bill suffered defeat in Congress:* setback, loss of a contest, failure to win. **4.** *Losing the scholarship meant defeat of all her hopes:* frustration, disappointment, thwarting; loss. **—Ant.** 1 lose, succumb, surrender, capitulate, bow, yield, submit. 3 success, triumph, victory.

defect *n.* **1.** *The television was returned because of a defect:* fault, flaw, imperfection; blemish, spot, blotch, stain; scar, crack, break. **2.** *Her insensitivity is a defect in her character:* deficiency, omission, incompleteness, shortcoming, fault, default; weakness, fraility, failing; foible, weak point. **—v. 3.** *The scientist defected to another country:* desert or forsake (one's country), leave or quit (one's land for another) without permission. **—Ant.** 1 perfection, completeness. 2 strength, forte.

defection *n.* *His defection from the team weakened their cause:* desertion, abandonment, dereliction, disownment, divorce, separation, rejection, repudiation, revolt.

defective *adj.* **1.** *May I return this toaster if it's defective?:* faulty, imperfect, lacking, deficient, flawed, impaired, inadequate, insufficient, wanting, broken; out of order, inoperative. **2.** *Due to brain damage, his speech was defective:* abnormal; subnormal; lacking in normal development. **—Ant.** 1 perfect, adequate; intact, entire, whole. 2 normal.

defend *v.* **1.** *A family must defend its home against attack:* protect, preserve; secure, shield, shelter, guard, safeguard; keep safe, watch over. **2.** *Freedom from tyranny is a principle we should always defend:* uphold, sustain, support, maintain; endorse, advocate, champion; stand by.

defense *n.* **1.** *Many men enlisted for the defense of their country:* protection, preservation, security, safeguard, guard; maintenance; care, safekeeping, custody. **2.** *We must strengthen our defenses on the western border:* fortification, stronghold, barricade; means of defending. **3.** *I want to speak in defense of antipollution laws:* upholding, justification, support, advocacy. **4.** *The defense rests its case:* the defendant(s) and their counsel in a legal situation. **5.** *Three people from our school played for the defense:* the side of a team which tries to prevent the other team from scoring. **—Ant.** 4 prosecution. 5 offense.

defenseless *adj.* *We were defenseless against the onslaught:* vulnerable, unprotected, powerless, exposed, helpless, indefensible, naked, open, unguarded. **—Ant.** safe, secure, guarded, protected, out of harm's way.

defensible *adj.* *The attorney attempted to prove to the jury that his client's conduct was defensible:* justifiable, warrantable, proper, valid, suitable, fit, tenable, sensible, vindicable, allowable, excusable, admissible, supportable, pardonable, forgivable, permissible, condonable. **—Ant.** unsound, senseless, unwarranted, unjustifiable, inexcusable.

defensive *adj.* **1.** *The troops took up a defensive position:* prepared, protective, protecting, safeguarding, vigilant, defending, foiling, forestalling, guarded, heedful, preventive, safeguarding, wary, watchful. **2.** *He was defensive about his stutter:* prickly, contentious, argumentative.

defer[1] *v.* *You may defer payment until next*

month: delay, postpone, table, shelve, suspend, put off. **—Ant.** expedite.

defer² *v. The child always deferred to his older brother:* yield, submit, obey, capitulate, accede; respect; give in; pay respect to. **—Ant.** disobey, disrespect.

deference *n. Out of deference to her age and position, the committee followed her suggestions:* consideration, respect, reverence, honor, esteem, regard; obedience, capitulation. **—Ant.** disrespect, contempt; defiance, disobedience.

deferential *adj. Her treatment of the elderly people was affectionate and deferential:* considerate, respectful, courteous, civil, polite, reverential, reverent, regardful; dutiful, obedient, submissive, acquiescent.

deferment also **deferral** *n. She arranged for the deferment of payment with the finance company. He is finishing college under a deferment from the army:* postponement, delay, extension, stay.

deferred *adj. Interest on the loan was deferred for a year:* postponed, prolonged, adjourned, delayed, held up, in waiting, on hold, protracted, put off, remanded, stalled, staved off.

defiance *n. The child showed defiance by refusing to eat:* disobedience, rebelliousness, rebellion, obstinacy, hostility.

defiant *adj. His defiant attitude was a challenge to fight:* rebellious, disobedient, provocative; aggressive, bold; truculent. **—Ant.** meek, timid; obedient, yielding, submissive.

deficiency *n.* **1.** *I have a calcium deficiency:* shortage, insufficiency, inadequacy. **2.** *In spite of her mental deficiencies, she manages to do a good job:* flaw, defect, imperfection, failing, frailty, shortcoming, weakness. **—Ant. 1** sufficiency, adequacy, abundance.

deficient *adj.* **1.** *A diet deficient in vitamins is unhealthy:* lacking, inadequate, insufficient, short on. **2.** *His tests indicate that he is mentally deficient:* flawed, defective, inferior, substandard, weak, unsatisfactory. **—Ant. 1** sufficient, adequate. **2** up to par.

deficit *n. After all those expenses we ended the year with a deficit:* shortage, shortfall, deficiency.

defile *v.* **1.** *Insults alone cannot defile a person's honor:* dirty, soil, befoul, besmirch, spoil, stain, smear, taint, tarnish, dishonor, debase, disgrace, degrade. **2.** *The infidels defiled the holy shrine:* desecrate, profane; treat sacrilegiously. **—Ant. 1** honor. **2** hallow, consecrate, sanctify.

define *v.* **1.** *Can you define the word* defile?: state the meaning of. **2.** *This booklet defines the committee's functions:* specify, describe, state, designate, delineate; spell out, explain, clarify. **3.** *The black tree was clearly defined against a yellow sky:* delineate. **—Ant. 3** obscure, hide, conceal, camouflage.

definite *adj.* **1.** *The club has a definite meeting time each week:* precise, exact, fixed, set. **2.** *She was definite about the caller's message:* sure, positive, certain; clear-cut. **—Ant. 1, 2** indefinite, undetermined, indeterminate, unclear, uncertain.

definitely *adv. John will definitely have a place on the team next season:* doubtless, indubitably, unquestionably, absolutely, undeniably, surely, certainly, unequivocally, assuredly, positively, inescapably, categorically, unavoidably, incontrovertibly, expressly, explicitly, decisively. **—Ant.** perhaps, maybe, possibly, potentially, plausibly.

definition *n.* **1.** *Write a clear definition for the word* deep: statement of meaning. **2.** *The club must give a clear definition of its goals:* description, as of nature, purpose, limits, etc. **3.** *The photograph has fine definition:* clarity, distinctiveness.

definitive *adj. She devised a definitive method for winning in Las Vegas:* complete, reliable, conclusive, decisive, perfect, consummate; exact, decided. **—Ant.** incomplete, unreliable, inconclusive; imperfect, inexact.

deflate *v. Her sarcastic remark deflated him:* debunk, chasten, dash, dispirit, humble, humiliate, knock down, squash, collapse. **—Ant.** inflate.

deflect *v. The policeman's badge deflected the bullet:* divert, swerve; cause to run aside, alter the course.

deform *v. Strip mining deforms the landscape:* mar, disfigure, distort, contort, twist; mangle, maim; make ugly.

deformed *adj. The monster's face was hideously deformed:* malformed, misshapen, crippled, disfigured.

deformity *n. She has a deformity that makes walking difficult:* deformation, malformation.

defraud *v. Land speculators tried to defraud her of her savings:* cheat, bilk, fleece, swindle, rook, *Slang* con, rip off.

deft *adj. The tennis player returned the serve with a deft backhand:* skillful, expert; dexterous, adroit, able, apt; quick, sure. **—Ant.** unskillful, inexpert, maladroit, gauche, inept; slow, unsure.

defunct *adj. The company has been defunct since the war. Bustles are defunct:* extinct, dead. **—Ant.** alive, live, living; in force, in vigor.

defy *v.* **1.** *They believe it is essential to defy convention:* challenge, confront, resist, stand up to, oppose; disregard, disdain, spurn. **2.** *The plane defied the laws of gravity:* resist, withstand; stand up under. **—Ant. 1, 2** encourage. **1** support, help.

degenerate *v.* **1.** *The debate degenerated into an angry shouting match:* deteriorate, disintegrate, worsen, decline, retrograde, backslide, revert, go downhill, sink, go to pot, decay, rot, hit the skids, hit rock bottom, fall on evil days, retrogress. **—adj. 2.** *Such degenerate behavior should never be tolerated:* debased, dissolute, depraved, decadent, perverted, base, profligate, debauched, immoral, corrupt, degraded. **—Ant. 1** improve, progress, flourish, advance, develop. **2** virtuous, moral, upright, ethical.

degradation *n. In his degradation he drank heavily and considered suicide:* humiliation, disgrace. **—Ant.** exaltation; honor, dignity, up-rightness.

degrade v. **1.** *The sergeant was degraded to buck private:* demote, lower, downgrade, lower in rank. **2.** *She wouldn't degrade herself by cheating:* lower, shame, debase, dishonor, disgrace; corrupt; bring contempt upon. **—Ant.** 1 promote, elevate, lift in rank. 2 dignify.

degree n. **1.** *The salesclerk worked his way up a degree at a time:* step, grade, mark, point; phase, stage. **2.** *She has a high degree of intelligence:* level, order, grade. **3.** *The summer months had an average temperature of more than 80 degrees. A right angle has 90 degrees:* division, interval, unit.

dehydrate v. *During the heat wave our skin dehydrated:* desiccate, dry, dry out, dry up, evaporate, parch.

deify v. *The Romans sometimes deified their emperors:* worship, adore, apotheosize, enthrone, exalt, glorify, idolize, immortalize, venerate.

deign v. *I would not deign to comment on such behavior:* stoop, condescend, think fit, consent, deem; see fit.

deity n. *The ancient Greeks and Romans had deities governing every phase of their lives:* god, God, supreme being, goddess, divinity, divine being, godhead, immortal, *Latin* deus, idol, pagan god, moon goddess, sun god, sea god, Olympian, Olympic god.

delay v. **1.** *The committee delayed action on the matter until next month:* postpone, suspend; retard; shelve, table, put off. **2.** *A snowstorm delayed the plane for two hours:* detain; hinder, impede; slow, check, suspend; inhibit, hamper, obstruct; hold up, keep back. **3.** *If you delay, you'll just have to do more later:* procrastinate, dawdle, tarry, linger. *—n.* **4.** *Please finish your work without delay:* loitering, tarrying, lingering, dawdling. **5.** *We were granted a delay of 48 hours to gather more evidence:* postponement, deferment, suspension, prolongation, stay, reprieve. **6.** *The delay was caused by a three-car accident:* stoppage, slowing; hindrance to progress. **—Ant.** 1–3 expedite, hasten, speed, hurry. 4 progress without hindrance.

delectable adj. *Both the dinner and the conversation were delectable:* delightful, enjoyable, pleasurable, pleasant, agreeable, gratifying; delicious. **—Ant.** offensive, repulsive, disagreeable, revolting; distasteful.

delegate n. **1.** *Every state will send a delegate to the convention:* representative, agent, deputy, envoy, proxy. *—v.* **2.** *We have delegated her to represent our city at the convention:* designate, name, authorize; appoint as a representative. **3.** *She delegated her power of attorney to her nephew:* entrust, assign, give, give over, charge, transfer; commit to the care of, commission.

delegation n. **1.** *We did not approve his delegation of so much responsibility to one person:* commissioning, entrustment, authorization; designation; act of delegating. **2.** *A delegation was sent to the capital to meet with the governor:* body of delegates, legation.

delete v. *It will be clearer if you delete that last paragraph:* remove; cut, cancel, erase; take out, strike out, omit, leave out.

deleterious adj. *Smoking cigarettes may be deleterious to your health:* harmful, hurtful, detrimental; dangerous, destructive, ruinous, injurious. **—Ant.** beneficial; healthy, healthful, helpful, advantageous.

deliberate adj. **1.** *It was a deliberate attempt to bring discredit on the minister:* intentional, premeditated, planned, prearranged, purposeful, express, willful; calculated. **2.** *It took weeks for the court to reach its deliberate opinion:* careful, considered, circumspect, cautious, wary, prudent, thoughtful. **3.** *The horse proceeded at a deliberate pace:* leisurely, slow, easy, unhurried, slow-paced; measured. *—v.* **4.** *He deliberated his decision for several days:* examine, consider, weigh; meditate, contemplate, cogitate; mull over, reason out. **5.** *The board deliberated for two days before they reached a decision:* confer, debate, discuss; talk over. **—Ant.** 1, 2 impulsive, rash, impetuous, sudden, hasty. 3 fast, hurried.

deliberately adv. *He deliberately neglected to call us:* intentionally, advisedly, by design, calculatingly, consciously, determinedly, knowingly, on purpose, pointedly, purposely, purposively, willfully, wittingly.

deliberation n. **1.** *The judge could not be hurried in her deliberation:* careful consideration before decision. **2.** *The board of directors held their deliberation in the conference room:* discussion, conference, debate. **3.** *He spoke with deliberation, choosing his words carefully:* care, carefulness, circumspection, steadiness. **4.** *The crime was planned with great deliberation:* forethought, premeditation, calculation, distinct intention, conscious purpose.

delicacy n. **1.** *We admired the delicacy of the imported cloth:* fineness, exquisiteness, elegance, softness, smoothness, lightness. **2.** *The carving was executed with great delicacy:* precision, perfection, accuracy; fine workmanship, savoir-faire. **3.** *Pheasant is a delicacy we seldom can enjoy:* choice food, something pleasing to the palate. **4.** *Religion is a subject that must be approached with great delicacy:* tact, taste, discrimination; consideration; sensitiveness, sensitivity, sensibility. **5.** *The delicacy of his health has alarmed us all:* weakness, frailness, frailty, fragility, unsoundness. **—Ant.** 1, 2 coarseness, roughness, inelegance, grossness. 4 insensitiveness, insensibility, inconsideration, rudeness. 5 strength, vigor, vitality; energy.

delicate adj. **1.** *She wore a long gown of delicate silk:* fine, dainty, exquisite, elegant. **2.** *The plate was so delicate I was afraid to wash it:* breakable, fragile, frail, flimsy, perishable; dainty. **3.** *We were concerned over his delicate condition:* frail, feeble, debilitated, weakened; infirm, unwell, sickly, ailing. **4.** *The hostess passed around a tray of delicate tidbits:* palatable, savory, delicious, appetizing, luscious, toothsome. **5.** *Paint the walls a delicate blue:* soft, muted, subdued. **6.** *Did you see the deli-*

cate workmanship on the bronze door?: exquisite, minute, detailed. **7.** *He handled the situation in a delicate manner:* tactful, tasteful, diplomatic, careful, sensitive, fastidious, scrupulous, refined. **8.** *Sex education is a delicate subject:* touchy, ticklish, sensitive; difficult, precarious. **—Ant.** 1 coarse, crude, rough, inelegant, gross. 2 unbreakable, strong. 3 strong, healthy, well; good. 4 unappetizing; disagreeable. 5 harsh, bright, glaring. 6 careless; crude, rough. 7 disregardful, inconsiderate, careless, insensitive, unrefined, vulgar.

delicately *adv.* *She delicately touched on the subject:* sensitively, carefully, daintily, deftly, elegantly, exquisitely, fastidiously, finely, gracefully, skilfully, softly, subtly, tactfully.

delicious *adj.* *Try some of this delicious chocolate cake:* delectable, palatable, savory, tasty, luscious, mouth-watering, appetizing; pleasant, pleasurable, delightful, joyful, charming. **—Ant.** distasteful, unpleasant, disagreeable.

delight *n.* **1.** *They got a good deal of delight from their children:* pleasure, happiness, rapture, enjoyment, joy, gratification. **2.** *The zoo is a delight for people of all ages:* something that gives joy or pleasure. *—v.* **3.** *Your visit last week delighted us:* please, gratify, cheer; charm, fascinate, enchant, amuse. **4.** *I delight in browsing through antique stores:* revel; take great pleasure in, take delight in. **—Ant.** 1 disappointment, discontent, pain; displeasure. 3 displease; irk, bother. 4 dislike; take no pleasure in.

delighted *adj.* *A delighted audience demanded four encores:* pleased, captivated, enthralled, enraptured, enchanted; elated, ecstatic. **—Ant.** displeased, disgusted.

delightful *adj.* *With dinner and the theater, it was a delightful evening:* enjoyable, pleasing, pleasurable, pleasure-giving; agreeable, charming, engaging, entertaining, amusing, enchanting, *Informal* peachy; amiable, congenial. **—Ant.** displeasing, unpleasant, distressing; disagreeable, distasteful.

delinquency *n.* **1.** *Your delinquency with regard to this bill must be explained:* negligence, dereliction; neglect of obligation. **2.** *There was no excuse for the wealthy boy's delinquency:* misbehavior, misconduct, misdeed.

delinquent *adj.* **1.** *He was delinquent in his responsibilities toward his family:* neglectful, negligent, derelict, remiss. **2.** *The executive was billed for delinquent taxes:* due, overdue, late; in arrears. *—n.* **3.** *The robbery was committed by a group of delinquents:* misdoer, miscreant, wrongdoer; hoodlum, juvenile delinquent. **—Ant.** 1 dutiful, mindful. 2 paid.

delirious *adj.* **1.** *She was delirious from the high fever:* incoherent; hallucinating, raving. **2.** *The crowd became delirious when the war hero appeared on the terrace:* frantic, frenzied, carried away, excited, ecstatic. **—Ant.** 1 coherent, rational. 2 calm.

delirium *n.* *His delirium made him difficult to look after:* deliriousness, delirium tremens, dementia, derangement, frenzy, hysteria, madness, mania, rage, ranting, raving.

deliver *v.* **1.** *I delivered the checks to the bank. This supermarket delivers only on Saturdays:* carry, bear, bring, convey; surrender; give over, hand over, turn over. **2.** *The congressman delivers his speech tomorrow:* give, utter, say, proclaim. **3.** *The champion delivered a series of punches to the challenger:* launch, aim, throw, direct, deal, strike. **4.** *They were delivered from slavery:* save, rescue, liberate, emancipate, free, release; set free. **—Ant.** 1 keep, hold. 4 enslave, oppress.

deliverance *n.* *The village owes its deliverance to the army:* liberation, release, emancipation; rescue, salvation.

delivery *n.* *We awaited the delivery of the documents:* transfer, transmittal, transferral, transmission, handing over, giving over.

delude *v.* *I may be deluding myself, but I think I'm losing weight:* mislead, deceive, fool, trick, dupe, *Slang* con, put on.

deluge *v.* **1.** *Noah built the ark in readiness for the Deluge:* flood, inundation. **2.** *A deluge of requests for autographed pictures was received daily by the star:* inundation, flood, barrage, torrent, overwhelming amount, spate. *—v.* **3.** *The spring thaw caused the river to deluge the town:* overwhelm with a flood of water, inundate, drown, submerge, engulf, flow over, overflow; bury, swamp, flood, glut. **—Ant.** 1 drought, dearth, aridity, aridness; ebb, abatement. 3 dry out.

delusion *n.* *He had the delusion that he was a young boy:* illusion, misbelief, misconception.

delusive *adj.* *The promise of quick riches was delusive:* deceptive, apparent, chimerical, deceiving, deluding, false, illusory, imaginary, misleading, seeming, spurious.

deluxe *v.* *It is one of New York's truly deluxe restaurants:* elegant, grand, fine, luxurious, splendid, choice, *Informal* posh, *Slang* classy.

delve *v.* *We delved into the newspaper files to find out the facts:* search, probe, examine, explore, look into.

demagogue *n.* *Demagogues further their own political ends by exploiting the public's fear and prejudices:* rabble-rouser, agitator, soapbox orator, haranguer, fomenter, political opportunist, tub-thumper, spouter, ranter, hothead, incendiary, malcontent, firebrand, inflamer, troublemaker.

demand *v.* **1.** *She demanded a room all to herself:* exact, order, require; insist upon, lay claim to. **2.** *The situation demands immediate attention:* need, require, call for. *—n.* **3.** *Her every demand was carried out:* command, order; act of demanding, something that is demanded. **4.** *There was a huge demand for experienced workers:* need, requirement, want, call.

demanding *adj.* *The demanding guest wanted her bed remade:* difficult, imperious, insistent, pressing, taxing, onerous, challenging, painful, complicated, tough, trying, wearing. **—Ant.** undemanding, easy, facile, painless, simple, uncomplicated.

demarcation *n.* *The demarcation was shown by yellow tape:* delimitation, bound, boundary, confine, differentiation, distinction, division, limit, margin, separation.

demean v. Could you demean yourself by committing treason?: debase, lower, degrade, humble, humiliate, disgrace, shame. —**Ant.** dignify, honor; glorify, elevate.

demeanor n. He's a young man of pleasing demeanor: conduct, behavior, deportment, manner, comportment, bearing, presence, appearance.

demented adj. With all her ranting, I thought she must be demented: insane, mad, lunatic, crazy, crazed, deranged, Slang cuckoo, nuts. —**Ant.** sane, rational.

demise n. **1.** His untimely demise was caused by a sudden heart attack: death, decease, passing, expiration. **2.** The demise of the empire was caused by various internal factors: end, fall, collapse, ruin. —**Ant.** 1 birth.

democracy n. **1.** What are the principles of democracy? A true democracy allows free speech: government by the people, representative government; state having government by the people. **2.** The democracy of the courts provides equal justice for all: fairness, equality, political equality.

democratic adj. **1.** He staunchly defended democratic principles: advocating democracy, characterized by principles of political equality. **2.** These democratic gatherings are attended by all kinds: characterized by social equality, tending to level distinctions in rank. **3.** The Democratic primary was held this month: of the Democratic party. —**Ant.** 1 autocratic, despotic, tyrannical. 2 socially unequal.

demolish v. **1.** They are going to demolish the old armory: wreck, destroy, level, raze; tear down, Slang total. **2.** The evidence demolished the attorney's case: ruin, devastate; put an end to. —**Ant.** 1 build, create; restore, repair. 2 strength-en.

demolition n. We watched the demolition of the old tower: destruction, wrecking, razing, leveling.

demon n. **1.** They held an elaborate ceremony to exorcise the demons: devil; evil spirit, malignant spirit. **2.** The demon held her prisoner in the tower: fiend, monster. **3.** She's a demon to have on any committee: go-getter, energetic person. —**Ant.** 1, 2 angel. 1 cherub; good spirit. 2 kind person, gentle person, good person. 3 lazy person.

demonic also **demoniac, demoniacal** adj. She attacked the problem with demonic energy: fiendish, devilish; frantic, frenzied, hellish, hectic. —**Ant.** calm, cool.

demonstrable adj. All the results were demonstrable: verifiable, ascertainable, attestable, provable. —**Ant.** unprovable, undemonstrable.

demonstrate v. **1.** The instructor demonstrated the proper way to sew in a zipper: teach, show; describe, illustrate, explain. **2.** The fireman demonstrated great courage in saving the child: show, reveal, display, exhibit, manifest. **3.** The lawyer demonstrated that the witness was lying: prove, show, establish; make clear by reason-

ing, make evident. **4.** The miners demonstrated for better working conditions: picket, parade, march, hold a protest meeting.

demonstration n. **1.** We attended a demonstration of the new manufacturing process: exhibition, display, presentation, illustration. **2.** His new book seems an ample demonstration of his patriotism: expression, manifestation, exposition, display. **3.** We watched the demonstration from our window: parade, march, picketing; protest meeting, rally.

demonstrative adj. **1.** The little pup was very demonstrative: affectionate; effusive, gushing, openly expressive. **2.** The exhibition of ghetto art is demonstrative of many problems in the city: serving to demonstrate, offering proof.

demoralize v. Talk of defeat had demoralized the team: discourage, dishearten, dispirit, undermine, disorganize, disconcert; break down the morale of. —**Ant.** stimulate, encourage.

demote v. As punishment, the corporal was demoted to private: lower in rank, degrade; Slang bust.

demur v. **1.** The majority were in favor of the plan, but a few demurred: object, disagree; take exception. —n. **2.** The lieutenant was a man who would follow any order without demur: hesitation, scruple, qualm, compunction, misgiving, objection, protest.

demure adj. She was demure when her parents were around: shy, modest, prim, reserved; overly modest, bashful. —**Ant.** brazen, brash, impudent, barefaced; shameless, immodest.

demurrer n. The resolution was passed without demurrer: objection, challenge, dissent, doubt, demurral, protest, stricture, question, remonstrance, misgiving, compunction, scruple, qualm, exception, rebuttal. —**Ant.** consent, agreement, endorsement, acceptance, acquiescence.

den n. **1.** The cave made a good den for the foxes: lair, shelter, retreat. **2.** The place is a den of thieves: haunt, hangout; hotbed. **3.** Mother won't let any of us into her den: study, library, private room, sanctuary.

denial n. **1.** The colonel issued a denial of any wrongdoing: disowning, disavowal, disclaimer. **2.** His denial of the petition caused the students to rebel: rejection, refusal. —**Ant.** 1 affirmation, avowal, acknowledgment, admission. 2 granting.

denigrate v. He has a mentality that denigrates everything it doesn't understand: defame, malign, slander, tear down, abuse, stigmatize, traduce, disparage, run down, besmirch, downgrade, blacken, call names, calumniate, backbite, smear, vilify, revile, asperse, soil, sully; Slang give a black eye, drag through the mud, stab in the back, badmouth, dump on. —**Ant.** praise, commend, acclaim, exalt, boost.

denizen n. The denizens of the forest came alive at night: inhabitant, resident, dweller.

denomination n. **1.** The various required subjects fall under several denominations: name, designation, category, class, grouping. **2.** He's a churchgoer, but I don't know what denomina-

tion: sect, religious group, persuasion. **3.** *The bank sent the money in three denominations:* value, size.

denote *v. The flashing lights denote dangerous roads ahead:* indicate, mark, signal, signify, mean, name.

denouement *n. The denouement was so ridiculous it ruined the whole play:* outcome, upshot, solution; finale, conclusion, termination, end.

denounce *v.* **1.** *The council denounced the new law:* condemn, criticize, censure, vilify. **2.** *She was denounced as a thief:* accuse; inform against. **—Ant.** 1 commend, praise, extol, laud. 2 vindicate, exonerate.

dense *adj.* **1.** *The crowd was so dense we could hardly move. It was difficult to see through the dense fog:* crowded, compressed, compact, close, concentrated, thick, impenetrable, heavy, intense. **2.** *He's so dense he'll never understand your message:* dumb, stupid, dull, ignorant, dimwitted, thick, thickheaded, slow. **—Ant.** 1 sparse, scattered, dispersed; thin, transparent, light. 2 alert, bright, intelligent, quick, quick-witted, clever.

density *n. Physicists deal with the density of matter:* denseness, mass, body, bulk, closeness, compactness, consistency, heaviness, impenetrability, quantity, solidity, substantiality, thickness.

dent *n. The body of the car is full of dents:* depression, pit, nick, hollow, indentation.

dentistry *n. She obtained a degree in dentistry:* dental care, dental medicine, dental surgery, oral surgery, orthodontics.

denunciation *n. The candidate's speech was a denunciation of dishonest government:* condemnation, censure, denouncement; attack against. **—Ant.** defense, apology; acclamation, recommendation.

deny *v.* **1.** *The senator denied ever making such a statement:* contradict, disavow, disaffirm, disclaim, refute. **2.** *He denied the students a chance to speak:* refuse, disallow; withhold from. **3.** *Atheists deny the existence of God:* refuse to acknowledge, not recognize; contradict, declare untrue. **—Ant.** 1 confirm, concede, admit, affirm, assert. 2 grant. 3 acknowledge, recognize; believe in.

depart *v.* **1.** *Before you depart, let me give you a word of advice:* go, leave; exit, go away, set out, start out, set forth, go forth. **2.** *He departed from the text to tell an anecdote:* digress, turn aside, deviate. **—Ant.** 1 arrive; remain, stay.

department *n.* **1.** *I work in the payroll department:* division, bureau, branch, section, unit. **2.** *Bordeaux, France, is in the department of Gironde:* district, division, province, sector.

departure *n.* **1.** *Our departure is scheduled for 6 A.M. tomorrow:* leaving, going, exit, exodus; going away. **2.** *His new work is a departure from anything he wrote before:* digression, divergence, deviation. **—Ant.** 1 arrival, return.

depend *v.* **1.** *The farmers here depend heavily on the weather forecast:* rely, count, believe in. **2.** *You can always depend on her:* place trust, have faith. **3.** *The party depends on whether or*

not we collect enough money: hinge, rest, be determined by, be contingent upon, hang on, be dependent on.

dependable *adj. My secretary is skillful and dependable:* reliable, trustworthy, unfailing, trusty, trusted; loyal, faithful, steady, steadfast; sure, true. **—Ant.** untrustworthy, unreliable, doubtful, questionable, unsteady, fickle, unstable.

dependence *n.* **1.** *The old lady's dependence on her children was absolute:* dependency. **2.** *Her dependence on religion is very great:* reliance, trust, confidence.

dependency *n. There is usually some kind of mutual dependency in a love relationship:* dependence.

dependent *adj.* **1.** *Too many young people are dependent on their parents:* needing help, needful of, reliant. **2.** *Good health is largely dependent on proper nourishment:* determined by; contingent on; subject to. **—Ant.** 1 self-reliant, independent.

depict *v.* **1.** *The painter depicted Napoleon at the Battle of Waterloo:* paint, portray, draw, sketch, limn, delineate, picture, sculpt, carve, represent, diagram, draft, map out, chart. **2.** *The story depicts the hero as a cynical opportunist:* describe, dramatize, narrate, record, chronicle, relate, recount, detail, define, verbalize, recite.

deplete *v. The drought has depleted our supply of water:* exhaust, use up, drain, impoverish; lessen, reduce, decrease, consume. **—Ant.** increase, augment.

depleted *adj. Midway into the camping trip, they realized their supplies were depleted:* used, consumed, destitute, devoid of, drained, emptied, exhausted, sapped, spent, vacant, wasted.

deplorable *adj.* **1.** *The family lived in a deplorable slum:* wretched, awful, miserable. **2.** *The soldier's actions were deplorable:* deserving reproach, reprehensible, blameworthy. **—Ant.** 1 acceptable, good.

deplore *v.* **1.** *The citizens deplored the death of their king:* lament, mourn, bemoan, bewail, grieve for. **2.** *We all deplored his lack of good manners:* censure, condemn; disapprove of.

deploy *v. The colonel deployed his troops along the hillside:* dispose, arrange, display, expand, extend, position, redistribute, set up, unfold, use.

deport *v.* **1.** *The federal authorities deported him for illegal entry:* oust, expel; banish, cast out, exile, expatriate. **2.** *The young children deported themselves in a mannerly way:* behave, act, carry; conduct oneself.

deportation *n. A hearing was held concerning the man's impending deportation:* extradition, banishment, displacement, exile, expatriation, expulsion, removal, transportation, eviction.

deportment *n. If her deportment doesn't improve, the school may expel her:* conduct, behavior; comportment, demeanor.

depose *v. The nobles deposed the king:* dethrone; oust; remove from office, unseat.

deposit *v.* **1.** *Deposit your lunch tray at the cafeteria door:* put, place; set down. **2.** *The soil* *was deposited on the banks:* accumulate, place; put down. **3.** *We deposited $300 on a car:* give as security, give as partial payment; put down. **4.** *I deposited $10 in my savings account:* place for safekeeping; put in the bank, give in trust, commit to custody. —*n.* **5.** *The flood left a large deposit of mud in the street:* accumulation, sediment, pile. **6.** *I left a $10 deposit on a new winter coat:* down payment, partial payment, installment.

deposition *n.* **1.** *The deposition of Charles I took place in 1649:* the act of deposing. **2.** *The witnesses gave their pretrial depositions:* testimony, declaration, statement. **3.** *There was a deposition of soil on the banks:* deposit, accumulation.

depot *n.* **1.** *I went to the depot to meet her train:* terminal, terminus; railroad or bus station. **2.** *Enemy bombs demolished our supply depot:* military storage place, dump.

depraved *adj.* *A person of such depraved appetites has no place in our community:* corrupt, perverted, wicked, debased, debauched, degenerate, vile, degraded. —**Ant.** moral, virtuous, wholesome.

depravity *n.* *In the annals of depravity, he came first:* perversion, baseness, corruption, criminality, debasement, debauchery, degeneracy, degradation, immorality, iniquity, vice, viciousness, wickedness.

deprecate *v.* **1.** *The townspeople deprecated the new exhibit:* protest, condemn; object to, take exception to, express strong disapproval of. **2.** *You should not deprecate your own worth:* belittle, play down, depreciate. —**Ant.** 1 approve, favor, endorse, sanction.

depreciate *v.* **1.** *Runaway inflation has depreciated the country's currency. The car depreciated $800 since last year:* reduce or lower the value of, diminish; lose value. **2.** *He depreciates all my efforts to help him:* belittle, disparage, downgrade, scorn, denigrate; run down. —**Ant.** 1 appreciate. 2 appreciate, cherish, esteem, prize.

depredation *n.* *The English coastal towns regularly suffered depredation at the hands of the Vikings:* sack, plunder, looting, pillage, rapine, spoiling, sacking, robbery, freebooting, desecration, devastation, laying waste, spoliation, marauding, ravishment, ravage, brigandage.

depress *v.* **1.** *Her sad news depressed me all day:* dispirit, sadden, dishearten, deject, lower in spirits. **2.** *The new highway depressed business along the old road:* lessen, weaken, diminish, reduce, cut back. **3.** *Depress the lever to start the machine:* lower; press down. —**Ant.** 1 elate, cheer, gladden, hearten. 2 heighten, increase, strengthen.

depressed *adj.* **1.** *Constant rejection made the children depressed:* dejected, downcast, sad, saddened, unhappy, miserable, morose, despondent, melancholy, gloomy, morbid, *Informal* blue. **2.** *The depressed economy began to recover:* disadvantaged, depreciated, destitute, devalued, distressed, humble, needy, plebeian, poor, poverty-stricken, underprivileged. **3.** *The*

depressed button was almost out of view: sunken, concave, hollow, indented, pushed down, recessed, set back. —**Ant.** 1 happy, cheerful.

depression *n.* **1.** *She went through a long depression after losing her job:* sadness, gloom, dejection, discouragement, downheartedness; melancholia, melancholy, despondency, desolation. **2.** *There was a depression in the carpet where the lamp had stood:* indentation, hollow, dimple. **3.** *During the 1930's we experienced a severe depression:* economic decline, recession. —**Ant.** 1 cheerfulness, gladness; lightheartedness, joyousness. 3 boom.

deprivation *n.* *Lack of decent clothing led to further deprivation:* deprival, destitution, denial, detriment, disadvantage, hardship, lack, need, want, privation.

deprive *v.* *She was deprived of her membership for nonpayment of dues:* dispossess, divest, strip, confiscate; take from.

depth *n.* **1.** *The lake has a depth of 300 feet in the middle:* downward measurement, perpendicular measurement. **2.** *Her latest poem has remarkable depth:* profundity, deepness. **3.** *The depth of his voice gives him a good tone for recording:* timbre, deepness. —**Ant.** 1 height. 2 superficiality.

deputy *n.* *The Secretary of State sent his deputy to the preliminary talks:* agent, substitute, alternate, representative, surrogate, proxy, second, delegate, envoy, go-between, messenger, emissary, ambassador, spokesperson, minister, middleman, pinch hitter.

deranged *adj.* *She became so deranged she had to be institutionalized:* insane, irrational, unbalanced, demented; crazy. —**Ant.** sane, normal, rational.

derelict *adj.* **1.** *He was fired for being derelict in his responsibilities:* negligent, neglectful, delinquent, remiss; careless. **2.** *There are many old derelict ships in the bay:* abandoned, deserted. —*n.* **3.** *They run a home for derelicts downtown:* bum, vagrant, outcast, tramp, hobo.

dereliction *n.* *The negligent soldier was charged with dereliction of duty:* neglect, negligence, delinquency, fault, abandonment, desertion.

deride *v.* *They derided the new music:* ridicule, mock, scoff, scorn, sneer at.

derision *n.* *The losing players were the target of derision from their classmates:* ridicule, mockery, disdain, scorn, sneering.

derisive *adj.* *The derisive nature of the allegations became apparent:* derisory, contemptuous, disdainful, jeering, mocking, ridiculing, scoffing, scornful, taunting. —**Ant.** appreciative.

derivable *adj.* *The one derivable element was gold:* extractable, attributable, deducible, determinable, inferable, reasoned, resultant, traceable, obtainable.

derivation *n.* **1.** *He is working on the derivation of a new plastic from chemicals:* deriving, acquiring, obtaining, getting. **2.** *The waltz is probably of German derivation:* origin, source. **3.**

The dictionary gives the derivation of many words: etymology; historical development.

derivative *adj.* **1.** *The derivative essay received low marks:* derived, unoriginal, borrowed, copied, evolved, imitative, inferred, not original, obtained, plagiarized, rehashed, secondhand. —*n.* **2.** offshoot, outgrowth, byproduct, derivation, descendant, product, spinoff. —**Ant.** l original, archetypal, authentic, genuine, seminal.

derive *v.* **1.** *She derives great satisfaction from her coin collection:* gain, obtain, glean, enjoy. **2.** *Many English words are derived from Latin and Greek words:* descend; originate, arise; stem from.

derogatory *adj.* *They made derogatory remarks about their opponents:* belittling, disparaging, uncomplimentary, unfavorable, unflattering, injurious. —**Ant.** flattering, complimentary, favorable.

descend *v.* **1.** *The elevator descended slowly to the ground floor:* drop, come down, go down, move downward. **2.** *The walk descends sharply:* incline, dip, slope, slant. **3.** *The house descended through the male heirs for two centuries:* be inherited, pass, be handed down. **4.** *The troops descended upon the village and destroyed it:* swoop, invade; come in force. —**Ant.** l ascend, climb, go up.

descendant *n.* *The British royal family are descendants of Queen Victoria:* offspring, issue, progeny. —**Ant.** ancestor, progenitor, forefather.

descent *n.* **1.** *The spectators watched the descent of the balloon:* fall, drop, coming down. **2.** *There is a gradual descent from the house to the lake:* slope, slant, decline, declivity. **3.** *She is very proud of her descent from a Confederate colonel:* ancestry, origin, lineage. **4.** *The town was destroyed by a descent of barbarians:* sudden visit, sneak attack, raid, assault, incursion. —**Ant.** l ascent, rise; upward climb.

describe *v.* **1.** *They described their journey in vivid detail:* detail, narrate, relate, recount, speak of, recite, explain; illustrate, characterize, portray; depict. **2.** *Describe a circle on the floor with a piece of chalk:* draw, trace, outline; delineate, mark out.

description *n.* **1.** *She gave an accurate description of the man's appearance:* account, depiction, portrayal, illustration, characterization; narration. **2.** *The show featured dogs of every description:* kind, sort, type, ilk, variety; species, class, genus, nature, manner, brand.

descriptive *adj.* *Her descriptive account delighted us:* depictive, elucidative, explanatory, explicative, expository, graphic, identifying, illustrative, indicative, detailed, specific.

desecrate *v.* *Vandals desecrated many tombstones in the cemetery:* defile, violate, profane, dishonor. —**Ant.** honor, esteem.

desecration *n.* *Guards were posted to prevent further desecration of the tomb:* defilement, violation, abuse, blasphemy, debasement, irreverence, sacrilege, impiety.

desert[1] *n.* **1.** *Some animals can survive in the desert on very little water:* wasteland; arid region, barren wilderness. —*adj.* **2.** *The speculators bought a large desert tract and sold lots:* barren, desolate; infertile, arid, waste, uncultivated, untilled, wild, uninhabited.

desert[2] *v.* *The police are looking for a woman who deserted her children:* abandon, forsake, leave; run away from.

deserted *adj.* *The deserted village looked forlorn:* forsaken, vacant, abandoned, bare, barren, bereft, cast off, derelict, desolate, isolated, left stranded, relinquished, uninhabited, unoccupied, empty.

deserter *n.* *Several deserters escaped:* defector, fugitive, absconder, derelict, escapee, escaper, refugee, shirker, slacker, traitor, truant.

desertion *n.* *Desertion from the cause will be punished:* defection, flight, abandonment, absconding, betrayal, dereliction, disavowal, forsaking, relinquishment, repudiation, truancy.

deserts *n. pl.* *The new film was praised beyond its deserts. The bad boy got his just deserts in the end:* worth; due, payment, reward.

deserve *v.* *He deserves the award for his acts of bravery:* merit, rate, warrant; be worthy of, be entitled to, qualify for, earn as due, be deserving of.

deserving *adj.* *She donated to the deserving cause:* admirable, exemplary, laudable, commendable, estimable, fitting, meritable, meritorious, praiseworthy, rightful, worthy, creditable, due. —**Ant.** undeserving, unworthy.

design *v.* **1.** *She designed a new generator that saved the company millions:* plan, conceive, fashion, devise; draw, draft, sketch; draw up plans for. **2.** *This fund is designed to help worthy students:* intend, destine, set up. —*n.* **3.** *He wasn't happy about the designs for the book:* sketch, drawing, outline, plan, blueprint, diagram. **4.** *The quilt has a sunburst design:* pattern, motif; form, arrangement. **5.** *He has a design for becoming a millionaire in five years:* plan, project, blueprint, intention, purpose, goal, target, objective, end, aim. **6.** *The group had designs against the government:* plan, scheme, plot; intrigue.

designate *v.* **1.** *He designated the place where we were to meet:* specify, indicate, name, signify, pinpoint; select. **2.** *I asked that Martha be designated cochairman:* appoint, choose, elect, select, name, nominate, assign. **3.** *The new shopping center is designated York Plaza:* name, call, term, label, identify.

designation *n.* *After remodeling, the vehicle received another designation:* identification, appellation, class, classification, denomination, description, specification, epithet, label, mark, moniker, name, naming, style, title, delegation, recognition, selection.

designing *adj.* *They are so designing you can't help questioning their motives:* scheming, conniving, crafty, cunning, wily, artful, plotting. —**Ant.** candid, frank, honest, open, guileless, artless.

desirable *adj.* **1.** *We're moving to a more desirable neighborhood:* pleasing, fine; worth desiring, worth having, in demand. **2.** *Such changes* *are desirable:* advisable, advantageous, beneficial. **—Ant.** 1 undesirable, disagreeable. 2 harmful, inadvisable, improper.

desire *v.* **1.** *I desired candy all the time I was dieting:* crave, want, wish; long for; yearn for, hunger for, thirst for. **2.** *We desire your early reply to this inquiry:* request, urge; ask for. *—n.* **3.** *The desire for fame drove him relentlessly:* longing, craving, need, wish, yearning, thirst, hunger. **—Ant.** 1 spurn, reject, refuse, decline, repudiate. 3 distaste, aversion, dislike.

desist *v.* *The company agreed to desist from false advertising:* cease, stop; discontinue, suspend; refrain from, leave off, *Slang* lay off. **—Ant.** begin, persist, continue, persevere.

desolate *adj.* **1.** *After the war the town was a desolate place:* deserted, uninhabited, empty, bare, barren, bleak, forsaken, abandoned. **2.** *She has been desolate since losing her job:* despondent, dejected, forlorn, downcast, downhearted, depressed, sad, melancholy; sorrowful, wretched, miserable. *—v.* **3.** *Many coastal towns were desolated by the hurricane:* ruin, ravage, devastate; destroy, demolish; lay waste. **4.** *We were desolated by the death of our good friend:* sadden, grieve, depress, distress, dishearten; discourage. **—Ant.** 1 inhabited, populous. 2 cheerful, lighthearted, joyous, happy, glad. 3 develop, nourish, cultivate. 4 cheer, hearten, encourage.

desolation *n.* **1.** *The desolation of the town was accomplished with one bomb:* ruin, devastation, destruction. **2.** *We couldn't stay out there in that desolation another day:* barrenness, emptiness, bleakness, dreariness, bareness, wilderness. **3.** *Her desolation is greater now that the children are away:* loneliness, seclusion, solitariness, solitude. **4.** *That's too much desolation for anyone to bear:* sadness, melancholy, unhappiness, sorrow, depression, dejection, distress, misery.

despair *n.* **1.** *He sank into despair after his business failed:* hopelessness, discouragement, de-spondency, gloom, depression. **2.** *That child has been the despair of all her teachers:* burden, ordeal, trial. *—v.* **3.** *I despair of ever finding her again:* have no hope, lose heart, lose faith in. **—Ant.** 1 hopefulness, cheerfulness. 2 delight, joy, pride. 3 have faith in, have confidence in.

despairing *adj.* *The despairing convict slashed his wrists:* distraught, hopeless, despondent, blue, brokenhearted, dejected, depressed, disconsolate, downcast, forlorn, inconsolable, melancholy, miserable, oppressed, sad, upset, wretched, suicidal, *Informal* at the end of one's rope.

desperado *n.* *The desperado was wanted by police in seven states:* bandit, outlaw, lawbreaker, brigand, terrorist, criminal, convict, fugitive, ruffian, hooligan, rowdy, thug, hoodlum, gunman.

desperate *adj.* **1.** *He was a desperate criminal on the loose:* reckless, dangerous, wild, frantic. **2.** *Even his desperate schemes could not save the project:* daring, rash. **3.** *She's in the hospital with a desperate illness:* grave, critical, danger-

ous, serious; hopeless, incurable. **4.** *She became so desperate we feared for her sanity:* despairing, despondent, wretched; beyond hope. **5.** *The family is in desperate need of help:* extreme, great, urgent, critical, dire. **—Ant.** 1 cautious, careful. 2 sensible, safe. 3 hopeful, promising; curable. 4 elated, joyful, happy; hopeful, optimistic.

desperately *adv.* *They desperately pounded on the window:* recklessly, wildly, dangerously, frantically.

desperation *n.* *In desperation, he finally broke down the door:* despair, hopelessness, recklessness.

despicable *adj.* *How can you forgive such despicable behavior?:* contemptible, detestable, vile, mean, base, disgraceful, reprehensible, outrageous. **—Ant.** praiseworthy, laudable, worthy.

despise *v.* *I despise anyone who is cruel to animals:* dislike, scorn, loathe, detest, abhor; contemn, disdain; look down on. **—Ant.** like, admire, appreciate, respect, esteem.

despite *prep.* *Despite heavy rain, the strikers walked the picket line:* notwithstanding, in spite of.

despoil *v.* *Barbarians despoiled the northern towns:* rob, plunder, ravage, pillage, loot.

despondency *n.* *Her child's illness threw her into profound despondency:* depression, dejection, discouragement, melancholy, gloom, desperation, despair, sadness, *Informal* blues. **—Ant.** elation, joy, happiness.

despondent *adj.* *It's easy to get despondent when plans go awry:* discouraged, depressed, dejected, downhearted, disconsolate, downcast, hopeless, disheartened, low, blue, *Slang* down. **—Ant.** encouraged, light-hearted, joyful, joyous, happy, glad.

despot *n.* *The citizens revolted against the despot's rule:* tyrant, dictator, autocrat, oppressor.

dessert *n.* *Does the price of the meal include dessert?:* final course; (*variously*) pie, tart, cake, sweet, ice cream, fruit, nuts.

destination *n.* *My destination is Los Angeles, but I'm stopping off in Chicago:* journey's end, goal, plan, purpose, ambition, objective, aim, target, end, object.

destined *adj.* *The destined arrangement came to pass:* determined, fated, appointed, assigned, certain, compulsory, consigned, delegated, designated, directed, doomed, foreordained, inescapable, inevitable, ordained, preordained, predestined, predetermined, sealed, scheduled.

destiny *n.* **1.** *Do you believe that our destiny is predetermined?:* future, fate, fortune, lot. **2.** *Are you willing to let your life be controlled by destiny?:* fate, necessity, fortune, karma, kismet, *Greek* moira.

destitute *adj.* *The collection will be used to aid destitute families:* poor, poverty-stricken, needy, indigent, penniless, broke, *Slang* busted. **—Ant.** rich, affluent, opulent, wealthy.

destroy *v.* *Fire destroyed several stores in the business district:* ruin, demolish, wreck, waste, ravage, devastate. —**Ant.** save, preserve, conserve; establish, found, institute; make, form.

destruct v. *The taped message is programmed to destruct itself:* destroy, demolish, ruin, raze, gut, decimate, devastate, wreck, tear down, pull down, desolate, wipe out, despoil, lay in ruins. —**Ant.** erect, build, put up, create, originate.

destruction n. *The fire caused the destruction of two landmarks:* destroying; ruin, demolition, wrecking, wreckage, devastation, havoc. —**Ant.** preservation, conservation; institution, organization.

destructive adj. **1.** *It was the most destructive storm in 30 years:* damaging, ruinous, detrimental, injurious, devastating; harmful, hurtful. **2.** *Criticism should not be destructive:* not constructive. —**Ant.** 1 beneficial, constructive, creative, restor-ative, preservative. 2 constructive.

detach v. **1.** *They detached their trailer and set up camp:* separate, disconnect, disengage, sever, unhitch, unfasten, disentangle, loosen. **2.** *A plane was detached to survey the area:* send on a special mission, assign to special service. —**Ant.** 1 attach, fasten, connect, engage, tie, bind.

detached adj. **1.** *The coupon is not valid if detached:* separated, disconnected; unfastened, disengaged, unhitched, unconnected, uncoupled, severed. **2.** *A judge must be detached when weighing evidence:* impartial, neutral, unbiased, unprejudiced, disinterested, objective, dispassionate, fair-minded, fair. **3.** *She's so detached it's hard to get to know her:* aloof, distant, reserved, indifferent. —**Ant.** 1 attached, joined, connected, fastened. 2 partial, biased, prejudiced. 3 concerned, involved; warm, close, inviting.

detachment n. **1.** *The wreck was caused by the detachment of two cars from the train:* separation, disconnection, disengagement, severing, severance, cutting off. **2.** *You need detachment to arrive at a just decision:* impartiality, objectivity, fairness, neutrality. **3.** *His air of detachment lost him many friends:* aloofness, indifference, coolness; isolation, preoccupation. **4.** *A detachment of guards was sent to investigate the trouble:* unit, force, special task force.

detail n. **1.** *The likeness was perfect in every detail:* particular, item, fact, component, iota, feature, aspect, respect. **2.** *The detail in the statue is very fine:* particulars or items seen as a group. **3.** *Twelve sailors were assigned to a work detail:* special duty, particular assignment, detachment; special service. —v. **4.** *The men were asked to detail their grievances:* itemize, enumerate, particularize, specify, delineate, designate; relate, recount. **5.** *She was detailed to act as special courier:* select for special duty; assign to a task, appoint. —**Ant.** 1 whole, aggregate, total, sum. 4 generalize.

detailed adj. *The secretary read the detailed minutes aloud:* minute, intricate, elaborate, all-inclusive, comprehensive, copious, exhaustive, itemized, meticulous, particular, thorough, in depth. —**Ant.** compact, brief, concise.

detain v. **1.** *The bad weather detained us for*

several hours: delay, stop; hinder, retard, slow, slow down, slow up. **2.** *The police detained the suspect at the border:* confine, hold, keep in custody; arrest.

detect v. *We detected the robbers as they entered the store. I detected a note of pity in her voice:* discover, uncover, notice, note, observe, perceive, see, spot, espy; catch.

detection n. *Detection of the crime proved impossible:* exposure, uncovering, disclosure, discovery, ferreting out, revelation, tracking down, unearthing, unmasking, apprehension.

detective n. *The police assigned several detectives to apprehend the murderer:* investigator; special investigator; sleuth, *Slang* gumshoe, private eye, shamus.

detention n. **1.** *The detention of the whole class was unfair:* detainment, holding, keeping in, holding back. **2.** *He was kept in detention until he could raise bail:* custody, confinement; imprisonment, incarceration. —**Ant.** release, liberation.

deter v. *Bad weather didn't deter us from starting our vacation:* discourage, hinder, prevent, dissuade, daunt, divert; stop, impede.

deteriorate v. *The air quality has deteriorated these past few days. The patient's condition has deteriorated since the operation:* worsen, degenerate, decline, wane, ebb, lapse, fade; disintegrate, decay, crumble, fall off. —**Ant.** improve, ameliorate, advance.

deterioration n. *There's been no deterioration in his condition:* decay, decaying, spoilage, spoiling, adulteration, atrophy, corrosion, crumbling, debasement, decline, decomposition, degeneration, degradation, depreciation, devaluation, disintegration, disrepair, downfall, downgrade, downturn, fall, rotting, vitiation, lapse. —**Ant.** improvement.

determination n. **1.** *That was one determination the judge never regretted:* decision, resolution, resolve; judgment, solution, verdict, conclusion, finding. **2.** *The determination of our slogan was arrived at by a contest:* determining, settling, resolving, reasoning, fixing, act of deciding. **3.** *If she had more determination, she could be a success at anything:* resolution, resoluteness, perseverance, tenacity, persist-ence, steadfastness, stick-to-it-iveness; boldness, spunk, power, pluck, grit. —**Ant.** 1, 2 irresolution, indecision, doubt. 3 instability, hesitancy, hesitation, weakness.

determine v. **1.** *I tried to determine the reason for her actions:* ascertain, discover, learn, establish, detect; find out, figure out. **2.** *Present decisions will determine the future of the company:* control, regulate, affect; decide, influence; give direction to. **3.** *She determined that they would vacation in Canada:* settle, decide, resolve, conclude; come to a decision.

determined adj. *The determined fire fighters broke down the door:* persevering, steadfast, staunch, resolute, unflinching, firm, intent, unfaltering, unwavering. —**Ant.** irresolute, vacillating, wavering, faltering, flexible.

deterrent n. *Punishment is not necessarily a*

deterrent to crime: restraint, curb, hindrance, check, discouragement.

detest *v. I detest looking at snakes:* abhor, despise, loathe, hate; dislike intensely, recoil from. —**Ant.** like, love, adore, relish, cherish.

detestable *adj. Selfishness is a detestable quality in anyone:* hateful, obnoxious, abhorrent, loathsome, odious; unpleasant, disagreeable; repulsive, vile, revolting, disgusting, offensive. —**Ant.** likable, lovable, agreeable, attractive.

dethrone *v. The president was dethroned at the annual meeting:* oust, topple, depose, dismiss, displace.

detonate *v. Workers detonated the charges that collapsed the building:* explode, set off, touch off, discharge, fire, shoot, ignite, fulminate; burst, erupt, go off, blow up.

detour *n. We took a detour around the obstruction:* bypass, alternate route, temporary route, circumvention, deviation, divergence, diversion, digression.

detract *v. The peeling walls detract from the beauty of the room:* diminish, reduce, lower, lessen; take away from, subtract from. —**Ant.** increase, heighten, enhance; add to.

detraction *n. The criticism wasn't meant to be a detraction from her good work:* detracting, disparagement, belittling, defamation, vilification, calumny, abuse, slander, aspersion, depreciation. —**Ant.** praise, commendation.

detriment *n. Lack of education is often a detriment to a good career:* injury, damage, harm, loss; impairment, disadvantage. —**Ant.** improvement, enhancement; aid, advantage.

devalue *v. The country devalued its currency by 10 percent. Time has devalued his stature as a writer:* revalue, devaluate, depreciate, demonetize, remonetize; mark down, lower, write down, underrate; cheapen, adulterate, debase, corrupt, pervert, degenerate, degrade, contaminate, defile, taint, pollute, infect. —**Ant.** raise, elevate, overrate, overestimate, enhance.

devastate *v. The hurricane devastated a large section of the coast:* waste, destroy, ravage, desolate, despoil, spoil, ruin, wreck, demolish, level, lay waste. —**Ant.** create, erect, develop; build up.

devastation *n. The explosion caused complete devastation of the factory:* ruin, ruination, destruction, demolition.

develop *v.* **1.** *The children developed their reading skills further during this year:* expand, broaden, augment, improve, advance; mature, cultivate, grow, flower, ripen. **2.** *If you develop the idea further, I will be interested in discussing it:* expand, enlarge, amplify; elaborate on. **3.** *I developed a cold this week:* acquire, contract, pick up, come to have. **4.** *It developed that they had an alibi for the night:* evolve, turn out, unfold, come to light. **5.** *The builders are developing that part of town:* build up, convert, energize. **6.** *Let's have these pictures developed:* process, finish, print.

development *n.* **1.** *Scientists have studied the development of the human species:* progress, growth, evolution, history. **2.** *What are the latest developments in medicine?:* event, advance. **3.** *There are several new developments in the case:* event, result.

deviant *adj. The deviant professor resigned his post:* irregular, abnormal, bizarre, anomalous, atypical, unrepresentative, untypical, wayward, deviate, different, divergent, perverse, perverted, heretical. —**Ant.** orthodox, conventional, normal, straight, straightforward.

deviate *v. The witness deviated from the truth:* part, stray, wander, depart, vary; turn aside, swerve, veer, go astray, sidetrack. —**Ant.** continue, remain; stick to.

deviation *n. The supervisor permitted no deviation from his rules:* departure, variation, variance, alteration, divergence, aberration, anomaly, deflection, difference, digression, discrepancy, disparity, diversion, fluctuation, inconsistency, irregularity, modification, shift, turning, breach, change.

device *n.* **1.** *She invented a device that automatically closes windows when it rains:* invention, contrivance, apparatus, contraption, gadget, mechanism. **2.** *He is full of devices for getting sympathy:* plan, plot, scheme, trick, ploy, design, artifice; strategy, stratagem, wile, ruse, gimmick, angle.

devil *n.* **1. the Devil.** *The preacher said that the Devil would take over their souls:* Satan, Archfiend, prince of darkness, chief enemy of God, Lucifer, Beelzebub, spirit of evil. **2.** *The window was broken by those young devils:* mischief-maker, hellion, scoundrel, rogue, villain, ruffian. **3.** *The poor devil never knew what hit him:* wretch, creature, unfortunate, thing; *Informal* fellow, guy.

devilish *adj. Police foiled the devilish plot:* satanic, diabolic, diabolical, demoniac, infernal, Mephistophelian, fiendish, hellish. —**Ant.** good, fine, upstanding, righteous, godly.

devious *adj. His devious business methods landed him in trouble:* dishonest, deceitful, sneaky, tricky, wily, sly, treacherous, dishonorable, crooked, double-dealing. —**Ant.** forthright, aboveboard, straightforward; open, frank, honest.

devise *v. He tried to devise a foolproof plan for getting rid of termites:* design, invent, conceive, concoct, contrive, think up, frame, prepare, formulate, map out, block out, plot, forge, construct.

devoid *adj. The judge was devoid of sympathy when I presented my case:* lacking, barren, wanting, bereft of, destitute, empty, without, unblest with. —**Ant.** full, abounding, replete, flush, rich, abundant, overflowing.

devote *v. She devoted her life to helping struggling actors:* dedicate, give over to, direct, apply, address, utilize, concentrate, center one's attentions on, give oneself up to; consecrate.

devoted *adj. Be wary of politicians who claim to be devoted public servants:* dedicated, earnest, strongly committed, staunch, zealous, steadfast, unwavering; ardent, fond, loving, passionate; faithful, true, loyal, adhering. —**Ant.** uncommitted, undedicated, indifferent, dispassionate, unimpassioned, inconstant, unloving; unfaithful, disloyal.

devotion n. **1.** *His wife resents his devotion to his mother:* attentiveness, dedication, commitment, devotedness, earnest attachment; regard, reverence, love, fondness, concern for; loyalty, adherence, faithfulness, fealty, allegiance, zeal, ardor. **2.** *His devotion led him to the priesthood:* devoutness, religious fervor, holiness, piety, reverence, godliness, spirituality; religiosity. **3.** (*Usually plural*) *Devotions are held every Sunday morning:* act of religious worship, prayer service, religious observance, meditation. **—Ant.** 1 indifference, unconcern, disinterest, disregard; irreverence, negligence, aversion; unfaithfulness, disloyalty, faithlessness, inconstancy, infidelity. 2 impiety, irreverence.

devour v. **1.** *He was so hungry he devoured several helpings:* eat voraciously, consume greedily, take in ravenously, gobble up, wolf down, stuff in, bolt down, gulp down. **2.** *She devours several historical novels a week:* read eagerly and swiftly, read widely or compulsively, knock off, go through; absorb oneself in, become engrossed in. **—Ant.** refuse, pass up, ignore, be indifferent to. 1 disgorge, vomit, regurgitate.

devout adj. **1.** *The more devout members of the sect were wary of changing the ritual:* religious, orthodox, pious, worshipful, reverent. **2.** *She is a devout admirer of French painting:* ardent, fervent, earnest, intense, serious, passionate, zealous. **—Ant.** 1 irreligious, impious, irreverent, sacrilegious. 2 passionless, insincere, passive, indifferent.

dew n. *Beads of dew still clung to the leaves and flowers:* moisture, condensation, film of precipitation, night or morning wetness; droplets of moisture.

dexterity n. *A surgeon must have dexterity to handle precision instruments:* manual skill, deftness, adroitness, handiness, nimbleness with the fingers, proficiency, facility.

dexterous adj. *Her dexterous fingers moved effortlessly over the piano keys. He solved the riddle easily with his dexterous mind:* skillful, nimble, agile, adroit, deft; ingenious, resourceful, active, quick, gifted, efficient, able. **—Ant.** clumsy, awkward, maladroit, inept.

diabolic also **diabolical** adj. *They were unaware of his diabolic intent to sabotage the factory:* devilish, satanic, fiendish, wicked, evil, malevolent, demonic, impious, villainous, nefarious, monstrous, heinous, vicious, foul, baleful. **—Ant.** angelic, good, saintly, pious.

diagnose v. *The doctor quickly diagnosed the problem:* investigate, interpret, analyze, determine, distinguish, identify, pinpoint, place, recognize, spot.

diagnosis n. *The doctor's diagnosis indicated heart disease. The committee undertook a comprehensive diagnosis of the city's problems:* identification of a disease, specification of illness, determination from examination, summary or conclusion from symptoms, medical or

scientific report; investigation, study, examination, analysis, scrutiny.

diagonally adv. *They crossed the road diagonally:* obliquely, angled, aslant, crosswise, kitty-corner, slantways.

diagram n. *The company sent us a diagram of the new airplane:* outline, representation, plan, drawing, map, line drawing, sketch, illustration, chart, rough projection, breakdown.

dialect n. *Cockney is the colorful dialect spoken in the East End of London:* variety of a language, vernacular, localism, regionalism, colloquialism, provincialism, idiom, lingo, jargon, argot, patois.

dialogue or **dialog** n. **1.** *The stubborn mayor finally consented to a dialogue with the strike leaders:* formal discussion, conference, talk, exchange of viewpoints, parley, conclave, personal meeting. **2.** *The dialogue of the play was hilariously stilted, but the plot was quite conventional:* direct or spoken discourse in literature, verbal exchange, conversation in a book or play, lines, speech; literary piece completely in the form of a conversation. **—Ant.** monologue, soliloquy.

diameter n. *The screen was nine inches in diameter:* width, bore, breadth, broadness, caliber.

diaphanous adj. *The fabric was as diaphanous as a spider's web:* translucent, transparent, sheer, filmy, gossamer, gauzy, flimsy, pellucid, lucid, limpid. **—Ant.** opaque, solid, thick, heavy.

diary n. *She writes faithfully in her diary every night:* daily journal, day-to-day record, journal, daybook; log, chronicle.

diatribe n. *In her diatribe she gave full vent to all her resentments against him:* verbal or written castigation, bitter harangue, tirade, violent denunciation, stream of abuse, accusatory language, invective, vituperation, contumely.

dicker v. *Several movie studios are dickering for the rights to her life story:* negotiate, bargain, haggle, wrangle, chaffer, quibble, drive a hard bargain, *Scot.* higgle; talk down, beat down, underbid, outbid.

dictate v. **1.** *I'm dictating an answer to your letter now:* say to a person for writing down, utter for another to record, speak into a machine for recording, transmit a message through. **2.** *The conqueror dictated the surrender terms:* lay down, set forth, ordain, determine, order, enjoin, direct, prescribe, impose, pronounce, decree, declare with directive authority. **—n. 3.** *All of us must follow the dictates of the law:* requirement, mandate, stricture, rule, ruling, order, edict, decree, ordinance, dictum; bidding, urging, inclination, counsel, prompting, exhortation. **—Ant.** 1 record, write down. 2 follow, submit to, obey.

dictator n. *Stalin was one of the most feared dictators in modern history:* absolute ruler, despot, autocrat, tyrant; (*variously*) emperor, czar, kaiser, duce, führer, caesar.

dictatorial adj. **1.** *A constitutional president has no dictatorial powers:* absolute, authoritative, unlimited, unrestricted, categorical, arbitrary. **2.** *I resent his dictatorial manner:* domineering, imperious, inclined to command, tyrannical, despotic, autocratic, magisterial, peremptory, lordly, willful, supercilious, overbearing, haughty, arrogant. —**Ant.** 1 democratic, constitutional, limited, restricted. 2 suppliant, agreeable, humble, considerate, tentative.

dictatorship *n. Once elected, he imposed dictatorship:* absolutism, totalitarianism, tyranny, unlimited rule, absolute rule, authoritarianism, autocracy, coercion, despotism, fascism.

diction *n.* **1.** *Bad diction marred the effectiveness of her speech:* choice of words, command of language, verbal style, rhetoric, wording, manner of expression, turn of expression, use of idiom, vocabulary, phraseology, verbiage. **2.** *The actor was told to improve his diction:* enunciation, distinctness of speech sounds, articulation, pronunciation, elocution.

dictionary *n. She looked it up in the dictionary:* lexicon, wordbook, glossary, vocabulary.

dictum *n.* **1.** *We must go along with the boss's dictum:* dictate, edict, decree, fiat, pronouncement, commandment, authoritative statement, order, dogmatic bidding. **2.** *There's an old dictum that blood is thicker than water:* saying, saw, adage, maxim, axiom, proverb, truism, precept.

didactic *adj.* **1.** *The sociologist's talk was didactic but entertaining:* instructive, prescriptive, educational, intended for instruction, expository, edifying, tutorial, doctrinal. **2.** *He couldn't shake his didactic manner after teaching for so long:* lecturelike, preachy, inclined to lecture, pedantic, pedagogic, academic, donnish; moralizing, homiletic; dogmatically overbearing.

die *v.* **1.** *Her husband died in the war:* perish, suffer death, expire, pass away, pass on, pass over, leave this world, depart, meet death, come to one's end, be heard of no more, draw the last breath, go the way of all flesh, go to one's glory, go from dust to dust; *Slang* croak, kick the bucket. **2.** *The chiming of the bells died out but seemed to linger in the air:* wane, ebb, decline, recede, fade away, subside, melt away, fade, gradually diminish, become fainter and fainter, slowly disappear, wither, pass, come to an end, die away. **3.** *The electric train stopped when the batteries died:* fail, expire, become inoperative or inactive, run out, lose power, stop, break down, degenerate, rot, wear away, go flat; go stale, lose force, run down. **4.** *I'm dying to see Jamaica:* yearn, be eager, be anxious, long, desire greatly, pine with desire, want keenly, wish ardently, be consumed with desire, ache, be beside oneself with desire. —**Ant.** 1 live, be born, survive, breathe, exist, flourish, begin, be immortal. 2 increase, build, become strong.

diet[1] *n.* **1.** *The doctor recommended a rice diet for her high blood pressure:* nutritional regimen, particular selection of food for health or other reasons, prescribed food and drink, limitation of fare. **2.** *A balanced diet is necessary for good health:* nutrition, nourishment, eating habits, eating regimen, nutriment, nurture,

board, sustenance, subsistence, victuals, provisions, edibles, comestibles. —*v.* **3.** *You will have to diet before you can wear that dress:* eat abstemiously, eat judiciously, take food according to a regimen, follow prescribed eating habits, regulate one's food, cut back on one's food intake, restrict one's intake; eat sparingly, eat restrictedly; abstain from overindulgence.

diet[2] *n. The measure was approved by a voice vote of the diet:* lawmaking body, legislature, bicameral assembly, representative body for acting upon public affairs; congress, convention, convocation, general assembly, parliament, synod; assemblage.

differ *v.* **1.** *This photograph differs markedly from the other one:* contrast, stand apart from, deviate from, depart from, diverge from; be unlike, be dissimilar, be distinct, be disparate. **2.** *I differ with my partner sometimes, but usually we agree:* disagree, take issue, be of a different opinion, be at variance, stand opposed to, fail to go along, demur, think differently; dissent, dispute. —**Ant.** 1 ape, mimic, copy. 2 concur, coincide, agree.

difference *n.* **1.** *She doesn't know the difference between asking and demanding:* distinction, contradistinction, lack of resemblance, dissimilarity, unlikeness, dissimilitude, contrast, variation, disagreement, contrariety, deviation, divergence, contradiction; distinguishing characteristic, point of dissimilarity. **2.** *The difference in their ages is six years:* discrepancy, disparity. **3.** *They haven't spoken since their difference last year:* dispute, argument, disagreement, clash, falling out, contretemps, quarrel, squabble, spat, set-to. —**Ant.** 1 resemblance, similarity, likeness, similitude, analogy, affinity, agreement, uniformity, unity, consonance, identity, harmony, sameness. 3 agreement, concurrence, harmony, compatibility.

different *adj.* **1.** *Her hat is different from yours:* unlike, dissimilar, not identical, not alike, distinct, disparate, other than, divergent, contrasting. **2.** *We put the cookies in three different boxes:* separate, distinct, individual. **3.** *I heard the news from different sources:* several, various, sundry, divers, variegated, manifold, miscellaneous, diversified, unrelated, separate. **4.** *He has a different outlook on things:* unconventional, unusual, not ordinary, uncommon, rare, unique, singular, distinctive, atypical, aberrant; foreign, strange, peculiar, anomalous, bizarre. —**Ant.** 1 identical, alike, same, similar, like. 4 ordinary, common, usual, typical, conventional.

differentiate *v.* **1.** *I learned to differentiate between the French white wines:* discriminate, distinguish, see the difference in. **2.** *The chrome trim differentiates the luxury model from the standard:* distinguish, set off, set apart, constitute a difference between, make different; contrast, separate, draw the line.

differently *adv. Others looked at the issue differently:* dissimilarly, abnormally, alternatively, antithetically, conflictingly, contrarily, discordantly, disparately, distinctively, divergently, diversely, incompatibly, incongruously, individually, otherwise, separately, uniquely, variously.

difficult *adj.* **1.** *Moving the boulders was a difficult task:* hard, onerous, laborious, strenuous, demanding, requiring much effort, arduous, not easy, burdensome, exhausting, tedious, wearisome, toilsome, formidable, troublesome, exacting, trying, uphill, Herculean, Sisyphean, tough; complex, complicated, intricate, problematical, hard to solve, thorny, ticklish, knotty, *Slang* hairy; enigmatic, perplexing, bewildering, hard to understand. **2.** *She was always a difficult child:* hard to please, hard to satisfy, hard to deal with; unpredictable, unaccommodating; hard to manage, unruly, froward, obstinate, stubborn, willful, perverse, unmanageable, rambunctious, recalcitrant, obstreperous, unyielding, intractable, fractious, inflexible; critical, fastidious. **3.** *Times were difficult during the Depression:* hard, grim, rough, full of hardship, not easy, tough, trying, troublesome. **—Ant.** 1 simple, easy, facile, light; clear, uncomplicated, lucid; plain, manifest. 2 easy, pleasant, amenable, cooperative, accommodating, manageable, flexible, tractable. 3 easy, pleasant, halcyon.

difficulty *n.* **1.** *I finally overcame the difficulty of meeting people:* trial, troublesomeness, arduousness, laboriousness, uphill work, rough going, tough job, hard sledding; obstacle, impediment, obstruction, barrier, snag, stumbling block, hindrance; problem, dilemma, puzzle, quandary, intricacy, perplexity. **2.** *Because of some difficulty with her husband she had to return the coat:* trouble, predicament, pickle, critical situation, crisis, straits, hot water, mess, jam, deep water, muddle. **—Ant.** 1 ease.

diffidence *n.* *His diffidence keeps him from making friends:* timidity, timidness, timorousness, shyness, meekness, insecurity, retiring disposition, reserve, constraint, introversion; bashfulness, extreme modesty, humbleness, want of self-confidence, unassertiveness, sheepishness, lack of self-assurance; hesitancy, reluctance. **—Ant.** boldness, audaciousness, forwardness, assertiveness, aggressiveness; self-confidence, confidence.

diffident *adj.* *She was diffident about asking for a raise:* shy, self-conscious, self-effacing, bashful, abashed, embarrassed, timid, sheepish, modest. **—Ant.** forward, bold, unabashed.

diffuse *adj.* **1.** *The room was bathed in soft, diffuse light:* scattered, spread out, unconcentrated, dispersed, extended widely; vaguely defined. **2.** *His talk was so diffuse I missed his point:* wordy, verbose, discursive, rambling, long-winded, lacking conciseness, disjointed, digressive, not concentrated, desultory, roundabout, wandering, meandering, maundering, circumlocutory. **—Ant.** 1 concentrated. 2 succinct, concise, terse, pithy, compact; methodical, organized.

diffusion *n.* **1.** *The diffusion of knowledge was accelerated by the invention of writing:* spread, dispersal, scattering. **2.** *The diffusion of his writing style is confusing:* verbosity, diffuseness, wordiness, prolixity, verbiage, profuseness; circumlocution, indirection, roundaboutness, rambling, maundering, disjointedness, discursiveness. **—Ant.** 1 concentration, centralization, congestion. 2 conciseness, succinctness, terseness, condensation, compactness.

dig *v.* **1.** *The kids dug a tunnel in the sand. We dug worms for bait:* excavate, scoop out, gouge, penetrate and loosen ground, hollow out; bring to the surface, disinter, unearth, exhume, retrieve from the soil. **2.** *Can you dig the material out of the archives?:* search and find, retrieve, extricate, find among, come up with, pinpoint, salvage, bring to view. **3.** *He dug his elbow into my ribs:* poke, drive, jab, thrust, prod. **—n. 4.** *He gave me a dig in the ribs:* poke, thrust, punch, jab, prod. **5.** *She couldn't resist a dig about my freckles:* cutting remark, gibe, jeer, slur, verbal thrust, wry comment, taunt, aside, *Slang* put-down.

digest *v.* **1.** *Some foods are hard to digest:* assimilate, convert into an absorbable form, transform for bodily use, dissolve. **2.** *It took her a while to digest the bad news:* grasp, comprehend, absorb, assimilate mentally, understand, realize, take in mentally, appreciate, take in wholly, fathom, *Slang* dig. **—n. 3.** *The digest of the two-volume novel included the most exciting scenes:* condensation, abridgment, summary, synopsis, précis, résumé, abstract.

digging *n.* *The digging did no good: they could find nothing:* excavating, delving, burrowing, tunnelling, unearthing.

dignified *adj.* *My father is too dignified to do anything so silly:* full of dignity, decorous, self-respecting, circumspect, reserved, distinguished, proper, upright, honorable, upstanding, proud, august. **—Ant.** undignified, crass, vulgar.

dignify *v.* *He did not dignify the absurd question with an answer:* honor, distinguish, glorify, elevate, ennoble, exalt, uplift, grace, build up, raise, promote, magnify. **—Ant.** demean, humble.

dignity *n.* **1.** *She maintained her dignity throughout the trial:* comportment, dignified behavior, respectful deportment, self-possession, solemnity, decorum; stateliness, lofty bearing, proud demeanor, impressiveness of character; majesty, augustness. **2.** *We must respect the dignity of the high court:* loftiness, high position, honor, station, official prerogatives, importance.

digress *v.* *Let me digress for a moment to tell you a little story:* depart from the subject, stray, go off on a tangent, wander, divagate, deviate, turn aside, back up. **—Ant.** proceed, advance, continue.

digression *n.* *His long digression made him forget his main point:* divergence, departure, deviation, detour, straying, wandering; diversion, obiter dictum, side remark, divagation.

dilapidated *adj.* *We bought a dilapidated house and tried to repair it:* run-down, decrepit, decaying, broken-down, tumbledown, falling to pieces, falling into decay, ruined, ramshackle, deteriorated, crumbling, in disrepair, shabby, rickety, falling apart, battered, worn-out; *Slang* shot, beat-up.

dilate *v. This medicine will dilate the blood vessels and prevent clotting:* expand, swell, enlarge, distend, inflate, puff out, extend; make wider, widen, broaden. **—Ant.** constrict, contract, shrink, compress, condense, narrow.

dilatory *adj. The younger girl was dilatory about doing her homework:* inclined to delay, slow, procrastinating, remiss, tardy, sluggish, phlegmatic, reluctant; dawdling, lackadaisical, negligent; indolent, slothful, lazy. **—Ant.** diligent, assiduous, sedulous, industrious, conscientious; punctual, prompt.

dilemma *n. The doctor's dilemma was whether he should tell the patient the truth:* plight, difficult choice, bind, problem, quandary, predicament; impasse, deadlock, stalemate; Hobson's choice, *Slang* crunch.

dilettante *n. His inheritance allows him to pursue the arts as a dilettante:* one who pursues various arts, cultured hobbyist; dabbler, amateur, trifler, experimenter. **—Ant.** artist, expert, professional.

diligence *n. She did her homework with great diligence:* industry, persistence, effort, application, assiduity, perseverance, assiduousness. **—Ant.** carelessness, laziness.

diligent *adj. He was a diligent worker and deserved the promotion:* industrious, hardworking, zealous, persevering, active, sedulous, assiduous, persistent, earnest, pertinacious, untiring, plodding, studious, painstaking; careful, thorough, well-intentioned, patient, concerted. **—Ant.** dilatory, lazy, careless, laggard, indifferent, inconstant, erratic.

dilute *v.* **1.** *Dilute the ammonia with water:* thin, make thinner, thin out, make less concentrated, make weak, weaken, adulterate; thin with water, water down, add water to; make more fluid, make more liquid. **2.** *His love for the boy tended to dilute his anger:* diminish, mitigate, temper, lessen the force of, decrease, weaken, attenuate, reduce, diffuse. *—adj.* **3.** *I've heard that the corner bar serves dilute whisky:* diluted, watered down, watery, weak, weakened, adulterated, thinned out, reduced in strength by admixture. **—Ant.** 1 thicken, concentrate, strengthen. 2 strengthen, intensify.

diluted *adj. The drink was diluted:* thinned, cut, watered down, watery, weak, weakened.

dim *adj.* **1.** *The room was too dim for me to read:* lacking light, not bright, lacking luminosity, unilluminated, obscure from lack of light, darkened, dusky, tenebrous, shadowy, murky, adumbrated, indistinct, obscured, clouded, ill-defined, faint, nebulous, hazy; blurry, blurred; muffled, low, soft, weak, muted, feeble. **2.** *I had a dim suspicion that trouble was near:* vague, intangible, faint, indefinite, indistinct, remote, foggy; gloomy. **—Ant.** 1 bright, brilliant, radiant, luminous, effulgent. 2 distinct, plain, clear, palpable, definite, pronounced, well-defined.

dimension *n.* **1.** Often **dimensions.** *The dimensions of the supposed flying saucer were quite improbable:* measurements, size, length,

width, height, thickness; proportion, physical extent, mass, massiveness, bulk, volume. **2.** Usually **dimensions.** *No one realized the dimensions of his problem:* range, scope, magnitude, extent, importance, volume, amplitude, measure, weight, greatness, massiveness.

diminish *v.* **1.** *The cold spell quickly diminished our firewood supply:* reduce, lessen, shrink, abate, decrease, make smaller, shorten, lower. **2.** *Time will never make our friendship diminish:* become smaller, lessen, shrink, dwindle, narrow, be reduced, shrivel, wane, decline, subside, fall off, ebb, peter out. **—Ant.** enlarge, augment, increase, amplify, enhance, heighten, magnify; expand, grow, burgeon, increase.

diminutive *adj.* **1.** *Gulliver then encountered a diminutive people:* tiny, little, small, short, slight, stunted, undersized, miniature, petite, minute, lilliputian, pocket-size, vest-pocket, *Slang* half-pint; teeny, wee, elfin, dwarfish; on a small scale, insignificant, unimportant, inconsiderable. *—n.* **2.** *Maggie is a diminutive for Margaret:* short form, affectionate expression, nickname, pet name, hypocoristic term. **—Ant.** 1 enormous, immense, gigantic, oversized, huge, vast, colossal, mammoth, monumental.

dimwit *n. Why did you employ some dimwit who knew nothing about the job?:* dummy, blockhead, dunce, simpleton, fool, nitwit, numskull, chowderhead, meathead, booby, dolt, dull-ard, dummkopf, dumbbell, knucklehead, pinhead, dingbat, yo-yo, ding-a-ling, jerk.

din *n. There was such a din I didn't hear the phone:* clamor, uproar, loud confused noise, hubbub, racket, hullabaloo, tumult, commotion, clangor, stir, to-do, babble, clattering, ruckus; *Archaic* bruit. **—Ant.** quiet, silence, calm, stillness.

dine *v. She dines with friends almost every night:* eat, sup, feast, break bread, banquet, partake, take a little nourishment, take sustenance, fall to, gourmandize, feed, gluttonize; eat (or have) dinner, supper, lunch, breakfast; *Slang* eat high off the hog.

diner *n.* **1.** *In the restaurant sat several diners:* eater, patron, gourmet, guest. **2.** *Some things are finer than dinner in a diner:* canteen, café, coffee shop, fast-food outlet, grill, lunch counter, lunchroom, lunch wagon, sandwich shop, snack bar *Slang* greasy spoon, hamburger joint.

dingy *adj. The meeting was held in a dingy storeroom in the old building:* dirty and drab, dusty, murky, lacking brightness, shabby, tacky, grimy, dreary, gloomy, dismal. **—Ant.** bright, burnished, radiant, glittering, luminous, shining, lustrous; gay, cheerful.

dinner *n. Six sat down to dinner:* main meal, principal meal, meal, repast, spread, supper.

dint *n. By dint of hard work he became a leader in his profession:* force, effort, struggle, strain, labor, exertion, will, stress, endeavor, energy, power, might, strength, determination, push, insistence, drive, forcefulness, charge, relentlessness.

dip *v.* **1.** *She dipped the blouse into the hot*

suds: dunk, place momentarily in a liquid, soak, submerge, immerse briefly. **2.** *He dipped the chowder into individual bowls:* take out with a ladle, scoop, lift by scooping, dish, dish up, dish out, ladle, spoon, bail; shovel. **3.** *The moon dipped behind the trees:* droop, descend, slope, incline downward, turn down, decline, sink, drop down. **4.** *I've only dipped into politics:* dabble, try tentatively, involve oneself slightly; study slightly, read here and there in a book, peruse, skim, take a cursory view of, glance at, run over. —**Ant.** 3 rise, climb, ascend. 4 involve deeply, immerse.

diploma *n. She earned her diploma in embalming:* certificate, award, certificate, charter, commission, credentials, degree, sheepskin.

diplomacy *n.* **1.** *He is highly experienced in international diplomacy:* conduct of international relations, statesmanship, national spokesmanship, discourse between nations, foreign affairs, foreign negotiation, international politics. **2.** *She used great diplomacy in handling the awkward situation:* tact, finesse, discretion, prudence, savoir-faire; artful management, skill, subtlety, delicacy, maneuvering, craft, artfulness. —**Ant.** 2 tactlessness, crassness, awkwardness, clumsiness, ineptness.

diplomat *n.* **1.** *He's a U.S. diplomat assigned to the embassy in London:* government negotiator with foreign countries, statesman, national representative, international affairs expert, negotiator, interlocutor; ambassador, consul, minister, envoy, attaché, emissary. **2.** *We need a diplomat to deal with these prima donnas:* tactful person, one who is artful in coping with situations, artful handler of people.

diplomatic *adj.* **1.** *He has a diplomatic post in Ethiopia:* involving diplomatic service, ambassadorial, foreign-service, state-department. **2.** *He's so diplomatic he can get along with anyone:* tactful, discreet, politic; sensitive, prudent, urbane, suave, attuned, smoothly skillful in handling others, skillful at attaining one's ends, strategic, artful, adept. —**Ant.** 2 tactless, rude, unthinking, clumsy.

dire *adj.* **1.** *Any refusal to meet their demands will result in dire consequences:* dreadful, awful, appalling, horrible, terrible, woeful, harrowing, grave; calamitous, catastrophic, ruinous, cataclysmic, disastrous; urgent, desperate, extreme, fearful, crucial, critical. **2.** *We were frightened by her dire prediction:* ill-boding, grim, ominous, portentous, dreadful, ill-omened, apocalyptic, dismal, inauspicious. —**Ant.** 1 happy, pleasing, good, favorable. 2 favorable, auspicious, promising.

direct *v.* **1.** *Mr. Kelley directs the activities of the community center. I was directed to cut the budget:* supervise, manage, oversee, head, serve as director for, handle, conduct, control, superintend, administer, lead, preside over; advise, urge, instruct, order, command, enjoin, charge. **2.** *The policeman directed us to the shopping center:* point the way, show the way, usher, indicate, put on the right track, conduct to, lead, guide, pilot, navigate. **3.** *She directed*

her remarks to the speaker: level at, aim, focus, train at, point toward, address, intend for, earmark, designate. —*adj.* **4.** *They insisted upon direct negotiations between the leaders of the two countries:* face-to-face, head-on, personal, firsthand, without intervening agent, without intercessor, unmediated. **5.** *He surprised me with several direct questions:* straightforward, without circumlocution, frank, candid, clear, explicit, plain-spoken, point-blank, going straight to the point; sincere, honest, pointed, forward, forthright, blunt. —**Ant.** 4 indirect, meandering, roundabout, circuitous; mediated, by proxy. 5 indirect, devious, subtle, ambiguous, sly, oblique.

direction *n.* **1.** *The research center will be under his direction:* management, superintendence, headship, supervision, surveillance, guidance, leadership, control, charge; administration, command, care. **2.** *In which direction is the beach?:* way, line along which anything moves or lies, path, track, route, line of march, alignment; point of compass, course, bearing. **3.** *You're thinking in the right direction:* line of thought or action, inclination, aim, tendency, bent, course, trend, track, bearing, drift, current. **4.** *(Usually plural) Follow the directions carefully:* instruction, order, regulation, prescription, guidelines, recipe.

directly *adv.* **1.** *She drove directly to school. He lives directly across the street from me:* straight, in a straight line, on a straight course, not obliquely, unswervingly, as the crow flies, in a beeline, without deviation from course; exactly, precisely. **2.** *The guests will arrive directly:* soon, presently, momentarily; forthwith, at once, immediately, right away, promptly, as soon as possible. **3.** *I spoke directly to the manager:* face-to-face, in person, personally. **4.** *I hope you will answer me directly:* openly, honestly, frankly, straightforwardly, candidly, without circumlocution, in plain terms, unambiguously, unequivocally. —**Ant.** 1 indirectly, circuitously, crookedly; imprecisely, obliquely, inexactly. 2 later, eventually. 3 indirectly. 4 ambiguously, equivocally, cryptically, deceitfully, dishonestly.

director *n. What the camp needs is a vigorous recreation director:* supervisor, manager, controller, superintendent, conductor, head, leader, organizer, overseer, administrator, boss, governor, chief, curator, foreman, commander, chairman, master.

directory *n. They searched for her name in the directory:* register, roster, listing.

dirge *n. He composed a dirge to honor the war dead:* funeral song, requiem, death song, death march, lament, burial hymn, threnody, mournful composition; mournful sound.

dirt *n.* **1.** *We need more sweepers to keep the gutters free of dirt:* mud, mire, dust, filth, filthy substance, impurity, foul matter, trash, sweepings, refuse, garbage, rubbish, muck, grime, soot, smudge, slime, scum, sludge, slop, leavings, dross, excrement, offal. **2.** *This is good dirt for growing vegetables:* soil, earth, loam, ground, humus. **3.** *Those shops still peddle* *their dirt to the tourists:* smut, filth, pornography, muck, obscenity, moral filth, vileness, squalidness, scurrility, scabrousness, salaciousness, indecency, profanity, unclean language. **4.** *Her column is filled with dirt about famous people:* gossip, defamatory talk, rumor, scuttlebutt, scandal, slander, sensational exposé.

dirty *adj.* **1.** *Scrape your dirty shoes on the doormat:* unclean, grimy, soiled, begrimed, muddied, grubby, filthy, foul, besmeared, messy, unwashed, untidy, smudgy, befouled, sullied, tarnished, polluted, unsterile. **2.** *He got involved in some dirty dealings in the stock market:* unscrupulous, illegal, illicit, base, mean, contemptible, despicable, low-down, devious, deceitful, vile, shabby, nasty, sordid, squalid, dishonest, fraudulent, crooked, dishonorable, corrupt, perfidious, villainous, treacherous. **3.** *His company publishes dirty books:* obscene, vulgar, off-color, scabrous, pornographic, morally unclean, indecent, prurient, immoral, smutty, coarse, lewd, filthy, licentious; risqué. **4.** *I seem to get all the dirty jobs:* distasteful, unpleasant, disagreeable, rotten, foul; hard, difficult. —*v.* **5.** *We certainly dirtied this floor:* soil, make dirty, slop up, mess up, sully, smear, besmear, smudge, muddy, stain, spot, tarnish, begrime, blacken; pollute, muck up. —**Ant.** 1 clean, washed, pure, spotless. 2 honest, respectable, aboveboard, honorable. 3 moral, respectable, decent, reputable. 4 easy, agreeable, pleasant. 5 clean, tidy up.

disability *n.* **1.** *His disability prevents him from holding a job:* handicap, particular incapacity, disablement, unfitness, infirmity, impairment, defect, affliction, debilitation, impediment, weakness, inadequacy. **2.** *Not speaking French in Paris is a real disability:* disadvantage, disqualification, handicap, shortcoming, minus. —**Ant.** 1 fitness, capability, ability, capacity, strength. 2 advantage, merit, qualification, plus.

disable *v.* *The plane was critically disabled when one of the engines caught fire:* incapacitate, render inoperable, damage, cripple, impair; deprive of strength, weaken, hinder, handicap.

disabled *adj.* *The disabled jeep could go no further:* incapacitated, broken down, crippled, hamstrung, handicapped, helpless, hurt, impotent, infirm, laid up, maimed, mangled, paralyzed, paraplegic, sidelined, stalled, weakened, wounded, wrecked, unable. —**Ant.** sound, able-bodied, fit, hale, healthy, robust, strong.

disabuse *v.* *Someone ought to disabuse him of those star-struck notions:* enlighten about, free from error, clear the mind of, disillusion, disenchant, rid of deception, relieve of, set straight, set right, open the eyes of, free of a mistaken belief.

disadvantage *n.* **1.** *His years of experience at the job put me at a disadvantage:* weak position, unfavorable condition, handicap; in arrears. **2.** *What are the disadvantages of owning your own home?:* drawback, handicap, detriment, weakness, weak point, inconvenience, impediment, hindrance, fly in the ointment, trouble, hardship, nuisance, burden, flaw.

—**Ant.** 1 advantage. 2 advantage, convenience, merit, desirability, benefit, perquisite; gain, profit.

disadvantaged *adj.* *Several disadvantaged countries need immediate help:* underprivileged, underdeveloped, impoverished, struggling, emerging, emergent, deprived, handicapped, troubled. —**Ant.** advantaged, privileged, affluent.

disadvantageous *adj.* *She decided it would be disadvantageous to stand for office:* harmful, detrimental, deleterious, unfavorable, unprofitable, adverse, damaging, inconvenient, inopportune, prejudicial, hindered. —**Ant.** advantageous.

disaffect *v.* *His high-handed conduct disaffected his staff:* estrange, alienate, antagonize, discompose, disquiet, disturb, disunify, disunite, divide, repel.

disaffected *adj.* *Their oldest boy became disaffected and ran away from home:* estranged, alienated, antipathetic, withdrawn, unfriendly, hostile, discontented, dissatisfied, disturbed, upset, agitated, disgruntled, discomposed, irreconcilable, quarrelsome, belligerent, inimical. —**Ant.** contented, serene, easygoing, satisfied, well-adjusted.

disaffection *n.* *The nasty memo further increased her disaffection:* estrangement, alienation, animosity, antagonism, aversion, breach, disagreement, discontent, repugnance, resentment.

disagree *v.* **1.** *My total disagrees with yours. We disagree completely on politics:* differ, be unlike, fail to agree, not coincide, vary, be at variance, conflict, be discordant, deviate, be dissimilar, diverge, depart; be of different opinion, think differently, stand apart, oppose one another, be unreconciled, differ in opinion, entertain contradictory views; be at loggerheads, clash. **2.** *Too much sun disagrees with her:* be injurious, cause problems, disconcert, distress, discomfit, make ill, be unfavorable in effect, upset. —**Ant.** 1 agree, coincide, correlate.

disagreeable *adj.* **1.** *The weather has been thoroughly disagreeable all week:* unpleasant, nasty, displeasing, distasteful, unpalatable, grating, repugnant, disgusting, harsh, repellent, repulsive, offensive; uninviting, uncomfortable, unwelcome. **2.** *She is always so disagreeable when we ask her to help:* unpleasant, ill-natured, irritable, difficult, uncongenial, unamiable, ill-tempered, churlish, nasty, bad-tempered, grouchy, cross, peevish, surly, petulant, testy, acrimonious, obnoxious, irascible. —**Ant.** 1 agreeable, pleasant, propitious, delightful, inviting, welcome. 2 agreeable, pleasant, congenial, amiable, personable.

disagreement *n.* **1.** *There was apparent disagreement between their stories:* difference, lack of agreement, variance, discrepancy, unlikeness, disparity, failure to correspond, lack of harmony, deviation, divergence, diversity, dissimilarity, incongruity, dissimilitude, discord, incompatibility. **2.** *They haven't spoken since their disagreement:* quarrel, squabble, fight, argument, difference, falling-out, misunderstanding, discord, dispute, clash. **—Ant.** 1 agreement, unity, likeness, similarity, correspondence, convergence, congruity, accord, harmony.

disallow v. The new regulation was disallowed by a narrow margin: deny, veto, reject, cancel, censor, disavow, disclaim, dismiss, disown, embargo, exclude, forbid, prohibit, proscribe, rebuff, refuse, repudiate.

disappear v. **1.** The sun disappeared behind the clouds: vanish from sight, become obscured, cease to be seen, pass out of sight, be lost to view, cease to appear; withdraw, retire, go, be gone, depart, exit, flee, leave, fade, fade away. **2.** The spot disappeared when the shirt was washed: melt away, vanish, evaporate, end, cease to exist, leave no trace, be no more, die out, cease to be known. **—Ant.** 1 appear, arrive. 2 appear, materialize.

disappearance n. The disappearance of the secret documents created a scandal: act of disappearing, vanishing, evanescence, sudden or unexplained loss, passing from sight. **—Ant.** appearance, materialization, manifestation.

disappoint v. You disappointed us by not coming to our party: fail to live up to the expectations of, let down, sadden, disillusion, chagrin, dishearten; thwart, frustrate, hinder, foil, mislead. **—Ant.** satisfy, gratify, fulfill.

disappointment n. **1.** Rover has been a disappointment to us as a watchdog: letdown, failure, dissatisfaction, something that disappoints, disillusionment, washout, dud, fiasco, disaster, fizzle, Slang bomb. **2.** She says she's finally learned to accept disappointment: thwarted expectation, miscarriage of plan, unrealization, unfulfillment, loss, frustration, setback, dissatisfaction, defeat, failure; Slang the knocks. **—Ant.** 1, 2 satisfaction, fulfillment.

disapproval n. His sloppiness earned much disapproval: condemnation, blackball, blame, boycott, castigation, censure, criticism, denunciation, deprecation, disfavor, dislike, displeasure, objection, opprobrium, reproach, stricture.

disapprove v. **1.** Her parents disapprove of her going to dances alone: view with disfavor, frown upon, discountenance, object to, find unacceptable, condemn, regard as wrong, think ill of, dislike, take exception to, look askance at; censure, criticize, deprecate, denounce, disparage, deplore, decry. **2.** His request for reinstatement was disapproved: refuse, turn down, withhold approval from, disallow, refuse assent to, veto, reject. **—Ant.** 1 approve, commend, recommend, applaud, compliment, endorse, sanction, like. 2 approve, allow, authorize, accept, assent to.

disarm v. She can always disarm me with one of her radiant smiles: persuade, win over, convince, sway, influence, prevail on, move, entice, bewitch, charm, captivate, attract, fascinate, enchant, take the wind out of one's sails. **—Ant.** alienate, estrange, vex, irritate, repel.

disarmament n. Disarmament came slowly in the postwar decades: pacification, arms limita-

tion, arms reduction, de-escalation, demilitarization, demobilization, neutralizing, reduction.

disarming adj. He has a disarming smile: winning, winsome, magnetic, charming, ingratiating, ingenuous, beguiling, melting, irresistible, captivating, entrancing, appealing, bewitching, seductive. **—Ant.** irritating, annoying, exasperating, infuriating.

disarrange v. My records were disarranged by the children: scramble, disorder, mix up, displace, put out of order, disarray, upset, jumble, scatter, disorganize, confuse, put askew, muddle, turn topsy-turvy, Slang mess up; rumple, dishevel, ruffle. **—Ant.** arrange, order, systematize, methodize.

disarray n. The room was in complete disarray after the party: disorder, messiness, sloppiness, upset, disarrangement, dishevelment, untidiness, confusion, disharmony, disorganization, chaos, jumble, clutter, scramble, shambles, mix-up. **—Ant.** order, arrangement, organization.

disaster n. The fire was the worst disaster ever to hit the town: catastrophe, calamity, adverse happening, misfortune, great mishap, cataclysm, tragedy, trouble, scourge, crushing reverse, accident, adversity, ruination, blight, harm, misadventure, wreck, fiasco. **—Ant.** blessing, benefit, good fortune, profit, gain, boon, windfall.

disastrous adj. Investing his savings in that dubious stock was disastrous: ruinous, catastrophic, calamitous, critically injurious, devastating, ill-fated, ill-starred, hapless, inauspicious, dire, harmful, destructive, fatal, dreadful, terrible, tragic, adverse, unfortunate, grievous, desolating, horrendous, harrowing.

disavow v. He disavowed the rumors that he would run for mayor: repudiate, deny, contradict, denounce, reject, abjure, retract, recant, gainsay; disclaim knowledge of, deny responsibility for, deny connection with, disown, divorce oneself from, refuse to acknowledge. **—Ant.** acknowledge, admit; claim, accept.

disband v. The war having ended, they disbanded his regiment: break up, demobilize, dissolve, disperse, dismiss, separate, scatter. **—Ant.** organize, unite.

disbelief n. My disbelief in his alibi was obvious: skepticism, lack of credence, doubt, doubtfulness, unbelief, dubiety, incredulity, distrust, mistrust. **—Ant.** belief, credulity, trust, faith, credence.

disbelieving adj. Her disbelieving eyes could not take in the miracle: unbelieving, cynical, doubting, incredulous, leery, mistrustful, questioning, sceptical, suspicious.

disburse v. Company salaries are disbursed by the paymaster: pay out, lay out, allocate, give out in payment, distribute; Slang shell out, fork out.

discard v. Let's discard some of these old newspapers: eliminate, get rid of, throw away, throw out, weed out, thrust aside, cast aside, remove; abandon, shelve, have done with, relinquish, drop, shed, junk, dispose of, dispense with, dump, scrap, throw overboard, jettison. —**Ant.** retain, keep, preserve.

discern v. *She could discern a faint light at the end of the forest:* detect, make out, perceive, espy, catch sight of, descry, see, observe, behold, notice, pick out, ascertain.

discerning *adj. The mediator was discerning in his analysis of the problem:* perceptive, acute, perspicacious, sharp, astute, penetrating, keen-sighted, sensitive, piercing, discriminating, shrewd, intelligent, wise, judicious, sage, sagacious, clear-sighted, sharp-sighted; showing discernment, quick to discern, having keen insight. —**Ant.** undiscerning, unperceptive, indiscriminate.

discharge v. **1.** *We feared he would discharge the bomb:* set off, shoot, activate, touch off, fire off, detonate, trigger, explode; send forth a missile from, eject, launch, propel, let fly. **2.** *The boiler discharged steam:* emit, throw off, pour forth, send forth, project, expel, give forth, exude, gush. **3.** *His boss discharged him because of habitual absenteeism:* fire, dismiss, release, expel, oust, let go, terminate, sack, get rid of, give the gate to, can, axe, give one his walking papers, bounce, lay off, send packing, cashier, remove from office. **4.** *The prisoners were discharged from the detention camp:* release, allow to go, let go, free, set free, liberate. —n. **5.** *The discharge of the revolver was accidental:* firing, discharging, detonating, triggering, firing off, activating, exploding; detonation, explosion, blast, fusillade, shot, report, burst. **6.** *He framed his honorable discharge from the army:* release, release document, walking papers; demobilization. **7.** *The discharge from the wound contained pus:* flow, suppuration, drainage, emission, ooze, issue, secretion, seepage.

disciple n. *She is an ardent disciple of yoga:* pupil, student, follower, devotee, aficionado, pursuer; adherent, believer, admirer, supporter, partisan; proselyte, neophyte, convert; *Informal* nut, freak. —**Ant.** master, teacher, leader, guru.

disciplinarian n. *The teacher was no disciplinarian and his class ran wild:* one who maintains discipline, enforcer of rules and order, stickler for rules, strict taskmaster, martinet, authoritarian, one who goes by the book.

discipline n. **1.** *The discipline at the military academy is extraordinary:* training, drill, drilling, schooling, indoctrination, enforcement of rules, rigor, diligent exercise, practice, preparation. **2.** *Daily practice is a discipline observed by most musicians:* method, regulated activity, prescribed habit, regimen, self-enforced practice, course of exercise. —v. **3.** *His dog was disciplined by a professional trainer:* train, instruct, teach by exercise, drill, prime, break in. **4.** *He disciplined his students by keeping them after school:* punish, chastise, chasten.

disclaim v. *He disclaimed responsibility for the accident:* disavow, disaffirm, deny, repudiate, renounce, decline, disown, forswear, abnegate, wash one's hands of. —**Ant.** claim, avow, affirm, acknowledge, accept, admit.

disclose v. **1.** *The lawyer disclosed the details of the merger:* tell, reveal, divulge, make known, lay bare, bare, uncover, unveil, leak, communicate, broadcast, publish, make public, impart. **2.** *Daylight disclosed a chain of mountains in the distance:* uncover, allow to be seen, reveal, show, expose, bring into view, cause to appear, bring to light. —**Ant.** 1 conceal, hide, withhold. 2 cloak, mask, cover, veil.

disclosure n. *Further disclosures of his indiscretions made his position untenable:* revelation, announcement, admission, advertisement, declaration, discovery, divulgence, enlightenment, exposure, leak, publication, tipoff, exposé.

discolor v. *Water discolored the carpet:* stain, spot, spoil the color of, change the color of, tarnish, streak, bleach, tinge.

discomfort n. **1.** *The discomfort from the stitches was not too great:* ache, hurt, pain, sore-ness, irritation, affliction; hardship, absence of comfort, uncomfortableness, trouble, trial, disquietude; vexation, annoyance, nuisance, distress, malaise, misery. —v. **2.** *We were discomforted by her cool manner:* make uneasy, embarrass, make uncomfortable, discomfit, distress, try, discompose, disquiet. —**Ant.** 1 comfort, ease, pleasure.

discommode v. *Unpleasant service in restaurants discommoded her:* vex, annoy, bother, burden, disoblige, disquiet, disturb, fluster, harass, inconvenience, irk, upset, trouble, perturb, put out.

discomposure n. *She was outwardly calm and betrayed no discomposure:* perturbation, agitation, uneasiness, distraction, disturbed condition, confusion, disquietude, discomfiture, embarrassment, discomfort, flurry, anxiety, nervousness. —**Ant.** composure, poise, equanimity, impassiveness, easiness, quietude.

disconcert v. **1.** *Dropping an earring momentarily disconcerted her:* disturb, confuse, perturb, ruffle, discompose, perplex, bewilder, frustrate, embarrass, abash; disarrange, disorder. —adj. **2.** *When the hotel turned them away, the disconcerted couple sought other lodgings:* fazed, bewildered, confused, distracted, disturbed, embarrassed, flustered, nonplussed, perturbed, rattled, ruffled, shaken, troubled, unsettled, upset, *Informal* thrown. —**Ant.** 1 calm; order, arrange.

disconcerted *adj. The performers were disconcerted by the latecomers:* distracted, fazed, ruffled, nonplussed, agitated, unsettled, confused; upset, annoyed, disturbed, troubled, perturbed, thrown off, rattled. —**Ant.** unruffled, impassive, undistracted, stolid.

disconnect v. *The electric company disconnected his power:* separate, cut, sever, detach, disassociate, disengage, dissever, divide, part, uncouple.

disconnected *adj. The plot was too disconnected to make sense:* confused, rambling, jumbled, disorganized, illogical, incoherent, mixed-up, disjointed, irrational. —**Ant.** connected, organized, logical, coherent.

disconsolate *adj. She is disconsolate over the loss of her job:* depressed, downcast, unhappy, inconsolable, desolate, sad, dejected, crushed, despondent, miserable, forlorn, brokenhearted, pessimistic, heavyhearted, sorrowful, dispirited, woeful, woebegone, discouraged, doleful, low-spirited, melancholy, wretched, blue, *Slang* down, down-in-the-mouth, down-in-the-dumps. **—Ant.** happy, joyous, cheerful, hopeful, optimistic, comforted.

discontent *n. Lack of talks on their contract led to the workers' discontent:* discontentment, dissatisfaction, uneasiness, inquietude, restlessness, displeasure. **—Ant.** contentment; satisfaction, pleasure, ease, restfulness.

discontented *adj. She was discontented with her dull life:* unhappy, dissatisfied, regretful, displeased, bored, disgruntled, miserable, malcontent, fretful. **—Ant.** contented, satisfied, happy.

discontinue *v. I had to discontinue my gymnastics class after spraining my ankle:* stop, break off, interrupt, terminate, suspend, drop, cease, desist, give up, quit, abstain, abandon, leave off, end, put an end to. **—Ant.** continue, further, extend.

discontinuous *adj. His discontinuous speech was hard to follow:* unconnected, broken, broken off, disconnected, disjointed, fitful, gaping, incoherent, intermittent, interrupted, irregular, spasmodic.

discord *n.* **1.** *The couple split up after years of discord:* dispute, disagreement, conflict, quarreling, contention, discordance, differences, dissension, disunity, division, lack of concord, being at odds, clashing, wrangling, friction, strife, incompatibility. **2.** *The discord of his music is hard on the ear:* discordance, dissonance, disharmony, harshness, grating noise, cacophony, unpleasant sounds. **—Ant.** 1 harmony, consonance, accord, agreement, amity, unity, solidarity, compatibility. 2 harmony, consonance.

discount *n. Students get a discount on air fares:* reduction, deduction, subtraction, concession, cut rate, cut, break, exemption, allowance, abatement; rebate.

discourage *v.* **1.** *The second failure discouraged him utterly:* daunt, lessen the self-confidence of, dishearten, deject, unnerve, do in, dispirit, dismay, depress, prostrate; dash one's hopes, dampen one's spirits, disparage, decimate, destroy confidence in, unman. **2.** *They discouraged him from investing in the stock:* dissuade, deter, divert from, restrain, keep back, disincline, advise against, express disapproval of, attempt to prevent. **—Ant.** 1 encourage, hearten, fortify, inspire, embolden. 2 encourage, urge, bid; welcome, support.

discouraged *adj. The discouraged search party returned to their camp:* disheartened, crestfallen, dashed, daunted, depressed, deterred, dismayed, dispirited, down, downbeaten, downcast, glum, pessimistic, sad, *Informal* blue.

discouragement *n.* **1.** *His discouragement over the divorce is damaging his health:* depression, dejection, melancholy, hopelessness, despair, despondency, low spirits, downhearted-

ness, gloom, dismay, pessimism, moroseness, lack of spirit, heaviness of spirit. **2.** *The athlete's weak ankle is a severe discouragement to him:* consternation, worry, damper, constraint, restraint, curb, hindrance, obstacle, impediment. **—Ant.** 1 encouragement, hopefulness, high spirits, optimism, cheerfulness. 2 encouragement, boost, uplift.

discouraging *adj. The stock market results were most discouraging:* unfavorable, bleak, dampening, daunting, depressing, deterring, disheartening, dispiriting, hindering, inopportune, unpropitious, oppressive.

discourse *n.* **1.** *The lawyers enjoyed hours of leisurely discourse at their club:* conversation, talk, intercourse, converse, discussion, colloquy, dialogue, chat, gab. **2.** *We listened to a discourse on the evils of drugs:* lecture, address, speech, sermon, oration; dialogue, formal discussion of a subject; harangue, diatribe; essay, dissertation, treatise. *—v.* **3.** *The professors discoursed on Mycenaean civilization for an hour:* talk, talk together, converse, confer, discuss.

discourteous *adj. I was offended by his discourteous reply:* rude, impolite, ungracious, uncivil, uncourteous, unmannerly, ill-mannered, ungallant, cheeky, surly, boorish, disrespectful, impertinent, fresh, insolent, impudent; ill-bred, ill-behaved, ungentlemanly, uncourtly, unladylike, uncouth. **—Ant.** courteous, civil, polite, gracious, mannerly, respectful; well-bred, well-behaved, gentlemanly, ladylike.

discover *v.* **1.** *Columbus discovered America in 1492:* come upon, find, learn of, detect, gain sight or knowledge of, stumble upon, chance upon, light upon, uncover, unearth, locate, bring to light, root out, ferret out, dig up; find out, ascertain. **2.** *I discovered my error too late:* realize, notice, see, become cognizant of, recognize, perceive, spot, discern, learn of, determine, find, detect, uncover, unearth, locate.

discovery *n. What discovery will change our lives next?:* revelation, breakthrough, determination, disclosure, find, finding, identification, innovation, invention, sensing, sighting, uncovering, unearthing, strike.

discredit *v.* **1.** *She discredited his good name with ugly gossip:* defame, abuse, dishonor, impair the reputation of, disgrace, vilify, disparage, smirch, smear, debase, degrade, demean, vitiate, tarnish, taint, undermine, slur, sully, stigmatize, drag through the mud. **2.** *The insurance investigator discredited his false claim:* prove false, deny, disallow, disprove, reject; destroy confidence in, shake one's faith in, undermine belief in; dispute, challenge, question. **—Ant.** 1 credit, praise, laud. 2 credit, prove, support, accept, verify.

discreet *adj. I made discreet inquiries about his credit rating:* prudent, careful, tactful, sensitive, thoughtful, judicious, cautious, circumspect, diplomatic, polite, politic. **—Ant.** indiscreet, rash, heedless, imprudent, careless, incautious, impetuous.

discrepancy *n. There is a great discrepancy between his version of the accident and yours:*

difference, inconsistency, variance, disagreement, discordance, lack of correspondence, disparity, dissimilarity, divergence, incongruity, gap. —**Ant.** correspondence, accord.

discrepant adj. The bookkeeper found that the discrepant figures were hard to reconcile: different, at variance, conflicting, contradictory, contrary, disagreeing, discordant, disparate, dissonant, divergent, diverse, varying, incompatible, incongruent, incongruous, inconsistent.

discrete adj. The Liberal Arts College has been reorganized into six discrete departments: separate, distinct, different, detached, disconnected, discontinuous, disjunctive, unattached, independent, unassociated; several, various. —**Ant.** merged, combined, interdependent, united, linked, connected.

discretion n. **1.** Use your own discretion in choosing a restaurant: good judgment, power of choosing, preference, individual choice, predilection, inclination, volition, option. **2.** He showed little discretion in handling the awkward situation: good sense, judgment, sound judgment, judiciousness, sagacity, acumen, discernment, prudence, discrimination, tact. —**Ant.** 2 indiscretion, rashness, thoughtlessness, recklessness, irresponsibility, insensitivity, heedlessness, tactlessness, carelessness.

discretionary adj. The discretionary funds were spent quickly: elective, optional, arbitrary, unobligatory, unrestricted, open.

discriminate v. **1.** Many businesses are accused of discriminating against women: demonstrate bias, set apart as different, show disfavor toward, make a distinction against, disfranchise, disdain, treat as inferior. **2.** Can you discriminate between good and bad art?: differentiate, draw a distinction, distinguish, separate.

discriminating adj. Discriminating shoppers choose carefully: discerning, astute, choosy, astute, careful, cultivated, judicious, particular, picky, refined, selective, sensitive, tasteful, fastidious, finicky, fussy. —**Ant.** indiscriminate, general, random, unselective, unsystematic.

discrimination n. **1.** Laws have been passed against religious discrimination: bias, prejudice, differential treatment, bigotry, distinction, inequity, favoritism. **2.** He shows fine discrimination in choosing wines: discretion, discernment, judgment, distinction; taste, refinement; astuteness, acumen, shrewdness, sagacity, keenness, perspicacity.

discursive adj. His discursive style makes his writing hard to follow: digressive, rambling, roundabout, wandering, meandering, circuitous, diffuse, long-winded. —**Ant.** direct, methodical, coherent, succinct.

discuss v. We were all eager to discuss yesterday's game: talk about, talk over, speak of, discourse about, review, exchange views on, converse about, parley, debate, consider, examine, dissect.

discussion n. All members are invited to a discussion of the proposed bylaws: talk, dialogue, discourse, debate, parley, argument, disputation, review, consideration, deliberation; inquiry, colloquy, scrutiny, investigation, analysis; Slang hashing-out, powwow, rap.

disdain v. **1.** The proud man disdained all offers of help: look down upon, frown upon, think unworthy of notice, spurn, despise, abhor, treat with contempt, loathe, detest, discountenance, snub, brush aside, deride; recoil from with pride, deem unbecoming, consider beneath oneself, deem unacceptable. —n. **2.** I have only disdain for bigots: scorn, contempt, abhorrence, dislike, disrespect, distaste; feeling of superiority, haughty indifference, icy aloofness, intolerance. —**Ant.** 1 favor, admit, admire, like, love. 2 regard, admiration, respect, esteem, reverence, awe, fear.

disdainful adj. She rejected his advances with a disdainful glance: haughty, superior, contemptuous, scornful, arrogant, supercilious, contumelious. —**Ant.** friendly, amiable, considerate, attentive.

disease n. Doctors hope that someday they can eradicate disease: illness, sickness, ill health, physical disorder, ailment, malady, infirmity, affliction, morbid condition. —**Ant.** health, salubriousness, healthiness.

diseased adj. The diseased children were immediately hospitalized: sick, sickly, afflicted, ailing, communicable, contagious, epidemic, indisposed, infected, infectious, infirm, tainted, unhealthy, unwell.

disembark v. The assault troops disembarked on the beach just before dawn: land, leave a ship, go ashore from a ship, get off a ship, debark; detrain, deplane; Informal pile out. —**Ant.** embark, go aboard; entrain, enplane.

disengage v. The railroad cars were hard to disengage: separate, loosen, cut loose, disassociate, disconnect, disentangle, disjoin, dissociate, extricate, free, liberate, unloose, opt out, release, withdraw, uncouple, undo, unfasten, unfix, untie.

disentangle v. We were glad to disentangle the mess: untangle, free, loosen, clear up, detach, disconnect, disencumber, disengage, part, resolve, separate, solve, sort out, unfold, unravel, unscramble, unsnarl, untie, unwind, extricate.

disfavor n. **1.** She incurred the doctor's disfavor by ignoring her diet: disapproval, disapprobation, displeasure, disesteem, dislike, disregard, dissatisfaction, odium, disrespect; disgrace, unacceptableness, ignominy. **2.** We did ourselves a disfavor by inviting the rude girl: disservice, harmful act, ill turn, discourtesy. —**Ant.** 1 favor, approval, approbation, esteem, respect. 2 favor, service, kindness, courtesy.

disfigure v. Was she disfigured by the accident?: mar the features of, deform, deface, cut up, injure the appearance of, render unsightly, maim, make ugly, scar, scarify, blemish; mutilate, damage, impair.

disgorge v. Her dog luckily disgorged the bone from his throat: dislodge, throw up, discharge, regurgitate, throw out from the throat or stomach, spout, vomit forth, spew, eject, expel, cough up, spew up, cast up.

disgrace n. **1.** That junkyard is a disgrace to

the neighborhood: shame, reproach, dishonor, blot, smirch, blemish, discredit, stain, embarrassment, tarnish, scandal, eyesore. **2.** *He is in disgrace for revealing defense secrets:* disfavor, ill favor, contempt, disrepute, discredit; *Slang* in the doghouse. —*v.* **3.** *She disgraced herself by passing out at the garden party:* embarrass, humiliate, dishonor, debase, bring reproach upon, shame, degrade, abase, bring shame upon, cause to lose favor, discredit; blot, smirch, taint, derogate, disparage. —**Ant.** 1 grace, honor, credit, glory. 2 grace, favor, esteem. 3 grace, honor, credit, distinguish.

disgraceful *adj. He was chastised for his disgraceful manners:* shameful, dishonorable, scandalous, shocking, appalling, disreputable, discreditable, outrageous, ignominious; unworthy, unseemly, unbecoming; degrading, low, mean, inglorious, base, obnoxious, detestable, reprehensible, opprobrious, infamous, odious, despicable, vile. —**Ant.** honorable, reputable, creditable, worthy, seemly, becoming.

disgruntled *adj. Father becomes disgruntled when dinner is late:* sulky, grumpy, vexed, peevish, displeased, irritated, discontented, malcontent, dissatisfied, sullen, petulant, grouchy, testy, shirty. —**Ant.** happy, contented, pleased, satisfied.

disguise *v.* **1.** *She came to the ball disguised as Marie Antoinette:* assume a false identity, camouflage one's outward appearance, dress up, garb, mask, cloak, camouflage, veil; simulate, counterfeit, feign. **2.** *She tried to disguise her real feelings:* conceal, hide, falsify, dissemble, cover up, muffle, mask, veil, shroud, misrepresent, gloss over. —*n.* **3.** *His disguise did not conceal his identity:* cover, counterfeit appearance, masquerade, getup, deceptive covering, camouflage, concealment, guise, costuming, false appearance; veil, cover-up, mask, screen, blind, false front, veneer, façade, sham, pretense, pose.

disguised *adj. The disguised commandos slipped through the enemy's defenses:* camouflaged, in disguise, unrecognizable, undercover, incognito, masked; cloaked, dressed up, veiled.

disgust *v.* **1.** *His crudeness disgusted us:* repel, revolt, be repulsive to, appall, put off, offend, fill with loathing, cause aversion; sicken, nauseate, turn one's stomach. —*n.* **2.** *He couldn't hide his disgust at the news:* revulsion, repugnance, loathing, distaste, abhorrence, repulsion, aversion, contempt, hatred, detestation, antipathy, disaffection, displeasure, dislike, disrelish. —**Ant.** 1 please, delight, impress. 2 liking, taste, relish, fondness, love, satisfaction, affection, pleasure.

disgusted *adj. The disgusted manager stalked out of the boardroom:* repelled, repulsed, appalled, displeased, dissatisfied, nauseated, offended, overwrought, queasy, scandalized, sickened. —**Ant.** attracted, delighted.

disgusting *adj. The campers left behind a disgusting mess:* offensive, offending, loathsome, sickening, nauseous, nauseating, repulsive, revolting, odious, hateful, repugnant, foul, abomi-nable, abhorrent, distasteful, detestable. —**Ant.** delightful, delectable, attractive, beautiful.

dish *n.* **1.** *Put the potatoes in the blue dish:* plate, saucer, serving dish, platter, shallow bowl, flat receptacle, vessel. **2.** *Wasn't that a dainty dish to set before a king?:* food, recipe, particular food, fare, article of food, victuals, edibles, comestible. **3.** *Would you like a dish of peaches?:* dishful, portion, plateful, bowlful, serving, helping. —*v.* **4.** *Dish the berries into the bowl:* place, transfer, scoop, spoon, ladle; dole, portion, serve, dispense.

disharmony *n. Our disharmony was soon apparent to all our friends:* friction, strife, clash, conflict, contention, difference, discord, dissension, discordance, dissonance, inharmoniousness.

dishearten *v. It disheartens any writer to get rejection slips:* dispirit, dismay, discourage, faze, daunt, deject, depress, dash, abash, weaken the resolution of, crush, take the heart out of, sadden. —**Ant.** encourage, uplift, hearten, make determined.

disheveled *adj. She awoke from her nap disheveled:* unkempt, ruffled, rumpled, disorderly, disarrayed, disarranged, mussed, messy, sloppy, untidy, in disorder, tousled, frowzy, blowsy, uncombed, bedraggled. —**Ant.** ordered, orderly, unruffled, neat, tidy; kempt, groomed.

dishonest *adj.* **1.** *I wouldn't do business with such a dishonest man:* corrupt, not honest, untrustworthy, disposed to cheat, false, lacking integrity, perfidious, destitute of good faith, faithless, crooked, unscrupulous, deceitful, insincere, dishonorable, disingenuous, unprincipled, false-hearted, two-faced, fraudulent, underhanded. **2.** *The commercial was taken off the air because of its dishonest claims:* not honest, misleading, specious, deceptive, false, fraudulent, mendacious, untruthful, spurious. —**Ant.** 1 honest, upright, honorable, forthright, aboveboard, law-abiding, principled, lawful. 2 honest, true, supportable, demonstrable.

dishonesty *n. Such dishonesty will not be tolerated by this government:* cheating, deceit, deceitfulness, mendacity, lying, chicanery, corruption, double-dealing, duplicity, faithlessness, falsehood, falsity, fraud, fraudulence, graft, treachery, knavery, knavishness.

dishonor *n.* **1.** *His collaboration with the enemy brought dishonor to the family:* shame, dishonorableness, disgrace, ill repute, discredit, ignominy, odium, disrepute, public disgrace, infamy, derogation, disfavor, humiliation, scandal; stigma, blot, blemish, stain. **2.** *Refusing the man's offer was a dishonor to him:* slight, affront, insult, offense, discourtesy. —*v.* **3.** *Rumors of corruption dishonored the congressman:* disgrace, shame, bring shame on, bring reproach upon, defame, deprive of honor, discredit, abase, blacken, tarnish, stain the character of, sully, debase, stigmatize, disparage, degrade, humiliate. —**Ant.** 1 honor, glory, renown, repute, fame; reverence, veneration;

esteem, respect, regard, admiration. 2 honor, compliment, courtesy. 3 honor, credit.

dishonorable *adj. Dishonorable conduct resulted in his dismissal:* ignoble, base, disgraceful, shameful, shameless, false, fraudulent, corrupt; infamous, notorious, unscrupulous, unprincipled, disreputable, disgraceful, scandalous, ignominious, discreditable. —**Ant.** honorable.

disillusion *v. I hate to disillusion you, but your chances of winning are nil:* undeceive, shatter one's illusions, free from illusion, open the eyes of, burst the bubble, clue in, disenchant, disenthrall, disabuse, bring one down to earth, break the spell. —**Ant.** deceive, lead on, beguile.

disingenuous *adj. Their disingenuous protests irritated us:* dishonest, insincere, artful, cunning, designing, duplicitous, false, feigned, guileful, shifty, sly, wily, two-faced, tricky. —**Ant.** ingenuous.

disinherit *v. She disinherited her nephew:* disown, dispossess, deprive, exclude, repudiate.

disintegrate *v. The plane would probably disintegrate at that high speed:* fall apart, break up, break apart, go to pieces, shatter, crumble, crumble to fragments, reduce to particles, reduce to fragments, splinter, cause to fall to pieces. —**Ant.** blend, fuse, merge, coalesce; unite, combine, link up, join, connect.

disinterested *adj. We need a disinterested party to settle the argument:* impartial, unbiased, neutral, free from bias, unprejudiced, impersonal, outside, uninvolved, dispassionate, free from self-interest. —**Ant.** partial, biased, prejudiced, selfish, having an axe to grind.

disjointed *adj.* 1. *The structure of the house seemed somehow disjointed:* disconnected, detached, having the joints separated, unconnected, unattached, split, divided, apart, disarticulated, helter-skelter. 2. *The movie was too disjointed to make sense:* rambling, mixed-up, confused, spasmodic, disconnected, disorganized, jumbled, tangled, chaotic, disharmonious, discontinuous, heterogeneous, incoherent, irrational, illogical. —**Ant.** 1 jointed, connected, attached. 2 sensible, coherent, logical.

dislike *v.* 1. *I dislike selfish people:* regard with disfavor, not like, feel repugnance toward, hold as disagreeable, regard with displeasure, have no taste for, object to, look on with aversion, consider obnoxious; loathe, abhor, despise, hate, detest, abominate, scorn. —*n.* 2. *Her dislike of the catty woman was obvious:* distaste, aversion, antipathy, disaffection; loathing, repugnance, hatred, repulsion, revulsion, abhorrence, abomination, detestation, disgust; antagonism, hostility, malice, animosity, disdain, animus, enmity, rancor. —**Ant.** 1 like, esteem, favor. 2 liking, relish, delight, inclination, attraction, esteem, admiration.

dislocate *v. He gave up pitching when he dislocated his elbow:* put out of joint, disjoint, disconnect, disarticulate, unhinge, uproot, disengage, separate, disunite.

dislocation *n. Many job changes brought dislocation to his family:* displacement, break, confusion, disarray, disconnection, misplacement, discontinuity, disengagement, disorder, disorganization, disruption, disturbance.

dislodge *v. It took a bulldozer to dislodge the rock:* dig out, remove, displace, force out, eject, disturb, oust, uproot, extricate, disentangle, expel, dispel. —**Ant.** lodge, situate, bury, embed, root, plant, establish, seat.

disloyal *adj. She felt disloyal for giving up her citizenship:* unfaithful, inconstant, untrue, false to one's obligations, recreant, dishonorable, undutiful; perfidious, seditious, treasonable, treacherous, traitorous, faithless, subversive. —**Ant.** loyal, faithful, constant, true, steadfast.

disloyalty *n. He proved his disloyalty by betraying my secret:* faithlessness, unfaithfulness, apostasy, betrayal of trust, infidelity, lack of fidelity, breaking of faith, recreancy, perfidy, deceitfulness, falseness, falsity, breach of trust, inconstancy, double-dealing; treachery, treason, subversion, subversive activity. —**Ant.** loyalty, fealty, allegiance, fidelity, constancy.

dismal *adj.* 1. *She works in a dismal little room in the attic. His dismal attitude is contagious:* gloomy, cheerless, somber, bleak, dreary, drab; doleful, mournful, dolorous, despondent, sad, joyless, dejected, pessimistic, hopeless, morbid, downcast, depressed, unhappy, lugubrious, sorrowful, disheartened, heavy-hearted, desolate, woeful, melancholy, in the dumps, disconsolate, rueful, down-in-the-mouth, woebegone, forlorn; grim-visaged, long-faced. 2. *The show was dismal and a waste of time:* poor, unmentionable, awful, terrible, abysmal, very bad, abominable, dreadful, horrible. —**Ant.** 1 cheerful, bright, inviting, gay, happy. 2 good, fine, excellent, admirable.

dismantle *v. The mechanic slowly dismantled the engine:* disassemble, take apart, strip, undo, break down, dismember.

dismay *v.* 1. *The boy's recklessness dismayed his mother:* fill with consternation, alarm, frighten, distress, appall, scare, unnerve, horrify; cow, daunt, dishearten, abash, intimidate, discourage; disillusion, disappoint, put off. —*n.* 2. *Imagine our dismay at the sight of the gun:* alarm, apprehension, anxiety, distress, concern, complete loss of courage, consternation, perturbation, trepidation; panic, terror, dread, fright, affright, horror, scare; utter disheartenment, discouragement, intimidation. 3. *I couldn't hide my dismay over her poor grades:* disappointment, disillusionment, discouragement, exasperation. —**Ant.** 1 cheer, reassure, relieve, encourage, hearten. 2 confidence, assurance, aplomb, self-possession, encouragement. 3 satisfaction, happiness, joy, reassurance, relief.

dismember *v. The psychopath dismembered his victims:* disjoint, amputate, cut, dislocate, dismantle, dissect, divide, mutilate, part, sunder, sever, rend.

dismiss *v.* 1. *The workers were dismissed for lunch. Dismiss the meeting:* allow to leave, permit to go, release, excuse, send forth, let go, disperse; dissolve, adjourn, disband; free, liberate. 2. *She was dismissed for loafing on the job:*

fire, oust, discharge from office, put out of a job, sack, can, let go, terminate, remove from service, bounce, send packing, give one his walking papers, cashier, *Slang* pink-slip, give the heave-ho. **3.** *I trust her and dismiss any suggestion of dishonesty:* put out of mind, reject, set aside, disregard, disclaim, discard, lay aside, repudiate, eliminate. **—Ant.** 1 hold, detain, recall. 2 hire, employ, accept, admit. 3 welcome, accept.

dismissal *n. Gross overspending led to her dismissal:* discharge, expulsion, banishment, deportation, deposal, displacement, ouster, release, removal, eviction, exile.

dismount *v. All the lancers dismounted from their ponies:* descend, alight, light, get down. **—Ant.** mount, get down.

disobedience *n. Disobedience was just one of his vices:* revolt, insubordination, rebellion, challenge, confrontation, contrariness, contumacy, dereliction, disobedience, insurgence, mutiny, noncompliance, opposition, recalcitrance, revolution, sedition. **—Ant.** obedience.

disobedient *adj. The disobedient boy seemed incorrigible:* insubordinate, unsubmissive, rebellious, noncompliant, unmanageable, ungovernable, obstinate, recalcitrant, intractable, contrary, stubborn, refractory, fractious, froward, defiant, wayward, haughty, undutiful, perverse, unruly, disorderly, unyielding, seditious, insurgent, mutinous. **—Ant.** obedient, submissive, compliant, manageable, governable, dutiful, yielding, well-behaved.

disobey *v. He was finally expelled for disobeying the headmaster:* disregard, ignore, defy, break, go counter to, refuse to obey, rebel against, violate, overstep, transgress, resist, refuse to submit to, fail to comply with, infringe on. **—Ant.** obey, follow, abide by.

disoblige *v. The child would do anything to disoblige me:* inconvenience, affront, disturb, offend, slight, trouble, annoy, bother, displease.

disobliging *adj. The disobliging staff was of little help to the customer:* unpleasant, uncooperative, ill-disposed, rude, uncongenial, disagreeable, discourteous.

disorder *n.* **1.** *I can't stand the disorder of this garage:* disarray, mess, clutter, jumble, muddle, disorderliness, disarrangement, disorganization, chaos, disruption, confusion. **2.** *He was hospitalized with a kidney disorder:* ailment, illness, sickness, affliction, disease, organic disturbance, malady, indisposition, complaint. **3.** *The campus disorder was on tonight's news:* commotion, disturbance, public disturbance, fracas, turmoil, riot, ruckus, uproar, dissension, minor uprising, disturbance of peace, breach of order. **—Ant.** 1 order, orderliness, organization, neatness.

disordered *adj. His papers were too disordered for me to handle alone:* disorganized, confused, disarranged, jumbled, haphazard, *Informal* messed up. **—Ant.** ordered, organized.

disorderly *adj.* **1.** *Help me straighten these disorderly files:* disordered, out of order, unsystematized, disarranged, disorganized, unsystematic, pell-mell, unsorted, chaotic, jumbled,

confused, topsy-turvy, helter-skelter; untidy, messy, sloppy, disheveled, slipshod, straggling, unkempt, careless, slovenly. **2.** *The demonstrators were jailed for disorderly conduct:* unlawful, lawless, disruptive, unrestrained, rebellious, wayward, violating constituted order, constituting a nuisance; unruly, undisciplined, wild, boisterous, obstreperous, riotous, noisy, rowdy, rowdyish, rough-and-tumble, improper, bad, disreputable. **—Ant.** 1 orderly, ordered, arranged, organ-ized, methodical, neat, tidy.

disorganization *n. Much disorganization had to be rectified when the new CEO took over:* mess, chaos, confusion, derangement, disarray, disjointedness, disorder, disruption, dissolution, disunion, incoherence, unconnectedness.

disorganized *adj. His plan is too disorganized:* confused, disordered, jumbled, muddled, mixed-up, unsystematic, disordered, chaotic. **—Ant.** organized, ordered, systematic, systematized, methodized.

disoriented *adj. Their lives have been disoriented since the war:* not adjusted, confused, distracted, mixed-up, out of touch, out of joint; unstable.

disown *v. He disowned his reprobate son:* disinherit, disclaim, disavow, repudiate, renounce, cast off, forsake, denounce, reject, refuse to acknowledge, refuse to recognize. **—Ant.** claim, accept, acknowledge, recognize.

disparage *v. Don't disparage his attempts to better himself:* belittle, ridicule, discredit, run down, put down, mock, denigrate, demean, undervalue, underrate, depreciate, slight, detract from, derogate. **—Ant.** applaud, praise, laud, extol, acclaim, commend, compliment, appreciate.

disparagement *n. We received little disparagement after the good job we did:* derogation, aspersion, backbiting, belittlement, blame, censure, condemnation, debasement, denunciation, depreciation, detraction, discredit, disdain, reproach, ridicule, scandal, scorn, slander, derision, degradation, contempt.

disparate *adj. Their views are unusually disparate for brothers:* dissimilar, different, unlike, contrasting, at odds, at variance, discrepant, discordant. **—Ant.** similar, like, homogeneous, parallel, accord-ant.

disparity *n. Too often there's a disparity between campaign promises and the actual reforms:* inequality, imparity, discrepancy, gap, dissimilarity, disproportion, divergence, contrast, difference, dissemblance, dissimilitude, inconsistency; disagreement, contradiction. **—Ant.** accord, correspondence, parity, equality, unity.

dispassionate *adj. He described the problem in a dispassionate and objective way:* unemotional, cool, unexcited, unimpassioned, undisturbed, imperturbable, unmoved, calm, serene, collected, composed, level-headed, unruffled, uninvolved, detached; impartial, unbiased, unprejudiced, fair, impersonal, disinterested, neutral. **—Ant.** passionate, impassioned, emotional, excited, apprehensive, concerned, disturbed, partial, biased, prejudiced, interested.

dispatch v. **1.** *They dispatched the report to the field commander:* send off, send on the way, transmit rapidly, post, forward. **2.** *The negotiations were dispatched in record time:* finish, complete, conclude, execute quickly, wind up, carry out, dispose of rapidly, expedite, settle, discharge speedily, carry out speedily, make short work of. **3.** *The injured horse was dispatched by its owner:* kill, finish off, execute, put to death, slay, put an end to; summarily shoot; murder, assassinate, bump off; slaughter, massacre. —*n.* **4.** *The correspondent sent his dispatch from Hong Kong:* message, report, missive, bulletin, official communication, flash; letter, story, news account, item, piece, telegraphic message, communiqué. **5.** *The deed must be done with dispatch:* promptness, haste, quickness, expedition, swift execution, swiftness, rapidity, speed, celerity, alacrity.

dispel v. *The surprise attack dispelled the enemy infantry. Let me dispel your doubts:* scatter, drive away, drive away by scattering, disseminate, diffuse, expel, repel, rout, drive off; put an end to, make disappear, dissipate, resolve, allay, eliminate, remove, dismiss, banish.

dispensable adj. *Trying to economize, they found many dispensable items in their budget:* unnecessary, expendable, nonvital, disposable, unessential, nonessential, unimportant, of secondary importance, accessory, extrinsic, superfluous, extraneous. —**Ant.** indispensable, necessary, essential, needed, important.

dispensation n. **1.** *She directed the dispensation of blankets and hot coffee. The crash victims received a maximum dispensation:* distribution, dispensing, allocation, designation, dealing out, meting out, apportioning, dissemination, diffusion, consignment, allotment, bestowal, conferment, division; reparation, remuneration. **2.** *Catholics may divorce only with a special dispensation from the Pope:* permission, authorization, decree, credential, exemption, relaxation of a law, approval. —**Ant.** 2 prohibition.

dispense v. *They dispense all the supplies for the hospital:* deal out, distribute, apportion, allot, dole.

disperse v. *A thunderstorm came up and dispersed the picnickers:* drive off, scatter, disseminate, dissipate, send scurrying, send off, rout, dispel, disband; distribute, spread throughout, diffuse. —**Ant.** assemble, gather, amass, call in, collect, pool, congregate, convene, summon, muster, concentrate, recall.

dispirited adj. *The team was dispirited after suffering a decisive defeat:* dejected, down, downhearted, discouraged, downcast, disheartened, crestfallen, forlorn, glum, moody, unhappy, sad, cheerless, morose, melancholy, depressed; *Slang* down-in-the-mouth, down-in-the-dumps. —**Ant.** cheerful, light-hearted, up, elated, joyful.

displace v. **1.** *The automobile quickly displaced the horse and buggy:* supplant, supersede, replace, take the place of, unseat, oust, bump; crowd out, force out. **2.** *Many of the inhabitants were displaced by the rising floodwaters:* dislocate, dislodge, move, shift; put out of the usual place, put in a wrong place. **3.** *An object in water will displace its own volume:* fill the space of, take the place of.

display v. **1.** *The fireman displayed great courage in saving the child. The boat displayed all her flags as she came into port:* exhibit, show, demonstrate, manifest, reveal, bring into view, make visible, put in plain sight. —*n.* **2.** *The store has a large display of gift suggestions:* exhibition, exhibit, show; presentation, demonstration; manifestation. —**Ant.** 1 disguise, cloak, hide, conceal.

displease v. *Nothing displeases me more than loud talking:* annoy, irritate, irk, pique, offend, disturb, provoke, incense. —**Ant.** please, gratify.

displeasure n. *The TV commercial incurred the displeasure of many viewers:* annoyance, vexation, irritation, wrath, indignation; dissatisfaction, dislike, disapproval. —**Ant.** pleasure, satisfaction, approval, endorsement.

disposal n. **1.** *We bought a compactor for the disposal of trash:* disposition, riddance, discarding, dumping, junking; clearance, settlement. **2.** *He has a fleet of airplanes at his disposal:* command, control, direction, power, authority, management, supervision, government, administration, regulation. **3.** *The designer offered us an interesting idea for the disposal of the living-room furniture:* arrangement, array, grouping, placement, disposition, distribution, configuration, pattern, order, juxtaposition, organization. —**Ant.** 2 acquisition, accumulation, collection, storage, accrual.

dispose v. **1.** *The committee was not disposed to hold another meeting:* incline, motivate; be willing. **2.** *The store disposed the jewelry in an attractive display:* arrange, array, place; organize, order, rank, classify. **3.** *His vast property was disposed of in his will:* distribute, deal out; get rid of. —**Ant.** 2 disarray, disarrange, disorganize.

disposition n. **1.** *Did you ever meet anyone with such a cheerful disposition?:* spirit, nature, temperament, mental constitution, characteristic mood. **2.** *She has a disposition to criticize that has lost her many friends:* tendency, inclination; predisposition. **3.** *The disposition of troops preceded the battle:* organization, arrangement, grouping, placement, distribution. **4.** *The foundation has funds at its disposition for the aid of colleges:* control, disposal, power to dispose of a thing. **5.** *Relatives challenged the disposition of the old man's will:* bestowal; final settlement of a matter. —**Ant.** 1 disaffection, unwillingness.

dispossess v. *If you pay your rent, they can't dispossess you:* deprive of, take away, take back; evict, oust, expel.

disproportion n. *There was a severe disproportion in the amounts handed out:* imbalance, asymmetry, difference, discrepancy, disparity, unevenness, inadequacy, inequality, lopsidedness. **—Ant.** proportion, balance, congruity, harmony, symmetry.

disproportionate *adj. The smaller cat got a disproportionate amount of food:* unbalanced, off-balance, unsymmetrical, asymmetric, different, discrepant, disparate, inordinate, overbalanced, unequal, uneven, lopsided.

disprove *v. Evidence has now disproved that theory:* refute, discredit; controvert, prove to be false or wrong, prove to the contrary. **—Ant.** prove, demonstrate; show to be true.

disputable *adj. It's disputable whether the two groups will agree to work together:* questionable, debatable, controvertible, doubtful, uncertain, dubious.

disputatious *adj. The disputatious group could not agree:* quarrelsome, argumentative, cantankerous, captious, contentious, controversial, litigious, pugnacious, polemical.

dispute *v.* **1.** *The expert disputed the authenticity of the document:* doubt, question, challenge, contradict; call in question, question the truth of, impugn. **2.** *The strikers began to dispute hotly with members of management:* argue, quarrel, wrangle, squabble, clash. *—n.* **3.** *The dispute concerns capital punishment:* controversy, debate, argument; quarrel, disagreement, squabble, bickering, clash, altercation, feud, wrangle. **—Ant.** l agree to, concede, concur with.

disqualification *n. Age was no disqualification for the job:* invalidation, disentitlement, debarment, disability, disablement, elimination, exclusion, incapacity, incompetence, incompetency, ineligibility, lack, unfitness.

disqualify *v.* **1.** *Lack of education will disqualify you for most good jobs:* disable, make unqualified, make unfit. **2.** *They disqualified her for being late to the finals:* pronounce unqualified, declare ineligible, deny participation.

disquieting *adj. He has a disquieting way of staring at people:* disturbing, upsetting, vexing, troubling; disconcerting, unsettling, distressing, perturbing, annoying, irritating, bothersome.

disregard *v.* **1.** *Disregard the mess and keep working:* overlook, ignore; pay no heed to, pay no attention to, take no notice of. *—n.* **2.** *His complete disregard of others lost him the respect of his friends:* lack of regard or respect, lack of attention, willful oversight. **—Ant.** l heed; pay attention to, regard. 2 consideration, esteem, appreciation.

disrepair *n. Our summer cottage was in disrepair:* ruin, ruination, deterioration, collapse, decay, decrepitude, dilapidation.

disreputable *adj.* **1.** *They used to run around with several disreputable people:* shady, dishonorable, unprincipled; notorious, infamous, having a bad reputation, not reputable, of bad character. **2.** *The condition of this house is disreputable:* shameful, disgraceful, shocking, scandalous; not respectable. **—Ant.** l reputable, honorable; principled. 2 respectable, admirable.

disrepute *n. Shady business dealings brought* him much disrepute: notoriety, disgrace, ill repute, discredit, disfavor, dishonor, ignominy, ill favor, infamy, ingloriousness, opprobrium, reproach, shame, taint, slur, smear, stigma.

disrespect *n. The disrespect she shows her parents is shocking:* contempt, dishonor, irreverence, disregard, impoliteness, rudeness, discourtesy, lack of respect. **—Ant.** respect, esteem, regard, reverence.

disrespectful *adj. He was sent to the principal's office for his disrespectful behavior:* rude, impolite, discourteous, impertinent, contemptuous. **—Ant.** respectful, courteous, polite.

disrobe *v. We disrobed before entering the sauna:* shed clothing, unclothe, undress, bare, denude, peel, strip, take off.

disrupt *v.* **1.** *The special TV report disrupted regular programming:* interrupt, interfere with. **2.** *The war disrupted many lives:* upset; throw into disorder.

disruptive *adj. The disruptive child was ejected from class:* disturbing, distracting, obstreperous, rowdy, troublemaking, troublesome, unruly, unsettling, upsetting. **—Ant.** docile, cooperative, obedient.

dissatisfaction *n. The rise in prices created much dissatisfaction:* discontent, displeasure, dislike, disappointment, disapproval, disapprobation, uneasiness. **—Ant.** satisfaction, approval, approbation.

dissatisfied *adj. She was dissatisfied with the results:* displeased, unhappy, discontented; not satisfied. **—Ant.** satisfied, pleased, content.

dissect *v.* **1.** *In biology we had to dissect a frog:* cut apart, anatomize, lay open, separate into pieces. **2.** *Dissect the poem and find the author's meaning:* analyze, study; examine part by part, break down.

dissection *n. The biology instructor started his dissection of the frog:* examination, autopsy, analysis, breakdown, inquest, inspection, investigation, resolution, review, scrutiny, study.

dissemble *v. He tried to dissemble his disappointment with a joke:* hide, mask, disguise, camouflage, feign, conceal, dissimulate. **—Ant.** show, manifest, evidence, reveal.

disseminate *v. Plato's philosophy has been disseminated throughout the world:* scatter, spread, diffuse, disperse, circulate, broadcast.

dissemination *n. The censor halted all dissemination of the broadcast:* spread, transmission, circulation, diffusion, dissipation, distribution, promulgation, propagation, publication.

dissent *v.* **1.** *If enough members dissent, the new bill won't be approved:* disagree, protest, object, oppose; withhold assent, withhold approval. *—n.* **2.** *A conclusion cannot be reached while there is dissent among the leaders:* disagreement, difference, opposition, dissension, discord. **—Ant.** l agree, concur; think in like manner. 2 agreement, concurrence, accord.

dissertation *n.* **1.** *In order to receive the degree she had to present a dissertation:* thesis. **2.** *The women's group is drawing up a dissertation on natural childbirth:* treatise, disquisition, tractate, monograph, memoir, discourse.

disservice n. He did you a disservice by refusing to help: hurt, wrong, injustice, injury, harm, bad turn. —**Ant.** service, favor; good turn.

dissidence n. She edited a journal expressing political dissidence: dissension, contention, disaccord, disagreement, disharmony, dispute, heresy, nonconformity, rupture, schism, strife.

dissident adj. **1.** The dissident members kept the measure from coming to a vote: disagreeing, differing, dissenting, opposing. —n. **2.** The dissidents are saying the plan is unproductive: dissenter, rebel, agitator. —**Ant.** 1 agreeing, consenting, contented, satisfied. 2 conformist.

dissimilar adj. Jane and Edna were so dissimilar you wouldn't believe they were sisters: unlike, different, distinct, disparate; not similar. —**Ant.** alike, similar, corresponding, akin; identical.

dissimilarity n. There was marked dissimilarity among their three her children: disparity, contrast, difference, variance, discordance, discrepancy, distinction, divergence, diversity, incomparability, inconsistency, otherness.

dissimulate v. They dissimulated their true intentions: hide, conceal, dissemble, mask, disguise, camouflage.

dissipate v. **1.** He dissipated his inheritance in less than six months: squander, waste, misspend, fritter away, deplete, spend foolishly. **2.** The police managed to dissipate the mob without any arrests. The fog dissipated when the sun came out: disperse, dispel, scatter; break up and drive off. **3.** In her youth she seemed to dissipate almost compulsively: carouse, overindulge, live dissolutely, be intemperate.

dissipated adj. **1.** The heir's dissippated wealth could not be recovered: exhausted, consumed, played out, scattered, spent, squandered, used up, wasted. **2.** Suddenly, the dissipated young man decided to reform: debauched, corrupt, dissolute, hellbent, intemperate, profligate, rakish.

dissociate v. His marriage forced him to dissociate himself from his former companions: separate, disonnect, break off with.

dissociation n. He suffered from dissociation of thought and feeling: disconnection, break, detachment, disengagement, disjunction, distancing, disunion, division, divorce, estrangement, segregation, separation, severance.

dissolute adj. He was a dissolute young man who thought only of his own pleasure: dissipated, corrupt, loose, debauched, immoral; unrestrained, abandoned. —**Ant.** moral, upright, temperate, sober, prudent, circumspect.

dissolve v. **1.** Dissolve the chocolate in the top of a double boiler: melt, liquefy, render, soften, deliquesce, thaw, run, thaw out. **2.** The final decree dissolved their marriage: end, terminate, finish, conclude, abrogate, disband, sever, break up, annul, void. **3.** The mysterious rider dissolved into the mists: vanish, disappear, fade, dematerialize, evanesce, disintegrate, dissipate. —**Ant.** 1 congeal, thicken, harden, solidify.

dissonance n. **1.** The experimental music seemed nothing but dissonance to us: discord, cacophony, discordance, harshness, jangle, jarring, noise. **2.** Dissonance in the merged companies broke out almost at once: disharmony, antagonism, breach, break, conflict, disagreement, discord, disparity, dissension, dissidence, disunion, division, divorce, hostility, incongruity, inconsistency, rift, rupture, schism, variance.

dissonant adj. **1.** The violins sounded dissonant until they were tuned: harsh, discordant, inharmonious, grating, raucous, jangling, unmelodious, cacophonous. **2.** There seemed no way to reconcile such dissonant opinions: incompatible, incongruous, incongruent, inconsistent, hostile, irreconcilable, clashing, jarring, disagreeing, discrepant, contradictory, warring. —**Ant.** 1 melodious, mellifluous, harmonious, pleasing, agreeable. 2 compatible, congenial, sympathetic, cooperative.

dissuade v. My teacher dissuaded me from accepting the job: discourage; persuade not to, advise against, urge not to. —**Ant.** persuade to, advise in favor of, urge to.

distance n. **1.** The distance between the store and my house is 3 miles: span, gap, interval, intervening space, stretch. **2.** There was some distance between them at the last meeting: reservation, restraint, reserve, formality; coldness, coolness, aloofness, stiffness. —**Ant.** 1 closeness, nearness. 2 warmth, friendliness, familiarity, closeness.

distant adj. **1.** I'd like to travel to distant lands: far, far-off, remote, faraway, far-removed. **2.** Her distant relatives lived in this town: remote; not closely related. **3.** She was so distant with me I thought she was angry: unfriendly, cool, cold, aloof, stand-offish, detached, restrained, reserved. —**Ant.** 1, 2 near, close. 2 close. 3 friendly, cordial, warm, affectionate.

distaste n. She had an intense distaste for licorice: dislike, disinclination, aversion, repugnance, disgust, displeasure, dissatisfaction. —**Ant.** taste, delectation, liking, love, satisfaction; relish.

distasteful adj. Asking people for money is distasteful to most of us. The medicine is distasteful but good for you: unpleasant, displeasing, disagreeable, repugnant, loathsome, disgusting. —**Ant.** pleasant, pleasing, delightful; tasty.

distend v. The children's stomachs were distended by malnutrition: swell, bloat, swell out, expand, bulge, inflate, billow, puff out.

distill v. **1.** The liquid distills when heated: evaporate, condense, vaporize. **2.** Whiskey is distilled from a fermented mash of grain. Impurities are removed by distilling water: separate by evaporation, produce by vaporization and condensation, purify by distillation; extract, draw out, draw forth.

distinct adj. **1.** Her business life is distinct from her social life: separate, different, dissimilar, diverse, individual, not identical. **2.** The photograph showed a distinct image: clear, lucid, plain; definite, well-defined, clear-cut, unmistakable. **3.** It was our distinct pleasure to entertain the ambassador: well-defined, unmitigated, explicit, unquestionable; extraordinary, supreme.

—**Ant.** 1–3 indistinct. 1 same, similar, identical; connected. 2 unclear, vague, obscure, indefinite, ambiguous, blurred. 3 usual, common.

distinction n. **1.** *Being color-blind, he can't make a distinction between red and green:* differentiation, separation, discernment, discrimination. **2.** *What is the distinction between theology and theosophy?:* difference, differential, contrast. **3.** *She has become a painter of distinction:* excellence, superiority; eminence, notability, prominence, renown, importance, preeminence, greatness.

distinctive adj. *She has a very distinctive way of speaking:* unique, different, characteristic, uncommon, individual, original, singular, atypical, special, extraordinary. —**Ant.** typical, common, ordinary.

distinguish v. **1.** *His red hair distinguished him from his brothers:* differentiate, set apart, single out, make distinctive, define, characterize. **2.** *You should be able to distinguish between right and wrong:* discriminate, discern, decide; note differences. **3.** *She distinguished herself as a great lawyer:* make well known, make famous, make celebrated, make prominent.

distinguished adj. **1.** *The award went to a distinguished playwright:* notable, renowned, famous, celebrated, acclaimed, illustrious, prominent, eminent; great. **2.** *The men looked distinguished in their custom-made suits:* dignified, refined, elegant, distingué; grand, splendid, magnificent, superb. —**Ant.** 1, 2 undistinguished. 1 unknown, uncelebrated. 2 inelegant, common, inferior.

distort v. **1.** *The bias of a reporter can easily distort the news:* misrepresent, misconstrue, twist the meaning of, give a one-sided meaning to. **2.** *Years of pain had distorted his face:* contort, disfigure, deform; misshape, twist out of shape.

distortion n. *She claimed his statement was a complete distortion of the facts:* twist, warp, contortion, crookedness, exaggeration, falsification, lie, misinterpretation, misrepresentation, perversion.

distract v. **1.** *The clowns distracted the children:* divert, entertain, amuse; draw away the attention of. **2.** *Fear distracted her so that she could hardly think straight:* disturb, trouble, perplex, agitate, worry, disorder, confuse, bewilder; torment, madden, craze.

distraction n. **1.** *Tennis is one of the distractions we can offer:* diversion, amusement, entertainment, pastime, recreation. **2.** *I was worried almost to distraction:* madness, desperation, frenzy, mental distress or upset.

distraught adj. *The distraught mother waited for news of her missing child:* distressed, agitated, anxious, distracted, frantic; beside oneself, extremely troubled; mad, seething, frenzied. —**Ant.** collected, calm, serene, cool, composed.

distress n. **1.** *His distress was shared by all his neighbors:* pain, torment, agony, anguish, torture; need, want, acute suffering; trouble, danger. —v. **2.** *The news of his death distressed us*

greatly: grieve, trouble, upset, disturb, torment. —**Ant.** 1 comfort, solace, relief; happiness; safety. 2 relieve, console, make happy.

distressed adj. *The distressed parents sought relief in the church:* distraught, perturbed, worried, afflicted, agitated, anxious, bothered, disconsolate, exercised, inconsolable, troubled, upset, distracted.

distribute v. **1.** *The agency will distribute the food among several countries:* divide, apportion, disperse, parcel, allot; scatter, dispense, dole out, give out. **2.** *The postal department distributes the mail by districts:* deliver, circulate, disseminate. **3.** *The lessons were distributed over 24 chapters:* classify, class, separate, spread out, arrange, systematize, catalog, tabulate, methodize. —**Ant.** 1, 2 collect, amass, accumulate, gather.

distribution n. **1.** *The distribution of news is vital for an informed public:* dissemination, dispersion, scattering, spreading, circulation. **2.** *The distribution of schools in our city has been criticized:* arrangement, grouping, disposition, sorting, organization. **3.** *The distribution of property is clearly stated in her will:* apportionment, allotment, allocation, division.

district n. *A person must vote in his or her own district:* neighborhood, ward, parish, precinct; area, region.

distrust v. **1.** *I have distrusted him ever since he sold me that defective refrigerator:* suspect, doubt, mistrust, question; feel distrust of, regard with suspicion. —n. **2.** *My parents' distrust of Bill has made our friendship difficult:* suspicion, doubt, mistrust, misgiving; lack of faith. —**Ant.** 1 trust; depend on; have confidence in, have faith in, believe in. 2 confidence, trust, reliance.

distrustful adj. *Having been stung once, she was very distrustful:* distrusting, doubtful, dubious, suspicious, chary, cynical, fearful, leery, sceptical, suspicious, uneasy, wary. —**Ant.** unsuspecting, trustful, trusting.

disturb v. **1.** *She will be angry if you disturb her while she's sleeping:* interrupt, bother, intrude on, annoy; destroy the quiet of. **2.** *Only bad weather can disturb our plans:* unsettle, disarrange, disrupt, dislocate, disorganize, put out of order. **3.** *The students' arrest disturbed their friends:* worry, distress, trouble, upset, unsettle, perturb. —**Ant.** 2 establish, organize; put in order.

disturbance n. **1.** *You can work in here without any disturbance:* interruption, distraction, bother, annoyance. **2.** *There was some kind of disturbance at City Hall:* outbreak, rioting, disorder, uproar, turmoil, tumult, hubbub, ruckus. **3.** *The family's disturbance was evident at the news conference:* worry, upset, perturbation, distress. —**Ant.** 1 calm, serenity, quiet. 2 order.

ditch n. **1.** *The car skidded and went into the ditch:* pit, trench; hollow, excavation. —v. **2.** *The robbers ditched the getaway car:* abandon, get rid of, discard; scrap, junk.

dive v. **1.** *The parachutists dived from the plane:* fall, plunge, leap, jump. —n. **2.** *The policeman* made a dive for the dropped weapon: lunge, dash, plunge; jump, leap. **3.** *Informal We had a few drinks in some South Side dive:* shabby bar, sleazy nightclub, gin mill, honky-tonk.

diverge *v.* **1.** *The path diverges right after the pond:* separate, deviate, split off, swerve, deflect. **2.** *Her politics and mine diverge greatly:* differ, conflict, disagree, be at odds. —**Ant.** 1 converge, agree, concur.

divergent *adj.* **1.** *The two roads run parallel for a mile, then become divergent:* separate, splitting off, drawing apart. **2.** *He tried to reconcile their divergent views:* different, disagreeing, conflicting. —**Ant.** 1 convergent. 2 agreeing, concurring, similar, like; identical.

diverse *adj.* **1.** *My sister and I have diverse ideas on how to raise children:* different, differing, dissimilar, disparate, contradictory, conflicting, opposite. **2.** *She has diverse interests:* varied, of many kinds, sundry, eclectic, far-flung. —**Ant.** identical, same.

diversify *v. Wise investors are careful to diversify their holdings:* vary; increase the variety of, variegate; diffuse, divide up, spread out.

diversion *n.* **1.** *The diversion of the stream changed the land:* drawing away, turning aside, deflection. **2.** *His only diversion is an occasional game of golf:* distraction, pastime, amusement; hobby, avocation.

diversity *n. Diversity of opinions makes for an interesting discussion:* difference, variance, diversification, divergence; heterogeneity, variety, assortment. —**Ant.** likeness, similarity, sameness, homogeneity.

divert *v.* **1.** *During the storm the controller diverted our plane to another airport:* deflect, sidetrack, turn aside from a path, draw away from a course. **2.** *The children were diverted by his funny stories:* distract, amuse, entertain; turn from serious thoughts, draw off to a different subject.

divest *v.* **1.** *He divested himself of his clothing:* strip or remove (clothing), disrobe; take off, get out of, peel off. **2.** *During the Depression, the family was divested of its home:* deprive, dispossess; rid, strip, free. —**Ant.** 1 clothe, dress, cover.

divide *v.* **1.** *The builder will divide the land into home sites:* separate, split, subdivide, part, partition, *Slang* divvy up. **2.** *We divided the pie among the three of us:* distribute, share; allocate, apportion, deal out. **3.** *The new proposal divided the committee members:* disunite, cause to disagree, split, cause to take sides. **4.** *She divided the shirts according to size:* classify, arrange, sort, separate, put in order. —**Ant.** 1 connect, unite, join, attach. 3 unite, cause to agree.

dividend *n. We have yet to receive a dividend from our investment:* bonus, allotment, allowance, check, coupon, dispensation, gain, interest, premium, prize, profit, yield, remittance, reward, share, portion.

divination *n.* **1.** *The high priest's power of divination held sway over the people:* augury, soothsaying, prophecy, prescience. **2.** *Not many* of her divinations have been accurate: guess, prediction, premonition, conjecture, foreboding.

divine *adj.* **1.** *Zeus gave his divine blessing to the union:* heavenly, holy, sacred, celestial. **2.** *She made the most divine chocolate cake I ever tasted:* heavenly, excellent, wonderful, marvelous, admirable. —*v.* **3.** *The oracles were expected to divine the future:* foretell, prophesy, predict, forecast; fathom, surmise, guess, suspect.

divinity *n.* **1.** *He was punished for challenging the divinity of Zeus:* holiness, divine nature. **2.** *He is a student of divinity and hopes to become a priest:* religion, theology, science of divine things, theosophy, science of God. **3.** *In ancient Greece the divinities ruled the life of mortals:* god, goddess, deity; divine being, celestial being.

division *n.* **1.** *There is a division of the course into 32 lessons:* separation, splitting up. **2.** *They put up a division between kitchen and dinette:* partition, divider, room separator, room divider. **3.** *I think he works for a division of the company:* part, branch, department, section, unit, wing. **4.** *A sharp division of opinion was evident among the members:* split, difference, disagreement, divergence, variance, discord, dis-union. —**Ant.** 4 agreement, accord, union.

divorce *n.* **1.** *Why must there be a divorce between feelings and actions?:* separation, split, rupture, breach, rift. —*v.* **2.** *Is he still unable to divorce fantasy from reality?:* separate, segregate, disunite, dissociate, divide. —**Ant.** 1 unity. 2 unite, join.

divulge *v. Did the president ever divulge the reasons for his decision?:* disclose, reveal, tell, impart, relate, communicate; make known. —**Ant.** conceal, hide; keep secret.

dizzy *adj.* **1.** *I always feel dizzy after riding the merry-go-round:* shaky, giddy, reeling, whirly, unsteady, light-headed, vertiginous. **2.** *The marchers kept up a dizzy pace:* rapid, quick, fleet, swift. —*v.* **3.** *The rapidly changing colors dizzied the spectators:* make unsteady, make giddy; confuse, bewilder. —**Ant.** 1 steady, calm, composed.

do *v.* **1.** *Has she agreed to do the work?:* perform, execute, administer, carry out, bring about. **2.** *Have you done what I told you?:* accomplish, conclude, finish, fulfill, complete, achieve. **3.** *They do the kitchen and bathrooms every day:* clean, put in order, prepare, arrange, organize. **4.** *You'd better get used to doing as you're told:* behave, act, comport oneself, conduct oneself. **5.** *We used to do business on Grand Street:* conduct, proceed, carry on. **6.** *Will this tablecloth do or should I use another?:* suffice, serve; be satisfactory, be enough. **7.** *She's doing as well as can be expected:* fare, get on, make out. **8.** *Last summer we did ten countries in three weeks:* cover, travel through, visit, look at, stop in.

docile *adj. We bought a docile old horse for the children:* manageable, tractable, compliant, tame, obedient, complaisant, agreeable, obliging, willing. —**Ant.** unruly, wild, ungovernable, disobedient, untrainable.

dock[1] n. **1.** We took the children down to the dock to see the ships: wharf, pier, quay, waterfront, landing. —v. **2.** The tanker will dock in San Pedro for installation of new equipment: berth, come into port, guide a ship into dock, go into dry dock for repairs. **3.** The two modules docked in outer space: couple, hook up, link up, join, fasten together.

dock[2] v. **1.** The tail of the colt was docked: crop, cut short; cut off. **2.** They docked his salary because of absence: deduct a part from; deduct from the wages of, subject to loss.

docket n. This is just one of several cases on today's docket: agenda, program, schedule, calendar, timetable, card, bill, slate, roster, lineup, program of operation, order of business, things to be done.

doctor n. **1.** If you're ill, you'd better see a doctor: physician, medical practitioner, person licensed to practice medicine; (variously) internist, general practitioner, GP, dentist, osteopath, pediatrician, podiatrist, opthalmologist. —v. **2.** Doctor that cut before it becomes infected: treat, apply medication to, give medical treatment to. **3.** He was jailed for doctoring his service record: falsify, change, alter, tamper with.

doctrinaire adj. He's so doctrinaire it's pointless to disagree with him: dogmatic, inflexible, dictatorial, rigid, arbitrary, absolute, opinionated, authoritarian, imperious, pontifical, overbearing; pigheaded, stubborn, bullheaded, mulish, stiff-necked, narrow-minded. —**Ant.** reasonable, temperate, moderate, mild, flexible.

doctrine n. The Church teaches the doctrine of free will: principle, belief, gospel, conviction, philosophy, tenet, precept, teaching, dogma.

document n. **1.** There are many documents containing the king's signature: official paper, record, instrument, legal form. —v. **2.** The lawyer gathered evidence to document the charges: support, back up, give weight to, verify, certify, substantiate.

doddering adj. He helped the doddering old man across the street: shaking, trembling, tottering, weak, feeble, decrepit, senile. —**Ant.** spry, agile, nimble; healthy, strong.

dodge v. **1.** He threw a chair at me, but luckily I dodged: duck, swerve, sidestep, turn aside. **2.** The reporters gathered around him, but he dodged their queries: evade, avoid, elude; equivocate, hedge, fend off. —n. **3.** A dodge behind a tree kept her from being run over: sidestep, duck, quick jump aside. **4.** Informal She found a new dodge to keep from paying taxes: trick, stratagem, wile, device, machination.

doer n. Bill is a talker, but Fred is a doer: active person, activist, go-getter, hustler, dynamo. —**Ant.** do-nothing, idler, loafer, good-for-nothing.

doff v. He doffs his hat to every lady he meets: remove, take off, cast off, put off, shed, toss off; strip, undress, throw off, bare, disrobe, drop, step out of; scrap, junk, do away with, eliminate,

discard, abandon, throw out. —**Ant.** keep, retain, save, maintain, conserve.

dog n. **1.** What kind of dog makes the best pet for a child?: canine; pup, puppy, mutt, mongrel, cur. **2.** Nobody but a dog would evict his own mother: heel, scoundrel, villain, beast, blackguard.

dogma n. You can't embrace a religion without accepting its dogmas: doctrine, teachings, set of beliefs, principles, philosophy; convictions, credo, tenet.

dogmatic adj. **1.** She's so dogmatic you can't tell her anything: opinionated, arbitrary, biased, prejudiced; imperious, dictatorial, domineering; stubborn, obstinate. **2.** The Nicene Creed is one of the most important dogmatic statements of the Christian faith: doctrinal, expressing dogma. —**Ant.** 1 diffident, vacillating, uncertain; docile, complaisant.

doldrums n. pl. I've been in the doldrums since she left town: depression, melancholy, gloom, blues, dumps.

dole n. **1.** Many families are living on the dole since the strike: welfare, allotment, apportionment, allocation, share, handout; food or clothing distribution. —v. **2.** The organization doled out many gifts to the needy during Christmas: give, hand out, distribute as charity, deal, parcel.

doleful adj. The funeral was a long, doleful ceremony: sad, gloomy, sorrowful, woeful, unhappy, joyless, dreary, dismal. —**Ant.** happy, joyful, cheerful, lighthearted.

doll n. **1.** She asked me to make some clothes for her doll: dolly, figurine, dummy; (variously) baby doll, rag doll, teddy bear, golliwog, puppet, marionette. **2.** (Informal) Cathy is a little doll: pretty child, beauty; honey, sweetheart, darling.

dolorous adj. It was a dolorous occasion when the business closed down: mournful, sorrowful, woeful, grievous, woebegone, miserable, anguished, wretched, pathetic, pitiable; calamitous, harrowing, distressing, lamentable, doleful, unhappy, mournful, rueful. —**Ant.** cheerful, happy, carefree, lighthearted, gay.

dolt n. Some dolt in the office mislaid my application: idiot, jerk, clod, imbecile, fool, blockhead, bonehead, moron, nitwit, numskull, jackass, half-wit. —**Ant.** whiz, brain, genius.

domain n. **1.** His domain extends for 20 miles in every direction: estate, land, territory, property, fief. **2.** The conspirators were banished from the king's domain: dominion, territory, province, kingdom, empire. **3.** The doctor works in the domain of public health: sphere, area, field, region, province, bailiwick.

dome n. The dome of the basilica was visible for miles: cupola, arch, bubble, bulge, covering, span, top, vault.

domestic adj. **1.** His second marriage has made him very domestic: devoted to home life, hearth-loving, given to the concerns of home. **2.** Most family pets are domestic animals: domesticated, tame; housebroken. **3.** Their new car is a domestic make: native, not foreign, not imported, indigenous, endemic, produced at

home, native-grown, home-grown, homemade.
—*n.* **4.** *It takes a staff of domestics to run that big house:* servant, attendant; household help; (*variously*) maid, cook, butler, houseboy. —**Ant.** 2 wild, ferocious, untame. 3 foreign, imported.

domesticate *v.* *I'll bet no one has tried to domesticate a hyena:* tame, train, subdue, break, gentle, naturalize, acclimatize.

domicile *n.* *For voting purposes his domicile is in Los Angeles:* residence, legal residence, dwelling, home, house, place where one lives.

dominance *n.* *His dominance of the fashion industry was complete:* mastery, ascendancy, authority, command, control, dominion, influence, preeminence, sovereignty, supremacy, rule, sway.

dominant *adj.* **1.** *The dominant powers took control of the conference:* ruling, controlling, predominating, predominant, superior, commanding, authoritative, major, principal, chief. **2.** *The new tower will be the dominant building in the city:* outstanding, most important, most prominent.

dominate *v.* **1.** *She completely dominates her family and makes all the decisions:* rule, govern, direct, control, domineer; preside over, be at the head of. **2.** *A ring of huge oak trees dominated the house:* occupy a commanding position, command visually; tower over, dwarf.

domination *n.* *She has been under the domination of her father since childhood:* rule, control, authority, command, power, mastery, superiority. —**Ant.** subjection, inferiority, subordination.

domineering *adj.* *He was a domineering man, allowing no one to overrule him:* tyrannical, oppressive, dictatorial, despotic, imperious, authoritative, commanding, dogmatic; overbearing, arrogant. —**Ant.** subservient, submissive; timid, shy.

dominion *n.* **1.** *"I have sole dominion over this land," declared the king:* rule, sovereignty, jurisdiction, supremacy, authority, command, mastery. **2.** *The law was put into effect throughout the dominion:* domain, empire, realm; territory, land, region.

don *v.* *We donned our best apparel for the party:* wear, put on, dress in, invest oneself with, get into, pull on.

donate *v.* *She donated a large sum to the college endowment fund:* contribute, give, present, bestow, bequeath; make a gift of.

donation *n.* *Many donations of money and clothing poured in for the flood victims:* present, gift, contribution.

done *adj.* *The pie isn't done until the crust has browned:* ready; cooked sufficiently, cooked enough, prepared, finished, completed.

Don Juan *In high school he was something of a Don Juan, paying attention to all the young ladies:* lothario, Romeo, Casanova, Lochinvar, gallant, paramour, suitor, wooer, pursuer, courter, swain, admirer, squire, lady-killer; *Slang* wolf, lover boy, steady; boyfriend, fellow, man, young man, gentleman caller, beau.

donkey *n.* **1.** *Donkeys are better than horses on mountain trails:* ass; (*variously*) mule, burro, jackass. **2.** *Don't be such a donkey about accepting help from your friends:* fool, idiot, ass, jackass.

donnybrook *n.* *A donnybrook resulted when the two teams got into an argument after the game:* brawl, fight, fray, affray, knock-down-and-drag-out, dustup, scuffle, free-for-all, fracas, melee, row, skirmish, set-to, ruckus, rumpus, ruction.

donor *n.* *The new arts foundation won't survive without more donors:* contributor, benefactor, giver; philanthropist, humanitarian.

doohickey *n.* *Is this the doohickey that holds the picture in place?:* thing, whatsis, whatchamacallit, doodad, object, device, gadget, gizmo, thingamajig, thingamabob, dingus, widget, thingummy, thingamadoodle, dojigger, dojiggy.

doom *n.* **1.** *The condemned woman could only await her doom:* fate, lot, portion, destiny; end, destruction, ruin, death. **2.** *He begged the judge to revoke his doom of exile:* pronouncement, judgment, verdict. **3.** *The preacher warned his congregation about the day of doom:* the Last Judgment, Judgment Day, doomsday, end of the world, Armageddon, resurrection day. —*v.* **4.** *Many landmarks are doomed because of the public's indifference:* mark for demolition, consign to ruin, consign to destruction. **5.** *The court doomed the accused to a long term of imprisonment:* condemn, convict; pronounce judgment against. —**Ant.** 2 acquittal, discharge, freedom.

doomed *adj.* *Everyone abandoned the doomed ship:* cursed, accursed, hopeless, damned, bewitched, condemned, ill-fated, ill-omened, luckless, ruined, sunk, suppressed, wrecked.

doomsday *n.* *On doomsday, the preacher said, we will have to account for our sins:* Day of Judgment, end of the world, Judgment Day, the Last Judgment.

door *n.* *Barbara stood in the door and greeted everyone:* doorway, entrance, portal, entranceway, entry, ingress, hallway; exit, egress.

dope *n.* **1.** *The curtain material has to be treated with some dope:* preparation, substance, additive; medication, astringent, antiseptic, disinfectant. **2.** *Slang He was accused of peddling dope:* narcotics, drugs, opiates; uppers, downers. **3.** *Slang He gave me some dope on the fifth race:* tip, news; inside information, scoop. **4.** *Slang The dope never knows when I'm kidding him:* dummy, fool, jerk, creep, nerd, drip, *Yiddish* klutz. —*v.* **5.** *Louise was heavily doped before the operation:* drug, sedate, anesthetize, narcotize.

dopey *adj.* **1.** *This dopey dog doesn't even know its own name:* dumb, stupid, dull-witted, slow-witted, mindless, witless, simple-minded, block-headed, idiotic, asinine, thickheaded, brainless. **2.** *These pills always make me feel dopey:* sluggish, lethargic, slow-witted, torpid, slumberous, leaden, comatose. —**Ant.** 2 brisk, energetic, peppy, vivacious, animated.

dormant *adj.* *The geyser has been dormant for*

five years: inactive, quiescent, idle; sleeping, somnolent; hibernating. —**Ant.** active, operative, moving, awake.

dose *n. The doctor says to double her dose of medicine:* measure, portion, share, ration, quota, allotment, daily dose, allowance, quantity; cut, division, percentage, segment, slice, section; shot, slug, nip, dram, injection, needle, pill, tablet, capsule; overdose, O.D.

dossier *n. The office keeps a dossier on every employee:* file, record, portfolio, brief, detailed report.

dot *n. 1. She bought a blue dress with white dots:* mark, speck, small spot, fleck; period, point. —*v.* 2. *Dot the pie filling with bits of butter:* dab, dapple, spot.

dotage *n. He's in his dotage and has difficulty remembering things:* senility, feeblemindedness, second childhood. —**Ant.** youth, heyday, salad days.

dote *v.* 1. *Grandparents often dote on their grandchildren:* bestow excessive love on, fuss over, lavish foolish fondness on. 2. *She began to dote right after her 91st birthday:* be in one's dotage, be senile.

doting *adj. His doting parents spoiled him outrageously:* indulgent, fond, adoring, affectionate, devoted.

double *adj.* 1. *The workers receive double pay for working on Sundays:* multiplied by two, twice as much, twice as great, again as much. 2. *The house has double windows in the dining room:* paired, twin, two-part. 3. *His statement had a double meaning:* two-sided, dual, ambiguous; twofold in character. 4. *We sleep in a double bed:* meant for two; accommodating two. —*n.* 5. *She is the double of her mother as a girl:* twin, counterpart, duplicate, replica, clone; *Slang* spitting image, dead ringer. —*v.* 6. *That new stock has doubled my income:* make twice as great, multiply by two, increase twofold.

double-cross *v. They say that he would even double-cross his own mother:* betray, deceive, abandon, run out on, two-time, break faith with, sell out, let down, inform on, snitch on, tell on, turn in, denounce, sell down the river, rat on, do dirt, blow the whistle on.

double-dealing *n. Severe penalties prevented further double-dealing:* duplicity, betrayal, cheating, chicanery, deception, dishonesty, fraud, mendacity, perfidy, treachery, trickery, bad faith.

double entendre *n. The speaker used several double entendres to enliven her talk:* double meaning, ambiguous statement, statement with two interpretations; risqué remark, off-color joke.

double-talk *n. When I asked about his work, all I got was double-talk about efficiency engineering:* mumbo jumbo, gobbledygook, gibberish, nonsense, flimflam, balderdash, hokum, hocuspocus, twaddle, blather, gabble, jabber, drivel, prattle, palaver, baloney, bunk, bunkum, *Slang* jazz.

doubt *v.* 1. *She doubts that anyone is truly clairvoyant:* question, wonder; be skeptical concern-

ing, have doubts about, be doubtful, feel uncertain, waver in opinion. 2. *He promised to repay the money, but I doubt his word:* distrust, mistrust, suspect; lack confidence in. —*n.* 3. *Is there any doubt about your willingness to accept the job?:* uncertainty, indecision, question, lack of conviction. 4. *She has her doubts about loaning him more money:* misgiving, mistrust, suspicion, apprehension, qualm. —**Ant.** 1 believe, feel certain. 2 trust, believe, rely on. 3 resolve. 4 trust, belief, confidence, faith.

doubter *n. After his extraordinary speech, the doubters were in the minority:* sceptic, nonbeliever, unbeliever, disbeliever, agnostic, cynic, questioner, *Informal* doubting Thomas.

doubtful *adj.* 1. *She's still doubtful about the wisdom of her choice:* undecided, uncertain, unconvinced, unsettled; hesitating, tentative, irresolute. 2. *I think the manuscript is of doubtful authenticity:* dubious, suspicious, suspect, questionable. 3. *The results of the experiment are doubtful:* unclear, vague, obscure, uncertain, inconclusive. —**Ant.** 1 decided, certain, positive. 2 indubitable, incontrovertible; definite.

doughty *adj. He was a doughty little man who could never be bullied:* courageous, brave, bold, intrepid, fearless, unafraid, dauntless, stouthearted; strong, confident, determined. —**Ant.** cowardly, timid.

dour *adj. She has a dour expression that discourages friendship:* gloomy, sullen, morose, sour; cheerless, unfriendly, solemn, forbidding. —**Ant.** happy, bright, sweet, cheerful; soft.

douse *v. He doused his hair in the sink and rinsed off the shampoo:* drench, submerge, immerse, soak, plunge into water, souse, saturate.

dovetail *v.* 1. *The sides of the drawer dovetail at the corners:* unite, join, fit together, connect by interlocking. 2. *If our schedules dovetail, I'll see you in San Francisco:* harmonize, coincide, match, tally, jibe.

dowdy *adj. She's much too young to look so dowdy:* drab, shabby, sloppy, slovenly, frumpy, unattractive, tacky. —**Ant.** smart, well-dressed, fashionable, chic; neat, trim, tidy.

down *adj.* 1. *I've been down ever since I heard the news:* downcast, disheartened, dispirited, dejected, depressed, blue; down-and-out. 2. *He's down with a nasty cold:* sick, ill, ailing. —*v.* 3. *He downed the champion with a left hook:* fell, floor, drop, knock down, *Slang* deck. 4. *She usually downs three martinis before dinner:* swallow, gulp; drink down, put away. —**Ant.** 1 gladdened, glad, happy, spirited.

downcast *adj. Don't be downcast because you lost:* unhappy, sad, disconsolate, disheartened, cheerless, depressed, dejected, low, blue, discouraged. —**Ant.** happy, glad, encouraged, spirited.

downfall *n.* 1. *The revolution brought about the dictator's downfall:* fall, ruin, ruination, destruction, collapse. 2. *A downfall is expected, so take an umbrella:* downpour, shower, rainstorm, rain shower.

downgrade *v. The corporation's bonds were sharply downgraded:* devalue, abase, declass, decrease, decry, degrade, demerit, demote, denigrate, depreciate, detract from, disparage, lower, mark down, minimize, reduce, run down, undervalue. **—Ant.** upgrade, advance, ameliorate, better, elevate, enhance, improve, promote, raise.

downhearted *adj. The student is downhearted because the professor rejected her thesis:* unhappy, sorrowful, depressed, sad, disheartened, dispirited, dejected, discouraged, downcast. **—Ant.** happy, glad, encouraged, spirited.

downpour *n. We got caught in a sudden downpour and were soaked:* shower, cloudburst, rainstorm, rain shower.

downright *adj.* 1. *She told a downright lie:* absolute, total, utter, thoroughgoing, complete, out-and-out. 2. *Her downright answer startled him:* direct, straightforward, candid, open, frank, blunt; sincere, honest, aboveboard, straight-from-the-shoulder. *—adv.* 3. *He was downright rude to us:* completely, thoroughly, unmistakably, unequivocally; utterly, plainly; actually, really, in truth. **—Ant.** 1 indefinite, unclear. 2 indirect, devious; insincere, dishonest.

down-to-earth *adj. Her years in the army had given her a down-to-earth approach to life:* realistic, hardheaded, pragmatic, matter-of-fact, hard-boiled, plain-spoken, sober, sensible, practical, unidealistic, no-nonsense, unsentimental; coarse, crass, earthy. **—Ant.** airy, romantic; pretentious, highfalutin, hoity-toity, snooty.

downtrodden *adj. He vowed to do all he could to help the downtrodden masses:* oppressed, tyrannized, subservient; harshly ruled; exploited.

downturn *n. The latest downturn in the stock market has cost him thousands:* decline, downward trend, downtrend, dwindling, dip, drop, downfall, downslide, downswing, waning, diminution, degeneration, deterioration, slide, slip, skid, slump, sag, depression. **—Ant.** upturn, boom, growth, expansion, recovery.

downy *adj. Her feet sank into the downy carpet:* soft, feathery, fleecy, fluffy, fuzzy, woolly.

doze *v.* 1. *She was dozing in the hammock when I phoned:* nap, snooze; sleep lightly. *—n.* 2. *There's nothing like a little doze after lunch:* nap, snooze, light sleep, siesta, forty winks, catnap.

drab *adj.* 1. *She works in a drab little office:* dreary, gloomy, dull, dingy, dismal, cheerless, lackluster, somber, gray. 2. *The color of my hair has gone from blond to drab:* dull brown, dull grayish brown. **—Ant.** 1 bright, cheery, cheerful, colorful.

draft *n.* 1. *She just finished the first draft of her new play:* sketch, outline, rough sketch; preliminary version. 2. *Close the window and stop that draft:* wind, breeze; current of air. 3. *When he was 18, he had to register for the draft:* conscription, induction; military service. 4. *This team of horses has a draft of 16 tons:* drag, pull, haul. 5. *He sent a draft for $100 to his cousin in Ireland:* postal order, money order. 6. *The knights drained their drafts of wine:* drawing from a cask; drink, gulp, swallow. *—v.* 7. *He*

drafted the model of the atomic engine: outline, diagram, sketch. 8. *He was drafted by the army and served for four years:* induct, conscript, call for military service.

drag *v.* 1. *Drag the chair over here so I can stand on it:* pull, haul, lug; draw with effort, pull for-cibly; bring. 2. *The bride's long train dragged behind her:* trail; be drawn, be pulled along. 3. *Traffic during the rush hour just drags:* crawl, creep along, inch along; move slowly. *—n.* 4. *Don't be such a drag—come along with us:* Slang spoilsport, party-pooper, wet blanket, bore.

draggy *adj. The draggy speech induced slumber:* tedious, boring, tiresome, wearisome, drawn-out, dull, humdrum, lengthy, long, monotonous, overlong, prolonged, protracted.

drain *v.* 1. *Drain the oil out of the crankcase:* draw fluid from, pump off; remove by degrees, empty out. 2. *Most of the river drains into the Gulf of Mexico:* discharge, flow off gradually, flow out, debouch. 3. *He drained his parents of every cent they had:* sap, empty, deplete, impoverish; dissipate, use up. *—n.* 4. *What could have stopped up the bathtub drain?:* tube, pipe, outlet; conduit, sewer, channel. 5. *This car has really been a drain on my income:* sap, drag, strain; depletion, continuous strain. **—Ant.** 3 fill, supply, replenish.

drama *n.* 1. *He has written a historical drama:* play, theatrical piece, dramatic composition. 2. *She wants to study drama and become an actress:* dramatic art, acting, direction, mise-en-scène, the stage, the theater. 3. *The movie had the drama of a true-life adventure:* excitement, suspenseful events; dramatic quality, intense interest, vividness.

dramatic *adj.* 1. *Dramatic talent, like any other, must be trained:* theatrical; of the drama, for the theater. 2. *There was a dramatic confrontation between the two leaders:* emotional, striking, sensational, climactic, melodramatic, suspenseful.

dramatize *v. She dramatized every minor event in her life:* perform, play up, act, amplify, enact, exaggerate, execute, melodramatize, overdo, overstate, playact, present, produce, show, splash, stage.

drape *v. She often draped a coat over her shoulders before taking a walk:* cover, wrap, swathe, enwrap, cloak, wrap up, swaddle, enswathe, veil, envelop, sheathe, shroud, enshroud; adorn, dress, garb, deck, attire, array, apparel, enrobe, bedeck, festoon, *Archaic* bedight.

drastic *adj. He's liable to do something drastic in his present state of mind:* extreme, radical, rash; bizarre, outlandish; dire, dreadful; dangerous, deleterious.

draw *v.* 1. *How many horses will draw the royal coach?:* pull, drag, haul, tow, pull along. 2. *They will draw the winner's name from the barrel:* extract, pull out, take out, draw out, pick, pick out. 3. *Cover the food so it won't draw the flies:* attract, lure; allure, entice, charm; evoke, elicit, bring forth, make appear. 4. *The assignment is* *to draw a horse in motion:* sketch, etch, limn, picture with pencil or crayon, make a picture of. **5.** *She agreed to draw a proper contract:* draft, write, make up, make out. **6.** *She drew the wrong conclusion from the meeting:* get, take, deduce, infer. **7.** *The strands of rubber were drawn to test their strength:* stretch, attenuate, elongate; extend, protract. **8.** *He drew up his face in an expression of disgust:* contract, distort, wrinkle. **9.** *The polluted pond will have to be drawn and refilled:* drain, siphon; suck dry, pump out. —*n.* **10.** *Free dishes used to be a big draw at the movie theaters:* attraction, lure, enticement, inducement, *Slang* come-on. **11.** *The bake-off was a draw, so they awarded two first prizes:* tie, stalemate; deadlock. —**Ant.** 1 push, shove. 2 put in. 7 contract. 10 repellent. 11 victory; defeat.

drawback *n. Lack of funds can be a drawback if you want to invest in a sure thing:* obstacle, hindrance, handicap, detriment, impediment, stumbling block, disadvantage.

drawing *n.* **1.** *His drawing of the village green was quite good:* sketch, picture, study, illustration, delineation, depiction. **2.** *The drawing for prizes will be held at 8 P.M.:* selection of winners, lottery.

drawn *adj. She was pale and drawn after her ordeal:* haggard, fatigued, tired, fraught, peaked, pinched, sapped, starved, strained, stressed, worn, careworn.

dread *v.* **1.** *I dread the thought of coming home late at night:* fear, be afraid of, anticipate with horror, shrink from, cringe at, cower at. —*n.* **2.** *Her dread of being home alone made her extremely nervous:* fear, fright, terror, fearfulness, apprehension, anguish, anxiety, trepidation. —*adj.* **3.** *He prepared to face the dread consequences:* frightening, alarming, terrifying, fearful, awful, horrifying. —**Ant.** 1 be unafraid. 2 confidence, courage, fearlessness, bravery.

dreadful *adj. She had a dreadful accident:* awful, terrible, horrible, tragic; fearful, frightful, alarming, shocking, distressing.

dream *n.* **1.** *I had another dream about a faraway place:* sleeping vision; nightmare, incubus. **2.** *Her dream of success kept her from concentrating:* daydream, fantasy, reverie, vision. **3.** *The Ambassador's dream is for lasting peace:* desire, wish, goal, hope; prospect, expectation. **4.** *That new sports car is an absolute dream:* joy, pleasure, delight. —*v.* **5.** *I dreamed I won a chariot race with Ben-Hur:* have a dream, have a sleeping vision. **6.** *Stop dreaming and get to work!:* daydream, be lost in thought, pass time in reverie, muse. **7.** *I wouldn't dream of asking her to my home:* consider, think, give serious thought to. **8.** *The delegates dreamed of peace:* desire, wish, hope for, have as a goal, look forward to.

dreamy *adj.* **1.** *There was a strange, surreal, dreamy quality to the movie:* fanciful, dreamlike, fantastic, illusory, imaginary, immaterial, impractical, misty, mythical, otherworldly, phantasmagorical, shadowy, unreal, unsubstantial. **2.** *Even as a child she had a dreamy air:* absent, abstracted, daydreaming, musing, in a reverie, preoccupied, *Informal* with one's head in the clouds. **3.** *Our vacation was simply dreamy:* romantic, relaxing, soothing. —**Ant.** 1 down-to-earth, common-sense, practical, realistic, unromantic.

dreary *adj. She rented a dreary little room on the top floor:* gloomy, depressing, cheerless, bleak, drab, sad, dismal, mournful, forlorn, melancholy. —**Ant.** cheerful, joyful, happy, bright.

dregs *n. pl.* **1.** *Let the coffee dregs settle to the bottom of the pot:* residue, sediment, settlings, grounds, deposit. **2.** *Some of his clients are really the dregs of humanity:* the coarse part, lowest and worst part, lower depths; riffraff, rabble, canaille.

drench *v. If you don't take your raincoat, you may get drenched:* douse, saturate, wet, soak.

dress *n.* **1.** *She buys several new dresses every season:* gown, frock, robe; costume. **2.** *The dress of the natives is quite unique:* clothing, clothes, costume, attire, apparel, garb. —*v.* **3.** *Try to dress appropriately for each occasion:* clothe oneself, attire, put on clothes. **4.** *The store dressed its display windows for the Christmas season:* trim, adorn, ornament, decorate, deck, embellish, garnish. **5.** *She often spends hours dressing her hair:* arrange, curl, groom; comb out, do up. **6.** *He was released after his wounds were dressed:* treat, bandage, apply a dressing to, cleanse, disinfect.

dressing *n. The nurse applied a dressing to the wound:* bandage, compress, adhesive tape, Band-Aid, plaster, poultice, tourniquet.

dressmaker *n. The dressmaker hemmed several of my dresses:* seamstress; couturier, (*fem.*) couturiere, *French* midinette.

dressy *adj. The dressy pair were conspicuous at the dance:* smart, stylish, chic, classy, dressed up, elegant, fancy, fashionable, formal.

dribble *v.* **1.** *Cereal dribbled from the baby's mouth:* drip, drizzle, trickle, fall in drops, run bit by bit. **2.** *She dribbled the ball down to the goal and scored:* bounce; kick.

drift *v.* **1.** *The boat drifted dangerously near the falls. Some people drift through life without caring very much:* be carried by a current, be borne along; wander, ramble, meander, amble, peregrinate. **2.** *The wind drifted the leaves across our yard:* pile up, amass, gather, accumulate; scatter. —*n.* **3.** *They reported an easterly drift of winds:* direction, course, current, flow, stream; movement. **4.** *Wind left the snow in 10-foot drifts:* heap, pile, mass, accumulation. **5.** *The drift of his question seemed to embarrass the speaker:* implication, meaning, gist, sense; object, objective, aim, direction, purpose, intention.

drill *n.* **1.** *I need a drill to make a hole for the rod:* machine for drilling, boring tool. **2.** *Vocabulary is taught to the children by daily drill:* practice, training, repetition, repeated exercises. —*v.* **3.** *You'll have to drill for each of the bolts:* punch, pierce, puncture, bore. **4.** *The teacher drilled the class in pronunciation of Latin words:* instruct by repetition, train, exercise, work with.

drink v. **1.** *Do you want to drink tea or coffee?:* imbibe, absorb, take in, ingest, partake of. **2.** *We drank each other's health for most of the evening:* toast, salute, drink in honor of. —n. **3.** *We stopped at the farmer's well for a cool drink:* beverage, liquid refreshment, libation. **4.** *He took to drink after his wife left him:* alcohol, alcoholic liquor; alcoholism, drunkenness, heavy drinking, *Informal* the bottle, booze. **5.** *Give me a drink of your lemonade:* sip, gulp, swallow, swig, taste.

drinker n. *She was a serious drinker, but is now sober:* imbiber, chronic drinker, inebriate, problem drinker, serious drinker, sot, tippler, *Informal* drunk, guzzler.

drip v. **1.** *He got out of the shower and dripped water onto the floor:* trickle, dribble; splash, sprinkle, drizzle; let fall in drops. —n. **2.** *We heard the drip of a leaky faucet:* trickle, dribble, dripping. **3.** *Slang That drip can't take no for an answer:* ass, jerk, creep, nerd, bore, dummy, *Yiddish* klutz.

drive v. **1.** *They drove the cattle along the Chisholm Trail:* move, advance; lead, guide, conduct; push forward, spur, urge along. **2.** *The boss drives her workers hard:* press, urge, prod, goad; incite, impel. **3.** *Our troops are driving toward the enemy stronghold:* advance, press forward; rush. **4.** *We usually drive to the country on Sunday. She drives a car skillfully:* go by car, ride, go driving, motor; guide, steer; operate. **5.** *His pride drove him to complete the job:* motivate; force, compel, coerce. **6.** *Just what are you driving at?:* suggest, intend, mean, insinuate. —n. **7.** *Come with us for a drive in the country:* ride, outing, excursion; trip by car. **8.** *The team did not relent in their drive toward the goal:* push, surge, advance, campaign, onward course. **9.** *She has tremendous drive toward success:* motivation, ambition, impulse, push.

drivel v. **1.** *The baby sat driveling in his highchair:* drool, dribble, slobber, slaver. **2.** *When I left she was still driveling on about her popularity in school:* ramble, babble, talk foolishly, talk nonsense. —n. **3.** *We listened to a lot of drivel about the sagging economy:* gibberish, rambling, babbling, nonsense, senseless talk.

driver n. **1.** *He hired a car and driver for the evening:* chauffeur. **2.** *The driver made sure the herd kept moving:* cowboy, drover, herdsman.

driving adj. *He was the driving force behind the enterprise:* dynamic, active, compelling, energetic, enterprising, forceful, galvanic, lively, sweeping, vigorous, urging.

drizzle v. *It began to drizzle as we walked home:* mist, drip, rain, shower, sprinkle, spray.

droll adj. *We found the play very droll, but others disliked it:* humorous, whimsical, oddly amusing, funny, laughable; offbeat, eccentric, strange. —**Ant.** ordinary, common; dull, boring.

drone[1] n. *He was a drone who took advantage of everyone's hard work:* parasite, idler, loafer, lazy person.

drone[2] v. **1.** *The air conditioner droned almost inaudibly:* hum, buzz, whir, vibrate. —n. **2.** *The*

drone of the machines distracted me: hum, buzz, whir, vibration, murmuring.

drool v. *The dog drooled in anticipation of his dinner:* slobber, slaver, dribble, water at the mouth, salivate, drivel.

droop v. **1.** *The branches of the tree drooped after the heavy rain:* sag, hang down, hang listlessly, incline downward. **2.** *Our spirits drooped as we watched our team lose:* weaken, wither, lower, dim; lose vigor, sink, flag, diminish. —**Ant.** 1 rise. 2 revive, rally, flourish, perk up.

droopy adj. **1.** *Our flowers were all droopy because we had neglected to water them:* hanging down, limp, sagging, dangling, bowed, bent. **2.** *The bad news put her in a droopy mood for the rest of the day:* downcast, depressed, dejected, downhearted, dispirited, cast down, spiritless, blue, doleful, down, subdued, dashed, down-in-the-mouth, world-weary, despondent, despairing, pining, languishing.

drop n. **1.** *Drops of water sparkled in the sunlight:* droplet, drip, driblet, globule, tear, bead. **2.** *Add a drop of Tabasco and mix well:* dash, dab, pinch, trace, smack, sprinkling, *Informal* smidgen, *French* soupçon. **3.** *It's about a 20-foot drop to the ground. The road ends abruptly in a drop to the sea:* descent, fall; declivity, slope, plunge; precipice, abyss. **4.** *The drop in temperature was a relief:* decline, fall, lowering, decrease. —v. **5.** *Water dropped from the ceiling into the pan on the floor:* drip, dribble, trickle, fall in drops. **6.** *The sky diver dropped toward the earth:* fall, plunge, plummet, dive, descend. **7.** *If it's going to start an argument, let's drop the subject:* abandon, leave, forsake, give up; bring to an end, terminate, cease to consider. **8.** *Sales always drop in the spring:* fall, lower, lessen, dwindle, decline, diminish, slacken, slide, sink. **9.** *The boss dropped him from the staff after two weeks:* discharge, dismiss, fire, *Informal* can, sack. **10.** *The challenger dropped the champion in the fifth round:* fell, floor, deck, knock down. **11.** *Don't drop the "g" in "dancing" and "walking":* leave out, omit, fail to include, fail to pronounce. —**Ant.** 2 much, lots, loads, quantities. 3 rise. 4 rise, increase. 6 rise, soar, shoot up. 7 take up, discuss, consider, talk over. 8 rise, increase, go up. 9 hire, sign on, add. 11 include, pronounce.

drought n. **1.** *The drought caused famine throughout the country:* aridity; period of dry weather, lack of rain. **2.** *Right now there's a drought of new playwriting talent:* scarcity, paucity, lack, shortage, deficiency, want, dearth, need, insufficiency.

drown v. **1.** *How many drowned when the boat capsized?:* asphyxiate, suffocate; go to Davy Jones's locker, go down for the third time, meet a watery end. **2.** *The crops were drowned by the heavy rainfall:* inundate, flood, deluge, immerse, submerge, drench, soak. **3.** *She was irked because the audience's coughing drowned out her playing:* overpower, overwhelm, overcome, engulf, swallow up. —**Ant.** 2 dry, drain.

drowsy adj. **1.** *That medicine made me drowsy:* sleepy, dozy, lethargic, languid, listless, sluggish, slow, lazy, tired. **2.** *The drowsy music was relaxing:* hypnotic, soporific, somnolent, soothing. **—Ant.** 1 alert, lively.

drub *v.* *The man was severely drubbed for stealing the horse:* beat, whip, bastinado, cane, thrash, flog, hit, whale.

drudge *n.* **1.** *He's merely a drudge in his uncle's office:* menial, lackey, toiler, hack, grubber, underling, subordinate, inferior. **—v. 2.** *She drudges daily with no hope of bettering herself:* toil, hack, grub, plod, labor, struggle, slave.

drudgery *n.* *Doing these monthly reports is sheer drudgery:* distasteful work, menial labor, toil, hack work, travail, grind.

drug *n.* **1.** *The new drug helped to cure her:* medication, physic, prescription, remedy. **—v. 2.** *Narcotics were sure to drug him:* stupefy, anesthetize, benumb, deaden, desensitize, dope, knock out, narcotize, numb, sedate.

drugged *adj.* *The drugged boy slumped to the floor:* comatose, dazed, doped, dopey, narcotized.

drum *n.* **1.** *Oil is shipped in large drums:* barrel, keg, cask, tub. **—v. 2.** *The rain drums on the windowpane:* rap, tap, beat, beat rhythmically, tattoo. **3.** *The sound of the surf drummed in our ears:* roll, roar, beat, rumble, reverberate, din, beat a tattoo; pulsate. **4.** *They will drum him out of the corps for insubordination:* expel, discharge, dismiss, drive out. **5.** *His father drummed it into him that he had to succeed:* repeat persistently, reiterate, drive home, force, hammer at, din, din in the ear, harp on.

drunk *adj.* **1.** *He was drunk and surly when he arrived at the party:* intoxicated, inebriated, sodden, besotted, tipsy, under the influence of alcohol; *Slang* soused, plastered, smashed, stewed, looped, zonked, zapped, three sheets to the wind. **—n. 2.** *A drunk was the only one in the bar at that time of day:* drunkard, lush, sot, soak, rummy, souse, toper, barfly; alcoholic, dipsomaniac. **3.** *She went on a three-day drunk after her divorce:* drinking spree, binge, beerbust, carousal, *Slang* bust, bender. **—Ant.** 1 sober, abstemious, abstinent, temperate.

drunkard *n.* *The drunkard consumed two bottles of whiskey a day:* alcoholic, toper, sot, tippler, drinker, inebriate, dipsomaniac. **—Ant.** teetotaler.

dry *adj.* **1.** *This dry weather is bad for the crops:* arid, rainless, free from moisture. **2.** *I'm so dry, let's stop in here for a soda:* thirsty; desiring liquid, suffering for water, dehydrated, parched. **3.** *He gives the driest speeches I've ever listened to:* uninteresting, dull, tedious, monotonous, boring, wearisome. **4.** *He has a dry wit that I don't always understand:* deadpan, low-key; droll, quietly humorous. **—v. 5.** *Dry the dishes and put them away. Dry your eyes, everything's all right:* blot, wipe; remove the moisture from, make dry. **6.** *The river dried up during the hot spell:* become dry, shrivel up, desiccate, dehydrate. **—Ant.** 1 wet, damp, moist, humid, dank. 3 interesting, fascinating, lively, entertaining.

dual *adj.* *The program has a dual purpose:* twofold, double, two-part. **—Ant.** single, singular.

dub *v.* *She dubbed him 'Lord of the Manor':* name, baptize, call, christen, confer, denominate, designate, term, title, bestow, tag.

dubious *adj.* **1.** *I was dubious about his ability to help:* doubtful, uncertain, unsure, skeptical, unconvinced. **2.** *She spends too much time with dubious friends:* questionable, suspicious, suspect, shady; unreliable, untrustworthy, undependable. **—Ant.** 1 sure, positive, certain, definite. 2 reliable, trustworthy, dependable.

duck *v.* **1.** *I ducked when I saw the rock falling:* swerve, veer, dodge, sidestep; crouch, stoop. **2.** *She ducked the interviewers by sneaking out the back door:* evade, avoid, elude, dodge, give the slip to.

duct *n.* *The plumber located the leaking duct:* tube, aqueduct, canal, channel, conduit, course, funnel, passage, pipe.

ductile *adj.* **1.** *When heated, the metal is one of the most ductile materials:* flexible, pliable, plastic, formable, malleable, elastic, pliant, stretchable, bendable, tensile, moldable, supple, shapable, extensible. **2.** *Politicians know that public opinion can be extremely ductile:* ma-nipulable, tractable, swayable, susceptible, manageable; compliant, amenable, docile, adaptable, complaisant, submissive. **—Ant.** 1 inflexible, rigid, set, fixed, firm, unbending.

dud *n.* *After years of development the new airplane turned out to be a dud. No one had the heart to tell him his new play was a dud:* failure, fiasco, debacle, disappointment, miscarriage, fizzle, botch; *Slang* flop, washout, dog, bust, bomb, bummer, lead balloon, lemon, clinker, loser, hash. **—Ant.** success, smash, sensation, triumph, winner.

due *adj.* **1.** *How much is still due on your car?:* unpaid, owing, owed, outstanding; in arrears. **2.** *She is entitled to all the respect due a distinguished scholar:* suitable, fitting, rightful, deserved, merited, appropriate, becoming, proper; sufficient, adequate. **3.** *The plane is due at 4:15 this afternoon:* scheduled, expected to arrive. **4.** *The child gave her parents due cause to be upset:* sufficient, adequate, enough, ample, plenty of. **—Ant.** 2 inappropriate, unbecoming. 4 insufficient, inadequate, scanty, scant.

dulcet *adj.* *The dulcet tones of her voice floated down the hall:* pleasing, mellifluous, melodious, sonorous; lyrical, musical, tuneful.

dull *adj.* **1.** *This knife is so dull the blade won't cut:* blunt; not sharp, not keen. **2.** *He was a dull man and you had to explain things very carefully and slowly to him:* slow, dense, thick, obtuse, dim-witted, stupid. **3.** *The trade center had a very dull day:* slow, inactive, uneventful; not brisk. **4.** *How did such a dull book become a best-seller?:* boring, uninteresting, vapid, vacuous, unimaginative, prosaic, trite. **5.** *The walls were painted in a dull blue:* lackluster, muted, subdued, quiet. **6.** *I thought I heard a dull sound in the kitchen:* muffled, indistinct, subdued, deadened. **—Ant.** 1 sharp. 2 intelligent, clever, bright. 3 active, lively, spirited. 4 interesting, imaginative, exciting. **5** bright. **6** distinct, clear, well-defined.

dullard *n. People took advantage of him because he was a dullard:* dunce, dolt, nitwit, halfwit, imbecile, dumbbell, dummy.

duly *adj.* **1.** *The hostess was duly thanked for her hospitality:* rightfully, properly, suitably, deservedly; correctly, appropriately. **2.** *The witness duly arrived and was put on the stand:* punctually; on time, at the proper time.

dumb *adj.* **1.** *She was a therapist to deaf and dumb children:* mute, aphasiac, incapable of speech. **2.** *Everyone else informed on the cheat, but Alan remained dumb:* silent, mute, mum, refusing to speak. **3.** *Informal She says she's tired of being called dumb:* stupid, unintelligent; foolish, dopey; dull, dense, dim-witted. —**Ant.** 1 articulate; capable of speech. 3 smart, intelligent, clever, bright.

dumbbell *n. She may be smart but her children are dumbbells:* dunce, ignoramus, fool, blockhead, oaf, clod, clown, dummy, numskull, simpleton, booby, nitwit, moron, imbecile, idiot, dimwit, *German* dummkopf; *Slang* dumb-dumb, meathead, lunkhead, noodlehead, lamebrain, birdbrain.

dumbfound or **dumfound** *v. We were dumbfounded by all the damage done by the storm:* stun, astonish, startle, amaze, flabbergast.

dumbfounded *adj. The dumbfounded students could not take in the announcement that the university was closing:* stunned, flabbergasted, agape, aghast, amazed, astonished, astounded, bewildered, confounded, confused, dismayed, overcome, overwhelmed, shocked, speechless, staggered, startled, stumped, stunned, surprised, taken aback, thunderstruck, *Informal* buffaloed, floored, thrown.

dummy *n.* **1.** *The store's display windows had dummies in beautiful silk gowns:* mannequin, model, form, figure. **2.** *Informal Some dummy mixed up the letters and we lost the bid:* blockhead, dolt, dumbbell, oaf, idiot, clown, simpleton, chowderhead, knucklehead, dunderhead, dumb-dumb, *Yiddish* klutz, *German* dummkopf.

dump *v.* **1.** *The delivery boy dumped the groceries on the back porch:* toss, drop heavily, unload carelessly. **2.** *The truck dumped three loads of gravel on the driveway:* unload, empty; dispose of, get rid of. —*n.* **3.** *This furniture is about ready for the dump:* dumping ground, rubbish heap, refuse pile, junkyard. **4.** *Slang How can anybody live in a dump like this?:* hovel, hole; shack, shanty, hut.

dunce *n. Who was the dunce that left the door open?:* dummy, idiot, fool, moron, imbecile, simpleton, dimwit, nitwit, blockhead, numskull.

dunk *v. Grandfather would never eat a doughnut without first dunking it in his coffee:* douse, immerse, dip, plunge, submerge, souse, sop, duck, saturate, soak, steep, slosh, drench, bathe, drown, inundate, engulf, deluge, baptize.

duo *n. Mutt and Jeff make a funny duo:* pair, twosome, couple; combination, *Slang* combo.

dupe *n.* **1.** *He was the dupe of the racketeers and may go to prison:* pawn, patsy, fall guy, cat's paw, *Slang* sucker. —*v.* **2.** *The agency duped her into signing up for $200 worth of lessons:* trick, fool, mislead, deceive; humbug, bamboozle, hoodwink.

duplicate *n.* **1.** *The duplicate looks like a Rembrandt, but it won't fool the experts:* facsimile, reproduction, replica, imitation; copy, carbon copy, photocopy, photostat. —*v.* **2.** *Do you think you could duplicate that chocolate fudge cake?:* match, parallel, repeat, make again, copy, clone. —**Ant.** 1 original.

duplicity *n. She discovered that he had behaved with duplicity:* deceit, deceitfulness, fraud, dishonesty, guile, cunning, falseness, deception. —**Ant.** straightforwardness, forthrightness, candor.

durability *n. For sheer durability, these are the best tires:* durableness, endurance, lastingness, persistence, stamina, sturdiness, staying power.

durable *adj. This raincoat is made of very durable material:* enduring, lasting, sound, substantial, sturdy, tough, strong, long-wearing. —**Ant.** fragile, frail, weak, flimsy.

duration *n. For the duration of the strike we will remain closed:* continuance, extent, term, period, continuation.

duress *n. He testified that he had signed the contract under duress:* force, constraint, threat, coercion; compulsion, pressure.

dusk *n. At dusk the lights of the city come on:* twilight, sunset, sundown, nightfall.

dusky *adj.* **1.** *I hardly recognized him in the dusky light:* dim, veiled, cloudy, gloomy, murky. **2.** *The island natives had dusky complexions:* dark, swarthy, dark-hued. —**Ant.** 1 bright, clear. 2 fair, light.

dust *n.* **1.** *Dust covered the table:* dirt, ashes, cinders, earth, filth, flakes, grime, grit, lint, sand, soil, soot —*v.* **2.** *They dusted the crop twice a week:* cover, dredge, powder, scatter, sift, spray, spread.

dusty *adj. We strolled down the dusty road:* powdery, dirty, chalky, crumbly, dirty, granular, grubby, sandy, sooty, unclean, unswept, untouched.

dutiful *adj. For many years she was a dutiful secretary:* diligent, faithful, loyal; obedient, compliant, conscientious. —**Ant.** uncaring; disrespectful; disobedient; careless, remiss.

duty *n.* **1.** *He felt it was his duty to report the matter to the police:* obligation, responsibility; onus; business, province. **2.** *One of her duties is to report any absentees:* function, task, assignment, charge. **3.** *How much duty did you have to pay on the camera?:* tax, tariff, customs, excise, levy.

dwarf *n.* **1.** *Snow White and the Seven Dwarfs is a charming story:* fairy, pixie, sprite, elf, gnome, leprechaun, imp, goblin, troll. —*adj.* **2.** *This border was planted in dwarf marigolds:* diminutive, small, bantam, tiny, pygmy, miniature, petite, baby. —*v.* **3.** *This present trouble dwarfs that other matter:* overshadow, dim, diminish. —**Ant.** 2 huge, gigantic.

dwell *v.* **1.** *He dwells in the country during most* *of the year:* reside, live, inhabit, abide. **2.** *She dwelt at length on the similarities in the two paintings:* linger over, continue for a time, harp on. —**Ant.** 1 roam.

dwelling *n. They occupy a three-story dwelling on Park Street:* house, home, residence, abode, domicile, habitation.

dwindle *v. Our food supply dwindled when we were lost in the woods:* diminish, decrease, decline, lessen, shrink, become smaller; wane, fade. —**Ant.** increase, grow; burgeon, flourish.

dye *n.* **1.** *Try some red dye on that old sweater:* color, coloring, tint, shade, coloration, stain. —*v.* **2.** *Maybe you could dye that skirt to match your blouse:* color, tint, stain.

dynamic *adj. We need a dynamic person to head the board:* active, vigorous, vital, energetic, forceful, driving, powerful.

dynamite *v. Dynamiting the log jam seemed to be the only solution:* destroy, demolish, blow up, wipe out, annihilate, devastate, raze, decimate, ruin, wreck, dismantle, shatter, obliterate, eradicate, extinguish, exterminate, *Slang* trash. —**Ant.** create, construct, erect, build, put up, make.

dynasty *n. The Bourbon dynasty ruled France for 200 years prior to the Revolution:* ruling house, line, regime, lineage, regnancy, regency, suzerainty, reign, monarchy, kingship, hegemony, crown; government, administration, dominion, authority, jurisdiction.

dyspeptic *adj. My aunt was kind but my uncle was dyspeptic:* bad-tempered, ill-natured, ill-humored, crotchety, hot- tempered, irritable, irascible, short-tempered, mean, choleric, touchy, sour-tempered, waspish, *Brit.* shirty, cantankerous, grouchy, crabby, grumpy, ornery, fractious, contentious. —**Ant.** good-natured, agreeable, imperturbable, even-tempered, calm, serene.

eager *adj.* **1.** *The children were eager to go on the picnic:* excited, avid, keen, desirous, yearning, longing, impatient, raring, athirst, thirsting, hungering, agog. **2.** *He is an eager student:* earnest, enthusiastic, intent, intense, fervent, fervid, ardent, impassioned, passionate, zealous, spirited; industrious, enterprising, hardworking, persevering, diligent, resolute; ambitious, aggressive. **—Ant.** 1 indifferent, unconcerned, uninterested; opposed, adverse. 2 indifferent, uninterested, apathetic, impassive, heedless, unmindful, inattentive, irresolute, unambitious, unenterprising, unaggressive; lazy, negligent.

eagerness *n.* *Her eagerness to succeed startled us:* keenness, enthusiasm, excitement, alacrity, anticipation, anxiousness, avidity, fervor, gusto, hunger, zeal, zest, impatience, impetuosity, intentness, gusto.

early *adv.* **1.** *The dental appointment is early in the week:* during the first part, near the beginning. **2.** *The speaker arrived early for the meeting:* ahead of time, in advance, beforehand; too soon, prematurely, before the usual time; betimes, in good time. *—adj.* **3.** *The Smiths were among the early arrivals:* first, initial. **4.** *The salesman was early for the appointment:* ahead of time, beforehand, premature. **5.** *The archaeologists uncovered an early Egyptian city:* ancient, very old, primal, primitive, prehistoric, archaic, primeval, primordial. **—Ant.** 1–5 late. 1 later, near the end. 2 late, tardily. 3 latter, later, last. 4 tardy. 5 modern.

earmark *n.* **1.** *That remark had all the earmarks of an insult:* characteristic, feature, trait, quality, attribute, peculiarity, sign, token, identifying mark, singularity, label, tag, distinctive feature, stamp, band. *—v.* **2.** *I've earmarked this amount for my vacation fund:* designate, tag, allocate, assign, reserve, set aside, put away, hold.

earn *v.* **1.** *The average skilled worker now earns over $10,000 a year:* make, receive, gain, get, collect, draw, realize, reap, clear, net, pick up, bring home. **2.** *You won't get a promotion unless you earn it:* deserve, merit, rate, warrant, be entitled to; attain, achieve, secure. **—Ant.** 1 waste, lose, spend, forfeit, squander. 2 lose, forfeit.

earnest *adj.* **1.** *Only earnest chess players become champions:* serious, intent, eager, determined, resolute, purposeful, diligent, hardworking, persevering, industrious, assiduous, ambitious, devoted. **2.** *The earnest young man had no use for jokes:* sober, serious, thoughtful, grave, solemn, staid, sedate; stable, constant, fixed, steady, firm. **3.** *She ignored his earnest request for forgiveness:* sincere, honest, heartfelt, deeply felt, wholehearted; impassioned, passionate, intense, ardent, zealous, fervent, fervid, urgent, insistent, vehement; spirited, eager, enthusiastic. **—Ant.** 1, 2 frivolous, capricious, trifling, irresolute, apathetic; sportive, jesting; unsteady, unstable; flippant, light. 3 insincere, indifferent, halfhearted, unimpassioned; unspirited, unenthusiastic.

earnestness *n.* *His earnestness persuaded us to give him a job:* seriousness, attentiveness, concentration, deliberation, determination, doggedness, gravity, intensity, perseverance, persistence, purposefulness, resolution, sincerity, sobriety, vehemence, tenacity. **—Ant.** flippancy.

earnings *n. pl. Income taxes are based on one's earnings:* money earned, income, wages, salary, pay, payment, compensation, profits, receipts, proceeds. **—Ant.** costs, expenditures, outlay.

earth *n.* *The farmer examined a handful of earth:* soil, dirt, ground, land, topsoil, sod, turf, loam, clay, dust.

earthly *adj.* **1.** *Is man too occupied with earthly matters?:* worldly, terrestrial, mundane; secular, nonspiritual, ungodly, temporal, material, materialistic; corporeal, physical, bodily. **2.** *This gadget is of no earthly value:* possible, practical; conceivable, imaginable, feasible. **—Ant.** 1 unearthly, celestial, heavenly, spiritual, divine, godly; nonmaterialistic.

earthquake *n.* *The San Francisco earthquake was one of the worst catastrophes of the century:* quake, tremor, earth tremor, shock, seism, tremblor, upheaval.

earthy *adj.* *The old actress had not lost her earthy sense of humor:* coarse, lusty, bawdy, rib-ald, crude, rough, unrefined, unblushing, robust, vulgar, primitive, uncultured, uncultivated, peasant; *Slang* raunchy, funky; smutty, dirty, filthy, obscene, indecent. **—Ant.** genteel, refined, dainty, elegant, polished.

ease *n.* **1.** *The salve brought ease to the athlete's aching body:* comfort, relief, assuagement, solace, easement, freedom from pain. **2.** *The retired couple lived a life of ease:* comfort, leisure, relaxation, restfulness, rest, quiet, repose, serenity, tranquillity, security, peace of mind, freedom from worry; prosperity, luxury, luxuriousness, abundance, plenty, affluence. **3.** *Our team won the game with ease:* easiness, effortlessness, facility, readiness. **4.** *The hostess greeted her guests with ease:* naturalness, relaxed manner, unaffectedness, unconstraint, aplomb, poise, composure, confidence. *—v.* **5.** *The aspirin eased his headache. The pilot's calm manner eased the passengers' fears:* relieve, assuage, mitigate, abate, allay, alleviate, mollify, palliate, lessen, lighten, diminish; comfort, soothe, console, quiet, still, calm, pacify, disburden. **6.** *The movers eased the piano through the door:* move carefully, maneuver gently, handle with care, slip, slide. **—Ant.** 1 pain, discomfort, misery, irritation. 2 hardship, difficulty, travail, misery, poverty, worry, concern, distortion; turmoil, disturb-ance, agitation, annoyance, toil, hard work, sweat. 3 difficulty, effort, exertion, great pains; clumsiness, awkwardness. 4 stiffness, formality, affectedness, tension, constraint; embarrassment, discomposure, self-consciousness, awkwardness. 5 worsen, irritate, aggravate, discomfort, make uneasy, make nervous, make tense.

easily *adv.* **1.** *A good carpenter can fix the chair easily. The porpoise swam easily in the pool:* with ease, without difficulty, without trouble; with facility, handily, without a hitch; readily, effortlessly, facilely, lightly, freely, smoothly. **2.** *He is easily the school's best student:* beyond question, certainly, surely, far and away, by far, clearly, plainly, undoubtedly, undeniably, beyond doubt, beyond the shadow of a doubt. **—Ant.** 1 with difficulty; awkwardly, clumsily. 2 by a hair, by the skin of one's teeth; questionably, doubtfully.

East, the *n. More Americans visit Europe than the East:* the Orient, the Far East, Asia; the Near East; Eastern Hemisphere. **—Ant.** the West, Western Hemisphere, the Occident.

easy *adj.* **1.** *It was an easy job:* not difficult, not hard, easily done, effortless, simple, not burdensome, light, painless. **2.** *With no worries and plenty of servants, she's always led an easy life:* comfortable, untroubled, unworried, carefree; leisurely, relaxed, restful, serene, tranquil, peaceful, calm, composed, secure; wealthy, luxurious, well-to-do, affluent; *Slang* cushy. **3.** *His easy manner made him many friends:* relaxed, unaffected, natural, easygoing, informal, friendly, outgoing, unconstrained, pleasant, gracious, open, candid, frank, unforced. **4.** *The students considered Mrs. Smith an easy teacher:* not strict, lenient, permissive, not harsh, not oppressive, indulgent, accommodating, yielding, tractable, compliant, soft, gentle, benign, mild, docile; unsuspicious, gullible, overly trusting, naïve. *—adv.* **5.** *Mother won't rest easy until all the children are home:* easily, comfortably, without worry, without anxiety, without tension, serenely, peacefully, calmly, scarcely, leisurely. **—Ant.** 1 difficult, hard, arduous, laborious, burdensome, exhausting. 2 hard, difficult, uncomfortable, impoverished, poor; troubled, worried, anxious, insecure. 3 stiff, rigid, formal, unnatural, affected, forced, tense, anxious; *Slang* uptight; introverted, constrained, self-conscious, embarrassed, secretive, mysterious. 4 hard, strict, harsh, rigid, difficult, demanding, exacting, authoritarian, dictatorial, oppressive, unyielding; suspicious, guarded. 5 uncomfortably, anxiously.

easygoing *adj. Easygoing people seldom get ulcers:* calm, relaxed, carefree, happy-go-lucky, nonchalant, casual, offhand, unexcitable, insouciant, unruffled; even-tempered, mild-tempered, patient, unconcerned, unworried. **—Ant.** tense, worrying, compulsive, rigid, excitable, volatile, impatient, explosive; *Slang* uptight.

eat *v.* **1.** *Did you eat? The boys ate a hearty lunch:* feed, take nourishment, take sustenance, take a meal, break bread; *(variously)* breakfast, lunch, dine, sup; feast, gormandize; consume, devour, take, ingest, dispatch, bolt, gulp, wolf down, gobble, nibble. **2.** *The harsh chemical had eaten into the metal:* corrode, waste away,

dissolve, rust, wear away. **—Ant.** 1 fast, abstain; starve, go hungry, famish.

eatable *adj. Everything on the buffet was eatable:* edible, appetizing, palatable, nutritious, digestible, dietary.

eater *n. Her two helpings showed that she was a serious eater:* feeder, consumer, diner, diner-out, luncher, eater-out.

eating *n. Eating was his chief joy in life:* feeding, dining, feasting, gorging, snacking, munching.

eavesdrop *v. We eavesdropped on the conversation at the next table:* listen surreptitiously, bend an ear, listen in, spy, overhear, attend, hark-en, pry, snoop, tap, monitor, wiretap, *Slang* bug; prick up one's ears, cock one's ear, strain one's ears, listen with both ears.

ebb *v.* **1.** *A crab was left stranded on the beach when the tide ebbed:* recede, go out, flow away, flow back, fall away, move back, go down, retreat, withdraw. **2.** *The old man's strength began to ebb:* decline, fade away, abate, subside, dwindle, shrink, slacken, lessen, diminish, decrease, weaken, deteriorate, waste away, degenerate. **—Ant.** 1 flood, rise, swell, ascend, flow. 2 increase, grow, mount, build, climb, advance, progress, improve, wax, flourish.

ebullience *n. Her ebullience could not be denied:* enthusiasm, exuberance, animation, buoyancy, effervescence, effusiveness, elation, excitement, exhilaration, vitality, vivaciousness, vivacity, liveliness, high spirits. **—Ant.** apathy, lifelessness.

eccentric *adj.* **1.** *Comets move in eccentric orbits:* off center, not circular, parabolic, elliptical. **2.** *Wearing evening gowns all day is just part of her eccentric behavior:* peculiar, odd, strange, queer, weird, bizarre, unusual, extraordinary, unique, singular, uncommon, offbeat, outlandish, freakish; quaint, whimsical, capricious, quixotic, rash; curious, unconventional, unorthodox, erratic, irregular; *Slang* funny, nutty, kooky, freaky, sick; abnormal, aberrant, unnatural; psychotic, insane. *—n.* **3.** *The old eccentric left a fortune to his pet cat:* character, peculiar person, odd person, unconventional person, crackpot; *Slang* curio, oddball, screwball, kook, nut, flake, weirdo, weirdie. **—Ant.** 1 concentric; circular, round, centered. 2 common, ordinary, usual, conventional, customary, normal, natural, typical, regular. 3 normal person, conformist; *Slang* square.

eccentricity *n. Every year the rich old man added some new eccentricity to his behavior:* idiosyncrasy, aberration, abnormality, anomaly, bizarreness, capriciousness, freakishness, irregularity, nonconformity, outlandishness, peculiarity, queerness, singularity, strangeness, unconventionality, unusualness, waywardness, weirdness, oddity, oddness.

ecclesiastic *n.* **1.** *The dean of the divinity school has to be an ecclesiastic:* clergyman, cleric, churchman, minister, priest, rabbi, preacher, pastor, parson, chaplain, curate, prelate, rector, vicar, deacon. *—adj.* **2.** See ECCLESIASTICAL.

ecclesiastical also **ecclesiatic** adj. The bishop is responsible for all ecclesiastical matters in this diocese: religious, churchly, clerical, parochial, pastoral, episcopal. —**Ant.** secular, lay.

echelon n. Major decisions are made in the higher echelons of the company: level, rank, hierarchy, authority, position, grade, office; file, tier, line, rung.

echo n. **1.** The canyon is famous for producing echoes: reflection of sound, reverberation. —v. **2.** The cowbells echoed across the valley: resound, reverberate, ring. **3.** His speech echoed my own feelings: match, follow, parallel, reflect, mirror, duplicate, reproduce, take after, simulate, imitate, copy, repeat; ape, parrot. —**Ant.** 3 contradict, be at odds with, differ from, oppose, deny.

eclectic adj. The disc jockey played an eclectic selection of music: mixed, assorted, catholic, diverse, heterogeneous, multifarious, wide-ranging, varied, general.

eclipse n. **1.** A solar eclipse occurs when the moon passes between the sun and the earth: obscuration, darkening, veiling, cloaking, masking, covering, shadowing. **2.** The scandal caused an eclipse of the governor's reputation: diminishing, clouding, loss; blotting out, obliteration, overshadowing, annihilation, erasing, eradicating, wiping out. —v. **3.** Tomorrow the moon will partially eclipse the sun: cast a shadow upon, obscure, darken, cover, mask, cloak, conceal, hide. **4.** The author's latest book eclipses all his previous ones: overshadow, outshine, dim, surpass, outdo, exceed, excel, transcend, tower above, outrival; wipe out, obliterate, blot out. —**Ant.** 2 brightening, increase, enhancement. 3 illuminate, unveil, uncover, expose, display, show.

economic adj. **1.** Good transportation is needed for the economic growth of the country: material, monetary, productive, distributive. **2.** We bought a small car for economic reasons: monetary, pecuniary, financial, fiscal, budgetary. **3.** See ECONOMICAL.

economical adj. Economical shoppers wait for special sales: thrifty, economizing, economic, saving, frugal, prudent, careful, not wasteful; tightfisted, closefisted, parsimonious, penurious, niggardly, chary, sparing, scrimping, spartan; low-priced, cheap, reasonable, modest. —**Ant.** extravagant, spendthrift, uneconomical, wasteful, imprudent; generous, liberal, lavish; expensive, high-priced, exorbitant.

economize v. Their reduced income forced them to economize: cut expenses, cut costs, be economical, practice economy, avoid waste, avoid extravagance, be prudent, be frugal, be parsimonious, tighten one's belt, save, conserve, skimp, scrimp, stint, pinch, use sparingly, husband. —**Ant.** be extravagant, squander, waste, dissipate, misuse.

economy n. **1.** To run a large household one has to practice economy: thrifty management, thriftiness, thrift, frugality, prudence, providence. **2.** Inflation dealt a blow to the nation's econ-omy: material well-being, financial status, monetary resources, productive power, financial management, resources management. —**Ant.** 1 extravagance, lavishness, wastefulness, imprudence, improvidence.

ecstasy n. The saint was in a state of ecstasy: rapture, exaltation, bliss, elation, euphoria, fervor, intoxication, rhapsody, transport. —**Ant.** agony, affliction, distress, misery, torment.

ecstatic adj. The couple was ecstatic at the birth of a son: full of ecstasy, joyful, joyous, overjoyed, happy, glad, delighted, rapturous, enraptured, rapt, transported, entranced, blissful, elated, exalted, ebullient, enthusiastic, excited, beside oneself, delirious. —**Ant.** unhappy, wretched, miserable, sorrowful, grief-stricken, downhearted, joyless, saddened, displeased; unexcited, unenthusiastic, indifferent, blasé.

ecumenical adj. The ecumenical conference included representatives from all nations: universal, worldwide, global, international, catholic, cosmopolitan, general, comprehensive, all-inclusive, all-including, heavenwide, planetary, all-embracing, all-pervading; communalist, collectivist, communitarian, communist.

eddy n. The river is dangerous for swimmers because of its eddies: countercurrent, whirling current, whirlpool, maelstrom, vortex. —**Ant.** flow, drift, course, stream.

edge n. **1.** The river runs along the edge of the property: boundary line, line, bound, border, outline, contour, periphery, margin, rim, fringe, side, extremity, limit; dividing line, brink, verge, threshold. —v. **2.** The blouses were edged with ribbon: border, trim, rim, bind, fringe, outline, hem. **3.** Toward the end of the speech some members of the audience began to edge toward the door: steal, sneak, move sideways, sidle, inch, move little by little, advance slowly, creep, move with caution, move slyly, slink. —**Ant.** 1 center, interior, middle. 3 rush, run, sprint, bound, leap, speed, hasten.

edible adj. Are those mushrooms edible?: eatable, fit to be eaten, suitable for eating, comestible, consumable; nonpoisonous, safe for eating; digestible. —**Ant.** inedible, uneatable; poisonous, dangerous, indigestible.

edict n. The dictator's edict forbids speaking against the regime: decree, proclamation, pronouncement, pronunciamento, fiat, ukase, dictate, command, order, ordinance, mandate, dictum, injunction, manifesto, public notice; law, statute, regulation, prescript, enactment, ruling; bull.

edification n. Some religious instruction is necessary for the edification of the young: enlightenment, uplifting, moral improvement, advancement, elevation, teaching, education, educational benefit, indoctrination, instruction, guidance, direction; information.

edifice n. A 50-story edifice will be built on this lot: building, structure, construction.

edify v. The sermon failed to edify us: enlighten, educate, illuminate, improve, better, transform, uplift, raise, boost, lift, elevate.

edit *v. Edit the manuscript and get it ready for typesetting. The movie has been edited for television:* revise, rewrite, correct, redact, annotate, polish, rephrase, adapt, emend, abridge, blue-pencil, copy-edit, condense, touch up, clean up; censor, bowdlerize, expunge, expurgate.

edition *n. He collected first editions:* issue, number, impression, imprint, installment, printing, program, publication, reissue, reprint, version, volume.

editor *n. The writer thanked her editor in the acknowledgments:* checker, corrector, reviser.

educate *v. The public schools educate the greatest number of children:* teach, instruct, train, school, develop, tutor, coach; enlighten, inform, edify, civilize.

educated *adj. An educated public relies on books:* taught, instructed, coached, enlightened, erudite, experienced, finished, fitted, informed, knowledgeable, learned, lettered, literate, nurtured, polished, prepared, schooled, shaped, trained, tutored, well-informed, well-read, well-taught, well-versed. **—Ant.** uneducated, unschooled, ignorant, illiterate.

education *n. 1. The job demands someone with a college education:* schooling, training, instruction, teaching, learning, academic learning, study; information, knowledge, enlightenment, edification, cultivation, culture, mental development, scholarship, erudition. *2. You need six more courses in education to earn your teacher's certificate:* art of teaching, teaching, pedagogics, pedagogy, tutelage, didactics.

eerie *adj. Seeing the old graveyard gave us an eerie feeling:* inspiring fear, fearful, frightening, ominous, portentous, ghostly, spooky, creepy, weird, bizarre, mysterious, odd, queer, uncanny, strange, uneasy, apprehensive. **—Ant.** soothing, comforting, consoling, relaxing; calm, tranquil, easy.

efface *v. Time had effaced the ancient inscription:* wipe out, obliterate, eradicate, erase, delete, blot out, rub out, expunge, excise, cancel, extirpate; destroy, annihilate, raze. **—Ant.** restore, replace, reinstate, renew, revive; keep, retain.

effect *n. 1. The farmers felt the effect of the drought for years:* result, consequence, upshot, outcome, development, aftermath, aftereffect, outgrowth, sequel. *2. The plea for clemency had no effect on the judge:* influence, power, force, effectiveness, efficacy, impact, impression, weight, validity. *3. The law went into effect yesterday:* operation, action, execution, force, enforcement; function, accomplishment. *4. In effect, her insult meant the end of our friendship:* fact, actuality, reality, truth; significance, meaning, gist, general idea, purport, import, intent, intention; implication, essence, drift, tenor. *5. (usually plural) Before moving, the family sold as many of their effects as possible:* personal property, possessions, things, goods, movables, furniture, trappings; personal estate, commodities, holdings, assets, chattels. *—v. 6. The new hairdo effected a startling change in her appearance:* produce, accomplish, bring

about, make, cause, achieve, carry out, execute, perform, create, realize, attain. **—Ant.** 1 cause, occasion, inducement, incitement, foundation, source; beginning, origin. 6 prevent, hinder, deter, block, obviate, cancel out, frustrate.

effective *adj. 1. The business needs a more effective sales program:* effectual, efficacious, efficient, productive, useful, serviceable, capable, competent, successful, forceful, forcible, dynamic, powerful, strong, influential, potent. *2. The new interest rate becomes effective next month:* operative, in operation, active, activated, in effect, a reality; actual, real; current. *3. The book has a very effective closing chapter:* impressive, cogent, telling, convincing, compelling, persuasive; striking, forceful, powerful, successful, strong, incisive, moving, eloquent. **—Ant.** 1–3 ineffective. 1 ineffectual, inefficient, unproductive, bootless, inadequate, incompetent, useless, insufficient, impractical; forceless, powerless, impotent, weak. 2 inoperative, inactive. 3 weak, wishy-washy, tame, unimpressive, unconvincing; disappointing, unsatisfactory.

effectiveness *n. The new remedy had more effectiveness than the old one:* effect, efficiency, capability, clout, cogency, influence, performance, point, potency, power, punch, strength, success, weight, validity, vigor.

effectual *adj. New antipollution laws proved to be effectual:* effective, efficient, successful, productive, useful, potent. **—Ant.** ineffectual.

effeminate *adj. To everyone's surprise, the husky man had an effeminate voice:* womanish, unmanly, sissyish, sissified. **—Ant.** manly, manlike, masculine, virile.

effervescence *n. 1. The bottle of soda had lost its effervescence:* bubbliness, bubbling, bubbling up, fizz, fizzle, fizziness, froth, foaming. *2. The old lady was full of spirit and effervescence:* liveliness, ebullience, buoyancy, enthusiasm, life, vitality, vigor, vivacity, animation, spirit, zip, dash, gaiety. **—Ant.** 1 flatness. 2 despondency, tiredness, lethargy; seriousness, gravity, sedateness.

effervescent *adj. 1. Champagne and sparkling burgundy are effervescent wines:* bubbling, bubbly, fizzy, fizzing, sparkling, foaming. *2. The effervescent youngsters brought life to the staid resort:* lively, vivacious, ebullient, animated, exuberant, sparkling, bubbling, gay, merry, irrepressible. **—Ant.** 1 flat. 2 subdued, sedate, sober, grave, staid.

effete *adj. Over the years the nation's aristocracy had grown effete:* decadent, morally corrupt, depraved, degenerate; unproductive, unprolific, barren, sterile, enervated, worn-out, wasted, spent, exhausted. **—Ant.** healthy, wholesome, vital, productive, vigorous.

efficacious *adj. None of the prescriptions were efficacious:* effective, capable, successful, serviceable, effectual, efficient. **—Ant.** ineffective.

efficiency *n. When it was cleaned, the engine's efficiency doubled at once:* ability, effectiveness, productiveness, productivity, proficiency, prowess, adeptness, capability, capableness, competence, competency, efficacy, expertise, facility, faculty, force, influence, performance, potency, power, readiness, resourcefulness, strength.

efficient *adj. A lawyer needs an efficient secretary:* effective, productive, proficient, businesslike, workmanlike, capable, competent, skillful, apt, *Slang* crackerjack; work-saving, timesaving, unwasteful, effectual, efficacious. —**Ant.** inefficient, ineffectual, ineffective, unproductive, unworkmanlike, unbusinesslike; useless, wasteful.

effigy *n. The mob burned an effigy of the dictator:* representation, image, likeness; (*variously*) statue, dummy, doll, puppet, mannequin, puppet, marionette, straw man, scarecrow.

effort *n.* **1.** *The chair can be lifted with little effort:* exertion, power, force, energy, labor, work, industry, strain, struggle, toil, stress, pains, travail, trouble, elbow grease. **2.** *The factory made an effort to provide better working conditions:* endeavor, attempt, try.

effortless *adj. A good player can make tennis look effortless:* easy, uncomplicated, simple, facile, smooth, graceful, not difficult, painless. —**Ant.** hard, difficult, complicated, tough.

effrontery *n. What effrontery to barge in uninvited!:* shamelessness, brazenness, brashness, impertinence, insolence, impudence, presumption, arrogance, audacity, temerity, cheek, nerve, gall, brass, *Yiddish* chutzpah. —**Ant.** modesty, reserve, shyness, timidity, bashfulness; respect, diffidence.

effusion *n. The poet's latest effusion appalled me:* outpouring, pouring, outflow, diffusion, discharge, effluence, effluvium, emanation, emission, gush, ooze, verbosity, wordiness.

effusive *adj. The effusive praise embarrassed the chef:* lavish, unrestrained, profuse, gushy, gushing, unreserved, extravagant, expansive, copious, overflowing, free-flowing; ebullient, exuberant. —**Ant.** restrained, reserved, sparing, sparse.

ego *n. He was talented but had a big ego:* self, character, individuality, personality, self-admiration, self-pride.

egocentric *adj. Most young children have an egocentric view of the world:* self-centered, egomaniacal, egoistic, egotistical, self-absorbed, self-concerned, self-involved, self-obsessed, self-serving, narcissistic, megalomaniacal, self-seeking; wrapped up in oneself, stuck on oneself, be on an ego trip. —**Ant.** altruistic, unselfish, modest, liberal, generous.

egoism *n. Extreme egoism prevented him from thinking of anyone but himself:* self-centeredness, self-importance, self-absorption, self-love, narcissism, overweening pride, vanity. —**Ant.** humility, modesty; self-distrust, self-doubt.

egoist *n. The egoist believes that everyone is motivated by self-interest:* self-centered person, narcissist; selfish person.

egotism *n. Her letters are filled with overwhelming egotism:* self-admiration, self-praise, bragging, boastfulness, braggadocio, immodesty, conceit, vanity, vainglory, smugness, arro-

gance. —**Ant.** modesty, humility, bashfulness, self-criticism, self-abnegation.

egotist *n. I couldn't bear listening to that egotist talk about himself a minute longer!:* self-admirer, boaster, braggart, swaggerer, peacock, gascon, braggadocio; *Slang* blowhard.

egotistic also **egotistical** *adj. The spoiled child became an egotistic adult:* egocentric, egoistical, self-centred, self-absorbed, self-important, conceited, inflated, narcissistic, proud, puffed up, superior, *Informal* stuck-up.

egregious *adj. Introducing the speaker by the wrong name was an egregious mistake:* conspicuously bad, gross, flagrant, glaring, outrageous, shocking, notorious, extreme, monstrous, heinous, insufferable, intolerable, grievous. —**Ant.** tolerable, moderate, minor, unnoticeable.

egress *n.* **1.** *The thieves made their egress through a rear door:* exit, departure, withdrawal, escape; discharge, issue, outflow, seepage, leakage. **2.** *Each apartment must have an egress to a fire escape:* way out, passage out, outlet, exit; aperture, vent. —**Ant.** 1, 2 entrance.

eject *v.* **1.** *The volcano ejected lava and ashes:* discharge, emit, spew, spit out, spout, disgorge, exude, throw out, cast out. **2.** *The police ejected the demonstrators from the hall:* oust, evict, expel, remove, force out, turn out, kick out, drive out, *Slang* bounce; exile, banish, deport, dispossess. —**Ant.** 1 take in, inject; retain, withhold, keep, house, store. 2 move in, bring in, receive, admit, introduce.

elaborate *adj.* **1.** *The elaborate lighting system took months to install:* complex, involved, complicated, intricate; painstaking, labored. **2.** *The actresses were dressed in elaborate costumes:* fancy, elegant, ornate; ostentatious, showy, flashy, gaudy, garish, overdone. —*v.* **3.** *The reporter asked the general to elaborate on his statement:* expand, add details, particularize, specify, clarify, embellish. —**Ant.** 1, 2 simple, plain. 3 digest, condense, abbreviate, summarize, sum up.

élan *n. She skated with much élan:* vivacity, vivaciousness, animation, panache, ardor, brio, dash, esprit, flair, impetuosity, impetus, life, spirit, style, verve, vigor, vim, zest, zing.

elapse *v. Twenty years have elapsed since our first meeting:* pass, pass by, lapse, intervene, go by, slip by, slip away, glide by, roll by, slide by.

elastic *adj.* **1.** *The slacks have an elastic waistband:* stretchable, flexible, resilient, supple, rubbery, recoiling, springy, rebounding. **2.** *People with elastic dispositions recover quickly from disappointment:* flexible, supple, pliant, pliable, tolerant, complaisant, yielding, accommodating, adaptable, responsive; recuperative, readily recovering. —**Ant.** 1 stiff, inflexible, rigid. 2 inflexible, intolerant, unyielding, unaccommodating.

elate *v. News of victory elated them:* cheer, cheer up, excite, exhilarate, inspirit, exalt, lift, uplift. —**Ant.** depress, discourage.

elated *adj. The ski jumper was elated at setting*

a new record: overjoyed, jubilant, exalted, exhilarated, in high spirits, ecstatic, excited, animated; happy, delightful, joyful, joyous, pleased, glad, gleeful, rejoicing; proud, blissful, flushed with success. **—Ant.** dejected, depressed, dashed, dispirited, discouraged, blue, sad, unhappy; humbled, abashed, chagrined.

elation *n. Our elation could not be contained:* exhilaration, joy, joyousness, buoyancy, rapture, delight, ecstasy, enthusiasm, euphoria, excitement, exultation, glee, happiness, high spirits, intoxication, jubilation, transport, triumph.

elbow *v. He elbowed his way through the crowd:* jostle, bump, press, shoulder, shove, push, push around, push aside, hustle, nudge.

elder *adj.* **1.** *The elder son is in college, the younger in kindergarten:* older, firstborn, senior. **—n.** **2.** *Young people should have respect for their elders:* senior, older adult, *Informal* old-timer. **3.** *All elders of the church are members of the Council:* patriarch, presbyter, head; church dignitary, church official. **—Ant.** 1, 2 younger, junior. 3 neophyte; layman.

elderly *adj. The elderly man lived on a small pension:* old, aged, venerable; old, past one's prime; *Slang* over the hill. **—Ant.** young, youthful.

elect *v.* **1.** *The United States elected Teddy Roosevelt in 1901:* select by vote, vote into office, choose by ballot; choose, pick, select. **2.** *Gauguin elected painting as a career when he was in his thirties:* choose, select, decide on, opt for, adopt, resolve upon, fix upon, settle on, single out, pick out, espouse, embrace, take up, determine in favor of. **—Ant.** 1 defeat, vote down, vote out. 2 reject, repudiate, decline, abjure, renounce, dismiss, turn one's back on.

election *n.* **1.** *The municipal election is in November:* voting, choosing by vote, vote, balloting, poll. **2.** *The election to merge or not is up to the board of directors:* choice, selection, decision, option, alternative, determination, resolution, resolve.

elective *adj.* **1.** *Many people feel that judgeships should never be elective positions:* chosen by election, filled by election, passed by vote. **2.** *In college, English was a required course and psychology an elective course:* optional, not required, not obligatory, voluntary, selective, discretionary, open to choice. **—Ant.** 1 appointed, named; inherited. 2 required, obligatory, necessary.

electric also **electrical** *adj.* **1.** *I got an electric shock from the metal railing:* of electricity, for electricity, operated by electricity, power-driven. **2.** *The band played an electric rendition of the national anthem:* thrilling, stirring, exciting, dynamic, electrifying, spirited, stimulating, exalting, rousing, inspiring, soul-stirring, full of fire, galvanizing. **—Ant.** 2 dull, flat, unexciting, spiritless, unmoving, uninspiring, tedious, boring, colorless, insipid, ordinary, prosaic.

electricity *n. They got electricity in that town in 1923:* power, current, voltage, light, electromagnetism, ignition, magnetism, service, spark, tension.

electrify *v.* **1.** *A neon sign must be electrified:* supply with electricity, equip for the use of electricity; pass an electric current through, charge with electricity. **2.** *The trapeze artist's act electrified the audience:* thrill, stir, excite, rouse, stimulate, galvanize, quicken, animate, fire up; fascinate, amaze, astound, astonish, startle, stun, daze, dazzle, surprise, take one's breath away.

eleemosynary *adj. The orphanage is an eleemosynary institution:* charitable, existing on donations; altruistic, benevolent, beneficent, philanthropic, nonprofitmaking. **—Ant.** profitmaking, business.

elegance *n. The old mansion was furnished with great elegance:* luxuriousness, exquisiteness, sumptuousness, grandeur, richness; *Slang* class; taste, refinement, delicacy, grace, gracefulness; purity, balance, symmetry. **—Ant.** plainness; bad taste, crudeness.

elegant *adj.* **1.** *The table was covered with an elegant lace cloth:* exquisite, fine, grand, rich, sumptuous, luxurious, ornate, artistic; tasteful, delicate, refined, graceful, classic, symmetrical, well-proportioned; beautiful, handsome, lovely, attractive. **2.** *His mother is an elegant lady in her seventies:* refined, genteel, well-bred, polished, cultivated, dignified, gracious, charming, polite, courtly; *Slang* classy; fashionable, stylish, debonair, urbane, dapper. **—Ant.** 1 plain, inelegant; tasteless, tawdry, crude, coarse, rough; ugly, hideous, misshapen; clumsy. 2 unrefined, coarse, low-bred, boorish, undignified, rude, ungraceful; unfashionable.

elegy *n. The poet laureate composed an elegy upon the death of the king:* poem of lamentation, lament for the dead, melancholy poem, sad poem; requiem, funeral song, song of lamentation, melancholy piece of music. **—Ant.** paean, jubilee, hallelujah, anthem.

element *n.* **1.** *Hydrogen is the lightest of all elements:* basic chemical substance, uncompounded substance, simple body; *Classical legend* earth, air, fire, water. **2.** *Cells are the elements of the human body:* basic part, basic unit, constituent, component part, component, ingredient, building block, member, subdivision. **3.** usually **elements** *The elements of physics are difficult to grasp:* principles, rudiments, foundations, basic ideas, origins, essence, features, factors; *Informal* basics. **4.** *The artist was out of his element among the bankers and financiers:* natural habitat, native state, natural medium, environment; milieu. **—Ant.** 1 compound. 2 whole, entity, total, sum, system. 3 advanced concept; frills, supplement.

elementary *adj. The student took a course in elementary math:* basic, basal, fundamental, rudimentary, elemental; simple, plain, uncomplicated, easy, primitive, primary, original, first, undeveloped, crude. **—Ant.** advanced, higher, complex, complicated.

elevate *v.* **1.** *A special device elevated the stage for the finale:* raise, upraise, raise aloft, lift up, uplift, move up, hoist, heave, boost, place high, heighten. **2.** *The vice president was elevated to president of the company:* raise, move up, promote, advance; improve, better, refine, dignify, ennoble, enhance. **3.** *The good news elevated everyone's spirits:* elate, boost, lift, raise, uplift, cheer, exhilarate, animate, excite, inspire, perk up. **—Ant.** 1–3 lower. 1 lower, drop. 2 demote, degrade; *Slang* kick downstairs, bust; humble, demean. 3 depress, sadden, deject; deaden, numb.

elevated *adj.* **1.** *The elevated platform was reached by a ladder:* raised, raised up, aerial, high, high-rise, lifted, stately, tall, towering, uplifted, upraised **2.** *Her elevated address inspired us:* lofty, dignified, eloquent, stately, superb, upright, virtuous, upstanding. **—Ant.** modest, humble, lowly, simple.

elevation *n.* **1.** *The elevation of Mexico City is 7,500 feet:* height, altitude, height above sea level; prominence, lift. **2.** *We picnicked on an elevation overlooking the entire park:* elevated place, high place, rising ground. acclivity, ascent, rise, hill, mountain. **3.** *The sergeant's elevation to lieutenant was deserved:* rise, promotion, advancement, boost; improvement, bettering, refinement, cultivation. **—Ant.** 1 depth. 2 low ground, valley, depression, dip. 3 demotion.

elf *n.* *Elves inhabited the enchanted forest:* pixie, puck, brownie, fairy, sprite, leprechaun, troll, gnome; gremlin, goblin, hobgoblin.

elicit *v.* *The mayor's remark elicited a flood of letters:* bring forth, draw forth, draw out, call forth, evoke, extract, exact, extort, derive, wrest, fetch, cause, educe, bring to light. **—Ant.** repress, discourage.

eligible *adj.* *Only native-born citizens are eligible for the U.S. presidency:* qualified, able to be chosen, acceptable, authorized, appropriate, proper, suitable, fitting, applicable; desirable, worthwhile. **—Ant.** ineligible, unacceptable, inappropriate, unsuitable.

eliminate *v.* *Can the government eliminate poverty?:* get rid of, do away with, banish, abolish, eradicate, erase, exterminate, cut out, annihilate, weed out, stamp out, rub out; remove, throw out, exclude, reject, drop, delete, except, leave out, omit; eject, expel, cast out, exile, dismiss, oust. **—Ant.** obtain, get, invite, establish; add, include, inject, accept, admit, incorporate.

elite *n.* *Rhodes scholarships are given only to the elite among students:* best, choice, best group, choice class, select body, the pick, top, cream, flower; crème-de-la-crème, upper class, wealthy, society, high society, aristocracy, blue bloods, *French* haut monde; notables, celebrities, personages; *Slang* bigwigs, big shots. **—Ant.** worst, dregs, scum; lower class, working class; rabble, hoi polloi, riffraff.

elliptical *adj.* *The planet's orbit was elliptical:* egg-shaped, ellipsoidal, oblong, oval, ovoid.

elocution *n.* **1.** *The actor is famous for his elocution:* manner of speaking, articulation, pronunciation, intonation, diction. **2.** *If you want to be a politician, you should take a course in elocution:* public speaking, oratory, speech, diction, articulation, enunciation, pronunciation.

elongate *v.* *The metal bar could be elongated*

under intense heat: lengthen, extend, make longer, draw out, stretch out, prolong, protract. **—Ant.** shorten, curtail, contract, abbreviate, abridge.

eloquence *n.* *Even his first speech bore marks of eloquence:* fluency, expressiveness, force, grandiloquence, loquacity, mellifluousness, oration, passion, persuasiveness, rhetoric.

eloquent *adj.* *The defense lawyer made an eloquent plea for his client's acquittal:* persuasive, forceful, striking, stirring, moving, spirited, emphatic, articulate, passionate, impassioned, vivid, poetic. **—Ant.** routine, ordinary, commonplace, pedestrian, unimpressive, weak, dull, prosaic.

elucidate *v.* *The footnotes elucidated the text:* clarify, explain, explicate, make plain, clear up, throw light upon, illuminate, illustrate, describe, expound, detail, interpret, spell out, delineate, comment upon. **—Ant.** confuse, bewilder, obscure, becloud, muddle.

elude *v.* *The robber eluded his pursuers:* evade, avoid, escape, escape the notice of, dodge, circumvent, shun, fight shy of, keep clear of, slip by, get away from. **—Ant.** confront, meet, encounter; challenge.

elusive *adj.* **1.** *Antelope are among the most elusive animals to hunt:* hard to catch, evasive; tricky, slippery, shifty, wily, crafty, foxy. **2.** *Metaphysics is full of elusive concepts:* hard to grasp, difficult to comprehend; baffling, puzzling, hard to express.

emaciated *adj.* *The survivors were emaciated after weeks without food:* undernourished, starving, underfed, sickly, thin, wasted, gaunt, haggard, skinny, lean, scrawny, lank, wizened, skeletal, cadaverous. **—Ant.** robust, hardy, stout, fat, plump, chubby, beefy.

emanate *v.* *The brook emanates from an underground spring. The command emanated from headquarters:* flow, issue, come forth, come from, send forth, spring, well, exude, give off; originate, stem, proceed, rise. **—Ant.** end, terminate, culminate.

emanation *n.* *The emanation seemed to have a spectral origin:* issuing, arising, beginning, emergence, emission, flowing, outflow, radiation.

emancipate *v.* *Lincoln's Emancipation Proclamation emancipated slaves in the Confederate states:* free, set free, liberate, set at liberty, release, manumit; unfetter, unchain, unshackle. **—Ant.** enslave, subjugate; chain, manacle, shackle.

emasculate *v.* **1.** *The SPCA has recommended emasculating male cats to reduce the overpopulation:* castrate, geld, alter. **2.** *The law against speeding is emasculated by fining offenders only $5:* weaken, make less forceful, undermine, devitalize, soften, render impotent. **—Ant.** 2 strengthen, reinforce, vitalize.

embalm *v.* *They decided to embalm their St. Bernard:* preserve, conserve, enshrine, mummify.

embargo *n.* *Congress considered placing an embargo on foreign cars:* ban, prohibition, restriction, interdiction, injunction, stoppage, impediment, proscription, restraint of trade, shutdown, inhibition, quarantine, standstill.

embark v. **1.** *The last passengers embarked at noon:* board ship, go aboard; board, put on board, entrain, enplane. **2.** *He is about to embark on a new business venture:* start, begin, commence, undertake, launch, enter upon, set out. —**Ant.** 1 disembark, go ashore; land, arrive. 2 conclude, finish, end, terminate.

embarrass v. *The mother was embarrassed by her child's bad behavior:* make self-conscious, make ill at ease, mortify, shame, abash, chagrin, discomfit, disconcert, agitate, upset, distress, discompose, discountenance; fluster, rattle, confuse, faze, nonplus. —**Ant.** put at ease, be self-confident.

embarrassment n. **1.** *Losing her shoe on stage was a major embarrassment:* discomposure, chagrin, abashment, perplexity, confusion, discomfort, mortification. **2.** *Bankruptcy is one form of financial embarrassment:* trouble, annoyance, vexation, distress, harassment, hindrance. —**Ant.** 1 comfort, composure 2 encouragement.

embattled adj. *The embattled troops called for reinforcements:* engaged in battle, hardpressed, fighting, embroiled; equipped for battle, battle-ready, arrayed in battle order, prepared for battle, fortified.

embed v. *They embedded the switch in the paneling:* insert, implant, deposit, drive in, enclose, fix, inlay, install, lodge, plant, ram in, root, set, sink, stick in.

embellish v. *He embellished his signature with a series of curlicues:* enhance, elaborate, exaggerate, ornament, decorate, adorn, beautify, garnish, gild, color, embroider, dress up, fancy up, set off, *Slang* gussy up. —**Ant.** simplify, strip bare.

embellishment n. *The music required no further embellishment:* elaboration, adornment, beautification, decoration, decorating, embroidering, enhancement, enrichment, exaggeration, ornamentation, ostentation.

ember n. *Stir the embers and the fire may revive:* live coal, smoldering remains; cinder, ash, clinker, slag.

embezzle v. *The girl's guardian embezzled the money that had been willed to her:* misappropriate, defalcate; defraud, swindle, cheat; *Slang* fleece, filch, bilk, rook.

embezzlement n. *He was sentenced to six years in prison for embezzlement:* fraud, larceny, misappropriation, pilferage, pilfering, purloining, skimming, stealing, theft, thieving.

embitter v. *Being fired without cause is enough to embitter anyone:* envenom, make bitter, make resentful, make rancorous, rankle, sour, make cynical, make pessimistic. —**Ant.** comfort, please; gladden, delight.

emblem n. *The fleur-de-lis is the armorial emblem of the kings of France:* insignia, badge, symbol, hallmark, device, sign, design, representative figure, colophon.

embody v. **1.** *The sculpture embodies the art-*

ist's love of animals: express, represent, personify, exemplify, symbolize, realize, typify, manifest, substantiate. **2.** *The testimony is embodied in the court record:* include, incorporate, consolidate, collect, contain, organize, bring together, embrace; assimilate, blend, merge, fuse. —**Ant.** 1 disembody. 2 exclude, except; scatter, disperse.

embrace v. **1.** *The two sisters embraced warmly:* hug, clasp in the arms; grasp, clasp. **2.** *Iceland embraced Christianity in about the year 1000:* accept, espouse, adopt. **3.** *The study embraced all aspects of the housing problem:* include, involve, contain, embody, consolidate, comprise, incorporate, cover, encompass, comprehend. —**Ant.** 2 spurn, reject, refuse, decline, repudiate, scorn, disdain, rule out. 3 omit, delete, exclude, except; ignore, disregard.

embroider v. **1.** *The seamstress embroidered a monogram on the dress:* decorate with stitches, make of decorative stitches. **2.** *The old soldier embroidered his adventures more and more as years passed:* embellish, elaborate, adorn with fictitious details, exaggerate, fabricate, color, dress up; romanticize.

embroil v. *They became embroiled in office politics:* implicate, involve, incriminate, mire, trouble, ensnare, tangle, entangle, enmesh.

embryonic adj. *The class observed the frog in its embryonic state. The plan is still in an embryonic stage:* undeveloped, beginning, rudimentary, incipient, immature; unfinished, imperfect, incomplete, rough.

emend v. *The report must be emended by inserting the right figure:* correct, revise, rectify, improve, change.

emerge v. **1.** *Venus emerged from the sea:* rise, surface, issue, come up, come forth, come into view; discharge, emit, stream, gush, run, escape, flow, pour. **2.** *After long study, a possible solution emerged:* develop, arise, dawn, become apparent, surface, appear, become visible, loom, become manifest, come to light, come out of hiding, crop up, turn up. —**Ant.** 1 submerge, sink, fall, recede. 2 disappear, hide, fade away; retreat, depart, withdraw.

emergency n. *Sound the alarm only in case of emergency:* unforeseen danger, pressing necessity, contingency, exigency, crisis, urgency, pinch, predicament.

emergent adj. *The emergent economic powers made their presence felt:* emerging, appearing, budding, coming, developing, emanating, issuing forth, outgoing, rising, resulting.

emigrant n. *The emigrants scattered to many countries:* émigré, expatriate; *(loosely)* wanderer, wayfarer. —**Ant.** immigrant.

emigrate v. *The young British doctor emigrated to Canada:* move, migrate, remove; leave, depart, quit. —**Ant.** immigrate.

émigré n. *Vienna was full of émigrés after the 1956 Hungarian uprising:* exile, emigrant, expatriate, refugee, political refugee, expellee, evacuee, defector, immigrant, alien, fugitive, displaced person, DP.

eminence n. **1.** *Toscanini's eminence as a con-*

ductor is undisputed: high position, elevated rank, repute, public esteem, preeminence, importance, standing, prominence, distinction, note, notability, fame, celebrity, conspicuousness, reputation, glory, greatness, excellence. **2.** *The hotel was built on an eminence overlooking the sea:* elevation, high place, height, high point, prominence, promontory, hill, hillock, summit, rise, upland, ridge, mountain, peak, bluff, cliff, knoll, hummock. **—Ant.** 1 lowliness, unimportance, lack of distinction; disrepute, dishonor, infamy, notoriety. 2 lowland, declivity, valley.

eminent *adj.* **1.** *Churchill was one of the world's most eminent statesmen:* illustrious, preeminent, high-ranking, top, important, elevated, esteemed, distinguished, famous, renowned, prominent, exalted, laureate, celebrated, well-known, outstanding, noted, notable, signal, great, glorious, grand, imposing, paramount. **2.** *The explosive situation was handled with eminent restraint:* extraordinary, remarkable, outstanding, notable, noted, noteworthy, unusual, utmost, memorable. **—Ant.** 1 lowly, unimportant, undistinguished; little-known, unknown; infamous, notorious. 2 unremarkable, ordinary; inconspicuous.

eminently *adv.* *She was eminently qualified for the post:* greatly, highly, notably, conspicuously, exceedingly, exceptionally, extremely, outstandingly, prominently, remarkably, strikingly, suitably, surpassingly.

emissary *n.* *The prime minister met with the queen's emissary:* delegate, ambassador, envoy, legate, representative, deputy, agent; go-between, messenger, courier, herald.

emission *n.* **1.** *All cars must have devices to reduce exhaust emissions:* discharge, ejection, emanation, voidance, expulsion, extrusion, excretion; (*variously*) smoke, fumes, pollutant, impurity, waste. **2.** *The emission of radio signals was interrupted by a power failure:* sending out, emitting, transmission, issuance; throwing out, ejection, expulsion. **—Ant.** 2 injection, reception.

emit *v.* *The old radiator emits little warmth:* send out, give forth, give, discharge, issue, secrete, transmit, pour forth, shed, dispatch, expel, excrete, throw out, cast out, vent, beam. **—Ant.** inject; receive, retain, withhold.

emollient *adj.* **1.** *The lotion had an emollient effect on my sunburn:* soothing, relieving, palliative, alleviative, healing, restorative, easeful, allaying, assuasive, lenitive, calming, relaxing, balmy. **—n. 2.** *The doctor prescribed an emollient for the skin rash:* balm, salve, lotion, lenitive, ointment, lubricant, oil. **—Ant.** 1 irritating, painful, exacerbating, chafing, aggravating.

emotion *n.* **1.** *The candidate addressed the crowd with emotion:* strong feeling, fullness of heart, excitement, agitation, passion, sentiment, zeal, ardor, vehemence, fervor, heat, warmth. **2.** *Jealousy can be a destructive emotion:* concern, strong feeling; (*variously*) love, hate, anger, jealousy, sorrow, sadness, fear, despair, happiness,

satisfaction, pride. **—Ant.** 1 indifference, impassiveness, apathy.

emotional *adj.* **1.** *Weddings are emotional occasions:* appealing to the emotions, sentimental, warm, moving, touching, stirring, soul-stirring, heartwarming, thrilling, heart-rending, *Slang* tear-jerking. **2.** *Adolescents are often emotional:* easily affected by emotion, temperamental, hypersensitive, vulnerable, responsive, demonstrative, sentimental; passionate, impassioned, fervent, fiery, ardent, zealous, enthusiastic, impetuous; excitable, hysterical, wrought-up, high-strung. **—Ant.** 1, 2 unemotional, cold, dull. 2 insensitive, unfeeling, indifferent, apathetic, dispassionate, undemonstrative, unsentimental, unresponsive, unexcitable.

emotionalism *n.* *The lawyer's emotionalism embarrassed the jurors:* show of emotion, demonstrativeness, sentimentality, mawkishness, gushiness, hysteria, hysterics; theatrics, melodramatics, melodrama. **—Ant.** impassivity, impassiveness, detachment, matter-of-factness.

emotionless *adj.* *His emotionless response surprised us:* unemotional, blank, chill, cold, cold-blooded, cool, detached, dispassionate, distant, frigid, glacial, impassive, impersonal, indifferent, matter-of-fact, undemonstrative, unfeeling, unimpassioned, remote, reserved, poker-faced.

empathy *n.* *She listened to his complaints with great empathy:* compassion, understanding, responsiveness, concern, caring, sensitivity, identification, involvement, sharing, fellow feeling, perceptiveness, sympathy. **—Ant.** callousness, indifference.

emperor, Fem. **empress** *n.* *The emperor of Japan is venerated by his subjects:* ruler, monarch, sovereign; (*variously*) caesar, czar, mikado, sultan, kaiser, shah; (*fem.*) czarina, sultana, dowager empress.

emphasis *n.* **1.** *The emphasis of the new plan must be on cutting costs:* stress, prominent point, focal point, feature, weight, underscoring. **2.** *In the word "pillow" the emphasis is on the first syllable:* stress, accent, accentuation.

emphasize *v.* *The biography emphasized the general's military years:* stress, accent, feature, dwell on, press home, iterate, underscore, underline, punctuate, accentuate, point up, bring into relief. **—Ant.** deemphasize, play down, underplay; equalize, balance.

emphatic *adj.* **1.** *The defendant made an emphatic denial of the charges:* strong, vigorous, forceful, assertive, decisive, flat, unqualified, absolute, unequivocal, unyielding, insistent, unwavering, categorical. **2.** *The writer's second novel was an emphatic success:* definite, unmistakable, undeniable, striking, certain, distinct, decided, telling, momentous, marked, express, pronounced, conspicuous, significant. **—Ant.** 1 hesitant, unsure, uncertain, weak, wishy-washy, irresolute, qualified, equivocal. 2 uncertain, indistinct, insignificant, unremarkable, commonplace, average.

empire *n.* *India was once part of the British*

Empire: sovereignty, rule, dominion, realm, domain, commonwealth, imperium.

empirical *adj. The old sailor had never studied navigation, but he had a good empirical knowledge of it:* practical, experiential, pragmatic; experimental, firsthand. **—Ant.** theoretical, secondhand.

employ *v.* **1.** *The mill employs a thousand workers:* hire, use, engage, commission, retain, take on. **2.** *Grandmother employs her time crocheting:* use, utilize, make use of, put to use, apply, engage, keep busy, occupy, devote, exercise. **—n. 3.** *The geologist is in the employ of a large oil company:* service, employment; hire, retainership. **—Ant.** 1 discharge, dismiss, fire, let go, *Slang* can, sack. 2 waste, fritter away; misuse, misapply.

employed *adj. He was employed as a truck driver:* working, active, busy, engaged, hired, in place, laboring, occupied, on duty, at work. **—Ant.** jobless, idle, laid off, out of work, unemployed.

employee *n. The management has authorized wage increases for all employees:* worker, wage earner, job holder, staff member, member; underling, hireling. **—Ant.** employer, boss.

employer *n. The secretary worked for the same employer for 20 years:* boss; proprietor, business owner; business, firm, company, establishment, organization, outfit. **—Ant.** employee, worker, wage earner, job holder, staff member; underling, hireling.

employment *n.* **1.** *The student was looking for summer employment:* work, job, employ, service; occupation, business, profession, vocation, calling, pursuit, trade, field, line; task, chore, preoccupation. **2.** *The scheme requires the employment of great ingenuity:* utilization, exertion, using, use, employing, application, exercise, service, engagement. **—Ant.** 1 unemployment, leisure, inactivity; avocation, hobby, sideline. 2 disuse, disregard, neglect, forgetting, putting aside.

emporium *n. If the emporium doesn't carry the item, no one will:* large store, department store, general store, store; market, bazaar, warehouse.

empower *v. French law empowers the police to search any suspicious person:* authorize, sanction, invest, vest, license, endow; permit, allow, enable; commission, delegate. **—Ant.** restrain, disbar, divest of power; disallow, forbid, enjoin.

emptiness *n. So much emptiness demanded to be filled:* vacuum, vacancy, vacuity, void, bareness, blankness, chasm, desolation, waste, hollowness.

empty *adj.* **1.** *Our voices echoed in the empty house:* vacant, unoccupied, uninhabited, bare, void. **2.** *He didn't want to retire and lead an empty life:* aimless, meaningless, without substance, vacuous, insignificant, worthless, purposeless, futile, unfulfilled, idle, hollow; shallow, banal, trivial, inane, insipid, frivolous. **—v. 3.** *Empty the glass before putting it in the dishwasher. The Mississippi empties into the Gulf of Mexico:* pour out, drain, dump, void, evacuate; discharge, flow, debouch. **—Ant.** 1 full,

stuffed, crammed, packed, jammed; occupied, inhabited. 2 meaningful, significant, substantial, useful, valuable, worthwhile, purposeful, fulfilled, busy, full, rich, vital, interesting, serious. 3 fill, pack, put in, stuff, cram, jam; receive.

emulate *v. Politicians would do well to emulate Abraham Lincoln:* take as a model, follow the example of, pattern oneself after, follow, copy, imitate; try to equal, rival; mimic, ape.

emulation *n. The computer software was plainly an emulation of its main rival:* imitation, impersonation, aping, copying, echoing.

enable *v. A college education enables a person to get a better job:* make able, empower, qualify, capacitate, make possible for, allow, permit; aid, assist, support, facilitate, benefit. **—Ant.** prevent, bar, disqualify, prohibit, incapacitate; hinder, thwart, frustrate, block, keep back, hold back.

enact *v. The Congress enacted the new farm bill:* pass into law, pass, legislate, vote to accept, authorize, ratify; institute, proclaim, decree; sanction, approve. **—Ant.** reject, turn down, vote down, fail to pass, veto; abolish, annul, repeal, rescind, cancel.

enactment *n. The enactment of the trial will be staged tomorrow:* performance, acting, depiction, impersonation, personification, playacting, playing, portrayal, representation, execution.

enamor *v. John is enamored of Mary. Most visitors to London are enamored with the city:* inflame with love, affect with fondness, enrapture, infatuate, allure, draw to, attach; enthrall, charm, enchant, entrance, captivate, bewitch, fascinate, excite, take a fancy to. **—Ant.** repel, repulse, revolt, disgust, disenchant, put off, *Slang* turn off.

enamored *adj. He was enamored of his leading lady:* in love, loving, amorous, attracted, besotted, bewitched, captivated, enchanted, enraptured, entranced, fond, infatuated, smitten, taken with.

enchant *v.* **1.** *The sorcerer enchanted the beautiful princess:* cast a spell over, place under a spell, bewitch, charm; hypnotize, mesmerize. **2.** *The family was enchanted with the cute little girl:* charm, delight, entrance, enthrall, captivate, enrapture, fascinate, bewitch, transport. **—Ant.** 1 release, free, exorcise. 2 repel, repulse, revolt, disgust, sicken, *Slang* turn off.

enchanting *adj. She was an enchanting sight in her ball gown:* enthralling, appealing, bewitching, alluring, appealing, beguiling, captivating, charming, entrancing, fascinating, glamorous.

enchantress *n.* **1.** *The enchantress turned the prince into a frog:* sorceress, witch, vampire, siren. **2.** *Men flocked around the beautiful enchantress:* seductress, temptress, vamp, charmer, femme fatale.

encircle *v. A heavy wire fence encircles the compound:* circle, ring, surround, wreathe, girdle, gird, circumscribe, encompass; enclose, fence, wall, hem in.

enclose or **inclose** *v.* **1.** *A high stone wall enclosed the estate:* surround, ring, circle, encircle, girdle, encompass, circumscribe, fence in, wall in, close in. **2.** *Please enclose a check with your order:* include, insert, send along, put in the same envelope, put in the same package.

encompass *v.* **1.** *High mountains completely encompass the little ski resort:* surround, circumscribe, encircle, circle, enclose, ring, girdle, fence in, wall in, hem in. **2.** *The encyclopedia encompasses scientific, historical, and cultural information:* include, cover, embrace, contain, comprise, incorporate, embody, hold, involve, take in, touch on. **—Ant.** 2 exclude, leave out, omit; ignore.

encore *n.* *The audience insisted on an encore:* reappearance, repeat, repeat performance, repetition, response, return.

encounter *v.* **1.** *She encountered an old friend on the street. The plane encountered a storm over the Rockies:* meet, meet with, chance upon; sustain, confront, run into, experience, come upon; endure, undergo, suffer. **2.** *Napoleon encountered Wellington in the Battle of Waterloo:* clash with, meet and fight, do battle with, contend against, confront, engage in combat, grapple with, skirmish with, measure swords with, face, come face to face with. *—n.* **3.** *Many men were lost in the encounter:* battle, combat, fight, confrontation, hostile meeting, bout, affray, engagement, fracas, skirmish, clash, brush. **—Ant.** 1 escape, shun, miss, elude, avoid. 3 retreat, withdrawal.

encourage *v.* **1.** *Letters of support encouraged the mayor to run again:* inspire, give confidence to, inspirit, embolden, induce, give hope to, hearten, rally, egg on; spur, exhort, impel, sway; reassure, hearten, cheer. **2.** *Good health encourages clear thinking:* foster, promote, favor, advance, further, boost, forward, assist, help, prompt, aid. **—Ant.** 1 discourage, dissuade, deter, depress, deject, dishearten, dispirit. 2 retard, hinder, prevent, inhibit, hamper.

encouragement *n.* *A little encouragement is all some people need to keep doing a good job:* encouraging, approbation, praise, backing, support, reinforcement, reassurance; boost, lift, *Slang* shot in the arm. **—Ant.** discouragement, criticism; disparagement, ridicule.

encroach *v.* *The neighbor's hedge is encroaching on our property. Wiretapping encroaches on a person's right to privacy:* intrude, infringe, invade, impinge, make inroads on, overrun, overstep, violate, break into, trespass, transgress, interfere. **—Ant.** respect, honor, recognize, observe; safeguard, protect.

encumber *v.* *The hiker was encumbered with a heavy pack:* burden, weigh down, load, load down, lade, saddle; tax, inconvenience, hinder, handicap, impede, slow down, obstruct. **—Ant.** unload, unburden, unencumber.

encyclopedic *adj.* *In matters of general science, his knowledge is encyclopedic:* comprehensive, all-encompassing, exhaustive, universal, wide-ranging, broad, scholarly, erudite.

end *n.* **1.** *Put the platter at the end of the table. The school is at the south end of town:* extremity, terminus; edge, limit, boundary, border. **2.** *We stayed at the concert to the very end:* con-

clusion, ending, termination, close, finish, expiration, cessation, completion, finale, windup, culmination, consummation, denouement. **3.** *What will be the end of their constant feuding?:* outcome, upshot, result, consequence, effect, issue, fulfillment, settlement. **4.** *He used unscrupulous means to achieve his end:* aim, goal, purpose, object, objective, result, intention, design. **5.** *Another world war could mean the end of civilization. He met an untimely end:* extinction, extermination, destruction, annihilation, termination, ruin; death, demise. **6.** *This end of cloth is enough for a dress:* remnant, leftover, fragment, scrap. *—v.* **7.** *The book ends on page 364. The chairman ended the meeting at ten o'clock:* conclude, halt, draw to a close, terminate, cease, finish, stop, leave off, put an end to, run out, wind up, close, bring down the curtain. **8.** *The Spanish Conquistadors ended the Aztec civilization:* destroy, eradicate, kill, annihilate, exterminate, extinguish, finish off. **—Ant.** 1–3, 5 beginning, start, commencement, inauguration; inception, birth. 7, 8 begin, start, commence.

endanger *v.* *The spread of urban areas endangers wildlife:* threaten, put in danger, imperil, jeopardize, hazard, risk, expose, compromise. **—Ant.** protect, safeguard, preserve, defend, shield, save.

endear *v.* *Smoking a cigar in an elevator won't endear you to the other passengers:* make beloved, make dear; create goodwill among, ingratiate with, make attractive. **—Ant.** alienate, estrange.

endearment *n.* *His letters to his fiancée were full of endearments:* loving word, fond utterance, sweet talk; pet name, affectionate term. **—Ant.** curse, malediction.

endeavor *v.* **1.** *We should all endeavor to be more considerate of others:* try, attempt, make an effort, strive, work at, undertake, take pains, labor, struggle, do one's best; aspire, aim, seek, *—n.* **2.** *The boy made an honest endeavor to do the work right:* attempt, aim, effort, try, essay, exertion, striving, struggle. **3.** *Portrait painting has been his lifelong endeavor:* undertaking, enterprise, work, preoccupation, interest; occupation, vocation, job, career. **—Ant.** 1 neglect, ignore, pass up, overlook; abandon, dismiss.

ending *n.* *The movie has a happy ending:* conclusion, end, close, finish, windup, finale, termination, cessation, expiration, completion, culmination, consummation. **—Ant.** beginning, start, opening, inception.

endless *adj.* *Endless desert stretched before us. Their endless bickering got on everyone's nerves:* without end, unending, uninterrupted, unbroken, interminable, boundless, infinite, measureless, unlimited; perpetual, everlasting, never-ending, eternal, constant, continuous, continual, persistent. **—Ant.** finite, limited, bounded, circumscribed; temporary, short-lived, brief, passing, transitory, transient.

endorse or **indorse** *v.* **1.** *I find it impossible to endorse a candidate with a record like his:* support, back, champion, approve, sanction, advocate, recommend, vouch for, subscribe to, stand behind, affirm, ratify, OK, second, lend one's name to. **2.** *Endorse the check on the back:* sign, countersign; authorize, validate, certify. —**Ant.** 1 disapprove, denounce, condemn, discredit, disavow, reject, repudiate, spurn.

endow *v.* **1.** *Grandfather endowed each child with a trust fund:* bestow a fund upon, provide with an income; bequeath, settle on, leave, will; award, confer, grant, bestow. **2.** *Nature endowed her with extraordinary beauty:* supply, equip, provide, accord, invest, bestow, grant, furnish; bless, grace, favor. —**Ant.** 2 divest, deprive, take.

endowment *n.* **1.** *The tycoon left an endowment of a million dollars to each son:* legacy, bequest, bestowed fund, willed income; benefaction, grant, gift, donation, award. **2.** *A natural bent for music is just one of her endowments:* natural gift, talent, flair, ability, capability, aptitude, faculty, attribute.

endurance *n.* **1.** *Sailing the Atlantic single-handed requires great endurance:* stamina, hardihood, durability, strength; fortitude, perseverance, tenacity, tenaciousness, persistence, staying power, resolution, stick-to-itiveness. **2.** *The old building has remarkable endurance:* permanence, durableness; immutability, changelessness, stability. —**Ant.** 1, 2 frailty, weakness.

endure *v.* **1.** *The company has endured tremendous losses:* sustain, bear, withstand, stand, experience, undergo, cope with, go through, weather, suffer, bear up under, brave; tolerate, countenance, brook. **2.** *They vowed their love would endure forever:* last, persist, prevail, live, live on, continue, remain. —**Ant.** 1 escape, evade, avoid, bypass, sidestep; lose to, be defeated by, surrender to. 2 perish, die, fail, succumb, subside, crumble, decay, end, wither away.

enemy *n.* **1.** *His thoughtless behavior earned him many enemies:* antagonist, detractor, opponent, adversary, nemesis, foe, rival, competitor. **2.** *The enemy was advancing toward the city:* opposing military force, armed foe; hostile nation, belligerent state; assailant, attacker. —**Ant.** 1 friend, supporter, well-wisher. 2 ally, confederate.

energetic *adj.* *I never saw such an energetic child. The old lady has an energetic mind:* full of energy, active, vigorous, lively, peppy, zippy, animated, restless, spirited; forceful, dynamic, brisk, robust, go-getting, high-powered, hardworking, industrious; alert, enthusiastic, quick-witted. —**Ant.** enervated, languid, inactive, lethargic, sluggish, listless; phlegmatic.

energize *v.* *Not even a round of aerobics could energize us:* electrify, activate, animate, empower, enable, enliven, excite, fortify, inspirit, invigorate, liven up, motivate, prime, pump up, quicken, stimulate, strengthen, trigger, vitalize *Informal* pep up, turn on.

energy *n.* **1.** *The new power plant supplies energy for the entire city:* power, force; (*variously*) hydroelectric power, electric power, atomic energy, nuclear energy. **2.** *Even after hours of work his energy never seems to give out:* vitality, vim, vigor, verve, zip, élan, pep, go, vivacity, dynamism, liveliness, animation, zest, zeal, enterprise, drive, hustle. —**Ant.** 2 inertia, lassitude, listlessness, sluggishness.

enervate *v.* *The long march in the sun enervated the soldiers:* exhaust, weary, weaken, debilitate, devitalize, enfeeble, disable, sap one's energy, deplete, wash out, fatigue, tire, prostrate, *Slang* bush, fag, tucker. —**Ant.** energize, invigorate, strengthen, vitalize, stimulate, quicken.

enervated *adj.* *The enervated team could barely lift a finger:* debilitated, tired, devitalized, enfeebled, exhausted, fatigued, feeble, incapacitated, limp, listless, prostrated, rundown, sapped, spent, spiritless, undermined, unnerved, weak, weakened, worn out *Informal* done in, washed out.

enfeeble *v.* *Lack of fresh air and exercise enfeebled us:* devitalize, attenuate, debilitate, deplete, diminish, exhaust, fatigue, incapacitate, sap, undermine, weaken, wear out.

enfold *v.* *She enfolded him in her arms:* encompass, envelope, enclose, surround, clasp, clasp, clinch, cover, drape, embrace, encase, enwrap, hold, hug, enshroud, shroud, swathe, wrap up.

enforce *v.* *The police must enforce the law:* carry out, administer, keep in force, compel obedience to, insist on, impose, implement, execute, apply, exact; support, defend. —**Ant.** ignore, disregard; waive, forgo.

enforcement *n.* *Law enforcement was his main concern:* enforcing, execution, administration, application, carrying out, fortifying, strengthening.

engage *v.* **1.** *The children are engaged in a great many outdoor activities. When otherwise unoccupied, the rancher engaged in hunting down coyotes:* involve, occupy, engross, absorb; take part, participate, partake, busy oneself; undertake, set about, enter into, embark on. **2.** *The house was so large it was necessary to engage an extra maid:* employ, hire, take on, retain, secure, take into service, commission. **3.** *The couple married after being engaged a month:* betroth, affiance, pledge, promise. **4.** *The battleship engaged the enemy at the mouth of the harbor:* begin conflict with, encounter in battle, fight with, give battle to, war with, combat. —**Ant.** 2 fire, lay off, let go, *Slang* can. 4 flee, retreat, withdraw.

engagement *n.* **1.** *Do you have a luncheon engagement?:* appointment, date, commitment, meeting, arrangement; obligation, duty. **2.** *The couple announced their engagement at the party:* betrothal, troth, banns, plighted faith, affiancing. **3.** *The singer had a brief engagement at a New York nightclub:* employment, job, position, situation, *Slang* gig; post, berth, billet. **4.** *The general had won three engagements with the enemy:* battle, fight, encounter, combat, conflict, action, skirmish, brush, bout, contest, scuffle, fray.

engaging adj. It's hard to scold a child who has such an engaging manner: winning, attractive, disarming, winsome, enchanting, charming, fetching, captivating, pleasing, likable, lovable, agreeable, appealing, ingratiating. —**Ant.** offensive, disagreeable, displeasing, unattractive, unpleasant, unlikable, unlovable; repulsive, repellent.

engender v. Respect can engender love: give rise to, cause, bring about, beget, breed, generate, produce, occasion, precipitate. —**Ant.** kill, end, crush.

engine n. The engine started after several tries: mechanism, agent, apparatus, appliance, contrivance, cylinder, device, diesel, dynamo, generator, instrument, means, motor, piston, powerhouse, turbine, power plant, power train.

engineer v. She managed to engineer his dismissal: contrive, angle, arrange, cause, concoct, control, create, devise, direct, effect, encompass, finagle, machinate, manage, maneuver, manipulate, mastermind, negotiate, operate, originate, plan, put over, put through, rig, scheme, superintend.

engrave v. He engraved the bracelet for her: cut, bite, burn, carve, chisel, embed, etch, impress, inscribe.

engross v. I was completely engrossed in the book when the phone rang: absorb, occupy, preoccupy, involve, immerse, engage, hold, arrest, take up. —**Ant.** bore, tire, weary; vex, annoy, irritate.

engrossed adj. He was engrossed in organizing his stamp collection: immersed, absorbed, assiduous, attentive, busy, captivated, caught up, consumed, diligent, engaged, enthralled, fascinated, gripped, occupied, preoccupied, rapt, Informal into, hooked.

engrossing adj. If anything, we found the engrossing documentary too short: compelling, absorbing, all-consuming, captivating, consuming, controlling, enthralling, exciting, fascinating, gripping, monopolizing, obsessing, preoccupying, provoking, riveting.

engulf v. The floodwaters engulfed the entire village: swallow up, envelop, bury, swamp, overrun, inundate, submerge, immerse, deluge.

enhance v. The splendid dress enhanced her beauty: intensify, heighten, magnify, make more attractive, make more appealing; elevate, lift, raise, boost; redouble, embellish, augment, add to, complement. —**Ant.** diminish, reduce, lessen, decrease, minimize, depreciate, detract from.

enigma n. Just why he suddenly switched political parties remains an enigma: puzzle, riddle, question, perplexity, conundrum, mystery, secret, hidden meaning.

enigmatic also **enigmatical** adj. The Mona Lisa has an enigmatic smile: mysterious, secretive, puzzling, indecipherable, unfathomable, cryptic, baffling, perplexing, inscrutable, elusive, ambiguous, equivocal, paradoxical. —**Ant.** candid, frank, open, straightforward, selfexplanatory, intelligible, lucid; explicit, expressive, express, definite, clear, manifest.

enjoin v. **1.** The fire fighters enjoined the onlookers to stand clear: advise, counsel, warn, admonish, command, bid, charge, direct, instruct, call upon; beg, entreat, ask, urge. **2.** The judge enjoined the strikers from picketing inside company property: prohibit, forbid, restrain, place an injunction on, restrict, ban, bar, proscribe, interdict. —**Ant.** 2 permit, allow, let.

enjoy v. **1.** The audience enjoyed the new opera: like, appreciate, admire, think well of, take pleas-ure in, be pleased with, rejoice in, delight in, fancy, relish; savor; Slang eat up, get a kick out of. **2.** Americans enjoy some of the world's most beautiful scenery: have the benefit of, be blessed with, have, possess, own. —**Ant.** 1 dislike, hate, detest, loathe, abhor, abominate, despise.

enjoyable adj. Was it an enjoyable movie? We all had an enjoyable evening: pleasant, pleasing, providing enjoyment, pleasurable, agreeable, fun-filled, delightful, satisfying, rewarding, gratifying. —**Ant.** unpleasant, disagreeable, unenjoyable, unpleasurable, unsatisfying; hateful, detestable, loathsome, abominable, despicable.

enjoyment n. **1.** The guests sipped the fine wine with enjoyment: pleasure, delight, satisfaction, happiness, gratification, joy, zest, gusto, relish; fun, entertainment, amusement, diversion, recreation, good time. **2.** Every citizen is guaranteed the enjoyment of life, liberty, and the pursuit of happiness: benefit, advantage, blessing, privilege, right, prerogative, exercise, possession. —**Ant.** 1 displeasure, dissatisfaction, detestation, loathing, abhorrence, aversion, repugnance, hatred, dislike. 2 disadvantage, handicap.

enlarge v. **1.** The magnifying glass enlarges the image 50 times. The hotel is being enlarged to accommodate more guests: make larger, increase, expand, swell, extend, inflate; augment, add to, multiply; magnify, amplify, lengthen, widen, broaden, elongate; become bigger, grow, develop. **2.** In the discussion period the speaker enlarged on his opening statement: expand, amplify, elaborate, expound, expatiate, discourse. —**Ant.** 1 decrease, shorten, curtail, shrink, contract, reduce, diminish, lessen. 2 condense, abridge, abbreviate, narrow.

enlighten v. The tour of our country enlightened the foreign visitors on the workings of democracy: inform, instruct, educate, edify, clarify, make aware, illuminate, cause to understand, apprise, advise; civilize, sophisticate, Slang wise up. —**Ant.** mystify, perplex, puzzle, bewilder, mislead, confound, confuse.

enlightened adj. The enlightened department head asked for our views: aware, broad-minded, civilized, cultivated, educated, informed, instructed, knowledgeable, learned, liberal, literate, open-minded, reasonable, refined, sophisticated. —**Ant.** unenlightened, ignorant, narrowminded, unaware, uneducated.

enlightenment n. She was unable to give us any more enlightenment on the problem: awareness, broad-mindedness, comprehension, cultivation, edification, education, insight, knowledge, learning, literacy, open-mindedness, sophistication, teaching, understanding, wisdom.

enlist v. **1.** *Were you drafted into the army or did you enlist?:* join, join up, enroll, register, sign up, volunteer. **2.** *The mayor tried to enlist every citizen in the clean-up campaign:* recruit, engage, obtain, secure, procure, gain the assistance of. **—Ant.** 1 withdraw, resign, retire, leave. 2 reject, refuse, dismiss.

enliven v. *His jokes enlivened the party:* make lively, animate, pep up, cheer up, brighten, excite, quicken, vitalize, vivify, wake up, fire; renew, rejuvenate. **—Ant.** dampen, chill, cast a pall over, deaden, make dull, make boring, subdue, depress, weigh down.

en masse adv. *The audience booed and then walked out en masse:* in a group, in a body, together, all together, as a whole, as a group. **—Ant.** individually, separately, one by one.

enmesh v. *They became enmeshed in doctrinal disputes:* ensnare, embroil, implicate, incriminate, involve, net, snare, snarl, entangle, tangle, trammel, entrap, trap.

enmity n. *Despite the truce, strong enmity remains between the two nations:* hostility, ill will, hatred, rancor, acrimony, animosity, animus, bitterness, antipathy, strife, malice, bad blood. **—Ant.** goodwill, amity, friendliness, friendship, amicability, love, affection, cordiality.

ennui n. *An idle life left the heiress in a state of ennui:* weariness, boredom, tedium, languor, listlessness, lassitude; apathy, indifference. **—Ant.** excitement, eagerness, interest, curiosity, commitment.

enormity n. **1.** *The enormity of the crime shocked the public:* monstrousness, atrociousness, outrageousness, offensiveness, vileness, villainy, depravity, viciousness, wickedness, evilness, malignity, heinousness, baseness. **2.** *The enormity of the task overwhelmed them:* immensity, hugeness, vastness, largeness, enormousness. **—Ant.** 1 inoffensiveness, innocuousness, harmlessness, innocence. 2 smallness, insignificance, meagerness.

enormous adj. *The banquet was held in an enormous room:* huge, vast, immense, tremendous, colossal, gigantic, mammoth, gargantuan, Brobdingnagian, titanic, elephantine; massive, prodigious. **—Ant.** small, little, tiny, minute, miniscule, Lilliputian, diminutive, trivial, insignificant, meager, midget, dwarf, peewee, itty-bitty, teeny, (*fem.*) petite.

enough adj. **1.** *Is there enough food for everyone?:* adequate, sufficient, ample, plenty, abundant, copious. **—pron. 2.** *The paint is the right shade, but did you buy enough?:* sufficient amount, sufficiency, ample supply, competence, plenty, plentitude, full measure. **—adv. 3.** *I'm hungry enough to eat a bear:* adequately, sufficiently, satisfactorily, amply, abundantly; passably, tolerably, reasonably. **—Ant.** 1 inadequate, insufficient; skimpy, scant, meager. 2 insufficiency, inadequacy, paucity, scarcity. 3 inadequately, insufficiently.

enrage v. *Sloppy work enrages a meticulous person:* infuriate, incense, make furious, anger, madden, inflame, aggravate, provoke the wrath of, throw into a rage, make one's blood boil, *Informal* make one see red. **—Ant.** placate, pacify, appease, mollify, conciliate, soothe, calm, allay, quiet, assuage.

enrapture v. *Her beautiful singing voice enraptured audiences everywhere:* enthrall, hold rapt, transport, entrance, enchant, captivate, beguile, charm, bewitch, delight, thrill. **—Ant.** bore, disinterest, put off.

enrich v. **1.** *The development of oil fields enriched the Arab nations:* make rich, make wealthy, *Slang* feather the nest of. **2.** *American culture has been enriched by European immigrants. The breakfast cereal is enriched with vitamins and minerals:* elevate, improve, enhance, upgrade, ameliorate, fortify, endow, refine; adorn, embellish. **—Ant.** 1 impoverish. 2 degrade, downgrade, bastardize, weaken, divest, strip.

enroll v. *The school will enroll new students the first week in September:* register, sign up, enter, take on; admit, accept, engage; enlist, join, join up, recruit. **—Ant.** withdraw, drop out, retire; dismiss, expel.

enrollment n. **1.** *Today is the last day for enrollment in the YMCA swimming classes:* enrolling, registration, matriculation, signing up; enlistment, recruiting, admittance. **2.** *The school has an enrollment of 3,000 students:* total number enrolled, registration, roster; enlistment. **—Ant.** 1 withdrawing, dropping out.

en route adv. *Try to visit Jacksonville en route to Miami:* in transit, on the way, on the road.

ensemble n. **1.** *Mixing antique and modern furniture in a room can make a striking ensemble:* totality, entirety, general appearance, overall effect; grouping, assembly, aggregate. **2.** *She wears a different ensemble every day of the week:* outfit, costume, attire, *Slang* getup. **3.** *At the end of the performance the entire ensemble of dancers and singers took a bow:* group of performers, company, troupe.

enshrine v. *The new government enshrined certain principles:* consecrate, bless, cherish, exalt, hallow, hold sacred, preserve, revere, sanctify, treasure.

ensign n. **1.** *The ship's ensign was flown at half-mast:* flag, banner, standard, pennant, pennon, colors, jack. **2.** *The new lieutenant proudly sewed his ensign on his uniform:* insignia, badge, emblem, sign, mark; identifying device, symbol.

enslave v. *The czar enslaved the peasants. There is a danger of patients' becoming enslaved to painkilling drugs:* make a slave of, hold in bondage, enthrall, indenture, enchain, shackle, put in shackles; subjugate, subdue, capture, control, dominate; addict. **—Ant.** free, emancipate, release, liberate.

ensue v. *After the heavy rains, floods ensued:* follow, result, come afterward, come to pass, derive, succeed. **—Ant.** herald, precede, introduce.

ensuing adj. The ensuing changes were for the better: consequent, consequential, following, later, next, posterior, resultant, subsequent.

ensure or **insure** v. **1.** Come early to ensure getting a good seat: assure, be sure of, make sure, make certain of, clinch; guarantee, warrant, secure. **2.** Some people used to think that carrying a rabbit's foot would ensure them from harm: protect, guard, safeguard, make safe, secure.

entail v. The new job entails selling and setting up sales conferences: require, necessitate, demand, call for; include, involve, incorporate, occasion. —**Ant.** eliminate, cut out; exclude, leave out.

entangle v. **1.** He awoke with a start, entangled in the collapsed mosquito netting: tangle, enmesh, ensnare, snare, enravel, snarl, encumber, intertwine, twist up. **2.** The witness entangled himself in a web of lies: tangle, catch, trap, ensnare, involve, embroil; complicate, mix up, confuse, muddle, foul up; implicate, compromise, embarrass. —**Ant.** 1 disentangle, free, extricate, extirpate, unravel.

entanglement n. He resisted any further entanglement in other people's troubles: imbroglio, complexity, complication, entrapment, involvement, jumble, knot, mesh, mess, mix-up, muddle, predicament, snare, tangle, trap, web.

entente n. The entente was subscribed to by all member nations: understanding, rapprochement, agreement, accord, conciliation, French entente cordiale, cordial understanding, mutual understanding, consortium, unanimity, likemindedness, general agreement, consensus, confluence of minds, pact, treaty, covenant. —**Ant.** disagreement, misunderstanding, conflict, dispute, discord, rift, split.

enter v. **1.** The thief entered by a rear window: come in, go in, pass into, proceed into, make an entrance, arrive, penetrate, intrude into, trespass. **2.** If you plan to enter the diplomatic corps, study history and foreign languages. I refused to enter the discussion: join, commit oneself to, embark upon, set out on, bind oneself, become a member of, participate in, take part in. **3.** Are you going to enter the pie-baking contest?: enroll in, sign up for, register for, enlist in, join; list, record, post, inscribe. —**Ant.** 1 exit, leave, depart, go out, go. 2, 3 leave, withdraw from, drop out of, take out of, resign from, retire from.

enterprise n. **1.** The firm's latest enterprise will require an enlarged staff: undertaking, venture, endeavor, project, campaign, program, operation, effort, attempt, task. **2.** The manager was pleased with the salesman's enterprise: initiative, drive, aggressiveness, push, ingenuity, ambition, industry, energy, enthusiasm, eagerness, zeal, willingness, spirit, vigor, alertness, daring, boldness, adventurousness. —**Ant.** laziness, spiritlessness, indolence.

enterprising adj. The company always has room for an enterprising young man: ambitious, aggressive, industrious, hardworking, active, energetic, venturesome, inventive, intrepid, self-reliant, bold, eager, up-and-coming, enthusiastic, zealous, earnest, alert, keen, wide-awake. —**Ant.** lazy, indolent, timid, cautious, wary, conservative.

entertain v. **1.** The magician entertained the children with a variety of tricks: amuse, divert, give enjoyment to, beguile, please, regale, delight, enthrall, charm, engage pleasantly, interest, absorb, engross. **2.** Diplomats entertain often: have guests, give a party, play host, keep open house, offer hospitality. **3.** We simply cannot entertain such outrageous ideas: consider, admit, contemplate, imagine, harbor, foster, support, nurture, think about, keep in mind, heed, muse over, dwell on, ponder, cogitate on. —**Ant.** 1 bore, weary, tire; displease, disgust. 3 reject, ignore, disregard.

entertaining adj. The entertaining talker kept us interested in the topic: engaging, enjoyable, diverting, affecting, amusing, captivating, charming, cheering, compelling, delightful, enchanting, engrossing, enticing, entrancing, fascinating, lively, moving, pleasant, stimulating, thrilling, fun, funny, humorous.

entertainment n. The city offers all kinds of entertainment for young and old: amusement, diversion, distraction, recreation, divertissement, fun, play, good time, pastime, novelty; pleasure, enjoyment, satisfaction. —**Ant.** work, job, preoccupation.

enthrall or **enthral** v. **1.** The acrobats enthralled a large audience: intrigue, spellbind, fascinate, enchant, captivate, charm, transport, transfix, rivet, enrapture, entrance, thrill, bewitch, beguile, hypnotize, seduce. **2.** The emperor enthralled all military captives: enslave, put into slavery, keep in bondage, subjugate, overpower. —**Ant.** 1 bore, disinterest. 2 free, emancipate, liberate.

enthusiasm n. **1.** We are looking forward with enthusiasm to your visit: eagerness, keenness, anticipation, excitement, fervor, zest, ardor, relish, zeal, exuberance, elation. **2.** One of her great enthusiasms is skiing: interest, passion, love, devotion, craze, mania, rage, pet activity; hobby, hobbyhorse, diversion, distraction. —**Ant.** 1 apathy, indifference, unconcern, detachment, aloofness, calmness, coldness, coolness.

enthusiast n. Dad's a baseball enthusiast: fan, buff, devotee, aficionado, fanatic, addict, Slang bug, nut, freak.

enthusiastic adj. Sam is an enthusiastic golfer. The diplomat received enthusiastic praise: wholehearted, ardent, fervent, fervid, eager, zealous, passionate, spirited, exuberant; unqualified, unstinting. —**Ant.** blasé, dispassionate, cool, lukewarm, unenthusiastic, disinterested, halfhearted, faint, feeble.

entice v. Isn't there any way we can entice you to come to the party?: induce, tempt, beguile, lure, allure, incite, attract, seduce; persuade, coax, inveigle, wheedle. —**Ant.** repel, discourage, dissuade.

entire adj. **1.** The entire school turned out for the football game: whole, total, full, gross; complete, all-inclusive, thorough, absolute, *Latin* in toto. **2.** *The ancient vase was found entire and unblemished:* intact, unbroken, undamaged, unimpaired, in perfect condition. —**Ant.** 1 partial, incomplete. 2 broken, fragmented, defective, damaged, impaired.

entirely *adv. He's entirely wrong:* completely, wholly, fully, totally, thoroughly, altogether, utterly, absolutely, unreservedly, unqualifiedly. —**Ant.** partially, somewhat, slightly, moderately, partly, tolerably.

entitle *v.* **1.** *This coupon entitles you to a free dance lesson:* give the right to, authorize, qualify, make eligible, allow, permit, enable. **2.** *The book is entitled* The American Experience: title, name, designate, call, style, dub, label, tag. —**Ant.** 1 disable, disqualify.

entity *n. The moon is an entity whose origin is unknown:* real thing, thing, object, article, structure, body, matter, substance, quantity; creature, being, individual, presence. —**Ant.** nonentity, fantasy, hallucination, illusion, mirage, delusion, chimera, phantom.

entourage *n. The king traveled with an entourage of 200 servants, courtiers, and guards:* retinue, attendants, train, cortege, escort, following, convoy, staff, court, suite; companions, followers, associates.

entrails *n. pl. The soothsayer tried to foretell the future by examining the entrails of sacrificial animals:* viscera, intestines, insides, innards, guts, bowels.

entrance[1] *n.* **1.** *The store placed a guard at the front entrance:* entry, entranceway, way in, access, approach, ingress; (*loosely*) door, doorway, gate, gateway, portal, passageway, opening. **2.** *Men without ties and jackets will be refused entrance:* permission to enter, entry, admittance, access, ingress, entrée. **3.** *Her entrance in the red dress caught everyone's attention:* entry, coming in, approach, ingress; appearance, introduction. —**Ant.** exit, departure, egress.

entrance[2] *v.* **1.** *It was a gift bound to entrance any child:* delight, gladden, enrapture, fill with wonder, spellbind, fascinate, transport, captivate, enthrall, charm, bewitch, beguile. **2.** *A hypnotist looks for subjects who are easily entranced:* put into a trance, hypnotize, mesmerize. —**Ant.** 1 bore, disinterest.

entrant *n. There were nine entrants in the race:* entry, aspirant, candidate, competitor, contestant, entry, participant, player.

entrap *v. He says the police entrapped him at the scene of the crime:* tempt, entice, allure, inveigle, beguile, seduce; capture, snare, catch, ensnare, draw in, drag in; *Slang* hook, bag, nail, rope in, land, suck in, nab, collar.

entreat *v. I entreat you to contribute generously to the building fund:* ask earnestly, beseech, implore, plead with, appeal to, exhort, request, beg, supplicate, adjure, enjoin, petition, importune. —**Ant.** command, direct, demand.

entreaty *n. The prisoner's entreaty for mercy deeply affected the king:* earnest request, plea, appeal, supplication, prayer, petition, importunity. —**Ant.** demand, ultimatum.

entrée or **entree** *n.* **1.** *His family's position gives him entrée into the best social circles:* admittance, admission, entry, entrance, ingress, access, *Slang* pull; acceptance, acknowledgment. **2.** *The price of the meal includes entrée, dessert, and coffee:* main course, main dish, principal dish.

entrench or **intrench** *v. Most habits are firmly entrenched during childhood. He has entrenched himself so thoroughly as president of the club that he can't be dispensed with:* establish solidly, fix, set, install; embed, implant, ingrain, anchor, dig in, ensconce, plant, root; put in a strong position.

entre nous *adv. Entre nous, I think they're getting married in May:* between us, between you and me, between ourselves, confidentially, privately, in strict confidence, between me and thee.

entrepreneur *n. He makes his living as entrepreneur for various musical groups:* impresario, manager, organizer, coordinator, director.

entrust or **intrust** *v. The manager is entrusted with full responsibility for running the office:* trust, put in trust of, charge with, authorize, give the custody of, hand over, turn over, commit, consign, assign, delegate.

entry *n.* **1.** *The entry to the estate is behind those trees:* entranceway, way, way in, approach, ingress, access; (*loosely*) door, doorway, gate, gateway, portal, passageway. **2.** *Please wait in the entry:* entrance hall, foyer, doorway, vestibule. **3.** *An ovation greeted the candidate's entry into the hall. Only persons with tickets will be allowed entry:* approach, introduction, appearance; entrance, entrée, admission, admittance, ingress. **4.** *Make an entry of your deposit in your bankbook:* record, account, registration; note, memo, memorandum, minute, item, jotting. **5.** *Only entries mailed before midnight will be considered. The stable's entry in the race is the black horse:* thing entered, person entered, contestant, competitor. —**Ant.** 1 exit, egress. 3 exit, departure, leaving, leave-taking, withdrawal.

entwine *v. The couple was entwined behind a potted palm:* intertwine, interlace, lace, braid, coil, curl, embrace, encircle, enmesh, entangle, knit, plait, spiral, twine, twist, weave, wind, wreathe.

enumerate *v.* **1.** *The teacher enumerated the students' spelling mistakes:* specify, numerate, cite, relate, detail, recount, spell out. **2.** *Enumerate the items again to be sure none is missing:* count, count up, add, add up, sum up, total, tally, tabulate, number, list, tick off.

enunciate *v. The boy must learn to enunciate his consonants:* pronounce clearly, utter distinctly; articulate, sound, speak, voice, vocalize. —**Ant.** mutter, mumble, stammer, stutter.

envelop *v. Fog enveloped the town. The plan is enveloped in secrecy:* wrap, enwrap, cover, encase, sheathe, enfold, enclose, engulf, encircle, blanket, cloak, shroud, veil, contain, swathe, swaddle, surround, encompass; hide, conceal, obscure. —**Ant.** unwrap, uncover, expose, reveal, lay bare.

envelope n. Fold the letter and put it in an envelope: letter covering, paper wrapper, gummed wrapper; wrapping, jacket, cover, covering.

enviable adj. He is in the enviable position of being able to choose between two high-paying jobs: worthy of envy, covetable; desirable, advantageous, agreeable, excellent, beneficial, salutary, fortunate, lucky.

envious adj. The woman was too envious to enjoy her friend's good fortune: jealous, filled with envy, green with envy, covetous; grudging, jaundiced, resentful, spiteful.

environment n. Mold grows best in a warm, damp environment. A happy family provides a loving environment for its children: medium, habitat, element; surroundings, setting, locale, scene, milieu, atmosphere, ambience, situation, background; circumstances, living conditions, climate.

environs n. pl. Louisville, together with its environs, has a population of more than three quarters of a million people: outskirts, suburbs, surrounding area, exurbs, outlying area, outer limits, vicinity, adjacent district, precincts, metropolitan area. —**Ant.** central city, core city, inner city; downtown.

envisage v. For her retirement she envisages a house in the Swiss Alps: picture, imagine, visualize, conjure up, conceive, envision, conceptualize, fancy, view in the mind's eye, contemplate, form a mental picture of, dream of, picture to oneself, dream up, have a picture of.

envoy n. The president sent a special envoy to the peace talks. My envoy will pick up the contract at your office tomorrow: representative, delegate, emissary, ambassador, agent, deputy, minister, attaché, legate, intermediary, middleman; courier, messenger.

envy n. **1.** He found it hard to suppress his envy of his brother's success: jealousy, enviousness, resentfulness, resentment, grudging, greed, covetousness, spite, malevolence, the green-eyed monster. —v. **2.** It's hard not to envy a woman who has everything: feel envious toward, be jealous of, resent, be spiteful toward, begrudge.

ephemeral adj. There is no point in lamenting the ephemeral joys of youth: brief, temporary, transient, short-lived, temporal, transitory, fleeting, impermanent, evanescent, momentary, passing, fugitive, unenduring, nondurable, inconstant, fly-by-night, flitting, fugacious. —**Ant.** permanent, lasting, enduring, everlasting, perpetual, abiding.

epic n. **1.** The Aeneid is one of the great epics of Western culture: epic poem, historic poem, heroic poem, saga; heroic adventure, drama. —adj. **2.** Ulysses is one of the epic characters of literature: heroic, great, majestic, imposing, superhuman, noble, exalted; legendary, fabled, storied, fabulous.

epicure n. Only an epicure would spend so much time choosing wine and cheese: gourmet, gastronome, fastidious connoisseur, bon vivant; gourmand, glutton; sybarite, hedonist.

epicurean adj. **1.** The senator's epicurean life has been harshly criticized: devoted to luxury, pleasure-seeking, voluptuous, sensual, libertine, hedonistic, sybaritic, self-indulgent, intemperate. **2.** The banquet was an epicurean feast: fit for an epicure, gourmet, luxurious, lavish, rich, sybaritic, Lucullan. —n. **3.** Nero was one of history's most famous epicureans: voluptuary, sensualist, libertine, hedonist, sybarite. —**Ant.** 1, 2 Spartan, austere, simple, plain, humble, modest. 3 Spartan; puritan, ascetic.

epidemic n. **1.** Thousands died in the flu epidemic of the First World War: outbreak, contagion, infection; plague, pestilence, scourge. —adj. **2.** Thanks to the Salk vaccine, polio is no longer an epidemic disease: dangerously contagious, pandemic, rampant, widespread, far-reaching, rife, prevalent, pervasive, prevailing; catching, infectious.

epigram n. The plays of Oscar Wilde are celebrated for their epigrams: witty saying, clever comment, bon mot, witticism, quip; maxim, apothegm, aphorism, adage.

epilogue n. The book's epilogue hints at what the author thinks the future will bring: final section, concluding addition, addendum, rider, codicil, supplement, afterword, Music coda; concluding speech. —**Ant.** preface, prologue, introduction, Music overture.

episode n. **1.** The completion of the transcontinental railroad was an important episode in our own history. We'll forget this little episode, but never let me catch you lying again!: milestone, event, occurrence, happening, period; incident, affair, experience, adventure. **2.** The little boy asking for "more" is one of the most famous episodes in Dickens's Oliver Twist: scene, passage, part, section, chapter; installment.

episodic adj. The book's episodic style made the plot hard to follow: rambling, wandering, loosely connected, meandering, digressive, discursive, halting, segmented, discontinuous.

epistle n. The courier brought an epistle from the king. The sermon was based on St. Paul's Epistle to the Ephesians: letter, formal letter, missive, encyclical, written communication, message; text in letter form.

epithet n. **1.** "The Conqueror" was an epithet of William I of England: appellation, designation, ascription, sobriquet, nickname. **2.** He screamed several epithets into the phone and slammed down the receiver: curse, abusive word, insult, expletive, obscenity, blasphemy.

epitome n. Money and good taste made her the epitome of fashion: embodiment, exemplification, model, typification, representation, essence, summation, summary, sum and substance; ideal, peak, height.

epoch n. The Renaissance was an epoch of unparalleled cultural achievement: period, age, era, time, interval.

equable adj. **1.** A good traveling companion should have an equable disposition: eventempered, easygoing, calm, tranquil, serene, placid, unexcitable, unruffled, imperturbable, *Slang* unflappable; good-natured, agreeable, pleasant, sunny. **2.** *Florida has a more equable climate than Maine:* uniform, constant, unvaried, unchanging, even, steady, regular, consistent, dependable, stable, predictable. —**Ant.** 1 fitful, nervous, tense, excitable, temperamental; disagreeable, unpleasant, harsh, gruff. 2 variable, fluctuating, changeable, uneven, varied, irregular, inconsistent, unstable, unpredictable.

equal *adj.* **1.** *The two men were of equal height. The calories in this piece of bread are equal to those in four crackers:* the same, even, like, uniform; identical, one and the same, matched, evenly matched, of a piece; equivalent, proportional, corresponding, correlative, symmetrical, balanced, evenly balanced, tantamount, comparable, commensurate. —*n.* **2.** *The young reporter was considered the equal of many veteran journalists. The French Minister of Foreign Affairs is the equal of the American Secretary of State:* peer, match; equivalent, counterpart, parallel, opposite number. —*v.* **3.** *The debits must equal the credits on the balance sheet:* be the same as, be even to, equate with, be identical to, accord with, agree with, tally with, match, square with, balance with, correspond to, parallel, *Slang* jibe with; equalize. —**Ant.** 1 unequal, different, uneven, unlike, dissimilar, varied, diverse, disparate, disproportionate, incommensurate, irregular, unbalanced. 3 be unequal, be uneven, be different, disagree, diverge.

equality *n.* **1.** *Democracy must offer everyone equality:* equal opportunity, justice, fairness, impartiality, fair treatment, fair play. **2.** *The organization seeks to insure equality of pay for men and women:* parity, coequality, evenness, sameness, uniformity, equivalency, correspond-ence; balance, similarity. —**Ant.** 1 inequality, injustice, unfairness, bias, prejudice. 2 inequality, dissimilarity, difference.

equalize *v.* *He did his best to equalize the weights:* even, balance, equal, level, match, parallel, smooth, square, standardize.

equanimity *n.* *We must keep our equanimity during times of crisis:* calmness, composure, self-possession, steadiness, poise, aplomb, coolness, imperturbability, presence of mind, self-control, tranquillity, sangfroid, *Informal* cool. —**Ant.** panic, hysteria, disquiet, perturbation, agitation, discomposure.

equate *v.* **1.** *You can't equate investment and profitability:* equal out, even out, match, be equivalent to, be proportionate to, be commensurate, equalize, average, balance. **2.** *Don't equate his failure with laziness:* think of as, consider as, draw a parallel between, compare, liken.

equilibrium *n.* *When the two weights match, the scale is said to be in equilibrium:* balance, stability, equipoise, symmetry; sense of balance.

equip *v.* *Equip yourself with everything you'll need on safari:* furnish, supply, outfit, fit out, appoint, prepare, provide, provision, stock, accou-

tre; rig, caparison. —**Ant.** divest, denude, strip.

equipment *n.* *A good sleeping bag is an essential part of every camper's equipment:* apparatus, gear, material, paraphernalia, outfittings, matériel, supplies, furnishings, accoutrements, equipage, tackle, stuff.

equitable *adj.* *The lawsuit ended with an equitable settlement:* fair, just, evenhanded, impartial, unbiased, unprejudiced, reasonable, proper, due. —**Ant.** inequitable, unfair, unjust, unreasonable.

equity *n.* **1.** *The Supreme Court must judge each case with complete equity:* impartiality, fairmindedness, fairness, justness, evenhandedness, reasonableness; fair dealings, justice. **2.** *The family has more than $35,000 equity in the house:* assets over liabilities, assets after mortgage, cash value; (*loosely*) cash, value, profit, assets, investment. —**Ant.** 1 unfairness, partiality, bias, prejudice, unreasonableness; injustice.

equivalent *adj.* **1.** *A dime is equivalent to ten pennies:* equal, the same as, comparable, commensurate with, tantamount, corresponding, correspondent, correlative; even, one and the same, of a piece. —*n.* **2.** *That dress cost the equivalent of a week's salary:* equal amount, comparable sum; correspondent, peer, counterpart, parallel, match. —**Ant.** 1 unequal, dissimilar, incomparable, incommensurate, different.

equivocal *adj.* *The senator has equivocal feelings about the new gun-control legislation:* ambivalent, ambiguous, indefinite, imprecise, vague, undecided, nonspecific, indeterminate, uncertain, hazy, doubtful, enigmatic. —**Ant.** precise, definite, specific, clear-cut, explicit, certain.

equivocate *v.* *Please stop equivocating and give me a straight answer:* evade, avoid the issue, hedge, stall, dodge, beat around the bush, fudge, pussyfoot, be ambiguous, mince words, prevaricate, straddle the fence.

equivocation *n.* *She handed it over without further equivocation:* hedging, evasion, ambiguity, avoidance, deceit, deception, deceptiveness, duplicity, evasion, prevarication, quibbling, spuriousness, stonewalling, waffling.

era *n.* *The birth of Christ ushered in the Christian era:* period, age, epoch, time, interval.

eradicate *v.* *Diligent police work will help eradicate crime:* eliminate, annihilate, exterminate, erase, expunge, extinguish, extirpate, destroy, wipe out, get rid of, do away with, abolish, remove, blot out, obliterate, liquidate. —**Ant.** establish, originate, implant, engender, create, breed.

erase *v.* *Erase the penciled notes in the margins:* wipe away, rub out, eradicate, expunge, remove, eliminate, delete, strike out, scratch. —**Ant.** write, draw, print, stamp, mark, record.

erect *adj.* **1.** *The old man had an erect posture:* upright, vertical, straight, unstooped, unbent; stiff, rigid. —*v.* **2.** *The town will erect a monument to its war heroes:* construct, build, put up, raise. **3.** *The flagpole toppled over, and a crane had to be used to erect it:* place upright, stand up, put in a vertical position, set right side up. —**Ant.** 1 horizontal, supine, leaning, stooped, bent; limp, relaxed, flaccid. 2 raze, demolish, tear down, destroy.

erode *v. Salt spray eroded the bridge. Wind eroded the loose topsoil:* corrode, eat away; wear away, waste, ravage, spoil, disintegrate, despoil. —**Ant.** build up, strengthen, reinforce.

erosion *n. The erosion of the sandbank was noticeable:* wear, abrasion, corrosion, decrease, deterioration, disintegration.

erotic *adj. At one time, women's short-sleeved bathing suits were considered erotic. John Donne wrote several famous erotic poems to his mistress:* unchaste, immodest, ribald, wanton, impure, suggestive, risqué; obscene, indecent, lascivious, lewd, bawdy, lusty, salacious, *Slang* raunchy; sexual, sexy, sexually stimulating, carnal, *Slang* hot, amorous, passionate, ardent, amatory, impassioned.

err *v.* **1.** *Banks rarely err in figuring a checking account balance:* make a mistake, slip up, be incorrect, be in error, be inaccurate, miscalculate, mess up, blunder. **2.** *"To err is human, to forgive divine":* lapse from virtue, transgress, sin, slip from grace, go astray, misbehave, do wrong, do a bad thing.

errand *n. The boy had to go downtown on an errand for his mother:* mission, task, assignment, undertaking, duty, office, minor chore.

erratic *adj. March weather is often erratic. The boy's erratic behavior worried his parents:* inconsistent, unpredictable, unstable, shifting, vacillating, changeable, variable, fitful, capricious, odd, eccentric, queer, strange, peculiar, unusual, unnatural, aberrant, wayward, abnormal. —**Ant.** consistent, unvariable, regular, undeviating, unchanging, stable, steady, certain, sure, reliable, predictable, dependable; typical, normal, customary, natural.

erroneous *adj. The facts are correct, but your conclusion is erroneous:* inaccurate, incorrect, untrue, wrong, false, fallacious, faulty, mistaken, unsound, unfounded, unsupportable, off base, spurious, *Slang* full of hot air, all wet. —**Ant.** correct, accurate, true, factual, wellfounded.

error *n. The bill contains an error in addition:* mistake, inaccuracy, miscalculation, fault, flaw, *Slang* bungle, botch, blooper, boo-boo, howler, boner; misconception, misunderstanding, misapprehension, misinterpretation, fallacy, oversight. —**Ant.** accuracy, flawlessness, correctness.

ersatz *adj. During the war we made do with ersatz coffee:* synthetic, artificial, imitation, not genuine, counterfeit, sham, fake, phony, bogus, pretended. —**Ant.** real, genuine, authentic, natural, the real McCoy.

erstwhile *adj. My erstwhile friend refused to lend me the money:* former, past, bygone, previous, *Informal* ex. —**Ant.** current, present.

erudite *adj. The professor was an erudite man. The TV newscaster was known for his erudite comments:* learned, well-informed, well-educated, well-versed, literate, well-read, cultured, cultivated, scholarly, thoughtful, intelligent, well-reasoned, wise, sapient. —**Ant.** uninformed, uneducated, illiterate, unscholarly; shallow, unthinking; rash, ill-advised.

erudition *n. Einstein was a man of formidable erudition:* learning, formal education, knowledge, learnedness, culture, scholarship, literacy, skill, expertise, cultivation, refinement, education, schooling, book learning, enlightenment. —**Ant.** illiteracy, ignorance, unenlightenment, dullness, dumbness.

erupt *v. Mount Vesuvius erupted in 79 A.D., destroying Pompeii. Laughter erupted from the audience:* burst forth, break out, explode, blow up, pour forth, belch forth, eruct, discharge, be ejected, throw off, emit, vent, flow forth, gush. —**Ant.** retain, contain, hold, hold back; be dormant, subside.

eruption *n.* **1.** *The eruption of Old Faithful is a major attraction of Yellowstone Park:* discharge, emission, ejection, venting, bursting forth, outburst, outbreak, pouring forth, flare-up, outpouring, belching forth, flowing forth, gushing, explosion, blowing up. **2.** *The patient has a painful skin eruption:* rash, inflammation, flare-up, breaking out; dermatitis, eczema, festering. —**Ant.** 1 retention, repression; dormancy, quiescence; inactivity, subsidence.

escalate *v.* **1.** *With prices escalating, a dollar buys a lot less:* rise, increase, advance, ascend, elevate, mount, accelerate, boost, swell. **2.** *The enemy escalated the war by sending more troops to the front:* intensify, step up, accelerate, expand, extend, enlarge, amplify, magnify, broaden, aggrandize. —**Ant.** 1 lower, decrease, fall, subside, descend, retreat. 2 deescalate, lessen, limit, narrow, contract, minimize.

escapade *n. The students' latest escapade was painting the town statue purple:* prank, caper, antic, trick, caprice, mischief; lark, fling, spree, adventure, revel, high old time.

escape *v.* **1.** *Three prisoners escaped from the jail:* break free, break loose, get away, make a getaway, make off, slip away, run away, flee, skip, bolt, cut and run, abscond, steal off, *Slang* fly the coop; avoid capture. **2.** *The skiers barely escaped the avalanche. There's no way to escape doing the work:* avoid danger, get away safely, avert; avoid, elude, dodge, skirt, shun, eschew. **3.** *Gas is escaping from the broken pipe:* issue, emerge, emanate, be emitted, be discharged, leak, seep, pour forth, flow, stream, gush. **4.** *The exact date of our meeting escapes me:* elude, be forgotten by, slip from the memory of. —*n.* **5.** *How did the prisoners manage their escape?:* breakout, exodus, gain of freedom, flight, decampment, getaway. **6.** *Her escape from the fire was miraculous. The back door is your only means of escape:* avoidance of danger, safe getaway, extrication, deliverance; means of fleeing danger, exit, egress. **7.** *Television programs are a favorite escape of many people:* diversion, distraction, evasion of worry, avoidance of problems, way of getting away from it all. **8.** *The escape of oil caused the mo-*

tor to break down: discharge, emission, outflow, leakage, seepage, outpour, issuing forth, pouring forth, outburst, egress, efflux, effluence. **—Ant.** 1 capture, recapture, apprehend; stay. 2 meet, encounter, face; seek, hunt, chase; trap, catch. 3 retain, hold, contain; inject, pour in. 4 come to mind, be on the tip of one's tongue; remember, recollect. 5 capture, recapture, apprehension. 8 retention, containment; injection, influx.

eschew *v. Eschew fattening foods if you want to lose weight:* abstain from, forgo, give up, forbear, avoid, shun, steer clear of, keep shy of. **—Ant.** seek, chase after, hunt out; indulge in, welcome, embrace.

escort *n.* **1.** *The king's escort totaled 50 men:* accompanying guard, guard, protective screen; attendant body, retinue, cortege, entourage, attendants, company, train. **2.** *Her cousin will be her escort to the dance:* date, squire; companion, conductor, chaperon. **—v. 3.** *Let me escort you to the door:* conduct, guide, lead the way, take, usher; squire, chaperon.

esoteric *adj.* **1.** *Some fields of science seem hopelessly esoteric to the layman:* incomprehensible, abstruse, recondite, arcane, cryptic, enigmatic, inscrutable, mysterious, obscure. **2.** *The tribe has an esoteric ritual that no outsider may witness:* secret, undisclosed, private, confidential, inviolable, hidden, concealed, covert, veiled, cloaked; mystical, occult. **—Ant.** 1 obvious, clear, plain, simple. 2 public, open, exoteric.

especial *adj.* See SPECIAL.

especially *adv.* **1.** *The cabinet was made especially for the dining room:* expressly, specifically, exclusively; principally, particularly, primarily. **2.** *The sunsets in the Pacific are especially beautiful:* exceptionally, outstandingly, particularly, uncommonly, extraordinarily, unusually, singularly, notably, really, intensely.

espouse *v.* **1.** *The council will espouse the cause of conservation:* adopt, take up, embrace; support, champion, back, advocate, promote, further, side with, stand up for, express belief in, boost, tout. **2.** *The bride will be espoused at an outdoor wedding in June:* marry, become married, wed, unite in marriage. **—Ant.** 1 reject, renounce, abjure; denounce, hinder, obstruct, block, thwart.

esprit de corps *n. An enthusiastic coach can give a team esprit de corps:* team spirit, group unity, fellowship, camaraderie, group enthusiasm, group pride, high morale, solidarity.

espy *v. From his lofty vantage point, he espied the man o' war:* catch sight of, descry, discover, perceive, make out. **—Ant.** overlook.

essay *n.* **1.** *The assignment was to write an essay on "What Democracy Means to Me":* short composition, theme, paper; dissertation, treatise, tract, editorial, article, commentary, critique. **2.** *His first essay at flying an airplane was a near disaster:* attempt, effort, try, venture, endeavor, undertaking, experiment. **3.** *Who will essay crossing the stream first?:* try, attempt, take on, undertake, venture, make an ef-

fort at, take a crack at, take a fling at, make a stab at.

essence *n.* **1.** *The very essence of justice lies in the right of every man to a fair trial. The essence of his long speech was that we must all work harder:* basic quality, essential character, quintessence, nature, principle, substance, lifeblood, spirit, heart, core, germ, soul; meaning, significance, gist, point, pith, sum and substance. **2.** *Use essence of turpentine to remove the paint spot:* concentrate, tincture, elixir, spirits, extract. **3.** *Her favorite essence smells like gardenias:* perfume, scent, cologne, fragrance, toilet water.

essential *adj.* **1.** *Water is essential to the growth of crops:* indispensable, requisite, necessary, needed, crucial, vital. **2.** *The essential purpose of a vacation is to relax:* basic, fundamental; main, key, principal, cardinal, leading, important, inherent, intrinsic, ingrained. **—n.** **3.** *(sometimes pl.) Petroleum is an essential of modern industry. The course teaches the essentials of French in just six weeks:* basic need, requisite, necessity, indispensable element, key element, vital part, primary constituent; basics, fundamentals, rudiments, principles, *Slang* nitty-gritty. **—Ant.** 1, 2 dispensable, superfluous, peripheral, unimportant, incidental, unnecessary, immate-rial, secondary, minor, lesser, minimal, trivial. 3 accessory, extra, option.

establish *v.* **1.** *Father established this business forty years ago:* institute, found, set up, bring about, bring into existence, form, organize, create, begin, start, inaugurate, open, initiate. **2.** *The young man established himself as an expert on foreign stamps:* gain recognition for, win accept-ance for, make secure, install, settle, sustain, situate, fix, implant. **3.** *The new evidence establishes the suspect's guilt:* prove, show, confirm, verify, corroborate, authenticate, demonstrate, sustain, uphold, validate, put to rest any doubts about; justify, warrant. **—Ant.** 1 close, disband, dissolve, liquidate, eradicate, destroy. 2 uproot, unsettle, dethrone. 3 refute, invalidate, deny, cast doubt on, bring into question, throw suspicion upon.

establishment *n.* **1.** *The committee will work toward the establishment of a school for the handicapped:* establishing, setting up, instituting, founding, bringing about, formation, institution, foundation, development, organization, creation, building. **2.** *The flour mill is the oldest establishment in town:* business, company, concern, firm, corporation, outfit, organization, institution, building, plant, factory, office. **3. Establishment** *The student protesters blame the Establishment for all social problems:* traditional leaders, entrenched leaders, ruling class; established order, entrenched social order, system, powers that be. **—Ant.** 1 closing, dissolution, disbanding, liquidation, eradication, destruction. 2 revolutionaries, rebels, activists, young Turks, radicals, upstarts.

estate *n.* **1.** *The estate consists of a main house, servants' quarters, stables, and 200 acres of woods:* country estate, large residential property, landed property, manor, country place, compound, plantation. **2.** *He left an estate of more than a million dollars to be divided among his children:* assets at death, assets, fortune, wealth, money, property, material possessions, belongings, holdings; inheritance, legacy, bequest, will. **3.** *At the age of 21 a boy reaches a man's estate:* state, station, condition, status, situation, period of life; rank, grade, class, order.

esteem *v.* **1.** *History esteems Sigmund Freud as the father of psychoanalysis:* venerate, revere, hold in high regard, value, honor, think highly of, attach importance to, set store by, prize, treasure, admire, respect, cherish, look up to. **2.** *Experts esteem it prudent to save 10 percent of one's income:* consider, regard, believe, think, hold, deem, judge, reckon, calculate. *—n.* **3.** *I have the highest esteem for your honesty:* regard, respect, favorable opinion, estimate, approval, admiration, veneration, appreciation, reverence. **—Ant.** 1 disdain, scorn, disparage, deprecate, discredit, *Slang* put down; decry, detest, despise, dislike, abominate, abhor, loathe; undervalue, belittle, underrate; devaluate, degrade. 3 disrespect, contempt, disdain, scorn, depreciation; aversion, dislike, detestation, abhorrence, repugnance, loathing.

esthetic or **aesthetic** *adj. The course in art history is designed to develop the student's esthetic judgment:* appreciative of beauty, appealing to artistic taste, having artistic tastes, artistic; sensitive, discriminating, cultivated, refined, fastidious. **—Ant.** unesthetic, unappreciative; insensitive, undiscriminating.

estimable *adj. Robert Frost was an estimable poet:* highly regarded, worthy of esteem, worthwhile, important, admired, reputable, treasured, prized, respected, revered, praiseworthy, commendable, laudable, honorable, admirable, good. **—Ant.** scorned, ridiculous, disdained, disparaged, deprecated, despised, disliked; unworthy, disreputable, undeserving, inferior, bad.

estimate *v.* **1.** *The dealer estimated the worth of the used car at $850:* evaluate, judge, reckon, calculate, appraise, value, assess, assay, figure. **2.** *The archaeologist estimated that the vase was 3,500 years old:* think, consider, believe, surmise, guess, conjecture, opine, conclude. *—n.* **3.** *The expert's estimate is that the painting is worth $2,500:* evaluation, estimation, assessment, appraisal, calculation, assay; opinion, judgment, reckoning, thinking, surmise, view, belief.

estimation *n.* **1.** *According to the estimation of the critics this is the best movie of the year:* opinion, judgment, appraisal, estimate, view, belief, consideration, evaluation, reckoning. **2.** *The dedicated doctor earned the estimation of his colleagues:* esteem, respect, regard, favorable opinion, admiration, approval. **—Ant.** 2 contempt, scorn, disrespect, disapproval.

estrange *v. Strong political differences estranged the two old friends:* alienate, drive apart, disaffect, dissociate, part, destroy the affection of; antagonize, make hostile. **—Ant.** unite, join, link, bind; reconcile; conciliate.

estrangement *n. Disputes over money led to their estrangement:* breach, alienation, disassociation, disunity, division, divorce, hostility, schism, separation, breakup.

estuary *n. The boat anchored in the estuary:* tidal basin, inlet, arm of the sea; river mouth, firth.

etc. *The cat show featured Persians, Siamese, calicoes, etc.:* and others, and the rest, and so forth, and so on, et al., *Informal* whatnot, whatever.

etch *v. Those hard times were indelibly etched in her memory:* incise, inscribe, carve, cut, delineate, eat into, engrave, execute, impress, imprint, ingrain, portray, represent.

etching *n. The new etchings were shown at the gallery:* carving, engraving, impression, imprint, inscription.

eternal *adj.* **1.** *The minister spoke of the soul's eternal life:* lasting forever, everlasting, infinite, timeless, endless, immortal, without end. **2.** *I can't stand any more of her eternal nagging:* continual, unending, never-ending, perpetual, ceaseless, constant, endless, interminable, abiding, persistent, relentless, uninterrupted. **—Ant.** 1 transient, transitory, fleeting, perishable, finite, evanescent, ephemeral, mortal, temporal. 2 occasional, infrequent, rare, spasmodic, irregular, scattered, random, temporary, spotty, on-and-off.

eternity *n.* **1.** *The stars will exist throughout eternity. The dull play seemed to last an eternity:* forever, infinity, time without end, endlessness, ages and ages, eons and eons. **2.** *The minister's sermon was about the joys of eternity:* everlasting life, immortality, the hereafter, the next world, the afterworld, the world to come; Heaven, paradise, nirvana, Zion, New Jerusalem. **—Ant.** 1 instant, moment, a second, a split second. 2 the here and now, life on earth, mortality.

ethereal *adj. Her ethereal beauty couldn't be captured by the greatest painter:* sublime, refined, celestial, exquisite, aerial, airy, unearthly, unworldly, delicate; elusive, rare, rarefied. **—Ant.** earthly, mundane, worldly; statuesque, monumental, solid.

ethical *adj. Forcing the farmer to sell his land wasn't illegal, but it wasn't ethical either:* moral, decent, virtuous, honorable, upright, right, proper, fitting, correct, just, fair, aboveboard, straightforward, open and aboveboard, scrupulous, *Slang* kosher. **—Ant.** unethical, underhanded, shady, improper, unfair, low-down, nefarious, crooked, unscrupulous, unbecoming, unseemly, indecorous, immoral, indecent.

ethics *n. pl. (Sometimes sing.) Her ethics would never allow her to betray a friend. The Protestant ethic is that each man must work for his own sustenance:* moral code, moral standards, rules of conduct, moral principle, principles, moral values, morality, integrity, moral philosophy, sense of right and wrong, sense of duty, conscience.

ethnic *adj. Every country has its own ethnic dishes:* native, national, indigenous; racial, cultural; original, unique.

etiquette *n. The book on etiquette detailed the wedding procedure:* rules of behavior, amenities, protocol, conventions, behavior, proprieties, civilities, manners, usage, decorum, politeness, courtesy; gentility, good form, good taste. **—Ant.** impropriety, boorishness, rudeness, impo-liteness, vulgarity, indecorum.

Eucharist *n. Members of the congregation took the Eucharist:* Communion, Holy Communion, Sacrament of the Lord's Supper; consecrated wafer, consecrated elements of bread and wine; (*when given to a person in danger of dying*) viaticum.

eulogize *v. The deceased was eulogized by his closest friend:* praise highly, laud, panegyrize, extol, glorify, acclaim, hail, exalt, celebrate, magnify; compliment, tout, boost, commend, pay tribute to. **—Ant.** malign, defame, vilify, slander, libel, criticize, condemn.

eulogy *n. Lincoln's Gettysburg Address is a great eulogy:* oration of praise, praise of the dead, encomium, panegyric; high praise, tribute, homage, hosanna, acclamation, laudation, citation, paean, plaudit. **—Ant.** condemnation, criticism; vilification, defamation, aspersion, calumny, slander, libel.

euphemism *n. "Maiden lady" is a euphemism for "old maid":* mild expression, restrained expression, inoffensive expression, delicate term, refined term; prudish phrase, overdelicacy, overrefinement, prudishness.

euphoria *n. His euphoria was palpable after she said she loved him:* bliss, ecstasy, elation, exhilaration, exultation, happiness, high spirits, intoxication, joy, jubilation, rapture. **—Ant.** gloominess, depression, despair, despondency, dolefulness.

evacuate *v.* **1.** *When the fire drill starts, students will evacuate the building:* leave, withdraw from, quit, vacate; abandon, desert, forsake. **2.** *The fireman evacuated the guests from the burning hotel:* remove, move out, take out, order out. **—Ant.** 1 enter, go in, occupy. 2 take in, move in.

evade *v. The thief evaded the police by dodging into an alley. The stranger evaded all questions about his past:* avoid, dodge, elude, steer clear of, duck, parry, shun, escape, eschew, sidestep, circumvent, fend off, hedge; equivocate. **—Ant.** face, face up to, meet eye to eye, confront; encounter, meet, meet head-on.

evaluate *v. The teacher evaluated the performance of each student:* appraise, rate, assess, weigh, judge, estimate, guage, size up, value, assay.

evaluation *n. Evaluation of the property took weeks to complete:* estimate, appraisal, appraisement, assessment, calculation, decision, interpretation, judgment, opinion, rating.

evangelist *n. Billy Sunday was a famous evangelist of the 1920's:* religious crusader, preacher, revivalist, missionary, soul-saver, minister of the Gospel, Bible Thumper, reformer, proselytizer, propagandist, missioner, apostolic.

evaporate *v.* **1.** *The spot of water evaporated in the sun:* dry up, vaporize, melt away; dehydrate, desiccate. **2.** *The magician made a handkerchief evaporate into thin air. When the fight was over the crowd evaporated:* disappear, vanish, fade away, melt away, dissolve, evanesce; scatter, dispel, dissipate. **—Ant.** 1 condense, concentrate; reconstitute, reconstruct. 2 appear, materialize, emerge, gather, collect, converge.

evasion *n. The witness's evasion of the question was obvious:* avoidance, dodging, eluding, attempt to escape, ducking, shrinking from, shunning, sidestepping, circumventing. **—Ant.** confronting, facing up to, meeting head-on; frankness, candor.

evasive *adj. The politician's evasive answers infuriated the reporters:* elusive, elusory, ambiguous, equivocal, equivocating, dodging, hedging, devious, dissembling, shifty, deceptive, misleading, deceitful. **—Ant.** candid, straightforward, frank, direct, open, honest, truthful, guileless.

even *adj.* **1.** *An even road makes driving easy. Plant the rosebushes in an even row:* level, smooth, flat, plane; plumb, straight, parallel, flush, true, uniform. **2.** *The plane flew at an even speed:* constant, regular, steady, uniform, unvarying, unwavering. **3.** *Pour even amounts of milk into each cup. You buy the tickets next time and we'll be even:* equal, identical, the same, uniform; equitable, matching, balanced, square. **4.** *A teacher should have an even disposition:* even-tempered, calm, steady, placid, equable, unruffled, unexcitable; balanced, fair, just, dispassionate, impartial, unbiased. *—v.* **5.** *The seamstress evened the hem of the dress:* straighten, make parallel, make flush, make uniform; smooth, level, flatten; equal, equalize, balance. **—Ant.** 1–4 uneven. 1 wavy, undulating, rough, bumpy; crooked, curving, twisting, turning; slanted, awry, irregular. 2 variable, changing, fluctuating, nonuniform, irregular. 3 unequal, different, unidentical, nonuniform, inequitable, unbalanced. 4 emotional, hot-tempered, quick-tempered, excitable, easily ruffled, biased, unfair, unjust, prejudiced.

evening *n. Evening in the country is a very peaceful time:* sundown, sunset, twilight, dusk, gloaming; day's end, close of day; eve, even, eventide, nightfall. **—Ant.** dawn, dawning, sunrise, sunup, daylight, morning.

event *n.* **1.** *Winning the scholarship was a great event in the boy's life:* occurrence, momentous occurrence, milestone; occasion, episode, happening, experience, incident. **2.** *Track and field events are held at the new stadium:* contest, competition, tournament, game, bout.

eventful *adj. The birthday party and the movie have made this an eventful day. The Supreme Court's decision was an eventful one:* noteworthy, notable, memorable, thrilling, exciting, unforgettable; momentous, historic, epochal, important, significant, weighty, consequential; critical, crucial, fateful. **—Ant.** ordinary, dull, unexciting, uninteresting, trivial, trifling, unimportant, insignificant, inconsequential, irrelevant.

eventual adj. My father bought a house in Florida for his eventual retirement: future, prospective, coming, later; impending, imminent, upcoming, ultimate, final; following, subsequent, consequent, resulting, ensuing. —**Ant.** past, previous, prior.

eventuality n. We must be prepared for any eventuality: outcome, aftereffect, aftermath, consequence, effect, issue, likelihood, result, sequel, happening, event.

eventually adv. The house will have to be repainted eventually: in the course of time, sometime, one day, ultimately, sooner or later, finally, in the end, in the long run, when all is said and done. —**Ant.** never; immediately, at once.

ever adv. **1.** Unchanging in its nature, it was ever thus: continuously, eternally, perpetually, constantly, always. **2.** If you ever get a chance, see that movie: by any chance, at all, at any time. —**Ant.** 1 never.

everlasting adj. **1.** Heaven will give him everlasting peace: eternal, immortal, perpetual, lasting, never-ending, infinite. **2.** The poet wrote of the everlasting beauty of the Rocky Mountains: long-lasting, ever-living, timeless, imperishable, durable, indestructible, undying, continual. **3.** Your everlasting complaints annoy everyone: constant, endless, ceaseless, unceasing, incessant, perpetual, continuous, interminable, wearisome, tiresome, tedious. —**Ant.** 1, 2 transitory, temporary, passing, fleeting, ephemeral, momentary, short-lived, transient. 3 intermittent, occasional.

everyday adj. **1.** Cooking breakfast is an everyday job: daily, day after day, quotidian. **2.** After church, change into your everyday clothes: routine, ordinary, common, commonplace, workaday, usual, customary, familiar, established, regular; conventional, stock, run-of-the-mill, dull, mundane, unimaginative; trite, hackneyed, stereotyped; Slang square. —**Ant.** 1 occasional, infrequent, irregular, now and then, incidental, periodic, sporadic. 2 original, imaginative, extraordinary, uncommon, unusual, unique, individual, exciting, interesting, fantastic, outlandish; Slang far-out.

everything n. Everything was somehow connected: all, aggregate, all things, business, entirety, lot, total, universe, whole, whole lot, Informal whole shebang.

everywhere adv. Flags flew everywhere to celebrate our great holiday: every place, in all places, far and wide, far and near; extensively, ubiquitously; universally, all over, the world over; throughout, to the four winds. —**Ant.** nowhere, here and there.

evict v. The landlord evicted the tenant for nonpayment of rent: turn out, remove, dispossess, dislodge, expel, eject, oust, kick out, throw out, get rid of.

eviction n. Non-payment of rent resulted in eviction: removal, clearance, dislodgement, dis-

possession, ejection, expulsion, ouster, throwing out, Informal boot, bounce, walking papers.

evidence n. The suspect's fingerprints on the gun were the main evidence against him. Her smile was evidence of her happiness: proof, grounds, material proof, fact; substantiation, documentation, corroboration, confirmation, affirmation, authentication; exhibit, testimony, indication, sign, token; illustration, exemplification.

evident adj. The applause made it evident the play was a hit: clear, plain, obvious, apparent, manifest, conspicuous, perceptible, noticeable, demonstrable, certain, patent, unmistakable, unquestionable, undeniable, plain as the nose on your face; visible, tangible. —**Ant.** unclear, obscure, inconspicuous, imperceptible, doubtful, uncertain, vague, questionable, dubious; secret, covert, undisclosed, unknown, hidden, concealed, undiscovered.

evidently adv. He's been sniffling all day and evidently has a cold: apparently, assumedly, to all appearances; obviously, clearly, plainly, certainly, unquestionably, unmistakably, undeniably, doubtless, doubtlessly.

evil adj. **1.** Shakespeare characterizes Richard III as an evil king: bad, wicked, iniquitous, immoral, sinful, base, unprincipled, sinister, malevolent, malicious, malignant, vile, villainous, vicious, nefarious, heinous, black-hearted, unscrupulous, pernicious, venal. —n. **2.** The minister preached against evil: sin, wickedness, immorality, wrongdoing, vice, baseness, iniquity, depravity, turpitude, corruption. —**Ant.** 1 good, honorable, worthy, moral, exemplary; wholesome, upright, virtuous, benevolent, kind, good, human, humane, merciful, sympathetic, benign. 2 good, goodness, virtue, morality, righteousness.

evoke v. The book evoked memories of his boyhood: bring forth, call forth, call up, summon, invoke, conjure up, elicit, invite, induce, produce, suggest, stimulate, provoke, excite, stir, arouse, rouse, waken, awaken. —**Ant.** repress, suppress, restrain, hold back, inhibit, stifle, curb, check, crush; prevent, subdue, silence, stop, extinguish.

evolution n. The 20th century has seen a startling evolution in medical research: growth, development, unfolding, progression, rise, increase, expansion, enlargement; maturation, fruition; change, metamorphosis. —**Ant.** deterioration, withering, contraction, shrinking, decrease, diminution, falling off.

evolve v. The simple plan evolved into a complicated scheme: develop, grow, expand, enlarge, increase, unfold, unroll, mature, ripen. —**Ant.** deteriorate, wither, contract, shrink, decrease.

exacerbate v. Offering your opinion will only exacerbate the situation: aggravate, exaggerate, intensify, inflame, heighten, worsen, magnify, sharpen, deepen, fan the flames, pour oil on the fire, add fuel to the flames, rub salt into the wound, add insult to injury. —**Ant.** relieve, soothe, comfort, alleviate, assuage, mollify.

exact *adj.* **1.** *Please give your exact age:* correct, accurate, specific, explicit, precise, right, true; clear-cut, unequivocal, on the head, on the nose, to the letter, literal. **2.** *Watchmaking is an exact skill:* meticulous, painstaking, exacting, strict; careful, punctilious, scrupulous, systematic, methodical. —*v.* **3.** *The victors exacted ransoms for their hostages:* demand, claim, extract, take, wrest, force, require, compel, squeeze, mulct, extort. —**Ant.** 1 approximate, imprecise, inaccurate, incorrect. 2 sloppy, careless, slovenly, devil-may-care.

exacting *adj.* **1.** *General Patton was an exacting commander:* demanding, meticulous, unsparing, critical, strict, rigid, unbending, stern, severe, harsh, hard, hard-headed, hard-nosed, no-nonsense. **2.** *Volunteers are needed for an exacting assignment:* demanding, hard, arduous, difficult, tough, trying, strenuous. —**Ant.** 1 easy, easygoing, carefree, nonchalant, devil-may-care, soft, softhearted, lenient, permissive. 2 easy, effortless, undemanding.

exactly *adv.* **1.** *Where exactly is the pain?:* precisely, specifically, explicitly; accurately, correctly, truly, literally. **2.** *You may do exactly as you like:* just, entirely, absolutely, fully, wholly, precisely, quite, strictly. **3.** *Exactly, we agree:* quite so, that's right, indeed, of course, certainly, definitely, assuredly, just so. —**Ant.** 1 approximately, loosely, more or less; inaccurately, incorrectly.

exactness *n.* *Her exactness in matters of detail was legendary:* precision, preciseness, carefulness, correctness, definiteness, definitiveness, exactitude, faultlessness, nicety, orderliness, painstakingness, regularity, rigor, rigorousness, scrupulousness, strictness, unequivocalness. —**Ant.** inexactness, imprecision, inaccuracy, incorrectness.

exaggerate *v.* *The fisherman exaggerated the size of his catch:* overstate, magnify, amplify, hyperbolize, enlarge on, stretch, embroider, embellish, overdo, boast, lay it on. —**Ant.** understate, minimize, disparage, qualify.

exaggerated *adj.* *The exaggerated descriptions compelled disbelief:* inflated, magnified, amplified, embellished, embroidered, excessive, extravagant, farfetched hyperbolic, melodramatic, overblown, overdone, overestimated, overstated, overwrought, preposterous, pretentious, strained, stylized, unrealistic.

exaggeration *n.* *To say we were crushed was no exaggeration:* inflation, magnification, amplification, boasting, coloring, elaboration, embroidery, enlargement, excess, extravagance, fancy, fantasy, hyperbole, overemphasis, pretension, pretentiousness, overestimation, overstatement. —**Ant.** restraint, underplaying, understatement.

exalt *v.* **1.** *The retiring professor was exalted by his colleagues:* laud, extol, praise, pay tribute to, honor, applaud, acclaim, cheer, celebrate, commend, make much of; glorify, venerate, magnify, worship. **2.** *The orchestra gave a performance that truly exalted the audience:* uplift, elevate, inspire, ennoble, elate, stimulate, exhilarate. —**Ant.** 1 damn, condemn, disgrace, degrade, dishonor, shame, debase, demean, lower, humble, humiliate, disparage, depreciate, belittle, *Slang* put down. 2 depress, dispirit, dishearten, weary; dismay, appall.

exaltation *n.* **1.** *The people welcomed the returning heroes with exaltation:* tribute, praise, celebration, praising, eulogizing, panegyric, honor, dignity, glory; grandeur, nobility; worship, veneration, deification. **2.** *Her exaltation at visiting the Vatican lasted many days:* elation, exultation, ecstasy, rapture, transport, exhilaration, *Slang* high, happiness, bliss. —**Ant.** 1 damnation, condemnation, depreciation, debasement, belittling, degradation, dishonoring, humiliation, *Slang* put-down, depression, dejection, melancholia, gloom, despondency, blues; sorrow, sadness, misery.

exalted *adj.* **1.** *Kings are the most exalted of men. The poet Milton wrote in an exalted style:* high-ranking, noble, lordly, august, lofty, illustrious; magnificent, glorious, grand, elevated, dignified, venerable, honorable, notable. **2.** *The play put us in an exalted mood:* ecstatic, rapturous, inspired, excited, happy, elated, blissful, heightened, lofty, uplifted, *Slang* up. —**Ant.** 1 lowly, vulgar, common, ignoble, base, modest, unassuming; lowborn, lowbred, plebeian, servile. 2 depressed, dejected, glum, gloomy, despondent, blue; sorrowful, sad, low, miserable.

examination *n.* **1.** *The appraiser made a thorough examination of the house:* inspection, scrutiny, survey, perusal, looking over, probe, analysis, investigation, review, study, assay, audit; physical checkup. **2.** *The examination consisted of 50 true or false questions:* exam, test, review, quiz; midterm, final.

examine *v.* **1.** *Examine the merchandise carefully:* look over, inspect, scrutinize, view, survey, observe, peruse, scan. **2.** *Examine the facts carefully:* study, probe, look into, inquire into, consider, investigate, explore, ponder, review; audit, take stock of. **3.** *The teacher examined the students in chemistry. The lawyer examined the witness:* test, quiz; question, query, interrogate, *Slang* pump, grill. —**Ant.** 1 ignore, overlook. 2 accept at face value.

example *n.* *Notre Dame cathedral is an outstanding example of Gothic architecture:* sample, illustration, representation, exemplification, specimen, case in point, archetype, prototype, pattern, model, ideal, standard, exemplar, paragon. —**Ant.** anomaly, paradox; abnormality, aberration, contradiction, incongruity.

exasperate *v.* *Constant interruptions exasperated the speaker:* irritate, annoy, rile, irk, anger, madden, incense, infuriate, enrage; rankle, aggravate, provoke, try the patience of; offend, ruffle, chafe, harass, vex, pique, bother; *Slang* bug, turn off. —**Ant.** mollify, pacify, placate, appease, propitiate, conciliate; calm, assuage, tranquilize.

exasperation *n.* *Her refusal to comply added to his exasperation:* irritation, aggravation, vexation, anger, annoyance, bother, exacerbation, nuisance, passion, pique, provocation, resentment, ire.

excavate v. The engineers excavated a chamber in the mountain. Heinrich Schliemann excavated the ruins of ancient Troy: make a hole in, hollow out, tunnel, dig, dig out, scoop out; gouge, mine, quarry, cut out; burrow, furrow, groove; unearth, uncover, dig up. **—Ant.** fill, fill in, fill up, bury, cover up.

excavation n. By now the excavation was very deep: cavity, mine, quarry, burrow, cut, digging, ditch, dugout, hole, hollow, trench, trough.

exceed v. 1. The police will give you a ticket if you exceed the speed limit: go beyond, go over, pass, overdo, outreach, outrun, outpace, outstrip, overshoot, transcend, surmount. 2. In the Olympic Games, Americans exceeded in basketball: excel, predominate, surpass, come first, be superior, outrival, outrank. **—Ant.** 1 stay within, keep in, keep under. 2 fail, be inferior.

exceedingly adv. The children were exceedingly well behaved: very, extremely, greatly, especially, notably, very highly; vastly, enormously, outstandingly, impressively, eminently, preeminently, supremely, surpassingly, immeasurably, excessively, superlatively, extraordinarily, unwontedly, unusually, inordinately, amazingly, astonishingly.

excel v. In international competition, the Australians excel at tennis: exceed, surpass, prevail, predominate, rank first, tower above, outstrip, outrival, outdo, walk off with the honors, Slang take the cake. **—Ant.** fail, fall behind, fall short, be inadequate, be inferior to.

excellence n. Swiss watches are renowned for their excellence: high quality, quality, superiority, perfection, greatness, merit, eminence, preeminence, transcendence, distinction. **—Ant.** inferiority, poor quality, imperfection, deficiency; fault, blemish, defect, flaw, shortcoming, inadequacy, failing, frailty.

excellent adj. Franz Liszt was an excellent composer and pianist: outstanding, superior, superlative, exceptional, superb, classic, choice, capital, sterling, great, tremendous, terrific, wonderful, fine, superfine, topnotch, first-rate, first-class; admirable, notable; matchless, peerless, preeminent, exemplary; Informal prime, super, swell, aces, tops, grade A, A-1, Slang nifty, bang-up. **—Ant.** bad, poor, imperfect, inferior, terrible, awful, substandard, second-rate, second-class, below par, incompetent, inexpert, unskilled, faulty, Slang lousy.

except prep. 1. Put everything except the vase in the box: excepting, excluding, exclusive of, but, save, saving, other than, barring, besides. **—v.** 2. The A students were excepted from taking the exam: exempt, excuse, exclude, omit, eliminate; bar, ban, shut out, enjoin, remove, pass over, count out, disallow, reject. **—Ant.** 1 including. 2 include, reckon, count.

exception 1. All the houses in the block are brick, with the exception of the corner house: exclusion, exemption, omission, elimination, removal, debarment; separation, segregation, seclusion, isolation; leaving out, shutting out, disallowment; rejection, renunciation, repudiation. 2. This case is an exception to the rule: devia-

tion, special case, anomaly, rarity, inconsistency, irregularity, oddity, peculiarity, difference. **—Ant.** 1 inclusion, taking in, counting in. 2 consist-ency, regularity, conformity.

exceptional adj. 1. Snow this late in the year is exceptional: unusual, extraordinary, unique, uncommon, rare, singular, irregular, atypical, anomalous, abnormal, peculiar, unwonted, unnatural, queer, strange, odd, aberrant, unprecedented, unheard of, phenomenal, freakish. 2. The movie was good but not exceptional: better than average, outstanding, superior, excellent, noteworthy, first-class; wonderful, terrific, great, marvelous, special, extraordinary, remarkable, incomparable, inimitable, Slang out-of-sight. **—Ant.** 1 common, ordinary, usual, normal, typical, regular, natural, expected, customary, familiar. 2 average, mediocre, so-so, bad, terrible, awful, second-rate; Slang lousy, crummy.

excerpt n. The minister read excerpts from the Book of Genesis: extract, selection, portion, fragment, section, piece, part, abstract, quotation, quoted passage.

excess n. 1. The child had an excess of ener-gy: surplus, overabundance, superabundance, undue amount, too much, oversupply, surfeit, plethora; profusion, fullness, lavishness, avalanche, flood, inundation, overflow; glut, repletion. **—adj.** 2. The excess furniture was stored in the cellar: surplus, extra, excessive, overflow; remainder, residue, spare. **—Ant.** 1 deficiency, lack, shortage, scarcity, dearth, paucity, inadequacy, insufficiency, scantness. 2 insufficient, inadequate, scanty, scarce.

excessive adj. Excessive spending can lead to bankruptcy: excess, overabundant, undue, too much, profuse; extreme, superfluous, extravagant, immoderate, inordinate, exaggerated, unreasonable, needless, unnecessary, disproportionate, senseless. **—Ant.** insufficient, deficient, inadequate, lacking, wanting, scarce, meager, scanty, scant, skimpy, sparse.

exchange v. 1. The trapper exchanged furs for flour, coffee, and gunpowder: trade, swap, barter, trade off, convert into. 2. My cousins and I always exchange Christmas gifts: swap, interchange, give and take, reciprocate. **—n.** 3. There was an exchange of greetings among the old friends: interchange, reciprocity, give-and-take; trade, swap, switch, bandying, tit for tat, Latin quid pro quo. **—Ant.** 1 keep, hold on to.

exchangeable adj. All our purchases were exchangeable: interchangeable, replaceable, returnable.

excise[1] v. Alcohol and tobacco are subject to excise: tax, duty, surcharge, impost.

excise[2] v. The surgeon excised the carbuncle with great skill: remove, cut out, cut off, eradicate, extract, pluck out.

excitable adj. The excitable manager yelled and waved his arms: emotional, passionate, fiery, quick-tempered, hot-tempered, hasty, irascible, irritable, choleric. **—Ant.** unemotional, cool, calm, serene, tranquil.

excite v. 1. News of the discovery of gold in California excited the nation: thrill, electrify, galvanize, rouse, arouse, spur on, stir up, agitate, move, stimulate, energize, kindle, fire, inflame, provoke, animate, incite, foment, instigate; titillate, get a kick out of. **2.** *The professor's lecture on G. B. Shaw excited our interest:* evoke, elicit, waken, awaken, stimulate, whet, pique. **—Ant.** 1 dull, lull, bore, soothe, quiet, calm, pacify. 2 allay, appease, mollify, diminish; deaden, kill, quench.

excited *adj. The excited brother embraced his long-lost sister:* eager, agitated, stirred up, impassioned, stimulated, ruffled, discomposed, perturbed, eager. **—Ant.** calm, unruffled, composed, pacific.

excitement *n. The canoe trip over the rapids was full of excitement:* thrill, adventure, *Slang* kicks; stimulation, interest, animation, enthusiasm, elation, action, activity, furor, ferment, commotion, ado, brouhaha, turmoil, tumult, agitation, flurry, flutter, frenzy, stir, *Informal* fireworks, *Slang* flap, to-do, hoopla. **—Ant.** serenity, peace; inactivity, lethargy, sluggishness; dullness, boredom.

exciting *adj. That was the most exciting film of the year:* thrilling, electrifying, breathtaking, hair-raising, spine-tingling, rousing, sensational, stirring, impelling, provocative, stimulating, moving, affecting, inspiring, dazzling, zestful; titillating, spicy, risqué. **—Ant.** unexciting, uninteresting, dull, quiet, stodgy, boring, monotonous, wearisome, humdrum, drab, dreary, soporific.

exclaim *v. "You're a liar!" she exclaimed:* cry out, call out, ejaculate, shout, yell, bellow, howl, proclaim, vociferate.

exclamation *n. With an exclamation of surprise she recognized her long-lost relative:* ejaculation, vociferation, outcry, cry, shout, yell, shriek, bellow, howl, squeal, screech, yelp; interjection, expletive. **—Ant.** whisper, mutter, murmur, mumble; statement, question.

exclude *v.* **1.** *The men's bowling league voted to exclude women:* keep out, bar, ban, shut the door on, shut out, prevent entrance of, blackball, boycott, reject, prohibit, forbid, disallow, refuse; evict, remove, banish, expel, oust, eject, throw out. **2.** *The doctor excluded food poisoning as the cause of the illness:* rule out, omit, except, set aside, leave out; repudiate. **—Ant.** 1 invite, welcome; admit, include, accept, allow.

exclusion *n. The court ruled that the exclusion of women from the school was illegal:* keeping out, barring, nonadmission, debarment, rejection, prohibition, refusal; restraint, prevention, preclusion; eviction, removal, banishment, dismissal, expelling, ouster, ejection, expulsion, throwing out. **—Ant.** admittance, inclusion, acceptance.

exclusive *adj.* **1.** *The millionaire belongs to an exclusive men's club:* select, elect, high-class, *Slang* posh; restricted, restrictive; closed, private; clannish, cliquish; aloof, snobbish. **2.** *The real estate agent has the exclusive right to sell the house:* sole, single, private, unshared, undivided; complete, entire, total, absolute, full. **—Ant.** 1 open, unrestricted; popular, common.

2 nonexclusive, shared, divided; partial, incomplete.

exclusively *adv. The gift was meant exclusively for you:* solely, singularly, alone, but, completely, entirely, only, particularly, wholly. **—Ant.** shared, common.

excommunicate *v. The church has the power to excommunicate heretics:* remove, exclude from sacraments, anathematize, divest of membership, unchurch; expel, eject, banish, ban, oust. **—Ant.** admit, enroll; readmit, reinstate.

excoriate *v. She took time to excoriate her employee:* vilify, attack, berate, blister, castigate, censure, chastise, condemn, denounce, flay, lambaste, lash, rebuke, reproach, reprove, revile, scold, upbraid.

excruciating *adj. The medication eased the excruciating pain:* extremely painful, unbearable, insufferable, unendurable, agonizing, torturous, racking, tormenting; acute, severe, extreme, fierce, intense, violent, cutting, lacerating. **—Ant.** bearable, tolerable, endurable; mild, slight, gentle, trivial.

excursion *n. The family made a weekend excursion to a campground:* outing, junket, trip, pleasure trip, short journey, tour, jaunt, sally, expedition, sortie; (*variously*) ride, drive, voyage, cruise, flight, walk, stroll, hike, tramp, ramble, trek.

excusable *adj. Minor lapses were excusable:* permissable, allowable, condonable, defensible, exculpatory, forgivable, justifiable, pardonable, reasonable, tenable, understandable, warrantable, within limits, explainable, fair.

excuse *v.* **1.** *Please excuse me for interrupting:* forgive, pardon, make allowance for, pass over, bear with, indulge, accept one's apology. **2.** *Don't excuse his rudeness by saying he was in a hurry:* apologize for, justify, explain, defend, vindicate, ask forgiveness for; condone, pardon, let one off, absolve, acquit, exonerate, exculpate, clear; mitigate, palliate, extenuate, disregard, gloss over, overlook, whitewash. **3.** *In some jurisdictions persons over 65 may be excused from jury duty if they desire:* release, exempt, free, spare, let off, relieve of. **—***n.* **4.** *Ignorance of the law is no excuse:* justification, defense, vindication, acceptable explanation, absolution, exoneration, exemption, reason, alibi, argument, plea for forgiveness. **—Ant.** 1, 2 censure, blame, criticize; chastise, castigate, discipline, chasten, correct, punish, charge, accuse, condemn, convict, sentence. 3 hold liable for, hold responsible for, subject to; compel, obligate, oblige, force into. 4 accusation, charge.

execrable *adj. His execrable conduct was unparalleled:* revolting, abhorrent, abominable, atrocious, accursed, cursed, confounded, despicable, detestable, hateful, disgusting, heinous, low, loathsome, monstrous, nauseous, obnoxious, odious, repulsive, offensive, sickening, wretched, horrible, horrific.

execrate *v. He execrated the others for their sins:* excoriate, abominate, censure, anathematize, condemn, curse, damn, denounce, deplore, detest, despise, hate, imprecate, objurgate, vilify, revile.

execration *n. The witch hurled a stream of execration:* malediction, curse, cursing, profanity, excoriation, imprecation, abhorrence, abomination, blasphemy, condemnation, contempt, damnation, denunciation, vilification, obscenity, loathing, hatred, detesting.

execute *v.* **1.** *The general's plans were executed by his subordinates:* carry out, effect, put into effect, discharge, administer, accomplish, fulfill, achieve, complete, effectuate, consummate, realize, carry through, perpetrate, enforce. **2.** *Nathan Hale was executed as a spy by the British in 1776:* put to death, inflict capital punishment on; kill, slay; murder, assassinate, massacre. **3.** *The violin concerto was executed with great flair:* perform, render, play, do; act, enact, sustain.

execution *n.* **1.** *The execution of our plans must be carried out quickly:* carrying out, effecting, accomplishment, administration, performance, discharge, implementation, transaction, realization, fulfillment, achievement, completion. **2.** *France uses the guillotine for executions:* putting to death, infliction of capital punishment; killing, slaying. **3.** *The diver's execution of the half gainer was flawless:* performance, doing, rendition, interpretation.

executive *n.* **1.** *An executive should have wide business experience:* administrator, administrative head, director, manager; (*variously*) president, chairman, superintendent, supervisor, overseer. —*adj.* **2.** *The company is always looking for young women with executive potential:* administrative, managerial, directorial, supervisory, leadership. **—Ant.** 1 laborer, worker, subordinate, hired hand, flunky, menial, underling.

exemplary *adj.* **1.** *The older boy's exemplary behavior had a good influence on the younger:* worthy of imitation, emulative, model; admirable, praiseworthy, commendable, laudable, noteworthy, estimable, sterling, nonpareil, ideal, meritorious. **2.** *The costumes were exemplary of Renaissance dress:* typical, characteristic, model, illustrative, representative, sample. **—Ant.** 1 objectionable, blameworthy, punishable. 2 atypical, unusual, uncommon, unique, peculiar.

exemplify *v. The novel* Tom Sawyer *exemplifies 19th-century life in the United States:* typify, epitomize, characterize, illustrate, depict, represent, demonstrate, instance, embody, personify. **—Ant.** misrepresent, falsify.

exempt *v.* **1.** *A doctor's note will exempt you from physical education:* except, excuse, pardon, relieve, free, release, spare, absolve, clear, privilege, grant immunity to. —*adj.* **2.** *Church property is usually exempt from taxation:* not subject to, immune, excepted, excused, relieved, freed, absolved, spared, cleared, not liable to, released from; privileged. **—Ant.** 1 subject, oblige, liable, expose. 2 liable, subject; responsible, chargeable, answerable.

exemption *n.* **1.** *Because of poor eyesight, Fa-*ther had an exemption from military service during World War II:* release, immunity, freedom, absolution, dispensation, exception, excuse. **2.** *Children may be listed as exemptions on your income tax return:* deduction, allowance; expense. **—Ant.** 1 responsibility, obligation, liability.

exercise *n.* **1.** *Exercise stimulates the flow of blood:* workout, warm-up, movement, physical activity; calisthenics, aerobics, isometrics, gymnastics, a daily dozen. **2.** *Singing the scales is the best exercise a singer can give her vocal cords. The army is having military exercises this week:* practice, training, schooling, drill. **3.** *The exercise of caution is necessary when driving. Will you attend the graduation exercises?:* use, practice, employment, utilization, application, discharge; ceremony, performance, program. —*v.* **4.** *If you want to stay healthy you must exercise:* work out, be physically active, do calisthenics; train, drill, follow a training regimen, discipline, school, break in, give lessons, tutor, teach, develop, prepare, inculcate, accustom. **5.** *The President exercises the office of Commander in Chief. To lose weight, exercise restraint in eating:* carry out, perform, execute, discharge, employ, utilize, wield; apply, practice, exert, display, demonstrate, show, exhibit. **—Ant.** 1 inactivity, idleness. 3 avoidance, evasion, ignoring, overlooking. 4 be sedentary, be inactive. 5 avoid, evade, ignore, overlook, eschew.

exert *v. If you exert all your strength you can move that rock:* put forth, put in action, set in motion, exercise, employ, wield, use, utilize, make use of, apply, expend, discharge, resort to, avail oneself of.

exertion *n. It took a great deal of exertion to push the car up the hill. Chess requires a lot of mental exertion:* effort, energy, strength, labor, toil, work, pains, trouble, struggle, travail, endeavor, industry, application, activity, *Slang* elbow grease. **—Ant.** idleness, inertia; rest, repose, ease, leisure.

exhale *v. When we exhaled in the cold we could see our breath:* breathe out, respire, expire, emit breath, breathe; pant, puff, huff. **—Ant.** inhale, breathe in.

exhaust *v.* **1.** *The soldiers had exhausted their supply of ammunition:* use up, run through, expend, deplete, dissipate, spend, consume, finish. **2.** *The fast game of tennis exhausted me:* wear out, tire, overtire, fatigue, drain, enervate, devitalize, sap one's energy; *Slang* poop, fag, bush; tax, strain, weaken, debilitate, disable. **3.** *The chemist made a vacuum in the bell jar when he exhausted the air from it:* empty, draw out, draw off, drain. **—Ant.** 1 amass, obtain, get, restock, replenish; save, conserve, preserve, keep, store, hoard. 2 invigorate, refresh, renew, revive, vivify, animate, enliven, innerve, strengthen.

exhausted *adj.* **1.** *The children were exhausted after the day's play:* tired out, dead tired, fatigued, worn out, played out, all in, done in, devitalized, enervated, drained, spent, wearied;

Slang beat, bushed, pooped. **2.** *The campers' supply of food was exhausted:* used up, finished, spent, gone, depleted, consumed, drained, expended, emptied; bankrupt, impoverished. **—Ant.** 1 full of pep, ready to go, full of vim and vigor; invigorated, refreshed, revived, vivified, animated, enlivened. 2 replenished, restored, saved, conserved, preserved, kept.

exhaustion *n.* **1.** *The joggers were ready to drop with exhaustion:* fatigue, weariness, tiredness, enervation. **2.** *The exhaustion of the army's rations caused its defeat:* using up, spending, consumption; depletion, draining. **—Ant.** 1 energy, pep, vim, vigor, new strength. 2 replenishment; conservation, preservation.

exhaustive *adj.* *The student did exhaustive research before writing the term paper:* comprehensive, profound, all-inclusive, thorough, intensive, complete, sweeping, in-depth, all-out, all-embracing. **—Ant.** hit-or-miss, catch-as-catch-can, incomplete, cursory, superficial.

exhibit *v.* **1.** *Manufacturers are exhibiting their new model cars:* display, show, put on view, present for inspection, reveal, make public, parade, demonstrate, unveil, bring to light, air, flaunt, brandish. **—n. 2.** *This month there's an exhibit of modern sculpture at the museum:* exhibition, display, exposition, show, public showing. **—Ant.** hide, conceal, suppress, repress, mask, secret, bury.

exhibition *n.* *There will be an exhibition of antique glassware at the fair:* exhibit, show, showing, public showing, display, exposition, public presentation, demonstration, unveiling, array.

exhilarate *v.* *The walk in the beautiful woods exhilarated the hikers:* fill with high spirits, excite, stimulate, invigorate, hearten, lift, perk up, enliven, animate, quicken, elate, gladden, delight, cheer. **—Ant.** depress, dispirit, sadden, deject.

exhilarating *adj.* *The climb to the mountaintop was exhilarating:* invigorating, animating, exciting, breathtaking, rousing, cheering, electric, enlivening, exalting, gladdening, inspiring, intoxicating, quickening, stimulating, stirring, thrilling, tonic, uplifting, vitalizing.

exhilaration *n.* *After winning the game, the team was full of exhilaration:* high spirits, exaltation, elation, liveliness, animation, excitement, vivacity, delight, gladness, joyousness, lightheartedness, gaiety. **—Ant.** dejection, depression, sadness, gloom.

exhort *v.* *The general exhorted his troops to stand fast:* encourage, spur, goad, press, prod, give a pep talk to; *Slang* egg on; urge, plead with, beseech, enjoin, implore, appeal to, persuade; advise, advocate, recommend, admonish, bid. **—Ant.** dissuade, discourage; forbid, prohibit, enjoin.

exhortation *n.* *His speech was part pep talk, part exhortation:* incitement, entreaty, warning, admonition, advice, beseeching, bidding, caution, counsel, encouragement, goading, persuasion, sermon, urging.

exhume *v.* *They received permission to exhume the body:* disinter, dig up, disentomb, resurrect, reveal, disclose, unearth. **—Ant.** entomb, bury, inter.

exigency *n.* **1.** *A ship's captain must be able to cope with any exigency:* emergency, contingency, crisis, circumstance, predicament, quandary, plight, strait, extremity, difficulty, hardship; *Slang* pickle, pinch, scrape, fix, jam. **2.** *We have to cope with the exigencies of daily living:* requirements, necessities, demands, needs, constraints, urgencies.

exigent *adj.* **1.** *Famine made action exigent:* critical, crucial, acute, burning, clamorous, crying, imperative, importunate, insistent, needful, necessary, urgent, pressing. **2.** *The exigent task was too much for her:* burdensome, exacting, demanding, difficult, grievous, hard, rigorous, oppressive, severe, weighty, strict, stringent.

exile *v.* **1.** *Russia exiled Alexandr Solzhenitsyn for writing political novels:* banish, deport, expel, eject, oust, expatriate, drive out, strip of citizenship. **—n. 2.** *The king drove his enemy into exile:* banishment, expulsion, expatriation. **3.** *Political exiles seek refuge in neutral countries:* exiled person, banished person, refugee, expellee, displaced person, D.P., émigré; outcast, pariah, expatriate. **—Ant.** 1 grant refuge, grant citizenship; welcome, accept, embrace.

exist *v.* **1.** *A few old whaling ships still exist:* be in existence, survive, endure, last, remain, stay, abide. **2.** *Humans could not exist on Mars:* live, survive, maintain life, breathe. **3.** *A life free from all worry just doesn't exist:* occur, have existence, prevail, happen, ensue, obtain. **—Ant.** 1 pass away, disappear, vanish. 2 die, perish.

existence *n.* **1.** *Do you believe in the existence of the Loch Ness monster?:* actuality, reality, presence, animation; tangibility, materiality. **2.** *The patient's very existence depends on the doctor's skill:* life, being, survival; subsistence, continuance, endurance. **—Ant.** 1 nonexistence, nothingness. 2 death, passing away.

exit *n.* **1.** *There is only one exit from the theater:* way out, egress, doorway out, passage out. **2.** *We made a hasty exit when the fight started:* departure, withdrawal, retreat, exodus, escape. **—v. 3.** *Please exit by the rear door:* leave, depart, go out, withdraw, escape; *Slang* take a powder, blow, cut out, split. **—Ant.** 1, 2 entrance. 3 enter, come in.

exodus *n.* *On summer weekends the highways are filled by the exodus from the city:* departure, going forth, exit, flight, hegira, migration; emigration, exile.

exonerate *v.* *New evidence exonerated the prisoner. The jury exonerated the accused:* clear, free, absolve, vindicate, exculpate; find innocent, acquit. **—Ant.** prove guilty, condemn, blame; find guilty.

exorbitant *adj.* *That restaurant charges exorbitant prices:* excessive, enormous, unreasonable, preposterous, outrageous, extreme, undue, out-of-line, inordinate, extortionate; overpriced, high-priced, expensive, extravagant, costly, dear. **—Ant.** fair, equitable; cheap, reasonable, inexpensive, dirt cheap.

exotic *adj.* **1.** *Palm trees are exotic to northern* *countries:* foreign, not native, not indigenous, from abroad, alien. **2.** *She was famed for her exotic hats:* unusual, different, unique, intriguing, striking, exceptional, quaint, colorful, peculiar, strange, unfamiliar, outlandish. **—Ant.** 1 native. 2 commonplace, run-of-the-mill, ordinary.

expand *v.* **1.** *The business has expanded by 50 percent this year:* grow, increase, enlarge, magnify, multiply, amplify, develop, evolve, heighten, aggrandize, augment; widen, dilate, swell, distend, fatten, inflate. **2.** *The eagle expanded its wings as it rose in the air:* stretch, spread, spread out, outspread, extend, open, unfold, unfurl, unroll, unravel. **—Ant.** 1 decrease, fall off, shrink, contract, curtail, condense. 2 close, fold, furl, roll up.

expanse *n.* *Covered wagons had to cross the vast expanse of the Great Plains:* extent, area, space, range, sweep, field, stretch, reach, breadth, magnitude, compass. **—Ant.** limit, confine, enclosure.

expansion *n.* *Future expansion of the business calls for two new factories. The runway is undergoing expansion to accommodate larger planes:* enlargement, enlarging, increase, augmentation, growth, development, magnifying, amplification, multiplying, amplifying; extension, spreading, lengthening, widening, stretching; swelling, distention, dilation. **—Ant.** decrease, shrinkage, contraction, reduction, shortening, curtailment, cutback.

expansive *adj.* **1.** *A good salesman usually has an expansive personality:* open, free, effusive, exuberant, extroverted, outgoing, unrestrained, liberal, genial, amiable, affable, uninhibited, unrepressed; generous, bountiful, bounteous. **2.** *A judge must have an expansive knowledge of the law:* extensive, broad, vast, comprehensive, wide-ranging, wide, far-reaching, general, voluminous, capacious. **—Ant.** 1 reserved, restrained, repressed, stiff, inhibited, introverted, shy, antisocial; taciturn, silent, reticent. 2 narrow, limited, restricted, circumscribed.

expatriate *n.* *During World War II, many German expatriates settled in the United States:* exile, émigré, refugee, displaced person, D.P., political refugee, banished person, deported person, outcast, pariah.

expect *v.* **1.** *The skiers expected deep snow in Vermont:* look forward to, plan on, look for, envision, anticipate, foresee, contemplate, reckon on, bargain for. **2.** *The company expects promptness of every employee:* demand, look for, require, trust, rely upon, reckon upon, count on, hope for. **3.** *I expect that she will be here soon:* assume, presume, guess, suppose, believe, surmise, imagine, calculate, contemplate, conjecture, *Informal* reckon. **—Ant.** 1 despair of, lose faith in; dread, fear.

expectancy *n.* *We were all tense with expectancy:* expectation, anticipation, surmise, assumption, assurance, belief, calculation, hope, likelihood, presentiment, probability, presumption, prospect, supposition, waiting, suspense.

expectant *adj.* *The expectant students awaited*

their grades: anticipating, alert, anxious, apprehensive, awaiting, breathless, eager, vigilant, hopeful, waiting, watchful; pregnant, with child.

expectation *n.* *The team has every expectation of winning the championship:* expectancy, anticipation, likelihood, prospect, chance, presumption, assurance, confidence, hope, trust, reliance, belief, contemplation. **—Ant.** memory, recollection; unlikelihood, despair, discouragement, hopelessness.

expediency *n.* *The path of expediency was much traveled:* expedience, advantage, advisability, desirability, appropriateness, convenience, aptness, effectiveness, efficiency, propriety, helpfulness, opportunity, profitableness, propitiousness, suitability, utility, usefulness.

expedient *adj.* **1.** *The professor found it expedient to lecture from notes:* useful, helpful, worthwhile, advantageous, profitable, beneficial, practical, effective; desirable, advisable, wise, judicious. **2.** *In an expedient move, the legislators voted to raise their salaries:* self-serving, self-seeking, conniving, calculating, selfish, self-interested; opportune, politic. **—n. 3.** *The neon sign is ugly, but it's a necessary expedient to our business:* practical aid, help, advantage, benefit, profitable practice, strategem, tactic, resort, means, measure; makeshift device, instrument, stopgap. **—Ant.** 1 inexpedient, impractical, ineffective, detrimental, disadvantageous, harmful, undesirable, inadvisable, unadvisable, futile, vain, fruitless. 2 unselfish, altruistic; just, ethical.

expedite *v.* *Using postal zip codes expedites the delivery of mail:* hasten, speed up, accelerate, quicken, promote, further, facilitate, forward, advance, precipitate, dispatch, push through, rush, hurry. **—Ant.** slow, slow down, retard, impede, hinder, block, obstruct.

expedition *n.* **1.** *The scientists are on an expedition into the Brazilian jungle:* scientific trip, exploration; journey, voyage, trek; mission, enterprise, campaign. **2.** *The expedition slept in tents on the desert:* travelers, voyagers, wayfarers, adventurers, explorers.

expeditious *adj.* *The emergency demands expeditious action:* prompt, speedy, hasty, ready, quick, fast, swift, rapid, immediate, instant, punctual; alert, awake, ready, snappy, bright-eyed, effective, efficacious. **—Ant.** slow, dilatory, sluggish, leisurely, deliberate, inefficient, ineffective, ineffectual.

expel *v.* **1.** *The whale expelled water from his blowhole:* force out, drive out, cast out, eject, discharge, excrete, evacuate, eliminate, void, dislodge, spew. **2.** *The treasurer was expelled from the club for breaking the rules:* eject, oust, remove, throw out; discharge, fire, dismiss, cashier, drum out; *Slang* bounce, sack; banish, exile, evict. **—Ant.** 1 take in, ingest, inhale. 2 admit, accept, invite, welcome; hire, engage.

expend *v.* **1.** *The class expended a great amount of time on the project:* use up, spend, consume, go through; dissipate, drain, exhaust, empty, wear out, squander. **2.** *The treasury expended $50,000 on the new clubhouse:* spend, pay out, pay, disburse, dispense, give, donate, contribute; *Informal* fork out, shell out, lay out. **—Ant.** 1, 2 conserve, save, preserve, hoard. 2 earn, receive, collect.

expendable *adj.* **1.** *The city has a million dollars of expendable funds for street repair:* spendable, available, disbursable, payable. **2.** *Lives must be saved, but the equipment is expendable:* able to be sacrificed, relinquishable, consumable, forgoable, replaceable; dispensable, superfluous, extraneous, nonessential.

expenditure *n.* **1.** *Expenditures should always be less than income:* expenses, money spent, spending, disbursement, outlay, paying out; payment, cost, price, charge. **2.** *The project entailed a great expenditure of energy:* spending, expending, exertion, application, output, use, employment, consumption. **—Ant.** 1 receivables, receipts, income, profit. 2 conservation, saving, preservation, hoarding.

expense *n.* *The expense of remodeling the house is more than we can afford:* cost, price, charge, outlay; amount, quotation, rate, figure; source of expenditure, item paid for; drain, depletion; financial burden. **—Ant.** income, proceeds, return, profit, receipts, gain.

expensive *adj.* *The shop carries very expensive clothes:* costly, high-priced, dear; overpriced, exorbitant, extravagant, excessive, unreasonable, immoderate, uneconomical, beyond one's means. **—Ant.** cheap, inexpensive, economical, reasonable, bargain-basement.

experience *n.* **1.** *Experience is the best teacher:* personal knowledge, personal involvement, firsthand knowledge, observation, doing, practice, training, seasoning, familiarity, exposure. **2.** *Meeting the Japanese emperor was a memorable experience:* event, episode, incident, adventure, happening, encounter, occurrence, affair. *—v.* **3.** *Few North Americans experience real hunger:* know, undergo, live through, go through, encounter, meet, endure, suffer, sustain, bear; feel, sense, perceive, see, behold, view, observe; withstand. **—Ant.** inexperience; theory. 3 escape, miss.

experienced *adj.* *This work demands an experienced bookkeeper:* accomplished, practical, trained, seasoned, qualified, well-versed, knowing, veteran, skilled, expert, able, capable, competent, efficient, master; sophisticated, wise, worldly-wise. **—Ant.** inexperienced, impractical, untrained, unqualified, untried, green, apprentice, unskilled; inept, incompetent.

experiment *n.* **1.** *As an experiment she substituted honey for sugar in the icing. The research institute conducts experiments on jet engines:* test, trial, tentative procedure, tryout, venture; *Informal* flier, feeler; research, investigation, examination, analysis, verification, assay, experimentation. *—v.* **2.** *The chemist experimented with a new formula for dyes:* test, tryout, explore, *Slang* mess around with; research, investigate, analyze, examine, assay, seek proof for.

experimental *adj.* *The architect rendered several experimental designs:* tentative, speculative, conjectural, conceptual, developmental, trial, test, trial-and-error, rough, first-draft, new, radical, fresh. **—Ant.** traditional, proven, tried-and-true; hackneyed, commonplace, routine.

expert *n.* **1.** *Jane has become a chess expert:* authority, specialist, master, professional, virtuoso, connoisseur, mavin, ace, veteran, wizard, *Informal* whiz, *Slang* shark. *—adj.* **2.** *The riders were all expert horsemen:* skilled, skillful, masterful, masterly, professional, experienced, master, accomplished, trained, practiced, knowledgeable, qualified, proficient, able, apt, adept, deft, adroit, competent, capable, first-class; *Informal* ace, crackerjack, A-1. **—Ant.** 1 amateur, tyro, novice; dabbler, dilettante. 2 unskilled, amateurish, inexperienced, untrained, unqualified, inept, incompetent.

expertise *n.* *Landing a plane in fog takes a great deal of expertise:* special skill, skill, know-how, expertness, specialization, professionalism, *Informal* savvy.

expiate *v.* *By confessing your sins and being truly repentant you may expiate them:* atone for, do penance, rectify, make up for, make amends, redeem, compensate, redress, make reparation, make good, pay the penalty, pay the piper, wash away one's sins, shrive, square things, set one's house in order.

expire *v.* **1.** *The magazine subscription expires next month:* come to an end, run out, lapse, cease, discontinue, end, terminate, conclude, finish. **2.** *In the old play the heroine expired of a broken heart:* die, pass away, perish, decease, succumb, *Informal* give up the ghost, *Slang* kick off, kick the bucket. **—Ant.** 1 continue, renew, begin, start, commence. 2 live; be born.

explain *v.* **1.** *Can you explain how an airplane flies?:* describe, demonstrate, make clear, make plain, spell out, explicate, illustrate, illuminate. **2.** *The students were asked to explain the meaning of the poem. How do you explain such rude behavior?:* clarify, clear up, resolve, elucidate, interpret, account, give a reason for, fathom, justify, rationalize, give an explanation for. **—Ant.** 2 confuse, obscure, misinterpret.

explanation *n.* **1.** *The astronomers gave an explanation of how the orbits of the planets are related:* explication, account, description, elucidation, clarification. **2.** *There doesn't seem to be any explanation for the boy's erratic behavior:* reason, warrant, accounting, answer, cause, motive, motivation; justification, rationale, alibi, excuse.

explanatory *adj.* *The book had explanatory material at the back:* explicative, elucidatory, analytical, annotative, critical, demonstrative, descriptive, diagrammatic, discursive, enlightening, expositional, expository, illuminative, illustrative, informative, informing, instructive, interpretive, exegetic, exegetical.

expletive *n.* *They deleted all the expletives from the report:* curse, swear word, oath, profanity, exclamation, interjection.

explicate *v.* *She explicated what had to be done:* elucidate, amplify, clarify, enunciate, construe, demonstrate, develop, enlarge upon, expand, expatiate, explain, illustrate, expound, interpret.

explicit *adj. She gave explicit directions about the way the rug should be cleaned:* specific, definite, precise, exact, express, certain, distinct, absolute, categorical, unequivocal, unqualified, clear, clearly expressed, straightforward; candid, frank, plain, direct, outspoken, blunt, pointed, unreserved. **—Ant.** vague, general, indefinite, inexact, ambiguous, equivocal, uncertain, enigmatic, cryptic, obscure; implicit, implied, indirect, oblique; suggested, hinted.

explode *v.* **1.** *Fortunately, no one was hurt when the gas main exploded:* blow up, burst loudly, burst violently, go off; erupt, blast, discharge violently; set off, detonate. **2.** *The boss exploded with anger when he saw the sales report:* burst out emotionally, erupt, utter noisily, express noisily. **3.** *New facts explode the theory that the moon was once part of the earth:* disprove, prove wrong, prove false, belie, refute, expose, discredit, repudiate, invalidate, burst, destroy. **—Ant.** 1 implode; fizzle.

exploit *n.* **1.** *Flying the Atlantic alone was just one of Lindbergh's exploits:* achievement, feat, accomplishment, heroic act, brave deed, adventure, daring deed. *—v.* **2.** *You must exploit every opportunity to learn new things:* use to advantage, turn to practical account, utilize, make use of, put to use, capitalize on, profit by. **3.** *The company exploited its workers with long hours and low pay:* take advantage of, make self-ish use of, abuse, misuse, take unfair advantage of. **—Ant.** 1 failure, defeat. 2 pass up, ignore. 3 pamper, coddle, spoil.

exploration *n. The exploration centered on the eastern sector:* expedition, examination, inquiry, inspection, investigation, study, probe, research, reconnaissance, search, scrutiny, survey.

explore *v.* **1.** *Lewis and Clark explored the Northwest:* scout, range over, travel over, travel to observe, survey, reconnoiter, travel and map, traverse, penetrate. **2.** *We must explore all possible ways to increase food production:* look into, examine, research, scrutinize, investigate, search into, delve into, plumb, analyze, probe, pry into, inquire into, feel out, try, try out, experiment with.

explosion *n.* **1.** *The explosion at the munitions depot shook the entire town:* blowing up, detonation, blast; violent bursting, eruption, discharge, fulmination; report, crack, clap. **2.** *She felt better after her explosion of anger:* burst, outburst, outbreak, eruption, paroxysm, fit, tantrum.

explosive *n.* **1.** *Dynamite and other explosives must be handled with care:* blasting material; ammunition; pyrotechnics. *—adj.* **2.** *The dirigible should never have been filled with an explosive gas:* liable to explode, capable of exploding, unstable, volatile. **3.** *The charge of spying created an explosive international situation:* dangerous, tense, volatile, perilous, critical, precarious, strained, touchy, ticklish, shaky; emotional, keyed up.

exponent *n. The congressman is a leading ex-*

ponent of free trade: advocate, supporter, champion, proponent, backer, promoter, expounder, spokesman, defender, propagandist. **—Ant.** opponent, foe, enemy, detractor, critic.

export *v.* **1.** *We export wheat to Russia and import silk from Japan:* sell abroad, ship overseas, send out, dispatch. *—n.* **2.** *Germany's export of small cars totaled two million this year:* foreign sale, selling abroad, marketing abroad, shipping overseas. **3.** *Cheese and watches are two of Switzerland's chief exports:* exported commodity, trade commodity, shipped wares, material sent abroad, article of foreign trade.

expose *v.* **1.** *The small craft was exposed to the dangers of the open sea:* subject, force to endure, leave unprotected, submit; endanger, imperil, jeopardize, hazard, risk. **2.** *In some Muslim countries women do not expose their faces in public:* bare, uncover, show, display, exhibit, lay open to view; strip, denude, divest, exhibit nakedness. **3.** *The child exposed the plans for the surprise party:* disclose, reveal, divulge, let out, let slip, uncover, bring to light, unearth. **4.** *Education should expose students to good art and music:* familiarize with, put in contact with, acquaint with, make conversant with, offer. **5.** *The magazine exposed the politician as a crook:* disclose to be, reveal to be, show in one's real light; denounce, brand, betray. **—Ant.** 1, 2 hide, conceal, mask, cover, shield. 1 protect, guard. 3 conceal, keep secret.

exposé *n. The newspaper printed an exposé of local crime:* exposure, scandalous disclosure, sensational report, divulgence, revelation, baring. **—Ant.** cover-up, whitewash.

exposed *adj.* **1.** *Down in the valley his position was exposed:* vulnerable, in danger *or* peril, laid bare *or* open, liable, open, prone, sensitive, subject, susceptible, threatened, unprotected. **2.** *The exposed rock showed a vein of gold:* laid bare, made manifest, apparent, bare, disclosed, bared, discovered, divulged, evident, exhibited, made public, manifest, naked, on display, unconcealed, open, peeled, resolved, shown, revealed, solved, uncovered, unmasked, unprotected, unsealed, stripped, visible, unveiled. **—Ant.** 1 hidden, concealed, covered, screened.

exposition *n.* **1.** *The antique exposition will be held in the local armory. The Eiffel Tower was built for the Paris Exposition of 1889:* exhibition, display, exhibit, bazaar, mart, market, trade show, show; fair, trade fair, world's fair, *Informal* expo. **2.** *He gave a clear exposition of his views:* explanation, explication, elucidation, clarification, account, interpretation, exegesis, commentary; presentation, demonstration, description, illustration, picture.

expostulate *v. I expostulated with him to reconsider his decision:* protest, object, remonstrate, inveigh against, cry out against, raise one's voice against, enjoin, plead with, exhort, forewarn, counsel, caution, reason against.

exposure *n.* **1.** *The company feared exposure of its shaky cash position:* disclosure, divulging, divulgence, revelation, laying open, bringing to light, bringing out in the open, exposé, public notice, unmasking, uncovering. **2.** *Her skin was dry after exposure to the wind:* subjection, submission, laying bare, laying open, making vulnerable. **3.** *The room has a southern exposure:* outlook, vista, frontage, prospect, perspective, view. **—Ant.** 1 hiding, concealment, cover-up. 2 cover, covering, shelter, refuge, protection, shield.

expound v. *The candidate expounded his views on foreign policy:* state in detail, give a full account of, hold forth, explain, describe, elucidate, make clear, explicate; defend, uphold.

express v. **1.** *It's not easy to express such a complex idea:* put into words, articulate, phrase, word, couch, relate, communicate, state, say, speak, utter, declare, describe, verbalize, voice, vocalize. **2.** *Her face expressed her bitter disappointment:* reveal, divulge, disclose, show, exhibit, evidence, evince, convey, communicate, make known. *—adj.* **3.** *The doctor gave express orders that the patient was to have no visitors:* explicit, definite, specific, unequivocal, categorical, exact, clear, lucid, precise, direct, plain, certain, particular; vivid, forceful. **4.** *The express train is an hour faster than the local:* nonstop, stopping infrequently; fast, high-speed, quick, swift, rapid. **—Ant.** 1 remain silent, be quiet, be still. 2 hide, conceal, cover, veil, mask, cloak; supress, repress. 3 implicit, implied, indirect, oblique, hinted, suggested, vague, general, indefinite, obscure, enigmatic, ambiguous, equivocal.

expression n. **1.** *Shelley's poems are famous for their beauty of expression. In a democracy everyone is entitled to the expression of his views:* wording, phraseology, style, language; stating, saying, speaking, voicing, airing, venting, telling, uttering, declaration, assertion, setting forth, relating, communication. **2.** *"Round the bend" is a colorful expression meaning "crazy":* term, word, phrase, turn of phrase, phrasing, phraseology, idiom, locution. **3.** *She always has such a happy expression on her face:* look, appearance, aspect, mien, countenance. **4.** *An actor must speak his lines with a great deal of expression:* eloquence, emotion, meaning; modulation, enunciation, articulation, tone. **—Ant.** 1 suppression, restraint, repression.

expressionless adj. *During his testimony he remained expressionless:* blank, deadpan, poker-faced, impassive, inexpressive, stolid, inscrutable, vacant, vacuous, unexpressive, wooden, dead.

expressive adj. *Her playing was most expressive in the Beethoven sonata:* eloquent, moving, meaningful, effective, telling, significant, poignant, thoughtful, indicative, forceful, vivid, powerful, compelling, striking.

expressly adv. **1.** *I expressly told him I wouldn't go:* explicitly, definitely, pointedly, unequivocally, categorically, decidedly, clearly, distinctly, plainly, in no uncertain terms. **2.** *The tourist went to the Alps expressly to ski:* specifically, particularly, specially, precisely. **—Ant.** 1

implicitly, indirectly, obliquely; vaguely, indefinitely, equivocally.

expropriate v. *The new government expropriated all property of foreigners:* confiscate, appropriate, take, take over; seize, commandeer.

expulsion n. *Expulsion from school is the penalty for cheating. The expulsion of gas from the engine made a loud noise:* expelling, ejection, ousting, removal; exile, banishment, eviction, exclusion, debarment, prohibition, pro-scription; discharge, elimination. **—Ant.** acceptance, entering, entrance, welcoming, inclusion; injection.

expunge v. *The student expunged her mistake:* erase, abolish, annul, cancel, cut, delete, eradicate, discard, exclude, exterminate, extinguish, extirpate, kill, raze, obliterate, wipe out, take out, remove.

expurgate v. *The local censors expurgated several passages from the book:* cut, cut out, remove, delete, excise, censor, remove as offensive, bowdlerize, purge, blue-pencil, edit, *Television* blip, bleep out.

exquisite adj. **1.** *She bought an exquisite china figurine:* delicate, fine, elegant; particularly beautiful, beautifully dainty, lovely, precious. **2.** *The bracelet was made with exquisite workmanship:* superb, superlative, consummate, matchless, peerless, flawless, incomparable, excellent, fine, choice, admirable, splended. **3.** *The hostess had exquisite taste in clothes:* discriminating, admirable, impeccable, faultless, perfect, fastidious, meticulous. **—Ant.** 1 clumsy, bulky, ugly, hideous, *Slang* klutzy. 2 sloppy, clumsy; mediocre, ordinary; inferior, bad. 3 common, unrefined, indiscriminate, careless, slovenly.

extant adj. *The Dead Sea Scrolls contain the earliest extant manuscripts of many sections of the Bible:* in existence, existing, existent, surviving, to be found; present, living.

extemporaneous adj. *When the guest speaker failed to arrive, the club's president gave an extemporaneous talk on conservation:* impromptu, spontaneous, improvised, extempory, ad-lib, without notice, extempore, unprepared, unpremeditated, unrehearsed, off the top of one's head, spur-of-the-moment, offhand, without notes, off the cuff. **—Ant.** well-rehearsed, prepared, planned; premed-itated.

extemporize v. *Without preparation, he could only extemporize:* improvise, ad-lib, improvise, invent.

extend v. **1.** *Extend the line to the edge of the paper. We extended the meeting another 15 minutes:* stretch out, draw out, lengthen, make longer, elongate; continue, protract, prolong. **2.** *He extended his hand in greeting. The professor extended an invitation to all the students to come to tea:* advance, submit, put out, stretch forth, reach out; offer, give, hold out, proffer, bestow, impart, grant. **3.** *The course will extend the students' knowledge of nature:* broaden, widen, expand, enlarge, increase, spread, stretch, amplify, augment. **—Ant.** 1 shorten, curtail, abbreviate, abridge, contract, shrink, condense. 2 withdraw, take back. 3 narrow, decrease, restrict, limit, reduce.

extended *adj.* **1.** *The birds began their flight with extended wings:* spread out, stretched out, unfolded, unfurled. **2.** *The play was so successful that it had an extended engagement at the local theater:* prolonged, long, continued, protracted, lengthened, drawn out. **3.** *An extended search turned up the missing ring:* wide-spread, extensive, comprehensive, thorough; widened, broadened, expanded, enlarged. **—Ant.** 1 folded, furled, contracted. 2 short, shortened, curtailed, abbreviated, abridged. 3 narrow, limited, restricted.

extension *n.* **1.** *The soldier was granted a two-day extension of his furlough:* lengthening, continuation, increase, prolongation; delay, postponement. **2.** *The toolshed was built as an extension of the house:* wing, branch, appendage, arm, annex, adjunct, addition, appendix, enlargement, expansion, continuation. **—Ant.** 1 shortening, curtailment, decrease.

extensive *adj.* **1.** *An extensive desert covers much of northern Africa:* wide, broad, large, vast, huge, extended, voluminous, enormous, great; lengthy, long, protracted. **2.** *The scholar had an extensive knowledge of Oriental history:* wide, broad, comprehensive, considerable, all-inclusive, far-flung, thorough, universal, capacious. **—Ant.** 1, 2 narrow. 1 small, little, tiny; short. 2 restricted, specialized.

extent *n.* *The extent of the forest was unknown to the settlers. The new laws limit the extent of the king's powers:* expanse, stretch, area; scope, range, compass, breadth, magnitude, size, sweep, dimensions, amplitude, reach, amount, degree; duration, time, length. **—Ant.** limitation, limits.

extenuating *adj.* *He was not fined for speeding because his need to get to the hospital quickly was an extenuating circumstance:* justifiable, serving as an excuse, explanatory; mitigating, attenuating, qualifying, tempering, moderating, lessening, diminishing. **—Ant.** unjustifiable, inexcusable; aggravating, intensifying.

exterior *adj.* **1.** *The seed has a hard exterior covering:* outside, outer, outermost, external, superficial, outward. **2.** *The nation must follow its own policy and not be influenced by exterior events:* external, foreign, alien, exotic, extrinsic, extraneous. *—n.* **3.** *The exterior of the house is red brick:* outside, outer side, surface; façade, face, coating, covering, finish, shell, skin. **4.** *Her calm exterior belied her agitation:* outward appearance, manner, demeanor, bearing. **—Ant.** 1 inside, internal, inner. 2 internal, domestic, native; intrinsic, inherent, ingrained. 3 interior, inside, core.

exterminate *v.* *The new chemical will exterminate the cockroaches:* destroy, wipe out, kill, slaughter, massacre, annihilate, eliminate, *Slang* waste, zap; eradicate, abolish, root out, erase, expunge; extinguish, demolish. **—Ant.** increase, develop, foster, build up; create, generate, originate, beget; replenish, restore.

external *adj.* **1.** *The external layer of skin is called the epidermis:* outside, outer, outermost, exterior, surface, superficial, outward. **2.** *The house needs better insulation to keep out external heat:* from the outside, extraneous, extrinsic; foreign, alien. **—Ant.** 1 internal, inner, innermost, interior, inward, inside. 2 internal; intrinsic, inherent.

extinct *adj.* **1.** *The passenger pigeon is extinct:* defunct, dead, vanished, lost, gone, no longer in existence, died out, no longer surviving. **2.** *Popocatepetl is not an extinct volcano but a dormant one:* no longer burning, quenched, extinguished, put out, gone out. **—Ant.** 1 extant, surviving, living; flourishing, thriving. 2 burning, active.

extinguish *v.* **1.** *Firemen extinguished the blaze quickly:* put out, douse, quench, smother, suffocate; blow out, snuff out. **2.** *Flunking out of medical school extinguished his hopes of becoming a doctor:* wipe out, destroy, end, abolish, eliminate, kill, demolish, dispel, eradicate, cancel, crush, quash, stifle, dash, *Slang* zap, do in. **—Ant.** 1 ignite, light, fire. 2 increase, foster, promote, forward, build up; secure, establish, confirm, maintain, support.

extol *v.* *The general extolled the bravery of his men:* praise, laud, commend, compliment, acclaim, celebrate, glorify, applaud, eulogize, sing the praises of. **—Ant.** decry, denounce, damn, curse, condemn, censure, criticize, belittle, denigrate.

extort *v.* *They extorted a lot of money from the shopkeepers:* coerce, blackmail, bully, cheat, demand, wrench, wrest, hold up.

extortion *n.* *The gangster was arrested for extortion:* blackmail, shakedown; threats, force, coercion; forced payments, hush money, graft, *Informal* payola; ransom, tribute.

extra *adj.* **1.** *The store hired extra clerks for Christmas. Why did you buy all those extra eggs?:* additional, supplemental, further, more, spare, auxiliary, accessory; superfluous, surplus, redundant, unnecessary. *—n.* **2.** *The new car has all the extras:* accessory, additional feature, special accompaniment, adjunct, appurtenance, attachment, complement. *—adv.* **3.** *The coffee is extra strong this morning:* unusually, uncommonly, exceptionally, especially, particularly, additionally, remarkably, extraordinarily. **—Ant.** 1 fewer. 2 basic necessity. 3 less.

extract *v.* **1.** *The dentist extracted her wisdom teeth:* pull out, take out, draw out, pry out, remove, extricate, pluck out, root out, extirpate. **2.** *He always manages to extract some humor from every situation:* get, gleen, obtain, derive, exact, wrest, evoke, bring out, elicit, deduce, educe. **3.** *The new process extracts oil from shale:* process chemically, separate, take out, draw out, squeeze out, press out, distill. **4.** *The newspaper extracted several passages from the speech and printed them on the front page:* excerpt, choose, select, cull, abstract, copy out; cite, quote. *—n.* **5.** *Add a teaspoon of vanilla extract to the milk shake:* concentrate, essence, distillate, juice. **6.** *The book contains extracts from famous poems:* excerpt, selection, passage, abstract; quotation, citation. **—Ant.** 1, 2 insert, embed, implant, inject, infuse.

extradite v. *The murder suspect was extradited to his native country:* send away, expel, deliver, give up, release, surrender.

extraneous adj. **1.** *The witness's extraneous remarks were struck from the record:* irrelevant, unrelated, not germane, not pertinent, inappropriate, nonessential, immaterial, incidental, superfluous, inadmissible. **2.** *Tropical plants are extraneous to this climate:* foreign, alien, exotic, extrinsic, strange, adventitious. **—Ant.** 1 relevant, pertinent, germane, appropriate, material, connected, related, essential. 2 native, intrinsic, inherent.

extraordinary adj. *What an extraordinary dress! Even for a Great Dane the dog is of extraordinary size:* unusual, uncommon, remarkable, phenomenal, unique, rare, out of the ordinary, exceptional, notable; amazing, fantastic, incredible, unbelievable, inconceivable, unheard of; strange, odd, queer, monstrous. **—Ant.** usual, common, average, ordinary, unremarkable, run-of-the-mill, everyday, familiar, customary.

extravagance n. **1.** *His extravagance led him into bankruptcy:* excessive spending, overspending, squandering, inordinate outlay; waste, wastefulness, improvidence, prodigality. **2.** *She was misled by the extravagances of the travel brochure. Dancing all night was an extravagance his health could not afford:* excess, excessiveness, unrestraint, immoderation; unreasonableness, absurdity, folly, caprice, capriciousness, recklessness, profligacy. **—Ant.** 1 economy, frugality, saving, stinginess, tightfistedness, miserliness. 2 moderation, restraint, reasonableness.

extravagant adj. **1.** *The car is much too extravagant for us to buy:* expensive, high-priced, costly, overpriced, exorbitant. **2.** *Extravagant people never save money. Watering the lawn daily is an extravagant use of water:* profligate, spending readily, prodigal, overspending, lavishly spending, openhanded, spendthrift; wasteful, squandering, imprudent, improvident. **3.** *The ad made extravagant claims for the new soap. Did the singer deserve such extravagant praise?:* excessive, immoderate, unrestrained, inordinate, unreasonable, outlandish, preposterous, outrageous, absurd, fantastic, fabulous, unreal, high-flown, foolish, wild. **—Ant.** 1 cheap, reasonable, economical, lowpriced. 2 thrifty, economical; frugal, stingy, tightfisted, miserly, close; conservative, saving, prudent. 3 moderate, restrained, reasonable, sensible, serious, realistic, sober, down-to-earth; careful, cautious.

extravaganza n. *The circus is always the biggest extravaganza of the year:* spectacle, pageant, spectacular, phantasmagoria; stage show, vaude-ville, wild west show, opera, ballet, carnival, Broadway show, opéra bouffe, operetta, opéra comique, sound and light show, *French* son et lumière, fair, exposition.

extreme adj. **1.** *Extreme cold will cause the engine to fail:* severe, intense, very great, excessive, immoderate, extraordinary, unusual, uncommon; inordinate, exaggerated. **2.** *Patrick*

Henry's political views were extreme for his time: radical, advanced, avant-garde; outrageous, extravagant. **3.** *Plant the tree in the extreme corner of the yard:* most distant, farthest, outermost, farthest removed. **—n. 4.** *She will go to any extreme to get her way:* ultimate limit, extremity, boundary, height, depth, end; excess, excessive degree, *Informal* nth degree. **—Ant.** 1 moderate, mild, reasonable, common, average, ordinary. 2 traditional, conservative. 3 near, nearest.

extremely adv. *It's extremely warm for this time of the year:* very, quite, unusually, exceptionally, especially, extraordinarily, uncommonly, exceedingly, excessively, immoderately, intensely, singularly, surprisingly, remarkably, terribly, awfully; unnaturally, abnormally, freakishly, peculiarly, curiously.

extremist n. *Some extremists urged violent action:* radical, fanatic, revolutionary, zealot, agitator.

extremity n. **1.** *They fenced in the western extremity of the ranch. The spacecraft reached the extremity of its orbit:* end, farthest end, terminus, extreme, edge, outer edge, tip, brink, margin; most distant point, reach, limit, boundary, bound, border, periphery, confine. **2.** *The illustrator was good at drawing faces and bodies but not at extremities:* hand, foot; limb, arm, leg; finger, toe. **—Ant.** 1 beginning, start, commencement; nearest point.

extricate v. *The fox tried desperately to extricate itself from the trap. Let's see how she extricates herself from this embarrassing situation!:* free, release, get out, loose, rescue, liberate, deliver; untangle, disentangle, disengage, disencumber, wriggle out of. **—Ant.** catch, trap, snare, ensnare, tangle, entangle, trip up, tie, tie up.

extrinsic adj. *All the causes proved to be extrinsic:* external, exterior, outer, outside, exotic, acquired, outward, alien, extraneous, foreign, imported, superficial.

extrovert n. *Jim is an extrovert who loves to meet people:* outgoing person, gregarious person, sociable person, hail-fellow-well-met; exhibitionist, show-off, *Informal* life of the party. **—Ant.** introvert; loner.

exuberance n. *The children are always full of exuberance:* enthusiasm, energy, vitality, liveliness, spirit, zeal, vigor, buoyancy, sprightliness, vivacity, animation, élan, life, eagerness, excitement, *Informal* zip; effervescence. **—Ant.** despair, dejection; lethargy.

exuberant adj. **1.** *The crew gave an exuberant shout when the boat got under way:* enthusiastic, lively, spirited, sprightly, animated, eager, excited, energetic, zealous, vigorous. **2.** *The hillside is covered with an exuberant growth of weeds:* growing thickly, lavish, profuse, copious, abundant, plentiful, superabundant, luxuriant, rich, lush, plenteous, bounteous. **—Ant.** 1 despairing, dejected, unenthusiastic, dispirited, dull, lethargic. 2 thin, sparse, scant, scanty, meager, sporadic.

exude v. *The substance exuded a foul odor:* issue, discharge, emit, give forth, exhibit, give off, ooze, leak, trickle, show, manifest.

exult *v. The students exulted at the last day of school:* rejoice, be jubilant, be elated, be delighted, be exhilarated, be in high spirits, glory; *Informal* jump for joy; crow, gloat. —**Ant.** be downcast, be gloomy, be blue, feel sad.

exultant *adj. She was exultant after winning the competition:* exulting, ecstatic, elated, delighted, joyous, jubilant, overjoyed, rejoicing, reveling, transported.

eye *n.* **1.** *She shaded her eyes from the sun:* (*variously*) eyeball, iris, pupil; *Informal* orb, peeper. **2.** *Are your eyes good enough for you to drive without glasses? He has an artist's eye:* eyesight, vision, sight; perception, discrimination, taste. —*v.* **3.** *She eyed the stranger with amusement:* glance at, look at, gaze at, view, scan, take in, observe, regard, study, inspect, scrutinize, survey, stare at, watch, behold.

eyewitness *n. Her testimony was supported by three eyewitnesses:* spectator, looker-on, bystander, passerby, onlooker, viewer, observer, beholder, witness, informer, gazer, testifier, attester or attestor, gawker, gaper, rubberneck.

F

fable *n.* **1.** *Tell them the fable about the fox and the grapes:* parable, tale, fairy tale, legend, romance, allegory, myth. **2.** *That story about his pirate ancestor is probably a fable:* tall story, untruth, fiction, fabrication, falsehood, invention, fib, hoax, lie; *Slang* whopper, yarn, leg-pull.

fabled *adj.* *Some people still believe in the fabled Loch Ness monster:* fanciful, imaginary, unreal, fictitious; legendary, mythical, mythological, fabulous, storied. —**Ant.** real, authentic, historical, factual, honest-to-goodness.

fabric *n.* **1.** *Wash this fabric in cold water:* cloth, textile, material, dry goods, yard goods, stuff. **2.** *The fabric of the nation is weakened when its citizens mistrust the government:* framework, structure, frame, makeup, superstructure, organization, substance; texture; foundation, substructure, infrastructure.

fabricate *v.* **1.** *All of the furniture is fabricated on the premises:* build, form, construct, assemble, frame, manufacture, produce, erect, fashion, shape, compose. **2.** *She fabricated a good excuse for staying home:* invent, concoct, make up, hatch, devise, design, contrive, formulate, *Slang* fake; embroider, counterfeit, falsify, simulate, forge, feign, *Informal* trump up. —**Ant.** 1 destroy, raze, demolish, dismember.

fabrication *n.* **1.** *Our company is engaged in the fabrication of airplane parts:* building, construction, constructing, manufacture, assemblage, production, erection, composition, makeup, fashioning, creation. **2.** *His alibi was a complete fabrication:* falsehood, invention, lie, untruth, fiction, fib, concoction, fable, prevarication, myth, forgery, cock-and-bull story, yarn, fairy tale. —**Ant.** 1 destruction, razing, breakdown. 2 truth, fact, actuality.

fabulous *adj.* **1.** *The explorer talked about his fabulous adventures in Africa:* amazing, marvelous, extraordinary, astonishing, astounding, incredible, unbelievable. **2.** *We're still talking about the fabulous party you gave:* marvelous, wonderful, fantastic, superb, great, spectacular, stupendous, *Informal* smashing. **3.** *The story is about the fabulous unicorn:* fabled, legendary, mythical, mythological, storied, fanciful, imaginary, apocryphal, fictitious, invented, fantastic. —**Ant.** 1 credible, ordinary, routine. 2 ordinary, common, fair, commonplace. 3 genuine, authentic, real, natural, historical, actual, true.

façade *n.* **1.** *The façade of our building is yellow brick:* building front, frontage, front view, face. **2.** *She puts on a façade of confidence to hide her uncertainty:* false appearance, pretense, superficial manner, false front, mask, veneer.

face *n.* **1.** *She powdered her face before going to dinner:* visage, countenance, features, facial features, physiognomy; *Slang* mug, pan, puss, kisser. **2.** *Put on a happy face. Don't make a face at me:* expression, aspect, look, countenance, air; grimace, facial contortion, pout, look of annoyance. **3.** *Pioneers cleared the forest and changed the face of the countryside:* appearance, look, semblance, external aspect. **4.** *The scandal was hushed up in an effort to save face:* reputation, good name, dignity, repute, image, prestige, self-respect. **5.** *I scratched the face of my belt buckle:* front surface, obverse side, principal side, finished side, façade, frontage, forepart. **6.** *After forgetting my lines, I didn't have the face to go back on stage:* nerve, boldness, daring, pluck, self-assurance, mettle, spunk, confidence, bravado, grit, hardihood; cheek, front, sand, brass, gall, effrontery, impudence. —*v.* **7.** *The opponents faced each other across the chessboard:* encounter, confront, meet face to face, turn toward, look toward. **8.** *The lodge faces the ski area:* front on, give toward, overlook. **9.** *The cabinet is faced with a walnut veneer:* surface, cover, coat, overlay. —**Ant.** 5 back, underside, reverse, side. 6 shyness, timidity.

facet *n.* **1.** *The many facets in the diamond make it sparkle:* surface, polished surface, plane, cut. **2.** *Generosity is one of the nicer facets of his character:* aspect, side, phase, part, angle.

facetious *adj.* *He kept us laughing with his facetious remarks:* humorous, funny, amusing, jocular, joking, jovial, jesting, witty, clever, jocose, droll, comic, comical, playful, wisecracking. —**Ant.** solemn, serious, sober, lugubrious, grave, sedate, staid, sad, dull.

facile *adj.* **1.** *The rug weaver was extremely facile with his hands. Our guide spoke facile English:* skillful, adroit, handy, quick, artful, clever, apt, adept, proficient; fluent, effortless, smooth. **2.** *I don't trust his facile way of passing over the weakest points in his argument:* glib, slick, careless, casual, superficial, shallow, cursory. —**Ant.** 1 clumsy, awkward, plodding, halting, maladroit, unskillful, slow. 2 determined, serious, careful, thoughtful, penetrating.

facilitate *v.* *An addressing machine facilitates the handling of bulk mail:* expedite, speed up, accelerate, ease, simplify, help in, make less difficult, make easier, assist the progress of, lessen the labor of, lighten, smooth; forward, help to advance, promote, further, advance, aid, foster. —**Ant.** hinder, hamper, complicate, encumber, slow down.

facility *n.* **1.** *She speaks German with facility:* ease, fluency, expertness, skill, proficiency, efficiency, readiness, effortlessness, adroitness, aptness, dexterity, knack, deftness, smoothness, bent, capability, competence. **2.** *Modern stoves can be used with greater facility than the old wood-burners:* ease, practicability, effortlessness, easiness, smoothness. **3.** *This kitchen has a garbage disposal and other modern facilities:* appliance, convenience, aid, advantage, resource, means. —**Ant.** 1 ineptness, clumsiness, awkwardness, maladroitness; rigidity, woodenness, effort, exertion, pains. 2 difficulty, hardship, labor.

facsimile *n.* *This is a facsimile of the original*

Declaration of Independence: copy, reproduction, replica, imitation, duplicate, reprint, likeness, clone, transcript; photostat.

fact *n. The lawyer tried to establish the facts in the case:* happening, deed, occurrence, event, act, circumstance, incident, thing done, particular, specific; reality, actuality, truth, certainty, verity. **—Ant.** fiction, supposition, fancy, opinion, unreality, falsehood, lie, delusion, invention.

faction *n.* **1.** *The liberal faction of the party is demanding reforms:* group, side, subdivision, section, unit, clique, combine, ring, set, circle, coterie, gang, cabal, bloc, sect, minority, splinter group. **2.** *The convention broke up in bitter faction:* discord, dissension, conflict, disagreement, dissidence, division, contention, strife, rebellion, insurgency, schism, split, incompatibility, breach, quarreling, sedition, rupture, clash, disruption. **—Ant.** 2 agreement, accord, harmony, concord.

factious *adj. The chairman tried to bring the factious elements of the committee into agreement:* contentious, divisive, quarrelsome, bickering, disputatious, disagreeing, dissentious, insubordinate, rebellious, mutinous, combative, belligerent, insurrectionary, contending, warring, fighting, at sixes and sevens, at loggerheads; alienated, estranged, disaffected. **—Ant.** consenting, agreeing, harmonious, assenting, acquiescing.

factor *n. Money was the main factor in my decision not to buy a car:* consideration, reason, circumstance, element, part, component, constituent, influence, cause.

factotum *n. Our factotum, John, has cared for our estate for years:* handyman, jack-of-all-trades, right-hand man, man Friday, girl Friday; *Informal* guy Friday, gal Friday.

factual *adj. The reporter gave a factual account of the accident:* full of facts, matter-of-fact, plain, circumstantial, literal; genuine, actual, authentic, real, correct, exact, faithful, true, scrupulous, accurate; unadorned, unembroidered. **—Ant.** fanciful, imaginary, embellished, figurative.

faculty *n.* **1.** *He joined the faculty of Columbia University:* teaching staff, teaching body, professors, teachers. **2.** *He has a faculty for putting people at ease:* knack, capacity, capability, special ability, skill, gift, talent, genius, quality, bent, penchant, power, skillfulness, aptitude, adeptness, flair. **3.** *The stroke deprived him of the faculty of speech:* power, capability of the mind, inherent physical capability, function, endowment. **4. faculties.** *The old shepherd at age 95 still enjoys the full possession of his faculties:* wits, reason, normal intelligence, mental powers. **—Ant.** 2 inability, incapacity, unskillfulness, weakness, failing.

fad *n. Miniskirts were a widespread fad in the 1960's:* craze, rage, fashion, mania, latest word, latest thing, vogue, mode, *French* dernier cri; whim, whimsy, fancy.

fade *v.* **1.** *The blue rug has faded over the years. The light faded as the sun went down:* pale, dim, dull, bleach, lose luster, lose color,

lose brightness, make pale, become colorless, make colorless, grow dim, become dull, lose clarity, whiten. **2.** *His strength seemed to fade after the operation:* decline, dwindle, flag, fail, diminish, wither, fall off, lessen, taper, ebb, shrivel, languish, crumble, droop, wane, blur, slowly disappear; dissolve, evanesce, evaporate, recede, melt away, dissipate; die gradually, pass away. **—Ant.** 1, 2 brighten. 2 flourish; rise, increase, bloom, grow; endure, abide, last, stand.

fail *v.* **1.** *He failed to reach the finals of the tennis tournament. Our plans failed:* not succeed, stop short of, be unsuccessful, miss the mark, fall short of; come to nothing, come to naught, abort, fall through, turn out badly, miscarry, founder, be defeated, run aground, meet one's Waterloo, collapse, misfire, meet with disaster, be in vain, prove of no use; *Informal* come to grief, fizzle out, go up in smoke, end in smoke, be stillborn, slip up; *Slang* lay an egg, bomb, flop. **2.** *I failed math. He failed no students this term:* flunk, get less than a passing grade; give less than a passing grade. **3.** *I thought I could depend on the neighbors for help, but they failed us:* disappoint, let down, forsake, desert. **4.** *The battery failed because the lights were left on. His energy failed after his illness:* decline, dwindle, fade away, waste away, die, wane, become weaker, languish, deteriorate, flag, droop, perish gradually, disappear, give out, ebb, lose vigor, collapse; stop working, stop operating. **5.** *Bad investments caused the company to fail:* go bankrupt, go under, become insolvent, go out of business, crash, *Informal* fold. **—Ant.** 1 succeed. 2 pass. 4 grow, bloom, strengthen, flourish, prosper, gain.

failing *adj.* **1.** *The failing cause got little support:* inadequate, declining, faint, deficient, feeble, insufficient, scant, scanty, scarce, unsuccessful, unavailing, wanting, vain, weak. **—n. 2.** *Each had one strength and one failing:* shortcoming, weakness, foible, deficiency, defect, frailty, imperfection, fault, flaw. **—Ant.** success, sufficiency; strength.

failure *n.* **1.** *Her failure to get the job surprised us:* failing, proving unsuccessful; lack of success, vain attempt, ill success, labor in vain; nonfulfillment, washout, botch. **2.** *The bank warned him about his failure to meet the payments:* neglecting, dereliction, negligence, nonperformance, remissness, delinquency, default, nonobservance. **3.** *The failure of the bank caused a panic in the town:* bankruptcy, crash, financial disaster, insolvency, ruin, ruination, folding, collapse, downfall. **4.** *The party was a failure. His wife thinks he's a failure:* nonsuccess, disappointment, washout, botch, muddle, mess, miscarriage, misfire, mishap, fizzle; *Slang* flop, dud, bomb; ne'er-do-well, loser. **5.** *The failure of her eyesight makes reading difficult:* decline, loss of strength, failing, deterioration, deteriorating, breakdown. **—Ant.** 1 success; fulfillment. 2 observance, care. 3 success, prosperity. 4 success, effectiveness, adequacy. 5 strength, strengthening, improvement.

faint *adj.* **1.** *The music was too faint to hear.*

There was a faint trace of lipstick on the glass: soft, inaudible, remote, low, dulcet, indistinct, weak, muffled, whispered, muted; dim, pale, almost imperceptible, faded, subtle, delicate, obscure, inconspicuous. **2.** *He needed more than faint encouragement:* feeble, weak, slight, small, inconsiderable, meager, thin, frail, fragile, little. **3.** *Climbing those stairs caused her to feel faint:* dizzy, lightheaded, vertiginous, about to swoon, giddy; feeble, weak, exhausted, lacking strength, drooping, torpid, lethargic, fatigued, languid, worn out. **4.** *Faint heart never won fair lady:* timorous, timid, fainthearted, lacking spirit, fearful, lacking courage, cowardly, lily-livered. —*v.* **5.** *She fainted when she read the telegram:* swoon, black out, pass out, lose consciousness, collapse. —**Ant.** 1 bright, brilliant, clear, conspicuous, fresh, hearty, vigorous, loud, blaring, distinct, glaring. 2 strong, considerable, vigorous. 3 strong, steady, sturdy, hearty. 4 strong, brave, bold, courageous.

fainthearted *adj. He made only a fainthearted attempt to win the race:* weak, feeble, irresolute, halfhearted, indifferent; lacking courage, cowardly, lily-livered, timid. —**Ant.** stronghearted, brave, courageous, bold.

fair *adj.* **1.** *The lottery was fair, since everyone had an equal chance to win:* unprejudiced, impartial, equitable, evenhanded, treating all sides alike, just, unbiased, affording no undue advantage, dispassionate, objective, legitimate, disinterested; honest, reasonable, square, upright, honorable, aboveboard; according to the rules, proper, justified, *Slang* kosher, on the up and up. **2.** *He is a good fielder, but only a fair hitter:* average, moderate, pretty good, middling, so-so, mediocre, passable, adequate, reasonable, satisfactory, decent, tolerable, respectable, medium, ordinary, indifferent, run-of-the-mill. **3.** *The day is warm and the sky is fair:* cloudless, unclouded, rainless, sunny, sunshiny, pleasant, fine, bright. **4.** *She has fair hair, unlike her darker sisters:* light-colored, not dark, pale, blond, creamy; fair-skinned, light-skinned. **5.** *The old song was about a fair maiden and her suitors:* attractive, lovely, good-looking, pretty, comely, well-favored, beautiful, bonny. —*adv.* **6.** *He was accused by his opponents of not playing fair:* justly, truthfully, honestly, honorably, legally, ethically, squarely, forthrightly, candidly. —**Ant.** 1 unfair, prejudiced, partial, inequitable, biased; dishonest, dishonorable, improper. 2 exceptional, poor, bad. 3 cloudy, stormy, dark, foul, threatening. 4 dark. 5 ugly, homely. 6 unfairly, dishonestly.

fairly *adv.* **1.** *We hope the case will be decided fairly:* justly, honorably, honestly, squarely, equitably, in a fair manner, evenhandedly, in a just way, rightly, impartially, dispassionately, objectively, legitimately, properly. **2.** *He's fairly bright but not scholarship material:* rather, tolerably, passably, moderately, reasonably, somewhat. **3.** *The children fairly raced out of school:* actually, really, fully, completely, absolutely, positively; so to speak, in a manner of speaking. —**Ant.** 1 unfairly, unjustly, inequitably, wrongly, partially,

dishonestly, improperly. 2 extremely, very, immoderately, exceptionally.

fairness *n. In the interests of fairness we flipped a coin:* fair-mindedness, decency, equitableness, equity, justice, impartiality, integrity, rightfulness, rightness, seemliness, uprightness, suitability.

fairy *n. She played the good fairy in a high school production:* pixie, fay, leprechaun, nixie, nix, brownie, sprite, elf.

faith *n.* **1.** *I have faith in Dick's integrity. You must have faith in God's wisdom:* belief, confidence, trust, security, certitude, reliance, assurance, certainty, credence, conviction. **2.** *He is a member of the Catholic faith:* religion, creed, persuasion, denomination, sect, church. **3.** *Keep faith by paying your debts:* obligation, verbal pledge, word of honor, promise; fidelity, constancy, loyalty, fealty. —**Ant.** 1 doubt, uncertainty, skepticism, dubiety; unbelief, disbelief; mistrust, suspicion; misgiving, apprehension, denial, dissent, distrust, incredulity, discredit, infidelity, rejection, agnosticism.

faithful *adj.* **1.** *She was a faithful employee for 40 years. She prided herself on being a faithful wife:* loyal, devoted, steadfast, steady in the performance of duty, tried, conscientious, staunch, true, constant, reliable, unwavering, trustworthy, dependable, worthy of confidence, incorruptible, unswerving, resolute, trusty, scrupulous, honest, upright, truthful. **2.** *She gave a faithful account of the accident:* exact, strict, truthful, factual, precise, accurate, verifiable; true-to-life, lifelike; close, similar. —**Ant.** 1 faithless; disloyal, false, perfidious, traitor-ous, treacherous; fickle, inconstant, unstable, unfaithful, untrue, untrustworthy, wavering. 2 inexact, imprecise, inaccurate, dissimilar.

faithfulness *n. The promotion was a reward for faithfulness:* loyalty, fidelity, adherence, allegiance, ardor, constancy, attachment, dependability, devotion, duty, trustworthiness, piety.

faithless *adj.* **1.** *The faithless officer in fact became a deserter:* disloyal, false, inconstant, fickle, treacherous, perfidious. **2.** *The faithless husband lied to his wife:* unreliable, untrustworthy, untrue. **3.** *The faithless followers soon departed:* untrusting; unbelieving, doubting. **4.** *Faithless souls sometimes turn to God:* atheistic, agnostic, heathen, infidel. —**Ant.** faithful.

faithlessness *n.* falseness, betrayal, disbelief, dishonesty, disloyalty, doubt, inconstancy, fickleness, perfidy, infidelity, scepticism, treachery, treason.

fake *v.* **1.** *He faked a nervous disorder to stay out of the army:* pretend, feign, simulate, fabricate, put on, dissemble, dissimulate, hoax, sham. **2.** *He was arrested for faking some famous paintings:* counterfeit, fabricate, contrive, forge, trump up, falsify. —*n.* **3.** *Only an expert could tell that the pearls were fakes:* counterfeit, imitation, forgery, fraud, sham, dummy, make-believe; contrivance, trick, hoax, fabrication, put-on, imposture, delusion, deceit, deception, artifice, ruse, dodge. **4.** *The traveling medicine men were fakes:* imposter, poseur, fraud, pretender, faker, quack, phony, charlatan, deceiver, humbug. —*adj.* **5.** *He wore a fake mustache to the party:* not real, false, bogus, counterfeit, phony, pseudo, spurious, sham, fabricated, put-on, contrived, forged, simulated, specious, artificial, invented, concocted, make-believe, fictitious. —**Ant.** 5 real, authentic, actual.

falderal or **folderol** *n.* **1.** *Hearing enough falderol, he turned off the TV:* nonsense, humbug, trumpery, balderdash, flummery, fiddle-faddle. **2.** *The shop sold novelties and other falderol:* ornament, decoration, trifle, bauble, frippery, gewgaw.

fall *v.* **1.** *The apple fell from the tree. He fell down the stairs:* drop, drop down, tumble, plunge, topple, plop, crumple, come down suddenly, collapse, crash down. **2.** *The cost of meat finally fell:* decline, come down, become less, decrease, diminish, become lower, cheapen, depreciate. **3.** *Her dress falls in pleats from the waist:* extend down, hang down, slope, droop, cascade; descend, drop. **4.** *On the third day of the attack, the town fell:* surrender, be captured, be overthrown, be defeated, be taken, pass into enemy hands, collapse, topple, capitulate, succumb; be destroyed, come to destruction; be wounded, be slain, perish, die. **5.** *How many innocents have fallen and become hardened sinners!:* transgress, give in to temptation, succumb, go astray, lapse, sin, depart from rectitude, err. **6.** *My birthday falls on Sunday:* occur, come to pass, happen, take place, come off, crop up, come around. —*n.* **7.** *The net broke the tightrope walker's fall:* plunge, descent, drop, falling, dropping, spill, tumble, slip, plummet. **8.** *Yesterday saw a sudden fall in stock prices:* drop, decline, lowering, sinking, diminution, decrease, reduction, slump, depreciation; ebb, subsidence, wane. **9. falls.** *We could see the spray from the falls downriver:* waterfall, cascade, cataract. **10.** *The leaves are always colorful in the fall:* autumn, Indian summer, harvest time. **11.** *The play was about the fall of an honest man:* corruption, ruin, loss of innocence, deviation from virtue, slip, going astray, lapse into sin, surrender to temptation, subversion; disgrace, downfall, comedown, loss of eminence, debasement. **12.** *The fall of the city followed heavy bombardment:* surrender, capitulation, overthrow, capture, downfall, collapse, defeat. —**Ant.** 1, 2 rise, climb, ascend, mount, soar, increase. 4 triumph, prevail, endure, hold out, survive. 7 rise, ascent. 8 rise, climb, increase, advance, appreciation.

fallacious *adj.* *The rumors were patently fallacious:* incorrect, false, deceptive, erroneous, deluding, fictitious, illusory, fraudulent, invalid, mistaken, misleading, off, sophistic, spurious, unfounded, ungrounded, wrong, unsound, untrue.

fallacy *n.* **1.** *It's a fallacy that everyone needs the same amount of sleep:* misconception, error, false notion, misleading notion, mistake, false belief, misbelief, delusion, illusion, misapprehension. **2.** *The fallacy in that argument is that taste is unpredictable:* fault, faultiness, flaw,

inconsistency, erroneous reasoning, mistake, pitfall, catch. —**Ant.** 1 truism, surety, verity, sureness, fact, certainty. 2 logic, proof, soundness, verity, truth, surety, certainty, consistency.

fallen *adj.* **1.** *The fallen king was exiled:* overthrown, deposed; ousted, discharged, turned out. **2.** *The fallen player was helped to his feet:* tumbled, sprawled, toppled, dropped, spilled. **3.** *The mission catered to derelicts and fallen women:* immoral, sinful, loose, disgraced, ruined, debased. **4.** *The fallen soldiers were eulogized as heroes:* dead, slain; massacred, slaughtered, butchered.

fallible *adj.* *He's usually right, but his judgment is fallible:* imperfect, frail, liable to error; human, mortal; faulty, unsure, unreliable. —**Ant.** infallible, perfect; divine, superhuman.

fallow *adj.* *The land has been fallow since the farm was deserted:* idle, inactive, inert, dormant, unproductive, untilled, unplanted, unused, unsowed, unfruitful, uncultivated; worn out, depleted, barren, arid, exhausted. —**Ant.** fecund, prolific, productive, fruitful, fertile.

false *adj.* **1.** *Columbus had a false impression of the size of the earth:* faulty, incorrect, untrue, wrong, fallacious, apocryphal, not correct, erroneous, mistaken, inaccurate, invalid, unsound, inexact, unfounded; delusive, misleading, deceptive, deceiving, spurious, factitious. **2.** *She trusted him till he proved to be a false friend:* disloyal, faithless, unfaithful, false-hearted, two-faced, untruthful, double-dealing, devious, hypocritical, dishonest, treacherous, perfidious, traitorous, inconstant, deceitful, tricky. **3.** *She removed her false eyelashes:* artificial, bogus, counterfeit, fake, make-believe, imitation, ersatz, forged, spurious, feigned, pseudo, sham, phony, unreal. —**Ant.** 1 true, correct, right, accurate, valid, sound, exact. 2 loyal, true, faithful, constant, sincere, steadfast, honest. 3 real, genuine, authentic, bona fide.

falsehood *n.* **1.** *He told a falsehood to keep from being punished:* lie, untruth, false statement, fabrication, falsification, canard, invention, fiction, story, figment; *Informal* fib, whopper; white lie. **2.** *The boy's father punished him for falsehood:* lying, untruthfulness, falseness, dishonesty, falsity, falsification, deceptiveness, deception, misrepresentation, inaccuracy, deceit, distortion, mendacity, perjury, misstatement, dissimulation, double-dealing, dissembling; perfidy, hypocrisy, duplicity, bad faith, two-facedness, insincerity. —**Ant.** 1 truth, verity, fact. 2 veracity, genuineness, honesty, honor.

falsify *v.* **1.** *He falsified his birth certificate to get a passport:* alter fraudulently, misrepresent, fake, distort, doctor, represent falsely, tamper with, pervert, misuse. **2.** *The old theory has been falsified by new evidence:* disprove, belie, rebut, show to be false, prove unsound, refute, confute. —**Ant.** 2 verify, confirm, certify, justify.

falsity *n.* *She didn't see the falsity of the rumor:* falsehood, lie, untruth, mendacity, canard, cheating, deceit, deception, deceptiveness, dishonesty, fallacy, fib, fraud, fraudulence, disingenuousness, duplicity, erroneousness, error, hypocrisy, misrepresentation, treachery, prevarication.

falter v. **1.** *Once his mind was made up, General Lee never faltered in his loyalty to the South:* hesitate, be undecided, waver, vacillate, fluctuate, demur, be irresolute, show weakness, shrink, lag; *Informal* dillydally, blow hot and cold. **2.** *The boy faltered when the policeman demanded his name:* stammer, speak haltingly, pause nervously, stutter, mumble, halt. **3.** *She faltered toward the door in the dark:* stumble, move unsteadily, teeter, stagger, totter, reel; shamble, shuffle, dodder. **—Ant.** 1 persevere, persist, proceed.

fame n. *Pablo Picasso achieved great fame as a painter:* eminence, prominence, repute, renown, reputation, celebrity, public esteem, glory, popularity, illustriousness, prestige, notoriety, notability, preeminence, distinction, note, laurels, glory. **—Ant.** obscurity, oblivion; disgrace, dishonor, disrepute, discredit, infamy, ignominy.

familiar adj. **1.** *The boy and his pony are a familiar pair around town:* often encountered, well-known, known, seen frequently, generally seen; frequent, habitual, commonplace, ordinary, everyday, common, proverbial, customary, accustomed, usual, general; conventional, accepted, stock, traditional. **2.** *Are you familiar with the South?:* acquainted, cognizant of, conversant, informed about, versed in, abreast of, no stranger to, apprised of, experienced at, at home in; skilled in, proficient at, seasoned. **3.** *After a good dinner, we all loosened up and became quite familiar:* friendly, informal, amicable, close, intimate, confidential, unreserved, cozy, snug, chummy, hand and glove, brotherly, fraternal, accessible, companionable, *Spanish* simpático, *German* gemütlich; forward, unduly intimate, free, bold, impertinent, taking liberties, disrespectful, intrusive. **—**n. **4.** *Not even his familiars knew of his marriage:* friend, close acquaintance, crony, buddy, intimate, chum, pal, confidant, boon companion. **—Ant.** 1 unfamiliar, unknown, uncommon, new, unusual, unconventional, infrequent, rare, unaccustomed, extraordinary. 2 unfamiliar, ignorant, unversed, unacquainted, uninformed; unskilled, unseasoned. 3 distant, detached, indifferent, formal, aloof, cold.

familiarity n. **1.** *I asked him to translate the words on the coin because of his familiarity with Latin:* knowledge, acquaintance, cognizance, acquaintanceship, intimacy, comprehension, understanding, skill, know-how, proficiency, mastery, conversance, experience. **2.** *She brags about her familiarity with the duchess:* closeness, intimacy, friendship, association, close acquaintance; fellowship, brotherhood, amity, fraternity, brotherliness; *Informal* coziness, chumminess. **3.** *He received us with familiarity:* informality, ease, absence of ceremony, casualness, naturalness, unconstraint, unreserve. **4.** *I dislike that shop clerk because of his familiarity:* impertinence, disrespect, impudence, forwardness, presumption, undue intimacy, overfamiliarity, undue liberty, intrusiveness, impropriety, unseemliness, indecorum. **—Ant.** 1 unfamiliarity, ignorance, inexperience. 2 unfamiliarity, distance. 3 formality, constraint, reserve. 4 propriety, properness, respect, decorum.

familiarize v. *Tammy needs to familiarize herself with her new camera:* acquaint, make familiar, accustom, make conversant, instruct, educate, edify, inculcate, teach, school, inform, tutor, enlighten; make used to, acclimatize, habituate, season.

family n. **1.** *Our family needs a larger apartment. Do you want a large family?:* parents and children; children of two parents, issue, offspring, progeny, brood. **2.** *Our family has a reunion in Chicago every year:* relatives, kin, kinsmen, kith and kin, kinfolk, kinsfolk, relations. **3.** *The Hapsburg family ruled Austria for years:* house, lineage, ancestry, line, dynasty, clan, tribe, breed; genealogy, race, stock, blood, extraction; forebears, parentage, forefathers. **4.** *Both English and Russian belong to the Indo-European family of languages:* group, division, class, classification, kind, order, set, category.

famine n. **1.** *Crop shortages are causing a famine in Asia:* general scarcity of food, half rations, starvation, famishment, extreme hunger. **2.** *There is a famine of executive talent in our industry:* acute shortage, want, deficiency, paucity, dearth, lack, scarcity, scantiness, insufficiency, exhaustion, meagerness, depletion, destitution, poverty, short supply. **—Ant.** 1, 2 abundance, surfeit, sufficiency, feast, bounty, glut.

famish v. *I'm famished because I missed lunch:* be eager for food, be ravenous, suffer extreme hunger, distress with hunger, deprive of nutriment.

famished adj. *After a day without food the famished hikers staggered home:* ravenous, empty, hungering, hungry, starving, voracious.

famous adj. *Elizabeth Taylor is a famous movie star:* well-known, noted, celebrated, prominent, renowned, far-famed; eminent, illustrious, notable, distinguished; conspicuous, notorious. **—Ant.** obscure, unknown, undistinguished, unsung, inglorious, obscure, forgotten, uncelebrated.

fan n. *He is such a devoted football fan that he travels with his team:* enthusiast, aficionado, follower, supporter, rooter, partisan, booster, zealot, fanatic, addict, buff; *Informal* fiend, *Slang* nut, freak, bug.

fanatic n. *The fanatics on both sides want a civil war:* zealot, enthusiast, extremist, maniac, hothead, member of the lunatic fringe, *Informal* crazy; activist, radical, militant. **—Ant.** unbeliever, cynic; passivist.

fanatical adj. *He was the party's most fanatical supporter:* zealous, enthusiastic, rabid, frenzied. **—Ant.** apathetic.

fanaticism n. *His religious fanaticism led him to execute heretics:* zealotry, enthusiasm, extreme zeal, fervor, intemperance, ruling passion, obsession, monomania, extremism, wild and extravagant notions; activism, militantism, radicalism; opinionatedness, dogmatism. —**Ant.** cynicism, skepticism, indifference, passivism; latitudinarianism.

fanciful *adj.* **1.** *She has a fanciful way of calling her plants by name:* whimsical, flighty, imaginative, capricious, humorous, inventive, quixotic, romantic, fantastic, bizarre, odd, eccentric, curious, unusual, unpredictable. **2.** *His stories for children are filled with fanciful characters:* unreal, imaginary, visionary, fictitious, fabulous, based on fancy, fantastic, chimerical, apocryphal, illusory, mythical, legendary. —**Ant.** 1 unimaginative, conventional, conservative, sensible, sober, ordinary; prosaic, predictable. 2 real, realistic, true.

fancy *n.* **1.** *It suited the little girl's fancy to give a tea party for her dolls:* imagination, whimsy, caprice, fantasy. **2.** *She had some fancy that Prince Charming would come along:* illusion, fantasy, figment, daydream, reverie, conceit, vagary, crotchet, vision, notion, idea, dream, caprice. **3.** *She has a fancy for rich desserts:* leaning, liking, longing, fondness, predilection, inclination, relish, penchant, partiality, capricious preference, taste, desire, *Informal* hankering, yen; weakness. —*adj.* **4.** *The stationery was decorated with a fancy border. The shop handles fancy foods:* showy, not plain, unusual, ornamental, decorative, ornate, intricately wrought, elegant, elaborate; florid, rococo, gingerbread, baroque; fine, special, distinctive, superior, superfine, custom, exceptional, specially selected, deluxe, epicurean, gourmet; expensive, high-priced, extravagant. —*v.* **5.** *Can you fancy her marrying an Indian prince?:* imagine, dream of, picture, conceive of. **6.** *I fancy he'll get the promotion:* suspect, suppose, think, assume, opine, conjecture, imagine, surmise, presume, be inclined to think, suspect, take it. **7.** *She fancies the man with the blue eyes:* like, have a mind to, take a liking to, be bent upon, take to, have an eye for, want, long for, favor, be fond of, be pleased with, crave, yearn for, *Informal* hanker after; relish, enjoy. —**Ant.** 2 conviction, certainty. 3 dislike, distaste, aversion. 4 plain, ordinary, undecorated; common, inferior; low-priced, cheap, modest, inexpensive.

fanfare *n. He was elected without fanfare:* display, ballyhoo, cheering, demonstration, flourish, parade, show, pomp *Informal* trumpet call.

fantasize *v. She fantasized she could take a tropical vacation:* daydream, envision, dream, imagine, hallucinate.

fantastic *adj.* **1.** *She had some fantastic idea that I was poisoning her:* weird, odd, queer, freakish, antic, bizarre, amazing, wild, extravagant, absurd, crazy, mad, ridiculous, preposterous, outlandish, grotesque, implausible, unbelievable, incredible, strange, irrational, extreme, far-fetched; romantic, visionary, imaginary, chimerical, fanciful, quixotic, illusory. **2.** *The writer received a fantastic amount of praise for his new play:* great, extravagant, extreme, huge, enormous, tremendous. **3.** *Informal This is a fantastic dessert:* marvelous, extremely good, wonder-

ful, sensational, fabulous, terrific, great, superb. —**Ant.** 1 reasonable, sensible, credible, ordinary, rational, common. 2 ordinary, moderate, limited. 3 common, ordinary, poor; *Slang* crummy.

fantasy *n.* **1.** *We all occasionally commit brave deeds in fantasy:* fancy, imagination, realm of dreams, mind, make-believe, unreality. **2.** *Some of the old fantasies about the space age are coming true:* fancy, illusion, daydream, imagining, dream, reverie, invention, fabrication, visionary idea, notion, fiction, figment, supposition, caprice, whimsy; nightmare, vision, chimera, apparition, mirage, phantasm, phantom, hallucination. —**Ant.** 1, 2 reality, actuality, fact.

far *adv.* **1.** *Our land extends far beyond the fence:* a long way, at a great distance, distantly, deeply, to a remote point, to a distant point, yonder, afar, beyond range. **2.** *The weather was far worse than we expected:* very much, much, incomparably, to a great degree, immeasurably, greatly, transcendently, a great deal, considerably. —*adj.* **3.** *I long to travel to far places:* distant, far-off, far-away, remote, way-off, yonder, out-of-the-way, far-removed. —**Ant.** 1 close, near, nigh. 2 less, little. 3 near, nearby, close.

faraway *adj. He read about faraway lands:* remote, distant, far, far-flung, far-off, far-removed, outlying, remote, lost. —**Ant.** nearby.

farce *n.* **1.** *His new farce got very good reviews:* satirical comedy, broad comedy, burlesque, harlequinade, parody, low comedy. **2.** *There is much farce in this novel:* buffoonery, horseplay, tomfoolery, ridiculousness, absurdity, nonsense, drollery. **3.** *Freedom of the press is a farce under a dictatorship:* sham, mockery, travesty, pretense, make-believe, absurdity, parody. —**Ant.** 1 tragedy. 2 seriousness. 3 reality.

farcical *adj. Her farcical explanations were dismissed out of hand:* risible, laughable, ludicrous, absurd, derisory, outrageous, preposterous, ridiculous, amusing, comic, comical, diverting, funny, nonsensical, slapstick.

fare *n.* **1.** *The bus fare has gone up another nickel:* charge, passage money, ticket price, fee, cost of transportation. **2.** *The taxi driver stopped to pick up a fare:* paying passenger, rider, customer, client. **3.** *The fare served on the cruise was excellent:* food, food and drink, provisions, victuals, diet, table, comestibles, menu, regimen, board. —*v.* **4.** *He has fared well in the construction business:* manage, get on, get along, experience good or bad fortune, go through an experience, turn out, do, make out, perform.

farewell *interj.* **1.** *Now we must say "farewell":* good-bye, so long, Godspeed; *French* adieu, au revoir, *Spanish* adios, *Italian* arrivederci, ciao, *German* auf Wiedersehen, *Japanese* sayonara. —*n.* **2.** *We exchanged hasty farewells and parted:* good-bye, parting wish, parting compliment, valediction. **3.** *It was a painful farewell:* leave-taking, departure, departing, parting, adieu. —**Ant.** 1 hello, greetings. 2 salutation, welcome, greetings. 3 meeting, arrival.

far-fetched *adj. His theory of a coming invasion from outer space is certainly far-fetched:* improbable, unlikely, implausible, doubtful, dubious, preposterous, unconvincing, strained, *Slang* cockamamie. **—Ant.** likely, probable, plausible.

farm *n.* **1.** *Her uncle grows corn and soybeans on a 200-acre farm:* tract, spread, truck farm, ranch, grange, plantation, country place. *—v.* **2.** *He now farms almost all of his land:* cultivate, have under cultivation, use for raising crops, produce crops, till the soil, plant, engage in agronomy, practice husbandry; (*variously*) plow, harvest, reap, sow.

farmer *n. His father is a tobacco farmer:* grower, raiser, planter, cultivator of land, agriculturist, person who runs a farm, agrarian, agronomist, tiller of the soil, agricultural laborer, husbandman, harvester, rancher, granger, reaper, sharecropper, truck gardener, truck farmer.

farming *n. She took up dairy farming:* agriculture, agronomy, crop-raising, breeding, cultivation, gardening, gleaning, harvesting, grazing, growing, homesteading, production, husbandry, ranching, reaping, seeding, tillage.

farsighted *adj.* **1.** *Farsighted people usually need glasses for reading:* long-sighted, hyperopic. **2.** *A more farsighted person would have anticipated war:* foresighted, forehanded, farseeing, long-sighted, foreseeing, prescient, clairvoyant, provident, wise, judicious, prudent, levelheaded, commonsensical, acute, shrewd; wisely planned. **—Ant.** 1 nearsighted, myopic, shortsighted. 2 shortsighted, improvident, injudicious.

farther *adv.* **1.** *Didn't you walk farther than you'd planned? I'm farther into the book than you are:* further, to a greater distance, past the point that, at a greater distance; beyond, at or to a more advanced point; to a greater degree or extent, deeper. *—adj.* **2.** *The bar is at the farther end of the room:* more distant, more remote, remoter, further, more removed. **3.** *The trip from Atlanta to Savannah is farther than I thought:* longer, lengthier. **—Ant.** 2 closer, nearer. 3 shorter.

farthest *adv. That is the farthest point from here:* furthest, distant, most extreme, outermost, outmost, farthermost, ultimate, last, lattermost, utmost, remotest.

fascinate *v. The magician fascinated the children. The snake was fascinated by the charmer's music:* charm, captivate, bewitch, attract and hold, beguile, entrance, enchant, allure, grip the attention of, engross, delight, enthrall, enrapture, allure, spellbind, absorb, interest greatly, enravish; transfix, hold motionless, rivet, overpower, spellbind, hold spellbound. **—Ant.** bore, repel.

fascinated *adj. The fascinated audience watched the mystery unravel:* enthralled, absorbed, beguiled, attracted, bewitched, captivated, charmed, dazzled, enamored, delighted, enchanted, enraptured, entranced, intoxicated, hypnotized, mesmerized, infatuated, seduced, titillated, smitten, transfixed.

fascinating *adj. The book is so fascinating I can't put it down:* gripping, engrossing, enthralling, absorbing, riveting, overpowering, charming, captivating, enchanting, bewitching, beguiling, entrancing, alluring, interesting, delightful, spellbinding. **—Ant.** boring, uninteresting, dull; repellent.

fascination *n. That place has no obvious fascination for me:* allure, appeal, charisma, attraction, enchantment, charm, glamor, enthralment, lure, magic, magnetism, power, obsession, sorcery, trance, spell.

fascism *n. Fascism is right-wing dictatorship with a government-controlled economy and no opposition:* right-wing dictatorship, corporate state, corporatism, corporativism; (*variously*) national socialism, Nazism; totalitarianism, police state; autocracy, plutocracy, oligarchy. **—Ant.** socialism, democracy.

fashion *n.* **1.** *She always dresses according to the latest fashion:* style, custom, mode, trend, general practice, usage, habit, prevailing taste, vogue, craze, fad, rage; conventionality, convention, form. **2.** *She moves in a graceful fashion:* way, manner, demeanor, air, mode of action, attitude; tenor, behavior. *—v.* **3.** *She fashioned a necklace from paper clips:* shape, create, make, form, contrive, design, frame, devise, forge, pattern, fabricate, hew, mold, construct; compose, produce, manufacture, carve.

fashionable *adj. We ate at a fashionable new restaurant:* in fashion, stylish, in style, modish, smart, in vogue, voguish, all the rage, chic, current, prevailing, popular; *Slang* in, with-it, hip. **—Ant.** unfashionable, old-fashioned, out-of-date, dated, unstylish, passé; *Slang* old hat.

fast[1] *adj.* **1.** *Cheetahs are very fast animals. She did a fast job. The clock is fast:* swift, quick, fleet, moving quickly, winged, able to move rapidly, rapid; brisk, hasty, flying, hurried; accelerated; taking only a short time, done in little time, speedy, expeditious, *Slang* lickety-split; ahead, in advance. **2.** *Does she still run around with that fast crowd?:* wild, reckless, pleasure-mad, immodest, extravagant, dissipated, profligate, intemperate, wanton, dissolute, self-indulgent, rakish, free in behavior and morals, immoral, loose, lustful, debauched, lascivious, licentious. **3.** *The wives soon became fast friends:* steadfast, firm, constant, unwavering, abiding, enduring, resolute, durable, steady, unswerving; loyal, devoted, staunch, stable, true, lasting, faithful. **4.** *The cargo was hoisted aboard and made fast in the hold:* secure, fastened, firm, steady, immovable, rigid, firmly fixed in place, firmly tied, resistant, securely attached, stationary, taut, tight. **5.** *Is the dye fast or will it run?:* permanent, ineradicable, lasting, durable, unfading. *—adv.* **6.** *With that extra glue the stamp ought to stick fast:* firmly, fixedly, tightly, securely, tenaciously, immovably, solidly. **7.** *The child was fast asleep:* soundly, fully, completely. **8.** *Don't drive so fast:* swiftly, rapidly, speedily, quickly, hastily, hurriedly. **9.** *My* *watch is running fast:* ahead, in advance. —**Ant.** 1 slow. 2 upright, respectable, moral, steady, sober, virtuous, *Slang* square. 3 unsteady, wavering, inconstant, irresolute, unstable, disloyal, unfaithful. 4 loose, weak, movable, insecure, unsteady. 6 loosely, insecurely. 8 slowly, slow, dawdlingly. 9 slow, behind, late.

fast² *v.* **1.** *They always fast during the religious holidays:* forbear eating, deny oneself food, go without food, abstain from food, go hungry; starve, famish. —*n.* **2.** *He will continue his fast until his demands are met:* fasting, starvation, doing without food, abstinence from food, hunger strike; fast day, period of fasting. —**Ant.** 1 eat. 2 eating, feast.

fasten *v.* **1.** *Fasten the mirror securely to the wall. Fasten the ends together. Fasten the lock:* attach, tie, fix firmly in position, make fast, hold fixed, hold immovable, secure, make secure, anchor, affix; *(variously)* lash, hitch, tether, moor, truss, pin, bolt, screw, rivet, weld, pinion, bind, stick, yoke, clamp, cement, solder, fuse; unite, join, wed, connect, adhere, put together, hold together, *(variously)* close, bar, hook, lock, latch, button, couple, clasp, clip, snap, dovetail, link, dowel. **2.** *She fastened her eye on the child:* fix, direct, focus, rivet, hold. —**Ant.** 1 unfasten; loosen, loose; separate, untie, part, sever, sunder, divorce, divide, undo, relax, remove, detach, unbolt, unhitch, disunite, uncouple, disconnect.

fastidious *adj. She's too fastidious to enjoy roughing it:* fussy, particular, excessively critical, hard to please, persnickety, picky, difficult, finicky, meticulous, proper, hypercritical, choosy, exacting, overprecise; overdelicate, dainty, overrefined, precious; squeamish, queasy. —**Ant.** remiss, neglectful, slack, casual, lax; uncritical, indulgent, easy; indelicate, unrefined, coarse.

fat *n.* **1.** *I try not to eat much fat:* grease, greasy substance, animal fat, adipose tissue. —*adj.* **2.** *He's too fat and needs to diet:* stout, heavy, plump, chubby, overweight, obese, thickset, fleshy, pudgy, rotund, paunchy, portly, beefy, potbellied, lumpish, corpulent. **3.** *The doctor told him to stay away from fat foods:* fatty, greasy, oily, containing fat, unctuous, suety, blubbery. **4.** *Informal His new venture is turning a fat profit:* lucrative, rewarding, remunerative; fortunate, palmy, productive, fruitful, fertile. **5.** *The gambler took out a fat wallet:* well-stocked, full, replete, plentiful, plenteous, flush, abundant, copious, well-furnished, chockful, stuffed. —**Ant.** 2 lean, spare, lank, lanky, skinny, gaunt, scrawny, rawboned, angular; thin, slender, slim, slight, cadaverous. 3 lean. 4 lean, unprofitable, unlucrative, poor, scarce, scanty, unrewarding, unremunerative, unfruitful, unproductive. 5 barren, empty, lean.

fatal *adj.* **1.** *Only her friends knew she had a fatal illness:* terminal, deadly, mortal, causing death, lethal; virulent. **2.** *Disagreement among the architects was fatal to the project:* ruinous, lethal, destructive, calamitous, disastrous, catastrophic. —**Ant.** 1 harmless, slight, minor,

nonlethal. 2 lifegiving, constructive, beneficial, vitalizing, restor-ative, helpful.

fatalism *n. She accepted her child's illness with a kind of fatalism:* submission to fate, passive acceptance, acquiescence, resignation, stoicism, predestination; helplessness, powerlessness.

fatality *n.* **1.** *The fatality of the disease is almost certain:* deadliness, mortality, lethality, malignancy, perniciousness, banefulness. **2.** *A number of fatalities resulted from the fire:* death, casualty, violent death, fatal accident.

fate *n.* **1.** *By a twist of fate, U.S. Presidents Thomas Jefferson and John Adams both died on July 4, 1826:* destiny, predestination, predetermination; providence, will of heaven. **2.** *Always losing at cards seemed to be his fate:* fortune, lot, destiny, karma, portion, doom, kismet, *Greek* moira. **3.** *The fate of the proposed bill in the Commons is uncertain:* future, outcome, upshot, prospect, ultimate fortune, chances; consequence, effect. —**Ant.** 1 will, choice, decision, independence, freedom, chance.

fateful *adj. Meeting you was a fateful moment in my life:* momentous, decisively important, critical, decisive, determinative, crucial, significant; ominous, portentous; fatal, disastrous. —**Ant.** unimportant, ordinary, insignificant.

father *n.* **1.** *He resembles his father:* male parent, sire, *(variously)* dad, daddy, papa, pater, pop, *Slang* old man. **2.** *They work the land as their fathers did:* forefather, ancestor, forebear, progenitor. **3.** *Alexander Graham Bell was the father of the telephone:* inventor, creator, architect, designer, begetter, originator, founder, author, maker. **4.** *I studied with the fathers at St. Joseph's Academy:* priest, padre, abbé, pastor, curé, parson, preacher, dignitary of the church, confessor. —*v.* **5.** *A son owes a debt to the man who fathered him:* sire, act as the father of, beget, engender, procreate. **6.** *The plan was fathered by a local banker:* found, originate, create, begin, hatch, author, design.

fatherland *n. After the war he returned to his fatherland:* homeland, native land, native soil, native country, mother country, motherland, birthplace; *Latin* patria, *French* patrie, *German* Heimat.

fatherly *adj. Let me give you a little fatherly advice:* paternal, fatherlike, parental; benevolent, beneficent, benign, tender, kindly, affectionate, demonstrative, sympathetic, forbearing, indulgent, protective.

fathom *v. Can anyone fathom the meaning of that story?:* penetrate, figure out, comprehend, understand, follow, hunt out, probe, divine, discover, get to the bottom of, ferret out, unravel, uncover, root out.

fatigue *n.* **1.** *My fatigue was great after looking unsuccessfully for a job all day:* tiredness, exhaustion, weariness, debilitation, lassitude, enervation, heaviness, listlessness, languor, drowsiness, tedium, overtiredness. —*v.* **2.** *Climbing the mountain fatigued the whole scout troop:* exhaust, tire, overtire, weary, wear out, enervate, debilitate, drain, weaken; *Informal* bush, fag, tucker. —**Ant.** 1 energy, alertness, vigor, indefatigability. 2 rest, refresh, restore, rejuvenate, renew, relieve.

fatness n. *His fatness had become more conspicuous:* corpulence, obesity, flab, fleshiness, breadth, bulkiness, girth, heaviness, inflation, largeness, plumpness, heft, portliness, overweight, size, weight, stoutness.

fatten v. *They fattened several hundred head of cattle:* augment, bloat, broaden, build up, gain weight, coarsen, cram, expand, distend, feed, fill, nourish, increase, plump, round out, spread, thicken, swell, thrive.

fatty adj. *Butter and bacon are fatty foods. The well-known old expression "fine as fatty bread" means "in tiptop shape":* greasy, containing fat, shortened, buttery, oily, suety, lardy, blubbery.

fatuous adj. *She's so fatuous she thinks all the fellows are flirting with her:* foolish, inane, silly, vacant in mind, simple, stupid, brainless, witless, vapid, vacuous, asinine, imbecile, idiotic, puerile, obtuse, besotted, senseless, moronic, ridiculous. —**Ant.** sensible, prudent, judicious, wise, sage, sapient, clever, bright, intelligent, smart, witty.

faucet n. *She turned the faucet on:* tap, spigot, spout, valve.

fault n. **1.** *His only fault is that he lacks ambition:* shortcoming, defect, deficiency, insufficiency, imperfection, impediment, snag, flaw, failing, infirmity, frailty, weakness, weak point, drawback; *Informal* bug, *Slang* glitch; taint, stain, foible, blemish. **2.** *It would be wise to confess your fault:* error, blunder, wrong, mistake, misdeed, mistake of judgment, transgression, sin, oversight, offense, wrongdoing, dereliction, indiscretion, slip, cause for blame, peccadillo, misdemeanor, crime. **3.** *Whose fault is it that the plan fell through?:* responsibility, guilt, answerability, accountability, culpability, blame, negligence, mistake of judgment. —v. **4.** *He's awfully short to be a basketball player, but we can't fault him for trying:* find fault with, blame, impugn, censure, criticize, reprove. —**Ant.** 1 merit, excellence, virtue, perfection, strength, sufficiency. 3 credit. 4 credit, praise.

faultfinder n. *Please don't think me a faultfinder, but aren't the walls a bit too blue?:* critic, quibbler, carper, complainer, censor, caviler, fussbudget, derogator, detractor, Mrs. Grundy, nitpicker, bear, sorehead, crab, grouch, crank, grouser, curmudgeon; *Slang* bellyacher, fuddy-duddy.

faultless adj. *She practiced the speech until her delivery and timing were faultless:* perfect, without blemish, free from imperfection, flawless, without fault, ideal, exemplary, irreproachable, immaculate, unblemished, impeccable, unimpeachable; correct, accurate. —**Ant.** faulty, incomplete, imperfect, incorrect, defective, inaccurate, erroneous.

faulty adj. *I'd better get that faulty muffler fixed:* unsound, defective, impaired, injured, awry, out of order, amiss, inadequate, deficient, inferior; incorrect, mistaken, erroneous, unsatisfactory, bad, unreliable, wrong, false.

—**Ant.** sound, perfect, complete, adequate, blameless, faultless, correct, accurate.

faux pas n. *Insulting the guest was a terrible faux pas:* breach of etiquette, mistake, blunder, gaffe, indiscretion, false step, error, impropriety, lapse; *Informal* slip-up, *Slang* goof, boo-boo, howler, boner.

favor n. **1.** *Would you do me a favor and mail this letter?:* good turn, kind act, good deed, service, accommodation; benefaction, largesse, courtesy, dispensation, act of grace. **2.** *Punctuality is a good way to win the boss's favor:* approval, goodwill, friendly disposition, esteem, kindly regard, good opinion, approbation; support, patronage, commendation, countenance; championship, advocacy, espousal. **3.** *She put nosegays by each plate as party favors:* gift, present, goodwill token, memento, souvenir. —v. **4.** *How many board members favor the merger?:* approve, be in favor of, support, endorse, back, be for, go in for, like, commend, sanction, esteem, countenance, encourage, smile upon, side with, uphold. **5.** *The teacher favors serious students. I must favor my weak ankle when I walk:* prefer, have a preference for, fancy, side with, patronize, be partial to; pamper, deal gently with, humor, indulge, use lightly, use gently. **6.** *They favored our program with a large contribution:* support, aid, help, assist, oblige, succor, foster, accommodate, abet, show favor to, do a kindness for. **7.** *She favors her grandmother more than her mother:* look like, resemble, take after, be the image of. —**Ant.** 1 injury, disservice, harm, hurt. 2 ill will, disfavor, malice, malevolence, antipathy, prohibition, animosity, enmity, hostility, disapproval, oppose, be against, disapprove, dislike. 5 dislike, object to. 6 hurt, harm, inconvenience, thwart, foil.

favorable adj. **1.** *With favorable winds, a sailing ship could outrun a steamship:* advantageous, good, giving help, affording aid, helpful, beneficial, serviceable, convenient, timely, fair. **2.** *The credit bureau gave him a favorable report:* approving, showing favor, commendatory, salutary, good, showing approval, well-disposed; friendly, kind, benign, amicable, sympathetic. **3.** *Indications are favorable for an upsurge in business:* promising, propitious, opportune, auspicious, good, hopeful, conducive, predisposed. —**Ant.** 1–3 unfavorable. 1 disadvantageous, unhelpful. 2 disapproving, ill-disposed, unfriendly, unsympathetic. 3 unpromising, inauspicious.

favorably adv. **1.** *They reacted favorably to the report:* agreeably, amiably, cordially, approvingly, enthusiastically, courteously, generously, fairly, genially, heartily, graciously, helpfully, willingly, kindly, positively, receptively, happily. **2.** *At last the wind began blowing favorably:* opportunely, advantageously, conveniently, auspiciously, fortunately, profitably, well, satisfyingly.

favored adj. *The favored horses all finished last:* preferred, advantaged, best-liked, chosen, blessed, elite, favorite, pet, lucky, popular, recommended, privileged, well-liked, selected.

favorite n. **1.** The oldest boy was her favorite: preferred one, choice, pet, fancy, jewel, darling, fair-haired one, apple of one's eye. **2.** The incumbent is the favorite in the election: probable winner, one favored to win, front-runner. —adj. **3.** I can't find my favorite tie: best-liked, preferred, pet, choice, most popular, special.

favoritism n. A wise teacher never shows favoritism: partiality, bias, favoring of one over others, one-sidedness, partisanship.

fawn v. The bellhop fawned over the rich guest in hopes of a large tip: be servile, be obsequious, ingratiate oneself, truckle, toady, pander, seek favor, bow and scrape, flatter, pay court. —**Ant.** be insulting, ignore.

fawning adj. In the movie he played a fawning courtier: sycophantic, obsequious, compliant, bootlicking, cowering, servile, cringing, deferential, crawling, flattering, ingratiating, scraping, kowtowing, subservient, submissive.

faze v. The roof could fall in and it wouldn't faze her: disconcert, fret, rattle, daunt, worry, disturb, upset, bother, discompose, perturb, discomfit, embarrass, abash, confound, fluster, flurry.

fear n. **1.** She feels great fear in the dark: dread, fright, foreboding, terror, panic, threat, horror, affright, apprehension, alarm, dismay, trepidation, consternation, disquietude, quaking, perturbation, qualm, anxiety, worry, concern, fearfulness, cowardice. **2.** High places are her biggest fear: qualm, phobia, apprehension, source of anxiety, dread; nightmare, bugaboo, bugbear, specter, bogey; worry, concern, care. **3.** The immense space and quiet inside the cathedral gave one a proper fear of God: reverence, awe, reverential regard, wonder, veneration, esteem, deep respect. —v. **4.** I fear his wrath more than anything: be afraid of, dread, be frightened of, regard with fear, be apprehensive of, take fright, be scared of, tremble at, shudder at. **5.** The children were taught to fear God: feel awe for, revere, respect deeply, honor humbly, venerate, reverence, esteem. —**Ant.** 1 fearlessness, bravery, intrepidity, courage, confidence, security, calm, assurance, aplomb; backbone, endurance, grit, guts, heroism, pluck.

fearful adj. **1.** A fearful bolt of lightning split the sky: frightening, frightful, dreadful, causing fear, terrible, dread, alarming, formidable, appalling, macabre, ominous, ghastly, terrifying, distressing, shocking, portentous, horrible, sinister, dire, horrid, eerie, lurid, awful. **2.** We were fearful that she might harm herself: afraid, frightened, apprehensive, alarmed, aghast, panicky, haunted with fear, anxious, worried, scared, full of fear, uneasy, concerned, nervous. **3.** Strangers alarm the fearful child: frightened, tremulous, nervous, showing fear, intimidated, diffident, timid, timorous, anxious, skittish, panic-stricken, panicky, scared, fainthearted, chicken-hearted, apprehensive. —**Ant.** 1 reassuring, encouraging, pleasant, benign. 2 fearless, unafraid, confident. 3 fearless, audacious, brave, courageous, bold, dauntless, valiant, intrepid.

fearless adj. The soldiers followed their fearless leader into battle: dauntless, bold, undaunted, unafraid, confident, intrepid, brave, courageous, undismayed, without fear, unflinching, unshrinking, gallant, daring, venturesome, adventurous, unabashed, valiant, indomitable, valorous, heroic, audacious, stout-hearted, doughty, lion-hearted, plucky, gritty. —**Ant.** fearful, cowardly, timorous, daunted, afraid, dismayed, apprehensive, flinching, shrinking, terrified.

feasible adj. It's not feasible to make the trip in one day: practicable, possible, conceivable, workable, achievable, attainable; desirable, advisable, appropriate, viable, reasonable, fitting, suitable, politic. —**Ant.** unfeasible, infeasible, unworkable, unachievable, impractical, impossible, unsuitable, impracticable.

feast n. **1.** Our host provided a feast fit for a king: banquet, sumptuous repast, festive board, large dinner, elegant meal, large spread, bacchanal; rich supply, surplus, bounty. **2.** When is the feast of San Gennaro?: holiday, festival, feast day, celebration, festal day, fete, jubilee, saint's day, Italian festa. —v. **3.** The lords and ladies feasted on venison: eat richly, dine, have a feast, fare sumptuously, wine and dine, banquet, gorge, gluttonize, eat one's fill, gormandize. **4.** How many guests were feasted at the château?: feed luxuriously, entertain expensively, wine and dine, entertain with a feast. —**Ant.** 1 fast, famine, fasting. 2 fast, fast day, fasting.

feat n. The circus acrobats performed feats of dexterity and strength: deed, act, action, task, achievement, accomplishment, exploit, performance, attainment; maneuver, stroke; adventure, enterprise, triumph, tour de force.

feature n. **1.** **features.** The veil she was wearing obscured her features: parts of the face, visage, aspect, lineaments, physiognomy. **2.** The landscaping is the dominant feature of the estate: attribute, quality, hallmark, trait, characteristic, mark, property, earmark, character, important part. **3.** The high-wire act is the feature of the circus: highlight, main item, special attraction, specialty, drawing card. —v. **4.** The variety show featured a ventriloquist: represent prominently, play up, display, spotlight, headline, highlight, star, present. **5.** Informal Can you feature her playing a nun?: imagine, see, picture, conceive of, envision, fancy.

febrile adj. Her febrile performance alarmed her colleagues: fevered, feverish, inflamed, hot, fiery, delirious, pyretic.

feckless adj. The feckless workers created much inefficiency: careless, aimless, futile, ineffective, good-for-nothing, irresponsible, hopeless, ineffectual, purposeless, useless, worthless, shiftless.

fecund adj. The artist began his most fecund period: fertile, breeding, productive, fruitful, prolific, propagating, rich, teeming, spawning.

federation n. He is president of the new federation of garment workers: union, united group, league, confederation, confederacy, alliance, association, coalition, combine, syndicate, amalgamation, brotherhood, sisterhood.

fee *n. The doctor's fee was higher than we expected:* charge, consideration, payment for professional services, compensation, price, commission, honorarium, stipend, emolument, remuneration, salary, wage, hire; toll, fare, tariff.

feeble *adj.* **1.** *The old woman is too feeble to do her own shopping:* enfeebled, weak, weakened, infirm, sickly, disabled, not strong, ailing, fragile, debilitated, delicate, frail, decrepit, enervated, powerless, impotent, puny, forceless, senile, doddering, declining. **2.** *We were embarrassed by his feeble attempts to be funny:* ineffective, poor, flat, spiritless, thin, frail, lacking force, tame, meager, vapid, faint, weak, flimsy, flabby, slight, insipid, lame, ineffectual, paltry, wishy-washy, colorless, inadequate. **—Ant.** 1 robust, strong, sturdy, stout, stalwart, vigorous, lusty, energetic, hale, healthy. 2 effective, effectual, successful; forceful, cogent, vehement, ardent; hearty, strong, spirited.

feebleminded *adj. The feebleminded child needed special tutoring:* mentally slow, retarded, backward, subnormal, half-witted, moronic, imbecilic; senile; weak-minded, stupid, dull, childish, senseless. **—Ant.** bright, intelligent, smart.

feebleness *n. As soon as we saw him walk haltingly, his feebleness was obvious:* exhaustion, frailness, debility, frailty, effeteness, decrepitude, enervation, weakness, etiolation, ineffectiveness, inability, inadequacy, incapacity, insufficiency, incompetence, lassitude, malaise, senility, infirmity, infirmnesss, sickliness.

feed *v.* **1.** *She must struggle to feed and clothe such a large family:* supply with nourishment, provide food for; feast, cater, wine and dine; give as food. **2.** *Pigs will feed on just about anything:* eat, take nourishment, consume, take food, devour, fare, graze, pasture. **3.** *Applause feeds his ego:* nourish, nurture, support, fuel, augment, encourage, maintain, strengthen, bolster, sustain, foster; gratify, satisfy, minister to. **—n. 4.** *I bought a bag of bird feed:* foodstuff, nourishment, food for animals, provisions, fodder, victuals, provender, viands, comestibles, forage, mash, pasture. **—Ant.** 1 starve. 3 starve, thwart, deny, stifle.

feel *v.* **1.** *I love to feel silk pajamas against my skin:* perceive by touch, sense, touch, examine by touching, have the feeling of; palpate, paw, handle, finger, manipulate, press. **2.** *He feels the cold more than most. I feel great guilt about what happened:* have a sensation of, experience, sense, perceive, suffer from, be aware of; understand, comprehend, know, see, discern, observe, notice. **3.** *He had to feel for the light switch in the dark. Can you feel your way in the dark?:* grope, find by touching, fumble, search with the hands; reach, probe. **4.** *I feel that he should resign:* be of the opinion that, believe, think, be convinced, sense, have an impression. **5.** *It's hard to feel for someone so selfish:* have sympathy, sympathize with, share the feelings of, have compassion, be moved by, be touched by, be stirred by. **—n. 6.** *Don't you like the feel*

of this material?: feeling, sensation, touch, texture, composition, character, makeup.

feeling *n.* **1.** *He has no feeling in his left hand. The feeling of warmth from the fire was lovely:* sense of touch, sensation, tactile sense, perception by touch, sensibility, awareness, consciousness. **2.** *He had a feeling of joy when his son was born:* emotion, sense, sensation, thrill, reaction, impression, response, sentiment; aura, atmosphere. **3.** *She has no feeling for the suffering of others. He played the piece with great feeling:* sympathy, compassion, concern, sensitivity, susceptibility, passion, pity; emotion, ardor, affection, sentiment, fervor, vehemence, zeal, earnestness, verve, enthusiasm, warmth, gusto, spirit. **4.** *My feeling is that we should postpone the meeting:* opinion, view, point of view, attitude, impression, instinct, intuition, inclination, sentiment. **—Ant.** 1 numbness, insensibility, insensateness. 3 insensitivity, unconcern, imperturbability, coldness, apathy. 4 unfeeling, unemotional, dispassionate, cold.

feelings *n. pl. He doesn't care about the feelings of others:* sensibilities, susceptibilities, emotions, passions, sensitivities; pride, ego, self-esteem.

feign *v.* **1.** *She feigned surprise and they believed her:* simulate, affect, assume, pretend, fake, make believe, sham, imitate deceptively, put on, make a show of. **2.** *He feigned an alibi for the missing time:* make up, invent, forge, concoct, counterfeit, devise deceptively, fabricate, fake, *Slang* cook up.

feint *n. The dogs made a few feints at each other, then backed off without fighting:* feigned attack, pass, bluff, deceptive movement, move; artifice, stratagem, pretense, maneuver, ruse, ploy, trick, gambit, hoax, subterfuge, wile, dodge, pretext; mask, blind.

felicitation *n. Please accept our felicitations on your forthcoming marriage:* congratulations, compliments, best wishes, good wishes, blessings, joy; greetings, salutations, cheers, pat on the back, wishes for happiness.

felicitous *adj.* **1.** *Champagne is for weddings and other felicitous occasions:* happy, joyful, joyous, fortunate, propitious. **2.** *The young man searched hard for a felicitous last line to his poem:* apt, appropriate, suitable, relevant, pertinent, germane, fitting, well-chosen, well-put, well-said, pleasing, happy, inspired; effective. **—Ant.** 1 infelicitous, solemn, inappropriate. 2 infelicitous, awkward, clumsy, unfortunate.

felicity *n.* **1.** *Being locked in an ice-cream parlor was the boy's idea of felicity:* happiness, blissfulness, bliss, ecstatic joy, delight, delectation, paradise, heavenly contentment, heaven, beatitude, ecstasy. **2.** *He usually expresses himself with felicity:* aptness, charm, grace, nicety, fitness, effectiveness, suitability, relevancy, appropriateness; skill, knack, ingenuity. **—Ant.** 1 sorrow, misery, sadness, unhappiness. 2 inappropriateness, clumsiness, awkwardness.

fell *v. The tower was felled by lightning:* knock down, cut down, cause to fall, hew down, level, prostrate; demolish, destroy, raze.

fellow n. **1.** Harry is certainly a nice fellow: boy, man, chap, Slang guy, dude. **2.** The boy went to join his fellows on the playing field: companion, associate, friend, comrade, consort, chum, co-worker, compatriot, colleague, pal; British mate; peer, equal. —**Ant.** 1 girl, woman, gal. 2 foe, opponent, antagonist, stranger.

fellowship n. He enjoys the fellowship of his co-workers: companionship, comradeship, friendliness, cordiality, friendship, sociability, amicability, intimacy, familiarity, amity, affability; society, association, fraternity, brotherhood. —**Ant.** unfriendliness, unsociability; antagonism, hostility.

felon n. The felon was apprehended a week later: lawbreaker, outlaw, delinquent, criminal, offender, convict, malefactor.

female adj. **1.** She is their oldest female child: girl, woman; offspring-bearing, childbearing. **2.** Sewing is considered a female occupation: feminine, womanly, ladylike, womanlike, distaff. —n. **3.** Females constitute a slight majority of the population: woman, girl. **4.** This litter produced 2 males and 7 females: female animal, offspring-bearing animal; (variously) mare, dam, sow, heifer, cow, bitch, tabby, hen. —**Ant.** 1 male. 2 male, masculine, manly, virile. 3 male, man, boy. 4 male.

feminine adj. **1.** Gentleness was long considered a feminine trait: womanly, female, female-like, like a woman, girlish, ladylike, gentle, soft; dainty, delicate. **2.** There are few feminine members of the committee: female, of the female sex, woman, distaff. —**Ant.** 1 masculine, male, manly, virile; indelicate, rough, mannish, unfeminine. 2 male.

femininity n. She was a tough-minded executive, but she never lost her femininity: womanliness, female quality, girlishness, femaleness, feminineness; softness, gentleness. —**Ant.** masculinity, manliness, virility; toughness, mannishness.

fence n. **1.** We built a fence around the yard to keep the dog in: barrier, protective enclosure, palings, palisade, rail, barricade, stockade. —v. **2.** It took miles of barbed wire to fence in the farm: enclose with a fence, surround, secure, encompass, gird, corral, hedge, pen, encircle, hem in, wall in, coop, confine. **3.** He fenced with his new sword: duel, cross swords, engage in swordplay.

fend v. **1.** The governor fended off a mass of reporters and got into a limousine: ward off, avert, push away, keep off, avoid, repel, repulse, parry. **2.** As a grownup, you must fend for yourself from now on: manage, provide, shift, do, make out; survive, take care of, support.

ferment v. **1.** We decided to let a jug of raw apple juice ferment into hard cider: turn partly into alcohol, undergo fermentation, turn; sour, seethe, bubble up, foam, froth, effervesce. **2.** Campus politics fermented during the late 1960's: seethe, be turbulent, smolder, fester, agitate, inflame. —n. **3.** What kind of ferment do the winemakers use?: fermentation, fermentation agent; yeast, mold, enzyme, leaven, leaven-ing. **4.** The ferment among the students caused the college to close: unrest, disquiet, disruption, agitation, inflammation, fomentation, turmoil, turbulence, tumult, commotion, uproar. —**Ant.** 4 calmness, quiet.

ferocious adj. Tigers are among the most ferocious animals: savage, bestial, rapacious, brutish, ravening, predatory, fierce, violent; relentless, merciless, barbarous, ruthless, atrocious, murderous, maddened, enraged, bloodthirsty, fiendish, brutal, cold-blooded, deadly. —**Ant.** tame, domesticated, subdued, submissive, mild, calm.

ferry v. They ferried the convoy across the river: convey, transport, ship, bear, carry, buck, move across, lug, pack, send, ship, tote, shuttle.

fertile adj. **1.** Anything grows in this fertile ground. We were surprised that the old mare was still fertile: productive, fruitful, fructuous, fecund, vegetative, plenteous, luxuriant, loamy, rich; generative, reproductive, capable of bearing offspring, prolific; capable of developing, fertilized, fecundated, fructified. **2.** His fertile mind keeps turning out new schemes: imaginative, productive, prolific, resourceful, inventive, creative; original, ingenious. —**Ant.** 1 infertile, barren, unproductive, unfertilized, poor, dry, unfruitful; impotent, sterile. 2 unproductive, uninventive, unimaginative, uncreative.

fertility n. Fertility is one characteristic of genius: fruitfulness, fecundity, virility, abundance, copiousness, luxuriance, plentifulness, potency, pregnancy, readiness, productivity.

fertilize v. The male fish fertilizes the female's eggs. The garden soil needs fertilizing: make fertile, render productive, impregnate, make fruitful, fructify, furnish with pollen, fecundate, pollinate, inseminate; enrich, feed with nutrients, manure.

fervent adj. The lawyer made a fervent plea for clemency: earnest, impassioned, fervid, warm-hearted, passionate, ardent, devout, zealous, intense, keen, eager, vehement, spirited, fierce, heartfelt, wholehearted, hearty, fiery, heated, burning, enthusiastic. —**Ant.** cool, cold, chilly, frigid; apathetic, impassive, phlegmatic, unfeeling, unimpassioned.

fervor n. The pilgrims arrived at the shrine and offered their prayers with fervor: ardor, passion, intensity, earnestness, vehemence, verve, zeal, animation, gusto, fire, enthusiasm, heartiness, eagerness, zest, warmth; piety, devoutness, seriousness, purposefulness. —**Ant.** boredom, ennui, apathy, detachment, dispassion.

fester v. **1.** Her boil festered and had to be lanced: form pus, suppurate, become infected, inflame, ulcerate, blister; rot, putrefy. **2.** Her resentment had festered for many years: rankle, torment, smolder, intensify, grow, grow virulent, plague; gall, irritate, chafe, fret, nettle, pique, rile, vex.

festival n. I wore a yellow dress in the May festival: feast, celebration, holiday, carnival, fete, festivities, jubilee, gala day, gala, jamboree, fiesta.

festive adj. We all wore festive costumes to the

ball: festal, joyous, gala, merry, jolly, gay, convivial, lighthearted, celebratory; larkish, playful, sportive, frolicsome. —**Ant.** funereal, gloomy; sad, lugubrious, glum, drab, dreary.

festivity *n. The festivity began on the weekend:* fair, feast, festival, *French* fête, *Spanish* fiesta, amusement, bash, carnival, celebration, entertainment, commemoration, gala, jubilee, merry-making, party, revelry, revel, treat, *Informal* hoopla.

fetch *v.* **1.** *Throw a stick and watch the dog fetch it:* get and bring back, go for, retrieve, get, obtain, bring. **2.** *The load of furniture should fetch a good price:* sell for, bring, procure, yield, realize, get; cost, afford, amount to, *Informal* go for.

fetching *adj. The fetching girl wore a tartan skirt:* charming, alluring, attractive, enchanting, beautiful, captivating, cute, enticing, winsome, pleasing.

fete *n.* **1.** *They held a lavish fete at their country house:* party, feast, celebration, gala, garden party, banquet, carnival; *French* bal masqué, fête champêtre; festival, holiday. —*v.* **2.** *The ambassador will fete the visiting dignitaries:* wine and dine, give a party for, feast, banquet; treat, regale.

fetid *adj. The room reeks of that fetid cigar smoke:* stinking, malodorous, rank, foul, ill-smelling, noisome, stenchful, stenchy, mephitic; rotten, putrid; gamy, nasty, tainted, rank, rancid; musty, fusty, moldy; suffocating, stifling. —**Ant.** fragrant, odorous, odoriferous, aromatic, redolent, balmy; perfumed, scented; clean, fresh, pure.

fetish *n.* **1.** *A rabbit's foot carried for good luck is a fetish:* charm, talisman, magic object; superstition; idol, image, golden calf, totem, amulet, scarab, joss, phylactery. **2.** *Cleanliness is admirable, but don't make a fetish of it:* preoccupation, obsession, craze, mania, passion, idée fixe.

fetter *n.* **1.** *The guards put fetters on all the prisoners:* foot shackle, ankle irons, bond, chain, tether, yoke, manacle, handcuff, *Slang* bracelet. **2.** *Education aims at removing fetters from the mind:* hindrance, obstruction, curb, restraint; confinement, imprisonment, durance, duress. —*v.* **3.** *We had to fetter the horse to keep it from straying:* shackle, hobble, put into bilbos, confine, tether, trammel, pin down, tie down, tie up, truss up, bind hand and foot; manacle, handcuff, chain. **4.** *Many people are fettered by lack of self-confidence:* hamper, hinder, hold back, impede, restrain, bind, encumber; confine, cage, shut in. —**Ant.** 3, 4 free, unfetter, liberate, release; extricate, disencumber. 4 encourage, promote.

feud *n.* **1.** *The feud caused many deaths in the two families:* bad blood, vendetta, dispute, quarrel, strife; conflict, altercation, disagreement, bickering, falling out, argument; hostility, animosity, ill will, enmity, hard feelings, bad blood, discord, controversy; schism, faction; breach, rupture; fracas, affray, clashing, brawl, wrangle; *Informal* spat, fuss, tiff, set-to, squabble. —*v.* **2.**

Martha and her sister have been feuding for years: quarrel, dispute, be at odds, disagree, argue, bicker; clash, brawl, wrangle; *Informal* squabble, spat, row.

feverish *adj.* **1.** *I've been feeling feverish all morning:* fevered, hot, febrile, flushed, pyretic; fiery, red-hot, inflamed, burning, parched. **2.** *He had a feverish desire to begin the race:* ardent, fanatic, impatient, overeager, passionate, fervent, zealous, impassioned; frenzied, excited, restless, wrought-up, high-strung. —**Ant.** 2 composed, collected, cool; calm, unruffled, serene, tranquil; offhand, nonchalant.

few *adj.* **1.** *Few countries can survive without trade:* not many, scarcely any, hardly any; scant, scanty, thin, sparse, skimpy, rare, exiguous, scarce; occasional, sporadic, infrequent, few and far between; limited, piddling, paltry, meager, inconsiderable, infinitesimal, insignificant, unusual, uncommon, unique. —*n.* **2.** *Don't give me any more pencils—I still have a few:* small number, some, several, handful. —**Ant.** 1 many, abundant, numerous, abounding, plentiful, bounteous; unstinted, inexhaustible.

fiancée or **fiancé** *n. He didn't introduce his fiancée to his parents until after he'd given her the engagement ring:* affianced, person to whom one is engaged, intended, prospective spouse, wife-to-be, husband-to-be.

fiasco *n. My attempt to get Bill and Jane acquainted was a fiasco:* complete failure, disaster; nonsuccess, debacle, labor in vain, miscarriage; *Slang* flop, botch, washout, bomb, fizzle. —**Ant.** success, triumph, smash, coup.

fiat *n. The emperor's fiat forbade assembly by more than three persons:* command, decree, law, act, rule, ukase, edict, commandment, mandate, order, ruling, dictum.

fib *n.* **1.** *That compliment was a fib, but it made her feel better:* harmless lie, half-truth, white lie; untruth, prevarication, misrepresentation, falsification, fiction, fabrication, invention. —*v.* **2.** *I fibbed and told him he'd be up and around in no time:* lie, tell a white lie, tell a half-truth, stretch the truth, prevaricate, equivocate, hedge.

fiber *n.* **1.** *The fibers in the carpet were closely-woven:* cord, filament, hair, nap, pile, shred, strand, string, tendril, thread, warp, web. **2.** *Her deeds testified to her moral fiber:* quality, texture, grain, tissue, vein, substance.

fibrous *adj. These oranges are fibrous:* pulpy, stringy, woody, coarse, hairy, muscular, ropy, sinewy, stalky, stringy, threadlike.

fickle *adj. She's so fickle she has a new boy-friend every week:* changeable, unpredictable, vacillating, inconstant, irresolute, inconsistent, mercurial; whimsical, capricious, volatile; giddy, feather-brained, frivolous, light-headed, flighty, erratic, fitful, spasmodic, feather-headed, wavering, fluctuating, unstable, unsteady, variable, shifting; unreliable, untrustworthy. —**Ant.** constant, true, faithful, loyal, staunch, steadfast, firm, resolute, changeless, invariable; settled, stable, steady, sure, reliable, trustworthy.

fiction *n.* **1.** *Hemingway and Steinbeck were masters of fiction:* imaginative literary work, prose narration, romance; (*variously*) narrative, novel, novella, short story, short novel, tale, play; invention, imagination, fantasy, storytelling. **2.** *That story about her rich grandfather was certainly a fiction:* falsehood, fabrication, prevarication, made-up story, fable, fib, tall tale, concoction, lie, forgery; *Slang* whopper, yarn, cock-and-bull story. **—Ant.** 1 nonfiction, journalism. 2 certainty, fact, history; reality, truth, verity.

fictitious *adj.* *The spy checked into a hotel under a fictitious name:* unreal, false, untrue, assumed, feigned, invented, fanciful, imaginary, unfounded, counterfeit, forged, fabricated, bogus, fraudulent, spurious, supposititious, not genuine; artificial, sham, fake, phony, made-up, trumped-up, simulated; legendary, mythical, apocryphal. **—Ant.** real, true, actual; genuine, authentic, veritable; veracious, truthful.

fidelity *n.* **1.** *My grandfather always votes for the straight ticket out of fidelity to the party:* devotion, loyalty, faithfulness, adherence, constancy, trueheartedness, fealty; trustworthiness, integrity, honesty, truthfulness, probity; honor, allegiance, staunchness; sincerity, good faith, earnestness. **2.** *The artist portrayed the lady with great fidelity:* accuracy, exactness, exactitude, faithfulness, correspondency, adherence to fact; closeness, precision; reliability. **—Ant.** faithlessness, unfaithfulness, perfidy, perfidiousness, falseness, falsity, disloyalty, treacherousness, treachery, traitorousness, untruthfulness; disaffection, infidelity; inexactness, inaccuracy.

fidget *v.* *They fidgeted while waiting for the movie:* fret, chafe, fuss, fiddle, jiggle, squirm, jitter, toss, stir, worry, twiddle.

fidgety *adj.* *The children get fidgety when we take them to church:* restless, restive, impatient; unquiet, jumpy, jittery, jerky, twitchy, squirmy, *Slang* antsy; nervous, uneasy, fussy, apprehensive; irritable; tremulous.

field *n.* **1.** *The horses were turned loose in the field:* meadow, grassland, pasture, grazing land, lea, mead, sward; lawn, green, common, yard, acreage; heath, clearing. **2.** *Soccer is played on a rectangular field:* playing field; arena, turf, court, course, diamond; lists. **3.** *The general serves better in the field than at a desk:* battlefield, battleground, theater of war, front, front lines. **4.** *She is a leader in the field of cosmetics:* realm, domain, province, territory, region, area, sphere, department, bailiwick; occupation, profession, calling, line. **5.** *The optometrist will examine your field of vision:* scope, range, area, extent, reach, expanse, sweep, stretch, orbit, circle, spectrum. **—v. 6.** *The shortstop fielded the ball and threw out the batter:* catch, pick up, run down, grab, retrieve, glove.

fiend *n.* **1.** *People used to blame illness and misfortune on fiends:* evil spirit, demon, dybbuk, incubus, succubus; devil, Satan, hellhound, prince of darkness. **2.** *The police will spare no effort to capture the fiend who murdered the children:* wicked person, villain, scoundrel, de-mon, monster, brute, beast, devil incarnate; barbarian.

fierce *adj.* **1.** *The bear, when cornered, is one of the fiercest of all animals:* wild, savage, ferocious, menacing, fearful, threatening, bloodthirs-ty, violent, brutal, cruel, fell, feral, barbarous, merciless; enraged, raging, furious, tigerish, leonine; truculent, bellicose; voracious, ravenous, ravening; horrible, terrible. **2.** *The wind was so fierce we could hardly stand up:* powerful, strong, violent, vehement, intense, overpowering, extreme, inordinate, immoderate, overwhelming; unrestrained, unbridled, uncurbed, untamed; passionate, fiery, fervent, fervid, intensely eager, impetuous. **—Ant.** 1 tame, docile, gentle, harmless, domesticated; cool, civilized; kind, patient; submissive, affectionate, sweet. 2 mild, peaceful, temperate, calm.

fiercely *adv.* *He fiercely defended the government's policy:* ferociously, forcefully, forcibly, angrily, frenziedly, passionately, frighteningly, furiously, irresistibly, mightily, violently, severely, tempestuously, stormily, vehemently, wildly, savagely, roughly.

fiery *adj.* **1.** *Shadrach, Meshach, and Abednego were thrown into the fiery furnace:* full of fire, flaming, burning; intensely hot, sweltering, torrid, blazing, alight, ablaze, afire; glowing, glaring, red-hot, flashing. **2.** *The doctor felt the patient's fiery cheek:* feverish, fevered, burning, febrile, inflamed, flaming, pyretic. **3.** *The lovers were reunited in a fiery embrace:* ardent, passionate, fervent, fervid, violent, impassioned; high-strung, impulsive, fierce, impetuous, demonstrative, temperamental; spirited, mettlesome, enthusiastic; zealous, vehement. **4.** *He'd better learn to control that fiery temper:* hotheaded, hot-tempered, easily angered, excitable, headlong, readily provoked, impetuous, precipitate, choleric, peppery, irascible; angry, irate, violent, wrathful, irritable. **—Ant.** 1 extinguished, quenched. 2 cool, chilly, cold, icy, frigid. 3 indifferent, passionless, phlegmatic, unimpassioned; dispassionate; mild, tame.

fiesta *n.* *Every fall the town holds a fiesta to honor its patron saint:* festival, party, gala, festive occasion, carnival, jamboree, fete; feast, picnic, street fair, fun-fair, block party; feast day, saint's day; celebration, commemoration, observance.

fight *n.* **1.** *The two gangs had a fight on the playground:* skirmish, struggle, fray, mêlée, strife, encounter, confrontation, contest, duel, tussle, scuffle, scrimmage, quarrel, fracas, brush, bout, dogfight; battle, combat, armed action, clash of arms, war, armed conflict, pitched battle, battle royal. **2.** *The former mayor always had plenty of fight:* spirit, pluck, grit, toughness, combativeness, disposition to struggle, mettle, gameness; belligerency, pugnacity, bellicosity. **3.** *She had an awful fight with the garbage collector:* dispute, altercation, discord, contention, encounter, confrontation, quarrel, feud, difference, controversy, wrangling, set-to, tussle, bickering, dissension; *Informal* squabble, brawl, scrap, row, brush, spat, tiff. **4.** *A fight was arranged between the champion and the challenger:* bout, match, prizefight, event, tournament, tourney, round; joust, tilt. —*v.* **5.** *The story tells how David fought Goliath:* battle, do battle with, join battle with, take up arms against, cross swords with, come to grips with, combat, struggle with, encounter, confront, engage, battle; rise up in arms, go to war, wage war, exchange blows, take up the cudgels, scuffle, brawl, skirmish, tussle, scrap, box, spar, duel; joust, tilt. **6.** *She fought back the tears as she spoke:* resist, contend against, strive with, struggle against, oppose, repulse. **7.** *They fought the war all across Europe:* wage, conduct, carry on. **8.** *I separate the children when they start fighting:* argue, dispute, clash, feud, wrangle, bicker, squabble. —**Ant.** 1 pacification, reconciliation, reconcilement; appeasement, compromise.

fighter *n.* **1.** *Will both fighters last 15 rounds?:* boxer, pugilist, prizefighter; sparrer. **2.** *If you come from the slums, you have to be a fighter just to survive:* person with spirit, scrapper. **3.** *The army decorated him as a brave fighter:* warrior, soldier, military man, combatant, fighting man; belligerent, militarist.

fighting *n.* *Fighting was forbidden in school hallways:* battle, combat, brawling, bloodshed, conflict, bout, contention, donnybrook, exchange, hostility, fracas, match, joust, mêlée, riot, row, scrap, strife, struggle, warfare, scrimmage, scuffle, *Informal* rhubarb.

figment *n.* *The prowler on the roof turned out to be a figment of my imagination:* product, fabrication, creation, fancy, fantasy, fiction, invention, concoction; story, fable, canard; falsehood. —**Ant.** fact, reality, actuality, certainty.

figurative *adj.* *She used the word "dead" in its figurative sense to mean "tired":* metaphorical, not literal, symbolic, involving a figure of speech; ironic, satirical, humorous; hyperbolical; allegorical; flowery, florid, ornate. —**Ant.** literal, precise, verbatim, faithful, exact; prosaic, unpoetical, plain.

figure *n.* **1.** *The figure for "one" is "1":* numerical symbol, digit, number, cipher, numeral. **2.** *He named a figure that was much more than we could pay:* price, amount, rate, cost, quotation, sum, value. **3. figures.** *I was never much good at figures:* arithmetic, sums, calculations, computations. **4.** *The gown showed off her lovely figure:* form, shape, outline, silhouette, body, physique, build; contour, cut, cast; configuration, frame, anatomy. **5.** *Michelangelo was one of the great figures of the Renaissance:* personage, character, person, notable, eminence, force, leader, factor, presence, man, woman. **6.** *She bought a scarf printed with a spiral figure:* pattern, design, device, motif, emblem; sign, symbol, plan, schema; diagram, illustration, drawing. —*v.* **7.** *Figure the total and I'll pay it with a check:* calculate, compute, count up, add up, sum, reckon, cast, find the amount of, total, tot up, foot; assess, appraise, estimate. **8.** *The wallpaper was figured with rosebuds:* embellish,

adorn, ornament, mark, pattern, variegate, diversify. **9.** *Informal I figure it must be close to three miles:* calculate, reckon, think, suppose, conjecture; presume, believe, judge, imagine, guess. **10.** *Real historical events figure in Tolstoy's novel,* War and Peace: have a part, play a part, be mentioned, appear; be conspicuous, be prominent, be placed, count, shine forth, appear.

figurehead *n.* *His title was "President," but he was only a figurehead:* authority in name only, token, ornament, puppet, dummy, front; cipher, nonentity, tool.

filch *v.* **1.** *When he was a kid he filched apples from the corner fruit stand:* steal, rob, purloin, pilfer, swipe, lift; *Slang* boost, heist, cop, hook. **2.** *The professor caught her filching phrases from Faulkner:* appropriate, pirate, copy, lift, expropriate, plagiarize, crib, arrogate, use as one's own.

file *n.* **1.** *This room has been set aside for the department files:* collection of papers or documents, information for reference, data; records, archives, stacks; filing cabinet, folder, drawer, dossier. **2.** *A file of customers was waiting when the store opened:* line, queue, rank, row; string, chain, tier. —*v.* **3.** *Please file these letters under "Smith":* store, put away, arrange for later reference, classify, catalog, index, place on file; record, list, chronicle, make an entry of. **4.** *Did you file for disability insurance?:* apply, submit a claim, petition, put in, request. **5.** *The students filed into the assembly hall:* walk in line, march in a file, follow the leader, walk Indian fashion, move forward in a line, advance in a queue.

filial *adj.* *There was much filial affection in the hug she gave her father:* befitting one's child, sonlike or daughterly; respectful, dutiful.

filibuster *n.* *The senator began his filibuster on Tuesday:* obstruction, delay, hindrance, opposition, postponement, stonewalling.

fill *v.* **1.** *Ask him to fill the bottle with turpentine:* make full, fill up; pervade, permeate, overspread, charge; saturate, impregnate, infuse, suffuse; load, lade, pack; crowd, cram, glut; feed fully, gorge, sate, satisfy, satiate. **2.** *Has that secretarial position been filled?:* occupy, take up, assign, fulfill, supply; function, serve, act; preside, do duty; execute, discharge, carry out. **3.** *Does Ed need help filling those orders?:* make up, furnish, replenish, supply, provide; provision, outfit, stock; lay in, lay by, store. **4.** *This new medication fills an urgent need:* satisfy, meet, supply, answer, take care of. **5.** *Breathe in until your lungs fill with air:* expand, inflate, dilate, distend; blow up, puff. —*n.* **6.** *Have you had your fill of cashew nuts?:* full amount, sufficiency, surfeit. —**Ant.** drain; empty, evaporate, shrink, diminish, ebb, subside; exhaust, vacate.

filling *n.* *The cake had a cream filling:* filler, contents, center, fill, liner, dressing, stuffing, packing, padding, wadding, inside, innards.

film *n.* **1.** *There seems to be a film of oil on the water:* thin layer, coat, coating, membrane, skin, sheet; veil, cloud, haze, mist. **2.** *Who stars in his* *latest film?:* motion picture, movie, moving pictures, *Slang* flick. **3. films.** *She always wanted to work in films:* the film industry, cinema, movies, screen, motion pictures, moving pictures, *Slang* flicks. —*v.* **4.** *The old woman's eyes filmed over as she thought of the past:* haze, veil, mist. **5.** *They're filming a detective drama here now:* make a movie of, shoot.

filmy *adj.* **1.** *She wore a dress of filmy material:* gauzy, gossamer, chiffon, diaphanous, wispy, sheer, cobwebby, dainty, delicate, fine, fine-grained, finespun, flimsy, insubstantial, fragile, transparent, see-through. **2.** *Our eyes grew filmy over the sentimental part of the movie:* dim, blurred, blurry, opalescent, cloudy, hazy, milky, misty, opaque, pearly, membranous.

filter *n.* **1.** *The lake water passes through a filter before it is piped to our homes:* strainer, sieve, screen, purifying device. —*v.* **2.** *The dehumidifier filters the moisture out of the air:* strain, pass through a filter, cleanse, refine, purify, clarify, filtrate. **3.** *Sunlight was filtering through the venetian blinds:* seep, dribble, leak, trickle; ooze, drain, well out, exude, effuse. —**Ant.** 2 muddle, disturb, befoul; thicken; mix, merge, combine.

filth *n.* **1.** *The sidewalks and gutters were full of filth:* foul matter, dirt, trash, ordure, sewage, muck, slime; contamination, squalidness, squal-or, nastiness, filthiness, pollution, defilement, impurity; dung, excrement, feces, excreta, manure; slop, refuse, garbage, offal, carrion, putridness; mud, mire, sludge, slush. **2.** *They're trying to shut down those shops that sell filth:* pornography, obscenity, smut; grossness, indecency, immorality, lewdness; foul language, dirty-mindedness, vileness, corruption; suggestiveness, indelicacy; ribaldry.

filthy *adj.* **1.** *The filthy house hadn't been cleaned in years:* dirty, grimy, begrimed, foul, unclean, defiled, squalid. **2.** *They led a campaign to ban filthy magazines:* obscene, vile, dirty, pornographic, licentious, lascivious. —**Ant.** 1 clean, spotless, immaculate.

final *adj.* **1.** *Our final meeting for the season is next Wednesday:* last, closing, concluding; rear, rearmost, hindmost, hindermost; ending, terminating, terminal; latest, last-minute; extreme, ultimate. **2.** *She said "No, and that's final":* decisive, conclusive, definitive, determinative; complete, thorough, finished, exhaustive; irrevocable, unchangeable, unappealable. —**Ant.** 1 opening, first, initial. 2 preliminary; inconclusive, incomplete, changeable.

finale *n.* *The finale of the pageant was a spectacular fireworks display:* last part, conclusion, close, end, epilogue, curtain, finish, finis, windup, termination, culmination, swan song, crowning glory.

finality *n.* *We cannot give the answer with any finality:* certitude, completeness, totality, conclusiveness, decisiveness, entirety, finish, inevitableness, intactness, irrevocability, integrity, resolution, unavoidability.

finally *adv.* **1.** *Finally, the report mentions a decline in profits:* in the end, lastly, at the last, in conclusion, ultimately; eventually, at length. **2.** *The gunman's fate was finally sealed when he resisted arrest:* conclusively, definitively, once and for all; inescapably, inexorably, incontrovertibly.

finance *n.* **1.** *The company needs a person who knows finance:* money management, banking, investment banking, investment counseling, fiscal matters, economics, accounts. —*v.* **2.** *The bank will help me finance my new car:* pay for, raise money for, supply money for, underwrite.

finances *n. pl.* *The company's finances were in deplorable shape:* assets, cash, money, funds, resources, budget, capital, affluence, backing, condition, estate, fortune, holdings, income, means, possessions, property, purse, reserves, revenue, savings, securities, wealth, riches, substance.

financial *adj.* *Business pages contain all the financial news you need:* monetary, fiscal, pecuniary, budgetary, commercial.

financier *n.* *The library got a large contribution from a wealthy financier:* expert in money matters, broker, banker, large-scale investor, underwriter, backer, angel; rich man, man of means, man of substance, moneyed man, millionaire, capitalist.

financing *n.* *The municipality sought new financing:* funding, funds, backing, sponsorship, expenditure, expense, expenses, matching funds, money, payment, outlay, support, stake, loan.

find *v.* **1.** *She found a diamond ring on the bus:* discover, come upon, light upon, stumble upon, come across, chance upon; meet with, encounter, bump into. **2.** *Eli Whitney found a new way to remove seeds from cotton:* uncover, discover, hit upon, come by; unearth, dig up, disinter; track down, ferret out; detect, expose, learn, ascertain, determine. **3.** *We were surprised to find you at the party:* discern, catch sight of, espy, spot, see, meet. **4.** *They all helped me find the ring I lost:* regain, recover, get back, retrieve, repossess, locate. **5.** *She found peace of mind through the study of yoga:* acquire, gain, attain, achieve, get, procure, win, earn. **6.** *The jury found for the plaintiff. She was found guilty of shoplifting:* declare a verdict, determine, pronounce; decide, rule, decree, judge, adjudge, adjudicate, award. —*n.* **7.** *That mahogany table was a real find:* bargain, good buy, discovery; bonanza, windfall; catch, acquisition; godsend, lucky hit. —**Ant.** 1 lose, miss, overlook; mislay, misplace.

findings *n. pl.* *The judge's findings will be announced next week:* judgment, verdict, award, data, decision, decree, pronouncement, recommendation, conclusion.

fine[1] *adj.* **1.** *This shop has some very fine furs:* high-quality, choice, top-grade, exceptional, first-class, superior, superb, splendid, admirable, excellent, flawless, exquisite, magnificent; tasteful, smart; rare; *Slang* dandy, nifty, neat, swell, spiffy. **2.** *Fine hair just won't keep its curl:* thin, slender; silky, silken, delicate; lightweight, flimsy, gossamer, cobwebby, diaphanous, sheer, transparent; airy, ethereal. **3.** *The hourglass contains fine sand:* powdery, pulverized, powdered, ground, refined. **4.** *See if you can put a fine edge on this knife:* keen, sharp; precise, perfect; skillful, polished, brilliant, highly skilled, accomplished, consummate. **5.** *Her new tea set is of fine china:* delicate, fragile, exquisite, dainty, ethereal, gauzy. **6.** *We complimented the child on her fine manners:* elegant, refined, fastidious, well-bred, exquisite; smart, chic, stylish, modish. **7.** *If those clouds drift away, we'll have a fine afternoon:* clear, bright; pleasant, sunny, rainless, cloudless, fair. **8.** *He says there's a fine distinction between "wealthy" and "rich":* subtle, hard to discern, minute, small, nice, hairsplitting; slight, tenuous, thin, unsubstantial. **9.** *Bob and Edna have two fine children:* handsome, attractive, comely, good-looking, well-favored, fair; beautiful, pretty, bonny, lovely. —*adv.* **10.** *Sam is doing fine in his new business:* very well, excellently, swimmingly. **—Ant.** 1 coarse, rough, unfinished, plain, crude. 2, 3 thick, coarse, rough, heavy, stout. 4 dull, blunt. 5 poor, inferior. 6 rough, crude, clumsy. 7 cloudy, dark, foul. 8 broad, clear, obvious. 9 ill-favored, disagreeable. 10 poorly, badly.

fine² *n.* **1.** *The fine for overtime parking is outrageously high:* penalty, sum demanded as punishment, assessment, charge, damages, forfeit, mulct. —*v.* **2.** *The judge fined her $25 for jaywalking:* punish by a fine, penalize, assess, charge, mulct.

finery *n.* *She bought lots of new finery for her Caribbean cruise:* showy dress, elegant clothing, fine things, frippery, frills; trimmings, gaudery, paraphernalia, trappings; gewgaws, tinsel, spangles, trinkets, baubles.

finesse *n.* *What could have been a nasty situation was handled with great finesse:* delicacy, tact, discretion, artful management, savoir-faire, artfulness, craft; wile, ruse, subterfuge, artifice, stratagem, *Slang* savvy; trickery, cunning, dodge, guile; intrigue, deception.

finger *n.* **1.** *How do you get a child to stop sucking his finger?:* organ of touch, digit; (*variously*) thumb, forefinger, middle finger, ring finger, little finger; pointer; *Slang* feeler. —*v.* **2.** *The grocer asked us not to finger the tomatoes:* handle, touch, feel, caress, toy with, manipulate, play with, meddle with; poke, punch, squeeze; *Informal* paw, twiddle.

finicky *adj.* *He's finicky about the way he keeps his accounts:* overparticular, fussy, meticulous, overprecise, overexacting, hair-splitting, nitpicking, picky, niggling, fastidious, pernickety, persnickety. **—Ant.** sloppy, slapdash, careless, slovenly, messy, slipshod.

finish *v.* **1.** *We finished dinner around 9 o'clock:* end, conclude, bring to a close, complete, wind up, bring to an end; terminate, discontinue; stop, cease; seal, clinch; draw to a close; get done, accomplish, carry out, carry through, achieve, fulfill, consummate, make good; close, put an end to; get out of the way, dispose of, *Informal* knock off; realize, discharge, do thoroughly, settle. **2.** *Finish these potato chips and*

I'll get some more: use up, dispatch; consume, devour. **3.** *What can we use to finish off these bugs?:* eradicate, exterminate, destroy, kill, get rid of, put out of the way; defeat, overcome completely. **4.** *Why not finish the table with a walnut stain?:* surface, veneer, face, glaze, gild; lacquer, varnish, coat. —*n.* **5.** *At the finish no one applauded:* conclusion, end, close, termination, completion; finale, finis, fall of the curtain, ending, curtain; epilogue, denouement; final event, windup, closing period, last, last stage; goal, objective. **6.** *Does all the furniture have that glossy finish?:* surface, exterior, coating, veneer, lacquer; polishing, finishing touches, last touch. **—Ant.** 1 begin, start, undertake, commence; originate, create. 5 beginning, commencement, genesis; inauguration, inception; birth, conception.

finished *adj.* **1.** *The finished job was a great satisfaction to him:* completed, concluded, ended; complete, final; consummated, perfect; entire, full, whole. **2.** *The portrait was executed with finished artistry:* faultless, flawless, consummate, accomplished, skilled, impeccable; elegant, refined, beautiful, shapely, well-set; classic, ideal; cultivated, urbane, exquisite, well-bred, trained, polished, well-mannered. **—Ant.** 1 unfinished, incomplete, imperfect; begun. 2 green, callow, raw; inexperienced, unskilled; unrefined, inelegant, inartistic; rough, rude, coarse, crude.

finite *adj.* *Distances between stars are immense, but finite:* measurable, limited, bounded, countable, circumscribed, terminable, subject to limitations, confined, restricted; not everlasting, temporal, short-lived. **—Ant.** infinite, unlimited, unbounded, boundless, measureless; endless, perpetual.

fire *n.* **1.** *Keep an extinguisher in case a fire breaks out in the house:* conflagration, blaze, flame, bonfire; flash, spark, flare; inferno, holocaust. **2.** *Napoleon roused his troops with a speech full of fire:* ardor, vigor; power, intensity, force, genius, inspiration, imaginativeness, vehemence, spirit, burning passion, fervor, fervency; enthusiasm, eagerness, vivacity, gusto, earnestness; dash, élan, punch, verve, vim; splendor, brilliance, effulgence, luster, radiance. **3.** *The soldiers were ordered to hold their fire:* discharge of firearms, firing; salvo, fusillade, bombardment, volley, cannonade, broadside, enfilade; sniping, sharpshooting. —*v.* **4.** *The guns began firing at daybreak:* shoot, discharge, project a missile, open fire, bombard, shell, fusillade, enfilade; fire off, make go off, hurl, project, eject. **5.** *It took several bundles of twigs to fire the logs:* ignite, kindle, light, set on fire, set fire to, set burning, inflame; burn, catch fire. **6.** *It was a speech to fire the heart of every true patriot:* arouse, stimulate, rouse, vivify, spark, inspire, animate, excite, inspirit; fill with ardor, inflame, incite, stir, stir up, quicken, instigate, foment, galvanize, trigger. **7.** *The pottery was glazed and then fired at intense heat:* bake, cook. **8.** *Informal She was fired for spending too much time on the phone:* dismiss, let go, oust, remove from service, cashier; *Slang* sack, boot, dump, bounce, can, give one his walking papers; depose.

firearm *n. The villagers are buying firearms to protect their homes:* gun, small arm, sidearm, *Informal* shooting iron; (*variously*) pistol, rifle, shotgun, revolver, machine gun, submachine gun, *Slang* rod, piece, Saturday-night special.

firm[1] *adj.* **1.** *The plastic was poured into the mold and left to set until it was firm:* stiff, hard, rigid; unbending, unyielding; solid, compressed, dense, compact; rocky, stony, adamantine; steely, flinty. **2.** *The price was firm and not subject to bargaining:* settled, fixed, definite, established, confirmed; unalterable, indissoluble. **3.** *Put another nail in the frame to make it firm:* steady, not shaking, stable, fast, secure; rooted, moored, anchored; immovable; close, taut, tight, rigid, inflexible. **4.** *Mother was firm in her resolve not to move west:* resolute, steadfast, determined, unwavering, resolved, staunch, persistent, unflinching, unshaken, unfaltering; earnest, serious, decided, intent, constant, definite, steady; strong-willed, strong-minded, dogged, dead set; tough, obstinate, bent, inflexible, inexorable, *Slang* hard-nosed; grim, tenacious, obdurate; fearless, invincible. **—Ant.** loose, flabby; soft, flaccid, limp, loppy; flimsy, sleazy; shaky, unsteady, unstable; wavering, irresolute, inconstant, unreliable.

firm[2] *n. Mildred has worked for our firm since high school:* company, concern, organization, business, establishment, house; commercial house, partnership, corporation, conglomerate.

firmament *n. It was a clear night, and we gazed in awe at the starry firmament:* sky, heavens, vault, welkin, the blue, air, ether, canopy, canopy of heaven; space, outer space, the void, interstellar space, intergalactic space.

firmly *adv. She firmly refused to go:* resolutely, unflinchingly, unwaveringly, adamantly, determinedly, doggedly, intently, fast, fixedly, immovably, inflexibly, motionlessly, perseveringly, persistently, rigidly, purposefully, securely, solidly, steadily, stiffly, strongly, stubbornly, obdurately, obstinately.

firmness *n.* **1.** *Length of cooking determined the custard's firmness:* compactness, durability, density, fixedness, resistance, hardness, impenetrability, impermeability, imperviousness, inflexibility, rigidity, solidity, substantiality, soundness, temper, tautness, stability, stiffness, tensile strength, toughness, tension. **2.** *Firmness was needed in dealing with their dog:* durability, immovability, solidity, steadiness, strength, constancy, determination, fixedness, inflexibility, obduracy, obstinacy, purposefulness, resoluteness, resolution, staunchness, resolve, steadfastness, strictness, consistency.

first *adj.* **1.** *This painting received first prize in the contest:* foremost, leading, chief among others, principal, main, prime, head, first-string, ranking, highest; superior, preeminent, supreme, paramount; vital, essential. **2.** *Norsemen may have been the first European settlers in the New World:* earliest, original, premier, eldest;

primitive, primal, primeval, primordial, aboriginal; beginning, maiden. **3.** *He teaches the first principles of lifesaving:* basic, fundamental, elementary, rudimentary, primary, introductory, beginning. —*n.* **4.** *We were friends from the first:* beginning, introduction, commencement, start, outset, inception, starting point. —*adv.* **5.** *She asked first if we were free Tuesday evening:* before anything else, to begin with, at the outset, initially; first and foremost. **6.** *They want me to apologize, but I'd shoot myself first:* by preference, by choice, before; rather, sooner, preferably. **—Ant.** 1 secondary, subordinate, lesser. 2 later, subsequent.

first-rate *adj. She wrote a first-rate report on the office management systems:* best, choice, excellent, very good, first-class, prime, finest, superior, ace, elite, outstanding, select, A-one, top-drawer, topflight, topnotch, incomparable, distinguished, exclusive, nonpareil; *Slang* tops, crack; *Brit. Slang* top-hole. **—Ant.** run-of-the-mill, mediocre, ordinary, so-so, indifferent.

fiscal *adj. The job as treasurer entails fiscal responsibility:* financial, monetary, pecuniary, budgetary, economic.

fish *v.* **1.** *Every morning we fished off the end of the pier:* attempt to catch fish, angle, cast; hook, net, troll, trawl, seine. **2.** *She opened her purse and began fishing for her lipstick:* search, hunt, grope, rummage, ferret, look about, cast about.

fishy *adj.* **1.** *Informal There's something fishy about his diplomatic background:* doubtful, dubious, improbable; suspicious, suspect, unreliable, questionable; peculiar, strange, odd, weird, queer; extravagant, exaggerated, farfetched; slippery, shady, dishonest, unscrupulous. **2.** *She fixed me with a fishy stare:* glassy-eyed, dull, vacant, expressionless, blank.

fit[1] *adj.* **1.** *Is this water fit to drink? The truck with four-wheel drive is fit for rough use on dirt roads:* suitable, good, adapted, appropriate; right, proper, meet, correct; seemly, fitting, becoming, befitting, decorous; pertinent, relevant, applicable, consonant; timely, seasonable; opportune, convenient; apposite, apropos. **2.** *Only fit applicants need apply:* qualified, competent, trained, able; capable, capacitated, efficient; prepared, primed, initiated; mature, ripe; ready, eligible. **3.** *These days he looks fitter than I've ever seen him:* healthy, hale, hardy, sound, well, in good physical condition, strong, robust, toned up, in trim. **4.** *She's not fit to associate with decent folk:* worthy, deserving, suitable, acceptable; good enough, sufficiently virtuous. —*v.* **5.** *The house fits nicely in that wooded environment. Does a noon lunch fit with your schedule?:* be suitable for, be adapted to; agree, harmonize, accord; conform, be adapted to; be the right size or shape for, correspond; become, befit; match, equal; coincide, concur. **6.** *After she fits the dress it should be ready in a week:* try on for size, adjust, make suitable, suit, adapt; shape, alter, fashion; graduate, calibrate; correct, rectify. **7.** *Money was needed to fit the expedition:* equip, outfit; prepare, ready, make qualified, qualify, make competent; enable, empower, capacitate, train. —**Ant.** 1 unfit, ill-suited, unsuitable, inappropriate; unprepared, ill-fitted, inadequate, improper, unseemly; inexpedient, ill-timed, untimely, amiss.

fit[2] *n.* **1.** *From early childhood she was subject to fits and loss of memory:* epileptic seizure, convulsion, spell; (*variously*) grand mal, petit mal. **2.** *She had a fit of coughing she couldn't control:* spell, sudden acute attack, spasm, paroxysm, seizure, outbreak. **3.** *In a fit of pique she told him to go home:* outburst, explosion, burst, access; passing mood, whim, caprice, crotchet, whimsical notion.

fitful *adj. The rain has been fitful all afternoon:* irregular, intermittent, periodic, sporadic, spasmodic, now-and-then, now-and-again; unsteady, changeable, erratic, fluctuating, uneven, random, variable, convulsive; weak, listless. —**Ant.** constant, steady, incessant; even, equable, regular, uniform; orderly, systematic, methodical; predictable, calculable; changeless, unchanging, immutable.

fitness *n.* **1.** *A marathon requires great physical fitness:* condition, physical condition, conditioning, tone, shape, fettle, health, healthfulness, trim, repair, order. **2.** *The interviewer questioned his fitness for the job:* appropriateness, suitability, applicability, aptness, cogency, propriety.

fitted *adj. She was fitted with braces:* outfitted, supplied, provided, accoutered, appointed, armed, equipped, furnished.

fitting *adj. The visiting head of state was given a fitting welcome:* suitable, proper, decorous, seemly, appropriate, apt, befitting, meet, fit, congruous. —**Ant.** unfitting, unsuitable, improper, unseemly, ill-suited.

fix *v.* **1.** *The workmen fixed the antenna to the roof of the house:* secure, fasten, attach, affix, moor, make fast, implant, rivet, anchor, place permanently, connect. **2.** *The dealer fixed the price at $50:* set, settle, determine definitely, decide, establish, stabilize, prescribe. **3.** *Is something added to fix the cement?:* harden, solidify, make rigid, make firm, become stable, become set; congeal, consolidate. **4.** *Investigators fixed the blame for the fire on the night watchman:* place, put, impose, affix. **5.** *You'd better call someone to fix that leak:* repair, mend, patch up, correct, set right, put to rights, adjust, renovate, put in good condition, rebuild; adjust, regulate. **6.** *Informal What time are you going to fix dinner?:* prepare, make, put together, assemble. **7.** *Informal If he tries that again I'll really fix him:* get even with, get revenge on, get back at; *Slang* fix one's wagon, settle one's hash, cook one's goose; retaliate, take action against. —*n.* **8.** *After accepting two invitations for the same evening he was really in a fix:* predicament, embarrassing situation, plight, difficulty, dilemma, awkward spot, quandary, impasse, ticklish situation; *Slang* spot, jam, pickle, bind, scrape, hot water; muddle, mess, entanglement, involvement.

fixation *n. She has some fixation about birds*

hating her: obsession, preoccupation, fixed idea; delusion, complex, monomania; quirk, crotchet, fetish.

fixed *adj.* **1.** *France's Maginot Line was a series of fixed fortifications:* stationary, immovable, fast, firmly implanted; firm, stable, fastened, set, rooted, motionless, still, rigid. **2.** *Store owners are protesting fixed prices. I was embarrassed by her fixed stare:* not varying, not fluctuating, constant, steady; intent, steadily directed, persistent, determined, resolute; unbending, unpliant, inflexible, firm, unwavering. —**Ant.** moving, mobile, wavering, unstable, unsteady, inconstant; bending, pliant; varying.

fixture *n.* **1.** *The light fixture was installed on the living room ceiling:* apparatus, appliance, equipment; attachment, appendage, appurtenance, appointment, equipage, paraphernalia. **2.** *We lunch there so often we're considered fixtures:* regular; devotee, habitué; *Informal* familiar sight, old reliable, *Slang* addict.

fizzle *v.* **1.** *The wet match fizzled but didn't light:* sputter, hiss; bubble, gurgle, fizz. **2.** *Informal The plan fizzled for lack of interest:* come to nothing, fail, abort, misfire, fall through, miscarry, come to grief, fall short, miss the mark; *Slang* flop, fizzle out; break down, collapse, founder. —*n.* **3.** *The hot coals made a fizzle as they hit the water:* hiss, sputter. **4.** *Informal The play was a fizzle according to the critics:* failure, washout, disaster, fiasco; *Informal* botch, muddle, mess, flop; *Slang* turkey, bomb, dud, dog.

flabbergast *v. The news that she would run for Congress flabbergasted us all:* amaze, confound, astound, astonish, shock, stun, stupefy, *Slang* knock for a loop, stagger, dumbfound, overcome, puzzle, bewilder, render speechless, bowl over, strike dumb.

flabby *adj.* **1.** *His muscles had become flabby from lack of exercise:* limp, flaccid, soft, yielding, inelastic; feeble, weak, hanging loosely, slack, floppy, drooping limply; doughy, baggy, spongy. **2.** *The author's ideas were flabby and entirely conventional:* feeble, enervated; adulterated, emasculated, spiritless, effete, impotent, listless, lame, flimsy. —**Ant.** 1 firm, hard, solid; tight, taut, tense; tough, sturdy, strong. 2 plucky, gritty, tenacious.

flaccid *adj. After the long illness his muscles were flaccid:* slack, soft, weak, weakened, debilitated, drooping, emasculated, enervated, sapped, enfeebled, flabby, lax, flimsy, limp, ineffective.

flag *n.* **1.** *The country's flag was displayed in every window:* banner, emblem, standard, ensign, streamer, pennant, colors; (*in the U.S.*) stars and stripes, Old Glory, stars and bars; (*in Great Britain*) Union Jack. —*v.* **2.** *The highway patrol flagged us away from the accident:* signal, warn, wave. **3.** *My energy flagged after climbing all those steps:* decline, grow weak, wilt, give way, languish; grow spiritless, fall off in vigor, abate, slump, succumb, subside, sag, pall; fade, grow weary, tire, totter, dodder; faint, sink, ebb, wane, fail. —**Ant.** 3 freshen, recover, brace up.

flagrant *adj. That was a flagrant abuse of his*

authority: shockingly bad, shameless, brazen, blatant, flaunting, audacious, immodest; glaring, gross, sheer, obvious, crying, arrant, barefaced; notorious, scandalous, conspicuous, outrageous, heinous, monstrous.

flair *n. Thelma has a great flair for designing hats:* bent, knack, talent, aptitude, gift, genius; keen perception, discernment, feel, feeling, touch, ingenuity, faculty, capacity; style, taste; verve, dash, panache.

flake *n.* **1.** *Snow was falling in large flakes:* flat thin piece, scale, sheet, bit, fleck, shaving, patch. —*v.* **2.** *This new coat of paint has already started to flake:* peel off, peel, layer, strip, come off in flakes, scale off, chip off, chip, crumble.

flamboyant *adj.* **1.** *The apartment was decorated in flamboyant reds and purples:* ornate, gaudy, garish, florid; baroque, rococo; showy, flashy, ostentatious, *Slang* jazzy. **2.** *She was one of the most flamboyant actresses in the theater:* dashing, colorful, exciting, sensational, theatrical, wild, *Slang* jazzy.

flame *n.* **1.** *The flame of the match was visible for miles:* flare, blaze, fire, burning vapor, light, conflagration; spark, glare, gleam, glow, flash. **2.** *The flame of his ambition seemed to grow with time:* ardor, passion, fervor, intensity, fervency, glow, excitement, burning zeal; enthusiasm, warmth, affection. **3.** *Informal His old flame turned up at the high school reunion:* sweetheart, girlfriend; beau, lover, swain, boyfriend. —*v.* **4.** *The gasoline flamed up instantly when touched by the match:* burst into flames, fire, flare, kindle, light, ignite, blaze, burn with a flame; glare, shine brilliantly, flash; flush, redden, blush.

flaming *adj.* **1.** *The flaming wreckage burned for hours:* blazing, burning, fiery, afire, ablaze, alight; igneous, inflammable, smoldering, glowing; bright, brilliant, shining. **2.** *The bad news put the boss in a flaming rage:* violent, stormy, ardent, intense, vehement, fervid, fervent, passionate; conspicuous, flagrant, glaring, egregious.

flammable *adj. Flammable material should not be stored next to the chimney:* inflammable, combustible, igneous, combustive, incendiary. —**Ant.** nonflammable, fireproof.

flank *adj.* **1.** *He slapped the horse on the flank to make it move:* side, haunch, loin, hip. **2.** *The attack was aimed at the army's left flank:* side, wing, edge, border. —*v.* **3.** *Long rows of soldiers flanked the avenue:* line, border, skirt; edge, fringe; lie along, wing; screen, shield, cover.

flap *v.* **1.** *That shutter flaps every time there's a wind:* wave about, swing loosely, flop, flutter; shake, beat, vibrate, oscillate, agitate, bat, move to and fro, bang. —*n.* **2.** *We heard the flap of the screen door on the back porch:* flop, flapping, bang, banging, flutter. **3.** *A flap covered the entrance to the tent:* hanging piece, lap, lappet, fly, tab; skirt, apron.

flare *v.* **1.** *The addition of another log made the fire flare:* flame, blaze, burn, gleam, coruscate; glare, glow, incandesce, ignite, flash. **2.** *Tem-*

pers flared as the accusations became more heated: erupt, explode, break out, burst forth, blow up, boil over. **3.** *His nostrils flared at the aroma of roasting beef:* widen, broaden, spread, expand, distend, stretch, dilate.

flash *n.* **1.** *A flash of lightning preceded the crash of thunder:* burst, streak, blaze, glare, gleam, flare, flame; radiance, coruscation, incandescence, fulmination. **2.** *The speech was lightened by some flashes of humor:* outburst, instance, occurrence, spark, glimmer, touch. **3.** *Informal The waitress was back in a flash with the menus:* instant, moment, jiffy, minute, second, split second, trice, twinkling of an eye, blink, shake, wink. —*v.* **4.** *The light on top of the police car was flashing:* blink, go on and off, flicker, sparkle, glitter; shine, blaze, glare, flame, glow, gleam; scintillate, coruscate; glisten, glimmer.

flashy *adj. Her closets are full of flashy clothes:* dazzling, flamboyant, showy; smart, sporty; pretentious, gaudy, garish, loud, tawdry, ostentatious, *Slang* jazzy; bedizened, tricked out, tinsel, raffish, vulgar, in bad taste. —**Ant.** plain, modest, simple, natural, unaffected.

flask *n. She bought a flask of perfume:* decanter, vial, beaker, bottle, carafe, chalice, ewer, crock, flagon, glass, jar, goblet, jug.

flat *adj.* **1.** *The lower meadow is absolutely flat:* level, horizontal, smooth; plane, planar, regular, equal, unbroken, flush. **2.** *They took their naps, lying flat on the floor:* recumbent, prostrate, prone, lying at full length, flush, low, reclining, supine; leveled, laid low. **3.** *The senator issued a flat denial of all charges:* unqualified, unequivocal, thorough, out-and-out, positive, definite, downright, absolute, complete, total, peremptory; clear, direct, plain, unmistakable. **4.** *The ginger ale went flat after being left open:* lacking effervescence; stale, tasteless, insipid, flavorless; dull, vapid, dead, unpalatable. —*n.* **5.** Often **flats.** *The hunters waded into the flats, looking vainly for ducks:* level land, flat ground, lowlands; open country, prairie, plain; shallow, shoal, marsh. **6.** *The thruway is the worst possible place to have a flat:* blowout, deflated tire, blown-out tire, puncture. —*adv.* **7.** *Lie down flat and breathe deeply:* horizontally, levelly, prostrate. **8.** *Dinner will be ready in two minutes flat:* exactly, precisely. —**Ant.** 1 uneven, rough, rugged, broken, irregular, scabrous, hilly, rolling; slanting, sloping; vertical, upright, perpendicular. 4 bubbly, effervescent, sparkling, fizzy; flavorful, flavorsome, tasty, savory; palatable.

flatten *v.* **1.** *Flatten the dough with the palms of your hands:* make flat, smooth, level; plane, even; press down, compress; deflate. **2.** *The champion flattened his opponent in the first round:* knock down, floor, fell, ground, prostrate, *Slang* deck; crush, defeat, overwhelm, overcome.

flatter *v.* **1.** *At the testimonial dinner everyone flattered him shamelessly:* overpraise, compliment, praise lavishly, gratify by praise; eulogize, adulate, laud, extol, panegyrize, honor; court, cajole, blandish, beguile, wheedle; curry favor with, cotton up to, truckle to, toady; *Informal* sweet-talk, *Slang* butter up, soft-soap, bootlick, brown-nose. **2.** *The movies flatter him--he's not really that handsome:* represent too favorably, become, show off well. **3.** *I flattered myself that they really wanted to know what I thought:* delude, deceive, mislead, fool.

flatterer *n. The boss is the type who needs a staff of flatterers:* yes man, fawner, sycophant, wheedler, truckler, toady, eulogist; *Slang* apple-polisher, bootlicker, lickspittle.

flattery *n. Thirty years of flattery got him nowhere when she made out her will:* excessive compliment, false praise, *Slang* snow job; sycophancy, toadyism, toadying, obsequiousness, fawning, wheedling, servility; cajolery, blandishment, soft soap, truckling, jollying, blarney; adulation, eulogy, panegyric, encomium.

flatulence *n. Beans and cabbage contribute to flatulence:* gas, wind, *Informal* fart.

flatulent *adj. The flatulent speech lasted two hours:* gassy, swollen, distended; inflated, windy, wordy, bombastic, long-winded, oratorical, pompous, overblown, pretentious, tedious, prolix, turgid.

flaunt *v.* **1.** *We know she has money, so she doesn't have to flaunt it:* show off, parade, exhibit, brandish, vaunt, air, make a show of, advertise, broadcast, strut; boast, brag. **2.** *Everyone along the parade route seemed to be flaunting a flag:* flourish, brandish, wave, sport, blazon, dangle. **—Ant.** conceal, hide, screen; cloak, mask, disguise, dissemble.

flavor *n.* **1.** *The shop sells ice cream in eight different flavors:* characteristic taste, savor; tang, piquancy; relish, gusto; seasoning, flavoring; lacing. **2.** *The novelist has captured the flavor of life in the cities today:* subtle quality, distinctive character, attribute, essence, soul, spirit; aspect, style, tenor, aura, ambience, tone. **—v. 3.** *Mother flavors her custards with lemon extract:* give flavor to, season, spice, lace; imbue, infuse, instill. **—Ant.** 1 tastelessness, flatness; odorlessness, scentlessness; insipidity, vapidity, mawkishness.

flavoring *n. The dish required little added flavoring:* seasoning, condiment, relish, spice, zest; essence, extract.

flaw *n.* **1.** *Her beauty is without flaw. Lack of civilian clothes was the one flaw in our escape plan:* defect, blemish, fault, imperfection, marring feature, weakness, weak spot, fallacy, shortcoming, frailty; error, mistake; deformity, injury, defacement, disfigurement; spot, speck; blot, smudge, stain, blotch; failing, foible, vice. **—v. 2.** *The artist's garish use of color flawed the painting:* mar, impair, harm; weaken, compromise, detract from, make defective, blemish, deface, injure, disfigure.

flawless *adj. We heard a flawless rendition of Beethoven's Ninth Symphony:* faultless, errorless, impeccable, perfect; sound, without blemish, immaculate. **—Ant.** defective, flawed, marred, impaired.

flay *v.* **1.** *Eskimos flay the caribou they kill and use the hides for garments:* skin, scalp, peel, decorticate, pare, bark; strip, fleece, plunder. **2.** *The headmaster flayed the boys for their irresponsible behavior:* chastise severely, castigate, excoriate, censure harshly; assail, scold, rebuke, upbraid, punish.

fleck *n.* **1.** *The calico cat has flecks of orange and black:* spot, patch of color, mark, speck, flake, freckle, dot, speckle; mole, blemish; small bit, drop, jot, tittle, particle. **—v. 2.** *The damask wallpaper was flecked with gold:* speckle, mark with flecks, spot, flake, spatter, dapple, bespeckle; bespot, dot, besprinkle; streak, stipple, mottle.

fledgling *n. As a pilot, he's still a fledgling:* inexperienced person, novice, beginner, tyro, freshman, apprentice; *Informal* greenhorn, tenderfoot.

flee *v.* **1.** *He fled the kidnappers and phoned the police:* escape from, run away from, get away from, hasten away from, make one's escape from; make a getaway, take to one's heels, take flight, abscond, skip, fly the coop, cut and run, *Slang* split; decamp, desert, make off, hasten off, speed off, fly away; vanish, disappear. **2.** *Why does she always flee any kind of responsibility?:* evade, avoid, shun, wriggle out of; elude, dodge.

fleecy *adj. The new detergent had made the blankets fleecy:* fluffy, downy, soft, woolly; hairy, hirsute, shaggy.

fleet *n.* **1.** *Thousands waited on the dock for the fleet to come in:* naval force, navy, naval division, group of warships, *Archaic* armada; flotilla, squadron. **2.** *He made his money with a fleet of moving vans:* large group, number, array, band, squadron. **—adj. 3.** *Antelopes are among the fleetest animals:* swift, rapid, speedy, fast, swift-footed, fast of foot, light-footed, nimble-footed, nimble; hurried, quick, expeditious, hasty, cursory; transient, brief, evanescent; sudden, instantaneous, momentary; short, transitory. **—Ant.** 3 deliberate, slow, laggard, tardy.

fleeting *adj. We caught only a fleeting glimpse of the presidential motorcade:* swiftly passing, brief, flitting, passing, momentary, evanescent, short-lived, quick; fugitive, transitory, transient, fugacious, ephemeral, temporary, temporal; perishable, impermanent; precarious, unenduring. **—Ant.** lasting, permanent, enduring, imperishable, durable, long-lived.

flesh *n.* **1.** *The wound was merely a superficial penetration of the flesh:* muscular tissue, soft tissue of a body, muscle and fat, brawn; meat, animal food; fat, fatness. **2.** *The spirit is willing, but the flesh is weak:* body, physical nature, physique, flesh and blood, materiality; strength, vigor, power, muscular energy, animal force; carnality, sensuality, bodily desire. **3.** *The minister said that such was the way of all flesh:* mankind, humanity, human race, man, people, living creatures. **4.** *The flesh of the peach was sweet and juicy:* pulp, substance, meat, edible part. **—v. 5.** *Three good meals a day should flesh him out in no time:* fatten, fill out, make plump, become plump. **6.** *The playwright often fails to flesh out his characters:* fill out, characterize fully, realize, individualize, particularize, give depth to, embody.

fleshly adj. He rejected all fleshly pleasures: bodily, sensual, corporal, physical, corporeal, earthly, human, material, mundane, secular, worldly, animal, animalistic, carnal, erotic, gross, profane.

fleshy adj. The long vacation had made her fleshy: plump, corpulent, obese, fat, beefy, overweight, stout, chubby, stocky, portly, thickset, paunchy, potbellied, well-padded, tubby, roly-poly. **—Ant.** thin, skinny, underweight, scrawny, lean.

flex v. First, they flexed their arms and legs: stretch, tighten, angle, bend, ply, contract, spring, crook, curve.

flexibility also **flexibleness** n. **1.** She showed great flexibility in adapting to change: adaptability, pliancy, adjustability, tractability, compliance. **2.** The gymnast had remarkable flexibility: limberness, elasticity, give, extensibility, litheness, springiness, plasticity.

flexible adj. **1.** The springs were made of flexible steel: easily bent, elastic, resilient, springy, extensible, bendable, ductile, plastic, malleable, tractable, pliable, pliant; supple, limber, lithe, soft. **2.** We need a foreign policy that is more flexible: adaptable, changeable, yielding, responsive, manageable, malleable, compliant, complaisant; docile, submissive, easily managed; amiable, genial; mild, gentle. **—Ant.** 1 inflexible, stiff, rigid, inelastic. 2 intractable, unyielding, inexorable; absolute, dogmatic.

flicker v. **1.** The candle flickered in the breeze: flutter; glow, glisten, glitter, glimmer, shimmer; flare, blaze, flash; sparkle, coruscate, wave to and fro, quiver, flit, vibrate; waver, quaver, wriggle, tremble; undulate, oscillate; shake, waggle; throb, pulsate; sway; fluctuate, vacillate. **—n. 2.** There was a brief flicker and the flashlight went dead: unsteady light, glitter, flare, gleam, spark, flash. **3.** While there is a flicker of hope we will continue the search: small amount, vestige, modicum, scintilla, flame, spark, glimmer, glint, trace.

flight n. **1.** Some birds are incapable of flight. Our cross-country flight took five hours: air travel, flying, winging, soaring; aeronautics, plane trip; space travel. **2.** A flight of ducks passed overhead: flock, flying group, squadron, wing. **3.** There is no way to stop the flight of time: rush, swift movement, quick passage. **4.** The defeated army took flight: hasty departure, running away, rout, fleeing, retreat, escape, withdrawal; exodus, hegira.

flightiness n. The actress's flightiness made her hard to direct: capriciousness, irresponsibility, dizziness, changeability, fickleness, flippancy, giddiness, frivolity, inconstancy, variability, instability, Informal flakiness, ditsiness.

flighty adj. Her parents decided she was too flighty to get much out of college: unstable, frivolous, irresponsible, fickle, impractical, whimsical, capricious, changeable, mercurial, inconstant, volatile, quixotic; scatterbrained,

harebrained, dizzy, reckless, thoughtless, light-headed, giddy; irresolute, indecisive.

flimsy adj. **1.** These shirts are so flimsy I'm afraid to have them laundered: unsubstantial, thin, slight, frail, fragile, delicate; diaphanous, sheer, filmy, gossamer, gauzy, cobwebby; shoddy, ill-made, jerry-built; ramshackle, shabby, sleazy, dilapidated, cheap, trashy. **2.** Does she really expect us to believe a flimsy alibi like that?: feeble, weak, inadequate; poor, worthless, foolish, trivial, trifling, petty, frivolous; shallow, superficial. **—Ant.** 1 stout, sturdy, strong; heavy, weighty. 2 sound, cogent; substantial, solid.

flinch v. **1.** She flinched as she touched the hot stove: wince, draw back, jerk back, shrink, recoil, start, cringe, blench, shy, shudder, falter, shiver, quiver, quake, quaver, cower, quail; grimace, contort; retreat, fly, give ground. **—n. 2.** He gave a flinch of pain as the doctor removed the bandage: start, blench, wince, jerk, shiver, grimace.

fling v. **1.** She flung her coat on the chair and stormed into the room: throw with force, hurl, heave, pitch, toss, cast, dash, let fly, precipitate, propel, sling; eject, emit, expel. **—n. 2.** Next weekend let's have a fling in Tijuana: spree, bit of fun; Slang ball, bash, lark. **3.** She always wanted to have a fling at acting: attempt, trial, go, try.

flip v. **1.** Let's flip a quarter to see who goes first: toss, flick, throw, spin. **2.** He flipped through the pages of the phone book looking for the number: turn, thumb, turn over. **—n. 3.** He removed the crumb with a flip of the thumb and forefinger: tap, flick, fillip; toss, throw, spin.

flippancy n. The situation did not call for flippancy: irreverence, waggishness, archness, cheek, cheekiness, freshness, cockiness, impertinence, sauciness, impudence, mischievousness.

flippant adj. The young man shocked everyone by making flippant remarks while the will was being read: impudent, brash, impertinent, disrespectful, saucy, insolent, pert, rude; Informal cheeky, flip, lippy; trifling, frivolous; presumptuous, bumptious. **—Ant.** respectful, considerate.

flirt v. **1.** She flirts with every man in the office: toy, play at love, dally, trifle in love, tease, Slang make eyes at. **2.** Uncle Ted flirted with the idea of opening a bookstore: toy, play, trifle; entertain an idea. **—n. 3.** He stopped going with her when she turned out to be a flirt: flirter, tease, heartbreaker; (fem.) coquette, vamp.

flirtatious adj. She was especially flirtatious with the tennis coach: teasing, flirty, coquettish, sportive, amorous, arch, coy, enticing.

flit v. The honeybees were flitting from flower to flower: dart, skim, move lightly and swiftly, flicker, flitter, flutter; fly rapidly, wing, hasten, speed, scurry, scud.

float v. **1.** When you're tired of swimming just float for a while: rest on water; be poised in air; drift, hover, waft, slide, move gently, bob, be buoyant, be buoyed up; levitate. **2.** Is there enough water in the tub to float your boat?: make buoyant, buoy up, bear up, hold up, keep afloat, give support to; launch. —**Ant.** 1, 2 sink, settle, go to the bottom, submerge.

flock n. **1.** A flock of sheep blocked the road: herd, pack, bunch, group, clique, troop, drove, multitude; band, company, bevy, coterie, collection, aggregation; brood (of young birds), school (of fish), swarm (of insects), pride (of lions), pod (of seals or whales), covey (of game birds), gaggle (of geese). **2.** A flock of customers waited for the store to open: crowd, mob, gang, throng, crush, large number; gathering, assemblage; congregation. —v. **3.** Birds of a feather flock together: go, run, gather, assemble, muster, converge, swarm, cluster, congregate, herd; crowd, surge, mass, throng, huddle, stream, rush.

flog v. The quartermaster flogged a sailor caught napping on watch: whip, lash, thrash, beat, horsewhip, scourge, flail, flagellate, drub; strike, smite, lambaste, cuff; club, maul, cudgel; cane, birch, paddle, switch; strap, hide.

flood n. **1.** During the flood many people were stranded in their homes: inundation, great overflowing of water, overflow; deluge, cloudburst, downpour. **2.** A flood of tears didn't make her story any more convincing: torrent, stream, flow, outpouring, tide, cascade, downpour, deluge, current, gush. —v. **3.** The rains flooded the farmlands and destroyed all the crops: inundate, deluge, submerge, cover with a flood, wash over, fill to overflowing, flow over. **4.** The market has been flooded with electronic gadgets: oversupply, overwhelm, glut, saturate, inundate, deluge; shower, drench. —**Ant.** 1 drought, scarcity, lack, shortage, subsidence, stoppage.

floor n. **1.** The glass fell off the table and shattered on the floor: bottom surface, bottom, flooring, base, ground; pavement, parquet. **2.** Her apartment is on the 14th floor: story, stage, level; tier, deck. **3.** The government has put a floor under certain farm prices: base rate, base, minimum, bottom. —v. **4.** The challenger was floored with a solid right hook: knock down, ground, fell, level, prostrate, Slang deck.

flop v. **1.** The puppy just flopped around on the slippery floor: move clumsily or heavily; fall heavily, tumble, topple, drop, plop, flap awkwardly. **2.** Informal After only three performances, the play flopped: fail, close, close down, go under, shutter, fold, wash out, Slang bomb, lay an egg. —n. **3.** Informal The dinner party was a flop because the guest of honor didn't show up: failure, fiasco, disaster, disappointment, labor in vain, washout; Slang fizzle, bust, bomb, turkey. —**Ant.** 2 succeed, triumph, make a hit; flourish, prosper. 3 success, triumph, hit.

floral adj. Her bedroom wallpaper had a floral pattern: of flowers, flowery, blossomy, bloomy; botanical, herbaceous; verdant.

florid adj. **1.** It may be his high blood pressure that gives him such a florid complexion: ruddy, rosy, reddish, high-colored, rubicund; ruddy-faced, red-faced, flushed, sanguine, red-complexioned; inflamed, blowsy, hectic. **2.** We

listened to a long florid speech about the greatness of our founder: flowery, showy, ornamented, elaborate, ornate, ostentatious, gaudy, highly embellished, flamboyant, high-flown, grandiloquent; rococo, baroque. —**Ant.** 1 pallid, anemic, bloodless. 2 unadorned, bare, prosaic, matter-of-fact.

flotsam n. We spotted a great deal of flotsam that could have been from the missing ship: floating wreckage, floating goods, debris; castoffs, odds and ends, refuse, garbage, junk.

flounce[1] v. **1.** She was so furious she turned and flounced off the stage: sashay, strut, hurl oneself, fling oneself, storm, stamp, stomp; bounce, spring, bound; trip, skip, prance, caper, gambol. —n. **2.** With an angry flounce he was gone from the house: flouncing movement, bound, spring, leap.

flounce[2] n. **1.** Her dress had so many flounces she kept getting them caught on things: ruffle, frill, ornament, furbelow; valance, fringe, trimming; hem, edging, skirting. —v. **2.** The gown was flounced with tiers of pink lace: trim, ruffle, frill, ornament, fringe, hem, edge.

flounder v. **1.** The car floundered in the icy slush: struggle, move unsteadily, proceed clumsily, stumble, stagger; toss about, plunge clumsily; wallow, welter; lurch, totter, flop, shamble, tumble; limp, hobble. **2.** When she forgot her speech she floundered hopelessly: falter, waver, hesitate, be uncertain, halt; lose oneself, miss one's way, blunder, muddle, wander aimlessly.

flourish v. **1.** His dry-cleaning business really flourished this year: prosper, thrive, grow, succeed, turn out well, fare well, be successful; get ahead, get on, rise in the world, go up in the world, Informal make one's pile; have a run of luck, feather one's nest; bloom, blossom, flower, burgeon. **2.** Flourishing their swords and muskets, the troops attacked: brandish, wave about in the air, swing, flaunt, wield, shake; twirl, sweep, swish. —n. **3.** The armies met with a flourish of swords and bayonets: waving, shaking, brandishing, agitation, wielding, twist, swinging, thrashing; ostentatious display, show, parade, ostentation; swagger, strut, swashbuckling; pomp, glitter, splash, dash. **4.** John Hancock signed the Declaration of Independence with a flourish: embellishment, decorative figure, curl, curlicue, decoration; musical ornament, turn, grace note, appoggiatura, cadenza. **5.** The senator always speaks with a lot of flourish: bravado, bluff, braggadocio, boasting, vaunting; rant, fustian, hot air, grandiloquence, magniloquence. **6.** The coronation got under way with a great flourish of horns and trumpets: trumpet call, fanfare, fanfaronade. —**Ant.** 1 decline, fail, fade.

flourishing adj She inherited a flourishing business: blooming, burgeoning, growing, lush, profuse, successful, prospering, prosperous, thriving, vigorous, doing well, going strong.

flout v. She flouted convention by wearing black at her wedding: scorn, show contempt for, scoff at, spurn, laugh at, jeer at, gibe at, sneer at, defy, treat with disdain, mock, poke fun at; twit, taunt, chaff, rag, insult. —**Ant.** revere; regard, respect, esteem.

flow v. **1.** *The Missouri River flows eastward into the Mississippi:* course, roll along, move in a stream, run, pour, stream, cascade; rush, gush, well out, issue, effuse; discharge, debouch, drain; surge, deluge, swirl; filter, seep; move gracefully, glide, sweep, pass, drift, float. **2.** *It was a party flowing with the best champagne:* abound, be full of, overflow, run, be copious. —*n.* **3.** *The flow of melted snow cascaded down the mountainside and into the river:* stream, course, torrent, flood; current, tide; rapids, mill-race. **4.** *A steady flow of good ideas has come from the publicity department:* outpouring, stream, cascade, effusion, outflow, flux, tide, discharge; efflux, effluence, emanation, debouchment; spurt, spout, gush, jet; train, succession, sequence, progression; abundance, plenty, plethora.

flower n. **1.** *He sent her flowers to mark their anniversary:* blossom, bloom, posy; floret, floweret, bud; nosegay, bouquet, floral tribute. **2.** *The army boasted that it had the flower of the nation's youth:* best, pick, choicest part, finest part, cream; elite, aristocracy. —*v.* **3.** *Your peonies will flower in late spring. Mozart's genius flowered at a very early age:* bloom, produce blossoms, produce flowers, blossom, open, be in flower, blow; burgeon; bud; develop fully, mature, ripen, flourish, prosper. —**Ant.** 2 dregs, residue.

flowery adj. **1.** *The rosebush was never this flowery before:* covered with blossoms, flowering, burgeoning, blooming, blossoming; florescent, efflorescent; decorated with flowers, floral. **2.** *His language was embarrassingly flowery:* ornate, ornamental, embellished, fancy, euphuistic, florid; rhetorical, figurative, grandiloquent, magniloquent.

flowing adj. *The flowing action made it a good movie:* unbroken, fluid, rolling, running, abounding, brimming, cursive, emitting, flooded, gushing, fluent, issuing, running, pouring out, rushing, spouting, streaming, rippling, sweeping.

fluctuate v. **1.** *With prices fluctuating so much, it's hard to plan a budget:* rise and fall, change often, vary irregularly, shift, bob up and down, wobble, veer; come and go, ebb and flow. **2.** *All year she has fluctuated between optimism and despair:* waver, vacillate, sway, oscillate, undulate, swing, be irresolute, be unsettled, hesitate, be undetermined, falter, shift, alternate, vary, be inconstant; dawdle, dillydally. —**Ant.** hold fast, persist, stand fast, stand firm, remain steady.

fluent adj. *Edna is fluent in both Spanish and German:* able to speak readily, ready in speech; glib, smooth-spoken, vocal, voluble, eloquent, articulate, smooth-tongued, silver-tongued; effortless, facile; effusive, garrulous, talkative; self-assured, well-versed. —**Ant.** hesitant, stammering, halting, tongue-tied.

fluffy adj. *Her divan is covered with fluffy pink pillows:* soft and light as fluff, feathery, downy; fuzzy, fleecy, woolly, nappy; light and airy.

fluid n. **1.** *A few drops of cleaning fluid should take out that spot:* liquid, solution. —*adj.* **2.** *The doctor prescribed a fluid diet for two weeks:* liquid, liquefied, of fluids, watery. **3.** *Keep your plans fluid until we decide what we're going to do:* flexible, adaptable, adjustable; changeable,indefinite; unstable, unfixed, unsettled, shifting, floating, liquid. —**Ant.** 1 solid. 2 solid, hard, firm. 3 fixed, settled, definite.

fluke n. *By some fluke the judges passed over the obvious choices and chose her:* accident, unlikely event, quirk of fate, chance, mischance, hap, vicissitude, freak; stroke of luck, piece of luck, windfall, miracle.

flurry n. **1.** *A flurry sent the paper plates flying all over the yard:* sudden wind, gust, windy blast, breeze, puff, squall; shower, light snowfall. **2.** *There was quite a flurry when the President visited the campus:* bustle, sudden excitement, commotion, fuss, ado, fluster, flutter, stir, pother; nervous hurry, agitation, turbulence, tumult, disturbance, perturbation, discomposure, restlessness, fidgets, confusion, trepidation; fever, heat, flush; haste, hurry-scurry. —*v.* **3.** *Don't be flurried by her checking on your work:* make nervous, put into a flurry, fluster, agitate, disquiet, disturb, perturb; rattle, confuse, discompose, disconcert, flutter, confound; panic, alarm.

flush[1] n. **1.** *Her complexion has a flush I never saw before:* blush, rosiness, rosy glow; bloom, tinge of color, high color, tint; redness, ruddiness. **2.** *Give the floor a flush, then scrub it down:* cleansing flow, watery gush, wash, rinse, swab, spray, douche, deluge. **3.** *In a flush of anger he hurled the chair across the room:* rush of emotion, impulse, access; tremor, flutter, quiver; thrill, shock; jubilation, exultation. **4.** *She was a beautiful girl in the flush of youth:* bloom, glow, glowing, strength, freshness. —*v.* **5.** *She flushed with pleasure when we complimented her:* blush, redden, color, grow crimson, glow. **6.** *Once a year they have to flush the city's sewers:* cleanse by flooding, wash out, flood, douche; rinse, scour, scrub, sponge, swab; drench, dampen, moisten. **7.** *The returning army was flushed with victory:* animate, elate, make proud, puff up; thrill, excite.

flush[2] adj. **1.** *I want the tabletop flush with the back of the sofa:* even, level, on the same plane. —*adv.* **2.** *Put the bookcase flush against the wall:* squarely, in contact with, so as to touch.

fluster v. **1.** *I was flustered when company arrived unexpectedly:* disconcert, ruffle, make nervous, disturb, perturb, upset, agitate, shake, startle, discompose, discomfit, befuddle, muddle, discombobulate, confuse; perplex, daze, bewilder, throw off balance. —*n.* **2.** *I've never seen so much fluster as when the boss came back two days early:* nervous excitement, confusion, flutter, agitation, turmoil, commotion, hubbub, flurry, dither, discomposure, discomfiture, bewilderment.

flutter v. **1.** *The flag fluttered from the top of the staff:* wave, toss about, flap, flitter, flit; throb, tremble, shake, pulsate; bob, wobble, quiver;

palpitate. **2.** *The butterfly fluttered from leaf to leaf:* flit, flitter; wing, soar. —*n.* **3.** *There was a great flutter of wings as the flock of gulls rose in the air:* agitation, vibration, flapping, beating; quiver, tremble, tremor. **4.** *Meeting celebrities always puts her in a flutter:* twitter, fluster; confusion, flurry, perturbation; hurry, hurry-scurry, commotion; thrill, sensation, tingling; ripple, stir.

flux *n.* **1.** *The boat battled the mighty flux of the river:* flow, current, course, flood, stream, tide; motion. **2.** *Scientific knowledge is always in a state of flux:* continuous change, fluctuation, alteration, modification; motion, unrest; shifting, transition, mutation, transformation.

fly *v.* **1.** *The new airplane flies at twice the speed of sound:* travel through the air; pilot a plane; wing, take wing, take the air, take off, soar, glide, sail, coast, swoop. **2.** *The king's banner was flying above his tent:* wave, flutter, float, undulate, flap, vibrate, hover, display in the air, hoist in the air. **3.** *The days really flew during our vacation:* move quickly, pass rapidly, go suddenly. **4.** *He was warned to fly from the emperor's wrath:* flee, run away, hasten away, make one's escape, make one's getaway, take flight, take to one's heels, hasten, hustle, hurry, *Informal* skip, *Slang* split.

fly-by-night *adj.* *He offered us a fly-by-night scheme for investing in real estate:* undependable, untrustworthy, untrusty, unreliable, irresponsible, unstable, disreputable; shady, shifty, crooked, dishonest. —**Ant.** honest, reliable, dependable, trustworthy, honorable, responsible.

flying *adj.* *The flying acrobats soared over the center ring:* aerial, aeronautical, airborne, winged, avian, in air, soaring, swooping, floating, gliding, hovering.

foam *n.* *The glass of beer was mostly foam:* mass of tiny bubbles, froth, head, fizz, sparkle, effervescence, bubbling; scum, spume; suds, lather.

foamy *adj.* *I'd like a cold, foamy glass of soda:* frothy, bubbling, effervescent, sparkling, fizzy; lathery.

focus *n.* **1.** *He took out the binoculars and adjusted the focus:* focal length, focal point, point of concentration, converging point. **2.** *The café is the focus of social life in many French towns:* center, hub, middle; meeting place, gathering place, headquarters, rallying point; spotlight, limelight; rendezvous, trysting place; haunt, retreat, resort; heart, core, nucleus. —*v.* **3.** *Focus the telescope on that distant lighthouse:* bring into focus, adjust, center; converge, bring to a point, concentrate; fix, center, direct, aim, bring to bear.

fodder *n.* *Alfalfa is a common fodder for cattle:* feed, food, silage, forage, provender, rations.

foe *n.* *Our foes made peace with us, and we became friends:* enemy, adversary, opponent, foeman, antagonist; attacker, assailant; rival, competitor, contender, disputant, combatant. —**Ant.** friend, comrade, companion; ally, confederate.

fog *n.* **1.** *When the fog closed in we couldn't see the top of the hill:* thick mist, haze, smog, murkiness, cloudiness, brume; *Slang* soup, pea soup. **2.** *That early in the morning my brain was in a fog:* daze, haze, stupor, trance, bewilderment. —*v.* **3.** *When foul weather fogged the port, the ships anchored outside:* cover with fog, enclose in mist or fog. **4.** *Lack of sleep had fogged his mind:* bewilder, muddle, daze, confuse, perplex, obscure, dim, cloud, darken. —**Ant.** 2 clarity, comprehension, perspicuity. 3 clear, brighten, clarify, purge, purify.

foggy *adj.* **1.** *At sunrise we walked through the foggy fields:* misty, hazy, brumous; clouded, cloudy, beclouded, filmy, overcast, murky, smoggy, *Slang* soupy; vaporous, nebulous. **2.** *He has only a foggy notion of what he wants to do:* unclear, confused, vague, fuzzy, musty, cloudy, dim, obscure, indistinct, *Slang* spacey; resembling fog, shadowy, dusky, dark. —**Ant.** 2 lucid, distinct, decisive, accurate, clear, bright; shrewd, sharp; alert, alive, awake.

foible *n.* *Is vanity a cardinal sin or merely a foible?:* minor fault, weakness, shortcoming, frailty, failing, imperfection, weak point, weak side, infirmity, defect, deficiency; quirk, kink, whimsy, crotchet. —**Ant.** strength, forte, virtue, perfection; crime, atrocity; sin, enormity, abomination.

foil[1] *v.* *The revolt was foiled by troops loyal to the king:* frustrate, balk, thwart; hinder, prevent, check, nip. —**Ant.** advance, further, forward; endorse, promote, abet, sustain, foment, incite, instigate.

foil[2] *n.* **1.** *The dome of the capitol was covered with gold foil:* leaf, flake, lamina, sheet, film, wafer. **2.** *Her wry humor is a perfect foil for his gushiness:* contrast, antithesis, complement, supplement, match, counterpart, correlative, backdrop, setoff. —*v.* **3.** *Black velvet foiled the ruby's brilliance and made it glow:* set off, enhance.

foist *v.* *Don't let them foist used merchandise on you:* pass off, palm off, impose, unload, get rid of.

fold[1] *v.* **1.** *Fold the napkins and put one by each plate:* double, crease, pleat, corrugate, lap; gather, tuck, dog-ear, pucker; wrinkle, rumple, crumple; crinkle, crimp, curl. **2.** *Fold the scarf in some tissue paper:* wrap, wrap up, envelop, enfold, encase. **3.** *She folded the child in her arms:* embrace, embosom, clasp, enfold, entwine, hug. —*n.* **4.** *The poison capsule was concealed in a fold of her dress:* gather, tuck, pleat, layer, crimp, crinkle, pucker, ruffle, flounce, furrow, overlap. **5.** *The map has begun to split along the fold:* crease, folding, doubling, bend. —**Ant.** 1, 2 unfold, unwrap, uncover; expose, exhibit, disclose, reveal.

fold[2] *n.* **1.** *How many sheep are kept in each fold?:* pen, enclosure, corral, close, yard, sty; barnyard, stockade, compound. **2.** *The preacher said that one of the brothers had strayed from the fold:* religious life, straight and narrow; the church, congregation, flock, parish, sect, group, community.

foliage n. The red and gold foliage of the trees was lovely: leaves, foliation, leafage, verdure.

folklore n. Paul Bunyan is a character in American folklore: legends, lore, traditions, folk tales, fables, myths.

folks n. pl. **1.** Folks are talking about her scene at the church social: people, the public, everyone. **2.** Informal My folks will be here for Christmas and New Year's: parents, family, family members, relatives, kinsfolk, kinfolk, kith and kin, kinsmen, blood relations.

follow v. **1.** "Q" follows "P" in our alphabet: come after, go behind, tread on the heels of, walk in the steps of, tread in the rear of, proceed in the wake of; bring up the rear. **2.** Who will follow the prime minister when he retires?: succeed, come next, come after, step into the shoes of; replace, supplant, take the place of. **3.** The citizens agreed to follow their civic leaders: accept as an authority, give allegiance to; follow the example of, emulate, imitate, copy, take after. **4.** There is no excuse for not following instructions: obey, heed, act in accordance with, comply with, observe, mind, conform to, be guided by; notice, watch, regard, note. **5.** The detectives followed the gang to their hideout: pursue, chase, go after, run after; track, stalk, trail, trace, hunt; Informal shadow, tail, dog, hound; attend, accompany. **6.** Everyone ought to have some ideals to follow: emulate, cherish, strive after, aim at; cultivate. **7.** He followed law after he returned from service: take up, engage in, practice, carry on; be concerned with, attend to, prosecute. **8.** Could you follow what he was saying?: understand, grasp, comprehend, catch on; keep up with. —**Ant.** 1 precede, lead, guide; pilot, steer. 3 forsake, desert, abandon. 4 disobey, ignore, flout. 5 elude, evade, escape. 7 avoid, shun; quit, abandon, renounce, give up.

follower n. **1.** He eluded his followers by crossing the river: pursuer, stalker, chaser; Slang tail, shadow; hunter. **2.** Mahatma Gandhi had many followers throughout the world: disciple, adherent, apostle, proselyte, convert; devotee, admirer, fan, partisan, supporter, advocate; pupil, protégé. **3.** The queen's retinue included 300 followers: attendant, servant, servitor, retainer, dependent; henchman, accessory, satellite, stooge; hanger-on, parasite, toady, sycophant. —**Ant.** 2 leader, teacher, guru; enemy, foe, antagonist, dissenter; rival, opponent, contender, detractor.

following n. **1.** I hated the show, but it has a large following: audience, public, patronage, body of followers, attendance, clientele; partisans, adherents; suite, retinue, train, entourage. —adj. **2.** She stayed with us until the following afternoon: next, succeeding, subsequent, ensuing; successive, consecutive; consequent, sequential. **3.** The President has issued the following statement: ensuing, subsequent, below, now to be mentioned, coming next.

folly n. **1.** It would be folly for you to try to lift that piano: foolishness, senselessness, idiocy, brainlessness, imbecility, inanity, asininity; fatuousness, silliness, doltishness, irrationality. **2.** Please talk to her about the folly of quitting school: imprudence, mistake, indiscretion; foolishness, frivolity, absurdity, tomfoolery, nonsense, giddiness, levity, trifling. —**Ant.** 1 wisdom, prudence, sound judgment, good sense; sobriety, sober-mindedness, level-headedness; sanity, rationality, lucidity.

foment v. He did his best to foment a quarrel between the brothers: stir up, incite, foster, promote, instigate, provoke, urge, excite, stimulate, galvanize, foster; rouse, arouse, kindle, inflame, spur, goad, agitate; irritate, aggravate, exacerbate, quicken, fan the fire, fan into flame, blow the coals. —**Ant.** quell, suppress, repress, quench; check, curb, restrain; allay, discourage, destroy, extinguish, extirpate.

fond adj. **1.** Did you ever see anyone so fond of desserts?: having a liking for, enamored, addicted to, crazy about. **2.** What can I do to discourage her fond looks?: loving, tender, affectionate, amorous, devoted, passionate, impassioned, ardent, enamored, infatuated, sentimental, desirous; doting, indulgent, overaffectionate, foolishly loving, overfond. **3.** She has fond hopes of becoming a movie star: cherished, held dear, preserved, harbored, sustained; naive, somewhat foolish. —**Ant.** 1 averse, indifferent. 2 unconcerned, aloof; unloving, unaffectionate, undemonstrative; strong-minded, rational, austere.

fondle v. She's been fondling that kitten all morning: caress, stroke, pet, touch fondly; cuddle, hug, embrace, nestle, fold in one's arms, clasp to one's bosom; nuzzle, spoon, bill and coo, Slang smooch, make out. —**Ant.** worry, annoy, chafe, irritate; ruffle, tease, heckle, badger, bait; torment, aggravate.

fondness n. **1.** Apparently her fondness for him is reciprocated: tenderness, affection, attachment, devotion, care; love, amorousness, desire, passion, ardor. **2.** If I could only curb my fondness for rich desserts!: partiality, predilection, penchant, preference, inclination, propensity, bent, desire, fancy, liking; weakness, suscepti-bility. —**Ant.** 1 antagonism, hostility, antipathy; hatred, contempt, loathing; harshness, brutality. 2 dislike, aversion, repulsion, revulsion.

food n. **1.** It takes most of his pay to buy food for the family: foodstuffs, provisions, rations, comestibles, victuals, viands, provender, eatables, edibles, nourishment, nurture, nutrition, sustenance, subsistence; Slang grub, chow; board. **2.** We use the clover as food for the live-stock: fodder, forage, feed, silage, provender; pasture, pasturage.

fool n. **1.** Only a fool would let his inheritance slip through his fingers: stupid person, idiot, dolt, blockhead, bonehead, simpleton, lunkhead, nitwit, half-wit, dummy, imbecile, moron, nincompoop, dunderhead, numskull, ignoramus, ass, dunce, ninny, oaf, clod, chump, goose, Slang meathead; German dummkopf, Yiddish klutz. **2.** The king relied on his fool for wise counsel: jester, clown, buffoon, dunce, merry-andrew, stooge; harlequin, Punchinello,

Pierrot, Scaramouch. —*v.* **3.** *I thought I bought a good car, but I was fooled:* trick, deceive, make a fool of, dupe, flimflam, hoodwink, cheat, defraud, hoax, bilk, fleece, gull, *Slang* con, rip off; beguile, bamboozle, cozen, humbug, diddle. **4.** *When he seems to be fooling he may be quite serious:* joke, jest, play the fool, cut capers, play the monkey, frolic, cut up; pretend, feign, make believe, tease. —**Ant.** l genius, wise man, savant, sage, pundit, guru; adept, expert, scholar, master.

foolhardy *adj.* *Walking a tightrope across the falls was a foolhardy venture:* rash, reckless, incautious, impulsive, impetuous, imprudent, daredevil, madcap, hotheaded, harebrained, headstrong, brash, hasty; heedless, careless, thoughtless. —**Ant.** wary, cautious, circumspect; prudent, careful, heedful, mindful, watchful, alert; calculating, shrewd, farsighted, judicious.

fooling *n.* *"Enough fooling!" she sternly ordered:* buffoonery, joking, clownishness, frolicking, jesting, joking, joshing, spoofing, kidding, making light, tricks, mockery, teasing.

foolish *adj.* *That was certainly a foolish thing to say:* unwise, imprudent, ill-considered, indiscreet, ill-advised, incautious, short-sighted, irresponsible; unintelligent, absurd, inane, fatuous, witless, senseless; stupid, half-witted, brainless, boneheaded, silly, simple-minded; moronic, asinine, idiotic, imbecilic; preposterous, ridiculous, ludicrous. —**Ant.** intelligent, bright, smart; quick-witted, brilliant, sane, rational, sensible; wise, sage, sagacious, sapient; judicious, prudent, circumspect, cautious; clear-sighted, perspicacious, strong-minded, sound; clever, calculating, sharp.

foolishly *adv.* *Foolishly, he touched the live wire:* idiotic, absurdly, idiotically, indiscreetly, mistakenly, incautiously, stupidly, unwisely, ill-advisedly, imprudently.

foolishness *n.* *Because of her foolishness they're now deeply in debt:* imprudence, folly, extravagance, irresponsibility, indiscretion; absurdity, preposterousness, ridiculousness, asininity; injudiciousness, senselessness, witlessness, brainlessness, unwisdom; childishness, silliness, puerility; stupidity, fatuousness, idiocy, lunacy, imbecility.

foot *n.* **1.** *She's been limping since she dropped the skillet on her foot:* terminal part of the leg, lower extremity; *Slang* tootsy, dog; (of animals) hoof, paw, trotter, pad. **2.** *Reinforcements of 1,000 foot were sent up to the front:* foot soldiers, infantry. **3.** *We placed a wreath at the foot of the statue:* base, lower part, bottom, foundation.

foothold *n.* *The hill was so slippery it was hard to get a foothold:* footing, grip, hold, purchase, toehold; firm place, stable position, firm footing, support.

footing *n.* *He sought to place the organization on a better footing:* position, place, capacity, standing, station, state, character, condition, grade, rank, relationship, situation, status.

foot-loose *adj.* *Now that her children are grown*

she's foot-loose: free, unattached, uncommitted, unencumbered, fancy-free, carefree.

fop *n.* *In olden days such a vain, conceited ass would have been called a fop:* dandy, coxcomb, dude, popinjay, beau, Beau Brummel, swell, prettyboy, fashion plate, silk stocking.

foppish *adj.* *He wears such foppish clothes the other youths laugh at him:* dandyish, foplike, showy, ostentatious, dandified; gaudy, ornate, overelaborate; vain, affected, finical. —**Ant.** unassuming, modest, unostentatious, unpretentious, unaffected; dowdy, seedy, slovenly, tacky; clownish, gauche, yokelish, rustic, provincial, hayseed, cornball.

forage *n.* **1.** *Do the cattle have enough forage?:* fodder, feed, provender, silage; food, provisions; pasture, pasturage. **2.** *The squad went out on a forage and returned with several chickens:* search for provisions, foray. —*v.* **3.** *The survivors of the plane crash had to forage for something to eat:* search, rummage, seek, hunt, explore, look about, cast about; scavenge, scrounge, come up with; raid, strip of supplies, plunder, despoil, ravage.

foray *n.* **1.** *The Vikings made regular forays on the weakly defended coastal towns:* raid, sudden attack, invasion, depredation, incursion, inroad; sally, thrust; expedition, venture. —*v.* **2.** *The soldiers forayed into the surrounding countryside when their provisions were low:* plunder, pillage, ravage, raid; invade, attack, make an incursion.

forbear *v.* **1.** *She should try to forbear from saying such cruel things:* refrain, desist, abstain, do without, hold back, give up; eschew, renounce, forgo, abnegate, discontinue, leave off, stop, cease, quit, break off. **2.** *I wanted to curse him, but I had to forbear:* restrain oneself, hold back, show self-control, be patient, be tolerant, tolerate, show indulgence; suffer, endure, bear.

forbearance *n.* *It takes considerable forbearance to overlook his faults:* patience, leniency, resignation, tolerance, indulgence, self-restraint, command of temper, endurance, longanimity; mildness, meekness, submission; mercy, mercifulness, clemency, pity, pardon; moderation, abstinence, temperance. —**Ant.** anger, impatience, intolerance.

forbearing *adj.* *Even after his disgracing her, she was forbearing:* tolerant, charitable, clement, forgiving, considerate, gentle, humane, indulgent, humanitarian, longsuffering, mild, merciful, moderate, patient, thoughtful, easy.

forbid *v.* *I forbid you to stay out after midnight:* prohibit, not allow, command not to, order not to, interdict, enjoin, proscribe; ban, veto, taboo, bar, exclude, disallow; hinder, prevent, render impossible, preclude, obviate, obstruct, inhibit, impede; oppose, gainsay; refuse, restrain, reject. —**Ant.** permit, allow, let, suffer; authorize, bid, license; approve, sanction, endorse; order, command.

forbidden *adj.* *The trail was forbidden to us:* outlawed, off limits, banned, closed, closed down, closed up, prohibited, proscribed, taboo, refused, verboten, vetoed, contraband.

forbidding *adj.* *When I saw that forbidding*

watchdog, I went no farther: disagreeable, unpleasant, dour, inhospitable, unapproachable, unfriendly; dangerous-looking, sinister, ominous, grim, threatening, prohibitive, prohibitory; ugly, repellent, odious, offensive, horrible, repulsive, abhorrent, hideous. **—Ant.** attractive, alluring, inviting.

force *n.* **1.** *The force of her personality can be seen in the way her friends imitate her:* energy, power, potency, vigor, strength; vim, vitality, animation; effectiveness, efficacy; attraction, magnetism, charisma. **2.** *A poet must carefully weigh the force of each word he uses:* significance, meaning, value, import, weight, weightiness, signification; effect, impact, clout; cogency, validity, emphasis. **3.** *Push with as much force as you can:* power, might, strength, potency, pressure, energy, momentum, stress, impact, puissance, stamina. **4.** *The police had to use force to hold back the crowd:* coercion, constraint, duress, compulsion, enforcement; violence. **5.** *How many employees are in your work force?:* group, body, team, unit, division, squad, gang, crew; army, corps, detachment, squadron, battalion. **—v. 6.** *Bad weather forced us to call off the picnic:* oblige, compel, push, make necessary, necessitate, require, constrain, enjoin, make, impel, drive, overpower; persuade, induce. **7.** *We forced water into the pipe to clean it:* thrust, propel, push, press, drive, coerce, urge, impel; impose, intrude, obtrude. **8.** *The police tried to force the truth from the suspect:* obtain by force, pull, wrest, squeeze, pry, wrench, drag; coerce, extort; coax, elicit. **9.** *He had forgotten his key and had to force the door:* break, break open, use violence on. **—Ant.** 1 weakness, frailty; ineffectiveness, inefficiency, inefficacy.

forced *adj.* **1.** *The bridge had been built with forced labor:* enforced, compelled, coerced, involuntary, unwilling, obliged, obligatory, required, constrained, compulsory, binding, mandatory; slave, enslaved, impressed. **2.** *Her forced smile indicated that something was wrong:* strained, labored, grudging, not natural; artificial, insincere, mannered, affected. **—Ant.** 2 easy, natural, simple, unforced, unpretending.

forceful *adj. Lincoln's Gettysburg Address was a brief but forceful speech:* powerful, strong, full of force, puissant, dynamic, intense, vigorous, potent, energetic, emphatic; impressive, effective, vivid, pithy, valid, cogent; robust, virile. **—Ant.** feeble, weak, spent, exhausted.

forcible *adj. Forcible restraint was the only answer:* forceful, active, cogent, assertive, compelling, telling, effective, efficient, energetic, mighty, intense, militant, persuasive, potent, strong, powerful, vehement, weighty, vigorous, aggressive.

forcibly *adv. She was forcibly kept out of the kitchen:* by force, powerfully, effectively, hard, energetically, mightily, strongly, vigorously, coercively, compulsorily.

fore *adj. He stood watch in the fore part of the ship:* front, forward, frontal, headmost, anterior. **—Ant.** rear, aft, posterior, back, hindmost.

forebear or **forbear** *n. Our forebears came from eastern Europe:* ancestor, forefather, progenitor, antecedent, forerunner; procreator, begetter.

foreboding *n. She had a foreboding that the trip would end in disaster:* premonition, presentiment, prescience, apprehension; omen, prognostic, forewarning, foreshadowing, intuition, augury, portent; dread, boding; misgiving.

forecast *v.* **1.** *Experts have forecast an upturn in the stock market:* predict, prognosticate, project; prophesy, augur, foresee; expect, anticipate, calculate, extrapolate; envision, envisage, divine; foretell, presage, portend, foreknow. **—n. 2.** *The forecast for tonight is rain changing to snow:* prediction, prognostication, prophecy, prognosis, outlook; projection, foreknowledge, precognition, prevision, prescience, presentiment; presage, augury; anticipation, conjecture.

forefather *n. He wants to visit Scotland where his forefathers lived:* ancestor, forebear, progenitor, primogenitor, antecedent; patriarch, forerunner, precursor; originator, begetter, procreator, author, father. **—Ant.** descendant, progeny, issue, child.

forefront *n. A new group of young popular singers is coming to the forefront:* lead, head, vanguard, position of prominence, fore; public attention, widespread acceptance, fame, celebrity.

foregoing *adj. The foregoing was a paid announcement:* prior, aforementioned, precedent, aforesaid, preceding, antecedent, former, anterior, past, previous, above.

foreign *adj.* **1.** *He's thinking of buying a new foreign car:* from another land, alien, not domestic, not native; imported, introduced; strange, exotic, outlandish; distant, remote; unfamiliar, unknown; heathenish, barbarous. **2.** *The doctor cleansed the wound of foreign matter. Spite is foreign to her nature:* extraneous, extrinsic, unconnected, unrelated; irregular, unusual, uncharacteristic, inappropriate, antipathetic, inconsistent, incongruous, incompatible, inconsonant; not pertinent, irrelevant, inapplicable, beside the point, inadmissible. **—Ant.** 1 domestic, native. 2 relevant, pertinent, applicable; intrinsic, characteristic; congenial, agreeable, suited.

foreigner *n. This year many foreigners are visiting our country:* alien, outlander, nonnative; immigrant, newcomer, émigré, outsider, stranger; barbarian, pagan. **—Ant.** native, citizen, aborigine.

foreknowledge *n. Did anyone have foreknowledge of the stock market crash?:* prior knowledge, advance notice; foresight, foresightedness; clairvoyance, second sight, precognition, prescience, intuition, prevision; presentiment, anticipation, apprehension, premonition.

foreman *n. For years he worked as a foreman in a shoe factory:* manager, overseer, supervisor, crew leader, chief workman, boss, coordinator, superintendent, *(fem.)* forewoman; spokesman, chairman, president, presiding juryman.

foremost *adj. Yellowstone Park is one of the foremost tourist attractions:* principal, leading, main, preeminent, chief, head; paramount, supreme, capital, cardinal; vital, essential.

forerunner *n.* **1.** *The Western Baseball League was a 19th-century forerunner of the modern major leagues:* precursor, predecessor, prototype; ancestor, forebear, forefather, progenitor; trial balloon, stalking-horse. **2.** *Warm rains are the forerunners of spring:* herald, harbinger, foretoken, omen, portent, sign, presage, precursor, prognostic, token, augury, premonition, forewarning.

foresee *v. The prophet foresaw a severe famine in the land:* anticipate, expect, look forward to, envision, look ahead to; prophesy, foretell, predict, prognosticate, forecast; be clairvoyant, be prescient, foreknow, have second sight; augur, presage; divine, forebode.

foresight *n.* **1.** *The oracle was believed to have foresight in predicting future events:* clairvoyance, foreknowledge, prescience, power of foreseeing, second sight, prevision, precognition. **2.** *Through lack of foresight, he found himself out of gas on a country road:* preparedness, prudence, farsightedness, forethought, anticipation, provision for the future, planning, forehandedness, provident care, providence, longsightedness; shrewdness, perspicacity, sagacity; discretion, precaution, wisdom; premeditation. **—Ant.** 1 hindsight, retrospection. 2 unpreparedness, carelessness, neglect, improvidence.

forest *n. The forest was so dense we couldn't see through the trees:* woods, wood, thick growth of trees and underbrush, timberland, wooded area, woodland, bush, wildwood; stand, grove, thicket, copse; wilderness, jungle.

forestall *v. Labor and management have agreed on a temporary settlement, thereby forestalling a strike:* prevent, thwart, ward off, avert, deter, avoid, head off, circumvent; counteract, block, preclude, obviate; anticipate, guard against; *Informal* steal a march on, beat to the punch.

foretell *v. Perhaps certain gifted persons can foretell the future:* predict, prophesy, foresee, prognosticate, divine, augur, forecast; apprehend, foreknow; presage, forebode, portend; tell fortunes, cast a horoscope, soothsay, act the seer.

forethought *n.* **1.** *One needs forethought to stay within a budget:* careful planning, prudence, carefulness, foresight, providence, farsightedness, sagacity, shrewdness; caution, heed, wariness, circumspection. **2.** *Part of the game is to answer impulsively, without forethought:* deliberation, prior thought, discretion, consideration, premeditation; precaution, prudence, anticipation. **—Ant.** 1 unpreparedness, carelessness, neglect, improvidence. 2 impulsiveness, spontaneity.

forever *adv.* **1.** *The lovers promised to be faithful forever:* eternally, for all time, always, everlastingly, to the end of time, ever, perpetually, undyingly, for aye, till the crack of doom, till doomsday. **2.** *She is forever asking to borrow something:* continually, perpetually, unremittingly, constantly, always, interminably, ceaselessly, unceasingly, incessantly. **—Ant.** never, at no time, sporadically, occasionally.

forewarn *v. Sentries were stationed to forewarn us of the enemy's approach:* caution, alert, put on guard, give warning, tip off, prewarn, give advance notice, *Slang* put a flea (or bug) in someone's ear, sound the alarm, cry havoc.

foreword *n. In the foreword the author states his intentions in writing the book:* preface, introduction, introductory statement, preliminary remarks, preamble, prologue; prelude.

forfeit *n.* **1.** *You'll have to pay a forfeit if you fail to keep the appointment:* penalty, fine, damages, assessment, forfeiture, waiver. —*v.* **2.** *She forfeited the match when she refused to play. He forfeited his freedom when he was convicted of the crime:* lose because of some offense, surrender, yield, default, waive; squander, waste, let slip, miss, allow to slip through the fingers.

forge *n.* **1.** *The blacksmith's forge was so hot we couldn't get near it:* furnace, hearth; blacksmith's shop, smithy, ironworks. —*v.* **2.** *The smith forged the horseshoe with great skill:* hammer out, beat into shape, shape, form, fabricate, make, manufacture, fashion, produce, turn out; devise, contrive. **3.** *My signature was forged on the check:* sign falsely, imitate fraudulently, counterfeit, falsify, fabricate; copy, imitate, simulate, clone.

forgery *n.* **1.** *He made a fortune with the forgery of paintings:* fraudulent imitations; falsification, counterfeiting, cloning, misrepresentation; deception, fraudulence. **2.** *The museum director discovered that the Greek vase was a forgery:* counterfeit, imitation, copy, clone, fraud, fake, sham; make-believe, hoax.

forget *v.* **1.** *Don't feel hurt because she forgot your name:* fail to recollect, not remember, have escape the memory, be forgetful of, be unable to recall, let slip from the memory, lose sight of, lose the memory of; neglect, slight, disregard. **2.** *I hope he doesn't forget the plane tickets:* leave behind, overlook, fail to take, omit unintentionally; think no more of, pass over, dispense with, be done with, consign to oblivion, let bygones be bygones. **—Ant.** 1 remember, recollect, recall; reminisce, think back on, bring to mind, acquire, learn, retain; treasure, mind.

forgetful *adj. She's so forgetful that she has to make a note of everything:* apt to forget, absent-minded; heedless, neglectful, inattentive, oblivious, unmindful, negligent, mindless, careless, remiss, *Slang* out of it; amnesiac. **—Ant.** retentive, unforgetting, unforgetful, attentive, careful, mindful.

forgive *v. We must forgive our enemies if we ourselves expect forgiveness:* pardon, excuse, absolve, reprieve, cease to feel resentment against, make allowances for, bear with; think no more of, allow for; bury the hatchet, pocket the affront; remit the penalty of; acquit, clear, exonerate, exculpate, condone, pass over, overlook; discharge, set free, release; *Informal* wipe the slate clean, let bygones be bygones. —**Ant.** blame, condemn, censure, charge.

forgiveness *n. He sought forgiveness for his sins:* absolution, amnesty, clemency, dispensation, exoneration, acquittal, grace, immunity, impunity, lenience, mercy, pardon, reprieve, respite, vindication, indemnity, justification.

forgo or **forego** *v. Because of other expenses, I'll have to forgo that new suit:* give up, do without, relinquish, renounce; surrender, yield, waive; abstain from, refrain from, eschew, skip, abnegate; sacrifice.

fork *n.* **1.** *Set the table with knives and forks:* pronged implement, eating utensil; pitchfork; trident. **2.** *When you get to the fork in the road, bear right:* division, branching, branch, bifurcation, divergence, separation, intersection; crotch, angle, bend, elbow; turning point. —*v.* **3.** *Fork the bales and lift them onto the wagon:* pierce, take hold of with a fork, stab, skewer, impale. **4.** *The river forks just before it reaches town:* diverge, divide, bifurcate, branch, branch out, split, ramify.

forked *adj. The forked road made us choose between forest and countryside:* branching, split, angled, bifurcated, divided, separated, dichotomous.

forlorn *adj.* **1.** *She looks forlorn since her children married and moved away:* unhappy, depressed, dejected, despondent, dispirited; brokenhearted, woebegone, bereft, bereaved, disconsolate, miserable, comfortless, hopeless, despairing, desperate, inconsolable; abject, pitiable, wretched, pathetic. **2.** *We stayed at a forlorn little inn outside the town:* forsaken, deserted, solitary; desolate, dreary, dismal; friendless, lonesome, lonely, lone; destitute, abandoned, helpless, forgotten. —**Ant.** 1 happy, cheerful, elated, hopeful. 2 thriving, bustling.

form *n.* **1.** *The cookies were in the form of squares:* shape, outline, figure, pattern, contour; figuration, configuration; formation, conformation; structure, format, design, style, plan. **2.** *This coat really fits one's form:* body, figure, shape, anatomy, build, physique, person; being, presence. **3.** *When the cement has hardened, the form is removed:* mold, cast, frame, framework, matrix. **4.** *Ice is water in another form:* appearance, phase, aspect, manifestation, arrangement, image, likeness, semblance, guise; incarnation. **5.** *The ant is a form of insect:* type, variety, kind, sort; genus, species, genre, class; description, denomination; model, brand, character, stamp. **6.** *You paint well, but your work lacks form:* order, system, structure, orderliness, harmony, arrangement, regularity; shapeliness, proportion, symmetry. **7.** *They didn't follow the traditional form of the marriage service:* prescribed method, order, format, rule, habit, proceeding, practice, liturgy, formality, ceremony, rite, ritual; formula, style, mode; way, manner. **8.** *It's not good form to insist on talking about oneself:* social behavior, manners, deportment, practice, conduct, custom, usage, propriety, decorum; etiquette, conventionality. **9.** *If she's in*

form, she can win the match easily: trim, fettle, fitness, shape, top condition, healthy condition. —*v.* **10.** *Form the plaster with your hands and allow it to harden:* fashion, shape, mold; carve, sculpt, cut, sculpture, chisel, model; rough-hew, hew, block out; cast, stamp, pattern; construct, structure, fabricate, forge, build; produce, make, create, devise, put together, manufacture; found, set up, establish. **11.** *The sofa is formed of three separate sections:* compose, comprise, make up, constitute; serve to make up. **12.** *He formed the habit of peering over his glasses:* develop, acquire, contract, pick up.

formal *adj.* **1.** *Lee offered his sword to Grant in the formal gesture of surrender:* ceremonial, official, conventional, ritualistic, prescribed, regular, customary, *Latin* pro forma; external, outward, perfunctory. **2.** *"Your signature on the lease will make our agreement formal," said the landlord:* definite, settled, fixed; explicit, positive; proper, in due form, authoritative; legal, lawful. **3.** *Her Highness's manner with commoners is gracious but quite formal:* reserved, decorous, proper, strict, cool, aloof, distant, standoffish, prim, straitlaced, prudish; stiff, starched, stilted; rigid, inflexible, uncompromising; solemn, pompous; ceremonious, punctil-ious. **4.** *He kept a black bow tie and tuxedo for formal occasions:* dressy, stylish, grand, smart; solemn, fancy, full-dress, *Informal* highfalutin. —**Ant.** informal, casual, spontaneous, folksy, easygoing, unceremonious.

formality *n.* **1.** *The old man bowed and shook the child's hand with mock formality:* observance of form, conventionality, propriety, decorum, etiquette, punctilio; reserve, coolness. **2.** *Once the terms had been hammered out, the signing of the treaty was just a formality:* ritual, rite, custom, convention, rule of procedure, ceremony, ceremonial, mere form, motion. —**Ant.** informality, ease, casualness.

formation *n.* **1.** *A formation of planes thundered overhead:* ordered group, configuration, arrangement, constellation, set; structure, composition, makeup. **2.** *The Pilgrims' goal was the formation of a colony in the New World:* creation, establishment, development, organization, genesis, generation; production, manufacture, fabrication, building.

formative *adj. One learns a lot during the form-ative years of adolescence:* impressionable, susceptible, accessible, sensitive; plastic, shaping, determinative.

former *adj.* **1.** *In former days this was a fashionable restaurant:* past, prior, bygone, gone by; elapsed, lapsed, gone, passed away; ancient, olden, old-time, of yore. **2.** *He had two daughters, Alice and Sarah, the former of whom married an archaeologist:* first-mentioned, before-mentioned, first-named; aforementioned, aforesaid. **3.** *The house was built by her former husband:* previous, earlier, anterior, preceding, prior; antecedent, foregoing; erstwhile, quondam; *Informal* ex; *Archaic* whilom. —**Ant.** 1 modern, coming, future. 2 latter, succeeding, following. 3 ensuing, subsequent; present.

formerly *adv. She was formerly head of a large department store:* once, at one time, in times past, originally, previously; long ago, of old, of yore, anciently, hitherto, lately, ere now; *Archaic* whilom.

formidable *adj. A charging rhinoceros is a formidable sight:* awesome, imposing, impressive; fearful, terrifying, alarming, dreadful, portentous, menacing, threatening, forbidding; overwhelming, terrific, overpowering; difficult, demanding, dangerous; taxing, onerous, mammoth.

formless *adj. She thought his essay was formless:* amorphous, unformed, shapeless, chaotic, incoherent, indefinite, indeterminate, indistinct, vague, nebulous, disorganized, unorganized, orderless, obscure, unclear, undefined.

formula *n.* **1.** *What's your formula for success?:* prescription, recipe, blueprint, plan, guideline, rule, principle, precept. **2.** *The magician recited a secret formula:* incantation, rigmarole, set phrase, slogan, saying, verbal form, chant; cliché, platitude, pleasantry, cant.

formulate *v. So far he has not been able to formulate his new plan:* express clearly, state, define, systematize; frame, draft, compose; specify, particularize, itemize; devise, invent.

forsake *v.* **1.** *He held her close and swore never to forsake her:* desert, abandon, leave, quit, vacate, cast off; abdicate, resign, lay down; fling away, part with, jettison, dispose of; flee, depart. **2.** *His new wife persuaded him to forsake his old drinking habits:* renounce, forswear, abjure, give up, have done with, repudiate, spurn, abandon; relinquish, yield, surrender; waive, drop; reject, discard; disclaim, disavow; deny, go back on.

forsaken *adj. The forsaken young man shed bitter tears:* abandoned, jilted, cast off, derelict, deserted, forlorn, isolated, left behind, marooned, outcast, thrown over, disowned, ignored.

forswear *v. The witness forswore his previous testimony:* retract, repudiate, recant, abjure, gainsay, take back, deny, disavow, disclaim, disown, reject, renounce, revoke, contravene. **—Ant.** reaffirm, uphold, confirm, support, champion.

fort *n. The fort was headquarters for the governor:* fortress, fortification, stronghold; bulwark, bastion, castle, citadel, fastness; garrison, base, station, camp.

forte *n. He can play classical and pop, but his real forte is jazz improvisation:* strong point, special gift, specialty, particular talent, strength, chief excellence; natural turn, unusual aptitude, bent, knack, skill, proficiency.

forth *adv.* **1.** *From this day forth you are my truest friend:* forward, onward, ahead, outward, on to the end. **2.** *He brought forth a proposition that we all liked:* into consideration, to notice, into view, before one's attention; out from concealment, from retirement, from confinement.

forthcoming *adj.* **1.** *His forthcoming play is about the Garden of Eden:* about to appear, upcoming, coming, approaching; prospective, im-

minent, impending. **2.** *Financial assistance from his friends is always forthcoming:* ready as needed, available, obtainable, accessible, at hand, handy, on tap; openhanded, cooperative, helpful.

forthright *adj.* **1.** *Don't ask his opinion unless you're ready for a forthright answer:* frank, open, blunt, outspoken, candid, direct, plain-spoken, straightforward, *Informal* up-front; painfully truthful, not mincing matters, downright; *Informal* calling a spade a spade. **—adv. 2.** *Tell me forthright what you think of the idea:* straightforwardly, straight, straight out, directly, frankly, openly, bluntly, outspokenly, candidly, truthfully. **—Ant.** 1 furtive, secret, underhand; dishonest, untruthful, deceitful.

forthwith *adv. We said good night and left forthwith:* immediately, without delay, at once, directly, instantly, right off, straightaway, quickly, promptly, in a jiffy, *Slang* pronto.

fortification *n. There were fortifications along the border to discourage invaders:* fortress, fort, citadel, garrison, bastion, tower, bulwark, rampart, stronghold; breastwork, earthwork.

fortify *v.* **1.** *The medieval town was fortified with a high wall and a deep moat:* strengthen against attack, defend with fortifications, protect, secure, shield; fortress, bulwark, garrison. **2.** *The wooden beams were fortified with steel rods:* make strong, strengthen, reinforce, add strength to, brace, shore up, buttress; harden, stiffen. **3.** *The bridegroom took a brandy to fortify himself for the ceremony:* sustain, make strong, build up, support, strengthen, buoy up, boost, brace, hearten, cheer, reassure; encourage, embolden, urge on; stimulate, invigorate. **4.** *The bread is fortified with various vitamins. The punch is well fortified with rum:* enrich, add nutrients to; add alcohol to, lace. **—Ant.** 2 weaken, undermine, debilitate, impair. 3 demoralize, dishearten, unnerve, discomfit.

fortitude *n. It takes a lot of fortitude to sail around the world alone:* endurance, courage, strength of mind, moral strength, resoluteness, mettle; *Informal* guts, grit, sand, spunk, backbone; spirit, firmness, resolution, determination, prowess, pluck, tenacity; hardihood, dauntlessness, fearlessness, intrepidity, heroism; valor, bravery, boldness; nerve, dash, daring. **—Ant.** cowardice, weakness, faintheartedness.

fortress *n. The soldiers attacked the fortress:* large fortified place, fort, citadel, stronghold, fortification, acropolis; bastion, rampart, bulwark, buttress.

fortuitous *adj. The impromptu celebration was the result of a fortuitous meeting with an old friend:* chance, accidental, random, casual, unexpected; undesigned, unpremeditated, unpurposed, unintentional, inadvertent, unintended; stray, hit-or-miss, haphazard, incidental; not meant, never thought of, adventitious; serendipitous, lucky, happy, fortunate. **—Ant.** prearranged, planned, purposed, intentional, premeditated.

fortunate *adj.* **1.** *That irritating man is fortu-*

nate to have such a tolerant wife: lucky, having good fortune, blessed, favored; successful, booming, flourishing, happy, felicitous; rich, prosperous, well-to-do, well-off; Informal on easy street, sitting pretty. **2.** It was a fortunate day when we opened that store: bringing good luck, auspicious, propitious, favorable, advantageous, profitable, resulting favorably; well-timed, timely, opportune, convenient; promising, encouraging, providential; palmy, bright, rosy, fair, benign, halcyon. —**Ant.** 1 unlucky, unfortunate. 2 ill-starred, baleful, unhappy, miserable, disastrous, calamitous.

fortunately adv. Fortunately, I had the solution: luckily, happily, auspiciously, favorably, opportunely, providentially, satisfyingly, seasonably, successfully, prosperously.

fortune n. **1.** Gold prospectors could make a fortune overnight if they hit a rich vein: immense amount of money, wealth, riches, ample stock of wealth; affluence, prosperity, opulence, easy circumstances; bonanza, windfall, godsend; substance, property, capital, estate, means; revenue, income; treasure, mint, gold mine, pile. **2.** Let's leave it to fortune where we spend our vacation: fate, destiny, luck, chance, providence, accident, fortuity, haphazard; good luck, lady luck; kismet. **3.** usually **fortunes** His fortunes have been more down than up the last few years: lot, portion, destiny, fate, luck, condition in life, circumstances; star; doom, fatality. —**Ant.** 1 poverty, destitution, indigence. 2 design, intent, intention, purpose.

fortuneteller n. A fortuneteller told her she would marry a handsome foreigner: clairvoyant, seer, crystal gazer, palmist, medium, magician, chiromancer, Gypsy; soothsayer, oracle, prophet, sibyl, augur.

forum n. **1.** The issues will be discussed at the town forum next month. He left the senate to seek a new forum for his ideas: public meeting place, public arena, assembly place; platform, rostrum, outlet, medium, lecture room. **2.** There is a forum on drug addiction tonight at 8 P.M.: open discussion, symposium, seminar, colloquium.

forward adv. **1.** The cars moved forward very slowly: ahead, onward, in advance, in front, toward the front, forth, frontward; before; toward the future. **2.** The proposal was brought forward at our last meeting: forth, into consideration, into discussion, into prominence; out, into view. —adj. **3.** The forward motion of the ticket line was barely perceptible: moving ahead, advancing, onward; frontal, fore; anterior; progressive, go-ahead, forward-looking, up-to-date; enterprising. **4.** Mother thought his behavior was rather forward: bold, brash, impudent, presumptuous, immodest, self-assertive, presuming, overconfident; fresh, im-pertinent, cheeky, sassy, insolent, unmannerly; brazen, shameless, offensive, barefaced; intrusive. —v. **5.** We asked the postman to forward our mail: send forward, readdress, send on, pass on, relay, reroute. **6.** The civic leaders helped to forward the project: advance, help to progress, promote, further; as-

sist, back, champion, accelerate, hasten, spread, quicken. —**Ant.** 1 backward, to the rear. 3 backward, regressive. 4 retiring, modest. 6 hinder, impede, obstruct, bar, block.

foster v. **1.** Early experience with bullies in school fostered in him a hatred of tyrants: encourage, promote, further, forward, advance, accommodate, aid, nurture, help forward, help onward; advocate, support, back, take up the cause of, befriend, patronize; side with, favor, countenance, sanction; foment, stimulate. **2.** They have fostered several children of various races: rear, bring up, raise, rear up; nurse, mother, care for, tend, take in, feed; nourish, nurture, support, sustain; cherish, treasure, hold dear, harbor, protect. —**Ant.** 1 oppose, combat, resist, withstand; curb, restrain, inhibit.

foul adj. **1.** The slaughterhouse was filled with a foul odor: disgusting, loathsome, obnoxious, putrid, putrescent, stinking, smelly, malodorous; hateful, odious, revolting, repulsive. **2.** Take off those foul clothes and let me wash them: dirty, soiled, filthy, nasty, unclean; begrimed, besmeared, bedraggled; smeared, stained, sullied; muddy, grimy, grubby; squalid, sordid. **3.** I wish we didn't have to go out in this foul weather: stormy, squally, blustery, gusty; wet, rainy, drizzly, misty; foggy, murky, cloudy; muddy, turbid. **4.** Many were shocked by his foul language: coarse, vulgar, lewd, smutty, indecent, obscene; profane, scurrilous, blasphemous, risqué, indelicate, immodest, unseemly, gross; abusive, insulting. **5.** It was a neighborhood accustomed to foul crimes: heinous, abominable, infamous, notorious; disgraceful, contemptible, detestable; vile, wicked, evil, monstrous, base, scurvy, nefarious, villainous, atrocious, flagitious. **6.** The ship was delayed an hour because of a foul anchor: tangled, entangled, ensnared, befouled, encumbered, impeded, choked. —v. **7.** Persons allowing their animals to foul the footpaths will be prosecuted: make foul, dirty, befoul, defile, sully, soil, begrime, besmirch, pollute, taint. **8.** Masses of seaweed had fouled the anchor: tangle, clog, entangle, befoul, ensnare. —**Ant.** 1 fair, fragrant, pleasing. 2 clean, spotless, stainless. 3 fair, clear. 4 mild, modest, seemly, pure. 5 admirable, exemplary; pleasant; honorable. 7 cleanse, purify; honor. 8 clear, untangle.

found v. **1.** His grandfather founded the business in 1909: establish, institute, organize, bring about, set up, originate, create, develop, give rise to, start, set going; settle, colonize. **2.** Most of her arguments were founded on fact: base, rest, sustain, locate, ground. **3.** The house was founded on solid rock: build, construct, erect, raise, rear.

foundation n. **1.** First the builders poured a solid foundation of cement: base, substructure, understructure, underpinning, ground, groundwork, bed, bottom, lowest layer, support, foot, pedestal; basement, cellar; rock. **2.** The charges of fraud against the corporation proved to be without foundation: basis, base, justification, cause, reason, rationale; root, ground, groundwork, source, origin, commencement; purpose, motive; premise, assumption, underlying principle, infrastructure. **3.** *He left money for the foundation of a music school:* founding, establishment, institution, setting up, installation, creation; settlement. **4.** *The foundation provides money for hospitals and medical research:* institution; charity, fund; philanthropy, benefaction, endowment.

founder[1] *v.* **1.** *The ship foundered during a Caribbean hurricane:* sink, go down, go under, go to the bottom, swamp; capsize, shipwreck; run aground. **2.** *The company foundered during the last recession:* fail utterly, come to grief, collapse, abort, miscarry, perish, succumb, drown, sink; disintegrate, break up, fall apart, topple, go under; come to nothing, end in smoke; hit rock bottom, turn out badly. **3.** *His horse foundered as they came down the mountain path:* go lame, stagger, limp, hobble, reel; trip, stumble, tumble, fall, lurch, topple, plunge, sprawl; break down; *Informal* come a cropper.

founder[2] *n.* *Our company is managed by the son of the founder:* originator, creator, builder, organizer, planner, architect, strategist; author, father.

fountain *n.* **1.** *The colored lights playing on the fountains were spectacular:* jet, stream of water; gush, flow, spout, upwelling. **2.** *Explorers traced the Nile River to its several fountains in Central Africa:* source of stream, fountainhead, wellspring, head of a stream, well, spring, fount; reservoir. **3.** *Ancient Greece was a fountain of wisdom and philosophy:* origin, source; genesis, beginning, cradle; birth, derivation, first principles; reason, cause; supplier, purveyor, feeder.

foxy *adj.* *He's so foxy I always wonder if I'm being cheated:* cunning, crafty, clever, artful, wily, tricky, slick, guileful, sharp, canny, shrewd, shifty, astute; sly, stealthy, insidious, devious, oblique, sneaky, underhand; deceitful, deceptive; designing, intriguing, conniving, scheming. **—Ant.** straightforward, aboveboard, forthright; candid, open, plain, frank; artless, guileless, ingenuous, naive.

foyer *n.* *The messenger waited in the foyer while the butler delivered the package:* antechamber, vestibule, anteroom, waiting room, hall; lobby; entrance porch, loggia.

fracas *n.* *Upon leaving the bar they got into a fracas:* affray, altercation, fight, battle, brawl, bickering, dispute, disturbance, feud, fight, fray, mêlée, mix up, quarrel, riot, row, scuffle, squabble, tumult, uproar, run-in, scrimmage.

fraction *n.* **1.** *The average number of children per family is two and a fraction:* part of a whole, fractional part; section, segment, piece, portion, subdivision; ratio, quotient, proportion. **2.** *Not more than a fraction of the members attended:* small part, bit, few; particle, fragment, trifle, morsel; shaving, cutting, chip; scrap, crumb.

fractional *adj.* *There were only fractional returns from the election:* part, partial, fragmentary, incomplete, parcelled, piecemeal, sectional, segmented, apportioned.

fractious *adj.* *Don't be fractious when I ask you*

to do something: cross, irritable, peevish, ill-tempered, grouchy, snappish, fretful, querulous, irascible; touchy, huffy, shirty, waspish, petulant, shrewish, pettish; quarrelsome, unruly, refractory, rebellious, wayward, perverse, contrary, disputatious; recalcitrant, willful, unmanageable. **—Ant.** complaisant, amiable, good-humored, genial, agreeable, good-natured.

fracture *n.* **1.** *When she fell, she suffered a fracture of her wrist:* break, severance, rupture, cleavage; breach, separation, division; split, rift, fault, crack. **—v. 2.** *A serious misunderstanding fractured their friendship:* break, crack, split, sever, shatter; disrupt, breach, rend, cleave.

fragile *adj.* **1.** *These wine glasses are much too fragile for every day:* easily broken, frangible, breakable; delicate, dainty, flimsy, brittle, shivery, splintery; crumbly, friable, crisp; ephemeral, evanescent. **2.** *She has been in fragile health all winter:* frail, infirm, delicate, feeble, weak, slight, decrepit; tender, soft; flimsy, rickety, sleazy, dilapidated, tumbledown, unsubstantial. **—Ant.** tough, strong, stout, sturdy; elastic, resilient, flexible; hardy, tenacious; durable, lasting.

fragment *n.* **1.** *The archaeologists examined the fragments of ancient pottery:* part broken off, piece, segment, section, remnant, fraction, portion; chip, shard, bit, snip, morsel, crumb, shred, scrap; trace, vestige, survival. **—v. 2.** *The Nazi tactic was first to fragment the opposition:* disunite, break apart, break up, splinter, shatter; divide, separate; chop up, cut up; crumble, chip, disintegrate. **—Ant.** 2 unite, bring together, combine.

fragmentary *adj.* *He could give us only a fragmentary account of the meeting:* incomplete, unfinished, scrappy, piecemeal, disconnected; choppy, broken, segmented, disjointed, fractional, detached, not entire, scattered.

fragrance *n.* *Do you remember the fragrance of lilacs after a rain?:* fragrant odor, perfume, scent, aroma; bouquet, sweetness, aura, redolence, incense, balm. **—Ant.** stench, stink, effluvium, miasma, offensive odor.

fragrant *adj.* *The cake baking in the oven made the whole house fragrant:* sweet-scented, sweet-smelling, redolent, odorous, odoriferous, aromatic, perfumed; balmy, spicy. **—Ant.** fetid, malodorous, stinking.

frail *adj.* **1.** *The climber dangled in midair, held by one frail rope:* easily broken or destroyed, fragile, frangible, brittle, breakable, shivery, splintery, crumbly; rickety, dilapidated; sleazy, flimsy, unsubstantial, puny; perishable, delicate; vulnerable, fallible. **2.** *Her health has been frail for months:* slight, weak, delicate, feeble, not robust, fragile, weakly; infirm, decrepit. **—Ant.** 1 strong, stout, sturdy, stalwart, tough. 2 healthy, sound, hale, robust, vigorous.

frailty *n.* *A liking for flattery was one of his frailties:* weakness of character, moral weakness, fault, sin, vice, failing, defect, blemish, flaw, weak point, fallibility, imperfection, weak side, foible, susceptibility. **—Ant.** strength, virtue.

frame *n.* **1.** *Wouldn't this picture look better in a black frame?:* mounting, case, housing; border, setting, backing, edging, rim. **2.** *The wooden frame of the house is already in place:* framework, skeleton, structure, form, framing, scaffolding, casing, mold, body, chassis. **3.** *John is a man of large frame:* physique, build, figure, shape, anatomy; system, scheme, constitution, make, construction; cast; outline, contour, set. **4.** *A good dinner always puts him in a pleasing frame of mind:* attitude, state, mood, humor, nature, temperament, disposition, temper. —*v.* **5.** *A new set of bylaws was framed by the board members:* devise, conceive, contrive, invent, plan; draft, sketch, indite; concoct, scheme, hatch; formulate, map out, design; organize, systematize. **6.** *He says he was framed by his ex-wife:* incriminate unjustly, give false evidence against, *Slang* set up.

framework *n.* *They decided on a framework for the project:* bare frame, core, foundation, groundwork, plan, schema, scheme, shell, skeleton, structure, bones.

franchise *n.* **1.** *At first, the franchise was restricted to male property owners aged 21 or over:* right to vote, voting power, ballot, suffrage, enfranchisement. **2.** *Railroads competed for the franchise to expand track to the new territory:* right, privilege, authorization, license, permission, official sanction; grant, charter; prerogative; freedom, immunity.

frank *adj.* *She decided to be frank in rejecting his proposal:* candid, plain-spoken, direct, outspoken, straightforward, free, downright, forthright, straight from the shoulder, *Informal* upfront; bold, round, plain, unreserved, sincere, open, genuine, natural, honest, openhearted, aboveboard; ingenuous, artless; undisguised, transparent, evident, clear, apparent, unmistakable, unambiguous, unequivocal; manifest, distinct, patent, explicit. —**Ant.** reticent, evasive, indirect, reserved, close, covert, secretive; dissembling, underhand, crafty, disingenuous.

frankly *adv.* *She spoke frankly for the first time:* candidly, without reserve, directly, freely, honestly, in truth, openly, plainly, bluntly.

frantic *adj.* *There was a lot of frantic activity just before the royal visitors arrived:* excited, agitated, hectic; frenzied, frenetic, distracted, overwrought, beside oneself, distraught, nerv-ous; raging, impassioned, rabid, raving, furious, infuriated; wild, violent, ungovernable; crazy, mad, insane, deranged, delirious, berserk. —**Ant.** calm, collected, cool, unruffled, composed.

fraternal *adj.* *There was always a lot of fraternal affection between the boys:* brotherly, kindred, friendly, amicable, social; hearty, warmhearted; loving, devoted, affectionate; related, consanguineous. —**Ant.** hostile, antipathetic, inimical.

fraternity *n.* **1.** *One of the writer's favorite themes is the fraternity of mankind:* brotherliness, brotherhood, brotherly relation, kinship, interrelation; consanguinity, ties of blood, blood connection; propinquity. **2.** *Nowadays there are fewer fraternities on college campuses:* club, society, circle; league, alliance, federation, confed-

eracy, coalition, united body; clique, coterie, clan, brotherhood; company, union, association.

fraternize *v.* *Soldiers were forbidden to fraternize with local citizens:* mingle, keep company, associate, socialize, mix, hobnob, consort, band together, cooperate, combine, unite, coalesce, *Slang* hang around, pal around; confederate; sympathize, harmonize, concur. —**Ant.** shun, avoid, keep away from.

fraud *n.* **1.** *He was charged with fraud for selling deeds to nonexistent land:* fraudulence, swindling, cheating, trickery, deceit, deception, dishonesty, misrepresentation, sharp practice, duplicity, guile, cozenage, double-dealing, chicanery, treachery, *Slang* monkey business, hype; craft, artifice, subterfuge, dissimulation, machination, imposture, stratagem; sham, hoax, ruse, trick, swindle, humbug. **2.** *As an actress, she's an absolute fraud:* impostor, charlatan, mountebank, sham, fake, counterfeit, pretender; knave, rascal, rogue; quack, swindler, cheat, fourflusher, con artist. —**Ant.** 1 fairness, good faith, honesty, integrity.

fraudulent *adj.* *Fraudulent business practices, such as shortchanging customers, are against the law:* deceitful, dishonest, deceptive, treacherous, underhanded, guileful, crafty, wily, tricky, unprincipled, dishonorable, cunning, knavish; crooked, cheating; spurious, sham, bogus, false, counterfeit.

fraught *adj.* *The expedition was fraught with danger:* filled, full, laden, charged, abounding, loaded, teeming, replete, pregnant, heavy; attended, accompanied. —**Ant.** devoid, lacking, wanting, empty.

fray[1] *n.* **1.** *Several vice presidents were involved in the fray:* quarrel, fight, dispute, disagreement, tiff, spat, controversy, squabble, bickering, fuss, set-to, altercation, contention, dissension; fracas, commotion, tussle, rumpus, scuffle; wrangle, brawl, riot, melee, tumult, *Slang* rumble. **2.** *The fray intensified when fresh troops arrived:* battle, conflict, contest, fight, combat, warfare; affray, skirmish, engagement.

fray[2] *v.* *Look how the cuffs on this shirt have frayed!:* ravel, frazzle, tatter, wear out, become threadbare; strain, chafe, fret, rub.

freak *n.* **1.** *P.T. Barnum made a fortune exhibiting freaks:* monstrosity, monster, oddity, curiosity, deviation, aberration, mutation, abnormality, marvel, wonder; abnormal organism, sport, freak of nature. **2.** *All this rain is a freak of the weather:* twist, quirk, vagary, irregularity, anomaly; kink, whim, caprice, crotchet, turn; fancy, humor, whimsy; craze, fad. —*adj.* **3.** *The cars were involved in a freak accident:* odd, strange, queer, unusual, erratic, freaky, freakish, peculiar, bizarre.

free *adj.* **1.** *Most of the former French colonies in Africa are now free nations:* self-governing, autonomous, self-directing, independent. **2.** *The Russian serfs and American slaves became free at about the same time:* emancipated, freed, liberated, enfranchised, at liberty, manumitted, delivered, released; unshackled, unfettered, unbound, unconfined, unconstrained, unbridled, unhampered, unmuzzled, unrestrained; bond-less, unchained, unattached; fancy-free, uncom-mitted, footloose. **3.** *Not very many imports are free of all duty. Her nature is free of jealousy:* exempted from, exempt from, not liable to, im-mune to, excused from, released from, ab-solved of; unaffected by, devoid of, lacking in. **4.** *You are free to go now:* allowed, permitted, able, at liberty. **5.** *A free dish is given with each $10 order:* complimentary, without cost, gratis, for nothing, on the house, costless, gratuitous, chargeless. **6.** *Tie a knot in the free end of the rope:* loose, unattached; not in use, spare, ex-tra; idle, unoccupied, available. **7.** *Sometimes his free manner seems merely rude:* open, abandoned, uninhibited, unrepressed, unre-strained, uncontrolled, familiar, informal, easy, expansive, unceremonious; forward, unreserved, bold, audacious, overfamiliar, daring; confident, assured, fearless; lax, careless; licentious, wan-ton, dissolute. **8.** *Very few people are free with their money:* generous, freehanded, liberal, openhanded, giving, lavish, prodigal, bounte-ous, big, big-hearted, handsome, bountiful, munifi-cent. **9.** *The halls should be kept free of furniture:* clear, devoid, not littered, unob-structed, uncluttered, unencumbered, unim-peded, unblocked, unclogged. **—adv. 10.** *The barn door was swinging free in the high wind:* without restriction, freely, loosely; leisurely, idly, carelessly. **11.** *The first 100 customers will be admitted free:* without charge, at no cost, gratis. **—v. 12.** *The enemy freed 12 of the prisoners:* set free, liberate, make free, set at liberty, re-lease, let loose, let go, emancipate, manumit, enfranchise, exempt; parole, discharge; redeem, save, ransom; unchain, uncage, unleash, un-shackle, unfasten. **13.** *He hoped to free his people from hunger:* release, disengage, extri-cate, rid of. **—Ant.** 1 occupied, dependent. 2 subservient. 6 bound, engaged, busy, preoccu-pied. 7 reserved, restrained, restricted. 8 stingy, niggardly, close. 9 clogged, obstructed, clut-tered. 12 imprison, jail, intern, incarcerate, con-fine, restrain, inhibit, restrict, limit.

freedom *n.* **1.** *The little country will gain its freedom next year:* political independence, au-tonomy, self-determination, sovereignty, self-government; civil liberty, enfranchisement, emancipation, manumission; liberation, release, exemption from control. **2.** *I like this jacket be-cause it gives me more freedom:* ease of move-ment, elbow room; latitude, scope, sweep, mar-gin, range, play, swing; unrestricted use, wide berth. **3.** *Alone at last, they could now speak with freedom of their love:* openness, frankness, unrestraint, abandon, abandonment, absence of reserve, unreservedness, candor, unconstraint; informality, naturalness; bluntness, directness, forwardness, downrightness. **4.** *The teacher re-sented the freedom with which the student ad-dressed her:* boldness, impudence, license, dis-respect, rudeness, impertinence; impropriety, indecorum. **—Ant.** 1 dependence, restriction; bondage, servitude, slavery, serfdom; imprison-

ment, captivity. 3 restraint, caution, reluctance, respectfulness, decorum.

free-for-all *n. The argument at the bar ended in a free-for-all:* brawl, fight, affray, fray, melee, fracas, wrangle, ruckus, ruction, row, scrap, donnybrook, brannigan, *Slang* rhubarb, rough-and-tumble, knock-down-and-drag-out, tussle.

freely *adv.* **1.** *Everyone can move freely here:* spontaneously, at will, openly, voluntarily, frankly, openly, plainly, spontaneously, unre-servedly, willingly, without urging, without prompting, candidly *Informal* fancy-free. **2.** ef-fortlessly, amply, bountifully, copiously, extrava-gantly, lavishly, liberally, readily, lightly, smoothly, unhindered, well, cleanly, effortlessly, easily.

freeze *v.* **1.** *Salt water freezes at a lower tem-perature than fresh water:* become solid, solid-ify, turn to ice, harden; chill, cool, refrigerate; glaciate, congeal; frost. **2.** *I can't skate any more, I'm frozen:* benumb, chill, stiffen with cold; nip, bite, sting, pierce; anesthetize. **3.** *When we heard the scream, we froze in our tracks:* become immobile, become paralyzed, stop; halt, arrest; chill with fear, terrify. **—n. 4.** *The weatherman is predicting a freeze for to-night:* frost, chill, below-freezing temperature. **5.** *I was due for a raise when they put a freeze on wages:* lawful control, ceiling, restriction.

freezing *adj. The freezing temperature called out for warm clothing:* arctic, glacial, chill, chilled, chilly, cold, glacial, polar, biting, bitter, cutting, frigid, frost-bound, frosty, gelid, icy, nippy, numbing, penetrating, wintry, raw, shiv-ery, Siberian.

freight *n.* **1.** *Nowadays the railways earn most of their profit from freight:* transportation of goods, shipment of merchandise, truckage, cart-age, portage, conveyance, transshipment. **2.** *Timber-hauling trucks can carry many tons of freight:* goods, lading, cargo, load, charge, bur-den; luggage, baggage. **—v. 3.** *The ship was freighted with machinery and grain:* load, lade, charge, burden; weigh down. **4.** *Freighting mer-handise is less expensive than mailing it:* send by freight, transport, ship, convey, transmit; carry, haul.

frenetic *adj. They embarked on a frenetic dance:* frenzied, delirious, demented, insane, mad, distraught, excited, obsessive, fanatical, frantic, maniacal, rabid.

frenzied *adj. The frenzied crowd began to throw rotten fruit:* feverish, berserk, frantic, fre-netic, delirious, convulsive, distracted, dis-traught, excited, mad, maniacal, hysterical.

frenzy *n.* **1.** *The baboon shook the bars of its cage in a frenzy of rage:* fit, seizure, transport, outburst, access, furor, delirium; madness, fury, distraction, hysteria; obsession, craze, mania. **2.** *She was in a frenzy because fifteen people were coming to dinner:* mental agitation, turmoil, state; mad rush, great haste. **—Ant.** 2 calm, composure, collectedness, coolness, equanim-ity; sobriety, sanity, judgment.

frequency *n. He uses slang words with great frequency. The newsletter comes out at a fre-*

quency of about once a month: frequent occurrence, regularity, repetition, recurrence, reiteration, iteration, persistence.

frequent *adj.* **1.** *We take frequent walks through the park:* occurring often, oft-repeated, at short intervals, numerous; continual, recurrent, habitual, reiterative; incessant, perpetual. **2.** *During the summer we were frequent guests in their home:* regular, constant, habitual; daily, everyday; ordinary, common, familiar; wonted, customary; usual, accustomed. —*v.* **3.** *On Sundays we frequent the art galleries:* haunt, go to frequently, attend regularly, go often to, resort to, visit repeatedly, be seen at regularly, *Slang* hang out at, hang around in. —**Ant.** 1 rare, occasional; few, scanty. 3 shun, avoid, eschew, steer clear of, keep away from, spurn.

frequently *adv.* *Thelma and I frequently have dinner together:* often, ofttimes, many times, repeatedly; recurrently, constantly, continually, incessantly, perpetually, over and over again; usually, habitually, customarily, generally, ordinarily. —**Ant.** rarely, seldom, hardly ever, infrequently.

fresh *adj.* **1.** *They have fresh bread every morning at the bakery:* newly made, not stale, recent; well-preserved, unfaded, unspoiled, in good condition, unwithered, unwilted, not deteriorated, undecayed; *(variously)* green, hot, sweet; unworn, unused; undimmed, untarnished. **2.** *There is a lot of fresh material in his new play:* new, original, creative, inventive, not used before, novel, brand-new; unusual, unfamiliar, untried, unaccustomed; rare, strange, unique; modern, modernistic, new-fashioned, newfangled; recent, late, just out, up-to-date. **3.** *It was so good to taste fresh meat and fresh water again:* not salted, unsalted; not preserved, unpickled, unsmoked, undried, uncured. **4.** *She was still fresh after working all day:* fit, alert, keen, lively, ready, active, energetic, unworn, not fatigued, unwearied; refreshed, freshened, rested, invigorated; unimpaired, unabated. **5.** *Ever notice what fresh complexions English girls have?:* wholesome, clear, youthful-looking; rosy, ruddy; blooming, gleaming, sparkling, glowing; fair, bright, flourishing. **6.** *Open the window and let in a little fresh air:* pure, refreshing, cool; chill, nipping, bracing, stinging, cutting, biting; stiff, brisk, keen. **7.** *She was sent to her room for being fresh:* impudent, rude, cheeky, pert, saucy, sassy, brazen, insolent, *Slang* snotty; forward, presumptuous, smart-alecky, flippant, nervy; bold, brassy, assuming; obtrusive, meddlesome. —**Ant.** 1 stale, old. 2 trite, ordinary, hackneyed, stereotyped, shopworn; secondhand. 3 salted, preserved, canned. 4 weary, fatigued, exhausted; dull. 5 sickly, wan, pallid, faded. 6 stale, impure, polluted, musty. 7 sweet, amiable, charming, well-mannered, courteous, respectful.

freshen *v.* *The light rain freshened the garden:* invigorate, sweeten, air, refresh, cleanse, purify, restore, revitalize, spruce up, revive, ventilate, enliven, rouse.

freshness *n.* *The prize-winning books had a freshness about them:* newness, novelty, bloom, brightness, cleanness, glow, dew, dewiness, greenness, originality, shine, sparkle, vigor, youth, clearness.

fret *v.* **1.** *Fretting about the problem won't help a bit:* worry, brood, agonize, fume, stew, chafe; be peevish, be angry, be vexed, be irritated, be fretful; mope, lament, pout, pine, sulk; distress, gall, vex, ruffle, irritate. **2.** *Constant use had fretted the sandal strap to the breaking point:* wear away, abrade, erode, corrode, rub, irritate, excoriate, gnaw, eat; tatter, fray. —*n.* **3.** *When she spoke, her fret was apparent to all of us:* vexation, annoyance, displeasure, irritation, peevishness, fretfulness; disquiet, discomposure, fidgets, sulks.

fretful *adj.* *He's always fretful when the morning paper doesn't arrive:* peevish, irritable, touchy, cranky, grouchy, crotchety, sulky, cross, ill-natured, ill-tempered, pettish, querulous, complaining, contrary, petulant, waspish, snappish, *Brit.* shirty, huffy. —**Ant.** good-natured, cheerful, easygoing, agreeable, congenial; patient, forbearing.

friction *n.* **1.** *Friction with the air causes damage to planes flying at high speeds:* rubbing, abrasion, grating, fretting, chafing; attrition; resistance, counteraction. **2.** *Reporters capitalized on the friction between the two delegates:* conflict, opposition, discord, dissidence, disagreement, clash of opinion, dissension, antagonism, animosity, hostility, resentment, bad feeling, bad blood; strife, quarrel, contention.

friend *n.* **1.** *A friend and I hitchhiked through Europe last summer:* acquaintance, comrade, companion, chum, confidant; partner, buddy, pal, amigo, sidekick, crony, mate; playmate, cohort, playfellow; consort; bedfellow, intimate, soul mate, *French* intime; boyfriend, girl friend, escort, beau, date; lover, mistress, favorite, paramour. **2.** *There was a special performance for friends of the orchestra:* patron, supporter, backer, benefactor; well-wisher, encourager; advocate, defender, partisan, adherent. **3.** *Can we count on our friends to support the legislation?:* ally, colleague, fellow, associate; copartner, partner, co-worker; confrere, brother, follower, retainer, minion; henchman, myrmidon. —**Ant.** 1 foe, enemy. 2 antagonist, opponent, adversary. 3 rival, competitor.

friendless *adj.* *The friendless woman joined several associations:* ostracized, shunned, abandoned, all alone, alone, deserted, estranged, forlorn, forsaken, isolated, lonely, lonesome, solitary.

friendliness *n.* *The neighbourhood was marked by friendliness:* affability, geniality, neighborliness, sociability, amiability, amity, benevolence, companionability, congeniality, conviviality, cordiality, kindliness, kindness, warmth, goodwill.

friendly *adj.* **1.** *He said he was giving me a friendly warning:* kindly, kind, helpful, well-disposed; amiable, neighborly, amicable; loving, familiar, affectionate, kindhearted, cordial, genial, warmhearted; ardent, devoted, intimate; sympathetic, gracious, generous, chummy, companionable, clubby, convivial. **2.** *Several* *friendly nations came to the conference:* allied, not hostile, on good terms, being friends, fraternal, brotherly; hospitable, social, accessible, affable. **3.** *A friendly tailwind helped the boat across the finish line:* favorable, helpful, auspicious, propitious, salutary, advantageous, beneficial, benign, fortunate, oportune. **—Ant.** 2 belligerent, hostile, contentious. 3 unfavorable, sinister, inauspicious.

friendship *n.* **1.** *John and I have maintained our friendship for thirty years:* acquaintanceship, fellowship, association as friends, relationship of friends, companionship, comradeship, brotherhood, friendly relations, fraternity; close tie, intimacy, familiarity. **2.** *The two nations signed a treaty of perpetual friendship:* good feeling, friendliness, harmony, accord, concord, amity, comity, amicableness, consonance, understanding, sympathy, good fellowship, cordiality, neighborliness, goodwill. **—Ant.** 1 enmity, animosity, hostility, antipathy, antagonism. 2 strife, conflict, combat.

fright *n.* *The child turned and ran in fright from the growling dog:* fear, alarm, terror, panic, fear of danger, consternation; scare, perturbation; dread, apprehension, dismay, trepidation; affright, horror; concern, anxiety, misgiving; cold feet, funk; fear and trembling, the jitters, intimidation, reign of terror, disquietude, *Slang* the creeps, the willies; quaking, tremor, flutter, quivering, palpitation. **—Ant.** bravery, boldness, courage, fortitude, stoutheartedness.

frighten *v.* *He jumped out of the closet and frightened the daylights out of me:* alarm, scare, make afraid, throw into a fright, terrify, terrorize, shock, horrify, disturb with fear, petrify, affright, frighten, startle; *Archaic* affray; intimidate, daunt; excite, agitate, disquiet. **—Ant.** calm, soothe, comfort, reassure.

frightened *adj.* *Any number of things frightened him:* alarmed, unnerved, cowed, petrified, scared, shaky, shivery, startled, terrified, terrorized, terror-stricken, spooked, jittery, jumpy.

frightful *adj.* **1.** *As the full moon rose, frightful howls pierced the air about the cemetery:* horrible, horrendous, horrid, terrible, awful, fearful, shocking, appalling, dreadful, alarming; terrific, horrific, fearsome; lurid, grisly, ghastly, macabre, gruesome, sinister, baleful. **2.** *The most frightful dog came bounding out at us:* offensive, loathsome, nasty, insufferable, hideous, disgusting, detestable; revolting, repulsive, repellent, abominable; monstrous, freakish, ogreish. **3.** *Informal She really is a frightful snob:* very great, terrific, terrible, extreme, awful, dreadful, insufferable. **—Ant.** 1 calming, soothing. 2 beautiful, attractive. 3 slight, partial, moderate.

frigid *adj.* **1.** *With the furnace out of order the house was frigid:* cold, freezing cold, bitter cold, freezing, icy; gelid, glacial; cool, chilly; bleak, raw, bitter, nipping, piercing, biting, cutting. **2.** *She seemed polite enough, but her manner was distinctly frigid:* stiff, unresponsive, distant, forbidding, aloof; prim, formal, rigid, austere, frosty, cold, cool, chilly, icy, straitlaced. **—Ant.**

1 hot, burning, sweltering, stifling. 2 cordial, friendly, warm, hospitable; ardent, passionate, impassioned.

frill *n.* **1.** *She liked to add little frills to her aprons and nighties:* ruffle, gathering, flounce, fringe, edging, furbelow. **2.** *Why can't she just serve dinner without all those silly frills?:* ornament, decoration, added touch, frippery, embellishment; affectation, superfluity, falderal; air, mannerism.

fringe *n.* **1.** *How would this shawl look with a six-inch fringe?:* edging, trimming, ornamental bordering, border, tassel, skirting, hem, margin, selvage; mane; edge, periphery, limit, frontier. *—v.* **2.** *A ring of grass fringed the pool:* border, edge, skirt; surround, rim, outline, enclose; decorate, embellish.

frisk *v.* **1.** *George was frisking about on the lawn with the dogs:* romp, frolic, caper, gambol, cavort, lark, prance, dance, bound, bounce, cut capers; disport, cut up, trip, sport, jump about; skip, leap, jump, spring, hop. **2.** *The Mounties frisked the two suspects at the roadblock:* search, examine, inspect; check quickly, look over; ransack, rummage through.

frisky *adj.* *That pony may be too frisky for the children:* lively, animated, spirited, agile, vivacious, nimble, light-heeled, active; spry, sportive, playful, frolicsome, in high spirits, peppy, rollicking; waggish, prankish, mirthful, jocular; *Informal* feeling one's oats. **—Ant.** demure, sedate; pensive, meditative; stodgy, stolid.

fritter *v.* *Before he was 30 he had frittered away his inheritance:* squander, waste, spend foolishly, use up, dissipate, deplete, run through, frivol away, trifle away, fool away, *Slang* blow, dribble away, diddle away, idle away, fribble away. **—Ant.** conserve, save, skimp, economize, budget.

frivolity *n.* *While their money lasted, they wined and dined with gay frivolity:* giddiness, flightiness, levity, lightness, emptiness, folly; triviality, frippery, fickleness, flippancy, airiness; wantonness, thoughtlessness, abandon; dallying, play, whimsy, sport, jest, fun. **—Ant.** seriousness, staidness, sedateness; gravity, solemnity; soberness, earnestness.

frivolous *adj.* **1.** *Once a year she bought something frivolous just to please herself:* impractical, trifling, trivial, worthless, imprudent, improvident, ill-considered, unimportant, insignificant, pointless, silly, petty, paltry; slight, piddling, flimsy, niggling, minor; empty, airy, light, frothy, light-headed, flighty, careless; vain, self-indulgent, extravagant. **2.** *Why would she marry such a frivolous young man?:* flighty, superficial, unserious, silly, harebrained, light-minded; flippant, insouciant; rattlebrained, dizzy, shallowbrained; careless, heedless; foolish, senseless, fatuous; brainless, barmy, witless, stupid, inane, silly, nonsensical. **—Ant.** 1 important, vital. 2 mature, adult; sensible, serious, earnest; intense, grave, solemn.

frock *n.* **1.** *It's just a little frock that my seamstress made:* dress, gown, suit, coat, cloak, robe, smock, blouse. **2.** *The monks wore frocks* *of coarse homespun:* clerical garb, canonicals, clericals, vestment, monk's robe; cassock, soutane, surplice, chasuble.

frolic *n.* **1.** *The clowns were full of frolic:* fun, gaiety, merriment, merrymaking, mirth, recreation, amusement; sport, play, festivity, entertainment; tomfoolery, buffoonery; jollity, joviality, pleasantry; antic, gambol, spree, romp, caper, lark, escapade, skylarking, prank. —*v.* **2.** *Children and dogs were frolicking on the lawn:* romp, frisk, skip, caper, gambol, cavort, sport, disport, play merrily, amuse oneself, make merry; cut capers, act up, play pranks; *Informal* have a ball, live it up, make hay.

frolicsome *adj.* *The spring air made the ponies frolicsome:* playful, coltish, frisky, antic, gleeful, impish, jocular, kittenish, lively, merry, mischievous, roguish, rollicking, sportive.

front *n.* **1.** *The front of the house faces the street:* face, forward part; façade, frontage. **2.** *The soldiers were shpped to the front as replacements:* head, lead, top, beginning; fore; advanced guard, trenches, front rank, vanguard, front lines. **3.** *She maintained a calm front throughout the ordeal:* external appearance, semblance, demeanor, carriage, mien, air, bearing, presence; mask, pretense, façade. —*adj.* **4.** *We sat in the front row:* located in front, fore, anterior; first, beginning, initial. —*v.* **5.** *The clubhouse fronts on the lake:* face, look out, look forward, stand opposite to, give on, regard. —**Ant.** 1, 2, 4 back, rear.

frontier *n.* **1.** *Soldiers guard the frontier against invasions:* border, boundary, boundary line; limits, verge, edge, perimeter, extreme, confines; march. **2.** *Families are being encouraged to settle the frontier:* outlying area, remote districts, hinterland, far country, backlands, backwoods, outskirts, outposts; territories; marches. —**Ant.** interior, settled region.

frost *n.* **1.** *We may have a frost tonight, so cover the tomato plants:* below-freezing weather, cold spell, chill; frozen moisture, covering of ice, ice crystals; hoarfrost, rime. **2.** *Did you detect a slight frost in her reply?:* frigidity, iciness, chill, chilliness, coldness of manner, glaciality; unfriendliness, aloofness, distance, want of cordiality, inhospitality, coolness.

frosty *adj.* *We skied that frosty afternoon:* icicled, icy, chill, chilly, frigid, cold, frozen, gelid, shivery, glacial, wintry, nippy.

froth *n.* **1.** *Wind whipped the waves into a green froth:* foam, spume, scum, head, fume, fizz, bubbles; lather, suds, yeast; whitecap, surf. **2.** *Critics dismissed the play as a bit of froth:* trivia, frippery, trumpery, flummery, frivolity, triviality, nonsense; *Informal* bosh, fiddle-faddle, balderdash; trash, rubbish.

frothy *adj.* *The drink was mild and frothy:* foaming, foamy, fizzing, fizzy, sudsy, bubbly.

frown *v.* **1.** *When she frowns, you know she's very angry:* wrinkle the forehead, scowl, knit the brow, glower, look displeased, glare, look stern; mope, sulk, pout, fret; ponder, muse. **2.** *Many people frown on that kind of behavior:* disapprove of, view with disfavor, look disapprovingly on, take a dim view of, discountenance, look askance at; show disapproval of, show displeasure at, look down on. —*n.* **3.** *With a frown he examined his son's report card:* frowning look, scowl, glower, black look, glare. —**Ant.** 1 smile, show pleasure, express satisfaction, show kindliness. 2 approve, support, advocate, foster, cherish; favor, countenance.

frozen *adj.* **1.** *The ship remained frozen in the ice fields for months. Keep the meat frozen until you are ready to cook it:* icebound, obstructed, clogged, immobilized; stymied, stalemated; refrigerated, chilled, cooled, iced, gelid, solidified by cold. **2.** *When my toes feel frozen, I know it's time to go inside:* benumbed, numb, cold; chill, chilly; gelid, icy, glacial; frostbitten; wintry, hibernal; arctic, polar. —**Ant.** 1 thawed, melted. 2 warm, hot; torrid.

frugal *adj.* **1.** *The frugal Scotsman never takes a cab when he can walk:* economical, thrifty, unwasteful, prudent with money, sparing, economy-minded, penny-wise; parsimonious, tight, penny-pinching, stingy, niggardly; ascetic, abstemious. **2.** *It was a frugal dinner, but very nourishing:* scant, not abundant, slim, sparing, skimpy. —**Ant.** 1 extravagant, wasteful, imprudent, spendthrift. 2 luxurious, lavish, profuse.

frugality *n.* *In middle age he was known for extreme frugality:* carefulness, economizing, conservation, moderation, economy, prudence, scrimping, saving, thrift, stinginess, miserliness, avariciousness, parsimony.

fruit *n.* **1.** *The Thanksgiving table was laden with all the fruits of the earth:* produce, product, crop, yield, production, harvest; young, offspring, progeny, issue. **2.** *I hope the old man lives to enjoy the fruits of his labor:* result, product, consequence, outgrowth, upshot, issue, effect, outcome; return, profit, benefit, advantage; revenue, remuneration, emolument, earnings; award, reward.

fruitful *adj.* **1.** *Cherry trees here in the city are seldom fruitful:* productive, fecund, prolific, fructiferous; blooming, yielding, fertile, abounding in fruit; fruit-bearing. **2.** *The anonymous tip proved fruitful, and the suspect was captured:* profitable, productive, advantageous, effective, successful, efficacious. —**Ant.** 1 unfruitful, barren, sterile, infertile, unproductive. 2 fruitless, pointless, useless, vain, futile, abortive, ineffectual; scarce, scanty.

fruition *n.* *The plan should reach fruition in another year:* fulfillment, achievement, realization, attainment; satisfaction, gratification, actualization, materialization, consummation; maturity, ripeness.

fruitless *adj.* **1.** *Further investigations proved fruitless:* unfruitful, pointless, purposeless, useless, bootless, unsuccessful, unavailing, empty, hollow, vain, futile; ineffective, ineffectual, inefficacious; unrewarding, unprofitable, profitless, nugatory; worthless; abortive, inoperative; inept, incompetent. **2.** *Why did we ever move to this fruitless land?:* unfruitful, barren, infertile, arid, sterile; unproductive, unprolific. —**Ant.** 1 useful, profitable, rewarding, fruitful; effective, worthwhile, productive. 2 fertile, fecund; abundant, prolific, fructiferous.

frustrate v. **1.** *Steady rains frustrated our efforts to put in a garden:* hinder, defeat, thwart, baffle, foil, circumvent, prohibit, inhibit, bring to naught, nullify, cancel, make of no avail, render invalid, make null and void, check, impede, block, bar; suppress; undermine, cut the ground from under; forestall, balk, obstruct, prevent, counter. **2.** *Giving the child problems he can't solve will only frustrate him:* discourage, fluster, upset, dispirit, disappoint, disconcert, dishearten; cripple, hamstring, clip the wings of. **—Ant.** 1 foster, promote, further, forward, advance; incite, instigate, abet, foment. 2 encourage, hearten, cheer; satisfy, gratify.

frustrated adj. *She was frustrated at being denied entrance:* foiled, irked, balked, checkmated, stymied, thwarted, crabbed, cramped, defeated, flummoxed, resentful.

frustration n. *Without public support our efforts ended in frustration:* defeat, failure, futility, nonsuccess, nonfulfillment, foiling, thwarting, hindrance, balking, inhibition, interference, bafflement; contravention, counteraction, obstruction; disappointment, dissatisfaction, letdown, chagrin, discomfiture.

fry v. *I always fry potatoes in hot fat with a bit of onion:* cook, sauté, brown, grill, frizzle, fricassee; pan-fry, French fry, deep fry.

fudge v. *He fudged his statement to the press:* fake, pad, slant, falsify, hedge, equivocate, evade, color, cook up, embellish, embroider, exaggerate, magnify, overstate, misrepresent.

fuel n. **1.** *Factories have been urged to switch from coal to a cleaner fuel:* combustible material; (*variously*) wood, coal, oil, natural gas; gas, gasoline, petroleum. **2.** *The newspaper article provided him with fuel for his speech:* material, fodder, ammunition, inspiration; sustenance, means, wherewithal, impetus, motivation, stimulus. **—v. 3.** *We have to fuel the furnace once a day:* provide with fuel, replenish with fuel, fill up, charge, recharge, stoke, kindle, fire, ignite, light, feed; activate, energize, stimulate, incite, fan, inflame; sustain.

fugitive n. **1.** *The fugitive was wanted by police in several countries:* runaway, deserter, outlaw; refugee, escapee; exile, expatriate; renegade, apostate; rover, wanderer, itinerant, straggler; vagrant, vagabond, nomad; tramp, loafer, hobo. **—adj. 2.** *Fugitive slaves sometimes escaped into Canada:* escaping, escaped, fleeing, running away, flying. **3.** *Poetic The fugitive hours were gone and would not return:* fleeting, short-lived, transitory, evanescent, transient, fugacious, ephemeral; brief, momentary, passing, impermanent; unstable, errant, erratic, elusive, volatile, flitting, uncertain; hurried, hasty, cursory, summary; short, temporary; fading, shifting. **—Ant.** 3 lasting, permanent, durable; changeless, immutable; endless, eternal.

fulfill v. **1.** *The dream of a world without war is yet to be fulfilled:* carry out, accomplish, achieve, realize, effect, implement, effectuate, bring to pass, bring about; establish, execute, consummate; perfect, bring to perfection. **2.** *Don't be lax about fulfilling your obligations:* obey, perform, do, abide by, keep, discharge, comply with, adhere to, be faithful to, live up to; keep faith with; redeem; observe, follow, heed. **3.** *The thesis will fulfill the requirements for your M.A.:* satisfy, suit, meet, fill out, make good, answer. **—Ant.** 1 neglect, ignore, slight, overlook, disregard; fail in. 3 fall short of, fail to meet; disappoint, dissatisfy.

fulfilled adj. *She was fulfilled in her job:* realized, satisfied, successful, happy, pleased; completed, concluded, consummated, accomplished, crowned, achieved, actualized, effected, attained, executed, matured, perfected, obtained, performed, reached. **—Ant.** 0 disappointed, dissatisfied; failed, neglected.

fulfillment or **fulfilment** n. **1.** *The little house in the country was the fulfillment of her dreams:* realization, accomplishment, effectuation, implementation, attainment, achievement; execution, establishment, completion, crowning, pinnacle, culmination; finishing touch. **2.** *What fulfillment could there ever be in a typing job?:* satisfaction, contentment, gratification; pleasure, delight, happiness, contentedness.

full adj. **1.** *Add a full cup of chopped nuts. The child is full of energy:* filled, heaping, brimming, brimful, flush; replete, abounding, fraught, crammed, bursting, packed, laden, loaded, chock-full; teeming, swarming, saturated; filled up, well-supplied, well-stocked; sated, surfeited, stuffed, gorged, glutted. **2.** *Do you have a full supply of firewood?:* complete, entire, whole, thorough, maximum, total; intact, unabridged, plenary; mature, perfect, up to the mark. **3.** *The dress has a full skirt:* ample, capacious, wide, broad, voluminous; comprehensive, all-inclusive; large, big; round, rotund, shapely, plump; rich, resonant. **—adv. 4.** *He knew full well what I was trying to say:* very, quite, perfectly; exactly, precisely. **—Ant.** 1 empty, void; vacant, devoid, blank, exhausted. 2 partial, incomplete, qualified; altered, abridged. 3 tight, restricted; limited, exclusive; thin, meager, angular, faint.

full-bodied adj. *We agreed that the beer was full-bodied:* concentrated, rich, full-flavored, heady, lusty, potent, robust, mellow, matured, strong, redolent.

full-fledged adj. *The certificate now makes him a full-fledged CPA:* complete, mature, full-blown, full-grown; trained, qualified, experienced, schooled, adept, proficient, skilled, expert, top-flight, authoritative, masterly. **—Ant.** untrained, unschooled, green, inept, untried.

full-grown adj. *All the horses were full-grown:* grown, grown-up, adult, developed, mature, full-blown, full-fledged, ready, prime, ripened, ripe.

fullness n. *We will know in the fullness of time:* abundance, ampleness, breadth, amplitude, comprehensiveness; distension, enlargement, congestion, copiousness, fill, profusion, glut, repletion, roundness, tumescence; vastness, wealth, wideness, plenitude, plenty, satiation, satiety, plenum, swelling, extensiveness; completeness, completion, totality, entirety.

full-scale *adj. The dictator decided on full-scale war:* full-blown, all-encompassing, all-out, unlimited, comprehensive, exhaustive, sweeping, thorough, total.

fully *adv.* **1.** *Are you fully aware of what may happen?:* completely, entirely, wholly, totally, altogether, quite; perfectly, in all respects, in every respect; from first to last, throughout, from top to toe, from head to foot; positively, utterly, at all points; substantially, on the whole; every inch, heart and soul. **2.** *Is he fully supplied with materials to do the job?:* sufficiently, amply; abundantly, plentifully, copiously; richly.

fulminate *v. He fulminated over his bad treatment:* rage, rail, swear at, berate, bluster, curse, fume, blow up, explode, thunder, inveigh against, vituperate, upbraid.

fulmination *n. We heard even more fulminations:* raging, railing, tirade, blast, curse, diatribe, invective, explosion, outburst, tirade, philippic, obloquy.

fulsome *adj. We grew tired of their fulsome compliments:* grandiloquent, inordinate, excessive, overdone; cloying, fawning, saccharine, smarmy, sycophantic, unctuous, oily.

fumble *v. She fumbled one opportunity after another:* mishandle, bungle, botch, butcher, mess up, spoil, mar, muff, bumble, muddle, boggle, bollix, bobble; *Slang* blow, louse up, goof up, screw up.

fume *n.* **1.** *The fumes from his cigar made dining disagreeable:* smoke, haze, exhalation; vapor, gas, billow, waft; unpleasant odor, reek, stench; scent; miasma. —*v.* **2.** *The smokestack fumed in great black billows:* smoke, send forth fumes, puff, smolder, emit, exude, belch forth; exhale; smell, reek, stink, stench. **3.** *When he hung up the phone, he was really fuming:* display anger, rage, seethe, lose one's temper, get steamed up, burn, rant, rave, fly off the handle, explode, flare up, foam, boil, flame up, *Informal* carry on, *Slang* blow one's top, blow one's stack.

fun *n. We had such fun playing tag at the swimming pool:* enjoyment, gaiety, pleasure, amusement, merriment, diversion; entertainment, recreation, distraction, relaxation; joking, jest, playfulness, waggishness, jollity, mirth, good humor, joviality; cheer, frolic, whoopee, skylarking, tomfoolery, buffoonery; game, sport, play, horseplay, romp, antic, prank, lark, spree, escapade, revelry, high jinks, good time; *Slang* ball, blast, trip, gas. —**Ant.** misery, melancholy, woe, gloom, tedium.

function *n.* **1.** *The chief function of the kidneys is to purify the blood:* purpose, role, activity, operation, job, business, task, duty; capacity, power, faculty; province, sphere, office, niche, place, scope, range, field; concern, objective, raison d'être. **2.** *It was a rather large function with all sorts of dignitaries and celebrities in attendance:* social gathering, fete, gala, affair, festivity, party, entertainment, reception, soiree; dinner party, feast, banquet; ceremony, occasion. —*v.* **3.** *This armchair also functions as a day-bed:* serve, act, perform, do duty; operate, behave, work, answer a purpose, help, benefit, render a service, serve one's turn.

functional *adj. Is that oil lamp functional or merely decorative?:* working, operative, operable, functioning; useful, serviceable, practical, utilitarian.

fund *n.* **1.** *The family contributed weekly to a vacation fund:* sum of money, accumulated amount, savings, accumulation, bank; nest egg; *Slang* kitty; pool, pot; foundation, endowment, investment. **2.** *That woman is a fund of local historical information:* store, supply, stock; repository, reservoir, well, fount, spring; treasure, storehouse, hoard, reserve; mine, lode, vein. —*v.* **3.** *We're hoping the government will fund the project:* finance, pay for, underwrite, foot, float; support, endow, patronize. —**Ant.** 1 expenditure, outlay, outgo, disbursement; payment, remuneration.

fundamental *adj.* **1.** *His book is on the fundamental principles of banking:* basic, underlying, essential, necessary, requisite, first, primary, elementary; key, crucial, vital, central; major, principal, main, chief; cardinal, indispensable, integral. —*n.* **2.** *Have you mastered the fundamentals of retail selling?:* principle, basic, primary rule, ABC's, essential, requisite, axiom, element, component; base, basis, foundation, cornerstone; groundwork. —**Ant.** 1 advanced; superfluous, accidental; secondary, subordinate, lesser.

funds *n. pl. I'd like to help, but I'm momentarily without funds:* money, cash, cash on hand, wherewithal, means, resources, assets, capital, property, wealth, finances, income; *Slang* jack, lucre, dough, green stuff, pelf, wampum, bread, scratch, moola.

funeral *n. The funeral consisted of a requiem mass and a graveside service:* rites, obsequies, requiem, memorial service, interment, burial, entombment, inhumation; cremation; wake.

funereal *adj. From the doctor's funereal expression, I expected the worst:* sad, mournful, gloomy, dismal, doleful, woeful, grieving, solemn, dirgeful, somber, dreary, depressing; weepy, woebegone, lachrymose, lugubrious, cheerless, long-faced, grim, grim-faced; desolate, brokenhearted. —**Ant.** happy, gay, cheery, merry, lively, joyous, festive.

funnel *n.* **1.** *Use a funnel to pour the oil into the bottle:* cone-shaped utensil; channel, conduit, duct, shaft. **2.** *The steamship has four large funnels:* smokestack; chimney, smoke pipe, stovepipe, ventilator, flue, air shaft. —*v.* **3.** *They funnel most of their income into investments:* pour, concentrate, channel, focus, direct; siphon, pipe, filter.

funny *adj.* **1.** *It's a very funny story, but I don't want to repeat it:* comical, amusing, humorous, diverting, laughable, hilarious, absurd, ridiculous, ludicrous; witty, droll, comic, facetious, waggish, jocular, jocose, sporting, jesting, antic, mirthful, merry; farcical. **2.** *That's a funny way to speak of a relative:* odd, strange, unusual, uncommon, weird, curious, bizarre, outlandish, queer, peculiar, offbeat. **—Ant.** 1 serious, sober, humorless; solemn, grave; mournful, melancholy.

fur n. Her new suit is trimmed with fine fur: pelt, animal skin; hair, fleece, down.

furious adj. **1.** She gets furious whenever you mention her weight problem: enrage, irate, angry, mad, irascible, hot under the collar, up in arms, on the warpath, infuriated, maddened, provoked, raging, wrathful, fuming; rabid, frenzied, wild, fanatical; unbalanced, frenetic. **2.** A furious gale blew the ship toward the rocky shore: tempestuous, turbulent, fierce, intense, violent, vehement, stormy, raging, tumultuous, rampant; fiery, savage, passionate; ungovernable, unrestrained; reckless, heedless, wild. **—Ant.** 1 calm, serene, pleased, placated. 2 mild, calm, tame.

furnace n. Why isn't the furnace sending up any heat?: heater, heating system; oven, stove, incinerator; forge, boiler, kiln.

furnish v. **1.** The company will furnish each contestant with an entry blank: provide, equip, supply, stock, accommodate; endow, vest; purvey, render; favor, indulge; provision; give, grant, bestow on. **2.** The house was furnished entirely with handmade items: equip, appoint, outfit, fit out, array, fit up; rig; accoutre, dress; gird, arm, prepare.

furniture n. Some articles of furniture were lost when we moved: household goods, house fittings, movables, appointments, chattels, possessions, property, furnishings, effects.

furor n. **1.** The doctor's new book has caused quite a furor. A Calvinist phrase for God's anger is "the furor of His wrath": commotion, uproar, excitement, to-do, reaction, noise; rage, fury, fit of anger, passion, frenzy, madness, brouhaha, agitation, raving, Slang hoopla, flap; lunacy, insanity; transport, fervor, fanaticism. **2.** The latest furor is snakeskin vests: craze, vogue, fad, rage, mania, obsession, enthusiasm, fashion, French dernier cri, Slang thing, word.

furrow n. **1.** The plow dug a series of furrows across the field: trench, channel, depression, cut, rut, groove, corrugation, trough, ditch, track; rift, crevice, crack, fissure, cleft. **2.** The furrows on his brow showed deep concentration: wrinkle, crease, deep line, crow's foot, ridge. **—v. 3.** In April we furrowed the fields for spring planting: plow, trench, dig. **4.** Years of worry had furrowed her face: wrinkle, line, seam, pucker, knit.

further adv. **1.** The Carters live a block further down the street: farther, yonder, at a greater distance, more remotely, farther on, more in advance; beyond, abroad, afar off, out of range. **2.** Let's not discuss the matter further. Let me say further that I couldn't agree more: more, additionally; again, yet, too, likewise, also; besides, furthermore, moreover; over and above, to boot. **—adj. 3.** Harry and Meg live in the further house of those two over there: more distant, yonder, farther, farther on. **4.** Where can I get further information?: additional, supplementary, more, extra, supplemental; spare, other,

auxiliary, ancillary; new, fresh; contributory, accessory. **—v. 5.** His support furthered my career: forward, aid, assist, help, advance, encourage; foster, back, back up, champion, promote, propagate, work for, favor, stand by; lend a hand, contribute to, strengthen; hasten, quicken, expedite, speed, accelerate, oblige, accommodate. **—Ant.** 1, 3 nearer, closer. 5 slow, retard; hinder, frustrate, thwart, impede, obstruct.

furtherance n. She is active in the furtherance of our cause: advancement, advance, promotion, support, aid, succor, help, assistance, lift; patronage, favor, interest; advocacy, championship, defense; countenance, cooperation. **—Ant.** opposition, hindrance, restraint; defeat, destruction.

furthermore adv. And furthermore she's devoid of talent as well as brains: also, moreover, besides, in addition, too, additionally, as well, likewise; Informal to boot, into the bargain; over and above.

furtive adj. I could tell by his furtive glances at his watch that he wished to go: secret, secretive, surreptitious, stealthy, hidden, clandestine, covert; masked, veiled, shrouded, cloaked, private, secluded, unrevealed, unseen; confidential, mysterious, undercover; collusive, conspiratorial; sly, shifty, wily, crafty, underhand, sneaking, sneaky, skulking, shady, elusive, evasive. **—Ant.** forthright, straightforward, aboveboard; unconcealed, unreserved; public, undisguised, brazen, barefaced.

fury n. **1.** He smashed his fist into the wall in a drunken fury: rage, unrestrained anger, frenzy, furor, wrath, ire, choler; outburst, fit, tantrum, pet, snit, huff, dudgeon; acerbity, acrimony, virulence, gall, spleen. **2.** South Florida felt the full fury of the storm: might, force, violence, fierceness, vehemence, ferocity, intensity, severity, turbulence; assault, attack; impetuosity, headlong rush; bluster, excitement. **3.** He wondered if she would turn into a noisy fury like her mother: spitfire, she-devil, violent person, hellcat, hag, shrew, termagant, virago, vixen, she-dragon. **—Ant.** 1 calm, serenity, tranquillity, quietude, peacefulness, composure, placidity, equanimity. 3 angel.

fuse[1] v. **1.** The heat of the fire caused the silverware to fuse: smelt, run together, meld, blend by melting together, liquefy by heat, weld, solder, melt. **2.** The chairman must fuse dissenting elements into a strong united party: consolidate, merge, blend, mingle, intermingle, meld, join, link, weld, combine, incorporate; solidify, federate, amalgamate, league, band together, confederate; assimilate, coalesce, associate. **—Ant.** 2 separate, disunite, disperse, diffuse.

fuse[2] n. The bomb had a long fuse that delayed the explosion: detonator, igniting tube, ignition, firing material, wick, torch.

fusillade n. The ships approached each other exchanging fusillades. The new book received a fusillade of unfavorable reviews: barrage, broadside, salvo, volley, bombardment, cannonade, enfilade; drumfire, raking fire, mortar barrage; shower, spray, hail.

fusion n. **1.** *After fusion the metal will be recast:* smelting, melting, liquefaction; dissolving. **2.** *Success in our efforts depends on the fusion of many talents:* combination, blending, blend, union, merging, amalgamation, synthesis, unification; commixture, commingling, intermixture; federation, confederacy, confederation, league, alliance, association, coalescence, coalition, combine.

fuss n. **1.** *Let's have a simple wedding with as little fuss as possible:* bustle, ado, anxious activity, stir, to-do, flutter, flurry, pother, bother; commotion, hurly-burly, disturbance, hubbub, confusion, turmoil, turbulence, perturbation; ceremony, ceremoniousness, pomp, superfluity; fret, stew, fidget; worry, agitation; much ado about nothing, tempest in a teapot; fluster, hustle, scurry. **2.** *The children had a fuss about using each other's toys:* quarrel, minor argument, dispute, set-to, spat, tiff. —v. **3.** *Too nerv-ous to sit still, she got up to fuss in the kitchen:* stir about, bustle, busy oneself, potter, putter, pother; tinker, fool, fidget, flutter about. **4.** *Don't waste energy fussing over such a minor matter:* fume, fret, worry; nitpick, nag; carp, cavil, quibble, niggle; trouble, take pains, labor. **5.** *He can be fussed by the least little thing:* fluster, disconcert, rattle, confuse, flurry; annoy, bother, pester, put into a fuss, trouble, perturb; excite, agitate. —**Ant.** 1 inactivity, peace, tranquillity, simplicity.

fussy adj. *She's very fussy when it comes to planning a menu:* particular, hard to please, exacting, demanding, compulsive, meticulous, nit-picking, finicky, finical; painstaking, assiduous, fastidious, squeamish, scrupulous; critical, persnickety, old-maidish, crotchety; bustling, busy, nervous; cluttered, ornate.

futile adj. *His efforts to save the business were futile:* useless, fruitless, vain, profitless, idle, worthless, valueless, bootless, unprofitable; ineffective, ineffectual, unsuccessful, unavailing, abortive, nugatory; trifling, trivial, insignificant, empty, petty, frivolous, unimportant. —**Ant.** effective, fruitful, successful; profitable, useful, worthy; important, significant.

future n. **1.** *In the future you'd better get his permission first:* time to come, time from now on, futurity; hereafter, tomorrow, *Spanish* maña-na, morrow, by-and-by, offing. **2.** *Does the job have any future?:* outlook, prospect, chance for advancement, opportunity; anticipation, expectation; hope. —adj. **3.** *Our future plans are still indefinite:* from now on, in prospect, coming, to come, impending, prospective, eventual, projected, ultimate, anticipated, hereafter; following, subsequent, ensuing, succeeding; later, latter, after. —**Ant.** 1 past, time gone by, antiquity. 3 past, gone, bygone, former, previous.

fuzz n. *The scarf left fuzz all over my jacket:* fluff, lint, bits of thread, down, downy fibers.

fuzzy adj. **1.** *These peaches have a very fuzzy skin:* downy, linty, fluffy; frizzy, woolly; pubescent. **2.** *When the lens isn't focused, you get a fuzzy picture:* blurred, indistinct, unclear, vague, ill-defined, out of focus, not clear, indefinite; shadowy, dim, obscure; misty, hazy, murky, foggy; confused. —**Ant.** 1 smooth, slick. 2 clear, sharp, in focus.

G

gab v. **1.** *We gabbed for hours about how we would spend the holidays:* chat, chatter, talk idly, jaw, babble, jabber, gibber, chitchat, blather, blab, patter, prattle, prate, gossip; *Informal* shoot the breeze, chew the fat, chew the rag; *Slang* rap. —n. **2.** *Informal A good salesman should have the gift of gab:* small talk, glib speech, chatter; conversation; blarney, baloney, balderdash; gossip, chitchat; idle talk, patter, prattle.

gabble v. **1.** *Don't spend so much time gabbling on the telephone:* chatter, gab, jabber, chitchat, gossip, babble, blather, prate, blab; *Slang* rap. —n. **2.** *It's hard to work with all that gabble in the room:* chatter, babbling, jabbering, gibbering, prattle, blathering, chattering, chitchat.

gad v. *For three months they gadded about Europe:* ramble, jaunt, roam, knock about, gallivant, traipse, cruise.

gadget n. *This new gadget peels potatoes in a jiffy:* contrivance, device, tool, contraption, mechanical invention; newfangled object, novelty, gimmick; attachment; accessory; *Slang* doohickey, doodad, jigger, thingamajig, thingamabob.

gag v. **1.** *The robbers tied him up and gagged him with a towel:* stop up the mouth of, silence, muffle, hush; suppress, smother, stifle, muzzle, choke; bottle up, close off, stop. **2.** *The smell of sulfur makes me gag:* retch, be sick, be nauseated, choke, heave. —n. **3.** *The burglar stuffed a handkerchief in her mouth as a gag:* restraint on mouth to prevent outcry, stoppage, block; cloture. **4.** *Slang He imitated the boss's voice, and we fell for the gag:* joke, practical joke, hoax, jest, horseplay, foolery, facetiousness.

gaiety or **gayety** n. **1.** *When she tossed back her head and laughed, the whole room seemed to reverberate with her gaiety:* gay spirits, cheerfulness, vivacity, joyousness, jollity, high enthusiasm, good humor, mirth, high spirits, liveliness, animation; jauntiness, effervescence, sprightliness, sportiveness, festive spirits, airiness; elation, exhilaration; frolic, amusement, celebration, merrymaking, merriment, fun. **2.** *We feasted our eyes on the gaiety of the Mardi Gras parade:* brightness, colorfulness, showiness, brilliance; gaudiness, garishness; frippery, frumpery; tinsel, glitter, show, brummagem. —**Ant.** 1 sadness, melancholy, misery, despair, gloom; gloominess, despondency.

gaily adv. *She gaily dressed for the party:* spiritedly, with spirit, lightheartedly, cheerfully, happily, merrily, sparklingly.

gain v. **1.** *If nothing more, you will gain experience in that job:* acquire, obtain, secure, achieve, attain, get; gather, collect, get possession of, capture, bag, net; reap, win, glean; pick up, procure. **2.** *Last week I gained another five pounds:* acquire, put on, add, build up. **3.** *After battling the blizzard, we finally gained our desti-*

nation: attain, reach, arrive at, hit, come to; fetch, overtake, close with. **4.** *The doctors say that she continues to gain:* improve, recover, make progress; thrive, prosper, flourish; bloom, blossom. —n. **5.** Often **gains** *The taxes will be high on this year's gains:* earnings, winnings, profit, compensation, wages, salary, bonus, income, revenue, remuneration, dividend; proceeds, produce, yield; plus, favorable balance, black ink. **6.** *The gain in volume this year is nearly 10 percent:* increase, return, accretion, increment, addition, accumulation; advantage, improvement, attainment, plus; leap, jump. —**Ant.** 1 lose, forfeit. 4 fail, decline, worsen. 5 loss, forfeiture, detriment; damage, injury; privation, deprivation.

gainfully adv. *How long has he been gainfully employed?:* profitably, lucratively, productively, remuneratively; usefully.

gait n. *She walked with the straight-backed gait of a woman of fashion:* walk, stride, step, pace, tread; carriage, bearing, deportment.

gala adj. **1.** *It's a gala occasion when the Smiths have a party:* festive, celebratory, glittering, ceremonial, gay; splendid, sumptuous, opulent, grand, spectacular, magnificent, majestic; glamorous, fancy-dress, star-studded. —n. **2.** *At the opera gala all the stars of the company appeared:* celebration, festive occasion, festival, party, festivity, fete, benefit.

gale n. **1.** *We thought we'd never reach port in that gale:* strong wind, windstorm, blow; gust, squall, tempest, cyclone. **2.** *When I told her my predicament, she went into gales of laughter:* uproar, outburst, outbreak, eruption, gust, flurry; stir, commotion, fit, agitation, tumult.

gall¹ n. **1.** *He has a lot of gall expecting me to finish his work:* impudence, effrontery, boldness, audacity, temerity, assurance, brazenness; brass, nerve, cheek; insolence, rudeness, presumption, sauciness, high-handedness. **2.** *Of their former friendship there is nothing left but gall:* bitterness, bile, rancor, spleen, venom, animosity, virulence, malignity, acrimony.

gall² v. **1.** *My shins were galled by walking through those brambles:* chafe, make sore, rub sore, abrade, bruise; flay, score, excoriate. **2.** *It galls me that she does nothing and gets all the credit:* annoy, irritate, irk, provoke, gripe, vex, miff, exasperate, fret, displease, exacerbate, harass, rile, anger, ruffle, enrage, nettle; incense, affront, offend; sting, injure; *Slang* bug. —**Ant.** 2 delight, please highly, amuse.

gallant adj. **1.** *Custer's army made a gallant last stand:* brave, valiant, heroic, noble, chivalrous, courageous, dauntless, fearless, intrepid, daring, bold, high-spirited, valorous; lionhearted, stalwart, stouthearted; high-spirited, plucky, *Slang* gutsy, game, resolute. **2.** *The gallant young man is popular with the women:* chivalrous, cavalier, courtly, attentive, dashing, mannerly, courteous, polite, gentlemanly, suave, urbane, well-bred; considerate, thoughtful, kindly, obliging. —n. **3.** *The town's gallants meet at the coffee house:* cavalier, dandy, dashing young man, blood, gay blade; *Slang* swell, dude, stud;

fop, Beau Brummel. **—Ant.** 1 cowardly, craven, fearful, afraid, ignoble. 2 impolite, discourteous, ill-mannered, rude, churlish, boring.

gallantry n. 1. *The soldier was rewarded for his gallantry in action:* bravery, heroism, valor, dashing, courage, courageousness, fortitude, fearlessness, dauntlessness, intrepidity, daring, mettle, derring-do; spirit, pluck, mettle, nerve, prowess, determination, resoluteness; *Slang* grit, sand. 2. *His gallantry made him an ideal escort:* courtly attention, attentiveness, courtliness, chivalry, good manners, politeness, courtesy; good breeding, gentility, suavity, urbanity. **—Ant.** 1 cowardliness, cowardice; irresolution. 2 boorishness, loutishness, churlishness; discourteousness, discourtesy, rudeness, ungraciousness, unattentiveness.

gallery n. 1. *The monastery garden was surrounded by a gallery:* covered walk, roofed promenade, arcade, portico, colonnade, cloister, passage, passageway, corridor, piazza, loggia, stoa; triforium, ambulatory. 2. *The old-time ham actors loved playing to the gallery:* balcony, mezzanine; *Slang* peanut gallery, grandstand, bleachers. 3. *The gallery is having a show of new American art:* art gallery, picture gallery, exhibition hall, salon; art museum.

galling adj. *The team suffered a galling defeat:* upsetting, provoking, nettlesome, irritating, aggravating, bitter, bothersome, vexatious, vexing, painful.

gallivant v. *That evening we gallivanted around town:* gad about, jaunt, meander, traipse, wander, ramble, knock around, roam, rove.

gallop n. 1. *The band of cowboys rode into the frontier town at a full gallop:* fast gait; rapid ride, run, fast clip, mad dash; jog, trot, sprint. **—v. 2.** *The horse galloped away before I could catch it:* go at a full gait, run, race; ride at a fast gait, ride at full speed. 3. *The boy galloped away to join his friends:* race, run, rush, hurry, hasten, make haste, hie, dash, speed, tear along, tear off, bowl along; bolt, bound, spring, fly, scurry, dart; *Informal* flit, scamper, whisk, scoot, skedaddle, whiz, skim, scuttle, scud, sprint, shoot. **—Ant.** 1 slow gait. 2 amble, walk. 3 crawl, creep, walk, saunter, amble.

gallows n. *The highwayman was hanged on the gallows at noon:* scaffold, gibbet; (*loosely*) noose, rope, halter, Tyburn tree.

galore adv. *The farmers have had rainfall galore this year:* in abundance, in great quantity, aplenty, to spare, as much as desired, *French* à gogo. **—Ant.** in short supply.

galvanize v. 1. *Batteries were hooked up to galvanize the doorbell:* electrify, charge, energize, activate, stimulate, treat. 2. *The alarm galvanized the firemen into action:* arouse, rouse, excite, stimulate, stir, move, electrify, bring to vitality, quicken; infuse new life into, vitalize, fire, inspire, thrill, wake, awaken, spur on, rally, foment, provoke. **—Ant.** 2 lull, soothe, pacify; dull, deaden.

gambit n. *Pretending to be sick was only a gambit to gain sympathy:* maneuver, ploy, strat-

agem, scheme, trick, feint, ruse, artifice; opening move, initial play; voluntary sacrifice.

gamble v. 1. *He gambles on horse races and at dice:* bet, wager, play for money; take a flyer, try one's luck, tempt fortune. 2. *I'll gamble on his honesty and lend him the money:* take a chance, risk, hazard, speculate, chance; back, trust in, have blind faith in. **—n. 3.** *Opening a restaurant now would be a big gamble:* risk, hazard, uncertainty, speculation, venture, flyer; leap in the dark, random shot, tossup, blind bargain. **—Ant.** 2 be conservative, conserve; play it safe, *Informal* play it close to one's vest. 3 surety, sure thing, safe bet, cinch.

gambling n. *He was addicted to gambling:* betting, gaming, games of chance, wagering.

gambol v. *The lambs gamboled in the field:* romp playfully, skip about, dance about, frolic, frisk, sport, caper, cut capers, cavort, disport, prance, jump about, rollick; leap, bound, spring, bounce, hop, vault.

game n. 1. *Hide-and-seek is a favorite child's game:* play, amusement, diversion, pastime, sport, entertainment, recreation, distraction; fun, merriment, frolic, merrymaking, gaiety, festivity; lark, romp, antic, gambol, spree. 2. *Who won the football game?:* match, contest, athletic contest, competition, tournament, tourney. 3. *A good hunter always has game on the table:* wild animals, wild fowl, game fish; hunted meat; prey, quarry. **—adj. 4.** *He was a game fighter even when he was losing:* resolute, determined, plucky, unflinching, willing, dauntless, intrepid, courageous, brave, fearless, spunky, spirited, heroic, valiant, valorous, gallant; daring, cocky. 5. *Ever since my skiing accident I've had a game leg:* disabled, incapacitated, lame, crippled, halt, limping, bad, *Informal* gimpy; deformed, crooked, hobbling. **—Ant.** 1 work, toil, labor; duty; job, chore, business. 4 irresolute; fearful, afraid, cowardly. 5 healthy, strong, well.

gamut n. *Her acting covers the gamut from comedy to tragedy:* full range, complete scale, entire sequence, compass, sweep, scope, reach, ken, extent, purview, complete series; series of gradations, graded series.

gang n. 1. *Most of our old high-school gang have left town:* crowd, group, band, flock, outfit, pack; clique, circle of friends, coterie; friends, comrades, chums, companions; *Informal* buddies, pals, cronies; associates, neighbors; fellow members; schoolmates, classmates; co-workers, fellow workers, crew. 2. *A gang of highwaymen held up the stagecoach:* band, mob, company, troop, party, pack, contingent, body; ring. 3. *The gang of workers finished the rail line in record time:* crew, squad, shift, team, relay; troop, company, detachment, phalanx.

gangster n. *Gangsters tried to take control of the local nightclubs:* gunman, mobster, hoodlum, bandit, racketeer; syndicate member, mafioso; criminal, crook, felon, thug, ruffian; *Informal* hooligan, tough, hood, *Slang* goon.

gap n. 1. *We could see the house through a gap in the wall:* opening, breach, empty space, hole, gape, aperture; crack, crevice, fissure, cleft, chink, break, slit, slot, cut, fracture, divide; puncture, rent, rift, gash, notch, cavity. **2.** *After his ridiculous remark, there was a gap in the conversation:* blank space, interval, pause, void, vacuum, interim, lacuna, hiatus; break, interruption, intermission, recess, interlude. **3.** *Early American settlers moved west through the Cumberland Gap:* mountain pass; valley, canyon, ravine, gulch, gully; chasm, crevasse, abyss. **4.** *How much of a gap is there in their ages?:* difference, disparity, divergence.

gape *v.* **1.** *The audience gaped as the magician sawed the girl in half:* stare open-mouthed, stare in wonder, stare stupidly, show astonishment, regard with awe, gawk, stare, look excitedly, peer, ogle, gaze; *Slang* rubberneck. **2.** *After the hard climb he gaped for breath:* open the mouth wide, gasp; yawn. **3.** *The shirt gapes where the button came off:* part, separate, split, fly open, cleave, expand, open wide, spread out.

gaping *adj.* *There was a gaping hole in the carpet:* open, yawning, broad, wide, cavernous, great.

garage *n.* *We got the tire changed at a garage:* service center, carport, *Informal* shop.

garb *n.* *The nurse's garb was very becoming:* uniform, outfit, apparel, attire, dress, costume, clothing, clothes, garments, togs, get-up, rig; raiment, habiliments, habit, vesture, vestment; gown, robe, suit, wardrobe, finery, gear, livery, trappings.

garbage *n.* **1.** *Put the garbage down the incinerator:* refuse, kitchen scraps; rubbish, trash, dirt, sweepings, waste; swill, offal, carrion. **2.** *Informal Why do you carry all that garbage around in your pockets?:* junk, useless things, odds and ends; rubbish, litter, debris. **—Ant.** **2** valuables, treasure.

garble *v.* *Somehow his instructions were garbled, and he went to the wrong address:* confuse, jumble, mix up, be unclear, misunderstand; distort; fragment. **—Ant.** make clear, clarify, straighten out.

garden *n.* **1.** *Don't plant your garden in sandy soil:* garden plot; *(variously)* flower garden, vegetable garden, kitchen garden, herb garden, truck garden, rock garden, yard, lawn, plot. **2.** *The historic house and garden are closed to the public at sunset:* small park, botanical garden, zoological park, natural park. **3.** *The settlers made a garden out of the desert:* fertile region, agricultural region; paradise, Eden, Arcadia, green oasis. **—v. 4.** *First thing every morning he gardens for an hour or so:* cultivate a garden, plant a garden, tend a garden, work in a garden, work the soil, use one's green thumb.

gargantuan *adj.* *They bought a gargantuan house with at least 30 rooms. England's King Henry VIII had a gargantuan appetite:* gigantic, enormous, immense, huge, great, unbelievably big; vast, colossal, tremendous, mammoth, massive, stupendous, monstrous; titanic, herculean, elephantine, prodigious, amplitudinous; overgrown, lubberly, hulking, towering. **—Ant.** small, little, tiny, diminutive, miniature; dwarf-

ish, puny, minuscule, pint-sized; compact, meager, scant, paltry, trivial, niggling.

garish *adj.* *That garish dress is inappropriate for church:* gaudy, loud, flashy, glaring, showy, blatant, bright; overelaborate, too colorful, extremely ornate, tastelessly showy, ostentatious, pretentious, cheap, brassy, obtrusive; tawdry, vulgar, flaunting, tinsel. **—Ant.** sedate, conservative, unobtrusive, modest; plain, simple, somber; refined, tasteful, elegant.

garland *n.* *Each shepherdess made a garland of flowers for her love:* wreath, lei, festoon, diadem, crown, chaplet, circlet, coronet, headband, fillet, halo, corona, bay, laurel.

garment *Often* **garments** *n.* *Overcoats and other winter garments are on sale:* article of clothing; apparel, attire, garb, dress, gear, costume, raiment, togs, outfit, habit, vestment, habiliment.

garnish *v.* **1.** *The chef garnished the lamb chops with sprigs of mint:* embellish, decorate, adorn, ornament, trim, beautify, deck, bedeck, array, spruce up, furbish, festoon, set off, smarten, gild, embroider, emblazon; *Informal* trick out, dress up, doll up, deck out. **—n. 2.** *The ham was given a garnish of parsley:* decoration, embellishment, adornment, ornament, trim, trimming, festoon. **—Ant.** **1** strip, make bare, denude, deprive, divest.

garret *n.* *The poet lived in poverty in an unheated garret:* attic, loft; topmost floor, floor under the eaves. **—Ant.** basement, cellar.

garrison *n.* **1.** *The garrison faced starvation during the long siege:* soldiers stationed at a fort, detachment; *(variously)* division, brigade, regiment, squadron, platoon, battery, escadrille. **2.** *The army built a garrison to defend the town:* fort, fortification; military camp, military base. **—v. 3.** *The 49th Cavalry was garrisoned at Fort Big Horn:* place on duty, station, assign to, bivouac, put on duty in a garrison. **4.** *The town was garrisoned by a detachment of the king's militia:* occupy with troops, provide with a garrison; guard, watch over, secure, patrol.

garrulous *adj.* *She's so garrulous you can't get a word in edgewise:* talkative, effusive, loquacious; wordy, windy, verbose, long-winded; gabby, voluble, chattery, chatty, prattling, prating, babbling; gossipy. **—Ant.** reticent, taciturn, quiet, reserved, closemouthed; terse, concise.

gas *n.* **1.** *Helium is a gas used in balloons. The army developed a deadly nerve gas:* gaseous mixture; vapor, fume. **2.** *Stop at the next filling station for gas:* gasoline, fuel, *British* petrol, *French* essence.

gash *n.* **1.** *The gash in his cheek required ten stitches:* long cut, slash, gaping wound, incision; split, cleft, slit, crack, fissure, rent. **—v. 2.** *The flying glass gashed her arm severely:* make a long cut in, cut deeply, slash, make an incision in, incise, lance, pierce, wound, lacerate, slice; split, slit, cleave, rend, tear, hack; carve, quarter, dissect.

gasp *v.* **1.** *The long-distance runner gasped for air:* struggle *(for breath)* with open mouth, inhale frantically, labor for breath; suck in (air), breathe convulsively; have trouble breathing, respire laboriously; gulp, pant, wheeze, puff, catch the breath. **2.** *The victim gasped out the name of the assailant:* utter with gasps, exclaim in short breaths, speak breathlessly, blurt, vociferate, cry hurriedly. —n. **3.** *Her words came in gasps and were barely audible:* sudden short breath, convulsive breathing, sharp inhalation, gulp.

gastronomy n. **1.** *The famous chef wrote a book on gastronomy:* art of good eating, epicurism, pleasures of food and drink. **2.** *Mr. Eguchi's new restaurant offers French gastronomy in a Japanese setting:* culinary practices; style of cooking and serving.

gate n. **1.** *Close that gate or the cows won't stay in the pasture:* enclosure door, entrance to a pen, opening through a fence; portal, gateway, hatchway, doorway. **2.** *We bought our tickets to the baseball game at the gate:* entrance door; box office, ticket seller's booth; turnstile. **3.** *The pond won't fill with water until the gate is closed:* sluice; tap, valve, spigot.

gather v. **1.** *Storm clouds gathered on the horizon. Gather the men together and we'll start the hike:* assemble, get together, bring together, marshal, muster, accumulate, collect, amass, mass, group, convene, cluster, come together, bunch together, concentrate, congregate; pile up, stack, heap up, lump together, stockpile. **2.** *From your remarks, I gather that you're not happy here:* infer, deduce, assume, be led to believe, conclude; learn, understand, observe. —n. **3.** *The dress had tiny gathers at each shoulder:* fold, pucker; pleat, ruffle, shirr. —**Ant.** 1 disperse, dissipate; separate.

gathering n. *The party was the largest social gathering of the season:* assembly, meeting, party, conference, conclave, convocation, concourse, convention; company, crowd, throng, assemblage, accumulation, congregation, aggregation, multitude, turnout; *Informal* gang, pack, mob, bunch, drove, flock, horde, crush, press, roundup; collection, concentration, convergence.

gauche adj. *He's so gauche he even addressed the President as "Old Buddy":* ill-mannered, uncouth, socially awkward, unpolished, lacking in social graces, inelegant, overly informal, tasteless, ungentlemanly, unmannerly, unrefined, uncultured, boorish, oafish, ill-bred; proletarian, plebeian; ungraceful, inept, blundering, clumsy, awkward, heavy-handed, bungling, maladroit. —**Ant.** polite, well-mannered, well-bred, elegant, polished, suave, urbane, smooth, gracious, formal, tasteful, refined; graceful.

gaudy adj. **1.** *She wears such gaudy clothes she must have no taste at all:* garish, flashy, loud, showy, overly fancy; cheap, vulgar, worthless, tasteless, tawdry, flimsy, sham, bespangled, tinsel. **2.** *A good circus has to be gaudy:* colorful, showy, eye-catching, striking, ostentatious, glaring, pretentious; brilliant, dazzling, glittering, vivid, intense; sparkling, lustrous. —**Ant.** 1 sedate, conservative, quiet; modest, tasteful, re-

fined, elegant, unpretentious, subtle. 2 dull, lackluster, colorless.

gauge v. **1.** *Can you gauge the distance to the top of that hill?:* estimate, judge, appraise, ascertain, guess; evaluate, calculate, adjudge, rate, assess. —n. Also (*technical*) **gage. 2.** *This gauge registers the pressure in pounds:* measuring instrument, measuring device, measure, meter; standard, criterion, yardstick. **3.** *What gauge is that shotgun?:* size, measurement, internal diameter, inner measurement, inner dimension.

gaunt adj. **1.** *Illness has left him pale and gaunt:* very thin, emaciated, scrawny, haggard; lanky, skinny, bony, lean, lank, slender, slim, scraggy, spindly, spare, meager, raw-boned, spindleshanked; starved, cadaverous, wasted, withered, pinched, skeletal, shriveled. **2.** *It's gaunt country once you leave the highway:* bleak, forsaken, desolate, deserted, barren; grim, forbidding. —**Ant.** 1 plump, fat, chubby, stout, portly, corpulent, obese, rotund, well-fed; sleek. 2 lush, luxurious, blooming, inviting; bustling, active.

gawk v. *Stop gawking and call a doctor!:* stare stupidly, gape, look with astonishment; gaze, peer; rubberneck.

gawky adj. *Somehow the gawky child grew into a beautiful woman:* awkward, ungainly, clumsy, lubberly, *Slang* klutzy, bungling, fumbling, blundering, ham-handed, ham-fisted, all thumbs, graceless, gawkish, unwieldy, maladroit, lumpish. —**Ant.** graceful, polished, comely, attractive, urbane, suave.

gay adj. **1.** *Martha is a gay, fun-loving person:* cheerful, cheery, happy, lighthearted, merry, joyous, joyful; jolly, sunny, lively, vivacious, sparkling, sprightly, gleeful, in good spirits, buoyant, dashing, sportive, insouciant, effervescent, frolicsome, jovial, jocular, jocose, hilarious, humorous, waggish; festive, convivial, social, jubilant, frivolous, playful, rejoicing, elated, exultant, glad, gladsome, blithe, genial, smiling, airy, bright; jaunty, skittish, chipper, frisky, animated, spirited, coltish, volatile, *Slang* fun. **2.** *What a gay new hat!:* bright, colorful, showy, brilliant, vivid, intense, glowing, lustrous; particolored, multicolored, variegated; eye-catching, sumptuous, splendid; glittering, flamboyant, theatrical. **3.** *He was active in promoting gay rights:* homosexual, homophile. —**Ant.** 1 grave, serious, somber, sedate, staid, solemn, sober; cheerless, joyless; quiet, still, silent; unhappy, morose, grim, miserable; heavy, sad, melancholy. 2 dull, somber, colorless, drab, lackluster; sedate, conservative. 3 straight, heterosexual.

gaze v. **1.** *My father often used to gaze into the distance:* look steadily, look intently, look fixedly, contemplate, stare, watch, eye, keep one's look fixed, rivet the eyes, look long, look earnestly, strain one's eyes; study, peruse; look with wonder, gape, ogle, peer, scrutinize, survey, inspect, examine, pore over, witness, observe; glance, scan, behold, regard, peek; glare, glower, lower; *Slang* rubberneck. —n. **2.** *He* looked at the woman with a gaze of admiration: intent look, stare, steady look, scrutiny.

gear n. **1.** *This large gear turns the small one to rotate the cylinder:* toothed wheel, cogwheel; flywheel, cam. **2.** *The scuba diving gear is in the car trunk:* equipment, paraphernalia, outfit, things, accessories, apparatus, material, rigging, trappings; implements, instruments, tackle, rig, tools, contrivances; personal effects, belongings, property; apparel, clothing, clothes, attire, dress, garments, garb; *Informal* duds, togs; accoutrements.

gelatinous adj. *We couldn't identify the gelatinous substance:* jellied, jelly-like, gluey, glutinous, mucilaginous, coagulated, sticky, viscous.

gem n. **1.** *The queen's crown was covered with diamonds, rubies, and other gems:* jewel, precious stone; semiprecious stone, bijou; *Slang* rock. **2.** *The critics say his new play is a gem. She's a gem to go to all this trouble:* jewel, prize, treasure, wonder, marvel, one in a thousand; *Slang* beaut, peach, dear, doll, sweetheart.

gender n. *The French language has masculine and feminine gender:* sex.

genealogy n. *She can trace her genealogy back to the Pilgrims:* family tree, ancestry, lineage, list of forebears, family descent, parentage, extraction, derivation, pedigree; stock; line, house, birth.

general adj. **1.** *General elections will be held next month. I have a general idea of how a car works:* comprehensive, collective, overall, generic, basic, taken as a whole; sweeping, blanket, extensive, panoramic; vague, nontechnical, imprecise, inexact; not special, not particular, not specific, not limited, nonexclusive; unspecified, miscellaneous, not partial. **2.** *The suggestion met with general approval:* widespread, popular, prevalent, prevailing, common, universal, broad, public, pandemic; worldwide, ecumenical. **3.** *His general mood is pleasant enough:* usual, customary, regular, habitual, normal, natural, typical, accustomed, wonted; ordinary, everyday, conventional, frequent; current, prevalent, prevailing, most common. **—Ant.** 1, 2 specific, concrete, definite, particular, individual; exact, precise, special, distinctive. 3 exceptional, rare, singular, uncommon, unusual, extraordinary, infrequent; peculiar, odd.

generality n. **1.** *Stop speaking in generalities and be specific:* general statement, sweeping statement, generalization; abstract thought, vague notion, imprecise thinking, unorganized idea; undetailed plan, inexact presentation. **2.** *The generality of his knowledge is awesome:* universality, all-encompassing reach, far-flung scale; collectiveness, miscellaneousness; indiscriminateness. **3.** *It's a generality that people want to improve their lot:* general rule, generalization, widespread principle, universal thing; obvious statement, truism, cliché, platitude. **—Ant.** 1 specific, detail. 2 specialization; limit.

generalize v. *Do you know enough about today's youth to generalize that they are all selfish?:* infer, conclude, judge, form an opinion; speak in generalities, make a sweeping statement, make a generalization.

generally adv. **1.** *Dinner is generally served at 7 P.M.:* usually, ordinarily, in general, as a rule, for the most part, in most cases, typically, mainly, in the usual course of things, habitually; often, frequently, repeatedly, currently; always, universally; extensively. **2.** *Generally speaking, women live longer than men:* without reference to particular persons or things, without particularizing, without noting the individual exceptions; for the most part, in the main, on the whole, largely, mainly, chiefly, principally, mostly. **—Ant.** 1 rarely, as an exception, occasionally, infrequently, in a few cases, unusually, especially, particularly. 2 specifically, individually.

generate v. **1.** *This plant generates electricity for the entire city. The mayor tried to generate enthusiasm for the plan:* produce, cause, make, form, bring about, engender, effectuate, induce, institute, bring into existence; construct, fabricate, invent, frame, fashion, contrive, coin, originate; develop, evolve, occasion. **2.** *The human race was generated by Adam:* beget, father, sire, spawn; procreate, create; breed, reproduce, engender, propagate, proliferate, fructify, fecundate; impregnate, fertilize, bear, yield. **—Ant.** 1 extinguish, end, terminate, annihilate, kill, stifle, crush, squelch, quash.

generation n. **1.** *Adam's generation populated the earth:* progeny, issue, offspring; family, tribe, race, clan, house, line, lineage, breed, strain, stock; kin. **2.** *The biology class studied the generation of fruit flies:* process of generating, reproduction, propagation, procreation, engendering, begetting, breeding; fertilization, impregnation; proliferation. **3.** *The generation of ideas is a valuable talent:* creation, origination, production, formation, genesis; causation; development, growth, evolution.

generic adj. *It's much cheaper to buy the medicine under its generic name:* general, common, universal, nonexclusive, nonrestrictive, generalized, comprehensive, all-inclusive, sweeping, unspecified, collective. **—Ant.** specific, restricted, proprietary, exclusive, distinctive, explicit.

generosity n. **1.** *The magnate was noted for his generosity:* liberality, munificence, charity, bounteousness. **2.** *Generosity of spirit was her greatest virtue:* nobleness, disinterestedness, magnanimity. **—Ant.** stinginess, niggardliness, parsimony.

generous adj. **1.** *Your father was very generous to give you so much money:* openhanded, willing to give, freehanded, bighearted, ungrudging; lavish, liberal, munificent, princely, bountiful, bounteous, unrestricted, unstinting, unstinted, spare-no-expense; extravagant, prodigal, effusive; charitable, beneficent, philanthropic, free-giving, hospitable. **2.** *This restaurant serves unusually generous portions:* plentiful, ample, bounteous, large, copious, plenteous, abundant, liberal; overflowing, plethoric. **3.** *Aunt Helen had a most generous* *spirit:* unselfish, humane, humanitarian, considerate, benevolent, noble, altruistic; accommodating, obliging; bighearted, largehearted, magnanimous; high-minded, lofty; honorable. **—Ant.** 1 stingy, tight, tightfisted, closefisted, cheap, niggardly, miserly, parsimonious, illiberal, penurious; avaricious, covetous, selfish. 2 small, little, tiny; scarce, picayune, scanty, minimal. 3 mean, ignoble, small, petty, churlish, rapacious, greedy.

genesis *n. A news item about a freak accident was the genesis of her story:* origin, beginning, commencement, creation, birth, inception, rise, root, generation, begetting, engendering. **—Ant.** end, termination, conclusion, finish.

genetic *adj. There appear to be genetic causes for his disease:* congenital, hereditary, eugenic.

genial *adj. The host's genial manner put everyone at ease:* cordial, friendly, good-natured, congenial, amiable, gracious, affable, agreeable, pleasant, convivial, neighborly, companionable, sociable, social, courteous, civil, warm, happy, glad, hearty, expansive, kind, kindly, well-disposed, cheerful, sunny, vivacious, merry, cheery, jovial, jolly, jocund, gay, in good spirits, sparkling, mirthful, bright, lighthearted, festive, joyous, joyful; jaunty, lively, chipper. **—Ant.** unfriendly, unpleasant, uncongenial, ungracious, unsympathetic, cool, cold; rude, discourteous, uncivil; harsh, sullen, morose; cutting, sarcastic, sardonic, ironical, cheerless, caustic.

geniality *n. He greeted us with great geniality:* warmth, affability, conviviality, cordiality, amiability, friendliness, good nature, pleasantness, sunniness.

genitals *n. pl. In the painting the saint's genitals were concealed:* sex organs, genitalia, private parts, crotch, pubic region.

genius *n.* 1. *Einstein was a great scientific genius:* mental giant, mastermind, brilliant intellect, prodigy; child prodigy; *Slang* brain, mind, whiz, ace; master, expert, mine of information, walking encyclopedia. 2. *Rembrandt's genius is obvious in his paintings. You have a genius for getting into trouble:* natural talent, creative power, faculty, gift, knack, natural endowment, aptitude, penchant, wizardry, proclivity, bent, propensity, flair, predilection, turn of mind; insight, perception, percipience, intuition; imagination, invention, ingenuity; wisdom, intelligence, sagacity, understanding, judgment, wit. **—Ant.** 1 idiot, imbecile, half-wit, moron; oaf, fool, simpleton, dunce, dullard, dolt; numskull, blockhead, booby, nitwit, ninny, nincompoop, *Slang* stupe. 2 ineptitude.

genre *n. Shakespeare's play* Macbeth *is an example of the tragic genre of drama:* style, category, kind, class, sort, type, classification, variety, genus, species; fashion, description; school.

genteel *adj.* 1. *My aunt Mary was the most genteel woman I ever knew:* refined, well-bred, courteous, mannerly, polite, civil, well-spoken, ladylike, gentlemanly, courtly, decorous, poised; polished, cultured, cultivated, urbane; aristocratic, thoroughbred, patrician, of gentle blood. 2. *White gloves are a must at such a genteel*

gathering: elegant, stylish, fashionable, modish, suited to high society, elite; silk-stocking; *Slang* high-class, hoity-toity, highfalutin, high-hat, swank, ritzy, high-toned, swell, tony; overrefined, pretentious. **—Ant.** 1 unrefined, uncultured, inelegant, unpolished; impolite, discourteous, unmannerly, uncivil, rude; boorish, plebeian, low-class, low-bred, ill-bred. 2 unaffected, natural, simple, plain, unsophisticated, unfashionable, inelegant.

gentility *n. The brothers were widely admired for their gentility:* refinement, polish, savoir-faire, breeding, mannerliness, polished behavior, chivalry, gallantry, decorum, propriety, punctilio, suavity, urbanity, cultivation, civility. **—Ant.** grossness, coarseness, vulgarity, boorishness, indelicacy.

gentle *adj.* 1. *She was a gentle woman who wouldn't hurt a fly:* gentle-hearted, kindly, kind, peaceful, compassionate, tenderhearted, tender, sympathetic, mild, meek; tolerant, benign, lenient, indulgent, merciful; thoughtful, considerate. 2. *She gave the baby a gentle pat on the back. A warm, gentle breeze was coming from the sea:* mild, soft, light, easy, slight; quiet, calm, serene, tranquil, placid; balmy, moderate, temperate, not violent, not rough, not severe; bland, smooth, untroubled, low. 3. *Is that horse gentle enough for the children to ride?:* docile, tame, manageable, easily handled, tractable; domesticated, broken, harmless, subdued, pacific, peaceful, calm. **—Ant.** 1 hard; cruel, unkind, heartless, hard-hearted, rough, harsh, offensive, aggressive. 2 rough, harsh, hard, intense, powerful, strong, sharp, violent, immoderate; sudden, abrupt. 3 wild, fierce, savage, intractable; unmanageable.

gentleman *n.* 1. *A gentleman would never use such language!:* well-mannered man, honorable man, refined man, civilized man, polished man; man of social position, man of good family, man of gentle birth, man of good breeding, aristocrat, patrician; *Slang* silk stocking, gent, swell; cavalier, caballero, don, hidalgo, chevalier, squire, esquire. 2. *Are you the gentleman who read the water meter last month?:* man, young man, fellow, chap, *Slang* guy; (*of a male*) person, individual, one. **—Ant.** 1 brute, lout, churl, boor, scoundrel, dastard, bum, low-life.

gentlemanly *adj. She thought he behaved in gentlemanly fashion:* polite, well-bred, well-mannered, mannerly, refined, suave, polished, urbane, civilized, courteous, cultivated, genteel, obliging.

gentry *n. Fox hunting is a sport associated with the English gentry:* aristocrats, aristocracy, upper class, nobility, blue bloods, society, gentlefolk, elite, country gentlemen. **—Ant.** lower class, working class, bourgeoisie, plebeians, commoners, *Slang* hoi polloi.

genuine *adj.* 1. *Is the bracelet genuine gold?:* real, authentic, true, bona-fide, proven, veritable, actual, honest, legitimate, true-blue, solid, pure, simon-pure, sterling, unalloyed, unadulterated, 100 percent. 2. *The audience applauded with genuine enthusiasm:* sincere, true, unaffected, earnest; frank, candid, open, straightforward, honest, heartfelt, natural; ingenuous, naive, artless, guileless, unsophisticated, simple, plain. —**Ant.** 1 fake, false; artificial, phony, bogus, counterfeit, imitation, ersatz, fraudulent, simulated, feigned, sham, spurious. 2 insincere, affected, hypocritical, pretended, fake, false, phony, artificial.

germ n. **1.** *Cover your cough so you won't spread germs:* microbe, virus, microorganism, bacterium, bacillus, *Informal* bug. **2.** *It's only the germ of an idea, but you ought to develop it:* beginning, first stage, spark, rudiment; origin, source, root, fountainhead, seed, embryo. **3.** *Wheat germ is very healthy:* bud, sprout, seed bud, offshoot; seed, ovule, ovum; egg, embryo; nucleus, germ cell, spore. —**Ant.** 2 outcome, upshot, result; end, termination, consummation.

germane adj. *That's an interesting point, but it's not germane to our discussion:* pertinent, relevant, appropriate, applicable, connected, relative, material, related, native, proper, intrinsic; apropos, appertaining, suitable, fitting, fit, to the point, to the purpose, apt. —**Ant.** irrelevant, inappropriate, unrelated, immaterial, unconnected, extraneous, incompatible, extrinsic, incongruous, inconsonant; incidental; foreign, alien.

germinate v. *Put the seeds in wet sand until they germinate:* sprout, put out shoots, push up, vegetate, spring up, generate, develop, burgeon, shoot; bud, flower, bloom, blow, burst forth, blossom, open. —**Ant.** wither, die, perish; stagnate.

gestation n. *The period of human gestation is 9 months:* full term of a pregnancy, life from conception to birth, pregnancy, maturation; development, evolution, incubation, propagation, generation, epigenesis.

gesticulate v. *The driver gesticulated for the police car to stop:* gesture; signal, motion, wave the hand, make a sign, beckon, pantomime, indicate; (*variously*) shrug, nod, nudge, wink.

gesture n. **1.** *The speaker's gestures seemed unrelated to the speech:* bodily movement, hand and arm movement, gesticulation, pantomime; signal, sign, motion, dumb show; (*variously*) shrug, nod, wave, nudge, touch, wink, body Eng-lish, high sign. **2.** *He said he would help, but I'm sure it was only a gesture:* polite action, empty offer, formality, courtesy, flourish, demonstration. —*v.* **3.** *She was gesturing so excitedly I knew something was wrong:* gesticulate, signal, motion, wave, beckon.

get v. **1.** *Get a copy of the book from the library. You'll get a spanking when your father comes home:* obtain, acquire, attain, receive, procure, fetch, pick up, come by, go after, secure, come into possession of, glean, meet with; achieve, win, gain, earn, realize, net, bag, reap, take; inherit, succeed to, pocket. **2.** *New Orleans gets awfully warm in the summer:* become, come to be, get to be, change to, be changed to, grow, turn, turn to, turn into, be converted into, wax. **3.** *Do you have time to get the car washed this morning? What time should I get lunch?:* have done, cause to be done, have, make ready, fix,

prepare. **4.** *I tried to get you, but your phone was busy. What time does the bus get to Chicago?:* reach, communicate with, contact; arrive, come to, get in to; meet with, transport. **5.** *Sorry, I didn't get your name. He didn't get the point of the joke:* understand, comprehend, grasp, learn, perceive, hear, catch; take in, fathom, figure out, follow, sense. **6.** *It gets me why she suddenly decided to sell the house:* baffle, bewilder, perplex, puzzle, confound, confuse, mystify; upset, annoy, irritate, disconcert, *Slang* beat. **7.** *The Opera Guild got the governor to serve as honorary chairman:* persuade, induce, influence, prevail upon, enlist, dispose, incline; coax, wheedle, bring round, sway, win over, talk around, suborn; predispose, move, prompt. **8.** *The goblins will get you if you don't watch out:* seize, grab, capture, lay hold of, take, snatch, grasp, collar, grip; ensnare, entrap. **9.** *The teacher got chicken pox from the students:* catch, contract, be afflicted with, suffer from, come down with. —**Ant.** 1 give, give up; dish out, mete out; avoid, forgo, eschew, forswear; lose, relinquish, abjure, quit. 2 stay, remain. 4 leave, separate from; avoid. 5 misunderstand. 6 make sense, be logical to; please, comfort, calm. 7 dissuade. 8 let go, give up, release, free. 9 cure, heal, mend.

getaway n. *The thieves made their getaway in a car:* escape, flight, breakout.

ghastly adj. **1.** *I was really alarmed by her ghastly complexion:* ghostlike, ghostly, deathlike, corpselike, spectral, cadaverous; deathly pale, pallid, ashen, colorless, wan, pasty, blanched; lackluster, glassy, haggard, bluish-white. **2.** *It was the most ghastly accident I've ever seen. The rug was a ghastly shade of green:* hideous, revolting, gruesome, grisly, repellent, repulsive, loathsome, ugly, dreadful, horrible, horrendous, horrid, odious, terrifying, frightful, terrible, shocking, appalling, grim, forbidding, dismal; uncanny, weird, fearful. —**Ant.** 1 ruddy, robust, healthy, fresh, blooming. 2 attractive, appealing, beautiful, lovely, charming, enticing.

ghost n. **1.** *The former owner's ghost is believed to haunt the house:* spirit of a dead person, disembodied spirit, departed spirit; phantom, apparition, phantasm, wraith, specter, supernatural being, shadow, shade, *Slang* spook; manifestation, materialization; banshee, sprite, demon, chimera, goblin, hobgoblin; phantasma, *German* doppelgänger. **2.** *Since the tragedy, she's just been the ghost of her former self. There was just a ghost of her perfume left in the room:* trace, suggestion, hint, semblance; shadow.

ghostly adj. *A ghostly light seemed to be moving through the trees:* ghostlike, spectral, wraithlike, phantom, phantasmal, phantomlike, unearthly, supernatural; *Slang* spooky; shadowy, illusive; weird, eerie, uncanny, unreal; ghastly, pale. —**Ant.** earthly, natural.

ghoulish adj. *Someone with a ghoulish sense of humor turned out the lights:* macabre, weird, eerie, scary, sinister, diabolic, hellish, infernal, satanic, fiendish, monstrous, demonic, horrifying, gruesome, hair-raising, zombielike, ogreish, necrophilic.

giant *n.* **1.** *Remember when Jack climbed the beanstalk and slew the giant?:* imaginary being of huge stature, colossus, titan, Brobdingnagian, Gargantua, Goliath. **2.** *Our basketball team didn't have a chance against those giants:* tall person, tall thing, colossus, behemoth, titan; *Slang* whopper, spanker, thumper, strapper. —**Ant.** 1 dwarf, pigmy, midget. 2 *Slang* shorty, half-pint, shrimp.

gibberish *n.* *With some words missing and others misspelled, the message was pure gibberish:* meaningless talk, senseless writing, nonsense, unintelligible language, babble, gobbledegook, drivel, gabble, inarticulate talk, meaningless words, foolish talk; *Informal* balderdash, stuff and nonsense, bosh, twaddle, fiddle-faddle, flapdoodle, hocus-pocus, double-talk, double-speak, blab, mumbo-jumbo, blather.

gibe or **jibe** *n.* **1.** *She bore her sister's gibes all through childhood:* taunt, taunting, jeer, criticism, sarcastic remark, sarcasm, cutting remark, scoff, sneer, ridicule, mockery, derision; quip, wisecrack; *Informal* slings and arrows; *Slang* knock, brickbat. —*v.* **2.** *The children gibed at her because of her dirty face:* jeer, taunt, poke fun, make fun of, scoff, mock, ridicule, laugh at, deride, sneer, twit, chaff, flout, rail at; *Slang* rag, roast, razz, needle. —**Ant.** 1, 2 compliment, praise. 2 applaud; salute.

giddy *adj.* **1.** *The medicine made her feel too giddy and she had to sit down:* dizzy, lightheaded; feeling faint, faint, fainting, affected with vertigo, vertiginous, reeling, whirling, swimming. **2.** *We viewed the parade from the giddy heights of the 90th floor:* causing dizziness, dizzying, awesome, overpowering. **3.** *How can such a serious man be interested in such a giddy girl?:* flighty, frivolous, capricious, erratic, fickle, changeable, impulsive, fitful, volatile, unsteady, inconsistent; careless, thoughtless, reckless, irresponsible, silly, mercurial, inconstant, fanciful, whimsical, vacillating, harum-scarum, hare-brained, rattlebrained, muddled, befuddled. —**Ant.** 1 steady, stationary, steady on one's feet. 2 steadfast, determined, resolute, single-minded; serious, earnest; calm, serene.

gift *n.* **1.** *The office makes a yearly gift to the Heart Fund. He claimed the stolen money was a gift from his employer:* present, something given; award, donation, favor, tip, gratuity, boon, benefaction; bonus, prize, grant, fee, consideration, premium; handout, largess, alms, dole, contribution, offering, aid, help; bribe, sop, graft, tribute; legacy, bequest, dot, dowry, dower, endowment. **2.** *Mother has a gift for making people feel at home. To be able to paint so well is a real gift:* special ability, talent, capacity, natural endowment, aptitude, flair, genius, knack, faculty, capability, facility; qualification, attribute, quality, power, forte, aptness, virtue, property, turn, bent; skill, expertise, inge-

nuity, adroitness, proficiency, competency, craft, power. —**Ant.** 1 penalty, fine, forfeiture.

gifted *adj.* **1.** *The composer is also a gifted pianist:* talented, naturally endowed, well-endowed, fitted for, cut out for, at home as; ingenious, clever, inventive, able, adroit, adept, resourceful; facile, proficient, accomplished, skilled, capable, qualified, expert, master, superior, masterly, polished, practiced, finished, experienced; deft, quick, handy, slick; *Slang* crack, crackerjack, wizard. **2.** *The youngest attends a school for gifted children:* especially intelligent, unusually smart, bright, brilliant, having a high IQ. —**Ant.** 1 talentless; amateur, unskilled, inept. 2 retarded; dumb, dull, slow, slow-witted, slow-learning.

gigantic *adj.* *Sprawling over 3 million square miles, China is a gigantic country:* very large, huge, vast, enormous, immense, giant, colossal, mammoth, massive, monstrous, tremendous, stupendous, jumbo, elephantine; mighty, unwieldy, ponderous, hulking, strapping, bulky, lumpish, lubberly, towering, voluminous; large-scale, prodigious; gargantuan, herculean, titanic. —**Ant.** small, little, tiny, miniature, compact; *Slang* teeny-weeny, itty-bitty; infinitesimal, microscopic; feeble, puny, weak; petty, insignificant; dwarfish, pigmy.

giggle *v.* **1.** *Why do teenage girls giggle so much?:* laugh in a silly way, laugh nervously, chuckle, cackle, titter, twitter, simper, snicker, snigger. —*n.* **2.** *Her nervous giggle annoys me:* silly laugh, titter, snigger, snicker, simper, chuckle, cackle; tee-hee, hee-hee.

gild *v.* **1.** *The decorator gilded the mirror to match the gold sconces:* coat with goldleaf, paint gold, gold-plate. **2.** *She gilds the truth to make it more palatable:* embellish with minor lies, exaggerate, twist; gloss over, touch up, cover up, slant, stretch, bend.

gimcrack *n.* *She has a shelf full of little gimcracks:* knickknack, bauble, gewgaw, trinket, ornament, curio, bagatelle, trifle, kickshaw, bijou, whatnot; thingamabob, thingamajig, contrivance, plaything.

gimmick *n.* *The gimmick is that you have to buy one of their cars before you can open a dealership:* scheme, stunt, plan, stratagem, ruse, wile, design, subterfuge, ploy; *Slang* angle, wrinkle, dodge; device, contrivance, gadget.

gingerly *adv.* *We walked gingerly over the newly waxed floor:* very carefully, cautiously, warily, carefully, guardedly, charily, watchfully, circumspectly, vigilantly, prudently, discreetly, heedfully; suspiciously, hesitantly, timidly, daintily, delicately, fastidiously, mincingly, finically, squeamishly. —**Ant.** boldly, confidently; rashly, brashly, carelessly, heedlessly.

gird *v.* **1.** *The warriors girded their loins and prepared for battle:* encircle with a belt, bind with a girdle, girdle, strap, belt, lace round; secure, tie, girt; hitch, truss, tighten, fasten. **2.** *Enemy troops girded the city:* surround, encircle, ring, encompass, hem in, circumscribe, circle, loop; enclose, confine, wall in, hedge in, pen; besiege, lay siege, blockade. **3.** *Gird yourself for* some bad news: brace, steel, strengthen, fortify, sustain, prepare; harden, stiffen, buttress.

girdle n. **1.** The woman needs a girdle with that tight knit dress: corselet, corset, foundation garment, waist cincher, bodice; stays. **2.** The king wore a girdle of gem-studded velvet: waistband, sash, cummerbund; circlet, girth, cincture; surcingle, baldric. **3.** A girdle of trees enclosed the park: ring, belt, circle, band, hedge, boundary, hem, contour.

girl n. **1.** The school is for girls of ages 12 through 18. The oldest girl is a doctor now: young female, schoolgirl, miss, lass, lassie, colleen, ingenue; daughter, female child; unmarried woman, maiden, maid, virgin, damsel, demoiselle; Informal nymph, wench, minx, baggage, nymphette, soubrette; Slang chick, bird, pigeon, kitten. **2.** We need a girl once a week to help with the housework: maid, maidservant, domestic, female servant, hired woman, hired girl, cleaning woman, cleaning lady, female employee, help, maid-of-all-work; cook, scullion; lady's maid, handmaid. **3.** Freddy's girl won't be in town for the dance: girlfriend, sweetheart; fiancée, betrothed, affianced; lady love, darling, angel, inamorata; mistress.

girlish adj. She's lost her girlish figure during the last ten years: girl-like, maidenlike, maidenly, youthful. **—Ant.** matronly, mature, womanly.

girth n. **1.** The girth of the tree trunk was over 100 inches: circumference, perimeter, length around. **2.** Tighten the girth or the saddle will slip: saddle girth, saddle band, cinch.

gist n. The gist of his long speech was that he is against the proposal: essence, main idea, main point, essential part, sense, force, significance, substance, sum and substance, implication, theme, burden, effect, drift; core, crux, heart, center, pith, kernel, marrow, meat, spirit, tenor, import, purport.

give v. **1.** What can I give you for your birthday?: present, present to, make a gift, make a gift of, bestow, offer, donate; grant, accord, deliver freely, hand over; award, confer; commit, entrust. **2.** Most people give to some charity at Christmastime. She gave her brother the bulk of her estate: contribute, donate, make a gift, bestow, consign, apportion, allot, dispense, distribute, subscribe, assign, settle money upon, transfer money or property to, entrust, vouchsafe, make over, vest in, enrich; endow, bequeath, leave; Slang hand out, shell out, fork out. **3.** Give your hat to the checkroom attendant: place in someone's care, give over, hand over, entrust; present, accord. **4.** Give me one good reason why I should do that. She gave a cry that brought us all running: put forth, show, provide, present, issue, convey, afford; utter, emit, offer, give vent to, voice, articulate, pronounce. **5.** Would you give me that magazine on the table?: hand to, accommodate with, provide with, supply with, equip with, present, furnish, deliver, hand over, indulge with, favor with, proffer, tender, offer. **6.** The shop will give $10 for your old golf bag. She gave the porter a dol-

lar for carrying her suitcase: pay, compensate, recompense, remunerate, allow, exchange, dispose of, requite; tip, bribe, grease the palm of; hire, buy; grant, accord, confer, hand over, dispense, distribute, present; Slang shell out, fork over. **7.** She gave them notice that she was quitting on the 15th: notify, announce, let know, communicate, impart; present, issue, render. **8.** The assignment gave him the chance to prove his talents: permit, allow, grant, enable; present, offer, accord, provide, supply, furnish, proffer, afford, confer, impart, vouchsafe, deign, concede; admit, yield. **9.** He gave himself to the job with tremendous enthusiasm: apply, devote; surrender, attach, lose oneself in, lend, offer; addict. **10.** The branch gave under the weight of the heavy snow: give way, break down, collapse; slacken, loosen, unbend, ease, relax, relent, bend; retreat, move back, recede; shrink, become soft, sink, deliquesce. **11.** Our picture window gives onto the patio: open on; lead on to, afford an entrance; look out on, provide a vista. **—**n. **12.** A good mattress shouldn't have much give: flexibility, resilience; bounce, springiness. **—Ant.** 1–8 receive, get, take, accept, keep, retain, withhold, hold; take back, withdraw, recall. 11 shut off, block, hide, screen, mask, conceal, obscure.

glacial adj. A glacial wind blew from the north. She greeted us with a glacial stare: cold, chill, freezing, frigid, bone-chilling, polar, arctic, icy, frozen, congealed, frosty, wintry, gelid; raw, bitter, piercing, biting; hostile, unfriendly, inimical, antagonistic, disdainful, contemptuous. **—Ant.** hot, warm, mild, balmy; friendly, cheery, cordial.

glacier n. We climbed to the top of the glacier: icecap, ice field, glacial mass.

glad adj. **1.** We were so glad you could visit us: happy, delighted, pleased, elated, joyful, joyous, gleeful, cheerful, exhilarated, contented, rejoiced; Slang tickled, tickled pink. **2.** Where were you when you got the glad news?: happy, delightful, pleasing, elating, joyous, joyful, joy-giving, exhilarating, cheerful, blissful, gratifying, entrancing, cheering. **—Ant.** 1 sad, unhappy, melancholy, sorry, sorrowful, depressed, displeased, dejected, miserable; disappointed, discontented. 2 depressing, sad, unhappy, unpleasant, displeasing.

gladden v. The children's happiness gladdened all our hearts: cheer, cheer up, please, hearten, elate, delight, gratify, pleasure, exhilarate, make happy, rejoice, inspirit, animate, raise the spirits of, enliven. **—Ant.** disappoint, depress, sadden, grieve.

gladly adv. I will gladly accept anything you can give me: cheerfully, gratefully, readily, willingly, happily, contentedly, enthusiastically, freely, heartily, pleasurably, warmly, with pleasure, zealously. **—Ant.** grudgingly, reluctantly, unwillingly, sadly, dolefully.

gladness n. Christmas was a time of gladness: cheer, cheerfulness, blitheness, delight, pleasure, felicity, gaiety, happiness, high spirits, jollity, joyousness, mirth.

glamorous or **glamourous** adj. Jean Harlow

was a glamorous movie star of the 1930's: fascinating, charming, bewitching, enchanting, dazzling, captivating, alluring; attractive; exciting, magnetic, charismatic. **—Ant.** unglamorous, unexciting, colorless, unattractive, dull, drab.

glamour or **glamor** *n. Do you still think there's glamour in the advertising business?:* fascination, excitement, adventure, romance, challenge; attractiveness, allure, charm, enchantment, magnetism; magic, illusion, glitter.

glance *v.* **1.** *He glanced at the newspaper and threw it aside:* look quickly, see briefly, view momentarily, observe quickly, scan, cast a brief look, snatch a glance, catch a glimpse of, glimpse, regard hastily; peek, peep. **2.** *Thrown rocks will only glance off the bulletproof windows of this limousine:* rebound, ricochet, careen, bounce; graze, brush, shave, skim, slip, touch, kiss. **—n.** **3.** *Do you have time for a glance at this report?:* quick look, brief look, quick view, glimpse; peek, peep, squint. **—Ant.** 1 study, contemplate, scrutinize, peruse, inspect fully. 3 long look, perusal, thorough examination, close scrutiny, full inspection.

glare *n.* **1.** *The glare of the headlights almost blinded us:* harsh light, gleam, glint, flash, flare, glitter, glisten, blaze, flame; brightness, luminosity, radiance, glow, resplendence; gloss, sheen, shimmer, sparkle. **2.** *He ignored his wife's glare and went on telling the story:* angry look, reproving look, black look, dirty look, threatening look, piercing stare, glower, scowl. **—v.** **3.** *The sunlight glared on the ice:* shine harshly, reflect brightly, glitter, flare, gleam, glimmer, dazzle; sparkle, glisten, shimmer, glow, flash, blaze; radiate, twinkle, flicker. **4.** *The teacher glared at the noisy student:* stare angrily, look fiercely, scowl, look blackly, glower, lower.

glaring *adj.* **1.** *Those glaring lights hurt my eyes:* harsh, bright, strong, brilliant, intense, blinding, dazzling, flaring, piercing, penetrating; glittering, shimmering; vivid, resplendent. **2.** *This bill contains a glaring error in addition:* conspicuous, obvious, blatant, flagrant, arrant, unconcealed, unmistakable, egregious, undisguised; outrageous, audacious, gross, rank. **—Ant.** 1 soft, subdued. 2 hidden, concealed, inconspicuous; subtle, discreet.

glass *n.* **1.** *Pour the milk into a clean glass:* drinking glass, tumbler, goblet; beaker, chalice. **2.** *Drink eight glasses of water every day:* glassful, tumblerful.

glassy *adj.* **1.** *One punch turned the boxer's eyes glassy:* blank, expressionless, dazed, dull, empty, fixed, glazed, vacant, lifeless. **2.** *The glassy surface was unscratched:* shiny, glazed, polished, smooth, clear, sleek, slick, slippery, vitreous.

glaze *v.* **1.** *How much did it cost to glaze that big window after it broke? The potter glazed the bowl after it was dry:* glass over, fit with glass, cover with glass; put a glassy finish on, enamel, coat with a glaze. **2.** *My eyes began to glaze after four hours of reading:* become glassy, film over, blur, grow dim. **—n.** **3.** *The glaze is baked on the pottery at very high heat:* glossy coating, glazing, vitreous surface, gloss, finish, enamel, varnish.

gleam *n.* **1.** *The searchlight sent its gleam into the night sky:* beam, ray, streak, glow, glitter, glimmer; spark, sparkle, flash. **2.** *A good waxing will give that old table a fine gleam:* sheen, luster, gloss, brightness, gleaming, radiance, effulgence, brilliance, coruscation, glitter. **3.** *The soldiers got an occasional gleam of humor from their sergeant:* trace, ray, inkling, glimpse, bit, drop, jot, iota, speck, grain, hint, least bit, tiny bit, glimmer, flicker. **—v.** **4.** *The car's headlights gleamed in the distance:* shine, glow, flash, glare, flare, shimmer, glitter, glisten, glimmer, sparkle, glint, scintillate, coruscate; blink, flicker, twinkle. **—Ant.** 1 darkness. 2 dullness, tarnish.

glean *v. The historian gleaned his data from old books and documents:* gather piecemeal, discover gradually, collect little by little, pick up, cull, accumulate, amass, gather, piece together, scrape together, harvest.

glee *n. The children shouted with glee when they saw the presents:* merriment, gaiety, joy, joyfulness, joyousness, exhilaration, exultation, rapture, delight, gladness, ecstasy; jollity, hilarity, mirth, laughter, verve, jollification, cheerfulness, joviality, jocularity; playfulness, liveliness, sprightliness, sportiveness. **—Ant.** sadness, gloom, dejection, depression, melancholy, sorrow, misery; *Slang* the blues, the dumps.

gleeful *adj. The boy gave a gleeful shout when he received the puppy:* happy, elated, glad, delighted, merry, gay, joyful, joyous, jolly, blissful, exultant, cheerful, exhilarated, mirthful, jovial, jocund, lighthearted, lively, festive. **—Ant.** sad, gloomy, dejected, melancholy.

glen *n. The trip includes a sightseeing tour through the mountains and glens of Scotland:* narrow valley, dell, dale, vale, hollow, bottom. **—Ant.** height, peak, summit, mountain, hill.

glib *adj. The salesman had a glib answer for every question:* facile, flippant, quick, ready, smooth, smooth-tongued, suave, fluent, talkative, gabby, voluble, nimble of speech, ready of tongue, easy of manner; insincere, devious; slippery, oily, unctuous. **—Ant.** well-considered, sincere, deliberate, artless, guileless; hesitant, hesitating; halting, silent, quiet, taciturn.

glide *v.* **1.** *The hawk spread its wings and glided down toward the mountain:* soar, float, coast, sail, drift, flow. **2.** *The dancers glided gracefully over the dance floor:* move smoothly, move effortlessly, slide, float, flow, skim, slip; skate, glissade; roll, drift, stream. **3.** *Isn't it amazing the way the years glide by?:* slip, pass quickly, go unnoticed, roll, steal, drift, run; elapse, proceed, issue. **—Ant.** 1 fall, plummet, sink. 2, 3 lurch, stagger, flounder, stumble, trip, hobble, shuffle.

glimmer *n.* **1.** *The candle made only a glimmer in the vast room:* faint gleam, small glow, flickering light, shimmer, glimmering, twinkle; ray, scintilla. **2.** *There is still a glimmer of hope that the drought will end this week:* trace, gleam, flickering, drop, speck, grain, bit, hint, glimpse, intimation, fleeting view. —*v.* **3.** *The lights of the town glimmered in the distance:* shine, shine faintly, flicker, twinkle, flash, blink; gleam, sparkle, glitter, glisten, shimmer, scintillate, coruscate; glare, glow, flare, beam. —**Ant.** 1 glare, flash, flare, blaze.

glimpse *n.* **1.** *The hunter had only a glimpse of the deer before it ran into the woods:* fleeting look, quick look, brief look, brief sight, momentary view, quick view, glance; peep, peek, squint. —*v.* **2.** *We glimpsed the diplomats as the motorcade passed:* see fleetingly, see briefly, catch sight of, catch a glimpse of, spy, see, spot, espy, sight briefly, view momentarily; peep at, peek at. —**Ant.** 1 long look, survey, observation, scrutiny, inspection. 2 survey, observe closely, scrutinize, study, inspect; drink in.

glisten *v. The street glistened in the rain:* shine, sparkle, glitter, glister, flash, scintillate, coruscate, shimmer, glow, glimmer, gleam, glint, twinkle, flicker, radiate.

glitter *v.* **1.** *The diamond glittered in the light:* sparkle, shine, glisten, gleam, glow, glimmer, flash, glint, radiate, flare, twinkle. —*n.* **2.** *A good polishing will restore the candlestick's glitter:* luster, shine, sheen, gleam, glow, sparkle, fire, radiance, brilliance, splendor; beaming, refulgence. **3.** *Theatergoers love the glitter of opening night:* glamour, splendor, grandeur, pomp, show, showiness, pageantry, display, tinsel; excitement, thrill, electricity. —**Ant.** 2 dullness. 3 drabness, dullness, dreariness, monotony.

gloat *v. Be a good winner and don't gloat over your victory:* crow over, vaunt, brag, revel in, triumph, bask, glory over, exult, preen oneself, rejoice selfishly, relish maliciously, be overly pleased; strut, swagger. —**Ant.** regret, deplore; belittle, disparage, deprecate, slight, detract from, deride, scoff at, sneer at; *Slang* run down, knock, put down.

global *adj. Another global war could destroy mankind:* worldwide, world, universal, planetary, intercontinental, international; general, widespread, comprehensive, all-encompassing, unlimited, unbounded, all-out. —**Ant.** local, neighborhood, regional, sectional, provincial, parochial; limited, restricted, confined, circumscribed.

globe *n.* **1.** *The earth is not a true globe but is slightly larger near the equator:* sphere, spherical body, spheroid, spherule, ball, orb, globule. **2.** *Sandy's travels took her all over the globe:* planet, celestial body, world, Earth, biosphere.

gloom *n.* **1.** *A fire in the fireplace quickly dispelled the gloom:* darkness, dark, blackness, dimness, dinginess, murkiness, murk, gloominess; shadows, shade, cloudiness, dusk, duskiness, obscurity. **2.** *Don't let defeat fill you with gloom:* depression, low spirits, despondency, dejection, sadness, melancholy, cheerlessness, unhappiness, moroseness, heavy-heartedness, heaviness of mind; doldrums, blues, mopishness, disconsolateness, despair, hopelessness, forlornness, distress; woe, misery, oppression, sorrow, grief, dolor. —**Ant.** 1 light, brightness;

daylight, sunlight, radiance. 2 joy, glee, delight, happiness, gladness, cheerfulness, high spirits, merriment, mirth, jollity, smiles.

gloomy *adj.* **1.** *It was a gloomy winter day:* dark, dim, dull, dismal, dreary, murky, shaded, shady, shadowy, somber, cloudy, overcast, sunless, dusky. **2.** *Can't you snap out of that gloomy mood?:* sad, unhappy, downcast, dejected, melancholy, despondent, depressed, cheer-less, glum, doleful, dispirited, low-spirited, disheartened, heavy-hearted, downhearted, moody, morose, crestfallen, chapfallen, woebegone, mopy, dismal, dreary, grim, desolate, somber, morbid, funereal, in the doldrums; *Slang* down in the mouth, down in the dumps, down; discouraged, pessimistic, miserable, sorrowful, heartsick, forlorn, disconsolate, comfortless; frowning, dour, sour, ill-humored. —**Ant.** 1 bright, light, sunny; radiant, brilliant, dazzling. 2 happy, glad, cheerful, joyful, jolly, joyous, gleeful, merry, jovial, jocund, blithe, gay, high-spirited, lighthearted, smiling, delighted; *Slang* on top of the world.

glorify *v. Wesley wrote hymns to glorify God. His new book glorifies the outdoor life:* give glory to, pay homage to, exalt, venerate, revere; deify, apotheosize, idolize, canonize, adore, worship, bow down and worship, enshrine, consecrate, sanctify, beatify, elevate, ennoble, dignify, immortalize, burn incense to, light candles before; praise, laud, extol, honor, celebrate, make more splendid, add luster to, sing the praises of; glamorize, romanticize. —**Ant.** desecrate, profane, blaspheme, defile, dishonor, debase, defame, degrade; condemn, mock.

glorious *adj.* **1.** *What a glorious spring day!:* gorgeous, beautiful, wonderful, marvelous, splendid, fine, great, grand, excellent, superb, delightful, divine; sparkling, brilliant, dazzling, shining, radiant, resplendent, glowing, lustrous. **2.** *Beethoven's Ninth Symphony is a glorious piece of music:* sublime, noble, magnificent, grand, supreme, majestic, august, imposing, impressive, stately, dignified, distinguished, famous, eminent, noted, celebrated, honored, preeminent, renowned, illustrious, notable, praiseworthy. —**Ant.** 1 awful, horrible, horrid, ugly, unpleasant, *Slang* lousy; dull, drab, dreary, gloomy. 2 minor, unimportant, unimpressive, trivial, trifling; undistinguished, unknown.

glory *n.* **1.** *The Psalmist sang glory to God:* adoration, worship, homage, veneration, praise, thanksgiving, gratitude, benediction, blessing, admiration. **2.** *The old soldier had won glory on the field of battle:* honor, renown, fame, eminence, preeminence, illustriousness, esteem, repute, distinction, celebrity, notability, prestige, mark, name. **3.** *The glory of the Grand Canyon can best be seen on a clear day:* grandeur, splendor, magnificence, majesty, gloriousness, resplendence, impressiveness, sublimity, stateliness, nobility, dignity, solemnity, excellence. —*v.* **4.** *The mother gloried in her son's success:* take pride, rejoice proudly, revel, take delight; be boastful, pat oneself on the back, preen oneself, plume oneself, boast, vaunt. —**Ant.** 1

blasphemy, profanity. **2** dishonor, disgrace, shame, infamy, ignominy, disrepute; condemnation, malediction, curse. **3** ugliness, meanness, triviality, paltriness.

gloss *n.* **1.** *The wax imparted a high gloss to the tabletop:* luster, shine, sheen, polish, glow, glaze, gleam, radiance, brightness, glossiness, brilliance, shimmer, luminousness. —*v.* **2.** *The chair was glossed to give it an expensive look:* shine, polish, give a sheen to; glaze, varnish, enamel, lacquer, japan, veneer. **3.** *Parents tend to gloss over their children's mistakes:* smooth over, treat lightly, mitigate; explain away, rationalize, excuse, whitewash, cover up, disguise, color, veil, mask, cloak. —**Ant.** 1 dullness, dull film. 3 exaggerate, overemphasize, blow up; accept, recognize, face.

glossy *adj. The horse's coat was glossy:* lustrous, shiny, shining, glazed, smooth, sleek. —**Ant.** dull, matte, subfusc.

glow *n.* **1.** *The glow from the embers warmed us:* soft light, gleam, afterglow, glimmer, shimmer, flicker, radiation; low flame, soft heat, heat, warmth. **2.** *The long rest put the glow back in her cheeks:* color, warmth, brightness, intensity, vividness, reddening; flush, bloom, blush. **3.** *The glow of her smile made the guests feel very welcome:* warmth, radiance; enthusiasm, fervor, ardor, earnestness, eagerness, gusto. —*v.* **4.** *The remains of the fire glowed for hours. The hands of this watch glow in the dark:* burn softly, smolder; shine, gleam, glitter, shimmer, be incandescent, be fluorescent, glisten, twinkle, flicker. **5.** *The boy glowed with pride when he caught a fish:* radiate, fill, flush, blush, thrill, tingle; feel intensely, be enthusiastic about, be eager, be animated. —**Ant.** 2 paleness, pallor, whiteness, wanness, ashenness, grayness, dullness, drabness. 3 coldness, chill, coolness, iciness; indifference, dispassionateness, halfheartedness.

glower *v. The policeman glowered at the driver who was blocking traffic:* scowl, look angrily, look fierce, glare, stare, frown, lower, look black, stare sullenly; pout, sulk. —**Ant.** smile, grin; laugh, snicker, smirk.

glowing *adj.* **1.** *The children had glowing cheeks after their walk in the snow. The room was decorated in glowing shades of red:* ruddy, flushed, red; bright, vivid, luminescent, florid, hot, flaming. **2.** *The critics wrote glowing reviews of the new movie:* enthusiastic, rave, raving, fervent, ardent, ecstatic; thrilling, sensational, exciting, stimulating, passionate, rhapsodic. —**Ant.** 1 pale, pallid, white, wan, ashen, gray, colorless, dull, drab. 2 unenthusiastic, cool, dispassionate, halfhearted, so-so; dull, boring; scathing, cruel, brutal, venomous, stinging, vit-riolic.

glue *n.* **1.** *You need a bit of glue to hold the two ends together:* mucilage, paste, library paste, cement, *Slang* stickum, epoxy, fixative; putty, mortar, concrete, plaster. —*v.* **2.** *You may have to glue the stamp onto the envelope:* paste, gum, stick, cement, fix, affix, plaster, agglutinate, fasten.

glut *v.* **1.** *Many people glut themselves with turkey and dressing on Thanksgiving:* stuff, gorge, cram, fill, overfeed, eat to excess, overeat, satiate, eat one's fill, eat out of house and home, gluttonize, gormandize; devour, gulp, gobble, gobble up, bolt. **2.** *The manufacturer glutted the market with cheap pocket radios:* oversupply, flood, deluge, overload, saturate, supersaturate, sate, surfeit, jade; choke, clog, congest, obstruct. —*n.* **3.** *During a gasoline shortage, big cars become a glut on the market:* oversupply, over-abundance, superabundance, saturation, supersaturation, surplus, excess, superfluity, surfeit, drug, burden, load, overdose, plethora, clog, obstruction. —**Ant.** 1 starve; nibble. 2 undersupply, empty. 3 scarcity, shortage, paucity, dearth, want, lack, scarcity.

glutton *n. Most gluttons are overweight:* voracious eater, overeater, trencherman, gourmand, gormandizer, gorger, stuffer; *Slang* pig, hog, belly-slave, chowhound. —**Ant.** small eater, fussy eater, dainty eater, finicky eater; dieter.

gluttonous *adj. The gluttonous cats devoured three bowls of food:* greedy, devouring, voracious, ravenous, grasping, insatiable, ravening, piggy, hoggish, piggish, avid, rapacious. —**Ant.** abstinent, abstemious, restrained.

gluttony *n. High blood pressure can be the result of gluttony:* excessive eating, overeating, voracity, voraciousness, ravenousness, gormandizing, gourmandism; intemperance, rapacity; *Slang* hoggishness, piggishness, eating like a pig. —**Ant.** dainty eating, eating like a bird; dieting.

gnarled *adj. That gnarled oak tree is 100 years old. The old farmer had large, gnarled hands:* knotty, knotted, full of knots, nodular, covered with gnarls, snaggy, leathery, wrinkled, weather-beaten, rugged; contorted, twisted, distorted, crooked. —**Ant.** smooth, sleek, unblemished; unwrinkled, silky; straight.

gnash *v. He gnashed his teeth in anger:* grind together, hit together, bite and grind, strike together, chomp, gnaw.

gnaw *v.* **1.** *The boy gnawed an apple while he watched television:* munch, eat away at, chew, nibble, nibble at, chomp, crunch, bite, masticate; graze, browse, ruminate. **2.** *Her unfair decision gnawed at her conscience:* trouble, worry, torment, rankle, distress, chafe, fret, grate, gall, harrow, eat at.

gnome *n. In fairy tales gnomes always guard hidden treasure:* dwarf, troll, shriveled little old man; elf, goblin; sprite, pixy, leprechaun.

go *v.* **1.** *What time will you go to the store today? On your mark, get set, go!:* move toward, set out for, start for, begin, proceed, progress, be off, advance, make headway, go on, get on, wend, repair, stir; press onward, forge ahead, gain ground, sally forth. **2.** *Please go now, I'm getting tired:* leave, depart, go away, take one's departure, withdraw, retire, decamp, move out, move away, quit; *Slang* scram, beat it, take off, vamoose, blow, split; steal away, steal off, slip off, sneak off, take French leave, flee, fly, take flight. **3.** *Does this road go to the city? This belt* *won't go around my waist:* lead, extend, reach, stretch to, spread to. **4.** *Is the machine going now?:* work, operate, function, run, be operative, act, perform; be in motion. **5.** *Time goes so fast when you're having fun:* pass, pass by, go by, elapse, lapse, expire, flow, slide, glide by, slip away. **6.** *Most of my money goes for rent. The award goes to a different actor each year:* be used, be applied on, be given, be awarded, be contributed. **7.** *How did things go at the office today?:* turn out, work out, fare, take place, come to pass, transpire; result, end, terminate, fall out. **8.** *Where do these cups go? That green hat doesn't go with the blue dress:* fit, have a place, belong; be compatible, be suited to, agree, harmonize, jibe, accord, blend; conform with, comport, tally. **9.** *Elizabeth prefers to go by the name of Betty. How does that old saying go?:* be known, be considered, be reckoned; be stated, be phrased, be expressed. —*n.* **10.** *The job requires a man with a lot of go:* ambition, drive, energy, vigor, vim, vim and vigor, vitality, force, initiative, steam, spirit, animation, vivacity, verve, pep, dash, élan, life, mettle, enterprise; *Slang* get up and get. **11.** *Let me have a go at fixing it:* try, attempt, turn, chance, whirl; effort, trial, endeavor, experiment. —**Ant.** 1 stay, remain; arrive, finish, end. 2 arrive, come, move in. 4 be inoperative, be broken; stop. 5 stand still. 6 be unused; keep, retain. 8 mismatch, be incompatible, be unsuited, disagree. 10 laziness, lifelessness, lethargy.

goad *n.* **1.** *The drovers used goads to keep the herd moving:* prod, cattle prod, prick, pointed stick. **2.** *Fear of failure can be a goad to hard work:* incentive, stimulus, stimulant, motive, motivation, driving motive, pressure, spur; inducement, encouragement, instigation, whet, fillip. —*v.* **3.** *His wife goaded him to ask for a raise:* prod, urge, exhort, constrain, incite, spur, push, pressure, drive, stir up, arouse, *Slang* egg on; stimulate, impel, propel, move, press, set on. —**Ant.** 2 detriment, curb. 3 deter, keep back, hold back.

goal *n.* **1.** *His goal in life is to own his own business:* aim, objective, ambition, purpose, object, intent, intention, design, end, target. **2.** *The fullback crossed the goal to score the winning touchdown:* goal line, end line, finish line, wire, home, mark, terminus. **3.** *The hockey team made three goals in the first period:* score, point, mark, tally.

goat *n.* **1.** *The farmer raised sheep and goats:* (*variously*) billy goat, nanny goat, nanny, buck, kid. **2.** *When something goes wrong, he always makes me the goat:* scapegoat, victim, fall guy, whipping boy, butt, laughingstock. —**Ant.** 2 hero; victimizer, instigator.

gobble *v.* **1.** *Did you hear that wild turkey gobbling in the woods?:* gabble, cackle, gaggle, caw. **2.** *The secretaries gobbled their lunch and ran back to the office:* gulp, gulp down, bolt, bolt down, swallow quickly, eat quickly, devour, stuff, cram down, raven, wolf.

gobbledygook *n.* *The speech seemed to me to be full of pseudo-scientific gobbledygook:* jar-

gon, gibberish, cant, balderdash, double-talk, bosh, nonsense, foolishness, buncombe, moonshine, bunk, rubbish, tommyrot, hocus-pocus, fiddle-faddle, mumbo jumbo, *Brit.* tosh, twaddle.

go-between *n.* *Our go-betweens will settle the time and place of the meeting:* intermediary, agent, middleman, representative, emissary, messenger, arbiter, arbitrator, fixer, mediator, interceder, intermediator, deputy, delegate, envoy, proxy, second.

goblin *n.* *Eat your spinach or the goblins will get you!:* wicked elf, evil sprite, bogeyman, bogey, demon, gremlin, troll, ogre.

God *n.* **1.** *In the beginning God created the heavens and the earth:* Lord, Our Father, God Almighty, the Almighty, the Supreme Being, the Deity, the Creator; the Godhead, the Omnipotent, the Omniscient, the All-Merciful; *Slang* the Man Upstairs. **2.** usually **god** *Apollo was the Greek god of sunlight:* deity, divine being, ruling spirit, divinity. —**Ant.** 1 the Devil, Prince of Darkness, Spirit of Evil, the Foul Fiend; Satan, Mephistopheles, Lucifer, Beelzebub; *Slang* Old Nick, Old Scratch, Old Harry. 1, 2 mortal, human, human being, flesh and blood.

godforsaken *adj.* *The little desert town was a godforsaken place:* desolate, deserted, remote; neglected, abandoned; bleak, wretched, lonely.

godless *adj.* *Bombing the defenseless town was a godless act. In time he repented his godless life:* evil, wicked, depraved; blasphemous, atheistic, agnostic, irreligious, sacrilegious, ungodly, impious, profane, heathen, unhallowed, unsanctified, unrepentant, unrighteous. —**Ant.** godly, God-fearing, pious, religious, devout, holy; sacred, hallowed, consecrated, sanctified; inspired.

godliness *n.* *Cleanliness, it's said, is next to godliness:* holiness, sanctity, righteousness, saintliness, purity.

godly *adj.* *The old patriarch was a wise and godly man:* devout, pious, reverent, reverential, religious, righteous, devoted, God-loving, God-fearing, pietistic, believing, faithful, pure in heart, saintly, holy, divine, moral, good, spiritual; sacred, hallowed, consecrated, sanctified. —**Ant.** ungodly, godless, atheistic, irreligious, sacrilegious, impious, unrepentant, profane, heathen; evil, wicked, depraved.

godsend *n.* *The inheritance was a godsend:* boon, blessing, advantage, manna, windfall, benediction, benefit.

gold *n.* **1.** *Many prospectors found gold in the hills of California:* (*variously*) gold dust, nugget, bullion, ingot, bar, *Chemistry* aurum. **2.** *The school's colors are green and gold:* bright yellow, yellow, gilt. **3.** *He tries to act mean, but he really has a heart of gold:* goodness, kindness, beauty, purity; goodwill, beneficence, humanity.

golden *adj.* **1.** *The child has blue eyes and golden hair. A golden sunset:* bright-yellow, gold-colored, gold, aureate, blond, gilt, gilded; bright, shining, resplendent. **2.** *Year after year he waits for a golden opportunity:* advantageous, opportune, favorable, timely, promising, auspicious, propitious, seasonable, well-disposed, *Slang* rosy. **3.** *Good health and peacefulness can make old age the golden years:* joyous, most joyous, happy, happiest, great, splendid, glorious, most glorious, best, blest, delightful, beatific; flourishing, halcyon, palmy; most precious, most valuable, priceless, richest, extraordinary, exceptional. —**Ant.** 1 black, dark, brunet; dull. 2 unfavorable, inauspicious, untimely, unpromising. 3 worst, sad, saddest, wretched, most wretched; lean, poorest.

gone *adj. They were gone for half an hour:* away, absent; decamped, astray, *Informal* AWOL, taken leave; dead, deceased, departed, disappeared, defunct, ended, done, elapsed, extinct, finished, over, no more, passed away, not present, vanished; lost, missing.

good *adj.* **1.** *Abraham Lincoln was a wise and good man. Florence Nightingale was renowned for her good deeds:* virtuous, worthy, honorable, morally excellent, righteous, upright; honest, reliable, conscientious; moral, wholesome, praiseworthy, exemplary; religious, pious, devout, pure, innocent, unsullied, untainted; humane, considerate, benevolent, kindhearted, kind, kindly, gracious, sympathetic, well-disposed, altruistic, beneficent, obliging. **2.** *Have you been a good boy today?:* dutiful, obedient, proper, seemly, well-mannered, decorous, well-behaved, orderly. **3.** *Where can we get some good pizza? William Faulkner's novels are particularly good:* satisfactory, excellent, fine, great, wonderful, splendid, first-rate, choice, select, sound, capital, tiptop; worthy, worthwhile; valuable, precious, priceless; admirable, commendable, *Slang* crack. **4.** *The office needs another good typist:* skilled, skillful, capable, efficient, proficient, adroit, thorough; topnotch, first-rate, excellent, first-class, ace. **5.** *Milk is good for you. It's a good day for swimming:* beneficial, healthful, healthy, salutary, advantageous; suitable, appropriate, favorable, right, proper, fitting, fit, qualified, useful, adequate, becoming, adapted, deserving. **6.** *Have a good time on your vacation. An entertainer has to have a good personality:* enjoyable, pleasant, agreeable; cheerful, lively, sunny, genial, convivial, sociable, companionable. **7.** *Why don't you wear your good suit to the party?:* best; new, newest, smartest, most dressy, most stylish, expensive, valuable, precious, priceless. **8.** *I would cash his check if I could be sure it was good:* valid, bona-fide, sound, real, genuine, authentic, honest, legitimate, proper; worthwhile, valuable. **9.** *The old farm is a good mile from here. She spends a good amount of time playing bridge:* full, complete, solid, entire; considerable, large, fairly great, substantial, sizable, ample; adequate, sufficient. —*n.* **10.** *No one's all bad--everyone has some good in him. More people should concern themselves with doing good:* goodness, virtue, merit, worth, value, excellence, kindness, righteousness, moral qualities; righteous acts, moral acts. **11.** *You must try harder for the good of the team:* benefit, advantage, gain, profit, prosperity, good fortune, success, welfare, interest, well-being, improvement;

service, favor, good turn, boon; enjoyment, happiness, wealth; blessing, godsend, prize, windfall. —**Ant.** 1–8, 10, 11 bad 1 evil, wicked, sinful, dishonorable, immoral, dishonest, unreliable; unworthy, unwholesome, blamable; sullied, fallen, corrupt, corrupted, tainted; mean, cruel, unkind, ill-disposed, selfish. 2 improper, unseemly, ill-mannered, indecorous, naughty, mischievous. 3 unsatisfactory, unsatisfying, awful, second-rate, unsound, valueless, worthless. 4 unskilled, incompetent, inefficient, amateurish, awful, horrible, *Slang* lousy. 5 disadvantageous; wrong, improper, unfitting, unseemly, unsuitable, inappropriate, unqualified, useless, inadequate; unbecoming, undeserving. 6 awful, *Slang* lousy; unpleasant, disagreeable; dull, boring, cheerless, drab. 7 worst, valueless, worthless; informal, sporty, old, oldest. 8 phony, counterfeit, sham, fraudulent, bogus; false, invalid, unsound, dishonest, worthless. 9 scant, short, incomplete; small, insubstantial; inadequate, insufficient. 10 evil, wickedness, badness, sinfulness, meanness, baseness; immorality, dishonesty, corruption, cruelty. 11 detriment, loss; failure, ill fortune; decline.

good-by or **good-bye** *interj.* **1.** *Good-by and write me as soon as you get settled:* farewell, so long, bye, bye-bye, bye-now, adieu, God be with you, Godspeed; till we meet again, be seeing you, see you later; *French* au revoir; *Spanish* adios, *Italian* ciao, arrivederci; *German* auf Wiedersehen; *Japanese* sayonara. —*n.* **2.** *He gave her a rose at their last good-by:* farewell, adieu, parting, leave-taking, departure, separation, send-off. —**Ant.** 1 hello, hi, hi there. 2 meeting, greeting, welcoming; reunion.

good-humored *adj. We always count on her for a good-humored reply:* cheery, amiable, good-natured, cheerful, genial, complaisant, pleasant, kindly, congenial, affable, gentle, mild, easygoing. —**Ant.** irritable, cranky, crotchety, morose, surly.

good-looking *adj. The room was filled with good-looking people:* handsome, clean-cut, nice-looking, well-favored, attractive; beautiful, lovely, pretty, comely, fair, bonny, pulchritudinous, beauteous, eye-filling, eye-catching, sexy, ravishing, alluring, captivating, bewitching, enchanting, *Slang* foxy. —**Ant.** homely, ugly, plain, unattractive, unsightly.

good-natured *adj. You'd have to be good-natured to raise eight children:* amiable, affable, friendly, pleasant, cheerful, congenial, agreeable, easygoing, genial, good-humored, good-tempered, obliging, complaisant, accommodating, warm-hearted. —**Ant.** cranky, cantankerous, cross, peevish, ill-natured, irritable.

goodness *n.* **1.** *She was a gentle woman of exceeding goodness:* moral excellence, worth, honor, righteousness, honesty, integrity, merit, wholesomeness, probity; virtue, virtuousness, morality, rectitude, purity, innocence, benevolence, kindness, kindliness, generosity; piety, devotion; propriety, decorum. **2.** *Eat the carrot raw if you want to get all its goodness:* benefit, advantage, value, worth, usefulness, profit; service, favor; nutrition, nourishment. —*interj.* **3.** *Goodness, what a big cake!:* gracious, goodness gracious, mercy, heavens, heavens to Betsy, sakes alive, landsakes, land alive; *Slang* wow, wowee, gee, gee whiz, boy, boy-oh-boy, say, hey. —**Ant.** 1 badness, evil, wickedness, sinfulness, immorality, dishonesty, unwholesomeness, corruption, worthlessness. 2 detriment, disadvantage, drawback.

goods *n. pl.* **1.** *The movers put all our goods on the moving van:* possessions, property, effects, worldly goods, movables, movable effects, chattels; paraphernalia, trappings, appurtenances, furnishings, things, gear, trappings. **2.** *All the store's goods are protected by insurance:* merchandise, stock, inventory, wares, articles of trade, commodities. **3.** *What kind of goods do you want for your dress?:* cloth, fabric, material, woven goods; textiles, dry goods, piece goods, fabrics.

good will *n.* **1.** *The gift created a lot of good will:* friendliness, benevolence, favor, kindness. **2.** *Much good will accompanied us on our journey:* acquiescence, heartiness, ardor, zeal, earnestness.

gooey *adj.* *After fingerpainting, the children's hands were gooey:* viscous, gummy, sticky, adhesive, gluey, glutinous, mucilaginous.

gore *n.* *Aunt Rose thinks there's too much gore in bullfighting:* bloodshed, butchery, slaughter, carnage; blood, dried blood, clotted blood.

gorge *n.* **1.** *The waterfall was at the far end of the gorge:* steep valley, canyon, chasm, ravine, cleft, gully, gulch, defile; hollow, abyss, crevasse, gap; glen, dell, dale, vale; pass. **2.** *The dog had a chicken bone caught in its gorge:* throat, gullet, craw, esophagus; mouth, muzzle. **3.** *It makes my gorge rise to see someone behave so badly:* disgust, revulsion, repugnance, repulsion, nausea; anger, wrath, blood, ire, animosity, hatred. —*v.* **4.** *The children gorged themselves on cake and candy:* stuff, fill, glut, sate, fill, cram, satiate; overeat, overindulge, eat greedily, indulge, gormandize, gluttonize; swallow greedily, devour, gulp, gobble, bolt.

gorgeous *adj.* *You never saw such a gorgeous mink coat in all your life. What a gorgeous day!:* beautiful, attractive, good-looking, glorious, lovely, exquisite, stunning, ravishing, splendid, elegant, magnificent, grand, fine, sumptuous, rich, rich-looking, imposing, impressive, splendorous, splendiferous, opulent, luxurious, costly; shining, brilliant, dazzling, bright, glittering, resplendent. —**Ant.** ugly, hideous, unsightly, unattractive, repulsive, plain, homely, cheap, tawdry, shabby, trashy, shoddy, scrubby, sorry; drab, dull; dreary, gloomy, murky, dismal, somber, bleak, gray.

gory *adj.* **1.** *The hunter's knife was gory. The gory feud lasted for years:* bloody, bloodstained, bloodsoaked, stained with gore, covered with gore, ensanguined; bloodthirsty, murderous, sanguinary. **2.** *The gory tale gave the children nightmares:* bloody, scary, bloodcurdling, frightening, terrifying, horrifying, *Slang* creepy.

gospel *n.* **1.** Often **Gospel** *Ministers devote their lives to preaching the gospel. A Gothic translation of the Gospels was made around the year 360:* the tidings of salvation proclaimed by Jesus Christ, the good news; any of the first four books of the New Testament: Matthew, Mark, Luke, or John. **2.** *Her husband's opinions are gospel as far as she's concerned:* the whole truth, ultimate truth, the final word, the last word; doctrine, creed, credo.

gossamer *adj.* *The spider's web was like gossamer:* delicate, diaphanous, sheer, fine, flimsy, gauzy, light, silky, thin, airy.

gossip *n.* **1.** *A career can be ruined by malicious gossip:* groundless rumor, hearsay, whispering behind one's back, backbiting, newsmongering, scandal; idle talk, prattle, twaddle, babble, tattle, tittle-tattle; comment, report, news. **2.** Also **gossiper** *She's such a gossip you don't dare tell her anything:* idle tattler, talebearer, idle talker, rumormonger, scandalmonger, gossipmonger, newsmonger, tattletale, blabbermouth, tattler, chatterbox, busybody, babbler, chatterer; snoop, snooper, meddler, magpie; *Yiddish* yenta. —*v.* **3.** *Don't you hate people who gossip about their friends?:* spread rumors, go about tattling, talk idly, tattle, prattle, prate, gabble, blab, talk one's arm off, give one an earful; snoop, pry, meddle, stick one's nose in other people's business. —**Ant.** 3 keep quiet, keep mum, keep a secret, keep one's lips sealed, keep one's counsel.

gourmand *n.* *A gourmand is somebody who likes good food and plenty of it:* trencherman, bon vivant, gormandizer, glutton, big eater; *Slang* chowhound. —**Ant.** small eater, nibbler, dainty eater, picky eater, fussy eater; dieter.

gourmet *n.* *A gourmet always wants the best food, not the most:* epicure, gastronome, gastronomer, gastronomist, connoisseur, bon vivant.

govern *v.* **1.** *Canada is governed by a prime minister and his cabinet:* administer, manage, rule, direct, head, lead, control, guide, steer, run, pilot, supervise, superintend, oversee, exercise authority over, be at the helm of; *Informal* be in the driver's seat, pull the strings. **2.** *She's never been able to govern that malicious tongue of hers:* control, restrain, check, hold in check, curb, bridle, tame, inhibit, hold in hand, keep under control; discipline, command, rule, dominate, boss. **3.** *What factors governed your decision?:* guide, influence, sway, lead, steer, incline, form, rule. —**Ant.** 1 be subject; follow, comply, obey, submit. 2 let loose, give free rein to; encourage.

government *n.* **1.** *Society could not exist without government:* governing system, rule, administration, authority, law, management, control, domination, regulation, command, direction, guidance, supervision; state, dominion, statesmanship, reins of government. **2.** *The prime minister and his government will resign and new elections will be held:* governing body, administration, regime.

governor *n.* *The governor declined to meet the committee:* administrator, overseer, chief, head, director, leader, manager, ruler, superintendent, supervisor, boss, *Informal* head honcho.

gown *n.* **1.** *The bride wore a white satin gown:* formal dress, long dress, fancy dress, party dress; dress, frock; nightgown, nightdress. **2.** *Everyone in the graduating class wore a cap and gown:* academic garb, robe, academic dress, academic attire.

grab *v.* **1.** *He jumped up from the table, grabbed his hat, and ran to the bus stop:* seize, snatch, grasp, pluck, lay hold of; clutch, grip, hold, clasp; capture, catch, nab, collar, bag. *—n.* **2.** *The boy made a grab at the frog, but it jumped away:* sudden grasp, snatch, lunge, pass. *—Ant.* 1 let loose, let go of, release, free; drop, put down, set.

grace *n.* **1.** *It's difficult to walk up and down stairs with grace:* gracefulness, elegance, supple ease, lissomeness, willowiness, fluidity; beauty, comeliness, pulchritude, good looks. **2.** *As a girl she learned the graces required of a good hostess:* charming quality, endowment, accomplishment, skill; charm, refinement, culture, cultivation, polish, urbanity, suavity, elegance, mannerliness, manners, savoir faire, decorum, etiquette, propriety, tact, taste. **3.** *The monks prayed daily for grace:* God's favor, God's love, divine goodness, divine influence; holiness, sanctity, saintliness, devoutness, moral strength; virtue, piety, excellence, merit, love, felicity. **4.** *By the king's grace, the traitor was permitted to leave the country:* mercy, pardon, clemency, lenience, forgiveness, charity, reprieve, indulgence, mercifulness. **5.** *Drivers have 30 days' grace to renew their licenses.:* extra time, exemption, reprieve, dispensation, indulgence. *—v.* **6.** *Borders of flowers graced the paths in the park:* adorn, decorate, beautify, ornament, trim, embellish, set off, garnish, deck, bedeck; spruce up, smarten, dress up, enhance, enrich. **7.** *His Eminence graced the banquet by his presence:* dignify, honor, glorify, elevate, aggrandize, exalt, favor, endow. *—Ant.* 1 clumsiness, awkwardness, inelegance, gawkiness, stiffness; ugliness. 2 bad habit, in-elegance, boorishness, coarseness, bad manners, tactlessness, tastelessness. 4 disfavor, ill will, enmity, animosity; sternness, harshness, cruelty. 6 desecrate, ruin. 7 insult, dishonor, shame.

graceful *adj.* *She just isn't graceful enough to be a good dancer:* easy-moving, naturally supple, limber, lithe, willowy, shapely, sinuous, lithesome, lissome, light-footed; attractive, comely, lovely, beautiful; delicate, elegant, sylphlike. *—Ant.* clumsy, awkward, ungainly, ungraceful, graceless, inelegant, gawky, lumbering, ponderous, stiff; ugly, homely, plain.

graceless *adj.* *We agreed that his speech was a graceless performance:* awkward, crude, clumsy, gauche, boorish, coarse, rude, ill-mannered, unmannered, gawky, inelegant, inept, loutish, rough, tasteless, *Informal* klutzy.

gracious *adj.* **1.** *She was the most gracious hostess I've ever known:* kindly, courteous, cordial, amiable, affable, good-natured, hospitable, obliging, civil; polite, chivalrous, courtly, pleas-

ant; kind, friendly, kindhearted, charitable, humane, tender, compassionate, benevolent, benign, benignant, merciful, lenient, clement. *—interj.* **2.** *Gracious, what an ugly house!:* good heavens, heavens to Betsy, mercy, goodness, goodness gracious, landsakes, my stars, ye gods, my; *Slang* wow, gee, gee whiz, boy, oh boy. *—Ant.* 1 ungracious, uncordial, unpleasant, ill-natured, haughty, unfriendly, cold, cool, remote, stiff, unkind, discourteous, rude, impolite, brusque, curt, gruff, surly, sullen; cruel, mean.

gradation *n.* *There were several gradations of size:* succession, sequence, series, calibration, measurement, grade, scale, progression, arrangement, classification, grouping, ordering, level, degree, difference, variation, distinction, divergence, modification, notch, step, position.

grade *n.* **1.** *The truck had a hard time going up the steep grade:* incline, slope, gradient, ramp, inclined plane, acclivity, declivity; hill, bank. **2.** *These pearls are of the highest grade. In the U.S. Navy, a lieutenant junior grade ranks next above an ensign:* rank, degree, level, standing, place; order, class, status, station, position; estate, condition, caste; stage, step, sphere; quality, value, intensity, brand, pitch. **3.** *The student got a grade of B on the spelling test:* mark; rating, standing. *—v.* **4.** *Poultrymen grade their eggs from small to extra large:* classify, sort; rank, order, gradate, value, rate, brand. **5.** *The teacher spent all weekend grading exams:* mark, give a grade to, rate. **6.** *Grading the road should minimize its slipperiness:* level, even, make horizontal, smooth, flatten.

gradient *n.* *The truck labored up the gradient:* grade, rise, slope, pitch, declivity, inclination, incline, acclivity, angle, bank, hill.

gradual *adj.* *Your work has shown a gradual improvement:* slow-but-steady, progressive, measured, regular, continuous, successive, graduated, incremental, slow, gentle, steady, imperceptible, deliberate; piecemeal, step-by-step, little-by-little, inch-by-inch, drop-by-drop. *—Ant.* sudden, abrupt, precipitate, instantaneous, overnight.

gradually *adv.* *We introduced the topic gradually:* unhurriedly, gently, evenly, steadily, imperceptibly, slowly, moderately, progressively.

graduate *n.* **1.** *Our French teacher is a graduate of the Sorbonne:* alumnus, alumna, recipient of a diploma, holder of a degree. *—v.* **2.** *My sister graduates from college this June. The medical school graduates 100 doctors a year:* receive a diploma, receive a degree, complete one's studies, award a diploma to, confer a degree on, grant a degree to. **3.** *The measuring cup is graduated in ounces:* mark with gradations, mark off, divide into degrees, calibrate, grade, measure out. *—adj.* **4.** *The teacher is taking a graduate course in mathematics:* postgraduate, postbaccalaureate. *—Ant.* 1 dropout. 2 drop out of, flunk out of. 4 undergraduate.

graft[1] *n.* **1.** *The graft on the apple tree is thriving:* inserted shoot, implant, implantation, transplant, splice; slip, sprout, scion. —*v.* **2.** *The surgeon grafted skin from the patient's back onto his burned arm. The hawthorn branch was grafted onto an older tree:* implant, transplant, ingraft; inset, infix, join; plant, bud.

graft² *n. Steps were taken to abolish graft in the city government:* corruption, bribery, plunder, booty, loot; payoffs, bribes, hush money, rake-off, kick-back, spoils; *Slang* payola, swag.

grain *n.* **1.** *Farmers raise millions of bushels of grain to feed the nation:* edible seed plants, cereal; (*variously*) wheat, rye, barley, oats, corn, maize, millet. **2.** *The grain was separated from the stalks by beating:* kernel, seed, ovule; cereal, grist; (*variously*) wheat, rye, barley, oats, corn, maize, millet. **3.** *The grains of sand run through the hourglass:* particle, granule; bit, pellet. **4.** *There isn't a grain of truth in his assertion:* bit, speck, particle, trace, spark, iota, jot, dot, scintilla, whit, tittle, atom, crumb, molecule, mite, morsel, fragment, granule; trifle, touch, pinch, dash, modicum. —**Ant.** 2 chaff, stalks.

grammar *n. She was an expert in transformational grammar:* parsing, sentence structure, syntactic structure, syntax, morphology, rules of language, *Informal* ABCs.

grand *adj.* **1.** *What could be more grand than Buckingham Palace?:* magnificent, majestic, stately, monumental, august, imposing, elegant, impressive, distinguished, striking, splendid, superb, glorious, noble, sublime, lofty, imperial, palatial, royal, luxurious, sumptuous, opulent; fancy, dashing, showy; pretentious, ostentatious; large, big, huge, mammoth. **2.** *The queen received her subjects in a grand manner:* stately, majestic, regal, noble, august, exalted, lofty, dignified, elevated, lordly, royal, kingly, queenly; princely; grandiose, arrogant, pompous, haughty, *Slang* highfalutin. **3.** *Going to the movies is a grand idea:* good, splendid, excellent, wonderful, fine, great, terrific, marvelous, fabulous, superb, sensational, smashing, admirable, first-rate, choice; *Slang* A-1, swell, keen, super, out-of-this-world, out-of-sight, real cool, groovy, real gone. **4.** *He was retired as Grand Marshal of the Army:* main, chief, head, principal, supreme, highest-ranking. **5.** *When they told us the grand total of our bill I was stunned:* complete, full, all-embracing, all-inclusive, comprehensive. —**Ant.** 1 petty, paltry, trivial, trifling, measly, puny, small, little, meager, unimposing, insignificant; unimportant, secondary, incidental, inferior. 2 undignified, common, low-class, boorish; base, mean, contemptible, small. 3 bad, poor, unsound, wretched, worthless, inferior, second-rate; *Slang* rotten, terrible, awful, lousy.

grandeur *n. The painting shows the grandeur of the royal palace in 1850:* magnificence, majesty, splendor, stateliness, impressiveness, resplendence, nobility, glory, sublimity; pomp, state, augustness, solemnity, dignity; importance, celebrity, eminence, fame, distinction; excellence, luster, loftiness. —**Ant.** paltriness, triviality, pettiness, smallness; insignificance, un-

importance, degradation, inferiority, commonness, meanness.

grandiloquent *adj. The grandiloquent speech went on for over an hour:* high-flown, high-sounding, flowery, florid, grandiose, pompous, pretentious, bombastic, inflated, turgid, swollen, stilted; magniloquent, lofty, rhetorical; *Slang* highfalutin. —**Ant.** simple, direct, unaffected, plain-spoken, matter-of-fact, low-keyed; base, lowly.

grandiose *adj. Renting a chauffeur-driven limousine was just one of his grandiose ideas:* grand, high-flown, flamboyant, splashy, theatrical, pretentious, pompous, affected, extravagant, *Slang* highfalutin.

grant *v.* **1.** *The general granted us permission to visit the military base. The government will grant land to anyone willing to farm it:* give, allow, consent to, permit, bestow, accord, confer, vouchsafe, agree to; allot, allocate, present, donate, cede, assign, award, endow; dispense, deal out, apportion. **2.** *Are you ready to grant that I was right?:* concede, admit, accede to, allow, consent, vouchsafe, yield. —*n.* **3.** *The college was built on a grant of land from the government:* allotment, appropriation, present, presentation, gift, donation, award, endowment, benefaction, contribution, bestowal, largess; bequest, subsidy, offering, allowance, assignment, gratuity, tribute; concession, indulgence, favor, boon. —**Ant.** 1 refuse, deny, withhold, withdraw. 2 refute, disagree.

graphic *adj.* **1.** *The reporter wrote a graphic description of the accident:* vivid, realistic, lifelike, illustrative, pictorial, picturesque, well-drawn, well-delineated, forcible, striking, trenchant, explicit, clear, lucid, distinct, expressive, descriptive. **2.** *The museum has an exhibition of the graphic arts:* visual, visible, seen; written, drawn, pictured, painted, printed. —**Ant.** 1 unrealistic, unpicturesque, hazy, obscure, vague, dull, indefinite; impressionistic, expressionistic. 2 abstract; performing.

grapple *n.* **1.** *The sailors used a grapple to retrieve the chest from the bottom of the sea:* grappling hook, grapnel, large hook. —*v.* **2.** *The friends thou hast, grapple them to thee with hoops of steel:* hold, hold tightly, clasp, fasten, make fast, grasp, grip, clutch, seize, catch, lay hold of. **3.** *Every man has to grapple with the problem of what he wants to do in life:* struggle, contend, combat, fight, wrestle, take on, do battle, encounter, engage, face, tackle, meet, confront, breast, deal with, try to overcome, *Slang* sink one's teeth into. —**Ant.** 2 free, let loose, let go, release. 3 avoid, evade, sidestep, run away from.

grasp *v.* **1.** *She grasped the letter and held it to her breast:* seize, seize upon, grab, snatch, catch, catch at, take, take hold of, lay hold of; hold, clutch, clasp, grip, clinch; grapple. **2.** *The student couldn't grasp what the teacher was trying to explain:* comprehend, understand, catch on to, get, take in, perceive, fathom, follow, master, *Slang* savvy; sense, infer, deduce. —*n.* **3.** *Take a firm grasp on the rope and pull. The* *mother held the child tightly in her grasp:* grip, hold, clasp, clutch; clutches, embrace, handclasp; seizure, seizing, gripping. **4.** *Soon a full partnership will be within his grasp:* reach, power, control, compass, scope, range, sweep, sway. **5.** *The course will improve the students' grasp of algebra:* comprehension, understanding, perception, ken, knowledge, mastery, talent, skill, sense. **—Ant.** 1 drop, release, free, let go, let loose, relinquish, surrender. 2 misunderstand.

grasping *adj. She's more than ambitious, she's grasping:* greedy, avaricious, rapacious, predatory, covetous, selfish, miserly, acquisitive, mercenary, venal, wolfish, hoggish. **—Ant.** unselfish, altruistic, generous, large-hearted, publicspirited.

grate[1] *n.* **1.** *Let's build a fire in the grate:* fireplace, hearth, firebox, firebed, firebasket. **2.** *The city installed grates over the roadside storm drains:* grating, grill, screen, bars, lattice, latticework.

grate[2] *v.* **1.** *The car's fender grated against the curb:* scrape, rasp, grind, rub, scratch, abrade; screech, scream, jangle, buzz, burr, clack. **2.** *Grate the cheese and sprinkle it on top:* shred, mince, pulverize. **3.** *His rudeness is beginning to grate on my nerves:* chafe, jar, gnaw at, irritate, annoy, rankle, gall, irk, vex, exasperate, go against the grain. **—Ant.** 1 slip, slide, glide. 3 calm, soothe, pacify, quiet, settle.

grateful *adj. We were grateful for your long, newsy letter:* thankful, full of gratitude, deeply appreciative, gratified; obliged, obligated, under obligation, beholden, indebted. **—Ant.** ungrateful, unappreciative, disobliged.

gratification *n.* **1.** *Collecting stamps gives him tremendous gratification:* satisfaction, pleasure, enjoyment, comfort, solace; happiness, contentment, delight, joy, relish, gladness, elation, exhilaration, glee, jubilation, thrill, kick, bliss, rapture, transport, enchantment, ecstasy. **2.** *The gratification of his appetite keeps him fat:* gratifying, satisfying, indulgence, humoring, soothing, pleasing. **—Ant.** 1 frustration, disappointment, dissatisfaction; sorrow, sadness, gloom, pain. 2 control, discipline, curbing, restraint; denial, abnegation.

gratify *v.* **1.** *Winning the tournament gratified the golf pro:* give satisfaction to, satisfy, give pleasure to, please, delight, make glad; regale, gladden, exhilarate; divert, entertain, refresh, recreate; thrill, interest, take one's fancy, amuse, tickle, tickle one's fancy, suit, entrance, transport, enrapture, enthrall, enchant. **2.** *Do you have some candy to gratify my sweet tooth?:* satisfy, indulge, humor, pamper, coddle, favor; give in to, appease, soothe, flatter, compliment. **—Ant.** 1 frustrate, disappoint, dissatisfy, displease, offend; sadden, pain. 2 control, discipline, curb, restrict, deny.

grating[1] *n. The entrance to the vault was blocked by a grating:* framework of bars, gate of bars, grate, grille, grid, gridiron; open latticework, trellis, lattice; tracery, fretwork, fret, filigree.

grating[2] *adj.* **1.** *The iron door made a grating sound as it closed:* rasping, scraping, raspy, creaky, squeaky, harsh, shrill, jangling, piercing, high-pitched, strident, raucous, discordant, jarring, cacophonous. **2.** *His incessant chatter can be grating:* annoying, irritating, abrasive, disagreeable, unpleasant, displeasing, offensive; exasperating, vexatious, exacerbating. **—Ant.** 1 musical, melodic, dulcet, mellifluous, soft. 2 pleasing, pleasant, agreeable; calming, soothing.

gratitude *n. How can I express my gratitude for all your help?:* gratefulness, appreciation, thankfulness, thanks, acknowledgment, recognition, obligation, beholdenness; giving thanks, thanksgiving. **—Ant.** ingratitude, ungratefulness, thanklessness, unthankfulness.

gratuitous *adj.* **1.** *His gratuitous insult flabbergasted me:* uncalled for, unprovoked, unwarranted, unjustified, groundless, unfounded; unproven, baseless, conjectural, presumptive; wanton, impertinent, irrelevant. **2.** *The flood victims are greatly indebted for the gratuitous help of nearby towns:* free, free of cost, gratis, given without charge, obtained without payment, donated, complimentary, unrecompensed, without compensation; voluntary, unasked for, freely bestowed, spontaneous, willing. **—Ant.** 1 justified, warranted, provoked; well-founded, wellgrounded, proven, real, relevant. 2 paid, compensated; compulsory, involuntary.

gratuity *n. We offered the attendant a small gratuity:* tip, gift, present, bonus, donation, benefit, largesse, offering, perk, perquisite, recompense, reward, sweetener, token, contribution, *Informal* little something.

grave[1] *n. The funeral procession arrived at the grave:* excavation for burial, burial place, place of interment, last resting place; tomb, sepulcher, mausoleum, vault, crypt, catacomb, cenotaph, mound, ossuary.

grave[2] *adj.* **1.** *His sister was happy and carefree, but he was always grave:* solemn, sedate, serious, earnest, thoughtful, subdued, quiet, dignified, sober, staid; somber, gloomy, dour, frowning, grim-visaged, long-faced; sage, philosophical. **2.** *The international situation is becoming a matter of grave concern:* serious, critical, crucial, urgent, pressing, acute, important, vital, momentous, of great consequence, consequential, significant, weighty, life-and-death. **—Ant.** 1 carefree, gay, joyous, happy, sunny, smiling, merry, boisterous; frivolous, facetious, flippant, flip, trifling, undignified; devil-may-care, dashing, exciting. 2 frivolous, trivial, unimportant, uncritical, inconsequential, insignificant, petty; mild.

graveyard *n. There are only a hundred tombstones in this graveyard:* cemetery, burying ground, memorial park, churchyard, necropolis, charnel, ossuary; potter's field, boot hill; *Slang* boneyard.

gravitate *v.* **1.** *The wet leaves gravitate to the bottom of the pool:* settle, settle down, sink, descend, fall. **2.** *We naturally gravitate toward people who are kind to us:* be drawn, be attracted, have a natural tendency, have a proclivity for, be prone to, incline; lean toward, converge, tend, move, head, point toward, zero in on.

gravity n. **1.** *An apple falls down instead of up because of gravity:* gravitation, gravitational attraction, attraction, mutual attraction of objects, pull, pull of the earth. **2.** *The surgeon announced his decision with the utmost gravity:* seriousness, solemnity, solemnness, earnestness, thoughtfulness, dignity, sobriety, sedateness, staidness, gloominess, somberness, grimness, calmness, serenity, tranquillity. **3.** *The international situation has reached a point of extreme gravity:* seriousness, urgency, concern, critical nature, crucial nature, danger, emergency; importance, import, moment, significance, consequence, consideration, magnitude, enormity. **—Ant.** 1 antigravity; escape velocity, momentum. 2 frivolousness, frivolity, facetiousness, flippancy, thoughtlessness; gaiety, merriment, glee, joy, happiness. 3 inconsequentiality, unimportance, insignificance, pettiness.

gray or **grey** adj. **1.** *Gray walls would set off your paintings better. His face was drawn and gray:* neutral, pearl-gray, grayish, silver, silvery, slate, dun, drab, dove-colored, mouse-colored; ashen, ashy, pale, hoary. **2.** *It's another gray winter day:* gloomy, dismal, somber, cheerless, depressing, dark, murky, overcast, sunless, cloudy, clouded, foggy, misty. **3.** *He was already gray at 30:* gray-haired, gray-headed, silver-haired, hoary-headed, grizzly, pepper-and-salt. **—Ant.** 2 bright, clear, sunny.

graze[1] v. *The cows grazed in the pasture:* eat grass, feed on herbage, browse, crop; turn out to pasture, pasture.

graze[2] v. **1.** *The child grazed his knee on the top step:* scrape, scratch, skin, abrade, bruise, rasp, rub, grind; touch lightly, brush, skim, glance, swipe. **—n. 2.** *Put a little iodine on that graze:* scrape, scratch, abrasion.

grease n. **1.** *Pour off some of the bacon grease before you fry the eggs. Put some grease on that squeaky door hinge:* fat, drippings, lard, tallow; oil, lubricant; ointment, salve, unguent, balm. **—v. 2.** *How often do you grease your car?:* lubricate, oil, apply grease to, smear with grease, lard; anoint.

greasy adj. **1.** *Wash this greasy plate again:* grease-covered, oily, lardaceous, buttery, waxy, oleaginous; slippery, slick, slithery. **2.** *This bacon is too greasy:* lardy, fat, fatty, grease-filled. **—Ant.** 2 lean.

great adj. **1.** *The Pacific is an ocean of great size. Great crowds of people came to the sale:* vast, immense, enormous, huge, large, big, tremendous, gigantic, colossal, stupendous, mammoth, prodigious, voluminous, gross, monstrous, cyclopean, titanic, gargantuan; many, countless, multitudinous, abundant, unlimited, boundless, inexhaustible, manifold. **2.** *He felt great happiness:* extreme, pronounced, decided, considerable, strong, high, extravagant, inordinate, prodigious. **3.** *It is a great decision for one person to have to make:* important, of much consequence, consequential, significant,

weighty, heavy, momentous, grave, serious, critical, crucial. **4.** *David Copperfield is one of the great books of all time. Joe DiMaggio was a great ballplayer. This cake is great!:* outstanding, remarkable, superb, superior, superlative, magnificent, notable, prominent, distinguished, glorious, leading, famous, noted, renowned, chief, illustrious, eminent, celebrated, esteemed; fine, good, excellent, marvelous; grand, splendid, wonderful, fabulous, fantastic, terrific, sensational, smashing, choice, first-rate; *Slang* A-1, swell, super, marvy, out of this world, out-of-sight, way out, groovy, real gone, real cool; expert, proficient, skillful, crack, able, apt, adroit; *Informal* crackerjack. **5.** *Our minister is a great man:* fine, noble, high-minded, of lofty character, magnanimous, altruistic, humane, loving, generous, kind, gracious. **—adv. 6.** *Informal We hope your new business is going great:* very well, well, fine, excellent, excellently, superb, superbly, magnificently, grandly, splendidly, wonderfully. **—Ant.** 1–4 small, little, tiny, diminutive, puny; insignificant, petty, paltry, trivial, trifling, measly, mean. 2 mild, weak, some. 3 unimportant, inconsequential, inconsiderable, insignificant, secondary, incidental. 4 poor, bad, worse, inferior, wretched, worthless, *Informal* rotten, terrible, awful, *Slang* lousy; second-rate, unnotable, undistinguished, average, inexpert, unskilled, inept. 5 mean, base, ignoble, low-minded; inhumane, wicked, hateful, unkind. 6 badly, poorly, terribly; *Slang* awful, lousy.

greatly adv. *His health has greatly improved:* very much, tremendously, immensely, enormously, vastly, largely, immeasurably, infinitely, mightily, powerfully, abundantly, considerably, remarkably, markedly, notably. **—Ant.** little, insignificantly, mildly, somewhat.

greatness n. **1.** *Greatness in leaders is rare:* illustriousness, glory, grandeur, importance, loftiness, majesty, stateliness, sublimity; merit, distinction, heroism, high-mindedness, idealism, nobility, note, prominence, renown; celebrity, fame, eminence. **2.** *The greatness of mineral wealth became apparent:* bigness, largeness, prodigiousness, magnitude, hugeness, vastness, bulk, immensity, mass, abundance, amplitude; force, potency, power, might, intensity, strength.

greed n. *The pirate's greed led him to cheat his partners out of their share:* greediness, money-hunger, avarice, avariciousness, covetousness, selfishness, avidity, craving, cupidity, rapacity, rapaciousness, piggishness, inordinate desire; itching palm. **—Ant.** generosity, munificence, liberality, altruism, unselfishness, benevolence.

greedy adj. **1.** *Greedy men cannot be trusted:* money-hungry, avaricious, grasping, acquisitive, covetous, rapacious, predatory, selfish, mercenary, *Informal* hoggish. **2.** *The greedy animals crowded around the feeding trough:* ravenous, gluttonous, voracious, insatiable, famished, hungry; devouring, gormandizing; *Informal* hoggish, piggish, swinish, wolfish. **3.** *How refreshing to see a student who is greedy for knowledge!:* eager, avid, full of desire, keenly desirous, ardent, fervent, burning, thirsting, hungry, craving, impatient, anxious. **—Ant.** 1 generous, munificent, liberal, altruistic, unselfish, benevolent. 2 sated, full. 3 uncaring, apathetic, indifferent.

green *adj.* **1.** *These green walls are hideous!:* green-colored, (*variously*) yellow-green, chartreuse, lime, lime-green, olive, olive-green, greenish, grass-green, verdant, pea-green, forest-green, kelly-green, cobalt-green, jade, emerald, sea-green, aquamarine, blue-green. **2.** *The apples are still too green to pick. Green lumber warps easily:* unripe, immature, not fully aged, underdeveloped, undeveloped; young, tender, unfledged, crude; raw, unseasoned, not dried, not cured; untanned, unsmoked, unmellowed. **3.** *The Army makes men of green recruits:* inexperienced, callow, raw, untrained, rough, undisci-plined, crude, awkward; unpolished, unsophisticated, unversed, immature; unskilled, inexpert, ignorant, uninformed; gullible, easily fooled, credulous. **—***n.* **4.** *The town's stores were built around the green:* village green, common, heath, lawn, grassplot, turf, sward, greensward, verdure; campus; putting green, golf course. **—Ant.** 2 ripe, mature, matured, aged, developed, seasoned, finished. 3 experienced, mature, sophisticated, seasoned, skilled, expert, trained.

greet *v.* **1.** *The host greeted his guests at the door:* welcome, bid welcome, salute, hail, receive, admit, meet, accost; recognize, tip one's hat to, doff the cap to, speak to, smile upon. **2.** *The class greeted my suggestion with boos and hisses:* meet, receive, welcome, accept. **—Ant.** 1 ignore, shun, give the cold shoulder to; bid farewell, wave good-by.

greeting *n.* **1.** *The greeting of all the guests took more than an hour:* welcoming, welcome, saluting, salutation, salute, reception; introduction, presentation. **2.** Often **greetings** *When you see Jane, give her my greetings:* salutation, hello, regards, respects, remembrance, friendly message, felicitations, well-wishing, compliments, best, best wishes, good wishes.

gregarious *adj. A gregarious person loves parties:* sociable, social, genial, outgoing, convivial, extroverted, companionable, affable, friendly; vivacious, lively, talkative. **—Ant.** unsociable, solitary, reclusive, introverted, retiring, shy.

grief *n.* **1.** *No one could console them in their grief:* grieving, sorrow, sadness, heartbreak, heartache, misery, agony, woe, wretchedness, suffering, anguish, distress, despondency, despair, desolation; affliction, tribulation. **2.** *That used car has been a grief since the day I bought it:* grievance, hardship, trouble, burden, ordeal, worry, anxiety, care, concern, vexation, inconvenience, nuisance; remorse, discomfort. **—Ant.** 1 consolation, comfort, solace; joy, happiness, bliss, cheer, delight, enjoyment, gaiety, gladness, glee, rejoicing. 2 joy, comfort.

grievance *n. The workers demanded a committee to handle grievances:* complaint, *Slang* beef; injustice, wrong, disservice, hurt, affliction, iniquity, outrage, hardship, injury; *Informal* bone to pick. **—Ant.** benefit, privilege, boon; compliment.

grieve *v.* **1.** *The nation grieved for its war dead:* feel grief, mourn, weep, lament, sorrow, be sad, be anguished, be heavy-hearted, rue, wail, shed tears, cry, cry one's eyes out, sob, moan, bemoan. **2.** *The loss of the pet grieved the child:* sadden, make sorrowful, make unhappy, distress, agonize; pain, break the heart, make the heart bleed, wound the feelings of, cut to the quick; torture, harass, discomfort, oppress, deject, depress, disquiet, afflict. **—Ant.** 1, 2 console, comfort, solace, soothe, ease. 1 rejoice, delight in, enjoy, be happy about, be glad of. 2 delight, please, gratify, gladden, cheer, amuse, entertain.

grievous *adj.* **1.** *The death of Martin Luther King in 1968 was a most grievous loss:* tragic, sorrowful, sad, heartbreaking, woeful, agonizing, distressing, painful, lamentable. **2.** *The number of grievous crimes keeps increasing. She suffered a grievous injury:* very bad, grave, severe, serious, heavy, harsh, acute, critical, crucial, significant; appalling, atrocious, heinous, iniquitous, shocking, outrageous, monstrous, nefarious, shameful, deplorable, glaring; intolerable, insufferable, unbearable, harmful, distressing, lamentable, burdensome, destructive, calamitous. **—Ant.** 1 delightful, pleasant, pleasing, welcome, joyous, happy, glad; laughable, amusing, entertaining. 2 trivial, trifling, facetious, frivolous, unimportant, inconsequential, insignificant, mild, light.

grill *n.* **1.** *Cook the hotdogs on the grill:* griddle, gridiron, grid, grating, crossbars; broiler. **—***v.* **2.** *Let's grill the steaks over charcoal:* broil, fry, griddle, sear, cook. **3.** *Informal The police grilled the suspect about the missing jewels:* interrogate, question, pump, quiz, query, give the third degree to; cross-examine.

grim *adj.* **1.** *The boss has looked grim all morning:* somber, gloomy, austere; sullen, grumpy, sulky, scowling, morose, cantankerous; stern, severe, harsh, fierce, ferocious, unyielding, unrelenting, hard, relentless, merciless, cruel, brutal, heartless, vicious, inhuman, fiendish; obstinate, implacable, determined, resolute, inexorable. **2.** *The subject is too grim to make jokes about:* horrible, ghastly, sinister, grisly, frightful, horrid, hideous, gruesome, macabre, lurid, dreadful, repellent, repulsive, repugnant, forbidding, loathsome, appalling, foul, odious, revolting, shocking, squalid, ugly. **—Ant.** 1 happy, cheerful, joyful, gay, merry; lenient, benign, merciful, sympathetic, soft, easy, kind, kindly, amiable, amenable, congenial, genial. 2 pleasant, pleasing; attractive.

grimace *n.* **1.** *She made a grimace when I mentioned his name:* face, wry face, ugly expression, expression of distaste, smirk, contemptuous face, sneer. **—***v.* **2.** *The boy grimaced when his father said he couldn't borrow the car:* make a face, scowl, smirk, glower, lower.

grime *n. It takes strong soap to wash the grime out of clothes:* oily grit, dirt, dust, soil, soot, smut, filth, smudge.

grimy *adj. The grimy boys returned from the*

soccer field: grubby, begrimed, dirty, filthy, soiled, mucky, dingy, grungy, smeared, sooty.

grin n. **1.** A big grin broke out on his face when I told him how nice he looked: smile, beam, rictus, gleaming smile, broad grin, toothy grin, idiotic grin; simper, smirk. —v. **2.** She grinned with pleasure when the letter arrived: smile, beam, crack a smile, grin from ear to ear, grin like a chessy-cat; smirk, simper.

grind v. **1.** Most of the wheat will be ground into flour: pulverize, powder, granulate, crush, triturate, mill. **2.** In the olden days knife grinders used to go from house to house to grind all the knives: sharpen, whet, file, rasp; polish, scrape, abrade. **3.** The child grinds his teeth in his sleep: grate, rasp, gnash, grit. —n. **4.** Informal Writing this report every month is a real grind: chore, drudgery, dull task, laborious work, slavery, hard job. **5.** Informal In school he was a grind, but he got a great scholarship: drudge, bookworm, crammer, plodder, burner of midnight oil. —**Ant.** 2 dull, take the edge off. 4 easy job, enjoyable task, pleasure, joy, Slang piece of cake. 5 playboy, Slang goof-off.

grip n. **1.** The carpenter held the hammer securely in his grip: grasp, clutch, clasp, hold. **2.** He shook my hand with an iron grip: handclasp, handshake; gripping power. **3.** The woman was in the grip of a strong emotion. A navigator must have a good grip of mathematics: grasp, control, hold, retention, clutches, mastery, domination; understanding, comprehension, perception. **4.** The sword has a gold grip: handle, hilt. **5.** Grandmother traveled with a trunk and two grips: valise, suitcase, bag, traveling bag, satchel, gladstone. —v. **6.** He gripped the hammer and started nailing the wood together: grasp, seize firmly, clutch, clench, hold fast, hold tight; seize hold of, catch hold of, seize, grab, snatch. **7.** The reporter's account of the trial gripped the readers' interest: hold, retain, take hold on, spellbind, rivet, attract, impress.

gripe n. **1.** Often **gripes**. Green apples gave him the gripes: stomachache, bellyache, colic, cramps, spasm; affliction, distress, twinge, pang, pain, twitch. **2.** The foreman wouldn't listen to the workers' gripes: grievance, protest, complaint, faultfinding, whining, grousing, grumbling; Slang beef, kick, squawk. —v. **3.** The waitress griped about the small tip: complain, grumble, mutter, whine, find fault, grouse, grouch, fret, cavil, carp, rail, protest, Slang beef, kick, squawk, bellyache, Yiddish kvetch. —**Ant.** 2 complaint, flattery. 3 thank, express appreciation; compliment.

gripping n. Gripping requires the right tool: holding, fixing.

grisly adj. It was the most grisly crime the town had ever seen: gruesome, horrible, horrid, horrendous, hideous, ghastly, macabre, lurid, frightful, dreadful, shocking, gory, abominable, grim; abhorrent, repugnant, repellent, forbidding, revolting, repulsive, loathsome, foul, odious, sinister, appalling. —**Ant.** pleasant, pleasing, innocuous, attractive, charming, nice.

grit n. **1.** Wipe the grit off the window sill: soot,

dirt, dust, filth, muck. **2.** It took a lot of grit to cross the plains in a covered wagon: spunk, pluck, fortitude, courage, nerve, guts, sand; mettle, backbone; determination, tenacity, doggedness, perseverance, resolution, indomitable spirit, stamina. —v. **3.** The patient gritted his teeth in pain: grind together, rub, grate, scrape, rasp, gnash, crunch. —**Ant.** 2 faintheartedness, cowardice, timidity; faltering, wavering, hesitation, vacillation.

gritty adj. **1.** There were gritty particles in their shoes: abrasive, scratchy, grainy, granular, sandy, gravelly, rasping, rough. **2.** Fighting off the mugger was a gritty thing to do: brave, courageous, game, plucky, mettlesome.

groan v. **1.** The patient groaned as he was lifted onto the stretcher. The class groaned when the teacher assigned the homework: moan, whimper; grumble, complain, murmur, wail, lament; roar, howl, bellow, bleat; bemoan. **2.** The old gate groaned on its hinges: creak, resound harshly; squeak, screech. —n. **3.** With a groan the boxer realized he had lost: moan, whimper, whine, sorrowful murmur, wail, lament. **4.** We could hear the groan of the roof under the weight of the snow: moan, creak, crack, squeak.

groggy adj. I'm always groggy when I first wake up: lethargic, punchy, dopey, sluggish, befuddled, bewildered, perplexed, dazed, unsteady, stunned, dizzy, punch-drunk, staggering, reeling, shaky, Slang woozy, stupefied, addled, muddled, confused. —**Ant.** alert, on the ball, sharp, aware, on one's toes.

groom n. **1.** The groom helped the king put on his robes: valet, manservant, servant, lackey, flunky; livery servant, British boots. **2.** The groom led the horse to the barn: stableboy, hostler; footman. **3.** The groom waited at the altar for the bride: bridegroom; newly married man, husband, spouse, consort. —v. **4.** The cowboy groomed his horse with loving care: curry, currycomb, brush, comb, rub down. **5.** The girl spent hours grooming herself before the party: clean up, wash, make tidy, make neat, spruce up, primp, preen, comb, freshen, refresh; dress. **6.** The mayor is being groomed for governor: prepare, prime, make ready; train, educate, develop, indoctrinate, familiarize with; initiate, drill, exercise, practice.

groove n. **1.** The groove on the school desk is for pens and pencils: rut, furrow, gutter, channel, trench, flute, hollow; cut, cutting, scoring, score, corrugation. **2.** A vacation is a good time to get out of one's groove and do something different: rut, habit, fixed routine, set way of doing things, beaten path, matter of course; convention, second nature, usage, procedure, rule, practice, custom, use. —**Ant.** 1 ridge, bump.

grope v. **1.** I groped for the light switch in the dark room: feel about, fumble, probe; fish for, paw, finger; move blindly, feel one's way, move stumblingly. **2.** He groped for the right answer to the problem: search blindly, fumble, probe; venture, try one's luck, see how the land lies, send up a trial balloon, throw out a feeler.

gross adj. **1.** The firm's gross profit was over a

million dollars last year: total, whole, entire, aggregate; total before deductions, before expenses, before taxes. **2.** *The accident was caused by gross negligence:* flagrant, downright, sheer, utter, complete, total, plain, glaring, obvious, manifest; rank, egregious, heinous, outrageous, unmitigated, unqualified, unequivocal. **3.** *His gross remarks made us cringe:* coarse, crude, unrefined, vulgar, indelicate, improper, uncouth, offensive, unseemly; lewd, lascivious, lecherous, carnal, smutty, foul-mouthed, earthy, ribald, indecent, obscene, licentious, sordid. **4.** *The man was so gross he could hardly get through the door:* fat, obese, overweight, heavy; big, large, bulky, unwieldy, huge, great, vast, immense, enormous, monstrous, gigantic, massive, stupendous, colossal, prodigious, titanic, gargantuan. —*n.* **5.** *What is the gross of your earnings?:* sum total, total, total amount, whole, aggregate, lump sum; bulk, mass, main body; total before deductions. —*v.* **6.** *A popular movie can gross 50 million dollars:* earn, take in, make a gross profit of, pick up, reap; *Slang* bag, bring home. —**Ant.** 1, 5 net; total after deductions, total after expenses. 2 partial, mitigated, qualified. 3 delicate, dainty, graceful; refined, cultivated, elegant; decent, proper, inoffensive, chaste. 4 thin, slim, svelte; small, little, tiny, petite. 6 net, clear; loose.

grotesque *adj.* **1.** *These grotesque statues are relics of prehistoric times:* distorted, deformed, odd-shaped, misshapen, contorted, unnatural, fantastic, weird, bizarre, fanciful, strange, outlandish, odd, peculiar, eccentric, incongruous; wild, extravagant, exotic, rococo, baroque. **2.** *She never appreciated his grotesque humor:* outlandish, absurd, odd, distorted, fantastic, antic, wild, extravagant, weird, bizarre, preposterous; *Slang* far-out, way-out. —**Ant.** 1 well-proportioned, graceful, classic; realistic, natural, naturalistic; familiar. 2 routine, average, standard, normal, typical, unimaginative; down-to-earth.

grotto *n.* **1.** *They stopped to pray at the roadside grotto:* cavelike shrine, grot; catacomb. **2.** *The children hid in a small grotto on the side of the hill:* cavern, cave, recess, hollow; tunnel, burrow.

grouch *n.* **1.** *Why did you have to be a grouch and spoil the party?:* complainer, grumbler, curmudgeon, sulky person, pouter, ill-humored person, sullen person, moper, mope, crab, crank; *Slang* wet blanket, killjoy, spoilsport. —*v.* **2.** *It doesn't do any good to grouch about the bad weather:* complain, find fault, gripe, grumble, mutter, whine, cry, growl, grouse, cavil, carp, rail, protest; *Slang* beef, kick, bellyache; sulk, fret, pout, mope. —**Ant.** 1 charmer, flatterer, prince charming; life of the party. 2 compliment, flatter.

grouchy *adj.* *He was always grouchy in the morning:* cantankerous, irritable, irascible, fractious, cross, crotchety, choleric, foul-tempered, mean-tempered, grumpy, ornery, testy, touchy, peevish, surly, vinegary. —**Ant.** even-tempered, gracious.

ground *n.* **1.** *After that bumpy plane ride it's good to be back on the ground:* the earth, firm land, terra firma; dry land. **2.** *The ground must be plowed in early spring:* earth, soil, dirt, sod, turf, loam. **3.** Sometimes **grounds** *Houses should be built on high ground. Now that you've seen the house, I'll show you around the grounds:* tract of land, land, terrain; region, habitat, area, territory, realm, province, district, bailiwick, domain, sphere; property, premises, real estate, estate, lawns, gardens; yard, campus; farm, field, acres. **4.** Usually **grounds** *What grounds do you have for firing him?:* basis, cause, reason, motive, excuse; purpose, rationale, object, account, principle, occasion, considerations, arguments, inducement, call; reason why, pros and cons, the whys and wherefores. **5. grounds** *Put the coffee grounds in the garbage:* sediment, dregs; settlings, deposit. —*v.* **6.** *A storm grounded the ship on a sandbar:* run aground, beach, strand, founder. **7.** *Your accusation must be grounded on facts:* base, establish, fix firmly, support, settle, found, set, secure, confirm, organize, institute. **8.** *All applicants must be well grounded in mathematics:* instruct, train, teach, familiarize with, educate, indoctrinate, inform, initiate; drill, exercise, practice, discipline, prepare. —**Ant.** 1 the air, the sky; the sea, the ocean, water. 6 float; launch.

groundless *adj.* *The accusation is groundless and can't be backed up by facts:* without basis, baseless, unjustified, unjustifiable, unwarranted, unfounded, unsupported, without reason, without cause, without foundation, uncalled for, needless, idle, gratuitous, illogical, not following, imaginary, chimerical, unreal, flimsy, empty; unproved, false, fallacious, faulty, erroneous, untrue. —**Ant.** well-founded, reasonable, justified, logical, true, proven, provable, supported, real, substantial.

groundwork *n.* **1.** *The framers of the Magna Carta laid the groundwork on which our freedom is based. Constant practice is the groundwork for success in playing the piano:* foundation, basis, base, ground, grounds, underpinning, footing, bedrock, cornerstone, keystone, root, taproot, spring, cradle, origin, source; first principle, fundamental, fundamentals. **2.** *It will take a lot of groundwork before we can start a new business:* preparation, planning, spadework, preliminary steps; apprenticeship, learning, training, practice, indoctrination.

group *n.* **1.** *A group of students asked to see the principal:* assemblage, aggregation, gathering, collection, congregation, representation; crowd, band, throng, party, company, cluster, bunch, pack, gang, troop, detachment; hoard, swarm, herd, flock. **2.** *Children and the elderly are two groups who watch TV regularly:* class, classification, variety, species, branch, division, subdivision, section; set, faction, clique, circle, coterie, association, league, brotherhood, fraternity; family, tribe, clan. —*v.* **3.** *Group the shoes together according to size:* sort, organize, range, marshal, line up, align, arrange, combine, cluster, coordinate, classify, class, assign, sift, catalog, place, file, register, alphabetize, index, size; grade, graduate. **4.** *At every party the same people group together:* associate, fraternize, mingle, cluster, marshal, hobnob, keep company, consort. —*Ant.* 1, 2 individual. 3 separate, disperse, scatter.

grouse *v. He's always grousing about his wife's cooking:* complain, grumble, fret, gripe, fuss, fume, grouch, mutter; *Slang* bellyache, crab, kick, beef, put up a squawk, take on, carry on. —*Ant.* praise, extol, laud, commend, acclaim.

grove *n.* **1.** *We had our picnic in a quiet grove:* thicket, copse, coppice, woodland, cluster of trees, small wood, bosk, wood lot, wildwood, brake; shrubbery, pinery; forest, timber. **2.** *The house looks out over a banana grove:* orchard, cluster of fruit trees, plantation.

grovel *v. I hate to see a man grovel before his superiors:* humble oneself, demean oneself, be servile, behave abjectly, cower, cringe; fawn, toady, crawl, kowtow, stoop, snivel, truckle, flatter, lick the boots of, bow and scrape. —*Ant.* be proud, be haughty, act superior; domineer, intimidate, browbeat.

grow *v.* **1.** *My, how that child has grown!:* become larger, grow taller, spring up, shoot up, fill out; expand, increase, swell, widen, stretch, spread, extend; magnify, amplify, aggrandize. **2.** *Orange trees won't grow in this climate:* develop, mature, come to fruition, ripen; germinate, vegetate, sprout, bud, fructify, blossom, flower, bloom. **3.** *This looks like good soil to grow wheat:* cultivate, raise, produce, propagate, breed; sow, plant, till, farm, garden. **4.** *The report shows how our business has grown this year:* thrive, flourish, progress, develop, prosper, succeed, advance, improve, enlarge, increase, expand, rise, surge, wax, boom, mushroom, skyrocket. **5.** *The patient grew weaker every day:* become, get to be, come to be. **6.** *Playing with the orchestra helped him grow as a musician:* mature, develop; obtain experience, get practice, have training; become worldly, become sophisticated. —*Ant.* 1, 4 shrink, decrease, diminish, lessen, dwindle. 2 die, fail, decline, decay. 4 decline, slacken, subside, wane.

growl *v.* **1.** *The dog growled when the stranger came close:* snarl, bark menacingly. **2.** *The boss won't growl at you for asking for a raise:* snap, speak harshly, reply gruffly, complain, grumble, grouse, gripe, fret; mutter, murmur, rumble, groan, grunt, whine, croak. **3.** *My stomach begins to growl around lunchtime:* rumble, whine, croak, grind; *Informal* talk back.

grown-up *n.* **1.** *The movie was for grown-ups only:* adult, mature person, man, woman, gentleman, lady, grown man, grown woman. —*adj.* **2.** *When she was grown-up she would be a doctor. That was not a very grown-up way to behave:* adult, mature, full-grown, of age, big, senior, ripe, full-fledged, full-blown, at the age of consent. —*Ant.* 2 little, small, juvenile; childish, immature.

growth *n.* **1.** *It's awesome to watch the growth of a child. Has that cherry tree reached its full growth?:* natural development, development; advancement, advance, progress, improvement; maturity, matureness, prime. **2.** *The growth of our business has been phenomenal. Our city's growth must be encouraged:* expansion, increase, development, extension, increment, enlargement, burgeoning, surge, spread, swell, amplification, augmentation; progress, improvement, advancement, advance, prospering, flourishing, rise, success. **3.** *Is all this wheat just one season's growth?:* crop, harvest, production, cultivation, produce, flowering, planting, sowing, propagation. **4.** *The doctor removed a small growth from the patient's chin:* mass of tissue, lump, gnarl, hump, tumor; excrescence. —*Ant.* 2 decrease, decline, lessening, dwindling, shrinking, shrinkage, slackening, subsiding, retreat, backsliding, failure; stagnation.

grubby *adj. He came to dinner in grubby jeans and T-shirt:* dirty, grimy, sloppy, slovenly, unkempt, messy, seedy, frowzy, filthy, nasty, squalid, foul, shoddy, shabby, tacky, frumpy, bedraggled, sordid, *Slang* beat-up. —*Ant.* neat, well-groomed, well-pressed, clean, tidy, spick-and-span.

grudge *n.* **1.** *Do you still bear him a grudge for cheating you?:* ill will, resentment, hard feelings, malice, spite, malevolence, rancor, pique, aversion, dislike, animosity, animus, hatred. —*v.* **2.** *I don't grudge her her good fortune, but she should share it with others:* begrudge, envy, resent, be provoked at, be indignant at, cast a jaundiced eye at. —*Ant.* 1 appreciation, thankfulness, goodwill, benevolence, friendliness, liking. 2 celebrate, be pleased for.

grudging *adj. He sent us a grudging apology:* reluctant, unenthusiastic, unwilling, begrudging, apathetic, indifferent, perfunctory, lukewarm, tepid, ungenerous, mean-spirited. —*Ant.* enthusiastic, generous.

grueling *adj. Working in a mine is a grueling job:* tiring, exhausting, fatiguing; hard, punishing, racking, torturous, brutal. —*Ant.* easy, soft, *Slang* cushy; enjoyable, pleasant; exhilarating, exciting.

gruesome *adj. The gruesome story of graves and ghosts frightened the child:* horrible, horrifying, hideous, horrid, horrendous, grisly, gory, ghastly, frightful, spine-chilling, bloodcurdling; revolting, repulsive, loathsome, repellent; grim, forbidding, shocking, fearful, terrible, awful, macabre. —*Ant.* pleasing, pleasant, cheery, cheerful, delightful, lovely, appealing, benign, sweet, sentimental.

gruff *adj.* **1.** *The sergeant always gave a gruff answer to the soldiers' questions:* surly, brusque, curt, blunt, short, abrupt, stern, bluff; uncivil, rude, impolite, discourteous, ungracious, insulting; snarling, grumpy, grouchy, bearish, sour, crabbed, churlish; caustic, tart, sharp, waspish, ill-humored, ill-natured, ill-tempered, sulky, sullen, peevish, bristling, crusty. **2.** *A slight cold had given the speaker a gruff voice:* hoarse, husky, rough, harsh, throaty, raspy, gutteral; cracked, croaky, ragged, strident. **—Ant.** 1 pleasant, kind, sweet, good-humored; courteous, polite, civil, gracious. 2 smooth, mellifluous, rich.

grumble v. The handyman wouldn't do anything without grumbling first: grouse, fret, murmur discontentedly, mutter, complain, grouch, gripe, growl, chafe, find fault.

grumpy adj. Many people are grumpy when they first wake up: surly, ill-tempered, crabby, cranky, grouchy, sullen, sulky, irritable, disgruntled, ill-humored, cantankerous, peevish, pettish, out of sorts, testy, out of humor, in a bad temper, in a bad mood, sour; churlish, ill-disposed, moody, splenetic, crusty. **—Ant.** in a good mood, in good humor, pleasant, cheerful, sweet, kindly disposed.

guarantee n. **1.** The new car has a one-year guarantee: warranty, written promise of quality, written assurance of durability; surety, endorsement, guaranty, affirmation, pledge, assurance, avowal, word, word of honor, security, testimony; bond, bail. **2.** Beauty is no guarantee of happiness: assurance, promise. **—v. 3.** The manufacturer guaranteed the new furnace for five years: give a guarantee on, warrant, vouch for; assure, endorse, insure, underwrite, sponsor; avow, testify. **4.** The travel brochure guarantees that you'll have the time of your life. Buying a train ticket doesn't guarantee you a seat: promise, pledge, give one's word, vouch for, assure, affirm, allege, avow, attest, swear, stand behind; be responsible for, make oneself answerable for, make certain, answer for, become surety for, bind oneself, contract.

guaranteed adj. A guaranteed job was far from certain: assured, ascertained, insured, certain, pledged, bonded, certified, confirmed, endorsed, protected, sealed, secured, sure, surefire.

guaranty n. **1.** Howard gave his guaranty that I would repay the loan: warrant, warranty, pledge, guarantee, formal assurance, security, surety, insurance, endorsement, covenant, promise; contract, agreement, voucher. **2.** The bank can't give the loan without some kind of guaranty: collateral, security, pledge, pawn; bail, bond; deposit.

guard v. **1.** Three soldiers guarded the prince whenever he left the palace. Wear a hat to guard your face against the sun: protect, safeguard, shield, shelter, defend; watch over, keep safe, preserve, secure; save; attend, tend, mind, escort, conduct, convoy. **2.** Policemen guarded the prisoner throughout the trial: keep under surveillance, keep watch over, keep under close watch, keep from escaping. **—n. 3.** The guard won't let anyone through the gate without a pass: sentinel, sentry, watchman, guardsman, warder, Slang watchdog; body of defenders, garrison, patrol, picket, watch, convoy, escort; protector, bodyguard, defender; guardian, custodian, gatekeeper, doorkeeper, concierge. **4.** All football players should wear face guards: shield, screen, safeguard; defense, protection, security, preservation. **—Ant.** 1 expose to danger, endanger, threaten; menace, imperil.

guarded adj. Her answers were guarded and noncommittal: cautious, chary, wary, careful, restrained, discreet, circumspect, prudent, cagey, leery, mindful, heedful, on one's guard; hesitant, tentative. **—Ant.** reckless, careless, daring, frank, rash, foolhardy.

guardian n. **1.** The churches are the guardians of the faith: protector, preserver, keeper, custodian, defender, guard, trustee, caretaker, shepherd, curator, conservator, watchdog, vigilante, warden, warder, wardsman; guard, escort, bodyguard, sentry, picket, sentinel, patrol, convoy, champion, safeguard, attendant, conductor. **2.** Children may go on the trip only with the consent of their parents or guardians: legal custodian, protector, patron, benefactor; guardian angel, champion, advocate, friend at court. **—Ant.** 1 enemy, foe, opponent, attacker; traitor. 2 ward, protégé.

guerilla n. The guerillas ambushed the platoon: partisan, irregular.

guess v. **1.** You win a prize if he doesn't guess your weight correctly: judge correctly, estimate correctly, correctly answer, answer with the facts; divine, figure out; speculate, conjecture, risk an opinion on, hazard a supposition, hypothesize, make a stab at. **2.** I guess we'll go to Florida on our vacation this year: think, suppose, believe, assume, suspect, daresay, venture, conclude, gather, deduce, surmise, opine, fancy, imagine; judge, deem, reckon, estimate, predict, theorize, regard. **—n. 3.** My guess is that the job will take four hours: estimate, supposition, assumption, speculation, opinion, belief, view, hypothesis, conjecture, presumption, surmise, prediction, suspicion, feeling, divination, theory, guesswork, postulation, postulate. **—Ant.** 1 know, prove. 3 certainty, fact.

guest n. **1.** How many guests are coming for dinner?: invitee, visitor, caller, friend; company. **2.** The motel can accommodate 400 guests: (variously) roomer, boarder, lodger, sojourner, diner; patron, customer, client, paying customer, habitué, frequenter; patient, inmate. **—Ant.** 1 host, hostess.

guffaw n. He let out a guffaw when I finished telling the joke: burst of laughter, peal of laughter, hearty laugh, boisterous laugh, roar of mirth, howl, scream, shout of merriment; Slang horse laugh, belly laugh.

guidance n. **1.** The young man sought guidance on the choice of a career: counsel, advice, help; information, instruction, intelligence, enlightenment, pointer, tip, suggestion, clue, hint. **2.** Funds will be spent under the committee's guidance: direction, leadership, management, conduct, supervision, auspices; escort, protection, lead.

guide v. **1.** The hunters need someone to guide them through the jungle: lead, pilot, steer, show the way to, direct, conduct; escort, usher, accompany, convoy, shepherd. **2.** Can the pilot guide the plane to a safe landing? My father guided this business to success: maneuver, manipulate, manage, handle, direct, conduct, control, command, engineer, steer, lead, pilot, regulate; rule, govern, preside over, oversee, superintend, have charge of. —*n.* **3.** *Their guide through the mountains was a young Indian scout:* pilot, escort, convoy; conductor, leader, helmsman, steerer, director, cicerone, usher; marshal, shepherd, attendant, chaperon. **4.** *Let your conscience be your guide. That old tree is a guide to where the gold is hidden:* counselor, adviser, monitor, mentor, teacher, master; model, example, rule, pattern; landmark, signpost, marker, beacon, guiding light, polestar, lodestar. —**Ant.** 1 misguide, mislead. 3 follower. 4 disciple, imitator, pupil.

guild *n.* *The musicians formed a guild to present concerts:* professional organization, association, society, league, fraternity, brotherhood, sisterhood, alliance, company, corporation, federation, confederacy, order, coalition; union, trade union, labor union, craft union.

guile *n.* *He's full of guile, so be careful he doesn't cheat you:* slyness, trickery, trickiness, cunning, craft, craftiness, artifice, chicanery, wiliness, artfulness, strategy, sharp practice; deceit, treachery, duplicity, fraud, fraudulence, deception, dishonesty, *Slang* hanky-panky; tricks, stratagems. —**Ant.** candor, frankness, honesty, sincerity, naiveté, veracity, truthfulness.

guileless *adj.* *The child gave a guileless answer to the question:* straightforward, candid, frank, open, natural, honest, sincere, truthful, aboveboard; artless, undesigning; ingenuous, naive, unsophisticated, innocent, simple, unaffected, unselfconscious; harmless, innocuous, unoffending. —**Ant.** sly, cunning, deceitful, crafty, tricky, deceptive, artful; treacherous, fraudulent.

guilt *n.* **1.** *The prosecuting attorney tried to establish the suspect's guilt:* guiltiness, guilty conduct, criminality, culpability; wrongdoing, misconduct, misdoing, misdeed, misbehavior, wrong, turpitude, transgression; sinfulness, sin, vice; trespass, delinquency, dereliction. **2.** *Nothing could erase the guilt from his conscience:* guilty feeling, shame, disgrace, self-disgust, humiliation, degradation, dishonor, infamy; stigma, blot, black mark. —**Ant.** 1 innocence, blamelessness, righteousness, sinlessness, good deed, virtue. 2 pride, honor, self-respect.

guiltless *adj.* *The court absolved the guiltless parties:* innocent, spotless, blameless, immaculate, pure, unsullied, unpolluted, untarnished. —**Ant.** culpable, guilty, sullied, tarnished.

guilty *adj.* **1.** *The jury found the defendant guilty:* justly charged, having committed a crime, culpable, blamable, blameworthy, responsible for a wrongdoing. **2.** *The thief sought forgiveness for his guilty acts:* criminal; immoral, sinful, wrong, corrupt, erring, offensive. **3.** *His guilty look gave him away:* sheepish, hangdog; contrite, sorry, regretful, ashamed, conscience-stricken, penitent, repentant. —**Ant.** 1–3 innocent. 1 blameless. 2 moral, righteous, virtuous. 3 proud, noble.

guise *n.* *The king traveled throughout the land in the guise of a monk:* dress, attire, garb, costume, habit, clothing, apparel, clothes, mode, fashion; disguise, pretense, masquerade.

gulf *n.* **1.** *A hurricane is forming in the Gulf of Mexico:* large bay, estuary, arm of the sea, firth, fjord, inlet, cove, lagoon. **2.** *The earthquake left a gulf in the field. The gulf between the two friends widened:* chasm, abyss, crevasse, canyon, gully, opening, rent, cleft; rift, split, separation.

gullible *adj.* *The youth was so gullible he bought the Brooklyn Bridge from a con man!:* easily fooled, easily deceived, easily cheated, easily duped; overtrusting, unsuspicious, credulous, trusting, trustful; naive, innocent, unsophisticated, inexperienced, green, simple. —**Ant.** cynical, suspicious, untrusting, hard to convince; sophisticated, worldly.

gully *n.* **1.** *When snow melts in the mountains the gully is flooded:* ravine, gulch, gap, small valley, defile, gorge, small canyon; watercourse, channel. **2.** *The road was constructed with a gully on each side:* ditch, drainage ditch, gutter; furrow, trench.

gulp *v.* **1.** *I was so thirsty I gulped three glasses of water. The boy gulped down his lunch and ran out to play:* swallow in large mouthfuls, swallow eagerly, swallow greedily, swill, guzzle, swig, quaff, wolf, toss off; bolt, devour. —*n.* **2.** *There's just one gulp of milk left in the glass:* mouthful, swallow, swig, large draft. —**Ant.** 1 sip, drink daintily; nibble, eat daintily.

gumption *n.* *It takes a lot of gumption to work and go to school at the same time:* initiative, spirit, drive, energy, resourcefulness, enterprise, courage, forcefulness, hustle, aggressiveness, verve, dash, spunk, push; *Slang* get up and go, pizazz, zip.

gun *n.* **1.** *The policeman drew his gun from its holster:* firearm; (*variously*) revolver, pistol, automatic, .45, .38, .22, six-shooter, Colt, derringer; rifle, shotgun, carbine, Winchester, musket, fowling piece, muzzle loader, blunderbuss, flintlock, Kentucky rifle, machine gun; *Slang* gat, shooting iron, iron, trusty-rusty, rod, piece, equalizer. **2.** *The antitank guns were wheeled into place:* cannon, fieldpiece, artillery piece, big gun, piece of ordnance; (*variously*) mortar, howitzer, Big Bertha, Long Tom. —*v.* **3.** *The hunters were gunning for deer:* hunt, go after, shoot, expect to shoot; try, attempt, aim.

gurgle *v.* **1.** *The cider gurgled from the jug into the glass:* flow noisily, bubble, burble, babble, plash, sputter, ripple. —*n.* **2.** *We listened to the soothing gurgle of the brook:* gurgling, bubbling, babble, burble, murmur, plash, sputter.

guru *n.* *She readily accepted him as her guru:* teacher, guide, instructor, tutor, coach, trainer, handler, preceptor, master, docent, expert. —**Ant.** student, acolyte, follower.

gush *v.* **1.** *Oil gushed from the well:* flow forth, pour out, spurt, spout, stream, jet, well, burst forth, rush forth, issue, run, splash, squirt. **2.** *She gushed so much I didn't get a word in edgewise:* talk effusively, be overenthusiastic, chatter, babble, burble, gab, prattle, blather, blabber, prate, rattle on, run off at the mouth; flatter excessively. —*n.* **3.** *A gush of water came out when the pump started:* sudden outflow, outpouring, spurt, torrent, stream, jet, spout, squirt, splash, rush, outburst. **4.** *Do we have to listen to that gush about your high-school days?:* foolish talk, boring talk, mawkishness, sentimentalism, emotionalism; nonsense, stuff and nonsense, twaddle, blabber, drivel, rubbish, chatter, blab; *Slang* hot air, gas, baloney, bull. —**Ant.** 1 drip, trickle, dribble, ooze. 2 be close-mouthed, be uncommunicative. 3 drip, trickle.

gust *n.* **1.** *A gust of wind scattered the leaves:* puff, blast, draft, breeze, wind; zephyr, squall, flurry, blow. **2.** *A loud gust of laughter came from the next room:* burst, outburst, outbreak, sudden rush, explosion, paroxysm, fit. —*v.* **3.** *When the wind gusts this way it's no good for sailing:* blow in bursts, blow intermittently, puff, blast.

gusto *n.* *The hungry man ate with gusto:* hearty enjoyment, relish, zest, enthusiasm, fervor, joy, exhilaration, zeal, delight, pleasure, appreciation, savor, satisfaction, appetite; personal liking, individual taste.

gusty *adj.* *A gusty wind almost blew us down:* blustering, windy, breezy, stormy, squally.

gut *v.* **1.** *The pheasants must be gutted before they're cooked:* eviscerate, clean, disembowel. **2.** *Fire gutted several houses in the block:* destroy the interior of; lay in ashes, level, ravage, raze, consume, lay waste, lay in ruins. —*n.* **3.** *Is catgut used to make violin strings? He complained to the doctor of a pain in his gut:* intestines, entrails, viscera; lower alimentary canal, bowels, *Slang* breadbasket. **4.** *Slang You're*
getting a big gut from overeating:* stomach, abdomen; paunch, belly; bay window, beer belly, spare tire. **5. guts** *Slang It really took guts to speak up to that bully:* courage, bravery, boldness, mettle, spunk; daring, bravado, spirit, nerve, backbone, audacity, dash.

gutless *adj.* *Fleeing his creditors was a gutless thing to do:* spineless, cowardly, craven, abject, fainthearted, feeble, weak, *Informal* chicken, lily-livered. —**Ant.** bold, determined, resolute.

guttural *adj.* *The actress was known for her guttural voice:* throaty, husky, deep, low; hoarse, harsh, raspy, croaking, gruff; thick, inarticulate. —**Ant.** nasal, high-pitched, high, squeaky.

guy *n.* Guys and Dolls *was an outstanding musical:* man, fellow, male, lad, *British* bloke, chap *Informal* cat.

guzzle *v.* *Don't guzzle your soda!:* drink greedily, gulp down; swill, swig, toss off, quaff, imbibe, tipple; eat greedily, bolt, devour. —**Ant.** sip, drink daintily; nibble, eat daintily.

gyp *v.* **1.** *He gypped me out of $50 on that deal:* cheat, swindle, defraud, take advantage of, cozen, bamboozle, hoodwink, bilk, diddle, rook, soak; *Slang* rip off, burn. —*n.* **2.** *That movie was a real gyp:* fraud, flimflam, trick, deception, hoax, cheat, con game, fake, phony, humbug; *Slang* ripoff, con, scam.

gyrate *v.* *The figure skater gyrated faster and faster:* spin around, rotate, revolve, circle, twirl, whirl, turn around, wheel, spiral, swirl, pirouette.

H

habit n. **1.** *Moles have the habit of burrowing in the earth. Where did the habit of shaking hands originate?:* practice, behavior pattern, habitude, custom, convention, matter of course, routine, beaten path, rut, groove; characteristic tendency, trait, proclivity, peculiarity, inclination, wont, second nature; rule, observance, manner, mannerism. **2.** *George has that awful habit of picking his teeth:* way, practice, acquired mode of behavior, habitual action, fixed practice, confirmed way; leaning, inclination, predisposition, predilection, partiality, fondness, propensity, prevailing tendency. **3.** *Each order of nuns wears its own special habit:* dress, attire, costume, garment, garb, apparel, raiment, clothes, clothing, outfit, uniform, robe, vesture, livery; gear, trappings, accoutrements, habiliments.

habitat n. **1.** *The Western plains were the habitat of the buffalo:* native environment, natural home, natural locality, area of distribution; terrain, territory, range, domain, realm, milieu, environment, haunt, place, spot, locale, setting, region, zone, precinct; *Slang* stamping ground, home base. **2.** *The hermit's habitat was a crude cabin:* dwelling, dwelling place, place of abode, abode, domicile, habitation; home, housing, lodging, lodgment, quarters; *Slang* digs, roost, pad.

habitation n. **1.** *These tenements are not fit for habitation:* occupancy, tenancy, occupation, dwelling, lodging, lodgment, residence; abode, temporary stay. **2.** *Their mountain habitation is far from the city's noise:* abode, place of residence, dwelling, dwelling place, home, habitat, place of abode, domicile, haunt, residence, house; housing, lodging, shelter, quarters; *Slang* digs, roost, pad. **3.** *The pioneers built a habitation near the mouth of the river:* settlement, community, colony.

habitual adj. **1.** *Singing in the shower is habitual with him. Grandfather sat in his habitual place near the fire:* customary, usual, accustomed, regular, normal, natural, common, fixed, established, traditional, typical, wonted, familiar, expected, conventional; routine, recurrent, inveterate, confirmed; continual, incessant; by force of habit, second nature. **2.** *Harold has become a habitual borrower:* chronic, confirmed, inveterate, constant, addicted, continual, frequent, repeated, periodic, recurrent, established, ingrained, deep-seated, deep-rooted, perpetual, systematic, methodical. **—Ant.** 1 rare, uncommon, unusual, exceptional, abnormal, extraordinary, strange, unexpected, occasional. 2 infrequent, sporadic, irregular, unconfirmed.

habituate v. *Working on the farm habituated him to rising early:* accustom, make used to, indoctrinate, inculcate; break in, inure, harden, instill, imbue, adapt, discipline, initiate, season, train, school, drill.

habitué n. *Mildred is a habitué of the city's museums:* frequenter, regular patron, frequent visitor, constant customer; *Informal* regular.

hack[1] v. **1.** *He hacked at the logs with his hatchet. Carve the turkey nicely—don't hack it:* cut roughly, cut, cut up, chop, hew, chip, mangle, mutilate, lacerate, notch, gash, slit, slice, cleave, slash; *Slang* whack. **2.** *The boy's been hacking ever since he caught cold:* cough repeatedly, cough drily, emit short coughs, rasp; *Slang* bark.

hack[2] n. **1.** *One needs a special license to drive a hack:* taxicab, taxi, cab. **2.** *My grandfather recalled hiring a hack to take him to his wedding:* hackney coach, horse-drawn carriage, coach; horse-drawn carriage for hire. **3.** *Grandmother owned her own carriage and had a hack to pull it:* medium-sized horse, common horse, carriage horse, hackney; *Slang* nag, plug; worn-out horse; hired horse, horse for common hire; cart horse, shaft horse, dray horse, draft horse, workhorse. **4.** *The need for money turned a talented writer into a hack:* scribbler, penny-a-liner, grubstreet writer. **—Ant.** 3 thoroughbred; pony.

hackneyed adj. *The play had a hackneyed plot:* commonplace, routine, common, stale, trite, banal, inane, insipid, vapid, stereotyped, clichéd, threadbare, pedestrian, stock, worn-out, worn, well-worn, shopworn, platitudinous, conventional, bromidic, ordinary, moth-eaten, humdrum, uninspired, unimaginative; dull, jejune. **—Ant.** original, new, fresh, novel, imaginative, creative, unusual, uncommon; striking.

hag n. *The old hag screamed that we were trespassing:* harridan, crone, harpy, ogress, virago, shrew, hellcat, gorgon, witch, nag, beldam, vixen, termagant, biddy, frump, drab, fury; *Slang* bat, battle-ax.

haggard adj. **1.** *The sailor was haggard from his long, lonely voyage:* tired-looking, hollow-eyed, gaunt, careworn, woebegone; exhausted, spent, weary, fatigued, tired, debilitated, drooping, fagged, toilworn, worn, wasted, overwearied, flagging; *Slang* tuckered out, beat, bushed, pooped. **2.** *She was haggard with fright and we hardly recognized her:* wild-eyed, wild-looking, wild, frenzied, overcome, overwrought, upset, raging, ranting, harassed, harrowed. **—Ant.** 1 full of pep, energetic, vigorous, jaunty, bright-eyed and bushy-tailed, well-rested; hale, hale and hearty, glowing with health, robust, sleek. 2 calm, serene, tranquil.

haggle v. **1.** *The women were haggling over the price of a fish:* dicker, bargain, barter, higgle, beat down. **2.** *We always haggle over who should wash the dishes:* squabble, quibble, bicker, wrangle, quarrel, dispute.

hail v. **1.** *An old friend hailed me from across the street. The host hailed the guests at the door:* call to, shout at, cry out to, address, greet, accost, salute; welcome, receive, usher in, shake hands with, make welcome, bid one welcome. **2.** *The people lined the streets to hail the returning heroes:* acclaim, cheer, applaud, exalt, honor, glorify, eulogize, extol, panegyrize, esteem, compliment, commend. —*n.* **3.** *Through the fog we heard a hail from another ship:* shout, call, accosting, calling out, hello, salutation, greeting, salute. **—Ant.** 1 ignore, avoid, shun, cut. 2 condemn, rebuff, insult, criticize, boo, hiss.

hair *n.* **1.** *She has the most beautiful red hair I've ever seen:* head of hair, tresses, locks, curls, ringlets, bangs; *Slang* mop, mane; *(of animal)* coat, fur, pelt, fleece; wool, down, mane. **2.** *The car just missed the pedestrian by a hair:* narrow margin, iota, hair's-breadth.

hairless *adj.* *His forearms were hairless:* depilated, bald, smooth, shaved, shaven.

hairsplitting *adj.* *I don't think that these hairsplitting differences matter in the least:* hairline, minute, subtle, delicate, fine, minuscule; unapparent, imperceptible, inappreciable, inconsequential, infinitesimal; carping, quibbling, niggling, caviling, nitpicking, faultfinding, overcritical.

hairstyle *n.* *She approved of her friend's hairstyle:* hairdo, haircut, coiffure.

hairy *adj.* *Keep that hairy dog off the couch!:* hirsute, pilose, shaggy, bushy, woolly, furry, fleecy.

halcyon *adj.* *Most adults look back on their school days as halcyon times:* calm, peaceful, serene, pacific, quiet, placid, hushed, untroubled, reposeful, tranquil, unruffled, unagitated; carefree, contented, happy, blithe, cheerful, joyous. **—Ant.** tempestuous, stormy, blustery, tumultuous; troubled, agitated.

hale *adj.* *You're looking hale again after that bout of flu:* healthy, hearty, hardy, well, robust, able-bodied, sound, vigorous, energetic, sturdy, fit, strapping, rugged, robustious, in fine fettle, in the pink, in shape, full of vim and vigor. **—Ant.** weak, sickly, infirm, frail, debilitated.

half *n.* **1.** *Pay half now and the rest later. You've only heard half of the story!:* one half, one of two equal parts, fifty percent; part, fraction, portion, section, some. —*adj.* **2.** *The dog eats a half pound of hamburger every day. His testimony was full of half-truths:* one-half, halved; partial, fractional, incomplete, divided; inadequate, imperfect, limited, insufficient, deficient, meager, slight, scanty, skimpy; moderate, middling, tolerable, passable. —*adv.* **3.** *You're only half trying:* partially, partly, in part, after a fashion, inadequately, insufficiently, slightly, barely, feebly, weakly, faintly; relatively, fairly, moderately, passably, tolerably, comparatively, rather; pretty nearly, all but. **—Ant.** 1 whole, total, sum total, all, aggregate, entirety. 2 whole, complete, entire, full. 3 wholly, completely, entirely, fully, totally; strongly, adequately, sufficiently.

half-baked *adj.* *Every idea he had was half-baked:* ill-conceived, senseless, witless, half-witted, dumb, brainless, foolish, silly, harebrained, idiotic, impractical, poorly planned, short-sighted, stupid.

half-hearted *adj.* *He acknowledged the gift with a half-hearted thank-you:* unenthusiastic, indifferent, lackluster, perfunctory, cool, cold,

blasé, spiritless, faint, tame, lukewarm, passive, unaspiring, irresolute, neither hot nor cold, ambivalent, neither one thing nor the other; listless, lackadaisical, lethargic, apathetic, languid, phlegmatic. **—Ant.** wholehearted, enthusiastic, eager, spirited, zealous, avid, animated, warm, emotional, concerned, moved, excited; ambitious, aspiring, energetic, red-hot.

halfway *adv.* **1.** *The house is halfway up the hill:* midway, half the distance, in the middle. **2.** *We halfway convinced him to go to the party:* partially, partly, in part, to a degree, in some meas-ure, to some extent, nearly, pretty nearly, almost; somewhat, rather, moderately. —*adj.* **3.** *Chicago is the halfway point on the journey:* middle, midway, intermediate, medium, medial, midmost, middlemost, equidistant, between two extremes.

half-wit *n.* *Who was the half-wit who left the refrigerator door open?:* fool, dunce, dummy, blockhead, dolt, ninny, nitwit, numskull, nincompoop, dimwit, dope, dumb-dumb; feebleminded person, moron, imbecile, idiot, simpleton, mental defective, mental deficient, dullard.

hall *n.* **1.** *Martha's room is at the far end of the hall:* hallway, corridor, passageway, passage; gallery, arcade. **2.** *Leave your boots and umbrella in the hall:* entrance hall, entry, lobby, foyer, vestibule; waiting room, reception room, anteroom, antechamber. **3.** *The concert will be given in Symphony Hall:* concert hall, auditorium, assembly room, meeting place, amphitheater, chamber, club room; dining hall, banquet hall.

hallmark *n.* *Meticulousness was the hallmark of her work:* trademark, sure sign, telltale sign, authentication, badge, certification, ratification, indication, mark, seal, sign, stamp, symbol.

hallowed *adj.* *The church graveyard is hallowed ground:* sacred, consecrated, dedicated, honored; holy, blessed, sanctified, beatified, sacrosanct. **—Ant.** profane, unsanctified.

hallucination *n.* *The high fever gave her hallucinations. You didn't see a ghost, it was just an hallucination:* delusion, fantasy, illusion, mirage, apparition, phantasmagoria, chimera, figment, aberration, vision, dream, nightmare.

hallucinogen *n.* *LSD is a well-known hallucinogen:* psychedelic, psychedelic drug, psychoactive drug.

halo *n.* **1.** *The saint was painted with a halo over his head:* ring of light, aureole, nimbus, corona, radiance. **2.** *Does a halo around the moon mean bad weather?:* aurora, chromosphere. **3.** *One always feels a kind of halo surrounding royalty:* atmosphere of glory, magnificence, splendor, resplendence, radiance, luminousness, luster, illustriousness, majesty, dignity, grandeur, holiness, sanctity, sublimity, spiritual aura, solemnity.

halt *v.* **1.** *The hikers halted at the stream to refill their canteens:* stop, come to a stop, come to a standstill, pull up, draw up, wait, rest, pause, tarry, linger, suspend, interrupt; terminate, quit, cease, discontinue, leave off; *Slang* knock off, shut up shop, shut down, hang fire, break off, call it a day, wind up; brake, check, rein in, throttle down, heave to. **2.** *Officials are working hard to halt inflation:* stop, end, bring to a standstill, defeat, choke off, prohibit, extinguish, prevent, cut off, vanquish, suppress, overthrow, overturn, put down, subdue, rout, quell, quash, crush, scotch; curb, check, hinder, impede, repress, restrict, restrain, balk, thwart, stem, stall, stay, delay, abate, frustrate, foil, hamper, hold in check, bridle, block, inhibit; *Slang* squelch, throw a wrench in the works, spike one's guns, cut the ground from under. —*n.* **3.** *The proceedings came to a halt around noon:* stop, cessation, standstill, discontinuance, suspension, termination, close, end; intermission, recess, respite, interval, pause, rest, interruption, delay, interlude; *Slang* breather, breathing spell, break, time out. —*interj.* **4.** *Halt! Who goes there?:* stop, stand still, don't move, come to a halt. —**Ant.** 1, 2 continue, go ahead, proceed; begin, start, resume. 2 support, encourage, forward, maintain, aid, abet, bolster, boost. 3 beginning, start; resumption, continuation. 4 proceed! move on!

halve *v. Halve the apple and we'll share it. Prices were halved during the sale:* cut in half, split in two, divide equally, bisect; lessen by one half, reduce 50 percent. —**Ant.** double, increase 100 percent.

hamlet *n. The boy grew up in a hamlet of 200 people:* small village, village, crossroads; *Slang* burg, one-horse town, jerkwater town, whistlestop, hick town, tank town. —**Ant.** metropolis, city, megalopolis.

hammer *n.* **1.** *The only tools in the house are a hammer and screwdriver:* (*variously*) claw hammer, ballpeen hammer, tack hammer; mallet, sledge hammer, sledge, steam hammer, pile driver, rammer; gavel. —*v.* **2.** *Hammer a hook in the wall and hang the picture on it:* nail; hit, pound, knock, strike, pummel, whack, tap, punch, bang, drive. **3.** *The blacksmith hammered a horseshoe from the red-hot metal:* forge, form with a hammer, beat out; fashion, shape, make.

hamper *v. Lack of equipment is hampering our work:* hinder, impede, interfere with, hold up, handicap, encumber, inhibit, thwart, prevent, frustrate, balk, stall, restrain, restrict, retard, curb, check, stem, block, obstruct, fetter, shackle, muzzle, gag, hog-tie. —**Ant.** help, aid, assist, further, promote, forward, facilitate, expedite, speed, accelerate, hasten, encourage, bolster, boost.

hand *n.* **1.** *Aren't your hands cold with no gloves on?:* manual extremity; palm, fist; *Slang* paw, mitt, meat-hook. **2.** *The foreman hired three new hands last week:* laborer, hired hand, hired man, man, worker, workman, workingman, employee, aide, assistant, associate, helper, menial, handyman; member of a crew. **3.** *Give me a hand with this ladder:* help, assistance, aid, support, lift. **4.** usually **hands** *The condemned man's fate is in the governor's hands:* care, keeping, charge, custody, control, possession, power, hold, authority, command, management,

guidance, dominion, jurisdiction, supervision, domination, auspices. **5.** *Aunt Edna writes a beautiful hand:* handwriting, penmanship, script, calligraphy, longhand. **6.** *Give the little girl a great big hand:* round of applause, burst of applause; ovation. —*v.* **7.** *Hand me the newspaper, please:* give, pass, hand over, present, deliver, convey, turn over to, furnish with, *Informal* reach. **8.** *Remember how Sir Walter Raleigh handed Queen Elizabeth across the mud puddle?:* give a hand to, hold out a helping hand to, help, assist, guide, aid, do a good turn for, minister to, come to the aid of. —**Ant.** 2 employer, boss, foreman, overseer, supervisor.

handbag *n. The thief grabbed her handbag:* purse, bag, pocketbook, reticule.

handbook *n. Before trying the modem she consulted a handbook:* how-to-book, guidebook, manual, Baedeker.

handful *n. Only a handful of people attended the dance:* small number, smattering, sprinkling, scattering; small quantity, tiny amount, minimum, scant amount, modicum, thimbleful. —**Ant.** horde, mob, crowd, throng, a large amount, a lot.

handicap *n.* **1.** *Her lack of a college degree is a definite handicap:* drawback, disadvantage, detriment, impediment, restriction, limitation, shortcoming, defect, obstacle, barrier, stumbling block, difficulty, inhibition, burden, encumbrance, inconvenience. **2.** *It takes great fortitude to learn to live with a handicap:* physical disability; (*variously*) lameness, loss of a limb, blindness, deafness, speech disability. —*v.* **3.** *Being overweight will handicap a boy in sports:* hinder, hold back, hamper, impede, encumber, shackle, retard, burden, restrict, limit, place at a disadvantage, inhibit, thwart, suppress, repress; restrain, curb. —**Ant.** 1 advantage, benefit, asset, edge, boost, boon. 3 help, benefit, give an advantage to, assist, aid, forward, promote, further, boost.

handicraft *n. All the handicrafts were displayed in the outer room:* craft, artifact, artwork; handiwork, craftsmanship, workmanship.

handle *n.* **1.** *Give me the rake with the long handle. The door handle just fell off:* shaft, shank, hilt; hold, grasp, pull, knob, grip. —*v.* **2.** *Don't handle the tomatoes, you'll bruise them!:* take in the hands, pick up, hold; finger, knead, pinch, poke, touch, feel; stroke, caress, fondle, massage; *Slang* paw, paw over. **3.** *The pilot really knows how to handle an airplane:* control, steer, guide, maneuver, pilot; operate, run, work, manipulate, ply, use, utilize, employ, bring into play, manage, command. **4.** *Can the new employee handle this job? Rembrandt handled lighting with dramatic effect in his paintings:* manage, deal with, *Slang* swing; take care of, care for; command, control, manipulate, conduct, treat. **5.** *The hardware store handles a complete line of power tools:* sell, offer for sale, carry, deal in, trade in, traffic in, market, merchandise.

handling *n. The bomb required careful handling:* manipulation, treatment, care, charge, approach, care, management, supervision, administration.

handmade *adj. Every object on the shelf was handmade:* handcrafted, do-it-yourself, self-made.

handsome *adj.* **1.** *Bill and Jane have four handsome children. What a handsome room!:* good-looking, attractive, fine-looking, sightly, comely, easy on the eyes, easy to look at, lovely, exquisite, stunning, beauteous, beautiful, pretty, comely, bonny, fair; splendid, tasteful, elegant, stately, impressive, imposing, well-formed, well-proportioned, well-arranged. **2.** *The waiter received a handsome tip:* generous, magnanimous, liberal, bountiful; ample, considerable, sizable, sufficient, abundant, moderately large. **3.** *Caring for the motherless child was another of her handsome deeds:* gracious, generous, bountiful, unselfish, noble, magnanimous, big-hearted, princely; humanitarian, benevolent, merciful, benign, compassionate. **—Ant.** 1 ugly, unattractive, homely, bad-looking, repulsive, unsightly; tasteless, inelegant; ill-proportioned, unshapely. 2 ungenerous, illiberal, stingy, niggardly, miserly, cheap; small, meager, skimpy, scant. 3 mean, base, selfish, ignoble.

handsomely *adv. He was rewarded handsomely for his efforts:* liberally, richly, amply, bountifully, generously, magnanimously, munificently, plentifully.

handwriting *n. The handwriting was large and angular:* writing, autography, penmanship, calligraphy, chirography, fist, hand, script, longhand, scrivening, style.

handy *adj.* **1.** *Keep the flashlight handy in case the fuse blows again:* accessible, close at hand, ready to hand, at hand, on hand, at one's elbow, within easy reach, easily accessible, available, obtainable, near, convenient, nigh, on call, in readiness, on tap, at one's beck and call. **2.** *Father was never very handy at fixing things:* skillful, skilled, expert, adroit, dexterous, deft, nimble-fingered, competent, proficient, capable, adept, accomplished, clever, efficient. **3.** *This electric egg beater isn't very handy:* easy to use, convenient to handle, manageable, wieldy, useful, practical, serviceable, helpful. **—Ant.** 1 out of the way, hard to get, inaccessible, unavailable, inconvenient, remote, far. 2 clumsy, awkward, inept, unskilled, all thumbs. 3 clumsy, awkward, unwieldy, cumbersome, inconvenient; useless, impractical.

hang *v.* **1.** *After you wash the windows, hang the curtains. This picture hangs over the mantle:* suspend, fasten from above, append, attach, affix; dangle, swing freely, be pendent, depend. **2.** *The outlaw was hanged by the posse:* lynch, execute by hanging, send to the gallows, die on the gallows, *Slang* string up. **3.** *His whole career hangs on his passing the bar exam:* depend, be dependent, be contingent, rest, turn upon, hinge, be subject to, lie in, revolve around, repose in. **4.** *The child hung his head in shame:* let droop, dangle, bow, lower, drop, incline, bend forward, bend downward, sag; lean over,

trail. **—n.** **5.** *Informal If you get the hang of needlepoint I wish you'd teach me:* knack; gist, point, meaning, thought. **—Ant.** 1 take down, detach. 4 lift, raise.

hangdog *adj. I was certain from his hangdog expression that he was guilty:* abject, defeated, intimidated, humiliated, browbeaten, wretched, degraded, hopeless, miserable, resigned, hopeless; ashamed, embarrassed, guilty-looking, crestfallen, shamefaced, chapfallen. **—Ant.** confident, assured, undaunted, bold, cocksure.

hangover *n. The next morning he suffered from a hangover:* aftereffects, delirium tremens, D. T.'s, *Informal* willies, morning after, shakes.

hankering *n. Informal The old man had a hankering to see his boyhood home again:* longing, craving, desire, yearning, yen, hunger, thirst, urge, itch, aching, pining.

haphazard *adj. You can't work in such a haphazard way if you want to get the job done:* unmethodical, disorganized, unsystematic, chaotic, unorganized, disordered, disorderly, random, arbitrary; careless, unthinking, indiscriminate, casual, chance, slapdash, fitful, sporadic, catch-as-catch-can, hit-or-miss, on-and-off; aimless, purposeless, fortuitous, undesigned, undirected, unpremeditated, accidental. **—Ant.** organized, methodical, systematic, orderly, ordered; careful, thoughtful, designed, planned, arranged, premeditated, purposeful, intentional, considered, deliberate.

hapless *adj. It was a hapless day when that murderer was born!:* unlucky, unfortunate, jinxed, ill-starred, ill-fated, star-crossed, unhappy, luckless, forlorn, hopeless, miserable, wretched, woeful, cursed, accursed; *Slang* rotten, lousy, no-good. **—Ant.** happy, fortunate, lucky, blessed, charmed.

happen *v.* **1.** *When did the accident happen?:* take place, occur, come about, come to pass, ensue, transpire, result, betide, befall, eventuate; arise, spring up, crop up, come into existence, present itself, appear. **2.** *I happen to be a close friend of the mayor's:* have the fortune to be, have the luck to be; be the case, turn out. **3.** *What will happen to her now?:* become of, befall, be one's fate, fall to one's lot, be one's fortune; be experienced by, be borne by, be endured by, be suffered by.

happening *n. It was an unfortunate happening:* event, occurrence, incident, incidence, episode, affair, experience, matter, proceeding, occasion, circumstance, happenstance, adventure, advent, case; accident, vicissitude, just one of those things.

happily *adv.* **1.** *Happily, the disaster did not occur:* felicitously, aptly, auspiciously, favorably, fortunately, propitiously, prosperously, providentially, satisfyingly, seasonably, successfully, appropriately. **2.** *She responded happily to his invitation:* enthusiastically, gladly, willingly, agreeably, blissfully, blithely, cheerfully, contentedly, delightedly, pleasantly, smilingly.

happiness *n.* **1.** *Imagine our happiness at having all the children home for Christmas!:* gladness, joy, delight, felicity, contentment, content, sense of well-being, pleasure, enjoyment, satisfaction, lightheartedness, rejoicing, elation, jubilation, high spirits, bliss, beatitude, blessedness, rapture, ecstasy, gaiety, exultation, transport, exuberance; merriment, cheer, cheerfulness, cheeriness, glee, jollity, mirth. **2.** *Her grandchildren are her greatest happiness:* pleasure, satisfaction, gratification, blessing, comfort. **—Ant.** 1 unhappiness, sadness, sorrow, grief, woe; depression, despondency, low spirits, misery, anguish, distress, discomfort. 2 bane, annoyance; calamity, misfortune, thorn in one's side, cross to bear.

happy *adj.* **1.** *I'm so happy you could visit us. My birthday was a happy occasion:* glad, pleased, delighted, content, contented, gratified, tickled, tickled pink; gay, cheerful, in high spirits, elated, joyous, overjoyed, exhilarated, blissful, rapturous, ecstatic, exultant, gleeful, transported, rhapsodic, jubilant, flushed with pleasure, exuberant, in seventh heaven; pleasant, pleasing, delightful, gratifying, cheering, joyful. **2.** *Wasn't it a happy coincidence that I bumped into you?:* fortunate, lucky, auspicious, favorable, felicitous, propitious; convenient, opportune, meet, timely, seasonable, fitting, fit, advantageous, agreeable. **—Ant.** 1 sad, unhappy, sorry, sorrowful, displeased, discontent; despondent, forlorn, miserable, gloomy, glum, melancholy, depressed, downcast, joyless, mournful, somber; down in the mouth, down in the dumps. 2 unfortunate, unlucky, luckless, inauspicious; unfitting, unseasonable.

happy-go-lucky *adj. She has such a happy-go-lucky attitude she mustn't have a care in the world:* carefree, easygoing, untroubled, devil-may-care, unconcerned, heedless, insouciant, free and easy, unworried, light-hearted, nonchalant, blithe; feckless, irresponsible; flighty, skittish, scatterbrained. **—Ant.** cautious, circumspect, prudent, careful, discreet.

harass *v.* **1.** *The wagon train was harassed by the Indians:* attack repeatedly, raid frequently, assault continually, beset, besiege. **2.** *If you'll stop harassing me I can finish this work:* torment, pester, badger, harry, worry, disturb, annoy, irritate, distress, bother, irk, vex, bedevil, plague, hound, discommode, exasperate, tease, bait, heckle, hector, ride, persecute, browbeat, bully, intimidate, cow.

harbinger *n. The return of the swallows is the harbinger of spring:* herald, precursor, forerunner, indication, announcer, signaler, proclaimer; first sign, omen, portent, token, clue, symbol.

harbor *n.* **1.** *The disabled ship was towed into harbor:* port, protected anchorage; (*variously*) dock, pier, wharf, quay, cove, bay, lagoon, inlet, basin; destination, goal, terminus, terminal point. **2.** *The library was a harbor from the city's noise:* haven, refuge, asylum, retreat, shelter, sanctuary, hideaway, concealment, hiding place. **—***v.* **3.** *The suspect is accused of harboring an escaped convict:* give refuge to, shelter, hide, conceal, give hiding place to, shield, protect, care for, keep safe; quarter, house, lodge, billet,

take in, keep. **4.** *For years she harbored a resentment against her stepmother:* nurture, foster, bear in the mind, hold, maintain, retain, feel, cling to; brood over, muse over.

hard *adj.* **1.** *This candy is so hard no one can chew it:* firm, solid, hardened, rocklike, stony, steely; rigid, stiff, unmalleable, inflexible, unpliable. **2.** *The hard rain flattened the tomato plants. The hard blow knocked the boxer down:* strong, powerful, forceful, heavy, intense, fierce, severe, violent. **3.** *The teacher asked a hard question. It is a hard book to read:* difficult, arduous, laborious, strenuous, tough, exacting, formidable, Herculean, troublesome, burdensome, wearisome; baffling, confusing, puzzling, perplexing, bewildering, unfathomable, cryptic; complex, complicated, involved, intricate, impenetrable, thorny, knotty. **4.** *That new employee is really a hard worker:* industrious, energetic, vigorous, enterprising, relentless, assiduous, diligent, persevering, persistent, unremitting, indefatigable, untiring, unflagging; earnest, zealous, eager, conscientious, willing, spirited, animated. **5.** *We work for a hard master:* strict, stern, severe, unyielding, stubborn, uncompromising, stringent, oppressive, unbending; hardhearted, cruel, cold, implacable, unrelenting, merciless, pitiless, inexorable, unremitting, callous, impervious, unsparing, ruthless, thick-skinned, hardened, insensitive; inhuman, brutal. **6.** *This has been a hard winter. Many families had a hard time during the Depression:* severe, harsh, rough, difficult; unpleasant, disagreeable, distressing, oppressive, disheartening, burdensome, onerous, intolerable, unbearable, tormenting; harmful, hurtful, lamentable, sad, melancholy. **7.** *Hard feelings existed between the neighbors. The lawyers exchanged hard words:* hostile, belligerent, unfriendly, antagonistic, bellicose; mean, ugly, bitter, vicious, rancorous, venomous, malicious, acrimonious, vindictive, spiteful, sullen, cantankerous, unkind, critical, insulting. **—***adv.* **8.** *The ice is frozen hard:* solidly, firm, firmly, tight, tightly, rigid, stiff, closely. **9.** *It rained hard. Hit the ball hard:* forcefully, forcibly, powerfully, strongly, heavily, fiercely, severely, violently, intensely, sharply, vigorously. **10.** *The farmer worked hard to gather the hay before the rains came. The student studied hard:* industriously, vigorously, rigorously, energetically, arduously, laboriously, furiously, intently, intensely, with all one's might, relentlessly, unsparingly, unceasingly, steadily, diligently, persistently, untiringly, determinedly, assiduously, unflaggingly, conscientiously, resolutely, earnestly, eagerly, keenly, seriously, closely. **11.** *Mother took the bad news very hard:* emotionally, to heart, with strong feelings, with much sorrow, distressfully, severely, painfully, agonizingly; with much anger, angrily. **—Ant.** 1-3, 5, 6, 8 soft. 3, 5, 6 easy. 1 mushy; flexible, pliant, pliable, malleable. 2 weak, light, mild. 3 light, simple, uncomplicated, straightforward, clear, direct; easy as pie. 4 lazy, lethargic; lax, careless. 5 softhearted, lenient, permissive, yielding, kind, kindhearted, warmhearted, merciful, sensitive, humane, gentle. **6** mild, pleasant, agreeable, enjoyable, good, salubrious. **7** friendly, loving, amiable, warm, kind, sweet, good; complimentary. **8** loose, loosely, lightly. **9** softly, weakly, gently, mildly, lightly, faintly. **10** easily, effortlessly; lazily, lethargically. **11** calmly, unemotionally, mildly, placidly, serenely.

hard-and-fast *adj. There are no hard-and-fast rules about human behavior:* set, strict, inflexible, irrevocable, unyielding, exacting, binding, obligatory, compulsory, uncompromising, rigorous, unremitting, compelling, mandatory, unalterable, unbending; indisputable, incontestable, undeniable. **—Ant.** flexible, lax, elastic, yielding, lenient, debatable.

hard-core *adj. She declared war on hard-core pornography:* explicit, dyed-in-the-wool, extreme, diehard, intransigent, resolute, uncompromising, unyielding, dedicated, determined.

harden *v.* **1.** *Over time the metal hardened:* solidify, indurate, ossify, petrify. **2.** *Adversity hardened her:* strengthen, confirm, fortify, steel, brace, nerve, toughen, inure; habituate, accustom, season, train, discipline.

hardened *adj. The hardened criminal received an extra term in prison:* callous, hardhearted, heartless, inaccessible, impenetrable, obdurate, resistant, unbending, uncaring, uncompassionate, unemotional, unfeeling; accustomed, habituated, case-hardened, inured, seasoned, steeled, toughened, *Informal* hard-bitten, hard-boiled.

hardheaded *adj.* **1.** *The job requires a hardheaded businessman:* practical, objective, shrewd, astute, pragmatic, realistic; down-to-earth; unemotional, unfeeling, impersonal, sensible, tough-minded; not easily deceived, not easily ruffled, cool, coolheaded, self-controlled, poised, *Slang* unflappable. **2.** *He's so hardheaded he won't listen to anyone else's ideas:* stubborn, obstinate, self-willed, willful, contrary, intractable, balky, unbending, inflexible, immovable, unyielding, refractory, mulish, pigheaded. **—Ant.** **1** softhearted, idealistic, impractical, theoretical, philosophical; emotional, volatile, hotheaded, excitable. **2** flexible, yielding, receptive; agreeable, amenable.

hardhearted *adj. Only a hardhearted person would fail to be sympathetic:* cruel, cruelhearted, unfeeling, mean, heartless, merciless, remorseless, unsparing, unforgiving, uncaring, insensitive, indifferent, unsympathetic, cold-blooded, ruthless, unpitying, pitiless, cold, stony, hard, callous, thick-skinned, inhuman, brutal. **—Ant.** kind, loving, sweet, compassionate, sympathetic, softhearted, warmhearted, understanding, sensitive, warm, gentle, humane, tender, merciful, forgiving.

hardly *adv.* **1.** *There is hardly a foot of water in the well. It is hardly possible that such a thing could have happened:* scarcely, barely, only, just, not quite, almost not, faintly; rarely, uncommonly, infrequently, not often. **2.** *That was hardly the way to greet a friend!:* by no means, not by any means, certainly not, in no manner,

in no way, not by a great deal. **—Ant.** **1** fully, easily, amply, more than, well over, abundantly; often, frequently, commonly, usually. **2** by all means, certainly, really, truly, indubitably.

hard-nosed *adj. We didn't expect him to be so hard-nosed about his decision:* stubborn, hardheaded, intractable, unyielding, inflexible, uncompromising, rigid, hard-line, unbending; tough, businesslike, unsentimental; shrewd, calculating, *Slang* one-way. **—Ant.** open-minded, flexible, amenable, reasonable, tractable.

hardship *n.* **1.** *His family endured great hardship during the war:* suffering, affliction, trouble, misfortune, adversity, ordeal, tribulation, misery, unhappiness, grief, sorrow, travail, woe, wretchedness, agony. **2.** *Having another mouth to feed would be a great hardship right now:* privation, burden, handicap, encumbrance, difficulty, load, problem, millstone round one's neck, load, cross to bear. **—Ant.** **1** comfort, ease, happiness; good fortune, benefit. **2** help, aid, blessing, boon, relief, load off one's back.

hardware *n. The store stocked the necessary hardware:* metalware, ironware, fittings, fixtures, appliances, implements, kitchenware, utensils, tools, plumbing.

hardy *adj. One has to be hardy to work as a lumberjack:* robust, rugged, sturdy, hearty, strapping, able-bodied, strong, tough, vigorous, mighty; healthy, fit, physically fit, stalwart, hale, in good condition, in fine fettle. **—Ant.** delicate, frail, fragile, dainty, soft, weak, feeble, sickly, debilitated.

harebrained *adj. Such a harebrained scheme hasn't a chance of working:* foolish, flighty, dim-witted, rattlebrained, skittish, scatterbrained, simple-minded, half-witted, silly, asinine, senseless, empty-headed, featherbrained, wacky, *Slang* wacko. **—Ant.** prudent, intelligent, sensible, wise, well-advised.

harlot *n. Thieves and harlots frequented the café:* prostitute, whore, strumpet, trollop, bawd, slut, doxy, tart, jade, chippy, wanton, streetwalker, scarlet woman, painted woman, fallen woman, jezebel, call girl; *Slang* pros, pro; mistress, courtesan, kept woman.

harm *n.* **1.** *They were accused of doing him bodily harm. The drought did a lot of harm to the crops. Bad publicity did a lot of harm to the actor's career:* injury, hurt, damage, suffering, pain, agony, trauma; impairment, detriment, mischief, adversity, hardship, misfortune, ill, destruction, abuse, defacement, deterioration, scourge, calamity, havoc, devastation. **2.** *What's the harm in having a little fun?:* wrong, wickedness, evil, sin, sinfulness, iniquity, immorality, vice, villainy; malice, malevolence, maliciousness. *—v.* **3.** *Don't harm your eyes by reading in dim light. Will this cleaning fluid harm the furniture?:* impair, injure, hurt, wound, maim, ruin, cripple, pain, abuse, maltreat, do violence to, misuse, ill-use; damage, blemish, mar, spoil, deface, disfigure; debase, degrade, undermine; wrong, aggrieve. **—Ant.** **1** good, benefit, help, aid, assistance; boon, blessing. **2** goodness, righteousness, blessing. 3 benefit, help, aid, assist; improve, better, ameliorate; cure, heal.

harmful *adj. Follow the directions carefully, or this medicine may be harmful:* injurious, dangerous, deleterious, hurtful, destructive, ruinous, damaging, counterproductive, unwholesome, unhealthy, unhealthful, detrimental, adverse, bad, pernicious, baneful. **—Ant.** beneficial, good, helpful, favorable, wholesome, healthful, healthy; harmless, safe.

harmless *adj. Garter snakes are absolutely harmless:* safe, not dangerous, not hurtful, benign, nontoxic, inoffensive, gentle, peaceable, mild, sinless, blameless, innocent, incorrupt, guiltless, innocuous, unobjectionable. **—Ant.** harmful, dangerous, unsafe, destructive, unhealthy, injurious, wholesome.

harmonious *adj.* **1.** *Harmonious sounds drifted across the fields. The room was decorated in harmonious shades of blue and green:* melodious, sweet-sounding, mellifluous, euphonious, sweet, dulcet, agreeable, agreeably combined, matching, compatible, harmonizing, coordinated, consistent, unified, synchronized. **2.** *The two families were very harmonious:* likeminded, in agreement, in harmony, cordial, in accord, compatible, congenial, agreeable, amiable, amicable, sympathetic, friendly. **—Ant.** 1 harsh, grating, unmelodious, cacophonous; clashing, incompatible, contrasting, uncoordinated, inconsistent. 2 incompatible, un-alike, different, discordant, dissident, unfriendly.

harmonize *v. The choir harmonized beautifully:* blend, chime with, agree, attune, coordinate, correlate, correspond, integrate, match, orchestrate.

harmony *n.* **1.** *The interior decorator chose the rugs and drapes for their harmony:* pleasing consistency, coordination, compatibility, agreement, concord, correlation, parallelism, matching, mutual fitness, balance, symmetry, order, proportion, unity, organic totality. **2.** *Bob and I worked together in harmony for years:* agreement, accord, concord, unanimity, likemindedness, conformity, unity, amicability, amity, congeniality, sympathy, compatibility, fellowship, friendship, cooperation, mutual regard, peace; good understanding, harmonious relations, concurrence in opinions. **—Ant.** 1 incongruity, inconsistency; conflict, disproportion. 2 disagreement, enmity, opposition, conflict, contention, discord, dissension, antagonism, hostility.

harness *n.* **1.** *Put the harness on the mare and hitch her to the plow:* tackle, trappings; (variously) halter, bridle, reins, straps, traces, caparison, lines, tugs. **—v. 2.** *Harness the pony and we'll go for a ride in the cart:* put in harness, hitch up, yoke, collar, rig up. **3.** *The dam harnesses energy of the river:* control and use, direct to a useful purpose, utilize, employ, exploit, render useful, make productive, turn to account; restrain, curb, muzzle, bridle, rein.

harridan *n. The old harridan screamed at the children for sitting on her doorstep:* mean old woman, crone, old crone, shrew, hag, virago; *Slang* battle-ax, witch.

harrowing *adj. After that harrowing experience I shook for a week:* distressing, disturbing, tormenting, traumatic, painful, upsetting; frightening, fearful, alarming, chilling, bloodcurdling, terrifying, threatening dangerous.

harry *v.* **1.** *Pirates often harried the coastal towns:* attack repeatedly, raid frequently, beset; raid, plunder, sack, pillage, terrorize. **2.** *She was harried by doubts of his honesty. The carpenter could finish the job quicker if you wouldn't harry him:* trouble, torment, distress, haunt, disturb, bother, worry; harass, pester, gall, badger, annoy, irritate, irk, vex, plague, hound, exasperate, distract; tease, bait, hector, heckle, ride, intimidate, bully. **—Ant.** 2 soothe, quiet, comfort, console, solace; support, help, aid, encourage.

harsh *adj.* **1.** *What a harsh voice the speaker has! The harsh light hurt my eyes:* unpleasant, piercing, jarring, grating, shrill, rasping, raspy, hoarse, strident, scratchy, discordant, raucous, unmusical, unharmonious, cacophonous, squawky, glaring, overbright, too bright. **2.** *Snow White received harsh treatment from her stepmother. The critics had nothing but harsh words for the new play:* cruel, pitiless, ruthless, merciless, mean, unsparing, severe, stern, ungentle, unkind, abusive, vindictive, heartless, Draconian, hardhearted, brutal; bitter, caustic, hard, rough, sharp, uncharitable. **—Ant.** 1 soft, gentle, mild, smooth, pleasant, pleasing, agreeable, soothing; harmonious, melodious, mellifluous. 2 kind, gentle, sweet, loving, merciful, charitable, lenient.

harum-scarum *adj.* **1.** *You should know better than to ask some harum-scarum kid to do the job:* disorganized, undependable, unreliable, inconsistent, erratic, careless, unsettled; foolish, giddy, scatterbrained, rattlebrained, featherbrained, harebrained, flighty, impulsive, impetuous, absent-minded, confused, bewildered; unplanned, haphazard. **—adv. 2.** *We ran harum-scarum all over town trying to find her a present:* haphazardly, impulsively, recklessly, wildly, aimlessly, capriciously. **—Ant.** 1 organized, well-planned, careful, efficient, consistent, settled, serious, methodical, responsible, conscientious. 2 thoughtfully, efficiently, carefully, wisely.

harvest *n.* **1.** *The neighboring farmers gathered to help with the harvest:* harvesting, reaping, crop gathering; (variously) mowing, cutting, picking, haying. **2.** *There was a large apple harvest this year:* crop, yield, season's growth, produce; gathering, collection, accumulation, amassment. **3.** *The new medicine is the harvest of 30 years of research:* result, product, fruit, fruition, reward, benefit, proceeds, gain, return, yield, gleaning, reaping; aftermath, outgrowth, output. **—v. 4.** *Try to harvest the fruit before the first frost:* gather, reap, pick, pluck, mow, cut; collect, amass, accumulate. **—Ant.** 4 plant, sow, seed.

hassle *n.* **1.** *There was a hassle over who should pay for the broken window:* squabble, quarrel, dispute, row, argument; fight, struggle, tussle, set-to, scrap, battle, conflict, contest. —*v.* **2.** *Slang If the cops hassled the panhandlers more, maybe they would stay off the streets:* harass, harry, persecute, vex, hound, bother, badger, annoy; *Slang* bug.

haste *n.* **1.** *The contract says the work must be completed with all possible haste:* speed, speediness, hurry, rush, swiftness, quickness, celerity, hurriedness, rapidity, fleetness; expedition, dispatch. **2.** *Haste makes waste:* undue speed, careless hurry, precipitateness; recklessness, rashness, impetuousness, impulsiveness. —**Ant.** 1 slowness, delay, procrastination, plodding, sluggishness, leisureliness, lagging, hanging back. 2 deliberation, care, carefulness, sureness, reflection, calmness.

hasten *v.* **1.** *She gobbled down lunch and hastened to her appointment:* hurry, rush, speed, make haste, race, run, hustle, dash, scurry, fly, whisk, jump, sprint, bolt, dart, scuttle, flit, scamper, hurry up, lose no time, make time, go on the double, go like lightning; *Slang* go hellbent for leather, go full blast, step on the gas, step right along; work against time, make short work of. **2.** *An electric typewriter would hasten the work:* accelerate, speed up, expedite, quicken, push forward, precipitate, advance, promote; hurry on, urge on, drive on, incite, impel, *Slang* egg on. —**Ant.** 1 move slowly, creep, crawl; plod, shuffle; lag, procrastinate, dally, dawdle. 2 slow, slow down, delay, decelerate, slacken, retard, impede, inhibit, check, arrest, curb, hold back.

hastily *adv.* **1.** *There wasn't much time, so I dressed hastily:* quickly, speedily, fast, hurriedly, promptly, straightaway, posthaste, apace; *Slang* pronto, on the double, like a shot, like greased lightning, lickety-split, hell-bent for leather, before one can say Jack Robinson. **2.** *Don't make important decisions hastily:* too quickly, rashly, recklessly, impetuously, impulsively, precipitately, thoughtlessly, summarily, carelessly, heedlessly, on the spur of the moment. —**Ant.** 1 slowly, at a snail's pace. 2 deliberately, carefully, thoughtfully, calmly.

hasty *adj.* **1.** *A hasty search turned up the missing earring:* fast, quick, hurried, rapid, speedy, swift, prompt, fleet, quick as a wink; cursory, brief, rushed, fleeting, passing, momentary, breathless, superficial. **2.** *One often regrets hasty decisions. Your hasty temper will get you into trouble one of these days:* unduly quick, rash, impetuous, impulsive, reckless, hurried, headlong, heedless, abrupt, precipitate, without deliberation. —**Ant.** 1 slow, leisurely, plodding; long, protracted, detailed, meticulous, thorough, exhaustive. 2 deliberate, careful, considered, studied, thoughtful, premeditated.

hat *n.* *She wore a new hat for the occasion:* headwear, headgear, (*variously*) cap, bonnet, beret, topper, derby, *French* chapeau.

hatch *v.* *The thieves hatched a plan to rob the bank:* think up, devise, concoct, plot, plan, contrive, make up, formulate, conceive, design,

evolve, create, frame, invent, fabricate, improvise, originate, construct, fashion, dream up, *Slang* cook up; manufacture, bring forth, produce, give birth to.

hate *v.* **1.** *Those girls have hated each other since high school. I hate mice!:* dislike, despise, detest, abhor, loathe, abominate, execrate, hold in contempt, bear malice toward, be hostile to, not be able to bear, have no use for, recoil from, shrink from, be repelled by, be sick of, be tired of, give one a pain, give one a pain in the neck. **2.** *Mother hated to move from such a nice neighborhood:* be sorry, be reluctant, be unwilling, feel disinclined to, be averse to, shrink from, not care to, would rather not, not have the heart to, dread, wish to avoid, feel sick at, have no taste for, have no stomach for, wince at, regard as distasteful. —*n.* **3.** *Never trust a man who is full of hate:* hatred, dislike, distaste, disliking, aversion, loathing, repugnance, abomination, abhorrence; enmity, hostility, detestation, rancor, malice, antipathy, animosity, animus, venom, malevolence, resentment, vindictiveness, revengefulness, acrimony. —**Ant.** 1–3 love, like. 1 be fond of, delight in, regard highly, esteem, treasure, prize, cherish, dote on, be attracted by. 2 be pleased, enjoy, relish, fancy, prefer, be inclined; wish, hope. 3 liking, fondness, affection, devotion, amity, goodwill.

hateful *adj.* **1.** *What a hateful thing to do!:* offensive, disgusting, detestable, repugnant, repellent, loathsome, despicable, revolting, contemptible, deplorable, abhorrent, odious, obnoxious, foul, abominable, monstrous, ugly, nasty, vile, unpleasant, distasteful, sickening; mean, villainous, infamous, heinous, atrocious, insufferable, wicked, sinful; irritating, objectionable, intolerable, unbearable, unendurable. **2.** *Did you see that hateful look she gave me?:* full of hate, expressing hate, evil, forbidding, scornful, contemptuous, disdainful. —**Ant.** 1 commendable, likable, desirable; pleasing, pleasant, charming, attractive, wonderful, lovable, good, sweet, kind, beautiful. 2 friendly, loving, affectionate, devoted, kind, sweet, pleasant.

hatred *n.* **1.** *The old man's hatred of people has made him a recluse:* dislike, disgust, aversion, hate, loathing, abomination, abhorrence, distaste, detestation, repugnance, revulsion. **2.** *Such hatred can only lead to bloodshed:* hostility, enmity, malice, rancor, animosity, antagonism, antipathy, animus, malevolence, ill will, venom, resentment, vindictiveness, revengefulness, acrimony, bitterness, bad blood. —**Ant.** 1, 2 love, affection, fondness, devotion, liking, attachment, affinity, attraction. 2 friendliness, amiability, affection, amity, goodwill, kindness.

haughty *adj.* *Her high social position has made her haughty:* arrogant, overly proud, scornful, disdainful, contemptuous, overbearing, high and mighty, high-handed, lordly, aloof, officious; snobbish, conceited, condescending, patronizing, hoity-toity, swell-headed; *Slang* stuck-up, snooty, uppity, uppish, high-hat, highfalutin. —**Ant.** humble, modest; *Slang* regular, hail-fellow-well-met, one of the boys; servile, subservient, obsequious, self-effacing.

haul v. **1.** *The fisherman hauled the fish into the boat. The truck hauled the garbage away:* pull, drag, draw, heave, yank, jerk, wrench, lug, tug; carry, transport, move, convey, tote, cart, tow, fetch, bring, take, truck, remove. —n. **2.** *Give a haul on this rope to get the anchor loose:* pull, tug, yank, jerk, heave, wrench. **3.** *The bank robbers got away with a $10,000 haul. The fisherman had a huge haul of fish:* take, catch, yield, gain, takings; profit, capture, reward, booty, spoils, swag, bag.

haunt v. **1.** *As a girl, she used to haunt the local movie house:* frequent, visit often, go to repeatedly, beat a path to; hover about, loiter near, linger around; *Slang* hang around, hang out at, live in. **2.** *Memories of her childhood haunted her:* obsess, weigh on, prey on, beset, obsess, preoccupy, trouble, torment, vex, distress, disturb, worry, plague; frighten, terrify, terrorize. —n. **3.** Often **haunts** *The snack bar was one of the students' haunts:* hangout, gathering place, meeting place, rendezvous, stamping grounds, hideaway; (*of animals*) lair, den, burrow, hole, cave, nest, waterhole.

have v. **1.** *I had everything I wanted:* hold, occupy, possess, own, contain. **2.** *I must have that dress in the window:* get, receive, take, obtain, acquire, gain, secure, procure. **3.** *She had a sudden heart attack:* experience, enjoy, suffer, undergo. **4.** *Have him return it at once:* make, force. **5.** *They had it that he was guilty:* assert, maintain, hold, aver, state, asseverate, testify. **6.** *The cat had six kittens:* give birth, bear, beget, bring forth, deliver. **7.** *He realized that he'd been had:* cheat, deceive, dupe, fix, fool, outfox, outmanoeuvre, outsmart, outwit, swindle, take in, trick.

haven n. *The ship sought a haven in the storm:* shelter, refuge, retreat, sanctuary, asylum, cover, hideaway, hideout; harbor, port.

havoc n. *The tornado wreaked havoc on the town:* widespread damage, destruction, devastation, ruin, wrack and ruin, disaster, catastrophe, cataclysm, ruination, chaos, disorder, calamity, upheaval.

hazard n. **1.** *Are you aware of the hazards of white-water canoeing?:* danger, risk, peril, threat, menace, endangerment, imperilment, pitfall, jeopardy. **2.** *By hazard he took a wrong turn and discovered a shortcut:* chance, accident, fluke, luck, stroke of luck, happenstance; mishap, mischance, misfortune, coincidence. —v. **3.** *If I may hazard a guess, she's at least 50. I'll hazard a dollar on the bingo game:* venture, chance, dare, risk, submit, throw out, advance, volunteer, offer, proffer; presume, daresay, suppose, guess, theorize, speculate, conjecture, hypothesize; gamble, bet, wager, stake, take a chance, chance it, tempt fate, trust to luck. **4.** *Don't hazard your reputation by supporting that crook:* endanger, risk, imperil, jeopardize, threaten, expose. —**Ant.** 1 protection, safeguard, safety. 2 design, plan, calculation, pre-

meditation. 4 protect, safeguard, make safe, preserve.

hazardous adj. **1.** *These steep stairs are hazardous:* dangerous, unsafe, perilous, precarious, risky, threatening. **2.** *Prospecting for gold is a hazardous way to earn a living:* chancy, precarious, unsure, uncertain, unreliable, insecure, speculative, dubious, doubtful, shaky, iffy, untrustworthy; unsound, unstable. —**Ant.** 1 safe, secure. 2 sure, certain, reliable, sound, stable.

haze n. **1.** *The mountain was barely visible through the haze:* mist, fog, smoke, pall; cloud, vapor, film, veil, screen, cloak, mantle. **2.** *Look where you're going—don't walk about in a haze!:* state of confusion, daze; befuddlement, muddle, bewilderment, fogginess.

hazy adj. **1.** *It was another of those hazy fall days:* misty, foggy, smoggy, smoky; overcast, cloudy, dim, murky, veiled; dusky, bleared, bleary, blurry, filmy, faint. **2.** *We have only a hazy idea how to get to your house:* vague, general, indefinite, ill-defined, uncertain, unclear, nebulous, faint, obscure, ambiguous, dim; confused, foggy, muddled. —**Ant.** 1 clear, bright; light, sunny; cloudless. 2 clear, certain, sure, detailed, well-defined, explicit.

head n. **1.** *She has a good head for arithmetic:* mind, brain, mentality, intellect, I.Q., *Slang* gray matter; talent, gift, bent, genius, aptitude, capacity, ability, perception, understanding, apprehension, discernment, judgment, cleverness, acuteness, quickness of mind. **2.** *The original founder is still head of the organization:* leader, chief, director, boss, administrator; *Slang* big wheel, guiding light; (*variously in business*) chairman of the board, chairman, chief executive officer, chief executive, president, manager, superintendent, foreman, supervisor; (*variously in government*) dictator, king, queen, monarch, sovereign, ruler, czar, potentate, suzerain, president, prime minister, premier; (*variously in the military*) commander-in-chief, commanding general, general, captain, commandant, commander, admiral, commodore, field marshal, marshal. **3.** *The tallest boy stood at the head of the line. The studious girl graduated at the head of her class:* front, first place, forward part, front rank, forefront, lead, highest rank, place of honor. **4.** *The head of the Mississippi River is in Minnesota:* source, origin, beginning, birthplace, rise, fountainhead, spring, wellspring, fountain, font, well. **5.** *Her burst of anger brought matters to a head:* climax, turning point, crisis, peak, extremity, utmost extent, conclusion, termination, culmination, inevitable result, end, fruition. **6.** *The head of a pin is the blunt end, but the head of a spear is the sharp end:* upper end, top, peak, tip, apex, crown, crest, vertex, acme, zenith, summit, pinnacle. —adj. **7.** *Take the bills to the head bookkeeper:* chief, highest ranking, ranking, managing, principal, main, foremost, first, highest, leading, dominant, supreme, superior, prime, premier, preeminent, paramount; governing, commanding, ruling, controlling. **8.** *The mayor rode in the head car of the cavalcade:* first, lead, leading, front, fore, foremost, headmost, highest, top, topmost, uppermost, primary, most prominent. —v. **9.** *Didn't Teddy Roosevelt head the charge up San Juan Hill?:* lead, go at the head of, go first, precede, lead the way, take the lead, be in the vanguard; start, begin, initiate, inaugurate, launch, introduce. **10.** *When the president died the vice president was chosen to head the firm:* be head of, direct, supervise, manage, take charge of, administer, superintend, lead, conduct, boss, command, govern, control, rule, be master of, have authority over, officiate at, preside over, be at the helm, take the reins, be in the driver's seat. **11.** *Head the boat toward shore. When the rain stops let's head for the picnic grounds:* steer, aim, turn, drive, pilot, guide, direct; move toward, direct one's course, go in the direction of, go, proceed, make for, hie, start off, make a beeline for. —**Ant.** 2 follower, subordinate; (*variously*) cog, menial, drone, underling, worker, hired hand, laborer, working man, enlisted man. 3 end, foot, bottom, tail, last place, lowest rank. 4 mouth; end, foot. 6 bottom, foot; shaft. 7 lowest, inferior, subordinate. 8 last, end, trailing, hindmost; bottom, bottommost. 9 follow, go behind, be last, bring up the rear; end, finish, terminate, conclude. 10 follow, be subordinae, be inferior. 11 move away, retreat, withdraw.

headlong *adj. Nothing deterred him in his headlong flight from justice:* rushed, precipitate, precipitous, hasty, abrupt, hurried, impetuous, sudden, impulsive, reckless.

headstrong *adj. She's so headstrong she's bound to get into trouble:* willful, bent on having one's own way, impulsive, rash, reckless, incautious, imprudent, hotheaded, intractable, ungovernable, froward, refractory, uncontrollable, contrary, defiant, unmanageable, incorrigible, unruly, recalcitrant; stubborn, obstinate, bullheaded, pigheaded, mulish, dogged, obdurate. —**Ant.** subservient, obedient, pliant, docile, submissive, impressionable, manageable; cautious, deliberate, methodical.

headway *n. They made no headway in curing the disease:* advance, progression, improvement, increase, promotion, progress.

heady *adj.* **1.** *This is very heady punch, so watch your step:* intoxicating, potent, strong, hard, *Slang* high-voltage, high-octane. **2.** *Being offered such a good job was very heady news:* exciting, exhilarating, intoxicating, thrilling, stirring; tempting, inviting, alluring, seductive, tantalizing. —**Ant.** 1 nonintoxicating, nonalcoholic, weak, soft. 2 depressing, disappointing, melancholy.

heal *v.* **1.** *This salve will help heal the wound. The doctor claimed to have healed a hundred similar cases:* cure, remedy, make well, get well, treat, make whole, heal over, heal up, knit, mend; return to health, recover, recuperate, improve, convalesce. **2.** *That long talk healed many of our differences:* reconcile, conciliate, settle, compose, rectify, right, set to rights, make harmonious, restore good relations; alleviate, soothe, relieve, salve. —**Ant.** 1 wound,

hurt, injure, harm; reopen, break; make worse, get worse.

health *n.* **1.** *How is the old man's health?:* physical condition, general condition. **2.** *You mustn't do anything to jeopardize your health:* good health, healthfulness, freedom from disease, fitness, clean bill of health; well-being, hardiness, robustness, vigor, strength, vitality, stamina, hardihood. —**Ant.** 2 sickness, illness, disease, ailment; weakness, debility, infirmity, frailty.

healthful *adj. There's nothing more healthful than a brisk walk every day:* healthy, good for one's health, wholesome, conducive to health, healthgiving, salubrious, salutary, invigorating, nutritious, beneficial, nourishing; hygienic. —**Ant.** unhealthy, unwholesome; detrimental, deleterious, dangerous.

healthy *adj. All the children are healthy and happy:* in good health, enjoying good health, able-bodied; hale, hearty, sound, strong, sturdy, robust, hardy, vigorous, sound of mind and limb, fit, in fine fettle, in the pink. —**Ant.** sick, sickly, ill, infirm, diseased, unhealthy, ailing; feeble, frail, weak, delicate, fragile, unsound, debilitated.

heap *n.* **1.** *This heap of dirty clothes is for the laundry:* pile, stack, mass, mound, cluster, bundle, batch, bunch; accumulation, collection, gathering, assemblage, agglomeration, aggregation; jumble, mess. **2.** *Informal As Edgar Guest wrote, "It takes a heap o' living to make a house a home":* large amount, lot, lots, good deal, great deal, load, abundance, profusion, great number, multitude, plenty, considerable amount, ocean, oceans, world, worlds, barrels, store, pack; *Informal* hunk, slew, slews; *Slang* gob, gobs, oodles. —v. **3.** *Rake the leaves and heap them by the garage:* pile, pile up, group, bunch, bundle, amass, mass, lump; collect, gather, concentrate. **4.** *The boss usually heaps work on me just at quitting time. The boy heaped his plate with turkey and dressing:* load, load up, pile, supply abundantly, give in profusion, mete out, shower upon, pour upon; fill, inundate, flood, deluge, engulf; accord, assign, award, present. —**Ant.** 2 little, drop, dab, touch, tiny bit. 3 scatter, disperse, dissipate, dispel.

hear *v.* **1.** *A large audience heard the concert last night:* listen to, be among the listeners at, be present at, be a spectator at, appear at, attend, witness, look on, be an auditor at. **2.** *I hear that you're moving to France:* understand, find out, be informed, be told, receive news, be led to believe, be made aware of, receive information, learn, gather, discover, ascertain; receive a letter; receive a phone call; *Slang* hear tell, get an earful. **3.** *Hear our plea, O Lord!:* listen to, heed, favor, approve, receive, hearken to, accede to, hold with, grant, admit, acknowledge; concede, acquiesce, give assent, be favorably disposed to. **4.** *The judge will hear the case next month:* judge, try; officially investigate, examine, inquire into. —**Ant.** 3 ignore, reject, disapprove, disagree with.

hearing *n.* **1.** *The school board is granting the*

parents a hearing on their complaints next month. The Senate is having a special hearing on organized crime: opportunity to be heard, interview, conference, audience, consultation, council; official investigation, inquiry, examination, review, probe; questioning, interrogation. **2.** The mother didn't realize the child was within hearing: earshot, hearing distance; range of hearing, carrying distance, reach of one's voice, sound.

hearsay n. It's only hearsay that the chairman is going to resign: rumor, gossip, report, grapevine, talk, idle talk; Slang scuttlebutt.

heart n. **1.** The old lady had a warm heart for children. Did you know in your heart that you'd never return?: feelings, emotion, sentiment, nature, temperament, mood, disposition, humor; innermost feelings, true nature, soul. **2.** The child's sad story won our hearts: sympathy, compassion, tenderness, gentleness, softheartedness; tenderness, affection, fondness, love; tolerance, indulgence, forgiveness, charity, clemency. **3.** I wanted to argue with him, but I hadn't the heart: courage, enthusiasm, desire, spirit, firmness, resoluteness, fortitude, pluck, spunk, gameness, resolution; bravery, valor, fearlessness, stoutheartedness, daring, boldness, audacity, audaciousness, gallantry, manfulness; Slang guts, backbone, stomach. **4.** The heart of the problem is a shortage of funds: essence, core, root, source, base, main part, crux, nub, soul, nucleus, center, kernel, pith, meat, quintessence; essentials, fundamentals, rudiments, principles, foundation; Slang nitty-gritty, brass tacks, guts. **5.** The dentist's office is in the heart of town: center, central part, middle, hub, busiest part, inner part, interior. —**Ant.** 2 dislike, hatred, hate, enmity; hardheartedness, cruelty. 3 timidity, cowardice, fear, yellow streak; shyness. 4 minor part, supplement, accessory; side issue, irrelevancy. 5 outskirts, periphery, environs.

heartbreak n. She was afraid of suffering further heartbreak: woe, broken heart, heartache, suffering, agony, grief, sorrow, anguish, desolation, despair, distress, misery, pain.

hearten v. The good news heartened us: cheer, encourage, buoy, inspire, rally, rouse, arouse, stir, animate, embolden, energize, incite, stimulate, strengthen.

heartfelt adj. Please accept my heartfelt sympathy: sincere, honest, profound, fervent, ardent, genuine, devout, earnest, deep, keenly felt, wholehearted, intense; complete, total, all-inclusive, thorough, entire, full. —**Ant.** feigned, superficial, shallow, insincere.

hearth n. **1.** Sweep the hearth before building the fire: fireplace, fireside, chimney corner. **2.** After weeks of traveling the salesman was happy to return to his own hearth: home, abode, household, house, family life, family circle.

heartless adj. Refusing food to that poor man was a heartless thing to do: cruel, cruelhearted, coldhearted, hardhearted, callous, unfeeling, insensitive, unkind, unmoved, unstirred, cold, uncaring, unresponsive, unsympathetic, pitiless,

unpitying, unmerciful; brutal, savage, mean, ruthless, inhuman, cold-blooded. —**Ant.** kind, generous, humane, compassionate, sympathetic, sensitive, merciful, sweet, soft-hearted, warmhearted.

hearty adj. **1.** The Smiths always give their guests a hearty welcome. Sounds of hearty laughter came from the next room: sincere, genuine, wholehearted, cordial, warm; profuse, ample, effusive, generous, thorough, complete, unrestrained, unbounded, unreserved; vigorous, enthusiastic, zestful, heartfelt, lively. **2.** The children are all lively and hearty: healthy, well, physically fit, hale, sound, vigorous, hardy, strong, robust. —**Ant.** 1 halfhearted, lukewarm, mild, cool, cold, reserved, stiff. 2 sickly, ill, unhealthy, delicate, frail, weak, puny; feeble, debilitated.

heat n. **1.** Father can't stand the heat of August: hotness, warmness, warmth, high temperature; hot weather, warm weather; hot spell, swelter, oppressive heat. **2.** Don't make any decisions in the heat of anger: stress, passion, fervor, fervency, excitement, intensity; height, climax; enthusiasm, eagerness, thrill, zeal, ardor; rapture, transport. —v. **3.** Heat the water and we'll have a cup of tea: make hot, warm, bring to a boil, warm up, heat up; (variously) cook, reheat, simmer, stew, roast, braise, steam, bake, fry, broil, boil, sear. —**Ant.** 1 cold, coldness, coolness, cold temperature; cold wave, cold spell. 2 composure, calmness, coolness. 3 cool, let cool, cool off, chill; freeze.

heated adj. The men had a heated argument about politics: vehement, impassioned, passionate, fervent, excited, frenzied, fierce, emotional, intense; stormy, tempestuous, raging, hot, fiery, violent, furious, angry, inflamed, irate, infuriated, bitter. —**Ant.** dispassionate, calm, mild, peaceful, quiet; friendly, sociable.

heathen n. **1.** Dr. Smith is a Baptist missionary among the heathen. The King James Bible translates the Hebrew term "goy" (non-Jewish nation) as "heathen." The Fula are Muslims and regard their animist neighbors as heathens: (variously) non-Christian, infidel; non-Jew, idolator, gentile, goy; non-Muslim, non-believer, unbeliever; any uncivilized denier of the God of the Old Testament; (loosely) pagan, savage, polytheist, barbarian, uncivilized native; atheist, agnostic. **2.** Heathen though he was, the old man never tired of boasting about his sculptor son: ignoramus, boor, troglodyte. —**Ant.** 1 (variously) Christian, true believer; Jew, adherent of Judaism; Muslim, adherent of Islam, believer. 2 civilized person, intellectual, sophisticate.

heave v. **1.** Heave this box onto the top shelf: hoist, haul up, pull up, drag up, draw up, yank up, lift, raise, elevate, boost; pry, lever. **2.** Heave the rocks into the ravine: throw, pitch, fling, hurl, cast, toss, chuck, sling, let fly, propel, fire, peg, launch. **3.** The ditchdigger heaved a great sigh of relief when the work was done: utter wearily, breathe heavily, emit, exhale, eject, discharge, blow, puff; groan, moan, sob; Informal retch, vomit, regurgitate, puke. **4.** The old *man's chest heaved alarmingly as he gasped for breath:* expand and contract, palpitate, surge; expand, swell, dilate, thrust up, bulge, be thrown upward, tilt up, arch; draw a deep breath, pant. —**Ant.** 1 lower, take down, put down, pull down.

heaven *n.* **1.** Often **Heaven** *May her soul rest in Heaven:* paradise, abode of God and the angels, dwelling place of the righteous after death, our external home, afterworld, afterlife, next world, world to come, world beyond; life everlasting, eternal bliss, life beyond; the kingdom of Heaven, the heavenly kingdom, the City of God, the heavenly city, the Holy City, the Celestial City, our Father's house, the abode of saints, Elysium, Elysian fields, Island of the Blessed, Isle of the Blessed, Zion, New Jerusalem, Beulah Land, Abraham's bosom; Valhalla; Olympus; the happy hunting ground. **2. the heavens** *The astronomer scanned the heavens through the telescope:* the sky, the firmament, the starry heavens, the vault of heaven, the celestial expanse, the celestial sphere; space, outer space, *Slang* the wild blue yonder. **3.** *Our weekend in the country was heaven:* complete happiness, bliss, sheer bliss, seventh heaven, heaven on earth, supreme happiness, paradise, nirvana, ecstasy, perfection, rapture, Shangri-la, utopia, dreamland, enchantment, glory, delight. —*interj.* **4.** *Heavens, what a gigantic birthday cake!:* heavens to Betsy, goodness, goodness gracious, good gracious, mercy, my stars, land sake, my oh my; *Slang* wow, boy oh boy. —**Ant.** 1 hell, hades, the infernal regions, purgatory, the underworld, the nether world, the abyss, eternal agony, eternal fire; limbo. 3 hell, pure hell, agony, misery, torment.

heavenly *adj.* **1.** *Heavenly angels came to him in a vision:* seraphic, divine, angelic, holy, beatific, blessed, beatified. **2.** *At night she studied the heavenly bodies:* celestial. **3.** *The layer cake was heavenly:* paradisiacal, scrumptious, sweet, wonderful, ambrosial, delectable, delicious, delightful, excellent, exquisite, lovely. —**Ant.** 1 hellish, satanic, diabolical, devilish. 3 appalling, horrible, miserable, terrible, awful, grim.

heavy *adj.* **1.** *What a heavy suitcase!:* weighty; cumbersome, cumbrous, burdensome, bulky, unwieldy, big, large, hefty. **2.** *The tornado was followed by heavy rains. The boat foundered in the heavy seas. Have you always been a heavy smoker?:* abundant, profuse, copious, extensive, excessive, intemperate, unrestrained, immoderate, inordinate, unstinting, extravagant, full, large, considerable; violent, strong, fierce, savage, forceful, raging, tempestuous, turbulent, rampaging, furious, seething, unrelenting, unremitting, roaring; hard, intense. **3.** *The taxes on personal property are getting heavy. Going bankrupt was a heavy blow to his pride:* burdensome, oppressive, hard to endure, onerous, harrowing, grievous, harsh, distressing, unbearable, intolerable, unendurable; damaging, injurious, detrimental, ruinous, calamitous, destructive, deadly, crushing, pernicious, deleterious. **4.** *My friends, it is with a heavy heart that I*

speak to you tonight: sorrowful, sad, gloomy, melancholy, full of care, pained, distressed, depressed, woeful, agonized, miserable, doleful, burdened; cheerless, joyless, downcast, dejected, forlorn, desolate, disconsolate, mournful, grieving, crestfallen, laden with sorrows, grief-stricken, tearful, stricken. **5.** *The job carries heavy responsibilities. This philosophy book is too heavy for me to enjoy:* serious, weighty, grave, solemn, momentous, important, overwhelming, of great import, of great consequence, consequential, impressive, awesome, imposing, notable, significant, noteworthy; profound, deep, difficult, complex; tedious, laborious, tiresome, wearisome; dreary, dull, monotonous, pedantic. **6.** *I recognized his heavy step on the stairs:* ponderous, lumbering, clumsy, lumpish, leaden, slow, sluggish, lethargic; listless, torpid, lazy, lifeless, apathetic, languid, phlegmatic. **7.** *The boy is so heavy he needs extra-large shirts. Heavy lines on the map indicate main roads:* fat, obese, stout, portly, plump, corpulent, overweight, hefty; thick, bulky, broad, massive; coarse, gross, dense, rough; rugged, sturdy. —**Ant.** light. 1 lightweight; compact, handy. 2 moderate, mild, soft, gentle, calm, weak; small, scant, sparse, slight, thin, little, skimpy, trifling, trivial. 3 easy, light, bearable, acceptable. 4 happy, gay, cheerful, exuberant, joyful, buoyant. 5 trivial, trifling; frivolous, gay; unimportant, insignificant, inconsequential; entertaining, exciting. 6 agile, brisk, spry, quick, rapid, buoyant, active. 7 thin, skinny.

heckle *v.* *Several students heckled the speaker:* jeer at, harass, harry, harrow, badger, bait, provoke, needle, molest, bully, mock, hector, twit, taunt, annoy, ride, hound, chivy, hoot, shout down, boo, hiss.

hectic *adj.* *Moving day was rather hectic:* frenetic, frantic, tumultuous, turbulent, furious, feverish, frenzied, wild, mad, stormy, headlong, breakneck; chaotic. —**Ant.** calm, serene, tranquil, relaxing, restful, orderly, peaceful.

hedge *n.* **1.** *The new owner planted a hedge around the garden:* fence of shrubs, hedgerow, row of bushes; fence, wall, barrier, border, ring, bound, margin, circumference, delineation. **2.** *A savings account is a hedge against misfortune:* protection, guard, insurance; compensation, counterbalance. —*v.* **3.** *We planted lilacs to hedge the yard:* enclose, surround, border, bound, edge, encircle, outline, fence, wall, ring, shut in, hem, hem in; limit, delineate, demarcate, mark off. **4.** *Answer the question fully--don't hedge:* equivocate, evade, be evasive, temporize, duck, dodge, beg the question; *Informal* waffle, pussyfoot, give the runaround, beat around the bush.

hedonist *n.* *"Eat, drink, and be merry, with no thought of tomorrow" is the code of a hedonist:* pleasure seeker, libertine, profligate, voluptuary, dissipater, debauchee, sensualist, Sybarite. —**Ant.** puritan; moralist.

heed *v.* **1.** *Heed the doctor's advice or you'll be sorry:* follow, be guided by, mind, obey, accede to, defer to, yield to, concur, comply with, hold to, be ruled by, bow to, submit to, observe, respect; take notice of, listen to, consider, bear in mind, pay attention to, take note of, give ear to, give a thought to, take to heart. —*n.* **2.** *I warned him, but he paid me no heed:* attention, notice, regard, mind, mindfulness, care, observation, attentiveness, heedfulness, carefulness, prudence, precaution, pains; conscientiousness, scrupulousness, meticulousness, fastidiousness; perusal, study, examination, scrutiny. —**Ant.** 1 ignore, disregard, slight, neglect, overlook; reject, refuse, turn a deaf ear to, be inattentive to, treat frivolously. 2 inattention, disregard, mindlessness; carelessness, neglect, thoughtlessness.

heedless *adj. Heedless people have the most accidents:* careless, thoughtless, mindless, unmindful, negligent, neglectful, uncaring, unthinking, inattentive, oblivious, unobserving, unobservant, unwatchful, unwary, unconcerned, unaware, unheeding; remiss, slack, lax, improvident, imprudent, incautious, rash, impetuous, foolhardy, reckless; harebrained, scatterbrained, foolish, witless; frivolous, happy-go-lucky. —**Ant.** careful, cautious, wary, prudent, circumspect, mindful, attentive, heedful, thinking, thoughtful, observant, watchful, vigilant; concerned, aware, alert.

hefty *adj. All the players on the team were unusually hefty:* husky, heavy, beefy, strapping, stout, strong, weighty, sturdy, bulky, substantial, burly, rugged, robust, powerful, massive, strong, hearty, muscular, stalwart. —**Ant.** small, puny, skinny, weak, feeble, fragile.

height *n.* **1.** *The mountain rises to a height of 12,000 feet:* altitude, elevation, upward extent; tallness, highness, loftiness. **2.** *The house on the height has a commanding view of town:* hilltop, vantage point, promontory, eminence; mountain, hill, highland, palisade, cliff, bluff, mound, rise, knoll, plateau; pinnacle, summit, peak. **3.** *Her remark was the height of rudeness:* extremity, utmost degree, limit, ultimate, maximum, peak; pinnacle, tower, high point, crest, summit, zenith, acme, apex, apogee, culmination; supremacy, perfection, consummation, flowering, heyday. —**Ant.** 1 depth, lowness. 2 valley, canyon, gulch, ravine, abyss; lowland. 3 depth, low point, nadir; minimum.

heinous *adj. The murder was a most heinous crime:* atrocious, abominable, abhorrent, repugnant, repulsive, reprehensible, despicable, deplorable, horrid, shocking, monstrous, inhuman, gross, detestable, loathsome, foul, hideous, contemptible, distasteful, objectionable, outrageous; disgusting, revolting, vile, sickening, nasty, beastly; infamous, villainous, iniquitous, nefarious, vicious, terrible, odious, grisly, ghastly, offensive; scandalous, outrageous, disgraceful; sinful, wicked, evil. —**Ant.** good, beneficial, worthwhile, attractive, charming, admirable, laudable, praiseworthy, meritorious; lovable, pleasing, pleasant.

heir, *Fem.* **heiress** *n. The millionaire's only heir was his son:* beneficiary, inheritor, (*fem.*) inheritress, inheritrix; heir apparent, heir presumptive.

heirloom *n. She inherited several precious heirlooms:* bequest, inheritance, legacy, antique.

hell *n.* **1.** Often **Hell** *The preacher warned us about punishment in Hell:* abode of the damned, infernal regions, lake of fire, bottomless pit, the pit, the abyss, the lower world, the underworld, the nether world, the shades below, place of the lost, home of lost souls, Satan's kingdom, the Devil's house; everlasting fire, hell fire; (*variously*) hades, inferno, perdition. **2.** *Her life has been hell since her husband fell ill:* torment, anguish, agony, wretchedness, suffering, misery; despair, hopelessness, grief, martyrdom, remorse. —**Ant.** 1, 2 heaven, paradise. 2 bliss, joy, felicity, rapture, enchantment, happiness, ecstasy.

help *v.* **1.** *Ted helped his brother build the bookcase. Please help the needy:* assist, give assistance to, aid, lend a hand, give a helping hand, cooperate with, collaborate with, contribute to, serve; support, back, champion, advance, uphold, further, promote, side with, endorse, encourage, advocate, take the part of, stand by, give moral support to, maintain, intercede for; *Slang* go to bat for, stick up for; befriend, guide, advise, minister to, succor, console, nurture; be of advantage; give to, contribute to, *Slang* chip in for. **2.** *Help me--I can't swim!:* save, rescue, aid, come to the aid of, snatch from danger, extricate, retrieve. **3.** *The shots helped the patient's hay fever:* relieve, alleviate, cure, soothe, calm, mitigate, ease, remedy, improve, lift, put at ease, ameliorate, allay, correct, make healthy, make whole, bring through, bring round, do a world of good for; rectify, emend. —*n.* **4.** *The movers need some help lifting the piano. The senator needs the help of the local politicians to be reelected. The city must give more help to the poor:* assistance, aid, helping hand, cooperation, collaboration, service; support, backing, advancement, promotion, furtherance, endorsement, encouragement, contribution, gift, protection, friendship, support; benevolence, guidance, advice, care, welfare, good offices, kind regard. **5.** *The cook is in charge of the kitchen help:* employees, workers, workmen, laborers, hands, hired hands, workhands, assistants, helpers, hired helpers; (*variously*) farmhand, domestic, servant, apprentice, underling, menial, retainer, factotum; staff, crew, work force, force. **6.** *Aspirin may be a help for that headache:* cure, remedy, corrective, preventive, restorative, aid, relief, balm, salve. —**Ant.** 1 hinder, impede, obstruct, hold back, block, bar, frustrate, thwart, foil, balk; oppose, fight, side against, discourage, *Slang* put down. 2 harm, hurt, injure, attack; kill, let die. 3 make worse, aggravate, irritate, discomfit. 4 hindrance, obstruction, block, bar, opposition, discouragement. 6 bane, aggravation, irritant.

helper *n.* **1.** *The carpenter and his helper built the garage in two days:* assistant, aid, aide, second, aide-de-camp, adjunct, right-hand man, right hand, man Friday, girl Friday, helping hand; auxiliary, deputy, subordinate; apprentice.

2. *The doctor needs a helper to take over half his practice:* partner, colleague, associate, accomplice, confederate, collaborator, co-worker, confrere. **3.** *The women's club needs more helpers to make the charity ball a success:* backer, supporter, patron, benefactor, angel, good samaritan, fairy godmother; advocate, champion.

helpful *adj. Some of her suggestions were very helpful:* beneficial, useful, constructive, advantageous, favorable, usable, practical, serviceable; valuable, profitable; fine, good, nice, excellent, splendid. **—Ant.** pointless, useless, worthless; harmful, destructive, injurious.

helping *n. He asked for an extra helping:* portion, share, serving, allowance, plateful, ration.

helpless *adj. The helpless plane went down in heavy fog:* defenseless, unprotected, vulnerable, impotent, incapable, weak, forsaken, friendless, disabled, feeble, infirm, powerless, paralyzed, unable. **—Ant.** capable, able.

hem *n.* **1.** *The coat's hem was ragged:* edge, edging, fringe, border, margin, periphery, skirting, trimming, verge, brim, rim. *—v.* **2.** *The enemy hemmed them in. She hemmed the new skirt:* circle, circumscribe, encircle, enclose, encompass, confine, bound, cage, corral, fence, girdle, pen, ring, surround; edge, fringe, border, rim.

henchman *n. The film producer never went anywhere without several henchmen:* right-hand man, lieutenant, retainer; bodyguard, strong-arm man, hatchet man, attendant; hireling, minion, flunky, lackey, yes-man, hanger-on; *Slang* stooge, gorilla, goon, thug.

henpecked *adj. The aggressive woman berated her henpecked husband:* wife-ridden, under the thumb of one's wife; submissive, meek, timid, docile, unassertive, browbeaten, obedient. **—Ant.** manly, dominating, *Spanish* macho; forceful, aggressive, assertive.

herald *n.* **1.** *The herald announced the king's approach:* messenger, crier, proclaimer, courier. **2.** *Shakespeare called the lark the "herald of the morn":* forerunner, harbinger, precursor, envoy, predecessor, foregoer, usher; omen, sign, augury, warning, token, indication, indicator, symbol, clue; forecast, portent. *—v.* **3.** *Trumpets heralded the king's approach:* announce, proclaim, report, foretell, prefigure, presage, make known, give tidings of, divulge, reveal, usher in; inform, communicate, publish, publicize, advertise, bruit abroad, give voice to.

herculean **1.** Sometimes **Herculean** *The herculean wrestler easily won the match:* strong, powerful, mighty, muscular, strong as Hercules, strapping, rugged, burly, brawny, sturdy, robust, hefty; hard, tough. **2.** *Moving the cartons from the attic to the basement was a herculean task:* strenuous, laborious, backbreaking, arduous, exhausting, wearying, fatiguing, toilsome, burdensome, difficult, onerous, prodigious, formidable. **—Ant.** 1 weak, feeble, frail, delicate. 2 easy, effortless, relaxing, restful.

herd *n.* **1.** *A herd of buffalo thundered across the plains:* pack, drove, flock, bunch, group, cluster, gathering. **2.** *There was a great herd of bargain hunters at the sale:* crowd, mob, throng, horde, swarm, drove, bunch, gang, band, pack, press, mass, host, tribe, swarm, flock, cluster, army, troop, legion; gathering, group, assemblage, assembly, company, body, multitude, number, lot, congregation, convocation, conclave, collection, array, party. *—v.* **3.** *The drovers herded the cattle into the pens:* drive, guide, force, goad, spur, lead. **4.** *The teacher herded the boys onto the playground before the games began:* bring together, collect, muster, round up, assemble, gather, call together; crowd, cluster, huddle, bunch, come together, flock together, rally, group, convene.

hereafter *adj.* **1.** *Hereafter I'll take your advice:* after this, from now on, in the future, henceforth, henceforward, subsequently, from this time forth; at a later date, at a later time, one of these days, ultimately. *—n.* **2.** *The pious man expected his reward in the hereafter:* afterlife, afterworld, next world, life after death, future life, life beyond, world to come, heaven, heavenly kingdom, paradise. **—Ant.** 1 heretofore, before this, before now, before, in the past. 2 mortal life, here, here and now.

hereditary *adj.* **1.** *Is baldness hereditary?:* inherited, inheritable, heritable; inbred, inborn, congenital. **2.** *The family has a large hereditary fortune:* inherited, handed-down, ancestral; traditional, established. **—Ant.** 1, 2 acquired. 2 earned, saved.

heredity *n. Heredity played a role in his temperament:* ancestry, genetics, genetic makeup, eugenics, inheritance, traits, congenital traits, constitution.

heresy *n. Pope Leo X excommunicated Martin Luther for heresy. A businessman who speaks in favor of lower profits is speaking heresy!:* heretical beliefs, apostasy, heterodoxy, unorthodoxy, unsound doctrine, fallacy, unorthodox belief, unorthodox opinion, nonconformity, irreligion, dissension, iconoclasm, dissent. **—Ant.** orthodoxy, catholicity; convention, con-formity, traditionalism.

heretic *n. In former times the Inquisition burned heretics at the stake:* dissenter, apostate, skeptic, misbeliever; nonconformist, recusant, deviationist, freethinker, renegade; backslider, recreant. **—Ant.** orthodox believer, true believer, adherent.

heretical *adj. Can any church tolerate heretical ideas? Some of the painter's ideas about art seem a bit heretical:* unorthodox, contrary to accepted standards; unconventional, iconoclastic, nonconforming, nonconformist, dissident, radical. **—Ant.** orthodox; conventional, conforming.

heritage *n. Fair play is part of our heritage:* tradition, birthright, inheritance, portion, patrimony; estate, family possession, legacy.

hermit *n. The hermit left his cave and came to town only once a year:* recluse, solitudinarian, solitary; religious recluse, eremite, anchorite, desert saint, cenobite, monastic.

hero, *Fem.* **heroine** *n.* **1.** *John Paul Jones is an*

American naval hero: brave person, valorous person, person of courage, champion, fearless fighter, intrepid warrior; great person, noble person, chivalrous person, gallant; daredevil, adventurer, daring person; legendary person, idealized person, popular figure, idol, star, person of the hour. **2.** *The hero gets the girl at the end of the movie:* leading man, principal male character, protagonist, male lead, main actor, male star. **—Ant.** villain. 1 coward, dastard, poltroon. 2 antagonist; heavy.

heroic *adj.* **1.** *King Arthur's heroic deeds are the subject of many stories:* brave, courageous, valiant, valorous, dauntless, undaunted, fearless, lionhearted, stouthearted, intrepid, resolute, unflinching, bold, daring; noble, gallant, chivalrous; legendary, mythological, mythical, Homeric. **2.** *The opera* Lohengrin *is in the heroic style:* classic, grand, epic, elevated, dignified, exalted; highbrow, extravagant, grandiose, highflown; ostentatious, pretentious; exaggerated, inflated, bombastic. **—Ant.** 1 cowardly, fainthearted, afraid, timid, fearful, timorous, irresolute, wavering; ignoble, mean, base, craven, pusillanimous. 2 simple, straightforward, unadorned; earthy, lowbrow.

heroin *n.* *She injected herself with heroin:* narcotic, *Informal* horse, junk, scag, smack.

heroism *n.* *Davy Crockett's heroism is well-known:* bravery, courage, courageousness, prowess, valor, dauntlessness, fearlessness, lionheartedness, boldness, daring, intrepidity, fortitude; gallantry, nobility, chivalry. **—Ant.** cowardice, timidity; meanness, baseness.

hesitant *adj.* *Why were you so hesitant about asking for help?:* hesitating, reluctant, halfhearted, faltering, lacking confidence, hanging back; undecided, doubtful, indecisive, uncertain, halting, unsure, tentative, diffident, loath, irresolute, wavering, vacillating, shilly-shallying, sitting on the fence. **—Ant.** eager, willing, avid, keen; resolute, determined, steadfast, staunch, firm, certain, sure, confident, decisive, decided.

hesitate *v.* **1.** *The driver hesitated at the intersection, then turned right:* pause, delay, stop briefly, halt, falter; be undecided, be uncertain, be unsure, be irresolute, waver, vacillate, shilly-shally, dillydally, straddle the fence. **2.** *I hesitate to pay so much for a suit:* shy at, be unwilling, stick at, stickle at; hang back, be reluctant, balk, shrink from; think twice, scruple. **—Ant.** 1 go pell-mell, go headlong, continue; be decisive, decide, be firm, be certain, be sure, be confident. 2 welcome, do willingly, embrace, be determined, resolve.

hesitation *n.* **1.** *We had no hesitation in recommending her:* hesitancy, indecision, vacillation, irresolution, delay, uncertainty, doubt. **2.** *His speech was full of hesitation:* halting, stammering, faltering. **—Ant.** resolution, certainty.

heterogeneous *adj.* *It was a heterogeneous group of rich and poor, old and young:* mixed, varied, diversified, diverse, assorted, jumbled, miscellaneous, motley, variegated, composite; dissimilar, unlike, unrelated, disparate, divergent. **—Ant.** homogeneous, uniform, matched; same, like, alike, identical, similar.

hew *v.* *The farmer spent a day in the woods hewing timber. The statue was hewn from one large block of marble:* chop, hack, cut, cut down, ax, chop down, sever, lop, prune; carve, chisel, cut out, sculpture, whittle, form, shape, fashion, mold, devise, model.

hiatus *n.* *There was a hiatus of two years before the student went back to college:* lapse, interval, interim, break, space, gap, void, blank, interruption, disruption, vacuum, lacuna.

hibernate *v.* *The bear crawled into a cave to hibernate:* winter, hole up, lie dormant, lie torpid, vegetate.

hick *n.* *He was dressed like a hick:* rube, hayseed, bumpkin.

hide *v.* **1.** *Hide your money in your shoe:* conceal, secrete, keep out of sight, prevent from being seen, prevent from being discovered, put in concealment, cache, seclude. **2.** *The robbers hid in a cave:* lie concealed, be hidden, hide out, conceal oneself, remain in a hiding place, keep oneself out of sight, lie low, go into hiding, *Slang* go underground. **3.** *I can't hide my feelings. Fog hid the mountain:* conceal, obscure, cover, veil, screen, cloak, curtain, shroud, cloud; repress, suppress; mask, disguise. **—Ant.** 1, 3 reveal, show, expose, display, exhibit, parade, flaunt; find, discover, uncover. 2 find. 3 divulge, disclose, bare, unmask, unveil; admit, confess, avow, lay open, expose.

hideous *adj.* *What a hideous wallpaper! Every day we hear of some hideous crime:* ugly, grotesque, dreadful, horrid, repulsive, repugnant, awful, abhorrent, abominable, frightful, ghastly, revolting, appalling, shocking, repellent, macabre, gruesome, grim, horrendous, horrible; monstrous, loathsome, detestable, disgusting, sickening, vile, odious. **—Ant.** beautiful, lovely, attractive, pleasant, pleasing, charming, captivating, entrancing, appealing.

high *adj.* **1.** *New York City has many high buildings:* tall, lofty, towering, soaring, high-reaching, sky-scraping, alpine, cloud-capped. **2.** *The car was traveling at high speed. Prices have never been so high:* great, extreme, excessive, inordinate, unreasonable, undue, intemperate, immoderate; extravagant, exorbitant, exaggerated, unrestrained, uncurbed, unbridled. **3.** *He holds a high position in the government. The spy was guilty of high treason. One must have high ideals:* important, serious, elevated, lofty, top, eminent, exalted, consequential, significant, notable, distinguished, prominent, preeminent, illustrious, august, superior, imposing, leading; prime, primary, foremost, chief, main, principal, capital, predominant, uppermost; peerless, ascendant, grand, excellent, noble. **4.** *The speaker had a very high voice:* high-pitched, soprano, in the upper register; shrill, sharp, strident, piercing, earsplitting. **5.** *The boss has been in high spirits all day:* excited, elated, exuberant, exhilarated, exultant; merry, joyful, joyous, gay, cheerful, lighthearted, playful, jubilant, overjoyed, jolly, gleeful, jovial, mirthful. **—adv. 6.** *The hawk* *was circling high in the sky:* at great altitude, at great height, way up, far up, aloft. —**Ant.** low. **1** short, stunted, dwarfed. **2** moderate, mild, average, reasonable, routine, reduced; subdued, suppressed, restrained. **3** low-ranking, lowly, unimportant, inconsequential, insignificant, undistinguished; secondary, common, routine, average; menial; debased, degraded, ignoble. **4** low-pitched, base, alto; deep, husky, gruff, hoarse. **5** sad, cheerless, gloomy, joyless, depressed, dejected, melancholy; angry, mad, irritable.

highbrow *n.* **1.** *The lecture series seemed to be designed for highbrows:* intellectual, scholar, mastermind, thinker, Brahmin, mandarin; elitist, snob; *Slang* egghead, brain, double-dome. —*adj.* **2.** *Her highbrow tastes are usually very expensive:* intellectual, scholarly, erudite, cultured, cultivated, bookish, knowledgeable; snobbish, elitist. —**Ant. 1** lowbrow, hard-hat, redneck, ignoramus, Philistine. **2** unschooled, illiterate, untutored, uncultivated.

high-flown *adj. The young man had high-flown ideas about saving the world. The senator made a long, high-flown speech:* lofty, elevated, grandiose; proud, self-important, lordly, presumptuous; pretentious, extravagant, inflated, high-flying, pompous, florid, flowery, high-sounding, sententious, exaggerated, flamboyant; bombastic, magniloquent, turgid, orotund, grandiloquent; *Slang* highfalutin. —**Ant.** down-to-earth, practical, realistic, pragmatic; straightforward, simple, to the point; terse, concise.

highland *n.* Often **Highlands** *This wool plaid skirt was made in the Highlands of Scotland:* uplands, hill country, tableland, plateau, mountainous region, heights, headland; rise, promontory. —**Ant.** lowlands; valley.

highlight *n.* **1.** *Rembrandt used highlights to focus attention in his paintings:* spot of intense light, strong illumination; focal point, prominent detail. **2.** *The highlight of the children's vacation was the visit to the White House:* climax, outstanding part, main feature, memorable part, high point, peak, most interesting aspect. —*v.* **3.** *The senator's speech highlighted the need for reduced tariffs. The portrait highlighted the queen's necklace:* emphasize, stress, accent, feature, accentuate, give prominence to, point up, underline, focus attention on; make light, make bright. —**Ant. 1** shadow. **2** low point; disappointment. **3** de-emphasize, play down, gloss over, slight, neglect, overlook.

high-minded *adj. Such a high-minded person would never lie:* honorable, honest, fair, ethical, principled, sincere, truthful, just, scrupulous, conscientious, upright, worthy, virtuous, reputable, uncorrupt, square-dealing; noble, idealistic, lofty. —**Ant.** unprincipled, unworthy, dishonorable, dishonest, unfair, unethical, corrupt, unscrupulous, ignoble, mean, base, low.

high-strung *adj. Thoroughbred horses are often high-strung:* nervous, excitable, easily agitated, tense, uneasy, skittish, temperamental, jumpy, edgy, wrought-up, restless, impatient; *Slang* jittery, uptight; neurotic, oversensitive,

moody. —**Ant.** phlegmatic, calm, collected, placid, stolid, even-tempered, *Slang* cool.

highway *n. The new highway will reduce the driving time to our cabin by two hours:* main road, thruway, expressway, freeway, speedway, turnpike; (*variously*) interstate, state highway, parkway, main artery, divided highway, four-lane road, thoroughfare, highroad; hard road, paved road; *British* royal road, coach road, King's Highway, Queen's Highway. —**Ant.** byway, back road, county road, side road.

hike *v.* **1.** *The Boy Scouts hiked out to the reservoir:* march, tramp, journey on foot, trek, walk; trudge, roam, wander, rove, ramble; *Informal* hoof it, leg it, go by shank's mare, put on one's hiking shoes. **2.** *Hike up your trousers and tuck in your shirt:* pull up, hitch up, draw up, raise up, jerk up. —*n.* **3.** *After the hike to the river the soldiers camped for the night:* march, tramp, journey by foot, walk. **4.** *There's been another hike in food prices:* increase, rise, raise, escalation, upward movement; expansion, addition, augmentation.

hilarious *adj.* **1.** *The comedian told several hilarious stories:* very funny, laugh-provoking, comical, uproarious, hysterical, riotous, highly amusing, laughable, rollicking. **2.** *Everyone at the party had a hilarious time:* lively, jubilant, jovial, jolly, gay, gleeful, joyous, mirthful, high-spirited, exuberant, exhilarated, jocund, joyful, merry, rollicking; boisterous, noisy, vociferous. —**Ant. 1** sad, serious, **2** dull, gloomy, depressed; quiet, sedate.

hilarity *n.* glee, mirth, merriment, levity, jollity, hilariousness, hysterics, joy, jocularity.

hill *n.* **1.** *The park is on a hill overlooking the town. The truck went up the hill in first gear:* hilltop, knoll, foothill, rise, hillock, hummock, mount, promontory, dune, butte, bluff, cliff, highland, height, elevation, prominence, eminence; slope, incline, acclivity, hillside, climb, grade, upgrade, ramp, bank; downgrade, declivity. **2.** *Make a hill around each bean plant:* mound of earth, mound; heap, pile. —**Ant. 1** low ground, valley, canyon, gorge, gully, ravine, bottom, basin, hollow, dale, glen, dell, vale.

hinder *v. Heavy snow hindered the bus's progress. Lack of a practice field hindered the team:* delay, slow down, hold up, hold back, detain, stop, stay, arrest, stall, check, curb, hamper, retard, encumber, obstruct, block, deter, impede, bar, restrain, handicap, inhibit, frustrate, interfere with, make difficult; stifle, stymie, thwart, foil, hobble, fetter, spike, hamstring, hog-tie, put a spoke in one's wheels. —**Ant.** help, aid, support, further, advance, promote, benefit, encourage; expedite, facilitate, accelerate, speed, hurry, hasten, quicken.

hindrance *n. Lack of education could be a hindrance to your career:* impediment, stumbling block, obstacle, obstruction, blockage, handicap, encumbrance, restriction, limitation, interference, constraint, restraint, retardant, difficulty, bar, snag, catch, curb; barrier, blockade, barricade, clog, fetter, shackle. —**Ant.** help, aid, benefit, assistance, support, furtherance, advancement, spur, boon.

hinge *n.* **1.** *This door has a squeaky hinge:* hinged joint, pivot. —*v.* **2.** *The whole business hinges on the boss's decision:* depend, hang, revolve around, be subject to, rest, turn, pivot, swing; be due to, result from, arise from, emanate from.

hint *n.* **1.** *Give me a hint so I can solve the riddle. There was a hint of anger in the statement:* clue, inkling, notion, idea, tip, tip-off, pointer; suggestion, indication, insinuation, implication, innuendo, allusion, intimation, impression, whisper, indirection, slight knowledge; *Informal* flea in the ear, word to the wise. **2.** *There was just a hint of garlic in the salad:* trace, little, slight amount, touch, tinge, whisper, smattering, bit, pinch, grain, whiff, iota, jot, suspicion, *French* soupçon. —*v.* **3.** *She hinted that it was time we left:* suggest, intimate, imply, signify, insinuate, indicate, *Informal* tip off. —**Ant.** 2 abundance, profusion, plethora, amplitude; excess, surplus. 3 assert, declare, announce, state in no uncertain terms.

hinterland *n.* *They traveled far into the hinterland:* backwoods, back country, wilds, wilderness, bush, bush country, forests, frontier, uninhabited region, virgin territory, *Australian* outback *South African* bushveld, *Informal* back of beyond, the boondocks, the boonies, the sticks.

hire *v.* **1.** *The store hired two more clerks for the sale:* employ, engage, give employment to, take on, retain, appoint, secure, obtain, get, procure. **2.** *During our vacation we hired a boat and went fishing:* rent, charter, lease, let, engage. —*n.* **3.** *The new farmhand is worth every cent of his hire:* salary, wages, pay, compensation, remuneration, stipend, fee, emolument, recompense, income, receipts, payment, profit, reward, gain, earnings; cost, charge, rent. —**Ant.** 1 fire, discharge, dismiss, let go, cashier; *Slang* sack, can, give the boot, kiss off.

hireling *n.* *The gangster sent his hirelings to do the dirty work:* menial, minion, flunky, lackey, retainer; henchman, stooge, gorilla, thug, goon, hatchet man, strong-arm.

hirsute *adj.* *Cavemen are often pictured as muscular and hirsute:* hairy; unshaven, unshorn, bearded, bewhiskered, whiskered; bushy, woolly, shaggy, downy, nappy, bristled, bristly, prickly. —**Ant.** hairless, smooth-shaven; bald, closecropped.

hiss *v.* *The audience hissed the villain of the play:* boo; *Informal* give a Bronx cheer, hoot at, razz; heckle, catcall, jeer at, scoff at, deride, shout down, mock, sneer at, revile; *Slang* give the raspberry. —**Ant.** applaud, clap, cheer, shout, approval.

historic *adj.* *Plymouth Rock is a historic spot. July 4, 1776 is a historic day:* important in history, famed, well-known, notable, outstanding, renowned, memorable, celebrated. —**Ant.** unimportant, unknown, uncelebrated, trivial.

historical *adj.* *The book is based on historical events. It is a historical fact that George Wash-*

ington had false teeth made of wood: in history, of history, grounded in history; authentic, actual, real, true, documented, factual, attested, recorded, chronicled, supported by historical evidence; bygone, ancient, belonging to the past, past, former. —**Ant.** present-day, current, contemporary; fictional, fictitious, legendary, mythical, fabulous.

history *n.* **1.** *The 1860's were full of history. Today's history is being made in Washington, London, and Moscow:* important events, major events, world events, national events, local events; political change, military action, human progress, development, growth, change; an interesting past, an unusual past; actual events, unalterable facts. **2.** *The local librarian is writing a history of western Canada:* narration of past events, factual story of the past, chronicle, account, record, saga, epic, annals; portrayal, recapitulation, review, résumé; narration, narrative, story, tale. **3.** *Way back in history, all this land belonged to the king:* the past, former times, bygone days, bygone times, olden times, old times, the old days, days of old, days of yore, yesteryear, yesterday; tradition. —**Ant.** 1 current events. 1, 2 fiction, fantasy, legend, myth, fable. 3 the present, today, now; the future, time to come.

histrionics *n.* *The play was filled with histrionics to disguise its lack of ideas:* dramatics, dramaturgy, theatrics, staginess, melodramatics; temper tantrum, ranting and raving, tirade, outburst, fuss, bluster, bombast, rodomontade, *Slang* hamminess; performance, acting, playacting, theatricality.

hit *v.* **1.** *The boxer hit his opponent with a solid right to the jaw. The golfer hit the ball 200 yards down the fairway:* strike, deal a stroke, deal a blow, sock, smash, slug, knock, jab, wallop, clip, punch, smack, slam, poke; *Slang* paste, clout, clobber, belt, slap, whack, thwack, baste, lambaste, bash; trounce, pommel, drub, pound, beat, flog, thrash, batter, pelt, punch, flail; smite, club, bat, cudgel. **2.** *The truck hit the car at the intersection:* collide with, smash into, bump, butt, bang into; strike together. **3.** *The arrow hit the target. The quarterback hit the tight end with a perfect pass. This car can hit 120 miles an hour:* strike, succeed in striking, go straight to, make a bull's-eye, send to the mark; attain, connect with, reach, achieve, realize, arrive at; effect, execute, bring off. **4.** *The bad news hit everyone hard:* affect, touch, move, impress; overwhelm, overcome, crush, upset, hurt, devastate, shatter, abash; arouse, rouse, incite, provoke, quicken, stir, inflame. **5.** *Our troops and planes will hit the enemy at dawn. The senator's speech hit at government spending:* attack, strike, strike out at, assault, assail, mount an offensive; denounce, damn, criticize, censure, condemn, revile, lash out at, reproach; *Slang* rap. —*n.* **6.** *Jim is still recovering from that hit on the head:* blow, impact, bump, knock, strike, rap, tap, whack, thwack, cuff, bang, thump; *Slang* clip, wallop, lob, bat, swat, clout, smash, crack, belt, sock; smash, paste, jab, punch, smack, slap. **7.** *The new play is the biggest Broadway hit in years:* success, popular success, sensation, triumph, winner, *Slang* smash; victory, boon, find, coup, blessing, godsend. **—Ant.** 1 caress, pat; block, parry, deflect, counterpunch. 2 miss. 3 miss, miss the mark; fail. 5 retreat, withdraw, surrender, give up; defend, support, champion, praise, acclaim, applaud, compliment. 7 flop, failure; *Slang* bomb, dog.

hitch *v.* **1.** *Hitch these two ropes together. Hitch the mule to the plow:* tie, tether, loop, loop together, make fast, couple, attach, fasten, connect, bracket, yoke, clamp, secure; put in harness, harness. **2.** *Hitch up your socks:* pull, tug, yank, hike, raise, haul, draw, jerk. **—n. 3.** *The horse was tied with a hitch to the post:* knot, loop; attaching, joining, coupling, connection, fastening, tying. **4.** *The pitcher gave a hitch to his trousers before throwing the ball:* pull, tug, yank, jerk. **5.** *The program went off without a hitch:* mishap, mischance, mistake, difficulty, complication, problem, catch, snag; trouble, delay, halt, obstacle, impediment, stumbling block, restraint, hindrance, restriction, curb, stop, check, interruption; handicap, limitation. **—Ant.** 1 untie, unfasten, uncouple, free, release, loose, loosen. 2 pull down.

hither *adv.* *Come hither and let us have a look at you:* here, over here, to this place, to the speaker, forward, onward, on, near, nearer, close, closer, close by, nearby. **—Ant.** thither, yon, there; away, farther, farther away.

hitherto *adv.* *Hitherto I have always liked your work:* till now, until now, up to now, thus far, up to this time, before this, heretofore, hereto, ere now, to the present time. **—Ant.** henceforth, henceforward, hereafter, in future, after this, subsequently.

hive *n.* *The hive followed the queen bee to a new tree. The stock exchange was a hive of activity:* swarm of bees, colony, cluster; busy place, hub, center, heart.

hoard *n.* **1.** *The trapper kept a hoard of canned goods at the cabin:* stockpile, cache, store, supply, reserve, fund; gathering, accumulation, collection, pile, heap, mass, amassment, quantity. **—v. 2.** *Before rationing in World War II, some people hoarded sugar:* stockpile, store away, lay away, lay up, cache, save up, store, amass, accumulate, collect, buy up, acquire. **—Ant.** 2 distribute, dispense, scatter, disperse; waste, squander, dissipate.

hoarse *adj.* *The actor's cold made his voice hoarse:* husky, harsh, rasping, raspy, raucous, scratchy, croaky, rough, gruff, cracked, throaty, gravelly, guttural. **—Ant.** full, rich, sweet, clear, mellow, melodious, mellifluous.

hoary *adj.* **1.** *The old prospector's hair and beard were hoary. The fields were hoary with snow:* gray with age, white with age; white, whitened, grizzled, grizzly, hoar, gray, grayed. **2.** *That's a hoary tale my grandfather used to tell!:* old, ancient, aged; antique, out-of-date, dated, passé, *Slang* old hat. **—Ant.** 2

brand-new, new, modern, up-to-date, recent, *Slang* with-it.

hoax *n.* **1.** *Telling the boy he could catch whales in that pond was just a hoax:* mischievous deception, humorous deception, absurd story, exaggerated tale, false alarm, yarn, fish story, fiction; spoof, trick, prank, chicanery, deception, fake, fraud, cheat, humbug, canard, hocus-pocus. **—v. 2.** *The radio audience was hoaxed into believing that Martians had landed:* hoodwink, deceive, delude, take in, fool, trick, mislead, bluff; defraud, swindle, cheat, bilk, dupe, victimize, gyp, cozen, gull; *Slang* bamboozle. **—Ant.** 1 truth, true story, fact, factual account. 2 undeceive, enlighten.

hobble *v.* **1.** *Hobble the horse so it won't run away:* fetter, shackle, bind, manacle. **2.** *The skier hobbled around on crutches for a month after the accident:* limp, halt, walk lamely; shuffle, lumber, stumble, shamble, stagger, toddle. **3.** *Bad luck hobbled him most of his life:* hold back, hinder, restrict, encumber, interfere with, inhibit, frustrate, hamper, thwart, impede, handicap, cramp, shackle, constrain, restrain, check, hamstring, hog-tie, block, obstruct, stymie. **—n. 4.** *Tie the hobble around the horse's two rear legs:* fetter, shackle, manacle. **5.** *After his stroke the old man walked with a hobble:* limp, gimp, lame gait, uneven gait, jerking motion, stumbling motion, shuffle, stagger. **—Ant.** 2 run, prance, walk briskly. 3 help, aid, assist, benefit, advance, further. 5 jaunty step, even gait.

hobby *n.* *Stamp collecting is an educational hobby:* diversion, pastime, leisure-time activity, relaxation, sideline, amusement, entertainment, pursuit, avocation, divertissement. **—Ant.** work, job, vocation.

hocus-pocus *n.* **1.** *The magician said some kind of hocus-pocus and a rabbit appeared. The children enjoyed the magician's hocus-pocus:* magic formula, magic words, chant, incantation, mumbo jumbo; magic spell, charm, spell, bewitchment; magic tricks, magic, sleight of hand, legerdemain, prestidigitation. **2.** *There's too much hocus-pocus going on in local politics:* deception, trickery, deceit, dishonesty, humbug, hoax, delusion, sham, rubbish, bunkum, fakery; cheat, swindle, subterfuge, confidence game; *Informal* con game; *Slang* hanky-panky, flimflam, bosh, hogwash, poppycock, fiddle-faddle, flapdoodle, moonshine, tommyrot, stuff and nonsense, bull.

hodgepodge or **hotchpotch** *n.* *The garden is just a hodgepodge of bushes and weeds:* jumble, mess, confusion, mixture, muddle, miscellany, conglomeration, medley, mélange, hash, patchwork, mix, composite, potpourri; *Yiddish* mishmash.

hoi polloi *The boss's wife is too proud to rub shoulders with the hoi polloi:* the common people, the plebs, the proletariat, the proles, the working class; the lower orders, the masses, the crowd, the mob, the herd, the multitude, the lower classes, the vulgar, the rank and file, commonalty, populace, every Tom, Dick, and Harry; riffraff, rabble, *French* canaille. **—Ant.**

aristocrats, blue bloods, the upper class, high society, the ruling class; the intelligentsia, the illuminati, The Beautiful People.

hoist v. Hoist the flag to the top of the pole: raise, raise up, pull up, run up, upraise, uplift, lift, elevate, heave, take up, bear up, bear aloft. —**Ant.** lower, pull down, drag down.

hold v. **1.** Hold the money tightly. The mother held the baby. A pile of sandbags held the bridge: keep in the hand, have in the hand, grasp, clutch, grip, clasp; keep in the arms, embrace, enfold; carry, bear, take; support, uphold, brace, prop, shore. **2.** The glue didn't hold. This rope won't hold in a strong wind: stick, stick fast, cling, adhere, cleave; remain tied, remain bound, stay fixed; lock, unite, clinch, stay, resist breaking. **3.** This box holds a pound of candy. Will that filing cabinet hold all these papers?: have a capacity of, contain, accommodate, take in, include, enclose. **4.** Please hold your applause until the last performer is finished. The police are holding the suspect: restrain, contain, control, defer, postpone, repress, suppress, suspend, withhold, desist from, hold back, hold off, hold up, hold in check, hold down, forestall, stall, hinder, inhibit, frustrate, thwart, check, curb, stay, keep, halt, block, prevent, limit, restrict; detain, confine. **5.** Please hold my seat until I return. The airline is holding two tickets for you: keep, retain, reserve, set aside; watch, protect, guard; keep valid, be in force. **6.** He's too lazy to hold a job. The governor has held public office for ten years: keep, maintain, hold down; have, possess, occupy. **7.** The club will hold its monthly meeting next Tuesday: conduct, carry on, have, execute, engage in, join in; preside over, direct, manage. **8.** We hold these truths to be self-evident. I will hold you responsible for all damage: maintain, assert, affirm, declare, profess, deem, consider, regard, think, believe, conceive, count, reckon, suppose, presume, assume, understand, surmise, conclude, deduct; propose, submit, offer, put forth, put forward, advance, present, tender, venture, advocate, urge; bind, obligate, enforce. —n. **9.** Take a firm hold on this line: grasp, grip, clasp, clutch; embrace. **10.** Doesn't this suitcase have a hold? The mountain climber couldn't find a hold to climb any higher: handle, knob, strap, grasp, hilt, shaft; foothold, toehold, handhold, stand, anchorage, advantage; leverage, purchase. **11.** Her brother has always had a strong hold over her. Legal documents give the present owner a legitimate hold on the property: influence, controlling force, control, authority, sway, domination, dominance, mastery, rule, command, power, ascendancy; bond, attachment; possession, ownership. —**Ant.** 1 let go, let loose, put down, let drop, droop; hand over, give over, give. 2 come undone, come unstuck, let go; come untied, loosen, let loose, break, give way. 4 give, bestow, accord, grant, tender, offer, release, let loose, free, let go. 5, 6 give over, turn over, give up. 5 cancel, let lapse. 7 cancel, call off; postpone. 8 disavow, disclaim,

deny, refute, repudiate, controvert, reject, abjure, forswear, gainsay.

hole n. **1.** The boys watched the baseball game through a hole in the fence: opening, aperture, breach, open space; break, gap, rent, slit, crack, slot; puncture, perforation. **2.** The bomb left a big hole in the ground. Set a trap over that mole hole: hollow place, depression, cavity, concavity, indentation, excavation, pocket, orifice; cave, cavern, tunnel, pit, shaft, dugout, crater; den, lair, burrow. **3.** The police discovered several holes in the suspect's alibi: fault, defect, fallacy, flaw, discrepancy, inconsistency. **4.** Informal The sailor was thrown in the hole for attempted mutiny: prison, keep, Navy brig; dungeon, dark cell, solitary confinement cell; Slang cage, slammer, lockup. —**Ant.** 1 cover, plug, stopper, closure. 2 projection, protuberance, prominence, convexity, mound.

holiday n. **1.** Easter is considered a high holiday: holy day; feast day. **2.** Is Labor Day a holiday in all countries?: celebration, jubilee, fiesta, festival, fete; vacation, vacation day, day of rest; Canadian, British vacation trip, outing, junket. —adj. **3.** The whole town was in a holiday mood: festive, celebrating, gala, merrymaking, gay, joyous, joyful, cheery, cheerful. —**Ant.** 2 workday. 3 serious, somber, sad, gloomy.

holiness n. Please remove your hats out of respect for the holiness of the shrine. Islam denies the divinity of Jesus without disputing his holiness: sanctity, sacredness, blessedness, godliness, saintliness. —**Ant.** worldliness, secularity.

hollow adj. **1.** These chocolate Santas are all hollow: empty inside, empty, unfilled, not solid, vacant. **2.** The boy has a thin frame and hollow cheeks: concave, rounded inward, curving inward, sunken, cavernous, depressed, indented. **3.** His voice was hollow: dull, expressionless, unresonant, nonresonant, muted, sepulchral; deep, low, rumbling, reverberating. **4.** The victory, won at too great a price, proved hollow: meaningless, unavailing, empty, vain, pointless, false, specious, deceptive, fruitless, profitless, useless, futile, unprofitable, worthless, valueless, unsatisfactory, disappointing, nugatory, inconsequential. —n. **5.** More gravel is needed to fill the hollow in the driveway: depression, concavity, cavity, hole, indentation, pocket, ditch, furrow, rut, dip, sink; dent, dimple; void, vacuum; cave, cavern, crater, crevasse. **6.** Let's have a picnic down in the hollow: valley, dale, dell, vale, glen. —v. **7.** Hollow out the pumpkin and make a jack-o'-lantern: gouge out, scoop out, dig out, empty out, excavate; groove, channel. —**Ant.** 1 solid, full, filled, occupied. 2 convex, protruding, rounded, raised. 3 vibrant, resonant; expressive. 4 worthwhile, profitable, useful, valuable, meaningful, significant; satisfying, gratifying, pleasing. 5 protuberance, projection, bump, hump, mound, knob. 6 hill, hillock, mountain, rise, hummock, knoll, bluff, height.

holocaust n. **1.** The mob set fire to the police archives, but some files escaped the holocaust: conflagration, deadly fire; devastating blaze; inferno; bonfire. **2.** *Millions of Jews perished in the Nazi holocaust:* devastation, ruin, havoc, ravage; vast slaughter, massacre, carnage, killing, annihilation, genocide, mass murder, butchery.

holy *adj.* **1.** *The Bible and the Koran are considered holy books:* of divine character, of divine origin, divine, divinely inspired, pertaining to God, from God, sacred, heavenly, spiritual, religious, from above, heaven-sent. **2.** *Francis of Assisi was a most holy man:* saintly, godly, dedicated to God, devoted to God, spiritual, pure, pure in heart, sinless, angelic, immaculate, unstained, profoundly good, moral, righteous, guileless, uncorrupted, undefiled, unspotted, faithful, virtuous, unworldly; devout, pious, religious, reverent. **3.** *In those days suicides could not be buried in holy ground:* consecrated, hallowed, sacred, blessed, sanctified; sacrosanct, inviolable, religious, solemn, venerated; worshiped, adored, revered. **—Ant.** unholy. 1, 2 secular, worldly, earthly, human; profane, sacrilegious, unreligious, blasphemous, impious; sinful, wicked, evil, corrupt, immoral, impure. 3 unconsecrated, unsanctified, unhallowed, desecrated, impure.

Holy Spirit also **Holy Ghost** *n.* *The Trinity consists of the Father, the Son, and the Holy Spirit. Praise Father, Son, and Holy Ghost:* presence of God, third person of the Trinity, Paraclete; *Latin* spiritus sanctus, *Greek* hagion pneuma.

homage *n.* *This statue was erected in homage to the town's war heroes:* honor, respect, reverence, regard, veneration; praise, tribute, exaltation, glorification, esteem, devotion, deference, obeisance; worship, adoration, adulation. **—Ant.** dishonor, disrespect, irreverence; condemnation, blame, criticism.

home *n.* **1.** *The neighbors bought a retirement home in Florida:* house, residence, place of residence, dwelling, dwelling place, domicile, abode, place of abode; *Informal* place where one hangs one's hat, home sweet home. **2.** *Alaska is the home of the Kodiak bear:* habitat, haunt, abode, habitation, native land, native region, natural environment; cradle, fountainhead; *Slang* stamping ground, hangout. **3.** *The old woman spent her last years in a home for the aged:* institution, residence; (*variously*) nursing home, sanatorium, hospital, orphanage, asylum, poorhouse; refuge, haven.

homeless *adj.* *The homeless couple was sent to a shelter:* unhoused, houseless; displaced, dispossessed, exiled, outcast, uncared-for; itinerant, unsettled, vagabond, vagrant.

homely *adj.* **1.** *The mother is beautiful, but the daughter is homely:* plain-looking, plain, not good-looking, ordinary, drab, unattractive, ill-favored, uncomely, unhandsome, graceless, ungraceful; rather ugly. **2.** *Even though he's famous, he hasn't forgotten his homely manners. What a warm, homely room!:* plain, simple, unassuming, unpretentious, unaffected, modest, ordinary, everyday, familiar, natural, artless, unsophisticated, rustic, provincial, homespun;

homelike, homey, snug, cozy, comfy, comfortable. **—Ant.** 1 beautiful, gorgeous, pretty, handsome, comely, lovely, attractive, good-looking, striking, eye-catching. 2 elegant, grand, splendid, regal, courtly, refined; pretentious, affected, ostentatious, showy, sophisticated.

homespun *adj.* *The braided rugs had a homespun look to them:* homemade, hand-loomed, hand-woven, hand-crafted, hand-wrought; simple, plain, unpretentious, unaffected, artless, modest, natural, homely, folksy, native, down-home.

homicide *n.* **1.** *The man was charged with homicide in the death of his brother:* murder, manslaughter, slaying, bloodshed, foul play; (*variously*) parricide (*killing one's parent or close relative*), matricide (*killing one's mother*), patricide (*killing one's father*), fratricide (*killing one's brother*), feticide or aborticide (*abortion*), infanticide (*killing an infant*), uxoricide (*killing a wife*), regicide (*killing a king*), vaticide (*killing a prophet*). **2.** *In Anglo-Saxon times a homicide often paid blood money to the relatives of the person he had killed:* murderer, slayer, killer, manslayer, man killer.

homogeneous *adj.* *It was a homogeneous crowd of teenage girls, all wearing jeans and sweaters:* of the same kind, all alike, of a piece; uniform, unmixed, unvarying, unadulterated; consistent, constant, pure; akin, kindred, similar, identical. **—Ant.** heterogeneous, mixed, varied, varying, variegated, different, diverse, divers, various, divergent.

homosexual *n.* *Most of the city's homosexuals marched in the parade:* gay, gay person, lesbian.

homosexuality *n.* *He wrote a book about his own homosexuality:* gayness, homoeroticism.

honest *adj.* **1.** *An honest man. Honest dealings:* law-abiding, ethical, truthful, decent, upright, fair, just, righteous, honorable, virtuous, principled, conscientious, scrupulous, blameless, proper, reasonable, faithful, true-blue, tried and true, reputable, fair and square, square, straight, straight-shooting, aboveboard, open and aboveboard, on the level, on the up-and-up, as good as one's word, honest as the day is long; legal, legitimate, lawful. **2.** *Give me an honest answer. I expect an honest day's work. He installed a scale with honest weights:* true, truthful, frank, straightforward, candid, blunt, plainspoken, forthright, clear-cut, trustworthy, dependable, reliable, solid; valid, genuine, real, authentic, bona fide. **3.** *The youth has an honest face. She appreciated my honest praise:* sincere, open, frank, candid, plain, guileless, ingenuous, unaffected, innocent, artless, unsophisticated; unreserved, undisguised. **—Ant.** dishonest. 1 unethical, untruthful, unfair, unrighteous, dishonorable, bad, immoral, unprincipled, unscrupulous, improper, unfaithful; illegal, illegitimate, unlawful, corrupt, fraudulent; crooked, base, low, vile. 2 false, lying, untruthful, deceitful, unreliable, untrustworthy, undependable, treacherous, invalid, fake, counterfeit. 3 guilty, insincere, artful, deceitful, hypo-critical, disguised, secretive.

honesty *n. Are you questioning my honesty?:* truthfulness, integrity, trustworthiness, probity, veracity, word, sincerity, uprightness, rectitude, incorruptibility, honor, reputability, faithfulness, morality, scruples, principles, fairness, just dealing, square dealing, straight shooting, good name; innocence, guiltlessness. **—Ant.** dishonesty, crookedness, corruption, deceitfulness, deception, untruthfulness, falseness, falsity, lying, mendacity, trickery, fraud, chicanery, duplicity, insincerity, deceit, guile; unfairness.

honor *n.* **1.** *George Washington was a man of honor:* honesty, high-mindedness, principle, honorableness, probity, decency, uprightness, nobleness of mind, scrupulousness, trustworthiness, conscientiousness, sincerity, faithfulness; honesty, integrity, virtue, fairness, justness, truthfulness, truth, veracity, rectitude, goodness, constancy. **2.** *I was taught to show honor to my elders. My great grandfather won honor in the Civil War:* respect, esteem, regard, deference, reverence, homage, veneration, admiration, approbation, tribute, adoration, worship, glorification, exaltation; fame, glory, acclaim, renown, greatness, importance, high standing, distinction, prestige, repute, commendation, praise, recognition, note, notability, celebrity, credit, eminence, prominence, illustriousness, good report, good name, a feather in one's cap. **3.** *It's an honor to meet you:* privilege, compliment, pleasure, favor; grant, authorization, permission, sanction, power, right, leave, liberty. **—v. 4.** *Honor thy father and thy mother:* esteem, revere, venerate, respect, value, regard, admire, praise, laud, extol, commend, exalt, glorify, worship, have regard for, look up to, think much of, show deference to, pay homage to, pay tribute to, bow down before; venerate, adore. **5.** *His Majesty will honor us with a visit:* confer honor upon, give one the privilege of, favor, compliment, grant, dignify, glorify. **6.** *Which credit cards does this restaurant honor?:* take, accept, credit, acknowledge; *(of a check or draft)* make payment on, pay, redeem, cash, credit, make good. **—Ant.** 1–5 dishonor. 1 bad character, meanness, lowness, baseness, dishonesty, unscrupulousness, insincerity. 2 low regard, disrespect, contempt, disdain, scorn, shame, disgrace, disrepute, condemnation, infamy, ignominy, degradation, debasement, bad name. 3 insult, disfavor. 4 condemn, hold in contempt, disrespect, disdain, scorn, insult, defame, shame, degrade, debase, discredit, slight, disobey. 5 insult, offend, affront. 6 refuse, reject; refuse payment on, *Slang* bounce.

honorable *adj.* **1.** *He received an honorable discharge from the army:* upright, honest, noble, highminded, just, fair, trusty, trustworthy, true, virtuous. **2.** *He was descended from an honorable line:* dignified, distinguished, noble, illustrious, great. **3.** *They reached an honorable settlement:* creditable, reputable, estimable, right, proper, equitable. **—Ant.** ignoble, untrustworthy, corrupt; undignified; disreputable.

hoodlum *n. A gang of hoodlums highjacked the truck. The young hoodlum stole the old lady's purse:* gangster, mobster, gunman, crook, criminal, desperado; *Slang* gorilla, hood, strong arm, thug, plug-ugly; tough, hooligan, bruiser, ruffian, rowdy, juvenile delinquent; *Informal* punk.

hoodwink *v. The gang hoodwinked several of us into investing in a nonexistent oil well:* deceive, trick, dupe, cheat, swindle, mislead, inveigle, defraud, gyp, victimize, cozen, gull; *Slang* rook, bamboozle; fool, hoax.

hook *n.* **1.** *The waterlogged chest was raised from the sea with a hook:* grapple, grapnel, gaff, crook, bill, pothook, fluke, crampon, *(in lumbering)* peavey. **2.** *The driveway makes a hook around an old tree:* bend, curve, crook, angle, arc, crescent, horseshoe, arch, loop, bow, curl, elbow. **—v. 3.** *Hook the screen door when you come in:* fasten, latch, secure, make fast, make secure; buckle, hitch. **4.** *The creek hooks past the barn and around the hill:* bend, curve, wind, crook, angle, arc, arch, loop, curl. **5.** *The fishermen were hooking bass as fast as they could get their lines in the water:* catch, take, bag, nab, seize, grab; *(variously)* net, snare, ensnare, trap, capture, *Informal* collar. **—Ant.** 2 straight line, beeline, perpendicular. 3 unhook, unfasten, unlatch. 4 go straight, run straight, make a straight line, go straight as an arrow, make a beeline. 5 let go, loose; throw back.

hoot *v.* **1.** *The owl hooted all night. The train hooted in the distance:* screech, shriek, scream, howl, wail, shrill, whoop, ululate; moan, whistle, blow, honk. **2.** *The crowd hooted its disapproval. The students hooted the speaker:* howl, shout, cry out, sing out, bellow, proclaim, bawl, wail, screech, scream, roar, yelp, whoop, yowl, din, chorus; boo, jeer, hiss, razz, scoff at, mock, cry down, sneer at, snicker at, taunt, deride, give a catcall; *Slang* give a raspberry, give a Bronx cheer. **—n. 3.** *The speaker was greeted with a chorus of hoots:* boo, jeer, hiss, catcall, sneer, snicker, taunt, cry of disapproval, caterwaul, *Slang* Bronx cheer, raspberry; shout, shouting, wail, wailing, screech, screeching, scream, screaming, yelp, whoop, yowl, outcry; uproar, tumult, commotion, racket. **—Ant.** 2 hail, cheer, applaud, clap for, give a standing ovation; encourage, yell bravo, *Slang* root for; welcome, salute; acclaim. 3 cheer, applause, clapping, standing ovation; encouragement, shout of bravo, hurray, hurrah, huzzah; welcome, acclamation.

hop *v.* **1.** *The rabbit hopped across the field. The boy hopped the mud puddle and ran down the walk:* jump, spring, leap, bound, vault, bounce, skip; prance, gambol, frisk, bob, caper, romp, trip; jump over, leap over, spring over, vault over, bound over, skip over. **—n. 2.** *With one hop the frog was back in the pond:* jump, spring, leap, bound, step, vault, skip, bounce.

hope *n.* **1.** *Today's young people give me hope for the future:* faith, confidence, belief, assurance, reassurance, encouragement, trust, reliance, conviction, optimism, expectation, great expectations, expectancy, anticipation, assumption, presumption. **2.** *Father's fondest hope is to retire to Florida:* desire, wish, aspiration, ambition, longing, craving, yearning, hunger, dream, daydream, fancy, heart's desire, *Informal* hankering, *Slang* yen. **3.** *Our only hope is that the Coast Guard heard our SOS:* chance, possibility, prospect; chance for survival, possible way out, help, rescue, salvation, saving grace. —*v.* **4.** *I hope you're feeling better. The Johnsons hope to buy a new house next year:* trust, feel sure, be confident, desire, wish, aspire, look forward to, count on, expect, believe, contemplate, anticipate, reckon on, long for, crave, yearn for, hunger for, dream of, daydream, have one's heart set on, be bent upon, have an eye to, have a fancy for, *Informal* have a hankering, *Slang* yen for. **5.** *The doctors are doing all they can, now we can only hope:* be hopeful, have faith, hope for the best, trust in the Lord, trust; look on the bright side, take heart, be optimistic. —**Ant.** 1 dread, despair, despondency, hopelessness, distrust, doubt, disbelief. 4 doubt, deem unlikely, despair of. 5 despair, dread, expect the worst.

hopeful *adj.* **1.** *The team is hopeful that it will win the championship:* full of hope, in hopes, expectant, anticipative, optimistic, confident, assured, trusting. **2.** *The patient's good appetite was a hopeful sign of recovery:* promising, favorable, propitious, auspicious, heartening, sanguine, reassuring, cheering, encouraging, fortunate, of good omen. —**Ant.** 1, 2 hopeless. 1 despairing, dejected, despondent, pessimistic, down in the mouth. 2 discouraging, depressing, unpromising, unfavorable, inauspicious, disheartening, unencouraging, adverse, unfortunate.

hopeless *adj.* **1.** *It's a hopeless situation:* without hope, past remedy, incurable, beyond recall, irrevocable, irreversible, irreparable, irredeemable, irretrievable, impossible, beyond help, lost, futile, vain, useless, pointless. **2.** *The wrestler felt hopeless when he saw how big his opponent was:* without hope, pessimistic, despairing, dejected, abject, despondent, disconsolate, downcast, depressed, downhearted; sad, forlorn, heartbroken, heavyhearted, sick at heart, sorrow-stricken, grief-stricken; down in the mouth, melancholy. —**Ant.** 1, 2 hopeful. 1 promising, encouraging, optimistic, favorable, propitious, auspicious, promising, heartening, reassuring, rosy; remediable, curable, redeemable, retrievable. 2 full of hope, confident, assured, encouraged, heartened, expectant, gay, cheerful, happy, uplifted, lighthearted, joyful.

horde *n.* *Every summer the valley was invaded by hordes of grasshoppers:* multitude, host, pack, crowd, throng, mob, bunch, crush, drove, swarm, assemblage, assembly, gang, party, congregation, company, gathering; tribe, legion, band, troop.

horizon *n.* *The course in philosophy opened up new horizons for the student:* limit of experience, limit of knowledge, frontier, world, domain, area, range, vista, purview, scope, outlook, sphere, expanse, compass, perspective, stretch, field, realm, bounds, prospect.

horizontal *adj.* **1.** *Draw a horizontal line from one side of the page to the other:* parallel to a base line, parallel to the horizon, level, parallel to the ground, level with the ground; flat, plane, even, plumb, flush. **2.** *After he wrenched his back he had to stay horizontal for a week:* recumbent, prone, supine, reclining, prostrate, lying down, *Informal* flat on one's back. —**Ant.** 1 vertical, up and down; inclined, uneven. 2 upright, on one's feet, standing.

horn *n.* **1.** *The young goat was just beginning to grow horns:* antler, cornu; tusk; excrescence, spike, point. **2.** *The tuba is the largest horn in the band:* (*brass instrument: variously*) cornet, trumpet, trombone, tuba, bugle, baritone, sousaphone, euphonium, mellophone, French horn, alto horn; (*woodwind instrument: variously*) saxophone, clarinet, oboe, English horn, bassoon.

horrendous *adj.* *The new secretary is a horrendous speller. Don't tell the children such horrendous stories:* horrible, horrid, awful, terrible, dreadful, appalling, frightful; revolting, repulsive, hideous, shocking, repellent, horrifying, ghastly, gory. —**Ant.** pleasing, pleasant, attractive, agreeable.

horrible *adj.* *The accident was a horrible sight. The sewer emitted a horrible smell. What a horrible thing to say!:* gruesome, harrowing, revolting, repulsive, sickening, awful, disgusting, loathsome, terrible, vile, repellent, hideous, grisly, nauseating, distasteful, detestable, disagreeable, unpleasant, unsavory, foul, rank, nasty, bad, horrid, abhorrent, odious, obnoxious, abominable, unbearable, insufferable, appalling, dreadful, atrocious, monstrous, ghastly, shocking, frightful, forbidding, unspeakable, disquieting, despicable. —**Ant.** pleasing, pleasant, agreeable, attractive, enchanting, appealing, delightful, wonderful, good, charming, enchanting, fetching, lovely.

horrify *v.* *Try not to horrify Mother with such gruesome stories:* shock, terrify, frighten, affright, petrify, make one's flesh creep, make one's hair stand on end; disgust, sicken, repel, revolt, appall, nauseate, make one sick, make one turn pale; daunt, dishearten, disconcert, disquiet, dismay. —**Ant.** charm, enchant, please, attract, delight; gladden, reassure, calm, soothe.

horror *n.* **1.** *I have a horror of snakes:* fear, terror, dread, panic, apprehension, alarm, trepidation, dismay; aversion, loathing, abhorrence, detestation, abomination, hatred, distaste, disgust, dislike, antipathy, repugnance, revulsion, repulsion. **2.** *The horrors of war are beyond description:* cruelty, outrage, inhumanity, crime, atrocity; awfulness, hideousness, terribleness, misery, woe, distress, wretchedness, hardship, suffering, anguish, torment, discomfort, privation, affliction. —**Ant.** 1 liking, affinity, delight, love, attraction. 2 pleasure, delight, gratification, happiness, joy, wonder, reward, goodness, benefit, boon.

hors d'oeuvre *n. Hors d'oeuvres and cocktails were served on the patio before dinner:* appetizer, canapé, tidbit; (*variously*) little sandwich, finger sandwich, dip, relish tray; *Slang* finger food; *Italian* antipasto.

horse *n.* **1.** *Saddle the horse:* (*young*) foal, yearling, pony; (*female*) filly, mare, broodmare; (*male*) colt, stallion, sire, stud, gelding; (*variously*) steed, charger, mount, equine, galloper, racehorse, trotter, pacer, mustang, cow pony, pinto, quarter horse, bronco, bronc, thoroughbred, draft horse, palfrey, dobbin, hackney, hack, jade; *Slang* plug. **2.** *The king's army had 1,000 foot soldiers and 200 horse:* horse cavalry, cavalry, cavalrymen, soldiers on horseback, horse soldiers, mounted troops, troopers, mounted troopers, mounted warriors, dragoons, horse marines, lancers, hussars, cossacks. **—Ant.** 2 infantry, foot soldiers.

horseman *n.* **1.** *A good horseman can ride any horse well:* rider, horseback rider, equestrian, (*fem.*) equestrienne; jockey, postilion; (*variously*) horse breeder, trainer, groom, stable owner, stable keeper, stableman, stableboy, hostler, ostler. **2.** *A detachment of horsemen rode into battle:* cavalry soldier, cavalryman, horse soldier, mounted trooper, trooper, roughrider, dragoon, horse marine, lancer, hussar, cossack.

hose *n. The shopper bought two pairs of nylon hose:* stockings, hosiery; socks.

hospitable *adj.* **1.** *Fred and Jane are always very hospitable to their guests:* gracious, cordial, sociable, gregarious, genial, friendly, warm, amicable, welcoming, convivial, neighborly, openhanded. **2.** *I pride myself on being hospitable to new ideas:* receptive, accessible, open, openminded, approachable, agreeable, responsive, amenable, tolerant. **—Ant.** 1, 2 inhospitable, antisocial, reserved. 2 close-minded, unreceptive, unapproachable.

hospital *n.* **1.** *The young doctor interned at the local hospital:* medical center, clinic, polyclinic, medical pavilion; infirmary, sick bay. **2.** *The state is building a new hospital for the mentally disturbed:* sanatorium; (*variously*) asylum, nursing home, home, rest home, state hospital.

hospitality *n. It was an evening of stimulating talk and warm hospitality:* welcome, hospitableness, friendliness, congeniality, amicability, cordiality, conviviality, heartiness, warmth, cheer, geniality, sociability, neighborliness, warmheartedness, kindliness, openness, *German* Gemütlichkeit.

host[1], *Fem.* **hostess** *n.* **1.** *Fred was host at the alumni banquet. A good hostess makes her guests comfortable:* master of ceremonies, mistress of ceremonies; party giver, welcomer. **2.** *Your host, John Smith, hopes your stay at the hotel will be a pleasant one:* hotel manager, hotel keeper, innkeeper, hotelier, hosteler, proprietor, (*fem.*) proprietress, landlord; restaurant manager, receptionist, maitre d', headwaiter, head waitress. **—Ant.** 1, 2 guest. 2 lodger, boarder, traveler; diner; customer, patron.

host[2] *n. A host of barbarians attacked the city:* multitude, horde, swarm, troop, legion, army, drove, array, throng, *Informal* lot; band, group, party, gathering, body, convention, meeting, congress, confluence, conclave, company, convocation, congregation; mess, mob, crowd, gang, crew. **—Ant.** handful, sprinkling, small group, scattering.

hostage *n. The hostages were released after a week in captivity:* captive, prisoner; pawn, pledge, guaranty, security, surety.

hostile *adj.* **1.** *The town was surrounded by hostile troops. The hostile forces fought for possession of the mountain pass:* enemy, belligerent, bellicose, opposing, opposed, fighting, battling, contending, clashing, warring, at war; dissident, on bad terms, at odds, at outs, at loggerheads, with crossed swords. **2.** *A hostile look. Hostile words:* belligerent, angry, antagonistic, contrary, contentious, quarrelsome, bristling, disputatious, argumentative, disagreeing; malicious, vicious, malevolent, venomous, spiteful, bitter, malignant, malign, mean, ugly; unfriendly, unkind, unsympathetic, ill-disposed, ill-natured, disagreeable, incompatible, cranky, cantankerous, snappish, truculent, testy, touchy; cold, chilly, icy. **—Ant.** 1 friendly, peaceful. 2 friendly, approving, agreeable, amiable, amicable, cordial, congenial, sweet, kind, kindly, warm, sympathetic.

hostility *n.* **1.** (*usually* **hostilities**) *Hostilities broke out between Germany and France in 1939:* war, warfare, act of war, state of war, warring, fighting, fight, conflict, combat, military operation, battle, battling, clash; contest, fray, fracas, scuffle, feud, duel, dispute, contention, argument, altercation, dissidence, disagreement, bickering. **2.** *I can't understand his hostility to our suggestions:* belligerence, animosity, antagonism, antipathy, enmity, opposition, contrariness; anger, malice, viciousness, malevolence, bitterness, spleen, unfriendliness, ill will, rancor, hatred, hate, vindictiveness, venom. **—Ant.** 1 peace; truce, treaty, alliance. 2 agreement, approval, sympathy, good will, amity, fellow feeling; love, friendship, amiability, cordiality, congeniality.

hot *adj.* **1.** *I detest hot weather. You're hot from all that exercise. Bake the cookies in a hot oven:* very warm, uncomfortably warm, warm, sweltering, sultry, torrid; at high temperature, highly heated, heated; simmering, steaming, burning, boiling, broiling, scalding, scorching, blistering, searing, baking, roasting, sizzling, piping hot, fiery, smoldering; melting, molten, red-hot, white-hot, incandescent. **2.** *Put some of this hot sauce on the barbecued ribs:* piquant, peppery, highly seasoned, sharp, nippy, biting, pungent. **3.** *You'd better learn to control that hot temper of yours. The men had a hot argument about politics:* intense, violent, furious, raging, vehement, agitated, fierce, fiery, ardent, passionate, fervid, frenzied, feverish, stormy, tempestuous, hectic, excited, emotional, animated, earnest, wrought-up, fast and furious. **4.** *The police are hot on the trail of the robbers:* very close, following very closely, in close pursuit, near. **5.** *Is there any hot news on the election results?:*

late, latest, new, recent, fresh. **6.** *Informal This is going to be the hottest new style of the year:* popular, most popular, successful, sought after, fast-selling; attractive, good, top, excellent. **7.** *Be careful not to touch a hot wire when you fix the fuse box:* live, carrying current, electrified; radioactive. —**Ant.** 1 cold, chilly, chilled, cool, cooled, frigid, freezing, icy, frosty. 2, 3 mild, bland, insipid. 3 peaceful; unemotional, objective, dispassionate. 4 cold. 5 old, out-of-date, old hat, stale.

hotel *n. The hotel can accommodate 300 guests:* inn, lodging, hostel, hostelry, lodge, hospice; motel, motor inn.

hotheaded *adj. She couldn't keep her hotheaded spouse under control:* reckless, rash, incautious, headstrong, impetuous, overemotional, hot-tempered, passionate, fiery. —**Ant.** cool, serene, phlegmatic.

hound *n.* **1.** *The hounds cornered the fox at the edge of the woods. The old hound has been chasing the cat again:* hunting dog; dog, canine; *Slang* pooch, mutt, poochie, doggy; (*young*) pup, puppy, whelp. —*v.* **2.** *The bill collector hounded the poor man until he paid the debt. Don't keep hounding me to cut the grass!:* chase, pursue, track, trail, stalk, dog, follow, hunt, tail; nag, keep after, keep at, hector, bait, harass, pester, harry, bedevil, badger, worry, annoy, needle. —**Ant.** 2 run from, flee, escape, evade, elude.

hour *n.* **1.** *At what hour did you tell them to come?:* time, particular time, fixed time. **2.** *When is your lunch hour?:* period, interval, span, space. **3.** *The rock singer is the teenage idol of the hour:* present time, current moment, day.

house *n.* **1.** *The new house has four bedrooms and a den:* home, dwelling, dwelling place, residence, abode, domicile, shelter, habitation. **2.** *You woke up the whole house!:* household, family. **3.** *He was the last ruler of the House of Hapsburg:* royal family, noble family, line, dynasty, clan; lineage, ancestry, descent, family tree, ancestors, strain. **4.** *A church is a house of worship:* building, meeting place, gathering place; (*variously*) church, temple, theater, opera house, concert hall, auditorium, hippo-drome, hall. **5.** *The actors counted the house from behind the curtain:* audience, spectators. **6.** Often **House** *The bill was passed by the House and sent to the Senate:* congress, lower chamber, legislature, assembly, council; *U.S.* House of Representatives; *British, Canadian* House of Commons, Commons. **7.** *John works for a brokerage house now:* business firm, company, concern, firm, business, organization, establishment, corporation, partnership; store, shop. —*v.* **8.** *Many volunteered to house the flood victims:* lodge, shelter, harbor, quarter, board, billet, put up, accommodate; furnish with a house. **9.** *The antique car was housed in a barn:* store, garage, shelter, keep, contain, accommodate. —**Ant.** 6 upper chamber; *U.S., Canadian* Senate; *British* House of Lords. 8 evict, eject, oust, expel. 9 discard, throw away.

household *n.* **1.** *The neighbors have a large household. Mother takes care of the household:* family, family circle, house; home, domestic establishment, hearth. —*adj.* **2.** *How much are your household expenses? This is a good household soap:* for a family, housekeeping; of a house, for a house, for home use.

housewife *n. It's hard to combine a business career with being a housewife:* homemaker, wife; housekeeper, family manager, home economist.

housework *n. She disliked all forms of housework:* housekeeping, domestic science, home economics, homemaking.

housing *n.* **1.** *Many families are in need of better housing:* house, home, dwelling, domicile; abode, shelter, lodging, lodgment, quarters, accommodations, residence, habitation. **2.** *That machine should be protected by a metal housing:* case, covering, casing, enclosure, shield, sheath, jacket, envelope.

hovel *n. You mean he's lived in that hovel for forty years?:* wretched dwelling, broken-down residence, cramped shelter, cabin, hut, ramshackle building; *Slang* dump, hole; shanty, shack. —**Ant.** mansion, palace, showplace, villa, castle, manor.

hover *v.* **1.** *The helicopter hovered over the trees:* pause in flight, hang suspended, hang, poise, float; flutter, flit, flitter. **2.** *I can't stand anyone hovering near me when I'm working:* linger about, hang about, hang around, wait near at hand, attend, haunt. **3.** *The patient hovered between life and death:* waver, hang, pause, falter, hang in doubt, seesaw, fluctuate, vacillate. —**Ant.** 1 fall, sink, drop. 2 leave alone; depart, go away, withdraw, retreat.

howl *v.* **1.** *The dog howled all night:* yelp, bay, cry, bark. **2.** *To howl with pain. To howl with glee:* cry out, yell, shout, bellow, roar, clamor, ululate, shriek, scream, hoot, yowl, yelp, wail. —*n.* **3.** *The mournful howl of a wolf woke the campers. A howl of protest went up when the voting was announced:* cry, bay, yelp, bark, whine; outcry, clamor, uproar, yell, shout, bellow, roar, shriek, scream, yowl, hoot, wail, groan. —**Ant.** 2, 3 whisper, murmur, mutter.

hub *n. Chicago is the hub of the midwest:* center, axis, pivot, core, focal point, heart, focus, nub, middle.

hubbub *n. What was all that hubbub about?:* uproar, pandemonium, tumult, ruckus, fuss, bustle, to-do, hullabaloo, disturbance, stir, commotion, hue and cry, disorder, confusion, turmoil, bedlam, ferment, fuss, perturbation, agitation, pother; racket, noise, clamor, din, hurly-burly, babble. —**Ant.** quiet, quietness, serenity, calm, calmness, tranquillity, peacefulness, repose, equanimity, stillness, hush.

huddle *v.* **1.** *The chilly campers huddled around the campfire:* crowd together, throng, cluster, gather closely, flock together, press together, converge, collect, bunch, herd. **2.** *The lost boy was found huddled in a doorway:* curl up, snuggle, nestle, cuddle, make oneself small. —*n.* **3.** *The executives had a quick huddle before the* stockholders' meeting: gathering, conference, meeting, discussion, think session, putting together of heads. **4.** *Please sort out that huddle of clothes in the middle of the floor:* heap, jumble, mass, mess, muddle, medley, hodgepodge; crowd, group, bunch; confusion, disarray, disorder. **—Ant.** 1 disperse, scatter. 2 stretch out, stand tall.

hue *n.* *The bedroom is painted in pale hues of green and gold:* color, coloration, shade, tint, tincture, tone; cast, tinge.

hue and cry *n.* *A great hue and cry went up from the striking union members:* clamor, hullabaloo, uproar, outcry, bellow, roar, yell, shout, yowl, shriek; cry of alarm, alarm; howl of protest, dissenting shout.

huff *n.* *After the incident she left the party in a huff:* bad mood, ill humor, fit of anger, fit of pique, fury, rage, resentment, outrage, vexation, annoyance, petulance, dudgeon; *Slang* pet, snit.

huffy *adj.* *Jane tends to be huffy when she doesn't get her way:* easily offended, touchy, sensitive, hypersensitive, angry, irate, waspish, quarrelsome, ill-humored, resentful, querulous, cranky, petulant, churlish, snappish, shirty, testy, thin-skinned, irritable, peevish, grumpy, cross, curt, rancorous, hard to live with, out of sorts, sulky, surly, sullen, resentful, offended, wounded, hurt, moping, glowering, disgruntled, discontented, moody, morose; *Informal* in a pucker, in a snit, in a lather. **—Ant.** calm, soothed; good-humored, cheerful, sunny, gay, friendly, pleasant, easy to live with.

hug *v.* **1.** *They hugged the child before putting him to bed:* embrace, hold, clasp, press to the bosom, hold close, clutch, squeeze, cuddle, snuggle, nestle; cling together. **2.** *The road hugs the side of the mountain:* keep close to, cling to, follow closely, parallel closely, hover near.

huge *adj.* *As suggested by its name, Mammoth Cave is huge. She spent a huge amount of money for that coat:* extremely large, immense, enormous, vast, extensive, colossal, giant, gigantic, titanic, mammoth, monstrous, elephantine, jumbo, gargantuan, leviathan, herculean, cyclopean, Brobdingnagian; massive, great, overwhelming, staggering, stupendous, imposing, mighty, spectacular, monumental, extravagant, prodigious. **—Ant.** small, little, tiny, dwarfish, Lilliputian, mi-nute; *Informal* wee, ittybitty, itsy-bitsy; microscopic, infinitesimal; petty, puny, insignificant.

hulk *n.* **1.** *After bombardment only a hulk remained of the castle:* shell, remains, ruins, shambles, hunk, hull, wreck, skeleton. **2.** *He stood in the doorway like a big hulk:* oaf, lout.

hulking *adj.* *The gorilla is a great hulking animal:* bulky, heavy, massive, powerful, big, husky, oversized, massive, unwieldy, cumbersome, ponderous.

hull *n.* **1.** *Don't throw the peanut hulls on the floor. The freighter's hull is made of steel plates:* husk, shell, skin, pod, coating, shuck, peel, rind, case; epidermis, carapace, integument, tegmen-

tum; body of a ship. **—v. 2.** *Hull a cupful of peas:* shell, husk, shuck.

hum *v.* **1.** *Do you know this tune I'm humming?:* croon, drone, intone. **2.** *The motor hummed pleasantly as the plane reached cruising speed:* whir, purr, drone, thrum, murmur, vibrate; buzz. **3.** *The market hummed as trading began:* be busy, be active, bustle, thrive, be in full swing. **—n. 4.** *The steady hum of the motor indicated that the car was working properly:* whirring, whir, drone, droning, purring, purr, vibration; buzzing, buzz; murmur, faint sound.

human *adj.* **1.** *To err is human. We all belong to the human race:* characteristic of mankind, like man; of man, of men, mortal, manlike, hominid, anthropoid. **2.** *If the employee must be let go, do it in a human way:* sympathetic, compassionate, humane, gentle, merciful, kindly; personal, individual; humanitarian. **—n. 3.** *Wolves usually will not attack humans:* human being, person; man, Homo sapiens. **—Ant.** 1 nonhuman; god; animal. 2 inhuman, beastly, brutish, unsympathetic, cruel; impersonal.

humane *adj.* *Helping that family was a very humane thing to do:* kind, kindly, compassionate, sympathetic, tender, goodwilled, benevolent, warmhearted, merciful, pitying, human, humanitarian, bighearted, philanthropic, charitable, magnanimous, unselfish. **—Ant.** inhumane, cruel, inhuman, harsh, brutal, barbarous, uncivilized, merciless, unmerciful, pitiless, ruthless; unkind, unsympathetic.

humanitarian *adj.* **1.** *Among his humanitarian deeds was assistance to refugees:* humane, giving, philanthropic, altruistic, beneficent, benevolent, charitable, compassionate, generous, idealistic, kindly, public-spirited **—n. 2.** altruist, benefactor, philanthropist, patron, *Informal* Good Samaritan, Boy Scout, do-gooder.

humanity *n.* **1.** *The Nazi war criminals were condemned for crimes against humanity:* the human race, mankind, man, humankind, Homo sapiens; mortals, human beings, people. **2.** *Our humanity unites us:* humanness, human nature, mortality. **3.** *There is a great humanity in all of Thoreau's writing:* kindness, kindliness, compassion, sympathy, gentleness, tenderness, benevolence, warmheartedness, charity, fraternal feeling, fellow feeling, brotherly love, goodwill, humaneness, magnanimity, mercy, love. **—Ant.** 1–3 inhumanity. 3 unkindness, cruelty, brutality, ruthlessness.

humble *adj.* **1.** *Many famous people are surprisingly humble:* modest, unassuming, unpretentious, unpresuming, self-effacing, without arrogance, unostentatious; demure, gentle, meek; subservient, obsequious, deferential, respectful. **2.** *It was a humble but comfortable house. The boss began in a very humble job:* poor, low, lowly, modest, wretched, shabby, miserable, inferior; plain, simple, common, ordinary, undistinguished, obscure, inglorious, insignificant, inconsequential, unimportant; low-ranking, plebeian. **—v. 3.** *The king's forces were humbled by the peasant revolt:* bring down, put down, subdue, chasten, make humble, bring low, humiliate, abash, put to shame, embarrass, disgrace, mortify, shame, take down a peg; conquer, crush, degrade, pull down, derogate, trample underfoot, dishonor, demean, abase, lower, debase, make lowly, cast dishonor upon. —**Ant.** 1 proud, arrogant, haughty, immodest, pretentious, vain, vainglorious, pompous, lordly, overbearing, snobbish, conceited, superior, boastful, assuming, ostentatious, presuming, presumptuous. 2 rich, wealthy, sumptuous, elegant; superior, out of the ordinary, distinguished, glorious, famous, illustrious, important, significant, consequential, high, high-ranking, aristocratic. 3 exalt, raise, elevate, magnify, aggrandize; extol, glorify.

humbug n. **1.** *The con men concocted a humbug to sell worthless desert land:* deception, deceit, trick, trickery, fraud, cheat, flimflam, swindle, gyp, artifice, double-dealing, forgery, fake, counterfeit, imposture, dodge; pretense, pretension, sham, make-believe, spoof, hoax, fiction. **2.** *His speeches are always full of humbug:* pretense, pretentiousness, pretension, sham, hypocrisy, flummery, equivocation, mendacity, lying, lies, falsification, falsehood; nonsense, poppycock; *Informal* bunk, bunkum, balderdash, blather, claptrap, hocus-pocus; *Slang* hokum, bull. **3.** *The humbug tried to pass himself off as a lawyer:* fraud, quack, fake, liar, impostor, charlatan, mountebank; swindler, cheat, cheater, confidence man, con man, sharper, trickster; liar, fibber, perjurer, hypocrite. —*v.* **4.** *He humbugged me into believing his story:* deceive, trick, fool, hoax, bamboozle, mislead, beguile, hoodwink, dupe, cheat, swindle, cozen, gull, take in; lie, fib; falsify, fabricate, misrepresent. —*interj.* **5.** *Christmas? Bah! Humbug!:* nonsense, rubbish, balderdash, *Slang* phooey. —**Ant.** 2 truth, truthfulness; the real McCoy. 4 undeceive, disabuse.

humdrum adj. *It was just another humdrum day:* dull, boring, monotonous, run-of-the-mill, uninteresting, routine, everyday, mundane, dreary, tiresome, tedious, wearisome, wearying, lifeless, flat, insipid, trite, trivial, banal, commonplace, hackneyed, mediocre, pedestrian, uninspired, uninspiring, indifferent, unexciting, uneventful, unvarying, common, ordinary, conventional, unexceptional; *Slang* blah, dumb. —**Ant.** stimulating, exciting, provocative, entertaining, interesting, lively, gay, animated, exceptional, extraordinary.

humid adj. *It's so humid today my clothes are sticking to me:* muggy, sticky, sultry, steamy, damp, moist, dank, clammy, soppy. —**Ant.** arid, dry, moistureless, parched.

humiliate v. *I was humiliated when I couldn't remember her name:* embarrass, make ashamed, shame, mortify, chagrin, abash, humble, disgrace, dishonor, discomfit, chasten, crush, subdue, debase, degrade, belittle, bring low, bring down a peg; *Slang* put down. —**Ant.** honor, make proud, elevate, exalt, elate, please.

humiliation n. *When accused of lying, she blushed in humiliation:* embarrassment, shame, mortification, chagrin, discomfiture; disgrace,

dishonor, degradation, abasement, debasement. —**Ant.** pride, honor, exaltation, elevation.

humility n. *With humility he thanked others for their help:* modesty, humbleness, lowliness, unpretentiousness, lack of proudness, self-abasement, diffidence, demureness; meekness, shyness, timidity, bashfulness. —**Ant.** pride, arrogance, haughtiness, pretentiousness, vanity, vainglory, pomposity, disdain, snobbishness, conceit, superiority, boastfulness, presumption, superciliousness.

humor n. **1.** *The humor of the situation had everyone laughing:* funniness, comedy, comicality, ridiculousness, ludicrousness, drollery, nonsense, jocularity, jocoseness, jocosity. **2.** *The book is cheerful and full of humor:* jokes, joking, wit, wittiness, witticisms, gags, wisecracks, jests, jesting, foolery, fooling, foolishness, tomfoolery, raillery, ridicule, buffoonery, waggery, monkeyshines, comedy, high comedy, low comedy, broad comedy, slapstick, low humor, broad humor, burlesque, farce, caricature, parody, travesty, satire, whimsy, wordplay, puns. **3.** *Dad's always in a good humor on payday:* mood, temper, disposition, spirits, frame of mind. —*v.* **4.** *You have to humor him when he's in one of those moods:* give in to, indulge, pamper, flatter, spoil, baby, go along with, comply with, give in to, put up with, suffer, tolerate, appease, soothe, placate, mollify, cajole. —**Ant.** 1, 2 seriousness, gravity, solemnity, sobriety; sadness, grief, sorrow, melancholy. 4 stand up to, oppose, fight; aggravate, rouse, arouse, excite.

humorous adj. *The play was so humorous that the audience laughed all through it:* funny, comic, comical, full of humor, witty, droll, mirthful, laughable, amusing, sidesplitting, rib-tickling, facetious, waggish, whimsical, sportive, jocular, jocose, farcical, satirical; ludicrous, ridiculous, nonsensical. —**Ant.** unfunny, grave, serious, solemn, sober; sad, melancholy; earnest, matter-of-fact.

hump n. **1.** *The dromedary camel has one hump, the Bactrian has two:* protuberance on the back, hunch; bulge, lump, bump, mound, prominence, rise, swelling, convexity, projection, excrescence; knob, knurl. —*v.* **2.** *When the cougar humps its back, it will attack:* arch, hunch, raise in a hump, lift, bend, put up; tense.

hunch n. **1.** *I have a hunch Jack will be there after all:* intuition, feeling, foreboding, premonition, presentiment; idea, good idea, suspicion, inkling, clue, glimmer. —*v.* **2.** *The boy hunched his shoulders against the wind:* bend, hump, arch, tense.

hunger n. **1.** *This meal ought to satisfy your hunger. Hunger is a major problem in the drought-stricken areas of Africa:* desire for food, hungriness, appetite, ravenousness, voracity; famine, starvation, malnutrition, lack of food. **2.** *The hunger for power has created many tyrants:* craving, greed, greediness, desire, lust, itch, yearning, yen, appetite, thirst, *Slang* hankering; fondness, liking, love, relish. —*v.* **3.** *A good stu-*

dent hungers after knowledge: long for, desire, crave, burn for, have an appetite for, wish, want, thirst after, lust after, yearn for; Informal itch for, pant for, have a yen for, hanker. —**Ant.** 1 satiety, fullness; overeating. 2 repulsion, revulsion, disgust, repugnance, loathing, abhorrence, aversion, detestation, disgust, hatred.

hungry adj. She was hungry after her long fast: ravenous, famished, starved, starving. —**Ant.** sated.

hunk n. The boy broke off a large hunk of bread and ate it: chunk, piece, block, gobbet, clod, lump; Informal wad, gob, glob; quantity, portion, mass.

hunt v. **1.** November is a good time to hunt pheasant: shoot, go after, chase, track, stalk, trail, seek; drive out, ferret out. **2.** Police are hunting an escaped convict in this area: pursue, chase, track, trail, trace, follow the trail of, stalk, follow the scent of, look for, search for, seek, try to find, look high and low for, go in quest of, follow; turn everything upside down, leave no stone unturned, peer into every corner; explore, probe, inquire into. —n. **3.** The hunt is scheduled to begin at sunup: chase, hunting; fox hunt, riding to hounds, course, coursing.

hurdle n. **1.** The racer cleared the last hurdle and dashed toward the finish line: barrier, obstacle; (in steeplechase racing) fence, hedge, wall. **2.** The final exam is the student's last hurdle before graduation: obstacle, barrier, difficulty, hindrance, impediment, obstruction, roadblock, hazard, stumbling block, snag, interference. —v. **3.** The horse hurdled the fence and ran into the woods: jump, leap, vault, bound, surmount, spring over, clear.

hurl v. The young track and field athlete could already hurl the discus 60 yards: throw, fling, cast, sling, pitch, heave, chuck, toss, project, let fly; propel, launch, discharge, fire off. —**Ant.** catch, capture, seize; grasp, clutch, grab; take, receive.

hurly-burly n. She sought some peace away from the hurly-burly: commotion, activity, busyness, excitement, whirl, hurry, hurry-scurry, ferment, tumult, turmoil, uproar, agitation, frenzy. —**Ant.** calm, torpor.

hurrah or **hurray** or **hooray** interj. **1.** Let's hear it for the team—hip, hip hurrah!: good, fine, wonderful, excellent, great, bravo, heaven be praised, hallelujah, hosanna. —n. **2.** Thousands of hurrahs greeted the homerun hitter when he crossed the plate: shout of joy, cry of acclaim, cheer, bravo, exaltation; acclaim, congratulation, salute; Archaic huzza, huzzah.

hurricane n. The hurricane hit with winds of 135 miles per hour: violent tropical storm, (in the western Pacific) typhoon; tempest, windstorm, cyclone, monsoon.

hurried adj. Be careful about making a hurried assessment of the problem: hasty, fast, speedy, rushed, pressed for time; impulsive, precipitate, headlong; frantic, frenetic, feverish, hectic, breakneck; cursory, superficial, slapdash, haphazard, slipshod, careless. —**Ant.** leisurely, slow, studied, thorough, deliberate.

hurry v. **1.** Hurry and get home before it gets dark: go quickly, come quickly, move fast, move hastily, hasten, make haste, speed, speed up, accelerate, rush, hustle, get a move on; bolt, dart, dash, scurry, scuttle, scramble, whiz, zip, make time, make tracks, step along, step on it, step on the gas, push on, press on, get hopping, get cracking, cover the ground, go like the wind, go like a shot, go like sixty, lose no time. **2.** Don't hurry the cook or she'll spoil the dinner: urge on, goad, prod, drive on, push on, pressure, Informal egg on; rush, speed up, accelerate. —n. **3.** There was so much hurry at the last minute that she forgot her hat: rush, haste, scurry; hustle and bustle, fuss, flurry, flutter, stew, hurry-scurry, tumult, turmoil, commotion, ado. —**Ant.** 1 delay, slow down, slacken; procrastinate, dawdle, dally; move slowly, creep, crawl. 2 delay, slow, slow down, retard, detain. 3 slowness; composure, calmness.

hurt v. **1.** These new shoes hurt. My feet hurt: pain, ache, smart, sting, burn; torment, distress, agonize, torture. **2.** The driver hurt himself badly in the accident. Don't put that hot cup on the table, it will hurt the finish: injure, harm, disable, maim, cripple, lame, mangle, mutilate, impair, damage, maul; bruise, cut, scratch, scar, mar, mark, disfigure, deface. **3.** A sloppy appearance hurt the youth's chances of getting a job: hamper, impair, hinder, hold back, encumber, impede, retard, restrain, limit, frustrate, inhibit, weaken, obstruct, oppose, spike, check, thwart, foil, block, preclude, exclude, balk, forestall; decrease, lessen, reduce, diminish, lower, narrow, minimize. **4.** It hurts me when you talk that way: offend, sting, wound one's feelings, aggrieve, grieve, distress, trouble, cut to the quick. —adj. **5.** The boy came home with a hurt knee: injured, bruised, cut, scratched; scarred, marked; disabled, crippled, lame; mangled, mutilated, damaged; painful, aching, smarting. **6.** She's hurt because she wasn't invited to the party: offended, resentful, indignant, pained, wounded, injured, stung, piqued, miffed, crushed; distressed, crestfallen, dismayed, disheartened, aggrieved, mortified, chagrined; morose, melancholy, heartbroken, miserable, wretched, heartsick, dejected. —n. **7.** This salve will make the hurt go away: pain, soreness, ache, pang, sting, discomfort. **8.** He never got over his hurt at being rejected: pain, discomfort, sting, pique, resentment, mortification, embarrassment, chagrin, aggravation, annoyance; distress, suffering, misery, dismay, dejection, grief, heartbreak, wretchedness, torment, agony. —**Ant.** 1 relieve, alleviate, assuage, soothe. 2 heal, cure; repair, fix, restore. 3 help, aid, abet, benefit, forward, promote, advance, expedite; increase, multiply, heighten, widen. 4 console, calm, soothe; please, compliment, compensate. 5 relieved, alleviated, assuaged, soothed; healed, cured; repaired, fixed, restored. 6 consoled, calmed, soothed, placated, complimented. 8 happiness, pleasure, joy, delight, ecstasy; pride, gratification, satisfaction.

hurtful adj. He made several hurtful remarks:

cutting, cruel, wounding, harmful, hurting, injurious, damaging, destructive, mean, nasty, stressing, pernicious, poisonous, spiteful, unkind, upsetting, deleterious, detrimental.

hurtle v. *The motorcycle hurtled along the road at 90 miles an hour:* speed, fly, race, plunge, charge, rush, spurt, shoot, tear, scoot, whiz, zip; run, hie, whisk, gallop, lunge, scamper, scurry, scuttle, bolt, dash, dart, bound; go like the wind, go like a shot, go lickety-split. **—Ant.** crawl, creep, inch, drag, go at a snail's pace.

husband n. **1.** *Her husband is a stockbroker:* spouse, hubby, mate, man, consort, *Slang* old man; groom, bridegroom; married man. —v. **2.** *The nation must husband its natural resources:* conserve, preserve, use sparingly, manage wisely; save, set aside, retain, store, save up, keep, maintain; hoard, accumulate, amass. **—Ant.** 1 bachelor. 2 waste, squander, spend.

hush interj. **1.** *Hush! Someone's coming!:* be quiet, be still, be silent, quiet down, silence, quiet; *Informal* shut up, shush, pipe down, keep mum, *Slang* knock it off. —v. **2.** *The mother hushed the baby by rocking it:* quiet, shush, quell, silence, still; soothe, calm, mollify. —n. **3.** *There was such a hush in the empty house it was eerie:* silence, stillness; quiet, quietude, quietness, peacefulness, tranquillity. **—Ant.** 3 racket, din, noise, clamor.

husk n. *She peeled off the husk:* bark, hull, pod, rind, shell, skin, covering.

husky adj. **1.** *The husky boy carried the heavy package easily:* big, strong, robust, muscular, brawny, sturdy, strapping, stocky, burly, hefty, thickset, solid, broad-shouldered, powerful, athletic, strong as an ox; stout, beefy, overweight, plump. **2.** *The teacher's voice is husky because she has a cold:* hoarse, harsh, rough, coarse, gruff, rasping, grating, guttural, throaty, raucous, croaking, cracked, thick. **—Ant.** 1 small, puny, weak; thin, slim, underweight. 2 shrill.

hussy n. *That hussy had the nerve to flirt with my husband!:* strumpet, brazen woman, brash girl, saucy miss, wench, minx; loose woman, jade, bawd, woman of easy virtue, adulteress, trollop, baggage, wanton; prostitute, harlot, tart, whore, lewd woman, fallen woman, scarlet woman.

hustle v. **1.** *If you're going to be ready in time, you'd better hustle:* hurry, hasten, make haste, rush, speed up, move quickly, bolt, dart, dash, scurry, scuttle, scoot, scramble, make time, step on it, step along, fly, lose no time. **2.** *Informal A salesman has to hustle for a living:* be aggressive, work energetically; *Slang* be an eager beaver, be on the ball. **3.** *When the man started to fight, they hustled him out of the bar:* push, shove, nudge, elbow, prod, jostle, shoulder, bounce, throw, toss. —n. **4.** *Before dinner there's always a hustle in the kitchen:* energetic action, bustle, stir, hurry, scurry, rush, flutter, flurry, fuss, tumult, turmoil, commotion, scramble, hubbub, ado, hurry-scurry. **—Ant.** 1 procrastinate, dawdle, dally. 2 relax, take it easy. 4 calmness, composure; peace, quiet, tranquillity.

hut n. *In summer the shepherd lived in a hut*

near the grazing lands: shack, shanty, shelter, hutch, shed, lean-to, log cabin, cabin, cottage. **—Ant.** mansion, palace, castle, manor.

hutch n. *The boy cleaned out the rabbit hutch once a week:* pen, coop, cage, enclosure, shed, sty, cote, stall, crib.

hybrid n. *Mules are a hybrid, the offspring of a male donkey and a female horse. The play was a hybrid of suspense and humor:* crossbreed, cross, half-breed; mixture, composite, amalgam; six of one and half a dozen of the other, neither one nor the other. **—Ant.** thoroughbred.

hygiene n. *His personal hygiene left much to be desired:* cleanliness, personal hygiene, hygienics, sanitation.

hygienic adj. *Public water fountains are not very hygienic:* clean, sanitary, germ-free, prophylactic, sterile, disinfected, pure, unpolluted, uncontaminated, disease-free, aseptic; healthful, healthy, salutary, salubrious, wholesome; harmless, uninjurious. **—Ant.** unsanitary, contaminated, infected, dirty, impure, polluted; unhealthy, harmful.

hymn n. *The church service ended with a hymn:* song in praise of God, anthem, psalm, paean, devotional song; song of praise.

hype n. *None of the hype persuaded us to buy the product:* ballyhoo, buildup, promotion, publicity, puffery, advertising, *Informal* razzmatazz.

hyperbole n. *"She's as big as a house" is an example of hyperbole:* overstatement, exaggeration, enlargement, magnification, extravagant statement, figurative statement, stretch of the imagination; figure of speech, metaphor. **—Ant.** understatement.

hypnotic adj. *The sermon had a hypnotic effect on us:* mesmerizing, spellbinding, trance-inducing, soporific.

hypnotize v. *He was able to hypnotize her the second time around:* mesmerize, spellbind, captivate, charm, drug, magnetize.

hypocrisy n. *The senator showed his hypocrisy by saying he was for the bill and then voting against it:* insincerity, falsity, two-facedness, fakery, dissembling, duplicity, *Slang* phoniness; dishonesty, deceit, mendacity. **—Ant.** sincerity, truthfulness, honesty, frankness, candor, forthrightness.

hypocrite n. *That hypocrite told her he liked her hat, then laughed at it behind her back:* insincere person, false person, two-faced person, pretender, *Slang* phony; deceiver, dissembler.

hypocritical adj. *It would be hypocritical to praise bad work:* insincere, false, two-faced, dishonest, deceitful, deceptive, truthless, feigning, feigned, counterfeit, false, *Slang* phony. **—Ant.** sincere, heartfelt, unfeigned, genuine, honest; forthright, plainspoken.

hypothesis n. *His book advances the hypothesis that whales are as intelligent as humans:* theory, thesis, theorem, premise, assumption, postulate, proposition, assertion, presumption, proposal, conjecture, speculation, supposition, explanation, conclusion, *Slang* guesstimate.

hypothetical adj. *The medical students were*

asked how they would treat a hypothetical case and were graded on their responses: supposed, assumed, presumptive, theoretical, speculative, conjectural, possible, imaginary, suppositional, contingent, postulated; conditional, uncertain, questionable, dubious. —**Ant.** real, actual, true; certain, proved, proven, demonstrated, tested, tried, confirmed, established, substantiated, verified.

hysteria *n. The doctor gave her a shot to calm her hysteria:* emotional outburst, hysterics, delirium, fit, frenzy; uncontrolled fear, panic, uncontrolled weeping.

hysterical *adj.* **1.** *Both parents grew hysterical when they couldn't find the child:* overcome with fear, distraught, beside oneself, distracted, uncontrollable, frenzied, crazed, raving, worked-up, wrought-up, overwrought; *Informal* carried away, crazy, out of one's wits. **2.** *The hysterical thing about the joke is the way the comedian told it:* wildly funny, uproarious, comical, laughable, farcical, ridiculous, absurd, ludicrous, amusing, droll. —**Ant.** 1 calm, composed, poised, self-possessed. 2 sad, somber, serious, grave, melancholy.

ice-cold *adj. The child's ice-cold hands showed she had been playing in the snow for too long:* icy, freezing, frigid, glacial, icelike, frosty, supercold, supercooled, gelid, freezing cold, cold as ice, stone-cold; subzero, arctic, hyperborean, Siberian, polar. —**Ant.** hot, sultry, torrid, blistering, scorching, white-hot.

icky *adj.* **1.** *The melted marshmallow made an icky mess on the rug:* sticky, gummy, gooey, gucky, tacky, gluey; viscid, glutinous, mucilaginous, viscous, syrupy. **2.** *An allergy gave me this icky rash. She wrote an icky message on her valentine:* repulsive, nasty, offensive, disgusting, revolting, *Slang* gross; maudlin, mushy, bathetic, weepy.

icon *n. The icon was mounted on the wall:* picture, image, symbol, idol, representation, sign.

iconoclast *n. He's an iconoclast who will have nothing to do with organized religion:* dissenter, rebel, nonconformist, upstart, radical, revolutionary. —**Ant.** conformist, assenter.

icy *adj.* **1.** *Drive with caution—the roads are icy:* frozen over, glazed, slippery, sleety; cold, frigid, frozen, freezing, bitterly chilly, wintry, glacial, arctic, raw, bitingly cold, frosty, gelid. **2.** *An icy reception greeted the late arrivals. She gave me an icy stare:* hostile, unfriendly, cold, forbidding, without warmth or feeling, frigid, frosty, distant, impassive, aloof, haughty, cool, unemotional, coldhearted, glacial, chilly, chilling. —**Ant. 2** warm, friendly, gracious, sympathetic, cordial.

idea *n.* **1.** *The idea of success as monetary gain is slowly changing:* concept, mental picture, notion, thought, something believed, conception, insight, interpretation, apperception, appreciation, conception. **2.** *We need some idea of the cost:* hint, inkling, clue, indication, intimation, impression, approximation, suggestion, notion. **3.** *The council approved the commissioner's idea for improving traffic conditions:* proposal, suggestion, approach, solution, recommendation. **4.** *It's my idea that a vacation means sun, sand, and ocean:* view, feeling, understanding, sentiment, opinion, impression, conclusion, outlook, conviction, belief.

ideal *n.* **1.** *The ideals of a free nation include liberty and justice for all:* aim, objective, ultimate aim, optimal goal, ultimate end, highest goal; level of perfection, highest attainment. **2.** *Sir Laurence Olivier is the ideal of many actors:* model, hero, idol, inspiration, standard, perfect model, epitome, standard of excellence; exemplar, last word, ultimate, criterion, paradigm, pattern, model, archetype; primary aim, objective, dream, chief hope, target of one's efforts. —*adj.* **3.** *The meadow is an ideal place for the children to play:* perfect, absolutely suitable, meeting every need or desire, exemplary, optimal, excellent, faultless, impeccable, matchless.

idealism *n. Not even this bitter disappointment crushed his idealism:* belief in noble goals, persistent hopefulness, optimism, meliorism; wishful thinking, romanticism, utopianism. —**Ant.** realism, pragmatism, cynicism.

idealist *n.* **1.** *It is the idealists among us who try to aid humanity:* persistent optimist, perfec-

tionist. **2.** *There are few idealists in politics:* utopian, visionary, romantic, romanticist, dreamer, Pollyanna, stargazer. —**Ant.** 1, 2 pragmatist, materialist, realist, skeptic, cynic.

identical *adj. Identical chairs flanked the fireplace:* twin, duplicate, exactly alike, uniform, perfectly matched, indistinguishable, precisely corresponding, interchangeable, alike feature for feature; very same, one and the same, selfsame; exactly as before, none other than. —**Ant.** diverse, different, disparate, contrary, divergent; distinct, separate, unlike, dissimilar.

identification *n.* **1.** *Identification of the jewels was made by the owner:* establishment of identity; recognition, verification, confirmation, ascertainment; pinpointing, detection, revelation. **2.** *The candidate's identification with organized crime cost him the election:* assumed relationship, connection, association, affiliation. **3.** *A driver's license is adequate identification:* certificate of identity, credentials; (*variously*) proper papers, passport, identity book, identifying badge, label, or button; item or means of recognition.

identify *v.* **1.** *You can identify me by a green carnation in my lapel:* recognize, know, distinguish, determine, place, designate, pick out, single out, tell the identity of, be sure of, verify, specify. **2.** *The world identifies Lincoln with emancipation:* associate, combine, attach by association, think of in connection, mention in the same breath, put in the same category; consider the same, consider to be intimately connected, regard as representative of. **3.** *The audience identified with the main character:* put oneself in the place of, feel empathy for, respond sympathetically to, take the point of view of. —**Ant.** 1 mistake, confuse, overlook. 2 confuse, dissociate.

identity *n.* **1.** *Fingerprints established the suspect's identity:* name, individuality, unique personal nature, delineation, social specificity. **2.** *The father and son share an identity of political philosophy:* exact similarity, exact likeness, duplication, precise correspondence; oneness, accord, harmony, rapport, unanimity. **3.** *Many people in a large city feel a loss of a sense of identity:* individuality, distinctness of character, self, personality, self-perspective, distinctiveness, differentiation, personal uniqueness, social role. —**Ant. 2** difference, separateness, distinctness, contrariety.

ideology *n. Communist ideology is impossible for individualists to accept:* set of beliefs, body of concepts, principles, ideals, doctrine, theory, dogma, program, rationale, ethos, political philosophy.

idiocy *n.* **1.** *Idiocy can be congenital or caused by some early childhood disease:* cretinism, mongolism. **2.** *It would be idiocy to antagonize such an influential politician:* folly, senselessness, stupidity, absurdity, foolishness, foolhardiness, fatuity, abject silliness, inanity, asininity, insanity, madness, lunacy, utter rashness, suicide. —**Ant.** common sense, sense, sanity, wisdom, sagacity, judiciousness.

idiom *n.* **1.** *Foreigners often have trouble with idioms like "take a powder":* phrase, characteristic expression, unique grammatical or semantic construction. **2.** *The play suffers in its translation from French into the Spanish idiom. The symphony is written in the modern jazz idiom:* language, mode of expression, characteristic style, parlance, speech; colloquialism, localism, dialect, argot, patois, vernacular, jargon, slang; lingo, brogue.

idiosyncrasy *n. Wearing earmuffs in and out of doors is one of her idiosyncrasies:* peculiar trait, quirk, unusual characteristic, unusual habit, peculiarity, anomaly, oddity, mannerism, eccentricity, distinction; personal mark.

idiot *n.* **1.** *An idiot has a mental age of three or four years:* helplessly feebleminded person, mental defective, cretin. **2.** *The fire started because some idiot ignored the No Smoking sign:* foolish person, fool, simpleton, halfwit, dope, moron, dolt, ninny, ass, blockhead, damn fool, nitwit, dimwit, nincompoop, jerk, dummy, dumbbell, boob, dunce, numskull; *Slang* cluck. —**Ant.** 1 genius, mastermind, prodigy.

idiotic *adj. Not seeing a doctor was idiotic!:* stupid, emptyheaded, absurd, asinine, moronic, feebleminded, imbecilic, stupidly clumsy or careless, ridiculous, rattlebrained, addled, doltish, halfwitted, foolish, foolhardy, irrational, senseless; *Informal* dopey, nutty, crazy. —**Ant.** intelligent, sensible, thoughtful, clever, sage, wise, brilliant, commonsensical.

idle *adj.* **1.** *The plant closed and left hundreds of employees idle:* unemployed, lacking work, inactive, doing nothing, not working, unoccupied, out of work, jobless. **2.** *The fuel shortage has left many airplanes idle:* not in operation, not being used, unused, not operating, doing nothing, gathering dust, inactive; fallow. **3.** *Spring makes everyone feel idle:* lazy, indolent, sluggish, slothful, languid, somnolent, enervated, lethargic, at leisure, inert, torpid, drowsy, listless, otiose. **4.** *Don't waste time on idle gossip:* baseless, worthless, empty, vapid, unsubstantiated, petty, trifling, trivial, valueless, vain, useless, unproductive; fruitless, futile, bootless, pointless, aimless, unimportant, good-for-nothing. —*v.* **5.** *We idled the summer away swimming and playing tennis:* fritter, spend in idleness, pass lazily, while, wait out, putter, loaf, fool away, laze, waste. —**Ant.** 1 active, employed, working, occupied, busy. 2 operative, operating, functioning, actuated, working, active. 3 energetic, industrious, busy, wide-awake, active. 4 important, meaningful, profitable, worthwhile, significant, advantageous, productive, beneficial, useful, purposeful, effective, fruitful.

idleness *n. He spent all his time in idleness:* lazing, shiftlessness, sloth, inaction, dawdling, loafing, trifling; joblessness, unemployment.

idol *n.* **1.** *The temple was filled with golden idols:* religious effigy, icon, graven image, statue, effigy, simulacrum; artifact, relic. **2.** *Rudolph Valentino was a famous matinee idol:* popular hero, popular figure, darling, public favorite; inspiration, adored person, hero, guiding light; person toward whom one directs one's aspirations; godlike figure.

idolatry *n.* **1.** *Idolatry was commonplace in many early pagan religions:* worship of an object, image-worship, reverence of idols, idolization. **2.** *Only a millionaire could satisfy that woman's idolatry of jewels:* inordinate love, worship, adoration, obsession, preoccupation, excessive fondness, passion, devotion, veneration, single-minded attention, infatuation, senseless attachment, madness, mania.

idolize *v.* **1.** *Some cults idolize the sun:* worship, adore, venerate, revere, reverence, bow down before, deify, apotheosize. **2.** *The boy idolized his father:* adore, love to excess, admire, honor, worship, dote loyally upon, treasure, give up one's heart to, prize; *Slang* go bananas over, be nuts about. —**Ant.** 2 despise, scorn, disdain.

idyllic *adj. The grazing cows made an idyllic picture:* peaceful, rustic, pastoral, arcadian, sylvan, bucolic, charmingly simple, unspoiled, romantic.

if *conj.* **1.** *If I were you, I'd take an umbrella. She spoke to an enthusiastic if small audience:* in case, provided, providing, granting, supposing, even though, though; whether, whether or not. —*n.* **2.** *There were a lot of ifs in the plan:* condition, supposition.

iffy *adj. The outcome of a horse race is always iffy:* doubtful, unsettled, uncertain, dubious, unresolved, speculative, problematical, moot, conjectural, unsure, questionable, chancy, risky; capricious, erratic, whimsical, unpredictable. —**Ant.** certain, sure, sure-fire, settled, decided.

ignite *v.* **1.** *A dropped cigarette ignited the straw:* set on fire, set fire to, fire, kindle, light, inflame, touch off; explode, blow up. **2.** *The wood must be dry to ignite:* catch fire, catch on fire, burn, take fire, blaze, flame. —**Ant.** 1 stifle, extinguish, quench, douse.

ignoble *adj. The assassination was one of history's most ignoble deeds:* despicable, infamous, heinous, shameful, dishonorable, base, contemptible, nefarious, vile, dastardly, low, unconscionable, foul, degraded, mean, depraved, cowardly, pusillanimous, craven, degenerate, disgraceful, debased, inferior, discreditable, unworthy, indecent. —**Ant.** admirable, commendable, laudable, meritorious, lofty, sublime, glorious, splendid, distinguished, honorable, superior, exalted, grand, notable, fine, worthy, praiseworthy.

ignominious *adj. The army's disorganized retreat was ignominious:* humiliating, shameful, inglorious, disgraceful, wretched, degrading, abject, sorry, low, dishonorable, causing dishonor, discreditable, disreputable, despicable, grievous, unbearable. —**Ant.** creditable, honorable, reputable, admirable, estimable, worthy.

ignominy *n. The scandal brought the family further ignominy:* disgrace, dishonor, disrepute, contempt, discredit, shame, infamy, obloquy, opprobrium, scandal, odium, abasement. —**Ant.** credit, honor, repute, fame, distinction.

ignoramus *n. Jim's quite knowledgeable but pretends to be an ignoramus:* simpleton, fool, dunce, know-nothing, low-brow, numskull, nitwit, illiterate.

ignorance *n. Combating ignorance among the underprivileged is a national priority. Ignorance of the law is no excuse:* illiteracy, lack of knowledge or education, lack of learning, backwardness, mental darkness; unawareness, obliviousness, unenlightenment, confusion, lack of perception, unacquaintance, unfamiliarity. —**Ant.** knowledge, education, wisdom, sense, learning, erudition; comprehension, insight, perception, empathy, understanding.

ignorant *adj.* **1.** *The mountain villagers are an ignorant but peaceable people:* uneducated, unlearned, illiterate, lacking knowledge, unschooled, unlettered, unenlightened, untaught, untrained, untutored; naive, unworldly. **2.** *The father was ignorant of the child's fears:* uninformed, unknowing, innocent, unaware, unperceptive, insensitive, unknowledgeable, blind to, uncognizant, in the dark about. **3.** *It was an ignorant remark for someone claiming to be an expert:* unintelligent, shallow, irresponsible, insensitive, foolishly uninformed; fatuous, asinine, dumb, stupid. —**Ant.** 1 educated, instructed, learned, well-informed, wise, lettered, literate, cultured, cultivated. 2 aware, conscious, informed, briefed, knowledgeable, knowing. 3 sagacious, perceptive, astute, knowledgeable, wise, brilliant, sage.

ignore *v. It's sometimes best to ignore a rude person:* take no notice of, refrain from noticing, disregard, be oblivious to, pay no attention to, turn one's back on, pay no heed to, shut one's eyes to, brush aside, scorn, neglect, slight, eschew, give the cold shoulder to, snub; pass over, skip, omit, overlook. —**Ant.** heed, acknowledge, notice, note, regard, recognize, mark, attend.

ill *adj.* **1.** *Is he ill enough to need a doctor?:* sick, sickly, unwell, ailing, unsound, poorly, afflicted, diseased, unhealthy, indisposed; failing, invalid, laid up, under the weather. **2.** *The perpetrator of this ill deed will be apprehended. Let's disregard any ill comments that are aimed our way:* evil, harmful, wicked, vile, foul, peevish, surly, cross; malicious, unkind, vengeful, acrimonious. **3.** *The unusually heavy rainfall was an ill omen for the travelers:* unfavorable, boding bad luck, sinister, disturbing, unpropitious, unlucky, inauspicious, threatening, foreboding, ominous. —*n.* **4. ills** *She would be happiest helping to cure the ills of humanity:* affliction, ailment, disease, plague, complaint, malady, infirmity; woe, trouble, sorrow, slings and arrows, misfortune, trial. **5.** *They remain a forgiving people, despite the ill done them:* wickedness, malice, evil, mischief, abomination, cruelty, abuse, outrage, ill-treatment, ill-usage, harm, injury, damage, malefaction. —*adv.* **6.** *The country can ill afford to wage a large-scale war:*

not well, scarcely, hardly; by no means, nowise, noway. —**Ant.** 1 well, hale, healthy, strong, vigorous, robust. 2 kind, generous, selfless; favorable, complimentary, flattering. 5 good, beneficence, decency, honor, kindness. 6 well, easily, effortlessly, handily.

ill-advised *adj. She's a charming actress, but her attempts at Shakespeare have been ill-advised:* ill-considered, imprudent, unwise, injudicious, shortsighted, indiscreet, impolitic, ill-judged, myopic, unthinking, misguided; foolish, irresponsible, senseless, dumb, stupid, silly. —**Ant.** wise, prudent, sensible, smart, judicious.

ill-at-ease *adj. Speaking in public always makes her ill-at-ease:* uneasy, uncomfortable, disquieted, bothered, nervous, troubled, perturbed, disturbed, discomfited, on edge, discomposed, edgy; shy, self-conscious, embarrassed, nonplused, abashed, disconcerted, discountenanced. —**Ant.** self-assured, self-confident, positive, poised.

illegal *adj. Parking a car in front of a fire hydrant is illegal:* unlawful, against the law, not legal, prohibited, unsanctioned, proscribed, forbidden, banned, illicit, unauthorized; illegitimate, criminal, felonious, actionable, outlawed; against the rules, wrong. —**Ant.** legal, licit, lawful, authorized, permissible, sanctioned.

illegible *adj. Parts of the document are faded and illegible:* unreadable, impossible to read, indecipherable, undecipherable, scribbled, unintelligible; obscured, hard to make out, unclear. —**Ant.** legible, readable, clear, intelligible.

illegitimate *adj.* **1.** *The agency made illegitimate use of public funds:* illegal, improper, not legitimate, unwarranted, unlawful, illicit, unauthorized, lawless, unsanctioned, prohibited. **2.** *The king's illegitimate son could not inherit the throne:* bastard, natural, baseborn, misbegotten. —**Ant.** 1 legitimate, lawful, legal. 2 legitimate.

ill-fated *adj. The ill-fated ocean liner* Titanic *was the subject of a movie:* unfortunate, doomed to disaster, ill-omened, ill-starred, doomed, luckless, blighted, unlucky, hapless, destined to end unhappily; jinxed.

illiberal *adj. Most of his illiberal opinions dated from childhood:* intolerant, narrow-minded, biased, prejudiced, hidebound, brassbound, small-minded, bigoted, short-sighted, small, narrow, opinionated, petty, ungenerous. —**Ant.** broad-minded, liberal, tolerant, unprejudiced.

illicit *adj. The police began to crack down on illicit drug traffic:* unlawful, not legal, illegal, against the law, illegitimate, impermissible, not permitted, criminal, felonious, lawless, prohibited, improper, unauthorized; clandestine; *Informal* under-the-counter, black-market. —**Ant.** licit, lawful, legal, legalized, legitimate, permissible, aboveboard.

illiterate *adj.* **1.** *Many backwoods people are completely illiterate:* unable to read and write, unlettered, ignorant, uneducated, unlearned, not educated, unschooled. **2.** *That illiterate re-*

port must have been prepared by a first-grader: badly written, ungrammatical, childish, amateurish, ludicrously bad, unscholarly, unreliable, witless, incoherent. **3.** *I am illiterate on the subject of modern art:* ignorant, unknowledgeable, uninstructed, untutored, uninitiated, unversed, uninformed, unenlightened. —**Ant.** literate, taught, instructed, educated, schooled, informed, knowledgeable, expert.

ill-mannered *adj. Her ill-mannered reply shocked everyone:* rude, impolite, discourteous, disrespectful, uncivil, ungracious, ungallant, ill-bred, ill-behaved; boorish, coarse, offensive, loutish, crude. —**Ant.** gracious, well-bred, well-mannered, courteous, respectful.

ill-natured *adj. Her ill-natured patients demand most of her time:* ill-humored, unfriendly, quarrelsome, antagonistic, cross, peev-ish, captious, contentious, grouchy, cranky, irritable, cantankerous, crotchety, surly, churlish. —**Ant.** congenial, agreeable, amiable, likable, cordial.

illness *n. An undiagnosed illness put him in the hospital:* sickness, malady, disorder, disease, indisposition, ailment, infirmity, disability, affliction; complaint, malfunction; ill health, poor health. —**Ant.** health, robustness, wholesomeness, salubriousness, salubrity, hardiness.

illogical *adj. In view of the facts, your conclusion is illogical:* inconsistent, unreasonable, fallacious, contradictory, erroneous, incongruent, incongruous; unsound, preposterous, absurd; *Slang* nutty, screwy, dopey, wacky, far-out. —**Ant.** orderly, coherent, logical, reasonable.

ill-suited *adj. Such heavy makeup is ill-suited to one with her delicate features:* inappropriate, unsuitable, unsuited, malapropos, inapt, ill-matched, mismatched, misjoined, mismated, unbecoming, unbefitting, ill-adapted, uncongenial, inconsistent, incompatible. —**Ant.** apt, becoming, suitable, appropriate, congenial.

ill-tempered *adj. My ill-tempered neighbor warned me never to use his driveway:* peevish, cross, petulant, waspish, cantankerous, crotchety, ill-humored, ill-natured, *Brit.* shirty, cranky, testy, irritable, grouchy. —**Ant.** amiable, agreeable, amenable, pleasant.

ill-timed *adj. The offer was singularly ill-timed:* badly timed, mistimed, inappropriate, inconvenient, inopportune, unseasonable, unseemly, unsuitable, unwelcome, awkward.

illuminate *v.* **1.** *Torches illuminated the picnic grounds:* light up, fill or supply with light, light, illumine, irradiate, brighten, cast light upon. **2.** *Footnotes illuminated the difficult passages of the book:* clarify, explain, make understandable or lucid, make clear, throw light on, elucidate, enhance, spell out; give insight into; edify, enlighten, instruct; exemplify. —**Ant.** 1 darken, obliterate, becloud, benight, cloud, obscure.

illumination *n.* **1.** *The illumination of the stage was done by footlights:* illuminating, irradiation, illumining, lighting up. **2.** *The library's reading rooms need better illumination:* lights, lighting, light fixtures, lighting equipment; source of light. **3.** *He sought illumination by reading the great philosophers. Illumination of the public is*

a major aim of the ecology group: enlightenment, knowledge, perception, revelation, insight, wisdom, comprehension; information, instruction, edification, education. —**Ant.** 1 darkening, adumbration, dimming, obscuring.

illusion *n.* **1.** *Mirrors give an illusion of more space in a room:* semblance, misleading visual impression, optical illusion, unreality, deceiving appearance; impression, vision, false image, mirage; chimera, hallucination, apparition, phantasm, delusion, deception; hocus-pocus, humbuggery. **2.** *The illusions of youth fade with maturity:* false belief, false idea, erroneous impression, mistaken idea, delusion, misconception, misimpression, fallacy, misbelief, error, misapprehension, fancy, caprice, vagary. —**Ant.** 1 reality, substantiation, actuality, truth.

illusory *adj. The illusory state of tranquillity soon erupted into war:* unreal, illusive, deceptive, delusive, false, fallacious, spurious, erroneous, misleading, imaginary, fanciful, unrealistic, hallucinatory, sham, counterfeit; ostensible, apparent, seeming. —**Ant.** substantial, real, true.

illustrate *v.* **1.** *The company's bank statements illustrate its success:* make clear, explain, make intelligible, elucidate, throw light on, illuminate, define, clarify; emphasize, bring home, point up; demonstrate, show. **2.** *The artist illustrated the book with stick figures:* ornament, provide with illustrations, decorate, adorn with pictures, pictorialize, portray, delineate; paint or draw illustrations for; represent, picture.

illustration *n.* **1.** *The magazine has illustrations in black and white and in color:* picture, photograph, portrayal, drawing, figure, representation, image; plate. **2.** *The speaker gave an illustration of the dangers of poor nutrition:* example, instance, typical occurrence, pertinent case, representative sample, specimen, exemplification.

illustrative *adj. The book had much illustrative material:* delineative, descriptive, exemplifying, explanatory, expository, illuminative, indicative, interpretive, revealing, representative; pictorial, imagistic, diagrammatic, emblematic, figurative, graphic, iconographic; symbolic, allegorical, metaphoric, typical.

illustrious *adj.* **1.** *Jackie Robinson was an illustrious athlete:* highly notable, famous, famed, eminent, renowned, celebrated, prominent, widely admired; of the first rank, distinguished, honored, acclaimed. **2.** *Helen Hayes has had an illustrious career in the theater:* distinguished, brilliant, splendid, lustrous, great, glorious, magnificent; exemplary, matchless, peerless.

ill-will *n. Though he betrayed her, she bore him no ill will:* malice, antipathy, hostility, enmity, aversion, dislike, animosity, rancor, spleen, antagonism, gall, abhorrence, animus, malevolence, hatred, loathing, bad blood. —**Ant.** goodwill, cordiality, friendliness, benevolence.

image *n.* **1.** *Chagall often uses contorted images of fiddlers in his paintings:* representation, likeness, facsimile, copy, picture, pictorialization; effigy, portrait, figure, delineation, depiction; artistic or mechanical reproduction, photograph, semblance, simulacrum. **2.** *The image of* *the trees in the lake made a lovely picture:* reflection, mirroring, reflected appearance, likeness, semblance, countenance, visage. **3.** *Only a faint image of the encounter remains:* memory, recollection, concept, idea, mental picture. **4.** *The girl is the image of her mother:* copy, duplicate, reproduction, replica, double, facsimile, incarnation. **5.** *The writer used the image of corn silk to describe the girl's hair:* literary comparison; figure of speech; simile; metaphor; symbol. **6.** *The missionaries rebuked the natives for worshiping images:* idol, fetish, icon, statue, effigy, graven image.

imagery *n. The painter's imagery was simple:* picture, pictures, pictorialization, illustration, visualization, iconography, representation, portrayal, depiction, rendering, rendition.

imaginable *adj. She committed every sin imaginable:* conceivable, possible, thinkable, comprehensible, calculable, supposable. **—Ant.** unthinkable, impossible, inconceivable, incredible.

imaginary *adj.* **1.** *All characters in the book are imaginary:* unreal, invented, made-up, fictitious, fancied, fanciful; illusory, fantastic, fabulous, mythical, legendary, figmental, factitious, dreamed up; sham, counterfeit; *Slang* phony. *—n.* **2.** *The heroine of* A Streetcar Named Desire *confuses the imaginary with the real:* fanciful, romantic; fiction, fancy, illusion, delusion, figment, make-believe. **—Ant.** 1 real, actual, corporeal, true, factual.

imagination *n.* **1.** *Fairy tales often help to develop a child's imagination:* inventiveness, fancy, invention; creativity, creative thought; power to picture mentally. **2.** *With a little imagination we should find a solution:* resourcefulness, thought, ingenuity, inventiveness, thoughtfulness, creativeness, enterprise, creative use of resources; cunning, astuteness.

imaginative *adj. An imaginative set designer can always enhance a play. The artist's imaginative use of color delighted the critics:* original, creative, innovative, inventive; inspired, clever, ingenious; off the beaten path; unusual, out of the ordinary; enterprising, resourceful. **—Ant.** unimaginative, unromantic, literal, uninventive, ordinary, pedestrian, commonplace, unoriginal, uncreative, uninspired, prosaic, mundane, run-of-the-mill.

imagine *v.* **1.** *Try to imagine being on the moon:* envision, picture, pretend, conceive, project, visualize, envisage, dream up, fantasize. **2.** *I imagine you are tired from the journey:* presume, gather, assume, suppose, should think, believe, guess, conjecture, infer, judge, surmise; take for granted; suspect, fancy.

imbecile *n.* **1.** *The captain was an imbecile to sail in this storm:* fool, foolish person, idiot, nitwit, ass, jerk, dumbbell, dummy, dope, simpleton, moron, dunce, nincompoop, ninny, blockhead, dolt; *Slang* dingbat. *—adj.* **2.** *Also* **imbecilic** *Lending someone your passport is an imbecilic thing to do:* foolish, dumb, stupid, asinine, silly, absurd, inane; careless, mindless, thoughtless.

imbibe *v. During the hot summer our family imbibes gallons of iced tea:* consume, drink, quaff, ingest, swallow; *Informal* tope, tipple, guzzle, swig, chugalug, toss down; partake, wash down.

imbroglio *n. They got involved in an imbroglio over water rights:* complication, entanglement, dispute, embroilment, involvement, altercation, argument, bickering, involvement, quarrel.

imbue *v.* **1.** *Churchill imbued his countrymen with enormous patriotism:* inspire, fill, endow, impress, instill, inculate, infuse, ingrain; fire, arouse, animate. **2.** *Sunset imbued the Caribbean skies with beautiful pastels:* tinge, tint, color, tincture, bathe, steep, suffuse, permeate, pervade.

imitate *v.* **1.** *Be your own person and don't imitate others:* follow the pattern of, copy in manner, fashion oneself after, mirror, take as a model, simulate, follow in the steps of, emulate, reproduce the image of. **2.** *The comedian imitated W. C. Fields:* mimic, impersonate, do a takeoff on, act in imitation of, ape, parrot, represent, mime, parody, caricature. **3.** *The vinyl upholstery imitates real leather:* simulate, have the appearance of, copy, reproduce closely, duplicate, pass for, look like, counterfeit.

imitation *n.* **1.** *The fabric isn't real silk, only an imitation:* simulation, copy of an original, counterfeit, fake, semblance, reproduction, facsimile, similarity; duplication. **2.** *He can do imitations of every nationally known public figure:* impersonation, impression, burlesque, mimicry, parody, takeoff, travesty, caricature, representation, adaptation, aping. *—adj.* **3.** *Conservationists urge the wearing of imitation fur:* simulated, fake, ersatz, phony, make-believe, mock, sham; synthetic, artificial, man-made. **—Ant.** 3 real, actual, true, genuine.

imitative *adj. The imitative comedian had no original material:* derivative, unoriginal, emulative, secondhand, copied, copycat, mimic, mimicking, plagiarized, simulated.

immaculate *adj.* **1.** *The maid left the house immaculate:* spotless, spic and span, impeccably clean and neat; unstained, unsoiled, stainless, untarnished, unsullied, shipshape. **2.** *The senator's record is immaculate:* above reproach, faultless, morally blameless, pure, clean, virtuous, guiltless, perfect, ideal, unexceptionable, unimpeachable, intact, flawless, irreproachable, unsullied; innocent, sinless, saintly, chaste, virgin, virginal. **—Ant.** 1 dirty, filthy, spotted, unclean, stained, sullied. 2 impure, corrupt, sinful, contaminated, defiled, polluted, tainted, spotted, filthy, tarnished, sullied, impeachable, blameworthy.

immanent *adj. Behavior patterns may be more immanent than acquired:* inherent, natural, inbred, innate, inborn, indigenous, intrinsic; ingrained, deep-rooted, congenital, instinctive, instinctual, deep-seated, indwelling. **—Ant.** extrinsic, alien, extraneous, acquired, superimposed.

immaterial *adj.* **1.** *What people wear to the party is immaterial. The testimony is immaterial to these hearings:* of no importance, not relevant, irrelevant, inconsequential, insignificant, extraneous, unimportant, of minor importance, trifling, trivial, matter of indifference, of no moment, having no bearing, of little account. **2.** *The medium claims that she is in contact with the immaterial world:* spiritual, incorporeal, noumenal, bodiless, insubstantial, unsubstantial, impalpable, intangible, unbodied, unearthly, extramundane, ghostly, ethereal, evanescent, spectral, disembodied, shadowy, extrasensory, mystical. **—Ant.** 1 relevant, significant, germane, important, essential, vital, crucial. 2 material, physical, real, tangible, corporeal, palpable, earthly.

immature *adj.* **1.** *The larva or caterpillar is the immature stage of the butterfly:* embryonic, unripe, young, youthful, rudimentary, infantile, pubescent, unformed, half-grown, not mature, undeveloped, unfinished; unmellowed, out of season, green. **2.** *Some adults remain emotionally immature:* childish, juvenile, callow, puerile, infantile, babyish; *Informal* wet behind the ears, kiddish. **—Ant.** 1 mature, adult, ripe, mellow, developed, full-fledged. 2 adult, mature, grown-up, responsible.

immeasurable *adj.* *These rocks have been here for immeasurable time:* beyond measure, limitless, inestimable, incalculable, measureless, fathomless, immense, unlimited, illimitable, infinite, unbounded, boundless, unfathomable; interminable, endless, never-ending, inexhaustible. **—Ant.** measurable, finite, limited, circumscribed, restricted, bounded, specific; exact.

immediate *adj.* **1.** *Please send an immediate answer:* prompt, undelayed, instant, instantaneous, express, done without delay, sudden, abrupt, swift, speedy, hasty, punctual. **2.** *The shopping center is in the immediate neighborhood. The immediate past:* next, near, adjacent, close, local, nearby, nearest, proximate, contiguous, nigh, not distant; recent. **—Ant.** 1 delayed, postponed, leisurely, unhurried, slow, relaxed, late, tardy. 2 distant, peripheral, far, remote.

immediately *adv.* **1.** *We must report to the supervisor immediately:* instantly, at once, without delay, presently, directly, instantaneously, forthwith. **2.** directly, closely, without intervention. **—Ant.** later, anon.

immemorial *adj.* *The Alps have towered majestically over Europe since time immemorial:* ancient, timeless, dateless, olden, time-honored, ancestral, venerable, ageless, mythological, legendary, long-established, hallowed, longstanding.

immense *adj.* *The Grand Canyon is immense. We cooked an immense quantity of food:* vast, enormous, monstrous, stupendous, extensive, measureless, great, tremendous, huge, massive, gigantic, prodigious, mammoth, colossal, Brobdingnagian. **—Ant.** small, tiny, minute, wee, diminutive, petite, sparse, spare.

immerse *v.* **1.** *Immerse the cloth in the dye for twenty minutes:* submerge, dip, lower, dunk, duck, douse, drench, steep, soak, bathe, sink, plunge. **2.** *The entire family is immersed in sci-*

entific research: involve deeply, absorb, occupy, be caught up in, engage, engross, preoccupy with, concentrate on.

immigrant *n.* *The immigrants found life hard in their new home:* migrant, emigrant, newcomer.

immigrate *v.* *Many Italians immigrated to the United States and Canada:* migrate, move to, relocate in; settle, colonize. **—Ant.** emigrate; leave, depart from.

imminent *adj.* *My departure is imminent. The mountain climbers were in imminent danger:* impending, approaching, close at hand, near, immediate, near at hand; threatening, perilous, looming, menacing. **—Ant.** distant, future; delayed.

immobile *adj.* **1.** *Bolt the table to the floor to make it immobile:* immovable, fixed, stationary, fast, secure, steadfast, riveted, rooted, unbudgeable, stable; rigid, stiff. **2.** *A back injury kept him immobile for weeks:* incapacitated, laid up, motionless, not moving, still, quiet, quiescent, static, at rest, stock-still, immobilized. **—Ant.** 1 mobile, portable, movable, transportable. 2 active, vigorous, up and about, on the move.

immoderate *adj.* *The young men consumed an immoderate amount of wine and fell asleep:* excessive, extravagant, prodigious, unreasonable, unbridled, inordinate, uncalled-for, intemperate, extreme, exorbitant, unconscionable, undue, unrestrained, gargantuan, whopping, mind-boggling. **—Ant.** moderate; temperate; restrained, curbed, checked, inhibited; reasonable, rational, prudent, cautious, judicious, sensible.

immodest *adj.* **1.** *Clothing once thought immodest is acceptable today:* indecorous, overly revealing, indecent, indelicate, shameless; lewd, loose, suggestive, indecent, risqué; coarse, gross, wanton, unchaste. **2.** *The actor made immodest claims about his talent:* vain, exaggerated, inflated, pompous, conceited, high-sounding, brazen, self-centered, self-aggrandizing, braggart, bombastic, boastful, pretentious, peacockish. **—Ant.** 1 modest, decent, delicate, decorous, pure, chaste. 2 modest, humble, genteel, restrained.

immoral *adj.* *Selling drugs to children is immoral. The court banned two immoral movies:* unethical, unprincipled, corrupt, evil, wrong, vicious, wicked, profoundly bad, iniquitous, sinful, infamous, nefarious, heinous, profligate, dissipated, dissolute; sexually arousing, lewd, prurient, debauched, depraved, obscene, licentious, salacious, indecent; pornographic; *Informal* dirty, raunchy. **—Ant.** moral, upright, virtuous, law-abiding, conscientious, good, honorable, ethical, chaste, pure, clean, inoffensive.

immortal *adj.* **1.** *Humans long to be immortal. The immortal works of Beethoven are listed by opus number in the Kinsky Beethoven-Verzeichnis:* undying, not mortal, eternal, everlasting, divine, deathless, imperishable, lasting through all time, enduring, abiding. *—n.* **2. Immortals** *In ancient Greek mythology the Immortals dwell on Mount Olympus:* the gods, (specifically) the members of the Greek and Roman pantheon. **3.** *Chaucer is a literary immortal:* monumental figure, titan, giant, all-time great; demigod, great, illustrious name. **—Ant.** 1 mortal; transitory, fleeting, fugitive, ephemeral, evanescent, transient, short-lived, passing; fly-by-night.

immovable *adj.* **1.** *The entrance is blocked by an immovable rock:* unmovable, fixed, set, settled, fast, secure, immobile, stationary, unbudgeable, fastened. **2.** *The governor was immovable in his determination to end the strike:* unyielding in purpose, unchangeable, stubborn, obdurate, not to be put off, fixed, inflexible, stolid, inexorable, unbendable, adamant, resolute, dogged; unfeeling, impassive, unimpressionable, heartless, steely, coldhearted, icy, cold, unsympathetic, unimpressible, detached. **—Ant.** 1 movable, portable, transportable, yielding. 2 flexible, persuadable, swayable, open-minded, reasonable, irresolute, changeable.

immune *adj.* **1.** *The inoculations made the children immune to measles:* resistant, unsusceptible, protected, safe, invulnerable, unthreatened by, not in danger of. **2.** *Income from certain bonds may be immune from taxation:* exempt, free, not affected by, not liable to, not subject to, at liberty, clear, not vulnerable. **—Ant.** 1 subject, vulnerable, exposed, susceptible; unprotected, unsafe. 2 subject, liable.

immutable *adj.* *Platinum is one of the most immutable of metals:* unchanging, unchangeable, changeless, unvarying, unaltered, unalterable, incontrovertible, unmodifiable, intransmutable; permanent, lasting, enduring, stable; firm, fixed, solid, constant, inflexible. **—Ant.** changeable, unstable, alterable, flexible, variable.

imp *n.* **1.** *The forest was said to be full of mischievous imps:* small demon, evil spirit, sprite, elf, pixie, gnome, hobgoblin, little goblin, little devil, leprechaun. **2.** *The little imp has hidden my eyeglasses again:* mischievous child, harmlessly naughty child, brat, scamp, devil, rascal, urchin, hoyden, upstart.

impact *n.* **1.** *The impact of the car cracked the telephone pole:* collision, crash, smash, violent blow, force, concussion, contact, jolt. **2.** *The full impact of the news hit us several days later:* effect, brunt, influence, burden, shock, thrust; implication, repercussion.

impair *v.* *The water shortage impaired the city's fire-fighting capacity:* hinder, damage, mar, hurt, vitiate, harm, cripple, subvert, injure, lessen, weaken, enfeeble, decrease, undercut, detract from, reduce; enervate, debilitate, worsen. **—Ant.** improve, amend; repair; better, ameliorate, enhance, facilitate, increase.

impaired *adj.* *His health was impaired by years as a miner:* defective, damaged, faulty, flawed, imperfect, harmed, hurt, marred, spoiled, broken, injured, unsound.

impairment *n.* *There was no impairment of his faculties:* defect, breakdown, damage, detriment, disrepair, harm, hurt, injury, malfunction, worsening.

impale *v.* **1.** *The mercenaries impaled their victims upon wooden stakes:* fix on a stake, stick, run through. **2.** *The collector impaled the butterflies on pins before framing them:* transfix, affix, tack, pin, stick.

impalpable *adj.* *Something impalpable in the atmosphere made her uneasy:* imperceptible, intangible, nebulous, disembodied, imprecise, inappreciable, indiscernible, tenuous, vague, unsubstantial, indistinct, insubstantial, shadowy.

impart *v.* **1.** *The President imparted the news of his trip in a special conference:* make known, tell, pass on, communicate, relate, report, confide, mention, reveal, disclose, divulge, share. **2.** *The red draperies impart a certain elegance to the room:* confer on, bestow on, give, lend, grant, render, contribute, deliver, offer, dispense, consign, accord, afford.

impartial *adj.* *Try to remain impartial until you have heard both sides of the story:* unbiased, fair, just, objective, equitable, nonpartisan, disinterested, dispassionate, detached, open-minded, evenhanded, neutral, unprejudiced, fair-minded. **—Ant.** partial, prejudiced, influenced, swayed, affected, biased, slanted, swayable, bigoted, unfair, unjust.

impasse *n.* *The city and the teachers' union have reached an impasse:* deadlock, stalemate, blind alley, bottleneck, cul-de-sac, dead end; snag; dilemma, predicament, quandary, standstill, standoff.

impassioned *adj.* *The leader roused the protesters with an impassioned speech:* ardent, animated, intense, fervent, excited, inspired, passionate, heated, earnest, eager, zealous, fiery, stirring, rousing, forceful. **—Ant.** dispassionate, objective, cool, impassive, apathetic, indifferent, detached.

impassive *adj.* *The moderator maintained an impassive manner throughout the furious debate:* emotionless, unemotional, unmoved, imperturbable, dispassionate, aloof, stoical, untouched, stony, calm, cool, sedate, reserved, unperturbed, unimpressible, inscrutable, impervious, stolid, apathetic, phlegmatic, unimpressionable, insensible, indifferent. **—Ant.** responsive, emotional, passionate, excited, perturbed.

impatience *n.* *She fidgeted with impatience:* restlessness, restiveness, agitation, anxiety, eagerness, edginess, fretfulness, nervousness; rashness, vehemence, haste; irritableness, shortness, snappiness. **—Ant.** forbearance, composure, calm.

impatient *adj.* *The class was impatient for vacation to begin. The teacher became impatient with the inattentive students:* restless, nervous, edgy, tense, irritated, agitated, excitable, fussy, restive; enthusiastic, eagerly desirous, feverish, high-strung, rabid, passionate, hurried, hasty, ardent, itchy, anxious; peevish, irritable, irascible, testy, brusque, annoyed, touchy, intolerant. **—Ant.** patient; composed, imperturbable, unruffled, cool; calm, serene, tranquil, placid, restful, quiet; gradual, slow; unperturbed.

impeach *v.* **1.** *There were rumors of a move-*

ment in Congress to impeach the President: accuse, indict, arraign, inculpate, charge, incriminate, prefer charges against, lodge a complaint against. **2.** *He was careless, but there's no need to impeach his honesty:* question, call into question, challenge, assail, attack, belittle, impugn, disparage, discredit, slur, slander, *Slang* badmouth.

impeccable *adj. She has impeccable taste in clothes. His character is impeccable:* flawless, faultless, immaculate, free from imperfection, unblemished, perfect, irreproachable, excellent, irreprovable, unassailable, blameless, above criticism, unexceptionable, unimpeachable. —**Ant.** deficient, defective; superficial, shallow, uncritical, cursory; culpable, blameworthy; faulty, tarnished, stained, corrupt, flawed.

impecunious *adj. She discovered that bad investments had made her impecunious overnight:* poor, penniless, *Slang* broke, indigent, destitute, needy, down-and-out, impoverished, poverty-stricken, *Slang* hard-up, bankrupt, insolvent, straitened, pinched. —**Ant.** affluent, well-off, well-heeled, prosperous, flush, well-to-do.

impede *v. A lumber shortage impeded construction on the house:* delay, slow down, block, interfere with, interrupt, check, retard, obstruct, hinder, thwart, frustrate, inhibit, arrest, sidetrack, stall, stymie, deter, hamper, hold back, halter, disrupt. —**Ant.** assist, promote, advance, further, forward; help, aid.

impediment *n. Lack of confidence is an impediment to success. He suffers from a speech impediment:* delay, slowing down, block, blockage, barrier, stumbling block, interference, obstruction, hindrance, interference, handicap, obstacle, drawback, detraction; defect, flaw, deformity. —**Ant.** advantage, bolster, help, aid.

impel *v. Financial woes impel the firm to cut back on spending:* force, require, drive, push, compel, urge, necessitate, prompt, prod, induce, constrain, spur, stimulate, motivate, goad, incite. —**Ant.** restrain, curb, check, inhibit, withhold, hinder.

impending *adj. The dark clouds suggest an impending storm:* approaching, immediate, coming, due momentarily, imminent, near, oncoming, forthcoming, in prospect, brewing, looming; threatening, menacing.

impenetrable *adj.* **1.** *The dense hedge of thorns formed an impenetrable barrier around the castle:* impervious, inviolable, unenterable, impassable, invulnerable, inaccessible; solid, thick, dense, sealed. **2.** *The motive for the crime was impenetrable:* incomprehensible, defying interpretation or understanding, insensible, elusive, mysterious, unfathomable, inscrutable, inaccessible, insoluble, unpalpable, inexplicable, intangible, obscure, puzzling. —**Ant.** 1 pierceable, penetrable, vulnerable, enterable, accessible, passable. 2 understandable, fathomable, soluble, explicable, clear, obvious, lucid.

impenitent *adj. The revival meeting was aimed at rescuing the town's impenitent sinners:* remorseless, unrepenting, unashamed, unrepen-

tant, uncontrite, unapologetic; defiant, obdurate; hardened, callous, inured, incorrigible; lost, irreclaimable. —**Ant.** regretful, contrite, ashamed, remorseful, apologetic, penitent.

imperative *adj. It is imperative that we reach the doctor:* urgent, vitally important, essential, of the utmost necessity, requisite, necessary, needful, mandatory, compulsory, obligatory, pressing, unavoidable, crucial, critical. —**Ant.** unnecessary, unimportant, nonessential, avoidable; nonobligatory.

imperceptible *adj. The difference between the two colors is imperceptible:* undetectable, unnoticeable, not readily apparent, inconsiderable, subtle, minimal, unappreciable, minute, small, scant, insignificant, hidden, indistinct, unperceivable; academic, slight, minor; infinitesimal. —**Ant.** manifest, obvious, clear, perceptible, palpable, noticeable, distinct.

imperfect *adj.* **1.** *The student's understanding of the material was imperfect:* defective, faulty, incomplete. **2.** *Flippers are imperfect legs:* rudimentary, undeveloped, underdeveloped, incomplete; immature.

imperfection *n.* **1.** *The price of the coat was reduced because of a few minor imperfections:* defect, flaw, blemish, fault, impairment, faulty detail, deformity, shortcoming, weakness. **2.** *The architect was disturbed by the imperfection of the construction:* faultiness, imperfectness, falling short, inadequacy, insufficiency, fallibility, incompleteness. —**Ant.** 2 perfection, perfectness, completeness, faultlessness.

imperial *adj. His term of office was sometimes referred to as an imperial presidency:* highhanded, imperious, dictatorial, despotic, authoritarian, domineering, lordly, feudal, magisterial, overbearing, *Slang* bossy, tyrannical, autocratic, arbitrary, peremptory, repressive.

imperil *v. Lack of attention to safety rules may imperil your job as well as your life:* endanger, risk, jeopardize, hazard, chance, gamble, expose, compromise, expose to danger, put in jeopardy; *Slang* put on the spot. —**Ant.** protect, defend, shield, guard, preserve, safeguard.

imperious *adj. She was a poor girl who became imperious after she inherited a fortune:* domineering, overbearing, dictatorial, lordly, despotic, imperial, autocratic, commanding, tyrannical, *Slang* bossy; peremptory, arrogant, haughty. —**Ant.** servile, humble, obsequious, submissive; kindly, gentle.

impermanent *adj. Physical beauty is impermanent and fades with age:* fleeting, temporary, transitory, unenduring, evanescent, ephemeral, fugitive, unstable, passing, not fixed, transient. —**Ant.** permanent, immortal, stable, fixed.

impersonal *adj.* **1.** *These suggestions are impersonal and not directed toward anyone in particular:* general, all-encompassing, applicable to all; impartial, objective, dispassionate, neutral, detached, disinterested; perfunctory, remote, impassive. **2.** *A machine is an impersonal object:* inanimate, inorganic; inhuman, soulless, spiritless, lifeless, dead. —**Ant.** 1 personal, specific. 2 personal, animate; human, alive, vital.

impersonate v. **1.** *Narcotics agents sometimes impersonate drug addicts:* pretend to be, pose as, dress up as, get oneself up as, take the role of, represent oneself as, act the part of, masquerade as, pass oneself off as. **2.** *Bert Lahr impersonated a lion in* The Wizard of Oz: portray, play the part of, imitate, represent, personify, mimic, mime, copy, take off on, ape.

impertinence n. *Talking back amounted to impertinence:* insolence, rudeness, effrontery, forwardness, freshness, backchat, boldness, brass, brazenness, disrespect, incivility, presumption, gall, *Informal* sass, sauce, cheek, lip, guff.

impertinent adj. **1.** *The impertinent youth was sent from the room:* rude, unmannerly, disrespectful, insolent, impudent, presumptuous, arrogant, uncivil, surly, brazen, peremptory, brassy, insulting, discourteous; *Informal* fresh, smarty. **2.** *The judge ruled the testimony impertinent to the case:* irrelevant, extraneous, unimportant, immaterial, not pertinent, extrinsic, not germane, beside the point, unrelated, inappropriate. **—Ant.** 1 polite, respectful, mannerly, deferential. 2 pertinent, relevant, germane, related; important, vital, crucial.

imperturbable adj. *The usually imperturbable man showed signs of fear:* unexcitable, calm, collected, cool, serene, undisturbed, unruffled, dispassionate, unflustered, levelheaded, sedate, composed; unsusceptible, impervious, impassive, unanxious, unfazable; *Slang* unflappable. **—Ant.** perturbable, choleric, touchy.

impervious adj. **1.** *The firemen wore masks that were impervious to the acrid smoke:* impenetrable, impermeable, inaccessible, allowing no passage to, unapproachable; sealed or closed against; invulnerable. **2.** *The beautiful actress seemed impervious to the usual ravages of age:* immune to, protected against; untouched by, unmarked by. **3.** *The stubborn man seemed impervious to reason:* unmoved by, unaffected by, untouched by, invulnerable, closed. **—Ant.** 1 susceptible, vulnerable. 2 open, exposed, susceptible, sensitive, liable, prone.

impetuous adj. **1.** *The impetuous man is constantly falling in love. Inviting everyone to spend the weekend was an impetuous move:* rash, impulsive, hasty, headlong, precipitate; abrupt, unpremeditated, capricious, unexpected. **2.** *The storm approached with impetuous speed:* headlong, violent, precipitate, forcible, rampant, stormy, vehement; relentless, inexorable. **—Ant.** 1 cautious, wary. 2 moderate, leisurely, slow, mild.

impetus n. *Children need an impetus to study:* stimulus, stimulation, spur, moving force, motive, impulse, impulsion, propulsion, boost, drive, momentum, force, start, push, prod; incentive, motivation.

impinge v. *I hate to impinge on your privacy:* encroach, intrude, infringe, trespass, transgress, violate, obtrude.

impious adj. *She sought forgiveness for her impious thoughts:* disrespectful, sacrilegious, blasphemous, irreverent, ungodly, profane, irreligious, godless, iniquitous, iconoclastic, renegade, apostate, immoral, perverted. **—Ant.** devout, reverent, pious, godly.

impish adj. *The impish boy is constantly teasing his brother:* implike, mischievous, puckish, elfin, playfully naughty, sportive, roguish, rascally, prankish.

implacable adj. *It was impossible to negotiate with such an implacable enemy:* irreconcilable, unappeasable, inexorable, unamenable, inflexible, intractable, unpacifiable, uncompromising, relentless, unrelenting. **—Ant.** reconcilable, appeasable, yielding, lenient, relenting, forbearing, indulgent, tolerant, flexible.

implausible adj. *No one fell for that implausible excuse:* unlikely, improbable, incredible, unbelievable, illogical, unreasonable, doubtful, inconceivable, barely conceivable, preposterous, senseless, ridiculous, outrageous, far-fetched. **—Ant.** plausible, credible, believable, reasonable, likely, conceivable, sensible.

implement n. **1.** *What implements are needed for gardening?:* tool, utensil, instrument, device, apparatus, appliance, article, piece; equipment, materials. *—v.* **2.** *Donations are needed to implement our child-care programs:* put into effect, begin, activate, enact, start, set in motion, carry out, bring about, fulfill, achieve, accomplish, realize.

implicate v. *The suspect implicated two others in the robbery:* involve, associate, connect, entangle, ensnare, embroil, entangle; incriminate, inculpate. **—Ant.** dissociate; exclude, eliminate, rule out; extricate, disentangle, untangle, disconnect; acquit, exculpate.

implication n. **1.** *The newsmen discussed the political implications of the war:* ramification, suggestion, outcome, effect, overtone, intimation, insinuation, inference, consequence, significance, connotation, innuendo. **2.** *We were judged guilty by implication:* association, connection, involvement, entanglement.

implicit adj. **1.** *Victory was implicit in the early election returns:* implied, hinted, suggested, tacitly expressed; inferred, deducible, understood. **2.** *The crew had implicit faith in the captain's judgment:* innate, inherent, unquestioning, absolute, complete, profound, certain, resolute, unshakable, unreserved, total, unshakable, steadfast, staunch.

implied adj. *Was his implied meaning that he disliked her, she wondered?:* implicit, alluded to, connoted, hinted, foreshadowed, insinuated, latent, tacit, tacitly assumed, suggested, undeclared, understood, unexpressed, unsaid, unspoken, unuttered, indicated, indicative.

implore v. *The prisoner implored the king for mercy:* beg, beseech, entreat, urge, plead with, importune, obtest, supplicate, go to on bended knee. **—Ant.** order, demand, command.

imply v. **1.** *The doctor's frown implied that something was wrong:* indicate, suggest, hint, insinuate, intimate, connote. **2.** *A fair trial implies an unbiased jury:* presuppose, indicate, bespeak, betoken, presume; signify, mean, denote, evidence.

impolite *adj. It's considered impolite for a man to wear a hat indoors:* discourteous, ill-bred, ungenteel, unmannerly, rude, unrefined, undecorous, unfitting, uncivil, inconsiderate, not polite, disrespectful, impolitic. **—Ant.** polite, courteous, mannerly, civil, respectful, considerate.

impolitic *adj. To bring up the subject was highly impolitic:* tactless, undiplomatic, injudicious, ill-advised, ill-judged, imprudent, inconsiderate, indiscreet, inexpedient, rash, untimely. **—Ant.** diplomatic, discreet, judicious, prudent.

import *n. The import of the situation hit me like a ton of bricks:* significance, importance, meaning, burden, implication, connotation, thrust, moment, ramification, overtones.

importance *n.* **1.** *The importance of loving care to a child cannot be overemphasized:* value, significance, import, weightiness, weight, momentousness, relevance, essentialness, worth, seriousness, consequence, moment. **2.** *The visitor must be one of great importance:* rank, position, influence, esteem, repute, stature, eminence. **—Ant.** 1 unimportance, pettiness, triviality, paltriness, insignificance; nothingness, immateriality. 2 unimportance, insignificance.

important *adj.* **1.** *The speech was an important one in the campaign:* meaningful, consequential, significant, weighty, momentous, great, influential, serious, imperative, distinctive, notable. **2.** *Pablo Picasso was one of the century's most important painters:* leading, foremost, major, preeminent, remarkable, prominent, influential, esteemed; distinctive, original, creative, seminal. **—Ant.** 1 unimportant, inconsequential, inconsiderable, indifferent, insignificant, slight, minor, unnecessary, needless, negligible, nonessential, secondary, trivial. 2 unimportant, insignificant, undistinctive, minor.

imported *adj. He loved imported wines:* foreign, introduced, produced abroad.

importunate *adj. The importunate suitor banged on the door:* insistent, urgent, clamorous, imperative, harassing, pressing, crying, demanding, troublesome.

impose *v.* **1.** *The mayor imposed a curfew until the disturbance was over. Tariffs have been imposed on all foreign goods:* institute, lay on, introduce, place on, set, levy; *Slang* slap on. **2.** *Don't try to impose your wishes on us:* force, inflict, enact, establish, prescribe, dictate, command, apply, peddle, foist, thrust upon; *Informal* palm off. **—Ant.** lift, remove.

imposing *adj. The Empire State Building is an imposing structure:* impressive, majestic, grand, outstanding, striking, massive, monumental, lofty, towering, awe-inspiring, commanding, stately. **—Ant.** unimposing, unimpressive, ordinary, insignificant.

impossible *adj.* **1.** *It's impossible to reach the airport in this traffic:* out of the question, not possible, unable to bring about, unachievable, unattainable; beyond belief, beyond reason, unimaginable, inconceivable. **2.** *That child is impossible! Inflation is an impossible problem:* in-

tractable, stubborn, unyielding, intransigent, unmanageable; intolerable, insufferable, unbearable; unsolvable, insoluble, unanswerable. **—Ant.** 1 possible, likely, probable, feasible.

impostor *n. The professor was denounced as an impostor who had no college degrees:* pretender, deceiver, trickster, impersonator, dissembler, mountebank, fraud, cheat, masquerader, defrauder, duper, bluffer, pettifogger, charlatan, counterfeit, sham, shammer; *Slang* phony, quack, con man, flimflam man.

imposture *n. The imposture began when he pretended to be a bank inspector:* deception, deceit, fraud, swindle, cheat, con, fabrication, hoax, impersonation, masquerade, ploy, pretence, ruse, sham.

impotence *n. The cutback in federal funds leaves the project in a state of impotence:* weakness, powerlessness, ineffectiveness, ineffectuality, inefficacy, helplessness, incapacity, disability, paralysis. **—Ant.** capacity, vigor, ability, power, potency, strength, effectiveness, efficacy.

impotent *adj. Low morale can render an army impotent. His reply was an impotent shrug:* unable to function; ineffective, powerless, frail, feeble, weak, disabled, helpless, paralyzed; feckless, hapless. **—Ant.** potent, powerful, puissant, forceful, vigorous.

impoverished *adj.* **1.** *Money and food were sent to the impoverished drought victims:* poor, destitute, abject, sorely wanting, without material resources, impecunious, indigent, without means, down-and-out, marked by extreme poverty, pauperized, wiped out. **2.** *The land became impoverished from years of irresponsible use:* exhausted, worn out, used up, wanting, depleted, bereft, sterile, effete, barren, drained, unproductive. **—Ant.** 1 rich, affluent, wealthy, well-to-do, well-off. 2 fertile, fecund, fructuous, rich, productive.

impractical *adj. Running a household without a budget is impractical. Why did he marry such an impractical person?:* unrealistic, unwise, unintelligent, lacking foresight, disorganized, loose-ended, helter-skelter; starry-eyed, romantic, quixotic; sloppy, careless. **—Ant.** sound, sensible, down-to-earth, practical, pragmatic, clear-eyed, realistic, systematic.

impregnable *adj. The impregnable mountains protected the tiny village. The prosecution had an impregnable case:* invincible, unattackable, unconquerable, invulnerable, unassailable; powerful, strong, sturdy, mighty, potent. **—Ant.** vulnerable, frail, flimsy, assailable, weak, defenseless.

impregnate *v.* **1.** *Pavlov impregnated the lab animals by means of artificial insemination:* make pregnant, cause to conceive, get with young, cause to bear offspring; fructify, fecundate, inseminate, fertilize. **2.** *Impregnate the cloth with cleaning fluid:* saturate, wet, moisten, soak, imbrue, permeate, drench, steep, infuse, dampen, suffuse, inundate.

impress *v. The painter impressed the critics as an important new talent:* affect, influence, sway, move, reach, stir, touch, excite, strike, capture one's imagination, fix in the mind, seize one's mind or imagination; *Slang* grab, sink in; overwhelm, electrify, bedazzle, overpower.

impression *n.* **1.** *The new principal made a bad impression on the parents:* effect, impact, sensation, feeling; reception, influence, imprint. **2.** *I had the impression that you were ready to leave:* feeling, opinion, belief, understanding, idea, notion, view, hunch, surmise, conviction. **3.** *The suspect's shoes had left deep impressions in the mud:* imprint, impress, mark, outline, track, indentation, stamp, mold, trace, contour.

impressionable *adj. The early years of a person's life are the most impressionable:* easily influenced, receptive, susceptible to impressions, sentient, passible, affective, emotionally affected; suggestible, gullible, vulnerable.

impressive *adj. The Canadian Rockies are an impressive sight:* imposing, thrilling, awe-inspiring, magnificent, moving, soul-stirring, exciting, grand, majestic, striking, august, overpowering, outstanding, memorable, unforgettable. **—Ant.** unimpressive, unimposing, tame, ordinary, unmoving, uninspiring, unmemorable.

imprint *n.* **1.** *She made her imprint on the entire company:* mark, impress, impression, effect, influence, signature, stamp *—v.* **2.** *They imprinted the design on the medal:* print, stamp, impress, engrave, etch, inscribe, mark.

imprison *v. The bank robber was imprisoned for 20 years:* place in prison, confine, incarcerate, jail, place in confinement, shackle, hold captive, restrain, engage, coop up, fence in, impound, lock up, constrain, pen, entomb, immure. **—Ant.** free, release, liberate.

improbable *adj. Rain seems improbable on such a clear day. His explanation was an improbable one:* not probable, unlikely, doubtful, unforeseeable; unreasonable, implausible, illogical. **—Ant.** probable, likely; reasonable, plausible, logical.

impromptu *adj.* **1.** *Our guest delivered an impromptu speech:* improvised, unprepared, extemporaneous, unrehearsed, done on the spur of the moment, unexpected, sudden, offhand, unpremeditated, makeshift, spontaneous, impulsive; *Slang* off the top of one's head, off the cuff. *—adv.* **2.** *Don't be surprised if they ask you to sing impromptu:* without warning, without advance notice, on the spot, with no preparation, off the cuff, extemporaneously, on a moment's notice, right then and there. **—Ant.** 1 considered, planned, prepared, rehearsed, premeditated, deliberate.

improper *adj. Blue jeans would be improper for the class tea:* not suitable, unsuitable, inappropriate, unfit, unseemly, unbefitting, malapropos, irregular, out of place, inapt, unconformable, contrary to accepted standards, unbecoming, indecorous; out of tune, inharmonious, ill-suited, being at odds; indecent, lewd, suggestive, off-color. **—Ant.** proper, right, correct, decorous, decent, fitting, apropos; *French* comme il faut, de rigueur.

impropriety *n. There was no hint of impropriety in his behavior:* incorrectness, mistake, blunder, break, *French* faux pas, gaffe, goof, slip, solecism, unseemliness, vulgarity. **—Ant.** propriety, suitability.

improve *v.* **1.** *Practice will improve your penmanship. The patient improved with the new treatment:* make better, help, make more desirable or attractive, better, correct, repair, enhance, ameliorate, make improvements on; develop beneficially, recuperate, come around, take a turn for the better, gain ground, rally. **2.** *Retired people can improve their lives by doing volunteer work:* enrich, enhance, put to good use, employ to a good or useful end, turn to account, make productive, cultivate, increase the resources of, develop. **—Ant.** 1, 2 impair; worsen; injure, harm, damage, mar.

improvement *n.* **1.** *There has been little improvement in the air pollution problem:* betterment, amelioration, beneficial development, progress, upswing, gain. **2.** *Putting a new roof on the house is a valuable improvement:* enhancement, repair, reconstruction, reclamation, additive, amendment, emendation, reform. **3.** *Electric typewriters are certainly an improvement over the manual type:* refinement, betterment, advance, advancement, step forward.

improvident *adj. The improvident heir quickly spent the family fortune:* thriftless, spendthrift, unparsimonious, unthrifty, extravagant, wasteful, prodigal, lavish; imprudent, shortsighted, reckless, negligent. **—Ant.** provident, cautious, thrifty, penny-wise; prudent, farsighted, foresighted, forehanded.

improvise *v. The singer forgot the words and had to improvise. We improvised bookcases out of orange crates:* perform without preparation; invent offhand, make up, extemporize, come up with, do a makeshift job, throw together, ad-lib; create off the top of one's head; *Slang* wing it.

improvised *adj. He accepted the award with a few improvised remarks:* impromptu, ad-lib, offhand, extemporaneous, extempore, unrehearsed, improvisational, off-the-cuff, spontaneous, devised, contrived, concocted, hatched-up, dreamed-up, originated, invented, spur-of-the-moment, extemporized. **—Ant.** rehearsed, prepared, perfected, polished, memorized.

imprudent *adj. It was imprudent of the doctor to discuss his patients. It's imprudent to drive with those worn tires:* incautious, unwise, rash, inadvisable, indiscreet, ill-advised, ill-considered, thoughtless, injudicious; heedless, untoward, foolish, foolishly impulsive, foolhardy; unthinking, mindless; *Slang* crazy, dopey. **—Ant.** prudent, wise, thoughtful, judicious, cautious, careful, discreet.

impudence *n. The little boy was full of impudence:* impertinence, effrontery, insolence, rudeness, brazenness, boldness, presumption, presumptiveness, sauciness, pertness, flippancy; *Informal* nerve, brass, face, lip. **—Ant.** politeness, courtesy.

impudent *adj. The impudent child antagonized her teachers:* rude, brash, disrespectful, insolent, discourteous, impolite, shameless, saucy, bold, brazen, impertinent, upstart, forward, bumptious; *Informal* nervy, fresh, cheeky, smart-alecky, wise acreish. —**Ant.** respectful, courteous, polite, deferential.

impugn *v. Her opponents impugned her motives as pure self-interest:* attack, assail, oppose, call in question, challenge, question, deny, contradict, negate, asperse, criticize, berate, denounce, *Slang* knock; libel, slander. —**Ant.** defend, support, uphold; back, advocate.

impulse *n.* **1.** *Both of them were creatures of impulse:* instinct, feeling, fancy, bent, spontaneity, disposition, drive, inclination, inspiration, passion. **2.** *An electrical impulse made itself felt:* vibration, stimulus, surge, drive, force, impetus, impulsion, momentum, pressure, propulsion, push, stroke, thrust, vibration, beat.

impulsive *adj.* **1.** *The impulsive force of the wind drove the boat from its mooring:* pushing forward; propelling, propellant, impelling, driving; forceful, forcible. **2.** *The impulsive teenagers jumped into the pool fully clothed. What an impulsive act!:* rash, capricious, whimsical, notional, devil-may-care, unpredictable; spur-of-the-moment, impromptu, offhand, unpremeditated, unplanned, involuntary, spontaneous, impetuous, incautious, extemporaneous. —**Ant.** 1 curbing, arresting, halting. 2 deliberate, premeditated, considered, cautious, prudent, circumspect, calculating, planned, rehearsed, contrived.

impunity *n. The children can pick berries here with complete impunity:* freedom from punishment, freedom from harm; immunity, clearance; absolution, dispensation; privilege, prerogative, exemption. —**Ant.** blame, retribution, hazard; culpability, punishment, loss, harm, danger, risk.

impure *adj.* **1.** *Our lungs are black from breathing impure air:* dirty, unclean, defiled, polluted; filthy, foul, sullied, vitiated, tainted, contaminated, noxious, noisome, unwholesome. **2.** *The addition of an alloy made the gold impure:* adulterated, degraded, debased, devalued, depreciated; unrefined. **3.** *The minister chastised his son for using impure language:* immoral, improper, indecorous, indelicate, coarse, smutty, unchaste, immodest, licentious; smutty, dirty, lustful, lecherous, libidinous, prurient, salacious, obscene, lewd, indecent. —**Ant.** 1–3 pure. 1 clean, unpolluted, untainted, uncontaminated, wholesome. 2 unmixed, unadulterated, unalloyed; perfect. 3 chaste, wholesome, moral, decent, decorous, clean, proper.

impurity *n.* **1.** *The impurity of the water made it unfit to drink:* taintedness, pollution, uncleanness, foulness, contamination, unwholesomeness, defilement, corruption, dirtiness, filth. **2.** *Milk is pasteurized to rid it of impurities:* adulterant, comtaminant, pollutant, foreign matter; adulteration, alloy, taint, dross. —**Ant.** 1 purity, cleanness, wholesomeness.

impute *v. The critics imputed the failure of the play to poor direction:* charge, ascribe, refer,

credit, attribute, assign, set down to, lay at the door of, relate, see as a result.

inability *n. He had an inability to make up his mind:* incapability, incapacity, impotence, incompetence. —**Ant.** ability, competence.

inaccessible *adj. The island is inaccessible except by boat. The papers were inaccessible to the public:* unapproachable, unreachable; beyond access, hopelessly remote, unattainable, unobtainable, not at hand. —**Ant.** accessible, reachable; approachable; attainable, obtainable.

inaccuracy *n.* **1.** *The inaccuracy of the news report was disgraceful:* inexactness, faultiness, incorrectness, fallaciousness, unreliability, imprecision, unclarity. **2.** *The novel was full of historical inaccuracies:* error, mistake, slip, fault, fallacy, blunder; erratum, wrong; *Slang* booboo, goof. —**Ant.** 1 accuracy, correctness, reliability, faultlessness, exactness, precision, preciseness.

inaccurate *adj. The inaccurate description threw the police off the track:* incorrect, faulty, erroneous, full of errors, wrong, false, fallacious, unreliable, imprecise, inexact; wide of the mark; mistaken; not on target, off the track, off, off target. —**Ant.** accurate, correct, true, faithful, flawless, exact.

inactive *adj.* **1.** *Those office machines have been inactive since the computer was installed:* idle, inoperative, inert, quiet, still, dormant, on the shelf, out of service, unused, static. **2.** *The inactive life of the tropics began to bore the couple:* sluggish, idle, torpid, languid, easygoing, somnolent, low-intensity, low-key, indolent, lazy, slothful, dormant, quiet, sedentary, dull, leisurely, otiose, do-nothing. —**Ant.** 1 active, operative, operating, functional. 2 active, bustling, dynamic, busy, industrious, vigorous.

inadequacy *n. She suffered from feelings of inadequacy:* failing, lack, shortcoming, shortage, insufficiency, inadequateness, unfitness, defect, defectiveness, deficiency, deficit, drawback, faultiness, flaw, imperfection, inability, incapacity, incompetence, incompleteness, ineffectiveness, ineptitude, meagreness, paucity, scantiness, skimpiness, weakness, poverty, dearth.

inadequate *adj.* **1.** *The fuel supply is inadequate for a long winter:* not adequate, deficient, insufficient, less than necessary or required, lacking, meager, wanting, below par, short, scanty. **2.** *If you feel inadequate for the job, go out and get some useful experience:* incompetent, incapable, unqualified, unfit, too raw, inept, not up to, imperfect, unfitted. —**Ant.** 1 adequate, sufficient, abundant, enough. 2 adequate, qualified, equal, experienced.

inadmissible *adj. The judge ruled the evidence inadmissable:* unallowable, objectionable, immaterial, improper, inappropriate, irrelevant, unfit, unsuited, unwelcome.

inadvertent *adj. The newspaper apologized for the inadvertent omission:* unintentional, unintended, not on purpose, accidental, fortuitous, unmeant, unthinking, involuntary, unpremeditated. —**Ant.** deliberate, premeditated, intentional, studied, considered, conscious, aware.

inadvisable *adj. It would be inadvisable to approach him while he's still angry:* unwise, injudicious, imprudent, ill-advised, not advisable, impolitic, inopportune, risky, chancy, inexpedient. **—Ant.** advisable, wise, prudent, politic, judicious, opportune, expedient.

inalienable *adj. Freedom of assembly is an inalienable right:* inviolable, unassailable, absolute, unimpeachable, unforfeitable, sacred, sacrosanct, inherent; protected, defended.

inane *adj. The embarrassed man made some inane remark about the weather:* foolish, senseless, vapid, silly, absurd, vacuous, void of intelligence, shallow, pointless, asinine, insipid, nonsensical, empty, ridiculous; unthinking, unintelligent; dumb, stupid, idiotic, meaningless, fatuous; *Informal* dopey. **—Ant.** meaningful, sensible, sound, thoughtful, significant, intelligent, wise, sage, deep, profound.

inanimate *adj.* **1.** *The inanimate object had no name:* lifeless, inorganic, vegetable, mineral, mechanical. **2.** *The audience was virtually inanimate:* spiritless, lifeless, sluggish, inert, spiritless; dead, defunct. **—Ant.** animate, alive; spirited.

inapplicable *adj. Your idea is exciting but inapplicable to our present needs:* not applicable, irrelevant, unsuited, unsuitable, not pertinent, not apt, inappropriate, unfit, incompatible, not germane, inapposite. **—Ant.** applicable, suitable, suited, relevant, germane, pertinent, appropriate, apposite.

inappropriate *adj. Wearing shorts to church is completely inappropriate:* unsuitable, unsuited, improper, out of place, ill-timed, incongruous, unfitting, inapt, incompatible, in bad taste, indecorous, infelicitous, unbecoming, out of fashion. **—Ant.** appropriate, fitting, proper, felicitous, suitable, meet, fit, decorous, becoming.

inapt *adj. It was, she thought, an inapt thing to say:* unsuited, unsuitable, inappropriate, not pertinent. **—Ant.** apt, suitable, appropriate, fit.

inarticulate *adj.* **1.** *The man answered with a strange inarticulate sound:* incoherent, unintelligible, mumbled, babbled; blurred, garbled, indistinct, confused. **2.** *Fear made him totally inarticulate:* incapable of speech, mute, dumb, tongue-tied, speechless, wordless; paralyzed. **3.** *The sophisticated actor was surprisingly inarticulate in person:* hesitant in speech, uncommunicative, poorly spoken, inexpressive. **—Ant.** 1 articulate, clear, intelligible, coherent, distinct. 2 articulate. 3 expressive, glib, verbal, voluble.

inattentive *adj. The singer was offended by the inattentive audience. An inattentive driver is a menace:* showing no interest; not attentive, careless, negligent, thoughtless, unmindful, unobservant, heedless, absentminded, distracted, forgetful, unaware, daydreaming. **—Ant.** attentive, heedful; mindful, careful, aware.

inaugurate *v.* **1.** *The city inaugurated the clean-air campaign with a bicycle parade:* begin formally, launch, set in action, undertake, initiate, institute, embark upon, usher in, set up, start, *Informal* kick off. **2.** *The United States inaugurates its President in January:* induct for-

mally into office, invest with office; induct, instate, install ceremoniously. **—Ant.** 1 terminate, end, conclude, finish.

inauguration *n. The inauguration of the president passed without incident:* inaugural, installation, investiture, commencement, induction, initiation, institution, launching, opening, setting up.

inauspicious *adj. I'm afraid you picked an inauspicious moment to arrive:* ill-chosen, badly timed, ill-omened, unpropitious, unfavorable, unlucky, unpromising, unfortunate, infelicitous, unlucky, disastrous. **—Ant.** auspicious, favorable, propitious, fortunate, lucky, happy, providential, well-timed, hopeful, promising.

inborn *adj. Children seem to have an inborn love for music:* inherent, innate, inbred, congenital, constitutional, natural, native, intuitive, instinctive, inherited, intrinsic; basic, fundamental. **—Ant.** acquired, nurtured, learned, conditioned, taught, inculcated.

inbred *adj. The child impressed the guests with her inbred grace and charm:* innate, natural, ingrained, inherent, congenital, hereditary, deepseated, deep-rooted, inborn, intrinsic, indwelling, constitutional; instinctive, instinctual, primal. **—Ant.** superimposed, acquired, learned, extraneous.

incalculable *adj.* **1.** *The number of galaxies in the universe is incalculable:* beyond counting or calculation, too great to be calculated, too numerous to count, inestimable, countless, measureless, immeasurable, uncountable, incomputable, innumerable, infinite. **2.** *The future is incalculable:* unknowable in advance, unforeseeable, uncertain, dubious, unpredictable. **—Ant.** 1 calculable, estimable, measurable, countable, computable; limited, finite. 2 calculable, predictable, certain, foreseeable, knowable.

incandescent *adj.* **1.** *As electrical force increased, the wire became incandescent:* glowingly hot, luminously hot, white-hot; brilliant, blindingly bright. **2.** *The language of the play was incandescent. The young man has an incandescent charm:* brilliant, electrifying, galvanic, electric; dynamic, magnetic, scintillating, high-powered, glowing, radiant.

incantation *n. Incantations were used to summon the spirits of the dead warriors:* charm, spell, sorcery, magic, witchcraft, voodoo, black magic, wizardry, necromancy; invocation, chant, conjuration; *Slang* hocus-pocus, mumbojumbo, abracadabra; hex, jinx.

incapable *adj.* **1.** *Incapable management ruined the company:* unskilled, inept, incompetent, inferior, unfit, unqualified, untrained, inadequate, inefficient, ineffective. **2.** *He would be incapable of committing such a cruel deed:* lacking the mettle for, unable, powerless, helpless, impotent. **—Ant.** 1, 2 capable, able. 1 competent, qualified; efficient, effective, skilled.

incapacitate *v. A bad back incapacitated the athlete for the season:* disable, render incapable, undo, make powerless, make unfit; cripple, maim, handicap, paralyze, enfeeble, lay up, put out of action; disqualify; *Informal* sideline.

incarcerate v. Soviet authorities often incarcerate political offenders in mental institutions: imprison, jail, confine, lock up, impound, immure, intern, commit; pen, restrain, Slang coop up. —**Ant.** free, release, liberate.

incarnate adj. She thought he was the devil incarnate: embodied, physical, bodily, tangible, materialized, human, personified, manifested, real, substantiated.

incautious adj. It was an incautious remark that nearly cost him his job: rash, brash, reckless, headstrong, impetuous, hotheaded; imprudent, thoughtless, unwary, injudicious, unthinking, careless, heedless, over-hasty. —**Ant.** calm, cool; wary, cautious; prudent, careful.

incendiary adj. 1. They disarmed the incendiary device: inflammatory, explosive; provocative, rabble-rousing, seditious, subversive. —n. 2. arsonist, pyromaniac, Informal firebug.

incense v. The unruly class incensed the teacher: enrage, inflame, anger, make angry, infuriate, madden, make indignant, provoke, Informal burn up.

incentive n. Profit sharing is a good incentive for employees: motivation, spur, motive, encouragement, stimulus, inducement, lure, enticement, Informal come-on; inspiration. —**Ant.** deterrent, prohibition, warning, dissuasion.

inception n. Memorial Day marks the inception of summer for most people: commencement, beginning, origin, start, birth, onset, arrival, inauguration; outset, debut. —**Ant.** termination, end, ending, completion, finish, finishing, conclusion.

incessant adj. Her incessant complaining is tiresome to everyone: constant, ceaseless, continuous, continual, unceasing, unremitting, unending, perpetual, everlasting, persistent, interminable, unbroken, unrelenting, uninterrupted. —**Ant.** intermittent, periodic, sporadic, occasional; rare, infrequent.

inchoate adj. The architect began with a vague, inchoate design and then worked out the details: beginning, budding, incipient, commencing, embryonic, nascent; shapeless, formless, unformed, unshaped, amorphous; unorganized, uncohesive, disjointed, disconnected. —**Ant.** formed, shaped; finished, completed.

incidence n. There's now a much lower incidence of childhood diseases than in bygone times: frequency, rate, occurrence, commonness, routineness; scope, range, extent; occasion, happening, phenomenon.

incident n. 1. The incident has long since been forgotten: particular event, episode, affair, occasion, occurrence, happening; small disturbance, scene, contretemps, clash. —adj. 2. The problems incident to starting a new business are numerous: occurring naturally, related, arising from, happening in the course of, going along with, incidental, connected with, likely to happen.

incidental adj. 1. The incidental costs of the car added up to a large sum: secondary, extraneous, accessory, minor, subordinate; unexpected, unlooked-for. —n. 2. **incidentals** When you are traveling, be sure to take along a small valise for incidentals: minor items; accessories, appurtenances, extras; odds and ends, minutiae. —**Ant.** 1 essential, fundamental, basic.

incidentally adv. Incidentally, the Joneses may come along: by the way; in passing, connected with that, by the by, apart from the main subject, apropos, speaking of that, parenthetically, while we're on the subject.

incipient adj. An incipient sore throat kept the child home. She is an incipient actress: beginning, becoming apparent; nascent, inchoate, half-formed, rudimentary, developing; barely starting; promising, budding, embryonic, fledgling. —**Ant.** realized, achieved, finished, full-blown; accomplished.

incisive adj. 1. The incisive command stopped the dog in its tracks: keen, sharp, biting, crisp, brisk, curt, cutting, piercing, acute, mordant, trenchant, express, summary. 2. Will Rogers was known for his incisive humor: penetrating, analytic, acute, sharp, precise; shrewd, well-aimed, perceptive, probing, penetrating, trenchant, intelligent, sharp.

incite v. The dictator's cruel decree incited the people to open rebellion: rouse, activate, stimulate, actuate, induce, prod, arouse, urge on, inflame, provoke, foment, instigate, excite, agitate, Slang egg on; stir, stir up, fire up, drive, impel, goad, prompt.

incivility n. She apologized to the audience for her incivility: rudeness, disrespect, discourtesy, impoliteness, misbehavior; coarseness, impudence, indecorum, boorishness, uncouthness, tactlessness, vulgarity, barbarism. —**Ant.** decorum, propriety, seemliness, mannerliness.

inclement adj. Inclement weather forced postponement of the picnic: stormy, violent, rough, harsh, bitter, raw, severe, tempestuous, foul, nasty. —**Ant.** clement, mild.

inclination n. 1. The motor has an inclination to race. People have an inclination to loaf in hot weather: tendency, propensity, penchant, leaning, proneness, predilection, proclivity, preference, disposition, predisposition; fondness, bent, liking. 2. The boss okayed the plan with an inclination of the head: nod, bow, bend, bending, lowering, inclining. 3. There is a steep inclination in the road ahead: slant, rise, dip, slope, acclivity, sloping, rake, pitch, hill, grade. —**Ant.** 1 dislike, antipathy, disinclination.

incline v. 1. The whole family inclines to rise early: tend, have a mind to, have a preference, prefer, enjoy, like, lean toward. 2. Older people incline to slow down: tend, be apt, be likely, have a propensity, seem, wont. 3. The roof inclines over the porch: slope, slant, tilt, rake, decline, cant, pitch, lean. 4. Incline your body from the waist when you bow: bend forward, lean, bend, tilt, bow. —n. 5. The house is perched on an incline: slope, hill, gradient, pitch, cant, inclined plane, acclivity. —**Ant.** 1 dislike, hate, abhor, be disinclined.

include v. The meal includes appetizer, main

course, dessert, and coffee: contain, comprise, embrace, enfold, cover, take in, incorporate, encompass, comprehend, involve, entail, subsume. —**Ant.** exclude, preclude; eliminate, rule out, omit, leave out, forget.

inclusion *n. His inclusion in the group aroused comment:* incorporation, admittance, involvement, insertion. —**Ant.** exclusion, exception, rejection, omission.

inclusive *adj. All prices quoted are inclusive of tax:* including, comprising, incorporating, embracing, comprehending, taking in, encircling, surrounding; comprehensive, overall, general, sweeping, encyclopedic, all-encompassing.

incognito *adj. To escape arrest, he tried to leave the country incognito:* unidentified, unnamed, disguised, concealed, unrevealed, undisclosed, unacknowledged, nameless, unknown, uncredited; protected. —**Ant.** well-known, famous; attributed, credited.

incoherent *adj. His account of the robbery was hysterical and incoherent:* disjointed, unintelligible, rambling, confused, bewildering, irrational, illogical, inconsistent, unclear, nonsensical, muddled. —**Ant.** coherent, intelligible, logical, connected, rational, consistent.

income *n. Mother receives a nice income from stock dividends:* revenue, earnings, livelihood, means, wages, salary, emolument. —**Ant.** expense, disbursement, outlay.

incomparable *adj. Have you seen the incomparable beauty of Lake Louise?:* peerless, matchless, unequaled, unrivaled, unapproachable, inimitable, superlative, transcendent, beyond compare. —**Ant.** ordinary, fair, mediocre, second-rate, average, inferior, run-of-the-mill.

incompatible *adj.* **1.** *The partners were too incompatible to stay in business together:* inharmonious, uncongenial, antagonistic, lacking rapport, at variance, at odds, mismatched, clashing, disagreeing. **2.** *That raucous voice is incompatible with her fragile appearance:* inconsistent, contrary, incongruous, jarring, discordant, at odds, contradictory, unsuited, not going well together, inappropriate. —**Ant.** compatible, accordant, consonant, consistent, congenial; harmonizing, harmonious, agreeing, appropriate.

incompetent *adj. The incompetent typist had to redo the letter five times:* inept, untrained, unskilled, lacking ability, ineffectual, ineffective, inefficient, unfit, incapable, inexpert, unqualified. —**Ant.** competent, apt, expert, efficient.

incomplete *adj. My set of china is still incomplete:* unfinished, lacking a part, partial, not total, containing omissions, broken, fragmentary; wanting, defective, deficient. —**Ant.** complete, finished, whole, unbroken.

incomprehensible *adj. Physics is incomprehensible to me:* baffling, bewildering, beyond understanding, ungraspable, beyond comprehension, befuddling, unintelligible, confusing, inscrutable, obscure, unfathomable, abstruse, impenetrable. —**Ant.** comprehensible, understandable, clear, plain, intelligible.

inconceivable *adj. It's inconceivable that peo-*

ple could be starving in such a wealthy country: unthinkable, unbelievable, incredible, beyond belief, contrary to reason or belief; highly unlikely, unimaginable, strange, improbable, unlikely, impossible to comprehend. —**Ant.** conceivable, believable, credible, plausible, reasonable, likely, imaginable, probable, comprehensible.

inconclusive *adj. The committee's inconclusive findings left the case up in the air:* undetermined, indeterminate, unresolved, unsettled, indefinite, open, up in the air, eluding settlement, indecisive, not definite, still doubtful, unconvincing. —**Ant.** conclusive, decisive, definite.

incongruous *adj.* **1.** *Bathing suits look incongruous on a ski slope:* inappropriate, odd, outlandish, out of keeping, out of place, unsuitable, not harmonious, *Slang* far-out. **2.** *The witness's incongruous testimony damaged his credibility:* conflicting, contrary, at variance, incompatible, contradictory, inconsistent, irreconcilable, discrepant, disagreeing. —**Ant.** 1 congruous, fitting, suitable, appropriate, consonant, consistent, accordant, agreeing, harmonious, becoming.

inconsequential *adj. The matter is too inconsequential to worry about:* trivial, trifling, of no moment, valueless, slight, unimportant, of no consequence, insignificant, negligible, nugatory, meaningless, piddling, petty, picayune. —**Ant.** consequential, important, momentous, significant, meaningful, crucial.

inconsiderate *adj. It was inconsiderate of him to play the music so loud:* thoughtless, rude, uncivil, impolite, insensitive, uncaring, unkind, uncharitable, disregardful, ungracious; rash, unthinking, remiss, negligent, careless, tactless, lacking regard. —**Ant.** considerate, thoughtful; kind; polite.

inconsistent *adj.* **1.** *His dissolute life is inconsistent with his puritan upbringing:* incompatible, dissonant, inharmonious, inaccordant, inconsonant, discrepant, contrary, contradictory, not in agreement, incongruous, irreconcilable. **2.** *An inconsistent parent can make a child feel insecure:* erratic, unstable, constantly changing, wayward, inconstant, changeable; fickle, notional, unpredictable, irresolute, variable, vacillating, changeful. —**Ant.** 1 consistent, consonant, coherent, compatible, congruous; according or accordant, agreeing, tallying, jibing, corresponding or correspondent, suitable. 2 consistent, unchangeable; stable, reliable; constant, steady.

inconsolable *adj. The inconsolable couple were unable to return to work:* heartsick, heartbroken, brokenhearted, comfortless, dejected, desolate, despairing, disconsolate.

inconspicuous *adj. The star preferred to remain inconspicuous by wearing a very simple outfit:* unnoticed, unnoticeable, unobtrusive, unostentatious, attracting little attention, not outstanding, not egregious; unassuming, modest; unapparent, dim, muted, faint. —**Ant.** conspicuous, noticeable; striking, prominent, egregious.

inconstant adj. As a spouse, he was notoriously inconstant: changeable, fickle, inconsistent, variable, moody, capricious, vacillating, wavering, mercurial, volatile, unsettled, unstable, mutable, uncertain. —**Ant.** constant, steady, invariant, settled, staid.

incontrovertible adj. The eyewitness testimony was incontrovertible: undeniable, indisputable, irrefutable, apodictic, beyond question, unquestionable, established, past dispute, unarguable. —**Ant.** disputable, questionable, debatable.

inconvenient adj. It's inconvenient to have to work on the weekend: unhandy, inopportune, untimely, bothersome, troublesome, tiresome, awkward, annoying; burdensome, distressing. —**Ant.** convenient, opportune, timely; advantageous, helpful.

incorporate v. The committee incorporated the investigator's findings in its report: include, embody, work in, consolidate, fuse, amalgamate, introduce into, assimilate.

incorporeal adj. The people prayed to their incorporeal gods: bodiless, unfleshly, spiritual, insubstantial, immaterial; unworldly, unearthly; ghostly, phantom, unreal, intangible, supernatural, occult, disembodied. —**Ant.** corporeal, bodied, solid, tangible, material.

incorrect adj. The article was filled with incorrect statements: wrong, inexact, erroneous, untrue, false, mistaken, false, fallacious, inaccurate. —**Ant.** correct, right, accurate, true.

incorrigible adj. The incorrigible boy was in and out of reform school for years: uncontrollable, unmanageable, unruly, beyond saving, hopeless, past changing, beyond help, intractable; delinquent, hardened, hard-core, thoroughly bad. —**Ant.** correctable, manageable, tractable, amenable.

incorruptible adj. The incorruptible policeman refused even a free cup of coffee: pure, righteous, upright, honest, reliable, beyond corruption, irreproachable, above temptation, faultless, trustworthy, unbribable. —**Ant.** corruptible, bribable, dishonest, unreliable.

increase v. 1. Travel increases one's knowledge of the world: make greater or larger, enlarge, expand, enrich, add to, augment, advance, enhance. 2. The membership increased 50 percent: enlarge, become larger, swell, expand, burgeon, grow, wax, become more numerous, multiply. —**Ant.** decrease, diminish, lessen, reduce, abate, dwindle; shorten, abridge, abbreviate, curtail, retrench; contract, condense, shrink, deflate, decline, lower.

increasingly adv. They found it increasingly difficult to concentrate: progressively, more, with acceleration.

incredible adj. The tiny woman had an incredible appetite: unbelievable, remarkable, unimaginable, awesome, hardly credible, inconceivable, preposterous, absurd, farfetched, amazing, astounding, astonishing, extraordinary. —**Ant.** credible, believable, unremarkable; ordinary, usual, common.

incredulous adj. The judge was incredulous when the defendant told his bizarre alibi. She gave me an incredulous glance: dubious, skeptical, unwilling to believe, not believing, disbelieving, distrustful, doubtful, suspicious; showing disbelief. —**Ant.** credulous, gullible, believing, trustful, trusting.

increment n. There will be a $100 increment in rent beginning next month: increase, gain, benefit, profit, addition, augmentation, growth, rise, supplement, accumulation, enlargement, accretion, raise, appreciation, proliferation.

inculcate v. She was determined to inculcate some basic values in her children: instill, impart, infuse, implant, infix, impress, imbue, teach, instruct, indoctrinate, enlighten; impress upon the mind, hammer into one's head, inscribe in the memory, etch indelibly in the mind; condition, brainwash.

inculpate v. He was inculpated for several crimes: charge, blame, accuse, incriminate, censure, impeach. —**Ant.** exonerate.

incur v. Do not incur unnecessary debts. The naughty child incurred his nanny's wrath: contract, become liable for, bring into being, assume, bring on, acquire, fall into, become subject to; arouse, incite, stir up, involve, provoke, bring out, bring on oneself.

incurable adj. Rabies is an acute and in many cases incurable disease. Jim's an incurable optimist: beyond cure, having no remedy, irremediable, cureless, uncorrectable; incorrigible, relentless, ceaseless, unflagging, inveterate, dyed-in-the-wool, hopeless. —**Ant.** curable, correctable, remediable.

incursion n. The enemy made a second incursion over neighboring borders: invasion, foray, sortie, attack; assault, encroachment, impingement, infiltration, raid; forcible entering, inroad, push; advance forward or into.

indebted adj. 1. The restaurant is heavily indebted to the bank: under obligation, in debt, burdened with debt; financially burdened; chargeable, accountable. 2. We are indebted to you for your loyal support: obligated, bound, beholden, bounden; deeply appreciative, grateful, full of thanks, thankful. —**Ant.** 1 unobligated, free and clear. 2 unobligated, unbeholden, ungrateful, unthankful.

indecency n. The dance was full of indecency: immodesty, impurity, crudity, drunkenness, grossness, indelicacy, lewdness, licentiousness, obscenity, pornography, smuttiness; vulgarity, inappropriateness, impropriety. —**Ant.** decency, modesty, purity, decorum, delicacy, propriety, seemliness.

indecent adj. 1. Talking business at the funeral seemed indecent: unseemly, improper, lacking common decency, indiscreet, unbecoming, rude, ignoble, ill-bred, uncivil, offensive, vulgar, in bad taste. 2. The indecent film was banned: immoral, immodest, indecorous, obscene, pornographic, lewd, licentious, bawdy, salacious; arousing lust, prurient, unwholesome, dirty, filthy, blue, smutty. —**Ant.** 1, 2 decent. 1 proper, seemly, becoming, tasteful, appropriate; polite, civil. 2 chaste, pure, modest, virtuous, moral, ethical; high-toned, elegant, decorous, tasteful.

indecisive *adj.* **1.** *The result of the race was indecisive, and we had to run it again:* not decisive, inconclusive, unsettled, indeterminate, doubtful, dubious, disputable, debatable; unclear, confusing. **2.** *An indecisive man could never run the country:* irresolute, vacillating, hesitant, hesitating, wavering, weak, mercurial, halfhearted, uncertain, blowing hot and cold, wishy-washy. **—Ant.** 1 decisive, conclusive, firm, clear; indisputable, undebatable, certain. 2 decisive, resolute, certain.

indecorous *adj.* *The low-cut dress seemed indecorous for church. We were shocked by her indecorous behavior:* immodest, unbecoming, unseemly, unfitting, improper, unsuitable, inappropriate, not in good taste; ill-bred, low-class, gross; wicked, sinful; reprehensible, blameworthy. **—Ant.** decorous, decent, nice, demure; ceremonious, formal, conventional, standard, proper, suitable.

indeed *adv.* *The garden is indeed beautiful:* in fact, truly, in reality, without question, certainly, for sure, veritably, in truth, undeniably, really, to be sure, with certainty, positively, strictly speaking, joking apart, as a matter of fact, to tell the truth, to be honest, in point of fact, actually, coming right down to it.

indefatigable *adj.* *The new man is an indefatigable worker and will go far:* tireless, inexhaustible, persevering, persistent, diligent, dogged, energetic, sedulous, unfaltering, unflagging, untiring, unwearying, staunch.

indefensible *adj.* **1.** *The indefensible village fell in a matter of hours:* unable to withstand attack, vulnerable, defenseless; open to attack, unprotected, pregnable, vincible. **2.** *Her purchase of a mink coat was an indefensible waste of money:* inexcusable, beyond justification, unjustifiable, unspeakable, unpardonable, without reason or rationale; open to criticism, improper, untenable. **—Ant.** 1 defensible, invincible, invulnerable, protected. 2 defensible, justifiable, excusable, pardonable, reasonable, rational, tenable.

indefinite *adj.* **1.** *The store will be closed for an indefinite period:* unspecified, having no fixed limit, undetermined, indeterminate, unknown, inexact, inexplicit; illimitable, measureless, limitless. **2.** *I gave him an indefinite answer:* unsettled, uncertain, indistinct, vague; not clearly defined, dim, ill-defined, amorphous, indecisive, doubtful, tentative, obscure, ambiguous, unsure. **—Ant.** 1 definite, clear-cut, certain, limited, known, specific. 2 definite, certain, settled, sure, unambiguous.

indefinitely *adv.* *They could carry on indefinitely:* continually, endlessly, forever, limitlessly.

indelible *adj.* *The book left an indelible impression on me. The ink made an indelible stain:* vivid, permanent, unforgettable, lasting, memorable; permanently fixed, fast, ineradicable, unerasable, unremovable, incapable of being deleted or wiped out, ingrained, deep-dyed.

indelicate *adj.* **1.** *His indelicate manners are the result of a rough upbringing:* coarse, crude,

rude, unrefined, unbecoming; clumsy, awkward. **2.** *That was an indelicate story to tell in mixed company:* offensive, lacking good taste, indiscreet, unseemly, unrefined; off-color, immodest, crude, indecent, vulgar, suggestive, indecorous, lewd, risqué, broad, obscene, coarse, gross, improper. **—Ant.** 1 delicate, refined, seemly, decorous, smooth, polite, polished. 2 decent, chaste, refined, discreet, proper.

indemnify *v.* *The company indemnified him for the theft of his car:* reimburse, repay, pay back, compensate, requite, remunerate, recompense, make right, make restitution, make up for, make good, rectify, make amends, satisfy, atone.

indentation *n.* **1.** *You can identify some trees by the indentations of the leaves. The map shows numerous indentations along the shoreline:* cut, notch, incision, cavity, furrow, score; recess, concavity, niche, pocket, bay, inset. **2.** *High heels made indentations in the linoleum:* dent, pit, gouge, depression, nick. **—Ant.** bump, protuberance, projection, prominence.

independence *n.* *The American colonies won their independence from England:* emancipation, liberty, freedom, self-determination, self-government, freedom from control, sovereignty, self-reliance, liberation, autonomy. **—Ant.** dependence; subordination, subjection; servitude, slavery, bondage; reliance, dependency.

independent *adj.* **1.** *Children should be encouraged to be independent thinkers:* self-reliant, uncontrolled, on one's own, autonomous, free, self-directing, individualistic, uncoerced; unconstrained, free from the control or influence of others. **2.** *The United States became an independent country in 1776:* free, self-governing, autonomous; self-determining, sovereign. **3.** *The medical college is independent of the university:* separate, not joined to or associated with, unattached to, distinct from, exclusive, apart from, unconnected with, unallied. **4.** *The inheritance made him independent for life:* solvent, well-to-do, well-off, in easy circumstances, well-fixed, affluent, *Informal* well-heeled. **—Ant.** 1 dependent; influenced, controlled, directed; subordinate, subject, tributary, subservient, servile, slavish, subject, attached, interrelated. 4 dependent, reliant, beholden, attached.

independently *adv.* *They arrived at their conclusions independently:* individually, separately, singly, solo, unaided, alone, apart, autonomously, by oneself, severally.

indescribable *adj.* *The artistry of Michelangelo's* Pietà *is indescribable:* beyond description, inexpressible, beyond words, ineffable, beggaring description; indefinable; overwhelming, unutterable.

indestructible *adj.* *Toys for toddlers should be as indestructible as possible:* unbreakable, damage-resistant, infrangible, enduring, permanent, everlasting, imperishable, incapable of being destroyed. **—Ant.** destructible, perishable, breakable, unenduring, fragile, frangible.

indeterminate *adj.* *The acting superintendent*

will serve for an indeterminate time: unspecified, undetermined, unstipulated, uncertain, unfixed in extent or amount, unclear, obscure, not clear, unresolved, vague, undefined; ambiguous, problematic, perplexing, indefinite. —**Ant.** specified, precise, definite, clear, certain, determined, fixed, defined.

index *n.* **1.** *The poems are given in the index by author:* alphabetical list, catalog, register, glossary. **2.** *Overeating is often an index of emotional stress:* sign, token, indication, indicator, symptom, clue, evidence, manifestation, proof, mark.

indicate *v.* **1.** *The patient's pallor indicates anemia:* be a sign of, be symptomatic of, show, designate, denote, imply, point to, suggest; evince, bespeak, reveal, symbolize, signify, stand for, mean, represent. **2.** *Indicate where the pain is with your finger:* point out, point to, specify, direct attention to. **3.** *A barometer indicates air pressure:* show, make known, register, reveal, tell, establish, record.

indication *n.* *There was no indication this morning that it would rain:* sign, hint, intimation, signal, manifestation, token, warning, evidence, mark, clue, suggestion, foretoken, hint, symptom, gesture, demonstration; portent, augury, omen, boding, foreboding, premonition, presage; signifying, telling, indicating, designation, mention, showing, pointing.

indicative *adj.* *Fever may be indicative of infection:* suggestive, indicatory, characteristic, evidential, symptomatical, symptomatic, expressive, significant, emblematic, symbolic, representative, denotative, connotative, designative.

indict *v.* *The grand jury indicted him for embezzlement:* arraign, accuse, charge, inculpate, criminate, impute, bring to justice, cite, impeach, prosecute; find an indictment against, prefer charges, have up, pull up, bring up.

indifference *n.* **1.** *He would have preferred anger to her cold indifference:* unconcern, absence of feeling, lack of interest, disinterest, neglect, inattention, impassiveness, impassivity, nonchalance, aloofness, carelessness, negligence, insensibility, insensitivity, disdain, insouciance, apathy, coldness. **2.** *Religion is a matter of indifference to many of today's youth:* unimportance, triviality, no import, insignificance, paltriness, inconsiderableness. —**Ant.** 1 concern, warmth, sensibility; attention, interest, eagerness, caring. 2 importance, magnitude, significance, greatness.

indifferent *adj.* **1.** *The writer was indifferent to criticism, good or bad:* unconcerned, not caring, insensible, without interest, impervious, uninterested, insusceptible, detached, unmindful, impassive, unmoved, insouciant, apathetic, nonchalant, cool, aloof. **2.** *The actor's indifferent performance left the audience cold:* perfunctory, mediocre, not very good, undistinguished, uninspired, ordinary, so-so, rote, commonplace, neither good nor bad, medium, middling, fair, modest, moderate, passable, average, betwixt and between; falling short of any standard of excellence, second-rate, rather poor. —**Ant.** 1

avid, eager, keen, agog; interested, sensitive, susceptible, caring, sympathetic, responsive, compassionate, enthusiastic. 2 choice, notable, remarkable, exceptional, rare, first-class, superior, excellent, fine.

indigenous *adj.* *Cotton is indigenous to the southern United States:* native, growing naturally, aboriginal, originating in, characteristic of, endemic, homebred, home-grown, domestic, autochthonous. —**Ant.** naturalized; exotic; foreign, alien, extraneous, imported.

indigent *adj.* *Many indigent people receive government aid:* needy, destitute, in want, lacking the necessities of life, poor, in need, pinched, poverty-stricken, impoverished, penniless, without resources, badly off, moneyless, without food and clothing; *Informal* unable to keep the wolf from the door, hard-up. —**Ant.** wealthy, moneyed, rich, affluent, comfortable, solvent, flush.

indigestion *n.* *The stew gave her indigestion:* dyspepsia, acid indigestion, heartburn, acidosis, gas, gaseous stomach, nausea, upset stomach.

indignant *adj.* *The actress was indignant at the columnist's personal questions:* incensed, offended, angry, mad, infuriated, displeased, piqued, peeved, resentful, irate, provoked, riled, wrathful, fuming; *Informal* miffed, huffy, put off, put out, worked up, sore, on one's high horse, steaming, wrought up. —**Ant.** pleased, delighted.

indignation *n.* *Reports of child abuse aroused public indignation:* resentment, displeasure, righteous anger, annoyance, vexation, dismay, irritation, pique, umbrage, ire, choler, huff, animus, rage, wrath, fury, uproar. —**Ant.** calm, pleasure, serenity, composure, complacency, approval.

indignity *n.* *The prisoners suffered many indignities:* abuse, insult, mistreatment, injury to dignity, outrage, affront, insult to one's self-respect, humiliation, injustice, contemptuous treatment, offense, dishonor, discourtesy, rudeness, slur, slight, *Informal* slap in the face. —**Ant.** dignity, honor, respect, deference, compliment, courtesy.

indirect *adj.* **1.** *We took a long, indirect route to the beach:* devious, roundabout, winding, rambling, circuitous, meandering, oblique, zigzag, digressive, crooked, tortuous. **2.** *The job offer was an indirect outcome of the meeting:* incidental, unintentional, unintended; ancillary, secondary, derivative; distant, remote. **3.** *The politician's indirect answers angered the press:* evasive, not straightforward, discursive, oblique, rambling, digressive, circuitous, roundabout, vague, hedging. —**Ant.** 1 direct, straight. 2 direct, connected, primary. 3 direct, forthright, straightforward.

indiscreet *adj.* *Repeating a confidence is indiscreet:* imprudent, incautious, injudicious, uncalled-for, improvident, unseemly, uncircumspect, unbefitting, foolhardy, foolish, impolitic, tasteless, ill-judged, thoughtless, inconsiderate, unwise, careless, tactless, untactful, undiplomatic. —**Ant.** discreet, judicious, prudent, circumspect, cautious, politic, tactful.

indiscriminate adj. **1.** The boy's indiscriminate choice of friends got him into trouble: promiscuous, undiscriminating, unchoosy, random, unselective, undistinguishing, choosing at random, haphazard, hit-or-miss, without rhyme or reason. **2.** An indiscriminate collection of furniture made the room look cluttered: haphazard, random, unsystematic, disorganized, slapdash, jumbled, thrown together, motley, mongrel, confused, aimless, chaotic; Informal higgledy-piggledy, hodgepodge.

indispensable adj. A good director is indispensable for a successful film: essential, crucial, vital, imperative, absolutely necessary, needed, required, requisite, not dispensable, needful, obligatory, mandatory, compulsory; fundamental, basic. —**Ant.** dispensable, expendable, disposable, unnecessary, nonessential.

indisposed adj. **1.** One of the guests was indisposed with a fever and couldn't come: ailing, sickly, ill, laid up, slightly sick, taken ill, not oneself, unwell, bedridden, Informal under the weather. **2.** She was indisposed to accept the dull job: averse, not disposed, reluctant, hesitant, disinclined, unwilling, not predisposed, loath, not in favor of, opposed. —**Ant.** 1 healthy, hardy, hale, well, hearty, sound. 2 disposed, eager, avid, keen, anxious, willing, desirous, inclined.

indisputable adj. By age 40 he was the indisputable leader of his profession: undeniable, irrefutable, incontestable, indubitable, incontrovertible, unassailable, unquestionable, evident, obvious, unmistakable, apparent, definite, conclusive, assured, beyond a shadow of doubt. —**Ant.** dubious, uncertain, questionable, doubtful, iffy.

indistinct adj. The radio program was indistinct because of the static. The point of the book was indistinct: muffled, vague, not distinct, unintelligible, unclear, inaudible, weak, faint, not clearly defined, not clearly perceptible; obscure, ill-defined, indefinite, cloudy, murky, shadowy, clouded, out of focus, dim, nebulous, blurred, muddy; indecipherable, illegible; uncertain, mysterious, enigmatic, puzzling, hidden, indeterminate, ambiguous; incomprehensible, incoherent, confused. —**Ant.** distinct, intelligible, comprehensible, clear, audible, articulate, well-defined, perceptible, definite.

indistinguishable adj. One twin is indistinguishable from the other. The sign was indistinguishable in the fog: not differentiable, identical with, not distinguishable; a carbon copy of, the perfect likeness of, Informal the spitting image of; indiscernible, unclear, imperceptible, unobservable, unnoticeable, inconspicuous, not capable of being made out, invisible, unapparent, indistinct, obscure. —**Ant.** distinguishable, differentiable; separate, unidentical, different; discernible, perceptible, observable, noticeable, visible, apparent, distinct, clear.

individual adj. **1.** Students can apply for individual tutoring: special, especial, separate, particular, exclusive, personal, private, independent, singular, one's own, specific, exclusive, personalized. **2.** The model has an individual way of dressing: special, distinctive, unusual, original, personal, different, uncommon, unconventional, singular, characteristic, distinct, unique. —n. **3.** Everyone should be recognized as an individual: person, somebody, single human being, self-determined being, distinct person, unique entity, autonomous being. —**Ant.** 1 general, universal, group, collective, common. 2 conventional, ordinary, common, indistinct.

individuality n. The actor's individuality makes him interesting: independent nature, uniqueness, distinction, distinctiveness, particularity, singularity; unique character, specialness, cachet.

indoctrinate v. The sergeant thoroughly indoctrinated the new recruits in military routine: teach, inculcate, instruct in a doctrine, propagandize, brainwash, initiate, train, school, educate, tutor, brief, familiarize with, drill, give instruction to, infuse, instill, implant.

indolent adj. The indolent boy was fired: lazy, slothful, habitually idle, inactive, easygoing, shiftless, slack, sluggish, inert, lethargic, do-nothing, listless, lumpish, lackadaisical, dawdling, dilatory. —**Ant.** industrious; busy, diligent, conscientious, assiduous, sedulous; energetic, strenuous, vigorous, active.

indomitable adj. The coach's indomitable spirit helped the team to victory: invincible, indefatigable, unconquerable, invulnerable, unyielding, insuperable, unassailable, staunch, steadfast, formidable, unwavering, irrepressible, resolute, stubborn, dogged, unflinching, fearless, dauntless, unshrinking, intrepid, stalwart, courageous, undaunted, persevering, doughty, valiant, cast-iron. —**Ant.** yielding, weak, feeble, languid, wavering, faltering, flinching, shrinking, cowardly.

indorse v. See ENDORSE.

induce v. **1.** My arguments induced him to vote for the bill: coax, persuade, influence, prompt, dispose, incline, impel, spur, prevail upon, bring round, encourage, get, sway, win over, prevail on. **2.** Alcohol can induce a loosening of the tongue: bring on, give rise to, lead to, occasion, prompt, cause, bring about, produce, motivate, inspire, sow the seeds of, set in motion, effect, instigate, incite, activate, actuate, provoke, arouse. —**Ant.** 1 dissuade, prevent, disincline, deter, hinder, restrain. 2 deter, hinder, stop, squelch, curb, suppress.

inducement n. The biscuit was an inducement for the dog to perform: incentive, enticement, allurement, incitement, goad, spur, bait, stimulus, inspiration, motive, ground, cause, reason, provocation, temptation, persuasion, instigation, attraction. —**Ant.** deterrent, discouragement.

induct v. We inducted new members into our club. Thousands of young men were inducted into the army: initiate, instate, install, introduce, inaugurate, establish, invest, lead in, usher in, bring in; frock, ordain, consecrate; crown, enthrone; conscript, enlist, draft, sign up, register.

induction *n.* **1.** *She arrived at the result by a process of induction:* inference, logical reasoning, rationalization, reason. **2.** *All the young men were subject to induction:* initiation, draft, entrance, introduction, taking in, selection; inaugural, inauguration, installation, investiture, ordination, consecration.

indulge *v. The nurse indulged the spoiled child too much. He indulged his fondness for candy:* cater to, serve, go along with, oblige, gratify, accommodate, give way to, yield to, give loose rein to, treat, appease, yield to the desires of, pamper the whims of, coddle, pander to, baby, favor, humor, mollycoddle, humor to excess, spoil, cosset. —**Ant.** deny, forbid, thwart, disappoint, discipline, abstain from.

indulgence *n.* **1.** *Rich desserts are an indulgence the overweight can't afford:* luxury, something indulged in, self-indulgence, extravagance, excess, self-gratification, intemperance, immoderation; dissipation, profligacy, debauchery. **2.** *The pilot asked for the passengers' indulgence during the delay:* sufferance, understanding, tolerance, forgiveness, forbearance, patience, lenience, compassion, permissiveness, allowance, kindness, graciousness, benignity. —**Ant.** 1 abstinence, self-sacrifice, repression, restraint. 2 condemnation, castigation, reprehension.

indulgent *adj. A first-grade teacher must be somewhat indulgent:* lenient, tolerant, understanding, forbearing, humoring, forgiving, permissive, easygoing, complaisant, clement, pampering, sparing, patient, yielding, obliging, benign, kind, tender, conciliatory. —**Ant.** strict, stern, severe, rigorous, stringent, harsh, rough, austere, intolerant, unmerciful, unforgiving, demanding.

industrious *adj. Most employers treasure an industrious employee:* hardworking, zealous, diligent, sedulous, assiduous, productive, purposeful; busy, occupied; active, energetic, indefatigable, unremitting, tireless, unflagging. —**Ant.** idle, lazy, shiftless, indolent, lethargic.

industry *n.* **1.** *Heavy industry suffers during an energy crisis:* business, commerce, field, manufacture, trade. **2.** *The clerk was rewarded for his industry:* hard work, zeal, diligence, industriousness, sedulousness, application, go, labor, assiduity, bustle, hustle, enterprise, energy, perseverance, toil, patient plodding, indefatigability, activity, assiduousness.

inebriated *adj. Both men were too inebriated to drive:* drunk, under the influence, intoxicated, besotted, befuddled, tipsy, drunken, drunk as a lord; *Slang* plastered, in one's cups, oiled, sozzled, tight, high, loaded, three sheets to the wind, potted, bombed, stoned, smashed, wrecked, zonked. —**Ant.** sober.

ineffable *adj. She seemed to radiate ineffable happiness:* indescribable, inexpressible, unspeakable, indefinite, indefinable, incommunicable; unutterable, untellable, unspeakable; ideal, transcendental, transcendent; divine, sacred, spiritual.

ineffective *adj. The air conditioner was ineffective in such a crowded room. He proved to be an ineffective administrator:* of little use, not much good, futile, vain, not producing results, fruitless; inefficient, unproductive, weak, powerless, inadequate, useless, impotent, inoperative; incapable, worthless. —**Ant.** effective; effectual, efficacious, efficient; useful, profitable, capable, productive, adequate.

ineffectual *adj. Charles I was a brave king but an ineffectual ruler:* inept, incompetent, ineffective, inefficient, unsatisfactory, inefficacious, unprofitable, useless, unavailing, not up to par, unsuccessful, unproductive, profitless, vain, futile; weak, impotent, hapless, feeble, inadequate, lame. —**Ant.** effectual, efficacious, effective, profitable, fruitful, useful, successful, productive, gainful; efficient, satisfactory, competent, adequate.

inefficient *adj. The inefficient operation cost the firm a lot of money:* ineffective, incompetent, slipshod, ineffectual, slack, unproductive, inadequate, not efficient, wasteful of time or energy, inefficacious, inept, unskilled, good-for-nothing, indifferent; futile, pointless. —**Ant.** efficient, competent, able, capable, qualified; skillful, skilled, proficient, expert, adept; effectual, efficacious; *Slang* crackerjack.

inelegant *adj. The expression was inelegant, he decided:* ungraceful, unpolished, ungainly, awkward, clumsy, gauche, graceless, gross, indelicate, raw, rough, rude, stiff, uncouth, uncultivated, unrefined, vulgar, coarse, crass, crude.

ineligible *adj. Poor grades made the student ineligible for the team:* unqualified, disqualified, not eligible, unentitled, unfit, unacceptable, unsuitable. —**Ant.** eligible, qualified, suitable, fit.

ineluctable *adj. That an earthquake will occur along this fault is ineluctable:* inevitable, inescapable, unavoidable, ineludible, irrevocable, unevadable, inevasible, unpreventable, unstoppable, inexorable; certain, sure, fated, sure as fate. —**Ant.** dubious, doubtful, improbable, questionable.

inept *adj.* **1.** *The soldiers were brave but inept:* inefficient, incompetent, unskilled, untrained, unqualified, without dexterity, bungling, ineffective, inefficacious, ineffectual, awkward, clumsy, maladroit. **2.** *The speaker's inept comparison simply bewildered the audience:* out of place, unapt, pointless, empty, inane, inappropriate, unsuitable, unfitting, foolish, senseless, asinine, silly, fatuous, nonsensical. —**Ant.** 1 efficient, skillful, apt, qualified, dexterous, competent, talented, effectual, effective, adroit, efficacious, able. 2 apt, germane, appropriate, pointed; sensible.

inequality *n. Women are fighting inequality in the business world:* unfairness, inequity, lack of equality, imparity, favoritism, prejudice; irregularity, difference, diversity, variableness, changeableness, dissimilarity, unequalness, dissimilitude, disparity, disproportion, inconstancy, divergence, unlikeness. —**Ant.** equality, fairness, impartiality, regularity, sameness, similarity, similitude, constancy, likeness.

inert *adj. The man was so inert he seemed dead:* motionless, static, immobile, stationary, inactive, quiescent, still, passive, inanimate, impassive; listless, phlegmatic, sluggish, dull, numb, leaden, supine, slack, torpid, languid. —**Ant.** dynamic; animated; active, alert, kinetic, brisk, lively, energetic, vigorous.

inertia n. Blame your inertia on the hot weather: inertness, listlessness, sluggishness, languor, disinclination to move, passiveness, inactivity, laziness, inaction, lethargy, lassitude, torpidity, apathy, indolence, supineness, passivity, torpor, dullness, stupor, weariness. —**Ant.** activity, action, liveliness, energy, vigor, vitality, animation.

inevitable adj. Traffic delays are inevitable on a holiday weekend: inescapable, unavoidable, unpreventable, ineluctable, destined, predetermined, certain, written in the book of fate, fated, predestined, sure, sure to happen, ineludible. —**Ant.** escapable, avoidable, eludible, evadable, preventable; uncertain, indeterminate.

inexcusable adj. Her rudeness was inexcusable: unpardonable, unforgivable, indefensible, unjustifiable, unallowable, intolerable, unbearable. —**Ant.** excusable, pardonable, forgivable, justifiable, defensible.

inexorable adj. The judge was inexorable in passing the maximum sentence: unyielding, relentless, firm, inflexible, stiff, unbending, immovable, irresistible, intractable, adamant, adamantive, determined, obdurate, dogged, uncompromising, inescapable; cruel, pitiless, merciless, ruthless. —**Ant.** sympathetic, tender, indulgent, compassionate.

inexpensive adj. The restaurant serves good, inexpensive meals: low-priced, not expensive, popular-priced, costing little, nominal-priced; reasonable, moderate, cheap, economical, good at the price; Informal light on the pocketbook. —**Ant.** expensive, costly, high-priced.

inexperienced adj. The crew felt unsafe with an inexperienced pilot: unseasoned, unskilled, inexpert, unpracticed, untrained, unschooled, uninitiated, untutored; untried, unfledged, green, callow, fresh; unfamiliar, unversed, unaccustomed, unconversant, unacquainted; unsophisticated, naive. —**Ant.** experienced, skilled, practiced, seasoned, trained, expert, schooled, aged, versed, accustomed, conversant; sophisticated, worldly, worldly-wise.

inexplicable adj. The flying saucer sighting was inexplicable: unexplainable, unfathomable, inscrutable, insolvable, incomprehensible, unaccountable, insoluble, undecipherable; mysterious, mystifying, abstruse, baffling, puzzling, perplexing, enigmatical. —**Ant.** explicable, explainable, fathomable, solvable, comprehensible, accountable, soluble; reasonable, understandable, obvious, clear.

infallible adj. The designer has an infallible eye for color. It looked like an infallible escape plan: faultless, flawless, free from error, unerring, incapable of error, unfailing, not liable to err, free from mistake, unimpeachable, apodictic, absolutely trustworthy, impeccable, perfect, inerrant, irrefutable, incontrovertible; dependable, foolproof, sure, certain, reliable, assured, positive,

perfect, surefire. —**Ant.** fallible, questionable, dubious, contestable, refutable, untrustworthy, controvertible, doubtful, unreliable, uncertain, unsure, undependable.

infamous adj. Bluebeard was an infamous character. I was shocked by her infamous behavior: notorious, disreputable, having a bad reputation, villainous, of evil fame, of ill repute, nefarious, outrageous, dishonorable, vile, scandalous, shameful, ignoble, foul, heinous, monstrous, evil, wicked, opprobrious, disgraceful, base, damnable, odious, perfidious, detestable, abhorrent, sordid, recreant, abominable, low, iniquitous, treacherous, shamefully bad, corrupt, scurrilous, immoral, sinful, knavish, profligate. —**Ant.** illustrious; glorious, splendid, sublime, reputable, honorable, noble, good.

infamy n. President Franklin D. Roosevelt said that the attack on Pearl Harbor was "a day that will live in infamy": dishonor, shame, disgrace, ignominy, disrepute, opprobrium, disesteem, discredit, scandal; evil, wickedness, villainy, corruption, abomination; notoriety, notoriousness. —**Ant.** integrity, honor, virtue, probity, nobility.

infant n. Infants in arms are admitted free: baby, babe, child, kid, newborn, toddler, nursling, neonate, suckling.

infantile adj. Temper tantrums in an adult are infantile: babyish, suitable to an infant, characteristic of an infant, childish, childlike, juvenile, infantlike, infantine, sophomoric. —**Ant.** mature, adult, manly, womanly, grown-up.

infatuated adj. Many men were infatuated with the beautiful young widow: enamored, enchanted, bewitched by, inspired with blind love for, inflamed by, beguiled by, spellbound by, carried away by, having a crush on, intoxicated by, smitten by, deprived of common sense by, obsessed by, entranced by, captivated by, charmed by, enraptured by, enthralled by.

infect v. **1.** The flu virus infected almost the entire class: contaminate, taint, poison, blight; afflict, indispose. **2.** The director's bad mood infected the whole cast: touch, influence, spread among, affect adversely, work upon, have an effect on, spread through, leave a mark on; damage, corrupt, spoil, ruin.

infection n. Infection was rampant in the hospital ward: contagion, contagiousness, contamination, corruption, germs, impurity, septicity, communicability.

infectious adj. **1.** Measles is an infectious disease: contagious, catching, communicable, inoculable, virulent, epidemic, spreading, infective, Informal catchable. **2.** The children's gaiety was infectious: catching, contagious, tending to affect others, irresistible, compelling, captivating. —**Ant.** **1** noncontagious, noncommunicable, incommunicable.

infer v. From the testimony, the jury inferred that the defendant was lying: conclude, deduce, reckon, reason, judge; opine, guess, conjecture, speculate, gather, consider probable, glean, suppose, surmise, form an opinion, deem, presume.

inferior adj. **1.** Brass is inferior to gold. A pri-

vate is inferior to a sergeant: worth less than, of lower quality than, less valuable than; lower in rank than, of less importance than, subordinate, subservient, secondary, junior, subsidiary. **2.** *Many hot dog makers use inferior meat:* poor, substandard, low-quality, low-grade, second-rate, less valuable, of less excellence, indifferent, mediocre, *Informal* not up to snuff. —**Ant.** 1 superior, higher, senior, greater. 2 superior, first-rate, first-class, top, prime, fine, excellent.

infernal *adj.* **1.** *The poet wrote of the infernal world of Satan:* hellish, Hadean, Plutonian, Stygian, lower, nether. **2.** *He should try to control that infernal temper:* damnable, hellish, devilish, horrible, fiendish, diabolical, demoniacal, awful, terrible, heinous, black, cursed, execrable, flagitious, vicious, accursed, malicious, nefarious, atrocious, vile, abominable, monstrous, iniquitous, horrendous. —**Ant.** 1 supernal, angelic, cherubic, heavenly.

inferno *n.* **1.** *The inferno is usually described as a place of eternal torment:* hell, Hades, netherworld, nether regions, the pit, lower world, underworld, abyss, perdition, *Bible* Tophet, the bottomless pit, infernal regions; hellfire, fire and brimstone. **2.** *Open a window, this room's an inferno:* oven, hellhole, hotbox, furnace, fiery furnace; sizzler, roaster, scorcher. —**Ant.** 1 heaven, paradise, Eden; bliss, nirvana.

infertile *adj.* *The climate was harsh and the soil infertile:* barren, unfruitful, sterile, unproductive, nonproductive, arid, bare, fallow, desolate, fruitless, impotent, unprolific, effete, infecund; depleted, exhausted, drained. —**Ant.** fertile, fruitful, productive, fecund.

infest *v.* *Cockroaches infested the apartment:* overrun, fill, invade, infect, plague, overwhelm, teem.

infidel *n.* *Richard I and Saladin considered each other to be infidels:* unbeliever, heathen, pagan, idolater, nonbeliever in God, atheist, agnostic, skeptic, apostate, heretic; savage, barbarian. —**Ant.** believer.

infidelity *n.* **1.** *Infidelity was the cause of the divorce:* adultery, breaking of the marriage vows, marital faithlessness, unfaithfulness, violation of the marriage bed, betrayal, perfidy, disloyalty. **2.** *Infidelity to any of the organization's tenets will not be tolerated:* nonobservance, nonadherence, breach, falsity, disregard, transgression, violation, infraction. —**Ant.** 1 fidelity, faithfulness, loyalty.

infinite *adj.* **1.** *Learning to ski requires infinite patience. Man's will to survive is infinite:* enormous, great, immense, tremendous; immeasurable, vast, measureless. **2.** *The universe seems infinite:* boundless, interminable, limitless, uncircumscribed, unlimited, illimitable, unbounded, endless, knowing no limit, without end, inexhaustible; incalculable, measureless. —**Ant.** 1 small, little, limited. 2 finite; circumscribed, definitive, restricted, limited, bounded, measurable.

infinitesimal *adj.* *The punch contained only an infinitesimal amount of alcohol:* tiny, inconsiderable, insignificant, microscopic, imperceptible,

immeasurably small, diminutive, puny, minute, extremely small, undiscernible, *Informal* wee; inappreciable, negligible. —**Ant.** enormous, vast, infinite, huge, immeasurable, large, great.

infinity *n.* *The powerful new telescope may give us a glimpse into infinity:* boundless time, eternity, eternal time, infinitude, endlessness, boundlessness, illimitability, limitlessness; immeasurability, measurelessness, inexhaustibility; incalculability, incomprehensibility; forever, perpetuity, everlastingness, sempiternity. —**Ant.** finiteness, transitoriness, limitedness, temporariness.

infirm *adj.* *The old man was too infirm to work:* weak, feeble, frail, weakened, unsound, ailing, decrepit, enfeebled, doddering, shaky, unstable, anile, poorly, worn, helpless, failing, ailing, sickly, fragile, ill, debilitated, strengthless, powerless, enervated, disabled, emaciated. —**Ant.** hale; strong, sturdy, stalwart, stout; healthy, robust, sound.

infirmity *n.* **1.** *A back infirmity kept the young man out of the army:* disability, ailment, debility, infirmness, debilitation, malady, illness, disorder, indisposition, physical weakness, frailness, sickness, loss of health, lack of strength, handicap, fragility. **2.** *Some infirmity of character led the policeman to take a bribe:* failing, moral weakness, deficiency, flaw, defect, fault, frailty, vulnerability, imperfection; instability, unstableness. —**Ant.** 1 strength, vigor, healthfulness, soundness. 2 strength, perfection; stability.

inflame *v.* *Rudolph Valentino inflamed thousands of silent-movie fans. The agitator tried to inflame the mob:* excite, electrify, intoxicate, arouse, provoke, rouse, ignite, kindle, fire, excite the passions of, incite, stir up, stimulate, agitate, work up, heat up, enkindle, craze; rile, incense, enrage, madden. —**Ant.** extinguish (a passion), quench, allay, cool, calm, pacify, quiet, squelch, suppress.

inflammable *adj.* **1.** *Don't light matches near inflammable liquids:* flammable, easily set on fire, capable of being set on fire, combustible, ignitable, incendiary. **2.** *An inflammable temper got the man in trouble:* fiery, volatile, excitable, sensitive, inflammatory, easily roused, incendiary, high-strung, choleric, impetuous, precipitate, overhasty. —**Ant.** 1 nonflammable, uninflammable. 2 placid, calm, easy, passive, even, cool.

inflammatory *adj.* *The speaker's inflammatory remarks almost started a riot. The argument created an inflammatory situation:* provocative, fiery, incendiary, rabble-rousing, enraging, inciting, rabid, arousing, tending to stir up strong feelings, intemperate, rebellious, insurgent, revolutionary, mutinous, demagogic; combustible, inflammable, explosive, fulminating, volcanic. —**Ant.** soothing, calming, pacifying.

inflate *v.* *Use a bicycle pump to inflate the balloons:* fill up, puff out, blow up, be blown up, swell, expand, bloat, pump up, fill with gas, distend, dilate. —**Ant.** deflate, empty, flatten.

inflated *adj.* *He had an inflated idea of his own importance:* exaggerated, overblown, overestimated, aggrandized, amplified, bloated, dilated, distended, enlarged, magnified, puffed, swollen, tumescent *Rhetoric* grandiloquent, bombastic, flowery, fustian, prolix, verbose, wordy *Informal* windy, pumped up.

inflection *n. She couldn't recognize the inflection in his voice:* modulation, accent, articulation, emphasis, enunciation, intonation, pitch, tone, timbre, tonality.

inflexible *adj.* **1.** *Marble is an inflexible material:* unbending, unyielding, rigid, hard, firm, solid, not flexible, fixed, taut, stiff, unplastic, unmalleable. **2.** *The committee was inflexible in its opposition to our request:* unchangeable, rigid, unyielding, unbending, hidebound, obstinate, obdurate, intractable, stubborn, tenacious, pigheaded, mulish, dogged, headstrong, determined, adamant, adamantine, resolute, uncompromising, inexorable, implacable, unwavering, immovable; impervious, ironbound, stringent, hard and fast, firm, immutable. —**Ant.** 1 flexible, elastic, resilient, supple, springy; pliable, pliant, yielding, plastic, malleable, ductile; fluid, liquid; expansive, buoyant, soft. 2 amenable, tractable, docile, biddable, flexible, yielding, changeable, compromising, irresolute, undetermined.

inflict *v. The hurricane inflicted severe damage on the island. Don't inflict your problems on me!:* lay on, visit upon, put upon, impose, administer, cause to suffer, bring to bear, perpetrate, wreak; *Slang* unload, dump. —**Ant.** spare, remove, alleviate, withdraw, suspend.

influence *n.* **1.** *Special-interest groups have too much influence on government:* weight, sway, power, pull, effect, pressure, hold, potency, mastery, ascendancy, authority, domination, dominion, control, leverage, advantage, prestige; *Slang* clout. —*v.* **2.** *My father influenced me to accept the job:* induce, persuade, impel, act upon, work upon, move, prompt, provoke, stir, inspire, incite, arouse, actuate, sway, exercise influence on, have a bearing on, play a decisive role in, incline, dispose, predispose, guide, be guided; bring pressure to bear on. —**Ant.** 1 ineffectiveness, impotency. 2 dissuade, restrain, hinder, impede.

influential *adj. The citizens' lobby was influential in changing the election laws:* effective, instrumental, having influence, consequential, effectual, forceful, powerful, efficacious, important, significant, momentous, potent, puissant, strong, weighty; leading, moving, inspiring, activating. —**Ant.** uninfluential, weak, ineffective, ineffectual, unefficacious, inoperative, inconsiderable, unpersuasive, ineffectual, powerless, impotent, unimportant.

influx *n. The influx of vacationing students enlivened the town. April brought an influx of warm air:* inflow, inundation, flowing in, indraft, infiltration, inpouring, ingress, entry, incursion, arrival, converging. —**Ant.** outflow, outpouring, exit, egress, exodus.

inform *v.* **1.** *The police must inform the prisoner of his legal rights:* tell, apprise, notify, let know, give notice to, advise, make known to, report to, give knowledge of, give information, acquaint, familiarize, send word to, disclose to, forewarn, communicate to, declare to, mention to, enlighten, edify, serve notice on, signify to, announce to, indicate to, tip off, *Slang* clue in. **2.** *Who informed on the killer?:* denounce, give damaging evidence, furnish incriminating evidence, report an offense, tell on, tattle; *Slang* snitch, squeal, fink, rat, blow the whistle.

informal *adj. The party will be informal, so don't dress up:* casual, simple, without formality, unceremonious, unconventional, familiar, unofficial, easy, unconstrained, natural, not formal, easygoing, offhand, spontaneous, come-as-you-are. —**Ant.** ceremonious, formal, official.

informant *n. My informant tells me the company is near bankruptcy:* informer, adviser, appriser, respondent, enlightener, notifier, source, tipster; reporter, announcer, spokesman, spokeswoman, *Slang* horse's mouth.

information *n. Information on witchcraft can be found at the library:* data, material, news, knowledge, report, facts, evidence, bulletin, communiqué, tidings, account, fact-finding; (*variously*) documents, papers, notes, materials; announcement, notice, intelligence, enlightenment; briefing, notification.

informative *adj. The broadcast was most informative:* educational, enlightening, instructive, communicative, edifying, explanatory, illuminating, revealing, advisory.

informed *adj. An informed public reads newspapers:* conversant, cognizant, abreast, acquainted, briefed, enlightened, erudite, familiar, knowledgeable, posted, primed, versant, versed *French* au courant, *Informal* savvy, wise to.

informer *n. The informer's identity was kept secret:* police informant, betrayer, tattler, *Slang* stool pigeon, squealer, blabber, snitcher, fink, stoolie, rat, canary; traitor, Judas; *French* mouchard.

infraction *n. He had his driver's license revoked for too many speeding infractions:* violation, breaking of a law, lawbreaking, infringement, breach, transgression, trespass, encroachment; disobedience, unobservance, nonobservance; insubordination; peccadillo.

infrastructure *n. The army has built up a sound infrastructure for the protection of Europe:* basis, groundwork, foundation, base, support; underpinning, bottom, bedrock, substructure, understructure, footing, substratum, *Geology* substrate, ground, root.

infrequent *adj. Fortunately, her asthma attacks are infrequent:* occasional, rare, seldom, not regular, few and far between, sporadic, uncommon, unusual, unique, few, not habitual, happening at long intervals, spasmodic, fitful, seldom happening. —**Ant.** frequent, usual, customary, ordinary, common, habitual.

infringe *v.* **1.** *Pirating the book infringed the author's copyright:* violate, transgress, break, commit an infraction of, act contrary to, disobey, commit a breach of, infract, contravene. **2.** *Don't infringe on my territory:* trespass, encroach, intrude, invade, impinge, overstep; interfere with, *Slang* butt in.

infuriate *v. The child's stubbornness infuriated the mother:* anger, make angry, inflame, madden, enrage, rile, kindle wrath, incense, provoke, exasperate, make furious, outrage, vex, gall, offend, aggravate, irritate, lash into a fury, chafe, try one's temper; *Informal* burn one up, raise one's dander.

infuse *v. The glowing reviews infused the performers with confidence. If only he could infuse his work with some enthusiasm!:* instill, inspire, imbue, fortify; pour into, impart to, insinuate, introduce into, cause to penetrate, implant, inculcate, introject, breathe into.

ingenious *adj. Not even the experts could figure out the magician's ingenious escape:* clever, cunning, artful, skillful, inventive, masterful, stunning, deft, adroit, dexterous, masterly, expert, exhibiting ingenuity, brilliant, shrewd, crafty, resourceful, original. **—Ant.** unoriginal, pedestrian, unimaginative, artless, unskillful, uninventive, unresourceful; clumsy, maladroit.

ingenuity *n. The student showed ingenuity in solving the difficult math problem:* cleverness, skill, skillfulness, inventiveness, resourcefulness, imagination, aptitude, good thinking, adroitness, ingeniousness, imaginativeness, adeptness, flair, mastery, expertise, know-how, sharpness, dexterity, deftness, cunning, shrewdness, facility, astuteness. **—Ant.** awkwardness, clumsiness, dullness, stupidity, unskillfulness, inability, ineptitude, maladroitness.

ingenuous *adj. She was so charming and ingenuous most people adored her at once:* natural, artless, guileless, unaffected, genuine, simplehearted, openhearted, honest, open, unsophisticated, frank, direct, trusting, straightforward; *Slang* up front, straight-shooting. **—Ant.** worldly-wise, jaded, disingenuous; wily, devious, tricky.

inglorious *adj. The pirate was hanged for his inglorious deeds:* disgraceful, dishonorable, shameful, ignominious, infamous, ignoble, despicable, contemptible, heinous, depraved, corrupt, atrocious, nefarious, evil, base; scandalous, shocking, outrageous, flagrant. **—Ant.** admirable, commendable, praiseworthy, exemplary, worthy.

ingrained *adj. The boy had an ingrained fear of heights:* fixed, inborn, inbred, inherent, innate, deep, deep-seated, deep-rooted, constitutional, implanted, rooted, indelible, thorough, intrinsic, inveterate, confirmed, firm.

ingratiate *v. She was able to ingratiate herself with the boss:* curry favor, insinuate oneself, blandish, captivate, charm, fawn, flatter, grovel, toady, truckle, *Informal* kowtow, bootlick, lick boots, brownnose.

ingratiating *adj.* **1.** *An ingratiating manner endeared him to his superiors:* winning, engaging, captivating, personable, likable, magnetic, attractive, appealing, enchanting, congenial, winsome, persuasive, charming, amiable, genial, pleasing, cordial, affable, sweet, lovable, gracious, friendly, good-humored. **2.** *His smile is*

phony and his voice sickeningly ingratiating: unctuous, gushing, oily, oleaginous, fulsome, smarmy, obsequious; self-serving, falsely disarming; presumptuous. **—Ant.** 1 forbidding, austere, unattractive, unappealing, displeasing, unpleasant, abrasive, unlovable, charmless.

ingredient *n. What ingredients went into the soup? Hard work is a vital ingredient of success:* element, part, component, constituent, integral part; feature, factor, aspect, essential, contributor, principle.

inhabit *v. No one inhabits that ramshackle house:* reside in, live in, dwell in, occupy, tenant, lodge, take up one's abode in; people, populate, settle.

inhabitant *n. The inhabitants of the flooded island were evacuated:* resident, native, dweller, occupant, inhabiter, denizen, inmate, tenant, renter, lessee, occupier; boarder, lodger; citizen, villager, settler.

inhale *v. The fireman inhaled a dangerous amount of smoke:* breathe in, inbreathe, suck in, draw into the lungs, snuff, sniff, respire. **—Ant.** exhale, expire.

inherent *adj. Freedom of religion is an inherent part of the Bill of Rights:* essential, innate, inseparable, hereditary, native, intrinsic, inborn, deep-rooted, inveterate, natural, inbred, ingrained, constitutional, inalienable. **—Ant.** foreign, alien, extrinsic, adventitious; subsidiary, superficial, supplemental.

inherit *v. She hopes to inherit the family silver:* fall heir to, come into, come in for, be bequeathed, be willed, be left, get, come by, acquire, become heir to, have fall into one's hands, accrue to, have fall to one's lot, have fall to one's share.

inheritance *n. A large inheritance made him independently wealthy:* legacy, bequest, bequeathal, estate, devise, bestowal, heritage, endowment; birthright, patrimony.

inhibit *v. The medicine inhibited the spread of the disease:* prevent, hold back, arrest, hinder, impede, restrain, suppress, check, stop, repress, smother, muzzle, harness, block, control, obstruct, curb, constrain, gag, restrict, hold in leash; forbid, prohibit, enjoin, bar. **—Ant.** allow, let, permit, suffer, further, encourage, support, abet.

inhibited *adj. A strict upbringing had made her inhibited:* repressed, restrained, constrained, guarded, reserved, reticent, self-conscious, shy, subdued, undemonstrative, withdrawn, uptight. **—Ant.** uninhibited, free, outgoing, relaxed, spontaneous.

inhibition Often **inhibitions** *n. He has no inhibitions about disagreeing with his boss:* mental reservation, guardedness, self-consciousness, mental block, holding back of an action or thought, misgiving, inhibiting or restraining influence, reserve, restriction, constraint, restraint of action; impediment, obstruction, blockage, stricture, constriction, check.

inhospitable *adj. Our welcome, if I can call it that, was most inhospitable:* aloof, unfriendly, unsociable, cool, distant, standoffish; rude, impolite, unkind, uncongenial, ungracious, discourteous, inconsiderate, unneighborly, unobliging, unaccommodating. **—Ant.** cordial, sociable, genial, congenial, obliging, accommodating.

inhuman *adj. Inhuman treatment of mental patients shocked the public:* cruel, unfeeling, merciless, pitiless, heartless, coldhearted, brutal, ruthless, barbarous, barbaric, monstrous, coldblooded, savage, malevolent, vicious, satanic, hardhearted, brutish, demoniac, diabolical, malignant, venomous, fiendish. **—Ant.** human, humane; benevolent, kind, humanitarian, charitable, altruistic, sympathetic, compassionate, tender.

inhumanity *n. War is the best example of man's inhumanity to his fellow man:* cruelty, savagery, brutality, bloodthirstiness, ruthlessness, barbarity, fiendishness, viciousness, brutishness, malevolence, coldbloodedness, heartlessness, sadism, mercilessness. **—Ant.** humaneness, consideration, altruism, kindness.

inimical *adj.* **1.** *Over-the-counter drugs can be inimical to your health:* harmful, detrimental, injurious, dangerous, deleterious, destructive, hurtful, ruinous; toxic, virulent, venomous, poisonous. **2.** *His words became more inimical the longer he spoke:* hostile, antagonistic, unfriendly, ill-disposed, acrimonious, antipathetic, rancorous, ill-willed, hateful. **—Ant.** 1 helpful, beneficial, salutary, propitious. 2 friendly, amiable, congenial, well-disposed.

inimitable *adj. Many have tried to copy the painter's inimitable style:* matchless, unmatched, incomparable, unique, incapable of being imitated, peerless, preeminent, unparalleled, rare, unequaled, unsurpassed, nonpareil, beyond compare, unrivaled, unexcelled; consummate, superlative, supreme. **—Ant.** common, ordinary, imitable.

iniquity *n.* **1.** *The iniquity of false testimony is universally recognized:* unfairness, gross injustice, dishonesty, violation of one's rights, immorality, unrighteousness, inequity, unjustness. **2.** *The corrupt politician's iniquities should not go unpunished:* wickedness, wrong, wrongdoing, evil, evildoing, sin, transgression, infamy, miscreancy, knavery, roguery, villainy, flagrancy; abomination, sinfulness, depravity, corruption, outrage, immorality, vice, profligacy, turpitude. **—Ant.** 1 justice, fairness, integrity, virtue, rectitude, probity, honesty, uprightness, goodness, morality.

initial *adj. The initial move must be to get the board's approval:* first, starting, beginning, opening, commencing, primary, introductory, incipient, initiatory, inaugural, maiden; original, germinal, primal. **—Ant.** last, ultimate, ending, final, closing, concluding, terminal.

initiate *v.* **1.** *The museum initiated the fund-raising drive with a gala:* begin, set afoot, start, be started, set going, get going, open, be opened, get under way, enter upon, commence, launch, be launched, originate, institute, found, start the ball rolling, kick off, inaugurate, take the lead, set up, break ground, lay the founda-

tion, establish, lead the way, lay the first stone, blaze the trail. **2.** *The Rotarians initiated 12 new members:* induct, usher in, receive, admit with special rites, inaugurate, install, give entrance to, take in, bring in, introduce, invest; haze. **3.** *A year in Florence, Italy, initiated the girl into the art world:* introduce, familiarize with, acquaint with; accustom to, habituate to. **—Ant.** 1 consummate; fulfill, execute, accomplish, achieve, terminate, conclude, finish, end, complete. 2 refuse, reject, expel.

initiation *n.* **1.** *An initiation will be held for all new members:* initiating, formal admission, introduction, induction, ushering in, admittance, entrance. **2.** *The composer owed his initiation into the music world to his father:* introduction, indoctrination, inculcation, guidance. **3.** *Who was responsible for the initiation of hostilities?:* commencement, opening, beginning, genesis, inception, outset, onset, start, starting, beginning, introduction, inauguration, outbreak. **—Ant.** 1 expulsion, rejection, exit. 3 end, finish, completion, finalization, termination, closure.

initiative *n.* **1.** *The mayor took the initiative in closing the park to automobiles:* lead, first step, first move, leading action, beginning step, introductory act. **2.** *Eleanor Roosevelt was a woman of great initiative:* enterprise, leadership, forcefulness, dynamism, ability in initiating action, originality, creativity, power to begin, aggressiveness, *Slang* get-up-and-go.

inject *v. Try to inject some life into the party:* insert, put, interject, throw in, interpolate, introduce, infuse, imbue, infix, instill, intromit; force; *Slang* pump.

injection *n.* **1.** *She received a flu injection:* inoculation, hypodermic, intravenous, needle, vaccination, *Informal* shot, dose, hypo, fix, jab, needle. **2.** *The proceedings needed an injection of humor:* introduction, infusion.

injunction *n. The court ordered an injunction:* order, decree, charge, command, dictate, ruling.

injure *v. The boy injured his shoulder. Drinking can injure one's health. A scandal's bound to injure someone's reputation:* harm, do injury to, wound, damage, do harm to, cause harm to, afflict, hurt, mar, impair; bruise, deface, disfigure, mangle, lacerate, maim, deform, mutilate, lame; wrong, violate, abuse, ill-treat, maltreat, affront, offend, misuse, sting, sully, stain, vitiate, malign, debase, spoil, blemish, scathe. **—Ant.** soothe, heal, pacify; aid, help, assist, benefit.

injurious *adj. Smoking is injurious to the lungs. Poor management is injurious to a business:* hurtful, damaging, harmful, causing injury, detrimental, destructive, deleterious, noxious, abusive, ruinous, calamitous, pernicious, disastrous, corrosive; inimical, adverse. **—Ant.** beneficial, helpful, advantageous, salutary; profitable.

injury *n. A severe head injury left the fighter unconscious for days. The harsh review was an injury to the singer's pride:* hurt, harm, wound, damage, bruise, mutilation, cut, lesion, gash, contusion, stab, blow, affliction, scratch, laceration; abuse, blow, injustice, outrage, indignity, affront; defamation, vilification, detraction, impairment, aspersion, disservice.

injustice n. The newspaper led a campaign against welfare injustice. Many injustices are committed in the name of progress: unjustness, unjust character, unfairness, inequality, bias, prejudice, partiality, inequity, bigotry, favoritism, partisanship; unjust act, wrong, disservice, infraction, injury, iniquity, wrongdoing, infringement, sin, persecution, unfair treatment, encroachment, tyranny, transgression, offense, foul play, evil, malpractice. —**Ant.** justice, equity, fairness, fair play, impartiality, lawfulness, rectitude, right, righteousness, equality.

inkling n. Did you have any inkling that he was coming? There was never any inkling of scandal about her: idea, vague idea, hint, suspicion, indication, tip, clue, suggestion, glimmer, glimmering, notion; cue, intimation, conception, supposition; whisper, insinuation, innuendo.

inlet n. Anchor the boat in the inlet in case of a storm: cove, harbor, bay, gulf, estuary; narrows, waterway, strait, bight, fjord, firth.

inn n. We'll find a cozy inn to stay in for the night: public house, lodge, hotel, motel, lodging house, roadhouse, country hotel, hostel, pension, hospice, hostelry, tavern; caravansary.

innate adj. Mozart had an innate genius for music. An innate flaw doomed the plan from the start: native, natural, inborn, inherent, inbred, instinctive, intuitive, natural, ingrained, intrinsic, essential, congenital, constitutional, inherited, hereditary, indigenous. —**Ant.** acquired, learned; accidental, adventitious, incidental, fortuitous; assumed, affected, cultivated, fostered, nurtured; unnatural.

inner adj. **1.** Hansel and Gretel were lost in the inner part of the forest: interior, inward, inside, internal, central, middle. **2.** The secret was locked in the inner recesses of his mind: more secret, more intimate, unobvious, concealed, hidden, private, esoteric. **3.** Most people struggle for inner peace: spiritual, psychological, mental, psychic, emotional. —**Ant.** 1 outer, outward, outside, exterior, external, outermost, open. 2 outer, external, open, public, obvious, exterior, exoteric.

innermost adj. She confided her innermost thoughts to me: most personal, most intimate, most private, deep-rooted, farthest inward, secret, deepest, inmost, deep-seated. —**Ant.** surface, superficial.

innocence n. **1.** The defendant's innocence is presumed until proved otherwise: guiltlessness, freedom from moral wrong, inculpability, blamelessness, impeccability, sinlessness, incorruption, clean hands, stainlessness; chastity, purity, spotlessness, immaculateness. **2.** The girl has the sweetness and innocence of a child: simplicity, artlessness, ingenuousness, guilelessness, freshness, freedom from cunning or trickery, naiveté, purity, chastity. —**Ant.** 1 guilt; offensiveness, contamination, sinfulness, impurity, corruption, wrongness. 2 artfulness, guile,

cunning, trickery, wiliness, disingenuousness, worldliness.

innocent adj. **1.** The jury found the defendant innocent: guiltless, inculpable, blameless, faultless, free from moral wrong, above suspicion; sinless, irreproachable, upright, unimpeachable. **2.** Jill is an innocent soul: guileless, open, unsuspicious, naive, unworldly, unsophisticated, simple, artless, ingenuous, childlike, honest, uncorrupt, uncorrupted, spotless, unblemished, clean, impeccable, undefiled, stainless, spotless, pristine, unstained, unsullied, virtuous, pure, immaculate, virginal, chaste. **3.** The question was innocent. An innocent lark turned into disaster: well-meant, meaning no harm, harmless, intending no damage, unmalicious, innocuous, inoffensive, unoffending. —n. **4.** Herod's slaughter of the innocents is recounted in the second chapter of Matthew: young child, baby, little one, tot. **5.** The fox's favorite trick was to play the innocent: naïf, unsophisticated person, artless one, (fem.) ingénue. **6.** The old soldier never forgets that he was once an innocent, too: tenderfoot, greenhorn, novice, tyro. —**Ant.** 1 guilty, culpable, blameworthy, responsible; immoral, iniquitous, nefarious, sinful, unlawful, vicious, vile, wicked, evil, wrong; impure, tainted. 2 worldly, sophisticated, disingenuous, dishonest, artful, scheming; corrupt, sullied. 3 harmful, malicious, offensive.

innocuous adj. **1.** The women exchanged innocuous gossip over lunch: harmless, not damaging, painless, not injurious, innocent, mild, inoffensive. **2.** The play was innocuous and quickly forgotten: meaningless, vapid, insipid, dull, pointless, empty, barren; trite, banal, commonplace. —**Ant.** 1 hurtful, deleterious, harmful, insidious, obnoxious, damaging, injurious, offensive, malicious. 2 powerful, trenchant, compelling, impressive.

innovation n. The innovation of jet flight has made the world seem smaller: introduction, institution, establishment, inauguration, commencement; departure from the old, introduction of new methods, modernization, shift, drastic change, breaking of precedent; new measure, novelty, alteration, latest thing, latest fashion; French dernier cri.

innovative adj. Her innovative designs won awards: inventive, new, original, avant-garde, creative, cutting-edge, leading-edge.

innuendo n. The gossip column was full of innuendos about famous people: insinuation, intimation, whisper, oblique hint, veiled allusion, sly suggestion, implication, inference, imputation, hint, indirect reference, overtone.

innumerable adj. There are innumerable stars in the sky: countless, incalculable, myriad, numberless, incapable of being counted, numerous, multitudinous, too many to be counted, unnumbered. —**Ant.** numerable, countable, computable; few, sporadic.

inoculation n. She had a series of inoculations before leaving for the Far East: injection, vaccination, immunization, hypodermic, shot, booster shot, booster, needle, hypodermic injection.

inoffensive *adj. The odor of gasoline is strong but inoffensive:* harmless, unobjectionable, unoffending, tolerable, innocuous, endurable, sufferable; innocent, bland, mild, neutral; safe. **—Ant.** offensive, harmful, objectionable, offending, obnoxious; noxious.

inopportune *adj. I'm afraid I caught you at an inopportune moment:* inconvenient, untimely, ill-timed, incommodious, badly timed, inappropriate, unpropitious, unsuitable, unseasonable; awkward, troublesome; undesirable, unfavorable, disadvantageous, inauspicious, unfortunate, ill-advised. **—Ant.** opportune, timely, convenient, appropriate, propitious, suitable, commodious; favorable, auspicious, fortunate.

inordinate *adj. An inordinate amount of time was spent on minor details:* excessive, immoderate, extravagant, disproportionate, lavish, undue, unreasonable, unconscionable, superabundant, exorbitant, superfluous, overmuch, extreme, intemperate, unnecessary, profuse, unrestrained, wanton, overflowing, supersaturated, surplus, needless, uncalled-for, irrational; outrageous, scandalous, disgraceful, deplorable, shocking. **—Ant.** temperate, moderate; restrained, inhibited; rightful, equitable, reasonable, sensible.

inquest *n. An inquest was held to determine the cause of death:* post mortem, autopsy, necropsy, coroner's inquest, ex post facto examination; inquiry, hearing, probe, investigation, probing, delving, inquisition.

inquire *v.* **1.** *The pilot inquired about the weather conditions:* ask, query, seek information, question, make inquiry. **2.** *The reporter inquired into the rumors of fraud:* investigate, probe, explore, study, look into, look deeper, inspect, examine, search, look behind the scenes of, scrutinize, look over, track down, *Informal* check out. **—Ant.** 1 reply, answer, respond, rejoin, retort; inform.

inquiring *adj. She had an inquiring mind:* questioning, probing, analytical, curious, inquisitive, examining, interrogative, investigative, prying, quizzical, searching, speculative.

inquiry or **enquiry** *n.* **1.** *The murder inquiry was handled by the chief of homicide:* investigation, seeking for truth, examination, questioning, inquisition, hunt, scrutiny, search, probe, interview, study, reconnaissance, inquest, quest, exploration, research, analysis, inspection, survey. **2.** *Personnel made an inquiry about the applicant's previous job:* query, question, interrogation, quiz.

inquisitive *adj.* **1.** *The student is bright and inquisitive:* eager for knowledge, searching, intellectually curious, inquiring, fond of investigation, investigative, questioning. **2.** *The inquisitive woman spread rumors about her neighbor:* prying, interfering, meddling, overcurious, unduly curious, intrusive, too curious, meddlesome, snooping; *Informal* snoopy, nosy. **—Ant.** 1 indifferent, unconcerned, incurious, uninterested, apathetic, inattentive.

inroad *n. They made inroads on the supplies:* incursion, advance, encroachment, impingement, intrusion, invasion, onslaught, raid, trespass, foray.

insane *adj.* **1.** *The psychiatrists declared the killer insane. The letter made her insane with jealousy:* mentally deranged, not sane, not of sound mind, mad, crazed, crazy, lunatic, unsound, demented, maniacal, out of one's mind, bereft of reason, not in touch with reality, mentally disordered, unbalanced; (*variously*) psychotic, manic, schizophrenic, paranoiac; *Informal* out of one's wits, out of one's head, touched, mad as a hatter, mad as a March hare, stark staring mad, unhinged; *Slang* loco, teched, bats, batty, nuts, bats in the belfry, nutty, nutty as a fruitcake, balmy, loony, off one's rocker, cracked, zany; *British* daft, round the bend, off one's chump, potty, bonkers; raving, frenzied, wild, berserk. **2.** *It's insane to fly in this weather:* idiotic, senseless, unreasonable, foolish, dumb, imbecilic, mad, crazy; imprudent, injudicious; absurd, ridiculous, insensate; bizarre, eccentric. **—Ant.** 1, 2 sane; sensible, judicious, wise, sapient, prudent, sound, reasonable.

insanely *adv. They raged insanely against the restrictions:* crazily, wildly, ferociously, fiercely, furiously, violently, wildly, extremely.

insanity *n.* **1.** *She feared that insanity ran in the family:* mental illness, madness, mental disorder, derangement, raving, loss of reason, unsoundness, aberrance, aberration, craziness, lunacy, (*variously*) dementia, mania, psychosis, paranoia, schizophrenia, monomania, hallucination. **2.** *Few people dispute the insanity of nuclear war:* idiocy, senselessness, foolishness, absurdity, stupidity, madness, craziness, folly, unreasonableness. **—Ant.** 1 sanity, good sense, rationality, lucidity, reason, intelligence, soundness.

insatiable *adj. The fat man has an insatiable appetite:* unappeasable, voracious, ravenous, gluttonous, incapable of being satisfied, unquenchable, unsatisfiable, insatiate, bottomless, limitless, implacable; omnivorous. **—Ant.** satiable, appeasable, satisfiable, quenchable.

inscribe *v. He inscribed a dedication on the flyleaf of the book. She inscribed the book to her friend:* write, sign, autograph, scribble, scrawl; imprint, engrave, incise, carve, chisel, impress, mark, pen, letter, etch, brand, seal, blaze.

inscrutable *adj. The Sphinx of Greek mythology had an inscrutable face:* unknowable, incomprehensible, indecipherable, not easily understood, impenetrable to understanding, unfathomable, mysterious, mystifying, arcane, past comprehension, beyond interpretation, puzzling, perplexing, baffling, inexplicable, unsearchable, enigmatic, elusive, unintelligible, unreadable, unrevealed; *Informal* pokerfaced, deadpan; hidden, concealed, veiled, masked. **—Ant.** obvious, palpable, plain, clear, manifest, open, evident, patent; penetrable, comprehensible, understandable; intelligible, explainable, self-evident, familiar, explicable, readable, knowable, revealing, transparent, lucid.

insecure *adj.* **1.** *The battalion's position on the hill was insecure:* unsafe, endangered, exposed to danger, in danger, vulnerable, defenseless, exposed, ill-protected, unshielded, unprotected, unsheltered, risky, perilous, precarious, hazardous, on slippery ground, not out of the woods, under fire, dangerous, critical. **2.** *The foundation of the house is insecure:* not firm, unsteady, weak, shaky, unstable, dilapidated, wobbly, frail, unreliable, rickety, unsound, infirm, ramshackle, tottering, built upon sand, hanging by a thread, in a bad way, dangerous. **3.** *She is insecure about her ability to do the job:* uncertain, doubtful, beset by doubt, diffident, dubious, not confident, unsure, not sure, unassured, in a state of uncertainty, full of misgivings. **—Ant.** 1 secure, safe, invulnerable, protected, shielded, sheltered, steady, trustworthy. 2 stable, sound, reliable, firm. 3 secure, confident, sure, certain, assured.

insecurity *n.* **1.** *The engineers warned us about the insecurity of the bridge in a storm:* insecureness, instability, precariousness, shakiness, unsteadiness, vulnerability, defenselessness, unsafeness, endangerment. **2.** *A feeling of insecurity kept the boy from making friends:* lack of assurance, lack of confidence, uncertainty, lack of sureness, lack of self-reliance, self-doubt, doubt, dubiousness, doubtfulness, diffidence, incertitude, apprehensiveness. **3.** Often **insecurities** *The insecurities of the venture kept investors away:* peril, hazard, danger, cause for alarm, risk, jeopardy, pitfall, contingency. **—Ant.** 1 security, secureness, stability, invulnerability, safeness. 2 security, assurance, sureness, confidence, certitude. 3 security, safeness, sureness, certainty.

insensibility *n.* **1.** *The patient lapsed into insensibility:* unconsciousness. **2.** *His insensibility to criticism was legendary:* indifference, apathy, insusceptibility. **—Ant.** consciousness; concern, sensibility.

insensitive *adj. He was always insensitive to the feelings of others. The fisherman's hands were insensitive to the cold:* unaware of, not sensitive, indifferent, unconcerned, apathetic, uncompassionate; hardened, unfeeling, callous, thick-skinned, blasé, cold; unaware of feeling, not capable of feeling, impervious, insensible, insensate, impassive, dead, numb. **—Ant.** sensitive, compassionate, tender; susceptible, subject, prone, open, exposed, hypersensitive, thin-skinned.

inseparable *adj. The blind man and his dog are inseparable:* constantly together, always in each other's company, attached, extremely intimate; not to be separated, incapable of being parted, indivisible, unseverable, indissoluble. **—Ant.** separable, unattached, divisible, sunderable, severable, soluble.

insert *v. Insert the key in the lock. He inserted a comment in the margin:* place in, put in, infix, set in, imbed, inject, inlay, inset, implant, put between, wedge in, push in, intersperse, slide in, infuse, interlard, press in, thrust in, stick in, stuff in, tuck in, drive in, *Informal* pop in; introduce, interpolate, interpose, interject, intrude, enter, add. **—Ant.** extract, disengage, detach, withdraw, remove, draw.

inside *n.* **1.** *The inside of the cabinet is wallpapered:* interior, inner part, inner space, interior part, inner surface, inner side. *—adj.* **2.** *The lead horse was on the inside track:* inner, innermost, inmost, inward; internal, interior. **3.** *That must be an inside joke. I have inside information:* private, confidential, cliquish, for the elect or knowledgeable, secret, esoteric, intimate, internal, *Slang* in. **—Ant.** 1 outside, exterior. 2 outside, outer, exterior, outermost, external, outward. 3 outside, public, open, exoteric.

insidious *adj.* **1.** *We were taken in by her insidious plan:* devious, treacherous, deceitful, guileful, intending to entrap, crafty, tricky, stealthy, sly, wily, cunning, foxy, artful, contriving, underhanded, perfidious, crooked, slippery, shady, designing; surreptitious, subtle, Machiavellian, sneaky; falsehearted, disingenuous. **2.** *Corruption within the government was insidious and widespread:* secretive, stealthy, surreptitious, underhand, undercover, furtive, sneaking, clandestine, covert, undetected, concealed, disguised; pernicious, deleterious. **—Ant.** 1 upright, forthright, artless, ingenuous, straightforward, sincere, open, honest, frank, candid. 2 open, conspicuous, innocuous, obvious; harmless.

insight *n. The teacher had unusual insight into children's emotions:* perception, spontaneous understanding, apprehension, acumen, innate knowledge, penetration, discernment, intuition, penetrating judgment, immediate cognition, perspicacity, perspicaciousness, perceptiveness, perceptivity, instinctive knowledge, intuitiveness, clear understanding, comprehension. **—Ant.** obtuseness, blindness.

insignia *n. Sew the insignia onto the shoulder of the uniform:* emblem, badge, badge of office, mark, distinguishing mark of honor, decoration, patch, sign, mark of authority, ensign of royalty, symbol; *(variously)* bar, star, oak leaf, medal, epaulet, chevron, stripe.

insignificant *adj. This problem was insignificant compared to others she faced:* unimportant, inconsiderable, petty, negligible, trivial, of little account, of no consequence, inconsequential, having little meaning, paltry, nugatory, of no moment, small, minute, minuscule, trifling, picayune, meaningless, meager, irrelevant, not vital, worthless, immaterial, flimsy, puny, nonessential, indifferent, niggling, not worth the pains, beneath consideration, second-rate, piddling, not worth mentioning, *Informal* small potatoes. **—Ant.** significant, considerable, important, momentous, large, meaningful, essential, vital, appreciable; relevant, material.

insincere *adj. His insincere offer fooled no one:* hypocritical, dishonest, dissembling, deceitful, disingenuous, emotionally dishonest, two-faced, uncandid, untruthful, untrue, false, guileful, disingenuous, dissimulating, fraudulent, perfidious, mealymouthed, devious, lying, evasive, equivocal, double-dealing. **—Ant.** sincere, honest, candid, truthful, true.

insinuate *v.* **1.** *The article insinuated that the fighter was bribed:* imply, suggest, hint slyly, allude remotely to, intimate, asperse, whisper, let fall. **2.** *The social climber insinuated herself into the group:* ingratiate, push artfully, worm one's way, gently incorporate, introduce subtly, wheedle, inject, insert. **—Ant.** 1 deny. 2 withdraw, remove, retreat; alienate.

insipid *adj.* **1.** *An insipid play like that won't last two weeks:* uninteresting, pointless, stupid, dull, characterless, banal, wearisome, bland, boring, trite, vapid, inane, barren, drab, prosaic, jejune, lifeless, zestless, arid, monotonous, lean, empty, commonplace; *Slang* blah, wishy-washy, namby-pamby. **2.** *The unsalted vegetables were insipid:* flat, tasteless, savorless, stale, vapid, unappetizing. **—Ant.** 1 interesting, zestful, pungent, spirited, spunky, provocative, engaging, lively, stimulating, exciting, piquant, colorful. 2 pungent, piquant, spicy, fiery, peppery, gingery; savory, flavorful, tasty, palatable, appetizing; gusty.

insist *v.* **1.** *She insisted that she heard someone in the house:* maintain, state firmly, asseverate, assert positively, vouch, contend, claim, hold, assert, aver, take a firm stand, stress, stick to one's colors, repeat, reiterate, stand one's ground, be pertinacious, persist, be determined; protest, remonstrate. **2.** *The doctor insisted that Don stop smoking:* demand, advise firmly, urge, lay down the law, require, exhort, command, be emphatic, be firm about, press earnestly; warn, caution, admonish. **—Ant.** 1 deny. 2 beg, plead, ask, request.

insistent *adj.* *The insistent audience clapped for an encore:* demanding, clamorous, assertive, imperative.

insolence *n.* *The foreman refused to put up with the worker's insolence:* insulting rudeness, impertinence, unmannerliness, disrespect, disobedience, overbearing contempt, overweening pride, lordliness, audacity, hauteur, arrogance, disdain, haughtiness, imperiousness, superciliousness, presumption, incivility, impoliteness, brazenness, bumptiousness, effrontery, gall, impudence, insulting disobedience. **—Ant.** deference, modesty, respect, politeness, bashfulness, humility, mannerliness, civility.

insolent *adj.* *The insolent child needs discipline:* disrespectful, insulting, impertinent, rude, discourteous, impolite, impudent, unmannerly, audacious, brazen, bumptious, outrageous, nervy, arrogant, presumptuous, defiant, fresh, overbearing, haughty, supercilious, disdainful, contemptuous, galling, *Informal* cheeky. **—Ant.** respectful, deferential; submissive, courteous, polite, civil, complimentary, mannerly.

insoluble *adj.* *The insoluble puzzle defied unraveling:* indecipherable, inexplicable, unfathomable, baffling, impenetrable, mystifying, unaccountable, unresolved, unsolved. **—Ant.** accountable, fathomable, penetrable, solvable.

insolvent *adj.* *The company became insolvent and had to declare bankruptcy:* incapable of discharging liabilities, penniless, impecunious, unable to satisfy creditors, unable to pay one's bills, short of money, destitute, ruined, out of money, bankrupt, overextended, impoverished, moneyless; *Informal* broke, wiped out, unable to make ends meet, down-and-out. **—Ant.** solvent, wealthy, flourishing, thriving, sound, moneyed, rich, *Informal* flush.

insomnia *n.* *She was forced to take sleeping pills because of her insomnia:* sleeplessness, wakefulness, insomnolence, tossing and turning, *Latin* pervigilium, *French* nuit blanche.

insouciant *adj.* *Her insouciant air always lifts my spirits:* lighthearted, happy-go-lucky, carefree, easygoing, buoyant, unconcerned, untroubled, jaunty, debonair, free and easy, airy, breezy, perky, devil-may-care, *French* sans souci; flippant, mercurial, whimsical, capricious. **—Ant.** troubled, careworn, agitated, perturbed, uneasy.

inspect *v.* **1.** *Ask the mechanic to inspect the tires. How often does the auditor inspect the books?:* examine, scrutinize, look over carefully, look carefully at, look intently at, regard carefully, view closely and critically; investigate, reconnoiter, peruse, observe, contemplate, peer at, eye; explore, pore over, scan, study, survey, probe. **2.** *The visiting president inspected the troops:* review, view formally, survey formally, examine officially. **—Ant.** 1, 2 ignore, overlook.

inspection *n.* *The building's inspection was done next:* examination, investigation, scrutiny.

inspiration *n.* **1.** *The painter's inspiration came from nature. Love was Robert Browning's greatest inspiration:* incentive, stimulus, influence, inspiring action, incitement, motivation, motive, prompting, compulsion, spur, encouragement, impulse, creative impulse. **2.** *The Gettysburg Address came to Lincoln as a sudden inspiration:* flash, creative thought, idea, afflatus, divine afflatus, fancy, flight of fancy, revelation. **—Ant.** 1 depressant, discouragement, disenchantment, deterrent.

inspire *v.* **1.** *Shakespeare has inspired generations of playwrights:* stimulate to creation, be an ideal for, fill with life or strength, infuse with inspiration, influence, exalt, illumine, illuminate, impel, motivate, prompt, occasion, galvanize, encourage, embolden, animate, vivify, fire, inspirit, hearten, enliven, quicken; cause, be responsible for. **2.** *A fair and kind employer inspires loyalty:* arouse, rouse, enkindle, engender, encourage, stimulate, prompt, induce, stir, excite, promote, inspirit, give rise to, provoke, cause, produce, occasion. **—Ant.** 1 stifle, squelch, dispirit, dishearten, discourage. 2 stifle, kill, squelch, discourage, suppress.

instability *n.* *His instability makes him a poor job risk:* unstableness, lack of stability, insecurity, lack of firmness, fluctuation, inconstancy, vacillation, unsteadiness, irresolution, indecision, wavering, changeability, capriciousness, flightiness, fitfulness, changeableness, inconsistency, mercurialness, vulnerability, weakness.

—**Ant.** stability, security, constancy, strength, steadiness, equilibrium, resolution, consistency.

install Also **instal** v. **1.** *The building installed a new boiler:* place in service, lodge, establish, station, set in place, emplace, locate, position, plant, arrange, situate, move in, make operative; embed, lay. **2.** *The club installed the new officers last night:* introduce into office, establish in an office or position, induct, invest, instate, receive, usher in, initiate, inaugurate, seat, crown, coronate, ordain. —**Ant.** 1 remove, dislodge. 2 fire; retire.

installment n. **1.** *How many installments did it take to pay off the loan? The first installment of his book was very exciting:* payment, successive portion, amount due, money payable; section, fragment, part, unit, division, chapter, segment, issue. **2.** *The installment of the phone didn't take long:* installing, installation, establishing in office or position, establishment, stationing, placing in service, locating, laying, connecting, hooking up. —**Ant.** removal, detachment.

instance n. *I can't think of an instance when Mother was unfair:* example, illustration, case, case in point, circumstance, time, occasion, exemplification; sample, antecedent, object lesson, specimen, prototype, precedent.

instant n. **1.** *The thunderclap lasted only an instant:* split second, very short time, moment, minute; twinkling, jiffy, flash, trice. **2.** *We liked each other the instant we met:* specific moment, particular time, point in time, very minute, second. —adj. **3.** *The telegram asked for an instant reply:* immediate, quick, prompt, instantaneous; sudden, abrupt, unhesitating; on the spot, splitsecond. **4.** *Space ships are stocked with a variety of instant foods:* premixed, precooked; ready-to-use. —**Ant.** 1 eon, age, eternity. 3 delayed, hesitant, slow.

instantaneous adj. *When the poor old fellow got hit by the truck, his death was instantaneous:* immediate, sudden, extremely fast, happening in an instant, imperceptibly fast, unhesitatingly quick, prompt, abrupt, direct; quick as a flash, speedy, swift, rapid. —**Ant.** delayed, slow, gradual.

instantly adv. *The boss wants the job done instantly!:* at once; without delay, instantaneously, without hesitation, immediately, promptly, directly, quickly; right now, here and now, instanter, in a flash; *Informal* quick as a wink, on the spot. —**Ant.** later, in the future; at one's leisure.

instead adv. *The roast beef is all gone, so have a steak instead:* as a substitute or equivalent, as a replacement, as an alternative, rather, in its place, in lieu of that.

instigate v. *Dissidents tried to instigate a rebellion:* provoke, urge; bring about, incite, start, begin, initiate, spur, goad, rouse, prompt, stimulate; foment, stir up, kindle, set in motion. —**Ant.** repress, quell, quash, check, restrain, discourage, stop, suppress.

instill or **instil** v. **1.** *The couple instilled a love of music in their children:* impart, introduce gradually, inculcate, teach, implant, inspire, in-

duce; sow the seeds of, engender. **2.** *Instill a few drops of oil in the cat's food:* add drop by drop, pour, mix in. —**Ant.** 1, 2 remove, eliminate, eradicate, drain, extirpate.

instinct n. **1.** *Instinct led the pigeons back to the roost:* natural or inbred behavior, natural tendency, nature, native aptitude, inborn drive; blind knowledge, blood knowledge, intuition, mother wit. **2.** *Some people have an instinct for saying the right thing:* aptitude, gift, genius, natural sense, faculty, intuition, knack, natural inclination, proclivity, predisposition, capacity, tendency. —**Ant.** 1 learned behavior, experience, reason, deliberation, judgment.

instinctive adj. *The will to survive is instinctive:* innate, inherent, inborn, inbred, instinctual, resulting from instinct, intuitive, inspired, natural, native, unlearned, unacquired; involuntary, spontaneous, automatic, impulsive; deepseated, ineradicable. —**Ant.** learned, acquired, voluntary, deliberate, willful.

institute v. **1.** *The government instituted a consumer protection agency:* establish, inaugurate, begin, found, originate, set up, bring into being, organize, constitute. **2.** *The police instituted a new investigation:* start, initiate, inaugurate, introduce, put into effect, prescribe, pass, enact, ordain; undertake, get under way, get going, commence. —n. **3.** *The university plans to establish an institute for Chinese studies:* institution, school, college, academy, professional school, graduate school, establishment; association, organization, society, foundation. —**Ant.** 1 abolish, end, terminate, conclude, close, finish, complete. 2 squelch, stop, close, finish, wind up, terminate, end.

institution n. **1.** *The institution of slavery was once widespread. Our annual barbecue has become a local institution:* custom, established practice, convention, unwritten law, rite, ritual, habit, usage, fixture. **2.** *Strong financial institutions are the foundation of a sound economy:* company, organization, establishment, association, organized society, foundation. **3.** *Our city boasts many excellent institutions:* institute, school, academy, college, university, seminary. **4.** *He should be locked up in an institution:* lunatic asylum, madhouse, mental hospital, *Slang* nuthouse, crazy house, bughouse; prison.

instruct v. **1.** *A private tutor instructed the prince and princess:* teach, tutor, educate, school, train, drill, indoctrinate, guide, coach, catechize. **2.** *Instruct the passengers on customs regulations:* give information to, notify, apprise, brief, advise, acquaint, inform, enlighten. **3.** *The captain instructed the soldiers to retreat:* command, direct, order, enjoin authoritatively, bid. —**Ant.** 1, 2 misinform, mislead, deceive, neglect.

instruction n. **1.** *Instruction of recruits was the responsibility of the first sergeant:* instructing, teaching; education, guidance, coaching, training, tutoring, tutelage, indoctrination; pedagogy. **2.** Usually **instructions** *The instructions for assembling the toy are very clear:* direction, information, guideline, prescription, recommendation, explanation, specification, advice, rule; lesson, maxim, precept, motto, moral, homily. **—Ant.** 2 misinformation, misdirection.

instructor *n. Working with an instructor greatly improved his French:* teacher, pedagogue, coach, professor, tutor, trainer, *British* don, lecturer, schoolteacher, schoolmaster, educator, mentor, preceptor, counsel, maestro, guide, guru; schoolmistress, governess, schoolmarm.

instrument *n.* **1.** *All surgical instruments must be sterilized:* implement, tool, device, utensil, appliance, apparatus, equipment, contrivance, machine, mechanism; gadget. **2.** *A police force is an instrument for keeping law and order:* agency, agent, means, medium, vehicle, tool; instrumentality; expedient. **3.** *The lawyers will draw up all the necessary instruments:* legal document; contract, deed, charter, paper, grant. **—Ant.** 2 obstruction, bar, stop, preventive; counteragent, opponent, neutralizer.

instrumental *adj. The newspaper was instrumental in bringing the problem to the public's attention:* helpful, serving as a means, useful, effective, effectual, active, contributory, functional, valuable, conducive, assisting; decisive, crucial, vital, essential. **—Ant.** ineffectual, useless; insignificant, negligible.

insubordinate *adj. Insubordinate sailors were thrown into the brig:* disobedient, refractory, insolent, defiant, intractable, recalcitrant, uncompliant, unsubmissive, unruly, rebellious, fractious, mutinous; disorderly, ungovernable. **—Ant.** obedient, docile, submissive, subdued; servile, obsequious.

insubstantial *adj.* **1.** *The experience seemed as insubstantial as a dream:* unreal, immaterial, intangible, bodiless, impalpable; baseless, groundless; imaginary, visionary, apparitional; airy, gossamer, ethereal. **2.** *The chair is too insubstantial to hold an adult:* slight, frail, flimsy, weak, delicate, fragile; shaky, unsound, unstable. **3.** *The donation was insubstantial but welcome all the same:* modest, trifling, paltry, small, inconsiderable, trivial, piddling. **—Ant.** 1–3 substantial. 1 real, material, tangible, palpable. 2 sturdy, hardy, sound, strong, stable. 3 large, great, considerable.

insufferable *adj. That child is an insufferable brat:* unendurable, intolerable, unbearable; dreadful, insupportable, unspeakable; detestable, disgusting, hateful, outrageous, abominable. **—Ant.** tolerable, bearable; pleasant, pleasing, attractive, charming, appealing, disarming, ingratiating.

insufficient *adj. The old car has insufficient power to get up the hill. He had insufficient funds:* inadequate, scanty, deficient, wanting, sparse, skimpy, lacking, not enough; unsatisfactory; impotent, incompetent. **—Ant.** sufficient, adequate, competent, enough; satisfactory.

insular *adj. The backwoods people had an insular approach to life:* narrow, narrow-minded, bigoted, biased, illiberal, prejudiced, intolerant, limited; provincial, parochial, isolated, petty, insulated. **—Ant.** broad-minded, liberal, catholic, cosmopolitan, sophisticated, worldly.

insulate *v. Thick walls insulated the house:* shield, protect, cocoon, cushion, line, wrap; isolate, keep apart, seclude, sequester, separate.

insult *v.* **1.** *The angry students purposely insulted the teacher:* treat with contempt, be rude to, slight, offend, treat insolently, abuse, scorn, deride, be discourteous to; cut, affront, disparage, belittle. **—n.** **2.** *The speaker's patronizing words were an insult to the audience:* affront, slight, offense, indignity, rudeness, discourtesy, outrage, slap; cheek, impudence; lese majesty. **—Ant.** 1 please, flatter, commend, praise. 2 compliment, flattery, honor, homage.

insulting *adj. The reviewer's criticism was unnecessarily insulting:* rude, discourteous, impolite, disrespectful, uncivil, insolent, offensive, nasty, abusive; derogatory, invidious, defamatory, disparaging, vicious.

insuperable *adj. We met with insuperable difficulties, and thus never finished the project:* insurmountable, overwhelming, impossible, unconquerable, invincible, inexpugnable, unbeatable, unyielding, impassable, overpowering, overmastering, crushing, defeating. **—Ant.** possible, doable, reachable, conquerable, attainable.

insurance *n. Does the company pay medical insurance?:* financial protection against loss, assurance; indemnity, coverage, policy; security, warranty, guarantee.

insure *v. The owner insured the house for $120,000:* obtain insurance for, cover by insurance; guarantee against loss or risk; secure, underwrite. **—Ant.** imperil, jeopardize.

insurgent *n.* **1.** *Insurgents tried to overthrow the government:* rebel, resister, mutineer, insurrectionist, dissident, renegade, revolter, revolutionist; guerrilla, partisan. **—adj.** **2.** *Insurgent activities will be dealt with harshly:* revolutionary, rebellious, mutinous, breakaway, dissident; lawless, insubordinate, disobedient, disorderly. **—Ant.** 1 patriot, loyalist. 2 obedient, loyal, patriotic, subordinate.

insurmountable *adj. The odds against winning seemed insurmountable:* incapable of being overcome, beyond reach, too great, insuperable, hopeless; unconquerable, unbeatable. **—Ant.** surmountable, beatable.

insurrection *n. The prison insurrection was suppressed by the guards:* revolt, rebellion, revolution, insurgence, mutiny, riot, rising, uprising, outbreak. **—Ant.** obedience, submission, subsidence, acquiescence.

intact *adj. The vase he dropped remained intact:* undamaged, in one piece, whole, unbroken, integral, complete, perfect; in good shape, untouched, without a scratch, unimpaired, unharmed, unhurt, uninjured, sound, safe. **—Ant.** impaired, damaged, injured, marred, broken, shattered.

intangible *adj.* **1.** *The soul is intangible:* incapable of being touched, untouchable, immaterial, abstract, ethereal, insubstantial, impalpable, imperceptible. **2.** *An intangible feeling of disaster filled the room:* vague, elusive, fleeting, evanescent, transient, fugitive, imperceptible, shadowy. —*n.* **3.** *The complex plan is full of intangibles:* abstraction, imponderable, accidental, unpredictable happening, unforeseen turn of events. —**Ant.** 1, 2 tangible, palpable, perceptible; material, concrete, physical.

integral *adj.* **1.** *The hedge forms an integral part of the landscaping:* essential, necessary, indispensable, component, constituent, inherent, basic, requisite. **2.** *The couple felt their life was integral even without children:* fulfilled, fulfilling, lacking nothing, whole, entire, full, complete, integrated, total, intact, perfect, finished, rounded, well-rounded. —**Ant.** 1 peripheral, unessential, unimportant, unnecessary. 2 lacking, incomplete, imperfect, deficient.

integrate *v.* **1.** *Integrate all the department reports into one annual statement:* blend, combine, amalgamate, mix, mingle, merge, bring together, unify, fuse, intermix, unite. **2.** *The city was ordered to integrate all public facilities:* make available to every race; open for use by all; desegregate. —**Ant.** 1 disperse, scatter, separate, divide. 2 segregate, separate.

integration *n.* **1.** *An electronic sound system represents an integration of thousands of components:* combination, combining, mixing, blending, fusion, synthesis, union. **2.** *Martin Luther King was a leading advocate of integration:* desegregation, assimilation. —**Ant.** 1 separation, dispersion. 2 segregation, separation, apartheid.

integrity *n.* **1.** *The judge's integrity is unquestioned:* honesty, probity, uprightness, moral soundness, moral stature, principle, character, virtue, purity, rectitude, decency, self-respect, straightforwardness, morality. **2.** *The integrity of a building depends upon a sound foundation:* structural soundness; unimpaired condition, reliability, completeness; wholeness, completeness, strength, unity, coherence, cohesion. —**Ant.** 1 duplicity; deceit, venality, corruption, dishonesty, immorality. 2 flimsiness, shakiness, fragility, faultiness, uncertainty, unsoundness.

intellect *n.* **1.** *Man's intellect distinguishes him from the beasts:* intelligence, mentality, mental power, power of comprehension, power of thinking, understanding, reasoning faculty, cognition, cognitive power, *Informal* brains; sense, mind, rationality, consciousness, perception; wisdom. **2.** *That fellow is a good athlete but not much of an intellect:* thinker, intellectual, *Slang* brain; wit. —**Ant.** 1 emotion, instinct; muscle. 2 idiot, moron.

intellectual *adj.* **1.** *Chess is a highly intellectual game. I admire her intellectual achievements:* cerebral, of the mind, using the intellect, mental, abstract; academic, scholarly. **2.** *The intellectual girl won a research grant:* intelligent, scholarly, studious; *Informal* bookish, brainy; reasoning, thoughtful, rational. —*n.* **3.** *Adlai Stevenson was considered an intellectual by most voters:* intellect, person interested in ideas; thinker, academic, scholar; pundit, sage, savant; mandarin, highbrow; *Slang* brain, longhair, egghead. —**Ant.** 1 physical, material, fleshly. 2

unintellectual, illiterate, unlearned, ignorant, stupid. 3 lowbrow, idiot, moron.

intelligence *n.* **1.** *The prime minister's intelligence and wit enlivened his press conferences:* intellect, mental power, comprehension, understanding, mental skill, power of reasoning, wisdom, acumen, sagacity, shrewdness, perspicacity, *Informal* brains. **2.** *Intelligence of a secret attack came over the wireless:* information, news, knowledge, advice, notice, report, notification, advisement, *Slang* dope; tidings. —**Ant.** 1 ignorance, stupidity, misapprehension, dullness. 2 concealment, suppression; misinformation.

intelligent *adj.* *An intelligent person would have been more careful. That was an intelligent question:* thoughtful, thinking, bright, alert, smart, clearheaded, sensible, informed, well-informed, sage, wise, perspicacious, perceptive, brilliant, keen, quick, knowing, sagacious, quick-witted, sharp-witted, clever, prudent, astute, canny, sharp, shrewd, *Slang* brainy. —**Ant.** unintelligent; foolish, idiotic, stupid, ignorant, dumb; irrational, unreasonable.

intelligentsia *n.* *The dictator jailed the intelligentsia of the country:* educated class, intellectual leaders, intellectual elite; thinkers, intellectuals, academe, ivory tower, academic community. —**Ant.** masses, hoi polloi; bourgeoisie.

intelligible *adj.* *He's a brilliant scientist but I wish his books were more intelligible:* understandable, clear, distinct, comprehensible, coherent, lucid, well-defined, clear-cut, apparent, evident, obvious, definite, unmistakable, unambiguous. —**Ant.** vague, confused, unclear, muddled, incomprehensible.

intend *v.* *What do you intend to do today?:* plan, aim, contemplate, have in mind, mean, determine, propose, design, set as a goal, aspire, expect, wish, project, resolve, calculate.

intense *adj.* **1.** *The heat from the furnace is intense:* extreme, very great, concentrated, acute, sharp, strong, powerful, forceful, considerable, forcible, potent, violent, keen. **2.** *The patient has an intense will to recover:* fervent, earnest, passionate, ardent, strong, powerful, extreme, deep, vehement, burning, deeply felt, emphatic. —**Ant.** 1 weak, mild, moderate, gentle. 2 subdued, relaxed, easy, moderate, casual, indifferent, cool, weak, mild.

intensify *v.* *Lying down only intensified the pain:* increase, heighten, quicken, aggravate, escalate, make more intense, sharpen, reinforce, strengthen, magnify, accelerate, boost, deepen, worsen, redouble. —**Ant.** reduce, lessen, diminish, mitigate, allay; abate; moderate, qualify; alleviate, lighten, relieve.

intensity *n.* **1.** *The intensity of the light depends on the bulb's wattage:* magnitude, power, strength, depth, severity. **2.** *The play's intensity left the audience drained:* passion, emotion, ardor, fervor, vehemence, energy, vigor, strength, power, force, potency, earnestness, zeal, forcefulness. —**Ant.** 2 relaxation, languor, coolness, indifference, weakness.

intent n. **1.** The prisoner was charged with intent to kill: intention, design, purpose, plan, determination, premeditation, aim, end. **2.** The intent of the speech escaped no one: meaning, significance, purport, import, burden, drift; gist, substance. —adj. **3.** The man's intent gaze caused the girl to lower her eyes: steady, steadfast, intense, fixed, highly attentive, undistracted, piercing; concentrated, preoccupied, engrossed, absorbed. **4.** She was intent on having her way: set, bent, insistent, earnest, tenacious, resolved, determined, unbending, unwavering. —**Ant.** 1 accident; chance, luck, fortune. 3 unsteady, wavering, wandering; casual, indifferent.

intention n. His intention is to spend a month in Spain: plan, aim, intent, objective, design, purpose, goal, resolution, target, object, resolve, end, determination.

intentional adj. The press agent's "slip" was intentional: deliberate, intended, willed, done on purpose, planned, purposeful, designed, premeditated, contemplated, voluntary, calculated. —**Ant.** accidental, fortuitous, inadvertent, unintentional, unplanned, unpremeditated.

intently adv. She stared at him intently: hard, searchingly, attentively, closely, fixedly, keenly, steadily.

inter v. Shakespeare said that the good that men do is often interred with their bones: bury, entomb, lay away, inhume, lay to rest, inurn, ensepulcher, Archaic inearth, Slang put six feet under. —**Ant.** exhume, dig up, disinter.

interact v. The two chemicals interact when mixed together in water: interreact, interwork, engage, mesh, dovetail, interplay, intermesh, interlace, coact; cooperate, coordinate, join, conjoin, combine, unite.

intercede v. **1.** Relatives interceded in behalf of the disowned son: offer support or help, lend a helping hand, put in a good word for, use one's influence; speak up, plead. **2.** A neutral nation volunteered to intercede in the interest of achieving peace: arbitrate, mediate, play intermediary, serve as go-between, intervene, interpose, step in. —**Ant.** 1, 2 withdraw, remain aloof, remain neutral.

intercept v. Try to intercept the letter before it falls into the wrong hands. He tried to intercept a forward pass: seize, get hold of, arrest, stay, detain, stop; block the passage of, catch, nab, take, grab, deflect, reroute, cut off; ambush. —**Ant.** transmit, relay; hasten, expedite; admit, permit.

interchange n. **1.** There was much interchange of ideas between departments: exchange, barter, trade, intersection, meshing, networking, reciprocation, switch, trade, transposition, variation, alternation, shift, change, crossfire. —v. **2.** They interchanged the parts: switch, swap, trade, barter, exchange, substitute, reverse, transpose, alternate.

interchangeable adj. "Hot dog" and "frank" are interchangeable terms. Most coffeepot cords are interchangeable: switchable, tradable, exchangeable, transposable; equivalent, closely similar, synonymous, corresponding, parallel, analogous. —**Ant.** unswitchable; unlike, opposite.

intercourse n. **1.** The war stopped commercial intercourse between the two nations: communications, dealings, trade, traffic, relations, connection, exchange, correspondence, commerce; conversation, discourse, talk, communion, colloquy, parley. **2.** Pregnancy is a result of intercourse: sexual relations, congress, copulation, coitus; coupling, pairing.

interest n. **1.** Often **interests** His interests include reading and tennis: preferred activity, absorption, engrossment, pursuit, avocation, preoccupation; pastime, hobby. **2.** The routine speech aroused little interest among political observers: notice, attention, concern, curiosity, regard; suspicion. **3.** Sometimes **interests** A good leader should act in the interests of the people: behalf, benefit, service, weal, advantage, good. **4.** The family has an interest in a chain of hardware stores: share, portion, stake, part, investment, holding, partial ownership. **5.** The loan was made at 6 percent interest: profit, bonus, yield, dividend, gain. —v. **6.** Geology interests him: absorb, engage the attention of, preoccupy, excite the curiosity of, divert, attract; touch, affect. **7.** The teacher tried to interest the students in current events: concern, involve, engage. —**Ant.** 2 unconcern, indifference. 3 disadvantage, detriment. 6 bore, Slang turn off.

interested adj. **1.** She was interested in biology: absorbed, attentive, attracted, caught, engrossed, roused, excited, fascinated, impressed, intent, keen, obsessed, occupied, stimulated, stirred, taken, moved, touched, Informal hooked, sold. **2.** The interested parties met to discuss the topic: partial, partisan, predisposed, prejudiced, involved, biased, concerned, implicated. —**Ant.** 1 bored, apathetic, indifferent, unconcerned.

interesting adj. The magazine's issue on marriage was especially interesting: absorbing, stimulating, arresting, striking; attractive, appealing, entertaining, engaging, pleasing; fascinating, magnetic, riveting; curious, suspicious. —**Ant.** uninteresting, dull, boring, flat, tedious, tiresome.

interfere v. **1.** The television interferes with my concentration: conflict, be a hindrance to, be inconsistent, not be conducive to, counter, get in the way, be an obstacle to, frustrate, jar. **2.** Don't interfere in the problems of others: mix, meddle, intervene, interpose, step in, rush in, intrude, intercede; Slang butt in, horn in, stick in one's oar. —**Ant.** 1 aid, help, assist.

interference n. He would tolerate no interference: hindrance, impedance, disruption, tampering, conflict, constraint, encroachment, hindrance, imposition, intervention, intrusion, meddling, prying, trespassing, Informal butting in.

interim n. **1.** The meeting isn't until noon, so in the interim I can make some phone calls: intervening time, interval, interlude, meantime. —adj. **2.** An interim government was appointed *until new elections could be held:* temporary, provisional, temporal, tentative, stopgap, *Latin* pro tempore. —**Ant.** 2 permanent.

interior *adj.* **1.** *The interior walls of the cabin were unpainted:* internal, inmost, inner, innermost, inside, located within, inward. —*n.* **2.** *The interior of the house is spacious and bright:* internal part, inside, inner space. **3.** *The terrorized tribes fled to the interior:* remote regions, inland parts, upcountry, bush, hinterland, heartland, backwoods. —**Ant.** 1 exterior; outer, outward, outside, external. 2 exterior, outside. 3 coast, borderland.

interject *v.* *The speaker interjected a funny story into his lecture:* insert, throw in, put in, interrupt with, interpose, interpolate, inject, force in, introduce, slip in, sneak in. —**Ant.** extract, remove, withdraw.

interloper *n.* *The host had the interloper thrown out:* intruder, outsider, trespasser; gatecrasher, unwanted presence, meddler, interferer, invader, persona non grata.

interlude *n.* *My evening at home was a pleasant interlude in a hectic week:* interval, intervening period, respite, intermission, recess, pause, break, breathing spell, letup; episode, event, incident.

intermediary *adj.* **1.** *Toronto was the intermediary stop between Montreal and Chicago:* intermediate, in-between, bridging, midway. **2.** *The intermediary agent in the dispute is to be a neutral diplomat:* mediating, acting as mediary, arbitrating, serving as mediator. —*n.* **3.** *He served as intermediary in the labor-management dispute:* mediator, arbitrator, middleman, intermediate, go-between; referee, umpire, adjudicator.

intermediate *adj.* **1.** *The intermediate part of the journey took us through Hungary:* middle, midway, intermediary, halfway, mid, mean, midmost, median, mediate, transitional, intervening. **2.** *This piano piece is of intermediate difficulty:* medium, moderate, average, middling, so-so; fair, mediocre. —**Ant.** 1 first; last. 2 beginning; advanced.

interment *n.* *The interment was at the national cemetery:* burial, burial ceremony, entombment, inhumation; funeral. —**Ant.** exhumation.

interminable *adj.* *People began to walk out on the interminable speech:* endless, unending, ceaseless, boundless, without a stopping point, tediously long, long-drawn-out, prolix, long-winded, limitless, unlimited, illimitable, infinite, perpetual, continuous, incessant. —**Ant.** brief, short, fleeting.

intermingle *v.* *The unlikely ingredients intermingled into a delightful dish:* mix, combine, commingle, blend, amalgamate, intermix, fuse, commix, unite, merge, interfuse, interlace, interblend, mix up, emulsify, mix together, conglomerate, homogenize. —**Ant.** disperse, scatter, break up, disband, separate.

intermission *n.* *The emergency crew worked all night without intermission. The play has two 15-minute intermissions:* interim, period of respite, pause, stoppage, suspension, halt, interlude, stop, rest, break, recess; *British* interval; hiatus,

gap. —**Ant.** continuance, prolongation, uninterruptedness.

intermittent *adj.* *The weatherman predicted intermittent showers:* recurrent, spasmodic, occasional, periodic, starting and stopping, discontinuous, sporadic, on and off, on-again-off-again, fitful, irregular. —**Ant.** steady, unceasing, continuous.

internal *adj.* **1.** *The bleeding must be coming from an internal injury:* interior, located inside, inner, inmost. **2.** *The nation's internal affairs are in turmoil:* domestic; governmental, administrative, state, executive, sovereign, political. —**Ant.** 1 outer, exterior, external, outside. 2 foreign.

international *adj.* *International trade benefits all participants:* between nations, involving two or more nations, cosmopolitan; worldwide, universal. —**Ant.** national, domestic.

interpolate *v.* *He interpolated some personal remarks in the middle of his speech:* insert, inject, put in, work in, stick in, throw in, add, introduce, interlard, intercalate, interline, interject, insinuate, intervene, intersperse, sandwich, implant, intrude, wedge in, *Slang* drag in by the heels.

interpret *v.* **1.** *The psychiatrist interpreted the patient's distress:* explain, make clear, clarify, explicate, explain the meaning of, assign a meaning to, decipher, define, elucidate, throw light upon; unravel, puzzle out, figure out, piece together. **2.** *I interpreted her smile as approval:* understand, construe, take, accept, make out, decipher, see, read, account for. **3.** *Please interpret the comments of our foreign guest:* translate, rephrase in one's native language; restate, paraphrase, reword, render. —**Ant.** 2 mistake, confuse, confound, misconceive, misunderstand.

interpreter *n.* *The diplomat's speech required an interpreter:* translator; clarifier, commentator, exegetist, explicator.

interrogate *v.* *The police interrogated the witness about the accident:* question, probe, examine, cross-examine; investigate, test, catechize, ask, query; *Informal* grill, give the third degree. —**Ant.** answer, retort, respond.

interrupt *v.* **1.** *The newscaster interrupted the quiz show for a flash:* stop, break off, halt temporarily, cause to stop, break in on, discontinue, cut in on, disturb, interfere with, obstruct the course of. **2.** *Sea walls interrupt the long stretch of beach:* block partially, interfere with, break the continuity of, disconnect, intersect, sever, disjoin, punctuate. —**Ant.** 1 continue, resume.

interruption *n.* *The interruption was caused by a group of hecklers:* halt, pause, stop, discontinuity, obstruction, hindrance, disconnection, interference; break, gap, hiatus, lacuna, intermission, rift, interlude. —**Ant.** continuance, resumption.

intersect *v.* **1.** *A beam of light intersected the room's darkness:* cut across, cross, traverse, crosscut, pass through, pass across, bisect, divide, transect. **2.** *The roads intersect a mile from here:* cross, interconnect, crisscross, meet and cross, have a common point; meet, come together, overlap.

intersection *n. The collision occurred at the intersection of Hollywood and Vine:* junction, meeting point, crossroads, crossing, interchange, corner.

intersperse *v. Illustrations are interspersed throughout the book:* interpose, interpolate, intercalate, interlard, interfuse, interject, wedge in; strew, scatter, sprinkle, pepper, bestrew, broadcast, dot, disperse.

interstice *n. There was dust in the interstices between the floorboards:* chink, crevice, cleft, crack, cranny, fissure, slit, space.

intertwine *v. They intertwined their arms:* entwine, interlace, weave, interweave, interknit, braid, crisscross, mesh.

interval *n.* **1.** *An interval of a year passed before another meeting took place:* intervening period, interim, pause, rest, recess, break, interlude, intermission; season, spell, hiatus, interruption. **2.** *An interval of 40 yards separated the house from the river:* space, opening, gap, interspace, separation, rift, cleft; gulf, breach.

intervene *v.* **1.** *Much had happened during the years that intervened:* occur between times, pass, take place, come to pass, befall. **2.** *The referee intervened before the players hurt each other:* step in, break in, interpose, intrude, interfere, mediate, arbitrate, intercede, come between, interrupt, *Slang* butt in.

intervention *n. The policeman's intervention broke up the fight. The two countries will not accept outside intervention:* stepping in, breaking in, mediation, intermediation, interposition, arbitration, intercession; interference, intrusion, *Slang* butting in.

interview *n.* **1.** *He was listening to a radio interview:* conversation, talk, chat; round table, conference, question-and-answer session, questioning. **2.** *Don't be late for your job interview:* professional examination, evaluation, in-person appraisal, consultation; conference, meeting, parley; audience.

intestinal *adj. Intestinal flu laid us low:* alimentary, bowel, abdominal, stomach, gut, ventral, visceral.

intestines *n. pl. Most digestion takes place in the intestines:* alimentary canal; insides, entrails, viscera, bowels, *Informal* guts.

intimacy *n. The two old friends visited together with great intimacy:* closeness, familiarity, caring, tenderness, fondness, dearness, affection, warmth, endearment; lovemaking, sexual relations, sexual intercourse; friendliness, amity, chumminess, brotherhood, camaraderie, fraternity. **—Ant.** separation, aloofness, alienation, estrangement, indifference.

intimate[1] *adj.* **1.** *Only the couple's most intimate friends were invited:* close, bosom, cherished, dear, familiar, personal, near and dear. **2.** *Some feelings are too intimate to discuss:* deeply personal, innermost, confidential, private, guarded. **3.** *An intimate knowledge of drugs enabled him to help the addicts:* detailed, deep, thorough, special, profound, personal, di-

rect, experienced, first-hand, close. **—n.** **4.** *Many famous artists were among Gertrude Stein's intimates:* close friend, close associate, confidant, familiar; *Informal* chum, crony, pal, buddy. **—Ant.** 1 distant, formal, remote. 2 open, public, known. 3 superficial, limited, slight. 4 stranger, outsider; enemy, foe.

intimate[2] *v. The report intimated that more was involved than met the eye:* hint, suggest, imply, indicate, insinuate, allude, refer to indirectly, rumor. **—Ant.** state, declare, assert, proclaim.

intimation *n. There are intimations that the director may be replaced:* hint, suggestion, inkling, clue, innuendo, indication, veiled comment, rumor, allusion, insinuation, sign, portent.

intimidate *v. The gang tried to intimidate the merchant:* terrorize, terrify, scare, cow, menace, make afraid, make timid, make fearful, frighten, fill with fear, alarm, subdue, bully, daunt, browbeat, buffalo; compel by threats, coerce. **—Ant.** encourage, inspire, embolden; reassure.

intolerable *adj. The noise of the drilling is intolerable:* unendurable, unbearable, insupportable, insufferable; excruciating, racking, torturous, agonizing; abominable, hateful, loathsome, abhorrent; unreasonable, excessive, outrageous. **—Ant.** tolerable, bearable, endurable, comfortable; reasonable.

intolerance *n.* **1.** *Racial intolerance is one of the greatest shames of mankind:* bigotry, bias, prejudice, narrow-mindedness, lack of forbearance; xenophobia, chauvinism, racism. **2.** *Albinos have an intolerance for bright light:* low tolerance, inability to bear, hypersensitivity; weak spot; *Informal* no stomach. **—Ant.** 1 tolerance, compassion, forbearance, liberality. 2 tolerance, endurance.

intolerant *adj. Some pious churchgoers are intolerant of other religions:* not tolerant, bigoted, prejudiced, narrow-minded, fanatical, closed-minded, parochial, sectarian, hostile, resentful, jealous, mistrustful; xenophobic, chauvinistic. **—Ant.** tolerant, liberal, forbearing, large-minded.

intone *v. The audience intoned the pledge of allegiance to the flag:* chant, drawl, singsong, hum, croon, vocalize, intonate; say, speak, utter, voice, mouth, murmur, pronounce, enunciate, articulate.

in toto *adv. The writer insisted that the study be published in toto:* as a whole, entire, uncondensed, uncut, unabridged, entirely, outright, completely, totally, in all, all together. **—Ant.** abridged, condensed, cut, in part, incompletely.

intoxicated *adj.* **1.** *How could she become intoxicated after only one glass of wine?:* drunk, inebriated, drunken, *Informal* in one's cups, high, tight, tipsy, *Slang* wrecked, smashed, loaded, bombed, oiled, stoned, plastered, zonked, stinko, stewed. **2.** *The couple were intoxicated by the beauty of the night:* transported, rapt, enthralled, infatuated, delighted, elated, exalted, entranced, enchanted, exhilarated. **—Ant.** 1 sober. 2 bored, indifferent.

intoxicating *adj. The musical was an intoxicat-

ing mixture of high drama and lavish production numbers: stimulating, exciting, exhilarating, heady, inspiring, provocative, rousing, stirring, thrilling.

intoxication *n. Intoxication was a social issue:* alcoholism, drunkenness, inebriation, dipsomania, intemperance, *Informal* boozing, guzzling, tippling, heavy drinking, hard drinking.

intractable *adj. The intractable child refused to obey:* stubborn, perverse, headstrong, ornery, hard to cope with, obstinate, willful, unmanageable, obdurate, incorrigible, mulish, unruly, fractious, froward, refractory, ungovernable, uncontrollable, contumacious, unmalleable, inflexible. **—Ant.** tractable, obedient, docile, submissive, subdued; compliant, acquiescent, amiable.

intransigent *adj. The intransigent strikers refused to negotiate:* uncompromising, stubborn, intractable, obdurate, iron-willed, steadfast, diehard, unyielding, unmovable, unbudgeable, inflexible. **—Ant.** compromising, yielding, flexible, open-minded, acquiescent, compliant.

intrepid *adj. Intrepid commandos led the raid:* fearless, bold, valiant, brave, courageous, audacious, heroic, valorous, dauntless, resolute, doughty, daring, adventurous, undismayed. **—Ant.** cowardly, timid, fearful, cautious, prudent.

intricate *adj. The intricate computer requires a skilled operator:* complicated, complex, sophisticated, involved, difficult to understand; *Informal* tricky, knotty; full of detail or difficulties, tangled, entangled; devious. **—Ant.** easy, simple, straightforward, effortless; obvious, plain, clear, patent.

intrigue *v.* **1.** *Fairy tales intrigue most children:* interest greatly, fascinate, appeal strongly to, arrest, attract, absorb, enthrall, arouse the curiosity of, capture the imagination of, fire, tickle one's fancy, titillate. **2.** *The dukes intrigued against the king:* plot, conspire, machinate, maneuver craftily, scheme, collude, spy. *—n.* **3.** *Politics is a field full of intrigue. The intrigue was exposed:* scheming, machination, secret plotting; underhanded or secret dealings; knavery, double-dealing, sharp practice, behind-the-scenes manipulation, plot, scheme, conspiracy. **4.** *King Arthur discovered the intrigue between Queen Guinevere and Lancelot:* love affair, romance, amour. **—Ant.** 1 bore. 3 sincerity, candor, honesty, openness, straightforwardness.

intrinsic *adj. The acting is good, but the play has little intrinsic value:* essential, innate, inherent, basic, fundamental, underlying, inborn, inbred, native, natural, ingrained, indigenous, per se. **—Ant.** extrinsic, accidental, incidental; added, appended; extraneous, alien, acquired.

introduce *v.* **1.** *Introduce me to your friends:* give an introduction, make acquainted, make known, present. **2.** *A trip to the museum introduced the class to modern art:* bring knowledge to, acquaint, inform, expose, familiarize, make familiar, initiate. **3.** *He wanted to introduce an alternative to the plan:* propose, advance, offer, put forward, present, originate, create, bring into notice; urge, sponsor, recommend. **4.** *The

MC introduced the program with a few jokes:* start, begin, lead off, lead into, *Informal* kick off. **5.** *Saint Patrick introduced Christianity to the Irish:* bring in, show, make familiar, import, bring into practice, institute, establish. **6.** *Shakespeare always introduced some comic relief in his tragedies:* put in, insert, interpolate, infuse, add, interject, interpose, *Informal* throw in. **—Ant.** 3 withdraw, remove, eliminate, exclude, delete, excise.

introduction *n.* **1.** *The union fought the introduction of automation:* introducing, instituting, institution, bringing in; conducting, ushering in; presentation; insertion. **2.** *Make the introductions while I take the coats:* presentation, acquaintanceship, meeting of strangers. **3.** *Modern introductions were resented by the old-timers:* innovation, change, novelty. **4.** *The book's introduction is brief:* preface, prefatory material, preamble, foreword, opening part, opening; prelude, precursor; preliminary speech, opening remarks, prologue. **—Ant.** 1 extraction, elimination, removal, withdrawal; completion, end, termination. 4 epilogue, afterword.

introductory *adj. The manufacturer made an introductory offer at a lower price:* serving to introduce, preliminary, acquainting, initial, beginning, initiatory, prefatory, precursory, *Informal* get acquainted. **—Ant.** final, concluding, last, conclusive, terminal.

introspection *n. After months of introspection he decided to become a priest:* self-analysis, self-examination, soul-searching, heart-searching, self-consultation, self-contemplation, self-observation, meditation, brooding, self-questioning, deliberation, rumination, reflection, self-scrutiny.

introvert *n. An introvert spends much time alone:* private person, withdrawn person; self-contained person; introspective person, inner-directed person; loner, thinker, contemplative, brooder. **—Ant.** extrovert, outgoing person.

intrude *v.* **1.** *The judge intruded his prejudices into the case:* thrust, interject improperly, interpose, push, impose. **2.** *Don't intrude in a family dispute:* enter uninvited, thrust oneself in, obtrude, interfere, intervene, interlope, come uninvited, trespass, encroach, meddle, *Slang* butt in.

intruder *n. An intruder broke into the house last night:* unlawful entrant, interloper, interferer, intervener; gate-crasher, trespasser, encroacher. **—Ant.** guest.

intuition *n. Intuition told me he would not show up. My intuition turned out to be correct:* innate knowledge, immediate cognition, instinct, instinctive feeling; extrasensory perception; telepathy, clairvoyance, precognition, second sight; insight, guesswork, surmise, sixth sense; *Informal* hunch, flash. **—Ant.** ratiocination, reasoning, deduction.

intuitive *adj. The child has an intuitive sense of music:* innate, instinctive, intuitional, natural, native, constitutional, inborn, inbred; resulting from intuition, based on a hunch; nonrational, extrasensory, telepathic, psychic, clairvoyant. —**Ant.** acquired, learned, rational.

inundate *v.* **1.** *Floodwaters inundated the valley:* engulf, overflow, fill with water, overspread, drench, submerge, flood, deluge, drown. **2.** *The visiting astronaut was inundated with invitations:* swamp, glut, flood, saturate, overcome; load down, overburden, overwhelm. —**Ant.** 1 drain dry, reclaim, desiccate, parch, empty.

inure *v.* *Growing up in Alaska inured him to cold weather:* accustom, habituate, familiarize, make used to, naturalize, custom; harden, strengthen, toughen, season, temper, desensitize, discipline, train, adapt, acclimatize, acclimate, get used to.

invade *v.* **1.** *Germany invaded many neighboring countries in World War II:* overrun, enter forcefully, swarm over, infest, enter as a conquering power, aggress upon, enter as an enemy, march into, strike at, assault, assail, attack. **2.** *Tourists invaded the city:* enter massively, overrun, engulf, flood, descend upon. **3.** *A measles epidemic invaded the school:* overspread, spread throughout, permeate, penetrate, infect, infest. **4.** *The state must not invade the freedom of the church:* intrude on, infringe upon, encroach on, trespass, violate, restrict, limit; *Informal* chip away at. —**Ant.** 1, 2 abandon, relinquish, vacate, evacuate. 3 bypass. 4 respect, honor.

invalid[1] *n.* **1.** *The invalid is confined to a wheelchair:* chronically ill person, disabled person, enfeebled person, stricken person, valetudinarian; (*variously*) cripple, paraplegic, paralytic, amputee. —*adj.* **2.** *We hired a nurse for our invalid mother:* infirm, enfeebled, unable to care for oneself, debilitated, disabled, sick, sickly, ailing, unwell, valetudinarian, incapacitated, powerless, weak, weakened. —**Ant.** 2 strong, well, healthy, vigorous.

invalid[2] *adj.* *This document is invalid unless officially stamped. That is an invalid argument:* not valid, void, null, nugatory, useless, forceless, ineffective, good-for-nothing, worthless; inoperative; dead letter; unconvincing, illogical, fallacious, unsupported, unsupportable, unsound, false. —**Ant.** valid, sound, legal, legitimate; correct, forceful, logical.

invalidate *v.* *Unauthorized changes invalidated the passport. Inaccuracies invalidated the speaker's position:* make invalid or worthless, make void, nullify, vitiate, annul, abrogate, repeal, countermand, cancel, deprive of legal force; weaken, discredit, undercut, undermine, refute. —**Ant.** validate, certify, authorize; strengthen, enhance.

invaluable *adj.* *Those invaluable ancient scrolls belong in a museum:* priceless, beyond price, very precious, of great worth, very valuable, extremely expensive, inestimable; rare, choice. —**Ant.** worthless, valueless.

invariable *adj.* *The students respected the teacher's invariable fairness:* constant, unfailing, uniform, unwavering, unvarying, unalterable, immutable, unchanging, changeless, undeviating, unchangeable, always the same, con-

sistent. —**Ant.** variable, changing, changeable, varying.

invasion *n.* **1.** *The military invasion was set for dawn:* infiltration, penetration, incursion, aggression, assault, attack, raid, foray, sortie, inroad; onslaught, juggernaut. **2.** *The illegal search was an invasion of their civil rights:* encroachment, breach, intrusion, infringement; trespass, overstepping, usurpation. —**Ant.** 1 evacuation, retreat. 2 respect, honoring.

invective *n.* *Invective poured from the speaker's mouth:* bitter language, harsh words, verbal abuse, venom, vilification, insult, contumely, diatribe, execration, sarcasm; vituperation, denunciation, revilement, censure, rant, railing, billingsgate. —**Ant.** praise, honor, commendation.

inveigh *v.* *Speaking to reporters he inveighed against unfair labor practices:* denounce, criticize, castigate, rail, abuse, belittle, rebuke, harangue, reproach, upbraid, revile, scold, censure, dress down, vituperate; *Slang* put down, run down, slam, knock. —**Ant.** commend, praise, acclaim, approve.

inveigle *v.* *The sponsors inveigled her into appearing on the benefit:* entice, ensnare, beguile, trick, tempt, allure, seduce, mislead, bamboozle, wheedle, coax, flatter, cajole; *Slang* rope in, suck in, sweet-talk, soft-soap.

invent *v.* **1.** *Alexander Graham Bell invented the telephone:* originate, create, develop, contrive, conceive, devise, put together, fabricate, fashion, formulate; *Informal* think up, come up with. **2.** *He invented some story about the train's being derailed:* make up, concoct, conceive, fabricate, contrive, conjure up, coin; *Informal* cook up, trump up. —**Ant.** 1 copy, imitate, reproduce.

invention *n.* **1.** *The invention of a space rocket took many years:* inventing, creation, fabrication, origination, discovery; production, development. **2.** *The electric can opener is a clever invention:* contrivance, gadget; implement, device, apparatus, machine, contraption; design. **3.** *Mozart is famous for melodic invention:* inventiveness, resourcefulness, originality, imagination, ingenuity, creativity, fertility. **4.** *The alibi was pure invention from start to finish:* fabrication, sham, fake, dissimulation, forgery, concoction, fiction, lie, prevarication, trumpery. —**Ant.** 3 uninventiveness. 4 truth, fact.

inventory *n.* **1.** *The company's inventory lists 2,000 items. The inventory was in perfect condition:* stock list, catalog, roster, roll, index, schedule, register; objects or items represented on the list, stock, merchandise, goods, supply. **2.** *The store is closed for inventory:* survey of goods on hand, accounting, stock-taking.

inverse *adj.* *Double-check by reading the figures in inverse order:* reversed, back to front, converse, backward, right-to-left, bottom-to-top, inverted, opposite, indirect, contrary. —**Ant.** forward; direct.

invert *v.* *They inverted the drawing:* reverse, double back, flip-flop, overturn, turn over, upend.

inverted *adj. In an inverted position, a 9 looks like a 6:* turned upside-down, reversed in position, inverse, bottom up. —**Ant.** upright, right side up.

invest *v.* **1.** *Everyone should invest some time in community service:* devote, give, allot, apportion, set aside, appoint. **2.** *According to the U.S. Constitution, only Congress is invested with the power to declare war:* endow, supply, license, enable. **3.** *The singer invested the songs with a bittersweet sadness:* endow, infuse, imbue, color, clothe, fill, enrich. **4.** *The designer invested the performers with sumptuous costumes:* clothe, garb, dress, cover, array, adorn. —**Ant.** 1, 2 withhold, deny. 2 withdraw.

investigate *v. The police are investigating the murder:* inquire into, explore, examine closely, study, scrutinize, research, probe, look into, search into, delve into; question, query, ask about; sift, pore over, dissect, analyze, inspect, anatomize; survey. —**Ant.** conjecture, guess; ignore.

investigation *n. The investigation may take months:* inquiry, investigating, thorough examination, search, study, scrutiny, probe, survey, review, research, fact-finding; analysis, inspection, dissection, anatomy.

investigator *n. An investigator produced a report:* agent, analyst, examiner, inquirer, inspector, researcher, tester; detective, private detective, private eye, plainclothesman.

investment *n.* **1.** *The man became rich through wise investments:* investing, allotment of funds, capital spending, stock acquisition; financial transaction. **2.** *Each partner's investment was $5,000:* money invested, contribution, offering, share; risk, venture, stake, ante.

inveterate *adj.* **1.** *Inveterate romantics are always falling in love:* confirmed, steadfast, constant, habitual, established, inured, hardened, ingrained, deep-rooted, deep-seated, diehard, adamant; incurable, unregenerate, unreconstructed. **2.** *An inveterate back problem kept him out of the army:* established, continuous, recurrent, chronic, long-standing. —**Ant.** 1 undeveloped, incipient; reformed. 2 superficial, passing.

invidious *adj. Likening my work to her own was an invidious comparison:* insulting, causing envy or hard feelings, inciting ill will, offensive, slighting; malevolent, resentful, malicious, vicious, rancorous, spiteful. —**Ant.** fair, just, placating; flattering.

invigorate *v. The cold invigorated him:* animate, enliven, fortify, energize, quicken, vitalize, strengthen. —**Ant.** enervate, enfeeble, weaken, devitalize.

invigorating *adj. An early morning swim is always invigorating:* refreshing, restorative, enlivening, animating, strengthening, energizing, bracing, healthful, stimulating, rejuvenating, vitalizing, quickening. —**Ant.** tiring, weakening.

invincible *adj. The Maginot Line was thought invincible. His invincible sense of humor helped him through hard times:* unconquerable, indomitable, impregnable, insurmountable, insu-perable, invulnerable, totally secure; irrepressible, unbeatable, undefeatable. —**Ant.** conquerable, vulnerable.

invisible *adj. H.G. Wells wrote a famous story about an invisible man:* not visible, not perceptible to the eye, imperceptible, undiscernible, unapparent, unseeable, unseen; covert, concealed, veiled, obscure, hidden. —**Ant.** visible, apparent, plain.

invitation *n.* **1.** *Have the party invitations been sent out yet?:* request for someone's presence, summons, solicitation, offer, call, bid, bidding. **2.** *Gloomy thoughts are an invitation to depression:* inducement, lure, enticement, allurement, temptation, open door; bid, bidding, call, summons; challenge. —**Ant.** 1 rebuff, repulse, response.

invite *v.* **1.** *Invite the family to stay for the weekend:* request the presence of, summon courteously, urge, call, bid. **2.** *The new hotel invited suggestions from the guests:* request politely, ask formally; encourage, welcome, solicit. **3.** *Some people seem to invite disaster:* tempt, induce, attract, entice, lure, encourage, welcome; act so as to cause. —**Ant.** 2, 3 repel, forbid, discourage.

inviting *adj. This is an inviting room. His proposal that we go swimming was an inviting suggestion:* tempting, attractive, appealing, magnetic, intriguing, alluring, engaging, enticing, charming, warm, welcoming. —**Ant.** uninviting, unattractive, forbidding, repellent.

invocation *n. The priest read a solemn invocation for divine blessing on the new church:* entreaty to a supernatural power, prayer, appeal, supplication, orison, petition, plea, summoning.

invoke *v.* **1.** *The sinner invoked the Lord's forgiveness:* entreat, call upon, petition, implore, appeal for, supplicate, pray for; beg, beseech, importune, ask for. **2.** *The president invoked the veto:* put into effect, have recourse to, resort to, use, implement, employ, apply, introduce. **3.** *The medium tried to invoke the spirits of the departed:* summon by incantation, call forth, conjure.

involuntary *adj.* **1.** *An involuntary confession was obtained through torture:* forced, coerced, unwilling, done without choice, unchosen, reluctant; compulsory, against one's will. **2.** *She gave an involuntary shiver:* spontaneous, reflex, unintentional, unconscious, instinctive, unwilled, automatic, inadvertent. —**Ant.** willing, voluntary, intentional.

involve *v.* **1.** *The plan involves the cooperation of young and old:* include, contain, be a matter of, comprise; entail, depend on, imply. **2.** *Treaty obligations involved the country in the war:* cause to be associated, implicate, embroil, entangle, mix up. **3.** *The senator is involved in a national health insurance bill:* absorb fully, preoccupy, commit, engage, wrap up. —**Ant.** 2 extricate, disentangle, liberate, release. 3 disengage.

involved *adj.* **1.** *The involved plans required much study:* complex, complicated, convoluted, elaborate, intricate, knotty, labyrinthine, tangled, tortuous, winding, confusing. **2.** *They were involved in several acts of fraud:* participating, taking part, concerned, embroiled, enmeshed, entangled, immersed in, implicated, incriminated, interested, occupied *Informal* into, heavily into, hooked into, really into, sucked into. —**Ant.** 1 uncomplicated, easy, simple, straightforward.

invulnerable *adj. The king built the fortress to be invulnerable:* unconquerable, unassailable, invincible, insuperable, unbeatable, undefeatable, inexpugnable, impregnable, formidable, indomitable, undestroyable, imperishable. —**Ant.** weak, vulnerable, fallible, defenseless, unprotected.

inward also **inwards** *adv.* **1.** *The door opens inward:* toward the inside, toward the interior, interiorly. **2.** *Nostalgia turned his reflections inward:* toward one's private thoughts, into the mind or soul, inwardly. —*adj.* **3.** *The explorers discovered an inward passageway. He has achieved inward peace:* directed toward the inside, ingoing, incoming, leading inside, going in, inner-directed, interior; personal, private, mental, spiritual, inner. —**Ant.** 1, 2 outward, outside. 3 outer, exterior, superficial.

iota *n. There's not an iota of truth to the story:* faint degree, small amount, particle, jot, smidgin, tiniest quantity, whit, shred, atom, scintilla, spark, bit, spot, speck. —**Ant.** mass, lot.

irascible *adj. The irascible old man is constantly picking fights:* easily angered, touchy, cantankerous, choleric, waspish, bad-tempered, ill-humored, hot-tempered, irritable, intractable, ornery, splenetic, cross, testy, cranky, grumpy, grouchy, peevish. —**Ant.** good-natured, amiable, gentle, mild, placid, serene, tranquil, easygoing.

irate *adj. The long wait at the checkout counter made the shoppers irate:* angry, angered, furious, rabid, enraged, infuriated; burned up, irritated, annoyed, livid, vexed, riled, galled, indignant, *Informal* mad. —**Ant.** good-humored, tolerant, pleased, tranquil.

ire *n. The strike stirred the community's ire:* anger, rage, outrage, fury, umbrage, wrath, vexation, indignation, resentment, choler. —**Ant.** goodwill, patience, forbearance, forgiveness.

iridescent *adj. The jewel was iridescent in the sun's rays:* changeable in color, colorful, glowing, shiny, reflecting many hues, rainbowlike, opalescent, prismatic. —**Ant.** blanched, neutral, colorless, dingy, dull, lusterless.

irk *v. Late arrivals irked the performers:* annoy, irritate, vex, gall, ruffle, bother, pester, provoke, *Slang* bug. —**Ant.** please, delight, cheer; overjoy.

ironclad *adj. The mill has an ironclad contract to supply the factory with steel for the next two years:* inflexible, unalterable, irrevocable, irreversible, unchangeable, immutable, fixed, unchanging, permanent, unmodifiable, strict, inexorable, rigoristic. —**Ant.** variable, changeable, impermanent, revocable.

ironic also **ironical** *adj.* **1.** *His praise of that awful play was ironic:* mocking, sarcastic, expressing or filled with irony, sardonic, facetious;

insincere, pretended; derisive, biting, cutting, stinging, sneering, caustic, abusive. **2.** *It's ironic that so many pacifists have died violent deaths:* incongruous, inconsistent, contradictory, surprising, unexpected, implausible; curious, strange, odd, weird; *Informal* funny. —**Ant.** 1 sincere, straightforward, direct. 2 natural, predictable, expected.

irony *n.* **1.** *Mark Twain's humor is filled with irony:* indirection, double meaning, facetiousness, sarcasm, mockery. **2.** *What irony to be offered three jobs after having none for so long!:* incongruity, contrariness, absurdity, implausibility, reverse state of affairs, unexpected outcome. —**Ant.** 1 sincerity, straightforwardness, directness.

irrational *adj.* **1.** *Animals and fish are irrational creatures:* incapable of logical thought, unthinking, unreasoning. **2.** *Both your fears and your behavior are irrational:* unsound, illogical, unreasonable, not based in reality, unfounded, baseless, nonsensical, absurd, foolish, ill-advised. —**Ant.** 1, 2 rational. 2 reasonable, wise, sensible, logical.

irreconcilable *adj. The partners' differences seem irreconcilable:* beyond reconciliation, unadjustable, unbridgeable, intransigent, implacably hostile, unappeasable; inconsistent, incompatible, opposed. —**Ant.** reconcilable, appeasable.

irrefutable *adj. The argument for better mass transit is irrefutable:* undeniable, not refutable, incontrovertible, indisputable; proof positive, unquestionable. —**Ant.** refutable, disputable, moot.

irregular *adj.* **1.** *Braces straightened the child's irregular teeth:* uneven, crooked, out of line, unaligned; not smooth, rough, broken, bumpy; asymmetrical. **2.** *Wearing shorts to the office is highly irregular:* nonconforming, unconventional, unusual, uncharacteristic, unexpected; improper, unsuitable, inappropriate, unfitting, indecorous; eccentric, peculiar, queer, odd, singular; abnormal, aberrant, anomalous; unsystematic, unmethodical, haphazard, desultory. —**Ant.** 1 regular, even, smooth, uniform. 2 regular, normal, typical; usual, customary; legitimate, proper, common, established; methodical, orderly, systematic, uniform.

irregularly *adv. She attended school irregularly:* at intervals, disconnectedly, erratically, fitfully, haphazardly, infrequently, intermittently, occasionally, spasmodically, sporadically, willy nilly, eccentrically.

irrelevant *adj. The question is interesting but irrelevant to the problem:* unconnected, unrelated, beside the point, inapt, unfitting, immaterial, nonpertinent, impertinent, malapropos, not apropos, extraneous, foreign, neither here nor there, not germane; *Informal* off base, out in left field. —**Ant.** relevant, pertinent, germane, apropos, related.

irreligious *adj. Communists are assumed to be irreligious people:* not religious, not holding religious beliefs, unbelieving, godless, atheistic, agnostic, impious, profane, sacrilegious, unholy, ungodly. —**Ant.** religious, pious, devout.

irreparable *adj. The hurricane caused irreparable damage:* beyond repair or salvage, uncorrectable, irreversible, beyond redress, uncompensable, irremediable, remediless, unfixable. —**Ant.** reparable, salvageable, reversible, remediable.

irrepressible *adj. Nothing could dampen the boy's irrepressible enthusiasm:* unrestrainable, uncontrollable, unsquelchable, unquenchable, undamped; bubbling, ebullient, vibrant, galvanic, boisterous, tempestuous, full of life. —**Ant.** repressible, restrainable; depressed, damped, squelched.

irreproachable *adj. The judge's record for fairness is irreproachable:* beyond reproach or criticism, above reproof, without fault, flawless, blameless, faultless, inculpable, impeccable; unblemished, stainless, unspotted, unimpeachable. —**Ant.** reproachable, flawed, blameworthy, faulty.

irresistible *adj.* **1.** *He felt an irresistible urge:* overwhelming, not resistible, not withstandable, overpowering, overmastering, superhuman. **2.** *The box of candy was irresistible:* extremely tempting, enticing, alluring, not to be resisted, tantalizing, seductive, enchanting, beckoning, highly desirable. —**Ant.** 1 resistible, withstandable, weak. 2 resistible, unattractive.

irresolute *adj. His irresolute nature made him a poor executive:* indecisive, wavering, hesitating, hesitant, faltering, unsettled, doubtful, undecided, uncertain, unsure, changeable, vacillating, fickle, weak, unsteady, unresolved. —**Ant.** resolute, determined, unwavering, decisive; decided, certain.

irresponsible *adj. She was an irresponsible mother. Turning down the scholarship was an irresponsible decision:* careless, not responsible, undependable, unreliable, indifferent, immature, untrustworthy, thoughtless; imprudent, incautious, reckless, rash, ill-considered, capricious, injudicious, overhasty; foolish, scatterbrained, harebrained. —**Ant.** responsible, careful, thoughtful, trustworthy, dependable.

irreverence *n. The comedian made a virtue of irreverence:* cheekiness, cheek, derision, disrespect, discourtesy, flippancy, impertinence, impudence, mockery, ridicule, rudeness, sauciness; blasphemy, impiety, heresy.

irreverent *adj. The deacon said that talking in church was irreverent:* disrespectful, lacking reverence, impious, irreligious, profane, blasphemous; impudent, brazen, shameless, saucy, sneering, nose-thumbing; disparaging, slighting, critical, skeptical, debunking.

irrevocable *adj. The decision to close the business is irrevocable:* final, conclusive, not subject to reversal, unchangeable, not commutable, irreversible, unalterable. —**Ant.** reversible, changeable, alterable.

irritable *adj. The heat made everyone irritable:* ill-humored, easily irritated, easily annoyed, ill-tempered, easily angered, irascible, easily vexed, touchy, oversensitive, testy, peevish, grouchy, grumpy, waspish, impatient, snappish, pettish, fretful. —**Ant.** easygoing, amiable, good-natured, agreeable, genial, affable.

irritate *v.* **1.** *The child's whining irritated the nurse:* annoy, vex, anger, make angry, make impatient, peeve, provoke, nettle, exasperate, irk. **2.** *Woolen clothing will irritate the rash:* make painful, aggravate, worsen, make sensitive, inflame, make sore, make swollen, rub against, chafe. —**Ant.** 1 appease, mollify, placate, pacify; gratify, please, delight. 2 soothe, balm, ease.

island *n.* **1.** *The island lies a mile offshore:* isle, islet, atoll. **2.** *The library is an island of quiet:* sanctuary, refuge, shelter, retreat, haven, place of tranquil isolation, isolated spot, oasis, enclave.

isolate *v. Researchers have isolated and identified the virus:* separate, segregate, place apart, set apart, insulate, quarantine, seclude, banish, sequester; disconnect, detach. —**Ant.** join, unite, combine, mix.

isolation *n. After a decade she emerged from isolation:* solitude, loneliness; separation, disconnection, segregation, detachment.

issue *n.* **1.** *The motor vehicle department handles the issue of drivers' permits. The magazine comes out in a monthly issue:* giving out, granting; sending out, putting forth, issuance, distributing, dispensation; number, publication. **2.** *The war was the main issue in the presidential campaign:* problem, question, dispute, matter for discussion, point of debate, matter to be settled, matter in dispute. **3.** *There was little hope that the negotiations would have a happy issue:* result, consequence, outcome; yield, product. **4.** *The king's legal issue inherited the throne:* offspring, progeny, children, descendants, heirs, heritors, posterity. **5.** *The issue of water from the cracked pipe grew so serious we called the fire department:* outpouring, gush, discharge, outflow, effluence, drainage, eruption. —*v.* **6.** *Lava issued from the volcano:* pour forth, go out, emanate, flow out, spout, gush, erupt, pass out, emerge. **7.** *The post office issued the new stamps last week:* put in circulation, circulate, distribute. **8.** *The authorities issued food to the flood victims:* give out, distribute, dispense, allot. **9.** *Her insecurities issue from an unhappy childhood:* result, proceed, follow, ensue, grow out of, rise, arise, emerge, stem, spring. —**Ant.** 3 start, beginning, inception, cause. 4 parent, sire. 7 withdraw, revoke, repeal. 8 withhold, withdraw. 9 cause; start, begin, initiate.

itch *v.* **1.** *Poison ivy makes the skin itch:* have an itch, feel the need to scratch, prickle, tickle, crawl, creep. **2.** *The girl itched to see the world:* long, yearn, hanker, have a yen, crave, desire, pine, ache. —*n.* **3.** *I have an itch on my back:* prickling sensation, tingling, itchiness, prickliness, pruritis. **4.** *Most people have an itch for romance:* strong wish, desire, yearning, restless urge, yen, appetite, hankering, craving, hunger, thirst.

item *n.* **1.** *There are ten items on my shopping list:* separate listing, article, notation, entry, detail, particular, unit, thing, matter, subject, point. **2.** *There is an item on the kidnapping in today's paper:* report, news article, notice, piece, story, account, dispatch, paragraph, feature.

itemize *v. Please itemize the purchases on the bill:* list individually, individualize, state one by one, particularize, detail, state by item, enumerate, spell out, specify. —**Ant.** combine, group, *Informal* lump together.

itinerant *adj.* **1.** *Itinerant minstrels strolled the country roads:* wandering, wayfaring, peripatetic, roving, roaming, migrant, traveling, nomadic, footloose, vagabond, vagrant, transient. —*n.* **2.** *A hobo is an itinerant:* person on the move; homeless traveler, transient, wayfarer, wanderer, roamer, rover, nomad, vagabond. —**Ant.** 1 stationary, settled, resident. 2 resident, stay-at-home.

itinerary *n.* **1.** *Leave an itinerary so we can reach you:* travel plan, schedule, detailed plan for a trip, list of places to be visited, timetable, course, route, circuit. **2.** *Father kept a lively itinerary of the trip:* log, record of a journey, travel record, journal, account, diary, day book.

J

jab *v.* **1.** *All during the game he kept jabbing me in the side:* poke, nudge, tap, bump, prod, dig, stab, strike, rap, hit, goad, elbow. —*n.* **2.** *His left jabs had taken their toll by the sixth round:* poke, short punch, quick thrust, pelt, cut, stroke, stab, dig, swing; hit, blow; *Slang* belt, sock, plug, clip, paste, lick, swat.

jabber *v.* **1.** *She was jabbering about nothing in particular and bored everyone:* babble, chatter, talk aimlessly, talk idly, maunder, prattle, prate, blather, drivel, gab, blab, talk nonsense, utter drivel, clack, ramble, gibber, rattle. —*n.* **2.** *Her endless jabber was infuriating:* jabbering talk, gibberish, nonsense, drivel, idle talk, maundering, ranting, prattle, chatter, blabber, babble, prating, patter, blather, gab, chitter-chatter, twattle, clack, palaver, raving, gossip, chitchat, gushing, twaddle, cackle; *Slang* gas, hot air.

jacket *n.* **1.** *You need a light jacket for the cool days of spring:* short coat, (*variously*) sport coat, blazer, smoking jacket, dinner coat or jacket, mackinaw, pea jacket, Windbreaker. **2.** *The notebook was protected by a jacket of clear plastic:* outer covering, wrapper, container, wrapping, cover, envelope, casing, case, coat, enclosure, folder, sheath.

jaded *adj.* **1.** *The movie dealt with the same old jaded themes of betrayal and revenge:* shopworn, worn-out, tired, played out, overused, stale; fatigued, exhausted, weary, wearied, dog-tired, fagged, spent, overwearied, tired out. **2.** *Parisians are said to be jaded and unimpressible:* blasé, bored, surfeited, spoiled, cloyed, dulled, satiate, satiated, sated, glutted, overindulged.

jagged *adj.* *I have a jagged tooth that has to be filed:* rough, snaggy, irregular, having uneven notches or points, indented, crenulated, ragged on the edges, jaggy, uneven, broken; knifelike, serrated, notched, sharp-toothed, saw-toothed, nicked, ridged, zigzag; angular, craggy, rugged, cragged, pointed; spiny, spinous, bristly, thorny; studded, spiked, barbed. —**Ant.** smooth, even, regular; level, straight.

jail or *British* **gaol** *n.* **1.** *He was sentenced to 90 days in jail:* prison, penal institution, penitentiary, prison house, house of correction; *Slang* pen, big house, hoosegow, lockup, jug, can, clink, cooler, slammer, stir, calaboose; reform school, reformatory, workhouse; station house, police station, detention house, halfway house, pound; *Military* guardhouse, guardroom, stockade, black hole, *Naval* brig; dungeon, keep, cell, bastille. —*v.* **2.** *The police jailed him with the rest of the protesters:* imprison, incarcerate, confine, lock up; hold in custody, take or make prisoner, take in, bring in, arrest, put under arrest, capture, seize, apprehend, arraign, book; *Informal* nab; *Slang* run in, pinch, collar, bust, bag. —**Ant.** 2 release, liberate, free, parole.

jam *v.* **1.** *He jammed his clothes into the old suitcase. The people were jammed into the small elevator:* press, cram, crowd, stuff, pack, overcrowd; squeeze, insert forcefully, ram, sandwich, wedge; work in, force in, edge in, worm in, foist in; put between. **2.** *The car picked up speed when she jammed on the accelerator:* hit suddenly, push, thrust, press, bear down on. **3.** *The accident jammed the access road for three hours. The gun jammed:* block, obstruct, congest, stick, suspend, stall, arrest, stop, interrupt, cease; become unworkable, become stuck, malfunction, break down momentarily. —*n.* **4.** *I'd rather walk than be in a traffic jam:* impassable mass of objects or persons, crowd, tie-up, multitude, throng, sea, agglomeration, mob, horde, pack, flock, herd, swarm, host, drove, army; crush, shove, push, press. **5.** *Informal He's in an awful jam with his boss:* fix, trouble, mess, predicament, strait, plight, dilemma, quandary; *Slang* pickle, scrape, pinch, hot water.

jamboree *n.* *At the men's club jamboree there were delegates from all over the world:* festival, fete, carnival, celebration, jubilee, frolic, festivity, gala, spree, party, carousal, *Spanish* fiesta, *French* fête champêtre, festive occasion, revel; *Slang* blowout, bash, do, shindig.

jangle *v.* **1.** *Gold and brass bracelets jangled on her wrist as she gestured:* rattle, clang, clatter, clank; tintinnabulate, chime, jingle, ring, make a plangent sound, reverberate; sound harshly, sound discordantly, make a racket, clash, crash. **2.** *The children's constant screaming jangles my nerves:* upset, jar, irritate, annoy, grate on. —*n.* **3.** *The jangle of the alarm bell woke the sleeping soldiers:* rattle, clang, clatter, clank, racket, clangor, wild pealing, harsh ringing, din, reverberation; cacophony, jumble of sound, confusion of noise. —**Ant.** 3 silence, quiet.

janitor *n.* *The janitor swept the halls every morning:* custodian, cleaning man, cleaning woman, cleaning lady, janitress, handyman, superintendent, *Slang* super, caretaker, porter.

jar¹ *n.* *There were jars of candy on the shelves of the store:* large earthen or glass vessel, container, receptacle, crock, pot, jug, bottle, canister, flask, decanter, beaker, urn, demijohn.

jar² *v.* **1.** *The news of their elopement jarred me:* disquiet, disturb, perturb, unsettle, upset, trouble, disconcert, distract, discompose, startle, shock, astound, stupefy, stun, take aback, shake up, confuse, fluster, bewilder, daze, befuddle; *Informal* give one a turn, throw, faze, floor. **2.** *The earthquake jarred the city and the surrounding countryside for miles:* shake, vibrate harshly, rock, cause to quake, jiggle, jolt, cause to quiver, agitate, make tremble, convulse, joggle, stir, upheave. —*n.* **3.** *The jar of the alarm made him bolt out of bed:* harsh sound, rattle, clang, clatter, clank, racket, clashing, crash, clangor, din, reverberation; cacophony, discordance, jangle, bray, brawl, blare, blast, bong, buzz, bleating. **4.** *The jar of the explosion was felt for miles:* concussion, reverberation, shake, jolt, agitation, impact, crash, shock, quake. —**Ant.** 2 soothe, calm, quiet.

jargon n. **1.** A legal secretary should be able to understand the elliptical jargon of law: specialized or professional language, idiom, parlance, phraseology, vocabulary, usage, vernacular, argot, lingo, cant, shibboleths. **2.** The report was full of jargon and completely useless: meaningless writing or talk, nonsense, gibberish, verbiage, grandiloquence, stuff and nonsense, prattle, drivel, prate, blather, twaddle, blabber, babble, jabberwocky, rigmarole, rubbish, fustian, tommyrot; Slang bunk, balderdash, hogwash, bosh, flapdoodle, folderol, hocus-pocus, abracadabra, poppycock, fudge, moonshine, gobbledygook, bull, hooey, baloney, malarkey, piffle. **3.** He learned to converse in the native jargon: simplified language, vernacular, lingo, dialect, patois, brogue, pidgin, lingua franca.

jaundiced adj. **1.** We take a jaundiced view of her professed naiveté: skeptical, cynical, doubting; blasé, bored, satiated. **2.** Other people's good luck always makes him jaundiced: jealous, envious, covetous, green-eyed; resentful, hostile, bitter, embittered, feeling ill will, mistrustful, suspicious, doubting. —**Ant.** 1 credulous, believing, trusting.

jaunt n. He had many souvenirs from his jaunts all over the world: short trip, excursion, junket, trip, tour, outing, expedition, ramble, adventure, flight; Informal spin, stroll, promenade, airing.

jaunty adj. It was pleasant to meet such a jaunty, smiling young man: lighthearted, high-spirited, buoyant, bouncy, perky, lively, sprightly, vivacious, airy, breezy, blithe, free and easy, carefree; sporty, debonair, dapper, high stepping, spruce, neat, trim; Informal natty. —**Ant.** staid, sober, sedate, dignified; dull, lifeless, pessimistic.

jazzy adj. The fashion show launched a jazzy selection of new outfits: snazzy, smart, animated, flashy, gaudy, lively, spirited, zestful, vivacious.

jealous adj. **1.** She was jealous of her friend's good figure: envious, resentful, covetous, green-eyed, grudging. **2.** She was extremely jealous of her boyfriend. They were ridiculously jealous of their social position: possessive, suspicious, mistrustful, mistrusting, wary, anxious, concerned, regardful, protective, watchful, apprehensive; conscious of, obsessed with, unduly proud of, zealous in maintaining or guarding something, mindful. —**Ant.** 1 trusting, trustful. 2 indifferent, uncaring.

jeer v. **1.** They jeered the first speaker: deride, sneer, mock, revile, laugh at, taunt, hoot, ridicule, scorn, harass, hound, make game or sport of, poke fun at, heckle, hector, gibe rudely, scoff, flout; hiss, boo, whistle at, whoop, catcall; Slang knock, bug, give the raspberry or Bronx cheer, razz. —n. **2.** The jeers from the crowd caused the senator to leave the podium: jeering utterance, derision, taunt, mockery, contumely, slur, barb, yell of contempt, hoot, insult, aspersion, abuse, obloquy, scoff, scoffing; Slang knock, rap, slam, dig. —**Ant.** 1 applaud, cheer. 2 encouragement, adulation, applause.

jeopardy n. You'll put yourself in jeopardy by crossing a man like that: danger, peril, openness to danger, imperilment, exposure, vulnerability, hazard, endangerment, unsafety, liability, risk, precariousness, insecurity. —**Ant.** security, safety.

jerk n. **1.** He gave a firm jerk on the rope and pulled in the rowboat. His hand moved in jerks because of his anger: pull, snap, tug, yank; shake, twitch, quiver, spasm, reflex, start, trembling, tic. **2.** Slang He was a jerk to fall for that old trick: idiot, fool, dupe, dope, dunce, ass, dummy, klutz. —v. **3.** He jerked on my lapel. His hands jerk when he's irritated: pull, tug, twist, thrust, pluck, yank, wrench; shake, convulse, twitch, quiver, tremble.

jerry-built adj. Workers lived in jerry-built shacks near the mine: flimsy, rickety, gimcrack, shoddy, unsubstantial, defective, faulty, weak, frail, shaky, thrown-together, thrown-up, run-up, unstable, ramshackle, slipshod, unsound; Slang tacky, sleazy, cheap-jack. —**Ant.** sound, sturdy, well-built, durable, substantial.

jest n. **1.** We don't need your jests at this moment: facetious remark, joke, jape, gibe, quip, wise crack, crack, pleasantry, pun; Informal gag, trick, prank, game; witticism, bon mot. —v. **2.** He jests at scars that never felt a wound: crack jokes, joke, quip, banter, fool, tease, act up, play the fool, laugh; Slang josh, wisecrack, horse around.

jester n. Royal jesters were welcome respites from the court formalities: clown, fool, zany, buffoon, joker, wag, motley fool, madcap, funnyman, merry-andrew, punchinello, Informal card; harlequin, wearer of the cap and bells; (variously) mime, pantomimist, mimic, mimer, mummer, comedian, comic, wit, humorist, quipster.

jet n. **1.** The firemen put jets of water on the blaze: stream, stream of liquid, fountain, spurt, spray, spout, squirt, swash, shoot, flush, gush, German Spritze. **2.** Turning the jet to the right he watered the lawn with the long hose: spout, nozzle, sprayer, sparger, sprinkler; atomizer, syringe, German Spritzer. —v. **3.** Oil suddenly jetted out of rig number four: spout, spurt, stream, shoot, shoot out, spray, squirt, issue, discharge, break or burst forth, gush, fountain, rush up, surge, effuse, vomit forth.

jettison v. During the storm the crew jettisoned much of the ship's cargo: throw overboard, toss overboard, pitch over, throw over, cast off, throw off ballast; eliminate, discard, throw out, dump, scrap, unload, eject, discharge.

jewel n. **1.** The jewels were kept in the safe: precious stone, cut and polished stone, gem, stone. **2.** She appeared at the reception wearing her finest jewels: ornament, piece of jewelry, bangle, bauble, bead, trinket, (variously) necklace, bracelet, earring, ring, tiara, lavaliere, locket, pendant, brooch. **3.** As a consultant, she was a jewel: treasure, prize, gem, one in a thousand, one in a million, first-rater, ace; Informal topnotcher, pearl, pearl of great price, pure gold, find, honey, dear, apple of one's eye, salt of the earth; Slang crackerjack, whiz, humdinger, pip, winner, knockout; work of art, masterpiece.

jewelry *n. Her jewelry was insured for one million dollars:* jewels, gems, precious stones, adornments, personal ornaments, regalia; articles of gold, silver, or gems; trinkets, gewgaws, bangles, costume jewelry.

jibe *v. My total doesn't jibe with the accountant's:* agree, conform, accord, fit, harmonize, tally, correspond, match, square, coincide, concur, mesh, go together, fit together, dovetail, fit in, go. **—Ant.** conflict, contradict, oppose, differ, disagree.

jiffy *n. Sit down, breakfast will be ready in a jiffy:* moment, minute, instant, trice, flash, second, twinkling, split second, wink of the eye, twinkling of an eye; *Slang* jiff, shake, two shakes of a lamb's tail; millisecond, microsecond, nanosecond; *British Slang* half a mo.

jiggle *v. He jiggled the key in the lock trying to get the door open. Please stop jiggling!:* shake, wiggle, joggle, agitate, jostle; wriggle, fidget, bounce, twitch, jerk.

jilt *v. She jilted him a week before the wedding:* cast off a lover or sweetheart, break an engagement, break off with, break one's word or promise; forsake, leave, leave in the lurch, desert; betray, let down, break one's heart.

jingle *v. 1. His keys jingled in his pocket:* jangle, ring, clank, clink, clatter, tinkle. *—n. 2. The jingle of bells announced the arrival of the ice cream truck:* ringing, clang, tinkle, tintinnabulation, jangle, reverberation. **3.** *That jingle has been played to death on every radio station:* a catchy poem or song, singing commercial, commercial tune, ditty, product theme; facetiae, burlesque poem or verse, trivial verse, doggerel, limerick.

jingoism *n. Patriotism is fine, but the jingoism of some politicians is self-serving:* chauvinism, nationalism, superpatriotism, flag-waving, blind patriotism, spread-eagleism, overpatriotism, patriotics, ultranationalism, wrapping oneself in the flag.

jinx *n. It was as if there were a jinx on her whole vacation:* evil spell, evil eye, hex, curse, plague, ill wind, *Slang* whammy; nemesis, bête noire, bugbear, bugaboo.

jitters *n. She had the jitters so bad she could hardly speak:* nervousness, shakes, shivers, fidgets, anxiety, tenseness, jumpiness, shakiness, uneasiness, quivering, fidgetiness, skittishness; *Slang* butterflies, willies, heebie-jeebies, whim-whams, jim-jams, the creeps, screamingmeemies. **—Ant.** calm, repose, ease, composure, serenity, poise.

job *n. 1. It was my job to see that all orders were filled quickly:* work, task, responsibility, charge, assignment, duty, business, affair; commission, mission, chore, errand, undertaking, function, role, part, stint, concern, care, trust; enterprise, activity, exercise, performance, accomplishment, achievement. **2.** *He took a job as a night watchman:* post of employment, position, situation, engagement, appointment, place, spot, opening; means of support, occu-

pation, career, living, livelihood, business, line of business; capacity, role, part, function, office; profession, vocation, field, province, calling, pursuit, métier, trade, craft, kind of work. **3.** *They were paid according to the number of jobs they completed:* unit of work, assignment, contract, commission; completed effort, piecework, lot, allotment, quota, portion, share, output, product.

jocose *adj. His jocose remarks had the audience roaring with laughter:* jocular, joking, teasing, playful, humorous, jesting, roguish, arch, facetious, witty, comic, comical, waggish, jovial, jolly, droll, quick-witted, nimble-witted, sportive, prankish, *Slang* fun. **—Ant.** serious, earnest, solemn, staid, humorless.

jocular *adj. He was a jocular man, especially around women:* humorous, lighthearted, given to joking or jesting, sportive, witty, jocose, joking, jesting, facetious, jolly, jocund, jovial, merry, gay, mirthful, laughter-loving, full of fun, funny, playful, rompish, prankish, roguish, frolicsome, waggish; entertaining, amusing, droll. **—Ant.** grave, earnest, sober, solemn.

jocund *adj. It was an evening of merriment among jocund companions:* cheerful, merry, pleasant, jovial, jolly, breezy, lively, lighthearted, elated, debonair, cheery, happy-go-lucky, easygoing, untroubled. **—Ant.** sober, serious, grave, sad, troubled.

jog *v. 1. The pony cart jogged down the bumpy road:* trot, bounce, jar, rock, jiggle, jounce, shake, jostle, joggle, bob, jerk. **2.** *The mention of his name jogged my memory:* nudge, stir, activate, energize, actuate, stimulate, prompt, animate, set going. *—n. 3. Give the pendulum a little jog to start the clock:* jerk, pull, twist, wrench, shake, twitch; *Informal* yank, tug.

join *v. 1. We joined the pieces of material by sewing their edges together:* bring together, connect, conjoin, fasten, tie together, marry, couple, bind, fuse, unite, piece together; splice, merge, mix, band, combine, pool; chain, link, bridge. **2.** *Use some mucilage to join the broken ends:* cement, glue, stick together, stick, hold fast, attach, paste; cohere, bind, connect, unify, unite, solder, affix. **3.** *Two rebel groups joined forces to overthrow the government:* unite, ally, combine, merge, bring together, consolidate; federate, amalgamate, conglomerate, associate, confederate, syndicate; hold together, get together, meet, fraternize, cooperate. **4.** *We joined the country club:* become a member of, associate oneself with, sign up with, enroll in, enlist in, enter, subscribe to. **5.** *The living room joined the patio:* adjoin, border on, verge on, be adjacent to, conjoin, be contiguous with; connect with, meet, reach, touch, abut; hug, skirt, scrape, brush, graze. **—Ant.** 1, 2 disjoin; part, separate, sever, sunder; detach, disengage; disentangle, untangle, divide, disconnect. 4 leave, resign, quit.

joint *n. 1. He suffers arthritis in his leg joints:* part where joining occurs, place of joining, connection, articulation, juncture, junction, coupling, hinge; nexus, link, knot; *(variously)* hock, knuckle, knee, elbow. —*adj.* **2.** *The canvassing was a joint effort by both organizations:* mutual, common, shared, sharing or acting in common, community, communal, hand-in-hand, collaborative, collective, cooperative, coalitional, conjoined, conjunctive; combined, allied, united, corporate, unified, associated, associate, consolidated; like-minded, unanimous. —**Ant.** 2 individual, solitary, lone.

jointly *adv. They took care of that problem jointly:* together, in common, by combined action, conjointly, mutually, by mutual consent, collectively, in conjunction, in association, unitedly, in unison; *Informal* arm in arm, hand-in-hand, side by side. —**Ant.** separately, individually, on one's own.

joke *n.* **1.** *A lampshade on the head was his idea of a joke:* jest, pleasantry, diversion, playful or mischievous trick or remark, play of wit, horseplay, facetiousness, whimsy, frolic; practical joke, gag, jape, monkeyshine, prank, caper, frolic, antic, lark; funny story, anecdote, shaggy-dog story, bon mot, wit, witticism, pun, quip, badinage, repartee, wisecrack, banter, satire, parody, lampoon, farce, travesty, burlesque, *Informal* put-on. **2.** *He was the joke of the town because of his tough-guy dress:* object of joking or ridicule, butt, target, laughing stock; simpleton, fool, buffoon, clown, town fool, village idiot, bumpkin. **3.** *The job was so easy it was a joke:* cinch, pushover, trifle, nothing, mere nothing, snap of the fingers, child's play, lark, farce, no great matter, a little thing, nothing to speak of, nothing worth mentioning. —*v.* **4.** *He was always joking around when there was work to be done:* jest, clown, crack jokes, banter, play the fool, frolic, gambol; *Slang* josh, goof, gibe, horse around, wisecrack. **5.** *They joked about his ineptitude:* poke fun at, make jokes about, mock, ridicule, make merry with, laugh to scorn, make game of, gibe at, laugh at, smile at, chortle, laugh up one's sleeve, snicker, deride, pooh-pooh, scoff at, jeer at; play a practical joke upon, send on a fool's errand, put on, dupe, gull, take in, fool, tease; *Slang* roast.

joker *n.* **1.** *He was the class joker:* clown, jester, comedian, funnyman, wit, wag, jokester, life of the party, madcap, zany, humorist, punster, mimic, *Slang* wisecracker. **2.** *Informal He was able to cheat the people by putting a joker in every contract:* hidden danger, pitfall, trap, exploitive device, obscure factor, catch, subterfuge, trick, hitch, snag, snare; fine print, escape clause, rider, codicil, supplement, addendum.

jolly *adj. We had a jolly time at the party. She's my jolliest aunt:* happy, merry, gay, mirthful, cheerful, sportive, funny, gleeful, delightful, rollicking, jocund, jocular, fun-loving, jovial, merry, droll, high-spirited, playful. —**Ant.** solemn, grave, serious; lugubrious, morose, dour, saturnine.

jolt *v.* **1.** *The news of his illness really jolted me. The bumpy road caused the old car to jolt and rattle:* startle, disturb, perturb, upset, take aback; shake, jar, shake up, shock, stun, *Informal* throw; jerk, jog, bump, bounce, convulse,

joggle, jump, bob, jiggle, jostle, bobble. —*n.* **2.** *The news about her nephew was a jolt to her. We felt the jolts of the car on the bumpy road:* shock, jar, start, thunderbolt, trauma; setback, reversal, shaking, bounce, jounce, twitch, jerk, joggle, jostle, jog, bump, lurch, agitation, jiggle, quiver, quake.

josh *v. Her friends joshed her about her freckles:* tease, jolly, ridicule, twit, poke fun at, guy, sport with, chaff, haze; *Slang* rib, jive, kid, razz, put on, rag, roast. —**Ant.** praise, flatter, compliment, adulate.

jostle *v. The students jostled each other on the staircase as they went to class:* shove, bump, crowd, push roughly, hit against, collide, run against, shoulder, elbow, butt, push, knock against, prod, jab, poke.

jot *v.* **1.** *She jotted down the main points the ecologist was making:* write quickly, put down, take down, set down, make a note of, make a memorandum of, note, scribble; list, record, register, enter. —*n.* **2.** *The fact that he was leaving didn't upset me a jot:* the least bit, one little bit, one iota, speck, whit, bit, dot, mite, trace, smidgen, trifle, particle, snip; modicum, scintilla, snippet, flyspeck.

journal *n.* **1.** *She kept a journal of her activities:* daily record, diary, register, chronology, almanac, record, daybook, notebook, calendar, chronicle, memorandum, record book, memory book, yearbook, history, scrapbook, album; memoir, autobiography, confession; *Naval* log, logbook; *Bookkeeping* ledger, account book. **2.** *We subscribe to the local journal:* newspaper, paper, gazette, chronicle, tabloid, sheet, daily, weekly; (*variously*) publication, periodical, magazine, monthly, quarterly, annual.

journalism *n. She studied journalism at Columbia:* coverage, news coverage, reportage, the press corps, the fourth estate, the press.

journalist *n. The journalists decided on a code of ethics:* reporter, newsman, newswoman, newswriter, representative of the press.

journey *n.* **1.** *His journeys took him all over the world:* trip, tour, junket, expedition, trek, excursion, outing, jaunt, wandering, divagation, peregrination, roving, odyssey, pilgrimage, quest; flight, voyage, course of travel, cruise; route, itinerary, transit, circuit, passage, way. —*v.* **2.** *He journeyed around the world:* travel, tour, take a trip, divagate, peregrinate, trek, sightsee, voyage, sail, navigate, cruise, fly, course, ramble, roam, rove, wander, pilgrimage, wend, meander, vagabond, tramp.

jovial *adj. He was a kind, jovial man:* cheerful, merry, gay, mirthful, gleeful, cheery, blithe, zestful, jocund, jolly, hearty, jocular, jocose, sunny, buoyant, delightful, sportive, playful, frolicsome, fun-loving, convivial, laughing, humorous, hilarious, rollicking. —**Ant.** saturnine, dour, morose, gloomy, lugubrious, melancholy.

jowl *n. Squirrels can carry nuts in their jowls:* jaw, cheek, flesh of the lower face, chops, mandible, muzzle (*of an animal*).

joy *n.* **1.** *She was filled with joy upon the birth of her grandchild:* delight, happiness, gladness, exultation, satisfaction, rapture, fullness of heart, ecstasy, elation, excitement, cheerfulness, glee, gaiety, exhilaration, delectation, jubilation, enjoyment, pleasure, contentment. **2.** *Her children were the joys of her life:* cause of gladness, source of pride or satisfaction, treasure, prize, pride, precious possession, gem, jewel. —**Ant.** 1 sorrow, misery, despair, unhappiness, grief. 2 bane, trouble, affliction, trial, tribulation.

joyful *adj.* **1.** *He was joyful to see his brother again:* delighted, jubilant, happy, glad, pleased, exultant, cheerful, elated, full of joy, ecstatic, overjoyed, enraptured, transported, beside oneself with joy, gladsome. **2.** *The birth of the baby was a joyful event:* happy, gladsome, pleasing, heartwarming, causing or bringing joy, delightful, blessed, rosy, cheerful, bright, pleasurable, heartening, gratifying.

joyless *adj. Reading the novel was a joyless experience:* sad, cheerless, unhappy, gloomy, dismal, miserable. —**Ant.** joyous.

joyous *adj. Their 50th anniversary was a joyous occasion:* happy, glad, gladsome, joyful, festive, wonderful, rapturous, gay, mirthful, merry, cheerful, gleeful, lighthearted, gratifying, pleasurable, heartening, heartwarming, delightful. —**Ant.** sad, unhappy, joyless.

jubilant *adj. When he won first prize, he was jubilant:* joyful, overjoyed, ecstatic, flushed with excitement or pleasure, in good or high spirits, exultant, rejoicing, rapturous, delirious, radiant, enraptured, exuberant, elated, exhilarated; cheerful, joyous, merry, mirthful, gay, gladdened, glad, gladsome, delighted, smiling, laughing, happy, gleeful, pleased, gratified, jolly, lighthearted, cheery; blithe, blithesome, buoyant, rhapsodic, enrapt, charmed, captivated, intoxicated; *Informal* happy as a lark, merry as a cricket, floating on cloud nine, tickled pink, happy as the day is long. —**Ant.** doleful, sorrowful, despondent, sad, melancholy, *Informal* down in the dumps.

jubilee *n. The diamond jubilee celebrated Victoria's 60 years as Queen of England:* festival, fete, gala, revelry, frolic, celebration, observance, festivity, revels, holiday, anniversary, commemoration, jubilation, party, conviviality, merrymaking; *Slang* bash, wing-ding, blast, do, blowout, shindig.

judge *n.* **1.** *They asked him to be a judge at the baking contest:* justice, magistrate; official, arbitrator, arbiter, moderator, juror, adjudicator; critic, reviewer, censor; referee, umpire. **2.** *She was a good judge of character:* critic, assessor, appraiser, evaluator, connoisseur; expert, authority. —*v.* **3.** *He's judged many cases in his 25 years at court:* rule on, settle, pass sentence, pronounce judgment on, administer justice, adjudge, adjudicate, arbitrate, sit in judgment on, determine, decide, find, announce a verdict; conduct, try, review, hear; referee, umpire. **4.** *I can't judge which one I like better. He judged the time to be about noon:* decide, ascertain, find, resolve, determine, discern, distinguish; estimate, surmise, guess, conjecture, suppose, believe, assume, imagine, fancy; consider, re-

gard, deem, conclude; infer, deduce; *Informal* reckon. **5.** *He was always judging people according to their taste in clothes:* appraise, rate, rank, assess, value, weigh, gauge, size up, analyze.

judgment or *chiefly British* **judgement** *n.* **1.** *In the jury's judgment he was guilty as charged:* decision, finding, ruling, verdict; decree, sentence; adjudication, arbitration. **2.** *She always had poor judgment in picking friends:* discretion, taste, judiciousness, discernment, discrimination; perceptiveness, perception, sense, shrewdness, acumen, percipience. **3.** *It was the reviewer's judgment that the play would be a success:* opinion, appraisal, belief, conviction, conclusion, deduction, persuasion, estimate, valuation, assessment, view.

judicial *adj.* **1.** *His guilt or innocence will be decided by judicial process:* judiciary, jurisdictional, juristic, legal, official. **2.** *He acted in a very judicial manner inside and outside the courtroom:* befitting a judge, judgelike, magistral, magisterial, majestic, imposing, distinguished.

judicious *adj. He was not judicious in the way he handled the interview:* sensible, wise, sagacious, sage, perspicacious, sound of judgment, just, discriminating, discerning, astute, knowing, sound, levelheaded, reasonable, clear-sighted, acute, shrewd, sober, sober-minded, percipient; diplomatic, politic, tactful, thoughtful, reflective, prudent, well-advised. —**Ant.** injudicious, imprudent, unsound; tactless, thoughtless, unreasonable.

jug *n. She filled the jug with wine:* vessel, pitcher, ewer, jar, urn, crock, decanter, bottle, flagon, carafe, demijohn, tankard, stein, container.

juggle *v.* **1.** *He was able to juggle five plates and sing at the same time:* practice jugglery, keep aloft, keep objects in play. **2.** *The accountant juggled the company's books and embezzled thousands of dollars:* manipulate, falsify, alter, misrepresent, modify, disguise, tamper with, fool with, redo, reorganize, meddle with, tinker with.

juice *n. We had coffee, eggs, and orange juice for breakfast:* drink, beverage, fluid, liquor, nectar, secretion, sap.

juicy *adj.* **1.** *The oranges are more juicy when they ripen on the tree:* juice-filled, fluid, moist, succulent, liquid, watery, wet, sappy, luscious, pulpy, lush, runny, flowing, fluent, dripping. **2.** *It was one of the juiciest scandals of the decade:* vivid, intriguing, exciting, picturesque, colorful, thrilling, racy, spicy, risqué, sensational, graphic, lurid, tantalizing, captivating, fascinating, provocative. —**Ant.** 1 dry, desiccated, arid, moistureless. 2 dull, vapid, colorless, lackluster, unimaginative.

jumble *v.* **1.** *Someone jumbled the files, and I can't find anything:* mix confusedly, mix up, throw together, toss at random, pitch, strew about, turn topsy-turvy, scatter, pile up, ball up, heap, bunch. —*n.* **2.** *His room was a jumble of clothes, newspapers, and soda bottles:* confusion, mixture, disarray, snarl, tangle, muddle, medley, conglomeration, mix, accumulation, aggregate, mélange, miscellany; mess, chaos, clutter, tumble, hodgepodge, gallimaufry, farrago, potpourri, stew, salmagundi, mishmash, patchwork, olio; *Informal* what the cat brought in, everything but the kitchen sink. —**Ant.** 1 separate, isolate; order. 2 order, system, arrangement.

jumbo *adj. The restaurant serves a jumbo steak that is a full 20 ounces:* huge, immense, gigantic, oversized, mammoth, colossal, stupendous, giant, elephantine, cyclopean, enormous, monumental, titanic, monstrous, mountainous, towering, mighty, vast. —**Ant.** small, tiny, minute, minuscule, wee.

jump *v.* **1.** *He not only avoided sidewalk cracks—he jumped over them:* leap, hop, skip, vault, spring, bounce, pitch, bound; buck, prance, gambol. **2.** *The car jumped the railing and went over the cliff:* skip, go over, hurdle, overrun, not be held back. **3.** *She jumped whenever someone came up behind her:* start, flinch, blench, wince, recoil. **4.** *The young thugs jumped the old man:* attack, ambush, spring upon, pounce upon, fall upon. **5.** *The professor was always jumping from one topic to another:* skip, pass, digress, maunder, switch, change abruptly, move quickly. **6.** *The price of meat jumped within one month:* increase or rise suddenly, climb rapidly, skyrocket, zoom up. —*n.* **7.** *One jump and you'll be over the fence:* bound, leap, vault, skip, hop, spring. **8.** *Though it was a small jump, his horse landed in the puddle:* obstacle, obstruction, barrier, barricade, impediment, hurdle. **9.** *In May there was a jump in sales:* sudden rise, increased volume, upturn; surge, swift increase, upsurge, advance, boost, increment, augmentation.

jumpy *adj. Being home alone at night makes her jumpy:* jittery, nervous, skittish, fidgety, agitated, shaky, nervy, fluttery, trembling, twitching, twitchy, aflutter; fretful, apprehensive, anxious, uneasy; *Slang* uptight, goosey; alarmed, panicky, frightened. —**Ant.** calm, unruffled, composed, serene, sedate.

junction *n. The policeman directed traffic at the junction of the two main thoroughfares:* juncture, convergence, linkup, joining place, concurrence, confluence, conflux, joining, connecting point, crossroads, intersection, interchange.

juncture *n.* **1.** *At that juncture, he decided to proceed with his original plans:* point of time, occasion, moment, interval, pass; critical point, crisis. **2.** *We placed the wiring at the juncture of the two walls:* junction, joining, joint, connection, seam, mutual edge, closure, point of contact, meeting, intersection. **3.** *The two signs were put at the juncture of the two mountain paths:* intersection, convergence, confluence, joining place, joining, junction, linkup, connection.

jungle *n. Tarzan lived in the jungle. Some parts of this city are a jungle:* rain forest, wilderness, wild impenetrable land, unexplored territory, virgin forest, bush, wild, woods, swampy forest; undergrowth, dense vegetation; uncivilized territory, lawless region, savage environment. —**Ant.** civilization, civilized territory.

junior *adj.* **1.** *I spoke with the junior Mr. Smith:* younger, minor. **2.** *He was the junior member of the committee:* lesser, subordinate, lower, secondary, inferior, minor, second-string; more recent, newer, later. —**Ant.** 1, 2 senior, elder, older; superior.

junk *n.* **1.** *We took all the junk out of the basement:* rubbish, litter, discarded material, clutter, trash, debris, refuse, waste, odds and ends, castoffs, oddments, rummage, scrap, *Slang* garbage. —*v.* **2.** *We junked the old TV set:* discard, throw away, dispose of, scrap, dump, throw out, pitch out.

jurisdiction *n.* **1.** *The university had no jurisdiction since the crime happened off campus:* judicial right, lawful power, authority, prerogative, legal right, say, control, dominion, command, sway, rule. **2.** *The sheriff's jurisdiction was only within his own county:* extent of authority, scope of power, precinct, bailiwick, province, dominion, hegemony, domain, district, circuit, sphere, compass, zone, range, reach, scope, bounds, beat, quarter, area, latitude, field.

jurist *n. Earl Warren was a famous jurist:* justice, judge, magistrate, legal authority; lawyer, attorney-at-law, attorney, counselor, counsel, advocate, legal adviser; *British* barrister, solicitor.

just *adj.* **1.** *He was a just man, listening to both sides of every complaint:* fair, equitable, even-handed, fair-minded, impartial, unbiased, unbigoted, unprejudiced; trustworthy, honest, moral, upright, uncorrupt, good, decent, blameless, ethical, principled, scrupulous, upstanding, high-minded, righteous, honorable, conscientious, aboveboard, open to reason; disinterested, dispassionate, objective. **2.** *His just beliefs led him through life:* reasonable, sensible, sane, sound, balanced, logical, based on knowledge and understanding, ethical, reputable, conscionable; well-grounded, well-founded, firm, solid, strong. **3.** *All in all, I think life imprisonment was a just sentence:* deserved, fair, justified, equitable, justifiable, worthy, merited, due, condign; suitable, appropriate, fitting, proper, befitting; logical, reasonable, adequate, acceptable. —*adv.* **4.** *She was just here:* a brief time ago, a moment ago, but a moment before, a little while ago; a short time ago, not long ago, recently, lately, only now. **5.** *The roast came out just right. That's just what he told me, too:* exactly, precisely, in all respects, completely, fully, entirely, perfectly, absolutely, quite. **6.** *He just did manage to place second:* by a narrow margin, narrowly, by a hair's breadth, barely, by a little, only just, no more than, hardly, scarcely. **7.** *He was just a poor man:* only, nothing but, merely, but, no more than, simply, at most. —**Ant.** 1–3 unjust. 1, 2 crooked, devious, corrupt; untrue, dishonest, prejudiced, unfair, unreason-able, partial, unlawful, inequitable. 3 undeserved, unfit, inappropriate.

justice n. **1.** *In the name of justice, all men should be equal:* righteousness, goodness, probity, right, uprightness, fairness, fair play, rightness, justness, equity, equitability, equitableness, honor, truth, honesty, integrity, probity, virtue. **2.** *He had justice on his side:* legality, right, proper cause, legitimacy, lawfulness, the law, constitutionality; justification. **3.** *Is there no justice after a crime like this?:* due punishment, reparation, penalty, chastisement, correction, atonement, amends, redress, satisfaction, just deserts, compensation, payment, remuneration. **—Ant.** 1–3 dishonesty, favoritism, inequity, injustice, partiality, unfairness, unlawfulness, unreasonableness, untruth, wrong.

justifiable adj. *They decided his actions were justifiable:* lawful, legitimate, valid, defensible, warrantable, admissible, allowable, acceptable, condonable, fair, fit, proper, reasonable, right, rightful, suitable, tenable, well-founded. **—Ant.** indefensible, inexcusable, arbitrary, unwarranted.

justification n. *She could give no justification for her conduct:* defense, validation, answer, account, advocacy, argument, basis, confirmation, explanation, grounds, rationale, rationalization, reason, reply, response, support.

justify v. *In some cases the end justifies the means:* vindicate, excuse, prove right, show to be just, warrant, support, validate, uphold, sanction, confirm, sustain, bear out, back up, defend, account for, explain, make explanation for.

justly adv. *We expected them to behave justly:* lawfully, legally, legitimately, befittingly, correctly, dutifully, fairly, fittingly, honorably, impartially, properly, reasonably, righteously, rightly, uprightly.

jut v. *The pier jutted out over a shallow bay:* extend, protrude, stand out, project, beetle, thrust forward, stick out, poke out, bulge, overhang, shoot out.

juvenile adj. **1.** *The movie was aimed at a juvenile audience. For a grown man he acted in a very juvenile manner:* young, youthful, adolescent, junior; immature, childish, childlike, pubescent, infantile, puerile, callow, boyish, girlish, sophomoric, unsophisticated. **—n. 2.** *Property may not be owned by a juvenile:* minor, youth, youngster, stripling, teenager, child, infant. **—Ant.** 1 adult, mature, matured, grown-up, full-fledged; senile; manly, womanly 2 adult, older person.

kaleidoscopic *adj. It was fascinating to watch the kaleidoscopic changes in the sunset:* many-colored, motley, rainbowlike, variegated, variable, changeable, fluctuating, ever-changing, checkered, protean, unstable, vacillating, shifting, mobile. —**Ant.** stable, constant, fixed, steady, uniform.

keen *adj.* **1.** *The knife was old, but the blade had a keen edge:* sharp, fine, finely honed, sharp as a razor, razorlike, paper-thin. **2.** *He had the keenest faculties and a phenomenal memory:* sharp, shrewd, astute, acute, penetrating, incisive, alert, quick-witted, clever, discerning, perspicacious, discriminating. **3.** *We were keen about going to the picnic. He had a keen appreciation of art:* eager, enthusiastic, impatient, excited; intense, fervid, ardent, earnest, fervent, avid, zealous, impassioned, fierce. —**Ant.** 1, 2 blunt, dull, flat, obtuse. 3 apathetic, indifferent, unexcited.

keep *v.* **1.** *We kept all the gifts Aunt Mary gave us. He kept the family name:* retain, hold, possess, preserve, maintain, conserve, *Informal* hang on to. **2.** *Try to keep your clothes in the closet. They kept a supply of fancy towels in their linen shop:* hold, store, place, deposit, accumulate, heap, stack, pile; have, lay in, furnish, carry, stock. **3.** *She kept her niece for a week:* care for, take care of, look after, mind; extend hospitality to, have as a guest; guard, watch over, safeguard, keep an eye on. **4.** *Peter Peter Pumpkin Eater had a wife and couldn't keep her:* support, provide for, supply with the necessities of life, sustain, pay for, maintain. **5.** *Keep the people away from the accident! The parade kept traffic from moving:* hold, hold back, keep back, restrain; encumber, stall, retard, impede, inhibit, arrest, constrain, prevent; obstruct, block, hinder, bar, hamper, hamstring, cramp, clog, hobble, tie up, shackle; detain, delay, hold up, deter. **6.** *Please keep moving! He kept at his studies and graduated with honors:* continue, carry on, keep up, persist in; stay, abide, stick, remain, stand, maintain, be constant, persevere, endure, be steadfast. **7.** *We keep the religious holidays:* observe, hold, pay heed to, celebrate, solemnize, honor, ritualize, commemorate, memorialize. —*n.* **8.** *He paid for his keep by doing odd jobs:* room and board, food and lodgings, sustenance, daily bread; subsistence, support, living, livelihood, maintenance. **9.** *The ruins of the medieval keep still stood after 600 years:* fortress, stronghold, donjon, fortification, fort, citadel, castle, tower. —**Ant.** 1 discard, abandon, give up, lose. 5 release, liberate, free; speed, expedite, hurry. 7 ignore, disregard.

keeper *n.* **1.** *Only the keeper was allowed in the animal cages:* gamekeeper, attendant, guard. **2.** *He was the keeper of the art collection. Am I my brother's keeper?:* curator, caretaker, guardian, warden, custodian, retainer, conservator; governess, chaperon, duenna, nurse, nurserymaid, nursemaid, wet nurse; protector, bodyguard, guardian angel; guard, sentinel, sentry, escort; jailer.

keeping *n.* **1.** *The gesture was in keeping with*

our friendship: congruity, harmony, conformity, consistency, agreement. **2.** *The child was delivered into their keeping:* custody, protection, care, charge, guardianship, trust.

keepsake *n. She kept the partially torn photograph as a keepsake of her trip:* memento, memory, token of remembrance, souvenir, remembrance, token, reminder, memorial, relic; symbol, emblem.

keg *n. Kegs of beer were delivered to the tavern:* barrel, cask, drum, butt, vat, tank, rundlet, container, tun, tub, puncheon, hogshead, kilderkin.

kerchief *n. She wrapped a kerchief around her head:* scarf, muffler, cloth, handkerchief, neckerchief, neckcloth, neckwear, headpiece, babushka.

kernel *n. The hickory nut has a very small kernel. There's a kernel of truth in his statement:* seed, grain, germ, pit, stone, pip, nut; core, center, nub, gist; marrow, pith, nucleus, center, quintessence.

kettle *n. The water boiled in the kettle:* teakettle, teapot, pot, pan, saucepan, cauldron, crucible, tub, vat, tureen, boiler.

key *n.* **1.** *He used his key to open the door:* opening device, opener; (variously) latchkey, master key, passkey, skeleton key, house key. **2.** *Her story gave the key to the mystery:* crucial determinant, solution, explanation, answer, meaning, translation, interpretation, elucidation, resolution, finding, explication, light, exposition; cue, clue, indicator, indication, indicant; point, pointer. **3.** *The instruments were tuned to the key of E. The arrangement involved her singing in different keys:* tonality; scale, mode. —*v.* **4.** *We tried to key the program to a younger audience:* adjust, fit, suit, adapt; address, direct, gear.

keynote *n. The keynote of the convention was "Better Health for All Americans":* theme, essence, main idea, gist, core, heart, substance, nub, nucleus, central point, sum and substance, salient idea, pattern, pith, marrow, quiddity, *Slang* nitty-gritty.

keystone *n. The presumption of innocence is the keystone of American law:* basis, base, principle, cornerstone, root, foundation, mainspring, linchpin, crux, central idea, cardinal point, main thing, gravamen; *Slang* bottom line; name of the game.

kibitz *v. He liked to kibitz when his friends played cards:* meddle, interfere, second-guess, pry, snoop; advise, counsel, coach, direct.

kibitzer *n. The kibitzer offered advice on every hand we played:* meddler, snoop, snooper, busybody, butt-in, prier, watcher, pry; *Slang* buttinsky, backseat driver.

kick *v.* **1.** *The football player kicked the ball over the goal:* strike with the foot, punt, boot, hit, strike. **2.** *Shotguns often kick after firing:* recoil, spring back, jump back, fly back, rebound. **3. kick out.** *The landlord kicked him out of his apartment for nonpayment of rent:* eject, throw out, cast out, turn out, remove, send packing, show the door, give the heave, give the gate, send about one's business; *Slang* give the boot to, boot out, give the bum's rush. **4.** *Informal What have you got to kick about?:* complain, fuss, make a fuss, protest, grouch, object, remonstrate, grumble, find fault, grouse, fret, fume, growl, gripe, beef. *—n.* **5.** *He gave the ball a hard kick:* a hit with the foot, boot, stroke; act of kicking. **6.** *The kick of the shotgun made him fall backward:* recoil, kickback, springing back, rebound, return, reaction, backlash. **7.** *Slang Sailing gave him quite a kick:* thrill, pleasure, excitement, amusement, fun, enjoyment; great satisfaction, gratification. **8.** *Slang The spices really gave the salad a kick:* flavor, pungency, high seasoning, tang, intensity, punch, sparkle, snap, dash, piquancy; pep, verve, zest, vigor, vim, power, force, vitality, life, animation. **9.** *Informal His kick was that he wasn't making enough money:* complaint, protestation, grievance, objection, remonstration, protest, gripe, beef.

kickback *n. He hinted that he should get a kickback for approving the contract:* bribe, cut, share, commission, percentage, protection, compensation, remuneration, recompense, protection money, graft, payoff; *Slang* payola, boodle, hush money.

kid *n.* **1.** *The kids were kept in the small corral:* young goat, yearling; *Informal* billy goat, nanny goat. **2.** *The gloves were made of kid:* goatskin, goat hide, goat leather. **3.** *Informal The kids had a great time at the movies:* child, little one, youngster, tot, moppet, shaver, tyke, little shaver, *Slang* squirt; juvenile, adolescent, teenager; baby, infant. *—v.* **4.** *Slang They kid him because he grew a beard. She was kidding him when she said she'd marry him:* tease, plague, harry, make fun of, mock, laugh at, make sport of, jest, josh, make game of, rag, rib, ride; ridicule, fool, mislead, delude, trick, deceive, hoodwink, gull, bamboozle, cozen, beguile, bluff, *Slang* put on. *—Ant.* 3 adult, grown-up.

kidnap *v. The criminals had planned to kidnap the wealthy man's son:* hold for ransom, abduct, carry off, capture, seize, impress, shanghai, bear away, lay hold of; hijack, skyjack; *Slang* snatch, put the snatch on, make off with.

kill *v.* **1.** *The prisoners killed a guard during the escape:* murder, slay, slaughter, cut down, put to death, assassinate, butcher, massacre, shoot down, shoot, mortally wound, injure fatally, end the life of, take the life of, dispatch, put an end to, get rid of, do in, silence, stop the breath of, wipe out, exterminate, deal out death, shed blood, spill blood, execute; *Slang* knock off, bump off, rub out, blow away, finish off, erase, waste, take for a ride; *(variously)* strangle, garrote, smother, asphyxiate, suffocate, drown, poison, electrocute, hang, lynch, string up, bring to the gallows, behead, guillotine, bring to the block, decapitate, cut the throat of, burn to

death, put to the stake, put to the sword, put to the knife, run through, dismember, hack or chop to pieces, tear limb from limb, draw and quarter, disembowel. **2.** *His constant failures killed his ambition:* extinguish, defeat, destroy, ruin, break, check, put a stop to, halt, stay, quell, stifle, smother, squelch. *—Ant.* 1, 2 enliven, bring to life, revitalize.

killing *n.* **1.** *The killing of the two children made headlines:* murder, slaying, slaughter, homicide, manslaughter, massacre, violent death, death by violence, annihilation, elimination, extermination, decimation, butchery, bloodshed, capital punishment, execution, electrocution, fatality; *(variously)* shooting, stabbing, strangulation, strangling, garroting, guillotining, decapitation, lynching, hanging, poisoning, impalement, flogging to death, beating to death, stoning to death, burning to death; patricide, matricide, regicide, fratricide, sororicide, uxoricide, infanticide, suicide; crucifixion, martyrdom, immolation. **2.** *His killing in a business venture made him a millionaire:* stroke of luck, master stroke, success, coup, windfall, bonanza; *Slang* big hit, smash hit; cleaning up, cleanup. *—adj.* **3.** *He raised his sword for a killing blow:* lethal, mortal, deadly, causing death, deathly, fatal, death-dealing. **4.** *He had a killing toothache:* extremely painful, excruciating, murderous, devastating.

killjoy *n. She was so depressed she was a real killjoy:* spoilsport, sourpuss, grouch, malcontent, crapehanger, worrywart, Cassandra, complainer, grumbler; *Slang* party-pooper, wet blanket, dog in the manger, sourball, gloomy Gus.

kin *n. All our kin were at the family reunion:* family, relatives, kinfolk, relations, folks, people, kith and kin, tribe, clan, flesh and blood, race, kinsmen, connections, next of kin, tribesmen, clansmen; *(female)* distaff side, spindle side; *(male)* spear side.

kind[1] *adj. Although he tried to act gruff, he was basically a kind man:* kindly, benign, generous, good-hearted, tenderhearted, soft-hearted, tender, gentle, compassionate, merciful, good-natured, affectionate, charitable, warmhearted, bighearted, sympathetic, understanding, well-meaning, considerate, thoughtful; amiable, obliging, cordial, gracious, accommodating, amicable, friendly, neighborly, good-humored, well-disposed, gentle, polite, courteous, civil. *—Ant.* unkind, cruel, harsh, merciless, severe.

kind[2] *n. What kind of dessert do you like?:* sort, type, class, brand, make, variety, style, description; cast, mold, nature, genus, genre, designation, breed, ilk, strain, caste, kidney.

kindhearted *adj. Her kindhearted deeds showed her generous nature:* kind, kindly, benign, good-hearted, tenderhearted, compassionate, kindly disposed, charitable, philanthropic, good, warmhearted, softhearted, good-natured, sympathetic, generous, humanitarian, humane, loving, affectionate, gentle, gracious, warm, merciful, accommodating, helpful; understanding, thoughtful, considerate, well-meaning, well-intentioned, altruistic, amicable. *—Ant.*

hardhearted, coldhearted, heartless, cold, selfish, unkind, cruel, harsh, severe, unsympathetic.

kindheartedness n. Her kindheartedness was shown in the many things she did for people: kindness, kindliness, benefaction, goodness, goodness of heart, tenderness, compassion, kindly nature, good nature, unselfishness, sympathy, understanding, benevolence, magnanimity, charitableness, philanthropy, altruism, humanitarianism, humaneness, love for mankind, goodwill, goodwill to man, humanity, mercy; graciousness, consideration. —**Ant.** unkindness, cruelty, meanness, selfishness, indifference, coldheartedness.

kindle v. **1.** He kindled the logs in the fireplace: enkindle, ignite, set on fire, set fire to, cause to start burning, light, apply a match to, Informal stick a match to. **2.** The orphan kindled the woman's maternal instincts: stir, arouse, rouse, stir up, inspire, call forth, waken, awake; enkindle, fire, stimulate, agitate, intensify, provoke, induce, incite, inflame, excite, invigorate, quicken, animate; sharpen, whet, foment, urge, prod, goad. —**Ant.** 1, 2 smother, stifle, extinguish, quench, dampen.

kindling n. **1.** We sent the boys to collect kindling for the bonfire: tinder, firewood, material that burns easily, fuel; (variously) brush, brushwood, twigs, small branches, paper, shavings. **2.** The kindling of the logs in the fireplace brought warmth to the room: setting fire to, igniting, ignition, enkindling, burning, flaming, lighting, firing, combustion.

kindly adj. **1.** He was a kindly man, helping those less fortunate than he: kind, benign, good, generous, warmhearted, softhearted, affectionate, devoted, tender, warm, compassionate, gentle, charitable, merciful, sympathetic, philanthropic, benevolent, magnanimous, humanitarian, bighearted, humane, friendly, understanding, patient, considerate, tenderhearted, good-natured, well-meaning, neighborly; amiable, gracious, cordial, good-humored, courteous, amicable. —adv. **2.** The nurse acted kindly toward her patients: benignly, generously, warmheartedly, warmly, softheartedly, affectionately, tenderly, compassionately, gently, charitably, mercifully, sympathetically, philanthropically, benevolently, magnanimously, humanely, bigheartedly, understandingly, considerately, tenderheartedly, good-naturedly, well-meaningly, neighborly, amiably, cordially, graciously, good-humoredly, amicably, well-manneredly, civilly. —**Ant.** 1 unkindly, malevolent, malign, malicious, spiteful, unsympathetic; mean, cruel, harsh, severe. 2 unkindly, malevolently, malignly, maliciously; spitefully, unsympathetically, meanly, cruelly, harshly, severely.

kindness n. **1.** One often depends on the kindness of strangers: kindliness, benevolence, generosity, benefaction, beneficence, mercy, charity, charitableness, philanthropy, humanity, humanitarianism, humaneness, magnanimity, goodness, goodness of heart, sympathy, compassion, unselfishness, consideration, under-

standing, patience, toleration, tolerance, grace, graciousness; goodwill, goodwill to men, brotherly love, friendly feelings, warm feelings. **2.** I've never forgotten her kindnesses in the past: kind act, humane gesture, kindly gesture, good deed, act of charity, act of generosity, good turn, act of grace, generosity, benefaction, bounty, gift, favor, kind office, help, aid, assistance, good treatment. —**Ant.** 1 unkindness, malevolence, harshness, cruelty, severity, sternness, roughness, austerity. 2 cruel or unkind act, evil deed.

kindred adj. We were kindred spirits and were very compatible: like, allied, closely related, similar, corresponding, alike, matching, resembling, analogous; united, harmonious, agreeing, accordant, congenial, sympathetic, Spanish simpático; consanguine, related, intimately related, akin, familial. —**Ant.** alien, unrelated, uncongenial, different.

king n. We arrest you in the name of the king: monarch, ruler, sovereign, liege, His Majesty, suzerain, crowned head, anointed ruler, royal personage, the anointed, royal person, potentate, protector, defender of the faith.

kingdom n. He ruled his small kingdom fairly and justly: realm, nation, country, dominion, domain, land, territory, state, principality, duchy, dukedom, empire, monarchy; sphere, field.

kingly adj. His Majesty received the visitors with kingly grace: majestic, kinglike, imperial, royal, regal, monarchal, sovereign, noble, princely, queenly; splendid, grand, magnificent, glorious, stately, awe-inspiring, august, patrician; autocratic, absolute, imperious, lordly, commanding, mighty; despotic, tyrannical.

kink n. **1.** He brushed the kinks from the horse's mane: twist, tangle, gnarl, coil, crimp, crinkle, frizz, knot, frizzle. **2.** All the hiking gave him a kink in his leg: local pain, pang, twinge, spasm, stiffness, knot, cramp; Informal crick, charley horse. **3.** It took us two days to smooth out the kinks in our plan: complication, hitch, defect, rough spot, difficulty, flaw, imperfection, loose end, tangle, snarl, knot, Slang glitch. **4.** An excessive fondness for the color black was the only kink in his personality: peculiarity, eccentricity, oddity, crotchet, mental twist, twist, idiosyncrasy, quirk, queerness, weirdness, foible; freakishness, singularity, vagary.

kinky adj. **1.** He wore his hair short because it was so kinky: knotted, tangled, twisted, matted, frizzled, wiry, crinkled, frizzly, twisty, frizzy. **2.** Inexperienced as we were, we thought her stories were a bit kinky: odd, eccentric, unusual, unorthodox, peculiar, bizarre, strange, queer, perverse, quirky, idiosyncratic; freakish, abnormal, aberrant, deviant, unnatural, Slang sick, kooky. —**Ant.** 2 standard, usual, orthodox, normal, ordinary. Slang square.

kinsman n. She awaited the arrival of her kinsmen from Europe: relative, blood relative, relation, blood relation, kin, sib, countryman, landsman, fellow citizen; (variously) father, mother, sister, brother, aunt, uncle, grandmother, grandfather, cousin, child, offspring, son, daughter, heir, parent.

kismet *n. The wise man said it was my kismet to be a leader of men:* destiny, fate, fortune, *Greek* moira, portion, lot, circumstance, Providence, predestination, one's lot in life; end, doom, God's will, will of Allah, inevitability.

kiss *v. She kissed her aunt when she arrived:* touch with the lips, greet with a kiss, kiss the cheek, kiss the hand, osculate; *Slang* buss.

kit *n. He took his kit from the trunk and began fixing the engine:* set of tools, instruments, implements, utensils; equipment, tools, supplies, devices, gear, tackle, outfit, necessaries, provisions, things, paraphernalia, accoutrements, trappings, impediments, furnishings, rig; *Slang* the whole kit and caboodle.

kitchen *n. All meals were prepared in the kitchen:* room equipped for cooking, cookroom, scullery, galley, cookhouse, *French* cuisine, *Spanish* cocina; bakery, bakehouse.

kittenish *adj. The kittenish actress got her first starring role:* frisky, frolicsome, coquettish, fun-loving, impish, mischievous, playful, sportive.

knack *n. I wish I had his knack for cooking. She had a knack for foreign languages:* skill, talent, facility, gift, ability, aptitude, adroitness, dexterity, dexterousness, finesse, expertise, genius, faculty, flair, natural endowment, cleverness, ingenuity, quickness, readiness, proficiency, efficiency, competence, capability, capacity, forte, bent, inclination, propensity, turn. **—Ant.** ineptitude, clumsiness, awkwardness; disability.

knave *n. The knave cheated her out of her savings:* rascal, scoundrel, blackguard, rogue, charlatan, swindler, varlet, reprobate, culprit, scalawag, scamp, rapscallion, cad, rotter, bounder, wretch, good-for-nothing; *Slang* rat, cur, dog, con man, con artist, phony. **—Ant.** hero, gentleman.

knead *v. The baker kneaded the bread vigorously:* manipulate, massage, shape, press, squeeze, twist, work, blend, form.

kneel *v. They all knelt when the king entered:* bow, bend the knee, bow down, genuflect, fall on one's knees, curtsy; make obeisance, prostrate oneself; *Slang* kowtow; salaam, fall at the feet of.

knickknack or **nicknack** *n. She had little knickknacks on shelves all over the house:* small object, trifle, bagatelle, bauble, trinket, toy, plaything, gewgaw, gimcrack, thingamajig, frippery, bric-a-brac, *French* bibelot.

knife *n.* **1.** *He took up his knife and began whittling:* cutting tool, blade, cutter, cutlery; *(variously)* pocketknife, penknife, jackknife, paring knife, switchblade knife, bowie knife, skinning knife, hunting knife, bread knife, butcher knife, table knife, carving knife, surgical knife, scalpel, palette knife, putty knife, pruning knife, machete, stiletto, dirk, dagger, *Slang* shiv. *—v.* **2.** *The thugs knifed him in the robbery attempt:* cut, stab, wound, lacerate, cut apart, slash, mutilate, cut down, run through, pierce.

knight *n. We read about King Arthur and his Knights of the Round Table:* soldier, man-at-arms, warrior, fighter, fighting man, arms bearer, horseman, equestrian, Templar; defender, protector, guardian, champion, paladin, Lancelot, hero, vindicator, brave person, gallant, cavalier; gentleman, man of rank.

knit *v.* **1.** *She knitted scarves while she was convalescing:* weave, do needlework, interweave, twist, intertwine, stitch, tat, plait, braid, crochet. **2.** *Our common interests knitted the group together:* draw, draw together, ally, join, attach, fasten, connect, unite, unify, bind, link. **3.** *He knitted his brow in contemplation:* wrinkle, knot, crease, furrow.

knob *n.* **1.** *We replaced the knobs on all the doors:* rounded handle, handle, handhold, hold, grip; lever, latch. **2.** *We used sandpaper to smooth out the knobs on the wood:* lump, hump, bump, knot, knurl, knur, snag, gnarl, bulb, tubercle, nub, nubbin, node, convexity, protuberance, protuberancy, protrusion, bulge, swell, swelling, projection, prominence.

knock *v.* **1.** *There was definitely somebody home when he knocked at the door:* rap, tap, hit, strike, bang, thump, thud. **2.** *They knocked the building down to make room for the superhighway:* pound, pummel, smash, batter, hammer, strike. **3.** *The assailant knocked the man to the ground:* hit, strike, smite, slam, slap, pummel, pound, beat, thwack, kick, push, jostle, dash, cuff, swat; *Informal* belt, bat, crack, smack, clout, wallop, sock. **4.** *Informal The critics knocked her last play:* criticize, find fault with, belittle, disparage, deprecate, peck at, cavil, carp at, abuse, lambaste, cry out against, decry, reprehend, inveigh against, censure, cut to pieces, condemn; *Slang* rap, bomb, murder. *—n.* **5.** *His amnesia was caused by a knock on the head:* stroke, hit, thump, thwack, bang, tap, rap, pat, slap; blow, smack, whack, punch, cuff, smash, bump, glancing blow, crash, crack; *Informal* sock, clip, clout, bat, lick. **6.** *Informal You have to take certain knocks in life:* criticism, faultfinding, setback, failure, defeat; reprehension, censure, condemnation.

knot *n.* **1.** *The rope was tied in a knot:* interlacement, twist, loop, braid, plait, intertwist; *(variously)* slipknot, square knot, half hitch, hitch, hawser fastening, slide knot, running knot, surgeon's knot, figure-eight knot, flat knot, single knot, double knot, overhand knot, midshipman's knot, hangman's knot, bowknot, cat's-paw. **2.** *The sweater was decorated with small knots of embroidery thread:* ornament, rosette, loop, braid, frog, star; shoulder knot, epaulet. **3.** *Knots of lilacs grew by the fence. The blow left a knot on his head:* cluster, bunch, clump; gathering, circle, group, assemblage, collection; bundle, pack, lump, heap, pile, mass; hump, bump, knurl. **4.** *She wore her hair in a knot:* bun, chignon, braid, plait, top-knot, tuft.

knotty *adj.* **1.** *We paneled the den in knotty wood:* knobby, full of knots, gnarled, nodular, unsmooth, rough, uneven, rough-grained, coarse, coarse-grained, rugged, bumpy, knurly, knurled; flawed, blemished, snaggy. **2.** *He delib-*

erated for hours over the knotty matter: difficult, thorny, tricky, complex, problematical, complicated, hard, tough, perplexing, puzzling, involved, intricate, baffling, ticklish, troublesome. —**Ant.** 1 smooth. 2 plain, simple, obvious, easy.

know *v.* **1.** *How did you know I'd be here? He knew the job was difficult:* be certain, be sure, apprehend, realize, discern, be positive, be confident, have no doubt, feel certain, be assured, have knowledge, have information about, be informed, recognize, perceive, notice, see, be cognizant of, be wise to, *Slang* get wise to; understand, make out, be aware of; be intelligent, be smart, be wise, be sagacious. **2.** *He knew the layout of the room:* have knowledge of, have in one's head, be acquainted with, be familiar with, have at one's fingertips; *Informal* have down pat, have down cold; know inside out, know backwards and forwards, know by rote, know by heart, know full well. **3.** *We know many people in show business:* be acquainted with, be familiar with, enjoy the friendship of, be on good terms with, be close to, be on intimate terms with; *Informal* be thick with, rub elbows with, have the ear of, be on a good footing with; have dealings with. **4.** *One should always know one's friends and enemies:* identify, distinguish, be able to distinguish, discern, discriminate, make out, perceive; perceive differences, recognize differences, tell one from the other. —**Ant.** 1 be ignorant or illiterate, overlook, misunderstand, misconstrue. 3 be unacquainted with, be unfamiliar with.

know-how *n. The company needed her know-how in computer programming:* technique, expertise, skill, ability, proficiency, expertness, *French* savoir-faire, competence, *Slang* savvy, art, craft, mastery, capability, adeptness, skillfulness, adroitness, deftness, knowledge, experience. —**Ant.** incompetence, inexperience, ignorance, unfamiliarity.

knowing *adj.* **1.** *Our professor was a very knowing man:* sagacious, wise, sapient, erudite, intelligent, intellectual, knowledgeable, enlightened, bright, brainy, widely read, literary, scholastic, academic, educated, schooled, learned, well-informed, clever, astute, shrewd, canny, smart, sharp, aware, conscious, perceptive, percipient, perspicacious, sophisticated; profound, deep, philosophical, *Slang* highbrow; understanding, comprehending, discerning, sound, sensible, judicious. **2.** *She gave us a knowing look when the subject was brought up:* meaningful, significant, expressive, revealing, eloquent, fraught; conscious, aware, perceptive. —**Ant.** 1 unknowing, unwise, unintelligent, uncomprehending. 2 blank, dull, empty.

knowledge *n.* **1.** *I was surprised by the breadth of her knowledge:* learning, scholarship, erudition, education, wisdom, intelligence, ken, schooling, cultivation, enlightenment, information, *Informal* book learning. **2.** *The populace received knowledge that the war was over:* communication, information, data, news, tidings, intelligence; pronouncement, declaration, statement, report, announcement, notice, notification; tip, hint, divulging revelation, intimation, mention. **3.** *He had no knowledge of his past actions:* awareness, realization, consciousness, perception, sense, cognizance, recognition, familiarity, memory, inkling, comprehension. —**Ant.** 1 ignorance, illiteracy, inexperience, misunderstanding, unfamiliarity, unawareness.

knowledgeable *adj. He was quite knowledgeable about current events:* well-informed, abreast of, conversant with, acquainted with, no stranger to, versed in, at home in, familiar with, *Slang* hip, *French* au courant.

known *adj. The mystery man was a known star of stage and screen. It is a known fact that he was once a millionaire:* recognized, acknowledged, familiar, popular, celebrated, famous, prominent, notorious, well-known, noted; apparent, obvious, evident, palpable, manifest, self-evident, plain, distinct, patent, definite, common. —**Ant.** unknown, unfamiliar, unrecognized; secret, unpublished, unrevealed.

knurled *adj. My grandfather was very proud of his old knurled walking stick:* knotted, gnarled, bumpy, lumpy, knurly, ridged, bulging, knobby, nodular, knotty, nubbly, gnarly.

kook *n. Some kook telephoned a bomb threat to the theater:* crackpot, eccentric, crackbrain, harebrain, cuckoo, loony; *Slang* ding-a-ling, nut, screwball, dingbat, crazy, weirdo, wacko, flake, fruitcake.

kowtow *v. The new mayor expected everyone to kowtow to him:* stoop, bend, genuflect, curtsy, bow low, salaam, bow and scrape, grovel, toady, truckle; *Slang* softsoap, butter up, apple-polish, bootlick; cringe, cower, fall on one's knees, prostrate oneself, bend the knee.

kudo *n. Slang A good fireman expects no particular kudo for saving someone's life:* award, prize, honor, plaudit, decoration, cita-tion.

kudos *n. Informal His brave deeds brought him kudos from the high command:* praise, laudation, admiration, honor, acclaim, commendation, high regard, esteem, glory, prestige, celebratedness, fame, celebrity, repute, renown, distinctive mark.

kvetch *v.* **1.** *He kvetched about his low pay:* complain, whine, find fault, grouse, gripe, bellyache. —*n.* **2.** *He was a real kvetch, with one complaint after another:* complainer, whiner, faultfinder, nitpicker.

L

label *n.* **1.** *All the sale items had special labels:* tag, ticket, sticker, slip, sign, stamp, mark, name, seal, docket, brand, tally; identification, designation, classification, appellation, characterization, specification, inscription; earmark. —*v.* **2.** *Be sure to label all the test tubes:* mark, note, tag, ticket, docket, mark off; name, classify, describe, designate, title, define, denominate, characterize, put a mark on, earmark, brand.

labor or *British* **labour** *n.* **1.** *Much labor went into the building of the pyramids:* exertion, effort, industriousness, laboriousness, plodding, toil, menial work, manual labor, travail, drudgery, struggle, sweat of one's brow. **2.** *Most of the nation's labor is on strike:* manpower, employees, workers, work force, workmen, laborers, blue-collar workers. **3.** *She went into labor two weeks early:* birth pangs, birth throes; parturition, childbirth, travail, accouchement. —*v.* **4.** *He labored in the mines for 30 years:* work, drudge, toil, travail, plod, sweat, slave, work like a slave, struggle, work day and night; *Informal* work one's fingers to the bone, grind away, plug away; occupy oneself with, busy oneself with, employ one's time. **5.** *He labored under some unfortunate delusion:* smart under, suffer, agonize, be the victim of, be affected by, be troubled by, be burdened by. —**Ant.** 1 rest, repose, relaxation, leisure, respite, ease. 4 rest, relax.

labored *adj.* **1.** *The old man moved in a labored manner:* ponderous, heavy, stiff, wooden; difficult, strained, forced, laborious, cramped, halting; awkward, maladroit, clumsy. **2.** *His so-called witticisms are so labored:* strained, studied, forced, contrived, unnatural, overdone, unspontaneous, drawnout, heavy, ponderous; self-conscious. —**Ant.** 1, 2 easy, natural, simple, light.

laborer *n.* *He began his career as a laborer in South America:* workman, worker, blue-collar worker, laboring man, workingman, workhand, toiler, manual worker, proletarian, wage earner; hand, hired man, menial, hired hand, hireling, drudge, plodder, roustabout, handyman, coolie.

laborious *adj.* *Digging rocks out of the soil was a laborious task:* strenuous, burdensome, onerous, labored, toilsome, wearisome, arduous, difficult, hard, effortful, uphill, herculean; tiresome, irksome, troublesome, oppressive; severe, rigorous, demanding, brutal; fatiguing, wearying, wearing. —**Ant.** simple, light, easy, effortless, undemanding.

labyrinth *n.* *The second floor was a labyrinth of tiny offices:* maze, complex, network, convolution, perplexity, complexity, intricacy; snarl, tangle, web, knot, morass, jungle, wilderness, mare's nest, riddle.

lace *v.* **1.** *The child has learned to lace his shoes:* tie, fasten, secure, bind, close, draw together, tie up, tighten, make fast; make taut, cinch, strap, truss, tether, lash, braid. **2.** *He verbally laced his son for his misbehavior:* punish, chastise; spank, give a whipping, whip, give a beating, beat, thrash, switch, cane, flail, lash. **3.** *Someone laced the punch with rum:* add liquor to, flavor, make more tasty, spice up, suffuse, infuse, fortify, strengthen, add spirits to, *Informal* spike; *Slang* dope, dope up. —**Ant.** 1 unlace, untie, unfasten.

lacerate *v.* *The broken glass lacerated her arm:* slash, cut, lance, gash, puncture, wound, stab, slice, tear, rip, sever, scratch, scar, deface; hurt, inflict pain, give pain, pain, torment, distress, torture, agonize, excruciate.

lachrymose *adj.* *Oddly, the lachrymose clown cheered us up:* tearful, weeping, teary, weepy, crying, sobbing, blubbering, blubbery; mournful, disconsolate, sorrowful, grief-stricken, woeful, anguished. —**Ant.** cheerful, happy, sunny.

lack *n.* **1.** *His lack of a college education rankled as he grew older. A lack of food caused her to grow weak:* want, absence, deficiency, need; neediness, privation, deprivation; scarcity, scantness, dearth, shortage, exhaustion, depletion; omission. —*v.* **2.** *He lacked the connections necessary to get his business started:* miss, need, be short of, fall short of, want, be found wanting, be deficient in, be inadequate, be insufficient, be missing, fail to reach the mark, be caught short. —**Ant.** 1 sufficiency, adequacy, competence; abundance, copiousness, plentifulness; excess, superfluity, surplus, plethora. 2 have, hold, possess, own, enjoy.

lackadaisical *adj.* *He was lackadaisical and his boss knew it. She dressed in a lackadaisical manner:* indifferent, mindless, listless, lifeless, inanimate, spiritless, unexcited, unexcitable, uninspired, unambitious, unaspiring, unmotivated, idle, loafing, dillydallying; languid, languishing, lethargic, phlegmatic, apathetic; uninterested, indifferent, unconcerned. —**Ant.** animated, spirited, excited, inspired, ambitious, intense, diligent.

lackey *n.* *The king was always surrounded by his lackeys:* attendant, servant, assistant, helper, retainer, employee, hireling, minion, hanger-on, toady, underling, inferior, slave, menial, flunky; follower, mercenary; (*variously*) waiter, usher, page, squire, steward, butler, valet, cupbearer.

lackluster *adj.* *Her lackluster performance ruined the play:* drab, dull, lifeless, pallid, lusterless, dead, leaden, dreary, somber, colorless, bland, uninteresting, prosaic, commonplace, ordinary, humdrum, run-of-the-mill, boring; *Slang* blah, nothing. —**Ant.** vivid, exciting, vivacious, brilliant, scintillating, radiant.

laconic *adj.* *Although his speeches were laconic, they were informative:* short, concise, brief, succinct, terse, compact, condensed, pithy, concentrated, sparing of words, pointed, to the point, summary; curt, blunt. —**Ant.** voluble, wordy, loquacious, garrulous, verbose.

lacuna *n.* *There seemed to be lacunae in her memory of recent events:* gap, hiatus, break, blank, interstice, interval, interruption, interim, void, omission, cavity, hole, fissure, space, vacancy, opening, gulf, breach, caesura, discontinuity, pause, suspension.

lacy *adj. Lacy patterns of frost decorated the windows:* lacelike, gossamer, filigree, webby, filigreed, netlike, retiform, reticulate, latticelike, gridded, barred, meshy; cobwebby, diaphanous, gauzy, netty, fine, delicate, sheer.

lad *n. Our newsboy was an enterprising lad:* boy, youth, juvenile, youngster, young man, schoolboy; stripling, shaver, sprig, kid, sprout; young fellow, young chap.

laden *adj. The laden donkey stumbled on its journey:* weighed down, weighted, burdened, encumbered, loaded, oppressed, taxed.

lady *n.* **1.** *Her bearing and appearance indicated that she was a lady:* well-bred woman, respectable woman, woman of refinement, woman of good family, gentlewoman; wife, spouse. **2.** *The ladies were dressed in their finest gowns:* woman, matron, female. **3.** *The lady of the manor received us:* woman of rank, noblewoman, peeress, aristocrat; (*variously*) duchess, countess, viscountess, marchioness, baroness.

ladylike *adj. That wasn't a very ladylike thing to say:* (*of a woman*) well-bred, well-mannered, courtly, polite, courteous, mannerly, genteel, decorous, modest, refined, dignified, well brought up; cultured, polished, cultivated, elegant, proper, respectable, civil. **—Ant.** unladylike, ill-bred, ill-mannered, impolite, discourteous, unmannerly, unrefined, uncultured.

lag *v.* **1.** *The littlest boy always lags behind:* trail, drag behind, drag, be behind, linger, loiter, dawdle, tarry, delay, be slow, slacken, hang back, inch, inch along, limp, trudge, falter, stagger, halt; procrastinate, dally, take one's time, bide one's time, be idle, be late, be tardy, be overdue. *—n.* **2.** *Bad weather caused a lag in the scheduled activities:* delay, slackening, falling behind, slowing down, slowdown, drag, hold up, setback; *Informal* snag, hitch. **—Ant.** 1 lead, go ahead, hurry along. 2 speeding up, step up, advance.

laggard *n. The drill sergeant shouted angrily at the laggards:* straggler, lingerer, loiterer, dallier, dawdler, idler, sluggard, do-nothing, mope, lounger, poke, loafer, slug, dilly-dallier, potterer, snail, slowfoot; *Informal* slowpoke; *Slang* stick-in-the-mud. **—Ant.** go-getter, live wire, self-starter, dynamo.

laic *adj. Older parishioners detested the introduction of laic elements into the worship:* secular, lay, secularistic, laical, worldly, civil, temporal, nonpastoral, nonecclesiastical, nonclerical, profane, popular; amateur, nonprofessional, inexperienced. **—Ant.** pastoral, clerical, spiritual; unworldly, nonsecular.

laid-back *adj. The laid-back athlete liked to sign autographs:* relaxed, easygoing, at ease, casual, off-hand, free-and-easy, dégagé, undemanding, loose, lax, nonchalant, blasé, flexible. **—Ant.** rigid, strict, severe.

lair *n. The Bible tells of Daniel in the lion's lair:* den, nest, retreat, resting place, sanctuary,

cover, hideout, hideaway, mew, lie, haunt, covert; hole, burrow, cavern.

laissez-faire or **laisser-faire** *n. The new administration will adopt a policy of laissez-faire toward industry:* nonintervention, noninterference, let-alone principle, let-alone policy; unconcern, indifference; live and let live, leave well enough alone, let them be.

lake *n. The lake was teeming with fish:* inland sea, landlocked water, tarn, pond, pool, lagoon, *Scottish* loch, *Irish* lough.

lambaste *v.* **1.** *The home team lambasted the visitors 16–0:* beat, thrash, trounce, whip, pummel, lick, pelt, defeat, subdue, vanquish, overwhelm, wallop, bludgeon, smear, drub; *Informal* shellac; *Slang* clobber. **2.** *She really lambasted me for being late again:* scold, berate, castigate, censure, reprimand, dress down, rebuke, cuss out, give one what for, denounce; *Informal* bawl out; *Slang* light into, chew out. **—Ant.** 2 praise, commend, extol, laud, approve, applaud.

lame *adj.* **1.** *He walked with an elegant cane, but he was not lame:* crippled, disabled, limping, halt, maimed, infirm, hobbled; game, unsound, deformed; feeble, faltering, weak, halting. **2.** *His lame alibi did not withstand close questioning:* weak, feeble, inadequate, sorry, clumsy, insufficient, deficient, flimsy, wanting, failing, unconvincing, unpersuasive, ineffectual, unsatisfactory. **—Ant.** 2 bold, convincing, persuasive, effectual, effective.

lament *v.* **1.** *He lamented the death of his friend:* mourn, weep, bewail; deplore, show concern for, complain about, express pity for, regret, sympathize with, commiserate with, condole with. *—n.* **2.** *We could hear her laments through the closed door:* lamentation, sob, plaint, cry, moan, wail, outcry, keening, wail, whimper; mourning. **3.** *The minstrels performed their laments before the king:* dirge, song of lamentation, death song, funeral music, requiem.

lamentable *adj.* **1.** *The jury felt that the judge's insensitivity to the defendant's rights was lamentable:* deplorable, dreadful, terrible, regrettable, woeful, grievous, unfortunate, distressing, shameful, disheartening. **2.** *There was little we could do to ease the lamentable plight of the refugees:* heartbreaking, distressing, dire, wretched, miserable, pitiable, piteous, pathetic. **—Ant.** 1 encouraging, heartwarming, satisfying. 2 happy, fortunate, cheering, blessed, felicitous.

laminate *v. We decided to laminate the picture:* veneer, coat, cover, face, layer.

lamp *n. I need a better lamp for reading:* light; (*variously*) electric lamp, battery lamp, gas lamp, oil lamp, lantern, reading light, headlight, ceiling light, ceiling fixture, floor lamp, table lamp, night light, chandelier, wall lamp; spotlight, klieg light, floodlight, searchlight, beacon, blinker, sunlamp, heat lamp; bulb; torch.

lampoon *n.* **1.** *The school's lampoon on the current political scene was outrageous:* satire, burlesque, broadside, parody, mockery, spoof, travesty, farce, pasquinade, diatribe, squib, caricature; *Informal* takeoff, put-on, *British* send up.

—*v.* **2.** *The school newspaper lampooned the current administration:* satirize, parody, ridicule, burlesque, caricature, make light of.

lance *n.* *All the king's soldiers were equipped with lances:* spear, javelin, assegai, pike, halberd, shaft, harpoon, gaff.

land *n.* **1.** *We live on the land, not the sea:* ground, earth, dry land, mainland, terra firma. **2.** *This land is good for growing vegetables. We own land in Vermont:* ground, soil, earth, subsoil, dirt, loam, humus; terrain; real estate, realty, property, real property, grounds, acres. **3.** *He wanted to visit the land his father came from:* country, nation, commonwealth, state, republic, dominion, realm, empire, domain, kingdom, colony, settlement; region, territory, terrain, zone, area, district, section, vicinity, location; fatherland, motherland, homeland, native land, native soil, the old country. **4.** *If you stood on the roof, you would see the land for miles:* country, county, district, countryside, region, province, shire, canton, precinct, parish, ward, acreage, acres, fields, tract, terrain, grassland, cornfield, wheat field, farmland, meadow, lea, pasture, grass, park, lawn, green, village green. —*v.* **5.** *We landed at the airport in Chicago:* come in for a landing, descend, come down, alight, light, settle down; *Informal* set down; make a three-point landing. **6.** *The ship landed on Saturday:* dock, come to land, put into port, make port, arrive at land, anchor, reach land, put into the harbor, put in, drop anchor, moor, tie up; put into shore, set foot on dry land, make land, debark, disembark, lay anchor. **7.** *His conduct will land him in jail one day. He landed six new accounts:* lead one to, carry one to, bring one to; lay hold of, catch, gain, secure, get, win over, clinch, seize, grab, capture, *Informal* nab; take, snare, net.

landlord *n.* *The landlord personally collected the rent every month:* landholder, landowner, landlady, property owner, owner, proprietor, possessor, holder, freeholder; lord of the manor; squire. —**Ant.** tenant, lessee, renter.

landmark *n.* *The court's decision is said to be a landmark. The President's birthplace has been designated a landmark:* milestone, keystone, high point, turning point, cornerstone, highlight, watershed, signpost, guidepost, benchmark; monument, historic building.

landscape *n.* **1.** *One look at the landscape convinced him to settle down there:* natural scenery, scenery, scenic view, scene, aspect, view, prospect, vista, spectacle, panorama, sight. **2.** *She preferred a good landscape to a portrait:* painting or drawing of countryside, scenic representation, rural scene.

lane *n.* *There were many small lanes in the quaint village:* narrow thoroughfare, path, passageway, footpath, way, road, avenue, roadway, drive, alley, alleyway, passage, pass, bypath, course, route, trail, track, access, approach, byway.

language *n.* **1.** *He spoke the language of his country:* speech, tongue, vocabulary, idiom, vernacular, mother tongue, native tongue, *Informal* lingo; dialect, patois, jargon; slang, colloquialism, cant, argot, *Slang* jive. **2.** *The average student has problems with language:* oral communication, self-expression, reading and writing, verbal intercourse, discourse, spoken language, elocution, public speaking; words, vocabulary. **3.** *I never could understand the language of the law:* vocabulary, wording, phraseology, speech, prose, parlance, verbiage, expression, idiom, rhetoric, use of words; manner of speaking or writing, diction, idiom, mode of expression. **4.** *Watch your language--there are ladies present!:* profanity, cursing, swearing, imprecation, profane talk, *Informal* cussing.

languid *adj.* **1.** *The illness made him feel languid:* faint, feeble, weak, weary, drooping, sickly, declining, indisposed, debilitated, unhealthy, unsound, unstable, doddering, infirm, on the decline, fatigued, exhausted, enervated, wornout, spent; rickety, shaky, trembling; lackadaisical, languorous, sluggish, torpid, apathetic, inert, inactive, supine. **2.** *It was one of those hot, languid days when moving around was an effort:* sluggish, listless, inanimate, inert, apathetic, lifeless, lethargic, languorous, spiritless, dull, heavy, torpid, slow, leaden. —**Ant.** 1 strong, tireless, active, energetic, vigorous, robust.

languish *v.* **1.** *He lost his accustomed vigor and languished in the tropical climate:* go into decline, droop, flag, faint, diminish, fade, wilt, wither, deteriorate, give away, break down, wane, ebb, waste away, become ill, take sick, sicken, go downhill, dwindle, fail. **2.** *He languished for the sight of his family:* pine for, sigh for, be desirous of, yearn for, hunger for, hunger after, long for, thirst for; *Informal* have a yen for, hanker for; desire, covet, hunger, thirst. —**Ant.** 1 luxuriate, thrive, prosper, flourish, bloom.

languor *n.* *The languor of life in the tropics is difficult for North Americans to adjust to:* listlessness, torpor, lassitude, inertia, sluggishness, torpidity, weariness, dullness, lethargy, hebetude, lifelessness, languidness, leisureness. —**Ant.** vitality, enthusiasm, vigor, verve, gusto, zest.

lanky *adj.* *His brother was stocky, but he was extremely lanky:* lank, tall and thin, rangy, lean, bony, scrawny, weedy, skinny, rawboned, angular, gaunt, spare, gangling, gawky. —**Ant.** burly, husky, brawny, muscular, sinewy; plump, portly, rotund, chubby, fleshy, stocky, stout, fat, short, full, rounded.

lantern *n.* *He carried a lantern that night:* lamp, light.

lap *v.* **1.** *The kittens lapped up the milk:* lick, lick up, tongue, drink, sip. **2.** *From the beach house we could hear the waves lapping at the shore:* ripple, slosh, wash, awash, splash, plash, babble, murmur, bubble, gurgle.

lapse *n.* **1.** *His lapse of manners was unforgivable:* breach, disregard, dereliction, error, slight mistake, omission, slip, peccadillo, oversight, fault, flaw, negligence, delinquency, laxity, infraction, blunder, faux pas, *Informal* boner; loss, failure, failing, shortcoming, fall, forfeiture. **2.**

His lapse into drunkenness followed a long run of bad luck: decline, descent, downfall, drop, backsliding, relapse, regression, wane, slump, deterioration, degeneration, falling off. **3.** *After a lapse of one century, the custom has been restored:* elapsing, period, interval, process of time, interim, interlude; intermission, interruption, passage, respite, pause, recess, *Informal* break; hiatus, gap. —*v.* **4.** *He lapsed into a coma and never recovered:* fall, slip, decline, subside, sink, collapse; worsen, backslide, relapse, recede, deteriorate, degenerate, wither, sag, droop; drop, slump down. **5.** *The warranty lapsed two months ago:* expire, become obsolete, run out, terminate, stop, cease, lose validity, fall into disuse. **6.** *Only five minutes had lapsed before she returned again:* pass by, elapse, slip by, run out, slip away, go by, expire.

larceny *n. The thief was charged with larceny:* stealing, theft, robbery, burglary; pilferage, pilfering, purloining, misappropriation, appropriation, looting, sacking, depredation, absconding, embezzlement, peculation, extortion, bilking, cheating, swindling, defalcation, fleecing, fraud, forgery, plagiarism; housebreaking, safecracking; petty larceny, petit larceny, grand larceny.

larder *n. The cook kept the canned goods in the larder:* pantry, food room, buttery, supply room, storage room, storeroom, cuddy; *British* spence, stillroom.

large *adj. They lived in a large house. He was given a large allowance. He had a large capacity for learning. He was of large build:* big, huge, great, grand, massive, immense, enormous, gigantic, spacious, capacious, vast, roomy, expansive, sizable, imposing, Brobdingnagian; substantial, considerable, ample, goodly, liberal, unstinted, copious, extravagant, exorbitant; comprehensive, extensive, wide, broad, sweeping, far-reaching, unlimited, limitless, boundless, high; mighty, towering, hulky, strapping, heavy, rotund, obese, fat, portly, plump, overgrown, outsized, ponderous, monstrous, giantlike, colossal, gargantuan; magnificent, stupendous; *Informal* kingsized, man-sized. —**Ant.** small, little, tiny, diminutive, minute; brief, inconsiderable, infinitesimal; narrow, paltry, petty, mean, scanty, sparse, short, trifling, trivial, slight, slender, slim, thin.

largely *adv. He owed his success largely to hard work:* mostly, mainly, chiefly, for the most part, by and large, on the whole, primarily, principally, generally, predominantly, to a great extent, greatly, substantially, considerably; extensively, widely.

large-scale *adj. A large-scale war broke out in Europe in 1914:* extensive, far-reaching, wide-ranging, broad, wide, far-flung, all-out, all-encompassing; big, huge, great, mighty, vast, gargantuan, colossal, gigantic, stupendous, monstrous, tremendous. —**Ant.** small-scale, limited, local, restricted.

largess or **largesse** *n. She was known for her largess to those less fortunate:* generosity, benefaction, kindness, benevolence, bounty, philanthropy; donation, gift, offering, bestowal, boon,

favor, assistance, aid, help, charity, mercy, benignity; reward, payment, remuneration, gratuity.

lark *n. The banker went to the amusement park for a lark:* escapade, frolic, fling, spree, caprice, whim; *Informal* gag, high old time; trick, prank, antic, romp, gambol, caper, game, sportiveness, jape.

lascivious *adj. He was blackballed by the club for lascivious conduct:* indecent, obscene, lewd, immoral, improper, lustful, ribald, bawdy, prurient; filthy, vulgar, gross, coarse, indelicate, salacious, squalid, foul, dirty, dirty-minded, impure, unwholesome, immodest, lecherous, sordid, lurid; shameless, wanton, unblushing, licentious, depraved, ruttish.

lash¹ *v. The robbers lashed the banker to a chair:* tie, bind, tie up, fasten, secure, leash, rope, make fast, truss, pinion, strap; tether, brace, moor, attach, fix, hitch.

lash² *n.* **1.** *The pirate captain beat his crew with a lash:* whip, scourge, cat-o'-nine-tails; strap, thong. **2.** *The criminal was sentenced to 50 lashes:* whip, blow, stroke, hit. —*v.* **3.** *The wagon driver lashed the horses:* whip, whip up, flog, thrash, lambaste, flail; horsewhip. **4.** *Rain lashed against the windowpane:* beat, strike, smack, hit, knock, buffet, pound, hammer. **5.** *The sergeant lashed the troops for their sloppy dress:* tongue-lash, berate, castigate, rail against, revile, curse, upbraid, scold, lecture, take to task. —**Ant.** 5 praise, compliment, commend, laud.

lass *n. All the young lasses were there in their finest dresses:* girl, young woman, damsel, schoolgirl, maiden, maid, female, miss, virgin; wench, colleen, lassie, lovely, pretty.

lassitude *n. His lassitude was caused by overwork:* weariness, weakness, debility, sluggishness, fatigue, tiredness, exhaustion, fatigue, lack of energy, enervation, lethargy, listlessness, inertia, feebleness, indolence, faintness, torpor, torpidity, drowsiness, languor, languidness, supineness, prostration, dullness, droopiness; apathy, indifference, ennui, doldrums, boredom; malaise. —**Ant.** vigor, energy, strength, robustness, freshness; verve, spirit, vitality; *Informal* get-up-and-go, push, vim, pep.

last¹ *adj.* **1.** *In the last act, the hero gets shot. She always had to have the last word. He was the last boy on line:* final, conclusive, closing, concluding, terminal, ultimate, extreme, farthest, furthest, utmost; rearmost, hindmost, behind, at the end, tailing, tagging along, bringing up the rear. —*adv.* **2.** *Our horse came last in the race:* after all others, after, behind, in back of, in the rear, trailing, in last place. **3.** *The speaker pointed out at last the many advantages of his plan:* finally, in conclusion, ultimately, eventually, once and for all, terminally. —*n.* **4.** *He was the last on my list of volunteers:* final one, concluding person or thing; rearmost one. **5.** *At the last, you will not be able to repent!:* end, conclusion, crucial time, closing, ending, finish, terminus, finale; crack of doom, end of the world, doomsday, Day of Judgment,

Armageddon. **—Ant.** 1 first, initial, foremost, opening, introductory, initiatory; best, highest. 2 first, ahead of all others, in front. 4 first.

last² v. *How long did the movie last? These shoes have lasted one year:* continue, go on, persist, extend, hold good, exist, survive, endure, stay, stand, remain, carry on, hold out, hold on, maintain, keep, persevere, abide, subsist, live; wear, stand up, hold up; outwear, outlive. **—Ant.** fail, die; end, stop, terminate, expire, depart, fade, cease; wear out, *Informal* give out.

lasting adj. *The diplomats tried to conclude a just and lasting peace. He had a lasting interest in art:* enduring, abiding, continuing, durable, long-term, permanent, never-ending, lifelong, perdurable, long-lived, protracted; continuing a long time, of long duration, firm, steadfast, constant, incessant, perpetual, unceasing, indissoluble, indestructible; deep-rooted, deep-seated, established, fixed, firmly established, solid; persistent, lingering, chronic; eternal, immortal. **—Ant.** fleeting, fugitive, passing, transitory, transient, short-lived, ephemeral, momentary.

lastly adv. *Lastly, let me stress the importance of everyone's cooperation in this plan:* finally, in conclusion, in the end, at last, after all; all things considered, on the whole, taking everything into consideration, to sum up. **—Ant.** firstly, at the outset, in starting, in the beginning, at the first.

latch n. **1.** *Please be sure the latch on the door is secure:* lock, catch, bolt, bar, fastening; hasp, clamp, hook, snap, loop, buckle, button, clip, clinch. —v. **2.** *Latch the gate carefully so the cows won't get out:* lock, bolt, fasten, hook, secure, make fast, close, shut. **—Ant.** 2 unlock, unlatch, unfasten, loose.

late adj. **1.** *He was always late for appointments. The movie was late in starting because of projection difficulties:* tardy, overdue, unpunctual, dilatory, behind time; slow, delayed, detained, postponed, put off, held up. **2.** *He was a late addition to the crew:* recent, new, fresh, newborn. **3.** *She was an admirer of the late president:* lately dead, recently deceased; departed, passed on, gone. —adv. **4.** *He arrived late for his appointment:* behind time, after time, behindhand, tardily, dilatorily. **—Ant.** 1 early, punctual, prompt, timely, ahead of time. 2 old, seasoned. 3 alive, still living, existing, extant. 4 early, ahead of time, in advance, beforehand.

lately adv. *Lately I've taken to making my own clothes:* recently, latterly, of late, not long ago, yesterday, a short time ago; just now, right now, presently, currently. **—Ant.** at first, originally.

latent adj. *Many of our deepest desires remain latent:* dormant, sleeping, quiescent, inactive, passive, suspended, in abeyance, abeyant, potential, undeveloped, unrealized, unaroused, not manifest, hidden, concealed, covert, lurking, intangible, unapparent, unexposed, inconspicuous, unexpressed. **—Ant.** activated, realized, developed; manifest, expressed, apparent, evident, obvious, conspicuous.

later adv. **1.** *The others will join us later:* after-

ward, at a subsequent time, in a while, thereafter, in time, presently, subsequently, tardily, thereupon, after a while, in sequel, successively, since, next, behind, from that moment, in the course of time. —adj. **2.** *The later arrivals had to stand in the back:* subsequent, ensuing, successive, following, succeeding, consequent, consecutive. **3.** *The later works are the composer's best:* occurring late in time, mature; more recent, most recent; toward the end, latter. **—Ant.** 2 earlier, antecedent, prior, beforehand.

lateral adj. *The path split off from the road in a lateral direction:* side, sideways, sidewise, sideward, sided, sidelong; flanking, flanked; slanting, sloping, oblique; edgewise, edgeways; skirting.

lather n. **1.** *This shampoo makes a lot of lather:* foam, shaving foam, froth, head, suds, soapsuds; spume, scum. **2.** *The exhausted horse was dripping with lather:* sweat, foam, froth. —v. **3.** *Lather your hair before rinsing:* soap, soap up; make froth, make foam.

latitude n. *The progressive school allowed great latitude in selecting courses:* scope, opportunity, freedom of action, freedom of choice, free play, amplitude, range, liberality, full swing, sweep, margin, independence, unrestrictedness, leeway, elbowroom, unrestraint, license, indulgence.

latter adj. **1.** *Of your two examples, I prefer the latter:* second-mentioned, most recent, latest, later; ensuing, successive, succeeding, subsequent; last-mentioned, last; modern. **2.** *Rain is predicted for the latter part of the day:* later, final, last, end, ending, terminal. **—Ant.** 1 former, previous; early, first, beginning. 2 first, initial, beginning, opening, commencing.

lattice n. *In June the lattice is covered with rose blooms:* trellis, openwork, latticework, network, grille, fretwork, webwork, reticulum, grating, framework, grid, screen, grate, fret, frame, framing, reticulation, trelliswork.

laud v. *They lauded the brave attempt:* praise, extol, applaud, celebrate, esteem, honor. **—Ant.** censure, condemn, criticize.

laudable adj. *Generosity is a laudable trait:* praiseworthy, estimable, admirable, commendable, worthy of admiration, deserving of esteem, meritorious, exemplary, model, unimpeachable, creditable, noble, sterling, excellent. **—Ant.** contemptible, lowly, base, unworthy, execrable, blameworthy, ignoble, reprehensible.

laudatory adj. *She introduced the speaker with a few laudatory remarks:* praising, adulatory, complimentary, approving, favorable, approbatory, commendatory, eulogizing, eulogistic, encomiastic, panegyrical, flattering, acclamatory, celebratory, glorifying, admiring. **—Ant.** critical, censorious, denigratory, scornful, abusive.

laugh v. **1.** *The clown made the children laugh with joy:* chuckle, giggle, express mirth, roar with laughter, roar, chortle, guffaw, snicker, titter, snigger, cackle, break up, split one's sides, roll in the aisle, howl. —n. **2.** *The comedian finally got a laugh from the unresponsive audience:* guffaw, giggle, chortle, burst of laughter, roar, cackle, peal of laughter, mirth, glee, snicker, snigger, horselaugh, bellylaugh, ha-ha, ho-ho. —**Ant.** 1 scowl, glower, frown; cry, mourn. 2 scowl, glower, frown; cry.

laughable *adj. The situation was so absurd it was laughable:* hilarious, funny, amusing, arousing laughter, worthy of laughter, risible, droll, merry, diverting, witty, comic, comical, farcical, sidesplitting, rib-tickling, tickling; worthy of scorn or derision, ludicrous, ridiculous, silly, stupid, asinine, inane, preposterous, outlandish, outrageous, dopey, grotesque, foolish, absurd. —**Ant.** solemn, serious, grave, somber, morose, sad, melancholy.

laughingstock *n. You'll be the laughingstock of the whole school in that silly outfit:* joke, butt, fool, ass, figure of fun, dupe, fair game.

laughter *n. It was an evening of good food, good company, and lots of laughter:* mirth, conviviality, merriment, joy, jollity, hilarity, glee, gaiety, joviality, exhilaration, revelry, merrymaking. —**Ant.** sorrow, lamentation, solemnity, gravity.

launch *v.* **1.** *The shipyard workers launched the freighter with a great splash:* float, set afloat, send down the skids, put to sea, slide from the stocks, set into the water. **2.** *The firm launched the new product with a big advertising campaign:* inaugurate, begin, initiate, start, introduce, unveil, premiere; embark upon, set forth on, venture upon; institute, found, establish. **3.** *We will launch the moon rocket tomorrow:* shoot, discharge, let fly, thrust forward, hurl, propel, project, cast forth, catapult, throw, eject, set in motion, impel, send off, fire off, fire. —**Ant.** 1 beach, ground; dock. 2 terminate, stop, withdraw, scrap. 3 withhold, retain, hold back.

launder *v. We'll have to launder these dirty work clothes:* wash, clean, cleanse, scrub, soak, rinse, scour, wash and iron, wash out.

laurels *n. He won his laurels as a research scientist:* glory, fame, renown, honor, award, reward, praise, kudos, acclaim, distinction, illustriousness, tribute, commendation, recognition, celebrity, applause, credit, accolade, citation, acclamation, popularity.

lavish *adj.* **1.** *He went through his inheritance with too lavish a hand. Such lavish praise was hard to believe:* free, profuse, plenteous, plentiful, abundant, extravagant, generous, effusive, prodigal, bounteous, bountiful, copious, without limit, overwhelming, intemperate, sumptuous, opulent, luxuriant, lush, plush, over-liberal, excessive, profligate, immoderate, unsparing, unstinting, munificent, greathearted; impetuous, wild, exuberant, unrestrained. —*v.* **2.** *The prince lavished money on show girls:* squander, spend freely, waste, dissipate, give overmuch, bestow generously, give in profusion, overindulge, pour out, shower, play Croesus with, fritter away. —**Ant.** 1 meager, parsimonious, sparing, scanty, frugal, cheap, thrifty, provident, stingy, niggardly, tightfisted, miserly. 2 withhold, stint, retain; begrudge.

law *n.* **1.** *The legislature passed a law against housing discrimination:* rule, governing princi-ple, regulation, mandate, commandment, established dictate, decree, legal form, enactment, precept, edict, standing order, statute, ordinance, canon, bylaw, act, bill. **2.** *There was no law in many parts of the Old West:* system of laws, collection of rules, rules of conduct, code; lawful behavior, conformity to rules, civil peace, orderliness, legal process and provision, justice, due process of law, legality, writ. **3.** *Newton's laws of motion form the foundation of classical mechanics:* principle, standard, criterion, axiom, postulate, dogma, precept, fundamental, convention, working rule, generalization, model, formulation, theorem, truth, absolute, invariable. **4.** *Will you go into law or medicine?:* jurisprudence, the practice or profession of a lawyer, legal profession. **5.** *There was so much commotion the neighbors called the law:* police, law-enforcing agency; *Slang* fuzz, gendarmes. —**Ant.** 2 chaos, anarchy, caprice, disorder.

lawbreaker *n. The county jail was filled with lawbreakers:* transgressor, outlaw, criminal, offender, delinquent, miscreant, culprit, perpetrator, malefactor, scofflaw, crook, felon, wrongdoer, convict, recidivist; *Slang* jailbird, con, thug, hood.

lawful *adj.* **1.** *Parking in front of a hydrant is never lawful:* legal, sanctioned by law, legally permitted, authorized, legitimate, legalized, legitimized, within the law, statutory, licit, allowed, warranted, permissible. **2.** *The lawful owner claimed the car:* rightful, proper, acknowledged by law, authorized, legally entitled, legitimate, prescribed, legally recognized, granted, titled, due. —**Ant.** 1 unauthorized, unlawful, illegal, illicit, prohibited, forbidden. 2 pretended, disputed, illegitimate.

lawless *adj.* **1.** *We must try to wipe out the lawless activities of the mob:* unlawful, contrary to law, indifferent to law, anarchic, lawbreaking, illegal, illegitimate, transgressive; insubordinate, disobedient, defiant, noncompliant. **2.** *A lawless crowd stormed the embassy:* disorderly, rebellious, mutinous, unruly, uncontrollable, ungoverned, chaotic, insurgent, disorganized, terroristic, refractory, riotous. **3.** *The mining town was lawless until the marshals arrived:* having no laws, heedless of law, ungoverned, chaotic, unrestrained, unbridled, wayward, freewheeling, wide open, out of hand, wanton, licentious. —**Ant.** 1 obedient, lawful, law-abiding, orderly, compliant, licit, legitimate. 2 civilized, docile, restrained, disciplined, regimented, orderly. 3 well-governed, law-abiding, tightly run.

lawn *n. The lawn needs mowing:* grass, yard, greensward, grassy ground, sward, glade, grassy plot, turf, grounds, park, meadowland, green field, terrace.

lawsuit *n. She brought a lawsuit against the company:* action, suit, case, arraignment, claim, contest, dispute, indictment, proceedings.

lawyer *n. The court appointed a lawyer for the accused:* attorney, attorney-at-law, counselor, counsel, advocate, legal advisor, jurist, counselor-at-law, prosecutor, legist, special pleader, pettifogger; *Slang* ambulance chaser, mouth-

piece, shyster; *British* solicitor, barrister.
—**Ant.** client; accused, defendant.

lax *adj.* **1.** *The coach was too lax about training, and the team did poorly:* negligent, neglectful, irresponsible, slack, loose, heedless, careless, unheeding, slipshod, remiss, derelict, yielding, indifferent, unconscientious, undutiful, unmindful, indifferent, casual, uncaring, unconcerned, thoughtless, oblivious; permissive, lenient. **2.** *The lax instructions left many of us confused:* careless, vague, hazy, nebulous, unstructured, slack, negligent, ill-defined, imprecise, incoherent, inexact, cryptic, confusing. **3.** *The old man spoke slowly and with a lax jaw:* slack, drooping, hanging open, not firm, weak, relaxed, flaccid, loose, agape, loose-muscled, limp, floppy, flabby. —**Ant.** 1 firm, scrupulous, strict, rigid, conscientious, unyielding, disciplined, severe, stern, austere, stringent. 2 exact, precise, careful, concise, specific. 3 tense, taut, rigid, firm, strong.

laxative *n.* *The doctor prescribed a laxative:* purge, purgative, cathartic, physic.

lay[1] *v.* **1.** *Lay the packages on the table:* put, place, set down, set, rest, repose, deposit, cause to lie. **2.** *The tornado laid the house flat:* prostrate, knock down, level, fell, beat down, knock over, floor, ground, raze, throw to the ground. **3.** *The nominating committee laid its slate before the board:* forward, present, offer, proffer, enunciate, elucidate, make a presentation of, place, put. **4.** *I'll lay you odds he will be late:* wager, bet, gamble, hazard; give odds. **5.** *A turtle lays many eggs at one time:* produce, bear, deposit, oviposit. **6.** *Lay the cartons one on top of the other. The tiles were laid in a geometric pattern:* place, arrange, set, align, lay out, dispose, assemble. **7.** *It's a mistake to lay too much emphasis on grades:* place, put, assign, allot, allocate, give, lend, apply; attribute, impute. **8.** *The first act was laid at a country estate:* set, locate, place, depict, seat, situate, stage, station. **9.** *The prisoners laid an escape plan:* arrange, formulate, form, make, devise, concoct, organize, plan, hatch, put together. **10.** *The town laid an assessment on property owners:* levy, charge, impose, exact, assess, demand, fine. —*n.* **11.** *He surveyed the lay of the land:* position, situation, arrangement, disposition, orientation, topography, configuration, contour, conformation. —**Ant.** 1 elevate, raise, lift. 2 pick up, set standing, erect, raise, lift. 3 withhold, withdraw, hide, keep secret. 6 disarrange, confuse, muddle.

lay[2] *adj.* **1.** *She serves as a lay teacher at the convent school:* nonecclesiastical, profane, secular, nonclerical, laic, laical. **2.** *The patient's lay diagnosis was close to the doctor's:* nonprofessional, unprofessional, amateur, inexpert, inexperienced, partly informed, nonspecialist. —**Ant.** 1 ecclesiastical, clerical, church. 2 professional, expert, specialized.

layer *n.* *A layer of smog settled over the city. The cake has three layers:* thickness, fold, lap, plate, leaf, sheet, coat, stratum, seam, tier, slab, stage, zone, level, story, bed; ply, lamina, scale.

layman *n.* *The Bishop wants every layman to participate in church affairs:* nonprofessional, laic, lay person, parishioner, member of the flock, catechumen, churchman, communicant, churchwoman, brother, sister, lay brother, lay sister; outsider, amateur. —**Ant.** professional, insider, specialist; cleric, clergyman.

layoff *n.* *Widespread layoffs affected much of the industry:* dismissal, ouster, discharge, firing, termination, cashiering, sacking, furloughing; *Slang* the boot, the heave-ho, the gate, the axe, the bounce, walking papers, pink slip, *British* the sack; unemployment, disemployment, idling, shutdown, closedown; depression, hard times.

layout *n.* *The layout for the ad was approved by the newspaper:* design, plan, model, blueprint, outline, diagram, sketch, drawing; arrangement, pattern, structure, form, motif.

laziness *n.* *The student's laziness passed belief:* sloth, slothfulness, idleness, apathy, dilatoriness, indolence, inertia, laxness, lethargy, negligence, remissness, slackness, sluggishness, unwillingness.

lazy *adj.* **1.** *She's too lazy to clean house:* idle, unwilling to work, shiftless, indolent, inert, inactive, slothful, slack, listless, lax, unindustrious. **2.** *The waiters seem lazy today:* sluggish, lethargic, torpid, languid, laggard, apathetic, languorous, slow, slow-moving; easygoing, sleepy, drowsy. —**Ant.** 1 industrious, quick, energetic, active, assiduous, diligent. 2 active, brisk, stimulated.

lead *v.* **1.** *The tug will lead the liner into the harbor:* guide, show the way, steer, draw, direct, head, command, conduct, pilot, convey, shepherd, marshal, precede, go before. **2.** *The candidate's integrity and strength led the voters to support him:* influence, persuade, attract, incline, induce, allure, lure, charm, tempt, seduce, draw, entice. **3.** *The path leads down to the river:* proceed, direct, guide, advance, go, stretch, extend, aim. **4.** *The vice-chairman will lead the meeting. The quarterback leads the football team:* direct, moderate, conduct, manage, preside over, control, head, command, domineer. **5.** *That nation leads in industrial output:* excel, rank first, outstrip, outdo, surpass, come first, set the pace; pioneer. **6.** *The drum major led the parade:* go first, head, be in advance, top. **7.** *He leads a full, active life:* pass, conduct, pursue, experience, live, have, undergo, go through. **8.** *The accident led to many lawsuits:* result in, produce, branch into, tend toward, issue in, bring on. —*n.* **9.** *The black horse took the lead. Your candidate has a slight lead:* precedence, precedency, advance, first place, foremost position, antecedence, priority; edge, margin, advantage; plurality. **10.** *The police haven't a single lead:* clue, hint, guide. **11.** *Most of the legislators followed the lead of the governor:* guidance, model, example, direction, indication, leadership. **12.** *A versatile actor is needed for the lead:* leading role, star part; protagonist, hero, principal performer, headliner;

leading man, leading woman. **—Ant.** 1 tail, trail. 2 disincline. 5 lag, trail.

leaden *adj.* **1.** *His arms felt leaden from the heavy burden:* numbed, deadened, dull, torpid, languid, sluggish, listless, unwieldy, cumbersome, hard to move, inanimate, inert; burdened, careworn, depressed, gloomy, glum, dreary. **2.** *The sky was leaden before the storm:* dark, gray, grayish, darkened, somber, murky, gloomy. **—Ant.** 1 light, feathery; active, energetic; strong, vital. 2 light, bright, clear.

leader *n.* *Harold was named leader of the fundraising drive:* head, director, conductor, chief, chieftain, supervisor, superior, commander, manager, captain, foreman, boss; forerunner, frontrunner, pacesetter, pacemaker, pioneer, torchbearer, guide, pathfinder, trailblazer; *Slang* bigwig, kingpin; magnate, mogul, tycoon; patriarch, godfather; master, prophet, mentor, guru; *Informal* honcho. **—Ant.** follower, adherent, henchman, partisan, disciple.

leadership *n.* **1.** *The vice-president took over the leadership of the country:* administration, directorship, managership, governorship, domination, hegemony, sway, stewardship, guardianship, superintendency, guidance, lead, supremacy, primacy, mastership, captaincy, headship; helm, wheel, reins. **2.** *The boy showed leadership as early as grammar school:* ability to lead, managerial skill, authoritativeness, command, supremacy, preeminence, charisma; self-assurance, self-reliance.

leading *adj.* **1.** *Monet was one of the leading French Impressionist painters:* foremost, most influential, most important, most significant, head, supreme, chief, prominent, notable, nonpareil, great, ranking, sovereign, prime, preeminent, unrivaled, unparalleled, unchallenged, principal, dominant, main, top, topmost, paramount, outstanding, stellar. **2.** *Platoon Four will be the leading group in the parade:* leadoff, foremost in position, advance, first, prime, initial, pacesetting, advanced. **3.** *My leading motive for writing the book was to enlighten the public:* principal, primary, guiding, directing, controlling, governing, ruling, motivating, prime, underlying, basic, essential, quintessential. **—Ant.** 1–3 secondary. 1 subordinate, inferior, supernumerary, minor, lesser, rank and file. 2 following, hindmost. 3 incidental, superficial.

leaf *n.* **1.** *The leaves of most plants are green:* frond, cotyledon, blade, needle, bract, foliole; petal. **2.** *The old book's leaves are dry and crumbling:* page, sheet, leaflet, folio. **3.** *The leather book is decorated with gold leaf:* foil, lamination, sheet of metal, lamella. **4.** *The table can be extended with three leaves:* insert, inset, extension. **—v. 5.** *Forsythia bushes leaf in early spring:* produce leaves, green, turn green. **6.** *Leaf through the book and look at the illustrations:* turn pages quickly, flip, thumb, glance, browse, skim.

leaflet *n.* *He handed me a leaflet advertising the nearby restaurant:* pamphlet, handbill, flyer, folder, brochure, booklet; advertisement, ad, circular; broadside, tract; handout, throwaway, broadsheet.

leafy *adj.* *The leafy trees shaded our heads:* leafed, green, verdant, abundant, covered, green, shady, springlike, summery, wooded.

league *n.* **1.** *Several nations formed a defense league. Faust was in league with the Devil:* alliance, association, group, collaboration, confraternity, partnership, guild, confederacy, confederation, federation, company, coalition, compact, cartel, union, fraternity, society, cooperative; conspiracy, cabal. **2.** *The local high schools formed a coed basketball league:* alliance, association, network, cooperative, group of competing teams. **—v. 3.** *The feminist groups leagued together to support a woman for mayor:* combine, merge, unite in a league, band, consolidate, ally, confederate, join forces. **—Ant.** 1 disunion, separation, secession. 3 divide, separate, part, secede.

leak *n.* **1.** *Water poured in through a leak in the ship's hull:* opening, gash, hole, aperture, puncture, fissure, crevice, cleft, crack, interstice, perforation, rupture, chink, break, breach, rent, fault, rift, rip. **2.** *The leak was so slow we barely noticed it:* leaking, leakage, draining, drain, outflow, efflux, seepage, escape, ebb. **—v. 3.** *Both the roof and the basement leak during heavy rains. The car leaks oil:* admit leakage, be permeable, exude, seep, take in; discharge, vent, ooze, filter, percolate, dribble, let enter or escape. **4.** *An informant leaked the news to the press:* divulge, reveal, disclose, let out, make public, give away, let slip, confide, allow to become known; *Slang* blab, spill. **—Ant.** 4 conceal, hide, suppress.

lean[1] *v.* **1.** *The exhausted runner leaned against the fence:* rest, rest one's weight, support oneself, prop oneself, recline. **2.** *See how the trees lean in the wind:* bend, incline, tilt, slant, tip, list, bow, cant, slope; lurch. **3.** *Many people lean on a personal philosophy in times of misfortune:* rely, depend, have faith in, seek solace in, resort to, take assurance from, set store by, trust in, count on. **4.** *Most of the writer's works lean toward satire. Kids today lean toward casual clothes:* tend, incline, aim, have a propensity for, suggest a preference for; be partial to, prefer. **—Ant.** 1, 2 stand erect, straighten up. 3 reject, withdraw from.

lean[2] *adj.* **1.** *Lean meat is healthier for you than fatty meat. The prisoners looked lean and pale:* nonfat, thin, spare, skinny, slender, willowy, svelte, slim, skeletal, angular, spindly, lank, lanky, rawboned, scraggy; emaciated, gaunt, weedy, scrawny. **2.** *The firm realized lean profits during the early years:* meager, scant, scanty, inadequate, small, poor, spare, sparse, insufficient, exiguous, barren, thin, modest, slender. **—Ant.** 1 fatty, brawny, fleshy, burly, plump, portly. 2 full, rich, abundant, plentiful, ample, profuse.

leaning *n.* *She had a leaning toward a medical career:* inclination, predilection, proclivity, proneness, propensity, aptitude, bent, bias, drift, tendency, weakness.

leap *v.* **1.** *The young deer were leaping about in the meadow:* jump, spring, bound, hop, hurtle, bounce, gambol, prance, caper, frisk, frolic, skip, romp, cavort. **2.** *The thief leaped the wall and escaped:* jump over, jump across, spring over, overleap, vault, bound over, hop over, hurtle over. **3.** *Don't leap to any conclusions:* rush, hasten, jump, arrive prematurely, make unjustified assumptions, come hastily. —*n.* **4.** *The boy cleared the fence in one leap:* bound, jump, spring, hurtle, hop, vault, saltation; *French* jeté. —**Ant.** 1 walk, run, crawl.

learn *v.* **1.** *Some people learn languages easily. All students here must learn to swim:* master, pick up, acquire knowledge of; receive instructions in, become able. **2.** *We must try to learn the answer:* find out, determine, discover, detect, unearth, uncover, ascertain; *Informal* ferret out. **3.** *When did you learn of Mary's divorce?:* hear, find out about, become apprised, become familiar with, become informed. **4.** *The actor had trouble learning his part:* memorize, commit to memory, con. —**Ant.** 1 forget; teach, instruct. 4 forget.

learned *adj.* *All these books were donated to the library by a learned woman:* wise, informed, educated, schooled, accomplished, erudite; profound, deep, scholarly, intellectual, well-educated, cultivated, cultured, literate, lettered, well-read, knowledgeable. —**Ant.** illiterate, unlettered, uneducated, unlearned, ignorant, *Informal* lowbrow.

learner *n.* *Get a permit for a learner before starting your driving lessons:* student, pupil, schoolchild, schoolboy, schoolgirl, apprentice, trainee, disciple, follower, proselyte, scholar; novice, tyro, tenderfoot, rookie, recruit, draftee, enlistee, freshman, neophyte, novitiate.

learning *n.* *Her writings reflected her immense learning:* education, scholarship, knowledge, schooling, culture, wisdom, erudition, enlightenment, information, understanding, comprehension, cultivation, edification, book learning. —**Ant.** ignorance, unenlightenment, uncomprehension, benightedness.

lease *v.* *We leased a car for six months:* charter, hire, loan, rent, rent out, sublease, sublet.

leash *n.* **1.** *Tie the dog's leash to the fence:* strap, thong, lead, harness, curb, rein, bridle, line, string, tether, choker. —*v.* **2.** *Leash the dog if you're going on the beach. Leash your anger until you've heard the whole story:* restrain, fasten, control, ruin, curb, harness, tether; hold in, suppress, contain, stifle. —**Ant.** 2 unleash; unharness, release, vent.

least *adj.* *The least problem troubled them:* slightest, smallest, tiniest, minutest, most trivial, fewest, lowest, minimal, minimum, nadir.

leathery *adj.* *The leathery turtle emerged on shore:* wrinkled, rough, tough, durable.

leave *v.* **1.** *Leave the room at once! The circus left town this morning:* go away from, separate from, quit, retire from, be off, depart, set out, go, exit, bid farewell, move on, start away from, embark from, decamp, fly, flee, abscond, venture away from, absent oneself; *Slang* shove off, push off, hotfoot it, bug out, take off, split. **2.** *Leave that window open, please. Just leave the dishes on the table:* let stay, let remain, keep, maintain, retain, sustain. **3.** *The boy left school in the middle of the year:* abandon, forsake, depart from, surrender, relinquish, desert, leave behind, yield, give up. **4.** *Leave the diagnosis to the doctor:* yield, entrust, allot, consign, give over, resign, cede, waive, eschew, forgo, release, surrender, commit, assign. **5.** *The cigarette left a bad taste in my mouth:* result in, produce, deposit, generate, cause. **6.** *He leaves a wife and three grown sons:* leave behind, be survived by. **7.** *The man left most of his money to charity:* bequeath, bequest, legate, will, commit, assign, consign, allot, apportion, endow. —*n.* **8.** *The senator asked leave to take the floor:* permission, consent, allowance, indulgence, sanction, approval, endorsement, understanding, tolerance, sufferance, concession. **9.** *He took leave after thanking his host:* parting, departure, farewell, going, retreat, leave-taking, withdrawal. **10.** *The platoon goes on leave for two weeks:* furlough, sabbatical, respite, liberty, recess, time off, vacation; *British* holiday. —**Ant.** 1 arrive, come, appear, emerge. 3 persist, gain, hold, retain, stay, continue. 4 assume, take over. 5 remove, erase, eradicate. 8 rejection, refusal, denial, forbiddance, prohibition, interdiction. 9 stay, continuance, persistence; arrival. 10 duty.

leave-taking *n.* *The train was coming in, so our leave-taking was mercifully brief:* farewell, parting, adieu, au revoir, send-off, good-bye.

lecherous *adj.* *His lecherous behavior scandalized the whole town:* lustful, lewd, libidinous, oversexed, lascivious, salacious, prurient, satyrlike, randy, erotic, licentious, carnal, lubricious, ruttish, goatish. —**Ant.** prudish, straitlaced, puritanical.

lechery *n.* *Don Juan led a life of lechery:* hypersexuality, carnality, lust, lustfulness, promiscuity, nymphomania, excessive sexual desire, satyriasis, salaciousness, lewdness, prurience, lasciviousness. —**Ant.** purity, chasteness, celibacy.

lecture *n.* **1.** *The sociology class heard a lecture on prison reform:* talk, address, speech, discourse, oral presentation, disquisition, oration; sermon, preachment, homily, reading, narration. **2.** *Mother gave us a lecture on keeping our rooms neat:* rebuke, reprimand, admonitory speech, harangue, chastisement, admonishment, moralizing talk, cautionary speech, warning, remonstrance, censure, talking-to, dressing down, reproof, reproach, chiding. —*v.* **3.** *The detective lectured in the city schools on drug abuse:* talk, give a talk, speak, expound, discourse. **4.** *The doctor lectured his patient about smoking too much:* reprove, rebuke, call down, take to task, harangue, rail at, scold, admonish, criticize at length, censure, chide, upbraid, moralize, preach, sermonize, hold forth. —**Ant.** 4 praise, compliment, applaud, laud.

ledge *n.* **1.** *The climbers advanced across a rocky ledge:* shelf, projection, offset, ridge, outcropping, sill, step, foothold, shoulder. **2.** *Potted* *plants lined the ledge in the living room:* shelf, sill, mantel, mantelshelf, mantelpiece.

leer *n.* **1.** *The stranger's leer frightened the children:* lewd look, lustful look, lascivious stare, ogle, goggle, sly glance, evil look, impolite gaze, insulting stare. —*v.* **2.** *The sailors leered at every passing girl:* stare suggestively, give the eye to, look knowingly, look with insulting familiarity, ogle, glance wantonly, look with a leer; smirk, fleer.

leery *adj.* *Almost everyone is leery of get-rich-quick schemes:* wary, suspicious, distrustful, circumspect, cautious, doubtful, unsure, skeptical, chary, guarded, mistrustful; hesitant, unsure, undecided, *Slang* cagey. —**Ant.** trusting, confident, credulous, gullible, unsuspecting.

leeway *n.* *Our schedule leaves no leeway for unexpected delays:* flexibility, extra time or resource, latitude, scope, margin, margin for error, allowance, cushion, reserve, elbowroom, room for choice or maneuverability; headroom, headway, clearance, play, slack, tolerance.

left *adj.* **1.** *She wrote with the left hand:* port, portside, sinistral. **2.** *We were left with nothing to do:* over, behind, left over, marooned, remaining, residual, abandoned. **3.** *The left triumphed in the election:* leftist, left-wing, socialist, radical. —**Ant.** 1 right, dextral 3 right, right-wing.

leftover *n.* **1.** *The canal project is a leftover from the previous regime. Save the leftovers for the dogs:* residue, excess, remainder, surplus, residual, legacy, oddments, overage, survivor, carry-over; remaining food, remaining odds and ends, leavings. —*adj.* **2.** *Use the leftover roast to make hash:* remaining, residual, surplus, excess; unused, uneaten.

leg *n.* **1.** *The girl jumped rope on one leg:* lower extremity, limb, member; *Slang* underpinning, stump, shank, pin, gam; (*bones*) femur, fibula, tibia. **2.** *One leg of the chair is cracked:* prop, support, upright, brace; post, column, pillar. **3.** *We're finally on the last leg of our journey:* portion, segment, part, stage, section, lap, stretch.

legacy *n.* **1.** *The man's legacy to the museum was his entire art collection:* bequest, devise, gift; inheritance, estate. **2.** *The Ionic style of architecture is a legacy from ancient Greece:* heritage, tradition; leftover, remaining portion, survivor, vestige, carry-over, throwback, transmission; heirloom, birthright; hand-me-down.

legal *adj.* **1.** *The judge's son plans to enter the legal profession. A legal question:* of law; juridical, jurisprudential, juristic; forensic, judicial, adjudicatory; courtroom. **2.** *Is it legal for bankers to serve on the municipal finance committee? Double parking is not legal:* permitted by law, lawful, permissible, rightful, sanctioned, constitutional, valid, licit, legitimate; fair, within bounds; *Slang* cricket, kosher. —**Ant.** 2 illegal, unlawful, illegitimate, illicit.

legality *n.* *The legality of the tax deduction is in question:* lawfulness, legitimacy, accordance with law; validity, licitness, constitutionality.

—**Ant.** illegality, unlawfulness, illegitimacy, illicitness.

legalization *n.* *He fought for legalization of marijuana:* decriminalization, legitimation, legitimatization.

legalize *v.* *They legalized drinking after the age of eighteen:* legitimate, legitimatize, legitimize, license, make legal, allow, permit, authorize, codify, declare lawful, decriminalize, legislate, ordain, permit, prescribe, put in force, regulate, sanction, validate.

legation *n.* *The nation's legation is housed near the UN:* diplomatic mission, consulate, delegation, ministry, embassy, chancellery, mission.

legend *n.* **1.** *The legend of his superhuman strength spread far and wide:* fable, myth, story, fiction. **2.** *She read the legend on the map:* caption, cipher, code, device, epigraph, epitaph, head, heading, inscription, key, motto, rubric, table, underline. —**Ant.** 1 fact, history.

legendary *adj.* **1.** *Babe Ruth performed legendary feats as a home run hitter:* famous, familiar to all, famed, known by tradition, storied, proverbial, worthy of legend, celebrated. **2.** *King Arthur is a legendary figure:* fabled, mythic, mythical, figuring in legends, fanciful, imaginary, unverifiable, fabulous, apocryphal, fictitious, unsubstantiated, unauthenticated. —**Ant.** 1 unknown. 2 historical, authenticated, genuine.

legerdemain *n.* **1.** *The magician's legerdemain drew a gasp from the audience:* sleight of hand, prestidigitation, deftness, adroitness; juggling, jugglery. **2.** *The coalition was accomplished by a brilliant piece of political legerdemain:* deception, trickery, artfulness, cunning, adroit manipulation, maneuvering.

legible *adj.* *The new edition is in larger, more legible type:* readable, easily read, plain, visible, decipherable, understandable, comprehensible, distinct, clear, clear-cut, neat. —**Ant.** illegible, undecipherable, unreadable, unclear, indistinct.

legion *n.* **1.** *The ancient Roman legion had from 3,000 to 6,000 foot soldiers:* military force, army, division, brigade, troops, corps. **2.** *Mahatma Gandhi had a legion of devoted followers:* multitude, mass, great number, throng, sea, swarm, spate, mob, drove, myriad, host, horde.

legislation *n.* **1.** *Legislation is the duty of a congress:* lawmaking, making law, passage of law; government. **2.** *Equal rights legislation has been passed that should benefit all:* legislative law, ordinance, enactment, regulation, bill, statute, amendment, act, measure, ruling.

legislative *adj.* *The legislative branch had failed to do its job:* lawgiving, lawmaking, legislatorial, statute-making, decreeing, enacting, congressional, parliamentary.

legislator *n.* *Members of Parliament and other legislators should be answerable to their constituents:* lawmaker, lawgiver, member of a legislature, representative, delegate, senator, representative, congressman, congresswoman, parliamentarian, councilman, assemblyman, alderman.

legislature *n.* *How members of the legislature*

voted should be made known to the public: law-making body; senate, parliament, congress, assembly, council, diet; house, chamber.

legitimacy n. The legitimacy of the nephew's claim to the estate is in question: legality, validity, lawfulness, rightfulness, correctness, appropriateness, genuineness, authenticity. —**Ant.** illegitimacy, illegality, unlawfulness.

legitimate adj. **1.** Which prince is the legitimate heir to the throne?: lawful, rightful, true, legal, licit. **2.** The workers' grievances are legitimate and must be remedied: genuine, justified, authentic, believable, plausible, logical, sound, well-founded, just, tenable, valid, reasonable, fair; proper, correct, appropriate. —**Ant.** 1 unlawful, illegal; fraudulent, sham, false. 2 unfounded, unjustified, unsound, unfair.

leisure n. Reading is a pleasant way to spend one's leisure: free time, spare time, time off, holiday, idle hours, periods of relaxation, ease, relaxation, recreation, respite, rest, vacation, recess, repose, diversion. —**Ant.** duty, work, occupation, employment, labor, business; obligation, responsibility, burden.

leisurely adj. **1.** We took a leisurely stroll after dinner: relaxed, restful, unhurried, without haste, slow-moving, slow, idle, casual; languid, lackadaisical. —adv. **2.** We walked leisurely, looking in all the windows: unhurriedly, slowly, lingeringly, without haste. —**Ant.** 1 hasty, rushed, rapid, fast. 2 hurriedly, quickly, rapidly, fast.

lend v. **1.** Can you lend me five dollars until payday?: loan, allow to use temporarily, make a loan of; Informal let one have, trust one for; advance. **2.** A fireplace lends coziness to a room: impart, furnish, give, invest, supply, contribute. **3.** The community lent full support to the mayor's plan: contribute, give freely, put at another's disposal. —**Ant.** 1 borrow. 2 deprive. 3 refuse, withhold, keep.

length n. **1.** The length of the track is one mile: reach, span, distance, end to end, extent, measure, longitude, range, compass, measurement. **2.** The lot is 200 feet in length and 50 feet in depth: longer dimension, longer side, lengthiest part; Informal the long way. **3.** The length of the movie is two hours: duration, extent, time; magnitude, period, stretch, term, elapsed time. **4.** We'll need several lengths of string to tie the package: piece, portion, segment, section, run, stretch. —**Ant.** 2 width, breadth, depth.

lengthen v. This year she had to lengthen all her hems: extend, elongate, stretch, protract, draw out, drag out, prolong, expand, spin out, string out, increase; fill out, flesh out, add to, pad. —**Ant.** shorten, curtail, abbreviate, abridge, decrease.

lengthy adj. Be prepared for a lengthy speech after dinner: very long, overlong, of great length, extended, prolonged, protracted, elongated, long-drawn, extensive; discursive, long-winded, windy, garrulous, wordy, rambling, prolix, drawn out, padded, digressive; interminable, endless. —**Ant.** short, brief, limited; condensed, succinct, terse, to the point.

lenient adj. The judge was lenient in sentencing the criminal: merciful, kind, clement, gentle, sparing, tenderhearted, indulgent, tolerant, forbearing, mild, soft, easygoing, kindhearted, softhearted, moderate, charitable, compassionate, sympathetic, benevolent, liberal, permissive, patient, forgiving. —**Ant.** harsh, stern, exacting, rigid, rigorous, stringent, strict, severe, cruel, merciless.

less adv. **1.** Father likes to take the less traveled roads: to a smaller extent, more limited way; little, meagerly, barely. —adj. **2.** The movie had less success than expected: smaller, not as great, more limited, slighter, not so significant. —n. **3.** People have been imprisoned for less: a smaller amount, lesser action, less serious offense. —**Ant.** 1–3 more. 2 greater, larger.

lessen v. Talking things out lessened the tension. The storm's fury is lessening: decrease, decline, diminish, abate, dwindle, sink, reduce, subside, shrink, contract, lower, depreciate, slacken, wind down, ease, wane, ebb, abridge; alleviate, lighten, mitigate; dilute, thin. —**Ant.** increase, raise, lengthen, enlarge, extend, heighten, multiply, mount, build.

lesser adj. **1.** The opera was pleasant, but it's one of the composer's lesser works: smaller, less important, secondary, slighter, humbler, inferior, minor. —adv. **2.** Of the two actors, he is the lesser known: to a smaller degree, less, secondarily. —**Ant.** 1 major, larger, primary, superior. 2 greater, primarily.

lesson n. **1.** The test will cover lessons 1 through 5: exercise, segment, assignment, matter to be learned, student's task, study, instruction, homework. **2.** The singer began taking lessons at age 12: class, instruction, drill, learning session. **3.** Her faith throughout the tragedy was a lesson to all: example, model, exemplar, advisement, notice, instruction, study, guide, moral, message, warning, admonition, deterrent, example, caveat, remonstrance, caution, rebuke, punishment. **4.** The lesson for today is from Paul's Epistle to the Ephesians: reading, recitation, Scriptures. —**Ant.** 3 misguidance, deception, bad example.

let v. **1.** Let the porter carry the bags: permit, allow, authorize, warrant, license, approve, give assent to; sanction, endorse; suffer, leave, tolerate; admit, concede. **2.** The family let a house for July and August: rent, lease, hire out, charter, sublease, sublet. **3.** Let the passengers know the plane will be late: cause, make, enable, allow, permit, grant, empower. —**Ant.** 1 forbid, prohibit. 2 buy; sell.

letdown n. I may have expected too much, but meeting her was a letdown: disappointment, anticlimax, disenchantment, discontent, dissatisfaction, comedown, disillusionment, mortification, discomfiture, disgruntlement, bafflement, frustration, balk, chagrin, regret, setback, rue, bitter pill; blighted hope, dashed hope, blow. —**Ant.** gratification, satisfaction, fulfillment, contentment.

lethal adj. Too many sleeping pills can be lethal: deadly, fatal, mortal, killing, mortally toxic;

dangerous, destructive; virulent, baneful, poisonous, venomous, malignant. **—Ant.** harmless, wholesome, healthful.

lethargic *adj. The hot, humid climate made everyone lethargic:* lazy, drowsy, sleepy, soporific, languid, indolent, idle, dull, somnolent, comatose, enervated, debilitated, dispirited, unspirited, torpid, lackluster, sluggish, slothful, indifferent, passive, inert, listless, apathetic. **—Ant.** energetic, vigorous, alert, active, responsive, bright, spirited; energized, animated, stimulated.

lethargy *n. My profound lethargy made work impossible:* languor, lassitude, apathy, indifference, drowsiness, sluggishness, dullness, inactivity, inertia, torpor, torpidity, stupor, laziness, indolence, listlessness, sloth, slothfulness. **—Ant.** vigor, alertness, liveliness, activity, eagerness.

letter *n.* **1.** *There are 26 letters in the alphabet:* orthographic character, alphabetic character, written symbol. **2.** *A letter was sent out asking for contributions:* epistle, dispatch, missive, note, message; memorandum, document, certificate; love letter, billet-doux. **3.** *Both sides obeyed the letter if not the spirit of the agreement:* actual terms, specific details, literal wording, strict meaning, substance, exact sense, literalness, preciseness. **4. letters** *He was a man of letters with no interest in current affairs:* literary accomplishment, learning, erudition, scholarly attainment; literature, belles lettres. **—Ant.** 3 spirit, tenor, heart.

letup *n. She watched television all day without letup:* stopping, slackening, relief, cessation, surcease, pause, slowdown, retardation, lessening, remission, abatement, decrease, respite, lull; interlude, interval, vacation. **—Ant.** increase, speedup, intensification, acceleration.

level *adj.* **1.** *The floors of the old house are remarkably level:* flat, even, horizontal, flush, plane; uniform, consistent; lacking roughness or unevenness, smooth, unwrinkled; on an even keel; parallel to the horizon, in line with the horizon. **2.** *The water rose level with the first landing. Supply is about level with demand:* even, on a line, aligned; equivalent to, comparable to, on a par with; together, tied, neck and neck. **—n.** **3.** *The water rose to the level of the porch:* height, elevation, vertical position, plane. **4.** *The whole class is at a third grade math level:* stage, station, rank, position, achievement. **5.** *The men's clothing department is on the second level. They discovered fossils in the lowest level of rock:* floor, story, landing, elevation; layer, bed, stratum, zone, vein. **—v.** **6.** *The bulldozer leveled the road before paving:* grade, make even, even out, make horizontal, align, plane, flatten, smooth, equalize. **7.** *A tornado leveled the entire business district:* flatten, raze, knock down, topple, lay low, wreck, tear down, reduce, devastate. **8.** *The hunter leveled his gun at the prey. You should level an accusation at the suspect:* aim, direct, point. **—Ant.** 1 slanted, tilted, uneven, warped, bumpy, hilly; vertical. 2

below, above. 6 roughen, furrow. 7 raise, erect; build, construct.

level-headed *adj. We need a person who's level-headed and wants to be a leader:* sensible, prudent, cautious, circumspect, steady, judicious, sage, dependable, practical, sound; composed, cool-headed, unruffled, self-controlled, balanced, poised, even-tempered. **—Ant.** foolish, skittish, flighty, thoughtless, senseless.

leverage *n. He had a lot of leverage over them:* influence, advantage, power, clout, ascendancy, authority, drag, edge, fix, hold, pull, weight, *Informal* bargaining chip.

levity *n. The situation is too grave for levity:* frivolity, lightness, lightheartedness, whimsy, lack of earnestness or seriousness, triviality, hilarity, foolishness, silliness, joking, mirth, jocularity, trifling, flippancy, flightiness; pleasantry, fun. **—Ant.** gravity, seriousness, sobriety, earnestness, solemnity, dignity.

levy *n.* **1.** *The government authorized a levy on cigarette sales:* duty, excise, tax, assessment, fee, toll, imposition, tariff. **2.** *National leaders demanded a levy of troops to meet the danger:* conscription, calling up, draft, muster. **—v.** **3.** *The court levied a fine on the defendant:* impose, demand, exact, assess, charge; collect. **4.** *The nation levied all ablebodied men for the war:* conscript, draft, call up, enlist. **5.** *In 200 BC the Syrians levied war against Egypt:* wage, start, carry on, make, prosecute, pursue.

lewd *adj. The film was considered lewd by some people. He uttered a lewd remark:* obscene, indecent, vulgar, lustful, lecherous, goatish, bawdy, Rabelaisian, ribald, risqué, pornographic, lascivious, excessively erotic, lubricious, libidinous, wanton, licentious, libertine, immoral, salacious, prurient. **—Ant.** chaste, decent, modest; proper, prim, pure, moral.

lexicon *n. That new word isn't in my lexicon:* wordbook, vocabulary, dictionary, thesaurus, glossary, index, gloss, code book, wordlist, concordance, synonymy, wordstock, onomasticon.

liability *n.* **1.** *Heavy liabilities forced the company into bankruptcy:* debt, obligation, indebtedness, debit, arrear, burden, duty, responsibility. **2.** *Shyness is a liability in politics:* disadvantage, drawback, onus, burden, obstacle, handicap, minus, impediment, hindrance, shortcoming, stumbling block, encumbrance, inconvenience, *Slang* drag. **—Ant.** 1, 2 asset. 2 bonus, plus, advantage, head start, boon.

liable *adj.* **1.** *Too much snacking between meals makes you liable to obesity:* vulnerable, susceptible, open, exposed, subject, prone, inclined, disposed, sensitive, ripe for. **2.** *The man was liable for his wife's debts:* legally responsible, answerable, accountable, chargeable, obligated. **3.** *If you disagree with him, he's liable to get angry:* likely, apt, inclined, prone. **—Ant.** 1 exempt, immune. 2 unaccountable, exempt. 3 unlikely, disinclined.

liaison *n.* **1.** *Our officers had close liaison with the general staff. The negotiator acted as liaison between labor and management:* contact, connection, association, communication, intercommunication; alliance, bond, link, coordination, union, cooperation, interchange; mediator, go-between. **2.** *For years the countess had kept up a secret liaison with a cabinet minister:* love affair, illicit romance, amour, entanglement, dalliance, flirtation, intrigue; *French* aventure.

liar *n. A compulsive liar finds it impossible to tell the truth:* falsifier, prevaricator, fabricator, perjurer; fibber, storyteller.

libel *n.* **1.** *The actor brought suit against the columnist for libel:* printed slander, defamation, malicious falsehood, calumny, smear, aspersion, slur, vilification, obloquy; unjust accusation. *—v.* **2.** *The candidate charged that his opponent libeled him in the article:* vilify, malign unjustly, slur, derogate, discredit, slander, defame, revile, disparage, blacken, calumniate, asperse. **—Ant.** 1 vindication, apology. 2 vindicate, apologize, retract. 2 set the record straight.

libelous *adj. The libelous statement was immediately challenged:* contumelious, defamatory, slanderous, scurrilous, aspersive, debasing, derogatory, injurious, malicious, opprobrious, pejorative, traducing.

liberal *adj.* **1.** *Liberal legislators hoped to improve the lot of the masses:* progressive, reformist, advanced, freethinking; civil libertarian, latitudinarian; left-wing. **2.** *Try to keep a liberal attitude and listen to both sides:* fair-minded, open-minded, broad-minded, tolerant, forbearing, magnanimous, unbigoted, unprejudiced, unbiased, impartial; enlightened, humanitarian. **3.** *Liberal donations enabled the hospital to build a new wing:* abundant, generous, lavish, openhanded, unsparing, extravagant, bounteous, bountiful, handsome, munificent, prodigal, unstinting, plenteous, ample. **4.** *The chairman gave a liberal interpretation of the rules:* lenient, broad, unrigorous, not strict, casual, flexible, tolerant, open to reason, not literal. *—n.* **5.** *Liberals did not like the government's conservative policies:* progressive, reformer, latitudinarian, libertarian; left-winger, leftist. **—Ant.** 1 conservative, reactionary, right-wing. 2 intolerant, narrow, bigoted, biased, prejudiced, provincial, limited. 3 skimpy, inadequate, small, cheap. 4 strict, unbending, fixed, inflexible, rigid, literal. 5 conservative, reactionary, right-winger.

liberate *v. Allied armies liberated France from the Nazis. Try to liberate yourself from preconceived ideas:* set free, deliver, release, discharge, disencumber, disengage, emancipate, manumit, redeem, absolve; rescue, extricate, let loose, let go, unshackle, let out; *Slang* spring. **—Ant.** imprison, intern, confine, restrict, limit; entrap, enthrall, enslave.

libertine *n.* **1.** *Casanova is known both as a literary figure and as a libertine:* profligate, debauchee, rake, voluptuary, reprobate, lecher, roué, sensualist, seducer; immoralist, moral iconoclast, immoral person; satyr, womanizer, goat. *—adj.* **2.** *His libertine behavior shocked the staid community:* immoral, dissolute, loose, unchaste, licentious, lewd, lustful, wanton, lascivi-

ous, libidinous, lecherous, morally unrestrained, profligate. **—Ant.** 1 prude, puritan. 2 straitlaced, moral, virtuous, chaste.

liberty *n.* **1.** *The constitution guards the liberty of the people:* freedom, self-determination, independence, autonomy; right, privilege. **2.** *Lincoln's Emancipation Proclamation gave slaves their liberty:* freedom, manumission, emancipation, liberation, delivery; citizenship, enfranchisement. **3.** *The entire crew can have a week's liberty once we reach shore:* leave, furlough, vacation, free time, shore leave. **4.** *Employees have liberty to use all the museum facilities:* freedom, permission, leave, sanction, license, dispensation; carte blanche. **5. liberties** *The fresh boy takes too many liberties with his elders. He takes liberties with the truth:* familiarity, license, impropriety, undue intimacy; distortion, misrepresentation, violation, misuse, falsification. **—Ant.** 1 tyranny, despotism; restraint, constraint, compulsion, duress, coercion. 2 slavery, subjugation, captivity, imprisonment, restraint, enslavement. 3 duty. 5 propriety, judiciousness, rigorousness.

libidinous *adj. His libidinous behavior in the workplace was extremely inappropriate:* wanton, lecherous, lustful, carnal, hot, lascivious, salacious, sensual, *Slang* horny.

license *n.* **1.** *The restaurant applied for a license to sell wine:* authorization, charter, leave, liberty, permit, right, allowance, sanction, warrant, privilege, carte blanche, grant, admission, free passage, freedom, dispensation, franchise. **2.** *The date on the license indicates that it expired a month ago:* permit, certificate, pass, passport, visa, safe-conduct. **3.** *Too much license was taken in translating the book:* liberty, latitude, departure from rule, deviation from custom, nonconformity, privilege; laxity, looseness, slackness; audacity, brazenness, presumptuousness. **4.** *Too much permissiveness may lead beyond liberty to license:* abused freedom, too much liberty, indifference to others' rights, irresponsibility, recklessness, licentiousness, temerity, presumption, arrogant self-indulgence, debauchery, libertinism, anarchy, lawlessness, unruliness, disorder. *—v.* **5.** *The county licensed the landowners to fish these waters:* authorize, issue a license to, certify, warrant, empower, enable, allow, let, sanction, accredit, commission; approve, endorse. **—Ant.** 1 forbiddance, denial, restriction. 3 strictness, restraint. 4 restraint, constraint, restriction, moderation, sobriety, submission. 5 prohibit, forbid; restrain, curb, check; disallow.

licentious *adj.* **1.** *The ruler's licentious practices led to a popular uprising:* irresponsible, unrestrained, amoral, unconstrained, excessive, lawless, unprincipled, unscrupulous, prodigal, ungoverned. **2.** *The licentious play was closed by the police:* lewd, libertine, lustful, lecherous, lascivious, immoral, libidinous, lubricious, debauched, wanton, abandoned, loose, promiscuous, salacious; goatish, profligate, dissolute, depraved, dissipated, ruttish, brutish; *Informal* dirty, sleazy, raunchy. **—Ant.** 1 law-abiding, lawful, responsible, principled, scrupulous. 2 chaste, pure, puritanical, proper, moral, prudish.

licit *adj. There are enough licit pleasures without running afoul of the law:* legal, lawful, authorized, allowable, acceptable, permissible, legitimate, admissible, constitutional, sanctioned, sanctionable, statutory, authorizable, valid; *Slang* legit, kosher. —**Ant.** forbidden, illegal, unlawful, illicit, banned, prohibited.

lick *v.* **1.** *Lick the ice cream cone so it won't drip:* pass the tongue over, touch with the tongue, tongue, lap, collect with the tongue. **2.** *The first flickers of fire licked the dry timber:* pass lightly over, lap, touch; ignite, fire, kindle. **3.** *Informal The Yankees licked the Dodgers in the World Series:* defeat, beat, conquer, vanquish, overcome, overthrow, overpower, drub, subdue, subjugate, rout, outmatch, master; *Informal* trounce, clobber. **4.** *Informal The father licked the boy for lying:* spank, beat, whip, thrash, hit, wallop. —*n.* **5.** *Informal May I have a lick off of your lollipop?:* taste, sample; lap, suck. **6.** *Informal John got a few licks in before the fight was broken up:* slap, blow, punch, hit, sock; verbal blow, denunciation, sally, crack. **7.** *You haven't done a lick of work today:* bit, speck, particle, modicum, touch, dab, jot, shred, snip, iota, hint, stroke, smattering, smidgen, trace, scintilla. —**Ant.** 4, 6 caress, pet. 7 lot, pile.

lid *n. Cover the pot with a lid and turn the gas down low. There was no lid on the amount one could bet:* top, cover, cap, stopper, plug, stopple, cork, operculum; curb, restraint; limit, ceiling, maximum.

lie[1] *n.* **1.** *The testimony was a pack of transparent lies:* falsehood, prevarication, falsification, untruth, fib, fiction, invention, fabrication, story, false story, perjury, deception, deceit, misrepresentation, equivocation. —*v.* **2.** *The witness lied to the jury:* perjure oneself, prevaricate, falsify, speak falsely, fabricate, tell untruths, forswear oneself; fib, embellish, embroider, romance, stretch the truth, equivocate, misstate. —**Ant.** 1 truth, veracity, fact, gospel.

lie[2] *v.* **1.** *Lie here until the dizziness goes away:* recline, rest, repose, be supine, be flat, be prone, sprawl, loll, lounge, stretch out. **2.** *The king lies now in his final resting place:* be buried, be interred, repose. **3.** *The village lies north of here. The responsibility lies with the driver:* be placed, be located, be found, exist, remain, abide, rest, stay, inhere, belong, be present, be established, obtain; range, extend. —**Ant.** 1 rise, arise, stand; be active, go, change, run.

life *n.* **1.** *There are many forms of life on earth:* living thing, living being, creature, organism, animal, plant; animate existence, being, substantiality, subsistence. **2.** *Many lives were lost in the explosion:* human, human being, person, individual, soul. **3.** *The mayfly has an average life of 24 hours:* lifetime, term of existence, life span, life expectancy; survival, longevity, duration; career. **4.** *Her life has been one of great accomplishment. Hermits lead a quiet life:* ca-

reer, lifework, path, course; existence, mode of living. **5.** *The author's life of Michelangelo was made into a movie:* biography, autobiography, story, life story, memoir. **6.** *The new musical bursts with life and humor:* liveliness, vitality, animation, spirit, energy, zest, vivacity, vigor, verve. —**Ant.** 1 death, lifelessness, nothingness. 6 lifelessness, spiritlessness, dullness, flatness.

lifeless *adj.* **1.** *The poor animal lay lifeless in the road:* dead, without life, defunct; deceased, departed, late; inert, inactive; inanimate. **2.** *Plays often make dull, lifeless movies:* static, lacking vitality, dull, spiritless, lifeless, torpid, vapid, sluggish, colorless, boring; stiff, wooden, flat, hollow, lackluster. —**Ant.** 1 living, alive; animate. 2 animated, vital; active, dynamic, live, spirited.

lifelong *adj. She was a lifelong believer:* enduring, lifetime, for life, longstanding, constant, deep-rooted, inveterate, lasting, long-lasting, longstanding, perennial, permanent.

lifework *n. Her lifework was service to the poor:* calling, mission, pursuit, vocation, work, business, career, occupation, profession, purpose.

lift *v.* **1.** *Please lift the packages onto the counter. Lift your head up and pay attention:* hoist, heave, move upward, raise, elevate, raise up, rear, upraise, uplift, boost. **2.** *The government lifted the ban on tourist travel:* cancel, revoke, rescind, put an end to, remove, banish, countermand. **3.** *The encouraging letter lifted our hopes:* elevate, uplift, exalt, raise, give a boost to. **4.** *With the rain, the smog lifted from the city:* rise, disperse, dissipate, scatter, vanish, disappear, float away, become dispelled; ascend, soar, move upward. **5.** *Informal Someone lifted his wallet on the bus:* steal, take, thieve, pilfer, pinch, purloin, filch, swipe, snatch, make off with, pick, palm, pocket; appropriate; pirate, plagiarize. —*n.* **6.** *With one great lift, the men moved the rock:* heave, hoist, boost, uplift, raising; ascent, gain in elevation, upward movement, climb, rise, ascendance. **7.** *The employer's praise gave the staff a lift:* sense of well-being, rising of spirits; encouragement, enheartenment, reassurance, boost, inspiration, elation, uplift; *Slang* shot in the arm, high. —**Ant.** 1 lower, drop. 2 establish, impose. 3 lower, disappoint, depress, crush, dash. 4 hang, descend, fall. 6 drop. 7 letdown, blow.

ligature *n. The surgeon tied a ligature:* tie, bond, band, binding, connection, knot, ligament, link, nexus.

light[1] *n.* **1.** *Light from the sun filled the darkened room:* radiance, illumination, shine, luminosity, brightness, blaze, glare, glow, luster, sparkle, brilliance, effulgence; beam, sunbeam, moonbeam. **2.** *Switch on a light so we can see better:* source of light; (*variously*) lamp, lantern, beacon, torch, candle. **3.** *Try to analyze the problem in a new light:* approach, aspect, manner of understanding, viewpoint, attitude, slant, side, vantage point, direction, angle, frame of reference. **4.** *The new facts throw some light on the matter:* elucidation, understanding, information, enlightenment, insight, illumination. **5.** *Do you have a light for my pipe?:* means of ignition; match, lucifer, lighter; flame. **6.** *Helen Keller was a light and inspiration to all sightless people:* model, exemplar, guide, paragon, paradigm, shining example, guiding light, beacon. —*adj.* **7.** *The room is not light enough for reading:* bright, well lighted, having light, illuminated, luminous, radiant, brilliant, sunny, aglow. **8.** *The living-room walls are a light yellow:* pale, light-toned, not deep or dark, light-hued, fair, bleached; blond, blondish. —*v.* **9.** *Light a fire for warmth:* ignite, set burning, set fire to, fire, catch fire, conflagrate, flame, spark, kindle. **10.** *Light the auditorium during intermission. To light one's way:* illuminate, illumine, give light to, irradiate, flood with light, brighten, floodlight; clarify. **11.** *A smile lit up his face:* brighten, make cheerful, lighten, radiate, make radiant, cause to shine. **12.** *Light some lamps in here:* turn on, switch on, put on. —**Ant.** 1 dark, darkness; shadow, shade, gloom, dusk, dimness. 4 obscurity, mystery, cloud, shadow. 7 dark, dim, gloomy, shadowy, dusky. 8 dark, deep. 9 extinguish, put out, damp, douse, turn off, quench. 11 darken, cloud, dull.

light² *adj.* **1.** *The suitcase is surprisingly light:* lightweight, underweight, not heavy, burdenless, weightless; gossamer, buoyant, ethereal. **2.** *A light breeze stirred the curtains. We had light rainfall for the month:* small, inconsequential, barely perceptible, inconsiderable, moderate, slight, puny, faint. **3.** *Let's see a light movie for a change:* lighthearted, amusing, funny, gay, carefree, frivolous, sprightly, blithe, nonintellectual, trifling; trivial, paltry, superficial, petty, inconsiderate, slight. **4.** *I heard a light tap at the window:* soft, moderate, slight, faint, gentle. **5.** *She is a light dancer:* light-footed, airy, graceful, sylphlike. **6.** *A light dinner is recommended for good digestion:* small, spare, frugal, modest in quality, not rich, slight, meager, scanty, restricted, not heavy, abstemious. **7.** *The beautiful day put us in a light mood:* high-spirited, gleeful, jolly, sportive, jaunty, jubilant, happy, chipper, bright, cheerful, gay, buoyant. **8.** *Some light exercise is healthy during convalescence:* easy, simple, manageable, effortless, moderate, untaxing, undemanding. —**Ant.** 1, 2, 4–6 heavy. 1 burdensome, weighty. 2 strong, substantial. 3 serious, intense, deep, profound. 4 forceful. 5 clumsy. 6 rich, gluttonous. 7 serious, despondent, somber. 8 hard, strenuous, taxing.

light³ *v.* **1.** *The passengers lighted from the train:* alight, descend, get down, get off, come off, step down, dismount. **2.** *The butterfly lit on a leaf:* come to rest, alight, stop, land, perch, fall, settle, roost. **3.** *I lit upon the ring while cleaning the drawers:* chance, discover, meet with, stumble on, encounter, come across, come upon, happen upon, find. —**Ant.** 1 ascend, mount, climb, get on, go aboard.

lighten¹ *v. More lamps will lighten the gloomy room:* brighten, cause to become lighter, light up, irradiate, illuminate, make bright, become

light; scintillate, shine, blaze, flare, flash, gleam, corruscate. —**Ant.** darken.

lighten² *v.* **1.** *We dropped ballast to lighten the balloon:* make lighter, make less burdensome, reduce in load, unload, ease, buoy up, unburden, disburden. **2.** *Extra help lightened the maid's work:* ease, lessen, reduce, make less harsh, mitigate, disencumber, alleviate, relieve, assuage, allay, abate, moderate, temper. **3.** *The grandchildren's phone call lightened our mood:* lift, gladden, elate, inspire, revive, enliven, buoy, uplift. —**Ant.** 1 weight. 2 increase, heighten, intensify, aggravate. 3 depress, sadden, oppress, weigh down.

lightheaded *adj. The burst of oxygen made her lightheaded:* dizzy, woozy, faint, giddy, punchy, reeling, vertiginous, whirling, light-headed.

lighthearted *adj. The children were lighthearted on the last day of school:* cheerful, cheered, cheery, gay, carefree, merry, joyous, jolly, joyful, glad, sunny, airy, free and easy, untroubled, blithe, chipper, buoyant, effervescent, insouciant, sprightly, lively, sanguine. —**Ant.** heavyhearted, cheerless, sad, depressed, dejected, despondent, melancholy, morose, glum, gloomy.

lightly *adv.* **1.** *The visitor tapped lightly on the door:* gently, hesitantly, weakly, faintly, timidly, softly. **2.** *The cake is lightly sprinkled with sugar:* thinly, slightly, meagerly, sparingly, sparsely, moderately. **3.** *Respect is not won lightly:* easily, facilely, readily, without effort. **4.** *Step lightly over the rocks:* nimbly, gingerly, airily; quickly, swiftly, buoyantly. **5.** *Responsibility must not be taken lightly:* carelessly, thoughtlessly, without concern, unconcernedly, frivolously, indifferently, slightingly, blithely, blandly, flippantly. —**Ant.** 1 heavily, firmly, forcefully. 2 heavily, thickly, abundantly. 3 difficultly, arduously. 4 heavily, awkwardly, ploddingly, slowly, ponderously. 5 carefully, seriously, earnestly.

lightweight *adj. He was a lightweight contributor to the magazine:* trivial, unimportant, inconsequential, insignificant, paltry, petty, slight, trifling. —**Ant.** important, substantial, momentous, serious, significant.

likable or **likeable** *adj. She has an outgoing and likable personality:* pleasing, genial, attractive, easily liked, charming, winsome, lovable, pleasant, amiable, agreeable, engaging, appealing, complaisant; nice, sympathetic; *Spanish* simpático. —**Ant.** unlikable, displeasing, unpleasant, hateful, odious, repellent, repulsive.

like¹ *adj. Each employee received a like bonus. The brothers have like personalities:* identical, similar, akin, same, much the same, comparable, corresponding; congruent, matched, analogous, homologous, cognate, equivalent, equal, uniform, parallel; selfsame; allied, related, resembling. —**Ant.** unlike, dissimilar, different, diverse, divergent.

like² *v.* **1.** *Most children like music:* enjoy, take pleasure in, find agreeable, relish, fancy, be partial to, dote, savor, relish. **2.** *The students like the new dean:* esteem, admire, find agreeable, have a friendly feeling for, be partial to, be fond of, fancy, approve, endorse; favor, support; *Informal* take a shine to, have a crush on. **3.** *Would you like to join us?*: care, think fit, feel inclined, wish, have a mind, choose. —*n.* **4.** **likes** *Everyone has different likes and dislikes:* partialities, favorites, inclinations, prejudices, preferences. —**Ant.** 1–3 dislike. 1, 2 hate, abhor, detest, loathe, abominate.

likelihood *n. There is a likelihood of rain today:* prospect, probability, strong possibility, good chance, reasonableness, potentiality, possibility. —**Ant.** improbability, unlikelihood.

likely *adj.* **1.** *An accident is likely to happen at that intersection:* inclined, apt, probable, liable, destined. **2.** *Your story is a likely one:* plausible, credible, reliable, believable, reasonable, rational, seemingly truthful, verisimilar. **3.** *The park is a likely spot for the picnic:* suitable, fit, proper, befitting, appropriate, qualified. **4.** *The former quarterback is a likely person for the coaching job:* promising, able, apt. —*adv.* **5.** *We will most likely be late:* probably, presumably, in all probability. —**Ant.** 1 unlikely, 2, 3 doubtful, dubious, questionable, problematic. 4 unpromising.

likeness *n.* **1.** *The artist sketched a good likeness of my father:* portrait, picture, representation, image, study, model, delineation, depiction, rendition, portrayal; replica, facsimile, effigy. **2.** *There is a likeness between the brothers:* resemblance, similarity, similitude, semblance, agreement; correspondence, analogy, affinity. —**Ant.** 2 dissimilarity, difference, divergence, disparity.

liking *n. Most children have a liking for animals:* affinity, preference, taste, appetite, inclination, proclivity, partiality, affection, fancy, fondness, penchant, appetite, leaning, predilection, soft spot, propensity, bent, weakness. —**Ant.** dislike, disinclination; hatred, abhorrence, loathing, repugnance, aversion.

lily-white *adj.* **1.** *I'm certain that her motives were lily-white:* blameless, guiltless, good, decent, exemplary, upstanding, inculpable, innocent, pure, virtuous, uncorrupted, righteous, irreproachable, faultless, proper, unimpeachable, upright, honorable, impeccable. **2.** *The lily-white country club has been widely criticized:* all-white, segregated, discriminatory, bigoted, biased, exclusive, prejudiced, racist, unintegrated. —**Ant.** 1 corrupt, depraved, wicked, degenerate, evil, immoral.

limb *n. The limb of an animal is vastly different from that of a tree:* appendage, member, part, extension; branch, projection, bough, sprig, spur, twig, shoot, outgrowth; wing, arm, leg; *Slang* gam, pin; prosthesis.

limber *adj.* **1.** *The dancer has a limber torso:* flexible, pliant, bending, pliable, malleable, lithe, agile, lithesome, supple, lissome, elastic, loose-jointed. —*v.* **2.** *Exercise will limber you up:* make limber, loosen, relax. —**Ant.** 1 stiff, rigid, unbending, inflexible, wooden. 2 stiffen.

limbo *n. Losing power, he found himself in limbo:* oblivion, nothingness, nowhere.

limelight *n.* public eye, public notice, cynosure,

fame, notoriety, exposure, publicity, réclame. —**Ant.** reclusiveness, seclusion.

limit *n.* **1.** *The climbers had reached the limit of their endurance:* end, furthest bound, greatest extent, end point, breaking point, ultimate. **2.** Often **limits** *These stakes mark the limits of the property:* edge, border, boundary, rim, fringe, frontier, margin, confines, periphery, perimeter. **3.** *Is there a speed limit on that thruway?:* limitation, restriction, maximum, greatest number allowed, ceiling, top; restraint, check, curb; quota. —*v.* **4.** *The nation must limit land development:* restrict, restrain, confine, delimit, curb, check, bound, keep within bounds, narrow, inhibit; define, prescribe, circumscribe, qualify.

limitation *n. The countries accepted limitation of arms:* restraint, constraint, check, circumspection, control, curb, modification, qualification, restriction; disadvantage, drawback, impediment, inhibition, obstruction.

limited *adj. Each branch of government has limited powers:* defined, delimited, confined, special, bounded, restrained, controlled, circumscribed, specified, fixed, finite; narrow, cramped, restricted, minimal. —**Ant.** unlimited, unbounded, unrestricted, limitless.

limitless *adj. The country's natural resources are not limitless:* endless, unlimited, unending, unbound, boundless, without measure, measureless, immeasurable, infinite, eternal, without limit. —**Ant.** limited, circumscribed, bounded, restricted, restrained, measured.

limp[1] *n.* **1.** *The war injury left him with a pronounced limp:* lameness, halting walk, gimp, jerky step, halt, lame movement, falter, hobble. —*v.* **2.** *The injured player limped off the field:* hobble, falter, halt; crawl, skulk.

limp[2] *adj. The runner went limp with exhaustion:* slack, loose, flabby, droopy, drooping, floppy, flaccid, yielding, lax, lacking vitality, lacking firmness, soft, dead tired, weak, lethargic, enervated, exhausted. —**Ant.** stiff, rigid, strong, hardy, robust.

limpid *adj. We could see ourselves in the limpid stream. He is a master of limpid prose:* lucid, clear, transparent, translucent, pure, pellucid; vitreous, crystalline; perspicuous, unambiguous, straightforward, clear-cut. —**Ant.** muddy, murky, cloudy, dark, dim, opaque.

line *n.* **1.** *Draw a line under the misspelled words:* underscore, long thin mark, score, long stroke, stripe, dash, streak, slash; demarcation, border, outline, contour. **2.** *Her face bore lines of worry:* wrinkle, mark, crease, furrow, crow's foot. **3.** *Is there a long line at the box office?:* queue, file, rank, tier, series, column, range, procession. **4.** *Drop us an occasional line during your travels:* note, brief message, letter, postcard, card, report, word. **5.** *Any deviation from the party line brought swift reprimands:* policy, stance, position, ideology, doctrine, idea, intention, scheme, system; course of action, belief, method; purpose, direction. **6.** *The calf comes from a long line of prize cattle:* lineage, stock, genealogy, race, family, house, strain, ancestry, breed. **7.** *The commuter rail line is in financial* *trouble:* transit company, transportation service or company, transit route. **8.** *Public relations is his line:* occupation, business, profession, vocation, calling, pursuit, métier, trade, means of living, livelihood, craft. **9.** *The fishing line became entangled in seaweed:* cord, strand, thread, cordage; fishline; cable, rope; towline. **10.** *Air conditioning will require a more powerful line:* circuit, conductor, conduit, power supply, electrical system. **11. lines** *The play does not try to be original but follows traditional lines:* pattern, habitual or fixed idea, convention, principle, model, example, general form or notion, routine. **12.** *Soldiers in the line suffer the most casualties:* front line, firing line, fighting front, front, vanguard; trenches, barricades; defensive perimeter. —*v.* **13.** *Line the pages for the graph both horizontally and vertically:* rule, mark or rule with lines, score, draw, inscribe. **14.** *People were lined up in front of the theater:* queue up, arrange in a line, align, array, form in a line, rank, marshal, file.

lineage *n. He is from a family of ancient lineage:* extraction, derivation, line, stock, pedigree, blood, descent, heredity, genealogy, ancestry, parentage.

linger *v.* **1.** *The last guests lingered until 2 A.M.:* stay, remain, tarry, persist, delay, delay departure, wait, dawdle, dillydally, procrastinate, dally; loiter, idle, lag, trail, *Informal* hang around. **2.** *He lingered on long after he could function normally:* last, persist in living, survive, hang on, die slowly, cling to life. —**Ant.** 1 leave hastily, rush, hasten, depart, disappear.

linguist *n.* **1.** *Mr. Kerenyi is our resident linguist--he speaks eight languages:* multilingual person, polyglot; interpreter, translator. **2.** *The Orientalist Sir William Jones was among the first modern linguists:* linguistics expert, language scholar; (*variously*) philologist, etymologist, lexicographer, semanticist, morphologist, grammarian, phonetician, phonologist.

liniment *n. The liniment eased the player's aching shoulder:* ointment, medicated lotion, soothing liquid preparation, balm, unguent, emollient, salve.

link *n.* **1.** *The bracelet is formed of silver links:* section of a chain, connective, bond, ring, loop, joint. **2.** *Old friends are a link with the past:* tie, bond, connecting part, connection, interconnection, junction, splice, association, relation, liaison, relationship. —*v.* **3.** *Fingerprints linked the suspect to the crime:* connect, conjoin, interconnect, tie, tie in, couple, combine, bind, fuse, unite; group, bracket, associate, relate, implicate, involve. —**Ant.** 3 separate, sever, divorce, split, part, divide; clear, vindicate.

lionize *v. Past members of the club were lionized at the annual banquet:* acclaim, admire, exalt, praise, glorify, flatter, adulate, revere, celebrate, deify, eulogize, glamorize, aggrandize, ennoble, enshrine, immortalize. —**Ant.** belittle, deprecate, criticize, disparage, ridicule, deride.

lip *n. Water beaded on the lip of the jug:* rim, border, brim, brink, edge, margin, spout.

liquid *adj.* **1.** *The river shone like liquid gold in the rays of the setting sun:* fluid, melted, thawed; molten, liquefied. —*n.* **2.** *The patient could only consume liquids:* drink, beverage, liquid substance, fluid, potable; solution. —**Ant.** 1 solid, gaseous; hard, frozen, congealed. 2 solid; vapor, gas.

liquidate *v.* **1.** *The inheritance allowed him to liquidate his debts:* settle, pay, discharge, dispose of, clear, pay off, wipe out, account for, put to rest, abolish, erase, cancel. **2.** *He decided to liquidate his restaurant business and start fresh:* close out, settle the affairs of, wind up, conclude, terminate. **3.** *The dictator brutally liquidated all opponents:* assassinate, kill, murder, eradicate, demolish, destroy, abolish, do away with, break up; *Slang* rub out, hit, waste.

liquor *n.* **1.** *You must be of legal age to buy liquor:* alcoholic beverage, alcoholic drink, spirits, intoxicants, inebriants, distilled spirits; (*variously*) whiskey, Scotch, bourbon, rye, gin, rum, vodka, brandy; *Slang* booze, hooch, sauce. **2.** *Use the liquor from the roast for the gravy:* liquid, juice, drippings, broth, extract.

lissome *adj. This year's champ in Ladies' Singles is a lissome teenager named Jill. The dancer moved with lissome grace:* lithe, limber, supple, flexible, pliant, lithesome, quick, nimble, agile, sprightly, lively, slender, graceful, light-footed. —**Ant.** rigid, stiff, wooden, inflexible; clumsy, awkward.

list¹ *n.* **1.** *Make up a shopping list. Does the club have a list of all its members?:* written series, register, roster, roll, muster, inventory, record, slate; index, schedule, enumeration, table, catalog. —*v.* **2.** *List all the things you need from the grocery:* write in a series, record, write down, catalog, tabulate.

list² *n.* **1.** *The ship has a list to the port side:* tilt, leaning, lean, inclination, slant, slope. —*v.* **2.** *The freighter listed as the cargo shifted:* tilt, lean, incline, slope, slant, heel, tip, careen, bend.

listen *v. Please listen carefully:* attend, hark, list, heed, hearken, hear, make an effort to hear, pay attention, give heed, take notice, keep one's ears open, give ear, note carefully, prick up the ears, strain one's ears, *Informal* be all ears, bend an ear; eavesdrop, listen in, overhear. —**Ant.** be deaf to, turn a deaf ear to; ignore, neglect, disregard, pay no heed to, take no notice of.

listless *adj. Many people feel listless on rainy days:* sluggish, lifeless, lazy, indolent, lacking zest, inactive, dull, spiritless, down, lethargic, lackadaisical, phlegmatic, leaden, soporific, torpid, enervated, sluggish; apathetic, uninterested, indifferent, unconcerned, mopish, languid, dreamy, drowsy. —**Ant.** lively, energetic, active, wide-awake, spirited; alert, interested, attentive.

listlessness *n. He was afflicted with listlessness:* indifference, inattention, inattentiveness, heedlessness; thoughtlessness, carelessness. —**Ant.** concern, care, attention, attentiveness.

litany *n.* **1.** *The priest led the congregation in a* *litany:* ceremonial prayer, prescribed prayer, formal prayer, invocation with responses, prayer of supplication. **2.** *She gave us a long litany of her woes:* recital, recitation, account, catalog, list, repetition, enumeration, rendition, description, narration, recapitulation.

literacy *n. True literacy is something more than just the ability to read and write:* learning, erudition, eruditeness, scholarship, learnedness, intelligence, enlightenment, edification, culture, intellectuality; store of knowledge, acquisition of knowledge, liberal education. **—Ant.** illiteracy, ignorance, unenlightenment, benightedness.

literal *adj.* **1.** *The students were asked to make a literal translation of the French story:* faithful, exact, precise, word-for-word, as close as possible to the original, verbatim, strict, accurate, direct, true, undeviating, *Latin* ad litteram. **2.** *The general wanted a literal report on the enemy's strength:* accurate, precise, factual, truthful, categorically true, without exaggeration, exact, correct, reliable, unimpeachable, trustworthy, honest, dependable, authoritative, undisputed, meticulous, scrupulous, conscientious, authentic, actual, real. **3.** *He's so literal he never knows when I'm kidding:* matter-of-fact, prosaic, unimaginative, taking everything at face value. **—Ant.** 1 free, liberal, general, figurative. 2 inaccurate, incorrect, wrong, erroneous, false, nonfactual, untruthful, unreliable, untrustworthy; careless, hazy, inexact, sloppy. 3 figurative; imaginative.

literary *adj.* **1.** *The literary club meets once a month:* of literature, of writings, of belles lettres, of books; fond of books, addicted to reading, bookish; artistic, poetic. **2.** *The Gotham Book Mart in New York City is a famous meeting place of literary folk:* bookish, intellectual, literate, lettered, belonging to the literati. **—Ant.** 2 uneducated, unlettered, untutored, untaught, unschooled, unenlightened.

literate *adj.* **1.** *Only a few of the nation's peasants are literate:* able to read and write, proficient in reading and writing. **2.** *A news commentator should be a highly literate man:* educated, learned, schooled, well-informed, well-read, cultured, literary, lettered, knowledgeable.

literature *n.* **1.** *Moby Dick is one of the classics of American literature:* literary work of lasting value, artistic writing, belles lettres, letters, classics. **2.** *We delved into the literature on colonial furniture:* writings, works, books, publications, papers, treatises, dissertations, theses; scholarship, lore.

lithe *adj. A pole-vaulter should be strong and lithe:* limber, supple, bendable, flexible, pliable, pliant, lissome, agile, nimble, graceful. **—Ant.** rigid, stiff, wooden, inflexible; clumsy, awkward.

litigate *v. The lawyer recommended that she litigate:* sue, file suit, prosecute, contest, dispute, press charges.

litigation *n. The neighbors resorted to litigation to determine their property boundaries:* lawsuit, legal proceedings, suit, prosecution, contention, legal action, filing of charges, disputation, day in court, judicial process; dispute, contest, controversy.

litter *n.* **1.** *Good campers don't leave litter on the campsite. What's this litter of clothes on the closet floor?:* scattered rubbish, rubbish, trash, refuse, debris; leavings, junk, mess, heap, jumble, pile. **2.** *The Chesapeake bitch had a litter of five pups:* group of animals born at one birth; offspring, young, issue, progeny. **3.** *The wounded were carried into the hospital on litters:* stretcher, portable bed, portable couch. **4.** *The squirrel made a litter of dried leaves:* bed, nest, lair; bedding, pallet. **—v. 5.** *Thoughtless vacationers had littered the beach with cigarette packages and beer cans. The reporter's desk was littered with news releases:* strew with rubbish, clutter with trash, strew, clutter, scatter; heap, pile, jumble. **—Ant.** 5 clean up, pick up; organize, order, arrange, tidy, tidy up, neaten up.

little *adj.* **1.** *The old man lived in a little house in the woods. The little dog followed the boy everywhere:* small, diminutive, petite, bantam, pint-sized, pocket-sized, miniature, wee, tiny, minute, *Slang* itty-bitty, itsy-bitsy; undersized, dwarfish, stunted; pygmy, elfin, Lilliputian; microscopic, infinitesimal. **2.** *A little group met to play bridge every Friday. The doctor has little hope for her recovery. There is little milk left in the pitcher:* small, scant, meager; skimpy, hardly any, not much, scarcely any, short, insufficient, deficient; few and far between, to be counted on one's fingers. **3.** *The tourists spent but a little time in Italy:* brief, short, hasty, quick, fleet, passing; short-lived, momentary. **4.** *She had a little cold last week, but she's fine now:* trivial, mild, slight, inconsequential, negligible, insignificant, unimportant, trifling, faint, piddling, paltry, of no account. **5.** *The criticism all came from people with little minds:* narrow, petty, mean, short-sighted, opinionated, inflexible; worthless, unworthy, inferior, third-rate, mediocre, commonplace, run-of-the-mill. **—adv. 6.** *I little thought he would take me seriously. The old woman slept little. The children visit the parents little now:* not at all, never, by no means, not in a thousand years; in only a small amount, in a small degree, not much, slightly, scarcely, hardly, somewhat; rarely, not often, seldom. **—n. 7.** *Just put a little on each plate:* small amount, small quantity; pittance, next to nothing, minimum, drop, crumb, iota, jot, dot, whit, bit, speck, fragment, particle, dash, pinch, trifle, modicum, drop in the bucket, trace, hint, suggestion. **—Ant.** 1, 2, 4 big, large, great, immense, huge, monstrous, enormous, colossal, giant, giant-sized. 2, 3 much, more than enough, abundant, ample, plentiful. 3 long. 4 major, important, momentous, grave, serious, considerable, significant, consequential. 5 broad-minded, farsighted. 6 always, certainly, surely, assuredly; much. 7 lot, much, many.

liturgy *n. The church has used the same liturgy for hundreds of years:* ritual, ceremony, religious ceremony, form of public worship, collection of formularies for public worship, rite, particular arrangement of services; services, worship, service, mass, communion, prayer meeting, sacrament.

livable or **liveable** *adj.* **1.** *Some of the houses are barely livable. This is a very livable summer cottage:* suitable for living in, habitable; homey, snug, cozy, comfortable, *Informal* comfy. **2.** *A few luxuries make life more livable:* worth living, worthwhile, agreeable, comfortable, convenient, enjoyable, pleasant, satisfying, gratifying; bearable, tolerable, endurable, acceptable, passable. **—Ant.** 1 uninhabitable, unfit, unsuitable. 2 unpleasant, unsatisfactory; unbearable, intolerable, unendurable, painful, disagreeable.

live[1] *v.* **1.** *Was he still living when the doctor arrived?:* be alive, have life, draw breath, breathe, have being; exist, be, be animate; see the light of day, come into existence, walk the earth. **2.** *Grandmother lived to the age of 93. The flowers will live longer if you put them in water. Tennyson's poetry will live forever:* remain alive, survive, endure, prevail; cling to life, persist, hold on, abide; stand, obtain, escape destruction, be permanent. **3.** *How can anyone live on that salary? Can he live as a painter?:* subsist, support oneself, provide for one's needs, maintain life, get along, make ends meet, make one's living; acquire a livelihood, earn money, follow a particular occupation, get ahead. **4.** *The castaways lived on fish and coconuts:* subsist, feed, be nourished, survive, get along, be supported; thrive, flourish; increase, multiply. **5.** *How long have you lived at this address? I've always wanted to live in Alaska:* reside, be in residence, dwell, abide, make one's abode, make one's home, occupy, lodge, stay, bunk, billet; settle, remain, take root, pass one's life. **—Ant.** 1, 2 die, pass away, decease, expire, perish, demise. 2 wither, fade, languish, decline, decay; depart, vanish. 3 be destitute, be indigent. 4 starve to death, starve.

live[2] *adj.* **1.** *The laboratory is conducting experiments with a dozen live monkeys:* alive, living, quick, animate, breathing, existent; vital, physical, corporeal, incarnate, bodily, fleshly. **2.** *Housing is still a live issue:* pertinent, of present interest, active, pressing, prevalent, prevailing; current, present-day, up-to-date, still in use, happening, going on, at hand, at issue, in question. **3.** *Use tongs to handle those live embers:* burning, afire, fiery, blazing, ablaze, aflame, flaming, aglow, glowing, alight, ignited; hot, red-hot, white-hot. **—Ant.** 1 dead, defunct, deceased, departed. 2 inactive, dormant, out-of-date, old hat.

livelihood *n. Can he earn a livelihood writing poetry? Farming has been the family's livelihood for three generations:* living, adequate income, support, maintenance, subsistence, sustenance, source of income; occupation, vocation, calling, business, line of work, trade, profession, career, métier; job, situation, position; venture, undertaking, enterprise. **—Ant.** destitution, indigence; avocation, hobby, entertainment, recreation, fun.

lively *adj. He may be 80, but he's still lively.*

The band played a lively tune: spirited, brisk, sprightly, vivacious, animated, bouncy, energetic, full of life, full of spirit, eager, excited, enthusiastic, buoyant; active, vigorous, alert, peppy, perky; ardent, intense, fervent, vivid, excitable. **—Ant.** lifeless, inactive, dull, slow, sluggish, phlegmatic, leaden, listless, apathetic; decrepit, disabled, debilitated.

liven *v. Uncle Bert livened the party with some magic tricks:* quicken, enliven, vivify, animate, invigorate, inspirit, energize, buoy; hearten, strengthen, embolden, fortify; *Slang* perk up, pep up, punch up; cheer, gladden, brighten, elate, delight, exhilarate. **—Ant.** delay, slow down; depress, dispirit, devitalize.

livery *n. The footmen wore red and gold livery:* uniform, costume, servant's uniform, vestments, regalia, garb, attire, dress, clothing, raiment, suit.

livid *adj.* **1.** *The skin was livid where he had been struck:* black-and-blue, discolored, purple; bruised, contused. **2.** *Her insulting remark made me absolutely livid:* enraged, irate, incensed, inflamed, furious, infuriated, raging, fuming, mad, angry, wrathful, indignant, *Slang* steamed up, ticked off; outraged, exasperated, vexed, riled, galled, provoked. **—Ant.** 2 mollified, assuaged, forgiving; delighted, enchanted, enraptured, blissful, overjoyed, happy, content, pleased.

living *adj.* **1.** *Are your grandparents still living? Every living creature has a place in nature's scheme:* alive, live, existing, existent, quick, breathing, this side of the grave; animate, in the flesh, fleshly, bodily, embodied, incarnate, material, corporeal, organic; on the face of the earth, under the sun. **2.** *English and French are living languages. The ideals of our country's fathers are part of our living heritage:* presently in use, alive, live, active, operative, existent, extant, of present interest, up-to-date, going on; surviving, enduring, prevailing, persisting, remaining, permanent. **—n. 3.** *The sheer joy of living makes up for one's troubles:* existing, existence, life, being, having life, drawing breath, subsisting, subsistence, animation. **4.** *Such reckless living can ruin your health:* way of life, mode of living, life-style. **5.** *The truck gardener makes a good living growing tomatoes. What do you do for a living?:* income, subsistence, sustenance, livelihood, means of support, maintenance; occupation, vocation, calling, business, trade, profession, career, line of work, job, work, employment; venture, undertaking, enterprise. **—Ant.** 1, 2 dead, deceased, expired, defunct, lifeless. 1 inanimate, inorganic. 2 vanishing, perishing, obsolescent; out-of-date, inactive. 3 dying, expiring. 5 destitution, indigence; avocation, hobby, entertainment, recreation, fun.

load *n.* **1.** *It took three loads of gravel to cover the driveway. The plane can carry a ten-ton load:* quantity carried; (*variously*) wagonload, truckload, carload, planeload, shipload; cargo, shipment, freight, lading, haul; capacity, contents. **2.** *The walls of the building carry the* load of the roof. That's a load off my mind!: quantity supported, burden, weight, deadweight, encumbrance, pressure; care, trouble, worry, oppression, misery, depression, affliction, tribulation; misfortune, unhappiness, unhappy lot. —v. **3.** The men loaded the truck with strawberries: fill, lade, pile, pack, heap, stack, stuff; weight, burden. **4.** She's been loaded down with family responsibilities all her life: weigh down, burden, overwhelm, crush, oppress, afflict, trouble, worry, vex, try; hamper, encumber, strain, handicap, hinder. —**Ant.** 2 support; solace, consolation. 3 unload, discharge, empty, lighten, unpack. 4 free, liberate.

loaf v. Don't just sit there and loaf--get to work!: waste time, idle, do nothing, kill time, fritter away time, take it easy, laze about, dally, loll, lounge around, twiddle one's thumbs, be lazy, malinger, Slang goldbrick, goof off. —**Ant.** work, toil, labor, slave.

loafer n. That loafer won't even look for a job!: lazy person, idler, loiterer, malingerer, ne'er-do-well, laggard, shirker, wastrel, sluggard, lazybones, Slang deadbeat, bum, no-good, goldbrick, lounge lizard, drugstore cowboy; Informal sponger. —**Ant.** hard worker, worker, workingman, laborer.

loan n. **1.** The neighbor asked for the loan of our binoculars: permission to borrow, lending; advance, advancing, giving credit, accommodation. **2.** The bank arranged a loan of $500 for home improvements: sum of money lent, thing lent, thing borrowed; credit, mortgage, advance. —v. **3.** Can you loan me $10?: lend, permit to borrow, advance, allow; mortgage, credit. —**Ant.** 3 pay back, give back, return.

loath adj. The salesman is loath to accept a job in a new territory: unwilling, averse, loth, reluctant, disinclined, indisposed, opposed, counter, resisting, set against, against, hostile, inimical. —**Ant.** willing, anxious, eager, keen, avid, enthusiastic, desirous, wanting.

loathe v. He's an art critic who loathes modern art: detest, hate, despise, dislike, find disgusting, abominate, abhor, deplore, be unable to bear, have a strong aversion to, have no stomach for; scorn, disdain, eschew, keep clear of, shrink from, recoil from, draw back from, blench from, flinch from, shy away from, view with horror. —**Ant.** love, adore; like, admire; relish, fancy, dote on, enjoy; desire, crave, hanker after, long for.

loathing n. She gave him a look of pure loathing: disgust, dislike, aversion, abhorrence, hatred, hate, antipathy; animus, animosity, hostility. —**Ant.** liking, love; friendship, regard.

loathsome adj. The villain of the play was completely loathsome: detestable, hateful, despicable, disgusting, repulsive, abominable, abhorrent, unbearable, revolting, repugnant, nasty, vile, obnoxious, offensive, sickening, odious, nauseating, rank, mean, invidious, distasteful, foul. —**Ant.** lovable, adorable, likable, engaging, attractive, alluring, charming, delightful.

lobby n. **1.** Wait in the lobby of the building until the rain stops: vestibule, entrance hall, foyer, reception hall, anteroom, waiting room, reception room, antechamber. —v. **2.** The mothers' group has been lobbying for gun controls for years: politick, urge legislative action, solicit legislative votes, seek to influence legislators, exert influence, bring pressure to bear, Informal pull strings.

local adj. The mayor is a local celebrity: citywide, regional, sectional, provincial, neighborhood, territorial, native, homegrown; geographically restricted, limited, circumscribed, confined, narrow, insular, parochial; nearby, adjoining. —**Ant.** international, worldwide, national, nationwide; foreign, exotic.

locale n. The play's locale is London: setting, place where events occur, location, locality, site, spot, area, quarter, zone, vicinity, region, neighborhood, section, province, precinct.

locality n. The two factories are in the same locality: neighborhood, area, district, section, province, precinct, zone, quarter, vicinity, region, territory, location; locale, place, site, spot.

locate v. **1.** The police are trying to locate the missing man: find, discover the whereabouts of, track down, ferret out, search out, unearth, uncover, pinpoint, discern, detect, hit upon, come upon, light upon, stumble on, meet with, lay one's hands on. **2.** The firehouse is located on Main Street. The dentist carefully located the filling in the cavity: situate, place, establish, set down, seat, deposit, put, fix, station, post. **3.** After Dad retires he's going to locate in California: settle, settle down, reside, take up residence, dwell, live, stay, establish one's home, put down roots, set up housekeeping; move to. —**Ant.** 1 lose, shake; hide, conceal. 2 dislodge, displace. 3 leave, quit, forsake, abandon, desert, vacate.

location n. No one knows the location of Captain Kidd's hidden treasure. This corner would make a good location for a gas station: whereabouts, position, site, spot, place, situation, locale; neighborhood, district.

lock[1] n. **1.** The front door needs a stronger lock: fastening device, securing device, fastening; (variously) bolt, padlock, safety catch, latch; clasp, hook, clamp, catch. **2.** The ship passed through several locks in the canal: canal gate, dock gate, floodgate, sluice gate, dam. —v. **3.** Be sure to lock the office door when you leave: fasten, secure, (variously) bolt, padlock, bar. **4.** You should lock the jewels in a wall safe. The convicts were locked up in their cells: secure, lock up, keep under lock and key; shut in, confine, jail, imprison, incarcerate, cage, pen, coop up, impound, put behind bars. **5.** The men locked arms and sang the old school song. Lock your hands together around the golf club: join, entwine, link, interlink, unite, intertwine; clinch, grip, hold, grasp, clasp, grapple, seize, hold, grab, embrace. —**Ant.** 3 unlock, unbolt, unbar, unfasten; open. 4, 5 free, release, let go.

lock[2] n. Grandmother still has a lock of my baby hair in her scrapbook: tress, ringlet, curl, hank, tuft, coil, skein, bang.

lockup n. The drunken driver spent the night in the lockup: jail, prison, penitentiary, reformatory, house of detention, house of correction; *Slang* slammer, jug, cooler, big house, pen, stir, clink, hoosegow.

locution *n.* "Cattywampus" is a midwestern locution for "diagonally opposite": expression, regionalism, term, idiom, saying, wording, verbalism, phrase, phrasing, usage, utterance, turn of phrase, turn of expression, set phrase, trope, figure of speech, phraseology, idiolect.

lodge *n.* **1.** The gatekeeper lived in a lodge near the main entrance: cabin, cottage; hut, shelter; hotel, motel, resort, camp; country house. —*v.* **2.** The travelers lodged in motels every night. The guest house can lodge five persons: stay, put up, obtain lodgings, sojourn, room, furnish with lodgings, house, billet, bed, quarter, shelter, harbor. **3.** The dime rolled across the floor and lodged in a crack: catch, become fixed, be positioned. **4.** Tell the manager I want to lodge a complaint: submit, file, register, enter formally, place on record, make known.

lodging *n.* Do you have lodging for tonight?: temporary quarters, place to stay, overnight accommodation, a room, bed for the night, temporary sleeping accommodations.

loft *n.* **1.** The artist rented a loft to use as a studio. The church has a beautiful choir loft: attic room, attic, garret, mansard; top floor, balcony, clerestory, gallery; belfry. —*v.* **2.** The batter lofted the ball into the bleachers: throw high, lob, pop up, hit high, strike in a high arc. —**Ant.** 1 basement, cellar. 2 ground.

lofty *adj.* **1.** Lofty towers flanked the town gate: soaring, towering, tall, high, elevated, high-reaching. **2.** Despite his lofty rank the Grand Vizier listened to poor men's grievances: exalted, imposing, stately, elevated, dignified, majestic, sublime, noble; high, high ranking, mighty, important, superior, distinguished, leading, illustrious, eminent, preeminent, glorious, grand, great. **3.** I didn't like her lofty treatment of the visitors: proud, haughty, arrogant, lordly, disdainful, scornful, insolent, aloof, distant, remote, cold, high-and-mighty, *Slang* hoity-toity; snobbish, imperious, patronizing, condescending, self-important, conceited; *Informal* puffed-up, stuck-up, snooty. —**Ant.** 1 low, short, stunted, dwarfed. 2 lowly, undignified, debased, mean, ignoble, degraded, cheap; low, low ranking. 3 modest, unassuming, humble; friendly, cordial, hospitable, warm, receptive, open.

log *n.* **1.** The cabin was built of logs: length of tree trunk, timber, part of tree limb; block, stump. **2.** The time of departure was entered in the ship's log: logbook; (*loosely*) daybook, journal, calendar, diary, docket, schedule, account, record. —*v.* **3.** The college student spent his summers logging in the north woods: cut timber, fell trees, work as a lumberjack, lumber.

logic *n.* **1.** Lawyers should be well-versed in logic: science of reasoning, syllogistic reasoning, inductive reasoning, organized thinking, argument, dialectics, deduction, induction, analysis. **2.** There is no logic in her argument: good sense, sound judgment, organized reasoning, reason, chain of thought, sense, coherence, cogency.

logical *adj.* **1.** The plan was presented in a logical manner: consistent, well-organized, cogent, coherent, clear, rational, sound, reasonable, intelligent; relevant, pertinent, germane; valid, deducible; analytical. **2.** He is the logical choice for governor: reasonable, likely, most likely, plausible, intelligent, enlightened, sensible. —**Ant.** 1 illogical, inconsistent, unorganized, incoherent, irrational, unreasonable; intuitive, instinctive. 2 illogical, unlikely, implausible.

logy *adj.* That heavy meal made me logy for the rest of the day: drowsy, lethargic, sleepy, tired, dull, torpid, sluggish, groggy, weary, inert, enervated, phlegmatic, drowsy, listless, lifeless, inanimate, hebetudinous, comatose. —**Ant.** active, energetic, lively, animated, spirited, vigorous.

loiter *v.* A suspicious character was loitering in the hall: linger idly about, hang around, hover around; skulk, lurk, slink; loll, laze, idle; tarry, dillydally, dally, dawdle, shilly-shally, loaf, procrastinate. —**Ant.** hasten, hurry, scurry, scuttle, scamper.

loll *v.* **1.** He's been lolling around the house all day. Sit up straight, don't loll in your chair: lounge, loaf, idle, dawdle, languish, take it easy, repose, relax; *Slang* goof off; recline, lean, slouch, slump, sprawl, flop over. **2.** The horse's tongue lolled as the animal gasped for breath: dangle, droop, hang loosely; flop, flap, sag, drop, drag.

lone *adj.* A lone bandit held up the restaurant: sole, single, solitary, individual, alone, only, unattended, unescorted, unaccompanied, unpaired, unabetted, companionless, isolated, unique, singular.

lonely *adj.* **1.** Robinson Crusoe spent many lonely days on the desert island before the man Friday appeared: by oneself, solitary, without company, unaccompanied, unattended, companionless; secluded, withdrawn, reclusive, hermitic, unsocial. **2.** The visiting nurse cheered the lonely shut-ins: lonesome, depressed by solitude, lacking companionship, friendless, forlorn, forsaken. **3.** The cabin was built in a lonely spot: isolated, secluded, remote, desolate, deserted, lonesome, unpopulated, uninhabited, unfrequented. —**Ant.** 1 accompanied, together. 2 popular, befriended. 3 crowded, mobbed, populous, frequented, teeming, swarming, bustling.

lonesome *adj.* He was very lonesome when he first went away to school: lonely, companionless, unfriended, alone, friendless, forlorn, desolate, forsaken, alienated; aloof, detached, withdrawn, insular. —**Ant.** sociable, gregarious, friendly, popular.

long[1] *adj.* **1.** There will be a long wait until the next bus: lengthy, extended, prolonged, protracted, drawn-out, spun out; interminable, unending. **2.** Alaska has a long coastline: lengthy, extended, extensive, elongated, protracted, far-reaching, outstretched. —*n.* **3.** It won't rain for long: a long time, an extended period. —*adv.* **4.** His election was long anticipated. It was below *freezing all winter long:* throughout a period of time; over an extended period; during the time, throughout the period. **5.** *The river is nearly 1,000 miles long:* in length, from end to end. **—Ant.** 1, 2 short, brief; little, small. 1 momentary, fleeting, short-lived, quick. 2 abridged, abbreviated, curtailed, compressed.

long² *v. The old man longs for the good old days:* yearn, crave, hunger, thirst, lust, hanker, sigh, pine, have a desire, have a yen for, hope, want, wish, aspire, have one's heart set on, covet, be bent upon. **—Ant.** despise, detest, loathe, abhor, abominate, hate, deplore, be repelled by; spurn, scorn, disdain, eschew, reject, renounce, forsake, refuse.

longing *n.* **1.** *After traveling abroad for so long, she had a longing to see her own hometown again:* strong desire, yearning, craving, hungering, thirst, wish; aspiration; *Informal* hankering, yen. *—adj.* **2.** *The child gave a longing look at the chocolate cake:* desirous, yearning, craving, hankering, hungering, wishful, pining, languishing, ardent. **—Ant.** 1 disinterest, indifference, unconcern, apathy; loathing, disgust, hatred, abhorrence, antipathy, repulsion, revulsion. 2 disinterested, indifferent, unconcerned, apathetic, cold, cool; loathsome, disgusting, hateful, scornful.

longstanding *adj. We have a longstanding friendship that goes back to our school days:* long-lived, long-lasting, enduring, long, lasting, durable, perennial, long-established, abiding, persisting, perpetual, ancient, rooted; hallowed, time-honored, venerable, hoary, unfading, hardy. **—Ant.** short, transient, passing, short-lived, transitory.

look *v.* **1.** *Look at the flock of geese up there. Look at all the facts before reaching a conclusion:* see, watch, turn the eyes upon, fix the eyes on, regard, contemplate, stare, gape, glance, peep, scan, peek, behold, give attention to, study, scrutinize, survey, examine. **2.** *Mother looks angry this morning. You look just like your father:* appear, seem, show, present evidence, exhibit, manifest, strike one as being, have the expression, cut a figure, carry the appearance. **3.** *The house looks toward the lake:* face, front, have a view of, be directed, be situated opposite. *—n.* **4.** *Let's have a look at the new car:* glance, glimpse, peek, peep, visual examination, once-over, contemplation, survey, scrutiny, visual search, reconnaissance, stare, view, observation, sight, gaze, ogle, glare. **5.** *Why such a woebegone look? The boss had a happy look on his face:* appearance, general aspect, countenance, presence, mien, expression, demeanor, air, guise, cast, bearing. **—Ant.** 1 be blind, be unseeing; close one's eyes to, overlook, miss, pass over, neglect, ignore, disregard.

lookout *n.* **1.** *Maintain a lookout for wolves attacking the sheep:* alertness, watchfulness, readiness, vigilance, surveillance, guardedness, vigil, awareness, attention, mindfulness, heed, precaution. **2.** *We posted several lookouts around the camp:* sentinel, watchman, guard,

sentry, watchdog, observer, spotter, patrol, scout, watchkeeper, forward observer.

loom *v. The Rocky Mountains loomed in front of the travelers:* tower, soar, ascend; come into view suddenly, emerge, rise, appear; stand forth, stand out, hulk, take shape. **—Ant.** vanish, disappear, melt away, fade away, dissolve from view.

loop *n.* **1.** *There are a lot of loops in this embroidery:* circle, spiral, whorl, convolution, twirl, coil; eye, eyelet, ring, ringlet, noose, opening, loophole, aperture; bend, twist, curve. *—v.* **2.** *Loop the rope over the post and tie it fast:* wind around, bend, twist, twirl, turn, curve around, encircle, circle, coil, curl, roll, furl; plait, braid.

loose *adj., adv.* **1.** *Her hair hung loose to her shoulders. The dog ran loose in the yard. The loose papers blew off the desk:* unbound, untied, unfastened, free, freed, freely, liberated; untethered, unchained, unfettered, unyoked, unleashed, uncaged, unimprisoned; unattached, unconnected, unjoined. **2.** *Is that shirt loose enough? He likes to wear his coats loose:* slack, free, not fitting tightly, not binding, not tight, not fastened; loosely. *—adj.* **3.** *Years of loose living made him soft:* wanton, profligate, abandoned, dissipated, debauched, wild, fast, dissolute, licentious, immoral, libertine, lewd, unbridled, unconstrained, unchaste, rakehell. **4.** *Her logic is too loose to make much sense:* inexact, unexacting, imprecise, inaccurate, vague, careless, slack, heedless. *—v.* **5.** *Loose the hounds. They loosed the prisoners' bonds and set them free:* untie, untether, unbind, unfasten, loosen, unloose, undo; free, set free, release, let go, liberate; unbridle, unshackle, unchain, unleash, unmanacle, unhandcuff; slacken. **—Ant.** 1 tied, bound, secured, fastened, tethered, fettered, chained; restrained, leashed, curbed. 2 tight. 3 moral, abstemious, virtuous, chaste, disciplined, puritanical, Spartan. 4 precise, exact, accurate, clear, meticulous. 5 tie, bind, fasten, tether, fetter, chain, manacle, handcuff; capture, cage, imprison.

loot *n.* **1.** *The pirate ships were loaded with loot:* spoils, plunder, booty, prize, take, stolen goods; *Slang* boodle, haul, swag. *—v.* **2.** *Vikings looted the Saxon coastal towns frequently:* plunder, pillage, ravage, sack, ransack, raid, rob, fleece, strip, pilfer.

lopsided *adj. Though the table was a priceless antique, it looked lopsided:* off-balance, askew, unequal, asymmetric, unbalanced, disproportional, irregular, uneven, disproportionate, crooked, *Slang* cockeyed, leaning, inclined, slanting, listing, tipped, tilting, slanted. **—Ant.** symmetrical, balanced, even, well-proportioned, straight.

loquacious *adj. He's so loquacious I can't get a word in edgewise:* talkative, talky, prolix, garrulous, wordy, verbose, voluble, windy, long-winded; prating, chatty, chattery, chattering, babbling, prattling; *Informal* gabby, blabby. **—Ant.** silent, reserved, taciturn, closemouthed, uncommunicative, reticent.

lord *n. The serfs vowed to do battle for their*

lord: king, ruler, sovereign, monarch, crown; master, superior, chief, overlord, leader, commander; feudal superior, seignior, landowner, landholder, proprietor.

lordly *adj.* **1.** *A lordly feast was provided:* fit for a lord, grand, majestic, regal, magnificent, elegant, sumptuous, stately, princely; lofty, imposing, magisterial, noble; eminent, august, exalted, dignified. **2.** *His lordly manners angered everyone:* haughty, arrogant, lofty, proud, disdainful, scornful, aloof, distant, remote, cold, high-and-mighty, hoity-toity, snobbish, imperious, patronizing, condescending, conceited, self-important, *Informal* stuck-up, puffed-up, snooty; tyrannical, despotic, domineering, dictatorial, bossy. **—Ant.** 1 lowly, plebeian, humble, modest, mean, abject. 2 modest, unassuming, humble; servile, submissive, gentle, mild.

lore *n.* *The lore of bears includes many fascinating stories about their habits:* popular knowledge, traditional knowledge, anecdotal knowledge; practical knowledge; traditions, beliefs, legends.

lose *v.* **1.** *The man lost his wallet. The enemy lost three ships in the naval battle. The ice skater lost his balance:* suffer loss of, incur the loss of, be deprived of, misplace, mislay; miss, be thrown off. **2.** *Don't lose your way in the storm. We lost all track of time:* stray from, miss, confuse; forget, ignore, fail to heed. **3.** *The team played well, but lost the game:* be defeated in, be the loser, fail to win, suffer defeat in, fail, have the worst of it, forfeit, take a licking, come out second best. **—Ant.** 1 keep, retain, hold; save, preserve; find, recover, get back. 2 find. 3 win, have the best of it.

loss *n.* **1.** *The loss of the ship ended his career as a captain:* wreck, wrecking, destruction, demolition, ruin, annihilation; extermination, extirpation, extinction, eradication; abolition, dissolution, removal. **2.** *Can the company bear the loss of a million dollars? He suffered a temporary loss of memory:* forfeiture, deprivation, privation, bereavement, expenditure, riddance; amount lost, number lost. **3.** *How did the boxer take the loss of the fight?:* losing, failure to win, defeat, undoing, overturn, vanquishment; *Slang* licking. **4.** *The loss of her purse caused her much inconvenience:* losing, misplacing, mislaying, being without. **—Ant.** 1 saving, preservation. 2 gain, acquisition; restoration, recovery, reimbursement. 3 winning, win. 4 finding, recovery.

lost *adj.* **1.** *The lost ring was never found. The family searched the neighborhood for the lost dog:* missing, mislaid, misplaced, gone out of one's possession; vanished, strayed, stray, astray, absent, lacking. **2.** *The lost hikers asked the Mountie for directions:* gone astray, unable to find one's way, off-course. **3.** *How many planes were lost in the battle?:* destroyed, wrecked, demolished, ruined, wiped out, abolished, obliterated, annihilated, exterminated, eradicated, extirpated; killed, murdered, perished. **4.** *Try to make up for lost time:* wasted, misapplied, squandered, misdirected, misused.

5. *She looked at the sunset, lost in thought:* absorbed, preoccupied, engrossed. **—Ant.** 1 found, recovered, reclaimed, returned. 3 saved, preserved.

lot *n.* **1.** *The boys drew lots to determine who would get to play first:* straw, counter. **2.** *It was her lot to suffer through life:* fate, allotted portion, share; apportionment, allowance, ration, measure, quota, proportion, allotment. **3.** *The neighbors bought a lot to build a house on. We could keep a pony in the back lot:* parcel of land, plot, property, tract, piece of ground, portion of land; field, patch. **4.** *We all like ice cream, so give everyone a lot:* great deal, much, many, *Informal* lots, lots and lots, oceans, oodles; *French* beaucoup.

lothario *n.* *He told all the women he was sincere, but they knew he was just a lothario:* lover, rake, Don Juan, Romeo, Casanova, seducer, roué, debauchee, debaucher, lecher, libertine, philanderer, sensualist, womanizer, sheik, lady-killer, skirt-chaser, profligate; *Slang* wolf, rip, lover-boy, swinger.

lotion *n.* *Some of this lotion should help your chapped hands:* ointment, cosmetic, balm, liniment, unction, wash, conditioner, unguent, salve, conditioner, skin cream, freshener, demulcent, emollient, moisturizer, embrocation, astringent, after-shave.

loud *adj.* **1.** *Who's making those loud noises?:* noisy, earsplitting, ear-piercing, deafening, clamorous, resounding, sonorous, stentorian, booming, thundering, blatant, intense; vociferous, loudmouthed. **2.** *What a loud shirt!:* garish, gaudy, splashy, flashy; bright, vivid, colorful; showy, ostentatious. **—Ant.** 1 soft, subdued; quiet, silent, inaudible. 2 sedate, somber, dull, colorless, conservative.

lounge *v.* **1.** *On Sundays a lot of people just like to lounge. The passengers lounged in deck chairs:* loaf, idle, take it easy, do nothing, relax, lie around, pass time idly, fritter away time, kill time, dawdle, dally, dillydally; recline, repose, stretch out, laze, languish, flop, loll, sprawl, slump, slouch; rest, sleep, slumber. *—n.* **2.** *Let's buy an easy chair to match the lounge:* sofa with headrest at one end; (*loosely*) sofa, couch, divan, davenport; daybed. **3.** *Shall we meet in the lounge by the clock?:* lobby, reception room, reception hall, vestibule; sitting room, reading room.

lousy *adj.* **1.** *The mattress is lousy and must be fumigated:* pediculous, infested with lice. **2.** *Slang That was a lousy thing to do to anyone. It was a lousy movie:* mean, shabby, nasty, crummy, unethical, unkind, hateful, vicious, contemptible, dreadful, unpleasant; inferior, bad, terrible, rotten, awful, second-rate, worthless.

lout *n.* *That lout doesn't even know that you're supposed to thank your hostess:* boor, churl, clod, oaf, dunce, clown, lummox, ape, booby, dullard, dummy, yokel, rustic, bumpkin; *Slang* klutz. **—Ant.** gentleman, sophisticate, dandy, swell.

loutish *adj.* *Loutish youths loitered around the*

entrance: boorish, unrefined, uncouth, ill-bred, rough, cloddish, clumsy, crass, churlish, coarse, crude, brutish, beastly. **—Ant.** refined, gracious, graceful.

lovable or **loveable** *adj. Isn't that the most lovable puppy?:* adorable, winsome, endearing, engaging, winning, enchanting, captivating, lovely, charming, taking, fetching, delightful, cute, sweet, cuddly, darling. **—Ant.** hateful, detestable, odious, obnoxious, abominable, abhorrent, loathsome, repugnant, revolting, repellent, offensive.

love *n.* **1.** *The engaged couple swore undying love. She felt a great love for her parents and her country:* passion, passionate affection, the tender passion, rapture, amorousness, ardor, amour, infatuation; devotion, adoration, fondness, tenderness, affection, affectionate regard, warm personal attachment, warm feeling, sentiment, emotion, esteem, admiration; friendship, amity, brotherhood, fellow feeling, compatibility, affinity, sympathy, concord, congeniality, cordiality; charity, goodwill, benevolence, solicitude. **2.** *He has always had a love of good food:* strong liking, fondness, devotion, relish, taste, predilection, attachment, penchant, leaning, partiality, inclination, proclivity, weakness, turn, bent, mind. **3.** *He's lonely because his love is out of town this weekend. The theater was his first love, but he became a radio announcer:* beloved, loved one, inamorata, truelove, paramour, lover, mistress, flame, light of one's life; sweetheart, darling, dear, dearest, precious, angel, sweetie, sweetie pie, honey; boyfriend, beau, fellow, man; girlfriend, girl, woman; fondness, attachment, penchant, choice. *—v.* **4.** *Romeo loved Juliet. Patrick Henry loved his country. Love thy neighbor:* have a passionate affection for, be filled with rapture by, feel amorous toward, be infatuated with, be enamored of, be devoted to, adore, be fond of, feel tenderness toward, lose one's heart to, hold dear, regard affectionately, feel warmly toward, admire, esteem, treasure, cherish; sympathize with, feel goodwill toward, feel solicitude for. **5.** *I've always loved opera:* like immensely, be fond of, be devoted to, relish, delight in, fancy, take pleasure in, enjoy, appreciate, savor, bask in, rejoice in, revel in, luxuriate in; *Slang* get a kick out of; have a penchant for, have a leaning toward, have a partiality for, have an inclination toward, be drawn to, have a weakness for. **—Ant.** 1–3 hate, hatred, dislike, distaste, aversion, abhorrence, repugnance, repulsion, disgust, loathing, abomination, detestation, contempt, scorn. 1 animosity, antipathy, antagonism, acrimony, animus, bitterness, resentment, hostility, opposition, malice, ill will, incompatibility, uncongeniality. 3 enemy, foe, rival. 4, 5 hate, dislike, abhor, be disgusted by, loathe, abominate, detest, scorn. 5 find distasteful, be averse to, find repugnant.

lovely *adj. What a lovely dress! The new nurse is a lovely person. We had a lovely time at the party:* attractive, handsome, comely, beautiful, adorable, exquisite, elegant; delightful, charm-

ing, enchanting, fascinating, enjoyable, agreeable, pleasing, pleasant; winsome, winning, lovable, cute, sweet, captivating, alluring, engaging, endearing, irresistible, fetching; good, fine. **—Ant.** ugly, hideous, unattractive, tasteless; hateful, detestable, odious, obnoxious, offensive, distasteful, abominable, abhorrent, loathsome, repugnant, revolting, repelling, awful, bad.

lover *n.* **1.** *The starlet's latest lover is a Hollywood director:* paramour, mistress; beloved, loved one, inamorata, truelove, love, sweetheart; dear, darling, sweetie, honey; boyfriend, beau, fellow, swain, lover boy, suitor, wooer, admirer, man; girlfriend, girl, woman. **2.** *Art lovers flocked to the gallery opening:* devotee, enthusiast, aficionado, follower; fan, buff, fanatic; *Slang* nut, freak.

loving *adj. She gave her husband a loving look. The child has a very loving nature:* affectionate, fond, tender, amorous, erotic, ardent, passionate, enamored, amatory, devoted, doting; warm, sympathetic, caring, kind, friendly, warmhearted, solicitous, benevolent. **—Ant.** unloving, hateful, distasteful, disgusting, contemptuous, scornful, angry, hostile; indifferent, unconcerned, aloof, detached, cold, chilly, frigid, mean, cruel.

low *adj.* **1.** *Low clouds hid the tops of the skyscrapers. It's hard to sit gracefully in these low chairs:* near the ground, not far above the horizon, low-lying; unelevated; near the floor, low-slung; lower. **2.** *A line of low hills was seen in the distance. The post office is in a low, two-story building:* short, of less than average height, having little elevation, squat, stumpy, stubby, dumpy, snubbed, sawed-off, truncated; small, little. **3.** *The low areas were inundated by floods:* low-lying, below sea level, near sea level, unelevated, coastal; concave, sunken, depressed; underwater, submerged, deep, undersea, submarine; underground. **4.** *I've been feeling low all week:* unhappy, depressed, dejected, disheartened, despondent, doleful, downcast, down, melancholy, gloomy, dispirited, glum, lethargic; *Informal* in the doldrums, blue, down in the mouth. **5.** *The limousine's license plate has a low number. The student passed with low grades. He works for low pay because he loves the job:* small, little; lowly, humble, insignificant, inconsequential, unimportant, low ranking, paltry, trifling, common, mediocre, inferior. **6.** *How could anyone do such a low thing?:* mean, base, vile, awful, terrible, scurvy, despicable, ignominious, dishonorable, unworthy, contemptible, abominable, repulsive, repugnant, heinous, cruel, brutal, outrageous, scandalous, disrespectful, nefarious, scoundrelly, corrupt, unethical, wicked, evil, cowardly, dastardly; degraded, depraved, sordid, squalid, gross, coarse, vulgar, obscene, dirty; *Slang* crummy, cruddy. **7.** *Speak in a low voice:* subdued, hushed, muffled, muted, quiet; whispered, murmured, faint, feeble; soft, gentle, soothing; low-pitched, of a low tone. *—adv.* **8.** *Bend low. Speak low:* in or to a low position, prone, prostrate; to a low degree;

in a low tone, quietly, softly; deep. —**Ant.** 1–5, 7, 8 high. 2 tall, lofty, soaring, towering. 3 elevated. 4 happy, elated, cheerful, gay, enthusiastic, peppy, full of pep, energetic, alert; *Informal* bright-eyed and bushy-tailed. 5 superior, grand, lofty, elevated, exalted, eminent, consequential, significant, important, illustrious, high ranking, above average. 6 wonderful, fine, admirable, commendable, praiseworthy, laudable, meritorious, creditable, honorable, worthy, uplifted, angelic; courteous; brave. 7 loud, noisy, strong, raucous; high-pitched.

lowbred *adj.* *Lowbred gatecrashers gorged on the buffet:* unrefined, vulgar, coarse, rude, lowborn. —**Ant.** refined, noble, highborn.

lower[1] *v.* **1.** *The carpenter should lower that shelf about two feet. Lower the window shade to keep out the sun. The deer lowered its head to drink from the pond:* make lower, decrease the height of, drop, pull down, let down, take down, put down, depress; submerge, immerse, duck, sink. **2.** *We must lower our expenses. The new plane lowers flying time from New York to Los Angeles by an hour:* decrease, reduce, diminish, make less, curtail, pare, pare down, cut, shorten, abbreviate, prune, lop off, render less, subtract from, detract from, deduct. **3.** *Please lower your voice. Can you lower those bright lights a little?:* tone down, soften, subdue, make less intense, dim, damp, muffle, mute, repress. —*adj.* **4.** *Congress wants lower tariffs:* reduced, decreased, diminished, lessened, curtailed, pared, pared down. —**Ant.** 1–3 raise. 1 elevate, lift up, pull up, hoist. 2 increase, enlarge, inflate, boost, magnify, amplify, augment, aggrandize; extend, protract, prolong. 4 higher, increased, enlarged.

lower[2] *v.* **1.** *The boss lowered when he saw all the workers standing around talking:* scowl, glare, look sullen, give a dark look, frown, sulk, glower. **2.** *The clouds lowered and the storm began:* grow dark, become threatening.

low-key *adj.* *The décor of the house was very low-key, being done mostly in pastels:* subdued, toned-down, restrained, modulated, subtle, understated, relaxed, low-pressure, muted, low-pitched, gentle, soft, muffled, softened; *Slang* laid-back, loose, soft-sell. —**Ant.** shrill, blatant, obvious, high-pitched, bold, obtrusive.

lowly *adj.* **1.** *Abraham Lincoln was not ashamed of his lowly origins. He rose from lowly birth to become the queen's consort:* humble, simple, modest, unassuming, unpretentious, obscure, lowbred, lowborn, baseborn, plebeian, proletarian, ignoble. —*adv.* **2.** *He bowed lowly before the queen. Speak lowly in the guru's presence:* low, in or to a low position, to a low degree; in a low tone, softly. —**Ant.** 1 exalted, elevated, lofty; proud, conceited.

low-priced *adj.* *Curiously enough, the low-priced tickets were the last to be sold:* cheap, inexpensive, reasonable, cut-rate, moderate, dirt-cheap, reduced, economical, budget, token, marked-down, closeout, bargain-basement, low-cost, nominal. —**Ant.** expensive, high-priced, costly, dear, exorbitant.

low-spirited *adj.* *It's a dreary kind of day that seems to make everyone low-spirited:* depressed, sad, dejected, heartsore, dispirited, melancholy, glum, gloomy, unhappy, crestfallen, blue, down, forlorn, downhearted, downcast, morose, down-in-the-mouth, woebegone. —**Ant.** happy, cheerful, upbeat, high-spirited.

loyal *adj.* *The king rewarded his loyal supporters. A good friend is always loyal:* faithful, steadfast, true, constant, reliable, trusty, trustworthy, devoted, dependable, resolute, unwavering, unswerving, staunch, firm, dutiful, scrupulous, true-blue, tried and true. —**Ant.** disloyal, false, faithless, unfaithful, perfidious, treacherous, untrustworthy; rebellious, traitorous, treasonous.

loyalty *n.* *Once he took the vow his loyalty never wavered:* faithfulness, fidelity, steadfastness, constancy, trustworthiness, reliability, devotion, dependability, staunchness, firmness, allegiance, adherence, fealty. —**Ant.** disloyalty, falsity, falseness, faithlessness, inconstancy, perfidiousness, perfidy, treachery; sedition, rebellion, insurrection.

lozenge *n.* *Take a throat lozenge to stop that cough:* pastille, small confection, drop, troche; cough drop, small medicated confection, tablet, pill.

lubricate *v.* *They lubricated the car's engine:* grease, oil, *Informal* lube.

lubricious *adj.* *The lubricious content of the magazine appalled us:* lewd, lascivious, licentious, salacious, wanton, unchaste, incontinent, lecherous, perverse, perverted, immoral, vulgar, lustful, carnal, libidinous, dissolute, libertine, profligate, depraved, corrupt, loose, sensual, concupiscent, impure, pornographic, obscene, dirty, filthy. —**Ant.** 0 prudish, chaste, moral.

lucid *adj.* **1.** *A lucid sky portended a fine day:* shining, bright, clear, transparent, crystalline, brilliant, resplendent, radiant, lustrous, luminous, scintillating, sparkling, dazzling; pellucid; illuminated. **2.** *The witness gave a lucid account of what happened:* clear, easily understood, crystal clear, intelligible, understandable, articulate, comprehensible; precise, direct, straightforward, accurate, specific, well-organized, to the point, apposite, positive, certain. **3.** *Although usually in a delirium, the patient has some lucid moments:* clearheaded, clear thinking, normal, rational; responsive, perceptive. —**Ant.** 1 dark, darkling, gloomy, dusky, obscure, opaque, turgid, muddy, murky; overcast. 2 unintelligible, incomprehensible, vague, indistinct, unclear, ambiguous, equivocal, garbled, mystifying. 3 confused, muddled, irrational; unresponsive, unperceptive.

luck *n.* **1.** *As luck would have it, we arrived just as they were leaving:* fortune, fate, lot, destiny, karma, kismet; chance, fortuity, happenstance, accident, Lady Luck, wheel of fortune. **2.** *With a little luck the team would have won. Did you have any luck in finding a job?:* good luck, good fortune, happy accident, piece of luck, smile of fortune; success, victory, triumph. —**Ant.** 1 design, cause and effect. 2 bad luck; failure, defeat.

lucky adj. **1.** I guess I'm just not lucky: fortunate, blest with good luck, in luck, favored, blessed, born under a lucky star. **2.** It was a lucky accident that the train was late. This is your lucky day!: fortunate, opportune, timely, beneficial, good, happy, felicitous, providential, auspicious, propitious, favorable, bringing good luck, of good omen, promising. —**Ant.** 1, 2 unlucky, luckless, unfortunate, ill-starred, ill-favored. 2 untimely, detrimental, bad, unhappy; inauspicious, unfavorable, unpromising, sinister, ominous.

lucrative adj. The oldest brother now has a very lucrative position: profitable, moneymaking, remunerative, high-paying, gainful, high-income; beneficial, fruitful. —**Ant.** unprofitable, low-paying, unremunerative.

ludicrous adj. It was so ludicrous to see the child throw away the banana and try to eat the peeling!: ridiculous, absurd, crazy, outlandish, preposterous, nonsensical; amusing, laughable, comic, comical, funny, farcical; Slang wild, far-out. —**Ant.** sensible, logical; tragic, grave, solemn, serious, sad, sorry, doleful, dolorous, melancholy.

lug v. Lug these boxes up to the attic: drag, tote, carry, carry with difficulty, heave, transport; pull, bear, tow, draw, haul, tug.

luggage n. Are you going to carry your luggage or check it through?: baggage, bags, suitcases, valises, trunks; effects, gear, accouterments.

lugubrious adj. The mourners all had lugubrious expressions on their faces as they expressed their sympathy to the family: melancholy, dolorous, mournful, sorrowful, downcast, rueful, woeful, dour, glum, gloomy, depressing, miserable, woebegone, funereal, somber, elegiac. —**Ant.** joyous, lighthearted, cheerful, ebullient, happy.

lukewarm adj. **1.** The yeast is added to lukewarm water: tepid, warm, mild, room-temperature, body-temperature, temperate. **2.** The reception we got was lukewarm at best: halfhearted, unenthusiastic, aloof, cool, unconcerned, detached, indifferent, uninterested, apathetic, uncaring, perfunctory, lackadaisical. —**Ant.** 2 impassioned, enthusiastic, wholehearted, caring.

lull v. **1.** The mother lulled the child to sleep: soothe, quiet, calm, pacify, hush, still, quell, subdue, compose, assuage, mollify, ease. —n. **2.** There was a sudden lull in the conversation. This is just the lull before the storm: hush, quiet, temporary stillness, brief silence, quiet interval, pause, break, interlude, interruption, halt, hiatus, gap, caesura, lacuna, short rest, respite, recess, breather, breathing spell; calm, calmness, tranquillity. —**Ant.** 1 excite, arouse, rouse, aggravate, provoke, incite. 2 continuation, resumption; flow, gush, spurt; excitement, tumult, turbulence, violence.

lumber[1] n. **1.** How much lumber is needed to build the shed?: wood, construction wood, building wood, boards, planks. —v. **2.** Many farmers used to lumber part time: log, work as a lumberjack, fell trees; cut timber into boards, prepare logs for market, operate a sawmill.

lumber[2] v. The hippopotamus lumbered into the water: waddle, trudge, move clumsily, barge, move heavily, plod, clump, stamp, shamble, shuffle, flounder.

lumbering adj. The lumbering elephants entered the ring: heavy-footed, lead-footed, awkward, blundering, bumbling, clodhopping, clumsy, clunking, hulking, ungainly, unhandy, unwieldy.

luminary n. **1.** The sun is only one of thousands of luminaries in the sky: light, luminosity, body that gives off light; source of light, illuminator. **2.** Many luminaries attended the opening of the opera season: celebrity, famous person, eminent person, personage, dignitary, notable, Slang bigwig, big shot, wheel, somebody.

luminescent adj. Children love to watch the luminescent light of fireflies: glowing, aglow, luminous, gleaming, glimmering, shimmering; glistening, twinkling, flickering; fluorescent, phosphorescent, not incandescent, glowing without heat. —**Ant.** incandescent, caused by heat, hot.

luminous adj. The watch has a luminous dial: reflecting light, luminescent, radiant, irradiated, glowing, lustrous, illuminated, shining; shining in the dark; bright, brilliant.

lump n. **1.** Break up these large lumps of dirt: mass, gob, chunk, clod, clump, cake, hunk. **2.** How did you get that lump on your head?: bump, swelling, protuberance, knot, knob, node, nodule, knurl, protrusion, excrescence; tumor, tumescence, growth. —v. **3.** Lump all our money together and let's see how much we have: heap, pile, unite, mass, amass, gather, bunch, batch, group, compile, assemble, aggregate, collect; combine, merge, pool, fuse, mix, blend. —**Ant.** 1 granule, grain, particle, bit. 2 depression, cavity, concavity, hollow, indentation, dent, pit, dip, dimple. 3 scatter, disperse; separate, divide.

lunacy n. **1.** Modern medicine and psychiatry can prevent certain forms of lunacy: insanity, insaneness, madness, mental derangement, dementia, mania, psychopathic condition. **2.** It's sheer lunacy to drive so fast: folly, foolishness, foolhardiness, imprudence, absurdity, silliness, senselessness, craziness; imbecility, idiocy, stupidity, asininity. —**Ant.** 1 sanity, reason. 2 good sense, prudence.

lunatic n. **1.** The lunatic was committed to a state asylum: madman, maniac, insane person, deranged person, crazy person; psychopath, demoniac; Slang nut, cuckoo, loony. —adj. **2.** The man's lunatic behavior is a menace to society: insane, crazy, mad, deranged, demented, maniacal, unhinged, unbalanced, daft, irrational, non compos mentis, of unsound mind, mentally ill, senseless, reasonless; Slang nutty, cracked, crackbrained, batty, screwy, loony, cuckoo, touched, loco, off one's rocker, touched in the head, out of one's mind, not all there, not right in the head, not in one's right mind; psychotic, psychopathic; British round the bend, crackers, bonkers, potty. **—Ant. 2** sane, sound, rational, reasonable; *Slang* all there.

luncheonette *n. We stopped in at a luncheonette for coffee and doughnuts:* café, diner, coffee shop, sandwich shop, lunchroom, beanery, eating house, snack bar, lunch counter, hash house.

lunge *n.* **1.** *The boxer made a lunge at his opponent:* charge, rush, plunge, lurch, dash, dive, thrust; lightning attack, jab, stab, pass, swing, swipe, cut. **—v. 2.** *The swordsman lunged at the foe:* thrust, jab, stab, strike at, hit at; attack, charge, pounce, make a pass, set upon, fall upon. **—Ant. 2** recoil, step back; parry.

lurch *v. The sailor lost his balance when the ship lurched. The sick man lurched forward and then fell:* roll, pitch, list, tilt, incline, cant, keel, slant, toss, swerve; jerk forward, lunge, plunge; stagger, stumble, sway, careen, reel, totter, teeter.

lure *n.* **1.** *Is cheese really a good lure for mice? The fisherman used a metal lure that looked like a minnow:* bait, decoy; trap, snare. **2.** *The sale on television sets was just a lure to get customers into the store:* enticement, allurement, inducement, allure, attraction, temptation; blandishment, cajolery, bribe; *Slang* come-on, drawing card. **—v. 3.** *The decoys lured the ducks to the pond. The travel brochure lured me into taking a Caribbean vacation:* entice, allure, attract, tempt, tantalize, fascinate, beguile, seduce; coax, cajole, persuade, induce. **—Ant. 1** repellent. **3** revolt, repel, deter.

lurid *adj.* **1.** *The painting was full of lurid colors:* fiery, bright-red, flaming, bloody, sanguine, scarlet, carmine, rubicund; glaring, glowing, shining. **2.** *The book told a lurid tale of crime in the big city:* sensational, graphic, dramatic, vivid, melodramatic, wildly emotional; appalling, shocking, grim, ghastly, eerie, gory, bloodcurdling. **—Ant. 1** pale, watery, pastel. **2** mild, lighthearted, gay, sunny, breezy, jaunty, carefree.

lurk *v. The thief lurked in the shadows:* skulk, slink, prowl, sneak, lie in wait, lie concealed, hide, lie in ambush; go furtively.

luscious *adj. Nothing is more luscious than wild strawberries:* delicious, mouth-watering, succulent, sweet and juicy, delectable, appetizing, flavorful, tasty, savory, toothsome; fragrant, scented, perfumed, aromatic. **—Ant.** sour, acid, vinegary, tart, bitter; bland, flavorless, tasteless.

lush *adj.* **1.** *A lush growth of ivy covered the path:* luxuriant, profuse, flourishing, dense, prolific, abundant, rich. **2.** *The hotel's presidential suite is exceptionally lush:* luxurious, grand, sumptuous, elegant, magnificent, elaborate, ornate, splendid, fancy; *Slang* posh. **—Ant. 1** sparse, thin, meager, scanty; barren, arid. **2** plain, simple, crude, Spartan.

lust *n.* **1.** *The dictator's lust for power knew no bounds. Lust is one of the seven deadly sins:* passion, strong desire, craving; bodily appetite, fleshly desire, sexuality, libidinousness, lasciviousness, lewdness, salaciousness, satyriasis,

nymphomania, carnality, lechery. **—v. 2.** *The old miser still lusts after money. Phaedra lusted after Hippolytus and caused his death:* desire intensely, crave, have a passion for, covet, hunger for; seek sexually, be lascivious, be libidinous, be lewd, be lecherous. **—Ant. 1** unconcern, apathy. **2** be indifferent; spurn, disdain, scorn.

luster *n.* **1.** *This polish brings out the luster of the silver:* shine, gleam, sheen, gloss, burnish, brightness, brilliance, resplendence, sparkle, radiance, refulgence, glow, glimmer, glitter, dazzle; radiation, luminosity, luminousness. **2.** *Winning the Nobel prize added even more luster to the poet's name:* glory, distinction, illustriousness, fame, prestige, honor, merit, notability. **—Ant. 1** dullness; tarnish. **2** ignominy, dishonor, shame, infamy, disrepute.

lustrous *adj. The coat was lined with a lustrous silk:* bright, luminous, radiant, glistening, illuminated, burnished, effulgent, incandescent, dazzling, coruscating, glossy, shining, gleaming, polished, glowing. **—Ant.** dim, drab, dull, dingy, lusterless.

lusty *adj. Robin Hood led a group of lusty men:* hearty, hale, full of life, vigorous, robust, virile, husky, brawny, rugged, sturdy, strapping, healthy, sound; exuberant, wholehearted, unrestrained, uninhibited, irrepressible. **—Ant.** lifeless, dull, lethargic, listless; effete, exhausted, feeble, weak, infirm, decrepit, frail, sickly.

luxuriant *adj.* **1.** *The jungle had a luxuriant growth of orchids:* lush, flourishing, dense, profuse, exuberant, abundant, overgrown, rank, teeming. **2.** *The building is covered with luxuriant scrollwork:* elaborate, ornate, fancy, elegant, magnificent, splendid, extravagant, luxurious, grand, sumptuous; florid, flamboyant, flowery. **—Ant. 1** sparse, thin, meager, scanty; barren, arid. **2** plain, simple, unadorned.

luxuriate *v. After a week of backpacking the campers luxuriated in hot baths and soft beds:* bask, delight, indulge in, relish, rejoice in, wallow in, live in luxury.

luxurious *adj.* **1.** *The house is full of luxurious appointments:* expensive, costly, rich, grand, elegant, sumptuous; enjoyable, comfortable, pleasurable, gratifying, pleasure-giving. **2.** *She's very fond of luxurious living:* costly, extremely comfortable, wealthy, given to luxury; loving luxury, indulgent, overindulged, pampered; effete, decadent. **—Ant. 2** ascetic, austere, Spartan, deprived; frugal, thrifty, economical, sparing, temperate; poor, squalid.

luxury *n.* **1.** *She's lived in luxury all her life:* luxuriousness, material abundance, extreme comfort; high standard of living, wealth, riches; *Slang* high living. **2.** *A long hot bath can be pure luxury:* delight, enjoyment, pleasure, satisfaction, gratification, bliss, heaven, paradise. **3.** *Buying a new coat before the old one wore out would just be a luxury:* extravagance, indulgence, nonnecessity, nonessential. **—Ant. 1** poverty, penury, destitution, straitened circumstances; deprivation, austerity, need, want, difficulty, distress. **2** deprivation, privation, hardship, affliction, burden, trial, infliction, misery. **3** necessity.

lying *adj. The lying politician lost the election:* untruthful, mendacious, dishonest, dissembling, dissimulating, falsifying, fibbing, inventing, misrepresenting. —**Ant.** truthful, veracious.

lynch *v. The mob lynched the cattle rustlers:* hang, gibbet, execute without due process of law; *Informal* string up.

lyric also **lyrical** *adj.* **1.** *The playwright has a lyric gift:* songlike, melodious, euphonious, musical, tuneful, melodic, lilting, sweet-sounding, mellifluous, singing, mellifluent; poetic. —*n.* **2.** Often **lyrics** *If you don't know the lyrics of the song, just hum along:* words of a song; poem.

M

macabre *adj. The macabre story of headless ghosts frightened the children:* gruesome, grisly, grim, ghastly, horrible, frightful, frightening, horrid, dreadful, horrific; eerie, weird, unearthly, ghostly, ghostlike. —**Ant.** pleasant, beautiful, lovely, appealing, inviting, delightful.

macerate *v.* **1.** *The tablets will macerate in warm water:* liquefy, dissolve, liquidize, fluidize, soften, mash, squash, pulp; soak, steep, souse, saturate, permeate. **2.** *She began to macerate after only one week of the diet:* become emaciated, waste away, shrink, shrivel, wither, lose weight; fade, decline, emaciate.

Machiavellian *adj. The prime minister has a Machiavellian scheme to be appointed the young king's guardian:* scheming, designing, self-serving, underhanded, amoral, treacherous, perfidious, unscrupulous, cunning, crafty, devious, deceitful, falsehearted. —**Ant.** naive, ingenuous, open, candid, frank, straightforward.

machinate *v. They machinated a plan to rob a bank:* plot, conspire, arrange, collude, connive, contrive, engineer, finagle, hatch, intrigue, manoeuvre, mastermind, plan, scheme, wangle.

machination *n. By a series of machinations one partner gained control of the business:* scheme, intrigue, design, crafty plan, rule, conspiracy, plot, artifice, device, stratagem, maneuver, contrivance, ruse, dodge.

machine *n.* **1.** *The washing machine needs repairing:* apparatus, appliance, device, mechanism, mechanical contrivance. **2.** *The mayor has a political machine working for his reelection:* organization, establishment, body, force, association, combine, union, society, pool, trust, faction, group, gang, crowd, ring, club, set, camp, coterie, army, corps; structure, machinery, system, setup.

machinery *n.* **1.** *The ship's machinery is being overhauled:* mechanical equipment, mechanism, apparatus, gear, contrivances; tools, tackle. **2.** *He is defying the machinery of school authority:* system, organization, structure, setup, makeup; *Slang* wheels; instrumentality, agency, resources.

machismo *n. He made a cult of machismo:* manliness, supermanliness, virility, potency, boldness, courageousness, dominance, primacy, arrogance.

macrocosm *n. The earth is but a speck in the macrocosm:* cosmos, universe, the great world, creation, nature; heavens, firmament. —**Ant.** microcosm.

mad *adj.* **1.** *Her haughtiness makes me mad:* angry, furious, irate, enraged, infuriated, incensed, wrathful, exasperated, provoked, miffed, fuming, foaming at the mouth, boiling over, seeing red, flushed with anger, in high dudgeon, wrought up, worked up, riled up, in a huff, up in arms; *Slang* teed off, ticked off, ticked. **2.** *Van Gogh had periods during which he was completely mad:* insane, crazy, demented, lunatic, crazed, deranged, maniacal, unbalanced, irrational, unhinged, bereft of reason, daft, balmy, not quite right, not all there, out of one's mind, not right in one's upper story; *Slang* nuts, nutty, nutty as a fruitcake, cuckoo, cracked, screwy, have a screw loose, off one's rocker, touched, loco; *British* crackers, round the bend; non compos mentis, *Informal* non compos. **3.** *The two sisters are mad about tennis. He's been mad about her for months:* enthusiastic, wild, excited, fanatic, avid, devoted to, frenzied, impassioned, ardent; infatuated, in love with, beside oneself, distracted, distraught. —**Ant.** 1 appeased, mollified. 2 sane, sound, rational. 3 calm, cool, collected, composed, unexcited, uncaring, nonchalant; disdainful.

madam *n. Madam, it is a pleasure to serve you:* lady, madame; matron, dowager, Mrs., *French* madame, *Spanish* señora, *Italian* signora, *German* Frau; *Archaic* dame, mistress.

madcap *adj. Her madcap ways were the despair of her parents:* wild, unruly, undisciplined, flighty, erratic, reckless, brash, thoughtless, inconsiderate, giddy, impulsive, hotheaded, rash, incautious, impractical, foolish, senseless. —**Ant.** cautious, prudent, careful, circumspect, practical.

madden *v. His indecision is enough to madden a saint:* enrage, anger, vex, pique, infuriate, provoke, upset, exasperate, frenzy, provoke, incense, outrage, inflame, aggravate, gall, craze, derange, unbalance, unhinge. —**Ant.** calm, soothe, appease, placate, mollify.

made *adj. Can you tell us how this chair was made?:* manufactured, fabricated, produced, constructed, built, assembled, formed; created, composed, developed.

made-up *adj. It was plainly a made-up story:* untrue, fabricated, false, fictional, imaginary, invented, make-believe, prepared, specious, trumped-up.

madhouse *n.* **1.** *Two inmates escaped from the madhouse:* insane asylum, lunatic asylum, mental hospital, mental institution, psychopathic hospital, state hospital; *Slang* loony bin, nuthouse. **2.** *I can't do any work--this place is a madhouse:* bedlam, scene of pandemonium, uproar, turmoil, wild confusion.

madly *adj. He loved her madly:* crazily, absurdly, irrationally, deliriously, dementedly, desperately, distractedly, excessively, rashly, recklessly, violently, wildly, excitedly, foolishly, frantically, extremely, frenziedly, furiously, insanely, intensely, passionately.

madman *n. Only a madman would rage and fume that way:* lunatic, insane person, maniac, deranged person, crazy person, demoniac, psychopath, psychotic, *Slang* loony, nut.

maelstrom *n.* **1.** *The canoe was caught in the maelstrom:* whirlpool, rapids, vortex, swirl, eddy, white water, undertow, riptide, torrent, shoot. **2.** *He's involved in the maelstrom of politics:* confusion, disorder, upheaval, tumult, uproar, pandemonium, bedlam, madhouse.

magazine *n.* **1.** *The student worked his way*

through school selling subscriptions to a maga-zine: periodical, journal; (*variously*) weekly, monthly, quarterly. **2.** *There was an explosion in the ship's magazine:* powder magazine, powder room, munitions room; arsenal, military store-house, military depot.

magenta *n.* *The evening sky was a magenta:* reddish purple, purplish rose, fuchsia; maroon, vermilion; crimson, carmine.

maggot *n.* *The bread was full of maggots:* larva, grub, worm, mealworm.

magic *n.* **1.** *Some Haitians still practice magic:* black magic, voodoo, voodooism, hoodoo, sor-cery, occultism, the black art, wizardry; witch-craft, witchery, demonology; spell, conjuration, divination. **2.** *The magician thrilled the audience with his feats of magic:* prestidigitation, legerde-main, sleight of hand, hocus-pocus, jugglery. **3.** *There was a magic in the great man's presence:* animal magnetism, fascination, captivation, cha-risma, charm, enchantment, lure, allurement, entrancement. **—Ant.** 1 science, facts and figures.

magician *n.* **1.** *Merlin was the famous magician of King Arthur's court:* wizard, sorcerer, necro-mancer, magus, shaman, warlock; witch doctor, medicine man; alchemist. **2.** *Harry Houdini was a famous magician in vaudeville:* prestidigitator, sleight-of-hand artist, expert in legerdemain, il-lusionist, escape artist; conjurer, juggler.

magisterial *adj.* **1.** *The magisterial professor liked to mark low:* dictatorial, dominating, dog-matic, doctrinaire, imperious, authoritarian, lordly. **2.** *He spoke in a magisterial tone:* mas-terful, masterly, authoritative, commanding, ex-pert.

magistrate *n.* *The couple were married by a magistrate:* justice of the peace, *Informal* j.p.; minor judge, judicial officer, civil officer, prefect, police judge.

magnanimous *adj.* *Only a truly magnanimous man could forgive such an insult:* forgiving, free of vindictiveness, generous, largehearted, libe-ral; charitable, beneficent, philanthropic, altruis-tic, unselfish, princely. **—Ant.** unforgiving, vin-dictive, resentful, small, petty, selfish; parsimonious, miserly.

magnate *n.* *Harry Sinclair was a magnate of the oil industry:* leader, dominant person, great man, empire builder, important person, VIP, gi-ant, mogul, influential person, notable, celebrity, *Slang* bigwig, big shot, big wheel, big gun; na-bob, tycoon, industrialist, giant of industry.

magnetic *adj.* **1.** *The North Pole has a strong magnetic force:* of a magnet, of magnetism. **2.** *She has a magnetic personality:* attractive, fasci-nating, persuasive; captivating, charismatic, en-chanting, alluring, entrancing, charming, irre-sistible, inviting, seductive. **—Ant.** 1 antimagnetic. 2 repellent, repulsive.

magnetism *n.* **1.** *Magnetism makes a compass needle point north:* magnetic force, magnetic attraction. **2.** *You could feel the magnetism of the singer's personality:* attraction, fascination, captivation, charisma, hypnotic appeal, enchant-ment, charm, enticement, allure, allurement,

animal magnetism, lure, mesmerism, seduction. **—Ant.** 1 repulsion. 2 repulsiveness, repellency.

magnificence *n.* *The magnificence of the pal-ace impressed us:* splendor, grandeur, impres-siveness, sumptuousness, pomp, state, majesty, luxury, luxuriousness, éclat. **—Ant.** squalor, poverty.

magnificent *adj.* *Mozart's* Don Giovanni *is a magnificent opera:* splendid, superb, sublime, grand, glorious, extraordinary, wonderful, fine, elegant, exquisite, noble, majestic, exalted, im-posing, commanding, impressive, stately, au-gust, transcendent, brilliant, resplendent. **—Ant.** modest, ordinary, undistinguished, un-imposing, unassuming, humble, mean, lowly, ignoble, poor, tawdry, trifling, trivial, petty, pal-try, bad; *Slang* awful, lousy.

magnify *v.* **1.** *This microscope magnifies the object 500 times:* enlarge optically, increase the apparent size of, *Informal* blow up. **2.** *She tends to magnify all her problems:* enlarge, expand, amplify, inflate, greaten, heighten, stretch, maxi-mize, boost, double; *Informal* blow up, puff up; exaggerate, depict extravagantly, overstate, en-large upon, overrate, embroider. **3.** *The Bible says to magnify the Lord:* laud, praise, acclaim, exalt, extol, glorify, revere, adore, worship, rev-erence. **—Ant.** 1, 2 reduce. 2 diminish, de-crease, deflate, lessen, lower, minimize, con-strict, shrink; understate, underplay; belittle, deprecate.

magniloquence *n.* *The senator's filibuster was marked more by magniloquence than persua-siveness:* bombast, pomposity, pretentiousness, grandiloquence, fustian, euphuism, turgidity, grandiosity, orotundity, tumidity, fanfaronade, high-soundingness.

magnitude *n.* **1.** *The auditorium is a building of great magnitude:* size, extent, expanse, dimensions, proportions, mass, bulk, amplitude, volume, measure; bigness, hugeness, enormity, largeness, vastness, immensity; brightness. **2.** *The professor is a scientist of considerable magnitude:* eminence, distinction, renown, re-pute, fame, celebrity, importance, consequence, significance, greatness. **—Ant.** 1 smallness, di-minutiveness, meanness. 2 insignificance, un-importance, paltriness, triviality, triflingness.

maid *n.* *It takes two maids and a gardener to keep up that big house:* housemaid, maidserv-ant, female servant, domestic, hired girl, (*vari-ously*) nursemaid, parlor maid, lady's maid, up-stairs maid, *British Slang* tweeny.

maiden *n.* **1.** *The prince fell in love with a fair young maiden:* girl, lass, maid, virgin, miss, las-sie, colleen, damsel, demoiselle, soubrette, in-genue, *Slang* chick. **—adj. 2.** Also **maidenly** *Her maiden blushes were most becoming:* girlish, youthful, chaste, virginal; unmarried. **3.** *The Ti-tanic sank on her maiden voyage:* first, initial, inaugural, untried, virgin, original, introductory, initiatory. **—Ant.** 1 matron, dowager, lady, madam, grande dame. 2 matronly; unchaste; married, wedded, espoused.

mail[1] *n.* **1.** *Did we get any mail this morning?:* post; (*variously*) letters, postcards, packages. **2.**

The mail has been slow lately: mail delivery, postal service, post-office service; airmail, surface mail. —v. **3.** Mail the check today: put in the mail, post, get out, dispatch, drop in a mailbox; send by mail, send by post.

mail² n. Sir Lancelot donned his coat of mail: armor, arms, suit of mail, panoply, flexible armor of interlinked rings, defensive armor, harness.

maim v. The explosion maimed several bystanders: mangle, mutilate, cut, slash, lacerate, wound, injure, rend, tear, rip, gash, disable, maul, dismember, cripple, incapacitate, lame, deface, disfigure, savage, hobble, hamstring.

main adj. The administrative office is in the main building. The main thing is to keep costs low: leading, principal, central, chief, head, primary, foremost, prime, capital, predominant, paramount, outstanding, preeminent, supreme; vital, essential, necessary, indispensable, requisite, important, critical, crucial, urgent, pressing, consequential; special, particular. —**Ant.** subordinate, secondary, dependent, collateral, auxiliary, ancillary; unimportant, insignificant, trivial, minor, lesser, least, nonessential.

mainly adv. The book is mainly about the author's childhood: chiefly, principally, mostly, primarily, predominantly, for the most part, most of all, above all, in the main, on the whole, in great measure, first and foremost. —**Ant.** secondarily, subordinately; partially, slightly, least of all, minimally.

mainstay n. He was the mainstay of his aging parents: chief support, backbone, principal reliance; pillar, pillar of strength, bulwark, buttress, prop, anchor.

maintain v. **1.** The two classmates maintained their friendship for the next forty years: keep, keep up, keep alive, keep going, continue, sustain, preserve, conserve, uphold. **2.** How can they maintain such a large house? The candidate maintained his position despite stinging criticism: take care of, support, provide for, keep, keep up, care for, finance; stand by, defend, uphold. **3.** Each driver maintained that the accident was the other's fault: declare, affirm, assert, state, insist, contend; hold, swear, avow, aver, profess, allege, claim. —**Ant.** 1 end, terminate, conclude, discontinue, drop, finish, abolish, dissolve, suspend, break off. 2 give up, relinquish; abandon, desert. 3 retract, disavow.

maintenance n. **1.** Our foreign policy is maintenance of friendly relations with all countries. The superintendent was responsible for the building's maintenance: preservation, conservation, keeping, safekeeping, safeguarding, protection; upkeep, repair. **2.** The divorced father pays $200 a month for the maintenance of the children: support, upkeep, subsistence, sustainment, sustenance, living, livelihood, keep. —**Ant.** 1 destruction, dissolution, eradication, abolition, termination, discontinuance, suspension.

majestic also **majestical** adj. In the distance rose the majestic Alps: stately, august, grand, imposing, impressive, magnificent, splendid,

glorious, superb, sublime, noble, lofty, elegant; regal, imperial, royal, princely; distinguished, famous, esteemed, illustrious, eminent, renowned. —**Ant.** modest, ordinary, unimposing, unassuming, humble, lowly, mean, ignoble, tawdry, paltry, undistinguished.

majesty n. The majesty of the occasion thrilled us all: grandeur, splendor, magnificence, dignity, distinction, augustness, elevation, loftiness, eminence, stateliness, glory, pomp, gloriousness, impressiveness, illustriousness, elegance, mobility, luster, solemnity, sublimity. —**Ant.** meanness, shabbiness, paltriness, lowness; degradation, disgrace, shame, debasement.

major adj. **1.** The major part of the job is done: greater, larger, main, principal, chief. **2.** Walt Whitman is a major poet. Health care is one of the major problems of our time: leading, primary, foremost, predominant, principal, chief, main, capital, prime, paramount, outstanding, preeminent, ranking, supreme, most important, important, serious, significant, consequential; essential, vital, necessary, indispensable, requisite, critical, crucial, urgent, pressing. —**Ant.** 1 lesser, smaller. 2 minor, lesser, subordinate, secondary, collateral, auxiliary, ancillary, insignificant, unimportant, trivial, trifling, inconsequential, nonessential.

majority n. **1.** The majority of the union members voted to strike: mass, bulk, best part, greater part, preponderance, lion's share, greater than half the total, greater number, more than half. **2.** She attains her majority in three years: legal age, seniority, maturity, adulthood, womanhood. —**Ant.** 1 minority, lesser part. 2 childhood, infancy.

make v. **1.** The company makes shirts and blouses. This shirt is made of cotton: manufacture, construct, produce, fashion, form, fabricate, assemble, create, compose, devise, shape, frame, build, erect. **2.** Don't make trouble. That makes me mad! He made a speech: cause, produce, bring about, effect, engender, foment, beget; cause to be; deliver, utter, speak, pronounce. **3.** I won't go and you can't make me!: compel, force, oblige, constrain, require, impel, dragoon, press. **4.** Laws are made to be obeyed: establish, put into effect, draw up, pass, enact, legislate; render, fix, appoint. **5.** We have to make Phoenix by sunset. Hurry or you won't make the train: reach, attain, arrive at; meet, arrive in time for, catch. —n. **6.** What make of car did you buy? When buying a coat, look closely at its make: kind, brand, mark; structure, construction, composition, form, formation, makeup, fashioning. —**Ant.** 1 destroy, demolish, wreck, ruin, raze. 2 end, conclude; terminate, abolish, dissolve. 3 ask, beg, plead, entreat. 4 repeal, revoke, nullify, abolish, cancel, set aside. 5 leave, depart, withdraw from; be late for, miss.

make-believe adj. **1.** Halloween is a time of make-believe goblins and witches: imagined, imaginary, unreal, fantastic, simulated, pretended, invented, fictitious, artificial, made-up, assumed, feigned; phony, false, fake, spurious, counterfeit, sham. —*n.* **2.** *The children enjoyed the make-believe of the fairy tales:* pretense, fantasy, invention, fabrication, creation, fiction; fake, counterfeit, sham, falsification, charade.

maker *n. The maker of the object took a bow:* builder, fabricator, fashioner.

makeshift *adj. The campers slept in a makeshift lean-to. This is a makeshift plan until we decide what to do:* stopgap, temporary, provisional, expedient, make-do, alternate, standby, tentative, substitute; slapdash.

makeup *n.* **1.** *His makeup combined arrogance and humility:* character, constitution, nature, build, cast, character, complexion, disposition, fiber, grain, humor, individualism, individuality, make, mold, personality, stamp, stripe, temper, temperament. **2.** *She was skilled at page makeup:* layout. **3.** *She applied makeup to her face:* cosmetics, paint, powder, *Informal* war paint. **4.** *They gave much thought to the makeup of their group:* composition, configuration, constitution, construction, contents, design, form, format, formation, shape, spread, structure, style, arrangement, order, ordering, organization, layout, setup.

maladroit *adj.* **1.** *As a mechanic he was maladroit:* unskillful, awkward, clumsy, bungling, inept, *Informal* all-thumbs, klutzy. **2.** *The maladroit introduction did him no service:* tactless, gauche. —**Ant.** 1 adroit. 2 tactful, subtle.

malady *n. The old woman has been afflicted by one malady after another all winter long:* ailment, sickness, illness, disorder, disability, disease, complaint, affliction, affection, indisposition, infirmity, unhealthiness. —**Ant.** health, healthfulness, haleness.

malaise *n. Mother isn't really sick, but she's had a malaise all winter:* vague discomfort, minor complaint, twinge, throb, pang; discomposure, nervousness, uneasiness, lassitude, disquiet, anxiety.

malcontent *adj.* **1.** *She knew he was a malcontent young man when she married him:* habitually unsatisfied, dissatisfied, discontented, hard to please, faultfinding, restive, restless, uneasy; glum, morose, sullen, grumpy, grouchy, sour, irritable, dejected, downcast, despondent. —*n.* **2.** *Does the new employee have a real grievance or is he just a malcontent?:* complainer, fault-finder, grumbler, grouch, growler, repiner; insurgent, rebel. —**Ant.** 1 contented, content, satisfied, happy, cheerful; complacent, easygoing, untroubled, unconcerned, unworried. 2 optimist.

male *adj.* **1.** *On the average, male babies weigh more at birth than female ones:* masculine, of the sex that fathers young; manly, manlike. —*n.* **2.** *Males are generally taller than females:* a male person or animal; man, youth, boy; (*variously*) stallion, tomcat, billy goat, bull, rooster, ram. —**Ant.** 1, 2 female, woman. 1 feminine.

malediction *n. The old patriarch uttered a malediction against the rival clan:* curse, damnation, imprecation, execration, evil spell, anathema; denunciation, diatribe, fulmination, proscription.

—**Ant.** benediction, blessing; eulogy, praise, compliment.

malefactor *n. The malefactors were apprehended:* evildoer, culprit, criminal, felon, outlaw, offender. —**Ant.** benefactor.

malevolence *n. Her malevolence made us recoil:* ill will, rancor, malignity, resentment, malice, maliciousness, spite, spitefulness, grudge, hate, hatred, venom. —**Ant.** benevolence, good will.

malevolent *adj. What a malevolent remark!:* malicious, showing ill will, ill-disposed, spiteful, ill-intentioned, malignant, baleful, sinister, acrimonious, venomous, resentful, vicious, rancorous, revengeful, invidious, pernicious, malign; surly, sullen, ill-natured. —**Ant.** benevolent, benign, magnanimous, kind, gracious, friendly, amiable, warmhearted.

malfeasance *n. She took steps to prevent further malfeasance:* misbehavior, misconduct, misdemeanor, misdeed, badness, wrongdoing, malpractice, delinquency, criminality, illegality, wickedness. —**Ant.** lawfulness, honesty.

malformed *adj. The tree has a malformed trunk:* misshapen, deformed, not straight, distorted, contorted, twisted, irregular, grotesque.

malfunction *n. The engine's malfunction spoiled our trip:* breakdown, defect, failure, fault, flaw, slip, *Informal* bug, glitch.

malice *n. He had no malice toward anyone:* ill will, evil intent, malevolence, maliciousness, malignity, hatred, spitefulness, spite, grudge, rancor, resentment, animosity, antagonism, acrimony, enmity, hate, venom, bitterness; evil disposition, uncharitableness, hardheartedness. —**Ant.** benevolence, goodwill, charity, friendliness, amiability, kindness, graciousness.

malicious *adj. She was the victim of a malicious rumor:* vicious, spiteful, malevolent, malignant, ill-disposed, baleful, harmful, vindictive, revengeful, resentful, rancorous, hateful, invidious, acrimonious. —**Ant.** benevolent, benign, friendly, amiable, amicable, kind, kindhearted, well-disposed.

malign *v.* **1.** *A fair politician should debate the issues and not just malign his opponent:* slander, defame, speak ill of, revile, abuse, belittle, disparage, derogate, denigrate, deprecate, vilify, inveigh against, backbite, blacken the reputation of; *Informal* run down, put down; *Slang* bad mouth. —*adj.* **2.** *The defeated bully gave his subduer a malign look. We guessed that some malign influence was behind our misfortunes:* evil, bad, harmful, injurious, detrimental, deleterious, pernicious, baneful, noxious; ominous, sinister, black, malignant, malevolent, threatening, menacing, malicious, hateful. —**Ant.** 1 praise, extol, eulogize, compliment, commend. 2 benign, benevolent, good; kind, friendly, amiable, warmhearted.

malignant *adj.* **1.** *The doctors removed a malignant growth:* deadly, pernicious, virulent; fatal, toxic, poisonous. **2.** *Such malignant gossip must be stopped before it ruins someone's reputation:* malicious, malevolent, ill-disposed, vindictive, resentful, revengeful, spiteful, rancorous, hateful, vicious, invidious, acrimonious, bitter, venomous, hostile, fiendish, diabolical, evil, evil-minded. —**Ant. 1** nonmalignant. **2** benevolent, benign, friendly, amiable, amicable, kind, kind-hearted, well-disposed.

malinger v. In the army he would malinger by pretending to be ill: slack, shirk, procrastinate, loaf, dodge, evade, duck one's duty, lie down on the job; Slang goldbrick, goof off.

mall n. The band concert was in the park's mall: promenade, tree-lined walk, esplanade; square, plaza, piazza, court, quadrangle, yard, parade ground, circus; arcade, colonnade, cloister.

malleable adj. **1.** Tin is a malleable metal: workable, easily shaped, easily wrought; ductile, tractable, plastic, pliant, flexible. **2.** Since young children are malleable, one must be careful what one says in front of them: impressionable, easily influenced, moldable, tractable, teachable, manageable, governable, docile; adaptable, flexible, pliable, compliant. —**Ant. 1** rigid, stiff, hard, firm; unyielding, inflexible, unbending, inelastic. **2** refractory, intractable, recalcitrant, ungovernable.

malnutrition n. Children in the drought-stricken area suffered from malnutrition: undernourishment, lack of proper nutrition; starvation, emaciation.

malodorous adj. The garbage can was highly malodorous: evil-smelling, fetid, foul, gamy, off, putrid, rancid, rank, reeking, rotten, high, nauseating, noisome, noxious, odorous, skunky, smelly, stinking, stinky.

malpractice n. The doctor was sued for malpractice: professional negligence, improper professional practice, professional dereliction.

maltreat v. They maltreated their pets: mistreat, abuse, injure, ill-treat.

mammon n. Too many people worship mammon these days: wealth, riches, possessions, money, gold, profit, material goods, affluence, gain, the god of money.

mammoth adj. The Great Pyramids are mammoth structures: enormous, huge, immense, massive, monstrous, gigantic, colossal, very large, mighty, great, whopping, monumental, mountainous, prodigious, gargantuan, elephantine, herculean, cyclopean, stupendous, tremendous, ponderous. —**Ant.** small, little, tiny, miniature, minute, dwarf-ish; Informal wee, pee-wee; Slang itty-bitty, itsy-bitsy.

man n. **1.** Man cannot live by bread alone: mankind, the human race, men and women, human beings, humankind, people, humanity, Homo sapiens. **2.** Every man must follow his own beliefs: individual, person, human being, human, living being, living soul, soul, one; anyone, somebody, someone. **3.** The average man is taller than the average woman: male, masculine person; gentleman, chap, fellow; Slang guy, gent. **4.** The minister pronounced them man and wife: married man, husband, spouse, Informal hubby. **5.** Hire a man to take care of the garden: handyman, workman, hired hand, hand, laborer, day laborer; employee, worker; man-servant, male servant, boy, waiter, footman,

butler, male retainer; assistant, helper, right-hand man; male follower, subject, liegeman, henchman. —v. **6.** The crew was ordered to man the lifeboats: attend, staff, take up one's position in, take one's place at, get to one's post; supply with hands, furnish with men, people; equip, fit out, outfit; garrison. —**Ant. 3** woman, female. **4** bachelor.

manacle n. **1.** Usually **manacles** The sheriff put manacles on the prisoner's hands: handcuffs, hand-fetters, irons, shackles, chains, bonds, Slang bracelets. —v. **2.** The sheriff manacled the thief and took him to jail: handcuff, fetter, tie one's hands, put in chains, put in irons, shackle, Slang put bracelets on. —**Ant. 2** unbind, unfetter, unchain; set free, free, liberate, turn loose, let go.

manage v. **1.** She seems so young to manage three children and that big house. The prime minister really manages the government: run, direct, oversee, superintend, have charge of, take care of, look after, watch over, supervise, head, administer, conduct, preside over, rule, govern, control, command, order, dominate, guide, steer, pilot, be at the helm, hold the reins. **2.** It's hard to manage a sailboat in a narrow inlet: manipulate, maneuver, handle, control, work, operate, make go, run; guide, steer; use, wield, ply. **3.** How will you manage without a job?: survive, get along, get on, fare, shift, keep one's head above water, weather the storm. **4.** We don't have much time to do the job, but we'll manage it: succeed, accomplish, deal with, cope with, cope, work out, bring about. —**Ant. 1** be under the care of, follow. **3** be destitute, starve. **4** fail, botch, bungle, spoil, make a mess of, muff, make a hash of.

management n. **1.** The owner's son took over the management of the business. The plan failed due to bad management: administration, supervision, direction, overseeing, superintendence, generalship; operation, guidance, regulation, conduct, conducting, command, control, ordering, charge, running, handling, care, rule; planning, organization; strategy, tactics, manipulation; dealing, negotiation, transaction. **2.** Management has vetoed your suggestion: executives, executive board, executive committee, administrators, the administration, supervisors, supervisory board, board of directors, directors, bosses; Slang bigwigs, big shots, wheels, top brass. —**Ant. 2** labor; staff, employees, workers.

manager n. **1.** The store manager does all the hiring: head, boss, supervisor, foreman, superintendent, overseer, executive director, administrator, majordomo, chief; agent, impresario. **2.** Only a good manager can run a household on fifty dollars a week: planner, organizer, budgeteer; tactician, manipulator, negotiator. —**Ant. 1** employee, worker, laborer, Slang flunky.

mandate n. **1.** The island is a mandate of the U.S.: protectorate, dependency, mandated territory, subject territory. **2.** Work on the new bridge will begin as soon as an official mandate is received: order, edict, decree, command, dictate, bidding, behest, directive, direction, instruction, authorization, authority, approval, sanction, charge, requisition, commission. —**Ant.** 2 petition, request, entreaty, supplication, appeal, solicitation, suit.

mandatory *adj. Attendance at Sunday Chapel is no longer mandatory for students:* compulsory, required, requisite, obligatory, incumbent on, not optional, binding, called for; essential, imperative, peremptory, necessary, needful, exigent.

maneuver *n.* **1.** *The generals planned the maneuver carefully:* troop movement, troop deployment; movement of warships, planes, armored vehicles, etc.; training exercise. **2.** *The prime minister thwarted the opposition's maneuver to gain control of the government:* scheme, stratagem, gambit, move, ploy, tactic; plot, artifice, device, contrivance, machination, trick, dodge, intrigue. —*v.* **3.** *The ships maneuvered to block the channel. Can you maneuver the car into that parking spot?:* deploy, move; manipulate, steer, pilot, guide. **4.** *The vice-president is maneuvering to displace the president of the company:* contrive, work surreptitiously, bring about in an underhand way, pull strings; scheme, plot, plan artfully, devise a way, intrigue, *Informal* finagle.

mangle *v. The dog's leg was mangled in the accident:* mutilate, maim, disfigure, maul, press, crush, flatten; cut, lacerate, tear, slash; injure, damage, harm, hurt, lame, impair, ruin.

manhood *n.* **1.** *He had to support his family before he achieved manhood:* adulthood, maturity, prime, legal age, majority, mature age. **2.** *He had to avenge the insult to his manhood:* virility, manliness, manfulness, masculinity, machismo, maleness.

mania *n.* **1.** *Hitler's mania is often cited as the cause of World War II:* madness, violent derangement, insanity, lunacy, fanaticism, dementia; frenzy, delirium, raving, rage, hysteria, delusion, hallucination, aberration. **2.** *Kim has a mania for collecting seashells:* passion, craze, craving, enthusiasm, exaggerated love, infatuation; obsession, fascination, monomania, compulsion, fixation. —**Ant.** 1 sanity, rationality; self-control, equanimity, stability, levelheadedness, coolness, coolheadedness, calmness.

maniac *n. They arrested some maniac for setting the fire. That maniac should be arrested for speeding:* madman, lunatic, psychotic, crazy person, insane person, deranged person; *Slang* nut, screwball, crackbrain, loony, cuckoo; psychopath; reckless person, fool, simpleton, ass, nitwit, half-wit.

maniacal *adj. The maniacal gang destroyed all in its path:* wild, mad, amuck, berserk, frantic, frenzied, furious, violent, rabid.

manic *adj. When she was manic she often danced the night away:* frenzied, excited, agitated, hyperactive, worked up, frantic, wrought up; *Slang* up, high, hyped up, freaked out, switched on. —**Ant.** low, sluggish, down, depressed.

manifest *adj.* **1.** *The principal's displeasure was*

manifest: obvious, clear, evident, self-evident, plain, apparent, patent, visible, noticeable, palpable, unmistakable, transparent, unconcealed, undisguised; open, frank, candid. —*v.* **2.** *The boss manifested his disgust with a scowl:* indicate, show, exhibit, reveal, express, disclose, make known, demonstrate, evince, evidence, display, divulge, make visible, unveil, uncover, hold up to view, bare, expose. —**Ant.** 1 hidden, concealed, suppressed, masked, obscured, vague, cryptic, inconspicuous, unseen. 2 hide, conceal, cover up, mask, cloak, bury, obscure, camouflage.

manifestation *n. Fever is one manifestation of a cold. The political rally was a huge manifestation of support for the candidate:* indication, symptom, evidence, proclamation, revelation; demonstration, example, instance, show, display, exhibition, illustration, expression, presentation.

manifesto *n. The rebel soldiers issued a manifesto on their war aims:* proclamation, declaration, pronouncement, edict, ukase, announcement, communiqué, statement, pronunciamento, annunciation, notice, notification, broadside, position paper; *Cath. Church* bull, encyclical.

manifold *adj. A housewife has manifold responsibilities. The City Council has a manifold plan to beautify the city:* many, numerous, multitudinous, multiple, myriad, innumerable; varied, variegated, diversified, many-sided, diverse, complex, multiform, multifarious. —**Ant.** few, scant, limited; simple, uncomplicated, uniform.

manipulate *v.* **1.** *The magician manipulated the cards and the ace vanished:* handle, finger; feel, pinch, stroke, pat, massage, squeeze. **2.** *Do you know how to manipulate a computer?:* operate, work, use, employ, handle, manage, control; wield, ply, drive. **3.** *The treasurer was arrested for trying to manipulate the company's financial records:* tamper with, change fraudulently, manage by crafty means, influence deviously, control illegally, direct unethically; deceive, defraud.

mankind *n. Is mankind in danger of extinction?:* the human race, humankind, Homo sapiens, the human species, man, men and women, humanity, mortals, people, persons, society.

manly *adj.* **1.** *The boy has a very manly voice:* masculine, male, malelike, virile, manful. **2.** *Football is a manly sport. Each soldier must do his duty in a manly fashion:* vigorous, hardy, strong, robust, husky, sturdy, muscular, athletic, brawny, strapping, powerful, stalwart; brave, courageous, daring, bold, resolute, stouthearted, valiant, fearless, staunch, indomitable, plucky, self-reliant; noble, heroic, chivalrous, gallant, gentlemanly. —**Ant.** 1 unmanly, effeminate, womanish, boyish, juvenile, youthful, puerile, childlike, childish, babyish. 2 weak, frail, feeble; cowardly, faint-hearted, irresolute; villainous, dastardly.

man-made *adj. It's the largest man-made lake in the eastern U.S.:* artificial, manufactured, fabricated, synthetic, factitious, created, fashioned, formed, crafted, constructed, handcrafted, ready-made, originated, produced; mock, sham, simulated.

manna n. Our fathers did eat manna in the desert: miraculous food, spiritual nourishment, divine sustenance; boon, bonanza, sudden gain, unexpected gift, award, reward.

manner n. **1.** I love duck cooked in the Chinese manner: way, style, mode, fashion, method, custom, practice, habit; guise, aspect, appearance, character. **2.** Her manner seemed rather uneasy: behavior, conduct; bearing, carriage, air, presence, deportment, demeanor. **3.** What manner of bird is that?: kind, type, sort, variety; classification, genre, species, category, breed, race, strain, stamp, brand, caste, make, form, mold; grade, rank.

mannered adj. The mannered paintings sold badly: affected, self-conscious, artificial, campy, pretentious, stilted. **—Ant.** natural, unaffected.

mannerism n. Uncle Ned has an annoying mannerism of scratching his head while he talks. Her British accent is just a mannerism picked up on her visit to London: peculiar action, habit, habitual gesture, distinctive way, characteristic style, eccentricity, idiosyncrasy, singularity; affectation, pose, affected gesture, mannered style, artificiality, pretense, pretension; airs.

mannerly adj. The older boy's mannerly conduct was an example to the younger children: polite, well-mannered, civil, courteous, well-behaved; refined, well-bred, genteel, courtly, gentlemanly, gallant, chivalrous. **—Ant.** unmannerly, discourteous, rude, impolite, ill-mannered, gauche, boorish.

manners n. pl. **1.** His bad manners are inexcusable. Mind your manners: social behavior, behavior, decorum, deportment. **2.** Don't they teach any manners at that school?: good manners, politeness, etiquette, courtesy, deference; refinement, breeding, polish, gentility, gallantry, courtliness, politesse, propriety, amenities. **—Ant.** 2 rudeness, impoliteness, bad manners, discourtesy, boorishness.

mansion n. The old mansion is the town's showplace: stately residence, impressive house, imposing dwelling; manor, manor house, villa, château, castle, palace; estate. **—Ant.** hovel, shack, hut, cabin, cottage, Slang hole.

manslaughter n. The driver responsible for the accident was charged with manslaughter: accidental murder, unpremeditated killing, killing without malice aforethought; (loosely) murder, killing, homicide, spilling of blood.

mantle n. **1.** The actress wore a velvet mantle over her gown: cloak, cape, tunic, wrapper; scarf for the head and shoulders, mantilla. **2.** A mantle of fog settled over the city: covering, cover, veil, cloak, mask, envelope, curtain, blanket, canopy, screen, cloud, film, shroud, pall.

manual adj. **1.** The sports car has a manual transmission: hand-operated, nonautomatic. **2.** Years of manual labor had hardened his muscles: physical, done by hand, requiring physical strength. **—n. 3.** She bought a manual of home repairs: handbook, guidebook, instruction book;

textbook, primer, workbook. **—Ant.** 1 automatic; machine-operated, electric. 2 mental, intellectual.

manufacture v. **1.** The company manufactures toys: produce, mass-produce, make, fabricate, mold, form, fashion, devise, frame; assemble, put together, construct, build. **2.** You'll have to manufacture some kind of excuse: invent, fabricate, trump up, make up, concoct, create, think up, Informal cook up. **—Ant.** 1 destroy, demolish.

manufactured adj. Manufactured products rose in price: machined, fashioned, created, formed, cast, crafted, forged, milled, molded, shaped.

manufacturing n. Manufacturing is a major industry: manufacture, fabrication, making, assembly, casting, composing, composition, construction, creation, production, tooling.

manure n. The manure pile is behind the barn: dung, animal excrement, animal droppings, feces, ordure, excreta; fertilizer; compost, dressing.

manuscript n. He showed me the manuscript of his new play: typescript, script, written document; (motion pictures, television) shooting script.

many adj. **1.** I've told you many times that I hate liver: numerous, innumerable, numberless, countless, myriad, multitudinous; several, various, divers, sundry. **—n. 2.** Many are called but few are chosen: a considerable number, a lot, lots, a heap, heaps, piles, scores, dozens, numbers; a liberal quantity, a profusion, an abundance. **—Ant.** 1 few, rare, infrequent, once or twice. 2 few, hardly any, a handful; none, none at all.

map n. **1.** This is a map of North America: topographical chart, chart, graph, projection, elevation; plot, diagram, plan, representation. **—v. 2.** The expedition will map the South Pole: make a map of, chart. **3.** The agency mapped out an advertising campaign for the new product: plan, project, prepare, devise, design, contrive, arrange, plot, lay out, organize, ready.

mar v. **1.** A large scratch marred the table: disfigure, blemish, deface, mutilate, maim, damage, hurt, scar, mark, nick, scratch, stain; ruin, destroy. **2.** A series of sour notes marred her singing: spoil, taint, blemish, impair, hurt, botch, detract from, make imperfect, diminish; defile, blight. **—Ant.** 1 beautify, embellish, adorn, decorate, ornament; restore. 2 improve, enhance, restore.

maraud v. The horsemen marauded the countryside: raid, plunder, pillage, ravage, ransack.

marauder n. The marauders raided several coastal towns: plunderer, pillager, depradator, ravager, looter, despoiler, spoiler; pirate, buccaneer, privateer, corsair, freebooter; roving outlaw band; guerrilla, ranger.

march v. **1.** First World War veterans will march at the head of the parade. March right upstairs and change those wet clothes!: parade, walk with measured steps, walk in step, walk in a procession, file by; go, go directly, walk, step, tramp, proceed. **—n. 2.** The soldiers had a ten-

mile march before lunch. The students will have a march from the rally to the football field: hike, tramp, trek, group walk; parade, procession. **3.** *The book describes the march of civilization from ancient Egyptian times to the present:* progress, progression, development, advance, advancement, rise, growth. **4.** *The band concert closed with a Sousa march:* piece of music in march time; martial music, military tune; funeral march.

mare *n. The mare recently had a colt:* female horse, broodmare.

margin *n.* **1.** *The student wrote notes in the margins of the book:* border, boundary, edge, side, rim, verge, confine, bound, hem, fringe, skirt. **2.** *There is no margin for error in his plan:* leeway, safeguard, extra amount, added quantity, extra room, allowance. **—Ant.** 1 center, middle, interior.

marginal *adj.* **1.** *The book has small marginal illustrations:* in the margin, on the edge, along the border. **2.** *He owns a small, marginal business:* barely profitable; barely useful.

marine *adj.* **1.** *The school has an excellent course in marine biology:* oceanic, sea, saltwater; of the sea, aquatic, oceanographic, pelagic. **2.** *The steamship company's lawyer was a specialist in marine law:* maritime, of ships, naval, nautical; seagoing, oceangoing, seafaring. **—Ant.** 1 terrestrial, land, dry-land; fresh-water.

mariner *n. The old mariner had sailed the seas for 40 years:* sailor, deck hand, seaman, seafarer, seafaring man, able-bodied seaman, boatman; *Slang* salt, tar, sea dog, bluejacket, gob; navigator, pilot, helmsman; yachtsman. **—Ant.** landlubber.

marionette *n. The marionettes were called Punch and Judy:* puppet, articulated puppet, puppet on strings, *Italian* fantoccino.

marital *adj. The couple celebrated 25 years of marital bliss:* wedded, married, of marriage, matrimonial, conjugal, spousal, nuptial, connubial; husbandly, wifely. **—Ant.** single, unmarried, unwed, unwedded.

maritime *adj.* **1.** *The admiral is an expert in maritime history:* marine, naval, nautical, of ships, of the sea, of sea trade, seagoing, seafaring; oceanic, aquatic. **2.** *Nova Scotia is one of Canada's Maritime Provinces:* coastal, bordering on the sea; engaged in sea trade, making a living from the sea. **—Ant.** 1 land, terrestrial, dry-land; fresh-water. 2 inland.

mark *n.* **1.** *What made those marks on the wall?:* spot, streak, line, stain; scratch, scar, cut, nick, dent, impression; pock, pit, notch, score; bruise, blemish. **2.** *This vase bears the mark of a famous potter. Everyone stood as a mark of respect when the president entered the room:* hall-mark, sign, symbol, stamp, label, badge, emblem, brand, colophon, imprint; token, symbol, indication, evidence, measure, symptom, proof. **3.** *The student received passing marks in all subjects:* grade; rating. **4.** *If that was meant to be an apology, your words were way off the mark. The employee's work has been below the mark this week:* target, goal, objective, intent,

point, track, bull's-eye; standard, criterion, yardstick, touchstone. **—v. 5.** *That wet glass will mark the table:* spot, streak, stain; scratch, scar, cut, nick, dent, leave an impression on, pock, pit, notch, score; bruise, blemish; mar, deface, disfigure, harm, injure; make a line on, writeon, write in. **6.** *The teacher marked the examination papers:* grade, correct, judge, rate. **7.** *X marks the spot. Well-kept houses mark a good neighborhood:* indicate, reveal, disclose, show, point out, designate, denote, signify, stand for; characterize, typify, symbolize, evidence, evince, suggest, betoken, manifest, be a sign of, distinguish, differentiate; label, stamp, brand. **8.** *Mark my words!:* heed, attend, pay attention to, mind, note, regard. **—Ant.** 5 clean, remove, obliterate, erase; repair. 7 hide, conceal, mask, veil, cover, screen, disguise, camouflage. 8 ignore, overlook, disregard.

marked *adj. She is a woman of marked intelligence:* outstanding, distinct, conspicuous, striking, noticeable, obvious, prominent; exceptional, uncommon, noteworthy, extraordinary, unique, signal, singular, special, remarkable, particular, definite, decided. **—Ant.** ordinary, commonplace, everyday, undistinguished, routine, run-of-the-mill, mediocre.

markedly *adv. His talent was markedly undervalued:* decidedly, patently, clearly, considerably, conspicuously, distinctly, especially, evidently, greatly, manifestly, notably, noticeably, obviously, particularly, remarkably, strikingly.

market *n.* **1.** *We buy our vegetables at the farmer's market. There's a new fruit market on the corner:* marketplace, wholesale market; stand; grocer's shop, grocery; meat market, butcher shop. **2.** *Over a million shares of stock were traded on the market:* stock market, stock exchange, curb market, *French* bourse; financial center; commodity market. **—v. 3.** *The inventor is trying to market his new product:* sell, vend, merchandise, retail, *Informal* peddle, hawk; put up for sale, dispose of. **—Ant.** 3 buy.

marketable *adj. They agreed it was a marketable commodity:* saleable, sellable, for sale, merchandisable, commercial, bankable.

marksman *n. A good hunter has to be a good marksman:* sharpshooter, good shot, good target-shooter, crack shot, dead shot, sure shot.

maroon[1] *v. The pirates' victims were marooned on a small island:* strand, cast ashore, leave behind, put ashore, cast away, abandon, desert, forsake, jettison, *Informal* leave high and dry.

maroon[2] *adj. My new winter coat is maroon:* brownish red, wine, magenta, plum, terra cotta.

marriage *n.* **1.** *They have been through a lot together in their forty years of marriage:* matrimony, marital state, wedlock, holy wedlock, conjugal union, connubial state, nuptial state. **2.** *The marriage will take place in June:* wedding, marriage ceremony, nuptials, nuptial rites, tying the knot, leading to the altar, ringing of wedding bells. **—Ant.** 1 divorce, annulment; single life, bachelorhood, spinsterhood.

marrow *n. She got to the marrow of the issue:*

core, essence, quintessence, gist, substance, heart, kernel, meat, pith, soul, spirit, bottom.

marry v. **1.** *He married a girl from his home town:* wed, get married to, take in marriage, espouse, exchange wedding vows with, lead to the altar, bestow one's hand upon, take for a husband, take for a wife, take for better or for worse; *Slang* get spliced, tie the knot. **2.** *The minister has married over 400 couples:* wed, join in marriage, join in wedlock, unite in holy wedlock, make one. **—Ant.** 1 divorce, get an annulment from.

marsh n. *The hunters built a duckblind in the marsh:* swamp, bog, fen, bottoms, slough; marshland, wetland, quagmire, quicksand, everglade, morass.

marshal n. **1.** *U.S. marshals arrested the two hijackers. The fire marshal directed the hook-and-ladder units:* law officer; sheriff, police chief; fire chief. **2.** *The marshal of the Rose Bowl parade was a movie star:* master of ceremonies, honorary leader, ceremonial head; chief, leader, director, supervisor, manager. **3.** *The oldest general was appointed marshal of the armies:* field marshal, commander in chief, generalissimo, chief officer, *French* maréchal. **—v. 4.** *The general marshaled his army for battle. Marshal your arguments before debating:* gather, collect, muster, assemble, mobilize; arrange, order, organize, group, deploy, array, align, line up, draw up. **—Ant.** 4 scatter, disperse; disorganize.

marshy adj. *All the land below their house was marshy:* swampy, miry, muddy.

mart n. *The manufacturers' furniture exhibition was held in the Merchandise Mart in Chicago:* trade center, trading center, exchange; marketplace, market; trade fair, trade show, exposition, show.

martial adj. **1.** *The town was under martial law. The old veteran had a martial bearing:* military; soldierly, soldierlike. **2.** *The country maintains a martial attitude toward its neighbors:* warlike, belligerent, Spartan, disposed to war, hostile, militant, combative, bellicose, pugnacious, contentious; military-minded. **—Ant.** 1 civilian, civil. 2 peaceful, conciliatory.

martinet n. *The boss is such a martinet he'll dock you for coming in two minutes late:* taskmaster, severe disciplinarian, authoritarian, hard master, tyrant, despot, dictator, drill-sergeant, drill master, Simon Legree, *Slang* little Caesar.

martyr n. *The early Christian Church had many martyrs:* person willing to die or suffer for a cause; person killed for his beliefs; one who undergoes great suffering; one venerated for dying or suffering.

martyrdom n. *The painting depicts the martyrdom of St. Sebastian:* the suffering of a martyr, death of a martyr; suffering, agony, anguish, torment, torture, ordeal, affliction; (*literary*) crown of thorns, bitter cup, cup of sorrow. **—Ant.** ecstasy, bliss, joy, pleasure, happiness, delight, gratification.

marvel n. **1.** *His speech was a marvel of tact:* miracle, wonder, phenomenon, wonderful thing,

supreme example; rarity, spectacle. **—v. 2.** *The tourists marveled at the beauty of Lake Louise:* be awed, be overwhelmed, be struck with wonder, be staggered, be amazed, be astonished, be stupefied, gape. **—Ant.** 1 commonplace. 2 be bored; take in stride.

marvelous or **marvellous** adj. *It was a marvelous party:* wonderful, splendid, lovely, superb, outstanding, great, grand, fine, first-rate, fabulous, heavenly, divine, fantastic, extraordinary, stupendous, sensational, colossal, phenomenal, magnificent, remarkable, astonishing, amazing, *Slang* super, A-1, smashing. **—Ant.** terrible, awful, lousy, bad; ordinary, commonplace, routine, everyday, run-of-the-mill.

masculine adj. *He likes to show off his masculine physique:* manly, male, manful, virile, *Slang* macho; strong, vigorous, robust, sturdy, hardy, husky, powerful, muscular, strapping, brawny, athletic; brave, courageous, resolute, daring, bold, stouthearted, fearless, valiant, staunch, indomitable, plucky, intrepid, self-reliant, forceful. **—Ant.** weak, unmanly, effeminate, womanish, girlish; female, feminine, womanly, ladylike, womanlike.

mash v. **1.** *Mash the potatoes and add cream and butter:* puree, reduce to pulp, crush, pulverize, squash, smash. **—n. 2.** *The horses are fed a mash of bran and oats:* pulpy mass, soft mixture, paste, mishmash, mush.

mask n. **1.** *The children wore Halloween masks. Each diver has to wear a mask:* false face; face covering, domino; face guard. **2.** *The jokes were a mask to hide his sadness:* cover, cover-up, screen, cloak, shroud, veil, curtain, blind; disguise, camouflage. **—v. 3.** *The bank robbers masked their faces:* cover, put a mask over, obscure, hide, disguise. **4.** *A row of trees masked the junkyard from the eyes of passing motorists. She tried to mask her feelings:* hide, conceal, shield from view, cover, screen, veil, cloak, shroud, curtain, keep secret; camouflage, disguise. **—Ant.** 2 revelation, disclosure, display, manifestation, demonstration, show, exhibition. 3 unmask. 4 reveal, disclose, divulge, expose, show, display, exhibit.

masquerade n. **1.** *The masquerade was the biggest party of the year:* masked party, costume party, masked ball, masque, mask, *French* bal masqué; harlequinade. **2.** *His laughter is just a masquerade so you won't know how disappointed he is:* cover, cover-up, mask, screen, veil, cloak, shroud; camouflage, pretense, pretext, subterfuge, guise, trick, artifice, ruse. **—v. 3.** *All this time he's been masquerading as a real doctor!:* go under the guise of, pass oneself off as, pretend to be, pose as, impersonate, falsely claim to be; go disguised as. **—Ant.** 2 revelation, disclosure, display, manifestation, demonstration, show, exhibition. 3 unmask, find out; expose, reveal to be.

mass[1] n. **1.** *Einstein studied the relation of energy and mass:* the quantity of matter in a body; (*loosely*) matter, material; weight. **2.** *That hill is actually one solid mass of coal:* block, lump, chunk, hunk, knot, clot, cake, concretion. **3.**

The club women gathered a mass of used clothing for the rummage sale. A mass of people jammed into the arena: pile, heap, stack, pyramid, batch, lot, clump, bundle, pack, bunch; accumulation, cumulation, collection, assemblage, gathering, group, body, aggregate, aggregation, assortment, conglomeration; crowd, throng, mob, congregation, host, horde, corps, troop, crush, press, jam. **4.** The mass of public opinion is in favor of no-fault auto insurance: greater part, preponderance, majority, plurality, bulk, main body, best part, lion's share. —v. **5.** Protesters massed in front of the city hall: collect, amass, gather, assemble, consolidate, congregate, accumulate; pile, heap, stack, bunch. —**Ant.** 2 fragment, bit, chip, piece, portion, morsel. 3 scattering. 4 minority. 5 disperse, scatter, spread.

mass[2] n. Often **Mass** St. Patrick's Cathedral is famed for its midnight Mass on Christmas eve: celebration of the sacrament, Communion service, Holy Communion, holy sacrament, celebration of the Lord's Supper, Eucharist; offering of bread and wine, consecration of the elements.

massacre n. **1.** The massacre of some 200 Sioux by U.S. troops at Wounded Knee, South Dakota, on December 29, 1890, marked the end of the Indian Wars: mass slaughter, mass murder, indiscriminate killing, butchery, carnage, bloodletting, bloodbath. —v. **2.** Herod's soldiers massacred the male infants of Bethlehem: slaughter en masse, kill at random, butcher, decimate; put large groups to death, perpetrate genocide.

massage n. **1.** A brisk massage restores the body's vigor: rubdown; rubbing, kneading, stroking, manipulation. —v. **2.** Massage your cheeks so they won't get frostbitten. He massaged his jaw thoughtfully: rub, rub down, knead, chafe, stroke, manipulate, flex, handle, finger, stretch.

masses n. pl. The masses are the true makers of history: the common people, the crowd, the mob, the multitude, the populace, the many, hoi polloi, the common herd, the great unwashed; the working class, the proletariat, the lower classes, proles, plebeians, plebes, the riffraff, rabble, the man in the street, the rank and file, every Tom, Dick, and Harry. —**Ant.** the élite, the aristocracy, the gentry, the upper class, bluebloods, silk stockings, society, high society, the crème de la crème, the Beautiful People, the intelligentsia, the cognoscenti, the illuminati; the middle class, the bourgeoisie.

massive adj. A massive rock formation blocked the end of the valley: immense, huge, gigantic, monstrous, enormous, mammoth, colossal, great, stupendous, cyclopean, titanic, gargantuan, elephantine, whopping; monumental, impressive, imposing, vast, extensive, towering; hulking, heavy, hefty, ponderous, weighty, bulky, solid, massy, substantial, ample. —**Ant.** small, little, tiny, diminutive, minute; petty, trivial; flimsy, slight, frail, slender, light.

master n. **1.** The dog obeyed his master. Cortés was master of the Aztec empire: owner, lord, conqueror, ruler. **2.** Father was definitely the master of our house: head, head man, boss, chief, leader, dominant person, controller, authority, overlord, governor, director, supervisor, manager, overseer, superintendent. **3.** The first mate was studying to become a master: ship's captain, skipper, commanding officer. **4.** Grandfather was a master at silversmithing: expert, master hand, skilled artist, craftsman, wizard, genius, virtuoso, Slang ace, whiz. —adj. **5.** Father and Mother have the master bedroom: main, chief, principal, primary, prime, paramount, most important, predominant, supreme, choice, best. **6.** A cabinet maker must be a master craftsman: expert, skilled, masterly, proficient, first-rate, deft, able, practiced, accomplished, finished, talented, gifted, Slang ace, crack, A-1. —v. **7.** You must learn to master your temper: conquer, subdue, overcome, triumph over, control, regulate, govern, manage, dominate, tame, curb, suppress, check, bridle. **8.** He could never master mathematics: grasp, learn thoroughly, be adept in, be skilled at, be proficient in, excel at, get the hang of. —**Ant.** 1 slave; subject, vassal, servant, 3 crew; able-bodied seaman. 4, 6 amateur, novice, tyro, 5 minor, lesser, unimportant. 6 amateurish, incompetent, inept, unskilled, untalented, unaccomplished; bungling, clumsy. 7 surrender to, yield to, capitulate to, give in to, give way to.

masterful adj. **1.** He showed a masterful grasp of the problem. The violinist gave a masterful performance: masterly, skillful, skilled, expert, virtuoso, deft, able, accomplished, finished, superb, excellent. **2.** She could only love a masterful man: strong-willed, self-confident, self-reliant, resolute, dynamic, forceful; commanding, domineering, bossy, authoritarian. —**Ant.** 1 amateurish, incompetent, inept, unskilled, untalented, unaccomplished, bungling, clumsy. 2 weak, wishy-washy, irresolute, meek, spineless.

mastermind v. **1.** The police know who masterminded the robbery: plan, organize, conceive, engineer, direct. —n. **2.** The advertising manager is the mastermind of our new marketing policy: planner, organizer, engineer, initiator, moving force, director. **3.** It will take a mastermind to solve this problem: genius, mental giant, brilliant intellect, sage, wizard, pundit; expert, specialist, virtuoso, master, master hand, authority, past master, old hand. —**Ant.** 3 idiot, moron, imbecile, simpleton, fool; amateur, incompetent, novice, tyro.

masterpiece n. Rembrandt's paintings are masterpieces: great work of art, masterwork, classic, old master, monument, prize, jewel, treasure, prizewinner, paragon, nonpareil, brainchild, Latin ne plus ultra, French chef d'oeuvre.

mastery n. **1.** The sergeant had complete mastery over his men: control, command, domination, dominance, leadership, supremacy, superiority, sway, rule, upper hand, whip hand. **2.** It takes years to gain a mastery of Japanese: expert knowledge, expert skill, proficiency, ability, adroitness, deftness, grasp, acquirement, attainment, achievement, accomplishment. —**Ant.** 1 subservience, submission, obedience. 2 incompetence, ineptness.

masticate v. Masticate each bite thirty times before swallowing: chew; champ, munch, gnaw, nibble. —**Ant.** swallow whole, gulp, bolt.

match n. **1.** The blue shirt and gray tie are a good match. Can you find the match to this glove?: matching pair, corresponding twosome; mate, one of a pair, duplicate, double, twin, companion. **2.** Bill is no match for his brother at chess: equal, equivalent, peer; parallel, counterpart. **3.** Who won the tennis match?: game, contest, competition, tournament, meet, event. —v. **4.** The drapes match the rug. These two pieces of the jigsaw puzzle don't match: harmonize, correspond, be alike, suit, fit, go well with; combine, fit together, pair, couple, connect, join, unite, yoke, link together; agree, be equal, adapt. **5.** The promoters matched the young boxer with a more skillful fighter: pit against, oppose, set against, put in competition with; contend; enter the lists with, vie with. —**Ant.** 1 mismatch. 2 unequal, superior; inferior. 4 clash with, differ from; be unequal, be a mismatch.

matching adj. The government gave them matching funds to equal what they raised privately: corresponding, like, parallel, duplicate, identical, equal, equivalent, same, twin. —**Ant.** distinct, different, disparate.

matchless adj. The vase is of matchless workmanship: incomparable, supreme, unmatched, unparalleled, unequaled, unrivaled; peerless, unsurpassed, unexcelled, unbeatable, crowning, superior, superlative, first rate, paramount, preeminent, foremost; rare, priceless, invaluable, inestimable, sterling, exemplary. —**Ant.** comparable, equaled, surpassed, excelled; average, mediocre, common, commonplace, ordinary, everyday; inferior, lesser, lower, cheaper, second-class.

mate n. **1.** Where's the mate to this sock?: one of a pair, duplicate, match, twin, counterpart, companion, equivalent. **2.** The zoo is looking for a mate for its female panda. Her mate seems to like her cooking: one of a pair of mated animals; spouse, partner, consort, helpmate; husband, Informal hubby; wife, better half. **3.** British Informal In London I had a drink with my friend and his mates at a local pub: chum, pal, crony, buddy, friend, companion, comrade, sidekick; co-worker, fellow worker, associate, confederate, colleague, partner; classmate; roommate; messmate. **4.** The mate gave orders to swab the decks: first mate, second mate; ship's officer below the rank of captain, master mariner. —v. **5.** Some animals will not mate in captivity: pair off; couple, copulate, cohabit.

material n. **1.** The material in the earth's crust is very old: matter, substance, stuff, constituents, elements. **2.** Often **materials** The price of building materials has gone up: supplies, stores, stocks; timber, bricks and mortar; equipment, machinery, tools. **3.** Mother bought some material to make a dress: fabric, textile, dry-

goods; piece goods, yard goods, cloth. **4.** The reporter is collecting material for an article: facts, figures, data, observations, impressions, quotations, notes; references, citations. —adj. **5.** What do we know of the material universe?: physical, formed of matter, tangible, substantial, substantive, essential, materialistic, concrete; bodily, corporeal. **6.** He made a material contribution to the work: significant, important, substantial, consequential, essential, vital, indispensable; relevant, pertinent, germane, direct; grave, serious, weighty, momentous. —**Ant.** 1 spirit, soul; mind, intellect. 5 nonmaterial, intangible; spiritual. 6 insignificant, unimportant, unsubstantial, inconsequential, trifling, piddling, unessential, dispensable, superficial; irrelevant, facetious, cavalier.

materialism n. Crass materialism causes people to forget spiritual values: love of possessions, love of material things, concern for comfort, pursuit of wealth; acquisitiveness, covetousness. —**Ant.** asceticism; idealism.

materialistic adj. Our materialistic society values possessions: acquisitive, possessive, object-oriented, unspiritual, material.

materialize v. The ghost was said to materialize once a year: appear, emerge, show, become visible, turn up, come into view, rise, come to light, issue, come forth, burst forth, loom, issue, spring forth, put in an appearance, manifest oneself, expose oneself; Slang pop up, bob up. —**Ant.** disappear, vanish, evaporate, dissolve, fade away.

materially adv. **1.** Were things materially different in the old days?: significantly, substantially, essentially, vitally, emphatically, considerably, to an important degree, seriously, in the main, for the most part. **2.** Materially, the family is quite successful: financially, monetarily, concerning material things, with regard to material comforts; in substance, tangibly, palpably, corporeally. —**Ant.** 1 insignificantly, unsubstantially, on the surface, superficially; hardly, scarcely, barely, little. 2 spiritually; intellectually.

matériel n. The Quartermaster Corps sent more matériel to the troops: military supplies, gear, equipment, materials; supplies, stores, provisions.

maternal adj. **1.** She showed her daughter's picture with maternal pride: motherly, of a mother, motherlike; doting, fond; shielding, sheltering, protective. **2.** My maternal grandmother was a small woman: related through one's mother, on one's mother's side of the family. —**Ant.** 2 paternal.

maternity n. The pregnant woman looked forward to her maternity: motherhood, being a mother; child-bearing, childbirth, delivery, parturition, labor, accouchement; pregnancy.

mathematical adj. **1.** He's some kind of mathematical genius: of mathematics, of higher mathematics; computational. **2.** The hostess planned the seating arrangements with mathematical precision: precise, exact, accurate, unerring, scientific, well-defined, meticulous, scrupulous, strict, punctilious, rigid, rigorous.

—**Ant.** 2 careless, heedless, thoughtless, sloppy, inaccurate, inexact, loose, lax.

mathematics *n. pl. She was a whiz at mathematics:* math, figures, *British* maths.

matinee *n. There will be two evening performances and a matinee of Macbeth:* afternoon performance; early performance, early show.

matriarch *n. My grandmother was the matriarch of our family:* female head, female chieftain, female ruler, female leader, materfamilias, grande dame.

matriculate *v. Freshmen wishing to matriculate in the university were asked to go to the registrar's office:* enroll, register, sign up, enlist, enter, join, check in.

matrimonial *adj. The state of matrimonial bliss evaded him for many years:* married, wedded, bridal, nuptial, conjugal, marital, connubial, hymeneal, spousal, epithalamic, affianced, husbandly, wifely.

matrimony *n. Young couples should enter matrimony seriously:* marriage, marital state, sacrament of wedlock, holy wedlock, conjugal union, connubial state, nuptial state. —**Ant.** divorce, annulment; single life, bachelorhood, spinsterhood.

matrix *n. The sculptor poured the molten metal into a matrix that gave it the shape of a cross:* mold, cast, form, frame; die, punch, stamp.

matron *n.* **1.** *Most of the club members are matrons, though young girls are welcome:* married woman, middle-aged woman, stately woman, dowager, madam, dame. **2.** *Each floor of the women's prison was supervised by a matron:* female supervisor, overseer, superintendent; directress, mistress, forelady, forewoman, housekeeper. —**Ant.** 1 girl, maid, maiden, miss, lass, young woman.

matted *adj. The dog's hair was heavily matted:* tangled, snarled, kinky, knotted, uncombed, twisted.

matter *n.* **1.** *The physical world is composed of matter. He has some foreign matter in his eye:* material, substance, stuff, elements; object, thing. **2.** *The book contains some rather controversial matter:* subject matter, text, subject, content, theme, topic, thesis, gist, sense, purport, drift, argument, essence, sum and substance; printed matter, written matter. **3.** *The matter was resolved amicably. There's that little matter of the money you borrowed:* affair, business, situation, transaction, thing, proceeding, episode, occurrence, experience, adventure, scrape, circumstance, event, happening. **4.** *It is no matter that he didn't phone:* importance, consequence, significance, import, moment, difference. **5.** *What's the matter?:* trouble, difficulty, cause of distress; predicament, emergency, crisis, exigency, dilemma, quandary, perplexity, strait; obstacle, impediment, *Informal* fix, snag. —*v.* **6.** *It matters very much:* be of importance, be of consequence, count, be of concern, be noteworthy; import, signify, carry weight, have influence. —**Ant.** 1 spirit, soul; mind, intellect. 4 insignificance, unimportance, meaninglessness. 5 solu-

tion, answer, resolution. 6 be unimportant, inconsequential, be of no concern.

matter-of-fact *adj. She gave us a matter-of-fact appraisal of the situation:* practical, straightforward, realistic, factual, literal, down-to-earth, unaffected, real, natural, sensible, prosaic, hardheaded, unsentimental, mundane, pragmatic, commonplace, ordinary; straight-out, blunt, candid, outspoken, frank, direct. —**Ant.** speculative, vague, impractical, theoretical, impassioned, emotional.

mature *adj.* **1.** *He's a mature man who can make his own decisions:* grown, matured, fully developed, completely grown, grown-up, fullgrown, of age, adult, middle-aged, in one's prime; experienced, practiced, seasoned; marriageable, nubile, womanly; manly, virile; ripe, full-blown. **2.** *When the plan is mature we will proceed:* completed, perfected, ready, finished, full-fledged. —*v.* **3.** *Girls mature earlier than boys:* maturate, reach maturity, come of age, become adult, grow up, develop; ripen, bloom, blossom, flower; mellow. —**Ant.** 1 immature, unripe, undeveloped, half-grown, underaged, young, juvenile, adolescent, childish, childlike, youthful, boyish, girlish; green, *Slang* wet behind the ears; callow, unfledged; unripe. 2 incomplete, unperfected, unfinished.

maturity *n.* **1.** *The body reaches maturity earlier than the mind:* adulthood, maturation, manhood, womanhood, full growth, full development; legal age, age of consent, majority; ripeness, full bloom; completion, perfection, readiness, fulfillment, culmination. **2.** *This job calls for a man with a great deal of maturity:* experience, practice, seasoning; levelheaded-ness, composure, mature judgment, matureness, responsibility. —**Ant.** 1 immaturity, youthfulness, boyishness, girlishness, childishness, juvenility, puerility, callowness; incompletion, imperfection, crudeness. 2 irresponsibility, faulty judgment; excitability, hot-headedness.

maudlin *adj. Dickens was a great writer despite his maudlin plots:* emotional, overemotional, sentimental, weakly sentimental, mawkish, bathetic, teary, lachrymose, gushing, tearful, *Informal* gushy, mushy, slushy. —**Ant.** realistic, matter-of-fact, unemotional, unsentimental.

maul *v. Neighbors mauled the thief before the police could get to him:* manhandle, batter, beat, beat up, rough up, pummel, thrash, bruise, mangle, stomp, knock about.

maunder *v.* **1.** *His thoughts tended to maunder as he relived the past:* wander, ramble, drift, saunter, meander, stray, straggle, flounder, dawdle, loaf, dillydally. **2.** *She maundered on about the many injustices of her life:* babble, blather, ramble on, prattle, run on, hem and haw, gibber, go on and on, gabble.

mausoleum *n. This is the mausoleum of the royal family:* stately tomb, family tomb, sepulchral monument.

mauve *adj. The garden was full of mauve irises:* light purple, bluish purple, lilac, lavender, puce, plum, violet.

maverick *n.* **1.** *The cowboys rounded up the*

mavericks for branding: unbranded calf, year-ling; unbranded cow; motherless calf. **2.** *The young senator was regarded as a political maverick:* noncomformist, eccentric, independent, individualist, loner, independent thinker, one's own man; dissenter, dissident.

maw *n.* **1.** *The farmer crammed grain down the goose's maw:* gullet, throat, esophagus, mouth; jaws, muzzle. **2.** *Food is partially digested in a bird's maw:* crop, craw, first stomach of a bird.

mawkish *adj. Mother tends to get mawkish when she speaks of her childhood:* sentimental, oversentimental, maudlin, emotional, nostalgic, lachrymose, tearful, teary, *Informal* mushy, gushy, schmaltzy. **—Ant.** unsentimental, unemotional, matter-of-fact.

maxim *n. "A stitch in time saves nine" is a popular maxim:* adage, aphorism, axiom, proverb, apothegm, platitude, truism, saw, saying, old saw; motto, guiding principle, rule.

maximum *adj. The plane can fly at a maximum altitude of 75,000 feet. The car was going at its maximum speed:* greatest possible, optimum, greatest, utmost, top, highest, maximal; supreme, unsurpassed, paramount, foremost; most, largest. **—Ant.** minimum, minimal, least possible, least, lowest, bottom.

maybe *adv. Maybe we'll see you tomorrow:* possibly, perhaps, perchance, peradventure, mayhap; feasibly, conceivably, imaginably; God willing, wind and weather permitting.

maze *n. The messenger boy got confused in the maze of offices:* labyrinth, complex, network, meander, tangle, snarl, convolution, complex puzzle; jungle.

meadow *n. Cows were roaming the meadow:* grazing land, grassland, pasture, lea, savanna, pasturage, green, mead, meadowland, field, park; forage, herbage.

meager *adj. The campers took only a meager supply of food:* scanty, scant, slight, paltry, little, skimpy, scrimpy, sparse, bare, slender, slim, token, thin, lean; inadequate, insubstantial, insufficient, deficient, wanting, short, stinted, spare, scarce. **—Ant.** ample, abundant, plentiful, copious; adequate, sufficient, substantial.

meal¹ *n. It's time for the midday meal. This restaurant is known for its Chinese meals:* repast, spread, feast, banquet, refreshment, nourishment; food, cuisine, cooking, fare, victuals, bill of fare, menu, diet, *Slang* eats, grub, chow.

meal² *n. Simple pancakes can be made out of meal and water:* ground grain, flour; (*variously*) cornmeal, oatmeal, groats, bran, grits, farina.

mealy-mouthed *adj. The mealy-mouthed statement put us off:* devious, hypocritical, false, duplicitous, two-faced, insincere, smarmy. **—Ant.** straightforward, candid.

mean¹ *v.* **1.** *Father didn't mean to be a clerk all his life, but that's the way it turned out:* intend, have in mind; propose, plan, purpose, aspire to, want, wish, dream of, think of, resolve, determine upon, aim at, drive at, have in view. **2.** *What does "antidisestablishmentarianism" mean? A damp breeze from the sea usually means rain:* denote, signify, express, stand for, symbolize, say, tell of; indicate, point to, imply, suggest, intimate, hint at, betoken. **3.** *Did she really mean it?:* say truly, speak sincerely, feel honestly, express genuinely. **—Ant.** 2 hide, conceal, mask. 3 lie, pretend, feign, counterfeit.

mean² *adj.* **1.** *The shoes were of mean quality. He has some mean job at the local factory:* low, low-grade, poor, inferior, cheap, second-rate, flimsy, sleazy, gimcrack, jerry-built, trashy, rubbishy, squalid, wretched, miserable, sordid; menial, low-ranking, low-paying, trifling, petty, unimportant, trivial, paltry, piddling, insignificant, inconsequential, small, picayune. **2.** *How could anyone be so mean?:* malicious, vicious, malign, malevolent, evil, villainous, base, petty, low, small-minded, shameful, contemptible, despicable, disgraceful, dishonorable, vile, nasty, disagreeable, rude, cruel, hardhearted, merciless, pitiless, inhumane, inhuman, unfeeling, unsympathetic, uncaring, unfair. **3.** *He's a mean man to do business with:* stingy, miserly, pinchpenny, closefisted, tightfisted, niggardly, penurious; ungenerous, illiberal, tight, close, cheap; greedy, grasping, avaricious, venal, hoggish, selfish, self-seeking, mercenary. **—Ant.** 1 high, good, superior, excellent, superb, splendid, first-rate, choice, premium, deluxe; high-ranking, important, consequential, significant, big. 2 kind, goodhearted, warm, good, sweet, gentle, humane, sympathetic, compassionate; noble, honorable, praiseworthy, pleasing, attractive, agreeable, wonderful. 3 generous, liberal, openhanded, bountiful, munificent, princely; unselfish, altruistic.

mean³ *n.* **1.** *His income is $3,000 above the national mean. Can't we strike a mean and find a house that's not too big or too small?:* average, norm, par, median, rule; happy medium, golden mean, balance, compromise, midway point. —*adj.* **2.** *The mean income of American families is over $15,000 a year:* average; normal, standard, medium, regular; commonplace, run-of-the-mill. **—Ant.** 2 extreme, ultimate; best, highest, greatest, most; worst, lowest, smallest, least.

meander *v. The path meanders up the hill. The tourists meandered through the old section of San Juan:* wind, circle, loop, zigzag, corkscrew, twist, snake, convolute, undulate, spiral; wander, ramble, go aimlessly, stray, rove. **—Ant.** go straight, go directly, make a bee line.

meaning *n. Look up the meaning of the word in the dictionary. Did that long speech have any meaning at all? Since his wife died his life has had no meaning:* denotation, sense, signification; significance, substance, sum and substance, content, subject matter, essence, gist, pith, meat, upshot; implication, drift, suggestion, intimation, indication, hint, pointer; intention, intent, purpose, purport, thrust, force, burden, goal, aim, point, object; value, worth, end; view, design, scheme, plan. **—Ant.** meaninglessness, insignificance, irrationality, absurdity.

meaningful *adj.* **1.** *She gave her husband a meaningful look:* pointed, significant, having meaning, purposeful, eloquent, expressive, deep, portentous, pregnant, designing, suggestive, explicit, pithy. **2.** *Every person deserves a meaningful job:* worthwhile, useful, substantial, significant, consequential, important, serious, meaty; gratifying, emotionally satisfying. **—Ant.** 1, 2 meaningless, superficial, senseless, facetious. 2 worthless, useless, unsubstantial, insignificant, inconsequential, unimportant, pithy, trifling, trivial, paltry.

meaningless *adj.* **1.** *Italian is meaningless to me. It seems to be a completely meaningless riddle:* unintelligible, incomprehensible, incoherent, impenetrable, inexpressive, undecipherable, illegible; puzzling, baffling, inscrutable, inexplicable, mystifying, perplexing, bewildering, enigmatic. **2.** *Thoreau felt that many people live meaningless lives:* without meaning, without purpose, purposeless, worthless, valueless, useless, unsubstantial, aimless, insignificant, inconsequential, unimportant, unessential, trivial, trite, paltry, piddling, shallow, senseless, frivolous, facetious, foolish, fatuous, absurd, stupid, nonsensical, idiotic, preposterous. **—Ant.** 1, 2 meaningful. 1 intelligible, comprehensible, understandable, coherent, expressive, clear, obvious, evident, manifest, pithy, trenchant; legible, decipherable. 2 purposeful, worthwhile, valuable, useful, substantial, significant, momentous, consequential, important, deep, sensible.

means *n. pl.* **1.** *Many elderly people don't have the means to travel. Only a person of means could afford a house that big:* money, resources, wherewithal, funds, dollars, income, revenue, *Slang* jack, long green, dough, bread; wealth, riches, substance, capital, property, affluence, easy circumstances. **2.** *Taking a plane is the quickest means of getting there:* way, method, mode; resort, avenue, course, alternative; measure, process, modus operandi.

meantime *n. I'll call you Sunday, but in the meantime say nothing:* interim, interval, the period between, the intervening time.

meanwhile *adv. Meanwhile, across town, things were humming. Meanwhile, don't call us, we'll call you:* at the same time, simultaneously, concurrently; during the intervening period, in the interim, meantime, for the time being.

measurable *adj. The distances to the farthest stars are measurable:* computable, reckonable, capable of being measured, mensurable, determinable, appraisable, assessable. **—Ant.** immeasurable, indeterminate.

measure *v.* **1.** *Did you measure the windows before buying the curtains? The tablecloth measures 18 by 20 feet:* ascertain the dimensions of, find the size of, size, pace off, step off, plumb, sound; time, clock; to be the size of, be long, be wide. **2.** *It's hard to measure the importance of good manners:* evaluate, value, assess, appraise, gauge, survey, judge. **—n. 3.** *The measure is given in centimeters. Hold the measure up to the box:* measurement, unit of measurement; (*variously*) gauge, rule, scale, yardstick. **4.** *Flood victims received a full measure of aid:* share, allotment, quantity, amount, portion, quota, allowance, extent, degree, range, scope; necessary amount, required amount. **5.** *He loved her beyond measure:* limit, limitation, bound, restraint, moderation, temperance. **6.** *The measure is now before the legislature:* act, bill, proposal, law, enactment; plan, scheme, design, project, proposition. **7.** *What measures were taken to prevent fires?:* course, means, step, method, resort, proceeding, procedure.

measured *adj.* **1.** *The cars raced over a measured mile:* predetermined; precise, exact, verified. **2.** *The dignitaries advanced with a measured tread:* uniform, steady, regular, equal. **3.** *His reply was stated in measured phrases:* studied, deliberate, premeditated, intentional, calculated, well-planned, carefully thought-out, cold-blooded. **—Ant.** 2 haphazard, irregular, random. 3 spontaneous, rash, reckless, emotional, on the spur of the moment, unplanned.

measureless *adj. A measureless chasm loomed below us:* limitless, boundless, immeasurable, immense, vast, endless, infinite, unending. **—Ant.** limited, finite.

measurement *n.* **1.** *The measurement of individual intelligence is very difficult:* measuring, mensuration, surveying, sounding, plumbing; evaluation, assessment, appraisal, gauging, estimation, reckoning. **2.** *What are the measurements of the living-room rug?:* dimension, size, breadth, depth, length, height, width, area; capacity, volume, content; mass, weight; magnitude, amplitude, extent.

meat *n.* **1.** *Veal is a very tender meat:* edible animal flesh, animal tissue or organs. **2.** *The weary travelers were given meat and drink:* food, nourishment, victuals, sustenance, edibles, comestibles, fare, provisions, grub, provender. **3.** *The meat of his argument is that poverty cannot be cured by government aid:* gist, point, essence, substance, core, heart, kernel, nut, nucleus.

meaty *adj. The meaty report required time for study:* substantial, weighty, meaningful, factual, pithy, pointed, profound, significant.

mechanic *n. The mechanic fixed our van:* repairman, workman, machinist; craftsman, artificer, artisan.

mechanical *adj.* **1.** *She doesn't understand anything mechanical:* run by machinery, having to do with machinery; machine-driven, automatic, self-acting. **2.** *His gratitude seemed rather mechanical. Blinking is a mechanical action of the eyelids:* perfunctory, routine, unfeeling, impersonal, cold, machinelike; automatic, instinctive, involuntary, unconscious, unthinking. **—Ant.** 1 manual. 2 genuine, sincere, heartfelt, wholehearted, personal, warm; voluntary, conscious, thinking.

mechanism *n. The can-opener is a simple mechanism. The mechanism of this toy train is faulty:* apparatus, tool, instrument, implement, utensil, contrivance, appliance, machine; works, machinery, motor.

medal *n. The war hero received many medals for bravery:* citation, decoration, medallion, ribbon, award of honor; trophy, prize, award; honor, laurel, reward.

meddle v. *No one asked him to meddle in this affair:* interfere, intervene, intermeddle, intrude, concern oneself unasked, interlope, mix in, pry into, *Informal* butt in, horn in, stick one's nose in; tamper with; *Informal* kibitz. —**Ant.** keep out, *Informal* butt out.

meddlesome adj. *If I offered her advice, she'd think I was meddlesome:* intrusive, officious, impertinent, presumptuous, obtrusive, meddling, prying, pushing, interfering, snooping; *Slang* nosy, snoopy, pushy. —**Ant.** restrained, reserved; aloof, indifferent, standoffish.

median adj. *Median income rose sharply:* midway, medial, average, center, central, equidistant, intermediate, mean, mid, middle, middlemost, midpoint, halfway, intermediary.

mediate v. *The lawyer tried to mediate between the company and the union:* arbitrate, negotiate, moderate, intervene, intercede, interpose, settle a dispute, bring to terms, effect an agreement, bring about an agreement; make peace between, pacify, conciliate, reconcile, propitiate, restore harmony, step in, umpire, referee.

mediation n. *The dispute was settled by mediation:* arbitration, compromise, adjustment, conciliation, reconciliation, give-and-take, settlement of difficulties, coming to terms; negotiation, discussion, parley, intervention, intercession; pacification, peacemaking.

mediator n. *Who will act as mediator in the dispute?:* arbitrator, negotiator, moderator, reconciler, go-between, intermediary, referee, umpire, peacemaker.

medical adj. *Medical research may find a cure for cancer. Some herbs have medical value:* relating to medicine, medicinal, medicative, curative, healing, therapeutic, remedial, restorative, sanative, health-bringing, salutary. —**Ant.** unhealthy, unhealthful, toxic, poisonous, virulent.

medication n. *The doctor prescribed some medication:* remedy, medicine, medicament, healing application, curative substance; tonic, restorative, palliative, balm; panacea, nostrum, elixir.

medicine n. **1.** *What kind of medicine are you taking?:* curative agent, medication; drug, pill, remedy, nostrum, tonic, restorative; balm, salve. **2.** *Where did the doctor study medicine?:* science of medicine, practice of medicine, healing art, medical treatment, therapeutics, materia medica. —**Ant.** 1 poison, toxin, bane.

medieval adj. *Chaucer wrote in the late medieval period:* of the Middle Ages (the period between A.D. 476 and approximately 1450), pre-Renaissance.

mediocre adj. *The student tries hard, but his work is mediocre. He seems content with a mediocre job:* ordinary, run-of-the-mill, undistinguished, commonplace, pedestrian, indifferent, passable, tolerable, so-so, fair-to-middling, betwixt and between, average, medium, normal, common; unimportant, inconsequential, insignificant, negligible, inconsiderable, inappreciable, petty, slight, trifling, paltry, meager; inferior,

rather poor, second-rate. —**Ant.** extraordinary, uncommon, distinctive, distinguished, unique, unexcelled, unsurpassed, unrivaled, incomparable; superior, fine, excellent, superb; important, significant.

mediocrity n. *The old poet decried the mediocrity of today's writing:* commonplaceness, indifference, ordinariness, unimportance, insignificance, pettiness, paltriness, meagerness, triviality; low-quality, inferiority, poorness. —**Ant.** distinction, uniqueness; importance, significance, consequence; excellence, superiority, greatness, brilliance.

meditate v. **1.** *Modern men don't set aside enough time to meditate:* think, reflect, think quietly, think seriously, ruminate, muse, contemplate, ponder, study, cogitate, deliberate, collect one's thoughts, dwell upon, turn over in the mind, mull over. **2.** *The congressman is meditating a reply to his critics:* plan, devise, concoct, contrive, consider, propose, have in view, aim at, dream of, aspire to. —**Ant.** 1 act, do.

meditative adj. *The meditative student pondered his future:* pensive, thoughtful, reflecting, contemplative; studious. —**Ant.** impetuous.

medium n. **1.** *Fish live in an aqueous medium:* environment, surroundings, atmosphere; setting, milieu. **2.** *There has to be a medium between good and bad:* middle ground, midcourse, middle way; compromise, moderation, happy medium, mean, golden mean, balance. **3.** *Television can be an excellent medium for education:* agency, means, way, mode, form, channel, instrument, vehicle, tool, avenue, instrumentality, organ. **4.** *The medium supposedly called forth her long dead uncle:* spiritualist, psychic, clairvoyant, fortuneteller, diviner, crystal-gazer; go-between, intermediary, intermediate. —adj. **5.** *The boy is of medium height for his age:* average, common, normal, ordinary, middling, moderate. —**Ant.** 2 extreme limit. 5 extreme, utmost, extraordinary, uncommon, distinctive, unique, unusual, undue, unreasonable.

medley n. *The band played a medley of march tunes:* miscellany, olio, mixture, assortment, potpourri, mélange, pastiche, mosaic, patchwork; jumble, gallimaufry, hodgepodge, farrago, *Informal* mishmash, hash, mess.

meek adj. *The boss constantly mistreated his meek assistant. The meek shall inherit the earth:* submissive, deferential, complaisant, docile, yielding, tractable, acquiescent, unresisting, compliant, long-suffering, spineless, spiritless, weak-kneed, lamblike; humble, mild, gentle, modest, unassuming, unassertive, unpretentious, retiring, tolerant, tenderhearted. —**Ant.** domineering, bossy, willful, overbearing, self-assertive, bold, forward, presumptuous; spirited, *Informal* spunky; rebellious, insubordinate, unyielding; arrogant, lordly, proud, immodest, pretentious.

meet[1] v. **1.** *I'd like you to meet my brother:* be introduced to, be presented to, become acquainted with; welcome, greet. **2.** *I met an old* school friend today. A policeman could meet danger any minute of his working day: come across, encounter, run into, bump into, come into contact with, light upon; confront, face, come into the presence of, speak with. **3.** *The club meets at a different member's home every week:* assemble, convene, gather, collect, congregate, rally, muster, come together. **4.** *To join the army, one must meet certain physical standards. Father was poor, but he always met his financial obligations:* fulfill, comply with, satisfy, observe, abide by, adhere to, observe, execute, carry out, perform, discharge, heed, obey, be faithful to, follow, acknowledge, respect, keep one's pledge; equal, come up to, answer, match. **5.** *Turn left where the highway meets the dirt road. The two properties meet at the bottom of the valley:* cross, intersect, unite with, converge with; adjoin, abut, border. —**Ant.** 1 become estranged. 2 avoid, elude, escape, miss. 3 adjourn; disperse, scatter, dispel. 4 fail, fall short of; renege. 5 diverge.

meet[2] *adj. It is not meet for strangers to interfere:* proper, appropriate, opposite, fitting, fit, befitting, suitable, seemly, right, apt, good, felicitous, decorous, becoming; allowable, admissible, permitted, permissible, pertinent, relevant, compatible, agreeable, congruous. —**Ant.** improper, unfitting, inappropriate, unsuitable, unseemly, wrong, unbecoming; incongruous, incompatible.

meeting *n.* **1.** *Our meeting was arranged by a mutual friend. The two lawyers had an argument at their very first meeting:* introduction, presentation; encounter, confrontation; date, engagement, rendezvous, tryst, assignation. **2.** *The chairman called the meeting to order:* gathering, assembly, group, convocation, conclave, council, congress, caucus; conference, convention, get-together.

melancholy *n.* **1.** *Rainy days give me a feeling of melancholy:* melancholia; depression, gloom, gloominess, dejection, despondency, disconsolateness, despair, forlornness, moodiness, low spirits, doldrums; *Slang* blues, dumps. —*adj.* **2.** *Hamlet was a melancholy man:* suffering from melancholia; depressed, gloomy, dejected, despondent, disconsolate, forlorn, glum, moody, mopish, doleful, downhearted, heavyhearted, discouraged, dispirited, downcast, cheerless, heartsick, sick at heart, unhappy, morose, languishing, *Slang* down in the dumps, down in the mouth, blue. **3.** *What a melancholy day!:* depressing, gloomy, dreary, somber, dismal, desolate, joyless, plaintive, mournful, funereal; dolorous, doleful; unfortunate, calamitous. —**Ant.** 1 exhilaration, joy, delight, pleasure, cheer, happiness, gladness. 2 exhilarated, joyous, joyful, cheerful, lighthearted, happy, glad, vivacious, gay, lively, sprightly, merry. 3 exhilarating, joyous, delightful, cheerful, happy.

mélange *n. The quilt was a mélange of colors, shapes, and textures:* mixture, mix, medley, potpourri, pastiche, miscellany, jumble, hodgepodge, mishmash, gallimaufry, assortment, patchwork, pasticcio, assemblage, compound.

meld *v. The instructions said to meld the ingredients into a smooth paste:* merge, mix, blend, fuse, combine, consolidate, coalesce, unite, amalgamate, incorporate, mingle, join, commingle, intermingle, interweave, intertwine, intermix, jumble, scramble. —**Ant.** separate, dissociate, split, divide.

melee *n. Rival fans started a melee on the way to the ball park:* fistfight, brawl, row, free-for-all, fracas, fray, set to, scuffle, scrap, tussle, dogfight, altercation, commotion, rumpus, disorder, riot, pandemonium.

mellifluous *adj. We heard mellifluous bells across the lake:* sweet-sounding, sweet-toned, euphonious, mellifluent, musical, harmonious, sweet, dulcet, melodious, mellow, soft, smooth; resonant, full-toned. —**Ant.** harsh, discordant, grating, jarring, raucous, hoarse, unmusical.

mellow *adj.* **1.** *This is a good mellow cheese:* ripe, mature, matured; full-flavored, full-bodied, luscious, sweet, delicious; soft, rich. —*v.* **2.** *Age and responsibility mellowed the callow youth:* mature, season; make more understanding, make sympathetic, make compassionate, make more tolerant, soften, smooth the rough edges. —**Ant.** 1 unripe, immature, green; raw, sour, biting, harsh. 2 harden, brutalize, make callous, make unfeeling, make stubborn.

melodic *adj. The composer has quite a melodic gift:* of melody, creating melody, full of melody; melodious, tuneful, lyric. —**Ant.** unmelodic.

melodious *adj.* **1.** *The girl has a very melodious voice:* sweet-toned, mellifluous, mellifluent, euphonious, musical, sweet, dulcet, mellow, soft, smooth; clear, rich, full-toned, resonant, ringing. **2.** *The operetta was very melodious:* tuneful, full of melody, melodic, lyric. —**Ant.** 1 harsh, discordant, grating, jarring, raucous. 2 unmelodic, untuneful, cacophonous, unharmonious.

melodramatic *adj. The play was criticized for its melodramatic ending:* exaggerated, flamboyant, overly theatrical, sensational, stagy, sentimental, overemotional, overwrought, frenzied, mawkish, maudlin, histrionic, spectacular, *Slang* hammy, corny, cornball, hokey. —**Ant.** realistic, matter-of-fact; understated, low-key, deadpan.

melody *n.* **1.** *I'll hum the melody and you try to guess the words:* tune, air, strain, theme; song, aria, ballad, ditty. **2.** *The success of a popular composer depends on his melody:* tunefulness, melodiousness, musicality, musical invention, melodic gift, melodic invention; euphony, harmoniousness, mellifluence, mellifluousness, concord, sweetness of sound, timbre. —**Ant.** 1 harmony; rhythm. 2 dissonance; harshness, discordance, clashing, jarring.

melt *v.* **1.** *When the sun came out the snow melted quickly:* dissolve, liquefy, thaw. **2.** *When the police came the crowd melted away:* dissipate, scatter, dispel, dwindle, fade, dissolve, disappear, evaporate, vanish; waste away. **3.** *One week melts into the next:* blend, fuse, merge, pass, shade, fade, dissolve. **4.** *The little boy's tears melted her heart:* touch, soften, disarm, make gentle, affect, arouse pity; appease, conciliate, mollify, propitiate. **—Ant.** 1 freeze, solidify; congeal, jell, set, harden. 2 accrue, gather, grow. 4 harden, make callous.

member n. **1.** Her lower members were numb with cold: extremity, appendage; (variously) limb, leg, foot, toe, arm, hand, finger, digit; (animals) wing, pinion, tail; part, organ; (plants) shoot, bough, branch. **2.** All the members of the committee were present: constituent, person who belongs to a group; component, element, part, piece, section, segment, portion, fragment, ingredient.

membership n. **1.** Women are denied membership in the men's bowling league: fellowship, affiliation, league, fraternal union, connection. **2.** The membership of the club is now 500: roster, personnel, body of members, number of members; community, company, association; society, fraternity, brotherhood, club, fellowship.

membrane n. The toes of a frog are connected by a membrane: web, covering tissue; film, thin sheet, coating, thin skin, sheath, lining, envelope; integument, pellicle.

memento n. She gave him an autographed photo as a memento of his visit: souvenir, token, keepsake, reminder, favor, remembrance, record, trophy, memorabilia, remembrancer, memorial, relic, commemoration.

memoir n. The duchess's memoirs caused a sensation: autobiography, diary, journal, recollections, reminiscences, reflections, experiences, adventures, confessions, biography, intimate biography, life, life story.

memorable adj. The vacationers spent a memorable week in the Canadian Rockies. T. S. Eliot's The Wasteland is one of the most memorable poems of the 20th century: unforgettable, notable, noteworthy, impressive, illustrious, famous, celebrated, distinguished, eminent, prominent, important, significant, momentous, historic, outstanding, salient, remarkable, extraordinary, striking, stirring, red-letter. **—Ant.** unmemorable, forgettable, unimpressive, undistinguished, unimportant, insignificant, mediocre, commonplace, ordinary, pedestrian, prosaic, banal, trite, trivial, run-of-the-mill.

memorandum n. He sent us a memorandum about the meeting: memo, reminder, minute, note, brief report, record, brief, jotting; list of items, agenda.

memorial n. **1.** This statue is a memorial to the town's war dead: monument, testimonial. **2.** Friends gathered at a memorial for the late statesman: tribute, homage, commemorative service, memorial service. —adj. **3.** A memorial plaque in honor of the church's first minister was installed in the chapel: commemorative, monumental, testimonial.

memory n. **1.** Can a person improve his memory?: recall, ability to remember, power of recollection, mental retention, remembrance, remembering. **2.** Mother has lovely memories of her youth: recollection, mental impression, reminiscence, remembrancer, memento, souvenir, keepsake, reminder, token, memorial, com-

memoration, testimonial. **3.** He is gone, but his memory remains to guide the living: fame, renown, eminence, reputation, repute, glory, prestige, distinction, esteem, honor, estimation, name, note, mark, regard, respect. **—Ant.** 1 forgetfulness. 2 amnesia; a total blank. 3 oblivion, nothingness, void, nonexistence.

menace n. **1.** Icebergs are a menace to ships in the North Atlantic: threat, danger, peril, hazard, jeopardy, risk, endangerment, imperilment, pitfall, cause for alarm. —v. **2.** Overeating can menace a person's health. The hoodlum menaced the local merchants: endanger, imperil, be a hazard to, jeopardize, risk; terrify, intimidate, threaten, terrorize, bully, browbeat, cow, daunt; forebode, portend, presage. **—Ant.** 1 blessing, benefit, boon, advantage. 2 benefit, help, aid, promote, further, advance; protect, guard, safeguard; soothe, console, calm.

mend v. **1.** A good tailor can mend that coat. The broken bone is starting to mend: repair, fix, put in order, restore, renovate, overhaul, recondition, touch up, retouch, patch, darn; heal, knit, cure, remedy. **2.** The judge warned the youth to mend his ways: correct, reform, improve, better, ameliorate, meliorate, amend, rectify, revise. **—Ant.** 1 damage, harm, mar, injure, lacerate, tear, break, split; spoil, ruin, destroy.

mendacious adj. The mendacious retailer misled us: lying, untrue, false, untruthful, deceitful. **—Ant.** truthful, honest.

mendacity n. There's so much mendacity in the world one doesn't know whom to believe: lying, falsehood, falsity, untruthfulness, falsification, prevarication, misrepresentation; deceit, deception, duplicity, dishonesty, hypocrisy, perfidy, double-dealing, fraud, chicanery, insincerity. **—Ant.** truth, truthfulness, veracity, frankness, openness, forthrightness; honesty, trustworthiness, uprightness, sincerity.

mendicant n. The streets of Tangier are full of mendicants seeking alms. The Capuchins were founded as an order of mendicants: begging monk, begging friar; beggar, street beggar, alms-seeker, panhandler.

menial adj. **1.** No job is too menial for a hungry man. His menial behavior disgusts me: lowly, degrading, low, humble, ignoble, mean, abject; servile, subservient, slavish, obsequious, fawning, groveling, truckling, cringing, sycophantic, Informal apple-polishing, boot-licking. —n. **2.** The king was surrounded by menials who did his every bidding: servant, flunky, lackey, underling, subordinate; employee, apprentice, helper; slave, drudge, drone; sycophant, toady. **—Ant.** 1 noble, dignified, autocratic, aristocratic, high, elevated; overbearing, domineering, bossy, proud, haughty, conceited. 2 master, lord, overseer, superior, chief, commander, boss.

mental adj. **1.** He got the answer by mental arithmetic: of the mind, in the mind, done with the mind, intellectual, intelligent, cerebral, rational; psychic, psychological; abstract, metaphysical, subjective. **2.** How many mental patients does the hospital care for?: mentally ill, mentally disturbed, psychotic, neurotic; insane, crazy, lunatic, disordered, disturbed, unbalanced, *Slang* nutty, cracked, psycho.

mentality *n. Contrary to popular belief, chess does not demand a high mentality. The girl has the mentality of a much older child:* intellect, mental ability, intelligence, mental power, mental endowment, mind, brains, gray matter; perception, judgment, understanding, discernment, perspicacity, acumen, wisdom, sagacity.

mention *v.* **1.** *Before closing I want to mention all those who contributed so generously. I hate to mention this, but--:* allude to, speak of briefly, refer to, touch upon; name, specify, cite, disclose, make known, divulge; hint at, intimate, imply, insinuate; state, observe, remark, tell, say, tell of, report, recount, narrate. *—n.* **2.** *No mention was made of her illness:* allusion, suggestion, indication, hint, insinuation, inkling, reference, remark, statement, utterance, comment, communication, advisement, announcement, notice, notification, report, specification, observation, designation, acquaintance, enlightenment. **—Ant.** 1 omit, be silent about; forget, neglect, disregard, slight, ignore, drop, suppress. 2 omission, avoidance, neglect, silence, suppression.

mentor *n. The student wrote his thesis under the guidance of his mentor:* adviser, counselor, preceptor; teacher, instructor, professor, tutor; monitor, proctor; master, guru, guide.

mercenary *adj.* **1.** *Does he love his wealthy mother or only pretend to for mercenary reasons?:* selfish, greedy, venal; monetary, money-motivated, for gain, for pay; acquisitive, grasping, avaricious, covetous. *—n.* **2.** *Much of the fighting was done by mercenaries:* hired soldier, paid soldier in a foreign army, soldier fighting for spoils; hireling. **—Ant.** 1 idealistic, selfless, unselfish, altruistic; generous, liberal, philanthropic, benevolent, munificent.

merchandise *n.* **1.** *The store has the best merchandise in town:* manufactured goods, goods, wares, stock, stock in trade; commodities, staples; effects, belongings. *—v.* **2.** *There's no use in manufacturing an item unless you can merchandise it:* sell, market, distribute; trade, deal in, buy and sell, carry on commerce in, do business in, traffic in; advertise, publicize, *Slang* huckster.

merchant *n. He is a widely traveled diamond merchant. Some of the local merchants donated goods for the fair:* salesman, saleswoman, dealer, wholesaler, purchaser, broker, jobber, trader; shopkeeper, retailer, tradesman, tradeswoman, vendor, storekeeper, peddler, hawker, chandler, monger, street vendor.

merciful *adj. Your Honor is accounted a merciful man:* compassionate, humane, exercising mercy, kind, lenient, clement, sparing, sympathetic, forgiving, pitying, kindhearted, softhearted, understanding, feeling, benign, gracious, tender, benificent. **—Ant.** merciless, unfeeling, uncompassionate, cruel, inhumane, hardhearted, pitiless.

merciless *adj. The killer was merciless:* pitiless,

ruthless, unmerciful, inhumane, hardhearted, cold-blooded, inhuman, unrelenting, relentless, remorseless, cruel, fell; harsh, severe, fierce, unsparing, heartless, unpitying, callous, ferocious. **—Ant.** merciful, humane, forgiving, kindhearted, clement, lenient.

mercurial *adj. He is so mercurial he constantly changes his political outlooks:* flighty, impulsive, changeable, inconstant, erratic, fickle, unstable, unpredictable, capricious, volatile, mobile, kinetic, fluctuating, variable, protean, impetuous, lively, electric, spirited, irrepressible. **—Ant.** unchanging, stable, fixed, phlegmatic.

mercy *n.* **1.** *The caretaker showed no mercy to trespassers. He begged the judge's mercy:* compassion, kindness, forbearance, benevolence, pity, clemency, sympathy, humaneness, softheartedness, humanity, tolerance, charity, commiseration, grace, fellow feeling, tenderheartedness, forgiveness, lenity, leniency, lenience. **2.** *What a mercy he escaped the fire!:* good thing, piece of luck, lucky break, blessing. **—Ant.** 1 pitilessness, cruelty, harshness, rigor, severity, sternness, implacability, inhumanity, brutality.

mere *adj. It's a mere trinket:* common, ordinary, inconsiderable, insignificant, trifling, commonplace, mundane, nugatory, paltry, negligible, unappreciable, uneventful; nothing else but, nothing more than, pure and simple, utter, plain, bare; sheer, scant, unmitigated, bald, sole.

meretricious *adj. We determined that his credentials were meretricious:* spurious, specious, bogus, sham, false, tawdry, fraudulent, counterfeit, deceptive, misleading, mock, pseudo, delusive, *Slang* phony, shoddy. **—Ant.** genuine, authentic, bona fide, legitimate.

merge *v. The two failing companies eventually merged:* combine, amalgamate, consolidate, fuse, become one, converge, blend, integrate, join, intermix, coalesce, weld, synthesize, unite, interfuse, interconnect, interlock, confederate, associate, band together, unify, link up. **—Ant.** separate, diverge, sever, part, disjoin, disband.

merger *n. The merger of the companies went smoothly:* alliance, merging, fusion, consolidation, amalgamation, incorporation, combination, union, unification.

meridian *n. At noon the sun is at the meridian:* zenith, acme, peak, summit, pinnacle, apex, top, tip, crest, vertex, apogee, climax, culmination, heights, brow, ridge, crown, point. **—Ant.** nadir, low, depths, bottom.

merit *n.* **1.** *There is great merit in dealing fairly with your employees. She is a person of some merit:* value, worth, worthiness, desert, virtue, advantage, benefit, justification; efficacy, credit, quality, stature, ability, worthiness, excellence, talent, distinction. *—v.* **2.** *The suggestion merits serious consideration:* deserve, be entitled to, rate, be worthy of, have a right to, warrant, invite, prompt, have claim to, earn. **—Ant.** 1 fault, defect, worthlessness, weakness, imperfection, discredit.

meritorious *adj. He was praised for his meritorious service as governor general:* commendable, laudable, praiseworthy, noteworthy, exceptional, deserving of reward or commendation, worthy, creditable, well carried out, estimable, excellent, fine, exemplary, admirable. —**Ant.** unexceptional, unpraiseworthy, unworthy, discreditable, undeserving, dishonest, dishonorable, ignoble, unchivalrous, ungenerous.

merriment *n. You never saw such unbridled merriment at a party!:* mirth, laughter, gaiety, jollity, hilarity, frolic, fun, good fun, good spirits, revelry, glee, sportiveness, amusement, cheer, gleefulness, celebration, joviality, jocularity, lightheartedness, liveliness, jocundity, festivity, merrymaking, levity, good humor, jubilation, skylarking, exhilaration, conviviality, *Informal* whoopee, hoopla. —**Ant.** cheerlessness, joylessness, distress, misery, mourning.

merry *adj. We joined the merry crowd:* gay, jolly, cheerful, happy, cheery, gladsome, blithe, gleeful, jovial, joyous, sportive, carefree, mirthful, jocular, frolicsome, fun-loving, lighthearted, jocund, jolly, lively, high-spirited, partying, laughing, skylarking, festive, convivial, rollicking, animated, vivacious, reveling, sprightly. —**Ant.** sad, unhappy, gloomy, disconsolate, dismal, dejected.

merrymaking *n. The annual picnic was a time of great merrymaking:* gaiety, festivity, revelry, jollity, merriment, revels, conviviality, sport, funmaking, celebration; carousal, bacchanalia, saturnalia; *Slang* whoopee, high jinks, hoopla, whoop-de-doo. —**Ant.** gloom, sorrow, melancholy, woe, sadness.

mesh *n.* **1.** *The net was made of a fine mesh:* web, netting, network, grille, reticulation, openwork, screen, sieve, plexus, webwork, meshwork, grid, webbing, wickerwork, latticework, grillwork, lacework. —*v.* **2.** *The car moved forward as the gears meshed:* engaged, interlock, interweave, enmesh, intermesh, connect, dovetail, fit together, coordinate, interact.

mesmerize *v. They say that Hitler mesmerized his audiences:* spellbind, bewitch, fascinate, magnetize, entrance, transport, charm, enthrall; hypnotize, put in a trance, control another's mind.

mess *n.* **1.** *Pick up that mess of dirty clothes:* clutter, unsightly accumulation, jumble, litter, hodgepodge, confused mass, hash, mishmash, conglomeration; untidy condition, dirty state, disorder, disarray. **2.** *How did you get into a mess like this?:* predicament, difficulty, plight, muddle, mix-up, confusion, pickle, situation, quandary, fix, strait, stew, scrape, pinch, trouble, *Informal* hot water, pretty kettle of fish; dilemma, imbroglio, crisis. **3.** *The fight happened in the enlisted men's mess:* messhall, dining room, refectory, dining hall, commissary, cafeteria.

message *n.* **1.** *I received a message that she would be late:* notice, report, word, statement, news, communication, memorandum, communiqué, intelligence, tidings, dispatch, missive, note, letter, bulletin. **2.** *The play has a serious message:* point, theme, central idea, meaning, purport, moral.

messenger *n. The messenger brought your note today:* carrier, bearer, runner, deliverer, delivery boy, delivery man, courier, go-between, intermediary, emissary, envoy, delegate.

messy *adj.* **1.** *I can't find anything on this messy desk:* disordered, cluttered, untidy, littered, sloppy, chaotic, disarranged, confused, jumbled, topsy-turvy; bedraggled, sloppy, disheveled, unkempt, slatternly, frowsy, blowsy, grubby. **2.** *She found herself in a messy spot:* awkward, difficult, unpleasant, embarrassing, tangled, inextricable, unenviable, ugly, uncomfortable, tricky. —**Ant.** 1 ordered, neat, tidy, clean. 2 pleasant, comfortable, enviable.

metamorphose *v. She metamorphosed into a career woman:* transform, transmogrify, convert, mutate, remake, vary, alter, change.

metamorphosis *n.* **1.** *There are four stages in the metamorphosis of a mosquito:* transformation, change of form, mutation, transmutation, structural evolution, transfiguration, series of changes, modification, conversion, transmogrification. **2.** *This once-confident man underwent a complete metamorphosis after his business failure:* change in appearance or behavior, personality change, transformation, alteration, radical change, startling change, permutation.

metaphor *n. In poetry the rose is often a metaphor for love:* image, representation, figurative expression, poetic equivalent, sensory symbol, figure of speech, simile, trope, metonymy, analogy, parallel, equivalence.

metaphysical *adj.* **1.** *Trying to define God led us to even more metaphysical questions:* philosophical, speculative, abstract, unanswerable, intellectual; ultimate, essential, universal, eternal, fundamental, basic; ontological, cosmological, epistemological, existential; esoteric, mystical. **2.** *Their argument was too metaphysical for me to follow:* abstract, intangible, vague, impalpable, lofty, high-flown, abstruse, oversubtle, recondite, jesuitical, *Slang* far-out. —**Ant.** 1 physical, material, mundane. 2 concrete, tangible, clear, comprehensible, down-to-earth.

mete *v.* Usually **mete out** *The money was meted out only after it had been carefully counted:* allocate, disburse, distribute, dispense, measure out, apportion, administer, deal out, dole out, parcel out, allot, divide, assign.

meteoric *adj. Many a rock singer has enjoyed a meteoric rise to success:* flaming, fleetingly bright, transiently brilliant, fiery, flashing, blazing; rapid, speedy, fast, swift, unabated, sudden, instant; unstoppable, inexorable, ineluctable. —**Ant.** slow, sluggish, gradual, inconspicuous, obscure.

meter *n. The poem had a strict meter:* beat, cadence, rhythm, measure, pattern, swing, feet.

method *n.* **1.** *What guitar method did you study?:* system, technique, procedure, approach, process, way, course, means, scheme, form, routine, usage, program, tack, formula, fashion, modus operandi; style, mode, manner. **2.** *There's a method in his madness:* purpose, plan, design, order, scheme, system, efficacy, viability.

methodical also **methodic** *adj. He is methodical even when he's on vacation:* systematic, deliberate, precise, orderly, well-regulated, exact, tidy, uniform, regular, neat, careful, meticulous; logical, analytical; businesslike. **—Ant.** unmethodical, desultory, random, haphazard, casual, hit-or-miss, confused, disordered, chaotic, jumbled.

meticulous *adj. Our meticulous housekeeper never forgets a thing:* fastidious, scrupulous, exact, exacting, minutely careful, solicitous about details, painstaking, precise, nice, finical, finicky, fussy, particular; punctilious, perfectionist. **—Ant.** careless, inexact, imprecise, sloppy, negligent.

métier *n. The law was his métier for more than 40 years:* vocation, calling, occupation, employment, profession, trade, work, livelihood, job, lifework, craft, specialty, pursuit, business, field, line, area, activity.

mettle *n. The Norsemen had mettle, craftiness, and good ships:* courage, hardy temperament, nerve, spirit, gameness, grit, pluck, valor, backbone, intrepidity, spunk, fearlessness, audacity, fortitude, vigor, bravery, gallantry, vim, enthusiasm, determination, resolution, heroism, derring-do, boldness, temerity, manliness, *Informal* guts.

microbe *n. Doctors who tracked the cause of disease were called microbe hunters:* germ, virus, microscopic organism, microorganism, bacillus, bacterium; (*variously*) parasite, spirochete, streptococcus, staphylococcus, zygote, gamete.

microscopic also **microscopical** *adj.* **1.** *The flu virus is microscopic. You need a microscopic lens to see it:* so small as to be invisible without a microscope, infinitesimal, immeasurably small, atomic; of a microscope. **2.** *I can't read this microscopic print:* very little, tiny, minute, diminutive, imperceptible, extremely small, *Informal* teeny. **—Ant.** 1, 2 large, huge, immense; perceptible; macroscopic.

middle *adj.* **1.** *The middle section of the county is the least populated:* central, mid, midway, halfway, midmost, medial, middlemost, median; intermediate, not extreme, main. *—n.* **2.** *The painters moved the furniture to the middle of the room:* center, midpoint, central part, midst, main part; core, heartland, heart, hub, nucleus. **3.** *She wrapped the scarf around her middle:* waist, midriff, midsection, stomach, belly, *Slang* gut. **4.** *Are you in the middle of something?:* midst, course, process, act, throes. **—Ant.** 1 beginning, end, initial, final, extreme. 2 edge, periphery, outskirts.

middleman *n. The middleman arranged the deal and took a percentage of the profits:* intermediary, agent, broker, go-between, dealer, jobber, distributor, wholesaler, entrepreneur, intercessor, mediator, liaison.

middling *adj. He had only middling success as an architect:* average, ordinary, mediocre, fairish, passable, moderate, moderately good, so-so, fair, unremarkable, medium, just satis-

factory, pretty good, tolerable, indifferent, run-of-the-mill; second-rate, minimal.

midget *n. She's so tall she makes me look like a midget:* dwarf, Lilliputian, pygmy, manikin, *Slang* munchkin, Tom Thumb, hop-o'-my-thumb, homunculus; shrimp, runt, peewee, squirt, small fry, fingerling, half-pint, pipsqueak; puppet, doll. **—Ant.** giant, colossus, monster, titan.

midst *n.* **1.** *They wanted the picnic to be in the midst of the forest:* heart, middle, center, interior, middle part, hub, bosom, thick, depths, deepest part, core, eye. **2.** *She took ill in the midst of the ceremony:* heart, thick, most critical time, most important part, core, nucleus; halfway through, midway in.

mien *n. The president was a man of calm and refined mien:* bearing, air, demeanor, manner, behavior, carriage, presence, deportment, attitude, style, appearance, aspect, countenance, visage, look, feature, semblance, guise, expression.

miff *v. It miffed me that he wouldn't help with the chores:* annoy, provoke, irritate, vex, offend, irk, exasperate, anger, affront, rub the wrong way, rankle, nettle, rile, pique, make one sore, put one off, chafe, raise one's dander. **—Ant.** pacify, soothe, mollify, placate.

miffed *adj. She was miffed at her churlish reception:* offended, insulted, resentful, angry, annoyed, irritated, peeved, nettled, vexed, aggravated, put-out, *Informal* teed off, bugged. **—Ant.** pleased.

might *n. The tank battle was a test of armored might:* power, force, strength, potency, prowess, vigor, puissance, robustness, durability, forcefulness, energy, competence, brawn, toughness, sturdiness, capability, capableness, lustihood, muscle; influence, *Slang* clout. **—Ant.** weakness, inability, feebleness.

mightily *adv.* **1.** *He was mightily angered at his colleagues:* very much, intensely, exceedingly, extremely, greatly, highly, hugely, mighty, surpassingly, decidedly, notably. **2.** *He swung mightily at the ball:* vigorously, energetically, forcefully, forcibly, hard, laboriously, lustily, manfully, powerfully, strenuously, strongly, hard.

mighty *adj.* **1.** *He was a mighty warrior:* powerful, strong, hardy, vigorous, robust, stout, lusty, indomitable, stalwart, sturdy, potent, puissant, overpowering, invincible, forceful, able; courageous, brave, bold, valorous, valiant; strapping, brawny, husky, manful. **2.** *The mighty iceberg came into view:* huge, enormous, of great size, immense, massive, extremely large, titanic, colossal, gigantic, vast, monstrous, majestic, monumental, imposing, prodigious, monolithic, gargantuan, stupendous, towering, Brobdingnagian, elephantine. *—adv.* **3.** *Informal It's a mighty fine morning. That's mighty nice of you:* very, exceedingly, particularly, exceptionally; really, truly. **—Ant.** 1 feeble, weak, impotent. 2 small, tiny, unimposing, negligible, unimpressive.

migrant *adj.* **1.** *The migrant workers were underpaid:* migratory, transient, nomadic, wandering, impermanent, itinerant, mobile, peripatetic, ranging, roving, seasonal, shifting, temporary, transient, travelling, casual. —*n.* **2.** *The migrants sought whatever work they could find:* emigrant, immigrant, itinerant, nomad, transient, wanderer, rover.

migrate *v.* **1.** *When did the Irish migrate to the United States?:* emigrate, immigrate, trek, journey, transplant oneself, relocate, resettle. **2.** *Many birds migrate south every winter:* move, move periodically or seasonally, travel, go elsewhere, depart with others.

mild *adj.* **1.** *Her mild disposition is a marvel in this chaotic office:* gentle, calm, serene, placid, smooth, easygoing, good-tempered, docile, bland, easy, tranquil, moderate, pacific, pleasant, complaisant, forbearing. **2.** *That coat is too heavy for such a mild day:* temperate, moderate, warm, balmy, not extreme, not severe, springlike, summery, pleasant. **3.** *This mild soap won't irritate your skin. Please make my drink a mild one:* not strong, not sharp, soothing, soft, delicate, uninjurious, emollient, not severe, not astringent. —**Ant.** 1–3 harsh, severe. 1 fierce, unkind, unpleasant; stormy, turbulent; piquant, biting, bitter, savage, rough, wild, violent. 2 stormy, intemperate, cold. 3 strong, sharp, astringent, powerful.

milestone *n.* **1.** *The ancient road was dotted with crumbling milestones:* road marker, signpost, milepost. **2.** *Their moving out west proved to be a milestone in her life:* significant event, crucial occurrence, turning point; decisive achievement, memorable moment, jubilee, red-letter day; anniversary.

milieu *n. Gallery openings tend to be part of a snobbish milieu:* environment, culture, ambience, setting, background, backdrop, surroundings, mise-en-scène, element, scene, preferred company.

militant *adj. His political outlook is more militant than conciliatory:* combative, combatant, aggressive, belligerent, contentious, uncompromising, assertive, extreme, defiant, pugnacious, disputatious; engaged in or favoring warfare, warlike, warring, military, paramilitary, fighting, warmongering, bellicose, martial. —**Ant.** moderate, concessive; peaceable, pacific, pacifist, noncombative, nonmilitant.

military *adj.* **1.** *The military might of the superpowers is awesome:* armed, martial, warmaking, combative; defensive. **2.** *The old soldier never lost his military demeanor:* soldierlike, soldierly, strict, well-disciplined, crisp, Spartan, martial; belligerent, warlike. **3.** *He hated all military routine:* regimented, regulated, systematized. —*n.* **4.** *The military took over the government of Greece:* army, armed forces, soldiers, standing army, militia, troops; generals, military establishment.

milksop *n. I've never known what she saw in that milksop:* coward, weakling, mollycoddle, sissy, softy, milquetoast, namby-pamby, pansy, pantywaist, poltroon, mama's boy, baby, mouse, crybaby; wimp, scaredy-cat, fraidy-cat. —**Ant.** he-man, brute, Tarzan, Superman.

milky *adj. The sky was milky:* milk-white, white, whitish, frosted, opalescent, pearly, cloudy, clouded.

mill *v.* **1.** *We watched them mill the grain into flour:* grind, pulverize, crush, reduce to powder, granulate; shape, finish, groove, or polish with a milling tool. **2.** *The crowd was milling around the train station:* roam, meander, wander or converge en masse, move around aimlessly, swarm, teem.

mimic *v.* **1.** *Back in the barracks he would mimic their platoon sergeant:* ape, imitate, take off, impersonate, parrot; mirror, echo, simulate, counterfeit, copy, reproduce. —*n.* **2.** *The boy is an incredible mimic:* imitator, mime, impressionist, aper, copyist, copycat, burlesquer, feigner.

mince *v.* **1.** *Mince the celery for the tuna salad:* dice, chop fine, cut into tiny particles, cut into small pieces, shred, grate. **2.** *I can't stand the way she minces around here:* pose, posture, put on airs, give oneself airs, attitudinize; affect daintiness, affect delicacy, affect primness. **3.** *He is direct and never minces words:* soften, moderate, mitigate, refine, palliate, whitewash, soften one's speech, qualify, be mealymouthed about, hold back, gloss over.

mind *n.* **1.** *Fear of failure was in the back of his mind:* brain, intellect, mental capacity, apprehension, intellectual faculties, brains, thinking instrumentality, gray matter; reason, judgment, reflection, comprehension, understanding, sense, intelligence, rationality, ratiocination, cognition, awareness, perception, percipience. **2.** *The storekeeper behaved as though he had lost his mind:* mental balance, sanity, reason, faculties, rationality, understanding, judgment, sense, *Slang* wits, marbles. **3.** *To my mind he's extremely offensive:* judgment, opinion, point of view, outlook, reaction, response, way of thinking. **4.** *The judge's mind is made up:* opinion, conclusion, consideration, judgment, intent, intention, thought, notion, impression, sentiment, conception, liking, will, propensity, choice, inclination. **5.** *The old scrapbook brought his childhood to mind:* remembrance, memory, consciousness, recall, inward attention, recollection, retrospection, reminiscence, contemplation. **6.** *Spring makes it hard to keep one's mind on work:* attention, concentration, thought, thinking, focus, preoccupation. —*v.* **7.** *Good drivers are always careful to mind the speed limit:* obey, heed, pay attention to, observe, follow, comply with, submit to, bow to, acquiesce to, adhere to, be careful concerning, be wary of, regard, note, be conscious of, take cognizance of, watch, notice, take notice of. **8.** *My son can mind the store for me:* tend, attend to, look after, take care of, take charge of. **9.** *Tell her to mind how she uses that drill:* be cautious, be careful, take care, be wary about, watch. **10.** *I don't mind your being a little late:* dislike, object to, resent, feel offended about, disapprove of, feel inconvenienced by, eschew, look askance at; shrink from, recoil from, turn up the nose at, have an aversion to, abhor, detest, hate.

—**Ant.** 1 body. 2 insanity, irrationality. 7, 8 neglect, overlook, ignore, disregard, dismiss.

mindful *adj. Be mindful of the danger involved:* attentive to, alert to, regardful, cognizant, heedful, conscious, thoughtful, careful, watchful, aware, cautious, observant, alive to, open-eyed to, sensible, wary; taken up with, occupied with, engrossed in, absorbed in, preoccupied with. —**Ant.** mindless, heedless, inattentive, oblivious, unaware, incautious, unobservant, thoughtless.

mindless *adj.* **1.** *His mindless behavior is disturbing:* witless, asinine, stupid, unintelligent, unthinking, nonsensical, obtuse, disregardful, unreasoning, sophomoric, simple-minded, doltish, cretinous, imbecilic, idiotic, insane. **2.** *She is mindless of the feelings of others:* insensitive to, careless, regardless, thoughtless, unattuned, oblivious, heedless, indifferent, apathetic, inconsiderate, indiscriminate, unaware, inattentive, unheeding, neglectful, unobservant. —**Ant.** 1 intelligent, reasoning, thinking, reasonable, sane. 2 mindful, sensitive, considerate, aware, attentive, observant.

mine *n.* **1.** *There was a fire in the coal mine:* pit, excavation, tunnel, shaft, quarry. **2.** *His mine of anecdotes is inexhaustible:* supply, reserve, stock, store, fund, hoard, accumulation, cache, treasure, wealth, abundance. **3.** *An ordnance man tried to detonate the mine:* underground or underwater explosive, booby trap, land mine. —*v.* **4.** *How much ore did the nation mine last year?:* excavate, extract, take from the earth, remove from a mine, scoop out; dig for. **5.** *The soldiers mined the enemy fort:* burrow under, tunnel under, dig under; lay explosives under, booby-trap.

mingle *v.* **1.** *The thousand sounds of the city at night mingle in a curious melody:* blend, mix, intermix, combine, intermingle, merge, commingle, interfuse, coalesce, fuse, unite, interweave, amalgamate, intertwine, intersperse, interlard. **2.** *A good host mingles with his guests:* socialize, join, mix, associate, circulate, consort, intermix, fraternize, *Informal* hobnob, rub shoulders with. —**Ant.** 1 separate, part, divide, dissolve. 2 stay aloof, stay separate, avoid.

miniature *adj. We saw an exhibit of miniature paintings:* small-scale, petite, diminutive, tiny, little, bantam, elfin, pocket-size, Lilliputian, pygmy, minuscule, microcosmic, microscopic. —**Ant.** large, full-size, oversize, enlarged, big, gigantic.

minimal *adj. That loafer does a minimal amount of work:* minimum, least possible, lowest acceptable, smallest permissible, scarcely satisfactory, nominal, unappreciable, token. —**Ant.** maximal, maximum.

minimize *v. She minimized her troubles:* deprecate, depreciate, underestimate, underrate, curtail, decrease, diminish, discount, downplay, lessen, make smaller, prune, reduce, attenuate. —**Ant.** maximize, magnify, enlarge, increase, elevate.

minimum *n.* **1.** *These new floors require a minimum of care:* least possible amount, smallest amount possible, least possible degree, modicum, lowest quantity. —*adj.* **2.** *The mill owners still pay less than the minimum wage:* lowest amount allowed; least, smallest, least possible; basic, base. —**Ant.** 1, 2 maximum, largest, greatest.

minister *n.* **1.** *They resented a minister who brought politics to the pulpit:* clergyman, preacher, pastor, chaplain, cleric, priest, parson, ecclesiastic, padre, father, vicar, reverend, rabbi, abbé, evangelist, revivalist. **2.** *He sold his business to become Minister of Agriculture:* chief government administrator, secretary, cabinet member. —*v.* **3.** *He ministered to his wife's every need:* attend to, be solicitous of, serve, answer, oblige, tend, take care of, accommodate, care for; pander to, cater to. —**Ant.** 1 layman, congregant.

minor *adj.* **1.** *He received only minor injuries:* small, insignificant, slight, light, unimportant, petty, inconsiderable, trivial, paltry, nugatory, trifling, piddling, picayune, inconsequential, lesser, secondary, subordinate. —*n.* **2.** *They can't serve drinks to minors:* child, youngster, teenager, youth, adolescent, *Legal* infant. —**Ant.** 1 major, greater, main, important, significant. 2 adult, elder; grown-up.

minority *n.* **1.** *The minority doesn't have a chance in this election:* smaller portion, less, lesser, smaller amount. **2.** *He will inherit the money when he has passed his minority:* immaturity, adolescence, childhood, boyhood, girlhood, juniority, nonage, youth, *Legal* infancy.

minor-league *adj. Judging from these pictures, I'd say he's a minor-league artist:* bush-league, small-time, insignificant, secondary, second-rate, dinky, lesser, small-fry; inferior, shabby, seedy, common; *Slang* punk, cheesy, tacky. —**Ant.** major-league, topdrawer, first-rate, choice.

minstrel *n.* **1.** *In the Middle Ages there were many wandering minstrels:* troubadour, singer, songster, itinerant musician, bard, poet, player, serenader, entertainer, lyrist; versifier, poetaster. **2.** *The minstrel put on his blackface:* vaudevillian, comedian, singer, dancer, song-and-dance man, end man, blackface, interlocutor.

minute[1] *n.* **1.** *My watch is five minutes slow:* sixty seconds, sixtieth part of an hour. **2.** *This will only take a minute:* moment, second, instant, flash, shake, jiffy, twinkling, wink, trice, a short time, breath. —**Ant.** 2 forever, ages, eons.

minute[2] *adj.* **1.** *The scratch was almost too minute to see:* little, extremely small, imperceptible, tiny, diminutive, infinitesimal, miniature, Lilliputian, fine, scant, microscopic, minikin, petite, *Informal* teeny, wee; slight, negligible, inappreciable, trifling, puny, inconsiderable, insignificant, petty. **2.** *The second doctor made a minute study of the illness:* exhaustive, meticulous, close, detailed, scrupulous, itemized, precise, conscientious, careful, strict, exact. —**Ant.** 1 tremendous, huge, vast, monstrous, great, enormous, grand. 2 general, quick, tentative, rough, superficial.

minutiae n. pl. *He concerns himself with minutiae and not the substance:* trivia, trivialities, minor details, trifles, niceties, bagatelles, odds and ends, subtleties, particulars, particularities, pedantries.

miracle n. **1.** *Only a miracle could save the Children of Israel from Pharaoh's soldiers. Atheists don't believe in miracles:* divine act, supernatural happening; wonder, marvel, prodigy, mystery; portent, sign, omen. **2.** *Picasso's work is a creative miracle:* marvel, wonder, phenomenon, prodigy, sensation, spectacle, masterpiece.

miraculous adj. **1.** *The Revelation of St. John the Divine was a miraculous vision:* divine, supernatural, visionary, wonderful, phenomenal, prodigious, supernormal; wonderworking, thaumaturgical, magical; mysterious, inexplicable. **2.** *The wounded man made a miraculous recovery:* extraordinary, exceptional, remarkable, wonderful, marvelous, spectacular; amazing, astonishing, astounding; unbelievable, incredible; phenomenal, preternatural. **—Ant.** 1, 2 ordinary, normal. 1 human, natural, mundane, of this world. 2 routine, unexceptional, predictable, run-of-the-mill.

mirage n. *The travelers found that the oasis was only a mirage:* optical illusion, illusion, phantasm, unreality, imagined image, fancy, hallucination, delusion, wishful thinking, misconception, fantasy, will-o'-the-wisp, castle in the air.

mire n. **1.** *The wagon was stuck in the mire:* mud, muck, ooze, slime, slush, sludge; quagmire, bog, marsh, fen. *—v.* **2.** *The sudden torrent mired the truck and it couldn't be moved:* bog down, ensnare, enmesh, lock into mud, entangle, halt the progress of. **3.** *The children were mired from head to toe:* spatter, soil, begrime, besmirch, cake, smear, muddy.

mirror n. **1.** *She spends hours admiring herself in the mirror:* reflecting glass, looking glass, glass, cheval glass. **2.** *She is the very mirror of virtue:* model, example, exemplar, paragon, pattern for imitation, standard, epitome, paradigm, image, reflection, copy. *—v.* **3.** *The pond mirrors the surrounding trees:* reflect, show, manifest, image.

mirth n. *Thanksgiving Day combines reverence and mirth:* merriment, amusement, jollity, hilarity, gaiety, joviality, glee, laughter, cheerfulness, good spirits, levity, happiness, jocundity, jocularity, festivity, drollery, merrymaking, playfulness. **—Ant.** sadness, dejection, depression, melancholy, misery, moroseness.

misadventure n. *The poor kid has had one misadventure after another:* mishap, misfortune, reverse, failure, disaster, calamity, catastrophe, unfortunate accident, contretemps, slip, adversity, casualty, debacle, setback, mischance, stroke of ill luck, bad break, infelicity, ill.

misanthropic adj. *His unhappy childhood fostered his misanthropic personality:* antisocial, unfriendly, unsociable, distrustful, unneighborly, inhospitable, morose, unpersonable, cynical, surly, discourteous, unaccommodating, unapproachable, unresponsive, cold, distant. **—Ant.** personable, amiable, amicable, loving, sociable, cordial; humanitarian; philanthropic, charitable.

misapprehend v. *They misapprehended the message:* misinterpret, misread, confuse, misconceive, misconstrue, mistake, misunderstand.

misapprehension n. *We shared a misapprehension about the completion date:* misunderstanding, misconception, miscalculation, misinterpretation, false impression, communication breakdown, misjudgment, mixup, misconstruction, mistake.

misappropriate v. *He was indicted for misappropriating public funds:* misuse, embezzle, defraud, steal, peculate, misapply, channel selfishly, put to a wrong use, abuse, misemploy, bilk, mulct, defalcate, swindle, cheat, purloin, *Informal* dip one's hand into the till.

misbegotten adj. *As an idea it was misbegotten:* illegitimate, baseborn.

misbehave v. *If you misbehave once more you're going home!:* act up, disobey, behave improperly, deport oneself badly, do wrong, transgress, show poor manners, be rebellious, be defiant. **—Ant.** behave, toe the line.

misbehavior n. *Her misbehavior was an embarrassment to her parents:* bad behavior, bad conduct, misconduct, impropriety, delinquency, disrespect, acting up; misdemeanor, offense, dereliction, lapse, transgression, trespass, misdeed, indiscretion, bad manners, impudence; unmanageableness, obstreperousness. **—Ant.** good conduct, discretion, mannerliness.

miscalculate v. *He miscalculated the force of the blow:* misconstrue, misinterpret, misjudge, err, misunderstand, overlook, stumble, blunder.

miscarriage n. **1.** *The miscarriage of our plans was a great blow:* failure, undoing, misfire, failing, unrealization, collapse, nonsuccess, default, nonfulfillment, *Informal* fizzle, botch; washout, frustration, casualty, shipwreck, slip, short-circuiting, going awry. **2.** *His wife had two miscarriages:* premature stillbirth, spontaneous abortion, disruption of pregnancy.

miscellaneous adj. *The thrift shop is filled with miscellaneous goods:* varied, manifold, assorted, mixed, mingled, of mixed character, various, different, heterogeneous, motley, of many categories, diversified, diverse, divers, of every description, sundry. **—Ant.** homogeneous, uniform, identical.

miscellany n. *The little volume is a miscellany of thoughts, quotes, and bits of poetry:* collection, mixture, blend, medley, compilation, anthology, potpourri, mélange, pastiche, omnium-gatherum, gallimaufry, salmagundi, assortment; conglomeration, jumble, hodgepodge, mishmash.

mischance n. *It was my mischance that the car ran off the road:* misfortune, bad luck, unfortunate occurrence, ill luck, ill lot, mishap, adversity, accident, misadventure, infelicity, ill wind.

mischief n. **1.** *The child has a lot of mischief in him:* naughtiness, rascality, devilment, sportiveness, tendency to tease, devilry, deviltry, devil-

ment, prankishness, playfulness, orneriness, roguery, roguishness, shenanigans; capriciousness, willfulness. **2.** *We fear he is up to se-*
rious mischief: wrongdoing, knavery, scheming,
plotting, malice, villainy, wrong, foul play, injury,
evil, depravity.

mischievous *adj.* **1.** *The mischievous boy is*
very appealing: naughty, impish, prankish, teasing, playfully annoying, elfin, elfish, playful, frolicsome, sly, roguish, devilish, sportive, waggish.
2. *Her mischievous interference caused a lot of*
unhappiness: wicked, vicious, spiteful, malicious, malign, malignant, gratuitous, uninvited,
uncalled for, annoying, vexing, injurious, destructive, harmful, pernicious, wicked, noxious,
exacerbating, deleterious, detrimental.

misconception *n. Many people have miscon-*
ceptions about astrology: misapprehension, erroneous idea, mistaken notion, misinterpretation, fallacious notion, error, misunderstanding,
delusion, misconstruction, misjudgment, misinformation, misrepresentation.

misconduct *n. Because of his misconduct, he*
was asked to resign from the club: transgression, wrongdoing, misbehavior, dereliction, malefaction, misprision, impropriety, peccadillo, delinquency, misdeed, misstep, malfeasance,
misdemeanor. **—Ant.** uprightness, morality,
probity, propriety.

misconstrue *v. I'm sorry you misconstrued my*
meaning: misinterpret, take in a wrong sense,
construe wrongly, misreckon, misrender, misapprehend, mistranslate, distort, mistake, misunderstand, misjudge, miscalculate. **—Ant.** understand, apprehend.

miscreant *n. The miscreant never admitted his*
dastardly deed: villain, rascal, knave, scoundrel,
blackguard, evildoer, sinner, wretch, malefactor,
reprobate, lost soul, scamp, scalawag, black
sheep; *Slang* heel, bad egg, bum.

misdeed *n. His misdeeds were the scandal of*
the whole town: transgression, misdemeanor,
sin, offense, misconduct, faux pas, peccadillo,
indiscretion, misbehavior, lapse, slip, wrong,
trespass, violation, infringement, malfeasance,
crime, felony, atrocity, outrage.

misdemeanor *n. She was charged with a mis-*
demeanor: misbehavior, misdeed, transgression, fault, misconduct; offense, trespass.

miser *n. The miser wouldn't contribute a penny:*
pennypincher, stingy person, Scrooge, skinflint,
tightwad, skimper, pinchpenny, niggard,
hoarder, *Informal* piker, *Slang* cheapskate.
—Ant. spendthrift, profligate, spender.

miserable *adj.* **1.** *Their living conditions are*
miserable: wretched, impoverished, very poor,
deplorable, lamentable, sorry, pathetic, unbearable, sordid, mean, shabby, degraded, desperate, scurvy, pitiable, second-rate, beggarly, rubbishy, needy, hapless, feckless, unfortunate,
inferior; contemptible, despicable. **2.** *The loss of*
his dog made him miserable. Her face had a
miserable expression: forlorn, unhappy, heartbroken, woeful, crestfallen, disconsolate,
wretched in mind, doleful, dolorous, brokenhearted, sorrowful, desolate, crushed, woebe-

gone, despondent, dejected, heartsick, down in
the mouth, grieved, mournful, depressed,
cheerless, chapfallen, heavy-laden, sad. **3.** *We*
were disappointed by his miserable perfor-
mance: sorry, deplorable, inept, abysmal, far
from satisfactory, atrocious, appalling, abject;
contemptible, despicable. **—Ant.** 1 comfortable, good, respectable. 2 happy, gay, joyous,
cheerful. 3 admirable, laudable.

miserly *adj. She's so miserly she won't give an-*
ything to anyone: parsimonious, stingy, selfish,
avaricious, mean, tight, tight-fisted, grasping,
scrimping, penurious, pinching, penny-pinching,
frugal, illiberal, closehanded, close-fisted, selfish, ungenerous, greedy, niggardly, near, meager, grudging, mean, cheap. **—Ant.** generous,
unselfish, charitable, extravagant, prodigal, profligate.

misery *n.* **1.** *In North America we were spared*
the real misery of World War II: sorrow, affliction, distress, trouble, suffering, woe, wretchedness, hardship, exaction, ordeal, trial, tribulation, privation, misfortune, catastrophe, disaster,
calamity. **2.** *I can't seem to shake this feeling of*
misery: wretchedness, heartache, desolation,
extreme unhappiness, sorrow, sadness, grief,
suffering, agony, woe, melancholy, distress, anguish, despair, torment, depression, dejection,
despondency. **3.** *The failure of her second mar-*
riage was another misery to her: sorrow, chagrin, regret, blow, curse, *Informal* bitter pill, bad
deal, bad scene, bad news. **—Ant.** 1 luxury,
ease, comfort. 2 happiness, joy, contentment,
pleasure, enjoyment. 3 boon, comfort, benefit.

misfortune *n.* **1.** *At times the 1960's seemed*
to be a decade of misfortune: trouble, bad luck,
hard luck, ill fortune, hard times, calamity, adversity, hardship. **2.** *The quarterback's injury*
was a misfortune for the whole team: blow, calamity, mishap, catastrophe, disaster, unfortunate accident, tribulation, trouble, reverse, affliction, setback, downfall, tragedy, loss, misery,
ruination, casualty, misadventure, piece of bad
luck. **—Ant.** 1 good luck, good fortune. 2
stroke of luck, relief.

misgiving *n.* Usually **misgivings** *We had*
misgivings about flying near mountains in such
weather: anxiety, fear, doubt, mental reservations, apprehension, foreboding, presentiment,
lack of confidence, worry, suspicion, disquiet,
qualm, skepticism, uncertainty, dread, alarm,
mistrust, dubiousness, dubiety, doubtfulness,
second thoughts. **—Ant.** confidence, trust, assurance, certainty.

misguided *adj. He was thoroughly misguided in*
his notions about language teaching: mistaken,
misled, in error, faulty, misdirected, misadvised,
ill-advised, erroneous, led astray, injudicious,
adrift, misinformed, *Informal* on the wrong
scent, on the wrong track, wide of the mark, in
the woods, at sea, off course, indiscreet, unwise,
imprudent.

mishap *n. Try to get through this maneuver*
without one of your typical mishaps: misadventure, mischance, unfortunate accident, disaster,

reverse, casualty, setback, miscarriage, difficulty, misfortune, slip, slipup, botch, snag, fiasco.

mishmash *n. The acting was a mishmash of styles and accents:* hodgepodge, mélange, patchwork, medley, pastiche, miscellany, assemblage, conglomeration, crazy quilt, jumble, mix, muddle, scramble, hash, salmagundi, stew, salad, mixed bag, omnium-gatherum.

misinform *v. She misinformed me about the cost:* mislead, misdirect, misrepresent, give incorrect information to, apprise inaccurately, misguide, deceive, lead astray.

misjudge *v. I misjudged the time the side trip would take. I'm afraid I misjudged her abilities:* miscalculate, estimate incorrectly, judge wrongly, fail to anticipate, misconceive, misapprehend, underestimate, overestimate, misconstrue, misinterpret, exaggerate, understate, misunderstand; judge unfairly, show poor intuition about, mistake, err about.

mislead *v.* **1.** *Morning sunshine misled us into thinking it would be a warm day:* misguide, deceive, misinform, lead into error, misdirect, lead astray. **2.** *I was misled by the confidence man's respectable appearance:* delude, deceive, seduce, beguile, entice, inveigle, take in, take advantage of, victimize, play false, gull, dupe, hoodwink, betray, bamboozle, fool, double-cross, *Informal* lead down the garden path, string along.

mismanage *v. She mismanaged her inheritance and ended up penniless:* botch, mishandle, bungle, spoil, ruin, mess up, mar, make a mess of, make a hash of, monkey-wrench; *Slang* foul up, louse up, screw up, bollix, muff, flub.

misnomer *n. In the military, "gun" is considered a misnomer for "rifle":* unsuitable term, misapplied name, inapplicable title, wrong designation, misusage, solecism, misnaming, wrong nomenclature, malapropism, bastardization, barbarism.

misplace *v.* **1.** *It's pouring and I've misplaced my umbrella:* mislay, lose, lose track of. **2.** *Don't misplace your confidence by trusting that irresponsible man:* place unwisely, entrust wrongly, abuse.

misprint *n. The second-last word was a misprint:* typographical error, erratum, typo.

misrepresent *v. He misrepresented his credentials:* falsify, con, confuse, misreport, cover up, disguise, distort, equivocate, garble, mask, pervert, prevaricate, skew, stretch, twist, warp, belie.

misrepresentation *n.* **1.** *His misrepresentation of the facts caused trouble:* misstatement, distortion, falsification, falsifying, doctoring, adulteration, altering, incorrect picture, twisting, exaggeration. **2.** *The cartoon is a cruel misrepresentation of our prime minister:* bad likeness, wrong impression, poor likeness, incorrect picture, mockery, travesty; burlesque, caricature.

miss[1] *v.* **1.** *The batter missed the ball:* fail to hit, fail to reach, fail to strike; fall short, fail to attain, miss the mark, fly wide, fail to light upon; fail to receive, fail to obtain. **2.** *We missed the start of the movie:* fail to catch, fail to be present at, fail to meet, fail to get; be distracted from, be late for, be absent from. **3.** *He missed his only chance:* let slip, let pass, let go, skip, fail to take advantage of, forego, go without, disregard, pass over, overlook, neglect, surrender, *Informal* blow, muff. **4.** *On Wednesday she missed her deadline:* fail to perform, fail to meet, fail to accomplish. **5.** *When did you first miss the jewels?:* notice the loss of, note the absence of. **6.** *The child misses his mother:* want, long for, pine for, lack, feel the loss of, feel the absence of, yearn for. **7.** *I just missed burning my hand:* avoid, avert, escape. **8.** *I missed what you said because of the noise. He missed my meaning:* fail to perceive, fail to hear, fail to understand, fail to get, fail to see, lose. **9.** *The cleaning man missed the spot on the collar. We missed the turn in the dark:* overlook, pass by, leave out, disregard, neglect, slip up on, pass over, gloss over; bypass, overrun, overshoot. —*n.* **10.** *After three misses he gave up trying to hit the target:* failure, failure to hit, failure to reach, false step, default, error, slip, miscue, blunder; omission, neglect, oversight, delinquency, mistake, loss. —**Ant.** 1 hit, reach, strike, attain, obtain. 2 catch, meet, get, make. 3 seize, grasp, accept. 4 meet, fulfill, accomplish, make. 8 catch, hear, overhear. 10 hit, success.

miss[2] *n. She is a lovely young miss:* unmarried woman, maid, maiden, girl, young lady, mademoiselle, señorita, demoiselle, lass, colleen, lassie, schoolgirl, damsel; woman, lady; old maid, spinster.

misshapen *adj. The misshapen mug was awkward to use:* distorted, deformed, malformed, contorted, warped, misproportioned, disproportionate, ill-formed, crooked, twisted, unshapely, irregular. —**Ant.** shapely, well-formed.

missile *n. The missile hit right on target:* projectile, shell, object or weapon that is thrown or shot; (*variously*) stone, spear, javelin, lance, harpoon, arrow, dart, bullet, ball, shaft; guided missile, rocket.

missing *adj. The missing person later showed up:* absent, not present, omitted, away, disappeared, gone, lacking, left out, lost, mislaid, misplaced, removed, unaccounted for, wanting, astray, short, *Informal* AWOL. —**Ant.** present, accounted for, at hand, available, here, in attendance, on hand.

mission *n.* **1.** *The diplomat was sent on a mission of great secrecy. The mission to blow up the bridge failed:* charge, assignment, undertaking, enterprise, quest, task, commission, mandate, job, purposive military operation. **2.** *The head of the Irish mission is on home leave. Our church mission in Africa needs medicines:* delegation, legation, diplomatic representative, missionary post, ministry. **3.** *He believed that his mission was working with drug addicts:* calling, pursuit, life's object, objective, end, principal task; raison d'être.

missive *n. The missive contained nothing new:*

letter, note, communication, dispatch, message, epistle.

misspent *adj. He regretted especially his misspent youth:* misapplied, wasted, spent foolishly, thrown away, idled away, profitless, squandered; depraved, dissolute, debauched. —**Ant.** productive, fruitful, unwasted, profitable.

misstate *v. He was accused of misstating the facts in the case:* state wrongly, state falsely, misreport, state misleadingly, falsify, misrepresent, misquote, alter, distort, pervert, give a false impression of; garble, confuse, bollix.

misstep *n. The town never forgave her for that one misstep:* error, delinquency, shortcoming, fault, transgression, sin, vice, offense, defect, faux pas, gaffe, indiscretion, lapse, dereliction, breach of etiquette, slip; *Slang* blooper, booboo, goof, foul-up, screw-up, boner.

mist *n.* **1.** *Mist hung over the valley:* cloud, fog, fogbank, haze, smog; soup. **2.** *The future seemed a mist to her:* bewilderment, haze, perplexity, obscurity. —*v.* **3.** *The windshield misted over:* fog, cloud over. —**Ant.** clarity.

mistake *n.* **1.** *Anyone can make a mistake:* error, misstep, wrong action, slip, slipup, boner, blunder, miscalculation, slip of the tongue, gaffe, oversight, faux pas, *Informal* blooper. —*v.* **2.** *Did you mistake the margarine for butter?:* confuse, identify incorrectly, take one for another, wrongly accept, confound, mix up, misidentify. **3.** *Unfortunately she mistook his intentions:* misunderstand, miscalculate, misinterpret, misconstrue, misapprehend, misreckon, misjudge.

mistaken *adj.* **1.** *My belief in his integrity was, alas, mistaken:* wrong, erroneous, in error, false, fallacious, incorrect, inaccurate, faulty, at fault, unfounded, unsound, unjustified, untrue, groundless, ungrounded, illogical. **2.** *She's mistaken about the name of the inn:* in error, making a mistake or misjudgment, deceived, *Informal* at sea, off course, on the wrong scent. —**Ant.** 1 wise, accurate, true, well-advised, sound, logical. 2 correct, accurate, right, logical.

mistreat *v. The general was accused of mistreating prisoners:* maltreat, ill-treat, ill-use, abuse, oppress, persecute, misuse, treat unjustly, harm, harass, wrong, hound, manhandle, mishandle, outrage, brutalize, bully, torment, molest, pervert, violate, assault, injure, harass.

mistress *n.* **1.** *She is the mistress of the manor:* female head, matron, lady, headwoman, housewife, female owner. **2.** *Does his wife know he has a mistress?:* lover, paramour, concubine, doxy, kept woman, inamorata, girlfriend, sweetheart, ladylove. **3.** *"Mistress" is an archaic form of address for "Miss, Mrs., or Ms.":* Madam, Miss, Mrs.

mistrust *n.* **1.** *His mistrust of new ideas is comical:* distrust, skepticism, misgiving, qualm, suspicion, doubt, dubiety, presentiment, leeriness, wariness, chariness, uncertainty, apprehension. —*v.* **2.** *Aunt Alice mistrusted any man who wore a mustache:* distrust, suspect, disbelieve, doubt, have doubts about, question, challenge. —**Ant.** 1 reliance, faith, confidence, trust. 2

trust, rely on, accept, believe, have confidence in.

misty *adj. The park was misty with light rain:* hazy, clouded by mist, vaporous, dewy, foggy, steamy; overcast, murky, cloudy, nebulous, indistinct; filmy, opaque. —**Ant.** clear, unclouded.

misunderstand *v. He was offended only because he misunderstood her meaning:* misconstrue, misinterpret, understand wrongly, take in a wrong sense, misjudge, misconceive, misapprehend, mistake, misreckon, miscalculate, miss the point of, put a false construction on, misread, confuse. —**Ant.** understand, apprehend, perceive.

misunderstanding *n.* **1.** *His misunderstanding of the recipe resulted in a lopsided cake:* misreading, mistake as to meaning, failure to understand, misapprehension, misinterpretation, misconception, false impression, misjudgment, miscomprehension. **2.** *The brothers' heated misunderstanding spoiled the family party:* quarrel, disagreement, dispute, difference, rift, spat, discord, dissension, contretemps, conflict, squabble, altercation, wrangle, *Informal* set-to.

misuse *n.* **1.** *Writing ad copy was a misuse of her creative talent:* misemployment, wrong use, misappropriation, misapplication, waste, improper utilization, ill use; prostitution, perversion, squandering, abuse, desecration, corruption; ill treatment, maltreatment, mistreatment, profanation. —*v.* **2.** *She misuses so many words it seems like a put-on:* use improperly, misapply, use wrongly, misemploy; profane, prostitute, pervert, corrupt, put to wrong use. **3.** *An arrogant man generally misuses his friends:* ill-treat, ill-use, abuse, wrong, mistreat, hurt, harm, take advantage of, exploit, injure, outrage, debase, maltreat. —**Ant.** 3 respect, esteem, honor, cherish, treasure, prize, appreciate.

mitigate *v. There's no way to mitigate the effect of that unfavorable report:* lessen, relieve, moderate, moderate in severity, alleviate, abate in intensity, palliate, soften, assuage, allay, soothe, placate, weaken, mollify, ameliorate, ease, blunt, reduce, lighten, diminish, temper, extenuate. —**Ant.** increase, augment, heighten, enhance, strengthen.

mix *v.* **1.** *Mix flour and water to make paste. He never mixes business with pleasure:* combine, commix, join, put together, blend, unite, incorporate, interfuse, mingle, intermingle, commingle, compound, fuse, intermix, interlard, interweave, intersperse, intertwine, alloy, amalgamate; merge, coalesce. **2.** *Did you mix the cream into the sauce?:* add, admix, put in, include, introduce, incorporate; fold, stir, whip, beat. **3.** *He never mixes with the enlisted men:* fraternize, associate, consort, socialize, hobnob, club, be on intimate terms with, join. —*n.* **4.** *We got good results with this cake mix. The guests seemed an odd mix:* mixture, combination of ingredients; mingling, fusion, assembly.

mixed *adj.* **1.** *They are a people of mixed blood:* mingled, alloyed, composite, combined, put together, fused, blended, inmixed, interwoven; hybrid, mongrel, adulterated, half and half. **2.** *It's a mixed collection:* diversified, variegated, of various kinds, not pure, motley, heterogeneous, miscellaneous, hybrid, conglomerate, made up of different kinds. **3.** *That story shouldn't be told in a mixed crowd:* male-and-female, co-ed, heterogeneous. **4.** *My reaction was mixed:* indecisive, ambivalent, tending both ways, inconclusive, neither here nor there, uncertain, positive and negative. **—Ant.** 1 unmixed, pure, isolated, straight, unblended. 2 unmixed, homogeneous. 3 male, female, homogeneous.

mixture *n. Green is a mixture of blue and yellow. His painting is a grotesque mixture of styles:* intermixture, combination, blend, admixture, union, fusion, amalgamation, adulteration; association, mix, alloy, amalgam, composite, compound, medley, stew, hodgepodge, jumble, hash, salmagundi, mélange, commixture, pastiche, potpourri, mishmash.

mixup *n.* **1.** *I'm late because there was a mixup in the time:* misunderstanding, mistake, miscomprehension, misjudgment, miscalculation, failure in communication; muddle, tangle, confusion. **2.** Informal *Did you hear about the big mixup over at the Four Clover Bar?:* fight, melee, riot; disorder, fracas, imbroglio, mess.

moan *n.* **1.** *The patient's moans kept her roommate awake:* groan, wail, lament, plaint, sob, lamentation. *—v.* **2.** *He moaned when he read the bill:* groan, grumble; bemoan, lament, wail, bewail, keen.

mob *n.* **1.** *The police tried to control the mob:* riotous throng, disorderly crowd, rabble, horde, crush of people, gathering, assembly. **2.** *The politician geared his platform to the mob:* common people, masses, rank and file, hoi polloi, populace, proletariat, plebeians, lower classes, rabble, multitude, *Informal* the great unwashed, herd. **3.** *They say he's a member of the mob:* band or gang of criminals, organized crime, underworld network, syndicate, Mafia. *—v.* **4.** *The kids mobbed the star when he left the theater:* surround noisily, swarm around, flock to, converge on, crowd around excitedly.

mobile *adj.* **1.** *He converted his truck into a mobile snack bar:* movable, portable, transportable, traveling, ambulatory, locomotive, not permanent. **2.** *Americans are historically a restless, mobile people:* moving readily, moving easily, motile, active, kinetic; rootless, wandering, nomadic, footloose. **—Ant.** 2 immobile, immovable, firm, set, steady, permanent.

mobilization *n. He ordered mobilization of the militia:* call-up, call to arms, conscription, muster, levy.

mobilize *v. We may have to mobilize the reserves for the invasion:* muster, call up, summon, activate, assemble for action, make operative, organize, marshal, call to arms, put in motion, tap in emergency. **—Ant.** immobilize, disband, disarm, disorganize, retire.

mock *v.* **1.** *She mocked his awkward marriage proposal:* ridicule, make fun of, scorn, treat with contempt, be contemptuous of, deride, revile, jeer at, taunt, assail with ridicule, spurn, make sport of, laugh at, make game of, scoff at, sneer at, poke fun at; imitate, ape, copy, burlesque, parody, caricature, mimic. **2.** *His irresponsibility mocked my trust in him:* disappoint, frustrate, let down, show up, belie, insult, profane. **—Ant.** 1 praise, honor, laud. 2 fulfill.

mockery *n.* **1.** *Mockery was the only outlet for his jealousy:* ridicule, ridiculing, sarcasm, derision, scoffing, jeering, scorn, contumely, disrespect, raillery; mimicry, contemptuous imitation, burlesque, travesty. **2.** *The disclosure of bribery made a mockery of the contest:* sham, joke, laughingstock, farce; burlesque, travesty.

mode *n.* **1.** *His mode of doing business is offensive to me:* manner, way, fashion, course, method, practice, means, system, rule, approach, procedure, form, process, style, technique. **2.** *She dressed in an old-fashioned mode:* style, custom, fashion, manner, cut, appearance, taste, way, trend, vogue; rage, fad, craze.

model *n.* **1.** *The investors disapproved the model of the proposed shopping center:* replica, miniature representation, prototype, representation, pattern, facsimile, simulacrum, copy, dummy, mock-up. **2.** *The angelic child is a model of perfection:* archetype, paragon, standard, ideal, paradigm, example, exemplar, mirror, pattern, criterion. **3.** *Who was the model for Goya's Olympia? She's a photographic model:* source, subject, real-life version, prototype; mannequin. **4.** *What model is your sewing machine?:* design, style, version, type, variety. *—adj.* **5.** *We looked at the model rooms:* demonstrational, representative, simulated. **6.** *He tries to be a model father:* perfect, worthy of imitation, ideal, exemplary, peerless. *—v.* **7.** *She models herself after her mother:* fashion, form according to a model, create in emulation, mold, give shape to, design, shape, cast, build, outline. **8.** *The children modeled animals with papier mâché:* form, shape, build, fashion, cast, mold, give form to. **9.** *Will you model this coat for Mr. Jones?:* display, show, wear as a demonstration, sport. **—Ant.** 6 imperfect, flawed, unworthy.

moderate *adj.* **1.** *We did only a moderate amount of business today:* average, medium, middling, modest, of medium quantity or extent, ordinary, mediocre, passable, fair; inexpensive, medium-priced. **2.** *His moderate approach to the crisis kept everyone calm:* reasonable, temperate, mild, judicious, rational, not violent, dispassionate, unruffled, gentle, calm, cool, sober, peaceable, measured, careful. *—n.* **3.** *He's a political moderate:* middle-of-the-roader, mainstreamer. *—v.* **4.** *He might get ahead faster if he would moderate his shrill voice:* temper, control, soften, tone down, curb, make less severe, lessen, subdue, tame, abate, diminish, hush, restrain. **5.** *We need someone neutral to moderate the debate:* act as moderator, preside over, act as chairman; regulate, direct, manage, oversee, conduct. **—Ant.** 1 immoderate, excessive, extreme, inordinate, unusual; expensive. 2 unreasonable, extreme, intemperate, hysterical, violent, ruffled, radical, wild. 3 extremist, radical. 4 intensify, heighten, increase.

moderately adv. She praised the document moderately: in moderation, temperately, within limits, within reason, reasonably, somewhat, passably, averagely.

moderation n. Moderation in eating should keep your weight down. The new drug achieved some moderation of the pain: temperance, abstemiousness, restraint, avoidance of extremes, forbearance, continence, economy, temperateness, frugality, self-control, moderateness; abatement, lessening, abating, allaying, alleviation, diminution, relaxation, mitigation, palliation, remission. —**Ant.** excess, intemperance; increase.

modern adj. I'd rather stay in a modern hotel. She collects modern art: new, contemporary, present-day, up-to-date, modernized, modernistic, 20th-century, streamlined, of our time; recent, current, contemporaneous, in vogue, modish, fashionable. —**Ant.** antique, ancient, old, archaic, obsolete, past, antiquated, former, old-fashioned.

modernity n. One is immediately struck by the modernity of Brasilia: up-to-dateness, recentness, modernism, contemporaneity, French dernier cri, last word, latest trend, latest fad, new look, new fashionedness, novelty, newfangledness, vogue, fashion; Slang the rage, the in thing, latest wrinkle. —**Ant.** oldness, obsolescence, staleness, fustiness.

modernize v. The first thing we have to do is modernize the kitchen: renovate, rejuvenate, refurbish, revamp, regenerate, update, streamline, renew, recondition, do over, redo, redesign, restore, bring up to date, make modern, move with the times. —**Ant.** age, wear, outdate, antique, date.

modest adj. 1. Considering how he won the award, he should be modest about it: unassuming, humble, meek, not boastful, unassertive, self-effacing, unpretentious, free from vanity, devoid of egotism, unpretending. 2. She served a modest but tasty meal: simple, plain, unpretentious, unshowy, limited, unostentatious, quiet, unobtrusive. 3. He made only a modest donation: moderate, nominal, not excessive, not extravagant; medium-priced, inexpensive. 4. She's too modest to be seen in a bathing suit: reserved, discreet, bashful, shy, self-conscious, constrained, quiet, timid, demure, coy, diffident, blushing, shrinking, timorous, proper, straitlaced, prim, circumspect, prudish, puritanical. —**Ant.** 1 immodest, vain, boastful, ambitious; showy, pretentious, egotistic, ostentatious, fancy. 3 generous, magnanimous. 4 shameless, brazen, barefaced, impudent; immodest, indecent, indelicate, indecorous, unseemly, improper.

modesty n. 1. I respect modesty, but I don't like coyness: humility, humbleness, freedom from vanity, reserve, self-effacement, lack of

self-importance, lack of boastfulness, restrained behavior, restraint, freedom from presumption, constraint. 2. The modesty of their home belies their great wealth: simplicity, unpretentiousness, plainness, naturalness, lack of ostentation, inexpensiveness, reasonableness. 3. Her modesty kept her from wearing a miniskirt: reserve, bashfulness, shyness, constraint, timidity, demureness, coyness, diffidence, timorousness, reticence, propriety, decency or reserve in dress; prudery. —**Ant.** 1 immodesty, boastfulness, self-conceit, pride, sauciness, arrogance, vanity, confidence, egotism, presumption, vainness, assurance, boldness, haughtiness. 2 extravagance, pretentiousness, showiness, ostentation. 3 immodesty, indecency, forwardness, impropriety.

modicum n. If he had a modicum of intelligence, he'd accept the offer: minimum, drop, jot, fragment, sliver, smidgen, small quantity, mite, bit, pinch, trifle, small amount, dash, little bit, particle, dab, tinge, sprinkling, touch, speck, snatch, fraction, grain, iota, handful, crumb, morsel, whit, atom, scrap, inch.

modify v. 1. They modified their itinerary by eliminating Greece: alter, vary, change, make different, adjust, give a new form to, transform, transmute, convert, refashion, rework, redo, reshape, remold, remodel, reorganize, revise, adapt, transmogrify. 2. You'll have to modify the height of the table to make it fit: reduce, moderate, modulate, temper, restrain, tone down, narrow, lower, remit, soften; qualify, limit, restrict, condition, control, adjust.

modish adj. Clothes that were modish twenty years ago are suddenly back in style: fashionable, chic, stylish, faddish, voguish, smart, current, high-style, a la mode, up-to-the-minute, all the rage; Slang with it, now, trendy, today, in, sharp, nifty, snazzy, spiffy, hot stuff. —**Ant.** passé, old-fashioned, dated, Slang out.

modulate v. 1. Please modulate the sound on the TV: reduce, regulate, turn down, adjust to lesser intensity, tone down, moderate, lower, soften, temper. 2. He modulated his voice when he spoke of the tragedy: change, temper, vary in tune and accentuation, vary the inflection, inflect the voice. 3. In his horn solo, he kept modulating from key to key: shift gradually, pass, progress, shift harmonically, change; attune, accord, harmonize.

mogul n. Samuel Goldwyn was a movie mogul: magnate, tycoon, important person, power, powerful figure, notable, czar, potentate, lord, baron, personage, man of distinction, influential person, Slang big shot, bigwig, big wheel, wheel, VIP.

moil v. 1. They moiled in a mine: work hard, toil, drudge, labor. —n. 2. Work was entirely a moil to him: toil, drudgery, labor. —**Ant.** 2 indolence, laziness.

moist adj. Even the steering wheel was moist after passing through that carwash. Her moist expression belied her indifference: damp, watery, wettish, slightly wet, wet; muggy, humid, dewy, dank, clammy, rainy, drizzly, drippy, dripping, vaporous; tearful, aqueous, misty, lachrymose, wet-eyed. **—Ant.** dry, arid.

moisten v. Moisten the edges of the crust and pinch them together: wet, dampen, moisturize, damp, vaporize, dew, mist, saturate, soak, humidify, water, spray, splash, hose, sponge, irrigate, douche.

moisture n. The sun will take the moisture out of the clothes: dampness, moistness, wetness, damp, wet, wateriness; humidity, mugginess, dankness, dew, evaporation, vapor; perspiration, sweat, exudate; mist, drizzle.

mold[1] n. **1.** I made the mousse in my new copper mold: cast, form, shaper; matrix, die. **2.** I like the angular mold of the sculpture: shape, contour, line, formation, form, structure, frame, construction, cut, conformation, outline, turn, configuration. **3.** Women of her mold are easy to see through: quality, type, ilk, sort, kind, character, stamp, kidney, make, brand. —v. **4.** He molded a rabbit out of clay: model, shape, form, cast, fashion, create, knead, sculpt, figure, construct, pattern. **5.** Higgins tried to mold the cockney girl into an elegant lady: form, fashion, remodel, turn, render, convert, transform, transmute, develop, bring along, train, make, transfigure.

mold[2] n. The bread was covered with green mold: fungus, mildew, blight, rust, lichen.

molest v. That big kid is always molesting the children: bother, harass, vex, annoy, pester, disturb, harry, torment, plague, hector, beset, distress, trouble, fret, irritate, irk, worry, abuse, harm, attack, ill-treat, hurt, assault, injure, maltreat; sexually abuse.

mollify v. Flowers would not mollify her anger: appease, calm, moderate, placate, quell, still, lessen, mitigate, allay, reduce, palliate, conciliate, make less violent, decrease, soften, pacify, soothe, tone down, quiet, lighten, temper, abate, ease, assuage, curb, check, dull, lull, blunt. **—Ant.** exasperate, exacerbate, agitate, stir, increase.

mollycoddle v. **1.** The way they mollycoddle that boy, he'll never grow up: spoil, pamper, overindulge, baby, cater to, cosset, give in to, pet, indulge. —n. **2.** As a child he was a mollycoddle, and he never outgrew it: milquetoast, milksop, sissy, coward, weakling, mama's boy, crybaby; Slang cream puff.

molten adj. The molten lava ran down the mountain: liquefied, melted, smelted, fusible, igneous, magmatic; red-hot.

moment n. **1.** I'll be with you in a moment: minute, instant, twinkling, short period of time, second, jiffy, flash, split second, trice. **2.** At this moment I can't answer your questions: point of time, the present time, instant, particular time, juncture. **3.** Your opinion is of great moment to me: consequence, import, importance, worth, significance, weight, gravity, value, concern, interest, weightiness. **—Ant.** 3 insignificance, unimportance, triviality, inconsequence, unconcern.

momentarily adv. They paused momentarily: temporarily, briefly, shortly.

momentary adj. **1.** It was only a momentary infatuation: temporary, transitory, passing, fleeting, flashing, brief, short, hasty, quick, short-lived, transient, ephemeral, fugitive. **2.** We feared a momentary attack: sudden, imminent, instant, expected at any moment, instantaneous, immediate. **—Ant.** 1 permanent, lengthy, lasting, long-lived.

momentous adj. The conference was a momentous occasion for both countries: important, of great portent, significant, of great consequence, essential, critical, decisive, influential, eventful, fateful, earthshaking, far-reaching, consequential, salient; grave, serious, substantial, ponderous, weighty. **—Ant.** unimportant, insignificant, trivial, trifling, inconsequential.

momentum n. The spinning top was losing momentum: force, impetus, impelling force, energy, moment, property of a body that keeps it in motion, impulse, thrust, push, go, drive, headway, propulsion, velocity, dash, vigor, speed.

monarch n. The monarch was ousted by a military coup: hereditary sovereign, crowned head, majesty, prince; (variously) king, H.R.H., potentate, ruler, emperor, czar, kaiser; pharaoh, shah, khan, chieftain, doge, emir, rajah, (fem.) queen, princess; empress, czarina, kaiserin, rani.

monarchy n. It was first a monarchy, then a republic: kingdom, realm.

monastery n. The monks have vowed never to leave the monastery: place of contemplation, retreat, cloister, convent, abbey, nunnery, priory, friary; community of monks, community of nuns.

monastic adj. The monastic life is unsuitable for the gregarious boy: of monks, of monasteries; contemplative, solitary, monkish, secluded, cloistral, cloistered, unworldly, hermitic, hermitlike, sequestered, celibate, ascetic, recluse, reclusive.

monetary adj. The monetary value of the treasure is staggering. Is he having monetary problems?: in money, pecuniary, financial, budgetary; fiscal, measured or valued in terms of money; sumptuary.

money n. **1.** The money stolen from the bank was never recovered. Beads are used as money in some cultures: currency, cash, funds, revenue, paper money, coin, coinage, specie, hard cash, collateral, proceeds, assets, capital; Informal wherewithal, Slang dough, bread, scratch, greenbacks, long green, bucks; medium of exchange, measure of value, buying power, legal tender, payment. **2.** They live as though they have money: wealth, affluence, financial independence, hereditary wealth, riches, lucrative investments, great income, no financial problems.

moneyed or **monied** adj. That restaurant caters to a very moneyed crowd: wealthy, affluent, rich, prosperous, solvent, well-to-do, well-off, well-heeled, opulent, flush, elegant, Informal flashy, swell, Slang loaded.

moneymaking adj. He engaged in moneymak-

ing ventures: profitable, lucrative, gainful, paying, well-paying, lucrative, remunerative, successful, thriving.

mongrel *adj.* **1.** *The author depicts a nightmarish world of the future populated by mongrel subhumans:* mixed, of mixed breed, half-breed, crossbred, hybrid; bastard, anomalous. —*n.* **2.** *The little mongrel is the smartest of all the puppies:* mutt, cur, an animal of mixed breed, hybrid, half-breed, offshoot, crossbreed. —**Ant.** 1, 2 purebred, thoroughbred. 1 pedigreed.

moniker *n.* *She never liked the moniker Thelma and called herself "Tee":* name, appellation, designation, given name, surname, nickname, sobriquet, cognomen, title, epithet, denomination, eponym, taxonomy; *Slang* tag, label, handle.

monitor *n.* **1.** *Mary served as monitor at the College Board exams:* proctor, disciplinarian, overseer, stand-in, *Informal* watchdog. **2.** *I watched the program on the director's monitor:* television set, studio television receiver, TV set, TV, scanner, pickup, screen; warning device, sensor. —*v.* **3.** *He monitored the whole TV debate to be sure the contestants got equal coverage:* watch attentively, observe critically; censor. **4.** *I'm monitoring the class during the math exam:* supervise, oversee, tend, take charge of, teach, guide, direct; police.

monk *n.* *He gave up a lucrative business career to become a monk:* brother, holy man, religious recluse, friar, abbé, abbot, monastic; hermit, recluse, anchorite, cenobite.

monkey *n.* **1.** *The zoo has a little monkey that looks almost human:* primate, ape, simian, baboon. **2.** *He made a monkey of me on the tennis court:* fool, dupe, ass, laughingstock, butt, clown, buffoon, *Slang* jerk. —*v.* **3.** *I monkeyed with the pinball machine until I broke it:* meddle, toy, tamper, trifle, fool, fiddle, play around, dicker around; tinker, jimmy.

monologue or **monolog** *n.* *We had to listen for an hour to a veritable monologue about her wonderful grandchild:* soliloquy, speech, oration, discourse, holding forth, address, lecture, expatiation, disquisition; sermon, screed. —**Ant.** dialogue, conversation.

monopolize *v.* **1.** *The government forbade them to monopolize the textile industry:* control, regulate, dominate, manage, have a monopoly of, obtain exclusive possession of, corner, cartelize, appropriate, own, absorb, take over, consume. **2.** *The hostess thoroughly monopolized the guest's time:* appropriate, dominate, arrogate, take up, take advantage of, preempt. —**Ant.** 2 share, divide.

monopoly *n.* *Gradually he achieved a monopoly over the entire industry:* exclusive possession, dominion, corner, trust, cartel, consortium, syndicate, ownership, copyright, proprietorship, control, domination, jurisdiction, combine, bloc, sovereignty.

monotonous *adj.* **1.** *They'll diversify his job to make it less monotonous:* unvaried, boring, dull, dreary, humdrum, repetitious, flat, colorless, tedious, tiresome, wearisome, prosaic, pe-

destrian, routine, mundane, uninteresting, banal, dry, stodgy, routine, jejune, plodding, insipid. **2.** *The preacher's monotonous voice put me to sleep:* without inflection, with a narrow range, droning, singsong, toneless, flat, soporific, somniferous, dull, torpid. —**Ant.** 1 varied, diversified, interesting.

monotony *n.* *The monotony of the work was almost unbearable:* tedium, humdrum, monotonousness, dullness, ennui, boredom, predictability, flatness, sameness, dreariness, tediousness, rut, wearisomeness, redundancy, iteration, reiteration, prosaism. —**Ant.** variety, innovation, excitement, diversity, stimulation.

monster *n.* **1.** *This two-headed calf is a real monster:* deviant, variant, freak, freak of nature, *Latin* lusus naturae; phenomenon, anomaly, curiosity, oddity, wonder, marvel; miscreation, abnormality, monstrosity. **2.** *The Medusa is my favorite monster:* mythical or legendary being, semihuman creature; (*variously*) Chimera, Gorgon, dragon, gargoyle, Hydra, incubus, succubus, mermaid, satyr, Harpy, Fury, centaur; bogeyman, zombie, vampire, Frankenstein, werewolf, Jekyll and Hyde, golem, ghoul. **3.** *In the wrong hands freedom can become a monster:* dangerous creation, destructive force, uncontrollable force, threat. **4.** *The assassins of the two princes must have been monsters:* fiend, demon, devil, beast, brute, wretch, villain, scoundrel, cutthroat, savage, barbarian, blackguard, caitiff. **5.** *Believe it or not, this 90-pound monster was supposed to be a toy poodle:* giant, mammoth, titan, colossus. —**Ant.** 1 commonplace, everyday thing, routine thing. 3 boon, blessing. 4 paragon, saint. 5 dwarf, midget, pygmy, shrimp, runt, pipsqueak.

monstrous *adj.* **1.** *Two monstrous sharks crossed the bow of the boat:* huge, enormous, immense, gigantic, mighty, gargantuan, giant, titanic, tremendous, colossal, mammoth, hulking, stupendous, prodigious, Brobdingnagian; ghastly, revolting, gruesome, grisly, hideous, horrible. **2.** *What a monstrous lie!:* outrageous, cruel, vicious, flagrant, egregious, fiendish, heinous, evil, harried, obscene, villainous, nefarious, odious, atrocious, satanic, diabolical, shocking, scandalous; outright, obvious, bald.

monument *n.* **1.** *That statue is a monument to our war dead. His writings are a monument to the struggle of his people:* memorial, testament, testimonial, remembrance, memento, witness, token, commemoration, reminder. **2.** *A monument was placed over the grave:* memorial, shrine; tombstone, gravestone, obelisk, cenotaph, monolith, slab.

monumental *adj.* **1.** *The Great Sphinx is a fascinating example of Egyptian monumental art:* monolithic, cyclopean; statuary; gigantic, colossal, massive, heavy, huge, larger than life. **2.** *Lincoln's monumental Gettysburg Address will always live:* historic, epoch-making, classic, immortal, enduring, memorable, lasting, epochal, awesome, stupendous, unprecedented. **3.** *Speaking down to the people was a monumental mistake:* egregious, colossal, immense, decisive, inestimable; fatal, horrendous, catastrophic, shattering, mind-boggling. —**Ant.** 1 small, tiny, delicate, dainty, light, miniature. 2 unimportant, insignificant, petty, worthless; everyday, ephemeral.

mooch *v. The cat mooched some tuna from us:* beg, scrounge, cadge, panhandle, hit up, bum.

mood *n. This balmy weather puts me in a cheerful mood. I'm just in one of my moods:* humor, disposition, state of mind, temper, temperament, frame of mind, mental state, feeling, condition, spirit, emotional state, predisposition; state of dejection, depression, melancholia, melancholy, gloominess, bad spirits, doldrums, *Informal* dumps, blues; state of irritation, vexation, hypersensitivity.

moody *adj.* **1.** *Such a moody person can depress everyone:* melancholy, dejected, gloomy, pessimistic, lugubrious, despondent, saturnine, morose, morbid, dismal, brooding, mopish, unhappy, *Slang* down-in-the-mouth; mean, irritable, irascible, sulky, ill-humored, sullen, testy, surly, peevish, crabby, temperamental. **2.** *I'm too moody to know what I'll feel like doing next week:* changeable, fickle, variable, unpredictable, inconstant, inconsistent, flighty, notional, mercurial, temperamental, capricious, volatile, erratic, whimsical, impetuous, impulsive. —**Ant.** 1 happy, joyful, cheerful; amiable, personable, compatible. 2 stable, constant, consistent, steady.

moonstruck *adj.* **1.** *The moonstruck girl loved to read magazines:* romantic, starry-eyed, moony, sentimental, mushy. **2.** *The moonstruck peasants yielded to every superstition:* unbalanced, touched, daft. —**Ant.** 1 down-to-earth.

moor[1] *v. Let's moor at the next dock for the night. They moor the aircraft to the deck with cables:* tie up, dock, anchor, berth, secure; fix firmly, affix, fasten, tether, chain, anchor, tie down, attach, make fast, lash. —**Ant.** untie, unfasten, cast off, set adrift.

moor[2] *Hounds pursued the escaped convict across the moor:* moorland, wasteland, heath, wold, down, fell, upland, tundra, steppe, savanna; marsh, fen.

moot *adj. Whether life exists on other planets is a moot question:* debatable, questionable, unsettled, subject to argument, disputed, disputable, arguable, problematical, undecided, unresolved, open, controvertible, conjectural, controversial, eristic. —**Ant.** indisputable, self-evident, axiomatic.

mope *v. Stop moping and perk up!:* sulk, languish, be dejected, fret, worry, be gloomy, brood, pine, repine, lament, grieve, be downcast, pout, wear a long face, grouse, grumble.

moral *adj.* **1.** *He was asked to give his legal opinion, not to make a moral judgment:* ethical, of right and wrong, of proper conduct, personal. **2.** *It was not exactly moral for a practicing attorney to offer a bribe:* ethical, right, proper, virtuous, honorable, noble, estimable, meritorious, principled, just, fair, aboveboard; pure, honest, high-minded, saintly. **3.** *By declaring him sane, the jury implied that he had a moral sense:* eth-

ical, able to distinguish between right and wrong, conscionable. **4.** *He turns every subject into a moral discussion:* of morals, didactic, sermonizing, homiletic, preaching, moralizing, tendentious. —*n.* **5.** *Every story he tells has a moral:* lesson, message, tag, moral teaching; saying, proverb, maxim, adage, epigram, aphorism, motto. —**Ant.** 2 immoral, unmoral, amoral, wrong, sinful, unjust, unfair, dishonest, unethical, improper, dishonorable, unprincipled.

morale *n. The team's morale is on the rise:* spirit, disposition, mental attitude, mood, temper, level of optimism, moral strength, confidence, self-confidence, self-assurance, resolution, esprit de corps.

morality *n.* **1.** *I'm not concerned with the morality of the question:* ethical values, ethics, right or wrong. **2.** *It's obvious from his ruthless behavior that he has no morality:* goodness, righteousness, virtue, rectitude, honor, uprightness, fairness, probity, integrity; code of ethics, ethical philosophy, set of values. **3.** *Her private morality is her own business:* sexual behavior, habits, chasteness, modesty, tastes. —**Ant.** 2 immorality, wickedness, dishonor.

morals *n. pl. They had deplorable morals:* ethics, ethic, principles, ideals, scruples, standards; beliefs, mores.

morass *n. I'll have to wade through that morass to find the ball:* marsh, wetlands, slough, bog, quicksand, quagmire, swamp, mire, fen.

morbid *adj. Cheer up, and don't be so morbid! His love of cemeteries is morbid:* depressed, gloomy, glum, sad, morose, brooding, self-absorbed, dour, saturnine, moody, melancholic, lugubrious, despondent, somber, grim, pessimistic; unwholesome, preoccupied with death, suggesting an unhealthy mental state. —**Ant.** cheerful, optimistic, vital, life-centered.

mordant *adj. The critic used all his mordant wit in reviewing the play:* cutting, stinging, biting, incisive, sarcastic, acerbic, bitter, caustic, waspish, venomous, acrimonious, scornful, trenchant, scathing, piercing, virulent, malicious, acidulous. —**Ant.** soothing, pacifying, charitable; bland, innocuous.

more *adj.* **1.** *I have more cookies if we need them:* extra, additional, other, added, supplemental, supplementary, further; spare, reserve. —*adv.* **2.** *He is more energetic than his sister:* to a greater extent or degree. **3.** *If I have to work more tonight, I'll collapse:* further, longer, additionally. —**Ant.** 1, 2 less. 1 fewer.

moreover *adv. Bicycling is good exercise; moreover, it doesn't pollute the air:* further, besides, also, more than that, what's more, furthermore, too, in addition.

mores *n. It's wise to remember that other countries have other mores:* customs, conventions, practices, standards, traditions, observances, code, usages, rules, rituals, forms, ethos, morals, etiquette, morality, proprieties.

moribund *adj. Many of the early customs were moribund by the turn of the century:* dying, doomed, waning, stagnating, dying out, near death, fading out, phasing out, on its last legs.

morning n. **1.** I found it difficult to get up in the morning: morn, daybreak, dawn, sunrise, break of day, daylight, sunup, crack of dawn. **2.** He'll deliver the groceries some time this morning: forenoon, before 12 noon. —adj. **3.** We have a very light morning meal: matutinal, early, of the morning, forenoon. —**Ant.** 1, 2 afternoon, evening; dusk, sunset.

moron n. What a moron I was to let that bargain slip away!: fool, dope, ass, simpleton, nit-wit, ninny, dunce, dumbhead, dummy, loony, dolt, nut, oaf, numskull, idiot, dimwit, imbecile, half-wit, muttonhead, bonehead, blockhead, dumbbell, nincompoop, boob, sap, jackass. —**Ant.** genius, brain, mastermind, wizard, whiz.

morose adj. I feel very morose after reading that sad story: depressed, low, crestfallen, sad, melancholy, downcast, moody, glum, dour, Informal blue, down in the dumps; saturnine, mopish, gloomy, despondent, mournful, solemn; sullen, sulky, cross, surly, testy, waspish, sour, churlish, grumpy, cranky, ill-tempered, irascible. —**Ant.** cheerful, blithe, happy, good-natured, pleasant, genial, amiable, friendly.

morsel n. You must taste just a morsel of this cake: nibble, tidbit, taste, bite, swallow, crumb, snack, sliver, sip, piece, nip, drop, small amount, dollop, mouthful; bit, scrap, touch, speck, little piece, segment, scintilla, trace, whit, modicum, fragment, iota, particle, fraction, grain, drop.

mortal adj. **1.** Desire, like all things mortal, passes swiftly: human, earthly, corporeal, mundane; fleeting, ephemeral, temporal, transitory. **2.** He received a mortal blow: fatal, lethal, deadly, causing death. **3.** We were in mortal terror of being found out: extreme, severe, intense, enormous, deep, grave, unimaginable, living. —n. **4.** He was a strange and lonely mortal: human being, person, creature, individual, Informal type, character. —**Ant.** 1 immortal, undying, everlasting, eternal, divine, perennial.

mortality n. **1.** Man's mortality is all too obvious in time of war: transience, impermanence, evanescence, ephemeral, transitoriness. **2.** The mortality from the earthquake was devastating: human loss, loss of life, slaughter, fatality, extermination, carnage, bloodshed, death toll. —**Ant.** 1 immortality, permanence; divinity.

mortify v. **1.** Forgetting the introductory remarks really mortified me: shame, horrify, embarrass, appall, chagrin, discomfit, abash, disconcert, make red-faced. **2.** It is good for the soul to mortify oneself periodically: deny, discipline, self-discipline, be abstinent, practice continence, practice rigorous austerities; fast, do penance. **3.** The wound will mortify without care: become gangrenous, fester, rot, decay, putrefy; make rotten, cause to decay. —**Ant.** 1 gratify, satisfy, make confident, make proud. 2 indulge, satisfy.

most adj. **1.** Of the three girls, Susan has the most freckles: the greatest in number, degree, or quantity; maximum; in the majority. —n. **2.** Give the winner the most: largest amount, maximum; the majority. —adv. **3.** That's the most

beautiful cake I ever saw: in the greatest degree, extremely, to the greatest extent, very, in the highest degree, best.

mostly adv. The guests are mostly friends of the bride: primarily, chiefly, for the most part, predominantly, largely, mainly; especially, above all, specially, particularly, principally; as a rule, most often, generally, more or less, greatly.

mother n. **1.** A mother can be a girl's best friend: female parent, Informal mom, mama, momma, mommy, mum, mummy, mums, old lady, British mater. **2.** Necessity is the mother of invention: origin, source, wellspring, stimulus, inspiration. —v. **3.** She mothered two children and adopted a third: bear, give birth to, bring forth, beget, produce, conceive, breed. **4.** She mothers her plants as she does her children: care for, rear, raise, tend, mind, nurse, nurture, protect, indulge.

motherly adj. The sergeant is almost motherly to the young recruits: maternal, parental, tender, kind, loving, gentle, sheltering, protective, indulgent, devoted. —**Ant.** unmaternal, unkind, unloving.

motif n. My apartment will have a French Provincial motif: style, theme, artistic theme, topic, subject, treatment, idea, shape, form, design, pattern, figure; refrain, thread.

motion n. **1.** Put the engine in motion. He was enthralled by the water's ceaseless motion: movement, mobility, motility, act of moving, kinesis; drift, passage, stir, flow, stream, flux, progress, action. **2.** What's the proper motion for a left turn?: gesture, signal, sign, move, action, bodily movement, gesticulation, indication, cue. **3.** I made a motion to dispense with the minutes of the last meeting: formal proposal, suggestion, request, proposition, recommendation. —v. **4.** He motioned us to our seats: signal, beckon, nod, gesture, gesticulate. —**Ant.** 1 rest, repose, stillness, immobility; quiet, quiescence, stasis.

motionless adj. When the curtain rises, the dancers are motionless: still, stationary, inert, without motion, immobile, immovable, immobilized, unmoving, quiescent, calm, at rest, fixed, static, at a standstill, stable, tranquil, inactive, static; transfixed, riveted to the spot, frozen; lifeless, unresponsive, idle, dead. —**Ant.** mobile, active, alive.

motivate v. What motivated her to give up her career?: impel, induce, stimulate, stir, activate, move, arouse, provoke, influence, goad, prompt, persuade, actuate, stir up; Slang egg on, turn on, light a fire under. —**Ant.** discourage, dissuade, daunt, disincline.

motivation n. His motivation was so strong that we doubted he could fail: motive, reason, impulse, impetus, cause, driving force, impulsion, causation, provocation.

motive n. What was his motive for committing the crime?: reason, purpose, object, cause, motivation, intention, occasion, design, thinking, grounds, rationale; inducement, incentive, provocation, enticement, stimulus, prompting, instigation, spur, incitement, inspiration; goal, aim, end.

motley adj. **1.** It's amazing how well such a motley group got along: varied, different, heterogeneous, disparate, composite, mixed, assorted, miscellaneous, variegated, sundry, diversified, unlike, incongruous, dissimilar, divergent, hybrid. **2.** I'm covering my sofa with a beautiful motley fabric: of different colors, varicolored, checkered, multicolored, polychrome, dappled, pied, piebald, particolored, speckled, watered, tabby, brindled, kaleidoscopic, mottled, iridescent, harlequin. —n. **3.** The dancers wore motley: varied colors, patchwork, rainbow pattern; clown's costume, jester or buffoon's garish apparel, clownish trappings. —**Ant.** 1 uniform, homogeneous, identical, like, similar. 2 monochromatic, solid, plain. 3 monochrome.

mottled adj. The draperies are a mottled fabric of yellow, green, and pink: motley, particolored, variegated, multicolor, piebald, polychromatic, iridescent, kaleidoscopic, pied, varicolored, flecked, brindled, blotchy, specked, speckled, stippled, tabby.

motto n. The motto of the state is "Let justice be served": slogan, watchword, maxim, proverb, precept, byword, rule, principle, saw, aphorism, saying, adage, catchword, dictum, axiom, proverb, mot, epigram, truism.

mound n. **1.** The archaeologist excavated an ancient burial mound: pile, rampart, ridge, entrenchment, embankment, bulwark, earthwork; rick, stack, heap. **2.** Only a jeep could handle the mounds on that terrain: knoll, hillock, hill, dune, mount, hummock, mogul, bump. —**Ant.** 2 dip, valley, dell, sinkhole.

mount v. **1.** You'll have to mount the ladder to reach the top shelf: ascend, climb, go up, climb up, scale, get over, climb over. **2.** The death toll mounted for days after the fire: rise, ascend, go up, increase, intensify, grow, soar, swell, surge, wax, multiply, augment. **3.** The Arab mounted the camel and rode away: climb up on, get astride, get upon, straddle. **4.** The navy mounted 8-inch guns on its warships. He mounted the diamond in a platinum setting: install, fit, equip, outfit, rig, fit out; put in position on, set into, affix, frame, fix, set, set off. —n. **5.** He urged his mount on: riding animal; horse, saddle horse, steed, charger; (variously) pony, elephant, camel. —**Ant.** 1 drop, descend. 2 fall, decline, lessen, decrease, diminish. 3 dismount.

mountain n. The north face of the mountain was scaled for the first time: peak, massif, natural elevation of the earth's surface, eminence, very high hill, elevation, height, range, highland, butte, bluff, ridge, mount, alp; volcano.

mountebank n. **1.** The miracle remedy that mountebank sold me was colored water: quack, quacksalver, medicine man, huckster. **2.** The investors were taken in by a clever mountebank: confidence man, charlatan, fraud, swindler, cheat, humbug, sharper, con artist, con man, hustler, operator, flimflam man, Informal phony.

mourn v. **1.** She's still mourning his death after all these years: grieve, grieve for, express grief, lament, weep over, despair, sorrow, be sorrowful, bewail, wail, pine, languish, cry, wail, sob, weep, keen. **2.** I really mourn the loss of that old sweater: regret, rue, deplore, bemoan. —**Ant.** 1 rejoice, exult, laugh, triumph.

mourning n. **1.** Mourning is an emotional catharsis for the survivors: grief, woe, grieving, lamentation, lamenting, dolor, bereavement, sorrow, sorrowing, anguish, despair; period of mourning. **2.** He wore mourning for his deceased wife: weeds, crape, black, black apparel. —**Ant.** 1 rejoicing, celebration, merrymaking.

mousy adj. She's so mousy she's terrified of meeting strangers: timid, shy, fearful, bashful, timorous, withdrawn, self-effacing, self-conscious; dull, colorless, drab; unobtrusive, inconspicuous, unnoticed; Slang wimpy. —**Ant.** brazen, brassy, conspicuous, flamboyant, self-assertive.

mouth n. **1.** Open your mouth and close your eyes: oral opening, jaws, oral cavity, facial orifice. **2.** The mouth of the jar was chipped: opening, aperture, lips, bell. **3.** The regatta was held at the mouth of the Cooper River: inlet, bay, estuary, place where a river flows into another body of water, outlet, portal, wide opening, jaws. —v. **4.** All he does is mouth pompous truisms. She mouthed the words as the record played: pronounce, speak, declare, say, voice, propound; feign speech, feign singing, shape words, lip-synchronize.

movable adj. Everything in the house was movable: portable, mobile, ambulatory, conveyable, shiftable, transportable, removable, separable, transferable, adjustable.

move v. **1.** Please move out of the way: shift, stir, budge, change position, locomote, change place, proceed, advance, go; transpose, carry, pass, remove, transport, switch, bear, convey, transmit. **2.** She just moved here at the beginning of the term: transfer, relocate, change residence, change one's abode, shift, transplant. **3.** The clock doesn't move: go, have motion, function, operate. **4.** Curiosity moved me to open the box: cause, influence, induce, lead, impel, get, prompt, incite, drive, inspire, provoke, persuade, stimulate, motivate. **5.** I was truly moved by his tears: touch, affect; arouse, rouse, excite, stir, sway, interest, impress, impassion, fire, strike. **6.** I move that we accept the proposal: propose, suggest, recommend, request, ask, urge, exhort, plead. **7.** Let's move before it's too late: get started, start off, go, go ahead, begin; strike, attack. —n. **8.** One move and I'll shoot!: movement, motion, gesture, stirring, budging. **9.** Selling your car was a good move: action, deed, act, maneuver, ploy, measure, stroke, step. **10.** It's your move: turn, opportunity, Informal go. —**Ant.** 1 stop, stay, arrest. 4 prevent. 5 untouched, unmoved, unimpressed.

movement n. **1.** The room shakes with his every movement: motion, change of position, locomotion, stirring, progress, agitation, action. **2.** His movement was not in time with the music: bodily rhythm, motion, steps, gestures, execution. **3.** *The army's movements were kept secret:* activity, operation, maneuver. **4.** *We're starting a movement to clean up the city:* drive, crusade, undertaking, program, measure, effort. **5.** *The first movement of Beethoven's Fifth Symphony is familiar to most music lovers:* section, part, division. **6.** *This watch has a 21-jewel movement:* mechanism, action, works. —**Ant.** 1 inertia, stasis, quiescence.

movie *n. That movie is now being shown on TV:* motion picture, film, cinema, screening, moving picture, show, showing, picture show, picture, feature, *Slang* flick.

moving *adj.* **1.** *It has no moving parts:* movable, capable of moving, mobile, motile, interacting; motor, locomotive. **2.** *What's the moving force behind the team?:* motivating, spurring, inspiring, stimulating. **3.** *The song was so moving it made me cry:* touching, heart-rending, exciting, affecting, stirring, impressive, poignant. —**Ant.** 1 stationary, immobile, unmoving, still. 3 unaffecting, unexciting, unimpressive.

moxie *n. After all these years Al is still full of the old moxie:* guts, spunk, grit, sand, pluck, courage, dauntlessness, nerve, spirit, mettle, backbone, stamina, hardihood, pluckiness, toughness, audacity. —**Ant.** timidity, cowardliness, faintheartedness.

much *adj.* **1.** *We have much work ahead of us:* abundant, ample, plenteous, sufficient, considerable, appreciable, copious, plentiful, plenty of, a lot of. **2.** *In spite of all the publicity, the film's not much:* important, impressive, worthwhile, consequential, noteworthy, striking, satisfying. —*n.* **3.** *He doesn't think I've done much:* appreciable amount, great deal, good deal, sufficiency, quantity; lots, loads, heaps, scores. —*adv.* **4.** *The professor is much revered:* greatly, decidedly, indeed, to a great degree, far; excessively, overly, exceedingly. **5.** *He looks much the same as you:* somewhat, rather, nearly, approximately, about, almost. **6.** *Do you go there much?:* often, frequently, regularly, many times, oftentimes, a lot. —**Ant.** 1 little, small, scarce, few. 1, 3 little. 2 unimportant, inconsequential, trifling, unsatisfying.

muck *n. The pipes beneath the sink were clogged with muck:* mud, dirt, filth, dung, sewage, slop, garbage, slime, sludge, mire, ooze, compost, *Informal* guck, gunk.

mud *n. He knocked the mud off his boots:* muck, mire, ooze.

muddle *v.* **1.** *I muddled the recipe and had to begin again:* confuse, mix up, ruin, botch, bungle, blunder, mess up, spoil, fumble, *Informal* muff; *Slang* blow, goof up. **2.** *The drug muddled me so much I forgot where I was:* stupefy, mentally confuse, mix up, nonplus, daze, throw, confound, rattle, bewilder, boggle; act confusedly. —*n.* **3.** *He's in too much of a muddle to be of any help. Her affairs are in a terrible muddle:* confused state, disconcertion, pother, haze, fog, daze; jumble, mess, disorder, disarray, chaos, disarrangement, clutter.

muffle *v.* **1.** *Don't forget to muffle yourself against the cold:* wrap, cloak, swaddle, swathe, cover, enclose, conceal, mask, veil, envelop, shroud, gag. **2.** *The interrogator muffled the prisoner's screams with a gag:* suppress, stifle, cut off, silence, block off, blot out, quiet, hush, still, mute, quell, dull, deaden, dampen, soften.

muffled *adj. A muffled sound came through the wall:* dull, deadened, muted, stifled, subdued, strangled, suppressed, dampened.

mug *n.* **1.** *Give the baby a mug of milk:* cup, tankard, tumbler, toby, toby jug, chalice, beaker, stoup, stein, goblet, flagon. **2.** *Slang He has an ugly mug:* face, visage, countenance, kisser, puss.

muggy *adj. This muggy weather irritates my sinuses:* humid, clammy, sultry, vaporous, steaming, steamy, oppressive, stuffy, sweaty, sticky, close, sweltering.

mule *n. The miner used a mule to carry his equipment:* half donkey-half mare; (*loosely*) ass, burro, donkey, jackass.

mull *v.* Usually **mull over** *I'll mull over your proposal and let you know:* ponder, pore over, consider, reflect on, deliberate, think about for a while, give thought to, study, meditate, weigh, ruminate.

multicolored also **multicolor** *adj. The stained glass was multicolored:* polychrome, varicolored, kaleidoscopic, particoloured, prismatic, iridescent, opalescent.

multifarious *adj. My multifarious duties make my work interesting:* varied, diverse, different, diversified, various, divers, variegated, manifold, multiform, motley, miscellaneous, multiplex, protean, sundry, heterogeneous, of many kinds, mixed, numerous, many, several.

multiple *adj. His actions took multiple forms:* many, legion, manifold, numerous, populous; diverse, diversified, diversiform, heterogeneous, motley, miscellaneous, mixed, indiscriminate, multifarious, varied, variegated, various, multiform, multiplex.

multiply *v.* **1.** *We bought two kittens that multiplied till we had six:* procreate, propagate, reproduce, proliferate, breed, increase, beget, generate. **2.** *Her anxieties multiplied until they could no longer be endured:* increase, enlarge, magnify, intensify, augment; add to, enhance, raise, extend, spread, heighten. —**Ant.** 2 decrease, diminish, lessen, wane, reduce, abate, shrink; divide.

multitude *n. The multitude awaited the champion's arrival. A multitude of problems delayed the construction project:* crowd, throng, mob, legion, horde, scores, mass, array, conflux, host, large amount, great number, troop, flock, slew, flood, crush, drove, army, pack, herd, myriad.

multitudinous *adj. The multitudinous rabble stormed the gates:* numerous, populous, myriad, legion, profuse, teeming, abounding, abundant, copious, great, multifarious, uncountable, untold, voluminous.

mum *adj. Keep mum about the surprise party:* silent, still, quiet, wordless, closemouthed, taciturn, secretive, mute, tight-lipped, uncommunicative, tacit.

mumble v. **1.** *I mumbled to conceal my lack of information:* mutter, murmur, utter indistinctly, speak inarticulately, speak incoherently, stammer, hem and haw, mouth. —*n.* **2.** *He gave a mumble of disapproval:* indistinct utterance, mutter, rumble, murmur, inarticulate sound, growl, grunt. —**Ant.** 1 articulate, enunciate.

mumbo jumbo n. *He peppered his speech with technical mumbo jumbo that none of us understood:* hocus pocus, humbug, double-speak, gobbledygook, flummery, gibberish, double talk; cant, sophistry, obfuscation, obscurantism; *Slang* hot air, hokum, blah, Jabberwocky, tripe, rot, bosh, bilge, baloney, hooey, fiddle-faddle, *British* tosh.

mundane adj. *Artists often have trouble with the mundane affairs of life:* ordinary, prosaic, commonplace, worldly, terrestrial, earthly, down-to-earth, day-to-day, routine, humdrum, everyday, practical, pedestrian, petty. —**Ant.** heavenly, celestial, ethereal, empyrean, unearthly, unworldly, spiritual.

municipal adj. *The city is planning to build a municipal auditorium:* civic, community, city, administrative, public.

municipality n. *Our suburb is at last becoming a full-fledged municipality:* self-governing district, town, city, township, bailiwick, parish, village.

munificence n. *The munificence of the patrons has kept the symphony alive:* generosity, bountifulness, liberality, benevolence, beneficence, benefaction, largesse, bounty, bounteousness, humanitarianism, philanthropy, charity, charitableness, patronage. —**Ant.** parsimoniousness, stinginess, pennypinching, niggardliness, miserliness.

munificent adj. *The park is just one of their munificent gifts to the city:* generous, liberal, freehanded, open-handed, free, benevolent, beneficent, bountiful, magnanimous, bounteous, altruistic, kindly, philanthropic, humanitarian, charitable, eleemosynary; lavish, profuse, extravagant, princely. —**Ant.** stingy, penurious, mean, niggardly.

murder n. **1.** *Matricide is the murder of one's mother:* homicide, assassination, manslaughter, killing. —*adj.* **2.** *Informal This heat is murder!:* unbearable, intolerable, oppressive, agonizing; very difficult, impossible, formidable. —*v.* **3.** *According to the historians he murdered his rival in cold blood:* kill, slay, assassinate, commit homicide, butcher, slaughter, cut down, *Slang* knock off, waste. **4.** *The comedian gets laughs by murdering the English language:* use incorrectly, abuse, mangle, misuse, bastardize, corrupt.

murderer n. *The murderer was executed for his crime:* killer, assassin, slayer, homicide; butcher, cutthroat.

murky adj. *I can't see anything in this murky light:* dark, dim, gloomy; hazy, misty, foggy, cloudy, vaporous, dusky, gray, overcast, sunless, obscure, lowering; dreary, somber, dismal, cheerless. —**Ant.** bright, clear, unobscured.

murmur n. *Listen to the murmur of the brook:* purl, low sound, susurrus, rumble, soft utterance, whisper, undertone, rustle, swish, purr, hum, lapping, drone, buzz, sough, mumble; mutter, complaint, grumble, lament, whimper, sigh.

muscle n. **1.** *Larry exercises to develop his muscles:* bicep, flexor, sinew, tendon, thew. **2.** *It'll take a lot of muscle to move this piano:* power, brawn, muscular strength, prowess, potency, might, thew, force, grit, puissance, energy, vigor, stamina, sturdiness, virility.

muscular adj. *All that tennis has made me quite muscular:* strong, husky, powerful, burly, brawny, tough, strapping, well-developed, fit, athletic, sinewy.

muse v. *The old man mused over the harsh finality of life. If we buy a car, I mused, then we can't afford the trip abroad:* meditate, consider, ponder, deliberate, mull, speculate, ruminate, contemplate, cogitate, reflect, review; think reflectively, say reflectively.

museum n. *We found the museum to be exceptionally varied:* gallery, depository, showplace, showroom, archive, storehouse, treasury.

mushroom v. *The small village mushroomed into a metropolis:* grow, expand quickly, spread, flourish, proliferate, burgeon, increase, shoot up, spring up, sprout.

mushy adj. **1.** *The mushy story lost our attention:* sugary, saccharine, sloppy, sentimental, effusive, maudlin, weepy, corny, *Informal* schmaltzy, tear-jerking, lovey-dovey. **2.** *The apple pie was mushy:* pulpy, paste-like, squishy, slushy, muddy, semi-liquid, semi-solid, slushy.

music n. **1.** *Shall we have some music during dinner?:* harmonious sound, euphony, harmony, minstrelsy, song, tune, melody; melodiousness, tunefulness, lyricism. **2.** *He passed out the music to the orchestra:* printed music, score, sheet music.

musical adj. *The piece of bamboo makes a musical sound:* melodious, melodic, euphonious, harmonious, tuneful, dulcet, sweet, mellifluent, pleasant-sounding, lilting, lyric, lyrical. —**Ant.** unmusical, discordant, inharmonious, unmelodious, cacophonous.

musician n. *The musician could play the flute, the piano, and the harp:* music maker, player, performer.

muss v. *Don't muss the freshly made bed:* rumple, disturb, crumple, tousle, disorder, disarrange, ruffle, jumble, dishevel, mess, bedraggle, tangle, *Slang* foul up. —**Ant.** straighten, arrange, untangle, tidy.

muster n. **1.** *There will be a muster of volunteers on the village green:* assemblage, gathering, assembly, aggregation, company, agglomeration, meeting, rally, turnout, confluence. —*v.* **2.** *Muster all troops on the parade ground:* summon, assemble, mobilize, round up, convene, call, line up, convocate, rally, call together, marshal, gather, raise.

musty adj. **1.** *The musty curtains had to be aired out:* mildewed, moldy, stale, dusty, fusty, damp, dank, dirty, stuffy, *British* frowsty. **2.** *I've heard that musty joke a dozen times:* hackneyed, stale, worn, worn-out, staled by time, old, threadbare, banal, antiquated, commonplace, trite, familiar, *Informal* tired, old hat. —**Ant.** 2 new, novel, fresh, original.

mutable *adj. Base metal was not mutable into gold:* changeable, transformable, adaptable, convertible, variable, versatile, flexible, pliable, adjustable, metamorphic, modifiable, permutable; mercurial, volatile.

mutation *n. Mutation caused genetic changes in the animal. This pink rose is a mutation of the red variety:* change, alteration, permutation, variation, metamorphosis, transformation, transmogrification, deviation, transfiguration, modification; anomaly, mutant.

mute *adj.* **1.** *In horror movies the mad scientist's assistant is usually mute:* dumb, speechless, voiceless, aphasiac. **2.** *He's mute on the subject of religion:* noncommittal, silent, nonvocal, unwilling to speak, mum, reticent, closemouthed, tight-lipped, uncommunicative; reserved, tacit, quiet, speechless, inarticulate. **3.** *My name has a mute "e" in it:* unsounded, silent, unarticulated, unuttered, unpronounced. —**Ant.** 2 expansive, informative, loquacious. 3 audible, pronounced, articulated.

mutilate *v. The assassins often mutilated their victims:* butcher, maim, mangle, cut to pieces, lacerate, cripple, deform, disfigure, lame; deprive of bodily part, cut off, amputate, truncate, excise, dismember.

mutinous *adj.* **1.** *The population was mutinous:* seditious, insurrectionary, revolutionary, insurgent. **2.** *The mutinous crew threw the captain overboard:* rebellious, refractory, insubordinate, unruly, contumacious, turbulent, riotous. —**Ant.** 1 patriotic 2 obedient.

mutiny *n.* **1.** *Government troops were called in to put down the mutiny:* uprising, revolt, insurrection, rebellion, insurgency, takeover, overthrow, coup, upheaval. —*v.* **2.** *The cruelty of the captain caused the ship's crew to mutiny:* revolt, rebel, rise up, defy authority.

mutter *v. She muttered to herself in disagreement all through the speech:* mumble, grumble, murmur, grouse, grouch, grunt, rumble, growl, whisper; carp, complain, gripe; *Slang* kvetch.

mutual *adj.* **1.** *He is a mutual friend of ours:* shared by two parties, interchangeable, common, coincident, correlative, joint, communal, interactive, related. **2.** *He loves me, and the feeling is mutual:* reciprocated, reciprocal, shared, interchanged, returned. —**Ant.** 1 distinct, uncommon. 2 unreciprocated, unshared, disparate.

mutually *adv. They mutually agreed to go slower:* jointly, together, reciprocally, in conjunction, commonly, cooperatively, in collaboration, by agreement.

muzzle *v.* **1.** *The judge ordered him to muzzle his dog:* harness, gag, bridle; curb, bind, check, rein in. **2.** *The chair tried to muzzle the opposition speakers:* silence, quiet, still, suppress, throttle, stifle, strangle, gag.

myopic *adj. The myopic preacher peered at his text:* nearsighted, shortsighted.

myriad *adj. Myriad treasures are believed to be buried beneath the sea:* innumerable, multitudinous, countless, boundless, measureless, infinite, incalculable, immeasurable, untold, limitless, manifold, uncounted, endless. —**Ant.** few.

mysterious *adj. There is something mysterious about her early childhood:* strange, puzzling, enigmatic, cryptic, secret, inscrutable, obscure, hidden, covert, clandestine, baffling, impenetrable, perplexing, secretive, undercover, sphinxlike, cloudy, inexplicable, surreptitious, unfathomable, dark, unknown, supernatural, undecipherable. —**Ant.** clear, plain, apparent, manifest, palpable.

mystery *n.* **1.** *The mysteries of their religion uplifted them:* sacred rites, things unexplainable, mysticism, occult, sacramental rite, symbolism, ineffability, holy of holies. **2.** *The first one to solve the mystery of the lost glasses wins a prize:* puzzle, problem, secret, riddle, conundrum, enigma, obscurity. **3.** *Her mystery makes her charming:* enigmatic manner, ineffability, ineffableness, mysterious quality, elusiveness, mystification, secrecy, ambivalence, quizzicality, vagueness.

mystical also **mystic** *adj. The mystical element of the play came across well:* mysterious, inscrutable, obscure, unknowable, enigmatic, abstruse, esoteric, cabalistic, symbolic, symbolical, secretive, hidden, occult, cryptic; otherworldly, transcendental, ethereal, metaphysical, nonrational, inner.

mystify *v. I like it, and yet exactly why still mystifies me:* bewilder, fool, deceive, mislead, elude, confound, perplex, puzzle, baffle, confuse, *Slang* bamboozle.

mystique *n. The actress's mystique created fan clubs:* glamor, charisma, fascination, magic, spell, charm.

myth *n.* **1.** *Things happen every day that remind you of the classical myths:* story, legend, tale, fairy tale, fable, allegory, parable. **2.** *Her alleged trip to California was a sheer myth:* fiction, made-up story, fantasy; falsehood, lie, fib, tall tale, prevarication, canard, hearsay, story, yarn. **3.** *The myth that the earth was flat was argued for many years before Columbus:* illusion, delusion, falsehood, error, shibboleth. —**Ant.** 1 historical fact, real-life occurrence. 2 truth, fact, actuality.

mythical also **mythic** *adj.* **1.** *The French painters were drawn to historical and mythical subjects:* legendary, fabled, about myths, mythological. **2.** *Jennifer has a mythical horse:* imaginary, fantasized, fictitious, fabricated, unsubstantial, illusory, unreal, pretended, conjured-up. —**Ant.** 2 real, actual, real-life.

mythological also **mythologic** *adj. The poem is weighted down with mythological allusions:* drawn from mythology; legendary, mythical, mythic, unreal, unfactual, fabulous, imaginary, fictitious, fantastic, imagined, illusory.

mythology *n. Greek mythology has been a source of inspiration for countless poets:* myth, legend, lore, fable, folk tale, folklore.

N

nab *v. The police nabbed the robber as he ran out of the bank:* arrest, capture, apprehend, catch, seize, grab, snare, snag, lay hold of, take into custody, detain, pick up, pull in; *Slang* pinch, collar, snatch, nail, haul in, bust. —**Ant.** release, let go, liberate, loose, set free.

nadir *n. Being thrown out of Mary's house was the nadir of my career as a Don Juan:* lowest point, low point, apogee, zero, nothing, bottom, rock bottom, floor, base. —**Ant.** peak, apex, zenith, high point.

nag *v.* **1.** *I'll go if you'll just stop nagging:* pester, harass, badger, harp, hector, upbraid, scold, nettle, irritate, annoy, plague, importune, bedevil, pick at, pick on, heckle, devil, goad, rail at, peck at, bicker, *Slang* hassle. —*n.* **2.** *That woman is a frightful nag:* scold, shrew, virago, termagant, harpy, tartar, battle-ax, Xanthippe; vixen, fury.

nail *v. We nailed all the shutters closed for the winter:* hammer, pin, fasten, fix, secure.

naive *or* **naïve** *adj.* **1.** *Her big eyes and naive questions made everyone feel protective toward her:* innocent, unaffected, unsophisticated, childlike, unspoiled, simple, artless, unjaded, plain, ingenuous, guileless, unassuming, natural, candid, open, unworldly. **2.** *Don't be so naive as to be taken in by their lies:* gullible, foolish, simple, credulous, unsuspecting, unsuspicious, unwise, green, immature, unwary, susceptible. —**Ant.** 1 sophisticated, disingenuous, jaded, blasé. 2 artful, sly, suspicious.

naiveté *or* **naïveté, naivety** *n. His naiveté was obvious from the way he told everyone his life story:* innocence, artlessness, ingenuousness, candor, openness, simplicity, naturalness, frankness, sincerity, unaffectedness, modesty; credulity, wide-eyedness; inexperience, callowness, greenness; foolishness, simplemindedness, childishness. —**Ant.** sophistication, worldliness, experience.

naked *adj.* **1.** *Naked bathing is not allowed on this beach:* nude, unclad, undressed, unappareled, unclothed, undraped, disrobed, bared, *Informal* in the buff, in one's birthday suit, in the altogether. **2.** *We picnicked right on the naked sand:* uncovered, bare, laid bare, exposed, wide-open. **3.** *The naked truth is I don't want to go:* plain, simple, unvarnished, frank, blatant, sheer, bald, patent, pure, palpable, manifest, perceptible, unqualified. —**Ant.** 1 dressed, clothed, clad, covered. 3 euphemized, embellished, exaggerated.

namby-pamby *adj. Speak up, and don't be so namby-pamby!:* wishy-washy, indecisive, weak, insipid, colorless, vapid, dull, banal, inane, sapless, innocuous, characterless; prim, prissy, mincing, simpering, coy. —**Ant.** decisive, definite, forceful, dynamic.

name *n.* **1.** *Her name is Amanda. The scientific name of the woodchuck is* Marmota monax: appellation, cognomen, title, designation; signature, denomination; taxonomy, nomenclature, term. **2.** *The name for him is speedy!:* nickname, chief characteristic, sobriquet, epithet, label. —*v.* **3.** *What will you name the new baby?:* call, christen, baptize, designate, *Informal* tag, label. **4.** *When will they name a successor?:* choose, delegate, appoint, nominate, deputize, commission, ordain, authorize, select, specify.

nameless *adj.* **1.** *The new company is as yet nameless:* unnamed, having no name, undesignated, without a name, untitled. **2.** *The best entry was by a nameless poet:* unknown, anonymous; obscure, unhonored, unheard-of, minor. —**Ant.** 2 famous, well-known, renowned.

naming *n. The naming of the new models took time:* designation, appellation, denomination, dubbing, identifying, styling, terming, calling, christening.

nap *v.* **1.** *The baby naps every afternoon. Don't be caught napping when the monthly report is due:* doze, take a short sleep, drowse, slumber, have a catnap, doze off, drift off, drop off, nod, rest, *Informal* snooze, catch forty winks; not pay attention, be off guard, be unaware, *Slang* goof off. —*n.* **2.** *That six-minute nap really refreshed me:* short sleep, catnap, slumber, rest, doze, siesta, *Informal* shut-eye, forty winks, snooze.

narcissistic *adj. He has the narcissistic attitude that we're all envious of him:* self-centered, egoistical, egocentric, conceited, egomaniacal, vain, self-absorbed, smug, self-satisfied, selfish, swelled-headed, self-admiring; *Slang* puffed-up, stuck on oneself.

narcotic *n. The doctor prescribed a narcotic to ease the pain:* drug, opiate, pharmaceutical, medicine, medication, medicament, soporific, painkiller, sedative, tranquilizer, medicinal drug.

narrate *v. Around the campfire they would narrate tale after tale:* tell a story, retell, repeat, set forth, recount, relate, chronicle, detail, give an account of, describe, portray, recite, render.

narration *n. I will do the narration of the trip if you'll run the projector:* storytelling, relating, speaking, telling, recounting, description, recitation, recital, chronicling, voice-over.

narrative *n.* **1.** *The true narrative of his life was more exciting than fiction:* story, tale, chronicle, statement, account, report, recital. **2.** *Doesn't his narrative remind you of Hemingway's?:* storytelling, technique of writing, fictional style; dialogue. —*adj.* **3.** *The life of St. Francis is the subject of many narrative paintings:* telling a story, involving storytelling, anecdotal, having a plot, episodic, historical.

narrow *adj.* **1.** *The handle of the brush is long and narrow:* slim, not wide, slender, fine, attenuated, tapered. **2.** *How can anyone work in such narrow confines?:* small, pinched, incapacious, close, scant, cramped, tight, scanty, restricted, confined, squeezed, compressed, constricted. **3.** *It's hard to reason with such narrow minds:* bigoted, biased, opinionated, provincial, isolated, narrow-minded, illiberal, dogmatic, parochial, shallow, intolerant, set, hidebound; conservative, reactionary. —**Ant.** 1 broad, wide. 2 spacious, ample, big. **3** open, liberal, receptive; radical.

narrow-minded *adj. The narrow-minded city fathers refused approval for the dance:* provincial, bigoted, straitlaced, prudish, opinionated, narrow, small-minded, parochial, conservative, hidebound, reactionary, one-sided, petty; unworldly, unsophisticated. **—Ant.** broadminded, inquisitive, tolerant.

narrows *n. pl. The aircraft carrier was too big to pass through the narrows:* strait, narrow part of a body of water, passage, neck, channel, canal, pass, isthmus; ravine.

nasty *adj.* **1.** *What's that nasty smell?:* foul, odious, awful, nauseating, repellent. **2.** *Telling on your brother was a nasty thing to do:* vicious, beastly, mean, abominable, hateful, vile, horrible. **3.** *Firing people is a nasty job:* unpleasant, distasteful, disagreeable, disgusting, awful, revolting. **—Ant.** 1, 3 pleasant, enjoyable, nice. 2 kind, sweet, admirable, honorable.

nation *n.* **1.** *The people considered itself a nation:* race, stock, ethnic group, population, people, tribe. **2.** *The new nation drew up a constitution:* state, country, commonwealth, kingdom, realm.

nationality *n. Her nationality was uncertain:* citizenship, country, origin, birthplace, nation, native land.

native *adj.* **1.** *When he retired, he returned to his native land to live:* of one's place of birth, of one's homeland, natal, home, paternal. **2.** *His native musical ability impressed his teachers:* inherent, inborn, innate, inbred, inherited, hereditary, intrinsic, basic, congenital, elemental, natural, endemic, ingrained, instinctive. **3.** *To save money, we'll use only native building materials:* local, national, indigenous, autochthonous, domestic, homegrown. **—***n.* **4.** *The natives were friendly to the explorers:* aborigine, original inhabitant; primitive, savage. **5.** *He is a native of New York:* one born in a specific place, lifelong inhabitant, long-time resident, citizen, countryman, countrywoman. **—Ant.** 1 adopted. 2 acquired, learned. 3 imported, foreign. 5 foreigner, alien.

natural *adj.* **1.** *The natural history course included a study of local rocks:* of nature, earthly, terrestrial. **2.** *The Indian face in the mountain is a natural phenomenon:* naturally occurring, formed naturally, native, formed over time, made by nature. **3.** *It takes natural talent and lots of hard work. It's natural to be upset by his tantrums:* instinctive, inborn, inherent, native, god-given, intuitive; normal, characteristic, essential, to be expected, regular. **4.** *The actress hasn't one natural gesture:* unaffected, spontaneous, genuine, straightforward, plain, unstudied, unmannered, unpretentious. **—Ant.** 2 unnatural, artificial. 4 affected, assumed, counterfeited, feigned, calculated.

naturally *adv.* **1.** *Naturally she spoke up for herself:* of course, characteristically, normally, ordinarily, readily, typically. **2.** *She spoke very naturally:* by nature, spontaneously, freely, simply, unaffectedly, openly.

nature *n.* **1.** *I'd like to leave the city and rediscover nature:* the natural world, world apart from man, created world, physical world, creation, earth, globe; cosmos, universe. **2.** *A cat is by nature very clean:* instinct, constitution, disposition, bent, humor, mood; birth, character, spirit, essence; trait, characteristic, property, peculiarity, feature. **3.** *What is the nature of your business?:* kind, variety, sort, type, category, style, stamp, particularity.

naughty *adj.* **1.** *If you're naughty, you won't get any dessert:* bad, devilish, disobedient, misbehaving, mischievous, willful, wayward, perverse, bad, obstinate, recalcitrant, fractious, unmanageable, disrespectful. **2.** *His jokes are funny but naughty:* off-color, bawdy, vulgar, dirty, pornographic, blue, ribald, risqué.

nausea *n.* **1.** *The pitching and rolling of the ship filled me with nausea:* sickness, upset stomach, queasiness, biliousness; (*variously*) travel sickness, motion sickness, car sickness, seasickness, airsickness; retching, vomiting, heaving. **2.** *I felt nothing but nausea for that kind of politicking:* disgust, revulsion, repulsion, contempt, loathing.

nauseate *v. The fare they served would nauseate a vulture:* sicken, make sick, upset, make bilious, turn one's stomach, make sick to the stomach; disgust, repulse, revolt, offend, repel.

nauseated *adj. Several people became nauseated after eating the tainted food. Weren't you nauseated by that speech?:* sick to the stomach, sick, queasy, ill; disgusted, revolted, repelled, upset.

nauseous *adj.* **1.** *Rotten eggs are nauseous. His sense of humor is nauseous:* sickening, nauseating, disgusting, unappetizing, repulsive, revolting, repellent, offensive, abhorrent, upsetting. **2.** *I felt nauseous before the ship even sailed:* sick, nauseated, upset, queasy, sick at one's stomach.

nautical *adj. He dressed in a nautical getup for the sail:* seagoing, of the sea, marine, oceanic, maritime, boating, aquatic, yachting, naval.

navigate *v.* **1.** *We navigated the channel in record time:* cross, sail across, cover the body of water, sail, cruise, ride, voyage, ship, sail over, ride across, fly. **2.** *He was trained to navigate by the air corps:* chart a course, plot a course; sail, maneuver.

navigation *n. My course didn't include night navigation. His navigation of the globe took two years:* art of sailing, seamanship, piloting, sailing, navigating, traveling, boating, cruising, voyaging.

navy *n. The small country has no navy, only merchant ships:* warships, naval forces, fleet, armada, flotilla, task force, convoy.

near *adv.* **1.** *She came near when I called:* close, close by, proximately, in propinquity, hereabouts, at close quarters, alongside, next door, close to home. **2.** *Informal He was near frozen when they found him:* nearly, almost, about, practically, all but, just about, nigh. **—***adj.* **3.** *A storm is near, I'm afraid:* close, imminent, impending, looming, approaching, threatening. —*prep.* **4.** *Are you near the end of the book?:* close to, proximate to, in the vicinity of, not far from, in range of, in sight of. —*v.* **5.** *Throw out the lines when you near the dock:* approach, come close to, move toward, come up to, draw near, advance toward, close with. —**Ant.** 1 distant, remote, far.

nearly *adv. I'm nearly ready to go:* about, almost, near, nigh, approximately, all but, roughly, just about, close to, for the most part, practically.

nearness *n. It's the nearness of the museum that attracts me:* closeness, proximity, propinquity, contiguity, adjacency, immediacy; handiness, availability, accessibility; intimacy; neighborhood, vicinity, approximation. —**Ant.** remoteness, distance.

neat *adj.* **1.** *He keeps his desk neat:* orderly, straight, tidy, shipshape, organized, uncluttered; immaculate, clean. **2.** *He plays a neat but unimaginative game:* efficient, competent, purposive, intelligent, controlled, dexterous, methodical, systematic, succinct, concise, correct, accurate. **3.** *Slang What a neat idea for jeans!:* great, exciting, striking, imaginative, ingenious, original, groovy. —**Ant.** 1 messy, disorderly, untidy, disorganized, cluttered. 2 inefficient, uncontrolled, incompetent. 3 bad, awful, terrible, lousy.

nebulous *adj. Our plans for the trip are still nebulous:* vague, hazy, unclear, murky, obscure, cloudy, dark, dim, indistinct, confused, ambiguous, uncertain, intangible, impalpable, indefinite, indeterminate, uncertain. —**Ant.** distinct, definite, precise.

necessarily *adv. A hundred percent humidity doesn't necessarily mean rain:* automatically, naturally, inexorably, inevitably, axiomatically, accordingly, compulsorily, by necessity, of course, perforce, unqualifiedly, incontrovertibly.

necessary *adj. Take whatever tools are necessary to get the job done:* required, obligatory, needed, needful, requisite, compulsory, indispensable, essential, called for, fitting, desired, wanted; imperative, urgent, exigent, crucial. —**Ant.** unnecessary, dispensable, nonessential, optional.

necessitate *v. The extra guests necessitated our taking two cars:* require, make necessary, enforce, cause, oblige, demand, impel, force, constrain, create a need for, compel; prescribe, call for.

necessity *n.* **1.** Often **necessities** *We'll take only the necessities for the camping trip:* something needed, necessary, essential, *sine qua non,* indispensable, requirement, requisite, exigency, must. **2.** *What's the necessity of leaving so early?:* urgency, demand, pressure, need.

necromancer *n. She insisted that a necromancer had put a spell on her:* magician, wizard, sorcerer, witch, warlock, black magician, conjurer, exorcist, magus, enchanter, hexer, occultist, voodooist, thaumaturgist, soothsayer, charmer.

necromancy *n. The wizard performed his nec-* romancy: magic, enchantment, conjuration, sorcery, divination.

need *n.* **1.** *The old man has a daughter who looks after his needs:* want, requisite, requirement, necessity, demand, exigency; wish, longing; essential, desideratum. **2.** *Many of our citizens are in desperate need:* poverty, want, neediness, penury, indigence, impecuniosity, destitution, pennilessness; reduced circumstances, extremity, distress, straits; insolvency, bankruptcy. —*v.* **3.** *The boy needs a heavy coat for this weather:* require, lack, want, demand, find necessary, find indispensable; have use for, have need of, call for, have occasion for; exact, necessitate, make a demand of; crave, yearn for. —**Ant.** 2 wealth, affluence; superfluity, excess.

needless *adj. Taxicabs are a needless expense:* unnecessary, unneeded, unessential, uncalled-for, superfluous, dispensable, gratuitous; useless, purposeless, unavailing, pointless, redundant, pleonastic; excessive, overabundant. —**Ant.** essential, obligatory, required, needful; useful, beneficial.

needy *adj. There are many needy families in the city:* poor, penniless, moneyless, destitute, indigent, impoverished, poverty-stricken, badly off, in want, *Informal* strapped, *Slang* broke, hard-up, down-and-out. —**Ant.** rich, affluent, wealthy, well-to-do, well-off.

nefarious *adj. He was punished for his nefarious deeds:* evil, vile, infamous, atrocious, wicked, bad, foul, abominable, base, low, odious, iniquitous, execrable, despicable, detestable; vicious, depraved; unspeakable, unmentionable; hellish, devilish, infernal, ungodly; ghastly, beastly; scandalous, villainous, heinous; shameful, disgraceful, opprobrious, dishonorable. —**Ant.** good, honest, honorable, just; exalted, noble; admirable, praiseworthy, laudable.

negate *v. This year's losses negate last year's profits:* nullify, invalidate, void, reverse; quash, squash, quell, squelch; vanquish, defeat, overthrow, overwhelm, destroy, wipe out, blot out; deny, abrogate, revoke, gainsay, retract, disavow; rebut, refute, contradict; disallow, set aside; veto, repeal; disown, disclaim, repudiate. —**Ant.** affirm, confirm, attest to, ratify, endorse, corroborate, reinforce, support.

negation *n. It was the negation of everything he believed:* antithesis, antonym, cancellation, contradiction, contrary, converse, denial, disavowal, disclaimer, nay, negative, nullification, refusal, refutation, repudiation, reverse, veto, void.

negative *adj.* **1.** *The vote was overwhelmingly negative:* indicating "no," disapproving, refusing, declining, rejecting, opposing, opposed; disagreeing, objecting, dissenting, demurring. **2.** *You can't learn anything with a negative attitude:* antagonistic, uncooperative, opposed, contrary, inimical, at odds, dissident; doubtful, dubious, skeptical; reluctant, unwilling, unenthusiastic; gloomy, bleak, dark, pessimistic, fatalistic, jaundiced, *Informal* downbeat, blue. —**Ant.** 1 affirmative, positive, assenting; agreeing, approving; concurring. 2 positive, optimistic, cheerful.

neglect v. **1.** *He's been neglecting his bills for months:* ignore, disregard, overlook, take no notice of, take no note of; let ride, let slide, let slip, slight, pass over, pass up, let pass, omit, let go; forget, fail, lose sight of, be remiss, be inattentive; pass by, shirk; abandon, shake off. —*n.* **2.** *Neglect of his studies caused him to fail:* inattention, disregard, nonpreparation; neglectfulness, laxity, laxness, negligence, remissness, idleness, dereliction, slackness, noncompliance; indifference, carelessness, fecklessness, passivity; inaccuracy, slovenliness, inexactness; slight, omission, default, oversight; unfulfillment, underachievement. —**Ant.** 1 attend to, take care of, perform, notice, appreciate, regard, value, prize. 2 attention, care, notice; regard, esteem, consideration, respect.

neglectful *adj. Lately he's been neglectful of his family:* negligent, careless, thoughtless, remiss, heedless, forgetful, unmindful, unthinking, unheeding, inattentive, unobservant, unwatchful, oblivious, disregardant; lazy, slack, procrastinating; respectless, disregardful, derelict, happy-go-lucky, devil-may-care, indifferent; inconstant, untrue, unfaithful; improvident, thriftless. —**Ant.** attentive, thoughtful, considerate, regardful, careful.

negligee or **negligé** *n. Her trousseau included a black negligee:* dressing gown, robe, wrapper, housecoat, kimono, bathrobe, peignoir.

negligent *adj. He crashed into a parked car and was charged with negligent driving:* neglectful, careless, indifferent, forgetful; inconsiderate, thoughtless; unthinking, unmindful, unheeding, heedless, remiss, slack, lax; inattentive, unobservant, unwatchful, untidy, slovenly. —**Ant.** careful, strict, rigorous; thoughtful, considerate, attentive, mindful, heedful.

negligible *adj. The interest on my small savings is negligible:* unimportant, trifling, slight, inconsequential, insignificant, trivial, petty, minor, piddling, paltry, small, minute. —**Ant.** significant, important.

negotiate *v.* **1.** *The Arab and Israeli leaders met to negotiate a settlement:* confer over, discuss, transact, arrange, bargain for, contract; agree to arbitration, come to terms, settle, meet halfway, adjust differences; haggle, barter, dicker. **2.** *I'll need a hand to negotiate these steps:* cope with, get over, handle, deal with, manage, make. **3.** *Keep those bonds in a safe place because anyone can negotiate them:* sign over, transfer, convey, make over, transmit; pass, deliver, turn over, pass over; hand over, consign; redeem, cash, cash in.

negotiator *n. A negotiator was hired to handle the dispute:* bargainer; adjudicator, arbitrator, mediator, moderator, delegate, ambassador, broker, go-between, intermediary.

neigh *v. The horse neighed as though to hurry us up:* whinny, nicker, *Archaic* hinny.

neighbor *n.* **1.** *Maybe you can borrow an ax from the neighbors. Canada and the United States are neighbors:* person who lives nearby; adjoining country, borderer; friend, acquaintance, associate. —*v.* **2.** *Canada and Mexico neighbor the U.S.:* border, border on, adjoin, conjoin, abut; touch, meet, be near, verge upon; come into contact with, connect with.

neighborhood *n.* **1.** *She had to move out of that tough neighborhood:* district, quarter, place, area, locale, vicinity, region, community, part, section, purlieus, side, ward, confines, environs, precinct, parish. **2.** *His debts are in the neighborhood of a thousand dollars:* range, approximate amount, area, sphere, environs.

neighboring *adj. They're visiting here from the neighboring town:* nearby, adjacent, adjoining, close by; contiguous, abutting, bordering, lying close, close, near, next, at hand, near at hand; surrounding, circumjacent. —**Ant.** distant, faraway, far-off, remote.

neighborly *adj. The townsfolk were quite neighborly when we moved here:* friendly, courteous, polite, amiable, kindly, kind, civil, hospitable, warmhearted, affable, considerate, helpful, cordial, well-disposed, gracious, obliging, amicable, *Informal* chummy. —**Ant.** antagonistic, uncivil, unfriendly, remote, hostile.

nemesis *n. Billy the Kid finally met his nemesis when Pat Garrett went gunning for him:* undoing, destruction, overthrow, ruin, downfall, *Informal* Waterloo; justice, vengeance, retaliation, retribution, punishment, revenge, an eye for an eye; avenger, punisher, instrument of fate; rival, match.

neologism also **neology** *n. "Stickum" is a neologism for "glue":* nonce word, coinage.

neophyte *n. The neophyte learned the ropes very fast:* beginner, tyro, apprentice, trainee, novice, probationer, newcomer, recruit, learner; tenderfoot, rookie, greenhorn, student, pupil; convert, proselyte, entrant, disciple, no-viitate. —**Ant.** veteran, old hand, expert.

ne'r-do-well *n. That ne'er-do-well isn't even looking for a job:* idler, loafer, good-for-nothing, wastrel, bum, layabout, black sheep; *Slang* no-account, no-good, sad sack, do-nothing, goof-off, loser.

nerve *n.* **1.** *It takes a lot of nerve to work as a steeplejack:* courage, boldness, fearlessness, pluck, grit, mettle, endurance, determination, fortitude, hardihood, stoutheartedness, coolness, hardiness, steadiness, tenacity, dash, intrepidity, bravery, strength, resoluteness, *Informal* spunk, guts, backbone; gameness, spirit, confidence, self-assurance, self-reliance; valor, gallantry, derring-do. **2.** *She had some nerve to say that!:* gall, insolence, presumption, arrogance, impertinence, impudence, effrontery, *Slang* brass, crust, sass, cheek; assurance, assumption; sauciness, flippancy, brazenness. —**Ant.** 1 cowardice, faintheartedness, weakness, frailty, feebleness.

nerveless *adj.* **1.** *The nerveless troops fell back to their old position:* feeble, weak, enervated, flaccid, spiritless, flabby, cowardly, pusillanimous. **2.** *He was virtually nerveless when under attack:* calm, collected, composed, controlled, cool, impassive, imperturbable, intrepid, patient, self-possessed, tranquil, unemotional. —**Ant.** 1 strong, brave, bold, fearless.

nerves *n. pl. His nerves were shot:* nervousness, fretfulness, neurasthenia, strain, stress, tenseness, tension, anxiety.

nervous *adj. She's so nervous she jumps at the slightest noise:* excitable, jumpy, jittery, shaky, high-strung, sensitive, touchy; ruffled, disturbed, uneasy, excited, tremulous, skittish, fidgety, neurotic, unsettled, trembling, unstrung, tense; anxious, hysterical, wild, delirious, fearful, apprehensive, timorous, feverish; alarmed, startled; peevish, irritable, impatient. **—Ant.** steady, calm, tranquil, peaceful; constant, even, equable, uniform; confident, bold; serene.

nervousness *n. She's taking pills now for her nervousness:* excitability, flutter, shaking, hysteria, quivering, trembling, twitching; hypersensitivity, touchiness, timorousness, timidity; perturbation, disturbance, agitation, irritability, irascibility; tension, tremor, fidgetiness; stage fright, apprehension, anxiety, *Informal* the shakes, the creeps, the fidgets. **—Ant.** calm, composure, coolness, equanimity.

nestle *v. The kitten nestled in the child's arms:* lie snug, snug, snuggle, lie, lie close, dwell, stay, remain, settle, settle down; embrace, clasp, enfold, fondle, nuzzle, cuddle, huddle, bundle, caress, coddle, pet, cosset; live, lodge, inhabit, occupy.

net[1] *n.* **1.** *A low net stretched across the tennis court:* mesh, netting, meshwork, web, network, latticework, lattice; screen, screening; grid, gridiron; grate, grating; grillwork, grille; snare, trap. *—v.* **2.** *They spent the afternoon netting butterflies:* capture with a net, ensnare, snare, enmesh, trap, entangle; apprehend, seize, take, catch, lay hold of, get hold of, take captive, take prisoner, capture; snag, snap up, clasp, clutch, grab, grip.

net[2] *v. How much did the business net last year?:* realize in profit, gain, earn, clear a profit of, clear above expenses; accumulate, gather, pick up, collect, gather in, bring in, acquire, obtain, take in.

nether *adj. Sinners are condemned to the nether regions of Hell:* lower, lowest, below, under, inferior, subjacent, downward; basal, bottom, bottommost, nethermost. **—Ant.** upper, higher, above.

nettle *v. It nettles her the way I leave my clothes lying around:* annoy, irritate, exasperate, vex, gall, provoke, bother, perturb, beset, bait; chafe, sting, harry, harass, prickle; *Slang* get one's goat, burn one up, get on one's nerves, give one a pain, miff, get in one's hair, put one off.

network *n. The network linked all their computers:* complex, system, connections, web, net, chain, grid, interconnections, mesh, nexus, web, wiring, circuitry.

neurosis *n. He sought help to cure his neurosis:* mental illness, psychological disorder, mental illness, neurasthenia, derangement.

neurotic *adj. He has a neurotic fear of the dark:* unhealthy, nervous, anxious; psychoneurotic, sick, disturbed, abnormal, unstable, distraught, overwrought, emotionally disordered; obsessive, intense, immoderate.

neuter *adj. Some types of insects are neuter:* asexual, sexless, neutral; barren, fallow, sterile, infertile, impotent; spayed, gelded, fixed.

neutral *adj.* **1.** *Ireland was a neutral nation in World War II:* nonbelligerent, noncombatant, nonparticipating, noninterventionist, nonpartisan, noninterfering. **2.** *My uncle was neutral on the subject of women's rights:* impartial, disinterested, unbiased; indifferent, unconcerned, uninvolved; withdrawn, dispassionate, remote, aloof, unaffected; of two minds, fence-sitting; pacifist, peaceful, peaceable. **3.** *We painted the room a neutral color:* indefinite, in-between, middle, medium, intermediate, half-and-half; mean, normal, average; without hue, achromatic. **—Ant.** 1 belligerent, active, participating, interfering. 2 partial, interested, biased, predisposed; decided, decisive. 3 positive, affirmative.

neutralize *v. A good defense will neutralize the attack:* render ineffective, frustrate, balance, counterbalance, counterpoise, counteract, nullify, negate, offset, check, block, stymie; annul, cancel, stop, halt, impede, prevent; defeat, overcome, suppress, overpower; disable, incapacitate.

never *adv. I'll never speak to her again:* at no time, nevermore, not ever, under no circumstances, on no occasion, not at all, *Poetic* ne'er. **—Ant.** always, forever, eternally, evermore.

never-ending *adj. When will we see the last of this never-ending rain?:* everlasting, unceasing, incessant, interminable, nonstop, continual, continuous, unremitting, relentless, unbroken, persistent, repeated, recurring; constant, enduring, undiminished, steady.

never-failing *adj. She relied on the never-failing comfort of her religion:* sure, steadfast, abiding, firm, unfaltering, enduring, reliable, dependable, proven, undeviating, unhesitating, trustworthy, trusty, unfailing, tried-and-true. **—Ant.** precarious, chancy, iffy, unreliable, faltering.

nevertheless *adv. He's charming; nevertheless I don't quite trust him:* nonetheless, on the other hand, in spite of that, yet, but, regardless, anyhow, anyway, however, notwithstanding, though, although, in any event, even so, just the same, after all, for all that, contrarily, contrariwise, be that as it may, when all is said and done, at all events.

new *adj.* **1.** *Did you see Sam's new car?:* recently acquired, of recent make, brand-new, just out, spanking new, up-to-date, modern, current, up-to-the-minute, newly or lately issued, *Informal* newfangled; novel, original, late, fresh, recent. **2.** *We have several new clerks this week:* untried, unseasoned, unessayed, unaccustomed, unfamiliar; unused, unexercised, unventured; uncharted, unexplored; remote, out-of-the-way; untouched, ungathered, uncollected, *Informal* green, wet behind the ears. **3.** *He says he feels like a new man:* restored, reinvigorated, renewed, renovated, revivified, reborn, recreated, regenerated, refreshed; fixed, repaired; rebuilt, reconstructed, remodeled; resumed, reopened; changed, altered. —**Ant.** 1 old, ancient, antique; stale, hackneyed, trite, passé, outmoded, old-fashioned; aged, elderly. 2 used, experienced; familiar.

newcomer *n. She and her husband are newcomers to our town:* recent arrival, stranger, outsider; entrant, comer; foreigner, outlander, immigrant, alien; novice, tyro, neophyte; intruder, trespasser, interloper.

newly *adv. Don't sit on the newly painted chair:* freshly, recently, lately, anew, afresh, of late, not long ago, just now.

news *n. pl. Did you hear the news about the election?:* information, intelligence, tidings, bulletin, communiqué, announcement, disclosure, account; report, release, story, dispatch, article, piece; dope, lowdown, exposé, revelation, divulgence, exposure; statement, *Informal* flash; message, word, rumor, talk, gossip, hearsay, chatter, mention, babble; scandal, libel, slander, dirt.

next *adj.* **1.** *We can always catch the next bus:* following, ensuing, after, coming, subsequent, succeeding, consequent, later; neighboring, adjoining, adjacent, proximate, abutting, alongside, beside, close, hard by. —*adv.* **2.** *We don't know what happens next:* coming up, following, after, thereafter, afterwards, behind, latterly, subsequently, closely, immediately.

nib *n. The nib of the pen is gold-plated:* point, tip, peak, end; apex, vertex, top, pinnacle, tiptop; upper end, height; extreme, extremity.

nibble *v.* **1.** *She sat there nibbling a cookie:* eat sparingly, bite, eat in small bites, gnaw; munch, crunch, chew; nip, peck, peck at. —*n.* **2.** *I'll just try a nibble of this cheese:* bite, taste, small piece, morsel, tidbit; crumb, speck, particle, fragment.

nice *adj.* **1.** *That was a nice party you gave:* good, fine, pleasant, agreeable, excellent, pleasurable; amusing, marvelous, divine, fantastic, lovely, enchanting, wonderful, entrancing, *Informal* great, swell, dandy, jim-dandy. **2.** *We think Helen is a nice person:* friendly, sympathetic, warmhearted, good, kind, agreeable, amiable, cordial, genial, congenial, pleasant; charming, attractive, interesting, delightful, gracious; understanding, compassionate; winning, pleasing; cheerful, likable. **3.** *A nice girl would never go there:* proper, refined, well brought up, virtuous, respectable, genteel, well-bred, correct, ladylike, seemly. **4.** *The cabinetmaker does nice work:* careful, painstaking, scrupulous, precise, meticulous, skillful, sensitive, exact; correct, accurate, methodical, unerring; strict, rigorous; subtle, delicate, deft; fastidious, finicky, fussy, punctilious, overconscientious. —**Ant.** 1 dreadful, miserable, awful; unpleasant, disagreeable. 2 unfriendly, unkind, mean. 3 coarse, vulgar, illbred, vicious. 4 sloppy, crude, rough, careless, haphazard, undiscriminating, inaccurate.

nicely *adv. Your arrival was nicely timed:* carefully, accurately, faultlessly, exactly, precisely, unerringly; happily, fortunately, opportunely; critically, fussily; fastidiously; attractively, neatly; pleasantly. —**Ant.** carelessly, haphazardly, sloppily; unfortunately; unattractively, unpleasantly.

nicety *n.* **1.** *She understands the niceties of furnishing a home:* subtlety, delicacy, fine point, subtle detail, small distinction, particularity; good taste, tastefulness, flair; cultivated taste, culture, cultivation, refinement, refined feeling, fine feeling; polish, finesse, fastidiousness, grace, elegance, tact. **2.** *Notice the nicety of the artist's brushwork:* meticulousness, attention to detail, delicacy, exactness, precision, preciseness, care, accuracy, attention; subtlety, minute attention, elaborateness, sensitivity; insight, penetration, acumen, perspicacity, discrimination. —**Ant.** 2 coarseness, roughness, crudeness, inaccuracy, sloppiness, slovenliness, haphazardness.

niche *n.* **1.** *The statue was placed in a niche on the stairway:* recess, alcove, nook, cranny, cubbyhole, depression, hole in the wall; snug place, dugout, cove, cavity; corner, hollow. **2.** *He found his niche in foreign service:* proper place, calling, suitable occupation, congenial job, vocation, trade, métier, slot, position, pigeonhole, *Slang* berth.

nick *n.* **1.** *This vase has a nick on the base:* score, notch, cut, scratch, mar, scoring, mark, chip, dent, indentation, jag; wound, injury, incision, scar; cleft, depression, gash, gouge; marking. —*v.* **2.** *He nicked his chin while shaving:* cut, notch, scratch, lacerate, scarify, score, gash, injure, scar, damage, dent, indent; mar, deface, mark.

nickname *n. His nickname is "Jon" for "Jonathan":* sobriquet, agnomen, familiar name, cognomen, diminutive, *Slang* moniker, handle; appellation, designation, pseudonym, epithet; childhood name, pet name, baby name, school name.

nifty *adj. He bought the nifty gadget:* dandy, enjoyable, chic, smart, stylish, clever, keen, pleasing, swell, terrific, peachy, neat, sharp, cool.

niggardly *adj.* **1.** *Don't be so niggardly with the mayonnaise:* stingy, miserly, parsimonious, closefisted, tight, mean, cheap, stinting, ungenerous, illiberal, grudging, sparing, hardfisted, close, penurious; frugal, saving, thrifty; grubbing, mercenary. **2.** *That was a niggardly gift for an old friend:* wretched, mean, insufficient, paltry, poor, sorry, beggarly, second-rate, meager, scanty, scrubby, measly; cheap, flimsy, tawdry, miserable, contemptible, shabby. —**Ant.** 1, 2 bountiful, liberal, generous, munificent, handsome; profuse, lavish, prodigal, copious, ample, abundant, bounteous, plentiful.

niggling *adj. It's a niggling amount—let's just forget it:* small, trifling, petty, picayune, minor, piddling; quibbling, nit-picking, fussy, finicky, pettifogging, caviling, insignificant, inconsequential, negligible, nugatory. —**Ant.** important, considerable, sizable, consequential.

nigh *adv.* **1.** *Evening draws nigh:* near, close,

within sight, within view. **2.** *She is nigh onto 80 years old:* almost, nearly, practically, verging on, on the brink of. —*adj.* **3.** *The time for repentance is nigh:* close, close at hand, at hand, near; close by, handy; in the vicinity, adjacent, neighboring, bordering. —**Ant.** 3 far, distant, remote, removed.

night *n. The guard is on duty during the night:* nighttime, dark, darkness, tenebrousness; hours of sleep, bedtime; evening, eventide, nightfall, sundown, dusk; small hours, early morning; murkiness, obscurity.

nightclub *n. He met his wife in a nightclub:* club, entertainment spot, cabaret, lounge, night spot, supper club, *Informal* dive, joint, honky-tonk, after-hours joint.

nightfall *n. We walked in the countryside till almost nightfall:* twilight, dusk, day's end, evening, evenfall, eventide, sunset, sundown, moonrise, crepuscule, gloaming, dark, darkness. —**Ant.** daytime, dawn, daybreak, daylight.

nightly *adj.* **1.** *The theater gives a nightly performance. Nightly shadows enveloped the house:* night, evening, night after night; nocturnal, night-cloaked, night-mantled, night-veiled; dark, obscure. —*adv.* **2.** *The restaurant is open nightly:* every night, nights, night after night; at night, by night, nocturnally, through the night. —**Ant.** 1, 2 daily, during the day, every day. 1 diurnal. 2 diurnally.

nightmare *n. The child awoke suddenly from a nightmare:* bad dream; frightening vision, hallucination; incubus, succubus.

nightstick *n. The officer twirled his nightstick menacingly as he approached the loiterers:* baton, cudgel, billy club, truncheon, shillelagh, bludgeon, mace; rod, staff, wand, scepter.

nihilism *n. His rejection of all philosophies amounted to nihilism:* disbelief in anything, skepticism, universal doubt, agnosticism, amorality; nothingness, emptiness, nonexistence; anarchism, radicalism, iconoclasm; lawlessness, irresponsibility, license, chaos; terrorism; alienation, anomie.

nil *n. My interest in the plan is nil:* nonexistent, none, naught, null, nullity, nothing, nothing whatever, none whatever, zero, cipher.

nimble *adj. He was nimble enough to jump the fence. A nimble mind:* agile, light-footed, nimble-footed, spry, supple; animated, spirited, swift, quick, mercurial, fleet-footed, speedy, lively, sprightly, active, quick as lightning, fleet, rapid, light-legged, quick moving; light, deft, skillful, dexterous; expert, proficient; prompt, ready. —**Ant.** clumsy, slow, plodding, awkward, dull, heavy, inert, inactive; lethargic, lazy, indolent.

nincompoop *n. Slang That nincompoop put the papers in the wrong file:* ninny, dunce, harebrain, featherbrain, scatterbrain, simpleton, blockhead, jackass, bonehead, rattlebrain, knucklehead, noodlehead, muddlehead, fool, dumb bunny, dunderhead, dunderpate, numskull; dimwit, lummox, dolt, pumpkin head, nitwit, half-wit; moron, idiot, imbecile; dope,

dummy, jerk, lunkhead, klutz, *German* dummkopf, *Slang* boob.

nip *v.* **1.** *John nipped his finger with the pliers:* pinch, tweak, squeeze; clutch, seize, snag, grab, snare, grasp, clasp, clamp, grip, snatch; snap, compress. **2.** *Don't nip any stalks off the plant till it's through blooming:* cut off, lop, snip, cut, clip, dock, crop; cut short, abbreviate, curtail, shorten; snap, crack, shear, sever, sunder. **3.** *The government nipped the rebellion in the bud:* check, cut off, curtail, put an end to, demolish, finish off, quash, deal a knockout blow to, destroy, ruin, crush; blast, thwart, frustrate. **4.** *A sharp wind nipped our cheeks and noses:* freeze, chill, frost; pierce, bite, cut; chill, benumb, make one shiver.

nitwit *n. The nitwit who answered the phone forgot to give her the message:* fool, blockhead, dummy, dolt, clod, dunce, dimwit, nincompoop, booby, lamebrain; *Slang* meathead, chowderhead, bonehead, klutz, pinhead, birdbrain, numskull, noodlehead, peabrain.

nobility *n.* **1.** *The nobility favored the king's abdication:* noble classes, upper classes, aristocracy, ruling classes, elite, peerage, lords, patricians, patriciate; royalty; high society, *Informal* Beautiful People, upper crust, the four hundred, blue bloods, *French* noblesse. **2.** *He is remembered for the nobility of his character:* greatness, superiority, sublimity, exaltedness, dignity, loftiness, stateliness, mightiness; distinction, eminence, grandness, grandeur, prestige; preeminence, supremacy, primacy; majesty, splendor, magnificence. **3.** *Documents disclosed the nobility of his birth:* nobleness, aristocracy, gentility, exalted condition, high rank, high station, distinction, breeding, high breeding. —**Ant.** 1 lower classes, peasantry, plebeians, obscurity, insignificance, meanness. 2 lowness, meanness, baseness, ignobility.

noble *adj.* **1.** *The minstrel boy was really of noble birth:* exalted, highborn, patrician, gentle, high, high ranking, aristocratic, distinguished, pureblooded, blue-blooded, thoroughbred, superior; princely, royal. **2.** *In keeping with his noble character, he left his fortune to charity:* great, lofty, selfless, superior, magnanimous, excellent, exemplary, elevated, eminent; moral, virtuous, upright, meritorious, incorruptible, just, trustworthy, honorable, estimable, worthy, reputable, high-principled, honest, ethical. **3.** *Noble mansions line the river bank:* stately, grand, majestic, lordly, baronial, imposing, impressive, splendid, magnificent, superb, handsome; awesome, awe-inspiring; glorious, supreme, sublime; famed, renowned, famous, preeminent; dignified, courtly, lordlike, distinguished; lofty, regal, imperial. —*n.* **4.** *Many of the nobles joined the uprising:* aristocrat, nobleman, don, patrician, grandee, peer, lord, thoroughbred; gentleman, chevalier, knight, cavalier, squire; great man, man of distinction, personage. —**Ant.** 1 lowborn, lowly, humble, plebeian, peasant, mean. 2 ignoble, base, selfish, despicable, contemptible, vulgar, doubtful, dishonest. 3 insignificant, modest, drab, mean, paltry, plain. **4** peasant, commoner, serf; scoundrel.

nobody *n.* **1.** *Nobody is home:* no one. **2.** *She thought he was a nobody:* nonentity, nullity.

nocturnal *adj. Some animals are nocturnal feeders. Nocturnal clouds portended a storm:* night, nighttime, of the night, nightly; night-cloaked, night-veiled, night-hidden; dark, obscure, darkling. —**Ant.** diurnal, daily, by day.

nod *v.* **1.** *She nodded to us from across the room:* incline the head, bow one's head, bend the neck, make obeisance; shake up and down, lower and raise, bob; acknowledge, recognize, give salutation, greet, salute, hail, say hello, bid hello. **2.** *The judge nodded his assent:* express with a nod, indicate by nodding, reveal, show, signify, signal, beckon, motion, sign, gesture; agree, consent, assent, concur. **3.** *We nodded as the speech dragged on:* doze, fall asleep, go to sleep; drop off, fall off; drowse, be torpid or languid, be inactive; be forgetful, be negligent, lapse, let up. —*n.* **4.** *His nod means a higher bid:* quick bowing of the head; signal, sign, gesture.

node *n.* **1.** *The trunk of the oak tree is full of nodes:* knot, woody formation, burl, joint, bud. **2.** *He had some nodes removed from his vocal cords:* lump, bump, nodule, prominence, protuberance, swelling, knob, bulge, button, hump; tumescence, excrescence.

nodule *n. The roots of the bean plant are covered with nodules:* knob, outgrowth, protuberance, growth, bump, lump, node, wen, cyst, stud, knot, sac; projection, protrusion, prominence; swelling, tumescence, bulge; excrescence.

noise *n.* **1.** *Those planes make an awful noise:* sound, din, racket, clamor, uproar, pandemonium, clatter, bedlam, tumult, babel, hullabaloo, blare, wail, boom, blast, bang, rumble, rumbling; barrage, thunder, cannonade; hubbub, commotion, stir, ado; discharge, report, reverberation, echo; dissonance, cacophony; roar, vociferation; bluster, caterwauling; shouting, brawling, gabbling. —*v.* **2.** *Don't noise it around, but he's retiring:* spread as news, circulate, repeat, pass, voice, rumor, bruit, *Slang* blab. —**Ant.** 1 quiet, silence, hush, stillness; peace, serenity, calm; harmony, melody.

noiseless *adj. The noiseless guest tiptoed up to bed:* silent, quiet, still, inaudible, soundless. —**Ant.** noisy, clamorous, tumultuous.

noisome *adj.* **1.** *A noisome odor filled the compartment and frightened us all:* smelly, foul, malodorous, stinking, fetid, reeking, rank, rotten, nauseating, putrid, mephitic. **2.** *A noisome substance had seeped into the drinking-water:* harmful, noxious, injurious, hurtful, detrimental, unhealthy, deleterious, pernicious, toxic, baneful, poisonous. —**Ant.** 2 wholesome, beneficial, healthful, salubrious.

noisy *adj. The streets are always noisy at 5 P.M.:* loud, rackety, clamorous, deafening, earsplitting, uproarious, turbulent, blaring, strident, boisterous, thunderous, thundering, tumultuous, tempestuous, raging, stormy, resounding; alive, animated, lively; furious, rampageous; grating, jarring, harsh-sounding; dissonant, discordant; blatant, clangorous; shrill, piercing, cacophonous. —**Ant.** quiet, noiseless, silent, subdued, hushed, still; melodious, tuneful.

nomad *n. Many Lapps were nomads until the U.S.S.R. cut off their migration route:* wanderer, itinerant, mover, rambler, roamer, strayer, migrator, migrant, traveler, rover, vagabond, tramp, bohemian, gypsy, knight of the road, vagrant, hobo, stray, straggler; refugee, runaway, renegade; immigrant, emigrant.

nomadic *adj. The Bedouins of Arabia are a nomadic people:* traveling, wandering, roaming, roving, drifting, migratory, migrant, itinerant, strolling, peregrinating; vagabond, peripatetic, footloose, vagrant.

nom de plume *n. Samuel Clemens' nom de plume was "Mark Twain":* pen name, writing name; pseudonym, assumed name; false name, alias.

nomenclature *n. In the nomenclature of botany, a tomato is a berry:* terminology, phraseology, vocabulary, terms; naming, nomination, appellation, designation, taxonomy; language, jargon, lingo.

nominal *adj.* **1.** *The independence of Andorra from France and Spain is by no means merely nominal:* titular, ostensible, in name only, so-called, theoretical, official; purported, professed; pretended, suggested; baseless, groundless; puppet. **2.** *There will be a nominal charge for the box lunch:* small, low, minimum, moderate, reasonable, inexpensive, low-priced, cheap; unsubstantial, insignificant. —**Ant.** 1 veritable, actual, real, true. 2 considerable, substantial.

nominate *v.* **1.** *I nominate Bill for club president:* name as a candidate, propose, suggest, recommend, put forward; label, tag, call, term, style. **2.** *The Prime Minister nominated him Ambassador to France:* name, pick, choose; authorize, place in authority, elevate, elect, install, select, invest.

nomination *n. He has a good chance of winning the nomination:* choice of a candidate, selection, election, designation; submission of a name, suggestion; appointment, installation; accession, inauguration, investiture.

nonbeliever *n. The church tried to rescue the souls of the nonbelievers:* doubter, unbeliever, skeptic, cynic, freethinker, doubting Thomas, backslider, questioner, empiricist, agnostic, atheist; heathen, pagan, infidel. —**Ant.** follower, devotee, disciple, convert, fanatic.

nonchalant *adj. How can he be so nonchalant in all this trouble?:* unconcerned, blasé, unheeding, imperturbable, unexcited, unemotional, unmoved, unaffected, unstirred, unruffled, cool, collected; offhand, casual, easygoing; indifferent, apathetic, uninterested, insouciant; withdrawn, dispassionate, unmindful, heedless, insensible; languid, phlegmatic, listless, lethargic, lazy, indolent, idle, careless; slack, lax. —**Ant.** concerned, moved, affected, stirred; anxious, agitated.

noncommittal *adj. She gave me a noncommit-*

tal answer: indefinite, equivocal, indecisive, vague, evasive; reserved, guarded, cautious, wary, careful, circumspect; tentative, ambiguous, neutral, temporizing; safe, cool, politic, prudent, discreet; mute, mum, unspeaking. —**Ant.** definite, decisive, positive, conclusive.

noncompliant *adj. His noncompliant attitude threatened to ruin his career:* nonconforming, unorthodox, unconventional, iconoclastic, dissenting, disagreeing, noncooperating, differing, objecting, dissident; obstinate, rebellious, resistive, ungovernable, unruly. —**Ant.** agreeable, complaisant, obliging, obedient, compliant.

nonconformist *n. The Pilgrims were nonconformists who came to America for religious freedom:* dissenter, dissident, individualist, loner, free spirit, liberated person, protester, reformer, heretic, schismatic, rebel, revolutionary, radical, iconoclast; eccentric, exception, original, oddity; insurgent, maverick, deserter, renegade; freethinker, bohemian, vagabond, beat, hippy, *Informal* character, *Slang* oddball, crackpot, screwball, weirdo, freak, nut, card.

nonconformity *n. They couldn't accept his nonconformity:* heterodoxy, iconoclasm, unconventionality, eccentricity, nonacceptance, noncompliance, originality, heresy.

nondescript *adj. The thief was nondescript and no one could recall his face:* undistinctive, usual, ordinary, vague, unexceptional, characterless, unimpressive, colorless, amorphous, undistinguished, stereotyped. —**Ant.** distinctive, unusual, extraordinary, vivid, unique.

nonentity *n. We hear she married a nonentity:* nobody, unimportant person, unperson, mediocrity, small-fry, nothing, zero, cipher, nullity, *Informal* small potato, no-count; Tom, Dick, or Harry. —**Ant.** celebrity, somebody, VIP.

nonessential *adj.* **1.** *Candy and movies are nonessential expenses:* unessential, unnecessary, unimportant; extraneous, irrelevant, subsidiary, incidental, accidental, extrinsic, peripheral, secondary; dispensable, disallowable, unconnected, beside the point, impertinent, inappropriate; insignificant, trivial, inconsequential, inconsiderable. —*n.* **2.** *The new budget cuts out all nonessentials:* unessential thing, unnecessary item, incidental; luxury, (*plural*) trimmings, trivia. —**Ant.** 1 vital, essential, important; apt, appropriate; significant.

nonesuch *n. The nonesuch won his third batting title:* paragon, ideal, model, pattern, nonpareil.

no-nonsense *adj. She has a no-nonsense attitude where business is concerned:* earnest, ardent, diligent, resolute, purposeful, determined, intent, dedicated, committed, grave, sober, solemn, sobersided, serious-minded, severe, grim. —**Ant.** frivolous, giddy, slapdash, scatterbrained, offhand.

nonpareil *adj.* **1.** *She was a woman of nonpareil beauty:* unequaled, unique, unsurpassed, unmatched, unrivaled, one-of-a-kind; exceptional, supreme, extraordinary, elite, *Slang* super. —*n.* **2.** *As founder of the cult, he was the nonpareil of virtue:* paragon, epitome, apotheo-

sis, symbol, exemplar, ideal, pattern, model, representative, one of a kind, *Latin* ne plus ultra, *French* crème de la crème.

nonpartisan *adj. Tax collection agencies should be nonpartisan:* unaffiliated, nonpolitical, politically independent; unbiased, unprejudiced; impartial; unswayed, uninfluenced; equitable, fair, just; uninvolved, disinterested, unimplicated; impersonal, objective; freethinking, unbigoted. —**Ant.** partisan, political; biased, prejudiced; unfair, unjust, inequitable.

nonplus *v. The child was nonplussed by all the TV cameras:* confuse, confound, muddle, baffle, bother, abash, disconcert, discountenance, disturb, upset, dismay, embarrass, faze; perplex, puzzle, bewilder, stump, mystify; flabbergast, astound, dumbfound, put at a loss, astonish; stop, halt, bring to a standstill, stymie, deadlock, balk, foil.

nonsectarian *adj. The town wants to found a nonsectarian youth club:* interdenominational, interchurch, undenominational, nondenominational, ecumenical; all-embracing, all-inclusive, all-encompassing. —**Ant.** sectarian, schismatic, denominational.

nonsense *n. If you're going to talk nonsense, I won't listen:* foolishness, folly, ridiculousness, absurdity, stupidity, inanity, senselessness, silliness, childishness; fooling, tomfoolery, joking, shenanigans, monkey business, horseplay, high jinks, antics; ludicrousness, meaninglessness, facetiousness; triviality, frivolity, extravagance, flummery, trifles; prattle, babble, chatter, blather, drivel, gibberish, *Informal* twaddle, bunk, trash, garbage, rubbish, hogwash, moonshine, rot, fiddle-faddle, piffle, flapdoodle; bombast, claptrap, balderdash, bosh, *Slang* baloney. —**Ant.** sense, common sense, wisdom; fact, reality, truth; gravity, seriousness, reason.

nonstop *adj. Lindbergh made the first nonstop flight from New York to Paris:* continuous, endless, uninterrupted, unrelieved, unbroken, unremitting, constant, incessant, never-ending, interminable, round-the-clock. —**Ant.** sporadic, periodic, interrupted.

nonviolent *adj. She urged nonviolent resistance:* pacifist, without violence, peaceable, passive, peaceful, quiet.

nook *n. We made the alcove into a breakfast nook:* recess, niche, alcove, cranny, corner; depression, cubbyhole, cavity, dugout; cove, snug place, retreat, refuge, shelter, haven, lair; hiding place, den, hideaway.

noon *n. The workers ate lunch at noon:* midday, twelve o'clock, twelve noon, 12 M.; noonday, high noon, noontime, lunch time; zenith, meridian, highest point.

norm *n. A C-average is the norm in our grading system:* standard, average, rule, type; pattern, model, par; yardstick, gauge, barometer, criterion, measure, measuring rod.

normal *adj. His growth is normal for that age:* standard, average, usual, ordinary, expected, natural, regular; conformable, conforming, consistent; typical, par, representative, conventional; constant, steady, unchanging; steadfast, reliable, dependable; in good order, well-regulated, in shape, fit, sound, healthy; continuous, uninterrupted; incessant, unceasing, unremitting, unchanging, uniform; sane, reasonable, rational, right-minded; middling, mediocre. **—Ant.** abnormal, unusual, exceptional, irregular; peculiar, rare, singular, uncommon; unprecedented, remarkable; monstrous, unnatural.

normally *adv. Normally we rose early for breakfast:* habitually, typically, usually, commonly, regularly, ordinarily.

north *adj.* **1.** *That north wind is really a chiller:* coming from the north, northerly; moving toward the north, northward; northern; polar, arctic; northernmost; upper. *—adv.* **2.** *Leaving the city, we headed north:* toward the north, northward; northerly.

nose *n.* **1.** *He keeps sticking his nose in our business:* proboscis, *Informal* snoot, snout, beak. *—v.* **2.** *She could nose out any irregularity:* detect, sniff, smell, pry, scent, search, snoop.

nostalgia *n. Those old recordings give him a feeling of nostalgia:* longing for the past, bittersweet memory; remembrance; homesickness, longing for home; pining, languishing; regret, remorse, regretfulness.

nostrum *n. This is an old nostrum my grandmother used to treat a stomachache:* remedy, medicine, formula, medicament; physic, balm, elixir, drug, potion; treatment, cure, cure-all, panacea; dose, draft, prescription; patent medicine.

nosy or **nosey** *adj. Don't be so nosy—this doesn't concern you:* inquisitive, all ears, curious, overcurious, prying, intrusive, snooping, eavesdropping, *Informal* snoopy.

notable *adj.* **1.** *There is a notable difference in their ages:* conspicuous, marked, pronounced, noticeable, salient, outstanding, remarkable, striking. **2.** *A notable doctor endorsed the book:* renowned, reputable, distinguished, famed, famous, celebrated, prominent, eminent, well-known. *—n.* **3.** *The convention attracted many notables:* celebrity, dignitary, luminary, personage, name, personality, *Informal* VIP, bigwig, *Slang* wheel, biggie. **—Ant.** 1 vague, ill-defined; imperceptible, concealed, hidden. 2 unknown, anonymous, obscure, little known.

notably *adv. The turnout at the lecture was notably small:* strikingly, markedly, noticeably, outstandingly, prominently, conspicuously, visibly; distinctly, unmistakably.

notation *n. He made a notation on his engagement calendar:* note, memorandum, entry.

notch *n.* **1.** *He had a notch on his six-shooter for each victim:* nick, cut, dent, indentation, score, scoring. **2.** *This restaurant is a notch above the others:* degree, level, grade, *Slang* cut. *—v.* **3.** *We notched our heights on the tree trunk:* nick, score, cut, mark, scratch.

note *n.* **1.** *Make a note to get some more milk:* memorandum, notation. **2.** *Drop Thelma a note and thank her:* brief letter, message, epistle, missive, communication; dispatch, communiqué; memorandum, *Informal* line. **3.** *He paid the bill in $50 notes:* bank note, bill, paper money; legal tender, money, currency; voucher, certificate, silver or gold certificate; draft, sight draft, bank draft; promissory note, mortgage note, *Informal* greenback, *Slang* folding money, green, scratch, bread, lettuce. **4.** *Take note of the lavish table decorations:* regard, notice. **5.** *Several persons of note were at the party:* importance, consequence, distinction, prominence, eminence, notability, reputation, fame, renown, celebrity. *—v.* **6.** *Note his name and address in your book:* make a note of, mark down, set down, put down, enter, write, write down, jot down, make a memorandum of, make an entry of. **7.** *We noted his reluctance to testify:* notice, mark, perceive, take cognizance of, give attention to, take notice of, be aware of, be conscious of. **—Ant.** 4 inattention, indifference, heedlessness, aloofness, unconcern. 5 obscurity, insignificance. 7 ignore, disregard, overlook.

noted *adj. A noted surgeon operated on him:* famous, renowned, eminent, celebrated, well-known, distinguished, prominent, illustrious, reputable; remarkable, notable, noteworthy, outstanding. **—Ant.** unknown, obscure, undistinguished; notorious, infamous.

noteworthy *adj. The book is a noteworthy addition to our library:* distinguished, outstanding, significant, important, remarkable, notable; substantial, considerable; exceptionable, unusual, singular. **—Ant.** negligible, trivial, inconsequential.

nothing *n.* **1.** *There is nothing for dinner. His latest play is nothing:* naught, no thing, nullity; insignificance, obscurity; trash, stuff, rubbish; bubble, air; bauble, bagatelle, trifle, gewgaw, trinket; trivia, inconsequentials. **2.** *The score was nine to nothing:* zero, naught, none, cipher, nix, *Slang* goose egg, duck egg, zilch, zip.

notice *n.* **1.** *The plan is not worth our notice:* attention, regard, cognizance, heed. **2.** *Did you receive any notice about the sale?:* information, mention, notification, specification; intelligence, knowledge, *Slang* goods, dope, info; statement, declaration, communication, disclosure; poster, handbill, circular, leaflet; pamphlet, brochure; advertisement, announcement. **3.** *She gave two weeks' notice when she quit:* warning, advisement, notification. **4.** *The paper gave the play a bad notice:* review, critique, appraisal, rating. *—v.* **5.** *Did you notice her engagement ring?:* see, catch sight of, observe, eye, take in, take notice of, mark, *Slang* get a load of. **—Ant.** 1 oversight, disregard, neglect, slight, connivance, omission, heedlessness; misinformation, ignorance. 5 ignore, slight, overlook, disregard, neglect; misjudge.

noticeable *adj. There's a noticeable difference in our totals:* definite, clear, plain, distinct, evident, obvious, conspicuous, unmistakable; striking, noteworthy, perceivable, perceptible, appreciable, observable, manifest, palpable.

notify *v. They notified us of a rent increase:* inform, acquaint, let know, send word, advise, tell, enlighten, apprise; warn, serve notice on.

notion n. **1.** *I have no notion of what he means:* idea, concept, suspicion, intimation, conception. **2.** *I never knew anyone with such odd notions:* belief, view, opinion; whim, quirk, caprice, fancy; whimsy, conceit, humor, vagary, crotchet, eccentricity.

notoriety n. *She sought fame, but achieved only notoriety:* disrepute, ill repute, shame, disgrace, discredit, dishonor, infamy, ignominy, scandal, degradation, stigma, stain, blot. —**Ant.** honor, nobility, esteem, goodness, standing.

notorious adj. *The guest was really a notorious jewel thief:* infamous, egregious, blatant, outrageous, glaring, arrant; widely known, renowned, notable, celebrated, outstanding.

notwithstanding prep. **1.** *Notwithstanding his efforts he was defeated:* despite, in spite of. —adv. **2.** *They tried to comfort us, but we were upset notwithstanding:* nevertheless, yet, however. —conj. **3.** *It was essentially the same statement, notwithstanding the different wording:* although, though, however, yet, nevertheless. —**Ant.** on account of, because of.

nourish v. *They needed good food to nourish their bodies:* nurture, feed, sustain; breast-feed, nurse, suckle. —**Ant.** starve, undernourish.

nourishing adj. *The cereal was very nourishing:* nutritious, wholesome, healthy, healthful, healthy, wholesome, beneficial.

nourishment n. *She's beginning to recover now and take a little nourishment:* food, sustenance, nutriment, nutrition, viands, victuals, comestibles, food and drink, meat, bread, *Slang* eats, chow, grub.

novel adj. *That's a novel way to do your hair:* unusual, original, new, different, innovative, out of the ordinary, uncommon, unorthodox, unconventional, singular, unique. —**Ant.** usual, customary, run-of-the-mill, habitual, ordinary, common, familiar; venerable, ancient, old-fashioned, time-honored, traditional.

novelty n. **1.** *There's little novelty in his writing:* originality, newness, uniqueness, variation, innovation, surprise, change. **2.** *The shop sells novelties to tourists:* trinket, gewgaw, gimcrack, bagatelle, bauble, knick-knack; token, souvenir, memento.

novice n. *He's a novice in the blacksmith's trade:* beginner, tyro, learner, apprentice, newcomer; greenhorn, tenderfoot, amateur; pupil, student, disciple. —**Ant.** master, old hand, past master, professional, *Informal* pro.

now adv. *Leave now, please:* immediately, at once, at present, directly, forthwith, instantly, straightaway, right away, right now, pronto; today, nowadays, these days, this day.

noxious adj. *The room was filled with noxious fumes:* harmful, poisonous, deleterious, injurious, baneful, damaging, pernicious, hurtful; lethal, deadly, virulent; putrid, putrescent, noisome, foul, foul-smelling, abominable, beastly, revolting, loathsome, disgusting. —**Ant.** wholesome, beneficial; sanitary, salutary, salubrious.

nuance n. *This poem admirably expresses different nuances of feeling:* subtle change, variation, nice distinction, delicate distinction; nicety, touch, shade, subtlety, refinement, modulation, delicacy, fineness, finesse; keenness, sharpness, discernment.

nub n. **1.** *The fabric has nubs on its surface:* hump, knot, lump, knob, node; bulge, swelling, tumescence, protuberance, prominence, projection. **2.** *The nub of the question is his guilt or innocence:* essence, crux, heart, core, gist, kernel, *Slang* nitty-gritty.

nucleus n. *Retired employees make up the nucleus of the club:* core, seed, nub, heart, kernel, center, pith. —**Ant.** exterior, face, integument; outer shell; appearance, features.

nude adj. *The nude statue caused considerable comment:* naked, stark naked, bare, bared, unclad, mother-naked, undressed, stripped, exposed, unclothed, wearing nothing, unarrayed, unadorned, uncovered, *Informal* stripped to the buff, without a stitch; *Slang* raw, in the raw, in one's birthday suit. —**Ant.** clothed, covered, dressed, appareled, clad.

nudge v. *She nudged me at all the funny lines:* elbow, poke, jab, punch; bump, jostle, jolt, jog; push, prod, touch, shove, press; motion, signal, indicate; nod.

nugatory adj. *Musicians know that undisciplined practice is of nugatory value:* inconsequential, trifling, trivial, piddling, paltry, worthless, useless, valueless, meritless, profitless; empty, idle, hollow, functionless, otiose, ineffectual. —**Ant.** valuable, useful; efficacious, profitable.

nuisance n. *That noisy fan is a real nuisance:* annoyance, bother, pest, bore, irritation, thorn, aggravation; inconvenience, botheration; worry, fret; scourge, affliction; handicap, misfortune; grievance, vexation; plague, pestilence, blight, curse; trouble, hurt, pain, torment, burden. —**Ant.** pleasure, delight, satisfaction, benefit, blessing, gratification, happiness, joy.

null adj. *The contract is null because of violations:* invalid, inoperative, void, nonexistent, null and void; worthless, unimportant, insignificant, valueless, no good, immaterial, *Slang* NG. —**Ant.** valid, lawful, binding.

nullify v. *Such an antiquated law should be nullified:* repeal, abrogate, void, make void, cancel, annul, declare null and void, abolish; set aside, retract, revoke, rescind, veto, invalidate, override. —**Ant.** enact, decree, legislate, ratify, confirm; establish, institute.

numb adj. *My thumb was numb after I hit it:* unfeeling, insensate, benumbed, insensible, dead, deadened, anesthetized, frozen, narcotized.

number n. **1.** *Assign a number to each box:* numeral, figure, character, symbol, integer, cipher, digit; round number, even or odd number; amount, quantity, sum, aggregate, tally, total. **2.** *A large number of guests came to the reception:* quantity, multitude, company, assemblage, group, crowd, *Informal* mob, mass, bunch, herd, swarm; abundance, preponderance; indefinite number, indeterminate number; a good many, a great number; scores, quantities; host, army; bevy, array. **3.** *There's a story about her in the current number:* issue, edition; book, magazine, quarterly; chapter, section, part, division; paragraph, passage. —*v.* **4.** *Number the pages in sequence. The guests numbered more than a hundred:* give a number to, enumerate; figure, cipher; paginate, foliate, numerate; tally, figure up, tot, reckon, count, total; compute, calculate; estimate, make an estimate of. —**Ant.** 2 scarcity, fewness, scantiness, paucity; want, lack; shortage, insufficiency. 4 guess, hazard, hypothesize, theorize, conjecture; lump, mass.

numberless *adj. Numberless children were begging in the streets:* countless, innumerable, numerous, multitudinous, myriad, uncountable, uncounted, unnumbered, immeasurable, plenteous, illimitable, copious, unbounded, unending; *Slang* umpteen, zillions. —**Ant.** few, scarcely any, a handful of, a couple of.

numeral *n. The numerals on the clock are painted gold:* number, symbol, character, figure, cipher, digit, integer; cardinal number, Arabic or Roman numeral; letter.

numeric also **numerical** *adj. The numeric calculations took effort:* arithmetical, mathematical, statistical, binary.

numerous *adj. The bride and groom received numerous gifts:* many, profuse, in profusion, copious, abundant, myriad, plentiful, a multitude of, multitudinous. —**Ant.** few, scarcely any, not many.

numskull or **numbskull** *n. Slang The numskull didn't even know the alphabet!:* dunce, ninny, scatterbrain, blockhead, bonehead, dolt, halfwit, knucklehead, dummy, dunderhead, silly ass, dimwit, dullard, nitwit, idiot, imbecile, chowderhead, muttonhead, noodlehead, fool, simpleton, jerk, dope, klutz, sap, lunkhead, dummkopf, nincompoop.

nuptial *adj. The nuptial ceremony was very brief:* matrimonial, marital; conjugal, connubial, hymeneal.

nuptials *n. pl. The nuptials were held in the bride's home:* wedding, marriage, marriage ceremony, matrimonials, espousals, hymeneals, exchange of vows.

nurse *n.* **1.** *The children were left with their nurse:* (*variously*) trained nurse, practical nurse, registered nurse, private nurse, *British* sister; district nurse, public health nurse; governess, nanny, nursemaid; nurserymaid, nurse girl; dry nurse, wet nurse; guardian, attendant. —*v.* **2.** *His wife nursed him back to health:* attend, care for, minister to, attend to; doctor, treat, remedy. **3.** *The mother cat refused to nurse her kittens:* suckle, feed at the breast, wet-nurse, give suck to; succor, nourish, feed; foster, nurture, cultivate. **4.** *He's been nursing a grudge for weeks:* keep in mind, bear in the mind, have in mind;

harbor, nurture, encourage, foster, promote. —**Ant.** neglect, disregard, slight; starve, kill, destroy.

nursery *n.* **1.** *The children spent their mornings at the nursery:* nursery school, day nursery, preschool; kindergarten, day school, infant school; children's room, schoolroom. **2.** *We bought a small tree at the nursery:* greenhouse, botanical garden; cold frame, conservatory, forcing house; breeding place, hotbed, incubator.

nurture *v.* **1.** *The book told us how to nurture the puppy:* feed, nourish, foster, tend, sustain, maintain, strengthen; provision, victual, mess. **2.** *The school is responsible for nurturing the child's mind:* train, discipline, develop, prepare, cultivate, tutor, school, educate, teach, instruct; bring up, rear, breed, raise. —**Ant.** 2 neglect, overlook, slight; disregard, ignore; deprive, dispossess.

nut *n.* **1.** *A bowl of nuts stood on the table:* edible kernel, nutmeat; seed, stone, pit. **2.** *Slang He's a nut about model airplanes:* enthusiast, fanatic, devotee, zealot, fan, buff, aficionado. **3.** *Slang That nut should be locked up:* eccentric, crackpot, screwball, oddball, freak; madman, lunatic, maniac, loony; idiot; psychopath.

nutriment *n. They invented a synthetic nutriment for space trips:* food, nourishment, foodstuff, *Slang* eats, chow; nutrition, nutrient, sustenance, subsistence, provisions, aliment; provender, feed, forage, mess, fodder, fare; groceries, victuals, edibles, eatables, board, daily bread, meat.

nutrition *n. A balanced diet gives one the proper nutrition:* food, nourishment, nutriment, foodstuffs, eatables, edibles, sustenance; groceries, provisions, rations, subsistence, *Slang* chow, grub; provender, pasturage, forage, fodder; silage, feed.

nutritious *adj. The diet is nutritious but low in calories:* nourishing, nutritive, body-building, wholesome, sustaining.

nuts *adj. You must be nuts to lend him more money:* crazy, wacky, bats, insane; *British* daft, potty; mad, unbalanced, cracked, demented; *Slang* wacko, round the bend, bonkers, dotty, balmy, loony, bananas.

nutty *adj. He's worked out some nutty scheme to make wire shoelaces:* foolish, senseless, crackbrained, inane, addlepated, lunatic, *British* daft, balmy, harebrained, silly; *Slang* goofy, wacky, screwy, cuckoo, dippy, wacko, squirrelly, meshuga, loony, bughouse, dotty, weirdo.

nuzzle *v. The child nuzzled the kitten:* cuddle, coddle, snuggle, nestle, caress, embrace, fondle; pet, cosset, pat; kiss, *Slang* buss, smack.

nymph *n. The painting showed nymphs and shepherds at play:* female nature spirit, naiad, dryad, sylph, wood nymph; belle, charmer, beauty.

oaf *n. That oaf wouldn't know a good job if he saw one:* dolt, lout, boob, booby, dunderhead, fool, numskull, bonehead, blockhead, dunce, dullard, simpleton, lummox, boor, ninny, nitwit, clod, ignoramus, nincompoop, moron, idiot, imbecile, half-wit, *Slang* jerk, sap, dope, dummy, klutz. —**Ant.** genius, intellectual, pundit, sage, guru, *Slang* egghead.

oasis *n.* **1.** *The road went through several oases in the desert:* watering place, water hole; fertile area, green spot. **2.** *The library was an oasis of quiet:* haven, refuge, harbor, sanctum, sanctuary, asylum, ivory tower, retreat, shelter. —**Ant.** 1 desert, arid region.

oath *n.* **1.** *Every U.S. President must take an oath to uphold the Constitution:* vow, avowal, pledge, adjuration, affirmation, attestation; declaration, deposition, affidavit. **2.** *The carpenter let out a stream of oaths when he hit his thumb with the hammer:* curse, curse word, profanity, blasphemy, obscenity, expletive, *Informal* cuss word, swear word; swearing, imprecation, malediction. —**Ant.** 2 benediction, blessing; prayer, invocation.

obdurate *adj.* **1.** *The child was obdurate in refusing to eat vegetables:* stubborn, obstinate, intractable, unyielding, inflexible, adamant, immovable, willful, headstrong, pigheaded, mulish, bullheaded; unmanageable, uncontrollable, ungovernable. **2.** *The tyrant was obdurate in his treatment of prisoners:* unmoved, uncaring, unfeeling, harsh, merciless, unmerciful, unpitying, pitiless, unsympathetic, uncompassionate, unsparing, untouched; hardened, callous, cruel, cold-blooded, hardhearted. —**Ant.** 1 obedient, agreeable, compliant, flexible, amenable; manageable, docile, tractable. 2 compassionate, sympathetic, caring, feeling, merciful, pitying, relenting, softhearted, kind, gentle, tender.

obedience *n. The dog was sent to school to learn obedience:* compliance, dutifulness, submissiveness, submission, subservience, docility, acquiescence, obeisance, deference, tractability, willingness, yielding, ductility, subjection; allegiance; conformance, conformability, compliance, accordance.

obedient *adj. An obedient child does what he's told:* obeying, dutiful, compliant, amenable, submissive, subservient, yielding, docile, acquiescent, faithful, loyal, law-abiding, devoted, deferential, respectful, obeisant, governable, tractable. —**Ant.** disobedient, disobeying, insubordinate, rebellious; contrary, perverse, wayward, recalcitrant, refractory, intractable, unruly, contumacious, disrespectful, undutiful, arrogant, unyielding, obstinate, obdurate, stubborn, ungovernable, unmanageable.

obeisance *n. The knights made obeisance to the queen. The king expects obeisance from all his subjects:* bow, curtsy, kneeling, genuflection, submission, subjection, prostration; homage, courtesy, deference, respect, veneration, esteem, regard, reverence, honor, obedience, humility, humbleness, self-abasement; loyalty, fidelity, fealty, allegiance. —**Ant.** disrespect, disregard, dishonor, irreverence; disloyalty, treachery.

obese *adj. The boy is too obese to take part in sports:* fat, overweight, gross, corpulent, heavy, stout, tubby, pudgy, plump, porky, fleshy, chubby, portly; paunchy, rotund, potbellied, big bellied. —**Ant.** skinny, thin, slim, slender, scrawny, lean, spare, angular, rawboned, lank, lanky, gaunt.

obey *v. A good citizen obeys the law:* comply with, be ruled by, follow orders, submit to, respect, observe, be regulated by, abide by, conform to, be governed by, mind, heed; acquiesce, serve, assent, concur, toe the line, submit to, bow to, yield to, succumb to, accede to. —**Ant.** disobey, defy, revolt, rebel, mutiny, resist, refuse, be insubordinate.

obfuscate *v. The questions he raised merely obfuscated the issue:* confuse, obscure, blur, muddle, garble, scramble, mess up, befog, complicate, distort, becloud, confound, fluster, stupefy. —**Ant.** clear up, clarify, simplify, elucidate.

obituary *n. The obituary appeared in the newspaper:* obit, death announcement, death notice, tribute, eulogy.

object *v.* **1.** *Mother objects to cigar smoking:* be averse, take exception, disapprove of, oppose, protest, be at odds with, balk at, look askance at, frown on, demur from, shudder at, revolt at; dislike, loathe, shrink from, abhor, abominate, criticize, condemn, denounce, remonstrate against, cavil at, carp at, find fault with, *Slang* knock. —*n.* **2.** *A bright moving object appeared in the sky at sunset:* thing, article, body, form, phenomenon; device, gadget, contrivance, *Slang* thingamajig, thingamabob, dingus, doohickey. **3.** *The principal has been the object of much criticism:* subject, target, recipient, cynosure; victim, butt, dupe, prey, quarry. **4.** *What is the object of the research?:* aim, goal, purpose, point, intent, intention, objective, design, end, target, mission, use; significance, reason, sense, meaning, explanation, substance, principle, essence, gist, pith, cause, motive, incentive, inducement, basis. —**Ant.** 1 approve, agree, welcome, admit, greet with open arms, accept, comply, concur, assert, consent, acquiesce, accede; like, love, fancy, relish, praise, applaud, laud, admire, compliment.

objection *n.* **1.** *Father's objection was that the trip was much too expensive:* complaint, criticism, opposing reason, contradiction, counter argument, rebuttal, protest, challenge, exception, demurral, cavil, *Slang* kick, beef. **2.** *The boy kept the dog despite his sister's objection:* disapproval, opposition, disagreement, dissension, reservation, disapprobation. —**Ant.** 2 approval, consent, agreement, endorsement, support, countenance, approbation.

objectionable *adj. He apologized for his objectionable behavior:* unacceptable, intolerable, unbearable, unendurable, disagreeable, unpleasant, displeasing, inappropriate, unseemly; offensive, obnoxious, nasty, foul, abominable, vile, odious, revolting, disgusting, abhorrent, loathsome, despicable, distasteful. —**Ant.** acceptable, agreeable, likable, pleasant, pleasing, appropriate, seemly, fit, meet.

objective adj. **1.** It's very difficult to give objective criticism: impartial, unprejudiced, detached, dispassionate, impersonal, unbiased, fair, just, uncolored, open-minded, disinterested, unswayed, uninfluenced; real, actual. —n. **2.** Her objective is to get a college education: aim, goal, purpose, object, intent, intention, design, end, mission; destination, target, mark. —**Ant.** 1 subjective, personal, biased, prejudiced, warped, unjust, unfair; abstract, theoretical.

objectively adv. She tried to look at life objectively: impartially, dispassionately, impartially, without prejudice, neutrally, open-mindedly.

obligate v. Posting bail obligated us to raise money: oblige, require, bind, constrain, force, restrict, bind.

obligation n. **1.** He has an obligation to help support his parents: duty, responsibility, a favor owed, debt, indebtedness, liability, onus, charge, care, constraint, accountability, answerability. **2.** The manufacturer has not fulfilled the terms of his obligation: agreement, contract, compact, bond, commitment, pledge, promise, oath, word, understanding; warranty, guaranty. —**Ant.** 1 choice, freedom.

obligatory adj. Paying taxes is obligatory: compulsory, mandatory, coercive, binding, required, enforced, requisite, imperative, peremptory, necessary, unavoidable. —**Ant.** noncompulsory, voluntary.

oblige v. **1.** Having been to their party, we were obliged to invite them to ours. The will obliges the heirs to live in the family mansion: obligate, to be duty bound, require, demand of, necessitate, make, impel, constrain, bind, compel, force, coerce. **2.** The pianist obliged the guests with a selection: accommodate, favor, do a favor for, do a service for, put oneself out for; help, aid, assist, support, serve. —**Ant.** 1 free, unfetter, liberate, release, acquit; persuade, induce. 2 disoblige, inconvenience.

obliging adj. A very obliging saleslady waited on me: accommodating, helpful, cooperative, solicitous, kind, considerate, well-disposed; sympathetic, friendly, amiable, agreeable, good-natured, cheerful, complaisant, courteous, gracious, polite. —**Ant.** disobliging, unaccommodating, uncooperative, unhelpful, ill-disposed, inconsiderate; rude, discourteous, curt, surly, sullen.

oblique adj. **1.** Draw an oblique line from one corner of the paper to the opposite: diagonal, slanting, slanted, inclined, sloping, tilted, aslant; askew, awry. **2.** The poem contains an oblique reference to Queen Elizabeth I: indirect, masked, covert, veiled, cloaked, sly, devious, underhand, furtive, sneaking, implied, hinted, suggested, allusive. —**Ant.** 1 vertical; horizon-

tal. 2 direct, frank, open, straightforward, forthright, candid, blunt, obvious, unveiled.

obliterate v. **1.** The bombardment obliterated the town: annihilate, eradicate, destroy, raze, level, wipe out. **2.** The eraser obliterated the writing. Try to obliterate the incident from your mind: erase, expunge, wipe out, rub out, efface, delete, remove, abolish; write over, strike over, cancel, blot out. —**Ant.** 1 construct, create, raise up; reconstruct, restore, rehabilitate. 2 write; add, keep.

oblivion n. **1.** The writer, once popular, is now relegated to oblivion: obscurity, limbo, a forgotten state, disregard, insignificance. **2.** Nonreligious people believe that death brings complete oblivion. He sought oblivion in liquor: nothingness, nonexistence, the void, blankness; forgetfulness, obliviousness, unconcern, unconsciousness, insensibility, blotting out. —**Ant.** 1 fame, popularity, celebrity, immortality. 2 being, existence, life; memory, remembrance, reminiscence, recollection, reminder.

oblivious adj. Concentrating on his work, the draftsman was oblivious to the noise. How can you be so oblivious to her rude remarks?: unaware of, unconscious of, undiscerning, insensible, unobservant; unmindful, disregardful, heedless of, unconcerned, forgetful, inattentive, careless. —**Ant.** aware, conscious, cognizant; heedful, concerned, troubled, worried, annoyed.

oblong adj. The oblong object couldn't be identified: ovate, egg-shaped, ellipsoidal, elliptical, oval, elongate, elongated.

obloquy n. **1.** The obloquy he received for his negligence was swift and scathing: censure, rebuke, denunciation, verbal abuse, vilification, calumny, dressing-down, opprobrium, defamation, billingsgate, scurrility, invective. **2.** The obloquy remained with her for the rest of her life: shame, disgrace, bad repute, ignominy, odium, infamy, humiliation, degradation, contempt, disfavor, discredit, opprobrium.

obnoxious adj. She's charming, but her husband is obnoxious: offensive, objectionable, disagreeable, unpleasant, displeasing, nasty, nauseating, repugnant, foul, vile, odious, revolting, disgusting, abominable, loathsome, despicable, abhorrent, repellent, hateful, detestable; unseemly, inappropriate, unbearable, unendurable, intolerable, insufferable. —**Ant.** agreeable, pleasant, pleasing, delightful, charming, engaging, likable, alluring, enchanting; acceptable, appropriate, seemly, fit, meet, in good taste.

obscene adj. The court must decide whether the movie is obscene: indecent, foul, morally offensive, pornographic, prurient, lewd, lascivious, lubricious, salacious, vulgar, scatological, dirty, filthy, Slang smutty, blue. —**Ant.** decent, modest, chaste, innocent, clean.

obscenity n. **1.** Many objected to the obscenity of the book: indecency, pornography, lewdness, prurience, lasciviousness, salaciousness, vulgarity, dirtiness, smuttiness, filthiness. **2.** His speech was full of obscenities: vulgarity, profanity, obscene expression, taboo word, Slang cuss

obscure to obstinate

word, swear word, four-letter word. **—Ant.** 1 decency, modesty, chastity, innocence.

obscure *adj.* **1.** *The point of his speech was obscure:* unclear, not easily understood, hidden, vague, uncertain, indefinite, indefinable, inscrutable, unfathomable, puzzling, perplexing, enigmatic, cryptic, confusing, confused. **2.** *The bus stopped at an obscure little town:* unknown, little known, nameless, unheard of, unsung, forgotten, unrenowned, unnoted, insignificant, inconsequential, unimportant, out-of-the-way, inconspicuous. **3.** *An obscure figure could be seen through the fog. The room is too obscure for reading:* indistinct, faint, dim, shadowy, murky, cloudy, dusky; dark, lightless, unlighted, unilluminated, somber, dingy. *—v.* **4.** *The large building obscured the hills behind:* hide, conceal, cover, block, eclipse; veil, blur, bedim, cloud, becloud; fog, befog; shroud, curtain, cloak, screen; mask, disguise; overshadow, shadow, darken. **5.** *The suspect tried to obscure the case against him:* confuse, obfuscate, muddle, befuddle, make hard to understand. **—Ant.** 1 clear, lucid, plain, transparent, obvious, evident, manifest, apparent, explicit, intelligible; straightforward, unmistakable. 2 well-known, famous, renowned, prominent, eminent, celebrated; important, major, significant. 3 distinct, conspicuous, prominent, well-defined; bright, light. 4 reveal, disclose, show, expose, exhibit. 5 clarify, explain.

obsequious *adj.* *The boss prefers obsequious underlings:* servile, fawning, toadying, sycophantic, subservient, menial, ingratiating, deferential, slavish, cringing, cowering, mealymouthed, truckling, *Slang* bootlicking, kowtowing, apple-polishing. **—Ant.** domineering, overbearing, swaggering, lordly, imperious, proud, haughty, arrogant, impudent, brash, bold, assertive, forceful, aggressive.

observance *n.* **1.** *Observance of the rules is important in this game:* obeying, following, compliance, adherence, attending, attention, heeding, keeping, regard, observation. **2.** *Christmas is one of our religious observances:* ceremonial, commemoration, celebration, memorialization, solemnity; ceremony, ritual, rite, custom, practice, formality. **—Ant.** 1 nonobservance, disobeying, noncompliance, inattention, disregard, omission.

observant *adj.* *Be observant for signs of danger:* watchful, vigilant, alert, on the lookout, awake, careful; mindful, attentive, aware, heedful, regardful, perceptive, wide-awake, conscious. **—Ant.** unobservant, inattentive, oblivious; unmindful, heedless, indifferent, unconcerned.

observation *n.* **1.** *This telescope is used for the observation of distant stars. Not even the slightest clue escaped the detective's observation:* observing, watching, viewing, seeing, beholding, eyeing, glimpsing, spotting, inspection, detection, examination, surveillance, scrutiny, survey, probe, search; notice, attention, interest, heed, watchfulness, heedfulness, cognizance. **2.** *The doctor examined the patient and wrote* down his observations. The speaker had some witty observations to make about modern politics: finding, firsthand information, discovery, description, diagnosis; remark, comment, statement, reflection, view, idea, opinion, theory, judgment, pronouncement, assertion, commentary.

observe *v.* **1.** *Thousands observed the ship leaving the harbor. Did you observe anything suspicious?:* see, watch, view, behold, peer at, catch sight of, stare at, make out, inspect, survey, glimpse, espy, spot, ogle, eye; notice, note, discover, detect, perceive, mark, heed, regard, pay attention to, size up, take stock of. **2.** *She observed that we were already late:* remark, comment, state, say, mention, announce, assert, declare; opine, reflect, theorize. **3.** *Observe the rules:* obey, comply with, conform to, follow, heed, abide by, adhere to, fulfill, keep, be guided by, acquiesce to, defer to, carry out, execute, perform, respect. **4.** *How many holidays do we observe?:* celebrate, commemorate, honor; sanctify, consecrate, solemnize; recognize, acknowledge. **—Ant.** 3 disobey, disregard, neglect. 4 profane.

obsessed *adj.* *He was obsessed with the idea of winning the race:* possessed, beset, dominated, controlled, having a fixation, maniacal, haunted, overwhelmingly desirous, overwhelmingly fearful, *Slang* hung up on.

obsession *n.* *Becoming a millionaire is an obsession with him:* overwhelming fear, all-encompassing desire, fixation, fixed idea, mania, phobia, quirk, neurotic conviction, ruling passion, monomania; preoccupation, infatuation, craze.

obsolescent *adj.* *Propeller-driven passenger planes are obsolescent:* becoming obsolete, becoming out-of-date, disappearing, declining, passing out of use, dying out, on the way out. **—Ant.** new, novel, modern, late, latest; up-to-date, current, fresh, new-fashioned, fashionable, in vogue, newfangled; in, mod, with-it.

obsolete *adj.* *Women's bloomers are obsolete:* out, out-of-date, out of fashion, out of use, old-fashioned, outdated, passé, outmoded, antiquated, antique, archaic, bygone, dated, extinct.

obstacle *n.* *A stone fence was the last obstacle in the steeplechase. Lack of education is an obstacle to success:* barrier, barricade, hurdle, blockade; impediment, interference, obstruction, hindrance, stumbling block, limitation, restriction, stoppage, check, bar, block, roadblock, curb, snag, catch, problem, difficulty. **—Ant.** help, aid, benefit, boon, spur, expedient, furtherance, support, encouragement.

obstinate *adj.* *The family was too obstinate to evacuate the house when the flood began:* stubborn, obdurate, unyielding, unbending, inflexible, willful, self-willed, headstrong, mulish, unreasonably stubborn, pigheaded; resolute, steadfast, staunch, dogged, tenacious; intractable, unmanageable, uncontrollable, ungovernable, refractory, recalcitrant. **—Ant.** compliant, complaisant, yielding, pliant, amenable, flexible; irresolute, undecided, wavering, wishy-washy;

tractable, manageable, docile, obedient, submissive.

obstreperous *adj. That obstreperous child must be punished!:* disorderly, unruly, refractory, uncontrolled, unrestrained, disobedient, perverse, unmanageable, ungovernable, uncontrollable; rampaging, uproarious, roistering, noisy, loud, boisterous, clamorous, vociferous. **—Ant.** orderly, restrained, obedient, well-behaved, manageable, tractable, docile; quiet, calm.

obstruct *v.* **1.** *A fallen tree obstructed the road. A fat spectator obstructed our view of the stage:* barricade, block, blockade, bar, debar, shut off, stop, dam up, choke off, close, close off, plug up; hide, eclipse, cover, shroud, mask, cloak. **2.** *Lack of funds obstructed the project:* delay, hinder, impede, curb, inhibit, stall, retard, check, hobble, restrict, limit; stop, block, arrest, halt, frustrate, thwart, stifle, throttle, suppress, bring to a standstill. **—Ant.** 1 unblock, clear, open. 2 help, aid, benefit, further, promote, advance, support, encourage, spur, expedite, facilitate, accelerate.

obstruction *n. There must be an obstruction in the drainpipe:* obstacle, encumbrance, barrier, blockage, block, stoppage, stop, barricade, hurdle, impediment, hindrance, hitch, check, curb, bar, snag, bottleneck. **—Ant.** clearing, opening, freeing, unblocking; help, aid, assistance.

obtain *v.* **1.** *How does one obtain a hunting license in this state? Where did you obtain your knowledge of Chinese history?:* acquire, get, attain, secure, procure, come by, pick up, get hold of; receive, earn, gain, glean, gather, achieve, get one's hands on, gain possession of, take, pick up. **2.** *The same rules obtain for everyone:* be in force, hold, stand, prevail, exist, be the case. **—Ant.** 1 lose, be deprived, forgo, relinquish, forfeit, surrender; give, grant, bestow, present, offer, proffer, confer, dispense, distribute, deliver, assign.

obtainable *adj. Everything was obtainable at the shop:* acquirable, procurable, attainable, available, derivable, in stock, on offer, purchasable, realizable, securable, achievable, *Informal* gettable.

obtrusive *adj.* **1.** *Don't be so obtrusive in other people's affairs. It's hard to be polite to obtrusive people:* interfering, intruding, intrusive, meddlesome, meddling, prying, *Informal* snoopy, nosy; interrupting; trespassing; forward, aggressive, brash, presumptuous, impertinent, familiar. **2.** *The red chair is too obtrusive in this room:* prominent, conspicuous, salient, outstanding, sticking out; jutting out, protruding, projecting, bulging, protuberant. **—Ant.** 1, 2 unobtrusive. 1 reserved, reticent, modest, unassuming, diffident, demure, timid, shy. 2 inconspicuous; concave, indented, hollow.

obtuse *adj.* **1.** *An obtuse angle is one of over 90°:* not sharp, not pointed; blunt, blunted, dull, unpointed, unsharpened. **2.** *She's so obtuse she never gets the point:* dull, dense, slow, slow-witted, thick, stupid, ignorant, simple; uncomprehending, insensitive, insensible, imper-

ceptive, thick-skinned. **—Ant.** 1 acute, sharp, pointed. 2 intelligent, bright, smart, clever, quick-witted, keen, sharp, alert, sensitive.

obviate *v. The suspect's confession obviates the necessity for a trial:* avert, avoid, make unnecessary, circumvent, remove, do away with, preclude, prevent; forestall, divert, parry, sidetrack, ward off, turn aside, stave off, fend off, *Informal* nip in the bud. **—Ant.** necessitate, require, make essential, oblige, impel, cause, make unavoidable.

obvious *adj. Her displeasure was obvious:* evident, self-evident, clear, plain, unmistakable, discernible, distinct, palpable, conspicuous, apparent, patent, manifest, undeniable, glaring, striking, *Informal* plain as the nose on your face; visible, perceptible, unconcealed, unhidden, unmasked, unveiled, undisguised, in plain sight. **—Ant.** concealed, hidden, obscure, unclear, indistinct, inconspicuous, unapparent, imperceptible, invisible.

occasion *n.* **1.** *The country's bicentennial was quite an occasion:* event, special event, important event, occurrence, happening, episode, situation, incident, advent, experience, adventure, venture; affair, celebration, time. **2.** *I want to take this occasion to thank you:* particular time, opportune time, opportunity, suitable time, convenient time, instance, circumstance, chance, opening. **3.** *There was no occasion for such behavior:* reason, cause, justification, provocation, motive, motivation, ground, grounds, base, basis, explanation, rationale. **—v. 4.** *The remark occasioned a burst of applause:* cause, elicit, bring about, prompt, lead to, provoke, inspire.

occasional *adj. The weather was good except for an occasional shower. She likes an occasional glass of wine:* taking place from time to time, recurring, now and then, sporadic, fitful, spasmodic, intermittent, random, irregular, scattered, infrequent, incidental, uncommon, rare; unreliable, uncertain. **—Ant.** constant, continual, continuous, incessant; customary, habitual, usual, regular, routine.

occasionally *adv. They occasionally stop by to see us. It snowed occasionally but not enough for skiing:* at times, sometimes, from time to time, now and then, every now and then, once in a while, infrequently, seldom, hardly ever, rarely, once in a blue moon; intermittently, sporadically, irregularly, periodically, fitfully. **—Ant.** always, constantly, continually, continuously, incessantly; often, frequently, regularly, again and again, over and over, habitually, customarily, generally, ordinarily, usually.

occlude *v. Waste materials seem to be occluding the drain:* obstruct, block, clog, shut off, shut up, choke, choke off, plug, close, barricade, congest, stopper, stop up, constrict, strangulate. **—Ant.** clear, unclog, open, ream, unplug.

occult *adj. The fortune-teller claims to have occult powers. The club has an occult initiation rite:* supernatural, magic, mystic, mystical, secret, mysterious, dark, arcane, cabalistic, esoteric, private, revealed only to the initiated, unrevealed, undisclosed, hidden, concealed, obscure, veiled, shrouded.

occupancy *n. The hotel room is twenty-five dollars a night for double occupancy. The lease gives us occupancy of the house until the first of the year:* tenancy, occupation, lodgment, habitation, habitancy, inhabitancy, possession, use, enjoyment, tenure, engagement. —**Ant.** eviction, dispossession, dislodgment; vacancy.

occupant *n. The new occupants of the house will move in tomorrow. Many of the early occupants of New York were Dutch:* dweller, householder, owner, resident, tenant, inhabitant, occupier; lessee, renter, roomer, lodger; addressee; settler, colonist, native.

occupation *n.* **1.** *He gave his occupation as bus driver:* job, trade, business, line of work, line, profession, work, capacity, vocation, craft; employment, livelihood, living; calling, pursuit, walk of life, lifework, career, sphere, activity; forte, specialty, specialization, métier. **2.** *The World War II German occupation of France lasted four years:* military occupation, military control, foreign rule, subjugation, subjection, control, seizure, conquest, possession.

occupied *adj.* **1.** *They were occupied all day:* busy, employed, engaged, tied up, working, active. **2.** *All the cubicles were occupied:* in use, taken, unavailable. **3.** *The occupied apartments were all on the tenth floor:* inhabited, lived-in, peopled, populated, settled.

occupy *v.* **1.** *Business occupies his mind most of the time. Grandmother occupies her time by knitting:* fill, fill up, engage, take up, employ, busy, engross, absorb, monopolize, saturate, permeate, pervade, overrun, concern, amuse, entertain. **2.** *Enemy troops occupied the country:* take possession of, have control, hold in thrall, conquer, subjugate, enslave. **3.** *The Smiths occupy the house on the corner. Is anyone occupying this seat?:* dwell in, reside in, be the tenants of, inhabit, lodge in, room in; sit in, use, hold, possess, be in, be on, be situated in. —**Ant.** 2 liberate, free. 3 vacate, quit, leave, evacuate; relinquish, give up, hand over.

occur *v.* **1.** *When did the accident occur?:* happen, take place, come about, come to pass, come off, befall, transpire, ensue, result, eventuate. **2.** *Tuberculosis occurs most often in damp climates:* appear, arise, rise, turn up, crop up, spring up, emerge, develop, materialize, show itself, manifest itself, be found, be met with. **3.** *It didn't occur to me that you would object:* enter one's mind, cross one's mind, suggest itself, *Slang* hit, strike. —**Ant.** 1 be avoided, be evaded, be thwarted, be nipped in the bud. 2 disappear, vanish, fade away, be suppressed.

occurrence *n. It was the strangest occurrence I can remember:* happening, event, incident, instance, episode, experience, business, proceeding, transaction, situation, venture, adventure, affair, occasion; appearance, circumstance, emergence, unfolding, development, manifestation, materialization.

ocean *n. The ship crossed the ocean in five days:* sea, high sea, deep, briny deep, main, water, flood, *Slang* pond, big pond.

odd *adj.* **1.** *1, 3, and 5 are odd numbers:* not divisible by two, not even. **2.** *What an odd shell!:* unusual, strange, queer, uncommon, unique, out of the ordinary, rare, peculiar, singular, curious, bizarre, freakish, outlandish, quaint, funny, weird, *Slang* far-out. **3.** *What shall I do with this odd sock?:* being one of a pair, having no mate, unmatched, single; leftover, surplus, remaining. **4.** *The youth earned pocket money doing odd jobs:* various, sundry, miscellaneous; occasional, casual, irregular, sporadic, spasmodic, periodic, spare, extra. —**Ant.** 1 even. 2 common, ordinary, usual, familiar, customary, habitual, regular, typical, normal, natural, unexceptional. 3 matched, paired, mated. 4 regular, constant, steady, permanent, full time.

oddity *n. An egg with two yolks is an oddity. We were attracted by the oddity of the painting:* rarity, phenomenon, curiosity, wonder, marvel, sight, freak, rara avis; strangeness, singularity, peculiarity, individuality, uniqueness, unusualness, outlandishness, freakishness; bizarreness, queerness, eccentricity, unnaturalness, abnormality.

odds *n. pl. The odds were in our favor:* chances, likelihood, probability, balance; favor, advantage, allowance, benefit, draw, edge, lead, superiority, head start.

odious *adj. The Nazi concentration camps were the most odious places in history:* evil, vile, abominable, hateful, hated, despicable, contemptible, detestable, invidious, heinous, repulsive, repugnant, revolting, disgusting, loathsome, obnoxious, infamous, offensive, nasty, foul, nauseating, rotten, sickening, monstrous, hideous, objectionable, intolerable, unendurable, unbearable. —**Ant.** likable, attractive, lovable, delightful, charming, pleasing, pleasant, agreeable, acceptable.

odium *n.* **1.** *He suffered the odium of a convicted traitor:* discredit, disgrace, dishonor, infamy, disrepute, shame, opprobrium. **2.** *She felt the odium of her fellow workers after crossing the picket line:* hatred, antipathy, abhorrence, disgust, contempt, repugnance. —**Ant.** 1 honor, repute, esteem. 2 love, affection, tenderness, fondness.

odor *n. I love the odor of freshly roasted coffee. What's that awful odor?:* smell, aroma; scent, fragrance, perfume, essence, bouquet; atmosphere, aura, flavor; stench, stink, effluvium.

odoriferous *adj. The fumigated house was odoriferous:* odorous, fragrant, aromatic, perfumed, redolent. —**Ant.** noisome, noxious.

odorless *adj. The kitty litter was odorless:* scentless, unscented, odor-free, unperfumed, deodorant, deodorizing.

odorous *adj. The odorous perfume overwhelmed us:* aromatic, fragrant, perfumed, pungent, redolent, reeking, scented, scent-laden, strong, heady.

off *adj.* **1.** *The hamburger was off:* bad, decomposed, rotten, rancid; disappointing, slack, displeasing, bad, substandard, unrewarding, unsatisfactory. —*adv.* **2.** *The village was off in the distance:* far, faraway, afar, away, away from, farther away, gone away, removed, above, ahead, apart, divergent, aside, elsewhere, out, over.

offal *n. The hunters took the meat and left the offal for the buzzards:* remains, carrion, carcass; garbage, refuse, junk, waste, rubbish, trash, debris, leavings, dregs, grounds, slag, residue.

offbeat *adj. The offbeat song appealed to us:* unusual, unconventional, uncommon, unexpected, out-of-the-ordinary, out-of-the-way, rare, special, eccentric, unique, way-out, far-out. —**Ant.** commonplace, conventional.

off-color *adj. After a few drinks he told some off-color jokes:* risqué, racy, spicy, indelicate, salty, earthy, blue, suggestive, naughty, wicked, improper, offensive, indiscreet, *Slang* raunchy, obscene, scabrous, indecent.

offend *v.* **1.** *He apologized for having offended her:* affront, displease, insult, wound, disgust, antagonize, anger, incense, inflame, madden, annoy, vex, aggravate, irritate, exasperate, rankle, nettle, rile, miff, fret, gall, chafe, pique, disgruntle. **2.** *She prayed that she would never offend:* sin, err, transgress, misbehave, lapse, stray from the straight and narrow, fall from grace. —**Ant.** 1 please, delight, beguile, captivate, charm, enchant, win over; soothe, calm, conciliate.

offense *n.* **1.** *For what offense was he arrested?:* crime, misdeed, misdemeanor, felony, breach of conduct, infraction, violation, malfeasance, delinquency; sin, transgression, wickedness, peccadillo, lapse, slip, shortcoming; outrage, enormity, atrocity, evil deed. **2.** *She meant no offense by the remark:* insult, affront, disrespect, insolence, impudence, rudeness, umbrage, harm, abuse, embarrassment, humiliation, indignity, outrage, slap, snub, twit, taunt, gibe, abuse. **3.** *Our football team has the best offense in the league:* offensive, attack, assault, aggression, charge; offensive unit. —**Ant.** 1 innocence, guiltlessness. 2 pleasure, delight, gratification, satisfaction. 3 defense, resistance, safeguard, guard, security.

offensive *adj.* **1.** *The youth's language was offensive:* insulting, disrespectful, insolent, impudent, rude, abusive, embarrassing, unmannerly, uncivil, ungallant; objectionable, rank, obnoxious, disgusting, unpleasant, disagreeable, distasteful, abominable, revolting, nasty, foul, horrid, hideous, repulsive, ugly, loathsome, repugnant, abhorrent, detestable, sickening, nauseating, intolerable, insufferable. **2.** *Offensive troops charged the hill position:* attacking, attack, assault, assaulting, assailing, belligerent, aggressive, charging, storming, bombarding. —*n.* **3.** *The team took the offensive and won:* offense, attack, assault, onslaught, onset, aggression. —**Ant.** 1 polite, courteous, respectful, deferential, diffident, civil, conciliatory; pleasing, pleasant, delightful, charming, agreeable, attractive, captivating, winning. 2 defensive, defending, resisting. 3 defense, defensive.

offer *v.* **1.** *She offered us some of her cookies:* proffer, tender, present, place at one's disposal, bestow on, bestow. **2.** *May I offer a suggestion? The neighbors offered to help:* propose, submit, render, advance, suggest, put forth, put forward, propound, volunteer, hold out, extend, make a motion, bring forward, be willing. **3.** *They offered their house for sale:* put on the market, put up. —*n.* **4.** *Shall I accept his offer to help?:* proposition, proposal, offering, bid, invitation, submission, overture, suggestion. —**Ant.** 1, 2 retain, retract, withdraw, withhold, deny; accept, take, receive; reject, refuse, decline. 4 withdrawal, retraction, revocation; acceptance, reception; refusal, denial.

offering *n. The second offering was the largest:* donation, alms, contribution, benefaction, beneficence, charity, sacrifice.

offhand *also* **offhanded** *adj.* **1.** *The senator asked the reporters not to quote his offhand remarks:* impromptu, extemporaneous, ad-lib, off-the-cuff, off-the-record, off the top of one's head, improvised, unpremeditated, unstudied, unprepared, unplanned, unrehearsed, spontaneous, chance, casual, random. **2.** *He works in a far too offhand manner:* casual, careless, thoughtless, heedless, haphazard, nonchalant, unconcerned, hasty; facetious, cavalier, relaxed. —**Ant.** 1 prepared, planned, premeditated, studied. 2 serious, intent, sober, grave, responsible, careful, thoughtful.

office *n.* **1.** *He was elected to the office of mayor:* position, post, job, capacity, function, occupation, role, commission, appointment. **2.** *usually* **offices** *Did he appreciate your good offices?:* favor, service, help, assistance; duty, charge, trust, function, task; province.

officer *n.* **1.** *The company promoted several new officers:* official, executive, manager, bureaucrat, head, administrator, officeholder, director, commissioner. **2.** *She asked information of the officer who was directing traffic:* policeman, police officer, officer of the law, law officer, patrolman, constable, detective, cop, *French* gendarme.

official *n.* **1.** *The company officials determine policy. The governor is a public official:* officeholder, officer, executive, director, manager, administrator, supervisor; functionary, dignitary, agent; chairman, administrative head. —*adj.* **2.** *The President's official duties include being Commander in Chief. There will be an official inquiry into the matter:* formal, administrative, vested; authorized, approved, sanctioned, authoritative, certified, accredited, authentic, warranted, licensed. —**Ant.** 1 underling, hireling; employee. 2 unofficial, unauthorized; informal, casual.

officiate *v. The judge agreed to officiate at the wedding:* preside, administer, oversee, direct, manage, run, head, superintend, be in charge of, moderate, emcee, chair, lead, handle, *Slang* call the shots for, regulate, supervise.

officious *adj. It's hard to be an office manager without being officious:* obtrusive, intrusive, interfering, meddlesome, meddling, prying, poking one's nose in, offering gratuitous advice or services, *Informal* kibitzing; overbearing, domineering, self-important, self-assertive, high-handed, high and mighty; pompous, patronizing. **—Ant.** unobtrusive, in the background.

off-key *adj. Everything seemed off-key to her that morning:* jarring, discordant, dissonant, inharmonious, unharmonious, irregular, unnatural, abnormal, anomalous, deviant, divergent.

offset *v. His A in math offset the D in art. Inflation will offset the pay raise:* compensate for, make up for, counteract, countervail, counterweight, counterbalance, balance; cancel out, nullify, neutralize, equalize, redeem, *Informal* knock out.

offshoot *n. The shop was an offshoot of her main enterprise:* branch, by-product, spinoff, adjunct, appendage, derivative, development, outgrowth, sprout.

offspring *n. The dictionary defines mule as "offspring of a male ass and a mare." The old man's offspring are wrangling over the estate:* children, progeny, descendants, posterity, succession, issue, increase; child, descendant, heir, scion; young, brood, family, litter, fry, spawn, seed.

often *adv. How often do you visit your parents? It rains often this time of the year:* frequently, regularly, repeatedly, habitually, periodically, recurrently, over and over, much, time and again, again and again, generally, usually, customarily, commonly, as a common thing, continually, constantly, oft, oftentimes, ofttimes. **—Ant.** never; rarely, seldom, infrequently, occasionally, irregularly, now and then, once in a great while, hardly ever.

ogle *v. The children ogled the cookies in the bakery window:* stare at greedily, gaze at with desire; stare at, gape at, gawk at, goggle at, scrutinize, eye, give the eye, give the once-over, leer at, cast sheep's eyes at, goggle.

ogre, *Fem.* **ogress** *n.* **1.** *I used to revel in stories about fearful ogres:* man-eating giant, monster, fiend, brute; bugbear, bogeyman; ghoul, harpy, demon. **2.** *The new supervisor is a real ogre:* tyrant, martinet, dictator, despot, slave driver.

oil *n.* **1.** *Oil and water won't mix:* petroleum; (*variously*) mineral oil, fuel oil, whale oil, vegetable oil, cooking oil, motor oil, lubricant; melted grease, melted fat; liniment, ointment, unguent, balm, salve; pomade, hair oil. **—v. 2.** *Oil that squeaky hinge. She oiled herself with suntan lotion:* lubricate; cream, grease, anoint, salve, cream, lard.

oily *adj.* **1.** *Use an astringent lotion to counteract oily skin:* greasy, slick, slippery, fatty, sebaceous, oleaginous, unctuous, slithery, buttery, lardy, lubricious. **2.** *His oily manner indicated that he was about to ask a favor:* unctuous, smarmy, lubricious, oleaginous; ingratiating, subservient, servile, fawning, groveling, bootlicking, toadying.

ointment *n. Every first-aid kit should contain an ointment for burns:* unguent, balm, pomade, spikenard, pomatum, salve, emollient, liniment, lotion.

old *adj.* **1.** *She's forty years old:* of age. **2.** *Father's an old man now. What an old car!:* elderly, aged, hoary, grizzled, gray-headed, gray with age, white with age, venerable; antiquated, ancient, vintage, timeworn, age-old, antique, old-fashioned, out-of-date, outdated, archaic, obsolete, obsolescent. **3.** *She and I are old friends. Do you remember the good old days?:* of long standing, long established, time-honored, traditional, age-old, of the past, from the past, of yore, bygone. **4.** *This old coat doesn't fit any more. That's an old joke:* worn-out, outworn, decrepit, dilapidated, used, much-used, timeworn, weathered, *Slang* beat-up; weather-beaten, deteriorated, battered, ramshackle, crumbling, tumbledown, rundown, broken-down; familiar, hackneyed. **—Ant.** 2–4 new, recent, current, late. 4 young, immature; brand-new, spanking new, modern, novel, up-to-date, modish, newfangled, new-fashioned, fashionable; mod, with-it.

old-fashioned *adj.* **1.** *It may be a new dress but it looks old-fashioned to me:* out-of-date, out of fashion, outmoded, unfashionable, behind the times, out of style, passé, from time gone by, antiquated, antique, outdated, obsolete, *Slang* corny. **2.** *She's an old-fashioned girl:* having time-honored values, traditional; time-honored, old-time, long-standing. **—Ant.** 1 modern, up-to-date, current, new-fangled, new-fashioned, in style, fashionable, in vogue, up-to-the-minute, chic, a la mode, avant-garde; *Slang* modish, mod, with-it.

old hat *adj. She uses a lot of expressions that are old hat:* out-of-date, antiquated, outmoded, outdated, old-fashioned, unfashionable, superseded, passé, stale, archaic, obsolete, obsolescent, outworn, *French* démodé, behind the times. **—Ant.** up-to-date, in, new, current, fashionable.

old-world *adj. There's still a lot of old-world courtliness in his manner:* European, continental; traditional, conservative, old-fashioned; formal, ceremonial, ceremonious, conventional, established, prescribed, orthodox, old-line; courtly, chivalrous, gallant.

omen *n. Some people believe a black cat's crossing one's path is a bad omen. Let's hope this glorious weather is a good omen for our vacation:* augury, sign, token, portent, auspice; indication, harbinger, herald, precursor, presage, foretaste, straw in the wind, handwriting on the wall; foreboding, warning.

ominous *adj. Ominous black clouds caused us to head the boat toward a harbor:* threatening, minatory, menacing, foreboding, sinister, dismaying, disquieting, portentous, unpromising, unpropitious, unfavorable, inauspicious, ill-starred, portending evil, unlucky, ill-omened, monitory. **—Ant.** encouraging, promising, favorable, propitious, auspicious.

omission *n.* **1.** *The student's omission from the honor roll was an oversight. There are sins of commission and sins of omission:* leaving out, exclusion, noninclusion, elimination, exception; neglect, negligence, delinquency, oversight. **2.**

The catalog has numerous omissions: something omitted, exclusion, neglected item, thing overlooked, gap, hole. —**Ant.** 1, 2 inclusion; addition, supplement.

omit *v.* **1.** *Be sure not to omit anyone's name from the list:* leave out, exclude, except, miss, skip, pass over, forget about, preclude, jump, ignore, elide, delete, drop, excerpt, cut, set aside. **2.** *You omitted telling me to buy bread:* neglect, fail, forget, overlook, let slip, ignore, avoid, shun, slight, bypass, leave undone. —**Ant.** 1 include, put in, add. 2 remember, recollect, recall.

omnipotent *adj. The Jews were the first nation on earth to worship a single omnipotent deity:* all-powerful, almighty, supreme; puissant, powerful, mighty. —**Ant.** powerless, helpless, impotent.

omnipresent *adj. The guards were omnipresent:* ubiquitous, present. —**Ant.** nowhere.

omniscient *adj. The Bible teaches that God is omniscient:* all-knowing, all-seeing, having infinite knowledge, all-wise; supreme, preeminent, infinite. —**Ant.** ignorant, unknowing, unaware, fallible, deceivable.

omnivorous *adj. Animals that feed on anything are omnivorous:* all-devouring, pantophagous, polyphagic, gluttonous, predacious, rapacious, voracious, ravenous, edacious, crapulous, hoggish.

on *adv. The shoes are on the mat:* in contact, touching, adjacent, against, close to, covering, leaning on, resting on, situated on, supported.

once *adv.* **1.** *She was once my best friend. Once dinosaurs walked these plains:* formerly, at one time, previously, some time back, some time ago, in times past, long ago, once upon a time, in other days, in the old days, in the good old days, years ago, ages ago; heretofore, hitherto. **2.** *We've been to Europe once:* a single time, one time, on one occasion; once and for all, for the nonce. —**Ant.** 1 in future, in time to come, after this, hereafter. 2 never, not at all, at no time; repeatedly, frequently, numerously, regularly, incessantly, continually.

oncoming *adj. The oncoming train missed the bus by inches:* approaching, advancing, looming, onrushing, imminent, impending, nearing, coming, bearing down, close. —**Ant.** receding, retiring, retreating, withdrawing.

one *adj.* **1.** *Put one piece of cake on each plate. He's the one man who can do it:* single, individual, a, an, sole, lone, solitary, only, singular, unique, unrepeated; entire, whole, complete. —*pron.* **2.** *One never knows what may happen:* a person, an individual, a man, a human being, a creature, somebody, someone, you, a body, a soul, a mortal, a thing.

onerous *adj. Holding down two jobs can be an onerous task:* oppressive, burdensome, hard to endure, arduous, not easy to bear, distressing, painful, wearisome, taxing, exhausting, crushing, heavy, weighty, demanding, grievous. —**Ant.** easy, light, simple, effortless, trivial, trifling.

one-time *adj. Guests included the city's one-*

time mayor: former, previous, earlier, erstwhile, ci-devant, quondam, past, recent, prior, early, old. —**Ant.** current, present, presentday, latest.

ongoing *adj. The patient requires ongoing care:* continuing, proceeding, forward-moving, uninterrupted, unbroken, unremitting, unending, endless, never-ending, lasting, enduring. —**Ant.** temporary, stopgap, sporadic, provisional.

onlooker *n. Onlookers crowded the sidewalk as the clown began to perform:* spectator, observer, eyewitness, sidewalk viewer, watcher, bystander, *Slang* sidewalk superintendent, kibitzer, rubberneck, gazer, ogler.

only *adv.* **1.** *Only Jennifer was left in the room:* alone, by oneself, by itself, solely, exclusively, individually, singly, without others, as the only one, without anything further. **2.** *She sees him only on Fridays:* no more than, merely, just, simply, purely; barely, nothing but, at least, to such an extent. —*adj.* **3.** *That was the only apple left. She's the only woman to be elected mayor of this town:* lone, sole, solitary, individual, single, singular, exclusive, unique, alone, one and only; unparalleled, unrepeated, unmatched. —**Ant.** 1 together, collectively, among, amongst. 3 many, several, numerous, innumerable, multitudinous, myriad, manifold.

onrush *n. Residents fled the onrush of the floodwaters:* onset, torrent, deluge, attack, assault, flood, flux, charge, storm, avalanche, cascade, wave, tide, stream, flow, current, spring, surge, gush.

onset *n.* **1.** *At the onset of the century this city was a small town:* start, beginning, outset, commencement, inauguration, initiation, outbreak; inception, genesis, birth, infancy, founding, incipience. **2.** *The bombardment began the final onset of the war:* attack, assault, onslaught, offensive, offense, raid, thrust, push, sally, charge, onrush, incursion, invasion, storming. —**Ant.** 1 end, close, conclusion, termination; old age, death. 2 defense, resistance, counterattack.

onslaught *n. The enemy onslaught overran the fort's defenders:* attack, assault, coup, charge, thrust, push, raid, foray, sally, onset, onrush, putsch, blitz, blitzkrieg; offensive, offense, invasion, incursion, aggression. —**Ant.** defense, resistance; counterattack.

onus *n. The prosecuting attorney must bear the onus of proving the suspect's guilt:* burden, burden of proof, responsibility, obligation, weight, load, strain, encumbrance, liability, duty, cross.

onward *adv.* **1.** Also **onwards** *Onward, march! The ship sailed onward through the night:* forward, ahead, toward the front, frontward, toward one's goal, along, en route, on the way. —*adj.* **2.** *The plane's onward movement was slowed by adverse winds:* forward, moving ahead, frontward, advancing, progressive, ongoing. —**Ant.** 1, 2 backward. 1 backwards; aback, to the rear. 2 retreating, regressive.

ooze *v.* **1.** *The water oozed from between the pipes:* seep, percolate, exude, trickle, dribble, drip, leak, transpire, discharge, drain, filter;

bleed, sweat. **—n. 2.** *After the flood subsided, the sidewalks were covered with ooze:* soft mud, slime, sludge, silt, muck, mire, alluvium; secretion, exudation; seepage, leakage. **—Ant.** 1 gush, stream, flood, cascade, pour, flow, effuse.

opalescent *adj. The opalescent pearls shone in the light:* iridescent, nacreous, polychromatic.

opaque *adj.* **1.** *Varnish is transparent, and paint is opaque. The once clear mountain stream is now polluted and opaque:* nontransparent, nontranslucent, impenetrable to light; dark, dull, murky, clouded, hazy, muddy, muddied. **2.** *The report was written in long, opaque sentences:* hard to understand, unclear, impenetrable, incomprehensible, difficult, obscure, abstruse, unintelligible, unfathomable. **—Ant.** 1, 2 clear. 1 transparent, translucent, pellucid; shiny, bright, sparkling, gleaming. 2 lucid, intelligible, comprehensible.

open *adj.* **1.** *An open window. An open boat. With open arms:* not shut, unshut, not closed, unclosed, ajar, agape, gaping, yawning; not covered, uncovered, coverless, unenclosed, unsealed, unfastened, unlocked; extended, unfolded; welcoming. **2.** *The boat headed for the open sea. Hunting is easiest in open country:* expansive, wide, unbounded, unfenced, unobstructed, uncluttered, exposed, clear; uncrowded, uninhabited, not built up. **3.** *The store is open from 9 till 5:* doing business, open for business, open to the public, available, accessible. **4.** *She's a very friendly, open person:* openhearted, forthright, sincere, natural, plain, artless, straightforward, honest, candid, outgoing, extroverted, frank, direct. **5.** *A juror must keep an open mind:* impartial, objective, unprejudiced, unbiased, unbigoted, disinterested, impersonal, fair, just; receptive, responsive. **—v. 6.** *Please open the door. Open the book to page 78. They can't open the road until the snow is cleared:* unclose, throw open, set ajar, move aside, swing aside; unlock, unfasten, unbar, unseal; unfold, expand, lay open, *Slang* crack; clear, unblock. **7.** *We'll open the meeting by singing the national anthem:* begin, commence, start initiate, inaugurate, originate, launch, embark upon, set in motion, get the ball rolling; institute, found, create, undertake, establish. **8.** *What time does the building open?:* open to the public, become available for use, permit access, afford entrance, receive customers, start business. **—Ant.** 1–3 closed. 6–8 close. 1 shut; covered, enclosed, sealed, fastened, locked; folded. 2 restricted, shut in, bounded, protected, narrow; obstructed, crowded, cluttered. 3 unavailable, inaccessible, out of bounds, off limits. 4 introverted, reticent, reserved. 5 prejudiced, biased, bigoted, subjective; unfair, unjust; stubborn, obdurate. 6 shut; lock, fasten, bar, seal; fold; block, obstruct. 7 end, conclude, finish, terminate, shut down.

open-handed *adj. The museum needs some open-handed patrons to help pay the bills:* generous, magnanimous, bountiful, bounteous, benevolent, liberal, beneficent, prodigal, lavish, unstinting, altruistic, ungrudging. **—Ant.** stingy, closefisted, niggardly, miserly.

opening *n.* **1.** *The bugs come through the opening in the screen:* hole, break, breach, gap, aperture, rent, rift, slit, cleft, crack, fissure, gash, slot, tear, vent, chink. **2.** *The opening of the highway is scheduled for next year. The book's opening is dull, but the last chapters are interesting:* inauguration, initiation, launching, installation; beginning, start, commencement, first part, preface, prelude, overture, introduction, *Slang* kickoff, send-off. **3.** *We have an opening for a file clerk:* job opening, vacancy, place, space, opportunity, possibility, chance, occasion; situation, position, job, *Informal* spot. **—Ant.** 1 obstruction, blockage. 2 closing, close, termination, end, ending, conclusion, finish, finale, finis, postscript.

openly *adv. They openly declared themselves:* aboveboard, forthrightly, frankly, artlessly, fully, honestly, ingenuously, naturally, plainly, publicly, in public, readily, unabashedly, unhesitatingly, unreservedly, willingly, without pretence, without reserve, unashamedly, wantonly, shamelessly. **—Ant.** secretly, covertly, furtively.

open-mouthed *adj. We stared at the mountain range in open-mouthed wonder:* dumbfounded, wide-eyed, astonished, amazed, flabbergasted, marveling, agape, aghast, surprised, confounded, staggered, thunderstruck, spellbound, awed, awestruck, bewitched, stupefied, wonderstruck. **—Ant.** bored, indifferent, apathetic, unmoved, unconcerned.

operate *v.* **1.** *Do you know how this toaster operates? Can you operate a bulldozer?:* work, go, function, run, behave, perform; manage, superintend, oversee, be in charge of. **2.** *The doctor says he may have to operate:* perform surgery, perform an operation, *Informal* go in, open up, do an exploratory.

operation *n.* **1.** *The students watched a printing press in operation. All his time is devoted to the operation of his business:* action, performance, operating, running, working, conduct, procedure, activity, pursuit; supervision, management, superintendence, overseeing. **2.** *How long has the plan been in operation?:* action, effect, force, influence, exertion; agency, instrumentality. **3.** *The doctors say the operation was a complete success:* surgery, *Informal* exploratory.

operative *n.* **1.** *She had several operatives at work:* worker, workman, artisan, hand, laborer. **2.** *A trained operative tracked down the suspect:* detective, investigator, private eye, agent. **—adj. 3.** *It was the operative ingredient in the mixture:* operating, exerting, influencing, influential. **4.** *The factory was operative:* effective, efficacious, efficient, effectual, serviceable. **—Ant.** inoperative; ineffectual, inefficient.

operator *n. The operator opened the bus door:* handler, driver.

opiate *n. The nurse gave her an opiate to deaden the pain:* sedative, hypnotic, narcotic, soporific, tranquilizer, somnifacient, anodyne, nepenthe, depressant, stupefacient, painkiller,

calmative, palliative; *Slang* dope, downer.
—**Ant.** stimulant, tonic; *Slang* upper, pep pill,
pick-me-up.

opine *v. He opined that we were in for a long
winter:* think, say, state, suggest, volunteer, conjecture, surmise, allow, reckon, consider, offer,
guess, imagine, speculate, deem, assume, conclude, presume, believe, *Slang* have a hunch.

opinion *n. It's my opinion that the plan won't
work:* belief, estimate, estimation, assessment,
evaluation, sentiment, judgment, view, impression, conviction, persuasion, notion, conclusion,
idea, surmise, suspicion, conception, assumption, thinking, conjecture, speculation, theory.
—**Ant.** fact, reality, actuality, certainty; act,
deed, event, occurrence, happening.

opinionated *adj. He's too opinionated to consider other people's views:* closed-minded, stubborn, bullheaded, obstinate, obdurate, headstrong, inflexible, unyielding, pigheaded,
unbending, dogmatic, uncompromising.
—**Ant.** open-minded, broad-minded, unprejudiced, receptive, responsive, persuadable.

opponent *n. The candidate criticized his opponent's record:* opposition, rival, competitor, adversary, contender, challenger, antagonist, foe,
enemy, assailant; disputant, resister. —**Ant.**
ally, colleague, co-worker, teammate, helper,
accomplice, cohort; friend, supporter, promoter,
backer.

opportune *adj. Now, before interest rates increase, would be an opportune time to buy a
new house:* timely, well-timed, advantageous,
favorable, appropriate, suitable, fitting, apt, seasonable, proper, propitious, auspicious, expedient, convenient, profitable, fortunate, lucky,
happy, felicitous. —**Ant.** inopportune, unfavorable, inappropriate, unsuitable, improper, unseasonable, unfortunate, inconvenient, untimely.

opportunity *n. A summer in France gave her
an opportunity to learn French. I'd like to take
this opportunity to thank everyone for helping:*
chance, good chance, favorable time, time, occasion, contingency, moment, means, situation,
turn, opening.

oppose *v. Several of the speakers opposed the
project:* act in opposition to, speak against,
fight, combat, battle, contest, contend against,
struggle against, resist, withstand, defy, be set
against, take a stand against, *Slang* buck; obstruct, thwart. —**Ant.** support, aid, help, abet,
champion, defend, advance, promote, advocate,
foster, back.

opposed *adj. The opposed factions made their
voices heard:* opposite, antagonistic, battling,
clashing, inimical, combatting, confronting, demurring, disagreeing, enemy, protesting, recalcitrant, refractory, resistant, unwilling, warring,
contrary, averse.

opposite *adj. 1. The two houses are on opposite sides of the street. What's on the opposite
side of this coin?:* facing, opposed, other; reverse, converse. **2. We have opposite views on
politics:* opposing, opposed, conflicting, differing, contradictory, contrary, antithetical, antagonistic, adverse; counteractive, counter. —**Ant.**

1 same. 2 alike, like, identical, uniform, similar,
analogous, synonymous, agreeing, consistent,
corresponding, parallel.

opposition *n. 1. I don't understand his opposition to the plan:* resistance, contention against,
disagreement, disapproval, rejection, aversion,
negativism, defiance, contrariety, antagonism,
hostility, enmity. **2. The opposition was quick to
reply to the charge:* opponent, competitor, rival,
adversary, contender, antagonist, foe, enemy,
other side. —**Ant.** 1 support, backing, approval, aid, help, assistance, advancement, promotion. 2 supporter, backer, promoter; ally, cohort, colleague, helper.

oppress *v. 1. She was oppressed by her many
woes:* trouble, vex, worry, burden, weigh down,
tax, try; depress, dispirit, cast down, dishearten,
deject, discourage, sadden, pain, grieve, sorrow.
**2. The tyrant oppressed the conquered peoples:*
tyrannize, despotize, persecute, treat harshly,
abuse, maltreat. —**Ant.** 1 unburden, relieve,
ease; gladden, cheer, cheer up, hearten, encourage.

oppression *n. 1. The new government proved
to be one of oppression:* cruelty, injustice, tyranny, despotism, persecution, severity; hardship, misery, suffering, calamity. **2. A feeling of
oppression kept her from drawing the curtains:*
depression, sadness, misery. —**Ant.** 1 kindness, justice 2 happiness, joy.

oppressive *adj. 1. The occupation by foreign
troops was extremely oppressive:* tyrannical,
despotic, repressive; cruel, brutal, harsh, severe,
hardhearted. **2. Obligations are often oppressive. Tropical humidity can be oppressive:* burdensome, onerous, wearing, trying, troublesome, worrisome, vexing, pressing; depressing,
discouraging; painful, grievous; uncomfortable,
distressing, unbearable. —**Ant.** 1 humane,
kind, gentle, compassionate, benevolent, tender, lenient, merciful, just. 2 soothing, relieving,
gladdening, joyful, pleasant, pleasing, encouraging, comforting; comfortable.

opprobrious *adj. 1. The editorial made an opprobrious attack on modern morals:* damning,
denunciatory, condemnatory, hypercritical, censorious, faultfinding; abusive, scurrilous, acrimonious, malicious, malevolent, maligning, vilifying, vitriolic, fulminating, reviling. **2. The
officer was reprimanded for his opprobrious
conduct:* disgraceful, dishonorable, shameful,
disreputable, objectionable, unbecoming, deplorable, reprehensible, base, outrageous,
shocking, scandalous, infamous, nefarious, despicable, corrupt, wicked. —**Ant.** 1 complimentary, flattering, approving, praising, laudatory,
uncritical. 2 honorable, noble, meritorious, upright, ethical, principled, virtuous, moral; becoming, praiseworthy, worthy, laudable, noteworthy, estimable.

oppugn *v. They oppugned everything he did:*
criticize, argue against, act against, dispute,
doubt, question, oppose. —**Ant.** favor.

opt *v. If it were up to me, I would opt for the
blue sedan:* choose, select, pick, decide on, go
for, elect, vote for, single out, prefer, take, settle

on, fix on, incline toward, tend toward. —**Ant.** reject, turn down, decide against, overrule.

optimism *n. Nothing can daunt his cheery optimism:* confidence, sanguineness, hopeful outlook, hoping for the best, hopefulness, bright outlook, seeing the good side of things, encouragement, cheerfulness, trust in the future, happy expectancy. —**Ant.** pessimism, cynicism; gloom, gloominess, glumness, depression, despondency.

optimistic *adj.* **1.** *The stockholders are optimistic about the company's future:* confident, sanguine, cheerful, disposed to take a favorable view, viewed favorably, hopeful, heartened, enthusiastic, encouraged, happily expectant, buoyed up. **2.** *There are optimistic signs for the company's future:* promising, auspicious, propitious, favorable, encouraging, bright, heartening, full of promise, roseate, rose-colored. —**Ant.** 1, 2 pessimistic. 1 cynical; despairing, depressed, despondent, discouraged, glum, gloomy. 2 unpromising, inauspicious, unfavorable, discouraging, disheartening.

optimum *n.* **1.** *Atmospheric conditions are at the optimum for a space probe:* ideal, peak, height, best point, most desirable, perfect degree, crest, zenith, perfection, quintessence, acme. —*adj.* **2.** *The experiment was conducted under optimum conditions:* ideal, best, perfect, most favorable, prime, choice, select, first-rate, first-class, flawless, faultless, unexcelled, superlative, supreme, capital, *Slang* A 1.

option *n.* **1.** *Every voter should exercise his option:* franchise, free will, right of choosing, freedom of choice, will, self-determination, voice, decision, discretion. **2.** *She has the option of entering graduate school or starting her professional career:* choice, alternative, selection, election; preference, partiality, liking, predilection, pleasure, will. **3.** *The publisher has an option on the author's next book:* first claim, right to buy, first choice to buy, right of first refusal, privilege. —**Ant.** 1 compulsion, coercion. 1, 2 requirement, obligation, necessity, must.

optional *adj. The car comes with a heater but air conditioning is optional:* left to one's choice, individually decided, elective, voluntary, nonobligatory, not required, volitional, unforced, discretionary, discretional; available at additional cost; open-ended, open; allowable. —**Ant.** mandatory, obligatory, required, compulsory.

opulence *n.* **1.** *The opulence of the pharaohs was awe-inspiring:* great wealth, riches, affluence, fortune, prosperity, ample means; luxuries, lavishness. **2.** *The opulence of the food served at the banquet overwhelmed the guests:* abundance, profusion, copiousness, plenty, plentitude, amplitude, bounty, overflowing quantity, wealth, cornucopia; elegance, lavishness, richness, sumptuousness. —**Ant.** 1 poverty, indigence, want, privation, impecuniousness, impecuniosity. 2 scarcity, scarceness, paucity, scantiness, dearth, lack, want, insufficiency.

opulent *adj.* **1.** *The opulent classes paid few taxes:* wealthy, rich, affluent, moneyed, sumptu-ous, luxurious. **2.** *The opulent dinner filled them to repletion:* abundant, copious, plentiful. —**Ant.** poor, squalid; scarce.

opus *n. The author's latest opus is his best book yet:* work, *oeuvre*, piece, production, product, composition, creation, handiwork, brainchild, invention, effort, attempt.

oracle *n. The oracle prophesied famine and war:* prophet, seer, augur, soothsayer, sage, clairvoyant, wizard, sibyl, diviner; predictor, forecaster, adviser.

oracular *adj.* **1.** *She spoke in oracular tones:* prophetic, portentous, auspicious. **2.** *The oracular professor delivered a lecture:* authoritative, inspired, inspirational, dogmatic, sententious.

oral *adj.* **1.** *Each student had to stand up and give an oral report in front of the class:* spoken, vocal, uttered, articulated, voiced, verbalized, using speech, viva voce, (loosely) verbal. **2.** *An oral surgeon removed the impacted wisdom tooth. Is it an oral vaccine or one given by injection?:* treating the mouth, of the mouth; swallowed, ingested, taken into the body through the mouth. —**Ant.** 1 written; unspoken, silent, tacit.

orate *v. The politician orated to the huge crowd:* declaim, hold forth, elocute, sermonize, preach.

oration *n. The students had to memorize Mark Antony's funeral oration from* Julius Caesar: address, formal speech, eulogy, talk; discourse, disquisition, peroration, recital, declamation, monologue, sermon, lecture, panegyric, *Informal* spiel.

orator *n. William Jennings Bryan was one of America's best known orators:* speaker, talker, elocutionist, rhetorician, declaimer, *Informal* spellbinder; public speaker, speechmaker, lecturer; preacher, sermonizer.

oratory *n. The senator was known for his oratory:* rhetoric, eloquence, delivery, declamation; grandiloquence, bombast, grandeur of style; art of public speaking, speech, speechmaking, speechifying; elocution; preaching.

orb *n. Her necklace was a string of crystal orbs:* sphere, spheroid, ball, globe, globule, moon. —**Ant.** cube; square.

orbit *n.* **1.** *The satellite was launched into orbit around the moon:* course, track, trajectory, path, pathway, circuit, cycle, way, route, channel. —*v.* **2.** *The earth orbits the sun:* circle, revolve around, travel around, circumnavigate.

orchestra *n.* **1.** *The orchestra played a Mozart symphony:* company of musicians, ensemble, band, chamber orchestra, symphony orchestra, Philharmonic. **2.** *Do you want to buy seats in the orchestra or the balcony?:* main floor of a theater, parquet, parterre, pit, *British* stalls; orchestra pit.

orchestrate *v. They were able to orchestrate a visit for her:* set up, put together, arrange, blend, compose, coordinate, harmonize, integrate, synthesize, unify, manage, organize.

ordain *v.* **1.** *He was ordained a priest two years ago:* confer holy orders upon, name, invest, frock, consecrate; appoint, commission, delegate, deputize, elect. **2.** *The king ordained that* *all forests belonged to the crown:* decree, rule, pronounce, will, prescribe, instruct, determine, adjudge, order, dictate, command, pass judgment; enact, legislate. **—Ant.** 1 unfrock, defrock; discharge, dismiss, relieve of one's duties, impeach. 2 countermand, revoke, rescind, reverse, annul, void, invalidate, cancel; repeal, nullify, overrule.

ordeal *n. Being lost in the wilderness for a week was an ordeal for the campers. The nation is just recovering from the ordeal of war:* nightmare, trial, harsh experience, trying experience, oppression, worry, vexation, trouble, burden, care, concern, pressure, strain, stress, tribulation, misery, torment, distress, agony, suffering, anguish, wretchedness, affliction, pain; unhappiness, sorrow, grief, heartache, tragedy, calamity. **—Ant.** delight, joy, happiness, elation, gladness, jubilation, ecstasy, rapture, bliss; relief, ease.

order *n.* **1.** *Loyal troops obeyed the duke's orders:* command, dictate, decree, rule, pronouncement, instruction, bidding, law, commandment, demand, dictum, imperative, ultimatum, ukase, fiat. **2.** *The files are kept in alphabetical order:* arrangement, organization, classification, system, categorization, tabulation, designation, codification, grouping, neatness, tidiness, orderliness; form, structure, pattern, framework. **3.** *The chairman tried to maintain order:* quiet, calm, law and order, peace and quiet, silence, peacefulness, harmony, tranquility; control, discipline. **4.** *Fish are a lower order of life than birds. Her singing talent is of the highest order:* classification, class, category, division, kind, species, family, caste, station, breed, sort, type, stripe; quality, caliber, position, standing, rank, status, degree, grade. **5.** *The girl joined a religious order:* society, sisterhood, brotherhood, organization, fraternity, sorority, guild, house, body, society, association, alliance, group, club, lodge, confederacy, company, federation. **—v. 6.** *She ordered the dog to sit:* command, bid, direct, instruct, charge, decree, dictate, adjure, enjoin, ordain, call for. **7.** *Let's order dessert when the waitress comes back:* request, call for, ask for, book, engage, reserve, contract for, agree to, purchase, authorize the purchase of. **—Ant.** 1 request, plea, entreaty; supplication. 2, 3 disorder, confusion. 3 anarchy. 6 plead, entreat, supplicate, beg.

orderly *adj.* **1.** *Keep your closets orderly:* neat, tidy, spruce, shipshape, uncluttered, systematic, organized, methodical, classified, in a regular sequence. **2.** *Let's proceed in an orderly manner:* disciplined, restrained, controlled, well-behaved, civil, quiet, well-mannered, proper, peaceable, peaceful, tractable, law-abiding. **—Ant.** 1, 2 disorderly. 1 messy, sloppy, unsystematic, disorganized, cluttered. 2 undisciplined, chaotic, uncontrolled, unregulated, riotous.

ordinance *n. The ordinance forbids fireworks inside the city limits:* law, rule, ruling, regulation, statute; command, decree, edict, canon, fiat, dictum, order, enactment, act, writ, mandate, commandment, bull.

ordinarily *adv. Ordinarily we eat breakfast at seven:* usually, generally, normally, customarily, commonly, as a rule, by and large, as a matter of course, routinely, in most instances, on the average, conventionally, habitually, regularly. **—Ant.** rarely, infrequently, hardly ever, as an exception, sporadically.

ordinary *adj.* **1.** *It was an ordinary lunch of soup and a sandwich. He's not a hero, just an ordinary man:* common, commonplace, usual, average, customary, standard, normal, everyday, routine, familiar, typical, conventional, traditional, habitual, unexceptional, stereotyped, run-of-the-mill. **2.** *The novelist's latest book is quite ordinary:* undistinguished, commonplace, mediocre, indifferent, unimpressive, uninspired, unimaginative, pedestrian, run-of-the-mill, so-so; uninteresting, dull, humdrum; unimportant, inconsequential, insignificant, trivial. **—Ant.** 1, 2 extraordinary, exceptional, outstanding, distinguished, unusual, uncommon, rare, unique, unfamiliar, novel, atypical, unconventional. 2 superior, impressive, imaginative, inspired; important, consequential, significant, exciting.

ordnance *n. The battle was lost through lack of proper ordnance:* artillery, cannon, field pieces; military weapons and equipment, arms, munitions, war matériel, armaments.

organ *n.* **1.** *The organ played as the bride came down the aisle:* pipe organ, reed organ, harmonium; hand organ, barrel organ, hurdy-gurdy. **2.** *The heart is one of the body's vital organs:* functional part, bodily part, bodily structure. **3.** *This magazine is an official organ of the teachers' union:* publication, journal, trade journal, group publication, special interest publication; instrument, vehicle, agency.

organic *adj.* **1.** *Organic compounds form the basis of life. Organic gardening uses no manufactured chemicals:* containing carbon; of living things, living, alive, animate, quick; natural, nonsynthetic. **2.** *The patient has an organic malfunction:* of an organ, physiological, physical, anatomical, constitutional. **3.** *Frank Lloyd Wright was praised for his organic architecture:* unified, ordered, harmonious, well-organized, patterned; systematic, planned, methodical, designed. **—Ant.** 1, 2 inorganic. 3 haphazard, chaotic.

organism *n.* **1.** *The amoeba is a very simple organism:* living thing, creature, animal, physiological unit; plant, organic structure; bacterium, microorganism, cell. **2.** *The army is an extremely complex organism:* organized body, organization, system, network, whole, entity, complex; institution, corporation, federation, association, society.

organization *n.* **1.** *The organization of the business took two years:* formulation, forming, formation, assembly, incorporation, coordination, arranging, structuring, constitution, making. **2.** *The most striking thing about this abstract painting is the organization of the shapes* *and colors:* arrangement, organization, design, pattern, composition, grouping, ordering, harmony. **3.** *The American Medical Association is a professional organization of physicians:* association, society, fraternity, federation, union, club, fellowship, order, league, group, alliance, corps, party; business organization, business, establishment, firm, company, corporation, outfit; sect. **—Ant.** 1 dissolution, disbanding, breakup. 2 disorganization, confusion, chaos.

organize *v.* **1.** *Let's organize a debating society:* form, formulate, establish, originate, found, create, set up, put together, lay the foundation of, develop. **2.** *I'm trying to organize these dresser drawers:* arrange, systematize, make orderly, order, neaten, tidy, tidy up; classify, catalog, coordinate, categorize, group, codify, tabulate, index, file. **—Ant.** 1 dissolve, disband, dismember, break up. 2 disorganize, disorder, confuse, mess up.

orgiastic *adj. The play ended in an orgiastic scene of drinking and dancing:* abandoned, bacchanalian, wanton, licentious, libertine, debauched, riotous, drunken, wild, Dionysian, undisciplined, dissolute, overindulgent, dissipated, unrestrained. **—Ant.** temperate, ascetic, moderate, restrained, disciplined.

orgy *n. We're planning a quiet New Year's Eve party, not an orgy!:* wild revelry, wild party, wanton celebration, drunken festivities, wassail, debauch, carousal, saturnalia, bacchanalia, bacchanal.

orient *n.* **1.** the Orient *We visited Japan and two other countries in the Orient:* Asia; eastern Asia, the Eastern Hemisphere, the Far East. *—v.* **2.** *The first days of school are meant to orient the freshmen to campus life:* accustom, familiarize, relate, acclimate, reconcile, make feel at home. **3.** *You can orient yourself by remembering that the big hill is due north:* locate, situate, set, fix, square, find, place with reference to the points of the compass, determine one's direction. **—Ant.** 1 the Occident; Europe, the Americas, the Western Hemisphere. 2 estrange, alienate. 3 disorient, lose, confuse.

orientation *n.* **1.** *New employees must go through a period of orientation before they can be expected to understand their job:* familiarization, acclimatization, acclimation, adjustment. **2.** *The winding trail caused the hikers to lose their orientation. The orientation of the building is such that the early morning sun shines on the façade:* sense of direction, direction; alignment, location, situation. **—Ant.** 1 estrangement, alienation; confusion, bewilderment, perplexity, mystification.

orifice *n. The mouth is the human body's largest orifice:* opening, hole, cavity, aperture, slot, slit, gap, cleft, vent, entrance, passage, inlet, cranny, fissure, crevice, lacuna, mouth, oral cavity, hollow, pocket, pit, socket, alveolus.

origin *n.* **1.** *The origin of the flood was three weeks of torrential rains. The reporter traced the story back to its origin:* source, cause, basis, base, foundation, derivation, reason, principle, agent, generator; originator, creator, father,

mother, author, producer, prime mover, spring, fountainhead, taproot, root, ground. **2.** *The students are studying the origins of jazz in America:* beginning, birth, genesis, inception, commencement; emergence, evolution, early development, growth, rise, derivation. **3.** *The family is of Scandinavian origin:* extraction, descent, ancestry, parentage, family, lineage, house, stock, race, strain, breed, line; birth, nativity. **—Ant.** 1 end, finish, termination, conclusion. 2 death, fall, extinction, finis. 3 posterity, issue, progeny, offspring.

original *adj.* **1.** *Philadelphia was the original capital of the United States. The original idea was good, but now the plan is too complicated:* first, initial, earliest, inaugural, introductory; basic, fundamental, essential, underlying, formative, germinal, seminal; aboriginal, primordial, primeval, primary, primal. **2.** *She won an award for the most original design:* having originality, imaginative, creative, inventive, ingenious, fresh, novel, new, new-fashioned, unique, unusual, different, bold, daring, out of the ordinary, extraordinary, singular; uncommon, unfamiliar, strange, atypical, unconventional, unorthodox, *Informal* newfangled. *—n.* **3.** *Many steam engines have been built since, but this is the original:* prototype, first or earliest model, pattern, example, basis, first form, first copy. **—Ant.** 1 last, latest, final; superficial. 2 unoriginal, common, commonplace, usual, typical, conventional, traditional, ordinary, average, standard, normal, familiar, banal, trite, stale; old, old-fashioned, antiquated, *Slang* old hat; derivative, borrowed, copied. 3 copy, reproduction.

originality *n. The design for the building shows a great deal of originality:* imagination, creativity, inventiveness, ingenuity, cleverness, individuality, freshness, newness, novelty, uniqueness, boldness, daring, unconventionality, unorthodoxy, singularity. **—Ant.** unoriginality, routineness, commonness, conventionality, averageness, familiarity, banality, triteness, predictability; derivativeness.

originally *adv.* **1.** *We are originally from Springfield:* by origin; by derivation, by birth. **2.** *The dress was originally $40:* at first, initially, at the outset, in the beginning. **3.** *The apartment is decorated quite originally:* imaginatively, creatively, inventively, uniquely, differently, unusually, in an original way, unconventionally. **—Ant.** 2 finally, in the end. 3 conventionally, traditionally, typically, routinely, unimaginatively, predictably, tritely.

originate *v.* **1.** *The cruise originates in Miami. The creek originates in a spring in the hills:* begin, start, commence, proceed, emanate; arise, rise, derive, come, germinate, flow, issue, spring up, crop up, sprout, emerge, stem; be based in. **2.** *He is credited with originating a new printing process:* create, invent, devise, initiate, inaugurate, formulate, fabricate, father, conceive, envision, design, draft; found, establish, organize, develop, evolve. **—Ant.** 1 end, conclude, terminate, finish, close, stop, cease. 2 copy, imitate, follow.

ornament *n.* **1.** *We bought ornaments for the Christmas tree:* decoration, adornment, trimming, accessory, embellishment, trim, furbelow, frills, garnish; ornamentation, finery, beautification, enrichment, elaboration. —*v.* **2.** *The seamstress ornamented the dress with lace:* adorn, decorate, bedeck, festoon, trim, furbish, deck, trick out, garnish, gild; embellish, beautify, enrich.

ornamental *adj.* *Ornamental gewgaws crowded the apartment:* decorative, dressy, elaborate, ornate, showy, adorning, festooned, florid.

ornate *adj.* *The gold frame is much too ornate for that simple picture:* elaborate, lavish, fancy, sumptuous, showy, flowery, florid, flashy, flamboyant, ostentatious, pretentious; decorated, adorned, embellished, baroque, rococo. —**Ant.** simple, plain, bare, unadorned, unembellished, undecorated.

ornery *adj.* *He's so ornery even his dog dislikes him:* mean, ill-tempered, ill-natured, irascible, surly, cantankerous, grouchy, quarrelsome, grumpy, snappish, crabby, dyspeptic, irritable, testy, peevish, curt, waspish, *Brit.* shirty.

orthodox *adj.* **1.** *The old folks cling to their orthodox beliefs:* traditional, established, following established doctrine, accepted, authoritative, official, approved, *Slang* hard-shell; religious, pious, devout. **2.** *Such orthodox thinking will not lead to a new solution to the problem:* conventional, traditional, customary, conformable, commonplace, usual, routine, standard, fixed, established, regular, ordinary, usual; narrow, circumscribed, limited. —**Ant.** 1, 2 unorthodox. 1 heretical, radical, liberal, heterodox, unconformable. 2 unconventional, unusual, uncommon, unique, original, novel; eccentric, nonconformist, independent.

oscillate *v.* **1.** *The clock's pendulum caught the sunlight as it oscillated:* swing, alternate, librate; pulsate, vibrate, pulse, move back and forth, seesaw, come and go, ebb and flow. **2.** *He's been oscillating between liberal and conservative all his life:* waver, vacillate, hesitate, fluctuate, vary, hem and haw, shilly-shally, change, equivocate.

ossify *v.* *At what age does cartilage ossify?:* harden into bone, fossilize; (*loosely*) harden, stiffen, become rigid, become fixed.

ostensible *adj.* *Bill is now the ostensible head of the company, but his father is still the real boss:* titular, nominal, apparent, implied, presumable, outward, surface, seeming, alleged, avowed, declared, professed, manifest, perceivable, visible; pretended, assumed, feigned, specious, illusory. —**Ant.** real, true, actual, genuine, de facto.

ostensibly *adv.* *He ostensibly paid the fine:* apparently, supposedly, evidently, outwardly, professedly, seemingly, superficially.

ostentation *n.* *She was a great one for ostentation:* pretension, pretentiousness, semblance, show, showiness, pretense, pretext, display, pageantry, pomp, pompousness, flourish.

ostentatious *adj.* *Grandfather warned us not to be ostentatious with our money. The dress is too ostentatious to wear to a reception:* flaunting wealth, fond of display, showing off, pompous, immodest, grandiose, affected, high-flown; conspicuous, pretentious, flamboyant, flashy, showy, gaudy, garish, loud, florid, overdone, exaggerated, obtrusive. —**Ant.** modest, reserved, conservative, somber, sedate; inconspicuous, simple, plain.

ostracize *v.* *After the scandal her old friends ostracized her:* shun, snub, avoid, refuse to associate with, reject, exclude, shut out, banish, expel, oust, disown, blacklist, blackball, give one the cold shoulder, turn one's back on, *Slang* cut. —**Ant.** welcome, embrace, accept, acknowledge.

other *adj.* **1.** *I'll take this and one other suit on the trip:* additional, more, further, added, extra, spare, supplementary, auxiliary. **2.** *Doesn't this dress come in other colors? Wait until you hear the other side of the story before blaming anyone:* different, additional, more, dissimilar, unlike, contrasted, differentiated; opposite, reverse, contrasting, contradictory, contrary, alternate, remaining.

otherwise *adv.* **1.** *Leave now; otherwise you'll be late:* if not, or else; under other circumstances, on the other hand. **2.** *She could not phrase the question otherwise. I think otherwise:* differently, in another manner; in opposition, in disagreement, in defiance, contrarily, contrariwise, inversely, in reverse. **3.** *He's too fat; otherwise he's nice looking:* in other respects, excluding this, barring this, excepting this, apart from this. —**Ant.** 2 similarly, alike, correspondingly.

otiose *adj.* **1.** *It was an era when everyone felt indifferent and otiose:* lazy, slothful, idle, indolent, sluggish, resting, inactive, somnolent, lethargic, listless, laggard. **2.** *In a modern society those who don't produce are considered otiose:* useless, ineffective, impotent, unavailing, worn-out, inoperative, incompetent, futile, fruitless, abortive, unproductive, unrewarding, powerless. —**Ant.** 1 energetic, active, dynamic. 2 effective, useful, rewarding.

oust *v.* *The umpire ousted the arguing player from the game. The lazy employee was ousted from the job:* expel, eject, evict, remove, banish, put out, cast out, throw out, kick out; dismiss, discharge, cashier, fire, unseat, *Slang* bounce, sack, give the gate, give the ax, send packing, boot out. —**Ant.** admit, invite, ask in, welcome; hire, engage, employ, appoint.

ouster *n.* *A vote of no confidence caused his ouster as prime minister:* ejection, overthrow, expulsion, dismissal, firing, discharge, dispossession, eviction, removal, banishment, dislodgment; *Slang* sacking, cashiering, drumming out, bouncing.

out *adv.* **1.** *We are out of flour:* depleted, finished, exhausted, used up, expired, extinguished, finished. **2.** *Let the cat out:* outside, outdoors, outward, without.

out-and-out *adj.* *She called him an out-and-out cad because of his conduct:* thorough, complete, absolute, utter, sheer, total, unconditional, unqualified, outright, straight-out; confirmed, inveterate, hardened, unregenerate, dyed-in-the-wool.

outbreak *n. Police quelled the outbreak of violence. There has been an outbreak of measles in town:* outburst, burst, eruption, explosion, outpouring, display, demonstration; sudden appearance, rapid spread, invasion, epidemic. —**Ant.** waning, ebbing, recession, decrease, decline, subsidence.

outburst *n. His outburst of anger shocked us all:* burst, eruption, outbreak, explosion, outpouring, display, demonstration; fulmination, blast, thunder. —**Ant.** suppression, repression, control, restraint, stifling.

outcast *n.* **1.** *The one-time star became an outcast:* exile, deportee, refugee, expatriate, displaced person, man without a country; pariah, castaway; outlaw, fugitive, runaway; lonely wanderer, roamer, rover, homeless man, vagabond, derelict, destitute person. —*adj.* **2.** *The Salvation Army mission was a haven for outcast souls:* rejected, discarded, expelled, castaway, ousted, banished.

outcome *n. What was the outcome of your interview?:* result, consequence, effect, upshot, issue, end, fruit, *Slang* payoff; aftereffect, aftermath, outgrowth.

outcry *n. The sentry's outcry warned the troops. There was a great outcry among consumers when prices rose:* crying out, cry, cry of alarm, cry of distress, cry of protest, shout, scream, shriek, caterwauling, screech, howl, yell, roar, bellow, whoop, yowl, yelp; clamor, uproar, commotion, noise, clangor, hubbub, hue and cry, hullabaloo; protest, complaint, objection, remonstrance. —**Ant.** whisper, murmur; quiet, stillness, silence, calm, tranquillity; assent, concurrence, ratification.

outdated *adj. His language was outdated:* dated, out-of-date, out-of-style, old-fashioned, outmoded, passé, anachronous, antiquated, archaic, obsolete, out, tired, unfashionable, *Informal* moth-eaten, old-hat, has-been, square. —**Ant.** contemporary, fashionable, in vogue.

outdo *v. No one can outdo her in stylishness:* excel, surpass, best, outshine, exceed, better, outclass, top, beat, eclipse, transcend, outstrip, outrank, outplay, defeat, overcome, worst, outfox, outwit, get the better of, steal a march on.

outer *adj. The outer surface is walnut veneer. The house is in the outer suburbs:* exterior, external, outward, outside, distal, without; farther, farther out, extreme, remote, outlying, outermost, peripheral. —**Ant.** inner, interior, internal, inward, inside, within; central, close-by, close-in, nearby, adjacent.

outfit *n.* **1.** *Mother bought a new outfit for Easter. A scuba diving outfit includes tanks, hose, mask, and flippers:* ensemble, costume, set of clothing, getup, wardrobe, habit; equipment, gear, paraphernalia, trappings, accoutrements, *Slang* rig. —*v.* **2.** *The expedition was outfitted with the latest scientific equipment:* equip, provision, supply, furnish, provision, appoint, fit,

accouter, *Slang* rig up; dress, clothe, costume, array.

outgoing *adj.* **1.** *Put the letter in the outgoing mail:* outbound, going out, outward bound, leaving, departing, exiting. **2.** *A good hostess should be very outgoing:* friendly, amiable, gregarious, convivial, genial, social, sociable, extroverted, sympathetic, cordial, warm, warmhearted. —**Ant.** 1 incoming, inbound, arriving, entering. 2 cold, austere, indifferent, distant, reserved, retiring, withdrawn.

outgrowth *n.* **1.** *The police investigation is an outgrowth of numerous complaints:* result, consequence, upshot, natural development, product, issue, fruit; end, conclusion, culmination, sequel, aftereffect, aftermath, offshoot. **2.** *The tree has outgrowths of fungus and mushrooms:* shoot, sprout, offshoot, outcropping, excrescence; protuberance, projection, bulge, node, knob, knot.

outing *n. The family enjoyed an outing at the beach last weekend:* excursion, expedition, trip, pleasure trip, holiday, junket; hike, tramp, ramble, walk; drive, ride, tour, spin, jaunt, airing.

outlander *n. The outlanders slowly adjusted to the customs of their new land:* stranger, alien, foreigner, *German* Ausländer; immigrant, settler, newcomer; wanderer, exile, displaced person, *French* émigré; barbarian, tramontane, ultramontane; intruder, invader.

outlandish *adj. Did you ever see such an outlandish hat?:* preposterous, incredible, outrageous, odd, bizarre, fantastic, freakish, ridiculous, eccentric, queer, weird, grotesque, strange, curious, peculiar, unusual, unconventional, unimaginable, unbelievable, inconceivable, unheard-of, unparalleled, *Slang* far-out, kooky. —**Ant.** commonplace, ordinary, everyday, routine, normal, familiar, standard, usual, run-of-the-mill.

outlast *v. A good suit like that will easily outlast a cheap one:* outwear, outstay, survive, endure, perdure, prevail, persist, stay on, keep on, hold on, carry on, continue, remain, hold out, persist, defy time.

outlaw *n.* **1.** *A posse was formed to track down the outlaws:* criminal, fugitive, felon, bandit, desperado, highwayman, miscreant; outcast, pariah. —*v.* **2.** *The new regulation outlaws the sale of bicycles without a headlight:* make unlawful, forbid, prohibit, ban, bar, proscribe, exclude, deny, disallow, suppress, stop, interdict. —**Ant.** 2 legalize, permit, allow; encourage, foster, welcome.

outlay *n. The swimming pool required an outlay of several thousand dollars:* expenditure, spending; amount spent, payment, disbursement, outgo, cost, expense, charge, fee; price. —**Ant.** profit, gain, yield, income.

outlet *n.* **1.** *Switzerland has no outlet to the sea:* opening, egress, passage, channel, path, way, avenue; exit, gateway, gate, portal, door; duct, conduit; means. **2.** *The child needs an outlet for all that energy:* vent, means of expression, means of satisfying, way of getting rid of, escape. —**Ant.** 1 entrance, ingress, entry.

outline *n.* **1.** *The hunter could see the outline of the deer against the trees:* profile, silhouette, contour, delineation, lineation; boundary line, limits, tracing, perimeter, periphery. **2.** *Just tell me the outline of the story now and fill in the details later:* synopsis, summary, résumé, brief report, brief, general sketch, thumbnail sketch, condensation, digest, abridgment, abstract, review, recapitulation. —*v.* **3.** *Outline the figure in red paint. Outline the story before trying to write it:* draw a line around, trace, delineate; diagram, write a synopsis, sketch out, blueprint, plot. —**Ant.** 1 bulk, mass, substance, volume; center, core, heart.

outlive *v.* *She outlived all her children:* survive, outlast.

outlook *n.* **1.** *The outlook from the top of the mountain is breathtaking:* view, vista, prospect, sight, aspect, panorama, spectacle, scene, picture. **2.** *His outlook has become quite pessimistic:* attitude, frame of mind, point of view, viewpoint, view, perspective. **3.** *The experts say that the business outlook for next year is good:* prospect, expectation, anticipation, forecast, assumption, presumption; probability, chance, promise. —**Ant.** 3 hindsight; recapitulation.

outlying *adj.* *A new shopping center is being built in an outlying area of the town. Some of the outlying districts have no medical service:* outer, exterior, peripheral; remote, distant, far-off, rural, suburban, exurban. —**Ant.** central, inner, internal, core; nearby, near, neighboring, close-by, adjacent.

outmoded *adj.* *He tried to revive political concepts that were outmoded years ago:* out-of-date, dated, old-fashioned, old-timey, démodé, passé, archaic, antique, vintage, antiquated, out-of-fashion, outdated, behind the times; *Slang* old hat, corny, tired. —**Ant.** up-to-date, stylish, modish; *Slang* with it, hip, cool.

output *n.* *The company has doubled its output in five years:* production, yield, productivity, achievement, produce, product, harvest, crop, accomplishment, turnout, profit, proceeds, take, gain, reaping, gathering, gleaning.

outrage *n.* **1.** *Bombing the church was an outrage:* atrocity, inhumane act, act of brutality, wanton violence, barbarity, barbarousness, iniquity, enormity, monstrosity, gross offense, gross crime; evil, wrong, transgression, gross indecency; desecration, profanation. **2.** *Such a lie is an outrage to anyone who loves the truth:* insult, affront, indignity, expression of contempt, disrespect, slap in the face. —*v.* **3.** *The speaker's remarks outraged the audience:* anger, incense, enrage, infuriate, madden, provoke, arouse, exasperate, gall, rile, ruffle, make one's blood boil, make one see red, steam up, get one's back up; insult, affront, make indignant, offend, shock, scandalize, disquiet, discompose. —**Ant.** 3 calm, soothe, quiet, pacify.

outrageous *adj.* **1.** *The gang committed several outrageous crimes:* atrocious, vile, base, heinous, grossly offensive, iniquitous, monstrous, barbarous, inhumane, inhuman, brutal, foul, despicable, contemptible, wicked, nefari-

ous, horrifying, odious, reprehensible, unspeakable. **2.** *I've never heard such an outrageous remark in my life!:* offensive, abusive, shameless, shocking, scandalous, disgraceful, insulting, insolent, rude, disrespectful, contemptuous, scornful; infuriating, maddening, galling, exasperating. **3.** *The cost of the repairs was outrageous:* monstrous, extreme, unreasonable, preposterous, flagrant, unwarranted, unconscionable, gross, rank, exorbitant, immoderate, immense, excessive, enormous. —**Ant.** 3 reasonable, moderate, mild, minor, trivial, paltry; equitable, fair, just; tolerable.

outright *adj.* **1.** *That statement was an outright lie:* utter, complete, total, downright, entire, full, unmitigated, unqualified, undiminished, unreserved, unconditional, absolute, sheer, thorough, thoroughgoing, out-and-out. —*adv.* **2.** *She was outright rude:* utterly, altogether, completely, absolutely, downright, thoroughly, entirely; openly, visibly, patently, manifestly, demonstrably. **3.** *The driver was killed outright:* instantly, immediately, at once, on the spot, promptly, forthwith. —**Ant.** 1 partial, incomplete; qualified, conditional. 2 somewhat, partially. 3 later, eventually, ultimately, finally, in due course.

outside *n.* **1.** *The outside of the house is painted white. The outside of the candy is chocolate:* exterior, surface, outer side, façade, face; covering, case, sheath, skin, coating. —*adj.* **2.** *The outside walls are brick:* outer, exterior, external, outward, outermost, outdoor. **3.** *National policy should not be determined by outside influences:* extraneous, foreign, alien, nonnative, nondomestic, unfamiliar, strange. **4.** *There's an outside chance it may rain today:* remote, distant, faint, obscure, slight. —*adv.* **5.** *Put the cat outside:* outdoors, out-of-doors, on or to the outside. —*prep.* **6.** *We took a trip outside the country:* beyond the bounds of, distant from, beyond the confines of. —**Ant.** 1, 2 inside, interior. 1 center. 2 inner, inmost, innermost, inward, internal. 3 native, domestic; familiar, known. 5 indoors. 6 inside.

outspoken *adj.* *She's so outspoken she's hurt the feelings of all her friends:* plainspoken, blunt, frank, honest, direct, straightforward, forthright, unreserved, opinionated, candid, unsparing; artless, ingenuous, guileless, undissembling, undissimulating. —**Ant.** tactful, diplomatic, gracious, judicious, reticent, guarded.

outstanding *adj.* **1.** *This is one of the outstanding paintings of the Renaissance period:* foremost, eminent, prominent, famed, celebrated, distinguished, famous, renowned, best known, remarkable, memorable, unforgettable, striking, notable, noteworthy; exemplary, exceptional, extraordinary, marvelous, most impressive, magnificent, great, phenomenal. **2.** *The outstanding bills must be paid by the first of the month:* unpaid, unsettled, due, in arrears, uncollected, payable, owing. —**Ant.** 1 commonplace, routine, ordinary, usual, everyday, run-of-the-mill; trite, banal. 2 paid, settled, collected.

outward *adj.* **1.** *There is no outward sign that*

the patient is improving. His outward appearance was calm but he was seething inside: external, exterior, outer, outside, surface, superficial, visible, perceivable, perceptible, apparent, ostensible; evident, manifest, observable. —adv. 2. Also **outwards** The ship was outward bound. This door opens outward, not inward: out, toward the outside, away, from here. —Ant. 1, 2 inward. 1 internal, interior, inner, inside, inmost, innermost; invisible, imperceptible, unobservable. 2 in; toward the inside.

outwardly adv. She was outwardly pleased with the idea: to all appearances, apparently, evidently, seemingly, ostensibly, on the face of it, manifestly, visibly, clearly. —Ant. inwardly, secretly.

outweigh v. 1. The boxer outweighed his opponent by ten pounds: weigh more than, be heavier than, exceed the weight of. 2. The good points outweigh the bad points: exceed, surpass, predominate, overshadow, eclipse, override, rise above, be more important than, prevail over, take precedence over.

outwit v. The store outwitted the robbers by putting phony jewels in the display case: outsmart, outfox, outmaneuver, take in, trick, fool, dupe, foil, thwart, baffle, circumvent, get around; trap, ensnare.

outworn adj. He still has the outworn concept that a woman belongs only in the kitchen: out-of-date, obsolete, passé, unfashionable, superseded, disused, extinct, antiquated, old-fashioned, dated; defunct, discarded, abandoned, rejected, bygone, forgotten. —Ant. current, fashionable, new, up-to-date, in.

oval adj. A large, oval rug would look nice in front of the fireplace: egg-shaped, ovoid, ovate, elliptical, ellipsoidal, ovular, curved, rounded, oviform, Botany obovate, almond-shaped.

ovation n. The singer was greeted with a standing ovation: enthusiastic applause, cheers, cheering, acclamation, adulation, homage, acclaim, tribute; hurrah, hurray, huzzah; fanfare. —Ant. jeering, taunts, catcalls, hoots, booing.

over adv. 1. Please look this contract over: from beginning to end, from top to bottom, all through, all over; from head to foot, from cover to cover; from stem to stern, from end to end; along the course of. 2. This work will have to be done over: again, a second time, once more, anew, afresh; repeatedly, time and again, often, in repetition. 3. Will there be any left over?: remaining, in addition, in excess, on top of the rest, beyond a certain amount, into the bargain, to boot; too, else, also; extra, over and above. —adj. 4. Is the meeting over?: at an end, finished, ended, concluded, done, terminated, completed, settled; lapsed, elapsed, expired, passed away, no more, gone, past, bygone. 5. I guessed the amount, but Jim was over by $10: in excess, in addition, above, extra, additional, excessive, surplus, too great, superfluous. —Ant. 2 once, only once. 3, 5 under, below, short, deficient, wanting, lacking, shy. 4 begun, started, commenced; in progress.

overabundance n. There is an overabundance of tomatoes this year: abundance, superabundance, excess, surplus, oversupply, superfluity, profusion, plethora, supersaturation, surfeit, glut, embarrassment of riches. —Ant. shortage, scarcity, dearth, scantiness, insufficiency, lack, want.

overall adj. The overall situation is encouraging: total, general, complete, entire, comprehensive, exhaustive, all-inclusive, all-embracing, sweeping, panoramic, extensive, thoroughgoing, widespread; long-range, long-term.

overbearing adj. He's so overbearing no one wants to work for him: arrogant, high-handed, self-assertive, self-important, cocky, lordly, high-and-mighty, know-it-all, disdainful, imperious, domineering, dictatorial, autocratic, tyrannical, despotic; egotistical, haughty, pompous, conceited, Informal stuck-up, snooty, high-hat. —Ant. modest, unassuming, humble, demure, meek, shy, timid, subdued, deferential, subservient; receptive, sympathetic, compassionate, gracious.

overblown adj. The overblown oratory amazed us: windy, bombastic, euphuistic, flowery, fulsome, grandiloquent, magniloquent, rhetorical, verbose, aureate; disproportionate, excessive, immoderate, inflated, overdone, pretentious, undue, profuse, superfluous, Informal hyped up.

overcast adj. The forecast is for overcast skies and a little rain: cloudy, overclouded, sunless, gray, dull, dreary, gloomy, dark, leaden, threatening, lowering, murky; misty, foggy, hazy. —Ant. cloudless, unclouded, clear, sunny, brilliant, bright.

overcome v. Someday we shall overcome racial intolerance. She was overcome with grief: conquer, best, get the better of, master, surmount, vanquish, defeat, beat, lick, suppress, overthrow, put down, overwhelm, overpower, subdue, crush, quell, prevail over, triumph over, win over, transcend; survive. —Ant. surrender to, give in to, capitulate to, submit to; give up, admit defeat.

overconfident adj. The chess player was so overconfident that he played carelessly: too confident, overly sure of succeeding, self-assured, egotistical, cocksure; impudent, arrogant, presumptuous, brash, immodest, conceited, cheeky. —Ant. self-effacing, fearful, modest, sheepish, shamefaced.

overdo v. 1. A little exercise is fine, but don't overdo it: do to excess, carry too far, not know when to stop, be intemperate in; overtax oneself by; indulge oneself in. 2. A simple "thank you" is enough; don't overdo it: exaggerate, overstate, hyperbolize, stretch a point, Informal lay it on thick; magnify, expand, amplify, embroider, gild, overact, overplay, Slang ham it up. —Ant. 2 understate, minimize, slight, neglect.

overdue adj. Your visit here is long overdue: past due, belated, late, tardy, unpunctual, behind time, behindhand, delayed, slow, dilatory, long delayed. —Ant. early, ahead of time, beforehand, premature.

overflow v. 1. Turn the water off or the bathtub will overflow. The flood overflowed the river val-

ley: flow over, run over, be filled to overflowing, overspill, slop over; overspread, inundate, flood. —*n.* **2.** *There is an overflow of cheap ballpoint pens on the market:* overabundance, superabundance, surplus, excess, superfluity, profusion, oversupply, plethora, copiousness, flood, glut. —**Ant.** 2 lack, want, scarcity, shortage, dearth, paucity, deficiency, insufficiency.

overhang *v.* **1.** *A banner overhung the entrance:* hang over, extend over, be suspended from, bulge, dangle over, droop over, jut out, project, protrude, rise above, stand out, stick out, tower above; impend, portend, loom. —*n.* **2.** *I'll wait for you under the overhang:* extension, bulge, protrusion, cantilever.

overhaul *v.* **1.** *The racing car had only one lap to overhaul the leader:* overtake, pass, catch up with, catch, beat. **2.** *How much will it cost to overhaul the motor?:* renovate, revamp, rebuild, reconstruct, remodel, recondition, inspect and repair, service, restore.

overhead *adv.* **1.** *There was a large skylight overhead. Look overhead!:* over one's head, above one's head; upward, up above, above; aloft, atop, on top. —*adj.* **2.** *Turn on the lamps and the overhead light:* ceiling, roof; overlying, overhanging; uppermost, upper, superior, topmost. —*n.* **3.** *To increase profits the business must reduce its overhead:* operating expenses, general expenses, *Slang* nut.

overjoyed *adj.* *She seemed overjoyed to see us:* delighted, deliriously happy, jubilant, elated, joyous, gratified, enthralled, enraptured, exultant, thrilled, euphoric, exuberant, enchanted, ecstatic, transported, *Informal* carried away, tickled pink, happy as the day is long, happy as a lark. —**Ant.** disappointed, unhappy, sad, depressed, dejected, downcast, sorrowful, despondent, blue.

overlap *v.* *One event overlapped the other:* overlay, overlie, lie over, overrun, extend along, lap over, fold over.

overlook *v.* **1.** *How could you overlook paying the rent?:* forget, neglect, leave undone, not trouble oneself about, omit, leave out, miss, slight, pass over, pass up, skip. **2.** *She overlooks most of his faults:* ignore, disregard, regard indulgently, pass over, blink at, wink at; excuse, forgive, shrug off, forget about, think no more of, let bygones be bygones, let ride. **3.** *The house overlooks the river:* have a view of, look over, give on, look out on, survey; tower above, command. —**Ant.** 1 remember, pay attention to, concentrate on, keep in mind. 2 complain, carp, nag, cavil, criticize, censure, find fault with, view with disfavor.

overly *adv.* *The book review seemed overly critical:* excessively, needlessly, exceedingly, too, immoderately, inordinately, unreasonably, unfairly, unduly, exorbitantly, disproportionately, overmuch, too much, to a fault; extremely, very, acutely, highly, severely, intensely. —**Ant.** insufficiently, inadequately, too little; moderately, reasonably, mildly.

overpower *v.* **1.** *The speaker was overpowered with emotion:* overcome, overwhelm, affect

strongly, move, sway, influence. **2.** *He overpowered his assailant and called the police:* subdue, overcome, get the better of, best, get the upper hand over, master, overwhelm, conquer, vanquish, defeat, worst, beat, triumph over, crush, quell. —**Ant.** 2 surrender, give up, give in, capitulate.

overrate *v.* *The critics certainly overrated that show:* overpraise, overestimate, overesteem, rate too highly, overvalue, overprize, praise undeservedly, make too much of, attach too much importance to. —**Ant.** underrate, underestimate, undervalue; belittle, minimize.

overriding *adj.* *Cost was an overriding consideration:* predominant, determining, dominant, major, main, major, central, compelling, overruling, paramount, pivotal, prevailing, primary, prime, principal, ruling, supreme, ultimate, cardinal. —**Ant.** negligible, immaterial, inconsequential, insignificant, minor, petty.

overrule *v.* **1.** *The judge overruled the council's objection:* disallow, rule against, reject, override, dismiss, preclude, set aside, waive, eject, throw out, deny, veto, refuse, repudiate, invalidate, countermand, overturn, repel, revoke, cancel, annul, nullify, make null and void. **2.** *One member wanted to raise the dues, but the rest of the club overruled him:* prevail over, outvote, outweigh, bend to one's will. —**Ant.** 1 accept, allow, permit, approve, grant, authorize, favor; sustain, support, promote, champion, back.

overrun *v.* **1.** *The Vandals of northern Europe overran the Roman Empire. Weeds overran the garden:* swarm over, infest, surge over, rove over, run riot over, overspread, pour in on, overwhelm, invade; raid, invade, swoop down on; sack, pillage, plunder, loot, despoil; engulf, inundate, deluge; overgrow, choke, flourish in. —*n.* **2.** *The overrun on the new bomber cost the government ten million dollars:* overproduction, surplus; additional cost, extra charge.

overseas *adv.* **1.** *Millions of American soldiers fought overseas in World War II:* abroad, in foreign lands, across the sea, beyond the sea; in foreign service. —*adj.* **2.** *Are you interested in an overseas job? Our oversea shipments go by freighter:* foreign, external, alien, exotic; transoceanic. —**Ant.** 1 at home, on native soil. 2 domestic, internal, native, indigenous.

oversee *v.* *While the owner is gone, his assistant will oversee the business:* supervise, superintend, overlook, have charge of, handle, attend to, see to, keep an eye on; administer, manage, direct, run, boss, command, govern, rule, guide, watch, preside over, carry on, pilot, steer, be at the helm of, regulate.

overseer *n.* *Their youngest daughter eloped with the overseer of the plantation:* supervisor, chief, head, boss, manager, director, foreman, superintendent, captain, taskmaster, governor, slave driver.

overshadow *v.* **1.** *Heavy clouds overshadowed the mountain:* cast a shadow over, eclipse, shade, darken; obscure, hide, conceal, cover, screen, mask, shroud, veil, fog. **2.** *His famous father always overshadowed him:* outshine, eclipse, dwarf, tower over, render insignificant by comparison, diminish the importance of, steal the limelight from.

oversight *n. Did you mean to leave the door unlocked or was it an oversight?:* omission, mistake, blunder, heedless mistake, inadvertence, careless error, slight; negligence, neglect, neglectfulness, carelessness, laxity, inattention, thoughtlessness, heedlessness, disregard, absent-mindedness. **—Ant.** care, attention, heed, heedfulness, diligence, alertness, vigilance, meticulousness, scrupulousness.

overstate *v. She tried to stress the urgency of her case by overstating the facts:* exaggerate, overstress, overdo, embellish, embroider, oversell, enlarge, overdraw, overpaint, increase, inflate, magnify, stretch, enlarge on; *Slang* touch up, play up, lay it on, spread it on thick. **—Ant.** understate, minimize, undervalue, underplay, soft-pedal.

overt *adj. There was no overt hostility between the two men:* apparent, obvious, noticeable, visible, observable, ostensible, plain, public, open, easily seen, unconcealed, perceptible, perceivable, palpable, evident, revealed, manifest, undisguised. **—Ant.** covert, unrevealed, unnoticeable, invisible, hidden, concealed, covered, masked, secret, undisclosed, disguised, private.

overtake *v.* **1.** *The champion slowly overtook the lead runner:* come abreast of, catch up with, catch, come up beside, gain on, reach, approach, run down; pass, overhaul, go by. **2.** *The storm overtook the sailors before they could take in sail:* take by surprise, come upon suddenly, befall, catch unprepared, catch off guard. **—Ant.** 1 fall back from, lose ground to.

overthrow *v.* **1.** *The rebels conspired to overthrow the regime:* overturn, topple, bring down, cast down from power, put an end to by force, overcome, overpower, defeat, abolish, undo, crush, do away with. **—n.** **2.** *The overthrow of the dictator was greeted with cheers:* toppling, bringing down, casting out of power, undoing, downfall, defeat, overturn, abolition; revolution, rebellion, insurrection, mutiny. **—Ant.** 1 preserve, conserve, maintain, uphold, support, keep, perpetuate; defend, protect, guard. 2 preservation, perpetuation; defense, protection.

overtone *n. There were overtones of distrust in his voice:* suggestion, intimation, insinuation, hint, implication, connotation, slight indication, innuendo, drift, coloring, hue.

overture *n.* **1.** *The opera was preceded by a short overture:* prelude, introduction, prologue; foreword, preface, preamble; beginning. **2.** *The losing army made a peace overture:* opening move, preliminary offer, receptive sign, invitation, approach, bid, offering, advance, tender, motion, signal, gesture, suggestion, proposal, proposition. **—Ant.** 1 finale, close; epilogue, afterword, coda. 2 rejection, spurning, repudiation, rebuke.

overturn *v.* **1.** *The mountainous waves nearly overturned the boat:* capsize, knock over, upset, knock down, upend, push over, topple, turn upside down, turn topsy-turvy. **2.** *The mobs*

stormed the palace and overturned the monarchy:* defeat, vanquish, overthrow, conquer, overcome, overpower, overwhelm, depose, turn out, crush, beat, thrash, oust.

overweening *adj. Given a measure of authority, he quickly becomes overweening:* overbearing, haughty, disdainful, arrogant, pompous, highhanded, patronizing, egotistical, overconfident, domineering, imperious, presumptuous, cocky, brassy, bigheaded, bossy, self-important, *Slang* pushy. **—Ant.** modest, shy, unassuming.

overweight *adj. An overweight person should reduce calorie intake and exercise more:* obese, fat, corpulent, pudgy, chubby, plump, chunky, well-padded, fleshy, overstuffed, fatty, fattish, potbellied, roly-poly, portly, tubby; *Slang* piggy, beer-bellied, gross. **—Ant.** underweight, skinny, bony, gaunt, emaciated, anorexic.

overwhelm *v.* **1.** *Invading armies overwhelmed the town:* overrun, overpower, overcome, overthrow, defeat, vanquish, subjugate, conquer, beat; quash, crush, quell, bury, swamp, engulf, inundate. **2.** *Sorrow overwhelmed the family:* overcome, overpower, devastate, crush, stagger, confound, bowl over. **—Ant.** 1 surrender, capitulate, give up, give in; rescue, deliver, save. 2 unaffect, leave indifferent; encourage, lift.

overwrought *adj. He was overwrought after the bitter argument:* overexcited, excited, agitated, wrought up, worked up, carried away, near hysteria, riled, greatly disturbed, distracted, inflamed, wild, frenzied, wild-eyed, uneasy, perturbed, ruffled; nervous, high-strung, oversensitive, touchy. **—Ant.** calm, tranquil, placid, unruffled, serene, unexcited, untroubled, cool, composed, *Slang* unflappable.

owe *v. After the latest loan the business will owe the bank $10,000. You owe your parents more respect:* be in debt, be indebted to, be obligated, have a loan from; be under obligation to, be bound in gratitude, be beholden to. **—Ant.** repay, pay back, reimburse, liquidate, amortize, compensate.

own *adj.* **1.** *Bring your own tennis racket. What I do with my spare time is my own business!:* belonging to oneself, belonging to itself; personal, private, individual, particular. **—v.** **2.** *Has the youth ever owned a car before?:* possess, have possession of, be in receipt of, be the owner of, have, retain, keep, maintain, hold. **3.** *She would never own to a mistake. Society must own the right of every man to speak his mind:* admit, acknowledge, confess to, concede, disclose, tell; grant, allow, yield, consent to, recognize; avow, assent, concur, acquiesce. **—Ant.** 1 someone else's, another's. 3 deny, disown, disclaim, repudiate, abjure; deprive, divest, disallow, refuse.

owner *n. The sign says the house is for sale by its owner:* possessor, landlord, landlady, proprietor, proprietress, holder, landholder, partner, copartner, landowner, master, mistress, titleholder, householder.

ownership *n. They claimed ownership of the property:* possession, title, deed, freehold, proprietorship, proprietary rights.

P

pace *n.* **1.** *Take three paces forward. The horse moved at an easy pace:* step, stride, gait, tread, slow gait, walk, amble, saunter. **2.** *The work progressed at a slow pace:* rate, speed, velocity, clip, motion, momentum, flow, gait. —*v.* **3.** *She paced the floor, waiting for the phone to ring. The horse paced around the ring:* walk nervously back and forth across; walk, go at a slow gait, amble, stroll, saunter. —**Ant.** 1, 2 trot, canter, run.

pacific *adj.* *There must still be some pacific places left in this busy world:* calm, serene, placid, peaceful, tranquil, quiet, restful, reposeful, smooth, undisturbed, untroubled, still, halcyon, unruffled, harmonious, peaceable; conciliatory, pacifying, gentle, dovelike, inoffensive. —**Ant.** agitated, troubled, overwrought; quarrelsome, belligerent, violent.

pacify *v.* *The king pacified the mob with promises of reform:* appease, calm, quiet, allay, bring to a state of peace, soothe, placate, propitiate, assuage, compose, mollify; restore to peace, restore harmony, conciliate, reconcile, settle differences, bring to terms, heal the breach. —**Ant.** make hostile, anger, enrage, madden, inflame, agitate, aggravate, provoke; begin hostilities, start a fight.

pack *n.* **1.** *The boy bought three packs of gum. That's a pack of lies!:* package, packet, parcel, bundle, kit, box, container; batch, bunch, set, lot, heap, mass, cluster, clump; accumulation, collection, assortment, miscellany. **2.** *A pack of angry shoppers demanded their money back:* crowd, throng, group, horde, mob, multitude, swarm, flock, herd, drove, covey, passel, bevy, gaggle. —*v.* **3.** *Spectators packed the stadium. Pack these books together and put them in the attic:* fill, load, jam, cram, stuff; bundle, bunch, batch, group, gather, assemble, tie, bind, truss. —**Ant.** 3 unpack, empty; unwrap, untie, unload.

package *n.* **1.** *How much is this package of detergent? Do you still have the package this came in?:* pack, parcel, packet; bundle, box, carton, case, container, kit, wrappings. —*v.* **2.** *Now they package the lettuce in cellophane:* wrap, wrap up, pack, encase; display in a container.

packet *n.* *A large packet of letters awaited me upon my return:* parcel, package, pack, bundle, pouch, bag, box, sheaf, bale, roll, quiver.

pact *n.* *Seven countries signed the trade pact:* treaty, international agreement, agreement, compact, contract, convention, concordance, concordat; bond, covenant, alliance, understanding.

pad *n.* **1.** *That carpet needs a pad under it. Get a pad to lie on:* cushion, cushioning, padding; mattress, mat, bolster. **2.** *Each student should have a pencil and pad:* tablet, writing tablet, notebook; desk pad, memorandum book, memo pad. —*v.* **3.** *The movers padded the furniture with mattresses and canvas:* cushion, protect; upholster; stuff, fill. **4.** *The author padded the book with long quotations:* fill out unnecessarily, expand needlessly, enlarge excessively, amplify freely, stretch out, inflate, fatten, blow up, puff out.

padding *n.* **1.** *Put plenty of padding around the vase when you pack it:* wadding, stuffing, filler, filling, lining, packing, wrapping. **2.** *It seemed to me there was a lot of padding in his speech:* wordiness, prolixity, verbiage, verboseness, verbosity, redundancy, superabundance, surplus, surfeit, extravagance. —**Ant.** 2 shortage, lack, dearth, want, scarcity.

paddle *n.* **1.** *They took a paddle down to the canoe:* oar, pole, propeller. —*v.* **2.** *We paddled to the middle of the lake:* row, oar, propel, pull, row, scull.

paean *n.* *The speech was a paean to the boss's virtues:* praise, encomium, hymn, anthem, hosanna, hallelujah, laudation, laud, tribute, homage, accolade.

pagan *n.* **1.** *The pagans worshiped the gods of fire and rain:* one who is not a Christian or Jew or Muslim; heathen, infidel, idolator, idol worshiper, polytheist; nonbeliever, unbeliever, atheist. —*adj.* **2.** *The pagan idols were destroyed by the missionaries:* heathen, heathenish, idolatrous, polytheistic; barbarian. —**Ant.** 1 Christian, Jew, Muslim; true believer, believer. 2 Christian, Jewish, Muslim, monotheistic, Christianized, civilized, enlightened.

page *n.* **1.** *The information was on the next page:* leaf, folio. **2.** *Each knight had a page in attendance:* attendant, squire, equerry, errand boy, servant, server. —*v.* **3.** summon, call.

pageant *n.* *The pageant commemorates the founding of the town:* spectacle, elaborate performance, show, exhibition, display, extravaganza; ceremony, ritual, pomp, rite; procession, parade.

pageantry *n.* *The pageantry of the coronation was spectacular:* display, pomp, pageant, ceremony, spectacle, drama, ritual, rite; grandeur, magnificence, splendor, glitter, show, theatrics, showiness, extravagance, ostentation, flashiness, flair, *Slang* splash.

pain *n.* **1.** *I have a pain in my shoulder:* ache, aching, soreness, hurt, hurting, smarting, pang, throb, twinge, pinch, stitch, discomfort, malaise. **2.** *May this country never again know the pain of war:* suffering, distress, anguish, agony, torment, torture, ordeal, hell, misery, grief, woe, heartache, heartbreak, sorrow, sadness, affliction, wretchedness, unhappiness. —*v.* **3.** *Does your ankle still pain you?:* hurt, ache, smart, throb, sting, discomfort. **4.** *The child's constant tantrums pained his mother:* distress, agonize, torment, torture, make miserable, trouble, worry, disturb, grieve, sadden; displease, annoy, vex, gall, harass, rile, chafe, pique, exasperate, try one's patience. —**Ant.** 1 comfort, relief. 2 delight, joy, pleasure, sweetness, satisfaction, gladness, enjoyment, ecstasy, happiness, rapture, comfort, peace, solace. 3 relieve, ease, comfort. **4** delight, please, gladden, enchant, enrapture, captivate, charm, satisfy, gratify; comfort, solace.

painful adj. **1.** The child has a painful earache: aching, very sore, agonizing, excruciating, throbbing, smarting, stinging, sharp, piercing, hurtful, torturous, racking, distressful; hurtful, afflictive. **2.** It was my painful duty to inform the next of kin: unpleasant, distressing, disagreeable, distasteful, difficult, trying, arduous, grueling, disturbing, disquieting; grievous, lamentable, sad, sorrowful, pathetic, dire, dismal, dreary. **—Ant.** 1 painless; soothing, comforting, alleviating, relieving. 2 pleasant, pleasurable, delightful, enjoyable, agreeable, happy, gratifying, satisfying.

painstaking adj. After years of painstaking research a cure was found: careful, thorough, thoroughgoing, conscientious, scrupulous, meticulous, punctilious, precise, exacting, fussy, finicky, diligent, persevering, assiduous, earnest, industrious, energetic, strenuous. **—Ant.** careless, haphazard, slapdash, Informal catch-as-catch-can; neglectful, negligent, feckless, heedless, thoughtless; halfhearted, lazy, frivolous.

paint n. **1.** The wall got a fresh coat of paint: coloring, pigment, stain, covering, dye, emulsion, tint. **—v. 2.** He painted mainly portraits: brush, coat, color, cover, cover up, daub; ornament, outline, compose, picture, portray, represent, delineate, depict, design, draft, draw, figure, limn.

painter n. This loft would make an ideal studio for a painter: artist, illustrator, old master, portrait painter, oil painter, watercolorist, drawer, sketcher, delineator, landscapist, miniaturist; house painter.

painting n. Her paintings were chiefly in acrylic: canvas, art, artwork, picture, piece.

pair n. **1.** What a lovely pair of shoes! The farmer hitched the pair of oxen to the wagon: two matched items, set of two, team, brace, yoke, span. **2.** The bride and groom are a good-looking pair: couple, duo, twosome, doublet, dyad; match, combination. **—v. 3.** Pair the socks and put them in the drawer: match, match up, mate, pair off, couple, combine, unite.

pal n. George and I were pals at school: buddy, bosom buddy, chum, comrade, companion, boon companion, crony, friend, intimate, intimate friend, confidant, British mate; sidekick, partner, alter ego, Informal pard; cohort, accomplice, associate, colleague.

palace n. Buckingham Palace is just one of the residences of the British royal family: royal residence, castle; (variously) mansion, stately residence, manor house, château, villa, hacienda.

palatable adj. The meal was most palatable: agreeable, savory, sapid, tasty, luscious, delicious, delectable, flavorsome. **—Ant.** unpalatable, distasteful, tasteless, flavorless.

palatial adj. The road was lined with palatial homes: luxurious, opulent, sumptuous, stately, plush, noble, splendid, rich, regal, monumental, magnificent, imposing, grand, grandiose, ele-

gant, showy; Slang posh, swanky, ritzy. **—Ant.** simple, humble, unpretentious, modest.

pale[1] adj. **1.** She looks so pale, she must be ill: colorless, white, pasty, ashen, ash-colored, wan, pallid, sallow, drained of blood, bloodless, anemic, cadaverous, deathly, deathlike, ghostlike, ghastly. **2.** The walls were painted a pale green: light, light-colored, light-toned, bleached, whitish. **—v. 3.** She paled when we told her the news: become pale, blanch, whiten. **—Ant.** 1 ruddy, rosy-cheeked, rosy, rubicund, high-colored, florid, flushed. 2 dark, deep, vivid. 3 flush, blush.

pale[2] n. **1.** Pales were driven into the ground to slow down the enemy: stake, post, picket, paling, upright, palisade. **2.** Prisoners were kept in the pale, awaiting trial: enclosure, pen, fold, confine, close, closure, fenced-in area.

palisade n. **1.** The fort was surrounded by a palisade: fence of stakes, fence of pales, enclosure, fence, close, stockade, bulwark, rampart. **2. palisades** The lighthouse is atop the palisades: line of cliffs, cliffs, bluffs; escarpment, ledge, crag, promontory.

pall[1] n. The smoke from the fire cast a pall over the town. The bad news cast a pall over the party: dark covering, darkness, shadow, haze, dimness; gloom, melancholy, depression, moroseness, cheerlessness, oppression, desolation. **—Ant.** light, brightness; joviality, gaiety, joy, cheer, merriment, exuberance, exhilaration, high spirits.

pall[2] v. We used to think gin rummy was fun, but now it's beginning to pall: become boring, become dull, be tiresome, weary, sicken, cloy; sate, satiate. **—Ant.** interest, excite, animate, create enthusiasm, delight.

palliate v. The nurse gave him a sedative to palliate the pain: relieve, sooth, ease, lessen, alleviate, mitigate, assuage, soften, moderate, temper, reduce, cushion; tame, check, curb, subdue; quiet, still, calm, hush, lull. **—Ant.** arouse, increase, intensify, exacerbate.

palliative adj. The remedy was palliative at best: alleviative, assuasive, soothing, emollient, lenitive.

pallid adj. **1.** After a week of the flu she was quite pallid: pale, anemic looking, sallow, wan, ashen, ghostly, peaked, pasty, colorless, ashy, waxen. **2.** The evening's entertainment was pallid beyond belief: dull, insipid, unimaginative, uninteresting, lifeless, boring, tedious, humdrum, monotonous, bland, vapid, Slang blah. **—Ant.** 1 rosy, hale, rubicund, glowing. 2 lively, exciting, imaginative, vivacious.

pallor n. The old man's pallor indicates some serious malady: paleness, pallidness, colorlessness, whiteness, pastiness, ashen color, wanness, bloodless coloring, bloodlessness, cadaverous color, ghostliness, gray complexion. **—Ant.** ruddy complexion, ruddiness, flush.

palmy adj. With the recession over, it looks like palmy days ahead: prosperous, bounteous, thriving, flourishing, successful, booming, blooming, golden, halcyon, balmy, sunny, rosy;

agreeable, pleasant, pleasurable, congenial. —**Ant.** failing, dwindling, fading, waning.

palpable adj. There is a palpable difference in their ages: tangible, obvious, plain, clear, noticeable, visible, discernible, manifest, apparent, perceivable, perceptible, recognizable, definite, distinct, evident, unmistakable; feelable, tactile, touchable. —**Ant.** intangible, unnoticeable, undiscernible, imperceptible, indistinct.

palpitate v. My heart is palpitating after all those stairs: throb, pound, pulsate rapidly, beat, beat quickly, pulse rapidly, flutter, quiver, quaver, go pit-a-pat; vibrate, shake, tremble, shiver.

palsied adj. The old woman's palsied hand could hardly hold the glass: palsy-stricken, spastic; shaking, trembling, quaking, uncontrollable.

paltry adj. The waiter was furious at being given such a paltry tip. He worked his way up from a paltry job to become president of the company: petty, trifling, trivial, of little value, piddling, puny, measly, picayune, shabby, scrubby, sorry; unimportant, insignificant, inconsequential, inconsiderable, wretched, inferior, poor, not worth mentioning. —**Ant.** important, significant, consequential, essential, major, valuable, worthy, considerable, grand, magnificent.

pamper v. She pampers her husband like a child: spoil, indulge, cater to, cater to one's every whim, humor, give in to, cosset, coddle, mollycoddle. —**Ant.** be stern with, lay down the law; mistreat; maltreat, abuse, tyrannize, domineer, oppress, intimidate, bully.

pamphlet n. This sixteen-page pamphlet tells how to care for your new car: booklet, brochure; (loosely) leaflet, circular, folder, bulletin, throwaway; tract, monograph.

pan v. She panned the book in her review: criticize, faultfind, deprecate, dispraise, censure, put down, fault, disparage, denigrate, disdain, despise, excoriate, reject, ridicule Informal knock, rap, flame. —**Ant.** praise, extol.

panacea n. There is no panacea for the world's problems: cure-all, universal cure, nostrum, elixir, sovereign remedy; easy solution, simplistic solution, final answer.

panache n. She showed much panache in her first exhibition: showiness, dash, flair, style, flamboyance, dazzle, showmanship, élan, verve, bravura, brilliance, virtuosity.

pandemic adj. The illness was pandemic: general, prevalent, universal, epidemic. —**Ant.** isolated, unique, singular.

pandemonium n. Pandemonium broke out when the teacher left the room: tumult, turmoil, chaos, bedlam, disorder, wild confusion, rumpus, commotion; uproar, clamor, racket, din, hubbub, disturbance, hullabaloo. —**Ant.** order, peace, quiet, calm, tranquillity.

pander also **panderer** n. The waterfront is frequented by panders and prostitutes: procurer, flesh-peddler, pimp; Slang hustler, cadet, mack; French souteneur, maquereau.

panegyric n. The retiring chairman received a panegyric from the new chairman: eulogy, laudation, praise, homage, tribute, extolment, citation, commendation, compliment, encomium, testimonial, good word. —**Ant.** condemnation, denunciation, censure, reproach, vituperation, diatribe.

panel n. **1.** The control panel of a modern jet is very complex. A light fixture was placed in the center of each wall panel: surface section; compartment, partition, piece, pane, insert, divider, bulkhead. **2.** A panel of artists will judge the contest: committee, board, group, expert group, advisory group, select group, jury; discussion group, round table.

pang n. She felt a pang of regret at leaving home. Except for a small pang his headache was gone: twinge, brief sensation; ache, pain, throb, smart, pinch, stick, stitch, sting, distress, discomfort; agony, anguish, suffering. —**Ant.** pleasure, delight, gratification, satisfaction, enjoyment, joy, happiness, comfort, solace, relief.

panic n. **1.** Panic swept through the swimmers as they saw the shark approaching: terror, overwhelming fear, fear and trembling, alarm, hysteria, scare, fright, affright, cold sweat; horror, dread, apprehension, anxiety, trepidation, nervousness, perturbation, consternation, confusion. —v. **2.** In case of fire, don't panic: give way to panic, succumb to fear, become hysterical, be overwhelmed by dread; Slang fall apart, go to pieces, go ape.

panorama n. The lookout tower gave us a panorama of the distant valleys. The book presents an excellent panorama of modern history: sweeping view, scenic view, scene, scenery, vista, prospect, tableau, picture, perspective, survey, overview, bird's-eye view, diorama; overall picture, long view.

panoramic adj. The hilltop house had a panoramic view of the valley: sweeping, extensive, all-embracing, all-encompassing, ide, far-ranging, far-reaching, extended, all-inclusive, bird's-eye, overall.

pant v. **1.** After jogging a quarter of a mile he was sweating and panting: breathe hard, gasp for breath, gasp, huff, puff, blow, wheeze. **2.** All his life he panted for wealth and luxury: long for, yearn for, lust after, hunger for, crave, desire, covet, want, have a yen for, hope for, wish for, aspire to, sigh for; Informal itch for, set one's heart on, lick one's chops for. —n. **3.** The dog's breathing was just a series of irregular pants: gasp, short intake of breath, puff, huff, wheeze.

pants n. pl. **1.** This sport jacket will match those pants nicely: trousers, pair of trousers, slacks, dungarees, knickers, denims, breeches; Informal britches, bluejeans, jeans. **2.** The child could put on his own undershirt and pants but needed help with his outer garments: underpants, drawers, underdrawers, undershorts, shorts, panties, British knickers.

pantywaist n. He was such a pantywaist everyone took advantage of him: weakling, milksop, sissy, Milquetoast, mama's boy, namby-pamby, weak sister, softy, crybaby, mollycoddle; Slang wimp, sissy-pants, sissy-britches.

pap n. **1.** Mothers used to feed infants pap:

mush, mash, gruel, cereal, soft food, paste, pulp, Pablum. **2.** *Informal How can anyone write such pap?:* childish nonsense, drivel, triviality, trivia, rubbish, rot, twaddle, junk, tosh, bosh, balderdash, *Slang* flapdoodle.

papal *adj. The church will announce a new papal decree tomorrow:* of the pope, pontifical, apostolic.

paper *n.* **1.** *Always bring a pen and paper to class. The picnic plates were made of water-resistant paper:* (*variously*) writing paper, notepaper, stationery, letter paper, bond, carbon paper, onionskin; cardboard, paperboard, construction paper; tissue paper, tissue, tracing paper; wrapping paper, gift wrap; printing paper, newsprint, stock, pulp; wallpaper. **2.** *This paper gives you title to the property:* document, instrument, certificate, deed, record, writing. **3.** *What does the paper say about tomorrow's weather?:* newspaper, journal, gazette, tabloid, news, chronicle; daily, weekly, monthly; publication, periodical, trade paper. **4.** *Each student must write a paper on what he learned from the course:* composition, essay, article, theme, report, work, opus; manuscript, typescript, draft; white paper. —*v.* **5.** *When did you last paper this room?:* wallpaper; line with paper, cover with paper.

papers *n. pl. He produced papers to show he was authorized:* documentation, certificate, certification, credentials, instrument.

par *n.* **1.** *For the first time the business's income and expenses are on a par:* equal footing, parity, equality, evenness, equilibrium, equivalency; balance, stability, level, identity, sameness, identicalness. **2.** *I'm not feeling up to par today:* average, normal, usual, standard, the norm.

parable *n. The New Testament recounts the parable of the loaves and the fishes:* allegory, story, tale, morality tale, fable, allegorical story, myth, legend, homily, apologue, folk story, folk tale.

parade *n.* **1.** *Over a dozen bands are marching in the St. Patrick's Day parade:* procession, march, march past, review; cavalcade, caravan, motorcade, cortege, column, line, progression, train, string. **2.** *I've never seen such a parade of jewelry as there was at the party:* show, display, array, exposition, demonstration, spectacle, flaunting, vaunting, ostentatious display; pageantry, pomp. —*v.* **3.** *Paris workers will parade on May Day:* march in a procession, march; go in a column, defile. **4.** *She loves to parade all her furs:* show off, make a show of, display, make a display of, vaunt, flaunt, strut, be ostentatious with; *Slang* grandstand, put on the ritz, put on airs, put on the dog. —**Ant.** 2 suppression, hiding, concealing, masking, cloaking. 4 suppress, secrete, hide, conceal, mask, cloak, veil.

paradigm *n. They always held his brother up as a sort of paradigm:* model, ideal, paragon, example, exemplar, pattern, matrix, standard, criterion, yardstick; prototype, archetype, original, sample.

paradise *n.* **1.** *Adam and Eve dwelt in paradise.*

Hawaii is called an island paradise: Eden, Garden of Eden, utopia, Shangri-la; happy valley, Land of Cockaigne; nirvana, heaven. **2.** *On a hot day a dip in the pool is sheer paradise:* delight, bliss, joy, enjoyment, ecstasy, rapture, transport, heaven, pleasure, happiness, satisfaction, gratification, seventh heaven. —**Ant.** 2 misery, torment, hell, agony, torture, pain.

paradox *n. It's a paradox, but the older she gets the more active she is:* self-contradiction, self-contradictory statement; seeming contradiction, incongruity, anomaly, inconsistency, oddity; enigma, puzzle, riddle, poser, seeming absurdity. —**Ant.** rule, axiom, maxim, truism, aphorism, proverb.

paragon *n. Aunt Sue has always been a paragon of virtue:* model, example, exemplar, prototype, archetype, paradigm, apotheosis, idea, symbol, pattern, standard, norm, criterion, yardstick.

parallel *adj.* **1.** *Parallel lines never meet:* running side by side, coextensive, lying side by side, equidistant, concurrent, alongside, abreast. **2.** *Stamp collecting and coin collecting are parallel hobbies:* similar, like, alike, analogous, comparative, comparable, collateral, corresponding, akin, correlative; twin, equivalent. —*n.* **3.** *The speaker pointed out the parallel between the French Revolution and the American Revolution:* comparison, analogy, likeness, correlation, identification, relation, connection, parallelism, correspondence, resemblance, similarity, coincidence. **4.** *The navy's able-bodied seaman is the parallel of the army's private:* counterpart, equivalent, equal, corollary, match, correspondent, correlative, analogue, same, twin. —*v.* **5.** *The stream parallels the road for several miles:* run parallel to, follow; run abreast of, keep pace with. **6.** *Your educational background parallels mine:* be equivalent to, be similar to, be alike, compare with, be comparable to, correspond to, be analogous to, amount to the same thing, duplicate, equal, match. —**Ant.** 1 nonparallel. 2 dissimilar, unlike, distinct, different, divergent, disparate. 3 dissimilarity, difference, divergence, unlikeness, disparity. 4 opposite, reverse, counter. 6 be dissimilar, be unlike, differ, diverge.

paralyze *v. Repeated bombings paralyzed the enemy's transportation:* stun, immobilize, benumb, incapacitate, stupefy, petrify, disable, debilitate, cripple, disarm, weaken, enfeeble, freeze, deaden; destroy, demolish, wipe out, neutralize, bring to a halt.

paramount *adj. Speed in finishing the job is of paramount importance:* main, chief, foremost, utmost, greatest, preeminent, highest, predominant, dominant, preponderant, supreme, leading, premier, principal, capital, essential, superior, peerless, leading, cardinal, outstanding, unmatched, incomparable, transcendent. —**Ant.** secondary, subordinate, least, smallest, negligible, insignificant, inconsequential, unimportant, slight, trifling, minor.

paramour *n. She was said to be the paramour of a wealthy businessman:* lover; mistress, kept woman, girl friend, doxy, lady friend, inamorata, courtesan, concubine; boyfriend, man, fancy man, lover boy, gigolo, inamorato, sugar daddy, lothario, Romeo, Don Juan, Casanova.

paranoid *adj. He has become paranoid about any criticism of his work:* paranoiac, affected by paranoia; having a persecution complex, having delusions of grandeur; oversuspicious, excessively wary, unreasonably distrustful.

parapet *n. The defenders of the castle fought from behind parapets:* defensive wall, breastwork, earthwork; rampart, bulwark, barricade, palisade, battlement, abutment.

paraphernalia *n. Bring along your fishing paraphernalia:* equipment, gear, outfit, implements, accoutrements, rig, stuff, regalia, apparatus, supplies, things, provisions, trappings, accessories, utensils, tackle, harness, fittings, material; personal effects, effects, properties, belongings, furnishings.

paraphrase *v. You needn't quote his exact words, just paraphrase what he said:* restate, reword, rephrase, state in other words, state in one's own words; recapitulate; *Slang* recap, rehash. —**Ant.** quote, state verbatim.

parasite *n.* **1.** *Spray the plant to rid it of parasites:* living thing that nourishes itself on another organism. **2.** *Don't be a parasite, earn your own way in life:* beggar, cadger, sponger, scrounger, freeloader, leech, bloodsucker; loafer, slacker, shirker, deadbeat, *Slang* goldbrick, moocher.

parcel *n.* **1.** *Send this parcel via airmail:* package, packet, bundle, pack, bale. **2.** *This parcel of land consists of 18 acres:* lot, tract, plot, piece of land, property. **3.** *Each guest was given a small parcel of the wedding cake to take home:* piece, part, portion, section, segment, division, fragment, fraction, allowance, allotment. —*v.* **4.** *The estate was parceled out to the heirs:* apportion, distribute, divide, allot, allocate, disperse, dispense, dole out, deal out, partition, carve up, split up. —**Ant.** 3 entirety, whole. 4 collect, gather, amass, accumulate; combine, merge, pool.

parch *v. The lack of rain had parched the land:* dry out, dry up, dessicate, shrivel, sun-dry, evaporate, dehydrate; wither, scorch, char, burn, blister, sear, singe, bake. —**Ant.** wet, moisten, water, flood, inundate.

parched *adj. The parched travelers found an oasis:* thirsty, dried out, dried up, dehydrated, dry, arid, waterless, shrivelled, withered.

parchment *n. Ancient manuscripts were written on parchment:* sheepskin, goatskin, papyrus, vellum; scroll, polished brown paper, parchment paper.

pardon *n.* **1.** *We asked his pardon for the unintentional rudeness. May God grant you pardon for your sins:* forgiveness, forbearance, indulgence; absolution, mercy, remission, deliverance, grace; release, exculpation, amnesty. —*v.* **2.** *Pardon the interruption:* forgive, excuse, forbear, indulge; overlook, disregard, blink at, wink at, shrug off, forgive and forget, let bygones be bygones. **3.** *The convict was pardoned after*

serving five years of his sentence: absolve, vindicate, exonerate, exculpate, grant amnesty; remit the penalty of, reprieve, set free, release, discharge. —**Ant.** 1 punishment, penalty, retaliation, retribution, vengeance, revenge, redress, reparation, condemnation, guilt. 2 punish; penalize, fine, discipline, correct. 3 condemn, doom, censure, blame, chasten, castigate, chastise, rebuke, admonish.

pare *v.* **1.** *Pare the apple and then slice it:* peel, skin, strip, trim, shuck, shell, hull, husk, decorticate. **2.** *To increase profits the firm must pare costs:* cut, cut down on, cut back, slash, shave, trim, prune, reduce, decrease, lessen, diminish, lower, curtail, shrink; crop, lop, dock, clip, shear. —**Ant.** 2 increase, inflate, enlarge, advance, raise, elevate, boost, step up.

parent *n. To have good children one must be a good parent. The Wright brothers' airplane is the parent of the modern jet:* mother, father; dam, sire, begetter, procreator; creator, originator, producer; ancestor, progenitor, predecessor, precursor, forerunner, antecedent; prototype, original, model, exemplar.

parentage *n. The birth certificate left no doubt as to her parentage:* ancestry, antecedents, forbears, genealogy, ancestors; lineage, descent, heredity, origin, background, birth, extraction, strain, pedigree, derivation, family tree, roots.

parenthetical *adj. The essay has too many parenthetical sentences. Stick to your speech and don't make parenthetical remarks:* in parentheses, bracketed, braced; incidental, interposed, inserted, intervening, aside, casual, extraneous, impertinent, irrelevant, immaterial, superfluous.

pariah *n. After the scandal he left his native land and became a pariah:* outcast, undesirable, untouchable, exile, expatriate, man without a country, stray, vagabond, rover, roamer, wanderer; outlaw.

parish *n.* **1.** *How are the parochial schools in this parish?:* church district, archdiocese, diocese, shire, canton; district, precinct, section, county, province, department; community, neighborhood. **2.** *The priest asked his parish to pray for peace:* congregation, parishioners, pastorate, fold, flock, church members, brethren.

parity *n. Workers sought parity in their pay:* equality; equivalence, correspondence, similarity, analogy, parallelism, likeness; sameness. —**Ant.** inequality, dissimilarity, difference.

park *n. One of the pleasures of London is walking through its many parks:* green, parkland, common, public park, sanctuary, woodland, grove, preserve, reserve, grassland, woods, picnic grounds; field, meadow, lawn, grounds, square, quadrangle.

parlance *n. "Computers" was a bad word in her parlance:* phraseology, language, idiom, diction, wording, words, phrasing, usage, grammar, wordage, locution, expression, formulation, tongue, lingo.

parley *n. The two prime ministers will have a parley to discuss peace:* discussion, conference, conclave, summit, meeting, council, exchange of views, talk, conversation, palaver, discourse, diplomatic consultation, *Slang* confab, powwow; peace talk, negotiation, arbitration, mediation.

parlor *n.* *The parlor had the best furniture and was used only by visitors:* sitting room, front room, living room, drawing room, salon, reception room, saloon, best room.

parochial *adj.* **1.** *The parochial schools are having a holiday:* parish, church, religious. **2.** *The candidate's views are too parochial for him to become a nationwide leader:* local, regional, sectional, provincial, insular, countrified, small-town; narrow-minded, limited, narrow, restricted, petty, small, little, illiberal, hidebound. **—Ant.** 1 public; lay. 2 international, worldwide, universal, national; sophisticated, cosmopolitan; broad-minded, open-minded, liberal.

parody *n.* **1.** *The student drama society gave a hilarious parody of* Hamlet: burlesque, takeoff, ludicrous imitation, caricature, lampoon, satire, travesty. **—v.** **2.** *Everyone laughed when the comedian parodied the senator's drawl:* burlesque, caricature, mimic, lampoon, satirize, travesty, *Informal* take off on.

paroxysm *n.* *The dog went into a paroxysm of delight:* fit, spasm, attack, access, seizure, throe, convulsion, outburst, eruption, irruption, explosion, storm.

parrot *n.* **1.** *Can that parrot talk?:* tropical bird of the *Psittaciformes* order; (*variously*) macaw, cockatoo, lory, parakeet. **2.** *The child is such a parrot he repeats everything:* mimic, mimer, imitator, *Slang* copycat; monkey, ape. **—v.** **3.** *She parrots every view her husband has:* repeat mindlessly, echo, reiterate, chorus; imitate, mimic, ape.

parry *v.* *The fencer parried his opponent's thrust. The actress parried all questions about her personal life:* fend off, ward off, repulse, stave off, repel, beat off; dodge, shun, avoid, elude, avert, sidestep, duck, circumvent, fight shy of, keep at a distance. **—Ant.** receive, take, welcome, face, confront, meet.

parsimonious *adj.* *Because the old couple was parsimonious they never had to ask for financial help:* frugal, saving, thrifty, economical, sparing, penny-pinching; miserly, penurious, tight, tight-fisted, close, closefisted, niggardly, ungenerous, stingy, money-grubbing. **—Ant.** extravagant, spendthrift, wasteful; lavish, liberal, munificent, generous, openhanded.

parsimony *n.* *Parsimony was his hallmark:* economy, frugality, niggardliness, stinginess, miserliness, sparingness, closeness, illiberality, close-fistedness, tight-fistedness, cupidity, meanness. **—Ant.** generosity, liberality.

part *n.* **1.** *The U.S. government is made up of three parts: executive, legislative, and judicial. This looks like part of a broken cup:* section, portion, division, subdivision, sector, branch, department, unit, component, element, member, constituent, ingredient, region; piece, segment, fragment, fraction, scrap, shred, bit, sliver, chip, shard, sherd, snippet, cutting, slice, crumb, morsel, *Slang* hunk; item, detail. **2.** *The young actress took the part of Joan of Arc:* role,

character; impersonation, personification, guise, disguise. **3.** *What was your part in the proceedings?:* role, function, capacity, share, concern, charge, care, place, business, assignment, job, chore, task, duty. **—v.** **4.** *The curtain parted and the show began. The rope parted and the load fell to the ground:* separate, disengage, open, disunite, divide; detach, disconnect, disjoin, break apart, split, slit, sunder, sever, rend, tear, tear assunder; cleave, break. **5.** *It's time to part:* depart, go, go away, leave, take one's leave, go one's way, set forth, set out, start out, take one's farewell, say good-bye, tear oneself away, get up and go, be on one's way; *Slang* mosey along, push off; end a relationship, break off, call it quits. **—Ant.** 1 whole, entirety, totality; mass, bulk, quantity. 4 unite, combine, join, close; hold, cling, stick, adhere. 5 arrive, come, appear; stay, remain, abide, tarry, linger.

partake *v.* *All the children will partake in the festivities. Everyone partook of the sumptuous meal:* share, take part, share in, enjoy, savor, sample; participate, engage in, join in, play a part in. **—Ant.** be excluded; abstain, forswear, forbear, forgo, refrain from, refuse, decline, eschew, relinquish, set out, pass up.

partial *adj.* **1.** *This is only a partial list of the books needed:* incomplete, fractional, limited, fragmentary, unfinished, uncompleted, inconclusive. **2.** *He's too partial to be a fair judge:* partisan, factional, biased, prejudiced, predisposed, slanted, prepossessed, subjective, one-sided, unbalanced, interested; unjust, unfair, inequitable. **—Ant.** 1 complete, entire, whole, total, full, final, finished. 2 impartial, unbiased, objective, balanced, disinterested, unprejudiced, equitable.

partiality *n.* **1.** *The referee's partiality toward the home team was obvious:* bias, prejudice, tilt, predisposition, slant, predilection, one-sidedness, partisanship, favoritism. **2.** *Father has a partiality for strawberry ice cream:* fondness, liking, inclination, predisposition, predilection, weakness, love, taste, affinity, propensity, penchant, fancy, bent, leaning, tendency, attraction, proclivity; choice, preference. **—Ant.** 1 impartiality, evenhandedness, objectivity, disinterest; justice, fairness. 2 dislike, disinclination, distaste, disgust, abhorrence, aversion, loathing, revulsion, detestation, antipathy.

partially *adv.* *The work is only partially finished:* partly, in part, partway, incompletely, fractionally, piecemeal, somewhat. **—Ant.** all, completely, entirely, wholly, totally.

participant *n.* *The participants in the race lined up at the starting gate:* participator, partaker, member, partner, party, sharer, helper, worker, contributor, shareholder, colleague, fellow, associate, confrere; accomplice, accessory.

participate *v.* *No professionals may participate in the amateur tennis tournament:* take part, engage in, join in, be a participant, perform, play a part, partake, share, form a part of, *Slang* have a finger in. **—Ant.** be excluded; abstain, forswear, forgo, forbear, refrain from, eschew, sit out, pass up.

particle *n. A particle of rock was wedged beneath the door. There's not a particle of truth in that statement:* small piece, small fragment, bit, speck, grain, shred, scrap, crumb, smidgen, morsel, granule, jot, iota, atom; trifle, trace, snippet, snip, whit, tittle, scintilla, modicum, mite.

particular *adj.* **1.** *The stores are closed on that particular day. Golf is his particular passion:* specific, exact, explicit, express, special, especial, fixed, concrete, individual; definite, well-defined, distinct, single, personal, separate, sole, particularized, itemized, detailed. **2.** *She's so particular that no one can please her:* hard to please, critical, demanding, exacting, picky, fussy, finicky, *Slang* persnickety; strict, fastidious, meticulous, painstaking, scrupulous, punctilious. **—n. 3.** Usually **particulars** *The lawyer must know all the particulars of the case:* detail, specific, item, fact, circumstance, event. **—Ant.** 1 general, universal; vague, unspecified, indefinite, undefined, impersonal. 2 easy to please, uncritical, undemanding, indifferent, heedless, inattentive; careless, slipshod, slapdash, haphazard, sloppy, inexact, carefree.

particularly *adv.* **1.** *The coffee is particularly good today:* especially, exceptionally, unusually, extraordinarily, strikingly, markedly, notably, eminently, supremely, prominently; mainly, principally. **2.** *He particularly asked that you be there:* in particular, explicitly, expressly, especially, specially, definitely, distinctly.

parting *adj.* **1.** *An insult was his parting shot:* departing, farewell, goodbye, valedictory, last, final. **—n. 2.** *Parting was sad for him:* departure, breakup, crossroads, departure, detachment, farewell, going, goodbye, leave-taking, separation, split, rift, break, breaking, rupture, severance. *Informal* swan song.

partisan *n.* **1.** *The hometown partisans cheered the local team:* supporter, follower, adherent, sympathizer, champion, advocate, ally, backer, upholder, enthusiast, fan, zealot, devotee, rooter, booster. **2.** *Even after the country was defeated, partisans fought the invaders in the hills:* freedom fighter, guerrilla, irregular, insurgent; (*U.S. Civil War*) bushwacker, jayhawker. **—adj. 3.** *The senator vowed not to engage in partisan politics:* favoring one political party, predisposed toward one group, favoring a cause, partial, biased, prejudiced, one-sided, slanted, unbalanced, subjective. **—Ant.** 1 detractor, defamer, censor, critic, backbiter, knocker; opponent, foe, adversary, rival, contender. 3 nonpartisan, bipartisan, unbiased, impartial, unprejudiced, disinterested, objective, broad-minded, open-minded.

partisanship *n. Partisanship overcame fair play:* partiality, factionalism, sectionalism.

partition *n.* **1.** *Citizens fought the partition of the town into two voting precincts:* division, dividing, separation, severance, splitting, parting; distribution, apportionment, allotment, allocation, assignment, demarcation, segregation. **2.** *Put up partitions to separate the living and dining areas:* dividing wall, non-supporting wall, wall, divider, separator, panel, screen, barrier, fence, *Nautical* bulkhead. **—v. 3.** *The dormitory was partitioned into cubicles:* divide, subdivide, separate, split up; distribute, disperse, dispense, apportion, allot, allocate, assign, parcel out, deal out, mete out.

partly *adv. The back door is only partly closed:* partially, in part, part way, fractionally, to a degree, in some measure, somewhat, incompletely, not wholly, to a limited extent; comparatively, relatively, in a manner of speaking, after a fashion. **—Ant.** fully, wholly, completely, entirely, totally.

partner *n.* **1.** *The business is owned by two partners. The teacher and some of his partners are taking the students on a field trip:* joint owner, co-owner, co-partner; associate, colleague, fellow worker, confrere, collaborator, accomplice, confederate, teammate, assistant, helper, aid, aider; accessory; friend, fellow, comrade, ally, confrere, companion, buddy, chum, sidekick, pal, mate; sharer, partaker, participant. **2.** *Are you sure you want him for your partner for life?:* spouse, mate, helpmate; husband; wife, better half.

partnership *n. Their partnership was highly successful:* alliance, amalgamation, cartel, coalition, combine, confederation, cooperation, coterie, fellowship, fraternity, gang, league, unification, union, association, affiliation, consolidation.

party *n.* **1.** *The family is giving a party on Grace's birthday:* social function, social gathering, gathering of friends, gathering, celebration, festivity, fête, get-together, affair, reception, at-home, soiree, *Slang* bash, blowout, do, wing-ding. **2.** *Is there need for a new political party? Forest rangers sent out a rescue party to bring back the injured hiker:* alliance, federation, confederacy, league, coalition, conclave, faction, wing, coterie; group, crew, team, band, body, company, squad, corps, unit, force, gang. **3.** *Both parties are to appear before the judge:* participant, paticipator, perpetrator, (*legal use*) participant in a lawsuit, (*variously*) contestant, litigant, petitioner, plaintiff, claimant, accused, defendant, appellant, respondent.

parvenu *n. The parvenu rose swiftly in society:* upstart, snob, Johnny-come-lately, climber.

pass *v.* **1.** *She never passes without stopping to say hello. The guard allowed the visitor to pass:* go by, go on, go past, go beyond, go ahead, go onward, move onward, progress, proceed. **2.** *Time passes quickly on vacation. Wait for the rain to pass:* go, go by, go away, elapse, glide by, slide by, slip by, flow, proceed, progress; pass away, be over, end, terminate, expire, die away, die, fade away, melt away, blow over, peter out, run its course, vanish, disappear, dissolve, evaporate, depart, leave. **3.** *Mother passes her time knitting:* spend, expend, use, consume, employ, engage, busy, occupy, fill, take up, devote. **4.** *Dick has already passed his father in height:* surpass, exceed, go by, go beyond, go ahead, best, excel, outshine, eclipse, overshadow, outstrip, outdo, top, cap. **5.** *Did* *you pass the chemistry course? To become a sergeant a policeman must pass certain requirements:* receive a satisfactory grade in, complete successfully, satisfy, qualify, meet, get through, achieve, accomplish, finish, come up to scratch, stand the test, meet the standard of. **6.** *Congress is expected to pass the bill:* exact, legislate, establish by law, vote approval on, approve, ratify, authorize, sanction, decree, ordain, legalize, accept; affirm, confirm. **7.** *Please pass me the salt. Pass the news along. The quarterback passed the ball fifty yards downfield to the wide receiver:* hand, hand over, hand along, give, pre-sent, turn over, let have, convey, transfer, transmit, deliver, throw, toss, hit, kick. —*n.* **8.** *The bus trip through the Brenner Pass was lovely:* mountain pass, gap, gorge, canyon, ravine, gulch; passageway, pathway, trail, way, lane, course, route, avenue; channel, narrows, canal. **9.** *The soldier had a weekend pass. Retired players get season passes to all the games:* permission to be absent, permission to leave, furlough; free ticket, complimentary ticket, *Slang* freebie, Annie Oakley; right of passage, permit, authorization. **10.** *Things have come to a pretty pass!:* state of affairs, situation, juncture, predicament, complication, difficulty, exigency, plight, juncture, strait, extremity, quandary, *Slang* pickle. —**Ant.** 1, 2 stop, halt, cease, standstill, pause, wait; withdraw, retreat. 2 begin, start, commence; continue. 3 waste, squander. 4 fall behind, falter, drag, pull back. 5 fail, flunk. 6 vote down, defeat, reject, veto; disapprove. 7 hold, keep, retain. 8 peak, summit; barrier, obstacle.

passable *adj.* **1.** *Are the roads passable in all this snow?:* traversable, fit for travel, clear, open, unobstructed; crossable, navigable, fordable. **2.** *This suit is worn, but it's still passable. The movie wasn't great, but it was passable:* presentable, respectable, allowable, acceptable, pretty good, adequate, not bad, so-so, better than nothing, fair, admissible, middling, mediocre, tolerable. —**Ant.** 1 impassable, impenetrable, closed, blocked, obstructed. 2 inadequate, unacceptable, insufficient; exceptional, extraordinary, unusual, uncommon.

passage *n.* **1.** *The newspaper quoted a long passage from the speech:* section, portion, piece, selection; clause, paragraph, sentence, column, verse, chapter. **2.** *The hunters needed a guide for their passage through the jungle. Bon voyage and have a pleasant passage:* progression, passing, movement; trip, journey, voyage, excursion, expedition, tour, junket, trek, transit; right to pass; cost of ship transportation, ship's fare. **3.** *Passage of the bill depends on public support:* passing into law, enactment, legislation, ratification, approval, authorization, ordainment, legalization, sanction, endorsement, acceptance; affirmation, confirmation. **4.** *Is there a passage through the mountains? The house has an underground passage:* pass, passageway, way, course, route, path, road, corridor, hallway, hall, aisle, tunnel, canal, channel; access, approach, right of access. —**Ant.** 3

veto, defeat, rejection, voting down. 4 barrier, obstacle, obstruction.

passageway *n. Don't leave your roller skates in the passageway:* corridor, hallway, hall, arcade, passage, aisle, tunnel; access, entrance, entryway, exit, doorway, gateway; path, walk, sidewalk, lane, *Nautical* gangway, companionway.

passé *adj. The idea of a chaperon for a dating couple is passé:* out of fashion, old-fashioned, out-of-date, outdated, outmoded, démodé, antiquated, antediluvian, superannuated, quaint; ancient, antique, archaic, obsolete, stale, hoary, *Slang* prehistoric; lapsed, disused, retired, outworn, faded, past. —**Ant.** modern, new, novel, current, up-to-date, new-fashioned, newfangled, *Slang* mod, hip, with-it, *French* au courant, á la page, dans le vent.

passion *n.* **1.** *He could never put any passion into his singing:* emotion, feeling, warmth, heart, ardor, fervor, fire, intensity, sentiment, rapture, transport, ecstasy, intoxication, enthusiasm, earnestness, gusto, eagerness, vehemence. **2.** *The newspapers called it a crime of passion:* lust, sexual desire, sexual appetite, carnality, carnal love, fleshly desire; amorousness, love. **3.** *Skiing is my current passion:* obsession, craze, mania, fancy, rage, craving, urge, desire, hunger, thirst; idol, beloved, loved one, infatuation, flame, inamorata. —**Ant.** 1 apathy, indifference, coldness, coolness, frigidity, unconcern.

passionate *adj. The two groups had a passionate debate. The groom gave the bride a passionate kiss:* impassioned, fervent, fervid, ardent, emotional, earnest, intense, fiery, fierce, furious, raging, tempestuous, excited, wrought-up, inflamed, feeling, heartfelt, enthusiastic, hot, heated, vehement, intoxicating, ecstatic; loving, amorous, desirous, lustful, sensuous, carnal, erotic, *Slang* sexy. —**Ant.** dispassionate, cold, cool, apathetic, passive, lethargic, indifferent; calm, soothing.

passive *adj. The townspeople remained passive throughout the occupation:* submissive, inactive, unassertive, apathetic, impassive, compliant, acquiescent, yielding, inert, quiescent, docile, pliable, tractable, lifeless, spiritless, listless, dormant, nonresistant, unresisting; patient, resigned, enduring. —**Ant.** active, domineering, dominant, forceful, aggressive, assertive, dynamic, energetic, alive, alert.

passport *n. Good looks became his passport to fame:* safe-conduct, visa, permit, travel permit, pass, authorization, credentials, identification, license.

password *n. No one was admitted to the society's meetings without giving the password:* watchword, keyword, shibboleth, *French* passe-parole, word, countersign; key, tessera, open sesame, catchword.

past *adj.* **1.** *The time for action is past. Forget past mistakes and start afresh:* gone by, passed away; elapsed, expired, ended, finished, gone, departed, dead and gone; belonging to the past, bygone, ancient, historical, former, previous, earlier, prior. —*n.* **2.** *The old man loved to talk about the past:* days gone by, days of yore, days of old, yesteryear, former times, previous times, times gone by, long ago, ancient times, olden times, antiquity, ancient history, history, events gone by. —*adv.* **3.** *Did you see a car go past?:* by, across one's field of vision; beyond, through. —**Ant.** 1 future, coming, later; present, now, begun, started, arrived. 2 future, time to come, days to come, tomorrow; present, today, now, this day and age.

paste *n. She applied paste to the back of the paper:* adhesive, glue, cement, fastening, fixative, glue, gum, mucilage, plaster, *Informal* stickum.

pastel *n.* **1.** *Many of the artist's drawings are done in pastels:* coloring stick; *(loosely)* coloring pencil, chalk, crayon. —*adj.* **2.** *The bedrooms were painted in pastel colors:* pale, faint, soft, light, muted, dim, washed-out, faded. —**Ant.** 2 bright, deep, dark, strong, vibrant.

pastime *n. Stamp collecting is an agreeable pastime:* diversion, hobby, avocation, sparetime activity, relaxation, distraction, amusement, divertissement, entertainment, fun, play, sport, game. —**Ant.** business, work, occupation, calling, employment, profession, job, chore, labor.

pastor *n. The pastor preached a lively sermon last Sunday:* minister, priest, cleric, preacher, parson, rector, clergyman, vicar, dean, curé; padre, father, chaplain.

pastoral *adj.* **1.** *Daphnis and Chloe is a pastoral tale written for city people. The orchestra played Beethoven's "Pastoral Symphony":* bucolic, rustic, rural, portraying country life, depicting the life of shepherds; arcadian, idyllic. **2.** *The new minister will take up his pastoral duties next month:* ministerial, ecclesiastical, clerical; priestly, episcopal, sacerdotal. —**Ant.** 1 worldly, sophisticated, cosmopolitan; urban, urbanized, city, citified, metropolitan. 2 secular, lay.

pasty *adj.* **1.** *Breakfast was a pasty mess of hot oatmeal:* like paste, gluey, mucilaginous, gummy, sticky, doughy; starchy, glutinous, *Slang* gooey. **2.** *The sickly man had a pasty complexion:* pale, ashen, ashy, wan, sallow, colorless, pallid, chalky, white, peaked, anemic, bloodless, ghostlike, deathly, gray. —**Ant.** 1 dry, powdery. 2 ruddy, rosy, florid, rosycheeked, rubicund.

pat *v.* **1.** *The children wanted to pat the bunny:* pet, stroke, caress, fondle. —*n.* **2.** *She gave the pillow several pats:* light blow, gentle stroke, tap, small spank; hit, thwack, slap, thump, rap. **3.** *Put a pat of butter on each plate:* little slab, small square, cake, dab, daub. —*adj.* **4.** *The salesman had pat answers to all my objections:* contrived, rehearsed, glib, facile, ready, easy, slick, smooth, flippant. **5.** *There are no pat solutions to all the world's problems:* perfect, ideal, exact, precise; appropriate, reliant, fitting, pertinent, suitable, apt, apropos, easy, simple; satisfactory. —**Ant.** 4 impromptu, spontaneous; sincere, well-considered, thoughtful, serious. 5 imperfect, inexact; irrelevant, unsuitable, difficult; unsatisfactory.

patch *n.* **1.** *The child's jeans had a patch at the knee. The soldiers wore the shoulder patch of the 145th Battalion:* mend, repair, small piece of material sewn on, reinforcement; insignia. **2.** *We chased the rabbits out of the cabbage patch. There was a patch of ice on the road:* plot, garden, tract, lot, field, clearing; area, spot, stretch, expanse, zone. —*v.* **3.** *Do you know how to patch an inner tube?:* mend, cover with a patch, repair, fix, darn, stitch, sew up, reinforce.

patchwork *n. Instead of an original work he gave us a patchwork of quotations:* jumble, medley, potpourri, pastiche, mélange, miscellany, omnium-gatherum, scramble, hodgepodge, conglomeration, mixture, muddle, tangle, hash, mess, gallimaufry, salmagundi, confusion, mishmash; *Slang* grab bag, mixed bag.

patchy *adj. They drove through patchy fog:* variable, varying random, sketchy, spotty, uneven, erratic, fitful, irregular. —**Ant.** even, regular, constant.

patent *n.* **1.** *Edison held the patent on the early phonograph:* government registration of an invention, certificate of invention, inventor's exclusive rights; registry, license, permit. —*adj.* **2.** *Try some of this new patent medicine:* protected by patent, trademarked, copyrighted, copyright; nonprescription, needing no prescription. **3.** *The charge against him was a patent falsehood:* obvious, manifest, evident, self-evident, apparent, open, plain, overt, transparent, express, palpable, decided, indubitable, downright, unreserved, glaring, unmistakable, pronounced, conspicuous, striking, rank, flagrant, bold, glaring, gross, prominent, clear, distinct, bald, undisguised, unconcealed, *Informal* plain as the nose on one's face. —*v.* **4.** *How long does it take to patent an invention?:* obtain a patent for, register as an original invention, obtain an inventor's exclusive rights to. —**Ant.** 2 unpatented. 3 imperceptible, subtle, hidden, concealed, disguised, questionable, dubious, equivocal, ambiguous, vague.

paternal *adj. His father never gave him much paternal affection:* fatherly, fatherlike, of a father, from the father's side of the family, patriarchal; of a parent, parental, tender, kind, indulgent, benevolent, solicitous; concerned, interested, watchful, vigilant.

path *n. We followed the path to the old mill. The path to success is never smooth:* walk, lane, pathway, trail, walkway, footpath, bypath; course, route, track, way, process, plan, approach, means.

pathetic *adj. The orphan's plight was quite pathetic:* pitiful, moving, affecting, touching, poignant, plaintive, distressing, arousing sympathy, calling forth compassion; to be pitied, piteous, pitiable, lamentable, sorrowful, rueful, sad, doleful, dolorous, miserable, woeful, wretched, deplorable, grievous. —**Ant.** amusing, funny, laughable, comical, humorous, ludicrous, ridiculous, droll, entertaining.

pathos *n. The book had so much pathos I wept all through it:* pathetic quality, power to affect, ability to touch, ability to arouse sympathy, poignancy, plaintiveness, sadness, feeling, sentiment, sentimentalism, sentimentality, pitiableness, anguish, heartache, agony, misery, distress, woe, desolation. —**Ant.** comicality, amusement, humor, fun.

patience n. **1.** *Have patience, the train will be here soon:* calm endurance, forbearance, uncomplaining nature, sufferance, tolerance, restraint, long-suffering, imperturbability, equanimity, longanimity, fortitude; composure, self-control, poise. **2.** *It takes a good deal of patience to learn to type:* persistence, perseverance, diligence, application, tenacity, determination, resolution, indefatigableness, tirelessness, stamina, industry, stick-to-itiveness. —**Ant.** 1, 2 impatience. 1 restlessness, exasperation, fretfulness, agitation, irritation, nervousness, peevishness, passion, frenzy. 2 vacillation, irresolution.

patient n. **1.** *The doctor has several patients waiting to see him:* person under medical care, case; sick person. —*adj.* **2.** *Just be patient, I think you're next:* persevering, enduring, long-suffering, uncomplaining, forbearing, unperturbed, serene, composed; persistent; persevering, diligent, determined, tenacious, resolute, tireless, indefatigable, industrious, unflagging, unfaltering, unwavering, unswerving, undaunted, dogged, dauntless.

patio n. *Breakfast was served on the patio:* terrace, porch, veranda, piazza, deck, *Hawaiian* lanai.

patrician n. **1.** *Only patricians may sit in the British House of Lords:* aristocrat, noble, nobleman, peer, lord, silk-stocking, blueblood, gentleman. —*adj.* **2.** *The old gentleman still retains his patrician manners:* aristocratic, noble, lordly, princely, imposing, stately, dignified, genteel, well-bred, upper-class, highborn. —**Ant.** 1 peasant, commoner, working man, member of the proletariat, hoi polloi. 2 peasant, plebeian, common, vulgar, ignoble, proletarian, working-class, lower-class, lowborn; bourgeois, middle-class, lowbrow, philistine.

patrimony n. *His patrimony was exhausted in less than two years:* inheritance, estate, legacy, endowment, bequeathal; *Law* devise, jointure, dower, hereditament; birthright, portion, share, lot; legacy, bestowal, heritage.

patriot n. *The patriots rose against the invaders:* nationalist, chauvinist, jingoist, *Informal* flag-waver.

patrol n. **1.** *She was assigned to night patrol:* rounds, lookout, guard, sentinel, vigilance, watch. —*v.* **2.** *Police patrolled the grounds:* watch, guard, keep guard, keep watch, police, protect, safeguard.

patron n. **1.** *Patrons requesting refunds should see the manager:* customer, client, buyer, shopper; frequenter, habitué, visitor; spectator, attender. **2.** *There will be a reception for patrons of the museum:* sponsor, supporter, backer, benefactor, *(fem.)* benefactress, financer, promoter, philanthropist, *Slang* angel; protector, defender, advocate, champion, upholder, encourager, helper, sympathizer, well-wisher,

friend. —**Ant.** 1 employee. 2 protégé, *(fem.)* protégée, ward.

patronage n. **1.** *The restaurant welcomes the patronage of anyone suitably attired:* business, trade, buying, purchasing, commerce, custom, dealing; clientele, customers, patrons, clients. **2.** *The scholarship fund depends on the patronage of the alumni:* financial support, support, sponsorship, charity, benefaction, philanthropy, backing, help, aid, assistance, favor; auspices, protection, advocacy, encouragement, fosterage, friendship. **3.** *The governor controls patronage in this state:* political favors, political appointments, spoils, government contracts, *Slang* pork barrel, plums.

patronize v. **1.** *I'll never patronize that store again:* do business with, trade with, deal with, shop at, buy from, frequent, be a habitué of, be a client of. **2.** *Don't patronize me, I'm not a child!:* treat in a condescending way, condescend, act superior toward, assume a lofty attitude toward, act disainfully toward, indulge unnecessarily, humor. —**Ant.** 2 flatter, toady to, be subservient to.

patter v. **1.** *The rain pattered on the window:* pat, beat, pound, tap, rap, drum, thrum, pad, go pitter-patter; tattoo, spatter, sprinkle. —*n.* **2.** *The parents heard the patter of little feet down the stairs:* pattering, pitter-patter, rat-a-tat, tattoo, pad, pat, tap, tapping, drumming; beat, palpitation.

pattern n. **1.** *The cloth had a checkered pattern:* design, decorative design, motif; form, shape. **2.** *A good seamstress can make a dress without a pattern:* guide, design, plan, draft, model; original, archetype, prototype, stereotype; standard, criterion, example, paradigm, exemplar, sample, specimen, illustration, ideal, apotheosis, paragon. —*v.* **3.** *The youth patterned his life on Benjamin Franklin's:* model, fashion, shape, mold, make resemble, form; imitate, emulate, copy, mimic, follow, simulate, parallel, duplicate.

paucity n. *There was a paucity of information on the reported invasion:* scarcity, dearth, lack, shortage, scarceness, scantiness, deficiency, poverty, sparsity, meagerness, puniness, thinness, poorness, insufficiency. —**Ant.** surfeit, overflow, excess, surplus, superabundance.

paunch n. **1.** *The baby raccoons clung to their mother's paunch:* stomach, abdomen, midsection, *Informal* tummy. **2.** *A little exercising would reduce that paunch:* potbelly, belly, *Slang* bay window, breadbasket, gut, pot, corporation, spare tire, beer belly.

pauper n. *After paying these bills I'll be a pauper!:* poor person, indigent, down-and-outer, bankrupt, insolvent; charity case, beggar, starveling, almsman, mendicant. —**Ant.** rich man, millionaire, magnate, tycoon, Midas.

pause n. **1.** *After a brief pause the speaker continued:* stop, halt, rest, break, cessation, interval, hiatus, time out, letup, gap, suspension, discontinuance, interlude, intermission, interim, interruption. —*v.* **2.** *The joggers paused to catch their breath:* stop briefly, halt, cease, rest, let up, take time out, break off; hesitate, wait, delay, deliberate. **—Ant.** 1 continuity, continuation, progress, progression, advancement. 2 continue, proceed, progress, advance.

pave v. One lane is closed while they're paving the road: surface, resurface, face; cement, tar, asphalt, black top, macadamize.

pavilion n. **1.** The reception was held in a pavilion on the lawn: tent, tentlike building, light open structure, temporary building; exhibition hall, exposition building; (variously) summerhouse, gazebo, pergola, arbor, kiosk, bandshell. **2.** The expectant mother was taken to the maternity pavilion: hospital building, hospital section, ward, wing.

pawn[1] v. **1.** The unemployed reporter pawned his typewriter to pay the bill: give as security, pledge, raise money on, borrow on, Slang hock. —n. **2.** He demanded her wristwatch as a pawn for the loan: security, pledge, assurance, bond, guarantee, guaranty. **—Ant.** 1 redeem, take out of hock.

pawn[2] n. He was merely the pawn of the racketeers: instrument, agent, puppet, tool, creature, dupe, cat's-paw; lackey, flunky, underling, hireling, henchman; Slang patsy. **—Ant.** leader, chief, head, boss, Slang kingpin.

pay v. **1.** They paid the cashier and left. Please pay this bill by the end of the month: give money owed to, give money for; pay in full, remit, settle, square accounts, foot, honor, meet, liquidate, make good on, Informal plunk down one's money for; Slang shell out, come across, cough up, ante up, chip in. **2.** It doesn't pay to waste time: be advantageous, be worthwhile, be useful, benefit, compensate, repay, serve, bear fruit, be a good investment, stand one in good stead. **3.** How much does that job pay? Does it pay to invest in municipal bonds now?: offer as remuneration, offer as compensation, offer as wages, bring in, reimburse; profit, yield, return, be a good investment. **4.** Please pay attention. He paid her a compliment on her cooking: give, grant, render, extend, proffer, present. —n. **5.** How much tax do they take out of your pay?: wages, salary, earnings, paycheck, income; compensation, recompense, fee, payment, reimbursement, stipend. **—Ant.** 1 collect, receive; owe, be in debt. 2 be disadvantageous, be worthless, be useless, be futile. 3 charge, cost. 4 withhold, retain, suppress, repress; receive.

payable adj. The bill is payable upon receipt: due, owed, owing, unpaid, outstanding, mature, demandable, receivable, in arrears.

payment n. **1.** Payment of the bill may be by check or money order. The bookkeeper is in charge of all payments: paying, remittance, settlement, liquidation, defrayal, discharge, outlay, expenditure, disbursement, debt, spending. **2.** Father makes a payment on the mortgage every month. What does he want in payment for that old car?: installment, partial payment, remittance, premium; remuneration, compensation, recompense, reimbursement, fee, pay, salary,

allowance, contribution. **—Ant.** 1 nonpayment, nonremittance; income, profit, return, credit.

payoff n. **1.** The payoff was when he finally admitted he hadn't read the book: clincher, outcome, climax, windup, upshot, result, finish, end, culmination, denouement, finale, resolution, conclusion; Slang crunch, bottom line. **2.** The mob demanded a payoff not to destroy his shop: bribe, protection, hush money, graft; Slang payola, grease, soap.

peace n. **1.** The country enjoyed 30 years of peace: harmony, accord, concord, amity, entente, agreement, pacification, reconciliation, armistice, truce. **2.** The peace of the countryside made for a perfect weekend: calm, serenity, tranquillity, ease, repose, placidity, content, composure. **—Ant.** 1 conflict, war, hostilities, belligerence. 2 turmoil, agitation, tumult, disorder, chaos.

peaceable adj. The inhabitants were peaceable: pacific, peaceful, amicable, friendly, amiable, mild, gentle; calm, tranquil, serene, quiet. **—Ant.** hostile, unfriendly; noisy.

peaceful adj. **1.** I want my children to be brought up in a peaceful world. Sweden is a peaceful nation: free from war, nonwarring, peacetime; peaceable, peace-loving, inclined toward peace, pacific, pacifistic, nonbelligerent. **2.** Labor and management reached a peaceful settlement of their differences: amicable, friendly, without violence, nonviolent, without hostility, free from strife, harmonious, agreeable. **3.** It's so peaceful in the woods: quiet, still, silent, tranquil, serene, restful, calm, placid, undisturbed, untroubled. **—Ant.** 1 warring, wartime; belligerent, bellicose, hostile, warlike. 2 violent, hostile, strife-torn, bitter, antagonistic, angry, unfriendly. 3 noisy, loud, raucous, tumultuous; disturbed, perturbed, disquieted, agitated, upset, nervous, restless.

peacemaker n. The President dispatched his team of peacemakers to the Middle East: conciliator, intermediary, diplomat, ambassador, negotiator, mediator, go-between, pacificator, placater, arbitrator, adjudicator; peacekeeper, peacemonger.

peak n. **1.** The mountain peak was covered with snow: summit, pinnacle, tip, top, apex, crown, crest; apogee. **2.** We drove through town at the peak of the rush hour: culmination, climax, maximum point, highest degree, acme, prime, zenith, crest, flood. —v. **3.** The flood waters should peak by midnight: reach a maximum, crest, climax, culminate. **—Ant.** 1 base, bottom, foot, foundation. 2 nadir.

peaked[1] adj. The suit of armor had a peaked helmet: with a peak, pointed, pointy, spiked, tapered; spiny, spiky.

peaked[2] adj. The patient was recovering but still looked peaked: pale, pallid, wan, sallow, ashen, white; sickly, ailing, ill, weak, infirm, debilitated, wizened; thin, lean, spare, skinny, scrawny, gaunt, emaciated, shriveled, pinched, haggard, drawn. **—Ant.** hearty, hale, hale and hearty, healthy; robust, hardy, sturdy, husky, strapping, brawny; ruddy, rosy-cheeked, florid, flushed, blushing.

peal n. **1.** *The peal of church bells filled the air. A peal of thunder woke us:* ringing, ring, reverberation, resounding, clang, clangor, toll, knell, din, tintinnabulation; clap, crash, crack, roar, blare, boom, blast, rumble, roll. —v. **2.** *All the bells in town pealed at noon:* ring, reverberate, resound, clang, toll, knell, tintinnabulate; crash, crack, roar, blare, boom, blast, rumble, roll.

pearly adj. *Pearly drops dripped from the cup:* opalescent, opaline, nacreous, iridescent, mother-of-pearl, pale, whitish, light, snowy, dove-gray, pearl-gray.

peccadillo n. *The book is full of the peccadilloes of Hollywood personalities:* misdemeanor, misdeed, lapse, slip, misconduct, misstep, petty sin, transgression, wrongdoing, trespass, wrong step, false move; faux pas, blunder, *Slang* booboo.

peck[1] v. **1.** *The bird pecked at the bread crumbs. Stop pecking on the window:* strike with the beak, bore with the beak, pick up with the beak; tap, strike, thump, pat. **2.** *The child just pecked at his food:* pick at, nibble, snack. —n. **3.** *Her husband gave her a peck on the cheek and left for the office:* light kiss, absent-minded kiss, *Slang* buss, smack; tap, rap, stroke, light jab. —**Ant.** 2 devour, gobble, wolf down, gulp, bolt.

peck[2] n. **1.** *How much do you pay for a peck of potatoes?:* a quarter of a bushel, the amount of eight quarts. **2.** *You're asking for a peck of trouble:* a great deal, a considerable quantity, lots, heaps, worlds, a slew, stack, scads, gobs, oodles, mess, bunch, batch, abundance. —**Ant.** 2 little, drop, crumb, grain.

peculiar adj. **1.** *Every bell has its own peculiar sound:* particular, individual, distinctive, distinct, distinguishing, characteristic, typical, representative, unique, singular, exclusive, private, personal, special, specific. **2.** *What a peculiar hat!:* odd, queer, strange, unusual, abnormal, curious, quaint, outlandish, unconventional, freakish, weird; eccentric, bizarre, idiosyncratic, erratic, capricious, whimsical, *Slang* far-out. —**Ant.** 1 common, general, unspecific, universal, indistinctive. 2 commonplace, usual, ordinary, expected, conventional, familiar, everyday.

peculiarity n. **1.** *The large fantail is a peculiarity of the peacock:* feature, trait, distinguishing quality, attribute, uniqueness, characteristic, quality, singularity, particularity, distinction, mark, badge, stamp. **2.** *Wearing nothing but blue clothing is only one of her peculiarities:* eccentricity, idiosyncrasy, odd trait, oddity; freakishness, strangeness, unnaturalness, weirdness, queerness, bizarreness, erraticism; abnormality. —**Ant.** 1 universality, common quality, general thing. 2 conventionality, normalcy.

pecuniary adj. *He was an expert in pecuniary matters:* monetary, financial.

pedagogic adj. *Few attempts were made to improve the school's pedagogic methods:* educational, tutorial, professorial, scholarly, instructional, academic; bookish, pedantic, didactic, donnish.

pedagogue or **pedagog** n. *A lover of learning, he wanted to be a pedagogue:* teacher, schoolteacher, schoolmaster, schoolmistress, schoolmarm, educator, educationist, tutor, instructor, professor, academic.

pedant n. *Is the professor really a brilliant scholar or just a pedant?:* ostentatious man of learning; bookworm, plodding scholar, doctrinaire scholar; methodologist, purist, dogmatist.

pedantic adj. *When you ask him a question you get a pedantic answer:* ostentatiously learned, pompous, academic, scholastic, didactic, doctrinaire, bookish, stilted, dogmatic, punctilious, hairsplitting, nitpicking, overly meticulous, fussy, finicky, overparticular. —**Ant.** succinct, pithy, straightforward; vague; general, comprehensive.

peddle v. *The boy peddles newspapers on the street corner. Stop peddling gossip all over the office!:* hawk, vend, sell, retail, carry about for sale; dispense, deal out, dispose of. —**Ant.** buy, purchase, get, obtain, acquire.

pedestrian n. **1.** *Pedestrians have the right of way at crosswalks:* walker, traveler afoot, foottraveler, stroller, *Informal* trekker. —adj. **2.** *The city built a pedestrian overpass over the highway:* for pedestrians, for walking; ambulatory, perambulatory, perambulating; peripatetic, itinerant. **3.** *His newest play is quite a pedestrian affair:* unimaginative, mediocre, commonplace, ordinary, prosaic, mundane, run-of-the-mill, tedious, unexciting, unimportant, inconsequential, insignificant, mediocre. —**Ant.** 1 driver, vehicle. 2 vehicular, for vehicles. 3 imaginative, exciting, interesting, intriguing, fascinating, compelling; important, significant, consequential, outstanding, remarkable, noteworthy.

pedigree n. *The poodle had an impressive pedigree:* record of ancestry, official record of descent, family tree, genealogical table; line of descent, descent, lineage, ancestry, family, parentage, line, bloodline, derivation, extraction, strain.

peek n. **1.** *Let me have a peek, please:* blink, gander, glance, glimpse, look, look-see, peep, sight —v. **2.** *She peeked under the covers:* peep, peer, pry.

peel v. **1.** *She peeled the apple:* strip, skin, pare, flay. —n. **2.** *The recipe called for diced orange peel:* skin, rind, bark.

peep[1] v. **1.** *No peeping! The girl peeped around the door and asked us in:* peek, look surreptitiously, steal a look, look from hiding; peer, give a quick look, give a cursory look, glimpse, skim. **2.** *The sun finally peeped out from behind the clouds:* peer out, come partially into view, begin to appear, emerge, come forth. —n. **3.** *The hunters just got a peep at the deer before it disappeared into the woods:* quick look, glimpse, glance, peek. —**Ant.** 1 scrutinize, inspect, examine, observe, contemplate; stare. 2 disappear, submerge, hide. 3 good look, examination, inspection.

peep[2] n. **1.** *The children were delighted by the peeps of the baby chicks. One more peep out of* *you and you'll get a spanking!:* peeping, cheep, chirp, tweet, twitter, chirrup, squeak; word, whisper, mutter, whimper, murmur. —*v.* **2.** *The birds peeped excitedly as we refilled the feeder:* cheep, chirp, chirrup, tweet, twitter, squeak.

peer¹ *v.* **1.** *She peered at the neighbors from behind the curtain:* look, gaze, stare, gape, peep, peek, squint. **2.** *The moon peered out from behind a cloud:* appear, come into view, emerge, become visible.

peer² *n.* **1.** *The defendant was tried by a jury of his peers:* equal, compeer; fellow citizen. **2.** *The peers of the realm defied the king's edict:* nobleman, noble, lord; aristocrat, gentleman, patrician, *Slang* blue blood.

peerless *adj. Paganini played with peerless artistry:* unsurpassed, matchless, unmatched, unexcelled, unequaled, incomparable, unrivaled, inimitable; superlative, surpassing, supreme, consummate, preeminent, transcendent; faultless, flawless. —**Ant.** commonplace, ordinary, mediocre, routine, indifferent, pedestrian; inferior, poor, second-rate.

peeve *v.* **1.** *What peeves me is the way she takes her friends for granted:* annoy, provoke, gall, irritate, chafe, exasperate, irk, vex, nettle, aggravate, rile, fret, perturb, *Slang* eat at, eat, gnaw at, gripe, bug, frost, give one a pain, give one a pain in the neck. —*n.* **2.** *Her pet peeve is discourteous people:* dislike, aggravation, annoyance, irritation, vexation, exasperation, provocation, complaint, grievance, gripe, *Informal* thorn in the side, pain in the neck. —**Ant.** 1 please, delight, charm, enchant, captivate, enrapture. 2 pleasure, delight, like.

peevish *adj. Father gets peevish when he's kept waiting:* cross, irritable, testy, grumpy, grouchy, ill-humored, sulky, petulant, surly, snappish, fractious, cantankerous, cranky, crabby, churlish, huffy, pettish; mean, ill-natured, ill-tempered, bad-tempered, splenetic, quarrelsome, querulous. —**Ant.** agreeable, easygoing, good-natured, affable, pleasant, genial, amiable.

peg *n* *The violin strings are wound around pegs and tightened:* pin, spike, skewer, nail, toggle; cleat, fastener, thole, dowel, tholepin.

pejorative *adj. In its pejorative sense, "light" means "weak":* belittling, disparaging, uncomplimentary, deprecatory, detracting, derogatory, scornful, negative, depreciatory, slighting, demeaning, unpleasant, downgrading, mocking, degrading, debasing, ridiculing, disdainful, contemptuous, disapproving. —**Ant.** complimentary, approving, praising, favorable, commendatory.

pellet *n. The rat poison comes in small pellets:* ball, drop, bead, sphere, pearl, globule, marble, pea, pill; pebble, stone.

pell-mell *adv. The assignment was thrown together pell-mell to meet the deadline:* helter-skelter, slapdash, recklessly, posthaste, impetuously, rashly, hastily, precipitately, hurry-scurry, hurriedly, heedlessly, thoughtlessly, carelessly, incautiously, imprudently, *Slang* at half cock.

—**Ant.** orderly, neatly, methodically; calmly, serenely.

pellucid *adj. The stream was pellucid:* translucent; limpid, clear, crystalline, crystal-clear, transparent. —**Ant.** dull, opaque.

pelt¹ *v. The boxers pelted each other in the middle of the ring. The boys pelted the tin can with rocks:* hit, strike, batter, pummel, pound, punch, buffet, whack, thwack, thrash, rap, pepper; *Slang* clobber, sock, belt.

pelt² *n. The coat was made of leopard pelts. The goat had a grayish pelt:* animal skin, skin, hide, fur; coat, fleece.

pen¹ *n. How many sheep are in the pen?:* enclosure, fold, pound, corral, paddock, compound, stockade; cage, coop, sty, crib, hutch, stall.

pen² *n.* **1.** *The contract must be signed with a pen, not a pencil:* fountain pen, quill; ballpoint pen. —*v.* **2.** *She penned a note to her mother:* write, write in ink, write by hand, scribble, scrawl, pencil; compose, draft.

penal *adj. Devil's Island was a famous penal colony:* of punishment, disciplinary, punitive, corrective, penalizing, punishing, castigatory, retributive; of jails, of prisoners.

penalty *n. The sign read "No trespassing under penalty of $50 fine":* punishment, forfeiture, retribution, infliction, assessment, suffering; fine, forfeit, handicap, disadvantage. —**Ant.** reward, prize.

penance *n. The faithful were required to do penance for their sins:* repentance, expiation, atonement, contrition, mortification, penitence, propitiation; self-flagellation, sackcloth and ashes, hair shirt.

penchant *n. The fat youth had a penchant for rich desserts:* fondness, partiality, liking, strong inclination, fancy, preference, predilection, proclivity, propensity, leaning, attraction, taste, relish, tendency, affinity, predisposition, disposition, proneness, prejudice, bias; flair, bent, readiness, turn, knack, gift. —**Ant.** hatred, dislike, loathing, aversion, abhorrence, disinclination, repulsion.

pendent or **pendant** *adj.* **1.** *The necklace was a gold band with pendent diamonds:* hanging, suspended, dangling, pendulous, pensile, swinging. **2.** *A pendent balcony overlooked the garden:* jutting, overhanging, protruding, extending, protuberant, sticking out, projecting.

pending *adj. Final disposition of the case is still pending:* awaiting decision, awaiting settlement, undetermined, undecided, unsettled, unresolved, unfinished, up in the air, in suspense; imminent, in the offing.

pendulous *adj. The pendulous vines made the jungle impassable:* hanging, suspended, dangling, pendent, swinging, pensile; drooping, sagging.

penetrate *v.* **1.** *The nail easily penetrated the soft wood:* pierce, puncture, cut into, bore, prick, perforate; cut through, pass through, traverse. **2.** *The foul odor penetrated the entire house:* pervade, permeate, saturate, impregnate, seep in; enter, invade, infiltrate. **3.** *Were you able to penetrate the author's symbolism?:*

understand, comprehend, perceive, discern, fathom, get, get to the bottom of, figure out, unravel, see through, catch; decode, decipher. —**Ant.** 1 ricochet, carom, rebound, glance off.

penetrating adj. **1.** Ammonia has an extremely penetrating odor: piercing, sharp, stinging, caustic, biting, acrid, strong, pungent, harsh, reeking; heady, redolent; pervading, pervasive, permeating, saturating. **2.** The book is a penetrating study of the labor movement: keen, sharp, sharp-witted, perceptive, discerning, thoughtful, perspicacious, shrewd, astute, intelligent, smart, clever, percipient, trenchant; alive, alert, aware. —**Ant.** 1 mild, sweet. 2 obtuse, unperceptive, uncomprehending, thoughtless, shallow, dull, stupid, dumb; indifferent, apathetic.

penetration n. **1.** The heavier the arrow the greater its penetration into the target: power of penetrating, foray, passage, invasion, intrusion, infusion, access; perforation, piercing, boring, puncturing. **2.** She showed great penetration in analyzing the problem: insight, keenness, sharpness, perception, discernment, perspicacity, shrewdness, astuteness, intelligence, cleverness, quickness, grasp. —**Ant.** 2 obtuseness, stupidity, shallowness, dullness.

penitence n. If a sinner feels penitence, he can be forgiven: repentance, remorse, self-reproach, compunction, regret, sorrow, humiliation, contrition; penance, attrition, expiation, atonement. —**Ant.** impenitence, unrepentance, obduracy; hardness, callousness.

penitent adj. **1.** Those who were penitent obtained absolution: penitential, repentant, contrite, atoning, remorseful, self-reproaching, compunctious, sorry, conscience-stricken, rueful, regretful. —n. **2.** The penitents were saying their prayers at early Mass: a penitent person, one who is remorseful for sin or fault; devotee, pilgrim. —**Ant.** 1 impenitent, unrepentant, obdurate; remorseless, callous.

penitentiary n. The murderer was sentenced to the penitentiary for life: federal prison, state prison; (loosely) prison, jail, penal institution, house of correction, house of detention, workhouse, reformatory; Slang pen, joint, slammer, stir, big house.

pennant n. The pennant flying from the mast indicated that the admiral was aboard: flag, banner, streamer, banderole, ensign, standard, colors, jack, pennon, burgee, bunting, ensignia, oriflamme.

penniless adj. Bad investments have left him penniless: moneyless, destitute, strapped, poverty-stricken, impoverished, indigent, poor, needy, pauperized; insolvent, ruined, bankrupt, down-and-out, wiped out; Slang broke, flat broke, busted. —**Ant.** rich, wealthy, affluent, moneyed, well-heeled, Slang in the chips.

pension n. He retired on a generous pension: retirement benefits, social security, annuity, reward.

pensive adj. What did you say to put him in such a pensive mood?: sadly thoughtful, reflective, meditative, contemplative, introspective,

musing, dreaming, daydreaming, dreamy; sad, wistful, melancholy, solemn, serious, somber, grave. —**Ant.** frivolous, joyous, happy, cheerful, gay, jovial, carefree, lighthearted.

pent-up adj. The children need to work off their pent-up energy: repressed, suppressed, restrained, stifled, checked, penned-up, penned-in, hedged-in, boxed-up, bottled-up, stored-up, held back, reined in.

penurious adj. The penurious traveler never carried money: mean, parsimonious, stingy, tight, tight-fisted, close-fisted, close, miserly, niggardly, mercenary. —**Ant.** generous.

penury n. She lived in penury during her last years: poverty, impoverishment, want, indigence, need, privation, destitution, straitened circumstances, dire necessity; financial ruin, insolvency, bankruptcy. —**Ant.** wealth, prosperity, opulence, luxury, elegance, abundance, affluence.

people n. pl. **1.** Will people ever live 200 years?: human beings, humans, mortals, men and women, individuals, humankind, homo sapiens, mankind, humanity. **2.** The people of the city want better schools. My people came from Ireland: citizens, citizenry, inhabitants, population, populace; family, ancestors, relatives, kin, kinfolk, Informal folks. **3.** A politician must appeal to the people: the public, the common people, the little people, the rank and file, the masses, the multitude, the millions, the man in the street, John Q. Public; commoners, the common run; the lower classes, the lower orders, the working class, the working man, the mob, the rabble, the herd, the crowd, the great unwashed, the hoi polloi. —**Ant.** 3 nobility, aristocracy, gentry, upper classes, blue bloods, silk-stockings.

pep n. She's always full of pep when she starts to work: vigor, vim, vitality, verve, energy, snap, zip, dash; Informal go, get-up-and-go; animation, vivacity, spirit, enthusiasm, life, ginger, gusto, liveliness.

peppery adj. This soup is too peppery: highly seasoned, spicy, hot, piquant, fiery, burning, pungent, sharp. —**Ant.** bland, mild, tasteless, insipid.

peppy adj. The band played a peppy tune: brisk, lively, spirited, energetic, vigorous, dynamic, animated, vivacious, sparkling, snappy, enthusiastic, perky, active. —**Ant.** listless, spiritless, lethargic, sluggish, slow, leaden, somber, dull.

perambulate v. Every evening the local people perambulate around the plaza: walk, stroll, saunter, promenade, amble, mosey, ramble, meander, pace, tour.

perceive v. **1.** The diners perceived a faint aroma of dill. Only an artist could perceive the fine shades of color in the painting: notice, be aware of, detect, note, discern, make out, recognize, distinguish, apprehend, discover; observe, see, hear, smell, taste, feel, sense. **2.** She gradually perceived that her parents had been right: understand, comprehend, apprehend, grasp, gather, realize, know, conclude, deduce, gain insight into; *Slang* savvy, get. **—Ant.** l overlook, ignore, miss, pass over.

percentage *n. She gained a percentage of the winnings:* proportion, portion, allotment, allowance, commission, cut, discount, percent, fraction, quota, rake-off, slice, split, division, piece, bite, chunk.

perceptible *adj. The difference in their heights is hardly perceptible:* perceivable, discernible, noticeable, apparent, detectable, observable, visible, discoverable, ascertainable; obvious, evident, manifest, distinct, conspicuous, clear, plain, palpable, tangible, prominent, notable, unmistakable, well-defined; unconcealed, unhidden. **—Ant.** imperceptible, indiscernible, unnoticeable, unapparent, undetectable, inconspicuous; concealed, hidden, obscured.

perception *n. A good driver must have a good perception of distance:* discernment, awareness, sense, faculty, apprehension, conception, recognition, cognizance, comprehension, consciousness, detection, discrimination, judgment, understanding, grasp.

perceptive *adj. She is very perceptive about the moods of others:* understanding, full of insight, sensitive, responsive, aware, discerning, penetrating; intelligent, keen, sharp, shrewd, astute, acute, sensible, quick, quick-witted. **—Ant.** insensitive, obtuse, callous, indifferent; stupid, thick, slow-witted, dull, dumb.

perch *n.* **1.** *The bird sat on its perch and sang lustily:* roost, roosting place, eyrie; resting place, rest, seat. *—v.* **2.** *The boy perched in the tree and called to his friends:* sit, roost, rest, settle; light, alight, land.

perdition *n. Sinners may suffer eternal perdition:* damnation, condemnation, destruction, ruin, ruination, loss of heavenly salvation, loss of one's soul; everlasting punishment, hellfire, Hell.

peregrination *n. After a year of peregrinations she settled down to a humdrum job:* journey, travel, wandering, trip, expedition, trekking, excursion, roaming, rambling, roving, hiking, jaunt, sally, junket, globe-trotting.

peremptory *adj.* **1.** *He was excused from the jury by a peremptory challenge:* absolute, final, irrevocable, irreversible, incontrovertible, undeniable, unquestionable, decisive, unequivocal; unavoidable, obligatory, imperative. **2.** *She's much too peremptory to cooperate with others:* domineering, overbearing, authoritative, dictatorial, assertive, aggressive, lordly, imperious, high-handed; opinionated, closed-minded, dogmatic, biased. **—Ant.** 1; 2 indecisive. 2 submissive, unassertive, passive, docile, tractable, compliant, meek; cooperative, open-minded.

perennial *adj. He sat there with that perennial grin on his face:* perpetual, everlasting, permanent, constant, incessant, unceasing, ceaseless, continual, continuous, unremitting, persistent; fixed, changeless, unchanging, immutable, durable, imperishable, indestructible, lasting, enduring, long-lasting, undying, timeless, unfailing, long-lived. **—Ant.** temporary, occasional, sporadic, intermittent, periodic, evanescent;

perishable, transient, fleeting, ephemeral, temporal.

perfect *adj.* **1.** *Can you draw a perfect circle?:* exact, accurate, precise, true, pure, correct in every detail, flawless, unerring, strict, scrupulous, faithful. **2.** *The athlete was in perfect health. The child has been a perfect angel all day:* faultless, flawless, without defect, unblemished, unimpaired, undamaged; complete, whole, entire, unbroken, finished, absolute, thorough, pure, consummate, unqualified, unmitigated, impeccable, matchless, unequaled, unrivaled, ideal, supreme, peerless, superlative, sublime; blameless, untainted, immaculate. *—v.* **3.** *The scientist perfected a method of desalting seawater:* bring to perfection, develop, complete, achieve, accomplish, effect, realize, evolve, fulfill, consummate. **—Ant.** 1, 2 imperfect. 2 faulty, flawed, defective, blemished, impaired, ruined, spoiled, damaged, incomplete, deficient, unfinished; partial, mixed, impure, qualified; inferior, poor, bad, worthless, *Informal* awful, *Slang* lousy.

perfection *n.* **1.** *The roast was cooked to perfection:* perfectness, excellence, faultlessness, flawlessness, impeccability, superiority, sublimity, ideal state; exactness, accurateness, precision, purity. **2.** *The perfection of the jet engine took many years:* development, completion, achieving, accomplishment, realization, evolution, fulfillment, consummation.

perfectly *adv.* **1.** *The cake was baked perfectly:* to perfection, superbly, wonderfully, flawlessly, faultlessly, without fault, without defect, without blemish, impeccably, consummately. **2.** *She's perfectly capable of taking care of herself:* entirely, thoroughly, completely, totally, fully, wholly, altogether, quite, utterly, absolutely, supremely, infinitely, preeminently, consummately, to the nth degree; downright, positively, purely. **—Ant.** 1 imperfectly, faultily, defectively, poorly, badly. 2 not; incompletely, partially; mistakenly, erroneously, inaccurately.

perfidious *adj. Benedict Arnold's perfidious act made him his country's first traitor:* treacherous, traitorous, treasonous, deceitful, false, disloyal, unfaithful, faithless, treasonable, dishonorable, untrustworthy, unscrupulous; dishonest, corrupt, untruthful, undependable, lying, cheating; *Informal* sneaky, double-dealing, shifty, two-faced.

perfidy *n. She couldn't abide his perfidy:* treachery, faithlessness, traitorousness, treason, disloyalty. **—Ant.** allegiance, faithfulness, faith, loyalty.

perforate *v. The nail perforated her coat and left an ugly rip:* pierce, prick, puncture, stab, bore, penetrate, punch, lancinate, drill, hole, stick; slit, gash, slash, split.

perform *v.* **1.** *A skilled worker can perform the task easily. A good citizen performs all his financial obligations:* do, accomplish, carry out, execute, perpetrate, achieve, effect, realize, attain, fulfill, bring to pass, bring about, finish, consummate, discharge, dispose of, meet; *Slang* knock off, pull off, polish off. **2.** *All of the musicians performed admirably. The actors per-*

formed Twelfth Night*:* play, present, render; act, enact, take part in; tread the boards, troupe; portray, represent, depict. **—Ant.** 1 fail, founder, neglect, forsake.

performance *n.* **1.** *He failed miserably in the performance of his duty:* discharge, accomplishment, execution, performing, doing, acquittal, exercise, transaction, fulfillment, realization, attainment, conduct, achievement, dispatch, perpetration, effectuation; completion, consummation. **2.** *The theater gives two performances a day:* show, presentation, rendering, production, exhibition; (*variously*) play, concert, opera, ballet, recital, entertainment, spectacle, ceremony.

perfume *n.* **1.** *Who's wearing that spicy perfume? Magnolias have a wonderful perfume:* fragrance, scent, extract, essence, cologne; aroma, smell, odor, bouquet. **—v. 2.** *Those roses perfume the whole garden:* imbue with odor, give fragrance to, aromatize, scent, sweeten. **—Ant.** 1 stench, stink, smell.

perfunctory *adj.* *That was certainly a perfunctory "hello" he gave us:* indifferent, casual, disinterested, offhand, careless, unconcerned, unthinking, cursory, inattentive, lax, hasty, superficial, routine, mechanical, halfhearted, lukewarm, apathetic, spiritless, listless, passionless; negligent. **—Ant.** careful, thorough, thoughtful, diligent, assiduous, attentive, warmhearted, effusive, spirited, ardent, keen, zealous.

perhaps *adv.* *Perhaps we could go to a movie tonight:* maybe, mayhap, possibly, God willing, conceivably, perchance, as the case may be, imaginably, for all one knows, *Archaic* peradventure, wind and weather permitting, *French* peutêtre. **—Ant.** definitely, certainly, unquestionably, surely.

peril *n.* *Does he understand the perils of mountain climbing?:* risk, danger, hazard, jeopardy, pitfall, threat, menace, cause for alarm; vulnerability, exposure to danger, openness to attack, defenselessness, insecurity, uncertainty, unsafety. **—Ant.** safety, security, secureness, certainty, surety; invulnerability, unassailability, impregnability.

perilous *adj.* *The floodwaters were perilous to cross:* risky, hazardous, dangerous, fraught with danger, unsafe, ominous, threatening; uncertain, unsure, chancy, venturesome, insecure, vulnerable, shaky, slippery, precarious, ticklish.

perimeter *n.* *Trees were planted on the perimeter of the garden:* periphery, border, borderline, circumference, bounds, confines; margin, edge. **—Ant.** center, middle, hub, heart, core, kernel, nucleus.

period *n.* **1.** *The student's lunch period is from twelve to one. Dinosaurs roamed the earth in an earlier period:* time, span of time, interval, interlude, duration, term, season; era, epoch, age, eon. **2.** *The suspect's confession put a period to the investigation:* end, stop, close, finish, termination, limit, discontinuance, halt, cessation, finale, *Slang* curtain.

periodic also **periodical** *adj.* *She makes periodic visits to the beauty parlor:* repeated, recurring, recurrent, frequent, intermittent, regular, routine, at fixed intervals, cyclic, seasonal.

periodical *n.* *The library subscribes to scores of periodicals:* publication; (*variously*) newspaper, paper, magazine, newsmagazine, newsletter, journal, bulletin, review, daily, weekly, monthly, quarterly, annual.

periodically *adv.* *You should have your eyes examined periodically:* regularly, routinely, at fixed intervals, repeatedly, often, frequently; occasionally.

peripatetic *adj.* *She was married to a peripatetic landscape gardener:* wandering, itinerant, traveling, roving, migrant, rambling, walking, ambulating, tramping, peregrinating, roaming, galivanting; migratory, nomadic.

peripheral *adj.* *She had other, more peripheral objections:* incidental, superficial, surface, borderline, minor, outer, outermost, secondary, tangential, unimportant.

periphery *n.* *Many houses have sprung up on the periphery of the town:* outskirts, fringes; boundary, edge, perimeter, circumference, border, bound. **—Ant.** center, middle, hub, heart, core, nucleus.

perish *v.* *Dozens perished in the storm. The ancient Aztec culture has all perished now:* die, expire, pass away; become extinct, cease to exist, vanish, disappear, wither away, decay, come to ruin, crumble, be destroyed. **—Ant.** be born, come into being, arise, appear; thrive, flourish, proliferate, prosper, fructify.

perishable *adj.* *Perishable foods must be kept refrigerated:* subject to decay, subject to spoiling, decomposable, unstable; short-lived, fleeting, transitory, ephemeral, evanescent. **—Ant.** nonperishable, stable, durable, long-lasting, long-lived, lasting.

perjure *v.* *The witness perjured himself:* commit perjury, lie, falsify, forswear.

perjury *n.* *The witness was charged with perjury for lying to the jury:* giving false testimony, lying under oath, false swearing.

perk *n.* *A company car was one of the job's perks:* perquisite, benefit, fringe benefit, bonus, dividend, extra, gratuity, largesse, tip.

perky *adj.* *We all like her because she's so perky:* jaunty, pert, lively, gay, vivacious, animated, sprightly, spirited, full of spirit, alert, saucy, brisk; cheerful, happy, sunny, smiling, lighthearted, free and easy. **—Ant.** passive, lethargic, spiritless, sluggish, phlegmatic; somber, grave, serious, dour, sullen, gloomy, glum, sour, morose, sad, cheerless.

permanent *adj.* **1.** *They built a permanent monument to the hero. Are these dyes permanent?:* lasting forever, lasting, perpetual, everlasting, eternal, infinite, endless, undying, never-ending, unending, immortal, deathless, abiding, indestructible, imperishable, unyielding, unalterable, unfailing, changeless, immutable; long-lasting, long-lived, durable, enduring, unfading, constant, stable. **—n. 2.** *She went to the beauty parlor for a permanent:* permanent wave, set, wave, perm. **—Ant.** 1 impermanent, temporary, brief, fleeting, momentary, finite, mortal, passing, short, short-lived, transitory, fugitive, unstable, variable, changing, inconstant, ephemeral, evanescent.

permeate v. *The rain permeated the old tent. That cigar smoke permeates the house:* penetrate, pass through, soak through, seep through; pervade, saturate, diffuse throughout, infuse, fill, imbue. —**Ant.** bounce off, ricochet, glance off, slide off.

permissible adj. *Hearsay is not permissible evidence in court. Is smoking permissible in the theater?:* permitted, allowed, allowable, unprohibited, tolerated, admissible, granted; sanctioned, authorized, licensed, lawful, legal, legitimate, licit. —**Ant.** forbidden, prohibited, banned, disallowed, proscribed; unauthorized, unlawful, illegal, illicit.

permission n. *May I have permission to use the car? The commanding officer must give his permission for all furloughs:* leave, consent, assent, approval, acquiescence, concession, agreement, compliance, approbation; authorization, sanction, allowance, dispensation, indulgence, endorsement, grant, license, permit. —**Ant.** refusal, denial, prohibition, ban, prevention, interdiction.

permissive adj. *Should parents be strict or permissive?:* indulgent, lenient, lax, assenting, consenting, acquiescent, tolerant, easygoing, forbearing; allowing, permitting, granting; unproscriptive, unprohibitive. —**Ant.** strict, rigid, authoritarian, domineering, proscriptive; refusing, denying, forbidding, withholding, grudging.

permit v. **1.** *Will you permit me to ask a question? The rules do not permit players to step out of bounds:* let, allow, give permission, give leave to, give assent to, agree to, consent to, tolerate, suffer, endure, bear with, put up with, let pass, approve, condone, OK; authorize, sanction, endorse, license. —n. **2.** *Do you have a driver's permit?:* license, official permission, authorization, warrant, authority, sanction.

permutation n. *The proposal underwent several permutations:* change, variation, modification, transformation, mutation, transmutation, transmogrification, metamorphosis, vicissitude, rearrangement, interchange, transposition, replacement, commutation. —**Ant.** sameness, regularity.

pernicious adj. *The common cold is usually not a pernicious disease:* harmful, injurious, serious, destructive, damaging, deleterious, detrimental, dangerous, disastrous, baneful, lethal, deadly, fatal, mortal, toxic, venomous, poisonous, noxious, malignant. —**Ant.** harmless, innocuous; beneficial, advantageous, helpful; healthful, healthy, wholesome, salutary, salubrious.

peroration n. *He delivered a peroration on the evils of tobacco:* speech, oration, declamation, discourse, address, sermon, lecture; tirade, exhortation, harangue, diatribe, jeremiad, filibuster, philippic.

perpendicular adj. *She stood at the edge of the perpendicular cliff:* vertical, plumb, sheer, straight-up, standing, upright, erect.

perpetrate v. *Only a madman would perpetrate such a crime:* commit, perform, carry out, execute, do, enact, transact, bring about, pursue, inflict, *Slang* pull off.

perpetual adj. *The will created a fund for perpetual care of the park. I'm tired of your perpetual nagging:* lasting forever, lasting, permanent, everlasting, eternal, abiding, enduring, constant, sustained, endless, never ending, unending; continuous, ceaseless, incessant, unceasing, interminable, uninterrupted, unremitting, inexhaustible, repeated, continual. —**Ant.** temporary, impermanent, brief, fleeting, momentary, passing, short-lived, transitory, transient, ephemeral.

perpetuate v. *We must perpetuate the free enterprise system:* cause to endure, make last, immortalize, make perpetual, make everlasting, eternalize, memorialize; preserve, save, sustain, maintain, continue. —**Ant.** destroy, obliterate, annihilate, exterminate, abolish, stamp out, snuff out; forget, ignore; avoid, eschew.

perpetuity n. *The estate was bequeathed to the heirs in perpetuity:* eternity, forever, permanence, time without end, infinity, all time, end of time, endlessness, timelessness, everlastingness, perpetuation, neverendingness, perdurability, perennialness. —**Ant.** transience, impermanence, ephemerality, transitoriness.

perplex v. *Mathematics perplexes me:* puzzle, baffle, confuse, bewilder, mix up, confound, dumbfound, muddle, befuddle, boggle, nonplus, stump, mystify; rattle, throw into confusion, *Informal* make one's head spin.

perquisite n. *The perquisites of the job included a house and car:* benefit, emolument, privilege, advantage, right, due, fringe benefit, *Slang* perk, gift, present, reward, inducement, recompense, honorarium.

persecute v. *The Pilgrims came to America after being persecuted for their religious beliefs:* harass, harry, annoy cruelly, pursue continually, oppress, tyrannize, victimize, plague, harrow, hector, hound, bully, badger, bait; torment, vex, annoy, maltreat, abuse. —**Ant.** pamper, indulge, humor; favor, accommodate; support, uphold, champion, back.

perseverance n. *Perseverance was at length rewarded:* persistence, tenacity, pertinacity, resolution, doggedness, determination, steadfastness, indefatigability. —**Ant.** irresolution.

persevere v. *Talent is worthless unless you persevere in developing it:* persist, be steadfast, be determined, be resolved, be resolute, be obstinate, work unflaggingly, not give up, keep on, maintain one's efforts, work hard, keep at it; *Informal* plug away, hammer away, stick to it, stick to one's guns, hang on, hang in there. —**Ant.** be irresolute, waver, vacillate, shilly-shally, falter, let down; give up, give in.

persist v. **1.** *Despite hardships, she persisted in her efforts to get a college education:* persevere, work unflaggingly, maintain one's efforts, pursue relentlessly, be tenacious, not give up, stop at nothing, be obstinate, hold steadfast, stand fast, be determined, be resolute, keep at it, not yield, work day and night; *Informal* stick to it, stick to one's guns, hang on, hang in there, move heaven and earth, leave no stone unturned, not take "no" for an answer, never say die. **2.** *The flowers persisted even in the driest weather:* last, endure, survive, remain, stay, continue, hold on, hold out, go on. —**Ant.** 1 be irresolute, waver, vacillate, shilly-shally; falter, quit, give up, surrender, stop, cease, end, leave off. 2 die, expire, wither away, fade, shrivel up.

persistent *adj.* **1.** *With persistent efforts we can finish on time:* stubborn, determined, obstinate, tenacious, relentless, persisting, obdurate, dogged, persevering, steadfast, resolute, unfailing, unswerving. **2.** *Her persistent criticism made everyone angry:* constant, unrelenting, unceasing, incessant, continual, continuous, endless, perpetual, eternal, sustained, interminable, inexhaustible, unremitting, unshakable; lasting, enduring, abiding.

persnickety *adj.* *The waitress knows how to deal with persnickety customers:* fussy, particular, nitpicking, finicky, overprecise, fastidious, meticulous, pernickety, punctilious, finical, choosy, overdemanding, fuddy-duddy, picayune. —**Ant.** sloppy, careless, indifferent, haphazard.

person *n.* *There will be 12 persons at our table:* individual, human being, human, being, creature, mortal, living soul, soul, living body, body; earthling.

personable *adj.* *We need a personable girl at the reception desk:* agreeable, affable, having a pleasing personality, likable, friendly, outgoing, sociable, amiable, warm, cordial, charming, attractive, pleasant, cordial, well-mannered, complaisant, tactful, diplomatic, amicable, sympathetic, well-disposed. —**Ant.** unpleasant, surly, ill-natured, sullen, rude, discourteous.

personage *n.* *The restaurant caters to personages of the entertainment world:* luminary, dignitary, VIP, notable, nabob, celebrity, public figure, leading light, popular hero; *Slang* bigwig, big shot, big name, somebody, heavyweight, high-muck-a-muck. —**Ant.** nothing, nobody, cipher, lightweight.

personal *adj.* **1.** *The library contains the president's personal papers:* private, own, individual, intimate, exclusive, confidential, secret, special, particular, privy; inward, inwardly felt, subjective. **2.** *The doctor lectured the class on personal hygiene:* bodily, physical, corporeal.

personality *n.* **1.** *Can one develop an agreeable personality?:* outward character, disposition, temperament, makeup, nature; identity, individuality, distinctiveness. **2.** *An entertainer has to have a lot of personality:* charm, personal attraction, friendliness, agreeableness, amiability, affability, magnetism, charisma.

personally *adv.* *She took care of it personally:* in person, individually, solely, independently, alone, by oneself, for oneself, privately, specially, subjectively.

personify *v.* *For years the Venus de Milo personified the ideal of female beauty:* embody, represent, exemplify, incorporate, characterize, express, symbolize; externalize, incarnate, personalize.

personnel *n.* *All personnel will receive an extra week's vacation:* employees, workers, staff, staff members, members, work force, crew, manpower, associates.

perspective *n.* **1.** *Primitive artists often paint without perspective:* the art of conveying distance, sense of depth. **2.** *From the top of the hill you can get a perspective of the entire park:* panoramic view, bird's-eye view, overview, vista, scene, scape, view, outlook, prospect. **3.** *I've been so close to the problem I have no perspective on it:* broad view, overview, comprehensive point of view, viewpoint, sense of proportion.

perspicacious *adj.* *The critic's remarks about the book were very perspicacious:* discerning, perceptive, astute, shrewd, penetrating, acute, keen, sharp, sharp-witted, keen-sighted, clearheaded, clear-sighted, clear-eyed, alert, awake, sagacious. —**Ant.** undiscerning, dull, dull-witted, stupid, thickheaded; dense, doltish, vacuous.

perspicacity *n.* *The investor's perspicacity was legendary:* perception, discernment, penetration, shrewdness, acuity, astuteness, insight, sharpness, acumen. —**Ant.** dullness, stupidity.

perspicuity *n.* *Her perspicuity during the crisis impressed us:* clearness, clarity, lucidity, transparency, plainness, distinctness, explicitness, intelligibility. —**Ant.** dimness, opacity.

perspicuous *adj.* *Her perspicuous summary clarified the issue:* clear, lucid, intelligible, plain, distinct, explicit, transparent, unequivocal. —**Ant.** opaque, unintelligible, indistinct, unclear, confused, clouded.

persuade *v.* *Can't we persuade you to come to the party?:* induce, influence, move, get, prevail upon, motivate, convince, win over, bring round, talk into, sway, prompt, coax, wheedle, cajole, inveigle; lure, tempt, entice. —**Ant.** dissuade, discourage, deter, repel, inhibit; forbid, prohibit.

persuasion *n.* *He was skilled in the arts of persuasion:* persuasiveness, winning over, seduction, conversion, enticement, exhortation, inducement, influencing, inveiglement, wheedling, blandishment, cajolery.

persuasive *adj.* *A good politician must be a persuasive speaker:* convincing, compelling, cogent, forceful, believable, plausible, logical, credible; effective, influential, winning, seductive, inviting, alluring, coaxing.

pert *adj.* **1.** *Don't be pert to your elders:* impudent, impertinent, insolent, brash, flippant, flip, fresh, saucy, nervy, cheeky, brazen, brassy, audacious, smart-alecky, impolite, discourteous, insulting. **2.** *The old lady walked with pert little steps:* lively, sprightly, brisk, perky, nimble, spry, chipper, alert, wide-awake, quick, energetic. —**Ant.** 1 shy, bashful, meek, retiring, demure, modest, reserved; respectful, diffident, polite, courteous.

pertinacious *adj.* *The pertinacious team even-*

tually won the day: tenacious, persevering, persistent, dogged. —**Ant.** relenting, flexible.

pertinacity *n. Because of his pertinacity he learned Arabic in just two months:* persistence, obstinacy, determination, stubbornness, bullheadedness; pigheadedness, mulishness, obdurateness, inflexibility, intransigence, contrariness, perverseness, willfulness, intractability. —**Ant.** tractability, submissiveness, compliance, flexibility.

pertinent *adj. The speaker's remarks on patriotism were pertinent to the independence day celebration:* relevant, to the point, germane, material, appropriate, fitting, concerning the matter at hand, befitting, apt, applicable, suitable, apropos, apposite, meet; related, congruent, concerned, connected, corresponding, consist-ent. —**Ant.** irrelevant, immaterial, inappropriate, unfitting, unsuited, unsuitable; unrelated, incongruous, unconnected, foreign, alien, discordant.

perturb *v. The teacher was perturbed by the student's lack of interest:* disturb, trouble, worry, distress, disquiet, upset, bother, fluster, discompose, disconcert.

perusal *n. A perusal of the document showed him it was of historic importance:* reading, examination, scrutiny, review, run-through, inspection, study, scanning, *Slang* look-through, contemplation, scrutinizing.

peruse *v. We perused our textbooks:* study, read, scrutinize, examine, survey, pore over, inspect, review, vet. —**Ant.** skim.

pervade *v. The aroma of fresh coffee pervaded the house:* permeate, spread through, diffuse throughout, saturate, suffuse, fill, infuse, imbue, penetrate.

pervasive *adj. Ill feeling was pervasive at the plant:* pervading, prevalent, permeating, widespread, common, extensive, general, omnipresent, ubiquitous, universal, inescapable.

perverse *adj. She takes a perverse delight in disagreeing with everyone:* contrary, stubborn, obstinate, obdurate, inflexible, balky, hardheaded, wrongheaded, mulish, ornery, dogged, pigheaded; headstrong, willful, wayward, intractable, disobedient, rebellious. —**Ant.** cooperative, complaisant, pliant, flexible; agreeable, good-natured, accommodating, obliging, amiable.

perversion *n.* **1.** *His statement was a perversion of the truth:* distortion, malformation. **2.** *The molester habitually engaged in several perversions:* sexual abnormality, sexual deviance, sexual pathology.

pervert *v. Forcing everyone to vote for the dictator perverts the very idea of democracy:* distort, warp, contort, abuse, misuse, corrupt, misrepresent, misapply, put a false interpretation on, falsify; desecrate, corrupt, subvert, degrade, debase, deprave.

perverted *adj. The child has a perverted sense of right and wrong:* distorted, twisted, warped, contorted, unbalanced, misconstrued, misconceived, misunderstood; false, faulty, untrue, fallacious, unsound, erroneous, imperfect, un-

sound; degraded, depraved, debased, corrupt, unnatural, abnormal, aberrant, deviant. —**Ant.** sound, true, valid, balanced, correct, natural, normal; good, straight, worthy, commendable.

pesky *adj. The pesky mosquitos attacked us in droves:* annoying, exasperating, irksome, bothersome, vexatious, troublesome, galling, pestiferous, nettlesome, chafing, aggravating, infuriating, maddening, disturbing; offensive, objectionable, disagreeable, distasteful, obnoxious. —**Ant.** agreeable, soothing, comforting, delightful.

pessimism *n. The pessimism in his writing is too depressing:* gloomy outlook, seeing only the gloomy side, belief that bad prevails; despair, hopelessness, discouragement, downheartedness, gloom, gloominess. —**Ant.** optimism, hopefulness, courage, dauntlessness, enthusiasm, cheerfulness.

pessimist *n. A pessimist never expects anything to turn out well:* defeatist, one who sees only the bad side, one who believes that bad prevails; *Slang* prophet of doom, Cassandra, crepehanger, gloomy Gus, sourpuss, kill-joy, spoilsport, wet blanket. —**Ant.** optimist, utopian, incurable romantic, Pollyanna.

pessimistic *adj. The pessimistic forecaster had little good to say:* cynical, gloomy, dark, foreboding. —**Ant.** optimistic, rosy, bright.

pest *n. The spray gets rid of mosquitoes and other pests. That child is a real pest!:* troublesome insect, troublesome animal, destructive plant; annoying person, nuisance, bother, scourge, blight, bane, annoyance, irritation, vexation, curse, *Informal* thorn in one's side, *Slang* pain in the neck.

pester *v. He's always pestering me to help him with his homework:* bother, annoy, torment, badger, plague, provoke, harass, harry, hector, taunt, nag, vex, irritate, irk, fret, nettle, disturb, trouble, worry, bait; try one's patience, get on one's nerves.

pestilent *also* **pestilential** *adj. The pestilent virus wiped out the population:* pernicious, contagious, infectious, dangerous, diseased, harmful, injurious, ruinous, troublesome, ruinous, destructive; evil, vicious, corrupting.

pet *n.* **1.** *Does a dog make a better pet than a cat?:* household animal, house pet. **2.** *Mother loved us all, but Clem was her pet:* favorite, darling, baby, *Slang* apple of one's eye; dear, beloved, loved one, sweetheart. —*adj.* **3.** *Improving the local park is the mayor's pet project:* favorite, choice, favored, preferred, cherished, dearest, dear to one's heart. —*v.* **4.** *Don't be afraid to pet the dog; he won't bite:* pat, stroke, caress, fondle.

petite *adj. The petite young lady wore a miniskirt:* dainty, elfin, small, little, smallish, wee, diminutive, little, miniature.

petition *n.* **1.** *The petition for a new traffic light had 500 names:* formal request, appeal, entreaty, plea; proposal, suit, solicitation; application, requisition; prayer, supplication, invocation, beseechment, orison; imploring. —*v.* **2.** *The condemned man petitioned the governor* *for clemency:* ask, beg, sue, beseech, entreat, call upon, appeal to, apply to, request of, plead with, urge, press, seek; pray, supplicate, invoke.

petrified *adj.* **1.** *After millenniums of absorbing minerals from water, the trees became petrified:* stony, rocklike, hard as a rock, solidified, turned to stone; hard, hardened, dense, solid. **2.** *She stood there, petrified with fear:* paralyzed, frozen, immobilized, transfixed, stupefied, dumbstruck, dumbfounded, numb, numbed, benumbed, dazed, shocked, terror-stricken, spellbound, *Informal* scared stiff.

petrify *v.* **1.** *We were petrified with fear:* freeze, chill, paralyze, benumb, daze, dumbfound, immobilize, numb, stun, stupefy, transfix, *Informal* scare silly, scare stiff **2.** *The clay had petrified:* harden, solidify, set, calcify, fossilize.

petty *adj.* **1.** *Don't bother the supervisor with such petty matters:* trivial, trifling, insignificant, unimportant, inconsequential, minor, paltry, slight, small, picayune, piddling, niggling, flimsy, inconsiderable. **2.** *It was petty of her not to accept the apology:* small-minded, narrow-minded, mean, ignoble, shabby, ungenerous. **—Ant.** 1 important, major, consequential, significant, momentous, considerable. 2 broad-minded, large-hearted, magnanimous, generous, tolerant.

petulance *n.* petulancy, irritability, peevishness, fretfulness, pettishness, testiness, waspishness.

petulant *adj.* *When he doesn't get his way, he can be quite petulant:* peevish, fretful, irritable, cross, snappish, sullen, sulky, surly, grumpy, grouchy, testy, huffy, pettish, irascible, fractious, gruff, cantankerous, sour, crotchety, crabbed, bearish, ungracious, ill-natured, ill-tempered, out of sorts, thin-skinned, touchy, tetchy, uncivil; faultfinding, complaining, contentious, quarrelsome. **—Ant.** agreeable, pleasant, good-natured, cheerful, happy, smiling, complaisant, cooperative, content, gracious, amenable.

phantasm *n.* *Scrooge was terrified by the phantasm of Christmas Past:* phantom, ghost, apparition, vision, specter, spirit, shade, incubus, succubus; figment, illusion, fantasy; delusion, mirage.

phantom *n.* *Had he actually seen his long-lost brother in the fog, or was it only a phantom?:* apparition, specter, spirit, ghost, wraith, phantasm, phantasmagoria, dream, mirage, chimera, figment of the imagination, hallucination, illusion, vision.

phase *n.* **1.** *The disease was discovered in an early phase:* stage, condition, period, degree, level, step, development, point of development, juncture. **2.** *Examine every phase of the problem:* aspect, facet, feature, side, angle, slant, circumstance, view, viewpoint, attitude, guise, appearance.

phenomenal *adj.* *John Stuart Mill was a man of phenomenal intelligence:* extraordinary, exceptional, outstanding, remarkable, superior, super, surpassing, uncommon, unusual, unprecedented, unparalleled, stupendous, prodigious, unique, singular, unheard-of, incredible, miraculous, marvelous, spectacular, fantastic, sensa-

tional, astonishing, amazing, overwhelming. **—Ant.** ordinary, common, unexceptional, usual, everyday, routine, normal, standard, average, familiar, customary, accustomed.

phenomenon *n.* **1.** *Snow is a phenomenon of winter:* occurrence, happening, visible fact, natural event, part of existence, contingency, thing, actuality, fact of life, proceeding, occasion, incident, episode. **2.** *Beethoven was a phenomenon among musicians:* rarity, marvel, miracle, wonder, remarkable person, exceptional thing, exception, singularity, sensation, nonpareil, curiosity.

philanderer *n.* *Every girl in the office knew he was a philanderer:* trifler, Don Juan, flirt, gallant, rake, libertine, womanizer, lothario, adulterer, lady-killer, rakehell, lecher, dallier, woman-chaser, wanton; *Slang* swinger, rip, wolf, lover boy, tomcat.

philanthropic also **philanthropical** *adj.* *The orphanage is just one of her philanthropic causes:* charitable, almsgiving, eleemosynary, benevolent, humanitarian, generous, liberal, bounteous, magnanimous, munificent, beneficent. **—Ant.** misanthropic; miserly, niggardly.

philanthropist *n.* *Andrew Carnegie was a true philanthropist, giving away millions to charity:* benefactor of charities, contributor, donor, giver, almsgiver, humanitarian, Good Samaritan, *Slang* do-gooder. **—Ant.** misanthrope; miser, niggard, pinchpenny.

philanthropy *n.* *Many organizations benefited from the wealthy man's philanthropy:* charity, charitableness, humanitarianism, almsgiving, benevolence, beneficence, largeheartedness, generosity, munificence, unselfishness, public-spiritedness, goodness, openhandedness, liberality, bounty.

philistine *n.* **1.** *He's too much of a philistine to patronize the arts:* lowbrow, cultural ignoramus, barbarian, savage, yahoo; bourgeois, conformist, conventionalist, Babbitt. **—***adj.* **2.** *For a college professor he certainly made some philistine remarks:* uncultured, uncultivated, unrefined, uneducated, unenlightened, untutored, unlettered, uninformed, ignorant; lowbrow, bourgeois, conventional, conformist, commonplace, prosaic; anti-intellectual. **—Ant.** 1 intellectual, highbrow; *Slang* egghead.

philosopher *n.* *Plato and Socrates were leading philosophers of ancient Greece:* student of basic truths, seeker of universal laws; seeker of wisdom, truth seeker, wise man, sage, savant; logician, rationalist, reasoner, philosophizer, metaphysician, thinker, dialectician, theorizer.

philosophic also **philosophical** *adj.* **1.** *The problem demands a philosophic approach:* reasonable, logical, rational, judicious, thoughtful, sagacious; theorizing, theoretical, abstract, learned, erudite. **2.** *She's very philosophical about all her bad luck:* stoic, stoical, resigned, complacent, fatalistic, patient, impassive, unemotional, self-restrained, composed, calm, serene, tranquil, imperturbed, unruffled, unexcited, quiet. **—Ant.** 1 illogical, irrational, thoughtless, careless, ill-considered; scientific, practical, factual, pragmatic. 2 emotional, excited, impulsive, hotheaded, rash, reckless, unrestrained; upset, perturbed, distraught.

philosophy n. **1.** *The judge's hobby is philosophy:* study of basic truths, search for universal laws, seeking after wisdom, love of wisdom; logic, rationalism, reason, reasoning, thought, thinking, philosophizing, theorizing, ideas; esthetics, metaphysics. **2.** *The book analyzes the philosophy of Bertrand Russell. My philosophy is live and let live:* system of beliefs, beliefs, convictions, conception, doctrine, basic idea, principle; opinion, view, viewpoint. **3.** *Accept bad news with philosophy:* stoicism, resignation, fatalism, patience, complacency, forbearance, restraint, impassivity, composure, calm, serenity, imperturbability, tranquillity.

phlegmatic adj. *Admiral Togo was always phlegmatic in the face of danger:* indifferent, apathetic, nonchalant, unemotional, unimpassioned, undemonstrative, unresponsive, imperturbable, unconcerned, unexcitable, cool, calm, serene, tranquil, impassive, stoical; spiritless, listless, languid, lethargic, sluggish, dull, passive, unfeeling, insensitive. **—Ant.** emotional, passionate, excited; active, demonstrative, alert, lively, animated, energetic, interested.

phobia n. *She has a phobia about heights:* unreasonable fear, terror, horror, dread, aversion, loathing, apprehension, overwhelming anxiety; *Slang* bugbear, bugaboo. **—Ant.** love, liking, fondness, fancy, bent, relish, penchant, inclination, predilection.

phonograph n. *Put a record on the phonograph and let's have some music:* record player, hi-fi, *Informal* phono, *British* gramophone; (*variously*) stereo, hi-fi; (*trademark*) Victrola.

phony or **phoney** adj. **1.** *The counterfeiter made phony ten-dollar bills:* not genuine, fake, counterfeit, forged, sham, spurious, bogus, specious, mock, pretended; artificial, imitation, synthetic, false, fraudulent, deceptive, trick, unreal, pseudo, unauthentic, untrue. *—n.* **2.** *He says he's a doctor, but I'm sure he's a phony. This painting isn't a Rembrandt, it's a phony:* fake, sham, fraud, counterfeit, imitation, make-believe, synthetic, fraud, hoax, forgery. **—Ant.** 1 real, authentic, genuine, original, bona fide, true. 2 the genuine article, *Slang* the real McCoy.

phrase n. **1.** *The speaker certainly has a way with a phrase:* expression, words, turn of phrase, word group, construction, utterance, remark, locution. **2.** *In the words of the old phrase, "Time's a-wasting":* figure of speech, saying, expression, truism, proverb, maxim, aphorism, cliché, platitude, banality, colloquialism, dictum; idiom, locution. *—v.* **3.** *The way he phrased the question I couldn't understand it:* express, word, put into words, find words, couch, put, state, declare, impart; say, voice, utter, enunciate, communicate, verbalize, articulate.

phraseology n. *His phraseology was highly distinctive:* diction, expression, style, language.

physical adj. **1.** *No one knows how large the physical universe is:* material, existing, existent, natural, tangible, substantive, palpable, solid, concrete, real, actual, apparent, external, essential. **2.** *He renounced the physical world and devoted himself to spiritual contemplation:* of the body, bodily, corporeal, corporal, human, living, fleshly, animal, carnal, sensual. **—Ant.** 1 nonmaterial, intangible. 2 spiritual, moral; mental, intellectual.

physician n. *You'd better see a physician about that cough:* doctor, M.D., medical doctor; medical examiner, GP, general practitioner, surgeon, specialist; *Slang* medic, medico, medicine man, doc, pill peddler, sawbones.

physiognomy n. *A person's physiognomy was formerly thought to reveal his character:* features, outward appearance, countenance, visage, face; shape, profile, outline, contour, silhouette, configuration, façade.

physique n. *He had a magnificent physique:* build, body, anatomy, constitution, figure, form, frame, muscles.

picaresque adj. *Don Quixote was a picaresque hero of Spanish fiction:* roguish, waggish, prankish, rascally, scampish, devilish, roistering, raffish, mischief-loving; adventuresome, daring, foolhardy.

picayune also **picayunish** adj. *Why quarrel over such a picayune matter?:* trifling, trivial, petty, paltry, insignificant, unimportant, inconsequential, inconsiderable, slight, measly, piddling, niggling, small, little, dinky, nugatory, flimsy.

pick v. **1.** *It took her an hour to pick a dress that suited her:* select, choose, decide upon, settle upon, single out, fix upon, elect, opt for. **2.** *Will you pick some flowers for the dinner table?:* pluck, pull off, pull out, detach, crop, cut; gather, collect, harvest. *—n.* **3.** *This pup was the pick of the litter:* choice, the best, prize, preference, favored one, elect, elite, flower, cream, *French* crème de la crème. **—Ant.** 1 reject, refuse, decline, spurn, scorn, disclaim, repudiate. 3 the worst, the booby prize.

picket n. **1.** *One of the pickets in the fence was loose:* stake, palisade, pale, pointed stick, paling; post, upright, stanchion; tether, restraint. **2.** *The picket warned the sleeping troops that the enemy was creeping near:* forward lookout, lookout, sentinel, watch, sentry, guard, patrol. **3.** *The pickets prevented nonstriking workers from entering the factory:* striker, protester, boycotter, blockader. *—v.* **4.** *A white fence picketed the yard on three sides:* enclose, fence, corral, pen in, shut in, wall in, hedge in, hem in; restrict, restrain. **5.** *The workers voted to picket the plant:* demonstrate against; (*loosely*) strike, walk out, go out, boycott, blockade.

pickle n. **1.** *Would you like a pickle with that sandwich?:* pickled cucumber, cucumber pickle; (*variously*) sweet pickle, dill pickle, gherkin, sour pickle, kosher dill, mixed pickle, bread-and-butter pickle, mustard pickle. **2.** *Informal If the car runs out of gas on this lonely road, we'll be in a pickle:* predicament, difficulty, tight spot, plight, jam, quandary, fix, mess, difficult position, extremity, emergency, crisis, dilemma, scrape; *Slang* hot water, pretty pickle, pretty pass, fine kettle of fish. —*v.* **3.** *Grandmother used to pickle peaches:* preserve in brine, preserve in vinegar, corn; treat with diluted acid.

picky *adj.* *She was picky about what she ate:* fussy, finicky, particular, fastidious, choosy; critical, faultfinding, pernickety, captious, carping.

picture *n.* **1.** *This is a picture of the view from our hotel window:* representation, delineation, portrayal, illustration; drawing, painting, sketch, study, etching; photograph, photo, snapshot; tintype, daguerreotype. **2.** *There's a good picture at the local movie house:* motion picture, moving picture, film, *Informal* movie, *Slang* flick, *British* cinema. **3.** *She is the picture of her mother as a girl:* likeness, image, duplicate, copy, facsimile, double; *Slang* dead ringer, spitting image, carbon copy. **4.** *He was the picture of health:* perfect example, model, paragon, mirror, exemplification, personification, essence, embodiment. —*v.* **5.** *The painter pictured the general sitting on a horse:* portray, represent, depict, illustrate, feature, delineate; paint, draw, sketch; photograph. **6.** *Can't you just picture Mother on a roller coaster!:* imagine, see, envision, call to mind, see in the mind, conceive of, fancy, believe.

picturesque *adj.* *On national holidays the Austrian peasants wear picturesque costumes:* quaint, exotic, colorful, striking, distinctive, unusual, interesting, imaginative, pictorial; attractive, charming, beautiful, artistic. —**Ant.** everyday, usual, commonplace, uninteresting, drab, dull, flat, tame, insipid; unattractive, inartistic.

piddling *adj.* *The clerk got a piddling raise of $2 a week:* trifling, trivial, insignificant, inconsequential, unimportant, picayune, paltry, skimpy, slight, measly, modest, niggardly, small, little, petty, puny, flimsy.

piebald *adj.* *The piebald horse had patches of white, brown, and black:* dappled, mottled, spotted, speckled, flecked; variegated, many-colored, particolored, motley, multicolored, varicolored, many-hued.

piece *n.* **1.** *Cook the beans with a piece of salt pork. The glass broke into pieces:* portion, quantity, amount, share, slice, cut, chunk, hunk, lump; pat, blob, bit, fraction, scrap; fragment, shard, part, shred, sliver; swatch, length, cutting, paring; component, member, section, segment, division. **2.** *This is a foul piece of treachery. This chair is an antique piece. The workers are paid by the piece:* instance, example, case, specimen, sample; unit, item, article, member, thing, entity. **3.** *The pianist played a piece by Chopin. The dramatist is writing a new piece for the theater. Did you read this piece in today's paper?:* selection, composition, work, creation, study; play, drama, sketch; story, article, essay, review, item. —*v.* **4.** *Do you think you can piece this torn curtain?:* piece together; patch, patch up, mend, repair, restore, fix. —**Ant.** 1 all, everything, total, sum total, entire amount, entirety, the whole; nothing, none, zero, naught, nullity. 4 tear, break, pierce, crack, shred.

piecemeal *adv.* **1.** *The stamp collection was gathered piecemeal:* gradually, bit by bit, inchwise, by degrees. **2.** *They undertook the tasks piecemeal:* separately, fractionally, disjointedly, spasmodically.

pier *n.* *The boat was tied up at the pier:* dock, jetty, wharf, berth, landing, levee, piling, quay, slip.

pierce *v.* **1.** *The nail completely pierced the tire:* perforate, puncture, penetrate, make a hole in, bore through, cut through, run through, drill, pass through; stick, prick, stab, spear, spike, lance, impale. **2.** *The strong soap pierced my skin. Her angry words pierced everyone:* sting, hurt, pain; cut, wound; affront, grieve, distress. —**Ant.** 1 glance off; patch, block, stop up. 2 soothe, calm, quiet; please, delight, gladden, cheer, gratify.

piercing *adj.* **1.** *We heard her piercing voice a block away:* shrill, grating, screeching, shrieking, strident; loud, earsplitting, ear-shattering, deafening. **2.** *She fixed him with a piercing glance. What a piercing sound!:* sharp, keen, penetrating, searching, probing; biting, cutting, intense, fierce, furious, raw, bitter, cruel, caustic; angry, painful, hurtful, agonizing, torturous, excruciating. —**Ant.** 1, 2 calm, soothing. 1 mellifluous, melodic; quiet, low. 2 vague, easy; pleasant, delightful, cheering, gratifying.

piety *n.* *The old woman expressed her piety by attending church daily:* piousness, religiousness, devoutness, devotion, godliness; reverence, respect, loyalty, dutifulness, humility; religiosity. —**Ant.** impiety, sacrilege, ungodliness, blasphemy, irreverence; disrespect, disloyalty, infidelity.

pig *n.* **1.** *The farm raises cows, chickens, and pigs:* small hog, swine, porker, (*male*) boar, (*female*) sow; (*young*) shoat, piglet, suckling pig, *Informal* piggy. **2.** *Informal We ate so much we made pigs of ourselves:* glutton, ravenous eater, large eater, guzzler, gourmand, gormandizer; *Slang* hog, chowhound.

pigheaded *adj.* *He's so pigheaded you can't reason with him:* stubborn, obstinate, wrongheaded, bullheaded, unyielding, unbending, inflexible, opinionated, obdurate, deaf to advice, blind to reason, mulish, dogged; willful, insistent, contrary, perverse, recalcitrant, refractory. —**Ant.** complaisant, flexible, open-minded, agreeable, tractable, docile, amiable, cooperative, obliging.

pigment *n.* *Add some red pigment to give the paint a pinkish cast:* color, coloring, coloring matter, tint, dye, dyestuff.

pike[1] *n.* *The king's sentry barred the doorway with his pike:* lance, bill, halberd, poleax, spear, spike, assegai; javelin; harpoon.

pike[2] *n.* *Grandfather used to call the highway the pike:* turnpike, toll road; superhighway, throughway, thruway, expressway, speedway, freeway, parkway, highway, hard road, interstate, *British* King's (or Queen's) highway, *German* autobahn. —**Ant.** secondary road, back road, country road.

piker *n.* *He's a piker when it comes to contrib-*

uting to charity: cheapskate, pinchpenny, penny pincher, tightwad, skinflint, miser; trifler, petty person, niggard. —**Ant.** big spender, spendthrift, squanderer.

pile[1] *n.* **1.** *A pile of dirty clothes lay by the washing machine. He made a pile of money in the stock market:* heap, stack, mass, batch, pyramid, mound; accumulation, collection, assortment, amassment, aggregation, hoard, store; large amount, quantity, profusion, abundance. —*v.* **2.** *Pile the leaves in the corner of the yard:* heap, mass, amass, stack, assemble; accumulate, collect, gather, agglomerate. —**Ant.** 2 scatter, disperse, strew, spread, broadcast.

pile[2] *n.* *The carpet has a soft, thick pile:* nap, shag, fluff; surface, plush, fleece, grain, warp, fibrousness.

pile[3] *n.* *Piles were driven into the ground to support the building:* piling, support, post, upright, pier, pillar, stanchion; foundation.

pilfer *v.* *He began his life of crime by pilfering pennies from the poor box:* steal, rob, thieve, purloin; plagiarize, pirate; *Slang* boost, hook, lift, pinch, heist, swipe, cop, snitch, finger.

pilgrim *n.* **1.** *The pilgrims approached the shrine:* palmer, crusader. **2.** *He was a pilgrim by temperament:* wayfarer, sojourner, traveler, wanderer.

pilgrimage *n.* **1.** *Devout Muslims must make a pilgrimage to Mecca:* religious journey to a shrine, religious journey, devotional trip, *Islam* hadj, penitential sojourn. **2.** *Sailing alone around the world was quite a pilgrimage:* journey, excursion, trek, long trip, sojourn, voyage; ramble, wandering, roving, roaming, peregrination.

pill *n.* *She took a pill after each meal:* tablet, pellet, capsule, lozenge, medicine.

pillage *v.* **1.** *The barbarians pillaged the town of all its wealth:* plunder, raid, sack, loot, rifle, rob, despoil, strip, fleece, ravage, maraud. —*n.* **2.** *The pillage of the occupying troops amounted to millions:* plunder, loot, booty, spoils, stolen goods, filchings; looting, robbery, plundering, sack, piracy.

pillar *n.* **1.** *The porch is supported by six immense pillars:* column, post, colonnade, upright, support, pile, piling, shaft, stanchion; pilaster, obelisk. **2.** *Father was a pillar of the club for over thirty years:* mainstay, tower of strength, important person, ranking personage, leading light, rock, support, champion; *Slang* VIP, somebody, wheel.

pillory *v.* *The pilloried him in the press:* mock, ridicule, deride, scorn, revile, sneer at, vilify, slur, stigmatize, brand, besmirch, smear, tarnish, blacken, skewer, crucify. —**Ant.** praise, esteem.

pillow *n.* *She put another pillow under her head:* cushion, pad, bolster.

pilot *n.* **1.** *The flying school graduates a hundred pilots a year:* flyer, aviator, airman, aeronaut; *Slang* birdman, sky jockey, fly-boy. **2.** *Samuel Clemens(better known by his pseudonym "Mark Twain")was a Mississippi riverboat pilot:* helmsman, wheelman, steersman, coxswain;

guide, leader. —*v.* **3.** *It's hard to pilot a boat in rough waters. Tourists need a guide to pilot them through the Casbah:* steer, be at the helm of, be at the wheel of, handle the tiller of, keep on course, control, manage, handle, navigate; direct, lead, conduct, escort, guide, accompany.

pimple *n.* *He put ointment on the pimple:* blemish, blackhead, pustule, spot, swelling, whitehead, *Informal* zit.

pin *n.* **1.** *The dressmaker used a pin to fasten the pattern to the cloth:* (variously) straight pin, common pin; safety pin, diaper pin; hatpin; pushpin; tine, skewer, prong; tholepin, dowel. **2.** *Did you see the diamond pin she got for Christmas?:* brooch, clasp, clip, stickpin, breast pin; medal, badge, decoration. —*v.* **3.** *The children played Pin the Tail on the Donkey:* attach with a pin, affix, secure, fasten, clasp. **4.** *The policeman pinned the thief's arms behind him:* pinion; hold fast, hold down; restrain, bind, fasten.

pinch *v.* **1.** *The girl pinched her little brother's arm out of meanness. These shoes pinch my feet:* tweak, squeeze, nip; cramp, crimp, compress, tighten, crush. **2.** *Slang The officer pinched the driver for going through a red light:* arrest, take into custody, apprehend, run in, *Informal* collar, *Slang* bust; nab, catch, grab, capture. **3.** *Slang The thief pinched her pocketbook and ran:* steal, snatch, swipe, snitch, lift, crib, purloin, cop, filch. —*n.* **4.** *The old man gave the boy a playful pinch on the cheek:* tweak, nip, squeeze. **5.** *Add a pinch of salt:* bit, speck, mite, jot, iota, spot, snip, trace, tittle. **6.** *Most North Americans have never felt the pinch of hunger. I'll be glad to help you out in a pinch:* pain, discomfort, hardship, ordeal, trial, affliction, misery, strait, plight; emergency, crisis, predicament, difficulty, exigency, squeeze, clutch, jam, pickle. **7.** *Slang Which policeman made the pinch?:* arrest, collar, capture, *Slang* bust.

pine *v.* **1.** *She pined for her native land:* yearn, long, hanker, sigh, languish; crave, hunger for, thirst after, desire, covet; *Informal* pant for, have a yen for. **2.** *After so much heartbreak she just pined away:* fail in health, decline, weaken, ebb, waste away, languish, wither, wilt, droop, dwindle, flag; die, expire.

pinnacle *n.* **1.** *The mountain climbers reached the pinnacle of the mountain. A writer who wins the Nobel prize has reached the pinnacle of success:* highest point, peak, summit, apex, crest, vertex, zenith, height, top, tiptop, acme, crown, cap. **2.** *The old church is topped with a pinnacle:* spire, steeple, tower; belfry, bell tower, campanile.

pinpoint *n.* **1.** *The hill was just a pinpoint in the distance:* dot, spot, speck, jot, iota. —*v.* **2.** *Engineers are trying to pinpoint the cause of the trouble:* locate exactly, localize, detect precisely, zero in on, home in on; describe precisely, detail, characterize.

pioneer *n.* **1.** *Pioneers from the East settled this region in 1870:* first settler, early immigrant, colonist; frontiersman, explorer. **2.** *Henry Ford was a pioneer in the auto industry:* leader, trailblazer, forerunner, pathfinder, innovator, developer, founder, founding father, father, establisher; predecessor, antecedent, precursor; herald, harbinger. —*v.* **3.** *The Wright brothers pioneered in early aviation:* be a leader, blaze the trail, lead the way, show the way, start, establish, found, discover, invent, create, develop.

pious *adj.* **1.** *His parents were pious churchgoers:* devout, religious, dedicated, faithful, reverent, reverential, worshipful; godly, spiritual, holy, divine, saintly, sainted. **2.** *The revivalist's pious statement that the meek shall inherit the earth was felt by some to be hypocritical:* sanctimonious, holier-than-thou, unctuous, pietistic, self-righteous, rationalizing; hypocritical, insincere. —**Ant.** 1 impious, irreverent, irreligious, ungodly, godless, unholy. 2 humble, meek; sincere, genuine.

pipe *n.* **1.** *The pipe behind the stove is for the gas:* tube, conduit; conveyor; main, duct, conductor. —*v.* **2.** *The birds began piping at daybreak:* whistle, sing, cheep, peep, trill, warble, twitter, chirp, tweet; play a flute, play a bagpipe.

piquant *adj.* **1.** *In Mexico, turkey is served with a piquant sauce:* pungent, spicy, sharp, tangy, zesty, savory, highly seasoned, hot, peppery, strong-flavored; bitter, acid, biting, stinging, piercing, mordant. **2.** *The play sparkled with piquant dialogue:* lively, peppy, sharp, zesty, vigorous, spirited, scintillating, sparkling, clever, bright, stimulating, animated, rousing, interesting, provocative, trenchant, incisive; racy, salty, spicy, peppery. —**Ant.** 1 bland, mild. 2 banal, inane, insipid, tame, jejune, uninteresting, boring, dull.

pique *v.* **1.** *It always piques him not to be consulted:* displease, offend, affront, hurt one's feelings, annoy, irritate, vex, irk, gall, nettle, incense, provoke, exasperate, disquiet, perturb; *Informal* put one's back up, miff, peeve, put one's nose out of joint. **2.** *The book piqued my interest:* arouse, kindle, stimulate, rouse, provoke, excite, stir, quicken, spur, goad. —*n.* **3.** *I saw your pique when he made that remark:* resentment, hurt feelings, displeasure, annoyance, irritation, vexation, exasperation, indignation, ire, umbrage, discomfort; grudge, snit, spite, malice, vindictiveness, ill feelings; embarrassment, humiliation, mortification. —**Ant.** 1 please, delight, gratify, satisfy, compliment. 2 deaden, dull, kill, quench.

pirate *n.* *Pirates ransacked the vessel:* plunderer, freebooter, picaroon, buccaneer, corsair.

pit[1] *n.* **1.** *Dig a pit and bury the garbage. The wood is full of pits and needs sanding:* hole, hollow, hole in the ground, cavity, crater, depression; gully, trough; indentation, gouge, concavity, furrow, dent, dimple, notch, dip, pock; scar, pockmark. —*v.* **2.** *The metal trivets are pitting the table:* gouge, dent, indent, nick, notch, pock, scratch, scar. **3.** *The managers want to pit the champion against an unknown:* match, set against, oppose, put in competition; contrast, juxtapose. —**Ant.** 1 mound, lump, bump, protuberance.

pit[2] *n.* *This type of cherry has a very small pit:* seed, stone, kernel, nut.

pitch *v.* **1.** *The Boy Scouts pitched their tent near the stream:* set up, raise, erect; set, place, fix, settle, plant, establish, locate, station. **2.** *He pitched the ball with a slight curve:* throw, hurl, heave, fling, cast, toss, lob, chuck, sling, fire, propel, shy, let fly. **3.** *The fisherman lost his balance and pitched into the lake:* fall headlong, fall headfirst, fall, topple, tumble. **4.** *The boat pitched in the storm:* rock from front to back, toss, plunge, lurch, bob, shake, jolt, jerk, oscillate, undulate. —*n.* **5.** *The roof has a steep pitch:* slant, slope, incline, declivity, grade, cant, angle. **6.** *The batter hit the pitch into left field:* throw, delivery, heave, toss, lob, cast, fling, chuck. **7.** *Her voice has a very high pitch:* tone, sound; harmonic, speed of vibration. **8.** *The children were in a high pitch of excitement:* level, degree, point; height, peak, apex, summit, zenith, pinnacle, crown, top. **9.** *The pitch of the ship threw the passengers off balance:* forward plunge, headlong fall, dip, rocking, lurch, lurching, bobbing, oscillation, undulation.

piteous *adj.* *The sound was like the piteous cry of a lost child:* pitiable, pitiful, sad, poignant, moving, heart-rending, deplorable, heartbreaking, distressing, woeful, pathetic, touching, affecting. —**Ant.** cheering, heart-warming, delightful, joyous.

pitfall *n.* *We warned her about the pitfalls of pursuing a career in politics:* hazard, risk, danger, peril, snare, quagmire, quicksand, stumbling block, trap, springe, booby trap, ambush.

pithy *adj.* *The Gettysburg Address is short and pithy:* to the point, meaningful, cogent, forceful, effective, expressive, trenchant; concise, terse, succinct, concentrated. —**Ant.** diffuse, vague; wordy, verbose, rambling, turgid.

pitiful *adj.* **1.** *The pitiful sobs of the child softened our hearts:* pitiable, piteous, arousing pity, deserving pity, heartrending, heartbreaking, moving, touching, poignant, pathetic; sad, lamentable, distressing, mournful, plaintive, miserable, forlorn, doleful. **2.** *The thief made a pitiful attempt to justify the crime. The movie wasn't just bad, it was pitiful!:* contemptible, deserving of scorn, miserable, despicable, pitiable, wretched, worthless, shabby, poor, sorry, abject, measly, insignificant, paltry, dreadful, abominable, god-awful. —**Ant.** 1 happy, cheerful, merry, glad, joyous, joyful. 2 commendable, praiseworthy, laudable; noble, lofty, sublime, exalted, dignified, great, grand, glorious; delightful, endearing, lovable, charming.

pitiless *adj.* *The tyrant was pitiless toward his subjects:* merciless, heartless, without pity, inhuman, unmerciful, unpitying, unsparing, hardhearted, cold-blooded, relentless, unrelenting, ruthless, cruel, brutal; unmoved, unresponsive, indifferent, untouched, insensitive, uncaring, implacable. —**Ant.** merciful, sparing, relenting, softhearted, compassionate, benign, kind; concerned, caring, responsive, touched.

pittance *n.* *He puts most of his money in the bank and tries to live on a mere pittance:* small amount, trifle, modicum, minimum, little, smidgen, crumb, mite; trifling sum, small allowance, minimal wage.

pity n. **1.** *The sad story aroused everyone's pity. It's a pity he didn't finish college:* sympathy, compassion, commiseration, condolence; cause for sorrow, regret, sad thing, shame; *Informal* crying shame. **2.** *The tyrant showed no pity:* mercy, charity, clemency, leniency, kindliness, humanity, tenderness, softheartedness, indulgence, forbearance, lenity, magnanimity. —v. **3.** *I pity the flood victims:* feel sorry for, have compassion for, commiserate with, sympathize with, lament, feel for, bleed for, weep for. —**Ant.** 1 anger, rage, wrath, fury; scorn, disdain, indifference, apathy, disinterest. 2 cruelty, brutality, hardheartedness, harshness, inhumanity, mercilessness, pitilessness, ruthlessness; severity.

pivot n. **1.** *The hands of the watch rotate on a pivot:* pin or shaft about which something turns; *(loosely)* axis, axle, swivel, hinge, fulcrum. —v. **2.** *The gyroscope pivoted on its stand:* rotate, revolve, wheel, swivel, circle, spin, twirl, turn, swing around, whirl, pirouette. **3.** *The passage of the bill pivots on the governor's support:* depend, hang, rely, be contingent on, hinge on, revolve around, turn, focus, center, be in the hands of.

pivotal adj. *The new job was offered him at a pivotal point in his career:* decisive, crucial, critical, vital, determining, climactic.

placate v. *No one can placate him when he's angry:* calm, soothe, pacify, quiet, lull, mollify, assuage, alleviate; appease, propitiate, win over, conciliate.

place n. **1.** *Is there any place to put this bowl of flowers? Beware of that slick place on the sidewalk:* space, spot, niche, point; site, location, position, whereabouts, *Law* venue. **2.** *There's a place on Main Street that has great hamburgers:* establishment, concern, business, store, shop, company, firm. **3.** *He was given an important place in the incoming government:* position, situation, post, appointment, job, office, niche, berth, station, commission; function, standing, duty, rank. **4.** *We're having a party at my place. He retired to a little place in the country:* residence, home, abode, house, dwelling, domicile, habitation, lodgings, quarters, premises, office, building, *Informal* digs; farm, ranch, plot, land, property. **5.** *New York's a nice place to visit. This is the place where the storm hit:* city, town, village; state, county, township, borough, district, neighborhood, vicinity, area, province, region, locality, locale, zone, quarter; country, territory. —v. **6.** *Place the chair in that corner:* put, set, rest, stand, situate, position, plant, deposit, settle, array, locate, ensconce, install; fix, affix, attach; house, lodge, harbor, shelter. **7.** *The employment agency placed her with an insurance firm:* get a job for, find hire, find work for, appoint, assign, install, commission, invest. **8.** *I remember her name but can't place her face:* identify, remember, recognize, classify. —**Ant.** 6 remove, take away, dislodge, dislocate; detach, take off.

placid adj. *The chalet overlooks a placid mountain lake. She has an amazingly placid disposition:* calm, quiet, tranquil, peaceful, pacific, serene, restful; untroubled, unruffled, smooth, undisturbed, collected, composed, self-possessed, poised, undemonstrative, unexcited, unexcitable, imperturbable; gentle, mild. —**Ant.** turbulent, agitated, rough; excitable, excited, tempestuous, emotional, passionate, impassioned, impulsive, disturbed, perturbed.

plagiarism n. *He accused her of plagiarism:* borrowing, copying, appropriation, cribbing, lifting, infringement, literary theft, piracy.

plague n. **1.** *In the 14th century the plague killed one-third of the population of Europe:* bubonic plague, Black Death; widespread epidemic, pandemic, fatal epidemic, pestilence; contagious disease, epidemic disease, *French* peste. **2.** *The plague of drought swept over the land:* affliction, scourge, visitation, calamity, hardship, misery, agony, suffering, woe, trouble, burden; evil, curse, bane, blight, cancer. —v. **3.** *The mistake plagued him for years:* torment, trouble, distress, worry, disquiet, perturb, persecute, harass, disturb, bother, vex, irk, peeve, nettle, gall, harry, chafe, fret, badger; pain, aggrieve, afflict, embarrass, haunt, prey on one's mind; try the patience of, get on one's nerves, go against the grain.

plain adj. **1.** *The figures aren't plain enough to read:* clear, distinct, legible, discernible, conspicuous, obvious, prominent, visible, apparent, glaring, pronounced, striking, outstanding, vivid, clear-cut, well-defined, well-marked, manifest, palpable. **2.** *Please rephrase the question in plain English:* easily understood, simple, clear, straightforward, direct, explicit, specific, unambiguous, unmistakable, understandable, comprehensible, unequivocal. **3.** *The plain truth is that he doesn't like you:* honest, frank, blunt, candid, open, sincere, forthright, straight, undisguised, undiluted, naked, bald, bare, unembellished, unvarnished, unadorned; plain-spoken, outspoken, unreserved. **4.** *Most of her relations are just plain folk. The hostess wore a plain blue dress:* simple, unaffected, unpretentious, unassuming; modest, everyday, ordinary, average, common, matter-of-fact; obscure, undistinguished, commonplace; unadorned, undecorated, unornamented, ungarnished, without frills. **5.** *The girl had a good figure but a plain face:* homely, not beautiful, unhandsome, unattractive, unlovely, uncomely, having plain features, not striking. —n. **6.** *The family crossed the plains in a covered wagon in 1860:* prairie, grassland, tableland, plateau, open country. —**Ant.** 1 indistinct, vague, blurred, illegible, indiscernible, inconspicuous; hidden, concealed. 2 obscure, abstruse, complex, difficult, indirect, ambiguous, incomprehensible; affected, pretentious. 3 deceptive, evasive, disguised, veiled, indirect. 4 affected, pretentious, assuming, snobbish; sophisticated, worldly, distinguished; decorated, ornamented, adorned, fancy, frilly. 5 beautiful, gorgeous, good-looking, attractive, comely, handsome.

plainly adv. **1.** Although wealthy, she dresses very plainly: simply, unpretentiously, unaffectedly, unassumingly, modestly, ordinarily; without adornment, without ornamentation. **2.** It's plainly the newest house on the block: clearly, obviously, conspicuously, prominently, markedly, visibly, strikingly, vividly, discernibly, manifestly, apparently, undeniably, unquestionably, undoubtedly, doubtless, definitely, without doubt, beyond doubt. **3.** She stated plainly that she didn't want to go: clearly, distinctly, explicitly, directly, unmistakably, unambiguously, comprehensibly, unequivocally, honestly, frankly, bluntly, candidly, openly, baldly, positively.

plain-spoken adj. He was a clean-cut plain-spoken young man: frank, direct, open, forthright, genuine, sincere, candid, plain, honest, straight, open-faced, aboveboard, straight-out.

plaint n. It's the same plaint she's had for 40 years: complaint, grievance, resentment, grudge, objection, gripe, grouse, grumble, regret, Slang beef, squawk; reproach, accusation, charge, reproof, remonstrance; lament, cry, wail, moan, sob.

plaintive adj. The widow gave a plaintive wail at the graveside: sad, mournful, sorrowful, lamenting, moaning, melancholy, doleful, dolorous, grievous, woebegone, tearful, wretched, heartrending, rueful, lugubrious, pathetic, piteous, pitiful.

plan n. **1.** The mayor has a plan for renewing the business district. The builder must follow the architect's plan: scheme, program, proposal, suggestion, idea, conception, proposition, procedure, method, way, strategy, stratagem; design, blueprint, sketch, map, diagram. —v. **2.** The entertainment committee will plan the dance: organize, devise, make arrangements, make preparations, conceive, think out, plot, contrive, prepare, fabricate, design; form, frame, outline, shape; block out, lay out, project, map out, diagram. **3.** Do you plan to stay late?: intend, aim, purpose, propose.

plane n. **1.** The roof was a perfect plane: flat surface, level surface. **2.** The discussion was on a high plane: level, elevation, standing, condition, position, status, station, degree. **3.** The plane took off from the airport at noon: airplane, aircraft; jet, Slang bird. —adj. **4.** The surface must be completely plane: flat, level, regular, plumb.

plant n. **1.** Living things are either animal, mineral, or plant. Are these plants tomatoes or beans?: vegetation, flora, herbage; (variously) tree, flower, bush, shrub, vine, herb, weed, wort, grass, moss, algae, fungi; seedling, slip, vegetable. **2.** The workers at the plant belong to the union: factory, shop, works, yard, mill, foundry; business, establishment. —v. **3.** Don't plant the flowers before mid-April: put in the ground, sow seed, broadcast, scatter, set in, set out; transplant. **4.** A good teacher plants the love of learning in students: implant, instill, engender, inculcate, infuse, inspire, propagate, establish, cultivate, foster, sow the seeds of.

plaster n. **1.** The painter will fill those holes with plaster before painting the wall: pasty mixture of gypsum or lime, sand, and water; calcined gypsum, grout, stucco, spackle, powdered gypsum; plaster of paris. —v. **2.** Will it take long to plaster the ceiling? The boy plastered the bread with butter: cover with plaster; coat, smear, spread thickly, overlay, lather, daub, bedaub.

plastic adj. **1.** Clay is a very plastic substance: capable of being molded, easily molded, shapable, formable, pliable, pliant, ductile, malleable, flexible, tractable, yielding, elastic, supple, soft. —n. **2.** Is this real leather or plastic?: moldable substance; synthetic organic compound. —**Ant.** 1 hard, rigid, stiff, inflexible, inelastic.

plate n. **1.** Put the plates in the dishwasher: dish; serving dish, platter, saucer. **2.** Stay for lunch, and I'll give you a plate of stew: serving, helping, platter, platterful, portion, dish.

plateau n. The ranch is in the middle of a large plateau: elevated plain, tableland, table, mesa; highland, upland. —**Ant.** valley, ravine; gulch, gully, savanna, swamp, lowland.

platform n. **1.** The mayor got up on the platform and welcomed us: speaker's platform, stage, stand, rostrum, dais, pulpit, podium. **2.** The candidate ran on a platform of better housing and equal rights for all: program, policy, plan, plank, set of principles, tenets, creed, goal; campaign promises.

plating n. The ship had heavy plating: plate, cladding.

platitude n. The speech was dull and full of platitudes: trite remark, stereotyped expression, cliché, banality, commonplace, truism, hackneyed saying, old saw, saw, threadbare phrase, Slang chestnut, bromide, old familiar tune, same old thing.

platonic adj. The platonic friendship lasted a lifetime: idealistic, ideal, spiritual, intellectual, nonphysical.

platoon n. The lieutenant was put in charge of an infantry platoon. The quarterback is the star of the team's offensive platoon: two or more squads; (loosely) unit, detachment, group, force, team, crew, corps, band, body.

plaudit n. Usually **plaudits** The play won the plaudits of the critics: praise, approval, acclaim, commendation, approbation, kudos, compliment, rave, bouquet; applause, ovation, cheer, cheering, hurrah, hallelujah, huzzah. —**Ant.** condemnation, jeer, taunt, hoot, Slang brickbat, rap, knock, slam, dig; boo, hiss, raspberry, Bronx cheer.

plausible adj. Did you find the ending of the story plausible?: believable, probable, credible, convincing, likely, persuasive, reasonable, rational, tenable, feasible, conceivable, possible, justifiable, acceptable, logical, sound, sensible, valid. —**Ant.** unbelievable, improbable, incredible, unlikely, implausible, unreasonable, inconceivable, impossible, illogical.

play n. **1.** Eugene O'Neill wrote several plays about the sea: drama, stage play, dramatic piece, dramatic performance; (variously) comedy, tragedy, farce, melodrama; show, spectacle, extravaganza, pageant, entertainment. **2.** *All work and no play makes Jack a dull boy:* amusement, recreation, entertainment, diversion, fun, merrymaking, pleasure, enjoyment; caper, romp, lark, gambol, frolic, jest, sport. **3.** *There's too much play between the door and the frame:* free motion, freedom of movement, swing, sweep; room, space, elbowroom, leeway. —*v.* **4.** *The children play indoors when it rains:* engage in games, amuse oneself, entertain oneself, divert oneself, have fun, make merry, enjoy oneself, gambol, romp, revel, frisk, frolic, sport, cavort, caper, skylark, antic, disport, while away the time; trifle, toy. **5.** *The teams will play each other Saturday. He played basketball in college:* contend against, compete with, vie with, perform in a game; participate in a sport, take part, be on a team. **6.** *Can you play the piano? Who's going to play Lady Macbeth?:* perform on, perform; act, act out, act the part of, take the part of, impersonate, personify, enact, represent.

playboy *n. The spoiled son grew into a playboy:* pleasure seeker, nightclub habitué, party goer, party boy, good-time Charlie, profligate, hedonist, jet-setter; rake, lecher, womanizer, ladykiller, ladies' man, Romeo, Lothario, Casanova, Don Juan, *Slang* wolf, swinger, sheik. —**Ant.** ascetic, monk, puritan; hermit, recluse.

player *n.* **1.** *The boy wants to be a baseball player when he grows up. Hide-and-seek can be played by as many players as one wants:* team member, performer, athlete, jock; participant, contender, competitor, contestant, opponent, antagonist, adversary, gamester. **2.** *The cast of players included several local actors:* actor, actress, thespian, trouper, mummer, mime, performer, entertainer.

playful *adj. Kittens are very playful. It was just a playful remark:* full of play, frolicsome, frisky, lively, rollicking, coltish, sprightly, sportive; not serious, amusing, jesting, humorous, mirthful, capricious, waggish, impish, prankish, funloving, lighthearted. —**Ant.** sedate, serious, somber, grave, morose, despondent, gloomy, glum.

plaything *n. The innocent plaything amused them:* bauble, doll, pastime, toy, trifle, trinket, amusement.

playwright *n. The play is the work of an outstanding playwright:* dramatist, dramaturgist, author, dramaturge, dramatic poet, dramatizer, melodramatist; librettist, play doctor; scriptwriter, scenarist.

plea *n.* **1.** *Their plea for aid went unanswered:* appeal, entreaty, prayer, suit, petition, supplication, solicitation, beseeching, begging, adjuration, request. **2.** *His plea was that he'd been unavoidably detained:* excuse, defense, explanation, argument, justification, vindication, apology, extenuation; pretext; alibi.

plead *v. She pleaded with the officer not to give her a ticket:* beg, beseech, implore, entreat, appeal to; petition, ask, request, importune, solicit, enjoin, supplicate, adjure.

pleasant *adj.* **1.** *Have a pleasant weekend. It was a pleasant spring day:* agreeable, pleasing, pleasurable, enjoyable, gratifying, satisfying, lovely, charming, attractive, inviting, felicitous, good, fine, nice; mild, gentle, soft. **2.** *The new intern is a pleasant young man:* likable, congenial, genial, friendly, affable, amiable, cheerful, good-humored, good-natured, companionable, sociable, gregarious, cordial, warm, amicable, tactful, polite. —**Ant.** 1 unpleasant, displeasing, disagreeable, distasteful, wretched, distressing, miserable, horrible, bad, awful. 2 unlikable, unfriendly, cold, offensive, repulsive, illhumored, ill-natured, rude, impolite, illmannered.

pleasantry *n. There wasn't much conversation, only an exchange of pleasantries:* polite remark, good-natured remark, greeting, salutation; quip, jest, witticism, sally, bon mot, humorous remark, joke, jape, *Slang* wisecrack.

please *v.* **1.** *The boy's good manners pleased his elders:* gladden, delight, give pleasure to, make happy, gratify, satisfy, suit, content, elate, charm, fascinate, enthrall, entrance, enrapture, thrill; tickle; amuse, divert, entertain. **2.** *The income allows her to live as she pleases:* like, wish, choose, desire, want, will, be inclined, elect, prefer, opt. —**Ant.** 1 displease, dissatisfy, repel, disgust, offend; sadden, depress, grieve; anger, madden, incense, annoy, provoke, pique, vex, nettle, chafe.

pleasing *adj. The audience found the movie pleasing. An entertainer should have a pleasing personality:* pleasurable, gratifying, satisfying, enjoyable, gladdening, delightful, amusing, diverting, entertaining; attractive, agreeable, inviting, likable, winning, captivating, charming, fascinating; friendly, affable, amiable, congenial, genial, cheerful, good-natured, good-humored, polite, mannerly, well-mannered. —**Ant.** displeasing, unpleasant, unpleasurable, unattractive, disagreeable, distasteful, disgusting, unlikable.

pleasure *n.* **1.** *The gift gave the child a great deal of pleasure:* enjoyment, happiness, joy, delight, gratification, cheer, bliss, elation, exultation, rapture; gaiety, mirth, lightheartedness, merriment, jubilation, high spirits. **2.** *All they seek in life is pleasure:* amusement, fun, gratification, diversion, entertainment, recreation, festivity, gaiety, beer and skittles. **3.** *What's your pleasure, coffee or tea?:* desire, choice, like, wish, will, inclination, preference, selection, option. —**Ant.** 1 displeasure, unhappiness, sorrow, sadness, suffering, pain, affliction, misery, anger, vexation. 2 work, labor, toil; self-denial, abstinence. 3 necessity, duty, obligation, compulsion; coercion.

plebeian *adj.* **1.** *She has such plebeian taste in furniture:* vulgar, coarse, common, lowbrow, low-class, unrefined, uncultivated, uncultured, commonplace, popular, banal, ordinary, low, mean, base; of the common people, lowborn, proletarian, bourgeois. —*n.* **2.** *He may act like an aristocrat, but at heart he's a plebeian:* common man, commoner, average man, average citizen, everyman, one of the masses; proletarian, bourgeoisie. **—Ant.** 1 highbrow, refined, cultivated, cultured, educated; upper class, aristocratic, royal, elevated. 2 aristocrat, blue blood, silk stocking, patrician, noble, nobleman, peer, lord; intellectual, highbrow.

pledge n. **1.** *I gave him my pledge I would vote for him:* vow, solemn promise, oath, word, assurance, adjuration, avowal, troth; agreement, pact, compact, covenant, contract. **2.** *The pawnbroker took the camera in pledge for the loan:* security, warranty, guaranty, collateral, surety; pawn, bond, bail. **—v. 3.** *I pledge allegiance to the flag:* promise solemnly, promise, vow, swear, bind by an oath, assert, guarantee, warrant, give one's word.

plenary adj. *The meeting was called into plenary session:* full, complete, entire, general, inclusive, whole.

plenitude n. **1.** *The symphony was realized to the plenitude of its form by Beethoven:* fullness, completeness, repletion, wholeness, entireness, amplitude, totality. **2.** *We purchased a plenitude of supplies for the trip:* abundance, bounty, mass, volume, profusion, quantities, quantity, cornucopia. **—Ant.** 1 scantiness, meagerness, paucity. 2 shortage, insufficiency, scarcity, inadequacy.

plentiful adj. *The town has a plentiful supply of food:* abundant, profuse, copious, bountiful, bounteous, prolific, lavish, ample, abounding, plenteous, overflowing, lush, liberal, generous, large, unsparing, unstinted, infinite, inexhaustible. **—Ant.** scant, scanty, sparse, inadequate, insufficient, deficient, scarce, skimpy, sparing, small, meager.

plenty n. **1.** *The car has plenty of room for everybody:* an abundant supply, ample amount, a full measure, abundance, sufficiency, profusion, plenitude, good deal, great deal, a wealth, enough and to spare, slew, *Slang* lots, oceans, worlds, oodles, gobs, scads. **2.** *For the New Year we wish you peace and plenty:* prosperity, good times, affluence, well-being, good fortune, riches, wealth, luxury, opulence. **—Ant.** 1 scarcity, sparsity, dearth, lack, shortage, scantiness, insufficiency, paucity, inadequacy, deficiency. 2 poverty, indigence, hard times.

plethora n. *The potluck supper had a plethora of desserts but no meat dishes:* excess, surplus, superfluity, surplusage, surfeit, overabundance, superabundance, glut, overage, redundancy. **—Ant.** shortage, lack, scarcity, deficiency.

pliable adj. **1.** *Before making the basket, soak the bark to make it pliable:* flexible, easily bendable, pliant, plastic, resilient, elastic, springy; supple, lithe, limber. **2.** *Be careful what you teach to pliable young children:* impressionable, pliant, compliant, receptive, willing, responsive, flexible, easily influenced; accommodating, manageable, adaptable, submissive, yielding, acquiescent, tractable. **—Ant.** 1 stiff, rigid, unbending. 2 stubborn, obstinate, inflexible, unyielding, willful, headstrong, dogged, intractable, dogmatic.

pliant adj. *She was pliant and gave in to all her parents' demands:* pliable, supple, flexible, flex-

ile, lithe, limber; compliant, easily influenced, yielding, adaptable, manageable, tractable, ductile, facile, docile. **—Ant.** inflexible; unyielding, rigid, intractable.

plight n. *The plight of the people in the drought-stricken area has not improved:* condition, situation, circumstance, state; poor condition, distressing situation, dangerous circumstances, predicament, dilemma, extremity, distress, trouble, difficulty, vicissitude, trial, tribulation; crisis, impasse, emergency, exigency, scrape, pinch, *Slang* pickle, straits, fix, muddle, jam.

plod v. **1.** *The soldiers plodded through the mud:* trudge, walk heavily, drag, slog, tramp, lumber, shuffle, waddle. **2.** *The youth just plodded along at his piano lessons:* work slowly, drudge, toil, moil, sweat, grind, struggle; persevere, be resolute, stick with it, peg away, *Slang* plug, grub.

plot[1] n. **1.** *The government uncovered a revolutionary plot:* conspiracy, intrigue, secret plan, evil plan, scheme, machination, maneuver, design, stratagem. **2.** *The plot of the novel is too silly to relate:* story, story line, tale, narrative, incidents, yarn, plan, action, design. **—v. 3.** *The criminals were plotting to rob the bank:* conspire, scheme, intrigue, design, plan, contrive, maneuver, collude, be in collusion. **4.** *The navigator plotted the ship's course:* chart, map, compute, calculate, determine; mark, draw, sketch, outline, diagram, blueprint, draft.

plot[2] n. *Tomatoes will grow easily on this plot:* area, space, section, area of ground, patch; lot, tract, field, clearing.

plow or **plough** v. **1.** *We will plow the field soon after the last frost:* dig up, turn up, spade, dig, till, break, break up, loosen, work; furrow, harrow, cultivate. **2.** *The ship plowed through the sea toward port:* push, press, plunge, drive, cut, shove, forge, *Slang* bulldoze.

ploy n. *Her ploy was to get me to invest in her latest wild whim:* stratagem, subterfuge, ruse, trick, artifice, game, maneuver, strategy, tactic, gambit, wile, scheme, game, design, *Slang* gimmick.

pluck v. **1.** *Please don't pluck the flowers:* pick, pull out, pull off, pull at, draw; jerk, grab, yank, snatch; uproot, extirpate. **—n. 2.** *The boxer showed a lot of pluck by fighting back even though badly hurt:* spirit, mettle, courage, bravery, valor, boldness, daring, *Slang* spunk, grit, sand, guts; resolution, temerity, determination, resolve, fortitude, doggedness, perseverance, persistence, tenacity.

plug n. **1.** *Stop up the leak with a plug:* stopper, stopple, bung, cork. **—v. 2.** *We temporarily plugged the hole with putty:* stop up, close, shut off, stanch, cork, fill up, stuff.

plumb n. **1.** *The fisherman used a plumb to find the depth of the lake:* plumb line, plummet, lead; plumb bob, level. **—v. 2.** *The geologist plumbed the depths of the ocean. She tried to plumb the depths of his mind:* take soundings, sound, fathom, measure, test, cast the lead; probe, penetrate, gauge, examine. **—adj. 3.** *The*

521

plummet to **poignant**

side of the garage doesn't look plumb: vertical, straight up and down; straight, true, sheer. —**Ant.** 3 horizontal; crooked, awry, askew, off-center, aslant.

plummet v. The hawk plummeted toward the earth: plunge, fall, fall headlong, drop straight down, dive, tumble, descend abruptly, nosedive. —**Ant.** rise, ascend, shoot upward, soar.

plump[1] adj. She's not grossly fat, but she's plump: chubby, pudgy, somewhat fat, fleshy, corpulent, obese, stout, portly, stocky, rotund; rounded, buxom. —**Ant.** slender, slim, lean; thin, skinny, scrawny, lanky, skeletal, cadaverous.

plump[2] v. 1. The youth plumped down in the chair and went to sleep: drop, plop, flop, plunk, sink, sprawl, collapse; spill, fall heavily, tumble. —adj. 2. The suspect answered with a plump denial of the charge: direct, straightforward, forthright, outright, downright, blunt, abrupt; unswerving, undeviating, firm, solid.

plunder v. 1. The invading soldiers plundered the town: sack, pillage, loot, ransack, raid, rifle, rob, pilfer, ravage, maraud, despoil, fleece, strip. —n. 2. The pirate ship was filled with plunder: loot, booty, pillage, takings, spoils, pilferings, filchings prize, Slang swag, haul, take.

plunge v. 1. The blacksmith plunged the red-hot horseshoe into a bucket of water. The boys plunged into the swimming pool: dip, thrust, cast, douse, immerse, duck; submerge, submerge, descend, sink; dive, jump, leap, throw oneself, fall headlong, tumble, pitch. 2. The firemen plunged into the building: rush, dash, run, dart, charge, speed, hurtle, bolt, sprint, scramble, lunge, hasten, scurry, scuttle, hustle, whisk, tear, shoot, fly, streak, scuttle; surge, push, press, drive, swarm. 3. The boat plunged in the high seas: pitch, toss, lurch, heave, reel, rock, jerk, roll, sway, tumble about, prance about. —n. 4. The sky diver had a plunge of more than 20,000 feet before his parachute opened: drop, fall, dive, headlong rush, jump, leap. —**Ant.** 1 emerge, rise, withdraw, take out. 2 stroll, amble, crawl.

plus adj. Typing is a requirement for the job, but knowing shorthand would be a plus factor: additional, extra, added, supplementary; supplemental, other, spare, auxiliary; helpful, desirable, useful, beneficial, advantageous.

plush adj. She spent years selecting the furnishings for her plush apartment: sumptuous, elegant, luxurious, opulent, deluxe, lavish, palatial, fancy, extravagant, grand, rich; Slang posh, classy, ritzy, lush, swank, swanky, snazzy. —**Ant.** spare, simple, Spartan, bare, austere.

ply[1] n. The boat has two plys of wood along the hull. The rug is made of four-ply yarn: layer, stratum, thickness, sheet, plate, leaf, sheath, lamina, slice; strand, twist, plait.

ply[2] v. 1. The old woman plied her shuttles in making lace: employ, wield, put to use, utilize, manipulate, operate, work, handle. 2. Father still plies his trade as a carpenter: practice, carry on, exercise, follow, labor at, pursue, occupy oneself with, persevere at, bend one's efforts to,

devote oneself to. 3. The salesman plied his customers with food and drink. Reporters plied the candidate with questions: besiege, press, thrust upon, urge upon, prevail upon, supply persistently, offer repeatedly. 4. The old ship plies the route between Hong Kong and Singapore: travel regularly, make repeated trips, go back and forth; sail, navigate, run, fly.

poach v. 1. They poached rabbits and pheasants: fish illegally, hunt illegally, filch, appropriate, encroach, infringe upon, pilfer, plunder, rob, steal. 2. We poached eggs for breakfast: simmer, seethe.

pocket n. 1. Do you have any change in your pocket? The briefcase has two pockets for papers: pouchlike part of a garment; compartment, envelope, receptacle, Archaic placket; chamber, cavity, hollow; pouch, bag, sack; purse, handbag, pocketbook. 2. The old prospector finally found a pocket of silver in the hill: isolated mass; vein, lode, pit, strip, streak, strain. —v. 3. The ticket seller was jailed for pocketing the box-office receipts: steal, pilfer, put into one's pocket, appropriate, arrogate, usurp, help oneself to, take possession of; attain, get, obtain, come by, gain, receive. —adj. 4. A pocket camera is easy to carry: pocket-size, for carrying in the pocket, small, compact, little, miniature, diminutive, vest-pocket, bantam, pygmy; portable; for the pocket.

pocketbook n. Didn't you put your glasses in your pocketbook?: purse, handbag, bag, shoulder bag, clutch; wallet, pocket secretary, notecase, money purse, coin purse, moneybag, pouch, satchel.

pod n. The peas must be stripped from each pod: husk, jacket, hull, shell, sheath, case, seed case, seed vessel, pericarp.

poem n. Rudyard Kipling wrote some of the best remembered poems in the English language: verse, rhyme, verse composition, jingle, doggerel; (variously) ballad, ode, sonnet, elegy, epic, madrigal, lyric, idyll, song, ballad, lay, limerick.

poet n. Emily Dickinson has been belatedly recognized as the greatest poet of the so-called New England Indian Summer: maker, singer; (variously) lyricist, lyrist, lyric writer, song-writer, librettist, improviser, reciter, minstrel, balladeer, balladist, sonneteer, verseman, versifier, rhymer, rhymester, poetaster, poet laureate, bard.

poetic also **poetical** adj. William Faulkner's novels have many poetic qualities: lyric, lyrical, imaginative, rhythmic, metrical, musical, melodic, songlike, lilting, melodious. —**Ant.** unpoetical, prosaic, routine, realistic, commonplace, matter-of-fact, unimaginative.

poetry n. Most of Alexander Pope's poetry is written in heroic couplets: verse, metrical composition, poesy, rhyme; versification.

poignant adj. The poignant words brought a tear to every eye. The critic wrote a poignant review of the movie: moving, affecting, touching, heartrending, pitiful, pitiable, piteous, distressing, pathetic, woeful, grievous, lamentable, sad, sorrowful, tearful, rueful, doleful; biting, trenchant, cutting, piercing, penetrating, sharp, pungent, piquant. **—Ant.** unaffecting, unmoving, cold, blunt, unfeeling; insipid, trite, vapid, banal, superficial.

point *n.* **1.** *Do you have a pencil with a sharper point? The lighthouse is on the northern point of the island:* sharp end, tapered end, tip, nib; spike, pike, apex, prong; projection, protuberance, prominence, extension, offshoot, promontory, outgrowth, spur. **2.** *The freezing point of water is 32 degrees Fahrenheit:* degree, stage, position, condition, place; limit, mark. **3.** *At that point the audience got up to leave:* instant, moment, time, very minute, juncture. **4.** *I think I missed the point of his story:* main idea, purpose, object, end, reason; gist, essence, heart, kernel, pith, core, meat, marrow, sum and substance. **5.** *There's no point in arguing further:* sense, reason, cause, object, objective, aim, intention, purpose, end, value, use. **6.** *Here's a point you may have overlooked:* detail, item, particular, aspect, feature, quality. **7.** *The team won by two points:* score, tally; unit, number; (*variously*) hit, basket, run, goal, game. **—v. 8.** *Point the gun at the target:* aim, train, direct; steer, guide, turn, bend, slant, level. **9.** *His conduct points to an ulterior motive:* indicate, suggest, imply, signify, intimate, hint at; portend, foreshadow, presage, bode, argue; testify; demonstrate, manifest, prove.

pointed *adj.* **1.** *The tree has a long, pointed leaf:* peaked, sharp, pointy, acute, acuminate, cuspidate, aciculate. **2.** *The teacher made a pointed remark about students who arrive late for class:* pertinent, incisive, fitting, telling, penetrating, trenchant, appropriate, accurate, piercing, cutting, biting; insinuating, hinting. **—Ant.** 1 blunt, dull, rounded. 2 pointless, irrelevant, inappropriate.

pointer *n.* **1.** *The guide used a pointer to indicate the towns on the map. The pointer on the speedometer indicated sixty miles an hour:* indicator, arrow, guide, stick; hand, arm, needle. **2.** *The old pro gave the youth a few pointers before starting him on the job:* piece of advice, bit of information, hint, suggestion, tip, advisement, recommendation; admonition, caution, warning.

pointless *adj.* **1.** *Fencers are required to use pointless foils:* without a point, unpointed, rounded, obtuse; blunt, dull, worn down, unedged, unsharpened. **2.** *Further discussions on this matter are pointless:* useless, purposeless, unproductive, unprofitable, bootless, unavailing, meaningless, fruitless, futile, worthless, aimless, invalid, ineffectual; unreasonable, irrational, illogical, absurd, preposterous, ridiculous, stupid, irrelevant, senseless, inapplicable, beside the point. **—Ant.** 1 pointed, sharp. 2 useful, profitable, meaningful, fruitful, productive, beneficial, worthwhile, valid, invaluable; appropriate, fitting, proper, to the point; reasonable, logical, sensible; desirable, advisable.

poise *n.* **1.** *A good hostess should have a lot of poise:* assurance, self-assurance, self-confidence, self-command, self-control, presence of mind, presence, aplomb, equanimity, calm, composure, *French* savoir faire, sangfroid. **—v. 2.** *The diver poised on the edge of the high board:* balance, be in equilibrium; hold aloft, raise, elevate.

poison *n.* **1.** *Strychnine is a deadly poison:* toxic chemical, harmful chemical, bane; (*loosely*) venom, toxin, harmful drug. **2.** *Hate is a poison for which there is no antidote:* evil, harm, curse, bane, disease, cancer, malignancy, malignity, canker, plague, pestilence; outrage, enormity, abomination, corruption. **—v. 3.** *Tainted food can poison your system. Lucretia Borgia poisoned many people:* kill with poison, harm with poison, give poison to; infect, contaminate, disease, make sick, impair, weaken, debilitate. **4.** *Industrial wastes are poisoning the atmosphere. Don't allow evil thoughts to poison your mind:* contaminate, pollute, taint, adulterate; corrupt, defile, debase, degrade, corrode. **—Ant.** 1 antidote. 2 good, benefit, salve, balm.

poisonous *adj.* *The leaves of many plants are poisonous:* lethal, fatal, toxic, venomous, noxious, deadly, pernicious, baneful, virulent, mortal, pestilential, deleterious. **—Ant.** beneficial, healthful, healthy, salubrious; harmless, innocuous.

poke *n.* **1.** *The bully gave the new boy a poke in the nose:* jab, thrust, punch, hit, push, prod, nudge, jolt, dig, thump. **—v. 2.** *Stop poking me with your elbow:* prod, jab, dig, nudge, jolt, thrust, push, butt, hit, punch, stick, stab, gore. **3.** *Stop poking along and get your work done!:* dawdle, idle, dally, dillydally, shilly-shally, fiddle, delay, potter; drag, shuffle, crawl, hang back, saunter, meander, shamble, *Slang* mosey.

polar *adj.* **1.** *It was the polar opposite of what we intended:* opposite, opposed, reverse, contradictory, antagonistic. **2.** *He explored in polar regions:* arctic, northern, north, frozen, freezing, glacial, icy.

pole *n.* *He levered the object out with a pole:* stick, bar, beam, pile, post, rod, shaft, spar, staff, stave, stake, standard.

police *n.* **1.** *Call the police!:* law-enforcement organization, police force, sheriff's office; law-enforcement officers, policemen, troopers, constabulary, *Informal* cops, gendarmes, men in blue, *Slang* fuzz. **—v. 2.** *Several watchmen police the factory at night:* patrol, guard, protect, go on one's beat; maintain law and order, keep in order, regulate, control. **3.** *The soldiers were ordered to police the parade ground:* clean, clean up, tidy, tidy up, pick up trash from, neaten, spruce up.

policeman, *Fem.* **policewoman** *n.* *Ask the policeman where the opera house is:* police officer, officer, officer of the law, law-enforcement officer, bluecoat, *Informal* arm of the law, gendarme, *Slang* cop, dick, flatfoot; (*variously*) patrolman, cop on the beat, motorcycle policeman, traffic cop; sheriff, marshal, constable.

policy *n.* *The store's policy is to exchange merchandise rather than give cash refunds. The Secretary of State carries out U.S. foreign policy:*

practice, procedure, course of action, mode of management, line of conduct, system, program, routine, habit, custom, rule, behavior, way, method, platform, principle, style; plan, scheme, strategy, tactics, design.

polish v. **1.** *Polish the silver before the guests arrive:* shine, buff, rub up, burnish, smooth, sand, pumice; wax, gloss, varnish, glaze. **2.** *The speaker spent several days polishing her lecture:* perfect, refine, improve, enhance, round out, touch up, emend, correct. —*n.* **3.** *Use brown polish on these shoes:* wax, shining substance, gloss, varnish, glaze, oil; abrasive, sandpaper, pumice, rouge. **4.** *Four years of college gave her considerable polish:* grace, culture, cultivation, refinement, elegance, finesse, sauvity, urbanity; good manners, politeness, politesse, courtesy, gentility, *Slang* class. —**Ant.** 1 tarnish, oxidize, discolor, dull, corrode, erode. 3 remover. 4 boorishness, clumsiness, awkwardness; indecorum, gaucheness, uncouthness.

polished adj. **1.** *The polished stone resembled a gem:* smooth, glossy, burnished, shining, shiny, shined, lustrous, brilliant. **2.** *The polished skating won top marks:* refined, cultured, finished, elegant, polite, poised; flawless, excellent, perfect.

polite adj. **1.** *What a polite young man!:* courteous, well-mannered, mannerly, well-behaved, cultivated, proper, civil, respectful, diffident, gentlemanly, courtly, gallant, ceremonious. **2.** *The wealthy matron was the leader of polite society:* refined, cultured, polished, genteel, well-bred, civilized, elegant, fashionable, high, elite, patrician. —**Ant.** 1 rude, impolite, discourteous, ill-mannered, unmannerly, uncouth; insulting, impudent, impertinent. 2 unrefined, uncultured, ill-bred, unpolished, crude, boorish.

politic adj. *Be politic and don't mention all the weight she's put on:* tactful, judicious, wise, prudent, circumspect, discreet, shrewd, diplomatic, artful, cautious, chary, perspicacious, mindful. —**Ant.** rude, tactless, blundering, rash.

politician n. *The mayor is a skilled politician:* professional in party politics, politico, political careerist; office seeker, campaigner, officeholder, incumbent, public servant, legislator, statesman.

politics n. pl. **1.** *The history of European politics is an interesting subject:* political science, art of government, administration of public affairs, practice of government; affairs of state, government policy, statecraft, statesmanship. **2.** *The Republican and the Democrat had an argument about politics:* political views, political matters, party policy, party leadership, political maneuvers.

poll n. **1.** *The election will begin at six A.M. when the polls open:* voting place; voting list; voting, vote, returns, tally, figures. **2.** *An independent poll shows that 60 percent of the people favor daylight saving time:* public opinion poll, public survey, sampling, census, canvass, nose count; public opinion. —*v.* **3.** *We polled the members about the change in rules:* take the vote of, register the vote of, solicit the vote of, canvass, survey, interview, sample the opinion of, count noses. **4.** *The winning candidate polled over a quarter million votes:* receive a vote; register, tally.

pollute v. *All those waste products are polluting the river:* contaminate, befoul, foul, dirty, soil, adulterate, sully, make filthy; defile, profane, desecrate, debase, deprave. —**Ant.** purify, clean, cleanse, clarify, purge.

pollution n. *The new law will reduce pollution of the air:* contamination, contaminating, befouling, fouling, dirtying, soiling, defiling; uncleanness, foulness, adulteration; pollutant, impurity.

pomp n. *The coronation of the new king was performed with great pomp:* stately display, ceremony, solemnity, pageantry, spectacle, splendor, grandeur, magnificence, brilliance, glory; flourish, style, show, display; pompousness, ostentation, pretentiousness, showiness, grandiosity, affectation, *Informal* front.

pompous adj. *He was a pompous, officious little bureaucrat:* self-important, ostentatious, pretentious, haughty, arrogant, patronizing, snobbish, condescending, overbearing, presumptuous, *Informal* uppish, puffed-up; vain, conceited, egotistic, supercilious, vainglorious, proud, imperious, blustering, swaggering, grandiose, lordly, high and mighty, affected, mannered, overdone. —**Ant.** simple, modest, inglorious; dull.

pond n. *We fed the ducks in the pond:* small lake, lagoon, pool, tarn; water hole; basin.

ponder v. *He pondered the problem for many hours:* consider, meditate on, reflect on, contemplate, think over, give thought to; cogitate, cerebrate, ruminate, deliberate, study, concentrate upon, puzzle over, rack one's brain, examine, *Informal* put on one's thinking cap; mull over, muse, reflect, speculate, wonder, brood over.

ponderous adj. **1.** *The boy struggled with a ponderous package:* heavy, weighty, burdensome, awkward, cumbrous, cumbersome, unwieldy; massive, bulky, enormous, big, large, *Informal* hefty. **2.** *The ponderous woman needed help getting up from the chair:* heavy, awkward, ungraceful, lumpish, hulking, graceless, lumbering, bovine, corpulent. **3.** *His ponderous speech put everyone to sleep:* dull, heavy, heavy-handed, labored, lusterless, boring, unexciting, dreary, unlively, sluggish; long-winded, wordy, tedious, droning, monotonous, wearisome. —**Ant.** 1 light, weightless; small, tiny, dainty. 2 graceful, light on the feet; dainty. 3 exciting, absorbing, lively; short, terse, brief, concise, succinct, to the point.

pontifical adj. **1.** *The Pope donned his pontifical robes:* churchly, priestly, ecclesiastical, clerical, episcopal, apostolic. **2.** *He can't make a simple statement without seeming pontifical:* pompous, pretentious, condescending, patronizing; imperious, overbearing, opinionated, dogmatic, authoritarian.

pool n. **1.** *Deer often come to drink at the pool. The corpse lay in a pool of blood:* pond, lake, tarn, mere, (variously) fishpond, millpool, swimming pool; puddle, splash. **2.** *He was employed* as a member of our typing pool. I joined the car pool: group, association, combine, coalition, confederation, cooperative, collective, alliance, union. **3.** *Who won the football pool this week?:* stakes, kitty, pot, bank. —v. **4.** *We pooled our resources and got the job done quickly:* combine, merge, amalgamate, share, consolidate, band together, unite, ally.

poor *adj.* **1.** *He was so poor, he couldn't even afford the carfare:* poverty-stricken, indigent, insolvent, destitute, impoverished, penniless, moneyless, pauperized, bankrupt, impecunious, *Slang* broke; needy, in need, in want, in straits, strapped, *Informal* badly off, hard up, on the rocks. **2.** *The farmlands were too poor to produce crops:* unfertile, infertile, barren, sterile; desolate, forlorn, meager, bare, exhausted, depleted, empty; uncultivable, fallow, unproductive, dead, wasted, worn. **3.** *It was a poor imitation of the real thing. His poor grades caused him to lose the scholarship. It was a poor attempt to win her affections:* inferior, inadequate, deficient, defective, imperfect, wanting, faulty, lacking something, devoid of; paltry, wretched, sorry, meager, beggarly, indifferent, worthless, fruitless, vain, futile, unprofitable, unworthy. **4.** *The poor man never knew what hit him:* pitiable, unfortunate, unlucky, pathetic, miserable, wretched, sorry; distressed, unhappy, sad, grieving. —n. **5.** *The state must care for the poor:* the unfortunate, the needy, the penniless, the destitute, the indigent. —**Ant.** 1, 2 rich. 1 affluent, wealthy, moneyed; fortunate, lucky, *Informal* well-off, *Slang* in the chips, on easy street; comfortable. 2 fertile, productive, fecund, cultivable, fruitful, fructiferous. 3 worthy, superior, excellent. 5 the rich, the affluent, the wealthy.

poorly *adj.* **1.** *She confessed she was poorly:* ill, sick, sickly, off-color, ailing, below par, indisposed, low, not well, unwell. —adv. **2.** *They did the job poorly:* badly, defectively, inadequately, incompetently, inexpertly, meanly, shabbily, unsatisfactorily, unsuccessfully. —**Ant.** 1 healthy, well, hale. 2 well, competently, expertly, satisfactorily.

pop *v.* **1.** *One of the balloons popped:* explode, burst; boom, bang, discharge, detonate, crack, snap. **2.** *The magician had real rabbits popping out of his hat:* appear, materialize, issue forth suddenly, burst, arise, come. —n. **3.** *We heard a pop and the champagne cork bounced off the ceiling:* explosion, detonation, boom, shot, discharge, bang, blast, report, crack, burst. **4.** *I love cherry pop:* soda, soda pop, soft drink.

poppycock *n. Informal Don't tell me you actually believe that poppycock!:* balderdash, bunk, bosh, tosh, nonsense, stuff, rubbish, trash, garbage, hogwash, rot, falderal, gibberish, *Slang* jive; jabberwocky, twaddle, blather, blabber, prattle, fustian, tommyrot, wish-wash, fiddlefaddle, flapdoodle, rigmarole, *Slang* gobbledygook; absurdity, drivel, inanity, froth, flummery, abracadabra, hocus-pocus, mumbo-jumbo, moonshine, hooey, fudge, baloney, applesauce.

popular *adj.* **1.** *Mary was a popular girl:* sought-after, well-received, in favor, in demand, ac-

cepted; preferred, approved, well-liked, favorite, admired; well-known, celebrated, famous. **2.** *Taxes are always a popular issue. The movie is back at popular prices:* public, of the people, general, communal, community, civic, democratic, social, sociological, civil, national; inexpensive, affordable, cheap. **3.** *As a senator he always voted the popular way:* current, prevalent, fashionable; accepted, approved, familiar, stock, conventional, established, orthodox. —**Ant.** 1–3 unpopular. 1 in disfavor, unaccepted; unliked, odious, displeasing. 3 uncommon, unusual, rare, unconventional, unorthodox.

popularity *n. The comedian enjoyed great popularity during the 30's and 40's:* favor, acceptance, approval, acclaim, vogue, fashion, fame, reputation, celebrity, repute, renown, note, notability; glory, *Informal* kudos; acclamation, esteem, regard, admiration; notoriety.

popularize *v. They popularized the novel in an abridgment:* make popular, catch on, disseminate, familiarize, give currency, spread, universalize.

population *n. The population of the city rose by 20 percent:* inhabitants, residents, habitancy; citizenry, public, citizens, body politic, commonality; people, folk, populace.

populous *adj. Cities are more populous than rural areas:* full of people, full of inhabitants, populated, peopled, crowded, teeming, jammed, swarming, thronged, thickly settled, dense.

pore[1] *v. He pored over the report, looking for the slightest error:* read, study, ponder, examine, scrutinize, peruse, inspect, scan, run the eye over; study, consider, search, probe, delve into, dig into, explore, survey, review.

pore[2] *n. Pimples occur when pores of the skin become clogged. Pumice is a rock with many pores:* tiny opening, hole, orifice, aperture, outlet.

pornographic *adj. One love scene in the book seemed rather pornographic to me:* obscene, indecent, lewd, gross, salacious, dirty, prurient, lascivious, smutty, filthy, off-color, blue, coarse, vulgar, bawdy, licentious.

porous *adj. Sponges are porous:* absorbent, permeable, penetrable, pervious; honeycombed. sievelike, cellular, riddled, lacy; spongy.

port *n. The ship will reach port tomorrow morning:* seaport, harbor, dock, pier, wharf, quay, landing, harborage, anchorage, mooring, dry dock; shelter, refuge, haven; destination.

portable *adj. I have a portable television set:* transportable, movable, haulable, conveyable, transferable, cartable, liftable; compact, folding, pocket, pocket-sized, vest-pocket, small, bantam; light, manageable, ready-to-go, handy, convenient.

portal *n. Usually* **portals** *Many great men have passed through these portals:* entrance, entranceway, door, gate, gateway, adit, doorway, wicket, approach, entry, threshold, arch, portcullis, vestibule, portico.

portend *v. The unemployment statistics portend*

bad times ahead: foretell, forecast, augur, bode, prophesy, predict, prognosticate; herald, signify, point to, warn of, forewarn, give token of, presage, prefigure, betoken, denote, suggest, forebode, foreshadow, foretoken, bespeak.

portent *n. The dark clouds were portents of a rough flight:* warning, sign, forewarning, boding, foreboding, threat, dire prospect; omen, sign, token, augury, presage, harbinger.

portentous *adj.* **1.** *Neighboring countries viewed the dictator's speech as portentous:* foreboding, threatening, intimidating, ominous, menacing, alarming, frightening; significant, fateful, prophetic; unpropitious, inauspicious. **2.** *She was a pianist of portentous talent:* prodigious, stupendous, amazing, astonishing, surprising, remarkable, extraordinary, incredible, superlative, exceptional, superb. **3.** *The book's style is portentous, but the substance is trivial:* pompous, self-important, pretentious, grandiose; bombastic, grandiloquent.

porter *n. The porter took our luggage into the terminal:* baggage carrier, redcap, skycap, carrier, transporter, bearer, conveyer, conductor; (*in the Far East*) coolie.

portfolio *n. All the papers were in her portfolio:* folder, attaché case, briefcase, case, bag.

portion *n.* **1.** *A portion of the contract dealt with royalties:* part, section, division, segment, sector; piece, fraction, fragment; measure, quantity, amount, sum. **2.** *Her portion of the inheritance amounted to $50,000:* part, division, allowance, allotment, share, apportionment, allocation; serving, helping, ration, percentage, *Slang* cut. **3.** *We must all accept our portion in life:* fortune, lot, destiny, fate, doom, luck, kismet, *Greek* moira; God's will. —*v.* **4.** *She portioned out the pie so everyone had a piece:* divide, distribute, deal out, disperse; cut up, slice, carve, separate, sever, split, segment, partition, demarcate; apportion, allocate, dole; parcel, break up.

portly *adj. He was a portly gentleman with an enormous appetite:* large, substantial, heavy, fat, big, corpulent, obese, fleshy, plump, pudgy, full-figured, rotund, stout, round, full, stocky, burly, chubby, beefy, brawny, tubby, endomorphic. —**Ant.** thin, slender, trim.

portrait *n.* **1.** *A portrait of his wife hung over the fireplace:* painting, sketch, drawing, photograph, picture, likeness. **2.** *From her portrait of you, I thought you'd be much shorter:* description, verbal picture, word painting, personal report, thumbnail sketch, impression, picturization, graphic account, depiction, representation, vignette, cameo.

portray *v.* **1.** *The artist portrayed her as almost saintly:* depict, describe, picture, delineate, model; sketch, draw, illustrate, paint, carve, sculpture, photograph. **2.** *Who portrayed King Lear?:* enact, play, represent, characterize, impersonate, pose as, simulate; imitate, mimic, ape. **3.** *The author portrayed his father as a vicious drunkard:* describe, depict, characterize, represent, detail; figure, set forth, narrate, delineate, picture.

pose *v.* **1.** *For the album cover, he posed them in front of a row of tenements:* position, arrange, group, order, set, line up. **2.** *She loves to pose when men are around:* posture, act self-consciously, act affectedly, show off, give oneself airs. **3.** *He posed as a newsman to get in:* pretend to be, pass oneself off as, impersonate. **4.** *Allow me to pose several questions:* state, put forward, submit, set forth, postulate, advance, throw out, present, propose, propound, bring up, suggest. —*n.* **5.** *He nervously assumed a stiff pose next to the fireplace:* attitude, posture, position, stance, bearing, carriage; mien, cast, air, mannerism, style.

posh *adj. Slang We were invited to a posh party at their country place:* elegant, fancy, refined, high-class, deluxe, classy, chic, swell, smart, stylish, extravagant, lavish, luxurious, opulent, swanky, ritzy, chi-chi. —**Ant.** plain, simple, modest, unpretentious, austere.

position *n.* **1.** *The hilltop was a perfect position for a watchtower:* place, location, placement, locus, situation, disposition; locality, site, station. **2.** *The sprinters lined up in a tense crouching position:* posture, stance, pose, attitude. **3.** *The guards were in position at all the exits:* at one's station, usual or proper place. **4.** *A man in his position might have done the same thing:* situation, predicament, condition, state, circumstances, plight; standing, place. **5.** *She was a woman of high position:* standing, status, station, elevation, prominence, eminence, distinction, importance, prestige, consequence, notability, class, caste, place, order. **6.** *I held an important position with the textile company:* job, place, career, post, capacity, function, role, charge, appointment, assignment, responsibility, duty, commission, office. **7.** *What's your position on foreign aid?:* opinion, viewpoint, outlook, point of view, stand, frame of mind. **8.** *He had good position and was sure to win:* location, vantage, ground, field position. —*v.* **9.** *She positioned the rooks on the wrong squares:* put, place, arrange, array, set; pose, establish, stand, fix, situate, locate, lodge, deposit.

positive *adj.* **1.** *He gave a positive identification of the killer:* conclusive, firm, absolute, decisive, unqualified, definite, definitive, leaving no doubt, unequivocal, explicit, corroborative, confirmatory, undisputed, irrefutable, incontrovertible. **2.** *She was positive she had seen him:* sure, certain, undoubting, confident, satisfied, assured, cocksure, dead certain, convinced. **3.** *He always has some positive ideas on company policy:* practical, practicable, effective, constructive, useful, helpful, serviceable, applicable; beneficial, gainful, good, salutary, contributory. **4.** *What we need is some positive thinking!:* forward-looking, optimistic, progressive, affirmative, cooperative. **5.** *Informal She's a positive sweetheart:* real, honest-to-goodness, absolute, complete, veritable, total, thoroughgoing. **6.** *His positive ways made him hard to live with:* dogmatic, opinionated, narrow, autocratic, overbearing, dictatorial; obdurate, unchangeable, immovable; assertive, self-assured, *Informal* cocksure. **—Ant.** 1 inconclusive, qualified, indefinite, disputable. 2 unsure, tentative, doubting, uncertain. 3 negative; impractical, speculative; wild, foolish, useless. 4 pessimistic; conservative, reactionary; neutral, indifferent; vain, idle. 6 amenable, tractable, self-effacing.

positively *adv.* **1.** *She positively identified him as the attacker:* absolutely, unhesitatingly, unquestionably, indisputably, decidedly, definitely, unmistakably, indubitably; emphatically, categorically, unqualifiedly, affirmatively, assuredly, confidently, certainly. **2.** *It's positively the worst movie I've ever seen:* definitely, literally, unquestionably, beyond question, without doubt, assuredly, absolutely.

possess *v.* **1.** *They possess eight acres of land:* own, have, have title to, hold, occupy, maintain. **2.** *She possesses a beautiful singing voice:* have, be endowed with, be blest with, boast; command; enjoy. **3.** *Nazi Germany possessed most of Europe during World War II:* conquer, vanquish, overrun, grab, control, occupy, absorb, take over, acquire. **4.** *Richard III was possessed by his wish to be king:* dominate, control, influence, obsess, consume; fascinate, fixate, mesmerize, enchant, be eaten up, hypnotize, bedevil, bewitch; dominate, make insane, drive crazy.

possessed *adj.* *The poor possessed woman tumbled on the ground:* under a spell, under the spell, bewitched, taken over, bedevilled; crazed, demented, enchanted, haunted, insane, mad, obsessed, raving; frenetic, frenzied, berserk.

possession *n.* **1.** *He's had possession of the adjoining lot for 10 years. Possession is nine-tenths of the law:* possessing, owning, ownership, proprietorship, vested interest; occupation, occupancy, control, custody, hold, title, tenancy. **2.** *He was a poor man with few possessions:* belonging, asset, material thing, effect, resource, accoutrement. **3.** *These islands were once possessions of Spain:* dominion, territory, province, protectorate. **4.** *With his usual possession, he answered all the questions:* self-possession, presence of mind, self-control, composure, even temper, calmness, unexcitability, coolness, placidity, sangfroid, poise, equanimity, equilibrium; control, command.

possibilities *n. pl. The proposal offered distinct possibilities:* potential, potentiality, capabilities, promise, prospects.

possibility *n.* **1.** *What's the possibility of having a sunny weekend?:* chance, likelihood, prospect, probability, hope, odds. **2.** *There's always the possibility that he won't come:* chance, eventuality, risk, hazard, gamble, contingency. **3.** *That idea has great possibilities:* potentiality, promise, prospects; feasibility, practicability, workability.

possible *adj.* **1.** *Here, for instance, is one possible educational program:* potential, contingent, conceivable, thinkable, imaginable, hypothetical; credible, thinkable, worth consideration, reasonable, compatible; admissible, cognizable. **2.** *Anything is possible with that man:* capable of being done, within reach, attainable, obtainable, achievable, practicable, workable, feasible, performable, manageable, conceivable; capable of happening. **—Ant.** 1, 2 impossible. 1 inconceivable, unimaginable, improbable; incredible, unthinkable, unreasonable, incompatible; unlikely. 2 unobtainable, inaccessible; unfeasible.

possibly *adv.* **1.** *Possibly we'll meet again soon:* perhaps, maybe, could be, may be, conceivably, as luck may have it, perchance, mayhap, God willing. **2.** *They give you all the food you can possibly eat for $5:* conceivably, normally, at the most. **3.** *She couldn't possibly have left without me:* by any means, in any way, at all, by the remotest chance.

post[1] *n.* **1.** *He spent the morning putting posts along the back boundary:* stake, picket, upright, pale, support, column, shaft, pole, mainstay, brace, splint, pile. **—v. 2.** *As soon as the principal posted the news, students began gathering in the yard. I'll keep you posted on further events:* put up, fasten up, tack up, publish, place in public view; make known, announce, broadcast, circulate, declare, disclose, report, advertise; proclaim; inform, notify, instruct, advise, acquaint, apprise, enlighten.

post[2] *n.* **1.** *The policeman was on his post until midnight:* place of duty, station, round, beat, routine. **2.** *He held an important post with the company:* job, position, office, situation, place, spot, station, seat; capacity, role, function, work, part; assignment, mission, appointment. **3.** *He returned to the post with a message for the general:* military camp, base, headquarters; settlement; trading post, post exchange, PX, exchange. **—v. 4.** *Post two soldiers at each gate:* station, situate, install, place, put, fix, set, establish; quarter, lodge, house, camp, settle; locate.

poster *n.* *They put a poster on every wall:* bill, notice, handbill, banner, advertisement, announcement, placard.

posterior *adj.* **1.** *The study is located in the posterior portion of the house:* rear, back, hindmost, aftermost, tail, hinder, rearward; dorsal, caudal. **—n. 2.** *I slipped on the ice and landed on my posterior:* rump, buttocks, backside, behind, seat, bottom; *Slang* butt, can, fanny, stern, tail, keister, tush, tushy, prat; *French* derrière, *Brit.* bum.

posterity *n.* *They preserved his writings for posterity:* future generations, succeeding ages, history; offspring, descendants, heirs, issue, successors, progeny; family, young, children; descent, lineage, succession.

posthaste *adv.* *They fled posthaste:* swiftly, at once, directly, expeditiously, hastily, promptly, quickly, rapidly, speedily, straightaway, *Informal* breakneck, double-quick, lickety-split, pronto.

postmortem *n.* *The coroner produced the postmortem results:* autopsy, coroner's report, death report; analysis, dissection, examination.

postpone *v.* *Would it be possible to postpone the party?:* defer, delay, put off, waive, lay over, adjourn, hold in abeyance, reserve, remand, suspend; stay, keep back, table, shelve.

postulate *v.* **1.** *He postulated first that good*

and evil exist in all men: propose, put forth, submit; assume, take as an axiom, presume, take for granted, presuppose; conjecture, guess, hazard, surmise, theorize, hypothesize, speculate. —n. **2.** He believed the postulate that virtue is its own reward: premise, assumption, fundamental principle, presumption, presupposition, axiom, theorem, theory, hypothesis.

posture n. **1.** These exercises will improve your posture: stance, carriage, bearing, pose, shape, contour; set, attitude, mien. **2.** A man of his posture should have known better: position, station, situation, status, standing, condition, post, place. **3.** The meeting took on a different posture after his moving speech: mood, tone, tenor, aspect, air, attitude, state, case, phase; situation, circumstance, predicament.

potency n. The potency of his appeal was undoubted: strength, power, capacity, command, control, effectiveness, efficacy, efficiency, force, might, muscle, puissance, punch, sinew, steam, sway, vigor, virility, virtue, capability, authority.

potent adj. **1.** He was a potent puncher: powerful, strong, mighty, forceful, vigorous, overpowering, formidable, solid, tough. **2.** Hitler was a potent demagogue: influential, convincing, persuasive, compelling, impressive; forceful, powerful, forcible, dynamic. **3.** Aspirin is one of our most potent drugs: effective, efficacious, operative. —**Ant.** 1, 2 impotent, weak; ineffectual, inefficient. 1 weak, frail, puny. 2 unconvincing, ineffective, unimpressive.

potentate n. The potentate wore a ruby as large as an egg: ruler, sovereign, sultan, suzerain, monarch, chieftain, mogul, satrap, lord, emperor, prince, head of state, crowned head.

potential adj. **1.** Always be on the lookout for potential dangers: possible, conceivable, latent, concealed, hidden, lurking, covert, unapparent; unrealized, dormant, quiescent, passive; unexerted, unexpressed, implicit, undisclosed. —n. **2.** Also **potentiality** You're wasting your potential on this job: ability, possibilities, capability. —**Ant.** 1 actual, real, manifest.

potion n. The potion turned the witch into a lovely princess: elixir, brew, concoction, dram, tonic, philter, draft, mixture, draft, potation, libation.

potpourri n. The meal was a potpourri of many international dishes: medley, mixture, mélange, pastiche, miscellany, olla podrida; hodgepodge, confused mass, mishmash, gallimaufry, olio, goulash, stew, hash, jumble, mess, farrago; mosaic, patchwork; salmagundi, motley.

pouch n. She kept her cigarettes in a leather pouch: bag, sack, satchel, receptacle, container; (variously) pocket, wallet, purse, pocketbook, handbag, carryall, reticule; rucksack, kit, ditty bag.

pounce v. **1.** The hawk pounced on the field mouse: swoop down on, fall upon, drop from the sky, plunge, strike at, spring upon, fly at, dash at, jump at, snatch; surprise, take unawares, ambush. —n. **2.** With one pounce, the leopard had killed its prey: swoop, downrush, spring, leap, jump.

pound v. **1.** He pounded so hard on the window that it broke. The boxer pounded his opponent: strike, hammer, drum, beat, batter, bang, Informal clobber; pummel, maul, trounce, thump, thwack, clout, cudgel, smack, wallop; drub, lambaste, thrash, paste, fustigate, bruise, beat black and blue. **2.** His head pounded from the headache: throb, beat, pulsate, palpitate. **3.** The natives pounded the grain into a fine powder: pulverize, crush, crumble, grind. **4.** They pounded down the stairs: stomp, thunder, march, tramp, clomp.

pour v. **1.** The wine steward poured champagne into the glasses: let flow, decant; tap, draw off; spill, squirt, effuse, slop; lade out. **2.** He worked so hard perspiration just poured from him: stream, issue, flow, gush, spout, cascade; seep, ooze, dribble, drop, drip; drain. **3.** It poured for 40 days and nights: rain heavily, rain hard, rain in torrents, Informal rain cats and dogs, come down in buckets, come down in sheets; flood, deluge, drench.

pout v. Stop pouting and do what I tell you: sulk, look sullen, grimace petulantly, have a hangdog look, make a long face, scowl, crab, fume, brood, brood over, fret, mope; be out of humor, frown, glower, lower.

poverty n. **1.** The family lived in poverty: privation, need, neediness, destitution, indigence, penury, impoverishment, pennilessness, insolvency, bankruptcy, pauperism; want, lack; beggary, mendicancy. **2.** There's a poverty of acting talent today: lack, deficiency, insufficiency, shortage, dearth, paucity, scarcity, deficit, meagerness. —**Ant.** 1 affluence, luxury, opulence, comfort; richness. 2 abundance, sufficiency, overabundance, plethora.

powder n. They ground it to powder: grain, grains, grit, dust, crumb, film, meal, particle, talc.

powdery adj. Powdery snow accumulated on the window sill: pulverized, ground, pestled, milled, floury, mealy, chalky, dusty, triturated, comminuted, crushed; shredded, grated.

power n. **1.** The doctors restored her power of speech: faculty, capability, capacity, competence, aptitude, talent, skill, genius, attribute, qualification, gift, endowment, property, quality. **2.** You could see the power in his big hands: strength, force, might, potency, energy, puissance, powerfulness, pressure, muscle, brawn, iron grip; vigor, vitality. **3.** The manager has the power to fire an employee: right, prerogative, status, influence, sway, prestige, authority, license. **4.** The cardinal was the real power behind the throne. The Western powers turned down the Soviet proposal: authority, ruler; dominant state, superpower, major nation. **5.** The lights flickered as the power was reduced: electricity, hydroelectric power, nuclear energy, solar energy, thermal energy. —v. **6.** Electricity powers all our appliances: energize, activate, operate, supply with power, give energy to. —**Ant.** 1 incapability, incapacity. 2 weakness, impotence, feebleness; enervation, listlessness.

powerful adj. **1.** The athlete should have a

powerful body: strong, able-bodied, mighty, potent, indomitable, unconquerable, invincible; vigorous, robust, sturdy, hardy, brawny, husky, athletic, muscular, strapping, stalwart, stout, herculean. **2.** *He's a powerful speaker:* commanding, authoritative, cogent, forceful, high-powered, energetic, rousing, moving, exciting, emphatic, incisive, intense, effective.

powerfully *adv. He spoke powerfully:* forcefully, forcibly, effectively, energetically, intensely, mightily, strongly, vigorously, authoritatively.

powerless *adj.* **1.** *Samson was powerless after Delilah cut his hair:* helpless, without strength, impotent, feeble, incapable, impuissant, feckless, weak, debilitated, incapacitated, disabled, prostrate, immobilized, crippled, infirm. **2.** *The town was left powerless and had to surrender:* defenseless, unarmed, weaponless, pregnable, vulnerable.

powwow *n.* **1.** *The committee scheduled a powwow of the leading authorities in the field:* meeting, conference, parley, talk, consultation, interview, palaver, discussion, huddle, discourse; forum, colloquy, round table, colloquium; council, congress, conclave, assembly, convention, summit conference. —*v.* **2.** *The boss wants to powwow about the fall schedule:* confer, consult, discuss, talk, parley, palaver, huddle, convene, caucus, meet.

practicable *adj. Adding a fireplace to the dining room may not be practicable:* practical, feasible, workable, attainable, doable, possible, achievable, functional, viable, performable, accomplishable, within one's powers, within the realm of possibility. —**Ant.** impracticable, impractical, unworkable, unfeasible, impossible.

practical *adj.* **1.** *Let me give you some practical advice:* useful, sound, sensible, realistic, functional, solid, down-to-earth, serviceable, utilitarian, pragmatic, pragmatical, systematic, efficient, businesslike; judicious, hardheaded, unsentimental, unromantic, matter-of-fact. **2.** *As a practical fund-raiser he knows how to get people to feel charitable:* working, practiced, seasoned, veteran, experienced, versed, accomplished, proficient, skilled, skillful, qualified, able, expert; trained, instructed. —**Ant.** 1, 2 impractical, unpractical. 1 theoretical, speculative, unsound, injudicious. 2 inexperienced, unversed, unqualified.

practically *adv. He was such a good friend he was practically a member of the family. I'm practically finished:* virtually, in effect, actually, essentially, nearly, in the main, almost, just about, all but, substantially; fundamentally, basically, to all intents and purposes.

practice *n.* **1.** *With practice he could speak French fluently:* training, drill, repetition, discipline, preparation, seasoning, exercise, rehearsal. **2.** *The new methods did not go into practice until last year:* operation, action, use, usage, effect, execution, performance, exercise, application, play. **3.** *It was her practice to rise every morning at dawn:* custom, wont, habit, procedure, rule, routine, process, method, manner, fashion, mode, way, ritual, ways, conduct,

observance, tendency, modus operandi. **4.** *His shady practices got him a prison term:* method, action, deed, maneuver, trick, ruse, dodge, device. —*v.* **5.** *He practiced the piano every day:* rehearse, drill, discipline, train; familiarize with, become proficient at, prepare for, qualify. **6.** *Why don't you practice what you preach?:* perform, do, carry out, follow, put into practice, put into action, apply, use, utilize, live up to, turn to use, bring into play, set to work. **7.** *He's only practiced dentistry for a year:* perform in, work at, engage in, pursue, be engaged in.

pragmatic *adj. The problem requires a pragmatic solution, not theories:* down-to-earth, matter-of-fact, practical, utilitarian, hardheaded, sober, businesslike, hard-boiled, sensible, realistic, unidealistic, hard-nosed, materialistic, unsentimental. —**Ant.** idealistic, theoretical; romantic, dreamy, sentimental.

praise *n.* **1.** *He had nothing but praise for his son:* good words, compliments; approval, appreciation, approbation, acclaim, congratulation, commendation, laudation; admiration, regard, esteem, respect; applause, accolade, plaudit, cheer, hurrah; eulogy, panegyric, encomium, tribute, testimonial. **2.** *The congregation raised their voices in praise:* worship by hymn-singing, adoration. —*v.* **3.** *The mayor praised him for his philanthropic activities:* commend, laud, approve, acclaim, extol, congratulate, compliment, applaud, cheer, root for; panegyrize, eulogize, exalt, *Slang* tout, build up. **4.** *Praise the Lord:* worship, celebrate, glorify, exalt; revere, venerate, honor.

praiseworthy *adj. His praiseworthy deed earned him a special citation:* worthy, estimable, excellent, fine, exemplary, commendable, admirable, laudable, meritorious.

prance *v. She pranced around when she heard the good news:* dance, skip, cavort, caper, gambol, romp, frolic; leap, spring, jump, vault; bounce, bound, frisk; strut, swagger.

prank *n. They thought that hiding his car keys was a harmless prank:* trick, caper, joke, escapade, antic, shenanigan, horseplay, lark, mischief, gambol, practical joke, stunt, spoof, tomfoolery.

prattle *n.* **1.** *The prattle increased as the crowd grew restless:* gab, babble, blab, prate, twaddle, chitchat; *Slang* hot air, yak; cackling, gibbering, jabbering, gabbling. —*v.* **2.** *They prattled endlessly about their rich friends:* jabber, chatter, babble, blather, gabble, blab, chitchat.

pray *v.* **1.** *I pray for your good health:* make devout petition to God, commune with God, address the Lord, offer a prayer, say one's prayers, invocate; fall on bended knee. **2.** *I pray you, please be kind:* beg, beseech, entreat, implore, plead, supplicate, make an entreaty for, importune, cry to; ask earnestly, request, solicit, call upon, petition, urge, sue, bid.

prayer *n.* **1.** *The priest led the congregation in prayer:* litany, orison, praise, thanksgiving, adoration, worship, glorification. **2.** *Often* **prayers** *You're the answer to my prayers!:* hope, dream, aspiration; request, appeal, plea, petition, solicitation; supplication, invocation; entreaty, suit, beseechment.

prayerful adj. She knelt and assumed a prayerful attitude during Communion: pious, devout, godly, religious, holy, pietistic, worshipful, reverent, solemn, spiritual, reverential. —**Ant.** blasphemous, impious, irreverent; disdainful, contemptuous.

preach v. **1.** He devoted his life to preaching the word of God: sermonize, proclaim, discourse, evangelize, homilize, preachify. **2.** Practice what you preach: advocate, urge, advise, counsel, profess, press urgently, exhort, propagate, stand for, hold forth, declare, pronounce, expound, admonish, promulgate, prescribe.

preacher n. He started his career as a country preacher: clergyman, minister, churchman, ecclesiastic, evangelist, reverend, pastor, man of the cloth, prebendary, parson, vicar, curate, chaplain, Informal sky pilot; sermonizer, homilist.

precarious adj. **1.** The situation was precarious politically: vulnerable, uncertain, problematical, ticklish, uncontrolled, critical, insecure, touch-and-go, not to be depended upon, unreliable, undependable, doubtful, dubious, questionable. **2.** Free-lance work can be a precarious occupation: hazardous, risky, perilous, unsafe, chancy, unsteady, unstable, shaky; alarming, sinister. —**Ant.** 1 certain, sure, secure, dependable, reliable, unquestionable. 2 safe, steady, stable.

precaution n. Take every precaution so as not to catch cold: safety measure, caution, care, safeguard, defense; protection, security; forethought, provision, prudence, foresight, anticipation, carefulness, heedfulness, circumspection, wariness.

precede v. A dance act preceded the star's performance: go before, go ahead of, come before, take place before, go on before; antedate, antecede.

precedence also **precedency** n. **1.** In any chronology, everything has precedence to something else: antecedence, priority in time, preexistence. **2.** My family takes precedence over my business: importance, preeminence, predominance, preference, prevalence; priority.

precedent n. She set a precedent as the first woman executive in the company: example, pattern, model, guideline, standard, criterion.

preceding adj. The preceding message was prerecorded: previous, earlier, prior, foregoing, preliminary, precursory, antecedent, anterior; preexistent, former, first-named or -mentioned, aforesaid, aforementioned, abovementioned.

precept n. His father gave him a few precepts before he left for college: maxim, principle, axiom, rule, teaching, motto, dictate, declaration, commandment; law, edict, dictum, decree, statute, regulation, canon, ordinance, bull, ukase.

precious adj. **1.** She owned many precious antiques: costly, dear, expensive, high-priced, valuable, priceless, invaluable, inestimable, beyond price, not to be had for love or money; rare, uncommon, choice, exquisite. **2.** A family is a precious blessing in life: valuable, highly esteemed,

cherished, choice, treasured, prized, valued, beloved, adored; sweet, darling, adorable, lovable. **3.** She was a precious, old-fashioned lady in her 90's: excessively nice, dainty, affected, pretentious, overrefined, fastidious, prissy, finicky, fussy, particular, meticulous, finical.

precipice n. The path ends at the precipice, which has a 50-foot drop: cliff, cliff edge, ledge, escarpment, bluff, headland, palisade, crag, declivity.

precipitate v. **1.** The war precipitated his induction into the army: hasten, bring on, quicken, expedite, speed up, accelerate, advance, spur. **2.** The explosion precipitated tons of snow from the mountain: throw, hurl, thrust, cast, fling, propel, drive, launch, catapult, discharge, let fly. —adj. **3.** She had to make precipitate choices as the test was only 5 minutes: hurried, hasty, abrupt, rushed, proceeding rapidly, speedy; headlong, reckless, rash, incautious, foolhardy, imprudent, thoughtless, impetuous, impulsive.

precipitous adj. **1.** The path was precipitous: steep, abrupt, sheer, perpendicular. **2.** Precipitous flight took her abroad: precipitate, precipitant, abrupt, breakneck, headlong, hasty, heedless, hurried, impatient, impetuous, madcap, quick, rapid, rash, reckless, rushing, sudden, swift; unanticipated, unexpected, unforeseen, without warning; ill-advised, indiscreet. —**Ant.** 1 gradual, sloping 2 thoughtful, considered.

précis n. The article is a précis of the poet's philosophy: summary, synopsis, brief, digest, condensation, abstract, résumé, compendium, abridgment, epitome, rundown, outline, sketch, recapitulation, French aperçu.

precise adj. **1.** Can't you be more precise in your answers?: exact, specific, strict, true, clear-cut, express, definite, explicit, accurate, incisive, unequivocal, to the point, distinct, literal; careful, painstaking, meticulous, fastidious. **2.** He had precise ways of doing things and would not change: exact, particular, unbending, inflexible, meticulous, distinct, rigid, strict, finicky, fussy. —**Ant.** 1 inexact, implicit, indefinite, ambiguous, equivocal, indistinct, vague, indeterminate, neb-ulous; careless, heedless, loose, lax, incautious. 2 flexible, changing, haphazard.

precisely adv. They calculated expenses precisely: exactly, accurately, correctly, definitely, literally, specifically, strictly.

precision n. He wrote with precision: exactness, preciseness, accuracy, meticulousness, scrupulous care, rigor, attention; authenticity, factualness, truthfulness, fidelity.

preclude v. Her full schedule will preclude a visit to our city: prevent, foil, thwart, hamper, hinder, stop, check, inhibit, curb, forestall, head off, stave off, deter, nip in the bud, debar. —**Ant.** encourage, help, facilitate, enable.

precocious adj. She's such a precocious little girl!: uncommonly smart, mature, advanced, smart, bright, brilliant, gifted, quick, clever, apt. —**Ant.** slow, backward, retarded, stupid.

preconception n. You have this preconception about New Yorkers and you're wrong: prejudg-

ment, predisposition, fixed idea, notion, presumption; bias, prejudice.

precursor *n. The polite letters were only precursors to blackmail:* vanguard, advance guard, forerunner; harbinger, messenger; usher, herald; predecessor, antecedent; sign, token, mark, omen, portent, warning; symptom.

predatory *adj. The pirates were predatory and unpredictable:* rapacious, raptorial, predacious, vulturine, plunderous, piratical, thievish, marauding, pillaging, larcenous.

predestination *n. It was predestination that we met and fell in love:* fate, fortune, kismet, destiny, providence, what must be, God's will, inevitability, force of circumstances; preordination, predetermination. —**Ant.** accident, chance.

predetermined *adj. The final vote at the conference was pretty much predetermined:* already settled, foreordained, preplanned, decided, predestined, calculated, premeditated, prearranged, deliberate, intentional, planned, destined, fated.

predicament *n. How'd I ever get into such a predicament?:* trying situation, dilemma, dangerous condition, trouble, crisis, difficulty, imbroglio, perplexity, sad plight, strait, corner, quandary, *Informal* hot water, jam, scrape, fix, bind, mess, hornet's nest, pinch, pickle.

predict *v. I predict that you will meet a handsome stranger:* prophesy, forecast, foretell, prognosticate, foresee, divine, read the signs, anticipate, envision; betoken, presage, augur, omen.

predictable *adj. Her reaction was predictable:* foreseeable, foreseen, anticipated, calculable, certain, expected, likely, sure, sure-fire. —**Ant.** unforseen, unexpected, surprising, unlikely.

prediction *n. It's uncanny, but all her predictions have come true:* prophecy, soothsaying, forecast, foretelling, prognostication, crystal gazing, augury, portent, divination; anticipation, announcement, proclamation, declaration.

predilection *n. I have a predilection for rich desserts:* preference, predisposition, partiality, proneness, proclivity, propensity, leaning, penchant, bent, inclination, tendency; attraction, love, liking, fondness, fancy, desire, taste, hunger, appetite, relish; prepossession, prejudice, bias, favor. —**Ant.** aversion, disinclination, dislike, hatred.

predispose *v. His mother's work as a nurse predisposed him to become a doctor:* incline, dispose, make of a mind to, bias, prejudice, sway, influence, prevail upon, prompt, induce, persuade, urge, encourage; seduce, win over, entice, lure, tempt.

predisposed *adj. The audience was predisposed to like the play:* biased, partial, prone, susceptible, eager, enthusiastic, inclined, liable, subject, willing, agreeable, amenable.

predominant *adj. English is one of the world's predominant languages:* dominant, important, major, reigning, sovereign, chief, main, leading, supreme, paramount; controlling, authoritative, ruling, influential, ascendant, powerful, strong, forceful, potent, vigorous. —**Ant.** subordinate,

secondary; minor, unimportant, lesser, inferior; uninfluential, weak.

predominate *v. Red predominated in the color scheme:* dominate, preponderate, prevail, outweigh, surpass, overrule.

preeminent *adj. Secretariat is the preeminent racehorse of recent years:* foremost, superior, supreme, paramount, second to none, unequaled, consummate, unrivaled, unparalleled, unsurpassed, matchless, peerless, incomparable, best, greatest, dominant, predominant; eminent, renowned, illustrious, famous, famed, celebrated, honored, distinguished.

preempt *v. The President's address preempted an hour of prime TV time:* appropriate, expropriate, arrogate, take, seize, usurp, confiscate, take over, commandeer, help oneself to. —**Ant.** give up, renounce, surrender, acquiesce.

preface *n.* **1.** *In his preface the author explains his purpose in writing the book:* foreword, prologue, preamble, introduction, prelude, overture, proem. —*v.* **2.** *He prefaced his talk with a humorous story:* begin, introduce, lead into, open, start, commence, initiate, launch, usher into. —**Ant.** 1 epilogue, postscript, appendix. 2 close, end, conclude, wind up.

prefer *v.* **1.** *I prefer to read mysteries:* choose rather, like better, fancy, single out, adopt, pick out, elect, make a choice of, select, have rather, favor, pick and choose, opt, make one's choice, think better, take to, fix upon. **2.** *He refused to prefer his claim as legal heir:* file, lodge, put forward, set forth, present, bring forward, offer, proffer, tender. **3.** *Archaic He was preferred to lieutenant:* promote, raise in office, advance in rank, graduate, elevate; aggrandize, exalt, dignify, ennoble. —**Ant.** 1 dislike, reject, eschew; hate, loathe, detest, abhor.

preference *n.* **1.** *Do you have a preference for a particular food?:* partiality, first choice, liking, fancy, predilection, inclination, bent, leaning, predisposition, bias, prejudice, proclivity, proneness, propensity; option, selection, pick. **2.** *College graduates generally get job preference over high school graduates:* favoring, precedence, advantage, favored treatment, priority; ascendancy, predomination, supremacy. —**Ant.** 1 dislike, aversion, eschewal; hatred, abhorrence.

preferred *adj. Taking a trip at home was the preferred option:* advantageous, approved, liked, well-liked; chosen, picked, adopted, culled, decided upon, elected, endorsed, fancied, favoured, handpicked, sanctioned, selected, set apart, settled upon, singled out.

pregnancy *n. Her pregnancy was in its sixth month:* gestation, gravidness, incubation, parturiency.

pregnant *adj.* **1.** *She was pregnant with their first child:* with young, parturient, gravid, gestating, with child, having a baby, *Informal* expecting, in a family way; about to become a mother. **2.** *The land was pregnant with lush growth:* full, replete, filled, fraught, abounding, teeming, plenteous, rich; fruitful, fertile, prolific, luxuriant, fecund, copious; productive, proliferous, fructiferous; life-giving. **3.** *He provided many preg-nant ideas:* meaningful, important, provocative, significant, weighty, seminal, momentous; suggestive, full of possibilities, impressive, forceful, potential.

prejudice *n.* **1.** *Her prejudices were many, her reasons few:* bias, preconception, slant, prejudgment, predisposition, one-sidedness, narrow-mindedness, bigotry; intolerance, unfairness, discrimination, partiality, predilection, favoritism. **2.** *Will you be able to judge without prejudice to the defendant?:* impairment, injury, detriment, damage, harm, hurt, ill; loss, disadvantage. —*v.* **3.** *He successfully prejudiced the audience with his demagoguery:* affect with a prejudice, influence against, sway, bias; predispose, jaundice, poison, infect, taint, contaminate. **4.** *His attempted escape seriously prejudiced any hopes for parole:* damage, harm, hurt, injure, mar, impair, spoil.

preliminary *adj.* *The judge held a preliminary hearing:* preparatory, initiatory, preparative, introductory, prefatory, prelusive, prelusory, precursory. —**Ant.** final, concluding; subsequent, following.

prelude *n.* **1.** *Months of training were a necessary prelude to the championship bout:* preliminary, introduction, preparation; opening, beginning, preamble, preface, prologue. **2.** *The pianist played several of Chopin's preludes:* short instrumental piece, brief musical selection; overture, introductory movement.

premature *adj.* **1.** *The candidate's announcement of victory was premature:* too soon, too early, hasty, abortive, overhasty, previous, too advanced, precipitate; untimely, ill-timed, inopportune, unseasonable. **2.** *The crop is too premature to harvest:* unripe, undeveloped, immature, raw, green; unfledged, unprepared, unready, callow; incomplete, embryonic, unhatched, vestigial; rudimentary. —**Ant.** l on time, well-timed, timely, opportune; too late, overdue. 2 mature, ripe; overripe.

premeditate *v.* *They premeditated the murder:* plan, deliberate, prearrange, predetermine, consider, precontrive, predesign.

premeditated *adj.* *He was charged with premeditated murder:* prearranged, predesigned, plotted, predetermined, predevised, studied, planned; deliberate, conscious, intended, intentional, purposeful, calculated, considered, contrived, willful, voluntary; in cold blood, with malice aforethought.

première *n.* *We attended the première:* first night, opening, opening night, debut, first performance, first showing.

premise *n.* **1.** *It was the lawyer's premise that his client was innocent:* hypothesis, basis for reasoning, proposition, argument, postulate, principle, theory; assumption, presumption, supposition, presupposition. **2. premises** *The police think the thief is still on the premises:* buildings and grounds, property, site; immediate area, vicinity, environs, precincts.

premium *n.* **1.** *If you buy two you get a premium of one more, free:* prize, gift, reward, bo-

nus, award, bounty, gain, return; remuneration, reparation, recompense, compensation, payment; incentive, encouragement; benefit, consideration. **2.** *Hard-to-get theater tickets can be bought at a premium:* inflated rate, overpayment, increased value, appreciation. **3.** *I put a premium on punctuality:* high value, great stock, priority.

premonition *n.* *She had a premonition that he had been injured:* forewarning, foreboding, prediction, omen, portent, presage, sign, augury, auspice, token, foretoken; indication, presentiment, feeling, inkling, *Informal* hunch.

preoccupied *adj.* *The preoccupied scholar didn't hear the doorbell:* absorbed, engrossed, concentrating, inattentive, in a brown study. —**Ant.** unthinking, thoughtless, frivolous.

preoccupy *v.* *I was too preoccupied to hear the bell:* engross, occupy wholly, absorb, immerse, arrest, engage the attention, take up, make uppermost in the mind, wrap up; fascinate, obsess.

preparation *n.* **1.** *He insulated the house in preparation for winter:* anticipation, precaution, prior measure, safeguard, provision, timely care; prudence, foresight, forethought, expectation. **2.** *The preparation of the banquet hall took six hours:* readying, preparing. **3.** Usually **preparations.** *We had only a week to make preparations for the wedding:* plan, arrangement, measure, preliminary. **4.** *The druggist suggested a preparation to relieve the ache:* concoction, composition, prescription, mixture, elixir, tincture, dressing; confection, prepared food. **5.** *His earlier preparation made him perfect for the job:* experience, qualification, training, apprenticeship, instruction, direction, education, guidance, tutelage, teaching, seasoning.

preparatory *adj.* *She took a preparatory course:* preliminary, introductory, preparative, elementary, basic, primary, elementary, opening, prefatory, previous, primary, prior to, before.

prepare *v.* **1.** *We prepared the playroom for the party:* ready, make ready, get ready, fix, adapt, arrange, rearrange. **2.** *Prepare yourself to take advantage of opportunity. They prepared themselves for the worst:* ready, prime, be resolved, make provision for, provide, be prepared, be ready; take steps, clear for action, put things in order, make all snug, set one's house in order.

prepared *adj.* *They were prepared for anything. The prepared mixture went down well:* in readiness, ready, able, adjusted, arranged, bagged, cinched, fixed, guard, packed, planned, predisposed, prepped, primed, qualified, ready, rehearsed, up on, on guard, *Informal* psyched up.

preponderance also **preponderancy** *n.* *The preponderance of factory buildings made the city ugly:* predominance, prevalence, profusion, domination, majority, greater numbers, dominance, mass, bulk, lion's share, plurality; excess, superabundance, glut, surplus, oversupply, surfeit, plethora, redundance.

prepossessing *adj.* *She was a lovely, prepossessing young woman:* attractive, striking, charming, pleasant, engaging, nice, personable, winsome; alluring, fascinating, bewitching, captivating, inviting, tantalizing, enchanting, entrancing, beguiling. **—Ant.** unprepossessing, unpleasant; uninviting.

preposterous *adj. That's the most preposterous idea I've ever heard:* outrageous, ridiculous, ludicrous, absurd, unthinkable, fatuous, foolish, silly, imbecilic, asinine, idiotic, stupid, inane, nonsensical, laughable, irrational, unreasonable, bizarre, *French* outré.

prerequisite *adj.* **1.** *The standard phone call is prerequisite to any personal meeting with him:* required beforehand; required, mandatory, called for, necessary, imperative, essential; indispensable, demanded, *French* de rigueur. *—n.* **2.** *Several years' experience is the minimum prerequisite for this job:* requirement, something needed beforehand, qualification, postulate, necessity, need, requisite, condition, exigency, stipulation, demand, *Latin* sine qua non.

prerogative *n. You have the prerogative of changing your mind:* privilege, warrant, right, license, claim; liberty, freedom, advantage, exemption; birthright, rightful power, authorization, legal power; grant, due, franchise; choice, option.

presage *n.* **1.** *We had no presage of the disaster:* presentiment, foreboding, foreshadowing, indication, premonition, foreknowledge. **2.** *Dark clouds were a presage of the storm:* portent, omen, sign, token, augury, warning, signal, prognostic. *—v.* **3.** *The economist presaged a recession:* portend, foreshadow, forecast, predict.

prescribe *v. The bylaws prescribed that membership should be limited. The doctor prescribed lots of rest:* legislate, enact, rule, direct, specify, stipulate, dictate, order, enjoin, command, decree, ordain, proclaim, require, impose, demand; institute, appoint, establish, settle, authorize, set, fix, assign; recommend, advocate, urge, require.

prescription *n.* **1.** *The doctor handed her a prescription:* decree, direction, formula, instruction; medicine, mixture, preparation, prescript, recipe, remedy. **2.** *She thought the new law was a prescription for disaster:* regulation, remedy, rule, decree, edict.

presence *n.* **1.** *Your presence at the meeting will help our cause:* attendance; existence, being, substantiality, subsistence; hypostatization, reification; entity, life. **2.** *There's a spy in our presence:* company, midst; neighborhood, immediate circle, group. **3.** *The speaker was a man of poor presence. He had a certain presence that made women fall in love with him:* personal appearance, features, lineaments, aspect, favor, look, figure; charisma, compellingness, character, vitality; air, manner, bearing, carriage, deportment, demeanor, mien, expression. **4.** *There's the presence of something evil in that old house:* spirit, shadow, ghost, curse, manifestation, specter, incorporeality, phan-

tasm, wraith, apparition, revenant, vision, phantom, eidolon.

present¹ *adj.* **1.** *The present state of affairs changes matters somewhat:* current, existent, existing, contemporary, at the moment, contemporaneous, now, prevalent, immediate, instant, coeval; now under consideration. **2.** *All the students are present today:* here, attending, in attendance, not absent, not away, accounted for; in, at hand, near, nearby, near, about, in the room, *Informal* on-the-spot, on hand; nigh, vic-inal; existing in a place or thing, embedded, unremoved, implanted, rooted, ensconced. *—n.* **3.** *I live in the present, not the past:* now, nowadays, here and now, today, this day and age, the time being, the moment. **—Ant.** 1 past; future. 2 absent. 3 the past, the future.

present² *v.* **1.** *It is my honor to present you with this token of our esteem. He presented the school with a check for one million dollars:* give, give a gift to, confer, bestow, award, grant, accord, hand over; make a present of, donate, place at one's disposal, provide, supply; proffer, offer, propose, submit, put forward, advance, tender; give away, give out, mete out, dole out, render; contribute, *Informal* chip in. **2.** *Please present your first witness:* summon, call up, introduce, show, exhibit, display, produce, bring on; offer, proffer, tender, bring forward, draw forth. **3.** *He presented his views and then sat down:* state, assert, declare, apprise of, tell, impart, make known, give by way of information, give notice of, communicate; propound, asseverate, frame, allege, profess, cite, pronounce, aver, hold forth; recount, relate, recite, deliver, read, *Informal* come up with; advance, offer, proffer, tender, propose, put forth, expound. **4.** *Present your bills on the first of the month:* submit, hand in, give over, turn in, surrender. *—n.* **5.** *I got many presents for my birthday:* gift, offering, thing presented; donation, endowment, bequest, legacy, benefaction, boon, largess, gratuity, perquisite, tip, grant, oblation, fee; alms, liberality, bounty.

presentable *adj.* **1.** *She looked quite presentable in her evening gown:* becoming, proper, fit to be seen, suitable, appropriate, acceptable, decent; fashionable, stylish, modish, chic. **2.** *The house was presentable but far from immaculate:* good enough, passable, respectable, not bad, suitable, decent, unobjectionable, so-so, tolerable, acceptable, better than nothing, fair-to-middling.

presentation *n.* **1.** *He gave his presentation for new marketing procedures:* offering, proposal, proposition, proffering, submission, offer, proffer; oveture, advance. **2.** *The awards presentation lasted four hours:* show, exhibition, exposition, production, demonstration, exhibit, display; materialization, appearance, unfoldment, unfolding, exposure, disclosure. **3.** *The check was the nicest presentation of all:* gift, present, bestowal, largess, grant, boon, oblation; benefaction, favor, gratuity, tip, compliment; fee; liberality, bounty.

presentiment *n. We had no presentiment he*

would turn up: anticipation, expectation, foreboding, forecast, forethought, premonition, presage, hunch, intuition, *Informal* vibes, funny feeling.

presently *adv.* **1.** *The speaker will begin presently:* soon, pretty soon, shortly, anon, forthwith, directly, before long, in a while, after a while, in no time now, any time now, in a short time. **2.** *We are presently reading Shakespeare's tragedies:* now, at present, at the present time, at the moment, currently, contemporaneously; *(variously)* this week, this month, this semester, this year.

preservation *n. We must strive for the preservation of our natural resources:* conservation, saving, salvation; safeguarding, safekeeping, protection, defense, maintenance. **—Ant.** abandonment, decay, ruin, destruction.

preserve *v.* **1.** *We must preserve our natural resources:* keep safe, guard, protect, watch over, care for, shield, shelter, conserve, save, defend, safeguard, maintain, keep intact, perpetuate, secure, keep sound, nurse, foster. **2.** *You can have strawberries in winter if you preserve them in the summer:* *(variously)* can, conserve, *Informal* put up; seal, insulate; freeze, refrigerate; cure, smoke, salt, season, marinate, corn, pickle; dehydrate, dry; embalm, mummify. **—n. 3.** Often **preserves** *I like peach preserves on my breakfast rolls:* jelly, jam, conserve, confection, compote, marmalade, comfit, sweetmeat, sweet. **4.** *No hunting is allowed in the preserve:* wildlife enclosure, sanctuary, haven, reservation, reserve, shelter, refuge, park, game preserve.

preserves *n. pl. She spent the morning making preserves:* jam, jelly, spread, confection, conserve, *French* confiture.

preside *v. Judge Johnson will be presiding at the trial. Father always presided over dinner:* be in authority, hold the chair, be at the head of, hold authority; wield authority, chair, chairman, preside at the board, preside at a meeting; direct, conduct, control, govern, administrate, administer, rule, command, *Informal* boss; supervise, manage, superintend, keep order, regulate; watch, overlook, oversee; host, hostess.

president *n.* **1.** Usually **President** *The President addressed the nation:* executive officer, chief executive, chief of state, head of the nation, head of government, commander in chief, chief magistrate, first citizen. **2.** *He succeeded his father as president of the company:* chief officer, chief official, head, executive head, chairman, ruler.

press *v.* **1.** *Press the "down" button. Press one clove of garlic:* push; depress, push down, force down, thrust down, push in, flick; condense, compress, mash, crush, reduce, squeeze, cram, jam, stuff, force, strain. **2.** *The tailor pressed the trousers:* iron, smooth, steam, flatten, hotpress; calender, mangle. **3.** *She pressed the puppy to her bosom:* hold closely, hug, squeeze, fold in one's arms, embrace, clasp; fondle, caress, pet, snuggle. **4.** *The problem pressed us sorely for weeks:* trouble, oppress, burden, bear upon, weigh heavily upon, bear down upon. **5.** *He keeps pressing me for money:* beg, implore, importune, urge repeatedly, entreat, plead, enjoin, supplicate, appeal, exhort; dun, tax; beset, *Informal* bug, hit, tap; urge insistently, prod, urge with force, compel, constrain, insist on, put the screws on; exact, extort, force from, hound, pressure, bear down on, set on. **6.** *The fans pressed around the rock group:* crowd, press in upon, surge, swarm, throng, mill, assemble, congregate, come together, gather, flock together, collect, cluster, herd, huddle. **7.** *I'm a little pressed for time:* push, rush, hurry, be in short supply of, constrict, be hard put. **—n. 8.** *Members of the press weren't allowed into the meeting:* the Fourth Estate, reporters, journalists, newsmen, public press, newspapermen; media, newspapers, periodicals, radio, TV, television, broadcasting, news services. **9.** *The manuscript goes to press next week. Put the duck meat through a press:* printing press, letter press, printing machine; machine for compressing; printing, publication, final form. **10.** *A press of fans greeted her at the stage door:* crowd, throng, mob, multitude, swarm, bunch, host, horde, pack, drove, legion, army, body, heap, crush. **11.** *The press of one-night stands tired the performer:* pressure, duress, stress, obligation, duty, compulsion; annoyance, bother.

pressing *adj. It was a pressing meeting and all members had to attend:* urgent, imperative, necessary, vital, critical, crucial, essential, indispensable, needed, needful, exigent, important; insistent, crying, clamoring, importunate, demanding. **—Ant.** unnecessary, nonessential, dispensable, unimportant, trivial; regular, customary, routine.

pressure *n.* **1.** *The pressure inside the old submarine was almost unendurable:* air pressure, compression, compaction, squeeze; weight, heaviness, gravity, density. **2.** *Having to cope with so many problems was a pressure hard to bear:* stress, strain, tension, difficulty, adversity, straits, trouble, trial, grievance, load, care, oppression, burden, affliction, anxiety, distress. **3.** *The pressure his father applied got him his position with the company:* influence, sway, pull, weight; power, potency, force, bias, interest. **4.** *The pressures of business were too much for him:* press, urgency, exigency, hurry; stress, strain, pinch; compulsion, coercion; need, necessity, want; demand, requirement.

prestige *n. He was an author of international prestige:* fame, celebrity, glory, renown, reputation, prominence, note, repute, mark, notability, distinction, significance, authority, account, import, importance, consequence, preeminence, eminence, honor, respect, esteem, regard, report.

prestigious *adj. She attended a prestigious university:* distinguished, illustrious, esteemed, honored, respected, reputable, notable, famed, prominent, renowned, eminent, acclaimed, famous, celebrated, well-known, important, outstanding. **—Ant.** inconsequential, unknown, insignificant, unimportant.

presumably *adv. He said he'd be here next week, presumably for Dad's birthday:* doubtless, probably, assumably, likely, presumptively, in all probability, all things considered, in all likelihood, ostensibly, to all appearances, apparently, unquestionably, to all intents and purposes.

presume *v.* **1.** *Dr. Livingstone, I presume?:* assume, guess, take for granted, take it, believe, postulate, posit, think likely, suspect, imagine, conceive, fancy; suppose, hypothesize, surmise, gather, deduce, have it. **2.** *She presumed to write him in her daughter's name:* dare, take leave, take a liberty, make free, venture, make bold, be so bold, act presumptuously, have the audacity. **3.** *She presumed on his good nature:* rely too much, take undue advantage of, impose.

presumption *n.* **1.** *Your presumption that he'd be here was wrong:* assumption, premise, belief, supposition, postulate; speculation, guess, surmise, conjecture; preconceived opinion, presupposition, prejudgment, preconception. **2.** *It took a great deal of presumption to insult the ambassador at his own party:* audacity, brass, effrontery, arrogance, gall; *Informal* cheek, nerve; *Slang* lip, chutzpah; impertinence, impudence, insolence, rudeness, flippancy, presumptuousness, pride, haughtiness, egotism; boldness, daring, forwardness. **—Ant.** 2 respect, deference, politeness.

presumptuous *adj.* **1.** *It was presumptuous of the young senator to challenge the leadership so soon:* bold, audacious, daring, overconfident, overfamiliar, forward, nervy, shameless, brash, brazen, brassy, fresh, cocky. **2.** *Her presumptuous airs made her disliked by many:* haughty, proud, snobbish, assuming, overbearing, lofty, patronizing, pompous, lordly, imperious; disdainful, contemptuous, domineering, dictatorial, arrogant.

pretend *v.* **1.** *Let's pretend we're grownups!:* make believe, take a part, fill a role, imagine, fancy, suppose; mimic, impersonate, masquerade, playact. **2.** *She pretended a headache so she wouldn't have to go:* feign, fake, affect, put on, assume, simulate, imitate, make a show of; counterfeit, sham, dissimulate, dissemble, put on a false front. **3.** *I pretended to know what they were talking about:* affect, claim, purport.

pretended *adj. The pretended reason for his absence was illness:* feigned, counterfeit, fake, avowed, affected, artificial, fictitious, imaginary, mock, ostensible, phony, professed, pseudo, purported, so-called, supposed, false, falsified, bogus.

pretense *n.* **1.** *The stage murder looked real, but it was only pretense:* make-believe, pretension, fake, hoax, invention, fabrication, imposture, sham, counterfeit; trick, trickery, deceit, deception. **2.** *By pretense the detective infiltrated the smuggling ring:* deception, subterfuge, guile, feint, camouflage, pretext, disguise, mask, cloak, cover. **3.** *Her mannerisms were affected and full of pretense:* show, pretentious-

ness, showing off, ostentation, display, fanfaronade, ostentatiousness, affectedness, affectation, false show, airs; boasting, bragging, vaunt, bombast, bluster, pomposity. **—Ant.** 1 reality, actuality, fact. 2 truthfulness, honesty. 3 simplicity, sincerity, candor, frankness, ingenuousness, openness.

pretension *n.* **1.** *His pretension to the crown was invalid:* claim, right, title, pretense; aspiration, ambition. **2.** *She talked of her rich friends with great pretension:* ostentation, affectation, snobbery, hypocrisy, pretense, airs, showing off, ostentatiousness, grandioseness, display, show, showiness, pretentiousness; pomp, bombast, self-importance, pomposity.

pretentious *adj. He was a pompous, pretentious man. Her grave is marked by a large, pretentious monument:* showy, ostentatious, pompous, fatuous, bombastic, pedantic, boastful, flaunting, overbearing, affected, unnatural, insincere, presuming, assuming; lofty, airy, snobbish, *Informal* high-and-mighty, hoity-toity, stuck-up; puffed-up, blown-up, inflated, exaggerated, theatrical, stagy; flashy, tawdry, ornate, gaudy, garish, florid, extravagant, overdone; self-glorifying, self-important, self-praising, smug. **—Ant.** unpretentious, modest, unaffected, natural, unassuming; plain, simple.

preternatural *adj. The revelations could only be explained by preternatural means:* supernatural, superhuman, supranatural, supernormal, miraculous, hypernormal, preterhuman; extramundane, unearthly, unworldly; metaphysical, transcendental; occult, mystical; esoteric, mysterious, arcane; bizarre, weird, strange, eerie, uncanny. **—Ant.** mundane, worldly, everyday, commonplace.

pretext *n. She used the ringing of the doorbell as a pretext to hang up:* excuse, alleged reason, professed purpose, basis, ground, pretense, subterfuge, semblance, bluff, feint, pretension; justification, vindication.

pretty *adj.* **1.** *She's such a pretty girl!:* attractive, beautiful, pleasing to the eye, lovely, comely, bonny, handsome, good-looking, beauteous, sightly, pulchritudinous, well-favored, fair, goodly; delicate, dainty, graceful; captivating, alluring, fetching, charming, engaging; well-proportioned, symmetrical, shapely, well-set, well-made. **—adv. 2.** *It was a pretty poor turnout for the meeting:* moderately, adequately, reasonably, satisfactorily, fairly, rather, somewhat. **—Ant.** 1 unattractive, ugly, plain, unsightly, clumsy, graceless, unseemly; unshapely, unsymmetrical.

prevail *v.* **1.** *A feeling of political indifference prevailed throughout the country:* abound, exist generally, be current, be widespread, obtain, exist, be prevalent. **2.** *Abstract Expressionism prevailed in the big international art shows of the 1950's:* predominate, be prevalent, preponderate, abound; have sway, hold sway, rule, reign. **3.** *The better fighter prevailed:* triumph, be victorious, win, win out, be a winner, be the victor, gain the palm, win the laurels; prove superior, succeed, conquer, overcome, carry the day, *Informal* bring home the bacon.

prevailing *adj.* **1.** *The prevailing fashion in evening wear was the tuxedo:* current, popular, in style; widespread, prevalent, general, usual, customary, normal, conventional, accustomed; definite, fixed, established, set. **2.** *The prevailing colors in her apartment are green and blue:* principal, main, prevalent, dominant, predominant, preponderant. —**Ant.** 1 dated, out-of-date, old-fashioned; unusual, rare, uncommon. 2 infrequent, uncommon; minor, subordinate, lesser, inferior.

prevalent *adj. Pigeons and squirrels are prevalent in city parks:* numerous, common, frequent, frequently occurring, prevailing, general, widespread, rife, pervasive, universal, abundant, extensive, rampant, ubiquitous, habitual, usual, normal, conventional, everyday, commonplace, familiar, customary, popular. —**Ant.** infrequent, rare, unusual, uncommon.

prevaricate *v. She may have prevaricated a bit about her illustrious forebears:* lie, fib, stretch the truth, dissemble, perjure, deceive, palter, be untruthful, tell a story, tell a tall story, be evasive; falsify, misstate, fake, hoodwink, counterfeit, misrepresent, mislead, distort.

prevent *v. Vitamin C is supposed to prevent colds. We prevented him from committing a gross error:* keep from occurring, defend against, counteract, fend off, hold back, stave off, ward off; block, bar, dam, deter, thwart, frustrate, foil, anticipate, balk, arrest, nip in the bud, forestall, avoid, preclude, avert; stop, halt, obviate, veto, prohibit, forbid, rule out; intercept, sidetrack, turn aside, deflect, draw off, turn away. —**Ant.** permit, allow, encourage, urge, incite.

prevention *n. Prevention of forest fires is up to you. As a prevention against disease you should be inoculated:* avoidance, stoppage, hindrance, inhibition, restraint, preclusion; obviation, deterrence, elimination, defeat; frustration, thwarting, forestallment, interception.

previous *adj. Have you had any previous experience?:* prior, preceding, earlier, early; foregoing, foregone, antecedent, former, erstwhile, before, aforesaid, aforementioned. —**Ant.** subsequent, consequent, ensuing, succeeding, following, later.

previously *adv. He stated previously that he didn't want the nomination:* before, earlier, at one time, once, a while back, a while ago, formerly, in times past, long ago, heretofore, earlier on, sometime back, back when.

prey *n.* **1.** *The huge bird flew off with its prey in its claws:* quarry, game, kill, food; victim; quest, prize. **2.** *She was the prey of unscrupulous lawyers:* victim, dupe, target, gull; *Slang* pigeon, fall guy, cat's-paw, sucker, patsy. —*v.* **3.** *Stronger animals prey upon weaker ones:* feed upon, devour, consume, eat, feast upon, fatten upon, gorge oneself upon; live off; fasten upon, fasten oneself to, parasitize, infest; suck the blood of.

price *n.* **1.** *What's the price of that car? He must pay the price of his folly:* cost, face value, amount, charge, fee, rate, expenditure, expense, outlay; selling price, current price, market value, list price, retail price, wholesale price; value, worth, exchange value, par value; penalty, punishment, fine, forfeiture. —*v.* **2.** *The coat was priced at $100. We priced various travel packages:* assess, evaluate, set a price on, appraise, value.

priceless *adj. He owned many priceless antiques:* without price, beyond price, invaluable, valuable, precious, dear, high-priced, costly, expensive, worth a king's ransom; irreplaceable, rare; incomparable, peerless; cherished, prized, treasured, valued. —**Ant.** worthless, cheap, inexpensive; common.

prick *n.* **1.** *It was a mere prick to draw blood:* perforation, jab, pinhole, prickle, puncture. —*v.* **2.** *They pricked the sausages:* perforate, pierce, puncture, cut, jab, lance.

prickly *adj. He was especially prickly by mid-afternoon:* grumpy, snappish, touchy, irritable, bad-tempered, cantankerous, edgy, fractious, peevish, petulant, waspish.

pride *n.* **1.** *She took great pride in her son's success:* satisfaction, pleasure, enjoyment, delight, joy, happiness; gratification, comfort. **2.** *A man with such pride rarely loses his temper in public:* self-esteem, dignity, self-respect, honor. **3.** *If you cannot admit you are wrong, you are guilty of pride:* self-importance, egoism, egotism, vanity, conceit, self-love, self-glorification, vainglory; immodesty, smugness, self-satisfaction; show, display, ostentation, parade, pomp, airs, pretension; swagger, arrogance, haughtiness, superciliousness, pomposity, imperiousness. —*v.* **4.** *He prided himself on being a man of self-control:* be proud of, be pleased with, have a feeling of pride in oneself, be satisfied with, be delighted at, be gratified at. —**Ant.** 3 humility, modesty, meekness.

priest *n. The priest gave a blessing:* cleric, churchman, clergyman, clergyperson, curate, pastor, padre, divine, ecclesiastic, father, father confessor, friar, reverend; nun, sister, mother.

prig *n. Don't be such a prig—let your hair down and enjoy the party!:* prude, puritan, bluenose, fuddy-duddy, bluestocking, *Informal* stuffed shirt; hypocrite, bigot; pretender; pedant, precisionist, formalist, attitudinarian; faultfinder, nitpicker.

prim *adj. She was a prim, old-fashioned schoolteacher:* particular, fussy, overprecise, strict, proper, tidy, fastidious, straitlaced, puritanical, prudish, squeamish; priggish, prissy, fuddy-duddy, starched, unbending, inflexible, stiff-necked, starched, no-nonsense, stuffy, haughty, smug. —**Ant.** careless, loose, untidy; informal, casual, easygoing, relaxed, carefree.

primarily *adv. The paintings are primarily from the 18th century:* chiefly, mainly, principally, mostly, largely, predominantly, first and foremost, essentially, fundamentally, for the most part, basically, in the main, generally.

primary *adj.* **1.** *He did well in primary school and better in high school:* first, introductory, beginning, initial, elementary, preparatory; rudimentary, nascent. **2.** *Your primary duties are outlined in this job description:* chief, main, principal, fundamental, basic, key, cardinal; prominent, predominant, dominant, ruling, star, leading, greatest, highest, utmost; important, necessary, vital, essential. **3.** *Love and hate are primary emotions:* primitive, primordial, primal, primeval; initial, original, prime, beginning, first; basic, fundamental, elementary, elemental, rudimental, rudimentary, key, basal; native, indigenous, aboriginal, natural, inherent, innate; oldest, earliest. **—Ant.** 1 secondary, following, subsequent, succeeding, ensuing, later. 2 lesser, unimportant, subordinate, inferior; indirect, supplemental.

prime *adj.* **1.** *He's the prime suspect in the murder case:* primary, chief, main, principal, cardinal, most important, leading, predominant; ruling, preeminent; greatest, highest, maximal, crowning, paramount, superlative, supreme, utmost; unsurpassed, unmatched, matchless, best, without peer, peerless; important, necessary, essential, vital. **2.** *Only prime foods are served at the hotel:* superior, quality, of the best quality, Grade A, choice, specially selected, select, first-class, unparalleled; *Slang* A1, top-drawer, top-flight, ace, top-hole. **3.** *Love is a prime emotion:* basic, fundamental, elementary, rudimentary, elemental, basal, essential; intrinsic, inherent, innate, congenital; native, indigenous, natural; primal, oldest, earliest, first, original. **4.** *Spring is the prime time for planting:* best, preferred, most advantageous, most favored, choice; timely, in good time, opportune, convenient; fit, seemly, suitable, fitting, propitious, befitting, expedient, well-timed, provident, auspicious, lucky; in good season, seasonable, early, bright and early. *—n.* **5.** *She's in the prime of health:* peak, perfection, ideal level, excellence; full strength, greatest strength; height, zenith, heyday, best days; maturity, full flowering, blossoming, bloom, flower, full beauty, pink. *—v.* **6.** *Her mother primed her for a life on the stage:* prepare, ready, fit, make ready, put into readiness, get ready, adapt, adjust; groom, coach, train, instruct, breed, raise, educate, school, tutor; inform, fill in, guide, prompt, brief. **—Ant.** 1 secondary, lowest, least important. 2 the worst, second-class, third-rate. 4 untimely, inconvenient, unfit, unsuitable, inauspicious; unseasonable.

primeval *adj. Longfellow's "Song of Hiawatha" takes place in the "forest primeval":* prehistoric, primordial, ancient, primitive, antediluvian, early, aboriginal, ancestral; legendary, mythological.

primitive *adj.* **1.** *Space travel is still in a primitive stage:* early, earliest, original, first, primary; beginning, elementary, introductory; undeveloped, unrefined, crude, rudimentary. **2.** *The Eskimos of the far north are primitive people:* uncivilized, native, aboriginal, backward; antique, archaic. **3.** *He had a primitive style of painting:* unsophisticated, simple, uncomplicated; artless, uncultivated, undeveloped, unskilled, unlearned. **4.** *The pioneers had to en-*

dure quite primitive living conditions: uncomfortable, inconvenient, crude; bare, Spartan, austere, ascetic. **—Ant.** 1 advanced, later; developed, sophisticated, refined. 2 civilized, modern. 3 sophisticated, artful, fashionable. 4 comfortable, elaborate.

primordial *adj. They traced it back to primordial times:* primeval, prehistoric, earliest, elemental, first, fundamental, original, primal, primary, prime, radical, basic.

primp *v. She primped for hours in front of the mirror:* groom oneself, dress carefully, dress fastidiously, preen, groom, plume, prettify, spruce up; make up, gussy up, doll up.

principal *adj.* **1.** *He's the principal stockholder:* chief, leading, foremost, most important, supreme, superior, capital, main, preeminent, dominant, prominent, predominant, outstanding, controlling, most considerable, cardinal; primary, prime, first; fundamental, essential, basic; greatest, ultimate, paramount. *—n.* **2.** *The principals were gathered on stage for rehearsal:* star, leading man, leading lady, protagonist, featured player, *Informal* first fiddle. **3.** *She was sent to the principal's office:* head of a school, headmaster, master, dean, preceptor; person in authority, chief person, chief authority, superior. **4.** *How much interest will there be on a principal of $5,000?:* original sum, original investment, capital sum, invested sum, fund; money. **—Ant.** 1 least important, inferior, minor, least powerful, weakest, inconsiderable; secondary, auxiliary, subsidiary, supplemental.

principally *adv. Though a composer, she is known principally as a pianist:* mostly, primarily, chiefly, mainly, largely, predominantly, for the most part, basically, fundamentally, first and foremost, particularly, especially, above all.

principle *n.* **1.** *He studied the principles of psychology:* rule, truth, law, assumption, precept, fact, basis, fundamental, rudiment, proposition, element, formula; regulation, canon, code, direction, dictum; theorem, axiom, maxim. **2.** *His principles wouldn't allow him to work on Saturday:* belief, article of faith, credo, tenet, theory, creed; dogma, doctrine, religious belief, scruple, way of thinking, system of belief; teaching, view, attitude, position. **3.** *He is too much a man of principle to compromise:* morality, standards, ethics, uprightness, honesty, probity, scruples; honor, integrity, incorruptibility, sense of honor; righteousness, rectitude, respectability; goodness, virtue, morals; conscientiousness. **—Ant.** 3 immorality, dishonesty; dishonor.

print *n.* **1.** *There were fresh prints in the snow:* imprint, impress, impression, stamp. *—v.* **2.** *They printed business cards:* imprint, impress, engrave, run off, issue, stamp.

prior *adj. Sorry, I'd love to go, but I have a prior commitment. Prior to her coming here she was in Paris:* previous, preceding in time, preexisting, preexistent, antecedent, anterior, earlier, former; precursory, erstwhile, going before, foregoing, prefatory, preparatory; aforementioned, aforementioned, aforesaid. **—Ant.** subsequent, following, later.

priority *n. This project has priority over all others:* precedence, greater importance, preference, urgency, immediacy, the lead, precedency, preeminence; antecedence, seniority, superiority, ascendancy.

prison *n. He was sent to prison for committing robbery:* jail, jailhouse, *British* gaol; house of detention, penitentiary, penal institution, reformatory, house of reform, house of correction, internment center; dungeon, tower, bastille, penal colony, *Navy* brig, *Slang* jug, clink, slammer, tank, brig, stir, can, cooler, pokey, calaboose, pen, big house, joint.

prisoner *n. The prisoners got an hour of exercise a day:* convict, detainee, captive, defendant, hostage, internee, *Informal* jailbird, con.

prissy *adj. His prissy behavior offended customers:* prim, finicky, fussy, fastidious, particular, pernickety, picky, squeamish, stuffy.

pristine *adj. It was a pristine part of the woods that few hikers had ever seen:* undefiled, unsullied, untouched, unspoiled, untarnished, virginal; uncontaminated, unpolluted, pure, unmarred. **—Ant.** sullied, defiled, contaminated, polluted, spoiled, tarnished.

privacy *n.* **1.** *A hidden microphone in a person's home is an invasion of privacy:* privateness, seclusion, security, integrity; solitude, solitariness, sequestration; isolation, dissociation; retirement, withdrawal, retreat. **2.** *The generals planned the overthrow in privacy:* secrecy, privity, secret, clandestineness.

private *adj.* **1.** *This is private property:* privately owned, personal, special, exclusive, express, restricted, closed, limited, confined, fixed; not public, nonpublic. **2.** *Plans for the takeover were kept private:* confidential, clandestine, privy, secret, inviolate; unofficial, nonofficial; undercover, covert, classified, undisclosed, off-the-record, concealed, unrevealed, hidden, underground, buried, invisible; *Informal* under wraps, hush-hush; mysterious, cryptic, obscure, esoteric, indistinct, dark. **3.** *He retired to his private retreat in the mountains:* secluded, isolated, remote, desolate, reclusive, privy, sequestered, lonely, solitary, lonesome, unfrequented. **—Ant.** 1, 2 public. 1 unrestricted, open, general, unlimited, unconfined. 2 known; official; disclosed, unconcealed, revealed; *Informal* out in the open. 3 unsecluded, frequented, visited.

privation *n. The family's privation was pitiable:* need, neediness, want, lack; poverty, impoverishment, indigence, penury, impecuniousness, pauperism, exigency, mendicancy, destitution, beggary, bankruptcy, reduced circumstances; distress, misery, hardship, straits, pinch. **—Ant.** ease, wealth, riches, affluence, success, good luck; sufficiency, gain, acquisition.

privilege *n.* **1.** *Big businesses enjoy certain privileges that smaller ones do not. It is my privilege to serve you:* right, due, entitlement, prerogative, prerequisite, birthright, freedom, liberty; license, power, authority, franchise, title, charter, patent; advantage, favor, boon, benefit; honor, pleasure. **—v. 2.** *This pass will privilege you to attend the closed hearings:* grant, permit, empower, allow, entitle.

privileged *adj. They belong to that privileged group of people who enjoy the "good life." Talks between lawyer and client are privileged and cannot be divulged:* limited, special; exempt, free, immune, excused; allowed, granted, permitted, licensed, sanctioned, warranted, empowered, entitled, authorized; unaccountable, not liable.

privy *adj. We were privy to his thoughts:* cognizant, aware, conscious, apprised, acquainted, informed.

prize *n.* **1.** *She won second prize in a beauty contest:* award, trophy, medal, medallion, cup; reward, citation, guerdon, premium; ribbon, decoration, blue ribbon, laurels, honors, accolade, crown. **2.** *As a secretary she was a prize:* jewel, pearl, gem, diamond, pure gold, treasure, masterpiece, choice bit, champion; *French* crème de la crème; *Slang* honey, catch, humdinger, dandy, crackerjack, lulu, pip, peach. **—adj. 3.** *Her prize recipe was printed in the newspaper:* honored, winning, award-winning, blue-ribbon. **—v. 4.** *She prized him for his good sense and understanding:* value, set store by; admire, respect, look up to, honor, esteem, regard, like, hold in esteem, appreciate; hold in affection, hold dear, treasure, cherish.

probability *n. We assessed the probability of winning:* likelihood, likeliness, chances, conceivability, credibility, expectation, feasibility, odds, plausibility, practicability, prospect.

probable *adj. The weather forecast is for probable showers. He's a probable candidate:* likely, possible, promising, presumable, presumptive, presumed, expected, supposed; encouraging, assuring, seeming, ostensible, apparent; *Informal* in the cards; credible, logical, reasonable, plausible, tenable, thinkable, conceivable, believable.

probably *adv. We will probably leave on Sunday:* in all probability, most likely, in all likelihood, as like as not, presumably, supposedly.

probe *v.* **1.** *Scientists probed the causes of the earthquake:* investigate, look into, inspect, pry into, delve into; scrutinize, study, examine, test; question, inquire, interrogate, quiz, query; hunt, pursue, follow up, seek after. **2.** *The surgeon probed for the bullet in the man's back:* look for, seek, explore with a probe, search; *Informal* fish for, rummage; penetrate. **—n. 3.** *His probe into the bribery charges proved futile:* investigation, inspection, exploration, examination, inquiry, inquest, study, search, research, survey, analysis, trial, test, review.

probity *n. Above all, the Presidency needs a man of probity for the Cabinet post:* integrity, uprightness, honesty, virtue, high-mindedness, morality, character, principle, honor, trustworthiness, incorruptibility, straightness, decency, goodness, righteousness. **—Ant.** dishonesty, duplicity, unscrupulous, corruption.

problem *n.* **1.** *I need help in solving this math problem. They ran into marital problems:* question, query, poser, puzzle, riddle, conundrum;

difficulty, disagreement, disputed point. —*adj.*
2. *The problem child needs special care. She
had problem hair:* unruly, difficult, hard to manage, uncontrollable, unmanageable; intractable,
incorrigible, stubborn. —**Ant.** 2 perfect,
model, manageable.

problematic *adj. The composition of Saturn's
rings is problematic:* uncertain, doubtful, questionable, dubious, unsettled, undetermined, enigmatic, unknown; perplexing, paradoxical, puzzling; difficult, troublesome, worrisome. —**Ant.**
certain, settled, known, undisputed, unquestionable.

procedure *n. The doctor developed a new procedure for liver transplants:* method, way, manner, course, process, strategy, modus operandi,
M.O., technique, approach, mode, methodology,
routine.

proceed *v.* **1.** *Proceed to the next light, then
turn left. Please proceed with your work:* go, go
forward, move ahead, move forward, go ahead,
move on, go on, continue, carry on, progress,
advance, make one's way; press on, push on,
keep moving. **2.** *After everyone was seated the
chairman proceeded to announce his plans:* undertake, set out, begin, commence, start; take
action, act, move, operate, function, work. **3.**
*His destitution proceeded from unwise spend-
ing:* result, arise, issue, take rise, come, follow,
ensue, succeed, be caused, spring, flow, emanate, start, derive, be derived, be produced,
originate, grow, stem. —**Ant.** 1 retreat, go
backward, get behind; discontinue, stop; regress, lose ground; stop moving.

proceedings *n. pl.* **1.** *Minutes of the
proceedings were written down by the club secretary:* activity, happenings, occurrences,
transactions, events, incidents, operations,
affairs, matters, actions, goings on, doings. **2.**
*His lawyer is representing him in the
proceedings:* legal action, legal process, lawsuit,
suit, action at law; litigation, trial, case, cause.
3. *He carefully read the proceedings from the
last meeting:* minutes, records, account, report,
returns, description, memoranda, archives.

proceeds *n. pl. The proceeds of the bazaar will
go to needy families:* profit, gain, receipts,
gross, net, gate, box office, yield, income, revenue, earnings, assets; reward, remuneration,
returns; money, lucre, pelf, winnings, take,
pickings.

process *n.* **1.** *Sherlock Holmes discovered the
murderer by a process of elimination:* method,
system, manner, practice, procedure, mode;
course of action, plan, scheme, project, line of
action, policy, ways and means; measure, step;
usage, function. **2.** *Adolescence is the process
of going from childhood to maturity:* procedure,
set of changes, proceeding, passage, course,
movement, motion, transformation; unfolding;
flux, flow, change, progress, progression. **3.** *The
server gave him a process to appear in court:*
summons, court order, writ, subpoena. —*v.* **4.**
*Grocery stores sell many foods that have been
processed:* prepare, treat, convert, alter, transform; *(variously)* freeze, preserve, freeze-dry,

smoke, dehydrate, dry, candy, can. **5.** *We will
process your order at once:* take care of, fill,
ship, handle, deal with, dispose of.

procession *n. The procession moved slowly
down Main Street:* parade, march, caravan, pageant, cavalcade, motorcade, cortege, train, file,
rank, column, array, line; sequence; course;
passage, progression, progress, succession.

proclaim *v. The salesman proclaimed that his
tonic would cure all ills:* declare, announce, herald, make known, make manifest, make public,
broadcast, give out; promulgate, assert, affirm,
set forth, state, profess; publish, advertise, circulate, blaze abroad, publicize, trumpet, blazon,
call out, blare, cry, sing out, hawk about; tell,
voice; report, enunciate, communicate; release,
disclose, divulge, reveal. —**Ant.** retract, recall;
suppress, repress, conceal, secrete.

proclamation *n. The proclamation was posted
everywhere:* promulgation, announcement,
broadcast, declaration, decree, edict, manifesto,
notice, notification, pronouncement, publication,
advertisement.

proclivity *n. She has a proclivity toward sweet,
rich desserts:* propensity, leaning, inclination,
disposition, affection, liking, proneness, affinity,
tendency, predilection, penchant, bent, bias,
prejudice, partiality, predisposition, turn of the
mind; appetite, taste, desire, impulse; *Informal*
yen, soft spot. —**Ant.** dislike, aversion, hatred,
loathing, disinclination.

procrastinate *v. Stop procrastinating and finish your homework!:* delay, stall, play for time,
temporize, kill time, dally, tarry, loiter, dillydally,
dawdle, waste time, twiddle one's thumbs, linger, drag one's feet; put off action, defer, postpone, adjourn, put on ice, wait till tomorrow;
hesitate, hold back, hang back, lag, be dilatory.
—**Ant.** expedite, hasten, hurry, speed, speed
up.

procreate *v. The Lord commanded them to
procreate children and replenish the earth:* beget, breed, engender, propagate, father,
mother, sire, bear, reproduce, generate, spawn,
give birth to, create, get, conceive, bring forth,
produce; multiply, proliferate.

procreation *n. Procreation outran subsistence:*
reproduction, begetting, generation, propagation, breeding.

procure *v. He was able to procure a Rembrandt
etching from the art dealer:* obtain, acquire, get,
secure, get into one's hands, lay hands on, attain, achieve, come by; take possession of, receive, pick up; take, appropriate, help oneself
to, seize, commandeer; win, earn, gain; get together, accumulate, gather; buy, purchase;
cause to occur, effect, bring about, contrive,
elicit, induce, evoke, incite.

prod *v.* **1.** *The shepherd prodded the sheep with
his staff:* poke, jab, prick, flog, whip, lash, needle; shove, push; accelerate, quicken, speed,
propel. **2.** *The teacher tried to prod the students to take more interest:* impel, stir, incite,
excite, stimulate, instigate, prompt; actuate,
rouse, stir up, set in motion, move, animate,
encourage, motivate; urge, exhort, goad, pro-

voke, egg on, nag, spur, bear down upon, pressure.

prodigal *adj.* **1.** *He had nothing left of his inheritance because of his prodigal ways:* wasteful, spendthrift, unthrifty, thriftless, overliberal, profligate, extravagant, exorbitant, lavish, excessive, gluttonous; improvident, dissipating, inordinate, intemperate, immoderate, reckless, impetuous, precipitate, wanton. **2.** *The prodigal amount of eggs laid by the fish insure the survival of the species:* bountiful, profuse, abounding, abundant, plentiful, bounteous, ample; lush, luxuriant, lavish, exuberant, generous; numerous, countless, numberless, innumerable, multitudinous; teeming, swarming, myriad, replete, copious. **—***n.* **3.** *The prodigal went through money as if it were water:* spendthrift, squanderer, spender, wastrel, profligate. **—Ant. 1** thrifty, frugal, economical, cautious, miserly, stingy; provident, temperate, moderate. **2** scarce, scanty, deficient, scant, meager, sparse, few, limited.

prodigious *adj. His knowledge of music was prodigious. A prodigious collection of modern art was on display:* exceptional, rare, singular, extraordinary, uncommon, unique, impressive, striking, noteworthy, renowned; surprising, startling, amazing, astounding, astonishing, dumbfounding, overwhelming, wonderful, remarkable, marvelous, wondrous, miraculous; enormous, vast, huge, immense, far-reaching, large, terrific, big, grand, great, monumental, mighty, stupendous, tremendous, gigantic, colossal, monstrous; inconceivable, unimaginable, unthinkable; uncustomary, unwonted, unprecedented. **—Ant.** unexceptional, ordinary, common, usual; unimpressive, unremarkable; small, negligible.

prodigy *n. Mozart was a prodigy who could read, play and improvise music at 5 years of age:* gifted child, great talent, child genius, young genius, wonder child, *German* Wunderkind; genius, wizard, master, mastermind, expert, whiz, whiz kid; marvel, wonder, sensation, phenomenon, *Informal* stunner; rare occurrence, rarity, *Latin* rara avis.

produce *v.* **1.** *They're thinking of producing a new synthetic fiber:* make, create, manufacture, construct, fashion, shape, compose, devise, fabricate, turn out, frame, evolve, form, concoct, conceive, develop; originate, institute, found, give birth to, beget, generate, invent, procreate, give life to, hatch, bring into being, give origin to, bring into existence, bring into the world. **2.** *The land produces enough to feed us:* provide, supply, furnish, give, bear, yield, afford; flower, sprout, bloom, bear fruit. **3.** *Can you produce evidence to clear him?:* show, exhibit, present, show forth, present for inspection, bring into view, advance, cause to appear, put on view, hold up to view, manifest, bring forward, bring in, adduce, evince, set forth, bring out, bring to light, display, put on display; materialize, reveal, divulge, uncover, disclose, unveil, discover, unmask, make plain, *Informal* come up with. **4.** *Dim lights and soft music are supposed to pro-*

duce a romantic atmosphere: cause, effect, give rise to, set up, put into effect, put in force, effectuate, bring about, bring off; achieve, accomplish, bring to pass, carry into execution. **—***n.* **5.** *He has a small store where he sells groceries and produce:* agricultural products, staple commodities, fruits, vegetables, greens, staples, greengrocery, foodstuffs. **—Ant. 3** conceal, hide, withhold. **4** prevent.

product *n. She showed us the product of his industry. Everyone agreed the company's product was good:* consequence, effect, goods, harvest, outcome, outgrowth, output, production, result, returns, spinoff, stock, upshot, yield, crop; merchandise, item, issue.

production *n.* **1.** *Japan is famous for the production of transistor radios:* making, producing, manufacture, manufacturing; building, construction, formation, origination, creation, fabrication; execution, effectuation, performance, fulfillment. **2.** *Several new productions will appear on Broadway this season:* presentation, theatrical offering, show, drama, play, stage show, entertainment, musical; motion picture, film, cinema, movie; carnival, circus. **3.** *With the production of an eyewitness, the man was convicted of murder:* introduction, appearance, showing, exhibit, display, materialization, show, presentation, manifestation, demonstration; disclosure, revelation.

productive *adj.* **1.** *He was president of a very productive firm:* producing, creating, creative, accomplishing much, prolific, effectual, efficacious; active, busy, vigorous, dynamic. **2.** *Through irrigation the desert was turned into productive land:* fruitful, fertile, fecund, proliferous, prolific, fructiferous; luxuriant, rich, plentiful, plenteous, copious, teeming, producing in abundance, yielding. **3.** *It was not a productive venture for him:* profitable, remunerative, gainful, worthwhile, paying, moneymaking. **4.** *Greed has been productive of many a man's downfall:* responsible for, bringing about, causing, bringing to pass. **5.** *After being released from prison he became a productive member of society:* useful, contributing, valuable, invaluable. **—Ant. 1**–3, **5** unproductive. **1** inactive; ineffectual. **2** unfertile, barren, sterile, unfruitful; poor, unyielding. **3** unprofitable, ungainful. **5** useless.

productivity *n. The new boss increased productivity:* output, productiveness, capacity, fertility, production, yield.

profane *adj.* **1.** *His profane language made the women blush:* irreverent, blasphemous, ungodly, godless, atheistic, agnostic, unbelieving, sacrilegious, irreligious, undevout, heretical, impious, unholy, unsaintly; foul, filthy, nasty, vile, abusive; wicked, evil, sinful, hellbound, diabolic, satanic, shameless, unchaste, unseemly, impure; crude, coarse, vulgar, obscene, lewd, bawdy, rib-ald, off-color. **2.** *Both sacred and profane music were played at the memorial service:* secular, nonreligious, lay, temporal, worldly, earthly, terrestrial. **—***v.* **3.** *The infidels profaned the holy shrine:* desecrate, debase, abuse, commit sacrilege, blaspheme; offend, outrage; misuse, misemploy, ill-use, waste; pollute, pervert, contaminate, prostitute, violate; mock, revile, scorn. —**Ant.** 1, 2 sacred, religious, spiritual. 1 holy, reverent, divine; decorous, proper, clean; delicate, seemly.

profanity n. Except for all the profanity, I liked the story: swearing, cursing, cussing, curse words, dirty words, expletives, four-letter words, obscenities, swearwords, oaths; scurrility, billingsgate, blue language, bad language, dirty talk; filth, scatology; obscenity, execration; blasphemy, irreverence, impiety, ungodliness.

profess v. **1.** He professed to be a member of royalty: claim, allege, lay claim, assume, purport; dissimulate, dissemble, sail under false colors, make a pretense of, pass oneself off, make out as if; simulate, act, pretend, put on, sham, feign, counterfeit, fake. **2.** He professed that he was, indeed, the masked bandit: confess, admit, own, acknowledge, affirm, confirm, certify, avow, vouch, aver, asseverate, depose; declare, state, proclaim, propound, announce; allege, assert, put forward, offer, advance; tell, say, enunciate; hold forth, contend, maintain. **3.** He professed Catholicism: declare one's faith in, embrace, believe in, practice.

profession n. **1.** What profession will you be studying for?: occupation, line of work, line, business, job, field, specialty, employment, work, vocation, walk of life, career, calling, métier, pursuit, undertaking, endeavor; office, position, situation, post, field, sphere; practice, service, industry, trade, craft. **2.** She wanted to marry a man in one of the professions: branch of learning, higher discipline; (variously) law, medicine, teaching. **3.** He gave a profession of eternal gratitude: declaration, statement, announcement, pronouncement; acknowledgment, confession, affirmation, confirmation, deposition, testimony, attestation; avowal, averment, promise, word, word of honor, troth, plight, pledge, vow, guarantee, assurance; assertion, claim, allegation. —**Ant.** 1 avocation, hobby. 3 denial, refutation, recantation.

professional adj. **1.** Professional athletes are not allowed in the Olympics: paid, receiving pay, in business as. **2.** You had better get professional advice before buying stocks or bonds: highly skilled, competent, knowledgeable, practiced, expert, experienced, adept, well-trained, well-informed. —n. **3.** Their house was decorated by a professional: expert, specialist, authority, adept. —**Ant.** 1, 3 amateur. 2 incompetent, inept.

professor n. The professor welcomed us to class: teacher, educator, faculty member, instructor, lecturer, pedagogue, sage, tutor.

professorial adj. His professorial attitude made him seem aloof: academic, bookish, donnish, pedantic, teachery, schoolmasterish, schoolmarmish, schoolteacherish, pedagoguish, preachy, didactic, Slang teachy.

proffer v. As a teacher, she proffered many suggestions for creative papers: offer, tender, volunteer, propose, suggest, hint. —**Ant.** refuse.

proficiency n. Her proficiency at gardening was remarkable: aptitude, ability, knack, accomplishment, competence, dexterity, efficiency, expertise, expertness, facility, know-how, knowledge, mastery, skill, skilfulness, talent, Informal the goods, the makings, savvy, the right stuff.

proficient adj. She was a proficient typist: skilled, skillful, capable, competent, able, good, adroit, deft, apt, adept, dexterous; expert, clever, sharp, masterly, masterful, efficient, effective, ready, quick, handy; trained, practiced, polished, accomplished, experienced, qualified, professional; talented, gifted, versatile. —**Ant.** unskilled, incapable, inept, incompetent, bad, maladroit, unaccomplished.

profile n. **1.** A profile of Washington appears on the U.S. quarter: outline, contour, delineation, lineaments, configuration, form, shape, figure; side view, side, half face, silhouette; skyline; picture, portrait, sketch, drawing. **2.** John Kennedy wrote Profiles in Courage: biography, short biography, tale, character sketch, portrait, vignette.

profit n. **1.** Did you make any profit last year?: gain, return, realization; (variously) gross profit, net profit, clear profit, marginal profit; money, remuneration, income, revenue, pay, earnings; proceeds, receipts; consideration, compensation, financial reward. **2.** Finishing college will be to your profit: advantage, benefit, interest, advancement, gain, improvement; good, benefaction, boon, favor; service, utility, use, avail, account, value. —v. **3.** Taking those extra courses profited me: benefit, help, serve, avail, stand in good stead. **4.** You must learn to profit by experience: make good use of, make the most of, be better for, be improved by, learn a lesson from, reap the benefit of, make use of, utilize, use, put to use. **5.** He hoped to profit from his investments: make money, earn, gain, come out ahead.

profitable adj. **1.** Selling that piece of property was quite profitable for me: gainful, rewarding, yielding profit, paying, moneymaking, remunerative, lucrative, well-paying; fruitful. **2.** It was a profitable experience: worthwhile, rewarding, productive, favorable, beneficial, advantageous, salutary, serviceable, useful; valuable, invaluable.

profligate adj. **1.** He's a profligate man, and no decent human being should have anything to do with him: dissolute, debauched, depraved, libertine, dissipated, degenerate, degraded, immoral, wicked, iniquitous; wanton, loose, abandoned, erotic, sybaritic, corrupt, evil, sinful, immoral, promiscuous, wild, fast, unprincipled, unbridled, unrestrained, licentious, lascivious, satyric. **2.** Your profligate ways are depleting your fortune: wasteful, prodigal, extravagant, lavish, unthrifty, spendthrift, improvident; unrestrained, unbridled, reckless. —n. **3.** I won't let my daughter go out with that profligate!: reprobate, profligate person, rake, satyr, debauchee, degenerate, dissipater, French roué; libertine, pervert, sinner, wrongdoer; spendthrift, wastrel, prodigal. **—Ant.** 1 moral, decent, upright; kind, good, virtuous, chaste.

profound *adj.* **1.** *That was a very profound statement:* deep, thoughtful, wise, sagacious, sage, penetrating, piercing, learned, erudite, intellectual, scholarly, educated; knowledgeable, comprehensive, recondite, omniscient, all-knowing; philosophical, reflective, thoughtful, well-considered, sober, serious, sober-minded; informed, well-informed, knowing, enlightened. **2.** *His death had a profound effect on her:* deep, severe, abject, extreme; thorough, thoroughgoing, far-reaching, radical, utter, out-and-out, complete, consummate; penetrating, piercing, pronounced, decided, positive. **3.** *Please accept my profound apologies:* deeply felt, heartfelt, keenly felt, sincere, heart-stirring, strongly felt, deep-seated, soul-stirring, moving; hearty, intense, keen, acute, abject. **—Ant.** 1 shallow, superficial, unwise, stupid, unlearned, uneducated, unknowledgeable, thoughtless, inconsiderate; uninformed, unenlightened; imprudent. 2 slight, superficial, shallow, surface, external. 3 insincere, shallow, hollow.

profundity *n.* *We all thought he was a young man of great profundity:* deepness, profoundness, reconditeness; erudition, wisdom, sagacity, learnedness; abstruseness, impenetrableness, abstractness. **—Ant.** superficiality, shallowness, frivolousness, triviality.

profuse *adj.* **1.** *She gave profuse thanks for our contribution. The island rejoiced in nature's profuse bounty:* generous, munificent, abundant, bountiful, bounteous, copious, ample, rich, lavish. **2.** *Your profuse spending has left you almost penniless:* wasteful, unthrifty, prodigal, improvident, spendthrift, intemperate, inordinate, immoderate, excessive, lavish, extravagant. **3.** *His acceptance speech was too profuse:* prolix, wordy, verbose, long-winded, garrulous, discursive, digressive, rambling, loquacious, diffuse. **—Ant.** 1 meager, scanty, inadequate, exiguous, sparse, cheap, stinting, skimpy, illiberal, close-fisted. 2 thrifty, penny-pinching, provident, temperate, moderate. 3 short, terse, pithy, brief, to the point.

profusion *n.* *The garden boasted a profusion of flowers:* great amount, great quantity, multiplicity, abundance, oversupply, plethora, multitude; superfluity, extravagance, excess, waste, surfeit, surplus, glut.

progeny *n.* *The castle passed into the hands of the duke's progeny and is still owned by the same family today:* descendant, offspring, young, child, children, issue, seed, offshoot; heir, heirs, scion, son, family, kin, kindred, blood, clan; posterity, race, stock, lineage, breed, line.

program *n.* **1.** *Today's program includes a tour of the Statue of Liberty:* schedule, order of events, things to be done, agenda, plan, order of business, curriculum, syllabus; timetable; card, bill, prospectus; book, slate, calendar, bulletin. **2.** *The ushers gave everyone a program for the evening's performance:* playbill, list of players, list of selections; notice, sketch, outline.

3. *New programs appear in the fall on television:* show, presentation, production; series. **—v. 4.** *We've programmed you to appear on his show next week:* schedule, arrange, book, slate, bill, calendar, docket, register, list; design, intend, expect; *Informal* line up.

progress *n.* **1.** *We made swift progress toward the mountains. He made progress with his work:* headway, advance, forward movement, advancement, furtherance; accomplishment, achievement; development, betterment, improvement, success. **2.** *Has the nation's progress been too fast?:* development, growth, rise, promotion; enrichment, enhancement, improvement; forward motion. **3.** *No one will be seated while the play is in progress:* process, development, course, unfolding, action, movement, stride. **—v. 4.** *He progressed within the company so fast he was made a vice-president in two years:* advance, proceed, move ahead, continue ahead, shoot ahead, go forward, get ahead, make headway, gain, make strides, gain ground, get on. **5.** *Have you progressed in your studies?:* advance, improve, become better, get better, make a turn for the better, grow better, make progress, make strides, make headway; increase, climb, mount; develop, grow, mature, grow up, ripen. **—Ant.** 1 regression; loss, failure, decline, retrogression, relapse, recession. 4 move backward, regress, retrogress, recede, go backward; lose ground, lose, get behind. 5 become worse, grow worse.

progression *n.* *The film showed the progression of events leading up to the incorporation of Austria in the Third Reich in April 1938:* sequence, succession, consecutiveness, continuance, order, series, continuation, continuousness; string, chain, strain; course, run; progress, advancement, furtherance, advance, ascent, climb, forward movement.

progressive *adj.* **1.** *He was an up-and-coming, progressive committeeman:* concerned with progress, supporting change; dynamic, forward-going, forward-looking, going ahead; advancing, advanced; enterprising; up-to-date; liberal, reformist. **2.** *It was a progressive disease and he would suffer more and more:* advancing step-by-step, gradual, increasingly severe, steadily going on, enlarging, incremental; traveling, spreading, ongoing. **—n. 3.** *Many young politicians are progressives:* liberal, reformist; ameliorist, activist; populist. **—Ant.** 1, 3 reactionary, conservative.

prohibit *v.* **1.** *The law prohibits occupancy by more than 250 persons:* forbid, disallow, proscribe, say no to, negate, disqualify, deny, veto. **2.** *He threw himself in front of the door and prohibited us from leaving:* prevent, inhibit, check, obstruct, impede, limit, hinder, block, curb, hamper, bar, interfere with; delay, stay, stop, preclude, obviate; ban, suppress, repress, withhold; restrict, enjoin, restrain. **—Ant.** 1, 2 permit, let, allow, suffer, tolerate; authorize, order. 1 endure, bear; command, consent to, give permission, license. 2 direct, empower, give consent, give leave; further.

prohibited *adj. The prohibited substance became legal:* illegal, banned, barred, forbidden, not approved, proscribed, refused, restricted, taboo, verboten, vetoed, wildcat.

prohibition *n. Age was no prohibition to taking part:* interdiction, prevention, embargo, ban, restriction. —**Ant.** permission.

prohibitive also **prohibitory** *adj. Prohibitive laws discouraged the drug trade. The project was abandoned because of prohibitive costs:* inhibitive, restrictive, circumscriptive, enjoining, restraining, forbidding; suppressive, repressive; preventive, injunctive; hindering, obstructive, disallowing, disqualifying, inadmissible, unacceptable.

project *n.* **1.** *My project this year is to refurnish the house:* undertaking, job, task, work, activity, assignment; plan, design, scheme, intention, ambition, aim, objective, goal. —*v.* **2.** *Could you project a new marketing technique for us?:* plan, design, draft, outline, propose, devise, frame, contrive, concoct, invent, map out. **3.** *Ledges project about one foot all around the building:* extend, jut out, stand out, stick out, protrude, overhang, beetle, bend over. **4.** *Remember to project your voice so that you're heard in the last row:* transmit, throw, throw out, cast, fling; eject, ejaculate, emit, expel, discharge, send; shoot, propel, hurtle, launch, fire. **5.** *He projected the weather for the coming week:* forecast, describe future conditions, calculate; predetermine. **6.** *Can you project next month's sales?:* forecast, plan ahead, predetermine, extrapolate.

projection *n.* **1.** *The narrow projection scarcely provided a foothold:* ledge, shelf, extension, jutty, overhang, eave, brow, extrusion, protrusion, protuberance, bulge, ridge, bump. **2.** *His projection shows what the population is likely to be in 1999:* estimate, estimation, approximation, guess, *Slang* guesstimate, prediction, prospectus, forecast, extrapolation.

proletariat *n. John Wanamaker rose from the proletariat to become a big businessman:* working class, laboring classes, laborers, rank and file, wage earners, the common people, the masses, the people, populace, the crowd; the multitude; commonalty, commoners, commonage; *Greek* hoi polloi; *Latin* plebs, populus, vulgus mobile; *Disparaging* lower classes, lower orders, the herd, the horde, the mob, rabble, the great unwashed, *French* canaille. —**Ant.** upper class, aristocracy, blue bloods, upper crust, gentry, nobility.

proliferate *v. Rabbits proliferated after they were introduced into Australia:* multiply, increase, reproduce rapidly, breed quickly, overproduce, procreate, regenerate, propagate, pullulate, teem, swarm; hatch, breed, spawn.

prolific *adj.* **1.** *My pet hamsters were so prolific they soon needed a larger cage:* reproductive, proliferous, proliferative, breeding, propagating, fertile, fruitful, yielding, fecund, procreative, multiplying, progenitive, germinative; luxuriant, copious, abundant, profuse, lush. **2.** *Haydn was a prolific composer who wrote 104 symphonies:*

very productive, creative. —**Ant.** 1 barren, unfruitful, unyielding, unproductive, unfertile, sterile. 2 unproductive.

prolong *v. We had to prolong our stay for another week:* lengthen, extend, make longer, stretch, elongate, attenuate, protract, draw out; maintain, sustain, continue, perpetuate, spin out, drag out; slow down, hold back, delay, retard. —**Ant.** curtail, shorten, abridge, abbreviate, limit, lessen; expedite, hurry, speed up.

prominence *n.* **1.** *His prominence in the music field is well known:* eminence, distinction, importance, preeminence, fame, renown, prestige, celebrity, notability, reputation, name; conspicuousness, salience, noticeability, significance; brilliance, greatness, illustriousness; grandeur, nobility, majesty, splendor; respectability, honor, dignity; mark, credit, popularity, notoriety; weight, influence, significance, might, superiority. **2.** *The doctor could feel a slight prominence on his skull:* projection, extrusion, protuberance, bulge, convexity, process, excurvature, excrescence, tumescence, rising, swelling, protrusion, hump, knurl, bump, knob, lump, node. **3.** *The house was built on a prominence overlooking the sea:* high point, height, promontory, precipice, pinnacle, summit, crest, cliff; elevation, high place, peak, mountain, hill, knoll, rise, hillock, rising ground, mound, mesa, tor, dune; overhang, bluff, extension, jutty, outshoot, spur.

prominent *adj.* **1.** *They opened a store on the most prominent site in town:* conspicuous, evident, noticeable, apparent, easily seen, salient, obvious, definite, well-marked, pronounced, remarkable; discernible, recognizable; glaring, staring, arresting, striking. **2.** *He has a prominent nose:* jutting out, extended, jutting, protruding, protrusive, standing out, protuberant, bulging, projecting, convex, excurved, swelling, swollen. **3.** *He's a prominent physician:* important, prestigious, preeminent, illustrious, distinguished, honored, respected, well-known, leading, eminent, outstanding, renowned, celebrated, notable, famous. —**Ant.** 1 inconspicuous, unnoticeable, indefinite; unrecognizable; secondary, insignificant, minor, indistinguishable, indistinct, unimportant. 2 receding, concave, indented. 3 unimportant, undistinguished, unknown.

promiscuous *adj.* **1.** *I simply have a promiscuous love of food:* indiscriminate, uncritical, indiscriminative, undiscriminating, undiscerning, unselective, indifferent, uncritical, undirected, helter-skelter, haphazard, desultory, casual, careless, aimless. **2.** *The closet contained a prom-iscuous array of things:* mixed, heterogeneous, intermixed, mixed together, mixed-up, mingled, commingled, medley, composite, miscellaneous, variegated, motley; diverse; sweeping, wholesale; jumbled, scrambled, disorderly, disordered, disorganized, disarranged; chaotic, perplexed, confused. **3.** *She could never live down her reputation as a promiscuous girl:* wanton, loose, lax, fast, rakish, wild, immoral, unchaste, unvirtuous, impure; licentious, lewd, lascivious, dissipated, satyric, dissolute, of easy virtue, intemperate, immodest, immoral, morally loose, incontinent. —**Ant.** 1 discriminating, discerning, selective, critical, distinguishing; careful, prudent. 2 unmixed, unmingled; orderly, neat, ordered, organized, arranged. 3 moral, upright, temperate, modest, chaste, virtuous, pure.

promise n. **1.** Give me your promise that you'll never do that again: word, pledge, word of honor, parole, vow, oath, troth, plight, avowal, covenant, agreement, stipulation; assurance, guarantee, warrant, warranty; declaration, profession. **2.** That rookie pitcher is full of promise: potential, capability, good prospects, cause for hope. —v. **3.** I promise never to tell anyone: give a promise, take an oath, give one's word of honor, pledge, vow, plight, aver, avow, vouch, guarantee, assure, warrant; covenant, agree, undertake, be bound, commit oneself, plight one's honor, make an avowal, swear, swear an oath, assert under oath. **4.** The skies promise better weather in the morning: indicate, give hope of, make one expect, lead one to expect, hint of, suggest, betoken, augur, imply; hold a probability, be probable.

promising adj. He's a promising new painter. It was a promising start in a new field: giving promise, full of promise; favorable, hopeful, reassuring, assuring, encouraging, rising, advancing, up-and-coming; inspiriting, bright, cheerful, cheering, rosy, optimistic, happy; propitious, auspicious, of good omen, lucky, fortunate, looking up. —**Ant.** unfavorable, unpromising, discouraging.

promontory n. The house was on a promontory overlooking the sea: headland, hill, high point of land, point, neck of land, spur, ness, cape, peninsula, embankment; projection, overhang, precipice, jutty; cliff, bluff, height.

promote v. **1.** He was in town to promote his new book: publicize, advertise, help the progress of, forward, help forward, further, advance, urge forward, Slang push, plug; work for, render a service to, work toward, clear the way for, ease, expedite; speak for, advocate, foster, encourage, support; cultivate, refine, develop, improve upon, enhance; aid, help, assist, abet. **2.** They promoted the corporal to sergeant: advance in rank, raise, elevate, upgrade, graduate; prefer. —**Ant.** 1 impede; hinder, obstruct, prevent.

promotion n. **1.** The salesman's promotion to general manager occurred without too much ceremony: advancement in position or rank, elevation, raise, upgrading, preferment. **2.** The singers were in town for the promotion of their new album: advertising, advertisement, publicity, fanfare, puffery, Slang ballyhoo; hype, advancement, furtherance, promulgation, advance, progress, encouragement, boosting. —**Ant.** 1 demotion, degradation. 2 denigration, depreciation, discouragement.

prompt adj. **1.** Thank you for your prompt attention to the matter: instant, immediate, quick, instantaneous, unhesitating; punctual, timely, on time. **2.** Policemen are trained to be prompt on the job: fast to react, ready, quick to act; Informal Johnny-on-the-spot; alert, sharp, bright, on one's toes, on guard, attentive, open-eyed, open-eared, eager, zealous, observant, wide-awake, vigilant, watchful; active, animate, lively, alive; efficient, intent, keen. —v. **3.** Whatever prompted you to act in such a way?: spur, impel, induce, inspire, stimulate, actuate, stir, excite, inspirit, activate, incite, move, motivate, instigate, goad, provoke, cause, occasion; push, thrust, press, propel, drive, force; incline, dispose, influence, determine, persuade. **4.** "Idiot" cards serve to prompt many an onstage actor: cue, assist one's memory, supply with a cue; remind, jog the memory, prod, set back on the track; assist, help out, put words in one's mouth. —**Ant.** 1, 2 remiss, lax, slack; dilatory, hesitating, slow, late, tardy. 2 inactive, sluggish, unready, inattentive, unobservant; inanimate; inefficient; unresponsive. 3 discourage, dissuade, deter.

promptly adv. We returned promptly: expeditiously, at once, directly, immediately, posthaste, pronto, punctually, quickly, rapidly, right away, speedily, straightaway, swiftly, unhesitatingly, Informal flat-out, lickety-split.

promulgate v. T. H. Huxley promulgated Darwin's theory of evolution: set forth, expound, present, communicate, enunciate, elucidate; teach publicly, instruct, explain, interpret; sponsor, foster, promote.

prone adj. **1.** She's prone to giggling at the most inopportune moments: inclined, susceptible, liable, tending, disposed, predisposed, apt, likely, subject, accustomed, habituated. **2.** He was lying prone on the couch, fast asleep: flat, face-down, recumbent, reclining, level, prostrate, horizontal. —**Ant.** 1 averse, disinclined. 2 erect, upright, vertical, face-up, supine.

prong n. Forks have three or four prongs: tine, point, projection; hook, tooth, horn, branch; spur, spike, barb.

pronounce v. **1.** Foreigners find it hard to pronounce many words in English: articulate, speak, say, enunciate, enounce, vocalize, sound; give forth, utter, emit; frame, form. **2.** I now pronounce you man and wife: declare, proclaim, decree, rule, announce, state, voice, orate; judge, pass judgment.

pronounced adj. He speaks with a pronounced Scottish burr: decided, distinct, unmistakable, broad, definite, well-defined, clear-cut, unquestionable, positive, clearly indicated, clear, plain, noticeable, obvious, conspicuous; apparent, strongly marked, outstanding, arresting, vivid, bold; patent, evident, recognizable, unhidden, visible, manifest, undisguised.

pronouncement n. The prisoner stood and heard the pronouncement of his sentence: official statement, formal statement, announcement, declaration, proclamation, decree.

proof n. **1.** Do you have any proof to substantiate your alibi?: conclusive evidence, corroboration, verification, certification, documentation, ratification, substantiation, confirmation, attestation. **2.** Will your theory stand up to proof?: trial, test, probation, essay, assessment, scrutiny, examination, ordeal, weighing. **3.** *The production manager OK'd the proofs:* (in printing) trial impression, proof, sheet, galley proof, galley.

prop *n.* **1.** *Beams were used as props to keep the wall from collapsing:* support, mainstay, pillar, buttress, reinforcement, stanchion, sustainer, supporter, stay, brace. —*v.* **2.** *They propped the stage scenery with several braces:* support, shore up, hold up, brace, bolster, shoulder, buttress, underpin. **3.** *She propped the broom against the chair:* rest, lean, set, stand.

propaganda *n. We weren't influenced by propaganda:* indoctrination, inculcation, newspeak, promotion, proselytism, publicity, advertising, *Informal* ballyhoo, hype, brainwashing.

propagate *v.* **1.** *It's necessary for the species to propagate in order to stay in existence:* multiply, reproduce, proliferate, breed, progenerate, procreate, increase, generate, engender, bear, bring forth, beget, give birth, hatch, spawn. **2.** *The missionaries propagated the teachings of Christianity throughout the islands:* spread, disseminate, make known, promulgate; publish, publicize, issue, give to the world, broadcast, noise abroad, trumpet, blazon; circulate; make public, give currency to, bring into the open, put forth, purvey, report, notify, proclaim, preach, give out; tell, repeat, enunciate, air, communicate, impart, herald; whisper about, rumor, hint abroad; scatter, disperse, bestrew, sow, spray; instill, implant, inculcate. —**Ant.** 1 reduce, diminish, decrease; extinguish. 2 hush up, silence, suppress, repress, stifle.

propagation *n.* **1.** *The "multiplication" spoken of in the first chapter of Genesis is what we now call "propagation of the species":* reproduction, procreation, breeding; siring, begetting; giving birth, pregnancy, gestation, bearing, yielding; hatching, laying, spawning; generation, engendering. **2.** *The Ministry of Information is concerned with the propagation of false information:* spreading, dispersion, diffusion, dissemination, circulation, distribution; transmission, publication, issuance.

propel *v. The bow serves to propel the arrow:* shoot, catapult, eject, set in motion, impel, drive forward, drive, force, push forward, push, prod, shove, goad, poke; start, launch, send, thrust, precipitate; send, discharge, project, toss, cast, hurl, pitch, heave, sling.

propensity *n. Children have a propensity for candy:* inclination, leaning, proclivity, predilection, liking, partiality, weakness, preference, penchant; attraction, liking, affinity, sympathy, favor, pleasure, taste, fancy; turn, bent, tendency, predisposition, bias, prejudice, disposition. —**Ant.** disinclination, aversion, loathing, dislike, hatred, antipathy, displeasure.

proper *adj.* **1.** *I was never taught the proper way to hold a pencil:* right, correct, appropriate, suitable, fitting, applicable, pertinent, germane, relevant; apropos, fit, apt, meet, conformable; conventional, orthodox. **2.** *Use proper language in the company of ladies:* decorous, decent, be-

coming, seemly, befitting, fitting, suitable, fit, acceptable; polite, courteous; modest, nice. **3.** *Please go to your proper seats:* individual, own, assigned, respective, particular, specific; distinguishing, peculiar, distinctive, characteristic, typical, appropriate, marked, representative. **4.** *The city proper is half the size of the metropolitan area:* strictly defined, in the limited sense, within legal limits, officially bounded, per se; express, particular, precise, correct, true. —**Ant.** 1 wrong, inappropriate, irrelevant, unfit, unsuitable, inapt, malapropos. 2 unseemly, unbecoming, impolite, discourteous, objectionable, rude, indecent, vulgar.

properly *adv.* **1.** *You conducted yourself properly:* in a proper manner, appropriately, suitably, aptly, acceptably; decently, decorously, politely, tastefully; conventionally. **2.** *If you do it properly the first time, you won't have to do it again:* correctly, exactly, right, without error, accurately, precisely, perfectly.

property *n.* **1.** *I leave all my property to my son:* belongings, effects, possessions, goods; estate, wealth, assets, resources, holdings, chattels; appointments; funds, means, investments, stock, treasure, capital, moneys; right of possession, ownership, hold, title, proprietorship. **2.** *We're interested in buying property in Vermont:* land, real estate, realty, acres, acreage, grounds, estates, territory. **3.** *Cheerfulness is a property of her personality:* quality, aspect, characteristic, trait, feature, particularity, attribute; peculiarity, idiosyncrasy, singularity, individuality; mark, point, badge, earmark.

prophecy *n.* **1.** *She had a knack for prophecy and was rarely wrong:* foretelling the future, prediction, forecasting, soothsaying, forecast, divination, prognostication. **2.** *Her prophecies nearly always came true:* prediction, forecast, prognostication; augury, portent; revelation, sign from God.

prophesy *v. The soothsayer prophesied that Caesar would meet his doom:* predict, foretell, presage, forecast, divine, soothsay, prognosticate, premonish, warn, forewarn, foresee, augur, portend, apprehend, forbode.

prophet, *Fem.* **prophetess** *n.* **1.** *He claimed to be a prophet of the Lord:* revealer of the word of God, proclaimer of holy truth; evangelist, inspired spokesman, guide, intercessor, interpreter, preacher. **2.** *Is she really a prophetess or is there a trick to her prophecies?:* predictor, foreteller, forecaster, prognosticator, prophesier, Cassandra, sibyl, soothsayer, oracle, clairvoyant, seer, seeress, diviner, divinator, augur; crystal gazer, palmist, fortune-teller, geomancer; sorcerer.

prophetic also **prophetical** *adj. Her remarks were prophetic:* predictive, presaging, Delphian, foreshadowing, oracular, sibylline.

propitiate *v. Offerings were made to propitiate the gods:* appease, placate, pacify, calm, assuage, mollify, conciliate, accommodate, soothe, allay. —**Ant.** anger, madden, infuriate, roil, pique, provoke.

propitious *adj. We have gathered together on*

this propitious occasion: favorable, fortunate, auspicious, opportune, well-timed; beneficial, fit, suitable, advantageous, promising, lucky; golden, happy, bonny, providential, benign. —**Ant.** adverse, harmful, deleterious, unlucky, pernicious.

proponent *n. She was a proponent of women's rights:* advocate, supporter, exponent, endorser, champion, espouser, spokesman, enthusiast, apologist, representative; defender, vindicator, backer, booster, partisan, upholder, votary, patron, friend.

proportion *n.* **1.** *The proportion of gin to vermouth is three to one in a martini:* relative amount, relationship, ratio, balance, distribution, correlation, correspondence. **2.** *The size of the furniture should be in proportion to the size of the room:* proper relation, balance, symmetry, perspective, proportionality, ideal distribution, evenness, consistency, commensuration, correspondence; harmony, agreement. **3.** **proportions** *The proportions of the room allowed us to put in a grand piano:* dimensions, size, extent, measurements, area, scope, expanse, range, span, spread, width, breadth; amplitude, magnitude, volume, capacity, greatness, bulk, mass. **4.** *A large proportion of the report was researched by someone else:* part, amount; division, segment, fraction, share, portion; ratio, quota, percentage, measure, lot, degree. —*v.* **5.** *Can you proportion the slacks to fit small, medium, and large sizes?:* adapt, adjust in size, adjust in relation, fit, form, shape, gauge, gear, measure, apportion, put in proportion; modulate, regulate, order, accommodate; equalize, equate, conform, match; poise, balance, harmonize, balance the parts of; rectify, correct, grade, graduate. —**Ant.** 2 disproportion, unevenness, inconsistency, disparity; disagreement, contrast, disharmony.

proportionate *adj. Rewards were proportionate to effort:* commensurate, comparable, comparative, corresponding, equal, equitable, equivalent, even, in proportion, just, proportional, uniform, symmetrical, balanced. —**Ant.** unequal, different, discordant.

proposal *n.* **1.** *The governor put forth a proposal to improve public transportation:* recommendation, proposition, plan, program, project, course, scheme, resolution, line of action; plot, design, conception, idea, stratagem; prospectus, prospect, presentation, outline, draft, sketch, theory. **2.** *I've decided to accept their proposal and spend my vacation on their yacht:* invitation, proposition, offer, suggestion, motion, appeal, proffer, bid, nomination, presentation, overture; marriage proposition, suit.

propose *v.* **1.** *He proposed a brand new system of accounting. He proposed his new neighbor for club membership:* recommend, suggest, present, submit, tender, proffer, come up with, offer for consideration, introduce, bring forward, put forward, put forth, advance, propound, set forth. **2.** *She proposes to move within the month:* plan, intend, set about, mean, design, plot, scheme, undertake, venture, purpose, de-

termine, expect, aspire, aim, hope, contemplate, have in mind, have in view, have a mind. **3.** *He proposed to her on bended knee:* press one's suit, woo, make one's suit; ask for one's hand, affiance; *Informal* pop the question.

proposition *n.* **1.** *The man wanted to buy our house and made us an attractive proposition:* offer, proposal, offer of terms, deal, bargain; negotiation, agreement, stipulation, contract, guarantee, assurance. **2.** *The membership voted on two major propositions:* proposal, suggestion, recommendation, scheme, resolution, plan, undertaking; subject, topic, issue, question, matter, point.

proprietor *n. The inn is for sale by its proprietor:* landlord, owner, proprietress, landowner, titleholder, landholder; master, lord of the manor; manager; possessor, holder.

propriety *n. Always conduct yourself with propriety:* correctness; courtesy, decorum, good behavior, decorousness, dignity, good manners, etiquette, formality, gentlemanly or ladylike behavior, respectability; savoir faire, appropriateness, becomingness, applicability, fitness, suitableness, seemliness, aptness, rightness. —**Ant.** impropriety, incorrectness, discourtesy, misbehavior, misconduct, bad manners, faux pas, inappropriateness, unsuitability, unseemliness, inaptness, wrongness.

prosaic *adj. The guests exchanged prosaic remarks and glanced at their watches:* dull, flat, tiresome, dry, stale, unimaginative, vapid, pedestrian, plebeian, hackneyed, platitudinous, uninteresting, unentertaining, tedious, monotonous, dull, spiritless, jejune, trite, common, matter-of-fact, humdrum, usual routine, ordinary; *Slang* blah; prosy, wordy, unpoetical. —**Ant.** exciting, imaginative, fascinating, interesting, entertaining, spirited; uncommon, unusual, extraordinary; poetical.

proscribe *v. During the Renaissance the church proscribed scientific works like those of Galileo:* denounce, condemn, censure, disapprove, repudiate; curse, damn, anathematize; outlaw, prohibit, forbid, interdict, ban, excommunicate; banish, exile; boycott. —**Ant.** allow, permit, encourage, aid.

prosecute *v.* **1.** *The state is prosecuting him for murder:* try, put on trial, arraign, indict, bring before a court, bring to justice, bring to trial; sue, bring action against, bring suit against, prefer charges against, go to law, take to court. **2.** *The dectective prosecuted his search for the ringleader:* persevere in, be resolute in, stick to, keep at or on, persist in, continue, prolong, maintain, sustain; follow up, pursue, go with, carry on, wage, see through. **3.** *Will you be able to prosecute your responsibilities effectively?:* carry on, conduct, perform, discharge, execute, administer, direct, deal with, manage, handle.

prospect Usually **prospects** *n.* **1.** *The prospects of a total disarmament treaty aren't too good:* chances, outlook, probability of success, likelihood, probability; anticipation, foretaste, expectation, hope, promise. **2.** *I delight in the prospect of visiting Quebec:* expectation, contemplation, anticipation, expectancy, hope, intention, ambition; plan, design, proposal. **3.** *The prospect from the balcony was breathtaking:* view, vision, picture; scene, scenery, landscape, vista, panorama; outlook, aspect. **4.** *The salesman worked hard at finding some new prospects:* potential client, potential customer, candidate, possibility. —*v.* **5.** *He prospected for gold in 1849:* explore, seek, search; go after, look for; work a mine.

prospective *adj.* **1.** *We are debating a prospective move to the surburbs:* future, coming, impending, approaching, to come, close to hand, to be, forthcoming, about to be, eventual, destined; in prospect, in view, foreseen, on the horizon, expected, looked-for, intended, hoped-for, in expectation; in the wind, looming, threatening. **2.** *Is she a prospective customer?:* likely, possible, potential, promising.

prospectus *n.* *The mutual fund sent us a prospectus:* outline, catalogue, list, plan, program, syllabus, announcement.

prosper *v.* *The store prospered under the new management:* thrive, gain, get on, get ahead, make good, be fortunate, fare well, come off well, run smoothly; be successful, flourish, succeed; advance, increase, progress, flower, bear fruit, fructify; make one's fortune, grow rich. **—Ant.** fail, lose, be unfortunate, be unsuccessful; decrease, be fruitless; grow poor.

prosperity *n.* *He enjoyed his new prosperity:* success, well-being, affluence, thriving condition, material comfort, ease, prosperousness; good fortune, run of luck, good luck, advantage; profit, gain, advance, progress, advancement; affluence, wealth, bounty opulence, luxury, abundance, plenty; blessings, welfare; palmy days, halcyon days, golden age, good times. **—Ant.** want, poverty, indigence, destitution, misfortune, bad luck, disadvantage; failure, reverses, adversity; shortage, depression.

prosperous *adj.* **1.** *He had the well-fed look of a prosperous businessman:* successful, thriving, flourishing; fortunate, lucky; rich, opulent, wealthy, affluent, moneyed; well-to-do, comfortable, well-off, in easy circumstances; *Slang* on easy street. **2.** *The auction got off to a prosperous start:* auspicious, propitious, providential, fortunate, of good omen, lucky, timely, opportune; good, favorable, promising, well-disposed, heartening, hopeful, encouraging, cheering, reassuring, pleasing; bright, rosy, golden, smiling, sunny, fair, happy. **—Ant.** 1 unsuccessful, unfortunate, unlucky; failing; poor, impoverished; defeated, beaten. 2 unpropitious, unfortunate, inauspicious, unlucky, untimely, inopportune; bad, unfavorable, unpromising.

prostitute *n.* **1.** *The mayor tried to rid the area of pimps and prostitutes:* whore, harlot, slut, hooker, hustler, streetwalker, lady of the night, lewd woman, loose woman, fallen woman, jade, bawd, tart, hussy, strumpet, trollop, call girl; *Informal* floozy, tart, chippy. —*v.* **2.** *The poet prostituted herself writing greeting card verses:* debase, cheapen, sell out, degrade, demean, lower, corrupt, pervert, spoil, defile,

debauch; abuse, misuse, misemploy, misdirect, misapply; profane, desecrate.

prostrate *v.* **1.** *The slaves were forced to prostrate themselves:* bow down, kneel down, abase, kowtow, fall to one's knees. **2.** *The wrestler prostrated his opponent:* throw flat, flatten; overthrow, overcome, *Informal* floor, *Slang* deck. —*adj.* **3.** *The prostrate slaves didn't get up until after the king left:* lying flat, lying full length, lying face down, stretched out, laid out, prone, horizontal, recumbent, flat; bowed low, supplicating, beseeching, crouching, on bended knee, on one's knees. **4.** *She was prostrate after hiking on that hot day:* overcome, worn out, bone weary, dead tired, exhausted, prostrated, spent, *Informal* fagged, on one's last legs.

prostration *n.* **1.** *The slaves, in their prostration, weren't allowed to set eyes on the emperor:* act of prostrating; bow, genuflection, kneeling; submission, subjection, lowliness, abasement. **2.** *In his prostration and grief he wasn't able to cope with funeral arrangements:* exhaustion, weakness, weariness, enervation, dejection, depression; paralysis, impotence, helplessness, depth of misery, desolation, despondency, despera-tion, despair, anguish, woe, distress, wretchedness, heartache, sorrow, misery, grief.

protagonist *n.* *The protagonist of* Hamlet *is a Danish prince:* hero, heroine, main character, central character, title role, principal, lead, leading man, leading lady, star, headliner, superstar; diva, prima donna; danseur noble, prima ballerina; *French* jeune premier, jeune première.

protect *v.* *The troops were there to protect the townspeople. Use an umbrella to protect yourself from the rain:* guard, shield, defend, watch over, safeguard, secure, take care of, care for, tend, look after; shelter, cover, hide, veil, harbor, screen; keep, maintain, sustain, conserve, save, preserve. **—Ant.** attack, assault, assail; expose.

protection *n.* **1.** *A policeman's first duty is the protection of the people:* protecting, guarding, safeguard, defense, championship, preservation, safekeeping, guardianship, custody, charge, care, keep, conservation, saving; support, aid, assistance; immunity, safety, security. **2.** *An umbrella serves as a protection against the rain:* protector, shield, guard, defense, preserver, safeguard, security; barrier, buffer, fence, wall, cover, shade, screen, shelter; asylum, refuge, haven, harbor, preserve, sanctuary.

protective *adj.* **1.** *Camouflage is man-made protective coloration:* protecting, guarding, safeguarding, safekeeping, preventive, shielding, defensive. **2.** *He felt protective toward his younger sister:* sheltering, shielding; watchful, vigilant, heedful, careful, solicitous; fatherly, motherly, paternal, maternal, sisterly, brotherly, big-brotherly, avuncular, grandfatherly, grandmotherly.

protest *n.* **1.** *The student protest was aimed at the policies of the administration:* demonstration, march, picketing, boycott, sit-in, strike; opposition, dissent, contradiction; dispute, disagreement, dissidence, resistance, disaffection, difference of opinion, demurral, discountenance, remonstrance, remonstration, deprecation, renunciation, formal complaint, disclaimer; objection, protestation; *Informal* kick, beef, gripe. —*v.* **2.** *Consumer groups are protesting against higher prices:* complain, express disapproval, cry out, object, take exception; oppose, disapprove, dissent, beg to differ, disagree, differ in opinion, contradict, deny, controvert. **3.** *The defendant protested his innocence:* assert, vow, avow, declare, contend, insist, announce, put or set forth, put forward, propound, hold out, maintain, offer; profess, speak, state, enunicate, pronounce; testify, attest, affirm, asseverate, aver, assure, allege, avouch. —**Ant.** 1 endorsement, agreement, sanction; acquiescence, approval. 2 approve, agree, sanction, endorse, acclaim, subscribe to.

protocol *n.* *In accordance with protocol the secretary of state met the visiting diplomat at the airport:* diplomatic code, diplomatic or court etiquette; proprieties, amenities, code of behavior, good form, decorum, formality, manners, usage, customs, standards, conventions, dictates of society.

prototype *n.* *The prototype of the new vehicle ran on electricity:* model, pattern, example, exemplar, original, archetype.

protract *v.* *The awards ceremony was protracted by many long-winded speeches:* prolong, extend, lengthen, draw out, stretch out, drag out, spin out, keep going, keep up. —**Ant.** shorten, curtail, abbreviate, condense, abridge.

protrude *v.* *Nails protruded from the board and had to be removed for safety:* jut out, project, stand out, stick out; bulge, swell, belly, push forward.

protuberance *n.* *The gunner's compartment formed a protuberance on the fuselage of the B-29:* bulge, swelling, prominence, projection, excrescence, *Archaic* protuberancy; knob, bump, hump, knot, lump, node, gnarl; convexity, excurvature, roundness, bow; elevation, rising, ridge, welt, weal.

proud *adj.* **1.** *He was a proud man who resisted his friends' offers of help:* independent, self-sufficient, dignified, scrupulous, honorable, self-respecting; strict, punctilious, principled, high-minded; lofty, elevated, reserved, distinguished; fine, admirable, august. **2.** *I'm so proud of you!:* filled with pride, pleased, satisfied, gratified, contented, delighted, happy. **3.** *He was one of those proud, boastful men you couldn't bear listening to:* conceited, vain, smug, self-satisfied, self-important; prideful, self-praising, bragging, boastful, braggart, egotistical, swollen, vainglorious, know-it-all, complacent; pompous, overbearing; assuming, affected, puffed up, inflated, bloated; arrogant, insolent, flaunting; patronizing, condescending, supercilious, disdainful, contemptuous, intolerant; haughty, aloof, snobbish, lordly, high-and-mighty, imperious; *Informal* uppish, uppity, snooty, cocky, stuck-up; *Slang* high-hat, snotty. **4.** *It was a proud time*

for his parents when he received his diploma: glorious, exalted, elevated, euphoric. **5.** *The young aristocrat bore a proud name:* stately, noble, majestic, magnificent, great, lordly, grand, august; revered, venerable, storied, cherished. —**Ant.** 1 humble, lowly, submissive; ignoble, dishonorable, undignified, servile, cringing, abject. 2 ashamed, displeased, dissatisifed, discontented. 3 humble, unassuming, modest, unobtrusive, meek, unpresuming, deferential. 4 ignominious, humiliating. 5 base, ignoble.

prove *v.* **1.** *Eyewitness testimony proved he was innocent. This document proves she has a legal claim to the estate:* verify, establish, substantiate, bear out, uphold, support, sustain, corroborate, document, witness, authenticate, confirm, affirm, attest, certify, warrant, testify to; justify, make good, validate, ascertain, show clearly, demonstrate, manifest, evidence. **2.** *He devised a system for proving new marketing techniques:* test, try, try out, put to the test, verify, make trial of, subject to trial; check, analyze, examine, probe, look into. **3.** *It proved a waste of time:* result in, turn out to be, be found to be, end up, wind up, eventuate, result. —**Ant.** 1 disprove, refute, negate, contradict, contravert, rebut, discredit, rule out.

proverb *n.* *He lives by the proverb, "Early to bed and early to rise makes a man healthy, wealthy, and wise":* saying, popular saying, adage, maxim, aphorism, truism, accepted truth; epigram, precept, apothegm, saw, axiom, moral; dictum, mot, byword, motto; cliché, bromide, platitude, commonplace.

provide *v.* **1.** *Was he able to provide you with the information? The Red Cross provides food and shelter for disaster victims:* furnish, give, place at one's disposal, offer, submit, present, tender, impart, render; yield, produce, grant, confer, bestow, donate, contribute, afford, pay, allow, accord, award, deliver, dispense; arm, equip, fit, outfit, supply. **2.** *He worked hard to provide for his old age:* prepare, make plans, take measures, anticipate needs; get ready, arrange, plan, accumulate, save up; make arrangements, make provision, cater. **3.** *The contract provides that he cannot work for another studio:* state, stipulate, postulate, specify, require. —**Ant.** 1 deprive, withhold, refuse, disallow. 2 neglect, overlook.

provided *conj.* *We will go provided we aren't busy:* on the condition that, if, in case, granted. —**Ant.** lest.

providence *n.* *Because of her providence she survived on her savings during the months of unemployment:* prudence, farsightedness, foresight, forethought, provision, forehandedness, circumspection, husbandry. —**Ant.** shortsightedness, improvidence, imprudence, heedlessness.

provident *adj.* *He was a provident man who made careful preparation for his future:* foresighted, well-prepared, farseeing, foreseeing, farsighted, forehanded, thoughtful, discreet, judicious, circumspect, discerning; cautious, wary, precautious, vigilant, careful; ready, equipped;

prudent, frugal, thrifty, economical, saving, parsimonious, chary. —**Ant.** improvident, unprepared, shortsighted; injudicious, undiscerning; incautious, unwary, reckless, heedless; imprudent, wasteful, uneconomical.

province n. **1.** *British Columbia is a province of Canada:* administrative division, state, territory, subdivision, department, zone, canton, county, arrondissement, region, area, section, part. **2.** *It's within his province to issue authorization:* area, field, sphere, bailiwick, territory, capacity, function, office, jurisdiction, domain, job, authority; responsibility, charge, business, duty, assignment, station, place, role, scope of duties.

provincial adj. **1.** *The dancers were wearing provincial costumes:* of a province, regional, territorial, local. **2.** *She was a farm girl with simple provincial manners:* rural, country, countrified, rustic, bucolic, small-town, backwoods; unsophisticated; homespun, homely, rude, rough; *Disparaging* crude; gauche; unpolished, unrefined, clumsy, loutish, boorish, oafish; clownish, awkward, cloddish, yokelish, clodhopping, hayseed, down-home, gawky. **3.** *The townspeople looked on with a provincial distrust of foreigners:* narrow, parochial, insular. —**Ant.** 1 standard, national. 2 big-city, citified, urban, fashionable, polished, refined, smooth. 3 cosmopolitan.

provision n. **1.** *Provision of shelter was the Red Cross's main concern for the disaster victims:* providing, supplying, furnishing, giving, endowment, donation. **2. provisions** *Provisions were kept in the storehouse:* supplies, food, eatables, edibles, comestibles, sustenance, stores, commons, groceries, victuals, viands, provender; feed, forage, fodder. **3.** *He made provision for their welfare in his will:* arrangement, anticipation, forehandedness, provident measures or steps, prearrangement, forethought, wherewithal; provident care, precaution, preparation, readiness. **4.** *According to the provisions of this agreement, you must continue to work for them another 2 years:* proviso, requisite, requirement, obligation, stipulation, condition, term, article, clause; restriction, limitation, reservation, modification, qualification; *Informal* string.

provisional adj. *The provisional agreement was later ratified:* tentative, conditional, contingent, interim, limited, makeshift, passing, rough-and-ready, stopgap, temporary, transient, transitional, experimental. —**Ant.** permanent, definite, fixed.

proviso n. *His will left everything to his daughter, with the proviso that she not marry:* condition, restriction, limitation, qualification, modification, stipulation, requirement; clause, amendment, addition, rider; *Informal* string.

provocation n. *She flared up at the smallest provocation:* cause, motivation, incitement, instigation, fomentation, goad, spur, prodding, stimulation, actuation, stimulus, vexation, irritation, pique, annoyance, perturbation, aggravation; excitation, slight, insult, affront, offense.

provocative adj. **1.** *Jack's provocative remark started an angry argument:* provoking, annoying, aggravating, irritating, vexing, vexatious,

irksome. **2.** *She wore a very provocative dress:* seductive, tempting, tantalizing, captivating, intriguing, entrancing, enchanting, fascinating, beguiling, bewitching, alluring, attractive, sexy; exciting, intoxicating, thrilling, stimulating, arousing, ravishing, irresistible, inviting.

provoke v. **1.** *Her constant nagging provoked him:* anger, enrage, incense, outrage, infuriate, madden, irritate, vex, agitate, annoy, gall, aggravate, irk, exasperate, rile, try one's patience, chafe, grate, move to anger, work into a passion, make one's blood boil, put out of humor, put out; *Slang* get one's goat, get under one's skin, get to one. **2.** *The cad's foul language provoked rage in the honest girl's breast:* cause, prompt, excite, incite, inspire, impel, instigate, induce, compel, arouse, stimulate, rouse, stir, animate, move, motivate. **3.** *The race provoked his spirit of competition:* arouse, stimulate, bring on, give rise to, cause, produce, bring about, effect, actuate, motivate, prompt, pique, put in motion, galvanize, foment, incite, generate, create, establish; stir, stir up, rouse, awaken, call forth, elicit, fire, inflame, kindle, quicken, excite, evoke. —**Ant.** 1 gratify, assuage, calm, soothe, mollify, ease, propitiate, please.

prowess n. **1.** *Richard the Lion Heart was known for his prowess:* bravery, valor, courageous deeds, heroism, fearlessness, intrepidity, gallantry, courage, grit, nerve, daring, boldness, derring-do, dauntlessness; strength, might, power, vigor, fortitude, stamina, endurance, mettle, spirit, hardihood, *Informal* spunk, *Slang* guts. **2.** *She had great prowess as a businesswoman:* ability, skill, skillfulness, competence, aptitude, know-how, knack, talent, faculty, genius, accomplishment, adeptness, expertness, proficiency. —**Ant.** 1 cowardice, cowardliness, fear, timidity, meekness. 2 incompetence, ineptness.

prowl v. *The neighbor's cat prowls around the garbage cans all night:* stalk, hunt, scavenge, roam, slink, steal, sneak, range, lurk, skulk, creep.

proximity n. *The proximity of the fire worried us:* closeness, contiguity, contiguousness, immediacy, juxtaposition, nearness, propinquity, adjacency.

prudence n. **1.** *The conduct of diplomacy requires prudence:* calculation, foresight, forethought, judgment, discretion, common sense, circumspection, caution, wisdom. **2.** *Her prudence concerning expenses proved decisive:* providence, care, economy, frugality, carefulness. —**Ant.** carelessness, imprudence, incaution.

prudent adj. *A prudent investor buys only sound stocks:* wise, sensible, careful, showing good judgment, judicious, expedient, discerning, sagacious, sage, politic, sapient, levelheaded, well-advised, rational, sane, self-possessed; thoughtful, considerate, reflecting, prudential, provident, heedful, vigilant, wide-awake, cautious, wary, circumspect, shrewd, guarded, chary; prepared, foresighted, discreet, farsighted, precautious; frugal, thrifty, saving, economical, sparing. **—Ant.** imprudent, indiscreet, unwise, irrational; thoughtless, inconsiderate, improvident, careless, heedless, reckless, rash, incautious, wasteful, extravagant, uneconomical.

prudish *adj. Catherine the Great was anything but prudish, while insisting on the most exact decorum:* prim, extremely proper and modest, Victorian, overmodest, priggish, puritanical, prissy, old-maidish, straitlaced; precise, fastidious, finical, particular; timid, shy, demure, skittish, queasy, squeamish; smug, sanctimonious, self-righteous, punctilious, pedantic, mincing; stilted, starched, stuffy.

prune *v.* **1.** *He spent the afternoon pruning the hedge:* trim, clip, snip, thin, thin out, shear, pull, crop, lop. **2.** *It's an editor's job to prune a manuscript:* reduce, curtail, trim, shorten, cut; abridge, condense, abbreviate; simplify, clarify.

prurient *adj. Unfortunately, the movie will appeal to prurient interests:* lustful, sexy, libidinous, concupiscent, hot-blooded, passionate, goatish, lascivious, licentious, lecherous, salacious, carnal, lubricious, lewd, obscene, priapic, satyric.

pry[1] *v. Stop prying into my affairs!:* snoop, poke, butt, nose, stick one's nose in, sniff, peek, peer; probe, explore, delve, inquire, search; meddle, interfere, mix in, butt in, intrude, intervene, *Slang* horn in.

pry[2] *v.* **1.** *We pried open the locked door with a crowbar:* force, break, prize, work, lever, crack, jimmy. **2.** *You'll never pry anything out of me!:* force, wring, squeeze; wrench, tear, wrest, extract; worm, winkle, ferret, smoke.

prying *adj. Prying neighbors annoyed them:* curious, inquisitive, peeping, peering, peeking; nosy. **—Ant.** blasé, unconcerned, uninterested.

pseudo *adj. He was a pseudo expert in karate:* false, spurious, mock, pretended, feigned, simulated, make-believe, fictitious, counterfeit, forged, sham, bogus, fraudulent, fake, phony; self-described, self-styled, *French* soi-disant. **—Ant.** genuine, real, authentic.

pseudonym *n. "Max" was a pseudonym for the French Resistance leader Jean Moulin:* alias, assumed name, false name, nickname, sobriquet; *French* nom de guerre, nom de plume, nom de théâtre; cognomen, anonym, pen name, professional name, stage name.

psyche *n. C. G. Jung had a lot to say about the human psyche:* soul, mind, spirit, makeup, personality, self; ego, superego, id; subconscious, unconscious, anima; *Archaic* bowels, penetralia.

psychiatrist *n. The psychiatrist spent an hour with her:* psychoanalyst, analyst, psychologist, psychotherapist, therapist, *Informal* shrink.

psychic *adj.* **1.** *A dream is a psychic event:* mental, psychological; cerebral, intellectual; spiritual. **2.** *The medium claimed to have psychic powers:* extrasensory, preternatural, telekinetic, supernatural, occult, mystic; supersensory, telepathic, clairvoyant. **—n. 3.** *She claimed to be a psychic:* clairvoyant, sensitive, telepa-

thist; prophet, soothsayer, diviner, augur; medium, paragnost, spiritualist; *French* voyant, *(fem.)* voyante.

psychology *n. Students of psychology try to predict behavior. The psychology of a hermit differs from that of a rock star:* mental processes, mind, makeup, attitude, feeling, head.

psychopath *n. The psychopath lied his way out of trouble:* psychotic, psycho, sociopath, antisocial personality, maniac.

psychotic *adj.* **1.** *Alexander the Great had psychotic tendencies, but sublimated them brilliantly:* insane, psychopathic, lunatic; mad, disturbed, demented, deranged, non compos mentis; *Slang* loony, crazy, nutty, kooky. **—n. 2.** *Psychiatrists try to help psychotics recover their lost sanity:* insane person, psychopath, madman, maniac, lunatic; *Slang* nut, kook, loony, loon.

pub *n. The town bus stopped at a pub for afternoon refreshments:* Brit. public house, tavern, barroom, bar, taproom, inn, saloon, grogshop, pothouse, rummery, rumship, bistro, *Slang* ginmill, alehouse, beer parlor, *Archaic* speakeasy.

puberty *n. Puberty ended early:* teens, teenage years, adolescence, juvenescence.

public *adj.* **1.** *Public opinion favors tax reform. He's running for public office:* common, general, popular, societal, social; political, civic, civil; state, statewide, national, nationwide, countrywide. **2.** *The zoo and gardens are public:* open to all persons, free to all, used by all, shared, not private or exclusive; unrestricted, available, accessible, passable, unbarred, unenclosed, unfenced, unbounded, not circumscribed, unobstructed; communal, community-owned. **3.** *The investigator made public his findings:* widely known, familiar to many people, notorious, recognized, acknowledged, disclosed, divulged, open, overt, outward, unabashed, unashamed, plain, frank, obvious, conspicuous, evident, visible, unconcealed, exposed, apparent, undisguised, revealed, patent, manifest, observable, discernible, perceivable, in sight or view, in broad daylight. **—n. 4.** *The museum is open to the public:* people, everyone, populace, community, nation, population, citizenry, commonality, society, body politic, proletariat, folk, bourgeoisie, multitude, masses, hoi polloi, rank and file, mob. **5.** *After years of TV, Hollywood is winning a new movie-going public:* following, attendance, audience, followers, those interested; buyers, purchasers, clientele, trade, patrons; constituency, supporters. **—Ant.** 1 private, personal, individual. 2 private, proprietary, exclusive, restricted, unavailable, inaccessible, barred, secluded, closed. 3 secret, unknown, unrecognized, hidden, unrevealed, mum.

publication *n.* **1.** *Publication of the cause reached an all-time high:* publishing, airing, announcement, appearance, communication, declaration, disclosure, dissemination, issuance, issuing, notification, proclamation, promulgation, reporting, revelation, writing, advertisement, publicity. **2.** *He launched a new publication:* serial, imprint, issue, emission; (*variously*) book, journal, newspaper, newsletter, magazine.

publicity *n. The movie received good publicity:* public notice, attention, currency, publicness, notoriety; circulation, promulgation, advertising, salesmanship, promotion; information, propaganda; build-up, puffery, write-up; *Informal* ballyhoo, plug, hype, flack, puff, blurb.

publicize *v. He was in town to publicize his new book:* promote, make known, make public, bring into public notice, give currency, spread word of, advertise, sell, circularize, propagandize, proclaim, acclaim, announce, broadcast, herald, emblazon, propagate, promulgate; *Informal* ballyhoo, push, plug, puff, hype. **—Ant.** keep secret, suppress, cover up, hush up, conceal, hide.

publish *v.* **1.** *The company has published all of that author's works:* print for sale, put to press, issue, bring out, put out. **2.** *Don't publish that-- it's strictly off the record:* print, make generally known, announce, make public, publicize, give publicity to, promote; disclose, release, give out, vent, air, broadcast, give to the world, tell, communicate, utter, impart, divulge, diffuse, disseminate, spread, propagate, promulgate, circulate; proclaim, declare, trumpet, herald, advertise, placard. **—Ant.** 2 conceal, hide, secrete; muffle, smother; bury, suppress; withhold, keep secret.

publisher *n. The publisher signed a contract with the author:* publishing house, press.

pucker *v.* **1.** *Lemons make your mouth pucker. The curtains were puckered at the top:* draw together, contract, shrink; pinch, crease, purse, compress, squeeze; wrinkle, crinkle; gather, fold, tuck, pleat, make a pleat. **—***n.* **2.** *She sewed little puckers in the sweater:* fold, tuck, gather, pinch, pleat, crease, wrinkle, crinkle, crumble, rumple, ruffle.

pudgy *adj. All that candy has made him pudgy:* fat, obese, stout, chunky, chubby, stocky, fleshy, paunchy, plump, buxom, rotund, thickset, tubby, roly-poly, squat, stubby, short and fat, dumpy.

puerile *adj. Stop being so puerile and act your age!:* childish, foolish, silly, immature, babyish, infantile, simple, childlike, callow, sophomoric, raw, green, juvenile; irrational, senseless, inane, nonsensical, ridiculous, frivolous, vapid, harebrained; trivial, piddling, petty, unimportant, worthless. **—Ant.** adult, mature; rational; intelligent.

puff *n.* **1.** *The locomotive let off puffs of steam:* short blast, abrupt emission, sudden gust, whiff, breath, exhalation, flurry, small cloud, wisp. **2.** *Her eye had a slight puff to it:* swelling, rising, bulge, elevation, node, inflammation, distention, inflation, dilation, excurvature, bow, convexity, hump, protuberance, extension, protrusion, protuberancy, excrescence, tuberosity. **3.** *Informal That speech was just so much puff:* exaggeration, overcommendation, sales talk, euphemism, overpraise, overlaudation, flattery, encomium, flummery, puffery, panegyric, much ado about nothing, misrepresentation, blurb, public-

ity; bluster, bombast; *Informal* plug, ballyhoo. **—***v.* **4.** *After running the mile, he was huffing and puffing:* breathe hard, be out of breath, pant, heave, wheeze, gasp, exhale, blow, be winded. **5.** *The dragon puffed fire:* blow in puffs, send forth, emit, discharge. **6.** *He puffed on his pipe:* draw, suck, inhale; smoke. **7.** *The prisoners' stomachs puffed out from malnutrition:* be inflated, be distended, swell, blow up, inflate, expand, extend, distend, dilate, stretch, bloat.

puffy *adj. Next morning his face was puffy with bruises:* swollen, inflated, puffed up, bloated, bulging, inflamed, distended, enlarged, expanded; round, corpulent, fat, fleshy.

pugnacious *adj. When he drank too much, he'd become quite pugnacious:* quarrelsome, given to fighting, antagonistic, unfriendly; aggressive, combative, defiant, warlike, hostile, menacing, militant; contentious, belligerent, bellicose, fractious, disputatious, argumentative; threatening, with teeth bared; with a chip on one's shoulder. **—Ant.** peaceful, calm, friendly, conciliatory, accommodating.

pulchritude *n. She was a vision of feminine pulchritude:* beauty, prettiness, comeliness, beauteousness, loveliness, fairness, *Scot.* bonniness, personableness, attractiveness, exquisiteness. **—Ant.** homeliness, plainness, drabness, ugliness.

pull *v.* **1.** *The child pulled a red wagon:* haul, drag, lug, tug, draw; take in tow, tow; troll, trawl. **2.** *He pulled a cord and the butler appeared:* tug, jerk, grab, yank. **3.** *The dentist may have to pull that infected tooth:* draw out, remove, detach, withdraw; extract, wrest, wring; uproot, extirpate, dig out, weed out. **4.** *He pulled the newspaper to shreds:* rip, tear, rend, split, sever, rive. **5.** *Pull over!:* go, move, drive. **6.** *She pulled a back muscle:* strain, stretch, twist, wrench, sprain. **7.** *The fight promoters hoped to pull record crowds:* draw, attract; lure, entice. **—***n.* **8.** *She gave the dog's leash a pull:* tug, jerk, yank, shake. **9.** *He couldn't resist the pull of her charm:* pulling power, drawing power; lure, allure, attraction, attractiveness, influence, enticement, fascination, appeal, allurement; gravity, magnetism. **—Ant.** 1, 2, 8 push, shove. 3 insert, plant. 7 repel.

pulp *adj.* **1.** *Pulp fiction was popular in the 1930's:* cheap, trashy, lurid, sensational, vulgar. **—***v.* **2.** *They pulped the fruit:* crush, macerate, mash, pulverize, squash.

pulsate *v. The heart pulsates. She was pulsating with excitement:* expand and contract rhythmically, throb, beat, palpitate, vibrate, reverberate, thump, pound, pulse, undulate, oscillate, tick, quiver, flutter, shake, shiver, quaver, shudder, tremble; wave, waver; come and go, alternate, ebb and flow.

pulse *n.* **1.** *The ship's engine beat with a steady pulse:* throb, regular beat, rhythm, cadence, pulsation, palpitation, recurrence, stroke, undulation, vibration, oscillation. **—***v.* **2.** *When he got angry, the veins in his temple pulsed:* beat, throb, palpitate, pulsate, thump, vibrate; quiver, shudder, tremble, oscillate.

pulverize *v. The mill pulverizes grain:* reduce to powder or dust, grind, pound, granulate, comminate, triturate, powder, atomize, mince, crush, crumble, crumb, mill, mash.

pump *v. They pumped air into the tire:* inflate, dilate, force, send, inject, drive, push, supply; siphon, draw, empty.

pun *n. The comedian was fond of puns:* double entendre, double meaning.

punch *n.* **1.** *He gave the bully a punch in the mouth:* blow, hit, jab, thrust, clout, stroke, cuff, slam, thump, box, poke, knock; *Informal* chop, sock; *Slang* roundhouse, haymaker. —*v.* **2.** *He punched the man in the nose:* hit with the fist, strike, smite, box, thwack, whack, jab, poke, pelt, wallop, clobber, clout, swat, cuff, slam, clip; *Informal* sock, conk, plug, paste; baste, pummel, pound, beat.

punctilious *adj. When drawing up a contract it pays to be punctilious:* exact, precise, correct, meticulous, painstaking, proper, scrupulous; exacting, rigid, strict, fussy, particular, demanding, finicky, picky, rigorous. —**Ant.** casual, indifferent, negligent, careless, slipshod.

punctual *adj. He was always punctual for appointments:* on time, not late, early, in good time, well-timed, prompt, ready, regular, steady, constant; quick, expeditious, instant, immediate, instantaneous; seasonable, timely; *Informal* on the dot. —**Ant.** unpunctual, late, tardy; irregular, unsteady.

punctuate *v.* **1.** *He did not bother to punctuate the telegraph message:* mark with punctuation marks; insert the stops, separate, break. **2.** *He punctuated his argument with phrases in his native Spanish:* interrupt, break, intersperse, pepper, sprinkle, scatter, lace.

puncture *n.* **1.** *A puncture in the balloon made it collapse:* hole, break, rupture, opening, perforation, nick, cut; wound, bite, sting. —*v.* **2.** *She punctured her finger with a sewing needle:* pierce, make a hole in, prick, pink, stick; wound, cut, nick. **3.** *Bad reviews punctured the young actor's ego:* deflate, depreciate; let down, knock down, shoot down, bring back to earth.

pundit *n. The pundit wrote a daily newspaper column on current affairs:* sage, expert, authority, savant, guru, wizard, master, guide, mentor, thinker, learned person.

pungent *adj.* **1.** *The ribs were served with a hot, pungent sauce:* sharp-tasting, highly flavored, savory, spicy, flavorful, piquant, flavorsome, palatable, tasty, highly seasoned, salty, peppery, hot; nippy, tangy, strong, stimulating, sharp; sharp-smelling, acrid, sour, acid, tart, astringent, vinegary, caustic, bitter, acetous, biting, stinging, smarting, penetrating. **2.** *His pungent ridicule made him quite a few enemies:* sharp, piercing, pointed, acute, trenchant, keen, poignant; stinging, biting, mordent, caustic, invidious, cutting, incisive, penetrating, sarcastic, smart, wounding, tart, acrimonious, bitter; stimulating, stirring, provocative, tantalizing, racy, spicy, scintillating; sparkling, brilliant, clever, snappy, keen-witted, witty. —**Ant.** 1 bland, mild; unsavory, unpalatable, flavorless, taste-

less; weak, unstimulating. 2 dull, mild, moderate, inane, vapid; pointless.

punish *v. His father punished him for disobeying:* subject to a penalty, penalize, chastise, correct, discipline; sentence, imprison, fine; give one his deserts; rebuke, reprove, admonish, castigate, chasten, take to task, dress down; avenge, take revenge, take vengeance on, bring to account, get even with, retaliate, settle accounts with; whip, flog, beat. —**Ant.** excuse, pardon, forgive; exonerate, absolve, vindicate; praise, laud, reward.

punishment *n. For a punishment, you'll get no allowance for two weeks:* penalty, punition; penance, penal retribution, price, penalization, payment, retribution, deserts; fine, forfeit, damages, reparation, redress; discipline, correction, chastisement, castigation, chastening, (*variously*) spanking, whipping, flogging, flaying, crucifying, hanging.

punitive *adj. The supervisor took punitive action:* punishing, penal, retaliative, in reprisal, in retaliation, retaliative, retaliatory, revengeful, vindictive, correctional, disciplinary.

puny *adj.* **1.** *Oliver Twist was an underfed, puny child:* small and weak, undersized, underdeveloped, slight, pint-sized, runty, sawed-off, little, bantam, mite-sized, miniature, diminutive, tiny; weakly, sickly, poor, feeble; thin, fragile, emaciated, delicate, frail, runtlike, infirm. **2.** *What a puny excuse!:* feeble, poor, weak, inadequate, insignificant, slight, impotent, light, inconsiderable, insufficient, meager; unimportant, picayune, picayunish, petty, trivial, worthless, trifling, paltry, piddling, shallow, flimsy, tenuous, measly. —**Ant.** 1 large, great, robust, healthy, strong, vigorous; colossal, gigantic. 2 significant, potent, strong, forceful, considerable, important; adequate, sufficient.

pupil *n. She taught a class of 27 pupils:* student learner, schoolgirl, schoolboy, coed; undergraduate, scholar; beginner, novice, tyro, initiate, probationer, apprentice, trainee, disciple. —**Ant.** teacher, master.

puppet *n.* **1.** *The children enjoyed the puppets:* animated doll, marionette, manikin; hand puppet; doll, toy. **2.** *Emperor Maximilian of Mexico was denounced as a mere puppet of Napoleon III:* tool, creature, pawn, cat's paw, dupe, instrument; lay figure, figurehead; man of straw, jackstraw; hireling, underling, subordinate, flunky, servant, lackey, henchman.

purchase *v.* **1.** *We purchased a new car:* buy, pay for, pick up. —*n.* **2.** *We're pleased with our purchase:* acquisition, buying, acquirement; buy. **3.** *The strong ropes gave us good purchase for getting up the side of the cliff:* advantage, hold, leverage; footing, foothold, toehold, support; power-exerting means, influence, edge. —**Ant.** 1 sell, dispose of, liquidate, divest, convert into cash. 2 sale, selling; disposal; liquidation.

pure *adj.* **1.** *These animals were bred from pure stock. Have you ever breathed pure oxygen?:* unmixed, full-strength, unadulterated, unmodified, unalloyed, unmingled, neat, straight; perfect, faultless, flawless, undefiled, uncorrputed, untainted, unblemished, unmarred; clean, fresh, immaculate, uncontaminated, uninfected, unpolluted, disinfected, antiseptic, germfree, sterilized, sterile, sanitary, healthful, wholesome, fit for consumption; purebred, of unmixed descent, thoroughbred, pedigreed, pure-blooded. **2.** *It was pure luck that he was home when we called:* mere, sheer, stark; absolute, complete, whole, entire, full, utter, downright, out-and-out, positive, perfect; unqualified, thorough. **3.** *She was a pure and wholesome girl:* innocent, guiltless, sinless, decent, uncorrupted, moral, righteous, ethical, upright; virtuous, chaste, undefiled, virgin, virginal, unsullied, unspoiled, spotless, immaculate, untainted, untarnished, unblemished, inviolable, inviolate; blameless, above suspicion, unimpeachable, true, sincere, guileless, angelic. **4.** *The academy debated the distinction between pure and applied sciences:* theoretical, abstract, hypothetical, conjectural, speculative, fundamental, basic, higher. **—Ant.** 1–3 impure. 1 adulterated, mixed, alloyed, mingled; imperfect, flawed, corrupted, tainted, blemished; unclean, dirty, contaminated; infected, polluted, unsterilized, unhealthful; mixed. 2 qualified. 3 guilty, culpable, sinful, corrupt, corrupted, immoral; unvirtuous, unchaste, defiled, sullied, spoiled, spotted, tarnished, blemished, contaminated; impeachable, untrue, insincere; immodest, indecent, filthy, gross, lewd, obscene. 4 applied, practical.

purely *adv.* **1.** *It's purely a matter of taste. The lecture was purely technical:* only, solely, merely, simply, essentially; completely, entirely, totally, absolutely, fully, wholly. **2.** *She always conducted herself purely and with propriety:* virtuously, chastely, virginally, incorruptibly, morally, innocently, cleanly, admirably, worthily, in all honor; piously, devoutly. **3.** *These animals are of a purely bred strain. The grammar of English is simple, but it's hard to speak English purely:* without admixture, cleanly, flawlessly, faultlessly. **—Ant.** 2 immorally, dishonorably, unwholesomely, impiously. 3 impurely, faultily.

purge *v.* **1.** *The mayoral candidate has promised to purge the police department:* clean up, cleanse, purify, clean out, sweep out, shake up. **2.** *Stalin purged his enemies from the Party:* remove, get rid of, do away with, oust, dismiss, kill, liquidate, eliminate, expel, uproot, discharge, banish, crush, rout out; eradicate, exterminate. **3.** *She purged her sins by devoting the rest of her life to prayer and good works:* wash away, expiate, atone for; obtain absolution, pardon, forgiveness, or remission from. *—n.* **4.** *Stalin conducted a purge of the officer corps:* purging, purgation, cleanup, shake-up, purification. **5.** *The medicine was an effective purge:* laxative, purgative, cathartic, aperient; clyster, physic, emetic.

purification *n. The milk required purification:* purifying, cleansing, ablution, disinfection, distillation, purgation.

purify *v. Purify the water before drinking it:* make pure, disinfect, decontaminate, sanitize, clear, clarify, (*variously*) boil, chlorinate, filter, distill, sterilize, pasteurize. **—Ant.** contaminate, pollute, dirty, infect.

puritanical *adj. D. H. Lawrence crusaded against puritanical censorship:* strict, severe, ascetic, austere, puritan, prim, prissy, prudish, priggish, straitlaced, stiff-necked, bluenosed, stilted, stiff, stuffy, rigid, dogmatic, fanatical, narrow, sanctimonious, bigoted. **—Ant.** permissive, broad-minded, latitudinarian.

purity *n.* **1.** *Exhaust fumes are a threat to the purity of the air we breathe:* pureness, clearness, clarity, lucidity, limpidity; cleanliness, cleanness, immaculateness, immaculacy, brilliance; excellence, fineness; homogeneity, uniformity. **2.** *She was a woman of purity and goodness:* guiltlessness, guilelessness, innocence, clear conscience; modesty, temperance, chastity, virginity, chasteness, virtuousness, virtue, decency, uprightness, morality, rectitude; piety, holiness, saintliness, sanctity; integrity, honesty, incorruptibility, honor; simplicity, plainness, directness. **—Ant.** 1, 2 impurity, impureness. 1 contamination, cloudiness; diversity. 2 vice, immodesty, unchasteness, immorality.

purport *v.* **1.** *The letter purported to be from the general himself:* claim, profess; declare, allege, or assert oneself. *—n.* **2.** *What is the purport of your visit here?:* meaning, import, significance, signification, implication, sense, reason, rationale, bearing; intention, purpose, design, end, aim, object, objective, intent, burden, point; gist, substance, drift, tenor, trend.

purpose *n.* **1.** *The purpose of a screen door is to keep flies out:* object, objective, function, point, rationale, intention, intent, raison d'être; meaning, reason, sense, aim, design. **2.** *His purpose was to graduate from medical school and become a great surgeon:* goal, aim, ambition, aspiration, object, objective, mission, intent, intention, target, resolution, plan, motive, design, scheme, project, proposal; disposition, desire, wish, expectation, hope. **3.** *He walked with a stride full of purpose:* resolve, determination, resolution, motivation, will, fixed intent. *—v.* **4.** *He purposed to become one of the world's leading conductors:* intend, mean, resolve, aim, aspire, drive at, persist, persevere; design, propose, plan, determine, conclude; endeavor, take upon oneself, set about, undertake, elect, choose; commit oneself, decide, make up one's mind; think to, contemplate, have a mind to. **—Ant.** 3 purposelessness, aimlessness; inconstancy.

purposeful *adj. He was a hardworking man whose every action was purposeful:* deliberate, intentional, calculated, conscious, considered, studied, premeditated; resolute, strong-willed, committed, decided, resolved, determined upon. **—Ant.** aimless, purposeless, vacillating, irresolute, faltering, wavering; undecided, unresolved, undetermined.

purposeless *adj. The purposeless campaign statement was a waste of time and effort:* pointless, aimless, worthless, useless, empty, good-for-nothing, meaningless, needless, nonsensical, senseless, undirected, unhelpful, unnecessary, unprofitable, desultory.

purposely *adv.* *The door was purposely left open:* deliberately, on purpose, intentionally, consciously, with intent, calculatedly, expressly, willfully, designedly, by design; knowingly, wittingly, advisedly, voluntarily, consciously. —**Ant.** accidentally, unintentionally, inadvertently, unknowingly, unconsciously, unthinkingly, unwittingly, by chance.

purse *n.* **1.** *Keep the money in your purse:* handbag, pocketbook, shoulder bag, clutch, bag; moneybag, wallet, pouch, sporran. **2.** *The purse for the next race is $25,000:* winnings, prize, award, stake; proceeds, fund, treasury, coffer. —*v.* **3.** *The sour taste made her purse her lips:* pucker, wrinkle, knit; pleat, pinch, gather, fold; bunch, contract.

pursue *v.* **1.** *The policemen pursued the bank robbers:* chase, follow in hot pursuit, go after, give chase to, race after, run after; chase after, track, trail. **2.** *She pursued the goal of perfection in her art:* seek, try for, try to accomplish, aspire to, aim for or at, contrive to gain, be determined upon; push toward, strive for, labor for, be intent upon, set one's heart upon, be after. **3.** *He pursued his studies with seriousness:* engage in, carry on, perform.

pursuit *n.* **1.** *He was employed in peaceful pursuits:* occupation, activity, employment, business, calling, career, interest, job, line, pastime, undertaking, venture, vocation, work **2.** *The pursuit of objectives took all her time:* quest, search, seeking, chase, following, hunt, hunting, pursuance, tracking, trail.

purview *n.* **1.** *Jurisdiction over such conduct does not come within the judge's purview:* range, scope, sweep, responsibility, compass, extent; dominion, realm, domain, reach, commission, territory, field, area. **2.** *A grasp of metaphysics is well beyond my purview:* ken, understanding, overview, experience, comprehension, viewpoint, outlook, horizon, *Slang* savvy, mental grasp.

push *v.* **1.** *Push the button if you want the elevator:* press, exert force on, move. **2.** *The celebrity pushed past the reporters and got into his car:* make one's way, work, drive, press, struggle, force one's way; shove, elbow, squeeze, worm, wiggle, wedge, shoulder, nudge; ram, butt, hustle, jostle, fight, forge. **3.** *We always have to push him to do his homework:* urge, encourage, egg on, goad, incite, prod, spur, instigate, rouse, inspire, induce, arouse, animate, motivate, impel, prompt, stimulate, provoke, move, propel, sway, persuade, importune, exhort; hound, dun, bear down hard upon, harass, browbeat, heckle, badger, harry, coerce, constrain, compel, force, drive, prevail upon; *Informal* put the screws on, strong-arm; *Slang* buffalo. **4.** *The salesman pushed the new product at every opportunity:* promote, publicize, propagandize, advertise, make known, boost; *Informal* hustle, plug. **5.** *The child pushed his fingers into the mud up to his wrist:* stick, thrust, drive, shove, stuff, plunge. —*n.* **6.** *Give the gate a*

push and it will open: shove, nudge, prod, jolt. **7.** *Informal The president of the company was a man with a lot of push:* energy, vitality, drive, go, get-up-and-go, vigor, vim and vigor, ambition, determination. **8.** *The army's push into enemy territory was successful:* thrust, advance, incursion, inroad, foray. —**Ant.** 1 pull, drag, haul, tow, lug, yank; pluck, withdraw, remove.

pushover *n.* *The game was a pushover; When the boy begged for candy, his father was a pushover and gave it to him:* child's play, walkover, *Informal* kid stuff, easy game, easy mark, picnic, smooth sailing, snap; chump, cinch, victim, *Informal* soft touch, stooge, sucker.

pushy *adj.* *Pushy newcomers came to the fore:* pushing, obtrusive, aggressive, assertive, self-assertive, bold, brash, bumptious, forceful, loud, militant, obtrusive, offensive, officious, presumptuous, aggressive. —**Ant.** meek, unassertive, diffident, inoffensive, reserved.

pusillanimous *adj.* *The brave hero scared off the pusillanimous villain:* cowardly, lily-livered, fainthearted, mean-spirited; timorous, fearful, apprehensive; spiritless. —**Ant.** courageous, brave, valorous; bold, daring, spirited.

pussyfoot *v.* *The mayor is pussyfooting and won't take a stand on the issue:* hedge, dodge, weasel, evade, sidestep, straddle the fence, evade the issue, beg the question; tread warily, tiptoe, walk on eggshells; sneak.

put *v.* **1.** *Put the milk in the refrigerator. Put the files in alphabetical order:* place, set, rest, lay, position, deposit. **2.** *The sergeant put the soldier to work on KP:* assign, set, employ. **3.** *He was put under arrest by the policeman:* place, bring. **4.** *The invading forces put our army on the defensive:* drive, force, throw. **5.** *I don't put much faith in his promises:* assign, place, fix, set, lay, attribute, ascribe, impute. **6.** *Let me put it to you this way:* express, phrase, word, state; articulate, enunciate. **7.** *The plan was put to the membership for consideration:* propose, submit, offer, bring forward, present; throw out, pose. **8.** *The athlete put the shot about 40 feet:* throw, heave, pitch, cast. —**Ant.** 1 remove, raise, withdraw, displace, misplace, transpose, transfer, change.

putative *adj.* *The putative hypothesis was rejected:* would-be, supposed, alleged, conjectural, imputed, presumed, reputed, assumed.

putdown *n.* *The introduction turned out to be a putdown:* snub, suppression, cut, dig, disparagement, gibe, humiliation, indignity, insult, jibe, rebuff, slight, sneer, criticism, *Informal* knock.

putrefy *v.* *The meat had been left out of the refrigerator too long and had begun to putrefy:* rot, decay, decompose, putresce, molder, deteriorate, disintegrate, biodegrade; spoil, taint, turn, stagnate.

putrid *adj.* *That awful smell was caused by putrid meat:* spoiled, rotten, decomposing, decaying, bad, purulent, putrefied, putrefactive, putrescent, polluted, contaminated, tainted, rancid, fetid, rank, foul, stinking. —**Ant.** pure, clean, wholesome, uncontaminated, fresh, untainted, good.

putter v. He puttered around the house on the weekend: fiddle, fool, dillydally, tinker, potter, piddle; loiter, dawdle, diddle, dally, drift, loaf, idle, lounge, lallygag, loll, laze.

puzzle v. **1.** The murder case continued to puzzle the police: perplex, nonplus, bewilder, confuse, confound, baffle, mystify, stump; outwit, foil, hoodwink. **2.** I keep puzzling over his strange behavior: wonder, mull, brood, ponder. —n. **3.** The murder case was a puzzle to the detective: mystery, problem, dilemma, bewilderment, bafflement, mystification, perplexity, complication, difficulty, enigma, conundrum, riddle.

pygmy n. **1.** The circus sideshow featured a giant and pygmy billed respectively as the tallest and smallest men in the world: midget, dwarf, homunculus, manikin, Lilliputian, Tom Thumb; shrimp, runt, pipsqueak, half-pint, bantam, mite, peewee, elf. —adj. **2.** The zoo acquired a pygmy hippopotamus: dwarf, dwarfish, miniature, diminutive, short, tiny, small, wee, midget, toy, bantam, undersized, elfin.

quack *n.* **1.** *When legitimate doctors couldn't help his back trouble, he resorted to quacks:* ignorant pretender, medical impostor, fake doctor, charlatan, quacksalver. —*adj.* **2.** *He was a quack psychiatrist:* fake, fraudulent, phony, pseudo, sham, counterfeit.

quaff *v.* *After the day's work he would quaff a cold beer:* drink, swallow, gulp, guzzle, swig, toss off, down, swill, lap up, drink deeply, imbibe; *Slang* chug-a-lug, belt down, knock back.

quagmire *n.* **1.** *The horses were stuck in the quagmire:* soft muddy ground, marsh, bog, swamp, fen, morass, mire, quag, slough, sludge, ooze, sump. **2.** *You'll need more than diplomacy to get out of that quagmire:* predicament, difficulty, critical situation, crisis, dilemma, perplexity, Gordian knot, quandary, plight, involvement, intricacy, entanglement, strait, imbroglio, scrape, jam, fix, mess, muddle, morass, mire, quicksand, hot water, pickle, jam, pinch.

quail *v.* *We all quailed when the principal suddenly entered the room:* shrink with fear, blanch, lose courage, be cowardly, take fright, show a yellow streak, have cold feet, lose heart, lose spirit, recoil, flinch, run away, turn tail, shy, fight shy, cower; quake, shudder, tremble, shake, shiver in one's shoes, shake in one's boots.

quaint *adj.* *We enjoyed the village's quaint customs:* charmingly old-fashioned, out-of-the-way, picturesque, old-timey, antique, antiquated; unusual, strange, odd, bizarre, queer, eccentric, outlandish, peculiar, singular, curious, unique, original, unconventional, uncommon, rare, singular, extraordinary; droll, fanciful, whimsical. —**Ant.** modern, current, new, newfangled, modish, up-to-date, fashionable.

quake *v.* **1.** *The people quaked with fear when their village was invaded:* shake, shudder, quaver, stand aghast, tremble, shiver, blanch, quail, quiver. —*n.* **2.** *The quake caused much damage:* earthquake, tremor, seismic disturbance. **3.** *A quake of fear passed through him:* quiver, shiver, thrill, shudder, trembling, wave, ripple, spasm, throb.

qualification *n.* **1.** *Only applicants with the proper qualifications will be considered:* requisite, prerequisite, requirement; eligibility, fitness, suitableness; competency, capability, ability, capacity, faculty, endowment, talent, accomplishment, achievement, aptitude, gift, skill, property; attribute, forte; standard; credential, bona fide, certification. **2.** *The contract has several qualifications for both parties:* limitation, restriction, reservation, stipulation, condition, postulate, provision, proviso; exception, exemption, escape clause; objection; modification, arrangement.

qualified *adj.* **1.** *Take that dog to a qualified veterinarian:* experienced, trained, competent, practiced, versed, knowing; eligible, fit, fitted, equipped, suited, meet, equal; capable, adept, able, talented, skilled, skillful, accomplished, expert; certified, licensed, authorized; efficacious, proficient, efficient. **2.** *He gave a qualified an-*

swer when I asked for definite assurances: limited, indefinite, conditional, provisional, reserved, guarded; restricted, limited, hedging, equivocal, ambiguous. —**Ant.** 1 inexperienced, untrained, unpracticed.

qualify *v.* **1.** *Two years of experience qualified him for a promotion. She didn't qualify for the semifinals:* make fit, make eligible, fit, train, ground, prepare, adapt, ready, condition, equip, make competent or capable, enable, endow; license, sanction, permit; empower, entitle, authorize, give power, commission; certify, legitimate; be eligible, measure up, be accepted; *Informal* have what it takes. **2.** *The mayor said no but later qualified his answer:* limit, restrict, restrain, circumscribe, narrow; modify, moderate, alter, adapt, adjust, accommodate; temper, soften, assuage, mitigate, abate, ease, diminish, reduce. **3.** *Broadly speaking, adjectives are words that qualify nouns:* describe, characterize, modify.

quality *n.* **1.** *She has a quality of kindness that appeals to everyone:* characteristic, attribute, trait, mark, feature, aspect, property; character, nature, constitution, disposition, temperament; qualification, capacity, faculty. **2.** *The furniture was of poor quality:* value, worth, caliber, degree of excellence, grade, rank, class, merit. **3.** *You could tell he was a man of quality by his dress and behavior:* social status, rank, family, position, high station, standing, blood; eminence, distinction, dignity. —**Ant.** 3 inferiority, low rank, low station.

qualm *n.* **1.** *He had no qualms about robbing the poor:* scruple, misgiving, uneasiness, compunction, twinge of conscience, reservation; hesitation, reluctance, unwillingness, indisposition, disinclination. **2.** *Already on the boat train I felt a qualm, and by the time I got aboard ship I was seasick:* queasiness, faintness, dizzy spell, giddiness, vertigo, nausea, turn, sick feeling. —**Ant.** 1 willingness, inclination.

quandary *n.* *She was in such a quandary she didn't know to whom to turn:* dilemma, difficulty, predicament, strait, impasse, crisis, pinch, fix, entanglement, plight, imbroglio, involvement, morass, mire, quagmire, kettle of fish, pickle, jam, scrape, hot water.

quantity *n.* *Put a small quantity of sugar into the batter:* amount, sum, number; measurement, measure, size, extent, extension; abundance, aggregate, multitude; volume, mass, magnitude, bulk, greatness, amplitude, area, vastness, expanse, length; dosage, dose, portion, share, proportion, quota, apportionment, allotment.

quarantine *n.* **1.** *The health officials put the ship's crew in quarantine:* isolation, sequestration, medical segregation, *French* cordon sanitaire. —*v.* **2.** *Doctors quarantined the chol-*

era victims: isolate, confine, segregate, sequester.

quarrel *n.* **1.** *The couple's quarrel was so loud the police were called:* dispute, squabble, bickering, argument, conflict, spat, scrap, tiff, fuss, row, misunderstanding, falling out, open variance, difference, contradiction; disagreement, breach of peace, dissension, strife, contention, discord, dissidence, controversy. **2.** *My quarrel is with the underrepresentation of women here:* dispute, cause for complaint, complaint, objection, bone of contention, apple of discord. —*v.* **3.** *The couple quarreled constantly and finally got a divorce:* disagree angrily, argue, bicker, wrangle, fuss, have words, raise one's voice, squabble, spat, be at odds, dispute, be at variance, be at loggerheads, differ, dissent; altercate, brawl, contend, fight, row, be at each other's throats; fall out, misunderstand; clash, jar, feud, conflict; cavil, nag, carp, raise a complaint, find fault, pick a quarrel. —**Ant.** 1 agreement, accord, accordance, concurrence, concord, amity, concordance, harmony; understanding; peacefulness, congeniality. 3 agree, accord, concur, coincide, consent, assent.

quarrelsome *adj.* *Overwork and tension can make one quarrelsome:* belligerent, contentious, truculent, pugnacious, combative, militant, bellicose, disputatious, argumentative; antagonistic, fractious, captious, churlish, disagreeable, contrary, cantankerous, irascible, petulant, peevish, querulous. —**Ant.** friendly, easygoing, amiable, agreeable.

quarry *n.* *He sought his quarry in field and wood:* prey, chase, game, quest, victim; goal, objective, prize.

quarter *n.* **1.** *A quarter of the population voted for him. His allowance was a quarter a week. Insurance premiums are due every quarter:* one of four equal parts, fourth part, one-fourth, fourth, 25 percent; 25 cents, quarter dollar; three months. **2.** *Throughout the Latin quarter, Spanish is the predominant language. The troops attacked the city from all quarters:* area, place, part, location, locality, locale, district, region, province, precinct, zone, territory, terrain; specific place, spot, station, position, situation; sphere, domain, realm; direction, point of the compass, side. **3.** Usually **quarters** *We must find quarters before nightfall:* lodging, lodgings, housing, place to stay, place to live, board, shelter, billet. **4.** *The king gave no quarter to traitors:* mercy, pity, clemency; leniency, compassion, humanity, sympathy, indulgence. —*v.* **5.** *She quartered the sandwiches and put them on a serving tray:* cut into quarters, slice four ways, quadrisect. **6.** *The visiting diplomat was quartered at the embassy:* furnish with quarters, billet, lodge, house, install, put up; place, station, post.

quash *v.* **1.** *The dictator's army quashed the rebellion:* suppress, put down, crush, smash, quell, squelch, squash, quench, subdue, repress; stop, put an end to, extinguish, exterminate, obliterate, annihilate, ruin, destroy, wreck, devastate, strike out, blot out, delete, cancel,

expunge, erase, efface, dissolve, eradicate, dispel, extirpate; undo, overturn, overthrow, overwhelm. **2.** *The court quashed the previous ruling on the case:* set aside, annul, nullify, void, abrogate, declare null and void, invalidate, vacate; overrule, override, countermand; retract, rescind, recall, revoke, reverse, repudiate.

quasi *adj.* *The vegetarian restaurant offered a quasi hamburger, made of vegetables but no meat:* almost, near, virtual; somewhat, part, halfway, semi; apparent, seeming, resembling; imitation, so-called, synthetic, ersatz.

quaver *v.* **1.** *Her whole body quavered when she heard the sad news. I quaver when speaking to large audiences:* shake, quiver, shiver, tremble, shudder, quake; wave, wobble, totter, teeter, falter, waver; wriggle, writhe; oscillate, sway, vibrate, pulsate, throb, beat; trill. —*n.* **2.** *The broadcaster's voice had a quaver in it as he announced the sad news:* tremulous shake, quavering tone, tremor, trembling, quiver, throb, vibration; trill, vibrato, tremolo.

quay *n.* *The fishing boat was moored at the quay:* landing, wharf, pier, dock, levee, mole, jetty; waterfront, basin, marina.

queasy *adj.* *Violence makes me queasy. I felt queasy about going to the principal's office:* sick to the stomach, sickish, nauseous, nauseated, giddy, disposed to vomit; nauseating, sickening, bilious; qualmish, uneasy, uncomfortable, uncertain, troubled, upset.

queen *n.* *Elizabeth I was a beloved queen of England:* female monarch, empress, *Latin* regina, *French* reine, *Spanish* reina, *German* Königin; (*variously*) princess, czarina, ranee.

queer *adj.* **1.** *Her queer way of dressing attracted the stares of passersby:* strange, odd, funny, unusual, uncommon, peculiar; bohemian, unconventional, nonconforming, unorthodox, eccentric, erratic, *French* outré; extraordinary, exceptional, original, unique, rare; irrational, unbalanced, crazy, unhinged, touched, daft; unparalleled, unprecedented, unexampled; abnormal, unnatural, outlandish, freakish, bizarre, weird, grotesque, exotic; fantastic, preposterous, absurd, ludicrous, laughable, ridiculous, comical, droll, fanciful, capricious; curious, quaint, off the beaten track, out of the way; astonishing, remarkable. **2.** *He gave some queer answers to the policeman's questions:* suspicious, doubtful, questionable, irregular, farfetched; *Informal* shady, fishy. **3.** *Heights give me a queer feeling:* queasy, slightly ill, qualmy, faint, dizzy, giddy, light-headed, reeling, vertiginous, woozy. —*v.* **4.** *Informal His cheating on the final queered his chances of graduation:* ruin, wreck, spoil, thwart, damage, harm, hurt, impair, injure, disrupt, compromise. —**Ant.** 1 common, regular, conventional, customary, orthodox, ordinary, unexceptional, unoriginal; normal, natural; rational, sane. 2 straight, believable. 4 help, aid, boost, enhance.

quell *v.* **1.** *The dictator quelled the uprising:* crush, put down, put an end to, squelch, quench, quash, extinguish, ruin, destroy, stamp out; vanquish, wreck, conquer, defeat, beat down, worst, rout; overcome, overpower, over-throw, overwhelm; subdue, subjugate, suppress; reduce, scatter, disperse. **2.** *The lullaby quelled the restive baby. Aspirin will quell your head-ache:* quiet, still, silence, hush, stay, calm, lull, becalm, compose, tranquilize; pacify, appease; mitigate, mollify, palliate, allay, alleviate, as-suage, ease, soothe; deaden, dull, blunt, soften; stem, abate. **—Ant.** 1 encourage, foster, fo-ment, defend; enlarge. 2 agitate, disturb, per-turb, stir; annoy, bother.

querulous *adj. She divorced her nagging, quer-ulous husband:* complaining, grumbling, peev-ish, fretful, disagreeable, faultfinding, finicky, fussy, finical, exacting, difficult, obstinate; dissat-isfied, discontented, resentful, long-faced, sour; whining, whiny, shrewish, petulant, pettish, crabbed, grouchy, disputatious, captious, sple-netic, irascible, quarrelsome, nettlesome, irrita-ble, cross, cranky, touchy, testy, waspish. **—Ant.** uncomplaining, agreeable, good-tempered, complacent; contented, satisfied, pleased; genial, cheerful, easy, calm, equable.

query *n.* **1.** *Direct all queries to your nearest dealer:* question, inquiry; matter in dispute, problem, issue, question at issue; request, de-mand; inquisition, investigation, inquest; exami-nation, interrogation; search, quest. *—v.* **2.** *The police queried him on his whereabouts the night of the crime:* ask, question, put a query to, inquire of, make inquiry, quiz, interrogate, seek by asking, sound out; investigate, subject to ex-amination, examine, look into, inspect; cate-chize. **3.** *I query his trustworthiness:* consider questionable, question, doubt, have doubts about, suspect, harbor suspicions, distrust, mis-trust, impugn; dispute, controvert, challenge, impeach.

quest *n.* **1.** *Ponce de León discovered Florida in his quest for the fountain of youth:* search, pur-suit, exploration, hunt, seeking, crusade, pil-grimage, mission, voyage, journey, enterprise, adventure. *—v.* **2.** *Jason quested after the Golden Fleece:* seek, search; pursue, hunt.

question *n.* **1.** *Did you ask him a question?:* something asked, request for information, query. **2.** *The question was put to a vote:* matter of discussion, issue, point in dispute, moot point, question at issue, subject of investigation, proposal, proposition, motion, subject; bone of contention; uncertainty, doubt, dubiety, misgiv-ing, objection; dispute, controversy. **3.** *I'd like to travel more, but there's always the hard ques-tion of money:* problem, difficulty, considera-tion, matter, *Informal* rub. *—v.* **4.** *Stop ques-tioning me about my personal business!:* ask, inquire of, query, quiz, interrogate, put ques-tions to, sound out, *Informal* pump; grill, put through the third degree, examine, cross-examine, bombard with questions, subject to examination, investigate, look into; test, drill, cate-chize. **5.** *I question his leadership abilities:* consider questionable, be uncertain of, lack confidence in, doubt, have one's doubts about, call in question; hesitate to believe, harbor sus-picions about, suspect; distrust, mistrust, im-

pugn; refuse to believe, disbelieve; take excep-tion to, challenge, oppose, dispute. **—Ant.** 1, 4 answer, reply. 1 response. 3 solution, expla-nation. 4 respond. 5 trust, be certain of, have confidence in, have no doubts about; believe.

questionable *adj.* **1.** *Whether the machine will fly is still questionable:* doubtful, debatable, moot, unsure, undecided, ambiguous, unpro-ven, controversial, arguable, hypothetical, dis-putable. **2.** *The jury thought the defendant's actions were questionable:* dubious, puzzling, mysterious, perplexing, confusing, mystifying, enigmatic; suspicious, shady, *Slang* fishy, sus-pect, equivocal. **—Ant.** 1 certain, definite, as-sured, proven. 2 unimpeachable, aboveboard, proper, legitimate.

queue *n. The queue at the box office was nearly a block long:* line, column, file, row, train, chain, rank, string.

quibble *v.* **1.** *The children quibbled over who got the bigger piece of cake:* argue, bicker, squabble, hassle; raise trivial objections, carp, nag, cavil, nitpick, haggle, niggle; pick a fight, spar, fence; be evasive, dodge the issue, equiv-ocate, waffle, fudge. *—n.* **2.** *A quibble over exact wording delayed passage of the bill:* trivial ob-jection, cavil, petty distinction, nicety; evasion, equivocation, dodge, shift, shuffle, distraction, delaying tactic; subtlety, subterfuge; white lie, prevarication, pretense, artifice, duplicity.

quick *adj.* **1.** *After a quick courtship they mar-ried:* brief, rapid, fast, abrupt, sudden, precipi-tate, headlong; fleet, swift, whirlwind, hasty, ex-peditious, accelerated. **2.** *She ran with quick steps to the house when it started raining:* rapid, speedy, fast, expeditious, precipitate, brisk, swift, fleet, hasty, hurried; flying, nimble-footed, light-footed, winged; brisk, spirited, lively, sprightly, agile, spry, nimble, frisky, ani-mated, active, energetic, vigorous, vivacious. **3.** *My son is a quick student and always has high grades:* quick-witted, bright, apt, intelligent, dis-cerning, perspicacious; smart, clever, acute, keen, astute, sharp, alert, wide-awake, vigilant; sagacious, brainy; prompt, eager, shrewd, pene-trating; expert, skillful, facile, able, dexterous, adroit, deft, adept. **4.** *He has a quick tongue, but is usually sorry afterward:* excitable, impetu-ous, impulsive, high-strung, impatient; irritable, sharp, keen, snappish, fiery, peppery, hot-blooded, hot-tempered, irascible, choleric, sple-netic; waspish, petulant; testy, touchy, tempera-mental. **—Ant.** 1–3 slow. 1 long, lingering, gradual. 2 deliberate; sluggish, lazy, lethargic; heavy; inert, inactive; dull, wearisome. 3 dull, unintelligent, stupid, unresponsive, slow-witted; inexpert, unskillful, maladroit; sluggish, lazy. 4 calm, patient; restrained, temperate.

quicken *v.* **1.** *Is there any way we can quicken the preparation of dinner?:* make more rapid, speed, accelerate, expedite, hasten, hurry, hurry on, precipitate, hustle; further, advance, propel, drive, rush, dispatch; press, urge, egg on, im-pel. **2.** *A good debate can quicken one's mind:* excite, stimulate, activate, stir, pique, provoke, spur, goad, rouse, arouse, affect, instigate, galvanize, kindle, incite, enkindle, inspire, inspirit, fire; actuate, vitalize, vivify, animate, enliven, energize, revive, invigorate, move, sharpen, refresh. **—Ant.** 1 slow down, slacken, check, delay, hinder, impede, abstruct, retard. 2 deaden, put to sleep, enervate, dull.

quick-tempered *adj. If you're quick-tempered, count to 10 before you speak:* bad-tempered, cantankerous, quarrelsome, peevish, testy, ill-humored, touchy, *Brit.* shirty, waspish, churlish, choleric, temperamental, snappish, shrewish; cross, cranky, grouchy, irascible, irritable. **—Ant.** even-tempered, placid, serene.

quick-witted *adj. He's a quick-witted young man and should learn rapidly:* keen, perceptive, witty, smart, clever, brilliant, alert, bright, penetrating, shrewd, ready, intelligent, sharp, incisive, perspicacious. **—Ant.** slow-witted, stupid, dull, plodding.

quiet *adj.* **1.** *It was so quiet you could hear a pin drop. Why are you so quiet this evening?:* making no sound, silent, noiseless, soundless, hushed, soft, low, still, calm, not busy or active; reticent, saying little, taciturn, reserved, uncommunicative, mum, speechless, inarticulate, voiceless, mute. **2.** *My vacation was anything but quiet:* restful, untroubled, unruffled; calm, mild, halcyon, serene, tranquil, peaceful, peaceable, pacific, placid. **3.** *The dog lay quiet at his master's feet:* inactive, inert, passive, undisturbed, becalmed, at rest; dormant, sleeping, slumbering, dozing, comatose, lethargic; still, motionless, immobile, at a standstill, stock-still; unmoved, fixed, stable, stationary, immovable, stagnant. **4.** *He was a quiet man who didn't let small things upset him:* gentle, clement, mild, meek, docile, not rough or turbulent, retiring, easygoing, contented; sedate, composed, cool-headed, phlegmatic, collected, steady, unexcitable, imperturbable, unperturbed, patient; humble, modest, moderate, temperate; unobtrusive, undemonstrative, unimpassioned, dispassionate, even-tempered. **5.** *The quiet decor of her home made you feel comfortable and at ease:* not showy or loud, plain, simple, unostentatious, unassuming, unpresumptuous, unpretentious; not bright, soft, mellow, subdued. **—v. 6.** *The principal tried to quiet the students:* make quiet, silence, still, hush, mute; stifle, muffle, smother; bridle one's tongue. **7.** *The aspirin seemed to quiet the headache:* relieve, allay, mitigate, palliate, comfort, soothe, soften, alleviate, mollify, assuage, settle, set at ease, compose, calm, pacify, tranquilize; dull, blunt, deaden; lessen, decrease, weaken; still, abate, lull, quell, subdue, bring to a standstill; stay, stop, curb, check, arrest, put a stop to, suspend, discontinue, terminate, bring to an end. **—n. 8.** *In the quiet of my room I tried to think things through:* quietness, silence, still, stillness, hush, lull, quietude, soundlessness, noiselessness, muteness; calm, calmness, tranquillity, serenity, peace, peacefulness, placidity, rest, repose, relaxation; ease, gentleness. **—Ant.** 1 noisy, talky, verbose, loquacious. 2 excited, troubled, ruffled, agitated, upset, perturbed, tur-

bulent. 3 active, busy, disturbed, restless, agitated, disquieted; awake, alert. 4 turbulent, violent, mercurial, excitable, perturbable, impatient; immoderate, intemperate, passionate, high-spirited. 5 obtrusive, demonstrative, conspicuous, showy, blatant, loud, ostentatious, pretentious; bright, harsh, glaring. 6 stir, agitate, disturb, perturb. 7 worsen, heighten, enlarge, strengthen, intensify, increase. 8 noise, din, activity, disturbance, commotion.

quietly *adv.* **1.** *I want you to sit quietly:* silently, soundlessly, noiselessly, mutely, softly; speechlessly, inaudibly. **2.** *He waited quietly for his mother to return:* patiently, calmly, serenely, contentedly; composedly, collectedly, unexcitedly, unperturbedly, placidly, tranquilly, peacefully, pacifically; tamely, meekly, mildly; moderately, temperately; undemonstratively, dispassionately. **3.** *She was a quietly pretty woman:* unobtrusively, unpretentiously, unostentatiously, unassumingly, without ceremony; modestly, humbly, unboastfully, diffidently, bashfully; coyly, demurely.

quilt *n. She bought a quilt at the auction:* bedspread, blanket, comforter, counterpane, cover, bed covering, coverlet, eiderdown.

quintessence *n. Keen observation of nature is the quintessence of this painter's work:* essence, elixir, heart, core, pith, soul, gist, marrow, sum total, quiddity, distillation, sum and substance; embodiment, exemplar, personification.

quip *n. Dorothy Parker was known for her quips:* clever remark, witty saying, witticism, retort, repartee, wisecrack, *French* bon mot; banter, badinage, sally, spoof, riposte; play on words, wordplay, pun, epigram, double entendre; cutting remark, crack, barb, putdown, sarcasm, jest, taunt, gibe, jeer, raillery, jape, joke, gag.

quirk *n.* **1.** *Wearing that silly hat everywhere was a quirk of hers:* peculiarity, oddity, eccentricity, idiosyncrasy, mannerism, affectation, crotchet; odd fancy, foible, caprice, vagary, whimsical notion, whimsy, whim; aberration, abnormality; kink, fetish. **2.** *By a quirk of fate the brothers found themselves on opposite sides during the Civil War:* sudden twist, turn, freak accident.

quit *v.* **1.** *He can't quit smoking:* stop, desist, cease, cease from, forswear, make an end of, discontinue, end, terminate; give up, relinquish, yield, surrender; part with, let go, forgo, waive, set aside; lose interest in. **2.** *He quit the urban rat race and bought a farm in the country:* leave, go away from, take off, depart, get away from, withdraw, drop out, retire from; take wing or flight, skip or flee the coop from. **3.** *You can't quit your job now:* resign, leave a job, have done with, renounce reject, disavow, disown, relinquish, let go, part with, give up, abdicate; abandon, forsake. **—adj. 4.** *I wish I could be quit of these responsibilities!:* released from obligation, clear, free, rid, exempt, absolved, discharged; exculpated, exonerated, acquitted, all straight; clear of debt, owing nothing. **—Ant.** 1 start, begin, continue, persist, keep on. 2 arrive at, come to; remain, stay. 3 keep, maintain.

quite *adv.* **1.** *It is not quite dawn yet. The bottle* *is quite empty:* totally, completely, entirely, wholly, *Latin* in toto; fully, at all points, altogether; perfectly, utterly, positively; exactly, precisely; outright, out-and-out, in all respects, throughout. **2.** *It was quite a bargain:* actually, in fact, really, surely, in reality, indeed, truly, verily, in truth, veritably; certainly, assuredly; absolutely. **3.** *He was quite rude:* to a considerable extent, exceedingly, extremely, remarkably, very, excessively, considerably, in a great degree, to a high degree, highly; vastly, hugely, enormously, exceptionally, unusually.

quiver *v.* **1.** *The building quivered as the explosive went off:* shake slightly, shudder, tremble, shiver, quake, quaver, vibrate, convulse, twitch, jump, jerk, jolt; palpitate, throb, pulsate; oscillate, fluctuate; wriggle, wobble, totter; be agitated, pant. —*n.* **2.** *He could tell by the quiver in her lower lip that she was about to cry:* quivering, tremulous motion, vibration, tremble, shiver, shudder, shake, tremor, flutter, flicker; quaver, convulsion, seizure; throb, pulsation, palpitation; tic, spasm, twitching.

quixotic *adj. He had the quixotic idea of challenging all his enemies to a duel:* extravagantly chivalrous, absurdly romantic, starry-eyed, fanciful, impulsive, whimsical; chimerical, dreamy, sentimental, poetic, head-in-the-clouds, utopian, idealistic, unrealistic, visionary, impractical; ineffective, inefficacious; fantastic, wild, madcap, preposterous, absurd, ridiculous.

—**Ant.** realistic, down-to-earth, practical, serious.

quiz *v.* **1.** *The teacher quizzed the students on history. Father quizzed my boyfriend about his intentions:* question, examine, subject to examination, test; query, ask, inquire of, sound out, put to the proof; interrogate, investigate, cross-examine, *Informal* pump. —*n.* **2.** *The history quiz consisted of 10 questions:* test, examination, exam; investigation, interrogation, questioning, inquest, inquisition, inquiry; cross-examination; catechism.

quizzical *adj.* **1.** *His quizzical look told me I hadn't made myself clear:* inquisitive, questioning, puzzled, inquiring, perplexed, searching, curious, baffled. **2.** *His quizzical manner angered his teachers:* mocking, teasing, joking, impudent, bantering, arch, coy, derisive, insolent. —**Ant.** 1 comprehending, understanding, assenting. 2 serious, straight-faced, sincere.

quota *n. Each salesman has a quota of business to bring in each month:* portion, part, share, proportion; allotment, apportionment, distribution, allocation, assignment; quantity, measure, ration, percentage; minimum.

quotation *n. His talk was full of quotations from the author's work:* quote, excerpt, citation, extract, passage, selection, reference; cutting, clipping, illustration.

quote *v. You might quote Mark Twain's remark about the weather:* cite, refer to, repeat, extract, retell, excerpt; name, adduce, exemplify, paraphrase, instance; recall, reproduce, recollect.

R

rabble *n.* **1.** *The train station was swarming with a rabble of kids on their way to camp:* mob, swarm, disorderly crowd. **2.** *"Rabble" is an insulting term for "common people":* commoners, proletariat, lower classes, the masses, rank and file, populace, the great unwashed, riff-raff, hoi polloi, *German* Lumpenproletariat, the herd, *French* canaille. —**Ant.** 2 aristocracy, upper classes, nobility, elite, high society.

rabid *adj.* **1.** *Rabid dogs were destroyed by forest rangers in Maine last year:* suffering from rabies, hydrophobic, foaming at the mouth. **2.** *The enemy came on in a rabid "human wave" assault and we had to fall back:* fanatical, wild, wild-eyed, violent, raging, frenzied, frantic; maniacal, berserk, deranged, crazed. **3.** *She is a rabid basketball fan:* zealous, fervent, ardent.

race *n.* **1.** *It rained the day of the stock car races:* competitive trial of speed, contest, competition, heat. **2.** *He entered the mayoral race:* campaign, contest. —*v.* **3.** *Let's race from here to the corner. Sterling Moss and A. J. Foyt race cars professionally:* run a race, enter in a race, engage in a contest of speed, compete in a race; operate. **4.** *She overslept and had to race to the office:* hasten, hurry, run, run like mad, hie oneself, rush, hustle, make a mad dash, hotfoot it, dart, fly, dash. —**Ant.** 4 go slowly, crawl, creep.

racial *adj.* *He studied racial characteristics in his anthropology class:* genetic, ancestral, hereditary; ethnic, ethnological, folk, national.

racism *n.* *She refused to perform in any locality that practiced racism:* racial discrimination, racial bias, bigotry, racial prejudice, race hatred, segregation, color bar, color line.

rack *n.* **1.** *The rack held magazines:* frame, framework, crib. **2.** *The martyr was put to the rack:* torment, anguish, torture, pain, agony. —*v.* **3.** *She was racked with fever:* torture, distress, torment, agonize, excruciate. **4.** *They racked their brains:* strain, force, wrest, stretch.

racket *n.* **1.** *Who's making all that racket?:* loud noise, din, shouting, caterwauling, babel, clamor, clangor, commotion, clatter, uproar, vociferation, roar; hubbub, tumult, hullabaloo, hurly-burly, rumpus; pandemonium, disturbance, stir, turmoil, banging around, turbulence. **2.** *Loansharking is a racket:* illegitimate enterprise or occupation, game, underworld business undertaking. **3.** *Informal What's your racket?:* business, occupation, line, *Slang* game. —**Ant.** 1 quiet, silence, tranquillity, serenity, calm, peace.

raconteur *n.* *A toastmaster should be a poised raconteur:* skilled storyteller, anecdotist, narrator, spinner of yarns, teller of tales, fabulist, romancer.

racy *adj.* **1.** *Women were fascinated by him because he had a racy life style:* vigorous, exhilarating, heady, zesty, zestful, keen, energetic, spirited, fast-paced, lively, animated, exciting, stimulating, buoyant, sparkling, glowing. **2.** *It's quite a racy novel:* suggestive, lurid, risqué, bawdy, ribald, off-color, salacious, indecent, immodest, prurient, erotic, obscene, pornographic, vulgar, crude, smutty. —**Ant.** unexciting, dull, flat, bland, insipid, flat, stale, jejune.

radiance *also* **radiancy** *n.* **1.** *One of the gems had a deep, subtle radiance:* luster, sparkle, glitter, dazzle, iridescence, lambency, gleam, sheen, splendor, resplendence, brightness, brilliancy, brilliance, luminosity, effulgence, refulgence, luminousness, coruscation, incandescence. **2.** *Her face positively glowed with radiance after she won first prize:* animation, joy, happiness, rapture. —**Ant.** 1 dullness, dimness, murkiness, darkness. 2 sadness, glumness, dourness.

radiant *adj.* **1.** *The sky was radiant yesterday:* shining, bright, sunny, giving off rays of light, luminous, effulgent, refulgent, lustrous, glowing, aglow, incandescent; glittering, gleaming, dazzling, brilliant, sparkling, scintillating, flashing. **2.** *The bride was radiant. The lover looked at his sweetheart with a radiant smile:* bright with joy, beaming, glowing, happy, elated, ecstatic, overjoyed, joyous, blissful, rapturous, pleased, delighted, gladsome. —**Ant.** 1 dull, dark, somber, dismal, murky, lusterless, sunless, shadowy, cloudy, gloomy, overcast, black. 2 sad, sorrowful, unhappy, disconsolate, gloomy, somber, joyless, cheerless; displeased, unpleased.

radiate *v.* **1.** *The electric heater radiated warmth. Heat radiated from the fire:* emit heat, light, or other radiation; give out, circulate, give off, beam, shed, transmit; diffuse, scatter, disperse, spread, disseminate, shed, pour, spread, spread out, carry. **2.** *Spokes radiate from the hub of the wheel:* branch out, spread, diverge, go in all directions. —**Ant.** 1 absorb, soak up. 2 converge, come together, move together, meet, focus, center, concentrate, close in, zero in.

radical *adj.* **1.** *There are radical differences between binary and decimal numeration:* basic, fundamental. **2.** *Disbanding the congregation seemed a rather radical step:* severe, extreme, immoderate, drastic, precipitate, rash, inordinate. **3.** *When a society is polarized, the radical Left confronts the radical Right and there's nobody in between:* favoring drastic reforms, extreme, extremist, militant, revolutionary. —*n.* **4.** *When we use "radical" as a noun, we usually mean a left-winger:* revolutionary, extremist, left-wing militant; rebel, firebrand, freethinker, antiestablishmentarian. —**Ant.** 1 superficial, negligible, inessential, trivial. 2, 3 conservative, moderate, middle-of-the-road. 4 right-winger, rightist, reactionary, conservative, ultraconservative.

radioactivity *n.* *They measured radioactivity around the nuclear plant:* atomic *or* nuclear radiation, radioactive radiation.

radius *n.* *The flood encompassed a four-mile radius:* sweep, compass, ambit, boundary, expanse, span, extent, limit, orbit, range, reach, space.

raffish *adj.* *He had a raffish air about him:* rakish, jaunty, sporty, casual, fast, devil-may-care.

raffle *n.* *She won $100 in a raffle:* draw, drawing, lottery, sweep, sweepstake.

ragamuffin *n.* *Ragamuffins scavenged the war-torn streets for scraps of food:* urchin, waif, guttersnipe, street arab, hoyden, *French* gamin, (*fem.*) gamine; tatterdemalion, sloven, wretch; beggar, tramp, bum, derelict, itinerant, hobo, vag-abond, ragpicker, vagrant; panhandler.

rage *n.* **1.** *His rage over the crime was beyond words. The defeated candidate stamped up and down in a rage:* violent anger, wrath, extreme agitation, frenzy, indignation; fury, choler, vehemence, temper, furor, excitement; resentment, animosity, bitterness, spleen, madness, perturbation, ire, umbrage, high dudgeon, displeasure, irritation, pique; passion, violent emotional state, rampage, storm, frenzy, temper tantrum, ferment, paroxysm. **2.** *Big earrings are the rage now:* object of widespread enthusiasm, prevailing taste, current style, fashion, vogue, mode, craze, mania, fad, the latest thing, the thing, the "in" thing, the last word, *French* le dernier cri. —*v.* **3.** *She raged when her jewels were stolen while under police protection:* speak with anger, act with fury, storm, throw a fit, flare up, fly off the handle, lose one's temper, show violent anger, be violently agitated, be furious, vent one's spleen, blow one's top, explode, blow up, fulminate, rant, roar, raise cain, fume, seethe, boil, rave, froth at the mouth, blow one's stack, lose one's cool. **4.** *The war raged for several years:* continue violently, go at full blast. —**Ant.** 1 calm, calmness, coolness, equanimity; pleasure, gratification, joy, delight. 3 be pleased, be gratified; remain unruffled, keep one's cool.

ragged *adj.* **1.** *The ragged children begged the tourists for money:* clothed in tatters, wearing worn clothes, dressed in rags, seedy. **2.** *He wore an old ragged coat:* worn to rags, worn-out, worn, tattered, shaggy, shabby, torn, rent, threadbare, frayed, tacky, battered, shredded, the worse for wear, patched, shoddy, *Slang* beat up. **3.** *Jane's nerves were ragged by Sunday morning:* overtaxed, strained, exacerbated, aggravated, at the breaking point, run down.

raging *adj.* **1.** *We could not stop the raging boy's tantrum:* angry, incensed, enraged, beside oneself, furious, infuriated, frenzied, fuming, irate, mad, raving. **2.** *The raging current swept them along:* stormy, tempestuous, turbulent, violent, wild.

raid *n.* **1.** *In AD 844, Normans began raids on Spanish coasts:* surprise attack, sudden assault, razzia, onset, predatory incursion, invasion, inroad, sortie, sally, foray. **2.** *Nobody move—this is a raid!:* authorized police break-in, roundup, *Slang* bust. —*v.* **3.** *Tonight we raid Calais! Many speakeasies were raided in the 1920's:* attack, assault, swoop down on, pounce upon, invade, storm, enter suddenly, make a raid on, *Slang* bust.

rail[1] *n.* **1.** *The cowboy leaned against the fence rail:* horizontal support, bar, railing, barrier, fence, banister. **2.** *I'm afraid of flying—I prefer to go by rail:* railway, railroad, train, *Archaic U.S.* the cars.

rail[2] *v.* *He was always railing against the government:* vociferate, inveigh, fulminate, speak harshly, declaim, scold, talk angrily, raise one's voice, vituperate, rant, rant and rave, rage; shout abuse, take on, carry on; scream, gnash one's teeth, foam at the mouth, raise a hue and cry, *Slang* pitch a bitch, blow up, blow one's stack.

railing *n.* *A railing surrounded the sculpture:* rail, rails, balustrade, fence, banister, bar, barrier, post.

raillery *n.* *The raillery aimed at the guest of honor was all good-natured:* jesting, joking, kidding, banter, teasing, fooling, japing, badinage, sport, persiflage, pleasantry; satire, lampoonery; *Slang* razzing, roasting, ribbing, ragging.

railway *n.* *A railway linked the cities:* rail, railroad, railway, line, rail line, track.

raiment *n.* *He wore heavy raiment:* habiliment, clothes, clothing, garments, apparel, attire, dress, costume, habit, togs, toggery, *Informal* getup, duds, threads.

rain *n.* **1.** *Rain doesn't seem likely at the moment:* precipitation, rainfall, (*variously*) drizzle, mist, sprinkle, cloudburst, thundershower, rainstorm, shower, downpour, drencher, squall, hurricane, deluge, torrent. **2.** **rains** *We don't see many tourists when the rains come:* the rainy season, monsoon. **3.** *A rain of pamphlets fell from the plane:* shower, deluge, spate, plethora. —*v.* **4.** *It rained for 40 days and 40 nights:* (*variously*) pour, shower, drizzle, sprinkle, *Slang* come down in buckets, rain cats and dogs, come down in sheets. **5.** *The smokestacks rained black soot on the city:* shower, drop, send down, down. **6.** *He rained gifts on his future bride:* lavish, shower.

raise *v.* **1.** *The carpenter raised the shelf above the reach of children. The seamstress raised the hem of the dress:* erect, put up, elevate, lift. **2.** *The building was raised on level ground:* build, set up, construct, erect, put up. **3.** *The farmer raises cows and corn. We want to raise our children to be decent men and women:* grow, breed, produce, cultivate, develop, nurse, nurture, foster; rear, bring up. **4.** *That discussion raised my interest:* excite, stimulate, pique, sharpen, rouse, arouse, awaken, summon up, stir up, spark, urge, spur, inspire, boost, kindle, inflame. **5.** *There's one point I'd like to raise:* put forward, bring up, advance. **6.** *The landlord raised my rent:* increase, make higher, inflate, *Informal* hike up, hike, jack up. **7.** *We're trying to raise funds for the Red Cross:* collect, solicit, canvass, obtain, bring in, procure, amass. **8.** *The curfew was raised:* lift, end, terminate. —*n.* **9.** *He received a raise not only in salary but in position as well:* increase, elevation, promotion, advancement. —**Ant.** 1 lower, let down, drop; sink, depress. 2 destroy, ruin, raze, demolish, wreck, smash, tumble, level. 4 quell, quash, put to sleep, calm, soothe. 5 suppress, keep quiet, pass over in silence. 6 decrease, lessen, cut, reduce, diminish. 8 start, begin, initiate, establish, effect; reinstate. 9 decrease, cut, slash, demotion.

rake[1] v. **1.** *Mounties raked the district for a trace of the missing men:* comb, scour, ransack, go over with a fine-tooth comb. **2.** *Police bullets raked the getaway car:* sweep with gunfire, enfilade, pepper.

rake[2] n. *Don't have anything to do with that rake, young lady!:* dissipated man of fashion, playboy, voluptuary, sensualist, libertine, roué, lecher, satyr, goat, seducer, womanizer, Don Juan, Lothario, Casanova, immoralist, debauchee, rakehell, prodigal, profligate; rascal, rogue, *Informal* sport, swinger.

rakish adj. **1.** *He's a rakish old man:* loose living, profligate, depraved, lascivious, lecherous, lustful, libertine, dissolute, dissipated, immoral, debauched. **2.** *He had a rakish way of walking:* jaunty, sporting, breezy, sauntering, airy, dashing, dapper, sporty, cavalier, debonair, gallant, bumptious, swaggering.

rally v. **1.** *The teacher rallied the group before setting out for the museum:* reassemble, bring together again, reconvene, reunite, call together, unite, assemble, collect, gather, muster. **2.** *His brothers rallied to his side when he was in trouble:* come to the aid or support of a person or cause, rush, be at beck and call. **3.** *The patient rallied after the administration of the new medicine. The team rallied in the second half:* recover strength, revive, get well, get better, recuperate, improve, convalesce, *Archaic* recruit; take a turn for the better, pick up, pull through, come round, get one's second wind, catch up, score. —n. **4.** *Will you be attending tonight's political rally?:* gathering, caucus, meet, mass meeting, convention, assembly, assemblage, congregation, convocation, *Slang* powwow. **5.** *The patient's sudden rally surprised the doctors:* recovery, revival, recuperation, renewal of strength, restoration, convalescence, improvement. —**Ant.** 1 disband, dissolve, dismiss, muster out, discharge, release, disperse. 2 desert, abandon, forsake. 3 lose strength, become weaker, get worse, take a turn for the worse, sink, fail. 5 relapse, loss of strength, collapse.

ram v. **1.** *He rammed the stake through the rotting wood:* drive, force, jam, thrust, push firmly; strike, hit, beat, hammer. **2.** *The car rammed into a tree:* slam, crash, smash, run into, hurtle; dash, batter, butt, bump.

ramble v. **1.** *We like to ramble around the neighborhood on sunny afternoons:* wander, stroll, amble, saunter, meander, perambulate, peregrinate, traipse, rove, drift, roam, gad, gad about, range, gallivant. **2.** *The road rambles through a thick wood:* meander, zigzag, snake, wind, twist, go here and there. —n. **3.** *She likes taking a ramble through the woods on sunny afternoons:* idle walk, stroll, saunter, traipse, roam, hike.

rambling adj. *In a rambling two-hour speech the dictator promised to restore democracy:* di-

gressive, discursive, circuitous, prolix, diffuse, disjointed, uneven. —**Ant.** concise, to the point, direct.

rambunctious adj. *The rambunctious children were too much for their babysitter:* rowdy, boisterous, high-spirited, exuberant, rollicking, unrestrained, uninhibited, irrepressible, untamed, knockabout, uproarious, wild. —**Ant.** docile.

ramification n. *We have to examine every ramification:* consequence, upshot, sequel, development, result, offshoot, branching, extension.

rampage n. **1.** *The gang went on a rampage and shot several people:* violent spree, jag of violence. —v. **2.** *The terrified elephants rampaged through the jungle:* move or behave violently, storm, rage; go berserk, run riot, run amok.

rampant adj. **1.** *Malaria is still rampant in some swampy regions:* widespread, rife, prevalent, universal, unchecked, unrestrained, raging, ungovernable, uncontrollable; epidemic, pandemic. **2.** *The knight's coat of arms showed two leopards rampant on an azure field:* (of a four-legged animal) standing on the hind legs, standing up, erect. —**Ant.** 1 restrained, curbed, checked.

rampart n. *The enemy attacked the outer ramparts of the fort. The hill served as a rampart, protecting the town from floods:* protective barrier, defensive wall; fortification, barrier, barricade, protective wall, bulwark, earthwork, breastwork, parapet, bastion.

ramshackle adj. *They took shelter in an old ramshackle barn:* shabby, deteriorating, dilapidated, falling to pieces, tumbledown, decrepit, run-down, crumbling; shaky, rickety, flimsy, unsteady, unstable, tottering. —**Ant.** well built, solid, substantial; steady.

rancid adj. *Our tea was served with ghee, a liquid butter with a rancid taste:* rank tasting, rank smelling, malodorous, stinking, putrid, foul, mephitic, gamy; old, strong, high. —**Ant.** fresh, pure.

rancor n. *A victim of injustice is bound to be full of rancor:* resentment, bitterness, ill feeling, ill will, hostility, antagonism, malevolence, spleen, acrimony; hatred, animosity, spite, spitefulness, animus, antipathy, malice, enmity, hate. —**Ant.** amity, goodwill, friendship, friendliness, amicability.

random adj. *The two friends had a random encounter on the street. Father likes to take random walks round and about the town:* occasional, chance, unintentional, unplanned, undesigned, unpremeditated, unintended, unexpected, fortuitous, accidental, hit-or-miss, offhand, casual, haphazard, aimless, adventitious, stray. —**Ant.** deliberate, planned, designed, intentional, intended, premeditated.

range n. **1.** *The company puts out a large range of products:* variety, scope, gamut, selection. **2.** *Hiring and firing are within the range of his responsibilities. The enemy plane flew out of the range of our guns:* sphere, field, orbit, domain, province, reach, limit, radius, bounds, purview. **3.** *The Rocky Mountain range:* chain of mountains, ridge, sierra, massif. **4.** *Home, home on* *the range:* grazing land, pasture, plains. —v. **5.** *Her children's ages range from three to eighteen:* extend, run, stretch, reach. **6.** *He spent the summer ranging the countryside:* rove, wander, roam, explore.

rangy *adj. The rangy mare was broken to saddle:* leggy, long, long-legged, gangling, gangly, lanky.

rank[1] *n.* **1.** *It was a terrible play—of the very lowest rank:* grade, quality, class, order, type, sort. **2.** *His rank allowed him to join the most exclusive clubs. The captain was promoted to the rank of major:* social standing, position, class, standing, status, estate; echelon, professional grade, level, classification. **3.** *Soldiers stood in ranks for inspection:* line, row, file, column. —v. **4.** *Buying a boat ranks low on my list of priorities:* have rank, take rank, be ranked, have place, be classed, stand, rate, come out. **5.** *The headmaster ranks at that boarding school:* hold the highest rank, have supremacy, be number one, come first.

rank[2] *adj.* **1.** *The island was covered with rank greenery:* overgrown, overabundant, luxuriant, lush, lavish, dense, profuse, tall, high-growing, jungly, tropical, wild. **2.** *Throw all the rank food out, then get that refrigerator fixed!:* strong smelling, ill smelling; rancid, foul; stale. **3.** *It was a rank insult:* utter, absolute, total, complete, sheer, bald, unmitigated, downright, flagrant, arrant, rampant, glaring; gross, crass, coarse, filthy, nasty, scurrilous; outrageous, monstrous, atrocious. —**Ant.** 1 spare, scanty, sparse. 2 fresh, sweet smelling, unspoiled.

rankle *v. His harsh words rankled:* irritate, gall, chafe, gripe, rile, pique, fester, not sit well. —**Ant.** please; soothe.

ransack *v.* **1.** *We ransacked the attic for grandmother's photo album:* rummage through, rake comb, search, turn upside down, scour. **2.** *Vandals ransacked the cathedral:* pillage sack, vandalize, plunder, loot, rifle, raid, devastate, despoil, ravage, gut, strip, lay waste.

ransom *n.* **1.** *The parents could not afford the ransom:* redemption, deliverance, liberation, release. —v. **2.** *They ransomed the prisoners:* redeem, release, restore, deliver, deliver up.

rant *v.* **1.** *He ranted about the lack of respect shown him:* harangue, rave, orate, rage, bluster, storm, spout, bellow, yell, explode, scold, fume; *Slang* blow one's top, blow one's stack, shoot off one's mouth. —n. **2.** *Her complaint about the service was so much rant:* bombast, declamation, bluster, exaggeration, bravado. —**Ant.** 1 whisper, mutter, mumble, murmur.

rap *v.* **1.** *Nervous, he rapped the tabletop with his knuckles until they were sore. We rapped at the door, but there was no answer:* tap, thump, drum, knock. **2.** *Slang The talk-show panelists rapped for several hours about many subjects:* talk, speak, chat, converse, communicate; shoot the breeze, jaw. **3.** *Informal The critics rapped the new play:* criticize, knock, come down on, *Slang* pan, roast, clobber, dump on. —n. **4.** *We heard a rap at the door:* light quick blow, knock, tap, bang. **5.** *Informal I refuse to take the rap*

for something you did: blame, responsibility, adverse consequences. —**Ant.** 3 praise, eulogize, laud, flatter, rave about.

rapacious *adj. The pirates of old were a rapacious lot. His rapacious ways made him wealthy but friendless:* plundering, marauding, ransacking, thievish, pillaging, looting, predatory; greedy, avaricious, covetous, grasping, mercenary; insatiable, voracious, wolfish, ravenous.

rape *n.* **1.** *The rape of the city took a week. He was sent to prison for the rape of three women:* forcible violation, criminal attack, abuse, assault, defilement, violation; sexual assault. —v. **2.** *The corporate predator raped the company:* despoil, plunder, pillage, ravish, violate. **3.** *He raped in several neighborhoods:* sexually assault, force, forcibly violate, ravish.

rapid *adj. She made a rapid departure. It was an age of rapid strides in science:* quick, fast, fleet, express, swift, speedy; hasty, hurried, instant; brisk, active; expeditious, precipitate, prompt; feverish, agitated, rushing, galloping, flying; accelerated, unchecked. —**Ant.** slow, leisurely, gradual; deliberate; lazy, sluggish, dilatory.

rapidity *n. Rapidity was called for in dealing with the problem:* swiftness, speed, fleetness, quickness, haste, velocity, alacrity, celerity. —**Ant.** sloth, lethargy.

rapidly *adv. He was rapidly becoming the nation's number one movie star. She ran rapidly up the stairs:* swiftly, fast, speedily, expeditiously, with rapid strides, apace, quickly, at a great rate, by leaps and bounds, overnight, at full speed; briskly, hurriedly, hastily, pell-mell, helter-skelter, as fast as one's legs will carry one, like a house on fire, like a shot, in high gear. —**Ant.** slowly, gradually.

rapids *n. pl. They encountered rapids at the end of their canoe trip:* chute, rapid, white water.

rapport *n. He has great rapport with all his children:* relationship, camaraderie, understanding, affiliation, fellowship; connection, link, tie, interrelationship.

rapprochement *n. Diplomats tried to work out a rapprochement between the two nations:* reconciliation, reconcilement, understanding, accord, entente, détente, agreement, conciliation, settlement, harmonization, appeasement, accommodation, pacification.

rapt *adj.* **1.** *She was a rapt listener:* engrossed, enthralled, absorbed, interested, attentive, intent. **2.** *There was a rapt look on his face whenever he looked at his sweetheart:* transported, ecstatic, rapturous, enrapt, enraptured, spellbound, enchanted, charmed, bewitched, captivated, moonstruck, entranced, fascinated, delighted; bemused, dreamy. —**Ant.** 1 uninterested, disinterested, detached, indifferent, incurious; bored.

rapture *n. Seeing Rome for the first time filled the young visitor with rapture:* ecstasy, joy, elation, thrill, felicity, delight, euphoria, bliss, beatitude. —**Ant.** unhappiness, sorrow, woe, misery.

rare *adj. Friends like him are rare:* seldom

found, seldom to be met with, hard to find; scarce, few, few and far between, infrequent, uncommon, unusual, exceptional, out of the common run, unique. —**Ant.** plentiful, many, bountiful, abundant; ubiquitous, profuse, manifold, often found, easy to find; frequent, habitual, regular.

rarefied adj. The collectors had rarefied tastes: refined, esoteric, special, secret, recondite, inside, privileged.

rarely adv. He rarely studied, yet he passed every exam: seldom, not often, hardly ever, uncommonly, scarcely ever, infrequently, on rare occasions, only occasionally; hardly; once in a great while, once in a blue moon. —**Ant.** often, frequently, always, continually, ordinarily, usually.

rascal n. **1.** That rascal was always playing practical jokes on us: mischievous person, trickster, prankster, scamp, imp, devil, scalawag, rapscallion. **2.** Her second husband was something of a rascal: rake, rogue, devil, delinquent, reprobate, rakehell, scoundrel, knave, villain, cad, blackguard.

rash adj. I think you were too rash in accepting his proposal. Hotspur was a rash young man: precipitate, brash, abrupt, hasty, premature, imprudent, injudicious, indiscreet, incautious; irresponsible, reckless, headlong, impulsive, impetuous, adventurous, ungoverned, uncontrolled, unchecked, unadvised; careless, heedless, thoughtless, unthinking; harebrained, devil-may-care; foolhardy, foolish.

rasp v. He rasped at the metal with a file: abrade, scrape, grate, grind, rub down, scour, wear, file.

rate n. **1.** She can read at the rate of 100 words a minute: speed, pace, tempo. **2.** The room rates at the hotel ranged from $10 to $35 per day: price, charge, figure, fee, dues; cost, expense, levy, tariff, toll; assessment. —v. **3.** I rate that performance one of the best I've ever seen: classify, class, rank, count, measure; regard, deem, look on.

rather adv. I was rather surprised at her behavior: to a certain extent, quite, very, pretty; somewhat, a bit, slightly, in some degree, comparatively, relatively, fairly, in some measure, moderately, Informal sort of, kind of; after a fashion, more or less.

ratify v. A majority is needed to ratify the new resolutions: confirm, validate, approve, uphold, affirm, make valid, authenticate, make good, endorse, support, acknowledge, sanction; settle firmly, authorize, certify, Informal okay; consent to, agree to, accede to. —**Ant.** veto, disapprove, refute, disagree to; invalidate, disavow, repudiate.

ratio n. The ratio of hydrogen to oxygen in water is 2 to 1: proportional relation, interrelationship, proportion, proportionality, equation, fixed relation; arrangement, distribution, apportionment.

ration n. **1.** Each flood victim was provided with a stated daily ration: food share, allotment, apportionment, provision; measure, dole, due. **2.**

rations The besieged fort had rations for two more days: provisions, stores, food, provender. —v. **3.** If the fuel shortage continues, will gasoline have to be rationed?: distribute by restricted allotments, apportion, allocate, allot, mete out.

rational adj. **1.** It was a rational plan and bound to succeed: based on reason, sound, reasonable, logical; solid, wise, sage, sagacious; judicious, advisable, perspicacious; credible, feasible, plausible. **2.** The doctors found him to be rational and so able to stand trial: sane, compos mentis, in one's right mind, lucid, clearheaded, balanced, normal, sound, responsible, Slang all there. —**Ant.** 1, 2 irrational, unreasonable, unsound, insane.

rationale n. I simply don't understand the rationale of his plan: basis, underlying reason, explanation, logic, foundations, grounds; reasoning, philosophy, key concept.

rationalize v. **1.** The boy's mother rationalized his bad behavior as just a playful boyish prank: justify, account for, make allowance for, make excuses for, excuse, explain away, put a gloss upon, palliate, whitewash. **2.** They were unable to rationalize the appearance of ghosts: explain, interpret rationally; account for objectively.

rattle v. **1.** The engine rattled. The earth tremor rattled the dishes in the cupboard. The old car rattled down the street: clatter, clink, clank, roll loosely, jar, shake, bounce. **2.** He rattled on about his various ailments: chatter, maunder, gab, prate, blather. **3.** Word of the accident rattled her: shake, upset, disturb, perturb, agitate, jangle, faze, discomfit, fluster, flurry, discompose, disconcert, distract, throw; nonplus, bewilder, confuse. —n. **4.** The rattle of the shutters was caused by the wind: clacking, clatter, clang, clank. —**Ant.** 3 calm, compose, soothe, settle, relax.

raucous adj. Don't speak in such a raucous voice! The raucous yelling of the crowd could be heard for blocks: harsh, rough, jarring, grating, raspy, hoarse, grinding, jangling; discordant, strident, cacophonous, inharmonious, dissonant, stertorous, blaring, loud, earsplitting; shrill; piercing. —**Ant.** soft, dulcet, mellow, mellifluous, soothing, pleasant.

ravage v. The invaders ravaged the countryside: cause widespread damage to, ruin, lay in ruins, raze, gut, lay waste, waste, wreck, desolate, destroy, demolish, devastate, rape, spoliate, despoil, shatter; pillage, plunder, maraud, sack, loot, strip, ransack, raid, overrun.

rave v. **1.** The distraught man kept raving until finally he was led away: rant, rage; babble, ramble; make delirious utterances. **2.** Father raved when I disobeyed him: storm, fume, be furious, be mad, go on, be angry, lose one's temper, flare up, explode, thunder; sputter, bluster, run or go amok, Slang fly off the handle, blow one's top. **3.** He raved about Brando's performance: speak glowingly, gush, effervesce, bubble, wax, go on and on, expatiate, rhapsodize; rant, carry on. —n. **4.** His book has received raves from all the New York critics: an extravagantly good review, an extremely favorable criticism, *Informal* kudos, good press, compliments, words of praise, high praise, flattery. —*adj.* **5.** *The critics gave rave notices to that new play:* laudatory, highly favorable. —**Ant. 3** cavil at, deplore, score. 4 condemnation, disapproval, *Slang* knock. 5 condemning, faultfinding; bad, disparaging.

ravenous *adj. Scrooge was a grasping, ravenous miser. The children were ravenous after going all day without eating:* predatory, ravening, rapacious, covetous, greedy, avaricious, grasping, insatiable, insatiate; hungry, voracious, starved, starving, famished; gluttonous, piggish.

ravine *n. The floodwater rushed through the ravine, sweeping everything in its path:* valley, gulch, gorge, *Spanish* arroyo, chasm, gap, cleft, canyon, pass, *Brit.* clough, wadi, gully.

ravish *v.* **1.** *The slave traders ravished babes from their mothers' arms:* seize and carry away by force, make off with, snatch. **2.** *As it says in the Bible, their houses shall be spoiled and their wives ravished:* rape; outrage, violate, abuse, deflower, defile. **3.** *She was ravished by the sight of her first grandchild:* transport, enrapture, enthrall, overjoy, delight, gladden, cheer, captivate, enchant, charm, entrance, fascinate; tickle, *Slang* knock out. —**Ant. 3** displease, disgust, provoke, rile, pique.

ravishing *adj. You look simply ravishing, my dear:* enchanting, alluring, charming, fascinating, entrancing, captivating, bewitching; very pleasing, delightful, gorgeous, splendid, striking, beautiful, sensational, *Slang* smashing. —**Ant.** terrible, awful, disgusting, repulsive.

raw *adj.* **1.** *The main ingredient of steak tartare is raw chopped beef:* uncooked, unprepared, unbaked; underdone, undercooked, rare. **2.** *The raw materials arrived at the factory by the trainload:* natural, crude, unrefined, unprocessed, rough, not manufactured, not finished, basic. **3.** *The raw forces of the townspeople were no match for the well-trained invaders:* untrained, unskilled, undisciplined, unpracticed, unexercised, undrilled, unprepared, inexperienced, inexpert, amateurish, uninitiated, unseasoned, untried, untested, undeveloped, crude, unrefined; untaught, ignorant; fresh, green, unfledged, *Slang* rookie; immature, unripe, callow, young. **4.** *These are the raw facts:* frank, plain, brutal, unembellished, unvarnished, bare. **5.** *It's rather raw outside, so dress warmly:* chilly, damp, bleak; cold, harsh, nipping, pinching, biting, piercing, cutting, bitter, numbing, freezing; inclement, blustery, windswept. —**Ant. 1** cooked, prepared; baked; done, well-done, well cooked. 2 refined, manufactured, wrought, finished. 3 trained, skilled, disciplined, practiced, experienced, professional. 4 embellished, gilded, smoothed over, edulcorated. 5 warm, balmy, fair, sunny, mild.

ray *n. A ray of sunlight appeared through the crack:* beam, glint, gleam, glimmer, glitter, flicker, radiance, stream, sunbeam, moonbeam, radiance, light.

raze *v. They're going to raze this building to*

make way for the new highway: tear down, pull down, level, fell, flatten, knock down, topple, break down, dismantle, reduce; wreck, smash, demolish, destroy, ruin, wipe out, obliterate, remove.

reach *v.* **1.** *When will we reach Los Angeles? Can you reach his hand?:* arrive at, get to, come to, make, get as far as, set foot in or on, land at, enter, *Slang* make, *Nautical* put in or into; succeed in touching, contact, touch, go to, attain, get hold of, seize, grasp, secure, get to, come to. **2.** *He reached for the phone and quickly dialed a number:* stretch, stretch out, extend, out-stretch; strain after something, grab at; make an effort. **3.** *You can reach me at this number:* contact, get, find, get in touch with, communicate with. **4.** *Record sales this week reached well into the thousands. The temperature reached into the high 90's:* extend, climb, spread; approach, move, amount to, go to, hit. —*n.* **5.** *The climber slipped, made a reach for the rope, and was saved:* act of reaching, stretch; grab, grasp, clutch.

reaction *n.* **1.** *Water encourages the reaction of iron and oxygen to form rust:* chemical change, chemical transformation; nuclear change in an atom, change in the nucleus of an atom. **2.** *What was her reaction when you proposed to her?:* response, reply, answer, counteraction, reflex. **3.** *After radical political reform the forces of reaction are always a danger:* (*variously*) resurgent conservatism, right-wing comeback, counterrevolution, restoration, backlash.

reactionary *adj.* **1.** *Metternich's reactionary policy could not stop the movement for political and social reform:* reversionary, regressive, counterrevolutionary, diehard, right-wing, ultraconservative. —*n.* **2.** *The baron was a reactionary who favored a return to the feudal system:* ultraconservative, right-winger, counterrevolutionary, diehard, rightist, mossback. —**Ant. 2** radical, liberal, revolutionary, left-winger, leftist.

reactor *n. The reactor was shut down:* nuclear reactor, pile, atomic pile, reactor pile, chain-reacting pile, chain reactor.

read *v.* **1.** *He can read several languages. Can you read Morse Code? I read a good article in today's paper:* apprehend, understand, construe, comprehend, discern, perceive; make out the meaning or significance of, translate, interpret, explain; study, pore over, scan, analyze, decipher. **2.** *I read an interesting article in yesterday's newspaper:* peruse, scan, glance or run the eye over, note, study; pore over. **3.** *The actor read his lines well:* utter, render in speech, speak aloud something written, recite; give a public reading or recital; deliver, present. **4.** *Although it was a comedy, you could read biting social comment into the actors' lines:* adduce, extrapolate, construe. **5.** *The thermometer now reads 50 degrees. The invitation read "Open house—come one, come all!":* have a certain wording, be worded, say, go; show, indicate.

readable *adj. We finished his highly readable account of the event:* enjoyable, entertaining, easy, engaging, interesting, pleasant, pleasurable, inviting, lucid, coherent, flowing, fluent, clear, smooth, plain, straightforward, simple; understandable, comprehensible, intelligible, legible. —**Ant.** turgid, boring, dull, illegible, incomprehensible, indecipherable.

readily adv. **1.** The younger mechanic readily fixed the car. The call to arms was met readily: promptly, immediately, at once, straightway, instantly, quickly, expressly, in no time, without delay, speedily, pronto; easily, without difficulty, effortlessly, smoothly, with no effort, with one hand tied behind one's back, hands down; on the spur of the moment, at short notice, at the drop of a hat. **2.** She readily accepted his proposal of marriage: willingly, without reluctance or demur, in ready manner, freely, graciously, with good grace, with goodwill, ungrudgingly. —**Ant.** 1, 2 unreadily. 1 slowly, with difficulty. 2 unwillingly, reluctantly, grudgingly.

ready adj. **1.** It took us several hours to get the gymnasium ready for the school dance. I'll be ready to help you whenever you need me: completely prepared, in readiness, set, all set, duly equipped, fitted out, furnished; in condition for immediate action or use, fit, serviceable, in working order; immediately available for use, accessible, present, at hand, handy, on hand, on tap, in harness, primed; punctual, speedy, expeditious, prompt; equal to, up to; mature, ripe. **2.** I'm always ready to make new friends: willing, eager, disposed, inclined, prone, predisposed, apt. **3.** He was a ready pupil, quickly learning all his tutor had to teach him and more: prompt in understanding or comprehending, acquisitive, perceptive, discerning, quick in perceiving, attentive, alert, wide-awake, bright, astute, sharp, acute, keen, cunning, shrewd, showing quickness, quick-witted, clever, ingenious, resourceful; skillful, artful, masterly, expert, dexterous, apt, adroit, deft, facile, versatile. **4.** The bank was ready to foreclose unless he could raise enough money to pay the mortgage: likely at any time or moment, liable; tending; on the verge of, on the brink of, at the point of, set, just about. —v. **5.** The country wasreadied for war: prepare, put in order, make ready, equip, fit out. —**Ant.** 1–4 unready. 1 unprepared, unequipped, unfurnished; unfit, out of order; unavailable, inaccessible, unhandy; tardy, late, slow, inexpeditious; immature. 2 unwilling, loath, disinclined, indisposed, reluctant, hesitant. 3 slow, plodding, pedestrian, unexceptional.

ready-made adj. Ready-made clothes are usually cheaper than custom clothes: ready-to-wear, off-the-rack, store manufactured; Slang store-bought. —**Ant.** custom-made, handmade, tailor-made, made-to-order.

real adj. **1.** This jacket's made of real leather: genuine, actual, authentic, bona fide. **2.** These are the real facts: true, factual, valid, veritable, unquestionable, veracious, truthful; actual, well-grounded, solid, substantial, substantive, tangible; rightful, legitimate; absolute, positive, certain, unadulterated, unalloyed, unvarnished. **3.** His love was real: sincere, not affected, unaf-fected, genuine, unfeigned; true, honest, pure, unadulterated. —**Ant.** 1–3 unreal, fake, false. 1 imitation, counterfeit, factitious. 2 imagined, imaginary. 3 insincere, affected, feigned, faked.

realistic adj. He was realistic about his failure. It was such a realistic movie one could easily relate to it: pragmatic, down-to-earth; true-to-life, natural, naturalistic, objective, lifelike, graphic, representational, descriptive, depictive; real, authentic, genuine, truthful, faithful, precise. —**Ant.** unrealistic, impractical, idealistic, romantic, fanciful.

reality n. Forget your fantasies and face up to reality: actuality, fact, truth, verity; materiality, substantiality, physical existence, corporeality, tangibility. —**Ant.** unreality, pretense, illusion, myth.

realize v. **1.** I don't think you fully realize the importance of his speech: comprehend, apprehend, understand, gather, grasp, get, fathom, appreciate, absorb, feel strongly; perceive, see into, penetrate, make out, discern; be cognizant of, recognize, cognize; conceive, imagine. **2.** He realized his fondest dream when he won the Pulitzer prize: actualize, fulfill, complete, consummate, bring to pass, bring about, effectuate, carry out, execute, carry through, work out, discharge, do, produce, perform; attain, get, achieve, accomplish, make good. **3.** She realized very little by selling those stocks: get as profit, gain, acquire, profit, clear, net, obtain a return, make money, make capital of, accomplish.

really adv. Did he really say that? Really, he's the most exasperating person I know: actually, in fact, truly, truthfully, genuinely; literally, indeed; surely, certainly, veritably, verily, positively, unquestionably, absolutely, categorically.

realm n. **1.** His realm extended halfway into Asia: dominion, kingdom, domain, empire, royal domain, monarchy, demesne, land, country; nation, state. **2.** That plan is not beyond the realm of possibility: sphere, province, orbit, region, field.

reap v. Some who succeed in the arts reap great rewards: gather, glean, harvest, take in, bring in; earn, gain, obtain, acquire, procure, realize, derive, profit, get, win, secure, score. —**Ant.** waste, dissipate, lose, spend.

rear[1] n. **1.** Please move to the rear of the bus! Her terrace looks out on the front lawn, mine overlooks the park in the rear: back, end, tail end, heel, stern, hind part, back part, postern, posterior; after part, area or position behind. **2.** Three companies made up the rear: last or back part of an armed force, rear guard. —adj. **3.** The rear end of the car was dented, but we had no trouble getting the trunk open: at, of, in, or near the back; back, hindmost, aftermost, after, posterior, rearmost; dorsal; aft. —**Ant.** 1 front, fore, forefront, forepart; foreground; frontage. 2 front rank, front lines, advanced guard, vanguard. 3 front, frontmost, forward, foremost, leading.

rear[2] v. The boy's aunt reared him: bring up,

raise, care for; train, educate, cultivate, develop, nurture, nurse, foster, cherish.

reason *n.* **1.** *There was no reason for her rudeness:* cause, occasion, motive, grounds, justification, explanation, rationale. **2.** *Use the reason that God gave you:* brains, head, faculties, wit, comprehension, apprehension, understanding, perception, intelligence, intellect, perspicacity, acumen, sense, penetration, awareness, discernment, insight. **3.** *An obstinate person will not listen to reason:* common sense, logic, reasoning, appeal to reason, argumentation, exhortation. **4.** *There is no reason in a madman:* rationality, soundness of mind, reasonableness, mental balance, sanity, normality, sense, lucidity, clearheadedness. —*v.* **5.** *The solution is there if you care to reason it out:* think through, figure, solve. —**Ant.** 4 irrationality, unsoundness, mental unbalance, insanity, abnormality, incoherence.

reasonable *adj.* **1.** *Your proposal sounds reasonable, but we'll have to talk about it further:* judicious, wise, sensible, intelligent; logical, rational; sane, sound, credible, plausible, probable, possible, likely; well-grounded, well-founded, admissible, justifiable, understandable; legitimate, proper, suitable, fitting, equitable, fair, just. **2.** *Be reasonable in your dealings with people and you'll be respected:* of good sense or sound judgment, exercising reason, rational, logical, thinking, understanding, thoughtful, reflective; just, fair, impartial, objective, judicious, levelheaded, patient, coolheaded; moderate, prudent, circumspect; intelligent, sensible, wise, knowing, sage. **3.** *It was a reasonable request. My rent is reasonable:* not exceeding a reasonable limit, not unlikely, not excessive, not extreme, natural, predictable, moderate, lenient, temperate, fair, just, tolerable, equitable. —**Ant.** 1–3 unreasonable, irrational, unintelligent, unsound, impossible; unjust, unfair, outrageous.

reasoning *n.* **1.** *Thomas Aquinas's powers of reasoning were quite formidable:* ratiocination, logic, thought, cogitation, thinking; deduction, inference, analysis, penetration. **2.** *Can't you understand our reasoning here?:* argument, train of thought, rationale, analysis, interpretation, reflection, ground, basis.

reassure *v. Reassure the child that he has your confidence:* personally assure, bolster, inspire hope in, encourage, inspirit, uplift, buoy up, cheer; comfort, set one's mind at rest. —**Ant.** dishearten, discourage, unnerve, disconcert.

rebate *n. She got a rebate on her purchase:* remission, discount, allowance, kickback, reduction, reimbursement.

rebel *n.* **1.** *The rebels were arrested and tried for treason. The film director was a rebel among his peers:* insurgent, insurrectionist, traitor, turncoat, deserter; secessionist, seceder, separatist, anarchist; revolutionist, revolutionary, resister; iconoclast, nonconformist, dissenter, malcontent, maverick, upstart. —*v.* **2.** *The peasants rebelled but were ultimately powerless:* resist lawful authority, defy authority, rise up, take

arms against an established order, oppose by force, revolt, mutiny, riot. **3.** *He rebelled at the idea of teaching young children:* be repelled by, turn away from, pull or draw back from, flinch, wince, quail, react, shrink, shy, recoil, be unwilling, avoid.

rebellion *n. The junta soon crushed the leftist rebellion:* insurrection, revolt, insurgency, sedition, revolution, mutiny, uprising, upheaval, defiance; putsch, coup d'état. —**Ant.** resignation, submission.

rebellious *adj. The king retaliated against the rebellious earls by confiscating their lands. Many children are rebellious during their teens:* defiant, disobedient, insubordinate, intractable, refractory, contrary, recalcitrant, pugnacious, fractious, contumacious, quarrelsome; up in arms, mutinous, seditious, insurgent, insurrectionary, revolutionary, turbulent, truculent, unruly, unmanageable, ungovernable, uncontrollable, disorderly, alienated. —**Ant.** patriotic, loyal, dutiful, deferential; obedient, unresistant, subordinate, subservient.

rebuff *n.* **1.** *She met his innuendo with a sharp rebuff:* rejection, refusal, putting off; repulse, snub, slight, cold shoulder, *Slang* put-down, slap in the face. —*v.* **2.** *Workers rebuffed the union leader's plan:* snub, slight, reject, spurn, ignore, disregard, cold-shoulder, refuse, repel, repulse, deny, decline, *Slang* turn down; check, keep at a distance, put off. —**Ant.** 1 welcome, acceptance, encouragement, come-on, come hither; spur, aid. 2 welcome, encourage.

rebuke *v.* **1.** *The clerk was harshly rebuked for misplacing some important files:* scold, upbraid, reproach, admonish, take to task, reprimand, reprove, chide, remonstrate with, lecture; censure, berate, call down, dress down, *Slang* chew out, take down a peg; find fault with, blame, score. —*n.* **2.** *The sharp wounding rebuke came as a complete surprise:* scolding, reprimand, remonstrance, admonishment, upbraiding, admonition, reprehension, reproach, reproof, reproval, tongue-lashing; disapproval, censure, castigation, chiding, berating, *Slang* chewing out, dressing down. —**Ant.** 1, 2 praise. 1 laud, applaud, congratulate; commend, compliment, approve. 2 laudation, commendation, compliments, approval; *Informal* pat on the back, congratulation.

rebuttal *n. In his rebuttal he demolished his opponent's argument:* refutation, rejoinder, confutation, contradiction, disagreement, disproof, denial, retort, riposte, counter-argument, counterreply, disproval, negation, *Law* surrejoinder. —**Ant.** validation, corroboration, substantiation, verification.

recalcitrant *adj. The recalcitrant youth needed more understanding teachers:* stubborn, obstinate, unwilling, unsubmissive, headstrong, refractory, mulish, pigheaded, bullheaded, willful, contrary, balky, unruly, disobedient, intractable. —**Ant.** obedient, compliant, amenable, submissive, yielding; controllable, manageable, governable.

recall *v.* **1.** *I'm sorry, I don't recall your name:*

recollect, remember; recognize, place. **2.** *They recalled some reserve units after war broke out:* reactivate, remobilize, call back; reinstitute, revive, reanimate. —*n.* **3.** *Do you have any recall of the accident? She has total recall for lists of numbers:* recollection, memory, remembrance; faculty of memory, ability to remember.

recant *v. Under cross-examination she recanted her previous testimony:* retract, take back, deny, abjure, withdraw, unsay, repudiate, disavow, renege, recall, revoke, renounce, rescind, disclaim, disown, forswear, repeal, eat one's words, apostatize, change one's mind. —**Ant.** reaffirm, confirm, repeat, validate.

recapitulate *v. The newscaster recapitulated the Prime Minister's speech:* summarize, recap, repeat in essence, sum up; reiterate, recount, repeat, relate, restate, reword, rephrase, epitomize.

recede *v. As he got older his hairline began to recede. The floodwaters have receded:* retreat, go back, back up, regress, abate, ebb, subside; retire, retreat, retrogress. —**Ant.** advance, proceed, move forward, progress.

receipt *n.* **1.** *This bill is payable upon receipt:* arrival, receiving, reception, recipience, admission, admittance, acceptance, acquisition, possession. **2.** *The deliveryman asked me to sign a receipt:* written acknowledgment of payment or goods received, voucher, release, discharge, transferral. **3. receipts** *We just opened our store and our first day's receipts exceeded our expectations:* amount or quantity received, profits, net profits, return, returns, gain, proceeds, share, *Slang* take, split, gate; revenue, income, earnings; pay, wages, payment, reimbursement, remuneration, emolument. **4.** *This mince pie is made according to an old family receipt:* recipe, formula.

receive *v.* **1.** *Have you received my check yet? The patient received the best of care:* get, acquire, secure, come by, be in receipt of, obtain, be given. **2.** *The hotel receives guests from all over the world:* accommodate, take in; admit, put up. **3.** *The prisoners received harsh and unfair treatment:* encounter, meet with, experience, go or pass through, have inflicted on one, submit to, be subjected to, undergo, sustain, suffer. **4.** *Madam is not receiving callers today. He was received with open arms:* be at home to, entertain, admit; welcome, greet, meet. **5.** *The book was well received by the critics and the public:* regard, accept, approve, react to, adjudge.

recent *adj. I was surprised to see so recent a movie on television. The bicycle is a recent purchase. In recent times the price of just about everything has gone up:* new, modern, up-to-the-minute, contemporary, up-to-date, lately made, late; novel, fresh; not long past, of yesterday, latter-day. —**Ant.** old-fashioned, dated, old, long past, remote, long ago.

recently *adv. They arrived recently:* anew, afresh, freshly, currently, lately, latterly, newly, of late, just now.

receptacle *n. Throw your litter in that wire receptacle on the corner:* holder, container, vessel, depository, repository, receiver, carrier; (*variously*) box, bin, basket, hopper, hamper, compartment, bottle, jar, can, bag, file, tray.

reception *n.* **1.** *I couldn't fathom her cool reception—what had I done?:* act of receiving one, welcome, greeting, recognition. **2.** *We had a big reception for the new ambassador:* affair, social gathering; party, fete, soiree, *Informal* do.

receptive *adj. The inventor hoped to find the examiner at the U.S. Patent Office in a receptive mood:* favorably disposed, openminded, accessible, approachable, amenable, hospitable, friendly, responsive, interested, susceptible. —**Ant.** unreceptive, illiberal, unresponsive, closed-minded, narrow-minded, prejudiced, biased.

recess *n.* **1.** *The judge ordered a recess of two hours. The student went to Vermont during his school's winter recess:* suspension of business, intermission, break, coffee break, time out, respite, rest, breathing spell, hiatus, pause, lull, *Informal* letup; interim, interlude, interval; holiday, vacation. **2.** *The safe was set in a recess of the wall. The boat was anchored in a small recess of the island:* receding part of space, indentation, hollow, break, fold; alcove, cell, nook, niche, slot, pigeonhole, corner, bend; inlet, bay, cove, harbor, gulf; cleft, gorge, gap, pass. **3. recesses** *Outwardly he appeared forgiving, but in the recesses of his mind he planned revenge:* inmost part, depths, penetralia.

recession *n. He even prospered during the recession:* downturn, decline, reversal, slump, slide, slump, stagnation. —**Ant.** boom, upturn.

recherché *adj. The antique store specialized in recherché objects:* rare, exotic, unique, choice, select, special, uncommon, original, unusual, different, exceptional, superior, valuable, priceless, prize, scarce, one of a kind. —**Ant.** ordinary, commonplace, run-of-the-mill, routine.

recipe *n. The recipe called for too many ingredients:* directions, instructions, formula, method, procedure, process.

reciprocal *adj. Our relationship's based on reciprocal respect. Canada and the U.S. made reciprocal trade agreements:* mutual, common; shared; interdependent, returned, given in return, exchanged, equivalent, give-and-take, one for one; complementary, bilateral, corresponding, interrelated, interchangeable, interchanged, linked. —**Ant.** one-way, unilateral.

reciprocate *v. He reciprocated his friend's admiration. They've invited us to dinner so many times I must reciprocate:* return, feel, give in return, give or take mutually, requite, interchange; respond, return the compliment, act likewise, make return, retaliate.

recital *n.* **1.** *She played her first public recital at Town Hall when she was 14:* solo musical performance, concert. **2.** *His recital of the poem was flawless. Did she give you a recital of her woes?:* recapitulation, narration, recitation, rendition, delivery, performance, reciting; narrative, telling, talk, discourse, dissertation; report, description, detailed statement, particulars, graphic account; public reading, oral exercise.

recitation n. The recitation took half an hour: recital, address, monologue, rendering, soliloquizing, address.

recite v. I was called on to recite "the Gettysburg Address": declaim, perform, speak, narrate, recount, tell, deliver, repeat, relate, say by heart, quote, communicate, do one's number, give a recitation.

reckless adj. He was fined for reckless driving: incautious, heedless, unheeding, unmindful, careless, irresponsible, thoughtless, regardless, inconsiderate, mindless, unthinking, neglectful, negligent, unwatchful, unwary, unaware, oblivious, inattentive, unconcerned; wild, daring, cavalier, daredevil, devil-may-care, volatile; precipitate, rash, unsolicitous, indiscreet, imprudent, uncircumspect, hasty, impulsive, fickle, unsteady; foolhardy, foolish, insensible; flighty, madcap, scatterbrained, harebrained, giddy. —**Ant.** cautious, heedful, mindful, careful, wary, aware, observant, thoughtful, regardful, responsible, deliberate.

reckon v. **1.** The wages were reckoned by the amount of hours worked: count, add, add up, total, tally, balance, figure, calculate, compute, estimate. **2.** Because our family is happy and healthy we reckon ourselves fortunate. He reckoned that we were only a few miles from our destination: regard, esteem, consider, deem, think, judge, adjudge, estimate; count, account, class, rank, rate, appraise, assess, value; determine, surmise, estimate, come to or arrive at a conclusion regarding, figure, decide, guess, speculate. **3.** Informal I reckon you'll be able to leave the hospital soon: guess, fancy, expect, presume, surmise, suppose, imagine, figure. **4.** I didn't reckon on his arriving two days ahead of time: count, figure, bank, plan, bargain. **5.** I don't know how to reckon with this problem: deal, cope, handle.

reckoning n. **1.** A reckoning of all outstanding accounts was made: count, total, tally, adding, summation, calculation, computation; appraisal, estimate, estimation, evaluation, statement of an amount due, bill, account, charge, tab; settling of an account. **2.** Both Christianity and Islam predict a time of reckoning for mankind: judgment, final judgment, doom.

reclaim v. They reclaimed an acre of swamp: recover, bring back, regain, restore.

recline v. She was reclining on a couch: lie back, lie down, rest, rest in a recumbent position, repose; lean, take one's ease, lounge, loll, sprawl.

recluse n. The recluse emerged from his hideaway: hermit, solitary, ascetic.

reclusive adj. She became reclusive in old age: ascetic, solitary, cloistered, isolated, retiring, secluded, sequestered, unsociable, withdrawn, antisocial. —**Ant.** gregarious, sociable.

recognition n. **1.** In this disguise, you can walk into your own home without a chance of recognition even by your loved ones: identification, act of being recognized, discovery. **2.** Some art-

ists gain recognition after death. The controversy over the new regime held up recognition for several years: acceptance, acknowledgment, understanding, comprehension, notice; act by which one government recognizes the existence of another, validation, diplomatic relations.

recognize v. **1.** I didn't recognize you in that disguise: know, identify, place, make out, discern, pick out, sight, spot. **2.** We recognize your financial problems, but your account is overdue: be aware of, appreciate, understand, comprehend, respect, acknowledge, realize, see, discern, make out; admit, know. **3.** The chair recognizes Mr. Jones: acknowledge as entitled to speak, give the floor to, yield or submit to, concede to. **4.** Portugal recognized Guinea-Bissau in 1974: establish diplomatic relations with, acknowledge. —**Ant.** 2, 3 ignore, overlook, turn one's back on, close one's eyes to.

recoil v. **1.** Spiders always made her recoil: draw back, hang back, start, shrink back, jump back, retreat, blench, quail, revolt; wince, flinch, demur, falter, shirk, blink, fail; cower, cringe. **2.** The cannon recoiled when it went off: fly back, spring back, rebound, bound back, jump back, kick.

recollect v. I can't seem to recollect where we met: recall, call to mind, remember, place.

recommend v. **1.** The supervisor recommended me for a promotion: put forward, present as worthy of, mention favorably, speak well of, favor, endorse, advocate, vouch for. **2.** The doctor recommended a change of scenery: urge, suggest, encourage, propose, advise, prescribe, order, counsel. —**Ant.** 1 mention unfavorably, disapprove. 2 forbid, discourage.

recommendation n. It was on your recommendation that we hired that new typist: praise, commendation, good word, behest, approval, endorsement, reference, Slang plug. —**Ant.** condemnation, criticism, disapproval, rejection.

recompense v. **1.** The company recompensed him for working overtime: compensate, remunerate, pay, reimburse, repay, reward. —n. **2.** This money isn't enough recompense for all the time and effort I put into the job!: compensation, remuneration, payment, reparation, repayment, return, reward, indemnification.

reconcile v. **1.** Father was unable to reconcile my brothers: conciliate, propitiate, restore to friendship, reunite. **2.** A pacifist cannot be reconciled to war: conciliate, win over, persuade, resign. **3.** We had better reconcile accounts: settle, set straight, make up, square; harmonize, fix up, patch up, rectify, adjust, correct.

recondite adj. She submitted a recondite thesis for her Ph.D.: profound, deep, abstruse. —**Ant.** clear, obvious, patent.

reconnaissance n. Reconnaissance of enemy territory showed a heavy concentration of artillery: inspection, survey, scrutiny, viewing, observation, reconnoitering, scouting, investigation, exploration; surveillance.

reconsider v. We begged her to reconsider her decision: rethink, review, reexamine, reevaluate, modify, reassess, think over, mull over, ponder, think better of, sleep on, revise, amend, correct, take under advisement, think twice about.

reconstruct v. *They reconstructed the dinosaur:* rebuild, reconstitute, reassemble, overhaul, piece together, recast, recreate, refashion, restore, revamp, rework, make over.

record v. **1.** *You should record precious comments like that:* write down, set down in writing, put or place on record, make an entry of, register, transcribe, take down, note, copy, inscribe for posterity, jot down, make a memorandum of; enter, catalog, list, enroll, post, admit, introduce, log; chronicle; register, tape. **2.** *A cardiograph records the heartbeat:* register, show, indicate. —n. **3.** *A record of each child's birth was in the family Bible:* account, report, document, register; docket, file; journal, annals, chronicle, archive, history, proceedings; note, memorandum, memo, jotting. **4.** *His employment record has always been good. He has no record with the police:* facts known about a person or thing, history, report of actions, account; background, experiences, adventures; conduct, performance, career. **5.** *Mark Spitz broke several world swimming records at the 1972 Olympics:* best performance known, top performance, greatest achievement of its kind to date, unbeaten mark, ultimate example, best rate attained. —Ant. 1 erase, obliterate, expunge, cancel, delete; disregard, omit.

recount v. *They recounted their adventure:* relate, narrate, tell, recite, describe, enumerate.

recoup v. *He went back to the baccarat table, hoping to recoup his losses:* regain, reacquire, retrieve, redeem, recover, replace; make up for, make good, make amends for, atone; provide an equivalent for.

recourse n. *We have no recourse but to seek help:* resource, resort, refuge, hope, expedient, means, device, help, strength, last resort.

recover v. **1.** *The army was unable to recover any of the territory it lost. The stolen jewels were finally recovered:* get back, retrieve, recoup, regain, reacquire, repossess, reclaim, redeem, recapture, reconquer, retake, win back; make up for, make good, restore, offset, balance, compensate. **2.** *She's home now recovering from the operation:* return to good condition, regain strength, be restored to health, get well, recuperate, convalesce, return to health, take a turn for the better, improve, heal, mend; rally, come around, pull through; regain control of oneself, be oneself again, revive, revivify, resuscitate, rejuvenate, restore, pick up. —Ant. 2 relapse, fail, grow worse, worsen.

recreant adj. **1.** *The recreant troops threw down their arms:* cowardly, craven, dastardly, base, pusillanimous, fainthearted, *Informal* yellow. **2.** *The recreant managers betrayed company secrets:* unfaithful, disloyal, false, faithless, untrue, treacherous, apostate. —n. **3.** *The recreants gave no defense for their conduct:* coward, craven, dastard. **4.** *He was a recreant to his faith:* apostate, traitor, renegade.

recreation n. *What's your favorite recreation?:* diversion, leisure activity, pastime, play, hobby, sport, entertainment, amusement, avocation; diversion, relaxation.

recruit n. **1.** *The volunteer campaign got new recruits:* newcomer, novice, beginner, neophyte, rookie, tenderfoot, trainee, tyro; convert; draftee, serviceman, enlisted man. —v. **2.** *They recruited a speechwriter:* procure, obtain, draft, engage, enlist, enroll, gain, gather, induct, levy, mobilize, muster, raise, supply.

rectify v. *The accounting error was rectified before the ledgers were audited:* right, set right, put right, make right, correct, adjust, regulate, straighten, square; focus, attune; mend, amend, emend, fix, repair, revise; remedy, redress, cure, reform.

rectitude n. *The candidate must be a person of absolute rectitude:* integrity, probity, uprightness, righteousness, principle, decency, incorruptibility, honor, high-mindedness, morality, trustworthiness, virtuousness, irreproachability. —Ant. immorality, corruption, laxity, crookedness.

recumbent adj. *One sleeps in a recumbent position:* lying down, prone, prostrate, supine, flat, couchant, stretched out, horizontal; reclining, leaning. —Ant. upright, erect, standing, standing up, vertical; sitting.

recuperate v. *He's recuperating slowly after heart surgery:* recover, get well, get better, come around, come back, heal, mend, pull through, improve, convalesce, return to health, regain one's strength, be on the mend. —Ant. fail, sink, worsen, succumb.

recur v. **1.** *If this cheating recurs, you will be expelled:* occur again, repeat; return, come again, reappear; resume, persist, continue. **2.** *The good times of my college days frequently recur to me:* come back, come to mind, flash across the memory, be remembered, haunt one's thoughts.

recurrent adj. *I had a recurrent dream about a sunflower:* recurring, frequent, periodic, intermittent, regular, appearing again, reappearing, repeating, repetitive.

red adj. **1.** *She wore red lipstick:* blood-colored; (*variously*) maroon, wine, ruby, vermilion, crimson, cardinal, scarlet, cherry, rosy, rose; auburn; pink, coral, flame. **2.** *Her red cheeks showed her embarrassment:* blushing, reddened, ruddy, flushed, rosy, florid, blooming, rubicund, rubescent, aglow, glowing, inflamed, flaming, burning.

red-blooded adj. *Baseball is the ideal sport for any red-blooded American boy:* vigorous, sturdy, robust, strong, vital, energetic, intense, dynamic, forceful, powerful, peppy, spirited; passionate, lusty, ardent, hot-blooded.

redden v. *The leaves reddened on the maples:* glow, go red, color, dye, flush, crimson, paint, pink, pinken, rouge, tint, blush.

redeem v. **1.** *Present this pawn ticket and you can redeem your ring:* buy back, repurchase; ransom; reclaim, recover, retrieve, regain, repossess, recoup. **2.** *By getting the work done on time he redeemed his promise to me:* keep, fulfill, make good; discharge. **3.** *She worked* *weekends to redeem the lost time:* make up for, cover, defray, compensate for, make good, settle; make amends for, atone for, satisfy, recover, regain, retrieve. **4.** *The preacher went about the countryside trying to redeem lost souls:* rescue, save, deliver from sin and its consequences, evangelize, turn from sin, set straight again; convert, reform.   **—Ant.** 1 lose, forfeit, yield, give up. 2 break; shun, disregard, violate.

redolent *adj.* **1.** *It was a beautifully carved box, redolent of sandalwood:* fragrant, aromatic, balmy, perfumed, spicy, savory, odorous, odoriferous; smelly, stinking, reeking. **2.** *The inn was redolent of Elizabethan England:* reminiscent, suggestive, indicative, expressive, evocative, mindful.

redress *n.* **1.** *The ex-convict went straight and made full redress to society. Redress of a sort is obtained when a court grants damages to a victim of fraud:* reparation, compensation, recompense, payment, indemnification, restitution, rectification, amends, satisfaction, easement, relief. *—v.* **2.** *The king redressed past injustices by granting the peasants land:* correct, right, set right, rectify, make reparation for, compensate for, make retribution for, amend, make up for; reform; remedy, ease, relieve.

reduce *v.* **1.** *We've reduced the price of the coat from $100 to $65:* lessen, diminish, discount, mark down, slash, cut. **2.** *It's easy to reduce if you simply watch what you eat:* lose weight by dieting, slim down, diet, trim down, slenderize. **3.** *The military court reduced the major to captain. Poverty reduced him to begging for a living:* lower in rank, demote, *Slang* bust, break; force, lower. **4.** *Windstorms reduced the house to a shambles:* bring down, leave in; damage, bring to destruction. **5.** *Water reduces the potency of a highball:* minimize, lessen, lower, cut down, dilute, thin, water, blunt the edge of, dull; modulate, tone down, moderate, temper, ease, abate, mitigate, assuage, soften; checkmate, retard, slow down, curb, check; debilitate, atrophy, weaken, devitalize, enfeeble, cripple, incapacitate, undermine.   **—Ant.** 1, 3 increase. 1 add to, augment, enlarge, extend, mark up. 2 gain weight, put on pounds. 3 promote, elevate. 5 heighten, enhance, strengthen.

redundant *adj.* **1.** *I found the lecture redundant and quite boring:* repetitious, tautological, pleonastic. **2.** *The story doesn't need all this redundant background material:* superfluous, unnecessary, inessential, dispensable, overflowing, extra, excess, surplus, superabundant.   **—Ant.** 2 necessary, essential, indispensable.

reek *n.* **1.** *The reek of garbage came from the city dump:* unpleasant smell or odor, stink, stench, effluvium. **2.** *You could hardly see the doors for the reek of incense and spiced tobacco:* fume, emanation, cloud of smoke. *—v.* **3.** *She reeks of cheap perfume:* smell strongly, give off, smell, be malodorous, stink, smell to high heaven. **4.** *The newly upturned clods reeked in the sun:* smoke, fume, steam.

reel *v.* **1.** *The punch-drunk boxer reeled and grabbed his opponent's shoulder:* rock, move uncertainly, stagger, totter, teeter, wobble, sway, stumble, lurch, pitch, roll. **2.** *He knew he'd been drugged when everything started to reel around him:* turn round and round, rotate, whirl, swirl, spin, revolve, sway, waver. **3.** *I was reeling after getting off the Cyclone ride:* feel dizzy, be giddy, be in a vertiginous state.

refer *v.* **1.** *After filling out the forms I was referred to the personnel director:* direct, send. **2.** *We referred the proposal to the board of directors:* hand over, submit, deliver, transmit, transfer, pass along. **3.** *The speaker referred to the past to make his point:* advert, make reference; allude, mention, cite. **4.** *Please refer to the last page of the book for answers:* go, turn; consult.

referee *n.* **1.** *The court appointed a referee to settle the claim:* judge, umpire, arbitrator, arbiter, adjudicator, moderator, mediator, intermediary, intercessor. *—v.* **2.** *One of the teachers volunteered to referee the match:* umpire, arbitrate, settle, determine, judge, adjudicate, decree, pronounce, judgment; mediate, moderate, intervene, intercede.

reference *n.* **1.** *In her autobiography there's no reference to her years as a singer:* mention, allusion, suggestion, hint, intimation, innuendo, inkling, implication. **2.** *He gave her an excellent reference when she resigned:* recommendation, testimonial, credentials, endorsement, certification, deposition, affirmation, *Slang* good word.

refine *v.* **1.** *The purpose of an oil refinery is to refine crude petroleum:* strain, filter, process, free from impurities, purify, cleanse. **2.** *Pianists use five-finger exercises to refine their dexterity and touch:* develop, improve, cultivate, perfect. **—Ant.** 1 contaminate, adulterate. 2 coarsen.

refined *adj.* **1.** *Neat's-foot oil is a highly refined organic product used to dress leather:* purified, cleansed, clean, clarified. **2.** *Jane Austen's novels are full of refined people with refined manners:* well-bred, free from coarseness, genteel, gentlemanly, ladylike, courtly, polite, courteous, mannerly; discriminating, fastidious, elegant, cultured, cultivated, civilized, polished, suave, finished; urbane, gentle, graceful, delicate.   **—Ant.** 1, 2 unrefined. 1 impure, unpurified. 2 ill-bred, coarse, crude, vulgar, boorish, common, philistine, ungenteel, ungentlemanly, unladylike, unmannerly; undiscriminating; inelegant.

refinement *n.* **1.** *You could tell she was a woman of refinement by her behavior:* fine sensibilities, fineness, cultivation, urbanity, culture, finish, finesse, elegance, grace, polish, tastefulness, discrimination, discernment, fastidiousness; dignity, gentility, breeding; suavity, urbanity, *French* savoir faire; graciousness, gentleness, delicacy; politeness, civility, courtesy, good manners, courteousness, propriety; nicety, example of refined manners. **2.** *This plant was set up for the refinement of crude oil:* purification, cleaning, cleansing, filtration, distillation. **3.** *With several refinements your essay would be excellent:* improvement, revision, rectification, amendment; development, amelioration, enhancement, betterment; advance, progression, advancement, step up, step forward. **—Ant.** 1 vulgarity, crudeness, coarseness, boorishness, tastelessness, gracelessness, discourtesy.

reflect v. **1.** *The still water reflected the full moon:* mirror, cast back from a surface, cause to return or rebound, send back, throw back, return, give back or show an image of, image, copy, imitate, reproduce. **2.** *His cowardice reflected nothing but shame on his family:* cast, throw, bring upon, bring as a result of one's actions. **3.** *The book reflected the author's own thoughts on the matter:* show, display, express, exhibit, bring to light, reveal, disclose, indicate, evince, uncover, expose, manifest, set forth, present, demonstrate, register, represent, mirror. **4.** *Failure to pay your bills reflects upon your credit rating:* bring discredit, undo, undermine, betray, cast or bring reproach, condemn. **5.** *Reflect for a moment--is what you plan to do the right thing?:* think, think carefully, deliberate, reason, ponder, consider, study, muse, meditate, contemplate, speculate, revolve in the mind, mull over, cogitate, ruminate, cerebrate, dwell upon, concentrate. **—Ant.** 1 absorb, keep, retain. 3 conceal, mask, hide, cover.

reflection n. **1.** *She studied her reflection in the mirror:* image, mirror image, optical counterpart. **2.** *He gave much reflection to the problem but still had no answer:* serious thought, deliberation, thought, consideration, attention, thinking, pondering, meditation, musing, pensiveness, study, concentration, rumination, cogitation, cerebration. **3.** *The book included reflections by various people involved in the incident:* thought, notion, idea, sentiment, conviction, opinion, impression, view. **4.** *Your brother's irresponsibility is no reflection on you:* statement or action that brings doubt or blame, derogation, insinuation, imputation, insult, blot, unfavorable observation or remark, slur, reproof, reproach, disparagement.

reflective adj. *She was reflective after the sermon:* pensive, meditative, contemplative, thoughtful, pondering, deliberating, reflecting, reasoning, cogitating. **—Ant.** thoughtless, inconsiderate, unthinking.

reform n. **1.** *Reform of the whole campaign funding set-up is urgent:* correction, rectification, reformation, amendment. *—v.* **2.** *How can an indifferent society reform desperate men? The ex-convict had reformed and was now a productive member of society:* change for the better, better, improve, correct, rectify, set straight again, restore, rehabilitate, remodel, rebuild, remedy, repair; revise, convert, be converted, progress; mend, amend, repent, atone, abandon evil conduct, mend one's ways, turn over a new leaf, set one's house in order.

reformation n. *They embarked on a program of reformation:* improvement, betterment, correction, reform, amendment.

refractory adj. *The refractory horse stopped dead in its tracks:* stubborn, unmanageable, obstinate, perverse, mulish, headstrong, pigheaded, contumacious, intractable, disobedient,

recalcitrant, cantankerous, ungovernable, unruly. **—Ant.** obedient, tractable.

refrain v. *For better health you must refrain from eating too much:* abstain, restrain oneself, keep oneself, hold off, desist, stay one's hand, curb oneself; forbear, forgo, renounce, eschew, avoid, refuse, resist, leave off. **—Ant.** indulge in, be intemperate; continue, persist, go ahead.

refresh v. **1.** *The travelers stopped at an inn to refresh themselves. A shower always refreshes me on hot days:* freshen, invigorate, brace, vivify, restore, recruit, strengthen, revive, renew, energize, rejuvenate, cool off, recreate, reanimate. **2.** *Please refresh my memory as to where we've met before:* prompt, prod, jog, arouse, rouse, stimulate, stir up, activate, quicken; revive, renew, awaken. **—Ant.** 1 weaken, tire, weary, fatigue.

refreshment n. **1.** *The hostess served refreshments after the tennis matches:* food and drink, nourishment, snack, appetizer, hors d'oeuvre, *Informal* pick-me-up, bite, eats; beverage, drink, thirst quencher, bracer, restorative, refresher, cocktail, drinkable, potable, potation. **2.** *She looked forward to winter for the refreshment of long walks in snowy weather:* invigoration, restoration, reinvigoration, recreation, relaxation, rejuvenation.

refrigerate v. *Refrigerate the mousse for several hours before serving:* cool, chill, freeze, congeal, keep cool, keep cold, store in the refrigerator, put on ice, keep on ice. **—Ant.** warm, heat, cook, simmer.

refuge n. **1.** *We took refuge under an awning when it started to rain:* shelter, sanctuary, protection. **2.** *Churches and schools were refuges to the flood victims. North America has long been a refuge for exiles from the Old World:* place of shelter, haven, retreat, safehold, sanctuary, asylum, resort; harbor, harborage, anchorage, home, port in a storm. **3.** *Drinking was his refuge from unpleasant reality:* resort, hideout, means of self-defense, technique for escaping, help in distress. **—Ant.** 1 exposure, peril, danger, threat, menace; insecurity.

refugee n. *It was years before the refugees could return to their homeland:* fugitive, exile, emigrant, émigré, expatriate, escapee, DP, displaced person, evacuee; absconder, runaway, eloper, bolter.

refund v. **1.** *The government refunded the overpayment I made on my taxes:* give back (money), return, reimburse, pay back, repay, recompense, make compensation for, remunerate, remit, rebate, make restitution for. *—n.* **2.** *I'd like to return this merchandise for a refund or credit:* rebate, repayment, reimbursement, remittance; amount repaid. **—Ant.** 1 withhold.

refurbish v. *Refurbishing the old house has made it habitable again:* renovate, fix up, spruce up, remodel, improve, renew, redo, restore, recondition, overhaul, repair, mend; clean, tidy up, freshen.

refusal n. *His refusal was final—we couldn't change his mind:* rejection, denial, turndown, declination, declining, nonacceptance, noncon-

sent, disapproval, noncompliance, unwillingness, regrets; veto.

refuse[1] *v. Because of a prior engagement we
had to refuse the invitation. I wouldn't refuse
help to an old friend. We had a press pass but
were refused admittance anyhow:* not accept,
decline, say no to, reject, veto, turn down,
spurn, forbid, prohibit, disallow, withhold, deny.
—**Ant.** approve, accept, consent to, permit, allow, agree to, give.

refuse[2] *n. The refuse was unloaded at the city
dump:* rubbish, trash, garbage, waste, junk, litter.

refute *v. The accused was given no opportunity
to refute the accusations:* disprove, confute, give
the lie to, invalidate, counter, rebut, answer,
challenge, contradict, deny. —**Ant.** prove, vindicate, support, confirm, corroborate, substantiate.

regain *v. If you don't sue now, you'll never regain your property. The patient never regained
consciousness:* recover, retrieve, repossess, get
again, gain anew, get back, retake, reclaim, recapture, recoup, redeem, win back.

regal *adj. A regal welcome awaited us at the
farm. She was a lady of regal bearing:* royal,
kingly, queenly, noble, princely, lordly, proud,
kinglike, princelike, queenlike; stately, majestic,
splendid, magnificent, grand, imposing, august,
splendiferous.

regale *v.* **1.** *The jugglers regaled the king's
court:* amuse, entertain, divert; delight, please;
enthrall. **2.** *We regaled the dignitaries with the
best dishes the chef could cook:* feed sumptuously, feast, serve nobly, wine and dine, fete,
ply, banquet; lionize.

regard *v.* **1.** *I regard that movie as one of the
worst I've ever seen:* consider, look upon, view,
see, think, judge, account, believe, hold, set
down, put down, reckon, estimate, rate. **2.**
*Prince Hal regarded his father's advice and later,
as Henry V, proved to be an able ruler:* heed,
follow, accept, respect, esteem, show consideration for, consider, mind, note well, pay attention
to, listen to, hearken to. **3.** *His work is highly
regarded by other painters:* value, esteem, think
highly of, think well of, respect, look up to, admire, hold a high opinion of. **4.** *The condemned
prisoner regarded the jury with a look of outraged innocence:* gaze at, look at, view, look
upon, contemplate, behold, eye, turn one's eyes
toward, cast the eyes on; scan, survey, watch,
scrutinize, take the measure of, take in. —*n.* **5.**
He gave little regard to his parents' feelings:
thought, consideration, concern, attention, notice, note, observation, heed, mind, care, meditation, reflection. **6.** *I have little regard for liars:*
respect, esteem, admiration, estimation, appreciation. **7.** *In that regard, at least, we agree:* respect, matter, point, subject, aspect, detail; reference, relation, connection. —**Ant.** 1–6
disregard. 2, 3 reject, repudiate, despise, scorn,
disrespect, spurn, ignore, think badly of, look
down on, disparage, detest, loathe, dislike. 4
look away from, shun, ignore. 5 heedlessness,
indifference, contempt.

regardless *adv. I knew it was futile, but I talked
to him regardless:* nevertheless, nonetheless,
notwithstanding, anyway, anyhow, for all that, in
spite of everything.

regards *n. pl. Give them my regards:* good
wishes, compliments, greeting, respects, salutation, commendations.

regenerate *v.* **1.** *The congregation was spiritually regenerated by the preaching of the evangelist:* reform, rejuvenate, redeem, uplift, make a
new man of, enlighten. **2.** *Worldwide bumper
harvests regenerated hopes of resolving the economic crisis:* generate anew, give new life to,
revive, renew, reawaken, resuscitate, resurrect,
revivify; inspirit, restore, retrieve. **3.** *Certain
worms can regenerate after being cut in half:*
grow back an injured or lost part; revivify.

regime *n. The new regime threatens to impose
higher taxes:* government, rule, reign, administration, dynasty, power, leadership, command,
direction, control, jurisdiction, dominion, management.

regimentation *n. Daily life in Albania is said to
be characterized by strict regimentation:* discipline, order, uniformity, control, regulation, system, method, rigor, rigorousness, orthodoxy,
regimen, methodization, doctrinaire approach.

region *n.* **1.** *My cousin lives in a mountainous
region:* area, territory, space, expanse, tract,
range, country, land, district, neighborhood,
zone, province, locality, vicinity. **2.** *He is a well-
known authority in the region of physics:* area,
field, province, sphere, domain, realm.

register *n.* **1.** *We signed the hotel register when
we checked in:* record book; ledger, daybook,
diary, log, logbook, roll, registry. **2.** *A register
next to the turnstile indicated the number of
people who had gone through:* dial, meter, indicator, gauge; recorder, calculator, counter. **3.**
The singer's voice had a wide register: range,
scale, compass. **4.** *We turned the house registers off during the summer:* heat vent, heat outlet, hot-air vent, heater, heat duct, radiator. —*v.*
5. *The court stenographer registered the trial
proceedings:* write down, record, put in writing,
put on the record, make a record of, note down,
set down, take down. **6.** *I registered at a hotel
near the train station. You must register to be
able to vote:* enroll, sign up, check in, enlist. **7.**
*The Geiger counter registered a high concentra-
tion of radioactive particles. His face registered
disappointment over losing the contest:* show,
indicate, exhibit, disclose, manifest, mark, point
to, record; portray, express, betray, betoken.

regress *v.* **1.** *As he got older, his mind re-
gressed further into the past:* go back, ebb,
move backward, lose ground, withdraw, reverse,
retrogress, revert, retreat, backslide, recede,
back, fall, fall back, pass back; relapse, deteriorate. —*n.* **2.** *Soviet shipping has treaty-
guaranteed rights of ingress and regress
through the Dardanelles:* return, exit. —**Ant.** 1
progress, advance; climb, rise, ascend. 2 ingress, entrance.

regret *v.* **1.** *You'll regret having said those
words! He regretted his decision:* be sorry for,

feel sorrow for, feel remorse for, be ashamed of, be remorseful, rue, be rueful, rue the day, repent, bemoan, deplore, bewail, moan, mourn, grieve at, lament, weep over, feel distress over, reproach oneself for, have second thoughts about, *Informal* eat humble pie, eat one's words, eat crow. —*n.* **2.** *I've never had any regrets over anything I've done:* sorrow, grief, remorse, remorsefulness, regretfulness, rue, ruefulness, compunction, contrition, apology, apologies, repentance, grievance, lamentation; disappointment, dissatisfaction, anguish, woe, qualm, reservation, scruple, pang of conscience, twinge, second thought; self-condemnation, self-reproach; heartache. —**Ant.** 1 feel happy for, rejoice, laugh at; feel satisfaction over. 2 remorselessness, impenitence, satisfaction, pleasure, contentment.

regretful *adj. He was regretful he had to turn the job down:* apologetic, sorry, contrite, penitent, remorseful, repentant, rueful, ashamed.

regrettable *adj. Overpopulation has caused a regrettable situation. I find your tactlessness regrettable:* lamentable, pitiable, unhappy, grievous, woeful, unfortunate, deplorable, calamitous. —**Ant.** happy, joyous; fortunate, successful, lucky, fortuitous.

regular *adj.* **1.** *Getting up at dawn is part of his regular routine:* usual, normal, customary, standard, typical, ordinary, common, commonplace, familiar, daily, steady, constant, habitual, undeviating, invariable, unvarying, unchanging, set, fixed, established. **2.** *Jim's a regular customer. She made regular entries in her diary:* consistent, habitual, frequent, recurrent, recurring, periodic, periodical. **3.** *The pitcher used a regular overarm motion:* orthodox, correct, proper, classic, established, accepted. **4.** *Informal He was just a regular guy. Charlie is a regular ladies' man:* genuine, real, down-to-earth, plain, natural, typical, everyday; thorough, real, absolute, complete. **5.** *The model's face had small, regular features:* uniform, even, smooth, well-proportioned, fine, symmetrical, well-balanced. —*n.* **6.** *The bartender knew all the regulars by their first names:* regular customer, regular client, habitué, faithful, old reliable, dependable; loyalist, true blue, stalwart, trusty. —**Ant.** 1–3, 5 irregular. 1 unusual, abnormal, unconventional, exceptional, rare, uncommon, variable, inconsistent, inconstant, varied, deviating, varying; sloppy, disorderly, unmethodical. 2 occasional, infrequent, rare. 3 erratic, unorthodox. 4 phony, fake. 5 uneven, variable.

regulate *v.* **1.** *The policeman regulated traffic at the intersection:* control, govern, handle, manage, superintend, supervise, oversee, monitor, guide, organize, direct. **2.** *Please regulate the sound on that radio:* adjust, fix, regularize, rectify, moderate, balance, modulate. —**Ant.** 1 confuse, disrupt, disorganize; neglect, set free, decontrol.

regulation *n.* **1.** *The purpose of a thermostat is the regulation of temperature:* adjusting, adjustment, handling, control. **2.** *It's against regulations to leave camp without permission. Radio broadcasting is subject to government regulation:* rule, ordinance, decree, standing order, direction, statute, dictate, order, command, edict, commandment.

rehabilitate *v.* **1.** *The social worker tried to rehabilitate the juvenile delinquents:* restore to society, resocialize, straighten out, reeducate, set straight; redeem, save. **2.** *The old ship was rehabilitated and used as a floating casino:* salvage, renovate, make over, remake, reconstruct, restore, fix, readjust, refurbish, recondition. **3.** *The king rehabilitated the banished earl:* restore, reinstate.

rehash *v. They rehashed everything that happened:* reiterate, repeat, restate, reuse, rework.

rehearsal *n. The actors had three weeks of rehearsal before the play opened:* practice, reading, walk-through, run-through, dress rehearsal, drill, exercise, repetition, recapitulation; reiteration, preparation, polishing, perfecting, *Slang* recap; trial run, tryout, audition, test run, hearing.

rehearse *v.* **1.** *The actors rehearsed their parts. The conductor rehearsed the musicians before opening night:* prepare, practice, ready, drill, polish, train, go over, run through; read one's lines, study one's lines. **2.** *A spokesman for the migrant workers rehearsed their grievances at the hearing:* repeat, recite, give a recital of, recount, relate, narrate; reiterate, retell.

reign *n.* **1.** *Robin Hood is said to have lived during the reigns of King Richard Lionheart and King John:* regnancy, rule, tenure, regnum, incumbency, government, regime, dominion, sovereignty. **2.** *Under the reign of wise teachers, he learned quickly:* influence, dominance, tutelage, supervision. —*v.* **3.** *Queen Victoria reigned for over 60 years. Chef Henri reigns supreme in the restaurant's kitchen:* have royal power, wear the crown, occupy the throne, sit on the throne, exercise sovereignty; rule, govern, hold authority, exercise authority, hold sway, command.

reimburse *v. You'll be reimbursed for any supplies you have to buy on your own:* pay back, rebate, refund, repay, remunerate, indemnify, square up, pay up, remit, compensate, recompense, make restitution.

rein *n.* **1.** Usually **reins** *Use the reins to lead the horse's head and neck:* bridle. **2.** *A heavy person should keep a tight rein on his food intake:* restraint, check, hold, bridle, harness. —*v.* **3.** *You must learn to rein in your temper:* control, check, curb, hold back, bridle, harness; restrict, limit, suppress; watch, keep an eye on.

reinforce *v. The troops reinforced the fort for the battle. That concrete is reinforced with steel beams:* make stronger, strengthen, support, buttress, prop, bolster, brace up, fortify, steel. —**Ant.** weaken, debilitate; diminish, lessen, harm, hurt.

reinstate *v. The court reinstated the employees:* restore, rehabilitate, bring back, recall, redeem, reestablish, rehire, reintroduce, revive, put back.

reiterate *v. Let me reiterate my disappointment at your decision:* repeat, resay, reprise, iterate, retell, reword, rephrase, restate, recapitulate; stress, hammer, go over and over, pound away at; *Slang* rehash, pound into someone's head.

reject *v.* **1.** *She rejected his marriage proposal. The board rejected all our ideas:* refuse, say no to, decline, turn down; shrug off, dismiss, turn from, repudiate, repel, repulse, rebuff, disdain, spurn, disallow, deny. —*n.* **2.** *These convicts are society's rejects:* castoff, castaway, discard; flotsam. —**Ant.** 1 accept, say yes to, pay attention to, receive willingly, approve, countenance, be in favor of, agree with; allow, permit; select. 2 treasure, prize.

rejection *n.* *The publisher's rejection of his manuscript depressed him:* refusal, rejecting, declining, rebuffing, scorning, spurning, disdain, dismissal, rebuff, ruling out. —**Ant.** acceptance, approval, selection, espousal, affirmation.

rejoice *v.* *He rejoiced in his good fortune. The people rejoiced when the new king was crowned:* be glad, be happy, be pleased, be transported, be delighted, be overjoyed, exult, jubilate, glory, delight, sing for joy, be elated, make merry, revel, celebrate, exhilarate. —**Ant.** be sad, be unhappy, mourn, lament, grieve.

rejoicing *n.* *The streets were filled with rejoicing after the victory:* celebration, festivity, revelry, reveling, merrymaking, mirth, merriment, liveliness, gaiety, jubilee, jollity, good cheer; happiness, gladness, jubilation, jubilance, joyfulness, delight, pleasure; exultation, elation, ecstasy; triumph, cheering.

rejoinder *n.* *Her rejoinder was often cited as the perfect squelch:* answer, reply, response, retort, rebuttal, return, *Slang* comeback, back talk, riposte, remonstrance, refutation, repartee, counterblast, countercharge, counterstatement; *Law* surrebuttal, surrejoinder.

rejuvenate *v.* *The old man tried to rejuvenate himself by taking hormone shots:* make youthful again, restore, put new life into, reinvigorate, revive, revivify, revitalize, reanimate, restore. —**Ant.** age, make older; tire, weary, fatigue; weaken, debilitate.

relapse *v.* **1.** *The dog relapsed into doing his old tricks as soon as he was home from obedience school:* fall back, slip back, sink back, turn back, revert, backslide, degenerate, regress, retrogress, lapse, worsen. —*n.* **2.** *Just when we thought he had recovered, he suffered a relapse. To avoid a relapse, the ex-addict migrated to a place where drugs were unavailable:* lapse, fall, reversion, return to illness, turn for the worse, falling back, retrogression, reverse, regression, backsliding, deterioration, decline, recurrence, worsening.

relate *v.* **1.** *The witness related what he had seen:* tell, recount, recapitulate, give an account of, report, detail, particularize, describe, make known, reveal, disclose, divulge, impart, convey, communicate, state, say, utter, speak, narrate, recite. **2.** *Can you relate what happened in your childhood to your present state of mind? His remarks related to the topic under discussion:* connect, associate, attach, link, refer, have ref-

erence, pertain, concern, be relevant, appertain, apply, belong. **3.** *It's unfortunate when a father and son can't relate to each other:* feel close, have rapport, interact well, communicate, be sympathetic, be responsive, feel empathy with. —**Ant.** 1 keep to oneself, keep secret. 2 dissociate, disconnect, separate, divorce, detach; be unconnected, be irrelevant.

relation *n.* **1.** Also **relationship** *There's no relation between our department and the state-run department:* connection, tie-in, tie, link, bond, interrelationship, association, affiliation. **2.** *He's a distant relation of mine:* relative, kin, kinsman. **3.** *Your remarks have no relation to this conversation:* regard, connection, reference, bearing, relevance, concern, pertinence, correlation, application, applicability. **4.** *Her relation of the fairy tale fascinated the youngsters:* narrating, narration, telling, recital, recitation; narrative, account, report, description, version, retelling, communication. —**Ant.** 1 disconnection, dissociation, independence.

relative *n.* **1.** *Most of my relatives were able to attend the family reunion:* relation, cognate, kinsman, kinswoman, kinfolk, kin, kith, kith and kin, people, family, folks, blood relative, cousin, flesh and blood, connection, clan, tribe. —*adj.* **2.** *He weighed the relative advantages of buying a house and renting an apartment:* comparative, comparable, dependent, not absolute, relational. **3.** *He's had experience in electronics and other relative fields:* related, correlated, correlative, connective, connected, associated, affiliated, allied, interrelated, interconnected. **4.** *The slides were relative to the art lecture:* pertinent, appropriate, pertaining, having reference or regard, relevant, referable, respective, applicable, germane. —**Ant.** 1 stranger, alien, foreigner. 2 absolute. 3 unconnected, unrelated. 4 irrelevant, remote, inappropriate.

relatively *adv.* *Her complaints were relatively minor:* comparatively, rather, somewhat, approximately, proportionately, comparably.

relax *v.* **1.** *A good massage always relaxes me. Relax and enjoy yourself:* make less tense, loosen up, calm, soothe; cool off, unwind, unbend, ease up, let up. **2.** *The regulations can be relaxed only under unusual circumstances. The general didn't relax in his cruel treatment of the prisoners:* make less severe, make less strict, slack, slacken, loosen, soften, make lax, bend, unbend, ease, decrease. **3.** *The doctor told him to relax a month or so before going back to work:* rest, take it easy, enjoy oneself, vacation, holiday; be idle, idle, be lazy, laze, loaf, lie around, unbend. —**Ant.** 1 tense, tighten, alarm, alert, bear down. 2 tighten, intensify, heighten, increase. 3 work, be busy, be active.

relaxation *n.* **1.** *A relaxation of the rules permitted outsiders to compete in the contest:* remission, loosening, bending, abatement, slackening. **2.** *What do you like to do for relaxation?:* recreation, enjoyment, fun, amusement, entertainment, diversion, pleasure, refreshment; pastime, avocation, hobby, sport, games; rest from work, repose, leisure. **—Ant.** 1 tightening, stiffening. 2 work, toil, labor, strain.

relay v. They relayed the broadcast: transmit, pass on, spread, communicate, deliver, carry.

release v. **1.** The convict was released from prison after serving his sentence: free, set free, liberate, let out, let go, discharge, set at liberty. **2.** The driver started the engine, released the brake, and was on his way: relieve; set loose, loose, untie, unloose, unfasten, unbind; disengage, detach, extricate. **3.** Don't release this news to the public until we give you the go-ahead. The actor's new film will be released next month: distribute, circulate, present, communicate. **—n. 4.** They fought for the release of the political prisoners: releasing, liberating, freeing, liberation, setting free, emancipation, setting loose, letting go, extrication, dismissal. **5.** The date of release of the new movie has not been decided: distribution, publication, circulation. **—Ant.** 1 imprison, incarcerate; detain, hold, keep. 2 fasten, engage. 3 withhold, conceal, hide. 4 imprisonment, incarceration, internment, detention, holding.

relegate v. **1.** They relegated the task to her: entrust, hand over, turn over, charge, commit, consign, delegate, pass on, refer, assign. **2.** They relegated him to the second division: demote, banish, eject, displace, expel, ostracize.

relent v. Father objected at first but then relented and let us go camping by ourselves: grow lenient, grow less severe, become milder, weaken, melt, soften, unbend, relax, bend, yield, give in, let up, give way, capitulate, have pity, be merciful, give quarter, come around.

relentless adj. He was relentless in his pursuit of fame and fortune. The general was relentless in meting out punishment: unrelenting, remorseless, implacable, inexorable, unyielding, inflexible, uncompromising, undeviating, adamant, harsh, hard, stern, severe, stiff, rigid, rigorous, ruthless, pitiless, merciless. **—Ant.** relenting, remorseful, yielding, flexible, pliant, compromising; kind, sparing, gentle, compassionate, feeling, pitying, merciful, lenient, softhearted, sympathetic, forgiving.

relevant adj. The film was relevant to what was being discussed in class: related, pertinent, referring, bearing, concerning, connected, cognate, intrinsic, tied in, allied, associated; germane, material, significant, appropriate, apposite, applicable, apropos; apt, suitable, suited, fit, fitting, to the point, to the purpose, on the subject. **—Ant.** irrelevant, unrelated, unconnected; inappropriate, inapplicable, immaterial, extraneous, extrinsic, foreign, alien, beside the point.

reliable adj. The Pauly-Wissowa encyclopedia is a reliable source of information about classical antiquity. Jim is not a reliable employee: dependable, unfailing, faithful, trustworthy, trusty, responsible, solid, sound, conscientious, true, tried and true. **—Ant.** unreliable, capricious, undependable, untrustworthy, irresponsible, questionable.

reliance n. I place no reliance on anything he says he'll do: trust, confidence, dependence, faith, credence, credit, belief, assurance. **—Ant.** distrust; uncertainty.

relic n. In the attic, we found relics of Grandmother's childhood: remembrance, keepsake, token, memento, souvenir, records, reminder, fragment, remnant, scrap, vestige, trace; antique, heirloom, artifact.

relief n. **1.** In some cases of extremely painful injury, morphine is the only relief. For relief of headaches take aspirin: easement, alleviation, assuagement, palliation, abatement, amelioration, mitigation, reduction, remedy, cure, panacea, balm, anodyne, antidote, palliative, lenitive. **2.** Much to the student's relief, the exam was postponed: peace of mind, release from anxiety, cheer, encouragement, elation. **3.** The poor families survived on relief: dole, welfare assistance, welfare, public assistance. **4.** Vacationing in Hawaii was a welcome relief from work: respite, rest, break. **—Ant.** 1 discomfort, aggravation, intensification; oppression. 2 anxiety, upset, depression, mental suffering, discouragement. 4 hardship, burden.

relieve v. **1.** The ointment relieved her itching. His humorous remark relieved the tension in the room: ease, lighten, abate, alleviate, assuage, solace, palliate, mitigate, appease, pacify, mollify, temper, allay, subdue, soothe. **2.** I was relieved to hear you were all right: reassure, free from fear, comfort, calm, console, solace, cheer, encourage. **3.** Public funds relieved the poverty-stricken families: bring help to, aid, help, succor, assist, support. **4.** His arduous schedule was relieved by frequent though brief vacations: break up, punctuate, mark, interrupt; set off, put in relief, contrast. **5.** The night watch relieved the day watch at 6 P.M. The general was relieved of his command: remove, take out, release, let out, replace, free; spell, take the place of. **—Ant.** 1 increase, intensify, heighten, aggravate. 2 alarm, discourage, concern. 3 burden, oppress.

religion n. **1.** As she grew old, religion meant more and more to her. Art for art's sake was Mallarmé's religion: belief in God or gods, faith, belief, religious faith, worship, adoration, devotion, reverence, veneration, homage; piety, devoutness, godliness, religiousness, spirituality; theology, dogma, cult, creed, canon. **2.** Moses was the great lawgiver of the Jewish religion: system of faith, system of worship; creed, denomination, sect, cult, persuasion, affiliation, church. **—Ant.** 1 atheism, godlessness, impiety, irreligion, irreverence, sacrilege, unbelief.

religious adj. **1.** He went to Hebrew school for religious instruction. The revolutionary government forbade religious services: spiritual, holy, sacred, theological, divine, denominational, devotional. **2.** Though he wasn't a religious man, he believed there was a greater force controlling his destiny: religious-minded, devout, spiritual-minded, godly, god-fearing. **3.** She was religious about always arriving on time for an appointment: conscientious, unswerving, constant, staunch, steadfast, undeviating, unerring, faithful, devout, devoted, scrupulous, exact, rigid, fastidious, meticulous, punctilious; ardent, wholehearted. —**Ant.** 1, 2 irreligious. 1 secular. 2 impious, unfaithful, irreverent, profane, unbelieving, godless; atheistic, agnostic, freethinking. 3 unconscientious, feckless, unreliable, inconstant.

relinquish v. **1.** *He relinquished all rights to the property. Edward VIII relinquished his throne to marry Mrs. Simpson:* renounce, repudiate, deny, disclaim, dismiss, lay aside, shed, cast off, discard, put aside; surrender, cede, give up, deliver up, hand over, yield; forgo, forbear, waive, sign away; resign, abdicate, quit, withdraw from, leave, vacate, forsake, abandon, turn one's back on, wash one's hands of, rid oneself of, drop. **2.** *Parents are sometimes reluctant to relinquish the influence they have on their children:* release, let go, give up, break off. —**Ant.** keep, retain, hold, cling to; sustain, maintain.

relish n. **1.** *He has a relish for parades and carnivals:* liking, partiality, fondness, love, appreciation; enjoyment, zest, want, desire, wish, longing, penchant, propensity, predilection, hankering, fancy, taste, palate, stomach, appetite. **2.** *A spirit of adventure gives relish to life:* pleasure, delight, satisfaction, gratification, enjoyment, ebullience, exuberance, enthusiasm; pleasing quality, zest, gusto, savor, tang, spice, taste, flavor, accent, piquancy. **3.** *Give me a hot dog with mustard and relish:* condiment, (variously) sweet relish, pickle relish, tomato relish, chili sauce, corn relish, beef relish, chutney, piccalilli, horseradish. —v. **4.** *I don't relish the idea of telling him the bad news:* like, have a liking for, love, fancy, look forward to, dote on, take pleasure in, delight in, rejoice in, enjoy, be pleased with, appreciate, luxuriate in, *Informal* be crazy about, get a kick out of, *Slang* dig, groove on. —**Ant.** 1 dislike, hatred, distaste, antipathy. 2 displeasure, dissatisfaction; distaste. 4 dislike, hate, loathe.

reluctant adj. *King John of England was reluctant to sign the Magna Carta in 1215, but he was forced to do so:* unwilling, loath, averse, disinclined, indisposed; hesitant, diffident, slow, shy, laggard. —**Ant.** eager, enthusiastic, keen, willing, desirous, inclined.

rely v. *If you ever need a friend, you can rely on me:* depend, be dependent, feel sure of, rest, lean, count, bank, reckon, give credence, credit, believe, swear, bet, place one's trust in.

remain v. **1.** *He gave large sums of money to charity but preferred to remain anonymous. Her love for him remained all through her life:* stay, continue, persist, go on, linger, hang on, hold up, endure, abide, last, survive, subsist, prevail, remain alive. **2.** *She told the children to remain in the car while she went into the store. Only my brother now remains at the old house:* stay, stay behind, stay in the same place, not move, not stir, wait, *Informal* stay put, stand, stand pat; be left, be left behind, be left over. —**Ant.** 1 leave, die, pass, disappear. 2 go, leave, depart.

remainder n. *The remainder of the produce was used for feed:* balance, rest, remains, resid-

uum, excess, residue, residual, surplus, overage, leftovers, leavings, remaining part, remnant, superfluity, surplusage; waste, refuse, scourings, wastage.

remark v. **1.** *I remarked that she looked very pretty:* observe, say, say in passing, mention, comment. **2.** *The teacher asked the class to remark the author's style of writing:* mark, note, notice, take notice of, take note of, make note of, perceive, see, look at, behold, observe, espy, regard, survey, view; pay heed, give heed to, mind, pay attention to, fix the mind on, contemplate. —n. **3.** *Your remarks may have hurt her feelings:* commentary, reflection, comment, observation, word. **4.** *The movie was so bad it's not even worthy of remark:* consideration, note, notice, attention.

remarkable adj. *He was brevetted in the field for remarkable feats of courage. Gone With the Wind is a remarkable movie:* noteworthy, notable, conspicuous, unusual, singular, phenomenal, signal, extraordinary, exceptional, memorable, unforgettable, outstanding; distinguished, striking, impressive. —**Ant.** ordinary, usual, common, commonplace, everyday, unsurprising; mediocre, unexceptional; undistinguished, insignificant, inconspicuous, unimpressive.

remedial adj. *The course in remedial reading will improve your basic learning skills:* corrective, helpful, beneficial, correctional, advantageous; curative, reformative, therapeutic, restorative, prophylactic, healing, meliorative, mending, sanative, salutary. —**Ant.** harmful, baneful, pernicious, destructive.

remedy n. **1.** *I'll tell you my favorite remedy for a cold:* cure, medicine, relief, nostrum, medicament, medication, treatment, corrective. **2.** *Optimists saw in the League of Nations a remedy for the ills of the world:* corrective, preventive, panacea, cure-all, help, aid, assistance, relief, redress, rectification. —v. **3.** *Those pills will do nothing to remedy your sinus condition. It is easier to prevent than to remedy an injustice:* cure, heal, effect a remedy, relieve, ease, calm, alleviate, palliate, assuage, ameliorate, soothe, make easy, mitigate, mollify; restore to health, make sound, put into condition, set right, fix, regulate, improve, make better, help, aid, repair, mend; correct, rectify, restore, redress, right, amend, emend. —**Ant.** 1 toxin, poison; disease. 3 aggravate, exacerbate, heighten, intensify, worsen, make worse.

remember v. **1.** *I don't remember her name, but her face is familiar:* recall, recall to the mind, call to mind, bring to mind, recollect; keep in mind, have in mind, retain the thought of, not forget, bear in memory, bear in mind. **2.** *He remembered his faithful butler by leaving him a substantial sum in his will:* take note of, appreciate, recognize, take care of, do something for; reward, tip. —**Ant.** forget, disregard, ignore, neglect, overlook, *U.S. Regional* disremember; *Slang* draw a blank.

remembrance n. **1.** *Do you have any remembrance of your childhood?:* memory, recall, remembering, recollection, reminiscence, retention in the mind; recognition, recognizance; nostalgia. **2.** *The photograph was a remembrance of her wedding day:* reminder, souvenir, favor, keepsake, relic, memento, token; memorial, commemoration. **—Ant.** 1 forgetfulness, obscurity, oblivion.

remind *v. That story reminds me of an experience I had long ago:* bring to mind, bring back to, suggest to, bring to recollection, awaken memories of, put in memory, put in mind.

reminder *n. She sent him a reminder of the meeting:* notice, warning, remembrance.

reminisce *v. Old friends like to reminisce about the "good old days":* remember, recollect, hark back, think back, look back, exchange memories, swap remembrances, tell old tales; reflect, ponder, muse, mull.

reminiscent *adj. Your experience is reminiscent of one I had some time ago. The fire on the hearth put us in a reminiscent mood:* remindful, similar to, analogous to; remembering, recollecting, retrospective, nostalgic. **—Ant.** forgetful, oblivious, unremembering.

remiss *adj. He was fired for being remiss in his responsibilities:* careless, negligent, lax, undutiful, unmindful, unthinking, thoughtless, derelict, delinquent; sloppy, slipshod, slack, loose; slow, dilatory, indolent, slothful, lazy, laggard, do-nothing, shiftless, loafing, idle, inactive; neglectful, forgetful, inattentive, indifferent, uncaring, oblivious, unwatchful. **—Ant.** careful, dutiful, heedful, attentive, diligent; neat, meticulous, scrupulous, blameless.

remission *n.* **1.** *He sought remission for his sins:* pardon, forgiveness, absolution, indulgence, exoneration, discharge. **2.** *Remission of labor was what he sought:* abatement, diminution, lessening, relaxation, moderation, mitigation. **3.** *They got no remission from hardship:* release, relinquishment. **4.** *Her disease went into remission:* decrease, subsidence, respite, stoppage, pause, interruption, relief, hiatus, suspense, suspension, abatement. **—Ant.** 1 blame, censure, conviction. 2 increase. 4 intensification.

remit *v.* **1.** *Please remit the balance due upon receipt of this bill:* send in payment, pay; make good, reimburse, compensate, put to rights; discharge, send, forward, dispatch, ship, transmit. **2.** *It shouldn't be difficult to remit an accidental unkindness:* forgive, pardon, excuse, overlook, pass over, absolve, clear. **3.** *The prisoners were not remitted even when found to be innocent:* free, release, set free, let go, let out, liberate. **4.** *The cold wave finally remitted its icy grip on the city:* diminish, decrease, moderate, reduce; slacken, slack, relax. **—Ant.** 1 withhold. 2 condemn, accuse, punish. 3 retain, hold, keep, imprison. 4 increase, strengthen, maximize, heighten.

remnant *n. Some pieces of pottery were the only remnants found of the ancient civilization. A patchwork quilt is made up of cloth remnants:* remainder, relic, shred, token, leftover, trace, monument, vestige; piece, bit, scrap, fragment;

remains, odds and ends; leavings, discard, residue, residuum, survival.

remonstrate *v. He remonstrated with the traffic officer that he hadn't seen the stop light:* protest, dispute, object, complain, argue, dissent, demur, contend, differ, expostulate; reproach, chide, admonish, rebuke, reprove, scold. **—Ant.** agree, assent, accept, comply.

remorse *n. The killer had no remorse over what he had done:* regret, regretfulness, rue, ruefulness, guilt, feelings of guilt, self-reproach, self-reproof, compunction, qualm, pangs of conscience, second thoughts; contrition, repentance, penitence; sorrow, grief, lamentation, anguish. **—Ant.** satisfaction, guiltlessness, pride.

remorseful *adj. She was remorseful for her unkind words:* regretful, penitent, contrite, repentant. **—Ant.** impenitent.

remorseless *adj. The remorseless storm took a heavy toll:* relentless, pitiless, uncompassionate, unrelenting, merciless, unmerciful, ruthless, cruel, savage, implacable, inexorable. **—Ant.** merciful, relenting.

remote *adj.* **1.** *He dreamed of traveling to remote South Sea islands:* far, far-off, faraway, distant, far-removed, a long way off, out of the way; exotic, alien, strange, foreign. **2.** *He lived in a remote part of the forest:* secluded, set apart, isolated, God-forsaken, solitary, sequestered, segregated, separate; out-of-the-way; lonely, alone, quiet. **3.** *Space travel seemed only a remote possibility to our parents:* distant, slight, faint, slim, meager; unlikely, doubtful, dubious, implausible. **4.** *He seemed remote, uninterested in the conversation:* removed, distant, standoffish, aloof, withdrawn, detached, faraway, far-off. **—Ant.** 1 close, near, nearby; familiar. 2 prominent; busy. 3 immediate, imminent; accessible, approachable, attainable. 4 attentive, interested, involved, alert.

remove *v.* **1.** *Remove those muddy shoes! The rioters were forcibly removed from the plaza:* take off, doff; take away, take out, dislodge, expel, oust, eject, evacuate, cart off, take away, sweep out, carry off. **2.** *The accident victim had to have his leg removed:* amputate, cut away, chop off, cut off, lop off. **3.** *He removed his desk to another office. They have decided to remove to a warm climate:* move, transfer, transport, transplant; displace, change, shift; depart, leave, go away, take leave, quit, vacate, withdraw, make an exit, retreat, retire. **4.** *Bleach removes color. Remove my name from your mailing list:* wipe out, get rid of, take out, erase, extract, eliminate, cancel, delete, blot out, drop. **5.** *The corrupt official was removed from office:* dismiss, discharge, unseat, oust, eject, fire, *Slang* kick out, boot out. **—Ant.** 1 put on, don, put back; join, unite, combine; keep, retain, detain, hold. 3 keep, sustain, maintain, hold, retain; hang on, stay, remain. 4 install, establish, set, put in.

remunerate *v. He promised I would be remunerated for the extra work:* pay, recompense, reimburse, compensate, repay, reward, requite, indemnify, satisfy, grant, award, vouchsafe. —**Ant.** charge, tax, assess, fine.

renaissance *n. In recent years there has been a renaissance of interest in science:* rebirth, renewal, renascence, revival, resurrection, reestablishment, rejuvenation, revivification, resurgence, reawakening, reemergence, revitalization, regeneration, restoration, *Italian* risorgimento, rekindling.

rend *v.* **1.** *Rend your clothes, and gird you with sackcloth. The lightning rent the tree. And the earth did quake, and the rocks rent:* rip, tear, split, rive, divide, rupture, cleave, sunder, sever, dissever, splinter, fracture, break, crack, break into pieces, shatter, fall to pieces. **2.** *Rend your heart, and not your garments! They spit on us, they rend us with their scorn:* lacerate, afflict, sear, pain, tear, rip, cut, hurt, wound. **3.** *An explosion rent the air:* split, pierce with sound. **4.** *This debate has rent our community so long, there soon won't be anything left to rend:* tear, disintegrate, divide, polarize, split, splinter. —**Ant.** 1 join, reunite, unite, bind, secure; mend, heal, join.

render *v.* **1.** *The long recuperation rendered him healthy again:* cause to be, make, cause to become. **2.** *The piano concerto was rendered flawlessly:* do, perform, play, execute, interpret. **3.** *We call on you to render assistance:* give, present, make available, tender, accord, grant, donate; supply, dispense, deal out, dole out, hand out, allot, *Informal* come across with, shell out, fork over. **4.** *He was obliged to render a large sum in back taxes:* pay as due; make restitution of, remit, make payment of, make requital, pay back, give in return, requite. **5.** *The troops refused to render their position:* give up, yield, surrender, cede, turn over, relinquish, hand over. **6.** *The foreign ambassador's speech was rendered by an interpreter:* translate, construe, interpret. —**Ant.** 3 withhold, refuse, keep, retain. 4 hold, keep, hang on to.

rendezvous *n.* **1.** *We have a rendezvous at noon. The lovers arranged a secret rendezvous:* agreement to meet, prearranged meeting, date, appointment, engagement, encounter, assignation, tryst, tête-à-tête. **2.** *The restaurant was our rendezvous:* meeting place, gathering place, stamping ground, retreat, haunt, focal point, focus, mecca; *Informal* watering hole. —*v.* **3.** *The two patrols rendezvoused at noon:* meet by appointment, get together; tryst; assemble, gather, muster.

rendition *n. Can you imagine a Japanese rendition of* Jingle Bells?*:* rendering, translation, interpretation, arrangement, version, edition, reading, performance, portrayal, depiction.

renegade *n.* **1.** *He was considered a renegade when he switched political parties:* traitor, deserter, slacker, betrayer, defector, turncoat; recreant, apostate, heretic, forsaker, rebel, dissenter, insurgent, quisling, treasonist, mutineer; backslider; runaway, fugitive, outlaw. —*adj.* **2.** *The renegade policeman became a gangster:* traitorous, mutinous, apostate, recreant, unfaithful. —**Ant.** 1 adherent, follower, loyalist.

renege *v. Dad will never renege on a promise. It's bad form to renege on a bet:* break a promise, break one's word, go back on one's word, fall back, back out, back down, weasel out, turn one's back, repudiate, withdraw, pull out, *Informal* fink out, get cold feet. —**Ant.** fulfill, carry out.

renew *v.* **1.** *We renewed our old friendship:* begin again, resume, continue, take up again, pick up; reestablish, reinstate. **2.** *Do you want to renew our contract?:* extend, continue, prolong, sign again, offer again, maintain, retain. **3.** *He tried hard to renew his faith:* revive, rejuvenate, regenerate, reinvigorate, revitalize, refresh, save, salvage, redeem. **4.** *A good shampooing renewed the soiled carpeting:* restore, rejuvenate, revitalize, make sound, put back into shape. —**Ant.** 1 forget, discontinue, end. 2 discontinue, cancel, let lapse, drop. 4 age, depreciate, wear out.

renounce *v. He renounced all rights to the throne. Consider carefully before renouncing your faith:* give up, relinquish, resign, abdicate, give up claim to, cede, part with, quit, forgo, eschew, waive; abandon, abnegate, wash one's hands of, cast aside, put aside, lay aside, dismiss; repudiate, abjure, forswear, recant, abrogate, deny, disavow, disclaim, reject, disown, cast off, write off, turn from, discard. —**Ant.** avow, assert, proclaim, maintain, uphold, defend, claim; keep, retain, hold, accept, approve, acknowledge.

renovate *v. The new owner set about renovating the rickety old building:* repair, mend, fix, improve; make over, remake, revamp, modernize, redecorate, remodel, restore, refurbish.

renown *n. Ignace Jan Paderewski and Pablo Casals were musicians of renown:* fame, acclaim, repute, reputation, popularity, prominence, note, notoriety, celebrity; eminence, status, distinction, mark. —**Ant.** obscurity, unpopularity; disrepute, infamy, shame, disgrace.

renowned *adj. Robert Service was a renowned poet:* celebrated, well-known, popular, famous, famed, notable, noteworthy, noted, prominent, outstanding, acclaimed, eminent, distinguished. —**Ant.** obscure, unknown, forgotten, unpopular, insignificant, undistinguished.

rent[1] *n.* **1.** *Rent on the apartment is due the first of every month:* rental, payment; dues, fee. —*v.* **2.** *We rented the cabin to a young couple. They rented a cabin for their vacation:* sell the use of, let, rent out, lease; buy the use of, hire, charter, lease.

rent[2] *n.* **1.** *I tried to sew the rent in my dress:* opening, rip, tear, tatter, rift, hole, rupture, fissure, cleft, chink, breach, crack, slit; chasm, gash, gap, hiatus, crevasse; split, fracture. **2.** *The two opposing factions caused a rent in the club's membership:* breach, break, rift, split, wrench, division, schism, cleavage.

renunciation *n. The preacher urged renunciation of the things of this world:* renouncing, rejection, repulsion, spurning, refusal, repudiation; denial, disavowal, disclaiming, eschewing, forgoing, abandonment, relinquishment, forswearing, abjuration. —**Ant.** acceptance, retention.

repair¹ v. **1.** *These shoes have to be repaired:* fix, restore, mend, set right, make good, recondition, refurbish, renew, rebuild, patch. **2.** *I'd like to repair our differences:* make up for, remedy, redress, rectify, patch up, mend, amend, emend, correct. —*n.* **3.** *You could always go to Uncle Jim for the repair of a broken toy:* repairing, fixing, mending, patching, reconditioning, rebuilding; refurbishing, overhaul. **4.** *The child's clothes were in poor repair:* general condition, state, shape. —**Ant.** 1 break, destroy, ruin. 2 aggravate, exacerbate, worsen, deepen. 3 destruction, breaking.

repair² v. *The ladies repaired to the drawing room:* withdraw, retire, remove, move, betake oneself, go.

reparation n. *He made reparation by paying for the goods he damaged:* amends, redress, restitution, compensation, damages, requital, recompense, return, quittance, satisfaction, peace offering.

repartee n. *A good comedian should be skilled in repartee:* witty reply, witty retort, bon mot, clever rejoinder, snappy comeback, riposte; badinage, persiflage, word play, pleasantries, bandying of words, banter, chit-chat.

repast n. *A hearty repast was laid before the travelers:* meal, table, board, banquet, feast, spread; food, provision, victuals, nourishment, refreshment, snack.

repay v. *We can never repay your kindness. She repaid him for his insult by not inviting him to the party:* pay back, reimburse, make restitution, recompense, remunerate, indemnify, refund, requite, reward, make requital, make retribution, give in exchange, return, return the compliment, match; make a return for, pay in kind, reciprocate; get back at, get even with.

repeal v. **1.** *Parliament repealed the obsolete law:* cancel, abrogate, abolish, annul, nullify, void, declare null and void, invalidate, set aside, revoke, rescind. —*n.* **2.** *The year 1933 marked the repeal of Prohibition in the U.S.:* abrogation, cancellation, abolition, termination, annulment, nullification, voiding, invalidation, revocation. —**Ant.** 1 confirm, reestablish; validate. 2 confirmation, reestablishment; validation.

repeat v. **1.** *Please repeat the question. Repeat after me:* restate, say again, say over, reiterate; echo, imitate, mimic. **2.** *She repeated what she had heard to her mother:* tell, relate, recite, retell, recount, quote, pass on. **3.** *History repeats itself. The choral society will repeat their program next week:* duplicate, redo, perform again, reproduce. —*n.* **4.** *Today's lecture was a repeat of yesterday's:* repetition, reiteration, duplication, rerun, *Slang* retread.

repeatedly adv. *She repeatedly tried to get through:* over and over, regularly, often, frequently.

repel v. **1.** *The fort's defenders repelled the attacking enemy. Boric acid crystals repel cockroaches:* push back, force back, drive back, rout, beat back, repulse, rebuff; dispel, scatter, disperse, chase away, put to flight, drive away; *Informal* send packing; keep off, hold off, ward off, fend off, forfend, stave off, throw off, resist, be proof against, foil, frustrate, deflect, withstand, oppose; keep at bay, keep at arm's length, check, keep out. **2.** *The gory movie repelled me:* disgust, repulse, revolt, be offensive to, be repugnant to, put off, go against one's grain; sicken, nauseate, turn one's stomach, make one's flesh crawl, set one's teeth on edge, make one shudder; offend, alienate, *Slang* turn off. —**Ant.** 1, 2 attract, draw. 2 please, delight, captivate, invite, fascinate, entrance, enchant.

repellent adj. **1.** *This fabric is water-repellent:* repelling, resisting; impermeable, proof. **2.** *The sight of meat is repellent to some vegetarians:* repugnant, repulsive, disgusting, nauseating, sickening, distasteful, abhorrent, offensive, revolting, loathsome.

repent v. *The killer never repented the crime he committed. Repent, for the kingdom of heaven is at hand:* regret, deplore, be grieved for, lament, bewail, weep over, bemoan; feel remorse, be ashamed, be regretful, repine, reproach oneself, rue; be penitent, be contrite.

repentance n. *Saint Augustine wrote about his own repentance for a misspent youth:* remorse, regret, grief, sorrow; self-reproach, self-condemnation, compunction, guilt, pangs of conscience; penitence, contrition. —**Ant.** contentment, complacency, impenitence.

repercussion n. **1.** *Are you aware of the repercussions that could occur if we carry out this plan?:* result, effect, consequence, side effect, aftereffect, reaction, reverberation, backlash, boomerang effect. **2.** *The repercussion of the blast could be heard for miles:* reverberation, concussion, echo.

repetition n. *The play was a repetition of a theme used twenty years ago:* repeat, retelling, recapitulation, restatement, iteration, reiteration.

repetitious adj. *I found the lecture boring and repetitious:* redundant, repetitive, repeated, wordy, prolix. —**Ant.** concise, pithy, succinct, terse.

replace v. **1.** *He replaced Mr. Jones as director:* take the place of, fill the place of, succeed, supersede, supplant, displace, take over for, substitute for, spell. **2.** *Replace those books on the shelf:* put back, put back in place, return, restore.

replenish v. *Our dwindling supplies were replenished when the new shipment arrived:* fill up again, refill, restock, reload, replace, renew, refresh, restore, reorder. —**Ant.** dissipate, empty, drain.

replete adj. *The cabinets were replete with valuable antiques. The diners were replete after the eight-course dinner:* abundantly filled, filled to repletion, abounding, teeming, fraught, well-stocked, loaded, crammed, jam-packed, full to bursting, brimming; stuffed, full, gorged, sated, satiated, surfeited. —**Ant.** empty, bare, barren; hungry, starved, ravenous, famished.

replica n. *We asked the artist for a replica of*

the portrait, so that we both could have a copy: duplicate, copy, close copy, carbon copy, imitation, likeness, double, facsimile, replication, reproduction, model.

reply v. **1.** *Please reply to the question. I replied that I had never been there:* answer, respond, rejoin, make rejoinder, retort, come back with, counter, react. —*n.* **2.** *I'm waiting for a reply to my question. His only reply was an angry stare:* response, answer, retort, rejoinder, counter, reaction; acknowledgment. **—Ant.** 1 question, demand, ask. 2 request, question; invitation.

report n. **1.** *His report of the battle won a Pulitzer prize. Copies of the annual report were sent to the stockholders:* account, description, version, relation, narration, story, write-up, summary, record, article, news story, press release. **2.** *The messenger brought in a secret report from France:* dispatch, message, communiqué, note, memorandum, missive. **3.** *The report that he was going to resign was false:* information, word, gossip, hearsay, rumor, talk. **4.** *We could hear the report of cannons in the distance. The pistol went off with a sharp report:* noise, sound, boom, discharge, detonation, bang, crack. —*v.* **5.** *The newspaper reported the death of the statesman:* announce, communicate, relate, tell, divulge, disclose, reveal, state, recount, recite, put in writing, write down, put on the record, describe, detail. **6.** *He reported the student for misconduct:* denounce, inform against, expose, tell on, complain about. **7.** *The soldier reported for duty:* present oneself, appear; *Informal* show up, check in. **—Ant.** 5 keep secret, withhold, conceal.

reporter n. *The reporter wrote his story after interviewing several witnesses:* journalist, newsman, newspaperman, gentleman of the press, newswoman, newspaperwoman; *Slang* newshawk, newshound, newshen; member of the press, investigative reporter, roving reporter, correspondent, foreign correspondent, columnist; announcer, commentator, newscaster, anchorman, news analyst.

repose n. **1.** *A full day's work earned him an evening of repose:* rest, respite, ease, tranquillity, calm, quiet, quietude, quiescence, peacefulness, relaxation, leisure, inactivity. —*v.* **2.** *After lunch Father reposed in the hammock:* rest, be at rest, lie, lie at rest, recline; relax, be calm, settle.

repository n. *The warehouse served as a repository for the store's additional merchandise:* storage place, depository, depot, magazine, storehouse, warehouse, treasurehouse.

reprehensible adj. *Assassination is a reprehensible crime:* condemnable, unworthy, objectionable, shameful, disgraceful; heinous, villainous, opprobrious, nefarious, foul, infamous, despicable, ignoble, base, vile, wicked, evil, bad; unpardonable, inexcusable, unjustifiable; deserving of blame, deserving censure, censurable, blamable, blameworthy, culpable, guilty. **—Ant.** admirable, laudable, commendable, praiseworthy, blameless, guiltless, unobjectionable, irreproachable, pardonable, forgivable.

represent v. **1.** *In Morse Code, dots and dashes represent letters:* stand for, symbolize, designate, denote, be the equivalent of, express, indicate, be, mean, equal, serve as; typify, characterize, emblematize, betoken. **2.** *Her lawyer represented her at the estate sale. The foreign minister represented the country at the conference:* act in place of, stand in the place of, act as a substitute for, be proxy for, be an agent for, be deputy for, be in the position of; speak and act for. **3.** *His drawing represented a Parisian café:* portray, depict, show, show a likeness of, picture, illustrate, sketch, outline, delineate, describe; state, present. **4.** *She represented her girlfriend as being much prettier than she was:* describe, depict, give an account of, portray, delineate. **5.** *Which actor represented Hamlet? The man represented himself as a leading surgeon:* portray, impersonate, appear as, appear in the character of, enact, act the part of; pose as.

representative n. **1.** *The lawyer acted as her representative in the hearings:* agent, deputy, emissary, envoy, proxy, delegate, substitute, proctor, surrogate, spokesman, *Informal* mouthpiece. **2.** *Each U.S. congressional district sends one representative to Congress:* member of a legislature, legislator, delegate; congressman, congresswoman, assemblyman, assemblywoman, member of parliament, M.P. —*adj.* **3.** *The lion is representative of the feline family:* serving to represent, typifying, symbolic, symbolical; exemplary, exemplifying, typical, characteristic, illustrative, descriptive, emblematic, delineative, denotative. **4.** *Every democracy is proud of its own representative form of government:* representational, republican, democratic, elected, elective; delegated, delegatory, deputed. **5.** *The pollsters questioned a representative sample of the population:* representing the whole, balanced, varied, cross-sectional.

repress v. **1.** *It is often wrong to repress one's true feelings:* hold back, keep in check, control, keep down, curb, check, restrain, inhibit, hold in, hold back, suppress, hide, conceal, mask, cloak, cover, veil, stifle, muffle, smother, squelch, strangle; pen up, bottle up, shut up, box up. **2.** *Seasoned mercenaries were hired to repress the rebellion:* crush, quash, quell, subdue, put down, squash, silence. **—Ant.** 1 let out, release, express. 2 encourage, incite, foment.

reprieve n. *Scheduled for execution, the prisoner won a last-minute reprieve:* respite, delay, postponement, remission, adjournment, suspension, stay, moratorium; *Slang* breather, breathing spell; lull, pause.

reprimand n. **1.** *The speeding motorist received a reprimand and a ticket from the policeman:* sharp reproof, reproval, rebuke, reproach, admonition, admonishment, upbraiding, scolding, remonstrance, castigation, chiding, dressing down, berating, trimming, censure, criticism, obloquy, opprobrium, rebuff, denunciation, disparagement; *Informal* rap on the knuckles, chewing out. —*v.* **2.** *The teacher reprimanded* *the class for being noisy:* reprove severely, rebuke, admonish, reproach, scold, upbraid, rail at, chastise, castigate, chide, berate, trim, dress down, call to account, take down, tell off; *Informal* chew out, give a rap on the knuckles; give a tongue lashing, take to task, lecture, raise one's voice against, denounce, dispraise, disparage; reprehend, reprobate, revile, criticize, censure. **—Ant.** 1 commendation, compliment, praise, applause, approval. 2 commend, compliment, praise, applaud, approve, endorse.

reprisal *n. The gang expected reprisals for the sneak attack:* retaliatory act, retaliation, revenge, redress, counterattack, counterblow, counteroffensive, retribution, vengeance, requital; *Latin* quid pro quo; *Slang* tit for tat, blow for blow.

reproach *v.* **1.** *He was severely reproached for his rude behavior:* find fault with, chide, admonish, reprimand, rebuke, reprove; criticize, censure, condemn, stigmatize, malign, vilify, revile, blame; scold, upbraid, rail at, castigate, charge, tongue-lash, call to account, take to task; disparage, denounce, asperse; shame, disgrace. **—n. 2.** *Her behavior was above reproach. The workers feared their supervisor's reproaches:* blame, rebuke, reproof; upbraiding, scolding, remonstrance, criticism, censure, hard words, tirade, diatribe. **3.** *The youth's bad behavior is a constant reproach to his parents:* cause of blame, badge of infamy, stigma, taint, blemish, stain, blot, spot, tarnish, slur; indignity, insult, offense; shame, humiliation, degradation, embarrassment, scandal, disgrace, dishonor, discredit. **—Ant.** 1 praise, commend, applaud, compliment. 2 commendation, compliment, praise, applause, honor. 3 honor, credit.

reprobate *n.* **1.** *The old reprobate never reformed:* wicked person, degenerate, profligate, roué, prodigal, rake, rakehell, immoralist, voluptuary, wanton, abandoned person; rascal, scamp, black sheep, rapscallion, rotter; miscreant, sinner, transgressor, evildoer, wrongdoer, outcast, castaway, pariah, derelict, untouchable. **—adj. 2.** *He was a reprobate person with no redeeming qualities:* corrupt, incorrigible, depraved, profligate, degenerate, dissolute, abandoned, shameless; wicked, evil, evil-minded, low, base, bad, vile. **—Ant.** 1 angel, paragon, saint. 2 pure, virtuous, righteous, saintly, angelic.

reproduce *v.* **1.** *The machine in the hardware store can reproduce a key in two minutes. The bird watcher could reproduce the call of over fifty birds:* make a duplicate of, duplicate, replicate, copy, match, represent, redo; repeat, re-echo, mirror, reflect; imitate, counterfeit. **2.** *Rabbits reproduce quickly:* produce young, produce offspring, procreate, propagate, generate, proliferate, give birth, beget, sire, bring forth, multiply, breed, spawn.

reproduction *n.* **1.** *Wealthy Romans collected reproductions of Greek statues:* copy, carbon copy, likeness, duplicate, replica, facsimile, representation; imitation, simulation. **2.** *We studied the processes of reproduction in biology class:* generation, propagation, procreation, prolifera-

tion, progeneration, multiplication, breeding. **—Ant.** 1 original, prototype.

reproof *n. He received a gentle reproof from his girlfriend for forgetting to shave:* rebuke, reproach, remonstrance, scolding, dressing-down, reprimand, admonition, chiding, criticism, censure, blame, condemnation. **—Ant.** approval, commendation, praise, reward.

reprove *v. When the child giggled, her mother reproved her with a stern look:* reproach, rebuke, chide, admonish, reprimand; censure, castigate, chasten, scold. **—Ant.** praise, applaud, encourage.

republic *n. Andorra is a small mountain republic between France and Spain:* republican nation, representative government, popular government, democracy, constitutional government.

repudiate *v.* **1.** *The new government repudiated the treaty signed by the former rulers:* reject, disavow, deny, disclaim, protest; rescind, reverse, revoke, repeal, retract, void, nullify, annul, declare null and void, abrogate, cancel, abolish, dissolve. **2.** *The man repudiated the religion he was born into and became an atheist:* disown, disavow, reject, cast off, discard, wash one's hands of, abandon, desert, forsake, renounce. **—Ant.** 1 accept, approve; adopt, espouse. 2 acknowledge, accept, embrace, welcome.

repugnance *n. Everything he did was met with repugnance:* objection, distaste, aversion, dislike, reluctance, hatred, hostility, antipathy. **—Ant.** attractiveness, attraction, liking, sympathy.

repugnant *adj.* **1.** *What a repugnant odor! The very thought of eating squid is repugnant to me:* repellent, offensive, causing disgust, disgusting, nauseating, sickening, repulsive, foul, nasty, vile, obnoxious, revolting, objectionable, unacceptable, undesirable, disagreeable, unpleasant; distasteful, unpalatable, unsavory, unappetizing; odious, hateful, loathsome, detestable, abhorrent, abominable, insufferable. **2.** *Lying and cheating are repugnant to my way of thinking:* contrary, opposed, adverse, counter, antipathetic, uncongenial. **—Ant.** 1 attractive, pleasant, tasteful, unobjectionable, desirable, agreeable, favorable. 2 consistent, harmonious, compatible.

repulse *v.* **1.** *The army repulsed the attacking forces:* repel, throw back, drive back, beat back. **2.** *The neighbors repulsed our offers of friendship:* reject, refuse, rebuff, turn one's back on, be deaf to, ignore, be cold to, spurn, stand aloof from, avoid, shun, shrink from, recoil from; *Informal* cold-shoulder. **—n. 3.** *Her repulse of his proposal depressed him:* refusal, rebuff, rejection, spurning, shunning. **—Ant.** 2 welcome, accept, encourage. 3 encouragement, acceptance, welcome.

repulsion *n. Spiders fill me with repulsion:* revulsion, repugnance, disgust, distaste, indisposition, disinclination; dislike, antipathy, detestation, aversion, loathing, hatred, abomination, abhorrence.

repulsive *adj. His table manners are repulsive:* repugnant, repellent, offensive, abhorrent, disgusting, obnoxious, nauseating, nasty, vile, revolting, objectionable, disagreeable, distasteful, loathsome, hateful, detestable, abominable, odious. —**Ant.** attractive, agreeable, pleasant, tasteful.

reputable *adj. If you want good service, go to a reputable dealer:* respectable, respected, creditable, trustworthy, held in good repute, esteemed, honored, reliable, of good name. —**Ant.** disreputable, untrustworthy, shady.

reputation *n. The scandal badly injured her reputation. That critic has a reputation as an excellent judge of talent:* standing, stature, repute, name.

repute *n.* **1.** *Blackstone was a jurist of high repute:* respectability; standing, reputation, renown, prominence, fame, regard, esteem, celebrity, notoriety. —*v.* **2.** *He was reputed to be a heavy gambler:* consider, regard, hold, esteem, estimate, judge, deem; believe, think, suppose, account, reckon, view, say.

request *n.* **1.** *Put in a request for a transfer to another department. This is not a request, it's an order!:* application, solicitation, petition. —*v.* **2.** *Did you request a new desk? He requested her hand in marriage:* ask, ask for, apply for, call for; solicit, bid for, seek, sue for, make suit for, petition for, make entreaty for, entreat, desire, importune.

require *v.* **1.** *What material do you require to complete the job?:* need, stand in need of, have need of; want, lack, miss; desire, hope for, wish for, long for, crave. **2.** *The subpoena requires you to appear in court:* command, charge, enjoin, order, oblige, constrain, compel, direct, dictate, bid. **3.** *This plan required secrecy:* necessitate, make imperative, entail, imply. —**Ant.** 1 dispense with, forgo.

required *adj. The required equipment was lacking:* necessary, needed, needful, vital, obligatory, compulsory, essential, imperative, indispensable, mandatory, prerequisite, requisite, rightful, set, suitable, unavoidable, vital, prescribed, called for. —**Ant.** elective, noncompulsory, optional.

requirement *n.* **1.** *Experience in a related field is a requirement for this job:* prerequisite, essential, requisite, must, desideratum, *Latin* sine qua non. **2.** *The product met all requirements set by the government:* guideline, specification, standard, criterion.

requisite *adj.* **1.** *Past experience is requisite for this job:* required, mandatory, compulsory, obligatory, prerequisite, necessary, essential, imperative, needed, indispensable. —*n.* **2.** *Steady nerves are a requisite for high-rise construction work:* prerequisite, requirement, need, necessity, essential, must, desideratum, *Latin* sine qua non. —**Ant.** 1 unnecessary, superfluous, unessential, superfluity, luxury.

requisition *n. She filled out the requisition:* request, call, demand, summons.

requite *v.* **1.** *They requited him for his trouble:* recompense, reimburse, repay, remunerate, satisfy, compensate. **2.** *The enemy requited their setback:* retaliate, avenge, revenge, punish. —**Ant.** 1 dissatisfy 2 forgive.

rescind *v. The judge rescinded the court's previous decision:* revoke, reverse, retract, repeal, recall, take back, invalidate, countermand, overrule, counterorder, override, set aside, discard, get rid of, sweep aside; void, annul, abrogate, abolish, declare null and void, nullify, cancel, quash, dissolve. —**Ant.** uphold, support; validate.

rescue *v.* **1.** *The fireman rescued three people from the burning building:* save, recover, salvage, extricate, deliver, liberate, ransom. —*n.* **2.** *An attorney arranged for the rescue of the hostage. The survivor credited his rescue to quick work by the ski patrol:* rescuing, saving, recovery, liberation, deliverance, freeing, extrication, release. —**Ant.** 1 abandon. 2 loss, abandonment.

research *n.* **1.** *You may conduct your research for the term paper in the library:* inquiry, investigation, search, factfinding, analysis, scrutiny, study, inspection, examination, probe, exploration, scholarship, delving. —*v.* **2.** *The scientist researched the cause of the disease:* do research on, study, investigate, conduct an examination on, probe.

resemblance *n. You bear a striking resemblance to Harry Truman. There's no resemblance between the two paintings:* likeness, similarity, closeness in appearance, affinity, similitude, semblance, analogy, correspondence, parallel, congruence. —**Ant.** unlikeness, dissimilarity, difference.

resemble *v. I resemble my mother, but my brother resembles my father:* bear a resemblance to, look like, appear like, favor, take after, be like, be similar to, correspond to, be akin to, parallel.

resent *v. I resent that remark!:* feel bitter anger at, be indignant at, be provoked at, be in a huff about, be piqued at, view with dissatisfaction; dislike, feel displeasure at, be offended at, take exception to, take amiss, take offense at, take umbrage at, be insulted by, be jealous of, bear a grudge against. —**Ant.** like, approve; welcome.

resentment *n. Her words were full of hatred and resentment:* indignation, bad feelings, anger, outraged spirit, ire, crossness, bad temper, dudgeon, huff, asperity, ill will, rancor; acrimony, bitterness, acerbity, sourness, soreness, irritation, irritability; pique, wounded pride, umbrage, offense, hurt feelings, displeasure; animosity, animus, malice, vindictiveness, vengefulness, spite; jealousy.

reservation *n.* **1.** *I have no reservation about hiring him. The professor gave the student a passing grade, subject to certain reservations:* reluctance, doubt, hesitancy, uncertainty; compunction, scruple; qualification, strings, condition, stipulation, provision, proviso. **2.** *The army reservation was five miles from Detroit:* reserved land, reserve; preserve, encampment, installation, establishment, settlement. **3.** *We made a* *reservation for dinner at the restaurant:* accommodation, booking, prearrangement, appointment, date, reserved place.

reserve *v.* **1.** *It's often wise to reserve judgment. Try to reserve energy:* keep, keep back, withhold, retain, hold, keep as one's own; preserve, spare, conserve, save, husband, lay up, store up, salt away, hoard up, amass, stock, stockpile, put by for a rainy day; postpone, delay, put aside, shelve, table. **2.** *Call ahead to reserve a room:* set apart, prearrange, provide for, engage, book; schedule. —*n.* **3.** *Keep the equivalent of six months' earnings as a reserve:* emergency fund, contingency fund, reservoir, savings, nestegg, hoard, stockpile. **4.** *A man of reserve seldom shows emotion:* reticence, reservedness, aloofness, retiring disposition. —*adj.* **5.** *We're running on reserve power:* stored up, unused, extra, spare, additional; second-string, backup. —**Ant.** 1 give, grant; squander, splurge, spend; throw away, waste. 4 sociability, warmth, affability, conviviality, openness, frankness.

reserved *adj.* **1.** *Be sure to get reserved seats:* kept in reserve, retained, booked, taken, engaged, spoken for, bespoken. **2.** *The English are supposed to be reserved, but we found them warm and friendly:* reticent, aloof, self-contained, undemonstrative, inhibited, restrained, constrained, formal, ceremonious, strained, distant, standoffish, unsocial, unsociable, unresponsive, uncommunicative. —**Ant.** 1, 2 unreserved. 2 demonstrative, open, uninhibited; sociable, warm, affable.

reservoir *n.* **1.** *The reservoir supplies the city's water:* water reserve; basin, millpond, well, fount, cistern. **2.** *Grandpa had his own backyard gasoline reservoir:* tank, receptacle, container, repository, depository. **3.** *The labors of scholars have put at our disposal an immense reservoir of facts:* supply, store, reserve, fund, stock, accumulation, pool, stockpile, hoard, backlog.

reside *v.* **1.** *I reside in Salt Lake City. Jim and Meg reside at the Grand Hotel:* dwell, live, occupy, inhabit, domicile, have residence, have one's abode, keep house, lodge, room, sojourn. **2.** *Does goodness reside in all of us?:* lie, rest, exist, belong, be present, be inherent, be ingrained, be intrinsic.

residence *n.* *His office is in town, but his residence is in the suburbs. I dread taking up residence in a new town. After a residence of ten years in Rio, she moved to Lisbon:* home, house, homestead, household, lodging, quarters, dwelling, dwelling place, habitation, domicile, abode, address, place, apartment, flat, room, *Informal* digs, *French* pied à terre, *Slang* pad; stay, sojourn.

resident *n.* *I'm a resident of Toronto. We joined the residents' committee:* inhabitant, resider, sojourner, dweller, housekeeper, citizen, denizen, townsman, local; tenant, occupant, lodger.

residual *adj.* *He was paid damages for his residual injuries:* remaining, continuing, abiding, lasting, enduring, lingering; extra, leftover, surplus, supplementary.

residue *n.* *A residue of coffee grounds remained in the pot:* remainder, remains, leavings, scraps, dregs, residuum, remnant, rest, balance.

resign *v.* **1.** *He resigned his position in the company:* give up, step down from, quit, relinquish, leave, abdicate, renounce, disclaim. **2.** *You must resign yourself to the fact that you'll never be rich or famous:* submit, reconcile.

resignation *n.* **1.** *His resignation left a vacancy on the board of directors:* quitting, retirement, withdrawal, departure. **2.** *He accepted his defeat with resignation:* submission, submissiveness, passiveness, nonresistance, acquiescence, equanimity, stoicism, fatalism, patience. —**Ant.** 1 retention. 2 rebellion, resistance, protest, impatience.

resigned *adj.* *The resigned prisoner accepted his sentence:* reconciled, philosophical, manageable, obedient, passive, patient, quiescent, stoical, submissive, subservient, tractable, unprotesting, unresisting, acquiescent, amenable, biddable, compliant, enduring, longsuffering.

resilient *adj.* *Rubber is very resilient. He's so resilient that his troubles never seem to get him down:* rebounding, elastic, flexible, springy, supple, rubbery; expansive, rapidly recovering, responsive, buoyant, resistant, irrepressible; hardy, tenacious, adaptable. —**Ant.** inflexible, stiff, rigid, tense; flaccid.

resist *v.* **1.** *He made an attempt to resist his attackers. This material resists stains:* fight against, oppose, strike back, beat back, fight, combat, contest, withstand, make a stand against, hold out against, bear up against, stand up to, weather, repel, counter, counteract, stop, stem, thwart, baffle, balk, foil, frustrate. **2.** *Try to resist chocolates and other rich foods:* not give in to, abstain from, refrain from, say no to, refuse, reject; turn down. —**Ant.** 1, 2 give in to, surrender to, submit to. 1 yield, comply with, succumb to, capitulate, acquiesce. 2 indulge in, enjoy.

resistance *n.* *The proposal met with resistance from the club members. Resistance sprang up all over Nazi-occupied Europe:* opposition, contention, noncompliance, obstinacy, defiance, recalcitrance, intransigence; rejection, rebuff, refusal, obstruction; struggle, armed struggle, insurgency, national liberation movement; insurrection, mutiny, rebellion.

resolute *adj.* *He was a serious, resolute student. Lord Beaverbrook was a resolute and energetic leader:* determined, purposive, set in purpose, deliberate, steadfast, staunch, steady, tenacious, pertinacious, earnest, zealous, industrious, assiduous, diligent, vigorous; persevering, relentless, persistent, dogged, untiring, unflagging, indefatigable; unyielding, unwavering, unfaltering, unflinching, inflexible, uncompromising, undeviating, unswerving, unbending, strong-minded, strong-willed, decisive, stern, stubborn, obstinate, intrepid. —**Ant.** irresolute, unresolved, doubtful, undecided, undetermined, unsteady, vacillating, weak.

resolution *n.* **1.** *The resolution passed by two*

votes: motion, formal proposition, proposal. **2.** *Have you made a New Year's resolution?:* resolve, promise, intent, intention, purpose, plan, design, ambition; objective, object, aim, goal. **3.** *He lacked the resolution to get through medical school:* resoluteness, firmness of purpose, fixed purpose, persistence, determination, tenacity, resolve, will power, perseverance, resilience, steadfastness, stability, steadiness, constancy; zeal, earnestness, energy, indefatigability, mettle, spirit, aggressiveness, follow-through. **4.** *He was faced with the resolution of a difficult matter:* solution, resolving, clearing up, working-out.

resolve *v.* **1.** *We resolved to visit Europe at least once a year:* make up one's mind, dedicate oneself to, determine, decide, form a resolution, purpose, plan, intend, design, set out. **2.** *We can resolve the matter to your satisfaction:* clear up, settle, solve, find the solution to, explain, answer, elucidate. **3.** *The jury was trying to resolve the defendant's guilt or innocence:* determine, settle, vote on, decide, adjudge, make up one's mind. —*n.* **4.** *It is our resolve never to surrender this fortress:* determination, resolution, decision, fixed intention, commitment, purpose. **5.** *Man is of soul and body formed for deeds of high resolve:* resoluteness, resolution, steadfast purpose, firmness of purpose.

resonance *n.* *The drum had great resonance:* sonorousness, sonority, vibrancy.

resonant *adj.* *For such a skinny person he's got an amazingly resonant voice:* full, rich, vibrant, sonorous, ringing; stentorian, bellowing, resounding, reverberant, booming, orotund, thunderous.

resort *v.* **1.** *Even saints have been known to resort to violence:* have recourse to, bring into play, avail oneself of, apply, take up, exercise, make use of, employ, use, utilize. —*n.* **2.** *We stayed at a resort in the Laurentians:* holiday retreat, vacation place, tourist spot. **3.** *In the face of defeat, suicide was the samurai's last resort:* recourse, expedient; avail, hope, chance.

resound *v.* *Church bells resounded throughout the Alpine valley:* peal, ring, sound, reverberate, resonate, tintinnabulate, clang, fill the air, echo, reecho, vibrate.

resource *n.* **1.** *A garden is a good resource of fresh vegetables:* source, recourse, expedient, wherewithal, means of supplying. **2.** Usually **resources** *We pooled our resources and bought a boat:* collective wealth, capital, funds, assets, means, money, revenue, income, collateral, wherewithal; belongings, effects, possessions.

resourceful *adj.* *He was a clever and resourceful young man:* inventive, creative, talented, imaginative, innovative, original, ingenious, smart, bright, sharp, cunning, shrewd, artful; adroit, skillful, able, competent, capable, effectual, proficient, ready, enterprising. —**Ant.** unresourceful, uninventive, uncreative, artless; unskillful, incompetent, incapable.

resources *n. pl.* *We mustered all our resources:* means, belongings, capital, holdings, property,

reserves, revenue, riches, savings, wealth, wherewithal, assets, property, possessions.

respect *n.* **1.** *In that respect, you're perfectly right:* detail, point, particular, matter, circumstance, feature, point of view, aspect, regard, sense. **2.** *In respect to your request, five dollars is being credited to your account:* relation, regard, reference, connection, bearing. **3.** *He had respect for his stepfather. Reporters have no respect for anyone's privacy:* regard, deference, veneration, reverence, esteem, appreciation, affection; praise, laudation, admiration, approval; notice, recognition; consideration. **4. respects** *It's proper to call on a new neighbor to pay one's respects:* expressions of friendship or esteem, compliments, personal observance, consideration, tribute, fealty, regards, greetings, remembrances. —*v.* **5.** *Respect your elders!:* honor, esteem, do honor to, revere, venerate, pay deference to, defer to, pay respect to, regard, pay attention to; look up to, be appreciative of, understand, set store by, admire, value, cherish, prize. **6.** *I respect your desire for privacy but am obliged to intrude. They respected the artist's last wishes and burned his letters:* consider, treat with consideration, treat with forbearance, refrain from interfering with, show consideration for, appreciate, regard, honor, comply with, obey, heed, follow, abide by, observe, adhere to, be faithful to, acknowledge. —**Ant.** 2, 3, 5 disrespect, disregard. 3 irreverence, contempt, scorn, disdain. 5 pay no attention to; think lowly of, have a low opinion of, scorn, hold in contempt, disdain. 6 neglect, ignore, disregard, disdain, abuse.

respectable *adj.* **1.** *My parents are respectable people. Can't you act in a respectable manner?:* worthy of respect, admirable, worthy, praiseworthy, reputable, estimable, honorable, noble, dignified, upright, honest, aboveboard; proper, decent, decorous, correct; becoming, presentable; refined, polished, courtly, civil, polite. **2.** *He earns a respectable salary:* ample, sufficient, fairly good, fairly large, considerable, fair, moderate, proper, passing, satisfactory, admissible, decent, worthy. —**Ant.** 1 unworthy, disreputable, dishonorable, ignoble, improper, indecent, indecorous, unbecoming, unpresentable; unrefined, impolite. 2 small, poor, paltry, inadequate, demeaning.

respectful *adj.* *You can be respectful without being obsequious:* deferential, polite, courteous, civil, showing politeness, mannerly, solicitous, regardful, gracious; decorous, reverent, reverential; ceremonious, formal, attentive, admiring, obliging, accommodating, genial, winning, amiable, personable. —**Ant.** disrespectful, impolite, discourteous, rude, uncivil, unmannerly, unrefined, ungracious, irreverent, indecorous; heedless, hostile, antagonistic.

respects *n. pl.* *We paid our respects to the couple:* deference, regards, salutations, compliments, best wishes, courtesies, greetings, wishes, best wishes, kind wishes.

respiration *n.* *Tadpoles use gills in respiration.*

In yoga you learn to control your respiration: breathing, respiratory action.

respite *n. The director gave the cast a short respite before the next scene. The condemned prisoner's lawyer got him a respite:* rest period, recess, break, breathing spell, intermission, pause, lull, letup; reprieve, postponement of execution, delay, extension, temporary suspension.

resplendent *adj. The light of the chandelier made her modest necklace look positively resplendent:* refulgent, brilliant, bright, sparkling, dazzling, splendid; gleaming, coruscating, glittering, glowing, radiant, beaming, blazing; luminous, lustrous, lambent. **—Ant.** dull, lusterless, lackluster, gray, somber, dimmed, flat, mat.

respond *v.* **1.** *Please respond to the question:* reply, answer, give answer, speak up; rejoin. **2.** *The Mounties are quick to respond to a call for help:* react, act in response, reply; recognize, acknowledge.

response *n.* **1.** *What's your response to these charges?:* answer, reply; rebuttal, counterstatement, countercharge; retort, return, rejoinder, riposte, comeback. **2.** *The mayor's response to our plan was encouraging:* reaction, impression, acknowledgment, feedback. **—Ant.** 1 query, question. 2 proposal, proposition.

responsibility *n.* **1.** *He accepted all responsibility for the mistake:* liability; accountability, answerability, blame, burden, culpability. **2.** *Taking care of a family is a big responsibility:* charge, trust, function, task, burden, obligation, duty, order. **3.** *I recognize her brilliance but question her responsibility:* dependability, reliability, trustworthiness, ability to come through. **—Ant.** 3 unreliability, undependability, untrustworthiness.

responsible *adj.* **1.** *Parents are responsible for the welfare of their children:* accountable, duty-bound, liable, answerable, under obligation. **2.** *A cabinet appointment puts one in a responsible position:* requiring maturity and ability, important, challenging, demanding; administrative, executive. **3.** *Who's responsible for this mess?:* liable to be called to account, culpable, guilty, at fault. **4.** *Betty's a responsible young lady:* conscientious, reliable, dependable, trustworthy, creditable; capable, mature, self-assured, adult, of age. **—Ant.** 1, 2, 4 irresponsible. 1 unaccountable, under no obligation. 4 unconscientious, immature, unreliable, undependable, untrustworthy.

responsive *adj. You weren't responsive enough at the interview. If we are not responsive to beauty, we will miss a lot in life:* reactive, retaliative, retaliatory, sharp, quick to answer, alive, awake; susceptible, impressionable, sensitive, sympathetic, compassionate, understanding, receptive, aware of. **—Ant.** unresponsive, apathetic, silent; slow to respond; impassive, dead, insensitive, unsympathetic.

rest¹ *n.* **1.** *We took a short rest before starting off on a second lap. If you have a cold, take aspirin, drink fluids, and get plenty of rest:* relief from work or exertion, respite, break, recess, pause, lull, intermission, interruption, suspension, quiet spell, breathing spell; *Informal* breather; vacation, holiday; ease, relaxation, leisure; peace, quiet, stillness; sleep, slumber, hibernation; bed rest, nap, siesta, *Slang* snooze, forty winks. **2.** *After a long illness he went to his final rest:* death, one's final peace, repose, the grave, demise, end, departure, decease, cessation. **3.** *The ball came to a rest inches from the corner pocket:* state of motionlessness, standstill, halt, stop. **4.** *The judge put the gavel on a small wooden rest:* supporting device, holder, support, prop, base, stand, platform, trivet. **—v.** **5.** *The hikers rested awhile. You can rest now, we're home. The joggers rested their legs:* relax, take one's ease, be at ease, take time out, take a breather, pause, let up; settle down, be quiet, be at peace; lie down; *Informal* cool one's feet, recline, loll, repose; sleep; give rest to, ease, laze, lounge, loaf. **6.** *The sleds rested at the bottom of the hill. Let's let the matter rest:* come to a standstill; stand, lie, be, remain. **7.** *He rested the box on the chair:* set down, deposit, set, place, lay; lean, prop. **8.** *The plan rests on your cooperation:* be founded, be based, depend, rely, hang, hinge; be found, reside, be, exist, lie. **—Ant.** 1 unrest, restlessness; work, toil, activity, bustle, exertion, stir, excitement, disquiet.

rest² *n.* **1.** *You may have the rest of the pie. Some agree with Jim, but the rest of us agree with Sam:* remains, remainder, remaining part, complement, that which is left, balance, that which remains, remnant, residue, residuum, the others; scraps, leftovers. **—v.** **2.** *Rest easy:* remain, go on being, continue to be, keep, stay.

restaurant *n. The new restaurant specializes in Spanish dishes:* café, dining room, lunchroom, luncheonette, cafeteria, diner, brasserie, bistro, steak house, chop house, coffeehouse, grillroom, tearoom; *Slang* beanery, hashhouse, eatery; *German* rathskeller.

restful *adj. I like a restful vacation:* relaxed, comfortable, giving rest, soothing, full of rest; unagitated, undisturbed, peaceful, tranquil, serene, calm, placid, quiet, pacific. **—Ant.** unrestful, unrelaxed, uncomfortable; agitated, disturbing, busy.

restitution *n. Restitution must be made for the loss of these paintings:* redress, satisfaction, atonement, amends, reparation, remuneration, compensation, recompense, indemnification, indemnity, reimbursement, requital, repayment, paying back, restoral, restoration, reinstatement; *Law* replevin, replevy.

restive *adj.* **1.** *The restive crew awaited orders:* uneasy, restless, nervous, impatient, ill at ease, recalcitrant, unquiet. **2.** *The restive horse refused to budge:* refractory, disobedient, obstinate, mulish, stubborn, pigheaded. **—Ant.** restful, patient, quiet, serene; obedient.

restless *adj.* **1.** *The patient has had many restless nights. Jimmy's a restless child:* restive, wakeful, sleepless, insomniac, fitful, awake, unquiet; agitated, uneasy, disquieted, ill at ease, uncomfortable; nervous, jittery, jumpy, fidgety, worried, fretful, anxious, highstrung, hyperactive, excitable, impatient. **2.** *Cagliostro was a restless wanderer:* always in motion, never at rest, on the go, on the move, transient, incessant, unsettled. **—Ant.** 1 restful, quiet, undisturbed, easy, comfortable, relaxed, carefree.

restlessness *n. Restlessness was a by-product of the fever:* restiveness, agitation, fretfulness, disquietude, inquietude, edginess, fitfulness, jitters, jumpiness, nervousness, uneasiness, unrest, discontent, *Informal* cabin fever.

restore *v.* **1.** *Angela, the monitor, finally shouted to restore quiet in the classroom:* bring back, get back, recoup, recover, retrieve, rescue, reclaim; reinstate, reestablish, reinstall; recreate. **2.** *We restored the antique desk. Mother restored the old jacket by putting patches on the elbows:* reconstruct, rebuild, recondition, rehabilitate, refurbish, convert, renew, renovate, remodel, make over, do over, fix, mend, repair, patch up, retouch, touch up. **3.** *The thermal treatments were somewhat effective in restoring her:* bring back to health, bring round, rally, pull through, make well, rehabilitate, set on one's feet; strengthen, energize, stimulate, exhilarate, reinvigorate, revitalize, reanimate, revive, revivify, resuscitate, refresh; cure, remedy, heal, treat, medicate, dose. **4.** *He was later restored to his former rank:* put back, reinstate, reinstitute, reestablish, reinstall; return, bring back, give back.

restrain *v. The leash restrained the dog:* keep under control, suppress, contain, withhold, hold back, inhibit, temper, chasten, restrict, limit, check, curb, bridle, arrest, muzzle, gag, constrain, hold, prevent, curtail, stop; bind, shackle, fetter, trammel, pinion, harness, tether, leash; handicap.

restrained *adj. The restrained speaker avoided retaliation:* in check, controlled, self-controlled, under control; quiet, reasonable, reticent, retiring, subdued, temperate, undemonstrative, unobtrusive, withdrawn; moderate, temperate, muted, cool. **—Ant.** intemperate, hot headed, wild.

restraint *n.* **1.** *The restraint held him in check:* deterrence, check, hindrance, impediment, captivity, arrest, confinement, constraint, cramp, curb, fetters, limit, limitation, obstacle, obstruction, restriction, rope, bar, curb, bondage, chains, bridle, rein, barrier. **2.** *She used restraint in shopping:* self-restraint, balance, constraint, discretion, economy, limitation, moderation, reserve, reticence, self-control, temperance, willpower, austerity, abstinence. **—Ant.** excess, intemperance.

restrict *v. The French police are legally entitled to restrict anyone's movements as they please. Firemen tried to restrict the area of the blaze:* confine, constrain, restrain, suppress, hold back, check, curb, impede, frustrate, thwart, squelch, crimp, cramp, hamper, obstruct, inhibit, prevent; keep within limits, limit, hem in, hold, circumscribe; narrow, constrict, straiten.

restriction *n.* **1.** *Restriction of the king's powers*
was the council's responsibility: curbing, limitation, control, restraint, regulation. **2.** *It is a club with rigid restrictions on its membership:* rule, regulation, provision, proviso, condition, stipulation, qualification, reservation, consideration, requirement.

result *v.* **1.** *His lameness resulted from an accident:* arise, ensue, eventuate, happen, stem, owe to, derive, originate, turn out, issue, spring. **2.** *Her singing lessons resulted in her getting a part in a musical:* culminate, wind up, end up, pan out. *—n.* **3.** *What was the result of the medical tests? The fire was the result of carelessness:* finding, decision, verdict, opinion, judgment, determination, resolution, solution, report; consequence, outcome, effect, upshot, eventuality, reaction, development, product, aftereffect, aftermath, outgrowth, sequel, fruit, issue. **—Ant.** 1 originate, prompt. 3 cause, determinant; antecedent, origin, source, seed, root.

resume *v. Please resume what you were doing:* take up again, begin again, go on, go on with, proceed, continue, recommence, reembark, reestablish.

résumé *n.* **1.** *I was assigned to do a résumé of the first three chapter:* summary, summation, epitome, summing-up, abstract, synopsis, digest, abridgment, condensation, précis, brief. **2.** *Be sure to take a copy of your résumé to the job interview:* work history, curriculum vitae, CV, biography, *Slang* bio.

resurgence *n. There's been a resurgence of the "Big Band" sound of the 1940's:* revival, appearing again, rising again, rebirth, renaissance, renewal, rejuvenation, recrudescence, return, renascence, reemergence. **—Ant.** passing away, decline, fading.

retain *v. Concentrated study will help you to retain knowledge:* keep, hold on to, hang on to, maintain, keep possession of, possess, grasp, absorb, hold; keep in mind, bear in mind, commit to memory, memorize, fix in the mind, remember, recall, recollect, call to mind; have at one's fingertips. **—Ant.** discard, lose, surrender, relinquish, abandon.

retaliate *v. When one of their soldiers was killed, the occupation army retaliated by killing hostages:* counter, reciprocate, take retribution, return like for like, repay in the same coin, give measure for measure, give one a dose of his own medicine, exact one's pound of flesh; return, repay, requite, return the compliment; pay back, pay off, avenge, revenge, take revenge, take vengeance.

retard *v. Lack of sunlight retards growth in many organisms:* slow up, slow down, impede, delay the progress of, detain, check, block, obstruct, clog, fetter, hamper, hinder, baffle, inhibit, arrest, prevent; delay, hold up, hold back, prolong, draw out, drag, slacken, decelerate, brake. **—Ant.** speed, speed up, accelerate, expedite, quicken, hasten, rush; advance, further.

retarded *adj. Their youngest child has been retarded since birth:* backward, disabled, dull, unsound, handicapped, simpleminded, slow, simple, subnormal, mentally defective, slow-witted; moronic, imbecilic, idiotic, mongoloid.

reticent *adj. T.E. Lawrence became an increasingly reticent man:* taciturn, quiet, uncommunicative, silent, sparing of words, close-mouthed, tight-lipped; reserved, retiring, shy, withdrawn, diffident, self-contained, restrained, subdued, closed. —**Ant.** voluble, talkative, communicative, unreserved, expansive, inclined to speak freely, candid, frank, open, plain.

retinue *n. The king always traveled with a large retinue:* entourage, train, suite, following, convoy, attendance, court; attendants, retainers, followers, associates, courtiers; employees, personnel, staff, hired help.

retire *v.* **1.** *For relaxation he retires to a hideaway in British Columbia:* go away, betake oneself, depart, retreat, withdraw, remove, resort. **2.** *I'm tired, so I'll retire now:* go to bed, turn in, go to sleep, lie down to rest, call it a day; *Informal* hit the sack, hit the hay, flake out. **3.** *He retired from the army:* withdraw from public life or business, give up office, resign, remove from active service, secede, abdicate, drop out. —**Ant.** 2 get up, arise, stay up; wake up, awaken. 3 join, sign on, enlist.

retiring *adj. Bill's a rascal with a deceptively retiring manner:* withdrawn, self-effacing, uncommunicative, unsocial, reticent, quiet; shy, diffident, bashful, modest, demure, shrinking, meek, sheepish, timid, timorous; unassuming, inconspicuous, unassertive, humble, unpretentious; reserved, self-contained. —**Ant.** outgoing, gregarious, sociable, bold, brazen, brassy, forward, audacious, *Informal* pushy.

retort *v.* **1.** *"Same to you!" he retorted:* reply sharply, counter, return, rejoin, rebut; give answer, say, respond, reply, answer, come back with, fire back. —*n.* **2.** *Her retort left me with nothing more to say:* sharp reply, pointed answer, counterblast, rebuttal, quip, rejoinder, witty reply, riposte.

retract *v.* **1.** *You may retract that statement or defend it with your life:* withdraw, take back, recant, recall, rescind, revoke, repeal, reverse, abnegate, abrogate, repudiate, disavow, disown, disclaim, deny, abjure, renounce, forswear. **2.** *The point of a ballpoint pen retracts:* draw back, pull back, peel back, draw in, recede, retreat, withdraw, recoil; reel in. —**Ant.** 1 offer, proffer. 2 poke out, protrude.

retreat *n.* **1.** *The general ordered a retreat:* strategic withdrawal, falling back, pulling back, backing out, retirement, evacuation, flight, departure, getaway, escape. **2.** *His retreat from social life was absolute:* withdrawal, retirement, seclusion, solitude, isolation, immurement, reclusion; hibernation, rustication. **3.** *They spent their honeymoon in a mountain retreat:* place of seclusion, privacy, or refuge; resort, haunt, refuge, hideaway, asylum, sanctum, sanctuary, den, haven, shelter, harbor, port. —*v.* **4.** *He retreated from reality:* withdraw, retire, fall back, move back, fall to the rear, draw back, back away, recoil, shy away, shrink, make a retreat, depart, go, leave, make a getaway, escape, turn

tail, make oneself scarce; flee, abscond, bolt, take flight. —**Ant.** 1 advance, charge. 2 entrance; participation. 4 advance, move forward, rush to, meet head on, engage.

retrench *v. If we're forced to retrench, there may be some layoffs:* cut back, cut down, economize, cut costs, conserve, tighten one's belt, scrimp, scrape, reduce, curtail, slash, reduce expenses, pinch pennies, *Slang* put the squeeze on. —**Ant.** fritter away, run through, squander, waste.

retribution *n. There will be retribution for his heinous crimes:* requital, retaliation, justice, satisfaction, redress, amends, restitution, return, reparation, reciprocation, recrimination, reprisal, penalty, punishment, reward; recompense, vengeance, revenge, an eye for an eye and a tooth for a tooth, measure for measure, vindication, just deserts.

retrieve *v. Interpol is busy trying to retrieve the stolen painting:* recover, regain, get again, get back, get back again, find again, recoup, reclaim, repossess, redeem, ransom, recapture, rescue, salvage; fetch, go and get, snag, find and fetch; *Hunting* find and bring back game.

retrospect *n. His youth was more enjoyable in retrospect than it had actually been when he was going through it. Each installment of the soap opera begins with a retrospect of the preceding episode:* contemplation of time past, review, retrospection, remembrance, reminiscence, flashback, looking backward; second thought, reconsideration, afterthought, hindsight.

return *v.* **1.** *We thought spring would never return. When will you return from Winnipeg?:* come back, go back, reappear, recur. **2.** *The electorate will return their favorite candidate to office. The thief returned the missing jewels:* send back, bring back, put back, restore; reinstate, reinstall, reestablish, reseat. **3.** *Permit me to return the compliment:* give back, repay, give in recompense, give in turn, requite, reciprocate. **4.** *The stocks more than returned ten percent a year:* repay, yield, provide, earn, produce, be profitable, give interest, render. **5.** *The jury is expected to return a decision shortly:* announce, hand down, come to, render. —*n.* **6.** *News of the astronauts' safe return to earth was delayed. Police announced the return of the stolen goods:* returning, coming back, homecoming, arrival, advent; reinstatement, restoral, reestablishment, restoration, recovery, retrieval; putting back. **7.** *We're headed for the return of rationing:* returning, recurrence, reappearance, reversion, happening again. **8.** *The bonds paid a handsome return:* profit, income, revenue, earnings, proceeds, yield, interest, gain, reward, advantage, benefit, compensation, gross, net. —**Ant.** 1 depart, leave, go away, disappear. 2 retain, keep, hold, withhold; remove. 4 lose, be unprofitable. 6 departure, leaving, removal.

reveal *v. Further investigation revealed the true facts:* make known, divulge, give out, disclose, impart, unearth, bare, lay bare, bring to light, unmask, unveil, expose, uncover, make public;

publish, come out with, let out, betray, give the lowdown, give inside information, point out; lay open to view, display, show, exhibit; manifest, evidence, unfold. —**Ant.** conceal, hide, keep secret, veil, mask, cover.

revel v. **1.** She thoroughly reveled in Jane's expulsion: take great pleasure, derive pleasure from, rejoice, take delight, delight, enjoy, relish; indulge, wallow in, bask in, be in seventh heaven. **2.** The villagers reveled far into the night: make merry, indulge in festivities, celebrate, take one's pleasure, Informal paint the town red; carouse, roister, have one's fling, go on a spree; frolic, gambol, romp, caper, skylark.

revelation n. **1.** "Spilling the beans" means confessing or making a startling revelation: disclosure, divulgation, divulgence, divulgement; confession, admission; bombshell, shocker, eyeopener, exposure, exposé; discovery, unveiling. **2.** Revelations concerning sin and baptism form the subject of an early Christian book titled The Shepherd: vision, apocalypse, prophecy, revelatory writing. —**Ant.** l coverup, concealment, veiling, smoke-screen.

revelry n. The streets were filled with revelry after the victory: boisterousness, boisterous festivity, reveling, merrymaking, merriment, celebrating, rejoicing, celebration, jollity, jollification, conviviality, exultation, festival, carnival, jamboree; celebrating; carousal, roistering, high jinks, spree.

revenge v. **1.** Mark my words—I shall revenge this abomination!: inflict punishment in return for a wrong done, exact expiation, take vengeance for, take revenge, avenge; wreak one's vengeance, have one's revenge, make reprisal for, vindicate, take an eye for an eye, give tit for tat, return like for like, undertake a vendetta, demand one's pound of flesh; reciprocate, retaliate, requite, repay, pay back, recompense. —n. **2.** He sought revenge for the harm they had done him: vengeance, paying back, retaliation, reprisal, satisfaction, retribution, requital, repayment, eye for an eye, tooth for a tooth.

revengeful adj. The revengeful pair vandalized his car: vindictive, spiteful, malevolent, resentful, malicious, malignant, implacable. —**Ant.** forgiving, benevolent.

revenue n. The grape harvest produced a sizable revenue each year: income, salary, earnings, pay, wages, compensation, emolument, profit, return, proceeds, gains, yield, receipts, interest, remuneration; pension, allowance, annuity, subsidy; Slang take, pickings.

reverberate v. Our voices reverberated in the cave. The sound of the bells reverberated through the valley: carry, echo, resound, ring, vibrate, be reflected, boom, rumble, thunder.

reverberation n. The reverberation could be heard for miles: resounding, rumble, rumbling, boom, booming, growl, growling, grumble, grumbling, thunder, thundering, echo, reecho.

revere v. One of the Ten Commandments enjoins us to revere our parents: honor, treat with veneration, venerate, esteem, defer to, show honor and devotion to, reverence, look up to,

show deep regard for, respectfully cherish, respect, deeply respect. —**Ant.** disrespect, dishonor; despise, scorn, disparage, mock, contemn, snap one's fingers at.

reverence n. Aeneas' reverence toward his father was one of our Latin teacher's favorite themes: deep respect, esteem, regard, honor, homage, deference, veneration, admiration, adoration, devotion, worship; awe, fear; devoutness, piety, gesture indicative of deep respect, observance; genuflection, prostration, religiosity. —**Ant.** irreverence, disrespect, disregard, scorn, contempt, dishonor; hatred.

reverie n. **1.** The child stopped crying and fell into a reverie: daydream, brown study, dreamy spell. **2.** Did you have reveries about what you'd do when you grew up?: fantasy, flight of fancy, musing, daydream, dream. **3.** She sat at the window, deep in reverie: meditation, abstracted preoccupation, woolgathering, musing, dreamland. **4.** The mayor's plan is pure reverie: fantasy, fancy, extravagance, castle-building, castles in the air, castles in Spain, woolgathering, wishful thinking, quixotism, fantasticality.

reverse adj. **1.** Sign your name on the reverse side of the contract: turned backward, reversed, opposite, backward, converse, inverse, inverted, back, rear. —n. **2.** His answer was just the reverse of what we expected: contrary, opposite, antithesis, counter, counterpart, converse, inverse. **3.** On the reverse are lines for your comments: back, rear, other side, posterior, tail. **4.** He's entitled to some success after all those reverses: reversal, change for the worse, adversity, setback, upset, disappointment, mischance, misfortune, mishap, hardship, trouble, hard times; frustration, failure, defeat. —v. **5.** If you'll reverse the placard you'll see what I mean: turn around, turn over, turn upside down, turn end for end, upend, upturn, turn topsy-turvy; turn inside out, invert, transpose. **6.** The umpire never reversed a decision: change, undo, unmake, revoke, rescind, repeal, retract, recall, recant, withdraw; overrule, override, set aside, countermand, invalidate, nullify, annul, declare null and void, void, negate, cancel, abrogate. —**Ant.** 3 obverse, front. 4 advance, benefit. 6 ratify, uphold, stick to.

revert v. Pressures made him revert to his old habit of smoking: go back, return, reverse, turn back, regress, recidivate, repeat, retrogress, backslide, lapse, relapse, fall back on.

review n. **1.** The review in the Christian Science Monitor panned the remake of the 1935 movie: critique, criticism, critical piece, notice, commentary, evaluation. **2.** The college publishes a drama review: magazine, journal. **3.** The committee has met for a final review of the facts: examination, reevaluation, reassessment, reconsideration, recapitulation, study, scrutiny, rehash, contemplation of past events, retrospection, reflection, survey. **4.** The soldiers were in full uniform for the review: military inspection, presentation, formal examination, military display; parade, procession; show, exhibition, exposition, demonstration. —v. **5.** Let's review the *situation:* look at again, go over again, look over again, reevaluate, reexamine, reassess, reconsider, retrace, hash over, scrutinize, study; reiterate, run over, recapitulate; restate briefly, summarize, sum up. **6.** *The local paper will review the new movie:* write a critique of, criticize, evaluate, report on, comment upon, discuss in a critical review, pass judgment on, analyze.

revile v. *She reviled the maid for not dusting the furniture:* scold, berate, tongue-lash, upbraid, bawl out, castigate, vilify, denounce, disparage, deride, scorn, abuse, lash out at, reproach, rebuke; *Slang* dress down, sail into, chew out. **—Ant.** praise, extol, laud, commend.

revise v. *Ben Jonson tells us that Shakespeare never had to revise a manuscript:* correct, change, alter, modify, edit, redact, rewrite, redo, amend, blue-pencil, rectify, emend, emendate, doctor, overhaul, recast, review, tinker with, fix up, revamp; bring up to date, make an up-to-date version of, update.

revision n. *Revisions were made to bring the text up to date. The aged poet published a final revision of his works:* change, alteration, modification, correction, improvement, emendation, amendment; revised version, recension, edition.

revival n. *The 1960's brought a revival of folk music:* reawakening, rebirth, rejuvenation, renaissance, freshening, invigoration, quickening, recovery, regeneration, renewal, restoration, resurgence, resuscitation, revitalization, enkindling.

revive v. **1.** *The smelling salts revived her:* restore to consciousness, bring back to life, resuscitate. **2.** *His interesting lecture revived my interest in volcanology:* bring back to life, reanimate, rouse again, reawaken, infuse new life into, give new life to, refresh, freshen, renew. **3.** *The repertory company revived plays from 30 years ago:* present again, bring back into use, produce again, set going again, bring back into notice, make operative again, resurrect; *Slang* dig up, drag up; restage, reproduce, repeat.

revoke v. *The authorities will revoke your license if you get another speeding ticket. There's a campaign afoot to revoke current restrictions on immigration:* withdraw, take back; negate, annul, nullify, invalidate, vacate, void, declare null and void, cancel, abrogate, abolish, expunge, erase, quash, do away with; repeal, rescind, reverse, recall, call back, retract; override, overrule, countermand, set aside, disallow, dismiss, abjure, renounce, disclaim, repudiate. **—Ant.** restore, give, maintain, grant; authorize, validate.

revolt v. **1.** *Several tribes revolted against the new government policy:* rise, rebel, rise up, mutiny. **2.** *The violence in the movie revolted me:* disgust, repel, repulse, offend, go against, sicken, make one sick, nauseate, turn the stomach; make the flesh crawl, horrify, appall, shock, distress, *Slang* turn one off. **—n. 3.** *The peasants' revolt was put down by the dictator's*

troops: rebellion, active resistance against authority, insurrection, insurgency, uprising, coup, putsch, revolution, opposition, disorder, mutiny, sedition, dissent, factiousness. **—Ant.** 1 give allegiance to, give loyalty to, support, obey, bow, submit to. 2 attract, lure; delight, amuse, please, fascinate.

revolting adj. *It was a revolting spectacle:* disgusting, repulsive, repellent, repugnant, disagreeable, offensive, objectionable, distasteful, obnoxious, nasty, vile, foul, odious, invidious, horrid, shocking, appalling, horrible, horrific, grim, frightful, dreadful, sickening, nauseating, abhorrent, abominable, loathsome, hateful; malodorous, noxious, noisome, stinking. **—Ant.** pleasant, agreeable, attractive, delightful, charming, unobjectionable; sweet-smelling, fragrant.

revolution n. **1.** *Wagner brought about a revolution in music and musical taste:* complete change, radical new departure, basic reformation, big shift. **2.** *The Russian Revolution occurred on November 7, 1917. Hitler attempted a Nazi revolution in 1923:* overthrow of an established regime, replacement of an old regime, coup d'état, coup, putsch. **3.** *The American Revolution took place between 1775 and 1783:* (variously) revolutionary war, armed struggle, war of national liberation, insurrection, uprising, rising, rebellion, revolt, mutiny. **4.** *The earth makes one revolution around the sun each year:* revolving, circling, movement in an orbit, circumvolution, circumrotation. **5.** *The "78 RPM" on the old record means "78 revolutions per minute":* single turn, rotation, gyration. **—Ant.** 1 reaction, retrogression, regression. 2, 3 counterrevolution, countercoup, reaction, restoration, backlash.

revolutionary adj. **1.** *Revolutionary factions wanted a complete overthrow of the government:* opposed to the established order, revolutionist, radical, extremist, insurrectionary, insurgent, rebellious, mutinous, subversive, seditious, dissenting. **2.** *The inventor had a revolutionary idea:* radically innovative, fundamentally novel, unprecedented, superadvanced. **—Ant.** 1 reactionary, counterrevolutionary; loyalist, conservative. 2 old, usual.

revolve v. *The moon revolves around the earth:* move in orbit, go around, circle, rotate, circumrotate, turn, gyrate, wheel, twist, spin.

revulsion n. *Talk of the operation aroused feelings of revulsion in all of us:* strong disgust, loathing, repugnance, aversion, distaste, abhorrence, detestation. **—Ant.** attraction, fascination, relish, taste.

reward n. **1.** *A large reward is offered for the return of the ring. Eventually all evildoers get their just reward:* prize, compensation, recompense, payment, bounty, guerdon, remuneration, quid pro quo, award, consideration, premium, bonus; token of appreciation, deserts, wages, due, reckoning, what is coming to one. **—v. 2.** *If you do well in Spanish I'll reward you with a trip to Spain. Nero was well enough rewarded for his crimes:* repay, requite, recompense, compensate, remunerate, take care of. —**Ant.** 1 penalty, fine, damages, punishment. 2 punish, penalize.

rhapsodic *adj. Critics were rhapsodic over the new violinist:* ecstatic, elated, thrilled, transported, rapturous, overjoyed, excited, walking on air, blissful, in seventh heaven, exhilarated, on cloud nine, beside oneself, beaming, delirious. —**Ant.** sad, morose, depressed, disenchanted.

rhetoric *n.* **1.** *Cicero was a master of rhetoric. Flaubert was a fanatical believer in the principles of rhetoric:* art of speaking or writing, rules of composition, classic style. **2.** *Churchill's "Blood, sweat, and tears" speech is a masterpiece of rhetoric:* effective use of formal language, verbal communication, elocution, discourse, oratory, eloquence, high style, mannered language. **3.** *The speaker used a lot of rhetoric but said nothing of importance:* eloquence, magniloquence, grandiloquence, flamboyance, figures of speech, hyperbole, euphuism, empty phrases, fustian, *Slang* hot air, wind, hocus-pocus, hokum, hooey, bunkum, bunk.

rhetorical *adj.* **1.** *The ancients loved rhetorical fireworks, so popular lecturers were idolized like present-day rock stars:* flamboyant, highflown, bombastic, grandiloquent, oratorical, eloquent, showy, inflated, windy, grandiose, magniloquent, silver-tongued, extravagant, highsounding, ornate, aureate, florid, purple, flowery, embellished, euphuistic. **2.** *Carlyle's language is often so heavily larded with rhetorical words it's impossible to understand:* used for stylistic effect, expressive, decorative, ornamental. **3.** *The politician took his speechwriter's copy and made a few rhetorical changes for ease of delivery, balance, and effect:* stylistic, elocutionary. **4.** *The violences of the 1966 upheaval in China were mainly rhetorical:* verbal, linguistic, discursive; disputative, disputatious, argumentative.

rhythm *n. Rhythm is a basic component of music and language. Our diet follows the rhythm of the seasons:* fluctuation, recurrence, natural flow, recurrent alternation, flow pattern, time, movement, meter, measure, accent, beat, pulse, pulsation, throb, stress, cadence, number, rhythmic pattern, accentuation, emphasis, swing, lilt, syncopation.

ribald *adj. It's a revue with racy songs and ribald humor:* bawdy, lewd, risqué, vulgar, off-color, indecent, improper, crude, rude, coarse, uncouth, earthy, unrefined, gross, shocking, lascivious, licentious, libidinous, salacious, racy, wanton, rakish, raffish, prurient, suggestive.

rich *adj.* **1.** *I'm not rich but I'm comfortable:* well-off, well-to-do, wealthy, affluent, flush, moneyed, on easy street, propertied, prosperous, well-heeled, *Informal* in clover. **2.** *Rich silks and other materials were brought back from the Orient:* valuable, estimable, highly valued, precious, opulent, luxurious, sumptuous, splendid, prodigal, lavish, expensive, costly, fine, priceless. **3.** *Plum pudding is a rich dessert:* heavy, filling, full-bodied; sweet. **4.** *The carpets were*

rich red. *His voice was a rich baritone:* intense, lush, dark, deep, bright, vivid; resonant, deeptoned, sonorous, euphonious, mellow, mellifluous. **5.** *Our home was always rich in love and understanding:* abundant, abounding. **6.** *Manitoba has lots of rich farmland:* productive, fruitful, fertile, fecund, loamy, luxuriant, lush. —**Ant.** 1, 5, 6 poor. 1 impoverished, destitute, penniless, indigent, impecunious, penurious, needy, poverty-stricken. 2 worthless, valueless, inexpensive, cheap. 3 bland, dull, flat. 4 weak, flat, dull; high-pitched, tinny. 5 wanting, lacking, scarce, rare, scanty, meager. 6 unproductive, unfertile, unfruitful, barren, sterile, dry.

rickety *adj.* **1.** *My kid brother spent the summer rebuilding a rickety old barn:* tumbledown, shaky, unsteady, wobbly, tottering, flimsy, brokendown, deteriorated, dilapidated, decrepit. **2.** *When Boswell met him, Voltaire was a rickety old man but still sharp:* decrepit, weakjointed, feeble, frail, fragile, infirm, debilitated, weak, weakly, tottering, withered, wasted. —**Ant.** 1 sturdy, durable, steady, solid, sound.

rid *v. I want to rid this city of corruption! Will I ever be rid of this cold?:* free, purge, clear, eliminate, remove, unburden, disburden, disencumber, disabuse, liberate. —**Ant.** burden, encumber, take on, adopt.

riddance *n. The exterminator promised complete riddance of the roaches. He's gone, and good riddance:* clearing out, clearance, removal, ejection, expulsion, ouster, dislodgment; relief, deliverance, freeing. —**Ant.** encumbrance, adoption.

riddle *n. The riddle of the Sphinx was at last disclosed:* mystery, enigma, secret; puzzle, poser, conundrum, puzzler, problem, brain twister, rebus, *Slang* stumper.

ride *v.* **1.** *Do you know how to ride a horse?:* manage, control, handle. **2.** *The bicycle rode roughly on the bumpy road. He rode a motorcycle to the station. The politician rode on a wave of popularity:* move, move along, travel, progress, journey; transport, drive, carry, support; move along, be supported, be carried.

rider *n. A rider was attached to the will:* additional clause, addition, amendment, codicil, supplement, appendage, suffix, affix, adjunct, addendum, appendix, attachment.

ridge *n.* **1.** *The settlement was just over that ridge:* hill, rise, crest, hillock, mound, spine, knoll, hump, bank, bluff, promontory. **2.** *The potato chips have ridges:* rib, ripple, crinkle, crimp, wrinkle, corrugation, rim, fret, bar, weal, welt, wale.

ridicule *n.* **1.** *The new bridge was generally a subject of ridicule:* mockery, sneering, derision, derogation, disparagement, aspersion, scorn, sarcasm, taunt, jeer, gibe, snicker, ribbing, teasing, caricature, burlesque, travesty, lampoonery. —*v.* **2.** *His classmates ridiculed him:* make fun of, make sport of, poke fun at, mock, mimic, imitate insultingly, laugh at, laugh to scorn, sneer at, scoff at, belittle, treat with disrespect, deride, ride, disparage, humiliate, taunt, jeer, gibe at, twit, razz, josh, guy, rib, tease, make a butt of, make sport of, play tricks on, make a monkey of, caricature, burlesque, lampoon, parody. —**Ant.** 1, 2 praise, honor; respect. 1 homage, veneration, deference.

ridiculous *adj. That's the most ridiculous thing I've ever heard!:* absurd, ludicrous, preposterous, asinine, nonsensical, foolish, silly, idiotic, fatuous, inane, irrational, destitute of reason, unreasonable, senseless, frivolous; incredible, astonishing, fantastic, outlandish, queer, odd, grotesque, bizarre, laughable, comical, funny, droll, amusing; *Informal* hysterical, farcical, crazy, nutty, screwy, screwball.

rife *adj.* **1.** *These marshlands were once rife with mosquitos:* teeming, swarming, alive with, thick, populous, crowded, packed, chockfull, *Informal* plumbfull; dense, close, solid, studded. **2.** *Poverty is rife on the small island:* prevalent, general, prevailing, predominant; extensive, universal, widespread, common, far-reaching; epidemic, pandemic.

riffraff *n. The prices were raised in an effort to keep out the riffraff:* mob, herd, masses, rabble, *French* canaille, crowd, peasantry, rank and file, proletariat, *Slang* proles, commonalty, lumpen proletariat; trash, scum, dregs, vermin, *Slang* the great unwashed. —**Ant.** gentry, upper crust, swells, bigwigs, high muck-a-mucks.

rifle *v. The burglar rifled the safe:* search and rob, rob, plunder, go through, pillage, ransack, ravage, burglarize, sack, loot, despoil, spoliate.

rift *n.* **1.** *The blast created a rift in the rock face:* cleft, split, crack, fissure, fracture, break, chink, breach, rent, cut, slit, aperture, gash, rupture; chasm, crevice, gap, cranny, fault, crevasse, abyss, gulch, gully, gulf, gorge, ravine. **2.** *There should be no rifts between good friends:* division, breach, rupture, break, breakup, misunderstanding, disagreement, quarrel, falling out.

rig *v.* **1.** *They rigged themselves out in finery:* clothe, costume, dress, arm, equip, furnish, kit, outfit, provision, set up, supply, array, attire. **2.** *The mayor rigged the election:* fix, manipulate, tamper with, trump up, doctor, engineer, fiddle with, gerrymander, juggle, manipulate, arrange.

right *adj.* **1.** *Nannies inculcate right behavior:* good, exemplary, proper, decent, morally excellent, virtuous, nice, fitting, seemly, rightminded, moral, upright, righteous, honest, aboveboard, ethical, scrupulous, honorable, unimpeachable, correct, punctilious, meet, square, fair and square, even-handed; equitable, just, fair. **2.** *That's not the right way to do it. Mussolini did not have the right answer:* valid, allowable, admissible, satisfactory; correct, accurate, free from error, unmistaken, perfect, infallible, exact, precise, true, factual, veracious, veridical, truthful. **3.** *He's not in his right mind:* rational, normal, regular, sane, sound, reasonable. **4.** *The right time to act is now:* most appropriate, suitable, seemly, fitting, proper, becoming; desirable, favorable, preferable, convenient, opportune, advantageous, ideal. **5.** *From these three identical "Rembrandts" pick out the right one, i.e., the true original:* actual, genuine, real, authentic; definite, clear-cut, certain; unquestiona-

ble, irrefutable, undisputed, incontestable; rightful, lawful, legal, licit, legitimate, valid. —*n.* **6.** *The Bourbon pretender pressed his right to the throne. You have the right to remain silent:* just claim, legal title, legal claim, due, moral claim, justification, birthright, inheritance; privilege, prerogative, liberty, power, license, freedom, grant, permission, sanction; authority, legal power, authorization, jurisdiction. **7.** *The defendant does not know right from wrong:* good, virtue, goodness, righteousness, moral excellence, good behavior, good actions, morality, morals; integrity, honor, nobleness, uprightness, propriety, rectitude, probity; what ought to be, what should be. **8.** Often **rights** *He bought the rights to the play:* ownership, deed, proprietorship, authorization, warrant, interest in property. —*adv.* **9.** *Losing no time, he went right to the heart of the matter:* directly, promptly, straight, straightaway, completely. **10.** *These shoes don't fit right. The curtains are hanging right:* correctly, appropriately, suitably, properly, accurately, perfectly; exactly, precisely, just. **11.** *Everything came out right in the end:* well, favorably, satisfactorily, *Informal* O.K. **12.** *I'll be right there:* immediately, at once, directly, presently, in a moment. —*v.* **13.** *A crane was used to right the toppled statue:* set upright, stand up, restore to the proper position. **14.** *The nationalist side wants to right many old grievances. The court ruling will right some existing injustices:* correct, put right, amend, solve, remedy, put in order; vindicate, redress, recompense, make up for, make restitution for. —**Ant.** 1, 2, 4, 5, 7, 10, 11 wrong. 1 bad, foul, sinful, iniquitous, nefarious, improper, indecent, unvirtuous, immoral; dishonest, unethical, unscrupulous, dishonorable; unjust, unfair, false, illegitimate. 2 unsatisfactory; incorrect, inaccurate, mistaken, invalid, erroneous, erring, imperfect, inexact, fallacious, untrue, unfactual, false, untruthful. 3 irrational, abnormal, insane, unsound. 4 inappropriate, unsuitable, unseemly, unfitting, unbecoming; undesirable, unfavorable, inconvenient, disadvantageous. 5 false, fake, phony, sham, counterfeit, fraudulent; indefinite, uncertain, questionable, contestable, unlawful, illegal, illicit, illegitimate. 7 evil, badness, venality, villainy, sinfulness, corruption, transgression, iniquity, bad behavior, immorality; dishonor, impropriety. 9 indirectly, circuitously, slowly; incompletely. 10 incorrectly, improperly; inaccurately, imperfectly. 11 badly, unfavorably, poorly. 13 set down, put down; make crooked, topple.

righteous *adj. The colonial governor, while severe, was a righteous man:* moral, honorable, ethical, honest, upright, elevated, just, fair, equitable, good; godly, pious, devout, God-fearing, religious, reverent, holy, spiritual, pure in heart; virtuous, chaste, incorrupt, unsullied, blameless, innocent. —**Ant.** unrighteous, immoral, bad, evil, wicked, sinful, villainous, dishonorable, disreputable, dishonest, corrupt, unscrupulous, unprincipled, false, iniquitous, unjust, unfair; ungodly, irreligious, unholy, irreverent, unvirtuous.

rightful *adj. The rightful heir to the throne is the Crown Prince:* having a right, having a just claim, deserving, right, true, proper, correct, legitimate, legal, lawful, held by a just or legal claim, allowed, sanctioned, authorized, valid, constitutional, designated, prescribed, inalienable, deserved, appropriate, fitting, condign. —**Ant.** unrightful, untrue, improper, unjust, incorrect, illegitimate, illegal, unlawful, usurping.

rigid *adj.* **1.** *Rubber bands are not rigid. Don't be so rigidrelax:* stiff, unyielding, inflexible, unpliant, unbending, inelastic, fixed, hard, set, firm, tense, taut; wooden. **2.** *The sergeant's a rigid disciplinarian:* strict, stringent, hard, stern, severe, harsh, austere, sharp, rigorous, exacting; stubborn, unrelenting, obdurate, uncompromising, inflexible, unbending, unyielding, strong, firm, fixed, set, cut and dried, clear-cut; straitlaced, formal, puritanical. —**Ant.** 1, 2 flexible, yielding. 1 pliant, supple, limber, bending, mobile, elastic, plastic. 2 lenient, soft, tolerant, indulgent, merciful, lax; informal.

rigorous *adj.* **1.** *The training involved rigorous exercises:* demanding, challenging, trying, stern, austere, harsh, exacting, tough, very harsh, severe, strict, stringent. **2.** *The Babylonians were capable of rigorous computations:* exact, accurate, correct, precise, scrupulous, meticulous, punctilious.

rile *v. Her haughtiness has always riled us all:* irritate, pique, vex, annoy, irk, provoke, gall, chafe, miff, nettle, gripe, plague, aggravate, bother, roil, peeve; *Slang* give someone a pain, get someone's goat, get in someone's hair, rub one the wrong way. —**Ant.** soothe, calm, cool, pacify, placate.

rim *n. The wagon wheel had an iron rim. We stood on the canyon's rim:* edge, outer edge, border, margin, side; brim, verge, brink, ledge, lip. —**Ant.** core, center, hub, inside.

ring[1] *n.* **1.** *The dancers formed a ring around the maypole:* circle, perimeter, circumference, loop, circuit, hoop; cordon. **2.** *The police just rounded up a ring of thieves:* gang, band, party, cabal, syndicate, combine, league, cartel, federation, bloc. —*v.* **3.** *She instructed the pupils to ring the correct answer:* draw a ring around, circle, circumscribe. **4.** *Ring the castle so no one can escape:* surround, encircle, encompass; enclose, seal off; blockade, besiege.

ring[2] *v.* **1.** *The bells rang throughout the valley:* sound, resound, reverberate, vibrate, fill the air, tintinnabulate, chime, peal, clang, knell, toll, jingle, jangle, tinkle; strike. **2.** *The airplane rang in a new era. You have to ring for service:* announce, make known, broadcast, proclaim, herald; call, summon, signal, buzz. **3.** *The arcade rang with gunfire:* reverberate, resound, echo. —*n.* **4.** *The ring of bells filled the air:* ringing sound, resonance, reverberation, tintinnabulation, chime, peal, clang, ringing, striking, vibration, toll, knell, tinkle, ting-a-ling. **5.** *His story had a suspicious ring to it:* quality, sound, tone, aura.

riot *n.* **1.** *The police tried to quell the riot:* public disturbance, disorder, violence, breach of the peace, lawlessness; tumult, strife, turbulence, outburst, turmoil, trouble, Donnybrook, rumpus, melee, fracas, commotion, uproar, pandemonium, confusion; revolt, rebellion, insurrection, uprising. —*v.* **2.** *The dissidents rioted in the capital:* break the peace, raise an uproar, be violent, kick up a row, act up, run amok, run riot, rage, rampage, take the law into one's own hands, rebel, resist, revolt, mutiny, rise in arms, arise.

rip *v.* **1.** *She ripped the drawing in half:* tear, rend, slash, rive, cleave, rupture, shred, cut apart. **2.** *His shirt ripped at the seam:* tear open, split, burst, sever. —*n.* **3.** *Sew that rip in your shirt:* tear, rent, rent made by ripping, split, cut, slash, laceration, rift, incision, cleavage, fracture, fissure, slit, gap.

ripe *adj.* **1.** *Are the tomatoes ripe?:* fully grown, fully developed, mature, maturated; mellow, seasoned. **2.** *The time is ripe for our departure:* come, due; timely; ideal, perfect; consummate, complete, accomplished, finished; fully prepared, fit, primed, ready. —**Ant.** 1 unripe, unready, underdeveloped, undeveloped, immature, green, raw, unseasoned. 2 incomplete, unaccomplished, unprepared, unfit, untimely, unready.

ripen *v. All the plants ripened:* mature, age, grow, develop, mellow, grow up, maturate, evolve, blossom, flower, come into season.

ripple *v.* **1.** *A breeze rippled the water:* wave, undulate, ruffle, purl. **2.** *Her long skirt rippled as she walked:* agitate, curl, dimple. —*n.* **3.** *There was a ripple of excitement in the crowd:* wavelet, wave, ruffling, undulation.

rise *v.* **1.** *He rose from the chair. I rise at dawn:* get up, stand, arise; get out of bed, meet the day. **2.** *The people rose against tyranny and injustice:* arise in opposition, rebel, revolt, resist, mutiny; go to war, take up arms; take the law into one's own hands; disobey, defy; strike, stand up, meet, face. **3.** *Heat rises. The mountains hereabouts rise to 2000 feet:* go up, move upward, ascend, climb; mount, soar, spire, tower; extend directly upward, slope upward. **4.** *Food costs rose sharply. The temperature kept rising:* increase, become greater, rocket, spire, surge, become larger, swell, burgeon, become louder. **5.** *He quickly rose to a position of importance:* reach a higher level or rank, rise in the world, work one's way up, be successful; climb, go up, succeed, prosper, thrive, flourish. **6.** *Our hopes rose after hearing the good news:* soar, surge, mount, grow, improve, lift, elevate, balloon. —*n.* **7.** *His rise in the company was meteoric:* rising, advance; progress, advancement, headway; growth, increase in rank, climb. **8.** *New cures for cancer are on the rise. I forecast another rise in food costs:* increase, upswing, march; addition, gain, augmentation, enlargement, expansion, extension. —**Ant.** 1, 3–7 fall. 1 sit, sit down; lie down, retire. 3–6 sink, descend, drop, plunge. 4 decrease, decline, shrink, lessen, abate. 6 descent. 8 decrease, drop, plunge, decline, lessening, contraction, downturn.

risible *adj. The thought of his doing the job is risible:* funny, amusing, comic, comical, laugh-provoking, laughable, droll, humorous, hilarious, rich, ludicrous, absurd, ridiculous, farcical, priceless, hysterical. **—Ant.** sober, solemn.

risk *n.* **1.** *You're taking a big risk driving so fast. Buying land you've never seen is a risk:* hazard, peril, danger, imperilment, endangerment, jeopardy; chance, venture, speculation, gamble, uncertainty. **—v. 2.** *It's senseless to risk other people's lives:* endanger, jeopardize, put in jeopardy, imperil, put in peril. **3.** *If we stop, we'll risk missing the train. It's foolish to risk money on a throw of the dice:* take the chance of, run the chance of; venture, hazard, speculate, dare, try one's luck, tempt Providence, have a fling at.

risky *adj. Stunt driving is a risky occupation:* hazardous, perilous, dangerous, fraught with danger, unsafe, unprotected, precarious, insecure, daring, venturesome, adventurous, daredevil; uncertain, ticklish, chancy, hit or miss, haphazard. **—Ant.** safe, sure, secure, certain.

risqué *adj. The risqué story made her blush:* off-color, improper, ribald, bawdy, indecorous, indecent; indelicate, immodest, immoral; racy, spicy, suggestive, daring, salacious, lascivious, lewd, licentious, offensive, vulgar, coarse, gross, dirty, obscene, smutty, pornographic, blue.

rite *n. The marriage rites were performed by a priest. The local tribes have curious initiation rites:* formal act or procedure, formality, ceremony, ceremonial, liturgy, ritual, service; solemnity, observance.

ritual *n.* **1.** *The priest performed the ritual:* ceremony, rite. **—adj. 2.** *For her, making tea was a ritual act:* ceremonial, formal, sacramental. **—Ant.** unceremonious, informal.

ritzy *adj. We lunched at that ritzy new hotel:* chic, elegant, stylish, luxurious, sumptuous; *Slang* classy, swank, high-class, posh, high-toned, tony, snazzy, spiffy, sharp. **—Ant.** *Slang* crummy, dumpy, schlocky, tatty.

rival *n.* **1.** *Although the boxers were rivals in the ring, they were really good friends:* competitor, contestant, disputant, contender, opponent, adversary, antagonist, foe, enemy. **—adj. 2.** *The rival companies tried to outsell one another:* contending, competing, adversary, opposing. **—v. 3.** *The two teams rivaled each other for the championship:* compete with, contend with, try to win from, clash with, do battle with, fight, strive. **4.** *Nothing can rival her cooking:* be an equal of, equal, be a match for, match, touch, approach; excel, surpass, outdo, eclipse, outshine. **—Ant.** 1 ally, friend; associate, helper, assistant, supporter, champion, abettor, backer. 2 allied, noncompeting. 3 aid, assist, help, support, back.

river *n. A river wound through the valley:* watercourse, waterway, artery, stream.

road *n. They live down the road:* way, thoroughfare, boulevard, avenue, street, route, roadway, parkway, expressway, highway, turnpike, freeway, throughway, byway, trail, lane, path.

roam *v. Troubadors roamed throughout medie-* val Europe: travel, ramble, rove, range, meander, jaunt, gad, stray, gallivant, wander, stroll, traipse, tramp, peregrinate, divagate, drift.

roar *v.* **1.** *The lions roared. The crowd roared for more:* howl, bellow, bay, growl, cry; thunder, boom, resound; shout, scream, bawl, cry aloud, yell, vociferate, bluster, clamor. **2.** *We roared at the comic's antics:* laugh loudly, guffaw; howl. **—n. 3.** *We heard the roar of a wild animal. The roar of airplane engines announced a coming air raid:* cry, howl, bellow, bay, growl, grunt, snort; yell, outcry, bawl, shout, shriek, scream, bluster, clamor, rumble, boom, uproar, outburst, thunder, roll, racket, blare, din, noise.

rob *v. The looters robbed everything they could lay hands on. To get rich quick, they decided to rob a bank:* hold up, stick up, raid; *(loosely)* steal from, thieve, burgle, burglarize, ransack, pillage, pilfer, sack, forage, despoil, plunder, loot, *Slang* heist; filch, steal, seize, purloin, rifle, lift, carry off, appropriate, help oneself to; skin, swindle, cheat, bamboozle, bilk, fleece, embezzle.

robber *n. The robber stole things you wouldn't have expected him to take:* thief, bandit, outlaw, crook, brigand; *(variously)* burglar, stickup-man, second-story man, yegg, embezzler, con man, sharper, swindler, larcenist, plunderer, highwayman, marauder, raider, pirate, buccaneer, despoiler, forager, pickpocket, rustler.

robe *n. Robes are standard apparel in the Middle East:* gown; *(loosely)* dress, garment, costume, vestment, habit; *(variously)* dressing gown, bathrobe, housecoat, negligee, smock, kimono, duster, lounging robe.

robust *adj. Such strenuous exercises could only be endured by a robust person:* hale, hardy, strong, tough, powerful, mighty, potent, forceful, puissant; healthy, well, wholesome, sound, healthful, hearty, fit, in fine fettle, able-bodied, rugged, sturdy, firm, athletic; virile, muscular, brawny, sinewy, wiry, husky, strapping; vigorous, lusty, stalwart, stout, staunch, energetic, active. **—Ant.** weak, unhealthy, infirm, unsound, unfit, sickly, frail, feeble, delicate, fragile, puny, anemic, slender, thin, emaciated.

rock¹ *v.* **1.** *The boat rocked on the rough seas:* sway to and fro, move backward and forward, move from side to side; swing, toss, roll, pitch, flounder; wobble, totter, bob, quake, shake, convulse, agitate; undulate, oscillate. **2.** *The explosion rocked the valley. The scandal rocked the community:* shake, jar, convulse; disturb, upset, stun. **—n. 3.** *The rock of the cradle quieted the baby:* rocking, undulation, sway; wobbling, tottering, bobbing; shaking; convulsion.

rock² *n. There are dangerous rocks in the road:* stone, boulder; *(variously)* crag, cliff, reef; pebble, flint; gravel, limestone, marble.

rocky *adj.* **1.** *The rocky fields yielded scant crops:* stony, rugged, flinty, hard, inflexible, jagged, petrified, rough, craggy. **2.** *The professor's reasoning was a little rocky:* dizzy, doubtful, ill, shaky, tottering, tricky, uncertain, undependable, unreliable, unsteady.

rod *n.* **1.** *He waved the rod over the hat and a*

rabbit appeared: stick, staff; (*variously*) wand, baton, scepter, mace, cane, crook, alpenstock, caduceus, stanchion, stake, pale, pole, swagger stick. **2.** *Spare the rod and spoil the child:* stick, cudgel; (*variously*) switch, birch, cane, rattan, lash, whip, scourge; (*loosely*) punishment, penalty, retribution.

rogue *n. He's nothing but a rogue who'd sell his own mother!:* dishonest person, deceiver, fraud, mountebank, rotter, rascal, scoundrel, scamp, rapscallion, cur, good-for-nothing, wretch, knave, varlet, blackguard, villain, snake in the grass, bad man, bounder, evildoer, malefactor; miscreant, reprobate, hellion; mischief-maker; scalawag, scamp, scapegrace, devil.

roil *v.* **1.** *The heavy rain roiled the stream:* muddy, foul, dirty, pollute, befoul, contaminate. **2.** *She roiled my peace of mind:* disturb, agitate, perturbate, stir, stir up, churn, whip, whip up. **3.** *They were roiled by the turn of events:* rile, anger, irritate, irk, vex, peeve, provoke. —**Ant.** clarify, calm.

role *n.* **1.** *What role did the actress play?:* character, part, characterization, impersonation, portrayal, representation, persona, personification; pose, posture, guise. **2.** *In his role as bailiff, he requested those in the courtroom to rise:* capacity, function, duty, service, chore, task, assignment, post; job, work.

roll *v.* **1.** *Roll the ball to me. Roll over, Fido!:* turn over and over; turn, revolve, rotate, gyrate; spin, go round, swirl, whirl; wheel, swing, flip, turn. **2.** *The car rolled to a stop. The tide rolled in:* wheel, coast; flow, swell, billow, surge. **3.** *The blast rolled throughout the valley:* boom, crack, rumble, thunder, roar, sound, resound, reverberate, echo. **4.** *Roll the yarn before you start knitting:* wind, curl, coil, loop, twist, twirl, furl, knot, entwine; form into a ball. **5.** *The ship rolled on the rough seas:* rock, undulate, toss, tumble, tumble about; lurch, pitch, reel, sway. —*n.* **6.** *The players watched the roll of the dice. You'll get used to the roll of the sea:* rolling, turning, tumble, toss, throw; rocking, tumbling, tossing, undulation. **7.** *Archeologists found papyrus rolls in the ancient ruins:* scroll, tube, cylinder, spool, reel. **8.** *The teacher read the roll of graduates:* list, catalog, inventory, roster, muster, schedule. **9.** *The roll of thunder presages a storm:* rumble, rumbling, boom, booming, thunder, drumming, drumbeat, reverberation.

rollicking *adj. We had a rollicking time at the picnic:* joyous, happy, gay, merry, cheerful, lighthearted, gleeful, mirthful, hearty, rip-roaring, jolly, jovial, jocular, jocund, hysterical, devil-may-care; lively, spirited, free and easy, exuberant, full of play, frolicsome, frolicking, playful, romping, gamboling, sprightly, bright, sparkling, sunny. —**Ant.** joyless, unhappy, sad, sorrowful, sorry, distressing, depressing, cheerless, mirthless; dull, somber, gloomy.

roly-poly *adj. He was a roly-poly little boy:* fat, plump, rotund, pudgy. —**Ant.** scrawny, gaunt, skinny.

romance *n.* **1.** *She liked to read romances:* love story; novel, fiction, melodrama, made-up fanci-ful story, fairy tale, fantasy. **2.** *Shakespeare immortalized the romance of Romeo and Juliet:* love affair, affair of the heart, relationship, affair, attachment; amour, idyll, tender passion; courtship, flirtation. **3.** *Much of what she says is pure romance:* invention, wishful thinking, self-delusion, imagination, illusion, flight of fancy; exaggeration, concoction, fiction, fabrication; *Informal* tall story, fish story, cock-and-bull story, moonshine, bosh. **4.** *Are you drawn by the romance of faraway places?:* romantic quality, exoticism, appealing quality, allure, pull, fascination, call.

romantic *adj.* **1.** *Judy Garland made many romantic movies:* concerning romance, conducive to romance, idyllic, sentimental; melodramatic. **2.** *They're such a romantic couple!:* loving, amorous, ardent, enamored, passionate, impassioned, warmhearted, fond, devoted; sentimental, tender, sensitive; ardent, fervent; *Informal* mushy, soppy. **3.** *Don't get carried away with romantic notions:* high-flown, idealized, impractical, improbable, rhapsodical; unreal, unrealistic, idealistic, utopian, flighty, whimsical, extravagant, fanciful, imaginary, dreamy, visionary; fantastic, preposterous, quixotic. —**Ant.** 1–3 unromantic. 1 realistic, prosaic, uninspiring. 2 unloving, unimpassioned, dispassionate, cold-hearted; unsentimental, insensitive; unaffectionate.

Romeo *n. Tell her Romeo is on the phone again:* lover, Lothario, Lochinvar, Don Juan, Casanova, paramour, beau, boyfriend, wooer, swain, gallant, inamorato, cavalier, sheik.

romp *v. The children romped in the park:* play in a lively manner, frolic, run around, frisk, rollick, caper, gambol, disport, disport oneself, sport, jump about, skip, hop, cut up.

rook *n.* **1.** *The poker player was a rook:* sharper, cardsharp, cheat, swindler. —*v.* **2.** *She was rooked out of her savings:* cheat, swindle, rob, fleece, defraud.

room *n.* **1.** *Go to the room at the end of the hall. There were no rooms at the inn:* chamber, cubicle, compartment; lodging, lodging place. **2.** *That cabinet takes up too much room:* space, extent, range, scope, expanse, territory, area, volume, elbow room. **3.** *There's no room for error here:* chance, provision, leeway, allowance, margin.

roomy *adj. The camper looks small but is really quite roomy:* spacious, capacious, generous, commodious, sizable, ample, expansive; wide, long, lengthy, broad, extensive, large, vast, immense, big, huge, boundless, unlimited. —**Ant.** small, tiny, uncomfortable, closed-in, cramped; short; bounded, limited, confined.

root[1] *n.* **1.** *The root of a flower is as delicate as its petals are. Don't pull out your hair by the roots:* underground part, stem, embedded part, bulb, tubes; radicle, radix; hidden base; lower part, bottom. **2.** *Let's get to the root of the problem:* basic part, basic element, fundamental, essential element, most important part, base, foundation. **3.** *The roots of his neuroses go back to childhood:* origin, source, spring, derivation, fount, fountain, fountainhead, foundation, basis, ground; starting point, motive, prime mover, determining condition, reason, rationale; rise, mainspring, occasion, inception, beginning, commencement, start. —*v.* **4.** *Root the bulbs in potting soil. Are you rooted to that spot?:* fix, set, establish; fasten, stick, nail, bind.

root² *v. Be sure to root for the home team:* cheer on, cheer, encourage, shout for, stick up for, bolster, boost, pull for, applaud, hail, acclaim, clap; support, back, second.

rope *n. They put a rope around the calf's neck:* strand, cable, cord, cordage, line, hawser.

roster *n. Her name was on the roster of night nurses:* muster, roll, list, register, listing, slate, panel, catalog, record, schedule, posting, agenda, docket, cadre.

rostrum *n. The orator stepped up to the rostrum:* stage, platform, dais, stand, pulpit, lectern, podium, soapbox, stump.

rosy *adj.* **1.** *My darling has such rosy cheeks:* pink, blushing, reddish, reddening, flushed, flushing, blooming, ruddy, rubicund, rubescent, florid, glowing, inflamed, high-colored. **2.** *The future is rosy:* rose-colored, hopeful, cheerful, cheering, inspiriting, encouraging, promising, full of promise, reassuring, hopeful, optimistic, looking up, bright, auspicious, favorable, of good omen, propitious, felicitous; confident. —**Ant.** 1 pale, pallid, ashen, gray, whitish; sickly. 2 cheerless, discouraging, unpromising, hopeless, pessimistic, inauspicious; insecure, unsure.

rot *v.* **1.** *The unrefrigerated food rotted:* spoil, go bad, decay, decompose, putrefy, putresce, disintegrate, wither up, molder; go to pieces, fall into decay, deteriorate, degenerate, break down, crumble. **2.** *Equally immoderate quantities of drink and ambition rotted his mind:* pervert, debase, defile, warp, deprave; infect, poison; corrupt, pollute, contaminate, tamper with; taint, stain; mar, impair, damage, injure, harm, hurt. —*n.* **3.** *The rot has only begun to set in:* rotting, decay, rottenness, dry rot, decomposition, deterioration, disintegration; putrescence, putrefaction, putridity, purulence; contamination, corruption. **4.** *Slang You don't believe that rot, do you?:* nonsense, tommyrot, bosh, bunk, bull, balderdash, poppycock, gobbledygook, twaddle, stuff and nonsense, moonshine, flapdoodle, inanity, absurdity, flummery, fiddlefaddle, trash, rubbish, gibberish, jabber, drivel, blather, folderol.

rotate *v.* **1.** *The moon rotates around the earth:* move about a center, turn around on an axis, go round, turn, revolve, spin, roll, circle, reel, circulate, whirl, gyrate, twirl, twist, swirl, wheel, eddy, pirouette, pivot, swivel. **2.** *The two guards rotated between the day and night shifts:* alternate, change, take turns, interchange, act interchangeably; go from one to the other.

rotten *adj.* **1.** *Don't buy rotten fruit!:* decomposing, decomposed, decaying, decayed, putrid, putrefied, putrescent, purulent, tainted, moldering, worm-eaten, bad, rancid, fetid, reeky, foul, rank. **2.** *To clear a town of rotten officials is*

easier said than done: dishonest, corrupt, deceitful, insincere, faithless, unscrupulous, dishonorable, disgraceful, contemptible, treacherous, untrustworthy, double-dealing, two-faced, devious, villainous, iniquitous, scurvy, crooked, criminal, vicious, venal, mercenary; immoral, indecent, dissolute. **3.** *Informal That was a rotten trick:* very bad, base, contemptible; unpleasant, nasty, dirty, filthy, scurrilous, unforgivable. —**Ant.** 1 wholesome, untainted, fresh, pure, unspoiled, good. 2 honest, scrupulous, honorable, trustworthy; moral, decent, incorruptible.

rotund *adj.* **1.** *A beanbag is of a generally rotund shape:* round, globular, bulbous, rounded, spherical, ball-like, circular, ring-like; ovoid, egg-shaped, ovate, curved. **2.** *The rotund woman needed to lose weight:* plump, fat, obese, full-fleshed, corpulent, fleshy, chubby, tubby, pudgy, lumpish, stout, portly, potbellied. —**Ant.** 1 angular, square, edged. 2 thin, slender, slim, trim, lean, lank, lanky, skinny, gaunt, scrawny, rawboned, emaciated, angular.

roué *n. His reputation as a roué was known to most of the coeds:* rake, libertine, lecher, cad, bounder, profligate, seducer, debauchee, womanizer, rakehell, wanton, rip, playboy, philanderer, dallier, trifler, Don Juan, Lothario, Casanova; *Slang* wolf, skirt-chaser.

rough *adj.* **1.** *Raw wool is a rough material. We rode over rough terrain:* coarse, unsmooth, uneven, jagged, ragged, rough-hewn, irregular, broken, craggy, unlevel, bumpy, rocky, scraggy; (*variously*) rugged, scratchy, knotty, stubbly, scaly, scabrous, chapped, gnarled. **2.** *Football is a rough game. We sailed in rough seas:* violent, rigorous, rugged; tough, violently disturbed, agitated, choppy, turbulent, turbid, roiled, tumultuous, tempestuous, stormy, raging; untamed, wild, savage, ferocious. **3.** *Ten lashes is mighty rough punishment:* sharp, harsh, tough, austere, stringent, severe, ungentle, hard, unfeeling, cruel, brutal; inconsiderate; extreme, drastic. **4.** *He had a rough manner:* boorish, rude, ill-mannered, unmannerly, ungentlemanly, uncourtly, ungenteel; unpolished, unrefined, raw, inelegant, ill-bred, ungracious, uncouth; bearish, loutish, churlish, crusty, gruff, bluff, surly, gauche, awkward, clumsy; blunt, brusque, abrupt; coarse, vulgar, indelicate, crude; callow, green. **5.** *The migrant workers have had a rough life:* without ordinary comforts, uncomfortable, unluxurious; difficult, unpleasant, tough, rugged, hard, difficult, austere. **6.** *This is just a rough plan:* not elaborated, unfinished, incomplete, not perfected, imperfect, crude, hastily done; quick, hasty; vague, sketchy, general, rudimentary, preliminary, approximate, not exact, inexact, vague, imprecise. **7.** *He had a rough voice:* gruff, husky, raspy, rasping, hoarse, grating, jarring, raucous, strident, harsh; inharmonious, discordant, cacophonous, unmusical. —*v.* **8.** *Hard work roughed his hands:* roughen, make rough, coarsen. **9.** *The collection agency paid hoodlums to rough up the "deadhead":* treat violently, manhandle, push around, physically intimidate, brutalize, beat, thrash; *Slang* beat on, do a number on, knock on. **10.** *The writer roughed out his next novel:* indicate in rough form, prepare hastily, do roughly, draft, outline, sketch out. —**Ant.** 1, 2, 4, 5, 8 smooth. 1 smooth-surfaced, regular, unbroken, level, plain, flat; soft, silky, satiny, velvety. 2 calm, easy, gentle, tender; tranquil, quiet; tamed, mild, halcyon. 3 soft, mild, kind, lenient, just, considerate. 4 polite, courteous, civil, well-mannered, mannerly, gentlemanly, courtly, genteel; polished, refined, urbane, elegant, well-bred; gracious, gentle; graceful, delicate, cultivated, sophisticated. 5 comfortable, luxurious, velvety, easy, cushy, pleasant, plush, nice. 6 elaborated, finished, well-made, complete, perfected, perfect, detailed, specific, exact, precise. 8 make smooth, smoothen, make soft, mollify, soften.

round *adj.* **1.** *Oranges are round:* circular, globular, globoid, cylindrical, orbed, spherical, spheroid, ball-shaped; elliptical, oval, ovate, ovoid, egg-shaped, pear-shaped; rounded, curved. **2.** *He was a short, round man:* rotund, full-fleshed, obese, corpulent, fat, full-formed, plump, chubby, tubby, pudgy, stout, portly. **3.** *Give me a round dozen and I'll pay in cash:* entire, full, whole, complete, perfect; unbroken, intact, undivided; thorough, total. **4.** *He spoke in round tones:* full and rich, sonorous, resonant, smooth, flowing, fluent; harmonious, mellifluent. —*n.* **5.** *A round of parties ushered in the New Year. Let's order a round of drinks:* complete course, circle, series, succession, procession, progression, cycle. **6.** Often **rounds** *The postman made his rounds:* circuit, beat, route, watch. —*v.* **7.** *The stagecoach rounded the bend:* travel around, go around, make a circuit, skirt. —**Ant.** 1 angular, rectangular, square, many-sided, polygonal. 2 slim, thin, trim, slender, skinny, lean, lank, gaunt, angular, rawboned, emaciated. 3 incomplete, broken, imperfect, divided. 4 rough, gruff, harsh, hoarse, grating, jarring, shrill, strident; inharmonious.

roundabout *adj.* *He arrived at the solution in a roundabout way:* indirect, meandering, labyrinthine, circuitous, sinuous, twisting, rambling, erratic, discursive, tortuous, devious, oblique, zigzag, winding, serpentine; circumlocutory, wordy; random, desultory. —**Ant.** straight, direct.

roundup *n.* *It was time for the fall roundup:* gathering, herding, assembly, collection, muster, marshalling, rally; summary, survey.

rouse *v.* **1.** *They had to rouse her from a deep sleep:* awaken, wake, awake, wake up, get up, arouse, activate, call, summon; arise, stir. **2.** *The speaker roused the mob to acts of violence:* excite, animate, incite, prod, stir up, provoke, arouse, inflame, move, goad, stimulate, pique, instigate, foment, galvanize, spur, *Slang* turn on. —**Ant.** 2 soothe, pacify, quell, restrain, curb.

rout *n.* **1.** *Napoleon's army suffered a complete rout at Waterloo:* disastrous defeat, total repulse, ruin, beating, drubbing, licking, disorderly retreat, disorderly flight, complete dispersal; panic, chaos, disorganization. —*v.* **2.** *Joan of*

Arc routed the English at Orleans: put to flight, scatter, throw into confusion; repel, drive off, repulse, chase away, drive away; defeat, vanquish, worst, overpower, overthrow, overcome, crush, subdue, conquer, quell; drub, lambaste, beat, thrash; *Informal* lick, trim, cream, clobber.

route *n.* **1.** *Which route do I take to Denver?:* course, way for passage, itinerary; pass, road for travel, passage; (*variously*) parkway, highway, thoroughfare, road, roadway, turnpike, throughway, artery, boulevard, path, track, run, tack. **2.** *A mailman's route can be a long hike:* fixed course or territory, beat, round, circuit. —*v.* **3.** *Cars were routed around the accident:* send by a particular route, forward by a specific route; direct, ship, dispatch, remit, transmit; detour.

routine *n.* **1.** *Getting up at dawn is part of his daily routine:* regular procedure, practice, established usage, custom, ordinary way; method, system, arrangement, order, operation, formula, technique. —*adj.* **2.** *A routine medical checkup is advisable at least once a year:* customary, conventional, usual; regular, typical, normal. **3.** *The story has a routine plot:* predictable, unexceptional, dull, habitual, boring, periodic, tedious, ordinary, run-of-the-mill. —**Ant.** 2, 3 special, uncustomary, unusual, irregular, abnormal, different, exceptional, extraordinary.

rove *v.* *My grandfather loved to rove the countryside:* wander, wander about, roam, ramble, travel, meander, gad about, range, drift, stroll, gallivant, traipse; prowl.

row[1] *n.* *Rows of tulips lined the street. The tin soldiers stood in a row:* line; file, tier, queue, string; echelon; series, sequence, succession, rank, range, chain, column; train.

row[2] *n.* *We had a small row but quickly made up:* noisy dispute, quarrel, spat, tiff, set-to, difference, squabble, altercation, argument, words, wrangle, wrangling, scrape, scrap, brawl; fracas, melee, imbroglio, disorder, contretemps.

rowdy *adj.* *The rowdy boys were chased by the police:* boisterous, disorderly, roughneck, unruly, obstreperous, rowdyish, raffish, mischievous; lawless. —**Ant.** peaceful, law-abiding, orderly, gentle; refined, mannerly, decorous.

royal *adj.* **1.** *Some of the royal family of Spain are resident in Portugal:* regal, sovereign, monarchal. **2.** *The millionaire treated us to a royal feast:* fit for a king, regal; majestic, august, stately, imposing, magnificent, grand, splendid, resplendent, superb; lavish, munificent.

royalty *n.* *Though the king abused his power, no one questioned his royalty:* sovereignty, majesty, regality, kingship, queenship, dominion, supremacy, divine right, hegemony, command, sway.

rub *v.* **1.** *The wood was rubbed to a glossy finish. We may have to rub polish on the floor:* polish, buff, burnish, smooth, wipe; scrub, braze, scour, clean, swab; smear, spread, slather. **2.** *He rubbed his aching legs with liniment:* massage, knead, stroke; handle, touch, finger, pass the fingers over; manipulate, move with pressure against something, abrade, chafe. —*n.* **3.** *The masseur gave me a back rub:* rubbing, rubdown, massage, kneading, handling, manipulation, stroke, stroking. **4.** *The plan is good, but how to make it succeed—there's the rub:* annoying circumstance, hitch, catch, problem, obstacle, secret, trick, thing, impediment, difficulty, trouble, strait, dilemma, hardship; pinch, setback.

rubbish *n.* **1.** *Throw the rubbish out:* refuse, trash, garbage, waste; waste matter, junk, rubble, debris, litter, worthless material, dross, offal, jetsam. **2.** *Informal I don't believe that rubbish:* nonsense, gibberish, inanity, balderdash, rot, rigmarole, drivel, bosh, flapdoodle, twaddle, babble, blather, silliness, idiocy, folderol.

ruckus *n.* *We heard a ruckus outside:* commotion, disturbance, fuss, row, to-do, hubbub, ruction, rumpus, uproar, racket, turmoil, brouhaha, foofaraw.

ruddy *adj.* *He has a ruddy complexion:* rosy, rosy-cheeked, red, reddish, florid, flushed, blushing, scarlet; of a red color, rubicund, roseate, sanguine. **—Ant.** pale, pallid, wan, colorless, ashen, gray, sallow.

rude *adj.* **1.** *Rude behavior will not be tolerated:* discourteous, inconsiderate, uncourteous, uncivil, disrespectful, impolite, impudent, insulting, abusive, impertinent, peremptory, insolent, saucy, fresh; unmannerly, bad-mannered, ungentlemanly, unladylike, uncourtly, ungallant, ungracious, undignified, ill-bred; indelicate, indecorous, indecent, profane; brusque, blunt, abrupt, gruff, surly, sullen, sulky, crusty; callow, green, uncouth. **2.** *We put up a rude shed and huddled under it:* roughly made, crude, roughly built, roughhewn, slapdash, makeshift, uneven, rough, rugged, scraggy, raw. **3.** *Many Bavarians pride themselves on their rude and rustic way of speaking:* blunt, without refinement, coarse, unrefined, inelegant, unpolished, artless, without culture, uncultured, ungraceful, awkward, gauche, clumsy; gross, uncouth, vulgar, boorish, loutish, churlish; uneducated, untaught, unlearned, untutored, untrained, ignorant, illiterate; primitive, rustic, provincial, countrified, homely, homebred, wild, uncivilized, brutish. **—Ant.** 1 courteous, polite, civil, respectful, considerate; mannerly, well-mannered, gentlemanly, ladylike, courtly, urbane, suave, gallant, gracious, dignified, well-bred; decorous, decent, affable, sociable, cordial, amiable. 2 well-made, well-built, well-formed; wrought, fashioned, formed, shapely, finished, even, smooth, slick. 3 refined, elegant, polished, artful, cultured, graceful; educated, taught, learned, tutored, trained, literate; urbane, civilized.

rudimentary *adj.* **1.** *My first piano teacher gave me a rudimentary knowledge of music:* elementary, basic, elemental, concerning first rules or steps, initial, primary, primitive, formative. **2.** *A tadpole is a rudimentary frog:* incompletely developed, undeveloped, prototypal, incomplete, imperfect, premature, simple; immature, vestigial, primitive. **—Ant.** 1 advanced. 2 completely developed, developed, finished, complete, perfect, mature.

rue *v.* *I rue the day I ever met you!:* feel sorrow

over, be sorry for, reproach oneself for, regret, repine, repent, wish undone, lament, mourn, bemoan; deplore.

ruffian *n.* *The ruffian frightened everyone in the neighborhood:* brute, bully, tough, rough, roughneck, villain, scoundrel, rogue, knave, blackguard, ugly customer, cutthroat; rowdy, roisterer, hooligan, hoodlum; *Informal* hood; mugger, thug, gangster, crook.

ruffle *v.* **1.** *The wind ruffled my hair:* muss, muss up, dishevel, disorder, disarrange, wrinkle, rumple, roughen, ripple. **2.** *The seamstress ruffled the skirt of the dress:* gather into folds, fold, pleat, rimple, flounce, furbelow, crinkle, ruff, plait, pucker, corrugate. **3.** *The near accident ruffled his composure:* disturb, trouble, upset, disquiet; perturb, disconcert, discompose, unsettle, confuse; agitate, excite, aggravate. **—n. 4.** *The wind made ruffles on the pond:* disturbance, agitation, commotion, wave, ripple. **5.** *The shirt had ruffles on the collar and cuffs:* pleat, flounce, frill, ruche, ruff, edging. **—Ant.** 1 arrange, order; smooth. 3 compose, calm, settle.

rugged *adj.* **1.** *Afghanistan is rugged mountainous territory:* rough, uneven, irregular, craggy, cragged, ridged, jagged, rocky, rock-strewn, bumpy, scraggy. **2.** *The old sailor had a rugged face:* wrinkled, furrowed, lined, worn, weathered, weather-beaten, hard-featured, roughhewn, coarse. **3.** *John Wayne portrayed a rugged cowboy:* hardy, hale, robust, vigorous, sturdy, stalwart, able-bodied, tough; husky, brawny, wiry, muscular, well-knit, sinewy, athletic; virile, masculine. **4.** *The obstacle course was a rugged test of our fitness. Homesteading is a rugged life:* harsh, tough, difficult, hard, severe, stern, trying, taxing, strenuous, arduous, onerous, laborious; rude, unrefined, uncultivated, graceless, uncouth. **—Ant.** 1 even, smooth, regular, level; easy, soft. 2 smooth, unmarked, delicate, youthful, refined, pretty. 3 weak, frail, fragile, sickly, puny, skinny, slim; effeminate. 4 gentle, tender; refined, graceful, elegant, cultivated.

ruin *n.* **1.** *ruins We saw the ruins of an ancient Maya temple in Mexico:* remains, remnants, wreckage; fallen structure, shell. **2.** *The boat went to rack and ruin:* disintegration, decay, disrepair, wreckage; pot, seed. **3.** *Military rule was the ruin of the Roman empire:* downfall, fall, undoing, breakdown, ruination, crack-up, failure, defeat, overthrow; decay, disintegration, dissolution, destruction, devastation, doom. **—v. 4.** *The fire ruined the house. The scandal ruined his chances of winning the election:* bring to ruin, reduce to wreckage, demolish, destroy, wreck, shatter, pull to pieces, devastate, lay waste, gut, ravage, raze, level, fell, cut down, pull down, upset, overthrow, overturn, defeat, crush, quell, quash, squash, spoil, harm, put an end to. **5.** *The stock market crash ruined many people:* make poor, reduce to poverty, bankrupt, impoverish, bring to want, beggar, pauperize, break. **—Ant.** 3 construction, creation, building up;

success. 4 construct, build, build up; improve, help, enhance. 5 enrich, profit.

ruinous *adj. The expense of maintaining two residences became ruinous:* calamitous, disastrous, catastrophic, ravaging, devastating, damaging, destructive, deleterious, cataclysmic; baneful, pernicious; fatal, deadly.

rule *n.* **1.** *You must obey the rules of the game:* law, regulation, order, ordinance, decree, canon, precept, principle; maxim, axiom, adage, golden rule, rule of thumb, doctrine. **2.** *Promptness is the rule here:* practice, method, system, routine, custom, policy, normal condition. **3.** *There's no set rule for us to follow in this case:* guide, guideline, precedent, criterion, model, precept, form, formula, prescription; standard, convention. **4.** *Queen Victoria's rule lasted 64 years:* reign, regnancy, sovereignty, suzerainty, regime, dominion, empire; control, command, authority, direction, administration, leadership, domination, supremacy, sway, influence, jurisdiction, government. —*v.* **5.** *George III ruled Great Britain for 60 years:* control, command, govern, regulate, direct, administer, manage, run; exercise dominion over, have authority over, reign, lead, preside over, be at the head of, head; sway, influence, dominate, domineer, prevail, predominate, have the upper hand. **6.** *The jury ruled that he was innocent of all charges:* decide, determine, conclude, settle, resolve, establish, find, judge, adjudicate, adjudge, pass upon; declare, pronounce, decree.

ruler *n.* **1.** *King Wenceslaus was a wise and beloved ruler:* leader, commander, head of state, (*variously*) president, sovereign, monarch, crowned head, emperor, king, queen, prince, czar; lord, viceroy, suzerain; potentate, dynast, sultan, satrap, emir, shah, pharaoh, sheik, chieftain, rajah, khan, shogun; chairman, governor, manager, director, administrator, supervisor, controller, coordinator; chief, head, boss; judge, arbiter, referee. **2.** *Use a ruler to measure the width of that cloth:* rule, yardstick, straightedge, measure, tape measure; slide rule.

ruling *n.* **1.** *The judge gave her ruling:* judgment, decree, edict, directive, finding, order, pronouncement, resolution, verdict, decision. —*adj.* **2.** *Modesty was his ruling principle:* prevailing, predominant, dominant, cardinal, central, chief, commanding, controlling, leading, main, overriding, preeminent, preponderant, prevailing, principal, reigning, sovereign, supreme, governing. —**Ant.** unimportant, minor, inferior, secondary.

rumble *v.* **1.** *Grandfather's voice rumbled heartily when he laughed:* boom, reverberate, resound, roar, thunder, roll. —*n.* **2.** *The rumble of cannon could be heard in the distance:* roar, thunder, boom, booming, drumming, resonance, reverberation, roll; clap, bang.

ruminate *v. He ruminated on the courses of action open to him:* ponder, mull, mull over, brood, think, reflect, think about, meditate, cogitate, deliberate, weigh, contemplate, think over, bring up again for consideration, consider, study, muse, speculate.

rummage *v. They liked to rummage through thrift shops:* search thoroughly, look through, root, examine, explore, poke around, delve into, probe, sift through; disarrange, ransack, turn over.

rumor *n.* **1.** *I don't believe any of those rumors about the Joneses:* unverified information, report, story, supposition, babble, gossip, whisper, hearsay, insinuation, innuendo, talk, *Slang* scuttlebutt. —*v.* **2.** *It was rumored that the old beggar was really a millionaire in disguise:* whisper, gossip, breathe about, buzz about, intimate, insinuate; circulate, spread abroad, bruit about, put into circulation, report.

rump *n. The rider gave the horse a slap on its rump:* hindquarters, rear, posterior, rear end, haunches, buttocks, backside, bottom, croup, seat, behind, stern, dorsum, breech, *French* derrière.

rumple *v.* **1.** *He rumpled his suit by sleeping in it:* wrinkle, crumple, crease, crinkle, rimple, crush, pucker, corrugate, ruffle; disarrange, disorder, dishevel, muss, tousle. —*n.* **2.** *His suit was all covered with rumples after he slept in it:* wrinkle, fold, crease, crumple, pucker, ruffle, crinkle, crimp.

rumpus *n. We heard there was a rumpus about the mixed-up reservations:* fuss, ado, to-do, disturbance, pother, stir; uproar, tumult, agitation, upheaval, fracas, confusion, noise, tempest; *Slang* ruckus, brouhaha, rhubarb.

run *v.* **1.** *I've got to run for my bus:* go quickly, step quickly, make off rapidly, move swiftly, race, dart, sprint, jog, trot, dash; hustle, hasten, hurry, hie, scamper, scurry, rush, scramble; speed, tear along, fly, bound. **2.** *It's been a nice visit, but now we have to run. The robbers took the money and ran:* leave, take flight, flee, fly, bolt; steal away, escape, decamp, abscond, take to one's heels, beat a retreat; *Informal* skedaddle, take off; *Slang* vamoose, hightail it, split. **3.** *The shuttle runs daily from New York to Boston:* go, ply. **4.** *Richard Roe will run for mayor:* compete, enter the lists, stand, campaign, make a bid. **5.** *The stream runs down the valley:* flow, pour, stream, course, roll, glide, sweep along; surge, issue; wander, meander. **6.** *He ran the car into a ditch:* cause to move, drive, propel, thrust, push, impel; direct, navigate, maneuver, pilot. **7.** *Teach me how to run the business:* operate, manage, direct, supervise, oversee, coordinate; head, preside over, boss. **8.** *She ran her fingers over the smooth material:* pass, glide. **9.** *The escaped prisoners ran the roadblock:* get past, get through, sweep past, break through, penetrate, pierce; defy. **10.** *The movie ran for 97 minutes:* extend in time, go by, pass, elapse, last, endure; proceed, move on, go, continue, advance. **11.** *The little pond ran dry:* become, get. **12.** *How much will the repairs run?:* cost, amount to, total, add up to. **13.** *Her red blouse ran on the lighter colored clothes in the wash:* bleed, lose color, mingle colors. **14.** *Will these hose run?:* come unraveled, separate, tear, ladder. **15.** *The prices run from $5 to $200:* vary, extend, be, go. **16.** *The ad was run in the paper* *for two days:* print, publish; display; make copies of. **17.** *She's not afraid to run a risk:* incur, bring on, court, invite; be liable to, be exposed to; encounter, meet, meet with; fall into. **18.** *The ice cream ran in the warm sun:* dissolve, melt, become fluid, liquefy; vanish, disappear, evanesce. —*n.* **19.** *We took a run around the track:* running, trot, canter, gallop, jog, sprint, dash. **20.** *Let's take a run upstate for the day:* trip, excursion, journey, pilgrimage, voyage, tour, drive, outing. **21.** *I'm darning up a run in my old ski sweater:* unraveled place, *Informal* ladder. **22.** *I can't keep up with the run of national events:* course, passage, tendency, direction, drift, flow, progress, onward movement. **23.** *You have the run of my office:* freedom, unrestricted use. **24.** Fiddler on the Roof *has the longest Broadway run to date. Gamblers always hope for a run of good luck:* continuous performance; series, course, continuance, continuation, perpetuation, duration; period, stretch, streak, spell, while. **25.** *The kids are building a rabbit run:* enclosure, pen. **26.** *We've had nothing exciting—just the usual run of applicants:* class, kind, sort, genre, type. **27.** *The run of water down a mountainside increases during spring thaw:* flow, flowing movement, stream, race, course, current, motion. **28.** *The home team scored two runs on that play:* point in baseball, score, tally, circuit of the bases. —**Ant.** 1 walk, crawl. 2 remain, stay. 10 stop, halt, cease. 18 solidify, congeal, harden. 19 walk, saunter. 24 discontinuance, stoppage.

runaround *n. When I ask him a direct question I always get the runaround:* slip, dodge, evasion, shunting off, evasiveness, avoidance, shunning, side step, bypass, elusiveness, equivocation.

runaway *n.* **1.** *The priest started a shelter for runaways:* fugitive, deserter, escapee, refugee, bolter, *Slang* skedaddler. —*adj.* **2.** *Her new novel is a runaway best-seller:* absolute, unqualified, complete, out-and-out, pure, perfect, unmitigated, unalloyed.

rundown *n. Give me a quick rundown on the President's news conference:* outline, summary, résumé, synopsis, abstract, précis, brief, review, condensation, digest, sketch, capitulation.

run-down *adj.* **1.** *They bought and renovated an old, run-down house:* broken-down, seedy, tacky, shabby, dilapidated, tired, deteriorated, tattered, rickety, tumbledown, *Slang* beat-up. **2.** *Despite her run-down condition, she won't see a doctor:* ailing, weary, exhausted, frail, feeble, fatigued, sickly. —**Ant.** 1 renovated, rebuilt, renewed, refurbished. 2 fit, robust, sturdy, able-bodied, stalwart.

running *adj.* **1.** *She gave us a running account of her vacation:* continuous, unbroken, uninterrupted, unceasing, incessant, flowing, fluent. —*adv.* **2.** *She lost two times running:* successively, consecutively, continuously, uninterruptedly. —*n.* **3.** *Running the office required shrewd judgment:* management, direction, supervision, control, coordination, leadership, organization,

regulation, administration; maintenance, operation.

run-of-the-mill *adj. This season's musicals are depressingly run-of-the-mill:* ordinary, commonplace, routine, everyday, mediocre, passable, banal, so-so, unimpressive, undistinguished, humdrum, middling, indifferent, modest, second-rate. —**Ant.** superior, superlative, prime, preeminent.

runt *n. He was too much of a runt to make the basketball team:* peewee, half-pint, chit, shrimp; dwarf, midget, Tom Thumb, Lilliputian, pygmy, homunculus, elf. —**Ant.** giant, colossus, behemoth, titan, monster.

rupture *n.* **1.** *A rupture in the water main flooded the street:* breaking, bursting, break, burst, split, fracture, crack, fissure, rent, severance, cleavage, cleft. **2.** *What caused the rupture between the two wings of the party?:* break, rift, split, breach, schism, separation, dissociation, disunion, disagreement, dissension, falling out, discord; friction, clash. —*v.* **3.** *The balloon ruptured:* break, burst, break up, sunder, crack, puncture, dissever, come apart, part, snap, pop, divide. **4.** *What ruptured their friendship?:* cause a break in, cause a breach in, disrupt, disunite, divide, break up. —**Ant.** 2 union; understanding, agreement; continuity. 4 unite, heal, knit.

rural *adj. We left the city for a rural home:* country, up-country, pastoral, bucolic, rustic, countrified, provincial, *Informal* hicR. —**Ant.** urban, city, citified, cosmopolitan.

ruse *n. The false telephone call was just a ruse to get me out of the way:* stratagem, machination, maneuver, device, shift, scheme, crafty device, contrivance, artifice, subterfuge, trick, hoax, deception, deceit, dodge, blind, feint.

rush *v.* **1.** *We've got to rush to the hospital:* speed, race, hasten, hie, hurry, run, dash, tear, scramble, dart, hustle, scurry, scamper. **2.** *The operation could not be rushed:* speed up, accelerate, dispatch, expedite, perform hastily, finish with speed; work against time, hurry. **3.** *Don't rush me!:* spur, whip, urge, goad, drive; pressure, push, press, keep at. **4.** *Don't rush into marriage:* go carelessly, go headlong, act thoughtlessly, leap, plunge, precipitate oneself. **5.** *The Indians rushed the settlers:* attack suddenly, storm, charge, descend upon, have at. —*n.* **6.** *The first shoppers made a rush for the bargain counter:* run, dash, sprint. **7.** *We have time to eat without rush:* haste, speed, dispatch, urgency. —*adj.* **8.** *This is a rush order:* urgent, emergency, top priority. —**Ant.** 1 walk, crawl. 2 slow. 7 leisure; dawdling, idling.

rust *n.* **1.** *The old sink pipes were full of rust:* corrosion, oxidation; stain, blight, rot, decay. **2.** *Her hair was a lovely shade of rust:* reddish-yellow, reddish-brown, russet, auburn. —*v.* **3.** *Exposed iron will rust. His talents had rusted over the years:* corrode, oxidize; decay, weaken with disuse, decline, deteriorate, crumble.

rustic *adj.* **1.** *Beaver Meadow is a rustic community:* country, rural, provincial, pastoral, agrarian, bucolic. **2.** *The folks around this neck of the woods have got down-home rustic* *manners:* simple, plain, unsophisticated; rough, countrified, rude, unpolished, unrefined, inelegant, uncouth, uncultured, crude, loutish, coarse, churlish, boorish; awkward, gauche, cloddish. —*n.* **3.** *Jeb is a rustic from the backwoods:* country person, countryman, provincial, peasant, bumpkin, hayseed, yokel, clodhopper, rube. —**Ant.** 1 urban, cosmopolitan. 2 sophisticated, fancy, polished, refined, elegant, courtly, urbane, citified. 3 sophisticate, cosmopolitan.

rustle *v.* **1.** *The taffeta skirt rustled when she walked:* move with soft sounds, swish, rustle, riffle, hiss, whish, stir, rub. —*n.* **2.** *We listened to the rustle of the leaves:* rustling, whispering sound, swish, hiss.

rusty *adj.* **1.** *The bottom of the boat was rusty:* covered with rust, rusted, corroded; rotten, moldy, tainted. **2.** *She had rusty hair:* reddish, rust-colored. **3.** *I'm a little rusty at ice-skating:*
out of practice, stiff, no longer agile, sluggish, inept through neglect.

rut *n.* **1.** *The heavy tanks left ruts in the road:* deep track, depression, furrow, hollow, ditch, gutter, cut, trench, channel, trough, tread, groove. **2.** *You're in a rut!:* fixed way of life, dull routine, monotonous round, narrow orbit, pattern, habit. —*v.* **3.** *Heavy rains rutted the road:* dig into, furrow, depress, hollow, groove, mark, channel, score.

ruthless *adj. Attila the Hun was a ruthless tyrant:* without pity, unmerciful, merciless, pitiless, unpitying, unforgiving, without compassion, unfeeling, heartless, callous, hardhearted, harsh, cruel, unsparing, remorseless, relentless, unrelenting; inhuman, vicious, barbarous, savage, ferocious, brutal, brutish, bestial, cold-blooded, murderous, deadly, bloodthirsty, sanguinary. —**Ant.** merciful, pitying, compassionate, forgiving, kind, tender, tender-hearted, gentle, sparing, lenient, remorseful, humane.

S

Sabbath *n. But the seventh day is the sabbath of the Lord thy God:* Sabbath day, day of rest, day of worship, (*Christian Church*) Lord's Day.

sable *adj. Stars twinkled in the sable night:* black, pitch-black, pitch-dark, ebony, inky, jet, raven.

sabotage *n.* **1.** *The enemy agent was arrested on charges of sabotage:* undermining of a cause, subversion; malicious destruction, malicious disruption. —*v.* **2.** *Enemy agents sabotaged the arms factory:* undermine, sap, conspire against, subvert, damage from within; disable, vandalize, paralyze, cripple, retard, incapacitate, destroy, disrupt.

saccharine *adj. Her saccharine words failed to sway the old man:* oversweet, cloying, syrupy, sugary, honeyed, sugared, candied; maudlin, sentimental, mawkish; *Slang* mushy, soppy, gooey; nauseating, sickening; offensive, revolting, disgusting. —**Ant.** sharp, sour, biting, acid, corrosive.

sack¹ *n.* **1.** *Give me a sack of potatoes. Santa brought a sack of toys. Each scout had a hiker's sack:* bag, (*variously*) pouch, knapsack, rucksack, haversack, gunnysack, duffel bag. —*v.* **2.** *I got hired one summer to sack grain:* put into a sack, bag; pack, store.

sack² *v.* **1.** *The invaders sacked the village:* pillage, plunder, loot, ransack, tear up, pull apart, lay waste, despoil, spoil, ravage, spoliate, prey upon, raid, maraud, depredate; steal from, rob. —*n.* **2.** *The sack of Palmyra took place in A.D. 273:* plundering, pillage, rapine, ravishment, ravage, devastation, depredation, waste, lay waste, despoliation; raid, marauding.

sacrament *n. He attended church for the sacrament of Holy Communion:* rite, ceremony, liturgy, solemnity, observance, ceremonial, ministration; pledge, promise, vow, covenant, troth, obligation, contract, plight, affirmation.

sacred *adj.* **1.** *Ethelred asked to be buried in sacred ground:* consecrated, hallowed, blessed, sanctified, holy. **2.** *Salzburg is sacred to Mozart-lovers:* venerable, awe-inspiring, revered. **3.** *The sacred books of the Essenes are contained in the Dead Sea Scrolls:* religious, ecclesiastical, hieratic, church; scriptural, holy, Biblical; hallowed, divinely inspired. —**Ant.** 1 unconsecrated, profane. 3 profane, secular, lay, temporal.

sacrifice *n.* **1.** *The pagans made sacrifices to their gods:* offering, oblation, homage; ritual slaughter, immolation, lustration. **2.** *Parents often make sacrifices for their children:* relinquishment, cession, concession, renunciation, surrender. **3.** *The furniture was sold at a sacrifice:* loss. —*v.* **4.** *The ancient Greeks sacrificed lambs or calves before engaging in battle:* make a sacrifice of, offer up, make an offering of; immolate. **5.** *We decided to sacrifice a trip for a new car:* give up, relinquish, forgo, forfeit, waive, re-

nounce, surrender, cede. **6.** *He was forced to sacrifice the house:* sell at a loss. —**Ant.** 3 profit, gain.

sacrilege *n. To start a fight inside a church is a sacrilege:* profanation, desecration, misuse of sacred things; blasphemy, profanity, profaneness, impiousness, impiety, irreligion, irreverence, mockery; sin, wickedness, sinfulness, violation, outrage, iniquity.

sacrosanct *adj. The burial grounds were considered sacrosanct. The general's orders were sacrosanct:* sacred, consecrated, hallowed, sanctified, solemn, holy, godly, religious, spiritual, divine, heavenly, celestial; inviolable, inviolate, immune from attack; unexamined, unquestioned, blindly accepted.

sad *adj.* **1.** *I was sad when I learned of her misfortune:* unhappy, cheerless, joyless, grieved, griefstricken; dispirited, downcast, low, crestfallen, heavyhearted, chapfallen, disconsolate, desolate, despondent, melancholy, inconsolable, depressed, dejected; *Informal* down in the mouth, down in the dumps, blue; distressed, miserable, pessimistic, troubled, full of care, despairing, brokenhearted, hurt, crushed; wretched, forlorn, sorrowful, doleful, mournful. **2.** *It was such a sad story, I cried:* pitiful, touching, pathetic, lamentable, dismal; lachrymose, maudlin. **3.** *Her sad circumstances made me unhappy:* unfortunate, grievous, serious, grave, calamitous, grim, dismal, solemn; lamentable, heartrending, heartrending, woeful, mournful, distressing; trying, taxing, difficult, hard, adverse, troublesome; tragic. —**Ant.** 1 happy, cheerful, smiling, joyful, glad, spirited, lighthearted, pleased, merry, optimistic. 2 happy, amusing, cheery, bright. 3 easy, fortunate, lucky, prosperous, flourishing, successful.

sadden *v. Her sudden departure saddened me beyond measure:* grieve, depress, dishearten, discourage, crush, deject, dispirit, sorrow, subdue, damp, dash, burden, aggrieve. —**Ant.** delight, cheer, gladden, please, encourage.

sadistic *adj. He was a sadistic killer. The prisoners received sadistic punishment at the hands of their captors:* deliberately cruel, brutal, vicious, fiendish, perverse, perverted, bloodthirsty.

safe *adj.* **1.** *The crystal was safe in its protective casing:* secure, out of danger, safe and sound, impregnable, out of harm's way; unharmed, unhurt, undamaged, unscathed, unscratched, unbroken, intact, whole. **2.** *The streets aren't safe at night:* secure, protecting, protected, guarded, defended, invulnerable, unexposed. **3.** *Five million dollars is a safe estimate:* cautious, prudent, circumspect, conservative, modest, discreet, noncommittal, wary; sure, certain. **4.** *The cab company wants to hire a safe driver. The train is a safe means of transportation:* not dangerous, dependable, reliable, trustworthy, to be trusted; sure, steady, firm, stable, sound, tried and true; harmless, innocuous. —*n.* **5.** *Put your valuables in the safe:* locked box, storage box, safe-deposit box; vault. —**Ant.** 1 harmed, damaged; imperiled; jeopardized, at risk. 2 unsafe, risky, hazardous, perilous. **3** wild, risky, extravagant; impetuous; speculative. **4** unsafe, undependable, unreliable; harmful, risky, pathogenic; lethal, toxic.

safeguard n. **1.** We need assurance of safeguards against nuclear holocaust: defense, protection, shield, armor, bulwark, guard, security, ward, buffer, screen, precaution; charm, amulet, talisman. —v. **2.** Car manufacturers are looking for new ways to safeguard passengers: guard, shield, defend, fortify, protect, screen, conserve, preserve, shelter, harbor, secure, armor, garrison. —**Ant.** 1 danger, hazard, peril, threat. 2 imperil, jeopardize, risk.

safety n. They sought safety in a cave: safeness, protection, security, immunity, asylum, cover, defense, impregnability, refuge, sanctuary, shelter.

sag v. **1.** The old mattress sagged in the middle: bend downward, droop, slump, bow, sink, drop, descend, decline, plunge, give way, settle; sway, keel, list, dip, lean, pitch, tilt. **2.** My mother's coat sagged on me: droop, flop, flap, hang loosely, billow. **3.** Her spirits sagged as the night wore on: weaken, diminish, decline, lose strength, break down; flag, weary, tire; fail, fizzle out.

saga n. The name of Admiral Robert Peary is famous in the saga of Arctic exploration: narrative, long narrative, tale, heroic tale, epic, legend, myth, adventure; chronicle, history; yarn, romance.

sagacious adj. The professor was a sagacious man. We pray that the Court will reach a sagacious decision: wise, shrewd, knowing, astute, intelligent, judicious, discriminating, sage, sapient, perspicacious, discerning, perceptive, practical, prudent; smart, clever, brainy, nimble-witted, sharp, acute, canny, cunning, calculating, foxy; sensible, sound, rational, tactful, discreet, diplomatic. —**Ant.** stupid, ignorant, dumb, obtuse, foolish, fatuous, silly.

sage n. **1.** The king brought difficult problems to a sage: wise man, magus, pundit, mage, philosopher, savant, scholar, guru, mandarin, solon, Slang egghead. —adj. **2.** He was sage in his judgment: wise, sapient, shrewd, prudent; sensible, sound, sagacious, knowing, astute, intelligent. —**Ant.** 1 fool, idiot. 2 stupid, foolish, senseless.

sail n. **1.** We took a sail around the islands: sailing trip, cruise, voyage, boat ride; journey by water, excursion. —v. **2.** We sailed around the world on a tramp steamer. The ship sailed at noon: cruise, go by water, navigate, ride the waves, boat, course, skim, scud, steam; set sail, set out on a voyage, put to sea, shove off, get under way. **3.** The balloon sailed upward: float, fly, drift, glide, soar.

sailor n. The old sailor had worked on many ships: mariner, yachtsman, seaman, deckhand, seafarer, seafaring man, navigator, voyager, Informal tar, salt, sea dog, Slang gob.

saintly adj. The man was praised for his saintly life: sainted, godly, holy, blessed, devout, pious, beatific, reverent, religious, spiritual, faithful, be-

lieving; virtuous, good, upright, moral, righteous, benevolent. —**Ant.** wicked, sinful, immoral, ungodly; corruptible, frail, flawed.

sake n. **1.** For the sake of your family, don't take so many risks: good, benefit, consideration, well-being, welfare, care, interest, concern, cause, behalf, regard, account, respect; advantage, profit, gain, enhancement. **2.** For argument's sake, let's assume the earth is flat: end, purpose, object.

salacious adj. The salacious remark offended her: lusty, lecherous, rakish, lewd, carnal, wanton, lascivious, libidinous, concupiscent; obscene, pornographic, prurient. —**Ant.** modest, prudish.

salary n. This position offers a weekly salary of $200: compensation for work, wages, pay, earnings, income; stipend, allowance; remuneration, recompense, emolument.

sale n. **1.** My agent arranged the sale of the house: selling, transfer, exchange. **2.** We're having a spring sale on winter coats: disposal of goods at reduced prices, markdown, reduction, discount, cut; bargain, special. —**Ant.** 1 purchase, acquisition.

salesman n. For a time he was a traveling salesman: salesperson, saleswoman, seller, vendor, Informal drummer.

salient adj. We stationed a lookout on the nearest salient point. The plan has several salient flaws: prominent, protruding, obvious, conspicuous, standing out, jutting up, striking, noticeable, easily noticed, palpable, outstanding, manifest, flagrant, egregious, arrant, glaring, marked, pronounced, important, remarkable, notable, noteworthy; considerable, substantial. —**Ant.** low-lying, depressed; inconspicuous, minor, trifling.

sallow adj. A gaunt man with sallow complexion coughed in the corner: yellowish, yellow, jaundiced, sickly, tallow-faced, anemic, bilious; pale, wan, ashen, livid, pallid, washed-out, gray, gray complected, green at the gills. —**Ant.** ruddy, rosy, flushed, blooming.

sally n. **1.** Joan of Arc was captured during a sally outside the walls: sortie, thrust, counterattack, bursting forth, foray, raid, attack. **2.** We made a lightning sally to the country and back: excursion, journey, expedition, trip, outing. **3.** Her quick sally made us laugh: clever remark, mot, ready reply, flash of wit, witticism, repartee, badinage, banter, retort, quip, wisecrack. —v. **4.** The troops sallied forth and broke through the encirclement: erupt, rush out, break out, issue suddenly, debouch, pour, surge, flow, spring; attack, charge, take the offensive, seize the initiative.

salon n. **1.** Large parties are held in the salon: large room, drawing room, hall, gallery. **2.** Alfredo will be opening a new beauty salon in Vancouver soon: stylish shop, beauty parlor, establishment.

saloon n. The temperance league wanted to close all the saloons in town: bar, tavern, pub, barroom, bistro, taproom, beer parlor, alehouse, cocktail lounge, inn, roadhouse, speak-easy, *Slang* ginmill.

salt *n.* **1.** *Her witty remarks added a little salt to the conversation:* wit, humor, pungency, piquancy; seasoning, smack, savor, flavor. **2.** *Your grandmother is the salt of the earth:* best, quintessence, choice, pick, select, elect, cream. —*adj.* **3.** *Salt water flows into the marsh:* saline, salty, salted, brackish, briny. —*v.* **4.** *The stew tastes flat; you'd better salt it:* season, flavor, savor, spice. **5.** *We salted the meat to preserve it:* cure, brine, marinate, pickle, corn, souse. **6. salt away.** *He's been salting away money for years:* save, store up, put away, lay away, set aside.

salubrious *adj. Regular exercise is salubrious:* healthful, healthy, health-promoting, therapeutic, good for one, salutary, bracing, beneficial, wholesome, lifegiving, invigorating. —**Ant.** unhealthful, unhealthy, harmful, unwholesome, insalubrious, deleterious.

salute *v.* **1.** *He saluted us heartily:* address, greet, hail, welcome; make obeisance to, bow to, nod to, wave to. **2.** *I salute my opponent's courage:* applaud, cheer, praise, honor, respect, pay tribute to, take one's hat off to. —*n.* **3.** *The hero acknowledged the salutes of the crowd with a wave of his hand:* expression of goodwill, salutation, greeting, recognition, honor, homage, reverence; applause, accolade, laudation, acclamation.

salvage *n.* **1.** *We're trying to finance the salvage of the Titanic:* recovery, reclamation, retrieval. **2.** *The salvage was piled upon the pier:* property saved from destruction, reclaimed materials, remains, scrap, junk, debris; flotsam and jetsam. —*v.* **3.** *We salvaged the cargo from the sunken ship:* save, rescue, retrieve, recover, rehabilitate, restore.

salvation *n.* **1.** *Think on your eternal salvation, friend!:* saving of the soul from sin, redemption, deliverance; election, grace. **2.** *Prayer was her salvation in times of stress:* means of surviving, protection, lifeline, mainstay, rock. **3.** *A loan from a friend aided in the salvation of his business:* saving, rescue, preservation, salvage, retrieval, reclamation, recovery, survival. —**Ant.** 1 perdition, damnation, condemnation. 2 downfall. 3 destruction, loss.

salve *n.* **1.** *She claimed that the salve helped her rheumatism:* unguent, ointment, balm, emollient, lotion, liniment, dressing, healing agent, alleviative, anodyne. —*v.* **2.** *My apology seemed to salve his injured feelings:* ease, assuage, alleviate, mitigate, relieve, temper, moderate, mollify, lessen, reduce, calm, pacify. —**Ant.** 2 irritate, exacerbate, inflame, aggravate.

same *adj.* **1.** *This is the same dress I wore to the other party:* identical, selfsame, one and the same, very, alike, twin, like, of like kind, similar. **2.** *Carol's house and Jane's house have the same number of rooms:* corresponding, equivalent, parallel; equal, on a par, on even terms. **3.** *You're still the same person I knew ten years ago:* unchanged, invariable, consistent, uniform.

—**Ant.** 1-3 different. 1 dissimilar, other. 3 changed, variable, inconsistent.

sameness *n. There was a sameness about all their comments:* identity, uniformity, monotony. —**Ant.** difference.

sample *n.* **1.** *The sketches were merely samples of her artwork. The doctor took a sample of the patient's blood:* representative, specimen, example, illustration, instance, cross section, portion, segment, exemplification, pattern, model, paradigm. —*v.* **2.** *She made us sample her cooking:* judge by a sample, test, examine; partake of, taste, try, dip into, experience.

sanctify *v. The bishops held a special service to sanctify the church:* bless, consecrate, hallow, anoint, make holy, enshrine, exalt, beatify, dedicate; purify, cleanse, absolve; sanction, legitimize, legitimate, legitimatize, uphold. —**Ant.** profane, desecrate, pollute, defile.

sanctimonious *adj. A true believer doesn't have to be sanctimonious about his beliefs. Our professor's always coming up with sanctimonious pronouncements:* making a show of sanctity, affectedly holy, belligerently pious, pietistic, aggressively devout, self-righteous, holier-than-thou, unctuous, pharisaical; solemn, overblown, pretentious, pompous, canting, preachy.

sanction *n.* **1.** *We received sanction to proceed with our plans:* approval, commendation, endorsement, assent, consent, permission, authorization; leave, liberty, license, authority; ratification, confirmation, support. **2.** *The international community imposed sanctions on Rhodesia for its illegal political actions:* penalty, pressure, punitive measure, coercion. —*v.* **3.** *Our plan wasn't sanctioned by the board of directors:* approve, endorse, authorize, legitimate, allow, permit, countenance, accept, agree to, favor, ratify, support. —**Ant.** 1 disapproval, forbiddance, refusal, ban, prohibition. 2 incentive, encouragement. 3 disapprove, reject, ban, prohibit.

sanctuary *n.* **1.** *Build ye the sanctuary of the Lord God:* holy place, consecrated place, house of worship, house of prayer, house of God, church, temple, chapel, shrine; sanctum, sanctum sanctorum. **2.** *The storm cellar was a sanctuary against the tornado. The outlaw claimed sanctuary in the church:* refuge, haven, retreat, safe place; safety, protection, asylum, shelter, immunity from pursuers; hiding place, cover. **3.** *The island is maintained as a sanctuary for endangered species:* protected area, reserve, preserve, park.

sane *adj.* **1.** *The killer was declared sufficiently sane to stand trial:* of sound mind, reasonable, in possession of one's faculties, compos mentis, clearheaded, sober, balanced, responsible, rational, lucid; *Slang* all there. **2.** *Have a safe and sane holiday!:* reasonable, well-founded, sensible, judicious, sagacious, logical, farsighted; credible, plausible. —**Ant.** 1 insane, unsound, mentally ill, non compos mentis, deranged, mad, irrational. 2 insane, senseless, stupid, foolish, injudicious, unreasonable, incredible, implausible.

sanguinary *adj. The sanguinary pillagers left no one alive:* bloody, murderous, bloodthirsty, cruel, savage, fell, ruthless, truculent, pitiless, unmerciful, merciless. **—Ant.** merciful, kind.

sanguine *adj.* **1.** *He had a sanguine outlook on life:* optimistic, hopeful, confident, happy, cheerful, sunny, bright; lighthearted, elated, buoyant, in good spirits. **2.** *Her cheeks were sanguine with excitement:* red, reddish, ruddy, crimson, scarlet; florid, rubicund, flushed, rosy, inflamed, glowing, blooming. **—Ant.** 1 pessimistic, doubtful, gloomy, depressed, despairing, heavy-hearted, dispirited, morose. 2 pale, ashen, pallid, white.

sanitary *adj. The Health Department checks on sanitary conditions. Hospital operating instruments must be sanitary:* health-promoting, healthful, salubrious, healthy, wholesome; sterile, sterilized, clean, germ-free, disease-free, hygienic, disinfected, aseptic, uninfected, prophylactic, unpolluted. **—Ant.** unhealthy, unwholesome; unsterile, dirty.

sanity *n. She managed to keep her sanity throughout the ordeal:* mental health, soundness of mind, saneness, mental balance, normality; soundness of judgment, reason, rationality, sensibleness, sense, lucidity, reasonableness, clearheadedness, coherence. **—Ant.** insanity, insaneness, madness, derangement; irrationality, incoherence.

sap *v. The ordeal sapped his energy and his spirit:* deplete, reduce, rob; weaken, undermine, tax, wear, enervate, enfeeble, exhaust, debilitate, devitalize; break down, impair, cripple, disable, afflict; subvert, destroy, ruin, devastate; bleed, drain.

sapient *adj. The sapient guru guided us:* wise, sage, sagacious. **—Ant.** stupid, dull, unwise.

sappy *adj. The sappy proposal was turned down:* foolish, absurd, silly, crazy, drippy, foolish, idiotic, stupid, preposterous; maudlin, mushy, slushy, drippy. **—Ant.** realism, hardheadedness.

sarcasm *n. His sarcasm hurt her feelings:* ridicule, irony, derision, contempt, scorn, mockery, scoffing, disparagement; cutting remark, sneer, taunt, gibe, jeer, rub, jest. **—Ant.** compliment, praise, enthusiasm, appreciation.

sarcastic *adj. He gave a sarcastic reply. Sarcastic people tend to lose friends quickly:* ironic, contemptuous, mocking, derisive, taunting; biting, cutting, piercing, stinging, bitter, caustic, mordant, acerb, sardonic, scornful, sneering, disparaging.

sardonic *adj. He watched his enemies turn against each other with sardonic amusement:* sarcastic, satiric, cynical, sneering, mocking, contemptuous, derisive, scornful, disparaging; caustic, mordant, biting, taunting, jeering.

Satan *n. Satan is the ruler of Hell:* the Devil, the Prince of Darkness, the Evil One, the Old Serpent, the Tempter, Beelzebub, Lucifer, Mephistopheles, the Foul Fiend, Old Nick, Old Scratch, Moloch, Belial, Apollyon.

satanic *adj. Dante's* Inferno *describes the satanic punishments of the damned:* befitting Satan, hellish, diabolical, demoniacal, demonic, infernal, devilish, fiendish, fiendlike; malicious, malignant, malevolent, bad, wicked, evil, infamous, inhuman, heinous, vicious, cruel, vile, sadistic. **—Ant.** angelic, heavenly, benevolent, good, humane, kind.

sate *v. The huge meal sated our hunger:* satisfy fully, satiate, fill; glut, stuff, surfeit, cloy, gorge.

satellite *n.* **1.** *How many satellites does Jupiter have?:* moon. **2.** *The king's satellites always accompanied him:* attendant, assistant, follower, disciple; companion, crony, retainer, servant; vassal, menial, underling, puppet, hanger-on, parasite, toady, sycophant. **3.** *In the rhetoric of the Cold War, dependent allies of the superpowers have been termed their satellites:* client state, vassal, tributary, puppet.

satiate *v. It was a banquet that more than satiated our need for food:* satisfy, fill, gratify, suffice, content; slake, quench; glut, stuff, sate, surfeit, overfill, overdo, cloy, saturate; sicken, disgust, nauseate; jade, bore, weary.

satire *n. Voltaire's* Candide *is a famous satire. The play is full of satire:* comic criticism, parody, takeoff, send up, burlesque, lampoon, travesty, caricature; mockery, ridicule, derision; pointed wit, sarcasm, irony, acrimony; raillery, banter, persiflage.

satirical *adj. He wrote a satirical piece on the government:* ironically critical, sardonic, sarcastic, mordant, ironical; derisive, mocking, sneering, biting, malicious, scornful, bitter, caustic; comic, humorous, tongue-in-cheek.

satisfaction *n.* **1.** *He gets a good deal of satisfaction from his grandchildren. The matter will be resolved to your satisfaction:* pleasure, comfort, gratification, happiness, fulfillment, pride, content, contentment. **2.** *The store owner received satisfaction for the damage:* reimbursement, repayment, compensation, recompense, restitution, remuneration, payment, remittance; settlement, quittance, damages, deserts; requital, redress, rectification, justice, amends, atonement, correction, reckoning, answering, measure for measure. **—Ant.** 1 dissatisfaction, grief, shame, unhappiness, discontent.

satisfactory *adj. The actress gave a satisfactory performance but could have been better:* good enough, competent, adequate, suitable, sufficient, all right, acceptable, passable, up to standard, up to the mark, OK. **—Ant.** unsatisfactory, inadequate, bad.

satisfy *v.* **1.** *Nothing satisfies her anymore! Do you satisfy the entry requirements for that college? The cold water satisfied our thirst:* make content, content, please, mollify, pacify, gratify, delight; meet, fill, fulfill, serve, suffice, be adequate to, answer; sate, satiate, slake, quench, appease, remove, put an end to. **2.** *We satisfied all overdue notices on our accounts:* pay off, settle, discharge, clear, annul; pay, remit, repay, reimburse, recompense, compensate, requite. **3.** *His persuasive talk still didn't satisfy me that the plan would succeed:* convince, free of doubt, persuade, assure, reassure. **—Ant.** 1 dissatisfy, displease, annoy; intensify, worsen. 3 dissatisfy, dissuade.

saturate *v.* **1.** *Heavy rain saturated the playing field:* soak thoroughly, drench, souse, douse; immerse, submerge. **2.** *Dust saturated the attic:* fill, infiltrate, cover, permeate, infuse, suffuse, pervade, impregnate, imbue. —**Ant.** 1 drain, dry.

saturnine *adj.* *When he's in one of his saturnine moods no one can cheer him up:* gloomy, sullen, glum, morose, moping, sulky, dour; downcast, downhearted, dejected; solemn, somber, grave, serious, staid, reserved, stern, taciturn, withdrawn, uncommunicative, apathetic. —**Ant.** genial, amiable, cheerful, cheery, happy.

saucy *adj.* **1.** *Her saucy remarks raised many eyebrows:* impudent, insolent, impertinent, forward, audacious, bold, brash, brazen, unabashed, barefaced, flippant, cheeky, fresh, smart-alecky, cocky, rude, impolite, discourteous, disrespectful. **2.** *She was a saucy little girl:* pert, lively; high-spirited. **3.** *Narcisse is modeling a saucy spring outfit:* jaunty, trim, smart, natty, spruce.

saunter *v.* **1.** *He sauntered into the house as if nothing had happened:* walk casually, amble, stroll, traipse, promenade; wander, ramble, roam, stray, meander; straggle, loiter, *Slang* mosey. —*n.* **2.** *We took a slow saunter around the park:* stroll, leisurely walk, amble, ramble, promenade.

savage *adj.* **1.** *The poor man received a savage beating from the thugs:* ferocious, fierce, brutal, barbaric, brutish, cruel, unkind, merciless, unmerciful, pitiless, sadistic, ruthless, relentless, bloody, murderous. **2.** *If you love savage beasts, leave them alone:* untamed, wild, undomesticated, feral. **3.** *The savage tribesmen were absolutely terrified of the helicopter:* uncivilized, primitive, uncultivated, uncultured, heathenish, barbaric, barbarous. **4.** *Savage winds whipped about the mountain climber's head:* violent, harsh, rough, rugged. —*n.* **5.** *If this is civilization, give me the savages any day! Do you believe in the myth of the noble savage?:* primitive, aborigine, aboriginal, native, barbarian. **6.** *Lock that savage up and throw away the key!:* fierce person, brute, fiend, maniac, barbarian, *Informal* animal; hoodlum, hooligan, ruffian; boor, yahoo. —**Ant.** 1 kind, merciful, lenient, gentle, tender. 2 tame, domesticated. 3 civilized, cultivated, cultured. 4 mild, soft, calm. 5 civilized person.

savant *n.* *He was one of the foremost savants of his time:* scholar, sage, intellectual, polymath, expert, authority, pundit, *British* boffin, *Informal* rocket scientist, maven, egghead, brain.

save *v.* **1.** *The firemen saved the family from the burning building:* rescue, recover, free, deliver, preserve, protect, safeguard, spare, salvage, redeem, help. **2.** *You'll save electricity by turning off lights not in use:* conserve, preserve, husband, spare. **3.** *I'm saving this dress for a special occasion:* set aside, store, reserve, set apart, withhold, hold, keep, conserve, preserve, put away, put aside. **4.** *Save your voice for to-*

night's performance: treat carefully, keep safe, protect, take care of, look after, safeguard, shield, defend, watch over, guard. **5.** *You must learn to save if you want to provide for the future:* be thrifty, avoid spending, curtail expenses, economize, retrench; provide for a rainy day, lay up, lay by, put by, hoard, amass, accumulate, husband, deposit, bank, heap up, garner, stock. —**Ant.** 1 endanger, imperil, risk, hazard. 2 use, consume, waste. 3 use, spend. 4 expose, risk, endanger. 5 spend, be extravagant.

saving *adj.* **1.** *His one saving grace was his sense of honor:* redeeming, redemptory, reclaiming, restoring, compensating, reparative. **2.** *Are you a saving sort of person?:* frugal, thrifty, penny-wise, careful, prudent, conservative, economical, sparing, provident; stingy, miserly, stinting, niggardly, close, illiberal; *Informal* tight. —*n.* **3.** *If you buy one now, you'll benefit from a saving of 20%:* amount saved, reduction in cost, price-cut, markdown. **4. savings** *It took all our savings to buy the house:* money laid aside, store of money, financial reserve, funds, bank deposit; nest egg.

savings *n. pl.* *We used all our savings to buy the house:* means, reserves, resources, stake, stockpile, accumulation, cache, *Informal* nest egg, kitty.

savior *n.* **1.** *Simon Bolivar was the savior of the South American peasants:* protector, champion, defender, preserver, guardian; rescuer, deliverer, salvation, liberator, emancipator, freer; redeemer, guiding light. **2. Saviour** *The birth of the Saviour is celebrated on Christmas Day:* Christ, the Messiah, Redeemer, Prince of Peace, the Son of God.

savoir faire *n.* *Diplomats should have a great deal of savoir faire:* social grace, social skill, tact, aplomb, graciousness, finesse, smoothness, adroitness, discretion; poise, complaisance; presence, assurance, composure, self-possession; polish, suavity, urbanity, worldliness. —**Ant.** awkwardness, clumsiness, ineptness, maladroitness.

savor *n.* **1.** *This cake has the savor of nutmeg:* taste, flavor, tang, spice, piquancy, pungency; smell, aroma, odor, scent, fragrance; smack, relish, zest. **2.** *His words had the savor of vengeance:* character, nature, particular quality, characteristic, property, particularity, distinctive feature, peculiarity, trait, aura, quality; substance, essence, gist, spirit, soul. —*v.* **3.** *Her sauce savored of garlic. This plan savors of treason:* taste, smell, smack, have a touch, show traces, have the earmarks, be suggestive. **4.** *He savored the cookies with cinnamon:* spice, season, flavor. **5.** *We ate the stew slowly, savoring it:* enjoy, relish, like; take pleasure in, delight in, luxuriate in, rejoice in, appreciate. **6.** *He had savored power during his first term in office:* experience, taste, sample, try.

savory *adj.* **1.** *We supped on a savory stew:* tasty, appetizing, mouth-watering, aromatic, fragrant, odorous; pungent, piquant, tangy, delectable, delicious, luscious, tasty, tasteful, palatable, toothsome, full-flavored, flavorous, *Informal* scrumptious, yummy. **2.** *He wasn't a very savory character:* reputable, respectable, edifying, in good odor, inoffensive, honest; attractive, alluring, charming. **—Ant. 1** ill-tasting, tasteless, insipid, malodorous, smelly. **2** unsavory, disreputable, shady.

say *v.* **1.** *How dare you say such a thing to me! He said he wouldn't go. What did the telegram say?:* speak, tell, utter, give utterance to, voice, verbalize, vocalize, articulate; express, word, mouth, phrase; state, declare, pronounce, announce; remark, comment, mention; communicate, convey; come out with, let out, divulge, repeat, reveal, make known, disclose. **2.** *The actors said their lines perfectly:* recite, read, speak, deliver, render, pronounce, mouth, repeat, rehearse, perform, do. **3.** *I'd say it's about two o'clock:* guess, suppose, surmise, assume, hazard a guess, conjecture, imagine; judge, reason; daresay; be sure, be certain, feel convinced. **4.** *It's been said that he's an impostor:* report, rumor, spread, circulate, bruit, noise abroad, put forth; allege, hold, claim, assert, maintain; contend, hint, imply, intimate, suggest, insinuate. **—***n.* **5.** *We should all have a say in the running of our government:* right to speak, voice, participation; vote, franchise. **6.** *You've had your say, now sit down:* opportunity to speak, chance, day in court; comment, expressed opinion; *Slang* two cents worth. **—Ant. 1** be quiet about, suppress.

saying *n.* *"A bird in the hand is worth two in the bush" is an old saying:* expression, proverb, saw, adage, maxim, truism, aphorism, dictum, motto, precept, apothegm, epigram, byword, moral.

scale[1] *n.* **1.** *Scrape the paint scales off the ceiling before repainting it:* thin piece, flake, chip; plate. **2.** *A scale of rust covered the steel plate:* coating, film, thin covering, skin, peel, lamina, membrane, layer, lamella, crust, shell. **—***v.* **3.** *You have to scale the fish before cooking it:* scrape, scour. **4.** *Scale the old paint from the ceiling:* chip off, flake, shave, rub off; delaminate; shell, peel, husk.

scale[2] *n.* **1.** Often **scales** *Weigh the fruit on the scale:* weighing machine, balance. **—***v.* **2.** *The baby scaled six pounds seven ounces:* have a weight of, weigh.

scale[3] *n.* **1.** *What's the scale of that ruler? I know how to convert Fahrenheit to the centigrade scale:* gradation, graduation, calibration, rule; measure. **2.** *We were graded on a scale from 1 to 10:* classification, range, series, progression; spread, spectrum, continuum, order, ladder. **3.** *What is the scale of that map?:* proportion, ratio. **4.** *The opera singer could sing in several scales:* register, range, octave; key. **—***v.* **5.** *Come with me and I'll teach you how to scale a rock face:* climb up, climb over, clamber, go up, ascend, mount, surmount, escalade, rise, progress upward, work upward. **6.** *Management agreed to scale wages according to the job specifications:* adjust, regulate, set; vary according to a scale.

scamp *n.* *I'll bet that little scamp has hidden your glasses:* rascal, scalawag, rogue, scoundrel, rapscallion, knave, scapegrace, villain, miscreant, imp, mischiefmaker, tease, prankster; *Slang* cut-up, rip; *British* bounder, rotter, blighter.

scamper *v.* **1.** *The children scampered out of the house after the rain stopped:* run, rush, hasten, fly, hurry, race, sprint, dart, dash, scuttle, scud, flit, zip, scurry; *Informal* scoot, skedaddle. **—***n.* **2.** *The child left the house with a scamper:* quick run, dash, sprint, hasty run; scurry, zip. **3.** *The dogs enjoyed a scamper in the open field:* frolic, running about playfully, gambol, frisk, romp.

scan *v.* **1.** *The lookout scanned the horizon for a sight of land:* examine, peruse, pore over, scour, probe, scrutinize, inspect, study, size up, take stock of; search, explore, sweep, survey, check. **2.** *He only scanned the letter but signed it anyway:* read hastily, glance at, browse through, skim. **3.** *The English teacher taught the class how to scan poems:* divide into feet, show the metrical structure of; analyze.

scandal *n.* **1.** *The Dreyfus Affair was the most famous political scandal in French history:* public disgrace, revelation of misconduct, exposure of wrongdoing, embarrassment, sensation, exposé. **2.** *She brought scandal to her family by her outrageous behavior:* dishonor, disgrace, disesteem, embarrassment, discredit; shame, outrage; smirch, stain, stigma, blot, debasement, odium, ignominy, opprobrium. **3.** *I will not listen to this scandal!:* malicious gossip, slander, libel, aspersion, defamatory talk, obloquy, calumny, detraction, disparagement, revilement, vituperation, abuse, evil-speaking. **—Ant. 2** honor, esteem, credit, praise.

scandalous *adj.* **1.** *I am shocked by his scandalous behavior:* disgraceful, shameful, disreputable, highly improper, offensive, shocking, outrageous, reprehensible. **2.** *That tabloid is full of scandalous stories:* slanderous, libelous, scurrilous, defamatory, gossiping. **—Ant. 1** proper, reputable, decent. **2** kind, praising, laudatory, sweet.

scant *adj.* **1.** *The surveyors found only a scant water supply:* limited, meager, exiguous, deficient, insufficient, inadequate; small, short, paltry, sparse. **2.** *My jailer offered me a scant cupful of water:* not full, bare, incomplete. **3.** *Since the husband died, the family has been scant of money:* ill-supplied, in need, short. **—***v.* **4.** *The general refused to scant the men's rations:* limit, stint, hold back, skimp on, reduce, cut. **—Ant. 1** plentiful, profuse, copious, abundant, ample, adequate. **2** full, overflowing. **3** well-supplied. **4** lavish.

scanty *adj.* *The beggar shivered in his scanty clothes:* inadequate, scant, insufficient; meager, deficient; thin, slender, sparse, skimpy, small, modest, short, stunted, undersized, paltry.

scapegoat *n.* *The mechanic became the scapegoat for the pilot's error:* victim, dupe, gull, whipping boy, laughingstock; *Slang* butt, fall guy, patsy, goat.

scar *n.* **1.** *He had a scar on his arm from an old*

accident. She bore the scars of an unhappy childhood. The boat had scars from hitting the reefs: mark left by an old wound, cicatrix, wound, seam, stitch mark, pit, pock; dent, gash; defect, flaw, blemish. —v. **2.** Falling on the rocks scarred his legs and arms. An unhappy childhood can scar you for life: leave a scar on, wound, cut, scratch, gash, lacerate, mutilate, mangle; mark, bruise, brand, deface, disfigure; hurt, impair, damage; influence, affect.

scarce adj. **1.** Qualified workmen were scarce during the strike: in short supply, hard to find, scanty, sparse, hard to obtain; wanting, insufficient, deficient, not abundant, not plentiful. **2.** Bald eagles are now fairly scarce in North America: rare, rarely seen, unusual, uncommon, exceptional. —**Ant.** 1 abundant, plentiful. 2 numerous, common.

scarcely adj. **1.** We scarcely had time for breakfast: hardly, barely, slightly, faintly, just, but just, at most, no more than, not easily. **2.** He was scarcely the type of person needed for the job: definitely not, certainly not, in no manner, in no way, by no means, not at all, not in the least, hardly, on no account.

scarcity n. **1.** The scarcity of supplies was alleviated when new shipments arrived: insufficient supply, insufficiency, shortage, scantiness, lack, dearth, deficiency, want, paucity, stint, thinness. **2.** Uranium is an expensive metal because of its scarcity: rarity, infrequency of occurrence, rareness, scarceness, sparsity, uncommonness, sparseness, fewness.

scare v. **1.** The thunder and lightning scared the child: fill with fear, strike terror into, make afraid, frighten, terrify, startle, terrorize, horrify, make one's flesh crawl, make apprehensive, panic, alarm, intimidate, harrow, daunt, disquiet, give a turn, disconcert, dishearten; become frightened. —n. **2.** The smell of gas gave me a scare: sudden fright, start, sudden terror, alarm, shock, panic; shake, palpitation, shiver, turn, nervousness, consternation; Slang jitters, the willies. —**Ant.** 1 reassure, calm, soothe, comfort. 2 calm, reassurance.

scared adj. The scared girl ran for her life: frightened, fearful, afraid, aghast, panicked, panicky, terrified, terror-stricken.

scary adj. When I saw his gun it became a very scary situation: frightening, terrifying, creepy, hair-raising, shocking, goosepimply, disturbing, discomfiting, menacing, alarming, threatening, fearful, Slang hairy; bad, awful, difficult. —**Ant.** cheering, reassuring, comforting, pleasant, pleasing.

scathing adj. She was in tears after the scathing criticism of her essay: brutal, cutting, scorching, lacerating, searing, mordant, stinging, caustic, vitriolic, biting, acrimonious, excoriating; savage, ferocious, rancorous, hostile, virulent; trenchant, sharp, tart, pointed, keen, incisive. —**Ant.** kind, gentle, considerate, mild.

scatter v. **1.** We scattered the rat poison around the cellar floor: spread loosely, distribute, disperse, throw, strew, sprinkle, spatter, cast, sow; circulate, broadcast, disseminate. **2.** The crows scattered when the farmer shot at them. A loud noise scattered the pigeons: disperse, flee; dispel, dissipate, rout, chase away. —**Ant.** gather, assemble, collect.

scatterbrained adj. The playboy was so scatterbrained he never had a serious thought. Going to Monte Carlo was a scatterbrained idea: hare-brained, muddleheaded, rattlebrained, birdbrained, featherbrained, light-minded, empty-headed, flighty, madcap, giddy, silly, zany, dizzy, stupid; absentminded, forgetful, foolish, foolhardy, wild, reckless, rash, heedless, careless, imprudent, frivolous, devil-may-care; irresponsible, unsteady, unstable; Informal crazy, nutty. —**Ant.** serious, intense, intelligent; careful, prudent; responsible, reliable, steady, stable.

scavenger n. **1.** Vultures are scavengers: carrion eater. **2.** The street urchins were scavengers: trash picker, garbage picker; salvager; collector, magpie.

scenario n. **1.** The writers were given two weeks to finish the scenario: screenplay, teleplay, working script, shooting script; manuscript, book. **2.** Have they worked out a scenario for launching the new car?: master plan, game plan, conception, scheme, plan, idea, concept; outline, summary, abstract, synopsis, précis.

scene n. **1.** Criminals are said to return to the scene of the crime: setting, site, location, locale, locality, whereabouts; place, spot, position, region. **2.** The setting of the sun over the lake was a beautiful scene: vista, view, vision, sight, panorama, prospect, picture, show, display, spectacle; survey. **3.** She made a scene and couldn't be quieted: display of temper, embarrassing spectacle, fuss, to-do, commotion. **4.** The scene of the story is Victorian England: setting, locale, milieu; backdrop, background, scenery. **5.** We missed the first few scenes of the movie: episode, part, division, sequence, act.

scenery n. **1.** The scenery up at the lake is just breathtaking!: landscape, terrain; general appearance, view, spectacle, vista. **2.** He painted scenery for the community playhouse productions: stage setting, backdrops, backgrounds, scenes, sets.

scenic adj. We paused before a scenic lookout: picturesque, panoramic, beautiful, breathtaking, dramatic, impressive, spectacular, striking.

scent n. **1.** The scent of lemons filled the grove: smell, odor, aroma, fragrance, bouquet, essence, perfume. **2.** The dogs followed the scent of the escaped convict. The thief managed to throw his pursuers off the scent: odor left in passing; trail, track, course, path, wake, wind, pursuit, spoor. —v. **3.** We could scent roses in the garden: smell, sniff, breathe, inhale; get wind of, get a hint of, detect, distinguish, recognize, discern, suspect; trace, trail, track. **4.** She used lemon juice to scent her hair: fill with an odor, give odor to, perfume, aromatize.

schedule n. **1.** What's on the schedule for today?: list of events, agenda, calendar, program; roll; inventory. **2.** Retailers have several price schedules. I need a train schedule: list, table;

timetable. —v. **3.** *The secretary is trying to schedule the month's appointments. We're scheduled to appear in court on Tuesday:* set the time for, slate, fix, plan, book; appoint, set down, fit in, put down.

scheme n. **1.** *He suggested several schemes to increase sales:* plan, design, program, project, course; method, means, system, way, device, procedure, policy; strategy, tactics. **2.** *The robbers devised a scheme to hold up the armored truck:* secret plan, conspiracy, plot, maneuver, ruse, shift; contrivance, connivance; intrigue, cabal, stratagem, machination. **3.** *The airport contains a scheme of crisscrossing runways:* arrangement, system, grouping, organization, network, disposition. **4.** *Follow this scheme to put the radio tubes back in order:* schematic diagram, outline, delineation, layout, sketch, design, drawing; chart, map. —v. **5.** *For months they had schemed to overthrow the government:* plan secretly, plot, conspire, connive, contrive, devise, concoct, study, design; frame, organize, maneuver, machinate, cabal, intrigue; *Archaic* complot.

scheming adj. *We were deceived by a scheming con man:* conniving, designing, contriving, calculating; Machiavellian, crafty, arch, sly, wily, artful, slippery, insidious, cunning, shrewd, tricky, intriguing. —**Ant.** naive, artless, ingenuous.

schmaltz n. *The screenwriter added a lot of schmaltz to the script:* sentimentality, sentimentalism, emotionalism, schwarmerei, mawkishness, bathos, mush, mushiness.

scholar n. **1.** *The art collector sought advice from eminent scholars:* learned person, erudite person, sage, wise man, man of letters, pundit, savant, mandarin; academic specialist, humanist, intellectual; *Slang* egghead, brain. **2.** *Several young scholars enrolled in the advanced mathematics course:* pupil, student, learner, studier, matriculant; schoolboy, schoolgirl, undergraduate, collegian; *Informal* coed; *Slang* bookworm, grind. —**Ant.** 1 dunce, dolt; ignoramus, illiterate.

scholarly adj. *The Library at Alexandria was organized by scholarly people. Scholarly disputes can be rather dull at times:* erudite, learned, informed, educated, well-read, academic, intellectual, lettered, literate, liberal, humane.

scholarship n. **1.** *Scaliger was renowned for his classical scholarship:* academic attainments, knowledge gained by study, learning, erudition, education, enlightenment, intelligence; thoroughness, accurate research, sound academic practice. **2.** *He won a scholarship to the state university:* aid granted a student, grant, endowment, maintenance for a student, stipend; assistantship, fellowship. —**Ant.** 1 stupidity, idiocy, foolishness.

scholastic adj. *A certain portion of our taxes is put aside for scholastic purposes:* of schools, educational, academic; scholarly, instructional, pedagogic, professorial, pedantic.

school n. **1.** *The children go to school every morning by bus:* place for instruction; academy, lyceum, institute; (*variously*) kindergarten, grade school, high school, college, university, seminary. **2.** *The old school refused to accept new ideas:* group of people who think alike, order, faction, denomination, way of thinking, thought, ism, system, method, style, view; persuasion, doctrine, theory, faith, belief; *Informal* bunch, crowd. —v. **3.** *She was schooled at Harvard:* teach, train, instruct, educate.

schooling n. *She received her schooling abroad:* education, training, instruction, tuition, tutelage, learning.

science n. **1.** *We studied several sciences in school. Chemistry is a science:* natural phenomena, empirical knowledge, organized knowledge, systematic knowledge; field of systematic inquiry. **2.** *We had the procedure down to a science. Boxing is called by its devotees the "sweet science":* art, technique, method, discipline; finished execution, skill, aptitude, acquirement, finesse, facility.

scintillating adj. *Conversation at the party was scintillating:* sparkling, lively, animated, ebullient, effervescent, exuberant, brilliant, dazzling, stimulating, glittering; charming, bright, witty. —**Ant.** dull, boring, lackluster.

scion n. *We heard he was the scion of a famous family:* offspring, child, heir, successor, descendant, son, daughter, heiress, offshoot; progeny, issue, seed, progeniture, posterity.

scoff v. *She scoffed at his attempts to improve himself:* mock, ridicule, deride, poke fun at, laugh at; deride, make sport of, make light of, belittle, make game of; flout, taunt, jeer, revile, contemn, rail at, run down; *Slang* knock, razz, put down. —**Ant.** praise, compliment, exalt; applaud, cheer.

scold v. **1.** *Dad scolded me for coming home late:* rebuke, upbraid, reprove, reprehend, remonstrate with, reprimand, chide, dress down, set down, take to task, bring to book, rake over the coals, put on the carpet, criticize, castigate, censure, blame angrily, berate, lash out at; find fault, nag, carp at, rail at, complain about. —n. **2.** *That old scold never has anything nice to say:* constant faultfinder, complainer, nagger, *Slang* kvetch; shrew, virago, termagant. —**Ant.** 1 praise, honor, compliment, applaud.

scoop n. **1.** *The storekeeper used a scoop to put the dry beans in a bag:* hand shovel; ladle, dipper, spoon, trowel. **2.** *The first paper with the scoop was the Herald:* exclusive news story, *Slang* beat. —v. **3.** *The shopkeeper bent over to scoop penny candy into the bag:* dish out; lade out, ladle, lift out, shovel, spoon; empty with a scoop, bail, clear, clean. **4.** *The bulldozer scooped out a deep hole:* hollow, dig out, excavate, burrow, shovel, render concave, gouge.

scope n. **1.** *The ministry is no place for a man of limited scope:* range or extent of view, vision; application, bearing; effect, force, influence, competence, breadth of knowledge, reach, grasp; aim, purpose, goal, motive, intention, ambition, destination, determination. **2.** *The scope of his property was enormous:* extent in space, area, span, stretch, spread, extension, compass, bounds, reach, confines. **3.** *Give your* child's creativity a wide scope: space for movement or activity, opportunity for operation; free course, rein, latitude, margin, range, field, room, elbow room, vent; freedom, liberty.

scorch v. A too-hot iron may scorch your clothes. The hot weather scorched the grass: burn the surface of, singe, sear; shrivel with heat, wither, parch, scathe, char; dry, dry out, dehydrate; blacken, discolor.

score n. **1.** The score is 2-0. Who made that last score?: record of points made, tally, count; (variously) point, goal, run, basket. **2.** My score on the test was 95: grade, test result, mark. **3.** The tree trunk had many scores in it: notch, incision, nick, scratch, mark, groove, cut, slash, gash, slit. **4.** "Fourscore and seven years ago...": set of twenty. **5. scores** Scores of people attended the special performance: large numbers, multitudes, throngs, hosts, lots, masses, legions, droves, swarms. **6.** I have to pay off this score before spending any more money: amount owed, amount due, account, bill, obligation, charge, debt, tab; grievance, grudge, difference. **7.** Informal He's a naive kid who doesn't know what the score is: facts, reality, truth, true situation. **8.** He wrote scores for many hit musicals: music (for a play, motion picture, etc.); written form of a musical composition. —v. **9.** How many points did he score in that basketball game?: make, gain, tally, register; pile up, amass. **10.** The professor hates to score exam papers: grade, mark, evaluate, judge; keep a tally, keep track of points. **11.** No good scout would score a tree trunk with a knife: notch, scratch, cut, groove; mar, damage, deface. **12.** Our team is sure to score a victory: achieve, win, strike, register. **13.** At the conservatory she learned how to score a musical composition: orchestrate, arrange.

scorn n. **1.** She regarded weaker people with scorn: contempt, scornfulness, disdain, haughtiness, arrogance; opprobrium, derision, contumely; scoffing, sarcasm, mockery, ridicule. —v. **2.** He scorned those who did not follow him into battle. The union leaders continue to scorn all of management's attempts at reconciliation: look down on, esteem lightly, contemn, be contemptuous of, despise, curl one's lip at, hold in contempt, disdain, treat with disdain, refuse to recognize, not countenance, care nothing for; spurn, refuse, rebuff, reject, repulse; ignore, disregard, refuse to deal with, have nothing to do with, refuse to listen to, turn a deaf ear to, slight; ostracize, spit upon. —**Ant.** 1 affection, deference, respect, esteem. 2 esteem, revere, look up to, admire; accept.

scotch v. She wants to scotch those rumors of an impending marriage: suppress, stop, kill, destroy, put down, thwart, quash, crush, stamp out, confound, foil, put to rest, undermine, obstruct, sabotage; Slang nip in the bud, short-circuit. —**Ant.** encourage, spur, stimulate, boost, promote.

scoundrel n. That scoundrel would sell his own mother!: villain, miscreant, rogue, cur, snake in the grass, weasel, ruffian, blackguard, knave, varlet, cad, bounder, rotter; mountebank, good-for-nothing, ne'er-do-well; thief, crook, swindler, sharper, trickster, four flusher; rascal, scamp, rapscallion, scalawag; turncoat, copperhead, carpetbagger, varmint.

scour[1] v. Use a scouring pad to scour the kitchen sink. Mother made me scour the family silver: clean by rubbing, scrub, scrape, cleanse, wash vigorously; abrade, polish, burnish, buff; shine, brighten.

scour[2] v. He scoured the bookstores looking for a particular volume of poetry. We scoured the countryside looking for the lost child: search through, comb, scan, rake, rummage, ransack; range over, pass over, traverse; move swiftly over, race through.

scourge n. **1.** The cruel captain used a scourge on disobedient sailors: whip, lash, flail, cat-o'-nine-tails, strap; switch, birch, rod, cane. **2.** Lack of rain is the scourge of certain parts of India and Africa. Genghis Khan was the scourge of Asia: cause of plague, bane, curse, terror; affliction, troublement, vexation. —v. **3.** Captain Bligh scourged his crew without mercy: flog, whip, lash, flail, thrash, beat; punish, discipline, flagellate; cane, switch, strap, birch, give the stick. **4.** Presidents sometimes fear being scourged by future historians: criticize severely, castigate, chastise, chasten, take to task, excoriate, rake over the coals, censure, Slang blast.

scout n. **1.** The scout reported that there was trouble on the road ahead: person sent ahead, reconnoiterer, vanguard, advance guard, advance man, point man, outrider, lookout; guide, pilot, escort. **2.** Baseball star Lou Gehrig was discovered by a Yankee scout: person employed to discover new talent, talent scout, recruiter. —v. **3.** Who scouted for Custer?: make reconnaissance, reconnoiter, survey, observe, put under surveillance, Slang case; spy, spy out.

scowl v. He scowled when I refused to lend him the money: frown, glower, lower, glare, look daggers, grimace, look sullen, pout, Slang give a dirty look.

scram v. Informal When he saw the bigger boy, he scrammed: go away, leave, depart, clear out, decamp, go away, quit, Informal skedaddle, vamoose, beat it.

scramble v. **1.** We scrambled for cover against the sudden rain: scurry, rush, race, run. **2.** The three of us had to scramble for the loose ball: scuffle, struggle, vie, fight, strive, engage, scrimmage, combat, battle, come to blows, scrap, tussle, jostle, collide, clash. **3.** The child can scramble eggs. In our code we scramble letters so words are unrecognizable: stir together; mix together, mix up, jumble, garble, disarrange, shuffle, disorganize, confuse, disorder; mess up, bring into disorder, upset, throw into confusion, unsettle, disturb, scatter. —n. **4.** We made a scramble for cover when it started raining: rush, race, run. **5.** There was a scramble to recover the dropped football: scuffle, struggle, tussle, free-for-all, competition, scrimmage.

scrap[1] n. **1.** There wasn't a scrap of evidence to convict him. Scraps of bread were thrown to the *birds:* small piece, small quantity, fragment, snippet, fraction, trace, sliver, particle; minimum, modicum, glimmer, smattering, sprinkling; bit, morsel, speck, dab, drop; atom, molecule, jot, iota, grain, crumb. **2.** *The old copper pipes were sold for scrap:* discarded material, reclaimable material, junk; trash, refuse. —*v.* **3.** *We decided to scrap the old car. I predict the Mayor will scrap the plan the minute he gets re-elected:* put in the scrap heap, sell as scrap; discard as worthless, junk, abandon, jettison. —*Ant.* 3 keep, repair, maintain.

scrap² *Informal n.* **1.** *The recruit got a black eye in his first barroom scrap:* fight, brawl, squabble, row; free-for-all, melee, fracas, brouhaha, *Slang* ruckus. —*v.* **2.** *Those two will scrap at the least provocation!:* fight, quarrel, spat, brawl, row, come to blows.

scrape *v.* **1.** *You can rent a machine to scrape floors:* rub hard, abrade, scour; clean, smooth, plane, buff, burnish. **2.** *I slipped and scraped an elbow:* graze, bruise, abrade, grate; scuff, skin. **3.** *The hungry troops tried to scrape up some food:* collect with difficulty, dig, forage, get by hook or crook; secure, procure, acquire, obtain, pick up, glean, gather, amass. **4.** *Don't scrape your fingernail across the blackboard!:* grate, rasp, grind, scratch. **5.** *We scraped for years to buy that house:* economize, be frugal, save, scrimp, stint, pinch pennies. —*n.* **6.** *How did you get that scrape on your arm?:* skin injury, abrasion, bruise; mark, score, gash, gouge, groove. **7.** *Her violent temper always got her into scrapes:* troublesome situation, predicament, difficulty, tough spot, tight spot, dilemma, pretty pickle, plight, straits; fight, scuffle, tussle, confrontation, run-in.

scratch *v.* **1.** *The car was only scratched in the accident:* make a mark on, graze, score, scrape, streak; cut, gash, lacerate; mar, blemish; damage slightly. **2.** *In Chinatown one may buy a scratcher to scratch one's back:* scrape, rub, dig at; claw; relieve the itching of. **3.** *He scratched a match on his boot heel:* draw along a rough surface, rub, scrape; strike. **4.** *Scratch out that last paragraph. Scratch his name from the finals:* strike out, cancel, cross out, delete, draw the pen through, withdraw, eliminate, remove, rule out, blot out, expunge, exclude, omit, erase, rub out. **5.** *The scout scratched a map in the dirt with a stick:* draw crudely, scrawl, scribble; incise, cut, etch. **6.** *Her fingernails scratched against the blackboard:* sound harshly, scrape, grate, rasp, grind. —*n.* **7.** *How did you get that scratch on your nose?:* slight flesh wound, laceration, abrasion, nick, cut, gash.

scrawny *adj.* *That husky man was once a scrawny boy:* extremely thin, spindly, skinny, spare, lean, sinewy, lank, lanky; bony, gaunt, angular, rawboned; scraggy; puny, undersized, underweight, stunted, runty; fleshless, skeletal, emaciated, drawn, wasted, attenuated. —*Ant.* fat, plump, chubby, brawny, muscular.

scream *v.* **1.** *She screamed when she saw the dead body:* shriek, howl, cry out, wail; screech, squawk, yowl, yelp, squeal, bellow, roar. **2.** *We screamed for help:* shout, yell, call out loudly, cry out, holler. —*n.* **3.** *We heard screams in the night. In New York you get used to the scream of sirens:* loud, shrill cry; shriek, outcry, shout, yell, holler; screech, squeal, whine, wail, yelp, squawk; bellow, roar; lamentation.

screen *n.* **1.** *She changed clothes behind a screen:* partition, room divider, curtain, lattice. **2.** *The fog acted as a screen for the smugglers:* concealment, protection, cover, coverage, veil, mask, curtain, shroud, cloak, mantle; buffer, safeguard, defense. **3.** *Sir Laurence Olivier is a star of stage and screen:* motion pictures, movies, cinema, the silver screen, films; the film industry. **4.** *Close the screen or the flies will get into the house:* screen door, window screen, screening, shutter, Venetian blind, jalousie, lattice. **5.** *The little child loves to sift sand through a screen:* sieve, strainer, sifter, filter, grate, colander; web, mesh. —*v.* **6.** *Sunglasses will screen your eyes from the harmful rays:* shield, shelter, protect, defend, secure, safeguard, guard; cover, shroud, shade, veil; keep hidden, conceal, hide from sight; withhold, secrete, keep secret. **7.** *The Personnel Department is here to screen applicants:* examine for suitability, size up, rate, grade; eliminate, get rid of, throw away, discard, throw out, eject, weed out; separate, sift, winnow, cull, filter, strain; sort, arrange, order, group, class. **8.** *They will screen a new movie at 9 PM:* project, show, present; see, view, preview.

screw *n.* **1.** *Use these screws to put the table together:* fastener, threaded nail, bolt. **2.** *The ship's screws stopped and it drifted helplessly:* propeller; driver. —*v.* **3.** *Screw this coat hook into the closet door. Screw the vise tighter:* fasten, bolt, rivet, attach, join, clamp; adjust, tighten; twist, turn. **4.** *He screwed the facts to suit his own purposes. She screwed up her eyes trying to see the shooting star:* twist, twist out of shape, contort, distort, pervert, warp; deform, misshape, garble; gnarl, knot. **5.** *The troopers screwed the information out of him somehow:* wring, wrench, wrest, force, exact, extort, twist, squeeze.

screwball *adj. Slang* **1.** *It turned out to be a screwball idea:* eccentric, off-center, whimsical, capricious, zany, *Informal* kooky, oddball, madcap, nutty, goofy, wacky. —*n.* **2.** *He was the screwball of his high school class:* oddity, character, oddball, zany, *Informal* kook, nut, nutcase.

screwy *adj.* *He had a screwy idea that he could find a buried treasure:* batty, daft, eccentric, unbalanced, queer, odd, peculiar, funny; *Slang* wacky, dotty, kinky, weird, weirdo, nutty, flaky, kooky, oddball.

scrimp *v.* *We scrimped for years until the house was finally paid for:* be sparing, skimp, be frugal, be parsimonious, be stingy, pinch, stint, save, be penurious, pinch pennies, hoard, cut corners, economize; dole out sparingly, use sparingly, begrudge.

script *n.* **1.** *She has a neat, precise script:*

handwriting, hand, longhand, cursive; penmanship, calligraphy, chirography. **2.** *The script was delivered to the director ahead of schedule. Several changes were made in the script:* manuscript, written text; dialogue, lines, book, scenario, libretto, score.

Scripture also **Holy Scripture** *n.* Often **the Scriptures, the Holy Scriptures.** *The text for the sermon was a passage from Scripture:* sacred writings, holy writ, inspired writings; the Bible, the Word of God, the Gospels, Old Testament, New Testament, *Informal* The Good Book; (*Judaism*) the Hebrew Scriptures, (*variously*) the Torah, the Law, the Pentateuch, the Septuagint.

scrub¹ *v.* **1.** *Scrub your back with this long-handled brush:* rub clean, scour, swab. —*n.* **2.** *She gave the floors a good scrub:* scrubbing, scouring; cleaning by rubbing.

scrub² *n.* *The land was cleared of scrub and deadwood:* low trees, brush, brushwood, stunted vegetation.

scrumptious *adj. Informal That was a scrumptious roast!:* delicious, flavorful, tasty, delectable, flavorsome, savory, appetizing, mouthwatering, toothsome, luscious, juicy, succulent, tender; agreeable, enjoyable, pleasant, pleasing, delightful.

scruple *n.* **1.** *He's a greedy person with no scruples when it comes to making a profit:* principle, ethics, moral restraint, compunction, misgiving; conscience, conscientiousness, scrupulousness, concern, care; qualm, anxiety, hesitation, uncertainty, apprehension, doubtfulness, protestation; squeamishness, fearfulness. —*v.* **2.** *She scrupled when it came to disobeying her father:* be ethical, have principles, hesitate, refrain, demur, pause, hang back, blench, balk, halt; waver, fluctuate, falter; have a qualm, feel qualms, be qualmish, have a bad conscience, be timorous, shy, fight shy, take exception.

scrupulous *adj. He's a sharp but fairly scrupulous businessman. The scientist described his observations with scrupulous accuracy:* having scruples, principled, honest, conscientious, honorable, upright; painstaking, sedulous, deliberate, careful, cautious; exact, exacting, precise, meticulous, fastidious, punctilious; dutiful. —**Ant.** unscrupulous, dishonest, unprincipled; careless, reckless, inexact.

scrutinize *v. The building inspector scrutinized the structure's foundation:* examine closely, study, observe, look at closely, peruse, scan, regard carefully, *Slang* give the once-over; inspect carefully, survey, look over, take stock of; inquire into, investigate, pry into, peer into; search, explore, probe. —**Ant.** neglect, disregard, overlook; glance at.

scrutiny *n. His testimony was given close scrutiny:* examination, attention, study, investigation, inquiry, inspection, perusal, close look, critical regard, watch, surveillance.

scuffle *v.* **1.** *The students scuffled in the school corridor:* struggle, fight, scrap, tussle, squabble, spar, jostle; come to blows, exchange blows, clash; *Slang* mix it up. —*n.* **2.** *The scuffle in the*

playground was soon over: struggle, scrap, tussle, row, fight, brawl, imbroglio; melee, donnybrook, free-for-all, fracas; rumpus, commotion.

scum *n.* **1.** *Don't use the pool until the scum is cleared off:* surface, film, crust, dross, deposit, slag, refuse. **2.** *According to the sheriff the demonstrators are the scum of society:* lowest of the low, trash, rubbish, dregs; riffraff, rabble.

scurrilous *adj. W.C. Fields was celebrated for his scurrilous remarks. The old salt was scurrilous but good-natured:* slanderous, derogatory, disparaging, detracting, derisive, reviling, offensive, contemptuous, insulting; coarsely abusive, coarse, gross, low, churlish, shameless, indecent, indelicate; vulgar, foulmouthed, obscene. —**Ant.** decent, proper, delicate, refined, well-bred, polite.

scurry *v.* **1.** *The bathers scurried across the hot sand toward the water:* move quickly, run with light steps, scamper, scramble, scuttle, make tracks, rush, speed, hasten, hurry, hie, hustle, scoot, spring, skim, race, tear along. —*n.* **2.** *We lifted the rock and watched a scurry of insects:* scamper, hasty running; rushing, hurrying, scooting; dispersal, scattering; haste, bustle, confusion.

scurvy *adj. The crew were a scurvy bunch of cutthroats:* mean, low, base, shabby, vile; contemptible, despicable, dishonorable, ignoble, worthless. —**Ant.** honorable, dignified, noble.

scuttle *v.* **1.** *The captain scuttled his ship rather than see it captured by the enemy:* sink, send to the bottom, send to Davy Jones's locker; sacrifice, abort, discard, dispatch, wreck, scrap, destroy. **2.** *The crab scuttled across the seafloor:* scurry, hurry, hasten, scamper, speed, scramble.

scuttlebutt *n. There's scuttlebutt that the company will move to Florida:* gossip, rumor, hearsay, talk, tittle-tattle, chitchat, small talk, prattle, scandal.

sea *n.* **1.** *It's my dream to sail the seas in a schooner. Many Muscovites vacation at resorts on the Black Sea:* ocean, deep, main, waves, waters, the briny deep; large body of water, bay, gulf, bight, lake. **2.** *The small boat struggled in a turbulent sea:* condition of the water's surface. **3.** *Enormous seas swept over the decks:* wave, swell, surge, flood, roller, breaker. **4.** *The business manager was deluged with a sea of complaints:* great deal, great quantity, multitude, slew, flood, spate, ton, leap, scads, lots, mass, legion, host, swarm, flock, scores, abundance, profusion. —**Ant.** land, terrain, terra firma.

seacoast *n. We stayed at a pleasant little resort on the seacoast:* shore, seashore, coast, seaside, seaboard, coastline, waterside, water's edge, shoreline, beach, littoral, lido, riviera, coastland; *French* côte.

seal *n.* **1.** *The document bore the king's seal:* figure, emblem, mark, symbol, distinctive design, insignia, stamp, impression, imprint, brand; signet, imprimatur; hallmark, colophon, trademark. **2.** *The envelope's seal was torn open:* fastening device, fastener; gummed flap. —*v.* **3.** *You must seal the document with the* *king's insignia:* certify, authenticate, confirm, verify, ratify, validate, endorse; affirm, approve, sanction, accept, OK. **4.** *We sealed our agreement with a handshake:* settle, conclude, make final; fix, establish, determine. **5.** *The jars were sealed with paraffin:* close, secure, fasten; shut, shut up, lock; plug, stop, stop up, cork, dam.

seam *n.* **1.** *Sew the split seams of the shirt:* line of stitches, juncture, joining, junction, joint, suture; interface. **2.** *Seams appeared on the dried-up riverbed:* wrinkle, incised line, furrow, scar; fissure, chink, crevice, break, breach, rupture, opening, crack, cleft, gap. **3.** *The prospectors found a seam of coal:* layer, stratum, vein, lode. —*v.* **4.** *Seam those two pieces and your skirt is finished:* join together in a seam, stitch together; suture. **5.** *Worry had seamed his forehead:* furrow, wrinkle, mark, line, cut into, incise, notch.

seamless *adj.* *Her seamless story could not be contradicted:* smooth, continuous, unvarying, integrated, indivisible, unbroken, uninterrupted, connected, uniform, homogeneous, jointless. —**Ant.** disjointed, fragmented.

seamy *adj.* *Policemen often see the seamy side of life:* unpleasant, nasty, disagreeable, coarse, sordid, unwholesome, rough, raw, dirty, unclean, dark, squalid. —**Ant.** pleasant, nice, wholesome, agreeable; gentle, tender, sweet.

sear *v.* **1.** *The flames seared her arms when she tried to put out the fire:* burn, scorch, char, singe; cauterize; blast, blister. **2.** *The bitter experience of betrayal seared his soul forever after:* harden, caseharden, scar, steel.

search *v.* **1.** *We carefully searched the attic for the old family album. The campers searched for a good place to pitch their tent. Police searched everyone present at the scene of the crime:* examine, scrutinize, explore, scour, scout out, investigate carefully, look over, inspect, overhaul, study, survey, check, check out, probe, sift, comb, drag, look into, pry into, delve into, pore over, ransack, rifle, rummage, turn inside out, turn upside down; snoop, fish; hunt, look, cast about, seek, quest; frisk, shake down. —*n.* **2.** *After a lengthy search we found the earliest patent for an electric blender. A search of the apartment produced several unregistered guns:* examination, inspection, scrutiny, study, close look, check, investigation, probe, inquiry, exploration; hunt, pursuit, quest; dragnet; tracer.

seashore *n.* *They rented a cottage on the seashore:* seaside, seashore, shorefront, coast, coastland, littoral, oceanfront, oceanside, seabank, seaboard, seacoast, seafront, tideland, tidewater, bayfront, bayside.

seasick *adj.* *As soon as the ship left the dock he got seasick:* nauseated, sick to one's stomach, queasy, squeamish, qualmish, vomitous; *Slang* barfy, green around the gills; ill, sick, giddy, faint, dizzy, lighthearted, vertiginous; *Slang* woozy, under the weather.

season *n.* **1.** *Spring and autumn are my favorite seasons. Peaches are out of season now. The young people have so much fun during the holiday season:* division of the year, *(variously)* spring, summer, the dog days, fall, autumn, Indian summer, winter, quarter; appropriate time, peak time, prime; period, term, stage, spell, stretch, interval, duration. —*v.* **2.** *She seasoned the stew with sage. His new play was seasoned with wit and humor:* flavor, spice, leaven, lace; enliven, heighten, color, accent, enhance, embellish, ornament. **3.** *The actor was seasoned by years of performing:* improve by experience, train, practice, discipline, drill; break in, tame; refine, mellow, soften, temper; accustom, inure, adapt; inform, shape, finish. **4.** *The carpenter taught us how to season wood:* age, dry, ripen, temper, mature, prime, cultivate, condition, prepare.

seasonable *adj.* *The weather was seasonable:* suitable, timely, opportune, fit, convenient, appropriate. —**Ant.** unseasonable, unsuitable, untimely, inopportune.

seasoning *n.* **1.** *This stew needs more seasoning:* flavoring, spice, condiment, relish, herb; *(variously)* salt, pepper, allspice, basil, thyme, oregano, rosemary, mace, sage, marjoram, clove, parsley, dill, paprika, garlic, onion, cinnamon, nutmeg, ginger; gusto, zest. **2.** *The pitcher was sent to the minors for a year of seasoning:* training, practice, preparation, orientation, familiarization; ripening, maturation; aging; drying.

seat *n.* **1.** *Won't you come in and have a seat? I forgot to reserve seats at the opera:* *(variously)* chair, sofa, couch, divan, bench, cushion, place, box. **2.** *The naughty child received several slaps on his seat:* buttocks, rear end, hindquarters, bottom, haunches, rump, posterior, croup, *French* derrière; *Informal* backside, behind, *Slang* fanny. **3.** *Hollywood is the seat of the film industry. That town is the county seat:* center, hub, axis, nucleus; heart, core; capital. **4.** *The castle was the seat of a noble family. The heart is regarded as the seat of the emotions:* residence, home, house, dwelling, abode, domicile, housing, address, quarters; site, locale, locus, location, habitat; family seat, ancestral hall. **5.** *He ran for a seat in Parliament:* place in a select group, membership; incumbency. —*v.* **6.** *The ushers will not seat latecomers:* show to a seat, provide with a seat; cause to sit, place on a seat; settle, situate.

secede *v.* *Soon after the Southern states seceded from the Union, the Civil War broke out:* withdraw, leave, pull out, quit, retire, resign, have done, disaffiliate, break with, forsake. —**Ant.** join, federate.

seclude *v.* *The old recluse secluded himself to escape the outside world:* place apart, keep apart, separate, dissociate, place in solitude, isolate, shut off, sequester, retire, retire from sight, hide, go into retreat.

secluded *adj.* *The naturalist built himself a secluded cabin in the forest. The ascetic led a secluded life:* isolated, sheltered, sequestered, cloistered; unvisited, seldom visited, unfrequented, remote, out-of-the-way, cut off, solitary, lonely, withdrawn, reclusive; shut in, confined; hidden from view, covert, shut away, closeted, private, screened off. —**Ant.** accessible, frequented; sociable; public, open.

seclusion *n. The millionaire went into seclusion to avoid interviewers. The mountain cabin was an ideal seclusion for quiet holidays:* isolation, solitude, hiding, concealment, retreat, reclusion, withdrawal, sequestration, cloister, retirement, exile, quarantine; secluded place, hiding place, sanctuary, asylum, hermitage, hideaway.

second[1] *adj.* **1.** *He was second in line. She was second in her class:* next after the first; runner-up. **2.** *They had a second house at the beach:* another, one more, additional. **3.** *Every second person was chosen:* alternate, alternating, other. **4.** *In beauty, the Rocky Mountains are second to none:* inferior, subordinate, second-rate, second fiddle, surpassed, exceeded, outdone. —*n.* **5.** *He was the second to be chosen:* second one; runner-up. **6.** *My second will call on you to arrange the duel:* helper, assistant, aid, attendant, lieutenant; agent, representative, deputy, delegate; substitute, alternate, fill-in, stand-in, understudy, pinch hitter, proxy. —*v.* **7.** *I second the nomination!:* support, endorse; back, stand by, back up, uphold, stand back of; side with, subscribe to, favor, work for, advocate; promote, encourage, further, advance; help, assist, aid, abet.

second[2] *n.* **1.** *He ran the race in 45 seconds:* sixtieth of a minute. **2.** *I'll be there in a second!:* moment, minute, instant, jiffy, trice, wink, flash; *Informal* bat of an eye, twinkling, shake of a lamb's tail, two shakes.

secondary *adj.* **1.** *Secondary school means junior high school and high school:* next after the first, second; following, subsequent, consequent, resultant. **2.** *That problem is secondary to the one now facing us:* lesser, inferior, smaller, minor, lower; subordinate, ancillary; mediocre, second-rate, middling, second-best, second-string, second fiddle. **3.** *"Moonlighting" means working at an extra job as a secondary source of income:* other, alternate; subsidiary, auxiliary; not primary, not original; backup. —**Ant.** 1–3 primary, first. 1 preceding. 2 superior, larger, bigger, major. 3 sole; original.

second-class *adj. The work was judged second-class:* second-rate, inferior, low-grade, low-quality, mean, mediocre, poor, shoddy, substandard, tacky, tawdry, common, cheap.

second-rate *adj. Let's trade in this second-rate TV on a good one:* inferior, mediocre, second-string, second-best, inadequate, middling, so-so, undistinguished, pedestrian, imperfect, outclassed, fair-to-middling, commonplace, everyday, average; cheap, shabby, low-grade, *Slang* tacky. —**Ant.** first-class, best, prize, A-one, excellent.

secrecy *n. The plotters were sworn to secrecy. She wrote to the enemy leader in secrecy:* secretiveness, silence, uncommunicativeness, muteness, confidentiality, closeness; covertness, clandestineness, mystery, stealth, furtiveness, underhandedness, surreptitiousness, dark dealing; private, solitude, concealment, privacy, hiding, sequestration, seclusion.

secret *adj.* **1.** *The president was elected by a secret ballot. A secret room was located behind the bookcase. The patent medicine is based on a secret formula:* private, confidential, unrevealable, unrevealed, undisclosed, unpublished, hush-hush; hidden, concealed, unseen, invisible, camouflaged, secluded; undercover, disguised; covert, clandestine, surreptitious; unknown, mysterious, mystic, dark, esoteric, arcane, occult. **2.** *He's a devious, secret person and I don't trust him:* keeping knowledge to oneself, secretive, close-mouthed, tight-lipped, mum, discreet; mysterious; furtive, stealthy, hugger-mugger. —*n.* **3.** *Can you keep a secret?:* confidential information, confidential matter, confidence. **4.** *Captain Cousteau lectured on the secrets of the deep:* mystery, enigma, puzzle. **5.** *What's your secret for looking so young?:* formula, key, recipe, unguessed-at reason, special method. —**Ant.** 1, 2 open. 1 public, revealed, disclosed; obvious, evident, apparent, undisguised; well-known, ordinary. 2 candid, frank, straightforward.

secrete *v. The escaped convicts secreted themselves in a cave:* hide, conceal, cache, *Informal* stash; cloak, curtain, screen, veil, disguise; keep secret, keep under wraps, cover, shroud. —**Ant.** reveal, show, display, exhibit.

secretive *adj. She was secretive about where she'd been last night:* unrevealing, uncommunicative, close-mouthed, tight-lipped, silent, mum, mute; reserved, discreet, withdrawn, reticent, private, taciturn, laconic, sparing of words; sly, stealthy, furtive, evasive, surreptitious, underhanded, covert, mysterious, cryptic, enigmatic. —**Ant.** open, communicative, talkative; candid, frank, plain, straightforward, direct.

secretly *adv. They met secretly by the waterfall:* in secret, by stealth, clandestinely, confidentially, covertly, furtively, in camera, surreptitiously, unobserved, *Latin* sub rosa.

sect *n. The Mennonite sect was founded during the 16th century:* religious subgroup, denomination, persuasion, school of thought, camp, affiliation, religious creed, religious order, cult; division, faction, splinter group.

sectarian *adj.* **1.** *The period was marked by sectarian squabbling:* clannish, cliquish, exclusive, insular, limited, narrow-minded, parochial, provincial, bigoted, doctrinaire, dogmatic; unorthodox, nonconforming, nonconformist, factional, schismatic, partisan. —*n.* **2.** *The sectarians formed a new church:* dogmatist, extremist, fanatic, bigot, zealot; nonconformist, partisan, schismatic, separatist. —**Ant.** broad-minded, catholic, freethinking, liberal, tolerant.

section *n.* **1.** *Do you separate your grapefruit sections with a knife? The class is divided into three sections:* part, division, piece, segment, unit, portion; share, installment, increment, allotment, measure, proportion; chapter, passage. **2.** *The smoking section of this theater is in the balcony. The residential section of the city is spacious and airy:* district, area, side, vicinity, province, sphere, region; sector, department; zone, ward, neighborhood; territory, range, terrain. **3.** *A section of tissue was sent to the lab for microscopic examination:* slice, cross section, cutting; specimen, sample.

sector *n. Which sector of the economy has been hardest hit by recession? After World War II, Berlin was divided into four sectors:* administrative division, zone, district; theater, area, sphere of action.

secular *adj. He was trained in sacred music, but prefers to write secular works:* worldly, profane, mundane, nonspiritual, nonsacred, nonreligious, temporal, earthly; lay, nonclerical, nonecclesiastical; fleshly, sensual, carnal. —**Ant.** sacred, divine, spiritual, ecclesiastical.

secure *adj.* **1.** *She felt secure only when both doors were locked. The child doesn't feel secure in the new school:* free from danger, free from harm, safe, unthreatened, invulnerable, immune, protected, defended, sheltered, out of danger; carefree, reassured, easy, at ease, composed, self-possessed, confident. **2.** *The citadel was secure:* unattackable, unassailable, impregnable. **3.** *His shackles were secure:* firmly fastened; set, fixed, tight. **4.** *Your future with the company is secure:* sure, certain, assured, guaranteed, definite, positive, absolute; *Slang* in the bag, surefire. —*v.* **5.** *First he secured a good location for his new business:* obtain, procure, acquire, get, get hold of, get possession of. **6.** *They say that our missiles and bombers secure us from attack:* free from harm, make safe, safeguard, defend, protect, shelter, insure. **7.** *The bank required collateral to secure the loan agreement:* ensure, guarantee. **8.** *The boat was secured to the dock:* make fast, fix firmly, fasten, lash tight, batten down, tie down, bind. —**Ant.** 1–4 insecure. 1 unsafe, endangered, threatened, in danger; unsure, uneasy, anxious. 2 weak, vulnerable. 3 loose, unfixed. 4 unsure, uncertain, unassured, indefinite; unsettled, undetermined; precarious. 5 lose, give up. 6 endanger, imperil, harm, leave unprotected. 8 loose, unloose, untie.

security *n.* **1.** *My family's health and security are of the utmost importance to me:* freedom from danger, freedom from harm, protection, safety, safekeeping; preservation, maintenance, support, care, keep. **2.** *The airport's system of security requires that every passenger be searched:* defense, safeguards, safety measures, protective devices; police, guards, troops. **3.** *The hostages were used by the robbers as security for escape:* assurance, guarantee, surety, pledge, bond, warranty; collateral; deposit. **4.** *You can look forward to your future in the company with security:* secureness, assurance, confidence, certainty, positiveness, sureness, absoluteness, definiteness, decisiveness; trust, peace of mind, reliance, promise, hope, faith, conviction. **5.** Usually **securities** *Your negotiable securities should be locked up:* stocks, bonds, certificates of title to property.

sedate *adj. The defendant remained sedate throughout the trial. We spent a sedate evening at home:* calm, composed, unruffled, collected, levelheaded, self-possessed, self-controlled, cool, coolheaded, imperturbable, impassive, undemonstrative, unexcited; serious, steady, solemn, sober, grave; poised, dignified, decorous, reserved, staid; subdued, quiet, still, serene. —**Ant.** nervous, perturbed, disturbed, impassioned, agitated, excited, noisy, active, restless, unsteady; flighty, frivolous, gay.

sedative *adj.* **1.** *Phenobarbital is prescribed for its sedative effects:* soothing, calming, relaxing, comforting, easing, tranquilizing, soporific, narcotic, composing; palliative, calmative, allaying, alleviative, assuasive, lenitive; anodyne, analgesic. —*n.* **2.** *The doctor gave the distraught woman a sedative:* tranquilizer, calmative; analgesic, anodyne, palliative, alleviative, mitigator, lenitive, assuasive; narcotic, opiate.

sedentary *adj. You may find that being a telephone operator is too sedentary a job:* sitting, seated, inactive, unmoving, unstirring, inert, fixed, stationary; quiescent, resting, still.

sediment *n. Sediment remained at the bottom of the coffeepot. After the flood the streets were covered with sediment:* settlings, lees, grounds; dregs, leavings, remains, residue; dross, scum; debris, waste, slag, sludge.

sedition *n. The sailors were tried for sedition and found guilty:* mutiny, revolt, insurrection, insurgency, rebellion, defiance, subversion, lawlessness, uprising, disloyalty; rebelliousness, disobedience, unruliness, subversiveness. —**Ant.** allegiance, loyalty, obedience, submission.

seduce *v.* **1.** *The vile man tried to seduce the young girl:* persuade to do wrong, lure, entice, lead astray; corrupt, defile, debauch, deflower, violate, ravish; deprave, pervert, disgrace, dishonor; abuse, ruin. **2.** *The homeless dog seduced us by whimpering and crying. The audience was seduced by the star's radiance:* attract, turn one's head, win over, conquer, persuade, overcome the resistance to, entice, charm, tempt, lure, allure, captivate. —**Ant.** 1 persuade to do right; save, protect; honor. 2 repel, repulse; disgust; dissuade.

seducer *n. He may be charming but the women avoid him as a seducer:* debaucher, cad, roué, womanizer, woman chaser, skirt-chaser, lady killer, playboy, philanderer, heartbreaker, Don Juan, Casanova, Lothario, Romeo, lover-boy; *Slang* wolf, letch.

seductive *adj. The starlet always wore a seductive dress:* alluring, enticing, tempting, sexy, provocative, voluptuous, come-hither; attractive, charming, disarming, enchanting, bewitching, beguiling, captivating. —**Ant.** repulsive, repellent; drab, staid, prim.

seductress *n. You may remember her as a seductress in early movies:* siren, temptress, enchantress, Jezebel, adventuress, vamp, mantrap, cocotte, Lorelei, woman of easy virtue.

sedulous *adj. The sedulous workers quickly finished the bridge:* diligent, industrious, assiduous, busy, hardworking, zealous, tireless, painstaking, meticulous, thoroughgoing, persevering, steadfast. —**Ant.** careless, lazy.

see *v.* **1.** *Can you see what that sign says? Did*

anyone see the accident? What you see is what you get!: make out, discern, distinguish, recognize; behold, observe, witness; hold in view, have in sight, notice, look at, regard, spot, catch sight of, sight, glimpse, spy, espy, descry; view, survey, contemplate, take in; eye, set one's eyes on, stare at, gaze at; *Slang* dig, get a load of. **2.** *Do you see now why I did that?:* perceive, understand, comprehend, apprehend, appreciate, grasp, take in, fathom, get the drift; know, be cognizant of, realize, be aware of, register, be conscious of. **3.** *I can't see you as a mother:* visualize, envision, picture, conceive, make out; regard, consider. **4.** *Let me see what I can do:* find out, ascertain, discover, determine; consider, meditate, contemplate, ruminate, give thought to, mull over. **5.** *The soldiers saw action:* undergo, experience, go through. **6.** *See that you arrive on time!:* make sure, take care, make certain, see to it, watch, mind, observe. **7.** *Please come to see us again soon. I can see the job applicants tomorrow:* call on, visit; meet, encounter, run into; speak to, consult, confer with; receive, attend to, entertain, listen to, interview. **8.** *How long have you two been seeing each other?:* date, court, woo; keep company with. **9.** *John always sees me to the door:* escort, accompany, attend. **—Ant.** 1 neglect, overlook, disregard, ignore. 2 misunderstand, mistake, be unaware of.

seed *n.* **1.** *The child planted marigold seeds in the window box:* grain, pit, stone, ovule; seedling. **2.** *A good teacher can plant the seeds of knowledge in students:* source, origin, basis, germ, embryo, beginning. **3.** *I will make thy seed as the dust of the earth:* descendants, progeny, issue, offspring, children; heirs, posterity. **—v. 4.** *I'm seeding some of my land to grass:* sow with seed, plant. **5.** *Seed the cherries before you put them in the pie:* remove the seeds from; pit.

seedy *adj.* **1.** *We found him living in a seedy hotel:* shabby, run-down, dilapidated, ramshackle, ragged, shoddy, shopworn, scruffy, tatty, ratty, down-at-heel, flyblown, moth-eaten. **2.** *She'd been feeling seedy for some time:* unwell, ailing, ill, sick, sickish, under the weather, run-down, exhausted, beat. **—Ant.** spruce, trim, smart.

seek *v.* **1.** *The police seek information as to the whereabouts of the robbers:* try to find, search for, look for, track down, look into, dig for, probe for, investigate, explore, examine, scrutinize, inspect; nose out, ferret out, pursue, be after, hunt, fish for, sniff out, scout out, trace. **2.** *Roderick Random sallied forth to seek fame and fortune. His lawyers are seeking a new trial:* try to obtain, strive for, aim for, aspire to, pursue; be after, go in for; request, inquire for, petition for, demand, call for; solicit, court, invite. **3.** *We sought to change her mind, but she said no:* try, attempt, endeavor, essay, set about, go about, try one's hand at, undertake, venture, *Informal* have a go at. **—Ant.** 1 neglect, ignore, abandon; avoid, shun; discard, relinquish, drop.

seem *v. He seems happy with his new job:* ap-

pear, look, give the impression of being, have the semblance of, look like, look as if, strike one as being.

seeming *adj. Her seeming indifference was only an act:* ostensible, apparent, evident, obvious; presumed, supposed, putative; superficial, surface.

seemly *adj. Young people should address their elders in a seemly manner:* suitable, felicitous, proper, appropriate, in good taste, fitting, becoming, befitting, due, acceptable, conventional, correct, prudent, polite, courteous, well-bred, decorous, right, decent, tasteful, refined; *French* comme il faut. **—Ant.** unseemly, unbecoming, improper, rude, impolite, impertinent, pert, forward.

seep *v. Rain seeped through the cracks in the roof:* leak, ooze, trickle, dribble, drip; suffuse, diffuse, penetrate, permeate, soak, soak through. **—Ant.** gush, flow, flood.

seer *n. The seer predicted a long war for the city of Athens:* prophet, sage, oracle, soothsayer, astrologer, stargazer, fortuneteller, psychic, augur, clairvoyant, medium, diviner, necromancer, sorcerer, sorceress, conjurer.

seethe *v.* **1.** *The water in the hot springs was seething:* boil, bubble, churn, roil; simmer, stew, brew, cook. **2.** *He seethed with frustration as the train left without him:* be greatly excited, be agitated, be upset, be irate, be livid, be angry, be indignant, rage, rant, rave, boil, storm, breathe fire, fume, smolder; carry on, foam at the mouth, bluster, raise a rumpus, stamp one's foot, throw a tantrum, raise Cain; *Slang* blow up, blow one's top, be in a tizzy.

segment *n.* **1.** *The magician cut the string and held up the two segments:* part, piece, section, division, portion; installment, increment; stage, leg. **—v. 2.** *That rod has been segmented for easy storage:* divide into parts, section, cut up, split up; cleave, separate, disjoin, disunite. **—Ant.** 1 whole, entity, entirety. 2 combine, meld, fuse; join, unite.

segregate *v. The library segregates oversized books and puts them on a separate shelf. Many Indian tribes have been kept segregated on reservations:* separate, isolate, cut off, detach, divide, divorce, disunite, disconnect; keep apart, sequester, set apart, set aside, single out, sort out; seclude, insulate, quarantine. **—Ant.** unite, blend, mix, desegregate, integrate.

seize *v.* **1.** *He seized his gun and ran out to investigate. The military junta seized power:* take hold of, take possession of, grab, snatch, pluck, grasp, clutch, embrace, lay hands upon; acquire forcibly, take possession of by force; usurp, arrogate, commandeer; confiscate, impound, appropriate. **2.** *She was quick to seize the meaning of his words:* grasp, comprehend, apprehend, understand, read, catch, gather, take in, glean. **3.** *Uncontrollable laughter seized us:* overwhelm, overpower; possess. **4.** *The escaped convict was seized outside the city:* capture, arrest, apprehend, take into custody, take captive; catch, nab, *Informal* bag, collar, pinch. **5.** *Seize every opportunity you can if you want* *to succeed:* take advantage of, make use of, utilize, profit from, act upon. **—Ant.** 1, 4 let go of, release; relinquish, give up; free, liberate, let go, loose. 5 waste, let pass, pass up.

seizure *n.* **1.** *The seizure of the criminal ended a three-month police chase:* act of seizing, taking, grasping; capture, apprehension, arrest; snatching, usurpation; possession, appropriation, confiscation; commandeering, impressment; abduction, kidnapping. **2.** *After his seizure, he needed round-the-clock care:* attack, convulsion, fit, stroke, throe, visitation, paroxysm; onset, access, spell, episode, crisis.

seldom *adv.* *I seldom get a chance to read:* rarely, scarcely, not often, not frequently, infrequently; hardly ever, now and then, sporadically, occasionally, once in a great while, uncommonly. **—Ant.** often, frequently, always.

select *v.* **1.** *Our class valedictorian was free to select the college she wished to attend. The decorator selected a delicate print for the wallpaper:* choose, pick, pick out, make one's choice, decide for, elect, single out, opt for, prefer; fix upon, settle upon, put aside, lay aside; *Informal* give the nod to, tap. *—adj.* **2.** *Only a select few were invited to the party:* choice, picked, privileged, chosen. **3.** *We only stay at select hotels:* superior, first-rate, first-class, élite; choice, preferred; exclusive, *Informal* topnotch, four-star, A1, posh, fancy. **—Ant.** 1 reject, refuse, repudiate, spurn. 2 indiscriminate; random. 3 inferior, second-rate; modest, ordinary, unremarkable, undistinguished.

selection *n.* **1.** *I made my selection, and the sales clerk charged it to my account:* choice, choosing, preference, pick, decision, election, option. **2.** *There's very little selection of winter clothes in the spring:* variety, choice, range, option. **3.** *The band played a selection of popular tunes:* selected number, collection, program; medley, miscellany, potpourri.

selective *adj.* *Learn to be a selective customer:* choosy, choosing carefully, discerning, discriminating, particular, fastidious, finicky, fussy, meticulous; cautious, careful, *Informal* picky. **—Ant.** unselective, promiscuous, careless, indiscriminate.

self-assured *adj.* *He was self-assured and bound to succeed:* confident, self-confident, assured, cocky, cocksure, brash. **—Ant.** self-doubting, insecure, unconfident.

self-centered *adj.* *A self-centered person isn't concerned with the needs of others:* selfish, self-seeking, self-absorbed, self-concerned, wrapped up in oneself, self-important; egotistic, egoistic, egocentric, conceited, narcissistic, vain, swell-headed, immodest.

self-confidence *n.* *Repeated failure in school was harming the boy's self-confidence:* self-assurance, self-reliance, positive self-image, resolution, mettle, pluck, spirit, nerve; cocksureness, boldness, cockiness, gameness.

self-confident *adj.* *The self-confident girl addressed the assembly:* assured, self-assured, poised, sanguine, secure, self-reliant, fearless.

self-conscious *adj.* *The self-conscious boy blushed when we complimented him:* uncomfortable, uneasy, discomfited, anxious, awkward, embarrassed, insecure, nervous, sheepish, shy, bashful, diffident, stilted.

self-consciousness *n.* *Her self-consciousness made it difficult for her to make friends:* shyness, modesty, timidity, bashfulness, reticence, reserve, diffidence, constraint, hesitancy, fearfulness, apprehension, constraint, abashment, demureness, self-effacement, sheepishness. **—Ant.** assurance, boldness, self-confidence, aggressiveness, self-assertion.

self-control *n.* *Counting to ten helps you maintain self-control when you're angry:* self-discipline, willpower, self-possession, composure, self-restraint, mental balance, levelheadedness, presence of mind, soberness, firmness, soundness, stability, coolheadedness, sobriety, poise, savoir faire, aplomb, unexcitability, imperturbability, sangfroid; patience, temperance, forbearance.

self-esteem *n.* *Self-esteem is a desirable form of self-love:* pride, self-respect, self-regard, confidence, self-confidence, self-assurance, self-sufficiency, self-reliance, independence, pardonable pride. **—Ant.** self-effacement, sheepishness; self-loathing, servility, abjectness.

self-evident *adj.* *The difference between rich and poor is self-evident:* obvious, plain, evident, manifest, apparent, palpable, glaring, distinct, patent, self-explanatory, incontrovertible, explicit, unarguable, undeniable. **—Ant.** doubtful, questionable, ambiguous, arguable.

self-government *n.* *The colony attained self-government:* self-rule, self-determination, autonomy.

selfish *adj.* *You must learn to share and not be so selfish:* self-seeking, self-concerned, self-centered, egocentric, egotistic; greedy, rapacious, avaricious, covetous, venal, mercenary, grasping; uncharitable, ungenerous, illiberal, grudging, stingy, parsimonious, miserly, mean, *Informal* tight. **—Ant.** unselfish, selfless, considerate; generous, bighearted, magnanimous, giving; altruistic.

self-love *n.* *With all that self-love he has no need of anyone else:* conceit, narcissism, vanity, haughtiness, amour propre, self-conceit, conceitedness, vainglory, self-satisfaction, complacency, egoism, egotism, self-importance, swellheadedness. **—Ant.** humility, modesty, unpretentiousness, self-deprecation.

self-reliant *adj.* *After her husband died, Mrs. Jones was as self-reliant as ever:* independent, assured, self-confident, self-possessed, self-sufficient, enterprising, spirited, plucky, mettlesome; resolute, hardy.

self-righteous *adj.* *Don't give me any of your self-righteous lectures!:* sanctimonious, righteous in one's own regard, smug, complacent, pharisaical, hypocritical, insincere, mealy-mouthed; pompous, pious, moralizing, pretentious, holier-than-thou, pietistic.

self-satisfaction *n.* *We all feel self-satisfaction after a job well done:* satisfaction with one's accomplishments, pride, self-pleasure, self-content, complacency, smugness, self-approval, self-admiration, self-righteousness; vanity; flush of success.

self-satisfied *adj. He's so self-satisfied he has no interest in improving his work:* complacent, smug, self-contented, priggish, overconfident, overproud, cocksure, self-approving, vain, vainglorious, self-righteous, egotistical, narcissistic. **—Ant.** self-critical, humble, modest, self-hating.

self-sufficient *adj. She was self-sufficient in her new job:* self-supporting, self-sustaining, independent, efficient.

sell *v.* **1.** *We sold the house for $50,000:* give up for a price, exchange for money; dispose of, dispense, unload, dump. **2.** *He sells vacuum cleaners:* deal in, trade in, handle; offer for sale, put up for sale, put on sale, effect the sale of; vend, market, barter, peddle, hawk, traffic in. **3.** *We tried to sell the toy manufacturer on our new plastic:* win the acceptance of, win over, persuade to buy, persuade to accept, convince, prevail upon, enlist. **4.** *He sold his country for a promise of power:* betray, sell out, deliver up, take a bribe for, play false, deceive.

seller *n. The sellers took their places on the floor of the stock exchange:* vendor, dealer, retailer, wholesaler, storekeeper, shopkeeper, tradesman, merchant, salesman, saleswoman, saleslady, salesgirl, salesperson, peddler, middleman, jobber, trader, *British* monger.

semblance *n.* **1.** *Her semblance of indifference was only an act. Let's try to maintain some semblance of order:* outward appearance, aspect, likeness, look, show, air, mien, bearing; unreal appearance, pretense, simulacrum. **2.** *The portrait was a perfect semblance of her face:* image, representation, copy, duplicate, replica, reproduction, facsimile, cast, counterpart, likeness.

seminal *adj. The ideal of social equality was one of the seminal ideas of the French Revolution:* originating, original, primary, germinal, germinative, formative; generative; creative, productive, fruitful.

send *v.* **1.** *Send this package by special delivery:* cause to go, have transported, have transmitted, dispatch, relay, forward, convey. **2.** *The ship sent out a message for help:* transmit, project, broadcast, disseminate; give off, emit. **3.** *We sent the man to the right address:* direct, refer, point the way to, indicate the course to, guide, show, lead, head, conduct. **4.** *The mortars sent shells across the enemy lines:* propel, throw, deliver, shoot, hurl, cast, discharge, drive, emit, launch, fling, toss. **—Ant.** 1 hold, keep, retain; receive. 2 get.

senile *adj. Though he was past 80, he was by no means senile:* doddering, superannuated, doting, foolish, senescent, infirm, decrepit.

senior *adj.* **1.** *Often* **Senior** *Mr. Jones, Junior, is the image of Mr. Jones, Senior:* older, elder, *French* père. **2.** *Mr. Gray is a senior officer in this bank:* superior, higher in rank; above, over. **3.** *Konrad Adenauer was already a senior statesman when first elected:* of long tenure, veteran,

doyen. **—n.** **4.** *My sister is the senior of the two of us:* one who is older, elder. **5.** *The three vice-presidents are my seniors:* person of higher rank, superior, better, higher-up, chief, head. **—Ant.** 1–5 junior. 1 younger. 2 subordinate, inferior. 5 subordinate, inferior.

seniority *n. The chief of surgery became committee chairman by virtue of his seniority:* precedence, longer service, tenure, longevity; superiority in rank; greater age.

sensation *n.* **1.** *After the accident he had no sensation in his left thumb:* perception, feeling, sensitivity, sensibility, perceptivity; consciousness, awareness, detection; responsiveness. **2.** *I have a dizzying sensation:* impression, sense, perception, feeling. **3.** *The moon landing in 1969 caused a worldwide sensation:* public excitement, uproar, stir, commotion, to-do, thrill, agitation; cause of excitement, thrilling event; hit; scandal.

sensational *adj.* **1.** *The acrobat performed a sensational feat of daring:* outstanding, striking, spectacular, extraordinary, exceptional; exciting, thrilling, electrical, galvanic; dramatic; excellent, superb. **2.** *The boy was reading a sensational paperback novel:* shocking, exaggerated, extravagant, emotional, heartthrobbing; lurid, cheap, meretricious, scandalous. **—Ant.** 1 ordinary, common, everyday, routine; mediocre. 2 prosaic, dull, bland.

sense *n.* **1.** *The word "tactile" refers to the sense of touch:* faculty, function, feeling, sensation; (*variously*) touch, smell, taste, sight, hearing. **2.** *A square meal gives one a sense of well-being:* impression, sensation, realization, awareness, recognition, consciousness. **3.** *The teacher tried to inculcate his pupils with a sense of beauty:* appreciation, understanding, intuition. **4.** *I can rely on his good sense:* mental ability, judgment, reason, mind, understanding, perspicacity, sagacity, wisdom, intelligence, reasonableness. **5.** *There is no sense in worrying:* value, worth, use, good, point, benefit, purpose, practicality, efficacy. **6.** *A sense of impending doom overwhelmed us:* impression, awareness, intuition, premonition, presentiment; aura, atmosphere. **7.** *Can you make any sense of these instructions? One sense of "secrete" means to hide or conceal:* meaning, signification, connotation, denotation, definition. **—v.** **8.** *The blindfolded prisoner could sense the breeze on his skin:* be aware of, perceive, feel; recognize, detect, discern. **9.** *She was quick to sense his difficulty:* grasp, understand, apprehend, comprehend, take in, descry, see, note, perceive, espy, regard, discern, realize. **10.** *We sensed that something was wrong:* have a vague impression, feel, suspect, divine, guess. **—Ant.** 4 stupidity, folly. 5 nonsense. 9 misunderstand; disregard, ignore, neglect, overlook, miss.

senseless *adj.* **1.** *The punch to the head left the boxer senseless:* unconscious, without sensation, insensible, insensate; deadened, comatose, numb; knocked out, stunned. **2.** *Quitting your job would be senseless:* useless, meaningless, purposeless; stupid, witless, brainless, harebrained, foolish, foolhardy, inane, silly, non-sensical, ridiculous, irrational, unreasonable, unwise, ill-advised, irresponsible, *Informal* crazy, dumb, nutty; without reason, illogical, groundless, meaningless, pointless, aimless; idle. —**Ant.** 1 conscious. 2 useful, meaningful, worthwhile; sensible, smart, intelligent, clever, wise; rational, reasonable, sound, logical.

sensibility *n.* **1.** *It is now possible to measure the sensibility of plants to light and heat:* ability to perceive, responsiveness, sensitiveness, sensitivity, perception. **2.** *The way she dressed suggested the sensibility of a painter:* artistic responsiveness, esthetic judgment, refined tastes; emotional makeup, temperament. **3.** Often **sensibilities** *Learn to have regard for other people's sensibilities:* sensitivity, sensitiveness, susceptibility; thin skin, sore spot, Achilles' heel. —**Ant.** 1 insensibility, insensitiveness, insensitivity; deadness, dullness, numbness, unconsciousness.

sensible *adj.* **1.** *Donald is a sensible young man. Our counselor offered a sensible approach to the problem:* sound, showing good sense, intelligent, thoughtful, perspicacious; wise, sage, sagacious, farsighted; discerning, discriminating, prudent, discreet, judicious, just; well-advised, well-grounded, logical, rational, reasonable, sane; plausible, credible, possible. **2.** *Animals are quick to be sensible of danger:* aware, perceiving, perceptive, cognitive, cognizant; conscious, knowing, enlightened, informed, apprised. **3.** *Her grief was sensible from her manner. There was a clearly sensible antipathy between the two brothers:* perceptible, noticeable, discernible; tangible, palpable, detectable, visible; plain, apparent, evident, obvious. **4.** *Are the natives of Tierra del Fuego sensible to extremes of heat and cold?:* capable of feeling or perceiving, sensitive, responsive, susceptible. —**Ant.** 1 unsound, unintelligent, stupid, unwise, foolish, absurd, senseless, imprudent, indiscreet, injudicious; illogical, irrational, unreasonable. 2 insensible, unaware, ignorant, blind. 3 undetectable, unnoticeable, invisible. 4 insensible, insensitive.

sensitive *adj.* **1.** *The tips of the fingers are particularly sensitive:* responsive, perceptive, sentient, sensing. **2.** *Don't be so sensitive, I was only joking:* easily affected emotionally, easily offended or hurt, touchy, thin-skinned; delicate, impressionable, susceptible; perceptive, keen, acute. **3.** *The cardiograph is a sensitive machine:* detecting slight change, delicate, fine; accurate, precise, exact; faithful. **4.** *That bruise is still sensitive:* sore, tender, painful. —**Ant.** 2 hard, tough, coarse, thick-skinned, callous, obtuse. 3 rough, coarse, inaccurate, approximate.

sensitivity *n.* *She had much sensitivity in dealing with the problem:* sensitiveness, awareness, consciousness, delicacy, feeling, impressionability, receptiveness, responsiveness, susceptibility, sympathy, acuteness; nervousness.

sensory *adj.* *The dish was a sensory delight:* sensual, perceptible; neural, neurological.

sensual *adj.* *Saint Paul reproves us for having sensual thoughts. He has a sensual appreciation of fine wine:* erotic, carnal, lustful, lewd, licentious, lecherous, sexy; earthy, fleshly, voluptuous, pleasure-seeking, pleasure-loving, hedonistic.

sensuous *adj.* *A meadow in spring is full of sensuous delights:* gratifying the senses, strongly appealing, delicious, exquisite, delightful.

sentence *n.* **1.** *He received a light sentence:* punishment, penalty, stretch, term, time, verdict, condemnation, decision, determination, dictum, edict, judgment, order, pronouncement. —*v.* **2.** *The judge sentenced her to five years in prison:* condemn, blame, penalize, punish, confine, convict, imprison, incarcerate, jail, pass judgment, adjudicate, *Informal.* put away, send up.

sententious *adj.* *The speaker's talk was boring and full of sententious platitudes:* preachy, didactic, pedantic, holier-than-thou, judgmental, sanctimonious, pietistic, self-righteous, moralistic; pompous, grandiose, high-sounding, high-flown, stilted, orotund.

sentient *adj.* *She loved all sentient creatures:* aware, alive, conscious, awake, cognizant, sensitive, sensible, witting, susceptible, feeling, perceptive, responsive, receptive, impressionable, sensate, reactive, discriminative, discriminatory. —**Ant.** dulled, insensible.

sentiment *n.* **1.** Often **sentiments** *We share the same sentiments on the matter:* opinion, attitude, point of view, viewpoint, feeling, thought, notion, idea. **2.** *Resisting sentiment, she threw out all her old letters:* feeling, emotion, sentimentality, nostalgia, tenderness, heart, soft-heartedness, emotionalism, romance, romanticism.

sentimental *adj.* **1.** *Sentimental movies always make me cry:* emotional, mawkish, pathetic, weepy, romantic, hearts-and-flowers, melodramatic, romanticized; *Informal* tear-jerking, mushy. **2.** *She gets sentimental whenever she thinks of her childhood:* emotional, nostalgic; tearful, maudlin, lachrymose.

sentimentality *n.* *When the author prolongs the heroine's death for two chapters, he is guilty of sentimentality:* emotionalism, mawkishness, sloppiness; sentimentalism, pathos, bathos, mush; emotional nature, heart, temperament, *Slang* kitsch.

sentinel *n.* *The sentinel walked up and down in front of the gate:* sentry, guard, lookout, watchman, watch, night watchman, ward, picket, patrol, scout, ranger, guardian, guardsman.

separate *v.* **1.** *A split rail fence separates the two farms. Separate the orange into sections:* keep apart, divide, mark off, come between, split, partition; subdivide, cut, sever, detach, break, sunder, bisect, part; disjoin, disunite, disconnect. **2.** *Separate the white clothes from the dark clothes before laundering:* set apart, put apart, segregate; sort out, remove, single out, isolate; pick out, cull, sift; distinguish. **3.** *We separated after ten years of marriage. Bear left when the road separates:* go separate ways, go different ways, go apart; divorce, split up; branch out, diverge, part, split, divaricate, bifurcate, fork, ramify, radiate, spread. **4.** *The delicate cake separates easily in one's fingers:* come apart, break away, break apart; crack, split, part, crumble. —*adj.* **5.** *The suite consisted of four separate rooms:* not joined, not connected, detached, disunited; not shared, single, individual, distinct, discrete; different, diverse, dissimilar. **6.** *Our newspaper and our printing business form separate corporate entities:* independent, existing by itself, autonomous. —**Ant.** 1 join, attach, link, unite, engage, connect. 2 combine, unite, mix, merge, integrate, consolidate. 3 meet, merge; convene. 4 adhere, cling. 5 joined, connected, united; shared; alike, similar. 6 affiliated, merged, interdependent.

separately *adv.* *We arrived separately:* independently, individually, alone, singly, severally, apart, distinctly. —**Ant.** together, collectively, jointly.

separation *n.* **1.** *Let us proceed to the separation of chaff from wheat:* separating, division, disjunction, disunion, disconnection, disengagement, divorce, severance; detachment, disassociation; sorting, removal, segregation, isolation. **2.** *Their separation at the railway station was emotional:* parting, farewell, good-bye, divergence, branching; separate residence, estrangement, divorce; breach, break, split, schism. **3.** *Fifth Avenue is the separation between the east and west sides of Manhattan:* partition, boundary, divide, divider, division; branching, fork, bifurcation. **4.** *There is a separation of 500 yards between the two houses:* gap, space, opening, distance, interval.

sepulcher *n.* *Each year, prior to the reign of Henry VIII, thousands of pilgrims visited the sepulcher of Saint Thomas Becket:* tomb, crypt, vault, ossuary, reliquary, resting place; mausoleum, cenotaph, necropolis, grave, burial place.

sequel *n.* **1.** *Rabbit Redux is a sequel to John Updike's Rabbit Run:* continuation, follow-up. **2.** *As a sequel to the encounter, he met the same beggar in an expensive restaurant that night:* subsequent event, aftermath, upshot, offshoot, outgrowth, product; epilogue, postscript, addendum; conclusion, end, finish, denouement, culmination; consequence, result, corollary, outcome.

sequence *n.* **1.** *Hitler rose to power in a strange sequence of events:* progression, order, succession, arrangement; series, run, course, flow, train, string, chain; consecutiveness, successiveness. **2.** *New employees had to attend a sequence of orientation meetings:* series, cycle, round; procession, parade, cavalcade, course; schedule, routine.

sequential *adj.* *The sequential tasks were done in correct order:* consecutive, successive, serial, continuous, incessant, ordered, persistent, regular, steady, subsequent.

sequester *v.* *The jury was sequestered while it deliberated over the murder case:* set apart, sequestrate, seclude, withdraw, isolate, banish, separate, segregate, retire, put aside, confine, lock up, quarantine.

sere *adj.* *The sere leaves gently floated to the ground:* dry, arid, moistureless, desiccated, droughty, dehumidified, dehydrated, waterless, unwatered, bone-dry, parched, scorched, dried-up, wizened.

serendipity *n.* *By serendipity we met at the airport:* happy chance, lucky chance, good luck, good fortune, happenstance, fortuitousness, adventitiousness.

serene *adj.* *The woods were reflected in the serene lake:* calm, tranquil, peaceful, quiet, still, untroubled, halcyon, unruffled, smooth; sedate, dignified, unperturbed, placid, composed, undisturbed, unexcitable, unimpassioned, poised, cool, nonchalant; clear, fair, bright, unobscured, pellucid, limpid. —**Ant.** disturbed, troubled, rough, agitated; excitable, anxious, discomposed.

serenity *n.* *Her serenity contrasted with everyone else's anxiety:* calmness, placidity, tranquillity, peacefulness, quietude, quiescence, composure, implicit confidence, dignity, equanimity, collectedness, coolness, complacence, nonchalance, *French* sangfroid. —**Ant.** anxiety, uneasiness, alarm, discontent.

serf *n.* *The feudal landowners had many serfs in their service:* slave bound to the land; vassal, villein; bondman, thrall; peasant, cotter. —**Ant.** master, lord.

serial *n.* **1.** *The Perils of Pauline was my grandmother's favorite movie serial:* story presented in installments. —*adj.* **2.** *Charles Dickens wrote his novels for serial publication:* in installments, in successive parts; continued, continuous, consecutive, sequential, successive; regular, recurring; incremental, piecemeal. **3.** *What is the serial number of that dollar bill?:* of a series, arranged in a series.

series *n.* *The coastline was hit by a series of violent storms:* succession, progression, sequence, order, procession; set, course, cycle, chain, string, parade; group, number.

serious *adj.* **1.** *The doctor emerged from the patient's room with a serious look on his face:* thoughtful, pensive, grave, solemn, frowning, long-faced, saturnine; sober, somber, sedate, staid, grim, rueful; sad, dejected, downcast. **2.** *If you're serious about becoming an actor, you must work hard:* sincere, earnest, not joking, not trifling, determined, decided, resolute, resolved, purposeful. **3.** *Buying a house is a serious matter:* demanding careful thought, important, consequential, far-reaching, momentous, weighty, heavy, crucial; fateful, portentous. **4.** *There's been a serious accident on the thruway. Europe is threatened with a serious fuel shortage:* dangerous, perilous, harmful, critical, severe, alarming, bad; incapacitating, crippling. —**Ant.** 1 thoughtless, careless; joyful, happy, jolly, gay, laughing, frivolous. 2 insincere, joking, trifling; undecided. 3 unimportant, insignificant, trivial. 4 slight, minor.

seriously *adv.* **1.** *She confronted the problem seriously:* earnestly, thoughtfully, purposefully, gravely, intently, resolutely, sincerely, soberly, with sobriety, solemnly, sternly, determinedly. **2.** *The swimmer was seriously in trouble:* acutely, dangerously, perilously, badly, critically, distressingly, menacingly, precariously, severely, threateningly, decidedly, gravely, grievously.

seriousness *n.* **1.** *In all seriousness we couldn't deal with the problem:* earnestness, gravity, humourlessness, intentness, sedateness, sincerity, solemnity, staidness, sternness, thoughtfulness, sober-mindedness, sobriety. **2.** *The seriousness of the dilemma alarmed her:* urgency, danger, enormity, gravity, importance, moment, significance, weight, criticalness.

sermon *n.* **1.** *The bishop preached a sermon from the pulpit:* speech containing religious instruction, preaching, preachment, exhortation, homily. **2.** *Don't give me a sermon on punctuality just because I'm five minutes late:* long tedious speech, lecture, harangue, tirade; reproof, admonition, rebuke; dressing-down, tongue-lashing, diatribe.

sermonize *v.* *He sermonized at the dinner table:* preach, lecture, evangelize, preachify, lecture, hold forth, discourse, dilate, expatiate, dogmatize, moralize, homilize.

serpent *n.* **1.** *The goddess is shown holding a serpent in each hand:* snake, viper, reptile, asp. **2.** *Don't trust that serpent:* traitor, trickster, deceiver, cheat, double-dealer; rogue, snake, snake in the grass; devil, the Devil, Satan.

serpentine *adj.* *A serpentine maze of tunnels and trenches provided shelter during the bombardments:* twisting, winding, snaking, meandering, tortuous, circuitous, coiling, devious, zigzag, roundabout, crooked, mazy, labyrinthine; spiral, convoluted, flexuous, sinuous; undulating.

serrated *adj.* *The serrated knife is good for cutting bread:* serrate, serriform, saw-toothed, notched, toothed, jagged.

servant *n.* **1.** *The millionaire had a staff of 30 servants:* employee, attendant, retainer, helper, domestic, factotum; (*variously*) maid, valet, footman, chauffeur, cook, butler, hired man, hired girl, household help, housekeeper; menial, flunky, lackey, slavey, scullion; henchman, underling, minion; man, girl, man Friday, girl Friday; help, hired help. **2.** *The mayor is a public servant:* public employee, public official, server; servitor. **—Ant.** 1 master, lord, employer.

serve *v.* **1.** *The butler served him faithfully for 25 years:* work for, act as a servant to, be in the service of, attend, take care of, wait on. **2.** *How may we serve you?:* be of help to, assist, render assistance, minister, tend, supply, provide for, aid, help, promote, further, oblige, attend; give aid or service, be of use. **3.** *Mr. Beauchesne will serve as mayor. The convict has to serve his sentence:* go through a term of service, work, act, perform, do duty, hold an office, fill a post, officiate; go through, carry out, spend, pass, complete. **4.** *She served in the restaurant to pay her way through college:* wait table, work as a waiter or waitress, *Slang* sling hash. **5.** *Dinner will be served in the main dining room:* provide

for customers or guests; supply with food, set food on a table. **6.** *This light dinner will serve me:* be enough for, content, satisfy, suit, suffice, do. **7.** *Her apartment also serves as her office. The table will serve as a desk:* act, be of use, be used, be functional, function, be instrumental; answer the purpose, answer the requirements, *Informal* fill the bill. **8.** *Her ingenuity has always served her well:* treat, work for, function for, avail. **9.** *The lawyer arrived to serve a writ:* deliver, present, hand over. **—Ant.** 1 command, order; deceive, betray. 2 obstruct, hinder, thwart, oppose. 6 be insufficient for; dissatisfy. 7 be useless.

service *n.* **1.** Sometimes **services** *May I be of service to you? Your services are no longer required:* labor; effort, ministration; attendance, assistance, help, aid; benefit, advantage, usefulness, use, utility, profit, accommodation; support, avail; employment, employ. **2.** *Bus service is free in some cities:* use, provision, system, accommodation, facility, utility, convenience. **3.** *An M.D. is chief officer of the health service:* department, agency, bureau. **4.** *He was in the service during World War II:* armed forces, military. **5.** *There's good money in TV service:* repair, servicing, maintenance, mechanical work. **6.** *The service in this restaurant is excellent:* attendance, waiting, accommodation, order-filling. **7.** Often **services** *The dentist sent a bill for his services:* professional work, treatment. **8.** *There is a church service this evening:* ritual, ceremony, ceremonial, rite, celebration, observance. **—v. 9.** *The repairman's gone to service a broken dishwasher:* repair, maintain, adjust, mend. **10.** *That power company services the entire southeast:* supply services to, serve.

serviceable *adj.* *The old coat is still serviceable:* usable, useful, utilitarian, functional, effective, operative, workable, practical; durable, lasting, rugged, strong, tough, sturdy.

servile *adj.* **1.** *A servile attendant accompanied the millionaire everywhere, opening doors and lighting cigars:* slavish, submissive, fawning, abject; unctuous, oily; obsequious, truckling, toadying, cringing, sycophantic, scraping, groveling, bootlicking. **2.** *The decayed gentleman was at last reduced to servile labor:* befitting a slave, menial; in bonds, abject, slavish, subservient, humble. **—Ant.** 1 masterly, commanding, overbearing, haughty.

servitude *n.* *To manumit means to release a slave or slaves from servitude. He was sentenced to ten years of penal servitude:* slavery, serfdom, thralldom, enthrallment, bonds, bondage, oppression, subjugation, enslavement, vassalage, fetters, shackles, chains; compulsory service, hard labor, imprisonment. **—Ant.** freedom, independence, emancipation.

session *n.* **1.** *Where was the first session of the U.N. General Assembly held?:* meeting, sitting, conference, convention, assembly, synod, conclave. **2.** *We urge you to enroll for the spring session now:* period, term, semester, quarter; course, round, bout.

set *v.* **1.** *Set the package on the table:* put,

place, position, move into position, lay, *Informal* plunk, plop; drop. **2.** *Set the timer for 20 minutes. Set the table. Can you set type?:* fix, adjust, regulate, calibrate; prepare, order, arrange, line up, align. **3.** *Let the pudding set:* harden, become hard or firm, solidify, consolidate, gel, jellify, congeal, thicken. **4.** *What time does the sun set?:* sink, pass below the horizon. **5.** *I can't set a value on friendship:* place, assign, establish, assess, attach, confer; estimate, rate. **6.** *Detectives were set at all the exits:* post, station, situate, install, assign. **7.** *Let's set the time of the meeting. I hate to set rules on anything:* decide upon, settle, fix, determine, establish, make, create; prescribe, decree, ordain. **8.** *The play is set in Venice:* put in a setting, locate, represent, suppose to take place. **9.** *The jeweler charges lots of money to set diamonds in a bracelet:* fix, mount in a frame; imbed; ornament, stud. **10.** *The composer set a prayer to music:* fit, arrange, adapt; style. **11.** *The hunters set the dogs on the cornered bear:* urge to attack, release, unleash; sic. —*n.* **12.** *The set of his chin suggested great tenacity:* setting, position, carriage, bearing, cut, line, profile; firmness, rigidity. **13.** *Alice wants a chess set for Christmas:* group, collection, assortment, array, suit, outfit, kit, service. **14.** *The so-called Beautiful People are today's fashionable set:* group of persons, crowd, clique, faction, coterie, club, bunch. **15.** *Want to buy a television set?:* apparatus, assembly, machine, complex. **16.** *Hollywood has many old movie sets:* scenery, scene, setting, backdrop; sound stage, studio; locale, location. —*adj.* **17.** *We have a set date for Tuesday:* definite, fixed, decided, firm, settled, prearranged, agreed upon; anticipated. **18.** *In the meeting we stuck to the set questions and answers we had already agreed upon:* established, usual, customary, accustomed; stock, common, commonplace, conventional, everyday, routine, regular, habitual, familiar; banal, trite, hackneyed, stale. **19.** *We're set for the picnic:* arranged, ready, prepared. **20.** *He's set in his ways:* stubborn, obstinate, steadfast, immovable, rigid, inflexible, frozen, hardened, stiff. —**Ant.** 1 remove, lift, pick up. 2 disarrange. 3 melt, soften. 4 rise. 7 change, break. 9 remove, extract. 17 undecided, tentative, vague. 18 unexpected, impromptu; unusual, uncommon, irregular. 19 unprepared. 20 flexible, adaptable.

setback *n. After a number of setbacks the business began to show a profit:* reversal, disappointment, misfortune, mischance, reverse, loss, adversity, defeat, relapse, regression, slump, undoing, failure, rebuff, mishap, *Slang* flop. —**Ant.** progress, advance, gain, advantage.

settle *v.* **1.** *Let's settle on a time for the meeting:* decide, agree, fix, choose, set, determine, establish. **2.** *Let's settle matters between us once and for all:* put in order, dispose properly, arrange, bring to order; reconcile, resolve, clear up, straighten out, rectify, put to rest. **3.** *It's wise to try to settle one's accounts monthly:* pay, discharge, acquit oneself of, dispose of,

make good, clear, satisfy. **4.** *The Pilgrims settled in Massachusetts:* move to, locate, situate, populate, establish oneself; colonize, put down roots, take root, lodge, inhabit, people, make one's home, set up housekeeping. **5.** *The sedative settled her nerves:* calm, bring to rest, soothe, quiet, compose, allay, pacify. **6.** *Bits of cork settled in the wine bottle:* deposit dregs, descend gradually, collect at the bottom, precipitate; clarify, clear. **7.** *The house is settling:* sink, drop, droop, sag, find one's level. **8.** *The bird settled on a high branch:* come to rest; land, alight, light; perch; sit down. —**Ant.** 1 disagree. 2 disarrange, upset; confuse. 4 wander; emigrate. 5 agitate, excite, disturb, roil. 7 rise, ascend.

settlement *n.* **1.** *After the settlement of our differences, we became friends:* adjustment, arrangement, reconciliation, resolution, working out. **2.** *We read all about the settlement of Saskatchewan. The first permanent settlement in North America was at Saint Augustine, Florida:* colonizing, colonization, peopling; community of settlers, colony, encampment, camp, post, outpost; small community, village, hamlet. **3.** *His father had to take on the settlement of his gambling debts. The court awarded her a handsome settlement:* payment, satisfaction, liquidation, discharge, amortization, clearing, clearance, acquittance; adjustment, compensation; bequest, sum, amount.

settler *n. Early settlers had a difficult life:* homesteader, squatter, pioneer, frontiersman; immigrant, colonist, colonizer.

sever *v.* **1.** *His arm was severed in the accident:* cut in two, cut off, separate, part, amputate, dismember, disconnect, dissever, lop off, truncate, bisect, cleave, split, slice, saw; rive, rend, tear. **2.** *Sometimes it's best to sever all family ties:* discontinue, dissolve, put an end to, terminate, do away with, disunite, disjoin, split up, break off, rupture. —**Ant.** 1 unite, join, bind. 2 continue; keep, maintain.

several *adj.* **1.** *We received several replies to our inquiry:* more than two, some, a number of, a few, divers. **2.** *They all had their several duties to perform:* separate, different, distinct, peculiar; individual, respective, own, particular, certain, specific, exclusive, special, express, private, personal, independent; single, distinctive; diverse, assorted, sundry. —*n.* **3.** *There are several here that I don't know:* several persons or things, a few, a number. —**Ant.** 2 joint, combined, communal.

severe *adj.* **1.** *Being put in the stocks was severe punishment:* strict, harsh, rigorous, taxing, demanding, vigorous, rough, stiff; cruel, brutal, merciless, ruthless, unsparing; drastic, draconian. **2.** *The general had a severe manner:* serious, stern, dour, strait-laced, grave, sober, grim, saturnine, sedate, somber, austere, forbidding, cold. **3.** *That coat is too severe to be worn anywhere but to a funeral:* restrained, plain, simple, conservative, uniform, unadorned, undecorated; chaste. **4.** *The blizzard of 1888 was a severe storm. The weatherman predicts* *severe cold:* intense, violent, extreme, unrelenting, raging, fuming; furious, fierce, savage, wild, brutal; turbulent, tumultuous; bitter, stinging, piercing, biting, cutting. **5.** *Appendicitis can be a severe illness:* serious, painful, dangerous, distressing, difficult. **—Ant.** 1 gentle, lenient, merciful, mild, moderate; easy; kind, considerate. 2 affable, genial, sweet. 3 gay, cheerful; decorative. 4 gentle, mild. 5 tolerable; easy; pleasant, mild.

severely *adv.* **1.** *The depression severely affected business:* badly, underminedly, acutely, extremely, dangerously, painfully, markedly. **2.** *We spoke to them severely:* sternly, strictly, critically, firmly, harshly, rigorously, seriously.

sew *v. She sewed several stitches in the hem:* stitch, bind, embroider, fasten, seam, tack, baste, tailor.

sex *n.* **1.** *What sex is the baby?:* gender, sexual classification, sexual identity, reproductive function; masculinity, maleness; femininity, femaleness. **2.** *"The birds and the bees" is a euphemism for "sex":* sexuality, generation, reproduction, procreation; sexual urge, sexual instinct, libido, Eros; sexual intercourse, love, lovemaking, coitus, coition, copulation.

sexual *adj. Sex hormones affect the growth and function of the sexual organs. Dr. Alfred Kinsey wrote a report on present-day sexual behavior. Don't confuse love with mere sexual attraction:* genital, generative, reproductive, procreative, venereal, copulatory, sex, coital; marital, conjugal, intimate; erotic, sexy, amatory, sensual, libidinous.

sexy *adj. The actor cashed in on his sexy voice. The celebrated chanteuse wiggled in a sexy way:* erotic, lewd, voluptuous, provocative, prurient, flirtatious, coquettish, suggestive, seductive, come-hither, bawdy.

shabby *adj.* **1.** *The beggar's clothes were shabby. The old house had grown shabby with age:* worn, ragged, raggy, threadbare, frayed, torn, ratty, tatty, the worse for wear; neglected, deteriorated, decaying, dilapidated, brokendown, ramshackle, tumbledown, rundown, seedy; impoverished, poverty-stricken. **2.** *He was a shabby dresser:* slovenly, ragged, wearing worn clothes, ill-dressed; dirty, mangy, scruffy, ratty, tatty, sorry; impoverished, down at the heels, down and out. **3.** *The mental patients received shabby treatment:* unfair; mean, wretched, sorry, miserable, contemptible, ignoble, dishonorable, sordid, low, inferior, unworthy; ungenerous, meager, cheap, poor, beggarly, illiberal, tight. **—Ant.** 1 pristine, new, neat, well-kept, well-to-do; grand, imposing. 2 well-dressed, fine, splendid; fashionable, chic, dapper. 3 fair, considerate, admirable, honorable; liberal, generous, handsome, lavish.

shack *n. The poorest lived in shacks:* shanty, hut, shed, hutch, hovel, cabin, crib, outbuilding, outhouse, lean-to, dump.

shackle *n.* **1.** *Shackles were placed on the prisoner's hands and feet:* fetter, irons, chains, bonds; handcuffs, cuffs, manacle; hobble. *—v.* **2.** *Shackle the captives so they can't escape:* fet-ter, chain, manacle, handcuff, cuff, secure, bind, tie, tether, pinion. **3.** *The soapbox orator told us we are shackled by ignorance and superstition. Lack of money shackled his plans for retirement:* restrict, thwart, retard, block, hamper, hobble, cramp, hinder, frustrate, foil, limit, impede, curb, check, rein, encumber, inhibit, circumscribe, stall, forestall, balk, bar, prevent, deter, hamstring, hogtie. **—Ant.** 2 unshackle, unchain; free, release. 3 aid, help, abet, promote, foster, further.

shade *n.* **1.** *It's cooler in the shade:* shadow, shadows; darkness, semidark. **2.** *The shades will keep the sun out:* (variously) window shade, blind; drape, curtain, awning, canopy, shutter, shield, screen, hood, veil. **3.** *A lighter shade of blue will make the room seem larger:* hue, tone, tint, color, cast. **4.** *There's only a shade of difference between the two candidates:* small degree, trace, tinge, touch, bit, whit, jot, iota, particle, scintilla, atom, modicum, soupçon, suggestion, hint. *—v.* **5.** *An awning shaded the porch:* shield from the sun, shield from the light, screen; make shady, darken, dim. **—Ant.** 1 sunlight, sunshine, direct light, light, glare, brightness. 4 great amount, full measure, lot, abundance, *Informal* heap, gobs, oodles. 5 light, lighten, illuminate, brighten; expose, uncover.

shadow *n.* **1.** *No shadow is cast when the sun is directly overhead:* silhouette, reflection; penumbra. **2.** Usually **shadows** *Someone was lurking in the shadows:* shade, partial darkness; gathering darkness. **3.** *Only a shadow of doubt remained. He was only a shadow of his former self:* trace, shade, bit, slight amount, small degree, touch, tinge; suggestion, whisper, hint, ghost, faint image. **4.** *The shadow of possible invasion hung over the country. The scandal left a shadow on his reputation:* threat, specter, cloud; dark spot, blight, taint, blot, blemish, smirch, smear, smudge, stain. *—v.* **5.** *Two detectives shadowed the suspect:* follow, tail, trail, dog the footsteps of, tag after, hound; track, stalk, pursue; keep tabs on.

shady *adj.* **1.** *It's cooler in the shady part of the yard:* shaded, shadowy. **2.** *Don't make any deals with that shady character:* disreputable, questionable, suspicious, fishy, dubious; unethical, dishonest, crooked, devious, underhanded; untrustworthy. **—Ant.** 1 sunny, sunlit, bright, unshaded, exposed. 2 upright, honest, honorable, moral, ethical, proper, aboveboard, straight, reputable, *Slang* square.

shaft *n.* **1.** *Grasp the knife firmly by the shaft:* handle, shank, hilt; spindle, trunk, stalk, stem. **2.** *The archers sent their shafts through the air:* (variously) arrow, dart, quill, spear, lance. **3.** *The candidates exchanged shafts in the debate:* sharp remark, barb, cut, gibe, insult, affront, aspersion, *Informal* brickbat. **4.** *A shaft of light came through the window:* ray, beam, streak, stream, gleam, patch. **5.** *The Washington Monument is an imposing marble shaft:* column, tower, obelisk, pillar, pilaster, pylon, monolith, minaret, spire, steeple. **6.** *The miners were* lowered into the shaft. The dumbwaiter was stuck in the shaft: excavation, cavity, pit, chasm, well, abyss; duct, vent, funnel, flue, chimney, conduit.

shaggy adj. Shaggy dogs require frequent grooming. A shaggy rug covered the floor: shagged, hairy, long-haired, hirsute, unshorn, bushy, fuzzy, woolly; downy, tufted, nappy, piled; whiskered, bewhiskered, bearded. —**Ant.** smooth, sleek, short-haired, close-cropped, shorn; flat-woven.

shake v. **1.** The house shakes when a train goes by. Shake the medicine well: vibrate, quiver, quake, quaver, totter, wobble, sway, tremble, shudder, shimmy, shiver, flutter, flicker, jiggle, joggle, jostle; agitate, mix. **2.** Don't shake your fist at me: wave, brandish, flourish, swing. **3.** The mining disaster shook the town: disturb, distress, unnerve, perturb; jar, jolt, rattle, unsettle, unstring, discompose, disquiet, ruffle, frighten; stun, startle, stagger, move, touch, affect, stir. **4.** The thief managed to shake the police. I can't seem to shake this cold: escape from, get away from, elude; get rid of, rid oneself of, throw off, slough. —n. **5.** Give the bottle a couple of shakes before pouring the juice: jiggle, jog, bounce, jounce, flourish. **6.** The shake of the speaker's hands betrayed his nervousness: trembling, tremble, shaking, shudder, quiver, quivering, quake, quaking, flutter, fluttering, shiver, shivering, flicker, flickering, jerk, twitch. —**Ant.** 3 calm, quiet, soothe, reassure, settle, compose, steady. 4 catch, capture, get; keep, retain. 6 steadiness, stillness.

shakeup n. Employees feared a shakeup when the company was sold: reorganization, turnover, cleanup, clean sweep, purge, rearrangement, realignment, restructuring, redistribution, redisposition.

shaky adj. **1.** Get down off that shaky ladder. I'm feeling a little shaky today: unsteady, trembling, shaking, quivering, wobbly, tremulous, tottering, teetery, teetering, weak, unstable, flimsy, frail, fragile; unsafe, hazardous, insecure, precarious; nervous, jumpy, jittery, fidgety. **2.** His determination to become a lawyer seems shaky: wavering, uncertain, unsure, dubious, unreliable, undependable, inconstant, vacillating, faltering, undecided, irresolute, unresolved, half-hearted, halting, hesitant.

shallow adj. **1.** The boat ran aground in the shallow water: shoal, of little depth, (variously) ankle-deep, knee-deep, waist-deep. **2.** They carried on a shallow conversation about parties and clothes: superficial, insubstantial, frivolous, frothy, trivial, slight, inconsequential, meaningless, unimportant, trifling, surface, skin-deep. —**Ant.** 1 deep, bottomless. 2 profound, serious, substantial, important, in-depth, intellectual, thoughtful, perceptive, keen, sharp.

sham n. **1.** Her illness was a sham to gain sympathy: fraud, fake, pretense, trick; imitation, counterfeit, copy, forgery, phony, put-on. —adj. **2.** The child's sham weeping fooled no one: feigned, fraudulent, fake, pretended, phony, false, make-believe, put-on; counterfeit, bogus,

forged, imitation, artificial, synthetic, simulated, spurious. —v. **3.** The girl's favorite trick was to sham tears: pretend, feign, fake, simulate, put on, act, imitate, affect, assume. —**Ant.** 1 original, the genuine article, Informal the real McCoy. 2 real, genuine, authentic, true; unfeigned, unpretended, natural.

shamble v. The tramp shambled along the street: shuffle, scuff, scuffle, plod, trudge, tramp, plug, lumber, stumble, stump, clump, slog, schlep, drag one's feet. —**Ant.** swagger, strut.

shambles n. **1.** The hurricane left the town in shambles: destruction, ruin, wreckage, ruination, devastation, holocaust, carnage, slaughter. **2.** The kitchen was a shambles: mess, disorder, confusion, chaos, turmoil, jumble.

shame n. **1.** The student felt great shame at having flunked the test: guilt, remorse, self-disgust, self-abomination; embarrassment, mortification, chagrin, shamefacedness, unworthiness. **2.** The corrupt politician brought shame to his party: disgrace, dishonor, contempt, ignominy, humiliation, mortification, disrepute, disrespect, degradation, debasement, odium. **3.** The way he abuses his dog is a shame: disgrace, scandal, stigma. **4.** What a shame that it rained the day of the picnic: disappointment, regretful thing, sorrowful happening. —v. **5.** The class's unruly behavior shamed the teacher: embarrass, humiliate, mortify, disgrace, humble. —**Ant.** 1 shamelessness, pride, self-respect, glory, worthiness. 2 honor, credit, renown, glory, esteem. 5 do credit to, make proud.

shamefaced adj. She was shamefaced after failing the exam: ashamed, embarrassed, chagrined, mortified, humiliated, sheepish, abashed, remorseful, blushing, sorry, humbled, Slang put-down, red-faced, crushed, disgraced, shamed. —**Ant.** proud, unashamed, shameless, unabashed.

shameful adj. What a shameful thing to do!: disgraceful, dishonorable, shameless, contemptible, ignoble, ignominious, opprobrious, inglorious, degrading, shocking, outrageous, despicable, deplorable, odious, reprehensible; dastardly, vile, villainous, base, mean, low, unworthy, iniquitous, heinous. —**Ant.** honorable, glorious, noble, worthy, praiseworthy, dignified, decent, virtuous, respectable; admirable, commendable, meritorious.

shameless adj. **1.** The shameless woman flirted with every man she met: without shame, disgraceful, dishonorable, degraded, abandoned, dissolute, immodest, wanton, immoral, indecent, indecorous. **2.** He's a shameless liar: brazen, forward, impudent, brash, pert, boldfaced, barefaced, unblushing, saucy, unabashed, unreserved, audacious, flagrant.

shanty n. They lived in a shanty deep in the woods: cottage, shack, cot, hut, hovel, cabin, house. —**Ant.** castle, palace.

shape n. **1.** The shape of Italy resembles a boot when you look at it on a map: outline, contour, figure, silhouette, profile, conformation, configuration; form, build, physique. **2.** Put those files *in shape:* order, array, orderly arrangement, state of neatness. **3.** *He's in good shape for a man of his age:* condition, physical condition, health, fettle, trim. —*v.* **4.** *The potter shaped the clay into a vase. A good teacher helps shape a child's character:* form, mold, model, fashion, frame; make, create, build, construct, develop; guide, determine. —**Ant.** 2 disorder, disarray, disarrangement, confusion, chaos. 4 destroy, ruin; warp.

shapeless *adj. She wore a shapeless dress:* unformed, formless, formless, indefinite, indistinct, nebulous, undeveloped, unformed, unmade, unshapely, unstructured, unsymmetrical, vague, amorphous. —**Ant.** shaped, well-proportioned, graceless.

shapely *adj. The shapely vase was on the mantle. The shapely young woman sat down:* curved, proportioned, regular, rounded, sightly, symmetrical, trim, elegant, well-formed, balanced, graceful, neat; well-proportioned, full-figured.

share *n.* **1.** *George's share of the inheritance was $40,000:* part, portion, allotment, apportionment, allowance, quota, percent, percentage, ration, *Informal* cut. —*v.* **2.** *Three doctors share the office:* own jointly, use jointly, receive together. **3.** *Share the candy with your brother:* divide and give out, split, cut up, divvy up, apportion, dole, allot, allocate, deal out, measure out, mete out.

sharp *adj.* **1.** *Be careful with that sharp axe. Hammer the sharp end of the peg into the ground:* keen-edged, fine-edged, fine, not blunt, razor-sharp; pointed, pointy, piked, edged, cutting; serrated, toothed, bristly, thorny, spiny, prickly. **2.** *After the storm there was a sharp drop in temperature. The sharp pain made the patient wince:* sudden, abrupt, precipitous, rapid; distinct, clear, clearly defined, extreme, acute, fierce, violent, keen, severe, intense, drastic, marked, excessive, immoderate, inordinate; vertical, steep, sheer, angular. **3.** *This salad dressing has a sharp taste:* biting, bitter, salty, acid, sour, vinegary, tart, caustic, acrid; piquant, strong; cutting, piercing, nippy, stinging, nipping. **4.** *She has such a sharp voice:* shrill, piercing, harsh, penetrating, raucous, strident; high, high-pitched, high-toned. **5.** *It takes sharp eyes to see the flaw. He's old but his mind is still sharp:* keen, acute, perceptive, quick; shrewd, astute, clever, penetrating, discerning, alert, awake, wide awake, vigilant. **6.** *His sharp business dealings earned him a bad reputation:* wily, crafty, cunning, sly, foxy, artful, calculating, conniving, contriving, unscrupulous, unprincipled, unethical, deceptive, tricky. **7.** *The angry men exchanged sharp words:* angry, harsh, scathing, unkind, spiteful, bitter, barbed, cutting, stinging; cruel, severe, vitriolic, rancorous, galling, venomous, acrid; abrupt, gruff, brusque, curt, blunt, crusty, bearish, crabbed. —*adv.* **8.** *Look sharp!:* sharply, keenly, acutely, alertly, quickly, closely, attentively. **9.** *The car stopped too sharp:* suddenly, abruptly, precipitously. **10.** *The meeting started at eight o'clock sharp:*

promptly, punctually, on the dot, on the nose, on the button; precisely, exactly, *Spanish* en punto, *French* juste. —**Ant.** 1 dull, blunt; round, rounded, straight, bulbous. 2 slow, gradual; gentle, easy, moderate, indistinct, blurred, unclear. 3 bland, mild, flat, insipid; sweet. 4 soft, mellow, soothing; well-modulated, low. 5 dull, dim, slow; unperceptive, obtuse, uncomprehending, unaware. 6 direct, straightforward, out in the open, aboveboard, ingenuous, guileless, artless; ethical, honest, scrupulous, principled. 7 sweet, gentle, kind, tender, soothing; polite, courteous, friendly, warm, loving. 8 dully; inattentively, carelessly, distractedly. 9 slowly, gradually, gently. 10 more or less, *Spanish* más o menos, *French* plus ou moins.

sharpen *v. Sharpen the knife on this whetstone:* make sharper, edge, put an edge on; whet, hone, grind, strop.

shatter *v.* **1.** *The plate shattered when it hit the floor:* break into pieces, break into smithereens, break into shivers, smash, crash, burst, explode, sunder, rive; splinter, crush, crumble, pulverize; break, crack, fracture, split. **2.** *Bad grades shattered the student's chances for a scholarship:* destroy, wreck, ruin, smash, devastate, crush, squash, quash, demolish, scuttle, spoil, upset, topple, overturn. —**Ant.** 2 increase, improve, enhance, heighten, better.

shave *v.* **1.** *Father finally shaved his mustache. Shave off the top branches of that bush:* cut off, cut, clip, crop, lop, prune, pare, trim, snip, barber, scissor, shear, fleece; dock; mow. **2.** *The bullet just shaved the Mountie's cheek:* graze, scrape, glance, brush, skin, touch lightly.

sheaf *n. He picked up a sheaf of grain:* bundle, stook, cluster, bunch.

shear *v.* **1.** *An experienced hand can shear a sheep in less than a minute. Shear the dead branches from the tree:* cut the fleece from, fleece; cut, clip, crop, trim, lop, prune, snip, scissor, shave. **2.** *The Provisional Government sheared Pétain of all his offices and honors:* deprive, relieve; take away, remove.

sheath *n. The pirate drew the dagger out of its sheath. The phonograph record came in a cellophane sheath:* scabbard; covering, sheathing, wrapper, wrapping, envelope, container, receptacle, jacket, coat, coating, case, slipcase, casing; membrane, skin, capsule, pod.

shed[1] *n. The farmer built a shed for his tractor next to the barn:* lean-to; hut, shack, hovel, shanty; toolshed, toolhouse; outbuilding.

shed[2] *v.* **1.** *Don't shed any tears over that scoundrel. Can anyone shed some light on the situation?:* let fall, let flow, spill, pour forth, give forth, emit, radiate, exude, discharge, shower; throw, cast, spread, distribute, scatter, strew, disperse, disseminate, broadcast. **2.** *Trees shed their leaves in autumn. An angora cat sheds more than a Siamese:* cast off, let fall, drop, discard, slough, doff; lose hair; molt. —**Ant.** 1 suppress, repress, withhold, hold back, choke back, stop; gather, collect, amass.

sheen *n. The sheen of the satin was enhanced by the candlelight:* luster, gloss, shine, glaze, polish, shininess, gleam, shimmer, effulgence, glossiness, glint, glitter, glister, brightness, radiance, burnish, glow, luminousness, refulgence. —**Ant.** tarnish, filminess, matte, dullness.

sheepish *adj.* **1.** *The sheepish mob followed the leader without question:* easily led, submissive, passive, docile, tractable, unassertive, obeisant, obedient, servile, subservient, unresisting, yielding. **2.** *The man offered a sheepish apology:* embarrassed, abashed, shamefaced, ashamed, hangdog, chastened, chagrined, mortified, guilty, blushing; timorous, fearful, bashful, shy, timid, meek, humble, diffident, shrinking. —**Ant.** 1 aggressive, strident, overbearing, assertive, masterful, independent; stubborn, obdurate, hardheaded, willful; disobedient, intractable, unyielding. 2 brazen, brash, unabashed, unashamed, unblushing, boldfaced, audacious, bold, immodest, confident, poised.

sheer *adj.* **1.** *That dress is too sheer to wear without a slip:* transparent, thin, fine, diaphanous, gossamer, gauzy, filmy. **2.** *Sheer alcohol will burn the lining of your throat. The clowns drew cries of sheer delight from the children:* unmixed, unadulterated, pure, one-hundred-percent, unalloyed; absolute, utter, total, complete, unlimited, unbounded, unrestrained, consummate, unconditional, unmitigated, unqualified, perfect, utter, out and out. **3.** *The mountain was too sheer to climb:* steep, vertical, perpendicular, plumb, straight up and down, bluff, sharp; abrupt, precipitous. —**Ant.** 1 opaque; thick, coarse. 2 mixed, impure, alloyed, adulterated, doctored; partial, fragmentary, incomplete, imperfect, conditional, mitigated, qualified, limited. 3 gradual, gentle, sloping; horizontal.

sheet *n.* **1.** *Fresh sheets were put on the beds. A sheet of frost covered the windshield:* bed sheet; coating, coat, layer, covering, blanket, film, membrane, sheath, overlay, top. **2.** *Cover the desk with a sheet of formica:* square, rectangle, slab, panel, leaf, piece, plate, pane.

shell *n.* **1.** *The turtle had an unusual pattern on its shell. Put the shells in the garbage:* carapace, case, hull, husk, shuck, pod. **2.** *Only the shell of the building stood after the fire:* framework, skeleton, hulk, walls and roof. **3.** *Shells burst over the enemy camp. The gun holds six shells:* artillery shell, cartridge shell, cartridge, bullet, round, shot; cannon shell, grenade, bomb, missile, projectile, rocket. —*v.* **4.** *Please shell some walnuts for the cake:* hull, husk, shuck. **5.** *Cannons shelled the fort:* fire on, bombard, rain shells on, pound, barrage, pepper.

shelter *n.* **1.** *The umbrella was a poor shelter from the heavy downpour. The ship sought shelter from the storm:* cover, protection, shield, refuge, safety, haven, asylum, sanctuary, security. **2.** *Most of our money goes for food and shelter:* housing, lodging, quarters, dwelling place, a roof over one's head. —*v.* **3.** *The overhanging roof sheltered us from the rain. Many Southerners sheltered runaway slaves during the Civil War:* protect, shield, cover; guard, safeguard, defend; harbor, take in, house, lodge,

care for, look after, provide for. —**Ant.** 2 exposure. 3 expose, lay bare; expel, turn out, evict; betray.

shelve *v.* *The committee decided to shelve the project for the time being:* lay aside, put aside, set aside, postpone, put off, suspend, defer, table, hold in abeyance, pigeonhole, *Slang* put on ice, put on the back burner. —**Ant.** begin, start, initiate, commence; activate, reactivate, revive; expedite.

shenanigans *n.* *Police tried to curb the shenanigans on Halloween:* hijinx, horseplay, mischief, sport, tomfoolery, antics, capers, sportiveness, deviltry, silliness, nonsense, buffoonery, roguishness, mischievousness.

shepherd *n.* **1.** *The shepherd tended the flock:* sheepherder, herder, herdsman. **2.** *The Lord is my shepherd:* protector, guardian, shelter, shield, defender, keeper, custodian, safeguard, champion, benefactor, patron, provider. —*v.* **3.** *The herdsman shepherded his flock through the winter. The guide shepherded the tourists through the Louvre:* tend, herd, watch over, protect, guard; guide, lead, pilot, direct, show, escort. —**Ant.** 1 rustler. 2 enemy, foe, rival.

sheriff *n.* *The sheriff arrested the suspect on the rural road:* chief law-enforcement officer of a county, county sheriff, constable.

shield *n.* **1.** *The sword glanced off the knight's shield:* (variously) buckler, aegis, escutcheon. **2.** *The policeman flashed his shield:* badge, emblem, medallion, ensign, insignia; button, star. **3.** *Dark glasses are an effective shield against the glare:* protection, protector, guard, safeguard, defense, buffer, cover, screen, shade, fender. —*v.* **4.** *Motorcyclists should wear helmets to shield them from injury. The motor is shielded in a shockproof housing:* protect, guard, safeguard, secure, preserve, keep, keep safe, shelter; house, harbor; screen, cover, shade. —**Ant.** 3 danger, risk, hazard. 4 expose, lay bare, uncover; endanger, imperil, risk, hazard.

shift *v.* **1.** *Shift the sofa so that it faces the fireplace:* move, transfer; switch, reposition, transpose, change, exchange, interchange, vary; swerve, veer. —*n.* **2.** *A sudden shift in the wind warned of the coming storm:* change, variation, shifting, alteration, modification, deviation, fluctuation, alternating, turning, move, switch, veering, swerve. **3.** *Bob works the day shift:* work period, stint, assignment, tour of duty, go, hitch. **4.** *She wore a light shift over her bathing suit:* straight, loose-fitting dress; camisole, chemise, slip.

shiftless *adj.* *This office has no place for a shiftless worker:* lazy, idle, inactive, lax, lackadaisical; careless, slothful, indolent, unconscientious; good-for-nothing, ne'er-do-well. —**Ant.** ambitious, willing-to-work, energetic, industrious, assiduous, active; conscientious, painstaking, scrupulous, careful.

shifty *adj.* *That shifty character needs watching:* crafty, foxy, cunning, wily, scheming, contriving, conniving, sneaky, slippery, maneuvering, tricky, deceitful; evasive, unreliable, untrustworthy, treacherous, dishonest. **—Ant.** open, straightforward, direct, artless, guileless; reliable, dependable, trustworthy, loyal.

shilly-shally *v. Stop shilly-shallying and make up your mind!:* waver, vacillate, procrastinate, hesitate, stall, falter, fluctuate, hem and haw, dillydally, dawdle, dither, go back and forth, seesaw, oscillate, straddle the fence, blow hot and cold. **—Ant.** be decisive, act, accomplish, perform, do.

shimmer *v.* **1.** *A light shimmered in the distance. The queen's lamé gown shimmered in the torchlight:* glimmer, twinkle, flicker, flutter, flash, blink, dance, sparkle, glisten, scintillate, coruscate, phosphoresce; gleam, glow, shine, beam. **2.** *The noonday air shimmered in the heat:* quiver, quake, shiver, shimmy, waver, vibrate, tremble. **—n. 3.** *In the telescope I glimpsed the shimmer of a far-distant star:* twinkle, glimmer, tremulous flickering, blinking, faint glimmering, wavering light.

shindig *n. Are you invited to the shindig on Saturday night?:* party, gala, ball, dance, fête, costume ball, affair, fancy-dress ball, soirée, festivity, revelry, masked ball, masquerade party, dinner dance, tea dance, prom, hop, barn dance, record hop; *Slang* bash, blowout, shindy; *French* thé dansant, bal masqué, bal costumé.

shine *v.* **1.** *The sun is shining. The diamond shone brightly:* emit light, shed light, reflect light, gleam, radiate, glow, beam, sparkle, shimmer, glitter, glisten, glister, twinkle, flicker, flash, blink, scintillate, coruscate, irradiate. **2.** *Shine the silver before the guests arrive:* polish, gloss, wax; buff, burnish, rub up; brighten. **—n. 3.** *We saw the shine of the night watchman's flashlight:* light, illumination, gleam, glow, beam, glare, glint, glitter, glimmer, sparkle, shimmer, twinkle, flicker, flash, blink; luminosity, luminousness, incandescence. **4.** *How does she get such a good shine on her silverware? Give these shoes a good shine:* gloss, luster, glow, sheen, brightness, radiance, brilliance, dazzle; polish, polishing, shining, wax, waxing, buffing, burnishing. **—Ant.** 2 dull, darken, dim; tarnish. 3 dark, darkness, blackness; dimness, murkiness. 4 dullness, tarnish.

shining *adj.* **1.** *Her shining hair looked especially beautiful:* radiant, gleaming, bright, brilliant, resplendent, glistening, effulgent, lustrous. **2.** *He is a shining example of good manners:* conspicuous, fine, outstanding, distinguished, eminent, prime, splendid, choice, excellent, select.

shiny *adj. The boy had a shiny new penny:* bright, brilliant, shining, gleaming, glistening, shimmering, sparkling, glittering, scintillating; luminous, radiant, lustrous, glowing, glaring, incandescent, effulgent; polished, burnished, glossy.

ship *n.* **1.** *Rough seas delayed the ship:* large boat, vessel, craft; (*variously*) steamship, steamer, ocean liner, liner, yacht, motorship, sailing ship, freighter, cargo ship, tanker, tramp steamer, tramp, packet, cruiser, battleship, destroyer, carrier, aircraft carrier. **2.** *The whole*

ship was given liberty: ship's company, crew; ship's passengers. **—v. 3.** *Ship the merchandise by air:* transport, send, dispatch, route, forward.

shipment *n. They arranged to pick up the shipment:* freight, consignment, cargo, lading.

shirk *v. Don't try to shirk your responsibilities:* get out of doing, avoid, evade, shun, duck, shrink from, sidestep, dodge, escape, elude, ignore, neglect, eschew; malinger, *Slang* goof off, goldbrick. **—Ant.** meet, face, confront; fulfill, perform, undertake, do, honor.

shiver *v.* **1.** *The child shivered from the cold:* shake, tremble, shudder, quiver, quaver, shimmy, quake. **—n. 2.** *A shiver of fear ran through me when the lights went out:* tremble, shudder, quiver, quaver. **3.** Often **shivers** *The goblet broke into shivers when I dropped it:* bit, piece, fragment, sliver, shard.

shock[1] *n.* **1.** *The shock of the earthquake was felt for miles:* impact, jar, jolt, rock, concussion; blow, collision. **2.** *The king's abdication was a shock to the nation. Oh, you gave me a shock:* surprise, blow, unexpected blow, disturbance, consternation, trauma, jolt, jar, bolt out of the blue; scare, start, turn. **—v. 3.** *We were shocked by the sad news. The parents were shocked by the child's foul language:* surprise, stun, stagger, shake, daze, stupefy, paralyze, jar, jolt, overwhelm, bowl over, give a turn; perturb, dismay, distress, disturb, upset, unsettle, disquiet, discompose, disconcert, astonish, astound, startle; appall, horrify, disgust, revolt, offend, outrage.

shock[2] *n. Shocks of wheat dotted the field:* sheaf, stack, bundle, pile; rick, cock.

shock[3] *n. The baby was born with a shock of black hair:* bush, bushy mass, mass, crop, mop, mane, thatch, mat.

shocking *adj.* **1.** *The failure of the bank was shocking news:* surprising, astounding, astonishing, startling, staggering, stupefying, jarring, jolting, overwhelming; disturbing, perturbing, upsetting, disquieting, unsettling, disconcerting. **2.** *Grandmother thought it shocking for girls to wear shorts. The hospital's treatment of mental patients is shocking:* scandalous, disgraceful, outrageous, indecent, offensive; appalling; horrifying, horrible, horrid, terrible, awful, disgusting, frightful, monstrous, insufferable, abominable, reprehensible, detestable, abhorrent, repugnant, repellent, odious, foul, wretched, hideous, revolting, ghastly, gruesome, grisly. **—Ant.** 1, 2 unsurprising, expected; gratifying, satisfying, pleasing. 2 acceptable, decent; good, excellent, fine, wonderful, marvelous, glorious, worthy, capital; admirable, honorable, praiseworthy, commendable, laudable; attractive, pleasant, desirable.

shoddy *adj.* **1.** *The carpenter did a shoddy job:* inferior, poor, second-rate, careless, sloppy, negligent, inefficient, haphazard, slipshod, *Informal* tacky. **2.** *Leaving his wife to do all the work was a rather shoddy thing to do:* nasty, mean, shabby, inconsiderate, low, low-down, base, reprehensible, contemptible, dirty; niggardly, miserly, ungenerous, stingy. **—Ant.** 1 excellent, first-rate, good, fine; precise, accurate, careful, meticulous, thorough, scrupulous, fastidious. 2 noble, gentlemanly, kind, thoughtful, considerate; sympathetic, compassionate.

shoot v. 1. *The policeman shot the mad dog:* hit, wing, nick, plug, riddle, pelt, pepper, shell, spray, pump full of lead; kill, pick off, drop, fell, blow one's brains out, *Slang* waste. 2. *Each archer shot three arrows at the target. The catapult shot hundred-pound rocks at the enemy. The reporters began to shoot questions at the congressman:* fire, open fire, discharge, let fly, hurl, propel, eject, sling, cast, fling, throw, toss, launch, catapult; detonate, explode, go off; bombard, shower, rain, pelt. 3. *The horses shot out of the starting gate:* move suddenly, charge, spring, dart, bolt, dash, sweep, spurt, jump, leap; race, speed, fly, tear, rush, hurry. —n. 4. *New shoots appeared on the bush:* new growth, young branch, twig, sprout, bud; stem, sprig, tendril; offshoot.

shop n. 1. *The local dress shop is having a sale:* store, retail store, small store, establishment, boutique; emporium, market, mart. 2. *He has an excellent woodworking shop in his basement:* workshop, studio, atelier; factory, plant, works, mill. —v. 3. *The newlyweds shopped for silver and china:* seek to purchase, go shopping for, windowshop, look, hunt, browse; buy, purchase, patronize.

shore[1] n. 1. *There are lighthouses all along the Eastern shore. We spend all our weekends at the shore:* coast, seacoast, seaboard; seashore, seaside, waterside, beach, strand; bank, riverbank; margin, brink. 2. *Finally, the sailors sighted shore:* land, dry land, terra firma.

shore[2] v. *Heavy posts shored the roof of the tunnel:* support, prop, hold, hold up, brace, reinforce, buttress, strengthen, bolster; bulwark, underpin, sustain, mainstay. —**Ant.** weigh down, burden, crush, overwhelm, push over, overturn.

short adj. 1. *Short hair is cooler for summer. A short person may have difficulty reaching the top shelves:* not long; not tall, stubby, squat, truncated; stunted, runty; small, little, pint-sized, pocket-sized, diminutive, slight, elfin, pygmy, bantam, Lilliputian, dwarfish. 2. *Our vacation was far too short. The mayor gave a short speech:* brief, short-lived, quick, fleet, fleeting, momentary, hasty, summary, cursory; concise, terse, succinct, compact; abridged, abbreviated, condensed; curtailed. 3. *The tired salesman was short with the customers:* curt, brusque, abrupt, gruff, impatient, sharp; cross, snappish, testy; illtempered, impolite. 4. *The plane had only a short fuel reserve:* low, scanty, scant, sparse, scarce, meager, skimpy, tight, niggardly, lean, slender, slim, thin; insufficient, deficient, wanting, lacking, limited, not abundant. —adv. 5. *Stopping the car short caused a pileup on the highway:* suddenly, abruptly, without warning, precipitously. 6. *The deadline was suddenly moved up, and I was caught short:* unawares, without preparation, by surprise, without warning. —**Ant.** 1 long; tall, high, reedy, rangy. 2

long, longish, lengthy, protracted, attenuated, elongated, extended; interminable, unending. 3 patient; polite, civil, mannerly; verbose, wordy, long-winded. 4 adequate, sufficient, ample, plenteous, plentiful, abundant, superabundant, copious, well-stocked, inexhaustible, profuse, lavish; overflowing, excessive, overstocked. 5 slowly, gradually, gently.

shortage n. *There is a shortage of food in the flooded areas:* lack, want, deficiency, shortfall, insufficiency, inadequacy, scantiness, scant supply, limited amount, scarcity, sparsity, sparseness, dearth, deficit, leanness. —**Ant.** abundance, superabundance, profusion, plenty, copiousness, plethora, sufficiency, adequacy; surplus, excess, overflow, overage.

shortcoming n. *Narrowmindedness is a serious shortcoming:* fault, flaw, defect, blemish, imperfection, failing, weakness, inadequacy, frailty, deficiency, foible; drawback, handicap, failure. —**Ant.** advantage, strength, strong point, virtue, merit.

shorten v. *Can the tailor shorten the coat by this evening? Shorten the report by five pages:* make shorter, cut short, cut down, curtail, trim, clip, pare, prune, shave, shear; abbreviate, cut, abridge, condense, contract, reduce, decrease, foreshorten, diminish, lessen. —**Ant.** lengthen, elongate; extend, protract, expand, increase, enlarge, inflate.

short-lived adj. *He had a short-lived assignment in Turkey:* impermanent, temporary, brief, ephemeral, evanescent, fugitive, passing, short-haul, short-run, short-term, temporary, transitory, fleeting.

shortly adv. *The guests will be arriving shortly:* soon, in a short time, in a little while, before long, by and by, presently, directly, promptly, anon, in a trice, immediately, forthwith. —**Ant.** later, much later.

shortsighted adj. 1. *A shortsighted person needs distance glasses:* unable to see far, nearsighted, myopic; amblyopic, weak-eyed, purblind. 2. *It was shortsighted not to plan for the possibility of rain:* lacking foresight, improvident, imprudent, ill-advised, unthinking, injudicious, undiscerning, uncircumspect; careless, heedless, reckless, rash, thoughtless, incautious, foolish. —**Ant.** 1, 2 farsighted. 2 foresighted, forehanded, prudent, wise, sagacious, circumspect.

short-tempered adj. *Grandpa is usually short-tempered around the children:* irritable, cranky, grouchy, hot-tempered, short-fused, ill-humored, irascible, testy, choleric, splenetic, snappish, cantankerous, crusty, sharp, peevish, waspish, *British* shirty, bearish, curt, abrupt. —**Ant.** calm, placid, temperate, sedate, pacific.

shot n. 1. *The shots quickly drew the police:* gunfire, report, discharge; volley, salvo, fusillade; detonation, blast, explosion. 2. *The cannon was out of shot:* ammunition, bullets, slugs, projectiles, balls. 3. *The hunter is an excellent shot:* marksman, shooter, rifleman, sharpshooter; archer, bowman. 4. *The golfer's tee shot traveled two hundred yards down the fair-*

way: stroke, throw, toss; play, move; hit, drive. **5.** *How about taking a shot at the answer?:* attempt, try, chance, go; guess, conjecture, surmise, essay; *Informal* crack. **6.** *A shot of penicillin should cure the infection:* injection; dose.

shoulder *n.* **1.** *Someone tapped me on the shoulder:* part of the body between the neck and upper arm; scapula, clavicle. **2.** *The disabled car was parked on the shoulder of the road:* edge, side, rim, margin, verge, border, brink, bank, skirt; crest, brow. —*v.* **3.** *The doctor shouldered his way through the crowd:* shove, elbow, push, thrust, lunge; jostle, bump. **4.** *The oldest son shouldered the burdens of the family:* assume, undertake, take on, bear, carry on one's shoulders, take, carry, uphold, sustain, support. —**Ant.** 2 middle, center. 4 shirk, shun, neglect, avoid, evade, eschew, duck, dodge.

shout *v.* **1.** *The drowning man shouted for help:* cry out, cry, call out, call, yell, holler, scream, shriek, howl, roar, bellow, bawl, clamor, thunder, exclaim, rend the air; whoop, hoot, yelp, hollo, huzzah. —*n.* **2.** *The shout brought everyone running. A shout of acclaim went up when the hero appeared:* cry, outcry, call, yell, holler, scream, shriek, howl, screech, roar, bellow, yelp; whoop, hoot, hollo, cheer, hurrah, huzzah; clamor, outburst, burst, chorus, hullabaloo, hue and cry.

shove *v.* **1.** *Stop shoving! Shove the chair closer to the table:* push, prod, jostle, elbow, shoulder, crowd, nudge; thrust aside, bump, jolt, joggle, butt; propel, drive, force, impel. —*n.* **2.** *Someone gave me a shove from behind:* push, prod, thrust, boost, nudge; jostle.

show *v.* **1.** *Does my slip show?:* be visible, be within view, come into view, appear, peep forth; be noticeable, attract attention. **2.** *The test will show how much each student knows:* reveal, disclose, make known, manifest, uncover, bare, lay bare, expose, unveil, bring to light; demonstrate, exhibit, display, prove, evidence, evince, suggest, intimate, hint at, represent, establish, bespeak; argue, testify to, attest, confirm, substantiate, certify, corroborate, bear out, bear witness to. **3.** *Show me how this lock works:* explain, indicate, make clear, point out, make known to, inform, teach, instruct, coach, school, tutor; demonstrate. **4.** *Show the guest into the study:* direct, lead, guide, usher, conduct. **5.** *The judge showed leniency to the prisoner:* grant, give, bestow, endow, tender, proffer, impart, favor, lavish; dispense, distribute. —*n.* **6.** *Many hands went up in a show of support. His face gave no show of fear:* display, demonstration, exhibition, sign, expression, token, mark, evidence, indication, manifestation, revelation, disclosure, testimonial, attestation, confirmation. **7.** *The painting was purchased at a sidewalk art show:* exhibit, exhibition, exposition, fair; display, demonstration. **8.** *There's a good television show on tonight. The local theater has a new show this week:* program, production, entertainment, performance; (*variously*) play, drama, comedy, musical, motion picture, pic-

ture, movie, opera, operetta, ballet, stage show, vaudeville show, variety show, bill; spectacle, ceremony, pomp. **9.** *Her headache was just a show to avoid going to work. He likes to put on a show of wealth for his guests:* display, pretext, pretense, pretension, affectation, pose, sham, front, counterfeit; impression, effect, appearance, illusion, delusion; vaunting, flaunting. —**Ant.** 1 hide, conceal, secrete, withhold, suppress, be invisible, be unnoticeable. 2 hide, conceal, obscure, veil, screen, mask, cloak, cover; disprove, deny, refute. 5 withhold, keep; withdraw. 6 hiding, concealing; disguise, camouflage.

showdown *n.* *The senator forced a showdown with his critics:* confrontation, conflict, climax, crisis, face-off, encounter, clashing, collision; battle, war, combat.

shower *n.* **1.** *It will take more than a shower to end the drought. A heavy shower turned the road into a quagmire:* brief fall of rain, sprinkle, drizzle; downpour, cloudburst, torrent, deluge. **2.** *A shower of acorns fell from the tree. A shower of contributions reached the Red Cross:* fall, pouring down, rain; deluge, flood, inundation, torrent, stream, rush, surge, profusion, plethora, wealth; salvo, volley, barrage, bombardment. —*v.* **3.** *The lawn sprinkler showered the children. Is it supposed to shower today?:* sprinkle, splash, spray, wet; rain, drizzle. **4.** *The grandparents showered gifts on the children:* give in abundance, bestow liberally, lavish, rain, deluge, pour, bombard.

showman *n.* *Barnum was a great showman:* impresario, producer, exhibitor, director.

showoff *n.* *Only a showoff would steer a bicycle with his feet:* exhibitionist, flaunter, swaggerer, strutter, cock of the walk; egotist, braggart, braggadocio, boaster, fanfaron, windbag.

showpiece *n.* *The sable cape was the showpiece of the fur collection:* masterpiece, masterwork, prime example, prize, gem, jewel, pearl; classic, paragon, prizewinner, rarity, pride, treasure, wonder; *French* chef d'oeuvre, pièce de résistance. —**Ant.** rubbish, trivia, trash.

showy *adj.* *The bush was covered with huge, showy blossoms:* brilliant, splendid, striking, gorgeous, ornate, vivid, florid, magnificent; gaudy, flashy, garish, loud, ostentatious. —**Ant.** dull, drab, lackluster, somber, dreary.

shred *n.* **1.** *The machine tore the paper into shreds:* strip, ribbon, band; fragment, sliver, piece, bit, scrap, snippet, rag, tatter. **2.** *There's not a shred of truth in that story!:* bit, particle, speck, grain, morsel, iota, jot, scrap, fragment, trace, atom, molecule, ion, whit, spot, scintilla, hair. —**Ant.** 2 mass, pile, heap, heaps, oceans, *Informal* gobs, oodles.

shrew *n.* *He suddenly realized he'd married a shrew:* nag, scold, virago, spitfire, vixen, harridan, hag, harpy, *Slang* battle-ax, fishwife, shewolf, termagant, Xanthippe; *Yiddish* kvetch, yenta.

shrewd *adj.* **1.** *He's too shrewd to trust in business matters:* sly, crafty, cunning, foxy, wily, cagey; artful, tricky, shifty, slippery, slick, smooth, disingenuous, contriving, designing, scheming, calculating, self-serving, Machiavellian. **2.** *Shrewd investors held their stock until prices rose again:* astute, smart, clever, sharp, sharp-witted, acute, keen, knowing, canny, discerning, quick, quick-witted, perceptive, sensible, farseeing, farsighted, probing, piercing, penetrating; wise, intelligent, sagacious, perspicacious, circumspect, prudent, cautious, careful, wary. **—Ant.** 1 straightforward, artless, guileless, ingenuous, candid, open, sincere, fair; innocent, naive, unsophisticated. 2 dull, unknowing, ignorant, undiscerning, slow-witted, slow, nearsighted, shortsighted, imprudent, careless; dumb, stupid.

shriek *n.* **1.** *The children greeted each other with shrieks of joy:* cry, outcry, call, yell, yelp, screech, squeal, squeak, howl, shout, scream, holler, whoop, hoot, peal. *—v.* **2.** *The girl shrieked when she saw the mouse:* cry out, scream, screech, squawk, yell, yelp, squeal, holler, howl.

shrill *adj.* *A radio announcer shouldn't have a shrill voice:* high, high-pitched, screeching, piercing, penetrating, strident, piping, loud, blaring, clamorous, raucous. **—Ant.** soft, mellow, mellifluous, dulcet, silvertoned, velvety, satiny; resonant, deep, low, well-modulated.

shrine *n.* **1.** *Every day the women come to pray at the shrine:* sacred place, consecrated place, sacred tomb; altar, sanctuary, sanctum, chapel, church, temple. **2.** *Gettysburg is a U.S. national shrine:* honored place, consecrated spot, monument.

shrink *v.* **1.** *Will this sweater shrink when washed? A bad harvest caused the farmer's income to shrink:* become smaller, make smaller, make less, lessen, shrivel, shorten, draw together, contract, pucker, constrict, deflate, compress, condense; decrease, diminish, decline, curtail, reduce, dwindle, dry up, wane, ebb. **2.** *The shy man shrank at the thought of being called on to speak. The boy shrank from the expected blow:* draw back, hang back, recoil, cringe, cower, quail, shudder, shy, blench, flinch, wince, duck, retreat, withdraw, retire; demur, stick, refuse, balk, bridle. **—Ant.** 1 stretch, swell, distend, dilate, inflate; increase, enlarge, amplify, grow, expand, mushroom, balloon. 2 welcome, meet head on, confront, stand up to.

shrivel *v.* *The peaches shriveled in the sun:* shrink, dry up, wither, wizen, wrinkle, pucker; parch, scorch; deteriorate, waste away.

shroud *n.* **1.** *The body was wrapped in a silk shroud:* burial cloth, graveclothes, winding sheet, cerements, cerecloth. **2.** *A shroud of mystery surrounded the case:* cover, covering, cloak, blanket, sheet, veil, mantle, pall, screen, cloud. *—v.* **3.** *The negotiations were shrouded in secrecy:* wrap, clothe, swathe, cover, envelop, cloak, veil; hide, conceal. **—Ant.** 3 uncover, unveil, reveal, expose.

shudder *v.* **1.** *The child shuddered from the cold. The plane shuddered and went into a tailspin:* tremble, shake, quiver, quaver, quake,

shiver; shimmy, twitch, jerk. *—n.* **2.** *She felt a shudder of fear when she remembered the near-accident:* trembling, tremor, shiver, quiver, quaver, shake, quake, flutter, paroxysm, spasm, pulsation, throb, pang, twitch, jerk, convulsion.

shuffle *v.* **1.** *Stop shuffling your feet!:* drag, scrape, slide, scuff, walk with clumsy steps, shamble. **2.** *Shuffle the cards and deal:* jumble, disarrange, rearrange, mix, scramble; exchange the positions of, interchange. *—n.* **3.** *His injured knee causes him to walk with a shuffle:* dragging gait, sliding gait, clumsy, step, scraping movement; limp, gimp. **—Ant.** 1 lift. 3 light step, high step.

shun *v.* *The recluse shunned all company:* avoid, evade, elude, dodge, keep away from, keep clear of, steer clear of, shy away from, fight shy of, shrink from, turn away from, circumvent; eschew, refuse, forgo, reject, disdain, boycott, ignore, have nothing to do with, have no part of. **—Ant.** welcome, embrace, encourage, seek, search out, solicit, court.

shut *v.* **1.** *Shut the door. Shut the drapes:* close, secure, fasten, snap, clasp, latch, lock; draw to, draw, fold. **2.** *Shut the cat in the kitchen for the night:* enclose, confine, constrain, cloister, closet, cage, coop, fence in, corral, box, lock in; barricade, impound, imprison, intern, incarcerate. *—adj.* **3.** *Is the window shut?:* closed, closed up; fastened, secured, latched, locked; drawn, drawn to. **—Ant.** 1 open, unshut; unfasten, unlock. 2 free, liberate, release, let out. 3 open, opened; unfastened, unlocked.

shy *adj.* **1.** *The child was too shy to enjoy parties:* self-conscious, bashful, shrinking, timid, diffident, timorous, meek, reserved, reticent, demure, modest; fearful, apprehensive, tremulous, nervous, anxious, skittish. **2.** *The charity drive is $2000 shy of meeting its goal:* short, under, deficient, lacking, wanting, needing, in need, scant, minus. **3.** *Always be shy of get-rich-quick schemes:* wary, leery, suspicious, distrustful, cautious, careful, *Slang* chary. *—v.* **4.** *The horse shied at a shadow on the road:* jump back, draw back, recoil from, balk, spring aside, swerve, dodge, shrink, blench, cower, flinch, wince. **—Ant.** 1 forward, brash, brazen, brassy; bold, fearless, unfrightened, unapprehensive. 2 over, ahead, above, showing a surplus. 3 rash, reckless, careless, unsuspicious, unsuspecting.

sibyl *n.* *They consulted the sibyl about their future endeavors:* oracle, prophetess, seer, augur, predictor, soothsayer, diviner, forecaster, fortune teller, sorceress, Delphic sibyl, prognosticator.

sick *adj.* **1.** *The actor was too sick to perform. Grandfather has been sick for years. Are you going to be sick?:* ill, unwell, ailing, laid up, indisposed; infirm, sickly, invalid, afflicted, unsound, unhealthy, poorly, frail, delicate, weak; nauseated, throwing up, queasy, under the weather; of a sick person. **2.** *The missing child's parents are sick with worry:* deeply upset, greatly affected, stricken, afflicted, suffering, distressed, grieved, wretched, heartbroken, crushed, miserable, troubled, uneasy, disturbed, perturbed, disquieted, discomposed. **3.** *I'm sick of the same old routine every day:* fed up with, disgusted with, tired, weary, bored with; adverse to, repelled by, displeased with, revolted by. —**Ant.** 1 well, fine, tip-top; healthy, hale, hale and hearty, sound, unimpaired, strong, robust, vigorous, blooming, fit as a fiddle. 2 unaffected, untroubled, undisturbed, unperturbed, unconcerned, unworried, easy, tranquil, calm.

sicken *v. The sight of blood sickened the young medical student. Within a week the captured whale sickened and died:* make sick, make ill, nauseate, turn the stomach, disgust, revolt, repel, repulse, horrify, upset, offend, shock; become sick, fall sick, take sick. —**Ant.** cure, make well; please, delight, enchant, gratify.

sickening *adj. What's that sickening odor?:* causing sickness, nauseating; disgusting, vile, horrible, nasty, foul, revolting, repugnant, noisome, repulsive, repellent, loathsome, abhorrent, distasteful, unsavory, offensive. —**Ant.** curative; agreeable, mouth-watering, delightful, pleasant, pleasing, heavenly, wonderful, inviting, tempting, attractive, lovely, enchanting, alluring, captivating.

sickly *adj.* **1.** *The sickly child missed many days of school. Did you notice her sickly complexion?:* ailing, in poor health, unhealthy, sick, ill, unwell, infirm, invalid, afflicted, unsound, frail, weak, delicate, poorly; pale, wan, ashen, drab, peaked, bloodless, leaden, cadaverous, lackluster. **2.** *His sickly excuse for being late convinced no one:* weak, feeble, flimsy, lame, faint, ineffective, unconvincing, lacking in fervor, insipid, spiritless, flat, uninspired, apathetic, torpid; simpering, smirking, snickering, sneaky, guilty, self-conscious, silly, namby-pamby, wishy-washy.

sickness *n.* **1.** *The worker was absent owing to sickness. Chicken pox is a common childhood sickness:* illness, ill health; disease, disorder, infirmity, ailment, malady, complaint, indisposition, affliction; poor health, sickliness, unsoundness, invalidism, frailness, delicate health, debility; disability. **2.** *Rough seas caused much sickness among the passengers:* nausea, queasiness, qualmishness; vomiting, throwing up, *Slang* upchucking.

side *n.* **1.** *Stand by my side. Please write on both sides of the paper:* flank; lateral surface, flat surface, surface. **2.** *Two sides of the property face the water. The boys stood at the far side of the room:* boundary, bound, limit, perimeter, border, edge, periphery, margin, rim, brim, skirt, hem; part, area, segment, section, sector, territory, region, division; half, quarter. **3.** *Both teams wanted the best pitcher on their side. Which side do you think will win the election?:* team; group, body, sect, faction, party, clique, coterie, circle; alliance, coalition, association, affiliation, federation. **4.** *Let's hear the defendant's side of the story. Look at the problem from both sides:* position, stand, attitude, part, belief, opinion, cause, behalf; viewpoint, point of view, view, standpoint, aspect, angle, slant, light, phase, facet, hand. **5.** *Harry is related on my father's side of the family:* part of a family;

line of descent, lineage, bloodline, strain, stock, house. —*adj.* **6.** *Plant the rose bushes in the side yard:* at one side, on one side, lateral, flanking; fringe, border, marginal, skirting. **7.** *Figure B shows the same device in side view. He gave her a side glance:* from the side, toward the side, lateral, postern; sideways, sidewise, sidelong, oblique, indirect, askance. **8.** *Does the job offer any side benefits? The car is parked on a side street:* minor, subordinate, lesser, incidental, secondary, subordinate, subsidiary, insignificant, unimportant, inconsequential; related, accessory, collateral, contingent, allied. —**Ant.** 1 front, back; top, bottom, edge. 2 middle, center, midpoint. 6 front, back, rear; top, bottom; center, central, middle. 7 frontal, direct, headlong; rear. 8 major, main, primary, principal, prime, first, leading, significant.

sidekick *n. He and his sidekick took charge:* partner, associate, confederate, cohort, henchman, subordinate, assistant, right hand, man Friday, girl Friday, gal Friday.

sideways also **sideway, sidewise** *adv.* **1.** *The pedestrian jumped sideways to avoid the cyclist. Try to slip sideways through the hole in the fence:* to the side, toward one side, from one side, sideward; with one side forward, laterally, sidelong, edgeways, edgewise, aslant, obliquely. —*adj.* **2.** *The boy gave the girl a sideways look:* sidelong, sidewise, oblique, lateral. —**Ant.** 1 forward, backward; head on. 2 direct, headlong.

siege *n. The siege of the city lasted two months:* blockade, besieging, attack.

sift *v.* **1.** *Sift the brown sugar onto the cookies. Dust sifted through the window frame:* sprinkle, scatter; drift, filter. **2.** *It's hard to sift the facts from the lies in his story. The jury sifted through the transcripts of the trial:* separate, sort out, sort, discriminate, distinguish, winnow, screen; study, scrutinize, inspect, examine closely, probe, search, investigate, analyze, review.

sigh *v.* **1.** *The laundress sighed with weariness. He sighed, "Too bad":* let out one's breath, breathe loudly, moan, groan, sob; say with a sighing sound, whine, hiss. **2.** *The soldiers sighed for home and family:* pine, yearn, long, brood; grieve, weep, lament, mourn, sorrow. —*n.* **3.** *The student gave a sigh of relief when the exam was over:* deep audible breath; moan, groan, sob, whine; hiss.

sight *n.* **1.** *Wearing glasses will aid poor sight:* eyesight, vision, visual perception. **2.** *We waved until the car was out of sight:* range of vision, field of vision, eyeshot, view, ken, scrutiny, gaze, survey. **3.** *The sight of land elated the ship's crew:* seeing, vision, appearance, visibility, viewing, glimpse, view. **4.** *The sun setting over the ocean was a sight to behold:* view, spectacle, display, pageant, exhibit, prospect, scene, vista, image, scenery; place of interest, thing of interest. **5.** *The rifle has a new sight:* peepsight, sighthole, bead; telescopic sight. —*v.* **6.** *The captain sighted a ship on the horizon:* see, observe, glimpse, spot, catch sight of, spy, espy, perceive, behold, view. —**Ant.** 1 blindness.

sign *n.* **1.** *A valentine is a sign of love. The dark* *clouds may be a sign of rain:* symbol, mark, figure, token, evidence, manifestation, emblem, badge, ensign; indication, indicator, omen, portent, prognostic, presage, warning, forewarning, forecast, herald, harbinger, signal, clue, symptom, hint, suggestion, intimation, note, index; characteristic, earmark, trademark, trait, feature, stamp, brand. **2.** *The conductor gave the engineer the sign to start. The winner made a thumbs-up sign:* signal, motion, gesture; go-ahead, wave, nod. **3.** *A "for sale" sign was in the window:* (*variously*) placard, advertising sign, electric sign, neon sign, signboard, signpost, billboard; road sign, street sign, guidepost; nameplate. —*v.* **4.** *Please sign both copies of the contract. Please sign my autograph book:* write one's signature, set one's hand to, countersign, underwrite, undersign, endorse, sign one's John Hancock; autograph, inscribe.

signal *n.* **1.** *The referee blew his whistle as a signal for the game to begin. Did the policeman give us a signal to go ahead?:* sign, high sign, indication, indicator, cue, warning, command; gesture, motion, nod; watchword, password. —*adj.* **2.** *Stop when the signal light is red:* indicating, direction, directing, guiding, pointing, warning. **3.** *The Aeneid is a signal example of literary epic as against oral epic:* singular, unique, exceptional, one-of-a-kind, distinctive, outstanding, extraordinary, exceptional, remarkable, noteworthy, notable, distinguished, eminent, illustrious, famous, honored, renowned, impressive, important, consequential, significant, momentous, considerable, memorable, unforgettable; conspicuous, striking, arresting, prominent, commanding. —*v.* **4.** *The conductor signaled the orchestra to rise:* motion, gesture, beckon, give a sign to. —**Ant.** 3 ordinary, commonplace, common, familiar, everyday, run-of-the-mill.

signature *n.* *He put his signature to the document:* autograph, hand, holograph, mark, seal, monogram.

significance *n.* *The Torah has great significance for all Jews. Do you understand the significance of the doctor's findings?:* consequence, importance, import, weight, meaning, signification, implication, relevance, moment, portent, gravity, force, influence, authority, concern, interest, note, notability, eminence, priority, prominence, distinction, excellence, value, merit, worth, virtue; sense, drift, intent, intention, aim, object, purpose, direction.

significant *adj.* **1.** *Penicillin was an extremely significant medical discovery. Does the report give all the significant facts of the case?:* consequential, important, substantial, meaningful, material, principal, great, paramount, major, chief, main, prime, vital, critical, serious, portentous, influential, considerable, momentous, grave, weighty, noteworthy, notable, eminent, prominent, distinct, outstanding, remarkable, pressive, exceptional, signal, eventful. **2.** *The hush was significant of the crowd's respect for the speaker. He gave her a significant look:* indicative, expressive, meaningful, suggestive, symbolic, symptomatic, emblematic, representative, demonstrative; eloquent, pregnant, cogent, telling, knowing. —**Ant.** 1 insignificant, inconsequential, trivial, unimportant, insubstantial, meaningless, immaterial.

signify *v.* *A white flag signifies surrender. Please signify agreement by raising your hands:* be a sign of, stand for, mean, import, indicate, represent, connote, convey, express, manifest, evidence, evince, demonstrate, exhibit, show, proclaim, declare, announce, communicate, set forth, designate, disclose, reveal, tell, give notice of; imply, intimate, suggest, hint at, denote, typify, symbolize, bespeak, betoken, import, argue; portend, predict, prognosticate, augur, omen, forebode, foretell, foreshadow, presage, herald, promise.

silence *n.* **1.** *The silence of the woods was broken by the cry of a loon. Father's silence indicated disapproval. Silence was the young man's key to success:* quiet, quietness, noiselessness, soundlessness, still, stillness, hush; peace, calm, tranquillity, serenity, placidness, placidity, repose; speechlessness, muteness, dumbness; reserve, reticence, uncommunicativeness, taciturnity, secretiveness, closemouthedness. —*v.* **2.** *The speaker tried to silence the angry crowd. There must be a way to silence the echoes in this room:* still, quiet, quieten, hush, calm, strike dumb, tongue-tie; deaden. **3.** *The dictator has silenced his opponents by jailing them. We must silence our fears and proceed:* gag, muzzle, muffle, choke off, suppress, repress, crush, quell, quash, put down, squelch, squash; stop, halt, stifle, check, curb, vanquish, overcome, defeat, rout, banish, subdue, conquer, extinguish, nullify, allay, quiet, still, put an end to, lay to rest. —**Ant.** 1 sound, noise, noisiness, din, roar, clamor, tumult, turmoil, commotion, agitation, excitement; speech, talking, talkativeness, verbosity, verboseness, loquaciousness, garrulousness, chatter, babel. 2 make noise; arouse, rouse, agitate, incite, inflame, stir up; make louder, amplify. 3 ungag, encourage, support, aid, help, abet, champion, broadcast, publicize.

silent *adj.* **1.** *The cat moved on silent feet. The house was as silent as a morgue:* making no sound, having no sound, soundless, noiseless, quiet, still, hushed, muffled, muted, mute; idle, inactive, unstirring, lifeless, inert, quiescent, dormant, calm, peaceful, tranquil, serene, placid. **2.** *The class was silent as the teacher explained the exam rules. Bill is the strong, silent type:* not speaking, saying nothing, wordless, mum, tongue-tied; speechless, mute, dumb; speaking but little, untalkative, reticent, uncommunicative, closemouthed, close-lipped, tight-lipped, taciturn, reserved; secretive, mysterious, discreet. **3.** *The "t" in "often" is silent:* not pronounced, unpronounced, not sounded, unsounded, unvocalized, mute. **4.** *Two men own the business, but one is a silent partner. The two nations have a silent understanding to come to each other's aid if either is attacked:* not taking an active part; tacit, understood, implied, implicit, inferred, intimated, insinuated, suggested, unspoken, unsaid, untalked-of, unmentioned, unexpressed, undeclared, unarticulated; unpublished, unwritten, unrevealed, hidden, covert, concealed. —**Ant.** 1 noisy, clamorous; active, stirring, lively, bustling, tumultuous, agitated, excited. 2 noisy, vocal, vociferous, talkative, talky, garrulous, loquacious, wordy, verbose, chatty, blabbering, babbling. 3 sounded, pronounced, articulated. 4 active; spelled-out, explicit, stated, declared, announced, expressed.

silhouette n. 1. He could see her face in silhouette: outline, profile, contour, delineation, lineation, lineaments, shape, configuration, shadow, gestalt. —v. 2. He was silhouetted against the wall: outline, profile, delineate, contour, limn.

silky adj. He ran his hand across the silky fabric: silken, silk, cottony, glossy, like silk, sleek, smooth, soft, delicate.

silly adj. 1. It's silly to drive without fastening one's seat belt. He's a vain, silly creature: lacking judgment, foolhardy, irrational, senseless, unwise, ill-advised, unwary, irresponsible, ridiculous, pointless, unwary; foolish, dumb, stupid, simpleminded, witless, brainless, featherbrained, harebrained, rattlebrained, muddlebrained, empty-headed, muddleheaded; shallow, fatuous, idiotic, absurd, asinine, inane, childish, frivolous, frothy, giddy, mad, insane, crazy. 2. That silly joke made everyone laugh: ridiculous, nonsensical, preposterous, absurd, farcical, ludicrous, laughable; meaningless, purposeless, inconsequential, inappropriate, aimless, unreasonable. —**Ant.** 1 judicious, rational, sensible, wise, reasonable, sane, sound, smart, bright, astute, clever, brainy, intelligent, perceptive, sharp, acute, sage; serious, deep, mature, stable. 2 serious, meaningful, purposeful, consequential, appropriate; sad, sorrowful.

silver n. 1. The prospector discovered a silver mine. The silver needs polishing: white shining precious metal, argentine, argent, Latin argentum; articles made of silver, silverware, silver jewelry. 2. I have only a dollar bill and some silver: change, coins. 3. The old man had hair of silver: grayish white, platinum.

similar adj. The two dresses are similar but not identical. The two men have similar political views: nearly alike, much the same, kindred, akin, parallel, like, equivalent, comparable, analogous, close, correspondent, corresponding, correlative, agreeing, approximate, resembling, allied, cognate; matching, duplicate, twin. —**Ant.** different, dissimilar, unalike, unlike, disparate, diverse, opposite, opposed, contrary, contradictory, antithetical, disagreeing, alien.

similarity n. There's a strong similarity between these two paintings: resemblance, likeness, correspondence, parallelism, kinship, similitude, semblance, sameness, oneness, comparability, equivalence, agreement, congruity, congruence, harmony, concordance, conformance, conformability, affinity, closeness, nearness, reciprocity. —**Ant.** dissimilarity, difference, unlikeness, dis-

similitude, disparity, diversity, incongruity, discordance, disagreement.

simmer v. 1. Simmer the meat in the sauce. I hear the kettle simmering: boil gently, stew, seethe; bubble, gurgle, burble. 2. He simmered with anger: seethe, fume, foam, boil, sizzle, burn; chafe, smart.

simper v. The children simpered behind the teacher's back: snigger, snicker, smirk, giggle, titter, tee-hee; smile sillily, grin self-consciously.

simple adj. 1. There are three types of sentences: simple, compound, and complex. Even a child can solve this simple puzzle: having few parts, not complex, uncomplicated, uninvolved, not elaborate, uncompounded; unsophisticated; basic, elemental, elementary, fundamental, rudimentary; easy, not difficult, manageable, soft. 2. She wore a simple black dress to the reception. The old farmer led a simple life: plain, not fancy, unadorned, undecorated, unembellished, untrimmed, modest, unaffected, unpretentious; unsophisticated, unworldly, natural, common, commonplace, ordinary, workaday; quiet, peaceful, rustic, homey, innocent, naive, guileless, artless, ingenuous. 3. The simple truth is that no one wants to do the job: plain, honest, true, sincere, candid, naked, stark, bare, unadorned, unvarnished, downright, sheer, absolute, straight, unfeigned, open, artless, guileless; blunt, frank, direct, plain-spoken, straightforward, out-and-out. 4. He's so simple he'll believe anything you tell him: innocent, naive, artless, guileless, ingenuous, green, callow, unworldly, inexperienced, unsophisticated; dumb, stupid, simpleminded, slow, dense, dull, thick, thick-witted, obtuse, foolish, weak in the upper story. —**Ant.** 1 complex, complicated, involved, intricate, elaborate, compound, sophisticated, advanced; difficult, hard, tough. 2 fancy, elaborate, ornate, adorned, decorated, embellished, pretentious, affected, ostentatious, flashy, showy; sophisticated, worldly, cosmopolitan; busy, hectic, bustling, confused, tumultuous. 3 dishonest, insincere, varnished, gilded, indirect, devious, artful, guileful; feigned, pretended, contrived. 4 worldly, sophisticated, knowing, wise, experienced; crafty, sly, cunning, foxy, clever, canny, shrewd, sharp, acute, keen, smart, bright, fast, fast on the uptake.

simpleminded adj. The maid is so forgetful I wonder if she's simpleminded: foolish, stupid, silly, fatuous, idiotic, dumb, asinine, emptyheaded, dull, slow, dull-witted, dim-witted, dense, thick, witless, half-witted, feebleminded. —**Ant.** clear-headed, bright, sharp, sensible, wise.

simpleton n. Anyone who believes that nonsense is a simpleton!: fool, numskull, nincompoop, dunce, blockhead, oaf, ignoramus, dolt, ninny, booby, dumbbell, idiot, dummy, dullard, imbecile, ass, jackass, donkey, dope, goose, Slang jerk, stupe; rustic, hick, rube, greenhorn.

simplicity n. 1. Modern architecture is marked by great simplicity. He spoke with great feeling and simplicity: lack of complexity; easiness, obviousness, directness, straightforwardness, plainness, clarity, clearness, purity, restraint, cleanliness, lack of adornment, austerity, serenity. **2.** *The child's simplicity was disarming:* openness, candor, directness, sincerity, honesty, guilelessness, truthfulness, artlessness, naturalness; innocence, naiveté, unworldliness, lack of sophistication. **—Ant.** 1 complexity, complicatedness, intricateness, difficulty; elaborateness, fanciness, ornateness, decoration, adornment, embellishment, pretentiousness, affectation, ostentation. 2 sophistication, worldliness; deviousness, insincerity, dishonesty, untruthfulness, guilefulness, guile, craftiness, slyness, cunning, conniving.

simplify *v. They tried to simplify their lives:* order, disentangle, boil down, break down, reduce, clarify, shorten, streamline, unscramble.

simply *adv. Give the directions as simply as possible. The poem is beautiful yet very simply expressed:* uncomplicatedly, plainly, directly, straightforwardly, explicitly, clearly, lucidly, intelligibly; without adornment, starkly, modestly, unaffectedly, unpretentiously, naturally, ingenuously.

simulate *v. She simulated tears to get our sympathy:* feign, put on, assume, pretend, dissemble, counterfeit, affect, fabricate, fake, sham; invent; act, play, playact, pose, make believe, imitate, ape, mimic, copy.

simulated *adj. The coat is made of simulated leopard skin:* imitation, synthetic, artificial, fabricated, manmade, pretend, make-believe, sham; fake, counterfeit, phony, forged. **—Ant.** real, authentic, actual, natural, true, bona fide.

simultaneous *adj. The two armies made simultaneous offensives on two fronts:* occurring at the same time, accompanying, concurrent, coincident, synchronous, synchronal, synchronic, concomitant; existing at the same time, coexistent, coexisting, coeval, contemporaneous, contemporary.

sin *n.* **1.** *May God forgive you your sins. The school considers disobedience a sin:* ungodly act, immoral act, irreligious act, sinfulness, iniquity, transgression, trespass; wrong, wrongdoing, evil, evil deed, villainy, vice, misdeed, violation, breach, crime, offense, infraction, error, slip, lapse. **2.** *It's a sin the way she wastes money:* shame, disgrace, scandal. *—v.* **3.** *Who has not sinned?:* offend against God, offend against morality, transgress, trespass, err, offend, fall, stray, do wrong, do evil, slip, lapse. **—Ant.** 1 virtue, goodness, righteousness, sinlessness, godliness, holiness, uprightness; good, honesty, ethics, morality.

since *adv.* **1.** *He has been unable to work ever since his breakdown:* after, subsequently. **2.** *He has been gone long since:* ago, before now. *—conj.* **3.** *I am unable to attend since I have a cold:* because, inasmuch as.

sincere *adj. Her sadness seemed sincere. The youth made a sincere effort to reform:* free from pretense, unfeigned, undeceitful, unaffected, real, honest, natural, genuine, authentic, artless, guileless, ingenuous, candid, frank, straightforward, forthright, truthful; earnest, wholehearted,

heartfelt, serious, in good faith. **—Ant.** insincere, feigned, pretended, deceitful, contrived, affected, devious, deceptive.

sincerely *adv. The boy was sincerely sorry:* really, genuinely, honestly, truly, truthfully; earnestly, seriously, wholeheartedly. **—Ant.** insincerely, falsely, dishonestly, deceptively, untruthfully, deceitfully.

sincerity *n. Everyone was touched by the sincerity of her apology:* honesty, probity, genuineness, earnestness, seriousness, candor, openness, frankness, straightforwardness, forthrightness, truthfulness, unaffectedness, artlessness, ingenuousness, guilelessness, wholeheartedness, good faith.

sinful *adj. Stealing is sinful. The people of Antioch in Syria were shamelessly sinful:* wicked, evil, unrighteous, unholy, impious, ungodly, irreligious, iniquitous, immoral, profligate, miscreant, corrupt, depraved, degenerate; villainous, vile, wrong, bad, heinous, despicable, wayward, errant, criminal, shameful, disgraceful. **—Ant.** sinless, righteous, upright, virtuous, moral, pure, godly; honest, ethical, honorable.

sing *v. The soprano sang beautifully. The birds sang all day:* utter musical sounds, intone, chant, croon, lilt, hum, perform a song, tell in song, melodize, tell in verse; warble, chirp, chirrup, trill, tweet, pipe, whistle; carol.

singe *v. Singe the chicken to remove any pin feathers before frying it:* scorch, sear, char, burn, burn slightly, burn superficially, brand.

singer *n. Caruso was a great singer:* vocalist, songster, songstress, crooner, diva, chantress, chanteuse; (*variously*) tenor, bass, soprano, contralto, baritone, countertenor, mezzo-soprano; minstrel, troubadour, bard; songbird, nightingale, lark.

single *adj.* **1.** *Put a single rose in the vase:* one, only one, individual, solitary, lone, sole, singular. **2.** *Is the new employee married or single?:* unmarried, unwed, spouseless, wifeless, husbandless, spinster, bachelor, maiden. **—Ant.** 1 accompanied; several, some, many, numerous. 2 married, mated, wed, wedded, espoused, *Slang* hitched, hooked-up.

single-minded *adj. She was single-minded in her pursuit of a career:* determined, persevering, inflexible, firm, resolved, unswerving, zealous, dogged, staunch, unwavering, devoted, tireless, intense, steadfast, relentless, unflinching, tenacious, dedicated, untiring, persistent. **—Ant.** wavering, irresolute, indecisive, vacillating.

singly *adv. They went to the party singly:* individually, apart, independently, separately, respectively.

singular *adj.* **1.** *The youngster has a singular ear for music:* unique, rare, unusual, uncommon, exceptional, extraordinary, unequaled, unparalleled, matchless, unprecedented, peerless, surpassing, choice, select, superior; remarkable, noteworthy, wonderful, marvelous, prodigious. **2.** *A singular glow came from the unidentified flying object:* unusual, unnatural, odd, strange, queer, peculiar, curious, freakish, bizarre, fantastic, outlandish, quaint, different, unconventional, eccentric, anomalous, unwonted, uncustomary, atypical, unfamiliar, abnormal, aberrant, unaccountable, out-of-the-ordinary, off the beaten track. —**Ant.** 1, 2 common, commonplace, familiar, ordinary, usual, everyday, routine, conventional.

sinister adj. **1.** Sinister rumblings came from the volcano. The villain's sinister laugh rang across the stage: threatening, ominous, menacing, dire, frightening, fearful, alarming, disturbing, disquieting, dismaying; inauspicious, unpropitious, unfavorable, unpromising, adverse, unlucky. **2.** The government discovered a sinister plot to take over the country: wicked, evil, villainous, vile, foul, treacherous, perfidious, malevolent, malign, malignant, insidious, Machiavellian, rascally, rank, dark, black, blackhearted, reprehensible, despicable, detestable, damnable, accursed, cursed, diabolical, infernal, hellish, devilish. —**Ant.** 1 calming, soothing, encouraging, heartening; favorable, auspicious, promising, propitious, opportune, advantageous; beneficial, kindly, benevolent, benign. 2 noble, heroic, honorable, worthy, virtuous, just, high-minded, exemplary, righteous, upright, reputable, principled, ethical.

sink v. **1.** The moon sank behind the mountains. The porch sinks a bit in the left corner: descend, go down, lower, drop, fall, plunge; decline, dip, slant, slope, tilt, sag, droop, slump. **2.** The ocean liner Titanic sank in 1912. The anchor sank to the bottom and held the ship: descend below the surface, submerse, submerge, go to the bottom, go under, go to Davy Jones's locker; become absorbed, seep, soak; engulf, drown. **3.** The farmer sank fence posts along the farm boundary. The engineers sank a tunnel into the ground: put down, set, lay, lower, bury; excavate, dig, bore, drill, drive, gouge, scoop out, hollow out. **4.** Prices sank to an all-time low. The patient's health seemed to sink overnight: lower, decline, fall, lessen, diminish, drop, shrink, subside, go down, reduce, depreciate; deteriorate, degenerate, worsen, regress, retrogress, wane, ebb, slump, slip, languish, give way, droop, sag, go from bad to worse, go downhill, go to pot, go to the dogs. **5.** I never thought he'd sink to cheating at cards: lower oneself, degrade oneself, debase oneself, stoop, fall, descend; succumb, give way, yield. —n. **6.** Wash your hands at the sink: basin, wash basin, bowl, washbowl, lavatory. —**Ant.** 1 rise, ascend, climb, mount, incline. 2 surface, emerge. 3 remove, dig up; fill in. 4 rise, increase, advance, ascend, climb, grow.

sinner n. The sinner was refused burial in holy ground: transgressor, evildoer, malefactor, wrongdoer, offender, apostate, backslider, reprobate, misfeasor, miscreant, trespasser, recidivist. —**Ant.** saint, holy person, exemplar.

sinuous adj. The sinuous trail wound up the mountainside: full of turns, winding, curving, curved, bending, volute, convoluted, folded, serpentine, labyrinthine, mazelike, twisted, twisting, coiling, zigzag, meandering, wandering, circui-

tous, roundabout, indirect, rambling, tortuous, undulating. —**Ant.** straight, direct, beeline.

sip v. **1.** Sip the coffee slowly until it cools off: drink bit by bit, drink slowly, lap, sup; sample, taste, savor, nip. —n. **2.** Try a sip of this lemonade: small mouthful, small draught, dram, swallow, drop, thimbleful, sup, soupçon, nip, drink, sample, taste. —**Ant.** 1 gulp, bolt, swill, swig, quaff, toss off. 2 gulp, swig.

siren n. **1.** The police siren woke everyone: warning signal; (variously) alarm, whistle, horn. **2.** Sometimes **Siren** According to Homer, the Sirens lured Odysseus' companions to shipwreck and death. Theda Bara played the siren in many early movies: nymph, sea nymph; seductress, enchantress, witch, temptress, vamp, deceiver; bewitching woman, charmer; Slang sexpot.

sit v. **1.** Sit on this chair near me. The bird sat on the top branch of the tree: be seated, have a seat; squat, sprawl, loll; settle, perch, roost; rest. **2.** The house sits high on a hill overlooking a lake. The old trunk sat in the attic for years: be situated, be located, be established, be seated, be placed, stand, rest, lie; remain, stay, endure, reside, abide, linger. **3.** The supreme court of this state sits twice a year. Have you ever sat on a jury?: convene, be in session, assemble, meet, gather, deliberate, conduct business; occupy a place, have an official seat, hold an official position; govern, rule, reign, officiate, preside, chair. **4.** A neighbor's daughter sat with the children: baby-sit, watch, watch over, care for, take care of, mind, attend, teach, keep company, chaperon, nurse. —**Ant.** 1 stand; lie. 2 move, remove. 3 adjourn, disperse, scatter.

site n. A new school occupies the site of the old armory. The Canadian Northwest is the site where we shot the movie: spot, place, point, ground, post, position, station; locale, locality, location, locus, whereabouts, territory, region, area, province, section, sector, district, zone, field, scene, setting.

situate v. The housing development must be situated near public transportation: locate, place, position, put, establish, station, set, settle, install, lodge, ensconce, billet, house; plant, post, stand; construct, build. —**Ant.** move, remove.

situation n. **1.** The international situation is headed toward peace. How did you ever get into such a bad financial situation?: state of affairs, state, circumstances, condition, status, case, position, posture; predicament, plight, fix, dilemma, quandary. **2.** The store is in an ideal situation to draw tourists: position, location, locality, locale, spot, place, site, station, seat. **3.** The situation as sales manager requires a great deal of traveling: job, position, post, assignment, place, seat, office, berth, capacity; role, function, duty, work, livelihood.

sizable adj. A sizable contingent marched to the front: large, largish, big, ample, big, capacious, substantial, comprehensive, considerable, extensive, gross, hefty, king-size, spacious, strapping, voluminous, goodly, comprehensive.

size *n.* **1.** *The size of the pool is 20 by 40 feet:* dimensions, measurement, extent, amplitude, stretch, proportions, area, volume, spread, expanse; magnitude, largeness, greatness, bigness, bulk, mass, scope; content, capacity. **2.** *What was the size of the research grant?:* amount, quantity, sum, aggregate, total, totality. —*v.* **3.** *Size the shoes from small to large:* arrange, array, sort, group, grade, classify.

sizzle *v.* **1.** *The steak sizzled on the grill:* hiss, sputter, splutter, spit, frizzle, crackle; fry. —*n.* **2.** *We awoke to the smell of fresh coffee and the sizzle of hot sausages:* hissing, hiss, sputtering.

skeleton *n. The medical students studied the skeleton of the human body. Only the skeleton of the house stood after the fire:* bony framework, bones; frame, underlying structure, hulk, shell. —**Ant.** skin; exterior, surface, covering, sheath.

skeptic or **sceptic** *n. He's too much of a skeptic to take anything simply on faith:* doubter, doubting Thomas, questioner, scoffer; agnostic, unbeliever, atheist.

skeptical or **sceptical** *adj. Ignorant people were skeptical of Columbus's theory that the earth was round. Nineteenth-century philologists tended to be overly skeptical:* inclined to question, questioning, dubious, doubting, doubtful, unsure, uncertain, unconvinced, incredulous; disbelieving, unbelieving, scoffing, hypercritical, cynical. —**Ant.** convinced, sure, certain, confident, unquestioning, undoubting; believing, credulous, gullible.

sketch *n.* **1.** *The artists made several sketches before beginning the final painting. The builder followed the architect's sketch:* drawing, preliminary drawing, preliminary painting; rough design, blueprint, graph, chart. **2.** *The budget committee gave the mayor a sketch of their long report:* outline, brief description, rough account, summary, abstract, précis, synopsis, digest. **3.** *The actors amused the audience with several impromptu sketches:* skit, short play, scene, vignette, characterization; lampoon, takeoff, burlesque, satire. —*v.* **4.** *A sidewalk artist sketched the passersby:* make a quick drawing of, draw; rough out, draft. **5.** *The historical article sketched the major events of the decade:* set forth briefly, describe quickly, outline, plot, summarize, abstract, map, mark out, picture, depict, delineate, portray, chart, graph, rough out.

sketchy *adj. The real-estate ad gives only a sketchy description of the property:* incomplete, cursory, rough, vague, bare, essential, outline, brief, short, hazy, slight, skimpy, slender, meager, light, shallow, superficial, undetailed; unfinished, preliminary, provisional, preparatory, unpolished, unrefined, crude, rough-hewn. —**Ant.** complete, full, detailed, lengthy, long, indepth, exact; finished, final, polished.

skew *v.* **1.** *The ship skewed from its mooring:* angle, slant, twist, turn, veer, sideslip, sheer, slew, slue, diverge, divagate. **2.** *All their plans were skewed:* distort, twist, alter, change, unbalance, upset. —**Ant.** 2 straighten, align.

skid *n.* **1.** *The car braked too quickly and went into a skid:* slip, sliding motion, slide; glissade. **2.** *The heavy crates were packed on skids and taken to the warehouse:* runner, platform with runners; sled, dray, sledge, drag. —*v.* **3.** *The truck's wheels skidded on the wet road:* slide, slip, slip sideways, sideslip; glide, glissade, skip, skate, ski, skim, skitter, coast.

skill *n.* **1.** *The antique cabinet had been made with great skill:* skillfulness, craft, adroitness, adeptness, expertness, deftness, dexterity, handiness, mastery, competence, artistry; acumen, cunning, cleverness, ingenuity, inventiveness. **2.** *Do you have the skill to ski such a difficult slope?:* ability, capacity, prowess, faculty, facility, proficiency, experience, knowhow, expertise, knack; talent, gift. —**Ant.** 1 incompetence, ineptness, ineptitude, awkwardness, clumsiness. 2 inability, nonproficiency, inexperience.

skillful *adj. Only the most skillful pilots are employed by airlines. The bricklayer did a skillful job in building the wall:* skilled, expert, able, competent, capable, proficient, qualified, accomplished, professional, masterful, masterly, experienced, veteran, practiced, trained, well-versed; apt, adept, adroit, dexterous, handy, facile, deft, talented, gifted, ingenious, clever, sharp, keen, cunning, slick. —**Ant.** unskillful, unskilled, inexpert, inept, incompetent, unqualified, unaccomplished, nonprofessional, amateurish, inexperienced, unpracticed, untrained; unqualified; clumsy, awkward, bungling.

skim *v.* **1.** *Skim the cream off the top of the milk:* take up from the surface, scrape, ream. **2.** *The water skier skimmed over the surface of the lake:* move lightly, glide, sweep, glissade, coast, skate, scud, skid, skip, bounce, float, sail, fly. **3.** *Don't read the report word for word now, just skim it:* read superficially, glance over, scan, flip, thumb through, dip into, leaf through. —**Ant.** 3 examine carefully, peruse.

skimp *v.* **1.** *Don't skimp on the butter when making these cookies:* be sparing of, be stingy with, scrimp, stint, slight, hold back, withhold. **2.** *By skimping a little we can stick to our budget:* be frugal, use economy, economize, be stingy, cut expenses, be parsimonious, be niggardly, pinch, scrimp, stint, scrape along. —**Ant.** 1 lavish, squander, be generous with, be profuse with, pour on, load on. 2 be extravagant, overspend, squander, be thriftless.

skimpy *adj.* **1.** *Why did you give me such a skimpy portion of ice cream? That sweater is too skimpy to wear over a bulky shirt:* not large enough, small, smallish, scant, scanty, spare, sparse, scrimpy, meager, exiguous, modest, slight; inadequate, insufficient, incomplete, wanting, inconsiderable. **2.** *She's a very skimpy contributor to the local charity:* stingy, too thrifty, parsimonious, miserly, niggardly, stinting, penurious, frugal, scrimping, sparing, pennypinching, grudging, illiberal, close, closefisted, tightfisted, *Informal* tight. —**Ant.** 1 big, too big, large, ample, full; abundant, profuse, copious, generous, lavish, considerable; adequate, sufficient. 2 extravagant, liberal, generous, openhanded.

skin n. 1. *Many Scandinavians have fair skin. The trappers sold bear skins to the trading post:* epidermis, body covering; complexion; hide, pelt, coat, fur, fleece. 2. *Boiled potatoes in their skins are delicious:* peel, rind, husk, hull, shell, pod, jacket, case, casing, sheath, integument, outer coating. —v. 3. *The hunter skinned the deer. The boy skinned his knee:* strip the skin from, peel, flay, remove the hide from, lay bare; scrape, bark, abrade.

skinflint n. *That skinflint wouldn't give a nickel to charity:* stingy person, miser, hoarder, niggardly person, niggard, penny pincher, pinchpenny, scrooge, *Slang* tightwad. —**Ant.** big spender, spendthrift, sport.

skinny adj. *The boy is skinny but surprisingly strong:* thin, slender, lean, scrawny, spindly, emaciated, spare, lank, lanky, wiry, angular, gawky, gangling, scraggy, gaunt, rawboned, skeletal, slight, shrunken. —**Ant.** fat, obese, corpulent, plump, chubby, hefty, husky, rotund, fleshy, robust.

skip v. 1. *The little girls skipped down the path. The speaker skipped from one topic to the next, confusing everyone:* leap lightly, hop, jump, trip, bob, spring, bounce, bound, flit, prance, gambol, caper, romp; jump lightly over, leap over. 2. *The autobiography skips the author's childhood and just tells of his early manhood. Let's skip dessert and just have coffee:* pass over, omit, leave out, overlook, ignore, eschew, neglect, disregard, do without; evade, elude, dodge, shun, miss. 3. *Informal The embezzler tried to skip the country. The boy skipped school two days in a row:* leave hurriedly and secretly, slip out of, escape, flee, make off, abscond, skedaddle, disappear, fly the coop; be absent from, be absent from without excuse, play hooky, cut. —n. 4. *The ice skater made two little skips and then did a pirouette:* light jump, leap, bound, spring, hop, bounce; prance, gambol, caper. —**Ant.** 1 shuffle, lumber, drag, trudge, plod, waddle. 2 include, cover, put in, contain, refer to, take into account; confront, meet. 3 stay, remain; be present, attend.

skirmish n. 1. *The major battle is over but there are still skirmishes along the front:* brief fight, encounter, clash, engagement, action, firefight; brush, fray, affray, scrap, tussle, scuffle, fracas, scrimmage, *Slang* set-to, run-in. —v. 2. *The soldiers skirmished at the border:* fight briefly, clash, battle; struggle, scrimmage, brush, scrap, tussle, tilt, joust.

skirt n. 1. *She wore a skirt and blouse. The dress has a full skirt:* (variously) overskirt, underskirt, hoop skirt, dirndl, crinoline, kilt; mini, maxi. 2. *There's a spot on the skirt of this tablecloth:* outer area, border, fringe, edge, rim, margin, perimeter, boundary, bounds, periphery, verge, hem. —v. 3. *The road skirted the lake for a few miles:* pass along the edge of, border, flank, lie along; circle, encircle, circum-

scribe, enclose, hem in, envelop, gird, girdle, ring. 4. *Politicians tend to skirt controversial questions:* avoid, evade, shun, fight shy of, keep away from; detour around, go around, circle, circumvent. —**Ant.** 1 pants, slacks, trousers. 2 center, middle, heart, core, hub. 3 diverge from, lead away from. 4 face, confront, meet.

skittish adj. 1. *The stable boy tried to calm the skittish horse. Too much coffee makes me skittish:* easily startled, easily frightened, fearful, nervous, jumpy, jittery, fidgety, excitable; restless, restive, unsteady, shaky, fitful, impulsive, flighty, mercurial, volatile, unstable. 2. *Some children are skittish about meeting strangers:* shy, bashful, timid, demurring; wary, cautious, chary, leery, guarded, distrustful, suspicious, unsure, reluctant. —**Ant.** 1 calm, relaxed, tranquil, serene, sedate, placid, unexcitable, composed, stable, steady, cool as a cucumber, unflappable; phlegmatic.

skulk v. 1. *A mugger skulked near the subway entrance:* lurk, slink, sneak, hide, lie in wait. 2. *The workers skulked all day:* shirk, malinger.

sky n. *There's not a cloud in the sky today. Astronomers scanned the sky for a sight of the comet:* atmosphere; upper atmosphere, the firmament, the heavens, the blue vault of heaven, arch of heaven, space, outer space.

slab n. *The walls of the building are made of slabs of marble. The boy helped himself to a slab of pie:* thick flat piece, slice, thick slice; hunk, chunk, wad, block; plank, board, slat; wedge. —**Ant.** bit, fragment, scrap, sliver, splinter, chip, shaving, shred.

slack adj. 1. *Keep the reins of the horse slack:* loose, relaxed, lax, limp, flaccid, not tight, not taut, not firm; pliant, flexible, flabby, baggy; free, untied, unfastened. 2. *The teacher was a slack disciplinarian. Living alone, he became slack about his appearance:* unexacting, lax, undemanding, not firm, easy, soft, loose, permissive; careless, slipshod, neglectful, negligent, dilatory, remiss, slapdash, offhand, inattentive, lazy, slothful, indolent, nonchalant, lackadaisical, thoughtless, unthinking, unconcerned, indifferent, heedless, unmindful. 3. *A slack stream ran through the property. Business has been slack because prices are too high:* slow, slow-moving, slow-paced, sluggish; not busy, inactive, lethargic, listless, dull; leisurely, lazy, quiet. —adv. 4. *The reins fell slack around the horse's shoulders:* limply, loosely, freely, easily; sluggishly, slowly. —v. 5. *Slack the rope before trying to untie the knot:* slacken, loosen, loose, make less taut, untighten, relax, make limp, free, let up on. —**Ant.** 1 tight, taut, rigid, stiff, firm, tense, inflexible; tied, fastened. 2 exacting, demanding, meticulous, firm, inflexible, hard; careful, diligent, attentive, sedulous, thoughtful, mindful, concerned, caring, heedful. 3 fast, fast-moving, rapid; busy, active, brisk, quick, bustling; pressing. 4 tight, tightly, taut, tautly, rigidly, stiffly, tensely. 5 tighten, stiffen, pull up, pull in, take up the slack.

slacken v. 1. *Wait for the rain to slacken before going out. Don't slacken your efforts when the* *job is only half done:* slack, slack off, slow, slow down, abate, taper off, dwindle, ease, let up, moderate, soften, weaken, mitigate, temper; relax, reduce, lessen, flag, decrease, diminish, curb, check, arrest, restrain, limit, retard, inhibit, keep back. **2.** *Don't slacken the reins or the horse may bolt:* loosen, loose, relax, untighten, slack, slack up on, let go limp, go limp; free, release, let go, let loose of. **—Ant.** 1 quicken, increase, rise, accelerate. 2 tighten, draw tight.

slacker *n.* *Don't count on that slacker to do any of the work:* malingerer, shirker, dodger, laggard, loafer, idler, dawdler, dallier, procrastinator, good-for-nothing, do-nothing, quitter, truant, *Slang* goldbrick, goof-off.

slake *v.* *The lemonade slaked my thirst. The encouraging words slaked everyone's fears:* quench, satisfy, sate, satiate, gratify, appease, relieve, mollify, assuage, allay, alleviate, decrease, take the edge off, curb, moderate, modify, ease, temper, mitigate; calm, soothe, compose, still, subdue, quell, hush, quiet, tranquilize, cool. **—Ant.** increase, heighten, intensify, stimulate, aggravate, inflame, fire, pique.

slam *v.* **1.** *The housewife slammed the door in the salesman's face:* shut with force and noise, bang. **2.** *Don't slam the cards down just because you lost!:* slap, hit, throw; strike forcefully, smack. **3.** *The waitress slammed into the swinging door:* crash, bang; strike with violent impact, collide with, bump, smash. **—n. 4.** *The slam of the shutter awoke me:* bang, crash; act or sound of slamming.

slander *n.* **1.** *When he called me a thief, I decided to sue him for slander:* defamation, vilification, falsehood; malicious fabrication, false statement, distortion, misrepresentation, calumny; (*loosely*) libel. **—v. 2.** *He slandered his opponent's good name:* defame, malign, vilify, revile; smear, sully, soil, besmirch; (*loosely*) libel.

slang *n.* *She used a lot of slang in her speech:* argot, jargon, patois, dialect, cant, colloquialism.

slant *v.* **1.** *The path slants down to the river here. Slant the desk top while you're writing:* incline, slope, angle, tilt; lean, list. **2.** *The writer slanted the story in favor of the candidate:* color, bias, prejudice, distort, angle. **—n. 3.** *The slant of the floor makes the table unsteady:* slope, tilt, rake, incline, pitch; slanting direction. **4.** *Bertolt Brecht's plays have a political slant:* bias, prejudice, angle, view, viewpoint, leaning, attitude. **—Ant.** 1 straighten, level off. 3 evenness, level.

slap *n.* **1.** *Her slap left red marks on his arm:* blow, smack, hit, whack, wallop, cuff, clap. **2.** *The Soviet attacks on Titoism were also a slap at China:* blow, insult, cut, rejection, snub, rebuff. **—v. 3.** *The baby slapped his sister when she tried to kiss him:* hit, strike, smack, cuff, whack, wallop, swat.

slapdash *adj.* *The house's construction was exceedingly slapdash:* careless, slipshod, sloppy, haphazard, any which way, hit-or-miss, hit-and-

miss, hasty, superficial, cursory, quick-and-dirty, once-over-lightly. **—Ant.** careful, meticulous.

slash *v.* **1.** *Vandals slashed the paintings with knives:* cut, gash, rip, lacerate, slit, rend, slice. **2.** *The shop plans to slash fur prices after Christmas:* cut, lower, drop, decrease, reduce, pare. **—n. 3.** *Make broad slashes through the words to be deleted. The slash in the painting made it virtually worthless:* stroke, mark, cut, gash, rip, rent, laceration, slit, tear. **4.** *The consumer welcomes a slash in meat costs:* cut, decrease, reduction, drop, lowering.

slate *n.* **1.** *A floor of slate would be handsome in the den:* dark blue-gray rock. **2.** *I hang a slate in my kitchen for memos:* blackboard, chalkboard, tablet. **3.** *The board approved the nominating committee's slate:* ballot, ticket, list of candidates.

slaughter *n.* **1.** *Beef slaughter methods are under attack by the humane society:* killing, butchering. **2.** *The attack resulted in a slaughter of the unarmed villagers:* massacre, bloodbath, mass murder, wholesale killing, pogrom. **—v. 3.** *I couldn't stand to watch them slaughter the cattle:* butcher, kill. **4.** *The killer slaughtered the entire family:* slay, massacre, destroy, annihilate, exterminate, wipe out.

slave *n.* **1.** *There were more slaves than citizens in ancient Athens:* serf, vassal, bond servant, bondsman, thrall, chattel. **2.** *He's a slave to alcohol:* addict, prey, victim. **3.** *She's just been a slave in that job and should have left the company long ago:* drudge, workhorse, menial, toiler, plodder. **—v. 4.** *Why do you slave at that unfulfilling job?:* drudge, toil, work like a slave. **—Ant.** 1 master, owner. 3 loafer, idler. 4 loaf, idle.

slavery *n.* **1.** *The natives were sold into slavery by their chiefs:* enslavement, bondage, captivity, penal servitude, enthrallment, vassalage, serfdom, subjugation, indentureship, compulsory service, impressment. **2.** *She was resigned to the slavery of a dreary job:* drudgery, toil, sweat, travail, labor, struggle, grind, strain, treadmill.

slavish *adj.* **1.** *Slavish devotion to another person is self-destructive:* servile, subservient, obsequious, slavelike, submissive. **2.** *The painting is a slavish imitation of Van Gogh's manner:* literal, strict, exact; unimaginative, derivative, imitative, unoriginal. **—Ant.** 1 masterful, willful, assertive. 2 original, imaginative, creative, inventive.

slay *v.* *David slew Goliath:* kill, slaughter, murder, do in, destroy, execute, annihilate, massacre.

sleazy *adj.* *That is a sleazy fabric, and it won't hold up long. His gothic novel is a sleazy piece of writing:* flimsy, shoddy, trashy, insubstantial, shabby; vulgar, cheap, tacky, *Slang* schlock.

sled *n.* *We pulled the sled up the hill:* sledge, sleigh.

sleek *adj.* **1.** *Your hair looks sleek and beautiful:* glossy, shiny, silky, satiny, velvety, lustrous. **2.** *The baroness was invariably attended by a sleek gigolo:* smooth, suave, unctuous, oily, slick, ingratiating, fawning.

sleep n. **1.** *I was awakened from a sound sleep:* slumber, snooze, nap, doze. **2.** *She went to her eternal sleep:* death, rest, peace. —v. **3.** *Everyone slept until dawn:* slumber, repose, nap, snooze, doze.

sleepy adj. **1.** *I'm too sleepy to watch the end of the show:* drowsy, weary, tired, fatigued, exhausted. **2.** *There was little to do in the sleepy fishing village:* quiet, inactive, dull. —**Ant.** 1 awake, energetic, spirited, animated, alert. 2 bustling, active, busy, thriving, lively.

slender adj. **1.** *She admired his slender build:* slim, lean, willowy, skinny, slight, delicate, thin, narrow. **2.** *The farm yielded only a slender crop this year:* little, small, meager, scant, spare. **3.** *Your chance of winning is slender:* slim, slight, feeble, faint, weak, poor, remote. —**Ant.** 1 large, fat, thick, stout, bulky, heavy. 2 large, profuse, considerable, appreciable, prolific. 3 strong, considerable, solid.

slice n. **1.** *Will you have a slice of pie?:* piece, portion, section, cut, segment. —v. **2.** *Slice the meat thin:* carve, cut, shave; whittle, pare; divide, separate, cut off, sever, dismember, segment.

slick adj. **1.** *A seal's coat is slick:* glossy, sleek, smooth, satiny, shiny. **2.** *Be careful not to slip on this slick floor:* slippery; oily, greasy, waxy, glassy. **3.** *A slick operator could sell anything:* sly, wily, cunning, tricky, foxy, clever, sharp, smooth-talking, fast-talking. —n. **4.** *The oil slick covered the beach:* film, coating, coat, scum. —v. **5.** *He slicked down his hair with oil:* smooth; make glossy. —**Ant.** 1 rough, bumpy, coarse. 2 rough, coarse. 3 honest, open, ingenuous.

slide v. **1.** *The boy likes to slide down the banister:* glide, coast. **2.** *The car slid into the ditch:* skid, slip, fall, veer, sideslip, slither. **3.** *The committee let the matter slide:* pass, slip, lapse. —n. **4.** *Let's take a slide on the toboggan:* coast, glide. **5.** *They need a rubber mat at the foot of the slide:* chute, ramp, slope. **6.** *Do you prefer prints or slides?:* small transparency, diapositive, lantern slide, transparent plate.

slight adj. **1.** *Only a slight change in temperature is predicted:* small, little, modest, moderate, limited, restricted, imperceptible, unimportant, inappreciable, negligible, tiny, infinitesimal. **2.** *He's too slight to play football:* slim, slender, frail, lean, thin, spare, fragile. —n. **3.** *I was hurt by the obvious slight:* snub, insult, slap, cut, rebuff, incivility. —**Ant.** 1 considerable, great, big, substantial, appreciable, tangible. 2 husky, muscular, sturdy.

slim adj. **1.** *Anything looks good on his slim figure:* slender, thin, lean, svelte, willowy, thready, skinny. **2.** *There's only a slim hope of survival for the crash victims:* slender, faint, remote, distant, slight, small, meager, negligible. —**Ant.** 1 chubby, fat; broad, broad of beam, wide, huge, elephantine. 2 great, strong, considerable.

slime n. *My boots are covered with slime from the marsh:* mire, muck, ooze, sludge; sticky mud.

slimy adj. **1.** *The rain made a slimy mess of the yard:* mucky, gummy, sticky, viscous, glutinous. **2.** *That slimy man gives me the creeps:* offensive, obnoxious, creepy; nasty, vile, repulsive, foul, putrid, loathsome. —**Ant.** 2 pleasant, appealing.

sling v. *She slung a knapsack on her back:* hoist, heave, chuck, cast, catapult, fling, hurl, launch, lob, pitch, suspend, swing, toss, bung.

slink v. *We caught the thief slinking out the back way:* slip, creep, steal, skulk, tiptoe; move in a furtive manner, prowl, sneak.

slip[1] v. **1.** *Slip the shoe on your foot:* slide, glide; put. **2.** *She slipped and fell down the stairs:* skid, slide, lose one's balance. **3.** *We slipped from the party unnoticed. Slip me the letter:* sneak, steal, go quietly; pass, hand stealthily. **4.** *The years have just slipped by:* pass quickly, pass imperceptibly. **5.** *The patient's condition is slipping:* fail, worsen, decline, sink, fall. **6.** *The burglar slipped from my grasp:* escape; break away, get clear of. **7.** *How did the news slip out?:* leak, escape, be revealed. —n. **8.** *She took a bad slip on the icy sidewalk:* skid, slide; fall. **9.** *That was an embarrassing slip about his brother's divorce:* blunder, indiscretion, imprudence, lapse, error, faux pas. **10.** *The slip in the market has been devastating:* drop, fall, decline. **11.** *You need a slip under that sheer dress:* petticoat, underdress, chemise. **12.** *The boat came untied and drifted out of the slip:* berth, dock. —**Ant.** 5 improve, rise. 10 rise, improvement, increase.

slip[2] n. **1.** *He gave me a slip from his plant:* cutting, sprig, sprout, shoot, offshoot. **2.** *He scribbled on a slip of paper:* scrap, strip, shred, small piece; receipt, voucher, ticket. **3.** *My nephew is a saucy young slip:* youngster, youngling, sprig, stripling, sapling.

slippery adj. **1.** *Be careful walking across this slippery floor. Wet soap is slippery:* slick, smooth, waxy, greasy, oily, glassy, soapy. **2.** *Don't trust that slippery character:* tricky, shifty, deceitful, untrustworthy, unreliable, treacherous, foxy, sneaky, wily, devious, crafty, contriving. —**Ant.** 1 rough, coarse; dry. 2 trustworthy, reliable, steady, dependable, responsible.

slipshod adj. *The cabinet was put together in a hurried, slipshod way:* careless, lax, sloppy; casual, thoughtless, offhand, slovenly, loose, untidy, messy. —**Ant.** careful, correct, meticulous, exact, fastidious; orderly, tidy, neat.

slip-up n. *There was a slip-up in mailing the invitations:* mistake, blunder, error, lapse, oversight, miscue, bungle, gaffe, faux pas; *Slang* goof, screw-up, foul-up, boo-boo, clinker, botch, flub, blooper.

slit n. **1.** *The coin fell through a slit in the floor:* cut, crevice, gash, incision, slash, crack, fissure. —v. **2.** *Slit holes in the mask for your eyes:* cut, slash.

slither v. *The belly dancers slithered like snakes:* slide, glide; move with a side-to-side motion.

sliver n. *She got the sliver out of his eye:* splinter, fragment, bit, thorn, shred, paring, piece, shaving, slice, snippet, flake.

slobber v. *The baby slobbered happily as he ate his cereal:* drivel, slaver, drool, dribble, slop, salivate, water at the mouth, splutter, sputter.

slogan n. *We need a new slogan for the advertising campaign:* motto, campaign cry, battle cry, catch phrase; byword, watchword, catchword.

slop v. **1.** *Don't slop water all over the floor:* slosh, splash, splatter, spatter, spill, swash. **2.** *Have you slopped the hogs yet?:* feed swill to. —n. **3.** *After the flood our rooms were full of slop:* slush, sludge, mire, ooze, mud, muck; filth. **4.** *Carry this bucket of slops to the pigpen:* swill, garbage; waste, refuse.

slope v. **1.** *The ski trail slopes down sharply here:* slant, angle, pitch, incline, lean, tip, tilt, bend, bank. —n. **2.** *The meadow has a gentle slope:* slant, incline, downgrade, inclination, descent. —**Ant.** 1 flatten, level. 2 plane.

sloppy adj. **1.** *I hate to drive on these sloppy back roads:* watery, sloshy, muddy, slushy, wet, sodden, swampy, marshy. **2.** *I can't find a thing on this sloppy desk:* messy, untidy, disorderly, soiled, dirty, unclean. —**Ant.** 1 dry. 2 neat, tidy, orderly, clean.

sloth n. *Her sloth keeps her from getting ahead in her job:* laziness, lethargy, torpor, indolence, lassitude, listlessness, do-nothingness, shiftlessness, torpidity, languor, phlegm, sluggishness, idleness. —**Ant.** energy, industriousness, diligence, assiduousness, activeness, get-up-and-go.

slothful adj. *The hot weather made the workers slothful:* lazy, indolent, do-nothing, otiose, sluggardly, lax, negligent, sluggish, idle, shiftless, inert, torpid, listless, drowsy, supine. —**Ant.** industrious, energetic, active, lively.

slouch v. **1.** *Straighten up and don't slouch!:* droop, slump, stoop, hunch, bend. —n. **2.** *She'd look taller if it weren't for her slouch:* stoop, droop, slump. **3.** *He's no slouch about helping with the dishes:* lazybones, laggard, sluggard, loafer, slacker, shirker, idler, *Slang* goldbrick. —**Ant.** 1 straighten up. 3 go-getter, eager beaver, ball of fire.

slovenly adj. **1.** *That outfit is too slovenly to wear to a job interview:* messy, sloppy, untidy, dirty, unclean, dowdy, frowzy, slatternly, disorderly, unkempt. **2.** *I shouldn't pay for that slovenly job he did:* slipshod, careless, slapdash, messy; indifferent, unconcerned. —**Ant.** 1 neat, tidy, trim, clean, orderly. 2 careful, meticulous, precise, conscientious, methodical, orderly.

slow adj. **1.** *The old car made slow progress. He is a slow runner:* slow-paced, slow-moving, slow motion, snail-like, tortoise-like. **2.** *Tree sloths climb with slow movements:* heavy, sluggish, torpid, lumpish. **3.** *The patient made a slow recovery:* long, prolonged, extended, stretched out, drawn out, protracted, time-consuming, lingering, tarrying, delayed. **4.** *My tenant's rent payments are always slow:* late, behind time, overdue, unpunctual, delayed, belated, backward. **5.** *John is a slow worker:* dawdling, dilatory, procrastinating, laggard, sluggish. **6.** *I'd be*

slow *about accepting those terms. He's slow to take a stand:* hesitant, cautious; halfhearted, backward, dragging; indisposed, loath, disinclined, reluctant, averse. **7.** *That game is a bit slow for my taste:* dull, tedious, boring, unexciting, uninteresting; slow-moving, sluggish, ponderous. **8.** *We enjoyed a slow Sunday at home. Ticket sales are slow this month:* leisurely, unhurried, unhasty, deliberate; inactive, quiet, not busy, not lively, *Informal* off. **9.** *Cousin Oscar is too slow for the advanced class:* slow-witted, dim-witted, dull-witted, slow on the uptake, backward, stupid, obtuse, dense, dumb, dim, dull; imperceptient, unperceptive. —v. **10.** *The train slowed as it approached the station:* slow down, reduce speed, decelerate, lose momentum; flag, falter. **11.** *The strike will slow our deliveries:* slow down, hold up, retard, check, curb, brake; handicap, hinder, obstruct, impede. —**Ant.** 1–3, 5 fast, quick, swift, speedy. 1 lightning-like. 4 prompt, punctual, on time. 6 eager, enthusiastic; inclined, disposed. 7 exciting, interesting; fast-moving. 8 hurried, hasty, active, busy, lively. 9 quick-witted, smart, bright, intelligent; perceptive. 10, 11 speed up, accelerate. 10 pick up speed. 11 spur, help, aid, abet.

slowdown n. *Business is going through a slowdown this winter:* slackening, slowing, slow-up, downturn, falloff, stagnation, decline, retardation, flagging, letup, letdown, ease-up, setback, deceleration, slump. —**Ant.** boom, upswing, upturn, peaking.

slowpoke n. *Hurry, slowpoke, we're going to be late!:* laggard, straggler, dawdler, lingerer, dallier, snail, slug, tortoise, stick-in-the-mud, idler, plodder, saunterer, *Slang* foot-dragger, lie-abed, slug-abed.

sludge n. *They drained the sludge from the bottom of the tank:* mud, mire, dregs, sediment, muck, ooze, slime, slop, slush.

slug v. *The two prizefighters slugged each other brutally:* hit, strike, punch, whack, thump, smite, pound, clout, bat, belt, whale, wallop, sock, bash, baste, batter, lambaste, *Slang* clobber.

sluggish adj. **1.** *Hot weather makes me sluggish:* lethargic, listless, languid, spiritless, soporific, phlegmatic; lazy, indolent, slothful; inert, inactive, lifeless, torpid. **2.** *The turtles ran a sluggish race:* slow, unhurried, leisurely, protracted. —**Ant.** 1 active, energetic, industrious, animated, spirited, lively. 2 rapid, fast, quick, brisk.

slum n. *The slum was on the city's south side:* ghetto, Bowery, skid row.

slumber v. **1.** *I was slumbering soundly when the alarm rang:* sleep; doze, snooze, nap. **2.** *How long did the volcano slumber? Bears slumber in the winter:* lie dormant, be inactive; hibernate, vegetate. —**Ant.** 1 be awake. 2 erupt; be active.

slump v. **1.** *The dying man slumped to the pavement:* collapse, fall, drop, slip, give way, sag, tumble. **2.** *Her work slumped because of personal problems:* dip, plunge, decline; fall off suddenly. —n. **3.** *I could tell from his slump how tired he was:* slouch, droop, sagging posture. **4.** *The economy went into a severe slump:* lapse, decline; falling off, reverse, setback. —**Ant.** 2 improve, increase. 4 improvement, rise, upsurge, upturn.

slur *v.* **1.** *I can't understand you when you slur your words like that:* mumble, mutter, run together, pronounce indistinctly. **2.** *She slurred over the unflattering comments:* overlook, skip, disregard, ignore, gloss over, pass over, slight, let pass; treat with indifference. **3.** *Don't slur my brother's reputation!:* blacken, smear, defame, malign, stain, taint, sully. —*n.* **4.** *Your slur makes it difficult for us to understand you:* mumbling, muttering, slurred speech, run-on words. **5.** *The neighbors talked about each other with ugly slurs:* insult, cut, dig, affront. **6.** *The rumors cast a slur upon my good name:* stain, mark, spot, blemish, taint. —**Ant.** 1 enunciate. 2 stress, accentuate. 3 praise, laud, compliment. 4 enunciation. 5 compliment, praise.

slut *n.* *He called her a slut for dating another man:* slattern, frump, sloven; hussy, jade, wanton, strumpet, trollop, wench, tramp, jezebel; whore, harlot, prostitute; *Slang* doxy, floozy, bimbo.

sly *adj.* **1.** *The dealer won the game with a sly maneuver:* wily, crafty, cunning, tricky, artful, conniving, sneaky, stealthy, foxy, shrewd; mischievous, playful, cunning; dissembling. **2.** *She gave me a sly wink:* secret, furtive, private, covert, confidential. —**Ant.** 1, 2 open, direct, straightforward.

smack¹ *v.* **1.** *She smacked him with her open hand:* slap, smite, hit, whack, spank; strike sharply. —*n.* **2.** *He gave the boy a smack on the leg:* slap, rap, blow, buffet, whack, spank, hit, cuff, clap. **3.** *He gave me a smack on the lips:* loud kiss, hearty kiss, buss. —**Ant.** 1 pet, caress.

smack² *n.* **1.** *I sometimes like a slight smack of cinnamon in my coffee:* trace, tinge; hint, suggestion, taste, flavor. **2.** *There's a smack of autumn in the air:* touch, trace, bit, suggestion, dash. —*v.* **3.** *This cake smacks of rum. That story smacks of prevarication:* taste; smell; savor, suggest, have a flavor.

small *adj.* **1.** *Are you small enough to squeeze through the hole?:* little, tiny, petite; diminutive, undersized, slight. **2.** *The business made only a small profit this year:* meager, scant, modest, not great. **3.** *Even the small details should be checked thoroughly:* minor, inconsequential, insignificant, trivial, superficial, unimportant, lesser, trifling; of no account. **4.** *Someone with a small mind usually believes the worst:* mean, petty, ignoble, narrow, opinionated, bigoted; provincial. **5.** *The kitten uttered a small cry:* feeble, weak, fragile, faint. —**Ant.** 1, 2 large, big, great, vast, huge, immense, enormous; appreciable, substantial. 3 major, important, significant, consequential, vital. 4 big, generous, lofty, farsighted, unbiased. 5 strong, powerful, solid, substantial; loud, noisy, heavy.

small-minded *adj.* **1.** *The small-minded instructor gave a low grade to the adventurous*

essay: narrow-minded, narrow, small, illiberal, mean, petty, close-minded, bigoted, intolerant. **2.** *The small-minded villagers thought only of themselves:* provincial, parochial, insular, limited, confined. —**Ant.** liberal, eclectic.

small talk *She ignored my small talk and had nothing to say:* chitchat, banter, repartee, bavardage, prattle, chatter, prattling, gossip, idle talk, tittle-tattle, table talk, tea-table talk, light conversation, casual conversation.

smarmy *adj.* *The smarmy manager took his bosses around the plant:* insincere, false, disingenuous, hypocritical, mealymouthed, sanctimonious; suave, sleek, smug, insinuating, unctuous, fulsome, oily, buttery; obsequious, flattering, sycophantic, ingratiating.

smart *adj.* **1.** *It's easy to teach smart students:* intelligent, bright, sharp, keen, clever, quick, brainy, astute. **2.** *These clothes are smart enough to put someone on the best-dressed list:* fashionable, chic, modish, elegant, stylish; trim, neat. **3.** *He's always ready with a smart retort:* witty, clever, shrewd, sharp; smart-aleck, brash, sassy. **4.** *The marchers moved at a smart pace past the reviewing stand:* energetic, vigorous, brisk, quick. **5.** *A red ant can give you a smart sting:* painful, sharp. —*v.* **6.** *Does your hand smart from the burn?:* hurt, sting, burn; feel pain, be painful. **7.** *I still smart each time I think of his rudeness:* ache, suffer, wince, flinch, blench. —**Ant.** 1 dumb, dull, slow, dense, thick, stupid. 2 sloppy, frowzy; old-fashioned, dowdy; out-moded, passé. 4 crawling, slow.

smart aleck *He could never answer a question without being a smart aleck:* know-it-all, showoff, smarty, wise guy, smarty-pants, braggart, grandstander, exhibitionist, windbag, wiseacre; blowhard, saucebox, wiseass.

smash *v.* **1.** *He smashed the window with a brick:* shatter, break, splinter, disintegrate, demolish. **2.** *The car smashed into a telephone pole. She smashed him with her fist:* crash, strike, hit, collide with; crack, break; batter, beat, *Slang* bash, clobber. **3.** *Our tanks quickly smashed the enemy infantry:* destroy, crush, demolish, shatter. —*n.* **4.** *He gave me a smash on the head:* blow, bang, clout, forceful hit. **5.** *The vibrations from the two-car smash could be felt inside the house:* crash, collision, accident, crack-up, smashup. **6.** *Informal Her performance was a tremendous smash!:* hit, winner, success, sensation, triumph. —**Ant.** 6 flop, loser, disaster.

smashing *adj. Informal That's a smashing outfit you're wearing:* terrific, sensational, marvelous, wonderful, super, stupendous, magnificent, superb, extraordinary, fabulous, fantastic, great.

smattering *n. He knows only a smattering of French:* drop, bit, scrap, slight amount, smidgen, snippet, dash, dab, sprinkling.

smear *v.* **1.** *The painter smeared the walls with plaster:* spread, rub, daub, coat, cover; lay on. **2.** *My clothes are smeared with mud:* stain, smudge, besmudge, splotch, soil, smirch, streak. **3.** *Water smeared the ink:* blur, smudge; obliterate, make indistinct. **4.** *My opponent tried* *to smear my reputation:* soil, stain, tarnish, mar, blacken, besmirch, blemish; malign, slander, denigrate, degrade, injure. —*n.* **5.** *You have a lipstick smear on your cheek. That's a filthy smear on his good name!:* blotch, smudge, streak, splotch, stain, smirch; libel, slander, accusation.

smell *v.* **1.** *We smelled the stew out in the hallway:* nose, scent, sniff, get wind of, be windward of, get scent of. **2.** *The room smells of incense:* have a scent, give out an odor, emit an odor. **3.** *This cheese smells!:* reek, stink, have an unpleasant odor, be malodorous. **4.** *I smell something funny about that plan:* detect, sense, perceive, feel, suspect. —*n.* **5.** *I love the smell of wisteria. A putrid smell drove us from the room:* aroma, scent, odor, fragrance; perfume, bouquet, emanation; reek, stink, stench, fetor.

smelly *adj. Informal Take the smelly fish out of the refrigerator!:* stinking, malodorous, odorous, fetid, reeking, noisome, rank, putrid. —**Ant.** fragrant, sweet-smelling, fresh-smelling.

smile *n.* **1.** *Wipe that smile off your face:* grin, smirk, simper. —*v.* **2.** *We smiled when we heard the good news:* grin, beam, show pleasure; simper, smirk. **3.** *Fortune smiles on those who are kind:* favor; shine; be benevolent toward.

smirch *v.* **1.** *The chimney was smirched with years of grime:* besmirch, soil, smudge, dirty, begrime, besmudge, stain, smear. **2.** *The gossip smirched his good standing in the community:* besmirch, tarnish, stain, damage, smear, sully, soil, blacken; slander, dishonor, discredit. —*n.* **3.** *There's a smirch on your white jacket:* stain, smudge, blotch, smear, spot. **4.** *The incident was a smirch on her perfect record:* smear, blemish, stain, taint, blot; mark, stigma; discredit, dishonor.

smirk *n.* **1.** *He gave a smirk when he heard her excuse:* sneer, simper, sarcastic smile, grin, unpleasant grin, leer. —*v.* **2.** *She smirked at my explanation:* sneer; simper; grimace.

smitten *adj. He's smitten with the new girl next door:* enamored, bewitched, infatuated, enraptured, stuck (on), gone (on), have a crush (on), soft (on), spoony (over), sweet (on), taken (with); *Slang* nuts (about), crazy (about).

smoke *n.* **1.** *Smoke is coming out of the chimney:* sooty vapor; exhalation, fumes. **2.** *I have to have a smoke after dinner:* something smoked; (*variously*) cigar, cigarette, pipe. —*v.* **3.** *Is the fireplace smoking?:* smolder, fume; give off smoke, billow, reek. **4.** *You can't smoke in this section of the theater:* use tobacco; draw, suck, inhale, puff; light up, *Informal* have a drag.

smoky *adj.* **1.** *You'd better clean that smoky oven:* smoldering, fuming; emitting smoke. **2.** *I can't breathe in this smoky car:* smoke-filled, reeking. **3.** *The walls are smoky from the incinerator:* sooty, dingy, grimy, smudgy, smoke-darkened.

smolder *v.* **1.** *The fireplace smoldered all night:* smoke; burn without flame. **2.** *I smoldered for days after our argument:* seethe, burn inwardly; rage silently, fume.

smooth *adj.* **1.** *The road is very smooth here.* *The fashion model has smooth skin:* even, flat, level; silky, velvety, sleek. **2.** *Stir the mixture until smooth:* without lumps. **3.** *The toboggan made a smooth run down the mountain:* even, steady; without abrupt turns, without jerks, without breaks. **4.** *The changeover in management was very smooth:* orderly, harmonious, well-ordered, well-regulated, methodical, uneventful; easy, calm, even, peaceful. **5.** *Nothing seems to upset his smooth disposition:* even, calm, serene, peaceful, placid, easygoing, pleasant, mild, composed, collected, self-possessed. **6.** *She is a smooth talker:* flattering, ingratiating, glib, facile, suave. **7.** *That's a smooth wine:* mellow, mild; without sharpness. —*v.* **8.** *Smooth the plaster before putting on the wallpaper:* make even, make level, flatten. **9.** *Money smoothed her way to the top:* pave, open; prepare; ease; facilitate, help. **10.** *He should smooth his sales pitch:* refine, cultivate, polish, perfect; soften, mellow, civilize. **11.** *The mayor was able to smooth the anger of the mob:* calm, soothe, mollify, appease, assuage, allay, mitigate. —**Ant.** 1 rough, bumpy, uneven, irregular. 2 lumpy. 3 jerky, uneven, bumpy, rough. 4 disorderly, difficult, turbulent, troublesome. 5 nervous, excitable. 6 rough, unpolished, abrasive. 7 harsh, sharp, pungent. 8 roughen, rough up. 9 hamper, hinder.

smother *v.* **1.** *The killer smothered the victim with a pillow:* suffocate, asphyxiate, strangle, choke. **2.** *Try to smother the flames with sand:* extinguish, snuff, deaden, quench. **3.** *They smothered the child with love. The steak was smothered with mushrooms:* shower, wrap, surround; envelop in. **4.** *We tried to smother our laughter:* hide, suppress, conceal, mask, quash; keep down, choke back.

smudge *n.* **1.** *You have an ink smudge on your forehead:* smear, smutch, blot, stain, spot, mark. **2.** *The smudge drove away the locusts:* heavy smoke, smoky fire, smoke cloud. —*v.* **3.** *She smudged her dress with chalk:* smear, stain, spot, dirty, soil. —**Ant.** 3 clean, cleanse.

smug *adj. He looked so smug about knowing the answer:* self-satisfied, complacent, self-righteous, superior, virtuous. —**Ant.** unsure, uncertain, insecure.

smuggle *v. They smuggled booze across the border:* bootleg, run contraband.

smuggler *n. During Prohibition, smugglers brought boatloads of rum into the cove:* bootlegger, runner, contrabandist, rumrunner, gunrunner.

smut *n.* **1.** *There is smut on the windowsill:* soot, smudge, dirt, grime. **2.** *The police promised to crack down on smut:* pornography, obscenity, scatology, lewd material, dirt, filth, *Slang* porn.

smutty *adj.* **1.** *My hands are all smutty from the coal:* sooty, dirty, grimy, soiled. **2.** *The children shouldn't read those smutty books:* dirty, lewd, obscene, vulgar, indecent; filthy, pornographic. —**Ant.** 1 clean, immaculate. 2 clean, pure; puritanical, straitlaced.

snack *n.* **1.** *Let's have a snack before going to*

the movie: refreshment, light repast, bite, collation, light lunch, pick-me-up, coffee break, tidbit, finger food, lap lunch; *Slang* nosh, munchies, snackies, crunchies, nibblies; *British* tea, elevenses; *French* casse-croûte. —*v.* **2.** *Try not to snack between meals:* nibble, munch, eat, take tea, *Slang* nosh.

snag *n.* **1.** *Our boat hit a snag in the water:* protrusion, projection; stub, stump; hidden obstruction. **2.** *The housing project encountered a financial snag:* hindrance, obstacle, hitch; difficulty, block, stumbling block, impediment, encumbrance, obstruction, barrier, bar. —*v.* **3.** *I snagged my stockings on the desk:* tear, rip; catch, grab, fasten upon.

snake *n.* **1.** *Garter snakes are harmless:* serpent, viper, ophidian, reptile, reptilian. **2.** *His behavior showed him to be a snake:* sneak, traitor, untrustworthy person.

snap *v.* **1.** *She snapped her fingers to get the child's attention:* crack, click, pop. **2.** *Snap the bolt tightly:* latch, catch, lock, secure, clasp; close. **3.** *He snapped the stick in two pieces:* break, crack, fracture. **4.** *The crab snapped at my toe:* bite, nip, grab. **5.** *The cadets snapped to attention:* jumped, clicked. **6.** *She snapped at me when I tried to comfort her:* snarl, growl, bark, yelp. —*n.* **7.** *We could hear the snap of the twigs as they neared:* crack, click, pop. **8.** *My dress snap is broken:* catch, clasp, fastener. **9.** *The dog made a snap at my finger:* nip, bite, grab, snatch. **10.** *We're having a sudden cold snap:* spell, period. **11.** *Informal Beating him at tennis was a snap:* cinch, breeze. —*adj.* **12.** *That was no snap decision on her part:* sudden, hasty, thoughtless, quick, careless, impulsive.

snappish *adj. She's always snappish when dinner is late:* peevish, surly, touchy, testy, grouchy, waspish, shirty, querulous, irascible, cross, captious, ill-natured, petulant, hottempered, quick-tempered, huffish, edgy, huffy. —**Ant.** affable, amiable, good-humored, pleasant.

snappy *adj.* **1.** *He drove up in a snappy new convertible:* classy, smart, tony, swank, ritzy, sharp, swish, stylish, dapper, spiffy, jaunty. **2.** *Get in here and make it snappy!:* fast, quick, hasty, speedy, swift, rapid, *Slang* lickety-split. —**Ant.** 1 dowdy, shabby, tacky. 2 slow, torpid, languid, lazy.

snare *n.* **1.** *We caught a rabbit in the snare:* trap, noose, net. **2.** *That advertisement is a snare for inexperienced people:* trap, pitfall, deception, trick, entanglement; lure, bait, decoy, ruse. —*v.* **3.** *Indians snared rabbits with vines:* capture, ensnare, trap, entrap, hook, catch, seize.

snarl[1] *v.* **1.** *Rover snarled when I took away the bone:* growl. **2.** *The boy snarled at his mother:* snap, lash out, bark. —*n.* **3.** *The dog's snarl was frightening:* growl.

snarl[2] *n.* **1.** *Try to comb the snarls out of your hair:* tangle, ravel, mat, twist, kink, knot. **2.** *These files are in a snarl:* tangle, jumble, mess, chaos, confusion, disorder. —*v.* **3.** *The wind snarled the streamers on the float. An accident can snarl traffic for hours:* tangle, entangle, twist, knot, disorder, jumble, muddle, confuse; hinder, clog, impede. —**Ant.** 2 order. 3 unsnarl, untangle, unscramble.

snatch *v.* **1.** *The rescuer snatched the boy out of the sea:* grab, seize, grasp; pluck, nab, pull, wrest. **2.** *Let's snatch an hour of sleep:* grab, catch, take. —*n.* **3.** *We saw only snatches of that show:* part, snippet, fragment, bit, piece.

sneak *v.* **1.** *Let's sneak out the back way:* slip, steal, creep. **2.** *Can you sneak the cake into the house?:* slip, spirit, smuggle. —*n.* **3.** *Don't trust that sneak:* skulker, lurker, slinker; rascal, knave, bounder, rogue, scalawag, scoundrel, rapscallion, scamp, miscreant. —*adj.* **4.** *The generals planned a sneak attack:* surprise, secret, secretive, furtive, surreptitious, sly, underhand.

sneaky *adj. I'd be ashamed of playing such a sneaky trick:* underhand, sly, devious, treacherous, traitorous; secretive, furtive; mean, malicious, vicious. —**Ant.** open, aboveboard.

sneer *v.* **1.** *The captive sneered at her attempt to be friendly:* scorn, mock, scoff, rebuff, jeer, deride, disdain, ridicule, belittle. —*n.* **2.** *An ugly sneer was all we got for our trouble:* smirk, scoff, leer.

snicker *v. The children snickered when the teacher tripped:* giggle, titter, snigger, simper, snort, cackle.

snide *adj. He was offended by her snide manner:* sarcastic, nasty, malicious, insinuating; mocking, scoffing, contemptuous.

sniff *v.* **1.** *This cold makes me sniff constantly:* snivel, sniffle, snuffle, snuff, snort. **2.** *You must sniff this lovely perfume:* smell, whiff, snuff. **3.** *He sniffed at the marriage proposal:* disdain, disparage; mock, scoff, jeer. —*n.* **4.** *Her sniffs kept me awake:* sniffle, snuffle, snort. **5.** *Did you get a sniff of that garlic?:* smell, whiff, odor, aroma.

snip *v.* **1.** *Please snip these uneven strands of hair:* clip, cut, crop, lop, trim, prune, shear, bob. —*n.* **2.** *I heard the snip of the scissors:* click, clack, snap. **3.** *Will you give me a snip of that material?:* scrap, swatch; bit, fragment, cutting, piece; sample. **4.** *Informal That child's nothing but a little snip:* twerp, brat, shrimp, punk.

snippy *adj. She was quite snippy when I was 10 minutes late:* curt, brusque, rude, impudent, cheeky, saucy, sassy, impertinent, insolent, illmannered, smart-alecky, flippant, short, snippety; *Slang* snotty. —**Ant.** polite, respectful, mannerly, deferential.

snob *n. He's too much of a snob to mix with that earthy crowd. She's an intellectual snob:* social climber, elitist, stuck-up person, pretentious person, condescending person.

snobbish *adj. She's much too snobbish to stay at that plain hotel:* pretentious, disdainful, condescending, patronizing, overbearing, superior, arrogant, vain, haughty, *Informal* stuck-up, snotty, high-hat, snooty. —**Ant.** unpretentious, humble.

snoop *v. She liked to snoop in other people's*

affairs: pry, interfere, pry, spy, nose around, peer.

snore *v. He snored all night:* snort, snuffle, breathe heavily, wheeze.

snort *v.* **1.** *We ran when the bull began to snort:* grunt, pant, puff, blast, blow, huff, gasp; storm, rage. **2.** *She snorted at our modest plan:* scoff, jeer, sneer. *—n.* **3.** *The pony gave a snort when she tried to saddle him:* grunt, gasp, pant, huff.

snub *v.* **1.** *The rich man snubbed his poor relations:* ignore, disdain, slight, scorn, rebuff; turn up one's nose at, cut, treat with contempt, give the cold shoulder. **2.** *The catch on the pole snubbed the rope:* check; stop suddenly. *—n.* **3.** *I was hurt by her obvious snub:* rebuff, slight, cut, repudiation, cold shoulder. *—adj.* **4.** *He had a snub nose:* short, blunt, stubby, retroussé.

snuff *v.* **1.** *Everyone seems to be snuffing from hay fever:* sniff, sniffle, snuffle. **2.** *The dogs snuffed the scent of the fox:* sniff, smell, scent; detect through the nose. *—n.* **3.** *Take a snuff of this strong cheese:* sniff, smell, whiff.

snug *adj.* **1.** *The bear was snug in the den. The hunters found a snug cabin in the woods:* cozy, comfortable; sheltered, safe, secure; tranquil. **2.** *She runs a snug office. The Mayflower was a tolerably snug ship:* tight, neat, well-organized; close, compact. **3.** *These shoes are too snug:* tight-fitting, tight, close-fitting; skin-tight. *—Ant.* **1** uncomfortable; unprotected. **2** disorganized, disorderly. **3** loose.

snuggle *v. The child snuggled in her mother's lap:* nestle, nuzzle, lie snug, cuddle, lie closely, curl up, nest, enfold, hug.

soak *v.* **1.** *The bedspread is soaking in the dye. Soak your feet in warm water and salt:* steep, bathe, wet, drench, saturate, immerse. **2.** *Paper towels will soak up the spilled milk:* absorb, take in, take up. **3.** *The wet snow soaked through my boots:* seep, penetrate, permeate, enter, pervade. **4.** *The full impact of the news will soak in later:* penetrate, pervade; sink in, be perceived, be absorbed, come home to.

soar *v.* **1.** *The bird soared through the air:* wing, glide, float, fly, take wing, go aloft. **2.** *Apartment rents soared, and many tenants had to relocate:* climb, rise, mount, increase swiftly; tower, thrust upward. *—Ant.* **1** fall, drop. **2** fall, drop, decrease.

sob *v.* **1.** *The child sobbed hysterically:* weep, cry, blubber, whimper, wail, snivel, howl, lament. *—n.* **2.** *The sobs of the baby were so sad:* cry, whimper, plaint, wail. *—Ant.* laugh, chortle.

sober *adj.* **1.** *He was a sober man who seldom smiled:* solemn, serious, somber, staid, grave, sedate. **2.** *A funeral is a sober event:* grave, grim, sad, serious, solemn, somber, joyless, sorrowful. **3.** *The room colors are sober and depressing:* drab, subdued, dull, somber, dreary. **4.** *She is sensible and will give a sober opinion of the facts:* realistic, sound, dispassionate, moderate; prudent, judicious; levelheaded, rational, cool, sane, steady. **5.** *He joined Alcoholics Anonymous and has been sober for five years:* temperate, dry, abstemious, not drunk.

—Ant. **1** gay, frivolous, lighthearted, merry. **2** happy, gay, joyous. **3** light, bright, showy, colorful, exciting, lively. **4** frivolous, unrealistic, immoderate, unsound, excessive, passionate, imprudent, injudicious. **5** drunk, intoxicated, inebriated.

so-called *adj. The so-called leader fled at the first sign of danger:* supposed, pretended, professed, ostensible, alleged, purported, commonly named, nominal, self-styled.

sociability *n. The bishop was known for his sociability:* sociableness, gregariousness, affability, camaraderie, clubbability, congeniality, companionability, friendliness, good-fellowship, communicativeness.

sociable *adj.* **1.** *She's very sociable and loves parties:* gregarious, social, congenial, affable, extroverted, outgoing, gracious, neighborly, companionable, agreeable. **2.** *The meeting was as sociable as it was businesslike:* social, friendly, cordial, convivial. *—Ant.* **1** unfriendly, withdrawn, forbidding, introverted, unsociable, cold, uncommunicative. **2** stiff, formal, businesslike; cut and dried.

social *adj.* **1.** *This is just a social call:* friendly, sociable. **2.** *My wife is a warm, social person:* sociable, gregarious, friendly, neighborly, pleasant, agreeable. **3.** *The ball was the social occasion of the year:* fashionable, smart, stylish, *Informal* in. **4.** *Bees are social insects:* gregarious, cooperative, interdependent. *—Ant.* **1** business. **2** antisocial, unfriendly, cold. **3** unfashionable. **4** solitary, reclusive, hermit.

socialism *adj. The political science course dealt with socialism:* public ownership, collectivization, nationalization.

socialist *adj. The socialists won the election:* collectivist, left of center, left-wing, social democratic.

socialize *v. The gathering gave them a chance to socialize:* consort, fraternize, hobnob, mingle, mix, be friendly, chum with, get together, keep company, associate.

society *n.* **1.** *Drug addiction is a major concern of society:* humanity, humankind, mankind, the general public. **2.** *Victorian society was prudish compared with present-day society:* social order, community. **3.** *She is president of the literary society:* group, body, club, association, organization, circle, alliance, league. **4.** *Every important member of society attended the wedding:* elite, aristocracy, nobility, gentry, blue bloods, high society, the 400.

sock[1] *n. Your socks don't match:* short stocking, ankle sock.

sock[2] *v.* **1.** *He socked his opponent in the eye:* hit, strike, box, punch, slap, wallop, smack, smash, *Slang* belt, clobber. *—n.* **2.** *I'll give you a sock on the jaw:* hit, punch, slap, wallop, smack, blow.

sodden *adj.* **1.** *The football field was sodden from last night's rain:* drenched, saturated, sopping, soppy, soaked, soggy, wet through, dripping. **2.** *This sodden soufflé must have too much flour:* mushy, pasty, doughy, lumpy, heavy, soggy. **3.** *He had a heavy, sodden look* *on his face:* listless, dull, expressionless, besotted. —**Ant.** 1 dry. 2 light, fluffy, crisp.

soft *adj.* **1.** *A soft mattress is bad for one's back. A soft wood is easier to whittle:* pliable, pliant, supple, malleable; not hard, easily penetrated, easily molded. **2.** *This silk scarf feels so soft:* smooth, sleek, velvety, satiny, downy, furry, silky, silken. **3.** *The doorbell is almost too soft to hear:* subdued, faint, muted, hushed, feeble; gentle, pleasantly low. **4.** *Those soft colors are very soothing. The lovers walked hand-in-hand in the soft rain:* gentle, mild, subdued, tranquil, restful, quiet; delicate, pale; not sharp, low intensity, shadowed, harmonious, shaded, twilight. **5.** *She has a soft spot in her heart for him:* tender, kind, lenient, tolerant, sympathetic, compassionate, pitying; sentimental. **6.** *His muscles are soft from lack of exercise:* weak; incapable of great endurance; not strong. **7.** *The "g" in "giant" gets a soft pronunciation:* not sharp, not hard; having a breathy sound. **8.** *Informal A soft assignment can be dull:* easy; requiring little effort. —**Ant.** 1, 5, 7, 8 hard. 1 unyielding, stiff, inflexible. 2 rough, harsh, coarse, abrasive. 3 loud, strong, noisy. 4 harsh, loud, sharp, glaring, bright. 5 unkind, unsympathetic. 6 strong, tough. 8 difficult, tough, rough.

soften *v.* **1.** *The landlord asked us to soften the music:* lower, subdue, moderate; tone down, make softer, turn down. **2.** *Soften the butter before adding it:* make soft. **3.** *She tried to soften the blow:* lessen, temper, ameliorate, mitigate, cushion, palliate, mollify. —**Ant.** 1 raise, intensify, increase; louden. 2 harden, freeze, set. 3 heighten.

softhearted *adj.* *She was so softhearted everybody borrowed money from her:* tender, kindhearted, sympathetic, warmhearted, compassionate, warm, generous, forgiving, humane, considerate, indulgent. —**Ant.** cold, heartless, unforgiving, unfeeling, hard-hearted.

softly *adv.* *He speaks too softly to be heard. Children find it hard to move softly:* quietly, weakly; gently, easily, mildly. —**Ant.** loud, loudly, blaringly, noisily; roughly; harshly, toughly, unkindly.

soggy *adj.* **1.** *The ground is soggy from the melting snow:* soaked, sopping, soppy, saturated, drenched, sodden, dripping. **2.** *Too much liquid made the cake soggy:* mushy, pasty, doughy, heavy, sodden. —**Ant.** 1 dry. 2 dry, fluffy, light.

soi-disant *adj.* *The soi-disant duchess was really a cleaning lady:* self-styled, so-called, pretended. —**Ant.** genuine, real.

soil[1] *n.* **1.** *This soil is good for growing things:* ground, earth, loam, humus. **2.** *It's good to have my feet on Canadian soil:* earth, land, region, country.

soil[2] *v.* **1.** *She soiled the carpet with her muddy shoes:* dirty, stain, smudge, grime, smear, spot, muddy, blacken. **2.** *His ugly innuendos soiled my reputation:* blacken, defile, disgrace, tarnish, debase, stain, ruin, sully, foul. —*n.* **3.** *What's that soil on your collar?:* stain, dirt, spot, grime, soot. —**Ant.** 1 clean, whiten, cleanse.

sojourn *v.* **1.** *We sojourned at my parents' home for the summer:* abide, visit, vacation; stay in a place temporarily, reside for a time, stay at, stay over. —*n.* **2.** *How long was your sojourn in Tibet?:* visit, stay, stopover, layover, pause, vacation, holiday.

solace *n.* **1.** *We drew solace from the many notes of sympathy:* comfort, consolation, reassurance; relief in affliction, help in need. —*v.* **2.** *The minister's words solaced the grief-stricken widow:* console, comfort, cheer, calm, assuage, reassure, soothe. —**Ant.** 1 pain, distress, discomfort, anxiety, anguish. 2 pain, distress, discomfort, dishearten.

soldier *n.* **1.** *Our soldiers will defend us against the enemy:* military man, enlisted man, serviceman, warrior, G.I., trooper, veteran. **2.** *He is a soldier for Christ:* militant leader, zealot, follower, partisan, worker, servant.

sole *adj.* **1.** *The hermit is the sole inhabitant of Goat Island:* only, exclusive, lone, solitary, single. **2.** *He has sole responsibility for the child:* exclusive. —**Ant.** 2 shared, divided, joint.

solely *adv.* **1.** *The boy was solely at fault for the broken window:* exclusively, alone, singly, single-handedly. **2.** *Porpoises live solely in salt water. It was solely a case of mistaken identity:* exclusively, purely, uniquely, merely.

solemn *adj.* **1.** *That solemn little girl never smiles:* somber, staid, grave, sedate, sober; quiet in demeanor. **2.** *He made a solemn decision never to drink again:* somber, grave, earnest, serious; determined, sincere, steadfast, absolute. **3.** *The inauguration was a solemn event:* formal, dignified, ceremonious, ceremonial, awe-inspiring. **4.** *A baptism is a solemn rite:* holy, religious, sacred, spiritual. **5.** *She always wears such solemn clothing:* dark, gloomy, somber, drab, grim, depressing. —**Ant.** 1 jovial, joyous, bright, lively, gay, happy, merry, spirited. 2 frivolous, halfhearted, insincere. 3 informal. 4 unholy, irreligious, sacrilegious. 5 gay, lively, bright, colorful.

solicit *v.* *They solicited our help in producing the school play. Campaign workers were busy soliciting votes:* seek, request, importune, ask, appeal for, entreat, plead, endeavor to obtain.

solicitous *adj.* **1.** *He was very solicitous about her office problems:* concerned, thoughtful, mindful, regardful, anxious, attentive. **2.** *The politicians do not seem overly solicitous to proceed in this investigation:* eager, zealous, desirous, longing, ardent, intense, keen, avid, enthusiastic, intent. —**Ant.** 1 unconcerned, undisturbed. 2 uninterested, unambitious, unenthusiastic.

solicitude *n.* *His solicitude about me was unnecessary and tiresome:* concern, anxiety, worry, care, uneasiness, disquietude, attention, overconcern, inquietude, fearfulness, apprehension. —**Ant.** indifference, heedlessness, neglect, unconcern.

solid *adj.* **1.** *A rock is a solid object. This figurine is solid:* real, substantial, concrete, tangible; dense, massy, not hollow. **2.** *We couldn't break through the solid line of tanks. What we want is* *a solid program of entertainment with no commercials:* unbroken, impenetrable, impermeable; constant, continuous, uninterrupted, without breaks. **3.** *Ice is solid, water is liquid:* hard, firm, solidified. **4.** *This old house has a remarkably solid foundation:* firm, well-constructed, strong, well-built, lasting, tough, sturdy, rugged, durable, substantial. **5.** *The curtains are solid green. The table is solid oak:* pure, unmixed, genuine, thorough, one-hundred-percent, real. **6.** *The book is a solid joy:* real, pure, complete, unalloyed. **7.** *My father is a solid member of the community:* sound, stable, steady, reliable, dependable, trustworthy; sober, sensible, levelheaded, rational. **8.** *The city council was solid in its decision to build a city center:* unanimous, undivided. **—Ant.** 1 hollow. 2 broken, permeable. 3 liquid, gaseous. 4 flimsy, shaky, unstable, unsteady, unsound. 5 mixed, variegated. 7 unsound, unstable, irresponsible, unreliable. 8 divided, undecided, split.

solidarity *n.* *A national emergency evokes solidarity among a nation's citizens:* closeness, unity, unification, union; harmony; cooperation; consolidation of interests and responsibilities. **—Ant.** divisiveness, factiousness, discord.

solitary *adj.* **1.** *The stranger ate a solitary meal. The old fisherman leads a solitary life:* lone, lonely, lonesome, companionless; avoiding the society of others. **2.** *The solitary boat looked tiny in the sea:* lone, isolated, single. **3.** *The thieves hid out in a solitary desert retreat:* secluded, cloistered, lonely, out-of-the-way, hidden, concealed; desolate, remote, isolated, uninhabited. **—Ant.** 1 companionable; gregarious, sociable, social. 3 bustling, busy, well-traveled.

solitude *n.* **1.** *The solitude of a hermit's life is not for me:* isolation, aloneness, loneliness, solitariness, desolation, seclusion, remoteness. **2.** *The hunters never saw a soul in that arctic solitude:* wasteland, wilderness, lonely place.

solution *n.* **1.** *The solution of the crime took three years:* solving, resolving, resolution; unraveling. **2.** *Have you found the solution yet?:* explanation, answer, key, cipher, resolution. **3.** *The marinade is a solution of wine and spices:* emulsion, suspension; mixture, blend.

solve *v.* *The clever child solved the riddle quickly:* resolve, decipher, unravel, find a solution to, find the answer, find the key, untangle, work out, figure out, decipher, unriddle.

solvent *adj.* **1.** *After years of saving, he was finally solvent:* in good financial condition, able to pay debts, financially sound. **2.** *Some saccharin is solvent only in hot liquid:* dissolvable, dilutable, dissoluble, soluble. **—n. 3.** *You need a solvent to soften that dried paint:* dissolving agent, dissolvent, diluent. **—Ant.** 1 bankrupt, broke. 3 hardener.

somber *adj.* **1.** *Why are schools painted in such somber colors? Wednesday was a somber day:* drab, toneless, gloomy, dark, gray, cheerless, dreary, grim. **2.** *His somber voice told us the news was bad:* grim, gloomy, depressing, mournful, funereal, grave, serious, sober, sol-

emn, melancholy. **—Ant.** 1 cheerful, gay, colorful, bright, sunny, lively. 2 cheerful, happy, gay, bright.

some *adj.* **1.** *Some viewers may find the movie disturbing:* any, one, anyone, unspecified. **2.** *He gained some twenty followers:* certain, specific, special, particular. **—Ant.** none.

somebody *n.* **1.** *Somebody answer the phone, please:* someone, some person, anybody. **2.** *Winning the lottery made her a somebody:* name, notable, celebrity, household name, luminary, public figure, star, VIP, dignitary, *Informal* bigwig.

somehow *adv.* *They somehow got out of the locked room:* anyhow, anyway, by some means.

something *n.* *Something was bothering her:* thing, item, article, being, entity, object, substance, commodity.

sometimes *adv.* *Sometimes they were forced to do painful things:* occasionally, on occasion, intermittently, now and then, periodically.

somewhat *adv.* *They were somewhat tired after their trip:* partially, in part, fairly, incompletely, kind of, moderately, quite, rather, to some extent, considerably, adequately.

somnolent *adj.* *After that immense meal we were somnolent all evening:* sleepy, drowsy, dozy, nodding, yawning, half-asleep, half-awake, torpid, slumberous, groggy, heavy-lidded, semiconscious, lethargic, languid, sluggish, dull; *Slang* dopey, out of it. **—Ant.** alert, active, energetic, wide-awake.

song *n.* **1.** *The band played our favorite song:* ballad, melody, tune, ditty, number. **2.** *The song of the robin woke me this morning:* piping, utterance, call, musical sound. **3.** *I enjoy reading Keats's love songs:* poem, lyric, verse.

sonorous *adj.* **1.** *The sonorous clang of the cymbals startled us:* resonant, full-toned, deep, vibrant, rich, reverberating, resounding, ringing. **2.** *The orator has a sonorous style:* eloquent, florid, flamboyant; impressive, grandiose. **—Ant.** 1 weak, tinny. 2 plain, weak, unadorned.

soon *adv.* *We hope to have a vacation soon:* directly, by and by, shortly, anon; instantly, quickly, pronto, right away, presently, forthwith, before long, ere long, betimes, without delay, early on, in a little while, any minute. **—Ant.** never, ne'er, at no time, never in the world.

soothe *v.* **1.** *He tried to soothe the crowd's rage:* pacify, comfort, calm, tranquilize, console, moderate, placate, mollify, relieve, appease. **2.** *The medication soothed her pain. The priest tried to soothe her doubts:* lessen, alleviate, relieve, ease, mitigate. **—Ant.** 1 upset, disturb, rouse, excite, disquiet. 2 increase, irritate.

soothsayer *n.* *A soothsayer predicted I would inherit a fortune:* fortune-teller, seer, diviner, prophet, forecaster.

sop *n.* **1.** *A doughnut is a good sop for coffee:* food for dipping. **2.** *The judgeship was given as a sop for his huge contributions:* tip, gratuity, baksheesh; bribe, payoff, hush money, payola. **—v. 3.** *Sop the cutlets in egg before flouring them:* dip, dunk, soak, drench, wet, saturate. **4.**

Use your bread to sop up the sauce: soak, absorb; take up. **5.** *My shoes were sopped through to my socks by the rain:* soak, wet, drench; become wet.

sophisticated *adj.* **1.** *The Duke of Windsor was a sophisticated world traveler:* seasoned, experienced, worldly, worldly-wise, cosmopolitan. **2.** *The play was too sophisticated for the country child:* intellectual, cultured, cultivated, *Informal* highbrow; studied, artificial, precious, mannered. **3.** *I can't work this sophisticated new equipment:* complicated, complex, difficult, subtle, advanced. **—Ant.** 1 unsophisticated, unseasoned, simple, unworldly. 2 unsophisticated, provincial. 3 simple, old-fashioned, uncomplicated.

sophistication *n.* *The fashion designer was the last word in sophistication:* urbanity, worldliness, worldly wisdom, social grace, refinement, composure, elegance, finesse, poise, refinement, grace, style, culture, *French* savoir faire, savoir vivre.

sophomoric *adj.* *We were disgusted by the grown man's sophomoric behavior:* juvenile, childish, infantile, adolescent; foolish, puerile, schoolboyish, callow; immature. **—Ant.** adult, mature, sophisticated, grown-up.

soporific *adj.* **1.** *His soporific voice almost put us to sleep:* hypnotic, somniferous, sleep-inducing, balmy, sluggish, heavy. **2.** *This warm weather makes me soporific:* sleepy, sluggish, drowsy, somnolent, slumberous, lethargic, lazy. *—n.* **3.** *Wine is a soporific for me:* sedative, hypnotic; sleep-inducer. **—Ant.** 1, 2 lively, animated. 3 stimulant.

sopping *adj.* *Take off those sopping clothes!:* drenched, wet, saturated, soppy, soaked.

sorcery *n.* *The witch used sorcery to turn the girl into a mouse:* witchcraft, witchery, wizardry, shamanism, black magic, necromancy, enchantment.

sordid *adj.* **1.** *This sordid slum isn't fit for a pig:* filthy, squalid, unclean, dirty; rank, putrid, rotten. **2.** *The prostitute wrote a book about her sordid life. The politician made a sordid business deal:* low, base, depraved, ignoble, vile, wicked, debauched, degraded, vulgar, gross, disreputable, corrupt. **—Ant.** 1 clean, pristine. 2 honorable, pure, noble.

sore *adj.* **1.** *The nurse bandaged my sore toe:* painful, tender, aching, sensitive, smarting, irritated; hurting, hurt, bruised. **2.** *Losing the election was a sore disappointment:* sharp, acute, harsh, painful, wounding; agonizing, distressing, unbearable. **3.** *His heart was sore at the news of war:* agonized, grieved, distressed, pained. **4.** *The farmers are in sore need of fuel:* severe, desperate, critical, grievous, extreme, great. **5.** *Informal I'm sore at you for being so late:* angry, indignant, irritated, irked, upset. *—n.* **6.** *Put some iodine on that sore:* inflammation, wound; sore spot. **—Ant.** 1 pain-free, painless. 2 painless. 3 happy, joyous, cheerful. 5 glad, happy, pleased, delighted.

sorely *adv.* *She is sorely in need of advice:* badly, severely, greatly, extremely, desperately, critically.

sorrow *n.* **1.** *The staff felt sorrow at the news of his retirement:* sadness, unhappiness, woe. **2.** *Too many sorrows crushed her spirit:* misfortune, loss, trial, trouble, hardship, affliction, travail, disaster, catastrophe; bad fortune. *—v.* **3.** *I sorrow for you in your loss:* grieve, weep, lament, despair, mourn; be sad. **—Ant.** 1 joy, gladness, delight, happiness. 2 good fortune, happiness, joy. 3 rejoice, revel.

sorrowful *adj.* **1.** *The tragedy made the entire town sorrowful:* grieved, sad, unhappy, melancholy, depressed, dejected, aggrieved, afflicted, mournful, plaintive, grievous, lamentable. **2.** *A sorrowful song ended the concert:* distressing, dismal, dreary, doleful, sorry, lugubrious, piteous. **—Ant.** happy.

sorry *adj.* **1.** *I'm sorry I made you cry:* regretful, contrite, sorrowful, sad, unhappy; remorseful, repentant. **2.** *Was she very sorry she missed the party?:* sad, melancholy, crestfallen, sorrowful; grieved, unhappy, brokenhearted. **3.** *What a sorry situation! The house is in a sorry mess:* miserable, sad, pitiful, pitiable, deplorable, wretched, woeful; pathetic, ridiculous. **—Ant.** 1 happy, unrepentant. 2 happy, joyous, elated, cheerful. 3 wonderful, uplifting.

sort *n.* **1.** *Is this the sort of car you want?:* kind, type; make, brand, species, variety, classification. **2.** *Trust him--he's a good sort:* person, individual. *—v.* **3.** *Let's sort the names alphabetically:* arrange, group, list, classify, class, divide, organize, systematize, grade, order, catalog, index, categorize; place in a category. **4.** *They tried to sort the fakes from the originals:* separate, segregate, take from, sift.

so-so *adj.* *Critics raved about the play, but we found it just so-so:* ordinary, mediocre, fair, modest, passable, average, commonplace, middling, run-of-the-mill, tolerable, adequate, bearable, humdrum, undistinguished, second-rate, indifferent, unexceptional; *Slang* blah, ho-hum.

sot *n.* *The old sot spent his life on skid row:* drunk, drunkard, toper, dipsomaniac, lush, souse, alcoholic, inebriate, soak, rumhound, *Slang* rummy. **—Ant.** teetotaler, abstainer.

soul *n.* **1.** *Her body died but her soul went to heaven:* spirit; spiritual part of a person, vital force. **2.** *He loved her with his heart and soul:* being, spirit; inmost feelings, inner core. **3.** *Won't someone help that poor soul?:* person, creature, individual; a living being. **4.** *The old farmer was the soul of honesty:* essence, embodiment, quintessence. **5.** *Some musicians lack soul:* inspiration, force, spirit, vitality.

sound[1] *n.* **1.** *I love the sound of rain on the roof:* noise; that which is heard, sensation produced by hearing. **2.** *He didn't like the sound of her telegram:* drift, tone, tenor, suggestion, implication. **3.** *Were you within sound of the explosion?:* range, earshot; hearing distance. *—v.* **4.** *The warning alarm sounded. Sound the whistle for lunch:* make a noise, produce sound, cause to sound, produce noise. **5.** *The bell sounded dismissal early today:* signal, announce. **6.** *Her* *voice sounds happy:* seem, convey a certain impression, come off as. **7.** *You must sound your words more clearly:* pronounce, articulate, enunciate, voice, utter.

sound² *adj.* **1.** *Her heart is as sound as a drum:* robust, sturdy, strong, good, fit, hardy, healthy. **2.** *The wiring in the old building is surprisingly sound:* undamaged, intact, unmarred; perfect; substantial, strong, well-built, lasting, sturdy, well-constructed; firm, solid, durable. **3.** *She has a sound, growing business:* solid, strong, stable, solvent. **4.** *You can depend on him to make a sound choice. The general presented a sound analysis of the situation:* sensible, solid, reliable, competent, sober, dependable, wise, penetrating, rational, reasonable, responsible. **5.** *I was in a sound sleep when you called:* deep, untroubled. **6.** *The officer gave him a sound reprimand:* thorough, thoroughgoing, severe, firm. **—Ant.** 1–4 unsound. 1 poor, ailing, weak. 2 damaged, defective. 3 failing, insolvent, insecure, shaky. 4 unreliable, incompetent, rash, irrational, irresponsible, frivolous. 5 light. 6 halfhearted.

soupçon *n. I detected a soupçon of garlic in the stew:* trace, dash, suspicion, bit, hint, vestige, suggestion, whiff, taste, tad, shade, drop, clue, taint, tinge, trifle, jot, touch.

sour *adj.* **1.** *These pickles are too sour:* tart, acid, vinegary, tangy, sharp, keen; acerbic, astringent. **2.** *Does the milk taste sour?:* spoiled, turned, fermented, rancid, curdled, bad; clabbered. **3.** *The baby's clothes have a sour odor:* offensive, nasty, repugnant, distasteful, unsavory, unpleasant. **4.** *She glanced at the noisy child with a sour expression:* disagreeable, nasty, unpleasant, peevish, surly, choleric, bad-tempered, bilious, crabbed, crabby, jaundiced, dour; petulant, uncivil, sullen, ill-humored, ill-tempered, cranky, waspish, tart, testy, acidulous, irritable, grouchy. **—v. 5.** *The cream soured in the trunk of the car. Too much heat soured the wine:* spoil, become spoiled, ferment, become fermented, curdle, turn. **6.** *A lonely childhood soured the boy. An unhappy romance soured her on men:* embitter, ill-dispose, make disagreeable, make unpleasant, jaundice, make bad-tempered; make cynical, make pessimistic, prejudice, alienate, *Slang* turn off. **—Ant.** 1 sweet, bland, mild. 2 fresh, unspoiled. 3 sweet, pleasant, agreeable, savory, fresh. 4 sweet, agreeable, pleasant, gracious, amiable, affable, good-natured, good-humored.

source *n.* **1.** *The reporter refused to name the source of his information. What is the source of his strength?:* origin, derivation, authority, basis; cause, prime mover, antecedent, fountain, fount, spring, wellspring, root, foundation; father, author, begetter. **2.** *The explorers searched for the source of the river:* beginning, rising, headwater, head, wellspring, place of issue, fount, fountain. **—Ant.** 1 outcome, result, effect, consequence, end, conclusion. 2 mouth, termination.

sourpuss *n. The old sourpuss yelled at us for walking across his yard:* grouch, crab, crank,

complainer, grumbler, bellyacher, griper, sorehead, grouser, bear, crosspatch, curmudgeon, killjoy, spoilsport, grump.

souse *v.* **1.** *The abrupt downpour soused us:* wet thoroughly, drench, soak, saturate; douse, inundate, immerse, submerge, duck, dunk, dip. **2.** *She soused the mushrooms in the marinade for two days:* pickle, steep, soak, marinate. **—n. 3.** *Slang He's been a souse all his life:* drunk, drunkard, alcoholic, inebriate, dipsomaniac, boozer, sot, tippler, lush. **—Ant.** 1 dry. 3 teetotaler, abstainer.

souvenir *n. She kept the pinecone as a souvenir of that weekend in the country:* memento, reminder, remembrance, relic, keepsake, token, emblem, trophy; scar, memory.

sovereign *n.* **1.** *He reigned as sovereign of the tiny kingdom:* supreme ruler, monarch; king, queen, prince, emperor, czar, potentate; crowned head, chief, chieftain, overlord, autocrat, lord. **—adj. 2.** *No one questions the queen's sovereign authority:* ruling, supreme, absolute; royal, monarchical, imperial, reigning, regal; powerful, all-powerful, prepotent, potent; kingly, queenly, princely. **3.** *Your welfare is my sovereign concern:* principal, chief, foremost, paramount, leading, governing, ruling, supreme, utmost, main, uppermost, highest, dominant, major, prime. **4.** *For a brief time Texas was a sovereign nation:* self-governing, free, independent, self-directing, self-ruling, autonomous. **—Ant.** 1 subject; peasant, serf. 2 subordinate; limited, partial. 3 minor, secondary, least, lowest.

sovereignty *n.* **1.** *The sovereignty of the monarch was under attack:* power, dominion, authority, supremacy, command, control, ascendancy, sway, jurisdiction, predominance, paramountcy, primacy; kingship, lordship; throne, scepter, crown. **2.** *The United States declared its sovereignty in 1776:* independence, autonomy, self-determination, self-rule, home rule, self-government, freedom.

sow *v.* **1.** *Sow the marigold seeds in early spring:* plant, seed, scatter, broadcast, disseminate, strew, disperse, cast, implant, sprinkle, set in. **2.** *Her strange behavior sowed suspicions of guilt in our minds:* plant, establish, inject, lodge, instill, introduce; spread, scatter, strew.

spa *n. She spent her holiday at a spa:* watering place, baths, springs.

space *n.* **1.** *The rocket was lost in space:* outer space, the universe, the void, the firmament, the heavens, sky, ether, nothingness, infinity, emptiness. **2.** *We need more space to set up the equipment:* room, area, sweep, range, territory, expanse, scope, spread, amplitude, swing, field, margin, compass, reach, latitude, breadth, width. **3.** *She has a wide space between her teeth:* gap, distance, span, chasm, separation, break, hiatus, interruption, interval, interstice, interspace, lacuna, omission, blank. **4.** *Can you finish eating in the space of an hour?:* period, interval, span, duration, term. **5.** *Luckily, there was an extra space on the plane:* seat, place, room, berth, spot, reservation, accommodation.

—v. **6.** *Space the paintings evenly on the wall. Space the meetings at one-hour intervals:* place, arrange, organize, distribute, order, set out, line up, range, rank, mark out; schedule, time. **7.** *He spaced the dancers so they wouldn't bump into each other:* separate, keep apart, part, spread. **—Ant.** 2 confinement, limitation. 3 closure. 7 crowd, bunch.

spacious *adj. Our yard is spacious enough for a swimming pool. We love the spacious western skies:* large, ample, wide, broad, sizable, commodious, capacious, roomy; immense, expansive, extensive, vast, enormous; uncrowded. **—Ant.** small, cramped, crowded, close.

span *n.* **1.** *The rescuers searched the entire span of the island. The span of human life is short:* distance, breadth, length, dimensions, reach, stretch, proportions, measure, scope, range, sweep, area, territory; extent, term, spell, duration, period, interval. **2.** *The car stalled on the second span of the bridge:* arch, vault, archway, trestle, wing, extension. *—v.* **3.** *The overpass spans the center of town:* bridge, bridge over, cross, extend across, reach over, vault. **4.** *Their friendship spanned a lifetime:* cover, reach over, stretch over, reach across; last, endure, survive.

spank *v.* **1.** *Mother spanked her for running into the street:* slap, paddle, whale, hide, tan, wallop; strike, beat, hit, flagellate, strap, belt, thrash, switch, whip, flog, cane, birch, *Slang* whop, lick. *—n.* **2.** *The spank hurt his hand more than it hurt me:* slap, strike, hit, blow, wallop, belt, paddling.

spare *v.* **1.** *The king spared the prisoner:* save from death, leave uninjured, refrain from hurting, deal leniently with, forgive, give quarter to, show mercy, be merciful to, have mercy on, show consideration for; exonerate, liberate, release, free; let off, reprieve, pardon, acquit. **2.** *The doctor tried to spare him from pain:* safeguard, protect, exempt, guard, shield, shelter, defend; save, relieve. **3.** *I can spare some time right now:* afford, part with, grant, give, donate, let go of, dispense with, relinquish, forgo, cede. **4.** *Spare your energy until the last lap:* conserve, withhold, not use, hold back, save, hoard, reserve, husband, lay up, set aside, amass, use frugally, keep. **5.** *She never spares the butter when baking:* use frugally, use economically, economize on, be parsimonious with, limit, pinch, conserve, skimp on, stint, be niggardly with. *—adj.* **6.** *Does the house have a spare room? I gave the beggar my spare change:* reserve, extra, auxiliary, supplementary, substitute, supplemental; unnecessary, superfluous, supernumerary, odd, additional, unused, surplus, unconsumed, extraneous, excess, leftover. **7.** *The suit hung limply on his spare frame:* fleshless, lean, bony, scrawny, scraggy, thin, emaciated, gaunt, skinny, lank, lanky, skeletal, haggard, weedy, rangy; slight, meager, skimpy, scanty, scant, slender. **—Ant.** 1 punish, condemn, destroy, hurt, harm, injure. 2 afflict, expose. 4 squander, use, spend. 5 squander, spend. 7 fat, fleshy, heavy, plump, large.

sparing *adj. She's sparing with the family's budget. The professor was sparing in his praise:* thrifty, economical, frugal, careful, saving; parsimonious, miserly, penurious, near, close-fisted, close, stinting, stingy, ungenerous, niggardly, tightfisted; grudging, meager, scanty, scant. **—Ant.** lavish, profuse, extravagant, generous, openhanded.

spark *n.* **1.** *A cigarette spark started the forest fire:* ignited particle, glowing particle, fiery particle; ember, brand. **2.** *Sparks flew from a short circuit in the toaster:* flash, flicker, sparkle, beam. **3.** *The dog showed not a spark of interest in food:* bit, iota, trace, jot, glimmer, atom, flicker. **4.** *Informal He has a lot of spark:* vitality, spirit, life, fire, animation, get-up-and-go. *—v.* **5.** *The fire is sparking:* sparkle, glitter; gleam, flash. **6.** *We need to spark some ambition in the lazy boy:* stimulate, incite, inspire, arouse, excite, pique, provoke, instigate.

sparkle *v.* **1.** *Her diamond tiara sparkled like fire:* shine, glitter, glint, glisten, flicker, twinkle, gleam, shimmer, scintillate, dazzle, flash; coruscate. **2.** *The champagne sparkled:* bubble, fizzle, effervesce, fizz, pop, foam, froth. **3.** *The children sparkled with excitement:* scintillate, shine, be vivacious, be witty, be cheerful, rejoice, be gay, effervesce. *—n.* **4.** *I see a sparkle in the ashes:* glint, glitter, twinkle, flicker, shimmer, scintillation, glimmer, flash; ember, brand. **5.** *Did you notice the sparkle in her eyes?:* gleam, radiance, brilliance, glow, dazzle, glimmer, glitter, light, glint, effulgence, luminosity, luminousness. **6.** *His sparkle made him the life of the party:* liveliness, animation, verve, dash, brilliance, élan, pep, vim; vivacity, life, exhilaration, ebullience, exuberance, vitality, spirit; quickness, alertness, briskness; cheerfulness, gaiety, jollity, cheer, effervescence. **—Ant.** 1 fade. 5 dullness, flatness. 6 dullness, tedium, cheerlessness, drabness, lethargy.

sparse *adj. Sparse trees provide poor shelter:* few, few and far between, spotty, thin, thinly distributed, uncrowded, scarce, infrequent; scattered, sporadic, dispersed, spaced-out, diffuse, strewn; meager, scanty, spare, exiguous, scant, skimpy. **—Ant.** plentiful, populous, crowded, numerous, dense, thick.

Spartan *adj. The monks lead a Spartan life:* plain, simple, austere, ascetic, frugal, abstemious, stark; disciplined, rigorous, restrained, restricted, stiff, stern, strict, exacting, severe, hard, stringent, inexorable, inflexible, self-denying, self-disciplined. **—Ant.** fancy, self-indulgent, luxurious, lavish, undisciplined, unrestrained, spendthrift, hedonistic, soft, easy, *Slang* cushy; lax.

spasm *n.* **1.** *A leg spasm cost her the race. A spasm of pain contorted the wounded man's face:* cramp, seizure, crick; twitch, tic, jerk, convulsion, shudder, start, grip, paroxysm; throe, pang. **2.** *What caused that spasm of tears?:* spell, fit, onset, burst, access, attack, frenzy, storm, flash, spurt, seizure, explosion, tempest, eruption.

spasmodic *adj. She shows only spasmodic*

bursts of affection: fitful, intermittent, occasional, periodic, fleeting, sporadic, capricious, desultory, flighty, mercurial, erratic, irregular, transient, inconstant, discontinuous. —**Ant.** constant, steady, regular, lasting.

spat *n.* **1.** *They had a little spat but made up quickly:* disagreement, misunderstanding, quarrel, tiff, difference, bicker, dispute, fight, dissent, scrap, set-to, squabble, altercation, wrangle. —*v.* **2.** *I can't remember what we spatted about:* quarrel, argue, bicker, fight, scrap, differ, contend, disagree, squabble, wrangle, tiff. —**Ant.** 1 agreement, concurrence, understanding. 2 agree, concur.

spatter *v.* **1.** *The painters spattered paint on the rug:* splash, plash, bespatter, splatter, sprinkle; spray, swash, slop, spurt; spot, mottle, fleck, stipple, speckle; shower. **2.** *Try not to spatter your dress with grease:* spot, stain, soil.

spawn *v.* **1.** *Salmon swim upriver to their birthplaces to spawn:* deposit eggs, lay eggs. **2.** *Lower species often spawn in great numbers:* reproduce, propagate, proliferate, multiply, teem, breed. **3.** *A good teacher can spawn a love of learning:* engender, generate, give rise to, propagate, give birth to, produce, bring forth, beget, yield. —*n.* **4.** *The polluted water harmed the spawn of the trout:* eggs, seed; offspring, brood; product, yield, fruit.

speak *v.* **1.** *The chief engineer speaks with an Italian accent:* talk, utter words, articulate, vocalize, sound, give utterance; enunciate, pronounce; mutter, mumble, murmur, whisper; call, shout, cry out; converse, confer, consult, exchange words, chat. **2.** *She spoke what was in her heart:* express, say, make known, communicate, tell, state, declare, recite, convey, relate, impart, put into words, voice, give voice to, bespeak; divulge, reveal, disclose, make disclosure, proclaim, announce, advise, air, report; imply, suggest, be expressive, indicate. **3.** *Is the governor going to speak at the rally?:* give a speech, deliver an address, discourse, lecture; sermonize, preach; expound, orate, declaim, hold forth, harangue, expatiate, dilate. **4.** *His letter spoke of his future plans:* mention, comment, refer, make reference, remark, treat, discuss, deal. —**Ant.** 2 repress, hide, conceal, suppress.

speaker *n.* *The senator is the opening speaker:* talker, lecturer, spokesman, spokeswoman, orator, speechmaker; valedictorian; reciter, reader; preacher, sermonizer; rhetorician, declaimer, discourser; monologist; mouthpiece, voice, advocate. —**Ant.** listener, audience.

spear *n.* **1.** *The spear pierced the lion's heart:* javelin, lance, harpoon, pike, bolt, dart, gaff, spike; shaft. —*v.* **2.** *Have you ever speared trout?:* impale, stab, run through, pierce, lance, spike, pike, gore, stick, transfix, spit, penetrate, puncture, prick.

spearhead *n.* **1.** *The whale broke the spearhead off the harpoon:* point of a spear, iron. **2.** *He was the spearhead of the ecology movement:* leader, establisher, pioneer, initiator, creator, spokesman, spokeswoman, begetter,

founder, prime mover, instituter, inaugurator, avant-guardist. —*v.* **3.** *Betty Friedan and others spearheaded the Women's Liberation Movement:* lead, pioneer, initiate, begin, start, launch, inaugurate, establish, originate, give birth to, institute, found, conceive, develop.

special *adj.* **1.** *The carpenter uses a special machine for routing:* especial, certain, specific, distinct, specialized, particular; proper. **2.** *This is a special day in my life:* out of the ordinary, unusual, uncommon, unique, select, distinctive, novel, unconventional, rare, singular, extraordinary, distinct, exceptional, especial, important, momentous, signal, outstanding, distinguished, noteworthy, remarkable. **3.** *The circus hired him for his special trapeze stunts:* distinctive, unique, peculiar; personal, individual, typical, endemic, representative. **4.** *Your apple pie is a special favorite of mine. David is a very special friend:* particular, great, outstanding, especial, exceptional; close, devoted, staunch, fast, steadfast, ardent, good, intimate. —*n.* **5.** *The juggling act is the special of the show. Today's special is the shoulder of lamb:* specialty, feature, attraction, high point, highlight, headliner, *French* pièce de résistance; extravaganza; bargain, sale item. —**Ant.** 1 ordinary, all-purpose, general, standard, unspecialized. 2 common, ordinary, undistinctive, unimportant, routine. 3 ordinary, unexceptional, usual.

specialist *n.* *My cousin is a specialist in Chinese studies:* expert, authority, connoisseur, master, maven, skilled hand, past master, adept, *Informal* buff. —**Ant.** amateur, generalist.

specialize *v.* *They decided to specialize in economics:* concentrate on, practice exclusively, study intensively, train for.

specially *adv.* *He was specially proud of his new car:* especially, expressly, particularly, specifically, distinctively.

specialty *n.* **1.** *Will your specialty be psychology or sociology?:* special field, focus, pursuit, special subject, major; special line of work, profession; hobby; faculty, aptitude, bent, talent, competence, genius, turn, endowment. **2.** *The restaurant's specialty is home-made soup:* special, distinctive product, distinction, particularity, earmark, badge, mark, trademark, stamp, feature, claim to fame, forte.

species *n.* *The flower looks like a species of rose:* type, sort, kind, class, category, breed, variety, genre, nature, kidney, order, stripe, make, division, form, subdivision, classification, designation.

specific *adj.* **1.** *What is the specific time of arrival? There are two specific questions we must answer:* precise, definite, exact, certain, fixed, specified, clearly stated, categorical, clear-cut, concrete, stated, unequivocal; confined, circumscribed, limited, bounded, pinned-down, tied-down, restricted; detailed, minute, determinate, relevant, pertinent, pointed, particular. **2.** *A specific attribute of the elephant is its long trunk:* especial, peculiar, special, distinctive, individual, unique, singular, particular, intrinsic, endemic, characteristic, typical, personal. —*n.* **3.** Often

specifics *The specifics of the accident were hazy:* particular, item, fact, relevant point, detail, datum, circumstance. **4.** *The doctor prescribed a specific for his stomach pains:* special remedy, cure, medication, physic. —**Ant.** 1 approximate, indefinite, uncertain, vague, hazy; general. 2 common, undistinctive, general.

specifically *adv. She specifically exempted him from the exam:* specially, expressly, concretely, definitely, distinctively, exactly, explicitly, particularly, peculiarly, pointedly, precisely, categorically.

specification *n.* **1.** *The vague charges against him lacked specification:* itemization, particularization, enumeration; precision; particularity; clarity, detail; concreteness, substance. **2.** *He fits all but one specification:* requirement, condition, stipulation, qualification.

specify *v. Please specify what the job will entail. The chef specified a dry white wine for the recipe:* detail, state in detail, define, indicate, designate, enumerate, name, be specific about, focus on, stipulate, cite, adduce, itemize, denote, particularize, describe, define, set forth; call for, order.

specimen *n. This is a perfect specimen of an American Beauty rose:* sample, model, representative, example, exemplar, instance, case, type, exemplification; prototype.

specious *adj. He reached the wrong conclusion by specious reasoning:* deceptive, misleading, fallacious, questionable, casuistic, dubious, false, invalid, faulty, sophistical, unsubstantiated, unsound, unfounded, incorrect, inaccurate, slippery, tricky, untrue, spurious, illogical. —**Ant.** valid, conclusive, undeniable, inescapable.

speck *n.* **1.** *Is that a speck of dust on the page or a period?:* particle, grain, mote, bit; dot, spot, mark, speckle, flyspeck, fleck. **2.** *I use just a speck of cream in my coffee. He doesn't care a speck about your opinion:* drop, trace, trifle, bit, pinch, modicum; whit, particle, mite, scintilla, iota, jot, hair, glimmer, shadow, pin, farthing.

speckled *adj.* stippled, brindled, dappled, flecked, mottled, peppered, dotted, spotted, sprinkled, studded, dappled.

spectacle *n.* **1.** *The eclipse was a spectacle not to be missed:* marvel, wonder, phenomenon, curiosity; sight, scene; rarity, rare sight. **2.** *The performers put on quite a spectacle:* exhibition, presentation, extravaganza, demonstration, production, exhibit, exposition, display, pageant, parade.

spectacular *adj.* **1.** *Princess Anne's wedding was a spectacular affair:* magnificent, gorgeous, glorious, striking, elaborate, sumptuous, impressive, showy, eye-filling, splendid, opulent, ceremonious, grand, rich, stately; jeweled, bespangled; theatrical; fabulous, marvelous, astounding, overwhelming. **2.** *The fireman made a spectacular rescue:* thrilling, daring, impressive, hair-raising, daredevil, dramatic, sensational. —*n.* **3.** *The charity ball was something of a spectacular:* spectacle, elaborate production, ostentatious show, extravaganza, gala. —**Ant.**

1 plain, unimpressive, modest, ordinary. 2 simple, easy.

spectator *n. Thousands of spectators jammed the stands:* onlooker, observer, viewer, witness, eyewitness, beholder, sightseer, rubberneck; kibitzer; theatergoer, fan, aficionado; audience, gallery, house; bystander. —**Ant.** performer, entertainer.

specter *n. The children thought they saw a specter in the deserted mansion:* ghost, phantom, spook, spirit, wraith, shade, apparition, demon, hobgoblin, sprite, ghoul, banshee, revenant, presence, phantasm; fantasy, vision.

spectral *adj. Cobwebs gave the place a spectral atmosphere:* ghostly, spooky, phantom, incorporeal; eerie, unearthly, uncanny, weird, creepy, supernatural, otherworldly; gossamer, ethereal, unreal, wraithlike, phantasmal, insubstantial, chimerical, airy, vaporous, shadowy; ghastly. —**Ant.** earthly, homey, tangible.

speculate *v.* **1.** *He often speculated about the purpose of life. Scientists only speculate about life on other planets:* meditate, consider, muse, contemplate, engage in thought, reflect, think, reason, deliberate, ponder, ruminate, study, cogitate, excogitate, wonder, brood; guess, surmise, conjecture, theorize, hazard an opinion, hypothesize, suppose, imagine, fancy, dream. **2.** *He speculated in foreign exchange and lost a lot of money:* buy and sell riskily, play the market, wager, take a chance, hazard, trade hazardously, gamble, chance, venture, play a hunch.

speculation *n.* **1.** *The man's identity was the object of much speculation:* conjecture, guesswork, hypothesis, opinion, supposition, guesswork; theory, reflection, meditation, thinking, thought, weighing, consideration, deliberation, contemplation. **2.** *Financial speculation was a way of life for him:* speculative enterprise, venture, gamble, hazard, risk, venture, risky venture, wager, *Informal* flutter, flier, plunge.

speech *n.* **1.** *We express ourselves through speech and writing:* speaking, oral communication, talking, talk, articulation, utterance, voice, vocalization; conversation, dialogue, converse, colloquy, discourse, verbalization, verbal intercourse, parlance, confabulation, oral commerce, discussion; remarks, statement, spoken words, observation, pronouncement, expression, declaration, comment; palaver, prattle, chatter, gossip, chitchat. **2.** *The candidate made a moving speech to his workers:* address, talk, oration, sermon, lecture, declamation, discourse, recitation, diatribe, tirade, salutation, valedictory, dissertation, appeal, harangue, exhortation, homily; soliloquy, monologue. **3.** *Her speech is informal and filled with colloquialisms:* style of speaking, manner of speaking, expression, utterance, rhetoric; articulation, pronunciation, enunciation, diction, elocution. **4.** *The speech of the islanders is hard to understand:* language, dialect, tongue, idiom; jargon, slang, colloquialism, *Informal* lingo. —**Ant.** 1 muteness, dumbness, speechlessness; silence.

speechless *adj.* **1.** *The loss left her speechless: Figurative* dumb, dumfounded, shocked, mute.

2. *The speechless children learned American Sign Language:* silent, mute, *Offensive* dumb. —**Ant.** loquacious, voluble, talkative.

speed *n.* **1.** *He finished the job with amazing speed:* quickness, dispatch, celerity, promptness, alacrity, swiftness, expedition, rapidness, rapidity, briskness, haste, hastiness; fleetness, velocity, dash, hurry, rush, acceleration. **2.** *The plane went faster than the speed of sound:* rate, velocity; tempo, momentum. —*v.* **3.** *The ambulance sped to the hospital:* hurry, rush, hasten, make haste, make time, lose no time, tear, tear off, barrel, hurtle, plunge; run, scurry, race, hie, gallop, hustle, dart, dash, bowl along, *Informal* go hell-bent, burn up the road, zip, zoom, hightail. **4.** *We'll never get there if he doesn't speed up:* hurry up, hurry, quicken, hasten, spurt ahead, step up, pick up, speed, put on a burst of speed, put on more speed, expedite, accelerate, *Informal* get a move on, step on it, gun it. **5.** *Good fortune sped her on her climb to the top:* hasten, assist, help, aid, boost, promote, advance, further, favor, give a lift, expedite, propel, impel, push forward, move along, dispatch. —**Ant.** 1 slowness, delay, sluggishness. 3 creep, crawl, dawdle, drag. 4 slow down. 5 hinder, slow, hamper, inhibit, block, bar.

speedy *adj.* *He made a speedy dash for the door. She wished him a speedy recovery:* swift, fast, rapid, hurried, hasty, quick, headlong, precipitate, sudden, abrupt, fleet, running, brisk; ready, without delay, early, not delayed, summary, with dispatch, express, quick-fire, rapid-fire, lively. —**Ant.** slow, sluggish, dilatory, laggard, lagging; delayed, late, tardy.

spell[1] *v.* **1.** *Children love to spell Mississippi. B-a-b-y spells baby:* write the letters of, say the letters of; form a word, make up. **2.** *Those dark clouds spell rain:* foretell, signify, mean, portend, indicate, typify, promise, forecast, denote, augur, stand for, betoken, suggest, symbolize, purport, bespeak, omen, forebode, imply, presage, herald, represent, amount to, connote.

spell[2] *n.* **1.** *The fairy godmother's spell transformed the pumpkin into a coach:* charm, enchantment, magic formula, magic, incantation, voodoo, hoodoo, sorcery, witchery, invocation, mumbo jumbo; open-sesame, abracadabra, hex. **2.** *Most women fall under the spell of his charm:* enchantment, fascination, rapture, glamour, bewitchment, allure, influence.

spell[3] *n.* **1.** *The long spell of sentry duty exhausted him:* stretch, turn, period, tour, term, bout, time, hitch, course, duration, round, tenure, assignment, stint, trick, go. **2.** *Just rest for a spell:* while, bit; interval, break, respite, lull, recess, pause. **3.** *We're expecting a cold spell:* period, wave, snap, interlude. —*v.* **4.** *Someone had better spell the night nurse:* relieve, take the place of, free, release, take over for, substitute for, cover for, pinch-hit for.

spellbound *adj.* *We were spellbound by the music:* fascinated, transported, enchanted, charmed, enraptured, entranced, enthralled, rapt, bewitched, transfixed, mesmerized, hypnotized, possessed; breathless, speechless, word-less, dumbstruck, tongue-tied, awestruck, agape, openmouthed. —**Ant.** unimpressed, indifferent, disenchanted.

spend *v.* **1.** *They spend more money than they make. What did you spend for that lamp?:* pay, pay out, expend, disburse, dispense, allocate, dole, outlay, *Informal* give, *Slang* fork out, shell out. **2.** *He spends too much energy worrying:* consume, use, employ, expend, devote, invest, squander, waste, dissipate. **3.** *He spent himself in years of dangerous police work:* burn out, drain, use up, exhaust, destroy, consume, dissipate, deplete, impoverish, wear out, waste; scatter, empty. **4.** *Let's spend tomorrow together:* occupy, pass, while away, take up, use, fill. —**Ant.** 1 earn, make, acquire, get, gain, take in; save, hoard, collect, gather. 2 save, conserve. 3 save, reserve, hoard, conserve, treasure up.

spendthrift *n.* **1.** *He's a spendthrift and can't save a penny:* wastrel, waster, big spender, spend-all, squanderer, prodigal, profligate. —*adj.* **2.** *My spendthrift brother pays a fortune for his clothes:* extravagant, wasteful, overgenerous, improvident, wastrel, profligate, prodigal, lavish. —**Ant.** 1 tightwad, penny pincher, cheapskate. 2 frugal, penny-pinching, stingy.

spent *adj.* *He was completely spent after two weeks of hard labor:* exhausted, weak, weary, wearied, used up, played out, worn out, debilitated, tired out, done, powerless, strengthless, ready to drop, drooping, fatigued, *Slang* bushed, beat; laid low, faint, on one's last legs, prostrate, enfeebled, done in, fagged out. —**Ant.** energetic, lively, strong, robust, vital.

spew *v.* *The volcano spewed out molten lava. The stove spewed smoke into the room:* vomit, disgorge, regurgitate, heave, throw out; cast up, spit out, eject, expel.

sphere *n.* **1.** *A ball is a sphere:* globe, round body, ball, globular mass, spheroid, globule, orb. **2.** *Poverty and slums were outside the rich boy's sphere:* orbit, domain, realm, range, area, pale, scope, compass, beat, territory, province, bailiwick; experience.

spice *n.* **1.** *Pepper is one of my favorite spices:* seasoning, pungent substance, herb, condiment, flavoring. **2.** *He's bored and needs a little spice in his life:* zest, tang, flavor, piquancy, relish, excitement, pungency, savor, zip, snap, kick, accent, *Slang* pizzazz. —**Ant.** 2 boredom, flatness, dullness.

spicy *adj.* **1.** *Mexican food is too spicy for me:* pungent, hot, piquant, sharp, strong, redolent, peppery, nippy, fiery, tangy, zippy, snappy, aromatic, gingery. **2.** *The comedian specialized in spicy remarks:* pungent, sharp, keen, piquant, witty, clever, spirited, provocative, pithy; sparkling, scintillating; piercing, trenchant, incisive, acute. **3.** *That French movie is too spicy for the children:* racy, ribald, risqué, scandalous, improper, indelicate, questionable, indecent, bawdy, off-color, suggestive, salty. —**Ant.** 1 bland, flat, tasteless, unsavory, insipid. 2 bland, boring, dull, insipid, tedious, spiritless, lifeless. 3 proper, prudish.

spike *n.* **1.** *Hammer the spike in straight:* large nail, hobnail, pin, skewer, rivet, peg, stake. **2.** *I tore my blouse on a spike of the fence:* point, prong, barb, tine; thorn, briar, spine, spur, bramble, bristle, spikelet, needle.

spill *v.* **1.** *Be careful not to spill the ice trays. Tears spilled from her eyes:* cause to overflow, allow to run over, overturn, slop, slosh, waste; drip, fall, drop, run, flow, overflow, splash. **2.** *The warrior spilled his opponent's blood:* let flow, shed, pour out. **3.** *The bronco spilled his rider:* dump, cause to fall, throw, toss. **4.** *Informal I knew he'd spill the whole story!:* disclose, reveal, tell, *Slang* blab.

spin *v.* **1.** *Few women spin their own yarn today:* make by twisting fibers; form into thread or yarn. **2.** *Children love to spin tops. The dancer spun around and around:* twirl, whirl, turn, rotate, revolve, swirl, wheel, pirouette, gyrate. **3.** *No one believed that fantastic tale he spun:* tell, narrate, render, relate, unfold, recount; invent, concoct, fabricate. —*n.* **4.** *Place your bets before the spin of the wheel:* turn, spinning, twirl, roll, rotation. **5.** *We took a spin around town:* quick drive, rapid ride, turn, fast circle, whirl.

spindly *adj.* **1.** *The spindly horse could scarcely carry him:* gaunt, bony, thin, lean, spare, skeletal, scrawny, skinny, lanky, gangly, gangling. **2.** *A spindly coffee table stood beside the sofa:* unsteady, shaky, rickety, teetery, teetering, tottery, tottering, wobbly. —**Ant.** robust, sturdy.

spine *n.* **1.** *He broke his spine in a fall from a horse:* backbone, vertebral column, spinal column, vertebrae. **2.** *Hedgehogs and porcupines protect themselves with their spines:* quill, horn, pointed projection, barb, spike, spur, point, prong, bristle, prickle; bramble, thorn, briar, needle.

spineless *adj.* *That spineless man will never speak up to his boss:* timid, fearful, fainthearted, weak, timorous, cowardly, pusillanimous, lily-livered, irresolute, chickenhearted, cowering, spiritless, cringing, vacillating, weak-willed, indecisive, wavering. —**Ant.** fearless, tough, strong, forceful, courageous, resolute.

spinoff *n.* *His new novel seems to be a spinoff of his long, narrative poem:* byproduct, outgrowth, offshoot, aftereffect, side effect, issue, adjunct, supplement, descendant, consequence, result, outcome.

spiral *n.* **1.** *A coiled spring forms a spiral:* helix, screw, whorl, whirl, gyre, coil, corkscrew; curl, curlicue, ringlet. —*adj.* **2.** *A spiral staircase takes up less space than a regular one:* helical, corkscrew, screw-shaped, spiroid, curled, coiled, whorled, winding, twisting.

spire *n.* **1.** *The view from the church spire was breathtaking:* steeple, belfry, turret, obelisk, minaret, tower, bell tower, campanile, shaft. **2.** *The spires of snow were beautiful against the blue sky:* peak, crest, summit, cap, cone, point, pinnacle, apex, vertex, tip.

spirit *n.* **1.** *They believe the spirit lives on after death:* soul, immortal part, vital essence; intellect, mind, psyche. **2.** *The haunted house was filled with spirits:* ghost, shade, spook, apparition, specter, phantom, phantasm, hobgoblin, wraith, banshee, presence; elf, fairy, bugbear, bugaboo, goblin, ghoul, sprite, dybbuk. **3.** *The spirit is willing but the flesh is weak:* will, motivation, resolve, resolution; mind, heart, animus, impulse, urge. **4. spirits** *He was deeply depressed and no one could lift his spirits:* mood, feelings, disposition, emotions, attitude, morale, sentiment, temper. **5.** *Even the children lacked spirit on that gloomy day. The troops attacked with spirit:* vigor, vim, zest, liveliness, animation, vitality, verve, élan, vivacity, enthusiasm, energy, eagerness; pluck, mettle, enterprise, drive, zeal, avidity; sprightliness, sparkle, ardor, fire, glow, warmth; courage, bravery, doughtiness, audacity, dauntlessness, stoutheartedness, daring, backbone, fortitude, boldness, stoutness, valor, staunchness, fearlessness, spunk, *Informal* sand, guts, grit. **6.** *The spirit of the country is one of disillusionment:* temper, feeling, disposition, frame of mind, vein, stripe, mood, humor, tone, tenor, turn of mind. **7.** *My father has great family spirit:* allegiance, devotion, loyalty, attachment, bond, fervor, ardor, enthusiasm, feeling. **8.** *I feel as bound by the spirit as by the letter of the agreement:* intention, significance, intent, meaning, essence, purport, substance; sense, gist, effect, purpose, aim. —**Ant.** 1, 3 body, flesh, materiality. 5 lifelessness, dullness, spiritlessness, timidity.

spirited *adj.* *The spirited horse will be a good racer. He gave a spirited reply:* high-spirited, full of spirit, lively, mettlesome, frisky, fiery; courageous, plucky, nervy, intrepid, fearless, bold. —**Ant.** spiritless, dispirited, timid, sluggish.

spiritless *adj.* *The spiritless team lost heavily:* dispirited, lifeless, apathetic, dejected, depressed, despondent, disconsolate, down, downcast, cast down, downhearted, draggy, droopy, indifferent, lackluster, languishing, lifeless, low, subdued, torpid, limp, listless, flat, broken, inanimate.

spiritual *adj.* **1.** *The medium tried to reach someone in the spiritual world:* ghostly, supernatural, supernal, psychic, metaphysical, phantom, incorporeal, immaterial, unearthly, otherworldly, spectral, insubstantial, intangible. **2.** *Her spiritual beauty outshone her physical beauty. Our friendship was strictly spiritual:* of the soul, psychic, psychological, mental, cerebral, inner, innermost; moral, unworldly, unfleshly, platonic. **3.** *He devoted himself to a spiritual life:* religious, holy, godly, pious, devotional, divine, ecclesiastical, priestly, Christian, sanctified, churchy, celestial, heavenly; blessed, hallowed, consecrated, sacrosanct. —**Ant.** 1 physical, earthly, material, corporeal. 2 fleshly, bodily, physical, carnal, sensuous. 3 earthly, temporal, secular, lay, worldly; atheistic, sacrilegious.

spit[1] *v.* **1.** *Don't spit on the sidewalk. The baby spit applesauce on his bib:* expectorate, spew, eject; slobber, drool, slaver, froth, foam, dribble. **2.** *The pan spit grease all over the stove. The butter was spitting furiously:* spew, spatter, throw out, eject, shower, scatter; pop, hiss, sputter. **3.** *He spat out angry words at his tormentors:* fling, eject, throw, express violently; hiss, shriek. —*n.* **4.** *Wipe the spit off the child's chin:* saliva, sputum, spittle, drool.

spit[2] *n.* **1.** *Put the meat on the spit:* turnspit, rod, skewer, brochette. **2.** *We went fishing off the end of the spit:* long narrow point of land, bar, peninsula, sandbank, headland, promontory, long shoal; atoll, reef.

spite *n.* **1.** *He tripped her out of spite, not accidentally:* malice, gall, hatred, hate, vindictiveness, bitterness, ill will, venom, maliciousness, resentment, malignity, animosity, animus, malev-olence, hostility, odium, antipathy, loathing, grudge, enmity, rancor, revengefulness, vengeance, vengefulness, detestation, bad blood; meanness, nastiness. —*v.* **2.** *You came late just to spite me!:* treat maliciously, annoy, humiliate, mortify, pain, injure, misuse, hurt, wound, ill-treat; sting, gall, slap in the face, provoke, irk, vex, harass, nettle, put out, irritate. —**Ant.** 1 kindness, kindliness, love, benevolence. 2 please, help, aid, assist, support, serve.

spiteful *adj.* *The story she spread about us was purely spiteful:* malicious, hateful, vicious, evil, malevolent, wicked, hostile, vindictive, rancorous, antagonistic, vengeful, unforgiving, acrimonious, merciless. —**Ant.** loving, affectionate, altruistic, kind, considerate.

spitefulness *n.* *Spitefulness marked her conduct:* spite, backbiting, backstabbing, belittlement, calumny, defamation, denigration, depreciation, detraction, disparagement, malice, obloquy, slander, aspersion.

splash *v.* **1.** *The diver splashed water all over the sunbathers:* splatter, spatter, shower, scatter, slosh, dash, fling; spread, strew, bestrew, cast, plash, disperse. **2.** *The piglets splashed around in the muddy pen:* plunge, paddle, wallow, welter, bathe, swash. **3.** *He splashed his shirt with paint:* bespatter, spatter, splatter, shower, sprinkle, splotch, besmirch, soil, stain, daub, smear, streak, discolor. **4.** *The waves splashed against the rocks:* wash, dash, hit, buffet, surge, toss, break, strike, smack, batter. **5.** *The outbreak of war was splashed across the television screens:* show prominently, blazon, broadcast. —*n.* **6.** *Splashes from the oars soaked his jacket:* flying liquid, spattering, splattering, shower. **7.** *The news made quite a splash around here:* stir, commotion, ado, sensation, uproar; impact, effect.

splay *v.* **1.** *He splayed his fingers on the floor to do a handstand:* extend, stretch out, spread out. —*adj.* **2.** *Ducks have splay feet:* spread out, broad, outspread, fan-shaped, fanlike; turned outward. **3.** *The tumbledown shack has a splay roof:* crooked, awry, askew, irregular, distorted, warped, tilted, aslant, sloping, inclined, slanted, slanting; awkward, clumsy. —**Ant.** 1 narrow, compress. 2 narrow; straight. 3 flat, straight, level, even, symmetrical.

spleen *n.* *He was upset and vented his spleen on his wife:* bad temper, rancor, spite, peevishness, spitefulness, venom, bile, gall, acrimony, animosity, animus, malice, malevolence, ill hu-

mor, ill will, bitterness, enmity, resentment, hatred, vexation, hostility, irritability, anger. —**Ant.** cheerfulness, happiness, good humor, joy.

splendid *adj.* **1.** *The queen wore splendid jewels. This is a splendid house:* beautiful, magnificent, splendorous, splendiferous, flashing, costly, superb, gorgeous, resplendent, dazzling, glittering, effulgent, brilliant; rich, ornate, gleaming; grand, sumptuous, palatial, majestic, elegant, imposing, regal, royal, stately, glorious. **2.** *His reputation as a statesman is splendid:* exalted, lofty, high, august, noble, elevated, illustrious, eminent, distinguished, peerless, imposing, glorious, preeminent, brilliant, surpassing. **3.** *That's a splendid painting:* excellent, exceptional, outstanding, estimable, brilliant, surpassing, transcendent, marvelous, admirable, rare, fine, remarkable, terrific, wonderful. —**Ant.** 1 plain, somber, tawdry, poor; beggarly, squalid. 2 inglorious, ignoble, mean, low, sordid, tarnished, ignominious. 3 poor, ordinary, mediocre, unexceptional, unremarkable, mediocre, unexciting.

splendor *n.* **1.** *The splendor of the jewels made my eyes blink. White teeth enhance the splendor of her smile:* brilliance, dazzle, luminosity, light, luster, gleam, sheen, fire, glitter, burnish, shine, luminousness, radiance, luster, effulgence, resplendence, irradiance, incandescence, intensity. **2.** *We were dazzled by the splendor of the royal wedding. The splendor of the Grand Canyon is incomparable:* pomp, grandeur, gorgeousness, glory, resplendence, brilliance, beauty, magnificence, opulence, stateliness; sublimity, augustness, nobility; preeminence, renown. —**Ant.** 1 dullness, paleness, pallidness, drabness. 2 plainness, dullness, drabness.

splenetic *adj.* *The splenetic manager undermined their morale:* spleenish, spleeny, irritable, peevish, spiteful, vexatious, irascible, testy, fretful, touchy, edgy, petulant, snappish, waspish, cross, choleric. —**Ant.** moderate, temperate.

splice *v.* *Can you splice the broken ends of the rope?:* interweave, braid together, knit, plait, intertwine, dovetail, interlace, interconnect, connect, merge, unite, graft; join together, wed. —**Ant.** cut, break, sever.

splinter *n.* **1.** *Pull the splinter out with a tweezer:* sliver, fragment, shiver, chip, needle. —*v.* **2.** *The carpenter splintered the wood when he drove in the nail:* sliver, split, shiver, shatter, crumble, disintegrate, pulverize, smash, break up; fly apart, fragment; chip, fracture; explode.

split *v.* **1.** *Split the pineapple before peeling it. The board split as I sawed it:* divide lengthwise, bisect, halve; cleave, rive, hew; break, crack, snap. **2.** *The strike split the union members into angry factions:* divide, disunite, rupture, part, sever, come between, set at odds, sow dissension, set against, segregate, alienate; disagree, differ, diverge, part company. **3.** *When he bent over, he split his pants. The water pressure split the pipe:* tear, tear asunder, become torn; sunder, break, burst, rive, be riven, part, rupture, divide, break apart, dissever; shiver, splinter, fracture, snap, crack, give way. **4.** *The robbers split the loot evenly:* share, parcel out, divide, divvy up, apportion, disperse, portion, allocate, partition, dispense, dole, deal, distribute, allot, mete, subdivide. **—n. 5.** *Can you mend this split in my jacket?:* tear, rift, rent, breach, cleft, splitting, separation; break, crack, fissure, fracture, opening. **6.** *A split in the party could lose us the election:* rupture, breach, cleavage, disunion, rift, break, schism, dissension, cleavage, division; quarrel, divorce, disassociation, falling out, difference, divergence, disagreement, alienation, estrangement, parting of the ways. **—adj. 7.** *This split material is useless. A schizophrenic is sometimes said to have a split personality:* torn, severed, rent, ripped, riven; broken, segmented, ruptured, dissevered, splintered, fractured, cracked; divided, separated, dual, two-fold; mixed, varied; undecided, ambivalent. **—Ant.** 1–3 unite, join. 6 union, merger, junction, agreement, connection. 7 whole, unbroken, sound.

splurge v. **1.** *Let's splurge and have champagne!:* indulge oneself, be extravagant, throw caution to the winds, *Informal* live it up, shoot the works. **—n. 2.** *He'll regret that jewelry-buying splurge when he receives the bill:* indulgence, self-indulgence, binge, spree, bender; showy display, showing off.

splutter v. **1.** *She spluttered a nervous apology:* sputter, stammer, stutter, mumble, jabber, gibber, hem and haw, stumble; bluster. **2.** *The log was spluttering in the fireplace:* spit, hiss, seethe, sputter; spew, burst, spray, spatter, expectorate, slobber.

spoil v. **1.** *She spoiled the soup with too much salt. The auto accident spoiled her beauty:* ruin, botch, mess up, foul up, mar, bungle, impair, damage, muddle, blemish, flaw, blight, disrupt, disfigure, mutilate, destroy, harm, injure, deface. **2.** *Food spoils more quickly without preservatives:* go bad, decay, rot, taint, become tainted, sour, putrefy, decompose, addle, deteriorate, mold, mildew, turn. **3.** *He spoiled his son by giving him too much money:* overindulge, pamper, overgratify, coddle, mollycoddle, baby, humor. **—Ant.** 1 enhance, improve. 2 preserve, conserve, save. 3 deprive, overtax, discipline.

spoils n. pl. *To the victor go the spoils!:* benefits, prizes, loot, booty, plunder, swag, pickings, bounty, quarry; profits, take, acquisitions; perquisites, comforts, amenities; patronage; *Slang* haul.

spoken adj. *The spoken, not the written word, appealed to us:* verbal, voiced, oral, articulate, lingual, uttered.

spokesman n. *Through his spokesman the ambassador welcomed us to the embassy:* spokesperson, spokeswoman, deputy, mouthpiece, delegate, representative, press agent, public relations representative, P.R. man, negotiator, middleman, agent, surrogate, proxy, protagonist.

sponge v. **1.** *Sponge the wound with an antiseptic before bandaging it:* swab, wash, rub,

mop, moisten, clean, cleanse; blot, towel, dry. **2.** *Informal He eats well by sponging off friends:* leech, panhandle, obtain free, borrow, bum, cadge, impose on, live on, *Slang* freeload, mooch, scrounge.

sponger n. *He's a sponger who borrows but never returns:* cadger, freeloader, leech, sponge, bloodsucker, barnacle, borrower; *Slang* moocher, scrounger, deadbeat.

spongy adj. *We walked on the spongy forest floor:* elastic, springy, cushiony, resilient, rubbery, soft, yielding, absorbent.

sponsor n. **1.** *A large department store is the sponsor of the annual Christmas parade. The boy needs a sponsor to get him into the fraternity:* promoter, financer, backer, advertiser; patron, angel, protector, guarantor, supporter, defender, advocate, proponent, partisan, champion, upholder, guardian. **—v. 2.** *Our local legislator sponsored the new environmental bill. Who will sponsor your admission into the club?:* back, finance, advocate, promote; champion, support, guarantee, warranty, uphold, stand up for, vouch for; set up, start out, underwrite.

spontaneous adj. *Her remarks were spontaneous and obviously not planned:* unpremeditated, improvised, impulsive, impetuous, off the cuff, ad lib, extemporaneous; natural, unstudied, uncontrived, ingenuous; extempore, impromptu, unprompted, offhand, unconstrained, voluntary, unplanned, free, gratuitous; unbidden, willing, independent, automatic, unhesitating, instinctive. **—Ant.** premeditated, studied, contrived, forced, planned, calculated, involuntary, constrained.

spoof n. **1.** *The story was really a spoof of Hemingway's style:* parody, takeoff, burlesque, *British* sendup, satire, travesty, caricature, joke; *Slang* kidding, joshing, ribbing. **—v. 2.** *The comedian loved to spoof the Presidents:* satirize, lampoon, parody, caricature, take off on, twit; *Slang* kid, josh.

spook n. **1.** *She imagined all sorts of spooks in the empty house:* apparition, ghost, phantom, haunt, specter, bogey, shade, goblin, hobgoblin, spirit, shadow. **—v. 2.** *It really spooked me when the bridge began to tremble:* frighten, alarm, startle, scare, unnerve, terrorize, terrify; unsettle, disquiet, intimidate, disturb. **—Ant.** 2 calm, pacify, soothe, relax.

sporadic adj. *We've had only sporadic snow flurries this month:* irregular, spotty, scattered, sparse, spasmodic, fitful, widely spaced, now and then, occasional, infrequent, periodic, fragmentary, intermittent, discontinuous, few and far between, meager, few, thin, scarce, rare, isolated, uncommon; haphazard, random. **—Ant.** continuous, regular, steady, constant.

sport n. **1.** *Tennis is a popular sport:* athletic pastime, physical activity, game, competition, contest, athletics; diversion, recreation, fun, distraction, divertissement, entertainment, amusement, play, relaxation, hobby. **2.** *The kids' teasing was only sport:* play, jest, jesting, pleasantry, skylarking, trifling, kidding, jollity, gaiety, frolic, mirth, hilarity, antics, lark, fun; joviality, merrymaking, festivity; raillery, ridicule, mockery, scoffing, derision, chaff, badinage, persiflage, depreciation. **3.** *The pompous man was sport for the unfriendly crowd:* laughingstock, monkey, butt, fair game, scapegoat, buffoon, joke, goat. **4.** *(Informal) Dick's a sport--he'll try anything:* game person, gambler, daredevil. **—v. 5.** *The colts were sporting in the meadow:* play, disport, amuse oneself, play games; make merry, dally, caper, gambol, revel, frisk, trip, cavort, frolic, rollick, lark, romp, skylark. **6.** *He sported with her affection:* toy, trifle, take advantage of, play, be frivolous, dally, play cat-and-mouse, deal lightly, treat cavalierly, take in, illtreat, abuse, misuse. **7.** *He sports an ivory-handled cane these days:* display, exhibit, show off, flourish; carry, bear. **—Ant.** 1 business, job, duty, work. 2 cruelty, seriousness, respect, adoration. 4 sissy, coward, stick-in-the-mud. 5 work, toil.

sporting *adj. The shop sold sporting goods. He had a sporting chance to win the raffle:* athletic; reasonable, fair. **—Ant.** unfair, unsporting.

sportive *adj.* **1.** *They were in a sportive mood after dinner:* playful, frolicsome, jesting, jocose, merry, jocular, gay, sprightly, frisky. **2.** *He made several sportive remarks:* joking, prankish, facetious. **—Ant.** sober, serious.

spot *n.* **1.** *That's a coffee spot on your tie:* stain, mark, speck, splotch, smudge, soil, blot, daub, smirch, fleck, patch, speckle, blotch, dot, flyspeck, discoloration, blemish. **2.** *The dishonorable discharge was a spot on his reputation:* disgrace, stain, blemish, brand, taint, blot, defect, discredit, flaw, stigma, slur, imputation, aspersion, reproach. **3.** *We're going to build our home on this spot. The swimming hole is a popular spot:* place, locality, locale, location, point, site, tract, situation, space, seat, locus, premises, position; part, region, district, area, territory, quarter, neighborhood, station, section, sector. **4.** *Informal All these expenses coming at once have put me in a spot:* bad situation, difficulty, plight, dilemma, fix, bind, predicament. **—v. 5.** *Wine spotted the tablecloth:* stain, smudge, smirch, soil, sully, blot, dot, discolor, daub, speck, grime, blemish, smear, speckle, sprinkle, spatter, splash. **6.** *I finally spotted a redcap:* locate, see, pick out, recognize, discover, light on, espy, spy, discern, detect.

spotless *adj.* **1.** *The house was left in spotless condition:* clean, unsoiled, unspotted, immaculate, pristine, unstained, unmarred, flawless, unsullied, untarnished, pure, perfect, unblemished, gleaming, shining, untainted, snowy. **2.** *His military record was spotless:* perfect, unflawed, flawless, untarnished, immaculate, unblemished, untainted, unsullied, faultless, pure, clean, stainless, unmarred; impeccable, irreproachable, unexceptionable. **—Ant.** 1 filthy, dirty, messy, soiled. 2 tarnished, flawed, marred, blemished, tainted; reprehensible.

spotlight *n. The spotlight was on the newcomer:* attention, interest, public attention, publicity, center stage, light, floodlight, limelight.

spotty *adj.* **1.** *She has a spotty complexion from too much sun:* mottled, full of spots, dappled, spotted, flecked, freckled, variegated; blotchy, splotchy, pimply, broken out. **2.** *His work is so spotty he can't hold a job:* uneven, irregular, unmethodical, fitful, erratic, random, unsystematic, disorganized, variable, sporadic, intermittent, episodic, spasmodic, unsteady, capricious, desultory; inconstant, wavering, unreliable, undependable, uncertain. **—Ant.** 1 smooth, unmottled; clear. 2 even, regular, methodical, systematic, uniform, constant, dependable.

spouse *n. Both spouses paid income taxes:* mate, husband, wife, companion, helpmate, partner.

spout *v.* **1.** *The whale spouted water from the blowhole on his back. Lava spouted from the volcano:* spurt, discharge, emit forcibly, squirt, issue, spray, pour out, disgorge, vomit, erupt, spew, eject, expel, gush, jet, stream, flow, surge, shoot, well, exude. **2.** *Informal He spouts off about things he knows nothing about:* speak pompously, carry on, go on, pontificate, harangue, gush, hold forth, rant, bluster. **—n. 3.** *Something's clogging the spout of the tea kettle:* outlet, vent, mouth, pipe, nose, tube, nozzle, lip, conduit, trough, snout, channel, waterspout, beak, sluice. **4.** *The children ran through the spout of the fountain:* jet, spurt, shoot, stream, fountain, gush, spray.

sprain *v. He sprained his hand playing tennis:* strain, overstrain, wrench, injure, twist.

sprawl *v.* **1.** *Her writing sprawled all over the page:* spread out, straggle, meander, stretch out, gush out, reach out, wind, extend, branch. **2.** *Don't sprawl at the table:* slouch, stretch out, loll, flop, spread-eagle, slump, languish, recline, lean, sit awkwardly, lie awkwardly, lounge.

spray[1] *n.* **1.** *The spray from the fountain kept us back. Perfume spray scented the air:* droplets, mist, splash, moisture, vapor. **2.** *The shower spray is broken:* sprayer, nozzle, sprinkler, vaporizer, atomizer, syringe. **3.** *The running boy kicked up a spray of sand:* barrage, shower, burst, fusillade, volley, discharge. **—v. 4.** *She sprayed hairspray in her eye by mistake:* discharge, atomize, scatter, disperse, shower, drizzle, sprinkle, spatter; moisten, dampen; coat, treat.

spray[2] *n. A spray of mistletoe hung over the doorway:* sprig, bouquet, nosegay, shoot, switch, twig, bough, posy, blossom.

spread *v.* **1.** *Let's spread the blanket under that tree:* stretch out, open, unfold, untwine, unroll, unfurl, extend. **2.** *She spread her toys all over the room. Their friendship spread over many years:* scatter, be scattered, strew, bestrew, sprinkle, overspread, cast, distribute, diffuse, shed, be shed, disperse; extend, stretch, cover. **3.** *The radio spread the news as soon as it happened. The fire spread rapidly:* publish, communicate, circulate, divulge, make known, disseminate, proclaim, broadcast, propagate, make public, air, repeat, report, bruit, blazon, vent, noise abroad, publicize, herald, announce, distribute, issue, ventilate, trumpet, declare, promulgate, whisper about, radiate, diffuse; proliferate, penetrate, pervade, permeate; overrun, suffuse, advance. **4.** *Spread the wax thinly on the floor:* apply, coat, lay, smear, besmear, overlay, bedaub, overspread, cover, cloak, pave; spray, spatter; plaster. —*n.* **5.** *The spread of the disease frightened the villagers:* spreading, increase, expansion, dispersion, enlargement, diffusion, dissemination, advance, circulation, amplification, radiation, pervasion, permeation, suffusion, proliferation. **6.** *Those moose antlers have a spread of five feet. The spread of the prairies was breathtaking:* stretch, reach, extent, extension, span, scope, range, distance, breadth, length, area, field, width, circuit, compass; expanse, open land, sweep, tract. **7.** *Informal The caterers prepared a huge spread:* feast, array of food, table, banquet. **8.** *The wedding had a big spread in the* Times: notice, coverage, write-up, report, article, account, story; printed advertisement. —**Ant.** 1 fold, roll up, wind, furl. 2 collect, pile up, gather. 3 suppress, conceal, hush; localize, confine; diminish, die, abate. 5 halting, check, abatement, diminishing.

spree *n.* *He was hung over for days after his spree. She went on a buying spree:* carouse, carousal, revel, revelry, wassail, bacchanal, orgy, debauch; bout, *Informal* binge, bender, drunk; saturnalia, splurge, fling, toot.

sprightly *adj.* *He's unusually sprightly for a man of 85:* animated, lively, alive, lighthearted, playful, vivacious, gay, buoyant, sportive, blithesome, blithe, spry, jolly, chipper, cheery, merry, jovial, active, dashing, jaunty, frolicsome, cheerful, breezy, keen, spirited, dynamic, nimble, brisk, energetic, agile. —**Ant.** glum, lethargic, lifeless, sluggish, phlegmatic.

spring *v.* **1.** *He sprang out of bed when the alarm went off:* leap, bound, rise suddenly, jump, dart, vault, lunge, bounce, start, hop. **2.** *Taking the bait will spring the trap:* release, trigger. **3.** *Oil wells sprang up all over Texas. Shouts of protest sprang from the crowd:* rise, shoot up, arise, appear, mushroom, crop out; sprout, burgeon, pop, loom, start up; pour, issue suddenly, burst forth, stream, flow, well, surge, rush, break forth, gush, jet, spout, spurt, shoot, emanate. **4.** *I can't believe that man springs from the apes. Lassen Peak sprang from a volcanic eruption:* descend, be brought forth, emanate, originate, come forth, be descended, proceed, derive, be derived, come into existence, stem, sprout, start, flow, arise, rise, germinate, begin, commence, issue, come, result, ensue. —*n.* **5.** *The dancer's high springs dazzled the audience:* jump, leap, saltation, vault, bound, hop, caper, bounce, gambol, lunge; entrechat. **6.** *Fine weather can put a spring in your step. There's no spring left in this tennis ball:* springiness, buoyancy, elasticity, kick, bounce, resiliency, elastic force, flexibility, stretchability, reflex, stretch, recoil. **7.** *The spring was too cold for swimming:* small stream, pool, hot spring, well, waterhole, watering place, fount, fountain, wellspring; baths, spa. —**Ant.** 1 crawl, creep;

land, alight, drop, fall. 4 end, finish, terminate. 6 inflexibility.

sprinkle *v.* **1.** *Sprinkle some powdered sugar on the cake:* dust, powder, scatter, dash, strew, spread, bestrew; squirt, spray, water, moisten, spatter, splash, shower, diffuse, splatter. **2.** *Take your umbrella in case it sprinkles:* shower, rain lightly, drizzle.

sprinkling *n.* *The recipe calls for only a sprinkling of dill:* sprinkle, smattering, modicum, droplet, minimum, dash, drop, soupçon, hint, touch, pinch.

sprint *v.* **1.** *The players sprinted across the football field:* run, race, dash, tear, whisk, whiz, shoot, scamper, dart, rush. —*n.* **2.** *He crossed the finish line with a sprint:* dash, burst, spurt, kick. —**Ant.** 1 stroll, saunter, walk, creep, crawl. 2 walk, stroll.

sprout *v.* **1.** *New buds sprouted from the pussy willow:* shoot forth, begin to grow, come up, burgeon, spring up, grow, come up, bud, bloom, flower, blossom, put forth; spread, wax, thrive, multiply, germinate. —*n.* **2.** *Bean sprouts are very healthful to eat:* shoot, offshoot, sprig, outgrowth, germinated seed.

spruce *adj.* *You look so spruce in your new suit:* trim, tidy, neat, smart, sharp, chic, dapper, natty; spick-and-span, shipshape, well-groomed, kempt, elegant, *French* soigné. —**Ant.** sloppy, messy, seedy, shabby, tacky.

spry *adj.* *She's very spry for a woman her age:* lively, sprightly, animated, frisky, lightfooted, supple, active, nimble, brisk, agile, deft; spirited, jaunty, sportive, full of life, buoyant, vigorous, energetic, playful, chipper, vivacious, hearty, hale, full of spirit, quick. —**Ant.** doddering, slow, inactive, sluggish, lethargic.

spunk *n.* *Informal It took a lot of spunk to brave that sea:* guts, pluck, spirit, grit, sand, nerve, courage, boldness, daring, bravery, mettle, fire, pepper, ginger, salt, gumption, heart, backbone, feistiness. —**Ant.** cowardice, timidity, fear, squeamishness.

spur *n.* **1.** *The cowboy dug his spurs into the horse:* boot spike, goad, prod. **2.** *The encouragement was a helpful spur to his ego:* stimulus, incitement, inducement, incentive, stimulant, stimulation, goad, excitant, whet, provocation, impetus, prick, instigation, whip, fillip, motive, impulse, encouragement. **3.** *This railroad spur connects with the city:* branch, arm, wing, leg, fork; tributary, feeder; siding. —*v.* **4.** *Her loving care spurred his recovery:* stimulate, hasten, encourage; goad, prod. —**Ant.** 2 discouragement, hindrance, restraint, check, curb, deterrent.

spurious *adj.* *Imagine paying all that money for a spurious Rembrandt!:* not genuine, fake, forged, counterfeit, sham, imitation, unauthentic, bogus, phony, fraudulent; simulated, feigned, mock, make-believe; false, hollow, fallacious, faulty, unsound, specious, illegitimate. —**Ant.** genuine, real, authentic; sound, legitimate, solid.

spurn *v.* *She spurned his love:* reject, turn down, scorn, disdain, refuse, repulse, repudiate, repel, look down upon, treat with contempt, contemn, cast aside, dismiss, decline, sneer at, scoff at, disparage, trample upon, mock, flout, coldshoulder, rebuff, slight, turn up one's nose at, snub. **—Ant.** welcome, embrace, accept, encourage.

spurt *v.* **1.** *Blood spurted from the wound:* spout, jet, gush, issue, burst, spring out, stream, flow, pour out, surge, shoot, squirt, spray; emit, disgorge, discharge, vomit forth. **2.** *Our horse spurted ahead just at the finish line:* speed, sprint, burst, lunge, tear, scoot, whiz, spring, dart, dash, rush. *—n.* **3.** *A spurt of water came out of the hose:* rush, jet, gush, stream, shoot, spout, sudden flow, squirt, fountain, ejection, spray. **4.** *He threw the glass in a spurt of anger:* explosion, eruption, burst, outbreak, outburst, flash, outpouring, rush, access, gust. **—Ant.** 1 drip, ooze. 2 creep, crawl, dawdle, lag. 3 oozing, drip, dribble, drizzle.

spy *n.* **1.** *Foreign spies followed him to the airport:* espionage agent, secret agent, intelligence agent, operative, undercover man, Mata Hari, fifth columnist; saboteur, agent provocateur; informer. *—v.* **2.** *Government agents spied on the enemy submarines:* watch secretly, keep watch, engage in surveillance, shadow, scout, reconnoi-ter; snoop, pry, peep. **3.** *The hunter spied a rabbit in the bush:* see, observe, discover, descry, glimpse, spot, catch sight of, sight, make out, detect, recognize, perceive, behold, notice, find, view, discern.

squabble *v.* **1.** *They squabbled over who would pay the check:* wrangle, quarrel, bicker, clash, dispute, differ, spat; have words, argue, bandy words, set to, lock horns, brawl, row, fight, contest, contend, battle, war, tiff. *—n.* **2.** *Their squabble was over a woman:* spat, quarrel, tiff, dispute, difference, dissension, fight, disagreement, scrap; contention, words, argument, row, run-in, set-to, altercation, controversy. **—Ant.** 1 agree, concur, assent. 2 agreement, concurrence.

squad *n.* *The squad regrouped the next day:* squadron, band, crew, company, force, gang, team, troop, group.

squalid *adj.* *These squalid slums breed disease:* unclean, foul, dirty, filthy, decayed, slovenly, reeking, nasty, sloppy, disheveled, slatternly, horrid, run-down, tumble-down, deteriorated, dilapidated, ramshackle; degraded, wretched, sordid, rotten, miserable, poverty-stricken, abject, mean, shabby, battered, broken-down. **—Ant.** clean, attractive, well-kept, tidy.

squalor *n.* *The poor man lives in unbelievable squalor:* wretchedness, foulness, filth, squalidness, uncleanness, dirtiness, dirt, nastiness, uncleanliness; ugliness, degraded condition, sordidness, meanness, grubbiness, abjectness, poverty, seediness, dinginess, misery, neglect. **—Ant.** cleanliness, beauty, fineness, splendor, luxury, nobility.

squander *v.* *Don't squander your money on such a cheaply made dress:* waste, throw away, misspend, dissipate, fritter away, misuse, *Slang* blow; lavish, run through, exhaust, be prodigal with, spend, spend like water; consume, deplete. **—Ant.** save, conserve, hoard.

square *n.* **1.** *The sides of a square are of equal length:* quadrangle, quadrate, quadrilateral, box. **2.** *The meeting was held in the village square:* plaza, place, large intersection, *British* circus; block; park; marketplace; green, common. **3.** *Slang She won't go out with that square:* dull person, conservative, stick-in-the-mud, fogy; prig, prude; jerk, cornball, hick, apple knocker, clodhopper. *—v.* **4.** *Square the material in four parts:* reduce to square form, block out, quadrate, set at right angles; form into right angles. **5.** *That touchdown squared the score. This payment will square my debt:* even, make even, even up, balance; pay off, settle up, close, discharge, liquidate. **6.** *Can you square those crooked pictures?:* align, make straight, straighten, even out, make level, make even; flatten, plane, smooth. **7.** *Be certain your alibi squares with mine:* agree, tally, harmonize, blend, accord, fit, conform, match, correspond, jibe, be in unison, cohere, be congruous, concur, fall in, equal. **8.** *Did you square your differences with your brother?:* settle, resolve, reconcile, heal, rectify, adjust, set right, reach agreement on, compose, arbitrate, patch up, arrange, mend, straighten out, mediate, clear up. *—adj.* **9.** *Company policy on trade-ins is fair and square. Are you being absolutely square with me?:* honest, just, equitable; truthful, candid, straightforward. **—Ant.** 3 hippie, hipster, mod, sophisticate. 6 make crooked, distort. 7 disagree, contrast, contradict. 8 entangle, prolong, worsen.

squash *v.* **1.** *She sat on his hat and squashed it:* smash, crush, flatten, press flat, compress, pulp, mash, ram down, squish; squeeze, jam, cram, crowd; compact, concentrate. **2.** *The wage freeze squashed his hope of a raise:* put down, quell, quash, prostrate, crush, suppress, repress, dispel, squelch, dissipate, trample, upset, flatten, level, undermine, overthrow; destroy, annihilate, obliterate. **—Ant.** 2 aid, promote, enhance, support.

squat *v.* **1.** *If you squat behind the table he won't see you:* crouch, bend the knees, sit on the heels; kneel, *Informal* hunker; cringe, cower, lie low, shrink. **2.** *The migrant workers squatted on the unused farm:* settle without title, dwell, establish oneself, set up housekeeping, move in, make a home, take up residence, encamp, locate. *—adj.* **3.** *Her body is too squat to be attractive:* dumpy, stumpy, stocky, chunky, stubby, pudgy, thickset, square. **—Ant.** 3 lanky, tall, slim, reedy, willowy.

squawk *v.* **1.** *The hen squawked when the farmer took her eggs:* scream, squall, blare, screech, croak. **2.** *Slang The tenants squawked about the lack of heat:* complain, protest, grumble, gripe.

squeak *v.* *The mouse squeaked in the corner. The rusty hinges of the door squeaked when we opened it:* screech, squeal, shriek, grate, creak; cheep, peep, cry, shrill, chirp, yelp.

squeal *v.* **1.** *The puppy squealed when I*

stepped on his tail: wail, yelp, cry, whine, shrill, screech, shriek, peep, cheep, scream, yell, bawl, squeak. **2.** *Slang One of the thieves squealed to the police:* inform, turn informer, betray accomplices, *Slang* blab, sing, fink.

squeamish *adj.* **1.** *She's too squeamish to see a peep show:* priggish, puritanical, prudish, modest, prim, proper, easily shocked, demure, fastidious, straitlaced, coy, sanctimonious, mincing, finicky, finicking, finical, fussy. **2.** *That movie is too violent for someone so squeamish:* easily nauseated, qualmish, easily disgusted, weak-stomached, delicate, sick, sickish, queasy, nauseous. **—Ant.** 1 bold, immodest, brazen, brash. 2 coarse, tough, strong-stomached.

squeeze *v.* **1.** *Squeeze the walnuts together to crack them:* press, compress, clutch. **2.** *He squeezed the last bit from the toothpaste tube:* extract, press out, force out; elicit, wring, wrest, wrench; pry, pull out, tear out, draw out, withdraw, extricate; extort, compel, coerce. **3.** *We squeezed our whole party into the elevator:* crowd, cram, pack, jam, stuff, thrust, cramp, wedge; concentrate, compact, consolidate. **4.** *Mother squeezed me tightly when I left:* hug, embrace, clasp, hold. **5.** *Can you squeeze through that line of cars?:* press, push, force one's way, wedge, elbow, crowd, shove, shoulder, ram, drive, jostle, butt, edge. **—n. 6.** *He gave her hand a squeeze. I managed to park, but it was a tight squeeze:* clasp, grasp, grip, hold, embrace, hug, clutch; pressure, crushing, compression, pinching, constriction; narrowing, crowding, stricture, wedge; bottleneck; passage, defile.

squelch *v.* **1.** *The police squelched the uprising before it became violent:* crush, put down, squash, quash, smash, trample on, abort, suppress; quell, silence, hush, quiet. **—n. 2.** *That was a perfect squelch!:* retort, riposte, crushing reply, put-down, silencer. **—Ant.** 1 incite, encourage, provoke.

squire *n.* **1.** *The squire and his guests went foxhunting:* country gentleman, landowner, rich farmer, planter; member of the gentry, lord of the manor. **2.** *The ladies and their squires formed for the promenade:* escort, consort, attendant; gallant, cavalier, date, companion, *Informal* boyfriend. **—v. 3.** *He squired her around town that summer:* escort, attend, court, accompany, take, date; chaperon, chauffeur.

squirm *v.* **1.** *The patient squirmed in pain:* turn, twist, contort, wriggle, writhe, wiggle, jerk, bend, twitch, pitch, toss. **2.** *He squirmed with embarrassment:* show discomfort, be restless, fidget, writhe, shift, shrink, blench, be upset, smart, flinch, wince, sweat, agonize; flounder.

squirt *v.* **1.** *Juice from the grapefruit squirted in my eye:* spray, spurt, shoot, gush, spout, splash, discharge. **2.** *The elephant squirted water on the children:* spray, shower, spatter, sprinkle, splash, dash, besprinkle; shoot, discharge. **—n. 3.** *The squirt of the watergun took me by surprise:* spray, jet, spurt, stream. **4.** *Slang He's nothing but a little squirt!:* insignificant person, punk, piker, runt.

stab *v.* **1.** *The killer stabbed his victim with a carving knife:* jab, pierce, stick, spear, bayonet, impale, gore, wound, gash, cut, spike, lance, run through, thrust through, knife, transfix, lacerate, prick, spit, gouge, slash, cleave. **2.** *Her bitter words stabbed him:* wound, hurt, injure the feelings of, pierce, cut, pain. **—n. 3.** *The stab missed his heart:* jab, thrust, lunge, dagger, stroke, cut, prick, slash, wound, laceration, gash. **4.** *I felt a sudden stab of remorse:* pang, prick, painful sensation, ache, sting, twinge, bite, shiver, thrill, qualm. **5.** *Informal Just make a stab at writing a poem:* try, attempt, effort, pass; trial, essay, endeavor; shot, go. **—Ant.** 2 soothe, assuage, ease, comfort, please, delight.

stability *n.* **1.** *Her stability enables her to face almost any problem:* steadiness, constancy, solidness, soundness, poise, aplomb, balance, equilibrium, evenness, reliability, stableness, steadfastness. **2.** *I feel sure of the stability of the old staircase:* solidity, soundness, firmness, steadiness, solidness, sturdiness, security, fixedness. **3.** *The young nation has not yet attained political stability:* permanence, fixity, firmness, unchangeableness, abidingness, durability, changelessness, continuity. **—Ant.** 1 instability, inconstancy, weakness, unsteadiness, unreliability, irresolution. 2 frailty, instability, fragility, unsteadiness, weakness. 3 instability, impermanence, changeableness.

stabilize *v.* *Their income had stabilized the following year:* balance, equalize, firm, fix, maintain, settle, steady, stiffen, support, sustain, uphold, ballast, counterbalance; maintain, preserve, prop, secure.

stable *adj.* **1.** *He finally built a stable business operation:* established, reliable, durable, sound, secure, well-grounded, indissoluble, solid. **2.** *The building has a stable foundation:* sound, sturdy, solid, steady, fixed, stationary, firm, safe, secure, immovable, anchored, moored. **3.** *Our country has a stable government:* fixed, unchangeable, firm, unchanging, steady, abiding, persisting, enduring, constant, uniform, even. **4.** *John is a stable employee:* reliable, steady, steadfast, resolute, true, staunch, loyal, stalwart, dependable, unwavering, firm, constant, faithful, unfaltering. **—Ant.** 1–4 unstable. 1 impermanent, shaky, unsound, unsteady. 2 frail, shaky, unsteady, unsubstantial, unsound. 3 changeable, alterable, variable, shaky, wavering. 4 unreliable, unsteady, mercurial, volatile, erratic.

stack *n.* **1.** *Let's hide behind this stack of hay. They left me with a stack of dirty dishes:* pile, heap, bank, sheaf, mass, rick, clump, mound, mountain, bunch, load; accumulation, aggregation, amassment, batch, bundle. **2.** *Santa will have a tight squeeze if he comes down that stack:* smokestack, chimney, flue, funnel. **—v. 3.** *Stack the chips in equal piles:* heap, pile, arrange vertically, mound, bank; gather, bunch, lump, amass, assemble, batch, hoard, accumulate.

stadium *n.* *The stadium was packed for the homecoming game:* arena, bowl, coliseum, amphitheater, circus, ballpark, field, park, palaestra, hippodrome, stade.

staff *n.* **1.** *The old man needed his staff to climb the hill:* cane, stick, walking stick, rod, crutch, pole, alpenstock; cudgel, wand, stave, bludgeon, billy club, bat, shillelagh; scepter. **2.** *The flag was raised only halfway up the staff:* pole, flagpole, flagstaff, support. **3.** *How many are on the hotel staff?:* force, crew, personnel, help, employees, group, cadre, team; assistants, advisors, retinue. —*v.* **4.** *How many employees will it take to staff this resort?:* make up the staff of, man, work, tend, manage, service.

stage *n.* **1.** *The rocket is in its final stage of development:* period, phase, level, step, grade. **2.** *The actor almost fell off the stage:* raised platform, raised floor, *Slang* the boards; rostrum, pulpit, podium, dais, soapbox, scaffold, stump. **3.** *The stage was his whole life:* dramatic profession, show business, theater, stage playing, acting, drama, the footlights, *Slang* the boards, show biz. **4.** *Primarily Europe was the stage for the Second World War:* spot, surroundings, scene of action, setting, locale, locality, arena, whereabouts, position, theater, location, sight, bearings. —*v.* **5.** *The city of Charleston staged* Porgy and Bess *in honor of its tricentennial:* produce, put on the stage, present, put on; act, perform, dramatize, play.

stagger *v.* **1.** *She staggered out of bed:* stumble, sway, wobble, reel, hobble, totter, lurch, shamble, blunder, waver, flounder. **2.** *A punch like that would stagger an ox:* cause to sway, cause to reel, make unsteady, stun, knock silly, totter, throw off balance. **3.** *The news of his death staggered the country:* stun, jolt, shock, nonplus, astound, astonish, shake, amaze, dumbfound, unsettle, disconcert, jar, bowl over, overwhelm, strike dumb, take away the breath of, stupefy, startle, flabbergast, bewilder, confound, give a turn, consternate. **4.** *Stagger the seats so that everyone can see:* spread out, arrange in a zigzag order; alternate, overlap, take in turns. —**Ant.** 2 steady. 3 steady, stabilize; strengthen.

stagnant *adj.* **1.** *Stagnant water is more likely to be harmful:* still, not running, not flowing, motionless, inert, lifeless, close, standing, stationary, unstirring, dead, quiet, quiescent, inactive, uncirculating; filthy, polluted, foul, tainted, putrid, putrefied, slimy, stale. **2.** *The seaside resort becomes stagnant when the tourists leave:* lifeless, inactive, dull, listless, dormant, dead, sluggish, inert, static, languid, torpid, slow, leaden, lethargic; vegetative, lazy, supine, ponderous, dronish, monotonous. —**Ant.** 1 running, flowing, moving, circulating; clean, pure, fresh, unpolluted. 2 lively, active, busy, thriving.

stagnate *v.* *The air will stagnate if we don't get some ventilation. His mind stagnated from years of solitude:* remain motionless, cease to flow, lie still, be stagnant, not stir, stand still; putrefy, become foul, become contaminated, become polluted; become sluggish, vegetate, become dull, stop developing, stop growing, go to seed, dete-

riorate, go to pot; become inactive, lie idle. —**Ant.** flow, circulate; grow, bustle.

staid *adj.* *He's too staid for such a lively young wife:* sedate, sober, settled, somber, subdued, serious, dignified, reserved, undemonstrative, solemn, stiff, quiet, earnest, demure, grave, complacent, priggish, prudish; decent, decorous, seemly, proper. —**Ant.** exuberant, jaunty, wild, indecorous, flighty, frivolous, demonstrative, playful, capricious, loose.

stain *n.* **1.** *Will that stain come off your tie?:* spot, discoloration, blemish, tarnish, blot, smudge, soil, smear, blotch, splotch, speck, mark, taint, daub, patch, smirch. **2.** *His trial for embezzlement was a stain on his family's good name:* blot, spot, brand, stigma, blemish, taint, tarnish, flaw, imputation, soil, smudge, shame, disgrace, slur, dishonor. **3.** *We need a dark stain on the floor:* tint, dye, coloring, dye-stuff, tincture. —*v.* **4.** *The tomato sauce stained the tablecloth:* spot, discolor, blemish, smirch, tarnish, blotch, sully, soil, dirty, smear, smudge, mar, spoil, grime, daub, mark, splotch, blot. **5.** *Stain the table before you varnish it:* dye, color, tint, pigment. **6.** *He stained his military record by going AWOL:* blemish, taint, disgrace, bring reproach upon, tarnish, defile, blot, blacken, impair, besmirch, foul, debase, stigmatize, dishonor, befoul, sully, drag in the mud, spoil, subvert, ruin, undermine, detract from; vilify, slander, libel, malign, discredit, denigrate, disparage. —**Ant.** 2 honor, credit, accolade. 4 clean. 6 clear, honor, enhance.

stake *n.* **1.** *One of the stakes in the fence is broken:* post, picket, pale, pole, peg, spike, stick, pile, rod, bar; column, pillar, marker, standard. **2.** *What is the stake in your poker game? In international finance the stakes are high:* money risked, hazard, bet, ante, wager, play; prize, pot, kitty, jackpot, reward, spoils, take, haul, booty, winnings, purse, grab, pickings, loot, returns. **3.** *He has a big stake in the new play:* share, investment, risk, interest, speculation, venture, hazard. **4.** *I have no stake in how the trial comes out:* personal concern, interest, involvement. —*v.* **5.** *The city engineer staked out the new school site:* mark off, delineate, mark out, outline, demarcate, define, delimit. **6.** *Stake the sweet peas securely:* brace, support, hold up, prop, stay; tie to a stake, hitch, secure, fasten, tether, trammel, moor, make fast, fetter, lash, peg down. **7.** *I'd stake my life on his honesty:* bet, wager, hazard, risk, chance, jeopardize, pawn, speculate, venture. **8.** *Informal She offered to stake me to a new coat:* stand, treat; back, finance, underwrite, sponsor, subsidize.

stale *adj.* **1.** *These old peanuts taste stale. Open the windows and get rid of this stale air:* flat, not fresh, vapid, tasteless, savorless; fusty, musty, close, stagnant. **2.** *His style of writing has become stale:* trite, banal, hackneyed, insipid, flat, vapid, dull, common, commonplace, ordinary, mediocre, humdrum, unvaried, tedious, worn-out, threadbare, prosaic, pedestrian, unimaginative, monotonous, uninteresting. **—Ant.** 1 fresh, crisp. 2 original, imaginative, varied.

stalemate *n. The stubborn negotiators reached a stalemate:* deadlock, impasse, tie, standoff, dead heat, draw; halt, blockage, standstill; dead end, cul-de-sac. **—Ant.** decision.

stalk[1] *n. Hold the flower by its stalk:* stem, shaft, column, trunk, spire, pedicel.

stalk[2] *v.* **1.** *The mugger stalked his victim. There are sharks stalking in those waters:* approach stealthily, pursue quietly, creep up on, sneak up on, track, hunt; steal, lurk, prowl; threaten, menace. **2.** *She stalked angrily out of the room:* march, strut, swagger, walk stiffly, stamp, stomp, tramp, stride. **3.** *A fear of reprisals for the uprising stalked the prison camp:* haunt, go through, hang over, pervade.

stall *n.* **1.** *The horse got out of its stall:* booth, cubicle, cell, compartment, coop, pen, confine, shed. **2.** *The fish stall hasn't opened yet:* booth, stand, arcade, shop, kiosk. **3.** *We bought a stall at the opera:* enclosed seat, box, *British* orchestra seat. *—v.* **4.** *The cows were stalled in the barn for the night:* confine, pen, put in a stall; bed down. **5.** *The strike stalled our holiday plans. The cold weather made the car stall:* stop, halt, bring to a standstill, be brought to a standstill, arrest, impede, check, paralyze, incapacitate, pull up, stop short, stop running, trammel, block, interrupt, obstruct, disable, hobble; delay, put off, postpone. **6.** *The manager stalled for time while his relief pitcher was warming up:* delay, play for time, temporize; be evasive, equivocate.

stalwart *adj.* **1.** *He's stalwart enough to lift the piano:* sturdy, robust, sound, strong, muscular, strapping, hardy, brawny, powerful, vigorous, rugged, hefty, ablebodied, hale, mighty, beefy, husky. **2.** *The stalwart captain refused to desert the ship:* valiant, bold, heroic, intrepid, courageous, stouthearted, lionhearted, indomitable, gallant, brave, valorous, manly, strong-willed, unflinching, spunky, plucky, staunch, gritty. **3.** *He demonstrated a stalwart belief in human rights:* unwavering, steadfast, staunch, stable, firm, unshakable, resolute, constant, unswerving, unflagging, unbending, intransigent, uncompromising, indomitable, unfaltering, unflinching, undeviating, persistent, unyielding, undaunted, unshrinking. **—Ant.** 1 weak, feeble, frail, infirm, puny, unsteady, shaky. 2 cowardly, fearful, timorous, faint-hearted, weak. 3 faithless, weak, shaky, flagging, deviating, halfhearted, uncertain, fragile, feeble, frail.

stamina *n. She doesn't have the stamina for the long trip:* endurance, strength of constitution, vigor, sturdiness, hardiness, staying power, vitality, stoutness, ruggedness, pith, energy, perseverance.

stammer *v. He stammered most when he was nervous:* speak with breaks and pauses, speak hesitantly, falter, stutter, stumble; sputter, hem and haw, fumble, mumble, splutter.

stamp *v.* **1.** *The horse stamped the ground nervously. She peevishly stamped her foot:* step on, stomp, thump, pound; crush, smash, tram-

ple. **2.** Usually **stamp out** *They tried to stamp out the burning leaves:* extinguish, put out, crush, put down, squelch, suppress. **3.** *The soldiers stamped noisily through the town:* tramp, stomp, clump, trudge, stalk, stride, strut, march. **4.** *The bookbinder stamped the leather with a fleur-de-lis:* print, mark, imprint, brand, impress, engrave, seal, inscribe, label. **5.** *His wild youth stamped him as the black sheep of the family:* mark, characterize, brand, tag, identify; reveal, demonstrate, betray, exhibit, distinguish, manifest, display, expose, personify; stigmatize, typecast. *—n.* **6.** *My business stamp is broken:* engraved block, seal, die, mold, matrix, mint, intaglio, signet, punch. **7.** *The cabinet is authentic and bears the stamp of the original maker:* mark, engraving, character, seal, brand, hallmark, imprint, identification, signature, official mark, trademark, authentication, emblem, label; ratification, endorsement, imprimatur, attestation, certificate, certification, voucher, validation, *Informal* OK. **8.** *The old rancher is a kindly fellow, but his brother is a man of a different stamp:* mark, characteristic; type, variety, character, sort, kind, nature, order, make, strain, genre, cast, breed, brand.

stampede *n.* **1.** *Twelve horses were killed in the stampede:* frenzied rush, headlong flight, retreat, rout, sudden scattering, panic; chaos, pandemonium. **2.** *The fuel shortage caused a stampede to the gasoline stations:* race, rush, dash. *—v.* **3.** *The guests stampeded out of the burning hotel. They stampeded the box office for tickets:* take flight, flee, beat a retreat, scatter, race, bolt, rush, panic, take to one's heels; crowd around, overrun, flood, inundate, engulf.

stand *v.* **1.** *We stood because there were no seats:* be upright, be erect, hold oneself erect, be on one's feet; rise, rise to one's feet, get up. **2.** *Stand the ladder over here. The lamp stands next to the armchair:* put, place, be placed, set, set upright, be set upright, rear, raise, rest, put up, stick up, set on its feet, hoist, erect, mount. **3.** *Please stand aside:* step, move, remove, take a position, shift, draw. **4.** *He stands for home and country:* support, uphold, defend a cause, argue, champion, be in favor of, declare oneself for, commend, sanction, speak well or highly of, plead for, endorse, countenance, honor, advocate. **5.** *The church has stood in the same spot for a hundred years. My decision stands:* be present, be located, be situated, rest, remain, exist, have its seat, stay, continue, be permanent; persist, prevail, remain in force, remain valid, hold. **6.** *The seawall stood against the raging storm. I can't stand strong criticism:* endure, remain intact, abide, remain erect or whole, persist, sustain, survive, resist destruction, resist decay or change, prove good, hold, be indestructible, obtain, hold out, last, remain steadfast, remain firm, bear up, keep one's position, carry on, withstand, tolerate, take, suffer, submit to, undergo, brook, put up with, face, weather, stomach; stand one's ground, persevere, stand pat. **7.** *He stands last when it comes to her affection:* be, rank, place. **8.** *He stood* lunch for the three of us: pay for, undertake, provide, finance; treat. —n. **9.** His feet ached from the two-hour stand: standing, wait without a seat; stance. **10.** The army made a valiant stand against the fierce attack: defense, resistance, effort, hold. **11.** What is the senator's stand on the bill?: position, point of view, policy, opinion, viewpoint, sentiment, standpoint, stance, posture, disposition. **12.** Where's the vegetable stand?: booth, stall, counter, kiosk; tent, pavilion. **—Ant.** 1 sit, lie, lay, recline. 6 collapse, succumb, falter, waver, yield, give way. 9 repose, sit, sitting. 10 retreat, collapse, withdrawal.

standard n. **1.** New cars without seat belts do not meet Federal safety standards. Critics with different standards often disagree: requirement, specification, criterion, guideline, principle; prototype, measure, yardstick, touchstone, ideal, guide, canon. **2.** Two men carried the standard in the royal parade: flag, pennant, banner, streamer, ensign, jack. **3.** The deck will need six standards to make it secure: pillar, support, stanchion, upright, post, column; leg, foot; base, foundation. —adj. **4.** What is the standard size of a twin bed?: normal, basic, usual, customary, universal, accepted, common, ordinary, typical, regular, stock. **—Ant.** 4 abnormal, exceptional, irregular, unusual.

standardize v. The firm standardized its forms: order, make regular, stereotype, homogenize, institute, normalize, systematize, mass-produce.

stand-in n. The star's stand-in did all the dangerous stunts for the film: substitute, sub, fill-in, surrogate, agent, proxy, deputy, alternate, pinch hitter, replacement, understudy, assistant, second, double, backup.

standing n. **1.** His standing in the class is high: rank, order, position, place, footing, station, grade, status, importance, reputation. **2.** He finally paid a debt of ten-years standing: duration, length of existence, continuance, age, tenure, time, term, life. —adj. **3.** He looks bigger in a standing position: stand-up, vertical, upright, perpendicular, upended, erect. **4.** Standing water breeds mosquitoes: motionless, still, stationary, inactive, not flowing, inert, static, dormant, unstirring, stagnant, at rest, quiescent. **5.** They issued us a standing invitation: fixed, continuing, immovable, permanent, perpetual, lasting, renewable. **—Ant.** 3 sitting, reclining, recumbent, lying. 4 flowing, moving, running.

standoffish adj. We tried to be friendly, but she was standoffish: unsociable, distant, cool, aloof, reserved, detached, withdrawn, remote, uncompanionable, unfriendly, reclusive, solitary, misanthropic, antisocial, uncommunicative, taciturn. **—Ant.** friendly, gregarious, affable, extroverted.

standstill n. Production at the factory is now at a standstill: stop, halt, cessation, pause, end, termination, full stop, impasse, dead stop, stalemate, discontinuance, abeyance, suspension, breakdown, hiatus, dead end, deadlock. **—Ant.** continuation, resumption, growth, progress.

stanza n. The poem had seven stanzas: quatrain, stave, poem, staff.

staple n. **1.** Beethoven's Fifth Symphony is a staple of the orchestral repertoire: basic item, feature, leader, fundamental component, article of merchandise, resource, commodity, raw material, product, vendible. —adj. **2.** Bread is a staple food: chief, primary, basic, fundamental, main, essential, key, major, prime, necessary, vital, indispensable.

star n. **1.** The stars are out tonight: sun; (loosely) heavenly body, celestial body, planet, satellite, asteroid, meteoroid, meteor, comet; constellation, galaxy, Milky Way, nebula. **2.** **stars** If the stars are against us, we can achieve nothing: fortune, fate, destiny, predestination, the future, signs of the future, portents, omens; astrological chart. **3.** The stars of the movie all came to the premiere: principal actor, principal, lead; hero, heroine, protagonist; well-known actor, popular entertainer, main attraction, headliner, drawing card, top draw, top banana, starlet; superior performer, superstar, All-American, great, giant, idol, immortal, god, goddess; (variously) prima donna, diva, prima ballerina, virtuoso, soloist; prominent figure, famous person, celebrity, name, luminary, eminence, notable, lion, mainstay, cynosure, VIP, bigwig. —v. **4.** The late movie tonight stars Sidney Poitier. With Olivier starring, the play is bound to succeed: present in a leading role, feature, showcase, be a vehicle for; play the lead, take the lead role, head the cast, top the bill. **5.** I didn't exactly star at my first job: do well, excel, shine, succeed, gain approval, stand out, attract attention, be conspicuous.

stare v. **1.** She was just staring into space. Don't stare at me!: gaze intently, fix one's gaze, look intently, gape, gawk, ogle, peep, Slang rubberneck; goggle; glare, lower, peer, eye, watch; glower. —n. **2.** Her icy stare gave me a chill: glare, fixed look, long glance, glower, staring, gaze, gape, gaping, ogling; scrutiny, regard, inspection; once-over.

stark adj. **1.** Stark terror seized the passengers: downright, bare, utter, plain, sheer, simple, pure, bold, patent, obvious, flagrant, absolute, complete, unmistakable, glaring, unmitigated, outright, palpable, arrant, evident, blunt, staring, conspicuous, gross, total, out-and-out, unalloyed, unmitigated, veritable, consummate. **2.** The room was as stark as a monk's cell: bare, severe, naked, plain, unadorned, barren, chaste, austere, empty; cold, forsaken, harsh, grim, bleak, desolate, abandoned, deserted, vacant, forlorn. —adv. **3.** The infant posed on the bearskin rug stark naked: absolutely, fully, utterly, wholly, quite, downright, completely, altogether, entirely, clean, plain, out-and-out, plumb, to the nth degree, through and through. **—Ant.** 2 fancy, adorned, embellished; gay, bright; cozy, warm, inviting; cultivated.

start v. **1.** Let's start for Vermont early: commence, get going, begin to move, make off, set out, leave, set off, take off, venture out, sally forth, hit the trail, depart, set sail, push off, embark. **2.** *Start the engine and I'll be right there:* set in operation, put in motion, set going, set in action; touch off, ignite, kindle, propel. **3.** *She started cooking dinner two days ago:* begin, commence, undertake, set about, embark on, enter upon, venture on, break ground, put in execution, take the first step, fall to, initiate, take up, plunge into, broach, turn one's hand to, make a beginning, buckle down. **4.** *President John F. Kennedy started the Peace Corps in 1961:* initiate, be initiated, originate, be originated, institute, found, be founded, establish, launch, set up, organize, institute, set moving, begin, inaugurate, create, give birth to, form, give rise to, introduce, lay the foundation of, touch off, usher in, fabricate, bring about, forge, propagate, engender, generate, beget, father, be the cause of. **5.** *Suddenly a pedestrian started from between the cars. Blood started from the wound:* spring, move suddenly, bound, jump, rise suddenly, burst forth, leap; rush, issue suddenly, spurt, gush, erupt, break forth, issue, shoot, emerge; pop out. **6.** *The gunshot started the ducks:* flush, rouse, disturb, scatter; eject, displace, turn out, evict. **7.** *I started when you touched my arm:* jump, twitch, jerk involuntarily, recoil, wince, blink, blench, shy, flinch. —*n.* **8.** *The start of the trip was hectic:* beginning, outset, commencement, first step, opening, onset, setting in motion; inauguration, inception, birth, creation, origin, genesis, dawn, initiation. **9.** *She gave a start when I inserted the needle:* jump, spasm, jolt, jerk, wince, twitch, turn. **10.** *All that money gives him a start over his rivals:* lead, advantage, head start, inside track, edge, advance, odds, drop, jump, priority, leg up. **11.** *My father gave him his start in life:* opening, chance, introduction, opportunity; support, aid, assistance, backing, advocacy. —**Ant.** 1 delay. 2 stall, turn off. 3, 4 end, finish, terminate, stop, cease. 8 end, finish, finale, termination; windup. 10 disadvantage, handicap.

startle *v.* *The knocking at the window startled me:* frighten, surprise, shock, disturb suddenly, cause to start, cause to jump, scare, alarm, unnerve, disquiet, disconcert, shake, faze, perturb, intimidate, discompose, upset, give a turn, jar, unsettle, take off one's guard. —**Ant.** calm, soothe, reassure, compose, settle.

starve *v.* **1.** *The campers starved before rescuers could get to them:* perish from hunger, die from hunger; go hungry, suffer from lack of food, famish, hunger, fast. **2.** *The enemy soldiers starved the townspeople into surrendering:* cut off from food, weaken by lack of food, undernourish, underfeed; force by underfeeding. **3.** *The lonely man starved for companionship:* hunger, yearn, long, be hungry, pine, crave, desire earnestly, thirst, lust, burn, languish, gasp, yen, raven, aspire; deprive, make eager, make desperate, deny, refuse, cut off. —**Ant.** 1 glut, overeat, gorge. 2 feed, overfeed, surfeit, glut.

starving *adj.* *The starving population fled across the border:* starved, famished, emaciated, empty, hungry, malnourished, ravenous, underfed, undernourished.

state *n.* **1.** *Ice is water in its solid state. What is the financial state of his business?:* condition, position, constitution, form, mode, guise, shape, stage, phase, structure, aspect; circumstances, status, situation, posture; predicament, plight, pass. **2.** *The royal family always moves in state:* high style, luxury, comfort; pomp, full dress, ceremony, ritual, formality. **3.** *I was disturbed by his depressed state:* condition, attitude, mind, frame of mind, mood, state of mind, spirits, morale. **4.** *The prime minister resigned for the good of the state:* nation, republic, commonwealth, country, monarchy, dominion, kingdom, realm, land, principality; body politic, people, government. —*adj.* **5.** *We attended two formal state functions this week:* ceremonial, official, governmental. —*v.* **6.** *He stated his case before a judge. Please state the exact time of arrival:* declare, express, propound, recite, recount, narrate, set forth, offer, present, put, explain; report, relate, describe, expound, elucidate. —**Ant.** 6 repudiate, deny, contradict, refute; disclaim.

stately *adj.* **1.** *We were awed by Mt. Fuji's stately splendor:* impressive, majestic, awesome, imposing, grand, regal, glorious, lofty, lordly, proud, magnificent, august, noble, royal, imperial. **2.** *The wedding was a stately occasion:* formal, ceremonial, dignified, eminent, elegant, grandiose. —**Ant.** 1 unimpressive, humble, modest, poor. 2 ordinary, common.

statement *n.* **1.** *He made a flattering statement about her clothes:* utterance, avowal, pronouncement, speech, assertion, declaration, allegation, profession, claim, explanation, testimony, mention, comment, remark, observation, sentence. **2.** *The company prepared a statement of its profits and losses:* report, record, account, announcement, specification, delineation; relation, exposition, recitation, recital; bill, invoice, account, tally, check, charge, reckoning, tab; balance sheet, count, accounting, valuation; communiqué, manifesto.

static *adj.* **1.** *Life on campus seemed static, and the student longed for a change:* inactive, motionless, stagnant, unmoving, inert, still, suspended, immobile, stationary, fixed, changeless, unchanging. —*n.* **2.** *There's a lot of static on the radio:* crackling, interference. —**Ant.** 1 moving, mobile, dynamic, kinetic; lively, spirited, vigorous, brisk, active.

station *n.* **1.** *All men to your stations!:* assigned place, position, post, location, placement, emplacement, spot, site. **2.** *We met at the railroad station:* terminal, terminus, depot, stop, whistlestop. **3.** *The thief was booked at the police station. The fire station was painted red:* station house; (*variously*) headquarters, precinct station, guardhouse, firehouse. **4.** *The ski patrol took the injured child to a first-aid station:* facility, dispensary. **5.** *His station in life is not what it was:* social standing, rank, position, status, place, footing, grade, condition, level, class, sphere, degree, importance, prestige, caste. —*v.* **6.** *The army stationed him in West Ger-*

many. *The cashier was stationed at the exit:* assign, post; locate, place, install, ensconce.

stationary *adj.* **1.** *It is easier to aim at a stationary than at a moving target:* immovable, motionless, standing still, standing, immobile; fixed, riveted, firm, moored; inert, transfixed, stable, stock-still, dead-still. **2.** *Business has been slow but our profits have remained stationary:* constant, unchanged, not changing, steady, stable, fixed, even, intact, undeviating, firm, uniform, unvarying, unchangeable, immutable. **—Ant.** 1 moving, mobile. 2 varying, changing, unstable, volatile, irregular; changeable.

statue *n. The statue was erected in the town square:* statuary, bust, cast, effigy, figure, sculpture, statuette, marble, bronze.

statuesque *adj. A statuesque woman descended the stairs:* majestic, grand, imposing, stately, shapely, well-proportioned, regal.

stature *n.* **1.** *Napoleon was a man of small stature:* height, tallness, size. **2.** *Such pettiness was surprising in a person of his stature:* rank, standing, place, position, high station, eminence, prestige, distinction, regard, elevation, prominence, importance, reputation. **—Ant.** 2 low rank, inferiority, lowliness.

status *n.* **1.** *His status in the community suffered from the scandal. Jewels symbolize status to some people:* position, rank, grade, degree, caliber, standing, footing, condition, estimation, station, caste, class, place; eminence, distinction, prestige, social superiority. **2.** *What's the status of the peace talks?:* situation, state, condition.

statute *n. The statute was enacted that day:* law, bill, decree, edict, measure, ordinance, regulation, rule, act, enactment.

staunch or **stanch** *adj.* **1.** *He's a staunch supporter of the church:* firm, steadfast, true, steady, constant, zealous, strong, stout, solid, loyal, faithful, resolute, stalwart. **2.** *This is a staunch little cabin:* substantial, solid, sturdy, stout, rugged, well-built, well-constructed, sound. **3.** *When the boys finished caulking the boat, they soaked it to make it staunch:* watertight, sound. **—v. 4.** *The doctor applied a tourniquet to my arm to stanch the bleeding:* stop the flow of, check, dam, hold back, obstruct, stem, impede, contain. **—Ant.** 1 inconstant, unfaithful, fickle, capricious, lukewarm. 2 weak, shoddy, jerry-built, flimsy. 3 leaky.

stay[1] *v.* **1.** *She stayed until my mother came home:* remain, tarry, visit, hang around, linger. **2.** *How long did they stay with you?:* remain, reside, dwell, abide, sojourn, take up quarters, lodge, room, bunk, live. **3.** *Stay as sweet as you are!:* keep oneself, endure, continue to be, remain, go on being. **4.** *Yoga is a difficult art, but if you stay with it, you'll learn it:* remain, continue, persist, persevere, hold out, carry on, stick; last out, see through. **5.** *She stayed her tears until her lover was out of sight:* restrain, hold back, suppress, rein in, postpone, withhold, curb, check, keep in, stifle, quell. **6.** *Athenians stayed the Persians at Salamis:* block, foil,

frustrate, thwart, ward off, stem. **—n. 7.** *How long was your stay at the beach?:* sojourn, stop, stopover, temporary residence, halt, visit, vacation, holiday. **8.** *The attorney won for his convicted client a stay of sentencing:* postponement, suspension, delay, deferment, abeyance; reprieve. **—Ant.** 1 leave, go, depart. 4 quit, give up, succumb. 5 loose, free, release, express. 6 fall to; surrender to.

stay[2] *n. One of the tent stays has come loose:* support; (*variously*) brace, prop, buttress, reinforcement, stanchion, standard, rest, rod, pole, guy, splint, shore, aim, rib, mainstay, block.

steadfast *adj.* **1.** *The navigator steered the ship on a steadfast course. Pay steadfast attention to your teacher:* steady, fixed, undeviating, direct; unwavering, attentive, undistracted, unflinching, rapt, intent, keen, persevering, unfaltering, unflagging. **2.** *Oliver Cromwell had a steadfast faith in God:* resolute, indomitable, undaunted, intransigent, obstinate, tenacious, inflexible, unyielding, uncompromising, unchangeable, unchanging, unalterable, deep-rooted, deep-seated, single-minded. **—Ant.** 1 deviating, wavering, flagging, faltering; fragile, unstable. 2 unreliable, irresolute, wavering, vacillating, capricious, halfhearted, changeable, fickle.

steady *adj.* **1.** *Is that stool steady enough to stand on?:* stable, firm, substantial, immovable. **2.** *With the monsoon came a steady rain. The drummer maintained a steady beat:* constant, unremitting, continuous, continuing, persistent, incessant, unending, unceasing, ceaseless; regular, even. **3.** *He's a steady visitor to the art galleries:* habitual, constant, frequent, regular, faithful, devoted, confirmed. **4.** *She's steady in her commitment to her job:* steadfast, constant, undeviating, unwavering, firm, resolute, staunch, untiring, unfaltering, unflagging, persevering, tenacious, dedicated, devoted, unremitting, resolute, single-minded. **5.** *He's a steady pupil who always does his work on schedule. The chauffeur is a steady driver:* reliable, dependable, careful, serious, sober, deliberate, conscientious, methodical, stable; levelheaded, coolheaded, sure. **—v. 6.** *Steady that ladder for me, please:* stabilize, balance, hold fast, secure. **—Ant.** 1 unsteady, shaky, unstable, insecure. 2 sporadic, intermittent, uneven, irregular, syncopated, broken, varying. 3 infrequent, irregular, rare, sporadic, sometime. 4 irregular; on-again, off-again, erratic; undependable, unreliable; ambivalent, of two minds, vacillating, irresolute, faltering, uncertain. 5 unsteady, unreliable, careless, frivolous; unsteady, shaky. 6 shake, rock, tip, tilt.

steal *v.* **1.** *Someone stole a painting from the museum:* take, burglarize, purloin, filch, pilfer, lift, snatch; make off with, abscond with, swindle, embezzle, extort, usurp, misappropriate; defraud; thieve, copy, crib, plagiarize; abstract, borrow, appropriate, imitate, help oneself to; pocket, *Slang* rip off, liberate, pinch, snitch, swipe, cop. **2.** *The children stole a look at the Christmas presents:* take secretly, sneak. **3.** *Try to steal into the room without waking the chil-*

dren: slip, slide, sneak, creep, pass stealthily, slink, skulk, pass unobserved. **4.** *Time steals away from you when you're having fun:* slip, pass gradually, creep, slide, drift, elapse, escape, glide, happen gently, diffuse, flow, filter, flit.

stealth *n. Our cat is a model of patience and stealth when it comes to catching mice:* covertness, secrecy, clandestine procedure, secretiveness, furtiveness, sneakiness, stealthiness, slyness, subterfuge, surreptitiousness, unobtrusiveness. **—Ant.** openness, candidness.

stealthy *adj. His manner was stealthy, as though he didn't want to be seen:* surreptitious, covert, underhand, underhanded, sneaky, shady, furtive, sly, sneaking, clandestine, devious, secretive, hugger-mugger, slippery, shifty. **—Ant.** open, aboveboard, direct, obvious, forthright.

steel *n.* **1.** *Construction workers brought in a lot of steel for the new building:* tempered iron, steel articles. **2.** *The knight plunged his steel into the bandit's throat:* blade, bayonet, sword, knife, saber, foil, cutlass, dagger, dirk, rapier, machete, scimitar, falchion, broadsword. **—v. 3.** *Here's some unpleasant news, so steel yourself for the blow:* brace, fortify, gird, nerve.

steep[1] *adj. The slope is too steep for us to climb:* close to vertical, sheer, precipitous, abrupt, sharp. **—Ant.** flat, gentle, gradual.

steep[2] *v.* **1.** *She steeped the cucumbers in brine to pickle them:* soak, be soaked, immerse, be immersed, saturate, brew, souse, impregnate, suffuse, marinate. **2.** *She steeps herself in the problems of her students. The village is steeped in history:* immerse, plunge, bury, saturate, engulf, drench, imbue, submerge, infuse, fill, pervade. **—Ant.** 1 drain.

steer *v.* **1.** *The captain steered the yacht into the harbor. He steered the team to victory:* sail, navigate, direct, guide, pilot, run, conduct, govern, supervise, manage, lead, head, coach. **2.** *The ship steered for the open seas:* proceed, head, sail, make, lay, lay a course, take a course, aim, bear, run, be bound, make a beeline.

stem[1] *n.* **1.** *The stem of my rose is broken:* main stalk; (*variously*) trunk, spear, shoot, cane, stalk, leafstalk, stock, spire, peduncle, pedicel, petiole, tendril. **2.** *Don't hold the glass by its stem:* shank. **—v. 3.** *His back trouble stems from an old war injury:* come, derive, issue, result, proceed, arise, rise, originate, spring, ensue, grow.

stem[2] *v. Nothing could stem the glacier's irresistible advance. The government tried to stem the growing discontent of the people:* stop, hold back, curb, stay, restrain, check, quell, arrest, prevent, impede, obstruct, dam, withstand, oppose, hold one's own against, resist, stanch, thwart, stall, halt, block, surmount, hinder, bring to a standstill, buck, retard, deter, counter. **—Ant.** further, promote, encourage, stimulate, incite, excite, unleash.

stench *n. The stench of the packinghouse is terrible:* stink, bad smell, offensive odor, fetid-

ness, fetor, reek. **—Ant.** fragrance, aroma, perfume.

step *n.* **1.** *With two steps she reached the crying child. He walks with a measured step:* footstep, pace, stride, gait; (*variously*) strut, hobble, shuffle, shamble, swagger, clip. **2.** *Did you hear a step in the attic?:* footfall, tread, stepping sound. **3.** *There were children's steps in the cement:* footprint, track. **4.** *Glazing is the final step in making pottery:* stage, phase, move, process, measure, maneuver, proceeding, act, action, procedure. **5.** *The promotion put him three steps from the top:* grade level, stage, rank, rung, degree, point, gradation, notch, period, span, remove. **6.** *One of the back steps needs replacing:* stair, foothold, tread, riser, rung, footing, purchase. **—v. 7.** *The patient was able to step to the window:* move, walk, pace, tread, stride. **8.** *Ouch! You stepped on my foot:* tread, tramp, trample.

stereotype *n.* **1.** *The belief that the husband should "rule the roost" is an old-fashioned stereotype. She fits the stereotype of a "schoolmarm":* conventional image, received idea, popular preconception, cliché, formula. **—v. 2.** *The newscaster stereotyped the protesters as "longhaired crazies":* pigeonhole, typecast, type, categorize, crudely identify.

stereotyped *adj. Stereotyped attitudes got in the way of real discussion:* fixed, settled, conventional, hackneyed, overused, commonplace, trite, banal, dull, ordinary, lifeless, uninteresting, stale, boring, worn, pointless, insipid, inane. **—Ant.** rare, uncommon, unusual; interesting fresh, sensible.

sterile *adj.* **1.** *The infant was kept in a sterile incubator:* sterilized, disinfected, free from germs, pure, uncontaminated, sanitary, uninfected, aseptic, antiseptic. **2.** *The sterile couple adopted two children. The rocky earth was sterile:* barren, infertile, childless; unfruitful, infecund, fallow, bare, empty. **3.** *The negotiations proved to be sterile:* unproductive, unprofitable, worthless, fruitless, ineffective, profitless, unrewarding, ineffectual, bootless, impotent, abortive, futile, vain, useless, unavailing. **—Ant.** 1 unsterile, infected, germ-ridden, unsanitary. 2 fertile, prolific, productive; fecund, fruitful. 3 productive, profitable, fruitful, effective.

sterilize *v. They sterilized the instruments:* clean, disinfect, decontaminate, make sterile, sanitize, purify, fumigate.

sterling *adj. John is a sterling example of a concerned citizen:* noble, high-principled, estimable, meritorious, honorable, worthy, true, superb, admirable, superior, first-rate, invaluable, superlative; genuine, pure, perfect, flawless. **—Ant.** inferior, shoddy, shabby, tacky.

stern *adj.* **1.** *He's much too stern with his son:* severe, strict, hard, unfeeling, unreasonable, despotic, ironhanded, ironfisted, unmerciful, stringent, cruel, tyrannical, sharp, pitiless, harsh, coercive, cold-blooded, ruthless, austere, grim, brutal, ungentle, rigorous. **2.** *The teacher gave him a stern look:* grim, austere, forbidding, hard, unkind, severe, serious, somber, gloomy, cold, unapproachable, unsympathetic, sharp, rigid, grave, implacable, harsh, stiff, frowning, reproachful, reproving, admonishing. —**Ant.** 1 permissive, soft, lenient, flexible, gentle, benign, merciful, kind. 2 friendly, approachable, kind, smiling, amused, relaxed, warm, sympathetic.

stew v. **1.** *I stewed the vegetables in a covered pot for an hour:* boil slowly, cook in water, simmer, seethe, steep. **2.** *Informal The waiter ignored us as we sat there, stewing:* become irritated, get angry; fuss, fume, chafe, worry, agonize, fret, seethe; grumble, gripe, grouse. —n. **3.** *We had beef stew for dinner:* stewed food, ragout; mixture, miscellany. **4.** *Informal She's in a stew over finding a baby-sitter:* state of worry, mental agitation, fuss, fret, flutter, tizzy, fluster.

steward n. **1.** *His steward made poor investments for him:* manager, financial manager, administrator, supervisor; overseer, bailiff, agent, factor, executor, trustee, deputy, comptroller, controller, representative, proxy. **2.** *She rang for the steward:* (variously) ship's attendant, airplane attendant, (fem.) stewardess; waiter.

stick[1] n. **1.** *They made a bonfire of sticks:* branch, switch, twig, fagot. **2.** *Grandfather walks with a stick. Bill carries a stick to ward off dogs:* cane, staff; baton, swagger stick, wand, rod; bat, club, cudgel, shillelagh, billy, truncheon, bludgeon; cue; pole, shaft, stave, stake, bar, skewer; scepter, staff, caduceus, crosier.

stick[2] v. **1.** *The doctor stuck him with a hypodermic needle:* puncture, pierce, stab, jab, prick, poke, pink, spear, spike, perforate, punch. **2.** *He stuck a needle in my arm:* jab, thrust, dig, poke, insert, punch. **3.** *Stick this notice on the bulletin board:* fix, put, place, set, plant, fasten, tack, pin, affix, nail, attach. **4.** *Can you stick the torn pieces back together?:* join; (variously) glue, fasten, paste, seal, adhere, cement, fuse, attach, affix, weld, bind. **5.** *A bone stuck in my throat:* lodge, become fastened, catch, snag, be embedded. **6.** *The bus stuck fast in the snow. The heavy snow stuck traffic for hours:* stall, mire, be unable to proceed, be tangled, hinder, check, block, immobilize, bind, trammel, hold, obstruct, curb, snarl, impede, hog-tie, constrain, shackle, scotch, thwart, hamper, balk, detain, inhibit, bar, back up, checkmate, stop. **7.** *Stick to your guns!:* be true, keep steadily at, hold, be faithful, be constant. **8.** *The prizefighter stuck it out to the end, but lost on points:* endure, abide, stand, bear up under, last, continue, not give up on, carry on. **9.** *I was stuck over one word in that crossword puzzle:* stymie, balk, stump, bewilder, boggle, puzzle, perplex, confuse. **10.** *Informal They always stick me with the dirty work!:* impose on, leave, burden, make responsible, victimize. —**Ant.** 3 remove, dislodge, unfasten, untack, unpin, unscrew. 4 separate, detach, disengage. 6 release, free, unblock, untangle, unfasten. 10 relieve, free.

stickler n. **1.** *I'm a stickler for details:* purist, fanatic, martinet; devotee, enthusiast, *Slang* nut, bug, crank; monomaniac, zealot. **2.** *This ques-*

tion is really a stickler!: knotty point, tough proposition, mystery, enigma, hard nut to crack, poser, riddle, puzzle, dilemma, Gordian knot, *Informal* stumper. —**Ant.** 2 cinch.

sticky adj. **1.** *Tar is sticky:* gummy, sticking, adhesive, tenacious, adherent, gluey, tacky, viscid, viscous, clinging, clingy, pasty, gooey, glutinous, cohesive, gelatinous, mucilaginous. **2.** *This sticky weather makes my hair frizz:* clammy, humid, muggy, sultry, damp, moist, wet, steamy, dank. —**Ant.** 1 slick, slippery. 2 dry, crisp.

stiff adj. **1.** *The laundry made this shirt too stiff:* starchy, rigid, crisp, inelastic. **2.** *The steering wheel is stiff. My back is stiff:* unyielding, tight, resistant, hard to move; unlimber, inflexible, tense, taut, rigid. **3.** *A stiff gust blew the tree down:* vigorous, strong, intense, forceful, pounding, persistent, gusty, powerful, raging, violent, keen, brisk, smart, spanking. **4.** *We couldn't change his stiff determination to quit:* stubborn, tenacious, firm, steadfast, decided, determined, strong, indomitable, fixed, staunch, unfaltering, unflinching, iron, steely, steeled, dogged, steady, unswerving, grim, obstinate, persistent, strong-willed, uncompromising, stern, constant, settled, resolute, resolved, intense; valiant, brave, unshaken, courageous. **5.** *It's hard to relax in this stiff drawing room. The lawyer nodded a stiff greeting:* cold, austere, formal, precise, stately, aloof, ceremonious, prim, wooden, stilted, starchy, cool, chilly, constrained, straitlaced, distant, *Slang* uptight. **6.** *The acting was stiff, and we couldn't wait for the play to end:* wooden, graceless, awkward, uneasy, forced, clumsy, stilted, ungainly, inelegant, labored, cold, unnatural, affected, mannered, artificial. **7.** *That's a stiff assignment for a newcomer:* difficult, exacting, laborious, heavy, tough, hard, stringent, rigorous, formidable. **8.** *He makes stiff demands on his employees. The asking price is too stiff:* steep, high, excessive, heavy, exorbitant, undue, inordinate, immoderate, unwarranted, extravagant. **9.** *I don't think his offense deserved such a stiff penalty:* harsh, stern, severe, stringent, cruel, sharp, brutal, drastic, violent, fearful, austere, unreasonable, sore, awful, bitter, uncompromising, extreme, merciless, draconian, pitiless, ruthless, grievous. **10.** *The whipped cream is not stiff enough:* thick, firm, solid, solidified, heavy, dense, viscid, viscous, jellied, gelatinous, clotted. —**Ant.** 1 soft, loose, yielding, bendable, supple, flexible, pliant, pliable, elastic, malleable. 2 supple, loose, limber, relaxed. 3 gentle, easy, soft. 4 halfhearted, undecided, faltering, irresolute, shaky. 5 casual, informal, cozy, relaxed, unceremonious, warm. 6 smooth, graceful, easy, unforced, natural, unaffected. 7 easy, soft, cushy, cinchy. 8 easy, simple, soft, moderate. 9 mild, moderate, permissive, soft, sparing, merciful. 10 thin, soft, mushy, liquid.

stiffen v. *Adversity stiffened her resolve:* harden, cement, brace, cement, petrify, make hard, reinforce, anneal, solidify, fix, firm, freeze, set; coagulate, condense, congeal, crystallize, gel, stabilize, thicken.

stiff-necked *adj. He should apologize, but he's so stiff-necked he can't:* stubborn, obstinate, mulish, intractable, intransigent, pigheaded, willful, unyielding, pertinacious, refractory, bullheaded, obdurate, unbending, contrary, self-willed, unshakable. —**Ant.** indecisive, vacillating; reasonable, flexible.

stifle *v.* **1.** *The maniac stifled his victim with a cushion. I'm stifling in this overheated car:* asphyxiate, smother, choke, suffocate, strangle, throttle, garrote; gasp for air, swelter, gag. **2.** *She stifled her laughter:* suppress, repress, curb, subdue, restrain, keep back, smother, muffle, squelch, check, inhibit. —**Ant.** 2 release, express; encourage, further, foster.

stigma *n. There was no stigma attached to losing the election:* disgrace, shame, odium, dishonor; blot, blemish, brand, flaw, mark of shame, smirch, smudge, besmirchment, taint, tarnish. —**Ant.** glory, honor, distinction, credit, approval.

still *adj.* **1.** *The deer lay very still:* motionless, without movement, inert, stationary, at rest, unstirring, unmoving, immobile. **2.** *The restaurant was as still as a library:* silent, hushed, quiet, noiseless, soundless. —*v.* **3.** *The wind stilled down at sunset. All sirens are to be stilled when passing hospitals:* calm, quiet; hush, silence, turn off. **4.** *AA helps alcoholics to still their craving for drink:* restrain, overcome, repress, suppress. **5.** *Gargantua ate and ate, but nothing stilled his hunger:* assuage, appease, gratify, pacify. **6.** *De Gaulle stilled the May Revolution of 1968:* put an end to, restore to order, put down, settle. —**Ant.** 1 active, moving, disturbed, agitated, restless, turbulent. 2 noisy, loud.

stilted *adj. His introduction was stilted and self-conscious:* stiff, wooden, awkward, graceless, labored, unnatural, pompous, starched, starchy, stuffy, cold, mannered, studied, ceremonious, formal, rigid, prim, priggish, forced, artificial, constrained, *Slang* uptight. —**Ant.** relaxed, easy, graceful, informal, spontaneous, natural, unforced.

stimulant *n. Tea is a stimulant that keeps me awake all night:* energizer, tonic, bracer, excitant, *Slang* upper. —**Ant.** anesthetic, narcotic, depressant, tranquilizer, *Slang* downer.

stimulate *v. Visiting the Metropolitan Museum stimulated my interest in the Florentine masters:* incite, arouse, excite, awaken, enkindle, fan, rouse, spur, actuate, prompt, stir, alert, animate, quicken, activate, initiate, wake, inflame, vivify, inspire, inspirit, sharpen. —**Ant.** deaden; discourage, dull; calm, soothe, assuage.

stimulus *n.* **1.** *Excitement is a stimulus to the adrenal gland:* (*loosely*) stimulant, tonic, bracer, activator, energizer, excitant. **2.** *Nothing is a greater stimulus to pride than success:* incentive, spur, incitement, inducement, goad, impetus, provocation, encouragement, fillip, quickener, motive, whet. —**Ant.** 1 repressant, depressant, suppressant. 2 discouragement, damper, deadener, obstacle, handicap.

sting *v.* **1.** *A bee stung him on the arm:* prick, wound, stab, pierce, nettle, penetrate. **2.** *The*

blowing sand stung the back of my legs. His abrupt reply stung her: burn, pain sharply, chafe, hurt, cause to wince, irritate, prick, wound; anger, rack, pique, rasp, agonize, grate, offend, disturb, insult, provoke, inflame, rile, grip, gnaw, vex, nettle, incense, madden, torment, harrow, torture, infuriate, gall. **3.** *My eyes are stinging from the smoke:* burn, feel sharp pain, smart, prick, wince, itch, twinge, tingle. **4.** *His smug challenge stung her to action:* impel, incite, provoke, irritate, goad, prod, kindle, fire, excite, stir up, nettle, whip, egg on, shake, arouse, instigate, spur, actuate, quicken, lash, awaken, propel, motivate, pierce, prompt, move. —*n.* **5.** *Did you get the bee sting out?:* stinging organ, prick, stinger, barb. **6.** *The sting of coral can be very painful:* bite, wound, sore, burn, pinch, nip; pain, hurt, tingle, prickle, irritation. **7.** *I still feel the sting of her bitter words:* wound, pain, hurt, ache, blow, affliction, bite, irritation, gall, scourge, rub, venom, cut, vexation, bitter pill, bitter cup, bitter draft, cross, shock. —**Ant.** 2 soothe, caress; mollify, assuage, calm. 4 delay, hinder, obstruct, halt, thwart, deaden, paralyze. 7 balm, caress.

stingy *adj.* **1.** *That stingy man won't contribute a cent:* miserly, tight, tightfisted, close, penurious, parsimonious, closefisted, niggardly, ungenerous, penny-pinching, mean, sparing, illiberal, stinting, frugal, cheeseparing. **2.** *It's hard to support a family on that stingy salary:* meager, slender, scanty, scant, sparse, lean, scrimpy, skimpy, small, modest, insufficient, thin, paltry, piddling, niggardly, inadequate. —**Ant.** 1 generous, liberal, open-handed, bountiful, munificent; prodigal, extravagant, lavish, charitable. 2 large, lavish, huge, handsome, profuse, ample, abundant, bountiful.

stink *v.* **1.** *The stagnant swamp stinks! That factory stinks up the town:* reek, emit a bad odor, smell to high heaven, be malodorous, offend the nostrils, give a bad odor. **2.** *Slang That book really stinks:* be rotten, be boring, be worthless, be no good. —*n.* **3.** *The stink of sour milk filled the refrigerator:* stench, bad smell, unpleasant odor, reek, fetor. —**Ant.** 3 perfume, aroma, fragrance, sweetness.

stint *v.* **1.** *I'll have to stint my charity gifts this year:* restrict, set limits to, give in small amounts, limit, cut down on, reduce, be sparing with, restrain, constrain, circumscribe, check, curb. **2.** *One thing Mother never stints on is food:* be sparing, hold back, scrimp, be frugal, save, deny oneself, economize, pinch pennies, withhold, be parsimonious. —*n.* **3.** *She was assigned the most difficult stint. The band did a stint in Las Vegas:* job, chore, task, duty, work period, term, assignment, part, turn, shift, quota; engagement.

stipend *n. Scholarship students rarely enjoy a generous stipend:* income, allowance, fixed pay, salary, compensation, wages, pension, emolument, remuneration, recompense; grant, scholarship.

stipulate *v. Our contract with the decorator stipulates the maximum amount he can charge* *us:* specify, set forth, insist upon, state, designate, indicate, name, cite, make a point of, make provision; promise, pledge, guarantee, insure, grant, provide, allow, assure, agree, warrant.

stir *v.* **1.** *The branches began to stir as the breeze came up:* move, rustle, shake, shiver, twitch, flutter, quiver. **2.** *Stir the sauce:* move, mix, scramble, agitate, beat, whip, set in motion, commix, blend, mingle, intermix, commingle. **3.** *You'd better stir if you want to make the movie:* act, move; (*variously*) exert oneself, make an effort, bestir oneself, hustle, get moving, get a move on, scramble, bustle, be active, step lively, rush, scamper, hasten. **4.** *The coach's emotional pep talk stirred the team:* rouse, arouse, inspire, excite, animate, awaken, inspirit, energize, electrify, kindle, quicken, vivify, work up, stimulate, fire, enflame, jolt, goad, provoke, start, spur, prod. —*n.* **5.** *She lay awake, listening to the stir of the willow branches above the tent:* stirring, moving, movement, rustle, rustling, sough. **6.** *Don't forget to give the sauce an occasional stir:* stirring, mixing, prodding, agitation, mingling. **7.** *The movie company caused quite a stir in the quiet town:* commotion, tumult, flurry, pother, uproar, to-do. —**Ant.** 3 relax, settle down. 4 calm, pacify; lull, deaden. 5 stillness, immobility, quiet, silence.

stitch *n.* **1.** *Make your hem stitches closer together:* loop of thread; suture. **2.** *Every stitch she owns is at the dry cleaners:* bit of clothing, piece, garment, particle, shred, article, scrap. **3.** *I haven't done a stitch of packing yet!:* bit, slightest amount, particle, shred, scrap, jot, iota. **4.** *All that dancing gave me a stitch in my side:* pain, kink, pang, crick, twinge, twitch, tingle, ache, shoot; cramp, charley horse. —*v.* **5.** *The tailor stitched the split seam in seconds:* sew, fasten with thread, mend, baste, seam, tack; embroider; suture.

stock *n.* **1.** *The shop carries a large stock of gift-wrapping paper around Christmas:* supply, store, inventory, array, quantity, selection, assortment; cache, accumulation, stockpile, fund, reserve, hoard, provision, reservoir; wares, merchandise, goods. **2.** *How much stock do you have in the company?:* ownership, shares, capital, capital shares; investment. **3.** *We're running low on feed for the stock:* livestock, cattle, domestic animals, herd. **4.** *She comes from sturdy peasant stock:* descent, lineage, ancestry, strain, line, breed, parentage, family, heredity, birth, root, extraction, blood, race, house, tribe, progeniture, nationality, pedigree, caste, people, genealogy, family tree, clan, dynasty, origin, source, forebears, background. **5.** *That rose is the finest of its stock:* breed, type, kind. **6.** *Grab the rifle firmly by the stock:* handle, haft, grasp, shaft, butt, pull, hold. **7.** *You need a good rich stock for the gravy:* broth; bouillon. —*adj.* **8.** *Toothpaste is stock merchandise in a drugstore:* standard, basic, regular, staple. **9.** *He got only a stock response to his suggestion to the governor:* routine, standard, formal, form, pro forma.

—*v.* **10.** *The landlord stocked the house with plenty of linens:* supply, furnish, appoint, equip, store, provide, fit out, accoutre, provision. **11.** *Do they stock children's shoes?:* handle, keep in stock, offer. —**Ant.** 10 empty, drain, deplete.

stocky *adj.* *One brother is stocky and the other is tall and slim:* thickset, short and heavy, husky, solid, sturdy, stumpy, chunky, squat, blocky, stout, stubby, dumpy, pudgy. —**Ant.** slim, slender, lanky.

stodgy *adj.* **1.** *We almost died of boredom at that stodgy resort. Much technical writing is needlessly stodgy:* dull, stuffy, humdrum, boring, uninteresting, tiresome, dreary, wearisome, tedious, monotonous, lifeless; flat, prosaic, pompous, lumbering, prolix, clumsy, laborious, pedantic. **2.** *It was hard to swallow that stodgy pudding:* indigestible, starchy, heavy, thick, lumpy. **3.** *He's too young to have such a stodgy outlook:* old-fashioned, antiquated, dated, passé, narrow, inflexible; staid, serious, stuffy. —**Ant.** 1 exciting, lively, sprightly, interesting, vital, vivacious, animated. 2 light, fluffy, airy. 3 new, modern, up-to-date, flexible, *Slang* with-it.

stoic *n.* **1.** *He's a stoic and never shed a tear at the news:* fatalist, quietist; man of stone, man of iron. —*adj.* **2.** *Her stoic attitude helped us all to bear the tragedy:* stoical, detached, philosophic, impassive, unruffled, unimpassioned, imperturbable, calm, tranquil, dispassionate. —**Ant.** 2 uncontrolled, undisciplined, excitable, volatile, emotional, passionate, disturbed.

stoical *adj.* *She was stoical in defeat:* stoic, impassive, calm, austere, apathetic, imperturbable, cool, indifferent. —**Ant.** sympathetic, warm.

stoicism *n.* *We were impressed by his stoicism throughout the crisis:* impassivity, imperturbability, tranquillity, fortitude, philosophical attitude, fatalism. —**Ant.** emotionalism, excitability, hysteria.

stolid *adj.* *He's too stolid to show excitement about anything:* impassive, unemotional, apathetic, sluggish, lethargic, phlegmatic, dull, obtuse, lumpish, bovine, dense; insensitive. —**Ant.** excitable, emotional, passionate, energetic, lively, active, animated, acute.

stomach *n.* **1.** *That heavy meal feels like lead in my stomach:* belly, abdomen, tummy; craw, crop, gizzard, maw; paunch, midsection, midriff, middle, *Slang* guts, pot, potbelly, breadbasket. **2.** *How can you have any stomach for lunch after that huge breakfast?:* hunger, appetite, taste, thirst, keenness, relish. **3.** *I have no stomach for violent movies:* liking, taste, appetite, disposition, keenness, desire, fancy, inclination, hunger, pleasure, affinity, leaning, attraction, proclivity, predilection, relish, partiality, mind, bent, temper, bias, sympathy, propensity, humor. —*v.* **4.** *The sick man couldn't even stomach liquids:* keep down, hold in the stomach, retain. **5.** *He couldn't stomach the snobbery of some of the guests:* stand, bear, swallow, put up with, take, endure, suffer, bear with, tolerate, countenance, brook, abide, submit to, resign oneself to, reconcile oneself to, let pass, close the eyes to, overlook, make allowance for, pass over, be patient with. —**Ant.** 2 distaste, disrelish. 3 dislike, distaste, disinclination, abhorrence, aversion, displeasure. 4 regurgitate, vomit. 5 reject, condemn, discountenance.

stone *n.* **1.** *The building is made of stone. The boys threw stones in the pond:* rock, pebble. **2.** *She has a three-carat stone in her ring:* gem, precious stone, jewel, brilliant, birthstone, bijou, *Slang* rock. **3.** *The stones are removed from these canned cherries:* pit, kernel, seed, nut. —*v.* **4.** *Vandals stoned the new building, breaking all the windows:* throw rocks at, pelt with stones.

stony *adj.* **1.** *You'll need shoes to walk on this stony path:* full of rocks, rocky, pebbly, bumpy, gravelly, craggy, jagged, uneven, coarse, rough, rugged. **2.** *Coal is a stony substance, but it's not a rock:* stonelike, rocklike, rocky; *(variously)* adamantine, flinty, ossified, concrete, lithoid, marble, granite, fossilized, petrified, crystallized. **3.** *Her tears couldn't move his stony heart:* unfeeling, insensible, unsympathetic, cold, hardhearted, coldhearted, merciless, austere, severe, soulless, unresponsive, icy, heartless, callous, obdurate, frigid, stern, stolid, passionless, unemotional, indifferent, flinty, hardened, blank, expressionless, coldblooded, stoical, unyielding, heartless, inexorable, pitiless, chill, forbidding, indurate, steely, deadened, untouched, unaffected, uncaring, *Informal* hard-boiled; bloodless. —**Ant.** 1 smooth, even. 2 soft, flexible, yielding. 3 feeling, sensitive, sympathetic, warm, responsive, softhearted, tenderhearted, tender, compassionate, merciful, soft, mellow, kind, friendly.

stoop[1] *v.* **1.** *She stooped to pick up a piece of paper:* bend down, lean over. **2.** *He stoops from years of carrying heavy objects on his back:* slouch, slump, be round-shouldered, be bowed, be doubled over, lean forward. **3.** *I can't believe he would stoop to such nonsense:* lower oneself, degrade oneself, sink, descend, fall, deign, bow, condescend, resort, succumb, bend, prostrate oneself; acquiesce, concede, yield, submit. —*n.* **4.** *His stoop seemed more pronounced after his illness:* stooping posture, stooping carriage, slump, slouch, round-shoulderedness, bend, droop, sag. —**Ant.** 1 stand erect. 3 rise, ascend. 4 straightness, erectness.

stoop[2] *n.* *We sat on the stoop and chatted for a while:* entrance staircase, entranceway, doorstep, steps; porch, small veranda.

stop *v.* **1.** *Stop or I'll shoot! Stop what you're doing. A tourniquet stops heavy bleeding:* halt, stay, stand fast, hold; discontinue, suspend, put an end to, cut short, bring to a standstill, postpone; check, arrest, suppress, block, stem, stall, interrupt the flow of, stanch, cut off; curb, rein in. **2.** *The guards stopped him from escaping:* restrain, hinder, hold back, prevent, bar, obstruct, preclude, deter, thwart, hamper, frustrate. **3.** *He stopped the leak with cement:* plug, caulk, close, block, fill, stop up, fill the holes in, close up, occlude, stanch, seal. **4.** *The music stopped. The lightning stopped. The car stopped:* come to an end, cease, come to a

halt, discontinue, conclude, finish, be over, desist, leave off, break off, terminate, run its course, run out, wind down, peter out, quit, hold, reach completion, come to a standstill, pause, intermit, lapse, pass away, draw to a close, expire, surcease; draw up, brake, stall, pull up, alight, become inactive, idle, falter, rest, stand; drop anchor. **5.** *We stopped at a motel for two nights:* sojourn, stay, rest, dwell, lodge, stop over, put up, abide, take up quarters, visit, tarry, repose, suspend one's journey. —*n.* **6.** *The strike caused a stop in construction. We must put a stop to the fighting:* cessation, termination, halt, halting, stoppage, suspension, arrest, break, discontinuation, desistance, leaving off, pause, rest, respite, lapse, spell, interruption, intermission, abeyance, wait, interlude, recess, interval, hiatus, breathing spell; end, standstill, ban, curb, block, prohibition. **7.** *We made a stop at Mother's on our way to Vancouver:* visit, stay, stopover, sojourn, rest, respite, layover, pause. **8.** *I get off at the last stop:* stopoff; depot, station, terminus, terminal; destination. —**Ant.** 1 start, begin, commence, initiate, continue, set going, institute, originate, inaugurate. 2 speed, assist, expedite, facilitate, further, encourage, incite. 3 unplug, open, uncork, unseal. 4 start, begin, commence, continue, proceed, progress, advance. 6 start, commencement, beginning; resumption.

stopgap *adj.* *Stopgap measures are needed to reduce unemployment quickly:* provisional, makeshift, improvised, temporary, substitute, emergency, impromptu, stand-by, tentative, contrived; *Latin* pro tem, ad hoc. —**Ant.** permanent, well-established, unalterable.

stoppage *n.* *The explosion caused a stoppage of traffic throughout the downtown area:* blockage, obstruction, obstacle, barrier, stricture, impediment, hindrance, interruption, disruption, curtailment, tieup, gridlock, check, checkmate.

store *n.* **1.** *Mother went to the store to buy some household things:* shop, market, mart, supermarket, department store, emporium, establishment. **2.** *Our store of fuel is running low:* supply, provision, stock, pile, stockpile, hoard, accumulation, inventory, stock in trade, reserve, wares, effects, fund, reservoir, quantity, cache. **3.** *He puts great store in her advice:* faith, confidence, regard, value, credit, trust, reliance, dependence, estimation, esteem. **4.** *He always has a store of marvelous anecdotes:* abundance, multitude, plethora, full measure, wealth, overflow, plenty, large quantity, legion, luxuriance, fund, richness, satiety, array, lot, volume, pack, host, profusion, copiousness, plenteousness, hoard, scores, riches, prodigality, multiplicity, exuberance, cornucopia. —*v.* **5.** *Squirrels store nuts for the winter:* save, stow away, keep, lay aside, put away, deposit, salt away, sock away, hoard, amass, stockpile, reserve, lay up or by, husband, lay in, accumulate, gather, hold, heap up, store up, cache, put in storage, put in mothballs, *Informal* stash. —**Ant.** 3 disbelief, distrust, skepticism, doubt, suspicion. 4 paucity, lack, poverty, dearth, skimpiness. 5 waste, spend, squander.

storehouse n. *The harvested grain was taken to the storehouse for safekeeping:* repository, warehouse, depot, depository, store, magazine, arsenal; silo, elevator, granary; stockroom, storeroom; bank, treasury, vault.

storm n. **1.** *The islanders were warned that a storm was coming:* torrent, deluge, rainstorm, cloudburst, downpour; snowstorm, blizzard; windstorm, tempest, gale, squall, blow, hurricane, typhoon, cyclone; tornado, twister. **2.** *My criticism produced a storm of anger. The hated speaker caused a storm on campus:* outburst, eruption, outbreak, burst, explosion, roar, tumult, disturbance, agitation, commotion, clamor, hubbub, turmoil, furor, flurry, uproar, row, stir, ruckus, upheaval, pother, to-do, ado, hullabaloo, brouhaha, fuss, tempest. **3.** *The enemy took the place by storm:* sudden attack, violent assault, frontal attack, overwhelming onslaught. —v. **4.** *It stormed so hard that all the electricity went out:* rain heavily, snow heavily, blow violently. **5.** *He stormed at the waiter and embarrassed everyone at the table:* rage, rant, rave, lose one's temper, complain furiously, bluster, carry on, rampage, raise hell, vent one's rage, fly into a rage, snarl, raise the devil, fume, fulminate, *Slang* blow one's top, blow one's cool, fly off the handle. **6.** *She stormed out of the house:* rush, stamp, stomp, rage, tear, tramp, stalk. **7.** *Their only hope of victory was to storm the enemy camp at night:* charge, attack, assail, strike, rush, assault, make an onslaught, fall upon, besiege. —Ant. 1 calm, fair weather. 2 calm, peace, hush, tranquillity. 5 whisper, reason, cajole. 6 amble, saunter.

stormy adj. *Don't take the boat out in this stormy weather:* rainy; snowy; windy; turbulent, rough, blustering, tempestuous, inclement, blustery, raging, violent, squally, roaring, rugged, howling, wild, foul. —Ant. mild, calm, fair.

story n. **1.** *His story of the incident contradicts mine. I saw your name in a newspaper story:* report, account, allegation, version, statement, word, testimony, tidings, article, news, information, dispatch, news item, piece. **2.** *He won the fiction award for his short stories:* tale, narrative, romance, fable, yarn, sketch, allegory, anecdote, parable; plot, argument, legend. **3.** *Informal I know you're just telling a story!:* lie, white lie, falsehood, fib, fabrication, prevarication; excuse, alibi.

stout adj. **1.** *She's too stout to wear that clinging dress:* fat, corpulent, large, thickset, portly, rotund, plump, obese, big, round, heavy, tubby, pudgy, fleshy, bulky, chubby, stocky. **2.** *His stout self-confidence makes you feel you can depend on him:* brave, stouthearted, courageous, heroic, dauntless, lionhearted, valorous, valiant, intrepid, bold, daring, unshrinking, unflinching, stalwart, gallant, resolute, indomitable, plucky, doughty, fearless, confident, *Informal* spunky; steadfast, determined, staunch, resolved, firm, faithful, unwavering, true, unfalter-

ing, steady, constant, inflexible, untiring, unshakable, unswerving, enduring. **3.** *We need a couple of stout young fellows to move the piano. The henhouse needs a stout foundation:* sturdy, strapping, strong, husky, stalwart, hardy, robust, muscular, tough, vigorous, rugged, able-bodied, athletic, brawny, mighty, burly, fit, staunch, able, leathery, hefty, solid. —Ant. 1 lean, lanky, spare, skinny, slim, slender, thin. 2 cowardly, timid, irresolute, fearful, shrinking, apprehensive. 3 weak, frail, delicate, puny, feeble, fragile, unfit, unsound, flimsy, jerry-built, unsubstantial.

stouthearted adj. *The hero sang loudly about being a stouthearted man:* brave, fearless, bold, heroic, valiant, courageous, dauntless, hardy, lionhearted, spirited, unflinching, intrepid, undaunted, resolute, unblenching; *Slang* spunky, gutsy. —Ant. timid, fearful, afraid, cowardly.

stow v. *Stow the potatoes in a cool dark place:* store, put, place, set, pack, ensconce, cache, tuck, stuff, squeeze, jam, load, cram, crowd, wedge, salt away, deposit, *Informal* stash.

straggle v. *The children straggled to school:* ramble, drift, meander, loiter, meander, wander, dawdle.

straight adj. **1.** *They cut a straight trail from the top to the bottom of the mountain:* direct, unbent, unswerving, undeviating, not curved. **2.** *Make sure the rearview mirror is straight:* square, even, adjusted, aligned. **3.** *It's hard to get a straight report on the accident:* straightforward, honest, candid, forthright, true, truthful, reliable, veracious, square, frank, clear, aboveboard, accurate, four-square, right, sound, trustworthy. **4.** *He took a straight approach to the problem:* direct, unwavering, unswerving, undeviating. **5.** *We've had eight straight days of rain:* unbroken, solid, uninterrupted, continuous, successive, consecutive, incessant, sustained, ceaseless, persistent, unrelieved. **6.** *His desk is always straight:* orderly, tidy, in order, neat, shipshape; coordinated, sorted out, arranged, methodical. —adv. **7.** *Go straight to bed. Go straight home:* directly, immediately, instantly, forthwith; in a straight line, without wandering. **8.** *Stand up straight:* straightly, erectly, upright; evenly, on a level, squarely. —Ant. 1 curved, crooked, indirect, winding, bent, zigzag. 2 crooked, uneven, awry. 3 unreliable, confused, false, ambiguous, qualified, evasive, equivocal. 4 indirect, wavering, deviating, uncertain. 5 broken, interrupted, discontinuous, nonconsecutive. 6 messy, disorderly, untidy, mussed, disarranged, confused, disarrayed, in error. 7 eventually, later, afterward. 8 crookedly, unevenly, askew, awry.

straightforward adj. **1.** *We took a straightforward route to the beach:* direct, straight. **2.** *She gave a straightforward explanation for her mistake. He's completely straightforward in his business dealings:* open, candid, frank, honest, guileless, plainspoken, blunt, aboveboard, direct, forthright; trustworthy, square, upright, honorable, straight, ethical, scrupulous, creditable. —Ant. 1 indirect, roundabout, circuitous.

2 devious, sharp, guileful, unethical, deceitful, unscrupulous, shady.

strain¹ v. **1.** *If you strain the elastic any more, it will break:* draw tight, stretch, put under tension, pull, tug, make tense or taut, tighten; stretch, elongate, protract, distend, extend. **2.** *The prisoner strained to get away from his captors:* struggle, heave, exert one's strength, labor, toil, make a supreme effort, huff and puff. **3.** *The manufacturer strained to get his orders out in time. The doctor warned him against straining himself:* drive oneself, exert oneself, press, struggle, overwork, push to the utmost, work day and night, grind, overexert, tax, overtax, fatigue, wear out, exhaust, burden, overburden, drudge, burn the midnight oil, work one's fingers to the bone, work like a slave, work like a horse, burn the candle at both ends, overdo, do double duty; try hard, bear down, buckle down. **4.** *He strained his Achilles tendon playing tennis:* pull, sprain, impair by stretching, injure, wrench, weaken, twist, hurt by overexertion. **5.** *Some cooks strain their gravy:* sieve, filter, screen, sift, winnow, purify, drain, refine. *—n.* **6.** *Too much strain broke the rope:* stress, pressure, force, tension. **7.** *The strain of keeping awake was painful:* effort, exertion, struggle. **8.** *A heating pad might help that muscle strain:* sprain, pull, injury, wrench, twist. **9.** *He was under enormous strain during the trial:* tension, pressure, stress, hardship. **10.** *It seems to me I've heard that strain before. Jim whistled a familiar strain from Rodgers and Hart:* tune, song, melody, air. **—Ant.** 1 relax, loosen, slacken. 2 relax, yield. 3 idle; pamper, coddle. 7 effortlessness. 9 relaxation.

strain² n. **1.** *He comes of a tough peasant strain:* parentage, ancestry, lineage, descent, stock, derivation, family, people, extraction, breed, heredity, line, species, blood. **2.** *My uncle cultivated a rare strain of orchid:* type, breed, variety, kind, sort, group. **3.** *A strain of musical talent seems to run in the family:* streak, hereditary character, vein, natural capacity, tendency, trait, predisposition, grain, genius, inclination, disposition.

strained adj. *Strained relations between them got even worse:* forced, labored, stiff, tense, choked, constrained, difficult, embarrassed, self-conscious, stiff, taut, uncomfortable, uneasy, unnatural, difficult, artificial, awkward. **—Ant.** natural, comfortable, relaxed.

strait n. **1.** *Our boat went aground in the strait before we reached the sea:* narrow passage of water, narrows; channel. **2.** Often **straits** *His gambling debts put him in awkward financial straits:* predicament, difficulty, plight, distress, embarrassment, extremity, *Informal* fix, pickle, hole. **—Ant.** 2 ease, comfort, luxury.

straitened adj. *The death of her husband had left her in straitened circumstances:* distressed, pinched, restricted, needy, hard-up, strapped, penniless, embarrassed, poverty-stricken, destitute, bankrupt, broke, impoverished, penurious, indigent, pauperized, wiped-out. **—Ant.** comfortable, well-off, affluent, flush.

straitlaced adj. *He's too straitlaced to get out on a dance floor:* puritanical, proper, strict, prudish, prim, rigid, overscrupulous, narrow; formal, reserved, inhibited, undemonstrative, stiff, austere, severe, *Slang* uptight. **—Ant.** loose, immoral; relaxed, uninhibited, broadminded.

strand¹ v. **1.** *The hurricane stranded the sailboat on the reef:* run aground, go aground, beach, drive ashore, leave ashore, ground; shipwreck. **2.** *The loss of electricity stranded us without heat. The bus left, and we were stranded in a strange town:* leave, leave high and dry, leave in the lurch, maroon, desert. *—n.* **3.** *Hotels were going up all along the strand:* shore, coast, seashore, beach, seacoast, bank, riverside.

strand² n. **1.** *Separate the rope into its individual strands. Weave a love knot with a strand of hair:* filament, fiber, thread; cord, rope, string, tress, lock, braid, twist; ingredient, component. **2.** *Father gave Mother a strand of pearls for her birthday:* string, necklace.

stranded adj. *They were stranded on a desert island:* cast away, grounded, marooned, aground, run aground, shipwrecked, sidelined, sidetracked, wrecked, beached, ashore, abandoned.

strange adj. **1.** *His behavior seems strange:* peculiar, odd, unusual, queer, extraordinary, abnormal, curious, singular, uncommon, eccentric, irregular, outlandish, unnatural, unconventional, bizarre, unaccountable, freakish, erratic, out-of-the-way, unaccustomed, fantastic, aberrant, anomalous, farfetched. **2.** *Not being able to speak the language made me feel strange:* out of place, uncomfortable, ill at ease, uneasy, awkward, disoriented, estranged, lost, discomposed, bewildered, foreign, alien, alienated. **3.** *This area is strange to me:* unknown, unfamiliar, foreign, alien, unaccustomed, unexplored, undiscovered. **4.** *He is strange to the new machinery:* unfamiliar, unaccustomed, unused, new; unhabituated. **—Ant.** 1 regular, conventional, normal, commonplace, run-of-the-mill, usual, common, accustomed, ordinary. 2 at home, comfortable, at ease, easy. 3 known, familiar. 4 familiar, acquainted, experienced, used.

stranger n. **1.** *Everyone at the party was a stranger to me:* unknown person. **2.** *It's hard for a stranger to make friends in this town:* outsider, newcomer, foreigner, auslander, immigrant, alien, outlander. **—Ant.** 1 friend, acquaintance, buddy, chum. 2 native, insider, resident, habitué.

strangle v. **1.** *The killer strangled his victims with his bare hands:* choke, suffocate, stifle, smother, asphyxiate, throttle, garrote; *British* burke. **2.** *The dictator's first step was to strangle the free press:* stop, suppress, repress, stifle, throttle, choke off, squelch, quell, put a stop to, check, crush, put down, snuff out, extinguish, muzzle, gag, smother. **—Ant.** 2 assist, further, encourage, promote, forward, abet, aid, help.

strap n. **1.** *The strap on one of my old ski boots*

broke: fastening strip, thong, band, tie, cord, belt. —*v.* **2.** *Strap the suitcases on top of the car:* lash, tie, bind, truss, leash, tether. **3.** *He strapped the boy with a leather belt:* whip, thrash, beat, flog, belt, lash, flail, scourge.

strapped *adj.* *Heavy expenses left them strapped:* broke, poor, down-and-out, flat, impoverished, poverty-stricken, needy, penniless, penurious, derelict, destitute.

strapping *adj.* *Informal That frail boy grew up to be a strapping man:* robust, sturdy, strongly built, husky, stalwart, hardy, burly, muscular, brawny, powerful, stout, strong. —*Ant.* frail, weak, fragile, puny.

stratagem *n.* *The general's clever stratagem was successful against the enemy:* maneuver, scheme, plan, plot, trick, intrigue, ruse, artifice, tactic, trickery, device, contrivance, machination, game, deception, subterfuge, deceit, ploy, dodge, feint, blind, wile.

strategic *adj.* **1.** *The strategic operation was agreed to by all the top brass. The army made a strategic retreat:* tactical, military; calculated; politic, diplomatic; planned, well thought-out, deliberate, clever, cunning, cautious, careful, guarded, prudent, precautionary, vigilant, wary. **2.** *Refreshment stands were set up in strategic spots around the dance floor. Wait for the strategic moment, and then strike:* crucial, important, decisive, critical, vital, significant, momentous, key, principal, consequential, turning. —*Ant.* 1 nonstrategic; unplanned. 2 unimportant, inconsequential, trifling.

strategy *n.* **1.** *The strategy is to wear the enemy down by repeated attacks:* military plan, overall plan, grand design, scheme; tactics, maneuvering, devices, game, artifice, policy, machination, plotting. **2.** *He was an expert in strategy during the war:* military science, war planning, war policy, art of war. **3.** *He needs to improve his strategy before he can call himself a good tennis player:* artfulness, craft, cunning, craftiness, wiles, artifice, game plan, tactics.

straw *n.* **1.** *He was lazing in the sun chewing on a straw. The glasses were packed in straw:* stem of grain; hay, chaff. **2.** *May I have a straw for my drink?:* tube for sucking liquid; pipette.

stray *v.* **1.** *The kitten must have strayed from its mother:* go astray, roam, wander, drift, rove, straggle, lose one's way. **2.** *Her thoughts strayed to her childhood:* wander, drift, digress. —*n.* **3.** *The kind lady's house was always open to strays:* homeless person or creature, waif, lost person, lost animal, itinerant, vagabond, wanderer, drifter, straggler. —*adj.* **4.** *The dogcatcher went looking for stray dogs:* straying, lost, misplaced. **5.** *Only a few stray clouds dotted the sky:* scattered, set apart, separate, random.

streak *n.* **1.** *You have a streak of paint on your forehead:* long smear, line, stripe, strip, bar, band; (*loosely*) smudge, blotch, splotch, smirch, blur, daub, blot. **2.** *There are streaks of ore in the mountain:* layer, portion, vein, lode, bed, seam; level, stratum, plane. **3.** *He has a mean streak:* vein, cast, strain, touch. —*v.* **4.** *The win-*

ning horse streaked past the finish line: race, speed, rush, hurtle; whiz, tear, zoom, dart, dash, fly. —*Ant.* 4 creep, crawl, go at a snail's pace.

stream *n.* **1.** *The stream is full of trout:* narrow river, streamlet, brook, creek, rivulet, rill, branch, run, watercourse, tributary, feeder, freshet. **2.** *A stream of water ran off the roof. A stream of traffic crossed the bridge. The child kept up a steady stream of talk:* flow, torrent, run, course, rush, race, current, spout, sluice, river, gush, onrush, jet, flux, surge, deluge, flood, tide; effusion, spate, profusion. —*v.* **3.** *Blood streamed from the wound. Cars streamed from the parking lot:* flow, pour, run, issue, course, rush, surge, burst, spill, gush, spout, spurt, flood, fountain, shoot; move continuously, file, go on endlessly. **4.** *The streets were streaming with tourists:* teem, abound, flow, overflow. **5.** *Her hair ribbons streamed behind her as she ran down the hill:* wave, float, flutter, blow, waft, stretch out, extend.

street *n.* *The child ran into the street. Our street has had a number of burglaries:* road; (*variously*) thoroughfare, roadway, route, highway, turnpike, expressway, thruway, way, avenue, boulevard, lane, alley, mews, terrace; block.

strength *n.* **1.** *Does he have enough strength to lift these weights? She has great strength of character:* power, vigor, might, muscles, hardiness, force, brawn, *Slang* beef; robustness, puissance, potency, sturdiness, stoutness, sinew, lustiness, stamina, endurance, viability, vitality, pith, backbone; firmness, fortitude, toughness, solidity, vitality, spirit; tenacity, pluck, grit, mettle, bravery, stoutheartedness, spice, *Slang* sand. **2.** *What is the total strength of the enemy army?:* force, number, size. **3.** *This medicine has lost its strength:* potency, power, force, effectiveness, efficacy, kick, *Archaic* virtue. **4.** *The clouds diminished the strength of the sunlight. The sauce has lost some of its strength:* intensity, concentration, purity, vitality. **5.** *Her faith in God is her real strength. Math is her strength, languages her weakness:* source of power, support, security, anchor, mainstay, buttress, sustenance, succor; forte, strong point. —*Ant.* 1 weakness, frailness, powerlessness, impotence, spiritlessness, feebleness. 3 ineffectiveness, inefficacy, unsoundness. 4 flatness, dilution, adulteration. 5 frailty, flaw.

strengthen *v.* *His back strengthened with exercise. The new evidence strengthened his case:* make stronger, become stronger, give strength to, gain strength, grow stronger, reinforce; fortify, build up, buttress, support, brace, prop, shore up, sustain; harden, steel, restore, renew, enhance, improve. —*Ant.* weaken, debilitate, crush, enervate, destroy, devitalize.

strenuous *adj.* **1.** *You shouldn't take such strenuous exercise:* laborious, taxing, exhausting, physically demanding, arduous, difficult, punishing; intense, vigorous, hard, uphill. **2.** *He's a strenuous student and will do well at school:* energetic, dynamic, vigorous, zealous, active, industrious, intense, earnest, ardent, eager, enterprising, animated, spirited, assiduous, sedulous, diligent, hardworking, dogged, on one's toes, painstaking, indefatigable, untiring. —**Ant.** 1 easy, light, effortless. 2 lazy, indolent.

stress n. **1.** *They place too much stress on money and position:* emphasis, importance, weight, consequence, significance, meaning, gravity, value, seriousness, prominence, worth, urgency, necessity, concern, consideration, moment. **2.** *In the word* sawdust, *the stress is on the first syllable:* accent, accentuation, emphasis, beat. **3.** *The limb couldn't bear up under the stress of the heavy snow. The stress of not knowing was too great for her:* strain, tension, anxiety, force, burden, pressure, oppression. —v. **4.** *The speaker stressed the need for better education:* emphasize, lay emphasis on, accentuate, accent, underscore, underline, mark, assert positively, insist upon, feature, repeat, affirm, assert. **5.** *Stress the second syllable in* today: accent, emphasize, accentuate. —**Ant.** 1 unimportance, insignificance, de-emphasis. 5 de-emphasize, underplay, understate; ignore, neglect, pass over.

stretch v. **1.** *She stretched the clothesline between two trees. Will this material stretch?:* distend, extend, draw out, pull out, widen, lengthen, deepen, protract, expand, be expandable, elongate; strain, make tense or tight, draw tight, draw taut, put under tension, be elastic, be extendable, bear extension. **2.** *Stretch your hand through the window:* extend, put forth, reach, reach out. **3.** *The road stretches across the mountains:* lie over, cover, extend, reach, spread, span, traverse. **4.** *Let's stretch out on the sand for a while:* lie at full length; sprawl. **5.** *The cat stretched and arched its back:* strain the body, draw out the muscles. **6.** *I think you have stretched a point there. You stretch my patience:* exaggerate, strain, push to the limit, carry too far, push too far, run into the ground; overtax, overstrain, overwork, overburden, burden, overcharge, overtask, fatigue, tire, overexert. —n. **7.** *He spent a long stretch in jail:* spell, term, duration, period, interval, stint, while. **8.** *We drove fast along a stretch of empty highway:* expanse, spread, tract, distance. **9.** *The stretch has gone out of this waistband:* elasticity, elastic quality, resiliency, tautness, spring. —**Ant.** 1 shrink, loosen, relax, slacken, tighten, tauten, contract, condense, compress, narrow, shorten. 2 withdraw, retract.

strew v. *They strewed confetti on the newly married pair:* scatter, sprinkle, overspread, broadcast. —**Ant.** gather, reap.

stricken adj. *The region has long been stricken with poverty. All hands were rescued from the stricken ship. The stricken animal was put out of its misery:* afflicted, smitten; (*variously*) ill, sick, taken sick, diseased, blighted, incapacitated, wounded, injured, hurt.

strict adj. **1.** *Her strict father insisted that she be home by midnight. Our laws on speeding are very strict:* stern, rigid, severe, authoritarian, rigorous, uncompromising, austere, stringent, un-

yielding, exacting, inflexible. **2.** *The church demands strict loyalty:* perfect, absolute, complete, unerring, conscientious, fastidious, exact, meticulous, scrupulous, nice. —**Ant.** 1 lax, lenient, indulgent, permissive; loose, flexible; broad, approximate. 2 loose, inattentive, careless.

stride v. **1.** *He strode out of the house:* march, walk with long steps, take long steps, stalk, lope, step. —n. **2.** *He reached the house several strides before us:* pace, long step. **3.** *The dancer moves with a graceful stride:* gait, step. **4.** *He's made tremendous strides toward recovery:* step, advance, advancement, progress, headway, improvement.

strident adj. *His strident voice hurts my ears:* grating, harsh, piercing, jangling, jarring, raucous, discordant, rasping, grinding, shrill, high-pitched, screeching, dissonant, clashing, cacophonous, twanging. —**Ant.** soft, mellow, dulcet, mellifluous, soothing.

strife n. *A history of strife has left its mark on the tiny nation:* conflict, discord, dissension, turmoil, upheaval, fighting, trouble, unrest, disharmony, contention, altercation, disturbance, disquiet, convulsion, struggle, violence, warfare. —**Ant.** peace, accord, calm, agreement, harmony.

strike v. **1.** *He struck me with his fist. Strike the nail as straight as you can:* hit, slug, deal a blow to, bang, box, cuff, slap, club, thump, smash, pound, knock, tap, clap, bump, beat, cudgel, clout, slam, bat, sock, punch, wallop, pommel, pelt, smite, whack, buffet, hammer, clip, drub, belt; thrash, flog, batter, lash, whip, whale, lambaste, scourge, flail, flagellate. **2.** *The enemy struck at dawn:* attack, assail, hit, assault, charge. **3.** *The speeding car struck a telephone pole:* hit, dash against, meet head-on, run into, hurtle against, knock into, bump into, beat against, ram into, run or fall foul of, collide with. **4.** *Heavenly music struck our ears:* reach, fall upon, hit; burst upon. **5.** *The lateness of the hour suddenly struck us:* occur to, come to the mind of, dawn upon, reach. **6.** *His enthusiasm struck his teacher favorably:* impress, affect, appear to, seem to. **7.** *Prospectors finally struck gold. He struck upon the solution quite by accident:* hit, come, arrive, run, light, chance, meet, stumble, find, encounter, come upon, come across, reach, unearth, discover. **8.** *The negotiators failed to strike a compromise:* reach, achieve, make, effect, arrange. **9.** *The soldiers struck camp and slipped away:* take down, pull down, put away, fold up, take apart. **10.** *Strike that statement from the record:* remove, cancel, eliminate, erase, eradicate, delete, wipe, cross out, scratch. **11.** *The clock struck noon:* sound, ring, chime, knell, toll. **12.** *A blight struck the entire crop:* hit, afflict suddenly, assault, assail, affect severely, deal a blow to, devastate, smite. **13.** *The transit workers struck just before Christmas:* go on strike, walk out. —n. **14.** *The strike ended when the wage demands were met:* walkout, work stoppage, tie-up, labor dispute; protest, boycott.

striking adj. *She bears a striking resemblance*

to her mother: remarkable, noteworthy, noticeable, notable, conspicuous, prominent, marked, outstanding, impressive; astounding, extraordinary, surprising.

string *n.* **1.** *The string around the package broke:* cord, thread, twine, strand, line, binding. **2.** *Mother has a fine string of pearls:* strand, rope, necklace. **3.** *A string of children filed into the house. A string of hotels lined the beach:* procession, file, parade; row, chain, train, succession, column, line, sequence, series, queue. —*v.* **4.** *They strung these pearls too tightly:* thread, put on a string. **5.** *String the clothesline between the two trees:* stretch, extend, spread.

stringent *adj.* **1.** *Stringent laws are needed to protect the consumer:* strict, stiff, demanding, rigorous, exacting, compelling obedience, inflexible, unbending, uncompromising, unyielding, harsh, severe, stern. **2.** *He used the most stringent reasoning in pleading his case:* forceful, cogent, effectual, severe, rigorous. **3.** *Such a stringent budget allows for few luxuries:* tight, close, sparing, spare, frugal. —**Ant.** 1 flexible, loose; ineffective, relaxed. 2 ineffective, unconvincing, equivocal, unsound, inconclusive. 3 lavish, ample, generous.

stringy *adj.* *The stringy steak was left uneaten:* fibrous, gristly, muscular, tough; ropy, sinewy, wiry; lank, lanky, gangly, gangling.

strip¹ *v.* **1.** *The doctor told him to strip before getting on the scales:* unclothe, undress, remove one's clothes, disrobe, divest of clothing, undrape; lay bare, unwrap, uncover, disencumber. **2.** *We had to strip the old paint from the doors:* remove, shave, peel, flay, flake, draw off, pull off, tear, lay bare, skin, denude. **3.** *They stripped the prisoners of their dignity:* deprive, rob, divest. **4.** *The pirates stripped the cargo ship:* plunder, ravage, sack, rob, despoil, loot, ransack, desolate, spoliate, lay waste, raid, steal from, rifle. —**Ant.** 1 dress, clothe; cover. 2 apply, put on. 3 invest, furnish.

strip² *n.* **1.** *I need two strips of adhesive tape:* long narrow piece, length, slip, ribbon, band, stripe; measure. **2.** *The landing strip was covered with snow:* airstrip, field.

stripe *n.* **1.** *Vertical stripes on a dress are slenderizing:* band, streak, line, swath, strip, bar, striation. **2.** *His mother sewed the stripes on his uniform:* strip of material, tape, braid, ribbon; emblem of rank, insignia, chevron, bar.

strive *v.* **1.** *A desire to please his parents made him strive to do well:* struggle, try hard, attempt earnestly, exert oneself, apply oneself, make efforts, labor, do all one can, push, take pains, do one's utmost, strain; leave no stone unturned, do one's best, spare no pains, work like a Trojan, move heaven and earth; essay, undertake, endeavor. **2.** *The surrounded platoon strove against unbeatable odds:* fight, contend, vie, struggle, battle. —**Ant.** 1 take it easy, *Slang* goof off, goldbrick.

stroke *n.* **1.** *He felled his opponent with one stroke:* blow, punch, chop, whack, swat, sock, wallop. **2.** *Give your hair 50 strokes with a brush every day:* brush, massage, light touch, caress. **3.** *The stroke of midnight signaled the New Year:* striking, tolling, sounding, chime, ringing. **4.** *The stroke left his right side paralyzed:* paralytic stroke, brain hemorrhage, apoplectic fit, apoplexy, seizure. **5.** *The letter Y ends with a downward stroke:* movement, flourish. **6.** *He outmaneuvered the enemy by a bold stroke. A stroke of fate turned the beggar into a rich man:* hit, achievement, blow, feat, deed, transaction, coup; piece of luck, chance, fluke, coincidence, accident. —*v.* **7.** *The golfer stroked the ball into the cup:* hit lightly, tap, punch, slap, bat, swat, poke. **8.** *He stroked her hair gently:* caress, pat, pet.

stroll *v.* **1.** *A huge crowd strolled down Fifth Avenue in the Easter Parade:* walk slowly, amble, saunter, promenade, wander, dawdle along, ramble, meander, poke along, *Slang* mosey. —*n.* **2.** *Will you join us for a stroll in the park?:* walk, amble, promenade, ramble, saunter, turn, tour, constitutional. —**Ant.** 1 run, race, hurry, dash, scurry.

strong *adj.* **1.** *Is the boy strong enough to lift that box? There's a strong undertow in the river here:* powerful, having great strength, forceful, mighty, potent, puissant; muscular, sinewy, stalwart, stout, herculean, burly, hardy, brawny, robust, healthy, hearty, tough, athletic, vigorous, energetic; severe, intense, violent. **2.** *Handling people is one of his strong points:* able, competent, capable, skilled, well-qualified, well-endowed, proficient, advantageous. **3.** *She was strong enough to overcome her handicap:* firm in spirit, resourceful, plucky, gritty, stalwart, stout, courageous, sturdy, sound, tough, tenacious, persistent, persevering; resilient, buoyant; tireless, indefatigable. **4.** *He offered some strong reasons for abandoning the project:* convincing, compelling, forceful, powerful, moving, potent, effective, solid, sound, cogent. **5.** *There's a strong similarity between the two candidates:* close, clear, distinct, definite, emphatic, unmistakable. **6.** *Those colors are too strong for a bedroom:* bright, bold, vivid, intense, fiery. **7.** *His strong religious belief helped him through a bad time. The senator has a strong following:* keen, fervent, intense, deep, deep-seated, zealous, ardent, vehement, earnest, impassioned, fervid, fierce, confirmed, assiduous, faithful, devoted, sedulous, diligent, high-spirited, animated, spirited. **8.** *I like my coffee strong. The fortune-teller used strong perfume:* highly flavored, tangy, sharp, potent, concentrated, undiluted, highly seasoned, pungent, nippy, highly spiced, piquant, savory, tart, biting, hot. —**Ant.** 1 weak, frail, feeble, powerless, soft. 2 unqualified. 3 passive, spiritless, submissive. 4 unconvincing, ineffectual, unsound; meek, mild, conciliatory. 5 slight, vague. 6 faint, dull, colorless. 7 shallow, spiritless, apathetic, lethargic, halfhearted, faint, wavering, insecure, unfaithful. 8 diluted, watery; faint, subtle; bland, tasteless, insipid; soothing, balmy; odorless.

stronghold *n.* **1.** *The plan was to attack the enemy stronghold at midnight:* fortified place, fortress, fortification, fort, bulwark, battlement, citadel, bastion, fastness, stockade, bunker, blockhouse, rampart, keep, safehold, hold, redoubt. **2.** *Montreal is a stronghold of tradition:* center, refuge, home, locale; bulwark, bastion, citadel, rampart.

structure *n.* **1.** *A large structure is being erected on the old fairground site:* building, construction, edifice. **2.** *The structure of the song is very symmetrical:* arrangement, plan, form, makeup, organization, composition, interrelation of parts, configuration, conformation, formation, design, pattern. —*v.* **3.** *They structured the program to reach all ages:* put together, construct, organize, conceive, arrange, design, assemble.

struggle *v.* **1.** *He struggled with the intruder. He struggled against those who opposed his plan:* battle, fight, join issue, combat, contend, compete, vie, tussle, scuffle, skirmish, joust, tilt, brush, duel, engage, match, exchange blows, spar, cross swords, lock horns, brawl, jostle, grapple, scrap; clash, argue, oppose, resist, differ, feud, quarrel. **2.** *She had to struggle to meet the deadline:* strain, push, work hard, do all one can, exert oneself, labor, strive, take pains, endeavor, spare no pains, move heaven and earth, do one's utmost, leave no stone unturned, work like a Trojan. —*n.* **3.** *The emperor lost 1000 men in the struggle:* fight, conflict, battle, combat, war, engagement, encounter, altercation, action, strife, contest. **4.** *It was a struggle to stay awake:* strain, grind, trial, labor, long haul, exertion, effort, push, pull, endeavor, stress. —**Ant.** 1 surrender, give in, yield, succumb. 4 cinch, sure thing.

strum *v.* *She strummed the guitar:* pluck, pick, plunk, thrum, twang.

strut *v.* *He strutted into the restaurant as though he owned it:* swagger, walk pompously, parade, sail, sashay, peacock, promenade. —**Ant.** cringe, cower, slink, sneak.

stub *n.* **1.** *The ashtray is filled with cigarette stubs. I can't write with this pencil stub:* stump, dock, butt, end, fag end, broken remnant, remains; tail. **2.** *Keep your ticket stubs:* torn ticket, cancelled ticket, counterfoil; payment voucher, receipt. —*v.* **3.** *He stubbed his big toe on the pavement:* strike accidentally, scrape, bump, knock. **4.** *He quickly stubbed out his cigarette:* snuff, crush, tamp out, extinguish.

stubborn *adj.* **1.** *She's too stubborn to give in:* obstinate, unmovable, immovable, unyielding, obdurate, tenacious, opinionated, indomitable, unbending, intractable, perverse, refractory, recalcitrant, headstrong, self-willed, willful, uncompliant, inflexible, ungovernable, mulish, pigheaded, bullheaded, dogged. **2.** *He made a stubborn attempt to break the lock:* purposeful, persistent, resolute, sturdy, strong, forceful, concerted, wholehearted. **3.** *I can't shake this stubborn cold:* hard to handle or manage; unshakable, tenacious, resistant. —**Ant.** 1 pliable, adaptable, tractable, flexible; irresolute, yielding, docile, manageable; vacillating, wavering, undecided. 2 weak, feeble, frail, halfhearted. 3 manageable.

stubby *adj.* *The blacksmith was a short, stubby man:* short and thick, stumpy, pudgy, squab, squat, squatty, dumpy, thickset, chubby, tubby, stodgy, stocky, chunky. —**Ant.** slim, lean, long, slender.

stuck-up *adj.* *When she first met Ralph she thought he was stuck-up:* conceited, vain, arrogant, high-hat, snobbish, uppish, haughty, snooty, self-important, hoity-toity, uppity, swellheaded, egocentric, disdainful, bigheaded, self-satisfied, cocky, overbearing. —**Ant.** modest, humble, unassuming, unpretentious.

student *n.* **1.** *How many students attend the local high school?:* pupil, learner, scholar, matriculant; collegian, undergraduate, schoolgirl, schoolboy, *Informal* coed; disciple, follower. **2.** *A good reporter is a student of human nature:* observer, examiner, spectator, reviewer, watcher, interpreter, analyst, commentator, reader. —**Ant.** 1 teacher, professor, mentor, instructor.

studied *adj.* *The studied casualness of the stranger's manner put us on guard:* calculated, deliberate, measured, purposeful, intentional, premeditated. —**Ant.** spontaneous, impulsive, unplanned, instinctive.

studious *adj.* **1.** *The studious girl rarely goes to parties:* devoted to study, scholarly, academic, intellectual, erudite, brainy, cerebral, bookish, scholastic; well-read, literate. **2.** *He made a studious effort to make us feel welcome:* earnest, diligent, painstaking, purposeful, laborious, determined, intent. —**Ant.** 1 fun-loving, frivolous; unscholarly. 2 idle, indulgent, careless, inattentive, thoughtless, negligent, indifferent.

study *n.* **1.** *She got married and never finished her studies:* pursuit of knowledge, learning, education, work at school, academic work, scholarship, instruction, mental cultivation, reading. **2.** *The committee made a thorough study of the causes of civil disorders:* investigation, inquiry, survey, research, examination, search, consideration, analysis, scrutiny, inspection, exploration, probe. **3.** *The dictionary is in the study:* library, studio, reading room, office, den. —*v.* **4.** *He's studying for exams:* work at learning, educate oneself, school oneself, pursue knowledge, *Informal* cram, grind, read, hit the books. **5.** *The committee will study the tax plan thoroughly. Astronomers studied the heavens for the predicted new comet:* plunge into, read up on, delve into, investigate, examine, inquire into, consider, explore, observe, probe, survey, search through, research. **6.** *He studied the directions for putting up the tent:* examine, read closely, look at carefully, pore over, survey, review, glance over, peruse, scrutinize.

stuff *n.* **1.** *Do you have the stuff you need to make the rug? Hope is the stuff that dreams are made of:* raw material, material, staple; matter, substance, component, constituent, ingredient; essence, inmost substance, quintessence. **2.** *Informal I left some of my stuff in Mother's attic:* things, effects, gear, belongings, possessions, paraphernalia, tackle. **3.** *Informal That story is nothing but a lot of stuff:* nonsense, stuff and nonsense, spinach, bunk, empty talk, humbug, balderdash, rubbish, foolishness, trash, bosh, hooey, hokum, hogwash, falderal, twaddle. **4.** *Informal Now get out there and do your stuff!:* best, utmost, darndest; thing, bit, tricks, act, performance. **—v. 5.** *She stuffed the trunk with her summer clothes:* pile, fill, fill up, jam, cram, load, pack, wad, heap, burden. **6.** *It seems barbaric to stuff animals for decorative purposes. He stuffed the cushions with down:* fill with stuffing, fill, pad. **7.** *She stuffed herself with chocolate candy:* gorge, cram, overeat, feed gluttonously, gluttonize, overindulge, satiate, sate, make a pig of. **8.** *Just stuff the laundry into the machine:* load, pack, thrust, jam, cram, crowd, stash, cache, wedge, store, stow. **—Ant.** 3 facts, truth. 5 empty, unpack. 8 take out, remove.

stuffing n. **1.** *He used straw as stuffing for the dolls:* filling, padding, wadding, packing. **2.** *I add walnuts to my turkey stuffing:* dressing, filling, forcemeat, farce.

stuffy adj. **1.** *The subway is unbearably stuffy in the summer:* close, unventilated, ill-ventilated, fusty, suffocating, stagnant, heavy, stifling, muggy, musty, sultry, sweltering, stale-smelling, oppressive, airless. **2.** *My nose is stuffy:* congested, stopped-up, stuffed-up, clogged-up. **3.** *We expected and got a stuffy response from that snob:* smug, pompous, pretentious, high-flown, self-satisfied, supercilious, cold, reserved, straitlaced; stodgy, old-fogyish, staid. **—Ant.** 1 airy, well-ventilated, cool. 2 unclogged. 3 natural, modest, unpretentious.

stultify v. *Nothing stultifies a student's enthusiasm more than a dull teacher:* vitiate, make useless, cripple, hamstring, impair, impede, nullify, frustrate, suppress, thwart, hinder, inhibit, balk. **—Ant.** arouse, encourage, spark, enliven, animate, spur, inspire.

stumble v. **1.** *She stumbled over a stool in the darkened room:* trip, stagger, pitch forward; fall, take a spill, sprawl, lurch, topple. **2.** *He stumbled out of the bar to look for a cab:* stagger, reel, walk unsteadily, totter, sway, flounder, hobble, shamble, pitch, roll. **3.** *The actor stumbled over his lines:* blunder, slip up, make mistakes, falter; hash up, botch, mess up, bungle. **4.** *I stumbled upon the answer to the riddle:* happen, fall, blunder, hit, come by chance. **—n. 5.** *She broke her ankle in that stumble over the bike:* trip, stagger, misstep, spill, fall, topple, pitch.

stumbling block n. *The biggest stumbling block to peace is the reluctance to disarm:* obstacle, obstruction, hindrance, barrier, hamper, impediment, hurdle, interference, snag, block, bar, difficulty, hitch, drawback, catch, rub. **—Ant.** aid, support, encouragement, assistance.

stump n. **1.** *We used the stump as a table:* tree stump, stub. **2.** *I can't get a grip on this pencil stump:* stub, nubbin, butt, end. **3.** *The loud stump of jackboots on the stairs woke the household:* tramping, stomping, footfall, clunk, thud. **—v. 4.** *The crime stumped the entire*

homicide squad: mystify, baffle, dumbfound, perplex, foil, bewilder, confound, stymie, befog, confuse, nonplus, *Informal* bamboozle. **5.** *Try not to stump up the stairs:* stomp, stamp, tramp, thud, clonk, clump, clomp, walk heavily.

stun v. **1.** *The blow to his head stunned him for a few moments:* daze, stagger, stupefy, numb. **2.** *Her sudden temper tantrum stunned us:* shock, dumbfound, stupefy, startle, amaze, astonish, stagger, astound, flabbergast.

stunning adj. **1.** *The fighter received a stunning blow to his head. The news was stunning:* dazing, stupefying, numbing; dumbfounding, amazing, astounding, shocking, startling, flabbergasting, astonishing, staggering. **2.** *Her stunning outfit made everyone turn to look at her:* striking, strikingly attractive, beautiful, lovely, exquisite, electrifying. **—Ant.** 1 mild, harmless; expected, commonplace, ordinary. 2 plain, ordinary, run-of-the-mill, unimpressive, unremarkable.

stunt[1] v. *It used to be said that smoking would stunt one's growth:* check, curtail, dwarf, curb, impede, stint, limit, delimit, restrain, restrict, cramp, stifle, suppress, abort. **—Ant.** increase, stimulate.

stunt[2] n. *That last stunt on the trapeze brought cheers from the crowd:* trick, act, feat, number.

stupefy v. **1.** *The fall from the ladder stupefied him:* daze, stun, shock, make punch-drunk, make one feel punchy. **2.** *News of the bombing stupefied the nation:* daze, flabbergast, stagger, amaze, astound, dumbfound, astonish, confound, surprise, overwhelm, nonplus.

stupendous adj. **1.** *What a stupendous movie!:* remarkable, astounding, extraordinary, wonderful, astonishing, marvelous, terrific, great, fabulous, unusual, prodigious, incredible, stunning, amazing, surprising, unexpected. **2.** *The stupendous housing development dwarfed the rest of the neighborhood:* gigantic, huge, mammoth, vast, enormous, prodigious, phenomenal, tremendous, immense, massive, giant, colossal, very large, imposing, monumental, big, titanic, jumbo, very great, mighty, herculean, cyclopean, monstrous, gargantuan, elephantine. **—Ant.** 1 ordinary, unsurprising. 2 small, little, minuscule, modest, diminutive, Lilliputian, wee, tiny.

stupid adj. **1.** *A stupid class is difficult to teach:* dull, dumb, brainless, witless, unintelligent, dense, simpleminded, simple, slow-learning, backward, weak-minded, doltish, rattlebrained, empty-headed; muddleheaded, dimwitted, duncelike, obtuse, oafish; idiotic, half-witted, imbecilic, moronic, cretinous. **2.** *The boy's stupid behavior got him into trouble. The general made a stupid decision:* foolish, irresponsible, unwise, reckless, indiscriminating, imprudent, ill-advised, ill-considered, ill-judged, mistaken, absentminded, heedless, foolhardy, thoughtless, unintelligent, idiotic, silly, childish, inane, senseless, nonsensical, unreasonable, inappropriate, fatuous, asinine; tactless, indiscreet, boorish. **3.** *We left in the middle of the stupid movie:* senseless, meaningless, absurd, silly, nonsensical, pointless, irrelevant, inept, inconsequential, preposterous, aimless, purposeless, asinine. —**Ant.** intelligent. 1 bright, clever, shrewd, quick, sharp, responsive, *Slang* hip. 2 smart, sensible, wise, thoughtful, tactful, prudent, well-advised, adult, mature, reasonable, canny, appropriate. 3 meaningful, interesting, deep, relevant, consequential, purposeful, sensible.

stupor *n.* **1.** *The drug caused a state more like a stupor than natural sleep:* stunned condition, near-unconsciousness, insensibility, stupefaction, numbness, somnolence; blackout, faint. **2.** *The defeated nation recovered from its stupor and rebuilt:* torpor, apathy, inertness, inertia, lethargy, daze.

sturdy *adj.* **1.** *We need several sturdy men to push this car:* strong, mighty, muscular, rugged, powerful, robust, tough, burly, vigorous, stout, stalwart, forceful, sinewy, strapping, hardy, able. **2.** *This chair is not sturdy enough to stand on:* solid, substantial, sound, strong, heavy, secure, tough, rugged, lasting, durable, well-constructed, well-made, well-built. **3.** *He put up a sturdy fight to the end:* brave, courageous, gallant, resolute, stouthearted, intrepid, plucky, valiant, unshrinking, spirited, stout, indomitable, undaunted, dauntless, heroic, firm, daring, invincible, doughty, dogged, high-spirited, fearless, unabashed, gritty, determined, stubborn, enduring, defiant, *Informal* spunky, gutsy. —**Ant.** weak. 1 frail, feeble, powerless. 2 fragile, unsubstantial, light, flimsy. 3 cowardly, fearful, irresolute, shrinking.

stutter *v. He stuttered from an early age:* speak haltingly, stammer, splutter, sputter, stumble, falter, hesitate.

stygian *adj. We descended the stairway to the stygian depths of the castle's cellar:* infernal, hellish; dreary, somber, murky, dark, funereal, gloomy, dim, black, starless, tenebrous, unlighted. —**Ant.** bright, light, cheerful, sunny, lighted.

style *n.* **1.** *De Quincey's style is verbose and Hemingway's is terse:* typical mode of expression, manner, characteristic tone. **2.** *The wealthy couple really live in style:* luxury, elegance, pomp, comfort, affluence. **3.** *He handled the awkward situation with style:* grace, smoothness, polish, class, savoir faire, charm, taste, flair, *French* élan. **4.** *Argyle socks are back in style. Last year's style was too trendy for me:* fashion, vogue, currency, favor; trend, taste, craze, fad, mode, rage. **5.** *Which style of writing paper do you prefer?:* type, kind, sort, pattern, model. —*v.* **6.** *She styled my hair in a pageboy:* design, arrange, give style to. **7.** *He styles himself a revolutionary:* call, name, designate. —**Ant.** 1 substance, content, essence. 2 squalor, drabness. 3 awkwardness, tastelessness.

stylish *adj. My aunt is a stylish dresser:* fashionable, chic, voguish, in vogue, modish, up-to-date, up-to-the-minute, latest, in fashion, a la mode, new, modern, smart, elegant, sophisticated, *Slang* hip, with-it; dapper, natty, swank.

—**Ant.** unstylish, unfashionable, passé, out-of-date, outmoded, dowdy, old-fashioned.

stymie *v. The riddle stymied us all:* stump, mystify, confound, puzzle, baffle, confuse; block, balk, check, thwart, hinder, frustrate, obstruct.

suave *adj. He's as suave as a diplomat:* urbane, smooth, silken, polished, gracious, politic, diplomatic, charming, affable, mannerly, civilized, elegant; flattering, smooth-tongued, unctuous, diplomatic, ingratiating.

subconscious *adj. I had only a subconscious awareness of the seriousness of the problem:* subliminal, half-conscious, intuitive, instinctive, dim, dawning. —**Ant.** conscious, explicit, expressed, clear.

subdivision *n. The mayor's office approved the subdivision:* tract. development, annexe.

subdue *v.* **1.** *The police used tear gas to subdue the rioters:* overcome, crush, master, quell, put down, overpower, down, still, smash, subject, subjugate, oppress, defeat, foil, overwhelm, thrash, drub, whip, trim, rout, triumph over, conquer, vanquish, get the upper hand over, trample, floor, overrun, surmount, break, bow, reduce, get the better of. **2.** *His soothing words subdued her fears:* calm, reduce, curb, check, moderate, palliate, mellow, soften, temper, assuage, ease, allay, salve, soothe, tranquillize, slacken, mollify, relieve, appease, deaden, mitigate, ameliorate, meliorate. **3.** *Try to subdue your laughter:* tone down, moderate, quiet down, mute, muffle, soften, soft-pedal. —**Ant.** 2 awaken, quicken, arouse, provoke, inflame, agitate, irritate. 3 vent, unleash.

subdued *adj. The subdued crowd filed silently out of the stadium:* toned down, grave, hushed, low-key, muted, quiet, restrained, sober, soft, softened, solemn, submissive, subtle, tempered, unobtrusive; sad, serious; chastened, crestfallen, dejected, downcast. —**Ant.** loud, lively, strident, vivacious, bright; cheerful, enthusiastic, happy.

subject *n.* **1.** *Campaign financing was the subject of the seminar:* topic, matter, subject matter, matter in hand, theme, substance, issue, motif, point at issue, question, point in question; concern, case, affair, business; thesis, text; gist, pith. **2.** *How many subjects are you studying this semester?:* branch of knowledge, field, study, discipline. **3.** *The Queen has many loyal subjects:* follower, dependent, subordinate; liege, vassal; citizen. —*adj.* **4.** *We are subject to the laws of the country:* bound by, owing allegiance, owing obedience; subservient, subordinate, at another's command, answerable, subjected, obedient. **5.** *The date of our trip is subject to my firm's vacation schedule:* dependent upon, conditional upon, contingent on, stipulatory. **6.** *He is subject to violent fits of temper:* susceptible, vulnerable, open, liable, prone, disposed, exposed, at the mercy of, in danger of. —*v.* **7.** *The hurricane subjected the islanders to devastating floods:* expose, put through, cause to undergo or experience, submit. **8.** *His rude behavior subjects him to frequent rebuffs:* make liable, lay open, bare, expose. —**Ant.** 3 sovereign, ruler. **5** independent, unrelated. **6** invulnerable, unsusceptible, undisposed. **8** exempt, protect.

subjective *adj. Bill's never done anything wrong, so I guess my dislike of him is purely subjective:* personal, individual, emotional, inner, individual, partial, partisan, biased, prejudiced, nonobjective. **—Ant.** objective, impersonal; external, concrete, tangible; impartial, unbiased.

subjugate *adj. Conquistadors subjugated the Aztecs:* conquer, subdue, make subservient, vanquish, overmaster, reduce to submission, lay one's yoke upon, suppress, bring under the yoke, dominate, quell, tame, crush, put down. **—Ant.** release, free, liberate.

sublimate *v. She tried to sublimate her grief in her poetry:* redirect, divert, channel, shift, turn, transfer; convert, transform, transmute; spiritualize, purify, elevate, exalt, ennoble.

sublime *adj.* **1.** *A classic example of the sublime style in prose narrative is the opening chapter of the Book of Genesis:* lofty, exalted, imposing, elevated, noble, majestic, grand, stately, high, high-wrought, awe-inspiring. **2.** *Her performance was sublime. Baked Alaska is a sublime dessert:* excellent, splendid, superb, very good, marvelous; estimable, praiseworthy; wonderful, great, terrific. **—Ant.** 1 low, ordinary, everyday, commonplace. 2 poor, bad, ordinary, mediocre.

submerge *v.* **1.** *She submerged the clothes in the sudsy water. The submarine submerged:* plunge, put or go under water, immerse, submerse, sink, souse, douse, go under, dive, go down. **2.** *The raging waters submerged the tiny village:* inundate, cover with water, flood, engulf, cover completely, stream over, submerse, deluge, pour over, drown. **—Ant.** 1 surface, emerge. 2 uncover.

submission *n.* **1.** *In a gesture of submission, the rebel kissed the king's feet. Her present submission is animated solely by her fear of punishment:* submitting, yielding, giving in, surrender, capitulation; submissiveness, obedience, compliance, nonresistance, acquiescence, passivity, passiveness, meekness, tractability, subservience, tameness. **2.** *The deadline for submission of entries is June 1st:* handing in, presentation, remittance, submitting, tendering. **—Ant.** 1 resistance, rebellion, mutiny; rebelliousness, disobedience, defiance.

submissive *adj. Stand up and fight for your rights instead of being submissive:* obedient, yielding, meek, humble, mild, nonresisting, deferential, pliant, docile, compliant, complaisant, acquiescent, malleable, passive, capitulating, dutiful, unassertive, tractable, accommodating; truckling, toadying, obsequious, slavish, servile, fawning, ingratiating, subservient, crawling, bootlicking. **—Ant.** rebellious, disobedient, haughty, proud, arrogant, unyielding, defiant, refractory, resistant, assertive, masterful.

submit *v.* **1.** *The captain submitted to his mutinous crew:* give in, give up, surrender, yield, succumb, accede, bow, resign oneself, capitulate, cede, bend, back down, knuckle under, acquiesce, acknowledge defeat, kneel, stoop, lay down one's arms, defer, prostrate oneself, humble oneself, comply, hoist the white flag, throw in the towel. **2.** *He submitted to hypnotism in order to stop smoking:* subject oneself, expose oneself, acquiesce, agree; resort. **3.** *My cousin submitted his playground plans to the city council:* present, tender, put forward, put forth, commit, suggest, propose, hold out, volunteer, offer, proffer. **4.** *I submit that the prosecution's case is a tissue of lies:* claim, contend, assert, propose, argue. **—Ant.** 1, 2 resist, withstand, fight, defy. 3 withdraw.

subnormal *adj. The workers complained about subnormal housing conditions:* substandard, mediocre, inferior, second-rate, subpar, deficient, inadequate, insufficient; sorry, bad, wretched, abysmal, dismal; *Slang* shabby, seedy, sleazy, crummy.

subordinate *adj.* **1.** *A private is subordinate to a corporal:* lower in rank, of low rank, outranked, inferior, junior, subaltern; subservient, subject, ancillary, auxiliary, subsidiary, secondary; lesser, lower. **—n.** **2.** *He treated his subordinates like slaves:* person of lower rank, inferior, assistant, junior, help, worker, dependent, attendant; servant, underling, hireling, lackey, menial. **—Ant.** 1, 2 superior, senior. 1 higher, primary; leading, prominent. 2 chief, master, leader, supervisor, boss.

sub rosa *adv. We were suspicious because the deal was made sub rosa:* confidentially, secretly, in secret, privately, in private, covertly, behind closed doors, behind-the-scenes, off-the-record, *Informal* on the sly. **—Ant.** openly, publicly.

subscribe *v.* **1.** *He subscribed generously to the new school:* pledge money, promise to give, contribute, donate, open one's purse strings, lend one's aid, help, *Informal* chip in. **2.** *The lawyer invited his client to subscribe the affidavit:* sign, undersign, set one's name to, affix one's signature to. **3.** *Do you subscribe to many magazines?:* have a subscription, receive a periodical by mail. **4.** *I don't subscribe to the idea that money brings happiness:* lend approval, assent, consent; go along with, hold with, support, endorse. **—Ant.** 4 be opposed, dissent.

subsequent *adj. The first ticket cost $10, but all subsequent ones were $8:* ensuing, consequent, succeeding, following, proximate, next, successive. **—Ant.** previous, preceding.

subservient *adj.* **1.** *His subservient attitude to his boss makes me wince:* excessively submissive, fawning, obsequious, toadying, servile, slavish, ingratiating, sycophantic, bootlicking, menial, cringing, docile, truckling, prostrate. **2.** *A good leader's policies must be subservient to the needs of the people:* subordinate, subsidiary, subject, auxiliary, contributory, accessory, ancillary. **—Ant.** 1 domineering, overbearing, assertive, masterful; disobedient, rebellious. 2 superior.

subside *v.* **1.** *As the land subsides, the sea advances:* settle, sink; drop, cave in, sag, descend. **2.** *My nervousness subsided when the* *plane landed. The crowds subsided:* diminish, lessen, abate, decrease, wane, moderate, level off, ebb, calm, recede, melt away, let up, ease, shrink, dwindle. **—Ant.** 1, 2 rise; increase, swell. 2 grow, heighten, intensify.

subsidiary *adj.* **1.** *In addition to his salary, he receives subsidiary income from investments:* supplementary, supplemental, additional, extra. **2.** *He never got beyond a subsidiary position in the firm:* secondary, junior, subordinate, lower, lesser, minor, inferior. **—n. 3.** *That generator is a subsidiary to our main power supply:* auxiliary, addition, supplement, adjunct, accessory. **4.** *He works for the corporation's subsidiary in Boston:* subsidiary company, affiliate, division, branch. **—Ant.** 1, 2 primary, principal, main, chief, major, most important. 2 senior, leading, superior. 4 parent company, main office.

subsidize *v. The corporation decided to subsidize daycare:* finance, fund, bankroll, endow, sponsor, stake, underwrite, back.

subsidy *n. The city sought a government subsidy for its arts program:* grant, aid, appropriation, provision, backing, subvention, sponsorship, allotment, honorarium, award, gift, support, subsidization; scholarship, fellowship, grant-in-aid, assistantship.

subsist *v. The survivors of the crash subsisted on coconuts and bananas:* live, survive, exist, stay alive, sustain oneself, nourish oneself, support life, feed oneself; eke out a living, keep body and soul together, make ends meet. **—Ant.** die, perish, starve.

subsistence *n. The few dollars he took home every Friday were barely enough for the family's subsistence:* survival, continued existence, maintenance, nourishment, sustenance, support, upkeep; livelihood, living.

substance *n.* **1.** *Of what substance does a meteorite consist? There was a sticky substance on the floor:* material, matter, stuff; ingredient, constituent, element. **2.** *Our fears had substance--the house was indeed on fire:* corporality, substantiality, corporeality, corporealness, reality, actuality; solidity, body, real content. **3.** *The substance of her argument was that we had treated her unfairly:* burden, core, thrust, main point, essence, import, germ, soul, keynote, connotation, gist, basic idea, purport; intent, pith, marrow, heart; sum and substance, quintessence, backbone, sense, force. **4.** *Our elderly grocer was not exactly a person of substance:* affluence, property, money, means, wealth, riches.

substantial *adj.* **1.** *We had a substantial tobacco crop this year:* sizable, considerable, plentiful, plenteous, large, ample, big, full, abundant. **2.** *For an unschooled man, he exhibits a substantial understanding of economics:* firm, solid, sound. **3.** *The banker built himself a substantial home in Grosse Pointe:* big, bulky, monumental, massive, massy. **—Ant.** 1 unsubstantial, poor, meager, small, paltry, inconsiderable, scanty. 2 slight, weak, unsound, feeble. 3 small, tacky; lightweight, slender.

substantiate *v. You haven't substantiated your*

argument at all: verify, corroborate, prove, demonstrate, show to be true, confirm, authenticate, sustain, support. **—Ant.** disprove, refute, discredit, undermine, tear to shreds, explode.

substitute *n.* **1.** *At celebrations, there is no substitute for champagne. The regular teacher's ill, so a substitute is teaching today:* alternate, replacement, fill-in, surrogate, makeshift, stopgap, temporary, standby, understudy, backup, ersatz, *Slang* pinch hitter. **—v. 2.** *She substituted a fake diamond for the original:* exchange, change, switch. **3.** *Her brother substituted as host while her husband was away:* fill in, take over, stand in, pinch-hit, act, deputize. **—adj. 4.** *The School Board hired a substitute teacher:* surrogate, alternate, alternative, stand-in, replacement, temporary.

subterfuge *n. Why didn't they tell us immediately rather than resort to this subterfuge?:* scheme, artifice, trick, stratagem, dodge, deception, evasion, shift, smoke screen, ruse, blind, machination, wile, imposture; sham, chicanery, deviousness, sneakiness, gameplaying, intrigue, scheming, guile, duplicity, pretense, evasiveness, camouflage, sophistry, casuistry, make-believe. **—Ant.** straightforwardness, openness, honesty.

subtle *adj.* **1.** *The message of the film was subtle and indirect. There's a subtle hint of garlic in the sauce:* understated, indirect, delicate, elusive, light, refined, fine. **2.** *His subtle understanding of labor problems made him a natural for the job:* fine, keen, sharp, astute, skillful, masterly, discriminating, discerning, sophisticated, perspicacious, clever, ingenious, deft, expert, quick. **3.** *I fall for that subtle ploy every time!:* sly, tricky, crafty, wily, foxy, cagy, cunning, shrewd, artful, slick, designing, devious, deceptive, shifty, underhand. **—Ant.** 1 heavy-handed, blunt, obvious, direct. 2 unskillful, undiscerning, undiscriminating, unsophisticated. 3 obvious, artless.

subtract *v. They subtracted expenses and were left with a loss:* withdraw, take away, deduct, diminish, detract, lessen, lower. **—Ant.** add.

suburbia *n. They moved to suburbia from downtown:* suburbs, exurb, exurbia, fringe, outlying area, outskirts, precinct, purlieu, residential area, greenbelt, commuter belt.

subversive *adj.* **1.** *Subversive elements were known to have infiltrated the government:* seditious, traitorous, treasonous, insurrectionary, revolutionary, incendiary, insurgent. **—n. 2.** *The army attempted to identify and eliminate subversives:* traitor, quisling, collaborator, seditionary, fifth columnist, insurrectionary, insurgent, collaborationist, revolutionary, incendiary.

subvert *v. Radical groups attempted to subvert the peace talks:* overthrow, upset, disrupt, wreck, ruin, undermine, undo, overturn, destroy, spoil, devastate, demolish, shatter, smash; poison, contaminate, despoil, defile, mar, ravage. **—Ant.** support, endorse, back, encourage, promote.

succeed *v.* **1.** *The experiment succeeded. He didn't succeed in borrowing his father's car:* be fruitful, turn out successfully, be effective, be efficacious, do well, make a hit, bear fruit, click, hit, catch, strike oil, attain a goal, achieve one's aim, triumph, prevail, gain one's end, avail, win, hit the jackpot. **2.** *He finally succeeded as a playwright:* attain fame, prosper, attain wealth, come into one's own, make good, make a hit, triumph, find fulfillment, gain one's end, strike oil. **3.** *Louis XIV succeeded Louis XIII. Who will succeed to the throne?:* accede, move up, come next in order, become heir; assume the office of, take over, supplant, replace, come into possession of, inherit; follow, come afterward, be subsequent to, take the place of, replace. —**Ant.** 1, 2 fail, flop, fall short, miss. 3 precede.

succeeding *adj. The new law will apply to this and all succeeding cases:* subsequent, ensuing, consequent, successive, later, following, future, impending, coming, oncoming, posterior. —**Ant.** preceding, foregoing, earlier, previous, prior, former.

success *n.* **1.** *The success of the school fair was greater than we could have hoped:* happy outcome, triumph, fulfillment. **2.** *His success surprised those who remembered him as a poor student:* attainment, prosperity, good fortune, achievement, advancement, fame, conquest, triumph, ascendancy, affluence. **3.** *Was the charity ball a success?:* well-received venture, hit, triumph, victory, *Slang* smash. —**Ant.** 1–3 failure, disaster, downfall, collapse.

successful *adj.* **1.** *Because the timing was perfect, the surprise was totally successful:* triumphant, effective, efficacious, accomplished, achieved, complete, fruitful, perfect. **2.** *She is a successful businesswoman:* prosperous, flourishing, thriving, rich, well-off, affluent, wealthy; proven, acknowledged. —**Ant.** 1, 2 unsuccessful. 1 defeated. 2 unprosperous.

succession *n.* **1.** *The endless succession of parties wore us out:* series, procession, progression, sequence, chain, round, cycle, course, run, train. **2.** *His succession to the party leadership is in dispute:* taking over, assumption, accession, inheritance, stepping-up.

successive *adj. He underwent four successive operations in two weeks:* succeeding, ensuing, following one after another, consecutive, continuous.

successor *n. The board asked the president to name his successor:* follower, replacement, substitute; beneficiary, legatee; heir, heir apparent, heiress, heritor, heritress, joint heir; *Law* devisee, donee, reversioner, coparcener, parcener.

succinct *adj. His comments were detailed but succinct:* to the point, terse, expressed in few words, brief, direct, clipped, concise, neat, condensed, compact, sparing of words, epigrammatic, short, tight, summary, crisp, pithy, gnomic, aphoristic. —**Ant.** discursive, rambling, maundering, circuitous, prolix, wordy, verbose, long-winded.

succor *n.* **1.** *The volunteers gave succor to the wounded:* help, sustenance, relief, aid, accommodation, helping hand, comfort, assistance, support, maintenance. —*v.* **2.** *The local vicar was always quick to succor those in need:* aid, assist, comfort, lend a hand to, help, relieve, support, sustain, nurture, wait on, minister to, nurse, take care of, render assistance to, back up, give a lift to, protect, shield, befriend.

succulent *adj. The eggplant was succulent:* luscious, lush, juicy, mouthwatering, rich, tasty, delicious, yummy.

succumb *v.* **1.** *He succumbed after a long illness:* die, pass away, expire, go under. **2.** *He finally succumbed to her pleading:* give in, yield, give way, submit, comply with, accede, defer to, capitulate, surrender; fall victim to. —**Ant.** 1 live, survive. 2 resist, fight, hold firm.

sucker *n. Only a sucker would buy a used car from them:* dupe, chump, fool, gull, mark, sap, boob, pushover, victim, easy mark, pigeon, sitting duck, cat's-paw, fair game, patsy, butt, fall guy, soft touch, goat, schlemiel, jerk.

sudden *adj. He made a sudden stop. Don't make sudden decisions:* abrupt, quick, speedy, rapid, immediate, instant, instantaneous; hasty, impetuous, precipitate, rash; unlooked-for, unexpected, unanticipated, unforeseen, unforeseeable, surprising. —**Ant.** slow, gradual; extended, prolonged; deliberate; foreseen, anticipated, expected.

suddenly *adv. Suddenly the lights went out:* abruptly, all of a sudden, without warning, all at once, unexpectedly, at short notice, on the spur-of-the-moment, in an instant, quickly, instantly, before one knows it, on the spot, in the twinkling of an eye, in no time. —**Ant.** gradually, slowly, deliberately, not unexpectedly.

sue *v.* **1.** *They sued the movers for ruining the furniture:* bring a civil action against, litigate against, institute process in law against, prefer a claim against, start a lawsuit against. **2.** *The condemned man sued for mercy:* beg, plead, beseech, entreat, appeal, make appeal to, importune, implore, supplicate, petition, pray.

suffer *v.* **1.** *She suffered greatly as a child. Is he suffering much from his injuries?:* feel distress, lament, despair, go through a lot, bear the cross, pine, grieve; feel pain, agonize, ache, hurt. **2.** *His work suffers when he has problems at home:* deteriorate, fall off, be impaired, drop off. **3.** *If the watch wasn't insured, she'll have to suffer the loss. One must suffer some bad days:* endure, bear, sustain, go through, undergo, tolerate, bear with, withstand, stand, stomach, put up with.

suffering *n.* **1.** *She refused to talk about her family's suffering during the war:* sorrow, distress, travail, heartache, heavy heart, grief, misery, dolor, woe, tribulation, care, anxiety, anguish, trial. **2.** *The medication should ease the suffering:* ache, pain, hurt, soreness, irritation, torture, affliction, agony, discomfort, pang, misery, twinge, distress, throe, torment. —**Ant.** 1 pleasure, joy, happiness.

suffice *v. A brief word of thanks will suffice:* serve, suit, avail, be adequate, be sufficient, meet, meet requirements, satisfy, answer.

sufficient *adj. Do we have sufficient fuel for the*

trip?: enough, adequate, ample, plenty, abundant, copious, satisfactory, minimal, up to the mark, plentiful, plenteous. —**Ant.** insufficient, deficient, inadequate, wanting, meager, scant.

suffocate *v. I nearly suffocated in the heat. The murderer suffocated his victims:* choke, gag, smother, asphyxiate, stifle; strangle, throttle, garrote; extinguish, quench, snuff out.

suffuse *v. Bright sunlight suffused the room each morning:* cover, overspread, saturate, fill, overflow, pervade, diffuse, permeate, soak, transfuse, steep, impregnate, infiltrate, infuse, overrun.

sugary *adj. She was embarrassed by his sugary compliments:* sweet, honeyed, saccharine, syrupy, cloying; flattering, cajoling, blandishing, mushy, gushing, mawkish, fulsome, unctuous. —**Ant.** acid, tart, crusty, sarcastic, venomous.

suggest *v.* **1.** *I suggest that we leave early for the airport. The letter suggested that a new clinic should be built:* recommend, advocate, move, urge, advise, propose, bid, counsel, posit, submit, propound, advance. **2.** *His restlessness suggested that he wanted to leave:* intimate, hint at, imply, lead one to believe, indicate, give a clue.

suggestion *n.* **1.** *I followed his suggestion that I lose weight:* advice, prompting, counsel, urging, recommendation, exhortation; pointer, tip. **2.** *There's only a suggestion of rum in this cake:* suspicion, shade, hint, trace, touch, dash, grain, taste, tinge, tint, soupçon, dab, sprinkling, feeling, intimation.

suggestive *adj.* **1.** *This silly old song is suggestive of my youth:* reminiscent, evocative, expressive, allusive, remindful. **2.** *His suggestive remarks shocked the young lady:* improper, indelicate, unseemly, off-color; indecent, loose, shameless, lewd, wanton, seductive, sexual, licentious, risqué, racy, bawdy; stimulating, prurient, provocative. —**Ant.** 2 decent, delicate, decorous, chaste, clean.

suit *n.* **1.** *His new suit doesn't fit well. John wore a clown suit to the party:* set of garments, outfit; jacket and pants, jacket and skirt; clothing, garb, costume, clothes, apparel, habit, habiliment, raiment, trappings, duds, getup, attire, accoutrements, togs; livery, uniform. **2.** *She responded to her wooer's suit:* courtship, court, wooing, blandishment, addresses, lovemaking, attentions, overtures. **3.** *His suit for mercy was moving:* plea, appeal, solicitation, entreaty, begging, supplication, prayer, petition. —*v.* **4.** *The architecture of the house should suit the rugged landscape:* conform to, match, follow, befit, fit, beseem, correspond to, be proper for, harmonize with, fall in with, agree with, square with, go along with, be appropriate to, jell with, tally with, accord with, comply with, dovetail with, comport with. **5.** *Outdoor living suits you:* become, be appropriate for, befit, be suitable for, be becoming to, do one good. **6.** *A later flight suits me even better:* be acceptable to, be convenient to, accommodate, content, oblige, be agreeable to, seem good to; make glad, gratify, satisfy, please, gladden, delight. —**Ant.** 4 disa-

gree with, not go with, be inappropriate to. 6 inconvenience, displease, discommode.

suitable *adj. Is this gown suitable for such a fancy affair? The minister's words were suitable to the sad occasion:* proper, appropriate, meet, fitting, fit, befitting, seemly, right, adequate, apt, qualified, cut out for, becoming, worthy, apropos, applicable, congruous, seasonable, relevant, pertinent, germane, commensurate. —**Ant.** unsuitable, inappropriate, unbecoming, improper, incompatible, dissonant, inconsistent, unfit, unseemly.

suitcase *n. I packed my suitcase last night:* bag; (*variously*) valise, grip, satchel, traveling bag, overnight bag, two-suiter, gladstone, portmanteau; duffel bag, rucksack, knapsack.

suitor *n. She had many handsome suitors in her youth:* beau, boyfriend, young man, lover, admirer, love, flame, fellow, gallant, wooer, swain, sweetheart.

sulk *v. He sulked about not winning the race:* pout, be sullen, wear a long face, mope, brood, show ill temper, be in a huff, be disgruntled, be resentful, be in a pet, grumble, grump, fret, be out of humor, be miffed, fume, be put out, chafe, crab, grouch, scowl, frown, glower, look glum.

sulky *adj. She was sulky in defeat:* sullen, ill-humored, resentful, aloof, moody, surly, morose, cross, splenetic, churlish. —**Ant.** temperate, good-natured.

sullen *adj.* **1.** *She couldn't appease the sullen child:* ill-tempered, gloomy, ill-humored, brooding, grumpy, out of humor, out of sorts, surly, glowering, sulky, crabbed, resentful, grouchy, sour, morose, scowling, peevish, petulant, splenetic, sore, grim, ill-natured, temperamental, glum, saturnine, moody, unsociable, crabby, unamiable, cross, touchy. **2.** *This sullen weather is depressing:* gloomy, grim, dismal, somber, funereal, mournful, dolorous, depressing, melancholy, dark, blue, doleful, foreboding, dreary, heavy, cheerless, desolate, forlorn. —**Ant.** 1 cheerful, happy, gay, smiling, sociable, merry, amiable. 2 bright, cheerful, sunny.

sully *v. They accused him of sullying the family name:* soil, dirty, besmear, stain, spot, befoul, smudge, begrime, blemish, spoil, ruin; contaminate, defile, corrupt, adulterate; disgrace, dishonor, defame. —**Ant.** cleanse, purify, tidy, decontaminate; honor, glorify.

sultry *adj.* **1.** *No one feels like working in this sultry weather:* sweltering, suffocating, stifling, oppressive, close, stuffy, warm and damp, humid, hot and moist, muggy, sweaty. **2.** *The waitress brushed past the truck driver with a sultry sidelong glance:* erotic, hot, voluptuous, sexy, sensual, provocative.

sum *n.* **1.** *The sum of her achievements is impressive:* amount, quantity, sum total, measure, entire amount, entirety, totality, summation, aggregate, whole, tally, score. **2.** *The sum they demanded for damages was outrageous:* amount of money, cash, funds, currency, coin; *Slang* dough, bread, bucks, lettuce, jack, moolah.

summarily *adv. The foreman summarily dis-*

missed two of the workers: at short notice, unhesitatingly, on the spur of the moment, precipitately, arbitrarily, without delay, on the spot, promptly, with dispatch, immediately, straightaway, straightway, directly, at once, quickly, speedily, forthwith.

summarize v. Try to summarize the speech in a paragraph or two: condense, capsulize, abstract, abridge, compress, digest, sum up, recapitulate, epitomize, concentrate, synopsize, outline. —**Ant.** expand, flesh out, enlarge on, embroider.

summary n. **1.** His summary of the case omitted the most important facts: digest, concise statement, short version, brief, abstract, résumé, detailed outline, précis, survey, Informal rundown; abridgment, recapitulation, condensation, breakdown, epitome, syllabus, synopsis, sketch, abbreviation, sum and substance, analysis, aperçu. —adj. **2.** He had time for only a summary report: short, brief, hasty, concise, abridged, succinct, condensed, terse, curt, hurried; perfunctory, token, cursory. **3.** It was a summary verdict: unceremoniously fast, rapid, done without consideration, peremptory, conducted without delay, hasty, quickly performed, instantaneous, sudden. —**Ant.** 2 complete, full, detailed, lengthy. 3 deliberate, considered, slow.

summer n. That summer there was a heat wave: summertime, dog days, sunny season.

summerhouse n. They had tea in the summerhouse: conservatory, arbor, bower, gazebo, pergola.

summery adj. This summery weather is almost too much for me: summerlike, vernal, aestival, sunny, sunshiny; hot, muggy, humid, close, oppressive, sultry, stifling, stuffy, torrid, scorching, roasting. —**Ant.** cold, wintry, raw, blustery, freezing.

summit n. From the mountain camp they reached the summit in six hours. He is now at the summit of his career: peak, crest, crown, highest point, apex, vertex, tip, height, top, pinnacle, zenith, apogee; acme, crowning point, culminating point, culmination, climax. —**Ant.** base, bottom, depth, nadir, all-time low.

summon v. **1.** Summon the police quickly!: call for, beckon, send for, rouse; call together, muster, activate, call into action, gather, call out. **2.** The state summoned three witnesses: call, command to appear, subpoena, serve with a writ. **3.** She had to summon all her strength to face them again: call forth, call on, invoke, command, muster, call into action, gather, draw on, strain. —**Ant.** 1 dismiss, discharge.

sumptuous adj. A sumptuous meal was served to the visiting dignitaries: splendid, luxurious, magnificent, grand, regal, spectacular, elaborate, lavish, munificent, elegant, superb; dear, costly, expensive, exorbitant, plush, rich, deluxe, extravagant, Slang posh. —**Ant.** plain, ordinary, cheap.

sundry adj. He worked at sundry jobs to put himself through school: various, divers, several, manifold, many, numerous, myriad, diverse, varied, motley, assorted, miscellaneous, heterogeneous, multifarious, dissimilar, different. —**Ant.** uniform, unvarying, same, regular.

sunny adj. **1.** Let's sit in a sunny spot. Yesterday was a sunny day: sunshiny, bright, sunlit; cloudless, shining, clear, brilliant, unclouded, fair, fine. **2.** The waiter didn't exactly have a sunny disposition: amiable, affable, happy, smiling, cheerful, cheery, joyful, blithe, jolly, joyous, lighthearted, genial, sparkling, buoyant, optimistic, breezy, jovial, merry. —**Ant.** 1 shaded, dark, cloudy, overcast, dim, gloomy, gray, murky, somber, wintry. 2 glum, gloomy, dour, unhappy, morbid, unsmiling, uncheerful.

sunrise n. We got up at sunrise to go fishing: dawn, sunup, dawning, daybreak, daylight, aurora, break of day, cockcrow, dawn's early light, rosy-fingered day, crepuscule, newborn day.

sunset n. We met at sunset for drinks on the terrace: dusk, twilight, sundown, nightfall, eventide, gloaming, crepuscule, blue hour, close of day.

super adj. His new motorcycle is really super: outstanding, matchless, great, extraordinary, superlative, peerless, superior, incomparable, prime, prize, excellent, world-class, unexcelled, nonpareil. —**Ant.** commonplace, ordinary, mediocre, run-of-the-mill.

superabundance n. The weather has been so favorable we have a superabundance of tomatoes: overabundance, overflow, glut, surplus, excess, plethora, superfluity, oversupply, redundance, pleonasm, surfeit, deluge, flood, spate, avalanche, riot, extravagance, overdose, inundation, French embarras de richesses. —**Ant.** scarcity, lack, shortage, paucity.

superannuated adj. The work force was superannuated: old, aged, decrepit, obsolete, antiquated, antique, senile, passé. —**Ant.** young, youthful, new, voguish.

superb adj. **1.** His first novel was superb: very fine, first-rate, excellent, magnificent, admirable, laudable, praiseworthy, A1, first-class, top-notch, top-drawer, of the first water, tip-top, Slang crackerjack. **2.** They put up for sale a superb Persian rug: sumptuous, splendid, grand, magnificent, marvelous, luxurious, deluxe, gorgeous, exquisite, costly, rich, expensive, priceless, precious, elegant, choice, select, golden, elect, matchless, rare; majestic, breathtaking, imposing, peerless, regal, princely, stately, lordly. —**Ant.** 1 bad, awful, terrible, second-rate, inferior. 2 tawdry, ordinary, plain, mean.

supercilious adj. His small success made him supercilious and obnoxious: haughty, self-important, lordly, pompous, disdainful, condescending, patronizing, arrogant, high-and-mighty, proud, overbearing, vainglorious, egotistical, magisterial, Informal snooty, Slang stuck-up; uppity, snobbish, prideful.

superficial adj. **1.** The crack in the table is only superficial. Apart from superficial cuts and bruises, she is unhurt: on the surface, outer, surface, exterior, skin-deep. **2.** She has only a superficial understanding of economics: shallow, skin-deep, summary, incomplete, slight, faint, slim, flimsy, cursory, perfunctory, passing, partial, minimal, surface, nodding, desultory. **3.** *He's too superficial to appreciate the deep feelings in the play:* frivolous, shallow, hollow, empty-headed, narrowminded, lacking depth, mindless, silly, myopic, shortsighted, trite. **—Ant.** 1–3 deep, in-depth, profound. 1 substantial, pervasive. 2 thorough, complete, total. 3 serious, intent, earnest, farsighted.

superficially *adv. They only superficially dealt with the problem:* outwardly, lightly, externally, frivolously, hastily, partially, casually.

superfluous *adj. Giving her so many presents was really superfluous:* unnecessary, excessive, redundant, overgenerous, needless, nonessential, inessential; excess, surplus, extra, superabundant, supererogatory, pleonastic, supernumerary, extraneous, spare, gratutous. **—Ant.** essential, vital, indispensable, required, necessary.

superhuman *adj. With superhuman strength he lifted the piano onto the rug:* superior, supreme, transcendent, supernatural, godlike, herculean, omnipotent, unearthly, miraculous, supermundane, supranatural, preternatural, otherworldly, divine. **—Ant.** mundane, earthly, normal, natural, terrestrial.

superintendent *n. Our principal was appointed superintendent of schools:* supervisor, chief administrator; director, head, overseer, proctor, chief, custodian, guardian, foreman, boss, manager, warden, steward, headman.

superior *adj.* **1.** *John Drew was a superior actor. The new butcher will give you a superior cut of beef:* excellent, exceptional, fine, notable, incomparable, distinguished, preeminent, noteworthy, nonpareil, unrivaled, foremost, first-rate, illustrious, peerless, inimitable, matchless; deluxe, choice. **2.** *Her knowledge of French literature is superior to mine:* greater, better, more extensive, more advanced. **3.** *His superior manner makes people resent him:* haughty, lordly, imperious, condescending, patronizing, snobbish, arrogant, high-and-mighty, vainglorious. **—n. 4.** *His promotion was approved by his superiors:* senior, boss, chief, supervisor; leader, higher-up, better, commander. **—Ant.** 1 inferior, lower, worse, poorer, unexceptional, undistinguished, lesser, mediocre, ordinary, average, second-rate, common, unremarkable; inconspicuous, obscure. 2 inferior, less worthy. 4 inferior, subordinate, employee; underling, minion.

superiority *n. Her plain superiority won out:* eminence, preeminence, ascendancy, dominance, predominance, excellence, preponderance, prevalence, supremacy, upper hand, advantage.

superlative *adj. Our carpenter does superlative cabinetwork:* most excellent, of the highest order, greatest, of the first water, superior, surpassing, best, supreme, magnificent, preeminent, foremost, transcendent, unsurpassed, expert, prime, surpassing all others, paramount, crack, exquisite, consummate, first-rate; matchless, incomparable, unrivaled, peerless, une-

qualed, unmatched, unparalleled, nonpareil. **—Ant.** inferior, poor, unexceptional, undistinguished.

supernatural *adj. The medium claimed to have supernatural powers:* preternatural, otherworldly, occult, mystic, transcendental, unearthly, spiritual, psychic, paranormal, miraculous, superphysical, supranatural. **—Ant.** natural, explainable, worldly.

supersede *v. This new drug will supersede all others in the treatment of the disease:* supplant, replace, take the place of, substitute for, displace, succeed; discard, set aside.

supervise *v. Can you supervise a whole production line?:* superintend, watch over, oversee, look after, preside over, manage, regulate, direct, govern, survey, control, guide, conduct, have charge of, administer, head, boss, handle.

supervision *n. My house was built under an architect's supervision:* direction, guidance, regulation, control, superintendence, governance, government, surveillance, orders, management.

supervisor *n. Only the supervisor can authorize your leave:* overseer, manager, administrator, director, superintendent, foreman, boss, head, chief, steward, commander, man at the wheel.

supplant *v. Machines are supplanting men in many industries:* supersede, replace, take the place of, usurp the place of, displace, depose.

supple *adj.* **1.** *The tubing is supple and fireproof:* pliant, flexible, plastic, tractable, bendable, pliable, elastic. **2.** *She has the supple body of a gymnast:* lithe, limber, lissome, coordinated, graceful. **3.** *Her supple nature enables her to accept change:* adaptable, flexible, amenable, tractable, compliant, complaisant, yielding, acquiescent, submissive, malleable. **—Ant.** 1 stiff, rigid, firm, inflexible. 2 stiff, awkward, graceless.

supplement *n.* **1.** *The night courses are a supplement to his regular course work:* complement, annex, addition, augmentation, corollary, extra, extension, addendum, adjunct. **2.** *The newspaper publishes a special travel supplement twice a year:* section, insert, attachment; appendix, addendum, rider, postscript, codicil, added part. **—v. 3.** *He supplemented his earnings by taking a night job:* add to, extend, increase, augment.

suppliant *n. The king agreed to see a few suppliants each morning:* supplicant, petitioner, beseecher, beggar, entreater, seeker, suitor, supplicator, asker, claimant, appellant; mendicant, cadger, almsman, almswoman.

supplicate *v. They supplicated for a raise in pay:* pray, entreat, petition, appeal to, beg, implore, crave, importune, sue, solicit, beseech. **—Ant.** order, command.

supplication *n. The supplications of the homeless refugees was pitiful:* entreaty, petition, plea, appeal, beseechment, solicitation, application, request, invocation, prayer, orison, suit, cry, imprecation, imploration; cadging, panhandling; *Slang* bumming, mooching.

supplies *n. pl. We got all our supplies before setting out:* equipment, provisions, stores, necessities, provender, provisions, stock, materials.

supply v. **1.** *The Red Cross supplied the hospital with blood. Who will supply the champagne?:* provide, furnish, outfit, turn over to, stock, equip; present, give, contribute, bestow, yield, deal out, come up with, deliver, render, grant, provision. —n. **2.** *How will they arrange for a daily supply of food to the flood victims?:* provisioning, providing, furnishing, allocation; stock, reservoir, reserve, store, quota, provision, cache, fund. **3.** Often **supplies** *What supplies will we need for our mountain climb?:* equipment, needed items, goods, material, items, provisions; gear, trappings, accoutrements; foodstuff.

support v. **1.** *Large beams support the damaged wall:* bear up, hold up; prop, bolster, uphold, brace, sustain, buttress, stay, shore up. **2.** *That crate will never support your weight:* sustain, bear, hold. **3.** *He has to support his mother and his sister:* maintain, provide for, subsidize, keep, finance, pay for, underwrite, back financially, foster. **4.** *Her brother supported her throughout the tragedy:* help, sustain, succor, comfort, give hope to, aid, carry, be a source of strength, strengthen. **5.** *I support his right to speak out:* defend, back up, champion, uphold, stand up for, stick up for, second, advocate, go along with, say yes to, reinforce, espouse, sanction, favor, countenance; aid, boost, assist, further, patronize, bolster. **6.** *Your testimony will support his plea of innocence:* verify, confirm, make good, establish, substantiate, corroborate, accord with, bear out, vouch for, accredit, clinch, warrant, attest to, endorse, bolster, guarantee, ratify. **7.** *Grandfather could never support disobedience:* endure, tolerate, put up with, suffer, abide, bear, brook, stand. —n. **8.** *These beams are the main support of the building. One of the roof supports is cracked:* holding up, buttressing; supporter, brace, prop, underpinning, post, buttress, abutment, shore, pile, pedestal, stanchion, bolster, pillar, column, pilaster, base. **9.** *On her shoulders falls the support of the whole family. Joe provided emotional support for the children when their father died:* sustenance, maintenance, upkeep, livelihood, means, subsistence, keeping, nurture; comfort, succor, aid, help, strength, boost, encouragement, consolation, lift. **10.** *The candidate did not ask for our support:* backing, patronage, aid, help, assistance, espousal, defense, advocacy, boost, promotion, furtherance, involvement.

supporter n. *He's a supporter of many liberal causes:* backer, upholder, defender, champion, patron, adherent, benefactor, disciple, well-wisher, partisan, advocate, ally, helper, follower, sympathizer. —**Ant.** adversary, antagonist, opponent.

suppose v. **1.** *Suppose you're offered the job-- will you accept?:* assume, hypothesize, presume, predicate, posit, consider. **2.** *I suppose you're all hungry?:* guess, imagine, believe, reckon, take for granted, presume, assume, gather, judge, fancy, conceive, suspect, divine, surmise.

supposition n. *That was only supposition. He acted on the supposition that the public would applaud his feat:* presumption, assumption, conjecture, opinion, predication, surmise, guess, guesswork, suspicion, belief, theory, thesis, notion, view, speculation, hypothesis, proposition, postulate, idea, given. —**Ant.** certainty, surety, fact, knowledge.

suppress v. **1.** *The new government quickly suppressed the rebellion:* put down, overpower, crush, subdue, put an end to, quash, overcome, snuff out, squash, quench, quell, extinguish. **2.** *It was all I could do to suppress my anger:* repress, withhold, stifle, squelch, keep back, check, control, smother, restrict, restrain, muffle, still, hold back, put a damper on, hold in leash, inhibit, keep in, curb. **3.** *His father tried to suppress the scandal:* keep secret, keep private, cover up, conceal, hide, put under wraps, bury, silence. —**Ant.** 2 express, let out, unleash, unloose, pour forth. 3 reveal, uncover, expose, broadcast.

suppression n. *Suppression of the new party came immediately:* block, blockage, blocking, censorship, repression.

supremacy n. *His supremacy on the basketball court was unquestioned. The king's supremacy was under fire:* preeminence, superiority, primacy, paramountcy, precedence, transcendency; domination, power, sovereignty, mastery, absolute authority, ascendancy, power to command, absolute rule, supreme leadership, omnipotence.

supreme adj. **1.** *In the oligarchy, his position was unquestionably supreme. The Pope is the supreme leader of the Roman Catholic Church:* sovereign, dominant, uppermost, front-ranking, first, highest, chief, principal, paramount, foremost, peerless, all-powerful, topmost, leading, ruling; commanding, prime, unqualified, absolute, unconditional, unlimited. **2.** *The supreme craftsmanship of this vase makes it priceless:* perfect, consummate, nonpareil, peerless, superlative, matchless, unexcelled, incomparable, unsurpassed, unequaled, unparalleled, second to none, unmatched, tops, unrivaled; extreme, immeasurable.

sure adj. **1.** *I'm sure of his loyalty:* confident, assured, fully persuaded, convinced, positive, certain, undoubting. **2.** *He's a sure and eager employee. This investment's a sure thing:* trustworthy, never-failing, reliable, worthy of confidence, unfailing, dependable, firm, steady, fast, solid, true, faithful; surefire, fail-safe, infallible. **3.** *She has a sure eye for color:* unerring, certain, accurate, unfailing, flawless, infallible, dependable, reliable, sound, steady, stable, firm. —**Ant.** 1, 3 unsure. 1–3 uncertain. 1 insecure, unassured, unconvinced, doubtful, distrustful. 2 fallible, unsteady, inconstant, wavering, unworthy, faithless, undependable, untrue, unreliable. 3 erring, inaccurate, unreliable, unsteady, unstable.

surely adv. *You surely acquitted yourself well.*

Surely you'll stay for dinner: for certain, assuredly, without doubt, undoubtedly, certainly, doubtless, unquestionably, definitely, positively, indubitably, emphatically, by all means, come what may, without fail, no doubt, to be sure, infallibly, of course.

surface *n. The surface of the sphere is coated with aluminum:* outside, superficies, face, facade, outer face, exterior; (*variously*) covering, shell, coat, finish, coating, veneer, crust, skin, top.

surfeit *n. There's been a surfeit of cheap wine on the market:* glut, surplus, excess, overabundance, superfluity, plethora, extravagance, oversupply, exorbitance, surplusage, overmuch, profusion, prodigality, supersaturation. —**Ant.** shortage, dearth, lack, paucity, shortfall.

surge *n. A surge of impatient shoppers poured into the store. Bookstores report a surge of interest in astronomy this year:* wave, swell, torrent, flood, rush.

surgery *n. She performed surgery on the broken leg:* operation, medical procedure, surgical intervention, *Informal* the knife.

surly *adj. Neighborhood children were scared of the surly storekeeper:* sullen, rude, snarling, irascible, grouchy, discourteous, ill-humored, bad-tempered, testy, crabbed, ill-natured, abrupt, cross, crusty, uncivil, grumpy, touchy, waspish, snappish, peevish, churlish, unfriendly, gruff, petulant, sour, harsh, hostile, unamiable, splenetic, bearish, choleric, insolent. —**Ant.** amiable, gracious, cordial, affable, genial, nice, pleasant, courteous, friendly, civil.

surmise *v.* **1.** *I surmised that Robinson was up for promotion:* conjecture, imagine, guess, suppose, presuppose, think, presume, opine, judge, suspect, consider, theorize, believe, deem, infer, hypothesize, posit, conclude. —*n.* **2.** *It's only a surmise, but I think he'll barely win the election:* guess, supposition, notion, idea, conjecture, opinion, speculation, assumption, hypothesis, *Informal* shot in the dark; presumption, belief, suspicion, thought.

surmount *v.* **1.** *How will we surmount that high wall?:* get over, scale, climb, top, clear. **2.** *He surmounted his handicap and achieved great success:* conquer, defeat, master, overcome, prevail over, vanquish, best, get the better of, worst, triumph over.

surpass *v.* **1.** *He surpassed the goal he set for himself:* exceed, go beyond, outdo, top, best, outstrip, beat, outdistance, leave behind, triumph over, go one better, outrun, transcend. **2.** *This mousse au chocolat surpasses any restaurant dessert I've ever had:* excel, outdo, be superior to, rise above, outshine, eclipse, overshadow, override, outclass, take precedence over, be better than, have it all over.

surplus *n.* **1.** *The government paid the farmers for their potato surplus:* oversupply, surfeit, superfluity, overage, surplusage, excess, overflow, plethora, overproduction, glut. —*adj.* **2.** *Some use should be found for surplus crops:* excess, extra, superfluous, leftover, residual. —**Ant.** 1

deficiency, shortage, insufficiency, inadequacy, dearth, paucity, lack.

surprise *v.* **1.** *His facility with power tools surprised us:* astonish, astound, nonplus, startle, amaze, flabbergast, take aback, strike with wonder, shock, stun, dumbfound, stagger, strike with awe, defy belief, leave open-mouthed, stupefy, confound, boggle the mind. **2.** *Mother surprised me raiding the icebox:* catch in the act of, come upon unexpectedly, take unawares, discover, catch off one's guard, burst in on. **3.** *The outlaws surprised them in the foothills:* ambush, assail suddenly, set upon, make a sneak attack on, take by surprise, fall upon, pounce upon, take unawares. —*n.* **4.** *The surprise was difficult to plan. The promotion was a surprise:* something unexpected, bolt out of the blue, bombshell, revelation. **5.** *To my surprise a gigantic ape appeared at the door:* amazement, wonder, astonishment, wonderment, incredulity, shock.

surrender *v.* **1.** *They were the last rebel contingent to surrender in the war:* give up, yield, submit, capitulate, concede, lay down arms, show the white flag, throw in the towel. **2.** *She gradually surrendered her dream of becoming an actress. He surrendered all rights to the property:* give up, let go, abandon, relinquish, renounce, give over, yield, forgo, part with, forsake, vacate, waive, turn over, hand over, render, accede, cede, deliver up. —*n.* **3.** *The Allies broadcast the terms of the surrender. The surrender of the evidence was delayed:* yielding, capitulation, submission; relinquishment, giving up, delivery; forgoing, renunciation. —**Ant.** 1 resist, withstand, oppose. 2 retain, keep, hold on to.

surreptitious *adj. The conspirators held a surreptitious meeting:* secret, secretive, stealthy, undercover, furtive, clandestine, hidden, covert, *Informal* hush-hush; concealed, veiled. —**Ant.** open, aboveboard, candid, direct, straightforward.

surrogate *n.* **1.** *A surrogate stood in for the chairperson:* substitute, replacement, stand-in, fill-in, alternate, backup, locum tenens, deputy, agent, relief, proxy, pinch hitter, understudy. —*adj* **2.** *The surrogate parents took good care of the children:* substitute, alternate, alternative, backup. —**Ant.** original, prototype.

surround *v. The firemen surrounded the burning building. A picket fence surrounds the yard:* encircle, circle, enclose, ring, encompass, girdle, engird, enfold, belt, compass, circumscribe, envelop, hedge, hedge in, shut in, close in, hem in, fence in.

surroundings *n. pl. It's important to work in friendly surroundings:* circumstances, environs, conditions; environment, habitat, milieu, setting, scene, ambience, atmosphere.

surveillance *n. The police have him under constant surveillance:* watch, observation, vigil, scrutiny; eavesdropping, trailing.

survey *v.* **1.** *Let's survey the events leading up to the crime:* review, look over, view generally, pass in review, consider, contemplate, scan, examine, inspect, study, scrutinize. **2.** *The city engineer surveyed the property to amend the* *map:* measure, determine the extent of, verify the boundaries of, delimit, plot, graph, gauge, block out; fathom, plumb; reconnoiter, observe, scout. —*n.* **3.** *They ran a survey of the most popular television programs:* review, study, comprehensive view, overview, investigation, probe, poll, canvass, analysis.

survival *n.* **1.** *The explorer was an expert at survival in the wilderness:* living, keeping alive, subsistence. **2.** *This custom is a survival from my great-grandmother's days:* carry-over, relic, vestige, hangover, continuation, atavism, throwback. —**Ant.** 1 death, extermination, extinction, eradication.

survive *v.* **1.** *How long can the crash victims survive in the Arctic? How many of the country's early customs survive?:* keep alive, continue to live, subsist, last, hang on, hold out; live on, persist, endure, prevail, continue, abide, subsist, be extant, exist. **2.** *Miraculously, they survived the bombing:* live through, come through alive. **3.** *Insurance statistics show that most wives survive their husbands:* outlive, outlast, live longer than. —**Ant.** 1 perish, disappear. 2 succumb to. 3 predecease.

susceptibility *n.* *She had a susceptibility for melodrama:* sensibility, sensitivity, sensitiveness, susceptiveness, susceptibleness, impressibility, vulnerability. —**Ant.** insusceptibility.

susceptible *adj.* **1.** *A vague law is always susceptible to differing interpretations. Is the virus susceptible to treatment?:* open, prone, subject, vulnerable, receptive to, capable of being affected by, sensitive to, disposed to, conducive to, liable to. **2.** *He's susceptible to a woman's tears:* sensitive, alive to, responsive, easily moved by, vulnerable, readily impressed by, easily touched by, sympathetic, sensible. —**Ant.** 1, 2 unsusceptible. 1 immune, invulnerable. 2 insensitive, unresponsive, unmoved, invulnerable, insensible, resistant.

suspect *v.* **1.** *He suspected her sincerity:* mistrust, doubt, distrust, question, have no confidence in, have one's doubts about, harbor suspicions about, wonder about, misdoubt, be suspicious of, believe guilty. **2.** *We suspect they'll be a little late:* guess, imagine, conjecture, surmise, opine, fancy, hypothesize, believe, posit, theorize, judge, presume, speculate, suppose, think. —*n.* **3.** *The suspect is being held at police headquarters for questioning:* suspected person, alleged culprit. —**Ant.** 1 trust, believe. 2 know, know for sure, be sure, be certain.

suspend *v.* **1.** *Suspend the swing from the tree branch:* hang, dangle, swing, append, sling. **2.** *I'll suspend judgment until all the facts are in:* put off, postpone, delay, defer, table, reserve, shelve, stay, withhold. **3.** *They suspended construction during the strike:* discontinue, cease, stop, halt, arrest, interrupt, leave off, break off, bring to a stop, bring to a standstill, stop short, check, cut short, put an end to, quit.

suspense *n.* *I can't stand the suspense of not knowing!:* uncertainty, incertitude, indecision, unresolved situation, indetermination, expecta-

tion, anticipation, tension, anxiety, being on pins and needles, edginess, curiosity. —**Ant.** certainty, certitude, resolution.

suspicion *n.* **1.** *Suspicion was taking its toll on the jealous wife:* distrust, mistrust, jealous apprehension. **2.** *I have my suspicions about his part in this case:* conjecture, feeling, idea, surmise, guess, supposition, hunch, hypothesis, notion. —**Ant.** 1 trust, trustfulness, credulity, belief, confidence.

suspicious *adj.* **1.** *His behavior was at the very least suspicious:* open to doubt, questionable, dubious, suspect, doubtful, slippery, ambiguous, untrustworthy, shady. **2.** *The police are suspicious of his alibi because he already has a record:* inclined to suspect, mistrustful, distrustful, untrusting, wary, doubting, incredulous, disbelieving, jealously unbelieving. —**Ant.** 1, 2 unsuspicious. 1 open, aboveboard, clear, unambiguous. 2 trusting, confident, credulous.

sustain *v.* **1.** *These four posts sustain the entire building:* support, bear up, uphold, hold up, underpin, prop. **2.** *The trucking company was somehow able to sustain the severe fuel shortage:* bear, brook, endure, carry on under, hold out against, abide, stand, withstand, brave, tolerate. **3.** *He sustained a terrible head injury:* suffer, undergo, experience. **4.** *The runner was able to sustain the same pace for hours:* maintain, keep up, prolong, protract. **5.** *The prisoners sustained themselves on bread and water:* nourish, maintain; nurture, feed, keep alive.

sustenance *n.* *They only had sustenance to last a week:* livelihood, support, keep, maintenance, provender, provision, ration, subsistence, wherewithal, necessities.

svelte *adj.* *Two months of dieting gave her a svelte figure:* slender, slim, thin, lissome, lithe, lean, willowy, spare, sylphlike; shapely, trim, neat, graceful, elegant, fine. —**Ant.** plump, stocky, pudgy; dumpy, squat, obese.

swagger *v.* *He swaggered brazenly across the room:* strut, stride, stride insolently, sashay, swashbuckle, sweep, parade, saunter. —**Ant.** slink, sneak, creep.

swallow *v.* **1.** *Chew your meat thoroughly before you swallow it:* ingest; gulp, gobble, devour, gulp down; imbibe, guzzle, swig, down, swill, tipple, quaff. **2.** *He swallowed his anger and went on working:* repress, hold in, suppress, keep back, withhold, hold back. —*n.* **3.** *Take a swallow of my soda:* mouthful, drink, gulp, nip, sip, taste, bit.

swamp *n.* **1.** *We saw alligators in the swamp:* marsh, bog, morass, quagmire, mire, bottoms, quag, fen, bayou, everglade, marshland, swampland, slough, slew, slue, moor, ooze, swale. —*v.* **2.** *The huge wave swamped our canoe:* sink, submerge, fill; engulf, flood, wash over, inundate, envelop, deluge, swallow up. **3.** *The senator was swamped with speaking invitations:* overwhelm, flood, besiege, engulf, beset, snow under.

swanky *adj.* *She has a big new apartment in a swanky neighborhood:* smart, stylish, chic, elegant, fashionable, showy, fancy, dashing, sporty, swank, flashy, splashy, sumptuous, rich, grand; *Slang* ritzy, sharp, jazzy, plush, posh, snazzy, spiffy. **—Ant.** restrained, subdued, conservative, austere.

swap *v. The boys swapped baseball cards:* trade, dicker, exchange, switch, bargain, barter, give and take.

swarm *n.* **1.** *A swarm of locusts destroyed the crop. A swarm of fans ran onto the football field:* multitude; drove, throng, horde, cloud, mass, herd, press, great number, legion, stampede, host, crowd, myriad. *—v.* **2.** *The bargain hunters swarmed into the store:* flock, surge, throng, crowd, herd, overrun, cluster, rush, mass, stream. **3.** *The yard swarmed with mosquitoes:* abound, teem.

swarthy *adj. He looked swarthy after a month in the Caribbean:* dark-complexioned, dark-skinned, brunet, dusky, tawny, swart, brown-skinned, brown-colored, olive-skinned. **—Ant.** pale, light, fair, light-complexioned, fair-skinned.

swat *v. He swatted the ball over the fence for a home run:* hit, smack, knock, tap, strike, smite, wallop, belt, clout, buffet, clobber, sock, slam, bash, whack, slug.

sway *v.* **1.** *The sailboat swayed on the stormy sea. The seasick passenger swayed with dizziness:* rock, list, move to and fro, swing, roll, oscillate, wave, undulate, pendulate, fluctuate, waver; reel, totter, wobble, stagger. **2.** *The prospect of cold weather swayed them, and they decided to go south:* move, influence, prompt, persuade, motivate, rouse, lead, induce, bend the will of, stimulate, predispose, dispose, incite, encourage, spur, impel, prevail on, bring round. **3.** *He has never swayed in his loyalty to his family:* fluctuate, vacillate, change, shift, vary, hesitate, alter, swerve, bend. *—n.* **4.** *The sway of the hammock made him feel queasy:* swaying, swinging, waving, pulsation, oscillation, undulation, fluctuation, back and forth, to-and-fro. **5.** *The cabinet is completely under the sway of the Prime Minister:* control, authority, rule, domination, command, mastery, power, domain, jurisdiction, government, iron hand, dictatorship, reign, grip, suzerainty, hold. **6.** *His father has too much sway over the boy:* influence, control, domination, hold, command, grip, direction, power, manipulation, *Slang* clout.

swear *v.* **1.** *The witness swore to tell all he knew:* state under oath, take an oath, vow, vouch, avow, bind oneself by oath, certify, warrant, bear witness, attest, adjure, pledge oneself, aver, assert, promise. **2.** *He swore them to silence:* cause to promise, bind by an oath, pledge. **3.** *The boy swears like a trooper:* curse, cuss, use profanity, utter oaths, blaspheme.

sweat *v. They sweated in the hot sun:* perspire, drip, swelter, wilt, *Slang* sweat bullets.

sweaty *adj. The sweaty football players took a shower:* perspiring, sweating, drenched, drippy, soaked, sticky, wet, bathed in sweat.

sweep *v.* **1.** *Did you sweep up all the broken glass? Sweep the floor and make the beds:* whisk, gather. **2.** *The winner swept past the finish line:* race, dash, rush, dart, scurry, hurry,

charge, scud, fly, zoom, swoop, tear. *—n.* **3.** *There's a long sweep of empty road before you come to the inn:* stretch, distance, spell. **4.** *He cut the rope with one sweep of his machete:* swing, arc, stroke, swish, swoop.

sweeping *adj. The company's new president made sweeping changes in the office:* extensive, far-reaching, widespread, wide-ranging, broad, wholesale, radical, exhaustive, blanket, comprehensive, all-inclusive, large-scale, thoroughgoing, out-and-out. **—Ant.** small, modest, trifling, trivial, limited, superficial, narrow, slight.

sweet *adj.* **1.** *These cookies are too sweet:* sweet-tasting, sugary; saccharine, cloying. **2.** *There's a sweet spring only a hundred yards inland from the shore. Do you like sweet butter? This milk is too old to be still sweet:* not salt, not salty, nonsalt; fresh, nonfermented, wholesome, not spoiled, not rancid. **3.** *The soprano has a sweet voice:* melodious, dulcet, pleasing, mellifluous, tuneful, silver-toned, mellow, euphonious, smooth. **4.** *The baby smells so sweet after his bath:* fragrant, fresh. **5.** *The Jacksons are sweet people:* attractive, sympathetic, agreeable, nice, pleasant, good-natured, dear, kind, lovable, amiable, darling. *—n.* **6.** *Don't eat too many sweets:* candy, piece of candy, confection, sweetmeat, *British* dessert. **—Ant.** 1 sour, acid, acerbic, bitter, nasty. 2 saltwater, salt, salty, salted; stale, rancid, sour, decaying, tainted, turned. 3 harsh, shrill; raucous, discordant, unmelodious, displeasing, unmusical, inharmonious, dissonant, strident. 4 stale, bad-smelling, rank. 5 disagreeable, unpleasant, unattractive, nasty, ill-natured, unlovable, unamiable; dreadful, awful.

sweeten *v.* **1.** *They sweetened their coffee:* sugar, add sweetening, add sugar, candy, candy-coat, honey. **2.** *The company sweetened its offer to employees:* augment, better, soften up, mollify, soften up, soothe, beef up.

sweetheart *n. Her sweetheart gave her a ring for Christmas:* love, beloved, true love, dear, darling, flame, steady, girlfriend, lover; mistress, ladylove, lady friend, valentine, inamorata; boyfriend, beau, swain, suitor, gentleman friend; fiancé, (*fem.*) fiancée, *Slang* honey, old lady, old man.

swell *v.* **1.** *His eye swelled painfully after the blow. The guest list swelled to 100 people:* distend, puff, puff up, grow, blow up, fatten, bulge, inflate, extend, bloat, thicken; expand, increase, lengthen, stretch, widen, spread out, burgeon, rise. **2.** *The music swelled as the finale approached. The sea swelled as the storm approached:* intensify, amplify, heighten, rise, mount, throb; billow, surge, wax, heave. *—adj.* **3.** *Informal We had a swell time:* fine, first-rate, good, excellent, super, marvelous, terrific, great, delightful, splendid, pleasurable, first-class, okay, dandy, A1, fabulous, tremendous. *—n.* **4.** *The clipper ship scudded along over the long swells:* wave, billow; breaker, comber; undulation. **5.** *The young man imagined himself as a swell, dressed in the latest fashion:* fashion plate, smart dresser, dandy, fop, clotheshorse.

—**Ant.** 1 shrink, contract, condense, compress, constrict. 2 decrease, diminish, lessen, fall, wane, lower, ebb away. 3 horrible, awful, dreadful, lousy, bad, disgusting.

swelling *n. The ice pack brought the swelling down:* swell, puffiness, distension, dilation, bulge, bump, lump, swell, protuberance, enlargement.

swelter *v. We were sweltering on that stuffy bus:* be oppressed with heat, be hot, sweat, perspire, languish, *Informal* cook, fry, boil, broil. —**Ant.** freeze, shiver.

sweltering *adj. The coastal climate was sweltering:* broiling, broiling, close, humid, stewing, sticky, stifling, torrid, oppressive, airless.

sweltry *adj. Last summer we had 14 sweltry days in a row:* hot, sizzling, roasting, baking, broiling, boiling, torrid, scorching, blistering, sweltering, stifling, suffocating, humid, sultry, clammy, sticky, muggy, dank, steamy. —**Ant.** cold, blustery, raw, nippy.

swerve *v. The car swerved to avoid a squirrel:* diverge, deviate.

swift *adj. The thief made a swift exit:* hasty, fast, rapid, fleet, prompt, immediate, precipitate, headlong, speedy, brisk, quick, abrupt, expeditious, flying. —**Ant.** slow, sluggish, inexpeditious, late, tardy.

swiftly *adv. They swiftly answered the call:* speedily, quickly, rapidly, double-quick, flat-out, fleetly, full tilt, hastily, hotfoot, hurriedly, posthaste, promptly, apace.

swill *v.* **1.** *They swilled those drinks down in no time:* guzzle, drink greedily, gulp down, swallow noisily, quaff, soak up, swig, tipple, drain the cup, chugalug. —*n.* **2.** *The farmer fed his pigs swill:* slop, liquid food, mash; garbage, refuse, scraps, leavings, waste.

swimmingly *adv. The test went swimmingly:* effortlessly, smoothly, easily, prosperously, successfully, well, *Informal* like clockwork.

swindle *v.* **1.** *He swindled his brothers out of the inheritance:* cheat, defraud, gyp, hoax, trick, fleece, cozen, bilk, do, gull, hoodwink, bamboozle, con, dupe, deceive, delude, rook. **2.** *The company swindled money from its investors:* embezzle, mulct, steal, defalcate, *Slang* rip off. —*n.* **3.** *The housing development was a pure swindle:* fraud, hoax, cheat, steal, gyp, embezzlement, trick, confidence game, con game, racket, *Slang* rip-off.

swindler *n. He seemed a distinguished-looking man, but he was a swindler:* embezzler; con man; crook, charlatan, mountebank, gyp, fraud, sharper, cheat, faker, deceiver, *Slang* rip-off artist, chiseler.

swing *v.* **1.** *The pendulum stopped swinging:* move to and fro, oscillate, sway, rock, undulate, seesaw, move back and forth. **2.** *Swing the plants from the wooden beams. The horse thief will swing if they catch him:* hang, dangle, suspend, be suspended, drop, loop. **3.** *Informal Can you swing us an invitation to the party?:* manage, manipulate, handle, accomplish, maneuver, pull off, wangle, inveigh, extract. **4.** *He swung round on his heels and walked out:* pivot,

rotate, turn, whirl. **5.** *The mayor tried to swing public opinion in favor of his plan:* influence, sway, decide, determine, rally, move, manipulate. —*n.* **6.** *The swing of the ship made everyone seasick:* swaying, rocking, listing, pitching, rolling, oscillation. **7.** *It takes just one swing of the bat to hit a home run:* sweep, sweeping blow, stroke. **8.** *The foreman has full swing to do as he pleases:* liberty, license, freedom; scope, sweep, compass, rein.

swipe *n.* **1.** *He got a swipe across the head:* knock, blow, clip, clout, cuff, hit, lick, rap, slap, smack, swat, wallop, bash. —*v.* **2.** *She swiped the intruder with the back of her hand: Informal* clout, clip, lash out, slap, sock, strike, swat, wallop, bash. **3.** *Informal The burglars swiped everything:* steal, heist, lift, pilfer, pinch, purloin, appropriate, *Informal* cop, filch, nick, sneak, snitch.

swirl *v.* **1.** *A gust of wind swirled bits of paper down the street:* whirl, spin, twist, revolve, wheel, turn, roll, twirl; rotate, eddy, churn, gyrate, bowl. **2.** *Riding the roller coaster made my head swirl:* be dizzy, reel, spin, swim.

switch *n.* **1.** *The teacher whipped the bad boy with a hickory switch:* rod, small branch, stick. **2.** *The switch must be broken because the wiring's good and the bulb is brand-new:* actuator device, box, lever, handle, button. **3.** *The train was derailed when the switch failed to work. The general's private railroad car is standing on the switch:* shunting device, shunt, train switch; railroad sidetrack. **4.** *Someone accidentally made a switch in suitcases. We had to make a switch in our arrangements:* change, alternation, trade, shift. —*v.* **5.** *Grandpa switched us when we were disobedient:* whip, birch, lash, cane, tan. **6.** *The cow switched its tail:* whisk, jerk, move, swing, lash. **7.** *I switched pocketbooks with my sister:* exchange, change, trade.

swivel *v. He swiveled to pick up the book:* pivot, revolve, rotate, spin, swing around, turn, hinge, pirouette.

swollen *adj. Put an ice pack on that swollen eye:* puffed-up, puffy, swelled, distended, bloated, inflated, bulging. —**Ant.** shrunken, contracted.

swoop *v.* **1.** *The sea gull swooped down on the fish:* descend, pitch, drop, plunge, sweep down, plummet, nose-dive, dive; spring, pounce, rush headlong. —*n.* **2.** *With one swoop the falcon captured its prey:* dive, swooping, plunge, sweep, drop; pounce, rush.

sword *n. The duelists crossed swords:* blade, steel; (*variously*) saber, rapier, cutlass, foil, scimitar, épée, broadsword.

sybarite *v. The sybarites returned from the beach:* voluptuary, epicurean, sensualist.

sybaritic *adj. Her parents still criticize her for what they call her sybaritic life:* hedonistic, self-indulgent, pleasure-loving, pleasure-seeking, voluptuous, luxury-loving, sensual, epicurean, dissolute, dissipated, pleasure-bent. —**Ant.** austere, ascetic, self-denying, abstinent.

sycophant *n. Richard II surrounded himself with sycophants:* parasite, toady, flatterer, bootlicker, lickspitter, fawner, flunky, stooge, hanger-on, yes-man, truckler, rubber stamp, slave, lackey, cat's-paw, tool, jackal, puppet, *Informal* apple-polisher.

sylvan *adj. She loved the sylvan beauty of the eastern part of the country:* woody, forestlike, woodland, arcadian, wooded, woodsy, timbered, forested, thicket-grown, forest-clad, overgrown, luxuriant, bushy, leafy, moss-carpeted.

symbiotic *adj. The plants and animals had a symbiotic relationship:* mutual, reciprocal, cooperative, cooperating, synergistic, interacting, interactive, interrelating   **—Ant.** independent, isolated.

symbol *n.* **1.** *In math, x is the symbol for an unknown quantity:* sign, mark, figure, indication. **2.** *The ring was a symbol of his love. The lion is often used as a symbol of courage:* emblem, token, badge, mark, representation, exemplification, sign, signal, figure.

symbolic *adj. She decided to perform a symbolic act:* figurative, characteristic, emblematic, representative, suggestive, typical.

symbolize *v. The dove symbolizes peace:* stand for, mean, emblemize, represent, express, personify, connote, denote, emblematize, signify, betoken, symbol, signalize, imply, allego **—Ant.** , shadow forth, embody, exemplify.

symmetrical *adj. The formal garden is too symmetrical for my taste:* balanced, well-balanced, orderly, regular, congruent, well-proportioned.   **—Ant.** asymmetrical, unbalanced, irregular, uneven, unequal, disorderly.

symmetry *n. What poet praised the tiger's "fearful symmetry"? The snowflake is often cited as an example of perfect symmetry:* correspondence of parts, regularity, conformity, balance, congruity, proportionality, equilibrium, order, parallelism, orderliness, harmony; beauty of form, form, shapeliness.   **—Ant.** disproportion, disharmony, irregularity, disagreement, disparity, malformation.

sympathetic *adj.* **1.** *The students all tell their problems to one of the more sympathetic teachers:* sympathizing, compassionate, understanding, sensitive, tenderhearted, commiserative, warmhearted, softhearted, pitying, comforting, humane, kindly, merciful, benevolent, benign, benignant, feeling. **2.** *His mother was not sympathetic to his plan to leave school:* favorably disposed, well-disposed, agreeable, approving, friendly.   **—Ant.** 1, 2 unsympathetic. 1 uncompassionate, coldhearted, inhumane, insensitive, pitiless, unpitying, unfeeling, unmerciful.

sympathize *v.* **1.** *Her family sympathized with her desire to be a lawyer:* agree, be in accord, side, go along; understand, appreciate, approve, sanction, regard with favor, favor, back, support; bear goodwill toward, stand behind, take an interest in. **2.** *I sympathize greatly with the bereaved man:* feel compassion for, be sorry for, feel for, have pity for, pity, empathize, feel sympathy for; identify with, grieve with, share the sorrow of, commiserate with, lament with, condole with, mourn with.   **—Ant.** 1 disagree, op-

pose, fail to understand, misunderstand, disallow, reject.

sympathy *n.* **1.** *There was an instant sympathy between the two men:* concord, accord, harmony, congeniality, understanding, agreement, rapport, affinity, consanguinity, communion, consonance, unanimity, concert, regard, amity, fellow feeling, fellowship, friendship. **2.** *He felt tremendous sympathy for the war orphans:* concern, compassion, feeling, commiseration, tenderness, empathy, grief, sorrow, pity. **3.** *Your plan has my complete sympathy:* support, favor, sanction, approval, agreement, advocacy, well-wishing, partisanship, patronage.   **—Ant.** 1 antipathy, hostility, misunderstanding, antagonism. 2 coldness, mercilessness, pitilessness, insensibility, indifference, unconcern. 3 disfavor, disapproval, opposition.

symposium *n. We attended a symposium on ecology:* conference, parley, discussion, panel discussion, forum, round table, colloquy, congress, meeting, deliberation, synod, debate, *Slang* powwow.

symptom *n. A rash is one symptom of scarlet fever:* signal, sign, indication, evidence, token, warning, prognostication, mark, earmark, giveaway.

syndicate *n. A syndicate is buying up all the stock of the firm. The Associated Press is an important news syndicate:* combine, coalition, alliance, league, federation, union, merger, association, group, trust, cartel, consortium.

syndrome *n. Several doctors were amazed at the syndrome:* complex, complaint, condition, disorder, infirmity, malady, problem, sickness, ailment; sign, cluster.

synonym *n. "Volume" is a synonym for "book." William Penn's name lives after him as a synonym for philanthropy:* equivalent word, parallel word, analogue, equivalent; another name.   **—Ant.** antonym, opposite.

synonymous *adj. "Car" is synonymous with "automobile":* equivalent, similar in meaning, alike, like, same, equal, coequal.   **—Ant.** antonymous, opposite in meaning.

synopsis *n. It's good to read a synopsis of the opera before going to it:* outline, summary, précis, epitome, digest, brief, argument, abstract, abridgement, *Informal* rundown; aperçu, résumé.

syntax *n. His extensive diction was matched by a command of syntax:* word order, syntactic structure, structure.

synthesis *n. Synthesis of ideas went on apace:* fusing, integration, blend, coalescence, compound, making one, unification, union, amalgamation, welding.

synthesize *v. The chemists synthesized the new compound:* fused, blend, amalgamate, harmonize, incorporate, integrate, make whole, unify.

synthetic *adj. Synthetic suede is more durable than the real thing:* artificial, unnatural, man-made, manufactured, ersatz; fake, phony, counterfeit, sham.   **—Ant.** real, authentic, genuine, natural, organic.

system *n.* **1.** *The Superintendent is the chief administrator of the school system. Music lovers appreciate a good hi-fi system:* combination of parts, organization, organized entity, overall unit, unit, structure, setup. **2.** *Don't wreck your system by overwork and lack of sleep!:* constitution, body, organism. **3.** *The system underlying modern physics is not fully worked out:* theory, theoretical base, hypothesis, frame of reference. **4.** *Does the new clerk understand the filing system?:* method, procedure, arrangement, scheme, program, mode of operation, modus operandi, regimen, routine.

systematic *adj.* **1.** *The bank recommends that each family should have a systematic savings program:* planned, organized, systematized, orderly, ordered. **2.** *His books are kept in a highly systematic way:* methodical, precise, orderly, well-organized, businesslike, tidy, neat, well-regulated, constant, regular. **—Ant.** 1, 2 unsystematic. 1 arbitrary, haphazard, random. 2 unmethodical, disorderly, disorganized, unbusinesslike, messy, sloppy.

systematize *v.* *The librarian was able to systematize the collection:* systemize, order, put in order, organize, methodize, make uniform, marshal, pull together, order, rationalize, schematize, standardize, straighten up, array, arrange.

tab n. **1.** *Buy file dividers with alphabetical tabs:* short strip, loop, eyehole, flap, projection, lip, tongue. **2.** *Informal Our host picked up the tab for dinner. What's the tab?:* bill, check, cost, price, tally.

table n. **1.** *Set the table with the good china. A clock radio was on the table by the bed:* (variously) eating table, dining room table, kitchen table, breakfast table; stand, end table, coffee table, bedside table, display table. **2.** *The country squire had a big house and a bountiful table:* board, spread, fare. **3.** *The math book contained a multiplication table. Find Chapter 3 by looking in the table of contents:* list, chart, tabular arrangement, tabulation, schedule, record, inventory, catalog, register, roll, roster; synopsis, index, syllabus. —v. **4.** *The committee tabled the proposal until a later meeting:* lay aside, put aside, postpone, shelve. —**Ant.** 4 act on, vote on, activate, begin, start, initiate; continue.

tableau n. *The final curtain fell on a tableau of the characters:* scene, spectacle, still life, grouping, picture, illustration, stage picture, view, setting, arrangement, pageant, picturization, delineation, depiction, *French* tableau vivant.

tablet n. **1.** *Each student should have pencils and a tablet with lined paper:* pad of paper, writing pad, pad, memo pad. **2.** *The statue had a bronze tablet listing the town's war heroes:* plaque, panel, tablature; thin slab, surface, sheet, leaf. **3.** *Take two aspirin tablets and go to bed:* flat cake, lozenge, troche, wafer, pellet, bolus.

taboo or **tabu** adj. **1.** *Eating pork is strictly taboo among Orthodox Jews:* forbidden, banned, prohibited, proscribed, outlawed, anathema, unacceptable, disapproved, unthinkable, unmentionable, *German* verboten. —n. **2.** *The Polynesians have a taboo on mentioning certain sacred rites:* religious ban, social ban, ban, prohibition, proscription, interdiction, *Slang* no-no. —**Ant.** allowed, permitted, permissible; approved, sanctioned, encouraged.

tabulate *He wants us to tabulate the data according to source:* arrange, order, systematize, file, index, classify, rank, list, group, rate, organize, sort, grade, range, categorize, codify, rank, catalog, sort out. —**Ant.** mix, confuse, jumble, tangle, muddle.

tacit adj. *The neighbors had a tacit agreement not to park in front of each other's houses:* unexpressed, understood, assumed, implied, inferred, implicit, wordless, undeclared, unspoken, unstated, taken for granted.

taciturn adj. *He's so taciturn no one knew whether he enjoyed the party or not:* reserved, aloof, reticent, sparing of words, uncommunicative, close-mouthed, tight-lipped, laconic, silent, quiet, secretive. —**Ant.** talkative, loquacious, voluble, garrulous, chatty, open, unreserved, wordy, verbose.

tack n. **1.** *The calendar was held to the wall with tacks:* short nail; (variously) thumbtack, carpet tack; thole, tholepin, peg, spike. **2.** *The sailboat's sudden tack to starboard startled the passengers:* zigzag, change, swerve, shift, switch. **3.** *If this plan doesn't work, we'll try a new tack:* course of action, approach, method, way. —v. **4.** *Tack the notice on the bulletin board:* nail, pin; attach, fasten, affix. **5.** *Congress tried to tack the highway measure onto the housing bill. Tack on a dollar for the tip to the waiter:* add, attach, affix, append, *Slang* slap, clap. **6.** *The ship tacked to starboard:* change course, go about, veer, sheer, swerve, zigzag. —**Ant.** 4 untack, unnail, unpin; loose, take off, take down. 5 subtract, deduct, separate, detach, delete, cut.

tackle n. **1.** *The sporting goods store had a window full of fishing tackle:* equipment, gear, paraphernalia, apparatus, trappings, rigging, accoutrements, appointments, implements; tools, instruments, material, appliances. **2.** *The freighter was unloaded at the dock by heavy-duty tackle:* system of ropes and pulleys; (variously) hoist, lift, crane, derrick, winch, windlass, capstan, halyard, jenny. **3.** *The policeman nailed the suspect with a flying tackle:* throw, pinioning of the legs. —v. **4.** *The comedian wanted to tackle a serious role in his next movie. The boys tackled the job of painting the room enthusiastically:* undertake, attempt, try, assay, endeavor, attack, take on, take up, accept, embrace, assume, devote oneself to, turn one's hand to, embark upon, engage in, set about, go about, enter upon, begin. **5.** *The defensive end tackled the quarterback at the line of scrimmage:* seize and throw down, throw, wrestle to the ground. —**Ant.** 4 reject, spurn, shun, evade, forgo, forswear, eschew; postpone, set aside, shelve.

tacky adj. **1.** *Did you ever see such a tacky kitchen?:* slovenly, messy, sloppy, disordered, untidy, unkempt, slipshod, shabby, shoddy, tatty, ratty, frazzled, dowdy, seedy, grubby. **2.** *Don't sit on the chair, the paint is still tacky:* sticky, gluey, gummy, adhesive, viscous, stringy, viscid; *Slang* gooey, gucky. —**Ant.** 1 neat, orderly, tidy, immaculate.

tact n. *The hostess showed enormous tact in handling the touchy situation:* diplomacy, circumspection, delicacy, savoir faire, suavity, suaveness, finesse, discretion, consideration, sensibility. —**Ant.** tactlessness, crudeness, clumsiness, awkwardness, heavy-handedness, indiscretion, indelicacy, insensitivity.

tactful adj. *A diplomat must be very tactful. The tactful suggestion offended no one:* socially adroit, diplomatic, politic, smooth, suave, decorous, subtle, discreet, delicate, considerate, thoughtful; mannerly, sensitive, polite. —**Ant.** tactless, undiplomatic, unpolitic, unsubtle, indecorous, indiscreet; indelicate, tasteless, clumsy, untoward, awkward, gauche.

tactic n. **1.** *The best tactic is to confess and ask her forgiveness:* course of action, plan, stratagem, way, tack, method, scheme, policy, approach, line, means of getting one's way. **2.** Usually **tactics** *The general's brilliant tactics won the battle:* maneuvers, battle arrangements, military operations.

tactless *adj. She made some tactless remarks about her boyfriend's sister:* rude, thoughtless, undiplomatic, inconsiderate, insensitive, ill-considered, clumsy, ham-handed, untactful, brash, stupid, boorish, impolitic, imprudent, indiscreet, gauche, blundering, impolite. **—Ant.** tactful, polite, diplomatic, considerate, discreet.

tag *n.* **1.** *Each item in the store carries a printed price tag:* label, tab, ticket, slip, card, stub, mark, marker; pendant, appendage, attachment. **—v. 2.** *The clerks tagged the merchandise for the sale:* attach a tag to, label, ticket, tab, earmark, mark, identify; term, title, name. **3.** *Just tag a postscript to the end of the letter:* add, add on, tack on, attach, append, annex, affix; fasten, join to. **4.** *Informal Must your brother tag along with us everywhere we go?:* accompany, attend, follow, shadow, trail, tail, dog, heel, hound, hang on the skirts of.

tailor *n.* **1.** *A Savile Row tailor makes all of Bill's clothes. The tailor shortened the pants two inches:* garment maker, dressmaker, seamstress, costumer, clothier, *French* couturier; alteration man, alteration lady. **—v. 2.** *Her clothing is tailored by a famous couturier. We can tailor the house to suit the owner's needs:* fashion, make, create, design, devise, shape, construct, build, produce, fabricate; alter, adapt, convert, change, fit, modify, transform, redo; sew. **—Ant.** 2 destroy, tear up; leave alone, let be.

taint *n.* **1.** *The scandal was a taint on the family's good name:* stain, spot, blemish, blot, stigma, tarnish, smudge, flaw, defect, fault, imperfection. **—v. 2.** *Rumors of bribery tainted the politician's reputation. The beef tainted when the freezer broke down:* spoil, damage, ruin, sully, defile, debase, stain, spot, soil, tarnish, blemish, besmirch, dirty, smudge, smear, mar; become spoiled, go bad, putrefy, rot, turn. **—Ant.** 2 enhance, elevate, exalt, strengthen, reinforce, boost.

take *v.* **1.** *Please take a cookie from the bowl. Take the rope in your right hand and pull:* get, have, obtain, acquire, secure, avail oneself of, help oneself to; grip, grasp, clutch, clasp, hold, lay hold of, get hold of, lay hands on, seize, grab, snatch, nab. **2.** *The military took control of the government. The thieves took all the money that was in the safe:* seize, grab, usurp, appropriate, misappropriate, capture, commandeer, confiscate, deprive of, divest; steal, purloin, filch, pocket, pilfer, cheat, bilk, fleece; loot, plunder, sack, pillage. **3.** *Take this package to the post office. The teacher took the students on a tour through the art museum:* deliver, carry, bring, bear, tote, lug, convey, transport, move, transfer; conduct, guide, lead, escort, usher. **4.** *The customer tried on two dresses and took both. My sister has taken a house by the shore for the summer. Don't take cold:* buy,

purchase; rent, lease, hire, obtain, acquire, get, use, employ; catch. **5.** *If you take 6 from 10, you get 4:* subtract, deduct, take away, remove, eliminate. **6.** *We took your silence to mean that you agreed:* interpret, understand, regard, respond to, receive, look on, see, perceive, deem, suppose, believe, comprehend, hold, consider, conceive, conclude, deduce, ascertain, infer, make out, *Slang* read. **7.** *Take the doctor's advice and start exercising:* accept, comply with, accede to, agree to, consent to, assent to, heed, follow, mind, obey, mark, listen to, observe, respect, be ruled by, resign oneself to, go along with. **8.** *Becoming a doctor takes years of study. It took all his strength to lift the chair:* require, necessitate, need, demand, call for; use, use up, employ, consume, claim. **9.** *She won't take any more of his insults:* endure, bear, stand, tolerate, suffer, stomach, brook, submit to, undergo, put up with. **10.** *I take great pleasure in introducing our guest speaker:* feel, have, experience, know; derive, gain, attain, get, draw. **11.** *Bill took the blame for his brother's mistake:* accept, assume, undertake, shoulder, draw. **12.** *As soon as the medicine takes, the patient should improve:* take effect, begin to work; work, succeed. **—n. 13.** *The fisherman brought home a huge take:* catch, haul. **14.** *The day's take came to over $500:* proceeds, net; profit, gross. **—Ant.** 1 give, put; let go, put down. 2 surrender, give up, yield, let go; return, restore, give back. 5 add, tack on. 7 reject, refuse, spurn, decline, veto, turn down, dismiss, renounce, repudiate, scorn. 11 forgo, forswear, avoid, evade, eschew. 12 fail, flop. 14 loss.

takeoff *n.* **1.** *Takeoff occurred at six o'clock:* flight, ascent **2.** *The comedian's takeoff was hilarious:* burlesque, caricature, cartoon, comedy, imitation, lampoon, mockery, mocking, parody, ridicule, satire, send-up, spoof, travesty.

tale *n.* **1.** *The author told a tale of intrigue and adventure:* story, narrative, narration, recital, account, report, yarn, anecdote; (*variously*) novel, short story, romance, fable, legend, myth, epic, saga. **2.** *The woman told tales to make her life seem glamorous. Don't tell tales out of school:* fib, lie, falsehood, untruth, fabrication, fiction, falsification, tall story, cock-and-bull story, fish story; piece of gossip, scandal, rumor, hearsay, tittle-tattle, *Slang* scuttlebutt.

talent *n.* *The girl seems to have a talent for drawing:* special ability, natural gift, gift, faculty, facility, endowment, genius, aptitude, capacity, capability, proficiency, skill, knack, bent, flair, turn, forte, strength.

talented *adj. Their youngest girl is a talented musician:* gifted, artistic, accomplished, well-endowed, polished, brilliant, expert, proficient, competent, adept, capable, born for, cut out for, made for.

talisman *n. She wore a small talisman around her neck:* fetish, charm, amulet, mascot, lucky-piece, good-luck charm, phylactery, juju, rabbit's foot, four-leaf clover.

talk *v.* **1.** *Can the baby talk yet? We talked business for hours:* utter words, speak, speak about;

(*variously*) converse, exchange words, bandy words, communicate orally, discuss, chat, chatter, gab, gossip, palaver, prattle, prate, babble, rap, jaw, rattle on. **2.** *You'd better talk with a lawyer:* confer, consult, speak, take up; negotiate, parley. **3.** *He's talking nonsense!:* utter, speak, say, express, intone, enunciate, state, proclaim, pronounce, deliver, declare; preach, pontificate. —*n.* **4.** *Let's have a little talk together:* conversation, chat, tête-à-tête, chitchat, colloquy, confabulation; discussion, conference, consultation, parley, dialogue, *Slang* powwow, palaver, confab, rap session. **5.** *The speaker gave a short, humorous talk:* address, lecture, speech, oration, discourse, sermon; harangue, tirade, exhortation; declamation, recitation, utterance. **6.** *There's been some talk about closing the office. Some people are all talk and no action:* gossip, rumor, hearsay, noise, report, word, *Slang* tittle-tattle, scuttlebutt, watercooler talk; empty speech, hot air, empty words, blarney, verbiage, bunkum, prattle, chatter, chat, twaddle, blather, blatherskite, gab. **7.** *The kids' hip talk is sometimes hard for adults to follow:* idiom, language, lingo, dialect, patois, slang, cant, jargon, argot. —**Ant.** 1 be silent, be mute; listen.

talkative *adj. The talkative man monopolized the conversation:* loquacious, voluble, effusive, garrulous, talky, chatty, gabby, gossipy, babbly, prolix, long-winded, windy, wordy, verbose. —**Ant.** silent, mute, mum, speechless; reticent, reserved, taciturn, uncommunicative, secretive, close-mouthed, tight-lipped.

talker *n.* **1.** *The congressman is a marvelous talker:* conversationalist, converser; speaker, lecturer, orator, speechmaker, speechifier; spokesperson, *Slang* mouthpiece. **2.** *She's quite a talker—I could get in a word!:* loquacious person, voluble person, garrulous person, chatterbox, chatterer, windbag, gabber, prattler, babbler, blatherskite; magpie, gossip, rumormonger, scandalmonger.

tall *adj.* **1.** *The boy is four feet tall:* high, in height. **2.** *Professional basketball players are all very tall. A tall mountain loomed over the valley:* of more than average height, long-limbed, big, lanky, rangy, gangling, stringy; high, lofty, towering, soaring, elevated. **3.** *Informal The story of catching a 100-pound fish is a pretty tall tale:* hard to believe, implausible, incredible, unbelievable, preposterous, absurd, hard to swallow, exaggerated, embellished. —**Ant.** 1 wide, broad, long, deep. 2 short, squat, low, stubby, dwarflike; tiny, small, diminutive. 3 believable, credible, plausible, reasonable, unexaggerated, unembellished, unadorned; true, real, authentic.

tally *n.* **1.** *The golfer added up the strokes on his tally:* scorecard, scorepad. **2.** *The final tally was 200 votes for and 150 against:* count, reckoning, mark, score; total, sum, enumeration, muster, census, poll. —*v.* **3.** *The judges tallied the scores:* record, mark down, register, list, catalog, post; count, add, sum up, total, compute, calculate, tabulate, reckon. **4.** *The checkbook stubs don't tally with my bank statement:* match, jibe, square, correspond, agree, conform, coincide, accord, concur, harmonize.

tame *adj.* **1.** *Even a tame monkey can become a dangerous pet. Greg is too tame to stand up for his own rights:* domesticated, domestic, broken; docile, gentle, mild, tractable, unresisting, submissive, subdued, pliable, pliant, complaisant, amenable, meek, timorous, timid. **2.** *Country life was too tame for the city boy:* unexciting, uninteresting, dull, boring, tedious, prosaic, flat, lifeless; quiet, placid, serene, tranquil. —*v.* **3.** *The cowboys tamed the wild horses. She'd better tame that violent temper:* break, make docile, domesticate, subdue, train; control, conquer, overcome, master, dominate, govern, manage, restrain, repress, suppress, curb, bridle, rein, check, regulate, damp. —**Ant.** 1 wild, untamed, undomesticated, intractable, unsubmissive, stubborn, obdurate, strong-willed. 2 exciting, interesting, stimulating, spirited, lively, wild, frenzied, tumultuous.

tamper *v.* **1.** *Don't tamper with other people's affairs:* meddle, interfere, intrude, obtrude, intervene, horn in, butt in, mix, poke one's nose in. **2.** *Did anyone tamper with this lock?:* tinker, fool around, fiddle, *Informal* mess around, monkey around, *British* muck.

tan *v.* **1.** *It takes skill to tan cowhide:* convert to leather, treat with tanning solution. **2.** *Fairskinned people don't tan easily:* suntan; brown, bronze. —*adj.* **3.** *Marilyn came back from her vacation with tan arms and face:* suntanned, bronzed; sunburned, sunburnt. **4.** *The den walls are covered with tan paneling:* light brown, brownish, yellow-brown, beige, tawny, sandy, cinnamon, roan, sorrel, khaki. —**Ant.** 2 fade; peel. 3 white, pale, light. 4 dark brown, mahogany, nut-brown.

tang *n.* **1.** *The salad dressing has too much tang of garlic:* strong taste, flavor, savor, pungency, bite, punch, sharpness, sting, piquancy, spiciness, tartness, acridness, acridity; odor, smell, reek, aroma, scent. **2.** *There's a tang of fall in the air:* trace, tinge, hint, touch, suggestion, bit, smack.

tangible *adj.* **1.** *A ghost is not a tangible thing:* palpable, touchable, material, solid, physical, corporeal, substantial. **2.** *The jury needs tangible evidence to convict:* concrete, real, actual, material, verifiable, indubitable, positive, clearcut, obvious, manifest. —**Ant.** 1 intangible, untouchable, impalpable; immaterial, ethereal, spiritual, incorporeal, disembodied.

tangle *v.* **1.** *The puppet strings tangle easily. The wind tangled the girl's long hair:* twist, snarl, entangle, ravel, knot; disarrange, dishevel, muss, tousle, jumble, disorder, rumple, ruffle. —*n.* **2.** *A deer was caught in the tangle of vines. The negotiations were in a hopeless tangle:* snarl, knot, tanglement, entanglement, web, net, network, mesh, skein, jungle, labyrinth, maze; fix, impasse. —**Ant.** 1 untangle, unsnarl, unknot, unravel, loose, loosen, untwist; arrange, order, array, organize, straighten, disentangle.

tank *n.* **1.** *A fifty-gallon tank supplies water to* *the kitchen and bath:* storage tank, vat, container, receptacle; reservoir, cistern, boiler; fish tank, aquarium. **2.** *Each infantry company was supported by three machine guns, a howitzer, and two tanks:* armored vehicle on caterpillar treads; armored car.

tantalize *v. The speaker tantalized us with tales of exotic lands and buried treasure:* torment with unobtainable prospects, tease, provoke, taunt, torment, make one's mouth water, whet the appetite, tempt, bait, titillate, lead on, intrigue; fascinate, bewitch, charm, captivate, entice. **—Ant.** satisfy, gratify, fulfill, appease.

tantamount *adj. Retreat was tantamount to defeat:* equivalent, parallel, same, selfsame, synonymous, like, alike.

tantrum *n. The child's tantrums were caused by frustration:* burst of temper, rampage, fit of passion, flare-up, storm, conniption fit, outburst, fit, paroxysm, explosion.

tap¹ *v.* **1.** *Rain tapped on the windowpane:* strike lightly, touch lightly, rap, pat, beat softly, drum, peck, thud, hammer. **—n. 2.** *I felt a tap on my shoulder and turned to see Ed grinning:* light strike, gentle blow, touch, stroke, pat, rap, peck.

tap² *n.* **1.** *Who left the hot-water tap on?:* faucet, spigot, stopcock, cock, valve, spout. **—v. 2.** *The bartender tapped a new keg of beer:* put a tap in, unplug, unstopper, remove the stopple, uncork; open the stopcock of; draw liquid from, draw off, broach. **3.** *The country must tap new sources of energy:* draw upon, use, utilize, exploit, employ, put to work.

tape *n.* **1.** *She put tape on the cut:* band, strip, braid, edging, line, ribbon. **—v. 2.** *They carefully taped the package:* bandage, tie up, wrap, seal, secure, swathe, truss, wrap, fasten, bind. **3.** *The band taped a new song:* record, tape-record, video, videotape.

tar *n.* **1.** *The crew put tar on the cracked pavement:* pitch, creosote, asphalt. **2.** *The tars sang a jolly chantey:* sailor, seaman, seafaring man, gob, mariner, swab, seafarer.

tardy *adj.* **1.** *You'll be tardy for class if you don't hurry:* late, not on time, unpunctual, behind time, behindhand, belated; overdue, remiss, dilatory. **2.** *The tardy progress of the work discouraged the foreman:* slow, slow-paced, sluggish, slack, creeping, crawling, leisurely, languid, snail-like, slowpoke, slow as molasses; procrastinating, reluctant. **—Ant.** 1 punctual, on time, prompt; undelayed; early, premature. 2 fast, fast-moving, speedy, quick, rapid; industrious, eager, zealous.

target *n.* **1.** *The arrow hit the center of the target. The organization's target was to double its membership:* mark, object aimed at; objective, object, goal, aim, end, purpose, ambition; design, plan, intent, intention. **2.** *Paul was the target of the practical joke:* butt, goat, victim, prey, dupe, gull, patsy, pigeon, laughingstock.

tariff *n.* **1.** *The cigarette tariff has gone up:* duty, input tax, export tax, excise tax, excise, assessment, impost, levy; list of import-export taxes, customs list, trade controls. **2.** *The railroads increased their tariff by ten percent:* fare, freight-age; (*loosely*) charge, rate, fee, price, cost, expense, rent, commission.

tarnish *v.* **1.** *Silver tarnishes easily:* oxidize, corrode, discolor, blacken, dull, dim, darken, lose luster. **2.** *The charge of fraud tarnished the firm's reputation:* discredit, degrade, defile, defame, vilify, stigmatize, denigrate, disgrace, dishonor, taint, stain, sully, spot, blemish, blacken, foul, befoul, smirch, besmirch, soil, blot, erode, dirty, dull, dim, darken, drag through the mud. **—Ant.** 1 shine, gleam, polish, burnish, clean; brighten. 2 enhance, glorify, credit, exalt.

tarry *v.* **1.** *I mustn't tarry here a moment longer:* linger, dally, remain, stay, bide, abide, rest, pause, *Informal* hang around, cool one's heels. **2.** *Don't tarry too long in coming to a decision:* dawdle, delay, wait, take time, be tardy, lag, procrastinate, put off, postpone, stave off, tempo-rize, stall, hang back. **—Ant.** 1 leave, go, depart, be off, run, run along, move on, get moving. 2 rush, hurry, hasten, quicken, hustle, expedite, precipitate, spur.

tart¹ *adj.* **1.** *This lemon pie is very tart:* sour, sourish, sharp, astringent, acid, acrid, acetic, vin-egary; piquant, spicy, tangy, pungent, bitter. **2.** *The clerk's tart reply offended the customer:* sharp, caustic, cutting, barbed, biting, acerb, acrid, crusty. **—Ant.** 1 sweet, sugary, saccharine, cloying; mild, bland, mellow, flat. 2 sweet, kind, kindly, gentle, mild, pleasant, agreeable, benign, genial, polite, gracious, friendly, amiable, good-natured.

tart² *n. The hostess served tea and raspberry tarts:* individual pie, small fruit pie, small open-faced pie; pastry shell.

task *n. Each child is responsible for certain household tasks:* chore, job, duty, work, labor, stint, mission, assignment, charge, responsibility, errand, business, undertaking.

taskmaster *n. The major was a stern taskmaster:* martinet, slave driver, tyrant, disciplinarian, despot, Simon Legree, stickler; master, boss, supervisor, superintendent, overseer, foreman, director, headman, manager.

taste *v.* **1.** *Can you taste the mint in the icing? This punch just tastes like pineapple juice:* experience the flavor of; savor, discern; have a flavor of, savor of, smack of. **2.** *Taste some of this cake:* sample, eat a little of, take a bite of, try, test; drink a little of, take a sip of. **3.** *At last he tasted the joys of success:* experience, partake of, encounter, meet, undergo, feel, enjoy, relish, savor, have a foretaste of. **—n. 4.** *This coleslaw has a sour taste:* flavor, savor, relish, smack, tang, piquancy. **5.** *Have a taste of this delicious pie:* mouthful, bite, morsel, bit, crumb, sample, forkful, spoonful; sip, swallow, nip. **6.** *Rachel has a taste for sweets. Modern furniture is more to my taste than antiques:* liking, predilection, propensity, leaning, inclination, penchant, bent, partiality, disposition, fondness, craving, hankering, longing, desire, fancy, yearning, yen, whim, relish, appetite, thirst, hunger. **7.** *Sylvia has marvelous taste in clothes. The comic's jokes showed poor taste:* esthetic judgment, sense of beauty, discernment, artistic appreciation; sense of propriety, propriety, correctness, judgment, discrimination, insight, delicacy, decorum. —**Ant. 3** miss. **6** distaste, dislike, disinclination, disrelish; hatred, abhorrence, loathing. **7** tastelessness; impropriety, indelicacy, coarseness, crudeness.

tasteful *adj. Everyone admired the tasteful decor:* showing good taste, esthetic, artistic, attractive, elegant, exquisite, refined, cultured, well-chosen, handsome, beautiful, suitable, becoming. —**Ant.** tasteless, unesthetic, inelegant, ugly, loud, flashy, garish, tawdry, gaudy, unrefined, uncultured.

tasteless *adj.* **1.** *The soup was rather tasteless:* having no taste, flavorless, unflavored, without savor, bland, insipid, weak, flat, mild, watery. **2.** *No one laughed at the tasteless joke. Her wardrobe seems completely tasteless:* lacking good taste, cheap, common, crude, rude, coarse, crass, gross, uncouth, improper, inappropriate, unseemly, unsuitable, insensitive, indelicate, indecent, indecorous, low, ribald, disgusting, distasteful, offensive, gaudy, flashy, garish, inelegant, unrefined, uncultured, unesthetic.

tasty *adj. The stew was quite tasty:* good-tasting, delicious, delectable, luscious, toothsome, *Slang* scrumptious, yummy; savory, flavorful, flavorsome, full-flavored, appetizing; piquant, spicy, well-seasoned, hot, zestful, tangy, palatable.

tatters *n. pl. The old derelict was in tatters:* shreds, rags; ragged clothing, torn clothes, cast-off clothes; patches.

tattle *v.* **1.** *Teach the child not to tattle on his friends:* tell on, inform on, divulge secrets, blab, gossip; *Slang* snitch, rat, squeal; babble, prattle, gabble, prate, blurt out confidences, blather. —*n.* **2.** *Her conversation is always full of tattle:* gossip, prattle, blather, chatter, babble, rumor-mongering, tittle-tattle, twaddle, tongue-wagging, hearsay, mudslinging, loose talk.

tattletale *n. Some tattletale got the other boys in trouble:* tattler, talebearer, rumormonger, newsmonger, gossip, telltale, busybody, informer, betrayer, troublemaker, scandalmonger, blabbermouth; *Slang* snitch, squealer, fink, rat, stool pigeon, stoolie, ratfink, *Brit.* sneak.

taunt *v.* **1.** *The bully taunted the smaller boy:* jeer at, jeer, mock, insult, tease, rag, jive, gibe, twit, guy, snigger at, deride, sneer at, ridicule, make fun of, poke fun at, make game of; torment, provoke, harass. —*n.* **2.** *The older sister's cruel taunts drove the little girl to tears:* jeer, mockery, insult, teasing remark, ragging, chaffing, gibe, derision, sneer, scoff, snigger, ridicule, sarcastic remark, scornful remark, slur, verbal abuse; tormenting, provocation, harassment. —**Ant. 1** humor, flatter, jolly, coddle, court, pander to, truckle to, curry favor with, butter up; praise, compliment. **2** humoring, flattering, coddling, pandering, truckling, currying favor, buttering up, praise, compliment.

taut *adj.* **1.** *Keep the measuring tape taut:* drawn tight, tight, stretched out full, tense, not slack, not loose, rigid, unbending, inflexible, under strain, unrelaxed. **2.** *The captain runs a taut*

ship: well-regulated, orderly, businesslike, well-disciplined, tight, neat, tidy, trim, trig, spruce, smart, shipshape, snug, no-nonsense. —**Ant. 1** slack, loose, relaxed, flexible. **2** sloppy, slovenly, undisciplined, messy, untidy.

tavern *n. We stopped at a tavern for a bit of refreshment:* saloon, barroom, taproom, bar, alehouse, restaurant, brasserie, bistro, cocktail lounge; *Brit.* pub, public house; *Slang* watering hole, grogshop, drinkery, gin mill, beer joint, honky-tonk, dive.

tawdry *adj. That tawdry dress will never do for church:* showy, flashy, raffish, flamboyant, garish, meretricious, gaudy, loud, tasteless, inelegant, vulgar, crass, tacky, cheap, tinsel, gimcrack, pretentious, ostentatious, conspicuous, obtrusive. —**Ant.** tasteful, elegant, refined, *Informal* classy, high-class; simple, plain, quiet, reserved, understated.

tawny *adj. Her tawny skin tans easily:* tan, bronze, yellowish-brown, light brown, brownish, beige, fawn, sandy; dusky, swarthy, olive.

tax *n.* **1.** *The French kings used to levy a burdensome tax on salt:* payment of money to support a government and its services; (*variously*) income tax, property tax, sales tax, excise tax, luxury tax, inheritance tax, excess profit tax, state tax, county tax, city tax; impost, assessment, excise, levy, tariff, duty, custom, toll. **2.** *Racing to make the train was a tax on our nerves:* burden, strain, strenuous demand, load, exertion, drain; charge, obligation, duty. —*v.* **3.** *The government does not tax certain private foundations:* impose a tax on, assess, levy, exact a duty from. **4.** *The overactive child taxed the nurse's patience:* burden, overburden, weigh, weight, lade, load, saddle, strain, overwork, tire, stretch, try; drain, exhaust, sap, wear out, deplete. —**Ant. 1** deduction, nontaxable income.

teach *v. Mr. La Farge teaches French at the local high school. The professor prefers to teach graduate students:* give instruction in, conduct classes in, give lessons in, be employed as a teacher; give instruction to, conduct class for, give lessons to, instruct, educate, school, tutor, coach, drill, exercise, discipline, prepare, prime; inform, enlighten, edify, indoctrinate, inculcate, implant. —**Ant.** learn, study, attend school, be educated.

teacher *n. The teacher dismissed the class:* (*variously*) schoolteacher, schoolmaster, master, schoolmistress, schoolmarm, instructor, professor, don, tutor, maestro, educator, preceptor, trainer, mentor, coach.

teaching *n.* **1.** *The teaching of math has changed drastically in the last decade. Audio-visual aids revolutionized teaching:* instruction, instructing, schooling, tutoring, tutelage, training, preparation; the teaching profession, education, pedagogy; indoctrination, inculcation, nurture. **2.** *The teachings of Mao Zedong were widely published in China:* precept, doctrine, dogma, principle, tenet.

team *n.* **1.** *A team of oxen pulled the wagon:* harnessed pair, yoked group; pair, set, yoke, tandem. **2.** *A football team consists of eleven* *players:* sports team, side; (*football*) eleven, (*baseball*) nine, (*basketball*) five. **3.** *A team of heart specialists performed the surgery. He's a member of the mayor's economic advisory team:* group, unit, staff, crew, band, gang, company, squad, association, alliance, league, confederation, federation, coalition, combine, party, force, faction, circle, clique, coterie. —*v.* **4.** *Team the oxen to the plow. Several charities teamed to raise funds for the new hospital:* yoke, join, couple, rig; combine, unite, join together, band together, get together, ally, form an alliance, merge, incorporate, federate, unify, consolidate, amalgamate; cooperate, pool one's efforts. —**Ant.** 4 unjoin, unyoke, unhook, uncouple; separate, divide, part, go one's separate way.

tear[1] *n.* **1.** *A tear rolled down the child's cheek:* teardrop. —*v.* **2.** *The smoke made our eyes tear:* fill with tears, shed tears, swim, mist.

tear[2] *v.* **1.** *The kitten tore a hole in the curtain. Silk stockings tear easily:* rip, rend, rive, split, slit, cleave, sever, sunder, shred, pull apart, come apart, pull to pieces, run, snag. **2.** *The purse snatcher tore the bag from the woman's hand:* pull, grab, seize, wrench, pluck, snatch, yank. **3.** *Political conflict has torn the nation:* divide, disunite, split, splinter, rend, disrupt. **4.** *When the bell rang, the students tore out of the room:* speed, race, rush, hasten, run, bolt, dash, dart, sprint, spurt, shoot, fly, hie, scurry, scuttle, scoot, scud, whiz, gallop, sweep, whisk, plunge, scamper, scramble, skedaddle, hustle, hotfoot it, make tracks. —*n.* **5.** *The house withstood many years of wear and tear:* damage, destruction, ravage, hard treatment, abuse, hard use; impairment, injury. **6.** *Mother will sew the tear in your shirt:* rip, rent, slit, split, hole; gap, break, breach, crack, rift, fissure, fault, rupture, opening. —**Ant.** 1 mend, repair, sew, stitch up. 3 unite, reunite, bind, solidify, join, strengthen. 4 creep, crawl, amble, stroll, saunter. 6 patch, mend.

tearful *adj. The lovers bade a tearful farewell at the airport:* weeping, teary, crying, lachrymose, mournful, lamenting; weepy, wailing, bawling, sobbing, blubbering, whimpering, sniveling; heartbroken, inconsolable, crushed, brokenhearted.

tease *v.* **1.** *Everyone teased him about his affected accent. Don't tease that cat or it will scratch you:* taunt, gibe, ridicule, mock, chafe, vex, rag, needle, haze, make fun of, josh, laugh at, twit, guy, bait, goad, heckle, mimic, tantalize, bedevil, torment; pester, plague, worry, provoke, annoy, irritate, bother, aggravate; harry, badger, irk, persecute, harass, hector, rile, gall, pique, nag. —*n.* **2.** *The bully's teases upset the boy:* taunt, jeer, gibe, twit, ridicule, mocking remark, scornful remark, chafing, razzing, hazing, needling, derision, sneer, scoff, snigger, heckling, mimicking, harassment, persecution. **3.** *My uncle was a big tease, always making fun of us:* teaser, taunter, mocker, needler, tantalizer, tormentor; pest, nag, worrier. —**Ant.** 1 praise, laud, compliment; humor, flatter; comfort, con-

sole, soothe, placate. 2 praise, compliment; comforting, consoling, soothing, placating.

technical *adj. She got her technical know-how at school. The manual was highly technical:* technological, scientific, mechanical, professional, industrial, *Informal* hi-tech; involved, detailed, complicated, esoteric, restricted, specialized.

technique *n.* **1.** *The young artist has imagination but needs to improve his technique:* technical skill, form, style, skillfulness, craft, expertness, proficiency, facility, art, adroitness, know-how, knack. **2.** *Doctors are developing a new technique for treating diabetes:* procedure, method, way, technology, formula, approach, manner, system.

tedious *adj.* **1.** *Cleaning out the basement was a tedious job:* time-consuming, drawn-out, slow, long; tiring, wearying, fatiguing, exhausting, irksome, burdensome, onerous, oppressive, laborious, dreary, dismal. **2.** *The tedious play put the audience to sleep:* dull, boring, monotonous, unexciting, uninteresting, unimaginative, prosaic, humdrum, insipid, vapid, drab, dreary, dismal, dry, lifeless, tiresome, wearisome, jejune. —**Ant.** 1, 2 exhilarating, exciting, interesting, amusing, enthralling, stimulating. 1 quick, fast, short. 2 imaginative, stirring, lively, provocative, inspiring.

tedium *n. He couldn't face the tedium of twenty more years at the same job:* monotony, dullness, tediousness, sameness, routineness, boredom, rut, ennui, tiresomeness, drabness, dreariness. —**Ant.** excitement, interest, amusement, fascination, stimulation, liveliness, exhilaration; inspiration, challenge.

teem *v. Rome teems with tourists in the summer:* swarm, be overrun, overflow, abound, be full of, be inundated, brim, gush, bristle with, be well-stocked, burst at the seams. —**Ant.** be empty of, have a scarcity of.

teeming *adj. The pond was teeming with trout:* abundant, brimming, swarming, bristling, chock-full, crammed, crawling, filled, fruitful, full, multitudinous, numerous, overflowing, packed, plentiful, populous, replete, rife, swarming, thick, thronged, bursting, alive. —**Ant.** short, lacking, wanting.

teeter *v. The plank teetered as the boys walked across it. After being hit, the boxer teetered and then fell:* wobble, totter, sway, seesaw, stagger, lurch, reel; waver, hesitate, vacillate.

teetotaler *n. Max is a teetotaler himself but will serve his guests cocktails:* nondrinker, abstainer, prohibitionist, dry. —**Ant.** drunk, drunkard, alcoholic, dipsomaniac, sot, *Slang* boozehound, boozer, wino.

telepathy *n. He knew what I was thinking through telepathy:* thought transference, sixth sense, second sight, extrasensory perception, ESP; clairvoyance, spirit communication.

telephone *n. She was on the telephone:* phone, telephone set, house phone, mobile phone, cell phone, *Informal* horn, blower.

television *n. They bought a large-screen television:* TV, TV set, small screen, *British* telly, *Informal* box, boob tube, idiot box, the tube.

tell *v.* **1.** *Tell the truth:* narrate, declare, relate, recount, give an account of, report, set forth, recite, speak, utter, express, state, say, pronounce, mention, enunciate, advise, acquaint, apprise, communicate, make known, impart, reveal, divulge, disclose, unfold, let fall, spout, publish, broadcast, spread abroad, bruit, blab, blazon, babble, inform, betray, breathe a word about, describe, chronicle, write, detail, depict, portray, sketch, paint a picture; confess, own. **2.** *Fish lovers find it easy to tell fresh from frozen. Even the weatherman couldn't tell the tornado was coming:* tell apart, distinguish, discriminate, discern, identify, make out, recognize, perceive, ascertain, find out, figure, calculate, reckon, apprehend, see; predict, forecast, foretell. **3.** *Tell the orchestra to begin:* direct, instruct, order, command, bid, ask, request. **4.** *A six-year-old should be able to tell time. The nun sat telling her beads:* count, count off, number, enumerate; compute, calculate, reckon, estimate. **5.** *Years of dissipation finally told on his health:* take effect, influence, have force, weigh, carry weight, take a toll on, be potent, register, be of account. **—Ant.** 1 keep quiet, keep mum, be mute, keep secret, hide, conceal; listen. 2 confuse, mix up.

telling *adj.* *The court's decision was a telling blow for freedom of the press:* effective, effectual, efficacious, powerful, forceful, striking, potent, weighty, momentous, trenchant, significant, influential, cogent, material, definite, definitive, decisive, decided, positive, conclusive, valid, solid, important, impressive, consequential. **—Ant.** ineffective, unimportant, immaterial, insignificant, unmeaningful, trivial, inconsequential, indefinite, indecisive.

telltale *n.* **1.** *Don't rely on that telltale to keep a secret:* talebearer; tattletale, tattler, blabbermouth, gossip, busybody, scandalmonger, newsbearer; informer, squealer. *—adj.* **2.** *There were telltale fingerprints on the cookie jar:* revealing, giveaway, tattletale, betraying, divulging, disclosing, informative, enlightening; confirming, verifying, affirming.

temerity *n.* *Where does he get the temerity to ask such a personal question? No one had the temerity to ride those rapids:* audacity, insolence, gall, brazenness, brashness, nerve, cheek, brass, impudence, effrontery, forwardness, sauciness, freshness, impertinence, intrusiveness, pushiness, indiscretion, *Yiddish* chutzpah; foolhardiness, rashness, boldness. **—Ant.** reserve, reticence, politeness, tact, discretion, meekness, bashfulness, shyness; timidity, cowardice, caution, wariness.

temper *n.* **1.** *The mob was in no temper to listen to reason:* frame of mind, mood, disposition, humor. **2.** *She stalked out of the room in a burst of temper:* anger, rage, fury, wrath, ire, irritation, irritability, annoyance, vexation, bad humor, pique, peevishness, acrimony, choler, spleen, gall, bile, animus, dander, huffiness, irascibility, churlishness, dudgeon, indignation, displeasure, umbrage, passion, emotion, ferment. **3.** *Don't make me lose my temper!:* good

humor, kindly disposition; calmness, composure, equilibrium, balance. **—v. 4.** *It's a new process for tempering steel:* strengthen, harden, toughen, anneal. **5.** *Mother tried to temper Father's anger with soothing words:* soften, moderate, allay, appease, pacify, tranquilize, mitigate, palliate, calm, compose, quiet, soothe, still. **—Ant.** 2 goodwill, good humor, calmness, composure. 3 bad humor, bad disposition, anger, rage, fury, indignation, wrath, ire, irritation, vexation, pique, peevishness; fit of emotion, ferment. 4 soften, weaken. 5 intensify, heighten, aggravate, excite, increase, stir, rouse, arouse, pique.

temperament *n.* *The child has an easygoing temperament. The young actor has a true artist's temperament:* disposition, nature, mood, frame of mind; temper, makeup, character, personality, spirit, soul; humor, tone, cast, quality, tenor, complexion, leaning, tendency, bent.

temperamental *adj.* *She's as temperamental as an opera star:* high-strung, excitable, moody, thin-skinned, sensitive, explosive, mercurial, volatile, passionate, emotional, hotheaded, fiery, tempestuous, peppery, mettlesome, turbulent, hysterical; unpredictable, capricious, erratic, fick-le, unreliable, undependable, unstable; willful, headstrong. **—Ant.** even-tempered, easygoing, cool, coolheaded, calm, unexcitable, *Slang* unflappable; reliable, dependable, predictable, steady.

temperance *n.* **1.** *Use temperance in giving advice to friends:* moderation, forbearance, self-control, self-discipline, restraint, discretion, prudence; abstention, self-denial. **2.** *The restaurant serves no liquor because the owner believes in temperance:* teetotalism, abstinence, abstemiousness, sobriety, prohibition. **—Ant.** 1, 2 intemperance, immoderation. 1 unre-straint, abandon, wantonness, indulgence, extravagance. 2 drinking, imbibing; alcoholism, dipsomania, boozing.

temperate *adj.* **1.** *Be more temperate in your eating habits. A good teacher must have a temperate personality:* self-restrained, self-controlled, moderate, unextravagant, sparing, sedate, sober, sane, rational, reasonable; calm, even, cool, coolheaded, levelheaded, composed, collected, unruffled, steady, tranquil, easygoing, self-possessed, patient, dispassionate, unimpassioned. **2.** *Mexico City has a very temperate climate:* mild, gentle, soft, moderate, clement, pleasant, mellow; balmy, sunny, warm. **—Ant.** 1, 2 intemperate, immoderate. 1 unrestrained, uncontrolled, abandoned, inordinate, extreme, excessive, extravagant, unreasonable, irrational; temperamental, excitable, passionate, impassioned, explosive, volatile, hotheaded, hysterical, frenzied, wild. 2 inclement, harsh, severe, unpleasant.

temperature *n.* *The temperature sank overnight:* degrees fahrenheit, degrees centigrade, degrees celsius, thermal reading, weather, climate, heat, warmth.

tempest *n.* *A tempest was stirred up by the coach's resignation:* storm, uproar, commotion, furor, upheaval, disturbance, tumult, cataclysm, outbreak, turbulence, hurly-burly, chaos, agitation, hubbub, *Slang* brouhaha. —**Ant.** calm, serenity, peace, tranquillity.

tempestuous *adj. Tempestuous winds sometimes endangered the ship. The two candidates had a long, tempestuous debate:* stormy, turbulent, raging, violent, furious, agitated, tumultuous; passionate, impassioned, emotional, frenzied, overwrought, wrought-up, hysterical, frantic, excited, fiery, hot, explosive, feverish. —**Ant.** calm, placid, peaceful; relaxed, unagitated, easy, serene, tranquil, quiet, coolheaded, unemotional, disinterested.

temple *n. He blessed the new temple:* holy place, place of worship.

tempo *n. The march was played at too fast a tempo:* speed, pace, time, meter, momentum, rate, velocity, gait, stride, pacing, timing, *Slang* clip.

temporal *adj.* **1.** *The Pope represents spiritual rather than temporal authority:* civil, lay, secular, nonspiritual, nonclerical, nonecclesiastical, profane. **2.** *Most of us are too busy with temporal things to think about eternity:* noneternal, temporary, transient, fleeting, passing, ephemeral, evanescent, day-to-day, fugitive, impermanent, worldly, mundane, mortal. —**Ant.** 1 ecclesiastical, clerical; spiritual, sacred, religious. 2 eternal, everlasting, otherworldly, unearthly.

temporary *adj. We took temporary quarters until the house was ready. The book enjoyed temporary fame:* momentary, brief, impermanent, passing, fleeting, fleet, transitory, transient, fugitive, short-lived, ephemeral, evanescent, flash-in-the-pan; stopgap, provisional, provisory, interim. —**Ant.** lasting, everlasting, permanent, durable, enduring, long-lived, persisting, protracted.

temporize *v. The committee temporized instead of reaching a decision:* delay, hedge, stall, equivocate, tergiversate, tarry, hem and haw, maneuver, drag one's feet, play for time, waver, vacillate, procrastinate, hang back. —**Ant.** act, decide, execute, proceed.

tempt *v.* **1.** *Don't tempt a car thief by leaving the keys in the car. That chocolate candy tempts me:* seduce, entice, inveigle, lure, allure, woo, bait, decoy; appeal to, attract, pull, invite, take one's fancy, whet the appetite, draw, intrigue, tantalize; captivate, bewitch, charm. **2.** *Don't tempt death by driving recklessly:* put to the test, fly in the face of, try, risk, provoke, incite, goad, rouse, arouse, prick. —**Ant.** 1 discourage, repel, repulse, disgust.

temptation *n. He couldn't resist the temptation of her rosy lips. Dieters must avoid the temptation to snack:* tempting, allurement, snare, lure, enticement, attraction, seduction, pull, urge, draw, bait, inducement, incentive, incitement, provocation, stimulus, fascination, captivation, charm, spell.

tempting *adj. The tempting prospect attracted her:* enticing, inviting, seductive, attractive, alluring. —**Ant.** repulsive, repellent.

temptress *n. She had been a famous tempt-*

ress of the silent screen: seductress, siren, enchantress, femme fatale, sorceress, Circe, Lorelei, vamp, vampire, flirt, coquette, charmer, oda-lisque, Jezebel, Delilah.

tenable *adj. That kind of argument is no longer tenable:* defendable, defensible, warrantable, condonable, workable, viable, justifiable, excusable, vindicable, maintainable, arguable, rational, sensible. —**Ant.** unjustifiable, untenable, indefensible, irrational.

tenacious *adj. He held my hand in a tenacious grip. She was tenacious in her belief and could not be swayed:* fast, firm, clinging, iron, hard, set; persevering, persistent, determined, resolute, obstinate, stubborn, obdurate, inflexible, uncompromising, immovable, unchangeable, unbending, unyielding, adamant, intransigent, inexorable, unwavering, unfaltering, unswerving, undeviating, steadfast, staunch, unremitting, stalwart, constant, relentless, mulish, pigheaded, dogged. —**Ant.** loose, lax, limp, slack; unpersevering, undetermined, irresolute, flexible.

tenacity *n. Tenacity won the day:* perseverance, persistency, pertinacity, obstinacy. —**Ant.** transitoriness.

tenant *n. The landlord collects the tenants' rent monthly:* renter, lessee, leaseholder; lodger, paying guest, roomer, boarder; occupant, inhabitant, resident, householder, dweller, denizen. —**Ant.** landlord, lessor, leaser.

tend[1] *v.* **1.** *Children tend to like cozy corners:* be inclined, be disposed, have a tendency, be apt, be likely, be liable, have an inclination, lean, have a leaning, predispose, bid fair to. **2.** *At the junction, take the road that tends west:* lead, bear, extend, point, head, aim, be bound for, gravitate, move.

tend[2] *v. Who will tend the garden while you're on vacation? A practical nurse should have experience tending sick people:* attend to, care for, take care of, look after, keep an eye on, mind, watch over, watch; nurse, nurture, foster, wait on, minister to; supervise, manage, guide. —**Ant.** neglect, ignore.

tendency *n. He has a tendency to talk too much. Stock market prices are showing an upward tendency:* inclination, disposition, proclivity, proneness, propensity, trend, predisposition, readiness, penchant, bent, leaning, impulse, habit, set, drive, trend, turning, drift, direction, course, gravitation, heading, aim. —**Ant.** disinclination, indisposition, aversion, reluctance, unreadiness, hesitancy.

tender[1] *adj.* **1.** *The nurse bathed the patient with tender care. He talks tough but has a tender heart:* soft, gentle, delicate, dainty; kind, good, compassionate, sympathetic, considerate, understanding, thoughtful, caring, softhearted, warmhearted, loving, affectionate, fond, sentimental, merciful, benevolent, benign, generous. **2.** *Grandfather is recovering, but is still in tender health:* weak, weakly, fragile, frail, feeble, delicate, vulnerable. **3.** *She left home at the tender age of thirteen:* young, youthful, juvenile, underage, immature, inexperienced, unsophisticated, impressionable, callow, green. **4.** *The area around the wound is very tender. Since the scandal, bankruptcy is a tender subject in this office:* sensitive, painful, requiring delicacy; sore, aching, raw, swollen, inflamed. —**Ant.** 1 tough, hard; mean, cruel, brutal, inhuman, sadistic, vicious, unsympathetic, unkind, inconsiderate, uncaring, hardhearted, cold-hearted, hateful, merciless, pitiless, ruthless. 2 hardy, strong, robust, sturdy, rugged, vigorous, hale, flourishing, thriving. 3 old, elderly, advanced; full-grown, grown-up, mature, experienced, seasoned, practiced, worldly, worldly-wise, sophisticated. 4 insensitive.

tender² *v. If I may tender a suggestion to the committee—:* present, present formally, make formal offer of, proffer, prefer, submit, put forward, lay before, place, volunteer, give, hold out, advance, propound, propose, extend, suggest, hand in. —**Ant.** withhold; withdraw, retract.

tenderhearted *adj. The tenderhearted man wept at the news:* sympathetic, compassionate; softhearted, kindhearted, warm-hearted, considerate, understanding, thoughtful, responsive, gentle, mild, humane, benevolent, benign, merciful, generous, altruistic. —**Ant.** hardhearted, coldhearted, mean, cruel, brutal, sadistic, inhuman, vicious, merciless, pitiless, callous, unsympathetic, inconsiderate.

tenderness *n.* **1.** *The tenderness of her touch soothed the child:* softness, gentleness, delicacy, mildness; kindness, kindliness, lovingkindness, compassion, sympathy, goodness, benevolence, beneficence, humanity, humaneness, mercifulness; fondness, warmth, affection, lovingness, love. **2.** *The wound's tenderness made walking painful:* sensitivity, soreness, painfulness, aching, rawness, smarting. —**Ant.** 1 hardness, toughness; cruelty, meanness, brutality, viciousness, unkindness, hardheartedness, coldheartedness, coldness, harshness, severity, mercilessness. 2 insensitivity.

tenet *n. The tenets of his religion forbid divorce:* belief, doctrine, dogma, way of thinking, creed, credo, canon, teaching, conviction, position, persuasion, principle, maxim, rule, thesis, view, opinion, ideology.

tenor *n. Were you able to grasp the tenor of his speech?:* meaning, sense, import, argument, significance, essence, content, substance, gist, drift, course, nature, implication, connotation; intent, intention, object, purport, purpose, trend, direction, tendency.

tense *adj.* **1.** *Keep the rope tense:* stretched tight, tight, taut, drawn, rigid, braced, stiff; inflexible, unyielding. **2.** *The witness was extremely tense:* nervous, strained, taut, drawn, wrought-up, high-strung, tremulous, uneasy, restless, restive, fidgety, jittery, on edge, excited, agitated, shaky, fearful, apprehensive, anxious, timorous, *Slang* uptight. —*v.* **3.** *Tense the reins and the horse will stop. The woman tensed at the sound of footsteps:* tighten up, draw up, make taut, stiffen, brace. —**Ant.** 1 relaxed, slack, loose, limp, flaccid; pliant, flexible.

2 relaxed, loose, calm, cool, collected, self-possessed. 3 relax, loosen.

tension *n.* **1.** *Too much tension will break the string:* stretching, straining, stress, tugging, traction, pressure, pulling, exertion; spring, elastic force; tightness, tautness, rigidity, stiffness. **2.** *She collapsed under the tension of waiting for the news. You could feel the tension when the two rivals walked into the room:* strain, stress, anxiety, apprehension, dread, nervousness, restiveness, trepidation, misgiving, fearfulness, perturbation, hostility, combativeness, suppressed anger, *Slang* bad vibrations, bad vibes. —**Ant.** 1 slack, looseness, laxness. 2 relief, relaxation, ease, calmness, serenity, tranquillity.

tentative *adj. Our vacation plans are still tentative:* unconfirmed, not settled, unsettled, not final, under consideration, open to consideration, subject to change, provisional, conditional, speculative, contingent, not definite, indefinite, undecided, *Informal* iffy; experimental, trial, temporary, not permanent, ad interim, acting, probational, probationary, proposed. —**Ant.** confirmed, settled, final, set, firm, conclusive, definite, decided, closed, unchangeable.

tenuous *adj. Some legislators made a rather tenuous argument against the bill:* weak, flimsy, shaky, unsubstantial, unsupported, slight, slim, thin, slender, frail, fragile, delicate, gossamer, shallow, paltry, unconvincing, halfhearted, uncertain, indefinite. —**Ant.** strong, solid, valid, substantial.

tenure *n.* **1.** *His tenure of 16 years in the office was a record:* term, incumbency, rule, tenancy, occupancy, time, administration, possession, reign, retention, occupation. **2.** *After three years at the school the teacher was offered tenure:* permanent status, job security, employment guarantee, entitlement, permanency.

tepid *adj. I want my coffee hot, not tepid! Such an accusation demands more than a tepid response:* lukewarm, temperate, warmish; moderate, mild, unemotional, halfhearted, indifferent, cool, impassive, phlegmatic, languid, apathetic, nonchalant, lackadaisical, unenthusiastic.

term *n.* **1.** *A doctor's secretary must be familiar with medical terms:* word, phrase, expression, idiom, technical word, technical expression; name, designation, appellation. **2.** *The President of the Republic will complete his term next year. The lease is for a term of three years:* span of time, span, period, time, duration, course, spell, while, course, interval, stage, cycle; age, era, epoch, reign, administration, dynasty. **3.** *One of the terms of the contract calls for high-grade steel in the construction:* stipulation, condition, provision, proviso, clause, item, detail, requirement, prerequisite, requisite, *Slang* catch, string. **4. terms** *He's on good terms with his employer:* relations, standing, footing, status, state, position, circumstance. —*v.* **5.** *The local critic termed the picture the worst of the year:* call, name, designate, dub, tag, style, characterize, cite.

termagant *n. If you think his wife is a termagant, you should have met his mother:* shrew, scold, nag, virago, harridan, fury, vixen, fishwife, hellion, spitfire, Xanthippe, she-wolf, ogress, tigress, hellcat, battle-ax.

terminal *adj.* **1.** *Main Street is the terminal stop for this bus route:* last, final, concluding, end. **2.** *Doctors say he has a terminal disease:* causing death, mortal, fatal, deadly, lethal. —*n.* **3.** *We'll pick you up at the railroad terminal:* station, depot, terminus, stand. —**Ant.** 1 first, initial; beginning, opening. 2 nonfatal; temporary, passing.

terminate *v. Let's terminate this meeting by ten P.M. The lease terminates in May:* bring to an end, come to an end, end, conclude, finish, stop, cease, close, wind up, complete, discontinue, expire, lapse, run out. —**Ant.** begin, start, commence, initiate, open; continue, pursue, extend.

termination *n. A few people lingered after the termination of the meeting:* end, ending, close, closing, conclusion, concluding, finish, windup, completion, cessation, discontinuation, finis, finale, expiration, lapse, halt, stoppage. —**Ant.** beginning, start, commencement, initiation, opening, inception.

terminology *n. Computers have their own terminology:* language, nomenclature, lexicon, vocabulary, vernacular, jargon, dialect, lingo.

terminus *n. The northern terminus of the route is Bangor, Maine:* end, conclusion, stop, ending, furthermost part, last stop, boundary, extreme, limit, terminal, extremity.

terms *n. pl. They finally agreed to terms:* agreement, understanding, conditions, details, particulars, points, qualifications, specifications, stipulation, *Informal* fine print, small print, nitty-gritty, strings attached.

terrain *n. The mountainous terrain was too rugged to cross without a guide:* topography, ground, area, region, territory, tract, countryside; surroundings, environment, milieu, setting, zone, district.

terrestrial *adj.* **1.** *Although they can swim, polar bears are terrestrial animals:* land, ground, earthbound; riparian. **2.** *Terrestrial gravity is greater than lunar gravity:* earth's, earthly, worldly, global, mundane. —**Ant.** 1 marine, aquatic, sea, water. 2 celestial, astral, lunar, cosmic, space.

terrible *adj.* **1.** *A terrible storm destroyed many homes. We're paying a terrible rent now:* severe, fierce, intense, strong, harsh, brutal, rough; great, huge, tremendous, immoderate, extreme, excessive, inordinate, monstrous, enormous, terrific. **2.** *What's that terrible odor?:* extremely bad, horrible, horrid, awful, hideous, repulsive, revolting, obnoxious, offensive, odious, distasteful, unpleasant, objectionable, intolerable, insufferable, appalling, hateful, bad, heinous, dire, ghastly, shocking, beastly. **3.** *The roar of a lion can be a terrible sound:* alarming, frightening, terrifying, fearful, fearsome, scary, harrowing, awful, dreadful, horrifying, formidable, distressing, upsetting, disturbing. —**Ant.** 1 mild, moderate, harmless, gentle; small, insignificant, paltry. 2 wonderful, excellent, fine, good, great,

pleasing, pleasant, delightful, admirable, nice; worthy, praiseworthy, laudable, commendable. 3 comforting, reassuring, encouraging, settling, soothing, calming, easing.

terrific *adj.* **1.** *A terrific explosion woke the whole town:* severe, intense, fierce, harsh, terrible, extreme, excessive, monstrous, great, enormous, huge, inordinate, immoderate, tremendous; frightening, terrifying, fearful, fearsome, alarming, scary, harrowing, distressing, awful, dreadful, horrifying, upsetting, disturbing. **2.** *You must read this book; it's terrific:* great, fine, good, wonderful, superb, excellent, splendid, marvelous, sensational, fabulous, fantastic, stupendous, smashing, super, superduper, extraordinary, remarkable, exceptional, *Slang* bang-up, marvy, fab, sensash, out of this world. —**Ant.** 1 mild, moderate, harmless, gentle, slight, insignificant, paltry; comforting, reassuring, encouraging, settling, soothing, calming, easing. 2 bad, terrible, awful, lousy, stinking, horrible, dreadful, hideous, revolting, unpleasant, appalling, distasteful.

terrify *v. The thunderstorm terrified the child:* fill with terror, frighten, scare, alarm, horrify, panic, petrify, unman, abash, daunt, cow, intimidate, overawe, make one's hair stand on end, make one's blood run cold, make one's skin crawl; upset, disturb, appall, dismay, agitate, disquiet. —**Ant.** comfort, reassure, encourage, hearten, soothe, calm, ease, please, delight.

territory *n.* **1.** *The mountainous territory was impassable in winter:* terrain, region, land, acreage, area, zone, district, sector, clime, tract, countryside, locale. **2.** *The Aleutian Islands are part of Alaska's territory:* domain, realm, province, sphere of influence, dominion, commonwealth, state, nation, principality, kingdom, empire; protectorate, dependency, mandate, colony; bailiwick, pale, limits, confines, bounds.

terror *n. The rumble of the volcano caused terror among the natives:* fear, fear and trembling, fright, affright, horror, panic, alarm, dread; dismay, trepidation, perturbation, consternation, apprehension, awe, anxiety, agitation, disquiet, disquietude. —**Ant.** security, reassurance, encouragement, comfort, calm, quiet, tranquillity.

terrorize *v. The gang terrorized the neighborhood:* dominate, coerce, intimidate. —**Ant.** ameliorate, mollify.

terse *adj. The terse statement that "war is hell" says it all:* brief and to the point, concise, pithy, succinct, crisp, clipped, incisive, pointed, neat, compact, condensed, compressed, clear, clear-cut, unambiguous, summary, trenchant, laconic, epigrammatic, axiomatic; brief, short, abrupt, curt. —**Ant.** rambling, circuitous, roundabout, diffuse, discursive, verbose, wordy, lengthy, long, long-winded; vague, confused, ambiguous.

test *n.* **1.** *Chemical tests showed the presence of potassium. The maneuvers will be a test of the army's effectiveness:* analysis, investigation; trial, tryout, dry run, probe, check, feeler, flyer; proof, verification, confirmation, corroboration. **2.** *The teacher gives a test every Friday:* examination, exam, quiz; (*variously*) final, comprehensive, midterm; questioning, questionnaire, catechism. —*v.* **3.** *The teacher will test the class on spelling today. The drug company tested the new product for years before putting it on the market:* quiz, examine; analyze, investigate, probe, experiment with; try out, put to the proof, prove, verify, confirm, corroborate, substantiate, validate, send up a trial balloon, throw out a feeler.

testament *n.* **1.** *His last will and testament directed that all his property go to his eldest son:* final written will; bequest, legacy, settlement. **2.** **Testament** *The Apocrypha are Biblical writings belonging to neither Testament:* Old Testament, New Testament; Bible, Scriptures, the Book.

testify *v. The fingerprint expert was asked to testify at the trial. His hard work testified to his determination to succeed:* bear witness, give evidence, state as fact, declare, affirm, swear; attest, show, indicate, signify, demonstrate, evidence, evince, manifest, prove.

testimonial *n.* **1.** *His former employer wrote him a glowing testimonial:* recommendation, reference, commendation, endorsement, citation; certificate, affidavit, deposition. **2.** *The entire faculty attended the testimonial for the retiring dean. The statue is a testimonial to Daniel Boone:* testimonial dinner, banquet in someone's honor; memorial, monument, tribute; medal, ribbon, trophy.

testimony *n.* **1.** *The witness's testimony cleared the suspect:* declaration under oath, statement, attestation, avowal, averment, profession, acknowledgment, deposition, affidavit, evidence. **2.** *Winning the scholarship is testimony of her intelligence:* evidence, witness, indication, demonstration, manifestation, proof, verification, corroboration, confirmation, affirmation, certification, endorsement, documentation. —**Ant.** 2 denial, disavowal, refutation, disproof, contradiction, rebuttal.

testy *adj. Too little sleep put her in a testy mood:* irritable, ill-humored, quick-tempered, irascible, cross, cranky, grumpy, crabby, snappish, snappy, fretful, peevish, petulant, sullen, waspish, churlish, splenetic, choleric, snarling, cantankerous, contentious, touchy, temperamental, impatient, crusty, fractious, captious, caviling, faultfinding, sharp-tongued, perverse, acrimonious, moody, *Informal* filthy. —**Ant.** good-natured, good-humored, even-tempered, sweet, pleasant, amiable, genial, friendly, agreeable, kind, generous, patient, smiling, sunny, *Informal* smiley.

tête-à-tête *n. No one wanted to interrupt the couple's tête-à-tête:* private conversation, intimate conversation, confidential talk, private interview; chat, talk, parley, confabulation.

tether *n.* **1.** *The boy had a pet goat he led around on a tether:* leash, rein, halter; rope, chain, cord. —*v.* **2.** *The zoo keeper tethered the monkey to its perch:* put on a leash, tie with a rope, tie, chain, fasten, secure; hobble. —**Ant.** 2 untether, unleash, untie, unchain, unfasten; release, free, loose, loosen.

text *n.* **1.** *Did you just look at the pictures in the book or did you also read the text? All the city schools use the same history text:* main body of writing, words, wording, content; textbook, schoolbook, primer; manual, workbook. **2.** *The preacher took his text from Judges:* sermon, subject, subject matter, theme, motif, topic, thesis, argument; passage, quotation, verse, paragraph, sentence. —**Ant.** 1 illustration; notes, index, glossary; prologue, introduction, epilogue.

textile *n. New England weavers made this textile. The fabric is made of a very fine textile:* woven material, fabric, cloth, piece goods, yard goods; fiber, yarn, filament.

texture *n. Satin has a smooth texture. The fine texture of her hair makes it unmanageable:* weave, composition, structure, character, quality, makeup, surface, nap, grain, feel, touch, look; fineness, coarseness.

thank *v.* **1.** *Don't forget to thank the hostess:* express gratitude to, express appreciation to, make acknowledgment to, tender thanks to, be grateful to, bless. —*n.* **2. thanks** *Let's express our thanks to God for this wonderful harvest:* gratitude, gratefulness, appreciation, thankfulness; benediction, blessing, grace. —**Ant.** 2 ingratitude, ungratefulness.

thankful *adj. We were thankful for his help:* full of thanks, grateful, appreciative, feeling gratitude, expressing appreciation; obliged, beholden, indebted to.

thankless *adj.* **1.** *No one wanted to take on the thankless task:* not likely to be appreciated, unappreciated, unacknowledged, unrewarded; unrewarding, fruitless, useless, profitless, vain, bootless; undesirable, unwelcome, uninviting, unpleasant, disagreeable, distasteful. **2.** *A thankless employer inspires little loyalty:* ungrateful, ingrate, unappreciative, unthankful, thoughtless, inconsiderate, heedless, unmindful, ungracious; critical, faultfinding, caviling. —**Ant.** 1 appreciated, acknowledged, rewarded; rewarding, fruitful, useful, desirable, pleasant, agreeable. 2 appreciative, grateful, thankful.

thanks *n. pl. The speaker offered his thanks for the banquet:* thankfulness, thanksgiving, appreciation, gratefulness, gratitude, recognition, acknowledgment.

thaw *v.* **1.** *The ice thawed in the sun:* melt, dissolve, liquefy, soften; warm, warm up. **2.** *The little girl's smile thawed the crusty old man:* melt, warm, make friendly, make sympathetic, make affectionate, make forgiving; become genial, relax, unbend, break the ice, shed one's reserve. —*n.* **3.** *The spring thaw caused heavy flooding:* thawing, melting; period of above-freezing winter weather, first warm weather of spring. —**Ant.** 1 freeze, freeze solid, solidify, congeal, harden; cool, chill. 3 freeze, frost.

theater *n.* **1.** *The play was given in a small theater off Broadway. Medical students watched the operation from a glass-enclosed theater:* (*variously*) playhouse; movie theater, movie, cinema, movie house, music hall, amphitheater, colosseum, arena, lecture hall, auditorium, lyceum, odeum. **2.** *A good production of* Hamlet *is real theater:* drama, stage entertainment, theatricals, show business; theatricality, histrionics. **3.** *The entire theater gave the star a standing ovation:* audience, spectators, house, auditorium, assemblage, assembly, gallery. **4.** *The South Pacific was the theater for much of the action in World War II:* field of operations, site, arena, stage, setting, scene, place.

theatrical *adj.* **1.** *Most of the producer's friends belong to the theatrical world:* of the theater, stage, movie, film, entertainment, show-business, *Slang* show-biz; dramatic, thespian, histrionic. **2.** *His manner is too theatrical:* exaggerated, stilted, affected, artificial, stagy, unnatural, mannered; pretentious, ostentatious, extravagant, showy, flashy, grandiloquent, grandiose, magniloquent, fustian, *Slang* hammy.

theft *n.* *He was arrested for jewel theft:* stealing; (*variously*) robbery, burglary, thievery, larceny, filching, pilfering, purloining, shoplifting, hijacking, fraud, swindling, embezzlement, rustling, looting.

theme *n.* **1.** *Love is a major theme of Robert Browning's poetry:* subject, subject matter, topic, text, motif, thesis, general idea, focus, keynote, point, question, argument, proposition, premise. **2.** *Each student wrote a theme on environmental conservation:* essay, composition, treatise, discourse, tract, monograph, report, critique, commentary, review, thesis, dissertation. **3.** *Can you whistle the theme from the overture to* Don Giovanni*?:* melody, strain, tune, air, song, motif, leitmotif; theme song.

then *adv.* **1.** *She then handed me a key:* at that time, next, soon after. **2.** *She then lived in Venice:* formerly. **3.** *If the facts were true, then she must leave at once:* consequently, accordingly, hence, so, thence, thenceforth, therefore, thereupon, thus, whence, ergo.

theological *adj.* *He had a worldwide reputation as a theological scholar:* religious, spirit-ual, holy, sacred; ecclesiastical, apostolic, canonical, doctrinal, dogmatic; Biblical, scriptural.

theology *n.* *After majoring in theology he taught a course in comparative religion:* divinity; (*variously*) science of divine things, religion, dogma, doctrine, system of belief.

theorem *n.* *The math student had to master many theorems:* law, rule, axiom, principle, proposition, rule, formula.

theoretical *adj.* *The belief that the universe is expanding has been proven and is no longer theoretical:* consisting in theory, concerning theory, theoretic, conjectural, hypothetical, speculative, suppositional, postulatory, putative; abstract, academic, nonpractical. **—Ant.** proven, known, verified, corroborated, demonstrated, substantial, established; practical, applied.

theorize *v.* *Early astronomers theorized that the earth was flat:* speculate, hypothesize, conjecture, posit, propose, imagine, think, suppose, assume, infer, presume, propound, formulate, hypothecate, predicate.

theory *n.* **1.** *Einstein developed the theory of relativity:* principle, law; science, doctrine, philosophy, ideology. **2.** *The scientist's theory is that if matter exists so must antimatter. It's my theory that the dog will find its way home in a day or two:* idea, notion, concept, hypothesis, postulate, conjecture, thesis, speculation, surmise, supposition, guess, thought, opinion, persuasion, belief, presumption, judgment, conclusion, deduction, view. **—Ant.** 2 practice, application; proof, verification, corroboration, substantiation, demonstration, exhibit, example.

therapeutic also **therapeutical** *adj.* *Aspirin isn't therapeutic but it does ease pain:* healing, sanative, salutary, curative, remedial, ameliorative, restorative.

therapy *n.* *Speech therapy corrected the child's lisp:* treatment, remedial procedure, healing, rehabilitation.

thereafter *adv.* *On opening day all tickets are a dollar; thereafter they'll be two dollars:* after that, afterward, afterwards, subsequently, later, from that time on, from then on, thenceforth. **—Ant.** before, previously.

therefore *adv.* *The apartment house was being torn down; therefore we had to move:* in consequence, consequently, so, accordingly, hence, thus, ergo, for that reason, for which reason, on that account, on that ground.

thereupon *adv.* *The child murmured "good-night" and thereupon fell asleep:* then, thereon, forthwith, straightaway, directly, immediately, suddenly, upon that, upon which, at once, without delay, in a moment, in the twinkling of an eye.

thesaurus *n.* *You should keep a thesaurus right next to your dictionary:* synonym dictionary, synonymy, dictionary of synonyms and antonyms, synonym finder, word finder, word treas-ury, conceptual dictionary, semantic dictionary, synonymicon.

thesis *n.* **1.** *The engineer's thesis was that the new machinery would double production:* proposition, proposal, argument; theory, hypothesis, postulate, concept, notion, conjecture, speculation, surmise, supposition. **2.** *Every sen-ior must write a thesis as a requirement to graduate:* dissertation, long essay, research paper, term paper, paper, treatise, disquisition, discourse, formal composition, article, monograph, tract; critique, commentary; master's thesis.

thespian *n.* *He was a thespian known for his portrayals of* Hamlet *and* King Lear*:* actor, actress, trouper, performer, player, stage performer, stage player, *Slang* ham; star, guest star, co-star, leading man, leading lady, juvenile, ingenue, character man, character woman, bit player, walk-on, extra, supernumerary.

thick *adj.* **1.** *That little restaurant makes good thick sandwiches:* fat, deep, wide, broad, big, bulky; generous, lavish, unstinted, munificent, liberal. **2.** *Thick smoke impeded the firemen. This gravy is too thick:* dense, heavy, impenetrable; viscous, viscid, gelatinous, glutinous, concentrated, condensed, compact, solid, coagulated, clotted. **3.** *Grandfather spoke with a thick Scottish brogue:* strong, decided, pronounced, extreme, great, heavy, intense, deep, profound. **4.** *The illness made his speech thick:* inarticulate, indistinct, muffled, fuzzy, blurred; hoarse, husky, guttural, throaty. **5.** *You'll never get that through his thick head!:* stupid, dumb, dense, obtuse, slow, slow-witted, dull, dull-witted, doltish, *Informal* wooden, fatheaded. **6.** *Informal The two men are as thick as thieves:* close, intimate, chummy, familiar, friendly, inseparable, devoted; brotherly, sisterly. **7.** *The marsh was thick with mosquitoes:* swarming, teeming, dense, profuse, overflowing, packed, crowded; abundant, copious, plenteous, heaped, piled. —**Ant.** 1, 2 thin. 1 slim, narrow, shallow, slight, lean, spare, small. 2 light, watery, runny, diluted. 3 slight, faint, weak, vague. 4 articulate, distinct, clear; shrill, shrieking. 5 smart, clever, intelligent, keen, sharp, quick, quick-witted. 6 distant, unfriendly, hostile, estranged. 7 bare, barren, bereft, empty.

thicken *v.* **1.** *Add cornstarch to thicken the sauce:* make thick, become thicker, make dense; set, compact, clot, cake, congeal, coagulate, condense, gelatinize, jell, jellify. **2.** *The mystery thickened:* become more complicated, intensify, deepen, darken, muddy, muddle. —**Ant.** 1 thin, dilute, thaw. 2 solve, resolve.

thicket *n.* *The deer hid in the thicket:* thick bushes, bush, undergrowth, underbrush, brush, covert, shrubs, shrubbery; growth of small trees, brake, bracken, grove, copse, scrub, forest, wood.

thickheaded *adj.* *He depended on a thickheaded servant to help him run the ranch:* stupid, dumb, dim-witted, blank, dull-witted, half-witted, obtuse, thick, chuckleheaded, blockheaded, thick-witted, slow-witted, fatheaded, knuckleheaded, boneheaded, *Slang* dopey. —**Ant.** bright, clever, smart, intelligent.

thickset *adj.* **1.** *The thickset trees hid the sun:* close-planted, close-set, dense, packed, solid, close. **2.** *One brother was thickset and the other tall and thin:* stocky, husky, sturdy, chunky, bulky, heavyset, stout; squat, stubby, stumpy, tubby, dumpy, roly-poly. —**Ant.** 1 scattered, dispersed, sparse. 2 slim, slender; tall, rangy, reedy, gangling, lanky.

thickskinned *adj.* **1.** *A rhinoceros is thickskinned:* having a thick skin, pachydermatous. **2.** *He's too thickskinned to take offense at such an insult:* insensitive, insensible, unfeeling, unsusceptible, imperturbable, unmovable, unconcerned, impervious, callous, hardened, inured. —**Ant.** 1, 2 thinskinned. 2 sensitive, feeling; concerned, caring, passionate, emotional; vulnerable, soft, fragile.

thief *n.* *The police arrested the jewel thief:* robber, burglar, bandit, crook; (*variously*) purloiner, holdup man, filcher, pilferer, pursesnatcher, mugger, shoplifter, pickpocket, sneak thief, kleptomaniac, housebreaker, second-story man, highwayman, hijacker, rustler; swindler, confidence man, racketeer, larcenist, embezzler, defrauder.

thievish *adj.* **1.** *That thievish fellow is bound to wind up in jail:* thieving, given to stealing, larce-

nous, light-fingered, sticky-fingered, dishonest. **2.** *The boy's skulking, thievish manner aroused the shopkeeper's suspicions:* thieflike, stealthy, furtive, sneaky, surreptitious, secretive, sly. —**Ant.** 1 honest. 2 open, frank, direct, aboveboard, straightforward.

thin *adj.* **1.** *The boy was thin for his age. A light-bulb filament is very thin:* lean, not fat, slender, slim, skinny, slight, scrawny, emaciated, gaunt, lanky, lank, spindly, fine, finespun, narrow, threadlike, delicate; fragile, sheer, transparent. **2.** *This gravy is too thin:* watery, runny, diluted. **3.** *That's a pretty thin excuse. His hair is getting thin on top:* weak, unsubstantial, feeble, faint, inadequate, insufficient; scant, sparse, spare. —*v.* **4.** *Thin the tops of the bushes. The traffic begins to thin around seven P.M.:* make thin, thin out, prune, reduce, diminish, grow thin, curtail. **5.** *Thin the paint so it will spread easier:* dilute, water, water down. —**Ant.** 1–3 thick. 1 fat, obese, corpulent, chubby, rotund, plump, overweight. 2 viscous, concentrated. 3 strong, substantial, solid, forceful, adequate, sufficient; full, abundant, dense, plentiful. 4, 5 thicken. 4 increase, grow, heighten.

thing *n.* **1.** *A can opener is a very useful thing. What's that thing that fell out of the motor?:* object, article, gadget, *Slang* thingamajig, thing-amabob, gizmo, doohickey, dingus. **2.** *You mean thing, you! The kitten was such a cute little thing:* creature, living being, person, human being, entity. **3.** *What a wonderful thing to do! How are things with you?:* deed, act, feat, action; event, occurrence, eventuality, proceeding, happening, matter, affair, transaction, business, concern, circumstance. **4.** *I want to say one thing about your behavior. There's just one thing missing to make this perfect:* statement, thought; detail, particular, item, feature, point, aspect. **5.** Often **things** *She hasn't a thing to wear to the dance. Pack your things and go:* article of clothing, suitable outfit; clothing, clothes, possessions, belongings, effects, goods, movables, equipment, gear, paraphernalia.

think *v.* **1.** *Think before you act. We've been thinking about you all day:* use one's mind, apply the mind, reason, reflect, cogitate, deliberate, turn over in the mind, mull over, ponder, contemplate, meditate, ruminate, have in mind, make the subject of one's thought, dwell on, brood, keep in mind, remember, recall, recollect, use one's wits, rack one's brain. **2.** *I think it's going to rain. Mother thinks she'll vacation in Canada:* believe, have an opinion, deem, judge, surmise, presume, anticipate, conclude, guess, suppose, reckon, expect, speculate; imagine, conceive, fancy; intend, purpose, propose, plan, mean, design, contrive. —**Ant.** 1 be thoughtless, act rashly, act unreasonably; forget, slip one's mind.

thinkable *adj.* *A vacation was not thinkable that year:* conceivable, believable, conceivable, feasible, imaginable, possible, presumable, reasonable, supposable, comprehensible. —**Ant.** unthinkable, absurd, impossible.

thinker *n.* *It'll take a real thinker to figure out*

the solution: man of thought, intellect, sage, savant, mastermind, wizard, mental giant, smart person, bright person, scholar, philosopher, metaphysician, intellectual, *Slang* egghead. —**Ant.** man of action, dunce, dumbbell, dummy, ninny, nincompoop, dope, idiot, imbecile, moron, *Informal* dunderhead, noodlehead.

thinking *adj.* **1.** *This essay is written for the thinking person:* rational, reasoning, reflective, thoughtful, contemplative, meditative, philosophical; intelligent, smart, bright, studious, educated, cultured, cultivated, sophisticated. —*n.* **2.** *The driver averted an accident by quick thinking. What is your thinking on the matter?:* using one's head, thought, brainwork, judgment, deduction; conclusion, belief, inference; view, concept, position, stand, impression, surmise; contemplation, meditation, reflection, consideration, rumination, study, deliberation, speculation, mental absorption. **3.** *She crossed the street without thinking:* paying attention, using one's head, being heedful.

thinskinned *adj.* **1.** *Thinskinned potatoes are best for boiling:* having a thin skin. **2.** *Don't be so thinskinned; learn to shake off criticism:* easily offended, sensitive, hypersensitive, oversensitive, touchy, susceptible, squeamish; irritable, petulant, ill-tempered, snappish, peevish, irascible, testy, huffy, sullen, sulky, quarrelsome, cross, cantankerous, crabbed, grumpy. —**Ant.** 1, 2 thickskinned. 2 insensitive, callous, hardened; even-tempered, sweet-tempered, good-natured, sweet, kind, happy, content.

thirst *n.* **1.** *The baseball players worked up a tremendous thirst:* need of liquid, dryness in the mouth, thirstiness. **2.** *A good student has a thirst for knowledge:* desire, keenness, craving, hankering, yearning, yen, hunger, appetite, voracity, stomach, lust, passion, itch, relish, fervor, ardor. —*v.* **3.** *The children thirsted for ice-cold milk:* be thirsty for, desire to drink, be thirsty, be parched. **4.** *The avaricious man thirsted for wealth:* desire, covet, crave, hanker for, yearn, yen, lust, itch, hunger, pant. —**Ant.** 2 disinterest, apathy; dislike, distaste, hate, abhorrence, aversion, revulsion, repulsion. 4 scorn, disdain, be disinterested in, be apathetic toward; dislike, hate, detest, abhor.

thorn *n.* **1.** *These rosebushes have a lot of thorns:* sharp spine, spike, barb, spur, prickle. **2.** *The jibes of the other children were the thorn of his existence:* bane, curse, torment, affliction, infliction, care, woe, trouble, plague, scourge, sting, gall, bitter pill, nuisance, annoyance, irritation, vexation, crown of thorns, cross, sore point.

thorny *adj.* **1.** *This bush is very thorny:* full of thorns, overgrown with thorns; prickly, spiny, brambly, barbed, spiked, bristling. **2.** *How to reduce a company's costs without firing anyone is a thorny problem:* difficult, full of difficulties, full of dilemmas, hard, tough, arduous, troublesome, dangerous, dire, formidable, sticky, ticklish, critical, crucial; complex, perplexing, involved, complicated, annoying, trying, vexa-

tious, nettlesome, irksome. —**Ant.** 2 easy, simple, untroublesome, uncomplicated.

thorough *adj.* **1.** *She gave the house a thorough cleaning. The new employee seems to be a very thorough worker:* complete, thoroughgoing, careful, full, painstaking, meticulous, exhaustive, all-inclusive, all-embracing, definitive. **2.** *The entire vacation was thorough pleasure:* perfect, pure, utter, sheer, total, entire, absolute, unmitigated, unqualified, downright, out-and-out; uniform, consistent, of a piece. —**Ant.** 1, 2 partial, incomplete. 1 careless, slipshod, sloppy, lackadaisical. 2 marred, mitigated, qualified, imperfect, with reservation.

thoroughbred *adj.* **1.** *The rancher raises thoroughbred black Angus:* purebred, pure-blooded, full-blooded, unmixed, pedigreed. —*n.* **2.** *This merino sheep is a true thoroughbred:* purebred animal, pure-blooded animal. **3.** Sometimes **Thoroughbred** *Ten Thoroughbreds are entered in the Kentucky Derby:* horse of the Thoroughbred breed, racehorse. **4.** *Informal Bill is marrying a real thoroughbred:* aristocrat, blueblood, silkstocking, high-class person.

thoroughfare *n.* *The shopping center is located near the major thoroughfare entering the city:* through street, street, main road, road, avenue, boulevard, concourse, parkway; highway, thruway, expressway, turnpike, roadway, freeway, interstate, superhighway. —**Ant.** dead-end street, cul-de-sac; alley, lane, backstreet, sidestreet.

thoroughly *adv.* **1.** *Search the house thoroughly:* completely, fully, exhaustively, inclusively, from top to bottom, through and through, carefully, meticulously. **2.** *We had a thoroughly good time:* perfectly, in all respects, utterly, entirely, totally, completely, absolutely, downright, out-and-out; uniformly, consistently, from beginning to end, throughout. —**Ant.** 1, 2 partially, incompletely. 1 carelessly, sloppily, inconclusively, lackadaisically. 2 imperfectly, somewhat, in part; slightly.

thought *n.* **1.** *Give the matter careful thought. The man stared blankly, lost in thought:* thinking, mental activity, deliberation, cogitation, consideration, reflection; introspection, meditation, contemplation, rumination, musing, reverie, thoughtfulness, brown study. **2.** *What are your thoughts on the matter? The thought of measuring volume by displacement of fluid came as a sudden inspiration to Archimedes. Sir James Jeans made important contributions to scientific thought:* idea, notion; opinion, conclusion, judgment, belief, view, speculation, supposition, surmise, sentiment, fancy, imagination, concept, conception; doctrine, credo, tenet, dogma. **3.** *It's not the gift, it's the thought that counts. It's his thought to open a branch office next year:* thoughtfulness, consideration, concern, caring, attention, kindness, kindheartedness, regard; intent, intention, purpose, design, aim, plan, scheme, goal, object, objective, end, anticipation, expectation.

thoughtful *adj.* **1.** *The magazine has a thoughtful article on the international situation.*

Why are you so quiet and thoughtful today?: full of thought, serious, thinking, probing; contemplative, reflective, meditative, musing, introspective, pensive, wistful. **2.** *What a thoughtful gift!:* considerate, kind, kindhearted, neighborly, solicitous, attentive, caring, loving. —**Ant.** 1, 2 thoughtless. 1 shallow, facetious, unthinking, heedless, rash, reckless, irresponsible, remiss. 2 inconsiderate, insensitive, unkind, mean, cruel, coldhearted; rude, impolite, neglectful.

thoughtfulness *n.* **1.** *The problem calls for a lot of thoughtfulness:* thought, thinking, contemplation, meditation, reflection, consideration, probing, questioning. **2.** *We appreciate your thoughtfulness in sending flowers:* consideration, kindness, kindheartedness, solicitousness, attentiveness.

thoughtless *adj.* **1.** *Several thoughtless mistakes cost the man his job:* unthinking, careless, heedless, inattentive, imprudent, improvident, ill-considered, ill-advised, neglectful; stupid, dumb, silly, foolish, scatterbrained, rattlebrained, harebrained, absent-minded. **2.** *Her thoughtless remark offended everyone:* inconsiderate, insensitive, rude, impolite, unkind, indiscreet, inadvertent, rash, reckless, unreflecting. —**Ant.** 1, 2 thoughtful. 1 intelligent, smart, wise, sage, prudent, provident, well-advised, thinking, careful, alert. 2 considerate, sensitive, diplomatic, kindhearted, solicitous, polite, courteous, discreet.

thoughtlessness *n.* **1.** *The driver's thoughtlessness caused the accident:* carelessness, inattention, inattentiveness, heedlessness, neglect, negligence, oversight, absent-mindedness, rashness, recklessness, imprudence. **2.** *The son's thoughtlessness hurt the mother's feelings:* lack of consideration, unconcern, insensitivity, unkindness, rudeness, impoliteness.

thrash *v.* **1.** *Teachers used to thrash disobedient pupils:* whip, spank, cane, switch, birch, strap; lash, beat, flog, flail, scourge, flagellate; pommel, lambaste, trounce, maul, drub. **2.** *The child thrashed around so much he fell off the chair:* toss, plunge, wiggle, squirm, writhe, flounce, tumble, joggle, jiggle, heave, jerk. **3.** *Before threshing machines, farmers threshed their wheat by hand:* separate the grains of, flail, separate the wheat from the chaff. **4.** *Community leaders met with a police official to thrash out mutual problems:* thresh out, resolve, argue out, solve, conclude by discussion.

threadbare *adj.* **1.** *It's time to throw out that threadbare sweater:* worn, worn-out, frayed, raveled, shabby, ragged, tacky, napless, pileworn, worn to a thread, the worse for wear. **2.** *The television drama had a threadbare plot:* hackneyed, banal, trite, clichéd, bromidic, stereotyped, stock, overfamiliar, stale, well-known, commonplace, routine, everyday, conventional, prosaic, boring, dull, humdrum, jejune. —**Ant.** 1, 2 new, brand-new. 1 unused, unworn, good as new. 2 novel, fresh, unique, singular, exciting, surprising, different, unusual.

threat *n.* **1.** *Threats don't scare me:* menacing

statement, terrorizing statement, intimidation; ill omen, portent, warning sign, premonition, foreboding, handwriting on the wall. **2.** *The threat of an economic depression hangs over the world:* menace, danger, risk, hazard, peril, jeopardy. —**Ant.** 1, 2 promise. 1 bribe, enticement, reward.

threaten *v.* **1.** *The gangster threatened to burn down the store unless the owner paid extortion money. The foreman threatened the lazy worker with dismissal:* promise injury, promise harm; menace, intimidate, cow, terrorize; warn, forewarn. **2.** *Floodwaters are threatening the town:* menace, endanger, imperil, jeopardize; be imminent, impend, hang over. —**Ant.** 1, 2 protect, defend, safeguard, guard.

threatening *adj.* **1.** *The bully's threatening remarks frightened the child:* menacing, terrorizing, sinister, intimidating; warning, forewarning. **2.** *Threatening clouds appeared on the horizon:* ominous, menacing, sinister, baleful, grim, alarming, ill-omened, foreboding, forbidding, inauspicious, unpropitious; imminent, impending, approaching.

threshold *n.* **1.** *The cabin has a flat stone for a threshold. Don't just stand there in the threshold, come in!:* doorsill, sill, groundsel, limen; entranceway, entrance, doorway, door, gateway, portal. **2.** *The scientist is on the threshold of a great discovery. The treaty will be the threshold of lasting peace:* brink, verge, edge; beginning, onset, start, commencement, starting point, inception, opening, dawn, prelude. —**Ant.** 2 end, termination, conclusion, finish; destruction, disappearance.

thrift *n.* *To save money for your old age you must practice thrift now:* economy, prudence, frugality, thriftiness, husbandry, parsimony, parsimoniousness, sparingness, closefistedness; moderation, reasonableness. —**Ant.** extravagance, prodigality, thriftlessness, wastefulness; excess, immoderation, unreasonableness.

thrifty *adj.* *Even though she had plenty of money, the old woman was very thrifty:* economical, frugal, parsimonious, economizing, sparing, saving, closefisted, tightfisted, penny-pinching, penny-wise, niggardly, stingy. —**Ant.** extravagant, free-spending, prodigal, spendthrift, uneconomical, wasteful, improvident; openhanded, generous.

thrill *n.* **1.** *A thrill runs up and down my spine every time "The Maple Leaf" is played:* rush of excitement, tingle, quiver, throb, tremble, tremor, glow, flush. **2.** *Seeing the pyramids was a real thrill:* thrilling event, adventure, satisfaction, kick; thrilling story, exciting thing. —*v.* **3.** *The close soccer game thrilled the crowd:* electrify, galvanize, stir, rouse, arouse, stimulate, excite, inspire, fire; delight, enrapture, transport, impress, tickle. —**Ant.** 2, 3 bore, weary; irk, annoy.

thrilling *adj.* *Catching a 150-pound tarpon was the most thrilling part of the vacation. The spy story was thrilling:* exciting, stirring, awesome, sensational, electrifying, riveting, engaging, fascinating, absorbing, provocative, tantalizing, titillating; delightful, pleasurable, exquisite. —**Ant.** boring, dull, uninteresting, tedious, monotonous.

thrive *v.* **1.** *The garden seems to thrive on the new fertilizer:* grow vigorously, flourish, wax, bloom, burgeon, fatten. **2.** *Now that the highway is finished, the shopping center should thrive:* prosper, succeed, get ahead, get on, grow rich, boom; be successful, be fortunate, turn out well. —**Ant.** 1 languish, die, wither, fade. 2 fail, go bankrupt; be unsuccessful, be unfortunate.

thriving *adj.* **1.** *The thriving tomato plants are plentiful this year:* growing fast; blooming, blossoming, flowering, luxuriant, rank, lush. **2.** *The pizza parlor did a thriving business. One brother is poor, but the other is thriving:* flourishing, prospering, prosperous, successful, succeeding, busy, vigorous; wealthy, rich, well-to-do, well-off, *Slang* on Easy Street, in clover. —**Ant.** 1 languishing, dying, withering, fading. 2 failing, bankrupt, unsuccessful; poor, moneyless, penniless, destitute, poverty-stricken, impoverished, badly off, indigent, broke.

throaty *adj.* *The actor had a very throaty voice:* husky, deep, low, base, full-toned, sonorous, resonant; guttural, thick, gruff, hoarse, grating, rasping, croaking, cracked, dry. —**Ant.** high, thin, shrill, squeaky.

throb *v.* **1.** *Her heart throbbed with the strain of walking up the hill:* beat, beat abnormally fast, pulsate, palpitate, vibrate, flutter, quiver, tremble, shake, twitch, heave, pant. —*n.* **2.** *The throb of bongo drums could be heard through the park. Her nervousness was shown by a slight throb in her hand:* throbbing, beat, beating, pulsation, pulse, palpitation, vibration, oscillation, reverberation; flutter, fluttering, quiver, quivering, shake, shaking, tremble, trembling, twitch, jerk, tremor.

throes *n. pl.* **1.** *The company is in the throes of moving to new offices. The country is in the throes of a revolution:* upheaval, disorder, confusion, chaos, tumult, turmoil, disruption. **2.** *The young mother was in the throes of labor when she reached the hospital:* pangs, spasms, paroxysms; ordeal, anguish. **3.** *The dying man received extreme unction immediately before the final throes set in. In its death throes the whale spouted blood:* paroxysm, convulsion, agony.

throng *n.* **1.** *The pre-Christmas sale attracted a throng of shoppers:* great number, multitude, assemblage, crowd, horde, host, army, mass, swarm, flock, pack, jam, rush, crush, flood, deluge. —*v.* **2.** *Spectators thronged along the parade route:* crowd, jam, cram, pack, swarm, mass, bunch, flock, press, surge, stream, herd, huddle, mill; gather, congregate, assemble, collect, cluster, converge. —**Ant.** 1 smattering, sprinkling, few. 2 disperse, scatter, disband.

throttle *v.* **1.** *That villain ought to be throttled. The dictator throttled news of his regime's atrocities:* choke, strangle, strangulate, garrote, burke; choke off, block, check, smother, stifle, silence, gag, seal off, shut off, stop. **2.** *The young pilot had to learn to throttle more*

smoothly: work a fuel lever, feed the flow of fuel to an engine; (*variously*) change speed, reduce speed, increase speed. —*n.* **3.** *Step on the throttle and pass that bus:* fuel valve, fuel lever; gas pedal, gas. —**Ant.** 1 breathe, breathe easily; announce, proclaim, broadcast, reveal, disclose. 3 brake.

through or *Informal* **thru** *adj.* **1.** *Is the work through yet? Dinner was through by the time the guests arrived:* finished, done, completed, concluded, ended, terminated, past. **2.** *There are several through trains from Paris to Zurich:* direct, long-distance; express. —*adv.* **3.** *The tunnel is high enough to walk through. Did you read the book through?:* in one side and out the other, from one end to the other; from beginning to end, from first to last, from A to Z, all the way, to the end. —**Ant.** 1 begun, started, initiated. 2 local.

throughout *adv.* *The factory was painted green throughout. Our vacation was relaxing, but it rained throughout:* all over, in every part, everywhere; all the time, from beginning to end, all the way through. —**Ant.** here and there, in some places, in some parts; now and then, some of the time.

throw *v.* **1.** *Throw the ball to first base! Throw a sweater over your shoulders--it's chilly:* fling, hurl, toss, cast, pitch, heave, sling, let fly, lob, chuck, shy; propel, impel, launch, project, hurtle; put, place, put in, put on, put around. **2.** *The horse threw his rider:* throw off, throw down, cause to fall to the ground, unseat; knock down, floor. —*n.* **3.** *He picked up the horseshoe and pitched a ringer with his very first throw:* toss, hurl, fling, cast, pitch, heave, sling, chuck, lob, delivery, shot. **4.** *The stronger wrestler won the first throw:* act of causing someone to fall to the ground; act of throwing off. —**Ant.** 1, 3 catch. 1 receive; give, hand.

throwing *n.* *Throwing was something she could do well:* hurling, tossing.

thrust *v.* **1.** *Thrust this wedge under the door. The angry man thrust his way through the crowd:* shove, push, poke, prod, butt, drive, press, force, ram, jam, impel, propel. **2.** *The duelers thrust and parried. The pirate thrust the sword into the captain's back:* wield a sword, place a sword; stab, pierce, plunge, jab, lunge. —*n.* **3.** *The parachute instructor gave the student a hard thrust out the plane's door. The rocket has a million pounds of thrust:* shove, push, poke, prod, boost, impulse; propelling force, propulsion force, impetus, momentum. **4.** *With one thrust Saint George killed the dragon:* sword thrust, stab, stroke, lunge, plunge, pass, riposte, swipe. **5.** *Napoleon's armies made a thrust into Russia:* military advance, assault, attack, charge, drive, sally, raid, foray, sortie, incursion, aggression, strike. —**Ant.** 1, 3 pull, draw, drag. 2, 4 parry. 5 retreat, withdrawal.

thud *n.* *The book fell to the floor with a thud:* dull sound, thump, clunk, bang, knock, smack.

thug *n.* *The two thugs robbed the old man:* ruffian, hoodlum, hood; (*variously*) gangster, gunman, mobster, robber, bandit, killer, hit man, murderer, assassin, mugger, cutthroat.

thumb n. **1.** *The baby sucked its thumb:* inside finger, short finger next to the forefinger. —v. **2.** *He thumbed the address book looking for the number:* flip through, leaf through, glance through, run one's eye through; handle, finger. **3.** *Informal The student thumbed his way across country:* hitchhike, hitch, hitch a ride, catch a ride.

thump v. **1.** *The speaker thumped his fist on the desk for emphasis:* strike, beat, hit, pound, knock, whack, thwack, bang, punch, buffet, batter, pommel, lambaste, slap, cuff, clip, jab, poke. **2.** *He thumped into bed and went to sleep:* fall heavily, collapse, bounce, sit down heavily. —n. **3.** *Did you hear a thump in the attic? A piece of plaster fell and gave him a thump on the head:* clunk, thud, bang; heavy blow, heavy fall, knock, rap, slam, smack, clout, swat, whack, hit.

thunder n. **1.** *Lightning and thunder woke everyone before the rain started. The thunder of artillery could be heard in the distance:* loud rumbling noise accompanying lightning discharge, thunderbolt, thunderclap; rumbling, clap, explosion, discharge, roar, boom, crash, crack. —v. **2.** *It lightninged and thundered. Applause thundered through the concert hall:* give forth thunder, discharge thunder; rumble, reverberate, echo, resound, roll, peal, explode, boom.

thunderstruck adj. *The town was thunderstruck by news of the scandal:* astounded, astonished, dumbfounded, flabbergasted, aghast, agog, agape, awed, awestruck, overcome, amazed, surprised, bewildered, confused, perplexed. —**Ant.** unmoved, unexcited, indifferent, apathetic, calm.

thus adv. **1.** *Hold the golf club thus:* in this way, in this manner, like this, like so, so; as follows. **2.** *Costs and overhead are up; thus prices must rise:* therefore, so, hence, wherefore, consequently, accordingly, for this reason, ergo. —**Ant.** 1 the other way, the reverse way. 2 but, however, nevertheless, nonetheless, even so, in spite of this.

thwack n. **1.** *The branch sprang back and gave him a thwack across the shoulders:* blow, whack, rap, smack, wallop, thump, knock, slap, clout, slam. —v. **2.** *The boy accidentally thwacked his brother with the board:* whack, paddle, rap, strike, hit, bang, baste, smack, wallop, thump, slap.

thwart v. *The barbed wire will thwart an infantry assault:* stop, frustrate, foil, balk, check, hinder, obstruct, baffle, inhibit, prevent, bar, ward off, stave off; contravene, cross, oppose. —**Ant.** encourage, help, aid, support, abet; hasten, increase, aggravate, multiply, magnify.

tic n. *Grandfather had a tic in his right cheek:* involuntary twitch, facial twitch, twitch, *Medical* trigeminal neuralgia, tic douloureux.

tick v. **1.** *You can't even hear this clock tick:* make a slight, sharp sound; click, clack, tap; make a sharp sound over and over, ticktock, beat, vibrate, oscillate, swing. **2.** *Tick off the*

items on this list: check, mark; record, note, mark down, list, enter, register, chronicle. —n. **3.** *Is there a tick in the motor?:* ticking noise; slight, sharp repeated sound; ticktock, click, clack, tap; vibration, oscillation, throb, pulsation. **4.** *Put a tick by each item you want to order:* checkmark, check, mark, stroke, line, dot; scratch, notch, nick, blaze.

ticket n. **1.** *He had two tickets to the latest Broadway play. Please show your ticket to the stewardess when you board the plane:* ticket of admission, trip ticket, voucher, coupon, pass; stub. **2.** *The driver got a ticket for speeding:* traffic ticket, traffic summons; parking ticket. **3.** *The sales ticket says the coat is $50:* tag, label, slip, marker, card, sticker. **4.** *The governor ran on the Democratic ticket:* list of political candidates, list of nominees, slate, roster; ballot. —v. **5.** *The passenger is ticketed to San Francisco. Ticket the merchandise before putting it on display:* provide with a ticket, hold a ticket, buy a ticket, sell a ticket; put a ticket on, tag, label, mark. **6.** *The policewoman ticketed the parked car:* attach a traffic summons to, serve a traffic summons to, give a traffic ticket to, attach a parking ticket to.

tickle v. **1.** *She tickled the baby under the chin:* stroke with the fingertips, stroke lightly, rub lightly, stroke, titillate. **2.** *My jaw still tickles from the dentist's injection:* tingle, twitch, itch, prickle, sting, prick, throb. **3.** *The comedian tickled the crowd with his jokes. The puppy's antics tickled the children:* amuse, regale, divert, enliven, gladden, cheer, delight, please, fascinate, enchant, captivate, enthrall, entrance, excite agreeably, thrill, rejoice, gratify, do one's heart good. —n. **4.** *The little girl laughed when her uncle gave her a tickle:* teasing stroke, tingling rub. **5.** *A cough drop can ease that tickle in your throat:* tickling sensation, tingle, twitching sensation, itch, scratchiness, prickle, sting.

ticklish adj. **1.** *Are you ticklish?:* sensitive to tick-ling, easily tickled, tickly; tingling, itchy, scratchy, prickly. **2.** *Bringing the two enemies together will be a ticklish job:* delicate, awkward, requiring tact, touchy, sensitive, uncertain, critical; difficult, complicated, intricate, tricky, tough, hard, knotty, thorny. —**Ant.** 2 easy, simple.

tidbit n. *These smoked oysters are delicious tidbits. I know a juicy tidbit of gossip about her:* delicate bit, morsel, mouthful, delicacy, treat, choice bit, bit, item.

tide n. **1.** *The tide left delicate lines on the sandy beach. The tide left the driftwood high on the beach:* twice daily rise and fall of the oceans; (variously) high tide, ebb tide, neap tide, flood tide, low tide, riptide, undertow; tidal water, tidewater, wave, current, flow. **2.** *The tide of fortune may make you wealthy again. The tide of public opinion is now against the mayor's plan:* rise and fall, ebb and flow, wax and wane; drift, current, tendency, movement, direction, state.

tidings n. *The messenger arrived with tidings of the king's death:* news, information, word, advice, intelligence, report, announcement, declaration, good word, notification.

tidy *adj.* **1.** *Her desk was always tidy. The carpenter was a good example of a tidy worker:* neat, orderly, trim, shipshape, trig, in apple-pie order; methodical, systematic, organized, meticulous, precise, careful, regular, regulated, businesslike; clean, immaculate, spotless. **2.** *Informal That car must have cost a tidy sum of money:* considerable, fairly large, substantial, sizable, goodly, ample. —*v.* **3.** *Tidy the living room before the guests arrive:* tidy up, neaten, neaten up, put in order, straighten, straighten up, clean up, spruce up, arrange, array. —**Ant.** 1 messy, sloppy, untidy, slovenly, unkempt, disordered, disorderly, unmethodical, unsystematic, unbusinesslike, careless, slipshod; filthy, dirty. 2 inconsiderable, unsubstantial, small, little, tiny. 3 mess, mess up, disarrange, disorder; dirty.

tie *v.* **1.** *Tie the boat to the dock. Tie a knot in this string:* bind, fasten, make fast, attach, secure, engage, tether, clinch, truss, lash; draw together and knot, knot, make a bow. **2.** *The United States and Canada are tied by a common language and mutual interests:* bind, fasten, attach, join, unite, connect, link, yoke, ally, couple, marry. **3.** *I'd like to give you more time to finish the job, but I'm tied by the contract:* limit, confine, constrain, restrain, restrict, hinder, hamper. **4.** *Two teams tied for first place:* make the same score, have the same record of wins and losses, draw, come out even, match, divide the honors. —*n.* **5.** *Hold back the curtain with a tie:* fastener for tying, cord, rope, string, line, cable, fastening, belt, band, ribbon, cinch, girdle, cincture, sash, cummerbund. **6.** *Men are supposed to wear coats and ties to the party:* necktie, cravat; bow tie. **7.** *The two friends have strong ties. The senator is said to have a strong tie with the oil industry:* bond, link, affinity, connection, relation, relationship, kinship, affiliation, shared interest, mutual interest, allegiance; duty, obligation. **8.** *The game ended in a tie. The race was a tie:* tied score, tied record, tied vote; draw, dead heat. **9.** *The builder added more ties to the structure. Trains were delayed while the railroad ties were replaced:* brace, support, beam, rod, connecting rod; crossbeam. —**Ant.** 1 untie, unbind, unfasten, loose, loosen, disengage, unknot. 2 detach, separate, divorce, disunite.

tier *n.* *Our seats were up in the second tier of the balcony. The wedding cake had three tiers:* row, rank, line, file, step, level, range, bank; layer, story, stratum, stratification.

tie-up *n.* *The tie-up of traffic lasted for hours:* snag, jam, block, hitch, bottleneck, snarl, stoppage, blockage, gridlock, failure, malfunction, breakdown, disruption, slow-up, *French* embouteillage.

tiff *n.* **1.** *The couple had a tiff over which party to go to:* minor quarrel, petty quarrel, clash, scrap, run-in, spat, words, squabble, argument, dispute, wrangle, altercation, disagreement, difference, misunderstanding; *Slang* hassle, rhu-

barb. **2.** *Don't be in a tiff just because you didn't get your own way:* slight fit of anger, annoyed mood, huff, snit, tizzy, miff, rage, ill humor, bad mood.

tight *adv., adj.* Also *adv.,* **tightly 1.** *This lid is screwed on tight. Make a good tight knot:* firmly, securely, solidly, closely; firm, secure, solid. **2.** *Pull the rope tight. Hold the horse with a tight rein:* taut, tense, stretched out, stretched as far as possible, rigid, stiff, drawn tight. **3.** *This dress fits tight. Tight shoes can be painful:* too closely, fitting closely, fitting too closely, close-fitting, snug, skintight, not big enough, too small, uncomfortably small, constricted. **4.** *The suitcase was packed tight. The boss has a tight schedule today:* full, crammed, jammed, jam-packed, stuffed, gorged; crowded, busy. —*adj.* **5.** *The material has a tight weave. Destroyers kept a tight formation during the maneuver:* closely constructed, closely fitted, close, dense, compact, set closely together, solid, compressed, impermeable, impenetrable, impassable. **6.** *The sergeant maintained tight discipline:* strict, firm, stern, rigid, rigorous, severe, exact, stringent, austere, stiff, inflexible, unyielding, uncompromising, tyrannical, dictatorial, harsh. **7.** *Unless he gets some money soon he'll be in a tight spot:* difficult, worrisome, troublesome, hard, hard-up, tough, onerous, burdensome, trying. **8.** *The government believes tight money will stop inflation:* scarce, difficult to obtain, scant, sparing, skimpy; insufficient, inadequate, deficient. **9.** *Informal The mayor won in a tight election:* nearly even, nearly equal, nearly tied, close, well-matched, nip-and-tuck, nose-to-nose. **10.** *Informal Don't be so tight with your money:* stingy, miserly, tightfisted, close, close-fisted, parsimonious, frugal, niggardly, penurious, illiberal, ungenerous, sparing, grudging. **11.** *Informal Uncle Lou had too much eggnog and got tight:* drunk, drunken, intoxicated, inebriated, tipsy, happy, plastered, blind, smashed, soused, loaded, pickled, stewed, pie-eyed, glassy-eyed, juiced, sloppy, stiff, stoned, zonked, high, in one's cups, three sheets to the wind, feeling no pain, lit-up. —**Ant.** 1–3, 5, 6 loose. 1–3 loosely. 1 insecure, insecurely. 2 slack, relaxed, limp, free, flexible. 3 big, too big, loose-fitting. 4 empty; sparse. 5 open, porous, airy, lacy. 6–9 easy. 6 lenient, indulgent, soft, relaxed, undemanding, permissive, unexacting, slack, lax, mild, informal, flexible, yielding, easygoing, free-and-easy. 7 comfortable, enviable. 8 abundant, plentiful, profuse, rife, ready, ample, sufficient. 9 uneven, runaway, landslide. 10 extravagant, spendthrift, thriftless, prodigal, squandering, wasteful, lavish; generous, openhanded, liberal, munificent, charitable. 11 sober, sober as a judge.

tighten *v.* *Tighten the nut on this screw. Tighten the clothesline so it doesn't drop:* make tight, make tighter, fix firmly, fasten, anchor, make fast, secure; draw tight, make taut, make tense, take up the slack; narrow, squeeze, contract, constrict, pinch. —**Ant.** loosen, loose, slacken, slack off, relax, ease, ease off; free, release, untie, open.

tightfisted *adj. He's so tightfisted he won't donate to any charity:* stingy, parsimonious, niggardly, penny-pinching, tight, penurious, miserly, cheap, illiberal, mingy, closefisted, greedy, avaricious, cheeseparing. **—Ant.** openhanded, generous, liberal, unstinting.

tight-laced *adj. Her mother was very tight-laced and wanted her home by 10 P.M.:* prim, prudish, priggish, straitlaced, prissy, stuffy, Victorian, puritanical, self-righteous, standoffish, repressed, inhibited. **—Ant.** uninhibited, free, fast, promiscuous.

tight-lipped *adj. Soldiers are expected to be tight-lipped about troop movements:* closemouthed, reticent, discreet, reserved, taciturn, quiet, mum, uncommunicative, terse, brief, untalkative, unsociable, curt, short. **—Ant.** talkative, unreserved, indiscreet, reckless.

tightwad *n. Informal That old tightwad wouldn't give a nickel to charity:* stingy person, skinflint, miser, niggard, moneygrubber, pinchpenny, cheapskate, piker, lickpenny, Scrooge. **—Ant.** spendthrift, prodigal, squanderer, wastrel, big spender, big-time spender; philanthropist, good Samaritan.

tilt *v.* **1.** *Is the table uneven or does the floor tilt?:* slant, incline, lean, slope, tip, list, cant. **2.** *The two knights tilted until one was unhorsed. It's a priest's job to tilt against the forces of evil:* joust, fight on horseback with a lance; fight, oppose, contend against, battle, contest; fence, spar, skirmish. **—***n.* **3.** *The tilt of the roof prevents snow from accumulating:* slope, slant, incline, cant, rake, pitch, grade. **4.** *Don Quixote engaged in a famous tilt with a windmill:* joust, jousting match, tournament; fight, contest, combat, battle, skirmish, encounter, affray; dispute, argument, quarrel, altercation, squabble, row, brawl, tiff. **—Ant.** 1 be even, be flat, be plumb. 3 evenness, flatness.

timber *n.* **1.** *Stack the timber near the tool shed:* wood, wood for building, lumber, boards, logs. **2.** *A wolf howled back in the tall timber:* timberland, wooded land; forest, woods, trees, bush, thicket, copse. **—Ant.** 1 firewood, kindling. 2 clearing, field, pasture, grassland, meadow, prairie, savanna.

timbre *n. The singer's voice had a pleasant timbre:* tone, sound quality, pitch, resonance.

time *n.* **1.** *Time and tide stop for no man. It's been a long time since we've seen each other:* the passage of time, duration, continuation of all existence; period, interval, span of time, elapsed time, spell, term, while, stretch. **2.** Usually **times** *The Parthenon was built in ancient times. Toy rocket ships are a sign of the times:* epoch, era, period, age, eon; stage, season, cycle, day. **3.** *The time is 2:30 P.M. It's time to go. Christmas time is almost here. The time of the play was the 1890's:* particular point in time, appointed time, proper moment, appropriate period, high time; (variously) instant, moment, hour, part of the hour, day, part of the day, week, part of the week, month, part of the

month, year, part of the year, season, term, decade, century, period. **4.** *The time of man is three score years and ten:* lifetime, years, days, period, phase, season, generation. **5.** *I don't have the time to play golf:* leisure time, spare time, free time, liberty, opportunity, chance, freedom. **6.** *A good time was had by all:* experience, occasion, period, event, episode, incident. **7.** *The piece was written in waltz time:* tempo; rhythm, beat, measure. **—***v.* **8.** *The runner was timed for the mile in four minutes flat. The enemy timed their attack perfectly:* measure the speed of, clock; measure the duration of; choose the time of. **9.** *The marchers timed their steps to the drumbeat:* synchronize, keep time, set to the rhythm of, adjust, match.

timeless *adj. The astronomer pondered the timeless reaches of space. Styles come and go, but good taste is timeless:* without beginning or end, eternal, infinite, never-stopping, never-ending, unending, endless, everlasting, interminable, perpetual, ceaseless, incessant, boundless, continuous; enduring; lasting, persistent, durable, permanent, abiding, unchangeable, immutable, indestructible, immortal, undying, deathless. **—Ant.** brief, quick, short, short-lived, temporary, passing, fleeting, unenduring, evanescent, ephemeral, transient, transitory, impermanent, changing.

timely *adj. The timely loan saved the businessman from going bankrupt. I'd like to give you some timely advice:* occurring at the right time, well-timed, opportune, felicitous, convenient, seasonable, prompt, punctual, providential. **—Ant.** untimely, inopportune, inconvenient, ill-timed, unseasonable, late, tardy.

timeworn *adj.* **1.** *The rose was pressed in a time-worn volume of poetry:* aged, ancient, antique, old, age-old, worn, venerable, hoary, antediluvian, ravaged with age, the worse for wear, battered, dog-eared, shabby, weathered, *Slang* beat-up. **2.** *No one laughed at the timeworn joke:* passé, antiquated, dated, obsolete, out of date; hackneyed, stale, trite, overused, *Slang* old-hat. **—Ant.** 1 new, brand-new, in mint condition. 2 fresh, novel, original.

timid *adj. The boy is timid as a mouse:* lacking self-assurance, fainthearted, fearful, afraid, scared, timorous, apprehensive, cowardly, spineless, pusillanimous, weak-kneed, shy, bash-ful, coy, diffident, modest, overly modest, humble, sheepish, retiring, shrinking, unassuming. **—Ant.** self-assured, confident, daring, audacious, stouthearted, fearless, brave, bold, intrepid, courageous, adventuresome; brash, brazen, forward, impertinent, impudent, presumptuous, insolent, fresh, saucy, immodest, unabashed, shameless, cheeky.

timidity *n. His timidity prevented him from asking her to the dance:* timidness, timorousness, shyness, lack of self-assurance, faintheartedness, fearfulness, trepidation, cowardice, spinelessness; bashfulness, diffidence, modesty, humility, sheepishness, *Slang* cold feet. **—Ant.** self-assurance, self-confidence, daring, audacity, fearlessness, bravery, boldness, courage; brashness, brazenness, forwardness, impertinence, impudence, presumption, insolence, immodesty, cheek.

tinge v. **1.** *Just one drop of ink tinged the water blue. His smile was tinged with cruelty:* color slightly, color, tint, dye, stain; touch, infuse, imbue, instill, lace, season, flavor. —*n.* **2.** *The wallpaper has just a tinge of orange. The book has a tinge of unpleasantness:* slight coloration, tint, shade, cast, stain; tone, touch, trace, hint, dash, vein, nuance, suspicion, flavor, taste, smack, soupçon.

tingle v. **1.** *Don't your hands tingle in the cold?:* have a prickling sensation, sting, prickle, tickle. —*n.* **2.** *A tingle of excitement ran down his back:* prickling, thrill, tremor, flutter, throb, palpitation, pulsation.

tinker v. *He tinkered with the engine all afternoon:* potter, putter, dabble, play play around with, trifle with, amuse oneself, *Informal* mess about, monkey with.

tinkle v. **1.** *Sleigh bells tinkled in the distance:* ring lightly, jingle, clink, chink, clank, chime, ping, plink, peal, ding. —*n.* **2.** *The tinkle of a bell summoned the butler:* light ring, jingle, clink, chink, clank, chime, peal, ding, ting-a-ling. —**Ant.** 1, 2 boom, roar, bang, thunder.

tinny adj. **1.** *The tinny band got scant applause:* unresonant, reedy, thin, hollow, weak, feeble. **2.** *The tinny stereo was returned for a refund:* inferior, cheap, low-grade, insubstantial, flimsy, cheapjack. —**Ant.** 1 hearty, full-voiced. 2 sturdy, rugged.

tinsel n. **1.** *The children put the tinsel on the Christmas tree:* decorative foil, shiny metal strip, spangle, sequin, glitter. **2.** *The fancy offices are just tinsel--the firm is small and almost bankrupt:* show, decoration, gaudiness, ostentation; sham, pretense, masquerade, camouflage, gloss, false colors, affectation, make-believe, showy thing, gaudy thing.

tint n. **1.** *The blouse was striped in several tints of blue:* shade, hue, tone, nuance, tincture. **2.** *There is just a tint of green in the rug:* tinge, trace, hint, suggestion, touch. **3.** *Is her hair naturally blond or does she use a tint?:* dye, stain, coloring, pigment. —*v.* **4.** *Why not tint your hair red?:* color slightly, color, dye, stain, tone, wash; tinge, frost.

tiny n. *The bush has tiny red berries on it:* small, little, minute, miniature, diminutive, minuscule, microscopic, wee, *Informal* teeny, teeny-weeny, teensy-weensy, itsy-bitsy; undersized, pocket-sized, pint-sized, midget, pygmy, dwarf-ish, runty, Lilliputian, bantam, petite. —**Ant.** large, big, huge, enormous, immense, mammoth, oversized, giant, gigantic, monstrous, colossal, gargantuan, titanic.

tip¹ v. **1.** *The rowboat tipped when the fat man got in:* tilt, slant, incline, lean, list, slope, cant. **2.** Often **tip over** *The glass tipped over and milk ran down the table:* overturn, topple over, tumble over, upset, upturn, capsize, upend, turn turtle. —*n.* **3.** *The tip of the ship caused the dishes to slide across the table:* tipping, tilting, leaning, slanting; slant, incline, tilt, slope, list,

pitch, rake, cant. —**Ant.** 1 be even, be flat, be plumb. 2 upright. 3 flatness, evenness.

tip² n. **1.** *Do you have a needle with a finer tip? The tribe used flint tips on its arrows:* pointed end, tapering end, small end; point, head, prong, spike. **2.** *The tip of the iceberg was over half a mile wide:* top, peak, apex, vertex, acme, zenith, summit, crown, crest, pinnacle, cap; upper part, brow. —*v.* **3.** *The baton was tipped with gold:* furnish with a slender end, serve as a pointed end, top, cap, crown; sharpen, barb, hook, point.

tip³ n. **1.** *Many people give the garbage man a tip at Christmas:* gratuity, small gift of money for services rendered, small reward, lagniappe, baksheesh, small bones, *French* pourboire; perquisite. **2.** *Here's a useful tip on how to remove stains. The police got a tip that the bank would be robbed tonight:* hint, suggestion, pointer, clue, advice, word to the wise, warning, forewarning, admonition; secret information, inside information, inside dope, tip-off, lowdown. **3.** *The golfer gave the ball a tip with his putter:* tap, light blow, weak blow, stroke, pat. —*v.* **4.** *Let's tip the waiter generously:* give a gratuity, give a small gift of money for services rendered, reward. **5.** *The batter just tipped the ball and it bounced down the first-base line:* tap, hit lightly, strike weakly, stroke, pat.

tippler n. *W. C. Fields was quite a tippler:* heavy drinker, habitual drinker, hard drinker, sot, toper, boozer, booze hound, guzzler, swiller, imbiber, sponge, bibber, soak, tosspot; drunk, drunkard, alcoholic, inebriate, dipsomaniac, lush, souse, wino, rummy. —**Ant.** teetotaler, abstainer, nondrinker; moderate drinker, social drinker.

tipsy adj. *Even a little wine can make some people tipsy:* mildly drunk, slightly intoxicated, *Slang* high; drunk, drunken, intoxicated, inebriate, inebriated, tight, happy, plastered, blind, smashed, soused, loaded, pickled, stewed, pie-eyed, glassy-eyed, juiced, sloppy, stiff, stoned, sodden, awash, in one's cups, three sheets to the wind, half seas over, feeling no pain, lit-up. —**Ant.** sober, sober as a judge.

tirade n. *The principal delivered a tirade to the disobedient students. The political candidate let loose a tirade against his opponent:* long angry speech, harangue, diatribe, jeremiad, lecture, reprimand, scolding, dressing-down, screed, fulmination; denunciation, condemnation, castigation, vilification, invective, vituperation, curse. —**Ant.** good word, short eulogy, panegyric, complimentary speech, praising speech, laudation, commendation, homage, paean.

tire v. **1.** *Climbing to the top of the Statue of Liberty tired the tourists:* weary, wear out, fatigue, exhaust, fag, tucker; make sleepy. **2.** *Her constant chatter tired everyone. I'm tired of the same old breakfast every morning:* bore, exhaust the patience of, be fed up with, be sick of, lose patience, lose interest, irk, annoy, bother, disgust. —**Ant.** 1 refresh, stimulate; wake up. 2 delight, interest, excite, enchant, fascinate, please, soothe.

tired *adj. After a full day's work she was tired:* weary, wearied, fatigued, exhausted, enervated, worn out, all in, dog-tired, tuckered, fagged, played out, *Slang* beat, pooped, bushed; sleepy, drowsy. —**Ant.** energetic, full of pep, peppy, fresh, refreshed; raring to go; wide-awake.

tireless *adj. The winner of the marathon was a tireless runner. The chairman thanked the committee for its tireless efforts in organizing the dance:* untiring, never-tiring, unwearied; industrious, hard-working, unflagging, unfaltering, unswerving, unremitting, indefatigable, devoted, unceasing, steadfast, resolute, determined, staunch, steady, constant, persevering, determined, faithful. —**Ant.** halfhearted, lackadaisical, sporadic, random; flagging, faltering, wavering, irresolute.

tiresome *adj.* **1.** *Working in the garden all day is very tiresome:* fatiguing, wearying, wearing, tiring, exhausting, fagging; arduous, laborious, tedious, hard, difficult. **2.** *What a tiresome opera! Andrew's constant puns are getting tiresome:* boring, monotonous, uninteresting, dull, drab, dismal, wearisome, deadly, humdrum, tedious; annoying, bothersome, irksome, vexing, trying. —**Ant.** 1 refreshing; easy. 2 delightful, interesting, exciting, stimulating, fascinating, enchanting, pleasing, soothing.

titanic *adj. The explorer discovered a titanic mountain range. A titanic effort is needed to finish the job by Monday:* gigantic, huge, enormous, immense, vast, colossal, giant, mammoth, monumental, monstrous, gargantuan; great, strong, stout, prodigious, mighty, herculean; *Slang* humongous, whopping. —**Ant.** small, little, tiny, minute, diminutive, minuscule, wee, teeny, teeny-weeny, itsy-bitsy, pocket-sized, pint-sized, midget, pygmy, dwarf-ish, Lilliputian, bantam; weak, feeble.

titillate *v. The hint of scandal titillated everyone's curiosity:* excite, tickle, tease, provoke, stimulate, rouse, arouse, turn on, allure, tempt, seduce, entrance, captivate, attract, fascinate, charm, whet the appetite. —**Ant.** allay, quiet, quench, quell, still, dull, slake, blunt, satisfy, sate, satiate.

titillating *adj. The tale of buried treasure nearby was titillating. Boccaccio's* Decameron *is titillating and bawdy but not pornographic:* provocative, exciting, alluring, tempting, suggestive, seductive.

title *n.* **1.** *The full title of the book is* The Life and Strange Surprising Adventures of Robinson Crusoe, of York, Mariner*:* name, designation, appellation, epithet. **2.** *Hilda's new title is "Vice President of Marketing Research." She fell in love with the Count only because of his title:* rank, occupational rank, position, status, station, condition, grade, place; title of nobility, lordly rank, nobility, noble birth. **3.** *Who owns title to the property?:* legal right, legal possession, right, possession, ownership, tenure, deed, claim. **4.** *Joe Louis held the heavyweight title longer than anyone:* championship, crown. —*v.* **5.** *The youth titled his poem "My Lost Love":* entitle, name, designate, term, dub, label, christen.

titter *v.* **1.** *The audience tittered at the little joke:* laugh self-consciously, laugh nervously, giggle, laugh softly, chuckle, cackle, snigger, snicker, simper, smirk, chirp. —*n.* **2.** *That little titter of hers is annoying:* self-conscious laugh, nervous laugh, giggle, snigger, snicker, simper, smirk, chuckle, soft laugh, teehee. —**Ant.** 1, 2 roar, guffaw. 1 split one's sides, die laughing, roll in the aisles. 2 burst of laughter, horse-laugh.

titular *adj. The king was the titular head of state, but the prime minister had the power:* in name only, in title only, so-called, ostensible, nominal, known as. —**Ant.** actually, really, in fact, for all practical purposes.

toady *v.* **1.** *He gets good grades only because he toadies to the teacher:* flatter to gain favor, curry favor, fawn, grovel before, kowtow to, *Slang* apple-polish. —*n.* **2.** *That bunch of toadies won't even tell the boss when he's making a big mistake:* sycophant, flatterer, fawner, lickspittle, truckler, backscratcher, yes-man, *Slang* apple-polisher, bootlicker; servile follower, flunky, stooge, hanger-on, parasite. —**Ant.** 1 defy, confront, be hostile to, stand up to, oppose, resist, scorn, disdain, mock, taunt, twist the lion's tail. 2 defiant person, hostile person, opponent, enemy, foe, antagonist.

toast *v.* **1.** *Come toast your feet by the fire:* warm, warm up, heat; dry. **2.** *Toast the bread before making the bacon and tomato sandwiches. The children toasted marshmallows over the bonfire:* heat until crisp, brown; grill, cook over an open fire. **3.** *Let's all toast the bride and groom:* drink in honor of, salute with a drink, drink one's health, clink glasses; honor, celebrate, compliment, commemorate. —*n.* **4.** *Poached eggs on toast is a good breakfast:* toasted bread, browned bread; a slice of browned, crisp bread. **5.** *I propose a toast to our new president:* drink in honor of, drink to compliment, drink to commemorate. —**Ant.** 1 cool, cool off, chill.

today *n.* **1.** *Today is March 22nd. The songs of today aren't as tuneful as when I was a boy:* the present day, this day; the present age, the present, this epoch, this era, this time, modern times. —*adv.* **2.** *Let's go to the beach today. Children get a better education today than at any time in the past:* on this day; nowadays, now, in this day and age, in modern times, during the present age, in this epoch, in this era. —**Ant.** 1, 2 yesterday; tomorrow.

toddle *v. The child is just beginning to toddle:* take short, unsteady steps; walk unsteadily, wobble, waddle. —**Ant.** stride; run, skip, prance.

to-do *n. I never saw such a to-do over anyone's birthday:* fuss, commotion, hurly-burly, stir, disturbance, flurry, ado, turmoil, bustle, tumult, uproar, excitement, noise, racket, furor, hubbub, rumpus, ruckus. —**Ant.** peace, calm, serenity, tranquillity.

together *adv.* **1.** *The tunes all ran together:*

continuously, continually, without interruption, consecutively. **2.** *The new team met together for the first time:* collectively, as one, in concert, concertedly, concurrently, conjointly, contemporaneously, in cooperation, in unison, jointly, mutually, simultaneously, synchronically, unanimously, unitedly, as a group, *Informal* in sync. —**Ant.** 1 apart, separately. 2 singly, independently, individually, one at a time, one by one, singly, alone.

togs *n. pl. Informal Don't go to a job interview in your beach togs:* clothes, clothing, outfit, apparel, attire, duds, *Slang* threads.

toil *n.* **1.** *After much toil the furniture was all in the moving van:* hard work, work, labor, effort, exertion, application, industry, pains, drudgery, grind, struggle, sweat, elbow grease, hardship, travail. —*v.* **2.** *The farmer toiled in the field from dawn till dusk:* work hard, labor, drudge, slave, moil, grub, sweat, exert oneself, apply oneself, work like a horse. —**Ant.** 1, 2 play. 1 amusement, entertainment, recreation, indolence, idleness, cavorting, ease; *Slang* goofing off, goldbricking. 2 take one's ease, relax, enjoy oneself, amuse oneself, take one's pleasure, *Slang* goof off, goldbrick.

toiler *n. Toilers in the industry were in favor of the union:* worker, laborer, wage earner, drudge, peon, field hand, hired hand, menial, servant, workhorse, slave, serf, slavey, galley slave; *Slang* prole, flunky, slogger; *Brit.* navvy, swot.

toilet *n.* *"Half bath" means a room with toilet and sink:* water closet, W.C., flush toilet; latrine, lavatory, washroom, rest room; privy, outhouse; convenience, facility, commode; *Slang* john, can; *Brit.* loo; men's room, ladies' room.

toilsome *adj. The work was both time-consuming and toilsome:* laborious, wearisome, difficult, hard, arduous, strenuous, tough, tedious, tiring, wearying, fatiguing, burdensome, effortful, uphill, backbreaking, herculean. —**Ant.** easy, simple, light, soft.

token *n.* **1.** *The employees gave the retiring man a watch as a token of their esteem:* symbol, sign, expression, indication, proof, mark, index, evidence, manifestation; reminder, memento, keepsake, souvenir, remembrance, testimonial. **2.** *Bus riders in some cities must use exact change or tokens:* coinlike metal piece, *French* jeton. —*adj.* **3.** *Employing just one woman among fifty men is but token recognition of equal rights for the sexes:* superficial, passing, nodding, of no real value, perfunctory, symbolic, nominal, for show; minimal, serving as a sample, vestigial. —**Ant.** 3 real, actual, valuable, worthwhile, serious, equitable, deep.

tolerable *adj.* **1.** *Such rude behavior is not tolerable:* able to be tolerated, bearable, endurable, sufferable, abidable; acceptable, allowable, permissible. **2.** *That restaurant has tolerable food, but I wouldn't take a gourmet friend there:* fairly good, fair, passable, acceptable, adequate, innocuous, mediocre, average, ordinary, commonplace, indifferent, run-of-the-mill, so-so, middling, fair-to-middling, betwixt and between.

—**Ant.** 1 intolerable, unbearable, unendurable, insufferable; unacceptable. 2 excellent, outstanding, wonderful, terrific, superior, great, choice, exemplary, noteworthy, memorable; awful, dreadful, terrible, lousy, bad.

tolerance *n.* **1.** *Some people have greater tolerance to pain than others:* ability to tolerate, capacity to resist, power to endure, endurance. **2.** *Tolerance between the races of the world is a must:* an understanding attitude, fair treatment, fairness, lack of prejudice, freedom from bigotry, democratic spirit, goodwill, brotherly love, fellow feeling, live-and-let-live attitude; forbearance, patience, sufferance, compassion, sympathy, charity. —**Ant.** 1 sensitivity. 2 prejudice, bigotry, bias, predisposition, ill will, unfairness, discrimination; irritability, anger, irascibility.

tolerant *adj.* **1.** *Can't you be tolerant of other religions?:* understanding, unprejudiced, unbigoted, fair, having goodwill, having brotherly love, liberal, broad-minded, moderate; forbearing, patient, compassionate, sympathetic, charitable. **2.** *The teacher was too tolerant of disobedient behavior:* lenient, permissive, indulgent, soft, easy, easygoing, forbearing, forgiving, uncomplaining, kindhearted, soft-hearted, sparing. —**Ant.** 1 intolerant, prejudiced, bigoted, biased, unfair, illiberal, narrow-minded, closed-minded. 2 strict, rigid, harsh, stiff, severe, stern, exacting, uncompromising, unyielding, unbending, authoritarian, tyrannical, dictatorial, despotic.

tolerate *v.* **1.** *I can't tolerate that loud music:* bear, endure, put up with, stand, take, suffer, abide, brook, stomach, submit to, undergo. **2.** *The school cannot tolerate cheating on exams:* allow, permit, let, sanction, consent to, admit, recognize, vouchsafe, indulge, be soft on, be easy on, be sparing of, show mercy toward, wink at. —**Ant.** 2 forbid, prohibit, disallow, outlaw, proscribe, ban, prevent, oppose.

toll *n.* **1.** *Each car must pay a toll to cross the bridge:* fee, charge, payment, levy, duty, exaction, impost, assessment, tax, tariff, tribute. **2.** *The flood took a toll of a hundred lives:* loss, amount of loss, extent of damage, destruction, extermination, extinction, annihilation, sacrifice, penalty; undoing, disruption, depletion.

tomb *n. Grant's Tomb is in New York City:* burial chamber, mausoleum, vault, sepulcher, crypt, monument to the dead; resting place, burial place, grave.

tomfoolery *n. Stop the tomfoolery and get down to work!:* foolishness, silliness, prankishness, play, horseplay, drollery, high jinks, antics, monkeyshines, skylarking, nonsense, playing around, fooling around, messing around, goofing off, lollygagging.

tommyrot *n. The rumor of a surrender was pure tommyrot:* nonsense, balderdash, tomfoolery, bosh, rot, rubbish, bilge, stuff and nonsense, twaddle, humbug, fiddle-faddle; *Slang* hogwash, hooey, crap, poppycock, malarkey, bunk, *Brit.* tosh.

tomorrow *n.* **1.** *Tomorrow is Sunday. Today's youth will be the leaders of tomorrow:* the day after today, the morrow, *Spanish* mañana; the future, the next generation. —*adv.* **2.** *The county fair starts tomorrow. Tomorrow everyone will be vacationing on the moon:* on the day after today; in the future, in days to come. —**Ant.** 1, 2 yesterday; today.

tone *n.* **1.** *The shrill tone of the factory whistle rent the air:* pitch, sound quality, sound, quality, tonality; note, musical interval of two semitones, overtone, harmonic; intonation, modulation, accent, stress, inflection, cadence, lilt. **2.** *The tone of this letter is rather unfriendly:* attitude, mood, spirit, style, manner, means of expression, note, tenor, quality, temper. **3.** *The coat is a light tone of green:* shade, tint, hue, tinge, cast, color, chroma. —*v.* **4.** *Please tone your voice down:* pitch, sound, subdue, moderate, temper, modulate, soften; shade, tint. **5.** *Exercise will tone your muscles. Some people take vitamins to tone up the system:* make firm, firm up, make supple, make more elastic.

tongue *n.* **1.** *Stick out your tongue:* organ of speech, lingua, lingula. **2.** *The stranger spoke in a foreign tongue. Fear made him lose his tongue:* language, speech, dialect, vernacular, patois, vocabulary; style of speech; power of speech. **3.** *The shoelace caught on the tongue of his shoe. The tongue of this board fits into that groove:* flap, overhanging strip. **4.** *The dock is just around that tongue of land:* point, spit, promontory. **5.** *The wagon tongue rested in the mud:* shaft, harnessing pole. —*v.* **6.** *To make a trill, tongue the whistle as you blow:* touch with the tongue, move the tongue against; lick, lap.

tonic *n.* **1.** *In the old days people took spring tonics. Fresh air is a good tonic for melancholy:* strengthening medicine, restorative, stimulant, invigorant, analeptic, bracer, refresher, pickup, pick-me-up. **2.** *The melody began and ended on the tonic:* keynote; primary note of a diatonic scale.

too *adv.* **1.** *The pie was too rich for them:* excessively, beyond, exceptionally, exorbitantly, extremely, greatly, highly, immensely, in excess, inordinately, notably, over, overly, unduly, unreasonably, very, awfully. **2.** *She asked if she could come along too:* also, as well, in addition, additionally, along, besides, further, furthermore, in addition, likewise, more, moreover, *Informal* to boot.

tool *n.* **1.** *A carpenter is only as good as his tools:* implement, handheld instrument, instrument, device, utensil, contrivance, apparatus, appliance, machine, mechanism. **2.** *A good education is a necessary tool for succeeding:* agent, means, instrumentality, medium, vehicle, intermediary, wherewithal. **3.** *The mayor is just a tool of the governor:* person used by another, instrument, pawn, puppet, dupe, hireling, stooge, cat's-paw.

tooth *n.* **1.** *The dentist filled the tooth:* hard bony part growing from the jaw; (*variously*) incisor, molar, grinder, cuspid, canine, bicuspid, wisdom tooth; fang, tusk. **2.** *Who broke a tooth off this saw?:* serration; (*variously*) point, spike,

tine, tang, spur, barb, thorn, cusp, nib, cog, sprocket.

top *n.* **1.** *Let's climb to the top of that hill. There's a scratch on the top of the table:* highest point, summit, peak, apex, vertex, pinnacle, acme, zenith, tiptop; crest, crown, brow; upper surface, upper part. **2.** *Where's the top to this bottle? The top of this box is torn:* lid, cap, cover; cork, stopper. **3.** *Kay graduated at the top of her class. Only a hard worker can reach the top:* highest rank, highest position, head, lead, first place, fore, van, front, place of honor. —*adj.* **4.** *Put the book on the top shelf. The car's top speed is 120 miles per hour:* topmost, highest, uppermost, upper; greatest, best. **5.** *The top doctors in the country will attend the meeting:* highest-ranking, foremost, best, chief, principal, paramount, eminent, preeminent, renowned, noted, notable, celebrated, famous, greatest. —*v.* **6.** *Top the strawberries with whipped cream:* put a topping on, put a top on, put over, crown, cap, cover; complete, add a finishing touch to. **7.** *This state tops the nation in per capita income. The swimmer topped the world's record by two-tenths of a second:* be at the top of, be greater than, surpass, exceed, transcend, better, best, excel, outdo, eclipse, outshine, overshadow, outstrip. —**Ant.** 1–4 bottom. 1 base, foot, lowest point; underside, underneath. 3 foot, end, tail end, last place, rear. 4 lowest, lower, least, worst. 5 inferior, second-rate, inept, incompetent; unknown, anonymous. 7 trail, be at the bottom, be less than.

topic *n.* *The speaker's topic will be "Poetry in the Modern World." That's not a fit topic for dinner-table conversation:* subject, subject matter, theme, keynote, matter at hand; text, thesis.

topical *adj.* *The book is too topical to be of interest ten years from now:* about current matters, current, contemporary; local, localized, parochial, limited, restricted, particular. —**Ant.** historical, traditional; general, universal, comprehensive, all-inclusive.

topmost *adj.* *One apple grew on the topmost branch. The dentist had reached the topmost echelon of his profession:* top, highest, uppermost; supreme, chief, head, preeminent, leading, foremost, principal, paramount.

topnotch *adj.* *This latest collection of stories has some topnotch writing in it:* first-rate, outstanding, finest, supreme, prime, choice, nonpareil, superior, incomparable, tip-top, ace, unparalleled, preeminent. —**Ant.** so-so, ordinary, run-of-the-mill, commonplace.

topple *v.* **1.** *The vase toppled and broke into smithereens:* tip over, overturn, turn over, upset, fall over; fall, tumble, pitch forward, sprawl. **2.** *The rebels have toppled the regime:* overthrow, bring down, abolish; defeat, vanquish, overcome, overpower, crush, smash, shatter, quash, quell.

topsy-turvy *adv.* **1.** *We turned the room topsy-turvy looking for the ring:* upside down, inside out, into a confused state, in a disorderly state. —*adj.* **2.** *I've never seen such a topsy-turvy of-*

fice: confused, confusing, disorderly, disarranged, disorganized, untidy, messy, chaotic; upside-down, wrong side up, inverted, reversed. —**Ant.** 1, 2 right side up. 1 straight, into a state of order. 2 orderly, well-arranged, organized, systematic, tidy, neat, trim.

torch *n.* **1.** *The campers lit torches from the campfire:* burning brand, brand, firebrand, cresset, flambeau. **2.** *The rescuers needed an acetylene torch to cut through the wreckage:* portable device for producing a hot flame; welder's torch.

torment *v.* **1.** *Pain tormented him all day long. The thief was tormented by guilt:* cause to suffer, afflict, torture, rack, distress, pain; plague, worry, trouble, annoy, agonize, persecute, harass, harrow, vex, nag, irritate, pester. —*n.* **2.** *Mosquitoes and black flies caused the hikers much torment:* suffering, agony, torture, anguish, pain, distress, misery, worry, annoyance, irritation, despair; cause of suffering, source of agony, scourge, bane, curse. —**Ant.** 1, 2 delight, comfort, ease. 1 please, make happy; soothe, mitigate, allay, alleviate, assuage. 2 pleasure, happiness, joy.

torn *adj.* *The child wore a torn shirt:* ripped, rent, split, slit, ruptured; ragged, shredded, unraveled.

torpid *adj.* *The heat and lack of sleep made everyone torpid:* slow-moving, sluggish, inactive, inert, lethargic, lazy, listless, spiritless, indolent, languid, languorous, apathetic, lackadaisical, passive, slow-thinking, dull; half asleep, sleepy, drowsy, somnolent; dormant. —**Ant.** quick-moving, active, energetic, vigorous, peppy, full of pep, animated, lively, spirited, alert, *Slang* sharp, on, bright-eyed; wide-awake.

torpor also **torpidity** *Her torpor may be due to illness:* sluggishness, slow movement, inertia, lethargy, laziness, languidness, listlessness, lassitude, indolence, languor, apathy, passiveness, dullness; sleepiness, drowsiness, somnolence; inactivity, inertia. —**Ant.** energy, vigor, vim, pep, animation, liveliness, alertness; wide-awakeness.

torrent *n.* **1.** *The drought was broken by a torrent. The torrent carried the raft far downstream:* heavy rain, downpour, deluge, cloudburst, torrential rain, cascade, waterfall, cataract, Niagara; fast-flowing stream, rapids, violent stream of water, white water, strong current. **2.** *The angry man let loose a torrent of curse words:* stream, rapid flow, outburst, outpouring, discharge, effusion, rain, deluge, flood, volley, barrage, salvo, burst, eruption, gush, rush. —**Ant.** 1 shower, sprinkle, drizzle.

torrid *adj.* **1.** *Nothing will grow in this torrid climate:* hot and dry, scorching, parching, sweltering, boiling, burning, broiling, sizzling, fiery, sultry, tropical. **2.** *The movie has a torrid love scene:* passionate, impassioned, ardent, fervent, fervid, vehement, spirited, excited, hot, hot and heavy, heated, intense; amorous, desirous, erotic, sexy, sexual, lustful. —**Ant.** 1 cold, cool, chilly; mild, gentle. 2 dispassionate, unimpassioned, spiritless; serene, moderate, mild, cool, apathetic, lethargic.

tortuous *adj.* *A tortuous trail led up the mountain. The essay was so long and tortuous I couldn't make sense of it:* winding, twisting, full of curves, circuitous, sinuous, serpentine, zigzag, meandering, crooked; labyrinthine, convoluted, complicated, involved; indirect, roundabout, devious, ambiguous, hard to follow. —**Ant.** straight, straight as an arrow, beeline, direct; straightforward, simple.

torture *v.* **1.** *The secret police tortured the captive to obtain information:* subject to severe pain, put to the rack; mistreat, maltreat, abuse. **2.** *After sentencing the man the judge was tortured by doubts:* have anxiety, torment, distress, cause anguish; rack, harrow, wring, prick, smite. —*n.* **3.** *The dungeon was full of instruments of torture:* punishment by causing pain, extorting information by subjecting to pain, cause of severe pain, brutality. **4.** *Waiting for news of the lost boy was sheer torture to his parents:* torment, agony, anguish, suffering, distress, pain, ordeal, trial, tribulation, infliction, cruelty. —**Ant.** 1 persuade, coax, cajole, wheedle, entice, flatter, charm. 2 set at ease, disburden, calm, quiet, relax; cheer, comfort, solace. 3 pleasure, enjoyment, comfort, contentment, well-being, happiness, mirth, gaiety, cheer. 4 joy, delight, ecstasy, rapture, happiness, enjoyment, gratification.

tortured *adj.* *The tortured prisoner confessed to the crime:* tormented, agonized, convulsed, crucified, excoriated, impaled, lacerated, on the rack, racked, ripped, savaged, wrung, bloodied, clawed.

torturous *adj.* *He had a torturous toothache. The losing candidate spent a torturous night listening to the election returns:* torturing, painful, agonizing, racking, cruel, anguishing, tormenting, distressing, distressful, excruciating, miserable, harrowing, anguished, tormented, distressed, annoying, irksome, unpleasant, galling, disagreeable. —**Ant.** painless, pleasant, pleasing, delightful, enjoyable, agreeable, welcome, comforting, gratifying; contented, cheerful, joyous, happy.

toss *v.* **1.** *Toss the newspaper over here. The boys tossed a ball back and forth:* throw, throw carelessly, pitch, flip, fling, sling, heave, hurl, cast, lob, let fly, propel. **2.** *The child tossed and turned in his sleep. The storm tossed the small boat at its anchor:* pitch, jerk, sway, rock, shake, agitate, roll, joggle, churn, tumble about, wiggle, wriggle, writhe, flounce, undulate, oscillate. —*n.* **3.** *Give the ball a toss:* pitch, throw, heave, fling, sling, hurl, cast, lob, flip. **4.** *She gave her head a toss and walked away:* sudden upward raise, flounce, jerk, shake, flourish. —**Ant.** 1, 3 catch, grasp. 1 seize, snatch, clutch, take; hold, keep, retain.

total *n.* **1.** *Add up the bill and tell me the total:* sum, sum total, full amount, whole amount, whole, aggregate, totality, entirety; gross. —*adj.* **2.** *The total cost was over a hundred dollars. The total population of the town was only two thousand:* entire, whole, complete, combined, full, gross, integral. **3.** *The party was a total suc-*

cess. The enemy suffered total defeat: absolute, complete, utter, perfect, thorough, unconditional, unqualified, unlimited, unmodified, undisputed, sheer, sweeping, comprehensive, downright, outright, out-and-out, *Slang* solid, wholesale. —*v.* **4.** *Total the bill and add sales tax. The year's income totals fifteen thousand dollars:* total up, tote up, add up, add, sum up, reckon, compute, calculate, figure up, figure, find the sum; add up to. —**Ant.** 1 subtotal, partial amount, part. 2, 3 partial, limited, incomplete. 2 fractional. 3 slight, meager, hollow, fragmentary; conditional, qualified, mixed, uneven, halfway; marred, defective, wanting. 4 subtract, deduct.

totalitarian *adj. Under Mussolini, Italy was a totalitarian country:* strictly controlled, undemocratic, unrepresentative, fascistic, fascist, autocratic, dictatorial, despotic, tyrannous, tyrannical. —**Ant.** anarchistic; democratic, republican, representative, popular.

totality *n. The totality was less than she thought:* total, all, sum total, grand total, everything, entirety, all and sundry, the works, the lot, *Informal* whole nine yards, whole bit, whole schmear, whole shebang, whole shooting match, whole ball of wax, kit and caboodle.

totally *adv. The story is totally false:* completely, utterly, entirely, from beginning to end, throughout, thoroughly, absolutely, unconditionally, without qualification, perfectly, downright, out-and-out, *Slang* solidly. —**Ant.** partially, in part, incompletely, slightly, somewhat, halfway, conditionally, with qualifications.

tote *v. Informal Are you going to tote that suitcase all over Europe? The sheriff always toted a gun:* carry, carry around, lug, cart, drag, pull, haul, move, fetch, convey, transport; carry on one's person, bear, pack, *Slang* schlepp.

totter *v. The old man tottered down the street. The vase tottered and fell:* walk unsteadily, shuffle, waddle, stagger, stumble, reel, lurch, falter; wobble, sway, waver, teeter, shake, rock, oscillate, vacillate.

touch *v.* **1.** *Reach out and touch the wall:* put a hand against, put a finger against, handle, finger, paw, thumb, feel, stroke, rub, manipulate, caress, fondle, pet, stroke. **2.** *The two buildings touch at this point:* be in contact, meet, join, unite, be contiguous, abut, adjoin, border, converge, come together, bring into contact. **3.** *Don't touch the money in the savings account. The vegetarian won't touch meat:* use, utilize; consume; avail oneself of, resort to, have recourse to, have to do with, be associated with, deal with. **4.** *The beggar's plea for food touched us deeply. The hero's speech touched the entire audience:* affect, move, impress, work, soften, melt, sadden; influence, sway, strike, inspire, thrill, excite, arouse, rouse, stir, fire, inflame, inspirit, electrify. **5.** *The meeting touched on the problem of higher costs:* mention, discuss briefly, deal with in passing, allude to, refer to, broach, hint at, bear upon, concern, pertain to; note, cite. **6.** *No one in the family can touch Jeanette as a cook:* compare with, equal,

match, rival, come up to, come near, keep pace with. —*n.* **7.** *He located the light switch by touch. The slightest touch will bruise the flower:* the sense of touch; feel, feeling; touching, stroke, handling, fingering, pawing, thumbing, manipulation, palpation; caress, fondling. **8.** *The baby's skin has such a soft touch:* feel, texture, fineness, surface, quality. **9.** *The salesman kept in touch with the office by phone. The old man is out of touch with today's attitudes:* communication, contact; awareness, familiarity, acquaintance, realization, understanding, comprehension, perception. **10.** *The salad had a touch of garlic:* trace, tinge, tint, bit, pinch, dash, sprinkling, soupçon, smack, taste, speck, hint, suggestion, suspicion, intimation. **11.** *This symphony shows the touch of a master:* technique, deftness, adroitness, hand, style, manner, method, skill, art, artistry, form, mastery, finesse, flair, gift, finish, polish, virtuosity; guiding hand, influence, direction. —**Ant.** 2 separate, diverge. 4 leave one unaffected, leave unmoved, leave one cold; bore. 5 ignore, disregard, overlook, pass over, skip, omit, leave out, reject, slight.

touching *adj. The hero's funeral is the most touching scene in the play:* moving, affecting, stirring; emotional, dramatic, sentimental; saddening, sad, heartfelt, heartbreaking, heartrending, distressing, pitiful, poignant, tender, pathetic, sorrowful. —**Ant.** unmoving, unaffecting, unemotional.

touchstone *n. Her singing of the role remains the touchstone for all later sopranos:* standard, yardstick, measure, criterion, gauge, model, example, guide, rule, pattern, guideline, norm, principle, proof, benchmark.

touchy *adj.* **1.** *She's touchy about her prerogatives, so be extra tactful. Why are you so touchy today?:* sensitive, easily offended, easily hurt, thinskinned, concerned, resentful, bitter; irritable, huffy, grumpy, grouchy, cross, testy, crabby, peevish, snappish, petulant, surly, quicktempered, irascible, cantankerous, querulous, captious, waspish. **2.** *Both labor and management are angry, so the negotiator is in a touchy situation:* delicate, requiring diplomacy, requiring tact, sensitive, ticklish, awkward, critical, requiring caution, precarious, difficult, fragile. —**Ant.** 1 insensitive, thickskinned, callous, hardened, inured, impervious, indifferent, unconcerned, nonchalant; sweet, good-humored, happy, pleasant, cheerful, cheery, smiling, blithe, jaunty, friendly, even-tempered, in good spirits, lighthearted, sunny. 2 noncritical, easy, easily handled, stable.

tough *adj.* **1.** *The tabletop is made of very tough plastic. What a tough steak!:* strong, durable, lasting, enduring, hardy, sturdy, firm, resistant, rugged, solid, impenetrable, infrangible, heavy-duty; leathery. **2.** *Digging a tunnel under the river will be a tough job. How to balance the government's budget without raising taxes is a tough problem:* difficult, hard, laborious, arduous, strenuous, toilsome, exhausting, onerous, formidable, exacting, troublesome, trying, grievous, irksome, hard-to-solve, baffling, bewildering, puzzling, perplexing, confusing, complicated, intricate, complex, involved, thorny, knotty, ticklish, enigmatic. **3.** *Mr. West is known as a tough teacher. The boss is a tough man to convince:* hard, stern, strict, firm, rigid, exacting, unyielding, uncompromising, inflexible, unbending; stubborn, obstinate, obdurate, perverse, adamant, hardheaded, dogged, mulish, bullheaded, pigheaded; wily, crafty, canny, cagey, calculating, cold. **4.** *The bully's tough talk frightened the other boys:* rough, vicious, bloodthirsty, ruthless, mean, cruel, brutal, savage, barbaric, inhuman, cold-blooded, heartless, hardhearted, hard, unfeeling, insensitive, unsympathetic, pitiless, callous. —**Ant. 1, 2** soft. 1 weak, delicate, frail, fragile, flimsy, brittle, frangible, susceptible; tender. 2, 3 easy. 2 simple, effortless, slight. 3 lenient, indulgent, permissive, unexacting; accommodating, amenable, acquiescent, complaisant, compliant, compromising, flexible. 4 sweet, kind, humane, benign, gentle, mild, softhearted, sympathetic, compassionate, considerate, loving, merciful.

toughen *v. Part of athletic training is toughening the body:* strengthen, harden, firm, firm up, fortify, inure, stiffen, temper, steel, discipline; accustom, acclimate, acclimatize, habituate, season. —**Ant.** weaken, exhaust, enfeeble, enervate.

toupee *n. He bought a toupee to cover his bald spot:* small wig, hairpiece, wig, periwig, peruke; *Slang* carpet, rug.

tour *n.* **1.** *The neighbors are taking a three-week tour of France and Italy:* (*variously*) circular journey, sightseeing trip, jaunt, excursion, junket, peregrination, voyage, trek, safari; itinerary. —*v.* **2.** *A group of baseball stars will tour overseas army bases. The group is touring Mexico this summer:* visit, travel around, travel through, sightsee in, vacation through, travel and perform at, travel and work at, inspect.

tourist *n. Several busloads of tourists stopped at the U.N.:* sightseer, journeyer, traveler, voyager, excursionist, globetrotter, world traveler; wayfarer, wanderer, pilgrim, vagabond; *Slang* rubberneck, *Brit.* tripper.

tournament *n. She won the last bridge tournament:* tourney, competition, match, contest, meet, meeting, test, tilt, tourney, joust.

tousled *adj. Please comb that tousled hair of yours!:* uncombed, mussed, mussed-up, disheveled, unkempt, disordered, rumpled, messy, untidy, tangled. —**Ant.** combed, combed and brushed; unmussed, well-kempt, neat, tidy.

tout *v. You can see him on television touting that new detergent:* praise, publicize, advertise, vaunt, brag about, ballyhoo, promote, celebrate, extol, exalt, glorify, acclaim, aggrandize; *Slang* plug, talk up. —**Ant.** belittle, deprecate; *Slang* slam, run down.

tow *v.* **1.** *The car had to be towed to the garage. The winch towed the log out of the way:* haul, drag, drag along, draw, pull, lug, trail; hoist, lift. —*n.* **2.** *The disabled motorboat got a tow from a*

Coast Guard cutter: act of towing, towing. —**Ant. 1, 2** push, shove.

toward *prep. He moved toward her:* towards, approaching, close to, en route, facing, headed for, moving, near, nearing, proceeding, in the direction of, against.

tower *n.* **1.** *The town water tower was next to the reservoir. The city hall had a picturesque clock tower:* tall structure; (*variously*) water tower, clock tower, bell tower, belfry, prison tower, guard tower, lookout tower; steeple, spire, turret, minaret, skyscraper, column, obelisk; castle, keep. **2.** *Throughout the centuries, Oxford has been a tower of learning. Throughout the trouble, Joe has been a tower of strength:* pillar, mainstay, bulwark, stronghold, rock, foundation, wellspring, fountainhead, refuge. —*v.* **3.** *The Empire State Building towers into the sky. Charlemagne towered above other rulers of his day:* rise high, rise above, ascend, soar, mount, shoot up, loom, surge, extend above, overhang, overtop, overshadow, eclipse; surpass, exceed, outshine, transcend, outdo, outclass, leave behind. —**Ant. 3** fall, sink, descend, drop.

towering *adj.* **1.** *The towering hills cast deep shadows on the valley:* high, tall, lofty, ascending, soaring, mounting, overhanging, alpine, cloud-swept, cloud-capped, snowclad. **2.** *Beethoven was a towering musical genius:* surpassing, supreme, transcendent, preeminent, paramount, foremost, principal, dominant, sublime, superior, extraordinary, incomparable, peerless, unexcelled, unequaled, unrivaled, unparalleled, without parallel, unmatched, matchless, second to none. —**Ant. 1** low, low-lying, short, squat, dumpy, stubby, truncated; flat, deep, submerged. 2 lowly, lesser, inferior, sorry, poor, paltry, inconsequential, insignificant; ordinary, commonplace, common, average, mediocre, run-of-the-mill, everyday.

town *n.* **1.** *The town has only one grade school:* small town, large village, small city; (*loosely*) village, hamlet, burg, settlement. **2.** *Aunt Edith has a cabin at the beach and a house in town. Chicago is my favorite town:* self-governing populated place, municipality, borough, township, parish; city, urban area, population center, metropolis, cosmopolis. **3.** *The whole town turned out to welcome the returning heroes:* townspeople, inhabitants, citizenry, residents. **4.** *The main store is in town, but there are branches in the suburbs:* main business district, business district, shopping district, downtown, city center, central city, inner city.

toxic *adj. Carbon monoxide is toxic to humans:* poisonous, venomous, poisoned, deadly, fatal, mortal, lethal; pernicious, noxious, unhealthy. —**Ant.** nontoxic, nonpoisonous, nonlethal; healthy, salubrious, refreshing, invigorating.

toxin *n. They identified the toxin in the water supply:* poison, venom, virus. —**Ant.** serum, antitoxin.

toy *n.* **1.** *The boy's favorite toy was a wind-up car. A private plane is the millionaire's latest toy:* plaything; bauble, trinket, gadget, gewgaw, gimcrack, trifle. —*adj.* **2.** *Toy trains are being re-placed by toy racing cars:* for play, for amuse-ment. **3.** *Toy poodles are among the most popular breed of dog:* miniature, diminutive, small-scale, small-sized, bantam, midget, pygmy, stunted, dwarfed; little, tiny, Lilliputian. —*v.* **4.** *The teacher had an annoying habit of toying with a pencil while he lectured. He's just toying with her affections:* play, trifle, dally, sport, fiddle, amuse oneself with. —**Ant.** 1 neces-sity; tool, instrument, utensil. 2 real, actual. 3 full-sized; oversize, giant, large, big, huge, enormous, immense, colossal, gigantic, mam-moth, gargantuan.

trace *n.* **1.** *There is no trace of the missing jewels. These statues are the only traces of a once-great civilization:* sign left behind, sign, mark, indication, evidence, relic, vestige, token, remains; trail, track, footprint. **2.** *There was a trace of sadness in her smile. It rained a trace last night:* tinge, touch, hint, suspicion, sugges-tion, shade, flavor; small amount, little bit, bit, trifle, jot, iota, drop. —*v.* **3.** *Police are trying to trace the missing man. The post office is tracing the missing package:* follow the trail of, track, track down, hunt for, hunt, nose out, ferret out, search for, look for, seek; find, discover, come across, light upon, unearth, dig up, uncover. **4.** *Please trace the location of the lot for the new owner. The book traces the history of modern art:* map, diagram, draw, outline, delineate, de-scribe, depict, mark out. **5.** *Trace the drawing on a piece of tissue paper:* copy by drawing over, draw over, follow the outline of.

track *n.* **1.** *The train will leave on track number three. The garage door is off its track again:* rail, guide rail, parallel rails; (*variously*) train track, streetcar track. **2.** *The guide followed the tracks of the elephants. Police are on the track of the criminal:* footprint, mark, sign, spoor; trail, path, scent. **3.** *The track of the ship led from San Francisco to Honolulu to Pago Pago. Try to get off on the right track in your new job:* course, path, route, trail, tack, way. **4.** *The racing cars sped around the track. The athlete excelled at both track and baseball:* racetrack, running track; sports performed on a track. —*v.* **5.** *The hunters tracked the bear to its lair. Scientists are trying to track the lost satellite:* follow the track, follow the path, trail, follow, trace. **6.** *The children tracked the newly waxed floor with muddy shoes:* leave footprints on, mark, dirty.

tract[1] *n. The plane flew over the snowy tract of the Arctic. He owns a large tract of land in Ore-gon:* stretch, expanse, region, zone, area, quar-ter, district, territory; plot, lot, parcel.

tract[2] *n.* **1.** *Young members of the sect hand out tracts on street corners:* pamphlet, leaflet, brochure, booklet, monograph. **2.** *Das Kapital is Karl Marx's famous tract analyzing the capitalist system:* treatise, essay, disquisition.

tractable *adj. A dude ranch needs tractable horses for its guests:* amenable, easy to man-age, manageable, easy to control, controllable, governable, obedient, trainable, teachable, doc-ile, tame, submissive, compliant, yielding.

—**Ant.** intractable, unmanageable, uncontrolla-ble, ungovernable, disobedient, wild, unruly, re-fractory, headstrong, willful, stubborn, obstinate.

trade *n.* **1.** *Foreign trade kept the country's economy healthy. Members of the professions used to look down on people in trade:* com-merce, buying and selling, business, mercantile business, business dealings, transactions, mer-chandising. **2.** *Bricklaying was Father's trade. Jim's a dentist by trade but does fine sculpture, too:* manual occupation, skilled occupation, skilled labor, occupational skill, manual skill, craft, hand-icraft; occupation, profession, call-ing, vocation, line of work, line, business, pur-suit, employment. **3.** *The boy made a trade of a bag of marbles for a kite:* exchange, swap. **4.** *The jewelry store caters to the elite trade:* clien-tele, customers, patrons, buyers, shoppers. —*v.* **5.** *I'd love to trade this car for a pickup truck:* exchange, swap, barter. **6.** *Germany trades with all European nations:* carry on commerce, do business, buy and sell, deal. **7.** *Do you trade at the local store or buy from the mail-order house?:* shop, be a customer, be a client, pa-tronize, buy, deal.

trademark *n. The company's trademark was famous:* trade name, brand, brand name, iden-tification, label, logo, mark, stamp, symbol, tag, initials.

trader *n. He started as a trader in used furs:* merchant, dealer, seller, businessperson, mer-chandiser, trafficker, tradesperson, salesperson, wholesaler, shopkeeper, retailer, storekeeper; *Slang* drummer, *Brit.* monger.

tradition *n.* **1.** *The concept of "fair play" is an old British tradition. Celebrating Christmas at Aunt Jean's is a family tradition:* handed-down belief, custom, habit, typical way, practice, con-vention, usage, unwritten law, order of the day. **2.** *According to tradition, the author of the* Iliad *and the* Odyssey *was a blind poet named Ho-mer:* legend, myth, folk story, tale, saga; folk-lore, lore, superstition. —**Ant.** 1 novelty, inno-vation, new wrinkle, new idea, the latest thing; law, decree, dogma. 2 true story, biography, au-tobiography; fact.

traditional *adj. Birthday cakes are a traditional part of birthday parties. The house was fur-nished with traditional furniture:* handed down from generation to generation, customary, typi-cal, conventional, usual, habitual, accustomed, fixed, inveterate, established, acknowledged; old, ancestral, historic. —**Ant.** new, modern, unusual, novel, original, innovative, unusual, unconventional.

traduce *v. He traduced his friend in an attempt to evade prison:* slander, malign, defame, libel, disparage, vilify, abuse, calumniate, deprecate, smear, backbite, sully, besmirch; *Slang* bad-mouth, run down. —**Ant.** honor, praise, extol, defend.

traffic *n.* **1.** *This highway has a lot of traffic at noon. Most of the store's traffic is from the en-trance to the dress department:* vehicular move-ment; (*variously*) cars, trucks, buses, trains, planes, ships; pedestrian movement, pedestrians. **2.** *The nine o'clock flight to Washington carries a lot of traffic:* passengers, travelers, voyagers; (*variously*) riders, tourists, vacationists, excursionists, commuters; freight. **3.** *Customs must suppress the illegal drug traffic:* transportation of goods, trade, dealings, business, enterprise, commerce, buying and selling, barter, exchange, transactions; smuggling, bootlegging. **4.** *The family has never had any traffic with criminals!:* dealings, relations, doings, contact, proceedings, intercourse. —*v.* **5.** *The bootlegger was arrested for trafficking in illegal whiskey:* trade, deal, buy and sell, carry on commerce; smuggle, bootleg.

tragedy *n.* **1.** *The boy's death was a tragedy. The widow's life was full of tragedy. The hurricane was a major tragedy to the entire Gulf Coast:* dreadful happening, sad thing, unfortunate affair, shocking misfortune, pathetic occurrence, setback, reversal, affliction; misery, anguish, sorrow, grief, woe, heartache, unhappiness, heartbreak, blow, grievous day; accident, disaster, catastrophe, calamity. **2.** *Shakespeare wrote comedies, histories, and tragedies:* play with a disastrous ending, play about the downfall of a great man or woman. —**Ant.** 1 blessing, boon, kindness, wonderful thing, good fortune; happiness, joy, pleasure, satisfaction, gratification, bliss, contentment. 2 comedy.

tragic *adj.* **1.** *The tragic accident took eight lives:* dreadful, unfortunate, appalling, heartbreaking, sad, lamentable, pathetic, piteous, pitiful, pitiable, deplorable, mournful, grievous, dreary, woeful, unhappy, dire, shocking, awful, frightful, terrible, horrible; disastrous, calamitous, catastrophic, fatal, deadly; ruinous, devastating, destructive. **2.** *The matinee idol wanted to be a tragic actor:* of dramatic tragedy; serious, dramatic. —**Ant.** 1 fortunate, happy, felicitous, pleasant, satisfying, gratifying, agreeable, joyful, worthwhile, wonderful, lucky. 2 comic.

trail *v.* **1.** *The gasoline truck trailed a chain below it to reduce static electricity. The kite's tail trailed in the air:* drag, drag along, drag behind, tow, draw; dangle, hand down, float, stream, flow. **2.** *The little boy trailed along behind his father. The team trailed by one touchdown in the last quarter:* follow, lag behind, be behind, tread on the heels of, follow in the wake of, bring up the rear; move slowly, dawdle, poke; be losing, be down. **3.** *Police trailed the thieves to their hideout:* track, trace, follow, tail, hunt, hound, dog. **4.** *Her voice trailed to a whisper:* diminish, dwindle, shrink, subside, fall, grow faint, grow weak, grow small, lessen, decrease, taper off, peter out. —*n.* **5.** *The dogs followed the trail of the fox. The FBI is on the trail of the kidnapper:* track, course, footprints, scent, spoor; sign, mark, trace, path. **6.** *Follow the trail until you come to the cabin:* path, footpath, pathway, beaten track, way; bridle path. —**Ant.** 1 push, shove. 2 lead, go before, be winning. 3 flee, run away. 4 increase, rise, swell, grow, intensify, strengthen.

train *n.* **1.** *The train is pulling into the station*

now. *The original settlers came to this region by wagon train:* railroad train; subway train, subway, elevated, el; caravan, procession, column. **2.** *What train of events led to the discovery?:* series, succession, sequence, progression, chain, line, set. **3.** *The wedding gown had a long train:* trailing part, trail, queue, appendage, continuation, afterpart. **4.** *The king is always surrounded by his train:* retinue, attendants, escort, followers, entourage, cortege. —*v.* **5.** *You should train your dog not to bark. The country needs to train five thousand doctors a year:* teach good behavior, teach a habit, discipline, domesticate, break; instruct, teach, drill, tutor, educate, school, prepare. **6.** *The boxer trained for a month before the fight:* exercise, get in shape, prepare, practice, rehearse. **7.** *The army trained its cannon on the fort:* aim, point, direct, level, sight, focus, bring to bear.

trait *n.* *Boldness and resolution are two of the traits of a good leader:* characteristic, quality, mark, distinguishing mark, hallmark, earmark, attribute, feature; peculiarity, idiosyncrasy, quirk, mannerism.

traitor *n.* *In time of war any traitor will be shot. Judas was a traitor to Christ:* one who betrays his country, one who commits treason, turncoat, renegade, serpent, snake in the grass, wolf in sheep's clothing; (*variously*) deserter, mutineer, revolutionary, rebel; betrayer, double-crosser, double-dealer, deceiver, hypocrite, false friend, Judas, apostate, quisling, fifth columnist, *Slang* rat, ratter, ratfink. —**Ant.** patriot, loyalist; defender, supporter, true friend.

tramp *v.* **1.** *We tramped for hours through the snow:* trek, hike, march, trudge, walk, traipse, slog; (*loosely*) wander, ramble, roam, rove, meander, perambulate, gallivant, peregrinate, prowl. **2.** *He tramped angrily out of the house. The children tramped on the new plants:* stamp, stomp, walk noisily, tread heavily, trample. —*n.* **3.** *There's a tramp at the back door asking for a handout:* hobo, wandering beggar, panhandler, bum, vagrant, derelict, floater, knight-of-the-road, itinerant.

trample *v.* *The cowboy was almost trampled in the stampede. Don't trample the new grass:* grind under foot, run over, crush, flatten, squash; step heavily upon, stamp, stomp.

trance *n.* *The medium went into a trance to summon the dead spirits:* spell, daze, dazed condition, half-conscious state, hypnosis, hypnotic state, sleepwalking, coma, stupor; vision, daydream, reverie, dream, pipe dream; absorption, concentration, abstraction, brown study, preoccupation, woolgathering.

tranquil *adj.* *Twilight in the forest is a very tranquil period. Mother remained tranquil despite the confusion around her:* peaceful, calm, unperturbed, serene, restful, placid, still, halcyon, quiet, unruffled, unexcited, composed, self-possessed, cool, undisturbed, mild, gentle. —**Ant.** agitated, disturbed, confused, busy, restless; excited, rattled, distracted.

tranquilize *v.* *They tranquilized the unruly animal:* soothe, calm, relax, sedate, lull, make calm, pacify, quell, quiet, still, subdue, compose. **—Ant.** upset, agitate, distress, perturb, trouble.

tranquillity n. After the hubbub of the city, the tranquillity of the country was heavenly: peace, calm, quiet, serenity, peacefulness, repose, hush, placidity, stillness, restfulness, quietude, harmony, concord, composure. **—Ant.** uproar, tumult, commotion, disorder.

transact v. He transacts most of his business by phone: carry on, carry out, carry through, conduct, exact, perform, do, exercise, execute, handle, accomplish, manage, discharge, achieve, settle, take care of.

transaction n. Investors made millions on that real estate transaction: business dealing, dealing, deal, bargain, piece of business, venture, enterprise, affair, operation, exchange, settlement, negotiation.

transcend v. **1.** That bizarre tale of men from Mars transcends belief: exceed, go beyond, rise above, outdo, surmount, surpass, overstep, overleap. **2.** Cleopatra's beauty transcended all others': surpass, be greater than, be superior to, exceed, excel, outdo, outstrip, overshadow, outshine, eclipse, outrival, outdistance, outrank.

transcendent adj. Transcendent forces made themselves felt during the storm: transcending, boundless, consummate, exceeding, ideal, incomparable, matchless, peerless, perfect, supreme, surpassing, unequalled, unique, unrivalled, absolute.

transcendental adj. **1.** The mystic was concerned with transcendental realities: metaphysical, transcending experience, spiritual, mental, intuitive. **2.** The world agrees on the transcendental beauty of a Beethoven symphony: extraordinary, unusual, uncommon, superior, unrivaled, peerless, matchless, incomparable, unequaled, unsurpassed, supreme, great, exceeding, surpassing, elevated. **—Ant.** 1 physical, empirical. 2 ordinary, common, commonplace, usual, average; inferior, little.

transcribe v. The court recorder transcribed the testimony: record, copy out, render, reprint, reproduce, rewrite, take down, write out, note.

transfer v. **1.** Let's transfer these files to the new cabinets. He transferred the ownership of the house to his wife: move, remove, shift, relocate, change, convey, carry, bring, send, transport, transmit; consign, turn over, hand over, relegate, make over, deed, cede. **—n. 2.** The transfer of the ship's cargo onto the pier was halted by a severe storm: transferring, transferal, transference, moving, removal, shifting, shift, relocation, relocating, conveying, carrying, bringing, sending, transportation, transporting, transmittal, shipment; consignment, delivering, relegation, deeding. **—Ant.** 1 keep, retain; leave. 2 keeping, retention.

transfix v. **1.** The spear fisherman transfixed the bass with his first shot: impale, skewer, spear, run through, fix fast, pin, stick, stab, spike, pierce, penetrate. **2.** The magician transfixed the children with his fire-eating act: rivet the attention of, rivet, hold rapt, engross, hold,

absorb, fascinate, spellbind, mesmerize, hypnotize, bewitch, captivate, intrigue, enchant; stun, astound, astonish; terrify.

transform v. The caterpillar was transformed into a butterfly. The new owners transformed the old house into a showplace: change, turn, convert, transfigure, transmute, alter, make over, transmogrify, metamorphose; remodel, reconstruct, remold, recast, refurbish.

transgress v. **1.** They transgressed every regulation: violate, break, contravene, disobey, infringe. **2.** He transgressed, then confessed all: offend, sin, err, trespass. **—Ant.** obey.

transgression n. The sinner prayed that his transgressions would be forgiven. Eavesdropping is a transgression on another's privacy: offense, sin, misdeed, evil deed, trespass, lapse, iniquity, wrongdoing, wrong, immorality, error; infraction, infringement, breach, encroachment, contravention, overstepping; violation, infraction, crime, lawbreaking. **—Ant.** virtue, morality, probity, righteousness, grace, good deed, merit; observance, compliance, adherence.

transgressor n. The preacher warned all transgressors to repent. Transgressors will be fined $1000 or sentenced to 30 days in jail: sinner, evildoer, trespasser, offender; lawbreaker, violator, wrongdoer, culprit, malefactor, miscreant, felon, criminal. **—Ant.** innocent, exemplar; law-abider.

transient adj. **1.** Youthful beauty is transient: temporary, transitory, fleeting, brief, momentary, ephemeral, evanescent, impermanent, unenduring, not lasting, perishable, short-lived, temporal, soon past, passing, here today and gone tomorrow. **2.** New Orleans is filled with transient visitors during Mardi Gras: temporary, staying a short time, short-term, passing through. **—Ant.** 1, 2 permanent. 1 lasting, long-lasting, undying, unfading, imperishable, perpetual, persistent, durable, abiding.

transit n. Rapid transit has been extended to the city's suburbs: transportation, transport, travel, motion, movement, passage, transfer, transference, conveyance.

transition n. The transition from farm life to city life is often difficult: change, changeover, alteration, passing, passage, shifting, jump, leap, conversion, variation, transformation, transmutation; progression, gradation, graduation.

transitory adj. His first love was a transitory summer romance that ended when school began: temporary, transient, fleeting, brief, shortlived, passing, impermanent, fugitive, not lasting, unenduring, evanescent, ephemeral, here today and gone tomorrow. **—Ant.** long, longlived, lasting, persistent, durable, enduring, permanent, undying, imperishable, abiding, everlasting, perpetual, eternal.

translate v. **1.** Chinese is a difficult language to translate into English: render, convert; decode, decipher. **2.** It's time you translate your beliefs into actions!: change, turn, transform, apply, convert, transmute; recast, alter. **3.** Please translate the medical diagnosis into terms I can understand: explain, interpret, simplify, elucidate, clarify, make clear, spell out; paraphrase, rephrase, reword, express differently.

translation *n. She was skilled at translation to and from several languages:* paraphrase, version, interpretation, rendering, treatment.

translucent *adj. Stained-glass windows are translucent enough to admit some light:* semitransparent, semiopaque, pellucid, translucid. —**Ant.** opaque.

transmission *n.* **1.** *The FBI arrived in time to prevent the transmission of the secret documents:* transmitting, transfer, transferring, transference, passage, passing, handing over, changing of hands, transmittal, transmittance, sending, conveyance, dispatch, forwarding, transportation, delivery, remittance. **2.** *The transmission contained news of the enemy's retreat:* message, dispatch, communication, delivery, note, broadcast.

transmit *v.* **1.** *A telegram will be the quickest way to transmit the message. Certain mosquitoes transmit malaria:* send, convey, deliver, relay, transfer, dispatch, issue, forward, ship, remit, pass on, carry, spread, disseminate, communicate. **2.** *The station transmits from 6 A.M. until midnight:* broadcast, televise, send, relay a signal.

transparent *adj.* **1.** *The water was so transparent we could see the fish clearly:* clear, crystal-clear, lucid, limpid, pellucid, glassy. **2.** *Those transparent curtains will never keep the light out:* see-through, thin, sheer, gauzy, translucent, diaphanous, *Informal* peekaboo. **3.** *Her reason for leaving was transparent:* evident, self-evident, plain, obvious, apparent, perceptible, palpable, manifest, visible, patent, explicit, distinct, clear-cut, unmistakable, unambiguous, unequivocal. —**Ant.** 1, 2 opaque. 1 muddy, roiled, murky. 2 thick. 3 imperceptible, unapparent, hidden, concealed, unrevealed, invisible, undetectable; indistinct, confused, vague, mysterious, mystifying.

transpire *v.* **1.** *After a few days, it transpired that the accident had been more serious than at first supposed:* become known, be discovered, be revealed, be disclosed, come to light, come out, make public, become public knowledge, get abroad, show its face, leak out. **2.** *Informal Be sure to tell us what transpires:* occur, happen, come to pass, evolve, take place, eventuate, be met with; befall, arise, present itself, chance, appear, turn up, crop up.

transplant *v. The crack medical team successfully transplanted the new heart:* graft, relocate, displace, reorient, shift, transfer; resettle, emigrate, uproot.

transport *v.* **1.** *It took all day to transport the furniture to the new apartment:* transfer, move, remove, convey, carry, transmit, take, bring, send, deliver, dispatch, fetch, bear, cart, tote, lug; ship, truck, freight. **2.** *The beautiful music transported the audience:* carry away, move, thrill, enrapture, enchant, lift, enthrall, entrance, overpower, make ecstatic, electrify, captivate, delight, charm, bewitch, *Slang* send. —*n.* **3.** *The transport of explosives is a dangerous business:*

transporting, transportation, shipment, shipping, conveying, conveyance, moving, transfer, removal, carrying, sending, delivery, dispatch, bearing, carting, trucking. **4.** *The transport took off with its cargo at midnight:* vehicle, conveyance; (*variously*) ship, freighter, cargo ship, train, freight train, airplane, cargo plane, truck, bus.

transportation *n. The price of the tour includes transportation to and from all airports:* conveyance, transference, transferal, transport, shipment, transmission, delivery, dispatch, removal, movement, haulage, cartage, portage, transit, transmittance.

trap *n.* **1.** *The wolf was caught in a trap:* (*variously*) snare, springe, net, pit, pitfall. **2.** *Promising a fortune for nothing was just one of the con man's traps:* ruse, trick, artifice, stratagem, wile, feint, ploy, device, machination, maneuver; ambush, booby trap. —*v.* **3.** *Some yellow cheese helped us trap the mouse:* entrap, catch, snare, ensnare, enmesh, hunt down, lure, entangle. **4.** *The engineers tried to trap the gas in the pipes but some escaped:* seal, stop, lock in, hold back, compartmentalize.

trappings *n. pl. The trappings of a king include his robe, crown, and scepter. The house was filled with the trappings for a party:* dress, garb, costume, raiment, attire, clothing, clothes, apparel, vesture, investment, outfit, habiliment; gear, accoutrements, paraphernalia, trimmings, effects, array, things, fittings, ornaments, adornments, decorations, embellishments, adjuncts.

trash *n.* **1.** *Gather up the leaves and put them with the rest of the trash:* litter, rubbish, junk, rubble, refuse, garbage, waste matter, residue, sweepings, dregs, leavings, dross, debris; worthless stuff, odds and ends, castoffs. **2.** *Don't waste your time reading that trash!:* worthless writing, worthless talk, junk, drivel, rot, hogwash, balderdash, twaddle; *Slang* tripe, crap, poppycock; nonsense, foolishness. **3.** *Informal Her son runs around with that trash down at the poolroom:* disreputable persons, bums, unsavory element, shady types, scum, riffraff, good-for-nothings, tramps, ne'er-do-wells, idlers, loafers. —**Ant.** 1 valuables, treasure. 3 elite, worthies.

trauma *n. She wished to avoid the trauma of separation:* traumatization, ordeal, distress, wound, blow, hurt, injury, pain, shock, strain, stress, suffering, torture, upset, agony, anguish.

traumatic *adj. The battle was traumatic for everyone involved:* shocking, wrenching, upsetting, painful, stunning, devastating, excruciating, injurious, harmful.

travail *n.* **1.** *The pioneer's life was full of hardship and travail:* toil, drudgery, hard work, backbreaking work, burdensome work, exertion. **2.** *The travails of war left the country limp:* anguish, suffering, strain, stress, hardship, worry, distress, pain. **3.** *She underwent only a brief and painless travail with her second child:* labor, labor pains, birth pains; childbirth, delivery, parturition, accouchement. —**Ant.** 1 ease, relaxation, rest, loafing. 2 comfort, pleasure.

travel v. **1.** *Try to make the ball travel in a straight line:* move, proceed, progress, go, wend, press onward. **2.** *We traveled to Greece and Turkey last summer. Don't worry, the driver has traveled this road many times:* take a trip, journey, tour, sightsee, visit; pass over, traverse, cross, be on, pass through; roam, rove, wander, junket, trek, globetrot, range; (*variously*) voyage, cruise, sail, drive, hitchhike. **—Ant.** 2 stay, remain, settle, remain stationary.

traveler n. **1.** *The airport was filled with summer travelers:* one who travels; (*variously*) tourist, journeyer, vacationer, wayfarer, voyager, excursionist, tripper, trekker, sightseer, globetrotter, wanderer, itinerant, rover, vagabond, nomad, migrant, gypsy, pilgrim. **2.** *How many travelers does your sales manager oversee?:* traveling salesperson, commercial traveler; representative, drummer.

traverse v. **1.** *The hikers had to traverse the shaky bridge one at a time:* cross, go across, move over, move along, travel over, travel, cut across; move through, negotiate, pass through. **2.** *The superhighway traverses the business district:* cross, cross over, span, reach across, go across, extend over, reach over, overpass, bridge, intersect, run through.

travesty n. **1.** *The comedian's travesty of a senator making a speech was riotously funny:* ludicrous imitation, burlesque, spoof, takeoff, parody, caricature, lampoon, mockery, broad satire, farce. **2.** *The entire courtroom trial was a travesty of justice:* mockery, perversion, shameful imitation, shameful example, misrepresentation, distortion, sham, disgrace.

treacherous adj. **1.** *Brutus proved to be a treacherous friend to Caesar:* traitorous, treasonous, untrustworthy, faithless, falsehearted, unfaithful, disloyal, untrue, deceitful, deceptive, false, perfidious, tricky, misleading, devious, twofaced. **2.** *A freezing rain made the road treacherous:* dangerous, hazardous, unsafe, perilous, precarious, risky. **—Ant.** 1 loyal, true, true-blue, faithful, trusty, trustworthy, dependable, reliable. 2 safe, reliable.

treachery n. *The boss considers the buying of a rival product treachery to the firm:* disloyalty, treason, betrayal, faithlessness, untrustworthiness, falseness, deceit, deceitfulness, deception, perfidy, violation of faith, breach of faith, underhandedness, duplicity, trickery, guile, doubledealing, double cross, infidelity, apostasy.

tread v. **1.** *Tread softly on the stairs so as not to wake the baby. Many religious pilgrims have trod this same street to the shrine:* walk, walk along, walk on, step, step on, trudge along, tramp, hike, stroll; roam, rove, range, prowl. **2.** *The boys trod on the newly planted flowers:* trample, stomp, stamp, crush under foot. **—n.** **3.** *We heard father's tread on the steps:* step, sound of footsteps, footstep, footfall; walk; manner of walking, gait, pace, stride.

treason n. *In time of war, treason is a crime punishable by death:* betrayal of one's country, aiding an enemy, sedition, subversion, conspiracy, rebellion, revolt, revolution, insurgence, in-surrection, mutiny; disloyalty, treachery, perfidy, duplicity, apostasy. **—Ant.** loyalty, allegiance, patriotism; faithfulness, fidelity.

treasure n. **1.** *The divers discovered the pirate's treasure in the sunken ship:* stored wealth, riches, hoard, store, deposit, *Slang* gold mine; (*variously*) precious gems, jewels, gold, silver. **2.** *That new secretary is a real treasure:* gem, jewel, paragon, pride and joy, apple of one's eye, pearl of great price. **—v. 3.** *The boy treasured the teacher's good opinion above all else:* value, cherish, revere, esteem, prize, hold dear, count precious, regard, dote upon, care greatly for, bank upon. **—Ant.** 3 disclaim, scorn, disregard, hold for naught, take lightly.

treasurer n. *The club's treasurer collects the membership dues:* controller, auditor, bursar, cash-keeper, purser; secretary of the treasury, minister of finance, *Brit.* Chancellor of the Exchequer; teller, cashier; financier, banker, financial officer; bookkeeper, accountant.

treasury n. **1.** *How much money is in the company's treasury?:* place where funds are kept, exchequer, repository, depository, storehouse, bank; vault, till, coffer, safe, strongbox, money box. **2.** *The club treasury was $500:* amount on hand, purse, funds, bank account. **3.** *Does the library have a treasury of the poems of Robert Frost?:* collection, anthology, compendium, compilation, thesaurus.

treat v. **1.** *Her parents still treat her like a child:* act toward, behave toward, deal with, relate to, consider, look upon; manage, handle. **2.** *You'll need a doctor to treat that wound:* try to cure, try to heal, doctor, attend, minister to, prescribe for, remedy, medicate, patch up. **3.** *The book treats the problems of economic development:* discuss, have as a subject matter, write about, expatiate on, address oneself to, speak about. **4.** *The wood was treated with a termite repellent:* apply, cover, coat, imbue, impregnate. **5.** *Father treated everyone to dinner at a restaurant:* entertain as a guest, take out, give, *Slang* stand, blow, spring; favor, grant; divert. **—n. 6.** *After days of camping, a hot shower is a real treat:* pleasure, satisfaction, gratification, comfort, delight, joy, thrill. **7.** *On Halloween the children go from house to house asking for treats. Taking everyone to the movie is my treat:* small gift of food, small gift; favor, grant; entertainment paid for by another.

treatise n. *The doctor wrote a treatise on alcoholism:* systematic work, detailed article, discourse, essay, thesis, dissertation, study, monograph, exhaustive paper, extensive piece, tract, tractate, manual, report, memoir, textbook, text.

treatment n. **1.** *All visitors should receive courteous treatment. The mayor's sensitive treatment of the problem satisfied both sides in the dispute:* manner of dealing, handling, management, treating, manipulation, operation, conduct, approach, process, procedure, way, course. **2.** *The doctors decided upon a nonsurgical treatment of the tumor:* medical care, cure, remedy, therapy, doctoring; regimen; application, medication, antidote.

treaty *n. The warring nations will soon sign a peace treaty:* international agreement, formal agreement, accord, bargain, deal, pact, compact, covenant, concordat, entente, understanding.

trek *n.* **1.** *Join us for a trek through the woods:* trip, journey; tramp, hike, outing, march; jaunt, junket, voyage, sail, excursion, odyssey, expedition, peregrination, pilgrimage; passage, migration. —*v.* **2.** *We trekked through the stores looking for a gift for mother:* tramp, hike, rove, roam, march, trudge, range, wander, plod, *Slang* slog; travel, traverse, journey, peregrinate.

tremble *v. His hands were trembling from the cold. The girl's voice trembled and she started to cry:* shake, quiver, shiver, shudder, quake, quail, quaver, waver, flutter, pulsate, palpitate.

tremendous *adj.* **1.** *Tremendous redwood trees loom over the highway. Building the bridge was a tremendous undertaking:* huge, gigantic, immense, colossal, enormous, extremely large, great, mammoth, giant, monstrous, gargantuan, elephantine, titanic, vast, towering, *Slang* humongous; formidable, awesome, major, considerable, sizable; important, consequential. **2.** *Informal France is known for its tremendous restaurants:* wonderful, excellent, exceptional, unusual, uncommon, extraordinary, marvelous, fantastic, incredible, amazing, first-rate, noteworthy, great, fabulous, fine, terrific, stupendous. —**Ant.** 1 small, little, tiny, diminutive, wee, undersized, miniature, dwarfed, stunted, pygmy; easy, simple, minor, unimportant. 2 ordinary, fair, average, mediocre, unexceptional, unremarkable, run-of-the-mill; bad, poor, awful, terrible, lousy, second-rate.

tremor *n. The tremor in his hands was the only indication of his nervousness. A slight earth tremor was felt in California today:* shaking, shake, trembling, tremble, quiver, quivering, shiver, shivering, shudder, waver, flutter, quavering, pulsation, throb, spasm, paroxysm, convulsion, palpitation, vibration; quake, jolt, shock, jar. —**Ant.** steadiness.

tremulous *adj.* **1.** *After a tremulous start the singer settled down and gave a solid rendition:* hesitant, faltering, timid, irresolute, uncertain, fearful, wavering; jittery, wobbly, shaky, nervous, trembling, jumpy, quivering, quaking; panicky, panic-stricken. **2.** *The actress was often praised for her tremulous quality:* excited, aflutter, keyed-up, atremble, worked-up, aquiver, restless, stimulated, agitated, impatient, on tenterhooks. —**Ant.** calm, collected, composed, relaxed, cool, unperturbed.

trenchant *adj.* **1.** *The defense presented its case to the jury in a trenchant manner:* clearcut, incisive, keen, penetrating, distinct, well-defined, probing, crisp, concise, razor-sharp. **2.** *Hamlet shows his true feelings in some trenchant asides:* caustic, bitter, sarcastic, tart, acid, acrimonious, mordant, acerbic, scathing, scorching. —**Ant.** 1 vague, rambling, disorganized. 2 flattering, kind, soothing, complimentary.

trend *n. Today's trend is toward less formal clothing:* fashion, mode, style; drift, direction, movement, flow, bent, tendency, leaning, inclination, propensity, proclivity, impulse.

trendy *adj. He's conservative about clothing and shuns anything considered trendy:* stylish, fashionable, faddish, modish, voguish, current, popular, swank, tony, all the rage; *Slang* in, with-it; up-to-the-minute. —**Ant.** classic, dated, old-fashioned, passé, outmoded, *Slang* old hat.

trepidation *n. It's natural to have some trepidation before undergoing surgery:* apprehension, disquiet, uneasiness, anxiety, dread, alarm, panic, jitters, fear, consternation, worry, disquietude, nervousness, jitteriness, *Informal* cold feet, butterflies. —**Ant.** confidence, sureness, fearlessness, quietude, steadiness, poise, composure, calm, cool.

trespass *v.* **1.** *The farmer threatened to shoot anyone who trespassed on his property:* enter unlawfully, intrude, infringe, invade, encroach, impinge. —*n.* **2.** *The fishing boat was seized for its trespass into restricted waters:* wrongful entry, unlawful entry, encroachment, intrusion, infringement, invasion. **3.** *Forgive us our trespasses:* sin, wrongdoing, evildoing, immorality, iniquity, transgression, error, misdeed, violation, wrong, offense; misconduct, misbehavior, infraction, overstepping, delinquency. —**Ant.** 3 good deed, virtue.

trial *n.* **1.** *The trial ended in acquittal for the defendants:* court case, litigation, judicial contest, hearing. **2.** *The trial of the new plane was delayed by bad weather. The recipe didn't turn out well the first time, but I'll give it another trial:* test, testing, test run, tryout, trying, putting to the proof; try, attempt, essay, venture, go, shot, endeavor, effort, *Informal* flyer, whirl. **3.** *The poor man's life was full of trials and tribulations:* hardship, misfortune, trouble, distress, affliction, woe, misery, pain, adversity, burden, ordeal, vexation, suffering, wretchedness, agony, anguish, torment, care, worry, heartache, misadventure, accident, bad luck, cross to bear. —**Ant.** 3 ease, comfort, happiness, joy, delight, good fortune, good luck.

tribe *n. The tribe kept up its traditions:* ilk, people, clan, caste, class, dynasty, family, kin, lineage, race, stock, blood.

tribulation *n. Too many tribulations have left him a beaten man:* affliction, trouble, ordeal, suffering, wretchedness, misfortune, worry, care, hardship, heartache, agony, anguish, torment, pain, adversity, trial; woe, misery, distress, grief, vexation, sorrow, unhappiness; ill fortune, bad luck. —**Ant.** happiness, joy, delight, ease, comfort; good fortune, good luck.

tribunal *n. The case was tried before the highest tribunal in the land:* court, bar, bench, forum, seat of judgment, authority, judiciary, judges, ruling body; judge's bench, judge's chair.

tributary *adj.* **1.** *A tributary stream meandered south:* side, secondary, accessory, branch, satellite, subordinate, feeding, dependent, accessory. —*n.* **2.** *They took their canoe down a tributary:*

branch, fork, feeder, *Canadian* snye, *Australian* billabong.

tribute *n.* **1.** *We must give tribute to all those who helped make this a free country. The musician gave full tribute to his old teacher:* honor, respect, esteem, gratitude, acknowledgment, recognition; praise, compliment, accolade, kudos, commendation, laudation, eulogy, panegyric, extolling, encomium; testimonial, memorial. **2.** *The pirates demanded tribute from the captured island:* payment, settlement, ransom, bribe, peace offering, levy, excise, impost, assessment, tax, duty, toll, consideration, payoff, blood money, pound of flesh. **—Ant.** 1 dishonor, disrespect, ingratitude, disdain, scorn; blame, insult, condemnation, slur, slap in the face.

trice *n.* *The waiter said he would be back in a trice with our coffee:* instant, second, minute, moment, split second, shake, wink, flash, blink, twinkling, jiffy, *French* coup d'oeil; *Slang* jiff, sec.

trick *n.* **1.** *Pretending to be hurt is a trick many prizefighters use:* ruse, device, deception, deceit, stratagem, machination, artifice, wile, feint, blind, maneuver, ploy, gimmick, resort, hoax; underhanded act, chicanery, sophistry, trap, fraud, imposture, subterfuge, contrivance, dodge, hocus-pocus. **2.** *Telling someone his shoe is untied is an old April Fool's trick:* prank, joke, gag, antic, bluff, put-on, practical joke, caper. **3.** *Can the dog do tricks? Here's a new trick the magician did:* clever act, skilled act, stunt, feat, antic, number; magic demonstration, sleight of hand, prestidigitation, piece of legerdemain. **4.** *There's a trick to making good coffee:* knack, art, know-how, skill, deftness, gift, dexterity, adroitness, technique, secret. **—v. 5.** *Dad tricked Mother into believing he had forgotten her birthday—then surprised her:* deceive, take in, trap, hoax, gull, dupe, bait, outmaneuver, hoodwink, mislead, have, outwit, bamboozle, outfox, bluff; cheat, swindle, manipulate, flimflam. **—Ant.** 1 honesty, truth, sincerity, candor, frankness, openness, straightforwardness, guilelessness. 4 luck.

trickery *n.* *The con man obtained that money by trickery, not work:* deceitfulness, deceit, guile, chicanery, charlatanism, duplicity, deviousness, skullduggery, stratagem, wiliness, craftiness, artfulness, slipperiness, quackery, rascality, pretense, hocus-pocus, imposture, crookedness, deception, bunkum, flimflam, artifice, shiftiness. **—Ant.** honesty, straightforwardness, artlessness, candidness, candor, frankness, openness, truth, uprightness.

trickle *v.* **1.** *Blood trickled from the wound. The audience trickled back into the auditorium:* drip, dribble, seep, leak, exude, ooze, percolate; move slowly, pass bit by bit, go gradually. **—n. 2.** *Only a trickle of water came out of the pipe:* dribble, drip, seepage, slow stream; little bit, small amount, small quantity. **—Ant.** 1 splash, gush, stream, course, pour, spurt, surge. 2 stream, gush, flood, cascade, surge, spurt; lot, lots, much, many.

tricky *adj.* **1.** *Be careful of your opponent, he's*

pretty tricky: crafty, sly, cunning, foxy, slippery, wily, rascally, artful, deceptive, underhanded, shifty, devious. **2.** *The old car is tricky to start. Working out a compromise between the two sides will be tricky:* difficult, complicated, hard to handle, touch-and-go, temperamental. **3.** *Be careful crossing that tricky bridge:* unreliable, unstable, undependable, unpredictable, hazardous, unsafe, dangerous, risky. **—Ant.** 1 candid, straightforward, open, frank, artless, ingenuous, guileless, honest, truthful. 2 simple, easy. 3 reliable, dependable, stable.

tried *adj.* *Tried methods proved the best:* tested, demonstrated, dependable, faithful, proved, reliable, secure, staunch, steadfast, trustworthy, trusty, certified.

trifle *n.* **1.** *The lost ring was only a trifle. Don't cry over trifles:* trinket, bauble, gimcrack, knickknack, bagatelle, gewgaw, plaything, toy; triviality, thing of no importance, small matter, unimportant matter, nothing. **2.** *I'll have just a trifle of the dessert:* small quantity, little, morsel, bit, mite, dash, dab, drop, nip, pinch, speck, scrap, sliver, crumb, fragment, trace, iota, jot, modicum, sprinkling, tinge, touch. **—v. 3.** *He's just trifling with her affections:* treat lightly, deal lightly, amuse oneself, toy, play. **4.** *We trifled too long at the fair:* dally, dawdle, linger, idle, dillydally, pass the time of day, kill time, waste time. **—Ant.** 2 lot, lots, gobs, oodles.

trifling *adj.* *The owner offered but a trifling reward for the return of the lost dog:* insignificant, unimportant, inconsequential, trivial, negligible, small, slight, petty, puny, piddling, nugatory, picayune, inconsiderable, niggling, nominal, token, inappreciable, beneath notice, not worthy of mention, worthless, paltry, sorry, beggarly. **—Ant.** important, significant, consequential, major, worthwhile, considerable, appreciable, large.

trigger *v.* *The burglars triggered an alarm:* start, activate, bring about, cause, generate, produce, prompt, provoke, set off, spark, activate.

trill *n.* *A trill at the song's end was especially effective:* vibrato, flutter, quaver, tremolo.

trim *v.* **1.** *Be sure to trim the rosebushes:* prune, clip, crop, pare, lop, shave, shear, cut. **2.** *The seamstress trimmed the dress with red stitching:* decorate, ornament, adorn, deck, bedeck, array, garnish, embellish, furbish, trick out, beautify, bedizen, embroider. **3.** *The loaders trimmed the load of the truck so it wouldn't be top-heavy. The crew trimmed the sails of the ship to achieve greater speed:* balance, distribute, arrange, adjust, equalize; change, shift, adjust to the direction of the wind. **—n. 4.** *Your vacation seems to have put you in fine trim:* shape, condition, fitness, state, form, fettle, kilter. **5.** *The lace trim on the bride's dress is over a hundred years old:* trimming, adornment, embellishment, decoration, garnish, ornamentation, border, piping. **6.** *His sideburns need a trim:* trimming, cutting, evening-off, clipping, shearing, cropping, pruning, paring. **—adj. 7.** *Eat less to achieve a trim figure:* lean, slim, sleek, slender, svelte, shapely, streamlined, willowy, well-proportioned, thin, lissome, shipshape, compact; fit, limber, supple, lithe, athletic.

trinket *n. We bought a few trinkets for the children as souvenirs:* trifle, bauble, charm, small ornament, bijou, bit of jewelry, bagatelle, gewgaw, gimcrack, knickknack, odds and ends, notion, toy, plaything.

trio *n. The trio for strings had several encores:* three, threesome, trey, triad, trilogy, trinity, triple, triplet, triplicate, triptych, triumvirate, triune, troika.

trip *n.* **1.** *The trip was canceled because of the snowstorm:* journey, voyage, excursion, outing, tour, jaunt, cruise, pilgrimage, expedition, foray, junket, trek, safari; commute. —*v.* **2.** *The boy tripped over a roller skate and broke his arm:* stumble, fall over, miss one's footing, misstep, slip, cause to fall, throw off balance, lose one's balance, upset. **3.** *The little girl can read easy words but trips on the hard ones. The hard math problem tripped up most of the students:* make a mistake, err, blunder, slip up, bungle, flounder, fluff, flub, muff; cause to make a mistake, cause to err, throw off, disconcert, confuse, fool, catch, catch off guard, outdo, hoodwink, outfox. **4.** *She tripped down the stairs like a fairy princess:* skip, step lightly, tread gracefully, flounce, caper, prance, dance, gambol, bob, scamper, frolic. **5.** *The machine won't operate unless someone trips this lever:* release, undo, pull, flip, throw, activate, set off.

trite *adj. The critics denounced the play for its trite plot:* banal, stale, hackneyed, pedestrian, worn-out, shopworn, stereotyped, clichéd, bromidic, overdone, commonplace, routine, run-of-the-mill, platitudinous, oft-repeated, threadbare, everyday, common, humdrum, ordinary; silly, frivolous, shallow, unimportant. —**Ant.** original, fresh, unusual, new, novel, exciting.

triumph *n.* **1.** *Helen Keller's triumph over deafness, blindness, and muteness was a miracle. The new opera is a complete triumph:* victory, win, success, conquest, mastery, ascendancy, superiority, accomplishment, attainment, achievement, *Informal* hit, smash hit, smash, coup. —*v.* **2.** *The Allies triumphed over the Axis powers in World War II. Justice triumphs in the end:* be victorious, succeed, be successful, win, prevail, come out on top, get the better of, best, subdue, conquer, overwhelm, vanquish, overcome, surpass, gain the day, take the prize, have the best of it. —**Ant.** 1 defeat, loss; failure. 2 lose; fail; succumb.

triumphal *adj. Winning a gold medal in the Olympics was the triumphal moment in the athlete's career. The heroes were given a triumphal procession:* victorious, successful, ascendant, fulfilling, rewarding, gratifying; joyous, exultant; spectacular, proud, marking a triumph, triumphant.

triumphant *adj.* **1.** *The triumphant team celebrated its victory:* victorious, winning, successful, conquering, trophy-winning, prizewinning, laurel-wreathed, first-place. **2.** *The triumphant fans*

poured into the stadium: rejoicing, celebrating, exultant, jubilant, elated, joyful. —**Ant.** 1 defeated, beaten, unsuccessful. 2 despairing, disappointed.

trivia *n. She could retain vast amounts of trivia:* trifles, trivialities, niceties, details, fine points, minutiae, *Informal* peanuts, small potatoes.

trivial *adj. Don't let such trivial things upset you:* trifling, unimportant, inconsequential, petty, slight, piddling, paltry, picayune, insignificant, meaningless, unessential, flimsy, nugatory, inconsiderable, small, little, slim, meager, puny, niggling, beggarly, worthless, idle, foolish, inappreciable, of little value, incidental; *Slang* rinkydink, two-bit; everyday, ordinary, common, commonplace, pedestrian, trite, banal. —**Ant.** weighty, important, consequential, significant, essential, worthwhile, momentous, material, considerable, large, appreciable, substantial; unusual, extraordinary, uncommon, exceptional.

troop *n.* **1.** *A troop of Boy Scouts was camping by the river. A troop of shoppers descended on the store looking for bargains:* band, unit, company; throng, horde, drove, crowd, swarm, herd, flock, gathering, assemblage, aggregate, congregation, collection, crush, press, army, bunch, gang. **2. troops** *The nation must keep its troops on alert:* soldiers, soldiery, army, armed force, military force, infantry, fighting men, militia; cavalry, cavalry unit; uniformed men, police force, troopers. —*v.* **3.** *The children trooped into the yard in single file:* march, file, parade; walk briskly, stride, step, trudge, tramp.

trophy *n. The winning golfer received $10,000 and a silver trophy. The stuffed lion head was a trophy of an African hunt:* (*variously*) loving cup, award, medal, blue ribbon, prize, citation, honor, kudos, wreath, laurels, palm; testimonial, souvenir, relic, memento; spoil, booty.

tropical *adj. Bananas grow best in tropical climates:* in the tropics, of the tropics; hot and humid, torrid, sultry, stifling, sweltering, muggy. —**Ant.** arctic; cold, wintry, icy, frosty, frigid, chilly, cool.

trot *v. The horse trotted for a while, then went into a canter:* go at a gait between a walk and a gallop; jog, go briskly, walk smartly, step quickly. —**Ant.** gallop, run; plod, creep, crawl.

trouble *v.* **1.** *The student's failing grades troubled his parents deeply. May I trouble you for a drink of water?:* distress, worry, upset, dismay, grieve, disquiet, make uneasy, agitate, perturb, concern, discompose, disconcert, unsettle, oppress, torment, plague, harry, depress; bother, disturb, inconvenience, annoy, pester, badger, harass, discommode, put out. **2.** *Didn't you trouble to read the directions?:* exert oneself, take time, make the effort, attempt, think, attend, heed. **3.** *Grandmother's arthritis is troubling her again:* bother, afflict, affect, pain, annoy, vex, plague. —*n.* **4.** *Did you have much trouble getting tickets to the opera? Please take the trouble to read the contract thoroughly:* difficulty, bother, pains, inconvenience, annoyance, irritation, vexation, pother, fuss, strain, stress, struggle; effort, care, attention, exertion, work, labor. **5.** *If you can't pay the bill, you're going to be in trouble:* difficulty, predicament, dilemma, quandary, entanglement, pass, pinch, strait, crisis, *Informal* scrape, mess, pickle, fix, hot water, deep water; challenge, competition, opposition. **6.** *In a lifetime of trouble God was her only salvation:* woe, misery, distress, pain, suffering, affliction, agony, tribulation, ordeal, hardship, trial, misfortune, adversity, disaster, burden, difficulty, reverse, setback, grief, sorrow, worry, blow, hard times, ill wind, rainy day. **7.** *Political agitators tried to cause trouble:* unrest, instability, disorder, agitation, dissension, commotion, discord, row, disunity, disturbance, ferment, convulsion, embroilment; dissatisfaction, discontentment, discontent, strife. **8.** *Back trouble prevents him from diving. Car trouble made me late:* ailment, disability, defect, disorder, difficulty; breakdown, malfunction, snag. **—Ant.** 1, 3 relieve, ease. 1 calm, soothe, compose, please, delight. 3 assuage, mollify. 4 convenience, facility. 6 pleasure, delight, happiness, joy, ease, comfort; success, good fortune. 7 peace, peacefulness, calm, tranquillity, content, contentment; unity, accord, concord, harmony.

troublemaker *n. One troublemaker can cause havoc in an office:* agitator, *French* agent provocateur, mischief-maker, provoker, instigator, incendiary, fomenter, inciter, rabble-rouser, miscreant; gossip, rumormonger, scandalmonger, scaremonger. **—Ant.** peacemaker, peacelover, arbiter, pacifier.

troublesome *adj.* **1.** *The youth was a troublesome student. Troublesome financial problems depressed him:* distressing, worrisome, bothersome, demanding, trying, taxing, disturbing, annoying, vexing, irksome, irritating, exasperating, tormenting, harassing, pesky, inconvenient, difficult, tough, cursed; disobedient, undisciplined, uncontrolled. **2.** *The troublesome task of scraping the floors took days:* laborious, difficult, arduous, herculean, onerous, oppressive, burdensome, cumbersome, unwieldy, unpleasant, disagreeable, fatiguing, tiresome, tiring, tedious, wearisome, hard, tough, heavy, knotty, thorny. **—Ant.** 1, 2 easy, simple, undemanding; pleasant, pleasing, delightful. 1 soothing, calming; obedient, disciplined, accommodating, congenial.

trough *n.* **1.** *Lead the horse to the water trough:* boxlike receptacle, drinking box; tray. **2.** *The heavy rain made a trough in the hillside. The boat was in a trough between two waves:* depression, hollow, channel, watercourse, canal, flume, aqueduct, duct, furrow, trench, gully, gorge, ravine; moat, ditch, race.

trounce *v. The husky man trounced his would-be assailant. The basketball team trounced its opponent:* defeat decisively, win easily over, overwhelm, overpower, vanquish, beat, whip, drub, clobber, lick, trim, humble, carry the day, take care of, get the better of; *Slang* cream, skunk.

troupe *n. A troupe of players came to town:* troop.

truant *n. The officer is in charge of rounding up truants:* absentee, vagrant, hooky-player, delinquent, loafer, idler, shirker, evader, deserter, layabout, drifter, malingerer, dodger, slacker; *Slang* goldbrick, goof-off, boondoggler.

truce *n. The enemy rejected a Christmas truce, and the bombing continued:* temporary halt in fighting, cease-fire, suspension of hostilities, armistice; respite, lull, pause, rest, stay, break, interruption, breathing spell, discontinuance, stop, halt. **—Ant.** war, warfare, hostilities, fighting.

truck *n. The car collided with a truck:* (*variously*) delivery truck, van; pickup truck, panel truck, rig, eighteen-wheeler, trailer truck, *British* lorry.

truckle *v. She never fails to truckle to important people:* ingratiate oneself, fawn, flatter, submit, bow, yield, knuckle under, defer, take orders, pander, grovel, bootlick, curry favor, court; *Slang* suck up to, fall all over, apple-polish, shine up to, butter up. **—Ant.** resist, stand up to, oppose, disagree with.

truculent *adj. His truculent nature gets him into a lot of scrapes:* belligerent, bellicose, aggressive, pugnacious, hostile, defiant, fierce, nasty, ill-tempered, bad-tempered, ill-humored, ill-natured, snarling; surly, cross, touchy, peevish, snappish, petulant, sour, ungracious, churlish, sulky, insolent, rude. **—Ant.** peaceful, gentle, kind, diffident, accommodating, friendly, gracious, amiable, affable.

trudge *v. The losing team trudged wearily off the field:* plod, walk wearily, hobble, drag, lumber, clump, limp, shamble, march, tramp. **—Ant.** bound, skip, prance, scamper, trot.

true *adj.* **1.** *Is it true that Georgia is larger than Michigan? This is a true story:* in accordance with the facts, accurate, correct, right, exact, precise; factual, truthful, trustworthy, literal, strict, faithful. **2.** *The table is a true antique. Albert Schweitzer was a true humanitarian:* genuine, authentic, real, valid, bona fide, legitimate, actual; positive, absolute, in the true sense of the term, unquestionable, true-blue, pure, simon-pure. **3.** *You've been a true friend:* faithful, loyal, steadfast, trusty, devoted, firm, staunch, constant, dependable, reliable, unwa-vering, unswerving, steady. **4.** *The true heir to the throne is in exile:* rightful, lawful, legitimate, legal, official, proper, just, bona fide, real. **5.** *This coat is not a true size 8:* normal, regular, even, typical, usual, real, full. **—Ant.** 1–5 false. 1, 3 untrue. 1 inaccurate, incorrect, wrong, fallacious, inexact; nonfactual, fictitious, imaginary, figurative. 2 fake, phony, counterfeit, bogus, spurious, imitation, artificial, synthetic. 3 faithless, disloyal, treacherous, deceitful, untrustworthy, unreliable, inconstant, undependable. 4 illegal, unofficial, unlawful, illegitimate. 5 abnormal, atypical.

truly *adv.* **1.** *Mozart was truly a brilliant composer:* unquestionably, beyond question, beyond doubt, indubitably, no doubt, unequivocally, assuredly, verily, certainly, incontestably, without question, indisputably, absolutely, indeed, really, in truth, in actuality, in fact, surely, positively, definitely, to be sure. **2.** *You quoted Hamlet's soliloquy truly:* accurately, correctly, exactly, precisely, literally, actually, factually. **3.**

I'm truly sorry for the mistake. I love you truly: sincerely, truthfully, honestly, really, genuinely, faithfully, upon my word, so help me God, all kidding aside. **—Ant.** 1 questionably, dubiously, uncertainly. 2 inaccurately, incorrectly, inexactly, imprecisely. 3 insincerely, untruthfully, unfaithfully.

truncate *v. The author was asked to truncate his manuscript by at least half:* shorten, abbreviate, abridge, cut short, bob, prune, snub, trim, nip, lop, dock, crop, curtail, clip, amputate, condense. **—Ant.** lengthen, elongate, extend, protract.

trunk *n.* **1.** *The wrestler had a massive trunk:* torso, body, bole, butt, column, stalk, stem, thorax, stock, block. **2.** *The trunk was shipped by air:* chest, box, coffer, crate.

truss *v.* **1.** *Truss the suitcases securely on top of the car. Truss up that wound with a bandage:* tie, secure, strap, bind, fasten, make fast, hitch; tie up, bind up, pinion, constrict, confine. **—n.** **2.** *The bridge was built on steel trusses:* braced framework, brace, support, prop, underpinning, stay, shore, stanchion, beam, girder. **—Ant.** 1 untie, loosen, unbind, unfasten, unhitch.

trust *n.* **1.** *The people's trust in the government has been shaken:* confidence, faith, belief, credence, assuredness, reliance, certitude, certainty, sureness, conviction. **2.** *My life is in your trust:* care, custody, guardianship, safekeeping, protection, keeping, charge, hands. **3.** *Public office is a public trust:* responsibility, charge, obligation, duty. **—v. 4.** *Trust in God. Trust nothing that scheming gossip says:* have faith in, put confidence in, believe, rely on, depend upon, count upon, look to, place oneself in the hands of, swear by, pin one's faith upon; credit, accept, take on faith, give credence to, subscribe to, take stock in. **5.** *I trust that the accommodations will be satisfactory:* presume, assume, expect, hope, be confident, anticipate, feel sure, contemplate, reckon upon, count on, take for granted. **—Ant.** 1, 4 mistrust, distrust, doubt. 1 disbelief, incredulity, suspicion, uncertainty, misgiving, skepticism. 4 disbelieve, discredit, question.

trusting *adj. The confidence man bilked the trusting widow of her life savings:* trustful, believing, unsuspicious; credulous, gullible. **—Ant.** distrustful, doubting, suspicious, skeptical.

trustworthy *adj. Only trustworthy people can be considered for such a high position:* responsible, dependable, reliable, trusted; faithful, loyal, true, true-blue, tried and true, steadfast, honorable, high-principled, honest, ethical, aboveboard, upright, incorruptible, scrupulous, unimpeachable. **—Ant.** untrustworthy, irresponsible, undependable, unreliable, disreputable; unfaithful, disloyal, treacherous, dishonorable, dishonest, shady, slippery, crooked, corrupt, unscrupulous.

truth *n.* **1.** *The detective was determined to get at the truth. I'm not certain of the truth of his story:* facts, reality; truthfulness, trueness, veracity, verity, reliability, authenticity, actuality, trustworthiness, fidelity, integrity, faithfulness, accuracy, exactness. **2.** *The mortality of man is an unquestioned truth:* fact, proven principle, verity, reality, law. **—Ant.** 1, 2 untruth. 1 untruthfulness, falseness, falsity, mendacity, deceit, deception, dishonesty, inaccuracy. 2 fiction, fabrication, delusion, fallacy, error.

truthful *adj.* **1.** *Edith is too truthful to lie about anything:* honest, veracious, trustworthy, sincere, guileless, artless, undeceitful, candid, frank, open, straightforward, aboveboard. **2.** *The witness gave a truthful account of the incident:* factual, in accordance with fact, true, honest, correct, accurate, reliable, authentic, trustworthy, faithful, scrupulous, precise, exact, meticulous, unvarnished, unadulterated. **—Ant.** 1, 2 untruthful. 1 lying, deceitful, deceptive, dishonest, insincere. 2 false, untrue, dishonest, inaccurate, fictitious, fabricated, fallacious, incorrect.

try *v.* **1.** *Please try to finish the job by Friday:* attempt, strive, endeavor, make an effort, set one's sights on, essay, aim, seek, undertake. **2.** *The pilots were eager to try the new plane. Have you tried that new toothpaste?:* test, put to a test, prove, make trial of, tackle, have a fling at, have a go at, take a crack at; sample, use, partake of, avail oneself of. **3.** *I wouldn't try water-skiing without a life jacket:* risk, venture, take a chance on, undertake. **4.** *The conspiracy case was tried by the Supreme Court:* hear and decide, adjudicate, adjudge, sit in judgment, deliberate. **5.** *The unruly children tried our patience:* strain, tax to the limit, put to a severe test. **—n.** **6.** *Make a try to succeed on the new job. The contestant has one more try at the answer:* attempt, effort, endeavor, opportunity, turn, *Informal* shot, go, crack, fling, whack. **7.** *Give the new dishwasher a try and see if you like it:* trial, test.

trying *adj. Mother looks as though she's had a trying day:* difficult, tough, hard, arduous, taxing, irksome, bothersome, troublesome, onerous, burdensome, distressing, irritating, vexing, pesky, exasperating, aggravating, harrowing, tiresome, wearisome, tedious, fatiguing, exhausting.

tryst *n. The lovers arranged a tryst for midnight:* appointment, engagement, rendezvous, date, assignation, meeting, vis-à-vis, tête-à-tête, secret meeting.

tube *n. A rubber tube was used to siphon water from the fish tank. Buy a tube of toothpaste:* pipe, cylinder, conduit, duct, hose; cylindered container.

tuck *v.* **1.** *Tuck the scarf into your collar:* stick, insert, thrust, stuff, shove, cram, put; gather, gather in, roll up. **2.** *Tuck this blanket around the children:* wrap snugly, cover snugly, enwrap, swaddle, swathe, shroud. **—n.** **3.** *The tailor made the waist of the pants smaller by making a tuck:* gather, pleat, pucker; ruffle, crinkle.

tuft *n. The drought left the lawn with only a few tufts of grass. The bird had a beautiful blue tuft:* cluster, bunch, wisp, bundle, batch, sheaf, tassel, brush, clump; topknot, crest, plume.

tug v. **1.** *Tug hard at the door handle:* pull, yank, jerk, draw, wrench, wrestle; haul, drag, tow, lug. —n. **2.** *Give the drawer a tug and it will open:* pull, yank, jerk. —**Ant.** 1, 2 push, shove, poke.

tuition n. **1.** *Tuition in math was the school's specialty:* tutelage, tutoring, instruction, lessons, schooling, teaching, training, education. **2.** *The school has raised tuition again:* charge, fee, expense, payment (for instruction).

tumble v. **1.** *Jack and Jill tumbled down the hill:* fall end over end, fall, roll, topple, go sprawling, stumble. **2.** *The acrobats tumbled over the stage:* do forward rolls, somersault, cartwheel, flip, do acrobatics, bounce. **3.** *A clothes dryer works by tumbling the clothes:* toss, whirl, mix, shuffle, stir up, jumble. **4.** *The temperature tumbled to 30 degrees last night:* drop, fall, plunge, dive, descend. —**Ant.** 4 rise, ascend, soar, increase.

tumbledown adj. *He lives in a tumbledown cabin by the river:* dilapidated, decrepit, rickety, unstable, ramshackle, broken-down, falling-down, disintegrating, tottering, shaky, jerry-built, crumbling, run-down. —**Ant.** solid, substantial, sturdy, strong, invulnerable.

tumid adj. *He was alarmed at his tumid ankles:* swollen, puffy, enlarged, bloated, edematous, tumescent, dilated, expanded, inflated, distended, protuberant. —**Ant.** deflated, shrunken, detumescent, withered, shriveled.

tumult n. *The tumult in the streets awakened us:* uproar, commotion, hullabaloo, din, disorder, bedlam, pandemonium, clamor, racket, hubbub; disturbance, turmoil, upheaval, confusion, bustle, agitation, excitement, ado. —**Ant.** peace, quiet, stillness, calm, serenity, tranquillity.

tumultuous adj. *The crowd gave the Governor a tumultuous welcome:* boisterous, raucous, noisy, rowdy, turbulent, disorderly, unruly, tempestuous, stormy, riotous, chaotic, clamorous, uproarious. —**Ant.** quiet, restrained; cool, lukewarm, indifferent.

tune n. **1.** *The woodwinds carry the tune in this part of the composition. Irving Berlin wrote this tune:* melody, theme, motif; aria, song, air, strain, ditty, number. **2.** *The piano is out of tune. The design of the house is in tune with modern architectural thinking:* pitch; agreement, harmony, accord, concord, unison, concert, conformity, *Slang* step, line. —v. **3.** *The violinist tuned the violin for the next piece. How long has it been since you've had a mechanic tune this engine? Please tune the television set to Channel 4:* adjust to the correct pitch, pitch; adjust for proper functioning; adjust for proper reception, adjust the tone, adjust.

tuneful adj. *The tuneful ballad won the audience over:* musical, melodious, harmonious, dulcet, sweet. —**Ant.** discordant, sour, flat.

tunnel n. **1.** *They dug a tunnel to connect the buildings:* burrow, channel, passage, passageway, crawl space, crawlway, mine, pit, shaft, subway, underpass, drift. —v. **2.** *They tunneled their way out of prison:* burrow, dig, penetrate, scoop out.

turbid n. *The landslide partially filled the lake and left its waters turbid:* unclear, opaque, murky, clouded, cloudy, stirred up, full of sediment, roiled, muddy; disturbed, agitated, unsettled. —**Ant.** clear, crystal-clear, limpid, clean; calm, placid, smooth.

turbulent adj. *The sea is too turbulent for sailing. The turbulent meeting ended in a fist fight:* disturbed, agitated, tumultuous, tempestuous, blustering, violent, raging, fierce, stormy, furious; restless, chaotic, disorderly, uproarious, clamorous, unruly, boisterous, rowdy, riotous. —**Ant.** calm, smooth, placid, quiet, orderly.

turgid adj. **1.** *The wound was red and turgid:* swollen, puffed up, puffy. **2.** *The writer's turgid prose is hard to read:* pompous, bombastic, grandiose, overblown, inflated, pretentious, hyperbolic, grandiloquent; ostentatious, showy, florid, flowery, ornate. —**Ant.** 1 shrunken, puckered. 2 simple, modest, restrained, reserved; concise, succinct, pithy, terse, plainspoken.

turmoil n. *Ever since Mother went to the hospital the house has been in a turmoil:* state of confusion, confusion, disturbance, chaos, disorder, mess; tumult, commotion, uproar, pandemonium, ferment, agitation, convulsion. —**Ant.** order, peace, peacefulness, state of calm.

turn v. **1.** *Turn the wheel to the right. The path turns to the left at that big tree. Turn over or your back will get sunburned:* revolve, rotate, move in a circle, spin, whirl, wheel, roll, swivel, gyrate, pivot; move around, pass around, shift, swerve, veer, wing, twist, curve, bend, flex; roll over, overturn, invert, reverse. **2.** *In the fall the leaves turn red and gold. He turned fifty on his last birthday. Military school turned the youth into a self-confident leader:* change, change to, become; transform, metamorphose, convert, alter, make. **3.** *The outcome of the election turns on whether the voters believed the senator's speech or not. Everything turns on this last play of the game:* be contingent on, be decided by, depend, hang, hinge, pivot, rest, reside, lie. **4.** *Let's turn our attention to the matter at hand. You can always turn to me for help:* direct, apply, put; look, go, come. **5.** *The speaker certainly knew how to turn a phrase:* make skillfully, perform, execute, deliver, accomplish; carry out, do. **6.** *Kevin turned his ankle while ice-skating:* wrench, twist, sprain. **7.** *Turn the prisoners loose. How could the old man turn his own son out of the house?:* send, cause to go, discharge; eject, throw, drive. **8.** *Don't leave the milk out in the sun or it will turn:* sour, spoil, curdle, ferment, acidify. **9.** *The cabinetmaker turned the legs on a lathe:* make round, cut into a round form, grind into a cylinder. —n. **10.** *Give the dial a turn to the left:* rotation, revolution, spin, swing, twirl, whirl, roll, swivel, pivot, gyration, twist; change of direction. **11.** *The patient took a turn for the better:* change, shift, fluctuation, deviation, alteration. **12.** *The road is* *full of sharp turns. Take two turns of the rope around the fence post and tie a knot:* curve, bend, twist, zigzag, winding, arc; loop, coil. **13.** *Has each child had a turn riding the pony? Whose turn is it to keep the watch?:* opportunity, chance, go, crack, shot, whack, round, fling, attempt, effort; time, stint, shift, spell, period. **14.** *One good turn deserves another:* deed, act, action, service. **15.** *Let's take a turn in the garden before going to bed:* short walk, walk, stroll, constitutional; short drive, ride. **16.** *My, but you gave me a turn!:* shock, start, surprise, scare, fright. **—Ant.** 2 remain, stay, continue to be. 7 keep, retain, hold; capture, catch, secure.

turncoat *n. The general ordered that the turncoat be shot:* traitor, renegade, betrayer, double-dealer, quisling, apostate, Judas; deserter, defector, bolter. **—Ant.** patriot, loyalist.

turnout *n.* **1.** *There was a huge turnout for the dance:* gathering, crowd, throng, assemblage, assembly, audience. **2.** *The factory produced a record turnout this year:* output, production.

turpitude *n. He was discharged from the Army for moral turpitude:* wickedness, depravity, immorality, vice, vileness, corruption, baseness, lewdness, degeneracy, wrongdoing, perversion, defilement, evil, sinfulness, debauchery, dissoluteness, licentiousness.

tussle *v.* **1.** *The children tussled over the last piece of candy:* scuffle, grapple, fight, brawl, wrestle, struggle, battle. **—n.** **2.** *He received a black eye in the tussle:* fight, scuffle, scrap, brawl, fracas, fray, melee, altercation, conflict, donnybrook, set-to, free-for-all; struggle, battle.

tutelage *n. I learned to sail under the tutelage of my grandfather:* supervision, guidance, direction; instruction, training, teaching, coaching, schooling, education, tutoring, inculcation, discipline, indoctrination.

tutor *n.* **1.** *A tutor helped me prepare for the Spanish exam:* coach, private teacher, instructor, master, teacher, mentor, coach, guru. **—v.** **2.** *The football coach tutors math six hours a week:* teach privately, coach, instruct, give lessons in, teach, school, drill, prepare. **—Ant.** 1 pupil, student, disciple. 2 study, learn.

twaddle *n. Everyone is tired of listening to his twaddle:* idle talk, silly talk, drivel, prattle, tripe, nonsense, tommyrot, rubbish, babble, chatter.

twang *n.* **1.** *We heard the twang of a guitar from next door:* sharp vibrating sound, vibration, resonance, reverberation. **2.** *He speaks with a Midwestern twang:* nasal sound, nasal resonance.

twilight *n.* **1.** *I could hardly see in the twilight. Driving at twilight is dangerous:* dusk, gloaming, half-light, edge of darkness; nightfall, evening, eve, sundown, sunset, moonrise, eventide. **2.** *The old man is in the twilight of his career:* decline, last phase, ebb. **—Ant.** 1 dawn, sunrise, daybreak. 2 advent, beginning, unfolding; peak, height, crowning point, climax.

twin *adj.* **1.** *The twin sisters refused to dress alike:* born as one of a pair, forming a pair. **2.** *Twin love seats flanked the fireplace:* paired,

matched, identical, duplicate, like, alike. **3.** *The plan has a twin purpose:* double, dual, twofold.

twine *n.* **1.** *Wrap the bundle with strong twine:* string, cord, two-strand string, twisted thread; binding; rope, cable. **—v.** **2.** *She twined her hair into braids:* intertwine, interlace, weave, entwine, twist, plait, braid; wind, coil.

twinge *n.* **1.** *I had a twinge in my neck:* sudden sharp pain, pain, cramp, spasm, stab, pang, stitch; throb, tingle, twitch. **2.** *Didn't you ever feel a twinge of regret about dropping out of school?:* pang, stab.

twinkle *v.* **1.** *The pilot saw the lights of the city twinkling far below:* glimmer, shimmer, shine, flicker, flash, sparkle, gleam, glisten, glow, scintillate, blaze, flare. **—n.** **2.** *The sky was dark except for the twinkle of a distant star:* glimmer, shimmer, flicker, sparkle, gleam, glow, flare, flash.

twirl *v. The dancers twirled across the stage. The marching band was led by a girl twirling a baton:* spin, whirl, rotate, revolve, gyrate, wheel, pivot, twine, pirouette.

twist *v.* **1.** *The girl twisted her hair into a braid. Twist the tourniquet tighter. Twist the dial to the left:* wind, twine, intertwine, entwine, interlace, tangle, knot, ravel; coil, curl, roll, wrap; rotate, turn, swivel, pivot, whirl, spin. **2.** *The road twists to the right at the next intersection:* bend, curve, wind, arc, swing, swerve, veer, curl, snake, zigzag, meander. **3.** *Aunt Louise twisted her ankle when she fell. The boy twisted the toy from his brother's hands:* wrench, turn, sprain; wrest, yank, pull. **4.** *She twisted her words to suit her own purpose. His face was twisted in pain:* distort, contort, wrench out of shape. **—n.** **5.** *The prospector carried the gold dust in a twist of paper:* curl, coil, roll, corkscrew, spiral; tangle, knot, kink. **6.** *Give the knob a twist:* turn, rotation, spin, whirl, wrench. **7.** *The mountain road is full of twists:* bend, zigzag, winding curve, corkscrew curve, convolution, involution. **8.** *There's an unusual twist to the plot at the end of the book. An indoor picnic—there's a new twist!:* change, development, surprise, turn; notion, idea, approach, slant, treatment, way, system, method. **—Ant.** 1 untwist, unwind; straighten, uncoil, unroll, unwrap; untangle, disentangle, unknot, unravel.

twit *v.* **1.** *She was twitted about her fancy new dress:* taunt, gibe at, banter, tease. **2.** *They twitted him for his absenteeism:* deride, reproach, upbraid.

twitch *v.* **1.** *The general's hands twitched in anger. Stop twitching around and sit still!:* jerk, quiver, quaver, throb, shake, tremble; wiggle, squirm, writhe. **—n.** **2.** *Is the twitch in my eye noticeable?:* tic, involuntary movement, jerk, spasm, quiver, quaver, throb, shake, tremor; paroxysm, convulsion.

twitter *v.* **1.** *The wrens twittered madly when the cat came near the nest:* chirp, chirrup, cheep, tweet, chatter, peep, warble. **2.** *The twitter of birds filled the garden:* twittering, chirp, chirping, chirrup, chirruping, cheep, peep. **3.** *Everyone was in a twitter over the wedding:*

flutter, tizzy, flurry, fluster, whirl, bustle, ferment, stew, fuss, pother, uproar, turbulence.

twofaced adj. Indians accused the white man of being twofaced: hypocritical, duplicitous, perfidious, double-dealing, double-faced, deceitful, disingenuous, devious, treacherous, dishonest, insincere, false, dissembling, fork-tongued, underhanded, slippery, deceptive, untrustworthy. **—Ant.** honest, straightforward, open, candid, frank, sincere, aboveboard.

tycoon n. Samuel Goldwyn was one of the first movie tycoons: powerful businessperson, wealthy businessperson, magnate, mogul, nabob, potentate, captain of industry, entrepreneur, industrialist, Slang big shot, bigwig, big gun, big wheel, boss.

tyke n. The boy's a cute little tyke: tot, child, little one, tad, wee one, kid, squirt, shaver.

type n. **1.** The horticulturist developed a new type of rose: class, kind, sort, variety, category, order, species, genus, race, family, phylum, group, division, brand. **2.** Joel is one of those strong, silent types: typical person, typical thing, individual example, specimen, model, sample; prototype, archetype. **3.** The wedding invitations were printed in fancy type: typeface, printed letters, design, pattern, print, printing character, typography, font.

typical adj. **1.** A typical day at the office begins at nine o'clock. Jane is a typical teenager: representative, standard, normal, average, stock, regular, usual, ordinary; true-to-type, conventional, orthodox; prototypal, model, exemplary. **2.** That sarcastic reply is typical of him: charac-

teristic, in character, to be expected, in keeping, true to type; distinctive, individual. **—Ant.** 1 atypical, abnormal, unrepresentative, irregular, unusual, uncommon, unique, singular, unconventional, strange, weird. 2 uncharacteristic, out of keeping, unexpected.

typify v. She works a lot in TV commercials because she typifies the healthy American teenager: personify, represent, exemplify, characterize, embody, sum up, epitomize, stand for, betoken, incarnate, pass for, instance, connote.

tyrannical adj. The tyrannical law met widespread opposition: dictatorial, arbitrary, despotic, harsh, severe, oppressive, unjust, imperious, domineering, inhuman, cruel. **—Ant.** judicious, unbiased, just, humane.

tyranny n. The Russians revolted against the tyranny of the Czar: despotism, cruel authority, unjust rule, cruelty, harshness, severity, domination, oppression, repression, persecution, coercion; absolute rule, iron rule, iron fist, iron hand, reign of terror, dictatorship, fascism, totalitarianism. **—Ant.** humanity, kindness, benevolence, fairness; democracy, freedom.

tyrant n. The American colonies regarded George III as a tyrant: cruel and unjust ruler, despot, cruel master, uncompromising superior, slave driver, taskmaster, martinet, bully, persecutor; absolute ruler, dictator.

tyro n. The old pro gave the tyro some tips on how to do the job: beginner, novice, neophyte, tenderfoot, greenhorn, newcomer, rookie, initiate, recruit, apprentice, learner, trainee, intern. **—Ant.** veteran, master, expert, professional.

U

ubiquitous *adj. The fog seemed to be ubiquitous that day:* omnipresent, pervading, pervasive, prevalent, widespread, worldwide, universal, allover, everpresent, all-pervading, everywhere.

ugly *adj.* **1.** *One sister is beautiful, the other ugly. What an ugly dress!:* homely, unattractive, unsightly, unseemly, unbecoming, ill-favored, repulsive, hideous, frightful, grotesque, monstrous; evil-looking. **2.** *His ugly disposition gained him few friends. What an ugly thing to do!:* nasty, quarrelsome, cantankerous, unpleasant, mean, hostile, belligerent, difficult; disagreeable, obnoxious, repulsive, offensive, dreadful, unbearable, disgusting, foul, odious, vile, abominable, abhorrent, sickening, horrid, horrible, repellent, repugnant. **3.** *Ugly clouds gathered on the horizon:* forbidding, ominous, portentous, threatening, menacing, inauspicious, dangerous, troublesome. —**Ant.** 1 beautiful, pretty, handsome, fair, lovely, comely, attractive. 2 pleasant, agreeable, personable, good-natured, likable, friendly; good, nice, sweet, attractive. 3 promising, auspicious, fortuitous.

ukase *n. An official ukase forbade any kind of public assembly:* edict, directive, ruling, decree, order, proclamation, fiat, mandate, manifesto, pronouncement, statute, ordinance, pronunciamento, dictum.

ulterior *adj. She definitely had an ulterior motive in offering to help:* hidden, covert, concealed, secret, unrevealed, unexpressed, undisclosed, undivulged; selfish, self-serving, opportunistic. —**Ant.** obvious, manifest, evident, self-evident, plain; altruistic, public-spirited.

ultimate *adj.* **1.** *The ultimate cost of the job was over a hundred dollars. Becoming president is his ultimate goal:* final, last, resulting, terminal, definitive, conclusive, crowning, end, eventual, long-range. **2.** *An Oscar represents the ultimate accolade for a movie actor's performance:* greatest, utmost, highest possible, supreme, maximum, extreme, crowning, at the peak. —*n.* **3.** *That hat is the ultimate in ridiculousness:* height, final point, utmost, peak, apex, acme, high point, extreme, last straw. —**Ant.** 1 initial, first, beginning. 2 least, lowest, minimum.

ultimatum *n. They gave the assistant an ultimatum: shape up or lose your job:* warning, notice, threat, demand, insistence, final offer.

umbrage *n. She took umbrage at the suggestion:* offense, pique, resentment, displeasure, grudge. —**Ant.** pleasure.

umbrella *n. The rain reminded her she'd left her umbrella at home:* parasol, sunshade, *British Informal* brolly.

umpire *n.* **1.** *The fans disagreed with the umpire's decision. A federal umpire will try to settle the labor dispute:* referee, judge; arbiter, arbitrator, mediator, intercessor, negotiator, moderator, adjudicator, go-between. —*v.* **2.** *Uncle Joe umpired the children's baseball game:* referee; judge, arbitrate, mediate, adjudicate, moderate.

unabashed *adj.* **1.** bold, brazen, undaunted, fearless, doughty, confident, sure. **2.** shameless, brazenfaced, forward, immodest, unblushing. —**Ant.** timid, retiring; modest, prim.

unabbreviated *adj. The poem was published in its unabbreviated form:* unshortened, unabridged, complete, uncondensed, uncompressed, uncurtailed, untrimmed, unsnipped, unpruned, uncropped, uncut, undocked, unexpurgated, unreduced. —**Ant.** abridged, incomplete, condensed, expurgated.

unable *adj. They were unable to meet the deadline:* powerless, impotent, inadequate, incapable, incapacitated, incompetent, ineffectual, inefficient, inept, inoperative, unfitted, unqualified, unskilled, weak, helpless. —**Ant.** able, powerful, capable, competent, effective, potent, adept.

unabridged *adj. There's an unabridged dictionary on the library table:* not abridged, not shortened, full-length, entire, complete, uncut, intact, uncondensed. —**Ant.** abridged, shortened, condensed.

unacceptable *adj. Such behavior is totally unacceptable:* not acceptable, not allowable, unsatisfactory, unsuitable, unseemly, improper, displeasing, unwelcome, insupportable, not up to snuff.

unaccompanied *adj. The entire program consisted of works for unaccompanied violin:* solo, lone, unattended, solitary, single; unescorted, apart, separate, companionless, lonesome, all by one's self, alone, isolated, *Music* a cappella. —**Ant.** escorted, accompanied, squired, chaperoned.

unaccountable *adj.* **1.** *Many unaccountable things happened in that haunted house:* unexplained, inexplicable, baffling, strange, odd, queer, weird, peculiar, curious, bizarre, incomprehensible, unfathomable, mysterious; unusual, intriguing, extraordinary, astonishing, surprising, unheard-of. **2.** *The driver was held unaccountable for the accident:* not responsible, not answerable, not accountable, not liable, blameless, innocent, inculpable, free, clear, excused; exempt, immune. —**Ant.** 1 explainable, explicable, comprehensible; usual, ordinary, normal, natural. 2 accountable, responsible, answerable, liable, culpable, guilty, blamable, blameworthy.

unaccustomed *adj.* **1.** *The unaccustomed sights of Tibet were fascinating:* unusual, unfamiliar, uncommon, out of the ordinary, extraordinary, strange, foreign, quaint, unique, singular, curious, peculiar, odd, queer, bizarre, surprising, astonishing, unimaginable, startling, out-of-the-way, unheard-of, amazing, remarkable, fantastic, *Slang* wild; new, novel, original, rare. **2.** *The poor man was unaccustomed to such luxury. I'm still unaccustomed to skiing such steep slopes:* not used to, unused, not accustomed, unhabituated, strange, unacquainted, ungiven to; inexperienced, unpracticed, untried, green, a novice at, unfamiliar with, unversed in, new to. —**Ant.** 1, 2 accustomed, familiar. 1 ordinary, common, regular, run-of-the-mill. 2 used to, well-acquainted, given to; experienced, practiced, well-versed, seasoned.

unaffected *adj.* **1.** *Users of gas were unaffected by the heating oil shortage. Passersby were unaffected by the beggar's plea:* not affected, not influenced, untouched, unbothered, undisturbed; unmoved, unstirred, unresponsive to, indifferent to, insensitive to, unconcerned, unfeeling, impervious to, unsympathetic to. **2.** *The girl's unaffected manner charmed everyone:* natural, sincere, genuine, simple, wholesome, plain, open, honest, frank, candid, direct, straightforward, plain-spoken, unreserved, open-hearted, undesigning, guileless, ingenuous; naive, innocent, childlike, unsophisticated, unworldly. —**Ant.** 1, 2 affected. 1 influenced, touched, changed, disturbed; moved, stirred, responsive, interested, concerned, sympathetic. 2 unnatural, artificial, insincere, pretentious, assumed, *Informal* put-on, phony; indirect, devious, scheming, designing, Machiavellian; sophisticated, worldly.

unanimity *n. Unanimity was rare at the meetings:* unanimousness, agreement, harmony, unity, unison, concert, accord. —**Ant.** discord, disagreement.

unanimous *adj. The members were unanimous in approving the project:* showing complete agreement, in complete accord, with no dissent; united, allied, harmonious, like-minded, accordant, consonant, of one mind, of the same mind. —**Ant.** not agreed, dissenting, discordant, disagreeing, unharmonious, inharmonious.

unappetizing *adj. The main dish was singularly unappetizing:* unappealing, unpalatable, unsavoury, gross, unattractive, uninviting, unpleasant, distasteful, *Slang* grody. —**Ant.** appetizing, palatable, agreeable.

unapproachable *adj.* **1.** *The wide moat made the castle unapproachable. The judge was a stern, unapproachable man:* inaccessible, unreachable, beyond reach, unattainable; remote, aloof, distant, austere, stand-offish, cold, cool, forbidding, intimidating, awesome. **2.** *Shakespeare's genius as a playwright is unapproachable:* unequaled, unrivaled, matchless, unparalleled, peerless, incomparable, beyond compare, inimitable, unique, nonpareil; supreme, preeminent, superior, foremost, second to none.

unasked *adj. She's good about offering us her unasked ideas:* unsolicited, uninvited, unsought, unbidden, unrequested; unwanted, unwelcome, undesirable; unasked-for, gratuitous, uncalled-for, wanton. —**Ant.** wanted, invited, welcome, sought.

unassuming *adj. Despite his wealth and position, he has an unassuming personality:* modest, unpretentious, not vain, without airs, easygoing, unostentatious, natural, simple, plain, homely, unobtrusive, unassertive, muted.

unauthorized *adj. The area is off-limits to unauthorized persons:* unofficial, unsanctioned, unapproved, uncertified, prohibited; unlawful,

banned, outlawed, unwarranted, unpermitted, unallowed; covert, concealed, furtive, clandestine, underhand, under-the-table. —**Ant.** official, certified, sanctioned, permitted.

unavailing *adj. Efforts to revive the patient were unavailing:* futile, unproductive, useless, idle, ineffective, inept, weak, empty, unproductive, ineffectual, fruitless, vain, bootless, unsuccessful; impotent, worthless, invalid. —**Ant.** effective, valid, useful, productive.

unavoidable *adj. Some mistakes are unavoidable. Paying taxes is unavoidable:* inevitable, inescapable, unpreventable, uncontrollable, fated, sure, certain; necessary, requisite, compulsory, obligatory, imperative, fixed.

unaware *adj. He was unaware of how hostile the people were toward him:* unsuspecting, ignorant, unenlightened, unknowing, unconscious, unapprised, unacquainted, incognizant; unwarned, unalerted, heedless, in the dark about, off one's guard, unmindful. —**Ant.** aware, cognizant, knowing, conscious, acquainted, heedful, mindful, enlightened, suspicious, wary, on one's guard, *Slang* hip.

unawares *adv.* **1.** *He drove into the ditch completely unawares:* unknowingly, unwittingly, inadvertently, unintentionally, unconsciously, unthinkingly, accidentally, by accident, mistakenly, by mistake, involuntarily, by chance. **2.** *The squall took us unawares:* unexpectedly, abruptly, without warning, suddenly, by surprise, like a bolt from the blue, like a thunderbolt, like a thief in the night, out of nowhere. —**Ant.** 1 knowingly, wittingly, intentionally, purposely, on purpose, consciously, voluntarily. 2 prepared, forewarned.

unbalanced *adj.* **1.** *The scales are unbalanced. The unbalanced stack of books toppled over:* not balanced, unequal, uneven, unpoised, out of equilibrium, unadjusted, lopsided, leaning, unsteady, unstable. **2.** *The actress portrayed a woman with an unbalanced mind:* mentally disturbed, unsound, deranged, demented, mad, irrational, illogical, unsettled, unhinged, unstable, crazed, psychotic, psychopathic, warped, *Informal* cracked, daft, wacky, nutty, unglued, batty, not all there, loco, bonkers.

unbearable *adj. The thought of losing the race was unbearable to him:* intolerable, insufferable, unendurable, unacceptable, insupportable, inadmissible, unthinkable.

unbecoming *adj.* **1.** *Why did Claire wear such an unbecoming dress?:* unattractive, unappealing, ugly, tasteless, homely, unsightly. **2.** *The officer was demoted for unbecoming conduct:* unsuitable, improper, unsuited, inappropriate, unfitted, unbefitting, indecorous, unseemly; tasteless, offensive, vulgar.

unbelievable *adj. She found the results unbelievable:* incredible, inconceivable, astonishing, beyond belief, dubious, preposterous, suspect, unthinkable, inauthentic. —**Ant.** believable, credible, plausible, trustworthy, authentic.

unbelieving *adj. Her alibi fell on unbelieving ears:* doubting, nonbelieving, skeptical, disbelieving, questioning, quizzical, incredulous, distrustful, suspicious, dubious, unconvinced. —**Ant.** trusting, believing, gullible, credulous.

unbending *adj. The captain is an unbending disciplinarian:* rigid, stiff, inflexible, unyielding, severe, firm, strict, tough, obstinate, stubborn, uncompromising, *Informal* hard as nails, stone-faced. —**Ant.** soft, easy, flexible, compromising, pliant, adaptable; wishy-washy.

unbiased *adj. It was difficult to find a completely unbiased jury:* unprejudiced, impartial, neutral, disinterested, dispassionate, detached, open-minded, just, fair, uninfluenced, neutral, liberal, broad-minded, tolerant, unbigoted, undogmatic, fair-minded.

unblemished *adj. The actress has a fair, unblemished complexion. The mayor has an unblemished reputation:* flawless, perfect, unvitiated, immaculate, spotless, pure, uncontaminated, unadulterated, unsoiled, unmarred, unsullied, white as snow, clean as a whistle.

unbounded *adj. On seeing the pony, the boy's joy was unbounded:* boundless, unlimited, unrestrained, unconditional, unrestricted, absolute, unconstrained, uncontrolled, unbridled.

unbreakable *adj. The dishes were said to be unbreakable:* indestructible, nonbreakable, shatterproof, adamantine, durable, everlasting, incorruptible, invulnerable, unshakable, unyielding. —**Ant.** fragile, brittle, flimsy.

unbroken *adj.* **1.** *After the storm only three of the windows remained unbroken:* (*variously*) uncracked, unshattered, unsmashed, unruptured; whole, intact, complete, entire, undivided, undiminished. **2.** *The new year brought an unbroken series of successes:* continuous, uninterrupted, successive, consecutive; ceaseless, endless, incessant, continual, unremitting; progressive, sequential. —**Ant.** 1 broken, cracked, shattered, smashed, ruptured, damaged, incomplete. 2 intermittent, interrupted, occasional, irregular, fitful, uneven, disconnected.

unburden *v. I'll unburden you of those packages. The boy unburdened his troubles to his homeroom teacher:* relieve, disburden, free, unencumber, disencumber; disclose, confess, reveal, confide, *Slang* get off one's chest, get out of one's system; unbosom.

uncalled-for *adj. Those nasty remarks about his brother were certainly uncalled-for:* unnecessary, needless, unneeded, redundant, nonessential, unwanted; unsought, unsolicited, unprompted, uninvited, unasked; unjustified, gratuitous, supererogatory, wanton. —**Ant.** justified, needed, necessary, essential.

uncanny *adj.* **1.** *Sherlock Holmes's powers of observation were uncanny:* extraordinary, unimaginable, remarkable, unexampled, exceptional, astonishing, unbelievable, incredible, marvelous, fantastic, inspired, prodigious, unheard-of; intuitive. **2.** *An uncanny silence pervaded the old mansion:* curious, mysterious, strange, uncomfortable, unnatural, eerie, weird, unearthly, *Informal* spooky. —**Ant.** 1 average, normal, common, usual, unexceptional, unnoteworthy, unremarkable, mediocre, run-of-the-mill. 2 natural, obvious.

uncertain *adj.* **1.** *They are uncertain of the time they'll arrive. Whether the game will be held or not is uncertain:* not certain, not sure, unsure, not confident, doubtful, dubious; not definite, indefinite, speculative, unconfirmed, undecided, up in the air. **2.** *An uncertain number of people were waiting. The outcome of the election is still uncertain:* indeterminate, unpredictable, not known exactly, undetermined, indefinite, indistinct, unclear, hazy, obscure, nebulous, doubtful, not fixed, unsettled, in question, debatable, disputable, questionable, conjectural. **3.** *Uncertain weather postponed our beach trip. Uncertain people make poor leaders:* wavering, variable, vacillating, fluctuating, erratic, fitful, unresolved, irresolute, unsure, hesitant. —**Ant.** 1–3 certain, definite. 1 sure, assured, confirmed, decided, positive. 2 predictable, known, determined, clear, settled, indisputable, unquestionable. 3 firm, resolute, certain, staunch, unvarying, unwavering, unhesitating.

uncertainty *n.* **1.** *The uncertainty of her answer made me suspicious:* hesitancy, hesitation, indefiniteness, irresolution, unsureness, vagueness, indecision, doubt, ambiguity, vacillation, equivocation, ambivalence, confusion, perplexity, quandary, *Informal* shilly-shally. **2.** *The future is full of uncertainties:* something uncertain, chance, gamble, odds, risk.

unchangeable *adj. Unchangeable laws governed their conduct:* changeless, unalterable, inalterable, constant, immovable, unmovable, immutable, inevitable, inflexible, invariable, permanent, stable, firm, fixed. —**Ant.** changeable, inconstant, variable, wavering, irregular.

unchanging *adj. The rules of the game were unchanging:* changeless, abiding, unvarying, invariable, unchanged, consistent, constant, enduring, eternal, fixed, immutable, imperishable, inescapable, lasting, permanent, perpetual, static, unfading, unfailing, uniform, enduring.

uncharitable *adj. Scrooge was very uncharitable. The veteran violinist made several uncharitable comments about the young musician:* ungenerous, stingy, tight, niggardly, miserly, illiberal, parsimonious, tightfisted, closefisted; ungracious, unkind, unfriendly, unfeeling, uncompassionate, insensitive, unsympathetic.

uncivil *adj. Not shaking hands seemed uncivil:* ill-mannered, unmannerly, rude, impolite, discourteous, disrespectful, uncouth, boorish, brusque, curt, impudent. —**Ant.** civil.

uncivilized *adj.* **1.** *Some New Guinea tribes are still uncivilized:* savage, barbaric, barbarous, untamed. **2.** *What uncivilized manners!:* uncouth, brutish, churlish, rude, boorish, uncultured, unpolished, obnoxious, ill-bred, ungenteel, vulgar, uncultivated.

unclad *adj. Marble statues of unclad figures lined the museum walls:* unclothed, undressed, unrobed, disrobed, uncovered; nude, naked, bare, stripped, stark-naked, *Brit.* starkers, in the raw, in the altogether, exposed. —**Ant.** dressed, clad, clothed, covered.

unclean *adj.* **1.** *Her hands were unclean:* dirty, soiled, filthy, nasty, foul. **2.** *The was something* *unclean about his character:* evil, vile, base, impure, unvirtuous, unchaste, sinful, corrupt, polluted. —**Ant.** clean.

uncomfortable *adj.* **1.** *These shoes are uncomfortable:* causing discomfort, causing distress, painful, bothersome, irritating, distressful. **2.** *The boy felt uncomfortable with his new classmates:* uneasy, ill at ease, awkward, out of place, discomposed, edgy, nervous, disquieted, tense, keyed up, on tenterhooks, discomfited, troubled, on edge, strained, confused, upset.

uncommitted *adj. Most of the delegates were uncommitted:* nonaligned, unaffiliated, unattached, floating, free, nonpartisan, uninvolved, cut loose.

uncommon *adj.* **1.** *A solar eclipse is an uncommon occurrence:* unusual, rare, infrequent, unfamiliar, unique, scarce, extraordinary, exceptional, unconventional, few and far between, novel, peculiar, curious, bizarre, *Informal* once in a lifetime. **2.** *This rose has an uncommon loveliness:* exceptional, remarkable, outstanding, incomparable, unusual, unparalleled, notable, extraordinary; superior, superlative, matchless, peerless, unmatched, unexcelled, supreme.

uncommonly *adv.* **1.** *Our dog only wanders uncommonly:* infrequently, irregularly, rarely, scarcely ever, seldom, hardly ever. **2.** *The children were uncommonly dirty:* especially, distinctively. **3.** *You have always been uncommonly kind:* unusually, exceptionally, remarkably.

uncommunicative *adj. Gwen shows her anger by being uncommunicative:* unsociable, reticent, taciturn, close-mouthed, withdrawn, retiring, shy, reserved; speechless, inexpressive, mute, mum, silent, quiet, tongue-tied, dumb, secretive. —**Ant.** talkative, voluble, loquacious, garrulous, gregarious, sociable, communicative, open, extroverted, outgoing, expressive.

uncomplimentary *adj. The aging actress's remarks about the ingenue were very uncomplimentary:* disapproving, disparaging, unadmiring, unflattering, insulting, critical, negative, derisive.

uncompromising *adj. The candidate for President must be a person of uncompromising integrity. If both the union and management are uncompromising, a strike will result:* firm, strict, rigid, scrupulous; stiff, unrelenting, exacting, inflexible, unvarying, immovable, unbending, unyielding, hardline, obdurate, inexorable.

unconcern *n. She expressed unconcern about the news:* indifference, nonchalance, insouciance. —**Ant.** concern.

unconcerned *adj. The public seemed unconcerned about the impending fuel shortage. The children in the playground seemed unconcerned about the rain:* indifferent, oblivious, apathetic, insensitive, uninvolved, unaware, nonchalant, uncaring, unsympathetic, unfeeling, unmoved, unresponsive; aloof, distant, passionless, cold; serene, untroubled, unperturbed, unmindful, composed, impervious. —**Ant.** concerned, aware, mindful, involved, caring, interested, sympathetic, compassionate; anxious, worried, perturbed, troubled.

unconditional *adj. Only an unconditional surrender was acceptable to the Allies:* unlimited, unqualified, unrestricted, absolute, categorical, thoroughgoing, complete, entire, utter, conclusive; downright, outright. —**Ant.** conditional, provisional, restricted, qualified, limited; partial, incomplete, inconclusive.

unconquerable *adj. There is no such thing as an unconquerable fortress. The child has an unconquerable fear of dogs:* invincible, undefeatable, unvanquishable, unable to be overcome, insurmountable, unbeatable, invulnerable, impenetrable; inveterate, ingrained, innate.

unconscionable *adj. He went on at unconscionable length about his aches and pains:* excessive, extreme, unreasonable, immoderate, unwarranted, unjustifiable, unjustified, inordinate; outrageous, preposterous, unpardonable, unforgivable, inexcusable, indefensible. —**Ant.** moderate, reasonable, judicious, sensible.

unconscious *adj.* **1.** *The boxer was unconscious for several hours after the knockout:* without consciousness, senseless, insensate, without awareness, in a faint, in a coma, comatose, *Informal* out, out cold, dead to the world. **2.** *She had an unconscious hostility toward her sister:* unrealized, incognizant, unsuspecting, unknowing, unmindful, latent, suppressed. —**Ant.** 1, 2 conscious, aware. 2 cognizant, knowing, active.

unconventional *adj. In 1900 automobiles were an unconventional means of transportation. Wearing jeans and sandals to the wedding was thought unconventional:* uncommon, unusual, extraordinary, exceptional, unaccustomed, atypical, rare, original, unique, singular, irregular, quaint, newfangled, fantastic, strange, peculiar, odd, curious, queer, outlandish, bizarre; nonconformist, nonconforming, unorthodox, different, eccentric, individualistic, idiosyncratic, bohemian, freakish, weird, off the beaten path, aberrant, offbeat, *Slang* wacky, nutty, crazy, kinky, far-out.

uncouth *adj. The other guests were offended by his uncouth manners:* crude, rude, boorish, churlish, crass, coarse, rough, gross, uncivil, callow, indelicate, loutish, brutish, impolite, ill-bred, ill-mannered, unmannerly, unrefined, uncultured, uncivilized, barbaric; uncultivated. —**Ant.** refined, polite, genteel, cultivated, well-mannered, delicate, gentlemanly.

uncover *v.* **1.** *She uncovered the porch furniture for the summer:* remove the cover from, unwrap, undo, unsheathe; undress, disrobe, bare, uncloak, undrape, strip, unclothe, denude. **2.** *It was two young reporters who uncovered the whole plot:* bring to light, disclose, expose, reveal, lay bare, make known, unmask, unveil, make visible, dig up, dig out, unearth. —**Ant.** 1 cover, wrap, sheathe; dress, clothe, drape. 2 hide, conceal, cloak, veil, suppress.

uncritical *adj. The audience cheered the pianist with uncritical enthusiasm:* undiscriminating, unthinking, unreflecting; shallow, perfunctory, superficial, casual, offhand; inexact, imprecise, inaccurate; careless, slipshod; uneducated, unschooled, untutored; dumb, ignorant, stupid; dull, obtuse. **—Ant.** perceptive, discerning, thoughtful, penetrating.

unctuous *adj. His personality was unctuous and insincere:* too smooth, too suave, smug, ingratiating, flattering, sycophantic, obsequious, sanctimonious, oily, slippery, smarmy, honeyed, honey-tongued, fawning, servile, self-righteous, pietistic. **—Ant.** blunt, brusque, open, frank, candid, straightforward.

uncustomary *adj. He answered the question with uncustomary wit:* rare, unaccustomed, uncommon, singular, unwonted, exceptional, unique, unusual, extraordinary, unexpected, unanticipated; unheard-of, amazing, unbelievable, astonishing, incredible. **—Ant.** standard, normal, customary, usual.

undaunted *adj. Though behind by three touchdowns, the team was undaunted. We must face the future with undaunted spirits:* not discouraged, unperturbed, undismayed, not put off, unfazed; resolute, courageous, unshrinking, valiant, valorous, stalwart, intrepid, unflinching, stouthearted, heroic, brave, fearless, indomitable, *Informal* plucky, gritty. **—Ant.** daunted, discouraged, perturbed, dismayed, disconcerted, fazed; irresolute, vacillating, meek, cowardly, fearful.

undecided *adj.* **1.** *Our plans are still undecided:* not decided, undetermined, uncertain, unsure, indefinite, unsettled, unresolved, not final, pending, open, tentative, in abeyance, unformulated, vague, *Informal* up in the air. **2.** *I'm still undecided about whom to vote for:* unsure, irresolute, indecisive, of two minds, open-minded, fluctuating, wavering, vacillating, dubious, in a dilemma, *Informal* going around in circles, blowing hot and cold, hemming and hawing. **—Ant.** 1, 2 sure, resolved. 1 decided, determined, certain, definite, settled, final, firm. 2 resolute, decisive, closed-minded, steadfast, unwavering, certain.

undemonstrative *adj. The father loved his children but was very undemonstrative:* reserved, shy, inexpressive, not affectionate, not displaying emotions, unemotional, unresponsive, distant, cold, aloof, impassive; stoical, self-controlled. **—Ant.** demonstrative, affectionate, emotional, responsive, unreserved, expressive, warm, outgoing.

undeniable *adj. That he's telling the truth is undeniable. Rembrandt's "Night Watch" is an undeniable masterpiece:* unquestionable, indisputable, incontestable, irrefutable, indubitable, beyond a doubt, incontrovertible, sure, certain, established, demonstrable, proven, decisive, conclusive, obvious, manifest, patent. **—Ant.** questionable, debatable, dubious, disputable, refutable, uncertain, indecisive, inconclusive, up in the air.

undependable *adj. When it comes to being on time, Nancy is totally undependable:* not to be depended on, unreliable, untrustworthy, irresponsible, unpredictable, erratic, inconstant;

variable, wavering, changeable, fickle, unstable, flighty, capricious. **—Ant.** dependable, reliable, responsible, trustworthy, predictable, exact, unchanging.

under *adv.* **1.** *The key was under the mat:* beneath, below. **2.** *All the followers were under his control:* subject to, subordinate to, dependent on, following, governed by, inferior to, lesser than, lower than, obedient to, reporting to, secondary to, subjugated to, subservient to, included in.

undercover *adj. We thought he was doing undercover work for the government:* secret, hush-hush, covert, concealed, clandestine, unrevealed, surreptitious, disguised, hidden, sub rosa, confidential, undisclosed; sly, stealthy, furtive. **—Ant.** open, undisguised, unconcealed, aboveboard.

undercurrent *n.* **1.** *Swimming in the channel was dangerous because of the undercurrent:* undertow, riptide, crosscurrent. **2.** *You could almost feel the undercurrent of hatred in the room:* underlying attitude, hidden feeling, undertone, mood, atmosphere, aura, quality, intimation, suggestion, hint, sense, tinge, vibrations, *Informal* vibes.

underdog *n. The underdog came from behind to win:* loser, failure, *Informal* little guy, low man.

underestimate *v. Never underestimate the power of a woman:* rate too low, undervalue, underrate, misjudge, miscalculate, undersell, sell short; disregard, dismiss, minimize, discredit, detract from, belittle, depreciate, disparage, deprecate, *Slang* put down. **—Ant.** overestimate, overvalue, overrate, overstate, exaggerate.

undergo *v. She has to undergo minor surgery. The early settlers underwent many hardships:* go through, submit to, experience; withstand, stand, encounter, endure, sustain, weather, suffer, brave. **—Ant.** evade, shun, avoid, escape, forgo, sidestep, circumvent, steer clear of.

underground *adj.* **1.** *The power lines for the new houses are underground:* buried, belowground, below the surface, subterranean. **2.** *The spy never told his family about his underground activities:* secret, covert, undercover, clandestine, surreptitious, sub rosa.

underhand *also* **underhanded** *adj. He got the contract in an underhand way:* unethical, unscrupulous, unprincipled, devious, tricky, sneaking, sneaky, surreptitious, stealthy, covert, evasive, furtive, conniving, cunning, crafty; illegal, dishonest, crooked, fraudulent, corrupt. **—Ant.** open, aboveboard, ethical, scrupulous, principled; legal, honest.

underline *v. Famine underlined the crisis:* underscore, bracket, caption, off, emphasize, feature, give emphasis, highlight, italicize, mark, play up, point up, stress, accentuate.

underling *n. The volunteer workers resented being treated like underlings:* menial, flunky, hireling, servant, subordinate, lackey, minion, inferior, minor employee, domestic employee, hired hand; subject, vassal, serf, thrall, attendant. **—Ant.** executive, supervisor, boss, employer, chief.

underlying *adj. She sought the underlying cause for the dispute:* basic, essential, cardinal, critical, elemental, elementary, fundamental, intrinsic, primary, root, vital, bottom; concealed, latent.

undermine *v.* **1.** *The escaped convicts had undermined the prison walls. The shifting sands undermined the foundation of the beach house:* excavate under, tunnel under, burrow under; eat away at, erode, wear away the base of, riddle. **2.** *She jealously tried to undermine our friendship. The crooked politician tried to undermine attempts at reform:* subvert, weaken, injure, cripple, ruin, destroy, *Informal* torpedo; render powerless, thwart, foil, scotch, frustrate, neutralize, hamstring, sabotage, cut the ground from under. **—Ant.** 2 reinforce, strengthen, buttress, encourage, support, forward, help, aid, abet.

underprivileged *adj. Once a week she teaches underprivileged children:* disadvantaged, deprived, badly-off, unfortunate, hapless, ill-starred, ill-fated, unlucky, in adverse circumstances; poor, indigent, impoverished, needy, in need, pauperized, penurious, penniless, destitute. **—Ant.** advantaged, privileged, affluent, well-off.

underscore *v. Underscore the titles of the books you want. The speaker underscored his words by banging his fist on the table:* underline, draw a line under; stress, emphasize, accentuate, press home, accent, point up, mark, bring out forcibly, feature, intensify, play up, draw attention to, heighten, deepen. **—Ant.** de-emphasize, moderate, skip over.

understand *v.* **1.** *I didn't understand your message. She didn't understand what was happening to her:* grasp the meaning of, comprehend, absorb, make out, fathom, *Informal* get, *Slang* dig; know, recognize, appreciate, see, be aware, perceive, discern, apprehend, realize, grasp. **2.** *He understood my letter to be a subtle warning:* interpret, see, read, take, take to mean. **3.** *We understand that you'll be returning next year:* gather, hear, learn, presume, take for granted, take it, conclude, assume. **4.** *I understand your not wanting to discuss the matter:* sympathize with, appreciate, can see, see the reasons for, accept.

understanding *n.* **1.** *Few people have an understanding of nuclear physics:* knowledge, grasp, comprehension, appreciation, cognizance, perception, awareness, apprehension. **2.** *Because she has great understanding, people confide in her:* sympathy, compassion, appreciation, empathy, sensitivity, insight, perception, intuition. **3.** *Management has finally reached an understanding with employees:* agreement, meeting of the minds, pact, concordance, compromise. *—adj.* **4.** *The youth was fortunate in having understanding parents:* sympathetic, compassionate, appreciative, responsive, sensitive, tolerant, perceptive, discerning, knowing. **—Ant.** 1 misunderstanding, incomprehension,

ignorance. 2 insensitivity, lack of insight, obtuseness, aloofness. 4 unsympathetic, uncompassionate, unresponsive, unfeeling, insensitive; intolerant, strict, stiff, rigid.

understood *adj.* **1.** *His absence from work during the trial was understood:* understandable, axiomatic, clear, comprehensible, customary, implicit, incontrovertible, inferred, manifest, obvious, plain, self-evident, self-explanatory, tacit, undeclared, undeniable, unexpressed, unformulated, unmistakable, unquestionable, unrecorded, unsaid, unspoken, unstated, accepted, *Law* prima facie; traditional, customary. **2.** *Understood factors led to the result:* appreciated, assumed, axiomatic, inferential, inferred, presumed.

understudy *n. Her understudy never got a chance to play the role:* stand-by, alternate, replacement, substitute, surrogate, double, backup, pinch hitter, fill-in, stand-in, relief; *Slang* sub.

undertake *v. Who will undertake the job of decorating the auditorium?:* set about, take on, assume, enter upon, embark on, tackle, shoulder, agree to do, promise to do, obligate oneself to, commit oneself to, get involved in, attempt, strive, endeavor, essay, try; commence, begin, start, set about. **—Ant.** abandon, drop, desist, decline, forswear, eschew, avoid; discontinue, stop.

undertaking *n. Building one's own house is a tremendous undertaking:* endeavor, enterprise, project, task, job, effort, commitment, venture, pursuit, concern.

undertone *n.* **1.** *They spoke in undertones so as not to wake the baby:* low tone, subdued voice, whisper, murmur, mumble. **2.** *There was an undertone of danger in the air:* undercurrent, feeling, sense, quality, mood, coloring, implication, intimation, atmosphere, aura, nuance, inkling, suggestion, hint, trace, tinge, scent, flavor; connotation.

undertow *n. The sea had a treacherous undertow at that point:* undercurrent, riptide, crosscurrent.

underwear *n. Underwear has its own drawer:* underclothes, underclothing, undergarments, underthings, undies, intimate things, unmentionables.

underweight *adj. The child looks underweight to me:* gaunt, skinny, skin-and-bones, scrawny, lanky, bony, undernourished, spindly, underfed, lank; emaciated, skeletal, hollow-cheeked, spindle-shanked. **—Ant.** overweight, obese, flabby, *Slang* gross.

underworld *n.* **1.** *Most gambling is controlled by the underworld:* criminal element, criminals, organized crime, gangsters, mobsters, *Informal* the mob; *(loosely)* the syndicate, the Mafia, the Cosa Nostra. **2.** *Are sinners doomed to spend eternity in the underworld?:* Hell, Hades, purgatory, limbo, abode of the damned, bottomless pit, infernal regions, lake of fire and brimstone, place of departed spirits, shades below.

underwrite *v. Several local businessmen will underwrite the concert season:* subsidize, sponsor, back, support, guarantee, aid; approve, validate, sanction; endorse, countersign. —**Ant.** reject, veto, refuse, cancel, *Slang* nix.

undesirable *adj. The dock area was full of hoodlums and other undesirable characters. Declaring bankruptcy would be an undesirable course of action:* unsavory, offensive, unworthy, unattractive, objectionable, distasteful, disagreeable, unwelcomed, uninviting, unseemly, unsatisfactory; unacceptable, unsuitable, inadmissible, unwished-for, unwanted, unbidden, unpopular, disliked; inappropriate, unbefitting, unfit, improper, unbecoming.

undeveloped *adj. His undeveloped argument did not convince us:* abortive, amorphous, backward, embryonic, formless, immature, imperfect, inchoate, incipient, inexperienced, rudimentary, shapeless, underdeveloped, unfinished, unformed; untaught, untrained, beginning, preliminary, *Informal* half-baked.

undignified *adj. Arriving barefoot may have been undignified, but it was fun:* lacking dignity, indecorous, inappropriate, unbecoming, unsuitable, unseemly, inelegant, boorish, unladylike, ungentlemanly, unrefined, improper, unbefitting, tasteless, indelicate, in bad taste; low, discreditable, unworthy, degrading, shameful, beneath one, beneath one's dignity, *Latin* infra dignitatem, *Informal* infra dig.

undine *n. The undine whispered magical words to him:* sprite, water nymph, sylph.

undisciplined *adj. Undisciplined children annoy everyone. The violinist had natural talent, but his playing was completely undis-ciplined:* unrestrained, wayward, willful, obstreperous, wild, uncontrolled; undependable, unreliable, fitful, erratic, capricious, fickle, changeable, mercurial, unsteady, inconstant, unpredictable; untrained, untaught, unschooled, uneducated, untutored, unpracticed, unfinished.

undisguised *adj. Her undisguised enthusiasm somehow won all of us over to the idea:* open, unconcealed, unhidden, obvious, evident, unmistakable, manifest, evident, distinct, pronounced, clear; unreserved, wholehearted, utter, out-and-out, complete, thoroughgoing, plain as the nose on one's face, plain as day.

undismayed *adj. The Wright brothers were undismayed by their first failures to fly and tried again. We were undismayed by his threats:* undiscouraged, not disheartened, still confident, undaunted, not disconcerted, unabashed; unalarmed, not apprehensive, unfrightened, unscared, unafraid, unintimidated, not cowed, not put off.

undisputed *adj. His last will and testament was undisputed by the surviving relatives. Shakespeare's genius is undisputed:* uncontested, not disputed, unchallenged, unquestioned, accepted; indisputable, incontestable, undeniable, freely admitted, granted, undoubted, beyond doubt, past dispute, irrefutable, without question, beyond question, incontrovertible, a matter of fact, acknowledged, unquestionable, indubitable, conclusive, certain, sure.

undistinguished *adj. The play was undistin-*guished, but the acting was good:* ordinary, common, commonplace, mediocre, unexceptional, unremarkable, usual, plain, prosaic, nothing to rave about, unexciting, pedestrian, run-of-the-mill, everyday.

undisturbed *adj.* **1.** *She's easygoing and remains undisturbed when the children quarrel:* unruffled, unperturbed, unagitated, unexcited, untroubled, unbothered; composed, placid, serene, peaceful, tranquil, equable, self-possessed, calm, cool, collected, steady. **2.** *Give me an undisturbed hour and I'll finish the work. The accountant gave orders that the papers on his desk be left undisturbed:* uninterrupted, without interruption, quiet, of solitude; untouched, unmoved, not meddled with, left in order. —**Ant.** 1, 2 disturbed. 1 upset, perturbed, agitated, troubled, excited, nervous, ruffled. 2 interrupted, confused, busy; moved, meddled with, disordered.

undivided *adj. You may count on our undivided support in the coming election:* not divided, solid, whole, entire, complete, unstinting, wholehearted; unanimous, united, unified, unsplit, of one mind.

undo *v.* **1.** *It's almost impossible to undo the harm you've done:* offset, reverse, cancel, nullify, erase, annul, wipe out, neutralize, void, repair, counterbalance, counteract; compensate for, make up for, rectify. **2.** *Can you undo this knot?:* open, free, unfasten, loose, loosen; (*variously*) disentangle, unknot, unravel, unwrap, unfold, untie, unbind, unlace, disengage, unbutton, unchain, unlock, unhook. **3.** *The gossip is bound to undo his candidacy:* ruin, destroy, subvert, undermine, end, eliminate, demolish, wipe out, defeat, overturn, invalidate, quash. —**Ant.** 1 do, accomplish, effect, realize, produce, commit, manage. 2 fasten, close, tie, knot, tangle, button, lock, hook, close. 3 enhance, help, aid, abet, further.

undoing *n.* **1.** *Poor management resulted in the undoing of all we had accomplished:* reversal, cancellation, wiping out, erasure, negation, annulment, nullification, neutralization, invalidation, thwarting, counteraction, upset. **2.** *A surprise attack brought about the undoing of the air force:* ruin, ruination, collapse, downfall, destruction, doom, defeat, breakdown, overthrow. **3.** *Her other grades were good, but math was her undoing:* cause of ruin, nemesis, downfall, weakness, jinx, Achilles' heel. —**Ant.** 1 realization, accomplishment, establishment, furtherance. 2 victory, success, triumph. 3 strength, strong point, specialty.

undoubtedly *adv. You are undoubtedly right in thinking you were cheated:* doubtless, unquestionably, beyond question, without doubt, beyond a doubt, undeniably, indubitably; certainly, definitely, assuredly, decidedly, positively, absolutely.

undress *v.* **1.** *The patient undressed in the examination room:* take off one's clothes, disrobe, unclothe, strip, uncover, undrape. —*n.* **2.** *The hostess was in a state of undress when the first guests arrived:* nakedness, nudity; disarray, carelessness of attire, dishabille. —**Ant.** 1 dress, clothe, robe, drape, cover.

undue *adj. The parents felt undue concern about the child's illness. The widow remarried with undue haste:* excessive, too great, inordinate, uncalled-for, unwarranted, unnecessary, overmuch, unjustified, needless, superfluous; improper, unsuitable, inappropriate, not fitting, ill-advised, unseemly, tasteless, unmeet, indiscreet, unworthy, unbecoming, objectionable, impolite, in bad taste. —**Ant.** due, proper, necessary, needed, justified; suitable, appropriate, fitting, seemly, meet, well-taken.

unduly *adv. Difficulties bother me unduly:* excessively, disproportionately, extravagantly, immensely, improperly, indecorously, inordinately, overly, overmuch, unjustifiably, unjustly, unnecessarily, unreasonably, extremely. —**Ant.** reasonably, justifiably, moderately, properly, duly.

undying *adj. He vowed his undying love:* eternal, never-ending, unending, unceasing, unfading, perpetual, endless, everlasting, lasting, enduring, abiding, imperishable, perennial, perpetual, incessant, permanent, constant, continual, continuing, unremitting, unrelenting, inde-structible, unfaltering, never-failing, untiring, undiminished, uninterrupted, steady; deathless, immortal. —**Ant.** temporary, unlasting, impermanent, passing, ephemeral, transitory, transient, fleeting, temporal, brief, momentary; mortal, dying.

unearth *v.* **1.** *The treasure seekers unearthed a buried pirate chest:* dig up, dig out, dredge up, excavate; exhume, disentomb, disinter. **2.** *The police have unearthed new information in the case:* discover, uncover, find, come across, dig up, ferret out, bring to light, root out, come up with; divulge, disclose, reveal, expose, show, display, exhibit. —**Ant.** 1, 2 bury. 2 cover up, conceal, hide.

unearthly *adj.* **1.** *There were unearthly lights glowing in the haunted house:* not of this earth, not of this world, supernatural, extramundane, ethereal, spectral, ghostly, phantom; incorporeal, disembodied, preternatural, weird, eerie, uncanny. **2.** *What an unearthly time to come calling!:* strange, abnormal, unusual, absurd, extraordinary, extreme; terrible, horrendous, disagreeable, unspeakable, awful, unpleasant, ungodly. —**Ant.** 1 earthly, natural, mundane. 2 normal, usual, common, ordinary, typical; pleasant, agreeable.

uneasy *adj.* **1.** *The driver was uneasy about the icy roads:* worried, disturbed, upset, apprehensive, troubled, perturbed. **2.** *She felt uneasy with her new in-laws:* ill at ease, awkward, uncomfortable, strained, nervous, nervy, edgy, on edge, unsure, tense, constrained, disquieted, *Slang* uptight. **3.** *I have an uneasy sensation in the pit of my stomach:* upsetting, queasy, bothersome, unpleasant, disturbing, uncomfortable, worrying, irksome, disquieting.

uneducated *adj. Most of the children in the village were uneducated:* ignorant, untutored, unschooled, unenlightened, uninstructed, uncultivvated, untaught, uninformed, unlettered, illiterate. —**Ant.** cultivated, literate.

unemotional *adj. Unemotional people seldom laugh or cry. She gave him a quick unemotional kiss on the cheek:* unfeeling, passionless, apathetic, impassive, indifferent, unconcerned, unresponsive, undemonstrative, cold, cool, lukewarm, remote, distant, reserved, formal.

unemployed *adj. When the factory closed, half the town was unemployed:* jobless, laid-off, out of work, workless, idle, at leisure, at liberty, unoccupied; fired, discharged, dismissed; *Slang* axed, sacked, booted-out, canned, bounced, pink-slipped. —**Ant.** working, employed, engaged, busy.

unending *adj. The rainfall in the tropics seems unending:* incessant, unceasing, never-ending, perpetual, constant, endless, eternal, permanent, perennial, enduring, lasting, everlasting, unremitting, steady, undiminished, unwavering, continual, continuous, uninterrupted. —**Ant.** brief, short, fleeting, momentary, transitory, transient, temporary, passing; sporadic, intermittent, unsteady, interrupted.

unenlightened *adj. The primitive tribe was totally unenlightened about the outside world:* uninformed, unknowledgeable, ignorant, unfamiliar with, unlearned, uninitiated, uninstructed, uneducated, in the dark. —**Ant.** enlightened, well-informed, knowledgeable, knowing, familiar, learned.

unequal *adj.* **1.** *The two men do the same job but earn unequal salaries. Since the two teams are unequal, the game isn't exciting:* not equal, uneven, different, unmatched, unlike, dissimilar, not uniform, disparate. **2.** *The unequal treatment of minority groups is against the law:* unfair, unjust, not equitable, prejudiced, biased, partial, bigoted. —**Ant.** 1, 2 equal. 1 even, matched, uniform, similar, like, alike. 2 fair, just, right, unprejudiced, unbiased, unbigoted.

unequaled *adj. Babe Ruth's home-run record was unequaled until Hank Aaron came along. She grew roses of unequaled beauty:* unsurpassed, unmatched, unparalleled, matchless, beyond compare, incomparable, unrivaled, second to none, unapproached, beyond comparison, unexcelled, supreme, paramount, peerless, consummate, *Latin* ne plus ultra.

unequivocal *adj. The evidence is unequivocal. His refusal is unequivocal:* decisive, unambiguous, clear, clear-cut, absolute, definite, final, certain, incontestable, indisputable, incontrovertible, emphatic. —**Ant.** equivocal, ambiguous, indecisive, vague, doubtful, indefinite.

unerring *adj. The antique dealer has an unerring ability to spot a fake:* infallible, unfailing, faultless, certain, sure, precise, reliable, faithful, unchanging, constant.

unessential *adj. She decided the hair dryer was unessential for the trip:* nonessential, unimportant, dispensable, immaterial, unnecessary. —**Ant.** essential.

unethical *adj. The lawyer was disbarred for unethical practices:* unprincipled, dishonorable, disreputable, shoddy, shady, underhand, devi-

ous, *Informal* dirty; unfair, wrong, unconscionable, dishonest, questionable, unworthy, ungentlemanly, unladylike. —**Ant.** ethical,
principled, honorable, reputable, honest, clean,
fair, aboveboard, conscionable.

uneven *adj.* **1.** *The table wobbles because the
floor is uneven. The car jolted over the uneven
road:* not even, not level, not flat, not plumb,
slanted, angled, awry, sloping, tilted, bent,
crooked, curved; unsmooth, bumpy, lumpy,
craggy, jagged, rough, coarse. **2.** *I wouldn't bet
on such an uneven fight. The two fighters are
uneven in style:* unequal, one-sided, unbalanced, lopsided, ill-matched, unfair, unjust; disparate, dissimilar, different, unlike. —**Ant.** 1, 2
even. 1 level, flat, straight, plane, smooth, uniform. 2 equal, well-matched, well-balanced, fair,
just; similar, alike, like.

uneventful *adj.* *Our trip was uneventful:* not
eventful, quiet, unexceptional, routine, ordinary,
commonplace, average, usual, standard, conventional, insignificant; dull, tedious, boring,
humdrum, prosaic, tiresome, monotonous, uninteresting.

unexcelled *adj.* *The team has an unexcelled
record of ten wins and no losses. The beauty of
the Taj Mahal is unexcelled:* unsurpassed, unbeaten, supreme, peerless, transcendent, superior, consummate, flawless, faultless; unequaled, unrivaled, matchless, unmatched,
incomparable, beyond compare, unparalleled,
unapproached, second to none.

unexpected *adj.* *Well, this is an unexpected
development!:* unanticipated, unlooked-for, unforeseen, unpredicted, startling, astonishing,
surprising, out of the blue; undesigned, unplanned, sudden, accidental, unintentional, unintended.

unfailing *adj.* *The Bible is an unfailing source of
inspiration. Jerry has been an unfailing friend
for over twenty years:* inexhaustible, endless,
continual, continuous, constant, dependable, reliable, never-failing, faithful, unchanging, true,
loyal, unwavering, steady, infallible, enduring.
—**Ant.** undependable, unreliable, unfaithful,
treacherous, disloyal, untrue, inconstant, wavering, unsteady, faulty, fallible.

unfair *adj.* *It's unfair to accuse anyone without
evidence. The referee was unfair in favoring one
of the teams:* not fair, unjust, not right, inequitable, unreasonable, *Slang* not cricket; partial, biased, prejudiced, partisan, unequal, one-sided,
dishonorable, unconscionable, unscrupulous,
unprincipled, unethical, underhand, dishonest,
corrupt, dirty, foul, crooked.

unfaithful *adj.* **1.** *An unfaithful employee sold
the idea to a rival firm. Henry VIII beheaded two
of his wives for being unfaithful:* disloyal, treacherous, perfidious, untrustworthy, faithless, false,
falsehearted, deceitful; adulterous, inconstant,
untrue, unchaste. **2.** *The portrait is unfaithful to
her true beauty:* not accurate, inaccurate, erroneous, untrue, false, inexact, imperfect, faulty,
distorted. —**Ant.** 1, 2 faithful, true. 1 loyal,
trustworthy, steadfast, true-blue; constant,
chaste. 2 accurate, correct, exact, perfect.

unfaltering *adj.* *She always helped me with unfaltering kindness:* firm, steady, resolute, unwavering, wholehearted, unfailing, steadfast, unswerving, enduring, unflagging, undeviating,
never-failing, sure, dependable; persistent, obstinate, persevering. —**Ant.** irresolute, undependable, fickle, vacillating.

unfamiliar *adj.* **1.** *The classical musician was
unfamiliar with popular music:* unacquainted,
not acquainted, unconversant, unaccustomed
to, a stranger to, unexposed to, unversed in,
unenlightened about, ignorant of, uninformed
about, inexperienced in, unpracticed in, unskilled in, uninitiated. **2.** *This soup has an unfamiliar taste. The artist's name is unfamiliar to
most people:* unknown, unusual, strange, curious, unique, different, new, novel, out-of-the-
way, exotic, foreign; not well-known, little
known. —**Ant.** 1, 2 familiar. 1 acquainted,
conversant, accustomed, well-versed, versed,
knowledgeable, experienced, practical. 2 common, commonplace, normal, everyday, average,
run-of-the-mill; well-known, known, recognized.

unfathomable *adj.* **1.** *The unfathomable ocean
inspired her best poems:* unplumbed, bottomless, boundless, immeasurable, infinite, soundless, unending, unmeasured, deep. **2.** *His reasoning was unfathomable:* incomprehensible,
uncomprehensible, enigmatic, esoteric, impenetrable, indecipherable, inexplicable, obscure,
unintelligible, baffling.

unfavorable *adj.* *Icy roads made traveling
conditions unfavorable. I fear he's in an unfavorable position with his boss:* not favorable, adverse, poor, unsuited, ill-suited, unpropitious,
inauspicious, regrettable, unhappy, infelicitous,
bad, disadvantageous, untimely, inconvenient,
inopportune, unseasonable, unpromising, ill-
favored, unfortunate.

unfeeling *adj.* *The unfeeling nurse refused to
give him an injection:* insensible, insensate,
numb, callous, unsympathetic, hard, hardhearted. —**Ant.** feeling, sympathetic.

unfinished *adj.* **1.** *It's five o'clock and the work
is still unfinished:* not finished, uncompleted, incomplete, undone, unexecuted, unfulfilled; imperfect, immature, deficient, lacking, wanting. **2.**
*These unfinished sketches give a general idea
of what the house will look like. Buy unfinished
furniture and paint it yourself:* rough, sketchy,
crude, deficient, wanting, unpolished, unrefined;
unnatural, (*variously*) unpainted, unvarnished,
unstained, unlacquered.

unfit *adj.* **1.** *This water is unfit for drinking:* not
fit, unsuited, unsuitable, not suited, inappropriate, inadequate, not designed, ill-contrived, ineffective, inefficient, not equal to, useless. **2.**
The young boy is unfit to run that business: unqualified, inadequate, incompetent, unprepared,
untrained, unskilled, unequipped, ill-equipped,
incapable, unready, unequal, unsuited, not
equal to, not up to, not cut out for, ineligible. **3.**
The operation left her unfit for months: unsound, unhealthy, debilitated, sick, sickly, frail,
weak, infirm, incapacitated, delicate, disabled.
—**Ant.** 1–3 fit. 1 suitable, adequate, useful,

adaptable. 2 suited, qualified, competent, capable, able, equipped, prepared, ready, eligible. 3 healthy, sound, hale, in good health, strong, sturdy.

unflagging *adj. The fans cheered the team with unflagging enthusiasm. Her unflagging determination to be a concert violinist is admirable:* unfaltering, untiring, tireless, indefatigable, undrooping, unremitting, unswerving, steady, steadfast, firm, resolute, undeviating, unwavering, unshaken, unyielding, indomitable, relentless, uncompromising, persevering, constant, fixed, firm, staunch, determined, undaunted, enduring, tenacious, persistent. —**Ant.** faltering, wavering, flagging, drooping, irresolute, relenting, compromising, half-hearted.

unflappable *adj. The unflappable speaker ignored the hecklers:* unruffled, relaxed, composed, cool, impassive, nonchalant, relaxed, self-possessed, calm, collected. —**Ant.** excitable, hotheaded, nervous, volatile.

unflinching *adj. The captain's unflinching courage gave the passengers hope:* steady, unshaken, unshrinking, steadfast, unabashed, plucky, unfaltering, tenacious, persistent, strong, gritty, game, fearless, firm, indomitable, unhesitating, unwavering, unswerving, staunch, stalwart, undaunted, unyielding, resolute. —**Ant.** shaken, hesitant, faltering, weak, wavering, irresolute.

unfold *v. 1. Unfold the map and tack it on the bulletin board:* spread out, open up, open out, stretch out, unwrap, unroll, unfurl. 2. *The leader began to unfold his plan to his followers:* reveal, make known, disclose, divulge, unveil, uncover, show, bare, lay open, set forth, present, tell, explain, expound, explicate, describe, recount, elucidate. —**Ant.** 1 fold, close, roll up, furl. 2 conceal, hide, cloak, veil; keep secret, keep mum about.

unforeseen *adj. The unforeseen snowstorm tied up the railroads for days:* unexpected, unpredicted, surprise, unanticipated, unlooked-for, sudden, abrupt, out of the blue; unplanned, unintended, accidental, surprising. —**Ant.** foreseen, expected, anticipated, looked-for, predicted; planned, intended.

unfortunate *adj. His unfortunate career seemed doomed from the start. Her unfortunate remark caused Father to dislike her:* unlucky, luckless, ill-starred, hapless, unhappy, ill-fated, infelicitous, cursed, unsuccessful, unblest, jinxed, unprosperous; regrettable, wretched, sorry, disastrous, woeful, ill-advised, unfavorable, unpropitious, inopportune, untimely, ill-timed, inauspicious. —**Ant.** fortunate, lucky, happy, felicitous, successful, propitious, opportune, timely, auspicious.

unfounded *adj. Rumors that an escaped convict was on the plane proved to be unfounded:* baseless, groundless, without foundation, without substance, idle; false, untrue, erroneous, fabricated, spurious.

unfriendly *adj. Each nation accused the other of unfriendly acts:* antagonistic, hostile, warlike; disagreeable, unsociable, chilly, cold, unsympa-thetic, distant, inhospitable, ungracious, uncongenial; withdrawn, reclusive; snobbish, haughty, aloof. —**Ant.** warm, hospitable, agreeable, congenial, friendly.

unfruitful *adj. Most of the discussions we held were unfruitful:* fruitless, unproductive, unprofitable, unrewarding, unremunerative; unavailing, useless, futile, vain, purposeless; barren, infecund, impoverished, worn-out, fallow. —**Ant.** fruitful, productive, useful, rewarding, profitable.

ungainly *adj. Claire is too ungainly to be a ballerina:* ungraceful, clumsy, awkward, maladroit, uncoordinated, stiff, lumbering, *Slang* klutzy. —**Ant.** graceful, lithe, willowy, limber, supple, sylphlike.

ungodly *adj. 1. His ungodly life was a disgrace to his family:* not religious, godless; impious, blasphemous; wicked, sinful, immoral, heinous, iniquitous, depraved, degenerate, dissolute, dishonorable, corrupt, villainous, rotten, base, vile. 2. *Informal They woke us at an ungodly hour!:* dreadful, awful, horrendous, outrageous, terrible, ghastly, unreasonable. —**Ant.** 1 godly, religious, pious, moral, good, virtuous, wholesome, honorable. 2 agreeable, pleasant, acceptable, reasonable.

ungracious *adj. Surprisingly, she was most ungracious next time we met:* discourteous, rude, unmannerly, ill-mannered, uncouth, uncivil, churlish, impolite, disrespectful, impertinent, bad-mannered, boorish, ungentlemanly, unladylike; loutish, coarse, vulgar. —**Ant.** polite, courteous, well-bred, urbane, gracious.

ungrateful *adj. They were ungrateful for the gift:* unthankful, unappreciative, selfish, dissatisfied, heedless, oblivious, self-centered, selfish, unmindful. —**Ant.** grateful, appreciative, thankful.

unguarded *adj. 1. A politician must be careful about making unguarded remarks:* indiscreet, imprudent, ill-considered, tactless, undiplomatic, uncircumspect, careless, unmindful, incautious, unwary; unrestrained, overly candid, too frank. 2. *The unguarded camp was vulnerable to attack:* unprotected, unpatrolled, unwatched, defenseless, undefended. —**Ant.** 1, 2 guarded. 1 discreet, circumspect, cautious, wary, careful. 2 protected, patrolled, watched, defended.

unhandy *adj. John is always unhandy around machinery:* clumsy, awkward, ham-handed, all thumbs, maladroit, fumbling, inept, bumbling, gauche, unskillful, inexpert; *Slang* butterfingered, klutzy. —**Ant.** adroit, expert, deft, skilled, handy.

unhappy *adj. 1. Why are you so unhappy?:* not happy, sad, sorrowful, despondent, depressed, dejected, downcast, heavyhearted, doleful, gloomy, forlorn, melancholy, dispirited, joyless, crestfallen, woebegone, somber, blue, long-faced, down in the mouth. 2. *Investing in that swampy property was an unhappy venture. Telling the hostess that the pie was "almost perfect" was an unhappy choice of words:* unfortunate, hapless, unsuccessful, unwise, imprudent, foolish, injudicious, ill-advised, regrettable, sorry, infelicitous, adverse, poor, bad, unlucky, luckless, inappropriate, inapt, unsuitable, awkward, unseemly, unbecoming, unbefitting. —**Ant.** 1, 2 happy. 1 gay, cheerful, joyful, joyous, lighthearted, sunny, smiling, exuberant, effervescent, enthusiastic. 2 fortunate, successful, wise, prudent, smart, shrewd, good, fine, wonderful, lucky, blessed, favorable; appropriate, apt, suitable, seemly, becoming, correct, befitting.

unhealthful *adj. Air pollution contributed to an unhealthful environment:* insalubrious, unwholesome, unhealthy, noxious, poisonous, harmful. —**Ant.** healthy, healthful, hale, hearty.

unhealthy *adj.* **1.** *He's been unhealthy since childhood:* sickly, sick, infirm, ailing, not well, unwell, in poor health, indisposed, poorly, feeble, weak, unsound; invalid, diseased. **2.** *Air pollution is very unhealthy:* unhealthful, harmful to health, noxious, hurtful, detrimental, unwholesome, insalubrious. **3.** *There's an unhealthy atmosphere of greed and corruption throughout the country:* demoralizing, harmful, morally bad, undesirable, destructive, corrupting, contaminating, degrading, depraved, morbid, negative, bad; hazardous, dangerous, perilous. —**Ant.** 1–3 healthy. 1 well, sound, strong, robust. 2 healthful, salubrious, salutary, wholesome, beneficial. 3 moral, positive, constructive, desirable, good.

unheard-of *adj. The private answered the captain with unheard-of effrontery:* outrageous, preposterous, outlandish, unbelievable, unreasonable, inconceivable; unique, unprecedented, unusual, original, exceptional, unparalleled, incomparable, matchless. —**Ant.** reasonable, expected, believable, usual, ordinary.

unheralded *adj. The unheralded visitors arrived in the middle of the night. The novel is an unheralded masterpiece:* unannounced, unexpected, unanticipated, unforeseen, unlooked-for; unsung, unacclaimed, unproclaimed, unrecognized, unpublicized.

unhesitating *adj.* **1.** *The sergeant expects unhesitating obedience to his orders:* immediate, quick, instantaneous, prompt, without hesitation, without delay, ready, direct. **2.** *Their unhesitating support was heartwarming:* unreserved, wholehearted, unflinching, eager, without reservation.

unholy *adj.* **1.** *The unholy alliance between gangsters and the police is being investigated by the district attorney:* wicked, evil, ungodly, sinful, depraved, immoral, wicked, heinous, iniquitous, corrupt, villainous, dishonest, dishonorable; rotten, base, vile. **2.** *The room was an unholy mess:* dreadful, shocking, awful, ungodly, horrendous, outrageous, unreasonable. —**Ant.** 1 moral, good, virtuous, honest, honorable, wholesome; godly, religious, pious. 2 agreeable, pleasant, acceptable, reasonable.

unidentified *adj. The perpetrator of the crime got away and is still unidentified. The guests agreed the cake had a strange unidentified flavor:* unknown, nameless, anonymous, vague, unrecognized; unnamed, unspecified, undesig-

nated, unlabeled. —**Ant.** known, named, recognized; specified, designated, labeled.

unification *n. The Revolutionary War resulted in the unification of the thirteen American colonies:* uniting, union, consolidation, consolidating, unity, junction, alliance, merger, combining, combination, confederation, confederacy, coalition, coalescence, incorporation, amalgamation, fusion. —**Ant.** separation, division, splitting, disunion, disunity.

uniform *n.* **1.** *My daughter has a new cheerleader's uniform:* dress, apparel, attire, costume, garb, array; *(variously)* vestment, habit, livery, regalia, regimentals. —*adj.* **2.** *The windows in the house are all uniform. The residents were uniform in their attitude toward strangers:* alike, equal, identical, similar, consistent, consonant, of a piece, harmonious, agreeing, of one mind, conforming, at one, in accord, in step, in line. **3.** *The acoustics are uniform throughout the auditorium:* the same, even, equal, unvarying, unvaried, undeviating, unchanging, unaltered, constant, regular, consistent. —**Ant.** 2, 3 different. 2 unalike, unlike, dissimilar, nonstandard, multiform, mixed; disagreeing, discordant, individual. 3 uneven, unequal, mixed, variable, inconsistent, irregular, erratic, deviating, changed, altered.

unify *v. A common allegiance to the Crown unifies the British Commonwealth:* unite, combine, form into one, join, consolidate, bring together, confederate, federate, incorporate, ally, coalesce, amalgamate, fuse, merge; link up, couple, wed, blend, lump together. —**Ant.** disunite, separate, divide, part, split, cleave, sever, disband.

unimaginable *adj. The consequences were unimaginable:* incomprehensible, inconceivable, unbelievable, incredible, unthinkable, indescribable, mind-boggling, singular, unheard-of, unique, impossible, fantastic.

unimaginative *adj. Most of the costumes at the party were unimaginative:* uninspired, unoriginal, routine, uncreative, ordinary, prosaic, mediocre, trite, commonplace, clichéd, run-of-the-mill, stock, pedestrian, everyday, stale, hackneyed, usual, predictable, unromantic, dull, unexciting, tedious, uninteresting, vapid, humdrum, dreary, unremarkable. —**Ant.** imaginative, original, creative, inspired, extraordinary, unusual, different, fanciful, exciting, interesting, fresh, novel, new.

unimpeachable *adj. His unimpeachable record makes him a perfect political candidate. The reporter obtained his information from an unimpeachable source:* totally honest, beyond criticism, impeccable, irreproachable, above reproach, unassailable, beyond question, blameless, inculpable, faultless, perfect, unmarred, unblemished, spotless, stainless, untainted, clean, undefiled, inviolate, pure, immaculate; reliable, trustworthy, unquestionable, solid, unchallengeable, infallible. —**Ant.** questionable, dubious, debatable, controversial, suspect, faulty, imperfect, tainted, untrustworthy, unreliable.

unimportant *adj. Whether you wear the red dress or the blue is really unimportant! His brother-in-law has an unimportant job with the firm:* not important, inconsequential, of no consequence, insignificant, of no moment, immaterial, irrelevant, nugatory, nonessential, not vital; inconsiderable, negligible, minor, lesser, subordinate, inferior, trivial, trifling, paltry, meager, slight, piddling, low-ranking, second-rate, mediocre. —**Ant.** important, consequential, significant.

uninformed *adj. He was completely uninformed about world affairs:* ignorant, unread, unaware, uninstructed, unknowing, unlearned, unenlightened, unschooled, uneducated, unconversant, unadvised; *Slang* not with it, in the dark. —**Ant.** informed, enlightened; *Slang* with it.

uninhabited *adj. The house has been uninhabited for almost a year. The boat landed on an uninhabited island:* unoccupied, unlived in, vacant, empty, untenanted; unpopulated, unpeopled, unsettled, deserted, abandoned, forsaken. —**Ant.** inhabited, occupied, lived in; populated, peopled, settled.

uninhibited *adj.* **1.** *Only uninhibited people would think of joining a nudist colony. Her uninhibited remarks embarrassed her friends:* unself-conscious, not shy, open; spontaneous, impulsive, impetuous, rash, instinctive, *Informal* fast; heedless, unwary, unguarded, incautious, careless, indiscreet; outspoken, candid, frank, unreserved, plainspoken, straightforward, forthright; reckless, madcap, capricious, headstrong, abandoned, free, free-spirited, daring, flamboyant, immodest. **2.** *The uninhibited use of automobiles caused a gasoline shortage:* free, unrestrained, unconstrained, uncontrolled, unrestricted, unchecked, unobstructed, unhampered, unstopped, unimpeded, unhindered, uncurbed, unbridled, unreined. —**Ant.** 1, 2 inhibited. 1 self-conscious, shy, bashful, retiring, sheepish, modest, demure; wary, guarded, cautious, careful, discreet, self-controlled; stiff, rigid, *Slang* uptight. 2 restrained, constrained, controlled, restricted, checked, hampered, hindered, curbed, bridled.

uninspired *adj.* **1.** *The audience was left uninspired by the dull speech:* unmoved, unstirred, unimpressed, unexcited, unaffected, untouched, unemotional, unstimulated, uninfluenced. **2.** *The movie was so uninspired I went to sleep:* unimaginative, unoriginal, ordinary, prosaic, trite, commonplace, clichéd, run-of-the-mill, stock, pedestrian, stale, hackneyed, predictable, dull, unexciting, indifferent, uninteresting, vapid, humdrum. —**Ant.** 1, 2 inspired. 1 moved, stirred, impressed, excited, affected, touched, influenced, stimulated. 2 imaginative, creative, original, fresh, novel, new, extraordinary, unusual, different, exciting, interesting.

unintelligent *adj. That seems like an unintelligent way to approach the problem:* stupid, dumb, obtuse, asinine, simpleminded, blockheaded, thickheaded, half-witted, slow-witted, dull, dense, dull-witted, thick, slow, doltish, blank, *Slang* dopey. —**Ant.** intelligent, smart, brainy, sharp, brilliant.

unintelligible *adj. She was crying so hard her words were unintelligible. The code was unintelligible to anyone who didn't have the key:* impossible to understand, incoherent, inarticulate, incomprehensible, illegible, incapable of being understood, meaningless, unfathomable, baffling, confusing, puzzling, perplexing; undecipherable, impenetrable, insoluble. —**Ant.** intelligible, understandable, coherent, articulate, legible; comprehensible, clear, decipherable, soluble.

unintentional *adj. The boy didn't mean to bump into you; it was purely unintentional:* accidental, fortuitous, unpremeditated, unintended, undesigned, unplanned, not done purposely, unconscious, inadvertent, unthinking, unwitting, involuntary.

uninterested *adj. I tried to tell her about my trip, but she was uninterested:* unconcerned, heedless, indifferent, incurious, apathetic, unmindful, listless, blasé, uninvolved, *Slang* above it all; remote, aloof; uncaring, unimpressible. —**Ant.** concerned, interested, involved, curious, alive.

uninteresting *adj. Chess strikes me as a very uninteresting game:* boring, tiresome, dreary, dull, tedious, uneventful, monotonous, drab, wearisome, prosaic, dry, jejune, trite, insipid, humdrum, pedestrian, vapid, uninspiring, unmoving, insignificant, ordinary, lifeless, colorless, unsatisfying.

uninviting *adj. The house was drab and uninviting:* unappealing, unwelcoming, unalluring, untempting, unattractive, unpleasant, displeasing, undesirable, disagreeable, distasteful, offensive, unappetizing, annoying.

union *n.* **1.** *The book is a perfect union of humor and seriousness. The union of hydrogen and oxygen forms water:* combination, mixture, amalgam, amalgamation, consolidation, joining, blend, merger, unity, uniting, oneness, marriage, wedding; fusion, synthesis, unifying, unification. **2.** *Representatives from each state hoped to form a more perfect union:* federation, confederation, association, affiliation, alliance, league, partnership, corporation, fraternity. **3.** *Before working with the AFL, Samuel Gompers was a leader of the cigar-maker's union:* (variously) labor union, trade union, craft union, workers' association, guild. —**Ant.** 1 separation, division.

unionist *n. The unionists voted to strike:* union member, trade unionist, labor unionist.

unique *adj. The tranquil beauty of the Mona Lisa is unique:* singular, distinctive, one of a kind, by itself, incomparable, unrivaled, unparalleled, unequaled, matchless, unmatched, unexcelled, unsurpassed, peerless, unapproached, unexampled, inimitable, nonpareil, surpassing. —**Ant.** commonplace, common, usual, everyday, ordinary, average, routine, typical, run-of-the-mill.

unison *n. They spoke in unison:* unanimity, concert, concord, concordance, harmony, conjunction; consent, cooperation, federation, fellowship, league, fraternity, union, unity, agreement, alliance, community, accord, accordance. **—Ant.** dissonance, discord, disharmony; disagreement, dissension.

unit *n.* **1.** *The refrigerator needs a new cooling unit. The Hawaiian Islands form one political unit:* part, element, segment, section, component, constituent, member, division; entity, whole, quantity, group, package, detachment. **2.** *An ounce is a unit of weight:* measure, measurement, quantity, category, denomination, entity.

unite *v.* **1.** *The school united its music and theater departments:* unify, combine, join, consolidate, confederate, federate, incorporate, ally, coalesce, amalgamate, fuse, merge, couple, blend, homogenize, pool, lump together. **2.** *The people must unite against the tyrant:* join together, join forces, lock arms, stand together, organize, become one voice. **—Ant.** 1 divide, separate, disunite, split, part, sever, disjoin, detach, disengage.

united *adj.* **1.** *The city has a united bus and subway system:* unified, combined, consolidated, incorporated, amalgamated, fused, merged, joined, coupled, blended, allied, collective, pooled, lumped together; federated, leagued. **2.** *Her parents were united in their insistence that she go to college:* joined together, one, of the same opinion, unanimous, of one mind, in agreement. **—Ant.** 1, 2 divided. 2 split, on opposite sides of the fence, at odds.

unity *n.* **1.** *Would the unity of the nation be destroyed by stronger state governments? Some Puerto Ricans want unity with the United States while others want complete independ-ence:* oneness, wholeness, entity, unification, consolidation, amalgamation, fusion, synthesis, merger, joining, association, federation, confederation, affiliation, league, alliance, union, partnership. **2.** *The new prime minister begged for unity between the warring factions:* accord, concord, peace, harmony, cooperation, friendship, amicableness, unanimity, understanding, goodwill, fellowship, compatibility, like-mindedness, rapport. **—Ant.** 1, 2 disunity. 1 independence, individuality, heterogeneity, isolation, division, separateness, separation, severance. 2 disagreement, discord, disharmony, enmity, ill will.

universal *adj.* *Overpopulation is a universal problem:* concerning everyone, affecting all, worldwide, international, omnipresent, widespread, ubiquitous, existing everywhere; general, all-embracing, all-inclusive. **—Ant.** individual, personal, private, local, localized, parochial, limited, restricted, exclusive, confined, special, specific.

universe *n.* *He considered himself the master of the universe:* cosmos, macrocosm, world, everything, global village, nature, creation.

unjust *adj.* *The accusation of treason was unjust:* unfair, wrongful, unjustified, unwarranted, undeserved, unmerited, inequitable; prejudiced, biased, partisan, warped, one-sided, unbalanced. **—Ant.** just, impartial, fair, justified, deserved.

unkempt *adj.* *The child always has dirty nails and unkempt hair:* uncombed, tousled, disheveled, ungroomed, untidy, messy, sloppy, rumpled, disarranged, disordered, mussed-up, slovenly. **—Ant.** combed, well-groomed, neat, tidy, orderly.

unkind *adj.* *It was unkind of you to cancel the date on such short notice:* inconsiderate, thoughtless, unfeeling, unsympathetic, insensitive, uncaring, unfriendly, ungracious, inhospitable, uncharitable, ungenerous; mean, nasty, malicious, abusive.

unknown *adj.* *The poem was written by an unknown author of the 16th century:* anonymous, unidentified, undiscovered, unnamed, nameless, undesignated, undetermined; obscure, unrenowned, unheard-of, uncelebrated. **—Ant.** well-known, celebrated, famous, renowned.

unlawful *adj.* *Shooting off fireworks without a special permit is unlawful:* illegal, prohibited, unauthorized, forbidden, illicit, unconstitutional, unofficial, unlicensed, against the law, *Slang* illegit, lawless, criminal. **—Ant.** legal, lawful, licit, official, authorized.

unlike *adj.* *I've always felt the twins were completely unlike:* different, unalike, diverse, dissimilar, disparate, different as night and day, separate and distinct, not comparable, like apples and oranges. **—Ant.** like, similar, alike as two peas, identical.

unlikely *adj.* **1.** *Snow seems unlikely today. He may be right this time, but it's unlikely:* not likely, improbable, questionable, unbelievable, scarcely conceivable. **2.** *The fat youth was the most unlikely member of the track team:* unpromising, unpropitious, hopeless. **—Ant.** 1 likely, probable, unquestionable, sure, certain. 2 promising, propitious, encouraging.

unlimited *adj.* **1.** *The king was unlimited authority:* limitless, unrestricted, unrestrained, unchecked, uncontrolled, absolute, total, totalitarian, complete, unconstrained, unqualified, allencompassing, comprehensive. **2.** *They flew over the unlimited reaches of the Arctic. Life has unlimited possibilities:* endless, limitless, boundless, unbounded, infinite, inexhaustible, vast, immense, huge, immeasurable. **—Ant.** 1 limited, restricted, controlled, confined, checked, constrained; partial. 2 finite, limited, bounded, small, little, minute.

unload *v.* *They unloaded their belongings from the van:* off-load, disburden, unburden, clear out, disburden, disencumber, discharge, disgorge, dump, empty, jettison, lighten, relieve, unpack, remove, rid.

unlucky *adj.* *It was an unlucky day when they formed that partnership:* ill-fated, hapless, illomened, inauspicious, ill-starred, unfortunate, unhappy, star-crossed, jinxed, cursed, luckless, untoward, misfortunate. **—Ant.** happy, providential, auspicious, fortunate.

unmanly *adj.* **1.** *The Spartans considered retreat unmanly, regardless of circumstances:* faint-hearted, weak-kneed, lily-livered, weakhearted, chickenhearted, cowardly, timid, pusillanimous, *Slang* yellow. **2.** *The football coach*

despised ballet as an unmanly pursuit: effeminate, womanish, sissyish, sissified. **—Ant.** 1 courageous, brave, valiant, lionhearted, stouthearted; brash, bold, reckless, 2 masculine, manly, virile.

unmannerly adj. Who was that unmannerly clod at the entrance? The children are too unmannerly to be invited to the party: badly behaved, ill-mannered, ill-bred, ungracious, ungentlemanly, unladylike; discourteous, impolite, crude, gross, uncouth, coarse, boorish, loutish, uncivil, surly. **—Ant.** well-behaved, courteous, polite, gracious, well-bred, mannerly; gentlemanly, ladylike, refined, cultured.

unmarried adj. He remained unmarried until he was almost 40: single, unwed, spouseless, free, available, footloose and fancy-free; husbandless, wifeless, maiden, spinster, old maid, bachelor; divorced, widowed. **—Ant.** married, wed, mated; Slang hitched, yoked.

unmask v. 1. The guests will come in costumes and masks but everyone will unmask at midnight: remove a mask; take off one's disguise. 2. The investigation unmasked the true culprits: reveal, expose, show, disclose, uncover, discover, unveil, bare, lay open, bring to light, betray.

unmatched adj. 1. The necklace is made up of twenty unmatched diamonds: not matched, unmatching, not paired, unlike, differing, not uniform, unequal, dissimilar, disparate, diverse, variable. 2. The painting is of unmatched beauty: matchless, unequaled, unparalleled, peerless, supreme, second to none, beyond compare. **—Ant.** 1 matched, matching, paired, like, uniform, equal, similar.

unmeasured adj. 1. The unmeasured crowd surged into the square: unlimited, measureless, immense, vast, infinite. 2. His unmeasured anger surprised them: unrestrained, intemperate, unconstrained; unstinting, lavish. **—Ant.** measured, finite; temperate, constrained.

unmerciful adj. The unmerciful blizzard closed the highways: merciless, pitiless, unpitying, relentless, cruel, unsparing; unconscionable. **—Ant.** merciful.

unmindful adj. He's too unmindful of his responsibilities to be dependable: negligent, derelict, lax, remiss, heedless, unheeding, thoughtless, careless, oblivious, unaware, unconscious, forgetful. **—Ant.** careful, heedful, aware, unremiss.

unmistakable adj. His lack of sincerity was unmistakable. The girl has an unmistakable genius for music: clear, obvious, evident, manifest, plain, apparent, distinct, patent, palpable, pronounced, prominent, glaring, conspicuous, undeniable, indisputable, unequivocal, unquestionable. **—Ant.** vague, indistinct, dim, faint, unrecognizable, unclear; hidden, concealed.

unmitigated adj. 1. August was a month of unmitigated hot weather: unrelieved, unalleviated, unabated, unbroken, persistent, uninterrupted. 2. He's an unmitigated liar!: downright, out-and-out, absolute, unqualified, arrant. **—Ant.** 1 mitigated, relieved, alleviated, abated, eased,

lessened, softened, mild, soft; sporadic, intermittent, random, occasional. 2 partial, incomplete, qualified, limited, redeemed, regenerate.

unmixed adj. The inheritance was an unmixed blessing: pure, unalloyed, unmingled, unadulterated. **—Ant.** mixed, impure, mongrel.

unmoved adj. 1. Mother wants this chair left unmoved: not moved, not shifted, left in place, not transplanted. 2. After debating for hours both sides remained unmoved: firm, steadfast, unwavering, unswerving, unshaken, unfaltering, inflexible, undeviating; staunch, determined, resolute, resolved, persistent, obstinate, dogged, uncompromising, relentless; devoted, dedicated. 3. His appeal for a loan left me unmoved: unaffected, untouched, calm, unstirred, indifferent, uninterested, undisturbed, unresponsive, unconcerned, uncaring; cold, stonyhearted, aloof, unpitying, unfeeling. **—Ant.** 1 moved, transferred, shifted. 2 wavering, vacillating, shaken; compliant, flexible, yielding, adaptable, submissive. 3 moved, touched, stirred, affected, concerned, responsive, sympathetic.

unnamed adj. The money was donated from some unnamed source: anonymous, nameless, undisclosed, unrevealed, unidentified, uncredited, unacknowledged, pseudonymous, unsigned, incognito, undesignated, unspecified, undiscovered, unreported. **—Ant.** known, identified, disclosed, credited, signed.

unnatural adj. 1. She has an unnatural craving for salty foods: not natural, abnormal, aberrant, peculiar, freakish, unusual, anomalous. 2. Since attending that fancy school she has an unnatural way of talking: artificial, affected, mannered, stilted, studied, forced, assumed, contrived, phony, fake, put-on, self-conscious; theatrical. **—Ant.** 1, 2 natural, normal. 1 common, ordinary, typical. 2 unaffected, unpretentious, sincere, genuine, honest.

unnecessary adj. There's no sense in taking unnecessary risks. Buying the second cake was unnecessary: not necessary, needless, uncalled-for, dispensable, unessential, unrequired, expendable, gratuitous; overmuch, excessive, extra, surplus, excess, superfluous, supplementary, auxiliary.

unnerve v. Being alone in the woods at night unnerved us: upset, unsettle, unhinge, agitate, daunt, intimidate, frighten, scare. **—Ant.** encourage, reassure; nerve, steel.

unnoticeable adj. In any large group she was always unnoticeable: inconspicuous, unemphatic, obscure, unobtrusive, undiscernible, indistinct, unobserved, unassuming, faint, dim, unostentatious, insignificant. **—Ant.** clear, distinct, noticeable, visible, obvious.

unnoticed adj. 1. The boy slipped through the gate unnoticed by the guard: unseen, unobserved, undiscovered, unperceived; (variously) unheard, untasted, not smelled, unfelt. 2. Everyone had such a good time dancing that the lack of refreshments went unnoticed: overlooked, disregarded, unnoted, unheeded. **—Ant.** 1, 2 noticed. 1 seen, observed, witnessed, discovered, perceived; heard, tasted, smelled, felt. 2 noted, heeded, marked.

unobtrusive *adj. An unobtrusive gray rug was on the floor. Her father is a very unobtrusive man:* inconspicuous, unpretentious, modest, humble, unostentatious; unassuming, diffident, bashful, reserved, unassertive, reticent, retiring, shy. —**Ant.** conspicuous, prominent, eye-catching, glaring, noticeable; ostentatious, pretentious, assuming, bold, brash, brazen, assertive.

unorganized *adj. These unorganized papers must be sorted and filed:* unordered, orderless, unsystematized, unsystematic, unarranged, random, casual, haphazard, confused, loose, helter-skelter, harum-scarum, chaotic, unclassified, aimless, disjointed, undirected. —**Ant.** organized, ordered, systematized, systematic, arranged, classified.

unorthodox *adj. She was unorthodox in the way she did things:* heterodox, unconventional, abnormal, different, dissident, eccentric, irregular, nonconformist, unusual, weird. —**Ant.** orthodox, conventional, customary, established.

unpaid *adj. Unpaid workers helped finish the job:* honorary, voluntary, volunteer; free, gratuitous.

unparalleled *adj. The stunning victory was unparalleled:* matchless, unmatched, unequaled, unrivaled, peerless. —**Ant.** equaled.

unperturbed *adj. Napoleon was unperturbed in the face of defeat:* calm, tranquil, cool, collected, composed, poised, unruffled, unexcited, unagitated, undisturbed, untroubled, undismayed, levelheaded, coolheaded, unimpassioned, nonchalant. —**Ant.** perturbed, excited, discomposed, upset, disturbed, troubled, dismayed, impassioned.

unpleasant *adj. This medicine has an unpleasant taste. What an unpleasant man!:* disagreeable, displeasing, nasty, distasteful, offensive, repulsive, repugnant, obnoxious, objectionable, unlikable, unattractive, irksome, annoying, vexatious, noisome, pesky; ill-natured, churlish, ill-humored. —**Ant.** pleasant, pleasing, agreeable, attractive, likable; congenial, good-natured.

unpopular *adj. The cutworm is one of the most unpopular of garden pests:* disliked, unaccepted, disdained, unwanted, unacceptable, unwelcome, snubbed, slighted, rebuffed, neglected, disapproved, looked down on, undesirable, rejected. —**Ant.** loved, wanted, courted, sought-after.

unpractical *adj. They decided the proposal was unpractical:* impractical, visionary, speculative, theoretical. —**Ant.** practical.

unprecedented *adj. Customers came in unprecedented numbers:* hitherto unknown, unheard-of, unexampled, unparalleled, unique, extraordinary, exceptional, novel. —**Ant.** familiar, usual, regular, normal, routine.

unpredictable *adj. The patient's behavior is unpredictable:* not predictable, not foreseeable, erratic, unstable, fitful, variable, uncertain, eccentric, inconstant, arbitrary, changeable, mercurial, impulsive, capricious, whimsical, fanciful.

—**Ant.** predictable, stable, constant, undeviating, reasonable.

unprejudiced *adj. A judge must be completely unprejudiced:* without prejudice, impartial, objective, unbiased, unbigoted, fair, fair-minded, just, even-handed, uninfluenced, unswayed, undogmatic, disinterested, open-minded, broad-minded. —**Ant.** prejudiced, partial, biased, bigoted, unjust, unfair, closed-minded, narrow-minded.

unpretentious *adj. After becoming wealthy he lived in the same unpretentious house as before:* unassuming, simple, plain, modest, unostentatious, unelaborate, unimposing, unobtrusive, humble, homely.

unprincipled *adj. His lying shows that he is completely unprincipled:* without principles, unscrupulous, unconscionable, amoral, conscienceless.

unprofessional *adj. Failure to report to rehearsals is unprofessional conduct:* amateurish, amateur, unbusinesslike, unworkmanlike, undisciplined, inexperienced, unpracticed, inefficient; incompetent, careless, sloppy, bungling, shoddy; unethical, negligent, unprincipled. —**Ant.** efficient, meticulous, businesslike, workmanlike.

unqualified *adj.* **1.** *The youth is completely unqualified to be an accountant:* lacking the qualifications, untrained, unschooled, uneducated, unskilled, inexpert, inexperienced, unprepared, ill-equipped; unfit, unsuited, incompetent. **2.** *The play is an unqualified hit:* absolute, total, complete, positive, consummate, utter, downright, thorough, through and through, out-and-out, unconditional, undisputed.

unquestionable *adj. The senator's integrity is unquestionable:* beyond doubt, undeniable, indisputable, uncontestable, irrefutable, proven, unequivocal, unimpeachable, definite, certain, sure, clear, plain, obvious, self-evident, evident, perfect, flawless, faultless, impeccable, errorless, blameless, irreproachable, uncensurable.

unquiet *adj. The unquiet animals stirred in their stalls:* restless, restive, turbulent, tumultuous, disturbed, agitated, upset, uneasy, nervous, perturbed, fidgety. —**Ant.** quiet.

unreal *adj. She lives in an unreal world of make-believe:* not real, nonexistent, imaginary, imagined, illusory, illusive, chimerical, insubstantial, fictitious, legendary, fantastic; ghostly, shadowy, spectral, intangible, phantasmagorical, phantom, ethereal, dreamlike, dreamy, dream, airy, idealistic.

unrealistic *adj. Her plan of moving to New York to be a writer was unrealistic:* impractical, unreasonable, illogical, idealistic, improbable, infeasible; delusory, fanciful, starry-eyed, wild, silly, crazy, foolish, crackpot, asinine, absurd. —**Ant.** realistic, sound, sensible, reasonable, practical.

unreasonable *adj.* **1.** *It's unreasonable to expect snow in July:* contrary to reason, senseless, irrational, illogical, absurd, far-fetched, preposterous, nonsensical. **2.** *He's a spoiled, unreasonable young man:* obstinate, headstrong, stubborn, inflexible, unyielding, unbending, obdurate, mulish, bullheaded, pigheaded, unmanageable, hard to deal with, ungovernable, intractable; opinionated, closed-minded, bigoted, biased, prejudiced, fanatical. **3.** *Management considers the union's demands unreasonable:* excessive, too great, exorbitant, extravagant, inordinate, immoderate, unfair, unwarranted, unjustifiable, undue, uncalled-for. **—Ant.** 1–3 reasonable. 1 sensible, logical, plausible, rational, sober, wise, prudent. 2 complaisant, agreeable, flexible, tractable, open-minded. 3 moderate, temperate, restrained, equitable, fair, justified, warranted.

unreconstructed *adj. She was an unreconstructed feminist:* unapologetic, impenitent, unrepenting, stubborn, defiant, obdurate, diehard, standpat.

unrefined *adj.* **1.** *The unrefined sugar had to be broken into chunks:* unpurified, coarse, harsh, crude. **2.** *The unrefined visitors had few social graces:* unpolished, uncultured, ill-bred, rude, boorish, vulgar, gross. **—Ant.** refined.

unrehearsed *adj. Her talk was all the more charming for being unrehearsed:* spontaneous, improvised, extemporaneous, impromptu, informal, off-the-cuff, offhand, spur-of-the-moment, unplanned, unpremeditated, unstudied, improvisational, unprepared, impulsive. **—Ant.** planned, contrived, rehearsed, prepared, studied.

unrelated *adj.* **1.** *The two men look alike but are unrelated:* not related, not kin, not kindred; dissimilar, unlike. **2.** *Such personal remarks are completely unrelated to the matter under discussion:* extraneous, irrelevant, unconnected, non-germane, foreign, unassociated, unallied, inappropriate, inapplicable, incompatible. **—Ant.** 1, 2 related. 1 kin, akin; similar, like, equal. 2 relevant, pertinent, germane, connected, applicable, appropriate, associated.

unrelenting *adj. The Health Department waged unrelenting warfare against the epidemic:* relentless, unremitting, unrelieved, incessant, ceaseless, unbroken, endless, unabated, unwavering; steady, constant, unswerving, undeviating, unyielding, inflexible, unbending, rigid, adamant, tenacious, uncompromising, implacable, inexorable.

unreliable *adj.* **1.** *Rumors are always unreliable:* undependable, not to be trusted; questionable, uncertain, fallible, undependable; phony, fake, false, inaccurate, mistaken, erroneous. **2.** *The new worker proved to be completely unreliable:* undependable, irresponsible, not conscientious, untrustworthy, deceitful; unstable, changeable, fickle, inconstant, capricious. **—Ant.** 1, 2 reliable, dependable. 1 certain, sure, unquestionable, infallible; real, genuine, authentic, correct, accurate, true, right. 2 responsible, conscientious, trustworthy.

unrepentant *adj. The sinner died unrepentant. Should unrepentant criminals be given life sentences?:* without repenting, not contrite, uncontrite, not penitent, unexpiated, unatoned; unregenerate, remorseless, unashamed; hardened,

incorrigible, obdurate, callous. **—Ant.** repentant, penitent, expiated, atoned; contrite, regenerate, remorseful, ashamed.

unreserved *adj.* **1.** *Their gratitude was unreserved:* full, entire, complete, unlimited. **2.** *The unreserved guest was most likeable:* frank, open, ingenuous, candid, naive, artless, guileless, undesigning, sincere. **—Ant.** 1 reserved, incomplete. 2 artful.

unresolved *adj. Whether the budget will be increased or not is still unresolved:* undetermined, unsettled, undecided, unanswered, unsolved, unascertained, pending, tentative; doubtful, vague, uncertain, questionable, moot, problematical, speculative; disputable, contestable.

unrest *n. It was a time of unrest throughout the country:* restlessness, turmoil, disquiet, ferment, tumult, turbulence, upheaval; discontent, discord, agitation, dissatisfaction, protest, rebellion; anarchy, disorder, chaos. **—Ant.** peace, quiet, calm, tranquillity, serenity.

unrestrained *adj. The audience roared with unrestrained laughter:* uncontrolled, unrestricted, unchecked, uninhibited, irrepressible, unrepressed, unreserved, unsuppressed, uncurbed, unbridled, unhampered, unfettered, unchecked, ungoverned, unhindered; unlimited, boundless, excessive, extravagant, inordinate, immoderate, intemperate, abandoned.

unruffled *adj. The unruffled host mopped up the spill:* smooth, calm, unperturbed, tranquil, serene, collected, imperturbable, cool, composed, peaceful, controlled, undisturbed. **—Ant.** ruffled.

unruly *adj. The child is unruly because he's been spoiled:* disobedient, obstreperous, wild, willful, unmanageable, ungovernable, undisciplined, uncontrollable, intractable, wayward, headstrong, perverse, refractory, fractious, contrary, unbridled, restive, rowdy, disorderly, boisterous. **—Ant.** obedient, well-behaved, well-mannered, manageable, controllable, docile, tractable, submissive, compliant, sweet-tempered, agreeable; calm, reserved.

unsafe *adj. The bridge is unsafe for heavy loads. If the enemy attacks, this fort will be unsafe:* dangerous, not safe, hazardous, perilous, risky; treacherous, untrustworthy, unreliable, unprotected, vulnerable, defenseless, exposed, undefended, unguarded, insecure. **—Ant.** safe, secure, immune from danger, reliable, trustworthy, guaranteed; protected, guarded, defended.

unsaid *adj. Much in the conversation remained unsaid:* implied, inferred, tacit, implicit; understood, undeclared, unexpressed, unspoken, unstated, unuttered, unvoiced, wordless.

unsatisfactory *adj. The student's work was judged unsatisfactory:* not satisfactory, unacceptable, unworthy, inept; inadequate, deficient, below par, inferior, poor, unsuitable, inappropriate, unfit, inadmissible, ineligible.

unsavory *adj.* **1.** *The salad was wilted and the dressing unsavory:* flat, insipid, tasteless, without savor. **2.** *The natives ate sheep's eyes and other unsavory things:* distasteful, unpleasant, bad-tasting, unappetizing, unpalatable, nasty, foul, nauseating, disagreeable. **3.** *He has an un-savory reputation:* morally objectionable, unpleasant, bad, tainted. **—Ant.** 1, 2 savory, appetizing, tasty, agreeable, pleasing. 3 virtuous, good, moral.

unscathed *adj. How could he come out of that accident unscathed?:* unhurt, uninjured, unharmed, unscratched, untouched, unimpaired, whole, entire, perfect, sound, intact, all in one piece. **—Ant.** hurt, injured, harmed, damaged.

unscrupulous *adj. An unscrupulous acquaintance sold them some worthless stocks:* unprincipled, dishonorable, devious, unethical, immoral, amoral, sharp, crooked. **—Ant.** scrupulous, principled, moral, ethical, honorable, honest, just, fair, trustworthy.

unseasonable *adj. The unseasonable storm destroyed their garden:* inopportune, ill-timed, untimely, inappropriate. **—Ant.** seasonable, opportune.

unseat *v.* **1.** *The leader was unseated during the next election:* displace, depose. **2.** *The rambunctious game unseated her:* throw.

unseemly *adj. Everyone was shocked by his unseemly conduct:* improper, inappropriate, unbefitting, unbecoming, indecorous, ungentlemanly, unladylike, unsuitable, out of character, out of place, discreditable, undignified, unworthy, disreputable, reprehensible, tasteless, offensive, distasteful, vulgar, indelicate, incorrect, indecent, gross, crude, coarse, rude, discourteous, ill-mannered, boorish, churlish, loutish. **—Ant.** seemly, proper, appropriate, fit, befitting, becoming, suitable, dignified, tasteful, cultivated, polite, courteous, mannerly, genteel, gentlemanly, ladylike.

unseen *adj. Unseen factors came to the fore:* invisible, unperceived, veiled, dark, hidden, imaginary, impalpable, impenetrable, inconspicuous, obscure, undetected, undiscovered, unnoticed, unsuspected, shrouded, concealed.

unselfish *adj. It was very unselfish of you to help us:* selfless, altruistic, generous, munificent, considerate, big-hearted, liberal, openhanded, self-sacrificing, handsome, princely, charitable, philanthropic, benevolent, humanitarian, magnanimous.

unsettle *v. World conditions have unsettled the stock market. The lawyer's questioning unsettled the witness:* make unstable, unbalance, disturb, perturb, upset, disorder; disconcert, confuse, bewilder, fluster, confound, ruffle, bother, trouble, agitate, unhinge, throw off one's guard, *Slang* rattle.

unsettled *adj. Unsettled conditions in the marketplace did not augur well for the firm:* unstable, unsteady, shaky, undependable, unsure, unfixed, undetermined, indeterminate, changeable, wavering, vacillating, infirm, fickle, faltering, irresolute. **—Ant.** settled, stable, steady.

unshaken *adj.* **1.** *The father's trust in his son is unshaken:* undaunted, unaffected, undisturbed, undeviating, unwavering, unfaltering, unswerving, unflinching, steadfast, determined, resolved, staunch, constant, stable, inflexible, uncompromising, tenacious, relentless. **2.** *She*

remained *unshaken as we told her the bad news:* cool, calm, composed, controlled, poised, self-possessed, levelheaded, serene, unperturbed, untroubled, unmoved, unruffled, unemotional, unexcited. **—Ant.** 1, 2 shaken. 1 wavering, faltering; destroyed, ruined, demolished, smashed, shattered, undone. 2 disconcerted, upset, emotional, excited, uncontrolled, moved, perturbed, troubled, dismayed, ruffled.

unsightly *adj. Please clean up this unsightly mess:* ugly, unattractive, hideous, obnoxious, offensive, distasteful, repellent, repulsive, revolting, odious, horrid, revolting, sickening. **—Ant.** attractive, lovely, beautiful, appealing.

unskillful *adj. He was unskillful at everything he tried:* untrained, inexpert, awkward, bungling, clumsy, inept, maladroit. **—Ant.** skillful.

unsociable *adj. She was unsociable before breakfast:* unsocial, aloof, hostile, inaccessible, inhospitable, reclusive, reserved, retiring, secretive, standoffish, unapproachable, unbending, uncommunicative, uncongenial, unforthcoming, unfriendly, unneighborly, uppity, withdrawn, chilly, cold, cool. distant, **—Ant.** sociable, convivial, friendly, gregarious, neighborly.

unsolicited *adj. She gave me her unsolicited opinion of my hat:* unasked for, unrequested, unsought, uninvited, gratuitous, volunteered; unwanted, unwelcome, unwished for, undesired, unnecessary; voluntary, unforced, free, spontaneous. **—Ant.** requested, sought, invited, solicited, desired, welcomed; enticed, courted.

unsophisticated *adj. It was refreshing to talk to the unsophisticated youth:* natural, ingenuous, artless, unworldly, unpretentious, unaffected, unassuming, open, candid, straightforward, homespun, unstudied, uncontrived, undissembling; naive, green, innocent, trusting.

unsound *adj.* **1.** *The old horse was thin and unsound. The doctors judged him to be of unsound mind:* unhealthy, sickly, diseased, crippled, defective, ailing, in poor health, infirm, unfit, invalid; feeble, weak, decrepit, drooping, languishing; mentally ill, deranged, insane, mad, unbalanced, unhinged, unsettled, disordered, confused, *Slang* off, off one's rocker. **2.** *Too little cement was used in the foundation, making the building unsound:* not solid, shaky, unsteady, weak, unstable, unsubstantial, rickety, tottery; unsafe, hazardous, dangerous, precarious, risky, perilous, unreliable, uncertain, insecure. **3.** *I think your reasoning is unsound:* not valid, unfounded, groundless, weak, shaky, untenable, fallacious, faulty, incorrect, wrong, erroneous, illogical, defective, spurious, specious, marred, blemished, impaired, imperfect, flawed; senseless, irrational, foolish, absurd. **—Ant.** 1–3 sound, strong. 1 healthy, whole, well, fit, in good health, of strong constitution, vigorous, robust, hardy, hale and hardy, in the pink; sane, rational, reasonable, stable, clearheaded. 2 solid, sturdy, firm, safe, secure, durable, lasting. 3 valid, well-founded, convincing, cogent, correct, accurate, true, judicious, sensible, meaningful, reliable, authoritative.

unsparing *adj. The charitable woman was un-*

sparing of her time and money: ungrudging, unstinting, generous, giving, bountiful, munificent, magnanimous, liberal, big-hearted, lavish, profuse, plenteous, abundant, extravagant, copious, plentiful, full; unconditional, unqualified, unlimited.

unspeakable adj. **1.** The Grand Tetons are a mountain range of unspeakable grandeur: inexpressible, too wonderful to describe, undescribable, unutterable, inconceivable, unimag-inable, incredible, overwhelming, astonishing, extraordinary, immense, huge, vast, enormous, great, prodigious. **2.** It was a crime of unspeakable horror: too horrible to talk about, awful, shocking, frightful, fearful, unheard of, repulsive, repellent, disgusting, odious, loathsome, abhorrent, nauseating, sickening, revolting, abominable, monstrous.

unspecified adj. We agreed to meet at some unspecified time in the future: unnamed, unmentioned, unannounced, unpublicized, undetermined, undefined, undesignated, unindicated, unstipulated, unsettled; vague, general, indefinite.

unspoiled **1.** The girl was charming and completely unspoiled: unpampered, not coddled; natural, artless, unaffected, unassuming, unpretentious, open, unstudied, unself-conscious, unsophisticated, unworldly, uncorrupted, trusting. **2.** The wilderness had an unspoiled beauty. The politician's reputation is unspoiled by scandal: preserved, undamaged, unharmed, unimpaired, pristine, perfect; spotless, unspotted, unmarred, unblemished, unscarred.

unstable adj. **1.** That ladder is too unstable to hold you: unsteady, unsubstantial, shaky, insecure, tippy, wobbly, tottering; flimsy, rickety, fragile, frail, weak. **2.** The patient's condition was unstable. The youth has a very unstable personality: fluctuating, not constant, changing, changeable, vacillating, shifting, unsteady; erratic, volatile, emotional, mercurial, unpredictable, irrational, fitful, inconsistent, insecure, irresponsible, fickle, capricious, fly-by-night.

unsteady adj. **1.** The unsteady patient clutched the door: unfixed, infirm, faltering. **2.** The unsteady current made the light flicker: fluctuating, wavering, unsettled, vacillating, fickle, changeable, unstable. **3.** As a doctor, he was unsteady: irregular, unreliable. **—Ant.** steady.

unsuccessful adj. **1.** The army made an unsuccessful attempt to capture the enemy fort: without success, futile, vain, useless, unavailing, unfruitful, fruitless, abortive, unproductive, ineffectual. **2.** No matter what business he tried, he was always unsuccessful. Restaurants in this neighborhood have always been unsuccessful: unlucky, hapless, unfortunate, ill-starred, luckless, unprosperous; thwarted, foiled, baffled; poor, moneyless, penniless, strapped, hard up, badly off; profitless, unprofitable, unremunerative. **—Ant.** 1, 2 successful. 1 victorious, winning, trium-phant, unbeaten; useful, fruitful, productive, ef-fective, worthwhile. 2 lucky, fortunate; prosper-ous, thriving, flourishing, rich,

wealthy, well-to-do, well-off, affluent; profitable, remunerative.

unsuitable adj. That dress is unsuitable for a wedding. A car without air-conditioning is unsuitable for driving across the desert: inappropriate, inapt, unbefitting, unfit, unfitting, improper, unsuitable, unbecoming, unseemly, out of place, out of keeping, out of character, unhappy, infelicitous, indecorous, incongruous, inconsistent, incompatible; unacceptable, inadmissible, inadequate, worthless, useless.

unsullied adj. Her reputation is unsullied: unsoiled, clean, spotless, untainted, untarnished, unblemished, unblackened, uncorrupted, uninjured, uncontaminated, unpolluted, undefiled.

unsure adj. She remained unsure about which school to attend: undecided, hesitant, unconvinced, uncertain, in a quandary, unassured, insecure, unconfident, self-doubting, self-distrustful; bashful, shy, timid, reserved. **—Ant.** self-confident, secure, unhesitating, decisive.

unsurpassed adj. Keats' Endymion is a poem of unsurpassed beauty: supreme, consummate, superior, best, paramount, peerless, nonpareil, highest, greatest, transcendent, exceptional, unexcelled, incomparable, unparalleled, matchless, unmatched, unequaled, unrivaled.

unsuspecting adj. She tried the new dish on her unsuspecting guests. The unsuspecting youth was easily cheated: unsuspicious, unaware, off one's guard; credulous, trusting, believing; over-trustful, gullible, unwary, naive, overcredulous. **—Ant.** knowing, heedful, aware, alert; suspicious, cautious, wary.

unswerving adj. The general had an unswerving devotion to duty: dedicated, faithful, devoted, steadfast, unwavering, undeviating, unflinching, unyielding, unfaltering, untiring, unflagging, inflexible, uncompromising, resolute, resolved, determined, single-minded, staunch, strong, firm, steady, unremitting, unshaken, undaunted. **—Ant.** wavering, faltering, flagging, irresolute, weak, faint, halfhearted.

unsympathetic adj. **1.** She was surprisingly unsympathetic about my problem: unfeeling, indifferent, coldhearted, hardhearted, hard-boiled, heartless, uncompassionate, callous, pitiless, unmerciful, uncaring. **2.** As a person he's totally unsympathetic: uncongenial, antipathetic, repellent, repugnant, unlikable, displeasing, unattractive, unpleasant. **—Ant.** 1 sympathetic, warmhearted, understanding. 2 congenial, attractive, pleasing.

untangle v. Help me untangle this yarn. There was a mixup in delivery dates that the shipping clerk had to untangle: unsnarl, unravel, disentangle, untwist; straighten out, clear up, solve, extricate. **—Ant.** tangle, entangle, snarl, twist.

untarnished adj. **1.** Wrap the silverware tightly to keep it untarnished: unoxidized, unblackened, shining, bright, polished. **2.** The arbitrator should be a man of untarnished reputation: spotless, unsoiled, unstained, untainted, unsullied, unblemished, unbesmirched, undefiled, unimpeachable, undisputed, faultless, flawless, immaculate, impeccable, perfect. —**Ant.** 1, 2 tarnished. 1 oxidized, blackened, dull. 2 tainted, sullied, soiled, blemished, stained, besmirched, defiled, questionable, damaged, marred, discredited.

untenable adj. If you'll check the facts, you'll find your argument is untenable: indefensible, unmaintainable, unsustainable, unjustifiable, insupportable, baseless, groundless, unsound, invalid, illogical, erroneous, fallacious, faulty, flawed, weak, spurious, specious, unreliable; questionable, debatable, contestable. —**Ant.** justified, sustained, supported, well-grounded; valid, reasonable, sound, logical; unquestionable, uncontestable.

unthinkable adj. To go to the wedding uninvited would be unthinkable: out of the question, not to be considered, inconceivable, unimaginable, incomprehensible, insupportable, unjustifiable, unwarranted.

unthinking adj. His unthinking remark offended the visitors: thoughtless, inconsiderate, heedless, careless, inadvertent, tactless, insensitive, undiplomatic, uncircumspect; senseless, mindless, witless, imprudent, negligent.

untidy adj. Straighten up that untidy room. She is one of the most untidy people I've ever met: messy, disorderly, littered, cluttered, unkempt, chaotic, disarrayed, confused, helter-skelter, topsy-turvy; slovenly, sloppy, slatternly, disheveled, mussed, mussed up, dowdy, frowsy, rumpled, tousled, bedraggled; careless, slipshod, unmethodical.

untie v. They quickly untied the knot: unfasten, loose, unknot, undo, unbind. —**Ant.** tie.

untimely adj. The neighbors' untimely visit prevented her from finishing the job. Everyone was shocked by his untimely remark: ill-timed, mistimed, inconvenient, inopportune, unexpected, premature; inappropriate, inapt, unsuitable, unfitting, unseemly, unbecoming, unbefitting, imprudent, out of place, unhappy, malapropos, infelicitous, unfortunate, ill-advised.

untiring adj. **1.** None of the competitors could catch up with the untiring runner who was in the lead: not becoming tired, tireless, never tiring, unwearied, fresh. **2.** His untiring help has been a great blessing: unflagging, indefatigable, unfaltering, constant, unremitting, unceasing, wholehearted, determined, persevering, staunch, steadfast, resolute, steady, patient, persevering, persistent, tenacious, relentless, diligent, sedulous, assiduous; devoted, dedicated, zealous, earnest. —**Ant.** 1 tiring, tired, weary, exhausted, fatigued, spent, Slang dog tired, played out, blushed, beat. 2 flagging, faltering, wavering, irresolute, fainthearted, lukewarm, indifferent, perfunctory, sporadic.

untold adj. **1.** The book reveals the hitherto untold story of the actress's private life: unrevealed, secret, private, concealed, unknown, suppressed, withheld, hushed up; unrelated, unpublished, unreported, undisclosed, unsaid, unspoken, unexpressed. **2.** The quake left untold thousands of people homeless: innumerable, countless, uncounted, numerous, myriad, unde-

termined, numberless, unnumbered; incalculable, immeasurable, limitless, unbounded, endless, infinite.

untouched adj. The scroll was untouched: uncorrupted, unaffected, unblemished, undamaged, uninjured, unmarred, unharmed, unhurt, flawless, fresh, immaculate, intact, perfect, pure, shipshape, spotless, unbroken, unscathed, unspoiled, unstained, untried, virgin, virginal, entire, whole; unmoved, unimpressed.

untoward adj. Untoward action by the applicant lost him the job: inappropriate, improper, unseemly, unbecoming, indecent, uncouth, unfitting, unsuitable, indecorous, indelicate.

untroubled adj. She recalled the untroubled days of her childhood: calm, placid, serene, peaceful, tranquil, carefree, halcyon, undisturbed, unperturbed, easygoing, unbothered, relaxed. —**Ant.** troubled, agitated, disturbed, roiled.

untrue adj. **1.** His story is completely untrue: not true, untruthful, false, fallacious, falsified, groundless, unfounded, made up, fictitious, spurious, meretricious, fake, sham, fraudulent; incorrect, erroneous, inaccurate. **2.** Henry VIII had two of his queens executed on the charge that they were untrue: unfaithful, faithless, incon-stant, adulterous, unchaste, promiscuous, false, perfidious; disloyal, dishonest, treacherous, double-dealing. —**Ant.** 1, 2 true. 1 right, correct, accurate, authentic, genuine, real, valid, legitimate, Slang straight. 2 faithful, constant, chaste, pure, virtuous; loyal, honest, trustworthy, incorruptible, dependable, honorable, righteous, truthful.

untrustworthy adj. The report from the front is untrustworthy. His best friend proved to be untrustworthy: unreliable, undependable, unauthenticated, questionable, fallible, uncertain; unfaithful, disloyal, faithless, dishonest, false, insincere, untruthful, untrue, unprincipled, devious, deceitful, unscrupulous, disreputable, corrupted, treacherous, inconstant, two-faced, perfidious, irresponsible, shifty, slippery, capricious, fickle.

untruth n. The attorney uncovered more than one untruth in the testimony: lie, falsehood, fib, story, tale, canard, prevarication, fabrication, falsification, misrepresentation, invention, yarn, cock-and-bull story, deception, humbug, Slang flimflam.

untypical adj. This picture is untypical of the painter's work: atypical, abnormal, anomalous, aberrant, unrepresentative, deviant; odd, bizarre, unusual, rare, irregular, unnatural, strange, uncommon, alien, unfamiliar. —**Ant.** typical, common, usual, normal, ordinary.

unusual adj. The shape of this leaf is unusual. Kevin married a girl of unusual beauty: singular, rare, exceptional, extraordinary, remarkable, noteworthy, atypical, untypical, novel, phenomenal, unique, uncommon, unfamiliar, surprising; strange, curious, peculiar; unparalleled, unequaled, unprecedented, unmatched, incomparable, unheard-of, out of the ordinary, one of a kind, offbeat. —**Ant.** usual, common, commonplace, ordinary, unremarkable, unexceptional, average, typical, familiar, routine, normal, natural, traditional, conventional, orthodox, stock.

unusually *adv. Unusually high winds kept the boat tied up:* uncommonly, especially, extra, extraordinarily, extremely, mighty, powerfully, really, remarkably, terribly, terrifically, very, awfully; strangely, surprisingly, oddly, peculiarly, curiously.

unvarnished *adj. The unvarnished truth is that you'll never recover the money:* plain, frank, bare, naked, candid, direct, honest, sincere, straightforward, straight, straight-from-the-shoulder; unembellished, unadorned. **—Ant.** embellished, exaggerated; hypocritical, evasive, insincere, dishonest.

unveil *v.* **1.** *The mayor unveiled a new statue in the park:* uncover, unsheathe, uncloak. **2.** *In his speech, the governor unveiled his new tax plan:* disclose, reveal, divulge, bare, make known, announce, broadcast, publish, bring to light. **—Ant.** 1, 2 veil. 1 cover. 2 conceal, hide, disguise, camouflage.

unwarranted *adj. Such strong criticism was completely unwarranted:* unjustified, uncalled-for, indefensible, unreasonable, inexcusable, unfounded, groundless, arbitrary; unauthorized, unsanctioned, unapproved, culpable, censurable, unlawful, illegal.

unwary *adj. This is a task for the unwary:* unwatchful, incautious, unalert, heedless, reckless, hasty, uncircumspect, imprudent, rash, precipitate, indiscreet, careless, headlong, unguarded, disregardful. **—Ant.** wary, cautious, discreet, guarded, circumspect.

unwavering *adj. It takes years of unwavering determination to become a surgeon:* unswerving, unfaltering, untiring, unflagging, dedicated, single-minded, faithful, undeviating, unflinching, resolute, determined, steadfast, staunch, strong, firm, steady, persevering, unremitting, persistent, tenacious, uncompromising, unshaken.

unwelcome *adj.* **1.** *Although she said we weren't interrupting, her coolness made us feel unwelcome. He said he had the money, and my offer of a loan was unwelcome:* unwanted, unwished for, uninvited, undesirable, unacceptable, rejected, excluded, unpopular, outcast, uncared for; unnecessary, unessential, unrequired. **2.** *Telling the boy he can't go to camp after all is an unwelcome task:* disagreeable, unpleasant, displeasing, distasteful, undesirable, thankless.

unwell *adj. Grandfather has been feeling unwell this week:* ailing, low, indisposed, poorly, infirm, sickly, queasy, qualmish, ill, sick, run-down, laid up, having a malaise, frail, delicate; *Slang* under the weather, off one's feed, not feeling oneself. **—Ant.** well, fit, tiptop; *Slang* perky, chipper.

unwholesome *adj.* **1.** *Stay away from unwholesome foods:* unhealthful, unhealthy, insalubrious, deleterious, harmful, hurtful, detrimental; unnourishing, noxious, pernicious, poisonous, venomous, baneful, deadly, toxic. **2.** *Unwholesome friends lead the youth astray:* morally harmful, immoral, corrupting, evil, sinful, wicked, bad, depraved, dishonorable, degrading, ruinous, corrupted, demoralizing, undesirable; dangerous, polluting, contaminating, filthy, foul. **—Ant.** 1, 2 wholesome. 1 healthful, healthy, salubrious; nutritious, hygienic, sanitary. 2 moral, uplifting, edifying, inspiring.

unwieldy *adj. A heavy ax is too unwieldy for a Boy Scout:* hard to handle, not handy, awkward, clumsy, inconvenient, uncomfortable, incommodious, cumbersome, bulky, heavy, burdensome, weighty. **—Ant.** handy, convenient, comfortable.

unwilling *adj. Ed is unwilling to be transferred to the East Coast office:* reluctant, loath, disinclined, unfavorably disposed, indisposed, undesirous, averse, against, opposed, resistant, recalcitrant, dissenting, demurring, unenthusiastic, not in the mood.

unwind *v.* **1.** *They went to unwind the cables:* unravel, untangle, disentangle, free, loose, loosen, uncoil, undo, unfurl, unwrap, slacken, separate. **2.** *A couple of beers helped us unwind:* relax, calm down, let go, loosen up, sit back, slow down, wind down, ease off.

unwise *adj. Investing all the money in just one stock would be unwise:* imprudent, improvident, ill-advised, inadvisable, injudicious, unsound, unreasonable, short-sighted, foolish, senseless, unintelligent, reckless, foolhardy, irresponsible, silly, dumb, stupid, *Slang* crazy.

unwitting *adj. The cab driver became an unwitting accomplice in the bank robbers' getaway:* unknowing, unaware, unintentional, inadvertent, unthinking, unmeant, accidental, unpremeditated, undesigned, unplanned, unexpected; involuntary, unconsenting. **—Ant.** witting, knowing, premeditated, voluntary, intentional.

unwonted *adj. The normally shy man spoke with unwonted boldness:* unaccustomed, atypical, unusual, unfamiliar, unexpected, rare, infrequent, uncommon, exceptional, extraordinary, remarkable. **—Ant.** accustomed, customary, habitual, typical, routine, usual, normal, standard, predictable.

unworldly *adj.* **1.** *The unworldly young man was shocked by the greed of his associates:* unsophisticated, naive, innocent, inexperienced, provincial, overtrusting, trusting, idealistic, callow, green. **2.** *The monk set his mind on unworldly things:* spiritual, holy, sacred, divine, pious, religious, devout, godly, solemn, pure, celestial, heavenly, transcendental, ethereal, unearthly, immaterial; aesthetic, metaphysical, intellectual, moral, ethical, philosophical.

unworthy *adj. Such conduct is unworthy of an ambassador:* inappropriate, unbefitting, unfit, improper, unbecoming, unseemly, unsuitable, unacceptable; ignoble, dishonorable, unethical, shameful, discreditable, disreputable, degrading, objectionable. **—Ant.** worthy, honorable, noble, commendable, admirable, praiseworthy; appropriate, fitting, befitting, proper, becoming.

unwritten *adj.* **1.** *Until the invention of writing all language was unwritten:* not written down, not reduced to writing, unrecorded, unregistered; spoken only, oral, vocal, by word of mouth. **2.** *In the old days it was an unwritten law that children speak only when spoken to:* unformulated, unstated, unexpressed, implied, implicit, understood, inferred, tacit, assumed; traditional, customary.

unyielding *adj.* **1.** *The mattress was so firm it was unyielding:* stiff, hard, rigid, unbending, inflexible, unpliable, stony, wooden, rocklike, tough. **2.** *The union is unyielding in its demands for higher pay:* unbending, inflexible, unwavering, firm, steadfast, resolute, determined, uncompromising, unswerving, undeviating, inexorable; persistent, stubborn, obstinate.

upbeat *adj.* *She was upbeat on hearing the news:* optimistic, cheerful, cheery, encouraging, hopeful, positive, promising, rosy, sanguine, buoyant.

upbraid *v.* *The foreman upbraided the worker for being habitually late:* reproach, scold, rebuke, reprove, reprimand, censure, chastise, admonish, find fault with; berate, castigate, revile, denounce, tongue-lash, dress down, *Slang* bawl out, chew out. **—Ant.** praise, laud, compliment, command, applaud, eulogize.

upcoming *adj.* *We have tickets for his upcoming concert:* approaching, coming, forthcoming, nearing, pending, prospective, imminent, drawing nigh, nearby, impending, momentary, looming, in the offing. **—Ant.** distant, remote, far-off, postponed, delayed.

update *v.* *The travel guide is updated every two years:* revise, renew, bring up to date, emend, overhaul, revamp, rework, refurbish, renovate, restore, rejuvenate, streamline, recast, reorganize, touch up, upgrade.

upheaval *n.* **1.** *The mountain was created by an upheaval millions of years ago:* (variously) upthrust, volcanic eruption, explosion, blowup, earthquake, quake, flood, tidal wave; cataclysm, catastrophe. **2.** *The Great Depression caused an upheaval in many people's lives:* drastic change, disruption, disorder, revolution, disturbance, tumult, turmoil.

uphill *adv.* **1.** *It's tiring to walk uphill:* up the slope of a hill, upward. **—adj. 2.** *It's an uphill walk to the lookout tower:* going upward on a hill, ascending, rising, upward. **3.** *Making a success of the business was an uphill struggle:* difficult, arduous, strenuous, hard, tough, exhausting, taxing, toilsome, enervating, tiring, fatiguing, wearisome, wearying, backbreaking, burdensome, onerous.

uphold *v.* **1.** *Six pillars upheld the roof:* hold up, carry the weight of, support, bear, carry, prop, prop up, sustain, brace, shore, shore up, buttress, bolster, underbrace, underpin, elevate, raise. **2.** *In taking the oath of office the President swears to uphold the U. S. Constitution:* support, maintain, sustain, preserve, protect, defend, champion, advocate, stand up for; approve, endorse, confirm, acknowledge, corroborate, encourage.

upkeep *n.* *The upkeep on such a big house is ruinous:* maintenance, operating costs, running expenses, overhead; preservation, sustenance, keep, subsistence, living, support, management.

uplift *v.* **1.** *Listening to the sermon should uplift your thoughts:* raise, elevate, advance, better, improve, refine, upgrade, cultivate, civilize, edify, inspire. **—n. 2.** *Steel braces provide uplift for the building's dome:* support, lifting, propping, bracing, shoring, buttressing, bolstering, underpinning. **3.** *Lectures and good books can provide moral uplift for everyone:* betterment, elevation, advancement, improvement, enhancement, refinement, enrichment, edification, cultivation. **—Ant.** 1 degrade, debase; depress, demoralize. 3 degradation, debasement, lowering; dishonor, disgrace, discredit, ignominy.

uplifting *adj.* *The sermon was not particularly uplifting:* edifying, improving, bettering, educational, informative, informational, instructive, enlightening. **—Ant.** debasing, corruptive.

upper *adj.* **1.** *Put the book on one of the upper shelves:* top, topmost, high, higher; superior, greater. **2.** *He wants to be promoted to the upper ranks of the business:* top, elevated, high, superior, eminent, major, important. **3.** *She was born in upper Michigan:* northern, more northerly; inland, further from the sea.

uppermost also **upmost** *adj.* **1.** *The apartment is on the uppermost floor of the building:* highest, top, topmost, closest to the top, loftiest, crowning. **2.** *The captain's uppermost concern was the safety of the passengers:* most important, greatest, chief, foremost, major, main, principal, predominant, supreme, leading, prime, primary, first, essential, paramount, transcendent, preeminent, highest, dominant. **—Ant.** 1 lowermost, lowest, bottom. 2 least, last, lowliest, minor, slightest, unessential, insignificant.

uppity *adj.* *The uppity couple refused to help us out:* arrogant, haughty, disdainful, scornful, presumptuous, cocky, supercilious, snobbish, snobby, stuck-up, snooty, *British* toffee-nosed. **—Ant.** modest, unassuming, down-to-earth.

upright *adj.* **1.** *Some tribes bury their dead in an upright position:* erect, vertical, perpendicular, standing-up; upended. **2.** *It's a pleasure to do business with an upright man:* honest, ethical, honorable, moral, principled, trustworthy, upstanding, righteous, reliable, high-minded, good, fair, just, aboveboard, *Slang* on the up-and-up. **—n. 3.** *The porch is supported by a row of uprights:* post, pillar, column, shaft, support, prop, pier, pile, stanchion, standard, strut, rib; stake, picket, pale, pole. **—Ant.** 1 horizontal, prone, lying down. 2 dishonest, crooked, unethical, dishonorable, unprincipled, untrustworthy, unreliable, unscrupulous, shady. 3 beam, lintel, transverse.

uprising *n.* *Troops were called to quell the uprising:* rebellion, revolution, revolt, insurrection, insurgence, mutiny; riot, outbreak.

uproar *n.* *The prime minister's resignation caused an uproar:* state of confusion, clamor, agitation, ado, commotion, furor, stir, tumult, turmoil, disturbance, burst of excitement, to-do, pandemonium.

uproarious *adj.* **1.** *Times Square is uproarious on New Year's Eve:* full of commotion, tumultuous, turbulent, riotous, disorderly, tempestuous, raging, stormy, intense, wild, furious; boisterous, noisy, clamorous, loud. **2.** *The new play is an uproarious comedy:* very funny, hilarious, hysterical, sidesplitting. **—Ant.** 1 quiet, calm, peaceful, serene, tranquil, placid. 2 sad, tragic, melancholy, tearful, doleful, gloomy; solemn, grave.

uproot *v.* **1.** *Uproot all the weeds from the garden. We must uproot our bad habits:* pull up by the roots, extirpate, root out; do away with, cast out, banish, destroy, eliminate, abolish, exterminate, annihilate, wipe out. **2.** *Floods and famine uprooted many of the country's people:* force to move, force out, displace, dislodge. **—Ant.** 1 plant; establish, institute, found, create, form, build; encourage, further, aid, abet.

upset *v.* **1.** *The child upset the glass of milk:* overturn, turn over, upend, invert; tip over, topple over, turn topsy-turvy, capsize. **2.** *Losing the ring upset her:* disturb, distress, trouble, grieve, make miserable, annoy, bother, worry, perturb, unnerve, discompose, disconcert, discomfit, agitate, fluster, rattle; anger, enrage, incense, ire, irk, infuriate, pique, vex. **3.** *The rain upset our plans for a picnic. The unexpected visit upset our schedule:* cancel, reverse, change; disorganize, disorder, confuse, muddle, jumble, mix up, turn topsy-turvy. **4.** *The home team upset the local champions:* defeat a favorite, win against the odds; *(loosely)* defeat, beat, be victorious over, overthrow, vanquish, overcome, overwhelm, overpower, conquer, crush, quash, thrash, trounce, demolish, smash. *—adj.* **5.** *The upset truck blocked traffic for hours:* overturned, turned over, upside-down, upended, inverted, upturned, wrong side up, tipped over, capsized. **6.** *The files were so upset no one could find anything:* disorganized, disordered, disorderly, disarranged, chaotic, confused, jumbled, mixed-up; mussed, messy, disheveled, untidy, slovenly, topsy-turvy. **7.** *Was she upset by my phone call?:* perturbed, disturbed, distressed, bothered, annoyed, worried, agitated, troubled, worried, grieved, disquieted, unnerved, overwrought, hysterical, angered, enraged, furious, incensed, mad, irked, vexed. **—Ant.** 1 right. 2 calm, quiet, pacify, put at ease, comfort. 3 settle, steady, stabilize; organize, order, arrange, straighten. 4 be defeated, lose. 5 right side up. 6 organized, ordered, orderly, well-arranged, neat, tidy, straightened. 7 calmed, quieted, pacified, eased, comforted, composed, placated.

upshot *n.* *The upshot of the matter was that he was asked to resign:* outcome, result, effect, conclusion, culmination, end, final development, eventuality, consequence; sequel, aftermath, outgrowth, aftereffect, offshoot, *Slang* payoff.

upstanding *adj.* **1.** *The yard was graced by twelve upstanding oak trees:* tall, erect; upright, straight, perpendicular, on end, vertical. **2.** *Arthur is an upstanding member of the community:* upright, honorable, trustworthy, high principled, virtuous, incorruptible, righteous, good, honest, ethical, moral, truthful, true.

up-to-date *adj.* *The house has a hot tub, a* built-in vacuum system, and other up-to-date features: modern, current, au courant, up-to-the-minute, contemporary, timely, modish, stylish, abreast of the times; *Slang* trendy, today, in. **—Ant.** old-fashioned, out-of-date, passé, dated.

urban *adj.* *Los Angeles, Chicago, New York, Montreal, and Toronto are large urban areas. The small-town youth never got used to urban attitudes:* city, town, metropolitan, municipal, civic, heavily populated; citified, cosmopolitan, sophisticated, worldly-wise.

urbane *adj.* *The new art director is a consummately urbane man:* suave, elegant, polished, debonair, smooth, sophisticated, cosmopolitan, civilized, refined, cultivated, gracious, courtly, gallant, genteel, chivalrous, gentlemanly, diplomatic, tactful, politic, courteous, polite, mannerly, civil, well-mannered, well-bred. **—Ant.** crude, coarse, rough, rude, boorish, unrefined, unpolished, uncultivated, unsophisticated, tactless, discourteous, impolite; rustic, cloddish, countrified, provincial.

urchin *n.* *The urchins threw snowballs at passing cars:* young rogue, mischievous boy, whippersnapper, imp, gamin, (*fem.*) gamine, brat; homeless boy, waif, stray, street youth, young hooligan, young tough, young punk, juvenile delinquent, *Slang* guttersnipe; boy, lad, laddie, youth, youngster, stripling, young fellow, whelp, young pup. **—Ant.** young gentleman, goody-goody, little Lord Fauntleroy, sissy.

urge *v.* **1.** *The riders urged their horses up the steep hill:* drive, goad, prod, spur, push, force, press, poke, prick, *Slang* egg on; hasten, speed, accelerate, quicken. **2.** *She urged the members to pay their dues promptly:* beseech, implore, plead with, exhort, petition, entreat, request, appeal to, supplicate, importune, press, prevail upon, solicit; coax, persuade, convince, sway. **3.** *The senator urged adoption of the housing bill:* argue for, advocate, recommend, advise, counsel, prescribe, suggest, push for, champion, support strongly, back. *—n.* **4.** *Father has an urge to visit Africa. What urge ever caused him to quit his job?:* impulse, desire, yearning, longing, craving, hankering, itch, yen, wish, fancy, hunger, thirst, passion; motive, motivation, reason, incentive, stimulus, drive, provocation, dictate, inducement, prompting, pressure. **—Ant.** 1 hinder, hold back, deter, prevent, restrain. 2 order, demand, command, require, force, coerce; discourage. 3 oppose, object to.

urgent *adj.* **1.** *The operator said the call was urgent:* pressing, important, serious, requiring immediate attention, compelling, essential, grave, crucial, critical, momentous, weighty; imperative, obligatory, compulsory, necessary, required, indispensable. **2.** *The charity made an urgent appeal for funds:* earnest, intense, ardent, heartfelt, wholehearted, demanding, insist-ent, zealous, fervent, passionate, spirited, pleading, beseeching. **—Ant.** 1 unnecessary, unimportant, trivial, paltry, insignificant, inconsequential, trifling, facetious. 2 weak, feeble, halfhearted, lukewarm, indifferent, perfunctory, spiritless, laconic, apathetic, impassive, nonchalant, lackadaisical.

usable *adj. None of the tools were usable:* employable, useful, fit, operative, helpful, applicable, advantageous, at disposal, convenient, current, ready, running, serviceable, valuable, working, accessible, available.

usage *n.* **1.** *Usage dictates that the host sit at the head of the table:* custom, tradition, convention, etiquette, practice, good form, normal procedure, habit, habitude; system, method, mode, manner. **2.** *In British usage, "lift" means "elevator":* way of using words. **3.** *Due to careless usage, the car lasted only two years:* use, treatment, care, handling, operation, employment, manipulation; management, control.

use *v.* **1.** *Do you know how to use a chain saw? Please use the back door when making deliveries. You'll have to use all your strength to force open that door:* make use of, put to use, operate, employ, work, manipulate, handle, ply, wield; utilize, apply, exercise, exert, resort to, have recourse to, avail oneself of, take advantage of, profit by, capitalize on, make the most of, exploit. **2.** *The car used too much gas. She used all her money buying flashy jewelry:* consume, expend, spend; deplete, drain, exhaust, run through, devour, swallow up, sap; squander, waste, dissipate, fritter away, throw away. **3.** *He complains that she has used him badly:* treat, behave toward, act toward, deal with; handle, manipulate. —*n.* **4.** *We've gotten a lot of use out of that old TV set. The poet is noted for his use of alliteration:* service, serviceability, operation, usage, usefulness, employment, work, function, enjoyment; application, utilization, handling, exercise. **5.** *What's the use of working so hard if no one cares? An electronic typewriter would be of no use where there is no electricity:* good, value, worth, profit, benefit, advantage, avail; usefulness, service, help, aid, convenience. —**Ant.** 2 save, conserve, preserve. 4 disuse, unemployment. 5 bad, detriment, disadvantage, loss, drawback, obstacle, hindrance, futility.

useful *adj. An electric blender is useful if you bake a lot:* practical, serviceable, functional, utilitarian; helpful, beneficial, advantageous, worthwhile, rewarding, valuable, profitable; effective, convenient, handy, time-saving.

useless *adj. This knife is useless for cutting bread. It's useless to speculate what might have been:* of no use, unusable, worthless, unserviceable, nonfunctional, unhelpful, ineffectual, impracticable, inadequate, inefficient, incompetent, futile, vain, inefficacious, fruitless, unavailing, unproductive, profitless, bootless.

usher *n.* **1.** *The usher showed us to our seats:* person who escorts people to seats, escort; guide, conductor, leader, director; porter; doorkeeper, gatekeeper. —*v.* **2.** *The mayor ushered the visiting dignitaries through city hall:* escort, guide, show, conduct, convoy, attend, direct, steer, lead, squire. **3.** *The rising sun ushered in a new day:* herald, introduce, announce, proclaim; precede, preface, inaugurate, launch, *Slang* ring in.

usual *adj. He explained the situation with his usual tact. The play had the usual boy-meets-girl plot:* customary, accustomed, expected, familiar, habitual, normal, wonted, established, well-established; typical, ordinary, routine, common, commonplace, regular, standard, stock, traditional, conventional, orthodox, prescribed, oft-repeated, popular, run-of-the-mill, trite, hackneyed, threadbare. —**Ant.** unusual, uncommon, exceptional, unique, singular, individual, rare, extraordinary, unconventional, unorthodox, novel, new, fresh, one of a kind, out-of-the-way, offbeat, *Slang* far-out.

usually *adv. She can usually be found at home:* generally, in general, chiefly, commonly, consistently, customarily, for the most part, frequently, habitually, largely, mainly, most often, mostly, normally, on average, ordinarily, predominantly, primarily, principally, regularly, routinely, traditionally, typically, widely, broadly.

usurp *v. The duke tried to usurp the throne. Little by little the assistant began to usurp his boss's authority:* seize illegally, take unlawfully, steal, grab; take for oneself, appropriate, commandeer, preempt, arrogate, encroach upon, infringe upon. —**Ant.** give up, surrender, yield, relinquish, renounce.

utensil *n. The cupboard was full of kitchen utensils:* instrument, tool, implement, apparatus, appliance, equipment, gadget, device.

utilitarian *adj. A good cloth coat is more utilitarian than a fur one:* useful, practical, serviceable, functional, pragmatic, sensible; efficient, workable, effective; convenient, handy, usable, beneficial, advantageous, valuable, profitable.

utility *n.* **1.** *Living in an apartment, we miss the utility of a basement and an attic:* usefulness, serviceability, use, service, availability, function; benefit, advantage, aid, help, avail, convenience. **2.** *What are your monthly bills for utilities?:* public service; (*variously*) gas, electricity, telephone, public transportation. —*adj.* **3.** *Ray is a utility outfielder for the White Sox:* alternate, substitute, surrogate, secondary; extra, accessory, reserve, additional, backup, supplemental, auxiliary. —**Ant.** 1 uselessness, worthlessness, futility, folly; disadvantage, inconvenience, drawback. 3 main, primary, prime, first, first-string, original, basic, essential.

utilize *v. To prevent an oil shortage more machines must utilize solar energy:* use, make use of, put to use, employ, take advantage of, turn to account, make the most of, capitalize on, exploit, put into service, bring into play; avail oneself of, profit by, resort to, have recourse to.

utmost *also* **uttermost** *adj.* **1.** *I have the utmost confidence in his ability. Secrecy is of the utmost importance:* greatest, maximum, highest; foremost, chief, major, main, principal, predominant, paramount, prime, primary, first, leading, sovereign, supreme, preeminent, cardinal, capital. —*n.* **2.** *The cruise ship provided the utmost in luxury:* ultimate, last word, best, acme, zenith, peak, tiptop, *Slang* tops, the most.

utopia *n. Retiring to Hawaii is my idea of utopia:*

ideal life, perfect bliss, supreme happiness; perfect place, heaven, seventh heaven, Erewhon, paradise, Eden, Shangri-la. **—Ant.** hell, hell on earth.

utopian *adj. We never shared her utopian beliefs of an earthly paradise:* idealistic, visionary, impracticable, unrealistic, unfeasible, otherworldly, insubstantial, unrealizable, unworkable, unattainable, unfulfillable. **—Ant.** worldly, realistic, feasible, practicable.

utter[1] *adj. With Mother away the house is in utter confusion:* complete, total, absolute, thorough, downright, outright, out-and-out, sheer, entire, perfect, pure, unrelieved, unqualified, unequivocal, categorical, unmodified, unmitigated, unchecked. **—Ant.** partial, moderate, slight, relative, reasonable, limited, qualified, passable, tolerable.

utter[2] *v. He sat there without uttering a word. Don't utter a word of this to anyone:* speak, say, voice, pronounce, articulate, enunciate, vocalize, talk, express, emit, deliver; disclose, reveal, divulge, tell, state, proclaim, declare; mutter, whisper; shout, exclaim, yell. **—Ant.** be mute, remain silent, keep quiet, keep mum; keep secret, keep confidential, conceal.

utterance *n.* **1.** *He couldn't give utterance to his thoughts:* expression, speech, vocalization, articulation, talk, verbalization, declaration, pronouncement, proclamation. **2.** *We could hardly understand his garbled utterance:* statement, discourse, talk, word, remark, answer, exclamation, opinion, expression.

utterly *adv. The party was utterly delightful:* thoroughly, entirely, fully, completely, totally, wholly, absolutely, perfectly, downright, outright, extremely, just, to the nth degree. **—Ant.** partly, partially, somewhat, moderately, a little, rather, reasonably, passably, tolerably.

uttermost *adj.* **1.** *The explorers reached the uttermost limits of the ice pack:* outermost. **2.** *Security should be a matter of uttermost concern:* utmost, extreme, maximum, sovereign, supreme. **—***n.* **3.** *The oarsmen strained to the uttermost of their strength:* utmost, extreme limit, maximum.

V

vacancy n. **1.** *The vacancy between the walls was filled with rubble:* empty space, void, gap, opening, hole, hollow, cavity, breach, fissure, crevice. **2.** *The vacancy of the house dates from last year:* emptiness, vacantness. **3.** *There's a vacancy on the fifth floor front:* unoccupied place, vacant quarters, room for rent, apartment for rent, house for rent, office for rent, suite for rent; housing, lodging, abode. **4.** *The personnel department is trying to fill a vacancy in the filing department:* unfilled position, available job, opening, situation, place. —**Ant.** 2 occupation, occupancy.

vacant adj. **1.** *Do you know of a vacant apartment? By the end of the game the stadium was almost vacant:* unoccupied, empty, unfilled, unused, not in use, for rent, for lease, untenanted, tenantless; deserted, uninhabited, abandoned, forsaken; unfurnished, clear, open. **2.** *Since retiring, Father has had a great deal of vacant time on his hands:* leisure, unoccupied, free, idle, unemployed, unengaged, unencumbered. **3.** *Busy passersby gave the arguing men a vacant stare:* blank, expressionless, uncomprehending, empty, vacuous, vapid, wooden, dull, deadpan, poker-face; incurious, indifferent, unconcerned, oblivious, apathetic, aloof, detached, blasé. —**Ant.** 1, 2 occupied, filled, taken, engaged, full, booked-up, crowded, packed. 1 rented, leased, in use, inhabited; crammed, jammed. 2 busy, employed. 3 expressive, comprehending, meaningful, thoughtful, reflective; animated, alert, lively; interested, concerned, engrossed, rapt.

vacate v. *We have to vacate these offices by December 31st:* give up possession of, give up, quit, leave, withdraw from, depart from, evacuate, empty; relinquish, surrender, hand over, resign, abdicate. —**Ant.** occupy, move into, take possession of, fill, possess, employ, retain, keep, hold, hang on to.

vacation n. **1.** *All employees are entitled to three weeks of vacation each year:* leave, rest, holidays, intermission; academic intermission, judicial intermission, recess; furlough, *U.S. Military* rest-and-recreation, *Informal* R

vaccinate v. *The children were vaccinated against the flu:* inoculate, immunize, inject, prevent, protect.

vacillate v. **1.** *He seemed certain about it yesterday, but today he's vacillating:* waver, be irresolute, hesitate, be unsettled, be doubtful, be changeable, fluctuate, falter, not know one's own mind, shilly-shally, hem and haw, blow hot and cold. **2.** *The earthquake caused the entire house to vacillate:* sway, move to and fro, rock, roll, toss, pitch, shift, waver, totter, teeter, reel, oscillate, wobble, flutter, vibrate. —**Ant.** 1 be determined, be resolute, be steadfast, be certain, be settled.

vacuous adj. *We left the vacuous movie after fifteen minutes:* vacant, empty, hollow, void, bland, blank, insipid, fatuous, inane, emptyheaded, airheaded, vapid, foolish, silly, asinine, *Slang* bubbleheaded, bubblebrained. —**Ant.** serious, lofty.

vacuum n. *It's said that nature abhors a vacuum:* void, nothingness, vacuity, emptiness, free space, gap, nothingness, exhaustion.

vagabond n. **1.** *During the Great Depression of the 1930's many men became vagabonds:* wanderer, roamer, rover, rambler, wayfarer, itinerant, floater, drifter, nomad, gypsy, migrant; vagrant, tramp, hobo, beachcomber. —*adj.* **2.** *The students spent a vagabond year hitchhiking through Europe:* wandering, roaming, roving, rambling, wayfaring, footloose, itinerant, nomadic, journeying, traveling, transient, vagrant, homeless; carefree, bohemian. —**Ant.** 1 householder, homebody; worker, businessman. 2 nontraveling, settled, rooted, ensconced, resident.

vagary n. *It was her vagary that we have a picnic instead of a wedding dinner:* whim, caprice, notion, whimsy, fancy, crotchet, impulse, fantasy, daydream, quirk, kink, humor, passing fancy, idiosyncrasy, eccentricity, *Slang* brainstorm.

vagrant n. **1.** *Police kept a close watch on the skid row vagrants:* person with no permanent address, homeless person; person with no means of support; itinerant, floater, wanderer, roamer, rover, vagabond, knight-of-the-road, nomad, migrant; tramp, hobo; beggar, panhandler, loafer, bum. —*adj.* **2.** *The old prospector had led a vagrant life:* roaming, roving, rambling, wandering, itinerant, peripatetic, nomadic, vagabond; homeless, transient.

vague adj. *The agreement between the two countries is vague, but diplomats are working out the details. The man was rather vague about his past:* not definite, indefinite, inexplicit, unclear, imprecise, ill-defined, undetailed, uncertain, unsettled, undetermined, confused, unsure, fuzzy, hazy, nebulous, unspecific, unspecified, loose, general, random, casual. —**Ant.** definite, explicit, clear, clear-cut, precise, specific, distinct, well-defined, detailed, express, settled, determined, fixed.

vain adj. **1.** *Ruth is very vain about her appearance:* proud, too concerned, self-satisfied, self-admiring, conceited, arrogant, puffed-up, vainglorious, pompous, self-important, *Slang* stuck-up; egotistical, boastful, disdainful, cocky, swaggering, dandyish. **2.** *The rescuers made a vain attempt to reach the sinking boat. Playing cards seems a vain pastime to me:* unsuccessful, unavailing, useless, futile, fruitless, bootless, ineffectual, ineffective, unprofitable, profitless; nugatory, worthless, trifling, pointless, timewasting, without merit, idle, foolish, silly, supercilious, superficial. —**Ant.** 1 modest, humble, unconcerned, unsatisfied; meek, unsure, shy, bashful. 2 successful, victorious, useful, fruitful, effective, expedient, serviceable; profitable, beneficial, beneficent, worthwhile; serious, substantial, valid, worthy.

vainglorious *adj. He's so vainglorious, he's always telling us about his accomplishments:* conceited, stuck-up, narcissistic, haughty, affected, egotistical, cocky, swell-headed, boastful, bragging, supercilious, insolent. **—Ant.** humble, shy, reserved, modest, self-effacing.

vainglory *n.* **1.** *Vainglory was evident in the way he strutted about:* egotism, vanity, conceit. **2.** *The military parade was full of vainglory:* pomp, show, ostentation. **—Ant.** humility.

valedictory *adj.* **1.** *The graduation ceremony will end with a valedictory address by the highest-ranking student:* farewell, parting, leave-taking, departing; final, last, terminal, ultimate, conclusive. —*n.* **2.** *The painter depicted George Washington's valedictory to his troops:* farewell speech; oration for a graduating class, commencement address.

valiant *adj. No knight was more valiant than Sir Lancelot:* courageous, brave, dauntless, undaunted, intrepid, valorous, heroic, bold, bold-spirited, fearless, unafraid, daring, audacious, unflinching, lionhearted, great-hearted, stout-hearted, stalwart, resolute; chivalrous, gallant, knightly, noble. **—Ant.** cowardly, craven, fearful, timorous, timid, afraid, fainthearted.

valid *adj.* **1.** *Do you have a valid reason for being late? This seems to be a valid solution to the problem:* acceptable, suitable, proper, fitting, applicable, effective, accurate, truthful, genuine, sound, well-grounded, well-founded, substantial, realistic, logical, good, convincing, forceful, compelling, decisive, weighty, strong, powerful. **2.** *Such a contract is not valid in this state:* legally binding, having legal force, legal, legalized, lawful, licit, being in effect, official, legitimate, authoritative, authentic, constitutional. **—Ant.** 1 unacceptable, unsuitable, improper, unfitting, inapplicable, ineffective, false, inaccurate, untrue, *Informal* phony; bogus, sham, unfounded, baseless, insubstantial, illogical, unrealistic, unforceful, weak. 2 invalid, void, null, inoperative, illegal, unlawful, illicit, unofficial, illegitimate.

validate *v. This passport has to be signed before the official can validate it:* make valid, make legally binding, make legal, legalize, make lawful, make official, authorize, certify, stamp, ratify, confirm, countersign, witness, authenticate, verify, corroborate, substantiate, prove, sustain, sanction, warrant; enact, put into effect. **—Ant.** invalidate, cancel, void, annul, terminate.

validity *n.* **1.** *His argument seems to have a great deal of validity:* soundness, grounds, factual foundation, substance, logic, convincingness, force, weight, strength, power, potency, accuracy, truthfulness, authenticity, conclusiveness; acceptability, suitability, applicability, effectiveness. **2.** *The lawyer questioned the validity of the contract:* legality, legal force, power; authority, authenticity, legitimacy, right, properness. **—Ant.** 1 unsoundness, weakness, flaws, lies, falsity, inaccuracy, ineffectiveness. 2 illegality, illegitimacy.

valley *n. The town nestled in a valley:* flat region between mountains, river valley, river basin, basin; dell, dale, glade, glen, vale, hollow, bottom, dip, ravine, gully, gulch, gorge, canyon, divide, chasm, water gap, gap, cut. **—Ant.** mountain, mount, peak, cliff, bluff, butte, ridge, hill, hillock, hummock, knoll, rise, height.

valor *n. The soldier was decorated for his valor under fire:* bravery, courage, dauntlessness, intrepidity, fearlessness, heroism, boldness, daring, fortitude; mettle, grit, spunk, nerve, guts; pluck, gallantry, chivalry. **—Ant.** cowardice, fear, fearfulness, timidity, pusillanimity, baseness, ignobility.

valuable *adj.* **1.** *Friendship is the most valuable thing in the world. Let me give you some valuable advice:* invaluable, worthwhile, precious, important, significant, priceless, treasured, prized, valued, esteemed, admired, respected; useful, beneficial, helpful, advantageous, profitable, good, fruitful, serviceable, utilitarian. **2.** *Her grandmother left her a valuable ring:* of great monetary value, costly, expensive, high-priced, dear, precious, priceless. **—Ant.** 1 worthless, valueless, unimportant, insignificant, trivial, unesteemed, disliked; useless, pointless, fruitless, unprofitable, silly, trifling. 2 cheap, inexpensive, worthless.

value *n.* **1.** *Mother attaches a great deal of value to good manners. A knowledge of typing is of great value in this job:* merit, worth, importance, significance, esteem, respect, admiration; prestige, greatness, excellence, superiority; use, usefulness, benefit, help, advantage, profit, service, utility. **2.** *The expert set a value of $10,000 on the painting:* worth, monetary worth, face value, market price; amount, cost, charge, rate, appraisal, assessment, estimation. **3. values** *I've never understood his set of values. Primitive peoples have different values than we do:* ideals, standards, moral code, code of ethics; institutions, customs, rules, beliefs, practices, conventions. —*v.* **4.** *The tax assessor valued the house at $40,000:* assess, assay, appraise, evaluate, set a value on; fix the price of, price, compute; count, weigh, judge, size up, reckon, rate. **5.** *I value his opinion:* regard highly, prize, respect, treasure, esteem, hold in high esteem, cherish, revere, set store by, admire, appreciate. **—Ant.** 1 unimportance, insignificance, inferiority; disadvantage, worthlessness, uselessness. 5 disregard, disesteem, misprize, be contemptuous of; undervalue, underestimate.

valued *adj. Jennifer was my most valued friend:* highly regarded, esteemed, prized, treasured, respected, cherished, revered, appreciated.

valve *n. They were able to shut the valve:* faucet, tap, cock, plug, spigot.

van[1] *n. All the furniture had been put on the moving van:* large truck, covered truck, truck, wagon, cart, dray, trailer, *British* lorry; camper, trailer.

van[2] *n. Tanks were in the van of the army's advance. Maxine was in the van of women's liberation:* vanguard, advance guard, avant-garde, forefront, front rank, first line, foremost division, head; front of an army, scout, sentinel, picket.

vandal n. *Many city buses were defaced by vandals:* willful destroyer, despoiler, saboteur, wrecker, demolisher, barbarian, looter, plunderer, pillager, ravager, raider, marauder.

vanguard n. **1.** *The vanguard was sent ahead to clear the woods of enemy snipers:* advance guard, avant-garde, van, front rank, front line, forward troops, foremost division, first line, spearhead, forerank. **2.** *The vanguard praised the merits of the young painter:* avant-garde, forefront, tastemakers, trendsetters, pacesetters, modernists, leaders, leadership, trailblazers, innovators.

vanish v. **1.** *The airplane vanished into the clouds:* disappear, become invisible, be lost to sight, dematerialize. **2.** *His anger vanished and he burst out laughing:* disappear, cease, expire, perish, end, terminate, die, die away, die out, fade away, evaporate, melt away, pass away, dissolve. **—Ant.** 1 appear, loom, come into view; materialize. 2 arrive, commence, begin, start.

vanity n. **1.** *She's pretty, but that's no excuse for such vanity:* pride, conceit, self-conceit, self-love, self-admiration, self-praise, narcissism, egotism, vainglory. **2.** *The minister's sermon was on the vanity of amassing worldly goods:* lack of real value, worthlessness, uselessness, emptiness, hollowness, inanity, folly, idleness, futility, fruitlessness, unsubstantialness, superficiality, sham, falsity; mirage, delusion. **3.** *Let's put the vanity between the two windows:* dressing table, mirror table, makeup table. **4.** *She took out her vanity and began powdering her nose:* compact, vanity case, powder box, vanity bag. **—Ant.** 1 self-hate, self-abasement, masochism; humility, modesty, meekness. 2 value, worth, usefulness, meaningfulness.

vanquish v. *The king's army vanquished the rebels:* defeat, conquer, overcome, overpower, crush, overwhelm, triumph over, beat, thrash, best, drub, lick, rout, master, subdue, subjugate, overthrow, get the upper hand over. **—Ant.** be defeated, lose, surrender, capitulate, give up, yield, submit, succumb, bow down, knuckle under.

vapid adj. *What a vapid young man! She made some vapid remarks about the weather:* lifeless, dull, flat, insipid, bland, flavorless, empty; tame, uninspiring, unsatisfying, colorless, lame, stale, characterless, wishy-washy, pointless, meaningless. **—Ant.** lively, exciting, inspiring, satisfying, colorful.

vapor n. *A thin coat of vapor began to collect on the windshield:* moisture, mist, dew, haze, fog, miasma, steam; smoke, smog; fumes.

vaporize v. *All the water vaporized at once:* evaporate, gasify, distil, aerate.

variable adj. **1.** *It was a cloudy day with variable winds. Her affections tend to be variable:* changeable, changing, shifting, fluctuating, unstable, fitful, spasmodic, fickle, capricious, wavering, inconstant. **2.** *The precise shape of a chair is variable:* indefinite, unsettled, diverse, different, uneven, unlike; alterable, mutable. **—n. 3.** *There are several variables that could*

change our plans: changeable factor. **—Ant.** 1 constant, unchanging, stable, steady. 2 invariable, firm, settled, unalterable, immutable, alike. 3 constant.

variance n. *There was considerable variance in how to solve the problem:* divergence, discrepancy, difference; disagreement, controversy, dissension, discord, strife. **—Ant.** invariance, sameness.

variant adj. **1.** *"Travelling" is a variant spelling of "traveling":* derived, different, modified, altered, transformed, divergent. **—n. 2.** *The song is just a variant of an old folk tune:* variation, different form, modification, alteration, transformation, departure, takeoff. **—Ant.** 1, 2 original. 1 basic, fundamental, root, earliest, underived, intrinsic, prime, primary, first, preferred. 2 archetype, prototype, pattern, model, source.

variation n. *We need some variation in our daily routine:* variance, variety, change, difference, diversity, innovation, modification, transformation, alteration, departure, variant, aberration, mutation, metamorphosis; disagreement, discrepancy, divergency, deviation; rate of change, amount of change. **—Ant.** uniformity, sameness, regularity, consistency, permanence.

varicolored adj. *She worked for years to develop a varicolored rose:* multicolored, multihued, polychromatic, technicolor, motley, variegated, dappled, mottled, opalescent, iridescent, parti-colored, flecked, marbled, rainbowlike, tartan, piebald, calico. **—Ant.** solid, plain, uniform, monochromatic.

varied adj. *The store carries a varied selection of merchandise:* diversified; diverse, various; assorted, different, miscellaneous, mixed, heterogeneous, sundry, motley, variegated. **—Ant.** uniform, standardized, homogeneous.

variety n. **1.** *Variety is the spice of life:* change diversity, diversification, difference, variation, dissimilarity, nonuniformity, unconformity, innovation. **2.** *The Smithsonian Institution has a wide variety of objects on display:* assortment, medley, miscellany, mixture, collection, mélange, pastiche, motley, multiplicity, heterogeneity, hodgepodge, jumble, hash, patchwork, omnium-gatherum. **3.** *The orchard grows several varieties of apples:* kind, type, sort, classification; class, category, breed, strain, stock, species, subspecies, genus, genre, brand, group, division, subdivision, denomination; race, tribe, family. **—Ant.** 1, 2 sameness, uniformity, homogeneity, standardization, conformity; similarity, likeness.

various adj. **1.** *We've had various types of cars but prefer a station wagon:* different, sundry, varied, diverse, divers, assorted, dissimilar, miscellaneous, other. **2.** *Various people have expressed disagreement with his proposal:* numerous, many, countless, innumerable, myriad, manifold, multitudinous, multifarious; several, some, few. **—Ant.** 1 same, like, alike, identical, uniform.

varnish n. **1.** *What's the best kind of varnish for this chair?:* resin solution; stain, lacquer, gloss. **—v. 2.** *Varnish the bookcase and give it a coat* *of wax:* stain, lacquer, gloss. **3.** *She tends to varnish the truth to make a more interesting story:* gilt, embellish, adorn, disguise; mitigate, soften, make allowance for, gloss over, excuse, smooth over; cover, conceal. **—Ant.** 3 be frank, be candid, be open; bare.

vary *v.* **1.** *Let's vary the routine and drive to work by a different route:* change, alter, diversify, modify, shift. **2.** *Television sets vary widely in price. This marigold varies from the norm in being giant-sized:* differ, be unlike, contrast, fluctuate, deviate, diverge, depart, veer; disagree, disaccord, dissent. **—Ant.** 1 keep unchanged, keep uniform, regulate, standardize. 2 conform, be uniform, be similar, be alike, be constant, be stable, correspond, harmonize; agree, comply with, reconcile with, fall in with, go along with.

vast *adj.* *The camel caravan crossed the vast expanse of the Sahara:* extensive, wide, widespread, far-flung, far-reaching, boundless, unbounded, infinite, measureless, immeasurable, unlimited, limitless, endless, interminable, great, immense, huge, enormous, prodigious, tremendous, stupendous, gigantic, colossal, titanic, jumbo, monumental, very large, very big, substantial, significant, monstrous; spacious, capacious, voluminous. **—Ant.** limited, narrow; small, little, tiny; moderate-sized, modest.

vault[1] *n.* **1.** *The vault of the cathedral is 150 feet above the floor:* dome, arched roof, arched ceiling, arch; arcade, cupola. **2.** *The bank doesn't open its vault until 9 A.M.:* strongroom; wall safe, safe, strongbox. **3.** *The old patrician was buried in the family vault:* burial chamber, mausoleum, crypt, sepulcher, tomb; ossuary, catacomb.

vault[2] *v.* **1.** *The boy vaulted the fence and ran into the woods:* hurdle, jump, jump over, leap over, spring over, leapfrog, bound, clear; polevault. *—n.* **2.** *One vault and he was over the hedge and gone:* jump, leap, spring, bound, hurdle. **—Ant.** 1 crawl under, creep beneath.

vaunt *v.* *She always vaunts her father's wealth:* boast about, brag of, crow about, gloat over, exult in, talk big about, give oneself airs about, blow one's own horn, gasconade; flaunt, swagger, show off, make a display of, strut. **—Ant.** decry, disparage, detract; conceal, repress, suppress, keep quiet about.

veer *v.* *The car veered suddenly to avoid hitting the dog. The ball veered over the left field stands:* change direction, swerve, wheel, turn, zigzag, turn aside, shift, dodge, curve, drift, *Nautical* go about, come round, tack, yaw, jibe. **—Ant.** go straight, go in a straight line, make a beeline for; hold course.

vegetable *n.* *Dinner includes soup, entrée, salad, and two vegetables:* edible herbaceous plant; legume, produce, greens.

vegetate *v.* *With nothing to do, they just vegetated:* stagnate, decay, deteriorate, hibernate, idle, languish, weaken, be inert. **—Ant.** develop, grow, accomplish, react, respond.

vegetation *n.* **1.** *The abandoned property was overgrown with vegetation:* plant life, plants, flora, shrubbery, foliage, herbage, verdure, flowerage, leaves; grass, weeds, vegetable growth. **2.** *Complete vegetation is my idea of a real vacation:* inactivity, idleness, loafing, sloth, torpor, lethargy, sluggishness, languor, languidness, indolence, inert existence; dormancy, hibernation, rustication.

vehemence *n.* *She spoke with great vehemence:* eagerness, impetuosity, verve, fire, ardor, violence, fervor, zeal, passion, enthusiasm, fervency, fury. **—Ant.** coolness, apathy, antipathy.

vehement *adj.* *He's a vehement supporter of progressive education:* ardent, fervent, fervid, intense, fierce, passionate, impassioned, emotional, excited, violent, forceful, furious, heated, hot, hotheaded, fiery, frenzied, agitated, stormy, tempestuous; enthusiastic, zealous, vigorous, fanatic, fanatical, rabid, wild, eager, earnest. **—Ant.** indifferent, unconcerned, mild, weak, feeble, lukewarm, halfhearted, dispassionate, apathetic, impassive, subdued, calm, cool, quiet, placid, serene.

vehemently *adv.* *The two men argued vehemently:* ardently, fervently, intensely, passionately, excitedly, violently, furiously, fiercely, hotly, strongly, tempestuously, emotionally; enthusiastically, zealously, vigorously, fanatically, wildly, eagerly, earnestly. **—Ant.** indifferently, mildly, feebly, halfheartedly, impassively, calmly, cooly, quietly.

vehicle *n.* **1.** *No vehicles are permitted inside the park:* conveyance, means of transport, transportation; *(variously)* motor vehicle, car, truck, bus, train, plane, space vehicle, rocket ship, motorcycle, bicycle. **2.** *Television has become a major advertising vehicle:* medium, means, agent, agency, instrument, tool, device, mechanism, intermediary, organ.

veil *n.* **1.** *The hat had a mesh veil. A veil of fog covered the valley:* cloth facial covering; cover, covering, blanket, curtain, cloak, screen, cloud, mantle, shroud. *—v.* **2.** *A curtain of smog veiled the sun. The misleading report veiled the facts:* hide, conceal, cover, cloak, mask, screen, shroud, enwrap, envelop; dim, obscure, camouflage. **—Ant.** 2 expose, disclose, reveal, show, divulge; unveil, uncover, unwrap, strip, denude.

vein *n.* **1.** *He was so angry the veins stood out on his forehead:* blood vessel, capillary. **2.** *There was a vein of coal running through the mountain:* stratum, stria, layer, seam, lode; streak, line, stripe, thread, rib. **3.** *He spoke to the crowd in a humorous vein. The book has a vein of cynicism throughout:* mood, tone, manner, style; nature, character, disposition, complexion, temper, temperament, tendency, inclination, bent, predisposition, propensity, predilection; strain, streak, touch, hint. *—v.* **4.** *The dried mud was veined with cracks:* line, streak, mark, marble, stripe, furrow, rib, web, fleck.

velocity *n.* **1.** *Some hawks descend with terrific velocity on their prey:* rapidity, swiftness, speed, fleetness. **2.** *The velocity with which the coup was carried out stunned the opposition:* speed, haste, pace, quickness, speediness, celerity, alacrity, fleetness, expedition.

venal *adj. The venal politician had no thought of the public welfare:* willing to be bribed, bribable, corruptible, corrupt, unprincipled, unscrupulous, dishonest; greedy, rapacious, avaricious, covetous, grasping, mercenary, money-grubbing, selfish, *Slang* shady, crooked. —**Ant.** unbribable, incorruptible, honest; public-spirited, selfless, altruistic.

vend *v. The founder of the store got his start by vending old clothes from a pushcart:* peddle, hawk, huckster, sell; retail, merchandise, deal in, trade in, market; auction, trade, barter.

vendor or **vender** *n. The youth works as a hot-dog vendor at the ballpark. The company is the largest vendor of air conditioners in the country:* seller, hawker, peddler, street peddler, huckster, monger, salesman, trader; retailer, wholesaler, dealer, merchandiser, supplier, purveyor; merchant, tradesman. —**Ant.** buyer, purchaser, customer.

veneer *n.* **1.** *The front of the house has a stone veneer. Apply a veneer of shellac to the coffee table:* facing, façade, outer layer, layer, covering, coat, coating, overlay, wrapper, sheath, envelope, casing, jacket. **2.** *Underneath her veneer of haughtiness she's actually very kind:* outward appearance, façade, front, show, mask, pretense.

venerable *adj. Bede, the English historian (673-735), is called the "Venerable Bede":* worthy of respect, respected, venerated, revered, august, esteemed, honored, admired; deserving respect because of age, elderly, aged, old, patriarchal, ancient, hoary, white-haired. —**Ant.** dishonorable, disreputable, shameful, ignominious, inglorious, infamous, dishonored, discredited, disgraced; young, youthful, inexperienced, green, callow.

venerate *v. As a child he venerated his grandparents:* revere, esteem, respect, honor, admire, idolize, adore, cherish, extol, glorify, look up to, treat with deference, pay homage to, reverence, worship, hallow. —**Ant.** scorn, disdain, contemn, despise, detest, hate, execrate, dishonor; disregard, slight, spurn.

veneration *n. The saint inspired much veneration:* respect, reverence, awe. —**Ant.** disrespect, irreverence.

vengeance *n. He swore vengeance for the murder of his brother:* revenge, reprisal, retaliation, avenging, retribution, requital, revengefulness, a tooth for a tooth, an eye for an eye; vindictiveness, malevolence, implacability, ruthlessness.

venial *adj. He wasn't perfect, but all his sins were venial ones:* forgivable, pardonable, excusable; justifiable, warrantable, allowable, defensible; slight, minor, trivial, unimportant, not serious. —**Ant.** mortal; unpardonable, unforgivable, inexpiable; inexcusable, unwarrantable, unjustifiable, indefensible; flagrant, infamous.

venom *n.* **1.** *The rattlesnake secretes venom through its fangs:* poisonous fluid; toxin, *Archaic* virus. **2.** *He spewed out his venom in a series of poison-pen letters:* hate, hatred, bitterness, ill will, malevolence, maliciousness, malice, animosity, resentment, rancor, rancorousness, spite, spitefulness, acrimony, hostility, enmity, grudge, anger, ire, choler, spleen, gall; savagery, barbarity, brutality. —**Ant.** 1 antidote, antitoxin. 2 love, affection, friendliness, kindness, sweetness, goodwill, good feeling, amity, brotherly love, benevolence, humanitarianism, charity.

venomous *adj.* **1.** *Some jellyfish are venomous:* poisonous, noxious, toxic; lethal, deadly, fatal, virulent. **2.** *Why are some movie reviews so venomous?:* spiteful, malicious, malevolent, resentful, rancorous, hostile, ill-disposed, abusive, malign, malignant; caustic, bitter, vicious, cruel, brutal, savage, bloodthirsty. —**Ant.** 1 nonpoisonous, nontoxic. 2 loving, affectionate, friendly, kind, kindly, sweet, genial, benevolent, compassionate, charitable, magnanimous, forgiving.

vent *n.* **1.** *Smoke poured out of the vent in the cabin's roof:* opening, outlet, aperture, venthole, hole, orifice, air hole; (*variously*) ventilator, chimney, flue, smokestack, spout, pipe; faucet, tap, spigot. **2.** *The children need a vent for all that energy:* outlet, means of escape, means of exit. **3.** *She gave vent to her wrath in a furious tirade:* expression, utterance, voice; declaration, disclosure, revelation, exposure. —*v.* **4.** *This pipe vents smoke from the kitchen:* let out, let escape, serve as an exit for; emit, discharge, release, debouch, escape, pour forth, gush, spout, exude, effuse, drip, ooze. **5.** *He vented his enthusiasm in a series of shouts:* express, communicate, voice, utter, declare; disclose, reveal, divulge, bare, air. —**Ant.** 1 obstruction, closure, stoppage, impediment, check. 4 block, stop, obstruct. 5 suppress, repress, withhold, restrain, inhibit, check, curb, bridle; hide, conceal.

ventilate *v.* **1.** *Open the window and ventilate the room:* provide with fresh air, circulate fresh air, air, air out; aerate, oxygenate. **2.** *Members are asked not to ventilate club problems outside this meeting:* make widely known, broadcast, publicize, report, circulate, voice, declare, divulge, disseminate, spread abroad, spread, air, sow, bandy about, noise abroad; discuss, talk about, express, comment on, review, analyze, examine, criticize, dissent.

venture *n.* **1.** *Speculating in the commodities market can be a costly venture:* endeavor, undertaking, enterprise, project; gamble, risk, adventure, chance, uncertainty, speculation, flyer, plunge. —*v.* **2.** *Nothing ventured, nothing gained:* risk, hazard, dare, chance, gamble, wager, bet, undertake, endeavor, attempt, strive for, try. **3.** *If I may venture an opinion, he'll never succeed:* advance, put forward, offer, proffer, tender, volunteer, submit, hold out; presume, take the liberty, make free with, make bold. **4.** *Don't venture into the jungle without a guide:* travel, go, risk going, plunge, take a flyer. —**Ant.** 1 certainty, surety, security, stability, reliability; caution, safety, protection. 2 assure, secure, guarantee; save, safeguard, conserve, protect.

venturesome also **adventuresome** *adj.* **1.** *He's so venturesome he'll try anything:* adventurous, ready to take risks, daring, bold, daredevil, audacious, rash, impulsive, impetuous, reckless, foolhardy; enterprising, ambitious, energetic, aggressive. **2.** *Diving for sunken treasure is a very venturesome way to make a living:* dangerous, hazardous, risky, perilous, precarious, unsafe; uncertain, insecure, unsure, speculative, doubtful, dubious, questionable, ticklish, tricky. **—Ant.** 1 cautious, wary, timid, timorous, apprehensive, fearful, afraid, fearsome; reluctant, adverse, loath, unwilling. 2 safe, protected, guarded; certain, sure, secure, reliable, sound, dependable, stable, trustworthy, infallible.

venturous *adj.* **1.** *The venturous pair scaled the mountain:* venturesome, adventurous, intrepid, fearless, enterprising, daring, bold. **2.** *The venturous attempt to put out the fire themselves had dire consequences:* hazardous, dangerous, risky, perilous. **—Ant.** fearful, cowardly; secure, safe.

veracious *adj.* *The veracious reporter was a stickler for detail:* honest, truthful, accurate, dependable, faithful, genuine, reliable, trustworthy, straightforward.

veracity *n.* *I sometimes doubt his veracity. The veracity of the report is unquestionable:* truthfulness, adherence to truth, honesty, integrity, probity, candor, frankness, openness, sincerity, guilelessness, ingenuousness; truth, accuracy, correctness, exactness, verity, verisimilitude, exactitude. **—Ant.** untruthfulness, deception, deceit, duplicity, guile, mendacity; lie, falsehood, fiction, fabrication, error.

verbal *adj.* **1.** *The book gives a good verbal picture of life in China. A verbal agreement is not as binding as a written contract:* of words, in words, expressed in words; (*loosely*) oral, spoken, said, voiced, vocal, unwritten, expressed, uttered. **2.** *The "-ed" in "talked" is a verbal suffix:* of verbs; derived from a verb.

verbatim *adv., adj.* *The witness repeated the conversation verbatim. Give me a verbatim account of what was said:* word for word, exactly, in exactly the same words, letter for letter, chapter and verse; to the letter, literatim; literal, literally, exact, exactly, accurate, accurately, faithful, faithfully, precise, precisely.

verbiage *n.* *The speaker bored everyone with his verbiage:* wordiness, long-windedness, verbosity, verboseness, circumlocution, logorrhea, volubility, grandiloquence, effusiveness, loquacity, prolixity.

verbose *adj.* *The senator is so verbose it takes him an hour to tell a simple joke:* wordy, long-winded, voluble, circumlocutory, effusive, grandiloquent, prolix, talkative, garrulous, gabby, loquacious. **—Ant.** terse, concise, succinct, pithy; reticent, curt, brusque.

verdant *adj.* *We hiked along the verdant trails of the park:* green, grassy, leafy, shady, turfy, meadowy; lush, luxuriant, blooming, burgeon-

ing, flourishing, thriving; springlike. **—Ant.** fading, waning, dying, withering; autumnal.

verdict *n.* *Has the jury reached a verdict?:* decision, judgment, finding, opinion, determination, ruling, decree, sentence, assessment, estimation, valuation, answer; adjudication, arbitration, arbitrament.

verge *n.,* **1.** *Guttering was installed around the verge of the roof. The child was on the verge of tears:* edge, border, brink, margin, rim, brim, hem, skirt, fringe, lip, ledge, flange; limit, threshold, bound, boundary, frontier, extreme, confine, end, terminus. *—v.* **2.** *The farm verges on the county line:* border, be on the brink, fringe, skirt, edge; be near, approach, approximate. **—Ant.** 1 center, middle, midst, heart, depth.

verify *v.* *Several witnesses verified his alibi. Later findings verified the scientist's theory:* confirm, corroborate, substantiate, attest to, prove, establish, support, sustain; certify, guarantee, validate, authenticate, witness, document, testify to, vouch for, accredit. **—Ant.** disprove, deny, refute, dispute, confute, contradict, controvert, gainsay, discredit; invalidate, subvert, falsify, misrepresent.

verisimilitude *n.* *The story had little verisimilitude:* realism, genuineness, likeness, plausibility, resemblance, semblance, similarity, authenticity.

veritable *adj.* *The old professor is a veritable gold mine of information:* true, real, genuine, actual, bona fide, valid, authentic, absolute, complete, utter, through-and-through, positive, literal, unquestionable, incontestable, unimpeachable, true-blue. **—Ant.** sham, spurious, feigned, false, deceptive, supposed, questionable, so-called, figurative.

vermin *n. pl.* **1.** *The rancher carried a .22 rifle to shoot vermin:* noxious animals and birds, varmints, pests; (*loosely*) mice, rats, snakes, wolves, foxes, coyotes, weasels, owls, birds of prey, crows, etc. **2.** *At night all sorts of vermin crawled out of the walls of the old house:* pestiferous insects, (*variously*) roaches, lice, fleas, bedbugs, silverfish, centipedes, termites, water bugs, spiders, ants.

vernacular *n.* **1.** *The politician tried to appeal to the people by speaking in the vernacular:* common speech, everyday language, slang, natural speech, colloquial speech, informal speech; native language, native tongue, the vulgar. **2.** *The word "slammer" means "penitentiary" in prison vernacular:* jargon, lingo, parlance, slang, cant, idiom, dialect, patois, shoptalk. **—Ant.** 1 formal speech, educated speech, literary language; foreign language, second language. 2 standard speech, received speech.

vernal *adj.* *The vernal equinox occurs about March 21st each year. The vernal radiance of her smile captivated us all:* spring; springlike, fresh, new, green, youthful.

versatile *adj.* **1.** *In order to repair barns, build fences, grow crops, and care for animals a farmer must indeed be versatile. Leonard Bernstein is a versatile composer:* having many abilities, many-sided, all-around, multifaceted, many-skilled, handy, adaptable, resourceful, protean; gifted, talented, accomplished, ingenious, proficient, clever, adroit, apt, able, expert. **2.** *Have you seen this versatile new kitchen gadget?:* having many uses, having many applications. —**Ant.** 1, 2 specialized, limited.

verse *n.* **1.** *Most of Shakespeare's works are in verse:* poetry, measure, meter. **2.** *The child recited a verse:* little poem, rhyme, jingle. **3.** *Let's sing the first and last verses of the hymn:* stanza, stave, strophe; jingle. **4.** *The minister read several verses from the Book of Job:* Biblical chapter division, passage of Scripture, line of Scripture.

versed *adj.* *The factory needs a man who's well versed in auto mechanics. The school turns out students versed in the classics:* experienced, practiced, familiar with, having an intimate knowledge of, acquainted with, conversant with, at home with, skilled, skillful, expert, proficient, accomplished, competent, able, adept; schooled, taught, instructed, tutored, well-informed, well-read, enlightened, lettered, learned, scholarly, erudite. —**Ant.** inexperienced, unpracticed, unfamiliar, unacquainted, green, raw, unfledged, callow, unskilled, unaccomplished, incompetent, inept; ignorant, untaught, unschooled.

versifier *n.* *Critics contemptuously referred to her as a versifier:* rhymer, poetaster, rhymester, versemonger, balladmonger, versemaker, poetling, versesmith, rhymesmith.

version *n.* **1.** *The two men told different versions of the accident:* account, story, report, description, depiction, interpretation, side. **2.** *The author wrote an up-to-date version of the Romeo and Juliet story:* rendering, adaptation, restatement. **3.** *Keats read Homer in the Chapman version:* translation, rendering, paraphrase, re-creation.

vertical *adj.* **1.** *The cliff rose in a vertical wall from the sea:* perpendicular, straight up and down, upright, 90-degree, sheer, plumb. —*n.* **2.** *The wall slants 10° from the vertical:* perpendicular, upright position, upright. —**Ant.** 1, 2 horizontal. 1 level with the ground; prostrate, flat, prone, supine; slanting, sloping, inclined.

vertigo *n.* *She felt a touch of vertigo and steadied herself against the wall:* dizziness, lightheadedness, swimming of the head, giddiness, reeling, unsteadiness, loss of equilibrium; fainting.

verve *n.* *The pianist played the concerto with tremendous verve:* liveliness, animation, spirit, vivacity, vitality, sparkle, dash, vigor, energy, vim, élan, zip, gusto, zeal, relish, enthusiasm, eagerness, ardor, fervor, passion, fire, abandon, rapture, feeling, warmth, vehemence, force, drive, punch. —**Ant.** apathy, lethargy, languor, torpor, sluggishness, indolence, indifference, spiritlessness, calmness, halfheartedness, reluctance, dislike, disdain, scorn.

very *adv.* **1.** *A very large crowd turned out to watch the Fourth of July parade. We were very impressed by his ability to speak Japanese so fluently:* extremely, exceedingly, especially, unusually, exceptionally, uncommonly, abnormally, terribly, awfully; intensely, deeply, profoundly; definitely, certainly, assuredly, decidedly, unquestionably, emphatically, perfectly, absolutely; really, truly, obviously, undeniably, veritably; remarkably, notably, strikingly, markedly, significantly, eminently; greatly, vastly, hugely, immensely, tremendously, highly, most, much, mighty, quite, extra; completely, totally, entirely, thoroughly, abundantly, excessively, surpassingly. **2.** *The two childhood friends were both born on the very same day:* exactly, precisely, actually, really. —*adj.* **3.** *The very thought of eating snails was repugnant to him:* mere, sheer, bare, plain, simple, pure. **4.** *This is the very thing I was looking for:* precise, exact, specific, particular; perfect, appropriate, suitable, fitting; necessary, essential.

vessel *n.* **1.** *The* Queen Elizabeth II *is one of the largest vessels afloat:* ship, boat, craft; (*variously*) liner, steamship, steamboat, ocean liner, packet, freighter, tanker, collier, tugboat, barge, scow, houseboat, ferryboat, trawler, whaler, sailboat, cruiser, yacht, *French* paquebot. **2.** *Cook the meat in a large vessel with a tight-fitting lid:* utensil, receptacle, container; (*variously*) pot, bowl, jug, crock, jar, vase, tub, vat, barrel, keg, cask, butt, caldron; glass, tumbler, cup, mug, carafe, flagon, goblet, beaker, tankard, decanter, flask; platter, dish, plate. **3.** *The doctor said I'd severed a vessel in my leg:* blood vessel, vein, artery, capillary; duct, tube.

vest *n.* **1.** *Is the vest included with the suit?:* waistcoat, jacket, *Historical* jerkin, doublet. —*v.* **2.** *The bishop was vested with ceremonial robes:* dress, robe, attire, clothe, garb, accouter, apparel, array, deck out, fit out, rig; drape, enwrap, envelop. **3.** *Most of the authority is vested in the board of directors:* place in control of, put into the hands of, put in the possession of. —**Ant.** 2 divest, strip, unfrock, disrobe, unclothe; uncover, expose, lay bare; dismantle.

vestal *adj.* **1.** *Dresses with Peter Pan collars have a vestal look:* chaste, pure, virtuous, virginal; simple, unsophisticated, unworldly; undefiled, immaculate; maidenly, virgin, unmarried. —*n.* **2.** *In ancient Rome the vestals guarded the sacred fires:* virgin, maiden, chaste woman, pure woman.

vested *adj.* *Each country has vested rights to the waters off its shores:* permanent, complete, established, fixed, settled, guaranteed, inalienable, indisputable, unquestionable, absolute.

vestibule *n.* *I waited in the vestibule until the butler announced me:* entrance hall, entrance way, foyer, entry, lobby, antechamber, anteroom, waiting room, lounge; hall, hallway, corridor, passage, passageway.

vestige *n.* *The diamond ring was her last vestige of bygone wealth:* trace, remnant, sign, token, evidence, relic; record, memento, souvenir.

vestments *n. pl.* *The prince was dressed in royal vestments:* ritual garments, official attire, raiment, apparel, dress, garb, costume, outfit, regalia, clothing, clothes, livery, uniform, gear, trappings, accoutrements.

veteran *n.* **1.** *The baseball veteran loved to coach young players:* expert, master, campaigner, *Informal* old hand, old-timer, vet. **2.** *The American Legion is made up of veterans:* war veteran, ex-serviceman, ex-soldier, old soldier, *Informal* vet. —*adj.* **3.** *The veteran bookkeeper announced his retirement:* experienced, seasoned, long-practiced. —**Ant.** 1, 3 beginner, apprentice, novice, neophyte, tyro, greenhorn, tenderfoot. 2 recruit, raw recruit.

veterinarian *n.* *She took the cat to a veterinarian:* veterinary surgeon, animal doctor, veterinary, *Informal* vet.

veto *v.* **1.** *The chairman has the right to veto any of the board's proposals:* reject, turn down, turn thumbs down on, deny, negate, nullify, void, enjoin, prevent, forbid, disallow, prohibit. —*n.* **2.** *The President's veto of the bill was overridden by Congress. The mayor threatened to use his veto over the city council's proposal:* rejection, refusal, denial, disallowing, disallowance, prevention, prohibition. —**Ant.** 1 ratify, sign into law, approve, endorse, sanction. 2 ratification, signing, approval, endorsement, sanction.

vex *v.* *Nothing vexes me more than your constant criticism:* annoy, irritate, nettle, pique, exasperate, anger, irk, chagrin, provoke, rile, miff, ruffle, chafe, fret, ruffle one's feathers, displease, pester, bother, torment, gall, harass, plague, harry, badger; trouble, distress, worry, disturb, upset, grieve, pain, *Slang* hassle, bug. —**Ant.** please, delight, gratify, satisfy; calm, quiet, soothe, placate, pacify, appease, mollify, conciliate.

vexatious *adj.* *The party was fun, but the mosquitoes were vexatious:* bothersome, troublesome, pesky, harassing, pestiferous, thorny, troubling, hectoring, badgering, worrisome, annoying, irritating, nettling, provoking, vexing, disquieting. —**Ant.** soothing, calming, pacifying, relaxing.

vexed *adj.* **1.** *She was vexed at not getting an answer:* disturbed, troubled, annoyed. **2.** *The vexed question came up again:* disputed, discussed. —**Ant.** delighted.

viable *adj.* **1.** *The fetus is considered viable at six months. No crops are viable in this barren soil:* capable of independent life, able to live, able to develop, able to thrive, capable of growing. **2.** *If the plan doesn't succeed do you have a viable alternative?:* workable, practical, practicable, feasible, usable, applicable, adaptable. —**Ant.** 1, 2 nonviable. 2 unviable, impractical, useless, unworkable, unusable.

viaduct *n.* *The railroad viaduct arches over the old highway:* overpass, span, ramp.

vial *n.* *Grandmother always carried a vial of smelling salts in her purse:* small medicine bottle, phial; (*loosely*) ampul, ampoule, flask.

vibrant *adj.* **1.** *The leaves were vibrant in the breeze:* fluttering, vibrating, quivering, pulsing. **2.** *The room was decorated in vibrant colors:* bright, brilliant, vivid, colorful, intense, deep, florid, loud, glowing, shimmering, glittering, luminous, lustrous, radiant, resplendent. **3.** *The*

vibrant sounds of the violin carried the melody: resonant, reverberant, resounding, sonorous, deep-toned, orotund, throbbing; bell-like, quivering, pealing, ringing. **4.** *Critics agreed that the actress was charming and vibrant:* vivacious, lively, alive, vital, animated, spirited, electrifying, thrilling, full of vigor, energetic, forceful, vehement, eager, enthusiastic, ardent, fervent. —**Ant.** 1 still. 2 dull, drab, grayish; pale, soft, pastel. 3 shrill, piercing, screeching. 4 listless, sluggish, phlegmatic, spiritless, boring, dull.

vibrate *v.* *The entire house vibrates when a big truck goes by:* reverberate, quiver, quaver, quake, tremble, flutter, wobble; sway, waver, swing, oscillate, undulate, pendulate; palpitate, throb, pulsate, beat, ripple.

vibration *n.* *When the machinery is running you can feel the vibration in the floor:* tremor, quiver, quivering, quake, quaking, trembling, throbbing.

vicarious *adj.* *It gave me a vicarious thrill to hear about her trip:* secondhand, indirect, surrogate, sympathetic, at one remove, empathetic, imagined, imaginary, fantasized, mental, by proxy. —**Ant.** firsthand, direct, personal, on-the-spot.

vice *n.* **1.** *The police made several raids to clean up vice in the city:* sexual immorality, debauchery, depravity, corruption, iniquity, wickedness, wantonness, profligacy, degeneracy, licentiousness. **2.** *Gossiping is her only vice:* fault, shortcoming, failing, flaw, imperfection, blemish, defect, frailty, weakness, weak point. —**Ant.** 1 virtue, good morals, morality. 2 good point, accomplishment, attainment, strong point, gift, talent, facility, forte.

vice versa *Do you want the soup before the salad or vice versa?:* the other way round, in reverse, in the opposite order, contrariwise, conversely.

vicinity *n.* *The store is somewhere in the vicinity of 1st and Main:* proximity, neighborhood, region, area, environs, surroundings, precincts, adjoining, region, vicinage, propinquity.

vicious *adj.* **1.** *That vicious dog ought to be on a leash:* ferocious, savage, fierce, violent, dangerous, untamed, wild, predatory, bloodthirsty; cruel, brutal, barbarous, treacherous, ill-humored, ill-tempered, ill-natured, sullen, surly, churlish. **2.** *It was one of the most vicious crimes of the century:* wicked, evil, atrocious, heinous, monstrous, villainous, fiendish, inhuman, foul, gross, base, vile, terrible, awful, bad, nasty, depraved, nefarious, immoral, abominable, offensive, abhorrent, horrid, shocking, diabolical, hellish. **3.** *He made up a vicious story about me to get even:* spiteful, malicious, rancorous, mean, nasty, malevolent, venomous, acrimonious, invidious, vindictive, pernicious, hateful, defamatory, libelous, slanderous. —**Ant.** 1 tame, friendly, playful, good-humored, good-natured, sweet-tempered. 2 moral, virtuous, righteous, upright, good, noble. 3 sweet, genial, kind, kindly, complimentary, laudatory.

victim *n.* **1.** *The fire claimed 43 victims:* fatality, dead; casualty, injured, wounded. **2.** *One victim* *was swindled out of her life savings:* quarry, prey, target, dupe, gull, patsy, innocent, sucker, *Slang* mark, pigeon; butt, scapegoat, tool, pawn. —**Ant.** 2 offender, culprit, guilty party, crook.

victimize *v. The swindler victimized the entire community:* dupe, swindle, cheat, deceive, trick, defraud, cozen, fool, hoodwink, beguile.

victor *n. The victors won by a score of seven to two:* winner, champion, medalist, prizewinner; conqueror, vanquisher.

Victorian *adj. Her Victorian attitude caused the children to rebel:* proper, puritanical, stuffy, straitlaced, prudish, smug, priggish, prim, sanctimonious, narrow, pietistic, insular, hypocritical, conventional, stuffy, tight-laced. —**Ant.** broadminded, liberal, relaxed, *Slang* laid-back.

victorious *adj. The victorious team had a celebration:* conquering, winning, triumphant, successful, champion, championship, prizewinning, vanquishing. —**Ant.** defeated, beaten, bested, worsted; conquered, vanquished, overcome, repulsed.

victory *n. Each candidate claimed victory in the election:* triumph, conquest, success, superiority, supremacy, ascendancy, the prize, laurels, the palm. —**Ant.** defeat, loss, failure, overthrow; retreat.

victuals *n. 1. The truck drivers say the victuals are good here:* food, meals, repast, cooking, cuisine, edibles, comestibles, nourishment, fare, diet, viands, meat, refreshment; *Slang* eats, grub, vittles, chow, feed. *2. We laid in enough victuals to last a month:* supplies, stores, provisions, groceries, provender, rations, foodstuffs; fodder, forage.

vie *v. The two teams are vying for the championship:* compete, contest, contend, struggle, strive, challenge, fight, be a rival, tilt with. —**Ant.** cooperate, share; negotiate.

view *n. 1. The tourists crowded closer to get a view of the painting:* look, glimpse, peep, glance, peek, gaze, sight. *2. His view of the game was obstructed by a pillar. Finally the ship came into view:* range of vision, vision, sight, ken. *3. What a beautiful view!:* vista, outlook, scene, scenery, panorama, prospect, spectacle, perspective, bird's-eye-view, landscape, picture, diorama. *4. In the mayor's view the town budget must be increased:* opinion, notion, feeling, sentiment, attitude, belief, conviction, conception, thought, theory, judgment. —*v. 5. Thousands viewed the Thanksgiving Day parade. Have you viewed the museum's new coin collection?:* watch, see, look at, witness, observe, behold, eye, take in, scan, glance at, glimpse, note; gaze at, survey, inspect, examine, scrutinize, explore, study, contemplate, pore over. *6. Experts view the situation with alarm:* think about, regard, consider, perceive, judge.

viewpoint *n. Try to consider low food prices from the farmer's viewpoint:* perspective, standpoint, attitude, position, point of view, angle, slant, vantage point, frame of reference, orienta-tion, opinion, bias, conviction, belief, sentiment, feeling.

vigilance *n. Eternal vigilance is the price of liberty:* watchfulness, alertness, attention, heedfulness, heed, care, concern, guardedness, carefulness; caution, cautiousness, precaution, prudence, circumspection, forethought. —**Ant.** negligence, neglect, laxity, carelessness, unwariness, inattention, lackadaisicalness.

vigilant *adj. The guards must be vigilant at all times:* alert, on the alert, watchful, wide-awake, attentive, heedful, observant, on the lookout; careful, cautious, prudent, guarded, circumspect, wary, chary, on guard, on one's guard, on one's toes, on the qui vive. —**Ant.** negligent, neglectful, lax, slack, remiss, careless, heedless, inattentive, unmindful.

vigor *n. 1. The leader of the expedition must be a man of great vigor:* energy, vitality, drive, verve, spirit, dash, vim, pep, zip; strength, force, might, power, robustness, hardiness; haleness, stamina. *2. He presented his ideas with a great deal of vigor:* forcefulness, animation, enthusiasm, verve, vim, spirit, élan, liveliness, vivacity; ardor, fervor, zeal, fire, vehemence, intensity, earnestness, passion. —**Ant.** 1, 2 lethargy, apathy, torpor; weakness, feebleness. 1 frailty. 2 calmness, serenity, tranquillity.

vigorous *adj. The forest ranger was a vigorous man. Hemingway's writing is known for its vigorous style:* energetic, active, dynamic, intense, forceful, vibrant, vital, spirited, ardent, strong, powerful, mighty, sturdy, muscular, brawny, virile, robust, hale, hardy; lusty, bold, aggressive, assertive, lively. —**Ant.** inactive, lethargic, languorous, indolent, apathetic, torpid, spiritless; weak, feeble, frail, effete, enervated.

vile *adj. 1. Rotten potatoes have a vile odor:* disgusting, offensive, revolting, repugnant, repulsive, repellent, nasty, obnoxious, odious, foul, objectionable, abhorrent, loathsome, unpleasant, bad, awful. *2. Kidnapping is a vile crime:* vicious, sordid, gross, base, low, mean, ignoble, nefarious, wretched; wicked, evil, sinful, iniquitous, heinous, abominable, loathsome, ugly, shocking, invidious, contemptible, despicable, shameful, beastly, villainous, hateful, detestable, execrable; immoral, depraved, degenerate, perverted, disgraceful, degrading, humiliating. *3. There's no excuse for using such vile language!:* vulgar, gross, coarse, filthy, smutty, lewd, obscene, foulmouthed, salacious. —**Ant.** 1 pleasant, agreeable, attractive, appealing, appetizing, good, wonderful. 2 honorable, noble, elevated, exalted, sublime, admirable, worthy; moral, upright, righteous, sinless. 3 refined, polite, cultured; delicate, chaste.

vilify *v. Both speakers vilified their opponent:* defame, traduce, depreciate, slander, disparage, malign, calumniate, revile, abuse, blacken, asperse, slur, decry. —**Ant.** commend, honor, praise.

village *n. The village consisted of a general store, a gas station, and seven houses:* small town, suburb, municipality, hamlet, burg, farming village, rural community, *Slang* hick town, burg, whistle stop, wide place in the road. —**Ant.** city, big city, metropolis, megalopolis, urban center, metropolitan area.

villain *n. The villain in a melodrama always menaces the heroine. The villain cheated the old lady out of her life's savings:* wicked person, scoundrel, rascal, rogue, knave, rapscallion, varlet, rotter, cad, blackguard, cur, scalawag, snake in the grass, caitiff; evildoer, malefactor, miscreant, transgressor; *Slang* louse, stinker, rat. —**Ant.** hero, protagonist, leading man; gentleman, worthy, champion.

vim *n.* **1.** *How can you be so full of vim so early in the morning?:* pep, vigor, energy, vitality, zip, snap, dash, animation, liveliness, vivacity, verve, *Slang* go. **2.** *The team with the most vim will win:* enthusiasm, spirit, zeal, fervor, ardor, intensity, fire, passion, vehemence; drive, power, punch, force; strength, might, potency. —**Ant.** 1, 2 lethargy, apathy, torpor.

vindicate *v.* **1.** *The suspect is sure the jury will vindicate him:* exonerate, clear, absolve, acquit, discharge, free, excuse, exculpate. **2.** *The principal's speech vindicated the teachers' right to go on strike:* uphold, support, defend, champion, advocate, maintain, assert; justify, bear out, corroborate, substantiate, bolster. —**Ant.** 1 blame, accuse, charge; convict. 2 counter, contradict, oppose, refute.

vindictive *adj. After being fired, the vindictive typist spread vile rumors about the company:* vengeful, revengeful, avenging, punitive, retaliative, retaliatory, unforgiving, spiteful, bitter, malicious, malign, malevolent. —**Ant.** forgiving, relenting, generous, magnanimous.

vintage *n.* **1.** *The 1961 Bordeaux wines were a great vintage:* wine of a particular year, grape harvest for a particular year. **2.** *It's a marvelous old lamp of 1890 vintage:* date, period, era, epoch. —*adj.* **3.** *This was a vintage year for good movies:* choice, prime, rare, outstanding, wonderful, fine, superior, excellent, great, sterling, prize. **4.** *The millionaire owns a vintage Rolls-Royce:* antique, ancient, old, aged, old-fashioned, out-of-date. —**Ant.** 3 bad, inferior, awful, terrible, *Informal* lousy. 4 new, brand-new, modern, up-to-date.

violate *v.* **1.** *The actress violated the terms of her contract and was sued by the producer:* break, disobey, infringe, contravene, act contrary to, transgress, disregard; trespass, encroach upon, trample on, invade. **2.** *The revolutionaries violated the flag by tearing it down:* profane, desecrate, defile, commit sacrilege, blaspheme, dishonor; abuse, outrage, rape, ravish. —**Ant.** 1, 2 respect, honor. 1 obey, uphold. 2 revere; protect, defend.

violation *n. The driver was fined for a speeding violation. Listening to another's telephone conversation is a violation of privacy:* breach, infringement, infraction, transgression, trespass, encroachment; contravention, nonobservance, abuse; dishonoring, defilement, desecration, sacrilege. —**Ant.** obedience, compliance, honoring, revering, upholding.

violence *n.* **1.** *The violence of the hurricane caused widespread damage:* force, might, power, impact, onslaught; fury, ferocity, rage, fierceness, severity, intensity. **2.** *The violence of the murder shocked everyone:* physical force, brutality, bestiality, bloodthirstiness, ferocity, ferociousness, savagery; desecration, profanation, outrage. —**Ant.** 1 mildness, weakness, feebleness; calmness. 2 gentleness, tenderness, humaneness.

violent *adj.* **1.** *The violent earthquake left 3,000 homeless:* full of force, strong, intense, severe, furious, fierce, raging. **2.** *She can't seem to control that violent temper. The patient became violent and had to be strapped to the bed:* tempestuous, vehement, strong, fierce, furious, ferocious, fiery, hot, passionate, hotheaded, raging, explosive, uncontrollable, ungovernable, unbridled, unruly, intractable, savage, murderous; wild, insane, maniacal, berserk, rampant. **3.** *The rebel leader died a violent death:* resulting from the use of force, cruel, brutal. —**Ant.** 1 mild, weak, feeble. 2 gentle, calm, composed, collected, cool, quiet, serene, tranquil, unruffled, pacific; sane, rational. 3 peaceful.

virago *n. How did such a pleasant man ever marry such a virago?:* shrew, scold, nag, termagant, Xanthippe, harpy, vixen, fury, harridan, dragon, gorgon, she-wolf; fishwife, *Slang* battle-ax.

virgin *n.* **1.** *The virgin vowed she would never marry:* maiden, maid, damsel, lass, girl. —*adj.* **2.** *The wilderness was twenty square miles of virgin forest. This sweater is made of virgin wool:* unused, untouched, unpolluted, unsullied, uncontaminated; pure, pristine, unadulterated, undefiled, unalloyed, unmixed; chaste.

virile *adj. How could such a big, virile man have such a high, piping voice?:* manly, masculine, manful; vigorous, forceful, masterful, strong, powerful, muscular, robust, mighty, hardy, husky, strapping, brawny; courageous, brave, stouthearted, bold, fearless, undaunted, resolute, stalwart, valiant, heroic, audacious, lusty; potent, capable of fathering children. —**Ant.** effeminate, sissified, unmanly, womanish, emasculate, weak; feminine; impotent, sterile.

virtual *adj. His sending her a dozen roses was a virtual declaration of love:* tacit, implied, indirect, implicit; essential, practical, substantial. —**Ant.** explicit, direct, stated, expressed, definite, emphatic.

virtually *adv. With the boss out sick, the bookkeeper is virtually in charge:* substantially, practically, in essence, essentially, in effect, to all intents and purposes, in substance, for the most part, for all practical purposes.

virtue *n.* **1.** *Didn't Emerson say "Virtue is its own reward"?:* moral goodness, morality, goodness, righteousness, uprightness, honor, honesty, integrity, probity, high-mindedness, rectitude. **2.** *Honesty is but one of his virtues. Low operating cost is only one of the car's virtues:* moral quality, moral principle, strength, principle; benefit, advantage, value, reward, strong point, good point, favorable point. **3.** *The queen's virtue is unquestioned:* chastity, purity, virginity, innocence, modesty; good behavior, decency. **—Ant.** 1 vice, wickedness, evil, sinfulness, immorality, badness, dishonor, dishonesty, corruption. 2 weakness, weak point, frailty, failing, defect, deficiency, fault; disadvantage, drawback. 3 unchastity, promiscuousness, promiscuity, immodesty.

virtuoso n. She was a violin virtuoso at an early age: master, maestro, ace, champion, champ, expert, genius, professional, pro, prodigy, star, wizard. Informal crackerjack, whiz.

virtuous adj., **1.** Everyone should seek to lead a virtuous life: morally good, moral, good, righteous, upright, honorable, high-principled; ethical, just; meritorious, praiseworthy, commendable, laudable, exemplary. **2.** Samson knew that Delilah was not a virtuous woman: chaste, pure, virginal, innocent, continent, unsullied, modest, decent. **—Ant.** 1 wicked, evil, sinful, immoral, bad, dishonorable, dishonest, corrupt. 2 unchaste, promiscuous, loose, impure, immodest.

virulent adj. **1.** The virulent fever claimed many victims: dangerously infectious, deadly, lethal, poisonous, toxic, noxious, venomous, pernicious; hurtful, harmful, deleterious, injurious, unhealthy. **2.** A virulent rumor nearly ruined her reputation: malicious, spiteful, malevolent, rancorous, hostile, vicious, malign, bitter, resentful, acrimonious. **—Ant.** 1 harmless, nonpoisonous, nontoxic, innocuous. 2 benign, kind, gentle, sweet, good, friendly, amiable; charitable, sympathetic, compassionate, merciful.

virus n. The disease is caused by a virus: microorganism smaller than a bacterium; (loosely) germ, microbe, Slang bug.

visage n. She always has a cheerful visage. The travelers looked out at the bleak visage of a burnt-out forest: face, features, countenance; appearance, look, aspect, semblance, image, mien, demeanor, air; profile, physiognomy.

vis-à-vis adv., adj. **1.** That was the first time we'd chatted vis-à-vis in years: face-to-face, tête-à-tête, eye to eye, side by side; together, in company; confidentially, privately. **—prep. 2.** Our income vis-à-vis expenses caused us to go bankrupt: as compared with, in contrast to, as distinguished from, as opposed to.

viscera n. pl. Ancient priests foretold the future by examining an animal's viscera: intestines, bowels, insides, guts, entrails, Slang innards.

viscous adj. Molasses is a liquid, but an extremely viscous one: thick, viscid, sticky, gluey, syrupy, tacky, slimy, gummy, glutinous, Informal gooey.

visibility n. **1.** The bright orange jacket gave the hunter high visibility: capability of being seen, conspicuousness, prominence, discernibleness, clarity, perceptibility, distinctness, definition. **2.** Because of fog, the visibility is only 200 feet: field of observation, range of view, reach of sight; ceiling; horizon.

visible adj. **1.** The house was visible across the valley: capable of being seen, observable, perceivable, perceptible, discernible, seeable, in sight, in view; clear, distinct, prominent, well-defined, in focus. **2.** Her dissatisfaction was visi-

ble. The man had no visible means of support: plain, manifest, open, unmistakable, inescapable, revealed, salient, glaring, patent, conspicuous, marked, pointed, pronounced, blatant; obvious, noticeable, evident, apparent, palpable. **—Ant.** 1, 2 invisible, imperceptible, indiscernible, unapparent; hidden, concealed, obscured, buried.

vision n. **1.** With such poor vision he really needs glasses: eyesight, sight; perception, discernment. **2.** Urban planning requires great vision: foresight, ability to plan ahead, ability to foresee, imagination. **3.** He has a vision of what the business will be like 20 years from now: mental image, concept, conception, idea, notion; dream, daydream, fancy, fantasy, illusion. **4.** As a child the saint saw a vision of the Virgin Mary: apparition, supernatural appearance, materialization, revelation; ghost, phantom, specter. **—Ant.** 1 blindness. 2 hindsight; shortsightedness. 3 reality, fact, actuality.

visionary adj. **1.** Is "peace on earth" just a visionary idea?: impractical, idealistic, utopian, starry-eyed, dreamy; unreal, imaginative, imaginary, insubstantial, illusory, fanciful, fancied, unfounded, chimerical, delusive. **—n. 2.** Church officials were skeptical of the visionary's claims: person who has visions, seer. **3.** Columbus was a visionary who made the world accept his dream: imaginative thinker, theorist, speculative thinker; dreamer, daydreamer, idealist, romantic, utopian; fanatic, zealot. **—Ant.** 1 practical, pragmatic, realistic, hardheaded; substantial, material, real, true, actual, authentic.

visit v. **1.** We visited Aunt Marge this afternoon. The tourists visited the city's museum: pay a visit to, call on, drop in on, look in on; be a guest of, sojourn at, stay with, go to see. **2.** A series of misfortunes visited the family: afflict, affect, befall, happen to, assail, assault, attack, smite, punish, frequent, haunt. **—n. 3.** The neighbors dropped in for a short visit: stay, call; sojourn.

visitor n. The visitor was ushered into the parlor by the butler. The Johnsons are entertaining out-of-town visitors: caller, guest, house guest, company; sojourner, transient; tourist, vacationer, voyager, sightseer, traveler, journeyer, tripper.

vista n. **1.** At the end of the boulevard was a vista of the distant mountains: view, scene, picture, perspective, prospect, outlook; scenery, landscape, panorama. **2.** He told us of his vista of approaching success: mental picture, prospect, outlook, vision, view.

visual adj. Many classrooms have visual learning devices: conveying visible information, relating to sight, for the eye, optical, optic, ophthalmic, ocular; visible, noticeable, seeable, observable, perceptible.

visualize v. I can't visualize the coat as you describe it: envision, imagine, see in the mind's eye, picture, conceive of; foresee, image, fancy, daydream of, dream of.

vital adj. **1.** The patient's pulse and other vital signs are weakening: life, living, animate, vivifying; alive, live, existing, breathing, viable, quick. **2.** *She's one of the most vital people in the organization:* lively, energetic, animated, vibrant, dynamic, vigorous, spirited, forceful. **3.** *This is one of the most vital issues now before Congress:* important, significant, critical, crucial, urgent, pressing; serious, essential, necessary, indispensable, requisite, material, chief, basic, fundamental, paramount, cardinal, foremost, primary. **—Ant.** 1 dying, dead, inanimate. 2 lethargic, apathetic, torpid, listless, phlegmatic, uninvolved. 3 unimportant, insignificant, trivial, trifling, negligible, nonessential, unnecessary, dispensable, subordinate.

vitality *n. Good nutrition will improve your vitality:* strength, life force, vital power, dynamism, the vital spark, animal spirits, energy, vigor, *Informal* pep, vim, zip; animation, enthusiasm, vivacity, liveliness, exuberance, ebullience, zest, zeal, verve. **—Ant.** lifelessness, lethargy, torpor, sluggishness, listlessness, apathy.

vitiate *v. His nasty temper vitiates his good qualities:* weaken, dilute, thin; pollute, taint, contaminate, adulterate, depreciate, impair; undermine, corrupt, debase, spoil, mar, invalidate, undo; sabotage, injure, obliterate; poison, blight, infect. **—Ant.** strengthen, reinforce, fortify, enhance.

vitriolic *adj. The movie critic is famous for his vitriolic reviews:* caustic, acid, acrimonious, acerbic, acerb, cutting, sharp, biting, scathing, withering, hypercritical, abusive, nasty, sarcastic, sardonic, satirical. **—Ant.** kind, sweet, friendly, affable, amiable, sympathetic, compassionate; mild, bland.

vituperate *v. He vituperated about their wrongdoing:* abuse, revile, objuragate, censure, vilify, reproach, upbraid, berate, scold. **—Ant.** praise, commend.

vituperation *n. Her simple mistake hardly merited so much vituperation:* abuse, faultfinding, invective, scolding, denunciation, censure, blame, tongue-lashing, revilement, obloquy, scurrility, castigation, tirade, calumniation. **—Ant.** praise, acclaim, adulation, flattery.

vivacious *adj. The vivacious girl made a good cheerleader:* lively, buoyant, full of life, vital, animated, effervescent, sparkling, bubbling, bubbly, ebullient, sprightly, spirited, active; merry, gay, lighthearted, cheerful, cheery, sunny, bright, genial, convivial, jolly, frolicsome. **—Ant.** lifeless, languid, spiritless, lethargic, listless, impassive, stolid; somber, melancholy, sad.

vivid *adj.* **1.** *The barn was painted a vivid red:* bright, intense, brilliant, strong, rich, deep, distinct, conspicuous, garish, showy, loud, florid, gay, colorful; shining, shiny, radiant, luminous, luminescent, glowing, lustrous, effulgent, resplendent. **2.** *He made the story so vivid we all believed it. The youth has a vivid imagination:* lifelike, true-life, realistic, graphic, descriptive, dramatic, expressive, pictorial, picturesque, moving, stirring; lively, energetic, vigorous. **3.** *The tall blond actress made a vivid impression when she walked into the room. The old profes-*

sor has a vivid memory: striking, strong, powerful, remarkable, impressive, astounding, astonishing, marvelous, extraordinary, memorable; clear, distinct, definite, unmistakable, inescapable, forceful, emphatic. **—Ant.** 1–3 dull, colorless, pale, drab, vague, indistinct, indefinite, nondescript; weak, faint, dim. 1 pastel; somber. 3 average, usual, unremarkable, everyday, routine, run-of-the-mill.

vixen *n.* **1.** *The vixen carried the rabbit back to her den:* female fox. **2.** *After a few months he discovered he'd married a vixen:* ill-tempered woman, quarrelsome woman, fishwife, harridan, shrew, scold, virago, termagant, witch, fury; spirited woman, spitfire.

vocabulary *n.* **1.** *The child has a very large vocabulary for his age. English has a much larger vocabulary than French:* word stock, lexicon. **2.** *The vocabulary of skiing is peppered with borrowings from German and Norwegian. The play is written in the vocabulary of the workingman:* speech, language, vernacular, lingo, tongue, jargon, argot, cant, slang, dialect, patois, phraseology, phrasing, terminology, style, idiom.

vocal *adj.* **1.** *Don't strain your vocal cords. The teacher gives a lot of vocal praise but writes scathing comments on term papers:* of the voice, oral, spoken, voiced, vocalized, uttered, articulated. **2.** *I prefer symphonies to vocal music:* sung, for singing; lyric, choral, operatic. **3.** *She was extremely vocal about her dislike of the plan:* outspoken, plainspoken, blunt, open, frank, forthright, candid, direct, voluble. **—Ant.** 1 written; unvoiced, unspoken, unsaid. 2 instrumental. 3 reserved, reticent.

vocalize *v.* **1.** *It would be better if she vocalized her fears rather than suppress them:* put into words, utter, speak, say, express, articulate, air, vent, ventilate. **2.** *The soprano vocalizes for two hours each day:* sing without words. **—Ant.** 1 suppress, pass over in silence, say nothing of, leave unsaid, reduce to silence, hush, hold one's tongue about, keep secret. 2 sing words.

vocation *n. Nursing is a very satisfying vocation:* calling, profession, métier, field, career, line, pursuit, lifework; line of work, occupation, business, trade, job, employment, situation, assignment, task, stint, post, berth; role, station, estate. **—Ant.** avocation, hobby, distraction, diversion, leisure pursuit.

vociferous *adj.* **1.** *A vociferous group of boys rushed into the room:* crying loudly, loud, shouting, loud-voiced, clamorous, noisy, boisterous, uproarious; shrill, piercing. **2.** *She was very vociferous in criticizing my plan:* demanding to be heard, strident, blatant; importunate, vehement; vocal, outspoken. **—Ant.** 1 quiet. 2 reticent, soft-spoken, subdued, calm.

vogue *n.* **1.** *Will long skirts be in vogue this year? Big sunglasses are all the vogue this summer:* fashion, style, mode, prevailing taste; rage, fad, trend, craze, the latest thing, the last word, the thing; custom, practice. **2.** *The movie* Gone With the Wind *had a great vogue in its day:* popularity, acceptance, popular favor, currency.

voice *n.* **1.** *All that shouting caused him to lose* *his voice. Ted speaks with a deep rich voice:* vocal sound, speech, power of speech; mode of speaking, tone, delivery, intonation, modulation, articulation. **2.** *Will the club members have a voice in choosing the speakers? Politicians must heed the voice of the people:* right to express an opinion, vote, say, role, part, participation, representation; will, desire, wish, opinion, choice, preference, option. **3.** *The composition was written for voice and orchestra:* singer; (*variously*) tenor, soprano, alto, baritone, mezzo-soprano, contralto, bass; singers. —*v.* **4.** *Some people voice both r's in the word "library":* pronounce, articulate, enunciate, vocalize, utter, speak. **5.** *Please voice any objections you have now:* state, express, declare, proclaim, announce, communicate, utter, say, air, ventilate, vent, vocalize, divulge, disclose, reveal. —**Ant.** 1 dumbness, muteness, speechlessness, voicelessness. 5 keep silent, keep to oneself, keep one's own counsel, be quiet; stifle, suppress.

void *adj.* **1.** *The book was void of meaning. Suddenly the street was void of people:* devoid, empty, barren, blank, lacking, wanting; vacant, bare, destitute, clear, free; drained, depleted, exhausted, emptied. **2.** *That violation makes the contract void:* invalid, not legally binding, not legally enforceable, not in force, inoperative, null, nugatory. —*n.* **3.** *At one time outer space was believed to be a complete void:* empty space, emptiness, vacuum, vacuity, blank. —*v.* **4.** *The overloaded tanker voided oil from its hold:* discharge, evacuate, empty, emit, eject, purge, pass, drain, exhaust, throw out, pour out. **5.** *Both parties want to void the agreement:* invalidate, revoke, cancel, nullify, annul, abolish, repeal, repudiate, renounce, recant, reverse, countermand, rescind. —**Ant.** 1 full, filled, fraught; occupied, cluttered, jammed, mobbed, packed. 2 valid, in effect, binding, enforceable, operative. 4 take in, fill, replenish. 5 validate, enforce; reiterate, strengthen.

volatile *adj.* **1.** *Volatile liquids must be kept in very tightly closed containers:* evaporating quickly, evaporable, vaporizing, vaporous; gaseous. **2.** *The situation in the Middle East is volatile:* explosive, eruptive; unstable, unsettled. **3.** *Richard is too volatile to stick with one job very long:* changeable, erratic, unstable, variable, unsteady, irresolute, fitful, spasmodic, unpredictable, undependable, inconstant, capricious, mercurial, temperamental, moody, fickle, flighty, giddy, frivolous; brash, reckless, wild, rash. —**Ant.** 1–3 stable. 2 calm, peaceful. 3 constant, consistent, steady, even-tempered, dependable, resolute, determined, coolheaded, self-controlled, serious, sober.

volition *n.* *If you decide to climb the mountain, it must be of your own volition:* free will, will, choosing, conscious choice, choice, decision, resolution, discretion, option, determination. —**Ant.** coercion, compulsion, duress, force, necessity, unavoidability.

volley *n.* *The attack began with a volley of shots. A volley of criticism greeted the mayor's proposal:* salvo, fusillade, barrage, discharge,

broadside, curtain of fire; outburst, burst, outbreak, shower, outpouring.

voluble *adj.* *The voluble youth had plenty to say:* fluent, glib, talkative, loquacious. —**Ant.** taciturn, quiet, silent.

volume *n.* **1.** *What is the volume of water in the tank? The box has a volume of one hundred cubic feet:* cubic content, space occupied, capacity; measure, size, dimensions, bulk, magnitude, extent, vastness. **2.** *During the holiday season the post office handles a tremendous volume of mail:* quantity, mass, amount, aggregate, heap, abundance. **3.** *The girl carried a slim volume of poetry under her arm. The encyclopedia is in twenty volumes:* book, treatise, tract, monograph, quarto, folio; tome, one book of a series. **4.** *Please turn down the volume on that radio:* loudness, sound, amplification.

voluminous *adj.* *The Senator carries on a voluminous correspondence with his constituents:* of great volume, large, extensive, abundant, copious, ample, sizable, massive. —**Ant.** small, minimal, slight, sparse, scant, skimpy, restricted.

voluntarily *adv.* *She voluntarily gave up her office:* freely, by choice, by preference, intentionally, spontaneously, willingly, without prompting, deliberately.

voluntary *adj.* **1.** *The hospital is supported by voluntary contributions:* free-will, optional, volunteered, discretionary, noncompulsory, unforced. **2.** *Blinking is an involuntary muscular action, winking is voluntary:* deliberate, done consciously, intentional, intended, willed. —**Ant.** 1 forced, compelled, compulsory. 2 involuntary, instinctive, unconscious, automatic; unintentional, unpremeditated.

volunteer *n.* **1.** *Mother works on Tuesdays as a volunteer at the hospital:* charity worker, unpaid worker, nonprofessional. **2.** *Do volunteers make better soldiers than draftees?:* enlistee, recruit. —*adj.* **3.** *The town has a volunteer fire department:* of volunteers, by volunteers; voluntary; unpaid, nonprofessional. —*v.* **4.** *Three people volunteered to help decorate the gym for the dance:* offer willingly, offer, express willingness, step forward; take on a task willingly; place at one's disposal; be at one's service. **5.** *I volunteered the fact that the plan had been tried before:* tell voluntarily, offer willingly, proffer, tender, present, extend, advance, put forward. —**Ant.** 1 forced laborer, appointed agent. 2 draftee, conscript. 3 paid, professional; commercial. 4 draft, force, coerce, compel, constrain, necessitate; requisition, levy, confiscate.

voluptuary *n.* *The old voluptuary spent his fortune on a succession of beautiful women:* sensualist, hedonist, pleasure seeker, seeker of sensual pleasures; high liver, bon vivant, epicure, gourmet, gourmand, gastronome; libertine, debauchee, sybarite, rake, roué, womanizer, seducer. —**Ant.** ascetic, aesthete; self-denier, abstainer.

voluptuous *adj.* **1.** *Velvet has a voluptuous texture:* pleasing to the senses, sensuous, sensual; luxurious, soft, smooth. **2.** *The wealthy playboy* had a long and voluptuous life: sensual, pleasure-seeking, pleasure-loving, self-indulgent, hedonistic, sybaritic; erotic, sexual, wanton, fleshly, carnal, licentious, lascivious, lustful, profligate, dissolute, debauched, dissipated. —**Ant.** 1 rough, coarse, unpleasant. 2 ascetic, abstinent, abstemious, self-denying, austere, puritanical.

vomit v. **1.** In treating some poison cases, force the patient to vomit: throw up, regurgitate, retch, bring up, disgorge, Informal puke, Slang upchuck, barf, heave, toss one's cookies. **2.** The volcano vomited great clouds of smoke: spew forth, eject, emit, expel, belch forth, discharge, disgorge.

voracious adj. Teenagers often have voracious appetites. The boy has always been a voracious reader: ravenous, ravenously hungry, edacious, gluttonous; insatiable, greedy, hoggish, omnivorous. —**Ant.** satisfied, satiated, sated, replete; apathetic, indifferent; delicate, dainty, fastidious.

vortex n. The swimmer was caught in the vortex and perished: whirlpool, eddy, maelstrom; whirling mass, whirlwind, cyclone, twister.

votary n. The student became a votary of French drama: devotee, enthusiast, admirer, aficionado, partisan, buff, fan, fanatic, champion, zealot; disciple, follower, adherent, habitué.

vote n. **1.** Father's vote usually went to the party in power. Put your vote in the ballot box: election choice, ballot, selection; expression of opinion, choice, selection, preference, option, decision, determination, judgment, approval, voice, say; ballot, ticket. **2.** The vote will be held next Tuesday: election, plebiscite, referendum, poll. **3.** When did women win the vote?: right to vote, suffrage, franchise. —v. **4.** Vote for the candidate of your choice: cast a vote, cast a ballot; support by one's vote.

vouch v. Can you vouch for Fred's integrity?: swear to, attest to, affirm, confirm, guarantee, warrant, endorse, corroborate, verify, certify, witness, attest, authenticate; support, uphold, maintain, sustain, back, back up. —**Ant.** refute, repudiate, deny, abjure, denounce.

vouchsafe v. They vouchsafed he was right: give, grant, bestow, confer, accord, award, concede, allow, permit, condescend, stoop, deign. —**Ant.** deny, refuse.

vow n. **1.** The couple made their wedding vows before a parish priest. She took her vows as a nun before she was twenty: solemn promise, pledge, parole, oath, plight, troth, word, word of honor; solemn promise to God, religious pledge. —v. **2.** They vowed to love each other throughout eternity. She vowed she would never play tennis again: promise, pledge, pledge one's word, swear, resolve, contract; declare, assert, affirm, vouch, assure, emphasize, stress.

voyage n. **1.** The voyage to England took seven days: sea journey, cruise, passage, ocean trip, crossing, sail. —v. **2.** The yachtsman spent a year voyaging around the world: cruise, sail, navigate, journey by water, travel by water.

voyager n. Even the experienced voyagers were sick on the crossing: traveler, cruiser, wayfarer, rambler, rover, pilgrim, peregrinator, adventurer, journeyer, tourist, sightseer, excursionist, world traveler, jet-setter; Slang globe-trotter. —**Ant.** stay-at-home, recluse, hermit, shut-in.

vulgar adj. **1.** His vulgar manners shocked everyone: lacking good taste, tasteless, coarse, rude, rough, crude, gross, uncouth, low, base; ill-mannered, impolite, boorish, ill-bred, unrefined, uncultivated; indecent, offensive, obscene, pornographic, smutty, dirty, filthy, ribald, off-color, suggestive, risqué. **2.** Is the inscription in Classical or Vulgar Latin? The vulgar herd never appreciated Gustave Moreau: common, plebeian, proletarian, lowbrow, ordinary. —**Ant.** 1 elegant, refined, cultivated, tasteful, polite, mannerly, delicate. 2 aristocratic, noble, highborn, patrician; educated, cultured, highbrow.

vulgarity n. **1.** The vulgarity of the movie was shocking: bad taste, tastelessness, coarseness, crudeness, grossness, indecorum, indelicacy; indecency, smuttiness, obscenity, pornography. **2.** His vulgarity cost him many friends: ill manners, rudeness, impoliteness, boorishness, lack of refinement. —**Ant.** 1 good taste, tastefulness, decorum, delicacy, decency. 2 good manners, politeness, refinement, cultivation, good breeding, sensitivity.

vulnerable adj. All who have not been inoculated are vulnerable to the disease. The young girl has always been vulnerable to criticism: open to attack, defenseless, unprotected, insecure, undefended, unguarded, exposed, exposed to harm, liable to harm, susceptible; easily hurt, easily wounded, weak, sensitive, thin-skinned. —**Ant.** well defended, protected, guarded, unexposed, invincible, unassailable; impervious, insensitive, thick-skinned.

vying adj. The vying teams arrived at a draw: competing, competitive.

W

wacky *adj. Slang The wacky plot got our attention:* eccentric, irrational, whimsical, knockabout, zany, madcap, foolish, silly, crazy, *Informal* oddball, *Slang* screwball, goofy. —**Ant.** serious, sobersided.

waddle *v. She waddled down the street carrying a load of groceries:* wobble, totter, toddle, hobble, sway, wag.

wade *v.* **1.** *He waded into the river to test the current:* walk in the water, walk in mud, ford. **2.** *It took hours to wade through all that work:* trudge, trek, labor, toil, plod, drudge, plow.

waffle *v.* **1.** *They waffled about whether to buy a new sofa:* vacillate, dither, equivocate, hesitate, tergiversate, waver, seesaw, fluctuate, hem and haw, back and fill, yo-yo, *British* haver. **2.** *The debaters waffled at every point:* blather, babble, prattle, gabble, prate.

waft *v. The odor of pine wafted through the mountain air:* float, drift, blow, puff.

wag[1] *v.* **1.** *Heads wagged at the wedding announcement. The young Einstein caused beards to wag throughout the scientific community:* move from side to side, move up and down repeatedly, oscillate, move, stir, wave, shake, waggle, wiggle, jiggle, bob, switch, flutter, flicker, flick, twitch, wigwag. —*n.* **2.** *With a wag of his tail the dog went to the door:* switch, wave, shake, waggle, wiggle, jiggle, bob, flutter, flick, flicker, twitch, wigwag.

wag[2] *n. Some wag put the "just married" sign on the old couple's car:* joker, jokester, jester, clown, comedian, buffoon, life of the party, wit, humorist, farceur, wisecracker, droll, *Slang* card.

wage *n.* **1.** *The job is interesting, but it doesn't pay a living wage:* salary, payment, remuneration, compensation, recompense, stipend, emolument, earnings, income, fee, pay, revenue. —*v.* **2.** *England and Spain waged war for many years:* carry on, conduct, maintain, undertake, engage in, practice.

wager *n.* **1.** *Thousands of people made wagers on the Kentucky Derby. The most common wager on a horse race is two dollars:* bet; gamble, hazard, speculation; stake, venture, ante; pool, pot, jackpot. —*v.* **2.** *The Las Vegas gambler wagered $100 on each throw of the dice:* bet, make a bet, venture, hazard, risk, stake; gamble, speculate, take a flyer, tempt fortune, try one's luck. **3.** *I wager Kay will be late again:* speculate, guess, hazard an opinion, assume, suppose, presume, imagine, fancy, conjecture, surmise, theorize.

waggish *adj. Their waggish uncle had to have his little joke:* roguish, jocular, humorous, mischievous, tricky, sportive, merry, jocose, droll, comical, funny.

wagon *n. They hitched up the wagon and went out:* cart, van, truck, dray; lorry, wain; buckboard, dogcart.

waif *n. The waif was left on the steps of the or-phanage:* homeless child, foundling, stray, urchin, ragamuffin, gamin, (*fem.*) gamine, guttersnipe, street arab, tatterdemalion, mudlark.

wail *v.* **1.** *The women of the town wailed over the war victims. The siren wailed and woke everyone:* utter a long mournful cry, cry, weep, keen, bemoan, moan, groan, lament, bewail; cry out, howl, roar, yell, bellow, bawl, shout, caterwaul, rend the air, whine. —*n.* **2.** *A wail went up from the mourner's bench. The wail of air-raid sirens rent the night air:* mournful cry, plaint, loud weeping, wailing, keening, moaning, moan, lament, lamentation, groan; outcry, howl, roar, shout, yell, bellow, caterwaull, whine. —**Ant.** 1, 2 laugh. 1 be jubilant, be happy, rejoice, celebrate; whisper, murmur. 2 laughter; shout of joy; whisper, murmur.

waist *n.* **1.** *He's getting a bit thick around the waist:* middle part, middle, midsection, midriff, mid-region. **2.** *The waist should be taken in another inch or so:* waistline, waistband; shirtwaist, blouse, shirt, top, bodice.

wait *v.* **1.** *You'll have to wait until I finish this work. The contract is waiting for your signature:* bide one's time, remain inactive, *Informal* take it easy, cool one's heel's, hold one's horses; linger, tarry, dally, remain ready, rest in expectation. **2.** *Let the work wait until I get back from vacation. We waited dinner, hoping you would get here:* be postponed, be put off, be delayed, be tabled, be shelved, linger, hang fire; delay, stay, postpone, put off, suspend. —*n.* **3.** *The passengers had a wait of four hours between planes:* delay suspension, stay, pause, halt, stop, stopover, postponement, deferment, *Law* continuance.

waive *v.* **1.** *The ambassador waived his right to diplomatic immunity and paid the fine:* relinquish a legal right, surrender, give up, give up claim to, forbear, to insist on, yield, forgo, forswear, renounce, disclaim, let go, not use, dispense with. **2.** *The judge waived final decision for 60 days:* postpone, defer, put off, put aside, lay over, shelve, table, stay. —**Ant.** 1 claim, demand, press, insist on, exact, assert, pursue, maintain, defend. 2 hasten, hurry, speed up.

waiver *n. The younger son signed a waiver giving up all claims to the property:* relinquishment, disclaimer, renunciation, abdication, abandonment, dismissal.

wake[1] *v.* **1.** *She waked her father and told him the good news:* awake, awaken, waken, wake up, rouse from sleep. **2.** *The newspaper article waked my interest in archaeology:* arouse, rouse, awaken, waken, stimulate, provoke, kindle, fire, stir, excite, enliven, quicken, galvanize, rally; revive, resuscitate. —*n.* **3.** *The wake was held at the home of the deceased:* all-night vigil over corpse before burial, all-night watch over the dead. —**Ant.** 1 put to sleep, go to sleep; soothe, quiet, hush. 2 allay, quell, appease, calm; sate.

wake[2] *n. Seagulls followed in the wake of the ship:* wash, track of a vessel, backwash; trail, path, course, train.

wakeful *adj.* **1.** *Worry caused her to be wakeful*

much of the night: unable to sleep, sleepless, unsleeping, awake, wide-awake, insomniac; restless, astir. **2.** *The palace guards were ever wakeful:* alert, vigilant, watchful, wary, careful, heedful, observant; cautious, circumspect. —**Ant.** 1 sleepy, somnolent, drowsy; asleep, sleeping, restful. 2 off-guard, unalert, unvigilant, heedless, unwary.

waken *v. They wakened her at nine o'clock:* wake, rouse.

walk *v.* **1.** *Let's walk around the lake. We got off the bus and walked the last few blocks:* proceed by steps, go on foot, travel on foot; stroll, saunter, amble, perambulate, promenade, march, tramp, traipse, trek, trudge, take a turn, *Informal* foot it, go shank's mare. —*n.* **2.** *The guests took a long walk after dinner:* stroll, saunter, constitutional, promenade, perambulation, march, trek, hike, journey by foot. **3.** *Have you ever noticed that bouncy little walk of hers?:* way of walking, gait, step, stride. **4.** *The walk in front of the house is covered with ice:* place for walking; (*variously*) sidewalk, path, pathway, trail, road, way, lane, promenade, route, passage.

wall *n. Let's knock out this wall and make the room larger. Two prisoners escaped over the walls of the prison:* side of a room, partition, divider; side of a building; fence, barrier, confine, barricade, rampart, stockade, parapet, battlement, breastwork, fortification, bastion.

wallop *v.* **1.** *He walloped the child for running away. Mickey Mantle could really wallop a baseball:* hit hard, strike hard, lambaste, clobber, belt, punch, smack, slap, swat, cuff; beat, thrash, pummel, spank, buffet; whip, strap, switch, lash. **2.** *The opposition party was really walloped in the fall elections:* beat badly, defeat, trounce, rout, crush, clobber, best, worst, *Slang* lick, trim. **3.** *The boxer was floored by a wallop to the chin:* hard blow, punch, hit, smack, whack, cuff, belt, slap, swat.

wallow *v.* **1.** *Pigs love to wallow:* roll in mud, lie in mud. **2.** *Since the inheritance she's been wallowing in luxury:* luxuriate, indulge, revel, enjoy selfishly, live self-indulgently; bask in, swim in, riot in, feast on, relish.

wan *adj.* **1.** *The patient still looks thin and wan:* pale, sickly pale, pallid, white, pasty, colorless, livid, sallow, anemic, ashen; cadaverous, ghostly, ghastly. **2.** *She made a wan attempt to smile at the tasteless joke:* weak, feeble, sickly sad, halfhearted, forced, unconvincing, spiritless, vapid, lame, limp, ineffective, ineffectual, unavailing. —**Ant.** 1 ruddy, rosy, rosy-cheeked, pink-cheeked, florid, flushed. 2 strong, forceful, spirited, convincing, wholehearted, effective.

wand *n. The fairy godmother waved her magic wand:* rod, stick, staff, baton, mace, scepter.

wander *v.* **1.** *The boy wandered the neighborhood, looking for his dog. The college student wandered through Europe during the summer:* walk aimlessly, move about aimlessly, roam, ramble, meander, rove, range, prowl; travel, journey, trek, jaunt, *Slang* knock about. **2.** *The little stream wanders through the woods:* meander, curve, twist, zigzag; swerve, veer, alter

course. **3.** *The goat wandered from the yard and never came back:* stray away, become lost. —**Ant.** 1 stay, remain, settle; rest, pause, stop, halt. 2 go straight as an arrow, make a beeline. 3 be found; come home, return.

wanderer *n. Johnny Appleseed spent much of his life as a wanderer. The happy wanderers brought back many souvenirs from their trip:* roamer, rover, rambler, nomad, itinerant, vagrant, vagabond, beachcomber, gypsy, hobo, knight of the road; wayfarer, journeyer, traveler, voyager, globetrotter, gadabout. —**Ant.** homebody, stay-at-home, stick-in-the-mud.

wane *v.* **1.** *The school's good reputation has started to wane. The old man's health began to wane:* fade away, fade, decline, dwindle, weaken, decrease, diminish, subside, abate, ebb, lessen; wither, waste, droop, sink. —*n.* **2.** *The 1960's saw the wane of the steamship passenger trade:* fading away, fading, decline, decrease, dwindling, subsiding, abating, ebbing, lessening, recession, weakening, withering, wasting away. —**Ant.** 1 appear, rise, increase, expand, advance, strengthen, grow, develop, wax, improve, flourish, thrive, soar, blossom, brighten. 2 rise, increase, expansion, advancement, strengthening, growth, development, waxing.

wangle *v. I tried to wangle another ticket for the concert:* maneuver, finagle, engineer, machinate, manipulate, wheedle, scheme, worm, angle, jockey, trick, intrigue.

wannabe *n. The California beaches are filled with wannabes who would love to become famous movie stars:* aspirant, aspirer, emulator, hopeful, seeker, wisher, wanter, imitator, candidate, postulant, applicant, solicitant.

want *v.* **1.** *I want a pink sweater and a skirt to match:* desire, wish for, crave, fancy, hope for, long for, yearn for, pine for, covet, hanker for, hunger for, thirst for, hunger after. **2.** *The FBI wants him for espionage:* seek, search for, hunt; have a warrant for. **3.** *This book wants mending:* need, require, lack, be without; be deficient in, be destitute of, fall short in, come short of. **4.** *She has never wanted for money:* be needy, have a shortage of, be without, lack. —*n.* **5.** *Most people have simple wants:* need, necessity, requirement, desire, yearning, craving, wish, requisite, demand. **6.** *The country has a want of water. In the 1930's many people were reduced to want:* deficiency, lack, scarcity, shortage, dearth, insufficiency, paucity, need; privation, hunger, hard times; poverty, destitution, impoverishment, pauperism, indigence, penury, pennilessness, impecuniosity, insolvency, straitened circumstances. —**Ant.** 1 be sated, be satisfied; have, own, possess, enjoy; refuse, reject, decline, repudiate, spurn, relinquish, give up, give away, surrender; loathe, hate, dislike. 6 plenty, abundance, copiousness; sufficiency, adequacy; wealth, opulence, affluence, luxury.

wanting *adj. The car was tested for safety and found wanting. A motive for crime was wanting:* deficient, inadequate, substandard, lacking, insufficient; imperfect, defective, short; missing, absent. **—Ant.** adequate, sufficient, passable; perfect, complete, full.

wanton *adj.* **1.** *The juvenile delinquents were charged with wanton destruction of property:* deliberate, willful, malicious, malevolent, unjustified, unprovoked, needless, uncalled-for, groundless, senseless, inconsiderate, heedless, careless, mindless, irresponsible. **2.** *He was often seen in the company of wanton women:* loose, of loose morals, immoral, dissolute, fast, debauched, abandoned, promiscuous, unchaste, lewd, lecherous, lustful, libertine, licentious; gross, obscene, bestial. *—n.* **3.** *The waterfront bar was frequented by thieves and wantons:* immoral person, dissolute person, lewd person, debauchee, libertine, profligate, voluptuary, sensualist, sybarite; (*of a man*) lecher, seducer, adulterer, fornicator, womanizer, rake, satyr, roué, whoremaster; (*of a women*) hussy, trollop, slut, strumpet, whore, prostitute, harlot, tart, bawd, chippy, jade, concubine, fornicatrix.

war *n.* **1.** *The First World War lasted from 1914 to 1918:* state of armed conflict, armed conflict, warfare, hostilities, military operations, clash of arms; fighting, battle, combat. **2.** *The mayor continued his war against corruption:* fight, struggle, attack, battle, combat, opposition, conflict. *—v.* **3.** *The country warred with its neighbors for years. The church must war against vice:* wage war, make war, be at war, carry on hostilities, battle with, fight, combat, contend, struggle, clash, exchange shots, declare war, go to war, take up arms, attack, invade, march against. **—Ant.** 1 peace, peacetime; neutrality; treaty, armistice, truce, ceasefire. 2 acceptance, approval, assent, compliance, sanction, agreement. 3 make peace, call a truce.

warble *v.* *Birds warbled in the trees:* sing, trill, vocalize, carol, lilt, give voice, descant, croon, chant, intone, pipe, belt.

ward *n.* **1.** *He's running for councilman of our ward:* administrative district, voting district; municipal district, precinct, quarter, zone. **2.** *The patient was taken to the isolation ward:* section of a hospital, pavilion; section of a prison. **3.** *The orphan became a ward of the state:* charge, dependent; protégé. *—v.* **4.** *The boxer fought desperately to ward off his opponent's blows. Is there any way the firm can ward off bankruptcy?:* turn aside, turn away, fend off, stave off, keep at bay, block, repel, beat off, defend against, guard against; avert, prevent, thwart, forestall, hold at arm's length.

warden *n.* **1.** *The prisoner was ordered to report to the warden:* chief prison officer, prison superintendent. **2.** *The game warden examined the hunter's license:* keeper, ranger, guard, sentry, watchman, protector, guardian, manager, superintendent, warder, curator.

wardrobe *n.* **1.** *She bought a new wardrobe to take on the cruise:* collection of clothes, supply of clothing; apparel, clothing, wearing apparel, outfit, attire, togs, garments, habiliments. **2.** *Better put some mothballs in the hall wardrobe:*

clothes closet, clothes cabinet, clothespress, closet; bureau, chest, cedar chest, commode, chiffonier, armoire.

warehouse *n.* *The warehouse couldn't contain everything:* storehouse, store, depot, distribution center, stockpile, stockroom, storage, repository, depository.

wares *n. pl.* *The silversmith showed us his wares:* articles for sale, goods for sale, line, merchandise, stock-in-trade, stock, inventory, supplies, staples, commodities.

warfare *n.* *Warfare raged along the border for days:* state of war, war, armed conflict, hostilities, military operation, clash of arms, fighting, fight, battle, combat, conflict.

warlike *adj.* *Warlike tribes lived nearby:* martial, military; bellicose, belligerent, hostile, inimical, unfriendly. **—Ant.** peaceful.

warm *adj.* **1.** *April was a warm, sunny month. The freshly baked pie was still warm:* moderately hot, somewhat hot, lukewarm, tepid, heated, not cold; hot. **2.** *Wear a warm sweater:* providing warmth, warming, keeping in the body's heat. **3.** *The dining room was decorated in warm colors:* bright, sunny, vivid, brilliant, glowing. **4.** *Aunt Sue is a very warm person. The teacher had a warm smile for everyone:* loving, warmhearted, affectionate, kind, kindly, kindhearted, tender, tenderhearted, sympathetic, compassionate, friendly, outgoing, cheerful, joyful, joyous, pleasant, cordial, happy, affable, gracious. **5.** *The question prompted a warm discussion:* lively, vigorous, animated, fervent, earnest, passionate, heated, enthusiastic, spirited, intense, vehement. *—v.* **6.** *Warm the soup while I make the sandwiches:* heat, heat up, warm up, warm over, make hot; cook, simmer. **7.** *The child's happy smile warmed his heart:* cheer, make joyful, make happy; arouse affection in, arouse sympathy in, thaw, melt. **—Ant.** 1–4, 6, 7 cool. 1, 3, 4 cold. 1 chilly, frigid, icy, ice-cold. 3 dull, drab, austere. 4 unfriendly, frigid, remote, standoffish, aloof, haughty; cruel, hardhearted, coldhearted, unsympathetic, uncaring. 5 lethargic, apathetic, torpid, dull, boring. 6, 7 cool off, chill, freeze. 7 alienate; depress, sadden.

warmhearted *adj.* *The warmhearted woman took in the stray cat:* kind, kindly, kindhearted, tenderhearted, sympathetic, compassionate, affectionate, loving, cordial, genial, warm, solicitous. **—Ant.** unkind, coldhearted, hardhearted.

warmth *n.* **1.** *Sit by the warmth of the fire. The warmth of this thin blanket is amazing:* warmness, heat, hotness; feeling of being warm, warm sensation. **2.** *Everyone responds to the warmth of her smile:* lovingness, warmheartedness, kindliness, kindness, kindheartedness, tenderness, tenderheartedness, sympathy, compassion, cheerfulness, cheer, joy, joyfulness, cordiality, affability, graciousness, happiness, friendliness. **3.** *He expressed his views with a great deal of warmth:* heat, passion, fire, excitement, spirit, enthusiasm, vehemence, vigor, intensity, animation, earnestness, zeal, fervor, liveliness, verve, ardor. **—Ant.** 1, 2 chill, coolness, coldness, iciness. **2** sternness, austerity, severity; frigidity, remoteness, aloofness, unfriendliness. **3** lethargy, apathy, torpor, indifference; insincerity.

warn *v. The scout warned the fort of the imminent Indian attack. I warned you not to buy that old car:* alert, forewarn, give warning of danger, alert, forewarn, give warning of danger, alert to danger, put on one's guard, caution, notify, make aware, apprise, signal, inform; advise, counsel, admonish.

warning *n. The sentry's warning woke the fort's defenders. Didn't you have any warning that the house was being sold?:* warning signal, warning sign, alarm, signal, forewarning, notice: notification, intimation, hint, sign, token, omen, portent, foretoken, presage; appraisal, advice.

warp *v.* **1.** *The dampness warped the floorboards:* bend, twist, contort, distort, misshape, deform. **2.** *Years of living alone warped his personality:* pervert, twist, distort, corrupt, pervert, lead astray, debase, infect; misguide, bias, prejudice, mislead. —*n.* **3.** *This porch railing has a warp in it:* bend, twist, distortion, contortion, deformation. **4.** *Bitterness gave her outlook a peculiar warp:* quirk, twist, bent, leaning, tendency, disposition, inclination, proneness, propensity, proclivity, predisposition, one-sidedness, partiality. —**Ant.** **1** staighten, straighten out, unbend.

warplane *n. The warplanes went on several missions:* combat plane, military aircraft.

warrant *n.* **1.** *The police have a search warrant. There is a warrant out for the suspect's arrest:* authorization, permission, permit; license. —*v.* **2.** *Such actions warrant a severe reprimand:* justify, provide grounds for, give sufficient reason for; permit, authorize, license. **3.** *The manufacturer warrants that all parts are new:* guarantee, certify, vouch for, pledge, swear, attest, affirm, promise, vow, avow, assure, assert, declare, asseverate, aver.

warranty *n. The vacuum cleaner has a 5-year warranty:* written guarantee; pledge, agreement, certificate.

warrior *n. The warriors marched off with Hannibal to the Punic Wars:* soldier, legionnaire, fighting man, man-at-arms, military man, fighter, combatant; veteran, campaigner.

warship *n. Several warships were sunk:* armored vessel, war vessel.

wary *adj. It does no harm to be wary of new acquaintances:* cautious, careful, guarded, suspicious, chary, heedful, mindful, watchful, vigilant, on one's guard, alert, wakeful, wide-awake; discreet, circumspect, close-mouthed, prudent. —**Ant.** unwary, unsuspecting, unguarded, rash, reckless, foolhardy, careless, heedless, incautious; negligent, remiss.

wash *v.* **1.** *Wash your hands and come to supper:* clean with soap and water, clean, cleanse; (*variously*) launder, rinse, scrub, mop, swab, scour, sponge, wipe, rub, bathe, shampoo, lave. **2.** *You'd better wash that cut with some iodine:* wet, moisten, drench, soak, irrigate, immerse, flood, inundate. **3.** *A large piece of driftwood washed onto the beach:* float, be carried by the

tide; move by the flow of water, move in waves. —*n.* **4.** *This bedspread could use a good wash:* washing, cleaning, cleansing: (*variously*) laundering, mopping, scouring, bath, shower, shampoo, ablution, lavation. **5.** *Mother does the wash twice a week:* laundry, clothes washing; group of things laundered.

waspish *adj. Personal questions bring out her waspish side:* testy, huffy, fretful, pettish, peevish, irritable, petulant, snappish, fractious, querulous, cantankerous, cranky, crotchety, bearish, ornery, *Brit.* shirty. —**Ant.** good-natured, agreeable, cheerful, genial.

waste *v.* **1.** *Don't waste time on nonessentials. A badly tuned motor wastes gas:* squander, dissipate, throw away, fritter away, expend needlessly, consume extravagantly, use up fruitlessly, devour, burn up, run through, deplete, empty, drain, exhaust; misuse, use unwisely, misspend, misapply, misemploy. **2.** *Invading armies wasted the countryside:* lay waste, destroy, ruin, devastate, spoil, wreck, demolish, crush, smash, shatter, raze; despoil, ravage, pillage, plunder, loot, sack, strip, rob, prey upon. **3.** *The old man's strength was wasting away:* fade, dwindle, decline, weaken, decrease, diminish, subside, abate, ebb, wane, wither, crumble, decay; droop, sink, die; disappear, evaporate, melt. —*n.* **4.** *Industrial waste must be prevented from polluting our rivers:* waste material, refuse, garbage, trash, rubbish, debris, litter, sweepings, dregs; excrement; offal. **5.** *The seamstress used waste to make doll clothing:* remnants, leftovers, remainders, scraps, leavings. **6.** *The city budget can afford no waste. Such a routine job is a waste of her talents:* wastefulness, squandering, extravagance, needless, expenditure, prodigality, useless consumption, needless loss; misuse, misapplication, dissipation. **7.** *The explorers spent months in the Arctic wastes:* wasteland, barren expanse, emptiness, void; (*variously*) barren, wilderness, desert region, arid region, tundra, steppe, badlands. **8.** *Nothing could stop the waste of the city by the barbarians:* destruction, ruin, ruination, devastation, wreck, wrecking, demolition, razing; ravage, despoliation, pillage, plundering, looting, sack, rape. —**Ant.** **1** save, conserve, husband, economize; spend wisely, use well. **2** build, rebuild, restore; protect, defend, guard. **3** strengthen, develop, grow, improve, rally, increase, advance. **6** saving, economy, thrift, frugality, conservation.

wasteful *adj. It's wasteful to throw out meat bones that could be used for soup:* squandering, prodigal; extravagant, uneconomical, thriftless, unthrifty, spendthrift, improvident. —**Ant.** economical, thrifty, frugal, prudent, unwasteful.

watch *v.* **1.** *He kissed her while no one was watching. Watch the magician and try to figure out how he makes the rabbit disappear:* look, look on, look at, stare, stare at, gaze at, see, eye, keep an eye on, peep at, peer at, ogle; observe, notice, note, pay attention to, attend, mark, regard, rivet one's eyes on, examine, scrutinize, survey, contemplate, pore over. **2.**

Watch for an empty seat and grab it: look out for, be on the lookout, be on the alert, keep an eye out for. **3.** *Watch where you're going! Watch that he doesn't cheat you:* pay attention, be careful, be cautious, be on guard, be wary, take heed, be chary. **4.** *Who's watching the children while the parents are on vacation? Watch your money or it will be gone before payday:* look after, look out for, keep an eye on, tend, tend to, care for, take care of, mind, oversee, superintend; save, preserve, protect, guard. —*n.* **5.** *Keep a close watch on the kettle so it doesn't boil over:* eye, surveillance, observance, observation, watchfulness, supervision, superintendence, attention, notice, heed, vigilance; lookout, alert, guard, survey. **6.** *The watch is late making his rounds. The sailor had the midnight to 4 A.M. watch:* watchman, guard, guards, sentry, sentries, sentinel, patrol, foot patrol, patrolman, picket, scout; period of time for standing guard, period of time for being on duty. **7.** *This watch keeps good time:* wristwatch; pocket watch. —**Ant.** 2 overlook, ignore, disregard. 3 be rash, be reckless, be careless. 4 neglect. 5 inattention, disregard, heedlessness.

watchful *adj.* **1.** *The hunter kept a watchful eye on the valley below him:* alert, observant, vigilant, on the lookout, attentive, heedful, aware, mindful, open-eyed, wide-awake. **2.** *To live on a budget one must be very watchful of one's expenses:* careful, prudent, cautious, circumspect, wary, guarded, on one's guard, chary, canny, shrewd. —**Ant.** 1, 2 careless, inattentive, heedless, unaware, unmindful. 1 unobservant. 2 rash, reckless, unguarded, unwary, thoughtless.

watchman *n.* *The watchman saw the prowler and called the police:* guard, sentry, sentinel, watch, patrol, foot patrol, patrolman; picket, scout, lookout.

watchword *n.* *Silence was their watchword:* password, countersign, shibboleth; slogan, motto.

water *n.* **1.** *Eat properly and drink six glasses of water a day:* H_2O; drinking water. **2.** *The canoeist was out on the water all day:* body of water; (*variously*) sea, ocean, lake, pond, pool, lagoon, river, stream. —*v.* **3.** *Water the flowers every morning:* supply water to; (*variously*) sprinkle, wet, moisten, damp, dampen, souse, soak, drench, douse, dip, submerge, immerse, splash, irrigate, flood, inundate, deluge. **4.** *Water the livestock when you feed them:* give water to drink. **5.** *That bar waters its drinks:* add water to, dilute, thin, adulterate, cut. **6.** *My eyes water when I'm tired:* tear, fill with tears. —**Ant.** 2 land, dry land, terra firma. 3 dry, dry up; parch, dehydrate, desiccate; wipe up, sponge, blot, swab.

waterfall *n.* *They swam near the waterfall:* falls, fall, cataract, cascade, *Informal* Niagara.

waterfront *n.* *The best properties were on the waterfront:* shoreline, coastline, embankment, bank, foreshore, lakefront, lakeshore, bayfront, bayside, riverside.

watery *adj.* **1.** *The pirate went to a watery grave. What's that watery stain on the wall?:* of water, like water, wet, moist, damp, liquid, fluid, aqueous. **2.** *This gravy tastes watery:* thin, diluted, watered, wishy-washy, weak, adulterated. **3.** *We all had watery eyes in that smoky room:* teary, tearing, tearful, rheumy.

wave *n.* **1.** *A big wave swamped the rowboat:* swell, billow, breaker, comber, whitecap, roller; ripple, undulation. **2.** *Can strong magnets distort radio waves?:* pulse, pulsation, vibration. **3.** *The captain led the first wave of marines up the beach:* moving row, advancing, rank, file, line, string, train, column, tier. **4.** *Her hair has a natural wave:* curve, series of curves, curl; coil, winding, spiral, roll, twirl. **5.** *The neighbor gave me a wave from across the street. A wave of the teacher's hand silenced the class:* salutation, to-and-fro hand gesture of greeting; gesture, gesticulation, hand signal, motion, flourish. **6.** *There's been a wave of selling on the stock exchange:* surge, rush, deluge, flood; rise, increase, heightening. —*v.* **7.** *The flag waved in the breeze. Don't wave that book in my face!:* move to and fro, flutter, flap, swing, sway, shake, waver, tremble, quiver; oscillate, vibrate, undulate, pulsate; brandish, flourish, wield. **8.** *The boy waved good-bye. The highway patrolman waved us to a stop:* signal, gesture, gesticulate.

waver *v.* **1.** *The palm trees wavered in the strong breeze:* wave, move to and fro, sway, swing, shake, flutter, flap; tremble, quiver, undulate. **2.** *The old woman wavered on the top step and nearly fell:* totter, reel, stagger, wobble, sway, weave, careen, falter, begin to give way. **3.** *He never wavered in his determination to become a doctor:* falter, be irresolute, be undecided, be undetermined, be doubtful, vacillate, shilly-shally, dilly-dally, hesitate, pause, change, vary, fluctuate, sway. —**Ant.** 3 be resolute, be steadfast, be certain, be determined, be decisive, stand firm.

wavy *adj.* *A wavy pattern ran through the sand:* rippling, curved, sinuous, rolling, winding, curvilinear, serpentine, curly, coiled, undulating; tortuous, labyrinthine, meandering, mazelike. —**Ant.** straight, uncurved, unbending, rigid.

wax *v.* *The mayor waxed enthusiastic over the new education program. The moon is always the same size but seems to wax and wane according to the light it reflects:* grow, become; become larger, enlarge, increase, expand, develop, thrive, extend, widen, become fuller, fill out, swell, dilate, spread out, inflate, puff out, blow up, balloon. —**Ant.** wane, become smaller, diminish, decrease, contract, narrow, deflate.

way *n.* **1.** *It's hard for a traveler to get used to foreign ways. Being gruff is just his way:* custom, practice, manner, habit, usage, form; behavior, conduct, nature, wont. **2.** *What's the best way to make coffee?:* method, means, process, procedure, manner, system, technique, course of action. **3.** *It's already spring out our way:* direction; neighborhood, vicinity, area, region. **4.** *This is the shortest way to town. Hard work is* *the way to success:* route, course, road, path, pathway, trail, lane, pass, passage; distance. **5.** *Make way for the king!:* space, room, room to advance. *—adv.* **6.** *Go way!:* away, from this place, off. **7.** *Can't you see it way in the distance?:* far, far off, remotely.

wayfaring *adj. The wayfaring strangers headed home:* wandering, itinerant, journeying, voyaging, nomadic, peripatetic, rambling, roving, traveling, vagrant, drifting.

waylay *v. Six highwaymen waylaid the stagecoach:* ambush, fall upon from ambush, lie in wait for, lay a trap for; set upon, assail, assault, attack; lure, entrap, ensnare, decoy, inveigle.

wayward *adj.* **1.** *The judge sent the boy to a home for wayward youths:* disobedient, unmanageable, ungovernable, incorrigible, intractable, unruly, insubordinate, rebellious, refractory, troublesome; headstrong, self-willed, willful, contrary, perverse, obstinate, stubborn, recalcitrant, balky, mulish. **2.** *It's hard to sail in a wayward wind:* fitful, erratic, changeable, undependable, inconsistent, inconstant, variable, fluctuating; fickle, restive, mercurial, capricious, whimsical. **—Ant.** 1 obedient, manageable, docile, malleable, tractable, compliant. 2 steady, fixed, constant, regular, consistent, dependable.

weak *adj.* **1.** *The flu victim was too weak to walk:* lacking strength, weakened, feeble, faint, frail, debilitated; exhausted, spent, wasted, enervated; shaky, unsteady, helpless. **2.** *The walls are too weak to hold up the roof. He gave us a weak smile:* frail, flimsy, unsubstantial, puny, shaky, unsteady, fragile, breakable, brittle, frangible, delicate. **3.** *We need strong leaders, not weak ones. The baseball team has a weak pitching staff:* powerless, spineless, cowardly, soft, timorous, irresolute, unmanly, effeminate, namby-pamby, wishy-washy; ineffective, ineffectual, inefficacious, inefficient, unsatisfactory, poor, lame. **4.** *The arguments in favor of the proposal are very weak. The army's defeat leaves the country in a weak position:* vulnerable, exposed, defenseless, assailable, unprotected, unguarded, unsafe, wide open; untenable, unsupported, unconvincing, untrustworthy, lacking. **5.** *Don't make the coffee too weak:* watery, thin, diluted, adulterated; tasteless, insipid. **—Ant.** 1–5 strong. 2–4 strengthened, sturdy, powerful. 1–3 steady. 1 vigorous, hardy, hearty, hale. 2 substantial, sound, solid, hefty; unbreakable; vivid, beaming, radiant, brilliant; ardent, eager. 3 forceful, aggressive, vigorous, energetic; firm, hard, tough, brave, bold, stalwart, staunch, manly; able, capable, potent, effective. 4 solid, sound, substantial, forceful, convincing, trustworthy, valid, good, satisfactory, effective; impregnable, invulnerable, unassailable, well-guarded, protected, safe, secure. 5 potent.

weaken *v. Lack of food weakened his strength. Public support of the highway program began to weaken:* make weak, impair, undermine, cripple, emasculate, unman, soften, soften up, expose; diminish, lessen, lower, sap, mitigate, moderate, exhaust, waste, devitalize, enervate, dilute, water down, thin, thin out; fail, flag,

droop, dwindle, wane, fade, abate. **—Ant.** strengthen, increase, grow, develop, rise, improve, enhance, better; invigorate, energize, revitalize.

weakling *n.* **1.** *Before embracing an active outdoor life, the young Teddy Roosevelt was a weakling:* physically weak person, frail person, feeble person, physical wreck. **2.** *Stand up for your rights and don't be such a weakling:* weak-willed person, weak sister, coward, sissy, namby-pamby, milksop, pantywaist, jellyfish, mouse, chicken, cream puff, mollycoddle, milquetoast, *Slang* wimp, twit.

weakness *n.* **1.** *The patient's weakness is due to poor nutrition:* feebleness, lack of strength, frailty, debility, debilitation; shakiness, unsteadiness. **2.** *Can't you see the weakness of his argument?:* fault, defect, deficiency, imperfection, unsubstantiality, lack of force, ineffectiveness, lameness, flimsiness, failing, frailty; vulnerability, susceptibility, unconvincingness, untrustworthiness. **3.** *Jerry has a weakness for sports cars:* passion, fondness, intense liking, penchant, propensity, proclivity, tendency, inclination, proneness, leaning, prejudice, bias, bent, hunger, thirst, appetite, *Informal* soft spot in one's heart. **—Ant.** 1, 2 strength. 1 vigor, vitality, stamina; health, hardiness, soundness, sturdiness; power. 2 force, effectiveness, potency; validity, perfection, soundness, unassailability, impregnability, trustworthiness. 3 dislike, hatred, loathing, aversion, disgust, horror.

wealth *n.* **1.** *His wealth is estimated at fifty million dollars:* money, quantity of money, riches, fortune, assets, resources, means, capital, estate, property, goods, chattels. **2.** *The family always lived in great wealth:* affluence, prosperity; luxury, luxuriousness, opulence, independence, easy circumstances, easy street. **3.** *There is a wealth of detail in the painting:* abundance, profusion, richness, copiousness, plenitude, amplitude, fullness, bounty, fund, store, mine. **—Ant.** 2 poverty, penury, pauperism, destitution, indigence, privation, straitened circumstances, want, need, wretchedness. 3 want, lack, dearth, paucity, scarcity, shortage, scantiness, deficiency.

wealthy *adj. The debutante comes from a very wealthy family:* rich, prosperous, affluent, moneyed, well-to-do, well-off, well-heeled, well-fixed, flush, loaded. **—Ant.** poor, impoverished, poverty-stricken, destitute, indigent, needy, down-and-out.

weapon *n.* **1.** *The army completed testing the new weapon:* arm, armament, instrument of war, lethal instrument, deadly weapon. **2.** *Reduced spending is our best weapon against inflation:* defense, protection, guard, countermeasure, safeguard, security, bulwark; offense, offensive, attack; means, measure, resort, resource.

wear *v.* **1.** *Are you going to wear blue jeans or a dress? The policeman wore his badge proudly:* dress in, clothe oneself in, carry on the person, put on, don, slip on, attire oneself with, fit oneself with, costume oneself, garb oneself, array oneself, wrap, swathe, shroud, swaddle. **2.** *This sweater has worn thin at the elbows:* wear away, wear out; abrade, rub away, fray, frazzle, shred; erode, wash away; corrode, eat away. **3.** *This coat wears better than any I've had:* resist abrasion, stand up to wear and tear; last, endure. **4.** *The long wait wore everyone out:* exhaust, tire, fatigue, weary, drain; overwork, overburden, tax. —*n.* **5.** *There's a lot of good wear left in those shoes:* wearability, use, service; utility, utilization, employment, application, consumption. **6.** *That store has the best selection of beachwear in town:* clothing, clothes, apparel, wearing apparel, attire, garments, costumes, togs, duds. **7.** *You can see the wear on the corner of the rug:* worn place, rubbed place, deterioration, disintegration, disrepair, wear and tear; damage, injury, dilapidation.

wearisome *adj. She spent a wearisome afternoon tending the children:* tedious, irksome, tiresome, vexatious, annoying, trying, irritating, bothersome, oppressive, burdensome; dreary, boring, dull, monotonous; tiring, exhausting, fatiguing. —**Ant.** agreeable, pleasant, enjoyable, pleasurable.

weary *adj.* **1.** *I'm always weary after my day's work:* tired, exhausted, fatigued, wearied, spent, worn-out, drained, done in, tuckered out, fagged out, played out, all in, dog tired, ready to drop, *Slang* beat, pooped, bushed; sleepy, drowsy. **2.** *Carrying the furniture to the attic was a weary task. I thought that weary speech would never end:* tiring, fatiguing, wearying, wearing, tedious, exhausting; boring, monotonous, tiresome, wearisome, humdrum, dull, routine; soporific, somniferous. **3.** *He's weary of her constant nagging:* tired, sick and tired, impatient, annoyed, dissatisfied; dispirited, discontented, disgusted; bored, blasé, jaded, fed up. —*v.* **4.** *The long drive wearied the children:* tire, tire out, fatigue, exhaust, wear out, play out, fag, tucker; overtax, overwork, overburden. —**Ant.** 1 refreshed, revivified, invigorated; energetic, full of pep. 2 easy; refreshing, invigorating; interesting, exciting, amusing, delightful. 3 invigorated, refreshed; delighted, pleased, interested; patient, forebearing. 4 refresh, invigorate, revive; energize, enliven.

weather *n.* **1.** *What's the weather like this morning?:* atmospheric conditions; (*loosely*) climate, temperature, clime. —*v.* **2.** *Stack the lumber and let it weather before building the barn. Copper turns green as it weathers:* expose to weather, dry, season, toughen; bleach, tan; rust, oxidize. **3.** *The sun weathered the paint:* harm by exposure to the weather. **4.** *The ship weathered the hurricane with no casualties:* pass through safely, withstand, stand; brave, face, confront. —*adj.* **5.** *Don't build your house on the weather side of the hill:* windward, facing the wind.

weather-beaten *adj.* **1.** *The weather-beaten cottages looked uninhabitable:* weathered, weather-scarred, roughened, storm-tossed, battered, run-down, worn-down, faded, worn, washed-out, bleached, damaged, eroded, etio-

lated. **2.** *The sailor returned from the voyage with sun-bleached hair and weather-beaten skin:* tanned, bronzed, darkened, toughened, roughened.

weave *v.* **1.** *The Navajos weave beautiful rugs. Weave the two strings together to make a stronger cord:* loom, interlace, intertwine, interweave, twist, knit, entwine, braid, lace, plait, crisscross. **2.** *The composer wove three separate melodies into his composition:* interweave, combine, meld, blend, fuse, mingle, incorporate, unify, unite, join, link. **3.** *The small car weaved through the traffic. The river weaves through the woods:* zigzag, wind, curve, meander, writhe, snake, twist and turn. —*n.* **4.** *The fabric has a beautiful herringbone weave:* woven pattern; texture. —**Ant.** 1 unravel, untwist, disentangle. 2 isolate, segregate; separate, divorce, divide. 3 go straight as an arrow, make a beeline.

web *n.* **1.** *Why doesn't a spider get stuck in its own web?:* spiderweb; cobweb; snare, trap. **2.** *Campers had to sleep under mosquito webs:* webbing, net, netting, mesh, screening, screen, gossamer. **3.** *His whole story is a web of lies:* network, tissue, complex, tangle; maze, labyrinth.

wed *v.* **1.** *The couple will be wed in June. He will wed his secretary next month:* marry, join in marriage, unite in holy wedlock, mate, make one, couple, hitch, tie the knot, splice; take for husband, take for wife, espouse, take for better or worse, lead to the altar. **2.** *She is wedded to the idea of equal rights for women:* bind, attach, marry, commit, dedicate, devote, pledge; enamor of, captivate by, fascinate by, win over. **3.** *Try to wed all these ideas into one story:* blend, combine, unite, meld, weave, link, fuse, merge, incorporate, unify, tie. —**Ant.** 1, 3 divorce, separate. 3 isolate, segregate; unravel, disentangle.

wedded *adj.* **1.** *The couple had fifty years of wedded bliss:* married, united in marriage, marital. **2.** *The fifty states are wedded into one nation:* united, joined, bound, tied, connected, linked; fused, merged, unified, incorporated, blended, melded. **3.** *He seems wedded to his newspaper career:* devoted, committed, bound, deeply attached, married, pledged. —**Ant.** 1, 2 separated, divorced. 1 single, solitary, unwed, unmarried; bachelor, spinster.

wedding *n.* **1.** *It was the grandest wedding of the season:* wedding ceremony, marriage ceremony, marriage, nuptials, nuptial rite. **2.** *How long before they celebrate their golden wedding?:* wedding anniversary; wedding day, marriage day, the big day. —**Ant.** 1 separation, divorce.

wedge *n.* **1.** *Here's a wedge you can use as a doorstop. Buy a wedge of cheddar at the grocery:* V-shaped block, chock; pie-shaped piece, chunk. —*v.* **2.** *This log will have to be wedged in half. Wedge the cabinet at the base to keep it from tipping:* split, cleave, rend, rive, force; chock. **3.** *She couldn't wedge another item into* *the suitcase:* cram, jam, stuff, crowd, ram, squeeze, pack, press.

wedlock *n. They were united in wedlock at the bride's home:* marriage, matrimony, holy matrimony, marriage, nuptial state.

wee *adj. Put just a wee bit of liquor in the punch. The elf lived in a wee house in the enchanted forest:* tiny, very small, little, minute, minuscule, scant, scanty, *Informal* teeny, teeny-weeny, itty-bitty; diminutive, miniature, microscopic, pocket-size, petite; undersized, dwarf, Lilliputian. **—Ant.** big, large, huge, immense, enormous, gigantic, titanic.

weep *v. She wept at losing her son:* shed tears, cry, sob, lament, bewail, bemoan. **—Ant.** laugh, rejoice.

weigh *v. They weighed all the possibilities:* measure, consider, balance, ponder, contemplate, study.

weight *n.* **1.** *The weight of this car is over three thousand pounds:* heaviness, poundage, tonnage, mass, heft, ponderousness; relative density. **2.** *That package is a heavy weight for a child to carry. He's beginning to feel the weight of his financial problems:* load, burden, stress, strain, pressure. **3.** *The mayor's opinion carries great weight in this town. Tax reform is a matter of some weight:* importance, influence, import, magnitude, significance, consequence, value, consideration, emphasis, urgency, concern. **—v.** **4.** *The statue was weighted with a lead base:* add weight to, weigh down, make heavy, make heavier; ballast. **5.** *She seems to be weighted with the cares of the world:* weigh, weigh down, burden, oppress, encumber, saddle, tax, load. **—Ant.** 1 weightlessness. 3 unimportance, insignificance. 4 lighten. 5 buoy, lift up.

weighty *adj.* **1.** *The flatcar held a weighty shipment of ore:* heavy, massive, hefty; ponderous, cumbrous, cumbersome, burdensome. **2.** *How long has she had this weighty responsibility?:* burdensome, onerous, oppressive, crushing, trying, taxing, difficult, arduous, troublesome. **3.** *This is a weighty problem with no quick answer:* important, significant, consequential, serious, grave, earnest, solemn; substantial, considerable; urgent, crucial, critical, pressing, vital, essential. **—Ant.** 1–3 light, lightweight. 2 easy, easy to bear. 3 unimportant, insignificant, inconsequential, trivial, trifling, paltry, slight, frivolous.

weird *adj.* **1.** *Weird noises came from the haunted house at night:* eerie, mysterious, strange, unearthly, spooky, supernatural, ghostly, phantasmal; mystic, magical. **2.** *She certainly has a weird sense of humor:* odd, queer, eccentric, bizarre, freakish, grotesque, abnormal, unconventional, unnatural, unorthodox, strange, curious, peculiar, unusual, outlandish, irregular, *Slang* crazy, nutty, kooky, wild, far-out. **—Ant.** 1, 2 natural, normal. 2 usual, everyday, customary, routine, regular, common, familiar, conventional, orthodox, run-of-the-mill, *Slang* square.

welcome *n.* **1.** *The guests received a warm welcome:* greeting, salutation, salute; reception.

—v. **2.** *The mayor welcomed the visiting dignitaries at the airport:* greet, receive, bid welcome, meet; admit, usher in, treat hospitably, offer hospitality to, entertain, do the honors, embrace, hold out the hand to, shake hands with, roll out the welcome mat; receive with open arms, accept eagerly. **—adj.** **3.** *The host made us all feel welcome. What a welcome surprise!:* gladly received, wanted, accepted, at home, comfortable, hospitably entertained; agreeable, delightful, pleasant, pleasing, gratifying, inviting, engaging, winning, enticing, charming. **4.** *All guests are welcome to use the golf course. You're most welcome—don't thank me:* given full right to, free to enjoy, admitted; under no obligation. **—Ant.** 1 snub, rebuff, cold shoulder, brush-off. 3 unwelcome, unwanted, cold-shouldered, excluded.

weld *v. The plumber welded the joints:* fuse, bond, bind, cement, combine, connect, join, link, solder, unite.

welfare *n.* **1.** *Parents are concerned about the welfare of their children. I give you this advice for your own welfare:* well-being, happiness, good, good fortune, success, good circumstances, advantage, benefit, profit; health. **2.** *How long has the family been on welfare?:* relief, public assistance, the dole.

well[1] *n.* **1.** *They sank the well to a depth of 250 feet:* hole drilled in the ground to obtain water, oil, etc. **2.** *There's a natural well behind the cabin:* spring, pool, fountain. **3.** *The light is out in the stairwell:* shaft. **4.** *Sally is a well of information:* store, fund, mine, treasure chest; source, fount, wellspring. **—v.** **5.** *Petroleum suddenly welled out of the ground. Tears welled up in her eyes:* pour, flow, stream, surge, issue, run, rise, gush, spurt, spout, spring, jet, ooze.

well[2] *adv.* **1.** *Marty is getting along well at college. The poor man can't hear well:* fairly well, satisfactorily, nicely, adequately, acceptably, properly, agreeably; quite well, successfully, commendably, laudably, advantageously, splendidly, famously, capitally, first-rate; auspiciously, favorably, propitiously. **2.** *Dust the room well:* thoroughly, fully, completely, carefully. **3.** *We could not turn down her invitation very well:* properly, rightly, justly, fairly, correctly, suitably; readily, easily. **4.** *The new play was received well by the critics:* favorably, kindly, approvingly, warmly, sympathetically, enthusiastically. **5.** *The bracelet is worth well over a thousand dollars:* considerably, substantially, amply, abundantly, sufficiently, very much. **6.** *Do you know the neighbors well?:* intimately, familiarly, personally. **—adj.** **7.** *The doctor says you'll be well again in a few days:* in good health, healthy, strong, robust, vigorous, sound, hale, hearty, in fine fettle, chipper; rosy-cheeked. **8.** *It's well the children didn't see what happened:* good, right, proper, fitting; fortunate. **9.** *All is well with the family:* satisfactory, good, going well, faring well, happy, successful, prosperous, auspicious, felicitous; advantageous, favorable, promising, lucky. **—Ant.** 1, 2, 4 badly, poorly. 8, 9 bad. 1 unsatisfactorily, inadequately, imperfectly, unacceptably, unsuccessfully. 2 carelessly, indifferently, sloppily, incompletely. 3 unjustly, unfairly, incorrectly, improperly. 4 unfavorably, unkindly, disapprovingly, unsympathetically; unenthusiastically, mildly, coolly. 5 somewhat, not much, scarcely. 7 sick, sickly, ill, unwell, infirm, diseased, ailing; poorly; weak, feeble, frail. 8 wrong, improper, unfitting, unfortunate. 9 unsatisfactory, going badly, unsuccessful; inauspicious, unfavorable.

well-being *n. We were greatly concerned for your well-being. Carrying a good-luck charm will not insure your well-being:* welfare, weal, happiness, felicity, good; success, profit, advantage, benefit, luck, good luck, fortune, affluence, prosperity, ease, comfort; health.

well-bred *adj. Both men were well-bred products of the best schools:* cultivated, refined, genteel, polite, cultured, polished, urbane, civilized, well-mannered, well-brought-up, gentlemanly, ladylike, gallant, suave, sophisticated. —**Ant.** ill-bred, coarse, vulgar, uncouth.

well-built *adj.* **1.** *The well-built lifeguard dived into the sea:* able-bodied, well-knit, well-proportioned, muscular, well-muscled, athletic, brawny, burly, thickset, stacked, hunky. **2.** *The cabin was well-built:* sturdy, strong, durable, solid, rugged, well-constructed, well-made, well-finished. —**Ant.** scrawny, fragile.

well-known *adj. She's a well-known authority on home decoration:* prominent, famous, noted, popular, leading, outstanding, important, famed, celebrated, talked-about, big-time, eminent, illustrious; notorious, infamous, scandalous. —**Ant.** unknown, obscure, nameless, unheard-of.

well-off *adj. He's well-off after inheriting his uncle's estate:* prosperous, moneyed, wealthy, rich, affluent, comfortable, flush, well-fixed, well-to-do, well-heeled, *Slang* loaded. —**Ant.** broke, needy, penniless, indigent, poor.

welt *n. The blow from the falling branch left a large welt on the lumberjack's arm:* raised ridge on the skin, wale, weal, swelling, stripe, streak; lump, bump, mark, bruise, contusion.

welter *v.* **1.** *The huge waves weltered throughout the night. The dog weltered happily in the muddy puddle:* roll, toss, heave, writhe; wallow, grovel, tumble about. —*n.* **2.** *Sort this welter of dirty clothes for the laundry:* jumble, mass, heap, mess, pile, hodgepodge. **3.** *It's hard to hear above the welter of street noises:* confusion, tumult, commotion, turmoil, hubbub, racket, bustle; turbulence, storm, tempest.

wend *v. It's time to wend our way home:* direct one's path, proceed on, move along toward, betake oneself, hie to, steer toward, make.

wet *adj.* **1.** *Take off that wet jacket:* wringing wet, soaked, soaking, drenched, dripping, sodden, sopping, waterlogged, watery, soggy, squishy, moist, damp, dampened; dank, humid, clammy. **2.** *Wet weather is predicted for tomorrow:* rainy, showery, stormy. **3.** *The little boy wrote his name in the wet cement:* liquid, liquified, not dry, not dried; not set, not hardened. —*n.* **4.** *Air out the house to get rid of the wet:*

wetness, moisture, moistness, dampness, dankness, clamminess, condensation, exudation. **5.** *Button up your raincoat before going out in the wet:* rain, rainy weather, rainstorm, storm, bad weather, shower; precipitation, water. —*v.* **6.** *Do you wet your hair before combing it?:* moisten, dampen, damp, sprinkle, splash, soak, drench, immerse, submerge, dip, steep; water, irrigate, inundate. —**Ant.** 1–3, 6 dry. 1 bone-dry, parched. 3 dried; set, hardened; nonliquid, solid. 4 dryness. 5 dry weather, fair weather, good weather. 6 parch, desiccate, dehydrate, evaporate.

whack *v.* **1.** *The child whacked the puppy with a rolled-up newspaper:* strike, smack, clout, hit, belt, slug, sock, wallop, slam, smite, pound, baste, slap, cuff, box. —*n.* **2.** *The falling board gave him an awful whack on the head:* hit, blow, smack, clout, knock, belt, sock, wallop, thump, rap, bang; punch, slap, cuff, box. **3.** *Have a whack at opening this jar:* try, go, attempt, trial, turn, *Slang* crack, stab; endeavor, venture.

wharf *n. The shrimp boats unloaded their catch at the fishermen's wharf:* pier, dock, quay, marina, landing, landing dock, slip, jetty, breakwater.

wheedle *v. Mother tried to wheedle Father into going to the party:* coax, cajole, flatter, inveigle, charm, beguile, lure, entice, persuade, induce, *Slang* softsoap, butter up. —**Ant.** force, coerce, bully, browbeat, cow, intimidate, dragoon, bulldoze.

wheel *n.* **1.** *The American Indians had not discovered the wheel by the time European settlers arrived. The refrigerator is mounted on wheels:* disk mounted on an axle; roller, caster, drum. **2.** *Buy one of those big wheels of cheese:* ring, circle, hoop, round, disk. —*v.* **3.** *He wheeled about and saw a figure in the doorway. Dancers wheeled gracefully on the ballroom floor:* turn quickly, turn round, pivot, rotate, revolve, spin, swivel, whirl; circle, gyrate, swirl, twirl, pirouette. **4.** *Wheel the cart over to the checkout counter:* roll, push along on wheels.

wheeze *v.* **1.** *An allergy can make a person wheeze and sneeze:* breathe audibly, breathe with a whistling sound; breathe hard, gasp, puff, huff and puff, pant; hiss, whistle. —*n.* **2.** *The child had an asthmatic wheeze:* audible breath, whistling breath, gasp, puff, huffing and puffing, panting; whistle, hiss.

whelp *n.* **1.** *The mother wolf led her whelps out of the den:* pup, puppy; cub. **2.** *That young whelp needs a good whipping:* whippersnapper, cub, urchin, brat, mischievous boy; youngster, lad, youth, stripling, child, kid, boy.

wherewithal *n. They had no wherewithal to make headway:* means, resources, resorts, money, cash, funds, capital, bankroll, finances, purse, assets.

whet *v.* **1.** *The woodsman stopped chopping to whet his ax on the grindstone:* hone, grind, strop, sharpen, edge, put an edge on. **2.** *The smell of cooking whetted my appetite. The very first paragraph of the book whets the reader's interest:* arouse, excite, stir, awaken, kindle, stimulate, animate, quicken, pique, provoke, induce, tempt, allure, entice, make eager, make avid, make keen. —**Ant.** 1 dull, blunt. 2 quench, satisfy, sate, satiate, extinguish, deaden; slake, stifle, damp, dampen, cool.

whiff n. **1.** *A whiff of air stirred the leaves:* breath, puff, slight gust, draft; zephyr, breeze. **2.** *There's a whiff of honeysuckle in the air. Did you get a whiff of that awful cigar?:* faint smell, scent, odor, aroma, bouquet; sniff, smell, breath; hint, trace, soupçon.

while n. *They spent a while in the bar:* stretch, time, period, spell, bit, interim, interval, spell.

whim n. *The boy is spoiled because his mother caters to his every whim. Edith bought that dress on a whim:* fancy, fanciful notion, notion, quirk, whimsy, caprice, conceit, eccentricity, crotchet; sudden notion, urge, impulse, inspiration, vagary.

whimper v. **1.** *The child whimpered after he was spanked:* cry softly, sob brokenly, blubber; whine plaintively, snivel, sniffle, pule. —n. **2.** *The poet T. S. Eliot wrote that the world will end "not with a bang but a whimper":* sniveling, whine, sobbing, sob. —**Ant.** 1 whowl, bawl. 2 howl.

whimsical adj. **1.** *Jerry is much too whimsical to be a businessman:* fanciful, capricious, notional, eccentric, quixotic; fickle, fitful, inconsistent, erratic, changeable, chimerical. **2.** *Her essay on the care and feeding of husbands is pleasantly whimsical:* droll, amusing, waggish, fanciful, quaint. —**Ant.** 1 staid, serious, sedate, sober, practical, down-to-earth, pragmatic, matter-of-fact; steady, consistent.

whine v. **1.** *The child was whining because he was lost:* cry plaintively, whimper, snivel, mewl. **2.** *Don't whine about the low pay; ask for a raise:* complain, grumble, fret, grouse, gripe meekly. —n. **3.** *The little girl took the foul-tasting medicine without a whine. A whine of anguish came from the bereaved woman:* whimper, plaintive cry, snivel; wail, moan, cry, sob; murmur, complaint, mutter, grumble.

whip n. **1.** *Mule drivers need long whips:* horsewhip, rawhide, cowhide, thong, lash, strap, scourge, blacksnake, cat-o'-nine-tails, switch, birch rod, rod, rattan. —v. **2.** *The boy was whipped for playing hooky:* horsewhip, flog, strap, scourge, lash, switch, birch, cane; flagellate; beat, spank. **3.** *The team really got whipped in its last game:* trounce, drub, maul, beat decisively, defeat soundly, vanquish, rout, *Slang* lick. **4.** *The wind whipped through the trees:* lash, flick, flap; move violently, toss about. **5.** *The thief whipped the pen from my hand and ran off:* snatch, jerk, whisk, jolt. **6.** *Whip the cream and ladle it on top of the strawberries:* beat, beat into a froth, whisk.

whir v. **1.** *The machine whirred when he flipped on the switch:* run with a humming sound; drone, hum, buzz, whisper, purr. —n. **2.** *We heard the whir of the vacuum cleaner in the living room:* drone, hum, buzz, whisper.

whirl v. **1.** *The propeller began to whirl, and the small plane started down the runway:* turn, turn round, spin, rotate, revolve; twirl, pivot, gyrate, pirouette, wheel, circle, swirl. **2.** *Looking down from that height made my head whirl:* spin, reel; feel dizzy, feel giddy. —n. **3.** *The colorful whirl of the dancers was beautiful to watch:* turning, turn, spin, spinning, rotation, revolving, revolution, twirl, twirling, pivoting, pivot, gyration, pirouette, wheeling, circle, circling, swirling. **4.** *Christmas weekend was a whirl of parties:* rapid round, dizzy round, dizzying succession, flurry, merry-go-round; dither, state of excitement. **5.** *They said gardening was fun, so I gave it a whirl:* try, go, attempt, trial, whack, turn, fling, *Slang* crack, stab.

whirlpool n. *The swimmers were warned away from the whirlpool:* whirling current, maelstrom, vortex, whirl, swirl, eddy.

whirlwind n. **1.** *The whirlwind sucked up dust from the fields:* funnel-shaped column of rapidly rotating air; dust spout, waterspout; cyclone, twister. —adj. **2.** *The couple was married after a whirlwind courtship:* impetuous, headlong, breakneck, rash, impulsive, short, quick, rapid, swift, hasty. —**Ant.** 2 long, lengthy, plodding, leisurely; careful, thoughtful, well-considered.

whisk v. **1.** *Whisk the lint off your coat:* brush, sweep lightly, flick. **2.** *The visiting dignitary was whisked away to the mayor's office before reporters could question him. The car whisked past the intersection:* rush, speed, hasten, move quickly; race, spurt, shoot, tear, fly, whiz, sweep, zip, hurry, scurry, sprint, scoot, dash, bolt, dart, spring, bound, bowl along. **3.** *Whisk the egg whites until they are stiff:* beat, whip. —n. **4.** *With a whisk of his napkin the waiter removed the crumbs from the table:* sweep, brush, flick. **5.** *Either an eggbeater or a whisk may be used to whip the eggs and milk:* wire whisk, omelette whisk, French whisk. —**Ant.** 1 rub, scrape. 2 move slowly, crawl, creep, drag, inch.

whiskey or **whisky** n. **1.** *Whiskey can be distilled from corn, rye, barley, or other grains:* alcohol, liquor, hard liquor, spirits, moonshine, firewater, John Barleycorn, booze; *Slang* sneaky pete, redeye, mountain dew, juice, hooch, rotgut, white lightning, (*variously*) rye, Scotch, Irish, unblended, blended, bourbon, corn, vodka, gin, rum, *Irish & Scottish* usquebaugh, (*loosely*) aqua vitae, aquavit, eau-de-vie. **2.** *Give me a whiskey and soda:* shot of whiskey, *Informal* shot.

whisper v. **1.** *Whisper so no one else will hear. "I love you," he whispered:* speak softly, utter under the breath; murmur, mutter, sigh, breathe; confide, speak confidentially. **2.** *People have been whispering about those two for months. Don't whisper it to a soul:* gossip, make an insinuation, spread rumor, rumor, intimate, hint; reveal, divulge, disclose, tell, blurt, blab, bruit. **3.** *The wind whispered through the pines:* rustle, murmur, sigh; drone, hum, buzz. —n. **4.** *Don't talk above a whisper in here:* undertone, murmur, mutter; indistinct utterance. **5.** *There has never been a whisper about the banker's integrity:* insinuation, innuendo, rumor, piece of gossip, gossip; hint, suggestion, inkling. **6.** *Lis-*

ten to the whisper of the wind. This fire engine makes only a whisper when running at full speed: rustling sound, rustle, murmur, sigh; drone, hum, purr, buzz. —**Ant.** 1, 4 shout, scream, roar, bellow, yell, cry, whoop. 2 speak out; keep secret, keep confidential, keep under one's hat. 3, 6 roar.

whit n. He wasn't a whit sorry for what he'd done. Put some mustard on the sandwiches, but just a whit: least bit, little bit, speck, mite; dab, drop, dash, pinch, morsel, grain, smidgen, trifle, jot, tittle, dot, iota, modicum, scintilla; fragment, particle, crumb, snip, splinter, chip. —**Ant.** great deal, large amount, lot, heap, scads.

white adj. **1.** Kathy has beautiful white teeth: ivory, ivory-colored, pearl, pearly, snow-white, snowy, alabaster, milk white, cream-colored. **2.** She turned white with fear: colorless, pale, pallid, blanched, bleached, wan, ashen, ashy, pasty, ghostly, cadaverous, bloodless, sallow, gray, leaden. **3.** White hair can look distinguished. The fruit bowl was of white glass: gray, silver, silvery, hoary, frosty, snowy, grizzled; cloudy, smoky, filmy, translucent, chalky, milky, off-white. **4.** White settlers took the Indians' land: Caucasian, light-skinned; fair, blond. **5.** You told her a white lie when you said she looked good: harmless, unmalicious, benign, innocent. **6.** Her reputation is as white as snow: pure, spotless, unblemished, unsullied, unstained, unspotted, stainless, clean, immaculate; chaste, innocent, undefiled, virtuous. —**Ant.** 1 black, jet black, jet, coal black, ebony, raven, inky. 2 ruddy, flushed, rosy, rosy-cheeked, red, pink, florid, high-colored. 3 clear, colorless, transparent. 4 black, Negro; red, Indian; yellow, Oriental. 5 harmful, corrupting, sinister, malicious, vicious, venemous, malevolent, malign, pernicious, destructive. 6 evil, wicked, bad, nefarious, notorious; black, blemished, impure, sullied, stained, spotted, tarnished, besmirched.

whiten v. **1.** The new polish whitens shoes well. Use a stronger soap to whiten the wash: make white, make whiter, color white, frost, silver; clean, bleach, blanch, lighten. **2.** She whitened when she heard the bad news: pale, blanch, turn pallid, turn ashen, turn white. —**Ant.** 1 blacken; darken, dull. 2 flush, blush, color.

whitewash v. **1.** It's time to whitewash the basement walls again: paint with a mixture of lime and water, calcimine. **2.** The committee's report tries to whitewash the senator's misdeeds: excuse, justify, vindicate, absolve, exonerate; play down, downplay, minimize, soft-pedal, cover up, gloss over, glaze over, make allowance for.

whittle v. **1.** The old farmer loved to sit and whittle sticks. Grandfather whittled whistles from small sticks: cut away bit by bit, carve roughly, carve, pare, shave, chip away at. **2.** The company has whittled down its debt by about one-half. Faster planes have whittled an hour off the transatlantic crossing: reduce gradually, lessen the amount of, pare, cut, shave, slash, decrease, shorten, curtail, clip.

whiz v. **1.** The sentry heard a bullet whiz by his head: whistle, swish, sizzle, whir, whine, hiss, buzz, hum, drone. **2.** Trucks whizzed down the road past the slower cars: speed, race, shoot, tear, fly, spurt, zoom, zip, sweep, whisk, scoot, rush, hasten, scurry, scud, scuttle, dash, dart, sprint, bolt, bowl along, make time, make tracks. —n. **3.** The deer heard the whiz of the hunter's arrow and ran: swish, whistle, whir, whine, hiss, buzz, hum, drone. **4.** Informal Jean's really a whiz at bowling: expert, adept, prodigy, wizard, crackerjack, shark, genius; master, masterhand, skilled hand.

whole adj. **1.** The two boys ate a whole pizza by themselves. It rained the whole week: entire, complete, full, total, unabridged. **2.** Captive seals still prefer eating whole fish rather than pieces. Is whole milk healthier than skimmed?: in one piece, entire, undivided, uncut, unbroken; complete, intact, undiminished. **3.** After a month of recuperation he's whole again: sound, well, healthy, in good health, hale, robust, vigorous; unharmed, uninjured, unbroken, undiminished, perfect. —n. **4.** Buying the house will take the whole of your savings: entire amount, total, sum total, aggregate; bulk, major part, main part, body, essence, quintessence. **5.** The table and six chairs make up the whole. These items make up the whole of the contract: totality, entirety, ensemble, unit, system, assemblage, completeness. —**Ant.** 1 partial, incomplete. 2 divided, cut up, cut, broken, fractional. 3 sick, sickly, ill, ailing, unwell, diseased, feeble, faint, frail; injured, hurt, broken, flawed, imperfect. 4, 5 part, piece, segment, division, portion. 5 component, element, constituent; particular, detail, item.

wholehearted adj. The plan has my wholehearted support: sincere, unfeigned, true, heartfelt, deeply felt, complete, unreserved, unstinting, earnest, serious, enthusiastic, zealous, emphatic. —**Ant.** halfhearted, lukewarm, faint, indifferent, perfunctory, unenthusiastic.

wholesale adj. There was a wholesale evacuation of the city: mass, general, comprehensive, extensive, far-reaching, large-scale, sweeping, wide-ranging, widespread, overall.

wholesome adj. **1.** A wholesome diet is a must for energy and alertness: healthful, healthy, nutritious, nourishing, health-giving, strengthening, invigorating; sanitary, hygienic. **2.** The summer at camp gave the boy a wholesome look: healthy, hale, sound, well, hardy, vigorous; blooming, rosy-cheeked, clear-complexioned, fresh, chipper, bright-eyed, Informal bright-eyed and bushy-tailed. **3.** Wholesome friends, it is hoped, will never lead the girl astray. Little Women is a very wholesome book: morally healthy, moral, honorable, right-minded, responsible, virtuous, upright, nice, decent, pure, clean-minded, clean, innocent, uplifting, worthy, meritorious, exemplary, ethical, honest, principled, dutiful. —**Ant.** 1–3 unwholesome. 1 unhealthful, unhealthy, pernicious, harmful, detrimental, deleterious, noxious; unsanitary, unhygienic. 2 unhealthy, pale, wan, pallid, ashen, gray; sickly, ailing, diseased, feeble, frail, weak, exhausted, tired. **3** immoral, dishonorable, evil, evil-minded, wicked, sinful, bad, indecent, impure, dirty-minded, filthy, lewd, degrading, unworthy, unethical, dishonest, crooked, unprincipled.

wholly *adv. I'm wholly in agreement with you:* entirely, completely, fully, totally, *Latin* in toto; utterly, quite, perfectly, thoroughly, altogether, as a whole, in every respect, from beginning to end. **—Ant.** partially, incompletely, in part, somewhat, imperfectly, in some respects.

whoop *n.* **1.** *The Indian let out a bloodcurdling war whoop:* shout, yell, scream, cry, holler, shriek, roar, bellow, howl, screech, hollo, outcry, hue and cry; cheer, hurrah. *—v.* **2.** *The children whooped with joy:* shout, yell, cry, cry out, holler, shriek, screech, scream, howl, roar, bellow, hoot, rend the air; cheer, hurrah; hollo.

whopping *adj. She bought a whopping ice cream cone:* gargantuan, giant, gigantic, colossal, enormous, great, huge, immense, mammoth, massive, mighty, monstrous, mountainous, tremendous, prodigious.

whore *n. Daniel Defoe's novel* Moll Flanders *tells the story of a whore:* prostitute, hooker, woman of ill fame, woman of ill repute, fallen woman, harlot, bawd, hustler, strumpet, trollop, jade, doxy, woman of easy virtue, demimondaine, demirep, lady of the night, fancy woman, painted lady, tart, streetwalker, chippy, call girl, *Slang* pro, prosty; mistress, kept woman, courtesan, concubine; hussy, slut, wanton, tramp. **—Ant.** nice girl, good girl, honest woman, respectable woman, lady.

whorl *n. The petals of the flower are arranged in whorls around the center:* spiral arrangement, circular arrangement, spiral, circle, coil, convolution, curl, roll, corkscrew, helix.

wicked *adj.* **1.** *Wicked deeds must be repented:* evil, sinful, immoral, bad, iniquitous, reprehensible, vile, foul, base, gross, low, heinous, abominable, atrocious, hellish, fiendish, devilish, Satanic, nefarious, cursed, villainous, blackhearted, infamous, vicious, malicious, malevolent, evil-minded, shameful, scandalous, dishonorable, disgraceful, corrupt, depraved, degenerate, monstrous. **2.** *Wicked children should be punished:* naughty, mischievous, rowdy, impish, knavish, rascally, ill-behaved, incorrigible. **3.** *I have such a wicked toothache I'm in agony:* intense, severe, serious, acute, fierce, extreme, bad, raging, rampant, awful, dreadful, fearful, painful, bothersome, troublesome, galling. **—Ant.** 1 moral, wholesome, upright, righteous, honorable, good, noble, ethical, honest, principled, benevolent, worthy, exemplary. 2 well-behaved, well-mannered, obedient.

wide *adj.* **1.** *How wide is this living room? Canal Street is very wide:* broad, spacious, large. **2.** *The plane flew over the wide Arctic wastes. The group discussed a wide variety of subjects:* broad, extensive, vast, spacious, immense, great, boundless, far-flung, far-reaching, far-ranging, widespread. **3.** *Are the shoes wide enough for your feet?:* large from side to side, ample, roomy, commodious, capacious. **4.** *The children's eyes were wide with excitement as Santa Claus led the parade down the street. The girl's parents greeted her with arms wide:* wide open, fully open; expanded, dilated; extended, distended; outstretched, outspread. *—adv.* **5.** *The dentist said to "open wide." Leave the door wide open:* fully, completely, as far as possible. **—Ant.** 1–4 narrow. 1 long; deep. 2 restricted, constricted, limited, small. 3 tight, cramped, confined. 4 shut, closed, contracted. 5 barely, narrowly; partially.

widen *v. The city is going to widen Main Street. You ought to widen your circle of acquaintances:* make wider, broaden, spread, spread out, stretch; enlarge, expand, extend. **—Ant.** narrow, close, take in; reduce, decrease, contract.

widespread *adj.* **1.** *A widespread flu epidemic affected eighteen Western states:* affecting a large area, extending far and wide, far-flung, pervasive, far-reaching, extensive, broad; nationwide, worldwide. **2.** *She greeted her son with widespread arms:* wide open, fully extended, outspread. **—Ant.** 1 localized, narrow, restricted, confined, limited, small. 2 closed.

width *n. The lake's width was seven miles:* wideness, distance across, breadth, amplitude, broadness, diameter, extent, girth, measure, reach, span.

wield *v.* **1.** *Sir Lancelot was adept at wielding his sword:* handle, ply, manage, use, utilize, manipulate; brandish, flourish, wave, swing. **2.** *The sales manager wields tremendous power in this company:* exert, exercise, employ, apply, display, put to use, have and use.

wife *n. His wife is a business executive:* spouse, consort, companion, marriage partner; better half, helpmate, mate, helpmeet, rib, squaw, *Dialectal* woman, *Slang* missus, old lady; bride; married woman. **—Ant.** single woman, miss, spinster, old maid.

wig *n. The bald man bought a wig. The woman has a long blond wig for evening and a short one for daytime:* toupee, hairpiece; *Slang* carpet, rug, topper; fall, switch, wiglet, *Archaic* periwig, peruke.

wiggle *v.* **1.** *Can you wiggle your ears? Sit still, child, and stop wiggling!:* wag, waggle, shake, twitch, jerk, flutter, quiver; twist, squirm, writhe, wriggle. *—n.* **2.** *The squirrel made a little wiggle with his tail and jumped to another branch:* jerk, twitch, wag, waggle, flutter, shake; squirming, wriggling, writhing.

wild *adj., adv.* **1.** *Some wild horses still live in this valley. A pack of dogs runs wild in these woods:* living in a natural state, untamed, undomesticated, unbroken; feral, savage. **2.** *Have you ever eaten wild blueberries? Strawberries grow wild on this hill:* uncultivated; without cultivation, naturally, by themselves. **3.** *The National Park Service wants to leave the Everglades a wild region. After the settlers gave up, this area grew wild again:* untouched by man, uninhabited, uncultivated, natural; rugged, waste, bleak, desolate, abandoned; wooded, forested, overgrown. **4.** *Wild tribes still inhabit part of the Philippines. Aborigines still live wild in the jungle:* uncivilized, primitive, savage, barbaric; ferocious, fierce; in an uncivilized state, in a primitive state. **5.** *We ran into wild seas our third day out. The wind blew wild:* violent, furious, tempestuous, blustery, howling; rough, choppy, turbulent; wildly, violently, furiously. **6.** *A group of wild youths vandalized the school. His blazing eyes and wild talk frightened everyone. The mob ran wild in the streets:* unrestrained, disorderly, undisciplined, ungovernable, lawless, unruly, violent; frantic, frenzied, fanatical, rabid, raging, raving, berserk, crazed, insane, maniacal, mad, demented, unhinged; wildly, without restraint, lawlessly, violently, rampantly, insanely, maniacally, madly. **7.** *I took a wild guess at the answer. Is that another of his wild ideas to make us all rich?:* reckless, rash, uninformed, ill-advised, illogical; impractical, fantastic, bizarre, giddy, flighty, fanciful, madcap, harebrained, rattlebrained, *Slang* nutty, screwball; wide of the mark. —*n.* **8. the wild** or **wilds** *The hunter roamed the wilds for weeks at a time:* wilderness, bush; barren area, wasteland. —**Ant.** 1 domesticated, tame, broken. 2 cultivated, planted. 3 populated, inhabited, cultivated; bare, barren. 4 civilized, advanced; friendly. 5, 6 calm, mild, gentle, quiet; calmly, mildly, gently, quietly. 6 well-behaved, orderly, law-abiding, lawful, peaceful; serene, tranquil; rational, sane; politely, peacefully, serenely. 7 careful, thoughtful, well-advised; realistic, practical, logical, intelligent.

wilderness *n. The hunting cabin is far out in the wilderness:* wild, wilds, bush, unsettled area, remote area; wasteland, waste, barrens, badlands, desert, tundra, desolate tract.

wild-eyed *adj.* **1.** *The wild-eyed stranger fired his gun into the crowd:* wild, manic, maniacal, rabid, frantic, frenzied, raving, amuck, mad, crazy, berserk. **2.** *His wild-eyed schemes bore no fruit:* visionary, quixotic, unrealistic, extreme, fanatical, fanatic, harebrained, *Slang* far-out, off-the-wall. —**Ant.** calm, composed; sensible, practical.

wile *n.* **1.** Often **wiles** *She used all her feminine wiles to get him to go to the dance:* sly trick, trickery, artifice, ruse, subterfuge, contrivance, machination, chicanery, stratagem, maneuver, ploy, expedient, gambit, trap; cunning, artfulness, craftiness, guile, subtlety. —*v.* **2.** *Can't you wile Father away from the television set for one evening?:* lure, entice, seduce, charm; coax, cajole, persuade. —**Ant.** 1 frankness, openness, artlessness, simplicity, candor, straightforwardness, ingenuousness.

will *n.* **1.** *No one stands a chance against her will. The team has a strong will to win:* willpower, force of will, moral courage, self-discipline, strength of purpose, conviction; determination, resolution, resoluteness; desire, wish. **2.** *What is your will, my lord?:* desire, wish, preference, inclination, pleasure; longing, yearning, craving, hankering. **3.** *The store wants to keep its customers' goodwill. Woe to anyone who incurs her ill will:* feeling, personal feeling, disposition, attitude. **4.** *He died without leaving a will:* last will and testament, testament. —*v.* **5.** *You can succeed if you will it strongly enough:* be resolved for, resolve, desire, want, wish for, determine upon. **6.** *The deceased willed his vast estate to his daughters:* bequeath, endow, bestow, leave as an inheritance, confer, convey at death. —**Ant.** 1 irresolution, indecision, vacillation, wishy-washiness, indifference. 2 dislike, hatred, disinclination; loathing, detestation. 5 be irresolute, be indecisive, vacillate.

willful *adj.* **1.** *It wasn't accidental manslaughter; it was willful murder:* deliberate, purposeful, intentional, intended, planned, premeditated, studied, designed, contemplated. **2.** *There's no use arguing with such a willful person:* stubborn, obstinate, unyielding, uncompromising, inflexible, persistent, determined, headstrong, perverse, self-willed, intractable, obdurate, closed-minded, mulish, pigheaded; bullheaded; unruly, ungovernable, undisciplined. —**Ant.** 1 unintentional, unintended, accidental, involuntary, unpremeditated, unplanned. 2 compliant, acquiescent, manageable, submissive, amenable, agreeable; obedient, tractable, docile.

willing *adj. I'm willing to go if you are:* favorably inclined, content, favorably disposed, amenable, agreeable, responsive, compliant, not averse, game; ready. —**Ant.** unwilling, disinclined, reluctant, loath, averse.

willowy *adj. Most ballerinas are willowy:* gracefully slender, svelte, sylphlike, long-legged, lithe, lissome, supple, limber, pliant, flexible.

willpower *n. She had no willpower to give up drinking:* will, determination, drive, firmness, resolution, self-control, self-discipline, single-mindedness, strength, drive. —**Ant.** indecision, hesitancy; apathy, torpor, weakness.

willy-nilly *adv. It appears that inflation is going up willy-nilly:* whether or no, perforce, inevitably, unavoidably, inescapably, compulsively, irresistibly, helplessly, uncontrollably, come what may. —**Ant.** voluntarily, by design, intentionally, deliberately.

wilt *v.* **1.** *The roses were beautiful for a week, then wilted:* wither, droop, become limp; shrivel, die. **2.** *The old man's strength wilted away. His courage wilted when he saw the enemy:* wither, fade, wane, ebb, recede, subside, sink, dwindle, diminish, languish, decline, weaken, decrease, deteriorate, degenerate, flag, sag.

wily *adj. He's too wily to be trusted:* devious, sly, cunning, crafty, foxy, tricky, scheming, calculating, designing, intriguing, artful, deceptive, underhand, treacherous, deceitful, guileful, shifty, crooked; shrewd, sharp, alert. —**Ant.** open, candid, frank, sincere, honest, straightforward, aboveboard; innocent, simple, artless, guileless.

win *v.* **1.** *The team must win today. Unless the defenders are reinforced the invading troops will win:* be victorious, triumph, prevail, conquer, vanquish, overcome, master, carry all before one, win the day. **2.** *The actor won an Academy Award for his role in the film. The youth won his diploma in only three years:* earn, gain, attain, achieve, accomplish, realize, acquire, obtain, secure, get, procure, receive, collect, pick up; *Informal* bag, net. **3.** *Saint Olaf won Scandinavian converts to Christianity. Opponents of the plan must be won over:* convince, persuade, influence, convert, induce, sway, prevail on, bring round. —*n.* **4.** *Four more wins and the team will clinch the championship:* victory, triumph, success, conquest; winning game, winning contest. —**Ant.** 1–3 lose. 1 be defeated, be beaten, fail, miss. 3 alienate, estrange. 4 loss, defeat.

wince *v.* **1.** *The patient winced when he took the foul-tasting medicine. The boy winced when his father raised his hand to spank him:* grimace, make a face, flinch, shudder, draw back, recoil, shrink, quail, cower, cringe. —*n.* **2.** *She thought with an unpleasant wince of the money she had lost:* grimace, flinch, shudder, recoil, shrinking, quailing, cowering, cringing.

wind[1] *n.* **1.** *Is there enough wind to sail a kite today?:* air current, breeze, zephyr, draft, gust, blast, whiff, puff, *Regional* air. **2.** *The wind blew down several trees:* heavy wind, windstorm, gale, blow; (*variously*) tornado, twister, cyclone, hurricane, tempest, typhoon, whirlwind. **3.** **winds** *In this passage the winds carry the melody:* wind instrument, aerophone. **4.** *The blow knocked the wind out of him:* breath, air. **5.** *If the deer catches wind of us, he'll run into the woods. How could he have got wind of our plans?:* scent, smell; hint, suggestion, inkling, intimation, clue, whisper, information, intelligence, news, knowledge, tidings, report. **6.** *The challenger says he'll knock out the champ in the first round, but that's a lot of wind:* empty talk, idle talk, boasting, bombast, bluster, mere words, bluff, braggadocio, fanfaronade, twaddle, *Slang* hot air. —**Ant.** 1 calm, dead calm, calmness, stillness. 3 brass; percussions.

wind[2] *v.* **1.** *The stream winds through the valley. The hikers wound their way up the hill:* curve, bend, snake, wend, sinuate, twist, zigzag, ramble, wander, meander. **2.** *Wind the wire around the post. Wind the yarn into a ball:* coil, twist, curl, loop, twine, entwine, lap, fold; roll, twirl. —**Ant.** 1 go straight as an arrow, make a beeline.

winding *adj.* *A winding road led to the cabin:* twisting, turning, bending, circuitous, coiling, convoluted, deviating, intricate, involved, meandering, rambling, roundabout, serpentine, sinuous, snaky, tortuous, undulating, wriggly, writhing, zigzag, curving. —**Ant.** plumb, even, direct.

window *n.* *The room has windows on three sides:* opening to admit air or light; aperture, orifice, opening; (*variously*) dormer, bay, oriel, casement, transom, skylight, porthole.

windy *adj.* **1.** *March is usually a windy month. The house is on a windy hill:* breezy, blowy, gusty, blustery; windswept. **2.** *The senator always makes such windy speeches:* long-winded, wordy, rambling, meandering, verbose, garrulous, talkative, loquacious, gabby; empty, bombastic, grandiloquent, rhetorical. —**Ant.** 1

windless; calm, still. 2 terse, concise, pithy, succinct, pointed, trenchant.

wing *n.* **1.** *The goldfinch's wings are black with white bars. The gas tanks are in the airplane's wings:* pinion, pennon, ala; supporting surface, flap, aileron. **2.** *The master bedroom is in the east wing of the mansion:* section; annex, addition, extension, appendage, adjunct. **3.** *The actors stood in the wings waiting to go on stage:* side part of a stage, coulisse. **4.** *He belongs to the radical wing of the party:* faction, segment, fraternity, group, band, knot, clique, circle, set, coterie. —*v.* **5.** *The bird winged its way through the storm. The aircraft winged out over the Atlantic:* fly, soar, zoom; take wing, take to the air. **6.** *The shot winged the escaping convict:* hit in the arm, hit in the wing; wound slightly, graze, nick, clip.

wink *v.* **1.** *The comedian winked at his audience:* blink, nictitate. **2.** *The stars winked in the night:* twinkle, sparkle.

winner *n.* *The champ was winner by a knockout:* victor, champion, master, vanquisher, conqueror, *Slang* champ.

winning *adj.* *She had winning ways about her:* taking, engaging, charming, captivating attractive, winsome. —**Ant.** losing, repulsive.

winsome *adj.* *She is a very winsome young lady:* charming, engaging, winning, pleasing, attractive, agreeable, likable, amiable, sweet, appealing, comely, endearing, delightful, bewitching, lovable. —**Ant.** dull, boring; disagreeable, unpleasant; ugly, repulsive.

wintry *adj.* *The wintry weather didn't end until April:* cold, frosty, snowy, glacial, icy, chilly, frozen, arctic, polar, Siberian, ice-cold, ice-bound; stormy, bleak, harsh, cheerless, stark, dreary, gloomy. —**Ant.** summery, sunny, bright, warm, balmy.

wipe *v.* **1.** *Wipe your shoes on the mat. Wipe the crumbs off the table. Wipe wax on the scratched surface:* rub lightly; (*variously*) clean, swab, sponge, mop, scrub, scour, rub off; dry, towel; remove, take off, clean off; rub on, apply. **2.** *She told him to wipe the grin off his face:* remove, take away from, banish, get rid of, erase, eradicate. —*n.* **3.** *It takes more than a wipe or two to clean the oven:* swipe, rub, swab, stroke, brush.

wire *n.* **1.** *One of the connecting wires came loose:* metal thread, metal strand; electric wire, electric cable, filament. **2.** *The message came by wire. We received a wire saying they arrived safely:* telegraph, cable, radiotelegraph; telegram, cablegram. —*v.* **3.** *Wire the lid to the box. Is the garage wired for electricity?:* attach by a wire, fasten with wires, bind with wires; equip with wiring, install wires in. **4.** *Please wire me when you arrive:* telegraph, send by telegraph, cable.

wiry *adj.* **1.** *The child has black, wiry hair:* resembling wire, wire-like; stiff, brittle, kinky. **2.** *The gymnast was a wiry young man of twenty:* sinewy, lean, spare, lanky; strong and supple, agile, limber, pliant.

wisdom *n.* **1.** *Learning facts does not necessar-*

ily give one wisdom: good judgment, sagacity, understanding, profundity, judiciousness, discernment, comprehension, penetration, apperception, intelligence, brains. **2.** *The class will discuss the wisdom of Plato:* philosophy, teachings, principles. —**Ant.** 1 folly, foolishness, stupidity, nonsense, absurdity, senselessness, silliness.

wise[1] *adj. The judge is a very wise man:* having good judgment, sagacious, sage, sapient, understanding, profound, judicious, discerning, perceptive, perspicacious, intelligent, knowing, knowledgeable. —**Ant.** foolish, stupid, silly, injudicious, unwise.

wise[2] *n. This will in no wise infringe on anyone's rights:* way, manner, respect.

wish *v.* **1.** *I wish to retire next year. We wish you luck:* want, desire, hope, long, crave, yearn, pine, hunger, thirst, yen, aspire, set one's heart upon; desire one to have, want to come about. —*n.* **2.** *He tries to satisfy her every wish. Helen's wish is to visit Rome:* want, desire, hope, longing, craving, yearning, yen, aspiration, ambition; hunger, thirst, appetite, whim, fondness, love, penchant, inclination, leaning, partiality, predilection. **3.** *It is dangerous to go contrary to the king's wish:* request, command, will, desire, want. **4.** Usually **wishes** *Please accept our sincere wishes:* good wishes, best wishes, felicitations, congratulations, compliments.

wishful *adj.* **1.** *He is still wishful of becoming a millionaire:* hopeful, desirous, wanting, keen on, eager, bent upon, anxious, avid, ambitious, expectant, aspiring; longing, hankering after, craving, yearning, pining, hungering after, thirsting after. **2.** *His talk of going to Harvard is just wishful thinking:* wistful, fanciful, dreamy-eyed, overoptimistic.

wishy-washy *adj. He's so wishy-washy he can never make up his mind:* indecisive, irresolute, shilly-shallying, vacillating, tergiversating, equivocating, wavering, noncommittal, blowing hot and cold, straddling the fence; weak, ineffectual, ineffective. —**Ant.** decisive, resolute, unwavering.

wisp *n. There was a wisp of hair on the table:* snippet, tuft, strand, lock, piece, shock, shred, thread, tuft, twist, bit.

wistful *adj.* **1.** *The child gave a wistful look at the candy-store window:* desirous, yearning, longing, craving, hankering, pining. **2.** *Whenever she speaks of her youth, she has a wistful look on her face:* pensive, sadly thoughtful, reflective, musing, contemplative, meditative, introspective; melancholy, forlorn, sad, sorrowful, woebegone, doleful, mournful, disconsolate.

wit *n.* **1.** *A good after-dinner speech must contain some wit. Dorothy Parker's writing is known for its wit:* cleverness, sense of humor, humor, drollery, levity, jocularity, funniness, waggery, quickness at repartee; brightness, sparkle, vivacity. **2.** *The book is a collection of the wit of Will Rogers:* raillery, badinage, persiflage, banter, joking, witty sayings, witticisms, quips, jokes, gags. **3.** *The speaker is known as a wit:* witty person, humorist, joker, jokester, wag,

gagster, comedian, comic, wisecracker, jester, funster, epigrammatist, punster; satirist. **4.** *She showed a great deal of wit in handling the delicate situation:* intelligence, understanding, perception, comprehension, judgment, sense, good sense, common sense, wisdom, insight, penetration, perspicacity, acumen, sagaciousness, sagacity, discernment, astuteness, cleverness, shrewdness, cunning, intellect, *Informal* brains. **5. wits** *I was out of my wits with worry. Keep your wits about you when you're driving:* mind, sanity, composure, mental balance, coolheadedness; mental alertness. —**Ant.** 1 seriousness, gravity, solemnity, sobriety, dullness. 4 foolishness, stupidity, silliness, folly, dumbness, obtuseness.

witch *n.* **1.** *The witch put an evil spell on the young princess:* devil's consort, sorceress, female magician; (*loosely*) seeress, prophetess, enchantress, temptress. **2.** *She's nice but her sister's a witch:* hag, crone, harridan, ugly old woman, battle-ax, beldam, ogress; mean woman, shrew, virago, termagant, scold, fury, vixen.

witchcraft *n. The old woman was hanged for practicing witchcraft:* worship of the Devil, diabolism, the cult of Satan; sorcery, wizardry, necromancy, black magic, black art, witchery, voodoo, voodooism, hoodoo, conjuration, casting of spells, divination, enchantment, fetishism.

withdraw *v.* **1.** *He withdrew his hand from the back of her chair. Withdraw fifty dollars from the savings account. The knight withdrew his sword:* remove, take away, take off; extract, unsheathe. **2.** *The waiter withdrew after serving the meal:* retire, retreat, go away, go, move away, leave, depart, disappear, absent oneself, make oneself scarce, *Slang* vamoose, split. **3.** *I withdraw that last statement and ask that it be struck from the record:* retract, take back, recant; rescind, recall. —**Ant.** 1 put on; put in; sheathe. 2 arrive, come, come near, appear. 3 introduce, propose, advance, offer; repeat, reiterate.

withdrawal *n. They announced the offer's withdrawal:* retraction, relinquishment, removal, repudiation, departure, disavowal, disclaimer, disengagement, exit, exiting, exodus, resignation, retirement, retreat, secession, abandonment, abdication.

withdrawn *adj. The child is so withdrawn we're concerned about her:* retiring, reserved, uncommunicative, shy, reclusive, quiet, introverted, unsocial, unfriendly. —**Ant.** boisterous, extroverted, open, outgoing, sociable, friendly, gregarious, warm.

wither *v.* **1.** *Because of the drought, most of the fruit withered. Frosts withered the leaves until the trees were bare:* wilt, droop, shrivel, dry up, fade, dehydrate, desiccate, blast. **2.** *She withered him with one accusing look:* shame, cut down, humiliate, blast, abash, mortify. —**Ant.** 1 bloom, flower, blossom; flourish, thrive. 2 praise, compliment.

withhold *v.* **1.** *The company withholds part of its employees' earnings for income taxes:* hold back, hold, keep back, keep, retain. **2.** *The wit-*

ness was accused of withholding information: hold back, keep back, conceal, hide, refrain from disclosing, suppress, keep secret, cover up, hush up. **—Ant.** 1, 2 give, provide, furnish. 1 grant, bestow, confer, yield, let go; let loose, free, promote, advance, encourage. 2 reveal, disclose, divulge, expose, lay bare.

without *prep.* **1.** *We can't do without equipment:* not having, free from, in the absence of, lacking, outside of. *—adv.* **2.** *The carriage awaited without:* outside, out, externally, outdoors, out-of-doors, beyond.

withstand *v. A politician must be able to withstand public criticism. This dress material will withstand repeated washings:* stand up to, confront, resist, endure, bear, suffer, tolerate, weather, brave, defy; grapple with, cope with.

witness *v.* **1.** *Did anyone witness the robbery?:* see firsthand, see, observe, view, behold, look on; note, mark, notice, perceive; attend, be present at. **2.** *A notary public must witness the signatures on the contract. Severe damage witnessed the destructive force of the storm:* verify, certify, corroborate, authenticate, substantiate, document, validate, endorse, sign, countersign, initial; attest to, confirm, vouch for, testify to, give testimony of, evidence, establish, bear out. *—n.* **3.** *Were there any witnesses to the accident?* eyewitness, onlooker, observer, spectator, looker-on, beholder. **4.** *The attorney for the defense called his next witness:* person who gives testimony, person who gives evidence, testifier, attester, deponent. **5.** *His worried look is witness to the strain he's under:* evidence, testimony, proof, confirmation, corroboration, verification, authentication, substantiation, documentation, validation.

witty *adj. Mark Twain's writings are both witty and profound:* amusing, clever, funny, humorous, quick-witted, comic, jocular, jocose, mirthful, waggish, droll, whimsical; sparkling, bright, scintillating, brilliant. **—Ant.** serious, somber; sententious, dull, dry; sad, melancholy.

wizard *n.* **1.** *Merlin was King Arthur's wizard:* sorcerer, magician, conjurer, enchanter, medicine man; oracle, seer, soothsayer; necromancer, diviner, clairvoyant. **2.** *Informal That boy is a wizard at math:* genius, prodigy, expert, adept, virtuoso, *Slang* whiz, shark; sage; wise man.

wizened *adj. The wizened elf threatened the children:* withered, shrivelled, dried, gnarled, lean, mummified, shrunken, wilted, worn, wrinkled, reduced, diminished.

wobble *v.* **1.** *This ladder wobbles when you stand on it:* sway, teeter, totter, be unsteady, reel, stagger, waver, shake, quake, shimmy. *—n.* **2.** *Put something under the table leg to stop the wobble:* sway, swaying, teetering, tottering, unsteadiness, wavering, shake, shaking, shimmy, shimmying, quaking.

wobbly *adj. The wobbly chair couldn't bear his weight:* wavering, precarious, rickety, rocky, shaky, teetering, tottering, unbalanced, unstable, unsteady, unsure, vacillating, wavering, weak, rattletrap, insecure.

woe *n. Job's life was full of woe:* suffering, distress, affliction, trouble, misfortune, calamity, adversity, misery, trial, tribulation, wretchedness, torment, agony, torture, sorrow, grief, heartache, anguish, dejection, gloom, anxiety, worry, melancholy, depression, despair. **—Ant.** joy, delight, pleasure, good fortune, happiness, bliss, satisfaction.

woebegone *adj. The bankrupt man walked around with a woebegone look on his face:* woeful, suffering, distressed, troubled, miserable, wretched, agonizing, tortured, sorrowful, doleful, mournful, forlorn, grief-stricken, sad, anguished, dejected, gloomy, funereal, glum. **—Ant.** happy, cheerful, elated, smiling, joyful.

woeful *adj.* **1.** *The woeful news grieved the nation:* distressing, unhappy, tragic, wretched, agonizing, painful, cruel, sorrowful, doleful, grievous, sad, heartrending, heartbreaking, depressing, crushing, disheartening, lamentable, deplorable, calamitous, disastrous, dreadful, catastrophic. **2.** *I've never seen such a woeful bunch of job applicants:* of very poor quality, unpromising, unlikely, awful, hopeless, terrible, bad, dreadful, horrible, miserable, appalling. **—Ant.** 1 happy, joyous, joyful, delightful, glad, heartening, cheering, cheerful, ecstatic. 2 promising, likely, excellent, wonderful, fine.

woman *n.* **1.** *The girl dreamed of the day when she would be a woman:* adult female, lady; (*variously*) dowager, matron; damsel, maiden, maid. **2.** *Woman, like man, must strive for political freedom:* womankind, women, females, the female sex, the fair sex, the weaker sex. **3.** *The queen's women helped her put on the royal robe. A woman comes in twice a week to clean:* handmaiden, chambermaid, female attendant, lady-in-waiting, maid, maidservant, housekeeper, cleaning woman, charwoman. **4.** *According to the song, "Frankie and Johnny," she was his woman but he done her wrong:* paramour, lover, mistress, concubine, kept woman; sweetheart, ladylove, beloved, darling, inamorata, girl, girl friend, sweetie, sweetie pie, flame; wife, fiancée, steady girl. **—Ant.** 1–4 man. 1 girl. 3 butler, valet. 4 beau, boyfriend, *Slang* John; husband, fiancé.

wonder *v.* **1.** *I wonder what she sees in him. Joe says he didn't do it, but I still wonder:* be curious about, be inquisitive; speculate, conjecture, question, be doubtful, be uncertain; meditate, ponder, cogitate. **2.** *I wonder at her perennial youthfulness:* marvel, be wonderstruck, stand agog, be awed, be amazed, be dazed, be stunned, be stupefied, be dumbstruck, be surprised, be flabbergasted, gape, stare. *—n.* **3.** *The Rockies are but one of the natural wonders of the West:* phenomenon, marvel, miracle, wonderwork, rarity, spectacle, sight. **4.** *The audience watched the trapeze act in wonder:* amazement, astonishment, wonderment, awe, fascination, stupefaction. **—Ant.** 1 know, be sure, be certain, comprehend, understand, perceive, see, fathom, figure out; ignore, not care, be uninterested. 2 be unfazed, be unmoved, accept matter-of-factly. 3 common occurrence, commonplace, cliché. 4 apathy, unconcern, indifference; boredom.

wonderful *adj.* **1.** *The human brain is a wonderful part of the body:* causing wonder, awe-inspiring, miraculous, amazing, incredible, phenomenal, fabulous, fantastic, unique, singular, extraordinary, astonishing, astounding, staggering, fascinating, striking, surprising, spectacular. **2.** *We had a wonderful time:* excellent, admirable, marvelous, magnificent, good, fine, great, terrific, first-rate, capital, tiptop, smashing, super, sensational, fabulous, fantastic, superb, divine, crackerjack. **—Ant.** 1 ordinary, common, usual, mediocre, average, modest, paltry, indifferent, uninteresting. 2 awful, terrible, bad, dreadful, abominable, miserable, appalling, horrid, unpleasant, unpleasing, *Slang* lousy, god-awful.

wont *adj.* **1.** *She is wont to get up early:* accustomed, used, habituated, wonted. **—n. 2.** *It was his wont to jog every evening:* custom, habit, practice, use. **—Ant.** unaccustomed.

woo *v.* **1.** *Father wooed several girls before marrying Mother:* court, pay court to, seek the love of, seek the favors of, pay one's addresses to, pursue, chase, set one's cap for. **2.** *The mayor knew how to woo the voters:* try to persuade, solicit, petition, solicit the approval of, court, appeal to, pursue, address, sue, cajole, importune, entreat, curry favor with, *Slang* butter up.

wood *n.* **1.** *The room was paneled in the finest woods. Throw some more wood on the fire:* lumber, timber, boards, planks, siding, wallboard, clapboard; log, firewood, kindling. **2.** Usually **woods** *The cabin was in a clearing in the woods:* forest, timberland, woodland, wildwood, bush, brush, grove, copse, thicket, brake. **—Ant.** 2 prairie, grasslands, savanna, tundra, meadow, moor, mesa, desert, clearing.

wooden *adj.* **1.** *The books were packed in a large wooden crate:* made of wood, wood, frame. **2.** *I was amazed at how wooden she was on the dance floor:* stiff, rigid, unbending, inflexible, awkward, clumsy, ungainly, ungraceful. **3.** *She gave the stranger a wooden stare:* expressionless, dull, vacant, lifeless, unemotional, impassive, deadpan, poker-faced, glassy-eyed. **—Ant.** 2 lissome, supple, limber, lithe, pliant, pliable, flexible, graceful. 3 expressive, animated, lively, spirited, emotional, passionate, fervent.

woozy *adj.* *The blow on the head made him woozy:* giddy, befuddled, light-headed, muddled, faint, dizzy, fuzzy, hazy, foggy, shaky, punch-drunk, punchy. **—Ant.** clearheaded.

word *n.* **1.** *The baby said his first word today. Write your reply in as few words as possible:* meaningful combination of letters, articulate sounds, unit of discourse; term, expression, locution, appellation, designation, sobriquet. **2.** *Just let me say a word of thanks:* brief statement, remark, comment, utterance, phrase, pronouncement. **3.** *The department head wants to have a word with you:* short talk, chat, brief conversation, discussion, conference, consultation, audience, interview, tête-à-tête, chitchat,

dialogue, discourse, colloquy. **4. words** *They had words in the lobby and started to fight in the hall:* angry words, argument, quarrel, dispute, bickering, wrangling, altercation, contention, *Informal* set-to. **5.** *She sent word that she had arrived safely. What's the latest word from the war zone?:* message, communication, news, information, report, advice, tidings, intelligence; dispatch, bulletin, communiqué, letter, telegram, telephone call; rumor, gossip, hearsay, *Slang* scuttlebutt, tittle-tattle, poop, dirt, lowdown. **6.** *Ed gave me his word he would be here:* assurance, promise, word of honor, pledge, vow, avowal, assertion, declaration. **7.** *The troops got the word to begin moving out:* command, order, direction, decree, notice, summons, dictate, edict, mandate; decision, ruling, ultimatum; signal. **—v. 8.** *Try to word the letter in a friendly way:* phrase, put into words, find words for, express, articulate, voice, describe, explain.

wording *n.* *The wording of the law is ambiguous:* phrasing, phraseology, manner of expression, choice of words, language.

wordy *adj.* *Don't be so wordy, make the report as short as possible:* verbose, long-winded, windy, loquacious, garrulous, talkative, discursive, mumbling, roundabout, prolix, redundant, tautological; grandiloquent, bombastic, turgid, fustian, gushing, effusive, rhetorical. **—Ant.** concise, terse, succinct, pithy.

work *n.* **1.** *It took a lot of work to make that cabinet:* labor, effort, industry, exertion, toil, endeavor, drudgery, trouble, manual labor, elbow grease, sweat. **2.** *Cleaning out the attic is your work for this weekend:* piece of work, job, task, chore, employment, pursuit, assignment. **3.** *The unemployed man is looking for work. The youth decided to make retailing his work:* employment, job, paying job; line of work, occupation, profession, business, vocation, line, métier, trade, craft, calling, pursuit; function, duty, office. **4.** *This painting is one of Matisse's greatest works.* Treasure Island *is probably Robert Louis Stevenson's best-known work:* work of art, creation, composition, achievement, performance, handiwork, piece, product, production, endeavor, structure, output; (*variously*) painting, drawing, sculpture, book, opus, symphony, opera, concerto, song, building. **5.** *The old philanthropist will be long remembered for his good works:* deed, act, achievement, feat; exploit, enterprise, transaction. **6. works** *Before the days of pipelines, every town used to have its own gasworks:* plant, factory, mill, foundry, yard, shop, workshop. **7. works** *The jeweler opened the case and cleaned the works of the watch:* internal mechanism, moving parts, contents, insides, *Slang* innards. **—v. 8.** *The boy works part-time at the grocery. The mechanic had to work for hours to fix the car:* be employed, have a job, be occupied, do business, pursue a vocation; labor, toil, be industrious, exert oneself, apply oneself, endeavor, perform, drudge, slave, sweat, *Informal* use elbow grease, put one's shoulder to the wheel. **9.** *How* *does this machine work? It's a good idea, but it just won't work. It took six hours to work the jigsaw puzzle:* operate, function, perform, run, go, act; take effect, be effective, succeed; do, solve, execute, enact, transmit, achieve. **10.** *Work the dough into a ball:* shape, form, fashion, mold, make, manipulate. **11.** *Phil wants to work up to being a sales manager. The ship worked its way into the harbor:* make one's way, progress, move, maneuver, win, achieve, gain. **12.** *Even a great doctor can't work miracles. It's time to work some changes around here:* bring about, produce, cause, effect; originate, engender, beget. —*adj.* **13.** *Put on work clothes before beginning the job:* for working, of working. —**Ant.** 1, 2, 8 play. 1 child's play; ease, leisure. 2 recreation, entertainment, fun; rest, relaxation. 3 unemployment; vacation, leave, retirement; avocation, hobby, leisure-time activity. 8 entertain oneself, have fun, relax, take it easy, vacation. 11 remain, stay put, mark time. 12 nullify, counteract, reverse. 13 leisure, play.

workable *adj. It seemed a workable solution to everyone:* working, practicable, practical, applicable, functional, possible, usable, useful, viable, feasible. —**Ant.** impossible, hopeless.

worker *n. The plant employs 500 workers. The charity drive needs some more good workers to collect funds:* workingman, workingwoman, workman, laborer, toiler, laboring man, laboring woman, proletarian; hired hand, hand; employee, job holder, artisan, craftsman, wage earner, breadwinner; doer, performer, producer, achiever, *Slang* hustler, eager beaver; drudge, plodder, grind; workaholic. —**Ant.** employer; unemployed person, retiree; idler, loafer, good-for-nothing, do-nothing, *Slang* goldbrick, deadbeat, bum.

working *n.* **1.** *Working takes up about a third of the day:* labor, laboring, toil, industry, exertion, drudgery; employment, job, tasks, chores, assignments, business, profession, occupation, duty. **2.** *Do you understand the working of a computer?:* operation, action, functioning, performance. —*adj.* **3.** *Working mothers left their children at the day-care center:* employed, holding down a job, laboring. **4.** *The job requires a working knowledge of Spanish:* usable, useful, practical, effective, operative, functioning, fluent. —**Ant.** 1 play, playing, recreation, fun, entertainment; rest, relaxation, leisure. 3 nonworking, unemployed, jobless; retired, vacationing.

workmanship *n. The chair is a fine example of 18th-century workmanship:* craftsmanship, handiwork, manual skill, handicraft, handcraft; construction, manufacture, technique.

workout *n. She had a fifteen-minute workout:* exercise, drill, practice, rehearsal, session, training, tryout, warmup, conditioning.

world *n.* **1.** *China is the largest country in the world. Is there life on other worlds?:* the planet Earth, globe, Earth, wide world; planet, orb, heavenly body, celestial object, star. **2.** *Man cannot explain many things in the world:* creation, universe, cosmos, macrocosm; nature. **3.** *The world must unite in the war on pollution:*

mankind, humanity, men and women, the human race, humankind, people; the public, everyone, everybody. **4.** *The sequoia is the tallest member of the plant world. The news excited the world of science:* group, class, division, system, sphere, domain, realm; profession, industry. **5.** *It's nice to get away from the world once in a while:* human affairs, society, social intercourse, day-to-day living; material matters, secular things, mundane interests, worldly things. **6.** *The Egyptian pyramids are an outstanding achievement of the ancient world:* era, period, epoch, age, times, duration. **7.** *A vacation will do you a world of good:* a great deal, large amount, *Informal* lots, oodles, gobs, heaps. —**Ant.** 5 spiritual matters, aesthetic matters. 7 a little bit.

worldly *adj.* **1.** *Worldly things meant nothing to the monk:* earthly, terrestrial, mundane, temporal, secular, profane; material, mercenary; physical, corporeal, fleshly. **2.** *He's too worldly to be shocked by the scandal:* sophisticated, cosmopolitan, urbane, worldly-wise, blasé, knowing, shrewd, astute, experienced, callous, hard-boiled. —**Ant.** 1 spiritual, heavenly, celestial, divine, holy, sacred; ethereal, ephemeral, transcendental, nonmaterial. 2 innocent, naive, unsophisticated, artless, ingenuous.

world-weary *adj. The world-weary travelers arrived back:* apathetic, depressed, jaded, indifferent, uncaring, blasé, impassive, detached, listless, burned-out, downbeat, cynical. —**Ant.** optimistic, cheerful, hopeful.

worm *n.* **1.** *Worms are good bait for catfish:* small legless elongated animal; (*variously*) earthworm, angleworm, inchworm, tapeworm, intestinal worm. —*v.* **2.** *The hunters silently wormed their way toward the herd of antelope:* creep, crawl, wriggle, writhe, inch, edge, steal, infiltrate, penetrate, advance stealthily. —**Ant.** 2 run, dart, sprint, dash.

worn *adj.* **1.** *Those tires are too worn to be safe. Can you patch the worn place on this jacket?:* worn through, worn-down, worn-out, frayed, abraded, threadbare, worn to a thread, worse for wear; decrepit, dilapidated, shabby, weather-beaten, battered, tumbledown, rickety, seedy, timeworn; faded, dingy. **2.** *The patient looked worn and pale:* exhausted, fatigued, worn-out, weary, wearied, spent, tired, dog-tired, haggard, played out, ready to drop, drooping; weak, enfeebled, wasted, debilitated; pinched, drawn. —**Ant.** 1 new, brand-new, spanking new, none the worse for wear. 2 energetic, vigorous, peppy, alive, dynamic, refreshed, restored, rejuvenated.

worrisome *adj.* **1.** *That boy is so worrisome he'll be the death of me:* causing worry, troublesome, aggravating, annoying, irritating, tormenting, vexing, trying, irksome, bothersome, disturbing, pesty. **2.** *Aunt Sue is so worrisome she never has a moment's peace:* tending to worry, anxious, apprehensive, uneasy, despairing, fretful, fussy. —**Ant.** 1 soothing, calming, nonirritating. 2 confident, secure; carefree, nonchalant, devil-may-care, lackadaisical.

worry v. **1.** *Mother always worries when the girls stay out late. Don't worry, tomorrow will be better:* be anxious, feel uneasy, be apprehensive, be disturbed, be troubled, be distressed, agonize, fret, despair, lose heart, be downhearted, be heavyhearted, be afraid, dread, brood over, stew. **2.** *Lack of rain is beginning to worry the farmers. Stop worrying me and get to work:* make anxious, make uneasy, disturb, upset, perturb, agitate, trouble, distress, harass, harry, badger, hector, bother, pester, vex, beset, plague, torment, persecute. —n. **3.** *The wayward boy caused his parents a lot of worry:* anxiety, uneasiness, apprehension, concern, misgiving, consternation, dismay, trouble, distress, bother, grief, anguish, torment, agony, misery, woe, difficulty, care, vexation. **4.** *Cancellation of the game is our chief worry:* concern, care, problem, dread, *Slang* bugaboo. —**Ant.** 2 comfort, solace, console, soothe, calm, allay. 3 certainty, assurance, security, trust, certitude; calm, composure, equanimity, serenity, tranquillity, placidity, quiet, peace of mind; comfort, solace.

worsen v. *The patient's condition continued to worsen:* decline, deteriorate, slip, go downhill, slide, take a turn for the worse, degenerate, lapse, fail, retrogress, erode, disintegrate, go to pieces. —**Ant.** improve, better, get better, ameliorate.

worship n. **1.** *The worship of idols is called "idolatry" in the Bible:* adoration, veneration, exaltation, reverence. **2.** *Worship is on Sunday at 11 A.M.:* divine service, religious service, devotionals. —v. **3.** *Each religion worships God in its own way:* pray to, adore, revere, venerate, reverence; glorify, exalt, praise, extol. **4.** *He has worshiped his older brother since he was a kid:* idolize, adore, revere, esteem, admire, adulate, dote upon, lionize, put on a pedestal. —**Ant.** 4 hate, detest, loathe, despise, scorn, disdain.

worth n. **1.** *A college education will be of great worth to you later:* use, usefulness, utility, benefit, value, good, merit, worthiness, importance, consequence, justification. **2.** *The appraiser put a worth of a thousand dollars on the ring:* value, price, cost, selling price, market price, current price, going price; valuation, appraisal. **3.** *His net worth is reckoned at over a million dollars:* assets, wealth, resources, holdings, real property, possessions, effects, estate. —**Ant.** 1 uselessness, fruitlessness, futility, worthlessness, inutility; drawback, handicap. 3 debts.

worthless adj. *The plot of land he bought proved to be worthless. Joe's ideas are usually worthless:* without value, useless, unusable, unavailing, unproductive, ineffectual, pointless, fruitless, bootless, futile, meritless, meretricious; unimportant, inconsequential, insignificant, trivial, paltry, piddling, undeserving, of no account, good-for-nothing, not worth a straw. —**Ant.** worthwhile, worthy, valuable, precious, profitable, useful, usable, utilitarian, productive, effective, fruitful; important, consequential, significant.

worthwhile adj. *Here's some worthwhile advice to any young businessman. So few movies are worthwhile nowadays:* valuable, worthy, profitable, rewarding, useful, usable, beneficial, good; worth one's time, worth the effort. —**Ant.** worthless, unworthy, useless, pointless, valueless, time-consuming, unimportant, inconsequential, trivial, of no account.

worthy adj. **1.** *The people gave generously to support the worthy cause. The school has graduated many worthy young people:* worthwhile, deserving, praiseworthy, laudable, commendable, admirable, estimable, excellent, good, meritorious, suitable, fit, fitting, befitting, appropriate, proper, creditable, honorable, virtuous, moral, ethical, reputable, upright, decent, respectable, noble, honest, reliable, trustworthy. —n. **2.** *The mayor and other local worthies were at the hearing:* notable, dignitary, leader, official, person of distinction, great man, great woman, personage, name, immortal, luminary, a somebody, pillar of society, *Slang* VIP, bigwig, big shot, big wheel. —**Ant.** 1 unworthy, worthless, undeserving, useless, unproductive, ineffectual; dishonorable, disreputable, ignoble, dishonest, unethical, unreliable, untrustworthy, *Slang* no-account. 2 member of the rank and file, nobody, anonym, anonymity, one of the little people, obscure person, obscurity; everyman; Tom, Dick, and Harry, *Slang* Joe Blow.

wound n. **1.** *The blow made a wound over his left eye:* laceration, gash, cut, slit, lesion; contusion, bruise. **2.** *The argument caused a wound that has never healed:* hurt feelings, trauma, provocation, irritation, vexation, pain, sting, distress, affliction, anguish, torment; hurt, injury, damage. —v. **3.** *The bullet wounded the policeman in the left arm:* lacerate, gash, cut, slash, tear, pierce, bruise; hurt, injure. **4.** *Her nasty remark really wounded him:* hurt the feelings of, offend, pain, sting, distress, grieve, mortify, torment; harm, damage, hurt, injure. —**Ant.** 3, 4 heal. 4 appease, assuage, calm, soothe, comfort.

wraith n. *The wraith was said to appear at midnight on the stairs:* ghost, spirit, shade, specter, apparition, doppelganger, phantom, phantasm, banshee, spook, materialization, revenant.

wrangle n. **1.** *The wrangle over uniforms continued unabated:* squabble, bickering, altercation, argument, clash, dispute, flap, fracas, quarrel, row, rumpus, tiff, disagreement. —v. **2.** *They wrangled about where to take a vacation:* squabble, quarrel, argue, bicker, contend, disagree, dispute, fall out, quarrel, quibble, row, scrap, spat, tiff, *Informal* bump heads, cross swords, have words, lock horns.

wrap v. **1.** *Buy tissue paper to wrap the gift. Wrap a bandage around his arm:* wrap up, enclose, enwrap, bundle, encase; bind, wind, fold. **2.** *The valley was wrapped in a dense fog:* clothe, cover, envelop, enclose, swathe, enfold, surround, girdle, gird, shroud, cloak, veil, mask, hide, conceal. —n. **3.** *Take a wrap in case the weather turns cool:* (variously) shawl, cloak, cape, stole, mantle, wrapper, scarf; sweater, jacket, coat. —**Ant.** 1 unwrap, unbundle; unbind, unwind, undo. 2 uncover, expose, reveal, open.

wrapper also **wrapping** n. The phonograph record came in a colorful wrapper: paper wrapping, envelope; covering, case, slipcase, casing, sheath, jacket, container.

wrath n. Don't contradict her or you'll feel the full force of her wrath: anger, rage, fury, vexation, irritableness; ire, indignation, rancor, resentment, hostility, animosity, animus, irritation, displeasure, spleen, choler, gall, bile. —**Ant.** appeasement, calm; kindness, friendship, geniality, affability, tenderness, forgiveness.

wrathful adj. The wrathful leader punished his disciples: angry, ireful, irate, furious, enraged, raging, incensed, resentful, indignant. —**Ant.** equable, pleased.

wreak v. The hurricane wreaked havoc on the town. The angry troops wreaked vengeance on the civilian population: inflict, visit, work, execute; retaliate with, vent, indulge, give full rein to, unleash.

wreath n. The President placed a wreath on the tomb of the Unknown Soldier: garland, laurel, lei, festoon; coronet, crown, chaplet, diadem.

wreck v. **1.** The airplane skidded off the runway and wrecked two hangars. Lack of money wrecked our vacation plans: ruin, destroy, demolish, level, raze, smash, shatter, break, break to pieces, devastate, ravage, Slang total. —n. **2.** The new owners let the house become a wreck. After the scandal, Henry became a complete wreck: dilapidated structure, ruin, mess; sick person, ailing person, debilitated person; derelict, wretch. **3.** The wreck was towed into port for salvage: shipwrecked vessel, stranded ship, derelict, damaged remains, ruins. **4.** Budget cuts mean the wreck of all our plans: ruin, destruction, devastation, undoing, dissolution, disruption, overthrow, upset, breakup, crash, crack-up; end, death, finish, annihilation. —**Ant.** 1 build, create, construct; save, salvage, preserve, conserve, protect. 4 formation, formulation, creation; preservation, salvage, saving, conservation, protection.

wrench v. **1.** The policeman wrenched the knife from the attacker's hand: twist, wrest, wring, force, pull, jerk, tear, rip. **2.** The baseball player wrenched his ankle on the play: twist painfully, sprain, strain. **3.** Don't wrench the facts in order to make the report more exciting: distort, twist, warp, put in a false light, pervert, misrepresent. —n. **4.** The plumber took out a wrench and tightened a bolt on the pipe: (variously) monkey wrench, socket wrench, British spanner. **5.** With one quick wrench he opened the jar: twist, wring, jerk, pull; tear, rip. **6.** The ice skater had a wrench in his left ankle: sprain, strain, painful twist.

wrest v. **1.** The bully tried to wrest the ball from the smaller boy's hands: wrench, twist, wring, take, grab, pull, jerk, tear, rip, force. **2.** The settlers found it hard to wrest a living from the rocky soil: obtain, get, gain, attain, achieve, secure, earn, make, glean, extract, squeeze. —**Ant.** 2 yield, give, furnish, supply.

wrestle v. **1.** Mother forbade the boys to wrestle for fear they would tear their clothes: engage in wrestling; tussle, scuffle, grapple. **2.** I've been wrestling with this problem for weeks: struggling, grapple strive, contend, struggle, tussle, labor, toil, battle, attempt to find a solution.

wretch n. **1.** The poor wretch was shivering in the doorway: unfortunate, miserable being, unhappy person, sufferer; outcast, castoff, misfit, homeless person, vagabond, hobo, tramp, derelict, waif. **2.** The miserable wretch deserted his wife and children: contemptible person, vile fellow, villain, scoundrel, rotter, worm, blackguard, rascal, rogue, knave, scalawag, varlet, swine, pig, cur; Slang louse, rat, stinker.

wretched adj. **1.** The wretched man hadn't eaten in three days. Why does Jane have such a wretched look on her face?: pitiable, pitiful, unfortunate; pathetic, miserable, unhappy, hapless, woebegone, forlorn, downcast, doleful, cheerless, crestfallen, despondent, disheartened, depressed, dejected, abject, broken-hearted, inconsolable, disconsolate, crushed, melancholy, sorrowful, gloomy, worried, low-spirited, despairing, hopeless, sick at heart. **2.** The wretched landlord refuses to have the furnace repaired. What nerve to charge $10 for that wretched meal!: contemptible, despicable, mean, miserable, vile, low, base, niggardly; inferior, worthless, sorry, awful, terrible, dreadful, rotten, abominable, Informal lousy, shabby, scruffy, sleazy. —**Ant.** 1 fortunate, enviable, prosperous, flourishing, successful, thriving; happy, cheerful, gay, carefree, lighthearted, jovial. 2 noble, admirable, excellent, good, wonderful, fine, great, worthy.

wriggle v. The children wriggled under the porch: squirm, worm, writhe, crawl, slink, turn, twist, waggle, dodge.

wring v. **1.** Wring the water out of the bathing suit before hanging it up to dry. He wrung my hand in gratitude: twist, force by twisting; squeeze, press, compress, choke. **2.** Isn't there any way to wring the truth out of the suspect?: force, coerce, wrest, wrench, extract. **3.** His sad story wrung our hearts: affect sorrowfully, sadden, grieve, distress, agonize, rend, pain, hurt, torture, pierce, stab. —**Ant.** 2 coax, wheedle, cajole, entice, beguile, inveigle, charm. 3 gladden, fill with joy, cheer, uplift.

wrinkle[1] n. **1.** The shirt didn't have a wrinkle in it. After forty, many people get wrinkles around their eyes: crease, rimple, crinkle, crimp, pucker, furrow, crumple, corrugation, fold, gather, pleat; crow's-feet. —v. **2.** Hang up your dress so it won't wrinkle: crease, rumple, crinkle, crumple, pucker, crimp, furrow, fold, gather, pleat.

wrinkle[2] n. Putting wheels on a bobsled for summer use is a new wrinkle: trick, device, gimmick; idea, notion, fancy; viewpoint, point of view, slant.

writ n. The attorney got a writ so he could examine the company's books: court order, mandatory order, sealed order.

write v. **1.** Many six-year-olds already know how

to write. Write your name and address at the top of the page: be literate; set down, write down, jot down, record, put on paper, put in writing, put in black and white, scribble, scrawl, take pen in hand; transcribe, copy; inscribe. **2.** *He wrote his first novel at seventeen:* compose, produce, turn out, dash off, *Informal* author, pen. **3.** *The lawyer is writing a contract for the partnership:* draw up, draft, make out. **4.** *Deceit was written all over his face:* be evident, be manifest, be conspicuous, be apparent, be patient, show, stand out, be visible. **—Ant.** 1 be illiterate; say, speak, tell. 4 hide, conceal, mask, cloak, veil.

writer *n.* **1.** *I'm not much of a writer, so don't expect a letter. The boy can print, but he's still a poor writer:* letter writer; penman, calligrapher, scribe, copyist, scribbler, scrawler. **2.** *Tolstoy is a famous Russian writer. He's a sportswriter for the Tribune:* author, professional writer; (*variously*) novelist, playwright, dramatist, poet, essayist, littérateur, reporter, journalist, newspaperman, newspaperwoman, correspondent, reviewer, critic, columnist, scriptwriter, screenwriter, television writer, songwriter, librettist, *Informal* hack, penny-a-liner. **—Ant.** 2 reader; viewer; listener.

writhe *v. The patient was writhing in pain until the doctor gave him an injection:* twist about, flail, thresh, thrash, jerk, contort, toss about, squirm, wiggle, wriggle.

writing *n.* **1.** *The actual writing of the report took about two days:* writing down, jotting down, putting on paper, composing, drafting, turning out, dashing off, *Informal* authoring, penning; transcribing, recording, copying, inscribing. **2.** *I won't believe it until I see it in writing. Can you read his writing?:* written form, print, handwriting, penmanship, longhand, calligraphy. **3.** *According to this writing, the deed is valid. The class is studying the writings of 18th-century novelists:* (*variously*) document, letter, diary, journal, composition, publication, book, work, volume, tome, opus, novel, play, story, poem, essay, article, report, editorial, column, critique, manuscript, script, libretto. **—Ant.** 1, 3 reading; speech, talk, address.

wrong *adj.* **1.** *Cheating is always wrong:* immoral, evil, wicked, sinful, bad, iniquitous, wrongful, dishonest, unethical, dishonorable; unlawful, illegal, illicit, felonious, crooked, criminal, unfair, unjust; unwarranted, unjustifiable, inexcusable, blameworthy, reprehensible. **2.** *Three wrong answers and you fail the test:* incorrect, erroneous, untrue, false, inaccurate, mistaken, faulty, fallacious, inexact, wide of the mark; illogical, unsound. **3.** *Such dark wallpaper is all wrong for a playroom. Did I say the wrong thing?:* improper, incorrect, unsuitable, inappropriate, undesirable, unbecoming, unseemly, unfitting, unfit, unbefitting, indecorous, inapt, un-

happy, infelicitous, incongruous, malapropos; indelicate, immodest. **4.** *Something's wrong with the motor:* faulty, amiss, out of order, in bad condition, out of kilter, out of gear, awry; ruined, *Slang* kaput. **5.** *Iron the skirt on the wrong side:* inverse, reverse, opposite. **—n. 6.** *A sane man knows the difference between right and wrong. He was condemned by the community for his wrongs:* immorality, evil, wickedness, sinfulness, iniquity, unrighteousness, dishonesty, unlawfulness, illegality, unfairness, injustice; immoral act, evil deed, sin, vice, offense, crime, misdeed, wrongdoing, injury, villainy, transgression, trespass. **—adv. 7.** *You guessed wrong:* incorrectly, erroneously, inaccurately, mistakenly. **—v. 8.** *Does he really think I wronged him?:* ill-treat, mistreat, maltreat, treat unjustly, treat unfairly, abuse, dishonor, harm, injure, hurt, ruin; cheat, defraud, bilk, swindle, fleece; impose upon, encroach upon. **—Ant.** 1–3, 5–7 right. 1 moral, virtuous, righteous, rightful, godly, good, honest, ethical, highminded, honorable, lawful, legal, just, fair; admirable, commendable, praiseworthy, worthy, meritorious, laudable. 2 correct, true, accurate, exact, precise, perfect; logical, sound, sensible. 3 proper, correct, suitable, appropriate, becoming, seemly, fit, fitting, befitting, meet, happy, felicitous. 6 morality, righteousness, goodness, godliness, honesty, highmindedness, lawfulness, legality, justice, fairness; virtue, good deed. 7 correctly, accurately, truly, exactly, precisely.

wrongdoer *n. Police apprehended the wrongdoers:* malefactor, perpetrator, miscreant, knave, evildoer, villain, culprit, felon, lawbreaker, transgressor, sinner, scoundrel, blackguard, trespasser, offender, rogue, rascal.

wrongful *adj. She sued for wrongful dismissal:* unlawful, illegal, illegitimate, lawless, blameworthy, criminal, dishonorable, immoral, improper, reprehensible, unethical, unfair, unjust, wicked. **—Ant.** rightful, lawful, legal, ethical, fair, honest, honorable, just.

wrongheaded *adj. We were wrongheaded in not accepting the idea:* perverse, stubborn, contrary, ornery, balky, wayward, obstinate, unreasonable, froward.

wrought *adj.* **1.** *The woman bought a delicately wrought silver tray:* worked, formed, made, fashioned, crafted, handcrafted, constructed. **2.** *The tourist bought a tray of wrought brass in the native bazaar:* hammered, beaten.

wry *adj.* **1.** *When the foreman makes that wry face, he's displeased:* twisted, crooked, contorted, distorted, askew, awry, warped. **2.** *His wry remark was meant to make her laugh, but it hurt her feelings:* ironic, cynical, sarcastic, caustic, sardonic, satiric, bitter, perverse; amusing, droll, dry. **—Ant.** 1 straight, direct, symmetrical.

xenophobic *adj. The xenophobic faction wanted to restrict immigration:* ethnocentric, bigoted, biased, racist, restrictive, exclusive, exlusionary, chauvinist, chauvinistic, jingoistic, insular, prohibitionary, closed-door, discriminatory, intolerant, biased, bigoted, racist. **—Ant.** welcoming, inclusive.

x-rated *adj. The x-rated movie drew big crowds:* erotic, sexy, sexual, adult, salacious, lewd, bawdy, ribald, obscene, pornographic. **—Ant.** clean, wholesome, innocuous.

x-ray *v.* **1.** *They x-rayed the patient:* roentgenize. **—n. 2.** *The doctor took several x-rays of my broken ankle:* roentgenogram, roentgenograph, radiogram, radiograph.

yacht *n. She sailed a yacht in the Caribbean:* sailboat, sailing boat, sloop, racer.

yahoo *adj. All the yahoos hated the ballet:* boor, vulgarian, churl, lout, barbarian, know-nothing, ignoramus, redneck, ruffian, Neanderthal, slob; rube, yokel, hayseed, hick, groundling; dullard, dope, dunce, buffoon, *Slang* clown, dimwit, bozo.

yank *v.* **1.** *The boy yanked the jump rope out of the girl's hand and threw it in the tree. The dentist yanked the abscessed tooth:* pull suddenly, jerk, wrest, tug, snatch, wrench; pull out, pluck, extract, draw out. **—n. 2.** *Give the door a good yank to close it:* pull, jerk, tug, wrench. **—Ant.** 1, 2 push, shove.

Yankee also **Yank** *n.* **1.** *The whaling ship's crew consisted of Yankees and Kanakas:* New Englander. **2.** *Tex boasted he would knock the daylights out of the next Yankee he met:* Northerner, damn Yankee, *Historical* Union soldier. **3.** *The Yanks distinguished themselves at Belleau Wood. Yankee go home!:* US citizen, US serviceman, *Historical* doughboy, teddy, GI, American, *Spanish* yanqui; (*disparagingly*) gringo.

yap *v.* **1.** *The little Pekingese yapped all night long:* bark shrilly, yelp, yip, yawp. **2.** *Marilyn is always yapping about some new diet. What's the opposition party yapping about now?:* talk incessantly, talk foolishly, chatter, jabber, gabble, babble, blather, prattle, rave, rave on, gush, blab, gossip, tattle; talk, lecture, scold, complain; converse, palaver. **—n. 3.** *The puppy gave a series of yaps and ran out the door:* shrill bark, yelp, yip, yawp.

yard¹ *n. The children are playing in the yard:* ground surrounding a building, grounds; enclosure, compound, confine, close; courtyard, court; garden, lawn, pasture.

yard² *n.* **1.** *Will two yards of dress material be enough?:* three feet, 36 inches, .914 meter; *abbreviation* yd. **2.** *The captain threatened to hang the mutineers from the yard:* yardarm, horizontal spar.

yarn *n.* **1.** *Buy some yarn and Aunt Judy will knit you a sweater:* spun thread, knitting thread, weaving thread. **2.** *The old sailor told us some yarns about whaling:* tale, story, anecdote, adventure story, narrative, account, adventure, experience.

year *n.* **1.** *That incident happened two years ago. The company's fiscal year ends on October*

XYZ

15th: period of 365 days (or in leap year 366 days), 12-month period, 52-week period, period of Earth's revolution around the sun. **2.** *The Martian year is 687 of our days:* period of planet's revolution around the sun. **3. years** *The boy seemed very mature for his years:* age, time of life. **4. years** *The country went through years of turmoil:* period, time, era, epoch, cycle.

yearly *adj. They paid yearly dues:* annual, once a year, per annum, perennial, regular, yearlong.

yearn *v. Do pregnant women really yearn for sour pickles?:* crave, have a strong desire, want, long, hanker, ache, hunger, thirst, wish, languish, pine, sigh, have a fancy for, set one's heart upon, be bent upon, have a passion for. **—Ant.** detest, despise, hate, loathe, abhor, abominate, be repelled by, recoil from, be revolted by, shudder at.

yearning *n. The city dweller had a yearning to return to the wide-open spaces:* craving, longing, hankering, yen, hunger, thirst, ache, strong desire, fancy, wish, want, desire, passion, aspiration, inclination.

yell *v.* **1.** *The lost man yelled, hoping someone in the woods would hear him. The crowd yelled when the hometown team scored a touchdown:* cry out, shout, holler, scream, bellow, roar, howl, shriek, bawl, whoop, yowl, hollo, hoot, screech, squall, yelp, clamor, rend the air, raise one's voice; cheer, hurrah, huzzah; boo. **—n. 2.** *The girl gave a yell of delight when the dollhouse was delivered. The angry yells of the crowd drowned out the announcer's voice:* cry, outcry, shout, holler, scream, bellow, roar, howl, shriek, whoop, hoot, screech, squeal, yelp, hollo, clamor; cheer, hurrah, huzzah; boo.

yellow *adj.* **1.** *A yellow scarf would look nice with that dress:* yellow-colored, lemon, canary, gold, ocher, mustard-yellow, saffron, yellow-orange, flaxen, straw-colored, blond. **2.** *Informal They said that if he didn't fight he was yellow:* cowardly, timorous, pusillanimous, craven, faint-hearted, afraid, fearful, apprehensive, frightened, *Slang* chicken, lily-livered, chicken-hearted. **—v. 3.** *Bleach keeps the white clothes from yellowing:* turn yellow; make yellow. **—Ant.** 2 brave, courageous, fearless, bold, daring, audacious, venturesome, unafraid, stout-hearted, lionhearted, *Slang* game. 3 bleach, whiten, brighten.

yelp *n.* **1.** *The dog gave a yelp when I stepped on his paw:* sharp cry, yap, howl, yip, bark, squeal. **—v. 2.** *The girls yelped with glee when the singing star appeared:* cry shrilly, scream, shriek, screech, bark, squeal, clamor, holler, shout; yap, yip, howl.

yen *n.* **1.** *After two weeks of vegetarian meals, the man had a yen for a big thick steak:* craving, longing, hankering, yearning, hunger, thirst, appetite, aching, desire, fancy, wish, want, passion, aspiration, inclination, relish. **—v. 2.** *The* *miner yenned for fresh air and sunlight:* crave, long, hanker, yearn, ache, hunger, thirst, wish, pine, sigh, languish, desire, fancy, wish, want, set one's heart upon, be bent upon, have a passion for. **—Ant.** 1 hatred, loathing, abhorrence, revulsion. 2 detest, despise, hate, loathe, abhor, abominate, be repelled by, recoil from, be revolted by, shudder at.

yes *adv.* **1.** *Yes, you are right:* aye, yea, it is so, just so, true, granted, of course, surely, really, truly, verily, to be sure, assuredly, certainly, indeed, emphatically, no doubt, undoubtedly, doubtless, positively, precisely, exactly, so be it, amen; affirmatively, in the affirmative. **—n. 2.** *May we count on your yes?:* affirmative reply, affirmative vote, affirmation, consent, assent, okay, acquiescence, acceptance, agreement, authorization, approval. **—Ant.** 1, 2 no, nay. 1 not so, untrue, wrong, false, of course not, no indeed, doubtfully, negatively, in the negative. 2 refusal, rejection, veto, disapproval.

yes-man *n.* *The mayor was surrounded by yes-men:* flatterer, sycophant, toady, apple-polisher, stooge, boot-licker, flunky, lackey, rubber stamp, minion, myrmidon.

yesterday *adv.* **1.** *Where did you go yesterday?:* on the day preceding today. **—n. 2.** *Where's the paper from yesterday?:* the day before today; yestermorn, yestereve. **3.** *Remember the hair styles of yesterday?:* the recent past, bygone days, former times, the past, yesteryear, the good old days, days of yore, time gone by, olden times. **—Ant.** 1, 2 tomorrow.

yield *v.* **1.** *This old tree still yields apples every year:* bear, bring forth, produce, give forth, put forth; give birth to, beget, spawn, procreate, generate. **2.** *The stock yields 8% interest a year:* earn, return, generate, pay, provide, furnish, supply, render, give. **3.** *The town soon yielded to the attackers. Don't yield to temptation:* surrender, give up, give in, give way, capitulate, submit, succumb, accede, acquiesce, resign oneself, truckle, bow down, *Slang* kowtow, cave in, cry uncle. **4.** *Cars entering the highway must yield the right of way. Will the speaker yield five minutes of his allotted speaking time to the senator from California?:* relinquish, grant, concede, give up, give, give away, defer, forgo, waive, renounce, forbear. **5.** *The small chair yielded under his weight:* give way, sag, droop, cave in, collapse, break, split, burst. **—n. 6.** *Farmers had an exceptionally good yield this year:* harvest, crop, gleanings; produce, product. **7.** *The current yield on municipal bonds is 9%:* interest, return, earnings, proceeds, gain, payment, revenue, premium. **—Ant.** 3 resist, oppose, combat, counterattack, attack; repulse, repel. 4 keep, retain, maintain, reserve, hold on to; appropriate, take, seize, grab, arrogate, claim.

yielding *adj.* **1.** *The yielding magistrate accepted their statement:* acquiescent, accommodating, biddable, compliant, docile, easy, flexible, nonresistant, passive, pliable, pliant, submissive, tractable. **2.** *The yielding turf felt easy to walk on:* pliable, elastic, flexible, malleable, resilient, soft, spongy, springy, supple. **—Ant.** 1 obstinate, stubborn, dogged, headstrong, willful. 2 unyielding, stiff.

yoke *n.* **1.** *The two oxen were put into the yoke. A rubber yoke held the two wires together:* double harness, coupler, collar, bond, clasp. **2.** *It takes a yoke of oxen to pull that wagon:* pair, team, brace, couple, span. **3.** *Lincoln's Emancipation Proclamation freed the slaves from their yoke:* bondage, slavery, enslavement, servitude; serfdom, vassalage, thralldom. **4.** *The youth was not ready for the yoke of responsibility:* burden, weight, oppression, load, strain, pressure, tax, troubles, distress, trial, tribulation. **—v. 5.** *The farmer yoked the oxen to the plow:* couple, double harness; hitch, harness. **6.** *Do these parts of the toy yoke together? The nation's economic growth is yoked to that of its neighbors:* join, unite, couple, link, attach, fasten. **—Ant.** 3 freedom, liberty, independence. 4 joy, pleasure, delight, enjoyment, comfort, satisfaction. 5 unyoke, uncouple, unhitch, unharness. 6 separate, divide, divorce.

yokel *n.* *With modern transportation and communications there are very few yokels anymore:* bumpkin, country bumpkin, naive rustic, rube, provincial, clod, clodhopper, hayseed, peasant, plowboy, hick, country boy.

yolk *n.* *Separate the yolks from the whites before making the cake:* egg yolk, yellow. **—Ant.** white, albumen.

yonder *adj.* **1.** *The yonder barn is bigger than the near one:* more distant, farther, thither, yon, far-off. **—adv. 2.** *He was born way down yonder in New Orleans:* faraway, far-off, over the hills and faraway, over the horizon; over there, there, thither. **—Ant.** 1 near, nearer, closer; nearby, close, at hand. 2 nearby, near here, close-by; over here, here.

young *adj.* **1.** *You're still young. The major's too young to be made a general:* youthful, not old; younger, junior, juvenile, infantile, underage, minor, childish, boyish, girlish, puerile, adolescent, beardless, teenage; immature, wet behind the ears, inexperienced, undeveloped, callow, sophomoric; growing, budding. **—n. 2.** *Both young and old like ice cream:* young persons, young people, children, juveniles, youngsters, kids, youths, teenagers, adolescents. **3.** *The mother tiger guards her young fiercely:* baby, child, cub, pup, whelp, kitten; offspring, issue, progeny, descendant. **—Ant.** 1, 2 old, aged. 1 elderly, older, elder, senior, gray, hoary, old-mannish, old-womanish, ancient, venerable; adult, mature, grown-up, experienced, ripe, fully developed, full-grown. 2 the old, senior citizens, oldster, old-timers; adults, grownups. 3 parent, progenitor.

youngster *n.* *The youngsters are both in school:* child, boy, girl, youth, kid, young person, fledgling, minor, adolescent, juvenile, teenager; offspring, progeny, tot, baby. **—Ant.** oldster, old-timer, senior citizen; adult, grownup.

youth *n.* **1.** *I visited South America in my youth. She's trying frantically to maintain her youth:* early life, childhood, boyhood, girlhood, adolescence, growing years, teens, pubescence, juvenile period, minority, school days, salad days, younger days, springtime of life, prime, bloom, heyday; youthful condition, youthful appearance. **2.** *The youth ran away to join the circus:* boy, schoolboy, lad, youngster, child, kid, juvenile, minor, teenager, adolescent, young man, stripling, young shaver, fledgling. **3.** *The new TV program is aimed at youth:* young persons, young people, the young, children, boys and girls, youngsters, kids, juveniles, teenagers, adolescents, the rising generation, young men and women. **—Ant.** 1 old age, later life; adulthood, maturity. 2 man, old man, old coot, codger; adult. 3 senior citizens, oldsters, old-timers; adults, grownups.

youthful *adj. The magician loved to perform before youthful audiences. It was just a youthful prank. Outside interests keep one youthful:* young, juvenile, adolescent, teenage; childish, boyish, girlish, puerile, immature, inexperienced, callow, sophomoric; of the young, for the young; young-looking, enthusiastic, fresh, lighthearted, bright-eyed, starry-eyed, having young attitudes, young at heart. **—Ant.** old, aged, elderly, older, senior, hoary; adult, mature, grown-up, full-grown, experienced; old-mannish, old-womanish, old-looking, old-fashioned; senile, decrepit.

yowl *v.* **1.** *The cats were yowling on the back fence:* howl, bay, caterwaul, yelp, scream, shriek, screech, squeal, bawl, whine. **—n. 2.** *The handyman let out a yowl when he hit his thumb with the hammer:* howl, wail, yelp, cry, shout, holler, bellow, roar, scream, shriek, screech, squeal, whine, bawl, caterwaul.

yo-yo *v. Informal They yo-yoed between alternatives:* vacillate, fluctuate, vary, shift, dither, equivocate, waffle, hesitate, tergiversate, waver, seesaw, fluctuate, hem and haw, come and go, *British* haver. **—Ant.** stabilize.

yule *n. Grandmother always saved her best preserves for the yule:* Christmas season, Christmas, Noel, yuletide; the feast of Christmas.

zaftig *adj. Slang The classically zaftig opera singer won huge applause for her aria:* rounded, Rubenesque, full, plump, pleasingly plump, curvaceous, curvy, buxom, voluptuous, pneumatic, built for comfort. **—Ant.** gaunt, skinny, emaciated, shapeless.

zany *adj.* **1.** *I prefer zany comedy to sophisticated humor:* clownish, outlandish, foolishly comical, silly, inane, nonsensical, ludicrous, slapstick, daffy, dizzy, crazy, wild; *Slang* nutty, goofy, wacky, screwy, batty, balmy. **—n. 2.** *Don't be such a zany, be serious for a change:* clown, buffoon, jester, comic, cutup; harlequin, buffo, pantaloon, farceur. **3.** *That old zany ought to be in a circus or an asylum:* daffy person, dizzy person, eccentric, lunatic, *Slang* nut, crazy, weirdo; nitwit, half-wit, imbecile, noodlehead, blockhead, bonehead, nincompoop, numskull, simpleton, booby, lunkhead. **—Ant.** 1 droll, ironic, sarcastic, wry, dry.

zeal *n. The boys began the work of building a doghouse with zeal. His political zeal prevented* us from having a quiet discussion: zest, gusto, relish, eagerness, fervor, ardor, industry, enthusiasm, animation, vigor, verve, fierceness, intensity, earnestness, intentness, vehemence, fire, passion, devotion, fanaticism. **—Ant.** apathy, indifference, impassivity, nonchalance, coolness, torpor, languor, listlessness.

zealot *n.* **1.** *It takes a real zealot to be a top-notch car salesman:* believer, enthusiast, partisan, champion, devotee, fan, buff; go-getter, pusher, hustler, live wire, eager beaver. **2.** *Religious zealots wanted the entire population to wear sackcloth and ashes:* fanatic, true believer, obsessed person, bigot, extremist, crank, crackpot, nut.

zealous *adj. Bill is the most zealous worker in the whole office. The lawyer made a zealous plea for his client:* full of zeal, eager, fervent, fervid, vigorous, ardent, earnest, enthusiastic, gung ho, animated, intense, fierce, vehement, passionate, impassioned, devoted, industrious; fanatic, rabid, raging, raving. **—Ant.** apathetic, languorous, torpid, listless, unenthusiastic, dispassionate, passionless, indifferent, lackluster, lackadaisical, nonchalant, dull, calm, cool, quiet, low-key.

zenith *n.* **1.** *Is the North Star really at the zenith of the north pole?:* point in the sky directly overhead; twelve o'clock high. **2.** *Being elected mayor was the zenith of his political career. The British Empire was at its zenith in the 19th century:* peak, highest point, high point, crowning point, pinnacle, acme, summit, apex, vertex, apogee, maximum, best, culmination, culminating point, climax. **—Ant.** 1, 2 nadir. 2 lowest point, low point, depth, minimum, worst.

zephyr *n. A zephyr whispered through the palm trees:* light breeze, gentle wind, breath of air, puff of air; west wind. **—Ant.** gust, blast, gale, squall, blow, windstorm, tornado; east wind.

zero *n.* **1.** *Four subtracted from four leaves zero. All our efforts added up to zero:* nothing, nothingness, naught, aught, cipher, *Slang* goose egg, zilch, zip; *symbol* 0. **2.** *The thermometer says two degrees above zero:* the lowest positive point on a scale, zero degrees; lowest point, nadir. **—adj. 3.** *Our chances of making a profit are zero:* amounting to zero, nil, nonexistent, no, naught, aught, *Slang* zilch, zip. **—Ant.** 1 infinity; something, everything. 2 zenith, highest point. 3 perfect, excellent.

zest *n.* **1.** *Father has a great zest for living:* keen enjoyment, gusto, relish, appetite, zeal, eagerness, enthusiasm, verve, passion; exhilaration, excitement, thrill, delight, joy, pleasure, satisfaction. **2.** *The special zest of this soup is due to the saffron:* flavoring, flavor, savor, taste, tang, zing, zip, piquancy, seasoning; spice, salt. **—Ant.** 1 apathy, weariness, dullness, distaste, disrelish, displeasure, aversion, abhorrence, repugnance, loathing.

zilch *n. Slang We got zilch in the settlement:* nothing, zero, nil, naught, aught, *Informal* zip, nix, diddly, diddly-squat, squat, *Spanish* nada.

Zion *n.* **1.** *King David of Judah ruled from Zion. The Lord hath founded Zion:* City of David, hill in Jerusalem on which the Temple was built; ancient Israel; the Jewish people. **2.** *The colonists prayed that their settlement would become a Zion:* community under God's protection, godly community, city of God, utopia.

zip *n.* **1.** *The scout saw the flash of a gun and then heard the zip of a bullet:* hiss, whine, whistle, buzz. **2.** *The new Miss America has beauty and zip. The show was interesting but had no zip to it:* energy, vim, vigor, pep, dash, verve, animation, vivacity, liveliness, life, vitality, spirit, effervescence, exuberance, zest, gusto, enthusiasm; power, drive, force, strength, intensity, punch, impact. —*v.* **3.** *Zip down to the store and get a quart of milk:* run, go quickly, dash, dart, streak, rush, hurry, speed, fly. **4.** *Better zip your jacket—it's cold outside:* zip up, zipper, fasten with a zipper, close. —**Ant.** 2 lethargy, torpor, languor, sluggishness, lassitude, apathy, listlessness, coolness; dullness, weakness. 3 creep, crawl, inch. 4 unzip.

zone *n.* **1.** *Most of the world's wheat is grown in the North Temperate Zone. It's against the law to build factories in this residential zone:* region, territory, area, terrain, belt; district, quarter, precinct, ward, sector, section, locality, location, tract. —*v.* **2.** *The U.S. and Canada are zoned for postal delivery. The downtown area is zoned for commercial use:* divide into zones, designate as a zone.

zoo *n.* *San Diego has one of the largest zoos in the world:* zoological garden, zoological park, animal farm; menagerie, vivarium.

zoom *v.* **1.** *His racing car zoomed right past the stands:* speed, race, streak, flash, buzz, zip, shoot, fly. **2.** *Stock market prices zoomed on the good business news:* rise, climb, soar, advance, skyrocket, rocket, ascend, take off.